CRIMINAL PROCEDURE

PRINCIPLES, POLICIES AND PERSPECTIVES

Sixth Edition

■ ■ ■

Joshua Dressler
Distinguished University Professor
Frank R. Strong Chair in Law
Michael E. Moritz College of Law
The Ohio State University

George C. Thomas III
Rutgers University Board of Governors Professor of Law
Judge Alexander P. Waugh, Sr. Distinguished Scholar
Rutgers School of Law, Newark

AMERICAN CASEBOOK SERIES®

WEST
ACADEMIC
PUBLISHING

American Casebook Series is a trademark registered in the U.S. Patent and Trademark Office.

© West, a Thomson business, 1999, 2003, 2006
© 2010, 2013 Thomson Reuters
© 2017 LEG, Inc. d/b/a West Academic
    444 Cedar Street, Suite 700
    St. Paul, MN 55101
    1-877-888-1330

Printed in the United States of America

ISBN: 978-1-63460-316-4

To Dottie, my life's companion: thank you;
and to David, Jessica, Lucy, Maya, Gideon, and the new one
coming: may your futures be filled with much happiness.

— J.D.

To Gretchen, for our love and friendship, and for traveling
along with me.

— G.T.

PREFACE

It is a pleasure to teach Criminal Procedure. Much of the course features constitutional law, with its fascinating questions about theories of interpretation and about fidelity to text and history. Criminal procedure also brings students face to face with fundamental policy questions about the appropriate balance between protecting us *from criminals* and protecting us *from the government*. We want the criminal process to solve and prosecute crime but we also want controls that protect our privacy and autonomy. Most students have had contact with the police, if only to receive a traffic ticket. Even minor events like traffic stops can lead to a search of the car and can manifest racial profiling or other abuses of police authority. Students also "know" about policing from television shows like the late-and-great *NYPD Blue* and the endless variations of *Law and Order*.

Television shows over the years have also featured the criminal trial process and the role of lawyers in it. Think of *Perry Mason* in black and white, *Perry Mason* in color, *Law and Order*, and the real-life dramas of countless actual trials, some of which are going on as we write this Preface. From these shows, and news accounts, the country has acquired a set of beliefs and attitudes about the prosecution, defense, and adjudication of criminal defendants. The focus at this stage of the process shifts to finding the right balance between convicting the guilty in an efficient manner while freeing the innocent and providing fairness to all. Fundamental policy issues underlie much of the doctrine here as well. Does the Constitution permit non-unanimous verdicts or exclusion of jurors on the basis of race? Does the Constitution require prosecutors to turn over all favorable evidence to the defense or only that evidence likely to produce an acquittal?

If criminal procedure is as topical as today's newspaper, it is also deeply steeped in history. Criminal trials appear in Roman law and Hebrew law. The right to counsel surfaces in Roman law and reappears in the twelfth century laws of Henry I. English history is filled with criminal procedure controversies, from the dispute between Henry II and Thomas Becket in 1168 over the authority of church courts, to the confrontation between King John and his rebel barons that led to the Magna Carta, to the stormy reign of Henry VIII that produced the Reformation. A study of criminal procedure is not just a search of now but also of our past. In our past, we find the enduring values that shape court decisions today.

A casebook cannot be all things to all people, but it should offer sufficient flexibility to accommodate diverse teaching goals and pedagogical methods. We include materials that encourage students to think about constitutional theory and judicial craftsmanship as they read cases and learn doctrine. In the selection of cases, less can be more. We have chosen not to edit cases down to their bones in order to include more cases. We offer broad coverage but also give students and professors the chance to dig deep into the important constitutional cases.

Professor Anthony Amsterdam famously observed about Supreme Court jurisprudence, that "once uttered, these pronouncements will be interpreted by arrays of lower appellate courts, trial judges, magistrates, commissioners and police officials. *Their* interpretation * * * for all practical purposes, will become the word of god." Anthony G. Amsterdam, *The Supreme Court and the Rights of Suspects in Criminal Cases*, 45 N.Y.U. L. Rev. 785, 786 (1979). We seek the "word of god" by including empirical research data where it exists, political science analyses, and news accounts that illuminate how law works "in the trenches."

We believe that students should learn early, and think often, about the overarching principles of the subject matter they are learning. In Chapter 1 we display failures of the criminal process as a way to get students to identify appropriate goals for a criminal process. Then we invite them to return again and again to those goals to understand, and sometimes to critique, Supreme Court doctrine. Why does the Sixth Amendment require appointed counsel in almost every case while the Fourth Amendment receives a grudging interpretation? We believe this, and many other, interpretational issues are illuminated by considering the importance that a criminal process places on accurate outcomes, a goal that is hopefully advanced when counsel is appointed, but inevitably hindered when limitations are placed on the power of government to seek evidence.

As much as we would like the law to be neutral, we are realistic enough to know that it does not always achieve that goal. And we think it important for students to realize the ways in which law fails to achieve neutrality. Thus, we do not skirt—in fact, we confront—the effects of racism and other malignant-isms in the criminal process.

A casebook need not be forbidding to inspire students to display high standards of thought, analysis, and criticism. Users of our book will discover some informality, even humor (heresy!), in places. For us, this style has worked well. We seek balance between principal cases and the Notes and Questions that illuminate or expand on the principal cases. Thus, professors who want to teach the cases can rely on the Notes and Questions to facilitate a more traditional classroom discussion. Those who like the problem method will find Problems in conjunction with the Notes and Questions to keep a lively class discussion going. And those, like Dressler and Thomas, who blend the traditional case analysis with the problem method, will find the book especially well suited to that approach.

Outside reading materials. There are many useful sources for additional reading. Among the excellent general resources are Joshua Dressler & Alan C. Michaels, Understanding Criminal Procedure (6th ed. 2013); Wayne R. LaFave, Jerold H. Israel, Nancy J. King & Orin S. Kerr, Criminal Procedure (5th ed. 2009); and Charles Whitebread & Christopher Slobogin, Criminal Procedure, An Analysis of Cases and Concepts (5th ed. 2008). For those who want even more coverage of the Fourth Amendment, nothing can compare to Wayne R. LaFave, Search and Seizure (5th ed. 2012), a monumental six-volume treatise. For those who want a greater dose of history with their Fourth Amendment, we recommend Thomas K. Clancy, The Fourth Amendment, Its History and Interpretation (2008). We have also cited and quoted from other excellent books and articles throughout the casebook.

Editing policies. We prefer students to read judicial opinions in largely intact form. Nonetheless, deletions are necessary. Because the goal of this book is pedagogy, we have not followed all scholarly conventions in identifying omissions from the extracted materials. We have applied the following rules of thumb to extracted materials.

1. Most footnotes and citations have been omitted, always without use of ellipses to indicate their omission. Asterisks have been used, however, to indicate deletions of other textual materials.

2. Numbered footnotes are from the original materials and retain their original numbering. Our "editors' footnotes" are designated by letter.

Personal acknowledgments. Many people assisted us in producing this edition or its predecessors, or all six, including many colleagues on our respective faculties and throughout the United States and United Kingdom as well as members of the Bar and judiciary. We name a few people here: Phil Bates, Robert Batey, Doug Berman, Susan Brenner, Neil Cohen, Stan Cox, Thomas Davies, Michiael Dimino, John G. Douglass, Jim Ellis, Arnold Enker, Barry Feinstein, Stanley Z. Fisher, Clifford Fishman, Gary Francione, Jeffrey Froelich, Adam Gershowitz, Mark Godsey, Stuart Green, Kenneth Graham, David Harris, Stephen Henderson, Peter J. Henning, Charles Jones, Andy Leipold, Rory Little, Gerard Lynch, Michael Mannheimer, Bernie McShane, Alan Michaels, Sam Pillsbury, and Michael Vitiello. Special thanks to Rutgers student Annabel Pollioni for help with the sixth edition.

Author Thomas thanks co-author Dressler for his unflagging attempts to force discipline on the project, some of which succeeded.

Author Dressler offers heartfelt thanks to co-author George for his seemingly unlimited good humor, which was put to the ultimate test by Dressler's compulsive need to send thousands of e-mail messages raising endless manuscript issues. He also thanks George for his condolences for the Dodgers's poor play in recent years. Wait 'till next year.

JOSHUA DRESSLER
Michael E. Moritz College of Law
The Ohio State University
Columbus, Ohio

GEORGE C. THOMAS III
Rutgers University School of Law
Newark, New Jersey

August 2016

ACKNOWLEDGMENTS

Janet E. Ainsworth, *The Pragmatics of Powerlessness in Police Interrogation*, 103 Yale Law Journal 259 (1993). Copyright © 1993, The Yale Law Journal Company, Inc. Reprinted by permission of the Yale Law Journal Company and Fred B. Rothman & Company from *The Yale Law Journal*, Vol. 103, pages 259–322.

Albert W. Alschuler, *Preventive Pretrial Detention and the Failure of Interest-Balancing Approaches to Due Process*, 85 Michigan Law Review 510 (1986). Copyright © 1986, Michigan Law Review Association. Reprinted by permission.

Albert W. Alschuler, *The Changing Plea Bargaining Debate*, 69 California Law Review 652 (1981). Copyright © 1981 by California Law Review, Inc. Reprinted from California Law Review, Vol. 69, No. 3, pp. 652–723.

Akhil Reed Amar, *Fourth Amendment First Principles*, 107 Harvard Law Review 757 (1994). Copyright © 1994 by the Harvard Law Review Association. Reprinted by permission.

Akhil Reed Amar, *The Bill of Rights and the Fourteenth Amendment*, 101 Yale Law Journal 1193 (1992). Copyright © 1992, Yale Law Journal Company, Inc. Reprinted by permission of The Yale Law Journal Company and Fred B. Rothman & Company from The Yale Law Journal, Vol. 101, pages 1193–1284.

Vivian O. Berger, *The Supreme Court and Defense Counsel: Old Roads, New Paths—A Dead End?*, 86 Columbia Law Review 9 (1986). Copyright © 1986 by the Directors of the Columbia Law Review Association. This article originally appeared at 86 Colum. L. Rev. 9 (1986). Reprinted by permission.

Craig M. Bradley, *Murray v. United States: The Bell Tolls for the Search Warrant Requirement*, 64 Indiana Law Journal 907 (1989). Copyright © 1989, by the Trustees of Indiana University. Reprinted by permission.

Craig M. Bradley, *Two Models of the Fourth Amendment*, 83 Michigan Law Review 1468 (1985). Copyright © 1985, Michigan Law Review Association. Reprinted by permission.

Susan W. Brenner, *The Voice of the Community: A Case for Grand Jury Independence*, 3 Virginia Journal of Social Policy & Law 67 (1995). Copyright © 1995, Virginia Journal of Social Policy & Law. Reprinted by permission.

Stephen Breyer, *The Federal Sentencing Guidelines and the Key Compromises Upon Which They Rest*, 17 Hofstra Law Review 1 (1988). Copyright © 1988, by the *Hofstra Law Review Association*. Reprinted with the permission of *Hofstra Law Review*.

Alvin J. Bronstein, *Representing the Powerless: Lawyers Can Make a Difference*, originally published in the Maine Law Review, 49 Maine Law Review 1, 5–7, 12–13 (1997). Copyright © 1997, University of Maine School of Law. Reprinted by permission.

Paul D. Butler, *Race-Based Jury Nullification: Case-in-Chief*, 30 John Marshall Law Review 911 (1997). Copyright © 1997, The John Marshall Law School. Reprinted with permission from The John Marshall Law Review, Volume XXX, Issue 4 (Summer 1997).

Gerald M. Caplan, *Questioning Miranda*, 38 Vanderbilt Law Review 1417 (1985). Copyright © 1985, Vanderbilt Law Review. Reprinted by permission.

Morgan Cloud, *The Dirty Little Secret*, 43 Emory Law Journal 1311 (1994). Copyright © 1994, Emory Law Journal. Reprinted by permission.

Sherry F. Colb, *What Is a Search? Two Conceptual Flaws in Fourth Amendment Doctrine and Some Hints of a Remedy*, 55 Stan. L. Rev. 119 (2002). Copyright © 2002 by the Board of Trustees of the Leland Stanford Junior University. Reprinted by permission.

David Cole, No Equal Justice (1999). Copyright © 1999, by David Cole. Reprinted by permission of the author.

John G. Douglass, *Confronting the Reluctant Accomplice*, 101 Columbia Law Review 1797 (2001). Copyright © 2001 by the Directors of the Columbia Law Review Association. This article originally appeared at 101 Colum. L. Rev. 1797 (2001). Reprinted by permission.

Joshua Dressler, Understanding Criminal Law (Seventh edition 2015). Reprinted with permission. Copyright © 2015 Matthew Bender & Company, Inc., a member of the LexisNexis Group. All rights reserved.

Joshua Dressler & Alan C. Michaels, Understanding Criminal Procedure (Fourth Edition 2006) (Vol. 2). Reprinted from <u>Understanding Criminal Procedure Vol. 2, 4th Ed.</u> with permission. Copyright © 2006 Matthew Bender & Company, Inc., a member of the LexisNexis Group. All rights reserved.

Joshua Dressler & Alan C. Michaels, Understanding Criminal Procedure (Sixth Edition 2013) (Vol. 1). Reprinted from <u>Understanding Criminal Procedure Vol. 1, 6th Ed.</u> with permission. Copyright ©

2013 Matthew Bender & Company, Inc., a member of the LexisNexis Group. All rights reserved.

Sam J. Ervin, Jr., *Foreword: Preventive Detention—A Step Backward for Criminal Justice*, 6 Harvard Civil Rights—Civil Liberties Law Review 291 (1971). Copyright © 1971 by the President and Fellows of Harvard College. Reprinted by permission.

Martha A. Field, *Assessing the Harmlessness of Federal Constitutional Error—A Process in Need of a Rationale*, 125 University of Pennsylvania Law Review 15 (1976). Copyright © 1976 by the University of Pennsylvania. Reprinted by permission.

Barry Friedman, *A Tale of Two Habeas*, 73 Minnesota Law Review 248 (1988). Copyright © 1988, Minnesota Law Review Foundation. Reprinted by permission.

Ann Fagan Ginger, editor, Minimizing Racism in Jury Trials (1969). Copyright © 1969, Ann Fagan Ginger. Reprinted by permission of the editor

Steven H. Goldberg, *Harmless Error: Constitutional Sneak Thief*, 71 Journal of Criminal Law & Criminology 421 (1980). Copyright © 1980, Northwestern University School of Law. Reprinted by special permission of Northwestern University School of Law, Journal of Criminal Law and Criminology, volume 71, pp. 421, 429–30 (1980).

James Goodman, Stories of Scottsboro, Random House Times Book (1994). From Stories of Scottsboro by James Goodman. Copyright © 1994 by James E. Goodman. Reprinted by permission of Pantheon Books, a division of Random House, Inc.

Joseph D. Grano, *Probable Cause and Common Sense: A Reply to the Critics of Illinois v. Gates*, 17 University of Michigan Journal of Legal Reform 465 (1984). Copyright © 1984, by the University of Michigan Journal of Law Reform. Reprinted by permission.

Bruce A. Green, *Lethal Fiction: The Meaning of "Counsel" in the Sixth Amendment*, 78 Iowa Law Review 433 (1993). Copyright © 1993, by the University of Iowa (Iowa Law Review) (reprinted with permission).

Sandra Guerra, *The Myth of Dual Sovereignty: Multijurisdictional Drug Law Enforcement and Double Jeopardy*, 73 North Carolina Law Review 1159 (1995). Copyright © 1995, North Carolina Law Review. Reprinted by permission.

Peter J. Henning, *Prosecutorial Misconduct in Grand Jury Investigations*, 51 South Carolina Law Review 1 (1999). Copyright © 1999, South Carolina Law Review. Reprinted by permission.

Lenese C. Herbert, *Can't You See What I'm Saying? Making Expressive Conduct a Crime in High-Crimes Areas*, 9 Georgetown.Journal on Poverty Law & Policy 135 (2002). Reprinted with permission of the publisher, Georgetown Journal on Poverty Law & Policy © 2002.

Lawrence Herman, *The Supreme Court, the Attorney General, and the Good Old Days of Police Interrogation*, 48 Ohio State Law Journal 733 (1987). Copyright © 1987, Ohio State Law Journal

Graham Hughes, *The Decline of Habeas Corpus*, (NYU Center for Research in Crime and Justice, 1990). Copyright © 1990, NYU Center for Research in Crime and Justice. Reprinted by permission.

Randolph N. Jonakait, *Restoring the Confrontation Clause to the Sixth Amendment*, 38 UCLA Law Review 557 (1988). Originally published in 35 UCLA L. Rev. 557. Copyright © 1988, The Regents of the University of California. All rights reserved. Reprinted by permission.

Sanford H. Kadish, *Fifty Years of Criminal Law: An Opinionated Review*, 87 Calif. L. Rev. 943 (1999). Copyright © 1999 by Sanford H. Kadish. Reprinted by permission of the author.

Michael J. Klarman, *The Racial Origins of Modern Criminal Procedure*, 99 Michigan Law Review 48 (2000). Copyright © 2000, Michigan Law Review Association. Reprinted by permission.

Richard B. Kuhns, *The Concept of Personal Aggrievement in Fourth Amendment Standing Cases*, 65 Iowa Law Review 493 (1980). Copyright © 1980, by the University of Iowa (Iowa Law Review). Reprinted with permission.

Gerald B. Lefcourt, *Responsibilities of a Criminal Defense Attorney*, 30 Loyola of Los Angeles Law Review (1996). Copyright © 1996, Loyola of Los Angeles Law Review. Reprinted by permission.

Andrew D. Leipold, *Race-Based Jury Nullification: Rebuttal (Part A)*, 30 John Marshall Law Review 923 (1997). Copyright © 1997, The John Marshall Law School. Reprinted with permission from The John Marshall Law Review, Volume XXX, Issue 4 (Summer 1997).

Andrew D. Leipold, *Why Grand Juries Do Not (and Cannot) Protect the Accused*, 80 Cornell Law Review 260 (1995). Copyright © 1995, Cornell Law Review. Reprinted by permission.

Erik Luna, *Gridland: An Allegorical Critique of Federal Sentencing*, 96 Journal of Criminal Law & Criminology 25 (2005). Copyright © 2005, Northwestern University School of Law. Reprinted by special permission of Northwestern University School of Law, The Journal of Criminal Law and Criminology.

Tracey Maclin, *Terry v. Ohio's Fourth Amendment Legacy: Black Men and Police Discretion*, 72 St. John's Law Review 1271 (1998). Copyright © 1998, St. John's Law Review. Reprinted by permission.

Tracey Maclin, *"Black and Blue Encounters"—Some Preliminary Thoughts About Fourth Amendment Seizures: Should Race Matter?*, 26 Valparaiso University Law Review 243 (1991). Copyright © 1991, by Valparaiso University Law Review. Reprinted with the permission of the publisher and author.

Michael S. Moore, Act and Crime, Oxford University Press (1993). Copyright © 1993, Oxford University Press. Reprinted by permission of Oxford University Press.

Robert B. Mosteller, *Remaking Confrontation Clause and Hearsay Doctrine Under the Challenge of Child Sexual Abuse Prosecutions*, University of Illinois Law Review 691 (1993). Copyright © 1993. The copyright to the University of Illinois Law Review is held by The Board of Trustees of the University of Illinois.

Charles E. Moylan, Jr., *Hearsay and Probable Cause: An Aguilar and Spinelli Primer*, 25 Mercer Law Review 741 (1974). Copyright © 1974, Walter F. George School of Law, Mercer University. Reprinted by permission.

Eric L. Muller, *Solving the Batson Paradox: Harmless Error, Jury Representation, and the Sixth Amendment*, 106 Yale Law Journal 93 (1996). Copyright © 1996, The Yale Law Journal Company. Reprinted by permission of The Yale Law Journal Company and Fred B. Rothman & Company from The Yale Law Journal, Volume 106, pages 93–150.

William J. Powell & Michael T. Cimino, *Prosecutorial Discretion Under the Federal Sentencing Guidelines: Is the Fox Guarding the Hen House?*, 97 West Virginia Law Review 373 (1995). Copyright © 1995, West Virginia Law Review. Reprinted by permission.

Ric Simmons, *Re-examining the Grand Jury: Is There Room for Democracy in the Criminal Justice System?*, 82 Boston University Law Review 1 (2002). Copyright © 2002, Boston University Law Review. Reprinted by permission.

David Simon, Homicide, A Year on the Killing Streets (1991). Abridged from Homicide: A Year on the Killing Streets. Copyright © 1991 by David Simon. Reprinted by permission of Houghton Mifflin Co. All rights reserved.

Abbe Smith, *Defending Defending: The Case for Unmitigated Zeal on Behalf of People Who Do Terrible Things*, 28 Hofstra L. Rev. 925 (2000). Copyright © 2000 by the *Hofstra Law Review Association*.

Reprinted with the permission of the *Hofstra Law Review Association.*

Potter Stewart, *The Road to Mapp v. Ohio and Beyond: The Origins, Development and Future of the Exclusionary Rule in Search-and-Seizure Cases*, 83 Columbia Law Review 1365 (1983). Copyright © 1983 by the Directors of the Columbia Law Review Association, Inc. This article originally appeared at 83 Colum. L. Rev. 1365 (1983). Reprinted by permission.

Kate Stith and José A. Cabranes, Fear of Judging: Sentencing Guidelines in the Federal Courts (1998). Copyright © 1998, University of Chicago Press. Reprinted by permission.

Louis Stokes, *Representing John W. Terry*, 72 St. John's L. Rev. 727 (1998). Copyright © 1998, St. John's Law Review. Reprinted by permission.

William J. Stuntz, *Miranda's Mistake*, 99 Michigan Law Review. 975 (2001). Copyright © 1999, Michigan Law Review Association. Reprinted by permission.

Scott E. Sundby, *Fallen Superheroes and the Brady Mirage*, 33 McGeorge Law Review 643 (2002). Copyright © 2002, McGeorge Law Review. Reprinted by permission of the author and journal.

Scott E. Sundby, *An Ode to Probable Cause: A Brief Response to Professors Amar and Slobogin*, 72 St. John's Law Review 1133 (1998). Copyright © 1998, St. John's Law Review. Reprinted by permission.

Scott E. Sundby, A Return to Fourth Amendment Basics: Undoing the Mischief of Camara and Terry, 72 Minnesota Law Review 383 (1988). Copyright © 1988, Minnesota Law Review Foundation. Reprinted by permission.

George C. Thomas III, The Supreme Court on Trial: How the Supreme Court Sacrifices Innocent Defendants (Ann Arbor: The University of Michigan Press). Copyright © 2008, The University of Michigan Press. Reprinted by permission.

Sandra Guerra Thompson, *The Non-Discrimination Ideal of Hernandez v. Texas Confronts a "Culture" of Discrimination: The Amazing Story of Miller-El v. Texas,* 25 Chicano-Latino L. Rev. 97 (2005). Copyright © 2005, Chicano-Latino Law Review. Reprinted by permission.

H. Richard Uviller, *Evidence from the Mind of the Criminal Suspect: A Reconsideration of the Current Rules of Access and Restraint*, 87 Columbia Law Review 1137 (1987). Copyright © 1987 by the Directors of the Columbia Law Review Association, Inc. This article originally appeared at 87 Colum. L. Rev. 1137 (1987). Reprinted by permission.

Thomas Weigend, *Germany*. From Criminal Procedure: A Worldwide View, edited by Craig M. Bradley (1998). Copyright © 1998, Carolina Academic Press. Reprinted by permission of Carolina Academic Press, telephone (919) 489–7486, website www.cap-press.com.

SUMMARY OF CONTENTS

TABLE OF CONTENTS

TABLE OF CASES

The principal cases are in bold type.

CRIMINAL PROCEDURE

PRINCIPLES, POLICIES AND PERSPECTIVES

Sixth Edition

UNITED STATES CONSTITUTION
(SELECTED PROVISIONS)

■ ■ ■

ARTICLE I

Section 9.   * * *

[2] The privilege of the Writ of Habeas Corpus shall not be suspended, unless when in Cases of Rebellion or Invasion the public Safety may require it.

[3] No Bill of Attainder or ex post facto Law shall be passed.

ARTICLE III

Section 1.   The judicial Power of the United States, shall be vested in one supreme Court, and in such inferior Courts as the Congress may from time to time ordain and establish. The Judges, both of the supreme and inferior Courts, shall hold their Offices during good Behaviour, and shall, at stated Times, receive for their Services a Compensation, which shall not be diminished during their Continuance in Office.

Section 2.   [1] The judicial Power shall extend to all Cases, in Law and Equity, arising under this Constitution, the Laws of the United States, and Treaties made, or which shall be made, under their Authority;—to all Cases affecting Ambassadors, other public Ministers and Consuls;—to all Cases of admiralty and maritime Jurisdiction;—to Controversies to which the United States shall be a Party;—to Controversies between two or more States;—between a State and Citizens of another State;—between Citizens of different States;—between Citizens of the same State claiming Lands under Grants of different States, and between a State, or the Citizens thereof, and foreign States, Citizens or Subjects. * * *

[3] The trial of all Crimes, except in Cases of Impeachment, shall be by Jury; and such Trial shall be held in the State where the said Crimes shall have been committed; but when not committed within any State, the Trial shall be at such Place or Places as the Congress may by Law have directed.

Section 3.   [1] Treason against the United States, shall consist only in levying War against them, or, in adhering to their Enemies, giving them Aid and Comfort. No Person shall be convicted of Treason unless on the Testimony of two Witnesses to the same overt Act, or on Confession in open Court.

[2] The Congress shall have Power to declare the Punishment of Treason, but no Attainder of Treason shall work Corruption of Blood, or Forfeiture except during the Life of the Person attainted.

ARTICLE IV

Section 2.   [1] The Citizens of each State shall be entitled to all Privileges and Immunities of Citizens in the several States.

[2] A person charged in any State with Treason, Felony, or other Crime, who shall flee from Justice, and be found in another State, shall on demand of the executive Authority of the State from which he fled, be delivered up, to be removed to the State having Jurisdiction of the Crime.

ARTICLE VI

[2] This Constitution, and the Laws of the United States which shall be made in Pursuance thereof; and all Treaties made, or which shall be made, under the Authority of the United States, shall be the supreme Law of the Land; and the Judges in every State shall be bound thereby, any Thing in the Constitution or Laws of any State to the Contrary notwithstanding.

* * *

AMENDMENT I [1791]

Congress shall make no law respecting an establishment of religion, or prohibiting the free exercise thereof; or abridging the freedom of speech, or of the press; or the right of the people peaceably to assemble, and to petition the Government for a redress of grievances.

AMENDMENT II [1791]

A well regulated Militia, being necessary to the security of a free State, the right of the people to keep and bear Arms, shall not be infringed.

AMENDMENT III [1791]

No Soldier shall, in times of peace be quartered in any house, without the consent of the Owner, nor in time of war, but in a manner to be prescribed by law.

AMENDMENT IV [1791]

The right of the people to be secure in their persons, houses, papers, and effects, against unreasonable searches and seizures, shall not be violated, and no Warrants shall issue, but upon probable cause, supported by Oath or affirmation, and particularly describing the place to be searched, and the persons or things to be seized.

AMENDMENT V [1791]

No person shall be held to answer for a capital, or otherwise infamous crime, unless on a presentment or indictment of a Grand Jury, except in cases arising in the land or naval forces, or in the Militia, when in actual service in time of War or public danger; nor shall any person be subject for the same offence to be twice put in jeopardy of life or limb; nor shall be compelled in any criminal case to be a witness against himself, nor be deprived of life, liberty, or property, without due process of law; nor shall private property be taken for public use, without just compensation.

AMENDMENT VI [1791]

In all criminal prosecutions, the accused shall enjoy the right to a speedy and public trial, by an impartial jury of the State and district wherein the crime shall have been committed, which district shall have been previously ascertained by law, and to be informed of the nature and cause of the accusation; to be confronted with the witnesses against him; to have compulsory process for obtaining witnesses in his favor, and to have the Assistance of Counsel for his defence.

AMENDMENT VII [1791]

In Suits at common law, where the value in controversy shall exceed twenty dollars, the right of trial by jury shall be preserved, and no fact tried by jury, shall be otherwise re-examined in any Court of the United States, than according to the rules of the common law.

AMENDMENT VIII [1791]

Excessive bail shall not be required, nor excessive fines imposed, nor cruel and unusual punishment inflicted.

AMENDMENT IX [1791]

The enumeration in the Constitution, of certain rights, shall not be construed to deny or disparage others retained by the people.

AMENDMENT X [1791]

The powers not delegated to the United States by the Constitution, nor prohibited by it to the States, are reserved to the States respectively, or to the people.

AMENDMENT XIII [1865]

Section 1.   Neither slavery nor involuntary servitude, except as a punishment for crime whereof the party shall have been duly convicted, shall exist within the United States, or any place subject to their jurisdiction.

Section 2.   Congress shall have power to enforce this article by appropriate legislation.

AMENDMENT XIV [1868]

Section 1.   All persons born or naturalized in the United States, and subject to the jurisdiction thereof, are citizens of the United States and of the State wherein they reside. No State shall make or enforce any law which shall abridge the privileges or immunities of citizens of the United States; nor shall any State deprive any person of life, liberty, or property, without due process of law; nor deny to any person within its jurisdiction the equal protection of the laws. * * *

Section 5.   The Congress shall have power to enforce, by appropriate legislation, the provisions of this article.

AMENDMENT XV [1870]

Section 1.   The right of citizens of the United States to vote shall not be denied or abridged by the United States or by any State on account of race, color, or previous condition of servitude.

Section 2.   The Congress shall have the power to enforce this article by appropriate legislation.

MEMBERS OF THE SUPREME COURT

Justice	Appointed By	State	To Replace	Judicial Oath Taken	Date Service Ended
Jay Chief Justice	Washington	NY	New Seat	10/19/1789	6/29/1795
Cushing	Washington	MA	New Seat	2/2/1790	9/13/1810
Rutledge, J.	Washington	SC	New Seat	2/15/1790	3/5/1791
Rutledge,[1] Chief Justice	Washington	SC	Jay	8/12/1795	12/15/1795
Wilson	Washington	PA	New Seat	10/5/1789	8/21/1798
Blair	Washington	VA	New Seat	2/2/1790	10/25/1795
Iredell	Washington	NC	New Seat	5/12/1790	10/20/1799
Johnson, T.	Washington	MD	Rutledge, J./Jay	8/6/1792	1/16/1793
Paterson	Washington	NJ	Johnson, T.	3/11/1793	9/9/1806
Chase, S.	Washington	MD	Blair	2/4/1796	6/19/1811
Ellsworth, Chief Justice	Washington	CT	Rutledge, J.	3/8/1796	12/15/1800
Washington	Adams, J.	VA	Wilson	2/4/1799	11/26/1829
Moore	Adams, J	NC	Iredell	4/21/1800	1/26/1804
Marshall, J., Chief Justice	Adams, J.	VA	Ellsworth	2/4/1801	7/6/1835
Johnson, W.	Jefferson	SC	Moore	5/7/1804	8/4/1834
Livingston	Jefferson	NY	Paterson	1/20/1807	3/18/1823
Todd	Jefferson	KY	New Seat	5/4/1807	2/7/1826
Duvall	Madison	MD	Chase, S.	11/23/1811	1/14/1835
Story	Madison	MA	Cushing	2/3/1812	9/10/1845
Thompson	Monroe	NY	Livingston	9/1/1823	12/18/1843
Trimble	Adams, J.Q.	KY	Todd	6/16/1826	8/25/1828

---

[1] Recess appointment; nominated 7/1/1795; rejected by Senate 12/15/1795.

Justice	Appointed By	State	To Replace	Judicial Oath Taken	Date Service Ended
McLean	Jackson	OH	Trimble	1/11/1830	4/4/1861
Baldwin	Jackson	PA	Washington	1/18/1830	4/21/1844
Wayne	Jackson	GA	Johnson, W.	1/14/1835	7/5/1867
Taney, Chief Justice	Jackson	MD	Marshall, J.	3/28/1836	10/12/1864
Barbour	Jackson	VA	Duvall	5/12/1836	2/25/1841
Catron	Van Buren	TN	New Seat	5/1/1837	5/30/1865
McKinley	Van Buren	AL	New Seat	1/9/1838	7/19/1852
Daniel	Van Buren	VA	Barbour	1/10/1842	5/31/1860
Nelson	Tyler	NY	Thompson	2/27/1845	11/28/1872
Woodbury	Polk	NH	Story	9/23/1845	9/4/1851
Grier	Polk	PA	Baldwin	8/10/1846	1/31/1870
Curtis	Fillmore	MA	Woodbury	10/10/1851	9/30/1857
Campbell	Pierce	AL	McKinley	4/11/1853	4/30/1861
Clifford	Buchanan	ME	Curtis	1/21/1858	7/25/1881
Swayne	Lincoln	OH	McLean	1/27/1862	1/24/1881
Miller	Lincoln	IA	Daniel	7/21/1862	10/13/1890
Davis	Lincoln	IL	Campbell	12/10/1862	3/4/1877
Field[2]	Lincoln	CA	New Seat	5/20/1863	12/1/1897
Chase, S.P., Chief Justice	Lincoln	OH	Taney	12/15/1864	5/7/1873
Strong	Grant	PA	Grier	3/14/1870	12/14/1880
Bradley	Grant	NJ	New Seat	3/23/1870	1/22/1892
Hunt	Grant	NY	Nelson	1/9/1873	1/27/1882

---

[2] Longest-serving member until Douglas; apparently he was intent on remaining on the Court longer than the record held by John Marshall and he refused to step down even when asked to do so by the other Justices; he did increasingly less Court work through the 1890s, and by the time of his retirement he was practically useless to his colleagues. *See, e.g.,* CARL BRENT SWISHES, STEPHEN J. FIELD, CRAFTSMAN OF THE LAW (1930); G. EDWARD WHITE, THE AMERICAN JUDICIAL TRADITION (1976).

Justice	Appointed By	State	To Replace	Judicial Oath Taken	Date Service Ended
Waite, Chief Justice	Grant	OH	Chase, S.P.	3/4/1874	3/23/1888
Harlan I	Hayes	KY	Davis	12/10/1877	10/14/1911
Woods	Hayes	GA	Strong	1/5/1881	5/14/1887
Matthews	Garfield	OH	Swayne	5/17/1881	3/22/1889
Gray	Arthur	MA	Clifford	1/9/1882	9/15/1902
Blatchford	Arthur	NY	Hunt	4/3/1882	7/7/1893
Lamar, L.	Cleveland	MS	Woods	1/18/1888	1/23/1893
Fuller, Chief Justice	Cleveland	IL	Waite	10/8/1888	7/4/1910
Brewer	Harrison, B.	KS	Matthews	1/6/1890	3/28/1910
Brown	Harrison, B.	MI	Miller	1/5/1891	5/28/1906
Shiras	Harrison, B.	PA	Bradley	10/10/1892	2/23/1903
Jackson. H.	Harrison, B.	TN	Lamar, L.	3/4/1893	8/8/1895
White E.	Cleveland	LA	Blatchford	3/12/1894	12/18/1910
White, E., Chief Justice	Taft	LA	Fuller	12/19/1910	5/19/1921
Peckham	Cleveland	NY	Jackson, H	1/6/1896	10/24/1909
McKenna	McKinley	CA	Filed	1/26/1898	1/5/1925
Holmes	Roosevelt, T.	MA	Gray	12/8/1902	1/12/1932
Day	Roosevelt, T.	OH	Shiras	3/2/1903	11/13/1922
Moody	Roosevelt, T.	MA	Brown	12/17/1906	11/20/1910
Lurton	Taft	TN	Peckham	1/3/1910	7/12/1914
Hughes	Taft	NY	Brewer	10/10/1910	6/10/1916
Hughes, Chief Justice	Hoover	NY	Taft	2/24/1930	6/30/1941
Van Devanter	Taft	WY	White, E.	1/3/1911	6/21/1937
Lamar, J	Taft	GA	Moody	1/3/1911	1/2/1916

Justice	Appointed By	State	To Replace	Judicial Oath Taken	Date Service Ended
Pitney	Taft	NJ	Harlan I	3/18/1912	12/31/1922
McReynolds	Wilson	TN	Lurton	10/12/1914	1/31/1941
Brandeis	Wilson	MA	Lamar, J.	6/5/1916	2/13/1939
Clarke	Wilson	OH	Hughes	10/9/1916	9/18/1922
Taft, Chief Justice	Harding	CT	White, E	7/11/1921	2/3/1930
Sutherland	Harding	UT	Clarke	10/2/1922	1/17/1938
Butler	Harding	MN	Day	1/2/1923	11/16/1939
Sanford	Harding	TN	Pitney	2/19/1923	3/8/1930
Stone	Coolidge	NY	McKenna	3/2/1925	7/2/1941
Stone, Chief Justice	Roosevelt, F.	NY	Hughes	7/3/1941	4/22/1946
Roberts	Hoover	PA	Sanford	6/2/1930	7/31/1945
Cardozo	Hoover	NY	Holmes	3/14/1932	7/9/1938
Black	Roosevelt, F.	AL	Van Devanter	8/19/1937	9/17/1971
Reed	Roosevelt, F.	KY	Sutherland	1/31/1938	2/25/1957
Frankfurter	Roosevelt, F.	MA	Cardozo	1/30/1939	8/28/1962
Douglas[3]	Roosevelt, F.	CT	Brandeis	4/17/1939	11/12/1975
Murphy	Roosevelt, F	MI	Butler	2/5/1940	7/19/1949
Byrnes	Roosevelt, F.	SC	McReynolds	7/8/1941	10/3/1942
Jackson, R.	Roosevelt, F.	NY	Stone/Hughes	7/11/1941	10/9/1954
Rutledge, W.	Roosevelt, F	IA	Byrnes	2/15/1943	9/10/1949
Burton	Truman	OH	Roberts	10/1/1945	10/13/1958
Vinson, Chief Justice	Truman	KY	Stone	6/24/1946	9/8/1953
Clark	Truman	TX	Murphy	8/24/1949	6/12/1967
Minton	Truman	IN	Rutledge, W.	10/12/1949	10/15/1956

[3]   Longest serving member to date.

Justice	Appointed By	State	To Replace	Judicial Oath Taken	Date Service Ended
Warren,[4] Chief Justice	Eisenhower	CA	Vinson	10/5/1953	6/23/1969
Harlan II	Eisenhower	NY	Jackson, R	3/28/1955	9/23/1971
Brennan	Eisenhower	NJ	Minton	10/16/1956	7/20/1990
Whittaker	Eisenhower	MO	Reed	3/25/1957	3/31/1962
Stewart	Eisenhower	OH	Burton	10/14/1958	7/3/1981
White, B.	Kennedy	CO	Whittaker	4/16/1962	6/28/1993
Goldberg	Kennedy	IL	Frankfurter	10/1/1962	7/25/1965
Fortas	Johnson, L.	TN	Goldberg	10/4/1965	5/14/1969
Marshall, T.	Johnson, L.	NY	Clark	10/2/1967	10/1/1991
Burger, Chief Justice	Nixon	VA	Warren	6/23/1969	9/26/1986
Blackmun	Nixon	MN	Forks	6/9/1970	8/3/1994
Powell	Nixon	VA	Black	1/7/1972	6/26/1987
Rehnquist	Nixon	AZ	Harlan II	1/7/1972	9/26/1986
Rehnquist, Chief Justice	Reagan	AZ	Burger	9/26/1986	9/3/2005
Stevens	Ford	IL	Douglas	12/19/1975	6/28/2010
O'Connor	Reagan	AZ	Stewart	9/25/1981	1/31/2006
Scalia	Reagan	VA	Rehnquist /Burger	9/26/1986	2/13/2016
Kennedy	Reagan	CA	Powell	2/18/1988	
Souter	Bush	NH	Brennan	10/9/1990	6/29/2009
Thomas	Bush	GA	Marshall, T	10/23/1991	
Ginsburg	Clinton	NY	White, B.	8/10/1993	
Breyer	Clinton	MA	Blackmun	8/3/1994	

---

[4] Joined the Court as a recess appointment on opening day of the 1953 term, shortly after Chief Justice Fred Vinson died unexpectedly; appointment was not confirmed by the Senate until March 1, 1954.

Justice	Appointed By	State	To Replace	Judicial Oath Taken	Date Service Ended
Roberts, Chief Justice	Bush	MD	Rehnquist	9/29/2005	
Alito	Bush	NJ	O'Connor	1/31/2006	
Sotomayor	Obama	NY	Souter	8/8/2009	
Kagan	Obama	MA	Stevens	8/7/2010	

CHAPTER 1

THE CRIMINAL PROCESS: FAILURES, CHOICES, AND LEGITIMACY

■ ■ ■

A. FAILURES

1. INTRODUCTION

Fear of government is fused deep within the American soul. We were born of a violent revolution against a parliament and king that the colonists viewed as powerful and hostile. When the Articles of Confederation failed, America's leaders constructed a more tightly-knit central government. But the prospect of a federal government, as opposed to a loose coalition of states, reminded many of the yoke that they had just thrown off. The president could become a king, and the Congress could become the feared English parliament. The new central government was hotly debated and barely ratified in the key states of Virginia and New York. Part of the price of ratification was the promise of a Bill of Rights that would protect Americans from government. Today, we tend to think of rights as bestowing individual liberty. While that is true enough, the founders saw the Bill of Rights primarily as a barrier to the government created in the body of the Constitution.

It is difficult for us, over two centuries later, to understand the fear of the looming central government. With the writs of assistance and excise searches by British officials still fresh in their minds, the Anti-federalists saw potential abuses of federal power everywhere they looked. Arguing against ratification of the Constitution without a bill of rights, Patrick Henry worried that "any man may be seized, any property may be taken, in the most arbitrary manner, without any evidence or reason. Every thing the most sacred may be searched and ransacked by the strong hand of [federal] power." 3 Elliot's Debates 588 (1836) He also predicted that

> [t]he officers of Congress may come upon you now, fortified with all the terrors of paramount federal authority. Excisemen may come in multitudes; for the limitation of their numbers no man knows. They may, unless the general government be restrained by a bill of rights, or some similar restriction, go into cellars and

rooms, and search, ransack, and measure, every thing you eat, drink, and wear.

Id. at 448–49. An anonymous Anti-federalist said in 1787 that excise searches by the federal government would lead "our bed-chambers to be searched by the brutal tools of power." William J. Cuddihy, The Fourth Amendment 678 (2009).

The deep-seated fear of the central government led directly to the drafting and ratification of the Bill of Rights. Early Americans viewed the Bill of Rights as a wall between themselves and the central government. It guaranteed free speech, a free press, and freedom of religion, while forbidding a national religion; it guaranteed a criminal process that is difficult to manipulate; and, in the Ninth and Tenth Amendments, it specifically reserved rights and powers to the people and the States.

> The potential tyrant has been hobbled. The citizens of the States are free to criticize the central government, to petition it, and to close their doors against its agents. Moreover, the prosecutors and judges of the central government can reach the citizens of States only through a rigorous process that includes the right to nonexcessive bail, to trial by juries drawn from the community, to assistance of counsel, and to confront accusers who might not be telling the truth. The Supreme Court comprehends that the Bill of Rights was meant to limit severely the powers of the central government, erecting a formidable wall between the citizens and the government. The Court interprets these provisions to require federal prosecutors to walk through a narrow gate in the wall. The gate is hedged with a series of requirements designed to make convictions more difficult to obtain.

See George C. Thomas III, *When Constitutional Worlds Collide: Resurrecting the Framers' Bill of Rights and Criminal Procedure*, 100 Mich. L. Rev. 145, 149 (2001).

An example of how difficult it was to obtain convictions is the Supreme Court's early intervention in the Aaron Burr case. In 1806, President Jefferson uncovered what he thought was a plot by Burr to invade Mexico, "place himself on its throne," and annex the entire Louisiana Purchase to his empire that would then be far larger than the United States. Jean Edward Smith, John Marshall: Definer of a Nation 353 (1996). Two alleged co-conspirators were arrested and held on charges of treason. The prisoners filed a writ of habeas corpus and asked the Supreme Court to rule on the legality of their detention. Several affidavits were filed in federal court alleging the details of the plot. But the Supreme Court held that the most the affidavits showed was a conspiracy to commit treason, rather than treason, and ordered the prisoners released because the government had charged treason and not conspiracy to commit treason. Ex parte Bollman & Ex parte Swartwout, 8 U.S. (4 Cranch.) 75, 2 L. Ed. 554 (1807). It is easy for us today to dismiss Burr's plans as a fantasy, but the Republic was barely twenty years old, most of North America was unsettled by Europeans, and Burr was a charismatic politician befriended by ambitious military generals. Ordering the release of two admitted conspirators was both a brave act on the part of Chief Justice Marshall's Court and a demonstration of the barrier that the Bill of Rights posed to federal power.

Significance

But the Bill of Rights did not restrain the state governments. See Barron v. Baltimore, 32 U.S. (7 Pet.) 243, 8 L.Ed. 672 (1833). As the United States careened toward the Civil War and its aftermath, state governments replaced the federal government as the principal threat to liberty and privacy. This would, of course, eventually lead to the Civil War Amendments that included the rights to due process and equal protection that directly limited state power. Initially, however, the Court interpreted the Fourteenth Amendment narrowly. See, *e.g.*, Slaughter-House Cases, 83 U.S. (16 Wall.) 36, 21 L.Ed. 394 (1873) (holding that the privileges and immunities clause protected only rights that existed *by virtue of national citizenship*, which did not include the rights guaranteed in the Bill of Rights). This narrow compass of the Fourteenth Amendment permitted states to deny rights that existed against the federal government. These denials of liberty might be viewed as failures of state criminal processes.

Some of the failures went to the investigation of crime, where state courts sometimes permitted investigation techniques that would not be permitted if conducted by federal officers. In 1907, the Supreme Court refused to review a claim that a confession was compelled because made "while in the 'sweat box' of the St. Louis police department." The "sweat box" was a euphemism for physically coercive interrogation that was sometimes compared to torture used in the Spanish Inquisition. The Court rejected the idea that the federal Fifth Amendment privilege against compelled self-incrimination through the Fourteenth Amendment offered broader due process protection than state law: If "the admission of this testimony did not violate the rights of the plaintiff in error under the Constitution and laws of the state of Missouri, the record affords no basis for holding that he was not awarded due process of law." Barrington v. Missouri, 205 U.S. 483, 486–87, 27 S.Ct. 582, 51 L.Ed. 890 (1907).

Barrington stands in marked contrast to Bram v. United States, 168 U.S. 532, 18 S.Ct. 183, 42 L.Ed. 568 (1898), where the Court held in a federal case that "any degree of influence" on a prisoner made his confession inadmissible as a matter of federal law. In *Bram*, the Court found "that an influence was exerted, and, as any doubt as to whether the confession was voluntary must be determined in favor of the accused, we cannot escape the conclusion that error was committed by the trial court in admitting the confession under the circumstances disclosed by the record." As *Barrington* and *Bram* were separated by only nine years, and many of the same justices sat on both cases, the only explanation is that the federal right against compelled self-incrimination provided a broader protection than the Fourteenth Amendment due process clause.

Barrington was a narrow interpretation of the Fourteenth Amendment due process clause: If it provides no protection beyond that of state law, then it adds nothing to existing law. The *Barrington* interpretation would not last. States that permitted outrageous investigative methods and trial procedures eventually pushed the Court to recognize broad protections under the due process clause. Thirty years after *Barrington*, the Court was faced with a state investigative failure that it could not ignore. And this time the defendant lodged his constitutional claim under the Fourteenth Amendment due process clause rather than the Fifth Amendment privilege against compelled self-incrimination.

2. INVESTIGATION FAILURES

BROWN V. MISSISSIPPI
Supreme Court of the United States, 1936.
297 U.S. 278, 56 S.Ct. 461, 80 L.Ed. 682.

MR. CHIEF JUSTICE HUGHES delivered the opinion of the Court [joined by JUSTICES VAN DEVANTER, MCREYNOLDS, BRANDEIS, SUTHERLAND, BUTLER, STONE, ROBERTS, and CARDOZO].

Issue

The question in this case is whether convictions, which rest solely upon confessions shown to have been extorted by officers of the State by brutality and violence, are consistent with the due process of law required by the Fourteenth Amendment of the Constitution of the United States.

Petitioners were indicted for the murder of one Raymond Stewart, whose death occurred on March 30, 1934. They were indicted on April 4, 1934, and were then arraigned and pleaded not guilty. Counsel were appointed by the court to defend them. Trial was begun the next morning and was concluded on the following day, when they were found guilty and sentenced to death.

Trial court holding

Aside from the confessions, there was no evidence sufficient to warrant the submission of the case to the jury. After a preliminary inquiry, testimony as to the confessions was received over the objection of defendants' counsel. Defendants then testified that the confessions were false and had been procured by physical torture. The case went to the jury with instructions, upon the request of defendants' counsel, that if the jury had reasonable doubt as to the confessions having resulted from coercion,

Δ arguments

and that they were not true, they were not to be considered as evidence. On their appeal to the Supreme Court of the State, defendants assigned as error the inadmissibility of the confessions. The judgment was affirmed.

[handwritten: Appellate court affirmed.]

Defendants then moved in the Supreme Court of the State to arrest the judgment and for a new trial on the ground that all the evidence against them was obtained by coercion and brutality known to the court and to the district attorney, and that defendants had been denied the benefit of counsel or opportunity to confer with counsel in a reasonable manner. The motion was supported by affidavits. At about the same time, defendants filed in the Supreme Court a "suggestion of error" explicitly challenging the proceedings of the trial, in the use of the confessions and with respect to the alleged denial of representation by counsel, as violating the due process clause of the Fourteenth Amendment of the Constitution of the United States. The state court entertained the suggestion of error, considered the federal question, and decided it against defendants' contentions. Two judges dissented. * * *

[handwritten: Supreme court affirmed.]

The grounds of the decision were (1) that immunity from self-incrimination is not essential to due process of law, and (2) that the failure of the trial court to exclude the confessions after the introduction of evidence showing their incompetency, in the absence of a request for such exclusion, did not deprive the defendants of life or liberty without due process of law; and that even if the trial court had erroneously overruled a motion to exclude the confessions, the ruling would have been mere error reversible on appeal, but not a violation of constitutional right.

The opinion of the state court did not set forth the evidence as to the circumstances in which the confessions were procured. That the evidence established that they were procured by coercion was not questioned. The state court said: "After the state closed its case on the merits, the appellants, for the first time, introduced evidence from which it appears that the confessions were not made voluntarily but were coerced." There is no dispute as to the facts upon this point, and as they are clearly and adequately stated in the dissenting opinion of Judge Griffith (with whom Judge Anderson concurred)—showing both the extreme brutality of the measures to extort the confessions and the participation of the state authorities—we quote this part of his opinion in full, as follows:

"The crime with which these defendants, all ignorant negroes, are charged, was discovered about one o'clock p.m. on Friday, March 30, 1934. On that night one Dial, a deputy sheriff, accompanied by others, came to the home of Ellington, one of the defendants, and requested him to accompany them to the house of the deceased, and there a number of white men were gathered, who began to accuse the defendant of the crime. Upon his denial they seized him, and with the participation of the deputy they hanged him by a rope to the limb of a tree, and having let him down, they hung him again, and when he was let down the second time, and he still protested his innocence, he was tied to a tree and whipped, and still declining to accede to the demands that he confess, he was finally released and he returned with some difficulty to his home, suffering intense pain and agony. The record of the testimony shows that the signs of the rope on his neck were plainly visible during the so-called trial. A day or two thereafter the said deputy, accompanied by another, returned to the home of the said defendant and arrested him, and departed with the prisoner towards the jail in an adjoining county, but went by a route which led into the State of Alabama; and while on the way, in that State, the deputy stopped and again severely whipped the defendant, declaring that he would continue the whipping until he confessed, and the defendant then agreed to confess to such a statement as the deputy would dictate, and he did so, after which he was delivered to jail.

"The other two defendants, Ed Brown and Henry Shields, were also arrested and taken to the same jail. On Sunday night, April 1, 1934, the same deputy, accompanied by a number of white men, one of whom was also an officer, and by the jailer, came to the jail, and the two last named defendants were made to strip and they were laid over chairs and their backs were cut to pieces with a leather strap with buckles on it, and they were likewise made by the said deputy definitely to understand that the whipping would be continued unless and until they confessed, and not only confessed, but confessed in every matter of detail as demanded by those present; and in this manner the defendants confessed the crime, and as the whippings progressed and were repeated, they changed or adjusted their confession in all particulars of detail so as to conform to the demands of their torturers. When the confessions had been obtained in the exact form and contents as desired by the mob, they left with the parting admonition and warning that, if the defendants changed their story at any time in any respect from that last stated, the perpetrators of the outrage would administer the same or equally effective treatment.

threatened!

"Further details of the brutal treatment to which these helpless prisoners were subjected need not be pursued. It is sufficient to say that in pertinent respects the transcript reads more like pages torn from some medieval account, than a record made within the confines of a modern civilization which aspires to an enlightened constitutional government.

"All this having been accomplished, on the next day, that is, on Monday, April 2, when the defendants had been given time to recuperate somewhat from the tortures to which they had been subjected, the two sheriffs, one of the county where the crime was committed, and the other of the county of the jail in which the prisoners were confined, came to the jail, accompanied by eight other persons, some of them deputies, there to hear the free and voluntary confession of these miserable and abject defendants. The sheriff of the county of the crime admitted that he had heard of the whipping, but averred that he had no personal knowledge of it. He admitted that one of the defendants, when brought before him to confess, was limping and did not sit down, and that this particular defendant then and there stated that he had been strapped so severely that he could not sit down, and as already stated, the signs of the rope on the neck of another of the defendants were plainly visible to all. Nevertheless the solemn farce of hearing the free and voluntary confessions was gone through with, and these two sheriffs and one other person then present were the three witnesses used in court to establish the so-called confessions, which were received by the court and admitted in evidence over the objections of the defendants duly entered of record as each of the said three witnesses delivered their alleged testimony. There was thus enough before the court when these confessions were first offered to make known to the court that they were not, beyond all reasonable doubt, free and voluntary; and the failure of the court then to exclude the confessions is sufficient to reverse the judgment, under every rule of procedure that has heretofore been prescribed, and hence it was not necessary subsequently to renew the objections by motion or otherwise.

"The spurious confessions having been obtained—and the farce last mentioned having been gone through with on Monday, April 2d—the court, then in session, on the following day, Tuesday, April 3, 1934, ordered the grand jury to reassemble on the succeeding day, April 4, 1934, at nine o'clock, and on the morning of the day last mentioned the grand jury returned an indictment against the defendants for murder. Late that afternoon the defendants were brought from the jail in the adjoining county and arraigned, when one or more of them offered to plead guilty, which the court declined to accept, and, upon inquiry whether they had or desired counsel, they stated that they had none, and did not suppose that counsel could be of any assistance to them. The court thereupon appointed counsel, and set the case for trial for the following morning at nine o'clock, and the defendants were returned to the jail in the adjoining county about thirty miles away.

"The defendants were brought to the courthouse of the county on the following morning, April 5th, and the so-called trial was opened, and was concluded on the next day, April 6, 1934, and resulted in a pretended conviction with death sentences. The evidence upon which the conviction was obtained was the so-called confessions. Without this evidence a peremptory instruction to find for the defendants would have been inescapable. The defendants were put on the stand, and by their testimony the facts and the details thereof as to the manner by which the confessions were extorted from them were fully developed, and it is further disclosed by the record that the same deputy, Dial, under whose guiding hand and active participation the tortures to coerce the confessions were administered, was actively in the performance of the supposed duties of a court deputy in the courthouse and in the presence of the prisoners during what is denominated, in complimentary terms, the trial of these defendants. This deputy was put on the stand by the state in rebuttal, and <u>admitted</u> the whippings. It is interesting to note that in his testimony with reference to the whipping of the defendant Ellington, and in response to the inquiry as to how severely he was whipped, the deputy stated, 'Not too much for a negro; not as much as I would have done if it were left to me.' Two others who had participated in these whippings were introduced and admitted it—not a single witness was introduced who denied it. The facts are not only undisputed, they are admitted, and admitted to have been done by officers of the state, in conjunction with other participants, and all this was <u>definitely well known</u> to everybody connected with the trial, and during the trial, including the state's prosecuting attorney and the trial judge presiding."

1.   The State stresses the statement in *Twining v. New Jersey*, 211 U.S. 78, 114, 29 S.Ct. 14, 26, 53 L.Ed. 97, that "exemption from compulsory self-incrimination in the courts of the States is not secured by any part of the Federal Constitution," and the statement in *Snyder v. Massachusetts*, 291 U.S. 97, 105, 54 S.Ct. 330, 332, 78 L.Ed. 674, 90 A.L.R. 575, that "the privilege against self-incrimination may be withdrawn and the accused put upon the stand as a witness for the State." But the question of the right of the State to withdraw the privilege against self-incrimination is not here involved. The compulsion to which the quoted statements refer is that of the processes of justice by which the accused may be called as a witness and required to testify. Compulsion by torture to extort a confession is a different matter.

The State is free to regulate the procedure of its courts in accordance with its own conceptions of policy, unless in so doing it "offends some principle of justice so rooted in the traditions and conscience of our people as to be ranked as fundamental." The State may abolish trial by jury. It may dispense with indictment by a grand jury and substitute complaint or information. But the freedom of the State in establishing its policy is the freedom of constitutional government and is limited by the requirement of due process of law. Because a State may dispense with a jury trial, it does not follow that it may substitute trial by ordeal. The rack and torture chamber may not be substituted for the witness stand. The State may not permit an accused to be hurried to conviction under mob domination—where the whole proceeding is but a mask—without supplying corrective process. The State may not deny to the accused the aid of counsel. *Powell v. Alabama*, [p. 25]. Nor may a State, through the action of its officers, contrive a conviction through the pretense of a trial which in truth is "but used as a means of depriving a defendant of liberty through a deliberate deception of court and jury by the presentation of testimony known to be perjured." And the trial equally is a mere pretense where the state authorities have contrived a conviction resting solely upon confessions obtained by violence. The due process clause requires "that state action, whether through one agency or another, shall be consistent with the fundamental principles of liberty and justice which lie at the base of all our civil and political institutions." It would be difficult to conceive of methods more revolting to the sense of justice than those taken to procure the confessions of these petitioners, and the use of the confessions thus obtained as the basis for conviction and sentence was a clear denial of due process.

2.   It is in this view that the further contention of the State must be considered. That contention rests upon the failure of counsel for the accused, who had objected to the admissibility of the confessions, to move for their exclusion after they had been introduced and the fact of coercion had been proved. It is a contention which proceeds upon a misconception of the nature of petitioners' complaint. That complaint is not of the commission of mere error, but of a wrong so fundamental that it made the whole proceeding a mere pretense of a trial and rendered the conviction and sentence wholly void. We are not concerned with a mere question of state practice, or whether counsel assigned to petitioners were competent or mistakenly assumed that their first objections were sufficient. In an earlier case the Supreme Court of the State had recognized the duty of the court to supply corrective process where due process of law had been denied. * * * [T]he court said: "Coercing the supposed state's criminals into confessions and using such confessions so coerced from them against them in trials has been the curse of all countries. It was the chief iniquity, the crowning infamy of the Star Chamber, and the Inquisition, and other similar institutions. The constitution recognized the evils that lay behind these practices and prohibited them in this country. * * * The duty of maintaining constitutional rights of a person on trial for his life rises above mere rules of procedure and wherever the court is clearly satisfied that such violations exist, it will refuse to sanction such violations and will apply the corrective."

In the instant case, the trial court was fully advised by the undisputed evidence of the way in which the confessions had been procured. The trial court knew that there was no other evidence upon which conviction and sentence could be based. Yet it proceeded to permit conviction and to pronounce sentence. The conviction and sentence were void for want of the essential elements of due process, and the proceeding thus vitiated could be challenged in any appropriate manner. It was challenged before the Supreme Court of the State by the express invocation of the Fourteenth Amendment. That court entertained the challenge, considered the federal question thus presented, but declined to enforce petitioners' constitutional right. The court thus denied a federal right fully established and specially set up and claimed and the judgment must be

Reversed.

NOTES AND QUESTIONS

1. The Court in 1936 was loathe to meddle in state criminal procedure. But how could the Court have done anything other than reverse the Mississippi courts on the outrageous facts of *Brown*? A more difficult question is how could the state supreme court have affirmed the convictions. How did the state court justify that conclusion? Does the argument seem plausible?

2. Notice that the Court drew the facts of the coercion/torture exclusively from the dissent in the Mississippi Supreme Court. Why do you think the Court did this?

3. Whenever some historical fact seems unbelievable—the deputies' conduct and the state court's opinion in Brown, for example—we should seek to recover what might have been different about that historic period. Consider this observation about *Powell v. Alabama*, p. 25, an earlier failure of Southern justice: "If all of this seems extraordinary to modern eyes, one must remember that for white southerners defending mob-dominated trials, the relevant comparison was to lynchings rather than to elaborate court proceedings accompanied by all the trappings of due process." Michael Klarman, *The Racial Origins of Modern Criminal Procedure*, 99 Mich. L. Rev. 48, 56 (2000). Would it be fair to say that the defendants in *Brown* should be thankful for the torture because their confessions led to a court case rather than a lynching?

4. *Brown: the rest of the story.* Are you surprised to learn that, upon remand from the United States Supreme Court, the three defendants in *Brown* accepted plea bargains rather than risk a retrial? They served from three to seven years in prison. Klarman, *supra*, at 82.

Are you surprised to learn that the prosecutor in *Brown* later served forty-two years as a United States senator? He was John Stennis, who ran for office in Mississippi thirteen times and never lost. See http://bioguide. congress.gov/scripts/biodisplay.pl?index=s000852.

5. Racism, of course, is not limited to the South. Consider the New York City Draft Riots, which raged for five days in July of 1863. The riots were touched off by working-class hostility to the military draft, from which the affluent could purchase an exemption for a $300 fee. While rioters initially concentrated on institutions associated with the draft (the government, the elite, capitalism and the Republican Party), the mob's rage soon expanded to New York's African-American population, which it saw as competition for scarce employment. The Colored Orphan Asylum, located at Fifth Avenue and Forty-third Street, was burned and looted, although most

of the children were safely evacuated. One little girl was found by the mob hiding under a bed, and killed.

One newspaper reported, "A perfect reign of terror exists in the quarters of this helpless people, and if the troubles which now agitate our city continue during the week it is believed that not a single negro will remain within the metropolitan limits." New York Herald, July 15, 1863. Peter Houston, a Mohawk Indian, was mistaken for an African-American and beaten to death. Just off the Bowery, one crowd set a building ablaze where African-Americans lived, waited for their victims to fall from the eaves of the rooftop, and beat them to death. Ann Derrickson, a white woman married to an African-American, was beaten by the mob as she saved her son's life. She died of her wounds. On Eighth Avenue, the mob re-strung the bodies of its African-American victims from lampposts after the authorities had come by and cut them down. Mobs also looted and burned the homes of whites who offered African-Americans safe-harbor, as well as businesses that catered to a racially mixed clientele.

The Union Army arrived from Gettysburg, where ten days earlier it had defeated Lee's Army of Northern Virginia, and put down the uprising. In the aftermath, New York's African-American population shrank by as much as a quarter. Many left for Hoboken, the outer boroughs, and the suburbs. See James McCague, The Second Rebellion: The Story of the New York City Draft Riots of 1863 (1968); see also Racial Violence in the United States, Allen D, Grimshaw, ed. (1968) at 37–42.

6.   Nor is torture merely an unpleasant historical fact. We address contemporary uses in Chapter 6. In the next sub-section, we address a failure of the trial process.

3.   TRIAL FAILURES

JAMES GOODMAN—STORIES OF SCOTTSBORO
(1995) 4–6, 13–16, 19, 21–23.

The train from Chattanooga to Memphis passed through northern Alabama on the night of March 25, 1931. Nine black youths and several white youths were riding the freight train illegally. Four of the blacks were friends who had gotten on the train in Chattanooga. The black and white youths got into a fight, and the black youths "chased or threw" all but one of the whites from the train shortly after it pulled away from a station. At the next stop, Paint Rock, dozens of white men armed with pistols, rifles, and shotguns grabbed the blacks, "tied them to one another with a plow line," put them on a flatbed truck, and drove them to the jail in Scottsboro. * * *

[A deputy told them they were being held on assault and attempted murder charges.] They were in jail for hours before they found out that there would be another charge. Not until the guards took them out of their cell and lined them up against a wall and the sheriff brought two white women by and asked them to point to the boys who had "had them" did they realize that they had been accused of rape. One of the women, Victoria Price, pointed to six of them. When the other didn't say a word, a guard said that "If those six had Miss Price, it stands to reason that the others had Miss Bates." The boys protested, insisting they hadn't touched the women, hadn't even seen them before Paint Rock, when they saw them being led away from the train. Clarence Norris called the women liars. One of the guards struck him with his bayonet, cutting to the bone the hand that Norris put up to shield his face. "Nigger," the guard hollered, "you know damn well how to talk about white women."

"I was scared before," Norris recalled years later, "but it wasn't nothing to how I felt now. I knew if a white woman accused a black man of rape, he was as good as dead. My hand was bleeding like I don't know what * * * but I didn't even think about it. All I could think was that I was going to die for something that I had not done." * * *

Without some luck they would have been dead already. The night they were arrested they were nearly lynched by several hundred "crackers" who had gathered around the old, dilapidated two-story jail as the news of the arrest spread through the hills of Scottsboro and the neighboring towns. The men leading the mob threatened to break down the doors if the sheriff wouldn't let them in or let the "niggers" out. The boys could hear their voices through the window of their cell. * * *

They were saved by the Jackson County sheriff, M. L. Wann, who, unable to disperse the crowd, called the governor of Alabama, Benjamin Meeks Miller, who, in turn, called the National Guard. But the boys had no way of knowing that the National Guardsmen, white men with guns, distinguishable only by their uniforms from the men threatening to hang them, were not part of the lynching bee. Nor in the weeks that followed that sleepless night could they ever be certain that the guardsmen would protect them from the crowds that gathered every time they were moved from one prison to another or back and forth between prison and court. Men with uniforms had beaten or threatened them in every jail they had been in. * * *

Everything white Alabamans heard or read in the next few days confirmed the story that spread from Paint Rock and Scottsboro the day the posse stopped the train. The day after the arrest, newspapers reported that Price and Bates had identified the Negroes who had attacked them and that all of the Negroes had either confessed or been implicated by the others. Editors repeated these stories in every piece they ran about the case for a week; local reporters and editors, who lived in Scottsboro, Paint Rock, Huntsville, and Decatur and worked as stringers for the Associated Press, wrote the dispatches that the wire service carried all over the South, the first drafts of the newspaper articles most people read.

On April 6, twelve days after the crime, Judge A. E. Hawkins called the Jackson County Court to order. Three days in a row Price and Bates told their story to four different juries, and to a standing-room-only audience, from which women of all ages and men under twenty-one were excluded. At recess and adjournments the audience passed the story on to the crowd outside; reporters rushed to the nearest phone or telegraph office, ensuring that highlights of the testimony made the front pages of papers published later the same day. The white audience listened to Price and Bates tell the white jurors how all nine of the defendants held knives at their throats, pinned down their legs, tore off their clothes, and raped them.

"There were six to me," Price told the jury in the first trial, "and three to her, and three of hers got away. It took three of them to hold me. One was holding my legs and the other had a knife to my throat while the other one ravished me. It took three of those negroes to hold me. It took two to hold me while one had intercourse. The one sitting behind [the] defendants' counsel took my overalls off. My step-ins were torn off. * * * This negro boy tore them off. He held me while he took them off. Six of them had intercourse with me. The one sitting there was the first one. I don't know the name of the next one. * * * I know them when I see them. I can surely point out the next one. Yonder he sits, yonder. That boy had intercourse with me. The third one was the little bit of one; yonder he is. He held my legs while this one and that one ravished me and then he took my legs again." In what seemed like two or three hours, each of them was raped six times. They begged the Negroes to quit but the men ignored them, and even after they finished they stayed in the car with them, "telling us they were going to take us north and make us their women or kill us." * * *

Writers and editors all over the region agreed that it was the most atrocious crime ever recorded in that part of the country, perhaps in the whole United States, "a wholesale debauching of society * * * so horrible in its details that all the facts could never be printed," a "heinous and unspeakable crime" that "savored of the jungle, the way back dark ages of meanest African corruption." They were revolted by the story, but not surprised. Or if surprised, surprised only by the magnitude of the crime. They expected black men to rape white women. Blacks were savages, more savage, many argued (with scientific theories to support them), than they had been as slaves. Savages with an irrepressible sex drive and an appetite for white women. They were born rapists, rapists by instinct; given the chance, they struck. Two white women swore that they had been raped. Even if all nine of the boys had denied it and told the same story it is likely they would have been convicted; accusations much less serious and less substantiated had condemned black men. Bates and Price charged rape. Most of the boys denied it.[a] There was no question in anyone's mind about whom to believe. * * *

Victoria Price and Ruby Bates knew two versions of the events on that freight train, and they told one of them to the sheriff's deputies, local reporters, solicitor, judge, and jurors. In search of work, they had traveled to Chattanooga the only way they could afford. They had no luck in Chattanooga, and much worse luck on their way home, when they were brutally assaulted and repeatedly raped by nine black men. Had the posse not stopped the train in Paint Rock, the Negroes would have raped them again, or killed them, or taken them up north. "When I saw them nab those Negroes," Price told reporters, "I sure was happy. Mister, I never had a break in my life. Those Negroes have ruined me and Ruby forever. The only thing I ask is that they give them all the law allows." * * *

Price and Bates worked in the worst mills. They came from families that had been battered by underemployment and poverty in the best of times. They had meager schooling if any at all. They lived with their mothers in unpainted wooden shacks in the worst sections of town. Bates's family was the only white family on their block, and their block was in the Negro section of town.

Their lives mocked the white South's most sacred ideal. More prosperous southerners liked to boast that the color line extended from the top to the bottom of southern society, and often it did. Yet no one who looked carefully could fail to notice that by the time it reached cities like Huntsville it was frayed beyond repair. Price and Bates lived among black people, played with them as children, roamed the streets with them as teenagers, bootlegged liquor and got drunk with them as young adults. They also went out with them, slept with them, fell in and out of love with them, apparently unaware of the widespread wishful thinking that made it possible for many white southerners to call all sex between white women and black men rape. No white woman, one Mississippi editor put it, no matter how degraded or depraved, would ever willingly "bestow her favors on a black man." Price and Bates had heard the words *white supremacy, segregation,* and *white womanhood,* but they did not live by them. In the eyes of "respectable" southern whites, Price and Bates had sunk as low as two women with white skin could sink. Perhaps lower. One frustrated Huntsville social worker complained that the whites in the mill villages were "as bad as the niggers."

---

[a]   Two of the defendants, Wright and Patterson, testified on at least one occasion that some of the defendants (not they or their Chattanooga friends) had had intercourse with the women. Goodman, at 14–15.

Until they were thought to have been raped. When sheriff's deputies found Price and Bates alongside the train at Paint Rock and realized they had been on it alone with the Negroes who had thrown the white boys off, their first thought was of rape. Later, no one could say for sure what came first, Price and Bates's accusation or the sheriff's interrogation. Some said that the girls had offered the charge without encouragement; others said that they had said nothing about an assault until a deputy asked if the Negroes had bothered them. Either way, Price and Bates were not deluded. They knew that the black youths had not raped them or bothered them in any way.[b] But they also knew that if they had said nothing or no—"No, those Negroes didn't even speak to us"—the people who asked would have thought of them the way respectable white men and women had always thought of them: as the lowest of the low, vagabonds, adulterers, bootleggers, tramps. If, on the other hand, they complained or said yes, the same people would suddenly have thought of them as rape victims and treated them as white southern women, poor but virtuous, for the first time in their lives. It was a rare opportunity, and the choice was not a hard one for them to make. * * *

On the witness stand there were all sorts of things about the trip to Chattanooga and the rape that Bates could not remember. She contradicted herself when asked whether she and Price had known the white boys on the train or traveled with them the day before. And unlike Price, she couldn't say positively which of the defendants had raped her, which ones had raped Price, or in what order. But considering what she had gone through, neither juries nor spectators held her bad memory against her; she got the most important part of the story right. She remembered clearly that two of the Negroes had guns and the rest had knives and that after chasing the white boys off the train they had thrown them down in the gondola, held knives at their throats, and raped each of them six times. * * *

POWELL V. ALABAMA

Supreme Court of the United States, 1932.
287 U.S. 45, 53 S.Ct. 55, 77 L.Ed. 158.

MR. JUSTICE SUTHERLAND delivered the opinion of the Court [joined by CHIEF JUSTICE HUGHES and JUSTICES VAN DEVANTER, BRANDEIS, STONE, ROBERTS and CARDOZO].

---

[b] That Ruby Bates was lying when she testified that the defendants raped her is not open to serious doubt. She admitted in a letter dated January 5, 1932 that "those Negroes did not touch me or those white boys." Goodman, 195. Though she later recanted the letter, under police threat of one hundred days on the chain gang, *id.* at 195, she testified in a subsequent trial that "the defendants did not rape, touch, or even speak to her and Victoria." *Id.* at 132. Despite this testimony, it took the jury only moments to vote unanimously to convict (it took eleven hours to persuade one juror to vote for the death penalty). *Id.* at 145.

These cases were argued together and submitted for decision as one case.

The petitioners, hereinafter referred to as defendants, are negroes charged with the crime of rape, committed upon the persons of two white girls. The crime is said to have been committed on March 25, 1931. The indictment was returned in a state court of first instance on March 31, and the record recites that on the same day the defendants were arraigned and entered pleas of not guilty. There is a further recital to the effect that upon the arraignment they were represented by counsel. But no counsel had been employed, and aside from a statement made by the trial judge several days later during a colloquy immediately preceding the trial, the record does not disclose when, or under what circumstances, an appointment of counsel was made, or who was appointed. During the colloquy referred to, the trial judge, in response to a question, said that he had appointed all the members of the bar for the purpose of arraigning the defendants and then of course anticipated that the members of the bar would continue to help the defendants if no counsel appeared. Upon the argument here both sides accepted that as a correct statement of the facts concerning the matter.

There was a severance upon the request of the state, and the defendants were tried in three several groups, as indicated above. As each of the three cases was called for trial, each defendant was arraigned, and, having the indictment read to him, entered a plea of not guilty. Whether the original arraignment and pleas were regarded as ineffective is not shown. Each of the three trials was completed within a single day. Under the Alabama statute the punishment for rape is to be fixed by the jury, and in its discretion may be from ten years imprisonment to death. The juries found defendants guilty and imposed the death penalty upon all. The trial court overruled motions for new trials and sentenced the defendants in accordance with the verdicts. The judgments were affirmed by the state supreme court. Chief Justice Anderson thought the defendants had not been accorded a fair trial and strongly dissented.

In this court the judgments are assailed upon the grounds that the defendants, and each of them, were denied due process of law and the equal protection of the laws, in contravention of the Fourteenth Amendment, specifically as follows: (1) they were not given a fair, impartial and deliberate trial; (2) they were denied the right of counsel, with the accustomed incidents of consultation and opportunity of preparation for trial; and (3) they were tried before juries from which qualified members of their own race were systematically excluded. These questions were properly raised and saved in the courts below.

The only one of the assignments which we shall consider is the second, in respect of the denial of counsel; and it becomes unnecessary to discuss the facts of the case or the circumstances surrounding the prosecution except in so far as they reflect light upon that question. * * *

* * * The record does not disclose [defendants'] ages, except that one of them was nineteen; but the record clearly indicates that most, if not all, of them were youthful, and they are constantly referred to as "the boys." They were ignorant and illiterate. All of them were residents of other states, where alone members of their families or friends resided.

However guilty defendants, upon due inquiry, might prove to have been, they were, until convicted, presumed to be innocent. It was the duty of the court having their cases in charge to see that they were denied no necessary incident of a fair trial. With any error of the state court involving alleged contravention of the state statutes or constitution we, of course, have nothing to do. The sole inquiry which we are permitted to make is whether the federal Constitution was contravened; and as to that, we confine ourselves, as already suggested, to the inquiry whether the defendants were in substance denied the right of counsel, and if so, whether such denial infringes the due process clause of the Fourteenth Amendment.

First. The record shows that immediately upon the return of the indictment defendants were arraigned and pleaded not guilty. Apparently they were not asked whether they had, or were able to employ, counsel, or wished to have counsel appointed; or whether they had friends or relatives who might assist in that regard if communicated with. That it would not have been an idle ceremony to have given the defendants reasonable opportunity to communicate with their families and endeavor to obtain counsel is demonstrated by the fact that, very soon after conviction, able counsel appeared in their behalf. This was pointed out by Chief Justice Anderson in the course of his dissenting opinion. "They were nonresidents," he said, "and had little time or opportunity to get in touch with their families and friends who were scattered throughout two other states, and time has demonstrated that they could or would have been represented by able counsel had a better opportunity been given by a reasonable delay in the trial of the cases, judging from the number and activity of counsel that appeared immediately or shortly after their conviction."

It is hardly necessary to say that, the right to counsel being conceded, a defendant should be afforded a fair opportunity to secure counsel of his own choice. Not only was that not done here, but such designation of counsel as was attempted was either so indefinite or so close upon the trial as to amount to a denial of effective and substantial aid in that regard. This will be amply demonstrated by a brief review of the record.

April 6, six days after indictment, the trials began. When the first case was called, the court inquired whether the parties were ready for

trial. The state's attorney replied that he was ready to proceed. No one answered for the defendants or appeared to represent or defend them. Mr. Roddy, a Tennessee lawyer not a member of the local bar, addressed the court, saying that he had not been employed, but that people who were interested had spoken to him about the case. He was asked by the court whether he intended to appear for the defendants, and answered that he would like to appear along with counsel that the court might appoint.
* * *

It thus will be seen that until the very morning of the trial no lawyer had been named or definitely designated to represent the defendants. Prior to that time, the trial judge had "appointed all the members of the bar" for the limited "purpose of arraigning the defendants." Whether they would represent the defendants thereafter if no counsel appeared in their behalf, was a matter of speculation only, or, as the judge indicated, of mere anticipation on the part of the court. Such a designation, even if made for all purposes, would, in our opinion, have fallen far short of meeting, in any proper sense, a requirement for the appointment of counsel. How many lawyers were members of the bar does not appear; but, in the very nature of things, whether many or few, they would not, thus collectively named, have been given that clear appreciation of responsibility or impressed with that individual sense of duty which should and naturally would accompany the appointment of a selected member of the bar, specifically named and assigned.

That this action of the trial judge in respect of appointment of counsel was little more than an expansive gesture, imposing no substantial or definite obligation upon any one, is borne out by the fact that prior to the calling of the case for trial on April 6, a leading member of the local bar accepted employment on the side of the prosecution and actively participated in the trial. It is true that he said that before doing so he had understood Mr. Roddy would be employed as counsel for the defendants. This the lawyer in question, of his own accord, frankly stated to the court; and no doubt he acted with the utmost good faith. Probably other members of the bar had a like understanding. In any event, the circumstance lends emphasis to the conclusion that during perhaps the most critical period of the proceedings against these defendants, that is to say, from the time of their arraignment until the beginning of their trial, when consultation, thoroughgoing investigation and preparation were vitally important, the defendants did not have the aid of counsel in any real sense, although they were as much entitled to such aid during that period as at the trial itself.

Nor do we think the situation was helped by what occurred on the morning of the trial. At that time, as appears from the [record], Mr. Roddy stated to the court that he did not appear as counsel, but that he would like to appear along with counsel that the court might appoint;

that he had not been given an opportunity to prepare the case; that he was not familiar with the procedure in Alabama, but merely came down as a friend of the people who were interested; that he thought the boys would be better off if he should step entirely out of the case. Mr. Moody, a member of the local bar, expressed a willingness to help Mr. Roddy in anything he could do under the circumstances. To this the court responded, "All right, all the lawyers that will; of course I would not require a lawyer to appear if—." And Mr. Moody continued, "I am willing to do that for him as a member of the bar; I will go ahead and help do any thing I can do." With this dubious understanding, the trials immediately proceeded. The defendants, young, ignorant, illiterate, surrounded by hostile sentiment, haled back and forth under guard of soldiers, charged with an atrocious crime regarded with especial horror in the community where they were to be tried, were thus put in peril of their lives within a few moments after counsel for the first time charged with any degree of responsibility began to represent them.

It is not enough to assume that counsel thus precipitated into the case thought there was no defense, and exercised their best judgment in proceeding to trial without preparation. Neither they nor the court could say what a prompt and thoroughgoing investigation might disclose as to the facts. No attempt was made to investigate. No opportunity to do so was given. Defendants were immediately hurried to trial. Chief Justice Anderson, after disclaiming any intention to criticize harshly counsel who attempted to represent defendants at the trials, said: " * * * the record indicates that the appearance was rather *pro forma* than zealous and active * * * ." Under the circumstances disclosed, we hold that defendants were not accorded the right of counsel in any substantial sense. To decide otherwise, would simply be to ignore actualities. * * *

It is true that great and inexcusable delay in the enforcement of our criminal law is one of the grave evils of our time. Continuances are frequently granted for unnecessarily long periods of time, and delays incident to the disposition of motions for new trial and hearings upon appeal have come in many cases to be a distinct reproach to the administration of justice. The prompt disposition of criminal cases is to be commended and encouraged. But in reaching that result a defendant, charged with a serious crime, must not be stripped of his right to have sufficient time to advise with counsel and prepare his defense. To do that is not to proceed promptly in the calm spirit of regulated justice but to go forward with the haste of the mob. * * *

Second. The Constitution of Alabama provides that in all criminal prosecutions the accused shall enjoy the right to have the assistance of counsel; and a state statute requires the court in a capital case, where the defendant is unable to employ counsel, to appoint counsel for him. The state supreme court held that these provisions had not been infringed, and with that holding we are powerless to interfere. The question, however, which it is our duty, and within our power, to decide, is whether the denial of the assistance of counsel contravenes the due process clause of the Fourteenth Amendment to the federal Constitution. * * *

It never has been doubted by this court, or any other so far as we know, that notice and hearing are preliminary steps essential to the passing of an enforceable judgment, and that they, together with a legally competent tribunal having jurisdiction of the case, constitute basic elements of the constitutional requirement of due process of law. The words of Webster, so often quoted, that by "the law of the land" is intended "a law which hears before it condemns," have been repeated in varying forms of expression in a multitude of decisions. * * *

What, then, does a hearing include? Historically and in practice, in our own country at least, it has always included the right to the aid of counsel when desired and provided by the party asserting the right. The right to be heard would be, in many cases, of little avail if it did not comprehend the right to be heard by counsel. Even the intelligent and educated layman has small and sometimes no skill in the science of law. If charged with crime, he is incapable, generally, of determining for himself whether the indictment is good or bad. He is unfamiliar with the rules of evidence. Left without the aid of counsel he may be put on trial without a proper charge, and convicted upon incompetent evidence, or evidence irrelevant to the issue or otherwise inadmissible. He lacks both the skill and knowledge adequately to prepare his defense, even though he have a perfect one. He requires the guiding hand of counsel at every step in the proceedings against him. Without it, though he be not guilty, he faces the danger of conviction because he does not know how to establish his innocence. If that be true of men of intelligence, how much more true is it of the ignorant and illiterate, or those of feeble intellect. If in any case, civil or criminal, a state or federal court were arbitrarily to refuse to hear a party by counsel, employed by and appearing for him, it reasonably may not be doubted that such a refusal would be a denial of a hearing, and, therefore, of due process in the constitutional sense. * * *

In the light of the facts outlined in the forepart of this opinion—the ignorance and illiteracy of the defendants, their youth, the circumstances of public hostility, the imprisonment and the close surveillance of the defendants by the military forces, the fact that their friends and families were all in other states and communication with them necessarily difficult, and above all that they stood in deadly peril of their lives—we think the failure of the trial court to give them reasonable time and opportunity to secure counsel was a clear denial of due process.

But passing that, and assuming their inability, even if opportunity had been given, to employ counsel, as the trial court evidently did assume, we are of opinion that, under the circumstances just stated, the necessity of counsel was so vital and imperative that the failure of the trial court to make an effective appointment of counsel was likewise a denial of due process within the meaning of the Fourteenth Amendment. Whether this would be so in other criminal prosecutions, or under other circumstances, we need not determine. All that it is necessary now to decide, as we do decide, is that in a capital case, where the defendant is unable to employ counsel, and is incapable adequately of making his own defense because of ignorance, feeble mindedness, illiteracy, or the like, it is the duty of the court, whether requested or not, to assign counsel for him as a necessary requisite of due process of law; and that duty is not discharged by an assignment at such a time or under such circumstances as to preclude the giving of effective aid in the preparation and trial of the case. To hold otherwise would be to ignore the fundamental postulate * * * "that there are certain immutable principles of justice which inhere in the very idea of free government which no member of the Union may disregard." * * *

The judgments must be reversed and the causes remanded for further proceedings not inconsistent with this opinion.

Judgments reversed.

MR. JUSTICE BUTLER, dissenting. * * *

If there had been any lack of opportunity for preparation, trial counsel would have applied to the court for postponement. No such application was made. There was no suggestion, at the trial or in the motion for a new trial which they made, that Mr. Roddy or Mr. Moody was denied such opportunity or that they were not in fact fully prepared. The amended motion for new trial, by counsel who succeeded them, contains the first suggestion that defendants were denied counsel or opportunity to prepare for trial. But neither Mr. Roddy nor Mr. Moody has given any support to that claim. Their silence requires a finding that the claim is groundless, for if it had any merit they would be bound to support it. And no one has come to suggest any lack of zeal or good faith on their part.

If correct, the ruling that the failure of the trial court to give petitioners time and opportunity to secure counsel was denied of due process is enough, and with this the opinion should end. But the Court goes on to declare that 'the failure of the trial court to make an effective appointment of counsel was likewise a denial of due process within the meaning of the Fourteenth Amendment.' This is an extension of federal authority into a field hitherto occupied exclusively by the several States. Nothing before the Court calls for a consideration of the point. It was not suggested below and petitioners do not ask for its decision here. The Court, without being called upon to consider it, adjudges without a hearing an important constitutional question concerning criminal procedure in state courts. * * *

MR. JUSTICE MCREYNOLDS concurs in this opinion.

NOTES AND QUESTIONS

1.   In what sense did the defendants here lack a lawyer? The judge, after all, appointed all the members of the local bar.

2.   *Doubts about guilt.* The excerpt about the Scottsboro defendants cannot begin to capture the richness of the account in James Goodman, Stories of Scottsboro (1995), which we highly recommend. The *Powell* Court was without Goodman's historical account strongly suggesting that no rapes took place. Even without an independent historical account, the Court could easily have been skeptical of the story told by the State, given the locale and racial dimension. If you had been on the *Powell* Court, would doubt about guilt have made you more likely to find a violation of the right to counsel? Turning the question around, would you *still* have found a violation of the right to counsel on these facts, even if the evidence of guilt had been overwhelming? If not, why not?

3.   *Further proceedings not inconsistent with this opinion.* Look again at the order at the end of the majority opinion. It is a standard order when a court reverses a lower court. Alabama could then choose to dismiss the indictments or retry the defendants with effective counsel at their side. And there would be many retrials. A total of eleven trials involved the nine defendants during the 1930s. Alabama dropped charges against four of the defendants in 1937. The other five eventually received convictions that withstood appellate review; the sentences were twenty years, seventy-five years (two defendants), ninety-nine years, and death. The death sentence was commuted to life by Alabama Governor Bibb Graves. Three Scottsboro defendants were paroled in 1943, 1946, and 1950. One escaped from prison in 1948 and was arrested in Detroit in 1950. Michigan governor G. Mennen Williams refused Alabama's request for extradition, and Alabama abandoned extradition proceedings. In 1976, Governor George Wallace pardoned the last surviving Scottsboro defendant (the one who had been sentenced to death).

4.   The irony of Wallace pardoning one of the Scottsboro defendants may be lost on many readers. Wallace was best known for his staunch pro-segregation views when he was governor of Alabama in the 1950s and 1960s. In 1963, he sought to block "the school house door" and prevent two black students from enrolling at the University of Alabama. He moved out of the way when confronted by the Deputy Attorney General of the United States, federal marshals, and units of the Alabama National Guard that had been nationalized by President Kennedy. Dan T. Carter, The Politics of Rage: George Wallace, the Origins of the New Conservatism and the Transformation of American Politics 150 (1995).

Late in his life, Wallace sought reconciliation with black politicians and African-Americans in general (primarily conducted through predominantly black churches) in Alabama. As historian Dan Carter comments, "[b]lack Alabamians wanted Wallace to be forgiven." Carter, at 463. His pardon of one of the Scottsboro defendants might have been part of this effort at reconciliation.

5. *Predecessor 1 to Powell.* More than a quarter century prior to *Powell*, the Court sought to intervene in a racially-flawed Southern death penalty case. The rape of a young white woman by a black man in 1906 in Chattanooga, Tennessee unleashed a storm of fury and racism. The sheriff arrested two black men and the prosecutor chose Ed Johnson, the one the victim came closer to identifying. But at the trial, the rape victim refused to say for certain that Johnson was her attacker. She would only testify, "To the best of my knowledge and belief, he is the same man." The defense team, three white lawyers, mounted an aggressive alibi defense that put the State's case in doubt.

At one point, a member of the jury rose to his feet, "tears streaming down his face * * * and in a voice trembling with emotion, he cried: 'In God's name, Miss Taylor, tell us positively—is that the guilty negro? Can you say it—can you swear it?' "

She responded: "Listen to me. I would not take the life of an innocent man. But before God, I believe this is the guilty negro."

The jury initially voted 8–4 for conviction and the judge sent them home for the evening. When the jury returned the next day, the doubts of the four dissenting jurors had somehow been laid to rest. Ed Johnson was found guilty and sentenced to hang. The Supreme Court granted a hearing on a writ of habeas corpus to examine whether the trial met due process fairness standards. To permit the hearing to proceed, the Court granted a stay of execution and issued an order that the prisoner be kept safe. The intervention by the federal court proved too much for some in the community.

The headlines in the Chattanooga News the next day, March 20, 1906, told the whole story: " 'God Bless You All—I Am Innocent,' Ed Johnson's Last Words Before Being Shot to Death By a Mob Like a Dog, Majesty of the Law Outraged by Lynchers, Mandate of the Supreme Court of the United States Disregarded and Red Riot Rampant, Terrible and Tragic Vengeance Bows City's Head in Shame."

President Theodore Roosevelt condemned the lynching as "contemptuous of the Court." Using the bloodless language of formal judicial opinions, the Court dismissed Johnson's appeal on the ground that it was "abated by the death of the appellant." Johnson v. Tennessee, 214 U.S. 485, 29 S.Ct. 651, 53 L.Ed. 1056 (1909). But prior to dismissing the appeal, the Court did something extraordinary. It ordered a federal criminal trial that resulted in contempt convictions for the Chattanooga sheriff and several other law enforcement officers.

In 2000, a Chattanooga court granted a petition to clear Mr. Johnson of the rape. Leroy Phillips, a local lawyer, noted during the proceeding that 4,708 lynchings took place in the United States from 1882 to 1944, according to an archive at Tuskegee University in Alabama. For a fuller description of the Johnson case, the heroes and villains, and its aftermath, see Mark Curriden & Leroy Phillips, Jr., Contempt of Court (1999); George C. Thomas III, The Supreme Court on Trial: How the American Justice System Sacrifices Innocent Defendants (2008).

6. *Predecessor 2 to Powell.* A similar story of lawlessness played itself out in Georgia in 1915. The vicious murder of a young woman in Atlanta led to sensational newspaper coverage and to the arrest of Leo Frank, her employer. From the beginning, the case attracted nationwide attention, in part because Frank was Jewish and anti-Semitism was on the rise in the United States. Frank was convicted and sentenced to death based wholly on circumstantial evidence offered in a trial that took place, according to Justice Oliver Wendell Holmes, "in the presence of a hostile demonstration and seemingly dangerous crowd, thought by the presiding judge to be ready for violence unless a verdict of guilty was rendered." Leonard Dinnerstein, The Leo Frank Case 109 (1968). Despite Holmes's due process concern, the Court, 7–2, denied Frank's habeas corpus petition. Frank v. Mangum, 237 U.S. 309, 35 S.Ct. 582, 59 L.Ed. 969 (1915). Such was the reluctance of the Supreme Court in the early twentieth century to reverse the fact finding of state courts.

A petition seeking executive clemency was filed with Georgia governor John M. Slaton. Over 100,000 letters asking for commutation arrived in the offices of the governor and the Prison Commission. *Id.* at 122. The Prison Commission voted two-to-one not to recommend clemency. After holding his own hearings into the facts of the murder, Slaton commuted Frank's death sentence to life in prison. "Privately, Slaton confided to friends that he believed Frank innocent and would have granted a full pardon if he were not convinced that in a short while the truth would come out * * * ." *Id.* at 129.

Many Georgians were furious at the commutation. His political career ruined, Slaton had to call out an entire battalion of state militia to keep from being lynched. *Id.* at 132. The commutation failed to save Frank. Two months later, a mob of twenty-five men stormed the prison farm, abducted Frank, and hung him. "Hordes of people made their way to the oak tree" to view Frank's body and take pictures. *Id.* at 143. Those who planned and participated in this lawless act included a "clergyman, two former Superior Court judges, and an ex-sheriff." *Id.* at 139. The Marietta Journal and Courier wrote: "We regard the hanging of Leo M. Frank in Cobb County as an act of law abiding citizens." *Id.* at 145.

7. *Trying to make sense of it all.* How could clergymen, judges, and law officers have participated in the conduct described in Note 6? Consider these observations about the Scottsboro case:

White Alabamians seemed genuinely puzzled at outside criticism of their handling of the Scottsboro cases. Avoiding a lynching was "a genuine step forward," and thus was deserving of commendation, not condemnation. The state supreme court lauded the speed of the Scottsboro Boys' trials as likely to instill greater respect for the law. A state member of the Commission on Interracial Cooperation thought it odd that Alabama should be criticized for delivering exactly what the [Commission] had been fighting so hard to accomplish—replacement of lynchings with trials. Several southern newspapers warned in connection with Scottsboro that if outsiders continued to assail Alabama after juries had returned guilty verdicts, then there would be little incentive to resist a lynching on future occasions.

Michael J. Klarman, *The Racial Origins of Modern Criminal Procedure*, 99 Mich. L. Rev. 48, 57 (2000).

8. *The broader effect of Powell.* Look again at Justice Butler's dissent in *Powell*. Butler is correct that federal courts, particularly in the nineteenth and early twentieth centuries, were loathe to impose federal supervision over state criminal justice systems. And, as Justice Butler points out, the Court could have decided the case in favor of the defendants by finding insufficient time to prepare. Yet the Court also held that the failure to appoint counsel violated due process. Why do you think the Court went this additional step?

Even if *Powell* did ensure better legal representation for southern black defendants, how much this affected actual case outcomes is uncertain. The [Communist International Labor Defense] criticized *Powell* because the Justices apparently had selected the least significant ground for reversing the Scottsboro Boys' convictions. Indeed, the Communists accused the Court of simply providing Alabama with instructions on how properly to lynch the defendants. Even if appointed days before trial and afforded adequate opportunity to prepare a defense, counsel generally could do little to assist clients like the Scottsboro Boys. Black lawyers, who might have been willing aggressively to pursue their clients' defense, were few and far between in the South, and in any event were distinct liabilities owing to the prejudice they aroused among white judges and juries. White lawyers, on the other hand, generally refrained from pressing defenses that raised broader challenges to the Jim Crow system, such as race-based exclusion from juries. In any event, even the most earnest advocacy rarely could influence case outcomes when the system was so pervasively stacked against fair adjudication of the legal claims of black defendants. The Scottsboro Boys did enjoy outstanding legal representation in their retrials, yet it made absolutely no difference to the outcomes.

Michael J. Klarman, *The Racial Origins of Modern Criminal Procedure*, 99
Mich. L. Rev. 48, 78 (2000).

Indeed, it is not clear that the promise of *Powell* has been realized even
today. Consider the following description of what the criminal process looked
and felt like to one public defender.

GERALD B. LEFCOURT—RESPONSIBILITIES OF A CRIMINAL DEFENSE ATTORNEY

30 Loyola of Los Angeles Law Review 59 (1996), 59–63.

Our perspective as criminal defense lawyers is often based on a
pivotal experience. Mine was as a law school honors program participant,
sent to work with Legal Aid Society lawyers—New York City's public
defenders. I was assigned to help a young lawyer handling arraignments.
In New York City that meant a daily crush of cases. His job was to seek
bail as each defendant entered the system. In disgusting pens holding as
many as forty prisoners, I would interview clients. I was the first person
many prisoners saw after they had spent up to four days waiting to
appear before the court.

The holding pens were filled with huddling defendants, most of whom
were standing because there was only one bench. Virtually the entire
population of the pens was nonwhite and poor, without the resources or
stable families to allow them bail. Most were in shock or panic, yelling
questions and begging for help. "What am I charged with?" "When will I
ever get out?" "Can you call my mother?" "What if I didn't do it; will they
still keep me?" "Will you call my boss because if I don't show up I'll lose
my job?"

I came to see that most of them were not really represented at all.
Not only would they not make bail, but most would ultimately plead
guilty to something, anything, just to move out of the system. I realized
that with a lawyer who had a few days to spend with the client instead of
a few minutes, a proper fight could be waged, both to get the defendant
out on bail and ultimately, to get a favorable disposition. In many cases
defendants would not have ended up with criminal records, a millstone
that serves to keep the underclasses as underclasses.

I realized that the Legal Aid attorneys, like their counterparts across
the country, were not properly trained, had no resources, and were,
frankly, overwhelmed. The number of defendants was so great that there
was no time for the niceties of an interview long enough to establish any
relationship, much less one of trust.

So, there were two systems operating, one for the wealthy who had
the resources to seek vindication of their rights and one for the rest of

society, left haphazardly to lawyers who could ensure entirely less predictable results.

It was obvious that a system promising the right to counsel was a farce.

NOTES AND QUESTIONS

1.   Lefcourt's anecdotal experience is borne out by the data. Researchers McConville and Mirsky concluded in 1990 that in large cities "criminal courts are places of *mass* processing," which "arraign defendants twenty-four hours a day, seven days a week." On days set for docketing cases, "lower courts commonly docket 100 or more cases a day, while superior courts often docket 60 felony indictments a day. Court business is conducted in a swirl of activity as judges seek to 'move' crowded calendars." Michael McConville & Chester L. Mirsky, *Understanding Defense of the Poor in State Courts*, 10 Studies in Law, Politics, and Society 217, 217 (1990).

Any thoughts about why public defense in large cities has become mass processing?

2.   Do you think Justice Sutherland, the author of the majority opinion in *Powell*, would consider the system described by Lefcourt and in Note 1 to constitute the "Assistance of Counsel"? Does this description portend "the guiding hand of counsel at every step in the proceedings"? How is the representation described here better or worse than the representation provided by Mr. Roddy and the local bar in *Powell*?

3.   *Is indigent defense really that bad?* In 2009, the National Right to Counsel Committee issued a report entitled Justice Denied: America's Continuing Neglect of our Constitutional Right to Counsel. The report details systemic and endemic failures of indigent defense in this country. It found "overwhelming" evidence that, in most of the country, "quality defense work is simply impossible because of inadequate funding, excessive caseloads, a lack of genuine independence, and insufficient availability of other essential resources."

The report provides twenty-two recommendations for improvement and can be found at http://tcpjusticedenied.org/. See also Mary Sue Backus & Paul Marcus, The Right to Counsel in Criminal Cases, A National Crisis, 57 Hastings L. J. 1031 (2006).

The committee included prosecutors, judges, defense lawyers, and academics. The honorary co-chairs were Walter Mondale, former Democratic candidate for president, and William Sessions, former director of the FBI.

The right to counsel is considered in depth in Chapter 14.

B. THE NORMS OF THE CRIMINAL PROCESS

By the time a case gets into court, and certainly by the time a case makes it all the way to the United States Supreme Court, it is unlikely to be solved by an easy application of a clear legal rule. There is a clear legal rule about many things—for example, the speed limit on a particular stretch of road—but disputes about clear rules rarely make it into the courts. Instead, most cases present the judge with a range of outcomes that are plausible because they fit within the precedents that she has before her. Some judges will resist this truth, at least publicly, because they want to be seen as merely applying "the law" rather than making a quasi-legislative choice, but any realistic examination of case law will make clear that judges have choices. Otherwise, how can we explain dissents?

Once we accept that most cases present judges with a range of outcomes, we must then consider what factors move judges to choose among the possible outcomes. Many factors undoubtedly are at play here, some legitimate and some illegitimate. A prior generation of legal scholars sought to unmask the power that lies in judicial choices as well as the factors that influence how this power is wielded. See, *e.g.*, Felix Cohen, *Transcendental Nonsense and the Functional Approach*, 35 Colum. L. Rev. 809 (1935); Karl Llewellyn, *A Realistic Jurisprudence— The Next Step*, 30 Colum. L. Rev. 431 (1930). Today's scholarship about judicial choices has at least two different camps. One camp seeks to understand choices by drawing on other disciplines of knowledge—for example, law and economics, law and history, and law and philosophy. Judge *A* might think that economic principles best explain how to decide the case while Judge *B* is motivated by an historical understanding of the issue. A second camp focuses mostly on what it considers illegitimate factors and can be loosely referred to as "critical" scholarship. It seeks to show how race, sex, gender, class, and hegemony lead judges to shut the door on those who are not of the dominant political majority.

Identifying the full range of factors that move judges to make choices, and how those factors interact, is probably impossible and certainly beyond the scope of this comment. But the study of criminal procedure brings to the forefront three factors that move judges to choose one permissible outcome over another. First, American judges are citizens in a free democracy. Like every other citizen in the United States, judges bring to the task at hand a view about the importance of security and individual rights. Governments exist, in large part, to provide security from those who might harm us, but the very power of government also leads us to be fearful about how its power will be exercised when our individual rights and freedom are at stake. John Adams signed into law the Sedition Act that made it a crime to criticize the government. Richard Nixon used the Internal Revenue Service to attack his enemies. In the wake of 9/11, George W. Bush authorized wiretaps without court order. There are many possible ways to balance security and individual rights, and judges who decide criminal procedure cases will strike the balance at different points. Obviously, judges who put the balance nearer the security end of the scale will be more likely to vest discretion in police and prosecutors while judges whose tipping point is nearer the individual rights end will require more judicial supervision of those who enforce the law.

A second factor that affects criminal procedure cases is federalism. The United States has a federal government, in which states and the federal government share power in an uneasy, shifting balance. The battle over ratification of the Constitution between the Federalists and the Anti-federalists has played out in every generation since and continues to this day—think "red" states and "blue" states. The long-festering controversy over how much federal power should exist led federal judges for most of our history to be reluctant to interpose the federal Constitution in matters that might plausibly be considered "local." But where to locate the balance between too much federal supervision and not enough is also a contestable issue, one about which judges disagree.

Notice, in this regard, Justice Butler's dissent in *Powell*. He argued that the Court did not need to reach the issue of the denial of counsel, that it was enough to find a violation of due process in the failure to provide sufficient time to prepare the case. To fasten on the states some undefined obligation to provide counsel to ignorant defendants was, for Justice Butler and Justice McReynolds, "an extension of federal authority into a field hitherto occupied exclusively by the several States" that should not be done unless necessary to decide the case before the Court. This argument has, at its core, a respect for, and deference to, state actors.

Racism is a third factor that might explain the Alabama and Mississippi decisions in *Powell* and *Brown*. The range of choices that are available to judges in one state or region may be different from the acceptable range in other parts of the country. In the Mississippi Supreme Court in 1935, only two of the five judges were willing to reverse convictions obtained by torture. We will never know whether their decision was influenced by racism, but we do know that all nine members of the United States Supreme Court found the state court's decision to affirm the convictions to be an unacceptable choice. Outside the Deep South, the range of available choices was different in cases where race was a central factor.

As you read the cases in this book, you should ask yourself what range of acceptable choices the judges thought they had, how the judges came up with that range of choices, and why the judges chose one outcome over the others. You will often find the various choices best explained by the balance between security and liberty and the balance between robust and minimal federal intervention in state criminal justice. But modern judges tend to cloak their foundational views in other language—the language of (1) the accuracy of verdicts; (2) the fairness of the procedure; (3) honoring the presence of certain limitations on the power of government to find or use evidence; and (4) efficiency.

Accuracy

All systems that process and evaluate information will make errors in evaluation. If the system is indifferent to the "direction" of the error (indifferent to which party is harmed by the error), it would permit a verdict based on the slightest difference in the weight of the evidence presented by the two parties. This standard of proof, called "preponderance of the evidence," is the standard used in civil court. As a consequence, the plaintiff wins if she can show the slightest additional weight of evidence on her side of the balance; the defendant wins if the evidence is in equipoise or tilted ever so slightly in the defendant's direction.

Criminal law has adopted an "innocence-weighted" procedural approach that, in theory, protects innocent defendants. See Tom Stacy, *The Search for Truth in Constitutional Criminal Procedure*, 91 Colum. L. Rev. 1369. Blackstone put the rationale colorfully: "[T]he law holds that it is better that ten guilty persons escape than that one innocent suffer." 4 W. Blackstone's Commentaries *352 (1769). To create an "innocence-weighted" procedure, criminal law requires proof beyond a reasonable doubt.

As Professor Daniel Givelber notes, however, no one knows for certain that the reasonable-doubt standard operates to acquit a greater percentage of *innocent* defendants. It might just produce more acquittals randomly distributed among defendants generally. Daniel Givelber, *Meaningless Acquittals, Meaningful Convictions: Do We Reliably Acquit the Innocent?*, 49 Rutgers L. Rev. 1317 (1997). There are two ways in which a high standard of proof should differentially benefit innocent defendants—by encouraging more innocent defendants to stand trial rather than plea bargain, and by influencing juries to vote not guilty in cases involving innocent defendants. If more innocent defendants choose to stand trial because they have faith in the reasonable doubt standard, then even random acquittals will differentially benefit innocent defendants. But the most direct differential effect—and the one Blackstone likely meant—is that it should be more difficult to convict innocent defendants than guilty ones. This effect, however, depends crucially on whether the prosecution will have a weaker case against innocent defendants. If innocent and guilty defendants present cases of equal "strength," then the reasonable-doubt standard does not help innocent defendants any more than guilty ones. Many scholars and judges assume that our rules of procedure will permit innocent defendants to demonstrate the weakness of the prosecution case, but is it so clear?

It is not evident to Professor Givelber, who argues that our rules of adjudication "assume a guilty defendant, and focus on the task of creating a fair fight between the prosecution and the guilty defendant." For example, no current doctrine insists on "the availability of the most accurate information concerning the crime and its investigation"—such as guaranteed defense access to DNA testing. Instead, the system has "provided the defendant with a series of tactical opportunities to derail the prosecution's case." *Id.* at 1378.

Some of these opportunities to derail the State's case should, in theory, advance accurate outcomes. As we saw in Part A., providing indigent defendants with a lawyer should help avoid wrongful convictions. Other trial rights provide the lawyer with tools to test the State's case—the right to confront the prosecution witnesses, to call defense witnesses, and to have the case heard in a public trial before an impartial jury fairly soon after the events in question.

The right to confront and to call witnesses bears an obvious relationship to accuracy. The right to a speedy and public trial enhances accuracy in two ways. The sooner the trial occurs after the crime, the more accurate should be the memories of witnesses. Less obviously, the public nature of a trial should serve as a deterrent to judges who might be inclined to favor one party over another.

All of these trial rights are specifically guaranteed by the Sixth Amendment. Partly because they bear an obvious relationship to accuracy, they are much less controversial than some of the rights that are grounded more in fairness or in limited-government sentiment.

Fairness

No one denies that suspects and defendants should be treated fairly. Much debate centers, naturally, on what constitutes "fair" treatment. One famous example is Yale Kamisar's 1965 article that pre-dated the famous *Miranda* warnings requirement. Yale Kamisar, *Equal Justice in the Gatehouses and Mansions of American Criminal Procedure*, reprinted in Yale Kamisar, Police Interrogation (1980). According to Professor Kamisar, the Fifth Amendment gives everyone the right to refuse to answer police questions, but most criminal suspects do not know they have that right. Affluent suspects are able to retain counsel to advise them during interrogation. Fairness, in this context, thus meant for Kamisar that suspects should be told of their right to refuse to answer and should be provided the right to counsel during interrogation, an analysis the *Miranda* Court adopted. Fairness here implicates equality; the rich and the poor, the knowledgeable as well as the ignorant, should be able to deal with police interrogators on more or less equal terms. '.

Others take a different view of fairness in the interrogation room. As long as the police do not coerce a confession, one could argue that it is fair to question suspects who are under arrest, and even to take advantage of suspects who do not know of the privilege against self-incrimination. Assuming that an inconsequential number of innocent people confess when faced with non-coercive interrogation—of late, a questionable assumption—these commentators wonder why anyone cares that the police trick or encourage guilty people to confess their crimes. Moreover, to make lawyers available to all suspects, just because a very few suspects have a lawyer during interrogation, might be the wrong way to solve the inequality problem; why not ban lawyers from police interrogation, thus reaching the "equality" of zero lawyers?

To the extent equality means making all suspects as resistant to police investigation as the savvy affluent suspects, some commentators deride equality as a "sporting theory of justice"—turning the police investigation into a fox hunt where the fox must be given a fair chance. Perhaps law-abiding persons should rejoice when non-coercive police questioning causes a guilty defendant to confess.

These questions tend to divide courts and commentators because of the inherent difficulty in deciding what is fair. Of course, a procedure is not fair if it produces too many inaccurate verdicts (though defining "too many" may be difficult), but once we have identified accuracy as an independent requirement, it is much more difficult to give content to a fairness requirement. Fairness, then, is a controversial legitimacy factor precisely because fairness invites those with different views to ascribe what they please to the concept of "fairness."

Limited-Government Provisions

One could have an accurate criminal process that included the power to question defendants in court, whether or not they wished to testify, and the power to introduce evidence seized in a search later found to be too broad or too intrusive. The continental European systems typically permit the presiding judge to question the defendant at trial in front of the jury. The Canadian, European, and English systems permit evidence to be introduced even if it is seized in an unfair manner. While we may prefer our system, no one suggests that these other systems produce more inaccurate verdicts than the American system.

The reason is simple enough. Physical evidence does not need to have its accuracy tested by the adversarial process; visual examination or lab tests can disclose its true meaning. And, there is no reason to believe that a system that permits defendants to be questioned in court will be less accurate than a system that permits defendants to avoid testifying. Indeed, limitations on questioning defendants and using physical evidence found in searches make the overall set of outcomes *less* accurate. So, on balance, the Fourth Amendment and the privilege against self-incrimination are accuracy-impeding provisions.

It is more controversial to assert that a process can be *fair* when it requires defendants to submit to questioning, or uses reliable evidence that was seized wrongfully. But one could plausibly argue, as Justice Cardozo did, that the question of how police obtain physical evidence is separate from the question of whether the defendant is guilty; otherwise, "[t]he criminal is to go free because the constable has blundered." People v. Defore, 242 N.Y. 13, 150 N.E. 585 (1926). As to questioning defendants in court, one might ask why it is unfair to expect other witnesses to testify at trial but not the one witness who probably knows more about the facts of the case than anyone else—the defendant. Judge Henry Friendly even called for the Fifth Amendment privilege against self-incrimination to be repealed by constitutional amendment. Henry J. Friendly, *The Fifth Amendment Tomorrow: The Case for Constitutional Change*, 37 U. Cinn. L. Rev. 617 (1968).

However one decides the fairness question, something more than accuracy and fairness explains why the Bill of Rights includes the Fourth Amendment. Examination of the constitutional language helps here. (The full text of the Bill of Rights can be found on pages 2–3.) The Fourth Amendment begins by recognizing the "right of the people to be secure in their persons, houses, papers and effects against unreasonable searches and seizures." It then establishes strict standards for issuing warrants, standards that include probable cause and a "particular[ ]" description of "the place to be searched, and the persons or things to be seized."

The Fourth Amendment is part of an overall theme in the Bill of Rights that establishes "the people" as a separate entity from the government. The First Amendment forbids a state religion and creates the right to worship freely, to speak freely, and to assemble and to petition the government. The Second Amendment provides for a militia to exist separately from the government. The Ninth and Tenth Amendments retain power in the people and the states. Viewed as part of this broad canvas, the Fourth Amendment is a statement that the government must not interfere with our daily lives (our persons, houses, papers, and effects) absent good cause. The specific requirements for warrants will keep judges from taking lightly the command that the people be "secure." The Fourth Amendment's purpose thus seems to be to limit the power of government to intrude on "the people" in this particular way.

Most of the Fifth Amendment also consists of general rights against government: it forbids re-litigating the outcome of the first trial (by forbidding double jeopardy); it forbids governmental compulsion of defendants to testify against themselves; it requires the government to obtain assent of the community through a grand jury indictment before bringing a defendant to trial; it forbids government from denying "life, liberty, or property" without due process of law, or taking private property without "just compensation." Viewed in this context, the Fifth Amendment prohibition of compelling defendants to be witnesses against themselves seems like a restriction on the power of government to invade our autonomy.

If the Fourth and Fifth Amendment rights are fundamentally to control government, rather than to enhance accuracy or fairness, it would explain why the suppression of evidence under these two provisions is more controversial than the implementation of the Sixth Amendment trial rights. Society today likely does not feel as hostile toward government as the Framers felt anti-British in 1791.

Indeed, Professor Daniel Givelber argues that these provisions actually lessen the chance that an innocent defendant can prove her innocence. "Advantages which may enhance the case of the guilty defendant such as the right to silence and to exclude relevant inculpatory evidence, work no benefit for the innocent. Instead, those advantages justify the prosecution's withholding from the accused and the factfinder evidence which might undermine the prosecution's case." Daniel Givelber, *Meaningless Acquittals, Meaningful Convictions: Do We Reliably Acquit the Innocent?*, 49 Rutgers L. Rev. 1317, 1394 (1997).

Efficiency

The political and pragmatic legitimacy of the criminal process requires a threshold level of efficiency in solving and prosecuting crime. Unfortunately police do not solve, or clear, as many crimes as society would like. Because limited-government norms are necessarily inconsistent to some degree with police efficiency, the low clearance rate has led crime control adherents to urge abolition or restriction of the limited-government provisions in the Bill of Rights. Specifically, many have urged a rethinking of the principle requiring suppression of evidence seized in violation of the Fourth Amendment, and a few scholars have suggested rethinking the *Miranda* principle requiring that suspects must be warned prior to custodial interrogation.

The criminal process following police investigation is also currently dominated by the efficiency norm. Plea bargains are much more efficient than trials, and over 90% of felony charges are bargained to guilty pleas. Most lawyers and academics contend that the system could not survive without plea bargaining. If a mere 20% of felony defendants demanded a jury trial, that would more than double the present number of trials, with the complications of choosing a jury and all the rights that attend presenting a defense. Plea bargaining, in short, is the grease that permits the wheels of justice to turn smoothly.

hmm.

The Supreme Court explicitly approves of plea bargaining, and has held that prosecutors are bound by plea bargains once the defendant pleads guilty. *Santobello v. New York*, Chapter 15. These rulings have a double effect in encouraging more pleas: Judges know they can accept guilty pleas induced by plea bargains, and defendants can seek these pleas knowing that the prosecutor cannot withdraw from the bargain once the guilty plea is entered.

but what if it leads to more innocent going away? what about 1st + 2nd prong?

Efficiency is an important overlay on the legitimating norms of the American criminal process. But it must be tempered by the fairness norm and by the limited-government provisions of the Bill of Rights. How to balance these norms is always controversial. And the balance is subject to outside influences, as we witnessed in the aftermath of September 11, 2001.

The Norms Post-September 11

Larry Ellison, chief executive of Oracle Corporation, on the question of whether we should have National ID cards: "Those are political decisions that need to be made. I just think people need to ask themselves who they trust more, terrorists or the government." Robert O'Harrow Jr. & Jonathan Krim, *Is Big Brother Watching?*, The Washington Post National Weekly Edition, Dec. 24, 2001—Jan. 6, 2002, at 6, 7.

We tend to forget, when times are good, that the ultimate role of government is to protect its citizens—from crime, from anarchy, from attacks by enemies. It is particularly easy for this country to forget. From the very beginning of the Republic, we have tended to view ourselves as isolated from the political machinations in Europe and Asia. And, until Pearl Harbor, the great oceans protected us from surprise attack. But in the wake of September 11, we now know all too well that we are vulnerable. One question is how much liberty we are willing to surrender, as a society, in exchange for the hope or expectation of being made more secure.

Of course, if the relevant question when deciding how much civil liberty we should surrender is whether we trust government more than terrorists, we are likely to surrender just about all of our civil liberties. Perhaps a better way to phrase the question is how much of an intrusion is the proposed government action and how much safety will it buy, and are there any liberties or values so valuable—even sacred—that they are not susceptible to cost-benefit analysis?

A few hours after the hijacked commercial airliners struck the two World Trade Center towers and the Pentagon, the FBI was in federal court getting court orders to wiretap the phones of hundreds of persons suspected of having links with terrorist groups. Some of these phone taps produced evidence of support for the hijackers—some gave thanks to Allah for the great success of the hijackers and others gloated at the death and destruction. Did this indicate widespread conspiratorial involvement or only defiant, but lawful, speech? And we may assume that many of the phone taps produced nothing even slightly incriminating because the persons under surveillance were innocent.

Moreover, we now know that the National Security Agency soon began a two-pronged monitoring of telephone calls and e-mails, in many cases without warrants. One part included monitoring the phone calls and e-mails of people with known ties to al-Qaeda. The other aspect was described by the New York Times as mining a "vast data trove," consisting of volume and pattern phone data. Eric Lichtblau & James Risen, *Spy Agency Mined Vast Data Trove, Officials Report*, N.Y. Times, December 24, 2005, A1. These data included who called whom, how often, and how long the calls lasted. *Id.* at A12. In 2015, Congress allowed the NSA metadata surveillance program to lapse. A separate NSA program, PRISM, still allows NSA to intercept emails and cellphone calls made by foreigners. Fred Kaplan, The State of the Surveillance State, *Slate*, June 1, 2015.

In the hours and days following September 11, we did not know whether additional attacks would occur, and whether those attacks might be nuclear, chemical, or biological. Did that risk justify the government's actions? Does it still justify mining "vast data troves"? And what about coercive interrogation methods used at our military base at Guantanamo Bay and other, secret locations overseas? The horrors of September 11, and the Government's response to it, bring into stark clarity the questions that must be asked and answered in *every* criminal investigation and prosecution. What is the optimal trade-off between liberty and privacy, on the one hand, and security against those who would destroy us, on the other hand? In the final analysis, what is the meaning of the middle word in "criminal justice system"?

NOTES AND QUESTIONS

1.   *Narrow holdings and the range of permissible choices.* It is useful to distinguish the narrow holding of a case from the rationale that informs it.

If you read *Brown v. Mississippi*, p. 14, what is the narrow holding? Does it extend only to confessions induced by torture? Suppose, for example, that police interrogate a suspect for over forty hours, until he passes out and then the same officers interrogate him for ten hours a few days later, after which he confesses? Is this confession coerced? Or suppose the police interrogate a suspect for thirty-six hours, after which he confesses? Is either case included within the narrow holding of Brown? Does the rationale of *Brown* reach either case? Which hypothetical case seems more likely to be coercive? Should either or both be held to be coercive police interrogation?

If you read *Powell v. Alabama*, p. 25, what is the narrow holding? The Court stressed the role of the defense lawyer in helping achieve a more reliable outcome, but is that part of the narrow holding or the rationale? One way to ask this question is to ask whether the *holding* of *Powell* extends to a defendant who was not so young or uneducated and who was charged with a non-capital crime in a situation that did not involve racial hysteria. Another way to ask the question is to ask whether ruling against this new defendant is within the range of acceptable choices. Consider the following case.

> [T]here was no question of the commission of a robbery. The State's case consisted of evidence identifying the petitioner as the perpetrator. The defense was an alibi. Petitioner called and examined witnesses to prove that he was at another place at the time of the commission of the offense. The simple issue was the veracity of the testimony for the State and that for the defendant. * * * [T]he accused was not helpless, but was a man forty-three years old, of ordinary intelligence, and ability to take care of his own interests on the trial of that narrow issue. He had once before been in a criminal court, pleaded guilty to larceny and served a sentence and was not wholly unfamiliar with criminal procedure.

Does the narrow holding of *Powell* apply to this case? If not, should *Powell* be extended to cover these facts? Would denying counsel to this defendant be an acceptable outcome, given *Powell*? What if the defendant were described as "a farm hand, out of a job and on relief," "too poor to hire a lawyer," and "a man of little education"? If you were the judge, would this description make you *more* likely to provide him a lawyer? If so, you might be interested to learn that the "ordinary intelligence" description appears in a majority opinion refusing to extend *Powell* and the "little education" description is found in Justice Black's dissent, joined by Justices Douglas and Murphy. See Betts v. Brady, 316 U.S. 455, 62 S.Ct. 1252, 86 L.Ed. 1595 (1942). This tells us, of course, that both choices were permissible ways to read *Powell* and that the Court was not (yet) willing to make the choice that Black, Douglas, and Murphy supported. Black would have the final word on this issue some twenty-one years later. See *Gideon v. Wainwright*, p. 1043.

If you read both *Brown* and *Powell*, choose one to answer (unless your professor assigns both).

2. *Norms versus rules.* Another way to approach the precedential effect of *Powell* is to understand the distinction between rules and norms. Though the distinction between a norm and a rule is not always clear, it can be a useful way to classify legal argument and doctrine. Roughly, a rule requires a particular result and a norm is a way of organizing one's thinking to produce the best result in a particular case. A rule can be expressed "if X, then Y," but

a norm implies a softer relationship between X and Y, sort of "if X, then we should carefully consider whether Y." It is wrong to tell a lie—a norm—suggesting that one should tell the truth. But does that mean we should tell our best friend that his wife is having an affair? Perhaps not. On the other hand if it is perjury to tell a lie under oath—a rule—then a question about the affair requires a truthful answer.

Using this admittedly oversimplified description, look again at the language from *Betts* quoted in the last Note. Can you phrase both a rule and a norm that would have governed the case?

3. *Police investigation problems.* In "solving" the following problems, do not use any constitutional doctrine that you might have learned in other courses (or think you have learned from television). Attempt to use only the norms and values we have identified in this section.

A. *Radar searches.* Suppose scientists develop a type of "radar" gun that can identify with 100% accuracy the existence of chemical compounds. This radar can be tuned so that it will *only* signal the existence of substances that cannot be legally possessed under federal law. If the police aim this machine at residences while driving up and down the streets, to provide the basis for search warrants, does this raise a fairness concern? Any other concern?

B. *The morality of torture.* Police arrested a kidnaping suspect and tried to persuade him to provide information about where the victim was located. He requested counsel, and police permitted him to call counsel. When counsel arrived, he refused to represent the kidnaper (who said the lawyer would only be paid from the ransom money). The kidnaper then insisted on meeting with the victim's father and arranging some kind of cash settlement for lawyer's fees, bail, and expenses. By the time the kidnaper led the police to where he had buried the victim in a coffin-like box in a shallow grave, she had suffocated. Should the police have acted more aggressively? Should they have attempted to coerce from the suspect the victim's location? Should they have used physical coercion? Torture? What if police knew of the victim's fate and had every reason to believe she was clinging to life? See William J. Pizzi, *The Privilege Against Self-Incrimination in a Rescue Situation*, 76 J. Crim. L. & Criminology 567 (discussing People v. Krom, 61 N.Y.2d 187, 473 N.Y.S.2d 139, 461 N.E.2d 276 (1984)).

4. *Criminal process problems.* If you were a state legislator, would you support the following bills? Again, use the norms and values identified in the reading above, rather than anything you might know about existing constitutional or statutory provisions that are relevant to each problem.

A. *Speedy trial.* A proposed bill would require trials within 180 days after formal charges are filed. The sanction for failing to meet the deadline is dismissal of charges, which can be without prejudice to bring the same charges again if required in the interests of justice.

B. *Pretrial depositions.* A bill is proposed to require depositions of criminal defendants, on the model of civil depositions, with two differences: (1) a judge will oversee the process; (2) the defendant may refuse to answer questions. If the defendant refuses, however, the refusal is admissible in evidence at trial.

The bill also requires the State to make its witnesses available for the defense to depose, except when the prosecutor can show the potential for witness intimidation or reprisal. State funds will pay defense counsel's fee when the defendant is indigent.

C. *Pretrial detention.* A bill requires pretrial detention of all defendants charged with the most serious felonies if the hearing magistrate finds by clear and convincing evidence that no lesser restraint will reasonably assure the appearance of the defendant at trial or the safety of the community.

D. *Jury service.* A proposed bill would automatically exempt from jury service the following groups: (1) surgeons; (2) lawyers; (3) mothers with children younger than six; (4) college students. Any exempted individual can request to be included in the pool by filing a form with the court clerk.

E. *Jury composition.* The legislature is considering a bill to reduce the jury size to six, requiring unanimity, or, alternatively, to keep the number at twelve and permit verdicts by a vote of 9–3.

F. *Jury challenges.* The bill described in E. abolishes all peremptory challenges (those granted without the necessity of showing cause for dismissal).

5.   The United States Supreme Court could not have been happy with the range of choices that some state courts seemed to find legitimate early in the twentieth century. *Johnson, Frank, Powell,* and *Brown* paint a frightening picture of justice in the hands of men too biased to see innocence in those perceived to be different, perceived as threatening. Even so, the power of federalism in criminal justice matters made the Court's interventions sporadic and weak for many years. The next section discusses the origin of this strong version of criminal justice federalism and its gradual decline.

C. THE BILL OF RIGHTS AND THE FOURTEENTH AMENDMENT: THE INCORPORATION STORY

Dating back to colonial days, criminal law and criminal justice were viewed as almost exclusively state and local matters. Federal criminal law jurisdiction was tiny; the first federal criminal code made crimes of murder, robbery, and larceny but only when committed on federal property or the high seas or against federal property. The vast bulk of criminal law and criminal prosecutions were carried out by the states as had been done when they were colonies. Thus, it is not surprising that when the Supreme Court began to "incorporate" rights from the Bill of Rights into the Due Process Clause, the criminal procedure rights were the last incorporated.

1 JOSHUA DRESSLER & ALAN C. MICHAELS— UNDERSTANDING CRIMINAL PROCEDURE

(5th ed. 2010), § 3.01, pp. 41–43.

The Fourteenth Amendment, adopted in 1868, imposes limits on *state action.* Section 1 of that amendment limits the state in three ways:

No State shall [1] make or enforce any law which shall abridge the privileges or immunities of citizens of the United States; [2] nor shall any State deprive any person of life, liberty, or property, without due process of law; [3] nor deny to any person within its jurisdiction the equal protection of the laws.

The relationship between the Fourteenth Amendment and the Bill of Rights has been vigorously disputed. The legal battle, commonly called the "incorporation debate," centers on the second clause of section 1, namely, the Due Process Clause. The essential question is this: To what extent does the Fourteenth Amendment Due Process Clause "incorporate" (or "absorb") the Bill of Rights and, as a consequence, impose on the states the same restrictions the Bill of Rights impose on the federal government? * * * A related question is whether the Fourteenth Amendment guarantees any rights not enumerated in the Bill of Rights. * * *

The incorporation debate is important for various reasons. First, the extent to which individuals are protected from overreaching by agents of the state depends in large measure on the extent to which the Fourteenth Amendment incorporates the Bill of Rights. At one extreme, if none of the rights found in the Bill of Rights apply to the states, citizens may be subjected to, for example, warrantless invasions of the home by local police, coercive interrogation techniques, and felony trials without the assistance of counsel. On the other hand, if the Due Process Clause incorporates the Bill of Rights in its entirety, the latter charter becomes a national code of criminal procedure—federal and state action would be identically restricted.

Second, as the latter observation suggests, values of federalism are at stake in the incorporation debate. The broader the interpretation of the scope of the Fourteenth Amendment Due Process Clause, the less free are the states to develop their own rules of criminal procedure, and to adapt them to an individual state's particular social and political conditions.

Third, the incorporation debate raises important questions regarding the proper role of the judiciary in the enforcement of constitutional rights.

In particular, if the Due Process Clause of the Fourteenth Amendment incorporates some, but not all, of the Bill of Rights, then judges must use some standard to decide which doctrines apply against the states and which do not, thereby increasing the risk that judges will make these determinations based on personal policy predilections rather than on a legitimate and principled constitutional basis.

NOTES AND QUESTIONS

1. *Privileges or immunities.* The first clause of the Fourteenth Amendment forbids states from denying its citizens "the privileges or immunities of citizens of the United States." Would this not guarantee at least some of the rights granted in the first ten amendments? In 1873, the Court rejected this argument in dicta by a 5–4 vote. Slaughter-House Cases, 83 U.S. (16 Wall.) 36, 21 L.Ed. 394 (1873). The Court stated that this clause protected only those privileges and immunities that exist *by virtue of national citizenship*, which did not include the rights guaranteed in the Bill of Rights. A recent historical account of the *Slaughter-House Cases* describes in detail the purpose of the legislation that the Court upheld—to prevent the vast butchering operations from disposing of waste into the streets of New Orleans. At times, the streets of New Orleans were rivers of offal. Unsurprisingly, the city had cholera outbreaks every year. See Ronald M. Labbe & Jonathan Lurie, The Slaughterhouse Cases: Regulation, Reconstruction, and the Fourteenth Amendment (2003).

2. *Due process.* In 1884, the Court acknowledged that the Fourteenth Amendment due process clause applied to state criminal processes, though the Court held that the right to a grand jury indictment is not part of due process. Hurtado v. California, 110 U.S. 516, 4 S.Ct. 111, 28 L.Ed. 232 (1884). In 1900, the Court held that the right to a jury of twelve in a criminal case is not part of due process (the state constitution required a jury of eight). Maxwell v. Dow, 176 U.S. 581, 20 S.Ct. 448, 44 L.Ed. 597 (1900). Eight years later, the Court held that due process did not prohibit an instruction to the jury that it could draw a negative inference from the defendant's failure to testify. Twining v. New Jersey, 211 U.S. 78, 29 S.Ct. 14, 53 L.Ed. 97 (1908).

3. We have seen that the defendants won their due process claim in *Powell* p. 25, and *Brown*, p. 14, and that the defendants in *Hurtado*, *Maxwell*, and *Twining* (Note 2) lost. Can you develop an account of due process that would explain why the *Powell* and *Brown* defendants prevailed while Hurtado and Twining lost? How would you apply your account to the following motions by defendants: (a) to suppress an eyewitness identification as unreliable; (b) for money to pay a forensic expert to testify on behalf of an indigent defendant; and (c) to require that a jury verdict be unanimous?

4. *Developing standards of due process.* What test should the Supreme Court use to decide when a state trial or investigation has violated the Fourteenth Amendment due process clause? In Palko v. Connecticut, 302

U.S. 319, 58 S.Ct. 149, 82 L.Ed. 288 (1937), Justice Cardozo sought to articulate a test for what due process requires of a state criminal process.

> Our survey of the cases serves, we think, to justify the statement that the dividing line between them, if not unfaltering throughout its course, has been true for the most part to a unifying principle. On which side of the line the case made out by the appellant has appropriate location must be the next inquiry and the final one. Is that kind of double jeopardy to which the statute has subjected him a hardship so acute and shocking that our polity will not endure it? Does it violate those "fundamental principles of liberty and justice which lie at the base of all our civil and political institutions"?

The test announced by Cardozo was a restrictive one. Not many rights would qualify if the test were whether the lack of the right "subjected" the defendant to "a hardship so acute and shocking that our polity will not endure it." Nor would many rights qualify as "fundamental principles of liberty and justice which lie at the base of all our civil and political institutions." Which rights in the Bill of Rights do you think would qualify for inclusion under Cardozo's test?

5. *The inexorable march of incorporation.* One way to read the Fourteenth Amendment, which avoids having to develop an account of due process, is Justice Hugo Black's "total" incorporation approach. In Black's view, "one of the chief objects" of the Fourteenth Amendment "was to make the Bill of Rights applicable to the states." Adamson v. California, 332 U.S. 46, 67 S.Ct. 1672, 91 L.Ed. 1903 (1947) (Black, J., dissenting). On this view, the Fourteenth Amendment simply absorbs the entire Bill of Rights, and makes each right applicable to the states, but creates no rights other than those found in the Bill of Rights.

Justice Black never persuaded a majority to accept total incorporation, but he stayed on the Court long enough (thirty-six years) to see a step-by-step "selective" incorporation that, by Black's death in 1971, was almost complete. Here is the way the Court described the status of incorporation in 1968.

> The Fourteenth Amendment denies the States the power to "deprive any person of life, liberty, or property, without due process of law." In resolving conflicting claims concerning the meaning of this spacious language, the Court has looked increasingly to the Bill of Rights for guidance; many of the rights guaranteed by the first eight Amendments to the Constitution have been held to be protected against state action by the Due Process Clause of the Fourteenth Amendment. That clause now protects the right to compensation for property taken by the State; the rights of speech, press, and religion covered by the First Amendment; the Fourth Amendment rights to be free from unreasonable searches and seizures and to have excluded from criminal trials any evidence illegally seized; the right guaranteed by the Fifth Amendment to be

free of compelled self-incrimination; and the Sixth Amendment rights to counsel, to a speedy and public trial, to confrontation of opposing witnesses, and to compulsory process for obtaining witnesses.

Duncan v. Louisiana, 391 U.S. 145, 88 S.Ct. 1444, 20 L.Ed.2d 491 (1968).

6.   The Court has overruled *Twining v. New Jersey*, Note 2. See Malloy v. Hogan, 378 U.S. 1, 84 S.Ct. 1489, 12 L.Ed.2d 653 (1964). The Court has not, however, overruled *Hurtado v. California*, Note 2, and states are thus *not* required to provide grand juries. But what about trial juries? How would that right fit into the list in Note 5? Consider the next case.

DUNCAN V. LOUISIANA
Supreme Court of the United States, 1968.
391 U.S. 145, 88 S.Ct. 1444, 20 L.Ed.2d 491.

MR. JUSTICE WHITE delivered the opinion of the Court [joined by CHIEF JUSTICE WARREN, and JUSTICES BLACK, DOUGLAS, BRENNAN, FORTAS, and MARSHALL]. * * *

* * * Appellant sought trial by jury [on the charge of simple assault], but because the Louisiana Constitution grants jury trials only in cases in which capital punishment or imprisonment at hard labor may be imposed, the trial judge denied the request. Appellant was convicted and sentenced to serve 60 days in the parish prison and pay a fine of $150. * * *

I * * *

The test for determining whether a right extended by the Fifth and Sixth Amendments with respect to federal criminal proceedings is also protected against state action by the Fourteenth Amendment has been phrased in a variety of ways in the opinions of this Court. The question has been asked whether a right is among those "fundamental principles of liberty and justice which lie at the base of all our civil and political institutions," whether it is "basic in our system of jurisprudence," and whether it is "a fundamental right, essential to a fair trial." The claim before us is that the right to trial by jury guaranteed by the Sixth Amendment meets these tests. The position of Louisiana, on the other hand, is that the Constitution imposes upon the States no duty to give a jury trial in any criminal case, regardless of the seriousness of the crime or the size of the punishment which may be imposed. Because we believe that trial by jury in criminal cases is fundamental to the American scheme of justice, we hold that the Fourteenth Amendment guarantees a right of jury trial in all criminal cases which—were they to be tried in a federal court—would come within the Sixth Amendment's guarantee. * * *

The history of trial by jury in criminal cases has been frequently told. It is sufficient for present purposes to say that by the time our Constitution was written, jury trial in criminal cases had been in existence in England for several centuries and carried impressive credentials traced by many to Magna Carta. * * *

Jury trial came to America with English colonists, and received strong support from them. Royal interference with the jury trial was deeply resented. Among the resolutions adopted by the First Congress of the American Colonies (the Stamp Act Congress) on October 19, 1765— resolutions deemed by their authors to state "the most essential rights and liberties of the colonists"—was the declaration:

> "That trial by jury is the inherent and invaluable right of every British subject in these colonies."

The First Continental Congress, in the resolve of October 14, 1774, objected to trials before judges dependent upon the Crown alone for their salaries and to trials in England for alleged crimes committed in the colonies; the Congress therefore declared:

> "That the respective colonies are entitled to the common law of England, and more especially to the great and inestimable privilege of being tried by their peers of the vicinage, according to the course of that law."

* * * The Constitution itself, in Art. III, § 2, commanded:

> "The Trial of all Crimes, except in Cases of Impeachment, shall be by Jury; and such Trial shall be held in the State where the said Crimes shall have been committed."

Objections to the Constitution because of the absence of a bill of rights were met by the immediate submission and adoption of the Bill of Rights. Included was the Sixth Amendment which, among other things, provided:

> "In all criminal prosecutions, the accused shall enjoy the right to a speedy and public trial, by an impartial jury of the State and district wherein the crime shall have been committed."

The constitutions adopted by the original States guaranteed jury trial. Also, the constitution of every State entering the Union thereafter in one form or another protected the right to jury trial in criminal cases.

Even such skeletal history is impressive support for considering the right to jury trial in criminal cases to be fundamental to our system of justice, an importance frequently recognized in the opinions of this Court. * * *

The guarantees of jury trial in the Federal and State Constitutions reflect a profound judgment about the way in which law should be enforced and justice administered. A right to jury trial is granted to criminal defendants in order to prevent oppression by the Government. Those who wrote our constitutions knew from history and experience that it was necessary to protect against unfounded criminal charges brought to eliminate enemies and against judges too responsive to the voice of higher authority. The framers of the constitutions strove to create an independent judiciary but insisted upon further protection against arbitrary action. Providing an accused with the right to be tried by a jury of his peers gave him an inestimable safeguard against the corrupt or overzealous prosecutor and against the compliant, biased, or eccentric judge. If the defendant preferred the common-sense judgment of a jury to the more tutored but perhaps less sympathetic reaction of the single judge, he was to have it. Beyond this, the jury trial provisions in the Federal and State Constitutions reflect a fundamental decision about the exercise of official power—a reluctance to entrust plenary powers over the life and liberty of the citizen to one judge or to a group of judges. Fear of unchecked power, so typical of our State and Federal Governments in other respects, found expression in the criminal law in this insistence upon community participation in the determination of guilt or innocence. The deep commitment of the Nation to the right of jury trial in serious criminal cases as a defense against arbitrary law enforcement qualifies for protection under the Due Process Clause of the Fourteenth Amendment, and must therefore be respected by the States. * * *

MR. JUSTICE BLACK, with whom MR. JUSTICE DOUGLAS joins, concurring. * * *

* * * With [the Court's] holding I agree for reasons given by the Court. I also agree because of reasons given in my dissent in *Adamson v. California*, 332 U.S. 46, 68, 67 S.Ct. 1672, 1683, 91 L.Ed. 1903. In that dissent, I took the position, contrary to the holding in *Twining v. New Jersey* [p. 51, Note 2], that the Fourteenth Amendment made all of the provisions of the Bill of Rights applicable to the States. * * *

* * * The dissent in this case, however, makes a spirited and forceful defense of that now discredited [*Twining*] doctrine. I do not believe that it is necessary for me to repeat the historical and logical reasons for my challenge to the *Twining* holding contained in my *Adamson* dissent and Appendix to it. What I wrote there in 1947 was the product of years of study and research. My appraisal of the legislative history followed 10 years of legislative experience as a Senator of the United States, not a bad way, I suspect, to learn the value of what is said in legislative debates, committee discussions, committee reports, and various other steps taken in the course of passage of bills, resolutions, and proposed constitutional amendments. My Brother Harlan's objections to my *Adamson* dissent history, like that of most of the objectors, relies most heavily on a criticism written by Professor Charles Fairman and published in the Stanford Law Review. 2 Stan. L. Rev. 5 (1949). I have

read and studied this article extensively, including the historical references, but am compelled to add that in my view it has completely failed to refute the inferences and arguments that I suggested in my *Adamson* dissent. * * *

In addition to the adoption of Professor Fairman's "history," the dissent states that "the great words of the four clauses of the first section of the Fourteenth Amendment would have been an exceedingly peculiar way to say that 'The rights heretofore guaranteed against federal intrusion by the first eight Amendments are henceforth guaranteed against state intrusion as well.'" In response to this I can say only that the words "No State shall make or enforce any law which shall abridge the privileges or immunities of citizens of the United States" seem to me an eminently reasonable way of expressing the idea that henceforth the Bill of Rights shall apply to the States. What more precious "privilege" of American citizenship could there be than that privilege to claim the protections of our great Bill of Rights? I suggest that any reading of "privileges or immunities of citizens of the United States" which excludes the Bill of Rights' safeguards renders the words of this section of the Fourteenth Amendment meaningless. * * *

* * * [In Justice Harlan's view,] the Due Process Clause is treated as prescribing no specific and clearly ascertainable constitutional command that judges must obey in interpreting the Constitution, but rather as leaving judges free to decide at any particular time whether a particular rule or judicial formulation embodies an "immutable principl[e] of free government" or is "implicit in the concept of ordered liberty," or whether certain conduct "shocks the judge's conscience" or runs counter to some other similar, undefined and undefinable standard. Thus due process, according to my Brother Harlan, is to be a phrase with no permanent meaning, but one which is found to shift from time to time in accordance with judges' predilections and understandings of what is best for the country. If due process means this, the Fourteenth Amendment, in my opinion, might as well have been written that "no person shall be deprived of life, liberty or property except by laws that the judges of the United States Supreme Court shall find to be consistent with the immutable principles of free government." It is impossible for me to believe that such unconfined power is given to judges in our Constitution that is a written one in order to limit governmental power. * * *

MR. JUSTICE FORTAS, concurring.

* * * I agree that the Due Process Clause of the Fourteenth Amendment requires that the States accord the right to jury trial in prosecutions for offenses that are not petty. * * *

But although I agree with the decision of the Court, I cannot agree with the implication, that the tail must go with the hide: that when we hold, influenced by the Sixth Amendment, that "due process" requires that the States accord the right of jury trial for all but petty offenses, we automatically import all of the ancillary rules which have been or may hereafter be developed incidental to the right to jury trial in the federal courts. I see no reason whatever, for example, to assume that our decision today should require us to impose federal requirements such as unanimous verdicts or a jury of 12 upon the States. We may well conclude that these and other features of federal jury practice are by no means fundamental—that they are not essential to due process of law—and that they are not obligatory on the States.

I would make these points clear today. Neither logic nor history nor the intent of the draftsmen of the Fourteenth Amendment can possibly be said to require that the Sixth Amendment or its jury trial provision be applied to the States together with the total gloss that this Court's decisions have supplied. The draftsmen of the Fourteenth Amendment intended what they said, not more or less: that no State shall deprive any person of life, liberty, or property without due process of law. It is ultimately the duty of this Court to interpret, to ascribe specific meaning to this phrase. There is no reason whatever for us to conclude that, in so doing, we are bound slavishly to follow not only the Sixth Amendment but all of its bag and baggage, however securely or insecurely affixed they may be by law and precedent to federal proceedings. To take this course, in my judgment, would be not only unnecessary but mischievous because it would inflict a serious blow upon the principle of federalism. The Due Process Clause commands us to apply its great standard to state court proceedings to assure basic fairness. It does not command us rigidly and arbitrarily to impose the exact pattern of federal proceedings upon the 50 States. On the contrary, the Constitution's command, in my view, is that in our insistence upon state observance of due process, we should, so far as possible, allow the greatest latitude for state differences. It requires, within the limits of the lofty basic standards that it prescribes for the States as well as the Federal Government, maximum opportunity for diversity and minimal imposition of uniformity of method and detail upon the States. Our Constitution sets up a federal union, not a monolith. * * *

MR. JUSTICE HARLAN, whom MR. JUSTICE STEWART joins, dissenting.

Every American jurisdiction provides for trial by jury in criminal cases. The question before us is not whether jury trial is an ancient institution, which it is; nor whether it plays a significant role in the administration of criminal justice, which it does; nor whether it will endure, which it shall. The question in this case is whether the State of Louisiana, which provides trial by jury for all felonies, is prohibited by the Constitution from trying charges of simple battery to the court alone. In my view, the answer to that question, mandated alike by our constitutional history and by the longer history of trial by jury, is clearly "no."

The States have always borne primary responsibility for operating the machinery of criminal justice within their borders, and adapting it to their particular circumstances. In exercising this responsibility, each State is compelled to conform its procedures to the requirements of the Federal Constitution. The Due Process Clause of the Fourteenth Amendment requires that those procedures be fundamentally fair in all respects. It does not, in my view, impose or encourage nationwide uniformity for its own sake; it does not command adherence to forms that happen to be old; and it does not impose on the States the rules that may be in force in the federal courts except where such rules are also found to be essential to basic fairness.

The Court's approach to this case is an uneasy and illogical compromise among the views of various Justices on how the Due Process Clause should be interpreted. The Court does not say that those who framed the Fourteenth Amendment intended to make the Sixth Amendment applicable to the States. And the Court concedes [in an omitted part of the majority opinion] that it finds nothing unfair about the procedure by which the present appellant was tried. Nevertheless, the Court reverses his conviction: it holds, for some reason not apparent to me, that the Due Process Clause incorporates the particular clause of the Sixth Amendment that requires trial by jury in federal criminal cases— including, as I read its opinion, the sometimes trivial accompanying baggage of judicial interpretation in federal contexts. I have raised my voice many times before against the Court's continuing undiscriminating insistence upon fastening on the States federal notions of criminal justice, and I must do so again in this instance. With all respect, the Court's approach and its reading of history are altogether topsy-turvy.

I * * *

A few members of the Court have taken the position that the intention of those who drafted the first section of the Fourteenth Amendment was simply, and exclusively, to make the provisions of the first eight Amendments applicable to state action. This view has never been accepted by this Court. In my view, often expressed elsewhere, the first section of the Fourteenth Amendment was meant neither to incorporate, nor to be limited to, the specific guarantees of the first eight Amendments. * * * In short, neither history, nor sense, supports using the Fourteenth Amendment to put the States in a constitutional straitjacket with respect to their own development in the administration of criminal or civil law.

Although I therefore fundamentally disagree with the total incorporation view of the Fourteenth Amendment, it seems to me that

such a position does at least have the virtue, lacking in the Court's
selective incorporation approach, of internal consistency: we look to the
Bill of Rights, word for word, clause for clause, precedent for precedent
because, it is said, the men who wrote the Amendment wanted it that
way. For those who do not accept this "history," a different source of
"intermediate premises" must be found. The Bill of Rights is not
necessarily irrelevant to the search for guidance in interpreting the
Fourteenth Amendment, but the reason for and the nature of its
relevance must be articulated. * * *

Today's Court still remains unwilling to accept the total
incorporationists' view of the history of the Fourteenth Amendment. This,
if accepted, would afford a cogent reason for applying the Sixth
Amendment to the States. The Court is also, apparently, unwilling to face
the task of determining whether denial of trial by jury in the situation
before us, or in other situations, is fundamentally unfair. Consequently,
the Court has compromised on the ease of the incorporationist position,
without its internal logic. It has simply assumed that the question before
us is whether the Jury Trial Clause of the Sixth Amendment should be
incorporated into the Fourteenth, jot-for-jot and case-for-case, or ignored.
Then the Court merely declares that the clause in question is "in" rather
than "out."

The Court has justified neither its starting place nor its conclusion. If
the problem is to discover and articulate the rules of fundamental
fairness in criminal proceedings, there is no reason to assume that the
whole body of rules developed in this Court constituting Sixth
Amendment jury trial must be regarded as a unit. The requirement of
trial by jury in federal criminal cases has given rise to numerous
subsidiary questions respecting the exact scope and content of the right.
It surely cannot be that every answer the Court has given, or will give, to
such a question is attributable to the Founders; or even that every rule
announced carries equal conviction of this Court; still less can it be that
every such subprinciple is equally fundamental to ordered liberty.

Examples abound. I should suppose it obviously fundamental to
fairness that a "jury" means an "impartial jury." I should think it equally
obvious that the rule, imposed long ago in the federal courts, that "jury"
means "jury of exactly twelve," is not fundamental to anything: there is
no significance except to mystics in the number 12. Again, trial by jury
has been held to require a unanimous verdict of jurors in the federal
courts, although unanimity has not been found essential to liberty in
Britain, where the requirement has been abandoned. * * *

Even if I could agree that the question before us is whether Sixth
Amendment jury trial is totally "in" or totally "out," I can find in the
Court's opinion no real reasons for concluding that it should be "in." The

basis for differentiating among clauses in the Bill of Rights cannot be that only some clauses are in the Bill of Rights, or that only some are old and much praised, or that only some have played an important role in the development of federal law. These things are true of all. The Court says that some clauses are more "fundamental" than others, but it turns out to be using this word in a sense that would have astonished Mr. Justice Cardozo and which, in addition, is of no help. The word does not mean "analytically critical to procedural fairness" for no real analysis of the role of the jury in making procedures fair is even attempted. Instead, the word turns out to mean "old," "much praised," and "found in the Bill of Rights." The definition of "fundamental" thus turns out to be circular.

II

Since, as I see it, the Court has not even come to grips with the issues in this case, it is necessary to start from the beginning. When a criminal defendant contends that his state conviction lacked "due process of law," the question before this Court, in my view, is whether he was denied any element of fundamental procedural fairness. * * *

The argument that jury trial is not a requisite of due process is quite simple. The central proposition of *Palko* [Note 4, p. 51], a proposition to which I would adhere, is that "due process of law" requires only that criminal trials be fundamentally fair. * * * But it simply has not been demonstrated, nor, I think, can it be demonstrated, that trial by jury is the only fair means of resolving issues of fact. * * *

It can hardly be gainsaid * * * that the principal original virtue of the jury trial—the limitations a jury imposes on a tyrannous judiciary—has largely disappeared. We no longer live in a medieval or colonial society. Judges enforce laws enacted by democratic decision, not by regal fiat. They are elected by the people or appointed by the people's elected officials, and are responsible not to a distant monarch alone but to reviewing courts, including this one. * * *

* * * The Court recognizes [that trials to judges are fair]:

> "We would not assert, however, that every criminal trial—or any particular trial—held before a judge alone is unfair or that a defendant may never be as fairly treated by a judge as he would be by a jury."

I agree. I therefore see no reason why this Court should reverse the conviction of appellant, absent any suggestion that his particular trial was in fact unfair, or compel the State of Louisiana to afford jury trial in an as yet unbounded category of cases that can, without unfairness, be tried to a court. * * *

In sum, there is a wide range of views on the desirability of trial by jury, and on the ways to make it most effective when it is used; there is also considerable variation from State to State in local conditions such as the size of the criminal caseload, the ease or difficulty of summoning jurors, and other trial conditions bearing on fairness. We have before us, therefore, an almost perfect example of a situation in which the celebrated dictum of Mr. Justice Brandeis should be invoked. It is, he said,

> "one of the happy incidents of the federal system that a single courageous state may, if its citizens choose, serve as a laboratory * * *."

This Court, other courts, and the political process are available to correct any experiments in criminal procedure that prove fundamentally unfair to defendants. That is not what is being done today: instead, and quite without reason, the Court has chosen to impose upon every state one means of trying criminal cases; it is a good means, but it is not the only fair means, and it is not demonstrably better than the alternatives States might devise. * * *

NOTES AND QUESTIONS

1. Justices Hugo Black and John Harlan were on the Supreme Court together for sixteen years (1955–1971). As you can see from the exchange in *Duncan*, they disagreed fundamentally over how to interpret the Fourteenth Amendment. Can you articulate Justice Harlan's view of due process? What do you think Harlan means when he charges that the "Court has compromised on the ease of the incorporationist position, without its internal logic"?

2. Part of Black's argument in favor of total incorporation is that, otherwise, judges would be tempted "to roam at large in the broad expanses of policy and morals and to trespass, all too freely, on the legislative domain of the States as well as the Federal government." Adamson v. California, 332 U.S. 46, 67 S.Ct. 1672, 91 L.Ed. 1903 (1947) (Black, J., dissenting). Remember, Black's view of total incorporation was that the Fourteenth Amendment incorporated *all* of the Bill of Rights guarantees but otherwise created no rights against state authority. For example, he dissented in Griswold v. Connecticut, 381 U.S. 479, 85 S.Ct. 1678, 14 L.Ed.2d 510 (1965), which held that the due process clause prohibited Connecticut from enforcing its criminal law against the use of birth control. A fundamental-rights theorist could find, as the Court did, a right to privacy in the due process clause, but not an incorporationist who looked only at the relatively specific guarantees of the Bill of Rights. Can you see why?

3. Between the Harlan and Black positions in *Duncan*, which argument do you prefer? Does it matter on this issue that the Framers of the Bill of Rights considered, and rejected, an amendment that would have required states to provide jury trials?

4. *The role of precedent.* Justice Fortas concurred in the majority opinion in *Duncan*, yet his view seems closer to Harlan's. Suppose you joined the Court a few years after *Duncan*, and one of the first cases is a challenge to a state statute permitting verdicts by a 9–3 vote. Now assume you agree with Harlan and Stewart, who are still on the Court, that *Duncan* was wrongly decided. Fortas and another member of the original *Duncan* majority are willing to reverse *Duncan*. Alternatively, you can distinguish *Duncan* on the theory that a 9–3 jury is at least a jury, while Duncan had no jury at all. Would you press to overrule *Duncan*, since you have five votes, or would you decide the new case by distinguishing *Duncan*? Do you think precedent ought to stand until it is necessary to overrule it, or should the Court take the first opportunity to correct doctrine when it decides a mistake has been made?

5. *What goes around, comes around.* The case described in Note 4 came to the Court, after Fortas resigned, and the Court split 4–4 on whether the Fourteenth Amendment required a unanimous verdict in state criminal trials. Apodaca v. Oregon, 406 U.S. 404, 92 S.Ct. 1628, 32 L.Ed.2d 184 (1972). Justice Powell's crucial fifth vote was based on the Fortas view that unanimous jury verdicts are required by the *Sixth Amendment* but not by the *Fourteenth*. The Court, in effect, gave greater leeway to the states in interpreting the Fourteenth Amendment than it was willing to give to Congress under the Sixth Amendment.

6. Scholars have begun to question the Warren Court's decision to incorporate the Bill of Rights criminal procedure guarantees. Incorporation, Tracey Meares argued, has caused the Court to de-emphasize the "public-regarding" vision of fairness that once highlighted racial injustice in the application of criminal laws. When the Court asked itself whether convictions resulted from fundamentally fair processes, it often considered, explicitly or implicitly, the racial context of the case. Incorporation, however, led the Court to ask merely whether the defendant received the proper procedure, a focus that invited courts to ignore the racial context. Choosing incorporation "as the mechanism for criminal justice system reform" has ironically limited "prospects for addressing race-related perceptions of criminal justice system unfairness." Tracey L. Meares, *Everything Old is New Again: Fundamental Fairness and the Legitimacy of Criminal Justice*, 3 Ohio State J. Crim. Law 105, 106 (2005).

Morgan Cloud concluded that incorporation in effect replaced traditional theories of the Fourth Amendment with new doctrines that weakened protections of privacy, property, and liberty. See Morgan Cloud, *A Liberal House Divided: How the Warren Court Dismantled the Fourth Amendment*, 3 Ohio State J. Crim. L. 33 (2005). George Thomas argued that one effect of incorporation was to distract the Court from what should be its prime directive in criminal procedure—designing doctrines to protect innocent suspects and defendants. See George C. Thomas III, *The Criminal Procedure Road Not Taken: Due Process and the Protection of Innocence*, 3 Ohio State J. Crim. L. 169 (2005).

In Donald Dripps's view, incorporation prevailed because there was not a strong advocate for the due process alternative. Donald A. Dripps, *Justice Harlan on Criminal Procedure: Two Cheers for the Legal Process School*, 3 Ohio State J. Crim. L. 125 (2005). While Justice Harlan was a brilliant justice and gifted writer, his stubborn view that criminal process questions could be left largely to the state legislatures doomed any chance that a majority of the Court would embrace his due process theory. Dripps argued that the due process clause could be read as requiring "proportionate police practices and reliable trial procedures" and that this would be a better criminal procedure world than incorporation has given us. *Id.* at 168.

7.   *Don't forget state law.* The focus in criminal procedure books tends to be on the Bill of Rights provisions that now, mostly, apply to state suspects and defendants just as they do in federal cases. But don't make the mistake one of the casebook authors made. Fresh out of law school, the author was appointed to represent a defendant charged with second-degree murder based on a drunk driving accident. The police obtained a highly incriminating blood sample from the driver while he was unconscious in the hospital. When time came to file a motion to suppress, the young lawyer decided not to bother since the Supreme Court had decided this precise issue against the defendant in Breithaupt v. Abram, 352 U.S. 432, 77 S.Ct. 408, 1 L.Ed.2d 448 (1957). An older and wiser member of the local defense bar asked why no motion to suppress was being filed. The young lawyer said, with a touch of arrogance, "The Supreme Court has already decided this issue in *Breithaupt*."

"I don't know *Breithaupt*," sputtered the wise lawyer. "But I do know the Tennessee Code Annotated."

Yes, indeed, a Tennessee statute provided that a blood sample could not be used for any purpose if taken without consent. The motion was filed and argued on state law grounds. The judge suppressed the blood sample, and a very favorable plea offer followed. (Tennessee later amended the statute so that it did not apply in homicide cases.)

D. THE "BEST TRIAL IN THE WORLD"?

In some ways, we are back to the future, though with less Supreme Court oversight. The chapter began with cases from the Deep South where the Court was forced to intervene to prevent rank injustices. This part demonstrates injustices that are more subtle, but just as real, and the Supreme Court does not get involved. The Court's unwillingness to take modern cases of injustice stems from the subtlety of the injustices, from the Court's assumption that the system works to protect against wrongful convictions, and from the sheer volume of criminal cases. It is fair to ask, though, whether the turmoil of the mid-twentieth century—when the Court imposed almost all of the Bill of Rights procedure guarantees on the states—accomplished anything of lasting value.

1. CONVICTIONS OF INNOCENT DEFENDANTS

GEORGE C. THOMAS III—THE SUPREME COURT ON TRIAL—HOW THE AMERICAN SYSTEM OF JUSTICE SACRIFICES INNOCENT DEFENDANTS

(2008) 6–8.

At 8:10 in the morning on December 29, 1991, a female bartender was found, dead, in the men's room of the C.B.S. Lounge in Phoenix. She was nude. The killer left behind no physical evidence save bite marks on her breast and neck. The victim had told a friend that Ray Krone was going to help close the bar that night. Police asked Krone to make a bite impression, and an expert witness prepared a videotape that purported to show a match by moving Krone's bite impression onto the marks on the victim. According to the Arizona Supreme Court, the videotape "presented evidence in ways that would have been impossible using static exhibits." State v. Krone, 897 P.2d 621, 622 (Ariz. 1995). Although defense counsel had been given the opportunity to examine the dental expert, counsel was not informed of the existence of the videotape until the eve of trial.

The only other evidence against Krone was that he was "evasive with the police about his relationship" with the victim. *Id.* Of course, without the bite mark identification, being "evasive" about a relationship is practically worthless as evidence. The case turned on the bite mark evidence, and the court-appointed defense expert had no experience in video production. Accordingly, counsel moved for a continuance to obtain an expert who could evaluate the videotape. Alternatively, counsel moved to suppress the videotape or to allow testimony about an earlier case in which the same expert's testimony was successfully challenged as not sufficiently scientific. The trial court overruled all the defense motions. The prosecution expert used the videotape in his testimony, and no defense expert challenged his presentation. The jury convicted Krone of murder and kidnaping. The trial judge sentenced Krone to death.

On appeal, the Arizona Supreme Court held that the trial judge had acted improperly in refusing to allow a continuance. The jury had not yet been selected when the motion was made, the court noted, and the State would have suffered little prejudice. If substantial prejudice would have been caused, the right course of action, according to the state supreme court, was to preclude use of the videotape. What the trial judge could not do was what he did—allow use of the tape without giving defense counsel ample opportunity to prepare a defense.

So far, so good. The case was remanded for a new trial, the defense secured an expert, and the jury convicted again. This time, though, the judge sentenced Krone to life in prison, "citing doubts about whether or not Krone was the true killer." See Innocence Project web site (case of Ray

Krone). This borders on the unbelievable. A trial judge who had "doubts about whether or not Krone was the true killer" *sentenced him to life in prison.* Krone served over ten years in prison before DNA testing conducted on the saliva and blood found on the victim excluded him as the killer. The DNA matched a man who lived close to the bar but who had never been considered a suspect in the killing.

Ray Krone's case is an example of how the current system fails innocent defendants. Police seized on the first plausible suspect and looked no further. The prosecution built a case on a Styrofoam bite impression and mumbo-jumbo scientific evidence. That the case was so weak perhaps explains why the prosecutor did not want the defense to be able to challenge the videotaped "expert" testimony. If true, that violates the first rule of prosecution—to do justice rather than try to win all cases. "Doing justice" in Ray Krone's case meant allowing the defense to challenge the prosecution's expert testimony.

The first trial judge failed to give Krone a chance to demonstrate his innocence, and the second one sentenced him to life in prison even though he had doubts about his guilt. These are fundamental failures. To be sure, some parts of the system worked. Krone received what appears to have been effective representation by his counsel, and the Arizona Supreme Court recognized the errors of the first trial judge. Nonetheless, despite these successes, Ray Krone would have spent the rest of his life in prison for a crime he did not commit were it not for DNA testing and the Innocence Project at Cardozo Law School, founded by Barry Scheck and Peter Neufeld.

What has gone wrong? In a work published in 1713, Matthew Hale acclaimed the English common law jury trial as the "best Trial in the World." Matthew Hale, The History and Analysis of the Common Law 252 (1713). Several commendable qualities that Hale noted have truth as the goal, and three mention truth specifically. Hale said that having witnesses testify in person—subject to being questioned by the parties, the judge, and the jury—was the "best Method of searching and sifting out the Truth." Today * * * any rational system of justice should care more about protecting innocent defendants than any other value. But DNA testing has made plain that our modern adversary system just isn't very good at protecting innocent defendants.

NOTES AND QUESTIONS

1.   *Is Krone a rare case?* In a study of over 10,000 cases in which the FBI compared DNA of the suspect with DNA from the crime scene, the DNA tests exonerated the prime suspect in 20% of the cases. In another 20%, the results were inconclusive. Because the inconclusive results must be removed from the sample, the police were wrong in one case in four. The lab records do not indicate whether the 20% of excluded suspects were tried using other

evidence. Edward Conners, et al., Convicted by Juries, Exonerated by Science: Case Studies in the Use of DNA Evidence to Establish Innocence After Trial, in National Institute of Justice Report (1996). We don't know from these data how many innocent suspects are arrested for crimes that cannot be cleared through DNA testing.

The DNA evidence is bound to overstate the error rate in arrests overall. When the identity of the actor is known, and the argument is over whether what he did is a crime, there is no risk of convicting the wrong person and thus no reason to conduct a DNA test. These cases will not, of course, appear in the DNA database, making the error rate in all cases lower than that found in the Justice study. But even if the error rate is only 3%, that means almost half a million innocent defendants are arrested each year. See U.S. Department of Justice, Federal Bureau of Investigation, Crime in the United States, 2004, tbl. 4.1, p. 280 (showing fourteen million non-traffic arrests in 2004).

2.   *Is there a reliable estimate of system-wide wrongful convictions?* The short answer is no. By "wrongful convictions," we mean convictions of factually innocent defendants. In his book, excerpted above, Thomas drew on a statistical model and a study of English convictions to produce a rough overall estimate that two percent of convictions are of innocent defendants. Thomas, at 39–40.

Michael Risinger has made a compelling argument that it is a fool's errand to attempt an estimate of a general error rate, both because we lack a methodology and because the error rate will almost certainly vary dramatically by category. See D. Michael Risinger, *Innocents Convicted: An Empirically Justified Factual Wrongful Conviction Rate*, 97 J. Crim. L. & Criminology 761 (2007). So, for example, the error rate in armed robbery cases, where identification is a critical issue, will be much higher than in cases of failing to file income tax returns, where it should be almost zero.

But Risinger has developed a methodology for estimating the error rate in rape-murder capital cases. His rigorous methodology produced a minimum error rate of 3.3%. What is your reaction to being told that of 319 capital rape-murder convictions Risinger studied, at least 10 of the men sentenced to die were factually innocent?

3.   "There is no worse error in American criminal justice than the wrongful prosecution, conviction, and incarceration of an innocent person, especially in capital cases. . . ." Richard A. Leo, *False Confessions: Causes, Consequences, and Solutions*, in Wrongly Convicted: Perspectives on Failed Justice (Saundra D. Westervelt & John A. Humphrey, eds. 2001). Do you have any thoughts about how to avoid these miscarriages of justice?

2. UNJUST CONVICTIONS

A series of questions arise about American criminal justice. Protecting innocent defendants is one goal of the system but far from the only one.

Indeed, while trying to help innocent defendants is surely uncontroversial, the innocence *movement* has generated criticism. Margaret Raymond, for example, criticizes the movement for "elevating factual innocence" over other defenses. This could lead jurors to think "that anything short of factual innocence is simply not good enough to justify an acquittal." Margaret Raymond, *The Problem with Innocence*, 49 Clev. St. L. Rev. 449, 457 (2001). Another criticism is that a focus on innocence is a distraction that "may obscure more pervasive flaws in the criminal justice system and have a series of untoward effects on (1) the trial process, (2) legislative reform, and (3) other systemic critiques." Daniel S. Medwed, *Innocentrism*, 2008 U. Ill. L. Rev. 1549, 1555 (articulating, but not embracing, that critique).

Thus, it is perhaps equally important to assess the extent to which the system provides a fair procedure to decide guilt or innocence, irrespective of the defendant's factual innocence. This raises questions about the quality of defense representation in a public defense system that, in many parts of the country, is literally overwhelmed with cases. Recall Gerald Lefcourt's reaction to the huddling defendants he encountered in the holding pens in New York City, p. 36: "I came to see that most of them were not really represented at all." An exhaustive study of New York County in the mid-1980s revealed that private lawyers appointed to represent indigent defendants *did not interview their clients* in 82% of the non-homicide cases. Even in homicide cases, the lawyer interviewed the client only 26% of the time. Michael McConville & Chester Mirsky, *Criminal Defense of the Poor in New York City*, 15 N.Y.U. L. & Social Change 581, 758–62 (1986–87).

The Reporters for the National Committee on the Right to Counsel concluded in 2006 that a national crisis exists in indigent defense. Mary Sue Backus & Paul Marcus, *The Right to Counsel in Criminal Cases, A National Crisis*, 57 Hastings L. J. 1031, 1045–46 (2006). In 2009, the National Right to Counsel Committee issued a report entitled Justice Denied: America's Continuing Neglect of our Constitutional Right to Counsel. The report details systemic and endemic failures of indigent defense in this country. It found "overwhelming" evidence that, in most of the country, "quality defense work is simply impossible because of inadequate funding, excessive caseloads, a lack of genuine independence, and insufficient availability of other essential resources." The report is available at http://tcpjusticedenied.org/.

Even if counsel has adequate time and provides an adequate defense, the next question is how well the American criminal justice system protects against unjust convictions. Here, we use the term "unjust convictions" to include more than convictions of innocent defendants. It also includes convictions that result from the prosecution taking an unfair advantage of a defendant. While we recognize that "unfair advantage" is a pliable concept, at its core it manifests an important truth. As Stephen B. Bright has put it:

> The Bill of Rights is not a collection of technicalities. It is this nation's most fundamental guarantees of fairness and justice. For 200 years we have revered these rights. This nation is respected and

emulated throughout the world because we provide these safeguards of liberty and justice to even the least among us, even those who have offended us most grievously.

Stephen B. Bright, *Death By Lottery—Procedural Bar of Constitutional Claims in Capital Cases Due to Inadequate Representation of Indigent Defendants*, 92 W. Va. L. Rev. 679, 694 (1990).

Here, too, the American system seems to fall short. "Many features of the criminal justice system in the United States are often severely criticized, and fairly so." Backus & Marcus, at 1037. For example, a defendant who did not get access to favorable evidence in the prosecutor's file, to which he was entitled, and who was convicted because he lacked that evidence was also unjustly convicted, again whether or not he was factually guilty.

One procedural defect, according to Professor Shima Baradaran, is the failure of courts to give full effect to the presumption of innocence. See Shima Baradaran, *Restoring the Presumption of Innocence*, 72 Ohio St. L.J. 723 (2011). The United States Supreme Court has essentially restricted the presumption of innocence to the trial context, where it requires the State to carry the burden of proving the defendant guilty beyond a reasonable doubt. But Professor Baradaran argues that a critically important aspect of the presumption of innocence is in guaranteeing bail to all defendants except those who are unlikely to appear for trial:

> * * * In our modern system of U.S. criminal justice [unlike in Blackstone's day], we proclaim that all are innocent until proven guilty at trial but we allow judges to predict which ones are guilty long before trial. We have adopted practices allowing predictions of guilt and weighing of evidence against defendants before trial since defendants' rights have lacked steady constitutional rooting. * * *

> The practical results of the presumption's diminution are apparent and troubling. The number of defendants held pretrial has steadily increased such that the majority of people in our nation's jails have not been convicted of any crime. In the last fourteen years, the United States has gone from releasing 62% of defendants to only 40%, without much complaint, discussion, or even acknowledgement by legal scholars.

Id. at 724–25, 775 (2011). Unsurprisingly, studies show that defendants who are denied bail are less likely to obtain a favorable outcome, at least in part because they are less likely to offer assistance in preparing a defense. Thus, if a defendant was denied bail unjustly, and was convicted because of that denial, it would be fair to conclude that he was unjustly convicted even if he was factually guilty.

And there are other choke points that produce unjust convictions. There is much evidence that some over-zealous prosecutors are parsimonious in complying with the duty to disclose evidence that might help the defense. Jailhouse informants are notorious for telling whatever story will get them a benefit from the State. Eyewitness identifications are often wrong but readily accepted by juries as infallible. Attention has recently been given to what some call "junk science"—the use of highly-questionable prosecution experts (as in Ray Krone's case) to "prove" guilt. Fred Zain, when a serologist with the West Virginia Division of Public Safety, apparently testified falsely about scientific results in as many as 182 cases. All of these problems, and more, are discussed in Thomas, Supreme Court on Trial, supra, at 6–44. It is difficult to avoid a conclusion reached by George Thomas and Randy Jonakait, in separate works, that unjust convictions are all too often the result of failures in the American adversarial system. Thomas, at 39; Randolph Jonakait, The American Jury System, 282 (2003).

An indictment of the modern American criminal justice system would thus include failures along the entire temporal dimension of the process— failures in evidence gathering, failures of the defense system, bail denial, over-zealous prosecutors, and failures in the trial process itself. When one adds up the ways American justice seems to fail defendants, one wonders what happened to the criminal trial process that Matthew Hale claimed in 1713 to be the "best Trial in the World"? Matthew Hale, The History and Analysis of the Common Law 252 (1713).

NOTES AND QUESTIONS

1. You are on a commission to reduce the incidence of unjust convictions in your state. Part of the mandate is that only limited funds are available to spend on improvements to the system. Thus, you cannot recommend large sums be spent to improve indigent defense. What changes would you recommend, knowing that only modest sums of money are available?

2. What is your overall impression of American criminal justice, circa 2012? Do you suppose criminal justice was better, was more fair, in the eighteenth century? Than the systems that produced *Powell*, p. 25, and *Brown*, p. 14.

NOTES AND QUESTIONS

CHAPTER 2

FOURTH AMENDMENT: AN OVERVIEW

■ ■ ■

A. THE TEXT AND ITS MYSTERIES

The Fourth Amendment journey begins here. The first step in that journey, as is the case in evaluating *any* provision of a constitution, is to read the text being interpreted. The Fourth Amendment is just 54 words long:

> The right of the people to be secure in their persons, houses, papers, and effects, against unreasonable searches and seizures, shall not be violated, and no Warrants shall issue, but upon probable cause, supported by Oath or affirmation, and particularly describing the place to be searched, and the persons or things to be seized.

These 54 words appear to tell us a great deal, but do they? They tell us *who* is protected by the provisions of the Amendment, *i.e.*, "the people." But, who are "the people"? Only citizens of the United States? Anyone legally present in the United States? Anyone in the country, legally or not? And, are United States citizens protected when they are outside the country? These questions, always important, have grown in significance in the aftermath of terrorist attacks on the United States, the investigations of which have frequently focused on persons of foreign ancestry located in and outside the United States, as well as United States citizens.

What does the Fourth Amendment guarantee "the people"? The text tells us that the people are entitled "to be secure in their persons, houses, papers, and effects" (we will see that this phrase is not all-encompassing) "against unreasonable searches and seizures." But, what is an "unreasonable" search or seizure? For that matter, what are "searches" and "seizures"? These are matters of considerable complexity.

Perhaps the most controversial feature of Fourth Amendment jurisprudence relates to the relationship between the preceding language (often called the "reasonableness clause" of the Fourth Amendment) and the remaining language of the text ("no Warrants shall issue, but upon probable cause * * *"), which constitutes the "warrant clause." Does the warrant clause mean that searches conducted without warrants are (at least, presumptively) unreasonable and, consequently, in violation of the reasonableness requirement? Or did the drafters of the Fourth Amendment mean only that *when* a warrant is issued it must meet the requirements of probable cause, oath or affirmation, and particularity, but that there is no warrant requirement, as such? And, however *this* question is answered, what does the text mean by "probable cause," and with what particularity must the warrant describe "the place to be searched, and the persons or things to be seized"?

Finally, notice what the text does *not* say. Yes, the people have a right (in their persons, houses, papers, and effects) to be free from unreasonable searches and seizures, but what is the *remedy* for violation of this right? Did the Amendment's Framers have a particular remedy in mind? Or, did they expect the judiciary or legislatures to formulate one?

All of these questions suggest the aptness of Professor Anthony Amsterdam's characterization of the Fourth Amendment text as "brief, vague, general, [and] unilluminating." Anthony G. Amsterdam, *Perspectives on the Fourth Amendment*, 58 Minn. L. Rev. 349, 353–54 (1974). The judiciary, in particular the United States Supreme Court, has endeavored to illuminate the text. Justice Felix Frankfurter observed in 1961, however, that "[t]he course of true law pertaining to [the Fourth Amendment] * * * has not * * * run smooth." Chapman v. United States, 365 U.S. 610, 81 S.Ct. 776, 5 L.Ed.2d 828 (1961) (concurring opinion). Indeed, although the text of the Amendment has not changed over the years, the personnel of the Supreme Court and its interpretation of the Constitution, *have* changed. As a consequence, the path you will be following in your Fourth Amendment journey includes many significant turns, including some U-turns, as well as zigs and zags. At the conclusion of your voyage, you will have a basis for determining whether Professor Akhil Amar overstated the situation when he equated Fourth Amendment case law to "a sinking ocean liner—rudderless and badly off course." Akhil Reed Amar, *Fourth Amendment First Principles*, 107 Harv. L. Rev. 757, 759 (1994).

B. THE REACH OF THE FOURTH AMENDMENT

How far does the Fourth Amendment reach? Two issues relating to the Amendment's scope—one relating to the category of persons who are searched and seized, and the other regarding the nature of persons who do the searching and seizing—deserve attention.

Consider, first, the criminal investigations that occurred in the aftermath of the September 11 attacks on the United States. Apparently all nineteen hijackers of the four airplanes were of Middle Eastern descent. After the events, the federal government investigated hundreds of persons in order to try to identify possible co-conspirators in the crimes and to identify persons who might be planning future attacks. Initial reports suggested that these investigations primarily focused on four categories of individuals: (a) American citizens of Middle Eastern descent living in the United States; (b) citizens of other countries *lawfully* in the United States on student (or other) visas; (c) citizens of other countries *unlawfully* in this country (persons who came lawfully but whose visas had expired, as well as those who illegally entered the country); and (d) non-U.S. citizens residing in other countries suspected of planning criminal activities in the United States or against U.S. interests on foreign land. Obviously, category (a) individuals are covered by the Fourth Amendment, but what rights do the other classes of suspects possess? May federal law enforcement agents conduct unlimited surveillance of such persons? May their homes be searched and their property seized with impunity? Remarkably, the Supreme Court has rarely spoken on the subject.

The Fourth Amendment provides that "the people" should "be secure in their persons, houses, papers, and effects, against unreasonable searches and seizures." It turns out, however, that the term "people" is not all-inclusive. In United States v. Verdugo-Urquidez, 494 U.S. 259, 110 S.Ct. 1056, 108 L.Ed.2d 222 (1990), Verdugo-Urquidez, a Mexican resident, was arrested on drug charges and brought to the United States for trial. While he was in a San Diego federal correctional facility, United States Drug Enforcement Agency (DEA) agents entered and seized property from defendant's Mexican residences without a search warrant. The issue presented to the Supreme Court was "whether the Fourth Amendment applies to the search and seizure by United States agents of property that is owned by a non-resident alien and located in a foreign country."

A seriously splintered Court held that Verdugo-Urquidez could not object to the DEA action on Fourth Amendment grounds, because he was not among "the people" the Framers intended to protect from unreasonable searches and seizures. Specifically, a search or seizure of property located in a foreign country, which is owned by a nonresident who is only briefly on U.S. soil, is not covered by the Amendment, even if the search is conducted by U.S. law enforcement agents. According to Chief Justice Rehnquist writing for the majority, the words "the people" found in the Fourth Amendment (and elsewhere in the Constitution) "refer[ ] to a class of persons who are part of a national community or who have otherwise developed sufficient connection with this country to be considered part of that community." The defendant's connection to the United States—"lawful but involuntary [presence]—is not of the sort to indicate any substantial connection with our country."

The justices left a great deal open for future resolution in category (b) and (c) cases, including whether the Fourth Amendment applies if a non-citizen's involuntary "stay in the United States were to be prolonged—by a prison sentence, for example." Also undecided—and certainly of greater significance—is whether, and to what extent, the Fourth Amendment protects a person *voluntarily* but *unlawfully living* in this country, *i.e.*, one who has "presumably * * * accepted some societal obligations," such as paying taxes, who is subjected to a search or seizure on U.S. land. Indeed, *Verdugo-Urquidez* even leaves open the issue of the scope of rights of non-U.S. citizens *lawfully* in this country temporarily or with the intention of becoming citizens. (Obviously, category (d) individuals are not protected by the Fourth Amendment.)

The second coverage issue relates to the *searching*, not the searched, party. In *Verdugo-Urquidez*, the contested searches were conducted by law enforcement agents. But, what if a search or seizure occurs in the United States, of a United States citizen, by a *private* party? Suppose that Burglar John breaks into Jane's home while she is at work, and is arrested while fleeing the crime scene. In an effort to avoid prosecution, John hands over to the police a large quantity of illegal drugs he discovered in Jane's home. May Jane object to the Government's use of these drugs against her in a drug prosecution? Or suppose that a private detective, hired by Jack to discover evidence of wife Jill's adulterous behavior, searches through Jill's belongings and, to his surprise, discovers evidence linking Jill to a murder. If the private detective furnishes the evidence to the police, may Jill object on Fourth Amendment grounds?

The answer in both cases is "no." The Supreme Court ruled in *Burdeau v. McDowell*, 256 U.S. 465, 41 S.Ct. 574, 65 L.Ed. 1048 (1921), that the Fourth Amendment only limits governmental action. It does not reach private searches or seizures. Consequently, the Fourth Amendment is not violated if a landlord searches her tenant's possessions, or an airline employee searches luggage, or a private company monitors telephone calls of its employees without their knowledge. On the other hand, the Amendment *is* implicated if the police instigate or participate in the search or seizure, such as when an officer requests a landlord to search through her tenant's belongings or assists in the process.

C. THE BIRTH OF THE EXCLUSIONARY RULE

Introductory Comment

Suppose that federal law enforcement officers, without good cause and without a search warrant, enter your home without your permission, and search it for evidence of a crime. The search is thorough: They go through every room in your house, including your bedroom, opening desk and dresser drawers, reading your personal diary, rifling through your private files, searching through closets, and opening containers. They find nothing and leave. We may assume for current purposes (with good reason) that this police conduct constitutes an unreasonable search of your home, in violation of your Fourth Amendment rights.

What is your remedy for violation of your rights? The text of the Fourth Amendment provides no answer. Perhaps you can bring a civil suit against the police. Or, you might file a formal complaint with police authorities or seek to convince a United States Attorney to prosecute the officers for some criminal offense.

Now, suppose that the same events occur, but the federal agents *do* find evidence of a crime in your home, which they seize and seek to use against you in a criminal prosecution. The Fourth Amendment guarantees "the people"—not just those innocent of criminal activity—the right to be free from unreasonable searches and seizures. Therefore, in *this* case, what should your remedy be? The same as before? Or, should you have a right to have your property—unconstitutionally taken from your home—returned to you and, therefore, the Government denied the right to introduce it into evidence in your prosecution?

At common law, and for decades after ratification of the Fourth Amendment, your only remedy would have been a civil action against the agents. If the agents had no valid warrant, and entered and searched without your permission, they were automatically deemed trespassers and could offer no defense. As the North Carolina Supreme Court put the rule: "Every entry by one, into the dwelling-house of another, against the will of the occupant, is a trespass, unless warranted by such authority in law as will justify the entry." Gardner v. Neil, 4 N.C. 104 (1814). The most famous English search case from the colonial era was, after all, a tort case. See Entick v. Carrington, 19 How. State Trials 1029 (1765) (holding the king's messengers liable in tort to the victim of the search because even a specific warrant could not justify seizing private papers from private premises).

Does the Fourth Amendment itself offer a remedy? In Adams v. New York, 192 U.S. 585, 24 S.Ct. 372, 48 L.Ed. 575 (1904), the Supreme Court provided its initial answer. It stated that "the weight of authority" was that "testimony clearly competent as tending to establish the guilt of the accused of the offense charged" may be retained by the Government and used at a defendant's trial. According to *Adams*, "the courts do not stop to inquire as to the means by which the evidence was obtained."

Governmental misconduct, it may forcefully be argued, is a collateral matter in a criminal prosecution of one whom they have arrested. If the purpose of a trial is to determine the innocence or guilt of the accused, shouldn't the trial focus *exclusively* on *that* matter? If the evidence seized by the police serves to prove the defendant's guilt, why should a court exclude this probative evidence? Yet, as the following cases demonstrate, the Supreme Court turned away from the *Adams* approach and formulated a so-called "exclusionary rule."

Note: As explained in Chapter 1, the provisions of the Bill of Rights, including the Fourth Amendment, only limit the conduct of agents of the federal, as distinguished from state and local, government. State and local police are limited, *if at all*, by the Fourteenth Amendment due process clause. Therefore, in considering the materials that follow, pay attention to the federal/state distinction.

WEEKS V. UNITED STATES
Supreme Court of the United States, 1914.
232 U.S. 383, 34 S.Ct. 341, 58 L.Ed. 652.

MR. JUSTICE DAY delivered the opinion of the court [joined by CHIEF JUSTICE WHITE, and JUSTICES MCKENNA, HOLMES, LURTON, HUGHES, VAN DEVANTER, LAMAR, and PITNEY].

An indictment was returned against the * * * defendant * * * . The seventh count, upon which a conviction was had, charged the use of the mails for the purpose of transporting certain coupons or tickets representing chances or shares in a lottery or gift enterprise, in violation of [federal law]. * * *

The defendant was arrested by a police officer, so far as the record shows, without warrant, at the Union Station in Kansas City, Missouri, where he was employed by an express company. Other police officers had gone to the house of the defendant and being told by a neighbor where the key was kept, found it and entered the house. They searched the defendant's room and took possession of various papers and articles found there, which were afterwards turned over to the United States Marshal. Later in the same day police officers returned with the Marshal, who thought he might find additional evidence, and, being admitted by someone in the house, probably a boarder, * * * the Marshal searched the defendant's room and carried away certain letters and envelopes found in the drawer of a chiffonier. Neither the marshal nor the police officers had a search warrant. * * *

[The defendant unsuccessfully petitioned the district court for return of the items that were seized by the local police and United States Marshal on the ground that the property was obtained in violation of the Fourth Amendment.] Among the papers retained and put in evidence were a number of lottery tickets and statements with reference to the lottery, taken at the first visit of the police to the defendant's room, and a number of letters written to the defendant in respect to the lottery, taken by the Marshal upon his search of defendant's room. * * *

The history of this Amendment is given with particularity in the opinion of Mr. Justice Bradley, speaking for the court in *Boyd v. United*

States, 116 U.S. 616, 6 S.Ct. 524, 29 L.Ed. 746 (1886). As was there shown, it took its origin in the determination of the framers of the Amendments to the Federal Constitution to provide for that instrument a Bill of Rights, securing to the American people, among other things, those safeguards which had grown up in England to protect the people from unreasonable searches and seizures, such as were permitted under the general warrants issued under authority of the Government by which there had been invasions of the home and privacy of the citizens and the seizure of their private papers in support of charges, real or imaginary, made against them. Such practices had also received sanction under warrants and seizures under the so-called writs of assistance, issued in the American colonies. Resistance to these practices had established the principle which was enacted into the fundamental law in the Fourth Amendment, that a man's house was his castle and not to be invaded by any general authority to search and seize his goods and papers. * * *

In the *Boyd Case*, after citing Lord Camden's judgment in *Entick v. Carrington*, 19 Howell's State Trials, 1029, Mr. Justice Bradley said:

> "The principles laid down in this opinion affect the very essence of constitutional liberty and security. They reach farther than the concrete form of the case then before the court, with its adventitious circumstances; they apply to all invasions on the part of the government and its employés of the sanctity of a man's home and the privacies of life. It is not the breaking of his doors, and the rummaging of his drawers, that constitutes the essence of the offence; but it is the invasion of his indefeasible right of personal security, personal liberty and private property, where that right has never been forfeited by his conviction of some public offence,—it is the invasion of this sacred right which underlies and constitutes the essence of Lord Camden's judgment." * * *

The effect of the Fourth Amendment is to put the courts of the United States and Federal officials, in the exercise of their power and authority, under limitations and restraints as to the exercise of such power and authority, and to forever secure the people, their persons, houses, papers and effects against all unreasonable searches and seizures under the guise of law. This protection reaches all alike, whether accused of crime or not, and the duty of giving to it force and effect is obligatory upon all entrusted under our Federal system with the enforcement of the laws. The tendency of those who execute the criminal laws of the country to obtain conviction by means of unlawful seizures and enforced confessions, the latter often obtained after subjecting accused persons to unwarranted practices destructive of rights secured by the Federal Constitution, should find no sanction in the judgments of the courts which are charged at all times with the support of the Constitution and to which people of all conditions have a right to appeal for the maintenance of such fundamental rights. * * *

* * * If letters and private documents can * * * be seized and held and used in evidence against a citizen accused of an offense, the protection of the Fourth Amendment * * * is of no value, and, so far as those thus placed are concerned, might as well be stricken from the Constitution. The efforts of the courts and their officials to bring the guilty to punishment, praiseworthy as they are, are not to be aided by the sacrifice of those great principles established by years of endeavor and suffering which have resulted in their embodiment in the fundamental law of the land. The United States Marshal * * * acted without sanction of law, * * * and under color of his office undertook to make a seizure of private papers in direct violation of the constitutional prohibition against such action. * * * To sanction such proceedings would be to affirm by judicial decision a manifest neglect if not an open defiance of the prohibitions of the Constitution, intended for the protection of the people against such unauthorized action. * * *

We therefore reach the conclusion that the letters in question were taken from the house of the accused by an official of the United States * * * in direct violation of the constitutional rights of the defendant; that having made a seasonable application for their return, * * * the court should have restored these letters to the accused. In holding them and permitting their use upon the trial, we think prejudicial error was committed. As to the papers and property seized by the policemen, it does not appear that they acted under any claim of Federal authority such as would make the Amendment applicable to such unauthorized seizures. * * * What remedies the defendant may have against them we need not inquire, as the Fourth Amendment is not directed to individual misconduct of such officials. Its limitations reach the Federal Government and its agencies.

It results that the judgment of the court below must be reversed * * * .

NOTES AND QUESTIONS

1.　Why does the Court conclude that the letters seized by the United States Marshal should be excluded from the defendant's trial? Why did the Court not treat the papers and property seized by the local police in the same manner?

2.　Federal Rule of Criminal Procedure 41(g) provides that a "person aggrieved by an unlawful search and seizure of property or by the deprivation of property may move for the property's return." And, under Rule 41(h), "[a] defendant may move to suppress evidence in the court where the trial will occur * * * ."

Suppose the police unlawfully search Jane's home and seize contraband, such as illegal narcotics. Should Jane be able to seek its return under the federal rule quoted above? If not, is the contraband admissible at her trial?

3. *"Silver platter" doctrine.* Because the Court in *Weeks* only applied the exclusionary rule to evidence seized under "federal authority," this seemingly left local police free to conduct unreasonable searches and seizures and then deliver the evidence to federal prosecutors "on a silver platter," to be used in federal prosecutions. In Byars v. United States, 273 U.S. 28, 47 S.Ct. 248, 71 L.Ed. 520 (1927), however, the Court ruled that this "silver platter" doctrine did not apply to evidence obtained unlawfully during a search that "in substance and effect" was a joint state-federal venture. In *Byars*, state police conducted their search accompanied by a federal agent. And, in Gambino v. United States, 275 U.S. 310, 48 S.Ct. 137, 72 L.Ed. 293 (1927), state officers, acting alone, conducted a search solely on behalf of the federal government. In both cases, the Court applied the *Weeks* exclusionary rule to the state officers' actions.

4. *The exclusionary rule in the states.* What if state or local police officers want to use evidence in a *state* prosecution they obtained as a result of an unreasonable search or seizure? *Weeks* recognized an exclusionary rule in federal cases. Is there an equivalent exclusionary rule that applies in state courts through the Fourteenth Amendment due process clause? Consider the next case in this regard.

WOLF V. COLORADO

Supreme Court of the United States, 1949.
338 U.S. 25, 69 S.Ct. 1359, 93 L.Ed. 1782.

MR. JUSTICE FRANKFURTER delivered the opinion of the Court [joined by CHIEF JUSTICE VINSON, and JUSTICES REED, JACKSON, and BURTON.]

The precise question for consideration is this: Does a conviction by a State court for a State offense deny the "due process of law" required by the Fourteenth Amendment, solely because evidence that was admitted at the trial was obtained under circumstances which would have rendered it inadmissible in a prosecution for violation of a federal law in a court of the United States because there deemed to be an infraction of the Fourth Amendment as applied in *Weeks v. United States*, [p. 76 supra]? The Supreme Court of Colorado has sustained convictions in which such evidence was admitted, and we brought the cases here.

Unlike the specific requirements and restrictions placed by the Bill of Rights (Amendments I to VIII) upon the administration of criminal justice by federal authority, the Fourteenth Amendment did not subject criminal justice in the States to specific limitations. The notion that the "due process of law" guaranteed by the Fourteenth Amendment is shorthand for the first eight amendments of the Constitution and thereby incorporates them has been rejected by this Court again and again, after impressive consideration. * * * The issue is closed.

For purposes of ascertaining the restrictions which the Due Process Clause imposed upon the States in the enforcement of their criminal law, we adhere to the views expressed in *Palko v. Connecticut*, 302 U.S. 319, 58 S.Ct. 149, 82 L.Ed. 288. * * * In rejecting the suggestion that the Due Process Clause incorporated the original Bill of Rights, Mr. Justice Cardozo reaffirmed on behalf of that Court a different but deeper and more pervasive conception of the Due Process Clause. This Clause exacts from the States for the lowliest and the most outcast all that is "implicit in the concept of ordered liberty."

Due process of law thus conveys neither formal nor fixed nor narrow requirements. It is the compendious expression for all those rights which the courts must enforce because they are basic to our free society. But basic rights do not become petrified as of any one time, even though, as a matter of human experience, some may not too rhetorically be called eternal verities. It is of the very nature of a free society to advance in its standards of what is deemed reasonable and right. Representing as it does a living principle, due process is not confined within a permanent catalogue of what may at a given time be deemed the limits or the essentials of fundamental rights.

To rely on a tidy formula for the easy determination of what is a fundamental right for purposes of legal enforcement may satisfy a longing for certainty but ignores the movements of a free society. It belittles the scale of the conception of due process. The real clue to the problem confronting the judiciary in the application of the Due Process Clause is not to ask where the line is once and for all to be drawn but to recognize that it is for the Court to draw it by the gradual and empiric process of "inclusion and exclusion." * * *

The security of one's privacy against arbitrary intrusion by the police—which is at the core of the Fourth Amendment—is basic to a free society. It is therefore implicit in "the concept of ordered liberty" and as such enforceable against the States through the Due Process Clause. The knock at the door, whether by day or by night, as a prelude to a search, without authority of law but solely on the authority of the police, did not need the commentary of recent history to be condemned as inconsistent with the conception of human rights enshrined in the history and the basic constitutional documents of English-speaking peoples.

Accordingly, we have no hesitation in saying that were a State affirmatively to sanction such police incursion into privacy it would run counter to the guaranty of the Fourteenth Amendment. But the ways of enforcing such a rule raise questions of a different order. How such arbitrary conduct should be checked, what remedies against it should be afforded, the means by which the right should be made effective, are all questions not to be so dogmatically answered as to preclude the varying solutions which spring from an allowable range of judgment on issues not susceptible to quantitative solution.

In *Weeks v. United States, supra,* this Court held that in a federal prosecution the Fourth Amendment barred the use of evidence secured through an illegal search and seizure. * * * It was not derived from the explicit requirements of the Fourth Amendment; it was not based on legislation expressing Congressional policy in the enforcement of the Constitution. The decision was a matter of judicial implication. Since then it has been frequently applied and we stoutly adhere to it. But the immediate question is whether the basic right to protection against arbitrary intrusion by the police demands the exclusion of logically relevant evidence obtained by an unreasonable search and seizure because, in a federal prosecution for a federal crime, it would be excluded. As a matter of inherent reason, one would suppose this to be an issue as to which men with complete devotion to the protection of the right of privacy might give different answers. When we find that in fact most of the English-speaking world does not regard as vital to such protection the exclusion of evidence thus obtained, we must hesitate to treat this remedy as an essential ingredient of the right. The contrariety of views of the States is particularly impressive in view of the careful reconsideration which they have given the problem in the light of the *Weeks* decision.

[According to the Court's survey of the law, twenty-seven states prior to *Weeks* had passed on the admissibility of evidence obtained by unlawful search or seizure. Of these, all but one state rejected an exclusionary rule. After *Weeks,* forty-seven states passed on the *Weeks* doctrine. Of this number, only sixteen adopted the *Weeks* exclusionary rule. The Court also reported that of ten jurisdictions within the United Kingdom and the British Commonwealth, none had adopted a similar doctrine. The Court concluded that, although the exclusionary rule might "be an effective way of deterring unreasonable searches, it is not for this Court to condemn as falling below the minimal standards assured by the Due Process Clause a State's reliance upon other methods which, if consistently enforced, would be equally effective."] * * *

We hold, therefore, that in a prosecution in a State court for a State crime the Fourteenth Amendment does not forbid the admission of evidence obtained by an unreasonable search and seizure. * * *

Affirmed.

[JUSTICE BLACK'S concurring opinion is omitted. Also omitted are the dissenting opinions of JUSTICES DOUGLAS, MURPHY, and RUTLEDGE.]

NOTES AND QUESTIONS

1.   *Wolf* represented a classic "I have good news and I have bad news" story for the defendant: "Arbitrary searches and seizures by state and local police violate the concept of ordered liberty and, therefore, violate the Fourteenth Amendment due process clause, but—sorry!—the government can still use the fruits of its agents' unconstitutional conduct in your criminal prosecution." Is there any practical value in possessing the right to be free from arbitrary or unreasonable searches and seizures if a state may use the evidence unlawfully secured in a criminal prosecution?

2.   *The "Rochin" principle: the exclusionary rule in different clothing.* In Rochin v. California, 342 U.S. 165, 72 S.Ct. 205, 96 L.Ed. 183 (1952), Justice Frankfurter, author of *Wolf*, described the relevant facts in the case:

> Having "some information that [the petitioner here] was selling narcotics," three deputy sheriffs * * * made for the two-story dwelling house in which Rochin lived with his mother, common-law wife, brothers and sisters. Finding the outside door open, they entered and then forced open the door to Rochin's room on the second floor. Inside they found petitioner sitting partly dressed on the side of the bed, upon which his wife was lying. On a "night stand" beside the bed the deputies spied two capsules. When asked, "Whose stuff is this?" Rochin seized the capsules and put them in his mouth. A struggle ensued, in the course of which the three officers "jumped upon him" and attempted to extract the capsules. The force they applied proved unavailing against Rochin's resistance. He was handcuffed and taken to a hospital. At the direction of one of the officers a doctor forced an emetic solution through a tube into Rochin's stomach against his will. This "stomach pumping" produced vomiting. In the vomited matter were found two capsules which proved to contain morphine.

Rochin was prosecuted for possession of morphine. The chief evidence against him, admitted over defense objection, were the two capsules extracted from his stomach.

Although local police conducted the search and seizure, the Supreme Court ruled that the Fourteenth Amendment due process clause prohibited admission of the capsules. Justice Frankfurter explained:

> [W]e are compelled to conclude that the proceedings by which this conviction was obtained do more than offend some fastidious squeamishness or private sentimentalism about combatting crime too energetically. This is conduct that shocks the conscience. Illegally breaking into the privacy of the petitioner, the struggle to open his mouth and remove what was there, the forcible extraction of his stomach's contents—this course of proceeding by agents of government to obtain evidence is bound to offend even hardened

sensibilities. They are methods too close to the rack and the screw to permit of constitutional differentiation.

Is *Rochin* consistent with *Wolf*? If this had been a pre-*Weeks* federal prosecution, how would the case have been resolved?

3.   *Wolf* was not the end of the story. . . .

MAPP V. OHIO
Supreme Court of the United States, 1961.
367 U.S. 643, 81 S.Ct. 1684, 6 L.Ed.2d 1081.

MR. JUSTICE CLARK delivered the opinion of the Court [joined by CHIEF JUSTICE WARREN, and JUSTICES BLACK, DOUGLAS and BRENNAN.].

Appellant stands convicted of knowingly having had in her possession and under her control certain lewd and lascivious books, pictures, and photographs in violation of [state law].ᵃ * * *

On May 23, 1957, three Cleveland police officers arrived at appellant's residence in that city pursuant to information that "a person [was] hiding out in the home, who was wanted for questioning in connection with a recent bombing, and that there was a large amount of policy [gambling] paraphernalia being hidden in the home." Miss Mapp and her daughter by a former marriage lived on the top floor of the two-family dwelling. Upon their arrival at that house, the officers knocked on the door and demanded entrance but appellant, after telephoning her attorney, refused to admit them without a search warrant. They advised their headquarters of the situation and undertook a surveillance of the house.

The officers again sought entrance some three hours later when four or more additional officers arrived on the scene. When Miss Mapp did not come to the door immediately, at least one of the several doors to the house was forcibly opened² and the policemen gained admittance. Meanwhile Miss Mapp's attorney arrived, but the officers, having secured their own entry, and continuing in their defiance of the law, would permit him neither to see Miss Mapp nor to enter the house. It appears that Miss Mapp was halfway down the stairs from the upper floor to the front door when the officers, in this highhanded manner, broke into the hall. She demanded to see the search warrant. A paper, claimed to be a warrant,

---

ᵃ   The materials consisted of four books (*Affairs of a Troubadour, Little Darlings, London Stage Affairs, Memories of a Hotel Man*) and "a hand-drawn picture described in the state's brief as being 'of a very obscene nature.'" Potter Stewart, *The Road to* Mapp v. Ohio *and Beyond: The Origins, Development and Future of the Exclusionary Rule in Search-and-Seizure Cases*, 83 Colum. L. Rev. 1365, 1367 (1983).

²   A police officer testified that "we did pry the screen door to gain entrance"; the attorney on the scene testified that a policeman "tried * * * to kick in the door" and then "broke the glass in the door and somebody reached in and opened the door and let them in"; the appellant testified that "The back door was broken."

was held up by one of the officers. She grabbed the "warrant" and placed it in her bosom. A struggle ensued in which the officers recovered the piece of paper and as a result of which they handcuffed appellant because she had been "belligerent" in resisting their official rescue of the "warrant" from her person. Running roughshod over appellant, a policeman "grabbed" her, "twisted [her] hand," and she "yelled [and] pleaded with him" because "it was hurting." Appellant, in handcuffs, was then forcibly taken upstairs to her bedroom where the officers searched a dresser, a chest of drawers, a closet and some suitcases. They also looked into a photo album and through personal papers belonging to the appellant. The search spread to the rest of the second floor including the child's bedroom, the living room, the kitchen and a dinette. The basement of the building and a trunk found therein were also searched. The obscene materials for possession of which she was ultimately convicted were discovered in the course of that widespread search.

At the trial no search warrant was produced by the prosecution, nor was the failure to produce one explained or accounted for. At best, "There is, in the record, considerable doubt as to whether there ever was any warrant for the search of defendant's home." The Ohio Supreme Court believed a "reasonable argument" could be made that the conviction should be reversed "because the 'methods' employed to obtain the [evidence] * * * were such as to 'offend "a sense of justice," ' " but the court found determinative the fact that the evidence had not been taken "from defendant's person by the use of brutal or offensive physical force against defendant."

The State says that even if the search were made without authority, or otherwise unreasonably, it is not prevented from using the unconstitutionally seized evidence at trial, citing *Wolf v. Colorado* [p. 79], in which this Court did indeed hold "that in a prosecution in a State court for a State crime the Fourteenth Amendment does not forbid the admission of evidence obtained by an unreasonable search and seizure." On this appeal, * * * it is urged once again that we review that holding.

I. * * *

* * * [I]n the year 1914, in the *Weeks* [*v. United States*] case, this Court "for the first time" held that "in a federal prosecution the Fourth Amendment barred the use of evidence secured through an illegal search and seizure." This Court has ever since required of federal law officers a strict adherence to that command which this Court has held to be a clear, specific, and constitutionally required—even if judicially implied— deterrent safeguard without insistence upon which the Fourth Amendment would have been reduced to "a form of words." Holmes, J., *Silverthorne Lumber Co. v. United States*, 251 U.S. 385, 392, 40 S.Ct. 182, 183, 64 L.Ed. 319 (1920). It meant, quite simply, that "conviction by

means of unlawful seizures and enforced confessions * * * should find no sanction in the judgments of the courts * * * ," and that such evidence "shall not be used at all."

There are in the cases of this Court some passing references to the *Weeks* rule as being one of evidence. But the plain and unequivocal language of *Weeks*—and its later paraphrase in *Wolf*—to the effect that the *Weeks* rule is of constitutional origin, remains entirely undisturbed. * * *

II.

In 1949, 35 years after *Weeks* was announced, this Court, in *Wolf v. Colorado*, again for the first time, * * * decided that the *Weeks* exclusionary rule would not then be imposed upon the States as "an essential ingredient of the right." The Court's reasons for not considering essential to the right to privacy, as a curb imposed upon the States by the Due Process Clause, that which decades before had been posited as part and parcel of the Fourth Amendment's limitation upon federal encroachment of individual privacy, were bottomed on factual considerations.

While they are not basically relevant to a decision that the exclusionary rule is an essential ingredient of the Fourth Amendment as the right it embodies is vouchsafed against the States by the Due Process Clause, we will consider the current validity of the factual grounds upon which *Wolf* was based.

The Court in *Wolf* first stated that "[t]he contrariety of views of the States" on the adoption of the exclusionary rule of *Weeks* was "particularly impressive" * * * . While in 1949, prior to the *Wolf* case, almost two-thirds of the States were opposed to the use of the exclusionary rule, now, despite the *Wolf* case, more than half of those since passing upon it, by their own legislative or judicial decision, have wholly or partly adopted or adhered to the *Weeks* rule. Significantly, among those now following the rule is California, which, according to its highest court, was "compelled to reach that conclusion because other remedies have completely failed to secure compliance with the constitutional provisions * * * ." *People v. Cahan*, 44 Cal.2d 434, 445, 282 P.2d 905 [1955]. In connection with this California case, we note that the second basis elaborated in *Wolf* in support of its failure to enforce the exclusionary doctrine against the States was that "other means of protection" have been afforded "the right to privacy." The experience of California that such other remedies have been worthless and futile is buttressed by the experience of other States. * * *

It, therefore, plainly appears that the factual considerations supporting the failure of the *Wolf* Court to include the *Weeks* exclusionary rule when it recognized the enforceability of the right to privacy against the States in 1949, while not basically relevant to the constitutional consideration, could not, in any analysis, now be deemed controlling.

III.

* * * Today we once again examine *Wolf's* constitutional documentation of the right to privacy free from unreasonable state intrusion, and, after its dozen years on our books, are led by it to close the only courtroom door remaining open to evidence secured by official lawlessness in flagrant abuse of that basic right, reserved to all persons as a specific guarantee against that very same unlawful conduct. We hold that all evidence obtained by searches and seizures in violation of the Constitution is, by that same authority, inadmissible in a state court.

IV.

Since the Fourth Amendment's right of privacy has been declared enforceable against the States through the Due Process Clause of the Fourteenth, it is enforceable against them by the same sanction of exclusion as is used against the Federal Government. Were it otherwise, then just as without the *Weeks* rule the assurance against unreasonable federal searches and seizures would be "a form of words," valueless and undeserving of mention in a perpetual charter of inestimable human liberties, so too, without that rule the freedom from state invasions of privacy would be so ephemeral and so neatly severed from its conceptual nexus with the freedom from all brutish means of coercing evidence as not to merit this Court's high regard as a freedom "implicit in the concept of ordered liberty." * * * Therefore, in extending the substantive protections of due process to all constitutionally unreasonable searches—state or federal—it was logically and constitutionally necessary that the exclusion doctrine—an essential part of the right to privacy—be also insisted upon as an essential ingredient of the right newly recognized by the *Wolf* case. In short, the admission of the new constitutional right by *Wolf* could not consistently tolerate denial of its most important constitutional privilege, namely, the exclusion of the evidence which an accused had been forced to give by reason of the unlawful seizure. To hold otherwise is to grant the right but in reality to withhold its privilege and enjoyment. Only last year the Court itself recognized that the purpose of the exclusionary rule "is to deter—to compel respect for the constitutional guaranty in the only effectively available way—by removing the incentive to disregard it."

* * * This Court has not hesitated to enforce as strictly against the States as it does against the Federal Government the rights of free speech and of a free press, the right to notice and to a fair, public trial, including, as it does, the right not to be convicted by use of a coerced confession, however logically relevant it be, and without regard to its reliability. * * * The philosophy of each Amendment and of each freedom is complementary to, although not dependent upon, that of the other in its

sphere of influence—the very least that together they assure in either sphere is that no man is to be convicted on unconstitutional evidence.

V.

Moreover, our holding that the exclusionary rule is an essential part of both the Fourth and Fourteenth Amendments is not only the logical dictate of prior cases, but it also makes very good sense. There is no war between the Constitution and common sense. Presently, a federal prosecutor may make no use of evidence illegally seized, but a State's attorney across the street may, although he supposedly is operating under the enforceable prohibitions of the same Amendment. Thus the State, by admitting evidence unlawfully seized, serves to encourage disobedience to the Federal Constitution which it is bound to uphold. * * *

There are those who say, as did Justice (then Judge) Cardozo, that under our constitutional exclusionary doctrine "[t]he criminal is to go free because the constable has blundered." In some cases this will undoubtedly be the result. But, * * * "there is another consideration—the imperative of judicial integrity." The criminal goes free, if he must, but it is the law that sets him free. Nothing can destroy a government more quickly than its failure to observe its own laws, or worse, its disregard of the charter of its own existence. As Mr. Justice Brandeis, dissenting, said in *Olmstead v. United States*, 277 U.S. 438, 485, 48 S.Ct. 564, 575, 72 L.Ed. 944 (1928): "Our Government is the potent, the omnipresent teacher. For good or for ill, it teaches the whole people by its example. * * * If the Government becomes a lawbreaker, it breeds contempt for law; it invites every man to become a law unto himself; it invites anarchy." Nor can it lightly be assumed that, as a practical matter, adoption of the exclusionary rule fetters law enforcement. Only last year this Court expressly considered that contention and found that "pragmatic evidence of a sort" to the contrary was not wanting. * * *

* * * Our decision, founded on reason and truth, gives to the individual no more than that which the Constitution guarantees him, to the police officer no less than that to which honest law enforcement is entitled, and, to the courts, that judicial integrity so necessary in the true administration of justice. * * *

Reversed and remanded.

MR. JUSTICE BLACK, concurring. * * *

I am still not persuaded that the Fourth Amendment, standing alone, would be enough to bar the introduction into evidence against an accused of papers and effects seized from him in violation of its commands. For the Fourth Amendment does not itself contain any provision expressly precluding the use of such evidence, and I am extremely doubtful that such a provision could properly be inferred from nothing more than the basic command against unreasonable searches and seizures. Reflection on the problem, however, in the light of cases coming before the Court since *Wolf*, has led me to conclude that when the Fourth Amendment's ban against unreasonable searches and seizures is considered together with the Fifth Amendment's ban against compelled self-incrimination, a constitutional basis emerges which not only justifies but actually requires the exclusionary rule.

The close interrelationship between the Fourth and Fifth Amendments, as they apply to this problem, has long been recognized and, indeed, was expressly made the ground for this Court's holding in *Boyd v. United States*[, 116 U.S. 616, 6 S.Ct. 524, 29 L.Ed. 746 (1886)]. There the Court fully discussed this relationship and declared itself "unable to perceive that the seizure of a man's private books and papers to be used in evidence against him is substantially different from compelling him to be a witness against himself." * * * [A]lthough I rejected the argument [in *Wolf*], its force has, for me at least, become compelling with the more thorough understanding of the problem brought on by recent cases. In the final analysis, it seems to me that the *Boyd* doctrine, though perhaps not required by the express language of the Constitution strictly construed, is amply justified from an historical standpoint, soundly based in reason, and entirely consistent with what I regard to be the proper approach to interpretation of our Bill of Rights * * *.

[JUSTICE DOUGLAS's concurring opinion is omitted. JUSTICE STEWART, who concurred in the result expressed "no view as to the merits of the constitutional issue which the Court today decides." Instead, he would have reversed the conviction on the ground that it violated rights of "free thought and expression assured against state action by the Fourteenth Amendment."]

MR. JUSTICE HARLAN, whom MR. JUSTICE FRANKFURTER and MR. JUSTICE WHITTAKER join, dissenting.

In overruling the *Wolf* case the Court, in my opinion, has forgotten the sense of judicial restraint which, with due regard for *stare decisis*, is one element that should enter into deciding whether a past decision of this Court should be overruled. Apart from that I also believe that the *Wolf* rule represents sounder Constitutional doctrine than the new rule which now replaces it.

I.

From the Court's statement of the case one would gather that the central, if not controlling, issue on this appeal is whether illegally state-seized evidence is Constitutionally admissible in a state prosecution, an issue which would of course face us with the need for re-examining *Wolf*. However, such is not the situation. For, although that question was indeed raised here and below among appellant's subordinate points, the new and pivotal issue brought to the Court by this appeal is whether * * * the Ohio Revised Code making criminal the *mere* knowing possession or control of obscene material, and under which appellant has been convicted, is consistent with the rights of free thought and expression assured against state action by the Fourteenth Amendment. That was the principal issue which was decided by the Ohio Supreme Court, * * * and which was briefed[5] and argued[6] in this Court.

In this posture of things, I think it fair to say that five members of this Court have simply "reached out" to overrule *Wolf*. * * * I can perceive no justification for regarding this case as an appropriate occasion for re-examining *Wolf*. * * *

II.

Essential to the majority's argument against *Wolf* is the proposition that the rule of *Weeks v. United States*, excluding in federal criminal trials the use of evidence obtained in violation of the Fourth Amendment, derives not from the "supervisory power" of this Court over the federal judicial system, but from Constitutional requirement. This is so because no one, I suppose, would suggest that this Court possesses any general supervisory power over the state courts. Although I entertain considerable doubt as to the soundness of this foundational proposition of the majority, I shall assume, for present purposes, that the *Weeks* rule "is of constitutional origin."

At the heart of the majority's opinion in this case is the following syllogism: (1) the rule excluding in federal criminal trials evidence which is the product of an illegal search and seizure is "part and parcel" of the Fourth Amendment; (2) *Wolf* held that the "privacy" assured against federal action by the Fourth Amendment is also protected against state action by the Fourteenth Amendment; and (3) it is therefore "logically and constitutionally necessary" that the *Weeks* exclusionary rule should also be enforced against the States.

This reasoning ultimately rests on the unsound premise that because *Wolf* carried into the States, as part of "the concept of ordered liberty" embodied in the Fourteenth Amendment, the principle of "privacy" underlying the Fourth Amendment, it must follow that whatever configurations of the Fourth Amendment have been developed in the particularizing federal precedents are likewise to be deemed a part of

---

5 The appellant's brief did not urge the overruling of *Wolf*. Indeed it did not even cite the case. * * * The brief of the American and Ohio Civil Liberties Unions, as *amici*, did in one short concluding paragraph of its argument "request" the Court to re-examine and overrule *Wolf*, but without argumentation. * * *

6 Counsel for appellant on oral argument, as in his brief, did not urge that *Wolf* be overruled. Indeed, when pressed by questioning from the bench whether he was not in fact urging us to overrule *Wolf*, counsel expressly disavowed any such purpose.

"ordered liberty," and as such are enforceable against the States. For me, this does not follow at all.

It cannot be too much emphasized that what was recognized in *Wolf* was not that the Fourth Amendment *as such* is enforceable against the States as a facet of due process, a view of the Fourteenth Amendment which, as *Wolf* itself pointed out, has long since been discredited, but the principle of privacy "which is at the core of the Fourth Amendment." It would not be proper to expect or impose any precise equivalence, either as regards the scope of the right or the means of its implementation, between the requirements of the Fourth and Fourteenth Amendments. For the Fourth, unlike what was said in *Wolf* of the Fourteenth, does not state a general principle only; it is a particular command, having its setting in a pre-existing legal context on which both interpreting decisions and enabling statutes must at least build. * * *

I would not impose upon the States this federal exclusionary remedy. The reasons given by the majority for now suddenly turning its back on *Wolf* seem to me notably unconvincing.

First, it is said that "the factual grounds upon which *Wolf* was based" have since changed, in that more States now follow the *Weeks* exclusionary rule than was so at the time *Wolf* was decided. While that is true, * * * surely all this is beside the point, as the majority itself indeed seems to recognize. Our concern here, as it was in *Wolf*, is not with the desirability of that rule but only with the question whether the States are Constitutionally free to follow it or not as they may themselves determine, and the relevance of the disparity of views among the States on this point lies simply in the fact that the judgment involved is a debatable one. * * *

The preservation of a proper balance between state and federal responsibility in the administration of criminal justice demands patience on the part of those who might like to see things move faster among the States in this respect. Problems of criminal law enforcement vary widely from State to State. One State, in considering the totality of its legal picture, may conclude that the need for embracing the *Weeks* rule is pressing because other remedies are unavailable or inadequate to secure compliance with the substantive Constitutional principle involved. Another, though equally solicitous of Constitutional rights, may choose to pursue one purpose at a time, allowing all evidence relevant to guilt to be brought into a criminal trial, and dealing with Constitutional infractions by other means. Still another may consider the exclusionary rule too rough-and-ready a remedy, in that it reaches only unconstitutional intrusions which eventuate in criminal prosecution of the victims. Further, a State after experimenting with the *Weeks* rule for a time may, because of unsatisfactory experience with it, decide to revert to a non-exclusionary rule. And so on. * * * For us the question remains, as it has always been, one of state power, not one of passing judgment on the wisdom of one state course or another. In my view this Court should continue to forbear from fettering the States with an adamant rule which may embarrass them in coping with their own peculiar problems in criminal law enforcement. * * *

A state conviction comes to us as the complete product of a sovereign judicial system. Typically a case will have been tried in a trial court, tested in some final appellate court, and will go no further. In the comparatively rare instance when a conviction is reviewed by us on due process grounds we deal then with a finished product in the creation of which we are allowed no hand, and our task, far from being one of over-all supervision, is, speaking generally, restricted to a determination of whether the prosecution was Constitutionally fair. The specifics of trial procedure, which in every mature legal system will vary greatly in detail, are within the sole competence of the States. I do not see how it can be said that a trial becomes unfair simply because a State determines that evidence may be considered by the trier of fact, regardless of how it was obtained, if it is relevant to the one issue with which the trial is concerned, the guilt or innocence of the accused. Of course, a court may use its procedures as an incidental means of pursuing other ends than the correct resolution of the controversies before it. Such indeed is the *Weeks* rule, but if a State does not choose to use its courts in this way, I do not believe that this Court is empowered to impose this much-debated procedure on local courts, however efficacious we may consider the *Weeks* rule to be as a means of securing Constitutional rights.

Finally, it is said that the overruling of *Wolf* is supported by the established doctrine that the admission of evidence of an involuntary confession renders a state conviction Constitutionally invalid. Since such a confession may often be entirely reliable, and therefore of the greatest relevance to the issue of the trial, the argument continues, this doctrine is ample warrant in precedent that the way evidence was obtained, and not just its relevance, is Constitutionally significant to the fairness of a trial. I believe this analogy is not a true one. * * *

The point * * * must be that in requiring exclusion of an involuntary statement of an accused, we are concerned not with an appropriate remedy for what the police have done, but with something which is regarded as going to the heart of our concepts of fairness in judicial procedure. * * * What is crucial is that the trial defense to which an accused is entitled should not be rendered an empty formality by reason of statements wrung from him, for then "a prisoner * * * [has been] made the deluded instrument of his own conviction." That this is a *procedural right*, and that its violation occurs at the time his improperly obtained statement is admitted at trial, is manifest. For without this right all the careful safeguards erected around the giving of testimony * * * would become empty formalities in a procedure where the most compelling possible evidence of guilt, a confession, would have already been obtained at the unsupervised pleasure of the police.

This, and not the disciplining of the police, as with illegally seized evidence, is surely the true basis for excluding a statement of the accused which was unconstitutionally obtained. In sum, I think the coerced confession analogy works strongly *against* what the Court does today. * * *

I regret that I find so unwise in principle and so inexpedient in policy a decision motivated by the high purpose of increasing respect for Constitutional rights. But in the last analysis I think this Court can increase respect for the Constitution only if it rigidly respects the limitations which the Constitution places upon it, and respects as well the principles inherent in its own processes. In the present case I think we exceed both, and that our voice becomes only a voice of power, not of reason.

NOTES AND QUESTIONS

1.   *Counting votes.* You should grow accustomed to counting the votes in Supreme Court opinions. That is, you should determine how many justices signed an opinion of the Court. (We have helped you in this casebook, by summarizing each justice's vote.) A majority opinion of five justices does not carry the same symbolic weight as a unanimous opinion and, of course, is more susceptible to erosion or outright overruling, especially as new justices join the Court.

When counting votes, it is also important to distinguish between two types of concurring opinions. Sometimes, a justice will "concur in the judgment" or "concur in the result," as Justice Stewart did in this case. In such circumstances, the concurring justice has reached the same outcome as the majority (*e.g.*, reversal or affirmance of a lower court judgment), but does not want to attach his or her name to the main opinion, usually because the concurring justice reaches the result on different grounds.

Alternatively, concurring justices (here, Black and Douglas) may sign the Court's opinion, but still write separately. This is called a concurrence "in the opinion" of the Court. Typically, justices will write such a concurrence in order to clarify aspects of the main opinion that they believe need elucidation, or because they are unhappy with certain language in the principal opinion.

In view of this explanation, how many justices signed on to Justice Clark's opinion in *Mapp*?

2.   Do you consider Mapp an "innocent" or "guilty" person, who was subjected to police misconduct? In regard to the admissibility of the seized evidence, should such characterization matter?

3.   What was the Ohio Supreme Court getting at when it stated that a "reasonable argument" could be made that the conviction should be overturned because police methods "offended a sense of justice." Why do you think it rejected that "reasonable argument"?

4.   Why did Justice Harlan believe that this case was an inappropriate vehicle for overruling *Wolf*? Was he right? What should a justice who believed that *Wolf* was wrongly decided have done?

After his retirement, Justice Potter Stewart described the behind-the-scene events this way:

> At the conference following the argument, a majority of the Justices agreed that the Ohio statute violated the *first* and fourteenth amendments. Justice Tom Clark was assigned the job of writing the opinion of the Court.
>
> What transpired in the month following our conference * * * is really a matter of speculation on my part, but I have always suspected that the members of the soon-to-be *Mapp* majority had met in what I affectionately call a "rump caucus" to discuss a different basis for their decision.[12] But regardless of how they reached their decision, five Justices * * * concluded that * * * *Wolf* was to be overruled.
>
> I was shocked when Justice Clark's proposed Court opinion reached my desk. I immediately wrote him a note expressing my surprise and questioning the wisdom of overruling an important doctrine in a case in which the issue was not briefed, argued, or discussed by the state courts, by the parties' counsel, or at our conference following the oral argument.

Potter Stewart, *The Road to* Mapp v. Ohio *and Beyond: The Origins, Development and Future of the Exclusionary Rule in Search-and-Seizure Cases*, 83 Colum. L. Rev. 1365, 1368 (1983). For more on Justice Clark's behind-the-scenes role in *Mapp*, see Dennis D. Dorin, *Justice Tom Clark's Rule in* Mapp v. Ohio's *Extension of the Exclusionary Rule to State Searches and Seizures*, 52 Case W. Res. L. Rev. 401 (2001).

5.   Why did Justice Clark say that the "factual grounds upon which *Wolf* was based" were "basically [ir]relevant"? If so, why did he survey post-*Wolf* state law? Can it plausibly be claimed that the results of his survey actually supported the dissent?

6.   What is the purpose of an exclusionary rule? According to the majority, why is it required in state prosecutions? How did Justice Harlan answer the majority?

---

[12] Professor Schwartz reports that an impromptu caucus of the *Mapp* majority took place in an elevator at the Court immediately after the conference at which the case was discussed. [Bernard Schwartz, Super Chief: Earl Warren and His Supreme Court—A Judicial Biography 393 (1983).]

7. The majority supported its position by pointing out that coerced confessions are inadmissible at trial. What was Justice Clark's point in this regard? Why did Justice Harlan believe that this argument worked *against* the majority's position?

8. Just as *Wolf v. Colorado* was not the end of the story thanks to *Mapp v. Ohio*, *Mapp* is far from the end of the story about the Fourth Amendment exclusionary rule. The exclusionary rule has evoked considerable controversy, virtually from the day *Mapp* was handed down. And, because of the misgivings of a few, and later a majority, of Supreme Court justices, the scope of the Fourth Amendment exclusionary rule has been considerably narrowed. For an excellent behind-the-scenes look at the Court's growing distaste for the exclusionary rule, see Tracey Maclin, The Supreme Court and the Fourth Amendment's Exclusionary Rule (2013).

We will wait until Chapter 5, however, to look at the significant erosion of the exclusionary rule. For now, we turn to the Fourth Amendment itself, to identify the rights "the people" hold according to the Fourth Amendment, as interpreted by the United States Supreme Court. As you study the case law set out in Chapters 3 and 4, please keep in mind that violation of a person's search-and-seizure rights has generally required, since 1914 in the federal system, and since 1961 in the state courts, exclusion of the evidence obtained unconstitutionally by the police. Put another way, whenever a defendant has sought prior to trial to demonstrate that her Fourth Amendment rights were violated, her goal has been to convince a court that—because of the alleged constitutional violation—the evidence that incriminates her should be barred from introduction at her trial.

CHAPTER 3

PASSING THE THRESHOLD OF THE FOURTH AMENDMENT

■ ■ ■

The Fourth Amendment states that "[t]he right of the people to be secure in their persons, houses, papers, and effects, against unreasonable searches and seizures, shall not be violated * * * ." In these few words we are told what interests are protected (persons, houses, papers, and effects) and what the Government must do in regard to these protected interests (conduct only reasonable searches and seizures).

But notice: This amendment does not prohibit *all* unreasonable law enforcement practices. As far as the Fourth Amendment is concerned, *a police officer may act as arbitrarily or unreasonably as she wants,* as long as she does not conduct a "search" or "seizure"; and, even searches and seizures are unregulated by the Fourth Amendment unless the police search or seize a "person," "house," "paper," or "effect."

This chapter, therefore, considers the threshold of the Fourth Amendment. It focuses on the following question: What governmental conduct constitutes a *search* or *seizure* of a *person*, *house*, *paper*, or *effect* and, therefore, triggers Fourth Amendment protection?

A. WHAT IS A "SEARCH"?

1. GENERAL PRINCIPLES: FROM TRESPASS TO PRIVACY

Fourth Amendment "search" analysis is divisible into two historical periods. In the first period, * * * the justices treated Fourth Amendment "search" issues exclusively as a property-focused inquiry. * * *

Boyd v. United States [116 U.S. 616, 6 S.Ct. 524, 29 L.Ed. 746 (1886)] laid the seeds of a property-rights interpretation of the Fourth Amendment. * * * The Court quoted extensively from the "memorable discussion" * * * in *Entick v. Carrington* [19 Howell St. Tr. 1029, 1066 (1765) (Eng.)], in which Lord Camden stated that "every invasion of private property, be it ever so minute, is a trespass."

> According to Lord Camden, as quoted in *Boyd*, "[t]he great end for which men entered into society was to secure their property. That right is preserved sacred and incommunicable in all instances where it has not been taken away . . . by some public law for the good of the whole." * * *

Joshua Dressler & Alan C. Michaels, Understanding Criminal Procedure (Vol. 1: Investigation) (6th ed. 2013), at 68–69.

The so-called "trespass" approach to "search" law provided that there was no violation of the Fourth Amendment law in the absence of a trespass to private property. The second period of "search" law commenced eighty years later with the next case.

KATZ V. UNITED STATES

Supreme Court of the United States, 1967.
389 U.S. 347, 88 S.Ct. 507, 19 L.Ed.2d 576.

MR. JUSTICE STEWART delivered the opinion of the Court [joined by CHIEF JUSTICE WARREN, and JUSTICES BRENNAN, DOUGLAS, FORTAS, HARLAN, and WHITE].

The petitioner was convicted * * * under an eight-count indictment charging him with transmitting wagering information by telephone from Los Angeles to Miami and Boston, in violation of a federal statute. At trial the Government was permitted, over the petitioner's objection, to introduce evidence of the petitioner's end of telephone conversations, overheard by FBI agents who had attached an electronic listening and recording device to the outside of the public telephone booth from which he had placed his calls. In affirming his conviction, the Court of Appeals rejected the contention that the recordings had been obtained in violation of the Fourth Amendment, because "[t]here was no physical entrance into the area occupied by [the petitioner]." We granted certiorari in order to consider the constitutional questions thus presented.

The petitioner has phrased those questions as follows:

> "A. Whether a public telephone booth is a constitutionally protected area so that evidence obtained by attaching an electronic listening recording device to the top of such a booth is obtained in violation of the right to privacy of the user of the booth.

> "B. Whether physical penetration of a constitutionally protected area is necessary before a search and seizure can be said to be violative of the Fourth Amendment to the United States Constitution."

We decline to adopt this formulation of the issues. In the first place, the correct solution of Fourth Amendment problems is not necessarily promoted by incantation of the phrase "constitutionally protected area." Secondly, the Fourth Amendment cannot be translated into a general constitutional "right to privacy." That Amendment protects individual privacy against certain kinds of governmental intrusion, but its protections go further, and often have nothing to do with privacy at all.[4] Other provisions of the Constitution protect personal privacy from other forms of governmental invasion.[5] But the protection of a person's *general* right to privacy—his right to be let alone by other people—is, like the protection of his property and of his very life, left largely to the law of the individual States.

Because of the misleading way the issues have been formulated, the parties have attached great significance to the characterization of the telephone booth from which the petitioner placed his calls. The petitioner has strenuously argued that the booth was a "constitutionally protected area." The Government has maintained with equal vigor that it was not. But this effort to decide whether or not a given "area," viewed in the abstract, is "constitutionally protected" deflects attention from the problem presented by this case. For the Fourth Amendment protects people, not places. What a person knowingly exposes to the public, even in his own home or office, is not a subject of Fourth Amendment protection. But what he seeks to preserve as private, even in an area accessible to the public, may be constitutionally protected.

The Government stresses the fact that the telephone booth from which the petitioner made his calls was constructed partly of glass, so that he was as visible after he entered it as he would have been if he had remained outside. But what he sought to exclude when he entered the booth was not the intruding eye—it was the uninvited ear. He did not shed his right to do so simply because he made his calls from a place where he might be seen. No less than an individual in a business office, in a friend's apartment, or in a taxicab, a person in a telephone booth may rely upon the protection of the Fourth Amendment. One who occupies it, shuts the door behind him, and pays the toll that permits him to place a call is surely entitled to assume that the words he utters into the

---

[4] "The average man would very likely not have his feelings soothed any more by having his property seized openly than by having it seized privately and by stealth. * * * And a person can be just as much, if not more, irritated, annoyed and injured by an unceremonious public arrest by a policeman as he is by a seizure in the privacy of his office or home." *Griswold v. Connecticut*, 381 U.S. 479, 509, 85 S.Ct. 1678, 1695, 14 L.Ed.2d 510 [(1965)] (dissenting opinion of Mr. Justice Black).

[5] The First Amendment, for example, imposes limitations upon governmental abridgement of "freedom to associate and privacy in one's associations." The Third Amendment's prohibition against the unconsented peacetime quartering of soldiers protects another aspect of privacy from governmental intrusion. To some extent, the Fifth Amendment too "reflects the Constitution's concern for * * * ' * * * the right of each individual "to a private enclave where he may lead a private life." ' " Virtually every governmental action interferes with personal privacy to some degree. The question in each case is whether that interference violates a command of the United States Constitution.

mouthpiece will not be broadcast to the world. To read the Constitution more narrowly is to ignore the vital role that the public telephone has come to play in private communication.

The Government contends, however, that the activities of its agents in this case should not be tested by Fourth Amendment requirements, for the surveillance technique they employed involved no physical penetration of the telephone booth from which the petitioner placed his calls. It is true that the absence of such penetration was at one time thought to foreclose further Fourth Amendment inquiry, *Olmstead v. United States*, 277 U.S. 438, 457, 464, 466, 48 S.Ct. 564, 565, 567, 568, 72 L.Ed. 944 [(1928)]; *Goldman v. United States*, 316 U.S. 129, 134–136, 62 S.Ct. 993, 995–97, 86 L.Ed. 1322 [(1942)], for that Amendment was thought to limit only searches and seizures of tangible property. But "[t]he premise that property interests control the right of the Government to search and seize has been discredited." Thus, although a closely divided Court supposed in *Olmstead* that surveillance without any trespass and without the seizure of any material object fell outside the ambit of the Constitution, we have since departed from the narrow view on which that decision rested. Indeed, we have expressly held that the Fourth Amendment governs not only the seizure of tangible items, but extends as well to the recording of oral statements, overheard without any "technical trespass under * * * local property law." *Silverman v. United States*, 365 U.S. 505, 511, 81 S.Ct. 679, 682, 5 L.Ed.2d 734 [(1961)]. Once this much is acknowledged, and once it is recognized that the Fourth Amendment protects people—and not simply "areas"—against unreasonable searches and seizures, it becomes clear that the reach of that Amendment cannot turn upon the presence or absence of a physical intrusion into any given enclosure.

We conclude that the underpinnings of *Olmstead* and *Goldman* have been so eroded by our subsequent decisions that the "trespass" doctrine there enunciated can no longer be regarded as controlling. The Government's activities in electronically listening to and recording the petitioner's words violated the privacy upon which he justifiably relied while using the telephone booth and thus constituted a "search and seizure" within the meaning of the Fourth Amendment. The fact that the electronic device employed to achieve that end did not happen to penetrate the wall of the booth can have no constitutional significance.

The question remaining for decision, then, is whether the search and seizure conducted in this case complied with constitutional standards. [The Court went on to hold that they did not, as explained more fully in Note 6, *infra*.]

[JUSTICE DOUGLAS'S concurring opinion, with whom JUSTICE BRENNAN joined, is omitted.]

MR. JUSTICE MARSHALL took no part in the consideration or decision of this case.

MR. JUSTICE HARLAN, concurring.

I join the opinion of the Court, which I read to hold only (a) that an enclosed telephone booth is an area where, like a home, and unlike a field, a person has a constitutionally protected reasonable expectation of privacy; (b) that electronic as well as physical intrusion into a place that is in this sense private may constitute a violation of the Fourth Amendment; and (c) that the invasion of a constitutionally protected area by federal authorities is, as the Court has long held, presumptively unreasonable in the absence of a search warrant.

As the Court's opinion states, "the Fourth Amendment protects people, not places." The question, however, is what protection it affords to those people. Generally, as here, the answer to that question requires reference to a "place." My understanding of the rule that has emerged from prior decisions is that there is a twofold requirement, first that a person have exhibited an actual (subjective) expectation of privacy and, second, that the expectation be one that society is prepared to recognize as "reasonable." Thus a man's home is, for most purposes, a place where he expects privacy, but objects, activities, or statements that he exposes to the "plain view" of outsiders are not "protected" because no intention to keep them to himself has been exhibited. On the other hand, conversations in the open would not be protected against being overheard, for the expectation of privacy under the circumstances would be unreasonable.

The critical fact in this case is that "[o]ne who occupies it [a telephone booth], shuts the door behind him, and pays the toll that permits him to place a call is surely entitled to assume" that his conversation is not being intercepted. The point is not that the booth is "accessible to the public" at other times, but that it is a temporarily private place whose momentary occupants' expectations of freedom from intrusion are recognized as reasonable. *] m's p.o.v.*

In *Silverman v. United States*, we held that eavesdropping accomplished by means of an electronic device that penetrated the premises occupied by petitioner was a violation of the Fourth Amendment. That case established that interception of conversations reasonably intended to be private could constitute a "search and seizure," and that the examination or taking of physical property was not required. * * * In *Silverman* we found it unnecessary to re-examine *Goldman v. United States*, which had held that electronic surveillance accomplished without the physical penetration of petitioner's premises by a tangible object did not violate the Fourth Amendment. This case requires us to reconsider *Goldman*, and I agree that it should now be overruled. Its

Case overrules Goldman.

limitation on Fourth Amendment protection is, in the present day, bad physics as well as bad law, for reasonable expectations of privacy may be defeated by electronic as well as physical invasion. * * *

[JUSTICE WHITE'S concurring opinion is omitted.]

MR. JUSTICE BLACK, dissenting.

If I could agree with the Court that eavesdropping carried on by electronic means (equivalent to wiretapping) constitutes a "search" or "seizure," I would be happy to join the Court's opinion. * * *

My basic objection is twofold: (1) I do not believe that the words of the Amendment will bear the meaning given them by today's decision, and (2) I do not believe that it is the proper role of this Court to rewrite the Amendment in order "to bring it into harmony with the times" and thus reach a result that many people believe to be desirable.

While I realize that an argument based on the meaning of words lacks the scope, and no doubt the appeal, of broad policy discussions and philosophical discourses on such nebulous subjects as privacy, for me the language of the Amendment is the crucial place to look in construing a written document such as our Constitution. * * * The first clause protects "persons, houses, papers, and effects, against unreasonable searches and seizures * * * ." These words connote the idea of tangible things with size, form, and weight, things capable of being searched, seized, or both. The second clause of the Amendment still further establishes its Framers' purpose to limit its protection to tangible things by providing that no warrants shall issue but those "particularly describing the place to be searched, and the persons or things to be seized." A conversation overheard by eavesdropping, whether by plain snooping or wiretapping, is not tangible and, under the normally accepted meanings of the words, can neither be searched nor seized. In addition the language of the second clause indicates that the Amendment refers not only to something tangible so it can be seized but to something already in existence so it can be described. Yet the Court's interpretation would have the Amendment apply to overhearing future conversations which by their very nature are nonexistent until they take place. How can one "describe" a future conversation, and, if one cannot, how can a magistrate issue a warrant to eavesdrop one in the future? * * * Rather than using language in a completely artificial way, I must conclude that the Fourth Amendment simply does not apply to eavesdropping.

Tapping telephone wires, of course, was an unknown possibility at the time the Fourth Amendment was adopted. But eavesdropping (and wiretapping is nothing more than eavesdropping by telephone) was * * * "an ancient practice which at common law was condemned as a nuisance. 4 Blackstone, Commentaries 168. In those days the eavesdropper listened by naked ear under the eaves of houses or their windows, or beyond their walls seeking out private discourse." There can be no doubt that the Framers were aware of this practice, and if they had desired to outlaw or restrict the use of evidence obtained by eavesdropping, I believe that they would have used the appropriate language to do so in the Fourth Amendment. They certainly would not have left such a task to the ingenuity of language-stretching judges. * * *

Since I see no way in which the words of the Fourth Amendment can be construed to apply to eavesdropping, that closes the matter for me. In interpreting the Bill of Rights, I willingly go as far as a liberal construction of the language takes me, but I simply cannot in good conscience give a meaning to words which they have never before been thought to have and which they certainly do not have in common ordinary usage. I will not distort the words of the Amendment in order to "keep the Constitution up to date" or "to bring it into harmony with the times." It was never meant that this Court have such power, which in effect would make us a continuously functioning constitutional convention.

With this decision the Court has completed, I hope, its rewriting of the Fourth Amendment, which started only recently when the Court began referring incessantly to the Fourth Amendment not so much as a law against *unreasonable* searches and seizures as one to protect an individual's privacy. * * *

The Fourth Amendment protects privacy only to the extent that it prohibits unreasonable searches and seizures of "persons, houses, papers, and effects." No general right is created by the Amendment so as to give this Court the unlimited power to hold unconstitutional everything which affects privacy. Certainly the Framers, well acquainted as they were with the excesses of governmental power, did not intend to grant this Court such omnipotent lawmaking authority as that. The history of governments proves that it is dangerous to freedom to repose such powers in courts.

For these reasons I respectfully dissent.

NOTES AND QUESTIONS

1. Justice Stewart states that what "a person *knowingly* exposes to the public" is not protected by the Fourth Amendment. Should this be the rule? Would the scope of Fourth Amendment coverage have been enlarged if the Court had used the word "purposely," rather than "knowingly"?

Also, what is meant by the word "public"? If you knowingly expose your conversation to just one person, have you exposed it to the "public"? Keep these questions in mind as you proceed through this chapter.

2. *Variations on the theme.* Telephone booths are an endangered species—when did you last see one?—in the era of smartphones and other new methods of technological communication. One observer at the time of

Katz, perhaps thinking the question was merely rhetorical, asked, "Would the case have been different if the pay phone has not been surrounded by a booth?" Edmund W. Kitch, Katz v. United States: *The Limits of the Fourth Amendment*, 1968 Sup. Ct. Rev. 133, 140. Well, how would Justice Stewart have answered his question?

Or, suppose that the FBI, rather than conducting electronic surveillance, had positioned a lip reader immediately outside the telephone booth, who observed Katz's lips and recorded his words on paper? Would Justice Stewart consider *this* conduct a "search"?

What if police officers, in an effort to catch men in homosexual activity, install a peephole in the ceiling so they can secretly observe activities in a public toilet stall. Is this a "search" under *Katz*? Does it matter whether the stall has doors on it? See People v. Triggs, 8 Cal.3d 884, 106 Cal.Rptr. 408, 506 P.2d 232 (1973).

3.   Is a telephone booth a "person, house, paper, or effect"? If not, why does the Fourth Amendment apply to Katz's conversations there? Does the majority provide a suitable answer to Justice Black's textual argument that electronic surveillance falls outside the coverage of the Fourth Amendment?

4.   *The subjective prong in Justice Harlan's test: things to think about.* As the cases that follow will show, the two-prong formula set out in Justice Harlan's concurring opinion has become the primary standard for determining whether police conduct constitutes a search.

Do you see any problems with Harlan's subjective prong? Do *you* have an expectation of privacy in your home? Do you have an expectation of privacy in your belongings at the airport? Do you have an expectation of privacy regarding the Web sites you have visited on your computer, or the e-mails you have written? Have your answers to any of these questions changed in recent years in light of what you know about technology and/or news accounts of government surveillance? Why might the answers to these questions have motivated one scholar to write that "[a]n actual, subjective expectation of privacy obviously has no place * * * in a theory of what the fourth amendment protects." Anthony G. Amsterdam, *Perspectives on the Fourth Amendment*, 58 Minn. L. Rev. 349, 384 (1974).

5.   *The objective prong in Justice Harlan's test: things to think about.* How should a court apply the second prong of Justice Harlan's test? Should it consider whether the American people, in general, expect privacy in certain circumstances? If so, should a court consider public opinion polls and other reliable evidence of public attitudes in this regard? *E.g.*, Christopher Slobogin & Joseph E. Schumacher, *Reasonable Expectations of Privacy and Autonomy in Fourth Amendment Cases: An Empirical Look at "Understandings Recognized and Permitted by Society,"* 42 Duke L.J. 727 (1993) (surveying public attitudes regarding privacy, and concluding that "the Supreme Court's conclusions about the scope of the Fourth Amendment are often not in tune with commonly held attitudes about police investigative techniques"). And,

what if public expectations of privacy change over time—what then? Or, is Justice Harlan suggesting that courts should conduct a normative inquiry to determine what privacy rights people living in a democracy are entitled to possess?

All of these questions assume that a judge will determine what constitutes a "reasonable expectation of privacy" in a particular situation. But, is it desirable to permit judges to answer this question? Would it be better to leave this question to the jury, perhaps to re-litigate at the trial, if the judge first determines that the Fourth Amendment is not implicated? See Meghan J. Ryan, *Juries and the Criminal Constitution*, 65 Ala. L. Rev. 849 (2014).

6.   *If electronic surveillance is a search, what then?* Please keep in mind that in the excerpt of the *Katz* opinion set out above, the issue considered was whether the wiretapping constituted a Fourth Amendment "search," *i.e.*, whether the restrictions of the Fourth Amendment applied to the electronic surveillance. Having answered this question affirmatively, the Court next had to consider whether the FBI agents' actions complied with the Fourth Amendment.

The *Katz* Court, quoting prior case law, observed that the Fourth Amendment generally "requires adherence to judicial processes." Justice Stewart, using oft-quoted language, stated the rule that "searches conducted outside the judicial process, without prior approval by judge or magistrate [*i.e.*, in the form of a search warrant] are *per se* unreasonable under the Fourth Amendment—subject only to a few specifically established well-delineated exceptions." The Court proceeded:

> Accepting * * * the Government's [account of its] actions as accurate, it is clear that this surveillance was so narrowly circumscribed that a duly authorized magistrate, properly notified of the need for such investigation, specifically informed of the basis on which it was to proceed, and clearly apprised of the precise intrusion it would entail, could constitutionally have authorized, with appropriate safeguards, the very limited search and seizure that the Government asserts in fact took place.

All would have been well, in other words, had the FBI obtained a judicially authorized warrant to conduct the surveillance. Because no warrant was secured, however, the Court ruled that the Fourth Amendment was violated.

7.   *Obtaining a search warrant to conduct electronic surveillance: special problems.* Search warrants are considered in detail in the next chapter, but it is worth noting here that the search warrant process in electronic surveillance cases creates special constitutional issues. Notice that if the police want to search a suspect's home for a tangible object, let's say a stolen painting, they can tell the magistrate, with particularity, what it is they are looking for (the painting) and where they expect to find it. Once they

seize the object, the search ends. But, in an electronic surveillance case, the police must request permission to "search" and "seize" something that is not only intangible but does not even exist at the time of the warrant request, namely, a future conversation.

In Berger v. New York, 388 U.S. 41, 87 S.Ct. 1873, 18 L.Ed.2d 1040 (1967), the Supreme Court declared a New York wiretapping statute unconstitutional because it permitted law enforcement officers to obtain a judicial order to conduct electronic surveillance without particularizing the crime being investigated and the conversations they expected to hear; the statute also improperly permitted surveillance of *all* of the suspect's conversations for sixty days on the basis of a single showing of probable cause, and allowed renewal of the order without a further finding of probable cause; and the court order did not require the police to stop surveillance once the conversations they sought were "seized."

One year after *Berger* and *Katz*, Congress enacted legislation, the 1968 Omnibus Crime Control and Safe Streets Act, which includes warrant procedures for electronic surveillance that avoid the weaknesses in the invalidated New York statute. The complicated law is set out in Appendix A. of the Supplement to this casebook.

8.   *"So, do I really want to be a police officer?"* The police suspect a person of rape. The suspect denies his guilt but refuses to provide a DNA sample to the police. Later, an officer observes the suspect spit on a public sidewalk. The officer retrieves the saliva for DNA testing. Search? See Commonwealth v. Cabral, 69 Mass.App.Ct. 68, 866 N.E.2d 429 (2007).

9.   A student once asked one of the casebook authors how the police knew which telephone booth to wiretap. The answer is that they didn't precisely know, but they were aware that Katz regularly used one of two phone booths, so they obtained permission from the phone company to put one of the booths out of order, and then they installed the listening devices in the other booth! According to the attorney who argued Katz's case before the United States Supreme Court, when he informed his client "of the historic decision that now bears his name, his first response was not one of thanks or gratitude. Rather, he wanted to know if he could sue the telephone company for permitting the FBI agents to put the one telephone booth out of order." Harvey A. Schneider, *Katz v. United States: The Untold Story*, 40 McGeorge L. Rev. 13, 23 (2009).

2.   THE *KATZ* DOCTRINE: WHAT DOES PRIVACY MEAN?

UNITED STATES V. WHITE

Supreme Court of the United States, 1971.
401 U.S. 745, 91 S.Ct. 1122, 28 L.Ed.2d 453.

MR. JUSTICE WHITE announced the judgment of the Court and an opinion in which THE CHIEF JUSTICE, MR. JUSTICE STEWART, and MR. JUSTICE BLACKMUN join.

In 1966, respondent James A. White was tried and convicted under *charge* two consolidated indictments charging various illegal transactions in narcotics * * *. * * * The issue before us is whether the Fourth *issue* Amendment bars from evidence the testimony of governmental agents who related certain conversations which had occurred between defendant White and a government informant, Harvey Jackson, and which the agents overheard by monitoring the frequency of a radio transmitter carried by Jackson and concealed on his person. On four occasions the conversations took place in Jackson's home; each of these conversations was overheard by an agent concealed in a kitchen closet with Jackson's consent and by a second agent outside the house using a radio receiver. Four other conversations—one in respondent's home, one in a restaurant, and two in Jackson's car—were overheard by the use of radio equipment. The prosecution was unable to locate and produce Jackson at the trial and the trial court overruled objections to the testimony of the agents who conducted the electronic surveillance. The jury returned a guilty verdict and defendant appealed. * * *

I * * *

Katz v. United States * * * finally swept away doctrines that electronic eavesdropping is permissible under the Fourth Amendment unless physical invasion of a constitutionally protected area produced the challenged evidence. In that case government agents, without petitioner's consent or knowledge, attached a listening device to the outside of a public telephone booth and recorded the defendant's end of his telephone conversations. In declaring the recordings inadmissible in evidence in the absence of a warrant authorizing the surveillance, the Court overruled *Olmstead* [*v. United States*, 277 U.S. 438, 48 S.Ct. 564, 72 L.Ed. 944 (1928)] and *Goldman* [*v. United States*, 316 U.S. 129, 62 S.Ct. 993, 86 L.Ed. 1322 (1942)] and held that the absence of physical intrusion into the telephone booth did not justify using electronic devices in listening to and recording Katz' words, thereby violating the privacy on which he justifiably relied while using the telephone in those circumstances.

The Court of Appeals understood *Katz* to render inadmissible against White the agents' testimony concerning conversations that Jackson broadcast to them. We cannot agree. *Katz* involved no revelation to the Government by a party to conversations with the defendant nor did the Court indicate in any way that a defendant has a justifiable and constitutionally protected expectation that a person with whom he is conversing will not then or later reveal the conversation to the police.

Hoffa v. United States, 385 U.S. 293, 87 S.Ct. 408, 17 L.Ed.2d 374 (1966), which was left undisturbed by *Katz*, held that however strongly a defendant may trust an apparent colleague, his expectations in this respect are not protected by the Fourth Amendment when it turns out that the colleague is a government agent regularly communicating with the authorities.[a] In these circumstances, "no interest legitimately protected by the Fourth Amendment is involved," for that Amendment affords no protection to "a wrongdoer's misplaced belief that a person to whom he voluntarily confides his wrongdoing will not reveal it." No warrant to "search and seize" is required in such circumstances, nor is it when the Government sends to defendant's home a secret agent who conceals his identity and makes a purchase of narcotics from the accused, *Lewis v. United States*, 385 U.S. 206, 87 S.Ct. 424, 17 L.Ed.2d 312 (1966), or when the same agent, unbeknown to the defendant, carries electronic equipment to record the defendant's words and the evidence so gathered is later offered in evidence. *Lopez v. United States*, 373 U.S. 427, 83 S.Ct. 1381, 10 L.Ed.2d 462 (1963).

Conceding that *Hoffa*, *Lewis*, and *Lopez* remained unaffected by *Katz*, the Court of Appeals nevertheless read both *Katz* and the Fourth Amendment to require a different result if the agent not only records his conversations with the defendant but instantaneously transmits them electronically to other agents equipped with radio receivers. Where this occurs, the Court of Appeals held, the Fourth Amendment is violated and the testimony of the listening agents must be excluded from evidence.

To reach this result it was necessary for the Court of Appeals to hold that *On Lee v. United States* [343 U.S. 747, 72 S.Ct. 967, 96 L.Ed. 1270 (1952),] was no longer good law. In that case, which involved facts very similar to the case before us, the Court first rejected claims of a Fourth Amendment violation because the informer had not trespassed when he entered the defendant's premises and conversed with him. To this extent the Court's rationale cannot survive *Katz*. But the Court announced a second and independent ground for its decision; for it went on to say that overruling *Olmstead* and *Goldman* would be of no aid to On Lee since he "was talking confidentially and indiscreetly with one he trusted, and he

---

[a]   In *Hoffa*, the defendant talked in his hotel suite to a long-time labor associate, unaware that his colleague had become a government informant.

was overheard. * * * It would be a dubious service to the genuine liberties protected by the Fourth Amendment to make them bedfellows with spurious liberties improvised by farfetched analogies which would liken eavesdropping on a conversation, with the connivance of one of the parties, to an unreasonable search or seizure. We find no violation of the Fourth Amendment here." We see no indication in *Katz* that the Court meant to disturb that understanding of the Fourth Amendment or to disturb the result reached in the *On Lee* case, nor are we now inclined to overturn this view of the Fourth Amendment.

Concededly a police agent who conceals his police connections may write down for official use his conversations with a defendant and testify concerning them, without a warrant authorizing his encounters with the defendant and without otherwise violating the latter's Fourth Amendment rights. *Hoffa v. United States*. For constitutional purposes, no different result is required if the agent instead of immediately reporting and transcribing his conversations with defendant, either (1) simultaneously records them with electronic equipment which he is carrying on his person, *Lopez v. United States*; (2) or carries radio equipment which simultaneously transmits the conversations either to recording equipment located elsewhere or to other agents monitoring the transmitting frequency. *On Lee v. United States*. If the conduct and revelations of an agent operating without electronic equipment do not invade the defendant's constitutionally justifiable expectations of privacy, neither does a simultaneous recording of the same conversations made by the agent or by others from transmissions received from the agent to whom the defendant is talking and whose trustworthiness the defendant necessarily risks.

Our problem is not what the privacy expectations of particular defendants in particular situations may be or the extent to which they may in fact have relied on the discretion of their companions. Very probably, individual defendants neither know nor suspect that their colleagues have gone or will go to the police or are carrying recorders or transmitters. Otherwise, conversation would cease and our problem with these encounters would be nonexistent or far different from those now before us. Our problem, in terms of the principles announced in *Katz*, is what expectations of privacy are constitutionally "justifiable"—what expectations the Fourth Amendment will protect in the absence of a warrant. So far, the law permits the frustration of actual expectations of privacy by permitting authorities to use the testimony of those associates who for one reason or another have determined to turn to the police, as well as by authorizing the use of informants in the manner exemplified by *Hoffa* and *Lewis*. If the law gives no protection to the wrongdoer whose trusted accomplice is or becomes a police agent, neither should it protect him when that same agent has recorded or transmitted the conversations which are later offered in evidence to prove the State's case.

Inescapably, one contemplating illegal activities must realize and risk that his companions may be reporting to the police. If he sufficiently doubts their trustworthiness, the association will very probably end or never materialize. But if he has no doubts, or allays them, or risks what doubt he has, the risk is his. In terms of what his course will be, what he will or will not do or say, we are unpersuaded that he would distinguish between probable informers on the one hand and probable informers with transmitters on the other. Given the possibility or probability that one of his colleagues is cooperating with the police, it is only speculation to assert that the defendant's utterances would be substantially different or his sense of security any less if he also thought it possible that the suspected colleague is wired for sound. At least there is no persuasive evidence that the difference in this respect between the electronically equipped and the unequipped agent is substantial enough to require discrete constitutional recognition, particularly under the Fourth Amendment which is ruled by fluid concepts of "reasonableness."

Nor should we be too ready to erect constitutional barriers to relevant and probative evidence which is also accurate and reliable. An electronic recording will many times produce a more reliable rendition of what a defendant has said than will the unaided memory of a police agent. It may also be that with the recording in existence it is less likely that the informant will change his mind, less chance that threat or injury will suppress unfavorable evidence and less chance that cross-examination will confound the testimony. Considerations like these obviously do not favor the defendant, but we are not prepared to hold that a defendant who has no constitutional right to exclude the informer's unaided testimony nevertheless has a Fourth Amendment privilege against a more accurate version of the events in question. * * *

The judgment of the Court of Appeals is * * * reversed.

[JUSTICE BLACK concurred in the Court's judgment for the reasons set forth in his dissent in *Katz*. JUSTICE BRENNAN's concurrence in the result is omitted.]

MR. JUSTICE DOUGLAS, dissenting. * * *

The issue in this case is clouded and concealed by the very discussion of it in legalistic terms. What the ancients knew as "eavesdropping," we now call "electronic surveillance"; but to equate the two is to treat man's first gunpowder on the same level as the nuclear bomb. Electronic surveillance is the greatest leveler of human privacy ever known. * * * [T]he concepts of privacy which the Founders enshrined in the Fourth Amendment vanish completely when we slavishly allow an all-powerful government, proclaiming law and order, efficiency, and other benign purposes, to penetrate all the walls and doors which men need to shield them from the pressures of a turbulent life around them and give them the health and strength to carry on. * * *

Today no one perhaps notices because only a small, obscure criminal is the victim. But every person is the victim, for the technology we exalt today is everyman's master. * * *

It is urged by the Department of Justice that *On Lee* be established as the controlling decision in this field. I would stand by * * * *Katz* and reaffirm the need for judicial supervision under the Fourth Amendment of the use of electronic surveillance which, uncontrolled, promises to lead us into a police state. * * *

MR. JUSTICE HARLAN, dissenting. * * *

I

Before turning to matters of precedent and policy, several preliminary observations should be made. We deal here with the constitutional validity of instantaneous third-party electronic eavesdropping, conducted by federal law enforcement officers, without any prior judicial approval of the technique utilized, but with the consent and cooperation of a participant in the conversation * * * . The magnitude of the issue at hand is evidenced not simply by the obvious doctrinal difficulty of weighing such activity in the Fourth Amendment balance, but also, and more importantly, by the prevalence of police utilization of this technique. Professor Westin has documented in careful detail the numerous devices that make technologically feasible the Orwellian Big Brother. Of immediate relevance is his observation that " 'participant recording,' in which one participant in a conversation or meeting, either a police officer or a cooperating party, wears a concealed device that records the conversation or broadcasts it to others nearby * * * is used tens of thousands of times each year throughout the country, particularly in cases involving extortion, conspiracy, narcotics, gambling, prostitution, corruption by police officials * * * and similar crimes."[3] * * *

II * * *

A

On Lee involved circumstances virtually identical to those now before us. There, Government agents enlisted the services of Chin Poy, a former

---

[3] A. Westin, Privacy and Freedom 131 (1967). This investigative technique is also used to unearth "political" crimes. "Recordings of the private and public meetings of suspect groups [have] been growing. Police in Miami, Florida, used a hidden transmitter on a police agent to record statements made at meetings of a right-wing extremist group suspected of planning acts of terrorism. In 1964 a police undercover agent obtained recordings of incendiary statements by the leader of a Communist splinter movement in Harlem, at private meetings and at a public rally, which served as the basis for his conviction for attempting to overthrow the state government." *Ibid.*

friend of Lee, who was suspected of engaging in illegal narcotics traffic. Poy was equipped with a "minifon" transmitting device which enabled outside Government agents to monitor Poy's conversations with Lee. In the privacy of his laundry, Lee made damaging admissions to Poy which were overheard by the agents and later related at trial. Poy did not testify. Mr. Justice Jackson, writing for five Justices, held the testimony admissible. Without reaching the question of whether a conversation could be the subject of a "seizure" for Fourth Amendment purposes, as yet an unanswered if not completely open question, the Court concluded that in the absence of a trespass, no constitutional violation had occurred.

The validity of the trespass rationale was questionable even at the time the decision was rendered. In this respect *On Lee* rested on common-law notions and looked to a waning era of Fourth Amendment jurisprudence. * * *

III

A

That the foundations of *On Lee* have been destroyed does not, of course, mean that its result can no longer stand. Indeed, the plurality opinion today fastens upon our decisions in *Lopez, Lewis v. United States*, and *Hoffa v. United States*, to resist the undercurrents of more recent cases emphasizing the warrant procedure as a safeguard to privacy. But this category provides insufficient support. In each of these cases the risk the general populace faced was different from that surfaced by the instant case. No surreptitious third ear was present, and in each opinion that fact was carefully noted. * * *

The plurality opinion seeks to erase the crucial distinction between the facts before us and these holdings by the following reasoning: if A can relay verbally what is revealed to him by B (as in *Lewis* and *Hoffa*), or record and later divulge it (as in *Lopez*), what difference does it make if A conspires with another to betray B by contemporaneously transmitting to the other all that is said? The contention is, in essence, an argument that the distinction between third-party monitoring and other undercover techniques is one of form and not substance. The force of the contention depends on the evaluation of two separable but intertwined assumptions: first, that there is no greater invasion of privacy in the third-party situation, and, second, that uncontrolled consensual surveillance in an electronic age is a tolerable technique of law enforcement, given the values and goals of our political system.

The first of these assumptions takes as a point of departure the so-called "risk analysis" approach of *Lewis*, and *Lopez*, and to a lesser extent *On Lee*, or the expectations approach of *Katz*. While these formulations represent an advance over the unsophisticated trespass analysis of the common law, they too have their limitations and can, ultimately, lead to the substitution of words for analysis. The analysis must, in my view, transcend the search for subjective expectations or legal attribution of assumptions of risk. Our expectations, and the risks we assume, are in large part reflections of laws that translate into rules the customs and values of the past and present.

Since it is the task of the law to form and project, as well as mirror and reflect, we should not, as judges, merely recite the expectations and risks without examining the desirability of saddling them upon society. The critical question, therefore, is whether under our system of government, as reflected in the Constitution, we should impose on our citizens the risks of the electronic listener or observer without at least the protection of a warrant requirement.

This question must, in my view, be answered by assessing the nature of a particular practice and the likely extent of its impact on the individual's sense of security balanced against the utility of the conduct as a technique of law enforcement. For those more extensive intrusions that significantly jeopardize the sense of security which is the paramount concern of Fourth Amendment liberties, I am of the view that more than self-restraint by law enforcement officials is required and at the least warrants should be necessary.

B

The impact of the practice of third-party bugging, must, I think, be considered such as to undermine that confidence and sense of security in dealing with one another that is characteristic of individual relationships between citizens in a free society. It goes beyond the impact on privacy occasioned by the ordinary type of "informer" investigation upheld in *Lewis* and *Hoffa*. The argument of the plurality opinion, to the effect that it is irrelevant whether secrets are revealed by the mere tattletale or the transistor, ignores the differences occasioned by third-party monitoring and recording which insures full and accurate disclosure of all that is said, free of the possibility of error and oversight that inheres in human reporting.

Authority is hardly required to support the proposition that words would be measured a good deal more carefully and communication inhibited if one suspected his conversations were being transmitted and transcribed. Were third-party bugging a prevalent practice, it might well smother that spontaneity—reflected in frivolous, impetuous, sacrilegious, and defiant discourse—that liberates daily life. Much off-hand exchange is easily forgotten and one may count on the obscurity of his remarks, protected by the very fact of a limited audience, and the likelihood that the listener will either overlook or forget what is said, as well as the listener's inability to reformulate a conversation without having to contend with a documented record. All these values are sacrificed by a rule of law that permits official monitoring of private discourse limited only by the need to locate a willing assistant. * * *

Finally, it is too easy to forget—and, hence, too often forgotten—that the issue here is whether to interpose a search warrant procedure between law enforcement agencies engaging in electronic eavesdropping and the public generally. By casting its "risk analysis" solely in terms of the expectations and risks that "wrongdoers" or "one contemplating illegal activities" ought to bear, the plurality opinion, I think, misses the mark entirely. *On Lee* does not simply mandate that criminals must daily run the risk of unknown eavesdroppers prying into their private affairs; it subjects each and every law-abiding member of society to that risk. The very purpose of interposing the Fourth Amendment warrant requirement is to redistribute the privacy risks throughout society in a way that produces the results the plurality opinion ascribes to the *On Lee* rule. Abolition of *On Lee* would not end electronic eavesdropping. It would prevent public officials from engaging in that practice unless they first had probable cause to suspect an individual of involvement in illegal activities and had tested their version of the facts before a detached judicial officer. * * *

The Fourth Amendment does, of course, leave room for the employment of modern technology in criminal law enforcement, but in the stream of current developments in Fourth Amendment law I think it must be held that third-party electronic monitoring, subject only to the self-restraint of law enforcement officials, has no place in our society.

IV * * *

What this means is that the burden of guarding privacy in a free society should not be on its citizens; it is the Government that must justify its need to electronically eavesdrop. * * *

I would hold that *On Lee* is no longer good law and affirm the judgment below.

[JUSTICE MARSHALL'S dissent is omitted.]

NOTES AND QUESTIONS

1.   In *Katz*, the Supreme Court held that the electronic surveillance of Katz's conversations with others constituted a search and, therefore, was regulated by the Fourth Amendment. In *White*, however, the Court held that the Government's use of an informant "wired" with a transmitter fell outside the scope of the Fourth Amendment. As one scholar has observed:

> The law treats secret surveillance of speech or other behavior largely according to whether the surveilling agent is visible or invisible to the subject. An agent, visibly present though masquerading [as a confidant], is thought to gather evidence in a

fundamentally different manner than a concealed agent or a hidden electronic device. The theory is that the contents of the mind, deliberately revealed to another person, are willingly shared, while the secret eye or ear, possibly electronically enhanced, bypasses constitutional concern to spirit the evidence away.

H. Richard Uviller, *Evidence from the Mind of the Criminal Suspect: A Reconsideration of the Current Rules of Access and Restraint*, 87 Colum. L. Rev. 1137, 1151 (1987).

2. *False friends, false friends with tape recorders, and "wired" false friends.* Notice that there are various ways the Government listens to conversations of persons suspected of crime. First, it may surreptitiously eavesdrop on a conversation between *A* and *B*, as in *Katz*. Second, the Government may participate in the conversation itself, as when *A* talks to *B*, who turns out to be an undercover police officer or friend-turned-government-agent, as in *Hoffa*. In this latter case we may characterize *B* as a "false friend." Third, it is possible that false friend *B* will tape record the conversation (*Lopez*) or be "wired" with a transmitter (*On Lee, White*).

Consider first the pure false friend, *Hoffa*, situation. Should such a case fall outside the protection of the Fourth Amendment? Consider:

[T]he Court [has] viewed betrayal as an expected (if reprehensible) behavior among human beings * * * . Nosy neighbors and pretend friends are not unheard-of phenomena. We trust such people at our own risk. * * *

By allowing the police to send out pretend friends, however, the Court does more than simply mimic the sorts of betrayals that would inevitably occur from time to time in the real world of friendship. By planting moles in our midst, the government deliberately manipulates reality to create relationships for the sole purpose of betrayal. * * * By utilizing such spies, the government therefore adds a level of unusual risk to our private lives. Even for those of us who trust our own judgment in detecting pretend friends, the government-issue friend is peculiar enough to be more like the recording device on Katz's telephone booth than like a friend in the real world who fails to keep a secret. Such creatures are more difficult to discover (since they are not naturally occurring) and could therefore chill even the savvy individual, otherwise insulated by a sixth sense, from trusting other people.

Sherry F. Colb, *What Is a Search? Two Conceptual Flaws in Fourth Amendment Doctrine and Some Hints of a Remedy*, 55 Stan. L. Rev. 119, 141–43 (2002).

Do you agree with Professor Colb's observations? If so, are you prepared to set up constitutional obstacles to the use of undercover police agents in criminal investigations?

However you feel about *Hoffa* and false friends, is there something even worse about false friend *B* tape recording his conversations with *A* or transmitting them live to agents away from the scene, as in *White*? Do you think, for example, that if persons in the Nixon White House had known that their Watergate conversations were being taped by the President, that they would have been more careful with their words? Do you think *you* would be more cautious in *your* conversations if you knew that the government was listening? If so, is this a valid reason to provide Fourth Amendment protection to such conversations?

3.   *The objective prong of Harlan's "search" test.* Reconsider p. 102, Note 5. Based on his dissent here, how would Justice Harlan answer the questions raised in that Note?

In relation to the objective prong of the Harlan "search" test, Professor Anthony Amsterdam would phrase the issue this way:

> The ultimate question, plainly, is a value judgment. It is whether, if the particular form of surveillance practiced by the police is permitted to go unregulated by constitutional restraints, the amount of privacy and freedom remaining to citizens would be diminished to a compass inconsistent with the aims of a free and open society.

Anthony G. Amsterdam, *Perspectives on the Fourth Amendment*, 58 Minn. L. Rev. 349, 403 (1974). How would *you* decide *White* according to this standard?

4.   *Historical tidbit.* Timing sometimes matters a great deal. Consider: In 1938, Earl Warren's father was murdered in Bakersfield, California. The police had no leads until a San Quentin prisoner came under suspicion. The Bakersfield Chief of Police wanted to put a "stool pigeon" in the cell with the suspect and record their conversations. However, Warren, then District Attorney in Alameda County, rejected the use of the recorder, on the ground that he considered eavesdropping an inappropriate law enforcement technique. Therefore, no taping occurred, and the murder was never solved. Bernard Schwartz, Super Chief: Earl Warren and His Supreme Court—A Judicial Biography 11–12 (1983).

Warren joined the Supreme Court in 1953 upon the death of Chief Justice Fred Vinson, one year after the Court ruled, 5–4 (with Vinson joining the majority), in *On Lee v. United States, supra,* that use of a secret microphone by an undercover agent to transmit conversations to a third party did not implicate Fourth Amendment interests. Had the case come to the Court *after* Warren had joined the Court, the outcome might have been different. Had *On Lee* been decided differently, it is intriguing to consider how the law, culminating in *White,* might have evolved.

For a fuller examination of Chief Justice Warren's law enforcement background and its likely influence on his criminal justice opinions, see Yale Kamisar, *How Earl Warren's Twenty-Two Years in Law Enforcement Affected His Work as Chief Justice*, 3 Ohio St. J. Crim. L. 11 (2005).

5. *Justice Harlan and Big Brother.* Justice Harlan expressed his concern that the plurality's approach to the Fourth Amendment "might well smother that spontaneity—reflected in frivolous, impetuous, sacrilegious, and defiant discourse—that liberates daily life." He also pointed to the risks of "Orwellian Big Brother" technology that can be "used to unearth 'political' crimes."

One person's "political" crimes and free speech is another person's incipient terrorism. One post-September 11 commentator observed: "How the times have changed. Today the talk is of more, rather than less, surveillance. Instead of 'Big Brother is watching you,' we hear 'Big Brother is watching out for you.'" Editors, *Here's Looking at You*, Scientific American, Dec. 2001, at 8. Do you believe that the Supreme Court in *White* set the proper balance between security from crime and individual liberty?

6. The *White* plurality cited *Lewis v. United States*, a 1966 "consent" case, in which a federal agent, "misrepresenting his identity and stating his willingness to purchase narcotics, was invited into petitioner's home where an unlawful narcotics transaction was consummated." The Court found no violation in this conduct. It made the following observation about the use of undercover agents:

> Were we to hold the deceptions of the agent in this case constitutionally prohibited, we would come near to a rule that the use of undercover agents in any manner is virtually unconstitutional per se. Such a rule would * * * severely hamper the Government in ferreting out those organized criminal activities that are characterized by covert dealings with victims who either cannot or do not protest.

Does this represent a valid reason to uphold the *Hoffa-White* approach to false friends?

7. *Problem.* Undercover police officer Alice seeks to negotiate a drug sale with Barbara. Barbara informs Alice that she will only discuss the matter in a specified spot in a public park at 2:00 a.m., because "nobody is ever there at that hour." Alice agrees to meet her there. In the meantime, with Alice's knowledge, the police install a hidden transmitter in a tree near the meeting place, so that another officer can listen to the conversation. Is it a "search" when the officer listens to Alice's and Barbara's conversations via the transmitter? Put another way, is this *Katz* or *White?* What if agent Alice is herself unaware of the transmitter?

Suppose that the police leave the device in the tree and listen to other conversations in the park by passersby. Is the Fourth Amendment implicated by *this* surveillance?

SMITH V. MARYLAND

Supreme Court of the United States, 1979.
442 U.S. 735, 99 S.Ct. 2577, 61 L.Ed.2d 220.

MR. JUSTICE BLACKMUN delivered the opinion of the Court [joined by CHIEF JUSTICE BURGER, and JUSTICES WHITE, REHNQUIST, and STEVENS].

This case presents the question whether the installation and use of a pen register[1] constitutes a "search" within the meaning of the Fourth Amendment, made applicable to the States through the Fourteenth Amendment.

I

On March 5, 1976, in Baltimore, Md., Patricia McDonough was robbed. She gave the police a description of the robber and of a 1975 Monte Carlo automobile she had observed near the scene of the crime. After the robbery, McDonough began receiving threatening and obscene phone calls from a man identifying himself as the robber. On one occasion, the caller asked that she step out on her front porch; she did so, and saw the 1975 Monte Carlo she had earlier described to police moving slowly past her home. On March 16, police spotted a man who met McDonough's description driving a 1975 Monte Carlo in her neighborhood. By tracing the license plate number, police learned that the car was registered in the name of petitioner, Michael Lee Smith.

The next day, the telephone company, at police request, installed a pen register at its central offices to record the numbers dialed from the telephone at petitioner's home. The police did not get a warrant or court order before having the pen register installed. The register revealed that on March 17 a call was placed from petitioner's home to McDonough's phone. On the basis of this and other evidence, the police obtained a warrant to search petitioner's residence. The search revealed that a page in petitioner's phone book was turned down to the name and number of Patricia McDonough; the phone book was seized. * * *

Petitioner was indicted in the Criminal Court of Baltimore for robbery. By pretrial motion, he sought to suppress "all fruits derived from the pen register" on the ground that the police had failed to secure a warrant prior to its installation. The trial court denied the suppression motion, holding that the warrantless installation of the pen register did not violate the Fourth Amendment. * * * The pen register tape (evidencing the fact that a phone call had been made from petitioner's phone to McDonough's phone) and the phone book seized in the search of

---

[1] "A pen register is a mechanical device that records the numbers dialed on a telephone by monitoring the electrical impulses caused when the dial on the telephone is released. It does not overhear oral communications and does not indicate whether calls are actually completed." A pen register is "usually installed at a central telephone facility [and] records on a paper tape all numbers dialed from [the] line" to which it is attached.

petitioner's residence were admitted into evidence against him. Petitioner was convicted, and was sentenced to six years. * * *

II

A

* * * In determining whether a particular form of government-initiated electronic surveillance is a "search" within the meaning of the Fourth Amendment, our lodestar is *Katz v. United States*. In *Katz*, * * * [the] Court rejected the argument that a "search" can occur only when there has been a "physical intrusion" into a "constitutionally protected area," noting that the Fourth Amendment "protects people, not places." Because the Government's monitoring of Katz' conversation "violated the privacy upon which he justifiably relied while using the telephone booth," the Court held that it "constituted a 'search and seizure' within the meaning of the Fourth Amendment."

Consistently with *Katz*, this Court uniformly has held that the application of the Fourth Amendment depends on whether the person invoking its protection can claim a "justifiable," a "reasonable," or a "legitimate expectation of privacy" that has been invaded by government action. This inquiry, as Mr. Justice Harlan aptly noted in his *Katz* concurrence, normally embraces two discrete questions. The first is whether the individual, by his conduct, has "exhibited an actual (subjective) expectation of privacy"—whether, in the words of the *Katz* majority, the individual has shown that "he seeks to preserve [something] as private." The second question is whether the individual's subjective expectation of privacy is "one that society is prepared to recognize as 'reasonable' "—whether, in the words of the *Katz* majority, the individual's expectation, viewed objectively, is "justifiable" under the circumstances.[5]

B

In applying the *Katz* analysis to this case, it is important to begin by specifying precisely the nature of the state activity that is challenged. The activity here took the form of installing and using a pen register. Since the pen register was installed on telephone company property at the

---

[5] Situations can be imagined, of course, in which *Katz'* two-pronged inquiry would provide an inadequate index of Fourth Amendment protection. For example, if the Government were suddenly to announce on nationwide television that all homes henceforth would be subject to warrantless entry, individuals thereafter might not in fact entertain any actual expectation of privacy regarding their homes, papers, and effects. Similarly, if a refugee from a totalitarian country, unaware of this Nation's traditions, erroneously assumed that police were continuously monitoring his telephone conversations, a subjective expectation of privacy regarding the contents of his calls might be lacking as well. In such circumstances, where an individual's subjective expectations had been "conditioned" by influences alien to well-recognized Fourth Amendment freedoms, those subjective expectations obviously could play no meaningful role in ascertaining what the scope of Fourth Amendment protection was. In determining whether a "legitimate expectation of privacy" existed in such cases, a normative inquiry would be proper.

telephone company's central offices, petitioner obviously cannot claim that his "property" was invaded or that police intruded into a "constitutionally protected area." Petitioner's claim, rather, is that, notwithstanding the absence of a trespass, the State, as did the Government in *Katz*, infringed a "legitimate expectation of privacy" that petitioner held. Yet a pen register differs significantly from the listening device employed in *Katz*, for pen registers do not acquire the *contents* of communications. This Court recently noted:

> "Indeed, a law enforcement official could not even determine from the use of a pen register whether a communication existed. These devices do not hear sound. They disclose only the telephone numbers that have been dialed—a means of establishing communication. Neither the purport of any communication between the caller and the recipient of the call, their identities, nor whether the call was even completed is disclosed by pen registers."

Given a pen register's limited capabilities, therefore, petitioner's argument that its installation and use constituted a "search" necessarily rests upon a claim that he had a "legitimate expectation of privacy" regarding the numbers he dialed on his phone.

This claim must be rejected. First, we doubt that people in general entertain any actual expectation of privacy in the numbers they dial. All telephone users realize that they must "convey" phone numbers to the telephone company, since it is through telephone company switching equipment that their calls are completed. All subscribers realize, moreover, that the phone company has facilities for making permanent records of the numbers they dial, for they see a list of their long-distance (toll) calls on their monthly bills. In fact, pen registers and similar devices are routinely used by telephone companies "for the purposes of checking billing operations, detecting fraud, and preventing violations of law." * * * Although most people may be oblivious to a pen register's esoteric functions, they presumably have some awareness of one common use: to aid in the identification of persons making annoying or obscene calls. Most phone books tell subscribers, on a page entitled "Consumer Information," that the company "can frequently help in identifying to the authorities the origin of unwelcome and troublesome calls." Telephone users, in sum, typically know that they must convey numerical information to the phone company; that the phone company has facilities for recording this information; and that the phone company does in fact record this information for a variety of legitimate business purposes. Although subjective expectations cannot be scientifically gauged, it is too much to believe that telephone subscribers, under these circumstances, harbor any general expectation that the numbers they dial will remain secret.

[margin note: P. argues]

Petitioner argues, however, that, whatever the expectations of telephone users in general, he demonstrated an expectation of privacy by his own conduct here, since he "us[ed] the telephone *in his house* to the exclusion of all others." But the site of the call is immaterial for purposes of analysis in this case. Although petitioner's conduct may have been calculated to keep the *contents* of his conversation private, his conduct was not and could not have been calculated to preserve the privacy of the number he dialed. Regardless of his location, petitioner had to convey that number to the telephone company in precisely the same way if he wished to complete his call. The fact that he dialed the number on his home phone rather than on some other phone could make no conceivable difference, nor could any subscriber rationally think that it would.

[margin note: he assumed the risk!]

Second, even if petitioner did harbor some subjective expectation that the phone numbers he dialed would remain private, this expectation is not "one that society is prepared to recognize as 'reasonable.'" This Court consistently has held that a person has no legitimate expectation of privacy in information he voluntarily turns over to third parties. *E.g., United States v. Miller*, 425 U.S. [435, 442–444, 96 S.Ct. 1619, 1623–24, 48 L.Ed.2d 71 (1976)]; *United States v. White*, [p. 105]. In *Miller*, for example, the Court held that a bank depositor has no "legitimate 'expectation of privacy'" in financial information "voluntarily conveyed to * * * banks and exposed to their employees in the ordinary course of business." The Court explained:

> "The depositor takes the risk, in revealing his affairs to another, that the information will be conveyed by that person to the Government. * * * This Court has held repeatedly that the Fourth Amendment does not prohibit the obtaining of information revealed to a third party and conveyed by him to Government authorities, even if the information is revealed on the assumption that it will be used only for a limited purpose and the confidence placed in the third party will not be betrayed."

Because the depositor "assumed the risk" of disclosure, the Court held that it would be unreasonable for him to expect his financial records to remain private.

This analysis dictates that petitioner can claim no legitimate expectation of privacy here. When he used his phone, petitioner voluntarily conveyed numerical information to the telephone company and "exposed" that information to its equipment in the ordinary course of business. In so doing, petitioner assumed the risk that the company would reveal to police the numbers he dialed. The switching equipment that processed those numbers is merely the modern counterpart of the operator who, in an earlier day, personally completed calls for the subscriber. * * * We are not inclined to hold that a different constitutional result is required because the telephone company has decided to automate. * * *

We therefore conclude that petitioner in all probability entertained no actual expectation of privacy in the phone numbers he dialed, and that, even if he did, his expectation was not "legitimate." The installation and use of a pen register, consequently, was not a "search," and no warrant was required. * * *

MR. JUSTICE POWELL took no part in the consideration or decision of this case.

MR. JUSTICE STEWART, with whom MR. JUSTICE BRENNAN joins, dissenting. * * *

I think that the numbers dialed from a private telephone—like the conversations that occur during a call—are within the constitutional protection recognized in *Katz*. * * * The information captured by such surveillance emanates from private conduct within a person's home or office—locations that without question are entitled to Fourth and Fourteenth Amendment protection. * * *

The numbers dialed from a private telephone—although certainly more prosaic than the conversation itself—are not without "content." Most private telephone subscribers may have their own numbers listed in a publicly distributed directory, but I doubt there are any who would be happy to have broadcast to the world a list of the local or long distance numbers they have called. This is not because such a list might in some sense be incriminating, but because it easily could reveal the identities of the persons and the places called, and thus reveal the most intimate details of a person's life. * * *

MR. JUSTICE MARSHALL, with whom MR. JUSTICE BRENNAN joins, dissenting. * * *

Applying the standards set forth in *Katz v. United States*, the Court first determines that telephone subscribers have no subjective expectations of privacy concerning the numbers they dial. To reach this conclusion, the Court posits that individuals somehow infer from the long-distance listings on their phone bills, and from the cryptic assurances of "help" in tracing obscene calls included in "most" phone books, that pen registers are regularly used for recording local calls. But even assuming, as I do not, that individuals "typically know" that a phone company monitors calls for internal reasons,[1] it does not follow that they expect

---

[1] Lacking the Court's apparently exhaustive knowledge of this Nation's telephone books and the reading habits of telephone subscribers, I decline to assume general public awareness of how obscene phone calls are traced. Nor am I persuaded that the scope of Fourth Amendment protection should turn on the concededly "esoteric functions" of pen registers in corporate billing, functions with which subscribers are unlikely to have intimate familiarity.

this information to be made available to the public in general or the government in particular. Privacy is not a discrete commodity, possessed absolutely or not at all. Those who disclose certain facts to a bank or phone company for a limited business purpose need not assume that this information will be released to other persons for other purposes.

The crux of the Court's holding, however, is that whatever expectation of privacy petitioner may in fact have entertained regarding his calls, it is not one "society is prepared to recognize as 'reasonable.'" In so ruling, the Court determines that individuals who convey information to third parties have "assumed the risk" of disclosure to the government. This analysis is misconceived in two critical respects.

Implicit in the concept of assumption of risk is some notion of choice. At least in the third-party consensual surveillance cases, which first incorporated risk analysis into Fourth Amendment doctrine, the defendant presumably had exercised some discretion in deciding who should enjoy his confidential communications. See, *e.g.*, [*United States v. White, supra*]. By contrast here, unless a person is prepared to forgo use of what for many has become a personal or professional necessity, he cannot help but accept the risk of surveillance. It is idle to speak of "assuming" risks in contexts where, as a practical matter, individuals have no realistic alternative.

More fundamentally, to make risk analysis dispositive in assessing the reasonableness of privacy expectations would allow the government to define the scope of Fourth Amendment protections. For example, law enforcement officials, simply by announcing their intent to monitor the content of random samples of first-class mail or private phone conversations, could put the public on notice of the risks they would thereafter assume in such communications. Yet, although acknowledging this implication of its analysis, the Court is willing to concede only that, in some circumstances, a further "normative inquiry would be proper." No meaningful effort is made to explain what those circumstances might be, or why this case is not among them.

In my view, whether privacy expectations are legitimate within the meaning of *Katz* depends not on the risks an individual can be presumed to accept when imparting information to third parties, but on the risks he should be forced to assume in a free and open society. By its terms, the constitutional prohibition of unreasonable searches and seizures assigns to the judiciary some prescriptive responsibility. As Mr. Justice Harlan, who formulated the standard the Court applies today, himself recognized: "[s]ince it is the task of the law to form and project, as well as mirror and reflect, we should not * * * merely recite * * * risks without examining the desirability of saddling them upon society." *United States v. White, supra* (dissenting opinion). In making this assessment, courts must evaluate the "intrinsic character" of investigative practices with reference to the basic values underlying the Fourth Amendment. And for those "extensive intrusions that significantly jeopardize [individuals'] sense of security * * *, more than self-restraint by law enforcement officials is required."

The use of pen registers, I believe, constitutes such an extensive intrusion. To hold otherwise ignores the vital role telephonic communication plays in our personal and professional relationships, as well as the First and Fourth Amendment interests implicated by unfettered official surveillance. Privacy in placing calls is of value not only to those engaged in criminal activity. The prospect of unregulated governmental monitoring will undoubtedly prove disturbing even to those with nothing illicit to hide. Many individuals, including members of unpopular political organizations or journalists with confidential sources, may legitimately wish to avoid disclosure of their personal contacts. Permitting governmental access to telephone records on less than probable cause may thus impede certain forms of political affiliation and journalistic endeavor that are the hallmark of a truly free society. * * * I am unwilling to insulate use of pen registers from independent judicial review.

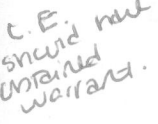

Just as one who enters a public telephone booth is "entitled to assume that the words he utters into the mouthpiece will not be broadcast to the world," *Katz v. United States, supra,* so too, he should be entitled to assume that the numbers he dials in the privacy of his home will be recorded, if at all, solely for the phone company's business purposes. Accordingly, I would require law enforcement officials to obtain a warrant before they enlist telephone companies to secure information otherwise beyond the government's reach.

NOTES AND QUESTIONS

1.   Is *Smith* consistent with *Katz*? Justice Stewart, author of *Katz,* dissented. Do his distinctions persuade you?

2.   Justice Stewart announced in *Katz* that what a "person knowingly exposes to the public" is unprotected by the Fourth Amendment. Is the implication of *Smith* that when a person exposes private information to one person or entity that she thereby altogether loses Fourth Amendment protection in that information? In this regard, consider:

A person going on vacation * * * might give a neighbor the key to her house and ask him to water her plants while she is gone. The neighbor now has explicit permission to observe what would otherwise be hidden from view * * *. By granting this permission that vacationer has forfeited a measure of privacy and has thus knowingly exposed part of her home to her neighbor. Still, if the neighbor were to invite his friends * * * into the apartment to see the vacationer's personal items, even just those things visible from where the plants are located, that act would go beyond the scope of the vacationer's permission and therefore represent an invasion of her privacy. There are degrees of privacy and, accordingly, degrees of exposure, and one might choose to forfeit some of her freedom of exposure without thereby forfeiting all of it.

Sherry F. Colb, *What Is a Search? Two Conceptual Flaws in Fourth Amendment Doctrine and Some Hints of a Remedy*, 55 Stan. L. Rev. 119, 122–23 (2002).

Do you agree? If so, how would *you* have the Court define "the public" in Justice Stewart's rule?

3.   *What the Court taketh away, Congress can giveth back. Smith* placed the installation and use of pen registers outside the scope of the Fourth Amendment. In 1986, however, Congress placed statutory limits on use of pen registers in law enforcement. See 18 U.S.C. §§ 3121–3126 (2008) (generally barring installation or use of pen registers without a court order).

4.   *"Dog sniffs."* You will remember that the *Smith* Court's analysis of pen registers relied in part on the "limited capabilities" of the device (it does not acquire the contents of communications). The Court has repeated this theme elsewhere. In United States v. Place, 462 U.S. 696, 103 S.Ct. 2637, 77 L.Ed.2d 110 (1983), federal drug authorities at LaGuardia Airport in New York subjected a passenger's luggage to a "sniff test" by a dog trained to identify narcotics by smell. One issue in the case was whether the dog sniff constituted a Fourth Amendment search:

> A "canine sniff" by a well-trained narcotics detection dog * * * does not require opening the luggage. It does not expose noncontraband items that otherwise would remain hidden from public view, as does, for example, an officer's rummaging through the contents of the luggage. Thus, the manner in which information is obtained through this investigative technique is much less intrusive than a typical search. Moreover, the sniff discloses only the presence or absence of narcotics, a contraband item. Thus, despite the fact that the sniff tells the authorities something about the contents of the luggage, the information obtained is limited. This limited disclosure also ensures that the owner of the property is not subjected to the embarrassment and inconvenience entailed in less discriminate and more intrusive investigative methods.

> In these respects, the canine sniff is *sui generis*. We are aware of no other investigative procedure that is so limited both in the manner in which the information is obtained and in the content of the information revealed by the procedure. Therefore, we conclude that the particular course of investigation that the agents intended to pursue here—exposure of respondent's luggage, which was located in a public place, to a trained canine—did not constitute a "search" within the meaning of the Fourth Amendment.

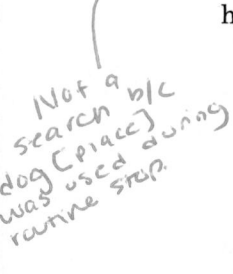

Not a search b/c dog (place) was used during routine stop.

The Supreme Court reaffirmed *Place* and explained it further in Illinois v. Caballes, 543 U.S. 405, 125 S.Ct. 834, 160 L.Ed.2d 842 (2005). In *Caballes*, police officers used a "well-trained narcotics-detection dog" to sniff the exterior of the trunk of an automobile, which was lawfully stopped on the highway for a traffic ticket. The Court, 6–2, per Justice John Stevens, wrote:

> Official conduct that does not "compromise any legitimate interest in privacy" is not a search subject to the Fourth Amendment. [*United States v.*] *Jacobsen,* 466 U.S. [109,] at 123, 104 S.Ct. 1652, 80 L.Ed.2d 85 [(1984)]. We have held [in *Jacobsen*] that any interest in possessing contraband cannot be deemed "legitimate," and thus, governmental conduct that *only* reveals the possession of contraband "compromises no legitimate privacy interest." This is because the expectation "that certain facts will not come to the attention of the authorities" is not the same as an interest in "privacy that society is prepared to consider reasonable." * * *

> Accordingly, the use of a well-trained narcotics-detection dog— one that "does not expose noncontraband items that otherwise would remain hidden from public view"—during a lawful traffic stop, generally does not implicate legitimate privacy interests. In this case, * * * [a]ny intrusion on respondent's privacy expectations does not rise to the level of a constitutionally cognizable infringement.

Justice Souter dissented:

> I would hold that using the dog for the purposes of determining the presence of marijuana in the car's trunk was a search * * * . * * *

> At the heart both of *Place* and the Court's opinion today is the proposition that sniffs by a trained dog are *sui generis* because a reaction by the dog in going alert is a response to nothing but the presence of contraband. Hence, the argument goes, because the sniff can only reveal the presence of items devoid of any legal use, the sniff "does not implicate legitimate privacy interests" and is not to be treated as a search.

> The infallible dog, however, is a creature of legal fiction. * * * [T]heir supposed infallibility is belied by judicial opinions describing well-trained animals sniffing and alerting with less than perfect accuracy, whether owing to errors by their handlers, the limitations of the dogs themselves, or even the pervasive contamination of currency by cocaine. Indeed, a study cited by Illinois in this case for the proposition that dog sniffs are "generally reliable" shows that dogs in artificial testing situations return false positives anywhere from 12.5 to 60% of the time, depending on the length of the search.

In practical terms, the evidence is clear that the dog that alerts hundreds of times will be wrong dozens of times.

Once the dog's fallibility is recognized, * * * that ends the justification claimed in *Place* for treating the sniff as *sui generis* under the Fourth Amendment: the sniff alert does not necessarily signal hidden contraband * * * . * * *

It makes sense, then, to treat a sniff as the search that it amounts to in practice, and to rely on the body of our Fourth Amendment cases * * * in determining whether such a search is reasonable.

What if the police use a narcotics-detection dog to sniff at the front door of a person's home? Should that be treated differently? The Supreme Court has now answered this question, but it is premature to disclose the result. (Trust us, we will get there in due time.)

5. *Open fields.* In Hester v. United States, 265 U.S. 57, 44 S.Ct. 445, 68 L.Ed. 898 (1924), the Supreme Court first enunciated the so-called "open fields" doctrine, which provides that police entry of an open field does not implicate the Fourth Amendment. In Oliver v. United States, 466 U.S. 170, 104 S.Ct. 1735, 80 L.Ed.2d 214 (1984), the Court held that this doctrine remains good law after *Katz*.

What is an "open field"? According to *Oliver*, it "may include any unoccupied or undeveloped area outside of the curtilage [of a home]. An open field need be neither 'open' nor a 'field' as those terms are used in common speech. For example, * * * a thickly wooded area nonetheless may be an open field as that term is used in construing the Fourth Amendment."

In *Oliver* and a companion case, law enforcement officers, without a warrant or probable cause, trespassed on defendants' rural property, even ignoring "No Trespassing" signs, and discovered fields of marijuana. In an opinion written by Justice Lewis Powell, the Court ruled, 6–3, that an open field does not constitute a "person, house, paper, or effect":

> The rule announced in *Hester v. United States* was founded upon the explicit language of the Fourth Amendment. That Amendment indicates with some precision the places and things encompassed by its protections. As Justice Holmes explained for the Court in his characteristically laconic style: "[T]he special protection accorded by the Fourth Amendment to the people in their 'persons, houses, papers, and effects,' is not extended to the open fields. The distinction between the latter and the house is as old as the common law."[6]

---

6 * * * Nor have subsequent cases discredited *Hester*'s reasoning. This Court frequently has relied on the explicit language of the Fourth Amendment as delineating the scope of its affirmative protections. * * * *Katz'* "reasonable expectation of privacy" standard did not sever Fourth Amendment doctrine from the Amendment's language. *Katz* itself construed the Amendment's protection of the person against unreasonable searches to encompass electronic

Nor are the open fields "effects" within the meaning of the Fourth Amendment. In this respect, it is suggestive that James Madison's proposed draft of what became the Fourth Amendment preserves "[t]he rights of the people to be secured in their persons, their houses, their papers, and their other property, from all unreasonable searches and seizures * * * ." Although Congress' revisions of Madison's proposal broadened the scope of the Amendment in some respects, the term "effects" is less inclusive than "property" and cannot be said to encompass open fields. We conclude * * * that the government's intrusion upon the open fields is not one of those "unreasonable searches" proscribed by the text of the Fourth Amendment.

The Court could have stopped at this point, but it did not. Five justices also concluded that entry of an open field does not constitute a "search" within the post-*Katz* meaning of that concept:

> [A]n individual may not legitimately demand privacy for activities conducted out of doors in fields, except in the area immediately surrounding the home. This rule is true to the conception of the right to privacy embodied in the Fourth Amendment. The Amendment reflects the recognition of the Framers that certain enclaves should be free from arbitrary government interference. For example, the Court since the enactment of the Fourth Amendment has stressed "the overriding respect for the sanctity of the home that has been embedded in our traditions since the origins of the Republic." *Payton v. New York*, [p. 205]

> In contrast, open fields do not provide the setting for those intimate activities that the Amendment is intended to shelter from government interference or surveillance. There is no societal interest in protecting the privacy of those activities, such as the cultivation of crops, that occur in open fields. Moreover, as a practical matter these lands usually are accessible to the public and the police in ways that a home, an office, or commercial structure would not be. It is not generally true that fences or "No Trespassing" signs effectively bar the public from viewing open fields in rural areas. And both petitioner Oliver and respondent Thornton concede that the public and police lawfully may survey lands from the air.[b] For these reasons, the asserted expectation of

---

eavesdropping of telephone conversations sought to be kept private; and *Katz'* fundamental recognition that "the Fourth Amendment protects people—and not simply 'areas'—against unreasonable searches and seizures" is faithful to the Amendment's language. As *Katz* demonstrates, the Court fairly may respect the constraints of the Constitution's language without wedding itself to an unreasoning literalism. * * *

b   Do you agree with a rule that "permits police to engage in what is criminal misconduct on the theory that they could have made the same observation by a legal, alternative means," such as viewing land from the air? Sherry F. Colb, *What Is a Search? Two Conceptual Flaws in Fourth Amendment Doctrine and Some Hints of a Remedy*, 55 Stan. L. Rev. 119, 131 (2002). Is the privacy in open fields is not an expectation that "society recognizes as reasonable."

The historical underpinnings of the open fields doctrine also demonstrate that the doctrine is consistent with respect for "reasonable expectations of privacy." As Justice Holmes, writing for the Court, observed in *Hester*, the common law distinguished "open fields" from the "curtilage," the land immediately surrounding and associated with the home. The distinction implies that only the curtilage, not the neighboring open fields, warrants the Fourth Amendment protections that attach to the home. At common law, the curtilage is the area to which extends the intimate activity associated with the "sanctity of a man's home and the privacies of life," and therefore has been considered part of the home itself for Fourth Amendment purposes. Thus, courts have extended Fourth Amendment protection to the curtilage; and they have defined the curtilage, as did the common law, by reference to the factors that determine whether an individual reasonably may expect that an area immediately adjacent to the home will remain private. Conversely, the common law implies, as we reaffirm today, that no expectation of privacy legitimately attaches to open fields.

Justice Marshall, writing also for Justices Brennan and Stevens, rejected the majority's "search" analysis:

If a person has not marked the boundaries of his fields or woods in a way that informs passersby that they are not welcome, he cannot object if members of the public enter onto the property. There is no reason why he should have any greater rights as against government officials. * * *

A very different case is presented when the owner of undeveloped land has taken precautions to exclude the public. * * * [A] deliberate entry by a private citizen onto private property marked with "No Trespassing" signs will expose him to criminal liability. I see no reason why a government official should not be obliged to respect such unequivocal and universally understood manifestations of a landowner's desire for privacy.

6. *Curtilage: what is it?* In *Oliver* (Note 5), Justice Powell defined and distinguished the curtilage of a house from an open field. In United States v. Dunn, 480 U.S. 294, 107 S.Ct. 1134, 94 L.Ed.2d 326 (1987), the Court explained the curtilage concept further. It stated that "curtilage questions should be resolved with reference to four factors: the proximity of the area claimed to be curtilage to the home, whether the area is included within an enclosure surrounding the home, the nature of the uses to which the area is

---

Court's analysis here consistent with *Katz*? Reconsider the lip-reader hypothetical raised on p. 102, Note 2.

put, and the steps taken by the resident to protect the area from observation by people passing by."

Dunn warned that the four factors do not produce a "fine tuned formula that, when mechanically applied, yields a 'correct' answer to all extent-of-curtilage questions. Rather, these factors are useful analytical tools only to the degree that, in any given case, they bear upon the centrally relevant consideration—whether the area in question is so intimately tied to the home itself that it should be placed under the home's 'umbrella' of Fourth Amendment protection."

In view of the four "curtilage" factors set out in *Dunn*, how would you characterize the area inspected by the police in that case? Here are the relevant facts:

> [Dunn]'s ranch comprised approximately 198 acres and was completely encircled by a perimeter fence. The property also contained several interior fences, constructed mainly of posts and multiple strands of barbed wire. The ranch residence was situated ½ miles from a public road. A fence encircled the residence and a nearby small greenhouse. Two barns were located approximately 50 yards from this fence. The front of the larger of the two barns was enclosed by a wooden fence and had an open overhang. Locked, waist-high gates barred entry into the barn proper, and netting material stretched from the ceiling to the top of the wooden gates.

> * * * [L]aw enforcement officials made a warrantless entry onto respondent's ranch property. A DEA agent accompanied by an officer from the Houston Police Department crossed over the perimeter fence and one interior fence. Standing approximately midway between the residence and the barns, the DEA agent smelled what he believed to be phenylacetic acid, the odor coming from the direction of the barns. The officers approached the smaller of the barns—crossing over a barbed wire fence—and, looking into the barn, observed only empty boxes. The officers then proceeded to the larger barn, crossing another barbed wire fence as well as a wooden fence that enclosed the front portion of the barn. The officers walked under the barn's overhang to the locked wooden gates and, shining a flashlight through the netting on top of the gates, peered into the barn.

Were the police standing in the "curtilage" or in an "open field"? What if the government agents had actually entered the barn? Should that change the Fourth Amendment analysis?

7. *Aerial surveillance of a curtilage (part 1).* It does not follow from the fact that an area is identified as a curtilage that police surveillance of it inevitably constitutes a Fourth Amendment search. That lesson is learned from two cases of aerial surveillance of curtilages. Consider the first case, California v. Ciraolo, 476 U.S. 207, 106 S.Ct. 1809, 90 L.Ed.2d 210 (1986):

On September 2, 1982, Santa Clara Police received an anonymous telephone tip that marijuana was growing in respondent's backyard. Police were unable to observe the contents of respondent's yard from ground level because of a 6-foot outer fence and a 10-foot inner fence completely enclosing the yard. Later that day, Officer Shutz, who was assigned to investigate, secured a private plane and flew over respondent's house at an altitude of 1,000 feet, within navigable airspace; he was accompanied by Officer Rodriguez. Both officers were trained in marijuana identification. From the overflight, the officers readily identified marijuana plants 8 feet to 10 feet in height growing in a 15- by 25-foot plot in respondent's yard; they photographed the area with a standard 35mm camera.

Based on this surveillance, the police obtained a warrant to search the premises. The issue was whether the information secured from the aerial surveillance properly was used to secure the warrant. That, in turn, raised the question of whether the surveillance was, itself, a search that may have required a warrant. The Court, per Chief Justice Burger, declared, 5–4, that the surveillance of the curtilage of Ciraolo's home was *not* a search and, therefore, fell outside the protections of the Fourth Amendment. The Court dealt briefly with the subjective prong of Harlan's "search" test before turning to the critical objective prong:

Clearly—and understandably—respondent has met the test of manifesting his own subjective intent and desire to maintain privacy as to his unlawful agricultural pursuits. * * * It can reasonably be assumed that the 10-foot fence was placed to conceal the marijuana crop from at least street-level views. * * *

Yet a 10-foot fence might not shield these plants from the eyes of a citizen or a policeman perched on the top of a truck or a two-level bus. Whether respondent therefore manifested a subjective expectation of privacy from *all* observations of his backyard, or whether instead he manifested merely a hope that no one would observe his unlawful gardening pursuits, is not entirely clear in these circumstances. * * *

We turn * * * to the second inquiry under *Katz*, *i.e.*, whether that expectation is reasonable. * * *

That the area is within the curtilage does not itself bar all police observation. The Fourth Amendment protection of the home has never been extended to require law enforcement officers to shield their eyes when passing by a home on public thoroughfares. Nor does the mere fact that an individual has taken measures to restrict some views of his activities preclude an officer's observations from a public vantage point where he has a right to be and which renders the activities clearly visible. "What a person knowingly exposes to the public, even in his own home or office, is not a subject of Fourth Amendment protection." *Katz, supra.*

The observations by Officers Shutz and Rodriguez in this case took place within public navigable airspace, in a physically nonintrusive manner; from this point they were able to observe plants readily discernible to the naked eye as marijuana. That the observation from aircraft was directed at identifying the plants and the officers were trained to recognize marijuana is irrelevant. * * * Any member of the public flying in this airspace who glanced down could have seen everything that these officers observed. On this record, we readily conclude that respondent's expectation that his garden was protected from such observation is unreasonable and is not an expectation that society is prepared to honor. * * *

* * * In an age where private and commercial flight in the public airways is routine, it is unreasonable for respondent to expect that his marijuana plants were constitutionally protected from being observed with the naked eye from an altitude of 1,000 feet. The Fourth Amendment simply does not require the police traveling in the public airways at this altitude to obtain a warrant in order to observe what is visible to the naked eye.

Are you persuaded? Four justices were not. Justice Powell, who wrote the open-fields *Oliver* decision, explained their disagreement:

As the decision in *Katz* held, and dissenting opinions written by Justices of this Court prior to *Katz* recognized, a standard that defines a Fourth Amendment "search" by reference to whether police have physically invaded a "constitutionally protected area" provides no real protection against surveillance techniques made possible through technology. Technological advances have enabled police to see people's activities and associations, and to hear their conversations, without being in physical proximity. Moreover, the capability now exists for police to conduct intrusive surveillance without any physical penetration of the walls of homes or other structures that citizens may believe shelters their privacy. Looking to the Fourth Amendment for protection against such "broad and unsuspected governmental incursions" into the "cherished privacy of law-abiding citizens," the Court in *Katz* abandoned its inquiry into whether police had committed a physical trespass. * * *

This case involves surveillance of a home, for as we stated in *Oliver v. United States*, the curtilage "has been considered part of the home itself for Fourth Amendment purposes." * * *

* * * [R]espondent's yard unquestionably was within the curtilage. Since Officer Shutz could not see into this private family area from the street, the Court certainly would agree that he would have conducted an unreasonable search had he climbed over the

fence, or used a ladder to peer into the yard without first securing a warrant.

The Court concludes, nevertheless, that Shutz could use an airplane—a product of modern technology—to intrude visually into respondent's yard. * * * It * * * relies on the fact that the surveillance was not accompanied by a physical invasion of the curtilage. Reliance on the *manner* of surveillance is directly contrary to the standard of *Katz*, which identifies a constitutionally protected privacy right by focusing on the interests of the individual and of a free society. Since *Katz*, we have consistently held that the presence or absence of physical trespass by police is constitutionally irrelevant to the question whether society is prepared to recognize an asserted privacy interest as reasonable.

The Court's holding, therefore, must rest solely on the fact that members of the public fly in planes and may look down at homes as they fly over them. * * *

This line of reasoning is flawed. First, the actual risk to privacy from commercial or pleasure aircraft is virtually nonexistent. Travelers on commercial flights, as well as private planes used for business or personal reasons, normally obtain at most a fleeting, anonymous, and nondiscriminating glimpse of the landscape and buildings over which they pass. The risk that a passenger on such a plane might observe private activities, and might connect those activities with particular people, is simply too trivial to protect against. It is no accident that, as a matter of common experience, many people build fences around their residential areas, but few build roofs over their backyards. Therefore, contrary to the Court's suggestion, people do not " 'knowingly expos[e]' " their residential yards " 'to the public' " merely by failing to build barriers that prevent aerial surveillance. * * * [T]he Court fails to acknowledge the qualitative difference between police surveillance and other uses made of the airspace. Members of the public use the airspace for travel, business, or pleasure, not for the purpose of observing activities taking place within residential yards. Here, police conducted an overflight at low altitude solely for the purpose of discovering evidence of crime within a private enclave into which they were constitutionally forbidden to intrude at ground level without a warrant. It is not easy to believe that our society is prepared to force individuals to bear the risk of this type of warrantless police intrusion into their residential areas.[10]

---

[10] The Court's decision has serious implications for outdoor family activities conducted in the curtilage of a home. The feature of such activities that makes them desirable to citizens living in a free society, namely, the fact that they occur in the open air and sunlight, is relied on by the Court as a justification for permitting police to conduct warrantless surveillance at will. Aerial surveillance is nearly as intrusive on family privacy as physical trespass into the

Notice that Powell stated that "[r]eliance on the *manner* of surveillance is directly contrary to the standard of *Katz*." Is it?

Justice Powell also was critical of the majority for failing "to acknowledge the qualitative difference between police surveillance and other uses made of the airspace." *Should* courts draw such a distinction? That is, even if we generally do not have reason to expect freedom from private invasions of our privacy, should the issue in Fourth Amendment cases be whether a person has a reasonable expectation of privacy from purposeful *governmental* surveillance?

8.   *Aerial surveillance of a curtilage (part 2)*. *Ciraolo* is not the Supreme Court's only effort to wrestle with the problems of aerial surveillance. In Florida v. Riley, 488 U.S. 445, 109 S.Ct. 693, 102 L.Ed.2d 835 (1989), a police officer observed the interior of a partially covered greenhouse in Riley's backyard, while circling 400 feet above the greenhouse in a police helicopter. Justice White, in an opinion joined only by Chief Justice Rehnquist and Justices Scalia and Kennedy, concluded that *Ciraolo* controlled the case:

> Under the holding in *Ciraolo*, Riley could not reasonably have expected the contents of his greenhouse to be immune from examination by an officer seated in a fixed-wing aircraft flying in navigable airspace at an altitude of 1,000 feet or * * * at an altitude of 500 feet, the lower limit of the navigable airspace for such an aircraft. * * *
>
>   Nor on the facts before us, does it make a difference for Fourth Amendment purposes that the helicopter was flying at 400 feet when the officer saw what was growing in the greenhouse through the partially open roof and sides of the structure. We would have a different case if flying at that altitude had been contrary to law or regulation. But helicopters are not bound by the lower limits of the navigable airspace allowed to other aircraft.

In dictum, the plurality suggested some additional limitations on aerial surveillance:

> This is not to say that an inspection of the curtilage of a house from an aircraft will always pass muster under the Fourth Amendment simply because the plane is within the navigable airspace specified by law. But it is of obvious importance that the helicopter in this case was *not* violating the law * * * . Neither is there any intimation here that the helicopter interfered with respondent's normal use of the greenhouse or of other parts of the curtilage. As far as this record reveals, no intimate details connected with the use of the home or curtilage were observed, and there was no undue noise, and no wind, dust, or threat of injury. In these circumstances, there was no violation of the Fourth Amendment.

---

curtilage. It would appear that, after today, families can expect to be free of official surveillance only when they retreat behind the walls of their homes.

What does Justice White mean by these limitations? For example, suppose that the surveillance of Riley's greenhouse had been conducted by *airplane* at 400 feet. Because an airplane should not ordinarily be at such a low altitude, has a search occurred, although the same surveillance by helicopter is permissible? Does such a distinction make sense?

Does Justice White also mean that if an officer in a helicopter simultaneously observes marijuana in a greenhouse and sexually intimate acts occurring in the same curtilage, the surveillance constitutes a search as to the latter, but not as to the former, sighting? Does such a distinction make sense? And, why is it a Fourth Amendment concern whether a helicopter is noisy or blows dust in a person's backyard?

Justice O'Connor concurred in the judgment in *Riley*, thus adding a fifth vote:

> In my view, the defendant must bear the burden of proving that his expectation of privacy was a reasonable one, and thus that a "search" within the meaning of the Fourth Amendment even took place.
>
> Because there is reason to believe that there is considerable public use of airspace at altitudes of 400 feet and above, and because Riley introduced no evidence to the contrary * * *, I conclude that Riley's expectation that his curtilage was protected from naked-eye aerial observation from that altitude was not a reasonable one. However, public use of altitudes lower than that—particularly public observations from helicopters circling over the curtilage of a home—may be sufficiently rare that police surveillance from such altitudes would violate reasonable expectations of privacy, despite compliance with F.A.A. safety regulations.

9. *Rifling through garbage: surveillance outside the curtilage, near a house, but not in an open field.* In California v. Greenwood, 486 U.S. 35, 108 S.Ct. 1625, 100 L.Ed.2d 30 (1988), officers searched through plastic garbage bags left on the curb in front of a house for trash pickup. The Court ruled that a person does not have a reasonable expectation of privacy in garbage left outside the curtilage of a home for trash removal. Justice White explained that the objective prong of *Katz* is not satisfied in such circumstances:

> It is common knowledge that plastic garbage bags left on or at the side of a public street are readily accessible to animals, children, scavengers, snoops, and other members of the public. Moreover, respondents placed their refuse at the curb for the express purpose of conveying it to a third party, the trash collector, who might himself have sorted through respondents' trash or permitted others, such as the police, to do so. * * *
>
> Furthermore, as we have held, the police cannot reasonably be expected to avert their eyes from evidence of criminal activity that

could have been observed by any member of the public. Hence, "[w]hat a person knowingly exposes to the public, even in his own home or office, is not a subject of Fourth Amendment protection." *Katz v. United States.* We held in *Smith v. Maryland* [p. 116], for example, that * * * [a]n individual has no legitimate expectation of privacy in the numbers dialed on his telephone * * * because he voluntarily conveys those numbers to the telephone company when he uses the telephone.

If you represented Greenwood, how would you try to distinguish *Katz* and *Smith* from the circumstances here?

10. After all of the Supreme Court "no search" decisions, it is worth noting one that went the other way. In Bond v. United States, 529 U.S. 334, 120 S.Ct. 1462, 146 L.Ed.2d 365 (2000), Border Patrol agents walked through a Greyhound bus that was stopped at a checkpoint. They routinely squeezed the soft luggage that passengers had placed in the overhead storage bins. In Bond's case, an agent felt a brick-like object. Bond then allowed the agents to open his luggage, at which point illegal drugs were discovered. At issue was the agents's pre-consent act of squeezing the luggage. Chief Justice Rehnquist, writing for seven members of the Court, held that this constituted a "search":

> [T]he Government asserts that by exposing his bag to the public, petitioner lost a reasonable expectation that his bag would not be physically manipulated. The Government relies on our decisions in *California v. Ciraolo* and *Florida v. Riley* [Notes 7–8] for the proposition that matters open to public observation are not protected by the Fourth Amendment. * * * But *Ciraolo* and *Riley* are different from this case because they involved only visual, as opposed to tactile, observation. Physically invasive inspection is simply more intrusive than purely visual inspection.

The Chief Justice went on to observe further that:

> When a bus passenger places a bag in an overhead bin, he expects that other passengers or bus employees may move it for one reason or another. Thus, a bus passenger clearly expects that his bag may be handled. He does not expect that other passengers or bus employees will, as a matter of course, feel the bag in an exploratory manner. But this is exactly what the agent did here. We therefore hold that the agent's physical manipulation of petitioner's bag violated the Fourth Amendment.

3. *KATZ* AND THE NEW TECHNOLOGY: BACK TO THE FUTURE?

KYLLO v. UNITED STATES

Supreme Court of the United States, 2001.
533 U.S. 27, 121 S.Ct. 2038, 150 L.Ed.2d 94.

JUSTICE SCALIA delivered the opinion of the Court [joined by JUSTICES SOUTER, THOMAS, GINSBERG, and BREYER].

This case presents the question whether the use of a thermal-imaging device aimed at a private home from a public street to detect relative amounts of heat within the home constitutes a "search" within the meaning of the Fourth Amendment.

I

In 1991 Agent William Elliott of the United States Department of the Interior came to suspect that marijuana was being grown in the home belonging to petitioner Danny Kyllo * * *. Indoor marijuana growth typically requires high-intensity lamps. In order to determine whether an amount of heat was emanating from petitioner's home consistent with the use of such lamps, at 3:20 a.m. on January 16, 1992, Agent Elliott and Dan Haas used an Agema Thermovision 210 thermal imager to scan the triplex. Thermal imagers detect infrared radiation, which virtually all objects emit but which is not visible to the naked eye. The imager converts radiation into images based on relative warmth—black is cool, white is hot, shades of gray connote relative differences; in that respect, it operates somewhat like a video camera showing heat images. The scan of Kyllo's home took only a few minutes and was performed from the passenger seat of Agent Elliott's vehicle across the street from the front of the house and also from the street in back of the house. The scan showed that the roof over the garage and a side wall of petitioner's home were relatively hot compared to the rest of the home and substantially warmer than neighboring homes * * *. Agent Elliott concluded that petitioner was using halide lights to grow marijuana in his house, which indeed he was. Based on tips from informants, utility bills, and the thermal imaging, a Federal Magistrate Judge issued a warrant authorizing a search of petitioner's home, and the agents found an indoor growing operation involving more than 100 plants. Petitioner * * * unsuccessfully moved to suppress the evidence seized from his home * * *. * * *

II

* * * "At the very core" of the Fourth Amendment "stands the right of a man to retreat into his own home and there be free from unreasonable governmental intrusion." With few exceptions, the question whether a

warrantless search of a home is reasonable and hence constitutional must be answered no.

On the other hand, the antecedent question of whether or not a Fourth Amendment "search" has occurred is not so simple under our precedent. The permissibility of ordinary visual surveillance of a home used to be clear because, well into the 20th century, our Fourth Amendment jurisprudence was tied to common-law trespass. Visual surveillance was unquestionably lawful because "'the eye cannot by the laws of England be guilty of a trespass.'" *Boyd v. United States*, 116 U.S. 616, 628 (1886) (quoting *Entick v. Carrington*, 19 How. St. Tr. 1029, 95 Eng. Rep. 807 (K. B. 1765)). We have since decoupled violation of a person's Fourth Amendment rights from trespassory violation of his property, but the lawfulness of warrantless visual surveillance of a home has still been preserved. As we observed in *California v. Ciraolo*, [p. 128, Note 7], "[t]he Fourth Amendment protection of the home has never been extended to require law enforcement officers to shield their eyes when passing by a home on public thoroughfares."

One might think that the new validating rationale would be that examining the portion of a house that is in plain public view, while it is a "search"[1] despite the absence of trespass, is not an "unreasonable" one under the Fourth Amendment. But in fact we have held that visual observation is no "search" at all * * * . In assessing when a search is not a search, we have applied somewhat in reverse the principle first enunciated in *Katz v. United States*. *Katz* involved eavesdropping by means of an electronic listening device placed on the outside of a telephone booth—a location not within the catalog ("persons, houses, papers, and effects") that the Fourth Amendment protects against unreasonable searches. We held that the Fourth Amendment nonetheless protected Katz from the warrantless eavesdropping because he "justifiably relied" upon the privacy of the telephone booth. As Justice Harlan's oft-quoted concurrence described it, a Fourth Amendment search occurs when the government violates a subjective expectation of privacy that society recognizes as reasonable. * * * We have applied this test in holding that it is not a search for the police to use a pen register at the phone company to determine what numbers were dialed in a private home, *Smith v. Maryland*, [p. 116], and we have applied the test on two different occasions in holding that aerial surveillance of private homes and surrounding areas does not constitute a search, *Ciraolo, supra*; *Florida v. Riley*, [p. 132, Note 8].

---

[1] When the Fourth Amendment was adopted, as now, to "search" meant "[t]o look over or through for the purpose of finding something; to explore; to examine by inspection; as, to search the house for a book; to search the wood for a thief." N. Webster, An American Dictionary of the English Language 66 (1828) (reprint 6th ed. 1989).

The present case involves officers on a public street engaged in more than naked-eye surveillance of a home. We have previously reserved judgment as to how much technological enhancement of ordinary perception from such a vantage point, if any, is too much. While we upheld enhanced aerial photography of an industrial complex in *Dow Chemical* [*v. United States*, 476 U.S. 227, 106 S.Ct. 1819, 90 L.Ed.2d 226 (1986)] we noted that we found "it important that this is *not an area immediately adjacent to a private home,* where privacy expectations are most heightened."

III

It would be foolish to contend that the degree of privacy secured to citizens by the Fourth Amendment has been entirely unaffected by the advance of technology. For example, as the cases discussed above make clear, the technology enabling human flight has exposed to public view (and hence, we have said, to official observation) uncovered portions of the house and its curtilage that once were private. The question we confront today is what limits there are upon this power of technology to shrink the realm of guaranteed privacy.

issue 2

The *Katz* test—whether the individual has an expectation of privacy that society is prepared to recognize as reasonable—has often been criticized as circular, and hence subjective and unpredictable. While it may be difficult to refine *Katz* when the search of areas such as telephone booths, automobiles, or even the curtilage and uncovered portions of residences are at issue, in the case of the search of the interior of homes— the prototypical and hence most commonly litigated area of protected privacy—there is a ready criterion, with roots deep in the common law, of the minimal expectation of privacy that *exists*, and that is acknowledged to be *reasonable*. To withdraw protection of this minimum expectation would be to permit police technology to erode the privacy guaranteed by the Fourth Amendment. We think that obtaining by sense-enhancing technology any information regarding the interior of the home that could not otherwise have been obtained without physical "intrusion into a constitutionally protected area" constitutes a search—at least where (as here) the technology in question is not in general public use. This assures preservation of that degree of privacy against government that existed when the Fourth Amendment was adopted. On the basis of this criterion, the information obtained by the thermal imager in this case was the product of a search.[2]

---

[2] The dissent's repeated assertion that the thermal imaging did not obtain information regarding the interior of the home is simply inaccurate. A thermal imager reveals the relative heat of various rooms in the home. The dissent may not find that information particularly private or important, but there is no basis for saying it is not information regarding the interior of the home. The dissent's comparison of the thermal imaging to various circumstances in which outside observers might be able to perceive, without technology, the heat of the home—for example, by observing snowmelt on the roof—is quite irrelevant. The fact that equivalent

The Government maintains, however, that the thermal imaging must be upheld because it detected "only heat radiating from the external surface of the house." The dissent makes this its leading point, contending that there is a fundamental difference between what it calls "off-the-wall" observations and "through-the-wall surveillance." But just as a thermal imager captures only heat emanating from a house, so also a powerful directional microphone picks up only sound emanating from a house—and a satellite capable of scanning from many miles away would pick up only visible light emanating from a house. We rejected such a mechanical interpretation of the Fourth Amendment in *Katz*, where the eavesdropping device picked up only sound waves that reached the exterior of the phone booth. Reversing that approach would leave the homeowner at the mercy of advancing technology—including imaging technology that could discern all human activity in the home. While the technology used in the present case was relatively crude, the rule we adopt must take account of more sophisticated systems that are already in use or in development.[3] * * *

The Government also contends that the thermal imaging was constitutional because it did not "detect private activities occurring in private areas." * * * The Fourth Amendment's protection of the home has never been tied to measurement of the quality or quantity of information obtained. * * * In the home, our cases show, *all* details are intimate details, because the entire area is held safe from prying government eyes. Thus, in [*United States v.*] *Karo*, [summarized in Note 5, pp. 145–146], the only thing detected was a can of ether in the home; and in *Arizona v. Hicks*, [p. 346], the only thing detected by a physical search that went beyond what officers lawfully present could observe in "plain view" was the registration number of a phonograph turntable. These were intimate details because they were details of the home, just as was the detail of how warm—or even how relatively warm—Kyllo was heating his residence.

---

information could sometimes be obtained by other means does not make lawful the use of means that violate the Fourth Amendment. The police might, for example, learn how many people are in a particular house by setting up year-round surveillance; but that does not make breaking and entering to find out the same information lawful. In any event, on the night of January 16, 1992, no outside observer could have discerned the relative heat of Kyllo's home without thermal imaging.

[3]   The ability to "see" through walls and other opaque barriers is a clear, and scientifically feasible, goal of law enforcement research and development. The National Law Enforcement and Corrections Technology Center, a program within the United States Department of Justice, features on its Internet Website projects that include a "Radar-Based Through-the-Wall Surveillance System," "Handheld Ultrasound Through the Wall Surveillance," and a "Radar Flashlight" that "will enable law officers to detect individuals through interior building walls." Some devices may emit low levels of radiation that travel "through-the-wall," but others, such as more sophisticated thermal imaging devices, are entirely passive, or "off-the-wall" as the dissent puts it.

potent. probs.

Limiting the prohibition of thermal imaging to "intimate details" would not only be wrong in principle; it would be impractical in application, failing to provide "a workable accommodation between the needs of law enforcement and the interests protected by the Fourth Amendment." To begin with, there is no necessary connection between the sophistication of the surveillance equipment and the "intimacy" of the details that it observes—which means that one cannot say (and the police cannot be assured) that use of the relatively crude equipment at issue here will always be lawful. The Agema Thermovision 210 might disclose, for example, at what hour each night the lady of the house takes her daily sauna and bath—a detail that many would consider "intimate"; and a much more sophisticated system might detect nothing more intimate than the fact that someone left a closet light on. We * * * would have to develop a jurisprudence specifying which home activities are "intimate" and which are not. And even when (if ever) that jurisprudence were fully developed, no police officer would be able to know *in advance* whether his through-the-wall surveillance picks up "intimate" details—and thus would be unable to know in advance whether it is <u>constitutional</u>.

The dissent's proposed standard—whether the technology offers the "functional equivalent of actual presence in the area being searched"— would seem quite similar to our own at first blush. The dissent concludes that *Katz* was such a case, but then inexplicably asserts that if the same listening device only revealed the volume of the conversation, the surveillance would be permissible. Yet, if without technology, the police could not discern volume without being actually present in the phone booth, Justice Stevens should conclude a search has occurred. * * * Thus the driving force of the dissent, despite its recitation of the above standard, appears to be a distinction among different types of information—<u>whether</u> the "homeowner would even care if anybody noticed." The dissent offers no practical guidance for the application of this standard, and for reasons already discussed, we believe there can be none. The people in their houses, as well as the police, deserve more precision.[6]

We have said that the Fourth Amendment draws "a firm line at the entrance to the house." That line, we think, must be not only firm but also bright—which requires clear specification of those methods of surveillance that require a warrant. While it is certainly possible to conclude from the videotape of the thermal imaging that occurred in this

---

[6] The dissent argues that we have injected potential uncertainty into the constitutional analysis by noting that whether or not the technology is in general public use may be a factor. That quarrel, however, is not with us but with this Court's precedent. See *Ciraolo* ("In an age where private and commercial flight in the public airways is routine, it is unreasonable for respondent to expect that his marijuana plants were constitutionally protected from being observed with the naked eye from an altitude of 1,000 feet"). Given that we can quite confidently say that thermal imaging is not "routine," we decline in this case to reexamine that factor.

case that no "significant" compromise of the homeowner's privacy has occurred, we must take the long view, from the original meaning of the Fourth Amendment forward. * * * Where, as here, the Government uses a device that is not in general public use, to explore details of the home that would previously have been unknowable without physical intrusion, the surveillance is a "search" and is presumptively unreasonable without a warrant. * * *

JUSTICE STEVENS, with whom THE CHIEF JUSTICE REHNQUIST, JUSTICE O'CONNOR, and JUSTICE KENNEDY join, dissenting. * * *

While the Court "take[s] the long view" and decides this case based largely on the potential of yet-to-be-developed technology that might allow "through-the-wall surveillance," this case involves nothing more than off-the-wall surveillance by law enforcement officers to gather information exposed to the general public from the outside of petitioner's home. All that the infrared camera did in this case was passively measure heat emitted from the exterior surfaces of petitioner's home; all that those measurements showed were relative differences in emission levels, vaguely indicating that some areas of the roof and outside walls were warmer than others. * * * [N]o details regarding the interior of petitioner's home were revealed. Unlike an x-ray scan, or other possible "through-the-wall" techniques, the detection of infrared radiation emanating from the home did not accomplish "an unauthorized physical penetration into the premises," nor did it "obtain information that it could not have obtained by observation from outside the curtilage of the house."

Indeed, the ordinary use of the senses might enable a neighbor or passerby to notice the heat emanating from a building, particularly if it is vented, as was the case here. Additionally, any member of the public might notice that one part of a house is warmer than another part or a nearby building if, for example, rainwater evaporates or snow melts at different rates across its surfaces. * * * [An] observation [similarly does not] become an unreasonable search if made from a distance with the aid of a device that merely discloses that the exterior of one house, or one area of the house, is much warmer than another. Nothing more occurred in this case.

Thus, the notion that heat emissions from the outside of a dwelling is a private matter implicating the protections of the Fourth Amendment * * * is not only unprecedented but also quite difficult to take seriously. Heat waves, like aromas that are generated in a kitchen, or in a laboratory or opium den, enter the public domain if and when they leave a building. A subjective expectation that they would remain private is not only implausible but also surely not "one that society is prepared to recognize as 'reasonable.'" * * *

* * * Just as "the police cannot reasonably be expected to avert their eyes from evidence of criminal activity that could have been observed by any member of the public," so too public officials should not have to avert their senses or their equipment from detecting emissions in the public domain such as excessive heat, traces of smoke, suspicious odors, odorless gases, airborne particulates, or radioactive emissions, any of which could identify hazards to the community. In my judgment, monitoring such emissions with "sense-enhancing technology," and drawing useful conclusions from such monitoring, is an entirely reasonable public service.

On the other hand, the countervailing privacy interest is at best trivial. After all, homes generally are insulated to keep heat in, rather than to prevent the detection of heat going out, and it does not seem to me that society will suffer from a rule requiring the rare homeowner who both intends to engage in uncommon activities that produce extraordinary amounts of heat, and wishes to conceal that production from outsiders, to make sure that the surrounding area is well insulated. * * *

Since what was involved in this case was nothing more than drawing inferences from off-the-wall surveillance, rather than any "through-the-wall" surveillance, the officers' conduct did not amount to a search and was perfectly reasonable.

II

* * * [T]he Court has fashioned a rule that is intended to provide essential guidance for the day when "more sophisticated systems" gain the "ability to 'see' through walls and other opaque barriers." The newly minted rule encompasses "obtaining [1] by sense-enhancing technology [2] any information regarding the interior of the home [3] that could not otherwise have been obtained without physical intrusion into a constitutionally protected area * * * [4] at least where (as here) the technology in question is not in general public use." In my judgment, the Court's new rule is at once too broad and too narrow, and is not justified by the Court's explanation for its adoption. * * *

Despite the Court's attempt to draw a line that is "not only firm but also bright," the contours of its new rule are uncertain because its protection apparently dissipates as soon as the relevant technology is "in general public use." Yet how much use is general public use is not even hinted at by the Court's opinion, which makes the somewhat doubtful assumption that the thermal imager used in this case does not satisfy that criterion.[5] In any event, putting aside its lack of clarity, this criterion

---

[5] The record describes a device that numbers close to a thousand manufactured units; that has a predecessor numbering in the neighborhood of 4,000 to 5,000 units; that competes with a similar product numbering from 5,000 to 6,000 units; and that is "readily available to the public"

is somewhat perverse because it seems likely that the threat to privacy will grow, rather than recede, as the use of intrusive equipment becomes more readily available.

It is clear, however, that the category of "sense-enhancing technology" covered by the new rule is far too broad. It would, for example, embrace potential mechanical substitutes for dogs trained to react when they sniff narcotics. But in *United States v. Place*, [p. 123, Note 4], we held that a dog sniff that "discloses only the presence or absence of narcotics" does "not constitute a 'search' within the meaning of the Fourth Amendment," and it must follow that sense-enhancing equipment that identifies nothing but illegal activity is not a search either. Nevertheless, the use of such a device would be unconstitutional under the Court's rule, as would the use of other new devices that might detect the odor of deadly bacteria or chemicals for making a new type of high explosive, even if the devices (like the dog sniffs) are "so limited in both the manner in which" they obtain information and "in the content of the information" they reveal. * * *

Because the new rule applies to information regarding the "interior" of the home, it is too narrow as well as too broad. Clearly, a rule that is designed to protect individuals from the overly intrusive use of sense-enhancing equipment should not be limited to a home. If such equipment did provide its user with the functional equivalent of access to a private place—such as, for example, the telephone booth involved in *Katz*, or an office building—then the rule should apply to such an area as well as to a home. See *Katz* ("[T]he Fourth Amendment protects people, not places"). * * *

The * * * reasons advanced by the Court as justifications for the adoption of its new rule are * * * unpersuasive. [T]he Court suggests that its rule is compelled by our holding in *Katz*, because in that case, as in this, the surveillance consisted of nothing more than the monitoring of waves emanating from a private area into the public domain. Yet there are critical differences between the cases. In *Katz*, the electronic listening device attached to the outside of the phone booth allowed the officers to pick up the content of the conversation inside the booth, making them the functional equivalent of intruders * * * . By contrast, the thermal imager here disclosed only the relative amounts of heat radiating from the house; it would be as if, in *Katz*, the listening device disclosed only the relative volume of sound leaving the booth, which presumably was discernible in the public domain.[6] * * * It is pure hyperbole for the Court to suggest that

---

for commercial, personal, or law enforcement purposes, and is just an 800-number away from being rented from "half a dozen national companies" by anyone who wants one. * * *

[6] The use of the latter device would be constitutional given *Smith v. Maryland*, [p. 116] which upheld the use of pen registers to record numbers dialed on a phone because, unlike "the listening device employed in *Katz* * * * pen registers do not acquire the contents of communications."

refusing to extend the holding of *Katz* to this case would leave the homeowner at the mercy of "technology that could discern all human activity in the home." * * *

III

* * * Instead of concentrating on the rather mundane issue that is actually presented by the case before it, the Court has endeavored to craft an all-encompassing rule for the future. It would be far wiser to give legislators an unimpeded opportunity to grapple with these emerging issues rather than to shackle them with prematurely devised constitutional constraints. * * *

NOTES AND QUESTIONS

1.   As a matter of public policy, whom do you believe has the better side of the argument, Scalia or Stevens? Or, do you agree with Professor Wayne LaFave, who suggested that "after reading both opinions * * * I feel as if I have witnessed a sword fight in which both sides drew blood"? Wayne R. LaFave, *The Fourth Amendment as a "Big Time" TV Fad*, 53 Hastings L.J. 265, 277 (2001).

In terms of privacy from governmental intrusion, what should matter more in Fourth Amendment analysis: (1) where the government surveilling agent is physically located; or (2) where the private information is physically situated? Do you agree with Justice Scalia that in regard to the home "*all* details are intimate details" that should be "held safe from prying government eyes"?

2.   Which opinion—the majority or the dissent—seems more faithful to the principles of *Katz*? To post-*Katz* case law?

3.   According to *Kyllo*, is it a "search" for the police to use a Geiger counter on public streets to locate plutonium (used in nuclear bomb-making) cached in someone's home?

What if some enterprising business tomorrow begins selling "pocket-thermal-imagers-'n'toenail-clippers" on cable television for $10.99 (but you get a second one free if you call within twenty minutes)? Would police use of a thermal imager *now* constitute a Fourth Amendment search? *See* John P. Elwood, *What Were They Thinking: The Supreme Court in Revue, October Term 2000*, 4 Green Bag 2d 365, 371 (2001).

4.   Do you sense that if he had the votes, Justice Scalia would seek to overrule some of the pre-*Kyllo* "search" cases? If so, which ones would seem to be on his potential "hit list"?

In regard to *Katz* itself, Justice Scalia previously observed in Minnesota v. Carter, 525 U.S. 83, 119 S.Ct. 469, 142 L.Ed.2d 373 (1998) (concurring opinion):

> In my view, the only thing the past three decades have established about the *Katz* test (which has come to mean the test enunciated by Justice Harlan's separate concurrence in *Katz*) is that, unsurprisingly, those "actual (subjective) expectation[s] of privacy" "that society is prepared to recognize as 'reasonable,'" bear an uncanny resemblance to those expectations of privacy that this Court considers reasonable. When that self-indulgent test is employed * * * to determine whether a "search or seizure" within the meaning of the Constitution has *occurred* (as opposed to whether that "search or seizure" is an "unreasonable" one), it has no plausible foundation in the text of the Fourth Amendment.

What does Scalia say about *Katz* in *Kyllo*?

5. *Primitive technology: the "beeper" cases.* In *Smith v. Maryland* (p. 116), the Supreme Court justified use of a technological device, the pen register, installed *outside* the defendant's home, in order to obtain information regarding an activity (telephone calls made) occurring *inside* his residence. But, technology can also assist law enforcement agents to determine the location of a suspect and/or to follow the suspect's movements. The Supreme Court has been called upon more than once to determine whether technologically-enhanced surveillance constitutes a search or seizure. (The "seizure" issues are considered in Section B. of this chapter.)

In the 1980s, "modern" surveillance technology included the use of a "beeper": In United States v. Knotts, 460 U.S. 276, 103 S.Ct. 1081, 75 L.Ed.2d 55 (1983), as part of an investigation of the manufacture of illicit drugs, federal agents installed a radio transmitter, which emitted periodic signals ("beeps"), in a five-gallon container of chloroform later purchased by defendant Petschen (presumably for use in the production of illicit drugs). By use of the beeper, the police monitored the suspect's movements from the point of purchase in Minneapolis, Minnesota along public roads to a secluded cabin in Wisconsin belonging to co-defendant Knotts. As is turned out, the police ended visual surveillance of the Petschen car when he made evasive maneuvers, but they picked up the signals from the beeper by helicopter, where the drum had been left outside the Knotts cabin. Based on this information, the police secured a warrant to search the cabin.

Defendants Petschen and Knotts sought to suppress evidence found in the cabin, on the ground that the surveillance, conducted without a warrant, was unconstitutional. The Court concluded that the surveillance did not constitute a Fourth Amendment search:

> A person traveling in an automobile on public thoroughfares has no reasonable expectation of privacy in his movements from one place to another. When Petschen traveled over the public streets he

voluntarily conveyed to anyone who wanted to look the fact that he was traveling over particular roads in a particular direction, the fact of whatever stops he made, and the fact of his final destination when he exited from public roads onto private property. * * *

Visual surveillance from public places along Petschen's route or adjoining Knotts' premises would have sufficed to reveal all of these facts to the police. The fact that the officers in this case relied not only on visual surveillance, but also on the use of the beeper to signal the presence of Petschen's automobile to the police receiver, does not alter the situation. Nothing in the Fourth Amendment prohibited the police from augmenting the sensory faculties bestowed upon them at birth with such enhancement as science and technology afforded them in this case. * * *

Respondent does not actually quarrel with this analysis, though he expresses the generalized view that the result of the holding sought by the Government would be that "twenty-four hour surveillance of any citizen of this country will be possible, without judicial knowledge or supervision." * * * [I]f such dragnet-type law enforcement practices as respondent envisions should eventually occur, there will be time enough then to determine whether different constitutional principles may be applicable. Insofar as respondent's complaint appears to be simply that scientific devices such as the beeper enabled the police to be more effective in detecting crime, it simply has no constitutional foundation. We have never equated police efficiency with unconstitutionality, and we decline to do so now. * * *

We think that respondent's contentions * * * to some extent lose sight of the limited use which the government made of the signals from this particular beeper. As we have noted, nothing in this record indicates that the beeper signal was received or relied upon after it had indicated that the drum containing the chloroform had ended its automotive journey at rest on respondent's premises in rural Wisconsin. * * * [T]here is no indication that the beeper was used in any way to reveal information as to the movement of the drum within the cabin, or in any way that would not have been visible to the naked eye from outside the cabin.

Notice the Court's observation in the last sentence. Didn't the pen register in *Smith v. Maryland* reveal information regarding activities *inside* a residence that was otherwise "hidden"? In any case, the *Knotts* Court's observation proved critical in a second "beeper" case, United States v. Karo, 468 U.S. 705, 104 S.Ct. 3296, 82 L.Ed.2d 530 (1984). In *Karo*, Karo ordered 50 gallons of ether from a government informant, to be used in drug offenses. With the permission of the informant, federal agents substituted their own ether can containing a beeper for one of those sold to Karo. They then monitored Karo's movements over public roads, as in *Knotts*, but also monitored the tracking device in Karo's home, as well as in two other houses. The Court held that the warrantless "monitoring of a beeper in a private residence, a location not open to visual surveillance, violates the Fourth Amendment rights of those who have a justifiable interest in the privacy of the residence." More specifically:

> In this case, had a DEA agent thought it useful to enter the * * * residence to verify that the ether was actually in the house and had he done so surreptitiously and without a warrant, there is little doubt that he would have engaged in an unreasonable search within the meaning of the Fourth Amendment. For purposes of the Amendment, the result is the same where * * * the Government surreptitiously employs an electronic device to obtain information that it could not have obtained by observation from outside the curtilage of the house. * * *
>
> * * * The case is thus not like *Knotts*, for there the beeper told the authorities nothing about the interior of Knotts' cabin. The information obtained in *Knotts* was "voluntarily conveyed to anyone who wanted to look * * *"; here, as we have said, the monitoring indicated that the beeper was inside the house, a fact that could not have been visually verified.[c]

Is *Karo* consistent with *Smith v. Maryland*? With *Kyllo*?

The 1980s "beeper" seems almost primitive by today's technological standards, particularly in view of the advent of Global Positioning System (GPS) tracking devices. Indeed, it is the latter technological "advance" that has required the Supreme Court to determine whether its interpretations of the Fourth Amendment announced in *Knotts* and *Karo*—and, for that matter, in *Katz*—adequately deal with the world in which we now live. Thus, we turn to. . . .

---

[c]   Consider:

[T]he Court's analysis here is counterintuitive. Imagine that police officers presented you with the option of having them follow you everywhere you travel, keeping track of when you leave your house each day, where you go for recreation and how often you visit various people and places. Now imagine that as an alternative, the police propose tracking exactly where inside your garage your car is parked at any given time. Which of the two would you choose? Which of the two represents the greater invasion of privacy?

Only the most formalistic analysis would consider the threshold of the home the place where privacy begins and ends, regardless of how trivial the "hidden" data and how absolute the "public" surveillance.

Sherry F. Colb, *What Is a Search? Two Conceptual Flaws in Fourth Amendment Doctrine and Some Hints of a Remedy*, 55 Stan. L. Rev. 119, 134 (2002).

UNITED STATES V. JONES

Supreme Court of the United States, 2012.
565 U.S. ___, 132 S.Ct. 945, 181 L.Ed.2d 911.

JUSTICE SCALIA delivered the opinion of the Court [joined by CHIEF JUSTICE ROBERTS, and JUSTICES KENNEDY, THOMAS, and SOTOMAYOR].

issue

We decide whether the attachment of a Global-Positioning-System (GPS) tracking device to an individual's vehicle, and subsequent use of that device to monitor the vehicle's movements on public streets, constitutes a search or seizure within the meaning of the Fourth Amendment.

I

In 2004 respondent Antoine Jones, owner and operator of a nightclub in the District of Columbia, came under suspicion of trafficking in narcotics and was made the target of an investigation by a joint FBI and Metropolitan Police Department task force. Officers employed various investigative techniques, including visual surveillance of the nightclub, installation of a camera focused on the front door of the club, and a pen register and wiretap covering Jones's cellular phone.

Based in part on information gathered from these sources, in 2005 the Government applied * * * for a warrant authorizing the use of an electronic tracking device on the Jeep Grand Cherokee registered to Jones's wife. A warrant issued, authorizing installation of the device in the District of Columbia and within 10 days.

probs

On the 11th day, and not in the District of Columbia but in Maryland,[1] agents installed a GPS tracking device on the undercarriage of the Jeep while it was parked in a public parking lot. Over the next 28 days, the Government used the device to track the vehicle's movements, and once had to replace the device's battery when the vehicle was parked in a different public lot in Maryland. By means of signals from multiple satellites, the device established the vehicle's location within 50 to 100 feet, and communicated that location by cellular phone to a Government computer. It relayed more than 2,000 pages of data over the 4-week period.

The Government ultimately obtained a multiple-count indictment charging Jones and several alleged co-conspirators with, as relevant here, conspiracy to distribute and possess with intent to distribute five *charge* kilograms or more of cocaine and 50 grams or more of cocaine base, in violation of [federal law]. Before trial, Jones filed a motion to suppress evidence obtained through the GPS device. The District Court granted the motion only in part, suppressing the data obtained while the vehicle was

---

[1] In this litigation, the Government has conceded noncompliance with the warrant and has argued only that a warrant was not required.

parked in the garage adjoining Jones's residence. It held the remaining data admissible, because " '[a] person traveling in an automobile on public thoroughfares has no reasonable expectation of privacy in his movements from one place to another.' " ([Q]uoting *United States v. Knotts*, [p. 144, Note 5]). * * *

* * * The jury returned a guilty verdict, and the District Court sentenced Jones to life imprisonment.

The United States Court of Appeals for the District of Columbia Circuit reversed the conviction because of admission of the evidence obtained by warrantless use of the GPS device which, it said, violated the Fourth Amendment. * * *

II

A

The Fourth Amendment provides in relevant part that "[t]he right of the people to be secure in their persons, houses, papers, and effects, against unreasonable searches and seizures, shall not be violated." It is beyond dispute that a vehicle is an "effect" as that term is used in the Amendment. We hold that the Government's installation of a GPS device on a target's vehicle, and its use of that device to monitor the vehicle's movements, constitutes a "search."

It is important to be clear about what occurred in this case: The Government physically occupied private property for the purpose of obtaining information. We have no doubt that such a physical intrusion would have been considered a "search" within the meaning of the Fourth Amendment when it was adopted. *Entick v. Carrington*, 95 Eng. Rep. 807 (C. P. 1765), is a "case we have described as a 'monument of English freedom' 'undoubtedly familiar' to 'every American statesman' at the time the Constitution was adopted, and considered to be 'the true and ultimate expression of constitutional law' " with regard to search and seizure. In that case, Lord Camden expressed in plain terms the significance of property rights in search-and-seizure analysis:

> "[O]ur law holds the property of every man so sacred, that no man can set his foot upon his neighbour's close without his leave; if he does he is a trespasser, though he does no damage at all; if he will tread upon his neighbour's ground, he must justify it by law."

The text of the Fourth Amendment reflects its close connection to property, since otherwise it would have referred simply to "the right of the people to be secure against unreasonable searches and seizures"; the phrase "in their persons, houses, papers, and effects" would have been superfluous.

Consistent with this understanding, our Fourth Amendment jurisprudence was tied to common-law trespass, at least until the latter half of the 20th century. * * *

Our later cases, of course, have deviated from that exclusively property-based approach. In *Katz v. United States*, [p. 96], we said that "the Fourth Amendment protects people, not places," and found a violation in attachment of an eavesdropping device to a public telephone booth. Our later cases have applied the analysis of Justice Harlan's concurrence in that case, which said that a violation occurs when government officers violate a person's "reasonable expectation of privacy."

The Government contends that the Harlan standard shows that no search occurred here, since Jones had no "reasonable expectation of privacy" in the area of the Jeep accessed by Government agents (its underbody) and in the locations of the Jeep on the public roads, which were visible to all. But we need not address the Government's contentions, because Jones's Fourth Amendment rights do not rise or fall with the *Katz* formulation. At bottom, we must "assur[e] preservation of that degree of privacy against government that existed when the Fourth Amendment was adopted." As explained, for most of our history the Fourth Amendment was understood to embody a particular concern for government trespass upon the areas ("persons, houses, papers, and effects") it enumerates.[3] *Katz* did not repudiate that understanding. * * *

More recently, in *Soldal v. Cook County*, 506 U. S. 56, 113 S.Ct. 538, 121 L.Ed.2d 450 (1992), * * * [we] established that "property rights are not the sole measure of Fourth Amendment violations," but [that *Katz*] did not "snuf[f] out the previously recognized protection for property." * * * We have embodied that preservation of past rights in our very definition of "reasonable expectation of privacy" which we have said to be an expectation "that has a source outside of the Fourth Amendment, either by reference to concepts of real or personal property law or to understandings that are recognized and permitted by society." *Katz* did not narrow the Fourth Amendment's scope.[5]

---

[3] Justice Alito's concurrence (hereinafter concurrence) doubts the wisdom of our approach because "it is almost impossible to think of late-18th-century situations that are analogous to what took place in this case." But in fact it posits a situation that is not far afield—a constable's concealing himself in the target's coach in order to track its movements. There is no doubt that the information gained by that trespassory activity would be the product of an unlawful search—whether that information consisted of the conversations occurring in the coach, or of the destinations to which the coach traveled.

In any case, it is quite irrelevant whether there was an 18th-century analog. Whatever new methods of investigation may be devised, our task, *at a minimum*, is to decide whether the action in question would have constituted a "search" within the original meaning of the Fourth Amendment. Where, as here, the Government obtains information by physically intruding on a constitutionally protected area, such a search has undoubtedly occurred.

[5] * * * [S]imilarly irrelevant is the concurrence's point that, if analyzed separately, neither the installation of the device nor its use would constitute a Fourth Amendment search. Of course not. A trespass on "houses" or "effects," or a *Katz* invasion of privacy, is not alone a search unless

The Government contends that several of our post-*Katz* cases foreclose the conclusion that what occurred here constituted a search. It relies principally on two cases in which we rejected Fourth Amendment challenges to "beepers," electronic tracking devices that represent another form of electronic monitoring. The first case, *Knotts*, upheld against Fourth Amendment challenge the use of a "beeper" that had been placed in a container of chloroform, allowing law enforcement to monitor the location of the container. We said that there had been no infringement of Knotts' reasonable expectation of privacy since the information obtained—the location of the automobile carrying the container on public roads, and the location of the off-loaded container in open fields near Knotts' cabin—had been voluntarily conveyed to the public.[6] But as we have discussed, the *Katz* reasonable-expectation-of-privacy test has been *added to*, not *substituted for*, the common-law trespassory test. The holding in *Knotts* addressed only the former, since the latter was not at issue. The beeper had been placed in the container before it came into Knotts' possession, with the consent of the then-owner. Knotts did not challenge that installation, and we specifically declined to consider its effect on the Fourth Amendment analysis. *Knotts* would be relevant, perhaps, if the Government were making the argument that what would otherwise be an unconstitutional search is not such where it produces only public information. The Government does not make that argument, and we know of no case that would support it.

The second "beeper" case, *United States v. Karo*, does not suggest a different conclusion. There we addressed the question left open by *Knotts*, whether the installation of a beeper in a container amounted to a search or seizure. As in *Knotts*, at the time the beeper was installed the container belonged to a third party, and it did not come into possession of the defendant until later. Thus, the specific question we considered was whether the installation *"with the consent of the original owner* constitute[d] a search or seizure * * * when the container is delivered to a buyer having no knowledge of the presence of the beeper." We held not. The Government, we said, came into physical contact with the container only before it belonged to the defendant Karo; and the transfer of the container with the unmonitored beeper inside did not convey any information and thus did not invade Karo's privacy. That conclusion is perfectly consistent with the one we reach here. Karo accepted the container as it came to him, beeper and all, and was therefore not entitled to object to the beeper's presence, even though it was used to monitor the

---

it is done to obtain information; and the obtaining of information is not alone a search unless it is achieved by such a trespass or invasion of privacy.

[6] *Knotts* noted the "limited use which the government made of the signals from this particular beeper"; and reserved the question whether "different constitutional principles may be applicable" to "dragnet-type law enforcement practices" of the type that GPS tracking made possible here.

container's location. Jones, who possessed the Jeep at the time the Government trespassorily inserted the information-gathering device, is on much different footing. * * *

Finally, the Government's position gains little support from our conclusion in *Oliver v. United States*, [p. 125, Note 5], that officers' information-gathering intrusion on an "open field" did not constitute a Fourth Amendment search even though it was a trespass at common law. Quite simply, an open field, unlike the curtilage of a home, is not one of those protected areas enumerated in the Fourth Amendment. The Government's physical intrusion on such an area—unlike its intrusion on the "effect" at issue here—is of no Fourth Amendment significance.[8]

B

The concurrence begins by accusing us of applying "18th-century tort law." That is a distortion. What we apply is an 18th-century guarantee against unreasonable searches, which we believe must provide *at a minimum* the degree of protection it afforded when it was adopted. The concurrence does not share that belief. It would apply *exclusively Katz's* reasonable-expectation-of-privacy test, even when that eliminates rights that previously existed.

The concurrence faults our approach for "present[ing] particularly vexing problems" in cases that do not involve physical contact, such as those that involve the transmission of electronic signals. We entirely fail to understand that point. For unlike the concurrence, which would make *Katz* the exclusive test, we do not make trespass the exclusive test. Situations involving merely the transmission of electronic signals without trespass would remain subject to *Katz* analysis.

In fact, it is the concurrence's insistence on the exclusivity of the *Katz* test that needlessly leads us into "particularly vexing problems" in the present case. This Court has to date not deviated from the understanding that mere visual observation does not constitute a search. * * * Thus, even assuming that the concurrence is correct to say that "[t]raditional surveillance" of Jones for a 4-week period "would have required a large team of agents, multiple vehicles, and perhaps aerial assistance," our cases suggest that such visual observation is constitutionally permissible. It may be that achieving the same result through electronic means, without an accompanying trespass, is an unconstitutional invasion of privacy, but the present case does not require us to answer that question.

---

[8] Thus, our theory is *not* that the Fourth Amendment is concerned with "*any* technical trespass that led to the gathering of evidence." The Fourth Amendment protects against trespassory searches only with regard to those items ("persons, houses, papers, and effects") that it enumerates. The trespass that occurred in *Oliver* may properly be understood as a "search," but not one "in the constitutional sense."

And answering it affirmatively leads us needlessly into additional thorny problems. The concurrence posits that "relatively short-term monitoring of a person's movements on public streets" is okay, but that "the use of longer term GPS monitoring in investigations *of most offenses*" is no good. That introduces yet another novelty into our jurisprudence. There is no precedent for the proposition that whether a search has occurred depends on the nature of the crime being investigated. And even accepting that novelty, it remains unexplained why a 4-week investigation is "surely" too long and why a drug-trafficking conspiracy involving substantial amounts of cash and narcotics is not an "extraordinary offens[e]" which may permit longer observation. * * * We may have to grapple with these "vexing problems" in some future case where a classic trespassory search is not involved and resort must be had to *Katz* analysis; but there is no reason for rushing forward to resolve them here.

III

The Government argues in the alternative that even if the attachment and use of the device was a search, it was reasonable—and thus lawful—under the Fourth Amendment because "officers had reasonable suspicion, and indeed probable cause, to believe that [Jones] was a leader in a large-scale cocaine distribution conspiracy." We have no occasion to consider this argument. The Government did not raise it below, and the D. C. Circuit therefore did not address it. We consider the argument forfeited.

* * *

The judgment of the Court of Appeals for the D. C. Circuit is affirmed. * * *

JUSTICE SOTOMAYOR, concurring.

I join the Court's opinion because I agree that a search within the meaning of the Fourth Amendment occurs, at a minimum, "[w]here, as here, the Government obtains information by physically intruding on a constitutionally protected area." * * * The Government usurped Jones' property for the purpose of conducting surveillance on him, thereby invading privacy interests long afforded, and undoubtedly entitled to, Fourth Amendment protection.

Of course, the Fourth Amendment is not concerned only with trespassory intrusions on property. Rather, even in the absence of a trespass, "a Fourth Amendment search occurs when the government violates a subjective expectation of privacy that society recognizes as reasonable." In *Katz*, this Court enlarged its then-prevailing focus on property rights by announcing that the reach of the Fourth Amendment does not "turn upon the presence or absence of a physical intrusion." As the majority's opinion makes clear, however, *Katz*'s reasonable-expectation-of-privacy test augmented, but did not displace or diminish, the common-law trespassory test that preceded it. * * * Justice Alito's approach, which discounts altogether the constitutional relevance of the Government's physical intrusion on Jones' Jeep, erodes that longstanding protection for privacy expectations inherent in items of property that people possess or control. By contrast, the trespassory test applied in the majority's opinion reflects an irreducible constitutional minimum: When the Government physically invades personal property to gather information, a search occurs. The reaffirmation of that principle suffices to decide this case.

Nonetheless, as Justice Alito notes, physical intrusion is now unnecessary to many forms of surveillance. With increasing regularity, the Government will be capable of duplicating the monitoring undertaken in this case by enlisting factory- or owner-installed vehicle tracking devices or GPS-enabled smartphones. In cases of electronic or other novel modes of surveillance that do not depend upon a physical invasion on property, the majority opinion's trespassory test may provide little guidance. * * * As Justice Alito incisively observes, the same technological advances that have made possible nontrespassory surveillance techniques will also affect the *Katz* test by shaping the evolution of societal privacy expectations. Under that rubric, I agree with Justice Alito that, at the very least, "longer term GPS monitoring in investigations of most offenses impinges on expectations of privacy."

In cases involving even short-term monitoring, some unique attributes of GPS surveillance relevant to the *Katz* analysis will require particular attention. GPS monitoring generates a precise, comprehensive record of a person's public movements that reflects a wealth of detail about her familial, political, professional, religious, and sexual associations. See, *e.g., People v. Weaver*, 12 N. Y. 3d 433, 441–442, 909 N. E. 2d 1195, 1199 (2009) ("Disclosed in [GPS] data . . . will be trips the indisputably private nature of which takes little imagination to conjure: trips to the psychiatrist, the plastic surgeon, the abortion clinic, the AIDS treatment center, the strip club, the criminal defense attorney, the by-the-hour motel, the union meeting, the mosque, synagogue or church, the gay bar and on and on"). The Government can store such records and efficiently mine them for information years into the future. And because GPS monitoring is cheap in comparison to conventional surveillance techniques and, by design, proceeds surreptitiously, it evades the ordinary checks that constrain abusive law enforcement practices: "limited police resources and community hostility."

Awareness that the Government may be watching chills associational and expressive freedoms. And the Government's unrestrained power to assemble data that reveal private aspects of identity is susceptible to abuse. The net result is that GPS monitoring—by making available at a relatively low cost such a substantial quantum of intimate information about any person whom the Government, in its unfettered discretion, chooses to track—may "alter the relationship between citizen and government in a way that is inimical to democratic society."

I would take these attributes of GPS monitoring into account when considering the existence of a reasonable societal expectation of privacy in the sum of one's public movements. I would ask whether people reasonably expect that their movements will be recorded and aggregated in a manner that enables the Government to ascertain, more or less at will, their political and religious beliefs, sexual habits, and so on. I do not regard as dispositive the fact that the Government might obtain the fruits of GPS monitoring through lawful conventional surveillance techniques. I would also consider the appropriateness of entrusting to the Executive, in the absence of any oversight from a coordinate branch, a tool so amenable to misuse, especially in light of the Fourth Amendment's goal to curb arbitrary exercises of police power to and prevent "a too permeating police surveillance."*

More fundamentally, it may be necessary to reconsider the premise that an individual has no reasonable expectation of privacy in information voluntarily disclosed to third parties. *E.g.*, *Smith* [*v. Maryland*, p. 116]; *United States v. Miller*, [p. 119]. This approach is ill suited to the digital age, in which people reveal a great deal of information about themselves to third parties in the course of carrying out mundane tasks. People disclose the phone numbers that they dial or text to their cellular providers; the URLs that they visit and the e-mail addresses with which they correspond to their Internet service providers; and the books, groceries, and medications they purchase to online retailers. Perhaps, as Justice Alito notes, some people may find the "tradeoff" of privacy for convenience "worthwhile," or come to accept this "diminution of privacy" as "inevitable," and perhaps not. I for one doubt that people would accept without complaint the warrantless disclosure to the Government of a list of every Web site they had visited in the last week, or month, or year. But whatever the societal expectations, they can attain constitutionally protected status only if our Fourth Amendment jurisprudence ceases to treat secrecy as a prerequisite for privacy. I would not assume that all information voluntarily disclosed to some member of the public for a limited purpose is, for that reason alone, disentitled to

---

* * * * *United States v. Karo* addressed the Fourth Amendment implications of the installation of a beeper in a container with the consent of the container's original owner, who was aware that the beeper would be used for surveillance purposes. Owners of GPS-equipped cars and smartphones do not contemplate that these devices will be used to enable covert surveillance of their movements. * * * In addition, the bugged container in *Karo* lacked the close relationship with the target that a car shares with its owner. The bugged container in *Karo* was stationary for much of the Government's surveillance. A car's movements, by contrast, are its owner's movements.

Fourth Amendment protection. See *Smith*, (Marshall, J., dissenting) ("Privacy is not a discrete commodity, possessed absolutely or not at all. * * * "); see also *Katz* ("[W]hat [a person] seeks to preserve as private, even in an area accessible to the public, may be constitutionally protected").

Resolution of these difficult questions in this case is unnecessary, however, because the Government's physical intrusion on Jones' Jeep supplies a narrower basis for decision. I therefore join the majority's opinion.

JUSTICE ALITO, with whom JUSTICE GINSBURG, JUSTICE BREYER, and JUSTICE KAGAN join, concurring in the judgment.

This case requires us to apply the Fourth Amendment's prohibition of unreasonable searches and seizures to a 21st-century surveillance technique * * * . Ironically, the Court has chosen to decide this case based on 18th-century tort law. By attaching a small GPS device to the underside of the vehicle that respondent drove, the law enforcement officers in this case engaged in conduct that might have provided grounds in 1791 for a suit for trespass to chattels. And for this reason, the Court concludes, the installation and use of the GPS device constituted a search.

This holding, in my judgment, is unwise. It strains the language of the Fourth Amendment; it has little if any support in current Fourth Amendment case law; and it is highly artificial.

I would analyze the question presented in this case by asking whether respondent's reasonable expectations of privacy were violated by the long-term monitoring of the movements of the vehicle he drove.

I

A

The Fourth Amendment prohibits "unreasonable searches and seizures," and the Court makes very little effort to explain how the attachment or use of the GPS device fits within these terms. * * *

The Court does claim that the installation and use of the GPS constituted a search, but this conclusion is dependent on the questionable proposition that these two procedures cannot be separated for purposes of Fourth Amendment analysis. If these two procedures are analyzed separately, it is not at all clear from the Court's opinion why either should be regarded as a search. It is clear that the attachment of the GPS device was not itself a search; if the device had not functioned or if the officers had not used it, no information would have been obtained. And the Court does not contend that the use of the device constituted a search either. On the contrary, the Court accepts the holding in *United States v. Knotts* that the use of a surreptitiously planted electronic device to monitor a vehicle's movements on public roads did not amount to a search.

The Court argues—and I agree—that "we must 'assur[e] preservation of that degree of privacy against government that existed when the Fourth Amendment was adopted.' " But it is almost impossible to think of late-18th-century situations that are analogous to what took place in this case. (Is it possible to imagine a case in which a constable secreted himself somewhere in a coach and remained there for a period of time in order to monitor the movements of the coach's owner?[3]) The Court's theory seems to be that the concept of a search, as originally understood, comprehended any technical trespass that led to the gathering of evidence, but we know that this is incorrect. At common law, any unauthorized intrusion on private property was actionable, but a trespass on open fields, as opposed to the "curtilage" of a home, does not fall within the scope of the Fourth Amendment because private property outside the curtilage is not part of a "hous[e]" within the meaning of the Fourth Amendment.

B

The Court's reasoning in this case is very similar to that in the Court's early decisions involving wiretapping and electronic eavesdropping, namely, that a technical trespass followed by the gathering of evidence constitutes a search. * * *

This trespass-based rule was repeatedly criticized. * * *

Katz v. United States finally did away with the old approach, holding that a trespass was not required for a Fourth Amendment violation. * * * [T]he *Katz* Court, "repudiate[ed]" the old doctrine and held that "[t]he fact that the electronic device employed * * * did not happen to penetrate the wall of the booth can have no constitutional significance." What mattered, the Court now held, was whether the conduct at issue "violated the privacy upon which [the defendant] justifiably relied while using the telephone booth."

Under this approach, as the Court later put it when addressing the relevance of a technical trespass, "an actual trespass is neither necessary *nor sufficient* to establish a constitutional violation." * * *

III

Disharmony with a substantial body of existing case law is only one of the problems with the Court's approach in this case.

---

[3] The Court suggests that something like this might have occurred in 1791, but this would have required either a gigantic coach, a very tiny constable, or both—not to mention a constable with incredible fortitude and patience.

I will briefly note * * * others. First, the Court's reasoning largely disregards what is really important (the use of a GPS for the purpose of long-term tracking) and instead attaches great significance to something that most would view as relatively minor (attaching to the bottom of a car a small, light object that does not interfere in any way with the car's operation). Attaching such an object is generally regarded as so trivial that it does not provide a basis for recovery under modern tort law. But under the Court's reasoning, this conduct may violate the Fourth Amendment. By contrast, if long-term monitoring can be accomplished without committing a technical trespass—suppose, for example, that the Federal Government required or persuaded auto manufacturers to include a GPS tracking device in every car—the Court's theory would provide no protection.

Second, the Court's approach leads to incongruous results. If the police attach a GPS device to a car and use the device to follow the car for even a brief time, under the Court's theory, the Fourth Amendment applies. But if the police follow the same car for a much longer period using unmarked cars and aerial assistance, this tracking is not subject to any Fourth Amendment constraints. * * *

[Third], the Court's reliance on the law of trespass will present particularly vexing problems in cases involving surveillance that is carried out by making electronic, as opposed to physical, contact with the item to be tracked. For example, suppose that the officers in the present case had followed respondent by surreptitiously activating a stolen vehicle detection system that came with the car when it was purchased. Would the sending of a radio signal to activate this system constitute a trespass to chattels? Trespass to chattels has traditionally required a physical touching of the property. In recent years, courts have wrestled with the application of this old tort in cases involving unwanted electronic contact with computer systems, and some have held that even the transmission of electrons that occurs when a communication is sent from one computer to another is enough. But may such decisions be followed in applying the Court's trespass theory? Assuming that what matters under the Court's theory is the law of trespass as it existed at the time of the adoption of the Fourth Amendment, do these recent decisions represent a change in the law or simply the application of the old tort to new situations?

IV

A

The *Katz* expectation-of-privacy test avoids the problems and complications noted above, but it is not without its own difficulties. * * * [J]udges are apt to confuse their own expectations of privacy with those of the hypothetical reasonable person to which the Katz test looks. In addition, the *Katz* test rests on the assumption that this hypothetical reasonable person has a well-developed and stable set of privacy expectations. But technology can change those expectations. Dramatic technological change may lead to periods in which popular expectations are in flux and may ultimately produce significant changes in popular attitudes. New technology may provide increased convenience or security at the expense of privacy, and many people may find the tradeoff worthwhile. And even if the public does not welcome the diminution of privacy that new technology entails, they may eventually reconcile themselves to this development as inevitable.

On the other hand, concern about new intrusions on privacy may spur the enactment of legislation to protect against these intrusions. This is what ultimately happened with respect to wiretapping. After *Katz*, Congress did not leave it to the courts to develop a body of Fourth Amendment case law governing that complex subject. Instead, Congress promptly enacted a comprehensive statute, and since that time, the regulation of wiretapping has been governed primarily by statute and not by case law. * * *

B

Recent years have seen the emergence of many new devices that permit the monitoring of a person's movements. In some locales, closed-circuit television video monitoring is becoming ubiquitous. On toll roads, automatic toll collection systems create a precise record of the movements of motorists who choose to make use of that convenience. Many motorists purchase cars that are equipped with devices that permit a central station to ascertain the car's location at any time so that roadside assistance may be provided if needed and the car may be found if it is stolen.

Perhaps most significant, cell phones and other wireless devices now permit wireless carriers to track and record the location of users—and as of June 2011, it has been reported, there were more than 322 million wireless devices in use in the United States. For older phones, the accuracy of the location information depends on the density of the tower network, but new "smart phones," which are equipped with a GPS device, permit more precise tracking. * * * Similarly, phone-location-tracking services are offered as "social" tools, allowing consumers to find (or to avoid) others who enroll in these services. The availability and use of these and other new devices will continue to shape the average person's expectations about the privacy of his or her daily movements.

V

In the pre-computer age, the greatest protections of privacy were neither constitutional nor statutory, but practical. Traditional surveillance for any extended period of time was difficult and costly and therefore rarely undertaken. The surveillance at issue in this case—constant monitoring of the location of a vehicle for four weeks—would have required a large team of agents, multiple vehicles, and perhaps aerial assistance. Only an investigation of unusual importance could have justified such an expenditure of law enforcement resources. Devices like the one used in the present case, however, make long-term monitoring relatively easy and cheap. In circumstances involving dramatic technological change, the best solution to privacy concerns may be legislative. A legislative body is well situated to gauge changing public attitudes, to draw detailed lines, and to balance privacy and public safety in a comprehensive way.

To date, however, Congress and most States have not enacted statutes regulating the use of GPS tracking technology for law enforcement purposes. The best that we can do in this case is to apply existing Fourth Amendment doctrine and to ask whether the use of GPS tracking in a particular case involved a degree of intrusion that a reasonable person would not have anticipated.

Under this approach, relatively short-term monitoring of a person's movements on public streets accords with expectations of privacy that our society has recognized as reasonable. But the use of longer term GPS monitoring in investigations of most offenses impinges on expectations of privacy. For such offenses, society's expectation has been that law enforcement agents and others would not—and indeed, in the main, simply could not—secretly monitor and catalogue every single movement of an individual's car for a very long period. * * * We need not identify with precision the point at which the tracking of this vehicle became a search, for the line was surely crossed before the 4-week mark. Other cases may present more difficult questions. But where uncertainty exists with respect to whether a certain period of GPS surveillance is long enough to constitute a Fourth Amendment search, the police may always seek a warrant. We also need not consider whether prolonged GPS monitoring in the context of investigations involving extraordinary offenses would similarly intrude on a constitutionally protected sphere of privacy. In such cases, long-term tracking might have been mounted using previously available techniques.

* * *

For these reasons, I conclude that the lengthy monitoring that occurred in this case constituted a search under the Fourth Amendment. I therefore agree with the majority that the decision of the Court of Appeals must be affirmed.

NOTES AND QUESTIONS

1.   Which opinion—Justice Scalia's or Justice Alito's—provides a broader interpretation of the Fourth Amendment? Which opinion do you find more faithful to *stare decisis*? As a matter of public policy, which of the three opinions (including that of Justice Sotomayor), do you prefer?

2.   *Thoughts about Jones.* There may be more going on in *Jones* than just the return of the trespass doctrine to "search" analysis. Professor Orin Kerr has observed that five justices—Justices Ginsburg, Breyer, Alito, Kagan, and Sotomayor—appear ready to adopt what Professor Kerr calls the "mosaic theory" of the Fourth Amendment, which would represent a "major departure from the traditional mode of Fourth Amendment analysis." Orin S. Kerr, *The Mosaic Theory of the Fourth Amendment*, 111 Mich. L. Rev. 311 (2012):

> Fourth Amendment analysis traditionally has followed what I call the sequential approach: to analyze whether government action constitutes a Fourth Amendment search or seizure, courts take a snapshot of the act and assess it in isolation. * * *

> Consider a few examples. If an officer inserts a key into the door of a residence and then opens the door to enter, a reviewing court will first consider the act of inserting the key and then analyze the distinct act of opening the door. If an officer sees expensive stereo equipment in an apartment, moves it to see the serial number, and then records the serial number, a court will treat moving the equipment as distinct from recording the number. * * *

> The sequential approach is not merely a minor aspect of Fourth Amendment doctrine. Rather, it forms the foundation of existing search and seizure analysis. * * *

> [In contrast, the] mosaic theory requires courts to apply the Fourth Amendment search doctrine to government conduct as a collective whole rather than in isolated steps. Instead of asking if a particular act is a search, the mosaic theory asks whether a series of acts that are not searches in isolation amount to a search when considered as a group. The mosaic theory is therefore premised on aggregation * * * .

Professor Kerr is critical of the mosaic approach. What was once considered "good police work" now becomes a "cause for [constitutional] alarm." That is, the use of a number of individual non-search acts by the police to develop a case against a suspect becomes a single Fourth Amendment "search" when aggregated.

3. Julia Angwin, *FBI Turns Off Thousands of GPS Devices After Supreme Court Ruling*, Wall Street Journal, Feb. 25, 2012:

> The Supreme Court's recent ruling overturning the warrantless use of GPS tracking devices has caused a "sea change" inside the U.S. Justice Department, according to FBI General Counsel Andrew Weissmann.

> Mr. Weissmann, speaking at a University of San Francisco conference called "Big Brother in the 21st Century" on Friday, said that the court ruling prompted the FBI to turn off about 3,000 GPS tracking devices that were in use. * * *

> After the ruling, the FBI had a problem collecting the devices that it had turned off, Mr. Weissmann said. In some cases, he said, the FBI sought court orders to obtain permission to turn the devices on briefly—only in order to locate and retrieve them.

4. The most recent generation of "smart phones" have a GPS transponder that sends signals about location periodically even when the phone is turned off. Those GPS units can thus be monitored without a trespass. How do you think the Court should ultimately resolve that issue? Recently, the New Jersey Supreme Court observed that "no one buys a cell phone to share detailed information about their whereabouts with the police." Therefore, applying the state constitution, the court held that police monitoring of a person's movements by means of an individual's smart phone GPS transponder constitutes a search. State v. Earls, 70 A.3d 630 (N.J. 2013).

5. What if a State wants to subject a recidivist sex-offender to nonconsensual, life-long satellite-based monitoring (SBM), by affixing a bracelet to the offender's ankle? SBM provides continuous tracking of the geographic location of the offender and reports violations of location requirements. Is *that* a search? The North Carolina Supreme Court thought it was not a search because *Jones* "considered the propriety of a search in the context of a motion to suppress evidence," rather than monitoring in a civil context.

In Grady v. North Carolina, 575 U.S. ___, 135 S.Ct. 1368, 191 L.Ed.2d 459 (2015) (*per curiam*), the Court unanimously reversed the North Carolina courts' opinion, The Court reaffirmed earlier decisions that Fourth Amendment protections extend beyond the sphere of criminal investigations. And, therefore, "it follows that a State also conducts a search when it attaches a device to a person's body, without consent, for the purpose of tracking that individual's movements."

The Court remanded the case to the State to decide the ultimate question of constitutionality: whether the SBM constitutes an *unreasonable* search.

6. The Supreme Court—and lower courts and lawyers—now have two ways to argue that particular police conduct is a Fourth Amendment

"search." Earlier in this chapter (p. 123, Note 4) we saw that the Supreme Court, applying *Katz*-ian privacy analysis, ruled that police use of a dog trained to identify narcotics does not constitute a "search" when the dog sniffs a person's luggage at an airport, or smells the exterior of an automobile stopped on the highway. But, what if the trained canine comes to the front door of your home to smell for possible narcotics? The next case demonstrates the Court's post-*Jones* approach to this question.

FLORIDA V. JARDINES

Supreme Court of the United States, 2013.
569 U.S. ___, 133 S.Ct. 1409, 185 L.Ed.2d 495.

JUSTICE SCALIA delivered the opinion of the Court [joined by JUSTICES THOMAS, GINSBURG, SOTOMAYOR, and KAGAN].

We consider whether using a drug-sniffing dog on a homeowner's porch to investigate the contents of the home is a search within the meaning of the Fourth Amendment.

I

In 2006, Detective William Pedraja of the Miami-Dade Police Department received an unverified tip that marijuana was being grown in the home of respondent Joelis Jardines. One month later, the Department and the Drug Enforcement Administration sent a joint surveillance team to Jardines' home. Detective Pedraja was part of that team. He watched the home for fifteen minutes and saw no vehicles in the driveway or activity around the home, and could not see inside because the blinds were drawn. Detective Pedraja then approached Jardines' home accompanied by Detective Douglas Bartelt, a trained canine handler who had just arrived at the scene with his drug-sniffing dog. The dog was trained to detect the scent of marijuana, cocaine, heroin, and several other drugs, indicating the presence of any of these substances through particular behavioral changes recognizable by his handler.

Detective Bartelt had the dog on a six-foot leash, owing in part to the dog's "wild" nature, and tendency to dart around erratically while searching. As the dog approached Jardines' front porch, he apparently sensed one of the odors he had been trained to detect, and "began energetically exploring the area for the strongest point source of that odor. As Detective Bartelt explained, the dog began tracking that airborne odor by * * * tracking back and forth," engaging in what is called "bracketing," "back and forth, back and forth." Detective Bartelt gave the dog "the full six feet of the leash plus whatever safe distance [he could] give him" to do this—he testified that he needed to give the dog "as much distance as I can." And Detective Pedraja stood back while this was occurring, so that he would not get knocked over when the dog was "spinning around trying to find" the source.

After sniffing the base of the front door, the dog sat, which is the trained behavior upon discovering the odor's strongest point. Detective Bartelt then pulled the dog away from the door and returned to his vehicle. He left the scene after informing Detective Pedraja that there had been a positive alert for narcotics.

On the basis of what he had learned at the home, Detective Pedraja applied for and received a warrant to search the residence. When the warrant was executed later that day, * * * the search revealed marijuana plants, and he was charged with trafficking in cannabis.

At trial, Jardines moved to suppress the marijuana plants on the ground that the canine investigation was an unreasonable search. * * *

We granted certiorari, limited to the question of whether the officers' behavior was a search within the meaning of the Fourth Amendment.

II

The Fourth Amendment * * * establishes a simple baseline, one that for much of our history formed the exclusive basis for its protections: When "the Government obtains information by physically intruding" on persons, houses, papers, or effects, "a 'search' within the original meaning of the Fourth Amendment" has "undoubtedly occurred." *United States v. Jones,* [p. 147]. By reason of our decision in *Katz v. United States,* [p. 96], property rights "are not the sole measure of Fourth Amendment violations,"—but though *Katz* may add to the baseline, it does not subtract anything from the Amendment's protections "when the Government *does* engage in [a] physical intrusion of a constitutionally protected area."

That principle renders this case a straightforward one. The officers were gathering information in an area belonging to Jardines and immediately surrounding his house in the curtilage of the house, which we have held enjoys protection as part of the home itself. And they gathered that information by physically entering and occupying the area to engage in conduct not explicitly or implicitly permitted by the homeowner.

A

The Fourth Amendment "indicates with some precision the places and things encompassed by its protections": persons, houses, papers, and effects. The Fourth Amendment does not, therefore, prevent all investigations conducted on private property; for example, an officer may (subject to *Katz*) gather information in what we have called "open fields"—even if those fields are privately owned because such fields are not enumerated in the Amendment's text. [*Olivier,* p. 125, Note 5.]

But when it comes to the Fourth Amendment, the home is first among equals. At the Amendment's "very core" stands "the right of a man to retreat into his own home and there be free from unreasonable governmental intrusion." This right would be of little practical value if the State's agents could stand in a home's porch or side garden and trawl for evidence with impunity; the right to retreat would be significantly diminished if the police could enter a man's property to observe his repose from just outside the front window.

We therefore regard the area "immediately surrounding and associated with the home"—what our cases call the curtilage—as "part of the home itself for Fourth Amendment purposes." That principle has ancient and durable roots. Just as the distinction between the home and the open fields is as old "as the common law," so too is the identity of home and what Blackstone called the "curtilage or homestall," for the "house protects and privileges all its branches and appurtenants." This area around the home is "intimately linked to the home, both physically and psychologically," and is where "privacy expectations are most heightened."

* * * Here there is no doubt that the officers entered it: The front porch is the classic exemplar of an area adjacent to the home and "to which the activity of home life extends."

B

Since the officers' investigation took place in a constitutionally protected area, we turn to the question of whether it was accomplished through an unlicensed physical intrusion.[1] While law enforcement officers need not "shield their eyes" when passing by the home "on public thoroughfares," an officer's leave to gather information is sharply circumscribed when he steps off those thoroughfares and enters the Fourth Amendment's protected areas. In permitting, for example, visual observation of the home from "public navigable airspace," we were careful to note that it was done "in a physically nonintrusive manner." *Entick v. Carrington,* 2 Wils. K.B. 275, 95 Eng. Rep. 807 (K.B.1765), a case "undoubtedly familiar" to "every American statesman" at the time of the Founding, states the general rule clearly: "[O]ur law holds the property of every man so sacred, that no man can set his foot upon his neighbour's close without his leave." As it is undisputed that the detectives had all four of their feet and all four of their companion's firmly planted on the constitutionally protected extension of Jardines' home, the only question

---

[1] At oral argument, the State and its *amicus* the Solicitor General argued that Jardines conceded in the lower courts that the officers had a right to be where they were. This misstates the record. Jardines conceded nothing more than the unsurprising proposition that the officers could have lawfully approached his home to knock on the front door in hopes of speaking with him. Of course, that is not what they did.

is whether he had given his leave (even implicitly) for them to do so. He had not.

"A license may be implied from the habits of the country," notwithstanding the "strict rule of the English common law as to entry upon a close." We have accordingly recognized that "the knocker on the front door is treated as an invitation or license to attempt an entry, justifying ingress to the home by solicitors, hawkers and peddlers of all kinds." This implicit license typically permits the visitor to approach the home by the front path, knock promptly, wait briefly to be received, and then (absent invitation to linger longer) leave. Complying with the terms of that traditional invitation does not require fine-grained legal knowledge; it is generally managed without incident by the Nation's Girl Scouts and trick-or-treaters. Thus, a police officer not armed with a warrant may approach a home and knock, precisely because that is "no more than any private citizen might do."

But introducing a trained police dog to explore the area around the home in hopes of discovering incriminating evidence is something else. There is no customary invitation to do *that*. An invitation to engage in canine forensic investigation assuredly does not inhere in the very act of hanging a knocker.[3] To find a visitor knocking on the door is routine (even if sometimes unwelcome); to spot that same visitor exploring the front path with a metal detector, or marching his bloodhound into the garden before saying hello and asking permission, would inspire most of us to—well, call the police. The scope of a license—express or implied—is limited not only to a particular area but also to a specific purpose. * * * Here, the background social norms that invite a visitor to the front door do not invite him there to conduct a search. * * *

III

The State argues that investigation by a forensic narcotics dog by definition cannot implicate any legitimate privacy interest. The State cites for authority our decisions in *United States v. Place,* and *Illinois v. Caballes,* [pp. 123–124, Note 4], which held, respectively, that canine inspection of luggage in an airport, * * * and canine inspection of an automobile during a lawful traffic stop, do not violate the reasonable expectation of privacy described in *Katz.*

---

[3] The dissent insists that our argument must rest upon "the particular instrument that Detective Bartelt used to detect the odor of marijuana"—the dog. It is not the dog that is the problem, but the behavior that here involved use of the dog. We think a typical person would find it " 'a cause for great alarm' " * * * to find a stranger snooping about his front porch *with or without* a dog. The dissent would let the police do whatever they want by way of gathering evidence so long as they stay on the base-path, to use a baseball analogy—so long as they "stick to the path that is typically used to approach a front door, such as a paved walkway." From that vantage point they can presumably peer into the house through binoculars with impunity. That is not the law, as even the State concedes.

Just last Term [in *Jones*], we considered an argument much like this. *Jones* held that tracking an automobile's whereabouts using a physically-mounted GPS receiver is a Fourth Amendment search. The Government argued that the *Katz* standard "show[ed] that no search occurred," as the defendant had "no 'reasonable expectation of privacy'" in his whereabouts on the public roads * * *. But because the GPS receiver had been physically mounted on the defendant's automobile (thus intruding on his "effects"), we held that tracking the vehicle's movements was a search: a person's "Fourth Amendment rights do not rise or fall with the *Katz* formulation." The *Katz* reasonable-expectations test "has been *added to,* not *substituted for,*" the traditional property-based understanding of the Fourth Amendment, and so is unnecessary to consider when the government gains evidence by physically intruding on constitutionally protected areas.

Thus, we need not decide whether the officers' investigation of Jardines' home violated his expectation of privacy under *Katz.* One virtue of the Fourth Amendment's property-rights baseline is that it keeps easy cases easy. That the officers learned what they learned only by physically intruding on Jardines' property to gather evidence is enough to establish that a search occurred. * * *

* * *

The government's use of trained police dogs to investigate the home and its immediate surroundings is a "search" within the meaning of the Fourth Amendment. The judgment of the Supreme Court of Florida is therefore affirmed.

JUSTICE KAGAN, with whom JUSTICE GINSBURG and JUSTICE SOTOMAYOR join, concurring.

For me, a simple analogy clinches this case—and does so on privacy as well as property grounds. A stranger comes to the front door of your home carrying super-high-powered binoculars. He doesn't knock or say hello. Instead, he stands on the porch and uses the binoculars to peer through your windows, into your home's furthest corners. It doesn't take long (the binoculars are really very fine): In just a couple of minutes, his uncommon behavior allows him to learn details of your life you disclose to no one. Has your "visitor" trespassed on your property, exceeding the license you have granted to members of the public to, say, drop off the mail or distribute campaign flyers? Yes, he has. And has he also invaded your "reasonable expectation of privacy," by nosing into intimacies you sensibly thought protected from disclosure? Yes, of course, he has done that too.

That case is this case in every way that matters. Here, police officers came to Joelis Jardines' door with a super-sensitive instrument, which they deployed to detect things inside that they could not perceive unassisted. The equipment they used was animal, not mineral. But contra the dissent, that is of no significance in determining whether a search occurred. Detective Bartelt's dog was not your neighbor's pet, come to your porch on a leisurely stroll. * * * [D]rug-detection dogs are highly trained tools of law enforcement, geared to respond in distinctive ways to specific scents so as to convey clear and reliable information to their human partners. They are to the poodle down the street as high-powered binoculars are to a piece of plain glass. Like the binoculars, a drug-detection dog is a specialized device for discovering objects not in plain view (or plain smell). And as in the hypothetical above, that device was aimed here at a home—the most private and inviolate (or so we expect) of all the places and things the Fourth Amendment protects. Was this activity a trespass? Yes, as the Court holds today. Was it also an invasion of privacy? Yes, that as well.

The Court today treats this case under a property rubric; I write separately to note that I could just as happily have decided it by looking to Jardines' privacy interests. A decision along those lines would have looked . . . well, much like this one. It would have talked about " 'the right of a man to retreat into his own home and there be free from unreasonable governmental intrusion.' " It would have insisted on maintaining the "practical value" of that right by preventing police officers from standing in an adjacent space and "trawl[ing]" for evidence with impunity. It would have explained that " 'privacy expectations are most heightened' " in the home and the surrounding area. And it would have determined that police officers invade those shared expectations when they use trained canine assistants to reveal within the confines of a home what they could not otherwise have found there

It is not surprising that in a case involving a search of a home, property concepts and privacy concepts should so align. The law of property "naturally enough influence[s]" our "shared social expectations" of what places should be free from governmental incursions. And so the sentiment "my home is my own," while originating in property law, now also denotes a common understanding—extending even beyond that law's formal protections—about an especially private sphere. Jardines' home was his property; it was also his most intimate and familiar space. The analysis proceeding from each of those facts, as today's decision reveals, runs mostly along the same path.

I can think of only one divergence: If we had decided this case on privacy grounds, we would have realized that *Kyllo v. United States* already resolved it. The *Kyllo* Court held that police officers conducted a search when they used a thermal-imaging device to detect heat emanating from a private home, even though they committed no trespass.

Highlighting our intention to draw both a "firm" and a "bright" line at "the entrance to the house," we announced the following rule:

> "Where, as here, the Government uses a device that is not in general public use, to explore details of the home that would previously have been unknowable without physical intrusion, the surveillance is a 'search' and is presumptively unreasonable without a warrant."

That "firm" and "bright" rule governs this case: The police officers here conducted a search because they used a "device * * * not in general public use (a trained drug-detection dog) to explore details of the home" (the presence of certain substances) that they would not otherwise have discovered without entering the premises.

And again, the dissent's argument that the device is just a dog cannot change the equation. As *Kyllo* made clear, the "sense-enhancing" tool at issue may be "crude" or "sophisticated," may be old or new (drug-detection dogs actually go back * * * only a few decades), may be either smaller or bigger than a breadbox; still, "at least where (as here)" the device is not "in general public use," training it on a home violates our "minimal expectation of privacy"—an expectation "that *exists,* and that is acknowledged to be *reasonable.*"[2] That does not mean the device is off-limits, as the dissent implies, it just means police officers cannot use it to examine a home without a warrant or exigent circumstance.

With these further thoughts, suggesting that a focus on Jardines' privacy interests would make an "easy cas[e] easy" twice over, I join the Court's opinion in full.

JUSTICE ALITO, with whom THE CHIEF JUSTICE ROBERTS, JUSTICE KENNEDY, and JUSTICE BREYER join, dissenting.

The Court's decision in this important Fourth Amendment case is based on a putative rule of trespass law that is nowhere to be found in the annals of Anglo-American jurisprudence.

The law of trespass generally gives members of the public a license to use a walkway to approach the front door of a house and to remain there for a brief time. This license is not limited to persons who intend to speak to an occupant or who actually do so. (Mail carriers and persons delivering packages and flyers are examples of individuals who may

---

[2] The dissent's other principal reason for concluding that no violation of privacy occurred in this case—that police officers themselves might detect an aroma wafting from a house—works no better. If officers can smell drugs coming from a house, they can use that information; a human sniff is not a search, we can all agree. But it does not follow that a person loses his expectation of privacy in the many scents within his home that (his own nose capably tells him) are not usually detectible by humans standing outside. And indeed, *Kyllo* already decided as much. In response to an identical argument from the dissent in that case, * * * the *Kyllo* Court stated: "[* * *] The fact that equivalent information could sometimes be obtained by other means does not make lawful the use of means that violate the Fourth Amendment * * * . [* * *]."

lawfully approach a front door without intending to converse.) Nor is the license restricted to categories of visitors whom an occupant of the dwelling is likely to welcome; as the Court acknowledges, this license applies even to "solicitors, hawkers and peddlers of all kinds." And the license even extends to police officers who wish to gather evidence against an occupant (by asking potentially incriminating questions).

According to the Court, however, the police officer in this case, Detective Bartelt, committed a trespass because he was accompanied during his otherwise lawful visit to the front door of respondent's house by his dog, Franky. Where is the authority evidencing such a rule? Dogs have been domesticated for about 12,000 years; they were ubiquitous in both this country and Britain at the time of the adoption of the Fourth Amendment; and their acute sense of smell has been used in law enforcement for centuries. Yet the Court has been unable to find a single case—from the United States or any other common-law nation—that supports the rule on which its decision is based. Thus, trespass law provides no support for the Court's holding today.

The Court's decision is also inconsistent with the reasonable-expectations-of-privacy test that the Court adopted in *Katz*. A reasonable person understands that odors emanating from a house may be detected from locations that are open to the public, and a reasonable person will not count on the strength of those odors remaining within the range that, while detectible by a dog, cannot be smelled by a human.

For these reasons, I would hold that no search within the meaning of the Fourth Amendment took place in this case, and I would reverse the decision below.

I

The opinion of the Court may leave a reader with the mistaken impression that Detective Bartelt and Franky remained on respondent's property for a prolonged period of time and conducted a far-flung exploration of the front yard. But that is not what happened. * * *

A critical fact that the Court omits is that, as respondent's counsel explained at oral argument, this entire process—walking down the driveway and front path to the front door, waiting for Franky to find the strongest source of the odor, and walking back to the car—took approximately a minute or two. Thus, the amount of time that Franky and the detective remained at the front porch was even less. The Court also fails to mention that, while Detective Bartelt apparently did not personally smell the odor of marijuana coming from the house, another officer who subsequently stood on the front porch, Detective Pedraja, did notice that smell and was able to identify it.

II

The Court concludes that the conduct in this case was a search because Detective Bartelt exceeded the boundaries of the license to approach the house that is recognized by the law of trespass, but the Court's interpretation of the scope of that license is unfounded.

A

It is said that members of the public may lawfully proceed along a walkway leading to the front door of a house because custom grants them a license to do so. * * *

Of course, this license has certain spatial and temporal limits. A visitor must stick to the path that is typically used to approach a front door, such as a paved walkway. A visitor cannot traipse through the garden, meander into the backyard, or take other circuitous detours that veer from the pathway that a visitor would customarily use.

Nor, as a general matter, may a visitor come to the front door in the middle of the night without an express invitation.

Similarly, a visitor may not linger at the front door for an extended period. The license is limited to the amount of time it would customarily take to approach the door, pause long enough to see if someone is home, and (if not expressly invited to stay longer), leave.

As I understand the law of trespass and the scope of the implied license, a visitor who adheres to these limitations is not necessarily required to ring the doorbell, knock on the door, or attempt to speak with an occupant. For example, mail carriers, persons making deliveries, and individuals distributing flyers may leave the items they are carrying and depart without making any attempt to converse. A pedestrian or motorist looking for a particular address may walk up to a front door in order to check a house number that is hard to see from the sidewalk or road. A neighbor who knows that the residents are away may approach the door to retrieve an accumulation of newspapers that might signal to a potential burglar that the house is unoccupied.

As the majority acknowledges, this implied license to approach the front door extends to the police. * * * [G]athering evidence—even damning evidence—is a lawful activity that falls within the scope of the license to approach. And when officers walk up to the front door of a house, they are permitted to see, hear, and smell whatever can be detected from a lawful vantage point.

B

Detective Bartelt did not exceed the scope of the license to approach respondent's front door. He adhered to the customary path; he did not approach in the middle of the night; and he remained at the front door for only a very short period (less than a minute or two).

The Court concludes that Detective Bartelt went too far because he had the *"objectiv[e]* * * * *purpose* to conduct a search." What this means, I take it, is that anyone aware of what Detective Bartelt did would infer that his subjective purpose was to gather evidence. But if this is the Court's point, then * * * most * * * police visits would likewise constitute searches. With the exception of visits to serve warrants or civil process, police almost always approach homes with a purpose of discovering information. * * *

What the Court must fall back on, then, is the particular instrument that Detective Bartelt used to detect the odor of marijuana, namely, his dog. But in the entire body of common-law decisions, the Court has not found a single case holding that a visitor to the front door of a home commits a trespass if the visitor is accompanied by a dog on a leash. On the contrary, the common law allowed even unleashed dogs to wander on private property without committing a trespass.

The Court responds that "[i]t is not the dog that is the problem, but the behavior that here involved use of the dog." But where is the support in the law of trespass for *this* proposition? Dogs' keen sense of smell has been used in law enforcement for centuries. The antiquity of this practice is evidenced by a Scottish law from 1318 that made it a crime to "disturb a tracking dog or the men coming with it for pursuing thieves or seizing malefactors." * * *

For these reasons, the real law of trespass provides no support for the Court's holding today. While the Court claims that its reasoning has "ancient and durable roots," its trespass rule is really a newly struck counterfeit.

III

The concurring opinion attempts to provide an alternative ground for today's decision, namely, that Detective Bartelt's conduct violated respondent's reasonable expectations of privacy. * * * I see no basis for concluding that the occupants of a dwelling have a reasonable expectation of privacy in odors that emanate from the dwelling and reach spots where members of the public may lawfully stand.

It is clear that the occupant of a house has no reasonable expectation of privacy with respect to odors that can be smelled by human beings who are standing in such places. And, I would not draw a line between odors that can be smelled by humans and those that are detectible only by dogs.

Consider the situation from the point of view of the occupant of a building in which marijuana is grown or methamphetamine is manufactured. Would such an occupant reason as follows? "I know that odors may emanate from my building and that atmospheric conditions, such as the force and direction of the wind, may affect the strength of those odors when they reach a spot where members of the public may lawfully stand. I also know that some people have a much more acute sense of smell than others, and I have no idea who might be standing in one of the spots in question when the odors from my house reach that location. In addition, I know that odors coming from my building, when they reach these locations, may be strong enough to be detected by a dog. But I am confident that they will be so faint that they cannot be smelled by any human being." Such a finely tuned expectation would be entirely unrealistic, and I see no evidence that society is prepared to recognize it as reasonable.

In an attempt to show that respondent had a reasonable expectation of privacy in the odor of marijuana wafting from his house, the concurrence argues that this case is just like *Kyllo v. United States,* which held that police officers conducted a search when they used a thermal imaging device to detect heat emanating from a house. This Court, however, has already rejected the argument that the use of a drug-sniffing dog is the same as the use of a thermal imaging device. * * *

Contrary to the interpretation propounded by the concurrence, *Kyllo* is best understood as a decision about the use of new technology. The *Kyllo* Court focused on the fact that the thermal imaging device was a form of "sense-enhancing technology" that was "not in general public use," and it expressed concern that citizens would be "at the mercy of advancing technology" if its use was not restricted. A dog, however, is not a new form of "technology" or a "device." And, as noted, the use of dogs' acute sense of smell in law enforcement dates back many centuries. * * *

The concurrence's *Kyllo*-based approach would have a much wider reach. When the police used the thermal imaging device in *Kyllo,* they were on a public street, and "committed no trespass." Therefore, if a dog's nose is just like a thermal imaging device for Fourth Amendment purposes, a search would occur if a dog alerted while on a public sidewalk or in the corridor of an apartment building. And the same would be true if the dog was trained to sniff, not for marijuana, but for more dangerous quarry, such as explosives or for a violent fugitive or kidnaped child. I see no ground for hampering legitimate law enforcement in this way.

IV

The conduct of the police officer in this case did not constitute a trespass and did not violate respondent's reasonable expectations of privacy. I would hold that this conduct was not a search, and I therefore respectfully dissent.

NOTES AND QUESTIONS

1.   Does this case make you more, or less, inclined to favor the direction Justice Scalia took in *Jones* in returning the Court's "search" analysis to pre-*Katz* trespass analysis? As a matter of *Katz* analysis exclusively, how do you believe this case should have been resolved?

2.   In light of *Jardines*, would the police have conducted a search if they had used Franky to walk through the second floor of an apartment building sniffing for the odor of marijuana? See State v. Nguyen, 841 N.W. 676 (N.D. 2013).

What if Franky had placed his paws on a vehicle (without the car driver's consent) and alerted the officer to a hidden cache of marijuana in the car trunk? See United States v. Thomas, 726 F.3d 1086 (9th Cir. 2013).

B. WHAT IS A "SEIZURE"?

UNITED STATES V. KARO

Supreme Court of the United States, 1984.
468 U.S. 705, 104 S.Ct. 3296, 82 L.Ed.2d 530.

JUSTICE WHITE delivered the opinion of the Court [joined by CHIEF JUSTICE BURGER, and JUSTICES BLACKMUN, POWELL, REHNQUIST, and O'CONNOR (as to the seizure issue)].

In *United States v. Knotts*, 460 U.S. 276, 103 S.Ct. 1081, 75 L.Ed.2d 55 (1983), we held that the warrantless monitoring of an electronic tracking device ("beeper") inside a container of chemicals did not violate the Fourth Amendment when it revealed no information that could not have been obtained through visual surveillance. In this case, we are called upon to address [a question] * * * left unresolved in *Knotts*: * * * whether installation of a beeper in a container of chemicals with the consent of the original owner constitutes a * * * seizure within the meaning of the Fourth Amendment when the container is delivered to a buyer having no knowledge of the presence of the beeper * * * .

I

In August 1980 Agent Rottinger of the Drug Enforcement Administration (DEA) learned that respondents James Karo, Richard Horton, and William Harley had ordered 50 gallons of ether from Government informant Carl Muehlenweg of Graphic Photo Design in Albuquerque, N. M. Muehlenweg told Rottinger that the ether was to be used to extract cocaine from clothing that had been imported into the United States. * * * With Muehlenweg's consent, agents substituted their own can containing a beeper for one of the cans in the shipment and then had all 10 cans painted to give them a uniform appearance. * * *

II

* * * It is clear that the actual placement of the beeper into the can violated no one's Fourth Amendment rights. The can into which the beeper was placed belonged at the time to the DEA * * * . The ether and the original 10 cans, on the other hand, belonged to, and were in the possession of, Muehlenweg, who had given his consent to any invasion of those items that occurred. Thus, even if there had been no substitution of cans and the agents had placed the beeper into one of the original 10 cans, Muehlenweg's consent was sufficient to validate the placement of the beeper in the can.

The Court of Appeals acknowledged that before Karo took control of the ether "the DEA and Muehlenweg presumably could do with the can and ether whatever they liked without violating Karo's rights." It did not hold that the actual placement of the beeper into the ether can violated the Fourth Amendment. Instead, it held that the violation occurred at the time the beeper-laden can was transferred to Karo. * * *

We * * * do not believe that the transfer of the container constituted a seizure. A "seizure" of property occurs when "there is some meaningful interference with an individual's possessory interests in that property." [*United States v. Jacobsen*, 466 U.S. 109, 104 S.Ct. 1652, 80 L.Ed.2d 85 (1984).] Although the can may have contained an unknown and unwanted foreign object, it cannot be said that anyone's possessory interest was interfered with in a meaningful way. At most, there was a technical trespass on the space occupied by the beeper. * * * Of course, if the presence of a beeper in the can constituted a seizure merely because of its occupation of space, it would follow that the presence of any object, regardless of its nature, would violate the Fourth Amendment. * * * .

[The concurring opinion of JUSTICE O'CONNOR, with whom JUSTICE REHNQUIST joined, is omitted.]

JUSTICE STEVENS, with whom JUSTICE BRENNAN and JUSTICE MARSHALL join, [dissented as to the seizure issue]. * * *

I

The attachment of the beeper, in my judgment, constituted a "seizure." The owner of property, of course, has a right to exclude from it all the world, including the Government, and a concomitant right to use it exclusively for his own purposes. When the Government attaches an electronic monitoring device to that property, it infringes that exclusionary right; in a fundamental sense it has converted the property to its own use. Surely such an invasion is an "interference" with possessory rights; the right to exclude, which attached as soon as the can respondents purchased was delivered, had been infringed. That interference is also "meaningful"; the character of the property is profoundly different when infected with an electronic bug than when it is entirely germ free. * * *

* * * By attaching the beeper and using the container to conceal it, the Government in the most fundamental sense was asserting "dominion and control" over the property—the power to use the property for its own purposes. And "assert[ing] dominion and control" is a "seizure" in the most basic sense of that term. * * *

NOTES AND QUESTIONS

1.   Reconsider *United States v. Jones* (p. 147). Was the installation of the GPS tracking device a seizure? In *Jones*, the Supreme Court requested the parties to brief the following issue: "Whether the government violated the Fourth Amendment by installing the tracking device without a warrant or consent." If the Court had focused on the Fourth Amendment "seizure" question, rather than analyzing the facts under "search" analysis, was there a way to distinguish it from *Karo* and rule that it *was* a seizure? If they had so determined, what would be the practical implications?

2.   Suppose that a police officer, properly inside a suspect's home, picks up a stereo turntable in order to record the serial number printed on the bottom. Is this a seizure of the turntable? See *Arizona v. Hicks*, Chapter 4.

3.   *Problem.* A package is shipped from outside the country to the United States containing a photo album and cocaine. Aware of this, the government takes custody of the package when it arrives in the country. It holds it for ten days until an electronic beeper can be hidden in the cover of the photo album, after which the package is delivered to the intended recipient. Seizure? See State v. Kelly, 68 Haw. 213, 708 P.2d 820 (1985).

4.   *Objects subject to seizure.* Law enforcement officers may seize what they have probable cause to believe is criminal evidence. Three categories of seizable items are: (1) contraband (evidence that may not lawfully be possessed by a private party); (2) fruits of a crime; and (3) instrumentalities used in the commission of an offense (*e.g.*, a weapon, an automobile for the get-away, etc.).

A fourth category of property is so-called "mere evidence," *i.e.*, an item of value to the police solely because it will help in the apprehension or conviction of a person for an offense. An example is a blood stained shirt in a homicide investigation. The item is not contraband, a fruit of the murder, or a criminal instrumentality. Its usefulness to law enforcement officers is limited to what it may provide in the way of evidence—such as the blood type of the killer—connecting a suspect to the crime.

Until 1967, "mere evidence" could not be seized by the police. Gouled v. United States, 255 U.S. 298, 41 S.Ct. 261, 65 L.Ed. 647 (1921). The Court's reasoning was that the Government could only seize property if it asserted a property interest superior to that of the possessor of the property. For reasons that need not detain us now, the Government was said to have a superior property interest in contraband and fruits and instrumentalities of criminal activity, but not as to "mere evidence."

The Supreme Court abandoned the "mere evidence" rule in 1967. It concluded that the doctrine was indefensible in light of the then-developing privacy principles of the Fourth Amendment. Warden v. Hayden, 387 U.S. 294, 87 S.Ct. 1642, 18 L.Ed.2d 782 (1967). Therefore, today (assuming sufficient grounds to do so) the police may seize contraband, fruits of a crime, criminal instrumentalities, as well as "mere evidence" (evidence that "will aid in a particular apprehension or conviction").

5. *Seizure of persons.* *Karo* involved seizure of property, but what constitutes a seizure of a person? According to the Supreme Court, "the quintessential 'seizure of the person' under our Fourth Amendment jurisprudence" is an arrest. California v. Hodari D., 499 U.S. 621, 111 S.Ct. 1547, 113 L.Ed.2d 690 (1991).

Although an arrest is the "quintessential" seizure of a person, a person can be "seized" for Fourth Amendment purposes short of an arrest. In Terry v. Ohio, 392 U.S. 1, 88 S.Ct. 1868, 20 L.Ed.2d 889 (1968), the Court stated that a seizure occurs "when the officer, by means of physical force or show of authority has *in some way* restrained the liberty of a citizen" (emphasis added). Even a temporary detention of a person by an officer constitutes a Fourth Amendment seizure. The law regarding seizures of persons is better understood in the context of other Fourth Amendment doctrines considered in the next chapter.

CHAPTER 4

THE SUBSTANCE OF THE
FOURTH AMENDMENT

■ ■ ■

A. PROBABLE CAUSE

Introductory Comment

The Fourth Amendment prohibits *unreasonable* searches and seizures. Very generally speaking, this means that searches and seizures must be supported by probable cause. Put differently, a search or seizure conducted *in the absence* of probable cause ordinarily is considered an *unreasonable one.* As the Court has put it, "probable cause" is the "traditional standard" of the Fourth Amendment. Arizona v. Hicks, 480 U.S. 321, 107 S.Ct. 1149, 94 L.Ed.2d 347 (1987).

It is easier to state the definition of "probable cause" than it is to determine whether it exists in a particular case. Probable cause to arrest "exists where 'the facts and circumstances within [the officers'] knowledge and of which they [have] reasonably trustworthy information [are] sufficient in themselves to warrant a man of reasonable caution in the belief that' *an offense has been or is being committed*" by the person to be arrested. Brinegar v. United States, 338 U.S. 160, 69 S.Ct. 1302, 93 L.Ed. 1879 (1949) (quoting Carroll v. United States, 267 U.S. 132, 45 S.Ct. 280, 69 L.Ed. 543 (1925)) (emphasis added). The same definition applies to "probable cause to search," except that the italicized language is replaced with "evidence subject to seizure will be found in the place to be searched."

Procedurally, the issue of probable cause typically arises in one of two circumstances. First, the police may apply to a magistrate for an arrest or search warrant. Warrants constitutionally may only be issued if there is probable cause to make the arrest or conduct the search. Therefore, the police must set out for the magistrate, under oath, the information in their possession that they believe justifies issuance of the warrant, *i.e.,* the facts that constitute probable cause for the arrest or search.

Alternatively, the police may conduct an arrest or search without a warrant. Assuming that it results in seizure of criminal evidence, the defendant may seek to have this evidence excluded from the trial at a suppression hearing. The defendant may argue that the police acted in violation of the Fourth Amendment because they did not obtain a warrant (an issue to which we will turn shortly), or she may argue that, warrant issues aside, the police lacked probable cause. In the latter case, the judge must decide whether the police had adequate evidence—probable cause—*before* they conducted the warrantless search or arrest. She must ask herself, in essence, "If the police *had* sought a warrant, would it properly have been granted?"

SPINELLI V. UNITED STATES

Supreme Court of the United States, 1969.
393 U.S. 410, 89 S.Ct. 584, 21 L.Ed.2d 637.

MR. JUSTICE HARLAN delivered the opinion of the Court [joined by CHIEF JUSTICE WARREN, and JUSTICES DOUGLAS, BRENNAN and WHITE].

William Spinelli was convicted under 18 U. S. C. § 1952 of traveling to St. Louis, Missouri, from a nearby Illinois suburb with the intention of conducting gambling activities proscribed by Missouri law. At every appropriate stage in the proceedings in the lower courts, the petitioner challenged the constitutionality of the warrant which authorized the FBI search that uncovered the evidence necessary for his conviction. * * * Believing it desirable that the principles of *Aguilar* [*v. Texas*, 378 U.S. 108, 84 S.Ct. 1509, 12 L.Ed.2d 723 (1964)] should be further explicated, we granted certiorari * * * . For reasons that follow we reverse.

In *Aguilar*, a search warrant had issued upon an affidavit of police officers who swore only that they had "received reliable information from a credible person and do believe" that narcotics were being illegally stored on the described premises. While recognizing that the constitutional requirement of probable cause can be satisfied by hearsay information, this Court held the affidavit inadequate for two reasons. First, the application failed to set forth any of the "underlying circumstances" necessary to enable the magistrate independently to judge of the validity of the informant's conclusion that the narcotics were where he said they were. Second, the affiant-officers did not attempt to support their claim that their informant was " 'credible' or his information 'reliable.' " The Government is, however, quite right in saying that the FBI affidavit in the present case is more ample than that in *Aguilar*. Not only does it contain a report from an anonymous informant, but it also contains a report of an independent FBI investigation which is said to corroborate the informant's tip. We are, then, required to delineate the manner in which *Aguilar*'s two-pronged test should be applied in these circumstances.

In essence, the affidavit * * * contained the following allegations:

1.   The FBI had kept track of Spinelli's movements on five days during the month of August 1965. On four of these occasions, Spinelli was seen crossing one of two bridges leading from Illinois into St. Louis, Missouri, between 11 a.m. and 12:15 p.m. On four of the five days, Spinelli was also seen parking his car in a lot used by residents of an apartment house at 1108 Indian Circle Drive in St. Louis, between 3:30 p.m. and 4:45 p.m. On one day, Spinelli was followed further and seen to enter a particular apartment in the building.

2.   An FBI check with the telephone company revealed that this apartment contained two telephones listed under the name of Grace P. Hagen, and carrying the numbers WYdown 4–0029 and WYdown 4–0136.

3.   The application stated that "William Spinelli is known to this affiant and to federal law enforcement agents and local law enforcement agents as a bookmaker, an associate of bookmakers, a gambler, and an associate of gamblers."

4.   Finally, it was stated that the FBI "has been informed by a confidential reliable informant that William Spinelli is operating a handbook and accepting wagers and disseminating wagering information by means of the telephones which have been assigned the numbers WYdown 4–0029 and WYdown 4–0136."

There can be no question that the last item mentioned, detailing the informant's tip, has a fundamental place in this warrant application. Without it, probable cause could not be established. The first two items reflect only innocent-seeming activity and data. Spinelli's travels to and from the apartment building and his entry into a particular apartment on one occasion could hardly be taken as bespeaking gambling activity; and there is surely nothing unusual about an apartment containing two separate telephones. Many a householder indulges himself in this petty luxury. Finally, the allegation that Spinelli was "known" to the affiant and to other federal and local law enforcement officers as a gambler and an associate of gamblers is but a bald and unilluminating assertion of suspicion that is entitled to no weight in appraising the magistrate's decision. *Nathanson v. United States*, 290 U.S. 41, 46, 54 S.Ct. 11, 12, 78 L.Ed. 159 (1933).

So much indeed the Government does not deny. Rather, * * * the Government claims that the informant's tip gives a suspicious color to the FBI's reports detailing Spinelli's innocent-seeming conduct and that, conversely, the FBI's surveillance corroborates the informant's tip, thereby entitling it to more weight. It is true, of course, that the magistrate is obligated to render a judgment based upon a common-sense reading of the entire affidavit. We believe, however, that the "totality of circumstances" approach taken by the Court of Appeals paints with too broad a brush. Where, as here, the informer's tip is a necessary element in a finding of probable cause, its proper weight must be determined by a more precise analysis.

The informer's report must first be measured against *Aguilar*'s standards so that its probative value can be assessed. If the tip is found inadequate under *Aguilar*, the other allegations which corroborate the information contained in the hearsay report should then be considered. At this stage as well, however, the standards enunciated in *Aguilar* must inform the magistrate's decision. He must ask: Can it fairly be said that the tip, even when certain parts of it have been corroborated by independent sources, is as trustworthy as a tip which would pass *Aguilar*'s tests without independent corroboration? *Aguilar* is relevant at this stage of the inquiry as well because the tests it establishes were designed to implement the long-standing principle that probable cause must be determined by a "neutral and detached magistrate," and not by "the officer engaged in the often competitive enterprise of ferreting out crime." A magistrate cannot be said to have properly discharged his constitutional duty if he relies on an informer's tip which—even when partially corroborated—is not as reliable as one which passes *Aguilar*'s requirements when standing alone.

Applying these principles to the present case, we first consider the weight to be given the informer's tip when it is considered apart from the rest of the affidavit. It is clear that a Commissioner could not credit it without abdicating his constitutional function. Though the affiant swore that his confidant was "reliable," he offered the magistrate no reason in support of this conclusion. Perhaps even more important is the fact that *Aguilar*'s other test has not been satisfied. The tip does not contain a sufficient statement of the underlying circumstances from which the informer concluded that Spinelli was running a bookmaking operation. We are not told how the FBI's source received his information—it is not alleged that the informant personally observed Spinelli at work or that he had ever placed a bet with him. Moreover, if the informant came by the information indirectly, he did not explain why his sources were reliable. In the absence of a statement detailing the manner in which the information was gathered, it is especially important that the tip describe the accused's criminal activity in sufficient detail that the magistrate may know that he is relying on something more substantial than a casual rumor circulating in the underworld or an accusation based merely on an individual's general reputation.

The detail provided by the informant in *Draper v. United States*, 358 U.S. 307, 79 S.Ct. 329, 3 L.Ed.2d 327 (1959), provides a suitable benchmark. While Hereford, the Government's informer in that case, did not state the way in which he had obtained his information, he reported that Draper had gone to Chicago the day before by train and that he would return to Denver by train with three ounces of heroin on one of two specified mornings. Moreover, Hereford went on to describe, with minute particularity, the clothes that Draper would be wearing upon his arrival at the Denver station. A magistrate, when confronted with such detail, could reasonably infer that the informant had gained his information in a reliable way.[5] Such an inference cannot be made in the present case. Here, the only facts supplied were that Spinelli was using two specified telephones and that these phones were being used in gambling operations. This meager report could easily have been obtained from an offhand remark heard at a neighborhood bar.

Nor do we believe that the patent doubts *Aguilar* raises as to the report's reliability are adequately resolved by a consideration of the allegations detailing the FBI's independent investigative efforts. At most, these allegations indicated that Spinelli could have used the telephones specified by the informant for some purpose. This cannot by itself be said to support both the inference that the informer was generally trustworthy and that he had made his charge against Spinelli on the basis of information obtained in a reliable way. Once again, *Draper* provides a relevant comparison. Independent police work in that case corroborated much more than one small detail that had been provided by the informant. There, the police, upon meeting the inbound Denver train on the second morning specified by informer Hereford, saw a man whose dress corresponded precisely to Hereford's detailed description. It was then apparent that the informant had not been fabricating his report out of whole cloth; since the report was of the sort which in common experience may be recognized as having been obtained in a reliable way, it was perfectly clear that probable cause had been established.

We conclude, then, that in the present case the informant's tip—even when corroborated to the extent indicated—was not sufficient to provide the basis for a finding of probable cause. This is not to say that the tip was so insubstantial that it could not properly have counted in the magistrate's determination. Rather, it needed some further support. When we look to the other parts of the application, however, we find nothing alleged which would permit the suspicions engendered by the informant's report to ripen into a judgment that a crime was probably being committed. * * * [T]he allegations detailing the FBI's surveillance of Spinelli and its investigation of the telephone company records contain no suggestion of criminal conduct when taken by themselves—and they are

---

[5] While *Draper* involved the question whether the police had probable cause for an arrest without a warrant, the analysis required for an answer to this question is basically similar to that demanded of a magistrate when he considers whether a search warrant should issue.

not endowed with an aura of suspicion by virtue of the informer's tip. Nor do we find that the FBI's reports take on a sinister color when read in light of common knowledge that bookmaking is often carried on over the telephone and from premises ostensibly used by others for perfectly normal purposes. Such an argument would carry weight in a situation in which the premises contain an unusual number of telephones or abnormal activity is observed, but it does not fit this case where neither of these factors is present. All that remains to be considered is the flat statement that Spinelli was "known" to the FBI and others as a gambler. But just as a simple assertion of police suspicion is not itself a sufficient basis for a magistrate's finding of probable cause, we do not believe it may be used to give additional weight to allegations that would otherwise be insufficient.

The affidavit, then, falls short of the standards set forth in *Aguilar*, *Draper*, and our other decisions that give content to the notion of probable cause. * * * [W]e cannot sustain this warrant without diluting important safeguards that assure that the judgment of a disinterested judicial officer will interpose itself between the police and the citizenry.

The judgment of the Court of Appeals is reversed * * * . * * *

MR. JUSTICE MARSHALL took no part in the consideration or decision of this case. * * *

MR. JUSTICE WHITE, concurring.

An investigator's affidavit that he has seen gambling equipment being moved into a house at a specified address will support the issuance of a search warrant. The oath affirms the honesty of the statement and negatives the lie or imagination. Personal observation attests to the facts asserted—that there is gambling equipment on the premises at the named address.

But if the officer simply avers, without more, that there is gambling paraphernalia on certain premises, the warrant should not issue, even though the belief of the officer is an honest one, as evidenced by his oath, and even though the magistrate knows him to be an experienced, intelligent officer who has been reliable in the past. This much was settled in *Nathanson v. United States*, [*supra*,] where the Court held insufficient an officer's affidavit swearing he had cause to believe that there was illegal liquor on the premises for which the warrant was sought. The unsupported assertion or belief of the officer does not satisfy the requirement of probable cause. What is missing in *Nathanson* and like cases is a statement of the basis for the affiant's believing the facts contained in the affidavit—the good "cause" which the officer in *Nathanson* said he had. If an officer swears that there is gambling equipment at a certain address, the possibilities are (1) that he has seen the equipment; (2) that he has observed or perceived facts from which the presence of the equipment may reasonably be inferred; and (3) that he has obtained the information from someone else. If (1) is true, the affidavit is good. But in (2), the affidavit is insufficient unless the perceived facts are given, for it is the magistrate, not the officer, who is to judge the existence of probable cause. With respect to (3), where the officer's information is hearsay, no warrant should issue absent good cause for crediting that hearsay. Because an affidavit asserting, without more, the location of gambling equipment at a particular address does not claim personal observation of any of the facts by the officer, and because of the likelihood that the information came from an unidentified third party, affidavits of this type are unacceptable.

Neither should the warrant issue if the officer states that there is gambling equipment in a particular apartment and that his information comes from an informant, named or unnamed, since the honesty of the informant and the basis for his report are unknown. Nor would the missing elements be completely supplied by the officer's oath that the informant has often furnished reliable information in the past. This attests to the honesty of the informant, but *Aguilar v. Texas, supra,* requires something more—did the information come from observation, or did the informant in turn receive it from another? Absent additional facts for believing the informant's report, his assertion stands no better than the oath of the officer to the same effect. Indeed, if the affidavit of an officer, known by the magistrate to be honest and experienced, stating that gambling equipment is located in a certain building is unacceptable, it would be quixotic if a similar statement from an honest informant were found to furnish probable cause. * * *

If the affidavit rests on hearsay—an informant's report—what is necessary under *Aguilar* is one of two things: the informant must declare either (1) that he has himself seen or perceived the fact or facts asserted; or (2) that his information is hearsay, but there is good reason for believing it—perhaps one of the usual grounds for crediting hearsay information. The first presents few problems: since the report, although hearsay, purports to be first-hand observation, remaining doubt centers on the honesty of the informant, and that worry is dissipated by the officer's previous experience with the informant. The other basis for accepting the informant's report is more complicated. But if, for example, the informer's hearsay comes from one of the actors in the crime in the nature of admission against interest, the affidavit giving this information should be held sufficient.

I am inclined to agree with the majority that there are limited special circumstances in which an "honest" informant's report, if sufficiently detailed, will in effect verify itself—that is, the magistrate when confronted with such detail could reasonably infer that the informant had gained his information in a reliable way. Detailed information may sometimes imply that the informant himself has observed the facts. Suppose an informant with whom an officer has had satisfactory experience states that there is gambling equipment in the living room of a specified apartment and describes in detail not only the equipment itself but also the appointments and furnishings in the apartment. Detail like this, if true at all, must rest on personal observation either of the informant or of someone else. If the latter, we know nothing of the third person's honesty or sources; he may be making a wholly false report. But it is arguable that on these facts it was the informant himself who has perceived the facts, for the information reported is not usually the subject of casual, day-to-day conversation. Because the informant is honest and it is probable that he has viewed the facts, there is probable cause for the issuance of a warrant.

So too in the special circumstances of *Draper v. United States*, the kind of information related by the informant is not generally sent ahead of a person's arrival in a city except to those who are intimately connected with making careful arrangements for meeting him. The informant, posited as honest, somehow had the reported facts, very likely from one of the actors in the plan, or as one of them himself. The majority's suggestion is that a warrant could have been obtained based only on the informer's report. I am inclined to agree, although it seems quite plain that if it may be so easily inferred from the affidavit that the informant has himself observed the facts or has them from an actor in the event, no possible harm could come from requiring a statement to that effect, thereby removing the difficult and recurring questions which arise in such situations.

Of course, *Draper* itself did not proceed on this basis. Instead, the Court pointed out that when the officer saw a person getting off the train at the specified time, dressed and conducting himself precisely as the informant had predicted, all but the critical fact with respect to possessing narcotics had then been verified and for that reason the officer had "reasonable grounds" to believe also that Draper was carrying narcotics. Unquestionably, verification of arrival time, dress, and gait reinforced the honesty of the informant—he had not reported a made-up story. But if what *Draper* stands for is that the existence of the tenth and critical fact is made sufficiently probable to justify the issuance of a warrant by verifying nine other facts coming from the same source, I have my doubts about that case.

* * * [T]he proposition is not that the tenth fact may be logically inferred from the other nine or that the tenth fact is usually found in conjunction with the other nine. No one would suggest that just anyone getting off the 10:30 train dressed as Draper was, with a brisk walk and carrying a zipper bag, should be arrested for carrying narcotics. The thrust of *Draper* is not that the verified facts have independent

significance with respect to proof of the tenth. The argument instead relates to the reliability of the source: because an informant is right about some things, he is more probably right about other facts, usually the critical, unverified facts. * * *

The tension between *Draper* and the *Nathanson-Aguilar* line of cases is evident from the course followed by the majority opinion. First, it is held that the report from a reliable informant that Spinelli is using two telephones with specified numbers to conduct a gambling business plus Spinelli's reputation in police circles as a gambler does not add up to probable cause. This is wholly consistent with *Aguilar* and *Nathanson*: the informant did not reveal whether he had personally observed the facts or heard them from another and, if the latter, no basis for crediting the hearsay was presented. Nor were the facts, as Mr. Justice Harlan says, of such a nature that they normally would be obtainable only by the personal observation of the informant himself. The police, however, did not stop with the informant's report. Independently, they established the existence of two phones having the given numbers and located them in an apartment house which Spinelli was regularly frequenting away from his home. There remained little question but that Spinelli was using the phones, and it was a fair inference that the use was not for domestic but for business purposes. The informant had claimed the business involved gambling. Since his specific information about Spinelli using two phones with particular numbers had been verified, did not his allegation about gambling thereby become sufficiently more believable if the *Draper* principle is to be given any scope at all? I would think so, particularly since the information from the informant which was verified was not neutral, irrelevant information but was material to proving the gambling allegation: two phones with different numbers in an apartment used away from home indicates a business use in an operation, like bookmaking, where multiple phones are needed. The *Draper* approach would reasonably justify the issuance of a warrant in this case, particularly since the police had some awareness of Spinelli's past activities. The majority, however, while seemingly embracing *Draper*, confines that case to its own facts. Pending full-scale reconsideration of that case, on the one hand, or of the *Nathanson-Aguilar* cases on the other, I join the opinion of the Court and the judgment of reversal, especially since a vote to affirm would produce an equally divided Court.

[The dissenting opinions of JUSTICES BLACK, FORTAS, and STEWART are omitted.]

NOTES AND QUESTIONS

1. Suppose that your professor announced in class that the dean of your law school "has cocaine in her office, which she uses every morning." Based exclusively on this statement, would you believe your professor's

claim? If not, why not? If you were a magistrate, and if you were told this under oath by your professor, would you issue a warrant to search the dean's office? If not, what more information would you demand? Are the factors you would consider in making a judgment in your dean's case similar to those set out by the Supreme Court in *Spinelli* and *Aguilar* (discussed in *Spinelli*)?

2.   One highly respected Maryland judge explained the magistrate's job, as set out in *Aguilar-Spinelli*, this way:

> The simple thrust of these decisions is that whatever rules govern the evaluation of information from the primary source—the affiant—govern also the evaluation of information from the secondary source—the non-swearing, non-appearing, off-warrant declarant, *i.e.*, the informant. Whether the magistrate is dealing with a primary, a secondary or even, theoretically, a tertiary source, he must still (1) assess the credibility of that source and (2) then weigh the information furnished if he believes it to be true.

> Whether the information being evaluated is the direct observation of the affiant or is hearsay information, the issuing magistrate is required to perform the same intellectual surgery. In determining the existence *vel non* of probable cause, the magistrate must make two distinct determinations. * * * He must:

>> (1) Evaluate the truthfulness of the source of the information; and

>> (2) Evaluate the adequacy of the factual premises furnished by that source to support the validity of the source's conclusion.

> In the first instance, he is judging the integrity of a person. In the second instance, he is judging the logic of a proposition. These functions are distinct. They are the direct analogues of those other functions performed by the ultimate finder of fact who (1) assesses the credibility of a witness and (2) then assesses the weight to be given the testimony of that witness.

Charles E. Moylan, Jr., *Hearsay and Probable Cause: An* Aguilar *and* Spinelli *Primer*, 25 Mercer L. Rev. 741, 750–51 (1974).

3.   What does Justice Harlan mean by the "two-pronged" test of *Aguilar*? What are the prongs?

4.   What does Justice White mean when he says that an informant's highly detailed information, such as existed in *Draper v. United States* (discussed in *Spinelli*), "will in effect verify itself." Do you agree?

5.   In what way did police corroboration of some of the claims made by informant Hereford in *Draper* strengthen the probable cause claim? Why does corroboration of entirely innocent conduct—*e.g.*, that Draper got off a particular train dressed in a particular way—support the critical finding that he was carrying heroin on his person?

6. In determining credibility, Judge Moylan has observed that "[t]estimonials from friends, neighbors, and business associates as to [an informant's] reputation for 'truth and veracity' would be highly relevant. As a practical matter, 'stool pigeons' are neither Boy Scouts, princes of the church, nor recipients of testimonials." Moylan, *supra*, at 758. How, then, does a police officer convince a judge that the typical informant is credible? How does the officer convince the magistrate that *she* (the officer-affiant) is credible?

7. *Bobo, a police officer's friendly four-legged informant.* In United States v. Florez, 871 F.Supp. 1411 (D.N.M.1994), a police officer's dog, Bobo, sniffed luggage in a train station and alerted the officer to the supposed presence of a controlled substance inside certain suitcases. The police seized the luggage, opened it, and discovered large quantities of cocaine.

Bobo got it right, but dogs, like humans, are imperfect. As Justice Souter stated in his dissent in Illinois v. Caballes, 543 U.S. 405, 125 S.Ct. 834, 160 L.Ed.2d 842 (2005), "[t]he infallible dog * * * is a creature of legal fiction." As a dog trainer testified in *Florez, supra,* "dogs are not unlike humans, dogs can have good and bad days just like we can." Indeed, reconsider the data on "dog sniffing" recounted by Justice Souter in *Caballes* (pp. 124–125). And, note the observation of the Seventh Circuit in a recent case regarding canine Lex: "Lex is lucky the Canine Training Institute doesn't calculate class rank. If it did, Lex would have been at the bottom of the class." United States v. Bentley, 795 F.3d 630 (7th Cir. 2015). So, how *should* a court go about evaluating the reliability of the Bobos and Lexes of this world?

The United States Supreme Court recently spoke to this issue, albeit in regard to one Aldo, rather than Bobo or Lex. In Florida v. Harris, 568 U.S. ___, 133 S.Ct. 1050, 185 L.Ed.2d 61 (2013), the state supreme court stated that the fact that a dog "has been trained and certified is simply not enough to establish probable cause." It ruled that the government in such a case must present evidence of "the dog's training and certification records, * * * field performance records (including any unverified alerts) and evidence concerning the experience and training of the officer handling the dog."

The Supreme Court, per Justice Kagan, unanimously reversed the Florida court. According to the Court, "evidence of a dog's satisfactory performance in a certification or training program can itself provide sufficient reason to trust his alert." Indeed, Justice Kagan observed that evidence of certification of successful training is apt to be more useful information than records of a dog's field performance:

> Errors may abound in such records. If a dog on patrol fails to alert to a car containing drugs, the mistake usually will go undetected because the officer will not initiate a search. Field data thus may not capture a dog's false negatives. Conversely, * * * if the dog alerts to a car in which the officer finds no narcotics, the dog may have not have made a mistake at all. The dog may have detected substances that were too well hidden or present in quantities too small for the

officer to locate. Or the dog may have smelled the residual odor of drugs previously in the vehicle or on the driver's person.

Justice Kagan stated that, "[i]n short, a probable-cause hearing focusing on a dog's alert should proceed much like any other."

ILLINOIS V. GATES

Supreme Court of the United States, 1983.
462 U.S. 213, 103 S.Ct. 2317, 76 L.Ed.2d 527.

JUSTICE REHNQUIST delivered the opinion of the Court [joined by CHIEF JUSTICE BURGER, and JUSTICES BLACKMUN, POWELL, and O'CONNOR]. * * *

II

* * * Bloomingdale, Ill., is a suburb of Chicago located in Du Page County. On May 3, 1978, the Bloomingdale Police Department received by mail an anonymous handwritten letter which read as follows:

> "This letter is to inform you that you have a couple in your town who strictly make their living on selling drugs. They are Sue and Lance Gates, they live on Greenway, off Bloomingdale Rd. in the condominiums. Most of their buys are done in Florida. Sue his wife drives their car to Florida, where she leaves it to be loaded up with drugs, then Lance flys down and drives it back. Sue flys back after she drops the car off in Florida. May 3 she is driving down there again and Lance will be flying down in a few days to drive it back. At the time Lance drives the car back he has the trunk loaded with over $100,000.00 in drugs. Presently they have over $100,000.00 worth of drugs in their basement.

> "They brag about the fact they never have to work, and make their entire living on pushers.

> "I guarantee if you watch them carefully you will make a big catch. They are friends with some big drugs dealers, who visit their house often.

> "Lance & Susan Gates

> "Greenway

> "in Condominiums"

The letter was referred by the Chief of Police of the Bloomingdale Police Department to Detective Mader, who decided to pursue the tip. Mader learned, from the office of the Illinois Secretary of State, that an Illinois driver's license had been issued to one Lance Gates, residing at a stated address in Bloomingdale. He contacted a confidential informant, whose examination of certain financial records revealed a more recent address for the Gateses, and he also learned from a police officer assigned to O'Hare Airport that "L. Gates" had made a reservation on Eastern Airlines Flight 245 to West Palm Beach, Fla., scheduled to depart from Chicago on May 5 at 4:15 p.m.

Mader then made arrangements with an agent of the Drug Enforcement Administration for surveillance of the May 5 Eastern Airlines flight. The agent later reported to Mader that Gates had boarded the flight, and that federal agents in Florida had observed him arrive in West Palm Beach and take a taxi to the nearby Holiday Inn. They also reported that Gates went to a room registered to one Susan Gates and that, at 7 o'clock the next morning, Gates and an unidentified woman left the motel in a Mercury bearing Illinois license plates and drove northbound on an interstate highway frequently used by travelers to the Chicago area. In addition, the DEA agent informed Mader that the license plate number on the Mercury was registered to a Hornet station wagon owned by Gates. The agent also advised Mader that the driving time between West Palm Beach and Bloomingdale was approximately 22 to 24 hours.

Mader signed an affidavit setting forth the foregoing facts, and submitted it to a judge of the Circuit Court of Du Page County, together with a copy of the anonymous letter. The judge of that court thereupon issued a search warrant for the Gateses' residence and for their automobile. * * *

At 5:15 a.m. on March 7, only 36 hours after he had flown out of Chicago, Lance Gates, and his wife, returned to their home in Bloomingdale, driving the car in which they had left West Palm Beach some 22 hours earlier. The Bloomingdale police were awaiting them, searched the trunk of the Mercury, and uncovered approximately 350 pounds of marihuana. A search of the Gateses' home revealed marihuana, weapons, and other contraband. * * *

The Illinois Supreme Court concluded—and we are inclined to agree—that, standing alone, the anonymous letter sent to the Bloomingdale Police Department would not provide the basis for a magistrate's determination that there was probable cause to believe contraband would be found in the Gateses' car and home. The letter provides virtually nothing from which one might conclude that its author is either honest or his information reliable; likewise, the letter gives absolutely no indication of the basis for the writer's predictions regarding the Gateses' criminal activities. Something more was required, then, before a magistrate could conclude that there was probable cause to believe that contraband would be found in the Gateses' home and car. See *Aguilar v. Texas*, 378 U.S. [108, 109 n. 1, 84 S.Ct. 1509, 1511 n. 1, 12

L.Ed.2d 723 (1964)]; *Nathanson v. United States*, 290 U.S. 41, 54 S.Ct. 11, 78 L.Ed. 159 (1933).

The Illinois Supreme Court also properly recognized that Detective Mader's affidavit might be capable of supplementing the anonymous letter with information sufficient to permit a determination of probable cause. In holding that the affidavit in fact did not contain sufficient additional information to sustain a determination of probable cause, the Illinois court applied a "two-pronged test," derived from our decision in *Spinelli v. United States*, [p. 178]. The Illinois Supreme Court, like some others, apparently understood *Spinelli* as requiring that the anonymous letter satisfy each of two independent requirements before it could be relied on. According to this view, the letter, as supplemented by Mader's affidavit, first had to adequately reveal the "basis of knowledge" of the letterwriter—the particular means by which he came by the information given in his report. Second, it had to provide facts sufficiently establishing either the "veracity" of the affiant's informant, or, alternatively, the "reliability" of the informant's report in this particular case.

The Illinois court, alluding to an elaborate set of legal rules that have developed among various lower courts to enforce the "two-pronged test," found that the test had not been satisfied. First, the "veracity" prong was not satisfied because, "[t]here was simply no basis [for] conclud[ing] that the anonymous person [who wrote the letter to the Bloomingdale Police Department] was credible." The court indicated that corroboration by police of details contained in the letter might never satisfy the "veracity" prong, and in any event, could not do so if, as in the present case, only "innocent" details are corroborated. In addition, the letter gave no indication of the basis of its writer's knowledge of the Gateses' activities. * * *

We agree with the Illinois Supreme Court that an informant's "veracity," "reliability," and "basis of knowledge" are all highly relevant in determining the value of his report. We do not agree, however, that these elements should be understood as entirely separate and independent requirements to be rigidly exacted in every case, which the opinion of the Supreme Court of Illinois would imply. Rather, as detailed below, they should be understood simply as closely intertwined issues that may usefully illuminate the commonsense, practical question whether there is "probable cause" to believe that contraband or evidence is located in a particular place.

III

This totality-of-the-circumstances approach is far more consistent with our prior treatment of probable cause than is any rigid demand that specific "tests" be satisfied by every informant's tip. Perhaps the central teaching of our decisions bearing on the probable-cause standard is that it is a "practical, nontechnical conception." "In dealing with probable cause, * * * as the very name implies, we deal with probabilities. These are not technical; they are the factual and practical considerations of everyday life on which reasonable and prudent men, not legal technicians, act." * * *

As these comments illustrate, probable cause is a fluid concept—turning on the assessment of probabilities in particular factual contexts—not readily, or even usefully, reduced to a neat set of legal rules. Informants' tips doubtless come in many shapes and sizes from many different types of persons. * * * Rigid legal rules are ill-suited to an area of such diversity. * * *

(handwritten margin note: Criticism of prong 2 test.)

Moreover, the "two-pronged test" directs analysis into two largely independent channels—the informant's "veracity" or "reliability" and his "basis of knowledge." There are persuasive arguments against according these two elements such independent status. Instead, they are better understood as relevant considerations in the totality-of-the-circumstances analysis that traditionally has guided probable-cause determinations: a deficiency in one may be compensated for, in determining the overall reliability of a tip, by a strong showing as to the other, or by some other indicia of reliability.

If, for example, a particular informant is known for the unusual reliability of his predictions of certain types of criminal activities in a locality, his failure, in a particular case, to thoroughly set forth the basis of his knowledge surely should not serve as an absolute bar to a finding of probable cause based on his tip. Likewise, if an unquestionably honest citizen comes forward with a report of criminal activity—which if fabricated would subject him to criminal liability—we have found rigorous scrutiny of the basis of his knowledge unnecessary. Conversely, even if we entertain some doubt as to an informant's motives, his explicit and detailed description of alleged wrongdoing, along with a statement that the event was observed firsthand, entitles his tip to greater weight than might otherwise be the case. Unlike a totality-of-the-circumstances analysis, which permits a balanced assessment of the relative weights of all the various indicia of reliability (and unreliability) attending an informant's tip, the "two-pronged test" has encouraged an excessively technical dissection of informants' tips, with undue attention being focused on isolated issues that cannot sensibly be divorced from the other facts presented to the magistrate.

As early as *Locke v. United States*, 7 Cranch 339, 348, 3 L.Ed. 364 (1813), Chief Justice Marshall observed, in a closely related context: "[T]he term 'probable cause,' according to its usual acceptation, means less than evidence which would justify condemnation * * * . It imports a seizure made under circumstances which warrant suspicion." More recently, we stated that "the *quanta* * * * of proof" appropriate in ordinary judicial proceedings are inapplicable to the decision to issue a warrant. Finely tuned standards such as proof beyond a reasonable doubt or by a preponderance of the evidence, useful in formal trials, have no place in the magistrate's decision. While an effort to fix some general, numerically precise degree of certainty corresponding to "probable cause" may not be helpful, it is clear that "only the probability, and not a prima facie showing, of criminal activity is the standard of probable cause."

We also have recognized that affidavits "are normally drafted by nonlawyers in the midst and haste of a criminal investigation. Technical requirements of elaborate specificity once exacted under common law pleadings have no proper place in this area." Likewise, search and arrest warrants long have been issued by persons who are neither lawyers nor judges, and who certainly do not remain abreast of each judicial refinement of the nature of "probable cause." The rigorous inquiry into the *Spinelli* prongs and the complex superstructure of evidentiary and analytical rules that some have seen implicit in our *Spinelli* decision, cannot be reconciled with the fact that many warrants are—quite properly—issued on the basis of nontechnical, common-sense judgments of laymen applying a standard less demanding than those used in more formal legal proceedings. Likewise, given the informal, often hurried context in which it must be applied, the "built-in subtleties" of the "two-pronged test" are particularly unlikely to assist magistrates in determining probable cause.

Similarly, we have repeatedly said that after-the-fact scrutiny by courts of the sufficiency of an affidavit should not take the form of *de novo* review. A magistrate's "determination of probable cause should be paid great deference by reviewing courts." *Spinelli, supra.* "A grudging or negative attitude by reviewing courts toward warrants" is inconsistent with the Fourth Amendment's strong preference for searches conducted pursuant to a warrant; "courts should not invalidate warrant[s] by interpreting affidavit[s] in a hypertechnical, rather than a commonsense, manner."

If the affidavits submitted by police officers are subjected to the type of scrutiny some courts have deemed appropriate, police might well resort to warrantless searches, with the hope of relying on consent or some other exception to the Warrant Clause that might develop at the time of the search. In addition, the possession of a warrant by officers conducting an arrest or search greatly reduces the perception of unlawful or intrusive police conduct, by assuring "the individual whose property is searched or seized of the lawful authority of the executing officer, his need to search, and the limits of his power to search." Reflecting this preference for the warrant process, the traditional standard for review of an issuing magistrate's probable-cause determination has been that so long as the magistrate had a "substantial basis for * * * conclud[ing]" that a search would uncover evidence of wrongdoing, the Fourth Amendment requires no more. We think reaffirmation of this standard better serves the purpose of encouraging recourse to the warrant procedure and is more consistent with our traditional deference to the probable-cause determinations of magistrates than is the "two-pronged test."

Finally, the direction taken by decisions following *Spinelli* poorly serves "[t]he most basic function of any government": "to provide for the security of the individual and of his property." The strictures that inevitably accompany the "two-pronged test" cannot avoid seriously impeding the task of law enforcement. If, as the Illinois Supreme Court apparently thought, that test must be rigorously applied in every case, anonymous tips would be of greatly diminished value in police work. * * * Yet, such tips, particularly when supplemented by independent police investigation, frequently contribute to the solution of otherwise "perfect crimes." While a conscientious assessment of the basis for crediting such tips is required by the Fourth Amendment, a standard that leaves virtually no place for anonymous citizen informants is not.

For all these reasons, we conclude that it is wiser to abandon the "two-pronged test" established by our decisions in *Aguilar* and *Spinelli*. In its place we reaffirm the totality-of-the-circumstances analysis that traditionally has informed probable-cause determinations. The task of the issuing magistrate is simply to make a practical, common-sense decision whether, given all the circumstances set forth in the affidavit before him, including the "veracity" and "basis of knowledge" of persons supplying hearsay information, there is a fair probability that contraband or evidence of a crime will be found in a particular place. And the duty of a reviewing court is simply to ensure that the magistrate had a "substantial basis for * * * conclud[ing]" that probable cause existed. We are convinced that this flexible, easily applied standard will better achieve the accommodation of public and private interests that the Fourth Amendment requires than does the approach that has developed from *Aguilar* and *Spinelli*.

Our earlier cases illustrate the limits beyond which a magistrate may not venture in issuing a warrant. A sworn statement of an affiant that "he has cause to suspect and does believe" that liquor illegally brought into the United States is located on certain premises will not do. *Nathanson v. United States.* An affidavit must provide the magistrate with a substantial basis for determining the existence of probable cause, and the wholly conclusory statement at issue in *Nathanson* failed to meet this requirement. * * * Sufficient information must be presented to the magistrate to allow that official to determine probable cause; his action cannot be a mere ratification of the bare conclusions of others. In order to ensure that such an abdication of the magistrate's duty does not occur, courts must continue to conscientiously review the sufficiency of affidavits on which warrants are issued. But when we move beyond the "bare bones" affidavits present in cases such as *Nathanson* and *Aguilar*, this area simply does not lend itself to a prescribed set of rules, like that which had developed from *Spinelli*. Instead, the flexible, common-sense standard * * * better serves the purposes of the Fourth Amendment's probable-cause requirement. * * *

IV

Our decisions applying the totality-of-the-circumstances analysis outlined above have consistently recognized the value of corroboration of details of an informant's tip by independent police work. * * *

Our decision in *Draper v. United States* * * * is the classic case on the value of corroborative efforts of police officials. [See pp. 180–181 for the facts.] * * *

The showing of probable cause in the present case was fully as compelling as that in *Draper*. Even standing alone, the facts obtained through the independent investigation of Mader and the DEA at least suggested that the Gateses were involved in drug trafficking. In addition to being a popular vacation site, Florida is well known as a source of narcotics and other illegal drugs. Lance Gates' flight to West Palm Beach, his brief, overnight stay in a motel, and apparent immediate return north to Chicago in the family car, conveniently awaiting him in West Palm Beach, is as suggestive of a prearranged drug run, as it is of an ordinary vacation trip.

In addition, the judge could rely on the anonymous letter, which had been corroborated in major part by Mader's efforts—just as had occurred in *Draper*. The Supreme Court of Illinois reasoned that *Draper* involved an informant who had given reliable information on previous occasions, while the honesty and reliability of the anonymous informant in this case were unknown to the Bloomingdale police. While this distinction might be an apt one at the time the Police Department received the anonymous letter, it became far less significant after Mader's independent investigative work occurred. The corroboration of the letter's predictions that the Gateses' car would be in Florida, that Lance Gates would fly to Florida in the next day or so, and that he would drive the car north toward Bloomingdale all indicated, albeit not with certainty, that the informant's other assertions also were true. "[B]ecause an informant is right about some things, he is more probably right about other facts," *Spinelli* (White, J., concurring)—including the claim regarding the Gateses' illegal activity. This may well not be the type of "reliability" or "veracity" necessary to satisfy some views of the "veracity prong" of *Spinelli*, but we think it suffices for the practical, common-sense

judgment called for in making a probable-cause determination. It is
enough, for purposes of assessing probable cause, that "[c]orroboration
through other sources of information reduced the chances of a reckless or
prevaricating tale," thus providing "a substantial basis for crediting the
hearsay."

Finally, the anonymous letter contained a range of details relating
not just to easily obtained facts and conditions existing at the time of the
tip, but to future actions of third parties ordinarily not easily predicted.
The letterwriter's accurate information as to the travel plans of each of
the Gateses was of a character likely obtained only from the Gateses
themselves, or from someone familiar with their not entirely ordinary
travel plans. If the informant had access to accurate information of this
type a magistrate could properly conclude that it was not unlikely that he
also had access to reliable information of the Gateses' alleged illegal
activities. Of course, the Gateses' travel plans might have been learned
from a talkative neighbor or travel agent; under the "two-pronged test"
developed from *Spinelli*, the character of the details in the anonymous
letter might well not permit a sufficiently clear inference regarding the
letterwriter's "basis of knowledge." But, as discussed previously, probable
cause does not demand the certainty we associate with formal trials. It is
enough that there was a fair probability that the writer of the anonymous
letter had obtained his entire story either from the Gates or someone they
trusted. And corroboration of major portions of the letter's predictions
provides just this probability. * * *

Reversed.

JUSTICE WHITE, concurring in the judgment. * * *

III

* * * Abandoning the "two-pronged test" of *Aguilar v. Texas* and
Spinelli v. United States, the Court upholds the validity of the warrant
under a new "totality of the circumstances" approach. Although I agree
that the warrant should be upheld, I reach this conclusion in accordance
with the *Aguilar-Spinelli* framework.

A * * *

In the present case, it is undisputed that the anonymous tip, by
itself, did not furnish probable cause. The question is whether those
portions of the affidavit describing the results of the police investigation
of the respondents, when considered in light of the tip, "would permit the
suspicions engendered by the informant's report to ripen into a judgment
that a crime was probably being committed." *Spinelli, supra.* The Illinois
Supreme Court concluded that the corroboration was insufficient to
permit such a ripening. * * *

In my view, the lower court's characterization of the Gateses' activity here as totally "innocent" is dubious. In fact, the behavior was quite suspicious. I agree with the Court that Lance Gates' flight to West Palm Beach, an area known to be a source of narcotics, the brief overnight stay in a motel, and apparent immediate return north, suggest a pattern that trained law enforcement officers have recognized as indicative of illicit drug-dealing activity.

Even, however, had the corroboration related only to completely innocuous activities, this fact alone would not preclude the issuance of a valid warrant. The critical issue is not whether the activities observed by the police are innocent or suspicious. Instead, the proper focus should be on whether the actions of the suspects, whatever their nature, give rise to an inference that the informant is credible and that he obtained his information in a reliable manner. * * *

As in *Draper*, the police investigation in the present case satisfactorily demonstrated that the informant's tip was as trustworthy as one that would alone satisfy the *Aguilar* tests. The tip predicted that Sue Gates would drive to Florida, that Lance Gates would fly there a few days after May 3, and that Lance would then drive the car back. After the police corroborated these facts, the judge could reasonably have inferred, as he apparently did, that the informant, who had specific knowledge of these unusual travel plans, did not make up his story and that he obtained his information in a reliable way. It is theoretically possible, as respondents insist, that the tip could have been supplied by a "vindictive travel agent" and that the Gateses' activities, although unusual, might not have been unlawful. But *Aguilar* and *Spinelli*, like our other cases, do not require that certain guilt be established before a warrant may properly be issued. * * * I therefore conclude that the judgment of the Illinois Supreme Court invalidating the warrant must be reversed.

B

The Court agrees that the warrant was valid, but, in the process of reaching this conclusion, it overrules the *Aguilar-Spinelli* tests and replaces them with a "totality of the circumstances" standard. As shown above, it is not at all necessary to overrule *Aguilar-Spinelli* in order to reverse the judgment below. Therefore, because I am inclined to believe that, when applied properly, the *Aguilar-Spinelli* rules play an appropriate role in probable-cause determinations, and because the Court's holding may foretell an evisceration of the probable-cause standard, I do not join the Court's holding.

The Court reasons that the "veracity" and "basis of knowledge" tests are not independent, and that a deficiency as to one can be compensated for by a strong showing as to the other. Thus, a finding of probable cause may be based on a tip from an informant "known for the unusual reliability of his predictions" or from "an unquestionably honest citizen," even if the report fails thoroughly to set forth the basis upon which the information was obtained. If this is so, then it must follow *a fortiori* that "the affidavit of an officer, known by the magistrate to be honest and experienced, stating that [contraband] is located in a certain building" must be acceptable. It would be "quixotic" if a similar statement from an honest informant, but not one from an honest officer, could furnish probable cause. But we have repeatedly held that the unsupported assertion or belief of an officer does not satisfy the probable-cause requirement. Thus, this portion of today's holding can be read as implicitly rejecting the teachings of these prior holdings.

The Court may not intend so drastic a result. Indeed, the Court expressly reaffirms the validity of cases such as *Nathanson* that have held that, no matter how reliable the affiant-officer may be, a warrant should not be issued unless the affidavit discloses supporting facts and circumstances. The Court limits these cases to situations involving affidavits containing only "bare conclusions" and holds that, if an affidavit contains anything more, it should be left to the issuing magistrate to decide, based solely on "practical[ity]" and "common sense," whether there is a fair probability that contraband will be found in a particular place.

Thus, as I read the majority opinion, it appears that the question whether the probable-cause standard is to be diluted is left to the common-sense judgments of issuing magistrates. I am reluctant to approve any standard that does not expressly require, as a prerequisite to issuance of a warrant, some showing of facts from which an inference may be drawn that the informant is credible and that his information was obtained in a reliable way. * * * Hence, I do not join the Court's opinion rejecting the *Aguilar-Spinelli* rules.

JUSTICE BRENNAN, with whom JUSTICE MARSHALL joins, dissenting. * * *

I * * *

In recognition of the judiciary's role as the only effective guardian of Fourth Amendment rights, this Court has developed over the last half century a set of coherent rules governing a magistrate's consideration of a warrant application and the showings that are necessary to support a finding of probable cause. We start with the proposition that a neutral and detached magistrate, and not the police, should determine whether there is probable cause to support the issuance of a warrant. * * *

In order to emphasize the magistrate's role as an independent arbiter of probable cause and to insure that searches or seizures are not effected on less than probable cause, the Court has insisted that police officers provide magistrates with the underlying facts and circumstances that support the officers' conclusions. * * *

Although the rules drawn from the cases * * * are cast in procedural terms, they advance an important underlying substantive value: Findings of probable cause, and attendant intrusions, should not be authorized unless there is some assurance that the information on which they are based has been obtained in a reliable way by an honest or credible person. As applied to police officers, the rules focus on the way in which the information was acquired. As applied to informants, the rules focus both on the honesty or credibility of the informant and on the reliability of the way in which the information was acquired. Insofar as it is more complicated, an evaluation of affidavits based on hearsay involves a more difficult inquiry. This suggests a need to structure the inquiry in an effort to insure greater accuracy. The standards announced in *Aguilar*, as refined by *Spinelli*, fulfill that need. * * *

II * * *

At the heart of the Court's decision to abandon *Aguilar* and *Spinelli* appears to be its belief that "the direction taken by decisions following *Spinelli* poorly serves '[t]he most basic function of any government': 'to provide for the security of the individual and of his property.'" This conclusion rests on the judgment that *Aguilar* and *Spinelli* "seriously imped[e] the task of law enforcement," and render anonymous tips valueless in police work. Surely, the Court overstates its case. But of particular concern to all Americans must be that the Court gives virtually no consideration to the value of insuring that findings of probable cause are based on information that a magistrate can reasonably say has been obtained in a reliable way by an honest or credible person. I share Justice White's fear that the Court's rejection of *Aguilar* and *Spinelli* and its adoption of a new totality-of-the-circumstances test, "may foretell an evisceration of the probable-cause standard * * * ." * * *

JUSTICE STEVENS, with whom JUSTICE BRENNAN joins, dissenting.

The fact that Lance and Sue Gates made a 22-hour nonstop drive from West Palm Beach, Florida, to Bloomingdale, Illinois, only a few hours after Lance had flown to Florida provided persuasive evidence that they were engaged in illicit activity. That fact, however, was not known to the judge when he issued the warrant to search their home.

What the judge did know at that time was that the anonymous informant had not been completely accurate in his or her predictions. The informant had indicated that "Sue * * * drives their car to Florida *where she leaves it to be loaded up with drugs * * * . Sue fl[ies] back after she drops the car off in Florida.*" Yet Detective Mader's affidavit reported that she "'left the West Palm Beach area driving the Mercury northbound.'"

The discrepancy between the informant's predictions and the facts known to Detective Mader is significant for three reasons. First, it cast doubt on the informant's hypothesis that the Gates already had "'over

[$100,000] worth of drugs in their basement.' " The informant had predicted an itinerary that always kept one spouse in Bloomingdale, suggesting that the Gates did not want to leave their home unguarded because something valuable was hidden within. That inference obviously could not be drawn when it was known that the pair was actually together over a thousand miles from home.

Second, the discrepancy made the Gates' conduct seem substantially less unusual than the informant had predicted it would be. It would have been odd if, as predicted, Sue had driven down to Florida on Wednesday, left the car, and flown right back to Illinois. But the mere facts that Sue was in West Palm Beach with the car, that she was joined by her husband at the Holiday Inn on Friday, and that the couple drove north together the next morning[3] are neither unusual nor probative of criminal activity.

Third, the fact that the anonymous letter contained a material mistake undermines the reasonableness of relying on it as a basis for making a forcible entry into a private home.

Of course, the activities in this case did not stop when the judge issued the warrant. The Gates drove all night to Bloomingdale, the officers searched the car and found 400 pounds of marihuana, and then they searched the house. However, none of these subsequent events may be considered in evaluating the warrant, and the search of the house was legal only if the warrant was valid. I cannot accept the Court's casual conclusion that, *before the Gates arrived in Bloomingdale*, there was probable cause to justify a valid entry and search of a private home. * * * I must surmise that the Court's evaluation of the warrant's validity has been colored by subsequent events. * * *[8]

NOTES AND QUESTIONS

1. *A bit more on Sue and Lance Gates and the anonymous informant.* According to Professor Thomas Davies, the anonymous informant was Sue Gates's beautician, who was infuriated at her client's frequent boasts about not working. Davies reports that "the hairdresser called the police after the

---

[3] Detective Mader's affidavit hinted darkly that the couple had set out upon "that interstate highway commonly used by travelers to the Chicago area." But the same highway is also commonly used by travelers to Disney World, Sea World, and Ringling Brothers and Barnum and Bailey Circus World. It is also the road to Cocoa Beach, Cape Canaveral, and Washington, D.C. I would venture that each year dozens of perfectly innocent people fly to Florida, meet a waiting spouse, and drive off together in the family car.

[8] The Court holds that what were heretofore considered two independent "prongs"— "veracity" and "basis of knowledge"—are now to be considered together as circumstances whose totality must be appraised. * * * "[A] deficiency in one may be compensated for, in determining the overall reliability of a tip, by a strong showing as to the other, or by some other indicia of reliability." Yet in this case, the lower courts found *neither* factor present. And the supposed "other indicia" in the affidavit take the form of activity that is not particularly remarkable. I do not understand how the Court can find that the "totality" so far exceeds the sum of its "circumstances."

case made the Chicago papers, and said that she would have signed the letter if she knew how much trouble she was causing!" (E-mail correspondence from Davies to author Dressler, January 24, 2001.)

Susan and Lance Gates pleaded guilty to the drug charges. "[N]ot exactly a Bonnie & Clyde operation," according to Professor Davies, and neither Sue nor Lance has reportedly been prosecuted in the intervening years.

2.   Is the *Gates* case an example of good law enforcement? The anonymous informant stated "I guarantee *if you watch them carefully* you will make a big catch. They are friends with some big drug *dealers, who visit their house often.*" According to one scholar, "[o]ut of the mouths of babes and anonymous informants sometimes comes wisdom." Yale Kamisar, Gates, *"Probable Cause," "Good Faith," and Beyond*, 69 Iowa L. Rev. 551, 576 (1984). Professor Kamisar reasons that if the police had been more patient they would have satisfied the two-pronged standard and, perhaps more importantly, have apprehended "big drug dealers."

3.   Suppose a friend you have known for years and who has proven to be a truthful individual alleges illegal behavior by another individual whom you do not know. Notice: here the veracity prong is satisfied, but the basis-of-knowledge prong has not been proven. Would you still believe your friend's allegations? *reputation*.

What if a stranger tells you he personally observed criminal behavior by *witness.* another individual (whom you also do not know), even setting out very specific details of what he observed. Here, the basis-of-knowledge is provided, but the veracity prong is not satisfied. Would you believe the stranger?

Do your answers suggest the *Gates* Court was right to abandon the strict two-pronged test of *Aguilar-Spinelli*?

4.   The police often use informants to obtain critical information in criminal investigations. In one study in the San Diego Judicial District, for example, 63.9% of search warrant affidavits contained information provided by informants. Laurence A. Benner & Charles T. Samarkos, *Searching for Narcotics in San Diego: Preliminary Findings from the San Diego Search Warrant Project*, 36 Cal. Western L. Rev. 221, 239 (2000). However, in half of the cases the affiant did not personally know the informant. That is, "the officer simply related information given him by another officer who did not join in signing the affidavit. Thus, Officer A swears under oath that Officer B told him that there was [a confidential informant] who gave him certain information." *Id.* at 241. Thus, the magistrate was receiving double hearsay. What problems do you see in this? *conspiracy*.

5.   *The "confidential informant": How confidential is he?* The police rarely disclose the identity of their informants—many of whom provide information on a regular basis—to magistrates in warrant applications. In McCray v. Illinois, 386 U.S. 300, 87 S.Ct. 1056, 18 L.Ed.2d 62 (1967), the Supreme Court ruled that the due process clause does not require a judge in

every probable cause or evidence-suppression hearing to compel disclosure of the informant's identity. In reaching this conclusion the Court quoted the following reasoning of the New Jersey Supreme Court in State v. Burnett, 42 N.J. 377, 201 A.2d 39 (1964):

> If a defendant may insist upon disclosure of the informant in order to test the truth of the officer's statement that there is an informant or as to what the informant related or as to the informant's reliability, we can be sure that every defendant will demand disclosure. He has nothing to lose and the prize may be the suppression of damaging evidence if the State cannot afford to reveal its source, as is so often the case. * * *
>
> The Fourth Amendment is served if a judicial mind passes upon the existence of probable cause. Where the issue is submitted upon an application for a warrant, the magistrate is trusted to evaluate the credibility of the affiant in an *ex parte* proceeding. * * * If the magistrate doubts the credibility of the affiant, he may require that the informant be identified or even produced.

6. *The "oath and affirmation" requirement of the Fourth Amendment.* A police officer-affiant is ordinarily considered reliable because she provides her information under oath. But, suppose that the defendant fears that the officer lied under oath to the judge who issued a search warrant? Perhaps the defense believes that the affiant lied to the judge as to what she personally observed, or made up the existence of an informant, or lied as to a real informant's reliability, or knew or should have known that the informant's claims were false. What may the defendant do to attack a warrant in such circumstances?

The Fourth Amendment provides that warrants, founded on probable cause, must be "supported by Oath or affirmation." The Supreme Court held in Franks v. Delaware, 438 U.S. 154, 98 S.Ct. 2674, 57 L.Ed.2d 667 (1978), that in view of this requirement, a defendant may challenge the truthfulness of statements made under oath in an affidavit supporting a warrant under limited circumstances. *Franks* explains the procedure:

> [W]here the defendant makes a substantial preliminary showing that a false statement knowing and intentionally, or with reckless disregard for the truth, was included by the affiant in the warrant affidavit, the Fourth Amendment requires that a hearing be held at the defendant's request. In the event that at that hearing the allegation of perjury or reckless disregard is established * * * by a preponderance of the evidence, and, with the affidavit's false material set to one side, the affidavit's remaining content is insufficient to establish probable cause, the search warrant must be voided and the fruits of the search excluded to the same extent as if probable cause was lacking on the face of the affidavit.

Franks does not authorize a special hearing if a defendant claims that the *informant* lied to an *innocent* affiant. Do you see why this is so?

7.   *Preference for the warrant process.* As noted in *Gates*, the constitutionally preferable arbiter of probable cause is a "neutral and detached magistrate," rather than a police officer "engaged in the often competitive enterprise of ferreting out crime." Johnson v. United States, 333 U.S. 10, 68 S.Ct. 367, 92 L.Ed. 436 (1948). In order to provide the police with an incentive to seek warrants, the Supreme Court has stated that "the resolution of doubtful or marginal cases [of probable cause] * * * should be largely determined by the preference to be accorded to warrants." United States v. Ventresca, 380 U.S. 102, 85 S.Ct. 741, 13 L.Ed.2d 684 (1965). In other words, in close cases, a search pursuant to a warrant may be upheld where, without one, it would not be.

8.   *How probable is "probable cause"?* *Gates* eschewed the quantification of any "precise degree of certainty corresponding to 'probable cause'." The Court has stated, however, that the standard does *not* "demand any showing that such a belief be * * * more likely true than false." Texas v. Brown, 460 U.S. 730, 103 S.Ct. 1535, 75 L.Ed.2d 502 (1983). As Professor Sherry Colb has put it:

> We do not know exactly what the phrase "probable cause" means, in strict numerical terms. We do, however, know what it does *not* mean: "probably." That is, probable cause does not—in the context of Fourth Amendment law—mean that the police must have evidence sufficient to conclude that a suspect is *probably* guilty or that she *probably* has evidence of a crime inside her home.

Sherry F. Colb, *Probabilities in Probable Cause and Beyond: Statistical Versus Concrete Harms*, 73 Law & Contemp. Probs. 69, 71 (2010).

Should this be the rule? What if the police have extremely solid evidence, amounting to near certainty, that one (but only one) of two identical twins committed a particular offense? (For real-life examples of this, see Jess Bidgood, *New DNA Test Sought in Identical Twin's Rape Case*, New York Times, Sept. 16, 2014; and Marc Lacey, *Identical Twins, One Charged in a Fatal Shooting, Create Confusion for the Police*, New York Times (National Edition), August 9, 2011.) In light of *Brown*, *supra*, should the police arrest *both* of the twins, even though they know one of them is innocent? If not, should they flip a coin and arrest the unlucky one? What if we are dealing with triplets? In this regard consider this true case recounted to the authors of this casebook by Professor Neil Cohen:

> A few years ago I got a call from a judge who had this case. Very late at night on a rural dark road a police officer spotted a car driving erratically. The officer * * * pulled over the car. * * * When the officer shined his flashlight in the car, he found three young men "asleep" in the back seat. No one was in the front seat. He "awakened" them and all said the same thing: They had been at a

party, drank too much, and fell asleep in the back seat of the car. Each denied knowing who the driver was. The officer had kept the car in eyesight the entire time and was confident that no one had gotten out of it. All three of the young men were drunk.

Was there probable cause to charge anyone with driving the vehicle under the influence of alcohol? What *should* the answer be? Do you believe, as one commentator has written about a one-in-ten, rather than one-in-three, situation, "[t]he question is whether one may reasonably expect—indeed, require—each suspect to sacrifice some liberty or privacy in order to unmask the offender. I think we can. In constitutional language, I would say that probable cause exists to arrest or search each suspect." Joseph D. Grano, *Probable Cause and Common Sense: A Reply to the Critics of* Illinois v. Gates, 17 U. Mich. J.L. Reform 465, 497 (1984).

Now consider Maryland v. Pringle, 540 U.S. 366, 124 S.Ct. 795, 157 L.Ed.2d 769 (2003). In *Pringle*, an officer lawfully stopped a speeding vehicle occupied by three men. As a result of a lawful search, the officer discovered a large amount of rolled-up money in the glove compartment, and five baggies of cocaine hidden in the back-seat armrest and elsewhere in the back seat. The officer questioned the men about the ownership of the drugs and warned them that if they did not answer he would arrest all three of them for possession of the cocaine, which he did when nobody admitted ownership. The Supreme Court unanimously upheld Pringle's arrest:

> We think it an entirely reasonable inference from [the] facts of the case that any or all three of the occupants had knowledge of, and exercised dominion and control over, the cocaine. [Under state law, "possession" of property exists if one or more persons has "actual or constructive dominion or control" over the property— Eds.] Thus a reasonable officer could conclude that there was probable cause to believe Pringle committed the crime of possession of cocaine, either solely or jointly.

Does this case resolve the triplet hypothetical or the three-drunks-in-the-back-seat case?

9. *A "sliding scale" of probable cause?* In Schmerber v. California, 384 U.S. 757, 86 S.Ct. 1826, 16 L.Ed.2d 908 (1966), the Supreme Court observed that the taking of a blood sample from a motorist arrested for drunk driving, because it involves an intrusion into a human body, is a more offensive type of search than the ordinary type and, therefore, requires "a clear indication that in fact such evidence [of intoxication] will be found." One can interpret this latter language as, perhaps, requiring "probable cause plus," i.e., a heightened degree of likelihood of discovering evidence when the police wish to conduct such a hyper-intrusive search. And, indeed, in Winston v. Lee, 470 U.S. 753, 105 S.Ct. 1611, 84 L.Ed.2d 662 (1985), a case in which the police sought a warrant to compel a surgical intrusion into a suspect's body in order to seize a bullet that might incriminate him, the Court stated that "when the State seeks to intrude upon an area in which our society recognizes a

significantly heightened privacy interest, a more substantial justification is required" to authorize such a search.

Does this suggest, therefore, a sliding scale of "probable cause"? And, if so, one may expect that the sliding scale could work in both directions. Might there be cases in which "probable cause" requires *less* than the ordinary degree of proof?

Consider this scenario: The police have a credible report that an atomic bomb, smaller than a suitcase, has been smuggled into New York City. The bomb, if detonated, will kill thousands of persons and make the city uninhabitable for generations. The report is confirmed by use of radiation sensors, which determine that the bomb is hidden in one of 100 homes. Therefore, Homeland Security officials search all 100 homes simultaneously. Ronald M. Gould & Simon Stern, *Catastrophic Threats and the Fourth Amendment*, 77 S. Cal. L. Rev. 777, 779 (2004). Did the government act with "probable cause"? Would your answer be the same if police instead searched the same houses for a small stash of cocaine, based on the same likelihood of success?

Does your response to these hypotheticals suggest that the Court is right in suggesting that "probable cause" should be a fluid concept—that there should be a sliding scale of probable cause? Can you suggest a plausible Fourth Amendment textual argument for such a distinction?

10. *Probable cause as an objective concept.* According to the Supreme Court, "evenhanded law enforcement is best achieved by the application of objective standards of conduct, rather than standards that depend upon the subjective state of mind of the [police] officer." Horton v. California, 496 U.S. 128, 110 S.Ct. 2301, 110 L.Ed.2d 112 (1990). Therefore, as will be developed more fully later, the Supreme Court has stated that an officer's "state of mind (except for the facts that he knows) is irrelevant to the existence of probable cause." Devenpeck v. Alford, 543 U.S. 146, 125 S.Ct. 588, 160 L.Ed.2d 537 (2004). As the Court held in *Devenpeck,* an arrest is lawful, even if an officer incorrectly believes he has probable cause to arrest a person for Crime A (and, therefore, makes such an arrest), if based on the facts known to the arresting officer, probable cause objectively exists to arrest for Crime B.

11. *Problem.* A mother reported to the police that her three-year-old son told her that *S*, an adult, had sexually touched him on his penis ("he touched my pee-pee"). Is this sufficient grounds to arrest *S* for child sexual abuse? United States v. Shaw, 464 F.3d 615 (6th Cir. 2006).

12. *Problem.* Ready for a little 1940s *film noir*? Here is how Chief Justice Roberts described the facts in Pennsylvania v. Dunlap, 555 U.S. 964, 129 S.Ct. 448, 172 L.Ed.2d 321 (2008) (dissenting from denial of certiorari):

> North Philly, May 4, 2001. Officer Sean Devlin, Narcotics Strike Force, was working the morning shift. Undercover surveillance. The neighborhood? Tough as a three-dollar steak. Devlin knew. Five years on the beat, nine months with the Strike Force. He'd made

fifteen, twenty drug busts in the neighborhood. Devlin spotted him: a lone man on the corner. Another approached. Quick exchange of words. Cash handed over; small objects handed back. Each man then quickly on his own way. Devlin knew the guy wasn't buying bus tokens. He radioed a description and Officer Stein picked up the buyer. Sure enough: three bags of crack in the guy's pocket. Head downtown and book him. Just another day at the office.

Do these facts support a finding of probable cause to arrest the man (who handed over cash) for the offense of possession of illegal drugs, although Officer Devlin did not see any drugs transferred? TOC.

13. *Problem.* Two adult men accused *B*, an Episcopal priest and former chaplain of a boarding school, of sexual abuse sixteen years earlier when they were teenagers. The police sought a warrant to search *B*'s home (a different home) for a footlocker that the complainants stated had, by their observation at the time of the crimes, contained pornographic material, photographs of sodomy performed on them, and sexual aids used on them in the sexual abuse. Probable cause? Behrel v. State, 151 Md.App. 64, 823 A.2d 696 (2003).

B. ARREST WARRANTS

PAYTON V. NEW YORK

Supreme Court of the United States, 1980.
445 U.S. 573, 100 S.Ct. 1371, 63 L.Ed.2d 639.

MR. JUSTICE STEVENS delivered the opinion of the Court [joined by JUSTICES BRENNAN, STEWART, MARSHALL, BLACKMUN, and POWELL].

These appeals challenge the constitutionality of New York statutes that authorize police officers to enter a private residence without a warrant and with force, if necessary, to make a routine felony arrest.

The important constitutional question presented by this challenge has been expressly left open in a number of our prior opinions. In *United States v. Watson*, 423 U.S. 411, 96 S.Ct. 820, 46 L.Ed.2d 598 [1976], we upheld a warrantless "midday public arrest," expressly noting that the case did not pose "the still unsettled question * * * 'whether and under what circumstances an officer may enter a suspect's home to make a warrantless arrest.' "a * * *

I

On January 14, 1970, after two days of intensive investigation, New York detectives had assembled evidence sufficient to establish probable cause to believe that Theodore Payton had murdered the manager of a gas station two days earlier. At about 7:30 a. m. on January 15, six

---

a   The Supreme Court held in *Watson* that as a matter of Fourth Amendment law, an arrest warrant is not required to make a felony arrest in a public place.

officers went to Payton's apartment in the Bronx, intending to arrest him. They had not obtained a warrant. Although light and music emanated from the apartment, there was no response to their knock on the metal door. They summoned emergency assistance and, about 30 minutes later, used crowbars to break open the door and enter the apartment. No one was there. In plain view, however, was a .30-caliber shell casing that was seized and later admitted into evidence at Payton's murder trial.

In due course Payton surrendered to the police, was indicted for murder, and moved to suppress the evidence taken from his apartment. The trial judge held that the warrantless and forcible entry was authorized by the New York Code of Criminal Procedure, and that the evidence in plain view was properly seized. * * *

On March 14, 1974, Obie Riddick was arrested for the commission of two armed robberies that had occurred in 1971. He had been identified by the victims in June 1973, and in January 1974 the police had learned his address. They did not obtain a warrant for his arrest. At about noon on March 14, a detective, accompanied by three other officers, knocked on the door of the Queens house where Riddick was living. When his young son opened the door, they could see Riddick sitting in bed covered by a sheet. They entered the house and placed him under arrest. Before permitting him to dress, they opened a chest of drawers two feet from the bed in search of weapons and found narcotics and related paraphernalia. Riddick was subsequently indicted on narcotics charges. At a suppression hearing, the trial judge held that the warrantless entry into his home was authorized by the revised New York statute, and that the search of the immediate area [as an incident of the arrest] was reasonable under *Chimel v. California*, 395 U.S. 752, 89 S.Ct. 2034, 23 L.Ed.2d 685. * * *

Before addressing the narrow question presented by these appeals, we put to one side other related problems that are *not* presented today. Although it is arguable that the warrantless entry to effect Payton's arrest might have been justified by exigent circumstances, none of the New York courts relied on any such justification. * * * Accordingly, we have no occasion to consider the sort of emergency or dangerous situation, described in our cases as "exigent circumstances," that would justify a warrantless entry into a home for the purpose of either arrest or search.

Nor do these cases raise any question concerning the authority of the police, without either a search or arrest warrant, to enter a third party's home to arrest a suspect. The police broke into Payton's apartment intending to arrest Payton, and they arrested Riddick in his own dwelling. We also note that in neither case is it argued that the police lacked probable cause to believe that the suspect was at home when they entered. Finally, in both cases we are dealing with entries into homes made without the consent of any occupant. In *Payton*, the police used crowbars to break down the door and in *Riddick*, although his 3-year-old son answered the door, the police entered before Riddick had an opportunity either to object or to consent.

II

It is familiar history that indiscriminate searches and seizures conducted under the authority of "general warrants" were the immediate evils that motivated the framing and adoption of the Fourth Amendment. Indeed, as originally proposed in the House of Representatives, the draft contained only one clause, which directly imposed limitations on the issuance of warrants, but imposed no express restrictions on warrantless searches or seizures. As it was ultimately adopted, however, the Amendment contained two separate clauses, the first protecting the basic right to be free from unreasonable searches and seizures and the second requiring that warrants be particular and supported by probable cause. * * *

It is thus perfectly clear that the evil the Amendment was designed to prevent was broader than the abuse of a general warrant. Unreasonable searches or seizures conducted without any warrant at all are condemned by the plain language of the first clause of the Amendment. Almost a century ago the Court stated in resounding terms that the principles reflected in the Amendment "reached farther than the concrete form" of the specific cases that gave it birth, and "apply to all invasions on the part of the government and its employees of the sanctity of a man's home and the privacies of life." *Boyd v. United States*, 116 U.S. 616, 630, 6 S.Ct. 524, 532, 29 L.Ed. 746. * * *

The simple language of the Amendment applies equally to seizures of persons and to seizures of property. Our analysis in this case may therefore properly commence with rules that have been well established in Fourth Amendment litigation involving tangible items. As the Court reiterated just a few years ago, the "physical entry of the home is the chief evil against which the wording of the Fourth Amendment is directed." And we have long adhered to the view that the warrant procedure minimizes the danger of needless intrusions of that sort.

It is a "basic principle of Fourth Amendment law" that searches and seizures inside a home without a warrant are presumptively unreasonable. Yet it is also well settled that objects such as weapons or contraband found in a public place may be seized by the police without a warrant. The seizure of property in plain view involves no invasion of privacy and is presumptively reasonable, assuming that there is probable cause to associate the property with criminal activity. The distinction between a warrantless seizure in an open area and such a seizure on private premises was plainly stated in *G. M. Leasing Corp. v. United States*, 429 U.S. 338, 354, 97 S.Ct. 619, 629, 50 L.Ed.2d 530:

"It is one thing to seize without a warrant property resting in an open area or seizable by levy without an intrusion into privacy, and it is quite another thing to effect a warrantless seizure of property, even that owned by a corporation, situated on private premises to which access is not otherwise available for the seizing officer."

As the late Judge Leventhal recognized, this distinction has equal force when the seizure of a person is involved. Writing on the constitutional issue now before us for the United States Court of Appeals for the District of Columbia Circuit sitting en banc, *Dorman v. United States*, 140 U.S.App.D.C. 313, 435 F.2d 385 (1970), Judge Leventhal first noted the settled rule that warrantless arrests in public places are valid. He immediately recognized, however, that

"[a] greater burden is placed * * * on officials who enter a home or dwelling without consent. Freedom from intrusion into the home or dwelling is the archetype of the privacy protection secured by the Fourth Amendment."

His analysis of this question then focused on the long-settled premise that, absent exigent circumstances, a warrantless entry to search for weapons or contraband is unconstitutional even when a felony has been committed and there is probable cause to believe that incriminating evidence will be found within. He reasoned that the constitutional protection afforded to the individual's interest in the privacy of his own home is equally applicable to a warrantless entry for the purpose of arresting a resident of the house; for it is inherent in such an entry that a search for the suspect may be required before he can be apprehended. Judge Leventhal concluded that an entry to arrest and an entry to search for and to seize property implicate the same interest in preserving the privacy and the sanctity of the home, and justify the same level of constitutional protection.

* * * We find this reasoning to be persuasive and in accord with this Court's Fourth Amendment decisions.

The majority of the New York Court of Appeals, however, suggested that there is a substantial difference in the relative intrusiveness of an entry to search for property and an entry to search for a person. It is true that the area that may legally be searched is broader when executing a search warrant than when executing an arrest warrant in the home. This difference may be more theoretical than real, however, because the police may need to check the entire premises for safety reasons, and sometimes they ignore the restrictions on searches incident to arrest.

But the critical point is that any differences in the intrusiveness of entries to search and entries to arrest are merely ones of degree rather than kind. The two intrusions share this fundamental characteristic: the breach of the entrance to an individual's home. The Fourth Amendment protects the individual's privacy in a variety of settings. In none is the zone of privacy more clearly defined than when bounded by the unambiguous physical dimensions of an individual's home—a zone that finds its roots in clear and specific constitutional terms: "The right of the people to be secure in their * * * houses * * * shall not be violated." That language unequivocally establishes the proposition that "[a]t the very core [of the Fourth Amendment] stands the right of a man to retreat into his own home and there be free from unreasonable governmental intrusion." In terms that apply equally to seizures of property and to seizures of persons, the Fourth Amendment has drawn a firm line at the entrance to the house. Absent exigent circumstances, that threshold may not reasonably be crossed without a warrant.

III

* * * New York argues that the reasons that support the *Watson* holding require a similar result here. In *Watson* the Court relied on (a) the well-settled common-law rule that a warrantless arrest in a public place is valid if the arresting officer had probable cause to believe the suspect is a felon; (b) the clear consensus among the States adhering to that well-settled common-law rule; and (c) the expression of the judgment of Congress that such an arrest is "reasonable." We consider each of these reasons as it applies to a warrantless entry into a home for the purpose of making a routine felony arrest.

A * * *

It is obvious that the common-law rule on warrantless home arrests was not as clear as the rule on arrests in public places. * * * [T]he weight of authority as it appeared to the Framers was to the effect that a warrant was required, or at the minimum that there were substantial risks in proceeding without one. The common-law sources display a sensitivity to privacy interests that could not have been lost on the Framers. The zealous and frequent repetition of the adage that a "man's house is his castle," made it abundantly clear that both in England and in the Colonies "the freedom of one's house" was one of the most vital elements of English liberty.

Thus, our study of the relevant common law does not provide the same guidance that was present in *Watson*. * * * [T]he absence of any 17th- or 18th-century English cases directly in point, together with the unequivocal endorsement of the tenet that "a man's house is his castle," strongly suggests that the prevailing practice was not to make such arrests except in hot pursuit or when authorized by a warrant. * * *

B * * *

* * * Only 24 of the 50 States currently sanction warrantless entries into the home to arrest, and there is an obvious declining trend. Further, the strength of the trend is greater than the numbers alone indicate. Seven state courts have recently held that warrantless home arrests violate their respective State Constitutions. That is significant because by invoking a state constitutional provision, a state court immunizes its decision from review by this Court. This heightened degree of immutability underscores the depth of the principle underlying the result.

C

No congressional determination that warrantless entries into the home are "reasonable" has been called to our attention. None of the federal statutes cited in the *Watson* opinion reflects any such legislative judgment. Thus, that support for the *Watson* holding finds no counterpart in this case. * * *

IV

The parties have argued at some length about the practical consequences of a warrant requirement as a precondition to a felony arrest in the home. In the absence of any evidence that effective law enforcement has suffered in those States that already have such a requirement, we are inclined to view such arguments with skepticism. More fundamentally, however, such arguments of policy must give way to a constitutional command that we consider to be unequivocal.

Finally, we note the State's suggestion that only a search warrant based on probable cause to believe the suspect is at home at a given time can adequately protect the privacy interests at stake, and since such a warrant requirement is manifestly impractical, there need be no warrant of any kind. We find this ingenious argument unpersuasive. It is true that an arrest warrant requirement may afford less protection than a search warrant requirement, but it will suffice to interpose the magistrate's determination of probable cause between the zealous officer and the citizen. If there is sufficient evidence of a citizen's participation in a felony to persuade a judicial officer that his arrest is justified, it is constitutionally reasonable to require him to open his doors to the officers of the law. Thus, for Fourth Amendment purposes, an arrest warrant founded on probable cause implicitly carries with it the limited authority to enter a dwelling in which the suspect lives when there is reason to believe the suspect is within.

Because no arrest warrant was obtained in either of these cases, the judgments must be reversed and the cases remanded to the New York Court of Appeals for further proceedings not inconsistent with this opinion. * * *

[JUSTICE BLACKMUN'S concurring opinion is omitted.]

MR. JUSTICE WHITE, with whom THE CHIEF JUSTICE BURGER and MR. JUSTICE REHNQUIST join, dissenting. * * *

I * * *

B

The history of the Fourth Amendment does not support the rule announced today. At the time that Amendment was adopted the constable possessed broad inherent powers to arrest. The limitations on those powers derived, not from a warrant "requirement," but from the generally ministerial nature of the constable's office at common law. Far from restricting the constable's arrest power, the institution of the warrant was used to expand that authority by giving the constable delegated powers of a superior officer such as a justice of the peace. Hence at the time of the Bill of Rights, the warrant functioned as a powerful tool of law enforcement rather than as a protection for the rights of criminal suspects.

In fact, it was the abusive use of the warrant power, rather than any excessive zeal in the discharge of peace officers' inherent authority, that precipitated the Fourth Amendment. * * *

* * * [T]he background, text, and legislative history of the Fourth Amendment demonstrate that the purpose was to restrict the abuses that had developed with respect to warrants; the Amendment preserved common-law rules of arrest. Because it was not considered generally unreasonable at common law for officers to break doors to effect a warrantless felony arrest, I do not believe that the Fourth Amendment was intended to outlaw the types of police conduct at issue in the present cases. * * *

II

A

Today's decision rests, in large measure, on the premise that warrantless arrest entries constitute a particularly severe invasion of personal privacy. I do not dispute that the home is generally a very private area or that the common law displayed a special "reverence * * * for the individual's right of privacy in his house." However, the Fourth Amendment is concerned with protecting people, not places, and no talismanic significance is given to the fact that an arrest occurs in the home rather than elsewhere. * * * The inquiry in the present case, therefore, is whether the incremental intrusiveness that results from an arrest's being made *in the dwelling* is enough to support an inflexible constitutional rule requiring warrants for such arrests whenever exigent circumstances are not present.

Today's decision ignores the carefully crafted restrictions on the common-law power of arrest entry and thereby overestimates the dangers inherent in that practice. At common law, absent exigent circumstances, entries to arrest could be made only for felony. Even in cases of felony, the officers were required to announce their presence, demand admission, and be refused entry before they were entitled to break doors. Further, it seems generally accepted that entries could be made only during daylight hours. And, in my view, the officer entering to arrest must have reasonable grounds to believe, not only that the arrestee has committed a crime, but also that the person suspected is present in the house at the time of the entry.

These four restrictions on home arrests—felony, knock and announce, daytime, and stringent probable cause—constitute powerful and complementary protections for the privacy interests associated with the home. The felony requirement guards against abusive or arbitrary enforcement and ensures that invasions of the home occur only in case of the most serious crimes. The knock-and-announce and daytime requirements protect individuals against the fear, humiliation, and embarrassment of being roused from their beds in states of partial or complete undress. And these requirements allow the arrestee to surrender at his front door, thereby maintaining his dignity and preventing the officers from entering other rooms of the dwelling. The stringent probable-cause requirement would help ensure against the possibility that the police would enter when the suspect was not home, and, in searching for him, frighten members of the family or ransack parts of the house, seizing items in plain view. In short, these requirements, taken together, permit an individual suspected of a serious crime to surrender at the front door of his dwelling and thereby avoid most of the humiliation and indignity that the Court seems to believe necessarily accompany a house arrest entry. Such a front-door arrest, in my view, is no more intrusive on personal privacy than the public warrantless arrests which we found to pass constitutional muster in *Watson*.

* * * The Court substitutes, in one sweeping decision, a rigid constitutional rule in place of the common-law approach, evolved over hundreds of years, which achieved a flexible accommodation between the demands of personal privacy and the legitimate needs of law enforcement. * * *

B

While exaggerating the invasion of personal privacy involved in home arrests, the Court fails to account for the danger that its rule will "severely hamper effective law enforcement." * * *

* * * [P]olice officers will often face the difficult task of deciding whether the circumstances are sufficiently exigent to justify their entry to arrest without a warrant. This is a decision that must be made quickly in the most trying of circumstances. If the officers mistakenly decide that the circumstances are exigent, the arrest will be invalid and any evidence seized incident to the arrest or in plain view will be excluded at trial. On the other hand, if the officers mistakenly determine that exigent circumstances are lacking, they may refrain from making the arrest, thus creating the possibility that a dangerous criminal will escape into the community. The police could reduce the likelihood of escape by staking out all possible exits until the circumstances become clearly exigent or a warrant is obtained. But the costs of such a stakeout seem excessive in an era of rising crime and scarce police resources.

The uncertainty inherent in the exigent-circumstances determination burdens the judicial system as well. * * * Under today's decision, whenever the police have made a warrantless home arrest there will be the possibility of "endless litigation with respect to the existence of exigent circumstances, whether it was practicable to get a warrant, whether the suspect was about to flee, and the like," *United States v. Watson*, *supra*. * * *

[JUSTICE REHNQUIST'S dissenting opinion is omitted.]

NOTES AND QUESTIONS

1.   Justice Stevens states that it is a "basic principle" of the Fourth Amendment "that searches and seizures inside a home without a warrant are presumptively unreasonable." Look again at the text of the Fourth Amendment: *Is* there a presumptive warrant requirement? Why does the majority conclude that there is one? How does the dissent answer the majority?

2.   What interest is served by the arrest warrant requirement? Does *Payton* protect the arrestee's person from unlawful seizure or, instead, the resident's interest in freedom from unlawful invasion of privacy in the dwelling?

3.   Warrant issues aside, *all* arrests, whether conducted in a public place (*Watson*) or made in a private residence (*Payton*), *must* be supported by probable cause. What is the Fourth Amendment textual basis for this rule?

4.   *Proceedings after a warrantless arrest: a "Gerstein hearing".* Most arrests occur outside a private residence. Therefore, in light of *United States v. Watson*, warrantless arrests are exceedingly common. This means that a police officer, and not a neutral and detached magistrate, usually makes the initial probable cause determination. Does this mean that an arrestee may be required to remain in custody pending trial without any judicial

determination that the arrest was lawful? No, the Supreme Court ruled in Gerstein v. Pugh, 420 U.S. 103, 95 S.Ct. 854, 43 L.Ed.2d 54 (1975):

> [A] policeman's on-the-scene assessment of probable cause provides legal justification for arresting a person suspected of crime, and for a brief period of detention to take the administrative steps incident to arrest. Once the suspect is in custody, however, the reasons that justify dispensing with the magistrate's neutral judgment evaporate. There no longer is any danger that the suspect will escape or commit further crimes while the police submit their evidence to a magistrate. And, while the State's reasons for taking summary action subside, the suspect's need for a neutral determination of probable cause increases significantly. The consequences of prolonged detention may be more serious than the interference occasioned by arrest. Pretrial confinement may imperil the suspect's job, interrupt his source of income, and impair his family relationships. Even pretrial release may be accompanied by burdensome conditions that effect a significant restraint of liberty. When the stakes are this high, the detached judgment of a neutral magistrate is essential if the Fourth Amendment is to furnish meaningful protection from unfounded interference with liberty. Accordingly, we hold that the Fourth Amendment requires a judicial determination of probable cause as a prerequisite to extended restraint of liberty following arrest. * * *

> [A]dversary safeguards are not essential for the probable cause determination required by the Fourth Amendment. The sole issue is whether there is probable cause for detaining the arrested person pending further proceedings. This issue can be determined reliably without an adversary hearing. The standard is the same as that for arrest. That standard—probable cause to believe the suspect has committed a crime—traditionally has been decided by a magistrate in a nonadversary proceeding on hearsay and written testimony, and the Court has approved these informal modes of proof. * * *

> * * * Whatever procedure a State may adopt, it must provide a fair and reliable determination of probable cause as a condition for any significant pretrial restraint of liberty, and this determination must be made by a judicial officer either before or promptly after arrest.

In order to satisfy the *Gerstein* timeliness requirement, a jurisdiction must provide a probable cause determination within 48 hours after a warrantless arrest, absent a bona fide emergency or other "extraordinary circumstance." County of Riverside v. McLaughlin, 500 U.S. 44, 111 S.Ct. 1661, 114 L.Ed.2d 49 (1991).

One question left unanswered by *Gerstein* and *McLaughlin* is what remedy is available if a timely hearing is *not* provided. Imagine that you are a prosecutor, and a defense lawyer files a motion to free her client from jail on the ground that no *Gerstein* proceeding has been held. Given that the hearing can be *ex parte* and based on hearsay evidence, what would be your likely response to this motion?

5.   *Exceptions to the Payton rule.* In Minnesota v. Olson, 495 U.S. 91, 110 S.Ct. 1684, 109 L.Ed.2d 85 (1990), two men robbed a gas station and killed the attendant. The gunman was quickly arrested and the murder weapon retrieved. His accomplice, however, escaped. The next day, the police learned that the second man was hiding with two women in the upper unit of a duplex. Hours later, the police surrounded the dwelling and, without permission or a warrant, entered the upper unit and arrested the suspect. The State sought to justify the warrantless entry on exigency grounds. Justice White, for seven justices, disagreed:

> In *Payton v. New York*, the Court had no occasion to "consider the sort of emergency or dangerous situation, described in our cases as 'exigent circumstances,' that would justify a warrantless entry into a home for the purpose of either arrest or search." This case requires us to determine whether the Minnesota Supreme Court was correct in holding that there were no exigent circumstances that justified the warrantless entry into the house to make the arrest.

> The Minnesota Supreme Court applied essentially the correct standard in determining whether exigent circumstances existed. The court observed that "a warrantless intrusion may be justified by hot pursuit of a fleeing felon, or imminent destruction of evidence, or the need to prevent a suspect's escape, or the risk of danger to the police or to other persons inside or outside the dwelling." The court also apparently thought that in the absence of hot pursuit there must be at least probable cause to believe that one or more of the other factors justifying the entry were present and that in assessing the risk of danger, the gravity of the crime and likelihood that the suspect is armed should be considered. Applying this standard, the state court determined that exigent circumstances did not exist.

> We are not inclined to disagree with this fact-specific application of the proper legal standard. The court pointed out that although a grave crime was involved, respondent "was known not to be the murderer but thought to be the driver of the getaway car," and that the police had already recovered the murder weapon. "The police knew that [two women] were with the suspect in the upstairs duplex with no suggestion of danger to them. Three or four Minneapolis police squads surrounded the house. The time was 3 p.m., Sunday. * * * It was evident the suspect was going nowhere. If he came out of the house he would have been promptly apprehended." We do not disturb the state court's judgment that these facts do not add up to exigent circumstances.

6. *Getting around Payton?* In *Payton*, suppose that Riddick, rather than his 3-year-old son, had come to the door. If the officers had said, "You are under arrest," would this warrantless arrest have been valid? What if they asked him to come outside, he complied, and *then* they arrested him?

Suppose that police surround an individual's residence and, with a bullhorn, order him out of the house, at which point they arrest him (again, without a warrant). Is *Payton* violated?

7. *Arrests in a third person's residence: the Steagald principle.* In Steagald v. United States, 451 U.S. 204, 101 S.Ct. 1642, 68 L.Ed.2d 38 (1981), the police secured a valid warrant to arrest Ricky Lyons, a fugitive, on drug charges. Based on information that Lyons could be found "during the next 24 hours" at the residence of acquaintance Gary Steagald, twelve officers proceeded to the house and entered without consent. They did not find Lyons, but they did observe cocaine belonging to Steagald. Steagald was later indicted on drug charges and sought to suppress the evidence discovered in the search on the ground that the officers entered the premises without a *search* warrant. The Court, per Justice Marshall, agreed:

> The question before us is a narrow one. The search at issue here took place in the absence of consent or exigent circumstances. Except in such special situations, we have consistently held that the entry into a home to conduct a search or make an arrest is unreasonable under the Fourth Amendment unless done pursuant to a warrant. * * * Here, of course, the agents had a warrant—one authorizing the arrest of Ricky Lyons. However, the Fourth Amendment claim here is not being raised by Ricky Lyons. Instead, the challenge to the search is asserted by a person not named in the warrant who was convicted on the basis of evidence uncovered during a search of his residence for Ricky Lyons. Thus, the narrow issue before us is whether an arrest warrant—as opposed to a search warrant—is adequate to protect the Fourth Amendment interests of persons not named in the warrant, when their homes are searched without their consent and in the absence of exigent circumstances.
>
> * * * [W]hile an arrest warrant and a search warrant both serve to subject the probable-cause determination of the police to judicial review, the interests protected by the two warrants differ. An arrest warrant is issued by a magistrate upon a showing that probable cause exists to believe that the subject of the warrant has committed an offense and thus the warrant primarily serves to protect an individual from an unreasonable seizure. A search warrant, in contrast, is issued upon a showing of probable cause to believe that the legitimate object of a search is located in a particular place, and therefore safeguards an individual's interest in the privacy of his home and possessions against the unjustified intrusion of the police.

Thus, whether the arrest warrant issued in this case adequately safeguarded the interests protected by the Fourth Amendment depends upon what the warrant authorized the agents to do. To be sure, the warrant embodied a judicial finding that there was probable cause to believe that Ricky Lyons had committed a felony, and the warrant therefore authorized the officers to seize Lyons. However, the agents sought to do more than use the warrant to arrest Lyons in a public place or in his home; instead, they relied on the warrant as legal authority to enter the home of a third person based on their belief that Ricky Lyons might be a guest there. Regardless of how reasonable this belief might have been, it was never subjected to the detached scrutiny of a judicial officer. Thus, while the warrant in this case may have protected Lyons from an unreasonable seizure, it did absolutely nothing to protect petitioner's privacy interest in being free from an unreasonable invasion and search of his home. * * * In the absence of exigent circumstances, we have consistently held that such judicially untested determinations are not reliable enough to justify * * * a search of a home for objects in the absence of a search warrant. We see no reason to depart from this settled course when the search of a home is for a person rather than an object.

8. *Problem: Payton versus Watson.* Police officers have probable cause to arrest Alice for a drug-related offense. The officers drive to Alice's residence without a warrant. Upon arrival in their police van, they observe Alice standing directly in the doorway ("one step forward would have put her outside, one step backward would have put her in the vestibule of her residence"). The officers get out of the van, guns drawn, shouting "police." Alice retreats into her residence. The officers follow her inside through the open door and arrest her. Inside, the police discover drugs in plain view. Should evidence of these drugs be excluded from her trial? See United States v. Santana, 427 U.S. 38, 96 S.Ct. 2406, 49 L.Ed.2d 300 (1976).

9. *Problem: Payton versus Steagald.* Police officers, armed with a warrant to arrest *B* for a felony, receive a tip that *B* is "staying" at a specific apartment building, in apartment #118; they show *B*'s picture to the apartment manager, who states that *B* "might be staying" in apartment #118; an occupant of the building informs them that *B* had been outside the building smoking a cigarette before the police arrived; another occupant tells the police that he observed *B* enter apartment #118 just before the police arrived; the officers knock at apartment #118; a female opens the door, but refuses to allow them to enter; police enter without her consent. State v. Blanco, 237 Wis.2d 395, 614 N.W.2d 512 (App.2000). Which case applies: *Payton* or *Steagald*? Suppose, instead, that the police had been informed by occupants of the apartment building that they believed *B* was at work, not at home at the time, but the police still go to the apartment and enter. Does this affect the constitutionality of the police entry?

10. *Executing an arrest: use of force.* Recent events in cities around the United States (e.g., Chicago, Illinois; Ferguson, Missouri; Cleveland, Ohio; and Charleston, South Carolina), in which unarmed citizens (frequently young African-American males) have been shot by law enforcement officers, have increased attention to the question of what level of force is justifiable in law enforcement, in particular, to make arrests. A 2008 Police Public Contact Survey conducted by the federal Bureau of Justice Statistics reported that, among persons who had contact with police, 1.4% "had force used or threatened against them during the most recent contact," that "men were more likely than females to have force used or threatened, * * * and blacks were more likely than whites or Hispanics to experience use or threat of force." Of those who had force used or threatened, 74% felt that the officer's actions were excessive in view of the circumstances. http://www.bjs.gov/index.cfm?ty=tp&tid=703. An April, 2016 Police Accountability Task Force report in Chicago similarly reported that its "own data gives validity to the widely held belief the police have no regard for the sanctity of life when it comes to people of color." https://chicagopatf.org/wp-content/uploads/2016/04/PATF_Final_Report_4_13_16-1.pdf. (at p, 7).

Of course, *believing* that force used was excessive does not make it so, but the Justice Department has determined that some police departments (*e.g.*, Albuquerque, New Mexico and Cleveland, Ohio) have been guilty of a pattern of use of excessive force. http://www.justice.gov/sites/default/files/crt/legacy/2014/04/10/apd_findings_4-10-14.pdf (April 10, 2014 letter from Jocelyn Samuels, Acting Assistant Attorney General, Department of Justice, Civil Rights Division, to Albuquerque Mayor Richard J. Berry); http://www.justice.gov/opa/pr/justice-department-and-city-cleveland-agree-reform-division-police (Justice Department Office of Public Affairs announcement that "Justice Department Reaches Agreement with City of Cleveland to Reform Division of Police Following Finding of a Pattern or Practice of Excessive Force").

The Fourth Amendment is relevant in this regard. After all, an arrest constitutes a seizure of the person, and the Fourth Amendment prohibits unreasonable seizures. This means that an arrest is constitutionally unreasonable, even if an arrest is based on probable cause, if it is executed in an excessive manner. But, what constitutes excessive force from a Fourth Amendment perspective?

The Supreme Court initially spoke to the issue in Tennessee v. Garner, 471 U.S. 1, 105 S.Ct. 1694, 85 L.Ed.2d 1 (1985), when it held that an officer's use of deadly force against a fleeing "young, slight, unarmed" burglary suspect violated the Fourth Amendment. As Justice White put it for the Court, "[i]t is not better that all felony suspects die than that they escape. Where the suspect poses no immediate threat to the officer and no threat to others, the harm resulting from failing to apprehend him does not justify the use of deadly force to do so."

More recent Supreme Court opinions have backed away from *Garner*. In Scott v. Harris, 550 U.S. 372, 127 S.Ct. 1769, 167 L.Ed.2d 686 (2007), the Court stated that the issue of what constitutes excessive force and, thus, what constitutes an unreasonable seizure of a person, is not susceptible to "an easy-to-apply legal test." Instead, "in the end we must still slosh though the factbound morass of 'reasonableness.' " The Court noted that "*Garner* does not establish a magical on/off switch that triggers rigid preconditions whenever an officer's actions constitute 'deadly force.' " Thus, the *Scott* Court held that a deputy sheriff did not use unreasonable force when he rammed a motorist's car from behind to end a long "public-endangering" car chase that began when the deputy sought to pull over the motorist for driving 73 miles-per-hour in a 55-mile zone. The deputy's action caused the speeding car to go off the roadway, turn over, crash, and leave its driver a quadriplegic. The Court reasoned that the fleeing driver posed a "substantial" and "immediate" risk of serious injury to innocent persons on the road, rendering the officer's action—seizure—reasonable.

As the Court put it in Graham v. Connor, 490 U.S. 386, 109 S.Ct. 1865, 104 L.Ed.2d 443 (1989), "what was implicit in *Garner*'s analysis" is "that *all* claims that law enforcement officers have used excessive force—deadly or not—in the course of an arrest, investigatory stop, or other 'seizure' of a free citizen should be analyzed under the Fourth Amendment * * * 'reasonableness' standard."

C. SEARCH WARRANTS

1. THE CONSTITUTIONAL DEBATE

The Fourth Amendment contains two clauses. The first one (the "reasonableness clause") declares a right to be free from unreasonable searches and seizures of persons, houses, papers and effects. The second clause, the "warrant clause," sets out the requirements of any valid warrant (most especially, that it be supported by probable cause, and that it particularly describe "the place to be searched, and the persons or things to be seized"). What is the relationship of these two clauses? Does the second inform the first, or are they independent? More specifically, what is the role of the search warrant in Fourth Amendment jurisprudence: If the police search and seize without a warrant, have they, at least presumptively, violated the Fourth Amendment?

Consider first Justice Jackson's observations for the Court in Johnson v. United States, 333 U.S. 10, 68 S.Ct. 367, 92 L.Ed. 436 (1948) (emphasis added):

> The point of the Fourth Amendment, which often is not grasped by zealous officers, is not that it denies law enforcement the support of the usual inferences which reasonable men draw from evidence. Its protection consists in requiring that those

inferences be drawn by a neutral and detached magistrate instead of being judged by the officer engaged in the often competitive enterprise of ferreting out crime. Any assumption that evidence sufficient to support a magistrate's disinterested determination to issue a search warrant will justify the officers in making a search without a warrant would reduce the Amendment to a nullity * * *. * * * *When the right of privacy must reasonably yield to the right of search is, as a rule, to be decided by a judicial officer, not by a policeman or government enforcement agent.*

There are exceptional circumstances in which, on balancing the need for effective law enforcement against the right of privacy, it may be contended that a magistrate's warrant for search may be dispensed with. But * * * [n]o reason is offered [in this case] for not obtaining a search warrant except the inconvenience to the officers and some slight delay necessary to prepare papers and present the evidence to a magistrate. These are never very convincing reasons and, in these circumstances, certainly are not enough to by-pass the constitutional requirement.

Johnson represents the traditional position that the Fourth Amendment is better served if police officers apply for warrants, rather than act on the basis of their own probable cause determinations. *Johnson*'s reasoning has led courts often to say that there is a "search warrant requirement" in the Fourth Amendment. Stated in its most extreme version, "[t]he command of the Fourth Amendment to the American police officer and the American Prosecutor is simple: 'You always have to get a warrant—UNLESS YOU CAN'T.'" Dyson v. State, 122 Md.App. 413, 712 A.2d 573 (1998). More traditionally, the constitutional "requirement" has been described as follows: "Searches conducted outside the judicial process, without prior approval by judge or magistrate, are *per se* unreasonable under the Fourth Amendment—subject only to a few specifically established and well-delineated exceptions." Katz v. United States, 389 U.S. 347, 88 S.Ct. 507, 19 L.Ed.2d 576 (1967).

The competing view is that the proper Fourth Amendment test "is not whether it is reasonable [or practicable] to procure a search warrant, but whether the search was reasonable." United States v. Rabinowitz, 339 U.S. 56, 70 S.Ct. 430, 94 L.Ed. 653 (1950). After all, the argument goes, the text of the Amendment bars unreasonable searches and seizures; nowhere does it state that warrants are required, only that when warrants *are* sought they must meet certain specifications.

These two alternative views of the relationship of the warrant clause to the reasonableness clause have co-existed uneasily for many years. As Justice Scalia, concurring in California v. Acevedo, 500 U.S. 565, 111 S.Ct. 1982, 114 L.Ed.2d 619 (1991), has observed:

Although the Fourth Amendment does not explicitly impose the requirement of a warrant, it is of course textually possible to consider that implicit within the requirement of reasonableness. For some years after the (still continuing) explosion in Fourth Amendment litigation that followed our announcement of the exclusionary rule in *Weeks v. United States*, [p. 76], our jurisprudence lurched back and forth between imposing a categorical warrant requirement and looking to reasonableness alone. (The opinions preferring a warrant involved searches of structures.) By the late 1960's, the preference for a warrant had won out, at least rhetorically.

The victory was illusory. * * * [T]he "warrant requirement" had become so riddled with exceptions that it was basically unrecognizable. In 1985, one commentator cataloged nearly 20 such exceptions * * * . Since then, we have added at least two more. * * *

* * * There can be no clarity in this area unless we make up our minds [about whether to impose a categorical warrant requirement or look to reasonableness alone], and unless the principles we express comport with the actions we take.

As you read the remaining cases in this chapter, you will see the Supreme Court moving (if not lurching, as Scalia described it) back and forth between an emphasis on the warrant clause and a more generalized reasonableness analysis.

NOTES AND QUESTIONS

1.   If the warrant clause does *not* inform the reasonableness clause—that is, if there is no Fourth Amendment "warrant requirement"—does this mean that Congress and the various states may abolish warrants altogether and thereby render the warrant clause useless? If so, does that mean that the requirement of probable cause, which is attached to the warrant provision, may also be avoided?

2.   One scholar has suggested a solution for the self-created quagmire in which the Supreme Court finds itself in the search warrant debate:

[C]urrent fourth amendment law, complete with the constant tinkering which it necessarily entails, should be abandoned altogether. Instead, there are two, and only two, ways of looking at the fourth amendment which will provide the police with reasonably coherent direction as to how they must proceed and the courts with a consistent basis for decision.

The two models, briefly, may be called the "no lines" and the "bright line" approaches. Model I, no lines, uses tort law as a guide in proposing that the hopeless quest of establishing detailed guidelines for police behavior in every possible situation be abandoned. It suggests that the Court adopt the following view of the fourth amendment: A search or seizure must be reasonable, considering all relevant factors on a case-by-case basis. If it is not, the evidence must be excluded. Factors to be considered include, but are not limited to, whether probable cause existed, whether a warrant was obtained, whether exigent circumstances existed, the nature of the intrusion, the quantum of evidence possessed by the police, and the seriousness of the offense under investigation. This model * * * is (roughly) the current practice in Germany and other European countries. Moreover, in most cases it reflects the result, though not the reasoning, of current Supreme Court cases.

The second model may be as shocking at first glance to "law and order" advocates as the first model is to civil libertarians. It is, basically, that the Supreme Court should actually enforce the warrant doctrine to which it has paid lip service for so many years. That is, a warrant is *always* required for *every* search and seizure when it is practicable to obtain one. However, in order that this requirement be workable and not be swallowed by its exception, the warrant need not be in writing but rather may be phoned or radioed into a magistrate (where it will be tape recorded and the recording preserved) who will authorize or forbid the search orally. By making the procedure for obtaining a warrant less difficult (while only marginally reducing the safeguards it provides), the number of cases where "emergencies" justify an exception to the warrant requirement should be very small.

* * * Model I, by presenting an unabashedly *unclear* rule that provides no guidelines, will never have to be modified to suit an unusual fact situation. While not an ideal solution, it will, it is argued, work considerably better than the present system where the Court purports to set forth clear rules but does not actually do so. Model II presents a clear rule which can be lived with. If the Court required a modified, easily obtainable warrant to be used in all but true emergencies, the police would know what is expected of them and would be able to conform their conduct to the requirement of the law, much as they have accommodated their behavior to the *Miranda* requirements.

Craig M. Bradley, *Two Models of the Fourth Amendment*, 83 Mich. L. Rev. 1468, 1471–72 (1985).

3. *A reality check. Does any of this debate really matter in day-to-day affairs: the warrant application process.* If it *is* better for magistrates, rather than "officers engaged in the often competitive enterprise of ferreting out crime," to make probable cause determinations, one is left with a nagging empirical question: *Does* the warrant application process serve its intended purpose? *Do* magistrates give warrant applications careful attention?

Perhaps not. In the most thorough national study of search warrant procedures ever conducted, the National Center for State Courts reported that in one city studied, the average length of magisterial review was a mere two minutes and forty-eight seconds; ten percent of the warrant applications were approved in less than one minute. Richard Van Duizend et al., The Search Warrant Process: Preconceptions, Perceptions, and Practices 31 (1984). In a more recent study in San Diego, only a few judges handled the great majority of warrant applications because of magistrate-shopping by the police. As a "veteran officer" candidly admitted, "some judges were known for being liberal in granting search warrants." Laurence A. Benner & Charles T. Samarkos, *Searching for Narcotics in San Diego: Preliminary Findings from the San Diego Search Warrant Project*, 36 Cal. West. L. Rev. 221, 227–228 (2000). As one scholar has put it, "warrants [are] commonly issu[ed] upon something more akin to 'possible cause' rather than 'probable cause.'" Fabio Arcila, Jr., *In the Trenches: Searches and the Misunderstood Common-Law History of Suspicion and Probable Cause*, 10 U. Pa. J. Const. L. 1, 58 (2007) (also suggesting that this approach does not appreciably differ from the Framers' era).

4. There is a lot of valuable scholarly literature dealing with the questions being considered here. *E.g.*, Akhil Reed Amar, *Fourth Amendment, First Principles*, 107 Harv. L. Rev. 757 (1994) (contending that the Framers of the Constitution did not intend that there be a "warrant requirement"); Tracey Maclin, *When the Cure for the Fourth Amendment is Worse than the Disease*, 68 So. Cal. L. Rev. 1 (1994) (responding to, and rejecting, Amar's position, and concluding that the warrant clause "defines and interprets" the reasonableness requirement of the Fourth Amendment); and Thomas Y. Davies, *Recovering the Original Fourth Amendment*, 98 Mich. L. Rev. 547 (1999) (concluding that although neither side of the debate adheres perfectly to the historical meaning of the Fourth Amendment, the "warrant-preference construction is more faithful to the Framers' concerns").

2. ELEMENTS OF A VALID SEARCH WARRANT

Warrants must meet constitutional specifications. They must be based on probable cause and supported by oath or affirmation, matters considered in Part A. of this chapter. Two other required features are considered here.

LO-JI SALES, INC. V. NEW YORK

Supreme Court of the United States, 1979.
442 U.S. 319, 99 S.Ct. 2319, 60 L.Ed.2d 920.

MR. CHIEF JUSTICE BURGER delivered the opinion of the Court [joined by JUSTICES BRENNAN, STEWART, WHITE, MARSHALL, BLACKMUN, POWELL, REHNQUIST, and STEVENS]. * * *

I

On June 20, 1976, an investigator for the New York State Police purchased two reels of film from petitioner's so-called "adult" bookstore. Upon viewing them, he concluded the films violated New York's obscenity laws. On June 25, he took them to a Town Justice for a determination whether there was reasonable cause to believe the films violated the state obscenity laws so as to justify a warrant to search the seller's store. The Town Justice viewed both films in their entirety, and he apparently concluded they were obscene. Based upon an affidavit of the investigator subscribed before the Town Justice after this viewing, a warrant issued authorizing the search of petitioner's store and the seizure of other copies of the two films exhibited to the Town Justice.

The investigator's affidavit also contained an assertion that "similar" films and printed matter portraying similar activities could be found on the premises, and a statement of the affiant's belief that the items were possessed in violation of the obscenity laws. The warrant application requested that the Town Justice accompany the investigator to petitioner's store for the execution of the search warrant. The stated purpose was to allow the Town Justice to determine independently if any other items at the store were possessed in violation of law and subject to seizure. The Town Justice agreed. Accordingly, the warrant also contained a recital that authorized the seizure of "[t]he following items that the Court independently [on examination] has determined to be possessed in violation of Article 235 of the Penal Law * * * ." However, at the time the Town Justice signed the warrant there were no items listed or described following this statement. As noted earlier, the only "things to be seized" that were described in the warrant were copies of the two films the state investigator had purchased. * * *

The Town Justice and the investigator enlisted three other State Police investigators, three uniformed State Police officers, and three members of the local prosecutor's office—a total of 11—and the search party converged on the bookstore. * * *

The search began in an area of the store which contained booths in which silent films were shown by coin-operated projectors. The clerk adjusted the machines so that the films could be viewed by the Town Justice without coins; it is disputed whether he volunteered or did so under compulsion * * * . The Town Justice viewed 23 films for two to three minutes each and, satisfied there was probable cause to believe they were obscene, then ordered the films and the projectors seized.

The Town Justice next focused on another area containing four coin-operated projectors showing both soundless and sound films. After viewing each film for two to five minutes, again without paying, he ordered them seized along with their projectors.

The search party then moved to an area in which books and magazines were on display. The magazines were encased in clear plastic or cellophane wrappers which the Town Justice had two police officers remove prior to his examination of the books. Choosing only magazines that did not contain significant amounts of written material, he spent not less than 10 seconds nor more than a minute looking through each one. When he was satisfied that probable cause existed, he immediately ordered the copy which he had reviewed, along with other copies of the same or "similar" magazines, seized. An investigator wrote down the titles of the items seized. All told, 397 magazines were taken.

The final area searched was one in which petitioner displayed films and other items for sale behind a glass enclosed case. When it was announced that each box of film would be opened, the clerk advised that a picture on the outside of the box was representative of what the film showed. Therefore, if satisfied from the picture that there was probable cause to believe the film in the box was obscene, the Town Justice ordered the seizure of all copies of that film. As with the magazines, an investigator wrote down the titles of the films seized, a total of 431 reels. * * *

After the search and seizure was completed, the seized items were taken to a State Police barracks where they were inventoried. Each item was then listed on the search warrant, and late the same night the completed warrant was given to the Town Justice. The warrant, which had consisted of 2 pages when he signed it before the search, by late in the day contained 16 pages. It is clear, therefore, that the particular description of "things to be seized" was entered in the document after the seizure and impoundment of the books and other articles. * * *

II

This search warrant and what followed the entry on petitioner's premises are reminiscent of the general warrant or writ of assistance of the 18th century against which the Fourth Amendment was intended to protect. Except for the specification of copies of the two films previously purchased, the warrant did not purport to "particularly describ[e] * * * the * * * things to be seized." Based on the conclusory statement of the police investigator that other similarly obscene materials would be found at the store, the warrant left it entirely to the discretion of the officials conducting the search to decide what items were likely obscene and to accomplish their seizure. The Fourth Amendment does not permit such action. Nor does the Fourth Amendment countenance open-ended warrants, to be completed while a search is being conducted and items seized or after the seizure has been carried out.

This search began when the local justice and his party entered the premises. But at that time there was not sufficient probable cause to pursue a search beyond looking for additional copies of the two specified films, assuming the validity of searching even for those. And the record is clear that the search began and progressed pursuant to the sweeping open-ended authorization in the warrant. It was not limited at the outset as a search for other copies of the two "sample" films; it expanded into a more extensive search because other items were found that the local justice deemed illegal. * * *

III

We have repeatedly said that a warrant authorized by a neutral and detached judicial officer is "a more reliable safeguard against improper searches than the hurried judgment of a law enforcement officer 'engaged in the often competitive enterprise of ferreting out crime.' " * * *

The Town Justice did not manifest that neutrality and detachment demanded of a judicial officer when presented with a warrant application for a search and seizure. We need not question the subjective belief of the Town Justice in the propriety of his actions, but the objective facts of record manifest an erosion of whatever neutral and detached posture existed at the outset. He allowed himself to become a member, if not the leader, of the search party which was essentially a police operation. Once in the store, he conducted a generalized search under authority of an invalid warrant; he was not acting as a judicial officer but as an adjunct law enforcement officer. When he ordered an item seized because he believed it was obscene, he instructed the police officers to seize all "similar" items as well, leaving determination of what was "similar" to the officer's discretion. Indeed, he yielded to the State Police even the completion of the general provision of the warrant. * * *

IV * * *

* * * Our society is better able to tolerate the admittedly pornographic business of petitioner than a return to the general warrant era; violations of law must be dealt with within the framework of constitutional guarantees. * * *

NOTES AND QUESTIONS

1. *"Neutral and detached magistrate" requirement.* What is it, precisely, that the Town Justice did wrong in *Lo-Ji Sales*? Is it that he left his regular office to make himself available to law enforcement personnel?

Should a search warrant be invalidated (and if so, why) in the following circumstances: (a) it is issued by the State Attorney General, see Coolidge v. New Hampshire, 403 U.S. 443, 91 S.Ct. 2022, 29 L.Ed.2d 564 (1971); (b) the magistrate is paid a fee for issuing a warrant, but is not paid if she denies an application for a warrant, see Connally v. Georgia, 429 U.S. 245, 97 S.Ct. 546, 50 L.Ed.2d 444 (1977); (c) the magistrate fails to read the warrant that she signs, see United States v. Decker, 956 F.2d 773 (8th Cir. 1992); or (d) she spends only 2 minutes, 48 seconds considering the warrant application (see p. 223, Note 3)?

2. *The warrant particularity requirement.* This requirement is intended to prevent general searches, the immediate evil "that motivated the framing and adoption of the Fourth Amendment," *Payton v. New York*, p. 205, and to prevent "the seizure of one thing under a warrant describing another." Andresen v. Maryland, 427 U.S. 463, 96 S.Ct. 2737, 49 L.Ed.2d 627 (1976).

Andresen also teaches that a court should read a search warrant in fair context. For example, in *Andresen*, a warrant authorized the police to seize a long list of specific items relating to a specific incident of false pretenses, "together with other fruits, instrumentalities, and evidence of crime at this [time] unknown." Although Andresen argued that the latter phrase permitted the search and seizure of *any* evidence of *any* crime—clearly a violation of the particularity requirement—the Court concluded that the challenged phrase, coming as part of the same sentence that included the long list of specific items, "must be read as authorizing only the search for and seizure of evidence relating to" the particular crime under investigation.

3. *Particularity by incorporation?* Suppose a search warrant fails to properly specify the property to be seized. May this constitutional failing be cured if the *application* for the warrant particularizes the items to be seized? In Groh v. Ramirez, 540 U.S. 551, 124 S.Ct. 1284, 157 L.Ed.2d 1068 (2004), the Supreme Court answered this way:

> The fact that the *application* adequately described "the things to be seized" does not save the *warrant* from its facial invalidity. The Fourth Amendment by its terms requires particularity in the warrant, not in the supporting documents. * * * We do not say that the Fourth Amendment forbids a warrant from cross-referencing other documents. Indeed, most Courts of Appeals have held that a court may construe a warrant with reference to a supporting application or affidavit if the warrant uses appropriate words of incorporation, and if the supporting document accompanies the warrant.

3. EXECUTION OF A SEARCH WARRANT

Introductory Note

Consider these facts: An informant reported to Atlanta police officers that he purchased two bags of crack cocaine from a man at a house the address of which he provided to the police. Based on this information, the officers obtained a warrant to search the residence. Armed with the warrant, eight members of the Atlanta police department went to the home where, in a military-type raid, broke into the house without warning—they did not knock at the door, nor did they announce their identity and purpose before breaking in. Inside the house was one person, Kathryn Johnston, a 92-year-old woman living alone.

Assume for current purposes (there is more to the story, which will be disclosed later) that the information the police received justified the search warrant. Thus, the police had a valid search warrant. And, surely the fact that the information proved wrong—this was not a house where drugs were sold—does not render the warrant invalid. Warrants are based on probable cause, not certainty. However, was the *means* of execution of the warrant unconstitutional? Specifically, does it violate the Fourth Amendment for agents of the government to enter a person's home forcibly, rather than giving the occupant(s) notice of their presence and allowing the resident(s) an opportunity to comply with the officers' demand for entry?

In Wilson v. Arkansas, 514 U.S. 927, 115 S.Ct. 1914, 131 L.Ed.2d 976 (1995), the Supreme Court, per Justice Clarence Thomas, ruled unanimously that the Fourth Amendment prohibition on unreasonable searches and seizures contains an implicit knock-and-announce rule previously embedded in the common law. However, the Court warned that "[t]his is not to say, of course, that every entry must be preceded by an announcement. The Fourth Amendment's flexible requirement of reasonableness should not be read to mandate a rigid rule of announcement that ignores countervailing law enforcement interests." Without "attempt[ing] a comprehensive catalog" of exceptions to the requirement, Justice Thomas suggested in dictum that the knock-and-announce principle does not apply

under circumstances presenting a threat of physical violence. Similarly, courts [have] held that an officer may dispense with announcement in cases where a prisoner escapes from him and retreats to his dwelling. Proof of "demand and refusal" was deemed unnecessary in such cases because it would be a "senseless ceremony" to require an officer in pursuit of a recently escaped arrestee to make an announcement prior to breaking the door to retake him. Finally, courts have indicated that unannounced entry may be justified where police officers have reason to believe that evidence would likely be destroyed if advance notice were given.

Soon after *Wilson*, the Supreme Court considered the exceptions to the knock-and-announce principle more fully.

RICHARDS V. WISCONSIN

Supreme Court of the United States, 1997.
520 U.S. 385, 117 S.Ct. 1416, 137 L.Ed.2d 615.

JUSTICE STEVENS delivered the opinion of the Court [joined by CHIEF JUSTICE REHNQUIST, and JUSTICES O'CONNOR, SCALIA, KENNEDY, SOUTER, THOMAS, GINSBURG, and BREYER]. * * *

In this case, the Wisconsin Supreme Court concluded that police officers are *never* required to knock and announce their presence when executing a search warrant in a felony drug investigation. In so doing, it * * * concluded that *Wilson* [*v. Arkansas*, Introductory Note] did not preclude this *per se* rule. We disagree with the court's conclusion that the Fourth Amendment permits a blanket exception to the knock-and-announce requirement for this entire category of criminal activity. * * *

I

On December 31, 1991, police officers in Madison, Wisconsin obtained a warrant to search Steiney Richards' hotel room for drugs and related paraphernalia. The search warrant was the culmination of an investigation that had uncovered substantial evidence that Richards was one of several individuals dealing drugs out of hotel rooms in Madison. The police requested a warrant that would have given advance authorization for a "no-knock" entry into the hotel room, but the magistrate explicitly deleted those portions of the warrant.

The officers arrived at the hotel room at 3:40 a.m. Officer Pharo, dressed as a maintenance man, led the team. With him were several plainclothes officers and at least one man in uniform. Officer Pharo knocked on Richards' door and, responding to the query from inside the room, stated that he was a maintenance man. With the chain still on the door, Richards cracked it open. Although there is some dispute as to what occurred next, Richards acknowledges that when he opened the door he saw the man in uniform standing behind Officer Pharo. He quickly slammed the door closed and, after waiting two or three seconds, the officers began kicking and ramming the door to gain entry to the locked room. At trial, the officers testified that they identified themselves as police while they were kicking the door in. When they finally did break into the room, the officers caught Richards trying to escape through the window. They also found cash and cocaine hidden in plastic bags above the bathroom ceiling tiles.

Richards sought to have the evidence from his hotel room suppressed on the ground that the officers had failed to knock and announce their presence prior to forcing entry into the room. The trial court denied the motion, concluding that the officers could gather from Richards' strange behavior when they first sought entry that he knew they were police officers and that he might try to destroy evidence or to escape. * * * Richards appealed the decision to the Wisconsin Supreme Court and that court affirmed.

The Wisconsin Supreme Court did not delve into the events underlying Richards' arrest in any detail, but accepted the following facts: "[O]n December 31, 1991, police executed a search warrant for the motel room of the defendant seeking evidence of the felonious crime of Possession with Intent to Deliver a Controlled Substance in violation of [state law]. They did not knock and announce prior to their entry. Drugs were seized."

Assuming these facts, the court * * * held that "when the police have a search warrant, supported by probable cause, to search a residence for evidence of delivery of drugs or evidence of possession with intent to deliver drugs, they necessarily have reasonable cause to believe exigent circumstances exist" to justify a no-knock entry. The court concluded that nothing in *Wilson*'s acknowledgment that the knock-and-announce rule was an element of the Fourth Amendment "reasonableness" requirement would prohibit application of a *per se* exception to that rule in a category of cases.

In reaching this conclusion, the Wisconsin court found it reasonable—after considering criminal conduct surveys, newspaper articles, and other judicial opinions—to assume that all felony drug crimes will involve "an extremely high risk of serious if not deadly injury to the police as well as the potential for the disposal of drugs by the occupants prior to entry by the police." Notwithstanding its acknowledgment that in "some cases, police officers will undoubtedly decide that their safety, the safety of others, and the effective execution of the warrant dictate that they knock and announce," the court concluded that exigent circumstances justifying a no-knock entry are always present in felony drug cases. * * * Accordingly, the court determined that police in Wisconsin do not need specific information about dangerousness, or the possible destruction of drugs in a particular case, in order to dispense with the knock-and-announce requirement in felony drug cases. * * *

II

We recognized in *Wilson* that the knock-and-announce requirement could give way "under circumstances presenting a threat of physical violence," or "where police officers have reason to believe that evidence would likely be destroyed if advance notice were given." It is indisputable that felony drug investigations may frequently involve both of these circumstances. The question we must resolve is whether this fact justifies dispensing with case-by-case evaluation of the manner in which a search was executed.

The Wisconsin court explained its blanket exception as necessitated by the special circumstances of today's drug culture, and the State asserted at oral argument that the blanket exception was reasonable in "felony drug cases because of the convergence in a violent and dangerous form of commerce of weapons and the destruction of drugs." But creating exceptions to the knock-and-announce rule based on the "culture" surrounding a general category of criminal behavior presents at least two serious concerns.

First, the exception contains considerable overgeneralization. For example, while drug investigation frequently does pose special risks to officer safety and the preservation of evidence, not every drug investigation will pose these risks to a substantial degree. For example, a search could be conducted at a time when the only individuals present in a residence have no connection with the drug activity and thus will be unlikely to threaten officers or destroy evidence. Or the police could know that the drugs being searched for were of a type or in a location that made them impossible to destroy quickly. In those situations, the asserted governmental interests in preserving evidence and maintaining safety may not outweigh the individual privacy interests intruded upon by a no-knock entry.[5] Wisconsin's blanket rule impermissibly insulates these cases from judicial review.

A second difficulty with permitting a criminal-category exception to the knock-and-announce requirement is that the reasons for creating an exception in one category can, relatively easily, be applied to others. Armed bank robbers, for example, are, by definition, likely to have weapons, and the fruits of their crime may be destroyed without too much difficulty. If a *per se* exception were allowed for each category of criminal

---

[5]   The State asserts that the intrusion on individual interests effectuated by a no-knock entry is minimal because the execution of the warrant itself constitutes the primary intrusion on individual privacy and that the individual privacy interest cannot outweigh the generalized governmental interest in effective and safe law enforcement. While it is true that a no-knock entry is less intrusive than, for example, a warrantless search, the individual interests implicated by an unannounced, forcible entry should not be unduly minimized. As we observed in *Wilson v. Arkansas*, the common law recognized that individuals should have an opportunity to themselves comply with the law and to avoid the destruction of property occasioned by a forcible entry. These interests are not inconsequential.

Additionally, when police enter a residence without announcing their presence, the residents are not given any opportunity to prepare themselves for such an entry. The State pointed out at oral argument that, in Wisconsin, most search warrants are executed during the late night and early morning hours. The brief interlude between announcement and entry with a warrant may be the opportunity that an individual has to pull on clothes or get out of bed.

investigation that included a considerable—albeit hypothetical—risk of danger to officers or destruction of evidence, the knock-and-announce element of the Fourth Amendment's reasonableness requirement would be meaningless.

Thus, the fact that felony drug investigations may frequently present circumstances warranting a no-knock entry cannot remove from the neutral scrutiny of a reviewing court the reasonableness of the police decision not to knock and announce in a particular case. Instead, in each case, it is the duty of a court confronted with the question to determine whether the facts and circumstances of the particular entry justified dispensing with the knock-and-announce requirement.

In order to justify a "no-knock" entry, the police must have a reasonable suspicion that knocking and announcing their presence, under the particular circumstances, would be dangerous or futile, or that it would inhibit the effective investigation of the crime by, for example, allowing the destruction of evidence. This standard—as opposed to a probable cause requirement[b]—strikes the appropriate balance between the legitimate law enforcement concerns at issue in the execution of search warrants and the individual privacy interests affected by no-knock entries. This showing is not high, but the police should be required to make it whenever the reasonableness of a no-knock entry is challenged.

III

Although we reject the Wisconsin court's blanket exception to the knock-and-announce requirement, we conclude that the officers' no-knock entry into Richards' hotel room did not violate the Fourth Amendment. We agree with the trial court * * * that the circumstances in this case show that the officers had a reasonable suspicion that Richards might destroy evidence if given further opportunity to do so.

The judge who heard testimony at Richards' suppression hearing concluded that it was reasonable for the officers executing the warrant to believe that Richards knew, after opening the door to his hotel room the first time, that the men seeking entry to his room were the police. Once the officers reasonably believed that Richards knew who they were, the court concluded, it was reasonable for them to force entry immediately given the disposable nature of the drugs. * * *

Accordingly, although we reject the blanket exception to the knock-and-announce requirement for felony drug investigations, the judgment of the Wisconsin Supreme Court is affirmed.

---

[b] To satisfy the "reasonable suspicion" standard, an officer must be able to articulate something more than an "inchoate and unparticularized suspicion or 'hunch.'" *Terry v. Ohio*, p. 389. There must exist "some minimal level of objective justification" for the police conduct. This is a less demanding standard than "probable cause." See generally, *Alabama v. White*, p. 433.

NOTES AND QUESTIONS

1.   As a practical matter, who are the big winners in this case, the police or home dwellers? Is it fair to assert that in virtually every drug-dealer case the police will possess reasonable suspicion that persons inside are armed or that contraband will likely be destroyed if they announce their presence and intention?

Why does the *Richards* Court permit the police to apply a less demanding standard than probable cause in determining whether an exception to the knock-and-announce requirement exists? Does Justice Stevens offer an explanation?

2.   *More to come.* There is much more to the story of the knock-and-announce rule, but as to that you will need to wait until we get to the next chapter. See p. 553, *infra.*

3.   What interests are served by the knock-and-announce rule? What reasons did Justice Stevens give for the rule?

4.   *The rest of the Atlanta story.* We promised you more to the story of the Atlanta police officers who entered a "drug house" only to find a 92-year-old woman inside. The story is more sordid than we suggested, and tragic. As it turned out, the informant lied to the police about purchasing drugs at that home. He had never been there and, it seems, picked that address at random. The police, in turn, lied to the magistrate when they applied for the warrant: an officer under oath falsely claimed that he had personally purchased drugs at that address in his undercover status. He further perjured himself by stating that he had seen surveillance cameras in the house. (Based on these false statements, *was* the warrant valid? What case or doctrine would come into play with this new information? Hint: see p. 201, Note 6.)

The sordid story now turns tragic. The elderly and infirm Kathryn Johnston, fearful of intruders, apparently kept a gun with her, which she fired at them when the intruders entered her small house. The outcome was inevitable: She was shot to death in the ensuing hail of police bullets. And, then to finish the ugly events, one or more of the officers planted a small quantity of drugs on the premises to try to justify their actions.

The family of the deceased has sued the city. Two police officers were charged with murder and pleaded guilty to manslaughter and federal civil rights violations. A third officer, who had been stationed at the rear of the house, was charged with violating his oath of office (acquitted), falsely imprisoning Johnston (acquitted), and lying in an official investigation (convicted). See, *e.g.*, Shaila Dewan & Brenda Goodman, *Atlanta Officers Suspended In Inquiry on Killing in Raid*, New York Times, Nov. 28, 2006, at A16; Steve Visser, *Officer in Fatal '06 Raid Guilty of One Charge*, The Atlanta Journal-Constitution, May 21, 2008, at 1A; *Former Atlanta Cop Gets 4½ Years*, Atlanta Journal-Constitution, May 23, 2008, at 16; and Christian Boone & Marcus K. Garner, *Family Offers to Settle in Notorious Raid*, Atlanta Journal-Constitution, July 18, 2008, at 5H.

5.   After knocking and announcing their presence, how long must the police wait before they forcibly enter a residence and execute a warrant to search for cocaine? In United States v. Banks, 540 U.S. 31, 124 S.Ct. 521, 157 L.Ed.2d 343 (2003), officers armed with a warrant to search Banks's two-bedroom apartment for cocaine, knocked loudly, announced their purpose, and waited fifteen to twenty seconds for a response. When nobody came to the door, the police broke open the door with a battering ram, entered, and executed their warrant. As it turned out, Banks was in the shower and had not heard the police knock.

The Court unanimously held that although the "call is a close one, * * * we think that after 15 or 20 seconds without a response, police could fairly suspect that cocaine would be gone if they were reticent any longer." In short, an exigency justified the forcible entry. The fact that Banks was in the shower was irrelevant: "[I]t is enough to say that the facts known to the police are what count in judging reasonable waiting time."

Does it matter to the analysis that the police entry required them to damage the property? The Court explained that where, as here, an exigency justifies immediate forcible entry, the police "may damage premises so far as necessary for a no-knock entrance without demonstrating the suspected risk in any more detail than the law demands for an unannounced intrusion simply by lifting the latch." However, the Court suggested that in some circumstances damage to property *could* be relevant to the reasonableness of an entry to execute a search warrant. Specifically, when immediate entry is *not* required as a result of an exigency, "the reasonable wait time" before causing damage to enter "may well be longer" than if the door to the house is open and they can enter without damaging the residence:

> Suffice it to say that the need to damage property in the course of getting in is a good reason to require more patience than it would be reasonable to expect if the door were open. Police seeking a stolen piano may be able to spend more time to make sure they really need the battering ram.

6.   *In anticipation of a warrant.* What, if anything, may the police do *before* they execute a warrant—indeed, before they even have a warrant—to ensure that criminal evidence they expect to find during the search will not be destroyed or moved while they apply for the warrant? For example, in Illinois v. McArthur, 531 U.S. 326, 121 S.Ct. 946, 148 L.Ed.2d 838 (2001), police officers who were already at McArthur's home, developed probable cause at the scene to believe that he had hidden marijuana in his trailer home. Two officers asked McArthur for permission to search the premises for marijuana, but he refused. As a consequence, one officer left to apply for a search warrant. The second officer informed McArthur, who by this time was standing on the porch, that he could not reenter his trailer unless accompanied by an officer. McArthur reentered his home two or three times, to make phone calls and get cigarettes, and each time the officer stood just

inside the door to observe McArthur. The first officer returned two hours later with a search warrant, which was promptly executed.

The Supreme Court, 8–1, approved the police action, although it conceded that by preventing McArthur or others from entering the trailer home, the police had effectively seized the premises without a warrant. Justice Breyer explained:

> We conclude that the restriction at issue was reasonable, and hence lawful, in light of the following circumstances, which we consider in combination. First, the police had probable cause to believe that McArthur's trailer home contained evidence of a crime and contraband, namely, unlawful drugs. * * *

> Second, the police had good reason to fear that, unless restrained, McArthur would destroy the drugs before they could return with a warrant. * * * They reasonably could have concluded that McArthur, * * * suspecting an imminent search, would, if given the chance, get rid of the drugs fast.

> Third, the police made reasonable efforts to reconcile their law enforcement needs with the demands of personal privacy. They neither searched the trailer nor arrested McArthur before obtaining a warrant. Rather, they imposed a significantly less restrictive restraint, preventing McArthur only from entering the trailer unaccompanied. They left his home and his belongings intact—until a neutral Magistrate, finding probable cause, issued a warrant.

> Fourth, the police imposed the restraint for a limited period of time, namely, two hours. As far as the record reveals, this time period was no longer than reasonably necessary for the police, acting with diligence, to obtain the warrant. Given the nature of the intrusion and the law enforcement interest at stake, this brief seizure of the premises was permissible.

7.   *Executing a warrant after entry: The scope of the search of the premises.* Once officers are lawfully on premises to execute a warrant, various search principles apply. First, the police may search containers large enough to hold the criminal evidence for which they are searching. For example, if a warrant authorizes a search of a suspect's bedroom for a stolen ring, the officer may, pursuant to the warrant, open dresser drawers, jewelry boxes, and other containers in the bedroom that could hold the ring. In contrast, if they are searching a bedroom for a stolen 60-inch television set, the police would not be authorized to open drawers or to open boxes smaller than the television.

Second, while officers execute a search warrant, they may seize an object *not* described in the warrant, if they have probable cause to believe it is a seizable item (contraband, or a fruit, instrumentality or evidence of a crime).

Third, as Maryland v. Garrison, 480 U.S. 79, 107 S.Ct. 1013, 94 L.Ed.2d 72 (1987), teaches, information that becomes available to officers immediately before or during the execution of a warrant may require them to cease or narrow their search, notwithstanding the dictates of the warrant. In *Garrison*, the officers obtained a warrant to search "the premises known as 2036 Park Avenue third floor apartment" belonging to one Lawrence McWebb. What the officers did not know when they sought the warrant, or even as they entered the third floor "apartment," was that the third floor was divided into *two* apartments, one occupied by McWebb, and a second by petitioner Garrison. The officers erroneously entered Garrison's premises; only after they discovered contraband there did they realize the mistake. They immediately ceased the search of Garrison's premises. However, they sought to prosecute him on the basis of the evidence they found before they discovered their error. The Court upheld the validity of the erroneous warrant and its execution:

> If the officers had known, or should have known, that the third floor contained two apartments before they entered the living quarters on the third floor, and thus had been aware of the error in the warrant, they would have been obligated to limit their search to McWebb's apartment. Moreover, as the officers recognized, they were required to discontinue the search of respondent's apartment as soon as they discovered that there were two separate units on the third floor and therefore were put on notice of the risk that they might be in a unit erroneously included within the terms of the warrant. The officers' conduct and the limits of the search were based on the information available as the search proceeded. While the purposes justifying a police search strictly limit the permissible extent of the search, the Court has also recognized the need to allow some latitude for honest mistakes that are made by officers in the dangerous and difficult process of making arrests and executing search warrants.

What is the essence of the Fourth Amendment lesson of *Garrison*?

8. *Searching persons during the execution of a warrant.* A warrant may authorize the search of a person, but it should be explicit. A warrant to search a home or other premises does not provide implicit authority to search persons found at the scene, even if the criminal evidence for which the police are looking might be on them.

For example, in Ybarra v. Illinois, 444 U.S. 85, 100 S.Ct. 338, 62 L.Ed.2d 238 (1979), the police obtained a valid warrant to search a tavern and "Greg," the bartender, for "evidence of the offense of possession of a controlled substance." Seven or eight officers proceeded to the tavern in the late afternoon. While most of the officers searched the premises and bartender Greg, one officer conducted cursory searches of a dozen or so customers present and, in the case of Ventura Ybarra, conducted a more extensive search. The latter search turned up a cigarette pack, inside which were six tinfoil packets containing a brown powdery substance that later turned out to be heroin. The Court held that the warrant did not authorize the Ybarra search.

Ybarra does *not* stand for the proposition that police officers may *never* search persons coincidentally at the scene during a warranted search. However, the police must have independent probable cause to search the person ("a person's mere propinquity to others independently suspected of criminal activity does not, without more, give rise to probable cause to search that person"), as well as some justification for conducting the search without a warrant, *i.e.*, they must be able to point to an exception to the "warrant requirement."

9. *Seizure of persons during warranted searches.* Although the police may not automatically *search* persons present at the scene during the execution of a search warrant (Note 8), the Supreme Court announced a bright-line rule in Michigan v. Summers, 452 U.S. 692, 101 S.Ct. 2587, 69 L.Ed.2d 340 (1981), regarding *seizure* of persons in such circumstances: "[A] warrant to search [a residence] for contraband founded on probable cause implicitly carries with it the limited authority to detain the occupants of the premises while a proper search is conducted."

The right of detention pursuant to *Summers* is automatic: it "does not require law enforcement to have particular suspicion that an individual [seized under the rule] is involved in criminal activity or poses a specific danger to the officers." Bailey v. United States, 568 U.S. ___, 133 S.Ct. 1031, 185 L.Ed.2d 19 (2013). Moreover, the right of the police under *Summers* to detain an occupant during a warranted search of a residence necessarily includes the right to use reasonable force to secure and maintain detention of the occupant. Muehler v. Mena, 544 U.S. 93, 125 S.Ct. 1465, 161 L.Ed.2d 299 (2005).[c]

On the other hand, because the right of detention is automatic and can result in a relatively lengthy detention while the search is conducted (see footnote *c*), the *Summers* rule is limited to the detention of occupants of the residence at the time of the search, and persons discovered "immediately outside a residence at the moment the police officers execute[ ] the search warrant." However, "[o]nce an individual has left the immediate vicinity of the premises to be searched," the bright-line *Summers* rule no longer applies. *Bailey, supra.*

In *Bailey*, the police observed *B* leave the residence that they intended to search pursuant to a warrant, but he was not detained until he was approximately a mile away from the premises. Because this detention was beyond "any reasonable understanding" of the term "immediate vicinity" of the residence, the Court held, 6–3, that *B*'s seizure fell outside the scope of *Summers*.

---

[c] The "reasonable force" used in *Mena*: when a SWAT team entered the premises, Mena was asleep in her bed. She was placed in handcuffs at gunpoint, moved to a garage, and detained there in that condition for two to three hours while the premises were searched pursuant to the warrant.

Justice Scalia, joined by Justices Ginsburg and Kagan, joined the Court's opinion, but added:

> It bears repeating that the "general rule" is "that Fourth Amendment seizures are 'reasonable' only if based on probable cause." *Summers* embodies a categorical judgment that *in one narrow circumstance*—the presence of occupants during the execution of a search warrant—seizures are reasonable despite the absence of probable cause. * * *

> *Summers'* clear rule simplifies the task of officers who encounter occupants during a search. * * * But having received the advantage of *Summers'* categorical authorization to detain occupants incident to a search, the Government must take the bitter with the sweet: Beyond *Summers'* spatial bounds, seizures must comport with ordinary Fourth Amendment principles.

Justice Breyer, joined by Justices Thomas and Alito, dissented, contending that the majority had "substituted a line based on indeterminate geography for a line based on realistic considerations related to basic Fourth Amendment concerns such as privacy, safety, evidence destruction, and flight."

D. WARRANT CLAUSE: WHEN ARE WARRANTS REQUIRED?

According to Katz v. United States, 389 U.S. 347, 88 S.Ct. 507, 19 L.Ed.2d 576 (1967), "searches conducted outside the judicial process, without prior approval by judge or magistrate, are *per se* unreasonable under the Fourth Amendment—subject only to a few specifically established and well-delineated exceptions." This chapter section considers the most important "exceptions" to the search warrant "requirement."

We primarily leave to Section E. of this chapter the Court's move away from "warrant requirement" jurisprudence to an explicit, flexible "reasonableness" balancing approach. Despite this sectioning of the topics, however, there is no absolute line separating the two lines of cases. One could treat the materials in Section E. as further "warrant exceptions," albeit discussed in "reasonableness" terms; or you could say that some of the "exceptions" here are, simply, examples of reasonable (warrantless) searches, albeit discussed in "warrant exception" terms.

1. EXIGENT CIRCUMSTANCES

Introduction

The facts in Warden v. Hayden, 387 U.S. 294, 87 S.Ct. 1642, 18 L.Ed.2d 782 (1967), provide a fairly classic example of the first warrant exception we will discuss. A robbery occurred. Almost immediately thereafter, police officers received information that the armed robber had entered a specified house. They rushed to the house. One officer knocked and announced their presence. A woman (as it turns out, the wife of suspect Hayden), answered the door. They explained that they believed a robber had entered the home and requested to search. As the Court put it, "[s]he offered no objection."

Multiple officers spread out throughout the first and second floors, as well as the cellar, looking for the suspect and any weapon used in the crime or which might be used against them. They did, indeed, discover weapons (in a bathroom flush tank adjoining the bedroom where Hayden, pretending to be asleep, was discovered; and under the mattress of the bed) and evidence relating to the crime (in a washing machine in the cellar).

Hayden sought to suppress the seized evidence on the ground that it was discovered without a search warrant. Justice Brennan, writing for the Court, stated that "neither the entry without warrant to search for the robber, nor the search for him without warrant was invalid. Under the circumstances of this case, 'the exigencies of the situation made the course imperative.' "

Hayden is a relatively uncontroversial application of the exigency exception to the "search warrant requirement." After all, they had probable cause to believe the robber was in the home they entered, and time was of the essence in this so-called "hot pursuit" situation. But, now, consider the next case.

KENTUCKY V. KING

Supreme Court of the United States, 2011.
563 U.S. 452, 131 S.Ct. 1849, 179 L.Ed.2d 865.

JUSTICE ALITO delivered the opinion of the Court [joined by CHIEF JUSTICE ROBERTS, and JUSTICES SCALIA, KENNEDY, THOMAS, BREYER, SOTOMAYOR, and KAGAN].

It is well established that "exigent circumstances," including the need to prevent the destruction of evidence, permit police officers to conduct an otherwise permissible search without first obtaining a warrant. In this case, we consider whether this rule applies when police, by knocking on the door of a residence and announcing their presence, cause the occupants to attempt to destroy evidence. The Kentucky Supreme Court held that the exigent circumstances rule does not apply in the case at hand because the police should have foreseen that their conduct would prompt the occupants to attempt to destroy evidence. We reject this interpretation of the exigent circumstances rule. The conduct of the police prior to their entry into the apartment was entirely lawful. They did not violate the Fourth Amendment or threaten to do so. In such a situation, the exigent circumstances rule applies.

I

A

This case concerns the search of an apartment in Lexington, Kentucky. Police officers set up a controlled buy of crack cocaine outside an apartment complex. Undercover Officer Gibbons watched the deal take place from an unmarked car in a nearby parking lot. After the deal occurred, Gibbons radioed uniformed officers to move in on the suspect. He told the officers that the suspect was moving quickly toward the breezeway of an apartment building, and he urged them to "hurry up and get there" before the suspect entered an apartment.

In response to the radio alert, the uniformed officers drove into the nearby parking lot, left their vehicles, and ran to the breezeway. Just as they entered the breezeway, they heard a door shut and detected a very strong odor of burnt marijuana. At the end of the breezeway, the officers saw two apartments, one on the left and one on the right, and they did not know which apartment the suspect had entered. Gibbons had radioed that the suspect was running into the apartment on the right, but the officers did not hear this statement because they had already left their vehicles. Because they smelled marijuana smoke emanating from the apartment on the left, they approached the door of that apartment.

Officer Steven Cobb, one of the uniformed officers who approached the door, testified that the officers banged on the left apartment door "as loud as [they] could" and announced, " 'This is the police' " or " 'Police, police, police.' " Cobb said that "[a]s soon as [the officers] started banging on the door," they "could hear people inside moving," and "[i]t sounded as [though] things were being moved inside the apartment." These noises, Cobb testified, led the officers to believe that drug-related evidence was about to be destroyed.

At that point, the officers announced that they "were going to make entry inside the apartment." Cobb then kicked in the door, the officers entered the apartment, and they found three people in the front room: respondent Hollis King, respondent's girlfriend, and a guest who was smoking marijuana. * * * [T]hey saw marijuana and powder cocaine in plain view. In a subsequent search, they also discovered crack cocaine, cash, and drug paraphernalia.

Police eventually entered the apartment on the right. Inside, they found the suspected drug dealer who was the initial target of their investigation.

B

* * * Respondent filed a motion to suppress the evidence from the warrantless search, but the Circuit Court denied the motion. The Circuit Court concluded that the officers had probable cause to investigate the marijuana odor and that the officers "properly conducted [the investigation] by initially knocking on the door of the apartment unit and awaiting the response or consensual entry." Exigent circumstances justified the warrantless entry, the court held, because "there was no response at all to the knocking," and because "Officer Cobb heard movement in the apartment which he reasonably concluded were persons in the act of destroying evidence, particularly narcotics because of the smell." * * *

The Supreme Court of Kentucky reversed. As a preliminary matter, the court observed that there was "certainly some question as to whether the sound of persons moving [inside the apartment] was sufficient to establish that evidence was being destroyed." But the court did not answer that question. Instead, it "assume[d] for the purpose of argument that exigent circumstances existed."

To determine whether police impermissibly created the exigency, the Supreme Court of Kentucky announced a two-part test. First, the court held, police cannot "deliberately creat[e] the exigent circumstances with the bad faith intent to avoid the warrant requirement." Second, even absent bad faith, the court concluded, police may not rely on exigent circumstances if "it was reasonably foreseeable that the investigative tactics employed by the police would create the exigent circumstances." Although the court found no evidence of bad faith, it held that exigent circumstances could not justify the search because it was reasonably foreseeable that the occupants would destroy evidence when the police knocked on the door and announced their presence. * * *

II

A * * *

Although the text of the Fourth Amendment does not specify when a search warrant must be obtained, this Court has inferred that a warrant must generally be secured. * * * But we have also recognized that this presumption may be overcome in some circumstances because "[t]he ultimate touchstone of the Fourth Amendment is 'reasonableness.'" Accordingly, the warrant requirement is subject to certain reasonable exceptions.

One well-recognized exception applies when " 'the exigencies of the situation' make the needs of law enforcement so compelling that [a] warrantless search is objectively reasonable under the Fourth Amendment."

This Court has identified several exigencies that may justify a warrantless search of a home. Under the "emergency aid" exception, for example, "officers may enter a home without a warrant to render emergency assistance to an injured occupant or to protect an occupant from imminent injury." [See p. 249, Note 5, for further discussion of the emergency exception.—Eds.] Police officers may enter premises without a warrant when they are in hot pursuit of a fleeing suspect. And—what is relevant here—the need "to prevent the imminent destruction of evidence" has long been recognized as a sufficient justification for a warrantless search.

B

Over the years, lower courts have developed an exception to the exigent circumstances rule, the so-called "police-created exigency" doctrine. Under this doctrine, police may not rely on the need to prevent destruction of evidence when that exigency was "created" or "manufactured" by the conduct of the police. * * *

* * * [L]ower courts have not agreed on the test to be applied. Indeed, the petition in this case maintains that "[t]here are currently five different tests being used by the United States Courts of Appeals," and that some state courts have crafted additional tests.

III

A

* * * Where, as here, the police did not create the exigency by engaging or threatening to engage in conduct that violates the Fourth Amendment, warrantless entry to prevent the destruction of evidence is reasonable and thus allowed.[4]

B

Some lower courts have adopted a rule that is similar to the one that we recognize today. But others, including the Kentucky Supreme Court, have imposed additional requirements that are unsound and that we now reject.

Bad faith. Some courts, including the Kentucky Supreme Court, ask whether law enforcement officers " 'deliberately created the exigent circumstances with the bad faith intent to avoid the warrant requirement.' "

This approach is fundamentally inconsistent with our Fourth Amendment jurisprudence. "Our cases have repeatedly rejected" a

---

[4]   There is a strong argument to be made that, at least in most circumstances, the exigent circumstances rule should not apply where the police, without a warrant or any legally sound basis for a warrantless entry, threaten that they will enter without permission unless admitted. In this case, however, no such actual threat was made, and therefore we have no need to reach that question.

subjective approach, asking only whether "the circumstances, viewed *objectively,* justify the action." * * *

The reasons for looking to objective factors, rather than subjective intent, are clear. * * * [T]his Court has long taken the view that "evenhanded law enforcement is best achieved by the application of objective standards of conduct, rather than standards that depend upon the subjective state of mind of the officer."

Reasonable foreseeability. Some courts, again including the Kentucky Supreme Court, hold that police may not rely on an exigency if " 'it was reasonably foreseeable that the investigative tactics employed by the police would create the exigent circumstances.' " * * *

Adoption of a reasonable foreseeability test would * * * introduce an unacceptable degree of unpredictability. For example, whenever law enforcement officers knock on the door of premises occupied by a person who may be involved in the drug trade, there is *some* possibility that the occupants may possess drugs and may seek to destroy them. Under a reasonable foreseeability test, it would be necessary to quantify the degree of predictability that must be reached before the police-created exigency doctrine comes into play. * * *

Probable cause and time to secure a warrant. Some courts * * * fault law enforcement officers if, after acquiring evidence that is sufficient to establish probable cause to search particular premises, the officers do not seek a warrant but instead knock on the door and seek either to speak with an occupant or to obtain consent to search.

This approach unjustifiably interferes with legitimate law enforcement strategies. There are many entirely proper reasons why police may not want to seek a search warrant as soon as the bare minimum of evidence needed to establish probable cause is acquired. Without attempting to provide a comprehensive list of these reasons, we note a few.

First, the police may wish to speak with the occupants of a dwelling before deciding whether it is worthwhile to seek authorization for a search. They may think that a short and simple conversation may obviate the need to apply for and execute a warrant. Second, the police may want to ask an occupant of the premises for consent to search because doing so is simpler, faster, and less burdensome than applying for a warrant. * * * Third, law enforcement officers may wish to obtain more evidence before submitting what might otherwise be considered a marginal warrant application. * * * And finally, in many cases, law enforcement may not want to execute a search that will disclose the existence of an investigation because doing so may interfere with the acquisition of additional evidence against those already under suspicion or evidence

about additional but as yet unknown participants in a criminal scheme.
* * *

Standard or good investigative tactics. Finally, some lower court cases suggest that law enforcement officers may be found to have created or manufactured an exigency if the court concludes that the course of their investigation was "contrary to standard or good law enforcement practices (or to the policies or practices of their jurisdictions)." This approach fails to provide clear guidance for law enforcement officers and authorizes courts to make judgments on matters that are the province of those who are responsible for federal and state law enforcement agencies.

C

Respondent argues for a rule that differs from those discussed above, but his rule is also flawed. Respondent contends that law enforcement officers impermissibly create an exigency when they "engage in conduct that would cause a reasonable person to believe that entry is imminent and inevitable." In respondent's view, relevant factors include the officers' tone of voice in announcing their presence and the forcefulness of their knocks. But the ability of law enforcement officers to respond to an exigency cannot turn on such subtleties. * * *

If respondent's test were adopted, it would be extremely difficult for police officers to know how loudly they may announce their presence or how forcefully they may knock on a door without running afoul of the police-created exigency rule. And in most cases, it would be nearly impossible for a court to determine whether that threshold had been passed. The Fourth Amendment does not require the nebulous and impractical test that respondent proposes.

D

For these reasons, we conclude that the exigent circumstances rule applies when the police do not gain entry to premises by means of an actual or threatened violation of the Fourth Amendment. This holding provides ample protection for the privacy rights that the Amendment protects.

When law enforcement officers who are not armed with a warrant knock on a door, they do no more than any private citizen might do. And whether the person who knocks on the door and requests the opportunity to speak is a police officer or a private citizen, the occupant has no obligation to open the door or to speak. And even if an occupant chooses to open the door and speak with the officers, the occupant need not allow the officers to enter the premises and may refuse to answer any questions at any time. * * *

Occupants who choose not to stand on their constitutional rights but instead elect to attempt to destroy evidence have only themselves to blame for the warrantless exigent-circumstances search that may ensue.

IV

We now apply our interpretation of the police-created exigency doctrine to the facts of this case.

A

We need not decide whether exigent circumstances existed in this case. * * * The Kentucky Supreme Court "assum[ed] for the purpose of argument that exigent circumstances existed," and it held that the police had impermissibly manufactured the exigency.

We, too, assume for purposes of argument that an exigency existed. We decide only the question on which the Kentucky Supreme Court ruled and on which we granted certiorari: Under what circumstances do police impermissibly create an exigency? Any question about whether an exigency actually existed is better addressed by the Kentucky Supreme Court on remand.

B

In this case, we see no evidence that the officers either violated the Fourth Amendment or threatened to do so prior to the point when they entered the apartment. Officer Cobb testified without contradiction that the officers "banged on the door as loud as [they] could" and announced either " 'Police, police, police' " or " 'This is the police.' " This conduct was entirely consistent with the Fourth Amendment, and we are aware of no other evidence that might show that the officers either violated the Fourth Amendment or threatened to do so (for example, by announcing that they would break down the door if the occupants did not open the door voluntarily). * * *

Respondent argues that the officers "demanded" entry to the apartment, but he has not pointed to any evidence in the record that supports this assertion. * * * There is no evidence of a "demand" of any sort, much less a demand that amounts to a threat to violate the Fourth Amendment. If there is contradictory evidence that has not been brought to our attention, the state court may elect to address that matter on remand. * * *

The judgment of the Kentucky Supreme Court is reversed, and the case is remanded for further proceedings not inconsistent with this opinion.[d]

---

[d]   Upon remand, the Supreme Court of Kentucky concluded that the "Commonwealth * * * failed to show circumstances establishing the imminent destruction of evidence." King v. Commonwealth, 386 S.W.3d 119 (Ky. 2012). It reversed the original ruling of the Circuit Court

JUSTICE GINSBURG, dissenting.

The Court today arms the police with a way routinely to dishonor the Fourth Amendment's warrant requirement in drug cases. In lieu of presenting their evidence to a neutral magistrate, police officers may now knock, listen, then break the door down, nevermind that they had ample time to obtain a warrant. I dissent from the Court's reduction of the Fourth Amendment's force. * * *

This case involves a principal exception to the warrant requirement, the exception applicable in "exigent circumstances." "[C]arefully delineated," the exception should govern only in genuine emergency situations. Circumstances qualify as "exigent" when there is an imminent risk of death or serious injury, or danger that evidence will be immediately destroyed, or that a suspect will escape. The question presented: May police, who could pause to gain the approval of a neutral magistrate, dispense with the need to get a warrant by themselves creating exigent circumstances? I would answer no, as did the Kentucky Supreme Court. The urgency must exist, I would rule, when the police come on the scene, not subsequent to their arrival, prompted by their own conduct.

I

Two pillars of our Fourth Amendment jurisprudence should have controlled the Court's ruling: First, "whenever practical, [the police must] obtain advance judicial approval of searches and seizures through the warrant procedure"; second, unwarranted "searches and seizures inside a home" bear heightened scrutiny. The warrant requirement, Justice Jackson observed, ranks among the "fundamental distinctions between our form of government, where officers are under the law, and the police-state where they are the law." The Court has accordingly declared warrantless searches, in the main, *per se* unreasonable." "[T]he police bear a heavy burden," the Court has cautioned, "when attempting to demonstrate an urgent need that might justify warrantless searches."

That heavy burden has not been carried here. There was little risk that drug-related evidence would have been destroyed had the police delayed the search pending a magistrate's authorization. * * * Nothing in the record shows that, prior to the knock at the apartment door, the occupants were apprehensive about police proximity.

(trial court), suppressed the evidence, and remanded the matter to that court, which then dismissed the indictment "with prejudice" (thus precluding any further prosecution). The government appealed, claiming that the trial court lacked authority to dismiss with prejudice. The Court of Appeals of Kentucky agreed with the government. It remanded the case still again (nine years after the original events) to the trial court, "whereupon, if the trial court deems it appropriate, the indictment may be dismissed without prejudice." Commonwealth v. King, 2014 WL 4667325 (Ky. Sept. 19, 2014).

In no quarter does the Fourth Amendment apply with greater force than in our homes, our most private space which, for centuries, has been regarded as " 'entitled to special protection.' " Home intrusions, the Court has said, are indeed "the chief evil against which * * * the Fourth Amendment is directed." How "secure" do our homes remain if police, armed with no warrant, can pound on doors at will and, on hearing sounds indicative of things moving, forcibly enter and search for evidence of unlawful activity?

II * * *

Under an appropriately reined-in "emergency" or "exigent circumstances" exception, the result in this case should not be in doubt. The target of the investigation's entry into the building, and the smell of marijuana seeping under the apartment door into the hallway, the Kentucky Supreme Court rightly determined, gave the police "probable cause * * * sufficient * * * to obtain a warrant to search the * * * apartment." As that court observed, nothing made it impracticable for the police to post officers on the premises while proceeding to obtain a warrant authorizing their entry. Before this Court, Kentucky does not urge otherwise. * * *

I * * * would not allow an expedient knock to override the warrant requirement. Instead, I would accord that core requirement of the Fourth Amendment full respect. * * *

NOTES AND QUESTIONS

1. Notice: Although the police did not obtain a pre-search determination of probable cause by a magistrate, i.e., a warrant, there *was* probable cause for the search. The point here is: An exception to the warrant requirement does *not* necessarily (or, even usually) dispense with the probable cause requirement.

2. Do you believe the police acted reasonably here? Why, or why not? If your answer is yes, and since the Fourth Amendment only prohibits unreasonable searches and seizures, isn't the Court correct in its ruling?

Let's look further. Suppose a police officer believes she has probable cause to search a suspect's house for drugs, but she is lazy and does not want to go to the effort of seeking a warrant. Or, maybe she just doesn't care about the Fourth Amendment, so she decides to act on her own. Therefore, she goes to the suspect's house and, just as in *King*, she bangs on the door as loud as possible, and announces, "This is the police," or "Police, police, police." The officer hears the sound of what may be drugs being flushed down the toilet. So, she breaks in without a warrant. Under *King*, is *her* warrantless entry constitutional? *Should* it be?

If *Katz* (p. 96) is right that warrantless searches "are *per se* unreasonable * * * subject to a few * * * well-delineated exceptions"—that is, if the default position truly is that police officers should almost always get warrants rather than act on their own belief that they have sufficient grounds for the search—and if it is true that "physical entry of the home is the chief evil against which the wording of the Fourth Amendment is directed," *Payton*, p. 205 (quoting United States v. United States District Court, 407 U.S. 297, 92 S.Ct. 2125, 32 L.Ed.2d 752 (1972)), then is Justice Ginsburg right that this case improperly reduces the force of the Fourth Amendment?

3.   *Warrantless entry of the home (part 1). King assumed* an exigency existed—albeit, arguably, a police-created one—for entry into the home. For what constitutes an exigent circumstance that justifies a warrantless entry of a home, look again at what the *King* court said, and look (again?) at *Minnesota v. Olson*, p. 215, Note 5 (in particular, the second paragraph of the opinion).

4.   *Warrantless entry of the home (part 2).* In Welsh v. Wisconsin, 466 U.S. 740, 104 S.Ct. 2091, 80 L.Ed.2d 732 (1984), the police received information that *W* had recently been driving his vehicle in a manner that suggested that he was inebriated or very sick. The police proceeded to *W*'s nearby home and entered without consent or an arrest warrant. They justified their action on the grounds of exigency—that they needed to accurately ascertain *W*'s blood-alcohol content before the evidence would naturally be "destroyed" by the passage of time. They placed him under arrest for operating a motor vehicle under the influence of an intoxicant, a noncriminal offense that could result in a monetary fine and subject *W* to civil forfeiture of his automobile. The Supreme Court held, however, that the warrantless entry of *W*'s house was unlawful:

> Our hesitation in finding exigent circumstances, especially when warrantless arrests in the home are at issue, is particularly appropriate when the underlying offense for which there is probable cause to arrest is relatively minor. Before agents of the government may invade the sanctity of the home, the burden is on the government to demonstrate exigent circumstances that overcome the presumption of unreasonableness that attaches to all warrantless home entries. When the government's interest is only to arrest for a minor offense, that presumption of unreasonableness is difficult to rebut, and the government usually should be allowed to make such arrests only with a warrant issued upon probable cause by a neutral and detached magistrate.

Although *Welsh* was interpreted by many as a virtual bar on any warrantless entry of a home, based on exigency, in a minor-offense investigation, this interpretation proved false.

In Stanton v. Sims, 571 U.S. ___, 134 S.Ct. 3, 187 L.Ed.2d 341 (2013), a civil case, the Court held unanimously that a warrantless hot pursuit entry into a residence can be constitutional, even if it is only based on the belief that a minor crime had been committed. The Court said that *Welsh* does not "lay down a categorical rule [requiring warrants to enter a home] for all cases involving minor offenses." It observed that *Welsh* said "only that a warrant is 'usually' required." It also observed that, unlike the facts in *Stanton*, *Welsh* did not involve a warrantless entry of a home in hot pursuit: "there was no immediate or continuous pursuit of [Welsh] from the scene of the crime [into the home]." Although the Court was not called upon in *Stanton* to announce a firm rule on the subject, it noted that "despite our emphasis in *Welsh* on the fact that the crime at issue was minor * * *[,] nothing in the opinion establishes that the seriousness of the crime is equally important *in cases of hot pursuit*."

5. *Warrantless entry of a home (part 3)*: *the "community caretaking" emergency doctrine.* Sometimes the police act in a "community caretaking" function. For example, suppose the police look through a window and see a person apparently having a heart attack. Under what circumstances may officers enter a home without a warrant (which, after all, is a document intended to be used in criminal investigations), in order to deal with such an emergency? What if the emergency has criminal law implications, as well? Consider the unanimous opinion of Chief Justice Roberts in Brigham City, Utah v. Stuart, 547 U.S. 398, 126 S.Ct. 1943, 164 L.Ed.2d 650 (2006):

> At about 3 a.m., four police officers responded to a call regarding a loud party at a residence. Upon arriving at the house, * * * they observed two juveniles drinking beer in the backyard. They entered the backyard, and saw—through a screen door and windows—an altercation taking place in the kitchen of the home. * * * [F]our adults were attempting, with some difficulty, to restrain a juvenile. The juvenile eventually "broke free, swung a fist and struck one of the adults in the face." The officer testified that he observed the victim of the blow spitting blood into a nearby sink. The other adults continued to try to restrain the juvenile, pressing him up against a refrigerator with such force that the refrigerator began moving across the floor. At this point, an officer opened the screen door and announced the officers' presence. Amid the tumult, nobody noticed. The officer entered the kitchen and again cried out, and as the occupants slowly became aware that the police were on the scene, the altercation ceased.
>
> The officers subsequently arrested respondents and charged them with contributing to the delinquency of a minor, disorderly conduct, and intoxication. In the trial court, respondents filed a motion to suppress all evidence obtained after the officers entered the home, arguing that the warrantless entry violated the Fourth Amendment. * * *
>
> It is a "'basic principle of Fourth Amendment law that searches and seizures inside a home without a warrant are presumptively unreasonable.'" Nevertheless, because the ultimate touchstone of the Fourth Amendment is "reasonableness," the warrant requirement is subject to certain exceptions. * * *

One exigency obviating the requirement of a warrant is the need to assist persons who are seriously injured or threatened with such injury. * * * [L]aw enforcement officers may enter a home without a warrant to render emergency assistance to an injured occupant or to protect an occupant from imminent injury. * * *

Respondents * * * contend that their conduct was not serious enough to justify the officers' intrusion into the home. They rely on *Welsh* v. *Wisconsin* [Note 4, *supra*], in which we held that "an important factor to be considered when determining whether any exigency exists is the gravity of the underlying offense for which the arrest is being made." This contention, too, is misplaced. *Welsh* involved a warrantless entry by officers to arrest a suspect for driving while intoxicated. There, the "only potential emergency" confronting the officers was the need to preserve evidence (*i.e.*, the suspect's blood-alcohol level)—an exigency that we held insufficient under the circumstances to justify entry into the suspect's home. Here, the officers were confronted with *ongoing* violence occurring *within* the home. *Welsh* did not address such a situation.

We think the officers' entry here was plainly reasonable under the circumstances. * * * [T]hey could see that a fracas was taking place inside the kitchen. A juvenile, fists clenched, was being held back by several adults. As the officers watch, he breaks free and strikes one of the adults in the face, sending the adult to the sink spitting blood.

In these circumstances, the officers had an objectively reasonable basis for believing both that the injured adult might need help and that the violence in the kitchen was just beginning. Nothing in the Fourth Amendment required them to wait until another blow rendered someone "unconscious" or "semi-conscious" or worse before entering. The role of a peace officer includes preventing violence and restoring order, not simply rendering first aid to casualties; an officer is not like a boxing (or hockey) referee, poised to stop a bout only if it becomes too one-sided.

The manner of the officers' entry was also reasonable. After witnessing the punch, one of the officers opened the screen door and "yelled in police." When nobody heard him, he stepped into the kitchen and announced himself again. Only then did the tumult subside. The officer's announcement of his presence was at least equivalent to a knock on the screen door. Indeed, it was probably the only option that had even a chance of rising above the din. Under these circumstances, there was no violation of the Fourth Amendment's knock-and-announce rule. Furthermore, once the announcement was made, the officers were free to enter; it would serve no purpose to require them to stand dumbly at the door awaiting a response while those within brawled on, oblivious to their presence.

6. *Problem*. A police officer drove to C's residence in order to talk to him about a noise complaint. When he arrived, he smelled the aroma of burnt marijuana coming from C's apartment. The officer testified that, at that moment, "he knew he lacked authority to enter." Therefore, to increase the chances C would open the door, he covered the front door peephole, moved to the side to ensure that he could not be seen through a nearby window, and knocked. C partially opened the front door to see who was there. The officer could see that C was holding a handgun (although not aimed at him). When C saw the officer, he shut the door. Now, perceiving C to be a threat, the officer shoved the door open and entered. Fourth Amendment violation? State v. Campbell, 300 P.3d 72 (Kan. 2013).

2. SEARCHES INCIDENT TO AN ARREST

a. General Principles

CHIMEL V. CALIFORNIA

Supreme Court of the United States, 1969.
395 U.S. 752, 89 S.Ct. 2034, 23 L.Ed.2d 685.

MR. JUSTICE STEWART delivered the opinion of the Court [joined by CHIEF JUSTICE WARREN, and JUSTICES DOUGLAS, HARLAN, BRENNAN, FORTAS, and MARSHALL]. * * *

The relevant facts are essentially undisputed. Late in the afternoon of September 13, 1965, three police officers arrived at the Santa Ana, California, home of the petitioner with a warrant authorizing his arrest for the burglary of a coin shop. The officers knocked on the door, identified themselves to the petitioner's wife, and asked if they might come inside. She ushered them into the house, where they waited 10 or 15 minutes until the petitioner returned home from work. When the petitioner entered the house, one of the officers handed him the arrest warrant and asked for permission to "look around." The petitioner objected, but was advised that "on the basis of the lawful arrest," the officers would nonetheless conduct a search. No search warrant had been issued.

Accompanied by the petitioner's wife, the officers then looked through the entire three-bedroom house, including the attic, the garage, and a small workshop. In some rooms the search was relatively cursory. In the master bedroom and sewing room, however, the officers directed the petitioner's wife to open drawers and "to physically move contents of the drawers from side to side so that [they] might view any items that would have come from [the] burglary." After completing the search, they seized numerous items—primarily coins, but also several medals, tokens, and a few other objects. The entire search took between 45 minutes and an hour.

At the petitioner's subsequent state trial on two charges of burglary, the items taken from his house were admitted into evidence against him, over his objection that they had been unconstitutionally seized. * * * [T]he appellate courts went on to hold that the search of the petitioner's home had been justified, despite the absence of a search warrant, on the ground that it had been incident to a valid arrest. * * *

Without deciding the question, we proceed on the hypothesis that the California courts were correct in holding that the arrest of the petitioner was valid under the Constitution. This brings us directly to the question whether the warrantless search of the petitioner's entire house can be constitutionally justified as incident to that arrest. The decisions of this Court bearing upon that question have been far from consistent, as even the most cursory review makes evident.

Approval of a warrantless search incident to a lawful arrest seems first to have been articulated by the Court in 1914 as dictum in *Weeks v. United States*, [p. 76], in which the Court stated:

> "What then is the present case? Before answering that inquiry specifically, it may be well by a process of exclusion to state what it is not. It is not an assertion of the right on the part of the Government, always recognized under English and American law, to search the person of the accused when legally arrested to discover and seize the fruits or evidences of crime."

That statement made no reference to any right to search the *place* where an arrest occurs, but was limited to a right to search the "person." Eleven years later the case of *Carroll v. United States*, 267 U.S. 132, 45 S.Ct. 280, 69 L.Ed. 543, brought the following embellishment of the *Weeks* statement:

> "When a man is legally arrested for an offense, whatever is found upon his person *or in his control* which it is unlawful for him to have and which may be used to prove the offense may be seized and held as evidence in the prosecution." (Emphasis added.)

Still, that assertion too was far from a claim that the "place" where one is arrested may be searched so long as the arrest is valid. Without explanation, however, the principle emerged in expanded form a few months later in *Agnello v. United States*, 269 U.S. 20, 46 S.Ct. 4, 70 L.Ed. 145—although still by way of dictum:

> "The right without a search warrant contemporaneously to search persons lawfully arrested while committing crime and to search the place where the arrest is made in order to find and seize things connected with the crime as its fruits or as the

means by which it was committed, as well as weapons and other things to effect an escape from custody, is not to be doubted."

[The Court then proceeded to summarize a long line of cases, including Harris v. United States, 331 U.S. 145, 67 S.Ct. 1098, 91 L.Ed. 1399 (1947) and Trupiano v. United States, 334 U.S. 699, 68 S.Ct. 1229, 92 L.Ed. 1663 (1948), in which the justices veered back and forth between an expansive and then narrow interpretation of the *Agnello* dictum (which subsequently became a holding) that police may, incident to an arrest, conduct a warrantless search of "the place where the arrest is made."]

In 1950 * * * came *United States v. Rabinowitz*, 339 U.S. 56, 70 S.Ct. 430, 94 L.Ed. 653, the decision upon which California primarily relies in the case now before us. In *Rabinowitz*, federal authorities had been informed that the defendant was dealing in stamps bearing forged overprints. On the basis of that information they secured a warrant for his arrest, which they executed at his one-room business office. At the time of the arrest, the officers "searched the desk, safe, and file cabinets in the office for about an hour and a half," and seized 573 stamps with forged overprints. The stamps were admitted into evidence at the defendant's trial, and this Court affirmed his conviction, rejecting the contention that the warrantless search had been unlawful. The Court held that the search in its entirety fell within the principle giving law enforcement authorities "[t]he right 'to search the place where the arrest is made in order to find and seize things connected with the crime * * * .' " * * * The opinion rejected the rule of *Trupiano* that "in seizing goods and articles, law enforcement agents must secure and use search warrants wherever reasonably practicable." The test, said the Court, "is not whether it is reasonable to procure a search warrant, but whether the search was reasonable."

Rabinowitz has come to stand for the proposition, *inter alia*, that a warrantless search "incident to a lawful arrest" may generally extend to the area that is considered to be in the "possession" or under the "control" of the person arrested. And it was on the basis of that proposition that the California courts upheld the search of the petitioner's entire house in this case. That doctrine, however, at least in the broad sense in which it was applied by the California courts in this case, can withstand neither historical nor rational analysis.

Even limited to its own facts, the *Rabinowitz* decision was, as we have seen, hardly founded on an unimpeachable line of authority. * * *

Nor is the rationale by which the State seeks here to sustain the search of the petitioner's house supported by a reasoned view of the background and purpose of the Fourth Amendment. Mr. Justice Frankfurter wisely pointed out in his *Rabinowitz* dissent that the

Amendment's proscription of "unreasonable searches and seizures" must be read in light of "the history that gave rise to the words"—a history of "abuses so deeply felt by the Colonies as to be one of the potent causes of the Revolution * * * ." The Amendment was in large part a reaction to the general warrants and warrantless searches that had so alienated the colonists and had helped speed the movement for independence. In the scheme of the Amendment, therefore, the requirement that "no Warrants shall issue, but upon probable cause," plays a crucial part. * * *

* * * Clearly, the general requirement that a search warrant be obtained is not lightly to be dispensed with, and "the burden is on those seeking [an] exemption [from the requirement] to show the need for it * * * ." * * *

* * * When an arrest is made, it is reasonable for the arresting officer to search the person arrested in order to remove any weapons that the latter might seek to use in order to resist arrest or effect his escape. Otherwise, the officer's safety might well be endangered, and the arrest itself frustrated. In addition, it is entirely reasonable for the arresting officer to search for and seize any evidence on the arrestee's person in order to prevent its concealment or destruction. And the area into which an arrestee might reach in order to grab a weapon or evidentiary items must, of course, be governed by a like rule. A gun on a table or in a drawer in front of one who is arrested can be as dangerous to the arresting officer as one concealed in the clothing of the person arrested. There is ample justification, therefore, for a search of the arrestee's person and the area "within his immediate control"—construing that phrase to mean the area from within which he might gain possession of a weapon or destructible evidence.

There is no comparable justification, however, for routinely searching any room other than that in which an arrest occurs—or, for that matter, for searching through all the desk drawers or other closed or concealed areas in that room itself. Such searches, in the absence of well-recognized exceptions, may be made only under the authority of a search warrant. The "adherence to judicial processes" mandated by the Fourth Amendment requires no less. * * *

It is argued in the present case that it is "reasonable" to search a man's house when he is arrested in it. But that argument is founded on little more than a subjective view regarding the acceptability of certain sorts of police conduct, and not on considerations relevant to Fourth Amendment interests. Under such an unconfined analysis, Fourth Amendment protection in this area would approach the evaporation point. It is not easy to explain why, for instance, it is less subjectively "reasonable" to search a man's house when he is arrested on his front lawn—or just down the street—than it is when he happens to be in the house at the time of arrest. As Mr. Justice Frankfurter put it:

> "To say that the search must be reasonable is to require some criterion of reason. It is no guide at all either for a jury or for district judges or the police to say that an 'unreasonable search' is forbidden—that the search must be reasonable. What is the test of reason which makes a search reasonable? The test is the reason underlying and expressed by the Fourth Amendment: the history and the experience which it embodies and the safeguards afforded by it against the evils to which it was a response." * * *

It would be possible, of course, to draw a line between *Rabinowitz* and *Harris* on the one hand, and this case on the other. For *Rabinowitz* involved a single room, and *Harris* a four-room apartment, while in the case before us an entire house was searched. But such a distinction would be highly artificial. The rationale that allowed the searches and seizures in *Rabinowitz* and *Harris* would allow the searches and seizures in this case. No consideration relevant to the Fourth Amendment suggests any point of rational limitation, once the search is allowed to go beyond the area from which the person arrested might obtain weapons or evidentiary items. The only reasoned distinction is one between a search of the person arrested and the area within his reach on the one hand, and more extensive searches on the other.[12]

The petitioner correctly points out that one result of decisions such as *Rabinowitz* and *Harris* is to give law enforcement officials the opportunity to engage in searches not justified by probable cause, by the simple expedient of arranging to arrest suspects at home rather than elsewhere. We do not suggest that the petitioner is necessarily correct in his assertion that such a strategy was utilized here, but the fact remains that had he been arrested earlier in the day, at his place of employment rather than at home, no search of his house could have been made without a search warrant. In any event, even apart from the possibility of such

---

[12] It is argued in dissent that so long as there is probable cause to search the place where an arrest occurs, a search of that place should be permitted even though no search warrant has been obtained. This position seems to be based principally on two premises: first, that once an arrest has been made, the additional invasion of privacy stemming from the accompanying search is "relatively minor"; and second, that the victim of the search may "shortly thereafter" obtain a judicial determination of whether the search was justified by probable cause. With respect to the second premise, one may initially question whether all of the States in fact provide the speedy suppression procedures the dissent assumes. More fundamentally, however, we cannot accept the view that Fourth Amendment interests are vindicated so long as "the rights of the criminal" are "protect[ed] * * * against introduction of evidence seized without probable cause." The Amendment is designed to prevent, not simply to redress, unlawful police action. In any event, we cannot join in characterizing the invasion of privacy that results from a top-to-bottom search of a man's house as "minor." And we can see no reason why, simply because some interference with an individual's privacy and freedom of movement has lawfully taken place, further intrusions should automatically be allowed despite the absence of a warrant that the Fourth Amendment would otherwise require.

police tactics, the general point so forcefully made by Judge Learned Hand in *United States v. Kirschenblatt*, 2 Cir., 16 F.2d 202, 51 A.L.R. 416, remains:

> "After arresting a man in his house, to rummage at will among his papers in search of whatever will convict him, appears to us to be indistinguishable from what might be done under a general warrant; indeed, the warrant would give more protection, for presumably it must be issued by a magistrate. True, by hypothesis the power would not exist, if the supposed offender were not found on the premises; but it is small consolation to know that one's papers are safe only so long as one is not at home."

Rabinowitz and *Harris* * * * are no longer to be followed.

Application of sound Fourth Amendment principles to the facts of this case produces a clear result. The search here went far beyond the petitioner's person and the area from within which he might have obtained either a weapon or something that could have been used as evidence against him. There was no constitutional justification, in the absence of a search warrant, for extending the search beyond that area. The scope of the search was, therefore, "unreasonable" under the Fourth and Fourteenth Amendments, and the petitioner's conviction cannot stand.

[JUSTICE HARLAN'S concurring opinion is omitted.]

MR. JUSTICE WHITE, with whom MR. JUSTICE BLACK joins, dissenting.

Few areas of the law have been as subject to shifting constitutional standards over the last 50 years as that of the search "incident to an arrest." There has been a remarkable instability in this whole area, which has seen at least four major shifts in emphasis. Today's opinion makes an untimely fifth. In my view, the Court should not now abandon the old rule. * * *

II

The rule which has prevailed, but for very brief or doubtful periods of aberration, is that a search incident to an arrest may extend to those areas under the control of the defendant and where items subject to constitutional seizure may be found. The justification for this rule must, under the language of the Fourth Amendment, lie in the reasonableness of the rule. * * * [T]he Court must decide whether a given search is reasonable. The Amendment does not proscribe "warrantless searches" but instead it proscribes "unreasonable searches" and this Court has never held nor does the majority today assert that warrantless searches are necessarily unreasonable.

Applying this reasonableness test to the area of searches incident to arrests, one thing is clear at the outset. Search of an arrested man and of the items within his immediate reach must in almost every case be reasonable. There is always a danger that the suspect will try to escape, seizing concealed weapons with which to overpower and injure the arresting officers, and there is a danger that he may destroy evidence vital to the prosecution. Circumstances in which these justifications would not apply are sufficiently rare that inquiry is not made into searches of this scope, which have been considered reasonable throughout.

The justifications which make such a search reasonable obviously do not apply to the search of areas to which the accused does not have ready physical access. This is not enough, however, to prove such searches unconstitutional. The Court has always held, and does not today deny, that when there is probable cause to search and it is "impracticable" for one reason or another to get a search warrant, then a warrantless search may be reasonable. This is the case whether an arrest was made at the time of the search or not.

This is not to say that a search can be reasonable without regard to the probable cause to believe that seizable items are on the premises. But when there are exigent circumstances, and probable cause, then the search may be made without a warrant, reasonably. An arrest itself may often create an emergency situation making it impracticable to obtain a warrant before embarking on a related search. Again assuming that there is probable cause to search premises at the spot where a suspect is arrested, it seems to me unreasonable to require the police to leave the scene in order to obtain a search warrant when they are already legally there to make a valid arrest, and when there must almost always be a strong possibility that confederates of the arrested man will in the meanwhile remove the items for which the police have probable cause to search. This must so often be the case that it seems to me as unreasonable to require a warrant for a search of the premises as to require a warrant for search of the person and his very immediate surroundings.

This case provides a good illustration of my point that it is unreasonable to require police to leave the scene of an arrest in order to obtain a search warrant when they already have probable cause to search and there is a clear danger that the items for which they may reasonably search will be removed before they return with a warrant. * * * There was doubtless probable cause not only to arrest petitioner, but also to search his house. He had obliquely admitted, both to a neighbor and to the owner of the burglarized store, that he had committed the burglary. In light of this, and the fact that the neighbor had seen other admittedly stolen property in petitioner's house, there was surely probable cause on which a warrant could have issued to search the house for the stolen coins. Moreover, had the police simply arrested petitioner, taken him off to the station house, and later returned with a warrant,[5] it seems very likely that petitioner's wife, who in view of petitioner's generally garrulous nature must have known of the robbery, would have removed the coins. For the police to search the house while the evidence they had probable cause to search out and seize was still there cannot be considered unreasonable. * * *

IV

* * * Like the majority, I would permit the police to search the person of a suspect and the area under his immediate control either to assure the safety of the officers or to prevent the destruction of evidence. And like the majority, I see nothing in the arrest alone furnishing probable cause for a search of any broader scope. However, where as here the existence of probable cause is independently established and would justify a warrant for a broader search for evidence, I would follow past cases and permit such a search to be carried out without a warrant, since the fact of arrest supplies an exigent circumstance justifying police action before the evidence can be removed, and also alerts the suspect to the fact of the search so that he can immediately seek judicial determination of probable cause in an adversary proceeding, and appropriate redress.

This view, consistent with past cases, would not authorize the general search against which the Fourth Amendment was meant to guard, nor would it broaden or render uncertain in any way whatsoever the scope of searches permitted under the Fourth Amendment. The issue in this case is not the breadth of the search, since there was clearly probable cause for the search which was carried out. No broader search than if the officers had a warrant would be permitted. The only issue is whether a search warrant was required as a precondition to that search. It is agreed that such a warrant would be required absent exigent circumstances. I would hold that the fact of arrest supplies such an exigent circumstance, since the police had lawfully gained entry to the premises to effect the arrest and since delaying the search to secure a warrant would have involved the risk of not recovering the fruits of the crime. * * *

---

[5] There were three officers at the scene of the arrest, one from the city where the coin burglary had occurred, and two from the city where the arrest was made. Assuming that one policeman from each city would be needed to bring the petitioner in and obtain a search warrant, one policeman could have been left to guard the house. However, if he not only could have remained in the house against petitioner's wife's will, but followed her about to assure that no evidence was being tampered with, the invasion of her privacy would be almost as great as that accompanying an actual search. Moreover, had the wife summoned an accomplice, one officer could not have watched them both.

NOTES AND QUESTIONS

1. Who has the better side of the argument, Justice Stewart or Justice White? Applying the majority's approach, what should the police have done about Chimel's wife?

2. According to Justice Stewart, what is the scope of a proper warrantless search incident to a lawful arrest (that is, *where* may the police search, and for *what* may they search)? Must the police have probable cause to search the permissible areas? Answer the same questions according to the dissent.

3. Justices Stewart and White apparently disagree with each other regarding the role of the warrant clause in Fourth Amendment analysis. What does each justice believe?

4. *"Principle of particular justification."* The majority opinion in *Chimel* applied what may be described as the "principle of particular justification" (James B. White, *The Fourth Amendment as a Way of Talking About People: A Study of Robinson and Matlock*, 1974 Sup. Ct. Rev. 165, 190). According to this principle, "the police must, whenever practicable, obtain advance judicial approval of searches and seizures through the warrant procedure," and "[t]he scope of [a] search must be 'strictly tied to and justified by' the circumstances which rendered its initiation permissible." Terry v. Ohio, 392 U.S. 1, 88 S.Ct. 1868, 20 L.Ed.2d 889 (1968).

Applying this doctrine, we start from the proposition—in computer terms, the "default" position—that warrantless searches are unreasonable and, therefore, unconstitutional. If the police seek to justify a warrantless search, the burden is on them to demonstrate the existence of a justification for dispensing with the warrant requirement. Assuming that a justification exists, the scope of the permissible warrantless search must be no broader than the justification for the warrantless conduct compels. Once the circumstances that justify the warrantless conduct no longer exist, or once the police go beyond the legitimate scope of the warrantless search, the original obtain-a-warrant default position returns.

Can you articulate how the principle of particular justification applies in *Chimel*?

5. *Bright versus fuzzy lines.* A recurring issue in criminal jurisprudence is whether the Supreme Court, in devising rules of criminal procedure, should announce bright-line rules or rules that are "fuzzy" in nature that require case-by-case adjudication. In *Chimel*, did the Court announce a bright-line rule? If Justice White had prevailed, would the search-incident-to-lawful-arrest rule have been brighter? (In Chapter 1, we offered a similar distinction between rules and norms. See p. 47, Note 2.)

6. *Problem.* Officers Gonzalez and Rogers believe they have probable cause to arrest Donald for murder. They come to Donald's home to arrest him, but nobody is home. They return to their car across the street, and await

Donald's arrival. Ninety minutes later, Donald arrives and enters his house. Fifteen minutes later, the officers come to the door, knock, and arrest Donald at the doorway when he opens the door. Donald is now shoeless but otherwise fully dressed. The police handcuff Donald at the door and move him into the living room, twelve feet from an open closet. The police search Donald, but they find nothing. Officer Gonzales, hoping to find the murder weapon, goes to the closet, pats down trousers on closet hangers, and shakes pairs of shoes. In one pair, the officer discovers a gun, later determined to be the murder weapon. Prior to trial, Donald moves to suppress the gun from evidence. Should the motion be granted? (The officers had neither an arrest nor a search warrant in the foregoing facts.)

7.   The Supreme Court has expanded the lawful scope of a warrantless search incident to an arrest in a home. See *Maryland v. Buie*, p. 454.

8.   *United States v. Robinson.* Four years after *Chimel*, the Supreme Court had another opportunity to consider the scope of the search-incident-to-lawful-arrest warrant exception. In United States v. Robinson, 414 U.S. 218, 94 S.Ct. 467, 38 L.Ed.2d 427 (1973), Officer Jenks had probable cause to believe that Robinson was operating his motor vehicle after revocation of his operator's permit. Therefore, *J* stopped *R*'s automobile, arrested *R* for the driving offense, and then patted down *R*'s outer clothing. *J* felt something in *R*'s breast pocket. Although he could not determine what it was, *J* reached inside R's pocket and pulled out a crumpled up cigarette package, which *J* then opened. He discovered a substance later determined to be heroin.

R unsuccessfully sought to have the heroin excluded at his subsequent trial. Notice how such an argument could be made: We saw in *Chimel* that the justification for a warrantless search incident to a lawful arrest is that a custodial arrest creates an emergency, namely, a need by arresting officers to seize any weapon that might be used against them, and to prevent destruction of any evidence relating to the crime. Here, however, these justifications seemingly did not exist: *R* was arrested for driving without a valid driver's permit, so there was no evidence of this crime that could be destroyed; and, as for a weapon, Officer *J* lacked probable cause to believe that *R*—at that point, a traffic violator and no more—was in possession of a weapon. Therefore, arguably, if warrantless searches *are* presumptively unreasonable absent a valid justification to forego the normal rule, the warrantless search here was unjustifiable. At most, *J* should have been permitted to pat-down *R*'s clothing for a weapon, as he did, and once he determined that what he felt in *R*'s clothing was not a weapon, he should have stopped the search. Finally, even assuming *arguendo* that *J* had a right to reach into *R*'s clothing and pull out the crumpled up cigarette package, the officer had no need to search that package. In the highly unlikely event a weapon was inside it (a razor blade?), *J* could simply have placed the unopened package in a locked glove compartment of the police vehicle, out of *R*'s reach.

The Supreme Court, per Justice Rehnquist, rejected these arguments:

[O]ur * * * fundamental disagreement [with these arguments] arises from [the] suggestion that there must be litigated in each case the issue of whether or not there was present one of the reasons supporting the authority for a search of the person incident to a lawful arrest. * * * A police officer's determination as to how and where to search the person of a suspect whom he has arrested is necessarily a quick *ad hoc* judgment which the Fourth Amendment does not require to be broken down in each instance into an analysis of each step in the search. The authority to search the person incident to a lawful custodial arrest, while based upon the need to disarm and to discover evidence, does not depend on what a court may later decide was the probability in a particular arrest situation that weapons or evidence would in fact be found upon the person of the suspect. A custodial arrest of a suspect based on probable cause is a reasonable intrusion under the Fourth Amendment; that intrusion being lawful, a search incident to the arrest requires no additional justification.

In short, in order to justify a warrantless search of a person incident to a lawful custodial arrest, an arresting officer does not need probable cause to believe that the arrestee has a weapon or criminal evidence on his person. The right to conduct the warrantless search is automatic: if the custodial arrest is based on probable cause, no more is needed.

Is this analysis consistent with *Chimel*?

9.   In Gustafson v. Florida, 414 U.S. 260, 94 S.Ct. 488, 38 L.Ed.2d 456 (1973), a decision handed down the same day as *Robinson* (Note 8), *G* was arrested for failing to be in possession of his driver's license. Unlike in *Robinson*, however, in which Officer Jenks was *required* to take *R* into custody for the traffic offense, the arresting officer here had a choice: take *G* into custody or simply issue a traffic citation and let *G* go. The officer chose to take *G* into custody. He conducted a search of *G*'s person and discovered marijuana. The Court upheld the search.

Is there an argument, however, for the view that the factual distinction between *Robinson* and *Gustafson* should have resulted in a different outcome? Hint: Look ahead to *Knowles v. Iowa* (p. 281, Note 4). And, now return to Justice Stewart's opinion in *Chimel*, specifically to the paragraph following footnote 12 (p. 255).

10.   *Arrest inventories: another warrant "exception."* Reconsider *United States v. Robinson* (Note 8). After Robinson is taken into custody, he had to be transported to the police station for booking, an administrative process that includes photographing and fingerprinting the arrestee (and, as we will see, p. 260, Note 8, sometimes taking a DNA sample). But there is more: any person who will be incarcerated, even temporarily, undergoes a second search: an "arrest inventory." This inventory search, which occurs without a

warrant and in the absence of probable cause, is constitutionally justified on various grounds: to protect the arrestee from theft of her valuables while in jail; to reduce the risk of false claims of theft by the arrestee; and to ensure that contraband and dangerous instrumentalities that might have been missed by the police in the initial search incident to the arrest are not smuggled into the jail. Illinois v. Lafayette, 462 U.S. 640, 103 S.Ct. 2605, 77 L.Ed.2d 65 (1983). To be valid, the inventory must follow procedures standardized in that jurisdiction.

Notice the significance of this warrant exception: Even if Officer Jenks had not searched Robinson's clothing at the scene and discovered the crumpled up cigarette package, it presumably would have been discovered in a routine inventory search. Although inventory operating procedures of police departments vary, the police typically open containers found on arrestees, such as wallets or, as here, cigarette packages. Therefore, as a practical matter, once Robinson's custodial arrest was made, his fate was virtually sealed: If one warrant exception didn't justify the search of his person, another would!

11. In *Robinson*, the Court permitted the arresting officer to search a container (a crumpled up cigarette package) found on the arrestee's person. What if, however, the container an officer pulls out of an arrestee's pocket is a smart phone? May the officer "open" *it* and search its "contents"? The next case speaks to this modern issue.

RILEY V. CALIFORNIA
Supreme Court of the United States, 2014.
573 U.S. ___, 134 S.Ct. 2473, 189 L.Ed.2d 430.

CHIEF JUSTICE ROBERTS delivered the opinion of the Court [joined by JUSTICES SCALIA, KENNEDY, THOMAS, GINSBURG, BREYER, SOTOMAYOR, KAGAN, and in part by JUSTICE ALITO].

These two cases raise a common question: whether the police may, without a warrant, search digital information on a cell phone seized from an individual who has been arrested.

I

A

In the first case, petitioner David Riley * * * was arrested for possession of concealed and loaded firearms * * * .

An officer searched Riley incident to the arrest and found items associated with the "Bloods" street gang. He also seized a cell phone from Riley's pants pocket. According to Riley's uncontradicted assertion, the phone was a "smart phone," a cell phone with a broad range of other functions based on advanced computing capability, large storage capacity, and Internet connectivity. The officer accessed information on the phone and noticed that some words (presumably in text messages or a contacts list) were preceded by the letters "CK"—a label that, he believed, stood for "Crip Killers," a slang term for members of the Bloods gang.

At the police station about two hours after the arrest, a detective specializing in gangs further examined the contents of the phone. The detective testified that he "went through" Riley's phone "looking for evidence, because * * * gang members will often video themselves with guns or take pictures of themselves with the guns." Although there was "a lot of stuff" on the phone, particular files that "caught [the detective's] eye" included videos of young men sparring while someone yelled encouragement using the moniker "Blood." The police also found photographs of Riley standing in front of a car they suspected had been involved in a shooting a few weeks earlier.

Riley was ultimately charged, in connection with that earlier shooting. * * * . * * * Prior to trial, Riley moved to suppress all evidence that the police had obtained from his cell phone. He contended that the searches of his phone violated the Fourth Amendment, because they had been performed without a warrant and were not otherwise justified by exigent circumstances. The trial court rejected that argument. * * * Riley was convicted * * * . * * *

B

In the second case, a police officer performing routine surveillance observed respondent Brima Wurie make an apparent drug sale from a car. Officers subsequently arrested Wurie and took him to the police station. At the station, the officers seized two cell phones from Wurie's person. The one at issue here was a "flip phone," a kind of phone that is flipped open for use and that generally has a smaller range of features than a smart phone. Five to ten minutes after arriving at the station, the officers noticed that the phone was repeatedly receiving calls from a source identified as "my house" on the phone's external screen. A few minutes later, they opened the phone and saw a photograph of a woman and a baby set as the phone's wallpaper. They pressed one button on the phone to access its call log, then another button to determine the phone number associated with the "my house" label. They next used an online phone directory to trace that phone number to an apartment building.

When the officers went to the building, they saw Wurie's name on a mailbox and observed through a window a woman who resembled the woman in the photograph on Wurie's phone. They secured the apartment while obtaining a search warrant and, upon later executing the warrant, found and seized 215 grams of crack cocaine, marijuana, drug paraphernalia, a firearm and ammunition, and cash.

Wurie * * * moved to suppress the evidence obtained from the search of the apartment, arguing that it was the fruit of an unconstitutional search of his cell phone. The District Court denied the motion. Wurie was convicted * * * . * * *

II * * *

As the [Fourth Amendment] text makes clear, "the ultimate touchstone of the Fourth Amendment is 'reasonableness.'" Our cases have determined that "[w]here a search is undertaken by law enforcement officials to discover evidence of criminal wrongdoing, * * * reasonableness generally requires the obtaining of a judicial warrant." Such a warrant ensures that the inferences to support a search are "drawn by a neutral and detached magistrate instead of being judged by the officer engaged in the often competitive enterprise of ferreting out crime." In the absence of a warrant, a search is reasonable only if it falls within a specific exception to the warrant requirement.

The two cases before us concern the reasonableness of a warrantless search incident to a lawful arrest. [The Court then proceeded to review "search incident to lawful arrest" case law, focusing in particular on *Chimel v. California* (p. 251), *United States v. Robinson* (p. 260, Note 8), and *Arizona v. Gant* (p. 286), a case involving the scope of a warrantless search of an automobile as an incident of the lawful arrest of a car occupant.]

III

These cases require us to decide how the search incident to arrest doctrine applies to modern cell phones, which are now such a pervasive and insistent part of daily life that the proverbial visitor from Mars might conclude they were an important feature of human anatomy. A smart phone of the sort taken from Riley was unheard of ten years ago; a significant majority of American adults now own such phones. Even less sophisticated phones like Wurie's, which have already faded in popularity since Wurie was arrested in 2007, have been around for less than 15 years. Both phones are based on technology nearly inconceivable just a few decades ago, when *Chimel* and *Robinson* were decided.

Absent more precise guidance from the founding era, we generally determine whether to exempt a given type of search from the warrant requirement "by assessing, on the one hand, the degree to which it intrudes upon an individual's privacy and, on the other, the degree to which it is needed for the promotion of legitimate governmental interests." Such a balancing of interests supported the search incident to arrest exception in *Robinson*, and a mechanical application of *Robinson* might well support the warrantless searches at issue here.

But while *Robinson*'s categorical rule [permitting an arresting officer to search containers discovered on an arrestee's person] strikes the appropriate balance in the context of physical objects, neither of its rationales has much force with respect to digital content on cell phones. On the government interest side, *Robinson* concluded that the two risks identified in *Chimel*—harm to officers and destruction of evidence—are present in all custodial arrests. There are no comparable risks when the search is of digital data. In addition, *Robinson* regarded any privacy interests retained by an individual after arrest as significantly diminished by the fact of the arrest itself. Cell phones, however, place vast quantities of personal information literally in the hands of individuals. A search of the information on a cell phone bears little resemblance to the type of brief physical search considered in *Robinson*.

We therefore decline to extend *Robinson* to searches of data on cell phones, and hold instead that officers must generally secure a warrant before conducting such a search.

A

We first consider each *Chimel* concern in turn. In doing so, we do not overlook *Robinson*'s admonition that searches of a person incident to arrest * * * are reasonable regardless of "the probability in a particular arrest situation that weapons or evidence would in fact be found." Rather than requiring the "case-by-case adjudication" that *Robinson* rejected, we ask instead whether application of the search incident to arrest doctrine to this particular category of effects would "untether the rule from the justifications underlying the *Chimel* exception."

1

Digital data stored on a cell phone cannot itself be used as a weapon to harm an arresting officer or to effectuate the arrestee's escape. Law enforcement officers remain free to examine the physical aspects of a phone to ensure that it will not be used as a weapon—say, to determine whether there is a razor blade hidden between the phone and its case. Once an officer has secured a phone and eliminated any potential physical threats, however, data on the phone can endanger no one.

Perhaps the same might have been said of the cigarette pack seized from Robinson's pocket. Once an officer gained control of the pack, it was unlikely that Robinson could have accessed the pack's contents. But unknown physical objects may always pose risks, no matter how slight, during the tense atmosphere of a custodial arrest. The officer in *Robinson* testified that he could not identify the objects in the cigarette pack but knew they were not cigarettes. Given that, a further search was a reasonable protective measure. No such unknowns exist with respect to digital data. * * *

The United States and California both suggest that a search of cell phone data might help ensure officer safety in more indirect ways, for example by alerting officers that confederates of the arrestee are headed to the scene. There is undoubtedly a strong government interest in warning officers about such possibilities, but neither the United States nor California offers evidence to suggest that their concerns are based on actual experience. The proposed consideration would also represent a broadening of *Chimel*'s concern that an *arrestee himself* might grab a weapon and use it against an officer "to resist arrest or effect his escape." And any such threats from outside the arrest scene do not "lurk[ ] in all custodial arrests." Accordingly, the interest in protecting officer safety does not justify dispensing with the warrant requirement across the board. To the extent dangers to arresting officers may be implicated in a particular way in a particular case, they are better addressed through consideration of case-specific exceptions to the warrant requirement, such as the one for exigent circumstances.

2

The United States and California focus primarily on the second *Chimel* rationale: preventing the destruction of evidence.

Both Riley and Wurie concede that officers could have seized and secured their cell phones to prevent destruction of evidence while seeking a warrant. That is a sensible concession. And once law enforcement officers have secured a cell phone, there is no longer any risk that the arrestee himself will be able to delete incriminating data from the phone.

The United States and California argue that information on a cell phone may nevertheless be vulnerable to two types of evidence destruction unique to digital data—remote wiping and data encryption. Remote wiping occurs when a phone, connected to a wireless network, receives a signal that erases stored data. This can happen when a third party sends a remote signal or when a phone is preprogrammed to delete data upon entering or leaving certain geographic areas (so-called "geofencing"). Encryption is a security feature that some modern cell phones use in addition to password protection. When such phones lock, data becomes protected by sophisticated encryption that renders a phone all but "unbreakable" unless police know the password.

As an initial matter, these broader concerns about the loss of evidence are distinct from *Chimel*'s focus on a defendant who responds to arrest by trying to conceal or destroy evidence within his reach. With respect to remote wiping, the Government's primary concern turns on the actions of third parties who are not present at the scene of arrest. And data encryption is even further afield. There, the Government focuses on the ordinary operation of a phone's security features, apart from *any* active attempt by a defendant or his associates to conceal or destroy evidence upon arrest.

We have also been given little reason to believe that either problem is prevalent. The briefing reveals only a couple of anecdotal examples of remote wiping triggered by an arrest. Similarly, the opportunities for officers to search a password-protected phone before data becomes encrypted are quite limited. Law enforcement officers are very unlikely to come upon such a phone in an unlocked state because most phones lock at the touch of a button or, as a default, after some very short period of inactivity. * * *

Moreover, in situations in which an arrest might trigger a remote-wipe attempt or an officer discovers an unlocked phone, it is not clear that the ability to conduct a warrantless search would make much of a difference. The need to effect the arrest, secure the scene, and tend to other pressing matters means that law enforcement officers may well not be able to turn their attention to a cell phone right away. * * *

In any event, as to remote wiping, law enforcement is not without specific means to address the threat. Remote wiping can be fully prevented by disconnecting a phone from the network. There are at least two simple ways to do this: First, law enforcement officers can turn the phone off or remove its battery. Second, if they are concerned about encryption or other potential problems, they can leave a phone powered on and place it in an enclosure that isolates the phone from radio waves. Such devices are commonly called "Faraday bags," after the English scientist Michael Faraday. They are essentially sandwich bags made of aluminum foil: cheap, lightweight, and easy to use. They may not be a complete answer to the problem, but at least for now they provide a reasonable response. In fact, a number of law enforcement agencies around the country already encourage the use of Faraday bags.

* * * If "the police are truly confronted with a 'now or never' situation,"—for example, circumstances suggesting that a defendant's phone will be the target of an imminent remote-wipe attempt—they may be able to rely on exigent circumstances to search the phone immediately. Or, if officers happen to seize a phone in an unlocked state, they may be able to disable a phone's automatic-lock feature in order to prevent the phone from locking and encrypting data. * * * Such a preventive measure could be analyzed under the principles set forth in our decision in [*Illinois v.*] *McArthur*, [p. 234, Note 6], which approved officers' reasonable steps to secure a scene to preserve evidence while they awaited a warrant.

B

The search incident to arrest exception rests not only on the heightened government interests at stake in a volatile arrest situation, but also on an arrestee's reduced privacy interests upon being taken into police custody. * * * Put simply, a patdown of Robinson's clothing and an inspection of the cigarette pack found in his pocket constituted only minor additional intrusions compared to the substantial government authority exercised in taking Robinson into custody.

The fact that an arrestee has diminished privacy interests does not mean that the Fourth Amendment falls out of the picture entirely. Not every search "is acceptable solely because a person is in custody." To the contrary, when "privacy-related concerns are weighty enough" a "search may require a warrant, notwithstanding the diminished expectations of privacy of the arrestee." One such example, of course, is *Chimel*. *Chimel* refused to "characteriz[e] the invasion of privacy that results from a top-to-bottom search of a man's house as 'minor.'" Because a search of the arrestee's entire house was a substantial invasion beyond the arrest itself, the Court concluded that a warrant was required.

Robinson is the only decision from this Court applying *Chimel* to a search of the contents of an item found on an arrestee's person. * * *

The United States asserts that a search of all data stored on a cell phone is "materially indistinguishable" from searches of these sorts of physical items. That is like saying a ride on horseback is materially indistinguishable from a flight to the moon. Both are ways of getting from point A to point B, but little else justifies lumping them together. * * * A conclusion that inspecting the contents of an arrestee's pockets works no substantial additional intrusion on privacy beyond the arrest itself may make sense as applied to physical items, but any extension of that reasoning to digital data has to rest on its own bottom.

1

Cell phones differ in both a quantitative and a qualitative sense from other objects that might be kept on an arrestee's person. The term "cell phone" is itself misleading shorthand; many of these devices are in fact minicomputers that also happen to have the capacity to be used as a telephone. They could just as easily be called cameras, video players, rolodexes, calendars, tape recorders, libraries, diaries, albums, televisions, maps, or newspapers.

One of the most notable distinguishing features of modern cell phones is their immense storage capacity. Before cell phones, a search of a person was limited by physical realities and tended as a general matter to constitute only a narrow intrusion on privacy. Most people cannot lug around every piece of mail they have received for the past several months, every picture they have taken, or every book or article they have read— nor would they have any reason to attempt to do so. And if they did, they would have to drag behind them a trunk * * * , rather than a container the size of the cigarette package in *Robinson*.

But the possible intrusion on privacy is not physically limited in the same way when it comes to cell phones. The current top-selling smart phone has a standard capacity of 16 gigabytes (and is available with up to 64 gigabytes). Sixteen gigabytes translates to millions of pages of text, thousands of pictures, or hundreds of videos. Cell phones couple that capacity with the ability to store many different types of information: Even the most basic phones * * * might hold photographs, picture messages, text messages, Internet browsing history, a calendar, a thousand-entry phone book, and so on. We expect that the gulf between physical practicability and digital capacity will only continue to widen in the future. * * *

Finally, there is an element of pervasiveness that characterizes cell phones but not physical records. Prior to the digital age, people did not typically carry a cache of sensitive personal information with them as they went about their day. Now it is the person who is not carrying a cell phone, with all that it contains, who is the exception. According to one poll, nearly three-quarters of smart phone users report being within five feet of their phones most of the time, with 12% admitting that they even use their phones in the shower. A decade ago police officers searching an arrestee might have occasionally stumbled across a highly personal item such as a diary. But those discoveries were likely to be few and far between. Today, by contrast, it is no exaggeration to say that many of the more than 90% of American adults who own a cell phone keep on their person a digital record of nearly every aspect of their lives—from the mundane to the intimate. Allowing the police to scrutinize such records on a routine basis is quite different from allowing them to search a personal item or two in the occasional case.

Although the data stored on a cell phone is distinguished from physical records by quantity alone, certain types of data are also qualitatively different. An Internet search and browsing history, for example, can be found on an Internet-enabled phone and could reveal an individual's private interests or concerns—perhaps a search for certain symptoms of disease, coupled with frequent visits to WebMD. Data on a cell phone can also reveal where a person has been. Historic location information is a standard feature on many smart phones and can reconstruct someone's specific movements down to the minute, not only around town but also within a particular building. * * *

In 1926, Learned Hand observed (in an opinion later quoted in *Chimel*) that it is "a totally different thing to search a man's pockets and use against him what they contain, from ransacking his house for everything which may incriminate him." If his pockets contain a cell phone, however, that is no longer true. Indeed, a cell phone search would typically expose to the government far *more* than the most exhaustive search of a house: A phone not only contains in digital form many sensitive records previously found in the home; it also contains a broad array of private information never found in a home in any form—unless the phone is.

2

To further complicate the scope of the privacy interests at stake, the data a user views on many modern cell phones may not in fact be stored on the device itself. Treating a cell phone as a container whose contents may be searched incident to an arrest is a bit strained as an initial matter. But the analogy crumbles entirely when a cell phone is used to access data located elsewhere, at the tap of a screen. That is what cell phones, with increasing frequency, are designed to do by taking advantage of "cloud computing." * * *

The United States concedes that the search incident to arrest exception may not be stretched to cover a search of files accessed remotely—that is, a search of files stored in the cloud. Such a search would be like finding a key in a suspect's pocket and arguing that it allowed law enforcement to unlock and search a house. But officers searching a phone's data would not typically know whether the information they are viewing was stored locally at the time of the arrest or has been pulled from the cloud. * * *

C

Apart from their arguments for a direct extension of *Robinson*, the United States and California offer various fallback options for permitting warrantless cell phone searches under certain circumstances. Each of the proposals is flawed and contravenes our general preference to provide clear guidance to law enforcement through categorical rules. * * *

The United States first proposes that * * * a warrantless search of an arrestee's cell phone [be permitted] whenever it is reasonable to believe that the phone contains evidence of the crime of arrest. * * *

* * * [This] standard would prove no practical limit at all when it comes to cell phone searches. * * * In the cell phone context, * * * it is reasonable to expect that incriminating information will be found on a phone regardless of when the crime occurred. * * * It would be a particularly inexperienced or unimaginative law enforcement officer who could not come up with several reasons to suppose evidence of just about any crime could be found on a cell phone. * * *

The United States also proposes a rule that would restrict the scope of a cell phone search to those areas of the phone where an officer reasonably believes that information relevant to the crime, the arrestee's identity, or officer safety will be discovered. This approach would again impose few meaningful constraints on officers. The proposed categories would sweep in a great deal of information, and officers would not always be able to discern in advance what information would be found where.

We also reject the United States' final suggestion that officers should always be able to search a phone's call log, as they did in Wurie's case.

The Government relies on *Smith* v. *Maryland*, [p. 116], which held that no warrant was required to use a pen register at telephone company premises to identify numbers dialed by a particular caller. The Court in that case, however, concluded that the use of a pen register was not a "search" at all under the Fourth Amendment. There is no dispute here that the officers engaged in a search of Wurie's cell phone. Moreover, call logs typically contain more than just phone numbers; they include any identifying information that an individual might add, such as the label "my house" in Wurie's case. * * *

IV

We cannot deny that our decision today will have an impact on the ability of law enforcement to combat crime. Cell phones have become important tools in facilitating coordination and communication among members of criminal enterprises, and can provide valuable incriminating information about dangerous criminals. Privacy comes at a cost.

Our holding, of course, is not that the information on a cell phone is immune from search; it is instead that a warrant is generally required before such a search, even when a cell phone is seized incident to arrest. Our cases have historically recognized that the warrant requirement is "an important working part of our machinery of government," not merely "an inconvenience to be somehow 'weighed' against the claims of police efficiency." Recent technological advances similar to those discussed here have, in addition, made the process of obtaining a warrant itself more efficient.

Moreover, even though the search incident to arrest exception does not apply to cell phones, other case-specific exceptions may still justify a warrantless search of a particular phone. * * *

In light of the availability of the exigent circumstances exception, there is no reason to believe that law enforcement officers will not be able to address some of the more extreme hypotheticals that have been suggested: a suspect texting an accomplice who, it is feared, is preparing to detonate a bomb, or a child abductor who may have information about the child's location on his cell phone. The defendants here recognize * * * that such fact-specific threats may justify a warrantless search of cell phone data. The critical point is that, unlike the search incident to arrest exception, the exigent circumstances exception requires a court to examine whether an emergency justified a warrantless search in seach particular case.

* * *

Our cases have recognized that the Fourth Amendment was the founding generation's response to the reviled "general warrants" and "writs of assistance" of the colonial era, which allowed British officers to rummage through homes in an unrestrained search for evidence of criminal activity. Opposition to such searches was in fact one of the driving forces behind the Revolution itself. In 1761, the patriot James Otis delivered a speech in Boston denouncing the use of writs of assistance. A young John Adams was there, and he would later write that "[e]very man of a crowded audience appeared to me to go away, as I did, ready to take arms against writs of assistance." According to Adams, Otis's speech was "the first scene of the first act of opposition to the arbitrary claims of Great Britain. Then and there the child Independence was born."

Modern cell phones are not just another technological convenience. With all they contain and all they may reveal, they hold for many Americans "the privacies of life." The fact that technology now allows an individual to carry such information in his hand does not make the information any less worthy of the protection for which the Founders fought. Our answer to the question of what police must do before searching a cell phone seized incident to an arrest is accordingly simple—get a warrant. * * *

JUSTICE ALITO concurring in part and concurring in the judgment.

I agree with the Court that law enforcement officers, in conducting a lawful search incident to arrest, must generally obtain a warrant before searching information stored or accessible on a cell phone. I write separately to address two points.

I

A

First, I am not convinced at this time that the ancient rule on searches incident to arrest is based exclusively (or even primarily) on the need to protect the safety of arresting officers and the need to prevent the destruction of evidence. * * *

* * * For example, an 1839 case stated that "it is clear, and beyond doubt, that * * * constables * * * are entitled, upon a lawful arrest by them of one charged with treason or felony, to take and detain property found in his possession which will form material evidence in his prosecution for that crime." The court noted that the origins of that rule "deriv[e] from the interest which the State has in a person guilty (or reasonably believed to be guilty) of a crime being brought to justice, and in a prosecution, once commenced, being determined in due course of law." * * *

The idea that officer safety and the preservation of evidence are the sole reasons for allowing a warrantless search incident to arrest appears to derive from the Court's reasoning in *Chimel* v. *California*, a case that involved the lawfulness of a search of the scene of an arrest, not the person of an arrestee. * * * *Chimel's* reasoning is questionable, and I think it is a mistake to allow that reasoning to affect cases like these that concern the search of the person of arrestees.

B

Despite my view on the point discussed above, I agree that we should not mechanically apply the rule used in the predigital era to the search of a cell phone. Many cell phones now in use are capable of storing and accessing a quantity of information, some highly personal, that no person would ever have had on his person in hard-copy form. This calls for a new balancing of law enforcement and privacy interests.

The Court strikes this balance in favor of privacy interests with respect to all cell phones and all information found in them, and this approach leads to anomalies. For example, the Court's broad holding favors information in digital form over information in hard-copy form. Suppose that two suspects are arrested. Suspect number one has in his pocket a monthly bill for his land-line phone, and the bill lists an incriminating call to a long-distance number. He also has in his a wallet a few snapshots, and one of these is incriminating. Suspect number two has in his pocket a cell phone, the call log of which shows a call to the same incriminating number. In addition, a number of photos are stored in the memory of the cell phone, and one of these is incriminating. Under established law, the police may seize and examine the phone bill and the snapshots in the wallet without obtaining a warrant, but under the Court's holding today, the information stored in the cell phone is out.

While the Court's approach leads to anomalies, I do not see a workable alternative. Law enforcement officers need clear rules regarding searches incident to arrest, and it would take many cases and many years for the courts to develop more nuanced rules. And during that time, the nature of the electronic devices that ordinary Americans carry on their persons would continue to change.

II

This brings me to my second point. While I agree with the holding of the Court, I would reconsider the question presented here if either Congress or state legislatures, after assessing the legitimate needs of law enforcement and the privacy interests of cell phone owners, enact legislation that draws reasonable distinctions based on categories of information or perhaps other variables. * * *

NOTES AND QUESTIONS

1. Are you persuaded by the Chief Justice's efforts to distinguish *Robinson*? If not, which case was wrongly decided, *Robinson* or *Riley*?

2. Rather than require a search warrant, should the Court have "permitted the police to conduct a [warrantless] brief field search of a cell phone incident to arrest, * * * when there is reason to believe that the phone contains useful evidence of the crime of arrest," as long as "the police limit their search to the places where such evidence might realistically be found"? Robert H. McAdams, Riley's *Less Obvious Tradeoff: Forgoing Scope-Limited Searches*, 48 Tex. Tech. L. Rev. 97, 131 (2015).

3. *Drunk driving and search-incident law.* In Birchfield v. North Dakota, 579 U.S. ___, 136 S.Ct. 2160, ___ L.Ed.2d ___ (2016), the Supreme Court for the first time considered the following question: may the police, who have arrested a motorist suspected of drunk driving, compel the motorist to submit to the taking of a blood sample or to a breath test as an incident of the arrest.

But, you might ask: why not simply justify such a warrantless search under the "exigent circumstances" warrant exception? Indeed, the Court has held that the natural dissipation of alcohol from the blood stream sometimes, *but does not always*, constitute an exigency justifying the warrantless taking of a blood sample. The constitutionality of such testing must be determined, as with all exigency cases, on a case-by-case, totality-of-the-factual-circumstances basis, sometimes justifying the warrantless search, *e.g.*, Schmerber v. California, 384 U.S. 757, 86 S.Ct. 1826, 16 L.Ed.2d 908 (1966), and sometimes not. Missouri v. McNeely, 569 U.S. ___, 133 S.Ct. 1552, 185 L.Ed.2d 696 (2013).

As we have seen, however, in contrast to the exigency exception, the search-incident warrant exception eschews the case-by-case approach in regard to searches of an arrestee: warrantless searches of the person are either allowed in all cases or they are barred in all cases. In *Riley*, the Court barred warrantless searches of cell phones discovered on the person of the arrestee.

In *Birchfield*, the search-incident exception issue arose in the context of drunk-driving investigations. In order to secure greater cooperation from drivers stopped on the highway, some states have recently enacted laws making it a criminal offense for the driver to refuse to undergo a breath test or the taking of a blood sample. In three cases consolidated on appeal, the *Birchfield* Court considered the constitutionality of two warrantless, nonconsensual blood tests and one similar breath test conducted after the drivers were arrested for their refusal.

Justice Alito, writing for five justices, held that warrantless breath tests, incident to a lawful arrest, are per se constitutional. (The arrests themselves were lawful: "it follows that a State may criminalize the refusal to comply with a demand to submit to the required testing, just as a State may make it a crime for a person to obstruct the execution of a valid search warrant.") As in *Riley*, the Court balanced the privacy interest of the individual against the interest of the government in combatting drunk driving.

Justice Alito, citing prior cases, noted that breath tests "do not 'implicate significant privacy concerns.'" The physical intrusion is "almost negligible." Although the testing requires the insertion of a mouthpiece connected to a machine into the individual's mouth, "there is nothing painful or strange about this requirement." The Court analogized this to use of a straw to drink beverages, "a common practice and one to which few object." Nor do people "assert a possessory interest in or any emotional attachment to *any* of the air in their lungs." Finally, the testing process does not result in "any great enhancement in the embarrassment that is inherent in any arrest."

Weighed against the minimal privacy interest of the arrestee is the government's "'paramount interest * * * in preserving the safety of * * * public highways.'" The Court noted that "[d]runk drivers take a grisly toll on the Nation's roads, claiming thousands of lives, injuring many more victims, and inflicting billions of dollars in property damage every year." Therefore, a warrantless breath test, as an incident to a lawful arrest in a drunk-driving case, is constitutional.

The Court majority, however, held that warrantless *blood* tests are *not* justifiable as an incident to a lawful arrest. "Blood tests are a different matter," Justice Alito wrote. They require piercing of the arrestee's skin as well as extraction of a part of the subject's body. Unlike air, which human exhale "many times per minute, humans do not continually shed blood." It is not a process people "relish." Moreover, "a blood test, unlike a breath test, places in the hands of law enforcement authorities a sample that can be preserved and from which it is possible to extract information beyond" the driver's blood alcohol content. The reasonableness of this more intrusive testing process "must be judged in light of the availability of the less invasive alternative of a breath test." The States here "offered no satisfactory justification for demanding the more intrusive alternative without a warrant."

Justices Sotomayor and Ginsburg, concurring and dissenting in part, would require warrants in both circumstances in search-incident cases: "no governmental interest categorically makes it impractical for an officer to obtain a warrant before measuring a driver's alcohol level * * * unless exigent circumstances exist in a particular case." If an exigency exists, of course the latter exception to the warrant requirement would apply.

Justice Thomas also concurred and dissented in part. He accused the majority of "contort[ing] the search-incident-to-arrest exception." He would apply the exigency exception, but he would adopt a bright-line rule justifying both warrantless breath and blood testing under *that* exception.

Notice: it can matter which warrant exception is asserted in a given case. Although a warrantless blood test is not justified as a search incident to an arrest, the prosecutor, with the proper facts, may still win a case by invoking a different warrant exception (*e.g.*, exigency). One exception might work when another doesn't. Keep this in mind as you learn about other exceptions to the warrant requirement.

b. Arrests of Automobile Occupants

NEW YORK V. BELTON

Supreme Court of the United States, 1981.
453 U.S. 454, 101 S.Ct. 2860, 69 L.Ed.2d 768.

JUSTICE STEWART delivered the opinion of the Court [joined by CHIEF JUSTICE BURGER, and JUSTICES BLACKMUN, POWELL, and REHNQUIST]. * * *

I

On April 9, 1978, Trooper Douglas Nicot, a New York State policeman driving an unmarked car on the New York Thruway, was passed by another automobile traveling at an excessive rate of speed. Nicot gave chase, overtook the speeding vehicle, and ordered its driver to pull it over to the side of the road and stop. There were four men in the car, one of whom was Roger Belton, the respondent in this case. The policeman asked to see the driver's license and automobile registration, and discovered that none of the men owned the vehicle or was related to its owner. Meanwhile, the policeman had smelled burnt marihuana and had seen on the floor of the car an envelope marked "Supergold" that he associated with marihuana. He therefore directed the men to get out of the car, and placed them under arrest for the unlawful possession of marihuana. He patted down each of the men and "split them up into four separate areas of the Thruway at this time so they would not be in physical touching area of each other." He then picked up the envelope marked "Supergold" and found that it contained marihuana. * * *. He then searched the passenger compartment of the car. On the back seat he found a black leather jacket belonging to Belton. He unzipped one of the pockets of the jacket and discovered cocaine. * * *

Belton was subsequently indicted for criminal possession of a controlled substance. In the trial court he moved that the cocaine the trooper had seized from the jacket pocket be suppressed. The court denied the motion. * * *

II

It is a first principle of Fourth Amendment jurisprudence that the police may not conduct a search unless they first convince a neutral magistrate that there is probable cause to do so. This Court has recognized, however, that "the exigencies of the situation" may sometimes make exemption from the warrant requirement "imperative." Specifically, the Court held in *Chimel v. California* [p. 251] that a lawful custodial arrest creates a situation which justifies the contemporaneous search without a warrant of the person arrested and of the immediately surrounding area. * * *

Although the principle that limits a search incident to a lawful custodial arrest may be stated clearly enough, courts have discovered the principle difficult to apply in specific cases. Yet, as one commentator has pointed out, the protection of the Fourth and Fourteenth Amendments "can only be realized if the police are acting under a set of rules which, in most instances, makes it possible to reach a correct determination beforehand as to whether an invasion of privacy is justified in the interest of law enforcement." LaFave, *"Case-By-Case Adjudication" versus "Standardized Procedures": The Robinson Dilemma*, 1974 S.Ct. Rev. 127, 142. This is because:

> "Fourth Amendment doctrine, given force and effect by the exclusionary rule, is primarily intended to regulate the police in their day-to-day activities and thus ought to be expressed in terms that are readily applicable by the police in the context of the law enforcement activities in which they are necessarily engaged. A highly sophisticated set of rules, qualified by all sorts of ifs, ands, and buts and requiring the drawing of subtle nuances and hairline distinctions, may be the sort of heady stuff upon which the facile minds of lawyers and judges eagerly feed, but they may be 'literally impossible of application by the officer in the field.'" *Id.*, at 141.

In short, "[a] single familiar standard is essential to guide police officers, who have only limited time and expertise to reflect on and balance the social and individual interests involved in the specific circumstances they confront."

So it was that, in *United States v. Robinson* [p. 260, Note 8], the Court hewed to a straightforward rule, easily applied, and predictably enforced: "[I]n the case of a lawful custodial arrest a full search of the person is not only an exception to the warrant requirement of the Fourth Amendment, but is also a 'reasonable' search under that Amendment." In so holding, the Court rejected the suggestion that "there must be litigated in each case the issue of whether or not there was present one of the reasons supporting the authority for a search of the person incident to a lawful arrest."

But no straightforward rule has emerged from the litigated cases respecting the question involved here—the question of the proper scope of a search of the interior of an automobile incident to a lawful custodial arrest of its occupants. * * *

When a person cannot know how a court will apply a settled principle to a recurring factual situation, that person cannot know the scope of his constitutional protection, nor can a policeman know the scope of his authority. While the *Chimel* case established that a search incident to an arrest may not stray beyond the area within the immediate control of the arrestee, courts have found no workable definition of "the area within the immediate control of the arrestee" when that area arguably includes the interior of an automobile and the arrestee is its recent occupant. Our reading of the cases suggests the generalization that articles inside the relatively narrow compass of the passenger compartment of an automobile are in fact generally, even if not inevitably, within "the area into which an arrestee might reach in order to grab a weapon or evidentiary ite[m]." In order to establish the workable rule this category of cases requires, we read *Chimel's* definition of the limits of the area that may be searched in light of that generalization. Accordingly, we hold that when a policeman has made a lawful custodial arrest of the occupant of an automobile, he may, as a contemporaneous incident of that arrest, search the passenger compartment of that automobile.

It follows from this conclusion that the police may also examine the contents of any containers found within the passenger compartment, for if the passenger compartment is within reach of the arrestee, so also will containers in it be within his reach.[4] Such a container may, of course, be searched whether it is open or closed, since the justification for the search is not that the arrestee has no privacy interest in the container, but that the lawful custodial arrest justifies the infringement of any privacy interest the arrestee may have. * * *

It is true, of course, that these containers will sometimes be such that they could hold neither a weapon nor evidence of the criminal conduct for which the suspect was arrested. However, in *United States v. Robinson*, the Court rejected the argument that such a container—there a "crumpled up cigarette package"—located during a search of Robinson incident to his arrest could not be searched:

> "The authority to search the person incident to a lawful custodial arrest, while based upon the need to disarm and to discover evidence, does not depend on what a court may later decide was the probability in a particular arrest situation that weapons or evidence would in fact be found upon the person of the suspect. A custodial arrest of a suspect based on probable cause is a reasonable intrusion under the Fourth Amendment; that intrusion being lawful, a search incident to the arrest requires no additional justification." * * *

III

It is not questioned that the respondent was the subject of a lawful custodial arrest on a charge of possessing marihuana. The search of the

---

[4] "Container" here denotes any object capable of holding another object. It thus includes closed or open glove compartments, consoles, or other receptacles located anywhere within the passenger compartment, as well as luggage, boxes, bags, clothing, and the like. Our holding encompasses only the interior of the passenger compartment of an automobile and does not encompass the trunk.

respondent's jacket followed immediately upon that arrest. The jacket was located inside the passenger compartment of the car in which the respondent had been a passenger just before he was arrested. The jacket was thus within the area which we have concluded was "within the arrestee's immediate control" within the meaning of the *Chimel* case. The search of the jacket, therefore, was a search incident to a lawful custodial arrest, and it did not violate the Fourth and Fourteenth Amendments. Accordingly, the judgment is reversed. * * *

[The concurrence of JUSTICE REHNQUIST and the concurrence in the judgment of JUSTICE STEVENS are omitted.]

JUSTICE BRENNAN, with whom JUSTICE MARSHALL joins, dissenting.

In *Chimel v. California*, this Court carefully analyzed more than 50 years of conflicting precedent governing the permissible scope of warrantless searches incident to custodial arrest. The Court today turns its back on the product of that analysis, formulating an arbitrary "bright-line" rule applicable to "recent" occupants of automobiles that fails to reflect *Chimel's* underlying policy justifications. While the Court claims to leave *Chimel* intact, I fear that its unwarranted abandonment of the principles underlying that decision may signal a wholesale retreat from our carefully developed search-incident-to-arrest analysis. I dissent.

I * * *

The *Chimel* exception to the warrant requirement was designed with two principal concerns in mind: the safety of the arresting officer and the preservation of easily concealed or destructible evidence. * * *

The *Chimel* standard was narrowly tailored to address these concerns * * *. It * * * places a temporal and a spatial limitation on searches incident to arrest, excusing compliance with the warrant requirement only when the search " 'is substantially contemporaneous with the arrest and is confined to the *immediate* vicinity of the arrest.' " When the arrest has been consummated and the arrestee safely taken into custody, the justifications underlying *Chimel's* limited exception to the warrant requirement cease to apply: at that point there is no possibility that the arrestee could reach weapons or contraband.

* * * [T]he Court today disregards these principles, and instead adopts a fiction—that the interior of a car is *always* within the immediate control of an arrestee who has recently been in the car. * * *

II

As the facts of this case make clear, the Court today substantially expands the permissible scope of searches incident to arrest by permitting police officers to search areas and containers the arrestee could not possibly reach at the time of arrest. These facts demonstrate that at the time Belton and his three companions were placed under custodial arrest—which was *after* they had been removed from the car, patted down, and separated—none of them could have reached the jackets that had been left on the back seat of the car. * * *

By approving the constitutionality of the warrantless search in this case, the Court carves out a dangerous precedent that is not justified by the concerns underlying *Chimel.* * * *

* * * [T]he crucial question under *Chimel* is not whether the arrestee could *ever* have reached the area that was searched, but whether he could have reached it at the time of arrest and search. If not, the officer's failure to obtain a warrant may not be excused. By disregarding this settled doctrine, the Court does a great disservice not only to *stare decisis*, but to the policies underlying the Fourth Amendment as well.

III

The Court seeks to justify its departure from the principles underlying *Chimel* by proclaiming the need for a new "bright-line" rule to guide the officer in the field. * * *

The standard announced in *Chimel* is not nearly as difficult to apply as the Court suggests. * * * Certainly there will be some close cases, but when in doubt the police can always turn to the rationale underlying *Chimel*—the need to prevent the arrestee from reaching weapons or contraband—before exercising their judgment. A rule based on that rationale should provide more guidance than the rule announced by the Court today. Moreover, unlike the Court's rule, it would be faithful to the Fourth Amendment.

JUSTICE WHITE, with whom JUSTICE MARSHALL joins, dissenting.

* * * The Court now holds that as incident to the arrest of the driver or any other person in an automobile, the interior of the car and any container found therein, whether locked or not, may be not only seized but also searched even absent probable cause to believe that contraband or evidence of crime will be found. As to luggage, briefcases, or other containers, this seems to me an extreme extension of *Chimel* and one to which I cannot subscribe. * * * Here, searches of luggage, briefcases, and other containers in the interior of an auto are authorized in the absence of any suspicion whatsoever that they contain anything in which the police have a legitimate interest. This calls for more caution than the Court today exhibits, and, with respect, I dissent.

NOTES AND QUESTIONS

1. Is *Belton* consistent with *Chimel*?

2. *Bright-lines (part 1).* Justice Stewart notes favorably the benefits to police of bright-line rules of criminal procedure. Are there benefits of such rules to *courts*? What are the *costs* of bright-line rules?

3. *Bright-lines (part 2).* The *Belton* majority quotes from an article written by Professor Wayne LaFave, apparently supportive of bright-line rules. In another article, this one written after *Belton*, LaFave explained his position more fully. According to him, a court should ask itself four questions before it adopts a particular bright-line rule:

> (1) Does it [the proposed rule] have clear and certain boundaries, so that it in fact makes case-by-case evaluation and adjudication unnecessary? (2) Does it produce results approximating those which would be obtained *if* accurate case-by-case application of the underlying principle were practicable? (3) Is it responsive to a genuine need to forego case-by-case application of a principle because that approach has proved unworkable? (4) Is it not readily subject to manipulation and abuse?

Wayne R. LaFave, *The Fourth Amendment In an Imperfect World: On Drawing "Bright Lines" and "Good Faith",* 43 U. Pitt. L. Rev. 307, 325–26 (1982).

> Does the *Belton* bright-line rule pass Professor LaFave's four-pronged test? If you believe a bright-line rule *is* desirable, did the Court fashion the best rule? Can you suggest a better bright-line rule?

4. *"Search incident to lawful citation"?* In Knowles v. Iowa, 525 U.S. 113, 119 S.Ct. 484, 142 L.Ed.2d 492 (1998), an Iowa police officer stopped *K* for speeding. State law authorized the police to arrest traffic violators and take them immediately before a magistrate, but the officer instead merely issued *K* a traffic citation. Although the officer had no reason to believe he would find a weapon or criminal evidence in the car, he conducted a full search of the vehicle, as expressly permitted by state law. During the search, the officer discovered marijuana and a "pot pipe" under the driver's seat.

The Supreme Court, per Chief Justice Rehnquist, unanimously held that the search of the car *violated* the Fourth Amendment:

> In [*United States v.*] *Robinson* [p. 260, Note 8], we noted the two historical rationales for the "search incident to arrest" exception: (1) the need to disarm the suspect in order to take him into custody, and (2) the need to preserve evidence for later use at trial. But neither of these underlying rationales for the search incident to arrest exception is sufficient to justify the search in the present case.
>
> We have recognized that the first rationale—officer safety—is "'both legitimate and weighty.'" The threat to officer safety from

issuing a traffic citation, however, is a good deal less than in the case of a custodial arrest. In *Robinson*, we stated that a custodial arrest involves "danger to an officer" because of "the extended exposure which follows the taking of a suspect into custody and transporting him to the police station." * * * A routine traffic stop, on the other hand, is a relatively brief encounter * * * . * * *

Nor has Iowa shown the second justification for the authority to search incident to arrest—the need to discover and preserve evidence. Once Knowles was stopped for speeding and issued a citation, all the evidence necessary to prosecute that offense had been obtained. No further evidence of excessive speed was going to be found either on the person of the offender or in the passenger compartment of the car.

5.   In *Knowles* (Note 4), the officer chose to issue a citation to the traffic violator although he could have taken the violator into custody under Iowa law. The Court disapproved the warrantless search of the car incident to the citation. However, may an officer skirt *Knowles* by simply taking a traffic violator into custody, and then seek to justify the search of the arrestee and the car on the basis of the "search incident to a lawful *custodial* arrest" rule? That question—and scenario—however, raises a preliminary Fourth Amendment question not considered in *Knowles*: *May* a legislature constitutionally authorize the police to take a person into custody for a petty offense, such as a minor traffic violation that carries only a small fine? Consider the next case.

In Atwater v. City of Lago Vista, 532 U.S. 318, 121 S.Ct. 1536, 149 L.Ed.2d 549 (2001), *A* was driving her pickup truck with her 3-year-old son and 5-year-old daughter in the vehicle. None of them was wearing a seatbelt. Officer *T*, who had on a previous occasion stopped *A* for the same reason but had let her go with a warning, again stopped *A*'s vehicle and yelled something at her, such as, "we've met before" and "you're going to jail." *A* pleaded to take her "frightened, upset, and crying" children to a friend's house nearby, but he told her, "you're not going anywhere." *T* handcuffed *A*, placed her in his squad car, and drove her to the police station where booking officers required her to remove her shoes, jewelry, and eyeglasses, and empty her pockets. Officers took *A*'s "mug shot," jailed her for an hour, after which she was taken before a magistrate and released on bond.

No criminal evidence was found on *A*'s person or in her vehicle during the warrantless searches. As a result, she pleaded no contest to the misdemeanor seatbelt offenses and paid a $50 fine. Later, she filed suit under a federal statute (42 U.S.C. § 1983) for violation of her Fourth Amendment rights. She claimed that the City lacked constitutional authority to permit a custodial arrest for such a minor offense.

The Court, 5–4, per Justice Souter, rejected *A*'s argument. First, it rejected the defense's historical claim that at common law (and, therefore, at the time of the framing of the Fourth Amendment), peace officers were forbidden to make warrantless misdemeanor arrests except for breaches of the peace. The Court went on to consider and reject the petitioner's non-historical argument, as well:

> Atwater does not wager all on history. Instead, she asks us to mint a new rule of constitutional law * * *, * * * forbidding custodial arrest, even upon probable cause, when conviction could not ultimately carry any jail time and when the government shows no compelling need for immediate detention.

> If we were to derive a rule exclusively to address the uncontested facts of this case, Atwater might well prevail. * * * In her case, the physical incidents of arrest were merely gratuitous humiliations imposed by a police officer who was (at best) exercising extremely poor judgment. Atwater's claim to live free of pointless indignity and confinement clearly outweighs anything the City can raise against it specific to her case.

> But we have traditionally recognized that a responsible Fourth Amendment balance is not well served by standards requiring sensitive, case-by-case determinations of government need, lest every discretionary judgment in the field be converted into an occasion for constitutional review. See, *e.g.*, *United States v. Robinson*. * * * See *New York v. Belton*.

> At first glance, Atwater's argument may seem to respect the values of clarity and simplicity * * * . But the claim is not ultimately so simple, nor could it be, for complications arise the moment we begin to think about the possible applications of the several criteria Atwater proposes for drawing a line between minor crimes with limited arrest authority and others not so restricted.

> One line, she suggests, might be between "jailable" and "fine-only" offenses * * * . The trouble with this distinction, of course, is that an officer on the street might not be able to tell. It is not merely that we cannot expect every police officer to know the details of frequently complex penalty schemes, but that penalties for ostensibly identical conduct can vary on account of facts difficult (if not impossible) to know at the scene of an arrest. Is this the first offense or is the suspect a repeat offender? Is the weight of the marijuana a gram above or a gram below the fine-only line? * * * And so on.

> But Atwater's refinements would not end there. She represents that if the line were drawn at nonjailable traffic offenses, her proposed limitation should be qualified by a proviso authorizing warrantless arrests where "necessary for enforcement of the traffic laws or when [an] offense would otherwise continue and pose a danger to others on the road." * * * The proviso only compounds the difficulties.

The dissenters, per Justice O'Connor, expressed concern about the long-term consequences of the Court's holding:

> The *per se* rule that the Court creates has potentially serious consequences for the everyday lives of Americans. A broad range of conduct falls into the category of fine-only misdemeanors. * * * In several States, for example, littering is a criminal offense punishable only by fine.
>
> To be sure, such laws are valid and wise exercises of the States' power to protect the public health and welfare. My concern lies not with the decision to enact or enforce these laws, but rather with the manner in which they may be enforced. Under today's holding, when a police officer has probable cause to believe that a fine-only misdemeanor offense has occurred, that officer may stop the suspect, issue a citation, and let the person continue on her way. Or, if a traffic violation, the officer may stop the car, arrest the driver, search the driver, search the entire passenger compartment of the car including any purse or package inside, and impound the car and inventory all of its contents. * * * [T]he majority gives officers unfettered discretion to choose that course without articulating a single reason why such action is appropriate.
>
> Such unbounded discretion carries with it grave potential for abuse. * * * [A] relatively minor traffic infraction may often serve as an excuse for stopping and harassing an individual. After today, the arsenal available to any officer extends to a full arrest and the searches permissible concomitant to that arrest. * * * [W]e must vigilantly ensure that officers' poststop actions * * * comport with the Fourth Amendment's guarantee of reasonableness.

6.   In *Knowles v. Iowa* (Note 4), as we saw, the officer who stopped Knowles for speeding had a choice: issue a traffic citation or take the driver into custody. Now, however, change the facts in *Knowles* as follows: Assume that the officer has only one option available to her under state law, namely, to issue a citation. However, further assume that the officer, *in violation of state law*, takes the driver into custody anyway. May the officer *now* conduct a search incident to this *custodial* arrest? No way, you might think. After all, the search warrant exception we are talking about applies to a search incident to a *lawful* custodial arrest, and the hypothetical arrest here was unlawful. Right?

Wrong. It turns out that when the Supreme Court speaks of a search incident to a "lawful" arrest, one must distinguish between an arrest that is lawful (or unlawful) under the Fourth Amendment and one that is lawful (or unlawful) under local law. According to a unanimous Court in Virginia v. Moore, 553 U.S. 164, 128 S.Ct. 1598, 170 L.Ed.2d 559 (2008), a custodial arrest based on probable cause, although in violation of state law, is "lawful" for purposes of Fourth Amendment analysis. A search conducted as an incident of such an arrest, therefore, satisfies the Fourth Amendment rules discussed in this chapter.

7. *Belton is extended * * * and questioned.* The Supreme Court extended the *Belton* rule in Thornton v. United States, 541 U.S. 615, 124 S.Ct. 2127, 158 L.Ed.2d 905 (2004). In *Thornton*, the police lawfully arrested *T*, who had just parked and exited his vehicle, for possession of illegal drugs. The police handcuffed *T* and placed him in the back seat of a patrol car, after which they conducted a warrantless *Belton* search of the car, resulting in discovery of a handgun under the driver's seat. *T* "argued that *Belton* was limited to situations where the officer initiated contact with an arrestee while he was still an occupant of the car." The Court disagreed, and ruled that the *Belton* rule applies "[s]o long as an arrestee is the sort of 'recent occupant' of a vehicle such as [*T*] was here."

Justice Scalia (joined by Justice Ginsburg), while concurring in the judgment, took the opportunity to criticize the *Belton* rule and suggest that it be recast:

> [One] defense of the [police] search is that, even though the arrestee posed no risk here, *Belton* searches in general are reasonable, and the benefits of a bright-line rule justify upholding that small minority of searches that, on their particular facts, are not reasonable. The validity of this argument rests on the accuracy of *Belton*'s claim that the passenger compartment is "in fact generally, even if not inevitably," within the suspect's immediate control. By the United States' own admission, however, "[t]he practice of restraining an arrestee on the scene before searching a car that he just occupied is so prevalent that holding that *Belton* does not apply in that setting would * * * 'largely render *Belton* a dead letter.'" Reported cases involving this precise factual scenario—a motorist handcuffed and secured in the back of a squad car when the search takes place—are legion. * * *
>
> The popularity of the practice is not hard to fathom. If *Belton* *entitles* an officer to search a vehicle upon arresting the driver despite having taken measures that eliminate any danger, what rational officer would not take those measures? If it was ever true that the passenger compartment is "in fact generally, even if not inevitably," within the arrestee's immediate control at the time of the search, it certainly is not true today. * * *
>
> If *Belton* searches are justifiable, it is not because the arrestee might grab a weapon or evidentiary item from his car, but simply because the car might contain evidence relevant to the crime for which he was arrested. * * *
>
> In this case, as in *Belton,* petitioner was lawfully arrested for a drug offense. It was reasonable for Officer Nichols to believe that further contraband or similar evidence relevant to the crime for

which he had been arrested might be found in the vehicle from which he had just alighted and which was still within his vicinity at the time of arrest. I would affirm the decision below on that ground.

In a separate concurrence, Justice O'Connor stated that she found Justice Scalia's proposed change in the law "on firmer ground" than "*Belton's* shaky foundation."

The two dissenters in *Thornton*—Justices Stevens and Souter—criticized *Belton* for allowing "the police to conduct a broader search than our decision in *Chimel v. California* would have permitted."

So, the law after *Thornton* sat in an odd position: *Belton* had been extended to recent occupants of automobiles, even as five justices expressed criticism of *Belton*. In 2005, Chief Justice Rehnquist (the author of *Thornton*) died and was replaced by John Roberts, and in 2006 Justice O'Connor retired and her seat was filled by Samuel Alito. It was not too long thereafter that the "new" Court took the opportunity to confront the *Belton* rule again, as we see immediately below.

ARIZONA V. GANT

Supreme Court of the United States, 2009.
556 U.S. 332, 129 S.Ct. 1710, 173 L.Ed.2d 485.

JUSTICE STEVENS delivered the opinion of the Court [joined by JUSTICES SCALIA, SOUTER, THOMAS, and GINSBURG].

After Rodney Gant was arrested for driving with a suspended license, handcuffed, and locked in the back of a patrol car, police officers searched his car and discovered cocaine in the pocket of a jacket on the backseat. Because Gant could not have accessed his car to retrieve weapons or evidence at the time of the search, the Arizona Supreme Court held that the search-incident-to-arrest exception to the Fourth Amendments warrant requirement, as defined in *Chimel v. California*, [p. 251] and applied to vehicle searches in *New York v. Belton*, [p. 276], did not justify the search in this case. We agree with that conclusion.

Under *Chimel*, police may search incident to arrest only the space within an arrestee's immediate control, meaning the area from within which he might gain possession of a weapon or destructible evidence. The safety and evidentiary justifications underlying *Chimel's* reaching-distance rule determine *Belton's* scope. Accordingly, we hold that *Belton* does not authorize a vehicle search incident to a recent occupant's arrest after the arrestee has been secured and cannot access the interior of the vehicle. Consistent with the holding in *Thornton v. United States*, [p. 285, Note 7], and following the suggestion in Justice Scalia's opinion concurring in the judgment in that case, we also conclude that circumstances unique to the automobile context justify a search incident to arrest when it is reasonable to believe that evidence of the offense of arrest might be found in the vehicle.

I

[The police had reliable information that there was an outstanding warrant for the arrest of Rodney Gant for driving with a suspended license. Officers proceeded to the house where they expected to find Gant. Shortly thereafter, Gant drove into the driveway. He was arrested after he got out of his car. Gant was handcuffed and placed in a locked patrol car. Two officers then searched his vehicle and discovered a gun, as well as a bag of cocaine in the pocket of a jacket on the backseat.]

Gant was charged with two offenses—possession of a narcotic drug for sale and possession of drug paraphernalia (*i.e.*, the plastic bag in which the cocaine was found). He moved to suppress the evidence seized from his car on the ground that the warrantless search violated the Fourth Amendment. * * * Gant argued that *Belton* did not authorize the search of his vehicle because he posed no threat to the officers after he was handcuffed in the patrol car and because he was arrested for a traffic offense for which no evidence could be found in his vehicle. When asked at the suppression hearing why the search was conducted, Officer Griffith responded: "Because the law says we can do it."

The trial court * * * denied the motion to suppress. * * *

After protracted state-court proceedings, the Arizona Supreme Court concluded that the search of Gant's car was unreasonable within the meaning of the Fourth Amendment. The court's opinion discussed at length our decision in *Belton* * * *. The court distinguished *Belton* as a case concerning the permissible scope of a vehicle search incident to arrest and concluded that it did not answer "the threshold question whether the police may conduct a search incident to arrest at all once the scene is secure." Relying on our earlier decision in *Chimel*, the court observed that the search-incident-to-arrest exception to the warrant requirement is justified by interests in officer safety and evidence preservation. When "the justifications underlying *Chimel* no longer exist because the scene is secure and the arrestee is handcuffed, secured in the back of a patrol car, and under the supervision of an officer," the court concluded, a "warrantless search of the arrestee's car cannot be justified as necessary to protect the officers at the scene or prevent the destruction of evidence." Accordingly, the court held that the search of Gant's car was unreasonable. * * *

The chorus that has called for us to revisit *Belton* includes courts, scholars, and Members of this Court who have questioned that decision's clarity and its fidelity to Fourth Amendment principles. We therefore granted the State's petition for certiorari.

II

Consistent with our precedent, our analysis begins, as it should in every case addressing the reasonableness of a warrantless search, with the basic rule that "searches conducted outside the judicial process, without prior approval by judge or magistrate, are *per se* unreasonable under the Fourth Amendment—subject only to a few specifically established and well-delineated exceptions." Among the exceptions to the warrant requirement is a search incident to a lawful arrest. * * *

In *Chimel*, we held that a search incident to arrest may only include "the arrestee's person and the area 'within his immediate control'—construing that phrase to mean the area from within which he might gain possession of a weapon or destructible evidence." That limitation, which continues to define the boundaries of the exception, ensures that the scope of a search incident to arrest is commensurate with its purposes of protecting arresting officers and safeguarding any evidence of the offense of arrest that an arrestee might conceal or destroy. If there is no possibility that an arrestee could reach into the area that law enforcement officers seek to search, both justifications for the search-incident-to-arrest exception are absent and the rule does not apply.

In *Belton*, we considered *Chimel*'s application to the automobile context. * * *

* * * [W]e held that when an officer lawfully arrests "the occupant of an automobile, he may, as a contemporaneous incident of that arrest, search the passenger compartment of the automobile" and any containers therein. That holding was based in large part on our assumption "that articles inside the relatively narrow compass of the passenger compartment of an automobile are in fact generally, even if not inevitably, within 'the area into which an arrestee might reach.'"

The Arizona Supreme Court read our decision in *Belton* as merely delineating "the proper scope of a search of the interior of an automobile" incident to an arrest. That is, *when* the passenger compartment is within an arrestee's reaching distance, *Belton* supplies the generalization that the entire compartment and any containers therein may be reached. On that view of *Belton*, the state court concluded that the search of Gant's car was unreasonable because Gant clearly could not have accessed his car at the time of the search. * * *

Gant now urges us to adopt the reading of *Belton* followed by the Arizona Supreme Court.

III

Despite the textual and evidentiary support for the Arizona Supreme Court's reading of *Belton*, our opinion has been widely understood to allow a vehicle search incident to the arrest of a recent occupant even if there is no possibility the arrestee could gain access to the vehicle at the time of the search. This reading may be attributable to Justice Brennan's dissent in *Belton*, in which he characterized the Court's holding as resting on the "fiction * * * that the interior of a car is *always* within the immediate control of an arrestee who has recently been in the car." * * *

* * * As Justice O'Connor observed [in *Thornton*], "lower court decisions seem now to treat the ability to search a vehicle incident to the arrest of a recent occupant as a police entitlement rather than as an exception justified by the twin rationales of *Chimel*." Justice Scalia has similarly noted that, although it is improbable that an arrestee could gain access to weapons stored in his vehicle after he has been handcuffed and secured in the backseat of a patrol car, cases allowing a search in "this precise factual scenario * * * are legion." * * *

Under this broad reading of *Belton*, a vehicle search would be authorized incident to every arrest of a recent occupant notwithstanding that in most cases the vehicle's passenger compartment will not be within the arrestee's reach at the time of the search. To read *Belton* as authorizing a vehicle search incident to every recent occupant's arrest would thus untether the rule from the justifications underlying the *Chimel* exception * * * . Accordingly, we reject this reading of *Belton* and hold that the *Chimel* rationale authorizes police to search a vehicle incident to a recent occupant's arrest only when the arrestee is unsecured and within reaching distance of the passenger compartment at the time of the search.

Although it does not follow from *Chimel*, we also conclude that circumstances unique to the vehicle context justify a search incident to a lawful arrest when it is "reasonable to believe evidence relevant to the crime of arrest might be found in the vehicle." In many cases, as when a recent occupant is arrested for a traffic violation, there will be no reasonable basis to believe the vehicle contains relevant evidence. But in others, including *Belton* and *Thornton*, the offense of arrest will supply a basis for searching the passenger compartment of an arrestee's vehicle and any containers therein.

Neither the possibility of access nor the likelihood of discovering offense-related evidence authorized the search in this case. * * * Because police could not reasonably have believed either that Gant could have accessed his car at the time of the search or that evidence of the offense [of driving with a suspended license] for which he was arrested might have been found therein, the search in this case was unreasonable.

IV

The State * * * asks us to uphold the search of his vehicle under the broad reading of *Belton* discussed above. The State argues that *Belton* searches are reasonable regardless of the possibility of access in a given case because that expansive rule correctly balances law enforcement interests, including the interest in a bright-line rule, with an arrestee's limited privacy interest in his vehicle.

For several reasons, we reject the State's argument. First, the State seriously undervalues the privacy interests at stake. * * * It is particularly significant that *Belton* searches authorize police officers to search not just the passenger compartment but every purse, briefcase, or other container within that space. A rule that gives police the power to conduct such a search whenever an individual is caught committing a traffic offense, when there is no basis for believing evidence of the offense might be found in the vehicle, creates a serious and recurring threat to the privacy of countless individuals. Indeed, the character of that threat implicates the central concern underlying the Fourth Amendment—the concern about giving police officers unbridled discretion to rummage at will among a person's private effects.

At the same time as it undervalues these privacy concerns, the State exaggerates the clarity that its reading of *Belton* provides. Courts that have read *Belton* expansively are at odds regarding how close in time to the arrest and how proximate to the arrestee's vehicle an officer's first contact with the arrestee must be to bring the encounter within *Belton*'s purview and whether a search is reasonable when it commences or continues after the arrestee has been removed from the scene. The rule has thus generated a great deal of uncertainty, particularly for a rule touted as providing a "bright line." * * *

* * * Construing *Belton* broadly to allow vehicle searches incident to any arrest would serve no purpose except to provide a police entitlement, and it is anathema to the Fourth Amendment to permit a warrantless search on that basis. * * *

V

Our dissenting colleagues argue that the doctrine of *stare decisis* requires adherence to a broad reading of *Belton* even though the justifications for searching a vehicle incident to arrest are in most cases absent.[9] The doctrine of *stare decisis* is of course "essential to the respect accorded to the judgments of the Court and to the stability of the law," but it does not compel us to follow a past decision when its rationale no longer withstands "careful analysis."

* * * The safety and evidentiary interests that supported the search in *Belton* simply are not present in this case. Indeed, it is hard to imagine

---

[9]   Justice Alito's dissenting opinion * * * accuses us of "overrul[ing]" *Belton* and *Thornton* v. *United States*, "even though respondent Gant has not asked us to do so." Contrary to that claim, the narrow reading of *Belton* we adopt today is precisely the result Gant has urged. That Justice Alito has chosen to describe this decision as overruling our earlier cases does not change the fact that the resulting rule of law is the one advocated by respondent.

two cases that are factually more distinct, as *Belton* involved one officer confronted by four unsecured arrestees suspected of committing a drug offense and this case involves several officers confronted with a securely detained arrestee apprehended for driving with a suspended license. This case is also distinguishable from *Thornton*, in which the petitioner was arrested for a drug offense. It is thus unsurprising that Members of this Court who concurred in the judgments in *Belton* and *Thornton* also concur in the decision in this case.

We do not agree with the contention in Justice Alito's dissent * * * that consideration of police reliance interests requires a different result. Although it appears that the State's reading of *Belton* has been widely taught in police academies and that law enforcement officers have relied on the rule in conducting vehicle searches during the past 28 years, many of these searches were not justified by the reasons underlying the *Chimel* exception. Countless individuals guilty of nothing more serious than a traffic violation have had their constitutional right to the security of their private effects violated as a result. The fact that the law enforcement community may view the State's version of the *Belton* rule as an entitlement does not establish the sort of reliance interest that could outweigh the countervailing interest that all individuals share in having their constitutional rights fully protected. * * *

The experience of the 28 years since we decided *Belton* has shown that the generalization underpinning the broad reading of that decision is unfounded. We now know that articles inside the passenger compartment are rarely "within 'the area into which an arrestee might reach,'" and blind adherence to *Belton*'s faulty assumption would authorize myriad unconstitutional searches. The doctrine of *stare decisis* does not require us to approve routine constitutional violations.

VI

Police may search a vehicle incident to a recent occupant's arrest only if the arrestee is within reaching distance of the passenger compartment at the time of the search or it is reasonable to believe the vehicle contains evidence of the offense of arrest. When these justifications are absent, a search of an arrestee's vehicle will be unreasonable unless police obtain a warrant or show that another exception to the warrant requirement applies. * * * Accordingly, the judgment of the State Supreme Court is affirmed.

JUSTICE SCALIA, concurring.

To determine what is an "unreasonable" search within the meaning of the Fourth Amendment, we look first to the historical practices the Framers sought to preserve; if those provide inadequate guidance, we apply traditional standards of reasonableness. Since the historical scope of officers' authority to search vehicles incident to arrest is uncertain, traditional standards of reasonableness govern. It is abundantly clear that those standards do not justify what I take to be the rule set forth in *Belton* and *Thornton*: that arresting officers may always search an arrestee's vehicle in order to protect themselves from hidden weapons. When an arrest is made in connection with a roadside stop, police virtually always have a less intrusive and more effective means of ensuring their safety—and a means that is virtually always employed: ordering the arrestee away from the vehicle, patting him down in the open, handcuffing him, and placing him in the squad car. * * *

Justice Stevens * * * would * * * retain the application of *Chimel* v. *California* in the car-search context but would apply in the future what he believes our cases held in the past: that officers making a roadside stop may search the vehicle so long as the "arrestee is within reaching distance of the passenger compartment at the time of the search." I believe that this standard fails to provide the needed guidance to arresting officers and also leaves much room for manipulation, inviting officers to leave the scene unsecured (at least where dangerous suspects are not involved) in order to conduct a vehicle search. In my view we should simply abandon the *Belton-Thornton* charade of officer safety and overrule those cases. I would hold that a vehicle search incident to arrest is *ipso facto* "reasonable" only when the object of the search is evidence of the crime for which the arrest was made, or of another crime that the officer has probable cause to believe occurred. Because respondent was arrested for driving without a license (a crime for which no evidence could be expected to be found in the vehicle), I would hold in the present case that the search was unlawful. * * *

No other Justice, however, shares my view that application of *Chimel* in this context should be entirely abandoned. It seems to me unacceptable for the Court to come forth with a 4-to-1-to-4 opinion that leaves the governing rule uncertain. I am therefore confronted with the choice of either leaving the current understanding of *Belton* and *Thornton* in effect, or acceding to what seems to me the artificial narrowing of those cases adopted by Justice Stevens. The latter, as I have said, does not provide the degree of certainty I think desirable in this field; but the former opens the field to what I think are plainly unconstitutional searches—which is the greater evil. I therefore join the opinion of the Court.

JUSTICE BREYER, dissenting.

I agree with Justice Alito that *New York* v. *Belton* is best read as setting forth a bright-line rule that permits a warrantless search of the passenger compartment of an automobile incident to the lawful arrest of an occupant—regardless of the danger the arrested individual in fact poses. I also agree with Justice Stevens, however, that the rule can produce results divorced from its underlying Fourth Amendment rationale. For that reason I would look for a better rule—were the question before us one of first impression.

The matter, however, is not one of first impression, and that fact makes a substantial difference. * * * Principles of *stare decisis* must apply, and those who wish this Court to change a well-established legal precedent—where, as here, there has been considerable reliance on the legal rule in question—bear a heavy burden. I have not found that burden met. * * * I consequently join Justice Alito's dissenting opinion with the exception of Part II-E.

JUSTICE ALITO, with whom THE CHIEF JUSTICE ROBERTS and JUSTICE KENNEDY join, and with whom JUSTICE BREYER joins except as to Part II-E, dissenting.

* * * Today's decision effectively overrules [*Belton* and *Thornton*], even though respondent Gant has not asked us to do so.

To take the place of the overruled precedents, the Court adopts a new two-part rule under which a police officer who arrests a vehicle occupant or recent occupant may search the passenger compartment if (1) the arrestee is within reaching distance of the vehicle at the time of the search or (2) the officer has reason to believe that the vehicle contains evidence of the offense of arrest. The first part of this new rule may endanger arresting officers and is truly endorsed by only four Justices; Justice Scalia joins solely for the purpose of avoiding a "4-to-1-to-4 opinion." The second part of the new rule is taken from Justice Scalia's separate opinion in *Thornton* * * *. * * * I would follow *Belton*, and I therefore respectfully dissent.

I

Although the Court refuses to acknowledge that it is overruling *Belton* and *Thornton*, there can be no doubt that it does so. * * *

The precise holding in *Belton* could not be clearer. The Court stated unequivocally: " '[W]e hold that when a policeman has made a lawful custodial arrest of the occupant of an automobile, he may, as a contemporaneous incident of that arrest, search the passenger compartment of that automobile."

Despite this explicit statement, the opinion of the Court in the present case curiously suggests that *Belton* may reasonably be read as adopting a holding that is narrower than the one explicitly set out in the *Belton* opinion, namely, that an officer arresting a vehicle occupant may search the passenger compartment "*when* the passenger compartment is within an arrestee's reaching distance." According to the Court, the broader reading of *Belton* that has gained wide acceptance may be attributable to Justice Brennan's dissent."

Contrary to the Court's suggestion, however, Justice Brennan's *Belton* dissent did not mischaracterize the Court's holding in that case or cause that holding to be misinterpreted. As noted, the *Belton* Court explicitly stated precisely what it held. * * * [The *Belton*] "bright-line rule" has now been interred.

II

Because the Court has substantially overruled *Belton* and *Thornton*, the Court must explain why its departure from the usual rule of *stare decisis* is justified. I recognize that stare decisis is not an "inexorable command," and applies less rigidly in constitutional cases. But the Court has said that a constitutional precedent should be followed unless there is a " 'special justification' " for its abandonment. Relevant factors identified in prior cases include whether the precedent has engendered reliance, whether there has been an important change in circumstances in the outside world, whether the precedent has proved to be unworkable, whether the precedent has been undermined by later decisions, and whether the decision was badly reasoned. These factors weigh in favor of retaining the rule established in *Belton*.

A

Reliance. * * *

* * * [T]here certainly is substantial reliance here. The *Belton* rule has been taught to police officers for more than a quarter century. Many searches—almost certainly including more than a few that figure in cases now on appeal—were conducted in scrupulous reliance on that precedent. It is likely that, on the very day when this opinion is announced, numerous vehicle searches will be conducted in good faith by police officers who were taught the *Belton* rule.

The opinion of the Court recognizes [this] * * * . But for the Court, this seemingly counts for nothing. * * *

B

Changed circumstances. Abandonment of the *Belton* rule cannot be justified on the ground that the dangers surrounding the arrest of a vehicle occupant are different today than they were 28 years ago. * * * [S]urely it was well known in 1981 that a person who is taken from a vehicle, handcuffed, and placed in the back of a patrol car is unlikely to make it back into his own car to retrieve a weapon or destroy evidence.

C

Workability. The *Belton* rule has not proved to be unworkable. On the contrary, the rule was adopted for the express purpose of providing a test that would be relatively easy for police officers and judges to apply. The Court correctly notes that even the *Belton* rule is not perfectly clear in all situations. Specifically, it is sometimes debatable whether a search is or is not contemporaneous with an arrest, but that problem is small in comparison with the problems that the Court's new two-part rule will produce. * * *

D

Consistency with later cases. The *Belton* bright-line rule has not been undermined by subsequent cases. On the contrary, that rule was reaffirmed and extended just five years ago in *Thornton*.

E

Bad reasoning. The Court is harshly critical of *Belton*'s reasoning, but the problem that the Court perceives cannot be remedied simply by overruling *Belton*. *Belton* represented only a modest—and quite defensible—extension of *Chimel*, as I understand that decision. * * *

* * * *Chimel* did not say whether "the area from within which [an arrestee] might gain possession of a weapon or destructible evidence" is to be measured at the time of the arrest or at the time of the search, but unless the *Chimel* rule was meant to be a specialty rule, applicable to only a few unusual cases, the Court must have intended for this area to be measured at the time of arrest.

This is so because the Court can hardly have failed to appreciate the following two facts. First, in the great majority of cases, an officer making an arrest is able to handcuff the arrestee and remove him to a secure place before conducting a search incident to the arrest. Second, because it is safer for an arresting officer to secure an arrestee before searching, it is likely that this is what arresting officers do in the great majority of cases. * * * Thus, if the area within an arrestee's reach were assessed, not at the time of arrest, but at the time of the search, the *Chimel* rule would rarely come into play. * * *

I do not think that this is what the *Chimel* Court intended. Handcuffs were in use in 1969. The ability of arresting officers to secure arrestees before conducting a search—and their incentive to do so—are facts that can hardly have escaped the Court's attention. I therefore believe that the *Chimel* Court intended that its new rule apply in cases in which the arrestee is handcuffed before the search is conducted.

The *Belton* Court, in my view, proceeded on the basis of this interpretation of *Chimel*. * * * Viewing *Chimel* as having focused on the time of arrest, *Belton*'s only new step was to eliminate the need to decide on a case-by-case basis whether a particular person seated in a car actually could have reached the part of the passenger compartment where a weapon or evidence was hidden. For this reason, if we are going to reexamine *Belton*, we should also reexamine the reasoning in *Chimel* on which *Belton* rests.

F

The Court, however, does not reexamine *Chimel* and thus leaves the law relating to searches incident to arrest in a confused and unstable state. The first part of the Court's new two-part rule—which permits an arresting officer to search the area within an arrestee's reach at the time of the search—applies, at least for now, only to vehicle occupants and recent occupants, but there is no logical reason why the same rule should not apply to all arrestees.

The second part of the Court's new rule, which the Court takes uncritically from Justice Scalia's separate opinion in *Thornton,* raises doctrinal and practical problems that the Court makes no effort to address. Why, for example, is the standard for this type of evidence-gathering search "reason to believe" rather than probable cause? And why is this type of search restricted to evidence of the offense of arrest? It is true that an arrestee's vehicle is probably more likely to contain evidence of the crime of arrest than of some other crime, but if reason-to-believe is the governing standard for an evidence-gathering search incident to arrest, it is not easy to see why an officer should not be able to search when the officer has reason to believe that the vehicle in question possesses evidence of a crime other than the crime of arrest.

Nor is it easy to see why an evidence-gathering search incident to arrest should be restricted to the passenger compartment. The *Belton* rule was limited in this way because the passenger compartment was considered to be the area that vehicle occupants can generally reach, but since the second part of the new rule is not based on officer safety or the preservation of evidence, the ground for this limitation is obscure.[2]

III

Respondent in this case has not asked us to overrule *Belton*, much less *Chimel*. Respondent's argument rests entirely on an interpretation of *Belton* that is plainly incorrect, an interpretation that disregards *Belton*'s explicit delineation of its holding. I would therefore leave any reexamination of our prior precedents for another day, if such a reexamination is to be undertaken at all. In this case, I would simply apply *Belton* and reverse the judgment below.

---

[2]   I do not understand the Court's decision to reach the following situations. First, it is not uncommon for an officer to arrest some but not all of the occupants of a vehicle. The Court's decision in this case does not address the question whether in such a situation a search of the passenger compartment may be justified on the ground that the occupants who are not arrested could gain access to the car and retrieve a weapon or destroy evidence. Second, there may be situations in which an arresting officer has cause to fear that persons who were not passengers in the car might attempt to retrieve a weapon or evidence from the car while the officer is still on the scene. The decision in this case, as I understand it, does not address that situation either.

NOTES AND QUESTIONS

1. In the second paragraph of the majority opinion, Justice Stevens states that a warrantless search incident to a lawful arrest is permissible, even if the arrestee no longer has access to the passenger compartment, "when it is reasonable to believe that evidence of the offense of arrest might be found in the vehicle." In Part VI, this portion of the *Gant* test is stated as follows: when it is "reasonable to believe the vehicle contains evidence of the offense of arrest." Are these two statements functionally the same? Furthermore, Justice Alito points out that the majority did not use the term "probable cause." In this context, is "reasonable to believe" a lesser standard than "probable cause"? Alito expresses puzzlement over the majority's failure to use probable but isn't the answer obvious?

2. *Problem.* In view of *Gant*, would a warrantless search of the passenger compartment of a vehicle be permissible to search for illegal weapons, after the driver of the vehicle (now handcuffed and in the police vehicle) is arrested for possession of a prohibited weapon? See United States v. Vinton, 594 F.3d 14 (D.C. Cir. 2010). What if the person is arrested for driving under the influence of alcohol: would it permissible to search the car for open containers of alcohol? United States v. Taylor, 49 A.3d 818 (D.C. Ct. of App. 2012).

c. Pretextual Stops and Arrests (Particularly in Automobiles)

Introductory Comment

Consider for a moment State v. Ladson, 138 Wash.2d 343, 979 P.2d 833 (1999):

> On October 5, 1995 City of Lacey police officer Jim Mack and Thurston County sheriff's detective Cliff Ziesmer were on proactive gang patrol. The officers explained they do not make routine traffic stops while on proactive gang patrol although they use traffic infractions as a means to pull over people in order to initiate contact and questioning. * * *

> On the day in question Richard Fogle attracted the attention of officers Mack and Ziesmer as he drove by. Fogle and his passenger Thomas Ladson are both African-American. Although the officers had never seen Ladson before, they recognized Fogle from an unsubstantiated street rumor that Fogle was involved with drugs. * * *

> The officers tailed the Fogle vehicle looking for a legal justification to stop the car. They shadowed the vehicle while it refueled at a local filling station and then finally pulled Fogle over several blocks later on the grounds that Fogle's license plate

tabs had expired five days earlier. The officers do not deny the stop was pretextual.

The police then discovered Fogle's driver's license was suspended and arrested him on the spot. After securing Fogle in handcuffs in the squad car, the police conducted a full search of the car "incident to Fogle's arrest." [The police proceeded to order passenger Ladson out of the vehicle, patted him down for weapons, and found a handgun resulting in his arrest and subsequent search. A search of his person turned up baggies of marijuana.]

Notice that this entire process began with an unsubstantiated rumor that could not justify the arrest or search of Fogle, his car, or Ladson. The police strategy, therefore, was to find lawful grounds to stop the vehicle. A traffic violation was the pretext. It gave the officers the opportunity to have forced contact with Fogle, visually peer inside the car in the hope of finding incriminating evidence of drugs, and perhaps find a way to "negotiate" consent to search the car. More conveniently in this case, the expired driver's license provided police with apparent authority to take Fogle into custody and use "search incident to lawful arrest" law to conduct a nonconsensual warrantless search of him and (in the pre-*Gant* era) his car, and then to turn their attention to Ladson. The police had the authority, that is, unless the pretextual aspects of the case affects the analysis.

The *Ladson* scenario is not rare. It is played out often on the sidewalks and highways of the United States. Sometimes the scenario even lacks the unsubstantiated rumor that triggered the car stop in *Ladson*. A person's race, ethnicity, or national origin may motivate the police conduct. The term "DWB"—Driving While Black—describes the phenomenon in which officers target persons based on race for traffic (or other) detentions in order to follow up on hunches of criminal behavior.

So, this brings us to the question: *Does* the Fourth Amendment bar pretextual police conduct? The next case considers this question.

WHREN V. UNITED STATES

Supreme Court of the United States, 1996.
517 U.S. 806, 116 S.Ct. 1769, 135 L.Ed.2d 89.

JUSTICE SCALIA delivered the opinion of the Court [joined by CHIEF JUSTICE REHNQUIST, and JUSTICES STEVENS, O'CONNOR, KENNEDY, SOUTER, THOMAS, GINSBURG, and BREYER].

In this case we decide whether the temporary detention of a motorist who the police have probable cause to believe has committed a civil traffic violation is inconsistent with the Fourth Amendment's prohibition against unreasonable seizures unless a reasonable officer would have been motivated to stop the car by a desire to enforce the traffic laws.

I

On the evening of June 10, 1993, plainclothes vice-squad officers of the District of Columbia Metropolitan Police Department were patrolling a "high drug area" of the city in an unmarked car. Their suspicions were aroused when they passed a dark Pathfinder truck with temporary license plates and youthful occupants waiting at a stop sign, the driver looking down into the lap of the passenger at his right. The truck remained stopped at the intersection for what seemed an unusually long time—more than 20 seconds. When the police car executed a U-turn in order to head back toward the truck, the Pathfinder turned suddenly to its right, without signalling, and sped off at an "unreasonable" speed. The policemen followed, and in a short while overtook the Pathfinder when it stopped behind other traffic at a red light. They pulled up alongside, and Officer Ephraim Soto stepped out and approached the driver's door, identifying himself as a police officer and directing the driver, petitioner Brown, to put the vehicle in park. When Soto drew up to the driver's window, he immediately observed two large plastic bags of what appeared to be crack cocaine in petitioner Whren's hands. Petitioners were arrested, and quantities of several types of illegal drugs were retrieved from the vehicle.

Petitioners were charged in a four-count indictment with violating various federal drug laws * * * . At a pretrial suppression hearing, they challenged the legality of the stop and the resulting seizure of the drugs. They argued that the stop had not been justified by probable cause to believe, or even reasonable suspicion, that petitioners were engaged in illegal drug-dealing activity; and that Officer Soto's asserted ground for approaching the vehicle—to give the driver a warning concerning traffic violations—was pretextual. The District Court denied the suppression motion, concluding that "the facts of the stop were not controverted," and "[t]here was nothing to really demonstrate that the actions of the officers were contrary to a normal traffic stop."

Petitioners were convicted of the counts at issue here. The Court of Appeals affirmed the convictions, holding with respect to the suppression issue that, "regardless of whether a police officer subjectively believes that the occupants of an automobile may be engaging in some other illegal behavior, a traffic stop is permissible as long as a reasonable officer in the same circumstances *could have* stopped the car for the suspected traffic violation." * * *

II * * *

Petitioners accept that Officer Soto had probable cause to believe that various provisions of the District of Columbia traffic code had been

violated. See 18 D. C. Mun. Regs. §§ 2213.4 (1995) ("An operator shall
* * * give full time and attention to the operation of the vehicle"); 2204.3
("No person shall turn any vehicle * * * without giving an appropriate
signal"); 2200.3 ("No person shall drive a vehicle * * * at a speed greater
than is reasonable and prudent under the conditions"). They argue,
however, that "in the unique context of civil traffic regulations" probable
cause is not enough. Since, they contend, the use of automobiles is so
heavily and minutely regulated that total compliance with traffic and
safety rules is nearly impossible, a police officer will almost invariably be
able to catch any given motorist in a technical violation. This creates the
temptation to use traffic stops as a means of investigating other law
violations, as to which no probable cause or even articulable suspicion
exists. Petitioners, who are both black, further contend that police officers
might decide which motorists to stop based on decidedly impermissible
factors, such as the race of the car's occupants. To avoid this danger, they
say, the Fourth Amendment test for traffic stops should be, not the
normal one (applied by the Court of Appeals) of whether probable cause
existed to justify the stop; but rather, whether a police officer, acting
reasonably, would have made the stop for the reason given.

A

Petitioners contend that the standard they propose is consistent with
our past cases' disapproval of police attempts to use valid bases of action
against citizens as pretexts for pursuing other investigatory agendas. We
are reminded that in *Florida v. Wells*, 495 U.S. 1, 4, 110 S.Ct. 1632, 1635,
109 L.Ed.2d 1 (1990), we stated that "an inventory search[1] must not be
used as a ruse for a general rummaging in order to discover incriminating
evidence"; that in *Colorado v. Bertine*, 479 U.S. 367, 372, 107 S.Ct. 738,
741, 93 L.Ed.2d 739 (1987), in approving an inventory search, we
apparently thought it significant that there had been "no showing that
the police, who were following standard procedures, acted in bad faith or
for the sole purpose of investigation"; and that in *New York v. Burger*, 482
U.S. 691, 716–717, n. 27, 107 S Ct. 2636, 2651, n. 27, 96 L.Ed.2d 601
(1987), we observed, in upholding the constitutionality of a warrantless
administrative inspection,[2] that the search did not appear to be "a
'pretext' for obtaining evidence of * * * violation of * * * penal laws." But
only an undiscerning reader would regard these cases as endorsing the
principle that ulterior motives can invalidate police conduct that is
justifiable on the basis of probable cause to believe that a violation of law
has occurred. In each case we were addressing the validity of a search

---

[1]   An inventory search is the search of property lawfully seized and detained, in order to
ensure that it is harmless, to secure valuable items (such as might be kept in a towed car), and to
protect against false claims of loss or damage.

[2]   An administrative inspection is the inspection of business premises conducted by
authorities responsible for enforcing a pervasive regulatory scheme—for example, unannounced
inspection of a mine for compliance with health and safety standards.

conducted in the *absence* of probable cause. Our quoted statements simply explain that the exemption from the need for probable cause (and warrant), which is accorded to searches made for the purpose of inventory or administrative regulation, is not accorded to searches that are *not* made for those purposes.

Petitioners also rely upon *Colorado v. Bannister*, 449 U.S. 1, 101 S.Ct. 42, 66 L Ed.2d 1 (1980) (*per curiam*), a case which, like this one, involved a traffic stop as the prelude to a plain-view sighting and arrest on charges wholly unrelated to the basis for the stop. Petitioners point to our statement that "there was no evidence whatsoever that the officer's presence to issue a traffic citation was a pretext to confirm any other previous suspicion about the occupants" of the car. That dictum *at most* demonstrates that the Court in *Bannister* found no need to inquire into the question now under discussion; not that it was certain of the answer. And it may demonstrate even less than that: if by "pretext" the Court meant that the officer really had not seen the car speeding, the statement would mean only that there was no reason to doubt probable cause for the traffic stop.

It would, moreover, be anomalous, to say the least, to treat a statement in a footnote in the *per curiam Bannister* opinion as indicating a reversal of our prior law. Petitioners' difficulty is not simply a lack of affirmative support for their position. Not only have we never held, outside the context of inventory search or administrative inspection (discussed above), that an officer's motive invalidates objectively justifiable behavior under the Fourth Amendment; but we have repeatedly held and asserted the contrary. In *United States v. Villamonte-Marquez*, 462 U.S. 579, 584, n. 3, 103 S.Ct. 2573, 2577, n. 3, 77 L.Ed.2d 22 (1983), we held that an otherwise valid warrantless boarding of a vessel by customs officials was not rendered invalid "because the customs officers were accompanied by a Louisiana state policeman, and were following an informant's tip that a vessel in the ship channel was thought to be carrying marihuana." We flatly dismissed the idea that an ulterior motive might serve to strip the agents of their legal justification. In *United States v. Robinson* [p. 260, Note 8] we held that a traffic-violation arrest (of the sort here) would not be rendered invalid by the fact that it was "a mere pretext for a narcotics search"; and that a lawful postarrest search of the person would not be rendered invalid by the fact that it was not motivated by the officer-safety concern that justifies such searches. And in *Scott v. United States*, 436 U.S. 128, 138, 98 S.Ct. 1717, 1723, 56 L.Ed.2d 168 (1978), in rejecting the contention that wiretap evidence was subject to exclusion because the agents conducting the tap had failed to make any effort to comply with the statutory requirement that unauthorized acquisitions be minimized, we said that "[s]ubjective intent alone * * * does not make otherwise lawful conduct illegal or unconstitutional." We described *Robinson* as having established that "the fact that the officer does not have the state of mind which is hypothecated by the reasons which provide the legal justification for the officer's action does not invalidate the action taken as long as the circumstances, viewed objectively, justify that action."

We think these cases foreclose any argument that the constitutional reasonableness of traffic stops depends on the actual motivations of the individual officers involved. We of course agree with petitioners that the Constitution prohibits selective enforcement of the law based on considerations such as race. But the constitutional basis for objecting to intentionally discriminatory application of laws is the Equal Protection Clause, not the Fourth Amendment. Subjective intentions play no role in ordinary, probable-cause Fourth Amendment analysis.

B

Recognizing that we have been unwilling to entertain Fourth Amendment challenges based on the actual motivations of individual officers, petitioners disavow any intention to make the individual officer's subjective good faith the touchstone of "reasonableness." They insist that the standard they have put forward—whether the officer's conduct deviated materially from usual police practices, so that a reasonable officer in the same circumstances would not have made the stop for the reasons given—is an "objective" one.

But although framed in empirical terms, this approach is plainly and indisputably driven by subjective considerations. Its whole purpose is to prevent the police from doing under the guise of enforcing the traffic code what they would like to do for different reasons. Petitioners' proposed standard may not use the word "pretext," but it is designed to combat nothing other than the perceived "danger" of the pretextual stop, albeit only indirectly and over the run of cases. Instead of asking whether the individual officer had the proper state of mind, the petitioners would have us ask, in effect, whether (based on general police practices) it is plausible to believe that the officer had the proper state of mind.

Why one would frame a test designed to combat pretext in such fashion that the court cannot take into account *actual and admitted pretext* is a curiosity that can only be explained by the fact that our cases have foreclosed the more sensible option. If those cases were based only upon the evidentiary difficulty of establishing subjective intent, petitioners' attempt to root out subjective vices through objective means might make sense. But they were not based only upon that, or indeed even principally upon that. Their principal basis—which applies equally to attempts to reach subjective intent through ostensibly objective means—is simply that the Fourth Amendment's concern with "reasonableness" allows certain actions to be taken in certain circumstances, *whatever* the subjective intent. But even if our concern had been only an evidentiary one, petitioners' proposal would by no means assuage it. Indeed, it seems to us somewhat easier to figure out the intent of an individual officer than to plumb the collective consciousness of law enforcement in order to determine whether a "reasonable officer" would have been moved to act upon the traffic violation. While police manuals and standard procedures may sometimes provide objective assistance, ordinarily one would be reduced to speculating about the hypothetical reaction of a hypothetical constable— an exercise that might be called virtual subjectivity.

Moreover, police enforcement practices, even if they could be practicably assessed by a judge, vary from place to place and from time to time. We cannot accept that the search and seizure protections of the Fourth Amendment are so variable, and can be made to turn upon such trivialities. The difficulty is illustrated by petitioners' arguments in this case. Their claim that a reasonable officer would not have made this stop is based largely on District of Columbia police regulations which permit plainclothes officers in unmarked vehicles to enforce traffic laws "only in the case of a violation that is so grave as to pose an *immediate threat* to the safety of others." Metropolitan Police Department—Washington, D. C., General Order 303.1, pt. 1, Objectives and Policies (A)(2)(4) (Apr. 30, 1992). This basis of invalidation would not apply in jurisdictions that had a different practice. And it would not have applied even in the District of Columbia, if Officer Soto had been wearing a uniform or patrolling in a marked police cruiser. * * *

III

In what would appear to be an elaboration on the "reasonable officer" test, petitioners argue that the balancing inherent in any Fourth Amendment inquiry requires us to weigh the governmental and individual interests implicated in a traffic stop such as we have here. That balancing, petitioners claim, does not support investigation of minor traffic infractions by plainclothes police in unmarked vehicles; such investigation only minimally advances the government's interest in traffic safety, and may indeed retard it by producing motorist confusion and alarm—a view said to be supported by the Metropolitan Police Department's own regulations generally prohibiting this practice. And as for the Fourth Amendment interests of the individuals concerned, petitioners point out that our cases acknowledge that even ordinary traffic stops entail "a possibly unsettling show of authority"; that they at best "interfere with freedom of movement, are inconvenient, and consume time" and at worst "may create substantial anxiety." That anxiety is likely to be even more pronounced when the stop is conducted by plainclothes officers in unmarked cars.

It is of course true that in principle every Fourth Amendment case, since it turns upon a "reasonableness" determination, involves a balancing of all relevant factors. With rare exceptions not applicable here, however, the result of that balancing is not in doubt where the search or seizure is based upon probable cause. * * *

Where probable cause has existed, the only cases in which we have found it necessary actually to perform the "balancing" analysis involved searches or seizures conducted in an extraordinary manner, unusually harmful to an individual's privacy or even physical interests—such as, for example, seizure by means of deadly force, see *Tennessee v. Garner*, 471 U.S. 1, 105 S.Ct. 1694, 85 L.Ed.2d 1 (1985), unannounced entry into a home, see *Wilson v. Arkansas*, 514 U.S. 927, 115 S.Ct. 1914, 131 L.Ed.2d 976 (1995), * * * or physical penetration of the body, see *Winston v. Lee*, 470 U.S. 753, 105 S.Ct. 1611, 84 L.Ed.2d 662 (1985). The making of a traffic stop out-of-uniform does not remotely qualify as such an extreme practice, and so is governed by the usual rule that probable cause to believe the law has been broken "outbalances" private interest in avoiding police contact. * * *

For the run-of-the-mine case, which this surely is, we think there is no realistic alternative to the traditional common-law rule that probable cause justifies a search and seizure. * * *

Here the District Court found that the officers had probable cause to believe that petitioners had violated the traffic code. That rendered the stop reasonable under the Fourth Amendment, the evidence thereby discovered admissible, and the upholding of the convictions by the Court of Appeals for the District of Columbia Circuit correct.

NOTES AND QUESTIONS

1.   *The "pervasive police practice" of pretextual stops and arrests (with race added in).* A police officer explains why he will pull over a car on the road: "I have what you might call a profile. I pull up alongside a car with black males in it. Something don't [sic] match—maybe the style of the car with the guys in it. * * * We go from there." Jeffrey Goldberg, *What Cops Talk About When They Talk About Race*, New York Times Magazine, June 20, 1999, at 51.

Race may explain why Peter Lawson Jones, an African-American lawyer was pulled over in his new Mercury Sable in a white neighborhood by a police officer for allegedly running a stop sign. When the officer learned that Jones was not only an attorney but a state legislator, no ticket was issued. Hope Viner Samborn, *Profiled and Pulled Over*, American Bar Association Journal, October, 1999, at 18.

Or consider Robert Wilkins, an African-American Harvard Law School graduate who was pulled over for speeding as he was returning home from a family funeral. Instead of issuing a speeding citation at that time, the officer sought consent to search the car. When Wilkins refused, he was held for thirty minutes until a drug-sniffing dog could be brought to the scene. Only when nothing was discovered did the officer get around to issuing a speeding citation. David Cole, No Equal Justice 34–35 (1999).

Statistical evidence seemingly reenforces these anecdotes. A survey conducted by the Justice Department of contacts between the police and the public in 2008 provided this data: (1) the most common reason for contact with the police was a traffic stop (44.1%); (2) whites (8.4%), African-Americans (8.8%), and Hispanics (9.1%) were stopped by police at statistically similar rates; but (3) African-American drivers were three times as likely as white drivers, and about twice as likely as Hispanic drivers, to be searched during a traffic stop. Bureau of Justice Statistics, Special Report, Contacts between Police and the Public, 2008 (NCJ 234599, Oct. 2011).

In a subsequent study, more African-American drivers were pulled over in a traffic stop (13%) than whites and Hispanics (10%); and, among those stopped, Hispanics (6.6%) and African-Americans (6.4%) had their person or vehicle searched more often than whites (2.3%). Bureau of Justice Statistics, Police Behavior During Traffic and Street Stops, 2011 (NCJ 242937, Sept. 2013).

2. The Supreme Court rarely rules unanimously on any controversial legal issue. Why do you think the justices were united on this subject?

3. *Subjective versus objective standards.* If you dislike the outcome in *Whren*, can you suggest a workable standard for adjudicating allegations of pretextual searches and seizures? The petitioners in *Whren* suggested an objective standard, *i.e.*, would a reasonable police officer have stopped and issued a ticket for the traffic violation in question. Why did the Court reject this standard? Is this a suitable standard?

Some critics eschew an exclusively objective standard. They favor a test that permits courts to consider whether the particular officer subjectively acted as the result of illegitimate motives. According to Professor Morgan Cloud, a "test that denies [judges] the power to examine important elements of the encounter—like the subjective motives of the actors—is misguided." Morgan Cloud, *Judges, "Testilying," and the Constitution*, 69 S. Cal. L. Rev. 1341, 1386 (1996). Thoughts?

Would it be appropriate for a court to hold that an officer's deviation from usual police practices in the jurisdiction constitutes prima facie evidence of an improper motive which, in the absence of a proven justification, renders a traffic stop constitutionally unreasonable?

3. CARS AND CONTAINERS

CHAMBERS V. MARONEY

Supreme Court of the United States, 1970.
399 U.S. 42, 90 S.Ct. 1975, 26 L.Ed.2d 419.

MR. JUSTICE WHITE delivered the opinion of the Court [joined by CHIEF JUSTICE BURGER, and JUSTICES BLACK, DOUGLAS, BRENNAN, STEWART, and MARSHALL]. * * *

I

During the night of May 20, 1963, a Gulf service station in North Braddock, Pennsylvania, was robbed by two men, each of whom carried and displayed a gun. The robbers took the currency from the cash register; the service station attendant, one Stephen Kovacich, was directed to place the coins in his right-hand glove, which was then taken by the robbers. Two teenagers, who had earlier noticed a blue compact station wagon circling the block in the vicinity of the Gulf station, then saw the station wagon speed away from a parking lot close to the Gulf station. About the same time, they learned that the Gulf station had been robbed. They reported to police, who arrived immediately, that four men were in the station wagon and one was wearing a green sweater. Kovacich told the police that one of the men who robbed him was wearing a green sweater and the other was wearing a trench coat. A description of the car and the two robbers was broadcast over the police radio. Within an hour, a light blue compact station wagon answering the description and carrying four men was stopped by the police about two miles from the Gulf station. Petitioner was one of the men in the station wagon. He was wearing a green sweater and there was a trench coat in the car. The occupants were arrested and the car was driven to the police station. In the course of a thorough search of the car at the station, the police found concealed in a compartment under the dashboard two .38-caliber revolvers * * * , a right-hand glove containing small change, and certain cards bearing the name of Raymond Havicon, the attendant at a Boron service station in McKeesport, Pennsylvania, who had been robbed at gunpoint on May 13, 1963. * * *

Petitioner was indicted for both robberies. * * * The materials taken from the station wagon were introduced into evidence * * * . [Petitioner was convicted of both offenses.] * * *

II * * *

* * * [T]he search that produced the incriminating evidence was made at the police station some time after the arrest and cannot be justified as a search incident to an arrest: "Once an accused is under

arrest and in custody, then a search made at another place, without a warrant, is simply not incident to the arrest." * * *

There are, however, alternative grounds arguably justifying the search of the car in this case. * * * Here * * * the police had probable cause to believe that the robbers, carrying guns and the fruits of the crime, had fled the scene in a light blue compact station wagon which would be carrying four men, one wearing a green sweater and another wearing a trench coat. As the state courts correctly held, there was probable cause to arrest the occupants of the station wagon that the officers stopped; just as obviously was there probable cause to search the car for guns and stolen money.

In terms of the circumstances justifying a warrantless search, the Court has long distinguished between an automobile and a home or office. In *Carroll v. United States*, 267 U.S. 132, 45 S.Ct. 280, 69 L.Ed. 543 (1925), the issue was the admissibility in evidence of contraband liquor seized in a warrantless search of a car on the highway. After surveying the law from the time of the adoption of the Fourth Amendment onward, the Court held that automobiles and other conveyances may be searched without a warrant in circumstances that would not justify the search without a warrant of a house or an office, provided that there is probable cause to believe that the car contains articles that the officers are entitled to seize. The Court expressed its holding as follows:

> " * * * [T]he guaranty of freedom from unreasonable searches and seizures by the Fourth Amendment has been construed, practically since the beginning of the Government, as recognizing a necessary difference between a search of a store, dwelling house or other structure in respect of which a proper official warrant readily may be obtained, and a search of a ship, motor boat, wagon or automobile, for contraband goods, where it is not practicable to secure a warrant because the vehicle can be quickly moved out of the locality or jurisdiction in which the warrant must be sought.

> " * * * [T]hose lawfully within the country, entitled to use the public highways, have a right to free passage without interruption or search unless there is known to a competent official authorized to search, probable cause for believing that their vehicles are carrying contraband or illegal merchandise. * * *

> " * * * The right to search and the validity of the seizure are not dependent on the right to arrest. They are dependent on the reasonable cause the seizing officer has for belief that the contents of the automobile offend against the law." * * *

Neither *Carroll* nor other cases in this Court require or suggest that in every conceivable circumstance the search of an auto even with probable cause may be made without the extra protection for privacy that a warrant affords. But the circumstances that furnish probable cause to search a particular auto for particular articles are most often unforeseeable; moreover, the opportunity to search is fleeting since a car is readily movable. Where this is true, as in *Carroll* and the case before us now, if an effective search is to be made at any time, either the search must be made immediately without a warrant or the car itself must be seized and held without a warrant for whatever period is necessary to obtain a warrant for the search.[9]

* * * Only in exigent circumstances will the judgment of the police as to probable cause serve as a sufficient authorization for a search. *Carroll* holds a search warrant unnecessary where there is probable cause to search an automobile stopped on the highway; the car is movable, the occupants are alerted, and the car's contents may never be found again if a warrant must be obtained. Hence an immediate search is constitutionally permissible.

Arguably, because of the preference for a magistrate's judgment, only the immobilization of the car should be permitted until a search warrant is obtained; arguably, only the "lesser" intrusion is permissible until the magistrate authorizes the "greater." But which is the "greater" and which the "lesser" intrusion is itself a debatable question and the answer may depend on a variety of circumstances. For constitutional purposes, we see no difference between on the one hand seizing and holding a car before presenting the probable cause issue to a magistrate and on the other hand carrying out an immediate search without a warrant. Given probable cause to search, either course is reasonable under the Fourth Amendment.

On the facts before us, the blue station wagon could have been searched on the spot when it was stopped since there was probable cause to search and it was a fleeting target for a search. The probable-cause factor still obtained at the station house and so did the mobility of the car unless the Fourth Amendment permits a warrantless seizure of the car and the denial of its use to anyone until a warrant is secured. In that event there is little to choose in terms of practical consequences between an immediate search without a warrant and the car's immobilization until a warrant is obtained. The same consequences may not follow where there is unforeseeable cause to search a house. But as *Carroll* held, for

---

[9]   Following the car until a warrant can be obtained seems an impractical alternative since, among other things, the car may be taken out of the jurisdiction. Tracing the car and searching it hours or days later would of course permit instruments or fruits of crime to be removed from the car before the search.

the purposes of the Fourth Amendment there is a constitutional difference between houses and cars. * * *

MR. JUSTICE BLACKMUN took no part in the consideration or decision of this case.

[JUSTICE STEWART'S concurring opinion is omitted.]

MR. JUSTICE HARLAN, concurring in part and dissenting in part. * * *

II

In sustaining the search of the automobile I believe the Court ignores the framework of our past decisions circumscribing the scope of permissible search without a warrant. * * *

Where officers have probable cause to search a vehicle on a public way, a * * * limited exception to the warrant requirement is reasonable because "the vehicle can be quickly moved out of the locality or jurisdiction in which the warrant must be sought." *Carroll v. United States.* Because the officers might be deprived of valuable evidence if required to obtain a warrant before effecting any search or seizure, I agree with the Court that they should be permitted to take the steps necessary to preserve evidence and to make a search possible. The Court holds that those steps include making a warrantless search of the entire vehicle on the highway * * * and indeed appears to go further and to condone the removal of the car to the police station for a warrantless search there at the convenience of the police. I cannot agree that this result is consistent with our insistence in other areas that departures from the warrant requirement strictly conform to the exigency presented.

The Court concedes that the police could prevent removal of the evidence by temporarily seizing the car for the time necessary to obtain a warrant. It does not dispute that such a course would fully protect the interests of effective law enforcement; rather it states that whether temporary seizure is a "lesser" intrusion than warrantless search "is itself a debatable question and the answer may depend on a variety of circumstances."[8] I believe it clear that a warrantless search involves the greater sacrifice of Fourth Amendment values.

The Fourth Amendment proscribes, to be sure, unreasonable "seizures" as well as "searches." However, in the circumstances in which this problem is likely to occur, the lesser intrusion will almost always be the simple seizure of the car for the period—perhaps a day—necessary to enable the officers to obtain a search warrant. In the first place, as this case shows, the very facts establishing probable cause to search will often also justify arrest of the occupants of the vehicle. Since the occupants

---

[8] The Court, unable to decide whether search or temporary seizure is the "lesser" intrusion, in this case authorizes both. * * * [T]he Court approves the searches without even an inquiry into the officers' ability promptly to take their case before a magistrate.

themselves are to be taken into custody, they will suffer minimal further inconvenience from the temporary immobilization of their vehicle. Even where no arrests are made, persons who wish to avoid a search—either to protect their privacy or to conceal incriminating evidence—will almost certainly prefer a brief loss of the use of the vehicle in exchange for the opportunity to have a magistrate pass upon the justification for the search. To be sure, one can conceive of instances in which the occupant, having nothing to hide and lacking concern for the privacy of the automobile, would be more deeply offended by a temporary immobilization of his vehicle than by a prompt search of it. However, such a person always remains free to consent to an immediate search, thus avoiding any delay. Where consent is not forthcoming, the occupants of the car have an interest in privacy that is protected by the Fourth Amendment even where the circumstances justify a temporary seizure. The Court's endorsement of a warrantless invasion of that privacy where another course would suffice is simply inconsistent with our repeated stress on the Fourth Amendment's mandate of " 'adherence to judicial processes.' " * * *

NOTES AND QUESTIONS

1.   *Carroll v. United States*, discussed in *Chambers*, involved a prosecution under the National Prohibition Act. The occupants of the car in question were not arrested (and could not lawfully have been arrested) until federal agents searched the car and discovered illegal liquor concealed inside the car. In contrast, the car occupants in *Chambers* were arrested *before* the search. If one considers the practicability of seeking a warrant, is this factual distinction relevant?

Now consider the two cases in terms of, simply, the reasonableness of conducting the respective searches without a warrant. In this regard, the driver has three interests at stake: an interest in locomotion (continuing to travel); an interest in control over his property; and a privacy interest in the car's contents. Note, *Warrantless Searches and Seizures of Automobiles*, 87 Harv. L. Rev. 835, 841 (1974). What are the competing legitimate interests of the police? Balancing these interests, do you think the police acted reasonably in *Carroll* in conducting the warrantless search on the highway (assuming, as the Court held, that the police had probable cause to believe the car was transporting contraband)? What about in *Chambers*, in conducting the warrantless search at the police station?

Why does Justice White believe that the *Carroll* principle applies in the *Chambers* circumstances? Are you persuaded by his explanation, or does Justice Harlan have the better side of the argument?

2.   *From Carroll to Chambers to another "C" car case.* Just a year after *Chambers*, the Supreme Court considered another case involving a warrantless automobile search. In Coolidge v. New Hampshire, 403 U.S. 443,

91 S.Ct. 2022, 29 L.Ed.2d 564 (1971), a police investigation of the murder of a fourteen-year-old girl focused on Edward Coolidge. Initially, the police questioned him and asked him to take a lie detector test, which he did. At all times, Coolidge was cooperative. Subsequently, the police determined that they had sufficient evidence to arrest Coolidge, which they did in his home.

At the time of the arrest, two Coolidge cars were parked in the driveway. More than two hours after Coolidge was taken into custody, the cars were seized without a warrant. One of the cars was searched and vacuumed for microscopic evidence two days later, again a year later, and a third time five months after the latter search. You may assume that the police had probable cause for these searches. Given that assumption, if you represented Coolidge, what would be the basis of your objection? If you were the prosecutor, how would you justify the warrantless searches of the car?

In a four-justice plurality opinion, Justice Stewart ruled that the warrantless car searches were unconstitutional, notwithstanding probable cause:

> [T]he most basic constitutional rule in this area is that "searches conducted outside the judicial process, without prior approval by judge or magistrate, are *per se* unreasonable under the Fourth Amendment—subject only to a few specifically established and well-delineated exceptions." * * * "[T]he burden is on those seeking the exemption to show the need for it." * * *

> * * * [E]ven granting that the police had probable cause to search the car, the application of the *Carroll* case to these facts would extend it far beyond its original rationale. * * *

> * * * As we said in *Chambers*, "exigent circumstances" justify the warrantless search of "an automobile *stopped on the highway*," where there is probable cause, because the car is "movable, the occupants are alerted, and the car's contents may never be found again if a warrant must be obtained." "[T]he opportunity to search is fleeting * * * ."

> In this case, the police had known for some time of the probable role of the Pontiac car in the crime. Coolidge was aware that he was a suspect in the * * * murder, but he had been extremely cooperative throughout the investigation, and there was no indication that he meant to flee. He had already had ample opportunity to destroy any evidence he thought incriminating. There is no suggestion that, on the night in question, the car was being used for any illegal purpose, and it was regularly parked in the driveway of his house. The opportunity for search was thus hardly "fleeting." * * *[18]

---

[18] It is frequently said that occupied automobiles stopped on the open highway may be searched without a warrant because they are "mobile," or "movable." * * * In this case it is, of course, true that even though Coolidge was in jail, his wife was miles away in the company of

The word "automobile" is not a talisman in whose presence the Fourth Amendment fades away and disappears. And surely there is nothing in this case to invoke the meaning and purpose of the rule of *Carroll v. United States*—no alerted criminal bent on flight, no fleeting opportunity on an open highway after a hazardous chase, no contraband or stolen goods or weapons, no confederates waiting to move the evidence, not even the inconvenience of a special police detail to guard the immobilized automobile. In short, by no possible stretch of the legal imagination can this be made into a case where "it is not practicable to secure a warrant," and the "automobile exception," despite its label, is simply irrelevant.

Since *Carroll* would not have justified a warrantless search of the Pontiac at the time Coolidge was arrested, the later search at the station house was plainly illegal, at least so far as the automobile exception is concerned. *Chambers* is of no help to the State, since that case held only that, where the police may stop and search an automobile under *Carroll*, they may also seize it and search it later at the police station.

Justice White and Chief Justice Burger concurred with the plurality that two of the three searches of the Coolidge car were improper:

Chambers upheld the seizure and subsequent search of automobiles at the station house rather than requiring the police to search cars immediately at the places where they are found. But *Chambers* did not authorize indefinite detention of automobiles so seized; it contemplated some expedition in completing the searches so that automobiles could be released and returned to their owners. In the present case, however, Coolidge's Pontiac was not released quickly but was retained in police custody for more than a year and was searched not only immediately after seizure but also on two other occasions: one of them 11 months and the other 14 months after seizure. Since fruits of the later searches as well as the earlier one were apparently introduced in evidence, I cannot look to *Chambers* and would invalidate the later searches * * * . It is only because of the long detention of the car that I find *Chambers*

---

two plainclothesmen, and the Coolidge property was under the guard of two other officers, the automobile was in a literal sense "mobile." A person who had the keys and could slip by the guard could drive it away. We attach no constitutional significance to this sort of mobility.

First, a good number of the containers that the police might discover on a person's property and want to search are equally movable, *e.g.*, trunks, suitcases, boxes, briefcases, and bags. How are such objects to be distinguished from an unoccupied automobile * * * sitting on the owner's property? It is true that the automobile has wheels and its own locomotive power. But given the virtually universal availability of automobiles in our society there is little difference between driving the container itself away and driving it away in a vehicle brought to the scene for that purpose. * * * [I]f *Carroll v. United States* permits a warrantless search of an unoccupied vehicle, on private property and beyond the scope of a valid search incident to an arrest, then it would permit as well a warrantless search of a suitcase or a box. We have found no case that suggests such an extension of *Carroll*.

inapplicable, however, and I disagree strongly with the majority's reasoning for refusing to apply it. * * *

For Fourth Amendment purposes, the difference between a moving and movable vehicle is tenuous at best. It is a metaphysical distinction without roots in the commonsense standard of reasonableness governing search and seizure cases. Distinguishing the case before us from the *Carroll-Chambers* line of cases further enmeshes Fourth Amendment law in litigation breeding refinements having little relation to reality. I suggest that in the interest of coherence and credibility we either overrule our prior cases and treat automobiles precisely as we do houses or apply those cases to readily movable as well as moving vehicles and thus treat searches of automobiles as we do the arrest of a person.

Is *Coolidge* consistent with *Chambers*? Whose reasoning—Stewart's or White's—do you find more persuasive?

3. *In search of a new rationale. Carroll, Chambers*, and *Coolidge* all focused on the mobility of motor vehicles (although notice in *Coolidge* how differently Justices White and Stewart viewed the concept of mobility) as the basis for warrantless searches. After *Coolidge*, the Supreme Court developed an additional, non-mobility-based rationale for warrantless car searches, as the next case demonstrates.

CALIFORNIA V. CARNEY

Supreme Court of the United States, 1985.
471 U.S. 386, 105 S.Ct. 2066, 85 L.Ed.2d 406.

CHIEF JUSTICE BURGER delivered the opinion of the Court [joined by JUSTICES WHITE, BLACKMUN, POWELL, REHNQUIST, and O'CONNOR].

We granted certiorari to decide whether law enforcement agents violated the Fourth Amendment when they conducted a warrantless search, based on probable cause, of a fully mobile "motor home" located in a public place.

I

On May 31, 1979, Drug Enforcement Agency Agent Robert Williams watched respondent, Charles Carney, approach a youth in downtown San Diego. The youth accompanied Carney to a Dodge Mini Motor Home parked in a nearby lot. Carney and the youth closed the window shades in the motor home, including one across the front window. Agent Williams had previously received uncorroborated information that the same motor home was used by another person who was exchanging marihuana for sex. Williams, with assistance from other agents, kept the motor home under surveillance for the entire one and one-quarter hours that Carney and the youth remained inside. When the youth left the motor home, the agents followed and stopped him. The youth told the agents that he had received marihuana in return for allowing Carney sexual contacts.

At the agents' request, the youth returned to the motor home and knocked on its door; Carney stepped out. The agents identified themselves as law enforcement officers. Without a warrant or consent, one agent entered the motor home and observed marihuana, plastic bags, and a scale of the kind used in weighing drugs on a table. Agent Williams took Carney into custody and took possession of the motor home. A subsequent search of the motor home at the police station revealed additional marihuana in the cupboards and refrigerator.

Respondent was charged with possession of marihuana for sale. At a preliminary hearing, he moved to suppress the evidence discovered in the motor home. The Magistrate denied the motion * * * .

Respondent * * * pleaded *nolo contendere* to the charges against him, and was placed on probation for three years. * * *

II

* * * There are, of course, exceptions to the general rule that a warrant must be secured before a search is undertaken; one is the so-called "automobile exception" at issue in this case. This exception to the warrant requirement was first set forth by the Court 60 years ago in *Carroll v. United States*, 267 U.S. 132, 45 S.Ct. 280, 69 L.Ed. 543 (1925). There, the Court recognized that the privacy interests in an automobile are constitutionally protected; however, it held that the ready mobility of the automobile justifies a lesser degree of protection of those interests. The Court rested this exception on a long-recognized distinction between stationary structures and vehicles * * * .

The capacity to be "quickly moved" was clearly the basis of the holding in *Carroll*, and our cases have consistently recognized ready mobility as one of the principal bases of the automobile exception. * * *

However, although ready mobility alone was perhaps the original justification for the vehicle exception, our later cases have made clear that ready mobility is not the only basis for the exception. The reasons for the vehicle exception, we have said, are twofold. "Besides the element of mobility, less rigorous warrant requirements govern because the expectation of privacy with respect to one's automobile is significantly less than that relating to one's home or office." [*South Dakota v. Opperman*, 428 U.S. 364, 96 S.Ct. 3092, 49 L.Ed.2d 1000 (1976).] * * *

These reduced expectations of privacy derive not from the fact that the area to be searched is in plain view, but from the pervasive regulation of vehicles capable of traveling on the public highways. As we explained in *South Dakota v. Opperman*, an inventory search case:

"Automobiles, unlike homes, are subjected to pervasive and continuing governmental regulation and controls, including periodic inspection and licensing requirements. As an everyday occurrence, police stop and examine vehicles when license plates or inspection stickers have expired, or if other violations, such as exhaust fumes or excessive noise, are noted, or if headlights or other safety equipment are not in proper working order."

The public is fully aware that it is accorded less privacy in its automobiles because of this compelling governmental need for regulation. * * * In short, the pervasive schemes of regulation, which necessarily lead to reduced expectations of privacy, and the exigencies attendant to ready mobility justify searches without prior recourse to the authority of a magistrate so long as the overriding standard of probable cause is met.

When a vehicle is being used on the highways, or if it is readily capable of such use and is found stationary in a place not regularly used for residential purposes—temporary or otherwise—the two justifications for the vehicle exception come into play. First, the vehicle is obviously readily mobile by the turn of an ignition key, if not actually moving. Second, there is a reduced expectation of privacy stemming from its use as a licensed motor vehicle subject to a range of police regulation inapplicable to a fixed dwelling. At least in these circumstances, the overriding societal interests in effective law enforcement justify an immediate search before the vehicle and its occupants become unavailable.

While it is true that respondent's vehicle possessed some, if not many of the attributes of a home, it is equally clear that the vehicle falls clearly within the scope of the exception laid down in *Carroll* and applied in succeeding cases. Like the automobile in *Carroll*, respondent's motor home was readily mobile. Absent the prompt search and seizure, it could readily have been moved beyond the reach of the police. Furthermore, the vehicle was licensed to "operate on public streets; [was] serviced in public places; * * * and [was] subject to extensive regulation and inspection." And the vehicle was so situated that an objective observer would conclude that it was being used not as a residence, but as a vehicle.

Respondent urges us to distinguish his vehicle from other vehicles within the exception because it was *capable of functioning as a home.* In our increasingly mobile society, many vehicles used for transportation can be and are being used not only for transportation but for shelter, *i.e.,* as a "home" or "residence." To distinguish between respondent's motor home and an ordinary sedan for purposes of the vehicle exception would require that we apply the exception depending upon the size of the vehicle and the quality of its appointments. Moreover, to fail to apply the exception to vehicles such as a motor home ignores the fact that a motor home lends itself easily to use as an instrument of illicit drug traffic and other illegal activity. * * * We decline today to distinguish between "worthy" and "unworthy" vehicles which are either on the public roads and highways, or situated such that it is reasonable to conclude that the vehicle is not being used as a residence.

Our application of the vehicle exception has never turned on the other uses to which a vehicle might be put. The exception has historically turned on the ready mobility of the vehicle, and on the presence of the vehicle in a setting that objectively indicates that the vehicle is being used for transportation.[3] * * *

JUSTICE STEVENS, with whom JUSTICE BRENNAN and JUSTICE MARSHALL join, dissenting. * * *

The hybrid character of the motor home places it at the crossroads between the privacy interests that generally forbid warrantless invasions of the home, and the law enforcement interests that support the exception for warrantless searches of automobiles based on probable cause. By choosing to follow the latter route, the Court * * * has accorded priority to an exception rather than to the general rule, and * * * has abandoned the limits on the exception imposed by prior cases. * * *

II * * *

In *United States v. Ross*, [456 U.S. 798, 102 S.Ct. 2157, 72 L.Ed.2d 572 (1982),] the Court reaffirmed the primary importance of the general rule condemning warrantless searches, and emphasized that the exception permitting the search of automobiles without a warrant is a narrow one. * * * Given this warning and the presumption of regularity that attaches to a warrant, it is hardly unrealistic to expect experienced law enforcement officers to obtain a search warrant when one can easily be secured.

* * * If the motor home were parked in the exact middle of the intersection between the general rule and the exception for automobiles, priority should be given to the rule rather than the exception.

III

The motor home, however, was not parked in the middle of that intersection. Our prior cases teach us that inherent mobility is not a sufficient justification for the fashioning of an exception to the warrant requirement, especially in the face of heightened expectations of privacy in the location searched. Motor homes, by their common use and

---

[3] We need not pass on the application of the vehicle exception to a motor home that is situated in a way or place that objectively indicates that it is being used as a residence. Among the factors that might be relevant in determining whether a warrant would be required in such a circumstance is its location, whether the vehicle is readily mobile or instead, for instance, elevated on blocks, whether the vehicle is licensed, whether it is connected to utilities, and whether it has convenient access to a public road.

construction, afford their owners a substantial and legitimate expectation of privacy when they dwell within. When a motor home is parked in a location that is removed from the public highway, I believe that society is prepared to recognize that the expectations of privacy within it are not unlike the expectations one has in a fixed dwelling. As a general rule, such places may only be searched with a warrant based upon probable cause. Warrantless searches of motor homes are only reasonable when the motor home is traveling on the public streets or highways, or when exigent circumstances otherwise require an immediate search without the expenditure of time necessary to obtain a warrant. * * *

In this case, the motor home was parked in an off-the-street lot only a few blocks from the courthouse in downtown San Diego where dozens of magistrates were available to entertain a warrant application. The officers clearly had the element of surprise with them, and with curtains covering the windshield, the motor home offered no indication of any imminent departure. The officers plainly had probable cause to arrest the respondent and search the motor home, and on this record, it is inexplicable why they eschewed the safe harbor of a warrant.[17] * * *

Unlike a brick bungalow or a frame Victorian, a motor home seldom serves as a permanent lifetime abode. The motor home in this case, however, was designed to accommodate a breadth of ordinary everyday living. Photographs in the record indicate that its height, length, and beam provided substantial living space inside: stuffed chairs surround a table; cupboards provide room for storage of personal effects; bunk beds provide sleeping space; and a refrigerator provides ample space for food and beverages. Moreover, curtains and large opaque walls inhibit viewing the activities inside from the exterior of the vehicle. The interior configuration of the motor home establishes that the vehicle's size, shape, and mode of construction should have indicated to the officers that it was a vehicle containing mobile living quarters. * * *

In my opinion, searches of places that regularly accommodate a wide range of private human activity are fundamentally different from searches of automobiles which primarily serve a public transportation function. Although it may not be a castle, a motor home is usually the functional equivalent of a hotel room, a vacation and retirement home, or a hunting and fishing cabin. These places may be as spartan as a humble cottage when compared to the most majestic mansion, but the highest and most legitimate expectations of privacy associated with these temporary abodes should command the respect of this Court. In my opinion, a

---

[17] This willingness to search first and later seek justification has properly been characterized as "a decision roughly comparable in prudence to determining whether an electrical wire is charged by grasping it." *United States v. Mitchell*, 538 F.2d 1230, 1233 (C.A.5 1976) (en banc).

warrantless search of living quarters in a motor home is "presumptively unreasonable absent exigent circumstances."

NOTES AND QUESTIONS

1.   What, if anything, is left of *Coolidge* (p. 310, Note 2) after *Carney*?

2.   *The reduced-expectation-of-privacy rationale.* Is the Court correct that we have a reduced expectation of privacy in our automobiles because of pervasive governmental regulation of them?

Are there other grounds for claiming that we have a lesser expectation of privacy in our cars than we do in our homes? Yes, according to Cardwell v. Lewis, 417 U.S. 583, 94 S.Ct. 2464, 41 L.Ed.2d 325 (1974):

> One has a lesser expectation of privacy in a motor vehicle because its function is transportation and it seldom serves as one's residence or as the repository of personal effects. A car has little capacity for escaping public scrutiny. It travels public thoroughfares where both its occupants and its contents are in plain view.

Do these arguments withstand scrutiny? Why, or why not?

3.   *Automobile inventories: another warrant "exception."* A warrantless search of a car may be permissible on various grounds. First, if the police have probable cause to search a car, the *Carroll-Chambers-Carney* "automobile exception" comes into play. Second, if an occupant (or recent occupant) of an automobile is arrested, the police may sometimes conduct, as an incident of the arrest, a contemporaneous search of the passenger compartment of the vehicle, even without probable cause to search.

A third basis for a car search is the "automobile inventory" warrant exception. In South Dakota v. Opperman, 428 U.S. 364, 96 S.Ct. 3092, 49 L.Ed.2d 1000 (1976), *O*'s automobile was towed to a city impound lot, as permitted by local ordinance, after it was ticketed twice for being parked in a restricted zone. Pursuant to standard operating procedures, officers unlocked the vehicle and, using a standard inventory form, inventoried the contents of the car. In the glove compartment, the police discovered marijuana. *O* was prosecuted for possession of the marijuana discovered during the warrantless, suspicionless search.

The Court determined that the probable cause and warrant requirements of the Fourth Amendment do not apply to routine inventory searches:

> The standard of probable cause is peculiarly related to criminal investigations, not routine, non-criminal procedures. The probable-cause approach is unhelpful when analysis centers upon the reasonableness of routine administrative caretaking functions, particularly when no claim is made that the protective procedures are a subterfuge for criminal investigations.

In view of the noncriminal context of inventory searches, and the inapplicability in such a setting of the requirement of probable cause, courts have held—and quite correctly—that search warrants are not required, linked as the warrant requirement textually is to the probable-cause concept. We have frequently observed that the warrant requirement assures that legal inferences and conclusions as to probable cause will be drawn by a neutral magistrate unrelated to the criminal investigative-enforcement process. With respect to noninvestigative police inventories of automobiles lawfully within governmental custody, however, the policies underlying the warrant requirement * * * are inapplicable.

With the warrant clause eliminated from analysis, the Court focused exclusively on the reasonableness requirement of the Fourth Amendment. In this regard, the Court balanced the competing interests. From the car owner's perspective there is his lesser expectation of privacy in the contents of the automobile. The Court then considered the government's side of the equation:

When vehicles are impounded, local police departments generally follow a routine practice of securing and inventorying the automobiles' contents. These procedures developed in response to three distinct needs: the protection of the owner's property while it remains in police custody; the protection of the police against claims or disputes over lost or stolen property; and the protection of the police from potential danger. The practice has been viewed as essential to respond to incidents of theft or vandalism. In addition, police frequently attempt to determine whether a vehicle has been stolen and thereafter abandoned.

Balancing the competing interests, the Court concluded that routine inventory searches are reasonable. Essential to this reasoning, however, is the requirement that the police follow standard procedures, *i.e.*, that they do not exceed the scope of their own rules. The police should not have unfettered discretion in conducting an inventory, in part to ensure that the inventory is "routine," rather than "a pretext concealing an investigatory police motive." *Id.*

For example, in Florida v. Wells, 495 U.S. 1, 110 S.Ct. 1632, 109 L.Ed.2d 1 (1990), the Court unanimously held that highway patrol officers were not permitted to open a locked suitcase they discovered during an inventory search because "the Florida Highway Patrol had no policy whatever with respect to the opening of closed containers encountered during an inventory search." A five-justice majority stated in dictum, however, that

in forbidding uncanalized discretion to police officers conducting inventory searches, there is no reason to insist that they be conducted in a totally mechanical "all or nothing" fashion. * * * A police officer may be allowed sufficient latitude to determine whether a particular container should or should not be opened in light of the nature of the search and characteristics of the container itself. Thus, while policies of opening all containers or of opening no containers are unquestionably permissible, it would be equally permissible, for example, to allow the opening of closed containers whose contents officers determine they are unable to ascertain from examining the containers' exteriors. The allowance of the exercise of judgment based on concerns related to the purposes of an inventory search does not violate the Fourth Amendment.

4. *Containers in cars.* In *Chambers*, the police discovered criminal evidence concealed in a compartment of the vehicle they searched. In *Coolidge*, the police found particles of gun powder, apparently on the car upholstery or floor. In *Carney*, drugs and related paraphernalia were in plain view on a table inside the motor home. That is, in each of these cases, the criminal evidence inside the car was in the open.

Suppose in an otherwise valid car search the police discover a closed container, such as a briefcase, an envelope, or paper bag. May the police open the container as part of the car search, or must they seize it, take it to the police station, and there hold it while they apply for a search warrant? We turn now to the container-in-car cases. We begin, appropriately enough, with another "C" case.

UNITED STATES v. CHADWICK

Supreme Court of the United States, 1977.
433 U.S. 1, 97 S.Ct. 2476, 53 L.Ed.2d 538.

MR. CHIEF JUSTICE BURGER delivered the opinion of the Court [joined by JUSTICES BRENNAN, STEWART, WHITE, MARSHALL, POWELL, and STEVENS]. * * *

(1)

On May 8, 1973, Amtrak railroad officials in San Diego observed respondents Gregory Machado and Bridget Leary load a brown footlocker onto a train bound for Boston. Their suspicions were aroused when they noticed that the trunk was unusually heavy for its size, and that it was leaking talcum powder, a substance often used to mask the odor of marihuana or hashish. Because Machado matched a profile used to spot drug traffickers, the railroad officials reported these circumstances to federal agents in San Diego, who in turn relayed the information, together with detailed descriptions of Machado and the footlocker, to their counterparts in Boston.

When the train arrived in Boston two days later, federal narcotics agents were on hand. Though the officers had not obtained an arrest or search warrant, they had with them a police dog trained to detect marihuana. The agents identified Machado and Leary and kept them under surveillance as they claimed their suitcases and the footlocker, which had been transported by baggage cart from the train to the departure area. Machado and Leary lifted the footlocker from the baggage cart, placed it on the floor and sat down on it.

The agents then released the dog near the footlocker. Without alerting respondents, the dog signaled the presence of a controlled substance inside. Respondent Chadwick then joined Machado and Leary, and they engaged an attendant to move the footlocker outside to Chadwick's waiting automobile. Machado, Chadwick, and the attendant together lifted the 200-pound footlocker into the trunk of the car, while Leary waited in the front seat. At that point, while the trunk of the car was still open and before the car engine had been started, the officers arrested all three. A search disclosed no weapons, but the keys to the footlocker were apparently taken from Machado.

Respondents were taken to the Federal Building in Boston; the agents followed with Chadwick's car and the footlocker. As the Government concedes, from the moment of respondents' arrests at about 9 p.m., the footlocker remained under the exclusive control of law enforcement officers at all times. The footlocker and luggage were placed in the Federal Building, where, as one of the agents later testified, "there was no risk that whatever was contained in the footlocker trunk would be removed by the defendants or their associates." The agents had no reason to believe that the footlocker contained explosives or other inherently dangerous items, or that it contained evidence which would lose its value unless the footlocker were opened at once. Facilities were readily available in which the footlocker could have been stored securely; it is not contended that there was any exigency calling for an immediate search.

At the Federal Building an hour and a half after the arrests, the agents opened the footlocker and luggage. They did not obtain respondents' consent; they did not secure a search warrant. The footlocker was locked with a padlock and a regular trunk lock. * * * Large amounts of marihuana were found in the footlocker.

Respondents were indicted for possession of marihuana with intent to distribute it * * * , and for conspiracy * * * . Before trial, they moved to suppress the marihuana obtained from the footlocker. In the District Court, the Government sought to justify its failure to secure a search warrant under the "automobile exception" of *Chambers v. Maroney*, [p. 306], and as a search incident to the arrests. * * * [T]he District Court rejected both justifications. The court saw the relationship between the footlocker and Chadwick's automobile as merely coincidental, and held that the double-locked, 200-pound footlocker was not part of "the area from within which [respondents] might gain possession of a weapon or destructible evidence." * * *

(2)

In this Court the Government * * * contends that the Fourth Amendment Warrant Clause protects only interests traditionally identified with the home. Recalling the colonial writs of assistance, which were often executed in searches of private dwellings, the Government claims that the Warrant Clause was adopted primarily, if not exclusively, in response to unjustified intrusions into private homes on the authority of general warrants. The Government argues there is no evidence that the Framers of the Fourth Amendment intended to disturb the established practice of permitting warrantless searches outside the home, or to modify the initial clause of the Fourth Amendment by making warrantless searches supported by probable cause *per se* unreasonable.

Drawing on its reading of history, the Government argues that only homes, offices, and private communications implicate interests which lie at the core of the Fourth Amendment. Accordingly, it is only in these contexts that the determination whether a search or seizure is reasonable should turn on whether a warrant has been obtained. In all other situations, the Government contends, less significant privacy values are at stake, and the reasonableness of a government intrusion should depend solely on whether there is probable cause to believe evidence of criminal conduct is present. Where personal effects are lawfully seized outside the home on probable cause, the Government would thus regard searches without a warrant as not "unreasonable."

We do not agree that the Warrant Clause protects only dwellings and other specifically designated locales. As we have noted before, the Fourth Amendment "protects people, not places," *Katz v. United States* [p. 96]; more particularly, it protects people from unreasonable government intrusions into their legitimate expectations of privacy. In this case, the Warrant Clause makes a significant contribution to that protection. The question, then, is whether a warrantless search in these circumstances was unreasonable.

(3) * * *

Although the searches and seizures which deeply concerned the colonists, and which were foremost in the minds of the Framers, were those involving invasions of the home, it would be a mistake to conclude, as the Government contends, that the Warrant Clause was therefore intended to guard only against intrusions into the home. First, the Warrant Clause does not in terms distinguish between searches conducted in private homes and other searches. There is also a strong historical connection between the Warrant Clause and the initial clause of the Fourth Amendment, which draws no distinctions among "persons, houses, papers, and effects" in safeguarding against unreasonable searches and seizures.

Moreover, if there is little evidence that the Framers intended the Warrant Clause to operate outside the home, there is no evidence at all that they intended to exclude from protection of the Clause all searches occurring outside the home. * * * What we do know is that the Framers were men who focused on the wrongs of that day but who intended the Fourth Amendment to safeguard fundamental values which would far outlast the specific abuses which gave it birth.

Moreover, in this area we do not write on a clean slate. * * *

* * * [Our] cases illustrate the applicability of the Warrant Clause beyond the narrow limits suggested by the Government. They also reflect the settled constitutional principle, discussed earlier, that a fundamental purpose of the Fourth Amendment is to safeguard individuals from unreasonable government invasions of legitimate privacy interests, and not simply those interests found inside the four walls of the home.

In this case, important Fourth Amendment privacy interests were at stake. By placing personal effects inside a double-locked footlocker, respondents manifested an expectation that the contents would remain free from public examination. No less than one who locks the doors of his home against intruders, one who safeguards his personal possessions in this manner is due the protection of the Fourth Amendment Warrant Clause. There being no exigency, it was unreasonable for the Government to conduct this search without the safe-guards a judicial warrant provides.

(4)

The Government does not contend that the footlocker's brief contact with Chadwick's car makes this an automobile search, but it is argued that the rationale of our automobile search cases demonstrates the reasonableness of permitting warrantless searches of luggage; the Government views such luggage as analogous to motor vehicles for Fourth Amendment purposes. * * * But this Court has recognized significant differences between motor vehicles and other property which permit warrantless searches of automobiles in circumstances in which warrantless searches would not be reasonable in other contexts.

Our treatment of automobiles has been based in part on their inherent mobility, which often makes obtaining a judicial warrant impracticable. Nevertheless, we have also sustained "warrantless searches of vehicles * * * in cases in which the possibilities of the vehicle's being removed or evidence in it destroyed were remote, if not nonexistent."

The answer lies in the diminished expectation of privacy which surrounds the automobile * * * .

The factors which diminish the privacy aspects of an automobile do not apply to respondents' footlocker. Luggage contents are not open to public view, except as a condition to a border entry or common carrier travel; nor is luggage subject to regular inspections and official scrutiny on a continuing basis. Unlike an automobile, whose primary function is transportation, luggage is intended as a repository of personal effects. In sum, a person's expectations of privacy in personal luggage are substantially greater than in an automobile.

Nor does the footlocker's mobility justify dispensing with the added protections of the Warrant Clause. Once the federal agents had seized it at the railroad station and had safely transferred it to the Boston Federal Building under their exclusive control, there was not the slightest danger that the footlocker or its contents could have been removed before a valid search warrant could be obtained.[7] The initial seizure and detention of the footlocker, the validity of which respondents do not contest, were sufficient to guard against any risk that evidence might be lost. With the footlocker safely immobilized, it was unreasonable to undertake the additional and greater intrusion of a search without a warrant.[8]

Finally, * * * the Government insists that the search was reasonable because the footlocker was seized contemporaneously with respondents' arrests and was searched as soon thereafter as was practicable. The reasons justifying search in a custodial arrest are quite different. * * *

* * * The potential dangers lurking in all custodial arrests make warrantless searches of items within the "immediate control" area reasonable without requiring the arresting officer to calculate the probability that weapons or destructible evidence may be involved. However, warrantless searches of luggage or other property seized at the time of an arrest cannot be justified as incident to that arrest either if the "search is remote in time or place from the arrest," or no exigency exists. Once law enforcement officers have reduced luggage or other personal property not immediately associated with the person of the arrestee to their exclusive control, and there is no longer any danger that the

---

[7]   This may often not be the case when automobiles are seized. Absolutely secure storage facilities may not be available, and the size and inherent mobility of a vehicle make it susceptible to theft or intrusion by vandals.

[8]   Respondents' principal privacy interest in the footlocker was, of course, not in the container itself, which was exposed to public view, but in its contents. A search of the interior was therefore a far greater intrusion into Fourth Amendment values than the impoundment of the footlocker. Though surely a substantial infringement of respondents' use and possession, the seizure did not diminish respondents' legitimate expectation that the footlocker's contents would remain private.

It was the greatly reduced expectation of privacy in the automobile, coupled with the transportation function of the vehicle, which made the Court in *Chambers* unwilling to decide whether an immediate search of an automobile, or its seizure and indefinite immobilization, constituted a greater interference with the rights of the owner. This is clearly not the case with locked luggage.

arrestee might gain access to the property to seize a weapon or destroy evidence, a search of that property is no longer an incident of the arrest.

Here the search was conducted more than an hour after federal agents had gained exclusive control of the footlocker and long after respondents were securely in custody; the search therefore cannot be viewed as incidental to the arrest or as justified by any other exigency. Even though on this record the issuance of a warrant by a judicial officer was reasonably predictable, a line must be drawn. * * * [T]he Warrant Clause places the line at the point where the property to be searched comes under the exclusive dominion of police authority. Respondents were therefore entitled to the protection of the Warrant Clause with the evaluation of a neutral magistrate, before their privacy interests in the contents of the footlocker were invaded. * * *

MR. JUSTICE BRENNAN, concurring.

I fully join the Chief Justice's thorough opinion for the Court. I write only to comment upon two points made by my Brother Blackmun's dissent.

First, I agree wholeheartedly with my Brother Blackmun that it is "unfortunate" that the Government in this case "sought * * * to vindicate an extreme view of the Fourth Amendment." It is unfortunate, in my view, * * * because it is deeply distressing that the Department of Justice, whose mission is to protect the constitutional liberties of the people of the United States, should even appear to be seeking to subvert them by extreme and dubious legal arguments. It is gratifying that the Court today unanimously rejects the Government's position.

Second, it should be noted that while Part II of the dissent suggests a number of possible alternative courses of action that the agents could have followed without violating the Constitution, no decision of this Court is cited to support the constitutionality of these courses * * * . In my view, it is not at all obvious that the agents could legally have searched the footlocker had they seized it after Machado and Leary had driven away with it in their car[1] or "at the time and place of the arrests."[2]

---

[1]   While the contents of the car could have been searched pursuant to the automobile exception, it is by no means clear that the contents of locked containers found inside a car are subject to search under this exception, any more than they would be if the police found them in any other place.

[2]   When Machado and Leary were "standing next to [the] open automobile trunk containing the footlocker," and even when they "were seated on it," it is not obvious to me that the contents of the heavy, securely locked footlocker were within the area of their "immediate control" for purposes of the search-incident-to-arrest doctrine, the justification for which is the possibility that the arrested person might have immediate access to weapons that might endanger the officer's safety or assist in his escape, or to items of evidence that he might conceal or destroy. I would think that the footlocker in this case hardly was " 'within [respondents'] immediate control'—construing that phrase to mean the area from within which [they] might gain possession of a weapon or destructible evidence."

MR. JUSTICE BLACKMUN, with whom MR. JUSTICE REHNQUIST joins, dissenting.

I think it somewhat unfortunate that the Government sought a reversal in this case primarily to vindicate an extreme view of the Fourth Amendment that would restrict the protection of the Warrant Clause to private dwellings and a few other "high privacy" areas. I reject this argument for the reasons stated in Parts (2) and (3) of the Court's opinion, with which I am in general agreement. * * *

I

One line of recent decisions establishes that no warrant is required for the arresting officer to search the clothing and effects of one placed in custodial arrest. The rationale for this was explained in *United States v. Robinson*, [p. 260, Note 8] * * * .

A second series of decisions concerns the consequences of custodial arrest of a person driving an automobile. The car may be impounded and, with probable cause, its contents (including locked compartments) subsequently examined without a warrant. *Chambers v. Maroney*, [p. 306]. * * *

I would apply the rationale of these two lines of authority and hold generally that a warrant is not required to seize and search any movable property in the possession of a person properly arrested in a public place. A person arrested in a public place is likely to have various kinds of property with him: items inside his clothing, a briefcase or suitcase, packages, or a vehicle. In such instances the police cannot very well leave the property on the sidewalk or street while they go to get a warrant. The items may be stolen by a passer-by or removed by the suspect's confederates. Rather than requiring the police to "post a guard" over such property, I think it is surely reasonable for the police to take the items along to the station with the arrested person. * * *

As the Court in *Robinson* recognized, custodial arrest is such a serious deprivation that various lesser invasions of privacy may be fairly regarded as incidental. An arrested person, of course, has an additional privacy interest in the objects in his possession at the time of arrest. To be sure, allowing impoundment of those objects pursuant to arrest, but requiring a warrant for examination of their contents, would protect that incremental privacy interest in cases where the police assessment of probable cause is subsequently rejected by a magistrate. But a countervailing consideration is that a warrant would be routinely forthcoming in the vast majority of situations where the property has been seized in conjunction with the valid arrest of a person in a public place. I therefore doubt that requiring the authorities to go through the formality of obtaining a warrant in this situation would have much practical effect in protecting Fourth Amendment values.

I believe this sort of practical evaluation underlies the Court's decisions permitting clothing, personal effects, and automobiles to be searched without a warrant as an incident of arrest, even though it would be possible simply to impound these items until a warrant could be obtained. The Court's opinion does not explain why a wallet carried in the arrested person's clothing, but not the footlocker in the present case, is subject to "reduced expectations of privacy caused by the arrest." Nor does the Court explain how such items as purses or briefcases fit into the dichotomy. Perhaps the holding in the present case will be limited in the future to objects that are relatively immobile by virtue of their size or absence of a means of propulsion. * * *

II

The approach taken by the Court has the perverse result of allowing fortuitous circumstances to control the outcome of the present case. The agents probably could have avoided having the footlocker search held unconstitutional either by delaying the arrest for a few minutes or by conducting the search on the spot rather than back at their office. Probable cause for the arrest was present from the time respondents Machado and Leary were seated on the footlocker inside Boston's South Station and the agents' dog signaled the presence of marihuana. Rather than make an arrest at this moment, the agents commendably sought to determine the possible involvement of others in the illegal scheme. They waited a short time until respondent Chadwick arrived and the footlocker had been loaded into the trunk of his car, and then made the arrest. But if the agents had postponed the arrest just a few minutes longer until the respondents started to drive away, then the car could have been seized, taken to the agents' office, and all its contents—including the footlocker—searched without a warrant.

Alternatively, the agents could have made a search of the footlocker at the time and place of the arrests. Machado and Leary were standing next to an open automobile trunk containing the footlocker, and thus it was within the area of their "immediate control." And certainly the footlocker would have been properly subject to search at the time if the arrest had occurred a few minutes earlier while Machado and Leary were seated on it.

In many cases, of course, small variations in the facts are determinative of the legal outcome. Criminal law necessarily involves some line drawing. But I see no way that these alternative courses of conduct, which likely would have been held constitutional under the Fourth Amendment, would have been any more solicitous of the privacy or well-being of the respondents. * * * It is decisions of the kind made by the Court today that make criminal law a trap for the unwary policeman and detract from the important activities of detecting criminal activity and protecting the public safety.

NOTES AND QUESTIONS

1.   What do you think of the Justice Department's interpretation of the Fourth Amendment? Is it "extreme," as Justice Blackmun asserted?

2.   Why did the district court describe the relationship between the footlocker and Chadwick's car as "coincidental"?

3.   *Cars versus containers.* At the time of the respective searches, was the Chambers car more mobile than the Chadwick footlocker? How does *Chadwick* distinguish *Chambers*? Are you persuaded?

4.   *Searches incident to lawful arrests.* According to Chief Justice Burger, exigencies aside, a warrant is required "at the point where the property to be searched comes under the exclusive dominion of police authority." If so, why didn't Officer Jenks have to obtain a warrant in *United States v. Robinson* (p. 260 Note 8), in order to open up the cigarette package he found on Robinson's person, once the container was in Jenks's possession?

5.   *Fortuities (part 1).* Justice Blackmun criticized the majority for devising a rule that permits fortuitous circumstances to control outcomes. He reasoned that if the police had searched the footlocker at the scene, a warrant would not have been required. Why does he say that? Is he right?

6.   *Fortuities (part 2).* Justice Blackmun also suggested that if the agents had delayed their arrests for a few moments until the car was on the road, they could then have seized the footlocker and searched it at headquarters without a warrant. Why does he say that? Is he right?

7.   *Containers "coincidentally" in cars.* In Arkansas v. Sanders, 442 U.S. 753, 99 S.Ct. 2586, 61 L.Ed.2d 235 (1979), the Supreme Court considered the Blackmun scenario mentioned in Note 6. In *Sanders,* the police had probable cause to believe that Sanders would arrive at the airport with a green suitcase filled with marijuana. The officers put the airport under surveillance. They observed Sanders, and later a second man, place a closed but unlocked green suitcase into a taxicab trunk and, shortly thereafter, drive away. The officers stopped the taxi within a few blocks, opened the taxi trunk, took out the suitcase, and opened it, all without a search warrant. At a subsequent trial, Sanders and his partner sought to exclude the marijuana found inside.

Notice that *Sanders* involves a container coincidentally in a car when it was seized. That is, as in *Chadwick,* the police in *Sanders* had probable cause to search a particular container before it was placed in an automobile. But here, unlike in *Chadwick,* the police did not confront the suspects until the vehicle was on the highway. As a consequence, unlike in *Chadwick,* the government in *Sanders* argued to the Supreme Court that the search was justifiable under the "automobile search" exception to the warrant requirement. As Justice Powell put it for the Court, "we thus are presented with the task of determining whether the warrantless search of respondent's suitcase falls on the *Chadwick* or the *Chambers/Carroll* side of the Fourth Amendment line." The majority concluded that it fell on the *Chadwick* side:

> [A] suitcase taken from an automobile stopped on the highway is not necessarily attended by any lesser expectation of privacy than is associated with luggage taken from other locations. One is not less inclined to place private, personal possessions in a suitcase merely because the suitcase is to be carried in an automobile rather than transported by other means or temporarily checked or stored. Indeed, the very purpose of a suitcase is to serve as a repository for personal items when one wishes to transport them. Accordingly, the reasons for not requiring a warrant for the search of an automobile do not apply to searches of personal luggage taken by police from automobiles. We therefore find no justification for the extension of *Carroll* and its progeny to the warrantless search of one's personal luggage merely because it was located in an automobile lawfully stopped by the police.

Do you agree? Why should the police be permitted to search a glove compartment or car trunk without a warrant on the highway or at the police station, but not be able to search a suitcase found in the same vehicle, assuming probable cause exists for either search?

8. *The relative Fourth Amendment worthiness of different containers.* *Chadwick* involved a double-locked footlocker. In *Sanders* (Note 7), the container was an unlocked suitcase. In both cases, the Court held that the police needed a warrant to search the container. However, are there containers that by their nature may be opened without a warrant? Yes, according to *Sanders*:

> Not all containers and packages found by police during the course of a search will deserve the full protection of the Fourth Amendment. Thus, some containers (for example a kit of burglar tools or a gun case) by their very nature cannot support any reasonable expectation of privacy because their contents can be inferred from their outward appearance. Similarly, in some cases the contents of a package will be open to "plain view," thereby obviating the need for a warrant.

These exceptions aside, however, all containers are treated alike. The Court has refused to draw a distinction between "worthy" and "unworthy" containers. The Court stated in United States v. Ross, 456 U.S. 798, 102 S.Ct. 2157, 72 L.Ed.2d 572 (1982):

> Even though * * * a distinction perhaps could evolve in a series of cases in which paper bags, locked trunks, lunch buckets, and orange crates were placed on one side of the line or the other, the central purpose of the Fourth Amendment forecloses such a distinction. For

just as the most frail cottage in the kingdom is absolutely entitled to the same guarantees of privacy as the most majestic mansion, so also may a traveler who carries a toothbrush and a few articles of clothing in a paper bag or knotted scarf claim an equal right to conceal his possessions from official inspection as the sophisticated executive with the locked attaché case.

9. *Cars with "coincidental" containers.* In *Chadwick* and *Sanders* (Note 7) the police had prior probable cause to search a container that was placed in a car. Suppose, however, the police have probable cause to search a car, during which search they inadvertently come across a container. We might call this a car-with-a-coincidental-container case, to distinguish it from *Chadwick* and *Sanders*, which were containers-coincidentally-in-car cases.

In Robbins v. California, 453 U.S. 420, 101 S.Ct. 2841, 69 L.Ed.2d 744 (1981), police officers stopped a car being driven erratically. When they approached the vehicle, they smelled marijuana smoke, which gave them probable cause to search the car. During the ensuing search the police found containers, which they opened. Writing for a four-justice plurality, Justice Stewart concluded that the warrantless search was impermissible under *Chadwick* and *Sanders*.

The Court quickly reversed directions, however, in United States v. Ross, 456 U.S. 798, 102 S.Ct. 2157, 72 L.Ed.2d 572 (1982). In *Ross*, the police had probable cause to believe that a particular individual was selling drugs from the trunk of his car at a specified location. When the police discovered the car and suspect, now on the road, they stopped the automobile and searched the car trunk. Inside, they found a closed brown paper bag, which they opened and in which they discovered heroin.

Justice Stevens, writing for a seven-justice majority, overruled *Robbins* and "rejected some of the reasoning in *Sanders*." Stevens pointed out that a warrant to search a home provides the police with implicit authority to open any container—for example, a dresser drawer, a jewelry box, a briefcase— that might contain the criminal evidence for which they are searching. Likewise, "[a] warrant to search a vehicle would support a search of every part of the vehicle"—including containers therein—"that might contain the object of the search." Therefore, the Court reasoned, the same rule should apply to *warrantless* car searches: When the police have probable cause to search a car without a warrant under the *Carroll-Chambers-Carney* line of cases, they may also search any container found during the car search that is large enough to hold the evidence for which they are looking.

Thus, immediately after *Ross*, an uneasy—and complicated— car/container distinction existed. If the police had probable cause to search a car, they could search fixed parts thereof (*e.g.*, glove compartments, trunks) as well as movable containers carried within it (assuming they could conceal the object of the search). But, if the police had probable cause to search a specific container, which coincidentally was found in a car, they could search the car on the highway (or tow it to the police station, per *Chambers v.*

Maroney), without a warrant in order to find and seize the container, but they needed a warrant to open the container (per *Chadwick* and whatever remained of *Arkansas v. Sanders* after *Ross*).

Then, along came the next case.

CALIFORNIA V. ACEVEDO
Supreme Court of the United States, 1991.
500 U.S. 565, 111 S.Ct. 1982, 114 L.Ed.2d 619.

JUSTICE BLACKMUN delivered the opinion of the Court [joined by CHIEF JUSTICE REHNQUIST, and JUSTICES O'CONNOR, KENNEDY, and SOUTER]. * * *

I

[Jamie Daza picked up a package from a Federal Express office, sent from Hawaii, that the police knew from prior inspection contained marijuana. Officers observed Daza take the package to his home. They kept the Daza residence under surveillance, while another officer left to obtain a warrant to search the Daza residence. Before a warrant could be obtained, the following events ensued.]

* * * [R]espondent Charles Steven Acevedo arrived. He entered Daza's apartment, stayed for about 10 minutes, and reappeared carrying a brown paper bag that looked full. The officers noticed that the bag was the size of one of the wrapped marijuana packages sent from Hawaii. Acevedo walked to a silver Honda in the parking lot. He placed the bag in the trunk of the car and started to drive away. Fearing the loss of evidence, officers in a marked police car stopped him. They opened the trunk and the bag, and found marijuana. * * *

The California Court of Appeal * * * concluded that the marijuana found in the paper bag in the car's trunk should have been suppressed. The court concluded that the officers had probable cause to believe that the paper bag contained drugs but lacked probable cause to suspect that Acevedo's car, itself, otherwise contained contraband. Because the officers' probable cause was directed specifically at the bag, the court held that the case was controlled by *United States v. Chadwick*, [p. 320] rather than by *United States v. Ross* [p. 330, Note 9]. Although the court agreed that the officers could seize the paper bag, it held that, under *Chadwick*, they could not open the bag without first obtaining a warrant for that purpose. * * *

We granted certiorari to reexamine the law applicable to a closed container in an automobile, a subject that has troubled courts and law enforcement officers since it was first considered in *Chadwick*. * * *

III * * *

This Court in *Ross* * * * recognized that it was arguable that the same exigent circumstances that permit a warrantless search of an automobile would justify the warrantless search of a movable container. In deference to the rule of *Chadwick* and [*Arkansas v.*] *Sanders* [p. 328, Note 7], however, the Court put that question to one side. * * * We now must decide the question deferred in *Ross*: whether the Fourth Amendment requires the police to obtain a warrant to open the sack in a movable vehicle simply because they lack probable cause to search the entire car. We conclude that it does not.

IV

Dissenters in *Ross* asked why the suitcase in *Sanders* was "more private, less difficult for police to seize and store, or in any other relevant respect more properly subject to the warrant requirement, than a container that police discover in a probable-cause search of an entire automobile?" We now agree that a container found after a general search of the automobile and a container found in a car after a limited search for the container are equally easy for the police to store and for the suspect to hide or destroy. In fact, we see no principled distinction in terms of either the privacy expectation or the exigent circumstances between the paper bag found by the police in *Ross* and the paper bag found by the police here. Furthermore, by attempting to distinguish between a container for which the police are specifically searching and a container which they come across in a car, we have provided only minimal protection for privacy and have impeded effective law enforcement.

The line between probable cause to search a vehicle and probable cause to search a package in that vehicle is not always clear, and separate rules that govern the two objects to be searched may enable the police to broaden their power to make warrantless searches and disserve privacy interests. * * * At the moment when officers stop an automobile, it may be less than clear whether they suspect with a high degree of certainty that the vehicle contains drugs in a bag or simply contains drugs. If the police know that they may open a bag only if they are actually searching the entire car, they may search more extensively than they otherwise would in order to establish the general probable cause required by *Ross*. * * *

To the extent that the *Chadwick-Sanders* rule protects privacy, its protection is minimal. Law enforcement officers may seize a container and hold it until they obtain a search warrant. *Chadwick.* "Since the police, by hypothesis, have probable cause to seize the property, we can assume that a warrant will be routinely forthcoming in the overwhelming majority of cases." *Sanders* (dissenting opinion). And the police often will be able to search containers without a warrant, despite the *Chadwick-Sanders* rule, as a search incident to a lawful arrest. * * *

Finally, the search of a paper bag intrudes far less on individual privacy than does the incursion sanctioned long ago in *Carroll*. In that case, prohibition agents slashed the upholstery of the automobile. This Court nonetheless found their search to be reasonable under the Fourth Amendment. If destroying the interior of an automobile is not unreasonable, we cannot conclude that looking inside a closed container is. In light of the minimal protection to privacy afforded by the *Chadwick-Sanders* rule, and our serious doubt whether that rule substantially serves privacy interests, we now hold that the Fourth Amendment does not compel separate treatment for an automobile search that extends only to a container within the vehicle.

V

The *Chadwick-Sanders* rule not only has failed to protect privacy but also has confused courts and police officers and impeded effective law enforcement. * * *

The discrepancy between the two rules has led to confusion for law enforcement officers. For example, when an officer, who has developed probable cause to believe that a vehicle contains drugs, begins to search the vehicle and immediately discovers a closed container, which rule applies? The defendant will argue that the fact that the officer first chose to search the container indicates that his probable cause extended only to the container and that *Chadwick* and *Sanders* therefore require a warrant. On the other hand, the fact that the officer first chose to search in the most obvious location should not restrict the propriety of the search. The *Chadwick* rule, as applied in *Sanders*, has devolved into an anomaly such that the more likely the police are to discover drugs in a container, the less authority they have to search it. We have noted the virtue of providing " ' "clear and unequivocal" guidelines to the law enforcement profession.' " The *Chadwick-Sanders* rule is the antithesis of a " 'clear and unequivocal' guideline." * * *

* * * We conclude that it is better to adopt one clear-cut rule to govern automobile searches and eliminate the warrant requirement for closed containers set forth in *Sanders*.

VI

The interpretation of the *Carroll* doctrine set forth in *Ross* now applies to all searches of containers found in an automobile. In other words, the police may search without a warrant if their search is supported by probable cause. The Court in *Ross* * * * went on to note: "Probable cause to believe that a container placed in the trunk of a taxi contains contraband or evidence does not justify a search of the entire cab." We reaffirm that principle. In the case before us, the police had probable cause to believe that the paper bag in the automobile's trunk contained marijuana. That probable cause now allows a warrantless search of the paper bag. The facts in the record reveal that the police did not have probable cause to believe that contraband was hidden in any other part of the automobile and a search of the entire vehicle would have been without probable cause and unreasonable under the Fourth Amendment.

Our holding today neither extends the *Carroll* doctrine nor broadens the scope of the permissible automobile search delineated in *Carroll*, *Chambers*, and *Ross*. It remains a "cardinal principle that 'searches conducted outside the judicial process, without prior approval by judge or magistrate, are *per se* unreasonable under the Fourth Amendment—subject only to a few specifically established and well-delineated exceptions.'" * * *

Until today, this Court has drawn a curious line between the search of an automobile that coincidentally turns up a container and the search of a container that coincidentally turns up in an automobile. The protections of the Fourth Amendment must not turn on such coincidences. We therefore interpret *Carroll* as providing one rule to govern all automobile searches. The police may search an automobile and the containers within it where they have probable cause to believe contraband or evidence is contained.

JUSTICE SCALIA, concurring in the judgment.

I agree with the dissent that it is anomalous for a briefcase to be protected by the "general requirement" of a prior warrant when it is being carried along the street, but for that same briefcase to become unprotected as soon as it is carried into an automobile. On the other hand, I agree with the Court that it would be anomalous for a locked compartment in an automobile to be unprotected by the "general requirement" of a prior warrant, but for an unlocked briefcase within the automobile to be protected. I join in the judgment of the Court because I think its holding is more faithful to the text and tradition of the Fourth Amendment, and if these anomalies in our jurisprudence are ever to be eliminated that is the direction in which we should travel. * * *

* * * Unlike the dissent, * * *, I do not regard today's holding as some momentous departure, but rather as merely the continuation of an inconsistent jurisprudence that has been with us for years. Cases like *United States v. Chadwick* and *Arkansas v. Sanders* have taken the "preference for a warrant" seriously, while cases like *United States v. Ross* and *Carroll v. United States* have not. There can be no clarity in this area unless we make up our minds, and unless the principles we express comport with the actions we take.

In my view, the path out of this confusion should be sought by returning to the first principle that the "reasonableness" requirement of the Fourth Amendment affords the protection that the common law afforded. I have no difficulty with the proposition that that includes the requirement of a warrant, where the common law required a warrant; and it may even be that changes in the surrounding legal rules * * * may make a warrant indispensable to reasonableness where it once was not. But the supposed "general rule" that a warrant is always required does not appear to have any basis in the common law, and confuses rather than facilitates any attempt to develop rules of reasonableness in light of changed legal circumstances, as the anomaly eliminated and the anomaly created by today's holding both demonstrate.

And there are more anomalies still. Under our precedents (as at common law), a person may be arrested outside the home on the basis of probable cause, without an arrest warrant. Upon arrest, the person, as well as the area within his grasp, may be searched for evidence related to the crime. Under these principles, if a known drug dealer is carrying a briefcase reasonably believed to contain marijuana (the unauthorized possession of which is a crime), the police may arrest him and search his person on the basis of probable cause alone. And, under our precedents, upon arrival at the station house, the police may inventory his possessions, including the briefcase, even if there is no reason to suspect that they contain contraband. *Illinois v. Lafayette*, [p. 262, Note 10]. According to our current law, however, the police may not, on the basis of the same probable cause, take the less intrusive step of stopping the individual on the street and demanding to see the contents of his briefcase. That makes no sense *a priori*, and in the absence of any common-law tradition supporting such a distinction, I see no reason to continue it.

* * *

I would reverse the judgment in the present case, not because a closed container carried inside a car becomes subject to the "automobile" exception to the general warrant requirement, but because the search of a closed container, outside a privately owned building, with probable cause to believe that the container contains contraband, and when it in fact does contain contraband, is not one of those searches whose Fourth Amendment reasonableness depends upon a warrant. For that reason I concur in the judgment of the Court.

JUSTICE WHITE, dissenting.

Agreeing as I do with most of Justice Stevens' opinion and with the result he reaches, I dissent and would affirm the judgment below.

JUSTICE STEVENS, with whom JUSTICE MARSHALL joins, dissenting.

At the end of its opinion, the Court pays lipservice to the proposition that should provide the basis for a correct analysis of the legal question presented by this case: It is " 'a cardinal principle that "searches conducted outside the judicial process, without prior approval by judge or magistrate, are *per se* unreasonable under the Fourth Amendment—subject only to a few specifically established and well-delineated exceptions." ' "

Relying on arguments that conservative judges have repeatedly rejected in past cases, the Court today—despite its disclaimer to the contrary—enlarges the scope of the automobile exception to this "cardinal principle," which undergirded our Fourth Amendment jurisprudence * * * . * * *

II

In its opinion today, the Court recognizes that the police did not have probable cause to search respondent's vehicle and that a search of anything but the paper bag that respondent had carried from Daza's apartment and placed in the trunk of his car would have been unconstitutional. Moreover, as I read the opinion, the Court assumes that the police could not have made a warrantless inspection of the bag before it was placed in the car. Finally, the Court also does not question the fact that, under our prior cases, it would have been lawful for the police to seize the container and detain it (and respondent) until they obtained a search warrant. Thus, all of the relevant facts that governed our decisions in *Chadwick* and *Sanders* are present here whereas the relevant fact that justified the vehicle search in *Ross* is not present.

The Court does not attempt to identify any exigent circumstances that would justify its refusal to apply the general rule against warrantless searches. Instead, it advances these three arguments: First, the rules identified in the foregoing cases are confusing and anomalous. Second, the rules do not protect any significant interest in privacy. And, third, the rules impede effective law enforcement. None of these arguments withstands scrutiny.

The "Confusion" * * *

The Court summarizes the alleged "anomaly" created by the coexistence of *Ross*, *Chadwick*, and *Sanders* with the statement that "the more likely the police are to discover drugs in a container, the less authority they have to search it." This juxtaposition is only anomalous, however, if one accepts the flawed premise that the degree to which the police are likely to discover contraband is correlated with their authority to search *without a warrant*. Yet, even proof beyond a reasonable doubt will not justify a warrantless search that is not supported by one of the exceptions to the warrant requirement. And, even when the police have a warrant or an exception applies, once the police possess probable cause, the extent to which they are more or less certain of the contents of a container has no bearing on their authority to search it.

To the extent there was any "anomaly" in our prior jurisprudence, the Court has "cured" it at the expense of creating a more serious paradox. For surely it is anomalous to prohibit a search of a briefcase while the owner is carrying it exposed on a public street yet to permit a search once the owner has placed the briefcase in the locked trunk of his car. One's privacy interest in one's luggage can certainly not be diminished by one's removing it from a public thoroughfare and placing it—out of sight—in a privately owned vehicle. Nor is the danger that evidence will escape increased if the luggage is in a car rather than on the street. In either location, if the police have probable cause, they are authorized to seize the luggage and to detain it until they obtain judicial approval for a search. Any line demarking an exception to the warrant requirement will appear blurred at the edges, but the Court has certainly erred if it believes that, by erasing one line and drawing another, it has drawn a clearer boundary.

The Privacy Argument

The Court's statement that *Chadwick* and *Sanders* provide only "minimal protection to privacy" is also unpersuasive. Every citizen clearly has an interest in the privacy of the contents of his or her luggage, briefcase, handbag or any other container that conceals private papers and effects from public scrutiny. That privacy interest has been recognized repeatedly in cases spanning more than a century.

Under the Court's holding today, the privacy interest that protects the contents of a suitcase or a briefcase from a warrantless search when it is in public view simply vanishes when its owner climbs into a taxicab. Unquestionably the rejection of the *Sanders* line of cases by today's decision will result in a significant loss of individual privacy.

To support its argument that today's holding works only a minimal intrusion on privacy, the Court suggests that "[i]f the police know that they may open a bag only if they are actually searching the entire car, they may search more extensively than they otherwise would in order to establish the general probable cause required by *Ross*." * * * [T]his fear is unexplained and inexplicable. Neither evidence uncovered in the course of a search nor the scope of the search conducted can be used to provide *post hoc* justification for a search unsupported by probable cause at its inception. * * *

The Burden on Law Enforcement

The Court's suggestion that *Chadwick* and *Sanders* have created a significant burden on effective law enforcement is unsupported, inaccurate, and, in any event, an insufficient reason for creating a new exception to the warrant requirement. * * *

Even if the warrant requirement does inconvenience the police to some extent, that fact does not distinguish this constitutional requirement from any other procedural protection secured by the Bill of Rights. It is merely a part of the price that our society must pay in order to preserve its freedom. * * *

NOTES AND QUESTIONS

1.   Does Justice Scalia's position remind you of any Fourth Amendment argument that the Court previously repudiated?

2.   *Acevedo* overruled *Sanders*. Did it overrule *Chadwick*? If not, why not? If not, what is left of the *Chadwick* doctrine?

3.   *Problem.* Would the following warrantless search variations on *Acevedo* be permissible?

A.   The police in *Acevedo* open the trunk, immediately spot the paper bag, open it, and find marijuana. The police proceed to search the remainder of the trunk. They find and seize transparent bags of cocaine hidden under a blanket. They search the passenger compartment. Under the front seat, they find a small quantity of marijuana.

B.   The same as A., except that when the police open the paper bag in the trunk they discover that it contains non-contraband lawful items. They proceed to search the remainder of the trunk, as in A.

C.   The police open the trunk, and do not immediately see the paper bag. They hunt through the trunk. They do not find the paper bag, but they do discover a briefcase. They open it, find the brown paper bag inside, and open it.

D.   The police stop Acevedo, but do not arrest him, before he enters the car. They seize and open the paper bag.

E.   The police stop Acevedo before he enters the car. They arrest him for possession of marijuana, seize the paper bag, and open it.

4.   What if, during an otherwise valid warrantless car search, the police come upon a smart phone. If they have probable cause to believe it contains incriminating evidence, may they turn the phone on and, for example, search the phone log? (Assume nobody in the vehicle is under arrest.) See United States v. Camou, 773 F.3d 932 (9th Cir. 2014).

5.   *Containers belonging to passengers.* Does probable cause to search a car entitle the police to open containers they have reason to know belong to an occupant whom they lack probable cause to arrest? In Wyoming v. Houghton, 526 U.S. 295, 119 S.Ct. 1297, 143 L.Ed.2d 408 (1999), the police lawfully stopped a vehicle containing a male driver and two female front seat passengers. The police uncontestedly obtained probable cause to search the car for drugs after they lawfully seized an illegal syringe from the driver, who admitted that he used it to take drugs. During the car search, the police

discovered a purse in the back seat that one of the passengers, Houghton, claimed belonged to her. At the time, the officers did *not* have probable cause to suspect her of drug use, nor was the driver under arrest.

The Supreme Court, 6–3, per Justice Scalia, announced that "police officers with probable cause to search a car may inspect [any] passengers' belongings found in the car that are capable of concealing the object of the search." According to Scalia, "[p]assengers, no less than drivers, possess a reduced expectation of privacy with regard to the property that they transport in cars * * * ." Moreover, "the degree of intrusiveness upon personal privacy and indeed even personal dignity" of a property search is less than the intrusiveness of a search of one's person. The Court concluded that the Government's legitimate interest in effective law enforcement justified a search of all car containers that might hold drugs, and not simply those containers apparently belonging to the driver.

4. PLAIN VIEW (AND TOUCH) DOCTRINES

HORTON V. CALIFORNIA

Supreme Court of the United States, 1990.
496 U.S. 128, 110 S.Ct. 2301, 110 L.Ed.2d 112.

JUSTICE STEVENS delivered the opinion of the Court [joined by CHIEF JUSTICE REHNQUIST, and JUSTICES WHITE, BLACKMUN, O'CONNOR, SCALIA, and KENNEDY].

In this case we revisit an issue that was considered, but not conclusively resolved, in *Coolidge v. New Hampshire*, 403 U.S. 443, 91 S.Ct. 2022, 29 L.Ed.2d 564 (1971): Whether the warrantless seizure of evidence of crime in plain view is prohibited by the Fourth Amendment if the discovery of the evidence was not inadvertent. We conclude that even though inadvertence is a characteristic of most legitimate "plain view" seizures, it is not a necessary condition.

I

Petitioner was convicted of the armed robbery of Erwin Wallaker, the treasurer of the San Jose Coin Club. When Wallaker returned to his home after the Club's annual show, he entered his garage and was accosted by two masked men, one armed with a machine gun and the other with an electrical shocking device, sometimes referred to as a "stun gun." The two men shocked Wallaker, bound and handcuffed him, and robbed him of jewelry and cash. * * *

Sergeant LaRault, an experienced police officer, investigated the crime and determined that there was probable cause to search petitioner's home for the proceeds of the robbery and for the weapons used by the robbers. His affidavit for a search warrant referred to police reports that described the weapons as well as the proceeds, but the warrant issued by the Magistrate only authorized a search for the proceeds, including three specifically described rings.

Pursuant to the warrant, LaRault searched petitioner's residence, but he did not find the stolen properly. During the course of the search, however, he discovered the weapons in plain view and seized them. Specifically, he seized an Uzi machine gun, a .38-caliber revolver, two stun guns, a handcuff key, a San Jose Coin Club advertising brochure, and a few items of clothing identified by the victim. LaRault testified that while he was searching for the rings, he also was interested in finding other evidence connecting petitioner to the robbery. Thus, the seized evidence was not discovered "inadvertently."

The trial court refused to suppress the evidence found in petitioner's home and, after a jury trial, petitioner was found guilty and sentenced to prison. * * *

II * * *

The right to security in person and property protected by the Fourth Amendment may be invaded in quite different ways by searches and seizures. A search compromises the individual interest in privacy; a seizure deprives the individual of dominion over his or her person or property. The "plain view" doctrine is often considered an exception to the general rule that warrantless searches are presumptively unreasonable, but this characterization overlooks the important difference between searches and seizures. If an article is already in plain view, neither its observation nor its seizure would involve any invasion of privacy. A seizure of the article, however, would obviously invade the owner's possessory interest. If "plain view" justifies an exception from an otherwise applicable warrant requirement, therefore, it must be an exception that is addressed to the concerns that are implicated by seizures rather than by searches.

The criteria that generally guide "plain view" seizures were set forth in *Coolidge v. New Hampshire*. The Court held that the police, in seizing two automobiles parked in plain view on the defendant's driveway in the course of arresting the defendant, violated the Fourth Amendment. Accordingly, particles of gun powder that had been subsequently found in vacuum sweepings from one of the cars could not be introduced in evidence against the defendant. The State endeavored to justify the seizure of the automobiles, and their subsequent search at the police station, on four different grounds, including the "plain view" doctrine. The scope of that doctrine as it had developed in earlier cases was fairly summarized in these three paragraphs from Justice Stewart's [plurality] opinion:

> "It is well established that under certain circumstances the police may seize evidence in plain view without a warrant. But it

is important to keep in mind that, in the vast majority of cases, *any* evidence seized by the police will be in plain view, at least at the moment of seizure. The problem with the 'plain view' doctrine has been to identify the circumstances in which plain view has legal significance rather than being simply the normal concomitant of any search, legal or illegal.

"An example of the applicability of the 'plain view' doctrine is the situation in which the police have a warrant to search a given area for specified objects, and in the course of the search come across some other article of incriminating character. Where the initial intrusion that brings the police within plain view of such an article is supported, not by a warrant, but by one of the recognized exceptions to the warrant requirement, the seizure is also legitimate. Thus the police may inadvertently come across evidence while in 'hot pursuit' of a fleeing suspect. And an object that comes into view during a search incident to arrest that is appropriately limited in scope under existing law may be seized without a warrant. *Chimel v. California* [p. 251]. Finally, the 'plain view' doctrine has been applied where a police officer is not searching for evidence against the accused, but nonetheless inadvertently comes across an incriminating object.

"What the 'plain view' cases have in common is that the police officer in each of them had a prior justification for an intrusion in the course of which he came inadvertently across a piece of evidence incriminating the accused. The doctrine serves to supplement the prior justification—whether it be a warrant for another object, hot pursuit, search incident to lawful arrest, or some other legitimate reason for being present unconnected with a search directed against the accused—and permits the warrantless seizure. Of course, the extension of the original justification is legitimate only where it is immediately apparent to the police that they have evidence before them; the 'plain view' doctrine may not be used to extend a general exploratory search from one object to another until something incriminating at last emerges."

Justice Stewart then described the two limitations on the doctrine that he found implicit in its rationale: First, that "plain view *alone* is never enough to justify the warrantless seizure of evidence"; and second, that "the discovery of evidence in plain view must be inadvertent."

* * * Before discussing the second limitation, which is implicated in this case, it is therefore necessary to explain why the first adequately supports the Court's judgment.

It is, of course, an essential predicate to any valid warrantless seizure of incriminating evidence that the officer did not violate the Fourth Amendment in arriving at the place from which the evidence could be plainly viewed. There are, moreover, two additional conditions that must be satisfied to justify the warrantless seizure. First, not only must the item be in plain view; its incriminating character must also be "immediately apparent." Thus, in *Coolidge*, the cars were obviously in plain view, but their probative value remained uncertain until after the interiors were swept and examined microscopically. Second, not only must the officer be lawfully located in a place from which the object can be plainly seen, but he or she must also have a lawful right of access to the object itself.[7] * * * [W]e are satisfied that the absence of inadvertence was not essential to the court's rejection of the State's "plain-view" argument in *Coolidge*.

III

Justice Stewart concluded that the inadvertence requirement was necessary to avoid a violation of the express constitutional requirement that a valid warrant must particularly describe the things to be seized. He explained:

> "The rationale of the exception to the warrant requirement, as just stated, is that a plain-view seizure will not turn an initially valid (and therefore limited) search into a 'general' one, while the inconvenience of procuring a warrant to cover an inadvertent discovery is great. But where the discovery is anticipated, where the police know in advance the location of the evidence and intend to seize it, the situation is altogether different. The requirement of a warrant to seize imposes no inconvenience whatever, or at least none which is constitutionally cognizable in a legal system that regards warrantless searches as '*per se* unreasonable' in the absence of 'exigent circumstances.'

> "If the initial intrusion is bottomed upon a warrant that fails to mention a particular object, though the police know its location and intend to seize it, then there is a violation of the express constitutional requirement of 'Warrants * * * particularly describing * * * [the] things to be seized.' "

We find two flaws in this reasoning. First, evenhanded law enforcement is best achieved by the application of objective standards of conduct, rather than standards that depend upon the subjective state of

---

[7] "This is simply a corollary of the familiar principle discussed above, that no amount of probable cause can justify a warrantless search or seizure absent 'exigent circumstances.' Incontrovertible testimony of the senses that an incriminating object is on premises belonging to a criminal suspect may establish the fullest possible measure of probable cause. But even where the object is contraband, this Court has repeatedly stated and enforced the basic rule that the police may not enter and make a warrantless seizure." *Coolidge*.

mind of the officer. The fact that an officer is interested in an item of evidence and fully expects to find it in the course of a search should not invalidate its seizure if the search is confined in area and duration by the terms of a warrant or a valid exception to the warrant requirement. If the officer has knowledge approaching certainty that the item will be found, we see no reason why he or she would deliberately omit a particular description of the item to be seized from the application for a search warrant. Specification of the additional item could only permit the officer to expand the scope of the search. On the other hand, if he or she has a valid warrant to search for one item and merely a suspicion concerning the second, whether or not it amounts to probable cause, we fail to see why that suspicion should immunize the second item from seizure if it is found during a lawful search for the first. The hypothetical case put by Justice White in his dissenting opinion in *Coolidge* is instructive:

> "Let us suppose officers secure a warrant to search a house for a rifle. While staying well within the range of a rifle search, they discover two photographs of the murder victim, both in plain sight in the bedroom. Assume also that the discovery of the one photograph was inadvertent but finding the other was anticipated. The Court would permit the seizure of only one of the photographs. But in terms of the 'minor' peril to Fourth Amendment values there is surely no difference between these two photographs: the interference with possession is the same in each case and the officers' appraisal of the photograph they expected to see is no less reliable than their judgment about the other. And in both situations the actual inconvenience and danger to evidence remain identical if the officers must depart and secure a warrant."

Second, the suggestion that the inadvertence requirement is necessary to prevent the police from conducting general searches, or from converting specific warrants into general warrants, is not persuasive because that interest is already served by the requirements that no warrant issue unless it "particularly describ[es] the place to be searched and the persons or things to be seized," and that a warrantless search be circumscribed by the exigencies which justify its initiation. Scrupulous adherence to these requirements serves the interests in limiting the area and duration of the search that the inadvertence requirement inadequately protects. Once those commands have been satisfied and the officer has a lawful right of access, however, no additional Fourth Amendment interest is furthered by requiring that the discovery of evidence be inadvertent. If the scope of the search exceeds that permitted by the terms of a validly issued warrant or the character of the relevant exception from the warrant requirement, the subsequent seizure is unconstitutional without more. * * *

In this case, the scope of the search was not enlarged in the slightest by the omission of any reference to the weapons in the warrant. Indeed, if the three rings and other items named in the warrant had been found at the outset—or petitioner had them in his possession and had responded to the warrant by producing them immediately—no search for weapons could have taken place. * * *

As we have already suggested, by hypothesis the seizure of an object in plain view does not involve an intrusion on privacy. If the interest in privacy has been invaded, the violation must have occurred before the object came into plain view and there is no need for an inadvertence limitation on seizures to condemn it. The prohibition against general searches and general warrants serves primarily as a protection against unjustified intrusions on privacy. But reliance on privacy concerns that support that prohibition is misplaced when the inquiry concerns the scope of an exception that merely authorizes an officer with a lawful right of access to an item to seize it without a warrant.

In this case the items seized from petitioner's home were discovered during a lawful search authorized by a valid warrant. When they were discovered, it was immediately apparent to the officer that they constituted incriminating evidence. He had probable cause, not only to obtain a warrant to search for the stolen property, but also to believe that the weapons and handguns had been used in the crime he was investigating. The search was authorized by the warrant; the seizure was authorized by the "plain-view" doctrine. The judgment is affirmed. * * *

JUSTICE BRENNAN, with whom JUSTICE MARSHALL joins, dissenting. * * *

I

* * * The Amendment protects two distinct interests. The prohibition against unreasonable searches and the requirement that a warrant "particularly describ[e] the place to be searched" protect an interest in privacy. The prohibition against unreasonable seizures and the requirement that a warrant "particularly describ[e] * * * the * * * things to be seized" protect a possessory interest in property. The Fourth Amendment, by its terms, declares the privacy and possessory interests to be equally important. As this Court recently stated: "Although the interest protected by the Fourth Amendment injunction against unreasonable searches is quite different from that protected by its injunction against unreasonable seizures, neither the one nor the other is of inferior worth or necessarily requires only lesser protection." *Arizona v. Hicks*, [p. 346].

The Amendment protects these equally important interests in precisely the same manner: by requiring a neutral and detached magistrate to evaluate, before the search or seizure, the government's showing of probable cause and its particular description of the place to be searched and the items to be seized. Accordingly, just as a warrantless search is *per se* unreasonable absent exigent circumstances, so too a seizure of personal property is *"per se* unreasonable within the meaning of the Fourth Amendment unless it is accomplished pursuant to a judicial warrant issued upon probable cause and particularly describing the items to be seized." * * * A decision to invade a possessory interest in property is too important to be left to the discretion of zealous officers "engaged in the often competitive enterprise of ferreting out crime." * * *

The plain-view doctrine is an exception to the general rule that a seizure of personal property must be authorized by a warrant. As Justice Stewart explained in *Coolidge,* we accept a warrantless seizure when an officer is lawfully in a location and inadvertently sees evidence of a crime because of "the inconvenience of procuring a warrant" to seize this newly discovered piece of evidence. But "where the discovery is anticipated, where the police know in advance the location of the evidence and intend to seize it," the argument that procuring a warrant would be "inconvenient" loses much, if not all, of its force. Barring an exigency, there is no reason why the police officers could not have obtained a warrant to seize this evidence before entering the premises. The rationale behind the inadvertent discovery requirement is simply that we will not excuse officers from the general requirement of a warrant to seize if the officers know the location of evidence, have probable cause to seize it, intend to seize it, and yet do not bother to obtain a warrant particularly describing that evidence. * * *

* * * The inadvertent discovery requirement is essential if we are to take seriously the Fourth Amendment's protection of possessory interests as well as privacy interests. The Court today eliminates a rule designed to further possessory interests on the ground that it fails to further privacy interests. I cannot countenance such constitutional legerdemain. * * *

NOTES AND QUESTIONS

1.   The dissent stated that, under the Fourth Amendment, "privacy and possessory interests [are] equally important"? Textual and historical issues aside, do *you* consider your personal possessory and privacy interests of equal magnitude? Why, or why not?

ARIZONA V. HICKS

Supreme Court of the United States, 1987.
480 U.S. 321, 107 S.Ct. 1149, 94 L.Ed.2d 347.

JUSTICE SCALIA delivered the opinion of the Court [joined by JUSTICES BRENNAN, WHITE, MARSHALL, BLACKMUN, and STEVENS]. * * *

I

On April 18, 1984, a bullet was fired through the floor of respondent's apartment, striking and injuring a man in the apartment below. Police officers arrived and entered respondent's apartment to search for the shooter, for other victims, and for weapons. They found and seized three weapons, including a sawed-off rifle, and in the course of their search also discovered a stocking-cap mask.

One of the policemen, Officer Nelson, noticed two sets of expensive stereo components, which seemed out of place in the squalid and otherwise ill-appointed four-room apartment. Suspecting that they were stolen, he read and recorded their serial numbers—moving some of the components, including a Bang and Olufsen turntable, in order to do so—which he then reported by phone to his headquarters. On being advised that the turntable had been taken in an armed robbery, he seized it immediately. It was later determined that some of the other serial numbers matched those on other stereo equipment taken in the same armed robbery, and a warrant was obtained and executed to seize that equipment as well. Respondent was subsequently indicted for the robbery. * * *

II

As an initial matter, the State argues that Officer Nelson's actions constituted neither a "search" nor a "seizure" within the meaning of the Fourth Amendment. We agree that the mere recording of the serial numbers did not constitute a seizure. To be sure, that was the first step in a process by which respondent was eventually deprived of the stereo equipment. In and of itself, however, it did not "meaningfully interfere" with respondent's possessory interest in either the serial numbers or the equipment, and therefore did not amount to a seizure.

Officer Nelson's moving of the equipment, however, did constitute a "search" separate and apart from the search for the shooter, victims, and weapons that was the lawful objective of his entry into the apartment. Merely inspecting those parts of the turntable that came into view during the latter search would not have constituted an independent search, because it would have produced no additional invasion of respondent's privacy interest. But taking action, unrelated to the objectives of the authorized intrusion, which exposed to view concealed portions of the apartment or its contents, did produce a new invasion of respondent's privacy unjustified by the exigent circumstance that validated the entry. This is why, contrary to Justice Powell's suggestion [in dissent], the "distinction between 'looking' at a suspicious object in plain view and 'moving' it even a few inches" is much more than trivial for purposes of the Fourth Amendment. It matters not that the search uncovered nothing of any great personal value to respondent—serial numbers rather than (what might conceivably have been hidden behind or under the equipment) letters or photographs. A search is a search, even if it happens to disclose nothing but the bottom of a turntable.

III

The remaining question is whether the search was "reasonable" under the Fourth Amendment. * * *

* * * "It is well established that under certain circumstances the police may *seize* evidence in plain view without a warrant," *Coolidge v. New Hampshire* (emphasis added). * * * It would be absurd to say that an object could lawfully be seized and taken from the premises, but could not be moved for closer examination. It is clear, therefore, that the search here was valid if the "plain view" doctrine would have sustained a seizure of the equipment.

There is no doubt it would have done so if Officer Nelson had probable cause to believe that the equipment was stolen. The State has conceded, however, that he had only a "reasonable suspicion," by which it means something less than probable cause. We have not ruled on the question whether probable cause is required in order to invoke the "plain view" doctrine. * * *

We now hold that probable cause is required. To say otherwise would be to cut the "plain view" doctrine loose from its theoretical and practical moorings. The theory of that doctrine consists of extending to nonpublic places such as the home, where searches and seizures without a warrant are presumptively unreasonable, the police's longstanding authority to make warrantless seizures in public places of such objects as weapons and contraband. And the practical justification for that extension is the desirability of sparing police, whose viewing of the object in the course of a lawful search is as legitimate as it would have been in a public place, the inconvenience and the risk—to themselves or to preservation of the evidence—of going to obtain a warrant. Dispensing with the need for a warrant is worlds apart from permitting a lesser standard of *cause* for the seizure than a warrant would require, *i.e.*, the standard of probable cause. No reason is apparent why an object should routinely be seizable on lesser grounds, during an unrelated search and seizure, than would have been needed to obtain a warrant for that same object if it had been known to be on the premises.

We do not say, of course, that a seizure can never be justified on less than probable cause. We have held that it can—where, for example, the seizure is minimally intrusive and operational necessities render it the only practicable means of detecting certain types of crime. No special operational necessities are relied on here, however—but rather the mere fact that the items in question came lawfully within the officer's plain view. That alone cannot supplant the requirement of probable cause.

The same considerations preclude us from holding that, even though probable cause would have been necessary for a *seizure*, the *search* of objects in plain view that occurred here could be sustained on lesser grounds. A dwelling-place search, no less than a dwelling-place seizure, requires probable cause, and there is no reason in theory or practicality why application of the "plain view" doctrine would supplant that requirement. Although the interest protected by the Fourth Amendment injunction against unreasonable searches is quite different from that protected by its injunction against unreasonable seizures, neither the one nor the other is of inferior worth or necessarily requires only lesser protection. We have not elsewhere drawn a categorical distinction between the two insofar as concerns the degree of justification needed to establish the reasonableness of police action, and we see no reason for a distinction in the particular circumstances before us here. Indeed, to treat searches more liberally would especially erode the plurality's warning in *Coolidge* that "the 'plain view' doctrine may not be used to extend a general exploratory search from one object to another until something incriminating at last emerges." In short, whether legal authority to move the equipment could be found only as an inevitable concomitant of the authority to seize it, or also as a consequence of some independent power to search certain objects in plain view, probable cause to believe the equipment was stolen was required.

Justice O'Connor's dissent suggests that we uphold the action here on the ground that it was a "cursory inspection" rather than a "full-blown search," and could therefore be justified by reasonable suspicion instead of probable cause. As already noted, a truly cursory inspection—one that involves merely looking at what is already exposed to view, without disturbing it—is not a "search" for Fourth Amendment purposes, and therefore does not even require reasonable suspicion. We are unwilling to send police and judges into a new thicket of Fourth Amendment law, to seek a creature of uncertain description that is neither a "plain view" inspection nor yet a "full-blown search." Nothing in the prior opinions of this Court supports such a distinction * * * .

Justice Powell's dissent reasonably asks what it is we would have had Officer Nelson do in these circumstances. The answer depends, of course, upon whether he had probable cause to conduct a search * * * . If he had, then he should have done precisely what he did. If not, then he should have followed up his suspicions, if possible, by means other than a search—just as he would have had to do if, while walking along the street, he had noticed the same suspicious stereo equipment sitting inside a house a few feet away from him, beneath an open window. It may well be that, in such circumstances, no effective means short of a search exist. But there is nothing new in the realization that the Constitution sometimes insulates the criminality of a few in order to protect the privacy of us all. Our disagreement with the dissenters pertains to where the proper balance should be struck; we choose to adhere to the textual and traditional standard of probable cause. * * *

[JUSTICE WHITE'S concurring opinion is omitted.]

JUSTICE POWELL, with whom THE CHIEF JUSTICE REHNQUIST and JUSTICE O'CONNOR join, dissenting. * * *

It is fair to ask what Officer Nelson should have done in these circumstances. Accepting the State's concession that he lacked probable cause, he could not have obtained a warrant to seize the stereo components. Neither could he have remained on the premises and forcibly prevented their removal. * * *

The Court holds that there was an unlawful search of the turntable. It agrees that the "mere recording of the serial numbers did not constitute a seizure." Thus, if the computer had identified as stolen property a component with a visible serial number, the evidence would have been admissible. But the Court further holds that "Officer Nelson's moving of the equipment * * * did constitute a 'search' * * *." It perceives a constitutional distinction between reading a serial number on an object and moving or picking up an identical object to see its serial number. * * * With all respect, this distinction between "looking" at a suspicious object in plain view and "moving" it even a few inches trivializes the Fourth Amendment.[4] The Court's new rule will cause uncertainty, and could deter conscientious police officers from lawfully obtaining evidence necessary to convict guilty persons. * * * Accordingly, I dissent.

JUSTICE O'CONNOR, with whom THE CHIEF JUSTICE REHNQUIST and JUSTICE POWELL join, dissenting.

The Court today gives the right answer to the wrong question. The Court asks whether the police must have probable cause before either

---

[4] Numerous articles that frequently are stolen have identifying numbers, including expensive watches and cameras, and also credit cards. Assume for example that an officer reasonably suspects that two identical watches, both in plain view, have been stolen. Under the Court's decision, if one watch is lying face up and the other lying face down, reading the serial number on one of the watches would not be a search. But turning over the other watch to read its serial number would be a search. Moreover, the officer's ability to read a serial number may depend on its location in a room and light conditions at a particular time. Would there be a constitutional difference if an officer, on the basis of a reasonable suspicion, used a pocket flashlight or turned on a light to read a number rather than moving the object to a point where a serial number was clearly visible?

seizing an object in plain view or conducting a full-blown search of that object, and concludes that they must. I agree. In my view, however, this case presents a different question: whether police must have probable cause before conducting a cursory inspection of an item in plain view. Because I conclude that such an inspection is reasonable if the police are aware of facts or circumstances that justify a reasonable suspicion that the item is evidence of a crime, I would reverse the judgment of the Arizona Court of Appeals, and therefore dissent.

* * * [T]he dispute in this case focuses on the application of the "immediately apparent" requirement; at issue is whether a police officer's reasonable suspicion is adequate to justify a cursory examination of an item in plain view.

The purpose of the "immediately apparent" requirement is to prevent "general, exploratory rummaging in a person's belongings." If an officer could indiscriminately search every item in plain view, a search justified by a limited purpose—such as exigent circumstances—could be used to eviscerate the protections of the Fourth Amendment. In order to prevent such a general search, therefore, we require that the relevance of the item be "immediately apparent." * * *

Thus, I agree with the Court that even under the plain-view doctrine, probable cause is required before the police seize an item, or conduct a full-blown search of evidence in plain view. Such a requirement of probable cause will prevent the plain-view doctrine from authorizing general searches. This is not to say, however, that even a mere inspection of a suspicious item must be supported by probable cause. When a police officer makes a cursory inspection of a suspicious item in plain view in order to determine whether it is indeed evidence of a crime, there is no "exploratory rummaging." Only those items that the police officer "reasonably suspects" as evidence of a crime may be inspected, and perhaps more importantly, the scope of such an inspection is quite limited. In short, if police officers have a reasonable, articulable suspicion that an object they come across during the course of a lawful search is evidence of crime, in my view they may make a cursory examination of the object to verify their suspicion. If the officers wish to go beyond such a cursory examination of the object, however, they must have probable cause. * * *

This distinction between searches based on their relative intrusiveness * * * is entirely consistent with our Fourth Amendment jurisprudence. We have long recognized that searches can vary in intrusiveness, and that some brief searches "may be so minimally intrusive of Fourth Amendment interests that strong countervailing governmental interests will justify a [search] based only on specific articulable facts" that the item in question is contraband or evidence of a crime. * * *

In my view, the balance of the governmental and privacy interests strongly supports a reasonable-suspicion standard for the cursory examination of items in plain view. * * *

Unfortunately, in its desire to establish a "bright-line" test, the Court has taken a step that ignores a substantial body of precedent and that places serious roadblocks to reasonable law enforcement practices. * * *

NOTES AND QUESTIONS

1. *Making sense of Hicks.* According to Justice Scalia, what element of "plain view" was not proven by the Government? Suppose that Officer Nelson had feared that a gun was hidden behind a closed curtain in the Hicks residence. Could he lawfully have opened the curtain, without a warrant, in the absence of probable cause?

In dictum, Justice Scalia stated that if Officer Nelson had had probable cause to believe that the stereo equipment was stolen, "he should have done precisely what he did." Does that seem correct? Why or why not?

2. *Plain touch.* The Supreme Court announced for the first time in Minnesota v. Dickerson, 508 U.S. 366, 113 S.Ct. 2130, 124 L.Ed.2d 334 (1993), that there is a comparable plain-*touch* doctrine:

> We think that [the plain-view] doctrine has an obvious application by analogy to cases in which an officer discovers contraband through the sense of touch during an otherwise lawful search. * * * If a police officer lawfully pats down a suspect's outer clothing [for weapons] and feels an object whose contour or mass makes its identity immediately apparent, there has been no invasion of the suspect's privacy beyond that already authorized by the officer's search for weapons; if the object is contraband, its warrantless seizure would be justified by the same practical considerations that inhere in the plain view context. * * *

Application of the plain-touch doctrine is considered in greater detail at p. 405, Note 7.

3. *Problem.* A police officer obtained a warrant to search *F*'s home and computer for marijuana and documents and computer files pertaining to marijuana sales. When the officer found the computer, he turned it on, went to the "Documents" sub-menu of the "Start" menu, and there discovered a list of recently opened files. He opened the first file and, to his surprise, it was a child pornography image. He then opened two or three more documents on the list, and they also contained child pornography. Does the plain-view doctrine justify the warrantless seizure of these photographs? Frasier v. State, 794 N.E.2d 449 (Ind. App. 2003).

4. *Problem*. A police officer, with consent, entered *H*'s residence to investigate an allegation of an abandoned minor at the residence. Inside, the officer observed a pipe sitting on a table that, based on his experience and training was "predominantly used to smoke marijuana." The officer picked it up and smelled the odor of marijuana. The officer seized the pipe and arrested *H* for possession of drug paraphernalia. Did the officer's actions violate *Hicks*? Commonwealth v. Hatcher, 199 S.W.3d 124 (Ky. 2006).

5. CONSENT

SCHNECKLOTH V. BUSTAMONTE

Supreme Court of the United States, 1973.
412 U.S. 218, 93 S.Ct. 2041, 36 L.Ed.2d 854.

MR. JUSTICE STEWART delivered the opinion of the Court [joined by CHIEF JUSTICE BURGER, and JUSTICES WHITE, BLACKMUN, POWELL, and REHNQUIST].

It is well settled under the Fourth and Fourteenth Amendments that a search conducted without a warrant issued upon probable cause is "*per se* unreasonable * * * subject only to a few specifically established and well-delineated exceptions." It is equally well settled that one of the specifically established exceptions to the requirements of both a warrant and probable cause is a search that is conducted pursuant to consent. The constitutional question in the present case concerns the definition of "consent" in this Fourth and Fourteenth Amendment context.

I

[While on routine patrol at 2:40 a.m., a police officer stopped a car containing six persons because he observed that one headlight and the car's license plate light were burned out. The driver could not produce a license. The officer requested the occupants to get out of the car, and the officer requested permission from Joe Alcala, who claimed to be the brother of the car owner, to search the vehicle. Alcala purportedly replied, "Sure, go ahead." Two reinforcement officers arrived at the scene. According to the officer's uncontradicted testimony, nobody was threatened with arrest prior to this time; it "was all very congenial." Wadded up under the left rear seat, the police discovered three stolen checks, later linked to one of the passengers, Bustamonte, who was prosecuted for theft. The trial court denied the defendant's pretrial motion to suppress the evidence, after which he was convicted at trial.]

II

* * * The respondent concedes that a search conducted pursuant to a valid consent is constitutionally permissible. * * * And similarly the State concedes that "[w]hen a prosecutor seeks to rely upon consent to justify

the lawfulness of a search, he has the burden of proving that the consent was, in fact, freely and voluntarily given."

The precise question in this case, then, is what must the prosecution prove to demonstrate that a consent was "voluntarily" given. * * * The Court of Appeals for the Ninth Circuit concluded that it is an essential part of the State's initial burden to prove that a person knows he has a right to refuse consent. The California courts have followed the rule that voluntariness is a question of fact to be determined from the totality of all the circumstances, and that the state of a defendant's knowledge is only one factor to be taken into account in assessing the voluntariness of a consent.

A

The most extensive judicial exposition of the meaning of "voluntariness" has been developed in those cases in which the Court has had to determine the "voluntariness" of a defendant's confession for purposes of the Fourteenth Amendment. * * * It is to that body of case law to which we turn for initial guidance on the meaning of "voluntariness" in the present context. * * *

In determining whether a defendant's will was overborne in a particular case, the Court has assessed the totality of all the surrounding circumstances—both the characteristics of the accused and the details of the interrogation. * * *

The significant fact about all of these decisions is that none of them turned on the presence or absence of a single controlling criterion; each reflected a careful scrutiny of all the surrounding circumstances. * * *

B

Similar considerations lead us to agree with the courts of California that the question whether a consent to a search was in fact "voluntary" or was the product of duress or coercion, express or implied, is a question of fact to be determined from the totality of all the circumstances. While knowledge of the right to refuse consent is one factor to be taken into account, the government need not establish such knowledge as the *sine qua non* of an effective consent. As with police questioning, two competing concerns must be accommodated in determining the meaning of a "voluntary" consent—the legitimate need for such searches and the equally important requirement of assuring the absence of coercion.

In situations where the police have some evidence of illicit activity, but lack probable cause to arrest or search, a search authorized by a valid consent may be the only means of obtaining important and reliable evidence. In the present case for example, while the police had reason to stop the car for traffic violations, the State does not contend that there was probable cause to search the vehicle or that the search was incident to a valid arrest of any of the occupants. Yet, the search yielded tangible evidence that served as a basis for a prosecution, and provided some assurance that others, wholly innocent of the crime, were not mistakenly brought to trial. And in those cases where there is probable cause to arrest or search, but where the police lack a warrant, a consent search may still be valuable. If the search is conducted and proves fruitless, that in itself may convince the police that an arrest with its possible stigma and embarrassment is unnecessary, or that a far more extensive search pursuant to a warrant is not justified. In short, a search pursuant to consent may result in considerably less inconvenience for the subject of the search, and, properly conducted, is a constitutionally permissible and wholly legitimate aspect of effective police activity.

But the Fourth and Fourteenth Amendments require that a consent not be coerced, by explicit or implicit means, by implied threat or covert force. For, no matter how subtly the coercion was applied, the resulting "consent" would be no more than a pretext for the unjustified police intrusion against which the Fourth Amendment is directed. * * *

The problem of reconciling the recognized legitimacy of consent searches with the requirement that they be free from any aspect of official coercion cannot be resolved by any infallible touchstone. * * * Just as was true with confessions, the requirement of a "voluntary" consent reflects a fair accommodation of the constitutional requirements involved. In examining all the surrounding circumstances to determine if in fact the consent to search was coerced, account must be taken of subtly coercive police questions, as well as the possibly vulnerable subjective state of the person who consents. Those searches that are the product of police coercion can thus be filtered out without undermining the continuing validity of consent searches. In sum, there is no reason for us to depart in the area of consent searches, from the traditional definition of "voluntariness."

The approach of the Court of Appeals for the Ninth Circuit finds no support in any of our decisions that have attempted to define the meaning of "voluntariness." Its ruling, that the State must affirmatively prove that the subject of the search knew that he had a right to refuse consent, would, in practice, create serious doubt whether consent searches could continue to be conducted. There might be rare cases where it could be proved from the record that a person in fact affirmatively knew of his right to refuse * * *. But more commonly where there was no evidence of any coercion, explicit or implicit, the prosecution would nevertheless be unable to demonstrate that the subject of the search in fact had known of his right to refuse consent. * * *

One alternative that would go far toward proving that the subject of a search did know he had a right to refuse consent would be to advise him of that right before eliciting his consent. That, however, is a suggestion that has been almost universally repudiated by both federal and state courts, and, we think, rightly so. For it would be thoroughly impractical to impose on the normal consent search the detailed requirements of an effective warning. Consent searches are part of the standard investigatory techniques of law enforcement agencies. They normally occur on the highway, or in a person's home or office, and under informal and unstructured conditions. * * * These situations are a far cry from the structured atmosphere of a trial where, assisted by counsel if he chooses, a defendant is informed of his trial rights. And, while surely a closer question, these situations are still immeasurably far removed from "custodial interrogation" where, in *Miranda v. Arizona*, [p. 625], we found that the Constitution required certain now familiar warnings as a prerequisite to police interrogation. * * *

In short, neither this Court's prior cases, nor the traditional definition of "voluntariness" requires proof of knowledge of a right to refuse as the *sine qua non* of an effective consent to a search.

C

It is said, however, that a "consent" is a "waiver" of a person's rights under the Fourth and Fourteenth Amendments. The argument is that by allowing the police to conduct a search, a person "waives" whatever right he had to prevent the police from searching. It is argued that under the doctrine of *Johnson v. Zerbst*, 304 U.S. 458, 464, 58 S.Ct. 1019, 1023, 82 L.Ed. 1461 [1938], to establish such a "waiver" the State must demonstrate "an intentional relinquishment or abandonment of a known right or privilege." * * *

The requirement of a "knowing" and "intelligent" waiver was articulated in a case involving the validity of a defendant's decision to forgo a right constitutionally guaranteed to protect a fair trial and the reliability of the truth-determining process. *Johnson v. Zerbst, supra,* dealt with the denial of counsel in a federal criminal trial. * * *

There is a vast difference between those rights that protect a fair criminal trial and the rights guaranteed under the Fourth Amendment. Nothing, either in the purposes behind requiring a "knowing" and "intelligent" waiver of trial rights, or in the practical application of such a requirement suggests that it ought to be extended to the constitutional guarantee against unreasonable searches and seizures.

A strict standard of waiver has been applied to those rights guaranteed to a criminal defendant to insure that he will be accorded the greatest possible opportunity to utilize every facet of the constitutional model of a fair criminal trial. Any trial conducted in derogation of that model leaves open the possibility that the trial reached an unfair result precisely because all the protections specified in the Constitution were not provided. A prime example is the right to counsel. For without that right, a wholly innocent accused faces the real and substantial danger that simply because of his lack of legal expertise, he may be convicted. * * *

The protections of the Fourth Amendment are of a wholly different order, and have nothing whatever to do with promoting the fair ascertainment of truth at a criminal trial. * * *

Nor can it even be said that a search, as opposed to an eventual trial, is somehow "unfair" if a person consents to a search. While the Fourth and Fourteenth Amendments limit the circumstances under which the police can conduct a search, there is nothing constitutionally suspect in a person's voluntarily allowing a search. The actual conduct of the search may be precisely the same as if the police had obtained a warrant. And, unlike those constitutional guarantees that protect a defendant at trial, it cannot be said every reasonable presumption ought to be indulged against voluntary relinquishment. * * * Rather, the community has a real interest in encouraging consent, for the resulting search may yield necessary evidence for the solution and prosecution of crime, evidence that may insure that a wholly innocent person is not wrongly charged with a criminal offense. * * *

In short, there is nothing in the purposes or application of the waiver requirements of *Johnson v. Zerbst* that justifies, much less compels, the easy equation of a knowing waiver with a consent search. * * *

D

Much of what has already been said disposes of the argument that the Court's decision in the *Miranda* case requires the conclusion that knowledge of a right to refuse is an indispensable element of a valid consent. The considerations that informed the Court's holding in *Miranda* are simply inapplicable in the present case. * * *

In this case, there is no evidence of any inherently coercive tactics—either from the nature of the police questioning or the environment in which it took place. Indeed, since consent searches will normally occur on a person's own familiar territory, the specter of incommunicado police interrogation in some remote station house is simply inapposite. There is no reason to believe, under circumstances such as are present here, that the response to a policeman's question is presumptively coerced; and there is, therefore, no reason to reject the traditional test for determining the voluntariness of a person's response. * * *

It is also argued that the failure to require the Government to establish knowledge as a prerequisite to a valid consent, will relegate the Fourth Amendment to the special province of "the sophisticated, the knowledgeable and the privileged." We cannot agree. The traditional definition of voluntariness we accept today has always taken into account evidence of minimal schooling, low intelligence, and the lack of any effective warnings to a person of his rights; and the voluntariness of any statement taken under those conditions has been carefully scrutinized to determine whether it was in fact voluntarily given.

E

Our decision today is a narrow one. We hold only that when the subject of a search is not in custody and the State attempts to justify a search on the basis of his consent, the Fourth and Fourteenth Amendments require that it demonstrate that the consent was in fact voluntarily given, and not the result of duress or coercion, express or implied. Voluntariness is a question of fact to be determined from all the circumstances, and while the subject's knowledge of a right to refuse is a factor to be taken into account, the prosecution is not required to demonstrate such knowledge as a prerequisite to establishing a voluntary consent. * * *

[The concurring opinions of JUSTICES BLACKMUN and POWELL, and the dissenting opinions of JUSTICES DOUGLAS and BRENNAN, are omitted.]

MR. JUSTICE MARSHALL, dissenting. * * *

I * * *

A

The Court assumes that the issue in this case is: what are the standards by which courts are to determine that consent is voluntarily given? It then imports into the law of search and seizure standards developed to decide entirely different questions about coerced confessions.

The Fifth Amendment, in terms, provides that no person "shall be compelled in any criminal case to be a witness against himself." * * * The inquiry in a case where a confession is challenged as having been elicited in an unconstitutional manner is, therefore, whether the behavior of the police amounted to compulsion of the defendant. Because of the nature of the right to be free of compulsion, it would be pointless to ask whether a defendant knew of it before he made a statement; no sane person would knowingly relinquish a right to be free of compulsion. Thus, the questions of compulsion and of violation of the right itself are inextricably intertwined. The cases involving coerced confessions, therefore, pass over the question of knowledge of that right as irrelevant, and turn directly to the question of compulsion. * * *

B

In contrast, this case deals not with "coercion," but with "consent," a subtly different concept to which different standards have been applied in the past. Freedom from coercion is a substantive right, guaranteed by the

Fifth and Fourteenth Amendments. Consent, however, is a mechanism by which substantive requirements, otherwise applicable, are avoided. * * * Thus, consent searches are permitted, not because * * * an exception to the requirements of probable cause and warrant is essential to proper law enforcement, but because we permit our citizens to choose whether or not they wish to exercise their constitutional rights. Our prior decisions simply do not support the view that a meaningful choice has been made solely because no coercion was brought to bear on the subject. * * *

II * * *

If consent to search means that a person has chosen to forgo his right to exclude the police from the place they seek to search, it follows that his consent cannot be considered a meaningful choice unless he knew that he could in fact exclude the police. * * * I would therefore hold, at a minimum, that the prosecution may not rely on a purported consent to search if the subject of the search did not know that he could refuse to give consent. * * *

If one accepts this view, the question then is a simple one: must the Government show that the subject knew of his rights, or must the subject show that he lacked such knowledge?

I think that any fair allocation of the burden would require that it be placed on the prosecution. * * *

The burden on the prosecutor would disappear, of course, if the police, at the time they requested consent to search, also told the subject that he had a right to refuse consent and that his decision to refuse would be respected. The Court's assertions to the contrary notwithstanding, there is nothing impractical about this method of satisfying the prosecution's burden of proof. * * *

The Court contends that if an officer paused to inform the subject of his rights, the informality of the exchange would be destroyed. I doubt that a simple statement by an officer of an individual's right to refuse consent would do much to alter the informality of the exchange, except to alert the subject to a fact that he surely is entitled to know. It is not without significance that for many years the agents of the Federal Bureau of Investigation have routinely informed subjects of their right to refuse consent, when they request consent to search. * * *

I must conclude, with some reluctance, that when the Court speaks of practicality, what it really is talking of is the continued ability of the police to capitalize on the ignorance of citizens so as to accomplish by subterfuge what they could not achieve by relying only on the knowing relinquishment of constitutional rights. Of course it would be "practical" for the police to ignore the commands of the Fourth Amendment, if by practicality we mean that more criminals will be apprehended, even though the constitutional rights of innocent people also go by the board. But such a practical advantage is achieved only at the cost of permitting the police to disregard the limitations that the Constitution places on their behavior, a cost that a constitutional democracy cannot long absorb. * * *

NOTES AND QUESTIONS

1. *A view from the trenches.* There are no precise data on how often searches are conducted on the basis of consent, but one study reported that the two most common warrant "exceptions" are consent and search incident to a lawful arrest, with one detective suggesting that as many as 98 percent of warrantless searches fall under the "consent" umbrella. Richard Van Duizend et al., The Search Warrant Process: Preconceptions, Perceptions, and Practices 21 (1984). Even if this figure is inflated, it suggests that consent issues are of profound importance in the "real world" of searches and seizures.

2. Warrant exceptions require a rationale. As we have seen, warrantless car searches are justified on the grounds of mobility and the lesser expectation of privacy we possess in vehicles. Warrantless searches incident to arrest are justified on the ground that the police must protect themselves from possible attack and prevent destruction of evidence. Why is a warrantless search based on consent allowed?

3. Arnold H. Loewy, *Cops, Cars, and Citizens: Fixing the Broken Balance*, 76 St. John's L. Rev. 535, 554 (2002):

> From the detainees' perspective [in *Schneckloth*], there was little that appeared voluntary. They were stopped at 2:40 in the morning, asked (ordered?) to exit the car, and witnessed the arrival of two reinforcement police officers. They were then asked to search the car without being told that "no" was an option. Can anyone not thoroughly steeped in legal fiction really believe that they thought "no" was one of their options?

Do you agree with Loewy?

4. *Why do guilty people consent?* "Every year I witness the same mass incredulity. Why, one hundred criminal procedure students jointly wonder, would someone 'voluntarily' consent to allow a police officer to search the trunk of his car, knowing that massive amounts of cocaine are easily visible there?" Marcy Strauss, *Reconstructing Consent*, 92 J. Crim. L. & Criminology 211, 211 (2001). Have you thought the same thing?

One court has gone so far as to observe that "no sane man who denies his guilt would actually be willing that policemen search his room for contraband which is certain to be discovered." Higgins v. United States, 209 F.2d 819 (D.C. Cir. 1954). Do you agree? If so, why *do* courts so often find, where criminal evidence was discovered by the police, that the consent to search was voluntary? Is it that judges "systematically overestimate the extent to which citizens in police encounters feel free to refuse [consent]"? Janice Nadler, *No Need to Shout: Bus Sweeps and the Psychology of Coercion*, 2002 Sup. Ct. Rev. 153, 156. Or, is there another explanation?

5.   *More of the same.* In Ohio v. Robinette, 519 U.S. 33, 117 S.Ct. 417, 136 L.Ed.2d 347 (1996), *O*, an officer, lawfully detained *R* for speeding. After checking *R*'s license and finding no outstanding violations, *O* asked *R* to get out of the car, after which he issued *R* a verbal warning for speeding and returned the license. *O* then said, "[o]ne question before you get gone. Are you carrying any illegal contraband in your car? Any weapons of any kind, drugs, anything like that?" After *R* responded in the negative, *O* sought and obtained consent to search the car. The search turned up a small amount of marijuana and, in a film container, a pill later determined to be a controlled substance.

R argued that his consent was involuntary because he was not informed that he was free to go after return of his driver's license. As in *Schneckloth*, the Court here ruled that, although knowledge is a factor to be taken into account in voluntariness analysis, there is no categorical requirement that police officers inform "detainees that they are free to go before a consent to search may be deemed voluntary."

6.   *Another view from the trenches.* The facts in *Robinette* (Note 5) repeat themselves often, with slight variations. Consider: A deputy sheriff pulled over three young men he saw drinking beer while driving in a rural area. Having open beer in the car was not a violation of state law, but the deputy surely had probable cause to think the driver might be intoxicated. The deputy ordered the driver to undergo a field sobriety test. Luckily for the driver, he had had only one beer and thus passed the test. Disgruntled, the deputy said (possibly a general question always to ask): "You boys mind if I take a look in your trunk." After a brief pause, the driver said, "No, sir." In the trunk, in plain view, was a modest amount of cocaine and some drug paraphernalia. The deputy seized these items and arrested all three men, who turned out to be college students.

Defendants retained one of the authors of this book to represent them. In the preliminary interview, their lawyer asked the obvious question: "You knew that stuff was in the trunk?" "Yes." "You're college students. College students are usually at least as smart as average people, so here it comes: why in the world did you consent?" 101.   to what?

The sheepish response was: "I thought if I didn't consent, the deputy would hold us and get a warrant; also, I thought if we were cooperative, he might overlook the small amount."

"You thought a deputy sheriff was going to overlook Schedule 2 drugs?"

Shrug: "I thought it was our only chance. If he got a warrant, I knew we were finished."

Is this valid consent under the majority opinion in *Schneckloth*? If so, does this case persuade you that Justice Marshall got the better of the argument in the case?

7. In *Bumper v. North Carolina*, 391 U.S. 543, 88 S.Ct. 1788, 20 L.Ed.2d 797 (1968), four white law enforcement officers went to the house of Hattie Leath, a 66-year-old African-American widow. According to the Court, the house was "located in a rural area at the end of an isolated mile-long dirt road." Ms. Leath met the officers at the front door. One of the officers told her, "I have a search warrant to search your house." She replied, "go ahead," and opened the door. At trial, the Government did not rely on a warrant to justify the search, but instead claimed that Ms. Leath voluntarily consented. The Supreme Court disagreed:

> When a prosecutor seeks to rely upon consent to justify the lawfulness of a search, he has the burden of proving that the consent was, in fact, freely and voluntarily given. This burden cannot be discharged by showing no more than acquiescence to a claim of lawful authority. * * *

> When a law enforcement officer claims authority to search a home under a warrant, he announces in effect that the occupant has no right to resist the search. The situation is instinct with coercion—albeit colorably lawful coercion. Where there is coercion there cannot be consent.

Is *Bumper* consistent with the totality-of-circumstances test of voluntariness announced years later in *Schneckloth*?

8. *Consent, race, and class.* Apparently most or all of the occupants of the Schneckloth vehicle were Hispanic. Should the Court have considered the possible disparate effect of the rule it was announcing in *Schneckloth* on persons of different races, cultures, and economic classes? Consider:

> Such reliance on ignorance and thinly veiled coercion is deeply troubling. * * * The current system created two Fourth Amendments—one for people who are aware of their right to say no and confident enough to assert the right against a police officer, and another for those who do not know their rights or are afraid to assert them.

> This doubtful standard would be problematic even if it did not closely parallel race and class lines. * * * [T]he consent doctrine in application is likely to reflect race and class divisions. Because a consent search requires no objective individualized suspicion, it is more likely to be directed at poor young black men than wealthy white elderly women. In addition, those who are white and wealthy are more likely to know their rights and to feel secure in asserting them.

David Cole, No Equal Justice 31 (1999). Is Professor Cole correct? If so, in light of *Schneckloth*'s announcement of a totality-of-circumstances test, should a court take into consideration the race and class of the suspect in determining the voluntariness of consent? In this regard, Professor Cole, *id.* at 33–34, reports:

> [O]ne of my students reports that when she attempted to teach the consent doctrine to prisoners at a federal prison in Virginia, her predominantly black and Hispanic students ridiculed the notion. They maintained that although it might be true that she, a white woman, had the right to consent, if they declined consent, the police would either beat them or go ahead and search anyway, and then testify that they had consented. It is of course difficult to verify such statements, but that perception itself will factor into a citizen's decision to assert her rights.

9.   Even if a person voluntarily consents to a search, she can set limits of a temporal nature ("You may search my house for exactly two minutes and no more.") or limit the scope of the search ("You may search my kitchen and living room, but not the bedroom."). The latter issue is considered more fully at p. 382, Note 4.

A person may also withdraw consent after it is granted. The police must honor the citizen's wishes, unless their pre-withdrawal search gives them independent grounds to proceed. But, the issue of whether a defendant has truly withdrawn consent, like voluntariness, can be a difficult one to resolve. Courts generally require that the withdrawal of consent be clearly given. For example, in State v. Wantland, 828 N.W.2d 885 (Wis. App. 2013), *W* consented to a police search of his automobile. When the officer picked up a briefcase in the vehicle, *W* asked, "Got a warrant for that?" Has *W* withdrawn his consent?

GEORGIA V. RANDOLPH

Supreme Court of the United States, 2006.
547 U.S. 103, 126 S.Ct. 1515, 164 L.Ed.2d 208.

JUSTICE SOUTER delivered the opinion of the Court [in which JUSTICES STEVENS, KENNEDY, GINSBURG, and BREYER joined].

The Fourth Amendment recognizes a valid warrantless entry and search of premises when police obtain the voluntary consent of an occupant who shares * * * authority over the area in common with a co-occupant who later objects to the use of evidence so obtained. *United States v. Matlock,* 415 U.S. 164, 94 S.Ct. 988, 39 L.Ed.2d 242 (1974). The question here is whether such an evidentiary seizure is likewise lawful with the permission of one occupant when the other, who later seeks to suppress the evidence, is present at the scene and expressly refuses to consent. We hold that, in the circumstances here at issue, a physically present co-occupant's stated refusal to permit entry prevails, rendering the warrantless search unreasonable and invalid as to him.

I

Respondent Scott Randolph and his wife, Janet, separated in late May 2001, when she left the marital residence in Americus, Georgia, and went to stay with her parents in Canada, taking their son and some belongings. In July, she returned to the Americus house with the child, though the record does not reveal whether her object was reconciliation or retrieval of remaining possessions.

On the morning of July 6, she complained to the police that after a domestic dispute her husband took their son away, and when officers reached the house she told them that her husband was a cocaine user whose habit had caused financial troubles. * * * Shortly after the police arrived, Scott Randolph returned and explained that he had removed the child to a neighbor's house out of concern that his wife might take the boy out of the country again; he denied cocaine use, and countered that it was in fact his wife who abused drugs and alcohol.

* * * Sergeant Murray asked Scott Randolph for permission to search the house, which he unequivocally refused.

The sergeant turned to Janet Randolph for consent to search, which she readily gave. She led the officer upstairs to a bedroom that she identified as Scott's, where the sergeant noticed a section of a drinking straw with a powdery residue he suspected was cocaine. * * * The police took the straw to the police station * * *. * * * Scott Randolph was indicted for possession of cocaine.

He moved to suppress the evidence, as products of a warrantless search of his house unauthorized by his wife's consent over his express refusal. The trial court denied the motion, ruling that Janet Randolph had common authority to consent to the search.

The Court of Appeals of Georgia reversed, and was itself sustained by the State Supreme Court * * *. * * *

We granted certiorari to resolve a split of authority on whether one occupant may give law enforcement effective consent to search shared premises, as against a co-tenant who is present and states a refusal to permit the search. We now affirm.

II

To the Fourth Amendment rule ordinarily prohibiting the warrantless entry of a person's house as unreasonable *per se,* one "jealously and carefully drawn" exception recognizes the validity of searches with the voluntary consent of an individual possessing authority. That person might be the householder against whom evidence is sought, or a fellow occupant who shares common authority over property, when the suspect is absent, *Matlock, supra.* * * * None of our co-occupant consent-to-search cases, however, has presented the further fact of a second occupant physically present and refusing permission to search, and later moving to suppress evidence so obtained. The significance of such a refusal turns on the underpinnings of the co-occupant consent rule, as recognized since *Matlock*.

A

The defendant in that case was arrested in the yard of a house where he lived with a Mrs. Graff and several of her relatives, and was detained in a squad car parked nearby. When the police went to the door, Mrs. Graff admitted them and consented to a search of the house. In resolving the defendant's objection to use of the evidence taken in the warrantless search, we said that "the consent of one who possesses common authority over premises or effects is valid as against the absent, nonconsenting person with whom that authority is shared." Consistent with our prior understanding that Fourth Amendment rights are not limited by the law of property, we explained that the third party's "common authority" is not synonymous with a technical property interest:

> "The authority which justified the third-party consent does not rest upon the law of property, with its attendant historical and legal refinement, but rests rather on mutual use of the property by persons generally having joint access or control for most purposes, so that it is reasonable to recognize that any of the co-inhabitants has the right to permit the inspection in his own right and that the others have assumed the risk that one of their number might permit the common area to be searched."

* * *

The constant element in assessing Fourth Amendment reasonableness in the consent cases, then, is the great significance given to widely shared social expectations, which are naturally enough influenced by the law of property, but not controlled by its rules. *Matlock* accordingly not only holds that a solitary co-inhabitant may sometimes consent to a search of shared premises, but stands for the proposition that the reasonableness of such a search is in significant part a function of commonly held understanding about the authority that co-inhabitants may exercise in ways that affect each other's interests.

B

Matlock's example of common understanding is readily apparent. When someone comes to the door of a domestic dwelling with a baby at her hip, as Mrs. Graff did, she shows that she belongs there, and that fact standing alone is enough to tell a law enforcement officer or any other visitor that if she occupies the place along with others, she probably lives there subject to the assumption tenants usually make about their common authority when they share quarters. They understand that any one of them may admit visitors, with the consequence that a guest obnoxious to one may nevertheless be admitted in his absence by another. As *Matlock* put it, shared tenancy is understood to include an "assumption of risk," on which police officers are entitled to rely, and although some group living together might make an exceptional arrangement that no one could admit a guest without the agreement of all, the chance of such an eccentric scheme is too remote to expect visitors to investigate a particular household's rules before accepting an invitation to come in. So, *Matlock* relied on what was usual and placed no burden on the police to eliminate the possibility of atypical arrangements, in the absence of reason to doubt that the regular scheme was in place.

It is also easy to imagine different facts on which, if known, no common authority could sensibly be suspected. A person on the scene who identifies himself, say, as a landlord or a hotel manager calls up no customary understanding of authority to admit guests without the consent of the current occupant. * * * And when it comes to searching through bureau drawers, there will be instances in which even a person clearly belonging on premises as an occupant may lack any perceived authority to consent; "a child of eight might well be considered to have the power to consent to the police crossing the threshold into that part of the house where any caller, such as a pollster or salesman, might well be admitted," but no one would reasonably expect such a child to be in a position to authorize anyone to rummage through his parents' bedroom.

C

Although we have not dealt directly with the reasonableness of police entry in reliance on consent by one occupant subject to immediate challenge by another, we took a step toward the issue in an earlier case dealing with the Fourth Amendment rights of a social guest arrested at premises the police entered without a warrant or the benefit of any exception to the warrant requirement. *Minnesota v. Olson,* [p. 215, Note 5, infra], held that overnight houseguests have a legitimate expectation of privacy in their temporary quarters because "it is unlikely that [the host] will admit someone who wants to see or meet with the guest over the objection of the guest." If that customary expectation of courtesy or deference is a foundation of Fourth Amendment rights of a houseguest, it presumably should follow that an inhabitant of shared premises may claim at least as much, and it turns out that the co-inhabitant naturally has an even stronger claim.

To begin with, it is fair to say that a caller standing at the door of shared premises would have no confidence that one occupant's invitation was a sufficiently good reason to enter when a fellow tenant stood there saying, "stay out." Without some very good reason, no sensible person would go inside under those conditions. Fear for the safety of the occupant issuing the invitation, or of someone else inside, would be thought to justify entry, but the justification then would be the personal risk, the threats to life or limb, not the disputed invitation.

The visitor's reticence without some such good reason would show not timidity but a realization that when people living together disagree over the use of their common quarters, a resolution must come through voluntary accommodation, not by appeals to authority. Unless the people living together fall within some recognized hierarchy, like a household of parent and child or barracks housing military personnel of different grades, there is no societal understanding of superior and inferior, a fact reflected in a standard formulation of domestic property law * * * . * * * In sum, there is no common understanding that one co-tenant generally has a right or authority to prevail over the express wishes of another, whether the issue is the color of the curtains or invitations to outsiders.

D

Since the co-tenant wishing to open the door to a third party has no recognized authority in law or social practice to prevail over a present and objecting co-tenant, his disputed invitation, without more, gives a police officer no better claim to reasonableness in entering than the officer would have in the absence of any consent at all. * * *

Disputed permission is thus no match for this central value of the Fourth Amendment, and the State's other countervailing claims do not add up to outweigh it. Yes, we recognize the consenting tenant's interest as a citizen in bringing criminal activity to light. And we understand a co-tenant's legitimate self-interest in siding with the police to deflect suspicion raised by sharing quarters with a criminal.

But society can often have the benefit of these interests without relying on a theory of consent that ignores an inhabitant's refusal to allow a warrantless search. The co-tenant acting on his own initiative may be able to deliver evidence to the police, and can tell the police what he knows, for use before a magistrate in getting a warrant. The reliance on a co-tenant's information instead of disputed consent accords with the law's general partiality toward "police action taken under a warrant [as against] searches and seizures without one" * * * .

Nor should this established policy of Fourth Amendment law be undermined by the principal dissent's claim that it shields spousal abusers and other violent co-tenants who will refuse to allow the police to enter a dwelling when their victims ask the police for help. It is not that the dissent exaggerates violence in the home; we recognize that domestic abuse is a serious problem in the United States.

But this case has no bearing on the capacity of the police to protect domestic victims. * * * No question has been raised, or reasonably could be, about the authority of the police to enter a dwelling to protect a resident from domestic violence; so long as they have good reason to believe such a threat exists * * * (And since the police would then be lawfully in the premises, there is no question that they could seize any evidence in plain view or take further action supported by any consequent probable cause.) Thus, the question whether the police might lawfully enter over objection in order to provide any protection that might be reasonable is easily answered yes. * * *

* * * We therefore hold that a warrantless search of a shared dwelling for evidence over the express refusal of consent by a physically present resident cannot be justified as reasonable as to him on the basis of consent given to the police by another resident.

E

There are two loose ends, the first being the explanation given in *Matlock* for the constitutional sufficiency of a co-tenant's consent to enter and search: it "rests * * * on mutual use of the property by persons generally having joint access or control for most purposes, so that it is reasonable to recognize that any of the co-inhabitants has the right to permit the inspection in his own right * * *." If *Matlock's* co-tenant is giving permission "in his own right," how can his "own right" be eliminated by another tenant's objection? The answer appears in the very footnote from which the quoted statement is taken: the "right" to admit the police to which *Matlock* refers is not an enduring and enforceable ownership right as understood by the private law of property, but is instead the authority recognized by customary social usage as having a substantial bearing on Fourth Amendment reasonableness in specific circumstances. Thus, to ask whether the consenting tenant has the right to admit the police when a physically present fellow tenant objects is not to question whether some property right may be divested by the mere objection of another. It is, rather, the question whether customary social understanding accords the consenting tenant authority powerful enough to prevail over the co-tenant's objection. The *Matlock* Court did not purport to answer this question, a point made clear by another statement (which the dissent does not quote): the Court described the co-tenant's consent as good against "the absent, nonconsenting resident."

The second loose end is the significance of *Matlock* * * * and [*Illinois v.*] *Rodriguez* [p. 376, infra] after today's decision. Although the *Matlock* defendant was not present with the opportunity to object, he was in a squad car not far away; the *Rodriguez* defendant was actually asleep in the apartment, and the police might have roused him with a knock on the door before they entered with only the consent of an apparent co-tenant.

If those cases are not to be undercut by today's holding, we have to admit that we are drawing a fine line; if a potential defendant with self-interest in objecting is in fact at the door and objects, the co-tenant's permission does not suffice for a reasonable search, whereas the potential objector, nearby but not invited to take part in the threshold colloquy, loses out.

This is the line we draw, and we think the formalism is justified. So long as there is no evidence that the police have removed the potentially objecting tenant from the entrance for the sake of avoiding a possible objection, there is practical value in the simple clarity of complementary rules, one recognizing the co-tenant's permission when there is no fellow occupant on hand, the other according dispositive weight to the fellow occupant's contrary indication when he expresses it. * * * Better to accept the formalism of distinguishing *Matlock* from this case than to impose a requirement [of seeking out any co-tenant to determine his wishes], time-consuming in the field and in the courtroom, with no apparent systemic justification. * * *

III

This case invites a straightforward application of the rule that a physically present inhabitant's express refusal of consent to a police search is dispositive as to him, regardless of the consent of a fellow occupant. * * * The State does not argue that she gave any indication to the police of a need for protection inside the house that might have justified entry into the portion of the premises where the police found the powdery straw * * * . Nor does the State claim that the entry and search should be upheld under the rubric of exigent circumstances, owing to some apprehension by the police officers that Scott Randolph would destroy evidence of drug use before any warrant could be obtained.

The judgment of the Supreme Court of Georgia is therefore affirmed.

JUSTICE ALITO took no part in the consideration or decision of this case.

[JUSTICE STEVENS's opinion, concurring, is omitted.]

JUSTICE BREYER, concurring.

If Fourth Amendment law forced us to choose between two bright-line rules, (1) a rule that always found one tenant's consent sufficient to justify a search without a warrant and (2) a rule that never did, I believe we should choose the first. That is because, as the Chief Justice's dissent points out, a rule permitting such searches can serve important law enforcement needs (for example, in domestic abuse cases) and the consenting party's joint tenancy diminishes the objecting party's reasonable expectation of privacy.

But the Fourth Amendment does not insist upon bright-line rules. Rather, it recognizes that no single set of legal rules can capture the ever changing complexity of human life. It consequently uses the general terms "unreasonable searches and seizures." And this Court has continuously emphasized that "[r]easonableness * * * is measured * * * by examining the totality of the circumstances."

The circumstances here include the following: The search at issue was a search solely for evidence. The objecting party was present and made his objection known clearly and directly to the officers seeking to enter the house. The officers did not justify their search on grounds of possible evidence destruction. And, as far as the record reveals, the officers might easily have secured the premises and sought a warrant permitting them to enter. Thus, the "totality of the circumstances" present here do not suffice to justify abandoning the Fourth Amendment's traditional hostility to police entry into a home without a warrant.

I stress the totality of the circumstances, however, because, were the circumstances to change significantly, so should the result. * * *

If a possible abuse victim invites a responding officer to enter a home or consents to the officer's entry request, that invitation (or consent) itself could reflect the victim's fear about being left alone with an abuser. It could also indicate the availability of evidence, in the form of an immediate willingness to speak, that might not otherwise exist. In that context, an invitation (or consent) would provide a special reason for immediate, rather than later, police entry. And, entry following invitation or consent by one party ordinarily would be reasonable even in the face of direct objection by the other. That being so, contrary to the Chief Justice's suggestion, today's decision will not adversely affect ordinary law enforcement practices.

Given the case-specific nature of the Court's holding, and with these understandings, I join the Court's holding and its opinion.

CHIEF JUSTICE ROBERTS, with whom JUSTICE SCALIA joins, dissenting.

* * * The rule the majority fashions does not implement the high office of the Fourth Amendment to protect privacy, but instead provides protection on a random and happenstance basis, protecting, for example, a co-occupant who happens to be at the front door when the other occupant consents to a search, but not one napping or watching television in the next room. And the cost of affording such random protection is great, as demonstrated by the recurring cases in which abused spouses seek to authorize police entry into a home they share with a nonconsenting abuser.

The correct approach to the question presented is clearly mapped out in our precedents: The Fourth Amendment protects privacy. If an individual shares information, papers, *or places* with another, he assumes the risk that the other person will in turn share access to that information or those papers *or places* with the government. And just as an individual who has shared illegal plans or incriminating documents with another cannot interpose an objection when that other person turns the information over to the government, just because the individual happens to be present at the time, so too someone who shares a place with another cannot interpose an objection when that person decides to grant access to the police, simply because the objecting individual happens to be present.

A warrantless search is reasonable if police obtain the voluntary consent of a person authorized to give it. Co-occupants have "assumed the risk that one of their number might permit [a] common area to be searched." *United States v. Matlock*. Just as Mrs. Randolph could walk upstairs, come down, and turn her husband's cocaine straw over to the police, she can consent to police entry and search of what is, after all, her home, too.

I

* * * One element that can make a warrantless government search of a home " 'reasonable' " is voluntary consent. * * * Today's opinion creates an exception to this otherwise clear rule: A third-party consent search is unreasonable, and therefore constitutionally impermissible, if the co-occupant against whom evidence is obtained was present and objected to the entry and search.

This exception is based on what the majority describes as "widely shared social expectations" that "when people living together disagree over the use of their common quarters, a resolution must come through voluntary accommodation." But this fundamental predicate to the majority's analysis gets us nowhere: Does the objecting cotenant accede to the consenting cotenant's wishes, or the other way around? The majority's assumption about voluntary accommodation simply leads to the common stalemate of two gentlemen insisting that the other enter a room first.

Nevertheless, the majority is confident in assuming—confident enough to incorporate its assumption into the Constitution—that an invited social guest who arrives at the door of a shared residence, and is greeted by a disagreeable co-occupant shouting " 'stay out,' " would simply go away. * * * But it seems equally accurate to say—based on the majority's conclusion that one does not have a right to prevail over the express wishes of his co-occupant—that the objector has no "authority" to insist on getting *his* way over his co-occupant's wish that her guest be admitted.

The fact is that a wide variety of differing social situations can readily be imagined, giving rise to quite different social expectations. A relative or good friend of one of two feuding roommates might well enter the apartment over the objection of the other roommate. The reason the invitee appeared at the door also affects expectations: A guest who came to celebrate an occupant's birthday, or one who had traveled some distance for a particular reason, might not readily turn away simply because of a roommate's objection. * * *

The possible scenarios are limitless, and slight variations in the fact pattern yield vastly different expectations about whether the invitee might be expected to enter or to go away. Such shifting expectations are not a promising foundation on which to ground a constitutional rule, particularly because the majority has no support for its basic assumption * * * beyond a hunch about how people would typically act in an atypical situation. * * *

* * * [T]he Fourth Amendment precedents the majority cites refer * * * to a "legitimate expectation of *privacy*." Whatever social expectation the majority seeks to protect, it is not one of privacy. The very predicate giving rise to the question in cases of shared information, papers, containers, or places is that privacy has been shared with another. Our common social expectations may well be that the other person will not, in turn, share what we have shared with them with another—including the police—but that is the risk we take in sharing. * * *

A wide variety of often subtle social conventions may shape expectations about how we act when another shares with us what is otherwise private, and those conventions go by a variety of labels— courtesy, good manners, custom, protocol, even honor among thieves. The Constitution, however, protects not these but privacy, and once privacy has been shared, the shared information, documents, or places remain private only at the discretion of the confidant.

II * * *

The common thread in our decisions upholding searches conducted pursuant to third-party consent is an understanding that a person "assume[s] the risk" that those who have access to and control over his shared property might consent to a search. In *Matlock,* we explained that this assumption of risk is derived from a third party's "joint access or control for most purposes" of shared property. And we concluded that shared use of property makes it "reasonable to recognize that any of the co-inhabitants has the right to permit the inspection in his own right."

In this sense, the risk assumed by a joint occupant is comparable to the risk assumed by one who reveals private information to another. If a person has incriminating information, he can keep it private in the face of a request from police to share it, because he has that right under the

Fifth Amendment. If a person occupies a house with incriminating information in it, he can keep that information private in the face of a request from police to search the house, because he has that right under the Fourth Amendment. But if he shares the information—or the house—with another, that other can grant access to the police in each instance.

To the extent a person wants to ensure that his possessions will be subject to a consent search only due to his *own* consent, he is free to place these items in an area over which others do *not* share access and control, be it a private room or a locked suitcase under a bed. * * *

III * * *

Just as the source of the majority's rule is not privacy, so too the interest it protects cannot reasonably be described as such. That interest is not protected if a co-owner happens to be absent when the police arrive, in the backyard gardening, asleep in the next room, or listening to music through earphones so that only his co-occupant hears the knock on the door. That the rule is so random in its application confirms that it bears no real relation to the privacy protected by the Fourth Amendment. What the majority's rule protects is not so much privacy as the good luck of a co-owner who just happens to be present at the door when the police arrive. Usually when the development of Fourth Amendment jurisprudence leads to such arbitrary lines, we take it as a signal that the rules need to be rethought. We should not embrace a rule at the outset that its *sponsors* appreciate will result in drawing fine, formalistic lines. * * *

While the majority's rule protects something random, its consequences are particularly severe. * * * Under the majority's rule, there will be many cases in which a consenting co-occupant's wish to have the police enter is overridden by an objection from another present co-occupant. What does the majority imagine will happen, in a case in which the consenting co-occupant is concerned about the other's criminal activity, once the door clicks shut? The objecting co-occupant may pause briefly to decide whether to destroy any evidence of wrongdoing or to inflict retribution on the consenting co-occupant first, but there can be little doubt that he will attend to both in short order. It is no answer to say that the consenting co-occupant can depart with the police; remember that it is her home, too, and the other co-occupant's very presence, which allowed him to object, may also prevent the consenting co-occupant from doing more than urging the police to enter.

Perhaps the most serious consequence of the majority's rule is its operation in domestic abuse situations, a context in which the present question often arises. * * * The Court concludes that because "no sensible person would go inside" in the face of disputed consent, and the consenting cotenant thus has "no recognized authority" to insist on the guest's admission, a "police officer [has] no better claim to reasonableness in entering than the officer would have in the absence of any consent at all." But the police officer's superior claim to enter is obvious: Mrs. Randolph did not invite the police to join her for dessert and coffee; the officer's precise purpose in knocking on the door was to assist with a dispute between the Randolphs—one in which Mrs. Randolph felt the need for the protective presence of the police. The majority's rule apparently forbids police from entering to assist with a domestic dispute if the abuser whose behavior prompted the request for police assistance objects.

The majority acknowledges these concerns, but dismisses them on the ground that its rule can be expected to give rise to exigent situations, and police can then rely on an exigent circumstances exception to justify entry. This is a strange way to justify a rule, and the fact that alternative justifications for entry might arise does not show that entry pursuant to consent is unreasonable. * * *

One of the concurring opinions states that if it had to choose between a rule that a cotenant's consent was valid or a rule that it was not, it would choose the former. The concurrence advises, however, that "no single set of legal rules can capture the ever changing complexity of human life," and joins what becomes the majority opinion, "[g]iven the case-specific nature of the Court's holding." * * * The end result is a complete lack of practical guidance for the police in the field, let alone for the lower courts. * * *

[The dissenting opinions of JUSTICES SCALIA and THOMAS are omitted.]

NOTES AND QUESTIONS

1. As a matter of policy (especially in light of the problem of domestic violence), whose opinion—Justice Souter's or Chief Justice Roberts'—do you find more persuasive? Which opinion seems more consistent with Fourth Amendment case law?

Justice Breyer states that if he were forced to choose one of the two bright-line rules he sets out in his concurrence, he would choose the first one he set out. If *you* had to choose one of the two bright-line rules, which one would *you* choose, and why?

2. *A variation on the theme.* Assume these facts: The police are investigating a criminal assault on the street. They come to an apartment in which *F*, a suspect, and *R* live. *F* tells the police, "You don't have any right to come in here. I know my rights." However, because the police have independent grounds to believe he had assaulted *R* in the apartment, they arrest *F* on that charge and take him to the police station. An hour later, they return to the apartment, inform *R* that *F* is under arrest, and obtain consent

from *R* to search their apartment. These are the facts from *Fernandez v. California*, 571 U.S. ___, 134 S.Ct. 1126, 188 L.Ed.2d 25 (2014). Does *Randolph* apply? After all, *F was* present in the apartment and *did* object to their entry an hour before the police obtained consent from *R*.

The Court, 6–3 per Justice Alito, held that *Matlock*, not *Randolph*, applied to these facts. Justice Alito stated that "consent by one resident of jointly occupied premises is generally sufficient to justify a warrantless search." He described *Randolph* as a "narrow exception," observing that Justice Souter's opinion in *Randolph* "went to great lengths to make clear that its holding was limited to situations in which the objecting occupant is present. Again and again, the opinion of the Court stressed this controlling factor. * * * The Court's opinion could hardly have been clearer on this point * * * ."

Justice Ginsburg dissented, joined by Justices Sotomayor and Kagan. She criticized the majority for not applying the general rule that "warrantless searches, in the main, [are] *per se* unreasonable. If this rule is to remain hardy, * * * exceptions to the warrant requirement must be 'few in number and carefully delineated.'" Here, the dissenters pointed out, the Court was permitting a warrantless search of a home, the most protected area of privacy. She noted, as well, that the police almost certainly had probable cause and, therefore, could have obtained a warrant. (Justice Alito responded that "the dissent's repeated references to the availability of a warrant * * * are beside the point.")

One other aspect of *Fernandez* is worth noting. *Matlock* and *Randolph* were decided under *Katz*-ian privacy analysis. But, does analysis of joint-authority consent cases now require consideration of trespass analysis, in light of the Court's resuscitation of that doctrine? Justice Scalia, in concurrence, stated that he believed *Randolph* was wrongly decided, but observed that the argument that "the search of petitioner's shared apartment violated the Fourth Amendment because he had a right under property law to exclude the police" was an argument that "can[not] be * * * easily dismissed." Justice Scalia observed that "I would * * * find this a more difficult case if it were established that property law did not give petitioner's cotenant the right to admit visitors over petitioner's objection." But, no case law was provided to Justice Scalia that "establish[es] that a guest would commit a trespass if one of two joint tenants invited the guest to enter and the other tenant forbade the guest to do so."

Do you agree with Professor Stuart Green who said, "I have always thought *Matlock* wrongly decided, because it insufficiently valued a co-tenant's interest in privacy. But if *Matlock* was correctly decided, then *Randolph* was wrongly decided because a co-tenant, under *Matlock*, has the right to vitiate the privacy interest of another co-tenant. But if *Randolph* is correctly decided, then *Fernandez* is wrongly decided because the co-tenant in *Fernandez* exercised his right to exclude the police. On my view, the Court is 0 for 3 in co-tenant consent cases."

3. *Originalism.* Issues of consent aside, Justices Stevens and Scalia got into an interesting debate in *Randolph* regarding "originalism"—the doctrine that the Constitution means whatever the framers of the text had in mind *and nothing else*, i.e., the meaning of the Constitution cannot properly change over time. Justice Stevens in his concurring opinion argued that property law had changed radically since the founding and thus originalism would provide an outcome different from what the Court held. Justice Scalia questioned Stevens's history but, more fundamentally, attacked Stevens's premise:

> Justice Stevens' attempted critique of originalism confuses the original import of the Fourth Amendment with the background sources of law to which the Amendment, on its original meaning, referred. From the date of its ratification until well into the 20th century, violation of the Amendment was tied to common-law trespass. On the basis of that connection, someone who had power to license the search of a house by a private party could authorize a police search. As property law developed, individuals who previously could not authorize a search might become able to do so, and those who once could grant such consent might no longer have that power. But changes in the law of property to which the Fourth Amendment referred would not alter the Amendment's meaning: that anyone capable of authorizing a search by a private party could consent to a warrantless search by the police.

> There is nothing new or surprising in the proposition that our unchanging Constitution refers to other bodies of law that might themselves change. * * * This reference to changeable law presents no problem for the originalist. * * *

4. Notice certain language in the last paragraph of the Chief Justice's dissent. He stated that Justice Breyer "joins *what becomes the majority opinion* * * *." What might this italicized language suggest about how the justices initially voted in this case?

5. *Problem.* W (Wife) and H (Husband) have joint authority over their home. *W*, outside the residence, consents to the search; *H*, inside the house and approached by the police, who intend to execute a warrant to arrest him, barricades himself inside. United States v. McKerrell, 491 F.3d 1221 (10th Cir. 2007). In view of *Randolph*, is a search of the home valid on consent grounds? (Ignore any other possible justifications for the entry.)

6. What if the driver of a car, lawfully stopped on the highway, consents to a search of the car, but his passenger, his common law wife, objects? Does *Randolph* apply outside the home? For one court's answer, see State v. Copeland, 399 S.W.3d 159 (Tex. Crim. App. 2013).

ILLINOIS V. RODRIGUEZ

Supreme Court of the United States, 1990.
497 U.S. 177, 110 S.Ct. 2793, 111 L.Ed.2d 148.

JUSTICE SCALIA delivered the opinion of the Court [joined by CHIEF JUSTICE REHNQUIST, and JUSTICES WHITE, BLACKMUN, O'CONNOR, and KENNEDY]. * * *

I * * *

On July 26, 1985, police were summoned to the residence of Dorothy Jackson on South Wolcott in Chicago. They were met by Ms. Jackson's daughter, Gail Fischer, who showed signs of a severe beating. She told the officers that she had been assaulted by respondent Edward Rodriguez earlier that day in an apartment on South California Avenue. Fischer stated that Rodriguez was then asleep in the apartment, and she consented to travel there with the police in order to unlock the door with her key so that the officers could enter and arrest him. During this conversation, Fischer several times referred to the apartment on South California as "our" apartment, and said that she had clothes and furniture there. It is unclear whether she indicated that she currently lived at the apartment, or only that she used to live there.

The police officers drove to the apartment on South California, accompanied by Fischer. They did not obtain an arrest warrant for Rodriguez, nor did they seek a search warrant for the apartment. At the apartment, Fischer unlocked the door with her key and gave the officers permission to enter. They moved through the door into the living room, where they observed in plain view drug paraphernalia and containers filled with white powder that they believed (correctly, as later analysis showed) to be cocaine. * * * The officers arrested Rodriguez and seized the drugs and related paraphernalia.

Rodriguez was charged with possession of a controlled substance with intent to deliver. He moved to suppress all evidence seized at the time of his arrest, claiming that Fischer had vacated the apartment several weeks earlier and had no authority to consent to the entry. The Cook County Circuit Court granted the motion, holding that at the time she consented to the entry Fischer did not have common authority over the apartment. The Court concluded that Fischer was not a "usual resident" but rather an "infrequent visitor" at the apartment on South California, based upon its findings that Fischer's name was not on the lease, that she did not contribute to the rent, that she was not allowed to invite others to the apartment on her own, that she did not have access to the apartment when respondent was away, and that she had moved some of her possessions from the apartment. The Circuit Court also rejected the State's contention that, even if Fischer did not possess common authority over the premises, there was no Fourth Amendment violation if the police *reasonably believed* at the time of their entry that Fischer possessed the authority to consent. * * *

II * * *

As we stated in [*United States v.*] *Matlock*, [415 U.S. 164, 94 S.Ct. 988, 39 L.Ed.2d 242 (1974)], "[c]ommon authority" rests "on mutual use of the property by persons generally having joint access or control for most purposes * * * ." The burden of establishing that common authority rests upon the State. On the basis of this record, it is clear that burden was not sustained. The evidence showed that although Fischer, with her two small children, had lived with Rodriguez beginning in December 1984, she had moved out on July 1, 1985, almost a month before the search at issue here, and had gone to live with her mother. * * * She had a key to the apartment, which she said at trial she had taken without Rodriguez's knowledge * * * . On these facts the State has not established that, with respect to the South California apartment, Fischer had "joint access or control for most purposes." * * *

III

A

The State contends that, even if Fischer did not in fact have authority to give consent, it suffices to validate the entry that the law enforcement officers reasonably believed she did. * * *

B

On the merits of the issue, respondent asserts that permitting a reasonable belief of common authority to validate an entry would cause a defendant's Fourth Amendment rights to be "vicariously waived." We disagree.

We have been unyielding in our insistence that a defendant's waiver of his trial rights cannot be given effect unless it is "knowing" and "intelligent." *Johnson v. Zerbst*, 304 U.S. 458, 58 S.Ct. 1019, 82 L.Ed. 1461 (1938). We would assuredly not permit, therefore, evidence seized in violation of the Fourth Amendment to be introduced on the basis of a trial court's mere "reasonable belief"—derived from statements by unauthorized persons—that the defendant has waived his objection. But one must make a distinction between, on the one hand, trial rights that *derive* from the violation of constitutional guarantees and, on the other hand, the nature of those constitutional guarantees themselves. * * *

What Rodriguez is assured by the trial right of the exclusionary rule, where it applies, is that no evidence seized in violation of the Fourth Amendment will be introduced at his trial unless he consents. What he is assured by the Fourth Amendment itself, however, is not that no government search of his house will occur unless he consents; but that no such search will occur that is "unreasonable." There are various elements, of course, that can make a search of a person's house "reasonable"—one of which is the consent of the person or his cotenant. The essence of respondent's argument is that we should impose upon this element a requirement that we have not imposed upon other elements that regularly compel government officers to exercise judgment regarding the facts: namely, the requirement that their judgment be not only responsible but correct.

The fundamental objective that alone validates all unconsented government searches is, of course, the seizure of persons who have committed or are about to commit crimes, or of evidence related to crimes. But "reasonableness," with respect to this necessary element, does not demand that the government be factually correct in its assessment that that is what a search will produce. Warrants need only be supported by "probable cause," which demands no more than a proper "assessment of probabilities in particular factual contexts * * * ." If a magistrate, based upon seemingly reliable but factually inaccurate information, issues a warrant for the search of a house in which the sought-after felon is not present, has never been present, and was never likely to have been present, the owner of that house suffers one of the inconveniences we all expose ourselves to as the cost of living in a safe society; he does not suffer a violation of the Fourth Amendment.

Another element often, though not invariably, required in order to render an unconsented search "reasonable" is, of course, that the officer be authorized by a valid warrant. Here also we have not held that "reasonableness" precludes error with respect to those factual judgments that law enforcement officials are expected to make. [Justice Scalia then recounted the facts in *Maryland v. Garrison*, p. 235, Note 7, in which the Court upheld a search in which the police mistakenly searched the wrong residence.] * * *

It would be superfluous to multiply these examples. It is apparent that in order to satisfy the "reasonableness" requirement of the Fourth Amendment, what is generally demanded of the many factual determinations that must regularly be made by agents of the government—whether the magistrate issuing a warrant, the police officer executing a warrant, or the police officer conducting a search or seizure under one of the exceptions to the warrant requirement—is not that they always be correct, but that they always be reasonable. As we put it in *Brinegar v. United States*, 338 U.S. 160, 176, 69 S.Ct. 1302, 1311, 93 L.Ed. 1879 (1949):

> "Because many situations which confront officers in the course of executing their duties are more or less ambiguous, room must be allowed for some mistakes on their part. But the mistakes must

be those of reasonable men, acting on facts leading sensibly to their conclusions of probability."

We see no reason to depart from this general rule with respect to facts bearing upon the authority to consent to a search. Whether the basis for such authority exists is the sort of recurring factual question to which law enforcement officials must be expected to apply their judgment; and all the Fourth Amendment requires is that they answer it reasonably. The Constitution is no more violated when officers enter without a warrant because they reasonably (though erroneously) believe that the person who has consented to their entry is a resident of the premises, than it is violated when they enter without a warrant because they reasonably (though erroneously) believe they are in pursuit of a violent felon who is about to escape.* * * *

* * * [W]hat we hold today does not suggest that law enforcement officers may always accept a person's invitation to enter premises. Even when the invitation is accompanied by an explicit assertion that the person lives there, the surrounding circumstances could conceivably be such that a reasonable person would doubt its truth and not act upon it without further inquiry. As with other factual determinations bearing upon search and seizure, determination of consent to enter must "be judged against an objective standard: would the facts available to the officer at the moment * * * 'warrant a man of reasonable caution in the belief'" that the consenting party had authority over the premises? If not, then warrantless entry without further inquiry is unlawful unless authority actually exists. But if so, the search is valid.

In the present case, the Appellate Court found it unnecessary to determine whether the officers reasonably believed that Fischer had the authority to consent, because it ruled as a matter of law that a reasonable belief could not validate the entry. Since we find that ruling to be in error, we remand for consideration of that question. * * *

JUSTICE MARSHALL, with whom JUSTICE BRENNAN and JUSTICE STEVENS join, dissenting. * * *

* * * The Court holds that the warrantless entry into Rodriguez's home was nonetheless valid if the officers reasonably believed that Fischer had authority to consent. The majority's defense of this position rests on a misconception of the basis for third-party consent searches.

---

*   Justice Marshall's dissent rests upon a rejection of the proposition that searches pursuant to valid third-party consent are "generally reasonable." Only a warrant or exigent circumstances, he contends, can produce "reasonableness"; consent validates the search only because the object of the search thereby "limit[s] his expectation of privacy," so that the search becomes not really a search at all. We see no basis for making such an artificial distinction. To describe a consented search as a noninvasion of privacy and thus a nonsearch is strange in the extreme. And while it must be admitted that this ingenious device can explain why consented searches are lawful, it cannot explain why seemingly consented searches are "unreasonable," which is all that the Constitution forbids. * * *

That such searches do not give rise to claims of constitutional violations rests not on the premise that they are "reasonable" under the Fourth Amendment, but on the premise that a person may voluntarily limit his expectation of privacy by allowing others to exercise authority over his possessions. Thus, an individual's decision to permit another "joint access [to] or control [over the property] for most purposes," *United States v. Matlock*, limits that individual's reasonable expectation of privacy and to that extent limits his Fourth Amendment protections. If an individual has not so limited his expectation of privacy, the police may not dispense with the safeguards established by the Fourth Amendment. * * *

I * * *

Unlike searches conducted pursuant to the recognized exceptions to the warrant requirement, third-party consent searches are not based on an exigency and therefore serve no compelling social goal. Police officers, when faced with the choice of relying on consent by a third party or securing a warrant, should secure a warrant and must therefore accept the risk of error should they instead choose to rely on consent.

II

Our prior cases discussing searches based on third-party consent have never suggested that such searches are "reasonable." In *United States v. Matlock*, this Court upheld a warrantless search conducted pursuant to the consent of a third party who was living with the defendant. The Court rejected the defendant's challenge to the search, stating that a person who permits others to have "joint access or control for most purposes * * * assume[s] the risk that [such persons] might permit the common area to be searched." As the Court's assumption-of-risk analysis makes clear, third-party consent limits a person's ability to challenge the reasonableness of the search only because that person voluntarily has relinquished some of his expectation of privacy by sharing access or control over his property with another person.

A search conducted pursuant to an officer's reasonable but mistaken belief that a third party had authority to consent is thus on an entirely different constitutional footing from one based on the consent of a third party who in fact has such authority. Even if the officers reasonably believed that Fischer had authority to consent, she did not, and Rodriguez's expectation of privacy was therefore undiminished. Rodriguez accordingly can challenge the warrantless intrusion into his home as a violation of the Fourth Amendment. * * *

III

* * * [T]he majority seeks to rely on cases suggesting that reasonable but mistaken factual judgments by police will not invalidate otherwise reasonable searches. * * *

* * * The cases the majority cites * * * provide no support for its holding. In *Brinegar v. United States*, for example, the Court confirmed the unremarkable proposition that police need only probable cause, not absolute certainty, to justify the arrest of a suspect on a highway. As *Brinegar* makes clear, the possibility of factual error is built into the probable cause standard, and such a standard, by its very definition, will in some cases result in the arrest of a suspect who has not actually committed a crime. Because probable cause defines the reasonableness of searches and seizures outside of the home, a search is reasonable under the Fourth Amendment whenever that standard is met, notwithstanding the possibility of "mistakes" on the part of police. * * *

The majority's reliance on *Maryland v. Garrison* is also misplaced. * * * As in *Brinegar*, the Court's decision was premised on the general reasonableness of the type of police action involved. Because searches based on warrants are generally reasonable, the officers' reasonable mistake of fact did not render their search "unreasonable." * * *

IV

* * * That a person who allows another joint access to his property thereby limits his expectation of privacy does not justify trampling the rights of a person who has not similarly relinquished any of his privacy expectation.

* * * [B]y allowing a person to be subjected to a warrantless search in his home without his consent and without exigency, the majority has taken away some of the liberty that the Fourth Amendment was designed to protect.

NOTES AND QUESTIONS

1. According to Justice Scalia, what is the justification for warrantless consent searches? Do you find the rationale in accord with *Schneckloth* and *Randolph*? Does Justice Marshall provide a plausible explanation of consent searches?

2. As developed at the trial court level and as is set out in the first paragraph of the Court's opinion, Gail Fischer told the police that she had clothing and some of her furniture at the apartment in question. Why would she have said this if it were her apartment? Don't these remarks put a reasonable officer on notice that this was not her apartment? In this regard, consider the following conversation between Michael R. Dreeben, who argued on behalf of the United States as *amicus curiae* in support of the State of Illinois, and Justices Stevens and O'Connor, during oral arguments in the *Rodriguez* case:

QUESTION: * * * [D]o you think the police officer had any duty to ask the young lady if she lived there? * * *

MR. DREEBEN: No. I don't think they did, Justice Stevens. And the reason that they didn't have a specific duty to ask that particular question is that they were summoned to the scene of what they understood was a battery victim. * * * They learned that she had been beaten by her boyfriend at an apartment that they—she described as "our apartment." There's testimony that she said that many of her things were there. * * *

QUESTION: Well, it would have been pretty simple for them to ask a few more questions, wouldn't it?

MR. DREEBEN: Yes, Justice O'Connor.

QUESTION: And, you're asking for an exception to the warrant requirement which is something paramount in the Fourth Amendment requirements. It seems to me you're suggesting that we just open the door wide without any corresponding obligation on the part of the police to make reasonable inquiry.

MR. DREEBEN: Justice O'Connor, I think it would be fully appropriate for this Court to hold that appropriate inquiry is necessary when the facts are ambiguous and clarification is what a reasonable police officer would do.

In your view, is this a case in which "the facts are ambiguous and clarification is what a reasonable police officer would do"?

3.   Does this case have Fourth Amendment implications that extend beyond consent searches? For example, suppose that when Rodriguez was arrested, the police conducted a search incident to the arrest and discovered additional contraband in a dresser drawer thirty feet away from the handcuffed arrestee. If you represented Rodriguez and sought to have that evidence suppressed, what would you argue? If you were the prosecutor, how would you respond, based on *Rodriguez*?

4.   *Scope of consent.* A consent search is invalid, even if the consent was voluntary, if the police exceed the scope of the consent granted. In Florida v. Jimeno, 500 U.S. 248, 111 S.Ct. 1801, 114 L.Ed.2d 297 (1991), Officer Trujillo, who had stopped Jimeno's car for a traffic violation, told Jimeno (based on earlier information) that he had reason to believe that Jimeno was carrying narcotics in the car. Trujillo asked permission to search the vehicle and reportedly received consent. In the search, the officer found a folded paper bag on the car's floorboard, which he opened. It contained cocaine. Jimeno moved to suppress the cocaine on the ground that his consent to search the car, even if voluntary, did not extend to the closed paper bag inside the car. The Court rejected the argument:

> The touchstone of the Fourth Amendment is reasonableness. The Fourth Amendment does not proscribe all state-initiated searches and seizures; it merely proscribes those which are unreasonable. *Illinois v. Rodriguez.* * * * The standard for measuring the scope of a suspect's consent under the Fourth

Amendment is that of "objective" reasonableness—what would the typical reasonable person have understood by the exchange between the officer and the suspect? The question before us, then, is whether it is reasonable for an officer to consider a suspect's general consent to a search of his car to include consent to examine a paper bag lying on the floor of the car. We think that it is.

The scope of a search is generally defined by its expressed object. In this case, the terms of the search's authorization were simple. Respondent granted Officer Trujillo permission to search his car, and did not place any explicit limitation on the scope of the search. Trujillo had informed Jimeno that he believed Jimeno was carrying narcotics, and that he would be looking for narcotics in the car. We think that it was objectively reasonable for the police to conclude that the general consent to search respondents' car included consent to search containers within that car which might bear drugs. A reasonable person may be expected to know that narcotics are generally carried in some form of a container. * * * The authorization to search in this case, therefore, extended beyond the surfaces of the car's interior to the paper bag lying on the car's floor.

The facts of this case are therefore different from those in *State v. Wells*, [539 So.2d 464 (1989)], on which the Supreme Court of Florida relied in affirming the suppression order in this case. There the Supreme Court of Florida held that consent to search the trunk of a car did not include authorization to pry open a locked briefcase found inside the trunk. It is very likely unreasonable to think that a suspect, by consenting to the search of his trunk, has agreed to the breaking open of a locked briefcase within the trunk, but it is otherwise with respect to a closed paper bag.

Did the Court adequately distinguish the facts in *Wells*? What if Trujillo had told Jimeno that he wanted to search the car for a stolen large-screen television set?

5.   *Problems*. In light of everything you have learned, what result in the following "consent" cases?

A.   *O* obtained consent to search *D*'s luggage at a train station. Inside the luggage, he found a can labeled "tamales in gravy." *O* shook the can and it seemed to contain a dry substance, like salt. *O* proceeded to break open the can and found a bag of methamphetamine. United States v. Osage, 235 F.3d 518 (10th Cir. 2000).

B.   A border agent received consent to "search" and "look in" the suspect's two mobile phones. When one phone rang, the agent answered it and pretended to be the defendant. This conversation produced evidence a prosecutor later sought to use in a smuggling prosecution. Is the evidence admissible? What if a text message, rather than a phone call, came during the mobile phone search: would the officer have a right to read the incoming message? United States v. Lopez-Cruz, 730 F.3d 803 (9th Cir. 2013).

C.   At 3:30 a.m., *S,* a passenger in a vehicle stopped in a public parking lot, voluntarily consented to a search of his person for drugs. As part of that search, one of the police officers pulled open the waistbands of *S*'s sweat pants and underwear and peered inside with a flashlight. *S* objected, but by the time he did, the officer has already observed the white cap of what appeared to be a pill bottle tucked in between *S*'s inner thigh and testicles. Should the pill bottle, which was seized, be suppressed? State v. Stone, 653 S.E.2d 414 (N.C. 2007).

D.   Police came to Victor's hotel room. They knocked. A woman answered. The officer asked, "Is Victor here?" According to the officer, the woman looked at him "funny—like a deer in the headlights type of look," and seemed "nervous" and "stunned." She replied, "I don't know." The officer told her truthfully that Victor asked for him to come to the hotel room. He asked consent to enter. She consented. The woman did not have authority over the premises. Is the consent valid? Commonwealth v. Lopez, 937 N.E.2d 949 (Mass. 2010).

E.   REASONABLENESS CLAUSE: THE DIMINISHING ROLES OF WARRANTS AND PROBABLE CAUSE

1.   THE *TERRY* DOCTRINE

a.   *Terry v. Ohio*: The Opinion

SCOTT E. SUNDBY—A RETURN TO FOURTH AMENDMENT BASICS: UNDOING THE MISCHIEF OF *CAMARA* AND *TERRY*
72 Minnesota Law Review 383 (1988), 383–95.

In its fourth amendment jurisprudence, the United States Supreme Court has struggled continually, and unsuccessfully, to develop a coherent analytical framework. * * *

* * * Many of the Court's present fourth amendment ills are symptoms of its failure to meet two basic challenges presented by the fourth amendment's text. First, the reasonableness clause's general proscription against "unreasonable searches and seizures" must be reconciled with the warrant clause's mandate that "no Warrants shall issue, but upon probable cause." Second, the concept of reasonableness must be defined to reflect the amendment's underlying values and purposes. * * *

The two challenges of fourth amendment interpretation are formidable standing alone, and the Court's decisions in *Camara v.*

Municipal Court[7] and *Terry v. Ohio*[8] have compounded the difficulty. Faced with novel fourth amendment questions, the Court in *Camara* and *Terry* turned to a broad reasonableness standard and an ill-defined balancing test for the immediate solutions. The combined effect of the *Camara* and *Terry* holdings, however, has proven to be something of a Faustian pact. The decisions allowed the fourth amendment's scope to extend to government activities like housing inspections, but in the process they significantly undermined the role of probable cause and set the stage for the long-term expansion of the reasonableness balancing test without proper justification or limits. * * *

I.   THE RISE OF REASONABLENESS IN FOURTH AMENDMENT ANALYSIS

A.   *When the Warrant Clause was King*

Prior to *Camara*, fourth amendment analysis had a relatively high amount of predictability: the Court presumed that a warrant based on probable cause was required before the police could perform a search or arrest. The Court's strong preference for the warrant requirement relegated the amendment's reasonableness clause, which bans "unreasonable searches and seizures," to a secondary role. The Court used the concept of reasonableness primarily to justify making an exception to the warrant requirement when exigent circumstances dictated excusing the police from procuring a warrant. Although reasonableness sometimes necessitated making an exception for obtaining a warrant, probable cause remained sacrosanct, immune from modification even in the name of reasonableness. * * *

The Court's almost exclusive focus on the warrant clause yielded predictability and strong protections, but it was not without costs. Because requiring a warrant based on probable cause would have precluded suspicionless government inspections, the Court did not extend the amendment's coverage very far beyond the context of criminal arrests and searches. When the fourth amendment governed, therefore, it provided the full protections of the warrant clause—but the protections generally did not apply to government intrusions other than criminal investigations.

The Court's warrant clause emphasis and corresponding reluctance to expand fourth amendment protections beyond criminal investigations largely explain its holding in *Frank v. Maryland*.[16] In *Frank* the Court

---

[7]   387 U.S. 523 (1967).

[8]   392 U.S. 1 (1968).

[16]   359 U.S. 360 (1959). In *Frank* a city health inspector looking for a source of rats in the neighborhood found the defendant's house in an "extreme state of decay" and asked the defendant's permission to inspect the basement. The defendant refused permission, and after a subsequent attempt to gain entry, the inspector swore out a complaint for the defendant's arrest based on a city code section providing:

addressed the issue whether the defendant's conviction for resisting a warrantless inspection of his house violated the fourth amendment. Upholding the conviction and fine, the *Frank* majority espoused the traditional view that if inspections like those at issue were subject to full fourth amendment protections, the search would have to satisfy the warrant requirement. Yet requiring a warrant based on probable cause for housing inspections would defeat the inspections' objective of maintaining community health. Resisting efforts to modify the warrant and probable cause requirements, the majority adopted an all-or-nothing view that if the Constitution required a search warrant, "the requirement [could not] be flexibly interpreted to dispense with the rigorous constitutional restrictions for its issue."

Consistent with the Court's warrant clause orientation, the *Frank* majority also argued that because Frank's asserted privacy interest did not concern a criminal investigation, his claim, at most, touched "upon the periphery" of the important fourth amendment interests protected against invasion by government officials. Stressing that the housing inspection was not a search for criminal evidence, Justice Frankfurter argued that the Constitution's prohibition against official invasion arose almost entirely from the individual's fundamental right to be secure from evidentiary searches made in connection with criminal prosecutions. The majority pointed to the historical acceptance of warrantless inspections, not as an enforcement mechanism of the criminal law, but "as an adjunct to a regulatory scheme for the general welfare." Consequently, the majority concluded that any legitimate liberty interest Frank had was overwhelmed by the government's need for inspection and the desirability of not tampering with the fourth amendment's rigorous protections.

B.   *Camara: Reasonableness Gets a Foot in the Door*

In *Camara v. Municipal Court*, the Court overruled its holding in *Frank* that the fourth amendment's full protections did not extend to housing inspections. Writing for the majority, Justice White rejected the "rather remarkable premise" in *Frank* that because housing inspections were not criminal investigations, they were merely on the periphery of the fourth amendment. He argued that inspection programs in fact went to the fourth amendment's central purpose of "safeguard[ing] the privacy and security of individuals against arbitrary invasions by government officials." Given that purpose, the majority concluded that it would be anomalous to suggest that an individual enjoys full fourth amendment protection only when suspected of criminal conduct.

"Whenever the Commissioner of Health shall have cause to suspect that a nuisance exists in any house, cellar or enclosure, he may demand entry therein in the day time, and if the owner or occupier shall refuse or delay to open the same and admit a free examination, he shall forfeit and pay for every such refusal the sum of Twenty Dollars."

Unshackling the fourth amendment from *Frank*'s restrictive reading of the amendment's purpose, however, was only the first step. The majority still had to address *Frank*'s perceived dilemma that application of the fourth amendment to administrative inspections would either dilute the amendment's protections or preclude blanket inspections altogether. In deciding how to apply the amendment, the Court did not adopt a new mode of fourth amendment analysis. Rather, it chose to assess the government inspection program within the traditional warrant and probable cause framework. Justifying its choice, the Court explained that it had adhered consistently to the governing principle that "[e]xcept in certain carefully defined classes of cases, a search of private property without proper consent is 'unreasonable' unless it has been authorized by a valid search warrant."

Having elected to continue its historical warrant clause emphasis, the necessity of modifying the clause's requirements to permit the housing inspections was evident. Traditional probable cause required facts sufficient to justify a reasonably cautious person in believing that another had committed or was committing a crime. Whether a search or arrest was reasonable depended at a minimum upon a showing of individualized suspicion amounting to probable cause. The fourth amendment would have precluded the government's power to conduct area housing inspections, a power all agreed was necessary, if probable cause required a showing of specific violations for each inspection. Consequently, the *Camara* majority redefined probable cause: rather than requiring individualized suspicion, probable cause was recast as standing for a broader concept of reasonableness based on a weighing of the governmental and individual interests. Under the new definition, probable cause existed and the warrant clause was satisfied once the Court concluded that the area housing inspections, although lacking individualized suspicion, were "reasonable." Probable cause, therefore, still served the formal function of a prerequisite for the issuance of a warrant, but its traditional requirement of particularized suspicion became merely one example of probable cause's meaning in a particular setting.

Ironically, in redefining probable cause as a flexible concept, the Court's effort to satisfy the warrant clause gave reasonableness a foot in the door as an independent factor in fourth amendment analysis. Prior to *Camara* the warrant clause had dictated the meaning of the reasonableness clause. A search or arrest was reasonable only when a warrant based on probable cause issued. *Camara*, in contrast, reversed the roles of probable cause and reasonableness. Instead of probable cause defining a reasonable search, after *Camara*, reasonableness, in the form of a balancing test, defined probable cause. Allowing reasonableness to define probable cause expanded the range of acceptable government behavior beyond intrusions based on individualized suspicion to include activities in which the government interest outweighed the individual's privacy interests. Reasonableness, in the form of a balancing test, had finally gained entrance into fourth amendment analysis, albeit through the back door of the warrant clause. * * *

Building upon *Camara*, the Court's decision in *Terry v. Ohio* provided reasonableness an even greater role as an independent factor in fourth amendment analysis.

JOSHUA DRESSLER & ALAN C. MICHAELS— UNDERSTANDING CRIMINAL PROCEDURE

(Volume 1) (Sixth edition 2013), 261–263.

The Fourth Amendment was once considered a monolith. "Probable cause" had a single meaning, and "searches" and "seizures" were all-or-nothing concepts. The monolith was cracked by the Supreme Court in *Camara v. Municipal Court*. In *Camara*, the justices recognized a different form of "probable cause," applicable to administrative-search cases, that does not require individualized suspicion and which is based on the general Fourth Amendment standard of "reasonableness." To determine "reasonableness," the *Camara* Court invoked a balancing test, in which the individual's and society's interests in a given type of administrative search were weighed against each other.

If *Camara* cracked the Fourth Amendment monolith, *Terry v. Ohio* broke it entirely. Although the issue in *Terry* was described by the Court as "quite narrow"—"whether it is always unreasonable for a policeman to seize a person and subject him to a limited search for weapons unless there is probable cause to arrest"—the significance of the case to Fourth Amendment jurisprudence is, quite simply, monumental. In terms of the daily activities of the police, as well as the experiences of persons "on the street," there is no Supreme Court Fourth Amendment case—not even *Katz v. United States*—of greater practical impact.

The significance of *Terry* will be seen in [the materials that follow], but a brief overview is appropriate. First, *Terry* transported *Camara*'s "reasonableness" balancing test from the realm of administrative searches to traditional criminal investigations, and used it to determine the reasonableness of certain warrantless searches and seizures, rather than merely to define "probable cause." The result has been a significant diminution in the role of the Warrant Clause in Fourth Amendment jurisprudence. That is, *Terry* provided the impetus, as well as the framework, for a move by the Supreme Court away from the proposition that "warrantless searches are *per se* unreasonable," to the competing view that the appropriate test of police conduct "is not whether it is reasonable to procure a search warrant, but whether the search was reasonable." Warrantless police conduct became much easier to justify after *Terry*.

Second, *Terry* recognized that searches and seizures can vary in their intrusiveness. The Court no longer treats all searches and all seizures alike. * * *

Third, as a corollary of the last point, because of *Terry* the police may now conduct a wide array of searches and seizures that are considered less-than-ordinarily intrusive, on the basis of a lesser standard of cause than "probable cause" * * * . * * *

At least one other aspect of *Terry* deserves note here. Professor Akhil Amar suggests that this case may provide "one of the most open Fourth Amendment discussions of race to date."[10] Whether or not this assertion is accurate,[11] there is no gainsaying that when the police forcibly stop persons on the street to question them or to conduct full or cursory searches, highly sensitive issues of racial profiling (and to a lesser extent, issues of ethnicity, class, and gender) come to the fore.

Some scholars believe that the *Terry* opinion (or, at least, the *Terry* doctrine as it has come to be interpreted over the years), and its move away from the warrant requirement, has done much to exacerbate racial tensions between the police and members of minority communities. Others believe that the Court's movement in this case to a reasonableness standard is good, in part because it will force courts to confront issues, such as race and class, "honestly and openly." Whoever is right in this regard, Chief Justice Earl Warren was surely correct when he observed in *Terry* that "[w]e would be less than candid if we did not acknowledge that this [case] thrusts to the fore, difficult and troublesome issues regarding a sensitive area of police activity."

TERRY V. OHIO

Supreme Court of the United States, 1968.
392 U.S. 1, 88 S.Ct. 1868, 20 L.Ed.2d 889.

MR. CHIEF JUSTICE WARREN delivered the opinion of the Court [joined by JUSTICES BLACK, HARLAN, BRENNAN, STEWART, WHITE, FORTAS, and MARSHALL]. * * *

Petitioner Terry was convicted of carrying a concealed weapon and sentenced to the statutorily prescribed term of one to three years in the penitentiary. * * * Officer McFadden testified that while he was patrolling in plain clothes in downtown Cleveland at approximately 2:30

---

[10] Akhil Reed Amar, *Fourth Amendment First Principles*, 107 Harv. L. Rev. 757, 808 (1994).

[11] It is not a universally held view. *E.g.*, Anthony C. Thompson, *Stopping the Usual Suspects: Race and the Fourth Amendment*, 74 N.Y.U. L. Rev. 956 (1999) (contending that the Supreme Court intentionally disguised the race-based aspects of the search and seizure in *Terry*).

in the afternoon of October 31, 1963, his attention was attracted by two men, Chilton and Terry, standing on the corner of Huron Road and Euclid Avenue. He had never seen the two men before, and he was unable to say precisely what first drew his eye to them. However, he testified that he had been a policeman for 39 years and a detective for 35 and that he had been assigned to patrol this vicinity of downtown Cleveland for shoplifters and pickpockets for 30 years. He explained that he had developed routine habits of observation over the years and that he would "stand and watch people or walk and watch people at many intervals of the day." He added: "Now, in this case when I looked over they didn't look right to me at the time."[e]

His interest aroused, Officer McFadden took up a post of observation in the entrance to a store 300 to 400 feet away from the two men. [He observed one of the men walk up the street, stop, peer into a store window, walk on, turn around, look in again, and then rejoin the second man and confer. The second man then repeated the process. This was done five or six times by each man.] At one point, while the two were standing together on the corner, a third man approached them and engaged them briefly in conversation. This man then left the two others and walked west on Euclid Avenue. Chilton and Terry resumed their measured pacing, peering, and conferring. After this had gone on for 10 to 12 minutes, the two men walked off together, heading west on Euclid Avenue, following the path taken earlier by the third man.

By this time Officer McFadden had become thoroughly suspicious. He testified that after observing their elaborately casual and oft-repeated reconnaissance of the store window on Huron Road, he suspected the two men of "casing a job, a stick-up," and that he considered it his duty as a police officer to investigate further. He added that he feared "they may have a gun." * * * Deciding that the situation was ripe for direct action, Officer McFadden approached the three men, identified himself as a police officer and asked for their names. At this point his knowledge was

---

[e]   Thirty years after the case, Terry's defense counsel remembers Officer McFadden's testimony as follows:

He was asked specifically what attracted him to them. On one occasion he said, "Well, to tell the truth, I just didn't like 'em." He was asked how long he'd been a police officer. "39 years." How long had he been a detective? "35 years." What did he think they were doing? "Well," he said, "I suspected that they were casing a joint for the purpose of robbing it." "Well," he was asked, "have you ever in your 39 years as a police officer, 35 as a detective, had the opportunity to observe anybody casing a place for a stickup?" He said, "No, I haven't." "Then what attracted you to them?" He indicated he just didn't like them.

Louis Stokes, *Representing John W. Terry*, 72 St. John's L. Rev. 727, 729–30 (1998).

As for McFadden himself, defense counsel Stokes respected him, *id.* at 729:

He was a real character—a tall, stately guy, and basically a good policeman. Mac, as we called him, was really a guy that we really liked. He was straight. One thing about him—as a police officer, he came straight down the line. You did not have to worry about him misrepresenting what the facts were.

confined to what he had observed. * * * When the men "mumbled something" in response to his inquiries, Officer McFadden grabbed petitioner Terry, spun him around so that they were facing the other two, with Terry between McFadden and the others, and patted down the outside of his clothing. In the left breast pocket of Terry's overcoat Officer McFadden felt a pistol. He * * * removed a .38-caliber revolver from the pocket and ordered all three men to face the wall with their hands raised. Officer McFadden proceeded to pat down the outer clothing of Chilton and the third man, Katz.[f] He discovered another revolver in the outer pocket of Chilton's overcoat, but no weapons were found on Katz. The officer testified that he only patted the men down to see whether they had weapons, and that he did not put his hands beneath the outer garments of either Terry or Chilton until he felt their guns. * * * Officer McFadden seized Chilton's gun, asked the proprietor of the store to call a police wagon, and took all three men to the station, where Chilton and Terry were formally charged with carrying concealed weapons. * * *

I * * *

* * * Unquestionably petitioner was entitled to the protection of the Fourth Amendment as he walked down the street in Cleveland. The question is whether in all the circumstances of this on-the-street encounter, his right to personal security was violated by an unreasonable search and seizure.

We would be less than candid if we did not acknowledge that this question thrusts to the fore difficult and troublesome issues regarding a sensitive area of police activity—issues which have never before been squarely presented to this Court. * * *

On the one hand, it is frequently argued that in dealing with the rapidly unfolding and often dangerous situations on city streets the police are in need of an escalating set of flexible responses, graduated in relation to the amount of information they possess. For this purpose it is urged that distinctions should be made between a "stop" and an "arrest" (or a "seizure" of a person), and between a "frisk" and a "search." Thus, it is argued, the police should be allowed to "stop" a person and detain him briefly for questioning upon suspicion that he may be connected with criminal activity. Upon suspicion that the person may be armed, the police should have the power to "frisk" him for weapons. If the "stop" and the "frisk" give rise to probable cause to believe that the suspect has committed a crime, then the police should be empowered to make a formal "arrest," and a full incident "search" of the person. This scheme is justified in part upon the notion that a "stop" and a "frisk" amount to a mere "minor inconvenience and petty indignity," which can properly be

---

[f]   Although the *Terry* opinion was not explicit, Terry and Chilton were African-Americans; Katz was white. *Id.* at 729.

imposed upon the citizen in the interest of effective law enforcement on the basis of a police officer's suspicion.

On the other side the argument is made that the authority of the police must be strictly circumscribed by the law of arrest and search as it has developed to date in the traditional jurisprudence of the Fourth Amendment. It is contended with some force that there is not—and cannot be—a variety of police activity which does not depend solely upon the voluntary cooperation of the citizen and yet which stops short of an arrest based upon probable cause to make such an arrest. The heart of the Fourth Amendment, the argument runs, is a severe requirement of specific justification for any intrusion upon protected personal security, coupled with a highly developed system of judicial controls to enforce upon the agents of the State the commands of the Constitution. Acquiescence by the courts in the compulsion inherent in the field interrogation practices at issue here, it is urged, would constitute an abdication of judicial control over, and indeed an encouragement of, substantial interference with liberty and personal security by police officers whose judgment is necessarily colored by their primary involvement in "the often competitive enterprise of ferreting out crime." This, it is argued, can only serve to exacerbate police-community tensions in the crowded centers of our Nation's cities.

In this context we approach the issues in this case mindful of the limitations of the judicial function in controlling the myriad daily situations in which policemen and citizens confront each other on the street. * * * Ever since its inception, the rule excluding evidence seized in violation of the Fourth Amendment has been recognized as a principal mode of discouraging lawless police conduct. * * *

The exclusionary rule has its limitations, however, as a tool of judicial control. It cannot properly be invoked to exclude the products of legitimate police investigative techniques on the ground that much conduct which is closely similar involves unwarranted intrusions upon constitutional protections. Moreover, in some contexts the rule is ineffective as a deterrent. Street encounters between citizens and police officers are incredibly rich in diversity. They range from wholly friendly exchanges of pleasantries or mutually useful information to hostile confrontations of armed men involving arrests, or injuries, or loss of life. Moreover, hostile confrontations are not all of a piece. Some of them begin in a friendly enough manner, only to take a different turn upon the injection of some unexpected element into the conversation. Encounters are initiated by the police for a wide variety of purposes, some of which are wholly unrelated to a desire to prosecute for crime. Doubtless some police "field interrogation" conduct violates the Fourth Amendment. But a stern refusal by this Court to condone such activity does not necessarily render it responsive to the exclusionary rule. Regardless of how effective the rule may be where obtaining convictions is an important objective of the police, it is powerless to deter invasions of constitutionally guaranteed rights where the police either have no interest in prosecuting or are willing to forgo successful prosecution in the interest of serving some other goal.

Proper adjudication of cases in which the exclusionary rule is invoked demands a constant awareness of these limitations. The wholesale harassment by certain elements of the police community, of which minority groups, particularly Negroes, frequently complain, will not be stopped by the exclusion of any evidence from any criminal trial. Yet a rigid and unthinking application of the exclusionary rule, in futile protest against practices which it can never be used effectively to control, may exact a high toll in human injury and frustration of efforts to prevent crime. No judicial opinion can comprehend the protean variety of the street encounter, and we can only judge the facts of the case before us. Nothing we say today is to be taken as indicating approval of police conduct outside the legitimate investigative sphere. Under our decision, courts still retain their traditional responsibility to guard against police conduct which is overbearing or harassing, or which trenches upon personal security without the objective evidentiary justification which the Constitution requires. When such conduct is identified, it must be condemned by the judiciary and its fruits must be excluded from evidence in criminal trials. And, of course, our approval of legitimate and restrained investigative conduct undertaken on the basis of ample factual justification should in no way discourage the employment of other remedies than the exclusionary rule to curtail abuses for which that sanction may prove inappropriate.

Having thus roughly sketched the perimeters of the constitutional debate over the limits on police investigative conduct in general and the background against which this case presents itself, we turn our attention to the quite narrow question posed by the facts before us: whether it is always unreasonable for a policeman to seize a person and subject him to a limited search for weapons unless there is probable cause for an arrest. * * *

II

Our first task is to establish at what point in this encounter the Fourth Amendment becomes relevant. That is, we must decide whether and when Officer McFadden "seized" Terry and whether and when he conducted a "search." There is some suggestion in the use of such terms as "stop" and "frisk" that such police conduct is outside the purview of the Fourth Amendment because neither action rises to the level of a "search" or "seizure" within the meaning of the Constitution. We emphatically reject this notion. It is quite plain that the Fourth Amendment governs "seizures" of the person which do not eventuate in a trip to the station house and prosecution for crime—"arrests" in traditional terminology. It must be recognized that whenever a police officer accosts an individual and restrains his freedom to walk away, he has "seized" that person. And it is nothing less than sheer torture of the English language to suggest that a careful exploration of the outer surfaces of a person's clothing all over his or her body in an attempt to find weapons is not a "search." Moreover, it is simply fantastic to urge that such a procedure performed in public by a policeman while the citizen stands helpless, perhaps facing a wall with his hands raised, is a "petty indignity."[13] It is a serious intrusion upon the sanctity of the person, which may inflict great indignity and arouse strong resentment, and it is not to be undertaken lightly.

The danger in the logic which proceeds upon distinctions between a "stop" and an "arrest," or "seizure" of the person, and between a "frisk" and a "search" is twofold. It seeks to isolate from constitutional scrutiny the initial stages of the contact between the policeman and the citizen. And by suggesting a rigid all-or-nothing model of justification and regulation under the Amendment, it obscures the utility of limitations upon the scope, as well as the initiation, of police action as a means of constitutional regulation. This Court has held in the past that a search which is reasonable at its inception may violate the Fourth Amendment by virtue of its intolerable intensity and scope. The scope of the search must be "strictly tied to and justified by" the circumstances which rendered its initiation permissible.

The distinctions of classical "stop-and-frisk" theory thus serve to divert attention from the central inquiry under the Fourth Amendment— the reasonableness in all the circumstances of the particular governmental invasion of a citizen's personal security. "Search" and "seizure" are not talismans. We therefore reject the notions that the Fourth Amendment does not come into play at all as a limitation upon police conduct if the officers stop short of something called a "technical arrest" or a "full-blown search."

In this case there can be no question, then, that Officer McFadden "seized" petitioner and subjected him to a "search" when he took hold of him and patted down the outer surfaces of his clothing. We must decide whether at that point it was reasonable for Officer McFadden to have

---

13   Consider the following apt description:

"[T]he officer must feel with sensitive fingers every portion of the prisoner's body. A thorough search must be made of the prisoner's arms and armpits, waistline and back, the groin and area about the testicles, and entire surface of the legs down to the feet." Priar & Martin, Searching and Disarming Criminals, 45 J. Crim. L. C. & P. S. 481 (1954).

interfered with petitioner's personal security as he did.[16] And in determining whether the seizure and search were "unreasonable" our inquiry is a dual one—whether the officer's action was justified at its inception, and whether it was reasonably related in scope to the circumstances which justified the interference in the first place.

III

If this case involved police conduct subject to the Warrant Clause of the Fourth Amendment, we would have to ascertain whether "probable cause" existed to justify the search and seizure which took place. However, that is not the case. We do not retreat from our holdings that the police must, whenever practicable, obtain advance judicial approval of searches and seizures through the warrant procedure, or that in most instances failure to comply with the warrant requirement can only be excused by exigent circumstances. But we deal here with an entire rubric of police conduct—necessarily swift action predicated upon the on-the-spot observations of the officer on the beat—which historically has not been, and as a practical matter could not be, subjected to the warrant procedure. Instead, the conduct involved in this case must be tested by the Fourth Amendment's general proscription against unreasonable searches and seizures.

Nonetheless, the notions which underlie both the warrant procedure and the requirement of probable cause remain fully relevant in this context. In order to assess the reasonableness of Officer McFadden's conduct as a general proposition, it is necessary "first to focus upon the governmental interest which allegedly justifies official intrusion upon the constitutionally protected interests of the private citizen," for there is "no ready test for determining reasonableness other than by balancing the need to search [or seize] against the invasion which the search [or seizure] entails." *Camara v. Municipal Court*, 387 U.S. 523, 534–535, 536–537, 87 S.Ct. 1727, 1735, 18 L.Ed.2d 930 (1967). And in justifying the particular intrusion the police officer must be able to point to specific and articulable facts which, taken together with rational inferences from those facts, reasonably warrant that intrusion. The scheme of the Fourth Amendment becomes meaningful only when it is assured that at some point the conduct of those charged with enforcing the laws can be subjected to the more detached, neutral scrutiny of a judge who must

---

[16] We thus decide nothing today concerning the constitutional propriety of an investigative "seizure" upon less than probable cause for purposes of "detention" and/or interrogation. Obviously, not all personal intercourse between policemen and citizens involves "seizures" of persons. Only when the officer, by means of physical force or show of authority, has in some way restrained the liberty of a citizen may we conclude that a "seizure" has occurred. We cannot tell with any certainty upon this record whether any such "seizure" took place here prior to Officer McFadden's initiation of physical contact for purposes of searching Terry for weapons, and we thus may assume that up to that point no intrusion upon constitutionally protected rights had occurred.

evaluate the reasonableness of a particular search or seizure in light of the particular circumstances. And in making that assessment it is imperative that the facts be judged against an objective standard: would the facts available to the officer at the moment of the seizure or the search "warrant a man of reasonable caution in the belief" that the action taken was appropriate? * * * Anything less would invite intrusions upon constitutionally guaranteed rights based on nothing more substantial than inarticulate hunches, a result this Court has consistently refused to sanction. * * *

Applying these principles to this case, we consider first the nature and extent of the governmental interests involved. One general interest is of course that of effective crime prevention and detection; it is this interest which underlies the recognition that a police officer may in appropriate circumstances and in an appropriate manner approach a person for purposes of investigating possibly criminal behavior even though there is no probable cause to make an arrest. It was this legitimate investigative function Officer McFadden was discharging when he decided to approach petitioner and his companions. He had observed Terry, Chilton, and Katz go through a series of acts, each of them perhaps innocent in itself, but which taken together warranted further investigation. There is nothing unusual in two men standing together on a street corner, perhaps waiting for someone. Nor is there anything suspicious about people in such circumstances strolling up and down the street, singly or in pairs. Store windows, moreover, are made to be looked in. But the story is quite different where, as here, two men hover about a street corner for an extended period of time, at the end of which it becomes apparent that they are not waiting for anyone or anything; where these men pace alternately along an identical route, pausing to stare in the same store window roughly 24 times; where each completion of this route is followed immediately by a conference between the two men on the corner; where they are joined in one of these conferences by a third man who leaves swiftly; and where the two men finally follow the third and rejoin him a couple of blocks away. It would have been poor police work indeed for an officer of 30 years' experience in the detection of thievery from stores in this same neighborhood to have failed to investigate this behavior further.

The crux of this case, however, is not the propriety of Officer McFadden's taking steps to investigate petitioner's suspicious behavior, but rather, whether there was justification for McFadden's invasion of Terry's personal security by searching him for weapons in the course of that investigation. We are now concerned with more than the governmental interest in investigating crime; in addition, there is the more immediate interest of the police officer in taking steps to assure himself that the person with whom he is dealing is not armed with a weapon that could unexpectedly and fatally be used against him. Certainly it would be unreasonable to require that police officers take unnecessary risks in the performance of their duties. American criminals have a long tradition of armed violence, and every year in this country many law enforcement officers are killed in the line of duty, and thousands more are wounded. Virtually all of these deaths and a substantial portion of the injuries are inflicted with guns and knives.

In view of these facts, we cannot blind ourselves to the need for law enforcement officers to protect themselves and other prospective victims of violence in situations where they may lack probable cause for an arrest. When an officer is justified in believing that the individual whose suspicious behavior he is investigating at close range is armed and presently dangerous to the officer or to others, it would appear to be clearly unreasonable to deny the officer the power to take necessary measures to determine whether the person is in fact carrying a weapon and to neutralize the threat of physical harm.

We must still consider, however, the nature and quality of the intrusion on individual rights which must be accepted if police officers are to be conceded the right to search for weapons in situations where probable cause to arrest for crime is lacking. Even a limited search of the outer clothing for weapons constitutes a severe, though brief, intrusion upon cherished personal security, and it must surely be an annoying, frightening, and perhaps humiliating experience. * * *

Petitioner * * * says it is unreasonable for the policeman to [frisk a suspect] * * * until such time as the situation evolves to a point where there is probable cause to make an arrest. * * *

There are two weaknesses in this line of reasoning, however. First, it fails to take account of traditional limitations upon the scope of searches, and thus recognizes no distinction in purpose, character, and extent between a search incident to an arrest and a limited search for weapons. The former, although justified in part by the acknowledged necessity to protect the arresting officer from assault with a concealed weapon, is also justified on other grounds, and can therefore involve a relatively extensive exploration of the person. A search for weapons in the absence of probable cause to arrest, however, must, like any other search, be strictly circumscribed by the exigencies which justify its initiation. Thus it must be limited to that which is necessary for the discovery of weapons which might be used to harm the officer or others nearby, and may realistically be characterized as something less than a "full" search, even though it remains a serious intrusion.

A second, and related, objection to petitioner's argument is that it assumes that the law of arrest has already worked out the balance between the particular interests involved here—the neutralization of danger to the policeman in the investigative circumstance and the sanctity of the individual. But this is not so. An arrest is a wholly different kind of intrusion upon individual freedom from a limited search for weapons, and the interests each is designed to serve are likewise quite different. An arrest is the initial stage of a criminal prosecution. It is intended to vindicate society's interest in having its laws obeyed, and it is inevitably accompanied by future interference with the individual's freedom of movement, whether or not trial or conviction ultimately follows. The protective search for weapons, on the other hand, constitutes a brief, though far from inconsiderable, intrusion upon the sanctity of the person. * * *

Our evaluation of the proper balance that has to be struck in this type of case leads us to conclude that there must be a narrowly drawn authority to permit a reasonable search for weapons for the protection of the police officer, where he has reason to believe that he is dealing with an armed and dangerous individual, regardless of whether he has probable cause to arrest the individual for a crime. The officer need not be absolutely certain that the individual is armed; the issue is whether a reasonably prudent man in the circumstances would be warranted in the belief that his safety or that of others was in danger. And in determining whether the officer acted reasonably in such circumstances, due weight must be given, not to his inchoate and unparticularized suspicion or "hunch," but to the specific reasonable inferences which he is entitled to draw from the facts in light of his experience.

IV

* * * We think on the facts and circumstances Officer McFadden detailed before the trial judge a reasonably prudent man would have been warranted in believing petitioner was armed and thus presented a threat to the officer's safety while he was investigating his suspicious behavior. The actions of Terry and Chilton were consistent with McFadden's hypothesis that these men were contemplating a daylight robbery—which, it is reasonable to assume, would be likely to involve the use of weapons—and nothing in their conduct from the time he first noticed them until the time he confronted them and identified himself as a police officer gave him sufficient reason to negate that hypothesis. Although the trio had departed the original scene, there was nothing to indicate abandonment of an intent to commit a robbery at some point. Thus, when Officer McFadden approached the three men gathered before the display window at Zucker's store he had observed enough to make it quite reasonable to fear that they were armed; and nothing in their response to his hailing them, identifying himself as a police officer, and asking their names served to dispel that reasonable belief. * * *

The manner in which the seizure and search were conducted is, of course, as vital a part of the inquiry as whether they were warranted at all. The Fourth Amendment proceeds as much by limitations upon the scope of governmental action as by imposing preconditions upon its initiation. * * *

We need not develop at length in this case, however, the limitations which the Fourth Amendment places upon a protective seizure and search for weapons. These limitations will have to be developed in the concrete factual circumstances of individual cases. * * * Suffice it to note that such a search, unlike a search without a warrant incident to a lawful arrest, is not justified by any need to prevent the disappearance or destruction of evidence of crime. The sole justification of the search in the present situation is the protection of the police officer and others nearby, and it must therefore be confined in scope to an intrusion reasonably designed to discover guns, knives, clubs, or other hidden instruments for the assault of the police officer.

The scope of the search in this case presents no serious problem in light of these standards. Officer McFadden patted down the outer clothing of petitioner and his two companions. He did not place his hands in their pockets or under the outer surface of their garments until he had felt weapons, and then he merely reached for and removed the guns. * * * Officer McFadden confined his search strictly to what was minimally necessary to learn whether the men were armed and to disarm them once he discovered the weapons. He did not conduct a general exploratory search for whatever evidence of criminal activity he might find.

V

We conclude that the revolver seized from Terry was properly admitted in evidence against him. At the time he seized petitioner and searched him for weapons, Officer McFadden had reasonable grounds to believe that petitioner was armed and dangerous, and it was necessary for the protection of himself and others to take swift measures to discover the true facts and neutralize the threat of harm if it materialized. The policeman carefully restricted his search to what was appropriate to the discovery of the particular items which he sought. Each case of this sort will, of course, have to be decided on its own facts. We merely hold today that where a police officer observes unusual conduct which leads him reasonably to conclude in light of his experience that criminal activity may be afoot and that the persons with whom he is dealing may be armed and presently dangerous, where in the course of investigating this behavior he identifies himself as a policeman and makes reasonable inquiries, and where nothing in the initial stages of the encounter serves to dispel his reasonable fear for his own or others' safety, he is entitled for the protection of himself and others in the area to conduct a carefully limited search of the outer clothing of such persons in an attempt to discover weapons which might be used to assault him. Such a search is a reasonable search under the Fourth Amendment, and any weapons seized may properly be introduced in evidence against the person from whom they were taken.

Affirmed.

[JUSTICE BLACK concurred in the judgment and CHIEF JUSTICE WARREN'S opinion except as to matters omitted from the excerpt above.]

MR. JUSTICE HARLAN, concurring.

While I unreservedly agree with the Court's ultimate holding in this case, I am constrained to fill in a few gaps, as I see them, in its opinion. * * *

In the first place, if the frisk is justified in order to protect the officer during an encounter with a citizen, the officer must first have constitutional grounds to insist on an encounter, to make a *forcible* stop. Any person, including a policeman, is at liberty to avoid a person he considers dangerous. If and when a policeman has a right instead to disarm such a person for his own protection, he must first have a right not to avoid him but to be in his presence. That right must be more than the liberty (again, possessed by every citizen) to address questions to other persons, for ordinarily the person addressed has an equal right to ignore his interrogator and walk away; he certainly need not submit to a frisk for the questioner's protection. I would make it perfectly clear that the right to frisk in this case depends upon the reasonableness of a forcible stop to investigate a suspected crime.

Where such a stop is reasonable, however, the right to frisk must be immediate and automatic if the reason for the stop is, as here, an articulable suspicion of a crime of violence. Just as a full search incident to a lawful arrest requires no additional justification, a limited frisk incident to a lawful stop must often be rapid and routine. There is no reason why an officer, rightfully but forcibly confronting a person suspected of a serious crime, should have to ask one question and take the risk that the answer might be a bullet. * * *

MR. JUSTICE WHITE, concurring.

* * * I think an additional word is in order concerning the matter of interrogation during an investigative stop. There is nothing in the Constitution which prevents a policeman from addressing questions to anyone on the street. * * * Of course, the person stopped is not obliged to answer, and answers may not be compelled, and refusal to answer furnishes no basis for an arrest, although it may alert the officer to the need for continued observation. * * *

MR. JUSTICE DOUGLAS, dissenting. * * *

The opinion of the Court disclaims the existence of "probable cause."
* * * Had a warrant been sought, a magistrate would * * * have been
unauthorized to issue one, for he can act only if there is a showing of
"probable cause." We hold today that the police have greater authority to
make a "seizure" and conduct a "search" than a judge has to authorize
such action. We have said precisely the opposite over and over again.

* * * [P]olice officers up to today have been permitted to effect arrests
or searches without warrants only when the facts within their personal
knowledge would satisfy the constitutional standard of *probable cause.*
* * * The term "probable cause" rings a bell of certainty that is not
sounded by phrases such as "reasonable suspicion." Moreover, the
meaning of "probable cause" is deeply imbedded in our constitutional
history. * * *

To give the police greater power than a magistrate is to take a long
step down the totalitarian path. Perhaps such a step is desirable to cope
with modern forms of lawlessness. But if it is taken, it should be the
deliberate choice of the people through a constitutional amendment. * * *

NOTES AND QUESTIONS

1.   *Follow-up tidbit.* At about the time the Court was hearing the *Terry*
case, Terry was confined to an asylum for the criminally insane; and prior to
the Court hearing, Chilton was shot to death while perpetrating a robbery in
Columbus, Ohio. Reuben M. Payne, *The Prosecutor's Perspective on Terry:
Detective McFadden Had a Right to Protect Himself*, 72 St. John's L. Rev.
733, 733 (1998). McFadden did take the third individual (Katz) into custody,
but no charges were brought against him.

2.   *What happened to probable cause?* Officer McFadden clearly did not
have time to obtain a warrant to search Terry, Chilton, and Katz. The
Supreme Court, therefore, could uncontroversially have justified the lack of a
warrant on the basis of exigency, but how does the Chief Justice explain
away the probable cause requirement?

3.   *Thinking about the implications of Terry.* Professor Akhil Amar has
written that there are "in effect two inconsistent *Terry* opinions," a "good
Terry" and "bad *Terry*." Akhil Reed Amar, *Terry and Fourth Amendment First
Principles*, 72 St. John's L. Rev. 1097, 1097 (1998). He has described the
"good *Terry*" opinion this way:

> First, it embraced a broad definition of "searches" and "seizures,"
> enabling the Fourth Amendment to apply to myriad ways in which
> government might intrude upon citizens' persons, houses, papers,
> and effects. Second, the good *Terry* did not insist that all such
> broadly defined searches and seizures be preceded by warrants.
> Third, and more dramatic still, the good *Terry* did not insist that all

warrantless intrusions be justified by probable cause. The stunning logical lesson of the good *Terry* is thus that a warrantless search or seizure may sometimes lawfully occur in a situation where a warrant could not issue (because probable cause is lacking). Fourth, in place of the misguided notions that every search or seizure always requires a warrant, and always requires probable cause, the good *Terry* insisted that the Fourth Amendment means what it says and says what it means: All searches and seizures must be reasonable. Reasonableness—not the warrant, not probable cause— thus emerged as the central Fourth Amendment mandate and touchstone. Fifth, the good *Terry* identified some of the basic components of Fourth Amendment reasonableness so that the concept would make common sense and constitutional sense. Reasonable intrusions must be *proportionate* to legitimate governmental purposes—more intrusive government action requires more justification. Reasonableness must focus not only on privacy and secrecy but also on *bodily integrity* and *personal dignity*: Cops act unreasonably not just when they paw through my pockets without good reason, but also when they beat me up for fun or toy with me for sport. Reasonableness also implicates *race*—a complete Fourth Amendment analysis, the good *Terry* insisted, must be sensitive to the possibility of racial oppression and harassment. If we wrongly think that the basic Fourth Amendment mandates are warrants and probable cause, we will have difficulty explicitly factoring race into the equation, but the spacious concept of reasonableness allows us to look race square in the eye, constitutionally.

Id. at 1098–1099.

Do you applaud some or all of these features of *Terry*?

Professor Scott Sundby is less enamored with *Terry,* particularly with its departure from the probable cause requirement:

It is mighty hard to argue with reasonableness. * * * After all, a flexible "reasonableness" based Fourth Amendment standard holds forth the promise of both accommodating a wide variety of governmental interests * * * while still being able to address a myriad of concerns about government overstepping * * * . * * *

Let me suggest, however, that when it comes to the Fourth Amendment there can be an unreasonable side to reasonableness, that "more can be less." * * *

My limited goal * * * is to suggest that if one looks at the Fourth Amendment's underlying values, in particular the value of mutual "government-citizen trust," probable cause should be viewed as a norm for a "reasonable" search or seizure. Consequently, any departures from probable cause should be deemed "reasonable" only as limited exceptions allowed under narrow circumstances. * * *

Viewing the Fourth Amendment as founded only upon privacy as a bedrock value * * * is to ignore that the Amendment is part of a larger constitutional setting. Once placed within a broader context of our whole constitutional system, the Amendment becomes much more than merely a constitutional outpost for individual privacy. Instead, the Amendment also becomes part of the mutually reinforcing consent that flows between the citizenry and the government, a form of reciprocal trust: The citizenry gives its consent and trust to the government to be governed and the government, in turn, trusts the citizenry to exercise its liberties responsibly. * * *

This idea of trust is why probable cause must be the center of the Fourth Amendment universe rather than * * * merely one satellite in orbit around a general reasonableness balancing test.

Scott E. Sundby, *An Ode to Probable Cause: A Brief Response to Professors Amar and Slobogin*, 72 St. John's L. Rev. 1133, 1133–1135, 1137–1138 (1998).

4. *Terry and race.* Professor Amar applauded *Terry* for bringing race into the Fourth Amendment picture (Note 3). Not everyone, however, believes that *Terry* handled the race issue adequately. Critics of *Terry* have argued that it effectively authorized disproportionate numbers of detentions and frisks of innocent persons of color. We will come back to this issue shortly (p. 443, Note 7), but consider here Tracey Maclin, *Terry v. Ohio's Fourth Amendment Legacy: Black Men and Police Discretion*, 72 St. John's L. Rev. 1271, 1275–1276, 1285–1287 (1998):

When one examines the history and modern exercise of police "stop and frisk" practices, the old adage "the more things change, the more they stay the same," aptly describes the experience of many black men when confronted by police officers. Before the "due process revolution" of the 1960s, a retired, white Detroit police officer told the United States Civil Rights Commission the following:

I would estimate—and this I have heard in the station also—that if you stop and search 50 Negroes and you get one good arrest out of it that's a good percentage; it's a good day's work. So, in my opinion, there are 49 Negroes whose rights have been misused, and that goes on every day.

* * * [T]hings have not changed much; black men continue to be subjected to arbitrary searches and "frisks" by police. * * *

The irony, of course, is that the police power to "frisk" suspicious persons is the product of a Supreme Court that did more to promote the legal rights of black Americans than any other court. The Warren Court, led by Chief Justice Earl Warren, played an instrumental role in ending racial * * * discrimination in the United States. * * *

Thus, it seems paradoxical to criticize the Warren Court as insensitive to the experience of blacks, particularly blacks targeted by police officials. Yet, the Court's ruling in *Terry v. Ohio*, which upheld the power of police to "frisk" persons they suspect are dangerous, merits criticism. * * *

My view that *Terry* was wrongly decided emanates from three propositions which bear emphasis. First, long before *Terry* came to the Court, the law was settled on the amount of evidence needed for a warrantless search. In a string of cases involving car searches, the Court left no doubt that the Fourth Amendment required probable cause of criminal conduct before officers could search the inside of a car. * * * If probable cause was the constitutional minimum to justify a car search, then surely an equivalent degree of evidence is required before that officer can undertake "a careful exploration of the outer surfaces of a person's clothing all over his or her body in an attempt to find weapons." * * *

Second, presenting the issue in *Terry* as a conflict between "police safety" and individual freedom, misunderstands the reality of street encounters. No matter how the Court ruled in *Terry*, police officers would continue frisking people they viewed as a threat to their safety. Once this pragmatic fact was conceded, the crucial question in *Terry* was who would bear the burden when officers searched without probable cause: The government, which would suffer the suppression of evidence, or the individual, who was the target of a search forbidden by the Constitution?

Finally, the *Terry* Court succumbed to pressure to weaken constitutional principle when it was clear that many politicians, and a large segment of the public, had signaled their disapproval of the Court's effort to extend meaningful constitutional protection to those who needed it the most: Poor and minority persons suspected of criminal behavior. A more confident Court would have surveyed the legal landscape, recognized that stop and frisk practices could not be reconciled with a robust Fourth Amendment, and begun the fight to ensure that blacks, the poor, and other "undesirables," would enjoy the same constitutional privileges possessed by the elite of American society.

Tracey Maclin, *Terry v. Ohio's Fourth Amendment Legacy: Black Men and Police Discretion*, 72 St. John's L. Rev. 1271, 1275–1276, 1285–1287 (1998).

5.   Suppose that a police officer, based on her personal observations, reasonably suspects (but lacks probable cause to believe) that a customer in a store is about to shoplift some merchandise. Applying *Terry*, may the officer

briefly detain the customer for questioning? May she pat down the suspected shoplifter?

6. *The "Terry doctrine" after a crime has been committed. Terry* and nearly all cases interpreting it have involved circumstances in which the police believed "crime was afoot." In United States v. Hensley, 469 U.S. 221, 105 S.Ct. 675, 83 L.Ed.2d 604 (1985), the Court unanimously ruled that the *Terry* doctrine also applies when an officer seeks to investigate a *completed* felony: Stops are allowed if the "police have a reasonable suspicion, grounded in specific and articulable facts, that a person they encounter was involved in or is wanted in connection with a completed felony." Left open is under what circumstances a *Terry* stop is justified to investigate a completed minor offense.

7. *Pat-downs (part 1).* When a frisk is permissible under *Terry*, what may the officer do when she feels some object during the pat-down? You will remember (p. 405, Note 2) that the Court recognized a "plain touch" doctrine in Minnesota v. Dickerson, 508 U.S. 366, 113 S.Ct. 2130, 124 L.Ed.2d 334 (1993). Consider how the officer in *Dickerson* conducted the frisk (you may assume the officer had a right to conduct the pat-down):

> The officers pulled their squad car into the alley and ordered respondent to stop and submit to a patdown search. The search revealed no weapons, but the officer conducting the search did take an interest in a small lump in respondent's nylon jacket. The officer later testified:
>
>> "[A]s I pat-searched the front of his body, I felt a lump, a small lump, in the front pocket. I examined it with my fingers and it slid and it felt to be a lump of crack cocaine in cellophane."
>
> The officer then reached into respondent's pocket and retrieved a small plastic bag containing one fifth of one gram of crack cocaine.

Although the officer in *Dickerson* had grounds to pat-down the suspect, the Court held that the crack cocaine here was improperly seized:

> [T]he dispositive question before this Court is whether the officer who conducted the search was acting within the lawful bounds marked by *Terry* at the time he gained probable cause to believe that the lump in respondent's jacket was contraband. * * * The Minnesota Supreme Court, after "a close examination of the record," held that the officer's own testimony "belies any notion that he 'immediately'" recognized the lump as crack cocaine. Rather, the court concluded, the officer determined that the lump was contraband only after "squeezing, sliding and otherwise manipulating the contents of the defendant's pocket"—a pocket which the officer already knew contained no weapon.
>
> Under the State Supreme Court's interpretation of the record before it, it is clear that the court was correct in holding that the police officer in this case overstepped the bounds of the "strictly

circumscribed" search for weapons allowed under *Terry*. * * * Here, the officer's continued exploration of respondent's pocket after having concluded that it contained no weapon was unrelated to "[t]he sole justification of the search [under *Terry*:] * * * the protection of the police officer and others nearby." It therefore amounted to the sort of evidentiary search that *Terry* expressly refused to authorize * * *.

8. *Pat-downs (part 2)*. Do you agree with the *Terry* Court that pat-down searches are less intrusive than so-called "full searches"? Forced to choose, would *you* rather be required to empty your trouser pockets (a full search) or have your body patted-down? In a concurring opinion in *Dickerson*, *id.*, Justice Scalia expressed misgivings with this aspect of *Terry*:

> I frankly doubt * * * whether the fiercely proud men who adopted our Fourth Amendment would have allowed themselves to be subjected, on mere *suspicion* of being armed and dangerous, to such indignity [as a frisk] * * *. * * * On the other hand, even if a "frisk" prior to arrest would have been considered impermissible in 1791, perhaps it was considered permissible by 1868, when the Fourteenth Amendment (the basis for applying the Fourth Amendment to the States) was adopted. Or perhaps it is only since that time that concealed weapons capable of harming the interrogator quickly and from beyond arm's reach have become common—which might alter the judgment of what is "reasonable" under the original standard. But technological changes were no more discussed in *Terry* than was the original state of the law.

> If I were of the view that *Terry* was (insofar as the power to "frisk" is concerned) incorrectly decided, I might—even if I felt bound to adhere to that case—vote to exclude the evidence incidentally discovered, on the theory that half a constitutional guarantee is better than none. * * * As a policy matter, it may be desirable to *permit* "frisks" for weapons, but not to *encourage* "frisks" for drugs by admitting evidence other than weapons.

What do you think of Scalia's half-a-constitutional-right suggestion?

9. *Pat-downs (part 3)*. In a state where it is not illegal to carry a firearm, what if a police officer asks a person on the street, "Are you carrying a firearm?," and the individuals says "yes." Under *Terry*, may the officer now non-consensually pat-down the individual? State v. Serna, 331 P.3d 405 (Ariz. 2014). Look carefully at the language in the *Terry* opinion. Can you see an argument for the view that such a pat-down violates the Fourth Amendment?

10. *Pat-downs (part 4)*. At 2:15 a.m., the police received a tip (not amounting to probable cause, but you may assume for current purposes constituting reasonable suspicion) that a man seated in a nearby vehicle was carrying narcotics and had a gun at his waist. The officer, *O*, approached the

vehicle to investigate. He tapped on the car window and asked the occupant, W, to open the door. Instead, W rolled down the window. When he did, O reached inside the car and—without conducting a pat-down—removed a revolver from W's waistband. (The gun was not visible to O, but it was in precisely the place indicated by his informant. W, charged with illegal possession of a handgun, moved to suppress the weapon.)

The Supreme Court in Adams v. Williams, 407 U.S. 143, 92 S.Ct. 1921, 32 L.Ed.2d 612 (1972), upheld O's actions. Why would the Court have authorized this non-pat-down search under the principles of *Terry*? Beyond the pat-down issue, if you had represented W, can you think of another argument you could have made, based solely on language found in the majority opinion in *Terry*, to argue that O acted unlawfully?

11. *When the purpose of the seizure changes: traffic stops that become something more.* The Court stated in *Terry* (end of Part II) that "in determining whether the seizure and search were 'unreasonable' our inquiry is a dual one—whether the officer's action was justified at its inception, and whether it was reasonably related in scope to the circumstances which justified the interference in the first place." In *Terry*, Officer McFadden seized Terry and the other suspects in order to investigate a possible imminent robbery; the subsequent pat-down weapons search was reasonably related in scope to the purpose of the initial seizure. In contrast, in *Minnesota v. Dickerson* (Note 7), a pat-down for weapons that turned into a pat-down for drugs fell outside the scope of the *Terry* doctrine and, therefore, was unreasonable.

What if the police temporarily detain a person lawfully on a traffic violation, and then use the opportunity to conduct an investigation unrelated to the reason for the original detention? For example, in Illinois v. Caballes, 543 U.S. 405, 125 S.Ct. 834, 160 L.Ed.2d 842 (2005), the police lawfully stopped C, an automobile driver, to write a warning ticket for speeding. While the vehicle was by the roadside, another officer used a "well-trained narcotics-detection dog" to sniff the vehicle for drugs. The police lacked reasonable suspicion to believe that the vehicle contained drugs.

Notice that use of the dog was unrelated to the original justification for the vehicle stop. According to the defense, therefore, "the use of the dog converted the citizen-police encounter from a lawful traffic stop into a drug investigation, and because the shift in purpose was not supported by any reasonable suspicion that [C] possessed narcotics, it was unlawful."

The Court, 6–2, rejected this argument. Writing for the majority, Justice Stevens stated that using a dog to sniff for drugs does "not change the character of a traffic stop that is lawful at its inception and otherwise executed in a reasonable manner, unless the dog sniff itself infringed [C's] constitutionally protected interest in privacy." Here, "any interest in possessing contraband cannot be deemed legitimate," and thus, governmental conduct that *only* reveals the possession of contraband "compromises no legitimate privacy interest."

Justice Ginsburg, joined by Justice Souter, disagreed:

A drug-detection dog is an intimidating animal. Injecting such an animal into a routine traffic stop changes the character of the encounter between the police and the motorist. The stop becomes broader, more adversarial, and (in at least some cases) longer. [C] * * * was exposed to the embarrassment and intimidation of being investigated, on a public thoroughfare, for drugs. Even if the drug sniff is not characterized as a Fourth Amendment "search," the sniff surely broadened the scope of the traffic-violation-related seizure.

Justice Stevens *did* warn in *Caballes* that "a seizure that is justified solely by the interest in issuing a warning ticket can become unlawful if it is prolonged beyond the time reasonably required to complete that mission." Here, however, the state courts determined that the dog-sniffing procedure did not extend the duration of *C*'s seizure.

In Rodriguez v. United States, 575 U.S. ___, 135 S.Ct. 1609, 191 L.Ed.2d 492 (2015), however, Justice Stevens's warning became doctrine. Here, a police officer stopped a vehicle containing two men because it had veered onto a highway shoulder for one or two seconds, in violation of a state law prohibiting driving on highway shoulders. The officer asked the driver why he had driven onto the shoulder (the driver said he was avoiding a pothole); he then gathered the driver's license, registration and proof of insurance, and conducted a records check (no problems found); and then he obtained the passenger's license for a records check (no problems found) and questioned him as to where the two men were coming from and where they were going. At that point, the police officer issues a written traffic warning and returned all of the documents. Twenty-two minutes from the initial stop had elapsed. At this point, although the officer lacked reasonable suspicion to suspect that the automobile contained narcotics, he ordered the occupants out of the car, and eight minutes later, a dog sniffed the vehicle and indicated the presence of drugs.

The Supreme Court, 6–3 per Justice Ginsburg, held that Rodriguez's Fourth Amendment rights had been violated. She stated that a routine traffic stop is comparable to a brief *Terry v. Ohio* seizure. As part of such a stop, Ginsburg explained, ordinary inquiries incident to a traffic stop—*e.g.*, checking the driver's license, determining whether there are any outstanding warrants against the driver, and inspecting the automobile's registration and proof of insurance—are permitted. Here, however, all of that had been completed before the dog was brought to the scene. This latter process (in the language of *Caballes*) "prolonged * * * the time reasonably required to complete th[e] mission" of issuing the warning ticket.

The Government argued (and the dissent agreed) that the officer effectively was being penalized because he had "expeditiously" completed all of the traffic-related tasks. As Justice Ginsburg put it, this argument meant that "an officer can earn bonus time to pursue an unrelated criminal investigation." But, she said, "[t]he reasonableness of a seizure * * * depends on what the police in fact do. * * * The critical question * * * is not whether the dog sniff occurs before or after the officer issues a ticket, * * * but whether conducting the sniff 'prolongs'—*i.e.*, adds time to—'the stop.' "

12. *Problem.* Consider the facts in Sibron v. New York, 392 U.S. 40, 88 S.Ct. 1889, 20 L.Ed.2d 917 (1968), a companion case to *Terry*: *O*, a police officer, observed *S* talk with known drug addicts over the course of an eight-hour period. Suspecting that *S* was selling drugs, *O* confronted *S* inside a restaurant, and told him to come outside. Outside, *O* said, "You know what I am after." *S* mumbled something and reached into his pocket, at which point *O* thrust his hand into the pocket and pulled out packets of heroin.

Should the heroin be suppressed at *S*'s trial? What if the officer had not thrust his hand in *S*'s pocket, but instead had ordered him to empty his pockets. Would this be permissible under *Terry*? See United States v. Reyes, 349 F.3d 219 (5th Cir. 2003).

b.   Drawing Lines: "*Terry* Seizures" Versus De Facto Arrests

DUNAWAY V. NEW YORK
Supreme Court of the United States, 1979.
442 U.S. 200, 99 S.Ct. 2248, 60 L.Ed.2d 824.

MR. JUSTICE BRENNAN delivered the opinion of the Court [joined by JUSTICES STEWART, WHITE, MARSHALL, BLACKMUN, and STEVENS]. * * *

I

On March 26, 1971, the proprietor of a pizza parlor in Rochester, N.Y., was killed during an attempted robbery. On August 10, 1971, Detective Anthony Fantigrossi of the Rochester Police was told by another officer that an informant had supplied a possible lead implicating petitioner in the crime. Fantigrossi questioned the supposed source of the lead—a jail inmate awaiting trial for burglary—but learned nothing that supplied "enough information to get a warrant" for petitioner's arrest. Nevertheless, Fantigrossi ordered other detectives to "pick up" petitioner and "bring him in." Three detectives located petitioner at a neighbor's house on the morning of August 11. Petitioner was taken into custody; although he was not told he was under arrest, he would have been physically restrained if he had attempted to leave. He was driven to police headquarters in a police car and placed in an interrogation room, where he was questioned by officers after being given the warnings required by *Miranda v. Arizona* [p. 625]. Petitioner waived counsel and eventually made statements and drew sketches that incriminated him in the crime. * * *

II * * *

* * * There can be little doubt that petitioner was "seized" in the Fourth Amendment sense when he was taken involuntarily to the police

station. And respondent State concedes that the police lacked probable cause to arrest petitioner before his incriminating statement during interrogation. Nevertheless respondent contends that the seizure of petitioner did not amount to an arrest and was therefore permissible under the Fourth Amendment because the police had a "reasonable suspicion" that petitioner possessed "intimate knowledge about a serious and unsolved crime." We disagree.

Before *Terry v. Ohio*, the Fourth Amendment's guarantee against unreasonable seizures of persons was analyzed in terms of arrest, probable cause for arrest, and warrants based on such probable cause. The basic principles were relatively simple and straightforward: The term "arrest" was synonymous with those seizures governed by the Fourth Amendment. While warrants were not required in all circumstances, the requirement of probable cause, as elaborated in numerous precedents, was treated as absolute. * * *

Terry for the first time recognized an exception to the requirement that Fourth Amendment seizures of persons must be based on probable cause. That case involved a brief, on-the-spot stop on the street and a frisk for weapons, a situation that did not fit comfortably within the traditional concept of an "arrest." * * * [S]ince the intrusion involved in a "stop and frisk" was so much less severe than that involved in traditional "arrests," the Court declined to stretch the concept of "arrest"—and the general rule requiring probable cause to make arrests "reasonable" under the Fourth Amendment—to cover such intrusions. Instead, the Court treated the stop-and-frisk intrusion as a *sui generis* "rubric of police conduct." * * * Thus, *Terry* departed from traditional Fourth Amendment analysis in two respects. First, it defined a special category of Fourth Amendment "seizures" so substantially less intrusive than arrests that the general rule requiring probable cause to make Fourth Amendment "seizures" reasonable could be replaced by a balancing test. Second, the application of this balancing test led the Court to approve this narrowly defined less intrusive seizure on grounds less rigorous than probable cause, but only for the purpose of a pat-down for weapons.

Because *Terry* involved an exception to the general rule requiring probable cause, this Court has been careful to maintain its narrow scope. * * *

Respondent State now urges the Court to apply a balancing test, rather than the general rule, to custodial interrogations, and to hold that "seizures" such as that in this case may be justified by mere "reasonable suspicion." *Terry* and its progeny clearly do not support such a result. * * *

In contrast to the brief and narrowly circumscribed intrusions involved in those cases, the detention of petitioner was in important respects indistinguishable from a traditional arrest. Petitioner was not questioned briefly where he was found. Instead, he was taken from a neighbor's home to a police car, transported to a police station, and placed in an interrogation room. He was never informed that he was "free to go"; indeed, he would have been physically restrained if he had refused to accompany the officers or had tried to escape their custody. The application of the Fourth Amendment's requirement of probable cause does not depend on whether an intrusion of this magnitude is termed an "arrest" under state law. The mere facts that petitioner was not told he was under arrest, was not "booked," and would not have had an arrest record if the interrogation had proved fruitless, while not insignificant for all purposes, obviously do not make petitioner's seizure even roughly analogous to the narrowly defined intrusions involved in *Terry* and its progeny. Indeed, any "exception" that could cover a seizure as intrusive as that in this case would threaten to swallow the general rule that Fourth Amendment seizures are "reasonable" only if based on probable cause.

The central importance of the probable-cause requirement to the protection of a citizen's privacy afforded by the Fourth Amendment's guarantees cannot be compromised in this fashion. * * *

In effect, respondent urges us to adopt a multifactor balancing test of "reasonable police conduct under the circumstances" to cover all seizures that do not amount to technical arrests. But the protections intended by the Framers could all too easily disappear in the consideration and balancing of the multifarious circumstances presented by different cases, especially when that balancing may be done in the first instance by police officers engaged in the "often competitive enterprise of ferreting out crime." A single, familiar standard is essential to guide police officers, who have only limited time and expertise to reflect on and balance the social and individual interests involved in the specific circumstances they confront. * * * For all but those narrowly defined intrusions, the requisite "balancing" has been performed in centuries of precedent and is embodied in the principle that seizures are "reasonable" only if supported by probable cause. * * *

* * * We accordingly hold that the Rochester police violated the Fourth and Fourteenth Amendments when, without probable cause, they seized petitioner and transported him to the police station for interrogation. * * *

MR. JUSTICE POWELL took no part in the consideration or decision of this case.

MR. JUSTICE WHITE, concurring.

The opinion of the Court might be read to indicate that *Terry v. Ohio* is an almost unique exception to a hard-and-fast standard of probable cause. As our prior cases hold, however, the key principle of the Fourth

Amendment is reasonableness—the balancing of competing interests. But if courts and law enforcement officials are to have workable rules, this balancing must in large part be done on a categorical basis—not in an ad hoc, case-by-case fashion by individual police officers. * * * It is enough, for me, that the police conduct here is similar enough to an arrest that the normal level of probable cause is necessary before the interests of privacy and personal security must give way.

[The concurring opinion of JUSTICE STEVENS is omitted.]

MR. JUSTICE REHNQUIST, with whom THE CHIEF JUSTICE BURGER joins, dissenting. * * *

I

* * * In my view, this is a case where the defendant voluntarily accompanied the police to the station to answer their questions.

* * * According to the testimony of the police officers, one officer approached a house where petitioner was thought to be located and knocked on the door. When a person answered the door, the officer identified himself and asked the individual his name. After learning that the person who answered the door was petitioner, the officer asked him if he would accompany the officers to police headquarters for questioning, and petitioner responded that he would. Petitioner was not told that he was under arrest or in custody and was not warned not to resist or flee. No weapons were displayed and petitioner was not handcuffed. Each officer testified that petitioner was not touched or held during the trip downtown; his freedom of action was not in any way restrained by the police. In short, the police behavior in this case was entirely free of "physical force or show of authority." * * *

* * * I do not dispute the fact that a police request to come to the station may indeed be an "awesome experience." But I do not think that that fact alone means that in every instance where a person assents to a police request to come to headquarters, there has been a "seizure" within the meaning of the Fourth Amendment. The question turns on whether the officer's conduct is objectively coercive or physically threatening, not on the mere fact that a person might in some measure feel cowed by the fact that a request is made by a police officer.

Therefore, although I agree that the police officers in this case did not have that degree of suspicion or probable cause that would have justified them in physically compelling petitioner to accompany them to the police station for questioning, I do not believe that the record demonstrates as a fact that this is what happened. No involuntary detention for questioning was shown to have taken place. The Fourth Amendment, accordingly, does not require suppression of petitioner's statements. * * *

NOTES AND QUESTIONS

1.   Does the dissent disagree with the majority's claim that the police may not compel a person to come to the police station for questioning on less than probable cause? What is the basis of the disagreement between the majority and the dissent?

2.   Would the seizure have been permissible if the police had found Dunaway in his front yard and had taken him to their police vehicle and questioned him there about the crime? What if they had taken him against his will from his front yard into his home for questioning?

3.   *Drawing lines: moving the suspect (part 1).* In Florida v. Royer, 460 U.S. 491, 103 S.Ct. 1319, 75 L.Ed.2d 229 (1983), two police detectives at Miami International Airport became suspicious of Royer, whose characteristics fit a drug-courier profile and who had paid cash for a one-way ticket to New York. Royer was about to embark on the flight when the detectives approached him. Upon request, he produced his airline ticket and driver's license. The ticket was under an assumed name. The detectives informed Royer that they were narcotics investigators and that they suspected him of transporting narcotics. Without returning the ticket or license, they asked him to accompany them to a small room, which was equipped with a desk and two chairs, adjacent to the airport concourse, where he was alone with the two officers. Meanwhile, one of the detectives retrieved Royer's luggage from the airline and brought it to the room. Royer consented to a search of his luggage that turned up marijuana. During the encounter, the police concededly lacked probable cause to arrest Royer.

Justice White, joined by Justices Marshall, Powell, and Stevens, concluded that the marijuana seized from the luggage had to be suppressed:

> We have concluded * * * that at the time Royer produced the key to his suitcase, the detention to which he was then subjected was a more serious intrusion on his personal liberty than is allowable on mere suspicion of criminal activity.
>
> * * * What had begun as a consensual inquiry in a public place had escalated into an investigatory procedure in a police interrogation room * * *. The officers had Royer's ticket, they had his identification, and they had seized his luggage. Royer was never informed that he was free to board his plane if he so chose, and he reasonably believed that he was being detained. At least as of that moment, any consensual aspects of the encounter had evaporated * * *. As a practical matter, Royer was under arrest. * * *
>
> We also think that the officers' conduct was more intrusive than necessary to effectuate an investigative detention otherwise authorized by the *Terry* line of cases. First, by returning his ticket and driver's license, and informing him that he was free to go if he so desired, the officers might have obviated any claim that the encounter was anything but a consensual matter from start to

finish. Second, there are undoubtedly reasons of safety and security that would justify moving a suspect from one location to another during an investigatory detention, such as from an airport concourse to a more private area. There is no indication in this case that such reasons prompted the officers to transfer the site of the encounter from the concourse to the interrogation room. * * *

Third, the State has not touched on the question whether it would have been feasible to investigate the contents of Royer's bags in a more expeditious way. The courts are not strangers to the use of trained dogs to detect the presence of controlled substances in luggage. There is no indication here that this means was not feasible and available. If it had been used, Royer and his luggage could have been momentarily detained while this investigative procedure was carried out. Indeed, it may be that no detention at all would have been necessary. A negative result would have freed Royer in short order; a positive result would have resulted in his justifiable arrest on probable cause.

4.   *Drawing lines: moving the suspect (part 2).* In Pennsylvania v. Mimms, 434 U.S. 106, 98 S.Ct. 330, 54 L.Ed.2d 331 (1977), *O* validly stopped *M* in his vehicle in order to issue him a traffic citation. *O* ordered *M* out of the car, as he routinely did with all traffic violators. When *M* complied, *O* observed a large bulge under *M*'s jacket. *O* frisked *M*, felt a gun, and seized it. The bulge would not have been observed had *O* not ordered *M* out of the car, so the issue in the case centered around that action.

The state court held that *O* did not have a right to order *M* out of the vehicle because he lacked a reasonable belief that the driver posed a threat to his safety. The Supreme Court disagreed. Balancing the competing interests, it ruled that when an officer legally stops a driver on the highway, he may order the driver out of the car without further justification. It described the interest in police safety as "legitimate and weighty." On the other side of the scale is the driver's interest, having been lawfully stopped, to be permitted to stay in his car:

> We think this additional intrusion [of getting out of the car] can only be described as *de minimis*. The driver is being asked to expose very little more of his person than is already exposed. The police have already lawfully decided that the driver shall be briefly detained: the only question is whether he shall spend that period sitting in the driver's seat of his car or standing alongside it.

What if a driver, stopped for a ticket, has a passenger in his car. Is the officer justified in ordering *her* out of the car, too? In Maryland v. Wilson, 519 U.S. 408, 117 S.Ct. 882, 137 L.Ed.2d 41 (1997), the Court, 7–2, said yes. "On the public interest side of the balance, the same weighty interest in officer safety is present regardless of whether the occupant of the stopped car is a driver or passenger."

"On the personal liberty side of the balance," the Court stated, "the case for the passengers is * * * stronger than that for the driver. There is probable cause to believe that the driver has committed a minor vehicular offense, but there is no reason to stop or detain the passengers." However, practically speaking, since innocent passengers are inevitably seized when the driver is stopped, the Court concluded that a change in circumstances—being ordered out of the car—was again too minor an additional intrusion to outweigh police safety.

Do you see the balance that way?

What if the speeding vehicle is a taxicab, and the passenger wants to leave to find another cab. May an officer order her to *remain* until he completes ticketing the driver?

5. *Drawing lines: length of the detention.* In *Terry v. Ohio*, Officer McFadden only detained Terry and Chilton briefly before he determined that he had grounds to arrest them for possession of concealed weapons. Does this mean, therefore, that a *Terry*-type seizure may not lawfully extend beyond a few minutes? Not necessarily.

In United States v. Sharpe, 470 U.S. 675, 105 S.Ct. 1568, 84 L.Ed.2d 605 (1985), federal drug agent Cooke patrolling a highway for drug trafficking observed a suspicious camper truck apparently traveling in tandem with a Pontiac. He radioed for assistance, and state highway patrolman Thrasher responded. They attempted to pull the cars over. The driver of the Pontiac pulled to the side, but the camper truck driver did not stop immediately. Thrasher successfully pursued the camper, which eventually pulled over.

Agent Cooke obtained identification from the Pontiac driver and then unsuccessfully attempted to reach Thrasher by radio. Cooke radioed for more assistance. When it arrived, he left the officers with the Pontiac and drove to the spot where Thrasher had pulled over the camper. When he smelled marijuana coming from the truck, he opened it, found bales of marijuana, and arrested the driver. The Court of Appeals held that the 20-minute detention of Savage, the driver of the camper, "failed to meet * * * [*Terry*'s] requirement of brevity." The Supreme Court, per Chief Justice Burger, saw it differently:

> Admittedly, *Terry*, *Dunaway*, [and] *Royer* [p. 413, Note 3], * * * considered together, may in some instances create difficult line-drawing problems in distinguishing an investigative stop from a *de facto* arrest. Obviously, if an investigative stop continues indefinitely, at some point it can no longer be justified as an investigative stop. But our cases impose no rigid time limitation on *Terry* stops. While it is clear that "the brevity of the invasion of the individual's Fourth Amendment interests is an important factor in determining whether the seizure is so minimally intrusive as to be justifiable on reasonable suspicion," we have emphasized the need to consider the law enforcement purposes to be served by the stop as well as the time reasonably needed to effectuate those purposes.

Much as a "bright line" rule would be desirable, in evaluating whether an investigative detention is unreasonable, common sense and ordinary human experience must govern over rigid criteria. * * *

In assessing whether a detention is too long in duration to be justified as an investigative stop, we consider it appropriate to examine whether the police diligently pursued a means of investigation that was likely to confirm or dispel their suspicions quickly, during which time it was necessary to detain the defendant. A court making this assessment should take care to consider whether the police are acting in a swiftly developing situation, and in such cases the court should not indulge in unrealistic second-guessing. * * * The question is not simply whether some other alternative was available, but whether the police acted unreasonably in failing to recognize or to pursue it.

We readily conclude that, given the circumstances facing him, Agent Cooke pursued his investigation in a diligent and reasonable manner. During most of Savage's 20-minute detention, Cooke was attempting to contact Thrasher and enlisting the help of the local police who remained with Sharpe while Cooke left to pursue Officer Thrasher and the pickup. Once Cooke reached Officer Thrasher and Savage, he proceeded expeditiously * * * .

* * * The delay in this case was attributable almost entirely to the evasive actions of Savage, who sought to elude the police as Sharpe moved his Pontiac to the side of the road. Except for Savage's maneuvers, only a short and certainly permissible pre-arrest detention would likely have taken place.

6.   *Problem.* Customs officials at L.A. International Airport had reason to suspect Rosa Montoya De Hernandez, who was a Colombian citizen, of being a "balloon swallower," *i.e.*, one who smuggles narcotics into the country hidden in balloons in her alimentary canal. The officials gave the suspect the option of undergoing an x-ray (she refused because she claimed that she was pregnant) or of being returned to her home country. She chose the latter option, but officials could not get her on a flight home due to visa problems. Therefore, "the officers decided on an alternative course: they would simply lock De Hernandez away in an adjacent manifest room 'until her peristaltic functions produced a monitored bowel movement.' The officers explained to De Hernandez that she could not leave until she had excreted by squatting over a wastebasket pursuant to the watchful eyes of two attending matrons."

The suspect was put incommunicado in a small room that contained only hard chairs and a table, where she remained for more than 16 hours during which she did not defecate. At that point, customs officials sought and received a court order authorizing a pregnancy test, which turned out negative, and a rectal examination that confirmed the existence of a balloon containing a foreign substance. Overall, the detention lasted nearly 24 hours.

Is this a *Terry* seizure or *de facto* arrest? Is it a border search? See United States v. Montoya de Hernandez, 473 U.S. 531, 105 S.Ct. 3304, 87 L.Ed.2d 381 (1985).

c.   Drawing Lines: Seizure Versus Non-Seizure Encounters

UNITED STATES V. MENDENHALL
Supreme Court of the United States, 1980.
446 U.S. 544, 100 S.Ct. 1870, 64 L.Ed.2d 497.

MR. JUSTICE STEWART announced the judgment of the Court and delivered an opinion, in which MR. JUSTICE REHNQUIST joined.**

* * *

I

* * * The respondent arrived at the Detroit Metropolitan Airport on a commercial airline flight from Los Angeles early in the morning on February 10, 1976. As she disembarked from the airplane, she was observed by two agents of the DEA [Drug Enforcement Administration], who were present at the airport for the purpose of detecting unlawful traffic in narcotics. After observing the respondent's conduct, which appeared to the agents to be characteristic of persons unlawfully carrying narcotics,[1] the agents approached her as she was walking through the concourse, identified themselves as federal agents, and asked to see her identification and airline ticket. The respondent produced her driver's license, which was in the name of Sylvia Mendenhall, and, in answer to a question of one of the agents, stated that she resided at the address appearing on the license. The airline ticket was issued in the name of "Annette Ford." When asked why the ticket bore a name different from her own, the respondent stated that she "just felt like using that name." In response to a further question, the respondent indicated that she had been in California only two days. Agent Anderson then specifically identified himself as a federal narcotics agent and, according to his testimony, the respondent "became quite shaken, extremely nervous. She had a hard time speaking."

After returning the airline ticket and driver's license to her, Agent Anderson asked the respondent if she would accompany him to the

---

** THE CHIEF JUSTICE [BURGER], Mr. Justice BLACKMUN, and Mr. Justice POWELL also join all but Part II–A of this opinion.

[1] The agent testified that the respondent's behavior fit the so-called "drug courier profile"—an informally compiled abstract of characteristics thought typical of persons carrying illicit drugs. In this case the agents thought it relevant that (1) the respondent was arriving on a flight from Los Angeles, a city believed by the agents to be the place of origin for much of the heroin brought to Detroit; (2) the respondent was the last person to leave the plane, "appeared to be very nervous," and "completely scanned the whole area where [the agents] were standing"; (3) after leaving the plane the respondent proceeded past the baggage area without claiming any luggage; and (4) the respondent changed airlines for her flight out of Detroit.

airport DEA office for further questions. She did so, although the record does not indicate a verbal response to the request. The office, which was located up one flight of stairs about 50 feet from where the respondent had first been approached, consisted of a reception area adjoined by three other rooms. At the office the agent asked the respondent if she would allow a search of her person and handbag and told her that she had the right to decline the search if she desired. She responded: "Go ahead." She then handed Agent Anderson her purse, which contained a receipt for an airline ticket that had been issued to "F. Bush" three days earlier for a flight from Pittsburgh through Chicago to Los Angeles. The agent asked whether this was the ticket that she had used for her flight to California, and the respondent stated that it was.

A female police officer then arrived to conduct the search of the respondent's person. She asked the agents if the respondent had consented to be searched. The agents said that she had, and the respondent followed the policewoman into a private room. There the policewoman again asked the respondent if she consented to the search, and the respondent replied that she did. The policewoman explained that the search would require that the respondent remove her clothing. The respondent stated that she had a plane to catch and was assured by the policewoman that if she were carrying no narcotics, there would be no problem. The respondent then began to disrobe without further comment. As the respondent removed her clothing, she took from her undergarments two small packages, one of which appeared to contain heroin, and handed both to the policewoman. The agents then arrested the respondent for possessing heroin. * * *

II

* * * Here the Government concedes that its agents had neither a warrant nor probable cause to believe that the respondent was carrying narcotics when the agents conducted a search of the respondent's person. It is the Government's position, however, that the search was conducted pursuant to the respondent's consent, and thus was excepted from the requirements of both a warrant and probable cause. Evidently, the Court of Appeals concluded that the respondent's apparent consent to the search was in fact not voluntarily given and was in any event the product of earlier official conduct violative of the Fourth Amendment. We must first consider, therefore, whether such conduct occurred, either on the concourse or in the DEA office at the airport.

A * * *

We adhere to the view that a person is "seized" only when, by means of physical force or a show of authority, his freedom of movement is restrained. Only when such restraint is imposed is there any foundation whatever for invoking constitutional safeguards. * * *

Moreover, characterizing every street encounter between a citizen and the police as a "seizure," while not enhancing any interest secured by the Fourth Amendment, would impose wholly unrealistic restrictions upon a wide variety of legitimate law enforcement practices. The Court has on other occasions referred to the acknowledged need for police questioning as a tool in the effective enforcement of the criminal laws. * * *

We conclude that a person has been "seized" within the meaning of the Fourth Amendment only if, in view of all of the circumstances surrounding the incident, a reasonable person would have believed that he was not free to leave.[6] Examples of circumstances that might indicate a seizure, even where the person did not attempt to leave, would be the threatening presence of several officers, the display of a weapon by an officer, some physical touching of the person of the citizen, or the use of language or tone of voice indicating that compliance with the officer's request might be compelled. In the absence of some such evidence, otherwise inoffensive contact between a member of the public and the police cannot, as a matter of law, amount to a seizure of that person.

On the facts of this case, no "seizure" of the respondent occurred. The events took place in the public concourse. The agents wore no uniforms and displayed no weapons. They did not summon the respondent to their presence, but instead approached her and identified themselves as federal agents. They requested, but did not demand to see the respondent's identification and ticket. Such conduct, without more, did not amount to an intrusion upon any constitutionally protected interest. The respondent was not seized simply by reason of the fact that the agents approached her, asked her if she would show them her ticket and identification, and posed to her a few questions. Nor was it enough to establish a seizure that the person asking the questions was a law enforcement official. In short, nothing in the record suggests that the respondent had any objective reason to believe that she was not free to end the conversation in the concourse and proceed on her way, and for that reason we conclude that the agents' initial approach to her was not a seizure.

Our conclusion that no seizure occurred is not affected by the fact that the respondent was not expressly told by the agents that she was free to decline to cooperate with their inquiry, for the voluntariness of her responses does not depend upon her having been so informed. We also reject the argument that the only inference to be drawn from the fact that the respondent acted in a manner so contrary to her self-interest is that she was compelled to answer the agents' questions. It may happen that a person makes statements to law enforcement officials that he later

---

[6] We agree with the District Court that the subjective intention of the DEA agent in this case to detain the respondent, had she attempted to leave, is irrelevant except insofar as that may have been conveyed to the respondent.

regrets, but the issue in such cases is not whether the statement was self-protective, but rather whether it was made voluntarily. * * *

B

Although we have concluded that the initial encounter between the DEA agents and the respondent on the concourse at the Detroit Airport did not constitute an unlawful seizure, it is still arguable that the respondent's Fourth Amendment protections were violated when she went from the concourse to the DEA office. Such a violation might in turn infect the subsequent search of the respondent's person. * * *

The question whether the respondent's consent to accompany the agents was in fact voluntary or was the product of duress or coercion, express or implied, is to be determined by the totality of all the circumstances, and is a matter which the Government has the burden of proving. The respondent herself did not testify at the hearing. The Government's evidence showed that the respondent was not told that she had to go to the office, but was simply asked if she would accompany the officers. There were neither threats nor any show of force. The respondent had been questioned only briefly, and her ticket and identification were returned to her before she was asked to accompany the officers.

On the other hand, it is argued that the incident would reasonably have appeared coercive to the respondent, who was 22 years old and had not been graduated from high school. It is additionally suggested that the respondent, a female and a Negro, may have felt unusually threatened by the officers, who were white males. While these factors were not irrelevant, neither were they decisive, and the totality of the evidence in this case was plainly adequate to support the District Court's finding that the respondent voluntarily consented to accompany the officers to the DEA office.

C

Because the search of the respondent's person was not preceded by an impermissible seizure of her person, it cannot be contended that her apparent consent to the subsequent search was infected by an unlawful detention. There remains to be considered whether the respondent's consent to the search was for any other reason invalid. * * *

III

We conclude that the District Court's determination that the respondent consented to the search of her person "freely and voluntarily" was sustained by the evidence and that the Court of Appeals was, therefore, in error in setting it aside. Accordingly, the judgment of the Court of Appeals is reversed, and the case is remanded to that court for further proceedings. * * *

MR. JUSTICE POWELL, with whom THE CHIEF JUSTICE BURGER and MR. JUSTICE BLACKMUN join, concurring in part and concurring in the judgment.

I join Parts I, II–B, II–C, and III of the Court's opinion. Because neither of the courts below considered the question, I do not reach the Government's contention that the agents did not "seize" the respondent within the meaning of the Fourth Amendment. In my view, we may assume for present purposes that the stop did constitute a seizure.[1] I would hold—as did the District Court—that the federal agents had reasonable suspicion that the respondent was engaging in criminal activity, and, therefore, that they did not violate the Fourth Amendment by stopping the respondent for routine questioning. * * *

II

[Justice Powell set out the reasons why, in the opinion of the concurring justices, the DEA agents possessed reasonable suspicion that Mendenhall was involved in illegal drug activities.] * * *

MR. JUSTICE WHITE, with whom MR. JUSTICE BRENNAN, MR. JUSTICE MARSHALL, and MR. JUSTICE STEVENS join, dissenting.

The Court today concludes that agents of the Drug Enforcement Administration (DEA) acted lawfully in stopping a traveler changing planes in an airport terminal and escorting her to a DEA office for a strip-search of her person. This result is particularly curious because a majority of the Members of the Court refuse to reject the conclusion that Ms. Mendenhall was "seized," while a separate majority decline to hold that there were reasonable grounds to justify a seizure. * * *

I * * *

Throughout the lower court proceedings in this case, the Government never questioned that the initial stop of Ms. Mendenhall was a "seizure" that required reasonable suspicion. Rather, the Government sought to justify the stop by arguing that Ms. Mendenhall's behavior had given rise to reasonable suspicion because it was consistent with portions of the so-called "drug courier profile," an informal amalgam of characteristics thought to be associated with persons carrying illegal drugs. Having failed to convince the Court of Appeals that the DEA agents had reasonable suspicion for the stop, the Government seeks reversal here by arguing for the first time that no "seizure" occurred, an argument that Mr. Justice Stewart now accepts, thereby pretermitting the question whether there was reasonable suspicion to stop Ms. Mendenhall. Mr.

---

[1]   Mr. Justice STEWART concludes in Part II–A that there was no "seizure" within the meaning of the Fourth Amendment. * * * I do not necessarily disagree with the views expressed in Part II–A. For me, the question whether the respondent in this case reasonably could have thought she was free to "walk away" when asked by two Government agents for her driver's license and ticket is extremely close.

Justice Stewart's opinion * * * addresses a fact-bound question with a totality-of-circumstances assessment that is best left in the first instance to the trial court, particularly since the question was not litigated below and hence we cannot be sure is adequately addressed by the record before us.

* * * Although it is undisputed that Ms. Mendenhall was not free to leave after the DEA agents stopped her and inspected her identification, Mr. Justice Stewart concludes that she was not "seized" because he finds that, under the totality of the circumstances, a reasonable person would have believed that she was free to leave. While basing this finding on an alleged absence from the record of objective evidence indicating that Ms. Mendenhall was not free to ignore the officer's inquiries and continue on her way, Mr. Justice Stewart's opinion brushes off the fact that this asserted evidentiary deficiency may be largely attributable to the fact that the "seizure" question was never raised below. In assessing what the record does reveal, the opinion discounts certain objective factors that would tend to support a "seizure" finding,[3] while relying on contrary factors inconclusive even under its own illustrations of how a "seizure" may be established.[4] * * *[T]he proper course would be to direct a remand to the District Court for an evidentiary hearing on the question, rather than to decide it in the first instance in this Court.

II

Assuming, as we should, that Ms. Mendenhall was "seized" within the meaning of the Fourth Amendment when she was stopped by the DEA agents, the legality of that stop turns on whether there were reasonable grounds for suspecting her of criminal activity at the time of the stop. * * *

None of the aspects of Ms. Mendenhall's conduct, either alone or in combination, were sufficient to provide reasonable suspicion that she was engaged in criminal activity. * * *

III

Whatever doubt there may be concerning whether Ms. Mendenhall's Fourth Amendment interests were implicated during the initial stages of her confrontation with the DEA agents, she undoubtedly was "seized" within the meaning of the Fourth Amendment when the agents escorted her from the public area of the terminal to the DEA office for questioning

---

[3]   Not the least of these factors is the fact that the DEA agents for a time took Ms. Mendenhall's plane ticket and driver's license from her. It is doubtful that any reasonable person about to board a plane would feel free to leave when law enforcement officers have her plane ticket.

[4]   MR. JUSTICE STEWART notes, for example, that a "seizure" might be established even if the suspect did not attempt to leave, by the nature of the language or tone of voice used by the officers, factors that were never addressed at the suppression hearing, very likely because the "seizure" question was not raised.

and a strip-search of her person. * * * Like the "seizure" in *Dunaway*, the nature of the intrusion to which Ms. Mendenhall was subjected when she was escorted by DEA agents to their office and detained there for questioning and a strip-search was so great that it "was in important respects indistinguishable from a traditional arrest." Although Ms. Mendenhall was not told that she was under arrest, she in fact was not free to refuse to go to the DEA office and was not told that she was. Furthermore, once inside the office, Ms. Mendenhall would not have been permitted to leave without submitting to a strip-search. * * *

* * * While the Government need not prove that Ms. Mendenhall knew that she had a right to refuse to accompany the officers, it cannot rely solely on acquiescence to the officers' wishes to establish the requisite consent. The Court of Appeals properly understood this in rejecting the District Court's "findings" of consent.

* * * [I]t is unbelievable that this sequence of events involved no invasion of a citizen's constitutionally protected interest in privacy. The rule of law requires a different conclusion. * * *

NOTES AND QUESTIONS

1.   How many (and which) justices believe that Mendenhall was seized? How many (and which) justices believe that the police had sufficient justification to seize Mendenhall?

Do *you* believe that Mendenhall was seized? If so, at what point did the seizure occur? Did it occur when the DEA agents first came up to Mendenhall and identified themselves? Would *you* have felt free to ignore the agents at this point and move on? If she was not seized then, was she seized when they asked for her ticket and license? Or, when they took her to the DEA office in the airport? If she was seized in your opinion, what level of seizure occurred—a *Terry*-level seizure or a *Dunaway*-type seizure (that is, a seizure tantamount to an arrest)?

2.   Reconsider the facts in *Florida v. Royer* (p. 413, Note 3) in light of *Mendenhall*. Since we know that the Court ruled that Royer was seized (indeed, virtually arrested) when he was taken to the small room, how do we distinguish that outcome from *Mendenhall*?

3.   *The potential role of race and other characteristics in "seizure" analysis.* To what extent is it relevant to the analysis that Mendenhall was an African-American woman, and that the police were white males? Consider the following:

> * * * [M]y thesis is that police encounters involving black men
> contain a combination of fear, distrust, anger and coercion that
> make these encounters unique and always potentially explosive.
> * * *

To be sure, when whites are stopped by the police, they too feel uneasy and often experience fear. Inherent in any police encounter, even for whites, is the fear that the officer will abuse his authority by being arrogant, or act in a manner that causes the individual to feel more nervous than necessary. * * *

But I wonder whether the average white person worries that an otherwise routine police encounter may lead to a violent confrontation. When they are stopped by the police, do whites contemplate the possibility that they will be physically abused for questioning why an officer has stopped them?

Tracey Maclin, *"Black and Blue Encounters"—Some Preliminary Thoughts About Fourth Amendment Seizures: Should Race Matter?*, 26 Val. U. L. Rev. 243, 243, 254–56 (1991).

If this mutual distrust exists, and if African-Americans, especially black males, fear the police, because of experiences in their community, in a way that white males do not, should the law take this difference into account in measuring police conduct? Specifically, if the question is whether a "reasonable person" in the suspect's situation would believe that he is not free to leave, should we incorporate the suspect's race in that analysis (as Professor Maclin ultimately recommends), or should the law apply a race-blind approach? Is the latter approach unfair because it would require people "to act as if they belonged to a completely different community, one whose experiences with government officials leads to the conclusion that it is safe to assert one's rights"? Susan F. Mandiberg, *Reasonable Officers vs. Reasonable Lay Persons in the Supreme Court's Miranda and Fourth Amendment Cases*, 14 Lewis & Clark L. Rev. 1481, 1502 (2010).

If the race of the suspect *should* be considered, are there other characteristics that should be included?

4. *Problem.* Officer, in police uniform, comes to *S*'s home at midnight and knocks at the door. *S*'s roommate opens the door. Officer asks if *S* is at home. Told that "he is, but is asleep," Officer insists that the roommate awaken *S*. When *S* arrives at the door, Officer tells him he is investigating a traffic violation and asks him to step outside the house. Seizure? State v. Scott, 138 N.M. 751, 126 P.3d 567 (2005).

5. *"Bus sweeps."* In *Terry* and *Mendenhall*, the general issue was whether (or when) a person who was in motion (walking back and forth on a Cleveland street, or moving through an airport concourse) was seized by a law enforcement officer. There is more to be said on this subject with the next case, but before we turn to it, let's turn things around a bit: when is a person seized if he or she is already in a stationary position? One example of this scenario is the so-called "bus sweep," described this way by Justice Marshall in Florida v. Bostick, 501 U.S. 429, 111 S.Ct. 2382, 115 L.Ed.2d 389 (1991):

At issue in this case is a "new and increasingly common tactic in the war on drugs": the suspicionless police sweep of buses in interstate or intrastate travel. Typically under this technique, a group of state or federal officers will board a bus while it is stopped at an intermediate point on its route. Often displaying badges, weapons or other indicia of authority, the officers identify themselves and announce their purpose to intercept drug traffickers. They proceed to approach individual passengers, requesting them to show identification, produce their tickets, and explain the purpose of their travels. * * * An "interview" of this type ordinarily culminates in a request for consent to search the passenger's luggage.

These sweeps are conducted in "dragnet" style. The police admittedly act without an "articulable suspicion" in deciding which buses to board and which passengers to approach for interviewing. By proceeding systematically in this fashion, the police are able to engage in a tremendously high volume of searches.

So, when is one of these bus passengers seized, if at all? At what point can we say that a reasonable person would believe that her liberty has been restrained by the officer? The Court, in United States v. Drayton, 536 U.S. 194, 122 S.Ct. 2105, 153 L.Ed.2d 242 (2002), explained:

> The proper inquiry necessitates a consideration of "all the circumstances surrounding the encounter." [We have noted] * * * that the traditional rule, which states that a seizure does not occur so long as a reasonable person would feel free "to disregard the police and go about his business," is not an accurate measure of the coercive effect of a bus encounter. A passenger may not want to get off a bus if there is a risk it will depart before the opportunity to reboard. A bus rider's movements are confined in this sense, but this is the natural result of choosing to take the bus; it says nothing about whether the police conduct is coercive. The proper inquiry "is whether a reasonable person would feel free to decline the officers' requests or otherwise terminate the encounter." * * * The reasonable person test * * * "presupposes an *innocent* person."

In *Drayton*, after a scheduled stop at a Greyhound terminal, passengers reboarded. After they did, three members of the Tallahassee Police Department boarded. The officers were dressed in plain clothes and carried concealed weapons but visible badges. One officer knelt on the bus driver's seat, facing the rear of the bus, and remained in that position. A second officer went to the rear of the bus and remained there. Meanwhile, the third officer worked his way through the bus, speaking to the seated passengers, asking their travel plans, and seeking to match passengers with their luggage in the overhead racks. As the Court explained, "[t]o avoid blocking the aisle [officer] Lang stood next to or just behind each passenger with whom he spoke." The Court went on:

> According to Lang's testimony, passengers who declined to cooperate with him or who chose to exit the bus at any time would

have been allowed to do so without argument. * * * Lang sometimes informed passengers of their right to refuse to cooperate. On the day in question, however, he did not.

Respondents were seated next to each other on the bus. Drayton was in the aisle seat, Brown in the seat next to the window. Lang approached respondents from the rear and leaned over Drayton's shoulder. He held up his badge long enough for respondents to identify him as a police officer. With his face 12-to-18 inches away from Drayton's, Lang spoke in a voice just loud enough for respondents to hear:

> "I'm Investigator Lang with the Tallahassee Police Department. We're conducting bus interdiction [sic], attempting to deter drugs and illegal weapons being transported on the bus. Do you have any bags on the bus?"

Both respondents pointed to a single green bag in the overhead luggage rack. Lang asked, "Do you mind if I check it?," and Brown responded, "Go ahead." Lang handed the bag to Officer Blackburn to check. The bag contained no contraband.

Officer Lang noticed that both respondents were wearing heavy jackets and baggy pants despite the warm weather. In Lang's experience drug traffickers often use baggy clothing to conceal weapons or narcotics. The officer thus asked Brown if he had any weapons or drugs in his possession. And he asked Brown: "Do you mind if I check your person?" Brown answered, "Sure," and cooperated by leaning up in his seat, pulling a cell phone out of his pocket, and opening up his jacket. Lang reached across Drayton and patted down Brown's jacket and pockets, including his waist area, sides, and upper thighs. In both thigh areas, Lang detected hard objects similar to drug packages detected on other occasions. Lang arrested and handcuffed Brown. Officer Hoover escorted Brown from the bus.

Lang then asked Drayton, "Mind if I check you?" Drayton responded by lifting his hands about eight inches from his legs. Lang conducted a patdown of Drayton's thighs and detected hard objects similar to those found on Brown. He arrested Drayton and escorted him from the bus.

The Court, 6–3, held that Drayton was not seized until his arrest, i.e., that everything was consensual until that point. It stated that bus passengers consent to searches of their luggage to "enhance[e] their own safety and the safety of those around them." Furthermore, according to Justice Kennedy, the officer at the front of the bus "did nothing to intimidate passengers, and he said nothing to suggest that people could not exit and indeed he left the aisle clear." He also rejected Drayton's claim that "a reasonable person would not feel free to terminate the encounter with the officers" after his seatmate, Brown, had been arrested. "The arrest of one person does not mean that everyone around him has been seized by the police. * * * Even after arresting Brown, Lang addressed Drayton in a polite manner and provided him with no indication that he was required to answer Lang's questions."

Do you agree with the Court's analysis?

CALIFORNIA V. HODARI D.
Supreme Court of the United States, 1991.
499 U.S. 621, 111 S.Ct. 1547, 113 L.Ed.2d 690.

JUSTICE SCALIA delivered the opinion of the Court [joined by CHIEF JUSTICE REHNQUIST, and JUSTICES WHITE, BLACKMUN, O'CONNOR, KENNEDY, and SOUTER].

Late one evening in April 1988, Officers Brian McColgin and Jerry Pertoso were on patrol in a high-crime area of Oakland, California. They were dressed in street clothes but wearing jackets with "Police" embossed on both front and back. Their unmarked car * * * rounded the corner, [and] they saw four or five youths huddled around a small red car parked at the curb. When the youths saw the officers' car approaching they apparently panicked, and took flight. The respondent here, Hodari D., and one companion ran west through an alley; the others fled south. The red car also headed south, at a high rate of speed.

The officers were suspicious and gave chase. [Officer Pertoso gave chase by foot. Just before he reached Hodari, the youth tossed away what appeared to be a small rock.] * * * A moment later, Pertoso tackled Hodari, handcuffed him, and radioed for assistance. Hodari was found to be carrying $130 in cash and a pager; and the rock he had discarded was found to be crack cocaine. * * *

As this case comes to us, the only issue presented is whether, at the time he dropped the drugs, Hodari had been "seized" within the meaning of the Fourth Amendment.[1] If so, respondent argues, the drugs were the fruit of that seizure and the evidence concerning them was properly excluded. If not, the drugs were abandoned by Hodari and lawfully recovered by the police, and the evidence should have been admitted. * * *

* * * From the time of the founding to the present, the word "seizure" has meant a "taking possession." For most purposes at common law, the word connoted not merely grasping, or applying physical force to, the animate or inanimate object in question, but actually bringing it within

---

[1]   California conceded below that Officer Pertoso did not have the "reasonable suspicion" required to justify stopping Hodari. That it would be unreasonable to stop, for brief inquiry, young men who scatter in panic upon the mere sighting of the police is not self-evident, and arguably contradicts proverbial common sense. See Proverbs 28:1 ("The wicked flee when no man pursueth"). We do not decide that point here, but rely entirely upon the State's concession.

physical control. * * * To constitute an arrest, however—the quintessential "seizure of the person" under our Fourth Amendment jurisprudence—the mere grasping or application of physical force with lawful authority, whether or not it succeeded in subduing the arrestee, was sufficient. * * *

To say that an arrest is effected by the slightest application of physical force, despite the arrestee's escape, is not to say that for Fourth Amendment purposes there is a *continuing* arrest during the period of fugitivity. If, for example, Pertoso had laid his hands upon Hodari to arrest him, but Hodari had broken away and had *then* cast away the cocaine, it would hardly be realistic to say that that disclosure had been made during the course of an arrest. The present case, however, is even one step further removed. It does not involve the application of any physical force; Hodari was untouched by Officer Pertoso at the time he discarded the cocaine. His defense relies instead upon the proposition that a seizure occurs "when the officer, by means of physical force *or show of authority*, has in some way restrained the liberty of a citizen." *Terry v. Ohio* (emphasis added). Hodari contends (and we accept as true for purposes of this decision) that Pertoso's pursuit qualified as a "show of authority" calling upon Hodari to halt. The narrow question before us is whether, with respect to a show of authority as with respect to application of physical force, a seizure occurs even though the subject does not yield. We hold that it does not.

The language of the Fourth Amendment, of course, cannot sustain respondent's contention. The word "seizure" readily bears the meaning of a laying on of hands or application of physical force to restrain movement, even when it is ultimately unsuccessful. ("She seized the purse-snatcher, but he broke out of her grasp.") It does not remotely apply, however, to the prospect of a policeman yelling "Stop, in the name of the law!" at a fleeing form that continues to flee. That is no seizure. Nor can the result respondent wishes to achieve be produced—indirectly, as it were—by suggesting that Pertoso's uncomplied-with show of authority was a common-law arrest, and then appealing to the principle that all common-law arrests are seizures. An arrest requires *either* physical force (as described above) *or*, where that is absent, *submission* to the assertion of authority. * * *

We do not think it desirable, even as a policy matter, to stretch the Fourth Amendment beyond its words and beyond the meaning of arrest, as respondent urges. Street pursuits always place the public at some risk, and compliance with police orders to stop should therefore be encouraged. Only a few of those orders, we must presume, will be without adequate basis, and since the addressee has no ready means of identifying the deficient ones it almost invariably is the responsible course to comply. * * *

Respondent contends that his position is sustained by the so-called *Mendenhall* test, formulated by Justice Stewart's opinion in *United States v. Mendenhall*, [p. 417], and adopted by the Court in later cases: "[a] person has been 'seized' within the meaning of the Fourth Amendment only if, in view of all the circumstances surrounding the incident, a reasonable person would have believed that he was not free to leave." In seeking to rely upon that test here, respondent fails to read it carefully. It says that a person has been seized "only if," not that he has been seized "whenever"; it states a *necessary*, but not a *sufficient*, condition for seizure—or, more precisely, for seizure effected through a "show of authority." * * *

In sum, assuming that Pertoso's pursuit in the present case constituted a "show of authority" enjoining Hodari to halt, since Hodari did not comply with that injunction he was not seized until he was tackled. The cocaine abandoned while he was running was in this case not the fruit of a seizure, and his motion to exclude evidence of it was properly denied. * * *

JUSTICE STEVENS, with whom JUSTICE MARSHALL joins, dissenting. * * *

II * * *

Whatever else one may think of today's decision, it unquestionably represents a departure from earlier Fourth Amendment case law. The notion that our prior cases contemplated a distinction between seizures effected by a touching on the one hand, and those effected by a show of force on the other hand, and that all of our repeated descriptions of the *Mendenhall* test stated only a necessary, but not a sufficient, condition for finding seizures in the latter category, is nothing if not creative lawmaking. Moreover, by narrowing the definition of the term seizure, instead of enlarging the scope of reasonable justifications for seizures, the Court has significantly limited the protection provided to the ordinary citizen by the Fourth Amendment. * * *

III

In this case the officer's show of force—taking the form of a head-on chase—adequately conveyed the message that respondent was not free to leave. * * * There was an interval of time between the moment that respondent saw the officer fast approaching and the moment when he was tackled, and thus brought under the control of the officer. The question is whether the Fourth Amendment was implicated at the earlier or the later moment.

Because the facts of this case are somewhat unusual, it is appropriate to note that the same issue would arise if the show of force took the form of a command to "freeze," a warning shot, or the sound of sirens accompanied by a patrol car's flashing lights. In any of these situations, there may be a significant time interval between the initiation of the officer's show of force and the complete submission by the citizen. At least on the facts of this case, the Court concludes that the timing of the seizure is governed by the citizen's reaction, rather than by the officer's conduct. One consequence of this conclusion is that the point at which the interaction between citizen and police officer becomes a seizure occurs, not when a reasonable citizen believes he or she is no longer free to go, but, rather, only after the officer exercises control over the citizen.

In my view, our interests in effective law enforcement and in personal liberty would be better served by adhering to a standard that "allows the police to determine in advance whether the conduct contemplated will implicate the Fourth Amendment." * * *

If an officer effects an arrest by touching a citizen, apparently the Court would accept the fact that a seizure occurred, even if the arrestee should thereafter break loose and flee. In such a case, the constitutionality of the seizure would be evaluated as of the time the officer acted. * * * It is anomalous, at best, to fashion a different rule for the subcategory of "show of force" arrests.

In cases within this new subcategory, there will be a period of time during which the citizen's liberty has been restrained, but he or she has not yet completely submitted to the show of force. A motorist pulled over by a highway patrol car cannot come to an immediate stop, even if the motorist intends to obey the patrol car's signal. If an officer decides to make [a random stop or one based solely on a hunch] * * *, and, after flashing his lights, but before the vehicle comes to a complete stop, sees that the license plate has expired, can he justify his action on the ground that the seizure became lawful after it was initiated but before it was completed? In an airport setting, may a drug enforcement agent now approach a group of passengers with his gun drawn, announce a "baggage search," and rely on the passengers' reactions to justify his investigative stops? The holding of today's majority fails to recognize the coercive and intimidating nature of such behavior and creates a rule that may allow such behavior to go unchecked. * * *

Some sacrifice of freedom always accompanies an expansion in the Executive's unreviewable law enforcement powers. A court more sensitive to the purposes of the Fourth Amendment would insist on greater rewards to society before decreeing the sacrifice it makes today. * * *

NOTES AND QUESTIONS

1.   In *Hodari D.*, the defendant tossed away rock cocaine during his flight from the officer. What is the lesson of the Court's ruling to officers who, as here, pursue individuals whom they lack reasonable suspicion to detain?

2. Justice Souter, writing for a unanimous Supreme Court in Brendlin v. California, 551 U.S. 249, 127 S.Ct. 2400, 168 L.Ed.2d 132 (2007), summarized the "seizure of person" line of cases this way:

> A person is seized by the police and thus entitled to challenge the government's action under the Fourth Amendment when the officer, " 'by means of physical force or show of authority,' " terminates or restrains his freedom of movement, *through means intentionally applied.*" Thus, an "unintended person * * * [may be] the object of the detention," so long as the detention is "willful" and not merely the consequence of "an unknowing act." [C]f. *County of Sacramento* v. *Lewis*, 523 U.S. 833, 844, 118 S.Ct. 1708, 140 L.Ed.2d 1043 (1998) (no seizure where a police officer accidentally struck and killed a motorcycle passenger during a high-speed pursuit). A police officer may make a seizure by a show of authority and without the use of physical force, but there is no seizure without actual submission; otherwise, there is at most an attempted seizure.

> When the actions of the police do not show an unambiguous intent to restrain or when an individual's submission to a show of governmental authority takes the form of passive acquiescence, there needs to be some test for telling when a seizure occurs in response to authority, and when it does not. The test was devised by Justice Stewart in *United States* v. *Mendenhall*, [p. 417], who wrote that a seizure occurs if "in view of all of the circumstances surrounding the incident, a reasonable person would have believed that he was not free to leave." Later on, the Court adopted Justice Stewart's touchstone, but added that when a person "has no desire to leave" for reasons unrelated to the police presence, the "coercive effect of the encounter" can be measured better by asking whether "a reasonable person would feel free to decline the officers' requests or otherwise terminate the encounter"; see * * * *United States* v. *Drayton*, [p. 425, Note 5].

Based on this summary of the law, the Court held that a car passenger, and not only the driver, is seized as the result of a police-ordered traffic stop:

> The law is settled that in Fourth Amendment terms a traffic stop entails a seizure of the driver "even though the purpose of the stop is limited and the resulting detention quite brief." And although we have not, until today, squarely answered the question whether a passenger is also seized, we have said over and over in dicta that during a traffic stop an officer seizes everyone in the vehicle, not just the driver. * * *

> * * * An officer who orders one particular car to pull over acts with an implicit claim of right based on fault of some sort, and a sensible person would not expect a police officer to allow people to come and go freely from the physical focal point of an investigation

into faulty behavior or wrongdoing. If the likely wrongdoing is not the driving, the passenger will reasonably feel subject to suspicion owing to close association; but even when the wrongdoing is only bad driving, the passenger will expect to be subject to some scrutiny, and his attempt to leave the scene would be so obviously likely to prompt an objection from the officer that no passenger would feel free to leave in the first place. * * *

[T]he * * * Supreme Court [of California] shied away from the rule we apply today for fear that it "would encompass even those motorists following the vehicle subject to the traffic stop who, by virtue of the original detention, are forced to slow down and perhaps even come to a halt in order to accommodate that vehicle's submission to police authority." But an occupant of a car who knows that he is stuck in traffic because another car has been pulled over (like the motorist who can't even make out why the road is suddenly clogged) would not perceive a show of authority as directed at him or his car. Such incidental restrictions on freedom of movement would not tend to affect an individual's "sense of security and privacy in traveling in an automobile." * * *

* * * Holding that the passenger in a private car is not (without more) seized in a traffic stop would invite police officers to stop cars with passengers regardless of probable cause or reasonable suspicion of anything illegal. The fact that evidence uncovered as a result of an arbitrary traffic stop would still be admissible against any passengers would be a powerful incentive to run the kind of "roving patrols" that would still violate the driver's Fourth Amendment right.

3.   *Problem*. Officers, in their police vehicle, flashed their red lights to stop a car. After two blocks, the driver pulled into the driveway of his home. Passenger *M* got out of the car. One officer called out, "Hold up." *M* replied, "What do you want?," began to back away slowly, and then fled. During pursuit, *M* threw down an object later determined to be contraband. Was *M* seized? If so, at what moment? See United States v. Morgan, 936 F.2d 1561 (10th Cir. 1991).

4.   *Problem*. In an area "infamous for racial tension," a suburban police officer observed three African-American youths riding their bicycle one block south of Eight Mile Road, the dividing point between largely-black Detroit and a nearly-white suburb. "After a quick interrogation and a racist joke, the officer allegedly ordered the youths to take their bicycles 'back across Eight Mile,' and watched while they did so." Stephen E. Henderson, *"Move On" Orders as Fourth Amendment Seizures*, 2008 B.Y.U. L. Rev. 1, 23. Assuming everything prior to this was constitutional, did the officer's "move on" order constitute a seizure?

d. "Reasonable Suspicion"

ALABAMA V. WHITE

Supreme Court of the United States, 1990.
496 U.S. 325, 110 S.Ct. 2412, 110 L.Ed.2d 301.

JUSTICE WHITE delivered the opinion of the Court [joined by CHIEF JUSTICE REHNQUIST, and JUSTICES BLACKMUN, O'CONNOR, SCALIA, and KENNEDY]. * * *

On April 22, 1987, at approximately 3 p.m., Corporal B. H. Davis of the Montgomery Police Department received a telephone call from an anonymous person, stating that Vanessa White would be leaving 235-C Lynwood Terrace Apartments at a particular time in a brown Plymouth station wagon with the right taillight lens broken, that she would be going to Dobey's Motel, and that she would be in possession of about an ounce of cocaine inside a brown attaché case. Corporal Davis and his partner, Corporal P. A. Reynolds, proceeded to the Lynwood Terrace Apartments. The officers saw a brown Plymouth station wagon with a broken right taillight in the parking lot in front of the 235 building. The officers observed respondent leave the 235 building, carrying nothing in her hands, and enter the station wagon. They followed the vehicle as it drove the most direct route to Dobey's Motel. When the vehicle reached the Mobile Highway, on which Dobey's Motel is located, Corporal Reynolds requested a patrol unit to stop the vehicle. The vehicle was stopped at approximately 4:18 p.m., just short of Dobey's Motel. Corporal Davis asked respondent to step to the rear of her car, where he informed her that she had been stopped because she was suspected of carrying cocaine in the vehicle. He asked if they could look for cocaine, and respondent said they could look. The officers found a locked brown attaché case in the car, and, upon request, respondent provided the combination to the lock. The officers found marijuana in the attaché case and placed respondent under arrest. During processing at the station, the officers found three milligrams of cocaine in respondent's purse.

* * * The Court of Criminal Appeals of Alabama held that the officers did not have the reasonable suspicion necessary under *Terry v. Ohio* to justify the investigatory stop of respondent's car, and that the marijuana and cocaine were fruits of respondent's unconstitutional detention. * * * We now reverse. * * *

Illinois v. Gates, [p. 188], dealt with an anonymous tip in the probable-cause context. The Court there abandoned the "two-pronged test" of *Aguilar v. Texas*, 378 U.S. 108, 84 S.Ct. 1509, 12 L.Ed.2d 723 (1964), and *Spinelli v. United States*, [p. 178], in favor of a "totality of the circumstances" approach to determining whether an informant's tip establishes probable cause. *Gates* made clear, however, that those factors that had been considered critical under *Aguilar* and *Spinelli*—an informant's "veracity," "reliability," and "basis of knowledge"—remain "highly relevant in determining the value of his report." These factors are also relevant in the reasonable suspicion context, although allowance must be made in applying them for the lesser showing required to meet that standard.

The opinion in *Gates* recognized that an anonymous tip alone seldom demonstrates the informant's basis of knowledge or veracity inasmuch as ordinary citizens generally do not provide extensive recitations of the basis of their everyday observations and given that the veracity of persons supplying anonymous tips is "by hypothesis largely unknown, and unknowable." This is not to say that an anonymous caller could never provide the reasonable suspicion necessary for a *Terry* stop. But the tip in *Gates* was not an exception to the general rule, and the anonymous tip in this case is like the one in *Gates*: "[It] provides virtually nothing from which one might conclude that [the caller] is either honest or his information reliable; likewise, the [tip] gives absolutely no indication of the basis for the [caller's] predictions regarding [Vanessa White's] criminal activities." By requiring "[s]omething more," as *Gates* did, we merely apply what we said in *Adams* [*v. Williams*, 407 U.S. 143, 92 S.Ct. 1921, 32 L.Ed.2d 612 (1972)]: "Some tips, completely lacking in indicia of reliability, would either warrant no police response or require further investigation before a forcible stop of a suspect would be authorized." Simply put, a tip such as this one, standing alone, would not " 'warrant a man of reasonable caution in the belief' that [a stop] was appropriate."

As there was in *Gates*, however, in this case there is more than the tip itself. The tip was not as detailed, and the corroboration was not as complete, as in *Gates*, but the required degree of suspicion was likewise not as high. We discussed the difference in the two standards last Term in *United States v. Sokolow*, 490 U.S. 1, 109 S.Ct. 1581, 104 L.Ed.2d 1 (1989):

> "The officer [making a *Terry* stop] * * * must be able to articulate something more than an 'inchoate and unparticularized suspicion or "hunch." ' The Fourth Amendment requires 'some minimal level of objective justification' for making the stop. That level of suspicion is considerably less than proof of wrongdoing by a preponderance of the evidence. We have held that probable cause means 'a fair probability that contraband or evidence of a crime will be found,' and the level of suspicion required for a *Terry* stop is obviously less demanding than for probable cause."

Reasonable suspicion is a less demanding standard than probable cause not only in the sense that reasonable suspicion can be established with information that is different in quantity or content than that required to establish probable cause, but also in the sense that reasonable suspicion can arise from information that is less reliable than that required to show probable cause. * * * Both factors—quantity and quality—are considered in the "totality of the circumstances—the whole picture," that must be taken into account when evaluating whether there is reasonable suspicion. Thus, if a tip has a relatively low degree of reliability, more information will be required to establish the requisite quantum of suspicion than would be required if the tip were more reliable. * * * Contrary to the court below, we conclude that when the officers stopped respondent, the anonymous tip had been sufficiently corroborated to furnish reasonable suspicion that respondent was engaged in criminal activity and that the investigative stop therefore did not violate the Fourth Amendment.

It is true that not every detail mentioned by the tipster was verified, such as the name of the woman leaving the building or the precise apartment from which she left; but the officers did corroborate that a woman left the 235 building and got into the particular vehicle that was described by the caller. With respect to the time of departure predicted by the informant, Corporal Davis testified that the caller gave a particular time when the woman would be leaving, but he did not state what that time was. He did testify that, after the call, he and his partner proceeded to the Lynwood Terrace Apartments to put the 235 building under surveillance. Given the fact that the officers proceeded to the indicated address immediately after the call and that respondent emerged not too long thereafter, it appears from the record before us that respondent's departure from the building was within the time frame predicted by the caller. As for the caller's prediction of respondent's destination, it is true that the officers stopped her just short of Dobey's Motel and did not know whether she would have pulled in or continued on past it. But given that the 4-mile route driven by respondent was the most direct route possible to Dobey's Motel, but nevertheless involved several turns, we think respondent's destination was significantly corroborated.

The Court's opinion in *Gates* gave credit to the proposition that because an informant is shown to be right about some things, he is probably right about other facts that he has alleged, including the claim that the object of the tip is engaged in criminal activity. Thus, it is not unreasonable to conclude in this case that the independent corroboration by the police of significant aspects of the informer's predictions imparted some degree of reliability to the other allegations made by the caller.

We think it also important that, as in *Gates*, "the anonymous [tip] contained a range of details relating not just to easily obtained facts and conditions existing at the time of the tip, but to future actions of third parties ordinarily not easily predicted." The fact that the officers found a car precisely matching the caller's description in front of the 235 building is an example of the former. Anyone could have "predicted" that fact because it was a condition presumably existing at the time of the call. What was important was the caller's ability to predict respondent's *future behavior*, because it demonstrated inside information—a special familiarity with respondent's affairs. The general public would have had no way of knowing that respondent would shortly leave the building, get in the described car, and drive the most direct route to Dobey's Motel. Because only a small number of people are generally privy to an individual's itinerary, it is reasonable for police to believe that a person with access to such information is likely to also have access to reliable information about that individual's illegal activities. When significant aspects of the caller's predictions were verified, there was reason to believe not only that the caller was honest but also that he was well informed, at least well enough to justify the stop.

Although it is a close case, we conclude that under the totality of the circumstances the anonymous tip, as corroborated, exhibited sufficient indicia of reliability to justify the investigatory stop of respondent's car. * * *

JUSTICE STEVENS, with whom JUSTICE BRENNAN and JUSTICE MARSHALL join, dissenting.

Millions of people leave their apartments at about the same time every day carrying an attaché case and heading for a destination known to their neighbors. Usually, however, the neighbors do not know what the briefcase contains. An anonymous neighbor's prediction about somebody's time of departure and probable destination is anything but a reliable basis for assuming that the commuter is in possession of an illegal substance—particularly when the person is not even carrying the attaché case described by the tipster.

The record in this case does not tell us how often respondent drove from the Lynwood Terrace Apartments to Dobey's Motel; for all we know, she may have been a room clerk or telephone operator working the evening shift. It does not tell us whether Office Davis made any effort to ascertain the informer's identity, his reason for calling, or the basis of his prediction about respondent's destination. Indeed, for all that this record tells us, the tipster may well have been another police officer who had a "hunch" that respondent might have cocaine in her attaché case.

Anybody with enough knowledge about a given person to make her the target of a prank, or to harbor a grudge against her, will certainly be able to formulate a tip about her like the one predicting Vanessa White's excursion. In addition, under the Court's holding, every citizen is subject to being seized and questioned by any officer who is prepared to testify that the warrantless stop was based on an anonymous tip predicting whatever conduct the officer just observed. Fortunately, the vast majority of those in our law enforcement community would not adopt such a practice. But the Fourth Amendment was intended to protect the citizen from the overzealous and unscrupulous officer as well as from those who are conscientious and truthful. This decision makes a mockery of that protection. * * *

NOTES AND QUESTIONS

1. Do you believe that the police had sufficient grounds to stop White?

2. The *White* Court unsurprisingly stated that reasonable suspicion "can be established with information that is different in quantity * * * than that required to establish probable cause." But, it also stated that "reasonable suspicion" is a less demanding standard "in the sense that reasonable suspicion can arise from information that is less reliable than that required to show probable cause." *Should* this be the rule?

3. The *White* Court quoted *Adams v. Williams*, the pertinent facts of which are summarized on p. 406, Note 10. Take another look at that Note. Now, here are some additional facts: The officer approached the Williams vehicle after "a person known to [the officer] * * * informed him that an individual seated in a nearby vehicle was carrying narcotics and had a gun at his waist." The officer knew the tipster because he had provided information once before, regarding homosexual activity. That information did *not* result in an arrest because the officer could not substantiate the claim. The *Williams* majority concluded, nonetheless, that reasonable suspicion in *this* case existed:

> [W]e believe that [the officer] acted justifiably in responding to his informant's tip. The informant was known to him personally and had provided him with information in the past. This is a stronger case than obtains in the case of an anonymous telephone tip. The informant here came forward personally to give information that was immediately verifiable at the scene. Indeed, under Connecticut law, the informant might have been subject to immediate arrest for making a false complaint had [the officer]'s investigation proved the tip incorrect. Thus, while the Court's decisions indicate that this informant's unverified tip may have been insufficient for a narcotics arrest or search warrant, the information carried enough indicia of reliability to justify the officer's forcible stop of Williams.

Are you persuaded that the officer had reasonable suspicion, justifying a seizure or search of Williams?

4. An important factor in *Alabama v. White*, one that put the police conduct on the proper side of the "reasonable suspicion" line, was that the anonymous informant accurately predicted future behavior of the suspect. Even with that, you will notice that the Court characterized the facts as

presenting "a close case" on the issue of reasonable suspicion. In this regard, consider Florida v. J.L., 529 U.S. 266, 120 S.Ct. 1375, 146 L.Ed.2d 254 (2000).

In *J.L.*, an anonymous caller told police that "a young black male standing at a particular bus stop and wearing a plaid shirt was carrying a gun." Two officers went to the location and observed three black males, one wearing a plaid shirt, "just hanging out [there]." Nothing about their behavior apart from the tip aroused suspicion, and no gun was visible. Nonetheless, the officers seized J.L., a minor, and frisked him. The Court *unanimously* held that the anonymous tip exhibited insufficient indicia of reliability to provide reasonable suspicion for the police action. Speaking for the Court, Justice Ginsburg wrote:

> The tip in the instant case lacked the moderate indicia of reliability present in *White* and essential to the Court's decision in that case. The anonymous call concerning J.L. provided no predictive information and therefore left the police without means to test the informant's knowledge or credibility. * * * All the police had to go on in this case was the bare report of an unknown, unaccountable informant who neither explained how he knew about the gun nor supplied any basis for believing he had inside information about J.L. If *White* was a close case on the reliability of anonymous tips, this one surely falls on the other side of the line.

> Florida contends that the tip was reliable because its description of the suspect's visible attributes proved accurate: There really was a young black male wearing a plaid shirt at the bus stop. * * *

> An accurate description of a subject's readily observable location and appearance is of course reliable in this limited sense: It will help the police correctly identify the person whom the tipster means to accuse. Such a tip, however, does not show that the tipster has knowledge of concealed criminal activity. The reasonable suspicion here at issue requires that a tip be reliable in its assertion of illegality, not just in its tendency to identify a determinate person.

Reconsider *Adams v. Williams* (Note 3). Is *J.L.* distinguishable?

5. The Supreme Court had another opportunity to consider the issues raised in *Alabama v. White* and *Florida v. J.L.* (Note 4). The facts in Navarette v. California, 572 U.S. ___, 134 S.Ct. 1683, 188 L.Ed.2d 680 (2014), were fairly simple: At 3:47 p.m., a 911 call relayed an anonymous tip from the caller to the effect that a Ford pickup had run the reporting party off the road five minutes earlier at a specified point on the highway. The caller described the Ford and provided a license plate number.

At 4:00 p.m., a highway patrol officer spotted the vehicle (roughly 19 miles away from the reported incident). He did not observe anything unusual about the way the pickup was being driven. Nonetheless, at about 4:05 p.m., the officer pulled the driver over. The officer smelled marijuana. A search of the truck bed revealed 30 pounds of marijuana. Driver Navarette and his passenger were arrested.

The issue was whether the initial stop, based as it was solely on the anonymous information provided by the caller, was founded on reasonable suspicion. The Court, 5–4, in an opinion authored by Justice Clarence Thomas, concluded that the stop was lawful. He stated that "under appropriate circumstance, an anonymous tip can demonstrate sufficient indicia of reliability to provide reasonable suspicion to make [an] investigatory stop."

Here, the Court found that "[b]y reporting that she had been run off the road by a specific vehicle, * * * the caller necessarily claimed eyewitness knowledge of the alleged dangerous driving. That basis of knowledge lends significant support to the tip's reliability." Thomas contrasted these facts to *J.L.*, "where the tip provided no basis for concluding that the tipster had actually seen the gun. Even in *White*, where we upheld the stop, there was scant evidence that the tipster had actually observed cocaine in the station wagon."

What about the other prong, namely, the anonymous caller's truthfulness? Justice Thomas said that there was "reason to think that the 911 caller in this case was telling the truth." The vehicle was in a location that was consistent with the call. Moreover, the "timeline of events suggests that the caller reported the incident soon after she was run off the road. That sort of contemporaneous report has long been treated as especially reliable." The Court offered still another justification for treating the call as reliable:

> A 911 call has some [technological] features that allow for identifying and tracing callers, and thus provide some safeguards against making false reports with immunity. * * * The caller's use of the 911 system is therefore one of the relevant circumstances that, taken together, justified the officer's reliance on the information reported in the 911 call.

But, even if so, what did it give the officers reasonable suspicion to believe had occurred? Actually, the Court said that the issue was not whether there was reasonable suspicion a crime had *occurred*—the Court again (see p. 405, Note 6) left open the issue of how the Court should deal with *Terry* stops for the purpose of investigating completed minor offenses—but rather whether there was reasonable suspicion that a crime was *occurring*, namely, drunk driving. But, does *that* follow?

> [T]he accumulated experience of thousands of officers suggests that * * * erratic behaviors [on the highway] are strongly correlated with drunk driving. Of course, not all traffic infractions imply intoxication. Unconfirmed reports of driving without a seatbelt or slightly over the speed limit, for example, are so tenuously connected to drunk driving that a stop on those grounds alone

would be constitutionally suspect. But a reliable tip alleging the dangerous behaviors discussed above generally would justify a traffic stop on suspicion of drunk driving.

The 911 caller * * * alleged a specific and dangerous result of the driver's conduct: running another car off the highway. That conduct bears too great a resemblance to paradigmatic manifestations of drunk driving to be dismissed as an isolated example of recklessness.

What about the fact that the officer did not observe erratic driving? Justice Thomas stated: "It is hardly surprising that the appearance of a marked police car would inspire more careful driving for a time." The Court concluded:

Like *White*, this is a "close case." * * * Under the totality of the circumstances, we find the indicia of reliability in this case sufficient to provide the officer with reasonable suspicion that the driver of the reported vehicle had run another vehicle off the road. That made it reasonable under the circumstances for the officer to execute a traffic stop.

Justice Scalia, joined by Justices Ginsburg, Kagan, and Sotomayor, dissented:

The tipster said the truck had "[run her] off the roadway," but the police had no reason to credit that charge and many reasons to doubt it, beginning with the peculiar fact that the accusation was anonymous. "[E]liminating accountability * * * is ordinarily the very purpose of anonymity." The unnamed tipster "can lie with impunity." Anonymity is especially suspicious with respect to the call that is the subject of the present case. When does a victim complain to the police about an arguably criminal act (running the victim off the road) without giving his identity, so that he can accuse and testify when the culprit is caught?

Justice Scalia described *Alabama v. White* as "extreme," but less so than the present case:

[In *White*], the reliability of the tip was established by the fact that it predicted the target's behavior in the finest detail—a detail that could be known only by someone familiar with the target's business * * *. Here the Court makes a big deal of the fact that the tipster was dead right about the fact that a silver Ford F-150 truck (license plate 8D94925) was traveling south on Highway 1 somewhere near mile marker 88. But everyone in the world who saw the car would have that knowledge, and anyone who wanted the car stopped would have to provide that information. Unlike the situation in *White*, that generally available knowledge in no way makes it plausible that the tipster saw the car run someone off the road.

Justice Scalia went on:

> The Court says that "[b]y reporting that she had been run off the
> road by a specific vehicle * * * the caller necessarily claimed
> eyewitness knowledge." So what? The issue is not how she claimed
> to know, but whether what she claimed to know was true. The claim
> to "eyewitness knowledge" of being run off the road supports *not at
> all* its veracity * * * .

As for the caller's veracity, the dissenters were similarly unimpressed.
What about the majority's point, however, that the tipster's identity can be
verified through the 911 system? Justice Scalia's response had a ring of
sarcasm:

> [T]he Court says that [an] * * * "indicator of veracity" is the
> anonymous tipster's mere "use of the 911 emergency system."
> Because, you see, recent "technological and regulatory
> developments" suggest that the identities of unnamed 911 callers
> are increasingly less likely to remain unknown. Indeed, the systems
> are able to identify "the caller's geographic location with increasing
> specificity." *Amici* disagree with this, * * * and the present case
> surely suggests that *amici* are right—since we know neither the
> identity of the tipster nor even the county from which the call was
> made. But assuming the Court is right about the ease of identifying
> 911 callers, it proves absolutely nothing in the present case unless
> the anonymous caller was *aware* of that fact. "It is the tipster's
> *belief* in anonymity, not its *reality*, that will control his behavior."
> There is no reason to believe that your average anonymous 911
> tipster is aware that 911 callers are readily identifiable.

But, Justice Scalia was not done:

> All that has been said up to now assumes that the anonymous caller
> made, at least in effect, an accusation of drunken driving. But in
> fact she did not. She said that the petitioners' truck " '[r]an [me] off
> the roadway.' " That neither asserts that the driver was drunk nor
> even raises the *likelihood* that the driver was drunk. The most it
> conveys is that the truck did some apparently nontypical thing that
> forced the tipster off the roadway, whether partly or fully,
> temporarily or permanently. Who really knows what (if anything)
> happened? The truck might have swerved to avoid an animal, a
> pothole, or a jaywalking pedestrian.
>
>   But let us assume the worst of the many possibilities: that it was
> a careless, reckless, or even intentional maneuver that forced the
> tipster off the road. [The driver] might have been distracted by his
> use of a hands-free cell phone, or distracted by an intense sports
> argument with [the passenger]. Or, indeed, he might have
> intentionally forced the tipster off the road because of some personal
> animus, or hostility to her "Make Love, Not War" bumper sticker. I

fail to see how reasonable suspicion of a *discrete instance* of irregular or hazardous driving generates a reasonable suspicion of *ongoing intoxicated driving*. What proportion of the hundreds of thousands—perhaps millions—of careless, reckless, or intentional traffic violations committed each day is attributable to drunken drivers? I say 0.1 percent. I have no basis for that except my own guesswork. But unless the Court has some basis in reality to believe that the proportion is many orders of magnitude above that—say 1 in 10 or at least 1 in 20—it has no grounds for its unsupported assertion that the tipster's report in this case gave rise to a *reasonable suspicion* of drunken driving.

It gets worse. Not only, it turns out, did the police have no good reason *at first* to believe that Lorenzo [Navarette] was driving drunk, they had very good reason *at last* to know that he was not. The Court concludes that the tip, plus confirmation of the truck's location, produced reasonable suspicion that the truck not only had been *but still was* barreling dangerously and drunkenly down Highway 1. In fact, alas, it was not, and the officers knew it. They followed the truck for five minutes, presumably to see if it was being operated recklessly. And *that* was good police work. * * * But the pesky little detail left out of the Court's reasonable-suspicion equation is that, for the five minutes that the truck was being followed (five minutes is a *long* time), [the] driving was irreproachable. * * *

Resisting this line of reasoning, the Court curiously asserts that, since drunk drivers who see marked squad cars in their rearview mirrors may evade detection simply by driving "more careful[ly]," the "absence of additional suspicious conduct" is "hardly surprising" and thus largely irrelevant. Whether a drunk driver drives drunkenly, the Court seems to think, is up to him. That is not how I understand the influence of alcohol. I subscribe to the more traditional view that the dangers of intoxicated driving are the intoxicant's impairing effects on the body—effects that no mere act of the will can resist.

The dissenters closed with a warning:

All the malevolent 911 caller need do [in light of this case] is assert a traffic violation, and the targeted car will be stopped, forcibly if necessary, by the police. If the driver turns out not to be drunk (which will almost always be the case), the caller need fear no consequences, even if 911 knows his identity. After all, he never alleged drunkenness, but merely called in a traffic violation—and on that point his word is as good as his victim's.

Whose analysis—Justice Thomas's or Justice Scalia's—do you find more persuasive in light of *White* and *J.L.*?

6.   In Illinois v. Rodriguez (p. 376), we saw that the Supreme Court observed that "in order to satisfy the 'reasonableness' requirement of the Fourth Amendment, what is generally demanded of the many *factual* determinations that must be regularly be made by [police officers] * * * is not that they always be correct, but that they always be reasonable." (Emphasis added.) What, then, about a reasonable mistake of *law* by a police officer?

The Court spoke to this question in Heien v. North Carolina, 574 U.S. ___, 135 S.Ct. 530, 190 L.Ed.2d 475 (2014). A police officer noticed that only one of a vehicle's brake lights was working, so he pulled over the driver. While issuing a warning citation, the officer became suspicious of the conduct of Heien, the car owner, and his passenger. Consequently, the officer sought and obtained consent to search the vehicle, which turned up cocaine. Heien moved to suppress the evidence of the cocaine on the ground that his seizure—the stop of the vehicle—was unconstitutional. Indeed, it turned out that the applicable North Carolina statute only required that vehicles be equipped with a single working brake light. Therefore, the officer had no legal basis to stop the vehicle.

The Court held, 8–1, that the officer's misunderstanding of the law was reasonable (in view of an ambiguity in the code provision) and, therefore, there was reasonable suspicion justifying the stop of the vehicle. Chief Justice Roberts stated that "[w]e have recognized that searches and seizures based on mistakes of fact can be reasonable." And, he said, "reasonable men make mistakes of law, too, and such mistakes are no less compatible with the concept of reasonable suspicion [and probable cause]." Justice Sotomayor dissented.

7.   *Racial profiling and reasonable suspicion.* Racial profiling (that is, the use of race or ethnicity as the primary criterion in conducting stops, searches, and other law enforcement investigative procedures) is a serious issue in light of the Supreme Court's ruling in *Whren v. United States*, p. 298, but it is magnified by *Terry v. Ohio* and the lower standard of cause that an officer may use to temporarily detain a person on the street or in a car.

For example, an officer might use something as minor as an apparent crack in a vehicle windshield as justification to stop an African-American (or Hispanic, etc.) driver on the ground that it constitutes reasonable suspicion that the driver is violating a statute that prohibits driving "in such unsafe condition as to endanger any person." Muse v. State, 146 Md.App. 395, 807 A.2d 113 (2002). The officer might then use this stop in order to seek consent to conduct a drug or weapons search of the car—a search that she might not have sought to conduct if the driver had been white. Indeed, the officer might not have stopped the car with the cracked windshield in the first place but for the fact the driver was black or Hispanic.

That racial profiling is a part of this nation's experience is not speculative. In Maryland, from 1995 through 1997, a survey indicated that 70% of drivers stopped on Interstate 95 were African-American, although 17.5% of the traffic and speeders on the road were black. David Cole, No

Equal Justice 36 (1999). Videotapes in one Florida county demonstrated that 5% of the drivers appeared to be dark-skinned, but 70% of the drivers stopped were African-American or Hispanic, and more than 80% of cars searched on the highway were persons of color. Traffic tickets, however, were given in less than 1% of the stops. *Id.* at 37. Or, consider the following uncontested findings of fact on stops-and-frisks in New York City, as reported in Floyd v. City of New York, 959 F.Supp.2d 540 (S.D.N.Y. 2013):

- Between January 2004 and June 2012, the NYPD conducted over 4.4 million *Terry* stops.

- The number of stops per year rose sharply from 314,000 in 2004 to a high of 686,000 in 2011.

- 52% of all stops were followed by a protective frisk for weapons. A weapon was found after 1.5% of these frisks. In other words, in 98.5% of the 2.3 million frisks, no weapon was found.

- 8% of all stops led to a search into the stopped person's clothing, ostensibly based on the officer feeling an object during the frisk that he suspected to be a weapon, or immediately perceived to be contraband other than a weapon. In 9% of these searches, the felt object was in fact a weapon. 91% of the time, it was not. In 14% of these searches, the felt object was in fact contraband. 86% of the time it was not.

- 6% of all stops resulted in an arrest, and 6% resulted in a summons. The remaining 88% of the 4.4 million stops resulted in no further law enforcement action.

- In 52% of the 4.4 million stops, the person stopped was black.

- In 31% of the stops, the person stopped was Hispanic.

- In 10% of the stops, the person stopped was white.

- In 2010, New York City's resident population was roughly 23% black, 29% Hispanic, and 33% white.

- In 23% of the stops of blacks, and 24% of the stops of Hispanics, the officer recorded using force. The number for whites was 17%.

- Weapons were seized in 1.0% of the stops of blacks, 1.1% of the stops of Hispanics, and 1.4% of the stops of whites.

- Contraband other than weapons was seized in 1.8% of the stops of blacks, 1.7% of the stops of Hispanics, and 2.3% of the stops of whites.

- For the years 2004 to 2009, the two most commonly [provided justifications] * * * for a stop were "Furtive Movements" and "Area Has Incidence Of Reported Offense Of Type Under Investigation" ("High Crime Area"). * * * [O]fficers marked "Furtive Movements" as a basis for the stop on 42% of the forms, and "High Crime Area" on 55% of the forms. In 2009, officers indicated "Furtive Movements" as a basis for the stop nearly 60% of the time.

- Both "Furtive Movements" and "High Crime Area" are weak indicators of criminal activity. For the years 2004 to 2009, stops were 22% more likely to result in arrest if "High Crime Area" was *not* checked, and 18% more likely to result in arrest if "Furtive Movements" was not checked.

District Judge Shira Scheindlin determined that because this police tactic was employed predominantly against young African-American and Hispanic males, the stops-and-frisks violated the Constitution.

Is there a way to justify disproportionate *Terry* stops of young, male racial minorities? One commanding officer in New York was tape recorded stating that his officers should frisk "the right people at the right time, the right location," and when asked what the "right location" meant, specified a particular location, stating "I told you at roll call, and I have no problem telling you this, male blacks 14, to 20, 21." Joseph Goldstein, *Bronx Inspector, Secretly Recorded, Suggests Race Is Factor in a Police Tactic*, New York Times, March 22, 2013, at A21. If the data supported the proposition that the "particular location" was a high crime area, and if the data supported the proposition that young males of color were more prone than others to commit offenses with weapons in that area, should that justify stops of persons fitting that category? Consider this remark:

> [M]ost criminologists who have studied the matter have concluded that blacks (and men and young people) do in fact commit crime in a higher per capita rate than whites (and women and older people). Thus, all other things being equal, it is rational to be more suspicious of a young black man than an elderly white woman. But that it may be rational does not make it right.

Cole, supra, at 42. If it *is rational* to be more suspicious of young black men than elderly white women, why isn't it also *right* and *constitutional* to be more suspicious? In this regard, suppose a small town near the Mexican border experiences a large influx of Hispanics into their community in a short period of time. Would it be rational for federal agents to suspect that many of them are in the country illegally? If so, should it be constitutional for the agents to briefly detain any person in that town who appears to be of Mexican descent, solely on that basis? Consider these remarks by Justice Sotomayor, in dissent, in Utah v. Strieff, 579 U.S. ___, 136 S.Ct. 2056, 195 L.Ed.2d 400 (2016):

> For generations, black and brown parents have given their children "the talk"—instructing them never to run down the street; always keep your hands where they can be seen; do not even think of

talking back to a stranger—all out of fear of how an officer with a gun will react to them. * * *

We must not pretend that the countless people who are routinely targeted by the police are "isolated." They are the canaries in the coal mine [who] * * * warn us that no one can breathe in this atmosphere. They are the ones who recognize that unlawful police stops corrode all of our civil liberties and threaten all of our lives. Until their voices matter too, our justice system will continue to be anything but.

For more on the subject, see Sherry F. Colb, *Profiling With Apologies*, 1 Ohio St. J. Crim. L. 611 (2004); Sharon L. Davies, *Profiling Terror*, 1 Ohio St. J. Crim. L. 45 (2003); Kent Greenawalt, *Probabilities, Perceptions, Consequences and "Discrimination": One Puzzle about Controversial "Stop and Frisk,"* 12 Ohio St. J. Crim. L. 181 (2014); and David A. Harris, Profiles in Injustice: Why Racial Profiling Cannot Work (2002).

8.   *Converting reasonable suspicion into an arrest?* May the police leap-frog from a *Terry* seizure based on reasonable suspicion into an arrest by simply asking the seized individual for her name and, if she refuses to answer, arresting her for that failure? Perhaps so if a state enacts a law requiring a properly detained individual to identify herself to the police.

In Hiibel v. Sixth Judicial District Court of Nevada, Humboldt County, 542 U.S. 177, 124 S.Ct. 2451, 159 L.Ed.2d 292 (2004), a deputy sheriff was dispatched to investigate a report of a man assaulting a woman. When the officer arrived at the scene, he found a man standing outside a truck, with a young woman sitting inside it. The man appeared intoxicated. The deputy asked the man, later identified to be Larry Hiibel, for identification. At least eleven times Hiibel refused to provide identification. Consequently, the deputy arrested him for "willfully resist[ing], delay[ing], or obstruct[ing] a public officer in discharging or attempting to discharge any legal duty of his office." The government reasoned that Hiibel had violated this statute because another statute, a so-called "stop and identify" statute, authorized police officers to "detain any person whom the officer encounters under circumstances which reasonably indicate that the person has committed, is committing or is about to commit a crime," and to "ascertain [the individual's] identity." The latter statute provided that "[a]ny person so detained shall identify himself."

Stop-and-identify statutes cannot be enforced if the stop—the initial seizure that presages the request for identification—is unlawful for want of reasonable suspicion. But, what about here, where Hiibel conceded that the deputy had grounds to conduct a *Terry*-level seizure?

Justice Kennedy, writing for the majority, explained that properly crafted and enforced stop-and-identify laws are constitutional:

Our decisions make clear that questions concerning a suspect's identity are a routine and accepted part of many *Terry* stops. * * *

The principles of *Terry* permit a State to require a suspect to disclose his name in the course of a *Terry* stop. The reasonableness of a seizure under the Fourth Amendment is determined "by balancing its intrusion on the individual's Fourth Amendment interests against its promotion of legitimate government interests." The Nevada statute [in this case] satisfies that standard. The request for identity has an immediate relation to the purpose, rationale, and practical demands of a *Terry* stop. The threat of criminal sanction helps ensure that the request for identity does not become a legal nullity. On the other hand, the Nevada statute does not alter the nature of the stop itself: it does not change its duration, or its location. A state law requiring a suspect to disclose his name in the course of a valid *Terry* stop is consistent with Fourth Amendment prohibitions against unreasonable searches and seizures.

Petitioner argues that the Nevada statute circumvents the probable cause requirement, in effect allowing an officer to arrest a person for being suspicious. According to petitioner, this creates a risk of arbitrary police conduct that the Fourth Amendment does not permit. * * * Petitioner's concerns are met by the requirement that a *Terry* stop must be justified at its inception and "reasonably related in scope to the circumstances which justified" the initial stop. Under these principles, an officer may not arrest a suspect for failure to identify himself if the request for identification is not reasonably related to the circumstances justifying the stop. * * * It is clear in this case that the request for identification was "reasonably related in scope to the circumstances which justified" the stop.

9.   *Problem.* Suppose that the police know that X is a drug dealer. Indeed, they observed a videotape of X selling drugs a few weeks earlier. Now they observe X talking to D, someone about whom they have no prior information. X is holding a plastic sandwich container and nervously looking around; their meeting lasts only two minutes, the same length of time as the drug sale in the videotape, and takes place in the interior of X's car. Do these facts justify a *Terry* stop of D after he leaves X? *Holt v. State,* 78 A.3d 415 (Md. 2013).

ILLINOIS V. WARDLOW

Supreme Court of the United States, 2000.
528 U.S. 119, 120 S.Ct. 673, 145 L.Ed.2d 570.

CHIEF JUSTICE REHNQUIST delivered the opinion of the Court [joined by JUSTICES O'CONNOR, SCALIA, KENNEDY, and THOMAS].

Respondent Wardlow fled upon seeing police officers patrolling an area known for heavy narcotics trafficking. Two of the officers caught up with him, stopped him, and conducted a protective patdown search for weapons. Discovering a .38-caliber handgun, the officers arrested Wardlow. We hold that the officers' stop did not violate the Fourth Amendment * * * .

On September 9, 1995, Officers Nolan and Harvey were working as uniformed officers in the special operations section of the Chicago Police Department. The officers were driving the last car of a four car caravan converging on an area known for heavy narcotics trafficking in order to investigate drug transactions. The officers were traveling together because they expected to find a crowd of people in the area, including lookouts and customers.

As the caravan passed 4035 West Van Buren, Officer Nolan observed respondent Wardlow standing next to the building holding an opaque bag. Respondent looked in the direction of the officers and fled. Nolan and Harvey turned their car southbound, watched him as he ran through * * * an alley, and eventually cornered him on the street. Nolan then exited his car and stopped respondent. He immediately conducted a protective pat-down search for weapons because in his experience it was common for there to be weapons in the near vicinity of narcotics transactions. During the frisk, Officer Nolan * * * felt a heavy, hard object similar to the shape of a gun. The officer then opened the bag and discovered a .38-caliber handgun with five live rounds of ammunition. The officers arrested Wardlow.

The Illinois trial court denied respondent's motion to suppress, finding the gun was recovered during a lawful stop and frisk. * * * Wardlow was convicted of unlawful use of a weapon by a felon. The Illinois Appellate Court reversed Wardlow's conviction, concluding that the gun should have been suppressed because Officer Nolan did not have reasonable suspicion sufficient to justify an investigative stop pursuant to *Terry v. Ohio.*

The Illinois Supreme Court agreed. While rejecting the Appellate Court's conclusion that Wardlow was not in a high crime area, the Illinois Supreme Court determined that sudden flight in such an area does not create a reasonable suspicion justifying a *Terry* stop. * * * [T]he court explained that although police have the right to approach individuals and ask questions, the individual has no obligation to respond. The person may decline to answer and simply go on his or her way, and the refusal to respond, alone, does not provide a legitimate basis for an investigative stop. The court then determined that flight may simply be an exercise of this right to "go on one's way," and, thus, could not constitute reasonable suspicion justifying a *Terry* stop.

The Illinois Supreme Court also rejected the argument that flight combined with the fact that it occurred in a high crime area supported a finding of reasonable suspicion * * * . Finding no independently suspicious circumstances to support an investigatory detention, the court held that the stop and subsequent arrest violated the Fourth Amendment. * * *

This case, involving a brief encounter between a citizen and a police officer on a public street, is governed by the analysis we first applied in *Terry*. * * *

* * * An individual's presence in an area of expected criminal activity, standing alone, is not enough to support a reasonable, particularized suspicion that the person is committing a crime. But officers are not required to ignore the relevant characteristics of a location in determining whether the circumstances are sufficiently suspicious to warrant further investigation. Accordingly, we have previously noted the fact that the stop occurred in a "high crime area" among the relevant contextual considerations in a *Terry* analysis.

In this case, moreover, it was not merely respondent's presence in an area of heavy narcotics trafficking that aroused the officers' suspicion but his unprovoked flight upon noticing the police. Our cases have also recognized that nervous, evasive behavior is a pertinent factor in determining reasonable suspicion. Headlong flight—wherever it occurs—is the consummate act of evasion: it is not necessarily indicative of wrongdoing, but it is certainly suggestive of such. In reviewing the propriety of an officer's conduct, courts do not have available empirical studies dealing with inferences drawn from suspicious behavior, and we cannot reasonably demand scientific certainty from judges or law enforcement officers where none exists. Thus, the determination of reasonable suspicion must be based on commonsense judgments and inferences about human behavior. We conclude Officer Nolan was justified in suspecting that Wardlow was involved in criminal activity, and, therefore, in investigating further.

Such a holding is entirely consistent with our decision in *Florida v. Royer* [p. 413, Note 3], where we held that when an officer, without reasonable suspicion or probable cause, approaches an individual, the individual has a right to ignore the police and go about his business. * * * But unprovoked flight is simply not a mere refusal to cooperate. Flight, by its very nature, is not "going about one's business"; in fact, it is just the opposite. Allowing officers confronted with such flight to stop the fugitive and investigate further is quite consistent with the individual's right to go about his business or to stay put and remain silent in the face of police questioning.

Respondent and *amici* also argue that there are innocent reasons for flight from police and that, therefore, flight is not necessarily indicative of ongoing criminal activity. This fact is undoubtedly true, but does not establish a violation of the Fourth Amendment. Even in *Terry*, the conduct justifying the stop was ambiguous and susceptible of an innocent explanation. * * * *Terry* recognized that the officers could detain the individuals to resolve the ambiguity.

In allowing such detentions, *Terry* accepts the risk that officers may stop innocent people. Indeed, the Fourth Amendment accepts that risk in connection with more drastic police action; persons arrested and detained on probable cause to believe they have committed a crime may turn out to be innocent. The *Terry* stop is a far more minimal intrusion, simply allowing the officer to briefly investigate further. * * *

The judgment of the Supreme Court of Illinois is reversed * * * . * * *

JUSTICE STEVENS, with whom JUSTICE SOUTER, JUSTICE GINSBURG, and JUSTICE BREYER join, concurring in part and dissenting in part.

The State of Illinois asks this Court to announce a "bright-line rule" authorizing the temporary detention of anyone who flees at the mere sight of a police officer. Respondent counters by asking us to adopt the opposite *per se* rule—that the fact that a person flees upon seeing the police can never, by itself, be sufficient to justify a temporary investigative stop of the kind authorized by *Terry v. Ohio*. * * *

Although I agree with the Court's rejection of the *per se* rules proffered by the parties, unlike the Court, I am persuaded that in this case the brief testimony of the officer who seized respondent does not justify the conclusion that he had reasonable suspicion to make the stop. Before discussing the specific facts of this case, I shall comment on the parties' requests for a *per se* rule.

I * * *

* * * A pedestrian may break into a run for a variety of reasons—to catch up with a friend a block or two away, to seek shelter from an impending storm, to arrive at a bus stop before the bus leaves, to get home in time for dinner, to resume jogging after a pause for rest, to avoid contact with a bore or a bully, or simply to answer the call of nature—any of which might coincide with the arrival of an officer in the vicinity. A pedestrian might also run because he or she has just sighted one or more police officers. In the latter instance, the State properly points out "that the fleeing person may be, *inter alia*, (1) an escapee from jail, (2) wanted on a warrant, (3) in possession of contraband, (*i.e.*, drugs, weapons, stolen goods, etc.); or (4) someone who has just committed another type of crime." In short, there are unquestionably circumstances in which a person's flight is suspicious, and undeniably instances in which a person runs for entirely innocent reasons.

Given the diversity and frequency of possible motivations for flight, it would be profoundly unwise to endorse either *per se* rule. The inference we can reasonably draw about the motivation for a person's flight, rather, will depend on a number of different circumstances. Factors such as the time of day, the number of people in the area, the character of the neighborhood, whether the officer was in uniform, the way the runner was dressed, the direction and speed of the flight, and whether the person's behavior was otherwise unusual might be relevant in specific cases. This number of variables is surely sufficient to preclude either a bright-line rule that always justifies, or that never justifies, an investigative stop based on the sole fact that flight began after a police officer appeared nearby. * * *

Even assuming we know that a person runs because he sees the police, the inference to be drawn may still vary from case to case. Flight to escape police detection, we have said, may have an entirely innocent motivation * * * . [Innocent people flee, *inter alia*, out of fear of being wrongfully arrested or forced to appear as a witness to a crime.]

In addition to these concerns, a reasonable person may conclude that an officer's sudden appearance indicates nearby criminal activity. And where there is criminal activity there is also a substantial element of danger—either from the criminal or from a confrontation between the criminal and the police. These considerations can lead to an innocent and understandable desire to quit the vicinity with all speed.

Among some citizens, particularly minorities and those residing in high crime areas, there is also the possibility that the fleeing person is entirely innocent, but, with or without justification, believes that contact with the police can itself be dangerous, apart from any criminal activity associated with the officer's sudden presence. For such a person, unprovoked flight is neither "aberrant" nor "abnormal." Moreover, these concerns and fears are known to the police officers themselves, and are validated by law enforcement investigations into their own practices. Accordingly, the evidence supporting the reasonableness of these beliefs is too pervasive to be dismissed as random or rare, and too persuasive to be disparaged as inconclusive or insufficient. In any event, just as we do not require "scientific certainty" for our commonsense conclusion that unprovoked flight can sometimes indicate suspicious motives, neither do we require scientific certainty to conclude that unprovoked flight can occur for other, innocent reasons.[12] * * *

II

Guided by that totality-of-the-circumstances test, the Court concludes that Officer Nolan had reasonable suspicion to stop respondent. In this respect, my view differs from the Court's. * * *

---

[12] As a general matter, local courts often have a keener and more informed sense of local police practices and events that may heighten these concerns at particular times or locations. Thus, a reviewing court may accord substantial deference to a local court's determination that fear of the police is especially acute in a specific location or at a particular time.

Officer Nolan and his partner were in the last of the four patrol cars that "were all caravaning eastbound down Van Buren." Nolan first observed respondent "in front of 4035 West Van Buren." Wardlow "looked in our direction and began fleeing." Nolan then "began driving southbound down the street observing [respondent] running through the gangway and the alley southbound," and observed that Wardlow was carrying a white, opaque bag under his arm. * * *

This terse testimony is most noticeable for what it fails to reveal. Though asked whether he was in a marked or unmarked car, Officer Nolan could not recall the answer. He was not asked whether any of the other three cars in the caravan were marked, or whether any of the other seven officers were in uniform. Though he explained that the size of the caravan was because "[n]ormally in these different areas there's an enormous amount of people, sometimes lookouts, customers," Officer Nolan did not testify as to whether *anyone* besides Wardlow was nearby 4035 West Van Buren. Nor is it clear that that address was the intended destination of the caravan. * * * Officer Nolan's testimony also does not reveal how fast the officers were driving. It does not indicate whether he saw respondent notice the other patrol cars. And it does not say whether the caravan, or any part of it, had already passed Wardlow by before he began to run.

Indeed, the Appellate Court thought the record was even "too vague to support the inference that * * * defendant's flight was related to his expectation of police focus on him." Presumably, respondent did not react to the first three cars, and we cannot even be sure that he recognized the occupants of the fourth as police officers. The adverse inference is based entirely on the officer's statement: "He looked in our direction and began fleeing."

No other factors sufficiently support a finding of reasonable suspicion. * * *

The State, along with the majority of the Court, relies as well on the assumption that this flight occurred in a high crime area. Even if that assumption is accurate, it is insufficient because even in a high crime neighborhood unprovoked flight does not invariably lead to reasonable suspicion. On the contrary, because many factors providing innocent motivations for unprovoked flight are concentrated in high crime areas, the character of the neighborhood arguably makes an inference of guilt less appropriate, rather than more so. Like unprovoked flight itself, presence in a high crime neighborhood is a fact too generic and susceptible to innocent explanation to satisfy the reasonable suspicion inquiry. * * *

NOTES AND QUESTIONS

1.   In your view, should "unprovoked flight" = "reasonable suspicion"? If not, in your view should "unprovoked flight" + "high-crime area" = "reasonable suspicion"? Can you posit a set of facts in which this is *not* an accurate formula?

2.   Lenese C. Herbert, *Can't You See What I'm Saying? Making Expressive Conduct a Crime in High-Crimes Areas*, 9 Geo. J. Pov. L. & Pol'y 135, 135–36, 165 (2002):

> As an eager young Assistant United States Attorney who "papered" countless complaints, conducted numerous hearings, and tried a substantial number of cases, I learned how to decode police officer jargon and law enforcement terminology. One of the most commonly used—yet seldom defined—phrases was "high-crime area." * * * Before court appearance, I would often question police officers about this characterization. In court, however, judges * * * never asked officers for data to support assertions that an area was high-crime. Even defense counsel seldom explored what this classification meant, the bases for it, or its relevance. * * *

> I suspected that the police were using a code language to suggest that their actions were justified because they were directed at "high-crime people": poor, undereducated, black and brown males who live in or frequent depressed * * * inner-city neighborhoods, or who look as if they do. In practice, police have the implicit authorization to create and apply an inferior set of rights to individuals in high-crime areas, presumably because those individuals are regarded as being less worthy than other citizens. * * *

> * * * The *Wardlow* Court * * * has virtually relinquished the protection and safeguarding of the rights of the policed to the police themselves.

Are these criticisms fair?

3.   *Problem*. Officers on patrol observed a car leaving the area with one headlight out and an expired inspection sticker. The officers signaled for the car to stop. The driver complied. As the officers approached the driver's side, *B*, a passenger in the front seat, jumped out and ran away. One officer gave chase and tackled him. Reasonable suspicion for *this* seizure? United States v. Bonner, 363 F.3d 213 (3d Cir. 2004). Does your answer depend on whether this occurred: (a) near a housing project in a poor part of town; or (b) in the Beverly Hills, California business district?

e.   Expanding the Scope of the *Terry* Balancing Approach

Introductory Comment

Notice that what we have covered so far regarding *Terry v. Ohio* has involved persons, rather than property—specifically, the warrantless "brief" seizures and, sometimes, "minimal" frisk-searches of persons. But, once one shifts the focus from the warrant clause to the reasonableness clause, and thus once a court balances the individual's Fourth Amendment interests against the government's interest in criminal law enforcement, there is nothing that conceptually limits this approach to stop-and-frisk (or stop-and-question) scenarios.

Indeed, as the following case and Notes demonstrate, it turns out that the *Terry* balancing approach extends to other criminal investigatory situations: to justify some warrantless, probable-cause-less, limited seizures and searches of *property*, as well as minimal *non*-frisk searches of persons, including some DNA searches.

MARYLAND V. BUIE
Supreme Court of the United States, 1990.
494 U.S. 325, 110 S.Ct. 1093, 108 L.Ed.2d 276.

JUSTICE WHITE delivered the opinion of the Court [joined by CHIEF JUSTICE REHNQUIST, and JUSTICES BLACKMUN, STEVENS, O'CONNOR, SCALIA, and KENNEDY].

A "protective sweep" is a quick and limited search of premises, incident to an arrest and conducted to protect the safety of police officers or others. It is narrowly confined to a cursory visual inspection of those places in which a person might be hiding. In this case we must decide what level of justification is required by the Fourth and Fourteenth Amendments before police officers, while effecting the arrest of a suspect in his home pursuant to an arrest warrant, may conduct a warrantless protective sweep of all or part of the premises. * * *

I

On February 3, 1986, two men committed an armed robbery of a Godfather's Pizza restaurant in Prince George's County, Maryland. One of the robbers was wearing a red running suit. That same day, Prince George's County police obtained arrest warrants for respondent Jerome Edward Buie and his suspected accomplice in the robbery, Lloyd Allen. Buie's house was placed under police surveillance.

On February 5, the police executed the arrest warrant for Buie. They first had a police department secretary telephone Buie's house to verify that he was home. The secretary spoke to a female first, then to Buie himself. Six or seven officers proceeded to Buie's house. Once inside, the officers fanned out through the first and second floors. Corporal James Rozar announced that he would "freeze" the basement so that no one could come up and surprise the officers. With his service revolver drawn, Rozar twice shouted into the basement, ordering anyone down there to come out. When a voice asked who was calling, Rozar announced three times: "this is the police, show me your hands." Eventually, a pair of hands appeared around the bottom of the stairwell and Buie emerged from the basement. He was arrested, searched, and handcuffed by Rozar. Thereafter, Detective Joseph Frolich entered the basement "in case there was someone else" down there. He noticed a red running suit lying in plain view on a stack of clothing and seized it.

The trial court denied Buie's motion to suppress the running suit * * * . * * *

II

It is not disputed that until the point of Buie's arrest the police had the right, based on the authority of the arrest warrant, to search anywhere in the house that Buie might have been found, including the basement. * * * There is also no dispute that if Detective Frolich's entry into the basement was lawful, the seizure of the red running suit, which was in plain view and which the officer had probable cause to believe was evidence of a crime, was also lawful under the Fourth Amendment. The issue in this case is what level of justification the Fourth Amendment required before Detective Frolich could legally enter the basement to see if someone else was there.

Petitioner, the State of Maryland, argues that, under a general reasonableness balancing test, police should be permitted to conduct a protective sweep whenever they make an in-home arrest for a violent crime. * * *

III

It goes without saying that the Fourth Amendment bars only unreasonable searches and seizures. Our cases show that in determining reasonableness, we have balanced the intrusion on the individual's Fourth Amendment interests against its promotion of legitimate governmental interests. Under this test, a search of the house or office is generally not reasonable without a warrant issued on probable cause. There are other contexts, however, where the public interest is such that neither a warrant nor probable cause is required.

The *Terry* [*v. Ohio*] case is most instructive for present purposes. * * * We stated [in *Terry*] that there is " 'no ready test for determining reasonableness other than by balancing the need to search * * * against the invasion which the search * * * entails.' " * * *

The ingredients to apply the balance struck in *Terry* * * * are present in this case. Possessing an arrest warrant and probable cause to believe Buie was in his home, the officers were entitled to enter and to search anywhere in the house in which Buie might be found. Once he was found, however, the search for him was over, and there was no longer that particular justification for entering any rooms that had not yet been searched.

That Buie had an expectation of privacy in those remaining areas of his house, however, does not mean such rooms were immune from entry. In *Terry* * * * we were concerned with the immediate interest of the police officer[ ] in taking steps to assure [himself] that the persons with whom [he was] dealing were not armed with, or able to gain immediate control of, a weapon that could unexpectedly and fatally be used against [him]. In the instant case, there is an analogous interest of the officers in taking steps to assure themselves that the house in which a suspect is being, or has just been, arrested is not harboring other persons who are dangerous and who could unexpectedly launch an attack. The risk of danger in the context of an arrest in the home is as great as, if not greater than, it is in an on-the-street or roadside investigatory encounter. A *Terry* * * * frisk occurs before a police-citizen confrontation has escalated to the point of arrest. A protective sweep, in contrast, occurs as an adjunct to the serious step of taking a person into custody for the purpose of prosecuting him for a crime. Moreover, unlike an encounter on the street or along a highway, an in-home arrest puts the officer at the disadvantage of being on his adversary's "turf." An ambush in a confined setting of unknown configuration is more to be feared than it is in open, more familiar surroundings.

We recognized in *Terry* that "[e]ven a limited search of the outer clothing for weapons constitutes a severe, though brief, intrusion upon cherished personal security, and it must surely be an annoying, frightening, and perhaps humiliating experience." But we permitted the intrusion, which was no more than necessary to protect the officer from harm. Nor do we here suggest, as the State does, that entering rooms not examined prior to the arrest is a *de minimis* intrusion that may be disregarded. We are quite sure, however, that the arresting officers are permitted in such circumstances to take reasonable steps to ensure their safety after, and while making, the arrest. That interest is sufficient to outweigh the intrusion such procedures may entail.

We agree with the State * * * that a warrant was not required. We also hold that as an incident to the arrest the officers could, as a precautionary matter and without probable cause or reasonable suspicion, look in closets and other spaces immediately adjoining the place of arrest from which an attack could be immediately launched. Beyond that, however, we hold that there must be articulable facts which, taken together with the rational inferences from those facts, would warrant a reasonably prudent officer in believing that the area to be swept harbors an individual posing a danger to those on the arrest scene. * * *

We should emphasize that such a protective sweep, aimed at protecting the arresting officers, if justified by the circumstances, is nevertheless not a full search of the premises, but may extend only to a cursory inspection of those spaces where a person may be found. The sweep lasts no longer than is necessary to dispel the reasonable suspicion of danger and in any event no longer than it takes to complete the arrest and depart the premises.

IV

* * * To reach our conclusion today * * * , we need not disagree with the Court's statement in *Chimel*, that "the invasion of privacy that results from a top-to-bottom search of a man's house [cannot be characterized] as 'minor,'" nor hold that "simply because some interference with an individual's privacy and freedom of movement has lawfully taken place, further intrusions should automatically be allowed despite the absence of a warrant that the Fourth Amendment would otherwise require." The type of search we authorize today is far removed from the "top-to-bottom" search involved in *Chimel*; moreover, it is decidedly not "automati[c]," but may be conducted only when justified by a reasonable, articulable suspicion that the house is harboring a person posing a danger to those on the arrest scene. * * *

We * * * remand this case to the Court of Appeals of Maryland for further proceedings not inconsistent with this opinion. * * *

JUSTICE STEVENS, concurring.

Today the Court holds that reasonable suspicion, rather than probable cause, is necessary to support a protective sweep while an arrest is in progress. I agree with that holding and with the Court's opinion, but I believe it is important to emphasize that the standard applies only to *protective* sweeps. Officers conducting such a sweep must have a reasonable basis for believing that their search will reduce the danger of harm to themselves or of violent interference with their mission; in short, the search must be protective.

In this case, to justify Officer Frolich's entry into the basement, it is the State's burden to demonstrate that the officers had a reasonable basis for believing not only that someone in the basement might attack them or otherwise try to interfere with the arrest, but also that it would be safer to go down the stairs instead of simply guarding them from above until respondent had been removed from the house. The fact that respondent offered no resistance when he emerged from the basement is somewhat inconsistent with the hypothesis that the danger of an attack by a hidden confederate persisted after the arrest. * * *

Indeed, were the officers concerned about safety, one would expect them to do what Officer Rozar did before the arrest: guard the basement door to prevent surprise attacks. As the Court indicates, Officer Frolich might, at the time of the arrest, reasonably have "look[ed] in" the already open basement door to ensure that no accomplice had followed Buie to the stairwell. But Officer Frolich did not merely "look in" the basement; he entered it. That strategy is sensible if one wishes to search the basement. It is a surprising choice for an officer, worried about safety, who need not risk entering the stairwell at all.

The State may thus face a formidable task on remand. However, the Maryland courts are better equipped than are we to review the record. * * * I therefore agree that a remand is appropriate.

[The concurring opinion of JUSTICE KENNEDY is omitted.]

JUSTICE BRENNAN, with whom JUSTICE MARSHALL joins, dissenting. * * *

* * * [T]he Court's implicit judgment that a protective sweep constitutes a "minimally intrusive" search akin to that involved in *Terry* markedly undervalues the nature and scope of the privacy interests involved.

While the Fourth Amendment protects a person's privacy interests in a variety of settings, "physical entry of the home is the chief evil against which the wording of the Fourth Amendment is directed." The Court discounts the nature of the intrusion because it believes that the scope of the intrusion is limited. The Court explains that a protective sweep's scope is "narrowly confined to a cursory visual inspection of those places in which a person might be hiding," and confined in duration to a period "no longer than is necessary to dispel the reasonable suspicion of danger and in any event no longer than it takes to complete the arrest and depart the premises." But these spatial and temporal restrictions are not particularly limiting. A protective sweep would bring within police purview virtually all personal possessions within the house not hidden from view in a small enclosed space. Police officers searching for potential ambushers might enter every room including basements and attics; open up closets, lockers, chests, wardrobes, and cars; and peer under beds and behind furniture. The officers will view letters, documents, and personal effects that are on tables or desks or are visible inside open drawers; books, records, tapes, and pictures on shelves; and clothing, medicines, toiletries and other paraphernalia not carefully stored in dresser drawers or bathroom cupboards. While perhaps not a "full-blown" or "top-to-bottom" search, a protective sweep is much closer to it than to a "limited patdown for weapons" * * *. * * * The "ingredient" of a minimally intrusive search is absent, and the Court's holding today therefore unpalatably deviates from *Terry* and its progeny.[6]

In light of the special sanctity of a private residence and the highly intrusive nature of a protective sweep, I firmly believe that police officers must have probable cause to fear that their personal safety is threatened by a hidden confederate of an arrestee before they may sweep through the entire home. * * * I respectfully dissent.

NOTES AND QUESTIONS

1.   On remand, the Court of Appeals of Maryland, 4–3, upheld the sweep. Buie v. State, 320 Md. 696, 580 A.2d 167 (1990).

2.   During a protective sweep, what may a police officer do if she finds a person hidden in a closet? Watching television in a family room? May she fully search the person? Automatically conduct a pat-down? May she conduct a search of the *grabbing area of that* person, even if this includes searching small areas, such as drawers, where a gun (but not another person) might be discovered?

3.   *Brief seizure of property?* In United States v. Place, 462 U.S. 696, 103 S.Ct. 2637, 77 L.Ed.2d 110 (1983), the Supreme Court extended the *Terry* analysis of temporary seizures of persons to personalty. In *Place*, law enforcement officers at Miami International Airport grew suspicious of Raymond Place's behavior and, after an initial investigation, alerted Drug Enforcement Administration (DEA) authorities in New York, where Place was traveling. When Place arrived at New York's LaGuardia airport, two DEA agents were waiting for him. Place's behavior there reasonably aroused the agents' suspicion. Therefore, they approached Place, identified themselves as federal narcotics agents, requested and received his identification, and then sought consent to search Place's two pieces of luggage. When Place refused, the agents informed him that would take the bags to seek a search warrant. Instead, they took the luggage to Kennedy Airport where they subjected the two bags to a "sniff test" by a trained canine, which reacted positively to one bag. This occurred about ninety minutes after the initial seizure of the luggage. Because it was late in the afternoon on Friday, the agents held both bags until Monday morning, at which time a magistrate issued a warrant to search one bag. Upon opening it, the agents discovered a large quantity of cocaine.

---

6   The Court's decision also to expand the "search incident to arrest" exception previously recognized in *Chimel v. California*, allowing police officers without *any* requisite level of suspicion to look into "closets and other spaces immediately adjoining the place of arrest from which an attack could be immediately launched," is equally disquieting. *Chimel* established that police officers may presume as a matter of law, without need for factual support in a particular case, that arrestees might take advantage of weapons or destroy evidence in the area "within [their] immediate control"; therefore, a protective search of that area is *per se* reasonable under the Fourth Amendment. I find much less plausible the Court's implicit assumption today that arrestees are likely to sprinkle hidden allies throughout the rooms in which they might be arrested. Hence there is no comparable justification for permitting arresting officers to presume as a matter of law that they are threatened by ambush from "immediately adjoining" spaces.

Justice O'Connor, writing for six members of the Court, held that the principles of *Terry v. Ohio* * * * applied to Place's luggage:

> We examine first the governmental interest offered as a justification for a brief seizure of luggage from the suspect's custody for the purpose of pursuing a limited course of investigation. The Government contends that, where the authorities possess specific and articulable facts warranting a reasonable belief that a traveler's luggage contains narcotics, the governmental interest in seizing the luggage briefly to pursue further investigation is substantial. We agree. * * *
>
> Against this strong governmental interest, we must weigh the nature and extent of the intrusion upon the individual's Fourth Amendment rights when the police briefly detain luggage for limited investigative purposes. On this point, respondent Place urges that the rationale for a *Terry* stop of the person is wholly inapplicable to investigative detentions of personalty. Specifically, the *Terry* exception to the probable-cause requirement is premised on the notion that a *Terry*-type stop of the person is substantially less intrusive of a person's liberty interests than a formal arrest. In the property context, however, Place urges, there are no degrees of intrusion. Once the owner's property is seized, the dispossession is absolute.
>
> We disagree. The intrusion on possessory interests occasioned by a seizure of one's personal effects can vary both in its nature and extent. The seizure may be made after the owner has relinquished control of the property to a third party or, as here, from the immediate custody and control of the owner. Moreover, the police may confine their investigation to an on-the-spot inquiry—for example, immediate exposure of the luggage to a trained narcotics detection dog—or transport the property to another location. Given the fact that seizures of property can vary in intrusiveness, some brief detentions of personal effects may be so minimally intrusive of Fourth Amendment interests that strong countervailing governmental interests will justify a seizure based only on specific articulable facts that the property contains contraband or evidence of a crime.
>
> In sum, we conclude that when an officer's observations lead him reasonably to believe that a traveler is carrying luggage that contains narcotics, the principles of *Terry* and its progeny would permit the officer to detain the luggage briefly to investigate the circumstances that aroused his suspicion, provided that the investigative detention is properly limited in scope.

Although the Government won *that* legal argument, it ultimately lost the Fourth Amendment claim in *this* case:

The precise type of detention we confront here is seizure of personal luggage from the immediate possession of the suspect for the purpose of arranging exposure to a narcotics detection dog. Particularly in the case of detention of luggage within the traveler's immediate possession, the police conduct intrudes on both the suspect's possessory interest in his luggage as well as his liberty interest in proceeding with his itinerary. The person whose luggage is detained is technically still free to continue his travels or carry out other personal activities pending release of the luggage. * * * Nevertheless, such a seizure can effectively restrain the person since he is subjected to the possible disruption of his travel plans in order to remain with his luggage or to arrange for its return. Therefore, when the police seize luggage from the suspect's custody, we think the limitations applicable to investigative detentions of the person should define the permissible scope of an investigative detention of the person's luggage on less than probable cause. Under this standard, it is clear that the police conduct here exceeded the permissible limits of a *Terry*-type investigative stop.

The length of the detention of respondent's luggage alone precludes the conclusion that the seizure was reasonable in the absence of probable cause. Although we have recognized the reasonableness of seizures longer than the momentary ones involved in *Terry*, * * * the brevity of the invasion of the individual's Fourth Amendment interests is an important factor in determining whether the seizure is so minimally intrusive as to be justifiable on reasonable suspicion. Moreover, in assessing the effect of the length of the detention, we take into account whether the police diligently pursue their investigation. We note that here the New York agents knew the time of Place's scheduled arrival at LaGuardia, had ample time to arrange for their additional investigation at that location, and thereby could have minimized the intrusion on respondent's Fourth Amendment interests. Thus, although we decline to adopt any outside time limitation for a permissible *Terry* stop, we have never approved a seizure of the person for the prolonged 90-minute period involved here and cannot do so on the facts presented by this case.

Although the 90-minute detention of respondent's luggage is sufficient to render the seizure unreasonable, the violation was exacerbated by the failure of the agents to accurately inform respondent of the place to which they were transporting his luggage, of the length of time he might be dispossessed, and of what arrangements would be made for return of the luggage if the investigation dispelled the suspicion. In short, we hold that the detention of respondent's luggage in this case went beyond the narrow authority possessed by police to detain briefly luggage reasonably suspected to contain narcotics.

Does any of the Court's analysis here seem to conflict with anything else you have read in the *Terry* materials?

4. *"Car frisks."* We have seen that the police may ordinarily search a car without a warrant if they have probable cause to do so. They may also search portions of it as an incident to a lawful arrest of a car occupant (or a recent one), even without probable cause, if the interior of the car is in the arrestee's grabbing area. But, now suppose the police conduct a lawful *Terry*-level stop of a driver. May the police, short of probable cause, search the car to protect themselves from possible weapons that might be hidden inside?

In Michigan v. Long, 463 U.S. 1032, 103 S.Ct. 3469, 77 L.Ed.2d 1201 (1983), two officers on patrol in a rural area of Michigan, shortly after midnight, observed a car driving erratically and swerve off into a shallow ditch. The officer stopped to investigate. Long, the only occupant of the car, exited his vehicle and, leaving the car door open, met the officers at the rear of his car. One officer asked Long for his driver's license, but Long—who now appeared to the officers to be "under the influence of something"—did not respond, but turned away and began walking to the open door of his car. The officers followed him, at which point they observed a large hunting knife on the floorboard of the driver's side of the car. At that point, the officers stopped Long from moving closer to the car. They subjected him to a *Terry* frisk, which revealed no weapons.

One officer then shone his flashlights into the car, "to search for other weapons." As the Court described it, "[t]he officer noticed that something was protruding from under the armrest on the front seat. He knelt in the vehicle and lifted the armrest. He saw an open pouch on the front seat, and upon flashing his light on the pouch, determined that it contained what appeared to be marihuana." A further search of the passenger compartment of the vehicle did not turn up other contraband. Long was arrested for possession of marijuana.

The Supreme Court granted certiorari in the case "to consider the important question of the authority of a police officer to protect himself by conducting a *Terry*-type search of the passenger compartment of a motor vehicle during the lawful investigatory stop of the occupant of the vehicle." The Court, per Justice O'Connor, upheld what has since been characterized as a *Terry* "frisk" of the passenger compartment of an automobile:

> Contrary to Long's view, *Terry* need not be read as restricting the preventative search to the person of the detained suspect.
>
> In two cases in which we applied *Terry* to specific factual situations, we recognized that investigative detentions involving suspects in vehicles are especially fraught with danger to police officers. In *Pennsylvania v. Mimms*, [p. 414, Note 4], we held that police may order persons out of an automobile during a stop for a traffic violation, and may frisk those persons for weapons if there is a reasonable belief that they are armed and dangerous. Our decision

rested in part on the "inordinate risk confronting an officer as he approaches a person seated in an automobile." In *Adams v. Williams*, [p. 407, Note 10], we held that the police, acting on an informant's tip, may reach into the passenger compartment of an automobile to remove a gun from a driver's waistband even where the gun was not apparent to police from outside the car and the police knew of its existence only because of the tip. Again, our decision rested in part on our view of the danger presented to police officers in "traffic stop" and automobile situations.

Finally, we have also expressly recognized that suspects may injure police officers and others by virtue of their access to weapons, even though they may not themselves be armed. * * *

Our past cases indicate then that protection of police and others can justify protective searches when police have a reasonable belief that the suspect poses a danger, that roadside encounters between police and suspects are especially hazardous, and that danger may arise from the possible presence of weapons in the area surrounding a suspect. These principles compel our conclusion that the search of the passenger compartment of an automobile, limited to those areas in which a weapon may be placed or hidden, is permissible if the police officer possesses a reasonable belief based on "specific and articulable facts which, taken together with the rational inferences from those facts, reasonably warrant" the officer in believing that the suspect is dangerous and the suspect may gain immediate control of weapons. "[T]he issue is whether a reasonably prudent man in the circumstances would be warranted in the belief that his safety or that of others was in danger."

Having announced the new rule, the Court turned to the question of whether the officers here had the requisite grounds to conduct the weapons search of the passenger compartment of the car:

The circumstances of this case clearly justified Deputies Howell and Lewis in their reasonable belief that Long posed a danger if he were permitted to reenter his vehicle. The hour was late and the area rural. Long was driving his automobile at excessive speed, and his car swerved into a ditch. The officers had to repeat their questions to Long, who appeared to be "under the influence" of some intoxicant. Long was not frisked until the officers observed that there was a large knife in the interior of the car into which Long was about to reenter. The subsequent search of the car was restricted to those areas to which Long would generally have immediate control, and that could contain a weapon. The trial court determined that the leather pouch containing marihuana could have contained a weapon. It is clear that the intrusion was "strictly circumscribed by the exigencies which justifi[ed] its initiation."

Do you agree with the Court's new rule? Even if you do, do you think the police needed to search the vehicle in *this* case? Justice Brennan, writing also for Justice Marshall, dissented:

> [T]he scope of a search is determined not only by reference to its purpose, but also by reference to its intrusiveness. Yet the Court today holds that a search of a car (and the containers within it) that is not even occupied by the suspect is only as intrusive as, or perhaps less intrusive than, thrusting a hand into a pocket after an initial patdown has suggested the presence of concealed objects that might be used as weapons.
>
> The Court suggests no limit on the "area search" it now authorizes. * * * Presumably a weapon "may be placed or hidden" anywhere in a car. A weapon also might be hidden in a container in the car. In this case, the Court upholds the officer's search of a leather pouch because it "could have contained a weapon." In addition, the Court's requirement that an officer have a reasonable suspicion that a suspect is armed and dangerous does little to check the initiation of an area search. In this case, the officers saw a hunting knife in the car, but the Court does not base its holding that the subsequent search was permissible on the ground that possession of the knife may have been illegal under state law. An individual can lawfully possess many things that can be used as weapons. A hammer, or a baseball bat, can be used as a very effective weapon. * * * Based on these facts, one might reasonably conclude that respondent was drunk. A drunken driver is indeed dangerous while driving, but not while stopped on the roadside by the police. Even when an intoxicated person lawfully has in his car an object that could be used as a weapon, it requires imagination to conclude that he is presently dangerous. Even assuming that the facts in this case justified the officers' initial "frisk" of respondent, they hardly provide adequate justification for a search of a suspect's car and the containers within it. This represents an intrusion not just different in degree, but in kind, from the intrusion sanctioned by *Terry*. In short, the implications of the Court's decision are frightening.

5.   *DNA testing of arrestees.* In Maryland v. King, 569 U.S. ___, 133 S.Ct. 1958, 186 L.Ed.2d 1 (2013), King was arrested for first-and second-degree assault. Pursuant to a Maryland statute,[g] the police used a cheek swab to take a DNA sample from King, uploaded the information to a Maryland DNA database, and later matched his DNA sample with one taken

---

g   The statute authorized the collection of DNA samples from "an individual who is charged with * * * a crime of violence or an attempt to commit a crime of violence; or * * * burglary or an attempt to commit burglary." Once taken, the sample may not be processed or placed in a database unless or until the arrestee is arraigned (which occurs approximately 48 hours after the arrest). The samples must be destroyed if the prosecution does not result in conviction of the individual or, after conviction, if the person is granted an unconditional pardon.

from the victim of an unsolved rape. Later charged in the rape, King moved to suppress the DNA match on the ground that the statute authorizing the suspicionless DNA collection violated the Fourth Amendment.

In an opinion authored by Justice Kennedy, the Supreme Court held, 5–4, that "[w]hen officers make an arrest supported by probable cause to hold for a serious offense and they bring the suspect to the station to be detained in custody, taking and analyzing a cheek swab of the arrestee's DNA is, like fingerprinting and photographing, a legitimate police booking procedure that is reasonable under the Fourth Amendment." The Chief Justice and Justices Thomas, Breyer, and Alito, joined the opinion.

Justice Kennedy conceded that the use of "a buccal swab on the inner tissues of a person's cheek in order to obtain DNA samples is a search. Virtually any 'intrusio[n] into the human body' will work an invasion of 'cherished personal security' that is subject to constitutional scrutiny." However, he went on, "[t]o say that the Fourth Amendment applies here is the beginning point, not the end of the analysis." The ultimate issue, he said, is whether the search is reasonable. Justice Kennedy then balanced the "privacy-related and law enforcement-related concerns to determine if the intrusion was reasonable."

To the Court majority, DNA testing is reasonable in view of the "need for law enforcement officers in a safe and accurate way to process and identify the persons and possessions they must take into custody. * * * When probable cause exists to remove an individual from the normal channels of society and hold him in legal custody, DNA identification plays a critical role in serving those interests."

How does DNA provide this benefit? Justice Kennedy explained that "a name is of little value compared to the real interest in identification at stake when an individual is brought into custody. Quoting a federal court, "[i]t is a well recognized aspect of criminal conduct that the perpetrator will take unusual steps to conceal not only his conduct, but also his identity. Disguises used while committing a crime may be supplemented or replaced by changed names, and even changed physical features." Justice Kennedy went on, "the only difference between DNA analysis and the accepted use of fingerprint databases is the unparalleled accuracy DNA provides."

Another benefit of DNA testing, Justice Kennedy claimed, is "ensuring that the custody of an arrestee does not create inordinate 'risks for facility staff, for the existing detainee population, and for a new detainee.' DNA identification can provide untainted information to those charged with detaining suspects [such as whether the suspect] has a record of violence or mental disorder."

The Court provided three additional law enforcement benefits of DNA testing:

> Third, looking forward to future stages of criminal prosecution, "the Government has a substantial interest in ensuring that

persons accused of crimes are available for trials." A person who is arrested for one offense but knows that he has yet to answer for some past crime may be more inclined to flee the instant charges, lest continued contact with the criminal justice system expose one or more other serious offenses. For example, a defendant who had committed a prior sexual assault might be inclined to flee on a burglary charge, knowing that in every State a DNA sample would be taken from him after his conviction on the burglary charge that would tie him to the more serious charge of rape. * * *

Fourth, an arrestee's past conduct is essential to an assessment of the danger he poses to the public, and this will inform a court's determination whether the individual should be released on bail. * * *

Finally, in the interests of justice, the identification of an arrestee as the perpetrator of some heinous crime may have the salutary effect of freeing a person wrongfully imprisoned for the same offense.

The Court found little on the other side of the scale to call into question the DNA sampling process: the procedure involves nothing more than a "brief and * * * minimal intrusion. A gentle rub along the inside of the cheek does not break the skin, and it 'involves virtually no risk, trauma, or pain.' A * * * swab of this nature does not increase the indignity already attendant to normal incidents of arrest."

Justice Scalia, who was joined by Justices Ginsburg, Sotomayor, and Kagan, wrote a fiery dissent. He analogized the DNA testing to the British use of general warrants that the "Americans despised" at the time of the founding of the nation, and which motivated the adoption of the Fourth Amendment:

The Fourth Amendment forbids searching a person for evidence of a crime when there is no basis for believing the person is guilty of the crime or is in possession of incriminating evidence. That prohibition is categorical and without exception; it lies at the very heart of the Fourth Amendment. Whenever this Court has allowed a suspicionless search, it has insisted upon a justifying motive apart from the investigation of crime.

It is obvious that no such noninvestigative motive exists in this case. The Court's assertion that DNA is being taken, not to solve crimes, but to *identify* those in the State's custody, taxes the credulity of the credulous.

Justice Scalia explained:

The portion of the Court's opinion that explains the identification rationale is strangely silent on the actual workings of the DNA search at issue here. To know those facts is to be instantly disabused of the notion that what happened had anything to do with identifying King.

King was arrested on April 10, 2009, on charges unrelated to the case before us. That same day, April 10, the police searched him and seized the DNA evidence at issue here. What happened next? Reading the Court's opinion, particularly its insistence that the search was necessary to know "who [had] been arrested," one might guess that King's DNA was swiftly processed and his identity thereby confirmed—perhaps against some master database of known DNA profiles, as is done for fingerprints. After all, was not the suspicionless search here crucial to avoid "inordinate risks for facility staff" or to "existing detainee population"? Surely, then— *surely*—the State of Maryland got cracking on those grave risks immediately, by rushing to identify King with his DNA as soon as possible.

Nothing could be further from the truth. Maryland officials did not even begin the process of testing King's DNA that day. Or, actually, the next day. Or the day after that. And that was for a simple reason: Maryland law forbids them to do so. A "DNA sample collected from an individual charged with a crime . . . *may not* be tested or placed in the statewide DNA data base system prior to the first scheduled arraignment date." And King's first appearance in court was not until three days after his arrest. (I suspect, though, that they did not wait three days to ask his name or take his fingerprints.)

This places in a rather different light the Court's solemn declaration that the search here was necessary so that King could be identified at "every stage of the criminal process." I hope that the Maryland officials who read the Court's opinion do not take it seriously. Acting on the Court's misperception of Maryland law could lead to jail time. See Md. Pub. Saf. Code Ann. § 2–512(c)–(e) (punishing by up to five years' imprisonment anyone who obtains or tests DNA information except as provided by statute). Does the Court really believe that Maryland did not know whom it was arraigning? * * * If the purpose of this Act is to assess "whether [King] should be released on bail," why would it *possibly* forbid the DNA testing process to *begin* until King was arraigned? Why would Maryland resign itself to simply hoping that the bail decision will drag out long enough that the "identification" can succeed before the arrestee is released? The truth, known to Maryland and increasingly to the reader: this search had nothing to do with establishing King's identity.

To the dissenters, the true purpose of DNA testing of arrestees is to create a database to solve previously unsolved crimes—to help solve "cold cases." But, what is wrong with that? Justice Scalia:

The Court disguises the vast (and scary) scope of its holding by promising a limitation it cannot deliver. The Court repeatedly says that DNA testing, and entry into a national DNA registry, will not befall thee and me, dear reader, but only those arrested for "serious offense[s]." I cannot imagine what principle could possibly justify this limitation, and the Court does not attempt to suggest any. If one believes that DNA will "identify" someone arrested for assault, he must believe that it will "identify" someone arrested for a traffic offense. This Court does not base its judgments on senseless distinctions. At the end of the day, *logic will out.* When there comes before us the taking of DNA from an arrestee for a traffic violation, the Court will predictably (and quite rightly) say, "We can find no significant difference between this case and *King.*" Make no mistake about it: As an entirely predictable consequence of today's decision, your DNA can be taken and entered into a national DNA database if you are ever arrested, rightly or wrongly, and for whatever reason.
* * *

Today's judgment will, to be sure, have the beneficial effect of solving more crimes; then again, so would the taking of DNA samples from anyone who flies on an airplane (surely the Transportation Security Administration needs to know the "identity" of the flying public), applies for a driver's license, or attends a public school. Perhaps the construction of such a genetic panopticon is wise. But I doubt that the proud men who wrote the charter of our liberties would have been so eager to open their mouths for royal inspection.

I therefore dissent, and hope that today's incursion upon the Fourth Amendment * * * will some day be repudiated.

6.   *Problem. R*'s live-in girlfriend called 911 to report that *R* was drunk and talking about committing suicide. While she was on the telephone, two gunshots were fired. The 911 dispatcher directed her to leave the house and wait for the police. A SWAT team arrived shortly thereafter and surrounded the house. The girlfriend informed them that *R* was the only person inside. After a lengthy standoff, an officer used a stun gun on *R*, who was sitting on a windowsill with his legs hanging out an open window as he drunkenly cursed at the officers. *R* was formally arrested outside the house for possession of a firearm. He told the officers that nobody else was inside the house. Nonetheless, the SWAT team secured the house and then broke through a barricaded door and entered the premises. Inside they seized a shotgun and made photographs of spent shells and the holes *R* had shot into the ceiling. The police justified the entry as a protective sweep. Was the entry valid on that or any other ground? Commonwealth v. Robertson, 275 Va. 559, 659 S.E.2d 321 (2008).

2. REASONABLENESS IN A "SPECIAL NEEDS" (AND NON-CRIMINAL?) CONTEXT

Introduction

It is necessary to draw a distinction between searches and seizures conducted by police in furtherance of their criminal law enforcement responsibilities and searches and seizures conducted by police, and by other public officials, in furtherance of "community caretaking functions" or, more generally, non-law enforcement purposes. It is necessary to draw this line because the Supreme Court sometimes does. Unfortunately, the line-drawing is exceptionally difficult, because the distinction, if it even exists, is not easy to draw.

If you think back over this chapter, nearly every case we have considered involved a search or seizure in a criminal investigation. But, there have been some exceptions. For example, we had a Note (p. 318, Note 3) relating to automobile inventories: When an automobile must be towed as the result of illegal parking, for example, the police may routinely inspect the contents of the car, not as part of a criminal investigation, but simply to make sure that belongings are properly inventoried for safekeeping and other purposes. South Dakota v. Opperman, 428 U.S. 364, 96 S.Ct. 3092, 49 L.Ed.2d 1000 (1976), held that because such inventories are not criminal investigations, the warrant clause including the probable cause requirement do not apply. The reasonableness clause, alone, must be considered, and the Court held that the police may inventory automobiles under specified circumstances in the absence of probable cause *or even reasonable suspicion*.

Opperman has come to be seen as stating a special inventory "exception" to the warrant "requirement." But that may primarily be a function of history. Over time, the Supreme Court has come to recognize another general warrant "exception," sometimes described as the "special needs" exception, which could easily encompass inventories. A search or seizure comes within the "special needs" category when a perceived need, *beyond the normal need for criminal law enforcement*, makes the warrant and/or probable-cause requirements of the Fourth Amendment impracticable or, simply, irrelevant. In "special needs" circumstances, the Court evaluates the governmental activity by applying the reasonableness balancing standard.

One scholar has observed that "little or no effort has been made to explain what these 'special needs' are; the term turns out to be no more than a label that indicates when a lax standard will apply." William J. Stuntz, *Implicit Bargains, Government Power, and the Fourth Amendment*, 44 Stan. L. Rev. 553, 554 (1992). An interesting feature of the doctrine is that, in this area, often "the Court [has] one of its rare opportunities to hear face-to-face, as Fourth Amendment claimants, those law-abiding citizens for whose ultimate benefits the constitutional restraints on public power were primarily intended." Stephen J. Schulhofer, *On the Fourth Amendment Rights of the Law-Abiding Public*, 1989 Sup. Ct. Rev. 87, 88. Yet, as we will see, in these cases not only are traditional warrants inapplicable, but the Supreme Court sometimes dispenses with the requirement of suspicion of wrongdoing on the part of the "victim" of the search or seizure.

NOTES AND QUESTIONS

1.   *Administrative searches.* In 1967 (long before recognition of a "special needs" doctrine), the Supreme Court considered the applicability of the Fourth Amendment in the enforcement of housing code regulations, Camara v. Municipal Court, 387 U.S. 523, 87 S.Ct. 1727, 18 L.Ed.2d 930 (1967), and safety code provisions affecting commercial buildings, See v. City of Seattle, 387 U.S. 541, 87 S.Ct. 1737, 18 L.Ed.2d 943 (1967). *Camara* and *See* were decided during the peak of the dominance of the warrant clause. In general, these cases provide that, except in the event of emergency or consent, residences and commercial buildings may not be entered to inspect for administrative code violations without an administrative search warrant. The "probable cause" for these administrative warrants can be supplied by a showing of non-arbitrary justification to inspect the particular premises, *e.g.*, that all the buildings in the area are due to being inspected. This kind of "probable cause" obviously does not require particularized suspicion of criminal wrongdoing or even of administrative code violations in a specific building.

Since the *Camara-See* doctrine was laid down, and as the Supreme Court's devotion to warrants has receded, the Court has approved *warrantless* administrative searches of "closely [governmentally] regulated industries," even in the absence of emergency or consent. As the Court explained in New York v. Burger, 482 U.S. 691, 107 S.Ct. 2636, 96 L.Ed.2d 601 (1987),

> [b]ecause the owner or operator of commercial premises in a "closely regulated" industry has a reduced expectation of privacy, the warrant and probable-cause requirements, which fulfill the traditional Fourth Amendment standard of reasonableness for a government search, have lessened application in this context. Rather, we conclude that, as in other situations of "special need," where the privacy interests of the owner are weakened and the government interests in regulating particular businesses are concomitantly heightened, a warrantless inspection of commercial premises may well be reasonable within the meaning of the Fourth Amendment.

Burger is an especially interesting case because, unlike most administrative searches that are conducted by employees of administrative agencies, the searches here were performed by police officers, who entered the defendant's automobile junkyard without a warrant or probable cause of criminal wrongdoing. Pursuant to statute, they asked to see Burger's business license and record of automobiles and parts on the premises. He admitted he had neither and thus was in plain violation of the administrative regulations for junkyards. The officers then searched the junkyard, where they discovered stolen vehicle parts that led to Burger's arrest for possession of stolen property.

The Court upheld the search. It did so despite the fact that the searches were conducted by police officers, and that the officers, serving as agents of an administrative agency, could have cited Burger for violation of administrative regulations once he admitted the lack of records to them, without ever conducting the search that turned up criminal wrongdoing. The Court did not focus on the motives of the officers in this case. All that mattered was that the administrative regulations had a non-penal purpose.

2.   *Birth of the "special needs" doctrine.* The Court gave birth to the "special needs" doctrine, although its express mention arose only in a concurring opinion, in New Jersey v. T.L.O, 469 U.S. 325, 105 S.Ct. 733, 83 L.Ed.2d 720 (1985). In *T.L.O.,* two public school students were caught smoking on school grounds, in violation of school rules. When one of them denied she smoked, the vice-principal demanded her purse, opened it, and observed a package of cigarettes. As he pulled them out, he discovered cigarette paper, which is often used to make marijuana cigarettes. This led to a full search of T.L.O.'s purse, which turned up evidence implicating her in marijuana sales. The criminal evidence was handed over to the police and used in a juvenile court proceeding against her.

The Supreme Court held that neither the warrant requirement nor probable cause applies to searches by public school officials. It quickly disposed of the warrant requirement, stating that it is "unsuited to the school environment," because it would "unduly interfere with the maintenance of the swift and informal disciplinary proceedings needed in the schools." As for probable cause, the majority observed that "[w]here a careful balancing of governmental and public interests suggests that the public interest is best served by a Fourth Amendment standard of reasonableness that stops short of probable cause, we have not hesitated to adopt such a standard." Here, the Court ruled, public school teachers and administrators may search students without a warrant if two conditions are met: (1) "there are reasonable grounds"—not necessarily "probable cause" in the criminal law context—"for suspecting that the search will turn up evidence that the student has violated or is violating either the law or the rules of the school"; and (2) once initiated, the search is "not excessively intrusive in light of the age and sex of the student and the nature of the infraction." The Supreme Court concluded that the initial search for cigarettes in this case, based on the report of her smoking, "was in no sense unreasonable for Fourth Amendment purposes."

3.   *A "special needs" school search that went too far.* In Safford Unified School District #1 v. Redding, 557 U.S. 364, 129 S.Ct. 2633, 174 L.Ed.2d 354 (2009), the Court confronted the issue of "whether a 13-year-old student's Fourth Amendment right was violated when she was subjected to a search of her bra and underpants by school officials acting on reasonable suspicion that she had brought forbidden prescription and over-the-counter drugs to school." The Court stated that characterizing the search—requiring the student "to remove her clothes down to her underwear, and then 'pull out' her bra and the elastic band on her underpants"—as a "strip search is a fair way to speak of it." (The search failed to turn up any pills.)

Every member of the Court except Justice Thomas concluded that the strip search violated the Fourth Amendment. The Court, per Justice Souter, stated that it violated the "rule of reasonableness as stated in *T.L.O.*":

> Here, the content of the suspicion failed to match the degree of intrusion. [The principal who ordered the search] knew beforehand that the pills were prescription-strength ibuprofen and over-the-counter naxproxen, common pain relievers equivalent to two Advil, or one Aleve. He must have been aware of the nature and limited threat of the specific drugs he was searching for * * * . * * *

> In sum, what was missing from the suspected facts that pointed to [the student] was any indication of danger to the students from the power of the drugs or their quantity, and any reason [specific to this student] to suppose that [she] was carrying pills in her underwear. * * *

> We * * * mean * * * to make it clear that the *T.L.O.* concern to limit a school search to reasonable scope requires the support of reasonable suspicion of danger or of resort to underwear for hiding evidence of wrongdoing before a search can reasonably make the quantum leap from outer clothes and backpacks to exposure of intimate parts. The meaning of such a search, and the degradation its subject may reasonably feel, place a search that intrusive in a category of its own demanding its own specific suspicions.

4.   *Airport searches.* Consider this scenario based roughly on the facts in United States v. Aukai, 497 F.3d 955 (9th Cir. 2007) (en banc): *A* goes to the airport and, because he has forgotten to bring his driver's license or other government-issued photographic identification, he is required to undergo a more intensive screening process in order to pass through security. First, *A* went through the ordinary screening process without difficulty. He then was informed he would have to undergo a second screening in which a Transportation and Security Administration (TSA) officer would pass a handheld "wand" close to *A*'s body. When the TSA officer used the wand, it sounded an alarm twice near one of *A*'s pockets. Although *A* continued to assert that his pockets were empty, he was ordered to empty his pockets. At this point, *A* told the TSA officer he had changed his mind and no longer wanted to board the plane and, instead, wanted to leave the airport. But, the

TSA agent refused to let him leave and required that he empty his pockets. When *A* complied, the officer discovered drug paraphernalia resulting in *A*'s arrest.

Was the latter warrantless search—after *A* asked to leave—constitutional? The Ninth Circuit in *Aukai* ruled, 15–0, that the search was constitutional. The court characterized the procedure as a valid "administrative search" (see Note 1), therefore not dependent upon *A*'s consent. The Ninth Circuit also invoked the "special needs" doctrine. In doing so, however, it ruled that "the scope of such searches is not limitless. A particular airport security search is constitutionally reasonable provided that it 'is no more extensive than necessary, in the light of current technology, to detect the presence of weapons or explosives * * * [and] that it is confined in good faith to that purpose.'" The Ninth Circuit concluded that the airport screening in *A*'s case satisfied these requirements.

5.   *Border searches.* Special rules also apply in the international border context. At the border and its functional equivalent (*e.g.,* at an airport where an international flight arrives), a person may be stopped and her belongings searched without a warrant and in the absence of individualized suspicion of wrongdoing, "pursuant to the long-standing right of the sovereign to protect itself" from the entry of persons and things dangerous to the nation. United States v. Ramsey, 431 U.S. 606, 97 S.Ct. 1972, 52 L.Ed.2d 617 (1977). In dictum the *Ramsey* Court did state, however, that "[w]e * * * leave open the question 'whether, and under what circumstances, a border search might be deemed "unreasonable" because of the particularly offensive manner it is carried out.'"[h]

The law of border searches is somewhat more complicated away from the border. Particularly on highways in the vicinity of the Mexican border, federal agents often stop vehicles to question occupants regarding their citizenship. The Court has distinguished here between seizures conducted by "roving border patrols" (where agents stop a car without notice on a little-traveled road) and those that occur at a fixed interior checkpoint (a permanent stop along a well-traveled highway). With *roving* border patrols, the Supreme Court has determined that the agents need reasonable suspicion of criminal activity to detain the car occupants briefly. United States v. Brignoni-Ponce, 422 U.S. 873, 95 S.Ct. 2574, 45 L.Ed.2d 607 (1975). However, in United States v. Martinez-Fuerte, 428 U.S. 543, 96 S.Ct. 3074, 49 L.Ed.2d 1116 (1976), the Court ruled that vehicle occupants may be

---

[h]   In United States v. Flores-Montano, 541 U.S. 149, 124 S.Ct. 1582, 158 L.Ed.2d 311 (2004), the Supreme Court unanimously held that a suspicionless international border search is constitutionally reasonable even when border agents, without reasonable suspicion, seize a person's car at the international border, remove the gas task (a process that took almost an hour), and search it. Chief Justice Rehnquist observed that "[t]he Government's interest in preventing the entry of unwanted persons and effects is at its zenith at the international border." He stated that "[i]t is difficult to imagine how the search of a gas tank, which should be solely a repository for fuel, could be more of an invasion of privacy than the search of the automobile's passenger compartment."

stopped for questioning at *fixed* interior checkpoints without individualized suspicion of wrongdoing.

The Court distinguished fixed checkpoints from roving patrols on two grounds. First, the subjective intrusion on the security of lawful travelers—their fear and surprise level—"is appreciably less in the case of a [fixed] checkpoint stop." Second, agents at fixed checkpoints have less discretionary enforcement authority than roving agents: the location of the checkpoint is fixed, and they may only stop those that pass through it.

MICHIGAN DEPARTMENT OF STATE POLICE V. SITZ
Supreme Court of the United States, 1990.
496 U.S. 444, 110 S.Ct. 2481, 110 L.Ed.2d 412.

CHIEF JUSTICE REHNQUIST delivered the opinion of the Court [joined by JUSTICES WHITE, O'CONNOR, SCALIA, and KENNEDY].

This case poses the question whether a State's use of highway sobriety checkpoints violates the Fourth and Fourteenth Amendments to the United States Constitution. We hold that it does not and therefore reverse the contrary holding of the Court of Appeals of Michigan.

Petitioners, the Michigan Department of State Police and its director, established a sobriety checkpoint pilot program in early 1986. The director appointed a Sobriety Checkpoint Advisory Committee comprising representatives of the State Police force, local police forces, state prosecutors, and the University of Michigan Transportation Research Institute. Pursuant to its charge, the advisory committee created guidelines setting forth procedures governing checkpoint operations, site selection, and publicity.

Under the guidelines, checkpoints would be set up at selected sites along state roads. All vehicles passing through a checkpoint would be stopped and their drivers briefly examined for signs of intoxication. In cases where a checkpoint officer detected signs of intoxication, the motorist would be directed to a location out of the traffic flow where an officer would check the motorist's driver's license and car registration and, if warranted, conduct further sobriety tests. Should the field tests and the officer's observations suggest that the driver was intoxicated, an arrest would be made. All other drivers would be permitted to resume their journey immediately.

The first—and to date the only—sobriety checkpoint operated under the program was conducted in Saginaw County with the assistance of the Saginaw County Sheriff's Department. During the 75-minute duration of the checkpoint's operation, 126 vehicles passed through the checkpoint. The average delay for each vehicle was approximately 25 seconds. Two drivers were detained for field sobriety testing, and one of the two was arrested for driving under the influence of alcohol. A third driver who drove through without stopping was pulled over by an officer in an observation vehicle and arrested for driving under the influence.

On the day before the operation of the Saginaw County checkpoint, respondents filed a complaint in the Circuit Court of Wayne County seeking declaratory and injunctive relief from potential subjection to the checkpoints. * * *

After the trial, at which the court heard extensive testimony concerning, *inter alia*, the "effectiveness" of highway sobriety checkpoint programs, the court ruled that the Michigan program violated the Fourth Amendment * * * . On appeal, the Michigan Court of Appeals affirmed the holding * * * . * * *

To decide this case the trial court performed a balancing test derived from our opinion in *Brown v. Texas*, 443 U.S. 47, 99 S.Ct. 2637, 61 L.Ed.2d 357 (1979). As described by the Court of Appeals, the test involved "balancing the state's interest in preventing accidents caused by drunk drivers, the effectiveness of sobriety checkpoints in achieving that goal, and the level of intrusion on an individual's privacy caused by the checkpoints." The Court of Appeals agreed that "the *Brown* three-prong balancing test was the correct test to be used to determine the constitutionality of the sobriety checkpoint plan." * * *

Petitioners concede, correctly in our view, that a Fourth Amendment "seizure" occurs when a vehicle is stopped at a checkpoint. The question thus becomes whether such seizures are "reasonable" under the Fourth Amendment.

* * * We address only the initial stop of each motorist passing through a checkpoint and the associated preliminary questioning and observation by checkpoint officers. Detention of particular motorists for more extensive field sobriety testing may require satisfaction of an individualized suspicion standard.

No one can seriously dispute the magnitude of the drunken driving problem or the States' interest in eradicating it. Media reports of alcohol-related death and mutilation on the Nation's roads are legion. The anecdotal is confirmed by the statistical. "Drunk drivers cause an annual death toll of over 25,000 and in the same time span cause nearly one million personal injuries and more than five billion dollars in property damage." For decades, this Court has "repeatedly lamented the tragedy."

Conversely, the weight bearing on the other scale—the measure of the intrusion on motorists stopped briefly at sobriety checkpoints—is slight. We reached a similar conclusion as to the intrusion on motorists subjected to a brief stop at a highway checkpoint for detecting illegal aliens. See [*United States v.*] *Martinez-Fuerte*, [p. 473, Note 5.] We see virtually no difference between the levels of intrusion on law-abiding motorists from the brief stops necessary to the effectuation of these two types of checkpoints, which to the average motorist would seem identical save for the nature of the questions the checkpoint officers might ask. The trial court and the Court of Appeals, thus, accurately gauged the "objective" intrusion, measured by the duration of the seizure and the intensity of the investigation, as minimal.

With respect to what it perceived to be the "subjective" intrusion on motorists, however, the Court of Appeals found such intrusion substantial. * * *

We believe the Michigan courts misread our cases concerning the degree of "subjective intrusion" and the potential for generating fear and surprise. The "fear and surprise" to be considered are not the natural fear of one who has been drinking over the prospect of being stopped at a sobriety checkpoint but, rather, the fear and surprise engendered in law-abiding motorists by the nature of the stop. * * * The intrusion resulting from the brief stop at the sobriety checkpoint is for constitutional purposes indistinguishable from the checkpoint stops we upheld in *Martinez-Fuerte*.

The Court of Appeals went on to consider as part of the balancing analysis the "effectiveness" of the proposed checkpoint program. Based on extensive testimony in the trial record, the court concluded that the checkpoint program failed the "effectiveness" part of the test, and that this failure materially discounted petitioners' strong interest in implementing the program. We think the Court of Appeals was wrong on this point as well.

The actual language from *Brown v. Texas*, upon which the Michigan courts based their evaluation of "effectiveness," describes the balancing factor as "the degree to which the seizure advances the public interest." This passage from *Brown* was not meant to transfer from politically accountable officials to the courts the decision as to which among reasonable alternative law enforcement techniques should be employed to deal with a serious public danger. Experts in police science might disagree over which of several methods of apprehending drunken drivers is preferable as an ideal. But for purposes of Fourth Amendment analysis, the choice among such reasonable alternatives remains with the governmental officials who have a unique understanding of, and a responsibility for, limited public resources, including a finite number of police officers. * * *

In *Delaware v. Prouse*, [440 U.S. 648, 99 S.Ct. 1391, 59 L.Ed.2d 660 (1979),] we disapproved random stops made by Delaware Highway Patrol officers in an effort to apprehend unlicensed drivers and unsafe vehicles. We observed that *no* empirical evidence indicated that such stops would be an effective means of promoting roadway safety * * * . * * *

Unlike *Prouse*, this case involves neither a complete absence of empirical data nor a challenge to random highway stops. During the operation of the Saginaw County checkpoint, the detention of the 126 vehicles that entered the checkpoint resulted in the arrest of two drunken drivers. Stated as a percentage, approximately 1.6 percent of the drivers passing through the checkpoint were arrested for alcohol impairment. In addition, an expert witness testified at the trial that experience in other States demonstrated that, on the whole, sobriety checkpoints resulted in drunken driving arrests of around 1 percent of all motorists stopped. By way of comparison, the record from one of the consolidated cases in *Martinez-Fuerte* showed that in the associated checkpoint, illegal aliens were found in only 0.12 percent of the vehicles passing through the checkpoint. The ratio of illegal aliens detected to vehicles stopped (considering that on occasion two or more illegal aliens were found in a single vehicle) was approximately 0.5 percent. We concluded that this "record * * * provides a rather complete picture of the effectiveness of the San Clemente checkpoint," and we sustained its constitutionality. We see no justification for a different conclusion here.

In sum, the balance of the State's interest in preventing drunken driving, the extent to which this system can reasonably be said to advance that interest, and the degree of intrusion upon individual motorists who are briefly stopped, weighs in favor of the state program. We therefore hold that it is consistent with the Fourth Amendment. * * *

[JUSTICE BLACKMUN'S concurrence in the judgment is omitted.]

JUSTICE BRENNAN, with whom JUSTICE MARSHALL joins, dissenting. * * *

* * * Some level of individualized suspicion is a core component of the protection the Fourth Amendment provides against arbitrary government action. By holding that no level of suspicion is necessary before the police may stop a car for the purpose of preventing drunken driving, the Court potentially subjects the general public to arbitrary or harassing conduct by the police. * * *

* * * That stopping every car *might* make it easier to prevent drunken driving is an insufficient justification for abandoning the requirement of individualized suspicion. * * * Without proof that the police cannot develop individualized suspicion that a person is driving while impaired by alcohol, I believe the constitutional balance must be struck in favor of protecting the public against even the "minimally intrusive" seizures involved in this case. * * *

JUSTICE STEVENS, with whom JUSTICE BRENNAN and JUSTICE MARSHALL join as to Parts I and II, dissenting. * * *

I

There is a critical difference between a seizure that is preceded by fair notice and one that is effected by surprise. That is one reason why a border search, or indeed any search at a permanent and fixed checkpoint, is much less intrusive than a random stop. A motorist with advance notice of the location of a permanent checkpoint has an opportunity to avoid the search entirely, or at least to prepare for, and limit, the intrusion on her privacy.

No such opportunity is available in the case of a random stop or a temporary checkpoint, which both depend for their effectiveness on the element of surprise. A driver who discovers an unexpected checkpoint on a familiar local road will be startled and distressed. She may infer, correctly, that the checkpoint is not simply "business as usual," and may likewise infer, again correctly, that the police have made a discretionary decision to focus their law enforcement efforts upon her and others who pass the chosen point. * * *

* * * [I]t is significant that many of the stops at permanent checkpoints occur during daylight hours, whereas the sobriety checkpoints are almost invariably operated at night. A seizure followed by interrogation and even a cursory search at night is surely more offensive than a daytime stop that is almost as routine as going through a toll gate. * * *

These fears are not, as the Court would have it, solely the lot of the guilty. * * * Unwanted attention from the local police need not be less discomforting simply because one's secrets are not the stuff of criminal prosecutions. Moreover, those who have found—by reason of prejudice or misfortune—that encounters with the police may become adversarial or unpleasant without good cause will have grounds for worrying at any stop designed to elicit signs of suspicious behavior. * * *

II

The Court, unable to draw any persuasive analogy to *Martinez-Fuerte*, rests its decision today on application of a more general balancing test taken from *Brown v. Texas*. In that case the appellant, a pedestrian, had been stopped for questioning in an area of El Paso, Texas, that had "a high incidence of drug traffic" because he "looked suspicious." He was then arrested and convicted for refusing to identify himself to police officers. We set aside his conviction because the officers stopped him when they lacked any reasonable suspicion that he was engaged in criminal activity. In our opinion, we stated:

"Consideration of the constitutionality of such seizures involves a weighing of the gravity of the public concerns served by the seizure, the degree to which the seizure advances the public interest, and the severity of the interference with individual liberty."

The gravity of the public concern with highway safety that is implicated by this case is, of course, undisputed. Yet, that same grave concern was implicated in *Delaware v. Prouse*. Moreover, I do not understand the Court to have placed any lesser value on the importance of the drug problem implicated in *Brown v. Texas* * * * . A different result in this case must be justified by the other two factors in the *Brown* formulation.

As I have already explained, I believe the Court is quite wrong in blithely asserting that a sobriety checkpoint is no more intrusive than a permanent checkpoint. * * * [T]he surprise intrusion upon individual liberty is not minimal. On that issue, my difference with the Court may amount to nothing less than a difference in our respective evaluations of the importance of individual liberty, a serious, albeit inevitable, source of constitutional disagreement. On the degree to which the sobriety checkpoint seizures advance the public interest, however, the Court's position is wholly indefensible.

The Court's analysis of this issue resembles a business decision that measures profits by counting gross receipts and ignoring expenses. The evidence in this case indicates that sobriety checkpoints result in the arrest of a fraction of one percent of the drivers who are stopped, but there is absolutely no evidence that this figure represents an increase over the number of arrests that would have been made by using the same law enforcement resources in conventional patrols. Thus, although the *gross* number of arrests is more than zero, there is a complete failure of proof on the question whether the wholesale seizures have produced any *net* advance in the public interest in arresting intoxicated drivers. * * *

III

The most disturbing aspect of the Court's decision today is that it appears to give no weight to the citizen's interest in freedom from suspicionless unannounced investigatory seizures. * * * [T]he Court places a heavy thumb on the law enforcement interest by looking only at gross receipts instead of net benefits. Perhaps this tampering with the scales of justice can be explained by the Court's obvious concern about the slaughter on our highways and a resultant tolerance for policies designed to alleviate the problem by "setting an example" of a few motorists. This possibility prompts two observations.

First, my objections to random seizures or temporary checkpoints do not apply to a host of other investigatory procedures that do not depend upon surprise and are unquestionably permissible. * * * It is, for example, common practice to require every prospective airline passenger, or every visitor to a public building, to pass through a metal detector that will reveal the presence of a firearm or an explosive. Permanent, nondiscretionary checkpoints could be used to control serious dangers at other publicly operated facilities. Because concealed weapons obviously represent one such substantial threat to public safety, I would suppose that all subway passengers could be required to pass through metal detectors, so long as the detectors were permanent and every passenger was subjected to the same search. Likewise, I would suppose that a State could condition access to its toll roads upon not only paying the toll but also taking a uniformly administered breathalyzer test. * * * This procedure would not be subject to the constitutional objections that control this case: The checkpoints would be permanently fixed, the stopping procedure would apply to all users of the toll road in precisely the same way, and police officers would not be free to make arbitrary choices about which neighborhoods should be targeted or about which individuals should be more thoroughly searched. * * *

This is a case that is driven by nothing more than symbolic state action—an insufficient justification for an otherwise unreasonable program of random seizures. Unfortunately, the Court is transfixed by the wrong symbol—the illusory prospect of punishing countless intoxicated motorists—when it should keep its eyes on the road plainly marked by the Constitution. * * *

NOTES AND QUESTIONS

1.   Is an otherwise permissible suspicionless checkpoint valid if there is no empirical data supporting its use? What if the data suggest that the checkpoints are useless or even counter-productive?

2.   In *Delaware v. Prouse*, distinguished by the Chief Justice in *Sitz*, the Court held that

> except in those situations in which there is at least articulable and reasonable suspicion that a motorist is unlicensed or that an automobile is not registered * * *, stopping an automobile and detaining the driver in order to check his driver's license and the registration of the automobile are unreasonable under the Fourth Amendment. This holding does not preclude * * * States from developing methods for spot checks that involve less intrusion or that do not involve the unconstrained exercise of discretion. Questioning of all oncoming traffic at roadblock-type stops is one possible alternative.

Why would be it less objectionable to stop and question everyone? Does this "misery loves company" approach to the Fourth Amendment make sense?

3. So checkpoints are constitutional, right? Well . . .

CITY OF INDIANAPOLIS V. EDMOND

Supreme Court of the United States, 2000.
531 U.S. 32, 121 S.Ct. 447, 148 L.Ed.2d 333.

JUSTICE O'CONNOR delivered the opinion of the Court [joined by JUSTICES STEVENS, KENNEDY, SOUTER, GINSBURG, and BREYER].

In *Michigan Dept. of State Police v. Sitz* [p. 474], and *United States v. Martinez-Fuerte* [p. 473, Note 5], we held that brief, suspicionless seizures at highway checkpoints for the purposes of combating drunk driving and intercepting illegal immigrants were constitutional. We now consider the constitutionality of a highway checkpoint program whose primary purpose is the discovery and interdiction of illegal narcotics.

I

In August 1998, the city of Indianapolis began to operate vehicle checkpoints on Indianapolis roads in an effort to interdict unlawful drugs. The city conducted six such roadblocks between August and November that year, stopping 1,161 vehicles and arresting 104 motorists. Fifty-five arrests were for drug-related crimes, while 49 were for offenses unrelated to drugs. The overall "hit rate" of the program was thus approximately nine percent.

* * * At each checkpoint location, the police stop a predetermined number of vehicles. Approximately 30 officers are stationed at the checkpoint. Pursuant to written directives issued by the chief of police, at least one officer approaches the vehicle, advises the driver that he or she is being stopped briefly at a drug checkpoint, and asks the driver to produce a license and registration. The officer also looks for signs of impairment and conducts an open-view examination of the vehicle from the outside. A narcotics-detection dog walks around the outside of each stopped vehicle.

The directives instruct the officers that they may conduct a search only by consent or based on the appropriate quantum of particularized suspicion. The officers must conduct each stop in the same manner until particularized suspicion develops, and the officers have no discretion to stop any vehicle out of sequence. * * *

The affidavit of Indianapolis Police Sergeant Marshall DePew * * * provides further insight concerning the operation of the checkpoints. According to Sergeant DePew, checkpoint locations are selected * * * based on such considerations as area crime statistics and traffic flow. The checkpoints are generally operated during daylight hours and are identified with lighted signs reading, " 'NARCOTICS CHECKPOINT ___ MILE AHEAD, NARCOTICS K-9 IN USE, BE PREPARED TO STOP.' "

* * * Sergeant DePew also stated that the average stop for a vehicle not subject to further processing lasts two to three minutes or less.

Respondents were each stopped at a narcotics checkpoint in late September 1998. * * * Respondents claimed that the roadblocks violated the Fourth Amendment of the United States Constitution * * *. Respondents requested declaratory and injunctive relief for the class, as well as damages and attorney's fees for themselves. * * *

II

The Fourth Amendment requires that searches and seizures be reasonable. A search or seizure is ordinarily unreasonable in the absence of individualized suspicion of wrongdoing. While such suspicion is not an "irreducible" component of reasonableness, we have recognized only limited circumstances in which the usual rule does not apply. For example, we have upheld certain regimes of suspicionless searches where the program was designed to serve "special needs, beyond the normal need for law enforcement." We have also allowed searches for certain administrative purposes without particularized suspicion of misconduct, provided that those searches are appropriately limited. See, *e.g.*, *New York v. Burger,* [p. 470, Note 1].

We have also upheld brief, suspicionless seizures of motorists at a fixed Border Patrol checkpoint designed to intercept illegal aliens, *Martinez-Fuerte, supra,* and at a sobriety checkpoint aimed at removing drunk drivers from the road, *Michigan Dept. of State Police v. Sitz.* In addition, in *Delaware v. Prouse*, we suggested that a similar type of roadblock with the purpose of verifying drivers' licenses and vehicle registrations would be permissible. In none of these cases, however, did we indicate approval of a checkpoint program whose primary purpose was to detect evidence of ordinary criminal wrongdoing. * * *

III

* * * [W]hat principally distinguishes these checkpoints from those we have previously approved is their primary purpose.

As petitioners concede, the Indianapolis checkpoint program unquestionably has the primary purpose of interdicting illegal narcotics. In their stipulation of facts, the parties repeatedly refer to the checkpoints as "drug checkpoints" * * *. In addition, the first document attached to the parties' stipulation is entitled "DRUG CHECKPOINT CONTACT OFFICER DIRECTIVES BY ORDER OF THE CHIEF OF POLICE." These directives instruct officers to "[a]dvise the citizen that they are being stopped briefly at a drug checkpoint." * * * Further, according to Sergeant DePew, the checkpoints are identified with lighted signs [announcing a "NARCOTICS CHECKPOINT"]. * * *

We have never approved a checkpoint program whose primary purpose was to detect evidence of ordinary criminal wrongdoing. * * * [E]ach of the checkpoint programs that we have approved was designed primarily to serve purposes closely related to the problems of policing the border or the necessity of ensuring roadway safety. Because the primary purpose of the Indianapolis narcotics checkpoint program is to uncover evidence of ordinary criminal wrongdoing, the program contravenes the Fourth Amendment.

Petitioners propose several ways in which the narcotics-detection purpose of the instant checkpoint program may instead resemble the primary purposes of the checkpoints in *Sitz* and *Martinez-Fuerte*. Petitioners state that the checkpoints in those cases had the same ultimate purpose of arresting those suspected of committing crimes. Securing the border and apprehending drunk drivers are, of course, law enforcement activities, and law enforcement officers employ arrests and criminal prosecutions in pursuit of these goals. If we were to rest the case at this high level of generality, there would be little check on the ability of the authorities to construct roadblocks for almost any conceivable law enforcement purpose. Without drawing the line at roadblocks designed primarily to serve the general interest in crime control, the Fourth Amendment would do little to prevent such intrusions from becoming a routine part of American life.

Petitioners also emphasize the severe and intractable nature of the drug problem as justification for the checkpoint program. * * * But the gravity of the threat alone cannot be dispositive of questions concerning what means law enforcement officers may employ to pursue a given purpose. Rather, in determining whether individualized suspicion is required, we must consider the nature of the interests threatened and their connection to the particular law enforcement practices at issue. We are particularly reluctant to recognize exceptions to the general rule of individualized suspicion where governmental authorities primarily pursue their general crime control ends.

Nor can the narcotics-interdiction purpose of the checkpoints be rationalized in terms of a highway safety concern similar to that present in *Sitz*. The detection and punishment of almost any criminal offense serves broadly the safety of the community, and our streets would no doubt be safer but for the scourge of illegal drugs. Only with respect to a smaller class of offenses, however, is society confronted with the type of immediate, vehicle-bound threat to life and limb that the sobriety checkpoint in *Sitz* was designed to eliminate.

Petitioners also liken the anticontraband agenda of the Indianapolis checkpoints to the antismuggling purpose of the checkpoints in *Martinez-Fuerte*. Petitioners cite this Court's conclusion in *Martinez-Fuerte* that the flow of traffic was too heavy to permit "particularized study of a given car that would enable it to be identified as a possible carrier of illegal aliens," and claim that this logic has even more force here. The problem with this argument is that the same logic prevails any time a vehicle is employed to conceal contraband or other evidence of a crime. This type of connection to the roadway is very different from the close connection to roadway safety that was present in *Sitz* and *Prouse*. Further, the Indianapolis checkpoints are far removed from the border context that was crucial in *Martinez-Fuerte*. * * *

The primary purpose of the Indianapolis narcotics checkpoints is in the end to advance "the general interest in crime control." We decline to suspend the usual requirement of individualized suspicion where the police seek to employ a checkpoint primarily for the ordinary enterprise of investigating crimes. * * *

Of course, there are circumstances that may justify a law enforcement checkpoint where the primary purpose would otherwise, but for some emergency, relate to ordinary crime control. For example, * * * the Fourth Amendment would almost certainly permit an appropriately tailored roadblock set up to thwart an imminent terrorist attack or to catch a dangerous criminal who is likely to flee by way of a particular route. The exigencies created by these scenarios are far removed from the circumstances under which authorities might simply stop cars as a matter of course to see if there just happens to be a felon leaving the jurisdiction. While we do not limit the purposes that may justify a checkpoint program to any rigid set of categories, we decline to approve a program whose primary purpose is ultimately indistinguishable from the general interest in crime control.

Petitioners argue that our prior cases preclude an inquiry into the purposes of the checkpoint program. For example, they cite *Whren v. United States* [p. 298], * * * to support the proposition that "where the government articulates and pursues a legitimate interest for a suspicionless stop, courts should not look behind that interest to determine whether the government's 'primary purpose' is valid." * * *

In *Whren,* we held that an individual officer's subjective intentions are irrelevant to the Fourth Amendment validity of a traffic stop that is justified objectively by probable cause to believe that a traffic violation has occurred. * * * In so holding, we expressly distinguished cases where we had addressed the validity of searches conducted in the absence of probable cause.

Whren therefore reinforces the principle that, while "[s]ubjective intentions play no role in ordinary, probable-cause Fourth Amendment analysis," programmatic purposes may be relevant to the validity of

Fourth Amendment intrusions undertaken pursuant to a general scheme without individualized suspicion. * * *

Petitioners argue that the Indianapolis checkpoint program is justified by its lawful secondary purposes of keeping impaired motorists off the road and verifying licenses and registrations. If this were the case, however, law enforcement authorities would be able to establish checkpoints for virtually any purpose so long as they also included a license or sobriety check. For this reason, we examine the available evidence to determine the primary purpose of the checkpoint program. * * * [A] program driven by an impermissible purpose may be proscribed while a program impelled by licit purposes is permitted, even though the challenged conduct may be outwardly similar. While reasonableness under the Fourth Amendment is predominantly an objective inquiry, our special needs and administrative search cases demonstrate that purpose is often relevant when suspicionless intrusions pursuant to a general scheme are at issue.[2]

It goes without saying that our holding today does nothing to alter the constitutional status of the sobriety and border checkpoints that we approved in *Sitz* and *Martinez-Fuerte,* or of the type of traffic checkpoint that we suggested would be lawful in *Prouse*. The constitutionality of such checkpoint programs still depends on a balancing of the competing interests at stake and the effectiveness of the program. * * *

Our holding also does not affect the validity of border searches or searches at places like airports and government buildings, where the need for such measures to ensure public safety can be particularly acute. * * * Finally, we caution that the purpose inquiry in this context is to be conducted only at the programmatic level and is not an invitation to probe the minds of individual officers acting at the scene.

Because the primary purpose of the Indianapolis checkpoint program is ultimately indistinguishable from the general interest in crime control, the checkpoints violate the Fourth Amendment. * * *

CHIEF JUSTICE REHNQUIST, with whom JUSTICE THOMAS joins, and with whom JUSTICE SCALIA joins as to Part I, dissenting.

I

* * * This case follows naturally from *Martinez-Fuerte* and *Sitz*. Petitioners acknowledge that the "primary purpose" of these roadblocks is to interdict illegal drugs, but this fact should not be controlling. Even

---

[2] Because petitioners concede that the primary purpose of the Indianapolis checkpoints is narcotics detection, we need not decide whether the State may establish a checkpoint program with the primary purpose of checking licenses or driver sobriety and a secondary purpose of interdicting narcotics. Specifically, we express no view on the question whether police may expand the scope of a license or sobriety checkpoint seizure in order to detect the presence of drugs in a stopped car.

accepting the Court's conclusion that the checkpoints at issue in *Martinez-Fuerte* and *Sitz* were not primarily related to criminal law enforcement,[2] the question whether a law enforcement purpose could support a roadblock seizure is not presented in this case. The District Court found that another "purpose of the checkpoints is to check driver's licenses and vehicle registrations," and the written directives state that the police officers are to "[l]ook for signs of impairment." The use of roadblocks to look for signs of impairment was validated by *Sitz,* and the use of roadblocks to check for driver's licenses and vehicle registrations was expressly recognized in *Delaware v. Prouse.* That the roadblocks serve these legitimate state interests cannot be seriously disputed * * * . * * *

Because of the valid reasons for conducting these roadblock seizures, it is constitutionally irrelevant that petitioners also hoped to interdict drugs. * * *

With these checkpoints serving two important state interests, the remaining prongs of the *Brown v. Texas* balancing test are easily met. The seizure is objectively reasonable as it lasts, on average, two to three minutes and does not involve a search. The subjective intrusion is likewise limited as the checkpoints are clearly marked and operated by uniformed officers who are directed to stop every vehicle in the same manner. * * * Finally, the checkpoints' success rate—49 arrests for offenses unrelated to drugs—only confirms the State's legitimate interests in preventing drunken driving and ensuring the proper licensing of drivers and registration of their vehicles.

These stops effectively serve the State's legitimate interests; they are executed in a regularized and neutral manner; and they only minimally intrude upon the privacy of the motorists. They should therefore be constitutional. * * *

JUSTICE THOMAS, dissenting.

Taken together, our decisions in *Michigan Dept. of State Police v. Sitz* and *United States v. Martinez-Fuerte* stand for the proposition that suspicionless roadblock seizures are constitutionally permissible if conducted according to a plan that limits the discretion of the officers conducting the stops. I am not convinced that *Sitz* and *Martinez-Fuerte* were correctly decided. Indeed, I rather doubt that the Framers of the Fourth Amendment would have considered "reasonable" a program of indiscriminate stops of individuals not suspected of wrongdoing.

Respondents did not, however, advocate the overruling of *Sitz* and *Martinez-Fuerte,* and I am reluctant to consider such a step without the benefit of briefing and argument. For the reasons given by The Chief

---

[2]   This gloss is not at all obvious. * * *

Justice, I believe that those cases compel upholding the program at issue here. I, therefore, join his opinion.

NOTES AND QUESTIONS

1. Look again at footnote 2 of the majority opinion. The footnote resulted in the following tongue-in-cheek observation of Professor Wayne LaFave, posing as David Letterman:

> Now, I'm no Supreme Court justice, nor one of them there high-priced lawyers with the shiny suits and ring on the pinky finger, or even one of those legal pundits that jabber on TV all the time. I'm just a simple late-show host and TV celebrity, but I think I've got about an ounce of common sense, which is all it takes to see that if these drug checkpoints are bad, it shouldn't make any difference what purpose is listed first and what is listed second. And if the Court doesn't make that clear when the time comes, I guarantee that you'll hear about it on this show during our occasional "Stupid Supreme Court Tricks" segment.

Wayne R. LaFave, *The Fourth Amendment as a "Big Time" TV Fad*, 53 Hastings L.J. 265, 274 (2001).

2. *How far does Edmond reach?* In Illinois v. Lidster, 540 U.S. 419, 124 S.Ct. 885, 157 L.Ed.2d 843 (2004), local police in Illinois set up a highway checkpoint designed to elicit information from motorists about a fatal hit-and-run accident that had occurred in roughly the same place a week earlier. The blockage resulted in a traffic slow-down, leading to lines of up to fifteen cars in each lane, a delay of a few minutes, and a brief ten-to-fifteen-second conversation with officers. Justice Breyer delivered the opinion of the Court:

> The checkpoint stop here differs significantly from that in *Edmond*. The stop's primary law enforcement purpose was *not* to determine whether a vehicle's occupants were committing a crime, but to ask vehicle occupants, as members of the public, for their help in providing information about a crime in all likelihood committed by others. The police expected the information elicited to help them apprehend, not the vehicle's occupants, but other individuals.

> *Edmond*'s language, as well as its context, makes clear that the constitutionality of this latter, information-seeking kind of stop was not then before the Court. * * * We concede that *Edmond* describes the law enforcement objective there in question as a "general interest in crime control," but it specifies that the phrase "general interest in crime control" does not refer to every "law enforcement" objective. We must read this and related general language in *Edmond* as we often read general language in judicial opinions—as referring in context to circumstances similar to the circumstances

then before the Court and not referring to quite different circumstances that the Court was not then considering.

Neither do we believe, *Edmond* aside, that the Fourth Amendment would have us apply an *Edmond*-type rule of automatic unconstitutionality to brief, information-seeking highway stops of the kind now before us. * * * The Fourth Amendment does not treat a motorist's car as his castle. And special law enforcement concerns will sometimes justify highway stops without individualized suspicion. Moreover, unlike *Edmond,* the context here (seeking information from the public) is one in which, by definition, the concept of individualized suspicion has little role to play. Like certain other forms of police activity, say, crowd control or public safety, an information-seeking stop is not the kind of event that involves suspicion, or lack of suspicion, of the relevant individual.

For another thing, information-seeking highway stops are less likely to provoke anxiety or to prove intrusive. The stops are likely brief. The police are not likely to ask questions designed to elicit self-incriminating information. * * *

Finally, we do not believe that an *Edmond*-type rule is needed to prevent an unreasonable proliferation of police checkpoints. Practical considerations—namely, limited police resources and community hostility to related traffic tie-ups—seem likely to inhibit any such proliferation. And, of course, the Fourth Amendment's normal insistence that the stop be reasonable in context will still provide an important legal limitation on police use of this kind of information-seeking checkpoint.

These considerations, taken together, convince us that an *Edmond*-type presumptive rule of unconstitutionality does not apply here. That does not mean the stop is automatically, or even presumptively, constitutional. It simply means that we must judge its reasonableness, hence, its constitutionality, on the basis of the individual circumstances.

The Court proceeded to apply *Brown* and determined that the relevant public concern was grave; the checkpoint advanced the grave public concern to a significant degree; and "[m]ost importantly, the stops interfered only minimally with liberty of the sort the Fourth Amendment seeks to protect." Justice Breyer found that, objectively, the seizures were brief and minimal, and even viewed subjectively, "the contact provided little reason for anxiety or alarm," as the police stopped all vehicles systematically and "there is no allegation here that the police acted in a discriminatory or otherwise unlawful manner while questioning motorists during stops."

3.   *Drug testing.* Suspicionless drug testing (by means of urinalysis, breathalyzer, or blood) has been upheld by the Supreme Court in various circumstances: drug testing of railroad personnel involved in train accidents,

Skinner v. Railway Labor Executives' Association, 489 U.S. 602, 109 S.Ct. 1402, 103 L.Ed.2d 639 (1989); random drug testing of federal customs officers who carry weapons or are involved in drug interdiction, National Treasury Employees Union v. Von Raab, 489 U.S. 656, 109 S.Ct. 1384, 103 L.Ed.2d 685 (1989); and random urine testing of school students involved in athletics, Vernonia School District 47J v. Acton, 515 U.S. 646, 115 S.Ct. 2386, 132 L.Ed.2d 564 (1995), or other extracurricular activities, Board of Education of Independent School District No. 92 of Pottawatomie County v. Earls, 536 U.S. 822, 122 S.Ct. 2559, 153 L.Ed.2d 735 (2002) (policy required all middle and high school students participating in any extracurricular activity to consent to drug testing).

In drug testing cases, the Court considers the "nature and immediacy" of the government's concerns regarding drug use. In some cases, the Court has found a "compelling," "substantial," or "important" governmental or societal need for drug testing that could not be accommodated by application of ordinary probable cause or reasonable suspicion standards. In *Skinner*, evidence was introduced that there was a link between drug and alcohol use by railroad employees and train accidents. In *Von Raab*, there was a felt need to ensure that federal officers involved in handling weapons or investigating drug offenses were themselves free of drugs. In *Vernonia*, the School District had experienced serious academic disruption due to drug use by students, especially student-athletes. In *Pottawatomie County*, the student drug problem was not as severe as in *Vernonia*, but the school district "provided sufficient evidence" of drug use in its schools "to shore up the need for its drug testing program."

Weighed against the interest in random drug testing is the privacy interest of those subjected to the testing. The *Skinner* Court concluded that the bodily intrusion involved in blood testing is minimal; and breath testing is less intrusive still. As for urine testing, however, the justices agreed that the excretory function "traditionally [is] shielded by great privacy." But, in each of the cases, the testing regulations ensured that the individuals were not observed while they urinated. Also weighing against the privacy interests of the individuals was the fact that, with the employees, their expectation of privacy was "diminished by reason of their participation in an industry * * * regulated pervasively to ensure safety"; and in *Vernonia*, the Court stated that "[c]entral * * * to the present case is the fact that the subjects of the [drug] Policy are (1) children, who (2) have been committed to the temporary custody of the State as schoolmaster."

Not all suspicionless drug testing is allowed. The Fourth Amendment "shields society" from urinalysis drug testing that "diminishes personal privacy [solely] for a symbol's sake." In Chandler v. Miller, 520 U.S. 305, 117 S.Ct. 1295, 137 L.Ed.2d 513 (1997), the Supreme Court ruled, 8–1, that Georgia's requirement that candidates for state office pass a drug test did "not fit within the closely guarded category of constitutionally permissible suspicionless searches." The statute required candidates for state office to submit to urinalysis testing within thirty days prior to qualifying for nomination or election. A candidate who tested positive for illegal drugs could not be placed on the ballot.

The Court found no special need for the testing. First, the law was not passed in response to any suspicion of drug use by state officials. Second, because the test date was no secret, a drug-taking candidate could "abstain for a pretest period sufficient to avoid detection." Thus, the scheme was "not well designed to identify candidates who violate antidrug laws." And, finally, unlike *Skinner* and *Von Raab*, in which it was not feasible to subject employees to day-to-day scrutiny for drugs, "[c]andidates for public office * * * are subject to relentless scrutiny—by their peers, the public, and the press." Consequently, all that was left to the testing regime was "the image the State seeks to protect." "However well-meant," the Court said, "the Fourth Amendment shields society against that state action."

What if the reason for the testing is, quite simply, to promote enforcement of criminal laws? And, is it relevant to the legitimacy of drug testing that law enforcement officials are involved in the testing process? In Ferguson v. City of Charleston, 532 U.S. 67, 121 S.Ct. 1281, 149 L.Ed.2d 205 (2001), the Supreme Court invalidated a program (Policy M-7) to identify and test pregnant mothers suspected of drug use, which program was formulated by a task force composed of representatives of the Charleston public hospital operated by the Medical University of South Carolina (MUSC), police, and local officials. The Court described the procedure as follows:

> The first three pages of Policy M-7 set forth the procedure to be followed by the hospital staff to "identify/assist pregnant patients suspected of drug abuse." The first section, entitled the "Identification of Drug Abusers," provided that a patient should be tested for cocaine through a urine drug screen if she met one or more of nine criteria. It also stated that a chain of custody should be followed when obtaining and testing urine samples, presumably to make sure that the results could be used in subsequent criminal proceedings. The policy also provided for education and referral to a substance abuse clinic for patients who tested positive. Most important, it added the threat of law enforcement intervention that "provided the necessary 'leverage' to make the [p]olicy effective." That threat was, as respondents candidly acknowledge, essential to the program's success in getting women into treatment and keeping them there.
>
> The threat of law enforcement involvement was set forth in two protocols, the first dealing with the identification of drug use during pregnancy, and the second with identification of drug use after labor. Under the latter protocol, the police were to be notified without delay and the patient promptly arrested. Under the former, after the initial positive drug test, the police were to be notified (and the patient arrested) only if the patient tested positive for cocaine a second time or if she missed an appointment with a substance abuse

counselor. [Subsequently], however, the policy was modified at the behest of the solicitor's office to give the patient who tested positive during labor, like the patient who tested positive during a prenatal care visit, an opportunity to avoid arrest by consenting to substance abuse treatment.

Justice Stevens, writing for five members of the Court, ruled that Policy M-7 did not fall within the "special needs" exception to the warrant requirement:

> The critical difference between [earlier] * * * drug-testing cases and this one * * * lies in the nature of the "special need" asserted as justification for the warrantless searches. In each of those earlier cases, the "special need" that was advanced as a justification for the absence of a warrant or individualized suspicion was one divorced from the State's general interest in law enforcement. * * * In this case, however, the central and indispensable feature of the policy from its inception was the use of law enforcement to coerce the patients into substance abuse treatment. * * *

> Respondents argue in essence that their ultimate purpose—namely, protecting the health of both mother and child—is a beneficent one. * * * In this case, a review of the M-7 policy plainly reveals that the purpose actually served by the MUSC searches "is ultimately indistinguishable from the general interest in crime control." *Indianapolis v. Edmond.*

> In looking to the programmatic purpose, we consider all the available evidence in order to determine the relevant primary purpose. * * * "[I]t * * * is clear from the record that an initial and continuing focus of the policy was on the arrest and prosecution of drug-abusing mothers * * * ." Tellingly, the document codifying the policy incorporates the police's operational guidelines. It devotes its attention to the chain of custody, the range of possible criminal charges, and the logistics of police notification and arrests. Nowhere, however, does the document discuss different courses of medical treatment for either mother or infant, aside from treatment for the mother's addiction.

> Moreover, throughout the development and application of the policy, the Charleston prosecutors and police were extensively involved in the day-to-day administration of the policy. * * *

> While the ultimate goal of the program may well have been to get the women in question into substance abuse treatment and off of drugs, the immediate objective of the searches was to generate evidence *for law enforcement purposes* in order to reach that goal. The threat of law enforcement may ultimately have been intended as a means to an end, but the direct and primary purpose of MUSC's policy was to ensure the use of those means. In our opinion,

this distinction is critical. Because law enforcement involvement always serves some broader social purpose or objective, under respondents' view, virtually any nonconsensual suspicionless search could be immunized under the special needs doctrine by defining the search solely in terms of its ultimate, rather than immediate, purpose. Such an approach is inconsistent with the Fourth Amendment. Given the primary purpose of the Charleston program, which was to use the threat of arrest and prosecution in order to force women into treatment, and given the extensive involvement of law enforcement officials at every stage of the policy, this case simply does not fit within the closely guarded category of "special needs."

The majority held that absent consent or an exigency, the urine testing here required a search warrant.

4.   *Problem.* A Missouri police department set up a narcotics roadblock, but with a twist. One evening, they put warnings on a highway: "DRUG ENFORCEMENT CHECKPOINT ONE MILE AHEAD" and "POLICE DRUG DOGS WORKING." In fact, however, the checkpoint was set up immediately following the signs, at an exit selected because it did not provide gas or food services. The only lawful purpose for getting off at that exit was to go to a local high school or church (where no events were occurring that evening), or one of several residences.

In this case, the defendant "suddenly veered off onto the off ramp." The police at the checkpoint stopped him (as they did all others who exited at that point). The defendant appeared nervous, had glazed and bloodshot eyes, and smelled of alcohol. The defendant consented to a vehicle search, which turned up large quantities of drugs. Are the drugs admissible in a criminal prosecution? State v. Mack, 66 S.W.3d 706 (Mo.2002).

5.   *Problem.* Consider the following New York City anti-terrorist checkpoint program for its subways: Officers are assigned to random-and-changing checkpoints. They are required to select every fifth or tenth person (based on passenger volume) and search the subway rider's belongings. Only belongings large enough to carry an explosive device may be opened, and the inspection is limited to "what is minimally necessary to ensure that [it] * * * does not contain an explosive device." The preferred inspection method involves physical manipulation of the contents by the subway rider or, if necessary, by the officer. The officer is not permitted to request or record a passenger's personal information (*e.g.*, name, address, demographic data). In general, the typical inspection lasts a matter of seconds. This program is conducted in the absence of any specific terrorist threat, and the City cannot provide studies demonstrating that such a program deters terrorists. Constitutional? MacWade v. Kelly, 460 F.3d 260 (2d Cir. 2006).

CHAPTER 5

REMEDIES FOR FOURTH AMENDMENT VIOLATIONS

■ ■ ■

A. STANDING

The Starting Point

There are two important Fourth Amendment rules considered in this chapter: the "exclusionary rule" and a doctrine that the Supreme Court used to call (and many lawyers still call) "standing."

As discussed more fully later in this chapter, the exclusionary rule—the rule that evidence obtained in violation of the Fourth Amendment is suppressed at trial—is typically justified on deterrence grounds: The police will be less likely to violate the Fourth Amendment if they know that the fruits of their unconstitutional conduct will be excluded from a criminal trial. Before evidence can be excluded, however, a court must determine whether the person seeking exclusion has the right to bring the Fourth Amendment claim. This is the "standing" requirement.

In this regard consider Alderman v. United States, 394 U.S. 165, 89 S.Ct. 961, 22 L.Ed.2d 176 (1969): Alderman and Aderisio were charged with conspiracy to transmit murderous threats in interstate commerce. They sought, as co-defendants and accused co-conspirators, to have incriminating statements they made excluded because one or both of them were the subject of unlawful governmental electronic surveillance. Justice White, writing for the Court, explained that the issue of exclusion had to be determined on an individual basis—*each* defendant would have to prove that he, *personally*, had "standing" to raise the Fourth Amendment claim. *Alderman* explained the law of standing this way:

> The established principle is that suppression of the product of a Fourth Amendment violation can be successfully urged only by those whose rights were violated by the search itself, not by those who are aggrieved solely by the introduction of damaging evidence. Coconspirators and codefendants have been accorded no special standing. * * *

The rule is stated in Jones v. United States, 362 U.S. 257, 261, 80 S.Ct. 725, 731, 4 L.Ed.2d 697 (1960):

"In order to qualify as a 'person aggrieved by an unlawful search and seizure' one must have been a victim of a search or seizure, one against whom the search was directed, as distinguished from one who claims prejudice only through the use of evidence gathered as a consequence of a search or seizure directed at someone else. * * *

"Ordinarily, then, it is entirely proper to require of one who seeks to challenge the legality of a search as the basis for suppressing relevant evidence that he allege, and if the allegation be disputed that he establish, that he himself was the victim of an invasion of privacy." * * *

We adhere to * * * the general rule that Fourth Amendment rights are personal rights which, like some other constitutional rights, may not be vicariously asserted. * * *

The necessity for [proving standing is] * * * not eliminated by recognizing and acknowledging the deterrent aim of the [exclusionary] rule. * * * The deterrent values of preventing the incrimination of those whose rights the police have violated have been considered sufficient to justify the suppression of probative evidence even though the case against the defendant is weakened or destroyed. We adhere to that judgment. But we are not convinced that the additional benefits of extending the exclusionary rule to other defendants would justify further encroachment upon the public interest in prosecuting those accused of crime and having them acquitted or convicted on the basis of all the evidence which exposes the truth.

NOTES AND QUESTIONS

1.   The Court ruled in *Alderman* that a person has standing to contest electronic surveillance, and thus is entitled to suppression of unlawfully heard conversations, if: (a) government agents unlawfully overheard that person's conversations, regardless of where they occurred; or (b) if the conversations occurred on that person's premises, whether or not she was present or participated in the conversations. In what way is a person a "victim" in each of these circumstances?

2.   *"Atomistic" versus "regulatory" perspectives of the Fourth Amendment.* The "standing" requirement can undercut the deterrence goal of the exclusionary rule. In this regard, consider Richard B. Kuhns, *The Concept of Personal Aggrievement in Fourth Amendment Standing Cases*, 65 Iowa L. Rev. 493, 495–96, 499, 501 (1980):

Supreme Court decisions interpreting and applying the fourth amendment reflect what Professor Anthony Amsterdam has characterized as two distinct perspectives of the prohibition against unreasonable searches and seizures.[20] The Court has often viewed the fourth amendment as a protection of certain individual rights. From this perspective the fourth amendment, in the words of Professor Amsterdam, is "a collection of protections of atomistic spheres of interest of individual citizens." In contrast to this "atomistic" perspective, the Court has sometimes discussed the fourth amendment from what Professor Amsterdam has characterized as a "regulatory" perspective—one that views the amendment as "a regulatory canon requiring government to order its law enforcement procedures in a fashion that keeps us collectively secure * * * against unreasonable searches and seizures." The most important question from the atomistic perspective is whether an individual's rights have been violated, whereas from the regulatory perspective, the critical question is whether the government has engaged in an activity that, if left unregulated, would pose a threat to the security of people generally.

The answers to these two questions will often be the same. For example, when the police make an arrest without probable cause to believe that the arrestee has committed a crime, the arrestee's rights have been violated, and the police have engaged in a type of conduct that the fourth amendment was designed to regulate. * * *

Nonetheless, * * * there are cases in which the result is likely to depend on which perspective of the fourth amendment is dominant in a court's thinking. * * *

Perhaps the clearest manifestation of the Supreme Court's adherence to the regulatory perspective of the fourth amendment appears in the Court's discussions of the exclusionary rule. In recent years, for example, the Court has urged that the rule's primary [regulatory] purpose "is to deter future unlawful police conduct and thereby effectuate the guarantee of the Fourth Amendment * * * ." * * *

In contrast to the regulatory objectives of the exclusionary rule, the concept of personal aggrievement, which is the core of the standing requirement, is essentially atomistic * * * .

3. Consider the facts in United States v. Payner, 447 U.S. 727, 100 S.Ct. 2439, 65 L.Ed.2d 468 (1980):

In 1965, the Internal Revenue Service launched an investigation into the financial activities of American citizens in the Bahamas. The project, known as "Operation Trade Winds," was headquartered in Jacksonville, Fla. Suspicion focused on the Castle Bank in 1972 * * * . Special Agent Richard Jaffe of the Jacksonville office asked Norman Casper, a private investigator and occasional informant, to

---

[20] Amsterdam, *Perspectives on the Fourth Amendment*, 58 Minn. L. Rev. 349, 362–72 (1974).

learn what he could about the Castle Bank and its depositors. To that end, Casper cultivated his friendship with Castle Bank vice president Michael Wolstencroft. Casper introduced Wolstencroft to Sybol Kennedy, a private investigator and former employee. When Casper discovered that the banker intended to spend a few days in Miami in January 1973, he devised a scheme to gain access to the bank records he knew Wolstencroft would be carrying in his briefcase. Agent Jaffe approved the basic outline of the plan.

Wolstencroft arrived in Miami on January 15 and went directly to Kennedy's apartment. At about 7:30 p. m., the two left for dinner at a Key Biscayne restaurant. Shortly thereafter, Casper entered the apartment using a key supplied by Kennedy. He removed the briefcase and delivered it to Jaffe. While the agent supervised the copying of approximately 400 documents taken from the briefcase, a "lookout" observed Kennedy and Wolstencroft at dinner. The observer notified Casper when the pair left the restaurant, and the briefcase was replaced. The documents photographed that evening included papers evidencing a close working relationship between the Castle Bank and the Bank of Perrine, Fla. Subpoenas issued to the Bank of Perrine ultimately uncovered [evidence that defendant Payner had falsified his tax records by denying that he maintained a foreign bank account at the Castle Bank, in the Bahama Islands].

The District Court found that the United States, acting through Jaffe, "knowingly and willfully participated in the unlawful seizure of Michael Wolstencroft's briefcase. * * * "

Based on the *Alderman* quote (The Starting Point), does Payner have standing to contest the Government's activities? *Should* he have standing? How would a court applying the atomistic perspective (Note 2) deal with the unlawful government conduct here? What would a court following the regulatory approach do about the evidence?

4.   If *Alderman* teaches us that a person may not successfully assert a Fourth Amendment claim unless she has standing to contest the search, *i.e.*, that she was the victim of the Fourth Amendment violation, the question to which we must now turn is, precisely, when *is* an individual a "victim" of an unlawful search. The materials that follow focus on this issue.

Rakas v. Illinois

Supreme Court of the United States, 1978.
439 U.S. 128, 99 S.Ct. 421, 58 L.Ed.2d 387.

Mr. Justice Rehnquist delivered the opinion of the Court [joined by Chief Justice Burger, and Justices Stewart, Powell, and Blackmun]. * * *

I

Because we are not here concerned with the issue of probable cause, a brief description of the events leading to the search of the automobile will suffice. A police officer on a routine patrol received a radio call notifying him of a robbery of a clothing store in Bourbonnais, Ill., and describing the getaway car. Shortly thereafter, the officer spotted an automobile which he thought might be the getaway car. After following the car for some time and after the arrival of assistance, he and several other officers stopped the vehicle. The occupants of the automobile, petitioners and two female companions, were ordered out of the car and, after the occupants had left the car, two officers searched the interior of the vehicle. They discovered a box of rifle shells in the glove compartment, which had been locked, and a sawed-off rifle under the front passenger seat. After discovering the rifle and the shells, the officers took petitioners to the station and placed them under arrest.

Before trial petitioners moved to suppress the rifle and shells seized from the car on the ground that the search violated the Fourth and Fourteenth Amendments. They conceded that they did not own the automobile and were simply passengers; the owner of the car had been the driver of the vehicle at the time of the search. Nor did they assert that they owned the rifle or the shells seized.[1] The prosecutor challenged petitioners' standing to object to the lawfulness of the search of the car because neither the car, the shells nor the rifle belonged to them. The trial court agreed that petitioners lacked standing and denied the motion to suppress the evidence. * * *

II * * *

A

[The Court rejected the petitioners' initial argument that, because they were targets of the search, *i.e.*, that the search was directed at obtaining incriminating evidence against them, they should have standing on that basis alone—even if they were not "victims" of the

---

[1] * * * The proponent of a motion to suppress has the burden of establishing that his own Fourth Amendment rights were violated by the challenged search or seizure. The prosecutor argued that petitioners lacked standing to challenge the search because they did not own the rifle, the shells or the automobile. Petitioners did not contest the factual predicates of the prosecutor's argument * * * . * * *

search—to contest the legality of the police action. The Court explained its reasoning:]

Conferring standing to raise vicarious Fourth Amendment claims would necessarily mean a more widespread invocation of the exclusionary rule during criminal trials. The Court's opinion in *Alderman* [p. 493] counseled against such an extension of the exclusionary rule * * * . Each time the exclusionary rule is applied it exacts a substantial social cost for the vindication of Fourth Amendment rights. Relevant and reliable evidence is kept from the trier of fact and the search for truth at trial is deflected. Since our cases generally have held that one whose Fourth Amendment rights are violated may successfully suppress evidence obtained in the course of an illegal search and seizure, misgivings as to the benefit of enlarging the class of persons who may invoke that rule are properly considered when deciding whether to expand standing to assert Fourth Amendment violations.

B

* * * [H]aving rejected petitioners' target theory and reaffirmed the principle that the "rights assured by the Fourth Amendment are personal rights, [which] * * * may be enforced by exclusion of evidence only at the instance of one whose own protection was infringed by the search and seizure," the question necessarily arises whether it serves any useful analytical purpose to consider this principle a matter of standing, distinct from the merits of a defendant's Fourth Amendment claim. We can think of no decided cases of this Court that would have come out differently had we concluded, as we do now, that the type of standing requirement * * * reaffirmed today is more properly subsumed under substantive Fourth Amendment doctrine. Rigorous application of the principle that the rights secured by this Amendment are personal, in place of a notion of "standing," will produce no additional situations in which evidence must be excluded. The inquiry under either approach is the same. But we think the better analysis forthrightly focuses on the extent of a particular defendant's rights under the Fourth Amendment, rather than on any theoretically separate, but invariably intertwined concept of standing. * * *

Analyzed in these terms, the question is whether the challenged search and seizure violated the Fourth Amendment rights of a criminal defendant who seeks to exclude the evidence obtained during it. That inquiry in turn requires a determination of whether the disputed search and seizure has infringed an interest of the defendant which the Fourth Amendment was designed to protect. We are under no illusion that by dispensing with the rubric of standing * * * we have rendered any simpler the determination of whether the proponent of a motion to suppress is entitled to contest the legality of a search and seizure. But by frankly recognizing that this aspect of the analysis belongs more properly under the heading of substantive Fourth Amendment doctrine than under the heading of standing, we think the decision of this issue will rest on sounder logical footing.

C

Here petitioners, who were passengers occupying a car which they neither owned nor leased, seek to analogize their position to that of the defendant in *Jones v. United States*[, 362 U.S. 257, 80 S.Ct. 725, 4 L.Ed.2d 697 (1960)]. In *Jones*, petitioner was present at the time of the search of an apartment which was owned by a friend. The friend had given Jones permission to use the apartment and a key to it, with which Jones had admitted himself on the day of the search. He had a suit and shirt at the apartment and had slept there "maybe a night," but his home was elsewhere. At the time of the search, Jones was the only occupant of the apartment because the lessee was away for a period of several days. Under these circumstances, this Court stated that while one wrongfully on the premises could not move to suppress evidence obtained as a result of searching them, "anyone legitimately on premises where a search occurs may challenge its legality." Petitioners argue that their occupancy of the automobile in question was comparable to that of *Jones* in the apartment and that they therefore have standing to contest the legality of the search—or as we have rephrased the inquiry, that they, like Jones, had their Fourth Amendment rights violated by the search.

We do not question the conclusion in *Jones* that the defendant in that case suffered a violation of his personal Fourth Amendment rights if the search in question was unlawful. Nonetheless, we believe that the phrase "legitimately on premises" coined in *Jones* creates too broad a gauge for measurement of Fourth Amendment rights. For example, applied literally, this statement would permit a casual visitor who has never seen, or been permitted to visit, the basement of another's house to object to a search of the basement if the visitor happened to be in the kitchen of the house at the time of the search. Likewise, a casual visitor who walks into a house one minute before a search of the house commences and leaves one minute after the search ends would be able to contest the legality of the search. The first visitor would have absolutely no interest or legitimate expectation of privacy in the basement, the second would have none in the house, and it advances no purpose served by the Fourth Amendment to permit either of them to object to the lawfulness of the search.[11]

We think that *Jones* on its facts merely stands for the unremarkable proposition that a person can have a legally sufficient interest in a place

---

[11] This is not to say that such visitors could not contest the lawfulness of the seizure of evidence or the search if their own property were seized during the search.

other than his own home so that the Fourth Amendment protects him from unreasonable governmental intrusion into that place. In defining the scope of that interest, we adhere to the view expressed in *Jones* and echoed in later cases that arcane distinctions developed in property and tort law between guests, licensees, invitees, and the like, ought not to control. But the *Jones* statement that a person need only be "legitimately on premises" in order to challenge the validity of the search of a dwelling place cannot be taken in its full sweep beyond the facts of that case.

* * * [T]he holding in *Jones* can best be explained by the fact that Jones had a legitimate expectation of privacy in the premises he was using and therefore could claim the protection of the Fourth Amendment with respect to a governmental invasion of those premises, even though his "interest" in those premises might not have been a recognized property interest at common law.[12] * * *

D

Judged by the foregoing analysis, petitioners' claims must fail. They asserted neither a property nor a possessory interest in the automobile, nor an interest in the property seized. And as we have previously indicated, the fact that they were "legitimately on [the] premises" in the sense that they were in the car with the permission of its owner is not determinative of whether they had a legitimate expectation of privacy in the particular areas of the automobile searched. It is unnecessary for us to decide here whether the same expectations of privacy are warranted in a car as would be justified in a dwelling place in analogous circumstances. We have on numerous occasions pointed out that cars are not to be treated identically with houses or apartments for Fourth Amendment purposes. But here petitioners' claim is one which would fail even in an analogous situation in a dwelling place, since they made no showing that they had any legitimate expectation of privacy in the glove compartment or area under the seat of the car in which they were merely passengers. Like the trunk of an automobile, these are areas in which a passenger *qua* passenger simply would not normally have a legitimate expectation of privacy.

Jones v. United States * * * involved significantly different factual circumstances. Jones not only had permission to use the apartment of his

---

[12] Obviously, however, a "legitimate" expectation of privacy by definition means more than a subjective expectation of not being discovered. A burglar plying his trade in a summer cabin during the off season may have a thoroughly justified subjective expectation of privacy, but it is not one which the law recognizes as "legitimate." His presence, in the words of *Jones,* is "wrongful"; his expectation is not "one that society is prepared to recognize as 'reasonable.' " And it would, of course, be merely tautological to fall back on the notion that those expectations of privacy which are legitimate depend primarily on cases deciding exclusionary-rule issues in criminal cases. Legitimation of expectations of privacy by law must have a source outside of the Fourth Amendment, either by reference to concepts of real or personal property law or to understandings that are recognized and permitted by society. * * *

friend, but had a key to the apartment with which he admitted himself on the day of the search and kept possessions in the apartment. Except with respect to his friend, Jones had complete dominion and control over the apartment and could exclude others from it. Likewise in *Katz* [p. 96], the defendant occupied the telephone booth, shut the door behind him to exclude all others and paid the toll, which "entitled [him] to assume that the words he utter[ed] into the mouthpiece [would] not be broadcast to the world." Katz and Jones could legitimately expect privacy in the areas which were the subject of the search and seizure each sought to contest. No such showing was made by these petitioners with respect to those portions of the automobile which were searched and from which incriminating evidence was seized.[17] * * *

MR. JUSTICE POWELL, with whom THE CHIEF JUSTICE joins, concurring.

I concur in the opinion of the Court, and add these thoughts. * * *

We are concerned here with an automobile search. Nothing is better established in Fourth Amendment jurisprudence than the distinction between one's expectation of privacy in an automobile and one's expectation when in other locations. We have repeatedly recognized that this expectation in "an automobile * * * [is] significantly different from the traditional expectation of privacy and freedom in one's residence." * * *

A distinction also properly may be made in some circumstances between the Fourth Amendment rights of passengers and the rights of an individual who has exclusive control of an automobile or of its locked compartments. * * * Here there were three passengers and a driver in the automobile searched. None of the passengers is said to have had control of the vehicle or the keys. It is unrealistic—as the shared experience of us all bears witness—to suggest that these passengers had any reasonable expectation that the car in which they had been riding would not be searched after they were lawfully stopped and made to get out. The minimal privacy that existed simply is not comparable to that, for example, of an individual in his place of abode; of one who secludes

---

[17] * * * [T]he dissenters repeatedly state or imply that we now "hold" that a passenger lawfully in an automobile "may not invoke the exclusionary rule and challenge a search of that vehicle unless he happens to own or have a possessory interest in it." It is not without significance that these statements of today's "holding" come from the dissenting opinion, and not from the Court's opinion. The case before us involves the search of and seizure of property from the glove compartment and area under the seat of a car in which petitioners were riding as passengers. Petitioners claimed only that they were "legitimately on [the] premises" and did not claim that they had any legitimate expectation of privacy in the areas of the car which were searched. We cannot, therefore, agree with the dissenters' insistence that our decision will encourage the police to violate the Fourth Amendment.

himself in a telephone booth; or of the traveler who secures his belongings in a locked suitcase or footlocker.[4] * * *

MR. JUSTICE WHITE, with whom MR. JUSTICE BRENNAN, MR. JUSTICE MARSHALL, and MR. JUSTICE STEVENS join, dissenting.

The Court today holds that the Fourth Amendment protects property, not people, and specifically that a legitimate occupant of an automobile may not invoke the exclusionary rule and challenge a search of that vehicle unless he happens to own or have a possessory interest in it. Though professing to acknowledge that the primary purpose of the Fourth Amendment's prohibition of unreasonable searches is the protection of privacy—not property—the Court nonetheless effectively ties the application of the Fourth Amendment and the exclusionary rule in this situation to property law concepts. Insofar as passengers are concerned, the Court's opinion today declares an "open season" on automobiles. However unlawful stopping and searching a car may be, absent a possessory or ownership interest, no "mere" passenger may object, regardless of his relationship to the owner. * * *

III

* * * Our starting point is "[t]he established principle * * * that suppression of the product of a Fourth Amendment violation can be successfully urged only by those whose rights were violated by the search itself * * * ." Though the Amendment protects one's liberty and property interests against unreasonable seizures of self[5] and effects,[6] "the primary object of the Fourth Amendment [is] * * * the protection of privacy." And privacy is the interest asserted here, so the first step is to ascertain whether the premises searched "fall within a protected zone of privacy." * * *

It is true that the Court asserts that it is not limiting the Fourth Amendment bar against unreasonable searches to the protection of property rights, but in reality it is doing exactly that.[14] Petitioners were in a private place with the permission of the owner, but the Court states that that is not sufficient to establish entitlement to a legitimate

---

[4] The sawed-off rifle in this case was merely pushed beneath the front seat, presumably by one of the petitioners. In that position, it could have slipped into full or partial view in the event of an accident, or indeed upon any sudden stop. As the rifle shells were in the locked glove compartment, this might have presented a closer case if it had been shown that one of the petitioners possessed the keys or if a rifle had not been found in the automobile. * * *

[5] * * * [P]etitioners of course have standing to challenge the legality of the stop, and the evidence found may be a fruit of that stop. Petitioners have not argued that theory here * * * . * * *

[6] * * * Petitioners never asserted a property interest in the items seized from the automobile. * * *

[14] The Court's reliance on property law concepts is additionally shown by its suggestion that visitors could "contest the lawfulness of the seizure of evidence or the search if their own property were seized during the search." What difference should that property interest make to constitutional protection against unreasonable searches, which is concerned with privacy? * * *

expectation of privacy. But if that is not sufficient, what would be? We are not told, and it is hard to imagine anything short of a property interest that would satisfy the majority. * * * The Court approves the result in *Jones*, but it fails to give any explanation why the facts in *Jones* differ, in a fashion material to the Fourth Amendment, from the facts here.[15] More importantly, how is the Court able to avoid answering the question why presence in a private place with the owner's permission is insufficient? * * *

IV

The Court's holding is contrary not only to our past decisions and the logic of the Fourth Amendment but also to the everyday expectations of privacy that we all share. Because of that, it is unworkable in all the various situations that arise in real life. If the owner of the car had not only invited petitioners to join her but had said to them, "I give you a temporary possessory interest in my vehicle so that you will share the right to privacy that the Supreme Court says that I own," then apparently the majority would reverse. But people seldom say such things, though they may mean their invitation to encompass them if only they had thought of the problem. If the nonowner were the spouse or child of the owner, would the Court recognize a sufficient interest? If so, would distant relatives somehow have more of an expectation of privacy than close friends? What if the nonowner were driving with the owner's permission? Would nonowning drivers have more of an expectation of privacy than mere passengers? What about a passenger in a taxicab? * * * Why should Fourth Amendment rights be present when one pays a cabdriver for a ride but be absent when one is given a ride by a friend?

The distinctions the Court would draw are based on relationships between private parties, but the Fourth Amendment is concerned with the relationship of one of those parties to the government. Divorced as it is from the purpose of the Fourth Amendment, the Court's essentially property-based rationale can satisfactorily answer none of the questions posed above. That is reason enough to reject it. The *Jones* rule is relatively easily applied by police and courts; the rule announced today will not provide law enforcement officials with a bright line between the protected and the unprotected. Only rarely will police know whether one private party has or has not been granted a sufficient possessory or other interest by another private party. Surely in this case the officers had no such knowledge. The Court's rule will ensnare defendants and police in

---

[15] Jones had permission to use the apartment, had slept in it one night, had a key, had left a suit and a shirt there, and was the only occupant at the time of the search. Petitioners here had permission to be in the car and were occupying it at the time of the search. Thus the only distinguishing fact is that Jones could exclude others from the apartment by using his friend's key. But petitioners and their friend the owner had excluded others by entering the automobile and shutting the doors. Petitioners did not need a key because the owner was present. * * *

needless litigation over factors that should not be determinative of Fourth
Amendment rights.

More importantly, the ruling today undercuts the force of the
exclusionary rule in the one area in which its use is most certainly
justified—the deterrence of bad-faith violations of the Fourth
Amendment. This decision invites police to engage in patently
unreasonable searches every time an automobile contains more than one
occupant. Should something be found, only the owner of the vehicle, or of
the item, will have standing to seek suppression, and the evidence will
presumably be usable against the other occupants. The danger of such
bad faith is especially high in cases such as this one where the officers are
only after the passengers and can usually infer accurately that the driver
is the owner. * * *

NOTES AND QUESTIONS

1.   *A procedural matter.* Judges hear Fourth Amendment suppression
motions prior to trial. Notice the problem potentially confronting a defendant
who seeks to have evidence seized by the police excluded from the trial: In
order to raise the Fourth Amendment claim, she must first prove standing
(or, after *Rakas*, must prove that it was *her* Fourth Amendment rights that
were violated). To do this, the defendant may need to testify at the
suppression hearing and, for example, assert ownership of a briefcase that
was searched (and in which contraband was discovered), allegedly without
probable cause.

The defendant's testimony that she owned the briefcase may benefit the
defendant in the suppression hearing by giving her a right to challenge the
police action, but what if she loses on her Fourth Amendment claim? May the
prosecutor now use at trial the defendant's inculpatory pretrial admission
that it was her briefcase in which contraband was discovered? If so,
defendants who need to testify to prove standing may be deterred from
raising legitimate Fourth Amendment claims for fear that their testimony
will be used against them at trial. To mitigate this problem, the Supreme
Court held in Simmons v. United States, 390 U.S. 377, 88 S.Ct. 967, 19
L.Ed.2d 1247 (1968), that "when a defendant testifies in support of a motion
to suppress evidence on Fourth Amendment grounds, his testimony may not
thereafter be admitted against him at trial on the issue of guilt unless he
makes no objection."

Does *Simmons* relieve a defendant of *all* risks from testifying at the
suppression hearing?

2.   Look carefully at the majority opinion. *Did* the Court state that the
petitioners lacked a legitimate expectation of privacy in the areas of the car
that were searched? Hint: Look at footnote 17 and the text linked to it. Why
does one of the authors of this casebook describe footnote 17 as the

"*chutzpah*" footnote. (Ask around if you need help on the meaning of *that* word.)

3. Do *you* believe that the front seat passenger had a reasonable expectation of privacy regarding the search under his seat, where the sawed-off rifle was discovered? Why or why not? What about the glove compartment search?

4. *Open season on automobiles*? The dissent in *Rakas* accused the majority of declaring "open season" on automobiles in regard to passengers therein. Is that so? Suppose the police lawfully stop a car on a public road. They search the trunk without consent or probable cause. The police find a blood-stained jacket in the trunk, which they seize. Subsequently, the prosecutor seeks to introduce the jacket in a murder prosecution of Bob, who was in the car. After *Rakas*, may Bob successfully challenge the search in the following circumstances? Why, or why not?

A. At the time of the search, Alice, the car owner, was driving the vehicle, and Bob, a friend, was her front seat passenger.

B. The same as A., but Bob was driving, while Alice sat in the front seat.

C. The same as A., but the two were driving across country. Alice and Bob alternated driving, and Alice furnished Bob with a spare car key for the trip.

D. The same as A., but Bob wants to contest the car stop, rather than the trunk search.

E. The same as A., but Bob claims ownership of the jacket.

5. *Are homes like cars when it comes to issues of standing*? In Minnesota v. Olson, 495 U.S. 91, 110 S.Ct. 1684, 109 L.Ed.2d 85 (1990), the police, without a warrant or consent, entered a residence in which they believed Olson, a robbery-murder suspect, was staying as an overnight guest. The officers searched the residence until they discovered him hiding in a closet. In an opinion written by Justice White, the Court held that Olson had standing to contest the warrantless search:

> To hold that an overnight guest has a legitimate expectation of privacy in his host's home merely recognizes the everyday expectations of privacy that we all share. Staying overnight in another's home is a longstanding social custom that serves functions recognized as valuable by society. We stay in others' homes when we travel to a strange city for business or pleasure, when we visit our parents, children, or more distant relatives out of town, when we are in between jobs or homes, or when we house-sit for a friend. We will all be hosts and we will all be guests many times in our lives. From either perspective, we think that society recognizes that a houseguest has a legitimate expectation of privacy in his host's home.

From the overnight guest's perspective, he seeks shelter in another's home precisely because it provides him with privacy, a place where he and his possessions will not be disturbed by anyone but his host and those his host allows inside. We are at our most vulnerable when we are asleep because we cannot monitor our own safety or the security of our belongings. It is for this reason that, although we may spend all day in public places, when we cannot sleep in our own home we seek out another private place to sleep, whether it be a hotel room, or the home of a friend. Society expects at least as much privacy in these places as in a telephone booth * * * .

That the guest has a host who has ultimate control of the house is not inconsistent with the guest having a legitimate expectation of privacy. The houseguest is there with the permission of his host, who is willing to share his house and his privacy with his guest. It is unlikely that the guest will be confined to a restricted area of the house; and when the host is away or asleep, the guest will have a measure of control over the premises. The host may admit or exclude from the house as he prefers, but it is unlikely that he will admit someone who wants to see or meet with the guest over the objection of the guest. On the other hand, few houseguests will invite others to visit them while they are guests without consulting their hosts; but the latter, who have the authority to exclude despite the wishes of the guest, will often be accommodating. The point is that hosts will more likely than not respect the privacy interests of their guests, who are entitled to a legitimate expectation of privacy despite the fact that they have no legal interest in the premises and do not have the legal authority to determine who may or may not enter the household. If the untrammeled power to admit and exclude were essential to Fourth Amendment protection, an adult daughter temporarily living in the home of her parents would have no legitimate expectation of privacy because her right to admit or exclude would be subject to her parents' veto.

Chief Justice Rehnquist and Justice Blackmun dissented, but did not write an opinion.

Is *Olson* consistent with *Rakas*?

6. *Is "standing" a relevant concept after Rakas*? Justice Rehnquist in *Rakas* dispenses with the concept of "standing," as such, in the Fourth Amendment context. Previously, a defense lawyer would seek to prove that her client had standing to challenge the police action; if that obstacle was overcome, she would raise the merits of the Fourth Amendment claim. Now, *Rakas* teaches, there is just one step: to answer the substantive question of whether *the defendant's* Fourth Amendment rights were violated. But, this approach of converting a two-step process into one can result in unintended confusion, as Justice Blackmun has observed:

In my view, *Rakas v. Illinois* recognized two analytically distinct but "invariably intertwined" issues of substantive Fourth Amendment jurisprudence. The first is "whether [a] disputed search or seizure has infringed an interest of the defendant which the Fourth Amendment was designed to protect"; the second is whether "the challenged search or seizure violated [that] Fourth Amendment righ[t]." The first of these questions is answered by determining whether the defendant has a "legitimate expectation of privacy" that has been invaded by a governmental search or seizure. The second is answered by determining whether applicable cause and warrant requirements have been properly observed.

I agree with the Court that these two inquiries "merge into one," in the sense that both are to be addressed under the principles of Fourth Amendment analysis developed in *Katz v. United States* and its progeny. But I do not read today's decision, or *Rakas*, as holding that it is improper for lower courts to treat these inquiries as distinct components of a Fourth Amendment claim. Indeed, I am convinced that it would invite confusion to hold otherwise. It remains possible for a defendant to prove that his legitimate interest of privacy was invaded, and yet fail to prove that the police acted illegally in doing so. And it is equally possible for a defendant to prove that the police acted illegally, and yet fail to prove that his own privacy interest was affected.

Rawlings v. Kentucky, 448 U.S. 98, 100 S.Ct. 2556, 65 L.Ed.2d 633 (1980).

Can you see why Justice Blackmun might be correct in this regard? If not, you will hopefully see why, after you read the next case.

MINNESOTA V. CARTER

Supreme Court of the United States, 1998.
525 U.S. 83, 119 S.Ct. 469, 142 L.Ed.2d 373.

CHIEF JUSTICE REHNQUIST delivered the opinion of the Court [joined by JUSTICES O'CONNOR, SCALIA, KENNEDY, and THOMAS].

Respondents and the lessee of an apartment were sitting in one of its rooms, bagging cocaine. While so engaged they were observed by a police officer, who looked through a drawn window blind. The Supreme Court of Minnesota held that the officer's viewing was a search which violated respondents' Fourth Amendment rights. We hold that no such violation occurred.

James Thielen, a police officer in the Twin Cities' suburb of Eagan, Minnesota, went to an apartment building to investigate a tip from a confidential informant. The informant said that he had walked by the window of a ground-floor apartment and had seen people putting a white powder into bags. The officer looked in the same window through a gap in the closed blind and observed the bagging operation for several minutes. He then notified headquarters, which began preparing affidavits for a search warrant while he returned to the apartment building. * * *

* * * A search of the apartment pursuant to a warrant revealed cocaine residue [and plastic baggies] on the kitchen table * * * . Thielen identified Carter, Johns, and Thompson as the three people he had observed placing the powder into baggies. The police later learned that while Thompson was the lessee of the apartment, Carter and Johns lived in Chicago and had come to the apartment for the sole purpose of packaging the cocaine. Carter and Johns had never been to the apartment before and were only in the apartment for approximately 2½ hours. In return for the use of the apartment, Carter and Johns had given Thompson one-eighth of an ounce of the cocaine.

Carter and Johns * * * moved to suppress all evidence obtained from the apartment * * * . * * * The Minnesota trial court held that since, unlike the defendant in *Minnesota v. Olson* [p. 215, Note 5], Carter and Johns were not overnight social guests but temporary out-of-state visitors, they were not entitled to claim the protection of the Fourth Amendment against the government intrusion into the apartment. The trial court also concluded that Thielen's observation was not a search within the meaning of the Fourth Amendment. After a trial, Carter and Johns were each convicted of * * * [two controlled substance] offenses. * * *

A divided Minnesota Supreme Court reversed, holding that respondents had "standing" to claim the protection of the Fourth Amendment because they had " 'a legitimate expectation of privacy in the invaded place.' " * * * Based upon its conclusion that the respondents had "standing" to raise their Fourth Amendment claims, the court went on to hold that Thielen's observation constituted a search of the apartment under the Fourth Amendment, and that the search was unreasonable. * * *

The Minnesota courts analyzed whether respondents had a legitimate expectation of privacy under the rubric of "standing" doctrine, an analysis which this Court expressly rejected 20 years ago in *Rakas*. * * * Central to our analysis [in *Rakas*] was the idea that in determining whether a defendant is able to show the violation of his (and not someone else's) Fourth Amendment rights, the "definition of those rights is more properly placed within the purview of substantive Fourth Amendment law than within that of standing." Thus, we held that in order to claim the protection of the Fourth Amendment, a defendant must demonstrate that he personally has an expectation of privacy in the place searched, and that his expectation is reasonable * * * . * * *

The text of the Amendment suggests that its protections extend only to people in "their" houses. But we have held that in some circumstances a person may have a legitimate expectation of privacy in the house of someone else. In *Minnesota v. Olson*, for example, we decided that an overnight guest in a house had the sort of expectation of privacy that the Fourth Amendment protects. * * *

Respondents here were obviously not overnight guests, but were essentially present for a business transaction and were only in the home a matter of hours. There is no suggestion that they had a previous relationship with Thompson, or that there was any other purpose to their visit. Nor was there anything similar to the overnight guest relationship in *Olson* to suggest a degree of acceptance into the household. While the apartment was a dwelling place for Thompson, it was for these respondents simply a place to do business.

Property used for commercial purposes is treated differently for Fourth Amendment purposes than residential property. "An expectation of privacy in commercial premises, however, is different from, and indeed less than, a similar expectation in an individual's home." And while it was a "home" in which respondents were present, it was not their home. Similarly, the Court has held that in some circumstances a worker can claim Fourth Amendment protection over his own workplace. See, *e.g.*, *O'Connor v. Ortega*, 480 U.S. 709, 107 S.Ct. 1492, 94 L.Ed.2d 714 (1987). But there is no indication that respondents in this case had nearly as significant a connection to Thompson's apartment as the worker in *O'Connor* had to his own private office.

If we regard the overnight guest in *Minnesota v. Olson* as typifying those who may claim the protection of the Fourth Amendment in the home of another, and one merely "legitimately on the premises" as typifying those who may not do so, the present case is obviously somewhere in between. But the purely commercial nature of the transaction engaged in here, the relatively short period of time on the premises, and the lack of any previous connection between respondents and the householder, all lead us to conclude that respondents' situation is closer to that of one simply permitted on the premises. We therefore hold that any search which may have occurred did not violate their Fourth Amendment rights.

Because we conclude that respondents had no legitimate expectation of privacy in the apartment, we need not decide whether the police officer's observation constituted a "search." The judgment of the Supreme Court of Minnesota is accordingly reversed * * * . * * *

JUSTICE SCALIA, with whom JUSTICE THOMAS joins, concurring.

I join the opinion of the Court because I believe it accurately applies our recent case law, including *Minnesota v. Olson*. I write separately to express my view that that case law * * * gives short shrift to the text of the Fourth Amendment, and to the well and long understood meaning of that text. Specifically, it leaps to apply the fuzzy standard of "legitimate expectation of privacy"—a consideration that is often relevant to whether a search or seizure covered by the Fourth Amendment is "unreasonable"—to the threshold question whether a search or seizure covered by the Fourth Amendment *has occurred*. If that latter question is addressed first and analyzed under the text of the Constitution as traditionally understood, the present case is not remotely difficult.

The Fourth Amendment protects "[t]he right of the people to be secure *in their* persons, houses, papers, and effects, against unreasonable searches and seizures * * * ." It must be acknowledged that the phrase "their * * * houses" in this provision is, in isolation, ambiguous. It could mean "their respective houses," so that the protection extends to each person only in his *own* house. But it could also mean "their respective and each other's houses," so that each person would be protected even when visiting the house of someone else. As today's opinion for the Court suggests, however, it is not linguistically possible to give the provision the latter, expansive interpretation with respect to "houses" without giving it the same interpretation with respect to the nouns that are parallel to "houses"—"persons, * * * papers, and effects"—which would give me a constitutional right not to have your person unreasonably searched. This is so absurd that it has to my knowledge never been contemplated. The obvious meaning of the provision is that *each* person has the right to be secure against unreasonable searches and seizures in *his own* person, house, papers, and effects. * * *

That "their * * * houses" was understood to mean "their respective houses" would have been clear to anyone who knew the English and early American law of arrest and trespass that underlay the Fourth Amendment. The people's protection against unreasonable search and seizure in their "houses" was drawn from the English common-law maxim, "A man's home is *his* castle." As far back as *Semayne's Case* of 1604, the leading English case for that proposition * * * , the King's Bench proclaimed that "the house of any one is not a castle or privilege but for himself, and shall not extend to protect any person who flies to his house." * * *

Of course this is not to say that the Fourth Amendment protects only the Lord of the Manor who holds his estate in fee simple. People call a house "their" home when legal title is in the bank, when they rent it, and even when they merely occupy it rent-free—*so long as they actually live there*. * * *

Thus, in deciding the question presented today we write upon a slate that is far from clean. The text of the Fourth Amendment, the common-law background against which it was adopted, and the understandings consistently displayed after its adoption make the answer clear. * * * We went to the absolute limit of what text and tradition permit in *Minnesota v. Olson*, when we protected a mere overnight guest against an unreasonable search of his hosts' apartment. But whereas it is plausible to regard a person's overnight lodging as at least his "temporary" residence, it is entirely impossible to give that characterization to an apartment that he uses to package cocaine. Respondents here were not searched in "their * * * hous[e]" under any interpretation of the phrase that bears the remotest relationship to the well understood meaning of the Fourth Amendment.

The dissent believes that "[o]ur obligation to produce coherent results" requires that we ignore this clear text and four-century-old tradition, and apply instead the notoriously unhelpful test adopted in a "benchmar[k]" decision that is 31 years old[,] citing *Katz v. United States*. In my view, the only thing the past three decades have established about the *Katz* test (which has come to mean the test enunciated by Justice Harlan's separate concurrence in *Katz*) is that, unsurprisingly, those "actual (subjective) expectation[s] of privacy" "that society is prepared to recognize as 'reasonable,'" bear an uncanny resemblance to those expectations of privacy that this Court considers reasonable. When that self-indulgent test is employed (as the dissent would employ it here) to determine whether a "search or seizure" within the meaning of the Constitution has *occurred* (as opposed to whether that "search or seizure" is an "unreasonable" one), it has no plausible foundation in the text of the Fourth Amendment. That provision did not guarantee some generalized "right of privacy" and leave it to this Court to determine which particular manifestations of the value of privacy "society is prepared to recognize as 'reasonable.'" Rather, it enumerated ("persons, houses, papers, and effects") the objects of privacy protection to which the *Constitution* would extend, leaving further expansion to the good judgment, not of this Court, but of the people through their representatives in the legislature.[3]

---

[3] The dissent asserts that I "undervalu[e]" the *Katz* Court's observation that "the Fourth Amendment protects people, not places." That catchy slogan would be a devastating response to someone who maintained that a *location* could claim protection of the Fourth Amendment—someone who asserted, perhaps, that "primeval forests have rights, too." The issue here, however, is the less druidical one of whether respondents (who are people) have suffered a violation of *their* right "to be secure in their persons, houses, papers, and effects, against unreasonable searches and seizures." That the Fourth Amendment does not protect places is simply unresponsive to the question of whether the Fourth Amendment protects people in other people's homes. In saying this, I do not, as the dissent claims, clash with "the *leitmotif* of Justice Harlan's concurring opinion" in *Katz*; *au contraire* (or, to be more Wagnerian, *im Gegenteil*), in this regard I am entirely in harmony with that opinion, and it is the dissent that sings from another opera. See [*Katz*] (Harlan, J., concurring): "As the Court's opinion states, 'the Fourth Amendment protects people, not places.' The question, however, is what protection it affords to those people. Generally, as here, the answer to that question requires reference to a 'place.'"

The dissent may be correct that a person invited into someone else's house to engage in a common business (even common monkey-business, so to speak) *ought* to be protected against government searches of the room in which that business is conducted; and that persons invited in to deliver milk or pizza (whom the dissent dismisses as "classroom hypotheticals," as opposed, presumably, to flesh-and-blood hypotheticals) ought *not* to be protected against government searches of the rooms that they occupy. I am not sure of the answer to those policy questions. But I am sure that the answer is not remotely contained in the Constitution, which means that it is left—as *many*, indeed *most*, important questions are left—to the judgment of state and federal legislators. We go beyond our proper role as judges in a democratic society when we restrict the people's power to govern themselves over the full range of policy choices that the Constitution has left available to them.

JUSTICE KENNEDY, concurring.

I join the Court's opinion, for its reasoning is consistent with my view that almost all social guests have a legitimate expectation of privacy, and hence protection against unreasonable searches, in their host's home. * * *

The dissent, as I interpret it, does not question *Rakas* or the principle that not all persons in the company of the property owner have the owner's right to assert the spatial protection. *Rakas*, it is true, involved automobiles, where the necessities of law enforcement permit more latitude to the police than ought to be extended to houses. The analysis in *Rakas* was not conceived, however, as a utilitarian exception to accommodate the needs of law enforcement. The Court's premise was a more fundamental one. Fourth Amendment rights are personal, and when a person objects to the search of a place and invokes the exclusionary rule, he or she must have the requisite connection to that place. * * *

The settled rule is that the requisite connection is an expectation of privacy that society recognizes as reasonable. The application of that rule involves consideration of the kind of place in which the individual claims the privacy interest and what expectations of privacy are traditional and well recognized. I would expect that most, if not all, social guests legitimately expect that, in accordance with social custom, the homeowner will exercise her discretion to include or exclude others for the guests' benefit. As we recognized in *Minnesota v. Olson*, where these social expectations exist—as in the case of an overnight guest—they are sufficient to create a legitimate expectation of privacy, even in the absence of any property right to exclude others. In this respect, the dissent must be correct that reasonable expectations of the owner are shared, to some extent, by the guest. This analysis suggests that, as a general rule, social guests will have an expectation of privacy in their host's home. That is not the case before us, however.

In this case respondents have established nothing more than a fleeting and insubstantial connection with Thompson's home. For all that appears in the record, respondents used Thompson's house simply as a convenient processing station, their purpose involving nothing more than the mechanical act of chopping and packing a substance for distribution. There is no suggestion that respondents engaged in confidential communications with Thompson about their transaction. Respondents had not been to Thompson's apartment before, and they left it even before their arrest. The Minnesota Supreme Court, which overturned respondents' convictions, acknowledged that respondents could not be fairly characterized as Thompson's "guests."

If respondents here had been visiting twenty homes, each for a minute or two, to drop off a bag of cocaine and were apprehended by a policeman wrongfully present in the nineteenth home; or if they had left the goods at a home where they were not staying and the police had seized the goods in their absence, we would have said that *Rakas* compels rejection of any privacy interest respondents might assert. So it does here, given that respondents have established no meaningful tie or connection to the owner, the owner's home, or the owner's expectation of privacy.

We cannot remain faithful to the underlying principle in *Rakas* without reversing in this case, and I am not persuaded that we need depart from it to protect the homeowner's own privacy interests. Respondents have made no persuasive argument that we need to fashion a *per se* rule of home protection, with an automatic right for all in the home to invoke the exclusionary rule, in order to protect homeowners and their guests from unlawful police intrusion. With these observations, I join the Court's opinion.

JUSTICE BREYER, concurring in the judgment.

I agree with Justice Ginsburg that respondents can claim the Fourth Amendment's protection. Petitioner, however, raises a second question, whether under the circumstances Officer Thielen's observation made "from a public area outside the curtilage of the residence" violated respondents' Fourth Amendment rights. In my view, it did not. * * *

[Justice Breyer summarized in greater detail the facts in the case, including that the apartment in question was partly below ground level, that families living in the building frequently used the grassy area just outside the apartment's window for walking and playing, and that the officer here stood for nearly fifteen minutes about a foot from the window looking through a closed set of Venetian blinds, observing the illegal activities.]

Officer Thielen, then, stood at a place used by the public and from which one could see through the window into the kitchen. The precautions that the apartment's dwellers took to maintain their privacy would have failed in respect to an ordinary passerby standing in that place. Given this Court's well-established case law, I cannot say that the officer engaged in what the Constitution forbids, namely, an "unreasonable search." * * *

For these reasons, while agreeing with Justice Ginsburg, I also concur in the Court's judgment reversing the Minnesota Supreme Court.

JUSTICE GINSBURG, with whom JUSTICE STEVENS and JUSTICE SOUTER join, dissenting.

The Court's decision undermines not only the security of short-term guests, but also the security of the home resident herself. In my view, when a homeowner or lessor personally invites a guest into her home to share in a common endeavor, whether it be for conversation, to engage in leisure activities, or for business purposes licit or illicit, that guest should share his host's shelter against unreasonable searches and seizures.

* * * First, the disposition I would reach in this case responds to the unique importance of the home—the most essential bastion of privacy recognized by the law. Second, even within the home itself, the position to which I would adhere would not permit "a casual visitor who has never seen, or been permitted to visit, the basement of another's house to object to a search of the basement if the visitor happened to be in the kitchen of the house at the time of the search." *Rakas.* Further, I would here decide only the case of the homeowner who chooses to share the privacy of her home and her company with a guest, and would not reach classroom hypotheticals like the milkman or pizza deliverer.

My concern centers on an individual's choice to share her home and her associations there with persons she selects. Our decisions indicate that people have a reasonable expectation of privacy in their homes in part because they have the prerogative to exclude others. The power to exclude implies the power to include. Our Fourth Amendment decisions should reflect these complementary prerogatives. * * *

Through the host's invitation, the guest gains a reasonable expectation of privacy in the home. *Minnesota v. Olson* so held with respect to an overnight guest. The logic of that decision extends to shorter term guests as well. * * * One need not remain overnight to anticipate privacy in another's home * * *. In sum, when a homeowner chooses to share the privacy of her home and her company with a short-term guest, the twofold requirement "emerg[ing] from prior decisions" has been satisfied: Both host and guest "have exhibited an actual (subjective) expectation of privacy"; that "expectation [is] one [our] society is prepared to recognize as 'reasonable.'" *Katz v. United States.*[2]

As the Solicitor General acknowledged, the illegality of the host-guest conduct, the fact that they were partners in crime, would not alter the analysis. * * * Indeed, it must be this way. If the illegality of the activity made constitutional an otherwise unconstitutional search, such Fourth Amendment protection, reserved for the innocent only, would have little force in regulating police behavior toward either the innocent or the guilty.

Our leading decision in *Katz* is key to my view of this case. * * * We were mindful that "the Fourth Amendment protects people, not places," and held that this electronic monitoring of a business call "violated the privacy upon which [the caller] justifiably relied while using the telephone booth." Our obligation to produce coherent results in this often visited area of the law requires us to inform our current expositions by benchmarks already established. * * * The Court's decision in this case veers sharply from the path marked in *Katz.* I do not agree that we have a more reasonable expectation of privacy when we place a business call to a person's home from a public telephone booth on the side of the street, than when we actually enter that person's premises to engage in a common endeavor.[3] * * *

NOTES AND QUESTIONS

1.   Count votes in this case. Although Carter and Johns, the respondents, lost on their appeal, did the Court narrow or expand on the protections provided to guests in residences, as originally announced in *Minnesota v. Olson?* After *Carter,* when does a guest in a home have standing to contest a police search of the residence?

2.   Why did Justice Breyer concur in the judgment, although he agrees with the dissent's observations on the "standing" issue? How did the dissenters respond to Breyer's opinion? In what way do the Breyer and Ginsburg opinions reinforce Justice Blackmun's observations (p. 506, Note 6)

---

[2]   In his concurring opinion, Justice Kennedy maintains that respondents here * * * "established nothing more than a fleeting and insubstantial connection" with the host's home. As the Minnesota Supreme Court reported, however, the stipulated facts showed that respondents were inside the apartment with the host's permission, remained inside for at least 2½ hours, and, during that time, engaged in concert with the host in a collaborative venture. These stipulated facts—which scarcely resemble a stop of a minute or two at the 19th of 20 homes to drop off a packet—securely demonstrate that the host intended to share her privacy with respondents, and that respondents, therefore, had entered into the homeland of Fourth Amendment protection. * * *

[3]   Justice Scalia's lively concurring opinion deplores our adherence to *Katz.* * * * Justice Scalia undervalues the clear opinion of the Court that "the Fourth Amendment protects people, not places." That core understanding is the *leitmotif* of Justice Harlan's concurring opinion. One cannot avoid a strong sense of *déjà vu* on reading Justice Scalia's elaboration. It so vividly recalls the opinion of Justice Black *in dissent* in *Katz.* * * *

about the confusion that can result from *not* analyzing cases under the rubric of "standing"?

3.　*Problem. S*, who was wanted by federal authorities in connection with a drug conspiracy and murder, drove all night from Michigan to Georgia. He arrived in the morning and promptly entered an apartment he had sublet from *L*, the leaseholder, for $2000. He went to sleep. Six hours later, the police entered, arrested *S*, and searched the premises, resulting in the seizure of evidence. United States v. Stuckey, 325 F.Supp.2d 793 (E.D. Mich. 2004). Standing?

4.　In *Rakas v. Illinois*, the Court repeatedly observed that the petitioners in that case had not claimed ownership of the property seized. The implication seemed to be that if a person owns seized property, she has standing to contest the search resulting in its seizure. That implication, however, has proved false. In Rawlings v. Kentucky, 448 U.S. 98, 100 S.Ct. 2556, 65 L.Ed.2d 633 (1980), the Court ruled that the test enunciated in *Rakas*—whether the petitioner had a reasonable expectation of privacy in the area searched—is the exclusive test for determining whether a defendant may successfully challenge a search.

In *Rawlings*, the police, armed with a warrant to arrest *X*, entered a residence occupied by five persons. While unsuccessfully searching for *X*, the police smelled burnt marijuana and observed some marijuana seeds on the mantel in one bedroom. While two officers left to obtain a search warrant, other officers detained the occupants of the house, allowing them to leave only if they consented to a body search. Two of the occupants consented to a search and left.

Less than an hour later, the two officers returned with a search warrant. One of them walked over to Cox, a female sitting on the couch, and ordered her to empty the contents of her purse, which she did. Among the contents was a jar containing 1,800 tablets of LSD. At that point, Cox turned to Rawlings, a male who had been sitting next to her, and told him "to take what was his." He claimed ownership of the controlled substances. The trial court determined that Rawlings had known Cox for a few days and had recently slept on her couch at least twice, and—although there was a factual dispute on the matter—Rawlings had dumped the drugs in Cox's purse, with her knowledge, on the afternoon of the search.

The Court agreed with the lower court that Rawlings had not made a sufficient showing that his legitimate expectation of privacy was violated by the search of Cox's purse:

> We believe that the record in this case supports that conclusion. Petitioner, of course, bears the burden of proving not only that the search of Cox's purse was illegal, but also that he had a legitimate expectation of privacy in that purse. At the time petitioner dumped thousands of dollars worth of illegal drugs into Cox's purse, he had known her for only a few days. According to

Cox's uncontested testimony, petitioner had never sought or received access to her purse prior to that sudden bailment. Nor did petitioner have any right to exclude other persons from access to Cox's purse. In fact, Cox testified that Bob Stallons, a longtime acquaintance and frequent companion of Cox's, had free access to her purse and on the very morning of the arrest had rummaged through its contents in search of a hairbrush. Moreover, even assuming that petitioner's version of the bailment is correct and that Cox did consent to the transfer of possession, the precipitous nature of the transaction hardly supports a reasonable inference that petitioner took normal precautions to maintain his privacy. * * *

Petitioner contends nevertheless that, because he claimed ownership of the drugs in Cox's purse, he should be entitled to challenge the search regardless of his expectation of privacy. We disagree. While petitioner's ownership of the drugs is undoubtedly one fact to be considered in this case, *Rakas* emphatically rejected the notion that "arcane" concepts of property law ought to control the ability to claim the protections of the Fourth Amendment.

Are you persuaded by the Court's reasoning?

5.   *Variations on Rawlings.* Assume the following variations on the facts in *Rawlings.* Would Rawlings have standing to challenge the police conduct in these circumstances?

A.   When Cox emptied her purse as ordered, a police officer observed the drug vial, picked it up, but was unable to determine what was in it. He removed the lid and inspected the contents. Based on his observations, he concluded that the vial contained controlled substances and, therefore, seized it.

B.   When Cox emptied her purse, the officer discovered a sealed envelope belonging to Rawlings. Based on a hunch that the envelope contained illegal drugs, the officer seized the envelope and, four days later, subjected it to a dog sniff, which confirmed his hunch. The officer then opened the envelope and seized the drugs inside.

B. EXCLUSIONARY RULE

1. THE RULE IS RECOGNIZED

MAPP V. OHIO

Supreme Court of the United States, 1961.
367 U.S. 643, 81 S.Ct. 1684, 6 L.Ed.2d 1081.

[See p. 83 for the text of the case.]

NOTES AND QUESTIONS

1. According to *Mapp*, is the exclusionary rule constitutionally required? Look carefully at the language in Justice Clark's majority opinion and Justice Harlan's dissent for clues.

2. *United States v. Calandra and the constitutionality of the exclusionary rule.* The Supreme Court held in United States v. Calandra, 414 U.S. 338, 94 S.Ct. 613, 38 L.Ed.2d 561 (1974), that the Fourth Amendment exclusionary rule does not apply in grand jury proceedings. The Court's reasoning is significant well beyond grand juries:

> [T]he [exclusionary] rule is a judicially created remedy designed to safeguard Fourth Amendment rights generally through its deterrent effect, rather than a personal constitutional right of the party aggrieved.
>
> Despite its broad deterrent purpose, the exclusionary rule has never been interpreted to proscribe the use of illegally seized evidence in all proceedings or against all persons. As with any remedial device, the application of the rule has been restricted to those areas where its remedial objectives are thought most efficaciously served. * * *
>
> Any incremental deterrent effect which might be achieved by extending the rule to grand jury proceedings is uncertain at best. Whatever deterrence of police misconduct may result from the exclusion of illegally seized evidence from criminal trials, it is unrealistic to assume that application of the rule to grand jury proceedings would significantly further that goal. Such an extension would deter only police investigation consciously directed toward the discovery of evidence solely for use in a grand jury investigation. The incentive to disregard the requirement of the Fourth Amendment solely to obtain an indictment from a grand jury is substantially negated by the inadmissibility of the illegally seized evidence in a subsequent criminal prosecution of the search victim. * * * We therefore decline to embrace a view that would achieve a speculative and undoubtedly minimal advance in the deterrence of police misconduct at the expense of substantially impeding the role of the grand jury.

What is the significance of the Court's statement that "the rule is a judicially created remedy * * *, rather than a personal constitutional right of the party aggrieved"? What are the implications of this assertion?

3. *The "judicial integrity" rationale of the exclusionary rule.* As seen in the last Note, the Court in *United States v. Calandra* weighed the purported costs of the exclusionary rule against the incremental deterrent benefits of invoking the rule in grand jury proceedings. As the dissenters pointed out there, however, the majority did *not* consider a second rationale for the exclusionary doctrine mentioned in *Mapp*:

For the first time, the Court today discounts to the point of extinction the vital function of the rule to insure that the judiciary avoid even the slightest appearance of sanctioning illegal government conduct. This rejection of "the imperative of judicial integrity," openly invites "[t]he conviction that all government is staffed by * * * hypocrites[, a conviction] easy to instill and difficult to erase." When judges appear to become "accomplices in the willful disobedience of a Constitution they are sworn to uphold," we imperil the very foundation of our people's trust in their Government on which our democracy rests.

Why might "extinction" of the judicial integrity rationale undermine the position of advocates of the exclusionary rule?

4.   As the Court has observed, even "[i]n the complex and turbulent history of the [exclusionary] rule, the Court never has applied it to exclude evidence from a civil proceeding, federal or state." United States v. Janis, 428 U.S. 433, 96 S.Ct. 3021, 49 L.Ed.2d 1046 (1976). According to *Janis*, the deterrence benefit of extending the exclusionary rule to non-criminal proceedings (*e.g.*, civil suits, deportation or disbarment proceedings, etc.) would be comparatively slight, whereas the social costs of exclusion would be severe.

Moreover, as we have already seen in the context of grand juries (Note 2), the exclusionary rule does not apply in all criminal proceedings. For example, courts have also allowed the introduction of unconstitutionally seized evidence at pre-trial preliminary hearings, after the guilt phase of a trial during sentencing, and at probation and parole revocation hearings.

And, for a long time, there has been one circumstance in which the exclusionary rule does not apply during the guilt phase of criminal trials: a prosecutor may impeach a defendant's testimony by introducing evidence previously excluded on Fourth Amendment grounds. For example, in Walder v. United States, 347 U.S. 62, 74 S.Ct. 354, 98 L.Ed. 503 (1954), the Supreme Court held that a defendant may not take advantage of a court's exclusion of narcotics found in his possession by testifying in direct examination that he has never possessed narcotics. In such circumstances, as Justice Frankfurter wrote for the Court:

> It is one thing to say that the Government cannot make an affirmative use of evidence unlawfully obtained. It is quite another to say that the defendant can turn the illegal method by which evidence in the Government's possession was obtained to his own advantage, and provide himself with a shield against contradiction of his untruths. Such an extension of the [exclusionary] doctrine would be a perversion of the Fourth Amendment.

In *Walder*, the prosecutor sought to impeach the testimony of the defendant given during *direct* examination. The exclusionary rule exception similarly applies if a prosecutor wishes to introduce unconstitutionally obtained evidence to impeach a defendant's *cross-examination* testimony. United States v. Havens, 446 U.S. 620, 100 S.Ct. 1912, 64 L.Ed.2d 559 (1980).

2. SCOPE OF THE EXCLUSIONARY RULE (WHEN IT APPLIES)

Introduction

The thrust of *Mapp v. Ohio* (p. 83) is straight-forward: When the police violate a defendant's Fourth Amendment rights—whether the violation is intentional, reckless, negligent, or even innocent—the evidence obtained in violation of the amendment may not be used at *that* defendant's (don't forget the standing requirement!) criminal trial in the case-in-chief. We will see in subsection 3, however, that this bright-line approach no longer applies. For now, however, let's look at the exclusionary rule in its robust form and consider the scope of the exclusionary rule when it otherwise applies.

a. In General

SILVERTHORNE LUMBER COMPANY v. UNITED STATES
Supreme Court of the United States, 1920.
251 U.S. 385, 40 S.Ct. 182, 64 L.Ed. 319.

Mr. JUSTICE HOLMES delivered the opinion of the court [joined by JUSTICES VAN DEVANTER, MCREYNOLDS, BRANDEIS, DAY, CLARKE, and MCKENNA]. * * *

The facts are simple. An indictment upon a single specific charge having been brought against the two Silverthornes mentioned, they both were arrested at their homes early in the morning of February 25, 1919, and were detained in custody a number of hours. While they were thus detained representatives of the Department of Justice and the United States marshal without a shadow of authority went to the office of their company and made a clean sweep of all the books, papers and documents found there. * * * An application was made as soon as might be to the District Court for a return of what thus had been taken unlawfully. It was opposed by the District Attorney * * * . * * * The District Court * * * found that all the papers had been seized in violation of the parties' constitutional rights. * * * The Government now, while in form repudiating and condemning the illegal seizure, seeks to maintain its right to avail itself of the knowledge obtained by that means which otherwise it would not have had.

The proposition could not be presented more nakedly. It is that although of course its seizure was an outrage which the Government now regrets, it may study the papers before it returns them, copy them, and then may use the knowledge [against the Silverthornes] * * * ; that the protection of the Constitution covers the physical possession but not any advantages that the Government can gain over the object of its pursuit by doing the forbidden act. * * * In our opinion such is not the law. It reduces the Fourth Amendment to a form of words. The essence of a provision forbidding the acquisition of evidence in a certain way is that not merely evidence so acquired shall not be used before the Court but that it shall not be used at all. Of course this does not mean that the facts thus obtained become sacred and inaccessible. If knowledge of them is gained from an independent source they may be proved like any others, but the knowledge gained by the Government's own wrong cannot be used by it in the way proposed. * * *

The CHIEF JUSTICE [WHITE] and MR. JUSTICE PITNEY dissent [without opinion].

NOTES AND QUESTIONS

1. Look again at this sentence by Justice Holmes: "The essence of a provision forbidding the acquisition of evidence in a certain way is that not merely evidence so acquired shall not be used before the Court *but that it shall not be used at all*"? What is he getting at by the words we have italicized? Walder v. United States, 347 U.S. 62, 74 S.Ct. 354, 98 L.Ed. 503 (1954) explained its meaning this way:

> The Government cannot violate the Fourth Amendment * * * and use the fruits of such unlawful conduct to secure a conviction. *Nor can the Government make indirect use of such evidence for its case, or support a conviction on evidence obtained through leads from the unlawfully obtained evidence.* All these methods are outlawed, and convictions obtained by means of them are invalidated, because they encourage the kind of society that is obnoxious to free men. (Emphasis added.)

In other words, if the police seize item A in violation of the Fourth Amendment, they also are barred from introducing item B at Citizen's criminal trial if B was obtained as a result of the unconstitutional seizure of item A. In this example, B is what lawyers call "a fruit of a poisonous tree." But, read on.

2. *"Independent source" doctrine.* The fruit-of-the-poisonous-tree doctrine is not as simple and straightforward as just stated. Notice what Justice Holmes wrote immediately after the words quoted in Note 1: "Of course, this does not mean that the facts thus obtained become sacred and inaccessible. If knowledge of them is gained from an independent source they may be proved like any others * * * ."

In other words, perhaps there *is* a poisonous tree (a Fourth Amendment violation), but we must consider the possibility that a particular "fruit" comes from a different, *un*poisoned tree. This is an expression of the so-called "independent source" doctrine. It and the related "inevitable discovery" (or "hypothetical independent source") rule are considered in subsection b. below.

3.   *"Attenuation" or "dissipation of taint" doctrine.* Even if particular evidence *is* a fruit of the poisonous tree, it may still be admissible, notwithstanding the sweeping italicized language in *Walder* (Note 1). As Justice Frankfurter explained in Nardone v. United States, 308 U.S. 338, 60 S.Ct. 266, 84 L.Ed. 307 (1939), "[s]ophisticated argument may prove a causal connection between information obtained through illicit [police conduct] and the Government's proof. As a matter of good sense, however, such connection may have become so attenuated as to dissipate the taint." At some point, in other words, the law stops looking backwards in time and essentially says, "enough is enough, we are prepared to eat this fruit," i.e., to allow use of the secondary evidence at trial even if it is causally linked to a previous Fourth Amendment violation. This attenuation factor in considered in subsection c. below.

4.   *Some help.* In analyzing any fruit-of-the-poisonous-tree case, study the facts carefully to: (a) identify the "tree" (the constitutional violation); (b) the fruit (the evidence the government seeks to introduce); (c) determine whether (b) comes from (a) (is there a causal link?); and (d) if the fruit *did* come from a poisonous tree, identify any facts that may justify the conclusion that the fruit no longer is poisoned (the "attenuation" or "dissipation" doctrine).

b.   "Independent   Source"   and   "Inevitable   Discovery" Doctrines

MURRAY v. UNITED STATES
Supreme Court of the United States, 1988.
487 U.S. 533, 108 S.Ct. 2529, 101 L.Ed.2d 472.

JUSTICE SCALIA delivered the opinion of the Court [joined by CHIEF JUSTICE REHNQUIST, and JUSTICES WHITE and BLACKMUN].

I

* * * [T]he facts are as follows: Based on information received from informants, federal law enforcement agents had been surveilling petitioner Murray and several of his co-conspirators. At about 1:45 p.m. on April 6, 1983, they observed Murray drive a truck and Carter drive a green camper, into a warehouse in South Boston. When the petitioners drove the vehicles out about 20 minutes later, the surveilling agents saw within the warehouse two individuals and a tractor-trailer rig bearing a long, dark container. Murray and [petitioner] Carter later turned over the truck and camper to other drivers, who were in turn followed and ultimately arrested, and the vehicles lawfully seized. Both vehicles were found to contain marijuana.

After receiving this information, several of the agents converged on the South Boston warehouse and forced entry. They found the warehouse unoccupied, but observed in plain view numerous burlap-wrapped bales that were later found to contain marijuana. They left without disturbing the bales, kept the warehouse under surveillance, and did not reenter it until they had a search warrant. In applying for the warrant, the agents did not mention the prior entry, and did not rely on any observations made during that entry. When the warrant was issued—at 10:40 p.m., approximately eight hours after the initial entry—the agents immediately reentered the warehouse and seized 270 bales of marijuana and notebooks listing customers for whom the bales were destined.

Before trial, petitioners moved to suppress the evidence found in the warehouse. The District Court denied the motion, rejecting petitioners' arguments that the warrant was invalid because the agents did not inform the Magistrate about their prior warrantless entry, and that the warrant was tainted by that entry. The First Circuit affirmed, assuming for purposes of its decision that the first entry into the warehouse was unlawful. * * *

II * * *

Almost simultaneously with our development of the exclusionary rule, in the first quarter of this century, we also announced what has come to be known as the "independent source" doctrine. * * * The dispute here is over the scope of this doctrine. Petitioners contend that it applies only to evidence obtained for the first time during an independent lawful search. The Government argues that it applies also to evidence initially discovered during, or as a consequence of, an unlawful search, but later obtained independently from activities untainted by the initial illegality. We think the Government's view has better support in both precedent and policy.

Our cases have used the concept of "independent source" in a more general and a more specific sense. The more general sense identifies *all* evidence acquired in a fashion untainted by the illegal evidence-gathering activity. Thus, where an unlawful entry has given investigators knowledge of facts x and y, but fact z has been learned by other means, fact z can be said to be admissible because derived from an "independent source." This is how we used the term in *Segura v. United States*[, 468 U.S. 796, 104 S.Ct. 3380, 82 L.Ed.2d 599 (1984)]. In that case, agents unlawfully entered the defendant's apartment and remained there until a search warrant was obtained. The admissibility of what they discovered while waiting in the apartment was not before us, but we held that the evidence found for the first time during the execution of the valid and untainted search warrant was admissible because it was discovered pursuant to an "independent source."

The original use of the term, however, and its more important use for purposes of these cases, was more specific. It was originally applied in the exclusionary rule context, [in *Silverthorne*,] with reference to that particular category of evidence acquired by an untainted search *which is identical to the evidence unlawfully acquired*—that is, in the example just given, to knowledge of facts *x* and *y* derived from an independent source * * *. * * *

Petitioners' asserted policy basis for excluding evidence which is initially discovered during an illegal search, but is subsequently acquired through an independent and lawful source, is that a contrary rule will remove all deterrence to, and indeed positively encourage, unlawful police searches. As petitioners see the incentives, law enforcement officers will routinely enter without a warrant to make sure that what they expect to be on the premises is in fact there. If it is not, they will have spared themselves the time and trouble of getting a warrant; if it is, they can get the warrant and use the evidence despite the unlawful entry. We see the incentives differently. An officer with probable cause sufficient to obtain a search warrant would be foolish to enter the premises first in an unlawful manner. By doing so, he would risk suppression of all evidence on the premises, both seen and unseen, since his action would add to the normal burden of convincing a magistrate that there is probable cause the much more onerous burden of convincing a trial court that no information gained from the illegal entry affected either the law enforcement officers' decision to seek a warrant or the magistrate's decision to grant it. Nor would the officer *without* sufficient probable cause to obtain a search warrant have any added incentive to conduct an unlawful entry, since whatever he finds cannot be used to establish probable cause before a magistrate.[2] * * *

III

To apply what we have said to the present cases: Knowledge that the marijuana was in the warehouse was assuredly acquired at the time of the unlawful entry. But it was also acquired at the time of entry pursuant to the warrant, and if that later acquisition was not the result of the earlier entry there is no reason why the independent source doctrine should not apply. Invoking the exclusionary rule would put the police (and society) not in the *same* position they would have occupied if no violation occurred, but in a *worse* one.

---

[2]   Justice Marshall argues, in effect, that where the police cannot point to some historically verifiable fact demonstrating that the subsequent search pursuant to a warrant was wholly unaffected by the prior illegal search—*e.g.*, that they had already sought the warrant before entering the premises—we should adopt a *per se* rule of inadmissibility. We do not believe that such a prophylactic exception to the independent source rule is necessary. To say that a district court must be satisfied that a warrant would have been sought without the illegal entry is not to give dispositive effect to police officers' assurances on the point. Where the facts render those assurances implausible, the independent source doctrine will not apply. * * *

We think this is also true with respect to the tangible evidence, the bales of marijuana. * * * So long as a later, lawful seizure is genuinely independent of an earlier, tainted one (which may well be difficult to establish where the seized goods are kept in the police's possession) there is no reason why the independent source doctrine should not apply.

The ultimate question, therefore, is whether the search pursuant to warrant was in fact a genuinely independent source of the information and tangible evidence at issue here. This would not have been the case if the agents' decision to seek the warrant was prompted by what they had seen during the initial entry,[3] or if information obtained during that entry was presented to the Magistrate and affected his decision to issue the warrant. [The District Court, however, did not explicitly determine whether the agents would have sought the warrant even if they had not illegally entered the warehouse.] * * *

Accordingly, we vacate the judgment and remand these cases to the Court of Appeals with instructions that it remand to the District Court for determination whether the warrant-authorized search of the warehouse was an independent source of the challenged evidence in the sense we have described. * * *

JUSTICE BRENNAN and JUSTICE KENNEDY took no part in the consideration or decision of these cases.

JUSTICE MARSHALL, with whom JUSTICE STEVENS and JUSTICE O'CONNOR join, dissenting. * * *

* * * In holding that the independent source exception may apply to the facts of these cases, I believe the Court loses sight of the practical moorings of the independent source exception and creates an affirmative incentive for unconstitutional searches. * * *

Under the circumstances of these cases, the admission of the evidence "reseized" during the second search severely undermines the deterrence function of the exclusionary rule. Indeed, admission in these cases affirmatively encourages illegal searches. The incentives for such illegal conduct are clear. Obtaining a warrant is inconvenient and time consuming. Even when officers have probable cause to support a warrant application, therefore, they have an incentive first to determine whether it is worthwhile to obtain a warrant. Probable cause is much less than certainty, and many "confirmatory" searches will result in the discovery

---

[3]   Justice Marshall argues that "the relevant question [is] whether, even if the initial entry uncovered no evidence, the officers would return immediately with a warrant to conduct a second search." We do not see how this is "relevant" at all. To determine whether the warrant was independent of the illegal entry, one must ask whether it would have been sought even if what actually happened had not occurred—not whether it would have been sought if something else had happened. That is to say, what counts is whether the actual illegal search had any effect in producing the warrant, not whether some hypothetical illegal search would have aborted the warrant. * * *

that no evidence is present, thus saving the police the time and trouble of getting a warrant. If contraband is discovered, however, the officers may later seek a warrant to shield the evidence from the taint of the illegal search. The police thus know in advance that they have little to lose and much to gain by forgoing the bother of obtaining a warrant and undertaking an illegal search.

The Court, however, "see[s] the incentives differently." Under the Court's view, today's decision does not provide an incentive for unlawful searches, because the officer undertaking the search would know that "his action would add to the normal burden of convincing a magistrate that there is probable cause the much more onerous burden of convincing a trial court that no information gained from the illegal entry affected either the law enforcement officers' decision to seek a warrant or the magistrate's decision to grant it." The Court, however, provides no hint of why this risk would actually seem significant to the officers. Under the circumstances of these cases, the officers committing the illegal search have both knowledge and control of the factors central to the trial court's determination. First, it is a simple matter, as was done in these cases, to exclude from the warrant application any information gained from the initial entry so that the magistrate's determination of probable cause is not influenced by the prior illegal search. Second, today's decision makes the application of the independent source exception turn entirely on an evaluation of the officers' intent. It normally will be difficult for the trial court to verify, or the defendant to rebut, an assertion by officers that they always intended to obtain a warrant, regardless of the results of the illegal search.[2] The testimony of the officers conducting the illegal search is the only direct evidence of intent, and the defendant will be relegated simply to arguing that the officers should not be believed. Under these circumstances, the litigation risk described by the Court seems hardly a risk at all; it does not significantly dampen the incentive to conduct the initial illegal search. * * *

* * * In the instant cases, there are no "demonstrated historical facts" capable of supporting a finding that the subsequent warrant search was wholly unaffected by the prior illegal search. The same team of investigators was involved in both searches. The warrant was obtained

---

[2] Such an intent-based rule is of dubious value for other reasons as well. First, the intent of the officers prior to the illegal entry often will be of little significance to the relevant question: whether, even if the initial entry uncovered no evidence, the officers would return immediately with a warrant to conduct a second search. Officers who have probable cause to believe contraband is present genuinely might intend later to obtain a warrant, but after the illegal search uncovers no such contraband, those same officers might decide their time is better spent than to return with a warrant. In addition, such an intent rule will be difficult to apply. The Court fails to describe how a trial court will properly evaluate whether the law enforcement officers fully intended to obtain a warrant regardless of what they discovered during the illegal search. The obvious question is whose intent is relevant? Intentions clearly may differ both among supervisory officers and among officers who initiate the illegal search.

immediately after the illegal search, and no effort was made to obtain a warrant prior to the discovery of the marijuana during the illegal search. The only evidence available that the warrant search was wholly independent is the testimony of the agents who conducted the illegal search. Under these circumstances, the threat that the subsequent search was tainted by the illegal search is too great to allow for the application of the independent source exception.[4] The Court's contrary holding lends itself to easy abuse, and offers an incentive to bypass the constitutional requirement that probable cause be assessed by a neutral and detached magistrate before the police invade an individual's privacy. * * *

In sum, under circumstances as are presented in these cases, when the very law enforcement officers who participate in an illegal search immediately thereafter obtain a warrant to search the same premises, I believe the evidence discovered during the initial illegal entry must be suppressed. Any other result emasculates the Warrant Clause and provides an intolerable incentive for warrantless searches. * * *

[The dissenting opinion of JUSTICE STEVENS is omitted.]

NOTES AND QUESTIONS

1. In *Murray*, the failure of the police to inform the magistrate of their unlawful confirmatory search strengthened their Fourth Amendment claim by avoiding possible taint in the warrant process. But, should an officer have a duty of candor that is violated by such non-disclosure when he seeks a warrant?

2. In *Murray*, suppose that a police officer had testified at the suppression hearing, "We were sure we had probable cause, so we planned on getting a warrant, but we were kinda worried that the defendants were going to come back and destroy the evidence. So, we went in, just in case, and then, when we saw we were wrong about the emergency, we went for the warrant. But, sure, if we had found nothing in the warehouse, we would not have applied for a warrant. Why would we have?" According to Justice Scalia, based on this testimony, would the independent source doctrine apply? Should it?

3. Consider Craig M. Bradley, *Murray v. United States: The Bell Tolls for the Search Warrant Requirement*, 64 Ind. L.J. 907, 915–18 (1989):

> While *Murray* will encourage the police to find evidence
> without a warrant, the most serious problem caused by the decision

---

[4] To conclude that the initial search had no effect on the decision to obtain a warrant, and thus that the warrant search was an "independent source" of the challenged evidence, one would have to assume that even if the officers entered the premises and discovered no contraband, they nonetheless would have gone to the Magistrate, sworn that they had probable cause to believe that contraband was in the building, and then returned to conduct another search. Although such a scenario is possible, I believe it is more plausible to believe that the officers would not have chosen to return immediately to the premises with a warrant to search for evidence had they not discovered evidence during the initial search.

affects the innocent rather than the guilty. The purpose of the warrant requirement is not to slow the police down in their pursuit of the guilty, but to require that the decision of a "neutral and detached magistrate" is interposed between the police's impulse to search and their action on that impulse.

* * * When * * * [non-exigent] warrantless searches are allowed to occur without any exclusionary sanction attaching, as in *Murray*, it greatly increases the chance that the police will search the innocent.

Consider the position of the rational police officer. Assume that it is true, as the Court avers, that if he has ample probable cause and ample time, he will go ahead and get a warrant in order to avoid the additional explanations that a warrantless search will entail. But suppose, as is frequently the case, that his probable cause is shaky or nonexistent. *Murray* positively encourages him to proceed with an illegal search. If he finds nothing, he simply shrugs his shoulders and walks away. If he finds evidence, he leaves his partner to watch over it, repairs to the magistrate, and reports that "an anonymous reliable informant who has given information on three occasions in the past that has led to convictions called to tell me that he had just seen bales of marijuana stored at a warehouse at 123 Elm Street." The warrant issues and the marijuana is seized. Before trial (assuming that the defense has found out about the illegal search), the officer admits it, chalks it up to a fear that the evidence would be lost if the warehouse were not immediately secured, apologizes for being wrong in this assessment, and introduces the warrant affidavit to demonstrate an independent source. The Court, in allowing such behavior, has missed the point of the warrant requirement and the exclusionary rule—that it "reduce[s] the Fourth Amendment to a nullity" to allow warrantless searches to go unpunished. * * *

Of course, it has always been the case that the police could make up the existence of "Old Reliable," the informant, and use his fictitious "tip" as the basis for a search warrant. The problem with this tactic is that, if the police are wrong and no evidence is found, they are forced to return to the magistrate empty-handed. This is embarrassing to the police department and would only have to happen a few times before the magistrates and defense attorneys would realize that the police were liars. After *Murray*, there is no such fear, because the fictitious "Old Reliable" will *always be right!* His "tip" will always lead to evidence because the police will have found it in advance.

4.   *Inevitable discovery doctrine.* In Nix v. Williams, 467 U.S. 431, 104 S.Ct. 2501, 81 L.Ed.2d 377 (1984), Williams was arraigned for the abduction of Pamela Powers, a 10-year-old girl who disappeared from a YMCA building

in Des Moines, Iowa, where she had accompanied her parents to observe a sporting event. While in custody, the police subjected Williams to a so-called "Christian Burial Speech" that motivated him to lead authorities to the victim's body, so that she could receive a "Christian burial." At the time, a search for her body was underway and one search team was within two-and-a-half miles of the victim, but the search effort was called off when Williams agreed to cooperate. Williams was convicted of first-degree murder, in part based on his incriminating statements to the police while leading them to the body.

Williams appealed his conviction. As examined in *Brewer v. Williams* [p. 764], the Supreme Court overturned the conviction because the police violated Williams's Sixth Amendment right to counsel when they conducted the Christian Burial Speech. Consequently, at Williams's second trial, the Government was not permitted to introduce the defendant's statements to the police, nor did they seek to show that Williams led the police to the body, but they presented evidence of the condition of the victim's body when it was found, as well as articles and photographs of her clothing, and the results of post mortem medical and chemical tests on the body, all of which were concededly a fruit of the poisonous Sixth Amendment tree.

Because the Government could not show that they found the body independently, the independent-source doctrine was unavailable. Instead, it reasoned that, if the search had *not* been suspended and Williams had *not* led the police to the victim, her body would inevitably have been discovered in essentially the same condition within a short time. Therefore, the Government argued, the contested evidence should be admissible.

The Supreme Court unanimously agreed that the fruit-of-the-poisonous-tree doctrine (here, the Sixth Amendment version, but similarly pursuant to the Fourth Amendment) is subject to an "inevitable discovery" rule. As the Court put the rule: "If the prosecution can establish * * * that the information ultimately or inevitably would have been discovered by lawful means—here the volunteers' search—then the deterrence rationale has so little basis that the evidence should be received." If it were otherwise, the Court concluded, the Government would be put in a worse position than if no illegality had transpired.

What divided the *Williams* Court is whether the Government should carry a heavier burden to prove inevitable discovery than when it claims an independent source. Seven justices ruled that the same burden of proof—preponderance of the evidence—applies in both circumstances. Justices Brennan and Marshall felt a higher burden should be placed on the Government when evidence, in fact, is a fruit of the poisonous tree:

> The inevitable discovery exception necessarily implicates a hypothetical finding that differs in kind from the factual finding that precedes application of the independent source rule. To ensure that this hypothetical finding is narrowly confined to circumstances that are functionally equivalent to an independent source, and to

protect fully the fundamental rights served by the exclusionary rule, [we] would require clear and convincing evidence before concluding that the government had met its burden of proof on this issue.

c. "Attenuation" (or "Dissipation of Taint") Doctrine

WONG SUN V. UNITED STATES

Supreme Court of the United States, 1963.
371 U.S. 471, 83 S.Ct. 407, 9 L.Ed.2d 441.

MR. JUSTICE BRENNAN delivered the opinion of the Court [joined by CHIEF JUSTICE WARREN, and JUSTICES BLACK, DOUGLAS, and GOLDBERG]. * * *

About 2 a.m. on the morning of June 4, 1959, federal narcotics agents in San Francisco, after having had one Hom Way under surveillance for six weeks, arrested him and found heroin in his possession. Hom Way, who had not before been an informant, stated after his arrest that he had bought an ounce of heroin the night before from one known to him only as "Blackie Toy," proprietor of a laundry on Leavenworth Street.

About 6 a.m. that morning six or seven federal agents went to a laundry at 1733 Leavenworth Street. The sign above the door of this establishment said "Oye's Laundry." It was operated by the petitioner James Wah Toy. There is, however, nothing in the record which identifies James Wah Toy and "Blackie Toy" as the same person. The other federal officers remained nearby out of sight while Agent Alton Wong, who was of Chinese ancestry, rang the bell. When petitioner Toy appeared and opened the door, Agent Wong told him that he was calling for laundry and dry cleaning. Toy replied that he didn't open until 8 o'clock and told the agent to come back at that time. Toy started to close the door. Agent Wong thereupon took his badge from his pocket and said, "I am a federal narcotics agent." Toy immediately "slammed the door and started running" down the hallway through the laundry to his living quarters at the back where his wife and child were sleeping in a bedroom. Agent Wong and the other federal officers broke open the door and followed Toy down the hallway to the living quarters and into the bedroom. Toy reached into a nightstand drawer. Agent Wong thereupon drew his pistol, pulled Toy's hand out of the drawer, placed him under arrest and handcuffed him. There was nothing in the drawer and a search of the premises uncovered no narcotics.

One of the agents said to Toy " * * * [Hom Way] says he got narcotics from you." Toy responded, "No, I haven't been selling any narcotics at all. However, I do know somebody who has." When asked who that was, Toy said, "I only know him as Johnny. I don't know his last name." However, Toy described a house on Eleventh Avenue where he said Johnny lived;

he also described a bedroom in the house where he said "Johnny kept about a piece" [an ounce—Eds.] of heroin, and where he and Johnny had smoked some of the drug the night before. The agents left immediately for Eleventh Avenue and located the house. They entered and found one Johnny Yee in the bedroom. After a discussion with the agents, Yee took from a bureau drawer several tubes containing in all just less than one ounce of heroin, and surrendered them. Within the hour Yee and Toy were taken to the Office of the Bureau of Narcotics. Yee there stated that the heroin had been brought to him some four days earlier by petitioner Toy and another Chinese known to him only as "Sea Dog."

Toy was questioned as to the identity of "Sea Dog" and said that "Sea Dog" was Wong Sun. Some agents, including Agent Alton Wong, took Toy to Wong Sun's neighborhood where Toy pointed out a multifamily dwelling where he said Wong Sun lived. Agent Wong rang a downstairs door bell and a buzzer sounded, opening the door. The officer identified himself as a narcotics agent to a woman on the landing and asked "for Mr. Wong." The woman was the wife of petitioner Wong Sun. She said that Wong Sun was "in the back room sleeping." Alton Wong and some six other officers climbed the stairs and entered the apartment. One of the officers went into the back room and brought petitioner Wong Sun from the bedroom in handcuffs. A thorough search of the apartment followed, but no narcotics were discovered.

Petitioner Toy and Johnny Yee were arraigned before a United States Commissioner on June 4 on a complaint charging a violation of 21 U.S.C. § 174. Later that day, each was released on his own recognizance. Petitioner Wong Sun was arraigned on a similar complaint filed the next day and was also released on his own recognizance. Within a few days, both petitioners and Yee were interrogated at the office of the Narcotics Bureau by Agent William Wong, also of Chinese ancestry. The agent advised each of the three of his right to withhold information which might be used against him, and stated to each that he was entitled to the advice of counsel, though it does not appear that any attorney was present during the questioning of any of the three. The officer also explained to each that no promises or offers of immunity or leniency were being or could be made.

The agent interrogated each of the three separately. After each had been interrogated the agent prepared a statement in English from rough notes. The agent read petitioner Toy's statement to him in English and interpreted certain portions of it for him in Chinese. Toy also read the statement in English aloud to the agent, said there were corrections to be made, and made the corrections in his own hand. Toy would not sign the statement, however; in the agent's words "he wanted to know first if the other persons involved in the case had signed theirs." Wong Sun had considerable difficulty understanding the statement in English and the agent restated its substance in Chinese. Wong Sun refused to sign the statement although he admitted the accuracy of its contents.

Hom Way did not testify at petitioners' trial. The Government offered Johnny Yee as its principal witness but excused him after he invoked the privilege against self-incrimination and flatly repudiated the statement he had given to Agent William Wong. That statement was not offered in evidence nor was any testimony elicited from him identifying either petitioner as the source of the heroin in his possession, or otherwise tending to support the charges against the petitioners.

The statute expressly provides that proof of the accused's possession of the drug will support a conviction under the statute unless the accused satisfactorily explains the possession. The Government's evidence tending to prove the petitioners' possession (the petitioners offered no exculpatory testimony) consisted of four items which the trial court admitted over timely objections that they were inadmissible as "fruits" of unlawful arrests or of attendant searches: (1) the statements made orally by petitioner Toy in his bedroom at the time of his arrest; (2) the heroin surrendered to the agents by Johnny Yee; (3) petitioner Toy's pretrial unsigned statement; and (4) petitioner Wong Sun's similar statement. The dispute below and here has centered around the correctness of the rulings of the trial judge allowing these items in evidence. * * *

We believe that significant differences between the cases of the two petitioners require separate discussion of each. We shall first consider the case of petitioner Toy.

I.

The Court of Appeals found there was neither reasonable grounds nor probable cause for Toy's arrest. * * *

* * * It remains to be seen what consequences flow from this conclusion.

II.

It is conceded that Toy's declarations in his bedroom are to be excluded if they are held to be "fruits" of the agents' unlawful action. * * *

The exclusionary rule has traditionally barred from trial physical, tangible materials obtained either during or as a direct result of an unlawful invasion. It follows from our holding in *Silverman v. United States*, 365 U.S. 505, 81 S.Ct. 679, 5 L.Ed.2d 734, that the Fourth Amendment may protect against the overhearing of verbal statements as well as against the more traditional seizure of "papers and effects." Similarly, testimony as to matters observed during an unlawful invasion has been excluded in order to enforce the basic constitutional policies. Thus, verbal evidence which derives so immediately from an unlawful entry and an unauthorized arrest as the officers' action in the present case is no less the "fruit" of official illegality than the more common tangible fruits of the unwarranted intrusion. Nor do the policies underlying the exclusionary rule invite any logical distinction between physical and verbal evidence. Either in terms of deterring lawless conduct by federal officers, or of closing the doors of the federal courts to any use of evidence unconstitutionally obtained, the danger in relaxing the exclusionary rules in the case of verbal evidence would seem too great to warrant introducing such a distinction.

The Government argues that Toy's statements to the officers in his bedroom, although closely consequent upon the invasion which we hold unlawful, were nevertheless admissible because they resulted from "an intervening independent act of a free will." This contention, however, takes insufficient account of the circumstances. Six or seven officers had broken the door and followed on Toy's heels into the bedroom where his wife and child were sleeping. He had been almost immediately handcuffed and arrested. Under such circumstances it is unreasonable to infer that Toy's response was sufficiently an act of free will to purge the primary taint of the unlawful invasion. * * *

III.

We now consider whether the exclusion of Toy's declarations requires also the exclusion of the narcotics taken from Yee, to which those declarations led the police. The prosecutor candidly told the trial court that "we wouldn't have found those drugs except that Mr. Toy helped us to." Hence this is not the case envisioned by this Court where the exclusionary rule has no application because the Government learned of the evidence "from an independent source"; nor is this a case in which the connection between the lawless conduct of the police and the discovery of the challenged evidence has "become so attenuated as to dissipate the taint." We need not hold that all evidence is "fruit of the poisonous tree" simply because it would not have come to light but for the illegal actions of the police. Rather, the more apt question in such a case is "whether, granting establishment of the primary illegality, the evidence to which instant objection is made has been come at by exploitation of that illegality or instead by means sufficiently distinguishable to be purged of the primary taint." Maguire, Evidence of Guilt, 221 (1959). We think it clear that the narcotics were "come at by the exploitation of that illegality" and hence that they may not be used against Toy.

IV.

[The Court determined that Toy's unsigned statement was inadmissible on non-constitutional grounds. Therefore, it did not reach the issue of "whether, in light of the fact that Toy was free on his own recognizance when he made the statement, that statement was a fruit of the illegal arrest."]

V.

We turn now to the case of the other petitioner, Wong Sun. We have no occasion to disagree with the finding of the Court of Appeals that his arrest, also, was without probable cause or reasonable grounds. At all events no evidentiary consequences turn upon that question. For Wong Sun's unsigned confession was not the fruit of that arrest, and was therefore properly admitted at trial. On the evidence that Wong Sun had been released on his own recognizance after a lawful arraignment, and had returned voluntarily several days later to make the statement, we hold that the connection between the arrest and the statement had "become so attenuated as to dissipate the taint." The fact that the statement was unsigned, whatever bearing this may have upon its weight and credibility, does not render it inadmissible; Wong Sun understood and adopted its substance, though he could not comprehend the English words. The petitioner has never suggested any impropriety in the interrogation itself which would require the exclusion of this statement.

We must then consider the admissibility of the narcotics surrendered by Yee. Our holding, *supra*, that this ounce of heroin was inadmissible against Toy does not compel a like result with respect to Wong Sun. The exclusion of the narcotics as to Toy was required solely by their tainted relationship to information unlawfully obtained from Toy, and not by any official impropriety connected with their surrender by Yee. The seizure of this heroin invaded no right of privacy of person or premises which would entitle Wong Sun to object to its use at his trial. * * *

[The concurring opinion of JUSTICE DOUGLAS, and the dissenting opinion of JUSTICE CLARK, joined by JUSTICES HARLAN, STEWART, and WHITE, are omitted.]

NOTES AND QUESTIONS

1.   What was the poisonous tree, *i.e.*, the initial illegality, in *Wong Sun*? What were the alleged fruits? Why did the Supreme Court treat Wong Sun differently than Toy?

2.   *Removing the taint: factors.* Typically, dissipation-of-taint claims are decided on their own facts, based on the totality of the circumstances. (But, see *Hudson v. Michigan*, p. 553.) The Supreme Court in Brown v. Illinois, 422 U.S. 590, 95 S.Ct. 2254, 45 L.Ed.2d 416 (1975), and lower courts apply various factors in determining whether the connection between the Fourth Amendment violation and the fruit has become so attenuated as to dissipate the taint: (1) the length of time that has elapsed between the initial illegality and the seizure of the fruit in question; (2) the flagrancy of the initial misconduct (dissipation of bad-faith violations takes longer than with good-

faith violations); (3) the existence or absence of intervening causes of the seizure of the fruit; and, closely related to the third factor, (4) the presence or absence of an act of free will by the defendant resulting in the seizure of the fruit.

For example, in *Brown*, he was arrested at his apartment without probable cause, in violation of the Fourth Amendment (the "tree"). While in custody, he made incriminating statements (the "fruit" from the poisonous tree) after being read the *Miranda* warnings and voluntarily waiving his constitutional rights pursuant to *Miranda*. Did the *Miranda* warning dissipate the taint? The Court rejected a proposed bright-line rule that *Miranda* warnings automatically untaint subsequent confessions. Whether a post-*Miranda*-warning statement, which is a fruit of a Fourth Amendment violation, is untainted is resolved like all other cases: on a case-by-case basis, based on the totality of the circumstances.

In *Brown*, the Court held that the State of Illinois had failed to sustain its burden of showing the requisite dissipation of taint, notwithstanding the *Miranda* warnings. The statement (the fruit) came less than two hours after the illegal arrest, and "there was no intervening event of significance whatsoever." Also, the Court noted that the illegality here (the unlawful arrest) "had a quality of purposefulness," in that the officers knew they were acting in violation of the Fourth Amendment. In essence, the purposefulness of the violation created substantial poison, and thus required more to be dissipated.

3.   In *Wong Sun*, the Court considered the admissibility of both tangible evidence (heroin) and verbal statements. The Court stated that "the policies underlying the exclusionary rule [do not] invite any logical distinction between physical and verbal evidence" in regard to the dissipation of taint.

But, it turns out, there *is* a distinction between verbal evidence and the existence of a witness who later provides verbal evidence. In United States v. Ceccolini, 435 U.S. 268, 98 S.Ct. 1054, 55 L.Ed.2d 268 (1978), the police unlawfully seized information that led them to a witness to a crime perpetrated by Ceccolini. Some months later, the witness agreed to testify against Ceccolini. According to the Court of Appeals, the witness's testimony should not have been permitted because "the road to [the] testimony from the [officer's] concededly unconstitutional search [was] both straight and uninterrupted."

The Supreme Court reversed. According to *Ceccolini*, "the exclusionary rule should be invoked with much greater reluctance where the claim is based on a causal relationship between a constitutional violation and the discovery of a live witness than when a similar claim is advanced to support suppression of an inanimate object." The Court reasoned as follows:

> The greater the willingness of the witness to freely testify, the greater the likelihood that he or she will be discovered by legal means and, concomitantly, the smaller the incentive to conduct an

illegal search to discover the witness. Witnesses are not like guns or documents which remain hidden from view until one turns over a sofa or opens a filing cabinet. Witnesses can, and often do, come forward and offer evidence entirely of their own volition. And evaluated properly, the degree of free will necessary to dissipate the taint will very likely be found more often in the case of live-witness testimony than other kinds of evidence. * * *

Another factor which * * * seems to us to differentiate the testimony of all live witnesses—even putative defendants—from the exclusion of the typical documentary evidence, is that such exclusion would perpetually disable a witness from testifying about relevant and material facts, regardless of how unrelated such testimony might be to the purpose of the originally illegal search or the evidence discovered thereby. Rules which disqualify knowledgeable witnesses from testifying at trial are, in the words of Professor McCormick, "serious obstructions to the ascertainment of truth" * * * . * * * In short, since the cost of excluding live-witness testimony often will be greater, a closer, more direct link between the illegality and that kind of testimony is required.

Are you persuaded?

4.   Assume the following general scenario. The police temporarily detain *D* without the requisite reasonable suspicion. Because of the unconstitutional seizure, the officer learns *D*'s name, which in turn leads to discovery of an outstanding warrant for *D*'s arrest. The officer arrests *D* pursuant to the warrant and conducts a warrantless search of *D*, which turns up contraband. Applying the attenuation factors set out in Note 2, is the contraband admissible against *D*? Federal and state courts reached conflicting answers to this question.

Now the Supreme Court has resolved the conflict, at least based on the facts presented to it in Utah v. Strieff, 579 U.S. ___, 136 S.Ct. 2056, 195 L.Ed.2d 400 (2016). In *Strieff*, based on an anonymous tip that drug activities were occurring at a specified residence, South Salt Lake City narcotics officers placed the residence under surveillance for a week. They observed "visitors who left a few minutes after arriving at the house." One of the visitors was Edward Strieff.

After Strieff left the home, and approached a nearby store, Officer Douglas Fackrell accosted him, identified himself, and asked Strieff what he was doing at the residence. The officer also requested identification, which he received, and then relayed that information to a police dispatcher who reported that Strieff had an outstanding arrest warrant for a traffic violation. The officer therefore arrested Strieff on the warrant, conducted a search incident to the arrest, and discovered a baggie of methamphetamine and drug paraphernalia on Stieff, resulting in his arrest on drug charges. At the suppression hearing, the officer acknowledged that the stop was designed for investigatory purposes—to "find out what was going on [in] the house"—and he admitted that he had no other basis for stopping Strieff. He also testified that it was "normal" practice by South Salt Lake City police to check for outstanding arrest warrants during all *Terry* stops.

It was conceded by the State that the initial stop of Strieff was unconstitutional, for lack of reasonable suspicion. The issue, therefore, was whether the drugs subsequently found on him were inadmissible as a fruit of the initial illegality. The Court, per Justice Thomas, by a vote of 5–3, held that "the officer's discovery of the [valid] arrest warrant attenuated the connection between the unlawful stop and the evidence seized incident to arrest."

Justice Thomas applied "three factors articulated in *Brown v. Illinois*" [Note 2 above]. First, the Court looked at the temporal proximity between the unconstitutional seizure of Strieff and the discovery of the drugs on his person. In view of the fact that the discovery occurred closely after Strieff's unlawful seizure, "such a short time interval counsels in favor of suppression."

The Court then turned to a second factor, "the presence of intervening circumstances." Here, Justice Thomas noted that the warrant was valid, "predated Officer Fackrell's investigation, and * * * was entirely unconnected with the stop." In view of the fact that, once discovered, the warrant obligated the officer to arrest Strieff, this factor "strongly favor[ed] the State." (Justice Thomas did not explain how this factor, which indeed predated the illegal seizure, could constitute an "intervening" circumstance).

Finally, the Court looked at "the purpose and flagrancy of the official misconduct." Justice Thomas found this "strongly" favored the State: "Officer Fackrell was at most negligent"; he "should have asked Strieff whether he would speak with him, instead of demanding that [he] do so." But the officer's "errors in judgment hardly rise to a purposeful or flagrant violation of Strieff's Fourth Amendment rights," meriting the exclusionary rule sanction.

Justice Kagan, joined by Justice Ginsburg dissented. She disagreed with the majority, which "chalks up Fackrell's Fourth Amendment violation to a couple of innocent 'mistakes.' But far from a Barney-Fife-type mishap, Fackrell's seizure of Strieff was a calculated decision, taken with so little justification that the State has never tried to defend its legality."

Justice Sotomayor, also joined by Justice Ginsburg, wrote a separate, stinging dissent. She wrote:

> Do not be soothed by the opinion's technical language: This case allows the police to stop you on the street, demand your identification, and check it for outstanding traffic warrants—even if you are doing nothing wrong. If the officer discovers a warrant for a fine you forgot to pay, courts will now excuse his illegal stop and will admit into evidence anything he happens to find by searching you after arresting you for a warrant.

Sotomayor observed that Utah listed over 180,000 misdemeanor warrants in its database. Therefore, she wrote, "[t]he warrant check * * * was not an 'intervening circumstance' separating the stop from the search for drugs. It was part and parcel of the officer's illegal 'expedition for evidence in the hope that something might turn up.'" She warned that, in light of this decision, "[t]he mere existence of a warrant * * * forgives an officer who, with no knowledge of the warrant at all, unlawfully stops that person on a whim or hunch."

Justice Sotomayor, then writing only for herself and "drawing on [her] professional experiences," indicated that "unlawful 'stops' have severe consequences much greater than the inconvenience suggested by the name":

> [T]his case tells everyone, white and black, guilty and innocent, that an officer can verify your legal status at any time. It says that your body is subject to invasion while courts excuse the violation of your rights. It implies that you are not a citizen of a democracy but the subject of a carceral state, just waiting to be catalogued.

Moreover, consider the following set of incentives created by *Strieff*: officers can stop anyone for any reason, run a warrant check, arrest and search those for whom there is an outstanding warrant, and let the rest go without searching them. In the latter case, there is a Fourth Amendment violation but no evidence to suppress and not much in the way of civil damages to deter the police. Presumably, this possibility was discussed by the justices because the majority found no indication that the stop was part of "systematic or recurrent police misconduct." But Justice Sotomayor pointed out that the majority offered no guidance as to how a defendant could prove such widespread misconduct.

3.   THE EXCLUSIONARY RULE IS NARROWED (AND ON LIFE SUPPORT?)

UNITED STATES V. LEON
Supreme Court of the United States, 1984.
468 U.S. 897, 104 S.Ct. 3405, 82 L.Ed.2d 677.

JUSTICE WHITE delivered the opinion of the Court [joined by CHIEF JUSTICE BURGER, and JUSTICES BLACKMUN, POWELL, REHNQUIST, and O'CONNOR].

This case presents the question whether the Fourth Amendment exclusionary rule should be modified so as not to bar the use in the prosecution's case in chief of evidence obtained by officers acting in reasonable reliance on a search warrant issued by a detached and neutral magistrate but ultimately found to be unsupported by probable cause. * * *

I

In August 1981, a confidential informant of unproven reliability informed an officer of the Burbank Police Department that two persons known to him as "Armando" and "Patsy" were selling large quantities of cocaine and methaqualone from their residence at 620 Price Drive in Burbank, Cal. [Based on this and other claims of the informant, the Burbank police initiated an investigation that focused on the Price Drive residence and, later, on two other residences.]

* * * Based on * * * observations summarized in the affidavit, Officer Cyril Rombach of the Burbank Police Department, an experienced and well-trained narcotics investigator, prepared an application for a warrant to search [three residences] and automobiles registered to each of the respondents for an extensive list of items believed to be related to respondents' drug-trafficking activities. Officer Rombach's extensive application was reviewed by several Deputy District Attorneys.

A facially valid search warrant was issued in September 1981 by a State Superior Court Judge. * * *

The respondents * * * filed motions to suppress the evidence seized pursuant to the warrant. The District Court held an evidentiary hearing and, while recognizing that the case was a close one, granted the motions to suppress * * *. It concluded that the affidavit was insufficient to establish probable cause * * *. In response to a request from the Government, the court made clear that Officer Rombach had acted in good faith, but it rejected the Government's suggestion that the Fourth Amendment exclusionary rule should not apply where evidence is seized in reasonable, good-faith reliance on a search warrant. * * *

The Government's petition for certiorari * * * presented only the question "[w]hether the Fourth Amendment exclusionary rule should be modified so as not to bar the admission of evidence seized in reasonable, good-faith reliance on a search warrant that is subsequently held to be defective." We granted certiorari to consider the propriety of such a modification. * * *

II * * *

A

The Fourth Amendment contains no provision expressly precluding the use of evidence obtained in violation of its commands, and an examination of its origin and purposes makes clear that the use of fruits of a past unlawful search or seizure "work[s] no new Fourth Amendment wrong." The wrong condemned by the Amendment is "fully accomplished" by the unlawful search or seizure itself, and the exclusionary rule is neither intended nor able to "cure the invasion of the defendant's rights which he has already suffered." The rule thus operates as "a judicially created remedy designed to safeguard Fourth Amendment rights generally through its deterrent effect, rather than a personal constitutional right of the party aggrieved."

Whether the exclusionary sanction is appropriately imposed in a particular case, our decisions make clear, is "an issue separate from the question whether the Fourth Amendment rights of the party seeking to invoke the rule were violated by police conduct." Only the former question is currently before us, and it must be resolved by weighing the costs and benefits of preventing the use in the prosecution's case in chief of inherently trustworthy tangible evidence obtained in reliance on a search warrant issued by a detached and neutral magistrate that ultimately is found to be defective.

The substantial social costs exacted by the exclusionary rule for the vindication of Fourth Amendment rights have long been a source of concern. "Our cases have consistently recognized that unbending application of the exclusionary sanction to enforce ideals of governmental rectitude would impede unacceptably the truth-finding functions of judge and jury." An objectionable collateral consequence of this interference with the criminal justice system's truth-finding function is that some guilty defendants may go free or receive reduced sentences as a result of favorable plea bargains.[6] Particularly when law enforcement officers have acted in objective good faith or their transgressions have been minor, the magnitude of the benefit conferred on such guilty defendants offends basic concepts of the criminal justice system. Indiscriminate application of the exclusionary rule, therefore, may well "generat[e] disrespect for the law and administration of justice." Accordingly, "[a]s with any remedial device, the application of the rule has been restricted to those areas where its remedial objectives are thought most efficaciously served."

B

Close attention to those remedial objectives has characterized our recent decisions concerning the scope of the Fourth Amendment exclusionary rule. The Court has, to be sure, not seriously questioned, "in

---

[6] Researchers have only recently begun to study extensively the effects of the exclusionary rule on the disposition of felony arrests. One study suggests that the rule results in the nonprosecution or nonconviction of between 0.6% and 2.35% of individuals arrested for felonies. Davies, A Hard Look at What We Know (and Still Need to Learn) About the "Costs" of the Exclusionary Rule: The NIJ Study and Other Studies of "Lost" Arrests, 1983 A.B.F. Res. J. 611, 621. The estimates are higher for particular crimes the prosecution of which depends heavily on physical evidence. Thus, the cumulative loss due to nonprosecution or nonconviction of individuals arrested on felony drug charges is probably in the range of 2.8% to 7.1%. * * * The exclusionary rule also has been found to affect the plea-bargaining process.

Many of these researchers have concluded that the impact of the exclusionary rule is insubstantial, but the small percentages with which they deal mask a large absolute number of felons who are released because the cases against them were based in part on illegal searches or seizures. * * * Because we find that the rule can have no substantial deterrent effect in the sorts of situations under consideration in this case, we conclude that it cannot pay its way in those situations.

the absence of a more efficacious sanction, the continued application of the rule to suppress evidence from the [prosecution's] case where a Fourth Amendment violation has been substantial and deliberate * * * ." Nevertheless, the balancing approach that has evolved in various contexts—including criminal trials—"forcefully suggest[s] that the exclusionary rule be more generally modified to permit the introduction of evidence obtained in the reasonable good-faith belief that a search or seizure was in accord with the Fourth Amendment." * * *

As yet, we have not recognized any form of good-faith exception to the Fourth Amendment exclusionary rule. But the balancing approach that has evolved during the years of experience with the rule provides strong support for the modification currently urged upon us. As we discuss below, our evaluation of the costs and benefits of suppressing reliable physical evidence seized by officers reasonably relying on a warrant issued by a detached and neutral magistrate leads to the conclusion that such evidence should be admissible in the prosecution's case in chief.

III

A

Because a search warrant "provides the detached scrutiny of a neutral magistrate, which is a more reliable safeguard against improper searches than the hurried judgment of a law enforcement officer 'engaged in the often competitive enterprise of ferreting out crime,'" we have expressed a strong preference for warrants and declared that "in a doubtful or marginal case a search under a warrant may be sustainable where without one it would fall." Reasonable minds frequently may differ on the question whether a particular affidavit establishes probable cause, and we have thus concluded that the preference for warrants is most appropriately effectuated by according "great deference" to a magistrate's determination.

Deference to the magistrate, however, is not boundless. It is clear, first, that the deference accorded to a magistrate's finding of probable cause does not preclude inquiry into the knowing or reckless falsity of the affidavit on which that determination was based. *Franks v. Delaware*, [p. 201, Note 6]. Second, the courts must also insist that the magistrate purport to "perform his 'neutral and detached' function and not serve merely as a rubber stamp for the police." A magistrate failing to "manifest that neutrality and detachment demanded of a judicial officer when presented with a warrant application" and who acts instead as "an adjunct law enforcement officer" cannot provide valid authorization for an otherwise unconstitutional search. *Lo-Ji Sales, Inc. v. New York*, [p. 224].

Third, reviewing courts will not defer to a warrant based on an affidavit that does not "provide the magistrate with a substantial basis for determining the existence of probable cause." "Sufficient information must be presented to the magistrate to allow that official to determine probable cause; his action cannot be a mere ratification of the bare conclusions of others." Even if the warrant application was supported by more than a "bare bones" affidavit, a reviewing court may properly conclude that, notwithstanding the deference that magistrates deserve, the warrant was invalid because the magistrate's probable-cause determination reflected an improper analysis of the totality of the circumstances, or because the form of the warrant was improper in some respect.

Only in the first of these three situations, however, has the Court set forth a rationale for suppressing evidence obtained pursuant to a search warrant; in the other areas, it has simply excluded such evidence without considering whether Fourth Amendment interests will be advanced. To the extent that proponents of exclusion rely on its behavioral effects on judges and magistrates in these areas, their reliance is misplaced. First, the exclusionary rule is designed to deter police misconduct rather than to punish the errors of judges and magistrates. Second, there exists no evidence suggesting that judges and magistrates are inclined to ignore or subvert the Fourth Amendment or that lawlessness among these actors requires application of the extreme sanction of exclusion.[14]

Third, and most important, we discern no basis, and are offered none, for believing that exclusion of evidence seized pursuant to a warrant will have a significant deterrent effect on the issuing judge or magistrate. Many of the factors that indicate that the exclusionary rule cannot provide an effective "special" or "general" deterrent for individual offending law enforcement officers apply as well to judges or magistrates. And, to the extent that the rule is thought to operate as a "systemic" deterrent on a wider audience, it clearly can have no such effect on individuals empowered to issue search warrants. Judges and magistrates are not adjuncts to the law enforcement team; as neutral judicial officers, they have no stake in the outcome of particular criminal prosecutions. The threat of exclusion thus cannot be expected significantly to deter them. Imposition of the exclusionary sanction is not necessary meaningfully to inform judicial officers of their errors, and we cannot conclude that admitting evidence obtained pursuant to a warrant while at the same time declaring that the warrant was somehow defective will in any way reduce judicial officers' professional incentives to comply with the Fourth Amendment, encourage them to repeat their mistakes, or lead to the granting of all colorable warrant requests.[18]

---

[14] Although there are assertions that some magistrates become rubber stamps for the police and others may be unable effectively to screen police conduct, we are not convinced that this is a problem of major proportions.

[18] * * * Federal magistrates * * * moreover, are subject to the direct supervision of district courts. They may be removed for "incompetency, misconduct, neglect of duty, or physical or mental disability." 28 U. S. C. § 631(i). If a magistrate serves merely as a "rubber stamp" for the

B

If exclusion of evidence obtained pursuant to a subsequently invalidated warrant is to have any deterrent effect, therefore, it must alter the behavior of individual law enforcement officers or the policies of their departments. One could argue that applying the exclusionary rule in cases where the police failed to demonstrate probable cause in the warrant application deters future inadequate presentations or "magistrate shopping" and thus promotes the ends of the Fourth Amendment. Suppressing evidence obtained pursuant to a technically defective warrant supported by probable cause also might encourage officers to scrutinize more closely the form of the warrant and to point out suspected judicial errors. We find such arguments speculative[a] and conclude that suppression of evidence obtained pursuant to a warrant should be ordered only on a case-by-case basis and only in those unusual cases in which exclusion will further the purposes of the exclusionary rule.[19]

We have frequently questioned whether the exclusionary rule can have any deterrent effect when the offending officers acted in the objectively reasonable belief that their conduct did not violate the Fourth Amendment. "No empirical researcher, proponent or opponent of the rule, has yet been able to establish with any assurance whether the rule has a deterrent effect * * * ." But even assuming that the rule effectively deters some police misconduct and provides incentives for the law enforcement profession as a whole to conduct itself in accord with the Fourth Amendment, it cannot be expected, and should not be applied, to deter objectively reasonable law enforcement activity. * * *[20]

---

police or is unable to exercise mature judgment, closer supervision or removal provides a more effective remedy than the exclusionary rule.

[a] Professor Tonja Jocabi asserts that the exclusionary rule actually *over*-deters, and thus leads to avoidance and under-enforcement. She reports that police avoid the exclusionary rule by perjury, among other means; and "judges resist and distort the rule for the same reason." This leads to under-enforcement of the Fourth Amendment, precisely the opposite, of course, of what the *Mapp* Court intended. Tonja Jocabi, *The Law and Economics of the Exclusionary Rule*, 87 Notre Dame L. Rev. 585, 675 (2012).

[19] Our discussion of the deterrent effect of excluding evidence obtained in reasonable reliance on a subsequently invalidated warrant assumes, of course, that the officers properly executed the warrant and searched only those places and for those objects that it was reasonable to believe were covered by the warrant.

[20] We emphasize that the standard of reasonableness we adopt is an objective one. Many objections to a good-faith exception assume that the exception will turn on the subjective good faith of individual officers. "Grounding the modification in objective reasonableness, however, retains the value of the exclusionary rule as an incentive for the law enforcement profession as a whole to conduct themselves in accord with the Fourth Amendment." The objective standard we adopt, moreover, requires officers to have a reasonable knowledge of what the law prohibits. As Professor Jerold Israel has observed:

"The key to the [exclusionary] rule's effectiveness as a deterrent lies, I believe, in the impetus it has provided to police training programs that make officers aware of the limits imposed by the fourth amendment and emphasize the need to operate within those limits. [An objective good-faith exception] is not likely to result in the elimination

This is particularly true, we believe, when an officer acting with objective good faith has obtained a search warrant from a judge or magistrate and acted within its scope. In most such cases, there is no police illegality and thus nothing to deter. It is the magistrate's responsibility to determine whether the officer's allegations establish probable cause and, if so, to issue a warrant comporting in form with the requirements of the Fourth Amendment. In the ordinary case, an officer cannot be expected to question the magistrate's probable-cause determination or his judgment that the form of the warrant is technically sufficient. "[O]nce the warrant issues, there is literally nothing more the policeman can do in seeking to comply with the law." Penalizing the officer for the magistrate's error, rather than his own, cannot logically contribute to the deterrence of Fourth Amendment violations.

C

We conclude that the marginal or nonexistent benefits produced by suppressing evidence obtained in objectively reasonable reliance on a subsequently invalidated search warrant cannot justify the substantial costs of exclusion. We do not suggest, however, that exclusion is always inappropriate in cases where an officer has obtained a warrant and abided by its terms. * * * [T]he officer's reliance on the magistrate's probable-cause determination and on the technical sufficiency of the warrant he issues must be objectively reasonable,[23] and it is clear that in some circumstances the officer[24] will have no reasonable grounds for believing that the warrant was properly issued.

---

of such programs, which are now viewed as an important aspect of police professionalism. Neither is it likely to alter the tenor of those programs; the possibility that illegally obtained evidence may be admitted in borderline cases is unlikely to encourage police instructors to pay less attention to fourth amendment limitations. Finally, [it] should not encourage officers to pay less attention to what they are taught, as the requirement that the officer act in 'good faith' is inconsistent with closing one's mind to the possibility of illegality."

[23] * * * [W]e * * * eschew inquiries into the subjective beliefs of law enforcement officers who seize evidence pursuant to a subsequently invalidated warrant. Although we have suggested that, "[o]n occasion, the motive with which the officer conducts an illegal search may have some relevance in determining the propriety of applying the exclusionary rule," we believe that "sending state and federal courts on an expedition into the minds of police officers would produce a grave and fruitless misallocation of judicial resources." Accordingly, our good-faith inquiry is confined to the objectively ascertainable question whether a reasonably well trained officer would have known that the search was illegal despite the magistrate's authorization. In making this determination, all of the circumstances—including whether the warrant application had previously been rejected by a different magistrate—may be considered.

[24] References to "officer" throughout this opinion should not be read too narrowly. It is necessary to consider the objective reasonableness, not only of the officers who eventually executed a warrant, but also of the officers who originally obtained it or who provided information material to the probable-cause determination. Nothing in our opinion suggests, for example, that an officer could obtain a warrant on the basis of a "bare bones" affidavit and then rely on colleagues who are ignorant of the circumstances under which the warrant was obtained to conduct the search.

Suppression therefore remains an appropriate remedy if the magistrate or judge in issuing a warrant was misled by information in an affidavit that the affiant knew was false or would have known was false except for his reckless disregard of the truth. *Franks v. Delaware.* The exception we recognize today will also not apply in cases where the issuing magistrate wholly abandoned his judicial role in the manner condemned in *Lo-Ji Sales, Inc. v. New York*; in such circumstances, no reasonably well trained officer should rely on the warrant. Nor would an officer manifest objective good faith in relying on a warrant based on an affidavit "so lacking in indicia of probable cause as to render official belief in its existence entirely unreasonable." Finally, depending on the circumstances of the particular case, a warrant may be so facially deficient—*i.e.*, in failing to particularize the place to be searched or the things to be seized—that the executing officers cannot reasonably presume it to be valid.

In so limiting the suppression remedy, we leave untouched the probable cause standard and the various requirements for a valid warrant. The good-faith exception for searches conducted pursuant to warrants is not intended to signal our unwillingness strictly to enforce the requirements of the Fourth Amendment, and we do not believe that it will have this effect. * * *

IV

When the principles we have enunciated today are applied to the facts of this case, it is apparent that the judgment of the Court of Appeals cannot stand. * * *

In the absence of an allegation that the magistrate abandoned his detached and neutral role, suppression is appropriate only if the officers were dishonest or reckless in preparing their affidavit or could not have harbored an objectively reasonable belief in the existence of probable cause. * * * Officer Rombach's application for a warrant clearly was supported by much more than a "bare bones" affidavit. The affidavit related the results of an extensive investigation and, as the opinions of the divided panel of the Court of Appeals make clear, provided evidence sufficient to create disagreement among thoughtful and competent judges as to the existence of probable cause. Under these circumstances, the officers' reliance on the magistrate's determination of probable cause was objectively reasonable, and application of the extreme sanction of exclusion is inappropriate.

JUSTICE BLACKMUN, concurring. * * *

As the Court's opinion in this case makes clear, the Court has narrowed the scope of the exclusionary rule because of an empirical judgment that the rule has little appreciable effect in cases where officers act in objectively reasonable reliance on search warrants. * * *

What must be stressed, however, is that any empirical judgment about the effect of the exclusionary rule in a particular class of cases necessarily is a provisional one. By their very nature, the assumptions on which we proceed today cannot be cast in stone. To the contrary, they now will be tested in the real world of state and federal law enforcement, and this Court will attend to the results. If it should emerge from experience that, contrary to our expectations, the good-faith exception to the exclusionary rule results in a material change in police compliance with the Fourth Amendment, we shall have to reconsider what we have undertaken here. The logic of a decision that rests on untested predictions about police conduct demands no less. * * *

JUSTICE BRENNAN, with whom JUSTICE MARSHALL joins, dissenting. * * *

I * * *

A

At bottom, the Court's decision turns on the proposition that the exclusionary rule is merely a " 'judicially created remedy designed to safeguard Fourth Amendment rights generally through its deterrent effect, rather than a personal constitutional right.' " The germ of that idea is found in *Wolf v. Colorado*, [p. 79], and although I had thought that such a narrow conception of the rule had been forever put to rest by our decision in *Mapp v. Ohio*, it has been revived by the present Court and reaches full flower with today's decision. The essence of this view * * * is that the sole "purpose of the Fourth Amendment is to prevent unreasonable governmental intrusions into the privacy of one's person, house, papers, or effects. The wrong condemned is the unjustified governmental invasion of these areas of an individual's life. That wrong * * * is *fully accomplished* by the original search without probable cause." This reading of the Amendment implies that its proscriptions are directed solely at those government agents who may actually invade an individual's constitutionally protected privacy. The courts are not subject to any direct constitutional duty to exclude illegally obtained evidence, because the question of the admissibility of such evidence is not addressed by the Amendment. This view of the scope of the Amendment relegates the judiciary to the periphery. Because the only constitutionally cognizable injury has already been "fully accomplished" by the police by the time a case comes before the courts, the Constitution is not itself violated if the judge decides to admit the tainted evidence. Indeed, the most the judge *can* do is wring his hands and hope that perhaps by excluding such evidence he can deter future transgressions by the police.

Such a reading appears plausible, because, as critics of the exclusionary rule never tire of repeating, the Fourth Amendment makes no express provision for the exclusion of evidence secured in violation of its commands. A short answer to this claim, of course, is that many of the Constitution's most vital imperatives are stated in general terms and the task of giving meaning to these precepts is therefore left to subsequent judicial decisionmaking in the context of concrete cases. * * *

A more direct answer may be supplied by recognizing that the Amendment, like other provisions of the Bill of Rights, restrains the power of the government as a whole; it does not specify only a particular agency and exempt all others. The judiciary is responsible, no less than the executive, for ensuring that constitutional rights are respected.

When that fact is kept in mind, the role of the courts and their possible involvement in the concerns of the Fourth Amendment comes into sharper focus. Because seizures are executed principally to secure evidence, and because such evidence generally has utility in our legal system only in the context of a trial supervised by a judge, it is apparent that the admission of illegally obtained evidence implicates the same constitutional concerns as the initial seizure of that evidence. Indeed, by admitting unlawfully seized evidence, the judiciary becomes a part of what is in fact a single governmental action prohibited by the terms of the Amendment. Once that connection between the evidence-gathering role of the police and the evidence-admitting function of the courts is acknowledged, the plausibility of the Court's interpretation becomes more suspect. * * * It is difficult to give any meaning at all to the limitations imposed by the Amendment if they are read to proscribe only certain conduct by the police but to allow other agents of the same government to take advantage of evidence secured by the police in violation of its requirements. The Amendment therefore must be read to condemn not only the initial unconstitutional invasion of privacy—which is done, after all, for the purpose of securing evidence—but also the subsequent use of any evidence so obtained. * * *

B * * *

* * * [T]he Court * * * has gradually pressed the deterrence rationale for the rule back to center stage. The various arguments advanced by the Court in this campaign have only strengthened my conviction that the deterrence theory is both misguided and unworkable. First, the Court has frequently bewailed the "cost" of excluding reliable evidence. In large part, this criticism rests upon a refusal to acknowledge the function of the Fourth Amendment itself. If nothing else, the Amendment plainly operates to disable the government from gathering information and securing evidence in certain ways. In practical terms, of course, this restriction of official power means that some incriminating evidence inevitably will go undetected if the government obeys these constitutional restraints. It is the loss of that evidence that is the "price" our society pays for enjoying the freedom and privacy safeguarded by the Fourth

Amendment. Thus, some criminals will go free *not*, in Justice (then Judge) Cardozo's misleading epigram, "because the constable has blundered," but rather because official compliance with Fourth Amendment requirements makes it more difficult to catch criminals. Understood in this way, the Amendment directly contemplates that some reliable and incriminating evidence will be lost to the government; therefore, it is not the exclusionary rule, but the Amendment itself that has imposed this cost.

In addition, the Court's decisions over the past decade have made plain that the entire enterprise of attempting to assess the benefits and costs of the exclusionary rule in various contexts is a virtually impossible task for the judiciary to perform honestly or accurately. Although the Court's language in those cases suggests that some specific empirical basis may support its analyses, the reality is that the Court's opinions represent inherently unstable compounds of intuition, hunches, and occasional pieces of partial and often inconclusive data. * * *

By remaining within its redoubt of empiricism and by basing the rule solely on the deterrence rationale, the Court has robbed the rule of legitimacy. * * * The extent of this Court's fidelity to Fourth Amendment requirements, however, should not turn on such statistical uncertainties. * * *

III

Even if I were to accept the Court's general approach to the exclusionary rule, I could not agree with today's result. * * *

At the outset, the Court suggests that society has been asked to pay a high price—in terms either of setting guilty persons free or of impeding the proper functioning of trials—as a result of excluding relevant physical evidence in cases where the police, in conducting searches and seizing evidence, have made only an "objectively reasonable" mistake concerning the constitutionality of their actions. But what evidence is there to support such a claim?

Significantly, the Court points to none, and, indeed, as the Court acknowledges, recent studies have demonstrated that the "costs" of the exclusionary rule—calculated in terms of dropped prosecutions and lost convictions—are quite low. Contrary to the claims of the rule's critics that exclusion leads to "the release of countless guilty criminals," these studies have demonstrated that federal and state prosecutors very rarely drop cases because of potential search and seizure problems. For example, a 1979 study prepared at the request of Congress by the General Accounting Office reported that only 0.4% of all cases actually declined for prosecution by federal prosecutors were declined primarily because of illegal search problems. If the GAO data are restated as a percentage of *all* arrests, the study shows that only 0.2% of all felony arrests are declined for prosecution because of potential exclusionary rule problems. Of course, these data describe only the costs attributable to the exclusion of evidence in all cases; the costs due to the exclusion of evidence in the narrower category of cases where police have made objectively reasonable mistakes must necessarily be even smaller. The Court, however, ignores this distinction and mistakenly weighs the aggregated costs of exclusion in *all* cases, irrespective of the circumstances that led to exclusion, against the potential benefits associated with only those cases in which evidence is excluded because police reasonably but mistakenly believe that their conduct does not violate the Fourth Amendment. When such faulty scales are used, it is little wonder that the balance tips in favor of restricting the application of the rule.

What then supports the Court's insistence that this evidence be admitted? Apparently, the Court's only answer is that even though the costs of exclusion are not very substantial, the potential deterrent effect in these circumstances is so marginal that exclusion cannot be justified. The key to the Court's conclusion in this respect is its belief that the prospective deterrent effect of the exclusionary rule operates only in those situations in which police officers, when deciding whether to go forward with some particular search, have reason to know that their planned conduct will violate the requirements of the Fourth Amendment. * * *

The flaw in the Court's argument, however, is that its logic captures only one comparatively minor element of the generally acknowledged deterrent purposes of the exclusionary rule. To be sure, the rule operates to some extent to deter future misconduct by individual officers who have had evidence suppressed in their own cases. But what the Court overlooks is that the deterrence rationale for the rule is not designed to be, nor should it be thought of as, a form of "punishment" of individual police officers for their failures to obey the restraints imposed by the Fourth Amendment. Instead, the chief deterrent function of the rule is its tendency to promote institutional compliance with Fourth Amendment requirements on the part of law enforcement agencies generally. Thus, as the Court has previously recognized, "over the long term, [the] demonstration [provided by the exclusionary rule] that our society attaches serious consequences to violation of constitutional rights is thought to encourage those who formulate law enforcement policies, and the officers who implement them, to incorporate Fourth Amendment ideals into their value system." It is only through such an institutionwide mechanism that information concerning Fourth Amendment standards can be effectively communicated to rank-and-file officers.

If the overall educational effect of the exclusionary rule is considered, application of the rule to even those situations in which individual police officers have acted on the basis of a reasonable but mistaken belief that their conduct was authorized can still be expected to have a considerable long-term deterrent effect. If evidence is consistently excluded in these circumstances, police departments will surely be prompted to instruct their officers to devote greater care and attention to providing sufficient information to establish probable cause when applying for a warrant, and to review with some attention the form of the warrant that they have been issued, rather than automatically assuming that whatever document the magistrate has signed will necessarily comport with Fourth Amendment requirements.

After today's decisions, however, that institutional incentive will be lost. * * *

JUSTICE STEVENS, [dissenting]. * * *

III * * *

The notion that a police officer's reliance on a magistrate's warrant is automatically appropriate is one the Framers of the Fourth Amendment would have vehemently rejected. The precise problem that the Amendment was intended to address was *the unreasonable issuance of warrants*. As we have often observed, the Amendment was actually motivated by the practice of issuing general warrants—warrants which did not satisfy the particularity and probable-cause requirements. The resentments which led to the Amendment were directed at the issuance of *warrants* unjustified by particularized evidence of wrongdoing. Those who sought to amend the Constitution to include a Bill of Rights repeatedly voiced the view that the evil which had to be addressed was the issuance of warrants on insufficient evidence. * * *

In short, the Framers of the Fourth Amendment were deeply suspicious of warrants; in their minds the paradigm of an abusive search was the execution of a warrant not based on probable cause. The fact that colonial officers had magisterial authorization for their conduct when they engaged in general searches surely did not make their conduct "reasonable." The Court's view that it is consistent with our Constitution to adopt a rule that it is presumptively reasonable to rely on a defective warrant is the product of constitutional amnesia.

IV * * *

* * * [T]he Court's creation of a double standard of reasonableness inevitably must erode the deterrence rationale that still supports the exclusionary rule. But we should not ignore the way it tarnishes the role of the judiciary in enforcing the Constitution. * * * Today, for the first time, this Court holds that although the Constitution has been violated, no court should do anything about it at any time and in any proceeding. In my judgment, the Constitution requires more. * * *

We could, of course, facilitate the process of administering justice to those who violate the criminal laws by ignoring the commands of the

Fourth Amendment—indeed, by ignoring the entire Bill of Rights—but it is the very purpose of a Bill of Rights to identify values that may not be sacrificed to expediency. In a just society those who govern, as well as those who are governed, must obey the law. * * *

NOTES AND QUESTIONS

1.   According to Justice White, what is the purpose of the exclusionary rule? Does Justice Brennan, in dissent, suggest another justification for the rule?

2.   Based on what you have learned this semester, and taking into consideration the various opinions in *Leon*, do you believe the Fourth Amendment exclusionary rule should be abolished? If so, how should the law deal with Fourth Amendment violations?

3.   However you answered the questions in Note 2, who has the better side of the argument on the narrow issue in *Leon*: Should "evidence obtained by officers acting in reasonable reliance on a search warrant issued by a detached and neutral magistrate * * * ultimately found to be unsupported by probable cause," be admissible in the prosecutor's case-in-chief?

4.   The Supreme Court applied the *Leon* exception in a second case decided the same day. In Massachusetts v. Sheppard, 468 U.S. 981, 104 S.Ct. 3424, 82 L.Ed.2d 737 (1984), the Court permitted introduction of evidence obtained from a search conducted pursuant to a warrant that violated the Fourth Amendment particularity requirement. The Court explained how the problem arose:

> Because it was Sunday, the local court was closed, and the police had a difficult time finding a warrant application form. Detective O'Malley finally found a warrant form previously in use in the Dorchester District. The form was entitled "Search Warrant—Controlled Substance G. L. c. 276 §§ 1 through 3A." Realizing that some changes had to be made before the form could be used to authorize the search requested in the affidavit, Detective O'Malley deleted the subtitle "controlled substance" with a typewriter. He also substituted "Roxbury" for the printed "Dorchester" and typed Sheppard's name and address into blank spaces provided for that information. However, the reference to "controlled substance" was not deleted in the portion of the form that constituted the warrant application and that, when signed, would constitute the warrant itself.

> Detective O'Malley then took the affidavit and the warrant form to the residence of a judge who had consented to consider the warrant application. The judge examined the affidavit and stated that he would authorize the search as requested. Detective O'Malley offered the warrant form and stated that he knew the form as presented dealt with controlled substances. He showed the judge

where he had crossed out the subtitles. After unsuccessfully searching for a more suitable form, the judge informed O'Malley that he would make the necessary changes so as to provide a proper search warrant. The judge then took the form, made some changes on it, and dated and signed the warrant. However, he did not change the substantive portion of the warrant, which continued to authorize a search for controlled substances; nor did he alter the form so as to incorporate the affidavit. The judge returned the affidavit and the warrant to O'Malley, informing him that the warrant was sufficient authority in form and content to carry out the search as requested. O'Malley took the two documents and, accompanied by other officers, proceeded to Sheppard's residence.

Although the warrant that was executed violated the Fourth Amendment, the Supreme Court concluded that the officers executing the warrant, which included Detective O'Malley, acted in objective good-faith.

The officers in this case took every step that could reasonably be expected of them. Detective O'Malley prepared an affidavit which was reviewed and approved by the District Attorney. He presented that affidavit to a neutral judge. The judge concluded that the affidavit established probable cause * * * . He was told by the judge that the necessary changes would be made. He then observed the judge make some changes and received the warrant and the affidavit. At this point, a reasonable police officer would have concluded, as O'Malley did, that the warrant authorized a search for the materials outlined in the affidavit.

Sheppard contends that since O'Malley knew the warrant form was defective, he should have examined it to make sure that the necessary changes had been made. However, that argument is based on the premise that O'Malley had a duty to disregard the judge's assurances that the requested search would be authorized and the necessary changes would be made. Whatever an officer may be required to do when he executes a warrant without knowing beforehand what items are to be seized,[6] we refuse to rule that an officer is required to disbelieve a judge who has just advised him, by word and by action, that the warrant he possesses authorizes him to conduct the search he has requested.

5. Is the *Leon* standard exclusively objective, or are there circumstances in which a court may inquire into the thought processes of the

---

[6]   Normally, when an officer who has not been involved in the application stage receives a warrant, he will read it in order to determine the object of the search. In this case, Detective O'Malley, the officer who directed the search, knew what items were listed in the affidavit presented to the judge, and he had good reason to believe that the warrant authorized the seizure of those items. Whether an officer who is less familiar with the warrant application or who has unalleviated concerns about the proper scope of the search would be justified in failing to notice a defect like the one in the warrant in this case is an issue we need not decide. We hold only that it was not unreasonable for the police in this case to rely on the judge's assurances that the warrant authorized the search they had requested.

officers seeking or executing a warrant? For example, suppose that an officer takes her warrant affidavit to the prosecutor for a legal judgment of its sufficiency. The prosecutor unequivocally states that it fails to show probable cause. Although the officer now believes that the affidavit is inadequate, she applies for a warrant anyway, "just in case" she finds a sympathetic magistrate. Based on the same affidavit, a magistrate improperly issues a warrant. In determining whether the *Leon* exception to the exclusionary rule applies, is the officer's visit to the prosecutor relevant? If so, may defense counsel inquire into the officer's reasons for seeking a warrant despite the advice? May the lawyer elicit testimony, for example, that the officer had doubted that she had probable cause, but went ahead because she believed that the magistrate was "police-friendly"? See 1 Wayne R. LaFave, Search and Seizure 71–73 (4th ed. 2004).

6. Does the *Leon* exception apply if a magistrate signs a warrant without looking at the supporting affidavit? What if she skims the affidavit and signs the warrant five seconds later?

HUDSON v. MICHIGAN

Supreme Court of the United States, 2006.
547 U.S. 586, 126 S.Ct. 2159, 165 L.Ed.2d 56.

JUSTICE SCALIA delivered the opinion of the Court [joined by CHIEF JUSTICE ROBERTS, and JUSTICES KENNEDY, THOMAS and ALITO], except as to Part IV [joined by CHIEF JUSTICE ROBERTS, and JUSTICES THOMAS and ALITO].

We decide whether violation of the knock-and-announce rule requires the suppression of all evidence found in the search.

I

Police obtained a warrant authorizing a search for drugs and firearms at the home of petitioner Booker Hudson. They discovered both. Large quantities of drugs were found, including cocaine rocks in Hudson's pocket. A loaded gun was lodged between the cushion and armrest of the chair in which he was sitting. Hudson was charged under Michigan law with unlawful drug and firearm possession.

This case is before us only because of the method of entry into the house. When the police arrived to execute the warrant, they announced their presence, but waited only a short time—perhaps "three to five seconds"—before turning the knob of the unlocked front door and entering Hudson's home. Hudson moved to suppress all the inculpatory evidence, arguing that the premature entry violated his Fourth Amendment rights.

The Michigan trial court granted his motion. On interlocutory review, the Michigan Court of Appeals reversed * * * . * * * Hudson was convicted of drug possession. He renewed his Fourth Amendment claim on appeal * * * . * * * We granted certiorari.

II

The common-law principle that law enforcement officers must announce their presence and provide residents an opportunity to open the door is an ancient one. See *Wilson v. Arkansas,* [p. 228]. Since 1917, when Congress passed the Espionage Act, this traditional protection has been part of federal statutory law * * * . * * * Finally, in *Wilson,* we were asked whether the rule was also a command of the Fourth Amendment. Tracing its origins in our English legal heritage, we concluded that it was.

We recognized that the new constitutional rule we had announced is not easily applied. *Wilson* and cases following it have noted the many situations in which it is not necessary to knock and announce. * * *

When the knock-and-announce rule does apply, it is not easy to determine precisely what officers must do. How many seconds' wait are too few? Our "reasonable wait time" standard, is necessarily vague. * * * [I]t is unsurprising that * * * police officers about to encounter someone who may try to harm them will be uncertain how long to wait.

Happily, these issues do not confront us here. From the trial level onward, Michigan has conceded that the entry was a knock-and-announce violation. The issue here is remedy. *Wilson* specifically declined to decide whether the exclusionary rule is appropriate for violation of the knock-and-announce requirement. That question is squarely before us now.

III

A

In *Weeks v. United States,* [p. 76], we adopted the federal exclusionary rule for evidence that was unlawfully seized from a home without a warrant in violation of the Fourth Amendment. We began applying the same rule to the States, through the Fourteenth Amendment, in *Mapp v. Ohio,* [p. 83].

Suppression of evidence, however, has always been our last resort, not our first impulse. The exclusionary rule generates "substantial social costs," which sometimes include setting the guilty free and the dangerous at large. We have therefore been "cautio[us] against expanding" it, and "have repeatedly emphasized that the rule's 'costly toll' upon truth-seeking and law enforcement objectives presents a high obstacle for those urging [its] application." We have rejected "[i]ndiscriminate application" of the rule, and have held it to be applicable only "where its remedial objectives are thought most efficaciously served"—that is, "where its deterrence benefits outweigh its 'substantial social costs.' "

We did not always speak so guardedly. Expansive dicta in *Mapp,* for example, suggested wide scope for the exclusionary rule. * * * But we have long since rejected that approach. * * *

* * * [E]xclusion may not be premised on the mere fact that a constitutional violation was a "but-for" cause of obtaining evidence. Our cases show that but-for causality is only a necessary, not a sufficient, condition for suppression. In this case, of course, the constitutional violation of an illegal *manner* of entry was *not* a but-for cause of obtaining the evidence. Whether that preliminary misstep had occurred *or not,* the police would have executed the warrant they had obtained, and would have discovered the gun and drugs inside the house. But even if the illegal entry here could be characterized as a but-for cause of discovering what was inside, we have "never held that evidence is 'fruit of the poisonous tree' simply because 'it would not have come to light but for the illegal actions of the police.' " Rather, but-for cause, or "causation in the logical sense alone," can be too attenuated to justify exclusion. * * *

Attenuation can occur, of course, when the causal connection is remote. Attenuation also occurs when, even given a direct causal connection, the interest protected by the constitutional guarantee that has been violated would not be served by suppression of the evidence obtained. "The penalties visited upon the Government, and in turn upon the public, because its officers have violated the law must bear some relation to the purposes which the law is to serve." Thus, in *New York v. Harris,* 495 U.S. 14, 110 S.Ct. 1640, 109 L.Ed.2d 13 (1990), where an illegal warrantless arrest was made in Harris' house,[b] we held that

> suppressing [Harris'] statement taken outside the house would not serve the purpose of the rule that made Harris' in-house arrest illegal. The warrant requirement for an arrest in the home is imposed to protect the home, and anything incriminating the police gathered from arresting Harris in his home, rather than elsewhere, has been excluded, as it should have been; the purpose of the rule has thereby been vindicated.

For this reason, cases excluding the fruits of unlawful warrantless searches say nothing about the appropriateness of exclusion to vindicate the interests protected by the knock-and-announce requirement. Until a valid warrant has issued, citizens are entitled to shield "their persons, houses, papers, and effects" from the government's scrutiny. Exclusion of the evidence obtained by a warrantless search vindicates that entitlement. The interests protected by the knock-and-announce requirement are quite different—and do not include the shielding of potential evidence from the government's eyes.

---

[b]   In *Harris*, police officers had probable cause to arrest Harris, but entered without a required arrest warrant. Harris received *Miranda* warnings, waived his rights, and made an incriminating statement in his home. Later, at the police station, Harris made a second inculpatory statement. The in-home statement was suppressed as tainted, pursuant to attenuation principles enunciated in *Brown v. Illinois* (p. 534, Note 2). The sole issue on appeal was the admissibility of Harris's statement at the station house.

One of those interests is the protection of human life and limb, because an unannounced entry may provoke violence in supposed self-defense by the surprised resident. Another interest is the protection of property. Breaking a house (as the old cases typically put it) absent an announcement would penalize someone who " 'did not know of the process, of which, if he had notice, it is to be presumed that he would obey it * * * .' " The knock-and-announce rule gives individuals "the opportunity to comply with the law and to avoid the destruction of property occasioned by a forcible entry." And thirdly, the knock-and-announce rule protects those elements of privacy and dignity that can be destroyed by a sudden entrance. It gives residents the "opportunity to prepare themselves for" the entry of the police. "The brief interlude between announcement and entry with a warrant may be the opportunity that an individual has to pull on clothes or get out of bed." In other words, it assures the opportunity to collect oneself before answering the door.

What the knock-and-announce rule has never protected, however, is one's interest in preventing the government from seeing or taking evidence described in a warrant. Since the interests that *were* violated in this case have nothing to do with the seizure of the evidence, the exclusionary rule is inapplicable.

B

Quite apart from the requirement of unattenuated causation, the exclusionary rule has never been applied except "where its deterrence benefits outweigh its 'substantial social costs.' " The costs here are considerable. In addition to the grave adverse consequence that exclusion of relevant incriminating evidence always entails (viz., the risk of releasing dangerous criminals into society), imposing that massive remedy for a knock-and-announce violation would generate a constant flood of alleged failures to observe the rule, and claims that any asserted * * * justification for a no-knock entry had inadequate support. The cost of entering this lottery would be small, but the jackpot enormous: suppression of all evidence, amounting in many cases to a get-out-of-jail-free card. Courts would experience as never before the reality that "[t]he exclusionary rule frequently requires extensive litigation to determine whether particular evidence must be excluded." * * * [W]hat constituted a "reasonable wait time" in a particular case (or, for that matter, how many seconds the police in fact waited), or whether there was "reasonable suspicion" of the sort that would invoke [one of] the [knock-and-announce] exceptions, is difficult for the trial court to determine and even more difficult for an appellate court to review.

Another consequence of the incongruent remedy Hudson proposes would be police officers' refraining from timely entry after knocking and announcing. As we have observed, the amount of time they must wait is necessarily uncertain. If the consequences of running afoul of the rule were so massive, officers would be inclined to wait longer than the law requires—producing preventable violence against officers in some cases, and the destruction of evidence in many others. * * *

Next to these "substantial social costs" we must consider the deterrence benefits, existence of which is a necessary condition for exclusion. (It is not, of course, a sufficient condition: "[I]t does not follow that the Fourth Amendment requires adoption of every proposal that might deter police misconduct.") To begin with, the value of deterrence depends upon the strength of the incentive to commit the forbidden act. Viewed from this perspective, deterrence of knock-and-announce violations is not worth a lot. Violation of the warrant requirement sometimes produces incriminating evidence that could not otherwise be obtained. But ignoring knock-and-announce can realistically be expected to achieve absolutely nothing except the prevention of destruction of evidence and the avoidance of life-threatening resistance by occupants of the premises—dangers which, if there is even "reasonable suspicion" of their existence, *suspend the knock-and-announce requirement anyway.* Massive deterrence is hardly required.

It seems to us not even true, as Hudson contends, that without suppression there will be no deterrence of knock-and-announce violations at all. Of course even if this assertion were accurate, it would not necessarily justify suppression. Assuming (as the assertion must) that civil suit is not an effective deterrent, one can think of many forms of police misconduct that are similarly "undeterred." When, for example, a confessed suspect in the killing of a police officer, arrested (along with incriminating evidence) in a lawful warranted search, is subjected to physical abuse at the station house, would it seriously be suggested that the evidence must be excluded, since that is the only "effective deterrent"? And what, other than civil suit, is the "effective deterrent" of police violation of an already-confessed suspect's Sixth Amendment rights by denying him prompt access to counsel? Many would regard these violated rights as more significant than the right not to be intruded upon in one's nightclothes—and yet nothing but "ineffective" civil suit is available as a deterrent. And the police incentive for those violations is arguably greater than the incentive for disregarding the knock-and-announce rule.

We cannot assume that exclusion in this context is necessary deterrence simply because we found that it was necessary deterrence in different contexts and long ago. That would be forcing the public today to pay for the sins and inadequacies of a legal regime that existed almost half a century ago. Dollree Mapp could not turn to 42 U.S.C. § 1983 for meaningful relief; *Monroe v. Pape,* 365 U.S. 167, 81 S.Ct. 473, 5 L.Ed.2d 492 (1961), which began the slow but steady expansion of that [civil rights] remedy, was decided the same Term as *Mapp.* It would be another

17 years before the § 1983 remedy was extended to reach the deep pocket of municipalities. Citizens whose Fourth Amendment rights were violated by federal officers could not bring suit until 10 years after *Mapp,* with this Court's decision in *Bivens v. Six Unknown Fed. Narcotics Agents,* 403 U.S. 388, 91 S.Ct. 1999, 29 L.Ed.2d 619 (1971).

Hudson complains that "it would be very hard to find a lawyer to take a case such as this," but 42 U.S.C. § 1988(b) answers this objection. Since some civil-rights violations would yield damages too small to justify the expense of litigation, Congress has authorized attorney's fees for civil-rights plaintiffs. This remedy was unavailable in the heydays of our exclusionary-rule jurisprudence, because it is tied to the availability of a cause of action. For years after *Mapp,* "very few lawyers would even consider representation of persons who had civil rights claims against the police," but now "much has changed. Citizens and lawyers are much more willing to seek relief in the courts for police misconduct." M. Avery, D. Rudovsky, & K. Blum, Police Misconduct: Law and Litigation, p. v (3d ed. 2005).[c] The number of public-interest law firms and lawyers who specialize in civil-rights grievances has greatly expanded.

Hudson points out that few published decisions to date announce huge awards for knock-and-announce violations. But this is an unhelpful statistic. Even if we thought that only large damages would deter police misconduct * * * , we do not know how many claims have been settled, or indeed how many violations have occurred that produced anything more than nominal injury. It is clear, at least, that the lower courts are allowing colorable knock-and-announce suits to go forward, unimpeded by assertions of qualified immunity. As far as we know, civil liability is an effective deterrent here, as we have assumed it is in other contexts.

Another development over the past half-century that deters civil-rights violations is the increasing professionalism of police forces, including a new emphasis on internal police discipline. Even as long ago as 1980 we felt it proper to "assume" that unlawful police behavior would "be dealt with appropriately" by the authorities, but we now have increasing evidence that police forces across the United States take the constitutional rights of citizens seriously. There have been "wide-ranging reforms in the education, training, and supervision of police officers." Numerous sources are now available to teach officers and their supervisors what is required of them under this Court's cases, how to respect constitutional guarantees in various situations, and how to craft an effective regime for internal discipline. Failure to teach and enforce

---

[c]   Justice Scalia failed to quote language from this book that immediately followed his quote: "But the development of the law has not been linear. In certain respects it is easier to challenge police misconduct in court. * * * In other respects, it is far more difficult." And, after *Hudson* was decided, the authors added a new footnote to their 2007 edition, characterizing the Court's quotation as "highly misleading."

constitutional requirements exposes municipalities to financial liability. Moreover, modern police forces are staffed with professionals; it is not credible to assert that internal discipline, which can limit successful careers, will not have a deterrent effect. There is also evidence that the increasing use of various forms of citizen review can enhance police accountability.

In sum, the social costs of applying the exclusionary rule to knock-and-announce violations are considerable; the incentive to such violations is minimal to begin with, and the extant deterrences against them are substantial—incomparably greater than the factors deterring warrantless entries when *Mapp* was decided. Resort to the massive remedy of suppressing evidence of guilt is unjustified.

IV

[The plurality proceeded to discuss three prior high court opinions it felt "confirms our conclusion that suppression is unwarranted in this case."]

* * *

For the foregoing reasons we affirm the judgment of the Michigan Court of Appeals.

JUSTICE KENNEDY, concurring in part and concurring in the judgment.

Two points should be underscored with respect to today's decision. First, the knock-and-announce requirement protects rights and expectations linked to ancient principles in our constitutional order. The Court's decision should not be interpreted as suggesting that violations of the requirement are trivial or beyond the law's concern. Second, the continued operation of the exclusionary rule, as settled and defined by our precedents, is not in doubt. Today's decision determines only that in the specific context of the knock-and-announce requirement, a violation is not sufficiently related to the later discovery of evidence to justify suppression. * * *

Today's decision does not address any demonstrated pattern of knock-and-announce violations. If a widespread pattern of violations were shown, and particularly if those violations were committed against persons who lacked the means or voice to mount an effective protest, there would be reason for grave concern. Even then, however, the Court would have to acknowledge that extending the remedy of exclusion to all the evidence seized following a knock-and-announce violation would mean revising the requirement of causation that limits our discretion in applying the exclusionary rule. That type of extension also would have significant practical implications, adding to the list of issues requiring resolution at the criminal trial questions such as whether police officers entered a home after waiting 10 seconds or 20.

In this case the relevant evidence was discovered not because of a failure to knock-and-announce, but because of a subsequent search pursuant to a lawful warrant. The Court in my view is correct to hold that suppression was not required. While I am not convinced that [the cases discussed in Part IV] have as much relevance here as Justice SCALIA appears to conclude, the Court's holding is fully supported by Parts I through III of its opinion. I accordingly join those Parts and concur in the judgment.

JUSTICE BREYER, with whom JUSTICE STEVENS, JUSTICE SOUTER, and JUSTICE GINSBURG join, dissenting. * * *

Today's opinion is * * * doubly troubling. It represents a significant departure from the Court's precedents. And it weakens, perhaps destroys, much of the practical value of the Constitution's knock-and-announce protection. * * *

II

Reading our knock-and-announce cases * * * in light of * * * foundational Fourth Amendment case law, it is clear that the exclusionary rule should apply. For one thing, elementary logic leads to that conclusion. We have held that a court must "conside[r]" whether officers complied with the knock-and-announce requirement "in assessing the reasonableness of a search or seizure." The Fourth Amendment insists that an unreasonable search or seizure is, constitutionally speaking, an illegal search or seizure. And ever since *Weeks* (in respect to federal prosecutions) and *Mapp* (in respect to state prosecutions), "the use of evidence secured through an illegal search and seizure" is "barred" in criminal trials.

For another thing, the driving legal purpose underlying the exclusionary rule, namely, the deterrence of unlawful government behavior, argues strongly for suppression. * * * [T]he Court [has] based its holdings requiring suppression of unlawfully obtained evidence upon the recognition that admission of that evidence would seriously undermine the Fourth Amendment's promise. [Prior] cases recognized that failure to apply the exclusionary rule would make that promise a hollow one, reducing it to "a form of words," "of no value" to those whom it seeks to protect. Indeed, this Court in *Mapp* held that the exclusionary rule applies to the States in large part due to its belief that alternative state mechanisms for enforcing the Fourth Amendment's guarantees had proved "worthless and futile."

Why is application of the exclusionary rule any the less necessary here? Without such a rule, as in *Mapp,* police know that they can ignore the Constitution's requirements without risking suppression of evidence discovered after an unreasonable entry. As in *Mapp,* some government officers will find it easier, or believe it less risky, to proceed with what they consider a necessary search immediately and without the requisite constitutional (say, warrant or knock-and-announce) compliance.

Of course, the State or the Federal Government may provide alternative remedies for knock-and-announce violations. But that circumstance was true of *Mapp* as well. What reason is there to believe that those remedies * * * , which the Court found inadequate in *Mapp,* can adequately deter unconstitutional police behavior here?

The cases reporting knock-and-announce violations are legion. Indeed, these cases of reported violations seem sufficiently frequent and serious as to indicate "a widespread pattern" (KENNEDY, J., concurring in part and concurring in judgment). Yet the majority * * * has failed to cite a single reported case in which a plaintiff has collected more than nominal damages solely as a result of a knock-and-announce violation. Even Michigan concedes that, "in cases like the present one * * * , damages may be virtually non-existent." And Michigan's *amici* further concede that civil immunities prevent tort law from being an effective substitute for the exclusionary rule at this time.

As Justice Stewart, the author of a number of significant Fourth Amendment opinions, explained, the deterrent effect of damage actions "can hardly be said to be great," as such actions are "expensive, time-consuming, not readily available, and rarely successful." The upshot is that the need for deterrence—the critical factor driving this Court's Fourth Amendment cases for close to a century—argues with at least comparable strength for evidentiary exclusion here.

To argue, as the majority does, that new remedies, such as 42 U.S.C. § 1983 actions or better trained police, make suppression unnecessary is to argue that *Wolf,* not *Mapp,* is now the law. * * * To argue that there may be few civil suits because violations may produce nothing "more than nominal injury" is to confirm, not to deny, the inability of civil suits to deter violations. And to argue without evidence * * * that civil suits may provide deterrence because claims *may* "have been settled" is, perhaps, to search in desperation for an argument. Rather, the majority, as it candidly admits, has simply "assumed" that, "[a]s far as [it] know[s], civil liability is an effective deterrent," a support-free assumption that *Mapp* and subsequent cases make clear does not embody the Court's normal approach to difficult questions of Fourth Amendment law.

It is not surprising, then, that after looking at virtually every pertinent Supreme Court case decided since *Weeks,* I can find no precedent that might offer the majority support for its contrary conclusion. * * *

I can find nothing persuasive in the majority's opinion that could justify its refusal to apply the rule. * * *

[The majority cannot] justify its failure to respect the need for deterrence, as set forth consistently in the Court's prior case law, through its claim of "substantial social costs"—at least if it means that those "social costs" are somehow special here. The only costs it mentions are those that typically accompany *any* use of the Fourth Amendment's exclusionary principle: (1) that where the constable blunders, a guilty defendant may be set free (consider *Mapp* itself); (2) that defendants may assert claims where Fourth Amendment rights are uncertain * * *, and (3) that sometimes it is difficult to decide the merits of those uncertain claims. * * * The majority's "substantial social costs" argument is an argument against the Fourth Amendment's exclusionary principle itself. And it is an argument that this Court, until now, has consistently rejected.

III

The majority * * * make[s] several additional arguments. In my view, those arguments rest upon misunderstandings of the principles underlying this Court's precedents.

A

The majority first argues that "the constitutional violation of an illegal *manner* of entry was *not* a but-for cause of obtaining the evidence." But taking causation as it is commonly understood in the law, I do not see how that can be so. Although the police might have entered Hudson's home lawfully, they did not in fact do so. Their unlawful behavior inseparably characterizes their actual entry; that entry was a necessary condition of their presence in Hudson's home; and their presence in Hudson's home was a necessary condition of their finding and seizing the evidence. At the same time, their discovery of evidence in Hudson's home was a readily foreseeable consequence of their entry and their unlawful presence within the home.

Moreover, separating the "manner of entry" from the related search slices the violation too finely. As noted [earlier], we have described a failure to comply with the knock-and-announce rule, not as an independently unlawful event, but as a factor that renders the *search* "constitutionally defective."

The Court nonetheless accepts Michigan's argument that the requisite but-for-causation is not satisfied in this case because, whether or not the constitutional violation occurred (what the Court refers to as a "preliminary misstep"), "the police would have executed the warrant they had obtained, and would have discovered the gun and drugs inside the house." As support for this proposition, Michigan rests on this Court's inevitable discovery cases.

This claim, however, misunderstands the inevitable discovery doctrine. * * * That rule does not refer to discovery that would have taken place if the police behavior in question had (contrary to fact) been lawful. The doctrine does not treat as critical what *hypothetically could* have happened had the police acted lawfully in the first place. Rather, "independent" or "inevitable" discovery refers to discovery that did occur or that would have occurred (1) *despite* (not simply *in the absence of*) the unlawful behavior and (2) *independently* of that unlawful behavior. The government cannot, for example, avoid suppression of evidence seized without a warrant (or pursuant to a defective warrant) simply by showing that it could have obtained a valid warrant had it sought one. Instead, it must show that the same evidence "inevitably *would* have been discovered *by lawful means.*" * * *

Case law well illustrates the meaning of this principle. In *Nix* [*v. Williams*, p. 528, Note 4], *supra*, police officers violated a defendant's Sixth Amendment right by eliciting incriminating statements from him after he invoked his right to counsel. Those statements led to the discovery of the victim's body. The Court concluded that evidence obtained from the victim's body was admissible because it would ultimately or inevitably have been discovered by a volunteer search party effort that was ongoing—whether or not the Sixth Amendment violation had taken place. In other words, the evidence would have been found *despite,* and *independent of,* the Sixth Amendment violation. * * *

Thus, the Court's opinion reflects a misunderstanding of what inevitable discovery means when it says, "[i]n this case, of course, the constitutional violation of an illegal *manner* of entry was *not* a but-for cause of obtaining the evidence." The majority rests this conclusion on its next statement: "Whether that preliminary misstep has occurred *or not,* the police * * * would have discovered the gun and the drugs inside the house." Despite the phrase "of course," neither of these statements is correct. It is not true that, had the illegal entry not occurred, "police would have discovered the guns and drugs inside the house." Without that unlawful entry they would not have been inside the house; so there would have been no discovery.

Of course, had the police entered the house lawfully, they would have found the gun and drugs. But that fact is beside the point. The question is not what police might have done had they not behaved unlawfully. The question is what they did do. Was there set in motion an independent chain of events that would have inevitably led to the discovery and seizure of the evidence despite, and independent of, that behavior? The answer here is "no."

B

The majority, Michigan, and the United States point out that the officers here possessed a warrant authorizing a search. That fact, they argue, means that the evidence would have been discovered independently or somehow diminishes the need to suppress the evidence. But I do not see why that is so. The warrant in question * * * was an ordinary search warrant. It authorized a search that *complied with,* not a search that *disregarded,* the Constitution's knock-and-announce rule.

Would a warrant that authorizes entry into a home on Tuesday permit the police to enter on Monday? * * * It is difficult for me to see how the presence of a warrant that does not authorize the entry in question has anything to do with the "inevitable discovery" exception or otherwise diminishes the need to enforce the knock-and-announce requirement through suppression.

C * * *

The majority * * * says that evidence should not be suppressed once the causal connection between unlawful behavior and discovery of the evidence becomes too "attenuated." But the majority then makes clear that it is not using the word "attenuated" to mean what this Court's precedents have typically used that word to mean, namely, that the discovery of the evidence has come about long after the unlawful behavior took place or in an independent way, *i.e.,* through " 'means sufficiently distinguishable to be purged of the primary taint.' " *Wong Sun v. United States* [p. 530].

Rather, the majority gives the word "attenuation" a new meaning * * * . "Attenuation," it says, "also occurs when, even given a direct causal connection, the interest protected by the constitutional guarantee that has been violated would not be served by suppression of the evidence obtained." The interests the knock-and-announce rule seeks to protect, the Court adds, are "human life" (at stake when a householder is "surprised"), "property" (such as the front door), and "those elements of privacy and dignity that can be destroyed by a sudden entrance," namely, "the opportunity to collect oneself before answering the door." Since none of those interests led to the discovery of the evidence seized here, there is no reason to suppress it.

There are three serious problems with this argument. First, it does not fully describe the constitutional values, purposes, and objectives underlying the knock-and-announce requirement. That rule does help to protect homeowners from damaged doors; it does help to protect occupants from surprise. But it does more than that. It protects the occupants' privacy by assuring them that government agents will not enter their home without complying with those requirements (among others) that diminish the offensive nature of any such intrusion. Many years ago, Justice Frankfurter wrote for the Court that the "knock at the door, * * * as a prelude to a search, without authority of law * * * [is] inconsistent with the conception of human rights enshrined in [our] history" and Constitution. How much the more offensive when the search takes place without any knock at all.

* * * The Court is therefore wrong to reduce the essence of its protection to "the right not to be intruded upon in one's nightclothes."

Second, whether the interests underlying the knock-and-announce rule are implicated in any given case is, in a sense, beside the point. As we have explained, failure to comply with the knock-and-announce rule renders the related search unlawful. And where a search is unlawful, the law insists upon suppression of the evidence consequently discovered, even if that evidence or its possession has little or nothing to do with the reasons underlying the unconstitutionality of a search. The Fourth Amendment does not seek to protect contraband, yet we have required suppression of contraband seized in an unlawful search. That is because the exclusionary rule protects more general "privacy values through deterrence of future police misconduct." The same is true here.

Third, the majority's interest-based approach departs from prior law. * * *

D

The United States, in its brief and at oral argument, has argued that suppression is "an especially harsh remedy given the nature of the violation in this case." This argument focuses upon the fact that entering a house after knocking and announcing can, in some cases, prove dangerous to a police officer. Perhaps someone inside has a gun, as turned out to be the case here. The majority adds that police officers about to encounter someone who may try to harm them will be "uncertain" as to how long to wait. It says that, "[i]f the consequences of running afoul" of the knock-and-announce "rule were so massive," *i.e.*, would lead to the exclusion of evidence, then "officers would be inclined to wait longer than the law requires—producing preventable violence against officers in some cases."

To argue that police efforts to assure compliance with the rule may prove dangerous, however, is not to argue against evidence suppression. It is to argue against the validity of the rule itself. Similarly, to argue that enforcement means uncertainty, which in turn means the potential for dangerous and longer-than-necessary delay, is (if true) to argue against meaningful compliance with the rule. * * *

IV * * *

There may be instances in the law where text or history or tradition leaves room for a judicial decision that rests upon little more than an unvarnished judicial instinct. But this is not one of them. Rather, our Fourth Amendment traditions place high value upon protecting privacy in the home. They emphasize the need to assure that its constitutional protections are effective, lest the Amendment "sound the word of promise to the ear but break it to the hope." They include an exclusionary principle, which since *Weeks* has formed the centerpiece of the criminal law's effort to ensure the practical reality of those promises. That is why the Court should assure itself that any departure from that principle is firmly grounded in logic, in history, in precedent, and in empirical fact. It has not done so. That is why, with respect, I dissent.

NOTES AND QUESTIONS

1.   Professor Wayne LaFave, author of the leading treatise on the Fourth Amendment is no fan of *Hudson*, which he says "deserves a special niche in the Supreme Court's pantheon of Fourth Amendment jurisprudence, as one would be hard-pressed to find another case with so many bogus arguments piled atop one another." 6 Wayne R. LaFave, Search and Seizure § 11.4(a), at 351 (5th ed. 2012). Putting aside your feelings for or against the exclusionary rule, do you believe the majority or the dissent is more consistent with exclusionary rule jurisprudence (specifically, independent-source, inevitable-discovery, and attenuation doctrines), as you learned it in this chapter?

David Moran, who represented Hudson in the United States Supreme Court, has written: "I have no idea whether my death will be noted in the *New York Times*. But if it is, I fear the headline of my obituary will look something like: 'Professor Dies; Lost *Hudson v. Michigan* in Supreme Court, Leading to Abolition of Exclusionary Rule.'" David A. Moran, *Waiting for the Other Shoe: Hudson and the Precarious State of Mapp,* 93 Iowa L. Rev. 1725, 1726 (2008).

2.   Suppose the police unconstitutionally seize Bill and, thereafter, unconstitutionally seize property in Bill's possession. Based on Justice Scalia's attenuation analysis in *Hudson*, how might the Government argue that the seized property is admissible? See James Tomkovicz, *Hudson v. Michigan and the Future of Fourth Amendment Exclusion*, 93 Iowa L. Rev. 1819 (2008).

Suppose the police have probable cause to conduct a search of a residence but they fail to secure one, enter without a warrant, and seize the evidence they expected to find. How might the police justify the admissibility of this evidence on the basis of language in *Hudson* relating to but-for causation?

3.   *Hudson* seemingly rejects application of the exclusionary rule when the police, armed with a search warrant, violate the knock-and-announce rule. What if the police, however, are armed instead with an *arrest* warrant, violate the knock-and-announce requirement, enter, and observe evidence in

plain view while seeking to execute the warrant? Is there a basis for distinguishing this situation? See United States v. Weaver, 808 F.3d 26 (D.C. Cir. 2015).

4. *Are the alternative remedies to the exclusionary rule really good enough?* Justice Scalia wrote in *Hudson* that "[w]e cannot assume that exclusion in this context is necessary * * * simply because we found that it was necessary * * * in different contexts and long ago. That would be forcing the public today to pay for the sins and inadequacies of a legal regime that existed almost half a century ago." Are things as rosy as he claims? According to Professor David Sklansky,

> systems of accountability for police misconduct have improved since the 1960s. But the particular system Justice Scalia talked about most in *Hudson*—civil damages action—is the one for which there is least evidence of significant improvement. * * * Chief among the new barriers to suing the police, of course, are the expanding doctrines of official immunity, which alone take [Avery, Rudovsky and Blum, the authors of the police misconduct book cited by Scalia] more than 120 pages to describe. More and more, these doctrines look like the Blob That Ate [Civil Rights] Section 1983.

David Alan Sklansky, *Is the Exclusionary Rule Obsolete?*, 5 Ohio St. J. Crim. L. 567, 571, 572 (2008).

One significant impediment to civil action is that government officials, including police officers, are immune from civil liability "insofar as their conduct does not violate clearly established statutory or constitutional rights which a reasonable person would have known." Messerschmidt v. Millender, 565 U.S. ___, 132 S.Ct. 1235, 182 L.Ed.2d 47 (2012) (quoting earlier cases). This is done to give officers "breathing room to make reasonable but mistaken judgments," *id.*, both of a legal and factual nature.

For example, FBI agents in November 1983 broke into the wrong house looking for a fugitive, subjected the innocent family to a SWAT-team raid and detention, and arrested the husband/father for obstruction of justice when he attempted to demonstrate that his family was innocent; he was released the next day without charges being filed. The FBI agent defended the Section 1983 civil suit on the ground that he believed that he had probable cause that the fugitive was in the house that was searched. The Eighth Circuit Court of Appeals held that the allegations presented an issue of fact for the jury. The Supreme Court reversed, 6–3, dismissing the lawsuit without a trial on the issue or discovery on the issue of the basis of the agent's belief in probable cause. Anderson v. Creighton, 483 U.S. 635, 107 S. Ct. 3034, 97 L. Ed. 2d 523 (1987).

Sklansky also is skeptical that civilian police review boards can satisfactorily replace the exclusionary rule. He writes that "[i]ronically, * * * one of the reasons citizens review panels have spread so broadly is that they have almost always proven much more sympathetic to rank-and-file officers than the [police] unions feared and than most of the original backers of the idea expected." *Id.* at 572.

HERRING V. UNITED STATES

Supreme Court of the United States, 2009.
555 U.S. 135, 129 S.Ct. 695, 172 L.Ed.2d 496.

CHIEF JUSTICE ROBERTS delivered the opinion of the Court [joined by JUSTICES SCALIA, KENNEDY, THOMAS, and ALITO].

* * * What if an officer reasonably believes there is an outstanding arrest warrant, but that belief turns out to be wrong because of a negligent bookkeeping error by another police employee? The parties here agree that the ensuing arrest is still a violation of the Fourth Amendment, but dispute whether contraband found during a search incident to that arrest must be excluded in a later prosecution.

Our cases establish that such suppression is not an automatic consequence of a Fourth Amendment violation. Instead, the question turns on the culpability of the police and the potential of exclusion to deter wrongful police conduct. Here the error was the result of isolated negligence attenuated from the arrest. We hold that in these circumstances the jury should not be barred from considering all the evidence.

I

On July 7, 2004, Investigator Mark Anderson learned that Bennie Dean Herring had driven to the Coffee County Sheriff's Department to retrieve something from his impounded truck. Herring was no stranger to law enforcement, and Anderson asked the county's warrant clerk, Sandy Pope, to check for any outstanding warrants for Herring's arrest. When she found none, Anderson asked Pope to check with Sharon Morgan, her counterpart in neighboring Dale County. After checking Dale County's computer database, Morgan replied that there was an active arrest warrant for Herring's failure to appear on a felony charge. Pope relayed the information to Anderson and asked Morgan to fax over a copy of the warrant as confirmation. Anderson and a deputy followed Herring as he left the impound lot, pulled him over, and arrested him. A search incident to the arrest revealed methamphetamine in Herring's pocket, and a pistol (which as a felon he could not possess) in his vehicle.

There had, however, been a mistake about the warrant. The Dale County sheriff's computer records are supposed to correspond to actual arrest warrants, which the office also maintains. But when Morgan went to the files to retrieve the actual warrant to fax to Pope, Morgan was unable to find it. She called a court clerk and learned that the warrant had been recalled five months earlier. Normally when a warrant is recalled the court clerk's office or a judge's chambers calls Morgan, who enters the information in the sheriff's computer database and disposes of the physical copy. For whatever reason, the information about the recall of the warrant for Herring did not appear in the database. Morgan immediately called Pope to alert her to the mixup, and Pope contacted Anderson over a secure radio. This all unfolded in 10 to 15 minutes, but Herring had already been arrested and found with the gun and drugs, just a few hundred yards from the sheriff's office.

Herring was indicted in the District Court for the Middle District of Alabama for illegally possessing the gun and drugs * * * . He moved to suppress the evidence on the ground that his initial arrest had been illegal because the warrant had been rescinded. The Magistrate Judge recommended denying the motion because the arresting officers had acted in a good-faith belief that the warrant was still outstanding. Thus, * * * there was "no reason to believe that application of the exclusionary rule here would deter the occurrence of any future mistakes." The District Court adopted the Magistrate Judge's recommendation, and the Court of Appeals for the Eleventh Circuit affirmed.

The Eleventh Circuit found that the arresting officers in Coffee County "were entirely innocent of any wrongdoing or carelessness." The court assumed that whoever failed to update the Dale County sheriff's records was also a law enforcement official, but noted that "the conduct in question [wa]s a negligent failure to act, not a deliberate or tactical choice to act." Because the error was merely negligent and attenuated from the arrest, the Eleventh Circuit concluded that the benefit of suppressing the evidence "would be marginal or nonexistent," and the evidence was therefore admissible under the good-faith rule of *United States v. Leon,* [p. 538].

Other courts have required exclusion of evidence obtained through similar police errors, so we granted Herring's petition for certiorari to resolve the conflict. We now affirm the Eleventh Circuit's judgment.

II * * *

A

* * * [O]ur decisions establish an exclusionary rule that, when applicable, forbids the use of improperly obtained evidence at trial. We have stated that this judicially created rule is "designed to safeguard Fourth Amendment rights generally through its deterrent effect."

In analyzing the applicability of the rule, *Leon* admonished that we must consider the actions of all the police officers involved. The Coffee County officers did nothing improper. Indeed, the error was noticed so quickly because Coffee County requested a faxed confirmation of the warrant.

The Eleventh Circuit concluded, however, that somebody in Dale County should have updated the computer database to reflect the recall of the arrest warrant. The court also concluded that this error was negligent, but did not find it to be reckless or deliberate. That fact is crucial to our holding that this error is not enough by itself to require "the extreme sanction of exclusion."

B

1.   The fact that a Fourth Amendment violation occurred * * * does not necessarily mean that the exclusionary rule applies. Indeed, exclusion "has always been our last resort, not our first impulse," and our precedents establish important principles that constrain application of the exclusionary rule.

First, the exclusionary rule is not an individual right and applies only where it " 'result[s] in appreciable deterrence.' " * * *[2]

In addition, the benefits of deterrence must outweigh the costs. "We have never suggested that the exclusionary rule must apply in every circumstance in which it might provide marginal deterrence." * * * The principal cost of applying the rule is, of course, letting guilty and possibly dangerous defendants go free—something that "offends basic concepts of the criminal justice system." "[T]he rule's costly toll upon truth-seeking and law enforcement objectives presents a high obstacle for those urging [its] application."

These principles are reflected in the holding of *Leon*: When police act under a warrant that is invalid for lack of probable cause, the exclusionary rule does not apply if the police acted "in objectively reasonable reliance" on the subsequently invalidated search warrant. We (perhaps confusingly) called this objectively reasonable reliance "good faith." In a companion case, *Massachusetts v. Sheppard,* [p. 551, Note 4], we held that the exclusionary rule did not apply when a warrant was invalid because a judge forgot to make "clerical corrections" to it.

Shortly thereafter we extended these holdings to warrantless administrative searches performed in good-faith reliance on a statute later declared unconstitutional. [Illinois v. Krull, 480 U.S. 340 (1987).] Finally, in [*Arizona v.*] *Evans,* 514 U.S. 1, 115 S.Ct. 1185, 131 L.Ed.2d 34 [(1995)], we applied this good-faith rule to police who reasonably relied on mistaken information in a court's database that an arrest warrant was outstanding. We held that a mistake made by a judicial employee could not give rise to exclusion for three reasons: The exclusionary rule was crafted to curb police rather than judicial misconduct; court employees

---

[2]   Justice GINSBURG's dissent champions what she describes as " 'a more majestic conception' of * * * the exclusionary rule," which would exclude evidence even where deterrence does not justify doing so. Majestic or not, our cases reject this conception, and perhaps for this reason, her dissent relies almost exclusively on previous dissents to support its analysis.

were unlikely to try to subvert the Fourth Amendment; and "most important, there [was] no basis for believing that application of the exclusionary rule in [those] circumstances" would have any significant effect in deterring the errors. *Evans* left unresolved "whether the evidence should be suppressed if police personnel were responsible for the error," an issue not argued by the State in that case, but one that we now confront.

2. The extent to which the exclusionary rule is justified by these deterrence principles varies with the culpability of the law enforcement conduct. As we said in *Leon,* "an assessment of the flagrancy of the police misconduct constitutes an important step in the calculus" of applying the exclusionary rule. Similarly, in *Krull* we elaborated that "evidence should be suppressed 'only if it can be said that the law enforcement officer had knowledge, or may properly be charged with knowledge, that the search was unconstitutional under the Fourth Amendment.'" * * *

Indeed, the abuses that gave rise to the exclusionary rule featured intentional conduct that was patently unconstitutional. In *Weeks* [*v. United States*], [p. 76], * * * the officers had broken into the defendant's home (using a key shown to them by a neighbor), confiscated incriminating papers, then returned again with a U.S. Marshal to confiscate even more. Not only did they have no search warrant, * * * but they could not have gotten one had they tried. They were so lacking in sworn and particularized information that "not even an order of court would have justified such procedure." * * *

Equally flagrant conduct was at issue in *Mapp v. Ohio,* [p. 83], which * * * extended the exclusionary rule to the States. Officers forced open a door to Ms. Mapp's house, kept her lawyer from entering, brandished what the court concluded was a false warrant, then forced her into handcuffs and canvassed the house for obscenity. An error that arises from nonrecurring and attenuated negligence is thus far removed from the core concerns that led us to adopt the rule in the first place. And in fact since *Leon,* we have never applied the rule to exclude evidence obtained in violation of the Fourth Amendment, where the police conduct was no more intentional or culpable than this.

3. To trigger the exclusionary rule, police conduct must be sufficiently deliberate that exclusion can meaningfully deter it, and sufficiently culpable that such deterrence is worth the price paid by the justice system. As laid out in our cases, the exclusionary rule serves to deter deliberate, reckless, or grossly negligent conduct, or in some circumstances recurring or systemic negligence. The error in this case does not rise to that level.[4] * * *

---

[4] We do not quarrel with Justice GINSBURG's claim that "liability for negligence * * * creates an incentive to act with greater care," and we do not suggest that the exclusion of this

The pertinent analysis of deterrence and culpability is objective, not an "inquiry into the subjective awareness of arresting officers." We have already held that "our good-faith inquiry is confined to the objectively ascertainable question whether a reasonably well trained officer would have known that the search was illegal" in light of "all of the circumstances." These circumstances frequently include a particular officer's knowledge and experience, but that does not make the test any more subjective than the one for probable cause, which looks to an officer's knowledge and experience, but not his subjective intent.

We do not suggest that all recordkeeping errors by the police are immune from the exclusionary rule. In this case, however, the conduct at issue was not so objectively culpable as to require exclusion. * * *

If the police have been shown to be reckless in maintaining a warrant system, or to have knowingly made false entries to lay the groundwork for future false arrests, exclusion would certainly be justified under our cases should such misconduct cause a Fourth Amendment violation. * * * Petitioner's fears that our decision will cause police departments to deliberately keep their officers ignorant are thus unfounded.

The dissent also adverts to the possible unreliability of a number of databases not relevant to this case. In a case where systemic errors were demonstrated, it might be reckless for officers to rely on an unreliable warrant system. But there is no evidence that errors in Dale County's system are routine or widespread. * * * Because no such showings were made here, the Eleventh Circuit was correct to affirm the denial of the motion to suppress.

* * *

* * * In light of our repeated holdings that the deterrent effect of suppression must be substantial and outweigh any harm to the justice system, we conclude that when police mistakes are the result of negligence such as that described here, rather than systemic error or reckless disregard of constitutional requirements, any marginal deterrence does not "pay its way." In such a case, the criminal should not "go free because the constable has blundered." *People v. Defore,* 242 N.Y. 13, 21, 150 N.E. 585, 587 (1926) (opinion of the Court by Cardozo, J.).

---

evidence could have *no* deterrent effect. But our cases require any deterrence to "be weighed against the 'substantial social costs exacted by the exclusionary rule,'" and here exclusion is not worth the cost.

JUSTICE GINSBURG, with whom JUSTICE STEVENS, JUSTICE SOUTER, and JUSTICE BREYER join, dissenting. * * *

II

A

The Court states that the exclusionary rule is not a defendant's right; rather, it is simply a remedy applicable only when suppression would result in appreciable deterrence that outweighs the cost to the justice system. * * *

B

Others have described "a more majestic conception" of the Fourth Amendment and its adjunct, the exclusionary rule. Protective of the fundamental "right of the people to be secure in their persons, houses, papers, and effects," the Amendment "is a constraint on the power of the sovereign, not merely on some of its agents." I share that vision of the Amendment.

The exclusionary rule is "a remedy necessary to ensure that" the Fourth Amendment's prohibitions "are observed in fact." The rule's service as an essential auxiliary to the Amendment earlier inclined the Court to hold the two inseparable.

Beyond doubt, a main objective of the rule "is to deter—to compel respect for the constitutional guaranty in the only effectively available way—by removing the incentive to disregard it." But the rule also serves other important purposes: It "enabl[es] the judiciary to avoid the taint of partnership in official lawlessness," and it "assur[es] the people—all potential victims of unlawful government conduct—that the government would not profit from its lawless behavior, thus minimizing the risk of seriously undermining popular trust in government."

The exclusionary rule, it bears emphasis, is often the only remedy effective to redress a Fourth Amendment violation. Civil liability will not lie for "the vast majority of [F]ourth [A]mendment violations—the frequent infringements motivated by commendable zeal, not condemnable malice." Criminal prosecutions or administrative sanctions against the offending officers and injunctive relief against widespread violations are an even farther cry.

III

The Court maintains that Herring's case is one in which the exclusionary rule could have scant deterrent effect and therefore would not "pay its way." I disagree.

A

The exclusionary rule, the Court suggests, is capable of only marginal deterrence when the misconduct at issue is merely careless, not intentional or reckless. The suggestion runs counter to a foundational premise of tort law—that liability for negligence, *i.e.,* lack of due care, creates an incentive to act with greater care. * * *

B

Is the potential deterrence here worth the costs it imposes? In light of the paramount importance of accurate recordkeeping in law enforcement, I would answer yes * * * .

Electronic databases form the nervous system of contemporary criminal justice operations. In recent years, their breadth and influence have dramatically expanded. Police today can access databases that include not only the updated National Crime Information Center (NCIC), but also terrorist watchlists, the Federal Government's employee eligibility system, and various commercial databases. Moreover, States are actively expanding information sharing between jurisdictions. As a result, law enforcement has an increasing supply of information within its easy electronic reach.

The risk of error stemming from these databases is not slim. Herring's *amici* warn that law enforcement databases are insufficiently monitored and often out of date. Government reports describe, for example, flaws in NCIC databases, terrorist watchlist databases, and databases associated with the Federal Government's employment eligibility verification system

Inaccuracies in expansive, interconnected collections of electronic information raise grave concerns for individual liberty. * * *

C

The Court assures that "exclusion would certainly be justified" if "the police have been shown to be reckless in maintaining a warrant system, or to have knowingly made false entries to lay the groundwork for future false arrests." This concession provides little comfort.

First, by restricting suppression to bookkeeping errors that are deliberate or reckless, the majority leaves Herring, and others like him, with no remedy for violations of their constitutional rights. There can be no serious assertion that relief is available under 42 U.S.C. § 1983. The arresting officer would be sheltered by qualified immunity, and the police department itself is not liable for the negligent acts of its employees. Moreover, identifying the department employee who committed the error may be impossible.

Second, I doubt that police forces already possess sufficient incentives to maintain up-to-date records. * * *

Third, even when deliberate or reckless conduct is afoot, the Court's assurance will often be an empty promise: How is an impecunious defendant to make the required showing? If the answer is that a defendant is entitled to discovery (and if necessary, an audit of police databases), then the Court has imposed a considerable administrative burden on courts and law enforcement.

IV

Negligent recordkeeping errors by law enforcement threaten individual liberty, are susceptible to deterrence by the exclusionary rule, and cannot be remedied effectively through other means. Such errors present no occasion to further erode the exclusionary rule. The rule "is needed to make the Fourth Amendment something real; a guarantee that does not carry with it the exclusion of evidence obtained by its violation is a chimera." In keeping with the rule's "core concerns," suppression should have attended the unconstitutional search in this case. * * *

NOTES AND QUESTIONS

1. What is Justice Ginsburg getting at with her "more majestic conception" of the exclusionary rule? Why might two commentators state that her vision is required to "ensure the continued viability of the Fourth Amendment and * * * prevent the reduction of this constitutional right to an 'empty promise.'" Robert M. Bloom & David H. Fentin, *"A More Majestic Conception": The Importance of Judicial Integrity in Preserving the Exclusionary Rule*, 13 U. Pa. J. Const. L. 47, 48 (2010).

2. With what level of culpability did Investigator Anderson conduct the arrest and search of Herring?

3. How do you expect post-*Herring* suppression hearings will differ from such hearings in the past? Will they take up more or less time than before *Herring*? Why do some observers predict that the case "threaten[s] to bring the development of Fourth Amendment law to an end"? Albert W. Alschuler, *Herring v. United States: A Minnow or a Shark?*, 7 Ohio St. J. Crim. L. 463, 512 (2009).

4. *Problem.* The police stopped *H* for riding his bicycle on a sidewalk in violation of a city ordinance. *H* provided the officers with his name, New Jersey address, and date of birth. The officers radioed dispatch with this information. The dispatcher reported that there was an outstanding warrant for *H*. Accordingly, the officer arrested *H* and conducted a search incident to the arrest, which turned up cocaine. The dispatcher was in error: the warrant in question, which was ten years old, was of a person with a different first name, a California address, and a different birth date. Is the cocaine admissible under *Herring*? State v. Handy, 18 A.3d 179 (N.J. 2011).

5.   *Problem*. A postal inspector in 2005, who was investigating threatening letters sent to a school, demanded a DNA buccal swab from *T*. Because the inspector acted in the absence of any independent determination "of whether *any* particular level of Fourth Amendment justification had been met," this search concededly violated the Fourth Amendment. The swab was sent to a private lab for profiling. The DNA results indicated that *T* was not the author of the threatening letters, so the case was closed. In 2011, however, in a similar investigation in the same geographical area, the same postal inspector obtained *T*'s DNA profile from the private lab, and this time the DNA matched the 2011 letters. *T* sought to have the DNA evidence excluded. Should the evidence be excluded? Do you need more information to answer this question? United States v. Thomas, 736 F.3d 54 (1st Cir. 2013).

6.   *Herring* was far from the last word on the exclusionary rule, as we see with the next case.

DAVIS V. UNITED STATES

Supreme Court of the United States, 2011.
564 U.S. 229, 131 S.Ct. 2419, 180 L.Ed.2d 285.

JUSTICE ALITO delivered the opinion of the Court [joined by CHIEF JUSTICE ROBERTS, and JUSTICES SCALIA, KENNEDY, THOMAS, and KAGAN]. * * *

I

[Davis was a passenger in an automobile subjected to a "routine traffic stop" that resulted in his arrest for giving a false name to the police. The driver of the car was arrested for driving while intoxicated. They were handcuffed and placed in separate patrol cars, after which the arresting officers conducted a warrantless search of the passenger compartment of the automobile, pursuant to the Fourth Amendment law set out in *Belton v. New York* (p. 276). A firearm was discovered in the pocket of Davis's coat in the automobile, resulting in his federal indictment and conviction on one count of possession of a firearm by a convicted felon. While Davis's appeal was pending in the Eleventh Circuit, the Supreme Court decided *Arizona v. Gant* (p. 286), which adopted a new rule relating to searches of automobiles incident to lawful arrests. The Eleventh Circuit held that, under the new law announced in *Gant*, the police search violated the Fourth Amendment.[d] However, based on *Herring v. United States* (p. 568), the appellate court concluded that "penalizing" the officers for following the law existed at the time of his conduct would not deter Fourth Amendment violations. It therefore refused to apply the exclusionary rule to the unconstitutional search and affirmed Davis's conviction.]

---

[d]   Under Teague v. Lane, 489 U.S. 288, 109 S.Ct. 1060, 103 L.Ed.2d 334 (1989), "a new [constitutional] rule * * * is to be applied retroactively to all cases, state or federal, pending on direct review or not yet final * * * ." (See p. 1554.)

II

The Fourth Amendment protects the "right of the people to be secure in their persons, houses, papers, and effects, against unreasonable searches and seizures." The Amendment says nothing about suppressing evidence obtained in violation of this command. That rule—the exclusionary rule—is a "prudential" doctrine, created by this Court to "compel respect for the constitutional guaranty." Exclusion is "not a personal constitutional right," nor is it designed to "redress the injury" occasioned by an unconstitutional search. The rule's sole purpose, we have repeatedly held, is to deter future Fourth Amendment violations. Our cases have thus limited the rule's operation to situations in which this purpose is "thought most efficaciously served." Where suppression fails to yield "appreciable deterrence," exclusion is "clearly * * * unwarranted."

Real deterrent value is a "necessary condition for exclusion," but it is not "a sufficient" one. The analysis must also account for the "substantial social costs" generated by the rule. Exclusion exacts a heavy toll on both the judicial system and society at large. It almost always requires courts to ignore reliable, trustworthy evidence bearing on guilt or innocence. And its bottom-line effect, in many cases, is to suppress the truth and set the criminal loose in the community without punishment. Our cases hold that society must swallow this bitter pill when necessary, but only as a "last resort." For exclusion to be appropriate, the deterrence benefits of suppression must outweigh its heavy costs.

Admittedly, there was a time when our exclusionary-rule cases were not nearly so discriminating in their approach to the doctrine. "Expansive dicta" in several decisions suggested that the rule was a self-executing mandate implicit in the Fourth Amendment itself. * * * In time, however, we came to acknowledge the exclusionary rule for what it undoubtedly is—a "judicially created remedy" of this Court's own making. * * * In a line of cases beginning with *United States* v. *Leon,* we also recalibrated our cost-benefit analysis in exclusion cases to focus the inquiry on the "flagrancy of the police misconduct" at issue.

The basic insight of the *Leon* line of cases is that the deterrence benefits of exclusion "var[y] with the culpability of the law enforcement conduct" at issue. When the police exhibit "deliberate," "reckless," or "grossly negligent" disregard for Fourth Amendment rights, the deterrent value of exclusion is strong and tends to outweigh the resulting costs. But when the police act with an objectively "reasonable good-faith belief" that their conduct is lawful, or when their conduct involves only simple, "isolated" negligence, the " 'deterrence rationale loses much of its force,' " and exclusion cannot "pay its way."

The Court has over time applied this "good-faith" exception across a range of cases. * * *

Other good-faith cases have sounded a similar theme. *Illinois* v. *Krull*, 480 U. S. 340 (1987), extended the good-faith exception to searches conducted in reasonable reliance on subsequently invalidated statutes. ("[L]egislators, like judicial officers, are not the focus of the rule"). In *Arizona* v. *Evans*, [514 U.S. 1 (1995),] the Court applied the good-faith exception in a case where the police reasonably relied on erroneous information concerning an arrest warrant in a database maintained by judicial employees. Most recently, in *Herring* v. *United States*, we extended *Evans* in a case where *police* employees erred in maintaining records in a warrant database. "[I]solated," "nonrecurring" police negligence, we determined, lacks the culpability required to justify the harsh sanction of exclusion.

III

The question in this case is whether to apply the exclusionary rule when the police conduct a search in objectively reasonable reliance on binding judicial precedent. * * * The search incident to Davis's arrest in this case followed [the Eleventh Circuit's] * * * precedent to the letter. Although the search turned out to be unconstitutional under *Gant*, all agree that the officers' conduct was in strict compliance with then-binding * * * law and was not culpable in any way. * * * The officers who conducted the search did not violate Davis's Fourth Amendment rights deliberately, recklessly, or with gross negligence. Nor does this case involve any "recurring or systemic negligence" on the part of law enforcement. The police acted in strict compliance with binding precedent, and their behavior was not wrongful. Unless the exclusionary rule is to become a strict-liability regime, it can have no application in this case. * * *

About all that exclusion would deter in this case is conscientious police work. * * *

* * * We have stated before, and we reaffirm today, that the harsh sanction of exclusion "should not be applied to deter objectively reasonable law enforcement activity." Evidence obtained during a search conducted in reasonable reliance on binding precedent is not subject to the exclusionary rule.

IV

JUSTICE BREYER's dissent and Davis argue that, although the police conduct in this case was in no way culpable, other considerations should prevent the good-faith exception from applying. We are not persuaded. * * *

Davis * * * contends that applying the good-faith exception to searches conducted in reliance on binding precedent will stunt the development of Fourth Amendment law. With no possibility of suppression, criminal defendants will have no incentive, Davis maintains, to request that courts overrule precedent. * * *

[A]pplying the good-faith exception in this context will not prevent judicial reconsideration of prior Fourth Amendment precedents. * * * This Court reviews criminal convictions from 12 Federal Courts of Appeals, 50 state courts of last resort, and the District of Columbia Court of Appeals. If one or even many of these courts uphold a particular type of search or seizure, defendants in jurisdictions in which the question remains open will still have an undiminished incentive to litigate the issue. This Court can then grant certiorari, and the development of Fourth Amendment law will in no way be stunted.

Davis argues that Fourth Amendment precedents of *this* Court will be effectively insulated from challenge under a good-faith exception for reliance on appellate precedent. But this argument is overblown. For one thing, it is important to keep in mind that this argument applies to an exceedingly small set of cases. Decisions overruling this Court's Fourth Amendment precedents are rare. * * * Moreover, as a practical matter, defense counsel in many cases will test this Court's Fourth Amendment precedents in the same way that *Belton* was tested in *Gant*—by arguing that the precedent is distinguishable.

At most, Davis's argument might suggest that—to prevent Fourth Amendment law from becoming ossified—the petitioner in a case that results in the overruling of one of this Court's Fourth Amendment precedents should be given the benefit of the victory by permitting the suppression of evidence in that one case. * * * Therefore, in a future case, we could, if necessary, recognize a limited exception to the good-faith exception for a defendant who obtains a judgment overruling one of our Fourth Amendment precedents.

But this is not such a case. * * *

* * *

It is one thing for the criminal "to go free because the constable has blundered." It is quite another to set the criminal free because the constable has scrupulously adhered to governing law. Excluding evidence in such cases deters no police misconduct and imposes substantial social costs. We therefore hold that when the police conduct a search in objectively reasonable reliance on binding appellate precedent, the exclusionary rule does not apply. The judgment of the Court of Appeals for the Eleventh Circuit is

Affirmed.

JUSTICE SOTOMAYOR, concurring in the judgment.

Under our precedents, the primary purpose of the exclusionary rule is "to deter future Fourth Amendment violations." Accordingly, we have held, application of the exclusionary rule is unwarranted when it " 'does not result in appreciable deterrence.' " In the circumstances of this case, where "binding appellate precedent specifically *authorize[d]* a particular police practice"—in accord with the holdings of nearly every other court in the country—application of the exclusionary rule cannot reasonably be expected to yield appreciable deterrence. I am thus compelled to conclude that the exclusionary rule does not apply in this case and to agree with the Court's disposition.

This case does not present the markedly different question whether the exclusionary rule applies when the law governing the constitutionality of a particular search is unsettled. As we previously recognized * * * , when police decide to conduct a search or seizure in the absence of case law (or other authority) specifically sanctioning such action, exclusion of the evidence obtained may deter Fourth Amendment violations * * * . * * *

The dissent suggests that * * * an officer who conducts a search in the face of unsettled precedent "is no more culpable than an officer who follows erroneous 'binding precedent.' " The Court does not address this issue. In my view, whether an officer's conduct can be characterized as "culpable" is not itself dispositive. We have never refused to apply the exclusionary rule where its application would appreciably deter Fourth Amendment violations on the mere ground that the officer's conduct could be characterized as nonculpable. Rather, an officer's culpability is relevant because it may inform the overarching inquiry whether exclusion would result in appreciable deterrence. Whatever we have said about culpability, the ultimate questions have always been, one, whether exclusion would result in appreciable deterrence and, two, whether the benefits of exclusion outweigh its costs.

As stated, whether exclusion would result in appreciable deterrence in the circumstances of this case is a different question from whether exclusion would appreciably deter Fourth Amendment violations when the governing law is unsettled. The Court's answer to the former question in this case thus does not resolve the latter one.

JUSTICE BREYER, with whom JUSTICE GINSBURG joins, dissenting. * * *

I

I agree with the Court about *whether Gant*'s new rule applies. It does apply. * * *

II

The Court goes on, however, to decide *how Gant's* new rule will apply. And here it adds a fatal twist. While conceding that, like the search in *Gant,* this search violated the Fourth Amendment, it holds that, unlike Gant, this defendant is not entitled to a remedy. That is because the Court finds a new "good faith" exception which prevents application of the normal remedy for a Fourth Amendment violation, namely, suppression of the illegally seized evidence. Leaving Davis with a right but not a remedy, the Court "keep[s] the word of promise to our ear" but "break[s] it to our hope."

* * * [T]he Court's rationale for creating its new "good faith" exception threatens to undermine well-settled Fourth Amendment law. * * *

If the Court means what it says, what will happen to the exclusionary rule, a rule that the Court adopted nearly a century ago for federal courts, and made applicable to state courts a half century ago through the Fourteenth Amendment, *Mapp* v. *Ohio,* [p. 83]? The Court has thought of that rule not as punishment for the individual officer or as reparation for the individual defendant but more generally as an effective way to secure enforcement of the Fourth Amendment's commands. This Court has deviated from the "suppression" norm in the name of "good faith" only a handful of times and in limited, atypical circumstances * * * .

The fact that such exceptions are few and far between is understandable. Defendants frequently move to suppress evidence on Fourth Amendment grounds. In many, perhaps most, of these instances the police, uncertain of how the Fourth Amendment applied to the particular factual circumstances they faced, will have acted in objective good faith. Yet, in a significant percentage of these instances, courts will find that the police were wrong. And, unless the police conduct falls into one of the exceptions previously noted, courts have required the suppression of the evidence seized.

But an officer who conducts a search that he believes complies with the Constitution but which, it ultimately turns out, falls just outside the Fourth Amendment's bounds is no more culpable than an officer who follows erroneous "binding precedent." Nor is an officer more culpable where circuit precedent is simply suggestive rather than "binding," where it only describes how to treat roughly analogous instances, or where it just does not exist. Thus, if the Court means what it now says, if it would place determinative weight upon the culpability of an individual officer's conduct, and if it would apply the exclusionary rule only where a Fourth Amendment violation was "deliberate, reckless, or grossly negligent," then the "good faith" exception will swallow the exclusionary rule. Indeed, our broad dicta in *Herring*—dicta the Court repeats and expands upon today—may already be leading lower courts in this direction. Today's decision will doubtless accelerate this trend.

Any such change (which may already be underway) would affect not "an exceedingly small set of cases," but a very large number of cases, potentially many thousands each year. And since the exclusionary rule is often the only sanction available for a Fourth Amendment violation, the Fourth Amendment would no longer protect ordinary Americans from "unreasonable searches and seizures." It would become a watered-down Fourth Amendment, offering its protection against only those searches and seizures that are *egregiously* unreasonable.

III

In sum, I fear that the Court's opinion will undermine the exclusionary rule. * * *

For these reasons, with respect, I dissent.

NOTES AND QUESTIONS

1.   Precisely, what is the holding of *Davis*?

2.   With what level of culpability did the arresting officers here conduct the warrantless search of the automobile?

3.   Justice Breyer stated that the majority in *Davis* did not just repeat the "broad dicta in *Herring*" but "expand[ed] upon" it. Is that true? If so, how does *Davis* expand on *Herring*?

4.   Consider again *Kyllo v. United States* (p. 135), where the police, on the street, beamed a "thermal imager" at a house in order to determine if it was emitting unusual levels of heat consistent with indoor marijuana growing. The information secured in that procedure was used to obtain a search warrant. The Court held, 5–4, that this constituted a search and, under the circumstances of the case, an improper intrusion on Kyllo's rights. If the case had arisen for the first time today rather than in 2001, would the evidence unconstitutionally seized in *Kyllo* be admissible?

What if the police conduct a warrantless search of your home because they believe they have probable cause to search it for weapons and that an exigency justifies the warrantless entry. The police don't find what they are looking for, but they do discover a small quantity of illegal drugs. Later, at a suppression hearing, a magistrate determines that the police lacked probable cause to search your home and that the facts available to the officers did not justify their belief that an exigency existed. After *Davis*, would the drugs be inadmissible at your trial?

5.   *Problem. H* challenged the introduction of evidence at his trial, obtained as a result of an arrest, pursuant to three misdemeanor arrest warrants. Here are the facts regarding the arrest warrants, as described by the Ohio Supreme Court, in State v. Hoffman, 25 N.E.3d 993 (Ohio 2014):

The deputy clerk who signed and issued the three arrest warrants had been employed by the Toledo Municipal Court for 17 years. She testified that when an officer came in for a warrant, she would verify that the complaint included the offender's correct name and address, the violation codes, the charge, the offense classification, the date of the offense, a description of the offense, and the signature of the officer. But she also stated that she never asked an officer any questions. With regard to the warrants issued against Hoffman, the deputy clerk specifically testified that she did not make a probable-cause determination. When asked if she knew what probable cause is, she said, "no, I don't." She denied that it was part of her job responsibility to make a finding of probable cause. She simply gave the officer the oath, issued the warrants, and placed them into the computer system.

It appears that, in 2000, an Ohio lower court had upheld an arrest warrant under similar factual circumstances in a one-paragraph analysis. The Ohio Supreme Court in that case declined to accept jurisdiction of the petitioner's appeal.

Based on everything you have learned to this moment, should the evidence seized in *Hoffman* be excluded from his trial?

6.   Consider where we have been and where we are now. For a long period of this nation's history, there was no remedy available to an individual who asserted that his "person, house, paper, or effects" were the subject of an unreasonable search of seizure. In the twentieth century, however, with the Supreme Court's rulings in Weeks v. United States (p. 76) and Mapp v. Ohio (p. 83), the Fourth Amendment exclusionary rule was recognized in the federal (*Weeks*) and, later, state (*Mapp*) courts.

Notice, as well, that the *Weeks-Mapp* rule was strict in its nature. It was essentially a strict liability rule: if a law enforcement agent violated the Fourth Amendment rights of a person, *even inadvertently*, the evidence obtained as a result of that violation (and subsequent, causally linked, tainted fruits thereof) was inadmissible in the prosecutor's case-in-chief.

What is the scope of the rule now? Do you believe the narrower or broader version of the rule is preferable, and why?

7.   *Where do we go now?* If the *Mapp* exclusionary rule in its robust form is no more, it is worth thinking about alternatives to the rule as it presently exists. Justice Scalia, in dictum, mused on the possibility of resolving Fourth Amendment violations through civil litigation, but there are obstacles to this approach (p. 567, Note 4). Can you think of any other remedy that would deter police misconduct at least as well as the exclusionary rule?

On a comparative note, Section 8 of the Canadian Charter of Rights and Freedoms provides that "[e]veryone has a right to be secure against unreasonable search or seizure." Unlike our Constitution, however, the

Canadian charter expressly recognizes a general exclusionary rule. Section 24 of the Charter provides that

> [w]here * * * a court concludes that evidence was obtained in a manner that infringed or denied any rights or freedoms guaranteed by this Charter, the evidence shall be excluded if it is established that, having regard to all of the circumstances, the admission of it in the proceedings would bring the administration of justice into disrepute.

What does "bring[ing] the administration of justice into disrepute" mean? Essentially it is linked to the concept of judicial integrity: "to exclude any evidence whose admission might be seen as judicially condoning a 'serious' violation of Canada's Charter." Apparently, the "seriousness" of the violation depends on whether it was deliberate or inadvertent. Craig M. Bradley, *Reconceiving the Fourth Amendment and the Exclusionary Rule*, 73 Law & Contemp. Probs. 211, 217 (2010).

In England and Wales, judges have discretion to exclude evidence if admitting it would make the proceedings unfair. The House of Lords, however, has not developed a body of search-and-seizure case law, nor guidelines for exclusion. *Id.* at 220–21.

In New Zealand, as a result of a 2002 court decision, "[e]vidence is now excluded * * * only if the exclusion is held to be a proportional remedial response to the breach of the Bill of Rights at issue in the case. In order to make that determination, judges have to settle on what best serves the due administration of justice." Scott Optican, *Lessons From Down Under: A Dialogue on Police Search and Seizure in New Zealand and the United States*, 3 Ohio St. J. Crim. L. 257, 269 (2005). New Zealand courts balance various factors, including the nature of the violation, the seriousness of the crime allegedly committed by the defendant, and the importance of the evidence to the prosecutor's case. *Id.* at 269–70.

CHAPTER 6

CONFESSIONS: THE VOLUNTARINESS REQUIREMENT

■ ■ ■

A. TORTURE AND CONFESSIONS

HECTOR (A SLAVE) V. STATE
Supreme Court of Missouri, 1829.
2 Mo. 166.

M'GIRK, C.J. * * *

* * * A part of the testimony was, that about half past ten o'clock at night, when the burglary was discovered, certain persons caught Hector and began to flog him to make him confess what he knew concerning the burglary and stealing of the money * * * . That they continued flogging all night, that he screamed under the lash, and said if they would release him he would find the money. The State then examined one McKinney, who said, that about day break he was awakened by a loud hollowing or screaming in the rear of his house; that he arose, and on inquiry was informed by some persons there, near his house, that certain persons were flogging the slave Hector, to compel him to discover [to reveal his crime; eds.]. That when Hector heard the witness' voice he called on him to come to his assistance; that then the witness went to Hector, and told him if he took the money he ought to confess, and then asked Hector if he took the money. That Hector replied that he took the money, and that he would show the witness where it was, but that he did not wish the persons who had been flogging him to accompany him. * * * [T]hen Hector, the witness, and the other persons, went to the house of Mr. Menard [Hector's master] and did not find any money. That witness conceiving that Hector had deceived him, gave him several lashes with a cowskin, and then left him.

The prisoner's counsel then moved the court to exclude McKinney's testimony from the jury, on the ground that the confession of Hector was not freely and voluntarily made, but extorted by pain, & c., which motion the court overruled; and the prisoner's counsel also prayed the court to exclude from the consideration of the jury, all the confessions which were extorted from him, which the court refused.

But instructed the jury that they should exclude from their consideration any confession made by Hector under the influence of torture or pain, or hope or fear, but that the confessions of the defendant, which, in their opinion, was given freely and voluntarily, should be taken as good evidence against the prisoner, which instruction was objected to, & c.

The first question to be considered is, did the court err in refusing to exclude the testimony of McKinney from the jury? I think in this the court did err. Hector had been under the lash the greatest part of the night. This circumstance might of itself be sufficient to subdue him into any confession required. No doubt when he saw McKinney he hoped for some relief, and asked him for it, but he was told that if he was guilty he should confess, and then was asked if he took the money, to which he replied he had taken it and offered to show where it was. This all might have been done, and most probably was, to gain a respite from pain; which view of the subject is strengthened by the fact that no money was found where the party and prisoner went to look for it.

The court erred in instructing the jury that all the confessions, freely and voluntarily made, were evidence. And those not of this character not evidence. Whether a confession is sufficiently free and voluntary to be competent testimony, is a matter of law to be decided by the court and not by the jury. In this case there was another confession other than that made to McKinney that he took the money, which I consider made under the influence of pain, which should by the court have been excluded from the consideration of the jury.

BROWN V. MISSISSIPPI

Supreme Court of the United States, 1936.
297 U.S. 278, 56 S.Ct. 461, 80 L.Ed. 682.

Brown begins on p. 14.

NOTES AND QUESTIONS

1.   Is the misconduct more heinous in *Brown* than in *Hector* because the torture in *Brown* was at least in part authorized and conducted by law enforcement officers sworn to keep the peace? Leaving aside the source of the misconduct, is the coercion more severe in *Brown* than in *Hector*? If your answer is that the coercion is either more severe or the same in *Brown*, notice a curious, and very sad, fact.

Hector and *Brown* were separated by a century and the Civil War, the bloodiest war in our history. Hector won his case in the courts of a slave state. Brown lost his case in state court seventy years after slavery was abolished. It seems that things had not changed all that much in Mississippi. What had changed, of course, was that the Thirteenth, Fourteenth, and

Fifteenth Amendments created legal tools to fight deep-seated racism. The Supreme Court in *Brown* relied on the due process clause of the Fourteenth Amendment to reverse the convictions and prevent the hanging of three probably innocent black defendants.

2.   Would you be even a bit more inclined to admit Hector's confession if the money had been found where Hector said it was?

If the reliability of Hector's confession does not matter in finding the confession inadmissible, then what is the rationale behind suppression? Is it the likelihood that some people might confess falsely even if a particular suspect did not? Or is the problem with the confession purely the means used to obtain it, without regard to whether a person in Hector's situation might confess falsely?

3.   Canvassing the authorities generally, John Henry Wigmore had no doubt that this kind of confession was inadmissible. 2 John Henry Wigmore, A Treatise on Evidence 159, § 833 (2d ed. 1923) (citing eight cases from 1829–1863). For more detail on how the law in slave cases generally tracked that of the law in cases involving whites, see Mark V. Tushnet, The American Law of Slavery: 1810–1860 (1981). At one point, Tushnet concludes that Southern courts "may have wished to relax various technicalities in slave cases, but they ran the risk that elimination of concern for technicality in slave cases would reflect back onto cases involving whites, which formed part of the permissible range of analogy." *Id.* at 122.

4.   *Is torture ever justified?* If one uses a purely utilitarian calculus, perhaps there are no limits on what can be done to obtain information if it would save more lives than it costs. This is the perhaps hackneyed "ticking time bomb" argument. If one is willing to use torture to save an entire city from destruction, or to find a kidnapping victim who is about to die, then why not use it to save those threatened by a bomb in a railroad station. Before insurgents in Sri Lanka were apparently defeated in 2009, they had waged a terror war on the country's democratically-elected government for twenty-five years. In 2002, *Atlantic Monthly* writer Bruce Hoffman interviewed a "battle hardened Sri Lankan army officer charged with fighting the [terrorists] and protecting the lives" of innocent Sri Lankans. The officer described a "code red" when intelligence indicated a pending terrorist attack against public places. Three terrorist suspects were in custody, suspected of having planted a bomb in the city. The officer asked for the location of the bomb, but the terrorists remained silent. The officer said he would kill them if they did not tell the location of the bomb. When they remained silent, he

> took his pistol from his gun belt, pointed it at the forehead of one of them, and shot him dead. The other two, he said, talked immediately; the bomb, which had been placed in a crowded railway station and set to explode during the evening rush hour, was found and defused, and countless lives were saved.

Bruce Hoffman, *A Nasty Business*, The Atlantic Monthly, January 2002, at 52. The officer "hadn't exulted in his explanation or revealed any joy or even a hint of pleasure in what he had to do."

5. The Sri Lankan officer in Note 4 assumed that threats or coercive interrogation techniques are often successful in producing the truth. There is at least considerable reason to doubt this assumption. Special agent Ali Soufan was involved in some of the early interrogations of al-Qaeda detainees after 9/11. Soufan claims that the use of nonthreatening techniques can confuse detainees and lead them to cooperate. "[E]ngaging and outwitting" detainees often proves more productive than coercion. Ali H. Soufan, The Black Banners 423 (2011). "Cruel interrogation techniques not only serve to reinforce what a terrorist has been prepared to expect if captured; they give him a greater sense of control and predictability about his experience, and strengthen his resistance."

Soufan gives as an example the interrogation of Abu Zubaydah, the first "high profile" detainee captured after 9/11. By befriending Abu Zubaydah and making him believe that Soufan knew about his friendship with Khalid Sheik Mohammed, Soufan got information that led to the thwarting of another attack. *Id.* at 387. The interrogation was "celebrated as a major breakthrough in Washington." *Id.* at 389. But shortly after that, the CIA turned the interrogations over to "contractors" hired specially to obtain information from the detainees. One of the contractors was Boris, a psychologist who believed that the detainees could be broken by using increasingly harsher techniques. In Soufan's view, these methods were counter-productive.

> Boris had to keep introducing harsher and harsher methods, because Abu Zubaydah and other terrorists were trained to resist them. In a democracy such as ours, there is a glass ceiling on harsh techniques that the interrogator cannot breach, so a detainee can eventually call the interrogator's bluff. And that's what Abu Zubaydah did.
>
> This is why the [harsh interrogation] proponents had to order Abu Zubaydah to be waterboarded again, and again, and again—at least eighty-three times, reportedly. The techniques were in many ways a self-fulfilling prophecy, ensuring that harsher and harsher ones were introduced.

Id. at 423.

6. *Ticking time bombs.* Sherry Colb has argued that the use of torture in the ticking time bomb situation presents a question of moral uniqueness that can be distinguished from the use of force in self defense. She identifies three conditions that must exist to justify the use of violence in either situation. The one that is always met in cases of self-defense but may, or may not, be met in the time bomb case is that there be a close link between the status of the target as a wrongdoer and the efficacy of the violence against

him in saving life or limb. In some cases, the target of the torture may be innocent but nonetheless possesses information that could be used to save lives. See Sherry F. Colb, *Why Is Torture "Different" and How "Different" Is It?*, 30 Cardozo L. Rev. 1411 (2009).

7.   *Torture warrants*. Noted civil libertarian and Harvard law professor Alan Dershowitz appeared on *60 Minutes* on January 20, 2002, to make a startling recommendation: The law should authorize torture warrants for the ticking bomb cases. Mike Wallace looked stunned and said that "sounds medieval." Dershowitz responded that torture should be brought "into the legal system so that we can control it" rather than pretending it is not happening and winking our approval when it does. For Dershowitz, the issue is not torture or no torture. "If you've got the ticking time bomb case, the case of the terrorist who knew precisely where and when the bomb would go off, and it was the only way of saving 500 or 1,000 lives, every democratic society would, has, and will use torture."

Torture warrants have a venerable history in English law. Torture to obtain confessions was unknown in England before 1540 (guess who was king) and then it required a warrant issued by the Privy Council. Luckily for historians, the English are good record-keepers and many of those warrants have survived. John Langbein found eighty-one Privy Council torture warrants, or an average of fewer than one per year. Unsurprisingly, for the most part they were issued in treason cases where the survival of the monarch was at risk. See John H. Langbein, Torture and the Law of Proof: Europe and England in the Ancien Regime (2006 edition) 94–123 (Table of Warrants).

What are the constitutional issues of reviving torture warrants?

"It's not against the Fifth Amendment if it's not admitted in a criminal case against the defendant," Dershowitz said. [Dershowitz was quite the prophet. A year later, in a splintered opinion, five justices said almost what Dershowitz said. See *Chavez v. Martinez*, Note 7, p. 613. Eds.] As for due process, "The process that an alleged terrorist who was planning to kill thousands of people may be due is very different from the process that an ordinary criminal may be due."

Do you agree with Dershowitz's proposal? Why or why not?

8.   Much of the discussion so far is utilitarian in cast. But there is another, perhaps more fundamental, rationale for suppressing the confessions in *Brown* and *Hector*—it is wrong, as a matter of morality or Kantian principles, to force someone to condemn himself. This rationale informs President Obama's position against torture. "I was clear throughout this campaign and was clear throughout this transition that under my administration the United States does not torture," Obama said, when asked at the news conference whether he would continue the Bush administration's policy of harsh interrogation. "We will abide by the Geneva Conventions. We will uphold our highest ideals." Associated Press, January 9, 2009, *Obama*

names intel picks, vows no torture, available at http://www.msnbc.msn.com/id/ 28574408.

9.   *And what of God's coercion?* In Colorado v. Connelly, 479 U.S. 157, 107 S.Ct. 515, 93 L.Ed.2d 473 (1986), Connelly approached a Denver police officer on the street and confessed to an unsolved murder. Connelly was suffering from chronic schizophrenia, including command hallucinations. One of his hallucinations involved the "voice of God" that "instructed [him] to withdraw money from the bank, to buy an airplane ticket, and to fly from Boston to Denver." When Connelly "arrived from Boston, God's voice became stronger and told [him] either to confess to the killing or to commit suicide. Reluctantly following the command of the voices," Connelly approached a police officer and confessed.

There was no dispute that Connelly confessed to the crime because he thought he had the grisly choice of confessing to murder or committing suicide. Did that make the confession involuntary? Focusing on the lack of state action, the Court held that the confession was, for purposes of the due process clause, voluntary.

> Our "involuntary confession" jurisprudence is entirely consistent with the settled law requiring some sort of "state action" to support a claim of violation of the Due Process Clause of the Fourteenth Amendment. The Colorado trial court, of course, found that the police committed no wrongful acts, and that finding has been neither challenged by respondent nor disturbed by the Supreme Court of Colorado. The latter court, however, concluded that sufficient state action was present by virtue of the admission of the confession into evidence in a court of the State.
>
> The difficulty with the approach of the Supreme Court of Colorado is that it fails to recognize the essential link between coercive activity of the State, on the one hand, and a resulting confession by a defendant, on the other. The flaw in respondent's constitutional argument is that it would expand our previous line of "voluntariness" cases into a far-ranging requirement that courts must divine a defendant's motivation for speaking or acting as he did even though there be no claim that governmental conduct coerced his decision.
>
> The most outrageous behavior by a private party seeking to secure evidence against a defendant does not make that evidence inadmissible under the Due Process Clause. We have also observed that "[j]urists and scholars uniformly have recognized that the exclusionary rule imposes a substantial cost on the societal interest in law enforcement by its proscription of what concededly is relevant evidence." Moreover, suppressing respondent's statements would serve absolutely no purpose in enforcing constitutional guarantees. The purpose of excluding evidence seized in violation of the Constitution is to substantially deter future violations of the

Constitution. Only if we were to establish a brand new constitutional right—the right of a criminal defendant to confess to his crime only when totally rational and properly motivated—could respondent's present claim be sustained.

10. *The implications of Connelly.* A neighborhood watch, with no connections to the local police or prosecutors, apprehended a man believed to be fleeing from an attempted rape. He refused to answer their questions, and the watch members began to torture him. When the pain became unbearable, he confessed to trying to force the victim to have sex with him. Will any right in the Bill of Rights lead to exclusion of the confession?

Justice Brennan in his *Connelly* dissent contended that, state action or not, Connelly's confession was unreliable and his conviction, therefore, a violation of due process on that ground alone. The *Connelly* majority conceded that a "statement rendered by one in the condition of respondent might be proved to be quite unreliable, but this is a matter to be governed by the evidentiary laws of the forum." For the "back story" on *Connelly*, see William T. Pizzi, *Colorado v. Connelly: What Really Happened*, 7 Ohio St. J. Crim. L. 377 (2009).

B. POLICE INTERROGATION WITHOUT TORTURE

LISENBA V. CALIFORNIA

Supreme Court of the United States, 1941.
314 U.S. 219, 62 S.Ct. 280, 86 L.Ed. 166.

MR. JUSTICE ROBERTS delivered the opinion of the Court joined by CHIEF JUSTICE STONE, and JUSTICES REED, FRANKFURTER, MURPHY, BYRNES, and JACKSON]. * * *

The petitioner, who used, and was commonly known by, the name of Robert S. James (and will be so called), and one Hope were indicted May 6, 1936, for the murder of James' wife on August 5, 1935. Hope pleaded guilty and was sentenced to life imprisonment. James pleaded not guilty, was tried, convicted, and sentenced to death. * * *

The State's theory is that the petitioner conceived the plan of marrying, insuring his wife's life by policies providing double indemnity for accidental death, killing her in a manner to give the appearance of accident, and collecting double indemnity.

James employed Mary E. Busch as a manicurist in his barber shop in March, 1935, and, about a month later, went through a marriage ceremony with her, which was not legal, as he then had a living wife. While they were affianced, insurance was negotiated on her life, with James as beneficiary. Upon the annulment of the earlier marriage, a lawful ceremony was performed. The petitioner made sure that the policies were not annulled by the fact that, when they were issued, Mary had not been his lawful wife.

The allegation is that James enlisted one Hope in a conspiracy to do away with Mary and collect and divide the insurance on her life. Hope testified that, at James' instigation, he procured rattlesnakes which were to bite and kill Mary; that they appeared not to be sufficiently venomous for the purpose, but he ultimately purchased others and delivered them to James; that James, on August 4, 1935, blindfolded his wife's eyes, tied her to a table, had Hope bring one of the snakes into the room, and caused the reptile to bite her foot; that, during the night, James told Hope the bite did not have the desired effect, and, in the early morning of August 5, he told Hope that he was going to drown his wife; that later he said to Hope, "That is that"; and still later, at his request, Hope aided him in carrying the body to the yard, and James placed the body face down at the edge of a fish pond with the head and shoulders in the water.

James was at his barber shop on August 5. On that evening he took two friends home for dinner. When they arrived the house was dark and empty, and, upon a search of the grounds, his wife's body was found in the position indicated. An autopsy showed the lungs were almost filled with water. The left great toe showed a puncture and the left leg was greatly swollen and almost black. Nothing came of the investigation of the death.

James attempted to collect double indemnity; the insurers refused to pay; suits were instituted and one of them settled. As a result of this activity, a fresh investigation of Mary James' death was instituted. On April 19, 1936, officers arrested James for the crime of incest.[a] He was booked on this charge on the morning of April 21, was given a hearing and remanded to jail. On May 2 and 3 he made statements respecting his wife's death to the prosecuting officials.

At the trial, in addition to that of Hope, testimony was adduced as to the finding and condition of the body, other evidence to connect James with the death, and expert testimony that the condition of the left leg could be attributed to rattlesnake bites. The purchase of snakes by Hope was proved by him and several other witnesses, one of whom said he sold the two snakes to Hope, one of which, Hope claimed, had bitten Mary James. Two snakes were brought into court, which the witness identified as those sold to Hope and by Hope resold to the witness.

James' statements were offered in evidence. Objection was made that they were not voluntary. Before they were admitted the trial judge heard testimony offered by the State and the defendant on that issue. He ruled that the confessions were admissible, and they were received in evidence.

---

[a]   No evidence appears in the opinion as to the basis for the charge of incest. Eds.

The State offered evidence with respect to the death of a former wife of James, in 1932. This tended to prove that, while driving down Pike's Peak, their automobile went off the road. James went for aid. When the persons called upon reached the automobile they found James' wife lying partly outside the car with her head badly crushed and a bloody hammer in the back of the car. James appeared unhurt. The woman recovered from her injuries, but, shortly afterwards, was discovered by James and another man, drowned in the bathtub in a house James had temporarily leased at Colorado Springs. James collected double indemnity from insurance companies for her death, the insurance having been placed at about the time he married her and her death having occurred within a few months thereafter. * * *

* * * The important question is whether the use of the confessions rendered petitioner's conviction a deprivation of his life without due process of law. Recital of the relevant facts is essential to a decision.

The petitioner, while having almost no formal education, is a man of intelligence and business experience. After his arrest, on the charge of incest, on the morning of Sunday, April 19, 1936, he was taken for a short time to the adjoining house and shown a dictaphone there installed. He was brought to the District Attorney's offices, where he was lodged in the Bureau of Investigation. He says that during the two or three hours he stayed there he was not questioned. He was taken into an office where the District Attorney showed him a statement made by a Miss Wright respecting the incest charge and asked him what he cared to say about it. He replied that he would not talk about it. He was questioned for about an hour. He says he was asked about his wife's death; others who were present deny this.

He was held in the District Attorney's suite until 5 or 6 o'clock, was given supper at a café, and then conducted to the house next door to his home, where he arrived about 7 or 7:30. Various officers questioned him there, in relays throughout the night, concerning his wife's death. He sat in a chair fully dressed and had no sleep. Monday morning he was taken out for breakfast and went with the officers to point out to them a house at 9th and Alvarado Streets, after which he was taken to the District Attorney's offices. He was brought back to the house next door to his home, and the questioning was resumed, and continued until about 3 o'clock Tuesday morning when, he says, he fainted; and others present say he fell asleep and slept until 7 or 8 o'clock. After he had breakfasted he was booked at the jail, arraigned before a magistrate, and committed on the incest charge.

James testified that about 10 P.M. Monday, April 20, the officers began to beat him; that his body was made black and blue; that the beating impaired his hearing, and caused a hernia; that later that night an Assistant District Attorney questioned him and that, after this ordeal, he collapsed. It is admitted that an officer slapped his face that night. This is said to have occurred as the result of an offensive remark James made concerning his wife; he denies having made the remark. In corroboration of James' testimony two witnesses said they noticed that one or both of his ears were bruised and swollen when he was lodged in the jail. All of this testimony is contradicted by numerous witnesses for the State, save only that it is admitted James was repeatedly and persistently questioned at intervals during the period from Sunday night until Tuesday morning. It is testified that, except for the one slap, no one laid a hand on James; that no inducement was held out to him; that no threats were made; that he answered questions freely and intelligently; and that he was at ease, cool, and collected. He admits that no promises or threats were made or maltreatment administered on the occasions when he was in the District Attorney's office. It is significant that James stated to one of the other officers that Officer Southard had slapped him and that when, May 2, the District Attorney asked how he had been treated he again referred to the slap. In neither case did he say anything of any other mistreatment. During the period April 19–21 James made no incriminating admission or confession.

* * * It is not suggested that James was not allowed to see his attorney as often as he desired or that any obstacle was interposed to the attorney's interviewing him between April 21 and May 2.

There is no claim that from April 21, when he was lodged in the jail, until May 2, he was interviewed, questioned, threatened, or mistreated by anyone. During this period his attorney told him that he would be indicted for his wife's murder and should not answer any questions unless his attorney was present.

May 1, Hope was arrested and made a statement. On the morning of May 2, James was brought from his cell to the chaplain's room in the prison and confronted with Hope. An Assistant District Attorney outlined Hope's story and asked James whether he had anything to say, to which he replied: "Nothing."

He went back to his cell and, about noon, an order of court was obtained to remove him from the prison. He was taken to his former home by two deputy sheriffs. The evidence does not disclose clearly either the purpose or the incidents of this trip. He was then brought to the District Attorney's office and that official began to question him. He requested that his attorney be sent for. In his presence a telephone call was made which disclosed that Mr. Silverman was not in Los Angeles. He asked that another attorney be summoned. He states that the District Attorney said it would take too long to acquaint any other attorney with the facts; others say that James did not give the name of the other attorney he wanted and it took some time to discover whom he had in mind. The attorney was not summoned.

The District Attorney and, at times, others questioned James until supper time. Sandwiches and coffee were procured. James says he had coffee but someone took his sandwiches. There is testimony that he had them. The questioning, based on Hope's confession, was continued into the night without James having refused to answer questions or having made any incriminating answers.

There is a sharp conflict as to how the session terminated. James says that Officer Southard, who had struck him on April 20, occupied the room alone with him, all others having left; that the officer told him he had been lying all evening and that if he did not tell the truth the officer would take him back to the house and beat him; that this so frightened him that he agreed to do his best to recite to the District Attorney the same story Hope had told. There is much evidence that no such incident occurred. Deputy Sheriff Killion says that sometime before midnight the others had left petitioner alone with him and that petitioner turned to him and said something to the effect: "Why can't we go out and get something to eat; if we do I'll tell you the story." To this Killion replied that they could go out. Killion and another Deputy Sheriff, Gray, a lady friend, and another person accompanied petitioner to a public café, where they had a supper and afterwards had cigars. James testified that neither Killion nor Gray nor the District Attorney ever laid hand on him, threatened him or offered him any inducement to confess.

The State's evidence is that after they started to smoke, James told a story, of which Killion took notes. Killion narrated at the trial what James had told him. * * *

Hope's statement laid on James the initiation of the murder plot, the attempt to consummate it with snake poison, the drowning and the disposition of her body. The account James gave Killion and the District Attorney, which he now says was an attempt to retell the tale Hope had told, which had been constantly dinned into his ears, is by no means a reiteration of Hope's story. On the contrary, James insisted that Hope suggested the destruction of Mary James, and the rattlesnake expedient, which Hope carried out; that when this failed Hope suggested that he, Hope, burn down the house to make it appear that Mrs. James died by accident; and that Hope also volunteered to commit an abortion on Mrs. James and also to do away with her. James asserted that, while he was absent from his home on the morning of August 5, 1935, Hope drowned his wife in the bathtub and told James that he had done so.

It is also to be noted that James' statement presents a lurid picture of the heavy drinking and intoxication of Hope, James, and Mary James during the three days anterior to the death of the latter. The effort evidently was to suggest that all were more or less irresponsible for their actions.

If Hope's story is true, James planned and accomplished the murder of his wife to obtain the insurance on her life. If James' statement is true, Hope planned the murder, James desired to abandon the scheme and thought that all Hope ultimately intended to do was to commit an abortion on James' wife and was shocked and surprised to learn that Hope had murdered her.

James said during supper at the café, and stated on another occasion, that there were not enough men in the District Attorney's office to make him talk, and if Hope had not talked he would never have told the story.

Scrutiny of the two statements indicates that James carefully considered what Hope had said and made up his mind to tell a story consistent with his intimacy with Hope, and with various incidents James could not deny, and then depict a drunken orgy as a result of which his will power was so enfeebled that he could not resist Hope's determination to make away with Mrs. James.

At the trial James contradicted the essential particulars of Hope's testimony and most of his own confession, including the evidence respecting the snakes. He swore all Hope was to do was to attempt an abortion; he believed Hope did not accomplish this, and that his wife died as a result of falling into the pond in a fainting fit due to her pregnancy.

The evidence as to the treatment of James and the conduct of officials and officers, from the moment of his arrest until the close of his statement to the District Attorney, was heard preliminarily by the trial judge in order to determine whether the State had, as required by California law, carried its burden of proving the confessions voluntary. The ruling was that it had; and the confessions were admitted. The trial judge, at defendant's request, charged the jury, in accordance with the State law, that the confessions must be utterly disregarded unless they were voluntary, that is, not the result of inducements, promises, threats, violence, or any form of coercion.

The failure of the arresting officers promptly to produce the petitioner before an examining magistrate, their detention of him in their custody from Sunday morning to Tuesday morning, and any assault committed upon him, were violations of state statutes and criminal offenses.

We find no authority for the issue of the court order under which the sheriff's deputies took the accused from jail to his former home, and to the District Attorney's office for questioning. The denial of opportunity to consult counsel, requested on May 2nd, was a misdemeanor. It may be assumed this treatment of the petitioner also deprived him of his liberty without due process and that the petitioner would have been afforded preventive relief if he could have gained access to a court to seek it.

But illegal acts, as such, committed in the course of obtaining a confession, whatever their effect on its admissibility under local law, do not furnish an answer to the constitutional question we must decide. The effect of the officers' conduct must be appraised by other considerations in determining whether the use of the confessions was a denial of due process. Moreover, petitioner does not, and cannot, ask redress in this proceeding for any disregard of due process prior to his trial. The gravamen of his complaint is the unfairness of the use of his confessions, and what occurred in their procurement is relevant only as it bears on that issue.

On the other hand, the fact that the confessions have been conclusively adjudged by the decision below to be admissible under State law, notwithstanding the circumstances under which they were made, does not answer the question whether due process was lacking. The aim of the rule that a confession is inadmissible unless it was voluntarily made is to exclude false evidence. Tests are invoked to determine whether the inducement to speak was such that there is a fair risk the confession is false.[14] These vary in the several States. This Court has formulated those which are to govern in trials in the federal courts. The Fourteenth Amendment leaves California free to adopt, by statute or decision, and to enforce, such rule as she elects, whether it conform to that applied in the federal or in other state courts. But the adoption of the rule of her choice cannot foreclose inquiry as to whether, in a given case, the application of that rule works a deprivation of the prisoner's life or liberty without due process of law. The aim of the requirement of due process is not to exclude presumptively false evidence, but to prevent fundamental unfairness in the use of evidence whether true or false. The criteria for decision of that question may differ from those appertaining to the State's rule as to the admissibility of a confession.

As applied to a criminal trial, denial of due process is the failure to observe that fundamental fairness essential to the very concept of justice. In order to declare a denial of it we must find that the absence of that fairness fatally infected the trial; the acts complained of must be of such quality as necessarily prevents a fair trial. Such unfairness exists when a coerced confession is used as a means of obtaining a verdict of guilt. We have so held in every instance in which we have set aside for want of due process a conviction based on a confession.

To extort testimony from a defendant by physical torture in the very presence of the trial tribunal is not due process. The case stands no better

---

[14] Wigmore, Evidence, 3rd Ed., §§ 823, 824.

if torture induces an extrajudicial confession which is used as evidence in the courtroom. * * *

The concept of due process would void a trial in which, by threats or promises in the presence of court and jury, a defendant was induced to testify against himself. The case can stand no better if, by resort to the same means, the defendant is induced to confess and his confession is given in evidence. As we have said, "due process of law * * * commands that no such practice * * * shall send any accused to his death."

Where the claim is that the prisoner's statement has been procured by such means, we are bound to make an independent examination of the record to determine the validity of the claim. The performance of this duty cannot be foreclosed by the finding of a court, or the verdict of a jury, or both. * * *

There are cases, such as this one, where the evidence as to the methods employed to obtain a confession is conflicting, and in which, although denial of due process was not an issue in the trial, an issue has been resolved by court and jury, which involves an answer to the due process question. In such a case, we accept the determination of the triers of fact, unless it is so lacking in support in the evidence that to give it effect would work that fundamental unfairness which is at war with due process. * * *

In view of the conflicting testimony, we are unable to say that the finding below was erroneous so far as concerns the petitioner's claims of physical violence, threats, or implied promises of leniency. There remains the uncontradicted fact that on two occasions, separated by an interval of eleven days, the petitioner was questioned for protracted periods. He made no admission implicating him in his wife's death during, or soon after, the interrogations of April 19, 20, and 21. If, without more, eleven days later, confessions had been forthcoming we should have no hesitation in overruling his contention respecting the admission of his confessions.

Does the questioning on May 2nd, in and of itself, or in the light of his earlier experience, render the use of the confessions a violation of due process? If we are so to hold it must be upon the ground that such a practice, irrespective of the result upon the petitioner, so tainted his statements that, without considering other facts disclosed by the evidence, and without giving weight to accredited findings below that his statements were free and voluntary, as a matter of law, they were inadmissible in his trial. This would be to impose upon the state courts a stricter rule than we have enforced in federal trials. There is less reason for such a holding when we reflect that we are dealing with the system of criminal administration of California, a quasi-sovereign; that if federal power is invoked to set aside what California regards as a fair trial, it must be plain that a federal right has been invaded.

We have not hesitated to set aside convictions based in whole, or in substantial part, upon confessions extorted in graver circumstances. These were secured by protracted and repeated questioning of ignorant and untutored persons, in whose minds the power of officers was greatly magnified; who sensed the adverse sentiment of the community and the danger of mob violence; who had been held incommunicado, without the advice of friends or of counsel; some of whom had been taken by officers at night from the prison into dark and lonely places for questioning. This case is outside the scope of those decisions.

Like the Supreme Court of California, we disapprove the violations of law involved in the treatment of the petitioner, and we think it right to add that where a prisoner, held incommunicado, is subjected to questioning by officers for long periods, and deprived of the advice of counsel, we shall scrutinize the record with care to determine whether, by the use of his confession, he is deprived of liberty or life through tyrannical or oppressive means. Officers of the law must realize that if they indulge in such practices they may, in the end, defeat rather than further the ends of justice. Their lawless practices here took them close to the line. But on the facts as we have endeavored fairly to set them forth, and in the light of the findings in the state courts, we cannot hold that the illegal conduct in which the law enforcement officers of California indulged, by the prolonged questioning of the prisoner before arraignment, and in the absence of counsel, or their questioning on May 2, coerced the confessions, the introduction of which is the infringement of due process of which the petitioner complains. The petitioner has said that the interrogation would never have drawn an admission from him had his confederate not made a statement; he admits that no threats, promises, or acts of physical violence were offered him during this questioning or for eleven days preceding it. Counsel had been afforded full opportunity to see him and had advised him. He exhibited a self-possession, a coolness, and an acumen throughout his questioning, and at his trial, which negatives the view that he had so lost his freedom of action that the statements made were not his but were the result of the deprivation of his free choice to admit, to deny, or to refuse to answer.
* * *

MR. JUSTICE BLACK, dissenting, with whom MR. JUSTICE DOUGLAS concurs.

I believe the confession used to convict James was the result of coercion and compulsion, and that the judgment should be reversed for that reason. The testimony of the officers to whom the confession was given is enough, standing alone, to convince me that it could not have been free and voluntary. * * *

NOTES AND QUESTIONS

1.   What violations of law did the state authorities commit in their treatment of the defendant? The Court concedes that these violations deprived James of due process of law and yet still affirmed his convictions. What role does the Court's concern with federalism play in its reasoning process?

2.   John Henry Wigmore, perhaps America's greatest evidence scholar, identified three possible tests for deciding when to suppress confessions.

> (1) The first is, Was the inducement of a nature calculated under the circumstances to induce a confession irrespective of its truth or falsity? (2) Another is, Was there a threat or a promise, a fear or a hope? (3) The third test, Was the confession voluntary? is practically colorless and unserviceable when the nature of the inducement is in the question, and is almost always translated secondarily, before application, into terms of one of the other two tests.

2 John Henry Wigmore, A Treatise on Evidence, § 831, pp. 154–55 (2d ed. 1923).

Wigmore gave as an example of the "unserviceable" nature of the voluntariness test: "As between the rack and a false confession, the latter would usually be considered the less disagreeable; but it is nonetheless voluntarily chosen." *Id.* at § 824, p. 145. The point is that all conscious choices are, in some sense, voluntary.

Aristotle saw the same problem over two thousand years earlier:

> Some acts are performed out of fear of greater evils or for some good thing. * * * This is the case with throwing cargo overboard in storms. In general, no one willingly throws things overboard; but all people of sense do so to save their own lives and those of other people. These actions are mixed, but they are more like voluntary acts. We choose or decide to do them at the time they are carried out, and the end or goal of the act is fitted to the occasion. * * * Such acts, then, are voluntary; but perhaps in a general way they are involuntary, since no one would choose any such act of itself.

Aristotle, *Ethics*, Book III § 1 (A. E. Wardman & J. L. Creed, trans. 1963).

Here is Professor Albert Alschuler's response to Aristotle's anguish over determining which acts are voluntary:

> Country lawyers are often better philosophers than philosophers are. Most lawyers have known for a long time that the term coercion cannot be defined, that judges place this label on results for many diverse reasons, and that the word coercion metamorphoses

remarkably with the factual circumstances in which legal actors press it into service.

Albert W. Alschuler, *Constraint and Confession*, 74 Den. U. L. Rev. 957 (1997).

Accepting the Wigmore-Aristotle-Alschuler skepticism about the definition of voluntariness, one is left with the question of whether courts should admit the confession.

Wigmore thought the only legitimate inquiry was:

> Human nature being what it is, *were the prospects attending confession* (involving the equalization or averaging of the benefit of realizing the promise or the benefit of escaping from the threat, against the drawbacks moral and legal of furnishing damaging evidence), *as weighed at the time against the prospects attending non-confession* (involving a similar averaging), *such as to have created, in any considerable degree, a risk that a false confession would be made?* Putting it more briefly and roughly, Was the inducement such that there was any fair risk of a false confession?

Id. at § 824, pp. 145–46 (emphasis in original).

3.   Using Wigmore's test, do you have reservations about the outcome of *Lisenba*—that is, did the police interrogation create a "fair risk" that the confession was false?

Using whatever due process test you think appropriate, do you agree with the *Lisenba* Court that James's confession is admissible? If not, how would you articulate the due process interest of the suspect that was violated? Is it relevant that James did not confess until confronted with Hope's statement that James had "planned and accomplished the murder of his wife to obtain the insurance"? Is it relevant that James did not "confess" in the full sense of taking all responsibility but sought, instead, to shift a large measure of the blame to Hope? Why might these facts be relevant to voluntariness?

4.   The English common law of evidence waxed and waned on the issue of admissibility of out-of-court statements. Justices of the peace were required, beginning in 1554, to examine those accused of a crime and make any statements available to the prosecutor for use at trial. Yet the earliest mention of any concern about those examinations does not appear in the English treatises until 1736. Hale's *Pleas of the Crown* cautions the justices to testify at trial that the prisoner confessed to them "freely and without any menace, or undue terror imposed upon him." 2 Matthew Hale, The History of the Pleas of the Crown 284 (1736).

Michael Foster's 1762 *Crown Pleas* noted that, in treason cases, "hasty Confessions made to Persons having no Authority to examine, are the Weakest and most Suspicious of All Evidence. Proof may be too easily procured, Words are often Mis-reported, whether through Ignorance, Inattention, or Malice, it mattereth not the Defendant * * * ."

Sir William Blackstone prepared eight editions of his *Commentaries on the Law of England*, probably the most influential treatise on English law. The first was published in 1765, two decades after Hale's treatise appeared, but it contains no concern about confessions beyond Parliament's 1547 ban on coercion in treason cases. Indeed, no additional concern appears until the eighth edition, published in 1778. A new insertion into the section about treason suddenly expresses profound skepticism. Tracking Foster, but expanding the concern beyond treason cases, Blackstone noted that out-of-court statements "are the weakest and most suspicious of all testimony; ever liable to be obtained by artifice, false hopes, promises of favour, or menaces; seldom remembered accurately, or reported with due precision; and incapable in their nature of being disproved by other negative evidence." 4 W. Blackstone, Commentaries 357 (8th ed. 1778). For a detailed treatment of English interrogation law from the thirteenth century through the end of the nineteenth century, see George C. Thomas III & Richard A. Leo, Confessions of Guilt: From Torture to Miranda and Beyond (2012).

Blackstone's skepticism about confessions manifests more than one rationale. Part of the concern is with reliability of the evidence ("seldom remembered accurately, or reported with due precision"). Concern about "menaces," and "false hopes [and] promises of favor," also suggests a reliability rationale. But it is not clear how a confession taken by "artifice" is unreliable. If police falsely tell a suspect that his fingerprints were found at the scene of the crime, this artifice would likely work only on suspects who are guilty. Indeed, police themselves acknowledge that lying about the evidence is a high-risk game; if the suspect knows he wasn't there (but his confederate was) or was there but wore gloves, he will see the falsehood and realize that the police need a confession. This awareness should stiffen his resolve not to confess.

Another rationale is needed to explain the common law concern with "artifice." One rationale might be called "mental freedom"—recognizing that even guilty suspects still retain their dignity and status as human beings, the State should not deprive them of the "mental freedom" to decide whether to confess. *Lisenba* seems to recognize this component of due process at the end of the opinion when it considered whether James had so lost "his freedom of action that the statements made were not his but were the result of the deprivation of his free choice to admit, to deny, or to refuse to answer." Some pressure to confess might fall short of coercion and still deny sufficient "mental freedom."

At least some trickery is also inconsistent with mental freedom. Consider the highly religious suspect who confesses to a "priest" who is a police detective. The confession is non-coerced and reliable (what highly religious person would falsely tell a priest that he had committed a crime?). Yet it was not made with the mental freedom to decide to confess to the police. You will see the mental freedom rationale in a highly-developed state in *Miranda*, p. 625.

Three rationales for suppressing confessions thus overlap and intertwine into an analytical stew: (1) to prevent unreliable evidence from reaching the jury; (2) to use only statements taken without overbearing police pressure; (3) to prove guilt only with statements that manifest a minimal level of mental freedom, whether or not police applied overbearing pressure. The Court has a more respectful term for its voluntariness inquiry than "analytical stew," noting that "a complex of values underlies the stricture against use by the state of confessions which, by way of convenient shorthand, this Court terms involuntary." Blackburn v. Alabama, 361 U.S. 199, 80 S.Ct. 274, 4 L.Ed.2d 242 (1960). "Complex" is a good word for the Court's involuntariness doctrine. Perhaps the best attempt to explain the complexity is Joseph D. Grano, Confessions, Truth and the Law (1993).

SPANO V. NEW YORK

Supreme Court of the United States, 1959.
360 U.S. 315, 79 S.Ct. 1202, 3 L.Ed.2d 1265.

MR. CHIEF JUSTICE WARREN delivered the opinion of the Court [joined by JUSTICES BLACK, FRANKFURTER, DOUGLAS, CLARK, HARLAN, BRENNAN, WHITTAKER, and STEWART].

This is another in the long line of cases presenting the question whether a confession was properly admitted into evidence under the Fourteenth Amendment. As in all such cases, we are forced to resolve a conflict between two fundamental interests of society; its interest in prompt and efficient law enforcement, and its interest in preventing the rights of its individual members from being abridged by unconstitutional methods of law enforcement. Because of the delicate nature of the constitutional determination which we must make, we cannot escape the responsibility of making our own examination of the record.

The State's evidence reveals the following: Petitioner Vincent Joseph Spano is a derivative citizen of this country, having been born in Messina, Italy. He was 25 years old at the time of the shooting in question and had graduated from junior high school. He had a record of regular employment. The shooting took place on January 22, 1957.

On that day, petitioner was drinking in a bar. The decedent, a former professional boxer weighing almost 200 pounds who had fought in Madison Square Garden, took some of petitioner's money from the bar. Petitioner followed him out of the bar to recover it. A fight ensued, with the decedent knocking petitioner down and then kicking him in the head three or four times. Shock from the force of these blows caused petitioner to vomit. After the bartender applied some ice to his head, petitioner left the bar, walked to his apartment, secured a gun, and walked eight or nine blocks to a candy store where the decedent was frequently to be found. He entered the store in which decedent, three friends of decedent, at least two of whom were ex-convicts, and a boy who was supervising the store were present. He fired five shots, two of which entered the decedent's body, causing his death. The boy was the only eyewitness; the three friends of decedent did not see the person who fired the shot. Petitioner then disappeared for the next week or so.

On February 1, 1957, the Bronx County Grand Jury returned an indictment for first-degree murder against petitioner.[b] * * *

On February 3, 1957, petitioner called one Gaspar Bruno, a close friend of 8 or 10 years' standing who had attended school with him. Bruno was a fledgling police officer, having at that time not yet finished attending police academy. According to Bruno's testimony, petitioner told him "that he took a terrific beating, that the deceased hurt him real bad and he dropped him a couple of times and he was dazed; he didn't know what he was doing and that he went and shot at him." Petitioner told Bruno that he intended to get a lawyer and give himself up. Bruno relayed this information to his superiors.

The following day, February 4, at 7:10 p.m., petitioner, accompanied by counsel, surrendered himself to the authorities * * * . His attorney had cautioned him to answer no questions, and left him in the custody of the officers. He was promptly taken to the office of the Assistant District Attorney and at 7:15 p.m. the questioning began * * * . The record reveals that the questioning was both persistent and continuous. Petitioner, in accordance with his attorney's instructions, steadfastly refused to answer. * * * Detective Farrell testified [about Spano]:

"Q. What did he say?

"A. He said 'you would have to see my attorney. I tell you nothing but my name.' * * *

"Q. Did you continue to examine him?

"A. Verbally, yes, sir."

He asked one officer, Detective Ciccone, if he could speak to his attorney, but that request was denied. Detective Ciccone testified that he could not find the attorney's name in the telephone book.[1] He was given two sandwiches, coffee and cake at 11 p.m.

---

[b]   *Spano* was decided before *Massiah v. United States*, p. 755. Today, as the concurring opinions in *Spano* anticipate, this case would be decided as a Sixth Amendment case and Spano would win easily. Eds.

[1]   How this could be so when the attorney's name, Tobias Russo, was concededly in the telephone book does not appear. The trial judge sustained objections by the Assistant District Attorney to questions designed to delve into this mystery.

At 12:15 a.m. on the morning of February 5, after five hours of questioning in which it became evident that petitioner was following his attorney's instructions, on the Assistant District Attorney's orders petitioner was transferred to the 46th Squad, Ryer Avenue Police Station. The Assistant District Attorney also went to the police station and to some extent continued to participate in the interrogation. Petitioner arrived at 12:30 and questioning was resumed at 12:40. * * * But petitioner persisted in his refusal to answer, and again requested permission to see his attorney, this time from Detective Lehrer. His request was again denied.

It was then that those in charge of the investigation decided that petitioner's close friend, Bruno, could be of use. He had been called out on the case around 10 or 11 p.m., although he was not connected with the 46th Squad or Precinct in any way. Although, in fact, his job was in no way threatened, Bruno was told to tell petitioner that petitioner's telephone call had gotten him "in a lot of trouble," and that he should seek to extract sympathy from petitioner for Bruno's pregnant wife and three children. Bruno developed this theme with petitioner without success, and petitioner, also without success, again sought to see his attorney, a request which Bruno relayed unavailingly to his superiors. After this first session with petitioner, Bruno was again directed by Lt. Gannon to play on petitioner's sympathies, but again no confession was forthcoming. But the Lieutenant a third time ordered Bruno falsely to importune his friend to confess, but again petitioner clung to his attorney's advice. Inevitably, in the fourth such session directed by the Lieutenant, lasting a full hour, petitioner succumbed to his friend's prevarications and agreed to make a statement. * * *

* * * [T]he officers also elicited a statement from petitioner that the deceased was always "on [his] back," "always pushing" him and that he was "not sorry" he had shot the deceased. All three detectives testified to that statement at the trial. * * *

At the trial, the confession was introduced in evidence over appropriate objections. The jury was instructed that it could rely on it only if it was found to be voluntary. The jury returned a guilty verdict and petitioner was sentenced to death. * * *

The abhorrence of society to the use of involuntary confessions does not turn alone on their inherent untrustworthiness. It also turns on the deep-rooted feeling that the police must obey the law while enforcing the law; that in the end life and liberty can be as much endangered from illegal methods used to convict those thought to be criminals as from the actual criminals themselves. Accordingly, the actions of police in obtaining confessions have come under scrutiny in a long series of cases. Those cases suggest that in recent years law enforcement officials have become increasingly aware of the burden which they share, along with our courts, in protecting fundamental rights of our citizenry, including that portion of our citizenry suspected of crime. The facts of no case recently in this Court have quite approached the brutal beatings in *Brown v. Mississippi*, [p. 14], or the 36 consecutive hours of questioning present in *Ashcraft v. State of Tennessee*, 322 U.S. 143, 64 S.Ct. 921, 88 L.Ed. 1192 (1944). But as law enforcement officers become more responsible, and the methods used to extract confessions more sophisticated, our duty to enforce federal constitutional protections does not cease. It only becomes more difficult because of the more delicate judgments to be made. Our judgment here is that, on all the facts, this conviction cannot stand.

Petitioner was a foreign-born young man of 25 with no past history of law violation or of subjection to official interrogation, at least insofar as the record shows. He had progressed only one-half year into high school and the record indicates that he had a history of emotional instability.[3] He did not make a narrative statement, but was subject to the leading questions of a skillful prosecutor in a question and answer confession. He was subjected to questioning not by a few men, but by many. * * * All played some part, and the effect of such massive official interrogation must have been felt. Petitioner was questioned for virtually eight straight hours before he confessed, with his only respite being a transfer to an arena presumably considered more appropriate by the police for the task at hand. Nor was the questioning conducted during normal business hours, but began in early evening, continued into the night, and did not bear fruition until the not-too-early morning. The drama was not played out, with the final admissions obtained, until almost sunrise. In such circumstances slowly mounting fatigue does, and is calculated to, play its part. The questioners persisted in the face of his repeated refusals to answer on the advice of his attorney, and they ignored his reasonable requests to contact the local attorney whom he had already retained and who had personally delivered him into the custody of these officers in obedience to the bench warrant.

The use of Bruno, characterized in this Court by counsel for the State as a "childhood friend" of petitioner's, is another factor which deserves mention in the totality of the situation. Bruno's was the one face visible to petitioner in which he could put some trust. There was a bond of friendship between them going back a decade into adolescence. It was with this material that the officers felt that they could overcome

---

[3] Medical reports from New York City's Fordham Hospital introduced by defendant showed that he had suffered a cerebral concussion in 1955. He was described by a private physician in 1951 as "an extremely nervous tense individual who is emotionally unstable and maladjusted," and was found unacceptable for military service in 1951, primarily because of "Psychiatric disorder." He failed the Army's FAQT-1 intelligence test. His mother had been in mental hospitals on three separate occasions.

petitioner's will. They instructed Bruno falsely to state that petitioner's telephone call had gotten him into trouble, that his job was in jeopardy, and that loss of his job would be disastrous to his three children, his wife and his unborn child. And Bruno played this part of a worried father, harried by his superiors, in not one, but four different acts, the final one lasting an hour. Petitioner was apparently unaware of John Gay's famous couplet:

> "An open foe may prove a curse,
> But a pretended friend is worse,"

and he yielded to his false friend's entreaties.

We conclude that petitioner's will was overborne by official pressure, fatigue and sympathy falsely aroused, after considering all the facts in their post-indictment setting. Here a grand jury had already found sufficient cause to require petitioner to face trial on a charge of first-degree murder, and the police had an eyewitness to the shooting. The police were not therefore merely trying to solve a crime, or even to absolve a suspect. They were rather concerned primarily with securing a statement from defendant on which they could convict him. The undeviating intent of the officers to extract a confession from petitioner is therefore patent. When such an intent is shown, this Court has held that the confession obtained must be examined with the most careful scrutiny, and has reversed a conviction on facts less compelling than these. Accordingly, we hold that petitioner's conviction cannot stand under the Fourteenth Amendment. * * *

MR. JUSTICE DOUGLAS, with whom MR. JUSTICE BLACK and MR. JUSTICE BRENNAN join, concurring. [omitted]

MR. JUSTICE STEWART, whom MR. JUSTICE DOUGLAS and MR. JUSTICE BRENNAN join, concurring.

While I concur in the opinion of the Court, it is my view that the absence of counsel when this confession was elicited was alone enough to render it inadmissible under the Fourteenth Amendment.

Let it be emphasized at the outset that this is not a case where the police were questioning a suspect in the course of investigating an unsolved crime. When the petitioner surrendered to the New York authorities he was under indictment for first degree murder.

Under our system of justice an indictment is supposed to be followed by an arraignment and a trial. At every stage in those proceedings the accused has an absolute right to a lawyer's help if the case is one in which a death sentence may be imposed. *Powell v. Alabama*, [p. 25]. Indeed the right to the assistance of counsel whom the accused has himself retained is absolute, whatever the offense for which he is on trial.

What followed the petitioner's surrender in this case was not arraignment in a court of law, but an all-night inquisition in a prosecutor's office, a police station, and an automobile. Throughout the night the petitioner repeatedly asked to be allowed to send for his lawyer, and his requests were repeatedly denied. He finally was induced to make a confession. That confession was used to secure a verdict sending him to the electric chair.

Our Constitution guarantees the assistance of counsel to a man on trial for his life in an orderly courtroom, presided over by a judge, open to the public, and protected by all the procedural safeguards of the law. Surely a Constitution which promises that much can vouchsafe no less to the same man under midnight inquisition in the squad room of a police station.

NOTES AND QUESTIONS

1.   What is the most important reason the Court ruled in Spano's favor? Is it the denial of counsel? Lack of sufficient mental freedom? Spano's "overborne will"? Doubts about the reliability of the confession (and thus the accuracy of the conviction)? Were you surprised that no one dissented?

It will likely come as no surprise to you that judges, being former advocates, tend to state the facts in a way that supports the holding. In *Spano*, for example, Chief Justice Warren wrote, "Inevitably, in the fourth such [interrogation] session * * * , lasting a full hour, petitioner succumbed * * * ." There was no dissent in *Spano*, but if you were writing a dissent, how would you describe these same facts?

2.   *Spano and the real world.* Spano's victim was a boxer of some repute. "He fought mostly as a welterweight, and had a number of victories to his credit" between 1945 and 1951. See *Former Boxer Slain*, The New York Times, January 23, 1957. This perhaps explains why the State sought the death penalty in a case where one could argue that Spano was still dazed from the beating he had suffered at the hands of the victim.

If you were the prosecutor, knowing that you could not use Spano's confession at a retrial, what charge and sentence would you consider an acceptable outcome?

3.   *When values and attitudes change over time, law changes.* Compare the Court's approach to state interrogation in *Spano* (1959) with that in *Lisenba* (1941). They are very different, almost diametrically opposed. Why would the Court so change its basic approach? It is easy to forget that judges are part of the culture, and change as the culture changes. One fundamental change in the world between *Lisenba* and *Spano* was the end of World War II, with the public revelation of Nazi atrocities. There is little doubt that these developments influenced the Supreme Court. Professor Carol Steiker provides an account of Justice Jackson's service as head of the American prosecution team at the Nazi war crimes trial in Nuremberg, which according

to Steiker made him a "fervent believer" that searches should be authorized by warrants in most cases. Carol S. Steiker, *Second Thoughts About First Principles*, 107 Harv. L. Rev. 820, 842 (1994). The same concern about totalitarian government probably moved the Court toward a voluntariness test that more easily condemned police interrogation.

Consider, in that regard, Justice Black's opinion for the Court in Ashcraft v. Tennessee, 322 U.S. 143, 64 S.Ct. 921, 88 L.Ed. 1192 (1944) (note the date):

> The Constitution of the United States stands as a bar against the conviction of any individual in an American court by means of a coerced confession. There have been, and are now, certain foreign nations with governments dedicated to an opposite policy: governments which convict individuals with testimony obtained by police organizations possessed of unrestrained power to seize persons suspected of crimes against the state, hold them in secret custody, and wring from them confessions by physical or mental torture. So long as the Constitution remains the basic law of this Republic, America will not have that kind of government.

4. *Involuntariness factors.*

A. *Spano.* What is the relevance of the facts about Spano (background, age, etc.)? Assume that Spano had been a contract killer for the mob. Would that change your notion of the mental freedom issue? Of the "overborne will" issue?

B. *Youth.* Suspecting that Christopher W., eleven years old, had set a fire at a church, a police officer took him into custody, and interrogated him for about an hour. Christopher continued to deny involvement. The officer produced the New Testament and asked if he believed in God and if he knew that church was God's home. When he answered yes, the officer asked him if he could place his hand on the Bible, look the officer in the eye, and say he had not been in the church that burned. At that point, Christopher confessed. Leaving *Miranda* issues to the next chapter, is this confession voluntary? See In re Christopher W., 329 S.E.2d 769, 769 (S. C. Ct. App. 1985).

C. *Mental incapacity.* A state trial judge held that *M*, whose I.Q. was "approximately 70 to 75 or below," was a "mentally retarded" person under state law, and thus ineligible for the death penalty. The suppression hearing showed that police had interrogated *M* intensely for six hours, often confronting him with assertions that he was guilty. They also lied about the evidence against *M*, telling him falsely that witnesses had seen him in the hallway outside the victim's office. Police showed him a fingerprint card and computer printout that proved his fingerprints were found in the victim's office; no fingerprint match had yet been made. After six hours, *M* admitted that he was in the office when the victim died. Voluntary? Though this is getting a bit ahead of ourselves, do you think it would matter if he was warned of his *Miranda* rights to remain silent and to have counsel? See Miller v. State, 770 N.E.2d 763, 766 n.3 (Ind. 2002).

D.   *Police methods.* To what extent is voluntariness an empirical "fact in the universe," as opposed to a normative judgment about police methods? For example, if the police intentionally exploit a suspect's highly religious nature, should courts be more likely to find the pressure overbearing than if the police were unaware of the suspect's religious nature but asked precisely the same questions in the same way? If you say "yes," you favor a normative view of voluntariness that turns, at least in part, on a moral judgment about what the police did. If you say "no, pressure is pressure regardless of police motives," you tend toward an empirical, Aristotelian view of voluntariness.

But the empirical approach ultimately suffers from a coherence problem. As the next chapter will explore in more detail, the notion of a disembodied "will" that exists independently from the interaction with police might be a fiction. Indeed, it might be that at the moment the suspect answers police questions, that is in fact his will—at least absent torture. On this view, it is incoherent to search for cases where the suspect's will is "overborne." The Court seemed to realize this in the 1940s as its terminology changed from whether coercion caused a suspect to confess to whether coercive methods were applied to the suspect. Perhaps the Court's clearest expression of the normative approach was to ask whether the suspect was "subjected to pressures to which, under our accusatorial system, an accused should not be subjected." See Rogers v. Richmond, 365 U.S. 534, 81 S.Ct. 735, 5 L.Ed.2d 760 (1961). A judgment about acceptable pressures is easy in some cases. Police shouldn't use torture or threaten to turn a suspect over to a mob or threaten to have a suspect's children taken away from her. See *Brown*, Payne v. Arkansas, 356 U.S. 560, 78 S.Ct. 844, 2 L.Ed.2d 975 (1958); Lynumn v. Illinois, 372 U.S. 528, 83 S.Ct. 917, 9 L.Ed.2d 922 (1963). Check, check, check. But making that judgment in more routine cases is not easy. Consider the next two Notes.

5.   Police suspected Oreste Fulminante of the brutal murder of his eleven-year-old stepdaughter, Jeneane Hunt. Before any charges were filed in the murder case, Fulminante was convicted of unrelated federal firearms charges. While in a federal correctional facility, Fulminante

> became friends with another inmate, Anthony Sarivola, then serving a 60-day sentence for extortion. The two men came to spend several hours a day together. Sarivola, a former police officer, had been involved in loansharking for organized crime but then became a paid informant for the Federal Bureau of Investigation. While [in prison], he masqueraded as an organized crime figure. After becoming friends with Fulminante, Sarivola heard a rumor that Fulminante was suspected of killing a child in Arizona. Sarivola then raised the subject with Fulminante in several conversations, but Fulminante repeatedly denied any involvement in Jeneane's death. During one conversation, he told Sarivola that Jeneane had

been killed by bikers looking for drugs; on another occasion, he said he did not know what had happened. Sarivola passed this information on to an agent of the Federal Bureau of Investigation, who instructed Sarivola to find out more.

Sarivola learned more one evening in October 1983, as he and Fulminante walked together around the prison track. Sarivola said that he knew Fulminante was "starting to get some tough treatment and whatnot" from other inmates because of the rumor. Sarivola offered to protect Fulminante from his fellow inmates, but told him, " 'You have to tell me about it,' you know. I mean, in other words, 'For me to give you any help.' " Fulminante then admitted to Sarivola that he had driven Jeneane to the desert on his motorcycle, where he choked her, sexually assaulted her, and made her beg for her life, before shooting her twice in the head.

Fulminate appealed his conviction and death sentence, arguing that his confession to Sarivola was the product of coercion. In Arizona v. Fulminante, 499 U.S. 279, 111 S.Ct. 1246, 113 L.Ed.2d 302 (1991), the Supreme Court agreed.

In applying the totality of the circumstances test to determine that the confession to Sarivola was coerced, the Arizona Supreme Court focused on a number of relevant facts. First, the court noted that "because [Fulminante] was an alleged child murderer, he was in danger of physical harm at the hands of other inmates." In addition, Sarivola was aware that Fulminante had been receiving " 'rough treatment from the guys.' " Using his knowledge of these threats, Sarivola offered to protect Fulminante in exchange for a confession to Jeneane's murder, and "in response to Sarivola's offer of protection, [Fulminante] confessed." Agreeing with Fulminante that "Sarivola's promise was 'extremely coercive,' " the Arizona Court declared: "The confession was obtained as a direct result of extreme coercion and was tendered in the belief that the defendant's life was in jeopardy if he did not confess. This is a true coerced confession in every sense of the word."[2] * * *

Although the question is a close one, we agree with the Arizona Supreme Court's conclusion that Fulminante's confession was coerced. * * * Accepting the Arizona court's finding, permissible on

_____

[2]   There are additional facts in the record, not relied upon by the Arizona Supreme Court, which also support a finding of coercion. Fulminante possesses low average to average intelligence; he dropped out of school in the fourth grade. He is short in stature and slight in build. Although he had been in prison before, he had not always adapted well to the stress of prison life. While incarcerated at the age of 26, he had "felt threatened by the [prison] population," and he therefore requested that he be placed in protective custody. Once there, however, he was unable to cope with the isolation and was admitted to a psychiatric hospital. The Court has previously recognized that factors such as these are relevant in determining whether a defendant's will has been overborne. In addition, we note that Sarivola's position as Fulminante's friend might well have made the latter particularly susceptible to the former's entreaties. See *Spano v. New York*, [p. 603].

this record, that there was a credible threat of physical violence, we agree with its conclusion that Fulminante's will was overborne in such a way as to render his confession the product of coercion.

Do you agree that Sarivola coerced Fulminante to confess? Four members of the Court dissented on the coercion issue.

> Exercising our responsibility to make the independent examination of the record necessary to decide this federal question, I am at a loss to see how the Supreme Court of Arizona reached the conclusion that it did. Fulminante offered no evidence that he believed that his life was in danger or that he in fact confessed to Sarivola in order to obtain the proffered protection. Indeed, he had stipulated that "at no time did the defendant indicate he was in fear of other inmates nor did he ever seek Mr. Sarivola's 'protection.'" Sarivola's testimony that he told Fulminante that "if [he] would tell the truth, he could be protected," adds little if anything to the substance of the parties' stipulation. The decision of the Supreme Court of Arizona rests on an assumption that is squarely contrary to this stipulation, and one that is not supported by any testimony of Fulminante.

> The facts of record in the present case are quite different from those present in cases where we have found confessions to be coerced and involuntary. Since Fulminante was unaware that Sarivola was an FBI informant, there existed none of "the danger of coercion resulting from the interaction of custody and official interrogation." * * * The conversations between Sarivola and Fulminante were not lengthy, and the defendant was free at all times to leave Sarivola's company. Sarivola at no time threatened him or demanded that he confess; he simply requested that he speak the truth about the matter. Fulminante was an experienced habitue of prisons and presumably able to fend for himself. In concluding on these facts that Fulminante's confession was involuntary, the Court today embraces a more expansive definition of that term than is warranted by any of our decided cases.

It might surprise you to learn that the five-justice majority finding in Fulminante's favor included Justice Scalia and that Justice Souter joined Chief Justice Rehnquist's dissent. Which opinion would you have joined? Can *Spano* be distinguished?

6.   *Problems of due process voluntariness.*

A.   *Physician 1.* Police call a physician to treat suspect *L*'s painful sinus condition. The physician, a psychiatrist who works for the police, tells *L* how much better he would feel if he unburdened himself about the crime of murdering his elderly parents with a hammer. *L* does not know that the physician is a psychiatrist. *L* confesses to the police shortly after the physician leaves. Is there any reason to think the confession is unreliable? *Cf.*

Leyra v. Denno, 347 U.S. 556, 74 S.Ct. 716, 98 L.Ed. 948 (1954). Would it matter to due process voluntariness if the psychiatrist did *not* work for the police? Does the case come out the same way if the police provide a police officer who pretends to be a physician? An officer who pretends to be a priest?

B.   *Physician 2.* Same as prior Problem, but this time, the physician engages in a lengthy interrogation (over an hour) during which he keeps suggesting details about how *L* killed his parents: his mother first, slipping up behind her, because *L* was going to kill his father when he came home, and he didn't want his mother to interfere. *L* responds over and over that he does not remember. The physician explains that he is "helping [him] think." As the interrogation becomes more intense, *L* responds to suggestions about how he killed his parents by saying, "That must have been the way I did it," or "It must have been me; no one else was in the house." After an hour, *L* says he is ready to talk to the police captain, and he gives a confession that contains the details suggested by the psychiatrist. Voluntary? What if, after confessing to the captain, *L* confesses within three hours to state prosecutors? Are these confessions consistent with due process?

C.   *Physician 3.* After three hours of questioning, *S* requests drugs to ameliorate the pain of narcotics withdrawal. According to later expert testimony, the drugs supplied by the police physician included a drug that functioned as a "truth serum." Neither the police interrogators nor the physician intended that effect; no one even had a reason to know that the drug would have this effect on *S*. Moreover, the police were unaware of the effect as they continued to question *S* and to take his confession. Does lack of bad faith have anything to do with the voluntariness inquiry? See Townsend v. Sain, 372 U.S. 293, 83 S.Ct. 745, 9 L.Ed.2d 770 (1963).

7.   Federal law, 42 U.S.C. § 1983, authorizes a civil lawsuit for damages if a state actor violates rights under the federal Constitution or federal law. In Chavez v. Martinez, 538 U.S. 760, 123 S.Ct. 1994, 155 L.Ed.2d 984 (2003), Oliverio Martinez brought suit under § 1983 against the police officer who caused him to confess. The issue was not whether the confession was admissible in a criminal trial, as in *Brown v. Mississippi*, p. 14, but whether the interrogation violated his due process rights at the moment that the questioning took place. The facts revealed a persistent interrogation of a suspect who had been shot and thought he was dying. Here is a portion of Justice Kennedy's opinion, concurring in part and dissenting in part:

> The District Court found that Martinez "had been shot in the face, both eyes were injured; he was screaming in pain, and coming in and out of consciousness while being repeatedly questioned about details of the encounter with the police." His blinding facial wounds made it impossible for him visually to distinguish the interrogating officer from the attending medical personnel. The officer made no effort to dispel the perception that medical treatment was being withheld until Martinez answered the questions put to him. There was no attempt through *Miranda* warnings or other assurances to

advise the suspect that his cooperation should be voluntary. Martinez begged the officer to desist and provide treatment for his wounds, but the questioning persisted despite these pleas and despite Martinez's unequivocal refusal to answer questions.

In a badly-splintered opinion, the Court held that the due process inquiry in civil cases, as here, was the "shock the conscience" test of Rochin v. California, p. 82, Note 2. It appears, therefore, that suspects have a due process right not to have involuntary confessions admitted in a criminal case against them but no right to sue for a due process violation unless the police conduct "shocks the conscience."

Five justices voted to remand *Martinez* to allow the lower courts to determine whether the *Rochin* standard was met. Is your conscience shocked? The Ninth Circuit remanded to the district court for "the resolution of contested facts." In 2007, a federal jury could not reach a verdict and the judge declared a mistrial. A newspaper article said a new trial would be held but we found no evidence of a second trial. See Stephanie Hoops, *Mistrial in civil rights suit*, Ventura County Star, April 27, 2007. Evidence at the trial revealed that Martinez lost his eyesight and was partially paralyzed as a result of the police shooting.

CHAPTER 7

POLICE INTERROGATION: THE SELF-INCRIMINATION CLAUSE

■ ■ ■

"No person * * * shall be compelled in any criminal case to be a witness against himself * * * ." U.S. Const. amend. V.

"The self-incrimination clause of the Fifth Amendment is an unsolved riddle of vast proportions, a Gordian knot in the middle of our Bill of Rights." Akhil Reed Amar, The Constitution and Criminal Procedure 46 (1997).

A. THE TEXT AND THE ROAD TO *MIRANDA*

BRAM v. UNITED STATES
Supreme Court of the United States, 1897.
168 U.S. 532, 18 S.Ct. 183, 42 L.Ed. 568.

MR. JUSTICE WHITE delivered the opinion of the Court [joined by JUSTICES HARLAN, GRAY, SHIRAS, and PECKHAM].

[A murder occurred on a ship in the North Atlantic. Crewman Brown was the initial suspect. When the ship made port, a Canadian customs official had a second suspect, Bram, stripped to search his clothes for evidence of the murder. The official, Power, questioned Bram either while his clothes were being removed or after he was "denuded." Power testified as follows. Eds.]

> "I said to him: 'Bram, we are trying to unravel this horrible mystery.' I said: 'Your position is rather an awkward one. I have had Brown in this office, and he made a statement that he saw you do the murder.' He said: 'He could not have seen me. Where was he?' I said: 'He states he was at the wheel.' 'Well,' he said, 'he could not see me from there.' "

The contention is that the foregoing conversation, between the detective and the accused, was competent only as a confession by him made; that it was offered as such; and that it was erroneously admitted, as it was not shown to have been voluntary. * * * In criminal trials, in the courts of the United States, wherever a question arises whether a confession is incompetent because not voluntary, the issue is controlled by that portion of the fifth amendment to the constitution of the United States commanding that no person "shall be compelled in any criminal case to be a witness against himself." The legal principle by which the admissibility of the confession of an accused person is to be determined is expressed in the text-books.

In 3 Russ. Crimes (6th Ed.) 478, it is stated as follows:

> "But a confession, in order to be admissible, must be free and voluntary; that is, must not be extracted by any sort of threats or violence, nor obtained by any direct or implied promises, however slight, nor by the exertion of any improper influence. * * * A confession can never be received in evidence where the prisoner has been influenced by any threat or promise; for the law cannot measure the force of the influence used, or decide upon its effect upon the mind of the prisoner, and therefore excludes the declaration if any degree of influence has been exerted." * * *

[The Court also quoted from Hawkins' Pleas of the Crown (6th Ed., by Leach, published in 1787). Eds.] In section 3, c. 46, it is stated that examinations by the common law before a secretary of state or other magistrate for treason or other crimes not within the statutes of Philip and Mary, and also the confession of the defendant himself in discourse with private persons, might be given in evidence against the party confessing. A note (2) to this section, presumably inserted by the editor (see note to Gilham's Case, 1 Moody, 194, 195), reads as follows:

> The human mind, under the pressure of calamity, is easily seduced, and is liable, in the alarm of danger, to acknowledge indiscriminately a falsehood or a truth, as different agitations may prevail. A confession, therefore, whether made upon an official examination or in discourse with private persons, which is obtained from a defendant, either by the flattery of hope, or by the impressions of fear, however slightly the emotions may be implanted, is not admissible evidence; for the law will not suffer a prisoner to be made the deluded instrument of his own conviction. * * *

* * * As said in the passage from Russell on Crimes already quoted: "The law cannot measure the force of the influence used, or decide upon its effect upon the mind of the prisoner, and therefore excludes the declaration if any degree of influence has been exerted." In the case before us we find that an influence was exerted, and, as any doubt as to whether the confession was voluntary must be determined in favor of the accused, we cannot escape the conclusion that error was committed by the trial court in admitting the confession under the circumstances disclosed by the record. * * *

[MR. JUSTICE FIELD retired before *Bram* was announced and took no part in the case.]

MR. JUSTICE BREWER, with whom concurred Mr. CHIEF JUSTICE FULLER, and Mr. JUSTICE BROWN, dissenting. * * *

The witness Power, when called, testified positively that no threats were made nor any inducements held out to Bram; and this general declaration he affirmed and reaffirmed in response to inquiries made by the court and the defendant's counsel. The court therefore properly overruled the objection at that time made to his testifying to the statements of defendant. It is not suggested that there was error in this ruling, and the fact that inducements were held out is deduced only from the testimony subsequently given by Power of the conversation between him and Bram. The first part of that conversation is as follows: "When Mr. Bram came into my office, I said to him: 'Bram, we are trying to unravel this horrible mystery.' I said: 'Your position is rather an awkward one. I have had Brown in this office, and he made a statement that he saw you do the murder.' He said: 'He could not have seen me. Where was he?' I said: 'He states he was at the wheel.' 'Well,' he said, 'he could not see me from there.'" In this there is nothing which by any possibility can be tortured into a suggestion of threat or a temptation of hope. Power simply stated the obvious fact that they were trying to unravel a horrible mystery, and the further fact that Brown had charged the defendant with the crime, and the replies of Bram were given as freely and voluntarily as it is possible to conceive.

NOTES AND QUESTIONS

1.   Do you agree that Bram's statements were compelled or is Justice Brewer right that his statements were given freely and voluntarily? How should a court weigh the fact that Bram was questioned while being "denuded"?

2.   *The "free agent" concept.* One way to understand *Bram* is to consider it the lineal heir of *Rex v. Thompson*, 168 Eng. Rep. 248 (Cent.Crim.Ct. 1783), in which the English trial judge suppressed a confession obtained by the "threat" to take the suspect before a magistrate if he did not provide "a more satisfactory account" of the events. The court wrote, "Too great a chastity cannot be preserved on this point. * * * It is almost impossible to be too careful upon this subject." The confession must be suppressed, the court held, because "[t]he prisoner was hardly a free agent at the time" he responded to the statement indicating that he might be taken before a magistrate. The statement "was certainly a strong invitation to the prisoner to confess."

But is a "strong invitation" to confess enough to create compulsion? Wigmore was harshly critical of cases like *Thompson* and *Bram*, concluding that they were among the "absurdities" that "have disfigured the law of the admissibility of confessions," giving it a "sentimental irrationality" that had "obstructed the administration of justice." 2 John Henry Wigmore, A Treatise on Evidence 159, § 865 (2d ed. 1923). For a thoughtful explanation of how English law came to develop the "free agent" concept in the law of confessions, see John H. Langbein, The Origins of Adversary Criminal Trial 229–233 (2003).

3. *Why not a federal rule of evidence?* None of the cases that *Bram* cited, including *Thompson*, were based on the privilege not to testify as a witness. Instead, they were based on a common-law rule of evidence that barred the use of involuntary confessions. The *Bram* Court could have reached the same result by reading the common law rule of evidence into the Fifth Amendment due process clause. Indeed, when the Court later began reviewing state court convictions based on confessions, as we saw in Chapter 6, it read the Fourteenth Amendment due process clause to forbid convictions based on compelled confessions. Why *Bram* chose the Fifth Amendment privilege to create a federal law of confessions is a mystery, one that has far-reaching consequences in the vast *Miranda v. Arizona* doctrine. We now pause to consider the relationship between the Fifth Amendment privilege and the due process right not to be coerced into confessing.

The Privilege and the Involuntary Confession Rule

"No person * * * shall be compelled in any criminal case to be a witness against himself * * *." Leaving aside for the moment the metaphysical difficulty of determining when a conscious utterance is compelled, the text of the Fifth Amendment appears clear enough. It seems to forbid the State from compelling a criminal defendant to testify against himself. While that is roughly its modern meaning, it cannot have been the Framers' meaning. In the eighteenth century, criminal defendants *were not permitted* to testify under oath, a rule of evidence based on a presumption that defendants would be tempted to lie. Lying would of course undermine the accuracy of the process, but the common law rule probably developed in part due to the religious nature of the period. Lying under oath condemned one to hell. That view probably explains why English magistrates were permitted to question suspects as long as they did not put them under oath.

Because defendants were not permitted to testify under oath in their own criminal trial, it would have made no sense for the Framers to prohibit compelling defendants to testify. This historical insight naturally leads to another question: What purpose *did* the privilege serve in the English common law? The answer is that it had nothing to do with the common law criminal courts and everything to do with the Star Chamber, a supervisory body that drew its authority from the monarch and thus had greater powers and more flexibility than the common law courts. Begun by Henry II in the twelfth century, the Star Chamber's original judicial role was to ensure fair enforcement of the laws. But in the sixteenth and seventeenth centuries, the Star Chamber became a tool in the seemingly endless conflict between English Protestants and Catholics. It was used ruthlessly by the Stuart monarchs to pursue and destroy their enemies. The test of wills between the religious dissenters and the Star Chamber was *not* about being compelled to confess to crimes. Rather, the objection was to the Star Chamber itself and its power to compel those called before it to swear an oath to tell the truth. Criminal defendants could not be required to testify in criminal cases under oath; many English subjects thought that the same rule should apply to the monarch's Star Chamber.

We know, from the First Amendment and from contemporaneous writings, that the Framers feared religious persecution. It would make sense, then, to include not only a guarantee of the freedom of religion but also a right not to have to respond to an accusation from a Star Chamber kind of court. Tom Davies argues that the Framers meant the privilege to provide a shield against government questioning under oath until a *prima facie* case was made to a justice of the peace and then a grand jury. See Thomas Y. Davies, *Farther and Farther from the Original Fifth Amendment: The Recharacterization of the Right Against Self-Incrimination as a "Trial Right" in Chavez v. Martinez*, 70 Tenn. L. Rev. 987 (2003). But so understood, the privilege would not prohibit defendants being questioned in court after the government had persuaded a justice of the peace and a grand jury that there was probable cause to believe them guilty of crime.

By the late nineteenth century, the criminal justice world had changed dramatically from the one the Framers knew. For example, the federal government and almost all states had, by statute, removed the common-law disability of criminal defendants to testify. When a witness before a grand jury in 1890 invoked the Fifth Amendment privilege, the government turned the likely historical meaning of the privilege on its head, arguing that the *only* role of the privilege was to prevent compelling testimony from defendants at their criminal trials. See Counselman v. Hitchcock, 142 U.S. 547, 12 S.Ct. 195, 35 L.Ed. 1110 (1892). The Court accepted the government's argument as a starting point but expanded the protection to include grand jury witnesses:

> It is impossible that the meaning of the constitutional provision can only be that a person shall not be compelled to be a witness against himself in a criminal prosecution against himself. It would doubtless cover such cases; but it is not limited to them. The object was to insure that a person should not be compelled, when acting as a witness in any investigation, to give testimony which might tend to show that he himself had committed a crime. The privilege is limited to criminal matters, but it is as broad as the mischief against which it seeks to guard.

Whatever the Framers might have intended, *Counselman* made the privilege available to criminal defendants and to witnesses called before formal bodies such as grand juries, congressional committees, or commissions. See, *e.g.*, Murphy v. Waterfront Commission, 378 U.S. 52, 84 S.Ct. 1594, 12 L.Ed.2d 678 (1964). The latter aspect of the privilege is considered in more detail in Chapter 13.

Decided five years after *Counselman*, *Bram* made the privilege the source of protection against compelled confessions in federal prosecutions. *Brown v. Mississippi*, p. 14, located in the due process clause a protection against coerced or involuntary confessions when the issue arose in state courts. These protections differ in two other ways. First, as to scope, the privilege offers a broader protection. As you will see in Chapter 13, it sometimes protects against subpoenas directed at documents and other tangible evidence while the due process clause protection in the confessions context is limited to interrogation by State agents.

In theory, the privilege could protect against being forced to provide *any* incriminating evidence, but the Court rejected that broad reading, by a 5–4 vote, in Schmerber v. California, 384 U.S. 757, 86 S.Ct. 1826, 16 L.Ed.2d 908 (1966). The police ordered a hospital to withdraw blood over Schmerber's objection. There is no doubt that Schmerber was compelled to give up his blood. The issue was whether Schmerber was being a "witness against himself" when he gave up his blood. Citing little authority, the Court held "that the privilege protects an accused only from being compelled to testify against himself, or otherwise provide the State with evidence of a testimonial or communicative nature." The Court noted that the

> distinction which has emerged [from the cases], often expressed in different ways, is that the privilege is a bar against compelling "communications" or "testimony," but that compulsion which makes a suspect or accused the source of "real or physical evidence" does not violate it.

> Although we agree that this distinction is a helpful framework for analysis, * * * [t]here will be many cases in which such a distinction is not readily drawn. Some tests seemingly directed to obtain "physical evidence," for example, lie detector tests measuring changes in body function during interrogation, may actually be directed to eliciting responses which are essentially testimonial. To compel a person to submit to testing in which an effort will be made to determine his guilt or innocence on the basis of physiological responses, whether willed or not, is to evoke the spirit and history of the Fifth Amendment.
> * * *

In the present case, however, no such problem of application is presented. Not even a shadow of testimonial compulsion upon or enforced communication by the accused was involved either in the extraction or in the chemical analysis. Petitioner's testimonial capacities were in no way implicated; indeed, his participation, except as a donor, was irrelevant to the results of the test, which depend on chemical analysis and on that alone. Since the blood test evidence, although an incriminating product of compulsion, was neither petitioner's testimony nor evidence relating to some communicative act or writing by the petitioner, it was not inadmissible on privilege grounds.

Thus, requiring a suspect to stand in a line-up, provide a writing sample, or speak certain words does not implicate the suspect's right not to be compelled to be a witness against himself.

The second difference between the due process right against coerced confessions and the Fifth Amendment privilege goes to *when* a violation occurs. The right not to be coerced into making an involuntary confession would seem to be violated when the coercion occurs, and the Court has held that this is correct. The Fifth Amendment privilege is slipperier. As the privilegee forbids "being a witness" against oneself, perhaps it is not violated until the evidence is offered in court. In Kastigar v. United States, p. 941, the Court held that witnesses called to testify before grand juries can be compelled to testify if they are given what is known as "use-and-derivative-use immunity." This doctrine forbids use of the compelled testimony, and everything derived from it, in a criminal case against the person providing the testimony. It applies to state and federal courts, regardless of which sovereign obtains the testimony by granting immunity. The underlying theory of *Kastigar* is that the witness is not being compelled to be a witness against himself if the compelled testimony is never used in a criminal case against him. Implicit in *Kastigar* is the premise that a violation of the Fifth Amendment privilege occurs only when the compelled testimony is used in a criminal case. That premise was ultimately accepted, at least in large part, in a controversial and splintered case in 2003.

In Chavez v. Martinez, 538 U.S. 760, 123 S.Ct. 1994, 155 L.Ed.2d 984 (2003), Martinez sued under 42 U.S.C. § 1983 the police officer who coerced him to make statements. The state chose not to prosecute Martinez and thus there was no evidence-admissibility issue. As you saw in the last chapter, Note 7, p. 613, the Court held that Martinez could prove that his substantive due process rights had been violated by showing that the interrogation methods "shocked the conscience." Martinez preferred, of course, to sue under the Fifth Amendment privilege where he would need merely to show that his confession was compelled.

Relying on the plain meaning of the text and on *Kastigar*, the four-justice plurality in *Chavez* concluded that no violation of the privilege would ever occur until the evidence was offered in a criminal case against the one claiming compulsion. Justice Souter, joined by Justice Breyer, concurred in the judgment on this issue, arguing that in some cases (*Miranda v. Arizona*, for example), the Court had extended the privilege beyond its core protection. But for Souter and Breyer, the burden was on Martinez to make "the 'powerful showing,' subject to a realistic assessment of costs and risks, necessary to expand protection of the privilege against compelled self-incrimination" beyond the core protection to reach civil liability. Concluding that Martinez could not make that "powerful showing," Souter and Breyer agreed with the plurality that he could not claim a violation of the privilege. Thus, for six members of the *Chavez* Court, a violation of the privilege occurs only when the evidence is offered in a criminal trial or a "powerful showing" is made that it is necessary to extend the privilege beyond its core meaning.

NOTES AND QUESTIONS

1.   The rest of this chapter focuses on the privilege against compelled self-incrimination in the context of statements being offered in criminal cases. As you undoubtedly know from watching police shows on television, *Miranda* applies in state as well as federal court. Since the Court had found in the due process clause a protection against the use in state court of coerced or involuntary confessions, why did the Court ultimately turn to the privilege in *Miranda v. Arizona*? In large part, the explanation can be found in the unsatisfying nature of a protection against involuntary confessions.

We saw in Chapter 6 that voluntariness is not an easy empirical or philosophical "fact" to determine. As Lawrence Herman has cogently put the problems with voluntariness:

> A careful reading of the Court's more than forty involuntary confession cases discloses not one but five different objectives. * * * (1) to deter the police from engaging in conduct that may produce an unreliable confession; (2) to deter the police from engaging in conduct so offensive to the minimum standards of a civilized society that it shocks the conscience of the Court; (3) to deter the police from engaging in less-than-shocking misconduct; (4) to deter the police from using the techniques of an inquisitorial system and to encourage them to use the techniques of an accusatorial system; and (5) to deter the police from overbearing the suspect's will.

> Your initial reaction may be that these objectives at last give us the definitional tool we need. Precisely the opposite is true, however. Each of the objectives is problematic in one or more ways, and the very number of them obfuscates rather than clarifies. * * *

* * * Small wonder, then, that in a period of thirty years or so, the Supreme Court granted review in over thirty-five cases in which confessions had been held voluntary. Small wonder, too, that the Court reversed the conviction in most of these cases. And small wonder that the Court became disaffected from its own work product. All students of the Court recognize that it cannot police the application of doctrine by lower courts. All it can hope to do is make doctrine intelligible and give illustrative examples. The Court tried to do that in the confession cases, and it failed. Given the inherent vagueness of the crucial concepts and the many rationales underlying the rule, failure was foreordained. So also was the search for an alternative.

Lawrence Herman, *The Supreme Court, the Attorney General, and the Good Old Days of Police Interrogation*, 48 Ohio St. L.J. 733, 749–50, 754–55 (1987).

2.   *Right to counsel as a limit on interrogation.* One attempt to provide limits on interrogation more precise than the voluntariness test was Escobedo v. Illinois, 378 U.S. 478, 84 S.Ct. 1758, 12 L.Ed.2d 977 (1964). Two years before *Miranda*, the Court held that the *Sixth Amendment* was violated when the police denied Escobedo's request to speak to his lawyer who was present in the police station; Escobedo was being interrogated before charges were filed but after the investigation had focused on him. The Sixth Amendment provides: "In all criminal prosecutions, the accused shall enjoy the right * * * to have the Assistance of Counsel for his defence." The dissents soundly criticized the majority for applying the Sixth Amendment right to counsel in a pre-indictment case. Do you see the interpretive difficulty?

Justice White's dissent in *Escobedo* presaged what the Court would do in *Miranda*:

> The Court may be concerned with a narrower matter: the unknowing defendant who responds to police questioning because he mistakenly believes that he must and that his admissions will not be used against him. But this worry hardly calls for the broadside the Court has now fired. The failure to inform an accused that he need not answer and that his answers may be used against him is very relevant indeed to whether the disclosures are compelled. Cases in this Court, to say the least, have never placed a premium on ignorance of constitutional rights. If an accused is told he must answer and does not know better, it would be very doubtful that the resulting admissions could be used against him.

Justice White lost the battle over the meaning of the Sixth Amendment but won the war. The Court would, in *Miranda*, change the textual basis for its interrogation rules from the Sixth Amendment to the Fifth Amendment. White dissented in *Miranda* as well.

3.   *Foreshadowing Miranda.* In Chapter 6 you saw *Lisenba v. California*, p. 591, which upheld a confession taken after over roughly hours

of interrogation in two sessions. Justice Black dissented, citing *Chambers v. Florida*, 309 U.S. 227, 60 S.Ct. 472, 84 L.Ed. 716 (1940), an opinion he had written for the Court a year earlier. In *Chambers*, an elderly white man was robbed and murdered, and the community was "enraged." The sheriff rounded up twenty-five to forty black men. Defendants claimed that they "were continually threatened and physically mistreated." The State, perhaps learning a lesson from *Brown*, denied the mistreatment. In the Court's view, however, it did not matter whether the authorities threatened the suspects. It was enough that they were arrested by "drag net methods" and then subjected to "protracted questioning * * * without friends, advisers or counselors, and under circumstances calculated to break the strongest nerves and the stoutest resistance." The "undisputed facts," the Court unanimously held, "showed that compulsion was applied." Notice that the critical inquiry was not whether compulsion *moved the suspect to confess*, as it surely did in *Brown*, but whether "compulsion was applied."

Similarly, in *Ashcraft v. Tennessee*, 322 U.S. 143, 64 S.Ct. 921, 88 L.Ed. 1192 (1944), the defendant could not point to any threat or promise of favor. But again it did not matter. Justice Black, writing for the Court, drew an explicit analogy to a criminal defendant on the witness stand, an analogy that Yale Kamisar would recreate in vivid fashion in 1965. See Note 4. Black wrote that no court would permit "prosecutors serving in relays to keep a defendant witness under continuous cross examination" for long periods. "Nor can we, consistently with Constitutional due process of law, hold voluntary a confession where prosecutors do the same thing away from the restraining influences of a public trial in an open court room."

The Court concluded that the interrogation by relays was "so inherently coercive that its very existence is irreconcilable with the possession of mental freedom by a lone suspect against whom its full coercive force is brought to bear." To be sure Ashcraft was interrogated for thirty-six hours, which made the case an easy one, but Justice Jackson's dissent saw the progression that would lead to *Miranda*: "If thirty-six hours is more than is permissible, what about 24? or 12? or 6? or 1? All are 'inherently coercive.'" Jackson recognized that Justice Black had wrested control over the interrogation issue from the justices who formed the majority in *Lisenba*. If *Ashcraft* prevailed, it would relieve future Courts from having to identify what external force overbore the suspect's will. It would be enough to conclude that pressure was applied. The latter is obviously far easier for the defendant to show than the former.

After Justice Black changed the focus from whether the suspect's will was overcome to whether pressure was applied, all that was left was to provide a doctrinal explanation for why *any questioning* was inherently coercive. The Court's due process voluntariness doctrine was not a good fit as it required substantial pressure before confessions were held to be involuntary.

4. *Enter the Fifth Amendment privilege, or Kamisar leads and the Court follows.* In 1965, a year after *Escobedo* attempted to ground

interrogation limits in the Sixth Amendment, and a year before *Miranda*, Professor Yale Kamisar argued that the Fifth Amendment privilege should be extended to the interrogation room. A privilege limited to the courtroom was not particularly valuable, Kamisar argued:

> The courtroom is a splendid place where defense attorneys bellow and strut and prosecuting attorneys are hemmed in at many turns. But what happens before an accused reaches the safety and enjoys the comfort of this veritable mansion? Ah, there's the rub. Typically he must first pass through a much less pretentious edifice, a police station with bare back rooms and locked doors.

Yale Kamisar, *Equal Justice in the Gatehouses and Mansions of American Criminal Procedure: From Powell to Gideon, from Escobedo to * * * *, in Criminal Justice in Our Time, 19 (A.E. Dick Howard, ed. 1965).

Noting that wealthy privileged suspects routinely faced police interrogators with counsel at their side, Kamisar argued that "respect for the individual and securing equal treatment in law enforcement" require the State to make counsel available to suspects who face police interrogation and to warn them that they need not answer. He concluded: "To the extent the Constitution permits the wealthy and educated to 'defeat justice,' if you will, *why shouldn't* all defendants be given a like opportunity?" *Id.* at 79–80.

5.   By 1966 it was clear to the Court that a more precise rule was needed to govern police interrogation. It was also clear that *Escobedo* was not a very good rule. Leaving aside the interpretive difficulty in grounding the rule in the Sixth Amendment, there was the problem that few suspects had counsel or would know to ask to speak to their lawyer as required before the *Escobedo* rule provided help. Moreover, by its terms, the *Escobedo* rule applied only when the investigation had focused on a particular suspect. No, what the Court needed was an all-encompassing rule. Enter *Miranda*.

B.   *MIRANDA* SPAWNS A NEW LAW OF CONFESSIONS

MIRANDA V. ARIZONA

Supreme Court of the United States, 1966.
384 U.S. 436, 86 S.Ct. 1602, 16 L.Ed.2d 694.

MR. CHIEF JUSTICE WARREN delivered the opinion of the Court [joined by JUSTICES BLACK, DOUGLAS, BRENNAN and FORTAS].

The cases before us raise questions which go to the roots of our concepts of American criminal jurisprudence: the restraints society must observe consistent with the Federal Constitution in prosecuting individuals for crime. More specifically, we deal with the admissibility of statements obtained from an individual who is subjected to custodial police interrogation and the necessity for procedures which assure that the individual is accorded his privilege under the Fifth Amendment to the Constitution not to be compelled to incriminate himself. * * *

We start here, as we did in *Escobedo* [p. 623, Note 2], with the premise that our holding is not an innovation in our jurisprudence, but is an application of principles long recognized and applied in other settings. We have undertaken a thorough re-examination of the *Escobedo* decision and the principles it announced, and we reaffirm it. That case was but an explication of basic rights that are enshrined in our Constitution—that "No person * * * shall be compelled in any criminal case to be a witness against himself," and that "the accused shall * * * have the Assistance of Counsel"—rights which were put in jeopardy in that case through official overbearing. These precious rights were fixed in our Constitution only after centuries of persecution and struggle. And in the words of Chief Justice Marshall, they were secured "for ages to come, and * * * designed to approach immortality as nearly as human institutions can approach it." * * *

Our holding will be spelled out with some specificity in the pages which follow but briefly stated it is this: the prosecution may not use statements, whether exculpatory or inculpatory, stemming from custodial interrogation of the defendant unless it demonstrates the use of procedural safeguards effective to secure the privilege against self-incrimination. By custodial interrogation, we mean questioning initiated by law enforcement officers after a person has been taken into custody or otherwise deprived of his freedom of action in any significant way.[4] * * *

I

The constitutional issue we decide in each of these cases is the admissibility of statements obtained from a defendant questioned while in custody or otherwise deprived of his freedom of action in any significant way. In each, the defendant was questioned by police officers, detectives, or a prosecuting attorney in a room in which he was cut off from the outside world. In none of these cases was the defendant given a full and effective warning of his rights at the outset of the interrogation process. In all the cases, the questioning elicited oral admissions, and in three of them, signed statements as well which were admitted at their trials. They all thus share salient features—incommunicado interrogation of individuals in a police-dominated atmosphere, resulting in self-incriminating statements without full warnings of constitutional rights.

An understanding of the nature and setting of this in-custody interrogation is essential to our decisions today. The difficulty in depicting what transpires at such interrogations stems from the fact that in this country they have largely taken place incommunicado. * * *

---

4   This is what we meant in *Escobedo* when we spoke of an investigation which had focused on an accused.

Again we stress that the modern practice of in-custody interrogation is psychologically rather than physically oriented. As we have stated before, " * * * [T]his Court has recognized that coercion can be mental as well as physical, and that the blood of the accused is not the only hallmark of an unconstitutional inquisition." Interrogation still takes place in privacy. Privacy results in secrecy and this in turn results in a gap in our knowledge as to what in fact goes on in the interrogation rooms. A valuable source of information about present police practices, however, may be found in various police manuals and texts which document procedures employed with success in the past, and which recommend various other effective tactics. These texts are used by law enforcement agencies themselves as guides.[9] It should be noted that these texts professedly present the most enlightened and effective means presently used to obtain statements through custodial interrogation. By considering these texts and other data, it is possible to describe procedures observed and noted around the country.

The officers are told by the manuals that the "principal psychological factor contributing to a successful interrogation is *privacy*—being alone with the person under interrogation." The efficacy of this tactic has been explained as follows:

> "If at all practicable, the interrogation should take place in the investigator's office or at least in a room of his own choice. The subject should be deprived of every psychological advantage. In his own home he may be confident, indignant, or recalcitrant. He is more keenly aware of his rights and more reluctant to tell of his indiscretions or criminal behavior within the walls of his home. Moreover his family and other friends are nearby, their presence lending moral support. In his own office, the investigator possesses all the advantages. The atmosphere suggests the invincibility of the forces of the law."

To highlight the isolation and unfamiliar surroundings, the manuals instruct the police to display an air of confidence in the suspect's guilt and from outward appearance to maintain only an interest in confirming certain details. The guilt of the subject is to be posited as a fact. The interrogator should direct his comments toward the reasons why the subject committed the act, rather than court failure by asking the subject whether he did it. Like other men, perhaps the subject has had a bad family life, had an unhappy childhood, had too much to drink, had an

---

[9]   The methods described in Inbau & Reid, Criminal Interrogation and Confessions (1962), are a revision and enlargement of material presented in three prior editions of a predecessor text, Lie Detection and Criminal Interrogation (3d ed. 1953). * * * Similarly, the techniques described in O'Hara, Fundamentals of Criminal Investigation (1956), were gleaned from long service as observer, lecturer in police science, and work as a federal criminal investigator. All these texts have had rather extensive use among law enforcement agencies and among students of police science, with total sales and circulation of over 44,000.

unrequited desire for women. The officers are instructed to minimize the moral seriousness of the offense, to cast blame on the victim or on society. These tactics are designed to put the subject in a psychological state where his story is but an elaboration of what the police purport to know already—that he is guilty. Explanations to the contrary are dismissed and discouraged.

The texts thus stress that the major qualities an interrogator should possess are patience and perseverance. One writer describes the efficacy of these characteristics in this manner:

> "In the preceding paragraphs emphasis has been placed on kindness and stratagems. The investigator will, however, encounter many situations where the sheer weight of his personality will be the deciding factor. Where emotional appeals and tricks are employed to no avail, he must rely on an oppressive atmosphere of dogged persistence. He must interrogate steadily and without relent, leaving the subject no prospect of surcease. He must dominate his subject and overwhelm him with his inexorable will to obtain the truth. He should interrogate for a spell of several hours pausing only for the subject's necessities in acknowledgment of the need to avoid a charge of duress that can be technically substantiated. In a serious case, the interrogation may continue for days, with the required intervals for food and sleep, but with no respite from the atmosphere of domination. It is possible in this way to induce the suspect to talk without resorting to duress or coercion. The method should be used only when the guilt of the suspect appears highly probable."

The manuals suggest that the suspect be offered legal excuses for his actions in order to obtain an initial admission of guilt. Where there is a suspected revenge-killing, for example, the interrogator may say:

> "Joe, you probably didn't go out looking for this fellow with the purpose of shooting him. My guess is, however, that you expected something from him and that's why you carried a gun—for your own protection. You knew him for what he was, no good. Then when you met him he probably started using foul, abusive language and he gave some indication that he was about to pull a gun on you, and that's when you had to act to save your own life. That's about it, isn't it, Joe?"

Having then obtained the admission of shooting, the interrogator is advised to refer to circumstantial evidence which negates the self-defense explanation. This should enable him to secure the entire story. One text notes that "Even if he fails to do so, the inconsistency between the subject's original denial of the shooting and his present admission of at least doing the shooting will serve to deprive him of a self-defense 'out' at the time of trial." * * *

The interrogators sometimes are instructed to induce a confession out of trickery. The technique here is quite effective in crimes which require identification or which run in series. In the identification situation, the interrogator may take a break in his questioning to place the subject among a group of men in a line-up. "The witness or complainant (previously coached, if necessary) studies the line-up and confidently points out the subject as the guilty party." Then the questioning resumes "as though there were now no doubt about the guilt of the subject." A variation on this technique is called the "reverse line-up":

> "The accused is placed in a line-up, but this time he is identified by several fictitious witnesses or victims who associated him with different offenses. It is expected that the subject will become desperate and confess to the offense under investigation in order to escape from the false accusations." * * *

[The Court described other strategies, including the "Mutt and Jeff" act in which one officer plays the good cop and one the brutal bad cop who can be kept under control only if the suspect cooperates with the good cop. Another strategy discourages silence: "Suppose you were in my shoes and I were in yours and you called me in to ask me about this and I told you 'I don't want to answer any of your questions.' You'd think I had something to hide, and you'd probably be right in thinking that." Finally, one strategy discourages requests to talk to a lawyer or to a relative: "Joe I'm only looking for the truth, and if you're telling the truth, that's it. You can handle this by yourself." The Court noted, "Few will persist in their initial refusal to talk, it is said, if this monologue is employed correctly."]

From these representative samples of interrogation techniques, the setting prescribed by the manuals and observed in practice becomes clear. In essence, it is this: To be alone with the subject is essential to prevent distraction and to deprive him of any outside support. The aura of confidence in his guilt undermines his will to resist. He merely confirms the preconceived story the police seek to have him describe. Patience and persistence, at times relentless questioning, are employed. To obtain a confession, the interrogator must "patiently maneuver himself or his quarry into a position from which the desired objective may be attained." When normal procedures fail to produce the needed result, the police may resort to deceptive stratagems such as giving false legal advice. It is important to keep the subject off balance, for example, by trading on his insecurity about himself or his surroundings. The police then persuade, trick, or cajole him out of exercising his constitutional rights. * * *

In the cases before us today, given this background, we concern ourselves primarily with this interrogation atmosphere and the evils it can bring. In No. 759, *Miranda v. Arizona*, the police arrested the defendant and took him to a special interrogation room where they secured a confession. In No. 760, *Vignera v. New York*, the defendant made oral admissions to the police after interrogation in the afternoon, and then signed an inculpatory statement upon being questioned by an assistant district attorney later the same evening. In No. 761, *Westover v. United States*, the defendant was handed over to the Federal Bureau of Investigation by local authorities after they had detained and interrogated him for a lengthy period, both at night and the following morning. After some two hours of questioning, the federal officers had obtained signed statements from the defendant. Lastly, in No. 584, *California v. Stewart*, the local police held the defendant five days in the station and interrogated him on nine separate occasions before they secured his inculpatory statement.

In these cases, we might not find the defendants' statements to have been involuntary in traditional terms. Our concern for adequate safeguards to protect precious Fifth Amendment rights is, of course, not lessened in the slightest. In each of the cases, the defendant was thrust into an unfamiliar atmosphere and run through menacing police interrogation procedures. The potentiality for compulsion is forcefully apparent, for example, in *Miranda*, where the indigent Mexican defendant was a seriously disturbed individual with pronounced sexual fantasies, and in *Stewart*, in which the defendant was an indigent Los Angeles Negro who had dropped out of school in the sixth grade. To be sure, the records do not evince overt physical coercion or patent psychological ploys. The fact remains that in none of these cases did the officers undertake to afford appropriate safeguards at the outset of the interrogation to insure that the statements were truly the product of free choice.

It is obvious that such an interrogation environment is created for no purpose other than to subjugate the individual to the will of his examiner. This atmosphere carries its own badge of intimidation. To be sure, this is not physical intimidation, but it is equally destructive of human dignity. The current practice of incommunicado interrogation is at odds with one of our Nation's most cherished principles—that the individual may not be compelled to incriminate himself. Unless adequate protective devices are employed to dispel the compulsion inherent in custodial surroundings, no statement obtained from the defendant can truly be the product of his free choice.

From the foregoing, we can readily perceive an intimate connection between the privilege against self-incrimination and police custodial questioning. It is fitting to turn to history and precedent underlying the Self-Incrimination Clause to determine its applicability in this situation.

II.

We sometimes forget how long it has taken to establish the privilege against self-incrimination, the sources from which it came and the fervor with which it was defended. Its roots go back into ancient times. * * *

Thus we may view the historical development of the privilege as one which groped for the proper scope of governmental power over the citizen. As a "noble principle often transcends its origins," the privilege has come rightfully to be recognized in part as an individual's substantive right, a "right to a private enclave where he may lead a private life. That right is the hallmark of our democracy." We have recently noted that the privilege against self-incrimination—the essential mainstay of our adversary system—is founded on a complex of values. All these policies point to one overriding thought: the constitutional foundation underlying the privilege is the respect a government—state or federal—must accord to the dignity and integrity of its citizens. To maintain a "fair state-individual balance," to require the government "to shoulder the entire load," to respect the inviolability of the human personality, our accusatory system of criminal justice demands that the government seeking to punish an individual produce the evidence against him by its own independent labors, rather than by the cruel, simple expedient of compelling it from his own mouth. In sum, the privilege is fulfilled only when the person is guaranteed the right "to remain silent unless he chooses to speak in the unfettered exercise of his own will."

The question in these cases is whether the privilege is fully applicable during a period of custodial interrogation. In this Court, the privilege has consistently been accorded a liberal construction. We are satisfied that all the principles embodied in the privilege apply to informal compulsion exerted by law-enforcement officers during in-custody questioning. An individual swept from familiar surroundings into police custody, surrounded by antagonistic forces, and subjected to the techniques of persuasion described above cannot be otherwise than under compulsion to speak. As a practical matter, the compulsion to speak in the isolated setting of the police station may well be greater than in courts or other official investigations, where there are often impartial observers to guard against intimidation or trickery.

This question, in fact, could have been taken as settled in federal courts almost 70 years ago, when, in *Bram v. United States*, p. 615, this Court held:

"In criminal trials, in the courts of the United States, wherever a question arises whether a confession is incompetent because not voluntary, the issue is controlled by that portion of the Fifth

Amendment * * * commanding that no person 'shall be compelled in any criminal case to be a witness against himself.' " * * *

III

Today, then, there can be no doubt that the Fifth Amendment privilege is available outside of criminal court proceedings and serves to protect persons in all settings in which their freedom of action is curtailed in any significant way from being compelled to incriminate themselves. We have concluded that without proper safeguards the process of in-custody interrogation of persons suspected or accused of crime contains inherently compelling pressures which work to undermine the individual's will to resist and to compel him to speak where he would not otherwise do so freely. In order to combat these pressures and to permit a full opportunity to exercise the privilege against self-incrimination, the accused must be adequately and effectively apprised of his rights and the exercise of those rights must be fully honored.

It is impossible for us to foresee the potential alternatives for protecting the privilege which might be devised by Congress or the States in the exercise of their creative rule-making capacities. Therefore we cannot say that the Constitution necessarily requires adherence to any particular solution for the inherent compulsions of the interrogation process as it is presently conducted. Our decision in no way creates a constitutional straitjacket which will handicap sound efforts at reform, nor is it intended to have this effect. We encourage Congress and the States to continue their laudable search for increasingly effective ways of protecting the rights of the individual while promoting efficient enforcement of our criminal laws. However, unless we are shown other procedures which are at least as effective in apprising accused persons of their right of silence and in assuring a continuous opportunity to exercise it, the following safeguards must be observed.

At the outset, if a person in custody is to be subjected to interrogation, he must first be informed in clear and unequivocal terms that he has the right to remain silent. For those unaware of the privilege, the warning is needed simply to make them aware of it—the threshold requirement for an intelligent decision as to its exercise. More important, such a warning is an absolute prerequisite in overcoming the inherent pressures of the interrogation atmosphere. It is not just the subnormal or woefully ignorant who succumb to an interrogator's imprecations, whether implied or expressly stated, that the interrogation will continue until a confession is obtained or that silence in the face of accusation is itself damning and will bode ill when presented to a jury. Further, the warning will show the individual that his interrogators are prepared to recognize his privilege should he choose to exercise it.

The Fifth Amendment privilege is so fundamental to our system of constitutional rule and the expedient of giving an adequate warning as to the availability of the privilege so simple, we will not pause to inquire in individual cases whether the defendant was aware of his rights without a warning being given. Assessments of the knowledge the defendant possessed, based on information as to his age, education, intelligence, or prior contact with authorities, can never be more than a speculation. More important, whatever the background of the person interrogated, a warning at the time of the interrogation is indispensable to overcome its pressures and to insure that the individual knows he is free to exercise the privilege at that point in time.

The warning of the right to remain silent must be accompanied by the explanation that anything said can and will be used against the individual in court. This warning is needed in order to make him aware not only of the privilege, but also of the consequences of forgoing it. It is only through an awareness of these consequences that there can be any assurance of real understanding and intelligent exercise of the privilege. Moreover, this warning may serve to make the individual more acutely aware that he is faced with a phase of the adversary system—that he is not in the presence of persons acting solely in his interest.

The circumstances surrounding in-custody interrogation can operate very quickly to overbear the will of one merely made aware of his privilege by his interrogators. Therefore, the right to have counsel present at the interrogation is indispensable to the protection of the Fifth Amendment privilege under the system we delineate today. Our aim is to assure that the individual's right to choose between silence and speech remains unfettered throughout the interrogation process. A once-stated warning, delivered by those who will conduct the interrogation, cannot itself suffice to that end among those who most require knowledge of their rights. A mere warning given by the interrogators is not alone sufficient to accomplish that end. Prosecutors themselves claim that the admonishment of the right to remain silent without more "will benefit only the recidivist and the professional." Even preliminary advice given to the accused by his own attorney can be swiftly overcome by the secret interrogation process. Thus, the need for counsel to protect the Fifth Amendment privilege comprehends not merely a right to consult with counsel prior to questioning, but also to have counsel present during any questioning if the defendant so desires.

The presence of counsel at the interrogation may serve several significant subsidiary functions as well. If the accused decides to talk to his interrogators, the assistance of counsel can mitigate the dangers of untrustworthiness. With a lawyer present the likelihood that the police will practice coercion is reduced, and if coercion is nevertheless exercised the lawyer can testify to it in court. The presence of a lawyer can also help to guarantee that the accused gives a fully accurate statement to the police and that the statement is rightly reported by the prosecution at trial.

An individual need not make a pre-interrogation request for a lawyer. While such request affirmatively secures his right to have one, his failure to ask for a lawyer does not constitute a waiver. No effective waiver of the right to counsel during interrogation can be recognized unless specifically made after the warnings we here delineate have been given. The accused who does not know his rights and therefore does not make a request may be the person who most needs counsel. * * *

Accordingly we hold that an individual held for interrogation must be clearly informed that he has the right to consult with a lawyer and to have the lawyer with him during interrogation under the system for protecting the privilege we delineate today. As with the warnings of the right to remain silent and that anything stated can be used in evidence against him, this warning is an absolute prerequisite to interrogation. No amount of circumstantial evidence that the person may have been aware of this right will suffice to stand in its stead. Only through such a warning is there ascertainable assurance that the accused was aware of this right.

If an individual indicates that he wishes the assistance of counsel before any interrogation occurs, the authorities cannot rationally ignore or deny his request on the basis that the individual does not have or cannot afford a retained attorney. The financial ability of the individual has no relationship to the scope of the rights involved here. The privilege against self-incrimination secured by the Constitution applies to all individuals. The need for counsel in order to protect the privilege exists for the indigent as well as the affluent. In fact, were we to limit these constitutional rights to those who can retain an attorney, our decisions today would be of little significance. The cases before us as well as the vast majority of confession cases with which we have dealt in the past involve those unable to retain counsel. While authorities are not required to relieve the accused of his poverty, they have the obligation not to take advantage of indigence in the administration of justice. * * *

In order fully to apprise a person interrogated of the extent of his rights under this system then, it is necessary to warn him not only that he has the right to consult with an attorney, but also that if he is indigent a lawyer will be appointed to represent him. Without this additional warning, the admonition of the right to consult with counsel would often be understood as meaning only that he can consult with a lawyer if he has one or has funds to obtain one. The warning of a right to counsel would be hollow if not couched in terms that would convey to the indigent—the person most often subjected to interrogation—the knowledge that he too has a right to have counsel present. As with the warnings of the right to remain silent and of the general right to counsel, only by effective and express explanation to the indigent of this right can there be assurance that he was truly in a position to exercise it.

Once warnings have been given, the subsequent procedure is clear. If the individual indicates in any manner, at any time prior to or during questioning, that he wishes to remain silent, the interrogation must cease. At this point he has shown that he intends to exercise his Fifth Amendment privilege; any statement taken after the person invokes his privilege cannot be other than the product of compulsion, subtle or otherwise. Without the right to cut off questioning, the setting of in-custody interrogation operates on the individual to overcome free choice in producing a statement after the privilege has been once invoked. If the individual states that he wants an attorney, the interrogation must cease until an attorney is present. At that time, the individual must have an opportunity to confer with the attorney and to have him present during any subsequent questioning. If the individual cannot obtain an attorney and he indicates that he wants one before speaking to police, they must respect his decision to remain silent. * * *

If the interrogation continues without the presence of an attorney and a statement is taken, a heavy burden rests on the government to demonstrate that the defendant knowingly and intelligently waived his privilege against self-incrimination and his right to retained or appointed counsel. This Court has always set high standards of proof for the waiver of constitutional rights, and we re-assert these standards as applied to in-custody interrogation. Since the State is responsible for establishing the isolated circumstances under which the interrogation takes place and has the only means of making available corroborated evidence of warnings given during incommunicado interrogation, the burden is rightly on its shoulders.

An express statement that the individual is willing to make a statement and does not want an attorney followed closely by a statement could constitute a waiver. But a valid waiver will not be presumed simply from the silence of the accused after warnings are given or simply from the fact that a confession was in fact eventually obtained. A statement we made in *Carnley v. Cochran*, 369 U.S. 506, 516, 82 S.Ct. 884, 8 L.Ed.2d 70 (1962), is applicable here:

> "Presuming waiver from a silent record is impermissible. The record must show, or there must be an allegation and evidence which show, that an accused was offered counsel but intelligently and understandingly rejected the offer. Anything less is not waiver."

Moreover, where in-custody interrogation is involved, there is no room for the contention that the privilege is waived if the individual answers some questions or gives some information on his own prior to invoking his right to remain silent when interrogated.

Whatever the testimony of the authorities as to waiver of rights by an accused, the fact of lengthy interrogation or incommunicado incarceration before a statement is made is strong evidence that the accused did not validly waive his rights. In these circumstances the fact that the individual eventually made a statement is consistent with the conclusion that the compelling influence of the interrogation finally forced him to do so. It is inconsistent with any notion of a voluntary relinquishment of the privilege. Moreover, any evidence that the accused was threatened, tricked, or cajoled into a waiver will, of course, show that the defendant did not voluntarily waive his privilege. The requirement of warnings and waiver of rights is a fundamental with respect to the Fifth Amendment privilege and not simply a preliminary ritual to existing methods of interrogation.

The warnings required and the waiver necessary in accordance with our opinion today are, in the absence of a fully effective equivalent, prerequisites to the admissibility of any statement made by a defendant. No distinction can be drawn between statements which are direct confessions and statements which amount to "admissions" of part or all of an offense. The privilege against self-incrimination protects the individual from being compelled to incriminate himself in any manner; it does not distinguish degrees of incrimination. Similarly, for precisely the same reason, no distinction may be drawn between inculpatory statements and statements alleged to be merely "exculpatory." If a statement made were in fact truly exculpatory it would, of course, never be used by the prosecution. In fact, statements merely intended to be exculpatory by the defendant are often used to impeach his testimony at trial or to demonstrate untruths in the statement given under interrogation and thus to prove guilt by implication. These statements are incriminating in any meaningful sense of the word and may not be used without the full warnings and effective waiver required for any other statement. In *Escobedo* itself, the defendant fully intended his accusation of another as the slayer to be exculpatory as to himself.

The principles announced today deal with the protection which must be given to the privilege against self-incrimination when the individual is first subjected to police interrogation while in custody at the station or otherwise deprived of his freedom of action in any significant way. It is at this point that our adversary system of criminal proceedings commences, distinguishing itself at the outset from the inquisitorial system recognized in some countries. Under the system of warnings we delineate today or under any other system which may be devised and found effective, the safeguards to be erected about the privilege must come into play at this point.

Our decision is not intended to hamper the traditional function of police officers in investigating crime. When an individual is in custody on probable cause, the police may, of course, seek out evidence in the field to be used at trial against him. Such investigation may include inquiry of persons not under restraint. General on-the-scene questioning as to facts surrounding a crime or other general questioning of citizens in the fact-finding process is not affected by our holding. It is an act of responsible citizenship for individuals to give whatever information they may have to aid in law enforcement. In such situations the compelling atmosphere inherent in the process of in-custody interrogation is not necessarily present. * * *

To summarize, we hold that when an individual is taken into custody or otherwise deprived of his freedom by the authorities in any significant way and is subjected to questioning, the privilege against self-incrimination is jeopardized. Procedural safeguards must be employed to protect the privilege, and unless other fully effective means are adopted to notify the person of his right to silence and to assure that the exercise of the right will be scrupulously honored, the following measures are required. He must be warned prior to any questioning that he has the right to remain silent, that anything he says can be used against him in a court of law, that he has the right to the presence of an attorney, and that if he cannot afford an attorney one will be appointed for him prior to any questioning if he so desires. Opportunity to exercise these rights must be afforded to him throughout the interrogation. After such warnings have been given, and such opportunity afforded him, the individual may knowingly and intelligently waive these rights and agree to answer questions or make a statement. But unless and until such warnings and waiver are demonstrated by the prosecution at trial, no evidence obtained as a result of interrogation can be used against him. * * *

V

Because of the nature of the problem and because of its recurrent significance in numerous cases, we have to this point discussed the relationship of the Fifth Amendment privilege to police interrogation without specific concentration on the facts of the cases before us. We turn now to these facts to consider the application to these cases of the constitutional principles discussed above. In each instance, we have concluded that statements were obtained from the defendant under circumstances that did not meet constitutional standards for protection of the privilege.

No. 759. *Miranda v. Arizona.*

On March 13, 1963, petitioner, Ernesto Miranda, was arrested at his home and taken in custody to a Phoenix police station. He was there identified by the complaining witness. The police then took him to "Interrogation Room No. 2" of the detective bureau. There he was questioned by two police officers. The officers admitted at trial that Miranda was not advised that he had a right to have an attorney present. Two hours later, the officers emerged from the interrogation room with a written confession signed by Miranda. At the top of the statement was a typed paragraph stating that the confession was made voluntarily, without threats or promises of immunity and "with full knowledge of my legal rights, understanding any statement I make may be used against me."

At his trial before a jury, the written confession was admitted into evidence over the objection of defense counsel, and the officers testified to the prior oral confession made by Miranda during the interrogation. Miranda was found guilty of kidnapping and rape. He was sentenced to 20 to 30 years' imprisonment on each count, the sentences to run concurrently. On appeal, the Supreme Court of Arizona held that Miranda's constitutional rights were not violated in obtaining the confession and affirmed the conviction. In reaching its decision, the court emphasized heavily the fact that Miranda did not specifically request counsel.

We reverse. From the testimony of the officers and by the admission of respondent, it is clear that Miranda was not in any way apprised of his right to consult with an attorney and to have one present during the interrogation, nor was his right not to be compelled to incriminate himself effectively protected in any other manner. Without these warnings the statements were inadmissible. The mere fact that he signed a statement which contained a typed-in clause stating that he had "full knowledge" of his "legal rights" does not approach the knowing and intelligent waiver required to relinquish constitutional rights. * * *

[The Court reversed the other three convictions as well. The opinion of JUSTICE CLARK, dissenting in three of the cases, including *Miranda*, and concurring in the result in one of the cases, is omitted.]

MR. JUSTICE HARLAN, with whom MR. JUSTICE STEWART and MR. JUSTICE WHITE join, dissenting. * * *

I * * *

While the fine points of [the majority's] scheme are far less clear than the Court admits, the tenor is quite apparent. The new rules are not designed to guard against police brutality or other unmistakably banned forms of coercion. Those who use third-degree tactics and deny them in court are equally able and destined to lie as skillfully about warnings and waivers. Rather, the thrust of the new rules is to negate all pressures, to reinforce the nervous or ignorant suspect, and ultimately to discourage any confession at all. The aim in short is toward "voluntariness" in a utopian sense, or to view it from a different angle, voluntariness with a vengeance.

To incorporate this notion into the Constitution requires a strained reading of history and precedent and a disregard of the very pragmatic concerns that alone may on occasion justify such strains. * * *

III * * *

What the Court largely ignores is that its rules impair, if they will not eventually serve wholly to frustrate, an instrument of law enforcement that has long and quite reasonably been thought worth the price paid for it. There can be little doubt that the Court's new code would markedly decrease the number of confessions. * * *

While passing over the costs and risks of its experiment, the Court portrays the evils of normal police questioning in terms which I think are exaggerated. Albeit stringently confined by the due process standards interrogation is no doubt often inconvenient and unpleasant for the suspect. However, it is no less so for a man to be arrested and jailed, to have his house searched, or to stand trial in court, yet all this may properly happen to the most innocent given probable cause, a warrant, or an indictment. Society has always paid a stiff price for law and order, and peaceful interrogation is not one of the dark moments of the law. * * *

MR. JUSTICE WHITE, with whom MR. JUSTICE HARLAN and MR. JUSTICE STEWART join, dissenting. * * *

III * * *

Although in the Court's view in-custody interrogation is inherently coercive, the Court says that the spontaneous product of the coercion of arrest and detention is still to be deemed voluntary. An accused, arrested on probable cause, may blurt out a confession which will be admissible despite the fact that he is alone and in custody, without any showing that he had any notion of his right to remain silent or of the consequences of his admission. Yet, under the Court's rule, if the police ask him a single question such as "Do you have anything to say?" or "Did you kill your wife?" his response, if there is one, has somehow been compelled, even if the accused has been clearly warned of his right to remain silent. Common sense informs us to the contrary. While one may say that the response was "involuntary" in the sense the question provoked or was the occasion for the response and thus the defendant was induced to speak out when he might have remained silent if not arrested and not questioned, it is patently unsound to say the response is compelled. * * *

On the other hand, even if one assumed that there was an adequate factual basis for the conclusion that all confessions obtained during in-custody interrogation are the product of compulsion, the rule propounded by the Court would still be irrational, for, apparently, it is only if the accused is also warned of his right to counsel and waives both that right and the right against self-incrimination that the inherent compulsiveness of interrogation disappears. But if the defendant may not answer without a warning a question such as "Where were you last night?" without having his answer be a compelled one, how can the Court ever accept his negative answer to the question of whether he wants to consult his retained counsel or counsel whom the court will appoint? And why if counsel is present and the accused nevertheless confesses, or counsel tells the accused to tell the truth, and that is what the accused does, is the situation any less coercive insofar as the accused is concerned? The Court apparently realizes its dilemma of foreclosing questioning without the necessary warnings but at the same time permitting the accused, sitting in the same chair in front of the same policemen, to waive his right to consult an attorney. It expects, however, that the accused will not often waive that right; and if it is claimed that he has, the State faces a severe, if not impossible, burden of proof. * * *

In sum, for all the Court's expounding on the menacing atmosphere of police interrogation procedures, it has failed to supply any foundation for the conclusions it draws or the measures it adopts.

IV * * *

The most basic function of any government is to provide for the security of the individual and of his property. These ends of society are served by the criminal laws which for the most part are aimed at the prevention of crime. Without the reasonably effective performance of the task of preventing private violence and retaliation, it is idle to talk about human dignity and civilized values. * * *

In some unknown number of cases the Court's rule will return a killer, a rapist or other criminal to the streets and to the environment which produced him, to repeat his crime whenever it pleases him. As a consequence, there will not be a gain, but a loss, in human dignity. The real concern is not the unfortunate consequences of this new decision on the criminal law as an abstract, disembodied series of authoritative proscriptions, but the impact on those who rely on the public authority for protection and who without it can only engage in violent self-help with guns, knives and the help of their neighbors similarly inclined. There is, of course, a saving factor: the next victims are uncertain, unnamed and unrepresented in this case. * * *

NOTES AND QUESTIONS

1.   What is the narrow holding of *Miranda*? Is the holding inconsistent with the Court's analytical approach in *Bram*?

2.   *Is Miranda legitimate?* The point to a Constitution, of course, is to enshrine certain principles so fundamental that they should stand even when a majority of the country thinks otherwise. This role is often called "counter-majoritarian" because it stands in the way of the ordinary democratic process. But when the Court seems to depart from the text or the meaning of the Constitution in implementing its view of fairness or justice, its counter-majoritarian function is potentially more controversial, and its legitimacy potentially weakened. We will shortly see, in Part C, both of those effects from *Miranda*.

When the Court is tempted to find new rights in old language, perhaps it should pause to consider how our society has become more partisan, the tenor of our discussions more shrill, the debates over Supreme Court nominees more contentious, and the decisions of the Court more indecipherable to the majority of our citizenry. Judging from the large percentage of our society that chooses not to take advantage of its right to vote, it appears that we have become increasingly disengaged from and cynical towards the democratic process as a means of effective societal change. Application of the Constitution as a counter-majoritarian check has not come without a price.

Assume, for the moment, that the Framers did not intend the privilege to apply to voluntary, pre-trial confessions, given in ignorance of a "right" to remain silent and in the absence of an attorney. Does that historical understanding make *Miranda* an illegitimate usurpation of the democratic process? Putting history to one side, do you think the text of the Fifth Amendment can be stretched to fit *Miranda* and thus give it legitimacy?

Does it matter to you in terms of legitimacy that in Wilson v. United States, 162 U.S. 613, 16 S.Ct. 895, 40 L.Ed. 1090 (1896), the Court squarely held that warnings of the right to remain silent were not required to secure admission of a statement? Or that the *Miranda* majority did not even mention *Wilson's* contrary holding?

3.   Does the *Miranda* Court see the interrogation problem as police compulsion or, rather, as the police cajoling suspects in a way that creates or exploits the natural tendency to appear co-operative? That tendency would naturally lead suspects to talk even when it is not in their best interests. Perhaps the *Miranda* warnings were intended to create a set of preferences that exist in opposition to the preferences that police wish suspects to have. See Louis Michael Seidman, *Rubashov's Question: Self-Incrimination and the Problem of Coerced Preferences*, 2 Yale J. L. & Human. 149 (1990).

Police are, of course, quintessential authority figures. Moreover, as Professor Kent Greenawalt provocatively argued in *Silence as a Moral and Constitutional Right*, 23 Wm. & Mary L. Rev. 15 (1981), the ordinary morality we apply in our day-to-day lives usually requires a response when someone accuses us of malfeasance or misfeasance. If your co-worker, for instance, asks why you failed to cover for her as you promised, the future working relationship will be strained if you respond, "I don't have to answer that question." If you do answer, moreover, it is odd to think of that answer as compelled by the questioner. It seems more likely that you evaluated the consequences of answering and not answering, and chose by an exercise of your will to answer. Why consider this choice to be "compulsion"? Examine the text of the Fifth Amendment. What is the textual basis for a "right to remain silent"?

4.   *The fox-hunt analogy.* The *Miranda* dissents raise, in one form or another, the normative question: What is wrong with taking advantage of the weakness of guilty suspects to obtain a confession? One answer is Professor William Stuntz's. He argued that the *Miranda* Court misread the self-incrimination clause as protecting privacy rather than freedom from coercion. *Miranda*'s limits on police questioning, on this view, began with the premise that "the information belonged to the defendant, it was private, and the government had no right to get it unless the defendant chose—*really* chose—to give it up." William J. Stuntz, *The Substantive Origins of Criminal Procedure,* 105 Yale L.J. 393, 441 (1995).

Professor Gerald Caplan put it as follows:

> Perhaps the impulse to allow even the unquestionably guilty some prospect of escaping detection or conviction is universal. Wigmore referred to this impulse as the "instinct of giving the game fair play." Pound characterized it as "the sporting theory" of justice, and Bentham derisively labeled it "the fox hunter's reason." Under this view, fairness is given that special definition that sportsmen reserve for their games. Bentham elaborated on his analogy to the fox hunt: "The fox is to have a fair chance for his life: he must have * * * leave to run a certain length of way, for the express purpose of giving him a chance for escape." Fairness, so defined, dictates that neither side should have an undue advantage; the police and the criminal should be on roughly equal footing and the rules of the game should be drawn to avoid favoring one side or the other. As Justice Fortas put it in a well-known article (written before he joined the Court), the accused and the accuser are "equals, meeting in battle." The state was sovereign, but so was the individual. The individual possessed the "sovereign right * * * to meet the state on terms as equal as their respective strength would permit * * * strength against strength, resource against resource, argument against argument." * * *

> [T]he *Miranda* approach reflects a bias against self-accusation on principle. This bias has roots in the desire to treat suspects equally. Suspects who do not know their rights, or do not assert them, as a consequence of some handicap—poverty, lack of education, emotional instability—should not, it is felt, fare worse

than more accomplished suspects who know and have the capacity to assert their rights. This "equal protection" appeal finds its way repeatedly into judicial opinions and legal commentary. In *Miranda* itself, Chief Justice Warren referred approvingly to [a] California Supreme Court's decision * * *, which stressed that "the defendant who does not realize his rights under the law and who therefore does not request counsel is the very defendant who most needs counsel." A few years earlier, Professor Beisel similarly argued that only the "frightened, the insecure, the weak, and untrained, the bewildered, the stupid, the naive, the credulous" confess. * * * To the extent that these observations are true—and they seem true enough—they suggest two distinct remedies. One would be to make it more difficult to convict those who are most vulnerable; the other would be to develop ways to bring those hardier, more knowledgeable persons—the hired killer, the calculating embezzler, the experienced burglar—to justice. The critics * * * have preferred the former. They do not see the lack of stamina and professionalism of the suspect as conferring a benefit on society by facilitating the identification of wrongdoers.

But guilt is personal. That another, equally guilty, person got away with murder because of some fortuitous factor—he was more experienced in dealing with the police, he had a poorly developed sense of guilt, he had a smart lawyer, he knew his rights—or even because of discrimination, does not make the more vulnerable murderer less guilty. To hold otherwise is to confuse justice with equality. "Both are desirable. However, neither can replace the other." Since sophisticated suspects ordinarily will choose not to confess (with or without knowledge of their rights), "[t]o strive for equality * * * is to strive to eliminate confessions." Thus, the *Miranda* Court elected to let one person get away with murder because of the advantage possessed by another.

Gerald M. Caplan, *Questioning Miranda*, 38 Vand. L. Rev. 1417, 1441–42, 1456–58 (1985).

5.   *Miranda: more pros and cons.* The Supreme Court has spoken of the privilege in stirring language. For example, "the roots of the privilege * * * tap the basic stream of religious and political principle because the privilege reflects the limits of the individual's attornment to the state and—in a philosophical sense—insists upon the equality of the individual and the state." In re Gault, 387 U.S. 1, 87 S.Ct. 1428, 18 L.Ed.2d 527 (1967). Before he joined the Court, Abe Fortas wrote: "A man may be punished, even put to death by the state, but * * * he should not be made to prostrate himself before its majesty. Mea culpa belongs to a man and his God. It is a plea that cannot be exacted from free men by human authority." Abe Fortas, *The Fifth Amendment: Nemo Tenetur Prodere Seipsum*, 25 Clev. B. Ass'n J. 91, 100 (1954).

The Court noted in 1964 that "the privilege, while sometimes 'a shelter to the guilty,' is often 'a protection to the innocent.'" Does the privilege only "sometimes" shelter the guilty but "often" protect the innocent? It does not seem likely. To be sure, an innocent defendant might make a poor witness or have a felony record that can be introduced to impeach his credibility if he testifies. Professor Stephen Schulhofer notes that the defendant "may look sleazy. He may be inarticulate, nervous, or easily intimidated. His vague memory on some of the details may leave him vulnerable to a clever cross-examination." Stephen J. Schulhofer, *Some Kind Words for the Privilege Against Self-Incrimination*, 26 Val. U. L. Rev. 311, 330 (1991). But Judge Henry Friendly concluded that the privilege "so much more often shelters the guilty" that its "occasional effect in protecting the innocent would be an altogether insufficient reason" to find the privilege beneficial. Henry J. Friendly, *The Fifth Amendment Tomorrow: The Case for Constitutional Change*, 37 U. Cin. L. Rev. 671, 687 (1968).

Professor Donald Dripps has remarked, with characteristic economy that "[t]he privilege is at best an anachronism and at worst a constitutional blunder." Donald Dripps, *Akhil Amar On Criminal Procedure and Constitutional Law: "Here I Go Down That Wrong Road Again,"* 74 N. C. L. Rev. 1559, 1635 (1996). As you proceed through this chapter, you should consider whether you agree more with Professor Dripps's characterization of the Fifth Amendment privilege or, instead, the sentiments in the first paragraph of this Note.

6.   Would *Miranda* apply to suspects who do not know that they are being questioned by police? Do you see the argument that it would not apply? With only Justice Marshall dissenting, the Court held in Illinois v. Perkins, 496 U.S. 292, 110 S.Ct. 2394, 110 L.Ed.2d 243 (1990), that encounters between suspects and undercover officers are not subject to *Miranda*, noting that "warnings are not required when the suspect is unaware that he is speaking to a law enforcement officer and gives a voluntary statement." The Court stated the rationale this way:

> Conversations between suspects and undercover agents do not implicate the concerns underlying *Miranda*. The essential ingredients of a "police-dominated atmosphere" and compulsion are not present when an incarcerated person speaks freely to someone that he believes to be a fellow inmate. Coercion is determined from the perspective of the suspect. When a suspect considers himself in the company of cellmates and not officers, the coercive atmosphere is lacking.

In his dissent, Justice Marshall raised the specter of the police posing as a priest or as the suspect's lawyer. Are those distinguishable from routine contacts with undercover officers? What arguments would you make on behalf of those suspects?

7.   *Where are they now?* The Court's sweeping judgment in *Miranda* was hardly the end of Ernest Miranda's contact with the criminal justice

system. The state re-prosecuted—without the confession given to the police, of course—and the second trial ended again in a conviction. The principal evidence was a confession Miranda made to his girlfriend when she visited him in jail a few days after he had confessed to the police. Liva Baker, Miranda: Crime, Law and Politics 291 (1983). Miranda's second conviction was affirmed on appeal, and the United States Supreme Court denied certiorari. Thus, Ernest Miranda served a prison term for the very rape that led to the most controversial criminal procedure ruling in the history of the Supreme Court.

But that is not the end of the story. After Miranda was paroled, he returned to Phoenix, and worked for a time as an appliance store deliveryman. On January 31, 1976, he played poker with two Mexican immigrants in La Ampola, a "dusty bar in the Deuce section of Phoenix." A fistfight escalated into a knife attack on Miranda. He was stabbed twice and was dead on arrival at Good Samaritan Hospital. Miranda was 34 years old. The police apprehended one of the immigrants, later charged as an accomplice in the killing of Miranda. The officers read the suspect his *Miranda* rights. Baker, at 408.

Thinking About *Miranda:* A Lawyer's (and Law Student's) Checklist

You have read *Miranda*, seen the *Perkins* clarification, p. 644, Note 6, and learned what happened to Miranda the man. Now we begin the road of learning what happened to *Miranda*—the doctrine—after the case was decided. Before we begin the story, it is worth setting out the basic issues that a lawyer or law student needs to consider when a *Miranda* issue potentially arises in a specific case.

First, there is the triggering mechanism for *Miranda* warnings—custodial interrogation. We will see later that the Supreme Court treats this concept as if it were two independent elements, "custody" and "interrogation." And, both elements can be difficult to discern in specific cases.

Second, assuming a finding of "custodial interrogation," *Miranda* warnings are ordinarily required. But, as *Miranda* teaches, a suspect may waive her "*Miranda* rights." What constitutes a valid waiver can also be a complicated matter. By far, waiver is the most litigated *Miranda* issue in criminal proceedings.

Third, if *Miranda* warnings are not given when they should be, or if they are given but a valid waiver is not secured, the suspect's statements received by the police are generally inadmissible. But, there is another question that may come to your mind: What about any "fruits" of the *Miranda* violation? Are *they* subject to exclusion as well, in the same way as "fruits of the poisonous tree" are handled in the Fourth Amendment? Wait until you see what the Supreme Court has said about that!

Fourth, are there exceptions to the *Miranda* rule? That is, are there circumstances in which the police do *not* have to give *Miranda* warnings in advance of custodial interrogation, or are there circumstances in which the remedy for violation of the *Miranda* rule does *not* include total exclusion of the original *Miranda*-less statement?

It would be nice if we could look at *Miranda* law in the organized manner set out above, but the Supreme Court's torturous path through the *Miranda* thicket hinders such a straight-forward approach. As it turns out, the Supreme Court, almost from the start of the post-*Miranda* era, began to back away from the case's implications, but did so in a somewhat odd way: It began to re-characterize *Miranda*'s relationship to the Fifth Amendment. As you will see, that re-characterization has an impact on how the *Miranda* doctrine is applied. Re-characterization led to reshaping. So, rather than turn to the *Miranda* issues in the order we set them out above—the way a lawyer might analyze a *Miranda* problem today—we will start with a description of the stormy seas in which the decision found itself, and see how those seas re-shaped the case. Warning: Even in the "stormy seas" there is law to learn. In particular, be on the lookout for the Court's approach to the "fruits" issue, and to the "exceptions to *Miranda*" question.

C. STORMY SEAS FOR *MIRANDA*

1. THE POLITICAL REACTION TO *MIRANDA*: NIXON, GEORGE WALLACE, AND THE OMNIBUS CRIME CONTROL ACT

The reaction to *Miranda* was intense. Police and district attorneys railed against what they saw as a major blow to their ability to solve crimes. Newspaper editorials were generally opposed. By the summer of 1968, both Richard Nixon and George Wallace sought to use the Warren Court as a campaign issue against Democrat Hubert Humphrey. George Wallace, running for president on the American Independent Party ticket, made the following remarks during a rally in Cicero, Illinois, remarks that were a standard part of his campaign speech. The Supreme Court, Wallace said, was a "sorry, lousy, no-account outfit." Murderers and rapists are "just laughing while the police are crying for help." If a criminal "knocks you over the head," he will be "out of jail before you're out of the hospital and the policeman who arrested him will be on trial. But some psychologist says, 'well he's not to blame, society's to blame. His father didn't take him to see the Pittsburgh Pirates when he was a little boy.'" Then, a promise from Wallace: "If we were President now, you wouldn't get stabbed or raped in the shadow of the White House, even if we had to call out 30,000 troops and equip them with two-foot-long bayonets and station them every few feet apart." Liva Baker, Miranda: Crime, Law and Politics 243–44 (1983).

According to Baker, Richard Nixon's strategy was to appear as a "more respectable alternative" to Wallace, "countering his rhetoric 'with a velvet-glove version of the mailed fist.' " Again according to Baker, although there were many contentious issues in the 1968 campaign (Vietnam, welfare, inflation, taxes, President Johnson's War on Poverty, Social Security), "the issue that stood out, its theme in every speech at every airport and on every makeshift stage, the one that was remembered most vividly years later, was [Nixon's] appeal for 'law and order.' " *Id.* at 244.

Focusing specifically on *Miranda*, Nixon said in Ohio two weeks before the election:

> I was in Philadelphia the other day. I found that a cab driver who had been cruelly murdered and robbed, and the man who murdered and robbed him had confessed the crime, was set free because of a Supreme Court decision. An old woman, who had been brutally robbed and then murdered—the man who confessed the crime was set free because of a Supreme Court decision. * * * And an old man who had been robbed and clubbed to death—and the man who confessed the crime was set free in Las Vegas. My friends, when that's happening in thousands of cases all over America, I say this. Some of our courts have gone too far in their decisions weakening the peace forces as against the criminal forces in the United States of America. And we're going to change that.

Id. at 248.

Just as telling as the attacks on the Court and on *Miranda* by Wallace and Nixon was Hubert Humphrey's failure to defend the Court. Only one position was presented to the American voter in 1968: The Court had gone too far in the direction of protecting criminals; the criminal forces were gaining an upper hand over the peace forces; something had to be done to right the ship. The voters spoke, giving 57% to Nixon and Wallace, and only 43% to Humphrey. In four years, Democratic votes for president declined from Lyndon Johnson's 61% to Humphrey's 43%. Many issues drove voters into the arms of Richard Nixon, including the hugely unpopular Vietnam War, the protests and counter-protests about the war, the race riots that erupted in over one hundred American cities in the summer of 1968, and the rioting at the Democratic convention that was put down by the heavy hand of Mayor Daley's police in riot gear. By the election in November, 1968, almost thirty thousand Americans had been killed in Vietnam and thousands more had been killed or injured in rioting throughout the country. Still, the unpopularity of the Warren Court played a part in the decline of Democratic fortunes. As Fred Graham put it:

> Where its predecessors had been bold, *Miranda* was to be brazen—*Gideon v. Wainwright* [p. 1043] had created a constitutional right to counsel in felony cases at a time when all but five states already provided it; *Mapp v. Ohio* [p. 83] had extended the exclusionary rule to illegal searches after roughly one-half of the states had adopted the same rule; *Miranda* was to impose limits on police interrogation that no state had even approached * * * .

Fred P. Graham, The Self-Inflicted Wound 158 (1970). Ultimately, the question was not so much whether "suspects should be warned of their rights, but whether *Miranda* was worth the price." *Id.* at 192.

In a 1968 campaign speech, Nixon promised "legislation to restore the balance" between the "peace forces" and "criminal forces." Baker, *supra*, at 245–46. Congress beat him to the punch, passing in the summer the Omnibus Crime Control and Safe Streets Act of 1968. What follows gives some sense of the rhetoric on the floor of the Congress.

[Senator McClellan:] [C]rime and the threat of crime, rioting, and violence, stalk America. Our streets are unsafe. Our Citizens are fearful, terrorized, and outraged. * * *

The war on crime must be fought on many fronts. * * * Court decisions that dispense "unequal" justice to society and which protect and liberate guilty and confirmed criminals to pursue and repeat their nefarious crimes should be reversed and overruled. * * * The confusion and disarray injected into law enforcement by [*Miranda* and other cases] are deplorable and demoralizing. * * *

* * * Look at that chart [of the crime rate]. Look at it and weep for your country. * * *

* * * [I]f this effort to deal with these erroneous Court decisions is defeated, every gangster and overlord of the underworld; every syndicate chief, racketeer, captain, lieutenant, sergeant, private, punk, and hoodlum in organized crime; every murderer, rapist, robber, burglar, arsonist, thief, and conman will have cause to rejoice and celebrate.

* * * [A]nd every innocent, law-abiding, and God-fearing citizen in this land will have cause to weep and despair.

114 Cong. Rec. 11,200–01, 14,146, 14,155.

Part of the resulting bill was 18 U.S.C. § 3501, a statute intended to "overrule" *Miranda*. We will return to § 3501 later in the chapter.

And Nixon was doing his part. His first appointment to the Court was conservative jurist Warren E. Burger to replace Chief Justice Earl Warren in 1969. Within the next three years, Nixon would replace Abe Fortas and Hugo Black with Harry Blackmun and Lewis Powell. Three-fifths of the *Miranda* majority would be gone by 1972. Nixon also replaced Justice Harlan with Justice William Rehnquist. Although Justice Harlan dissented in *Miranda*, he believed in an old-fashioned form of stare decisis in which he would follow a decision with which he disagreed unless he could persuade a majority to overrule the disfavored decision. Thus, he could be counted on to follow *Miranda*. Justice Rehnquist did not share Harlan's view of stare decisis. Many Court watchers and scholars thought it was just a matter of finding the right case, and *Miranda* would be overruled. Like many predictions of the future, this one was spectacularly wrong. Instead of being overruled, *Miranda* was limited by later Courts stressing that it was not required by the Fifth Amendment.

NOTES AND QUESTIONS

1.   For an account of the politics and debate surrounding § 3501, see Yale Kamisar, *Can (Did) Congress "Overrule" Miranda?*, 85 Cornell L. Rev. 883 (2000).

2.   One of the pre-*Miranda* efforts to regulate police interrogation was based on Federal Rule of Criminal Procedure 5(a), which requires officers to bring arrestees before a federal magistrate "without unnecessary delay." In 1943, the Court created a remedy of exclusion for violations of this rule. Statements taken after the permissible time period had passed had to be suppressed. See McNabb v. United States, 318 U.S. 332, 63 S.Ct. 608, 87 L.Ed. 819 (1943); see also Mallory v. United States, 354 U.S. 449, 77 S.Ct. 1356, 1 L.Ed.2d 1479 (1957).

Part of 18 U.S.C. § 3501 was a limitation on the *McNabb-Mallory* rule that, the Court held in 2009, makes the rule inapplicable when the statements are made in the first six hours after arrest. See Corley v. United States, 556 U.S. 303, 129 S.Ct. 1558, 173 L.Ed.2d 443 (2009). Notice the significance of this ruling: A statement obtained from an arrestee who has been held by federal agents longer than six hours before being brought before a federal magistrate is potentially inadmissible in a federal trial *even if Miranda warnings were given and properly waived, and even if the statement was not coerced under traditional due process or self-incrimination grounds!* To be sure, if the delay is longer than six hours, the *Corley* majority made plain that the government can argue that the delay was reasonable or necessary and thus avoid suppression.

2. THE DOCTRINAL REACTION TO *MIRANDA*: CLARIFYING *MIRANDA*'S STATUS

Introductory Comment

Revisit Note 1, p. 641. What was your answer? One statement of the narrow holding is that the convictions were reversed because the prosecution failed to demonstrate that the suspects had waived the rights that the Court found implicit in the Fifth Amendment. But, notice, that statement of the holding renders everything else in the opinion as dicta. As you know, dicta is technically not binding on future courts. So, for example, *Miranda* said that "the prosecution may not use statements, whether exculpatory or inculpatory, stemming from custodial interrogation of the defendant unless it demonstrates the use of procedural safeguards effective to secure the privilege against self-incrimination." Given this statement of the law (or is it dicta?), should the prosecution be able to use statements taken in violation of *Miranda* to impeach the defendant's testimony?

In 1971, Chief Justice Burger delivered a holding that statements taken in violation of *Miranda* could be used to impeach a defendant's testimony. Harris v. New York, 401 U.S. 222, 91 S.Ct. 643, 28 L.Ed.2d 1 (1971). Burger, for five members of the Court, noted: "Some comments in the *Miranda* opinion can indeed be read as indicating a bar to use of an uncounseled statement for any purpose, but discussion of that issue was not at all necessary to the Court's holding and cannot be regarded as controlling." Dicta ignored. The dissent argued, '[w]e settled this proposition in *Miranda*, but dicta settles nothing. Justice Harlan joined the majority opinion. Given his view of stare decisis, he must have believed that the impeachment issue was not part of the narrow holding in *Miranda*.

There is another problem with *Miranda*'s dicta. Perhaps because it was necessary to get five votes for the majority opinion in *Miranda*, the opinion contains dicta that are in conflict. Some language suggests that the *Miranda* warnings are *required* by the Fifth Amendment privilege against compelled self-incrimination. The second sentence of the opinion notes that "we deal with * * * the necessity for procedures which assure that the individual is accorded his privilege under the Fifth Amendment to the Constitution not to be compelled to incriminate himself." Later in the introduction, the Court said it was holding that no statement could be used unless the prosecution "demonstrates the use of procedural safeguards effective to secure the privilege against self-incrimination." And the Court spells out those procedures more than once as the warnings and waiver regime.

But the Court draws its punch in a major way in a paragraph reportedly inserted at the insistence of Justice Brennan. Return to the *Miranda* opinion and re-read the second paragraph in Part III:

This paragraph's invitation to separate the warnings and waiver requirement from the Fifth Amendment proved irresistible to later Courts. Eight years after *Harris* held that defendants could be impeached by statements taken in violation of *Miranda*, the Court held that statements taken in violation of the "pure" Fifth Amendment could *not* be used to impeach testimony. New Jersey v. Portash, 440 U.S. 450, 99 S.Ct. 1292, 59 L.Ed.2d 501 (1979), held that "a defendant's compelled statements, as opposed to statements taken in violation of *Miranda*, may not be put to any testimonial use against him in a criminal trial." To arrive at this doctrinal position, *Portash* drew an explicit distinction between a *Miranda* violation and a violation of "the constitutional privilege against compulsory self-incrimination in its most pristine form." Whatever *Miranda*'s status, it clearly was not a "pristine form" of the privilege.

Chronologically between *Harris* and *Portash* falls Michigan v. Tucker, 417 U.S. 433, 94 S.Ct. 2357, 41 L.Ed.2d 182 (1974). *Tucker* involved unusual facts. Police interrogated Tucker before *Miranda* was decided and thus the failure to provide warnings was truly a good-faith failure. Second, the evidence offered at a trial that took place after *Miranda* was not Tucker's statements but, rather, the statements of a witness whose name Tucker provided the police to substantiate his alibi. Clearly, the equities were in favor of permitting the witness to testify.

But instead of relying on an attenuation-of-the-taint argument to permit introduction off the witness' testimony, the Court chose to deny that Tucker's constitutional rights had been violated in the first place. The Court noted that *Miranda* warnings are "not themselves rights protected by the Constitution but [are] instead measures to insure that the right against compulsory self-incrimination [is] protected." The only harm the *Tucker* Court saw was that the police conduct departed "from the prophylactic standards later laid down by this Court in *Miranda* to safeguard" the Fifth Amendment privilege. Because the violation in *Tucker* was of a prophylactic rule, the Court balanced the additional deterrence that would result from not allowing the witness to testify— Tucker's statements to the police had been suppressed—against the value of having all relevant and trustworthy evidence presented to the fact-finder. That balance tilted in favor of having the witness testify.

By the end of the 1970s, *Miranda* was understood to be a "prophylaxis" designed to safeguard the Fifth Amendment privilege.

NOTES AND QUESTIONS

1.   Michael Mannheimer has developed an account of "testimonial evidence" that brings together the confrontation clause and the self-incrimination clause. Part of his unifying theory is that both clauses are implicated only when the statement is offered as evidence, as opposed to being offered simply to show that it was made. Using that theory, *Harris* correctly decided that statements taken in violation of *Miranda* were admissible to impeach because they were not being offered as evidence and thus did not implicate the self-incrimination clause. On the other hand, Mannheimer argues, *Portash* was incorrectly decided. It does not matter under Mannheimer's theory whether the violation was of the "pristine" constitutional provision or the *Miranda* prophylaxis. What is key is that the self-incrimination clause does not forbid the use of statements simply to show that they were made. See Michael J. Zydney Mannheimer, *Toward a Unified Theory of Testimonial Evidence under the Fifth and Sixth Amendments*, 80 Temple L. Rev. 1135 (2007).

2.   If the *Miranda* rights are not themselves "rights protected by the Constitution," might there be times when the warnings need not be given? Return to p. 48, Note 3.B. (the shallow grave case). If police did not give warnings and the suspect told the location of the grave, could that (should that) be admissible? The next case answers that question.

3.   After the *Harris-Tucker-Portash* start, the Court continued down the prophylaxis path. And what was the ultimate outcome? Read on and you will see.

NEW YORK V. QUARLES

Supreme Court of the United States, 1984.
467 U.S. 649, 104 S.Ct. 2626, 81 L.Ed.2d 550.

JUSTICE REHNQUIST delivered the opinion of the Court [joined by CHIEF JUSTICE BURGER, and JUSTICES WHITE, BLACKMUN and POWELL].
* * *

On September 11, 1980, at approximately 12:30 a.m., Officer Frank Kraft and Officer Sal Scarring were on road patrol in Queens, N.Y., when a young woman approached their car. She told them that she had just been raped by a black male, approximately six feet tall, who was wearing a black jacket with the name "Big Ben" printed in yellow letters on the back. She told the officers that the man had just entered an A & P supermarket located nearby and that the man was carrying a gun.

The officers drove the woman to the supermarket, and Officer Kraft entered the store while Officer Scarring radioed for assistance. Officer Kraft quickly spotted respondent, who matched the description given by the woman, approaching a checkout counter. Apparently upon seeing the officer, respondent turned and ran toward the rear of the store, and

Officer Kraft pursued him with a drawn gun. When respondent turned the corner at the end of an aisle, Officer Kraft lost sight of him for several seconds, and upon regaining sight of respondent, ordered him to stop and put his hands over his head.

Although more than three other officers had arrived on the scene by that time, Officer Kraft was the first to reach respondent. He frisked him and discovered that he was wearing a shoulder holster which was then empty. After handcuffing him, Officer Kraft asked him where the gun was. Respondent nodded in the direction of some empty cartons and responded, "the gun is over there." Officer Kraft thereafter retrieved a loaded .38-caliber revolver from one of the cartons, formally placed respondent under arrest, and read him his *Miranda* rights from a printed card. Respondent indicated that he would be willing to answer questions without an attorney present. Officer Kraft then asked respondent if he owned the gun and where he had purchased it. Respondent answered that he did own it and that he had purchased it in Miami, Fla.

In the subsequent prosecution of respondent for criminal possession of a weapon,[2] the judge excluded the statement, "the gun is over there," and the gun because the officer had not given respondent the warnings required by our decision in *Miranda v. Arizona* before asking him where the gun was located. The judge excluded the other statements about respondent's ownership of the gun and the place of purchase, as evidence tainted by the prior *Miranda* violation. * * *

[The New York Court of Appeals] * * * rejected the State's argument that the exigencies of the situation justified Officer Kraft's failure to read respondent his *Miranda* rights until after he had located the gun. * * * For the reasons which follow, we believe that this case presents a situation where concern for public safety must be paramount to adherence to the literal language of the prophylactic rules enunciated in *Miranda.*

The Fifth Amendment guarantees that "[n]o person * * * shall be compelled in any criminal case to be a witness against himself." In *Miranda* this Court for the first time extended the Fifth Amendment privilege against compulsory self-incrimination to individuals subjected to custodial interrogation by the police. The Fifth Amendment itself does not prohibit all incriminating admissions; "[a]bsent some officially coerced self-accusation, the Fifth Amendment privilege is not violated by even the most damning admissions." The *Miranda* Court, however, presumed that interrogation in certain custodial circumstances is inherently coercive and held that statements made under those circumstances are inadmissible unless the suspect is specifically informed of his *Miranda*

---

[2] The State originally charged respondent with rape, but the record provides no information as to why the State failed to pursue that charge.

rights and freely decides to forgo those rights. [As we said in *Michigan v. Tucker*, p. 651, the] prophylactic *Miranda* warnings therefore are "not themselves rights protected by the Constitution but [are] instead measures to insure that the right against compulsory self-incrimination [is] protected." Requiring *Miranda* warnings before custodial interrogation provides "practical reinforcement" for the Fifth Amendment right.

In this case we have before us no claim that respondent's statements were actually compelled by police conduct which overcame his will to resist. Thus the only issue before us is whether Officer Kraft was justified in failing to make available to respondent the procedural safeguards associated with the privilege against compulsory self-incrimination since *Miranda*.[5]

The New York Court of Appeals was undoubtedly correct in deciding that the facts of this case come within the ambit of the *Miranda* decision as we have subsequently interpreted it. We agree that respondent was in police custody * * * . Here Quarles was surrounded by at least four police officers and was handcuffed when the questioning at issue took place. As the New York Court of Appeals observed, there was nothing to suggest that any of the officers were any longer concerned for their own physical safety. The New York Court of Appeals' majority declined to express an opinion as to whether there might be an exception to the *Miranda* rule if the police had been acting to protect the public, because the lower courts in New York had made no factual determination that the police had acted with that motive.

We hold that on these facts there is a "public safety" exception to the requirement that *Miranda* warnings be given before a suspect's answers may be admitted into evidence, and that the availability of that exception does not depend upon the motivation of the individual officers involved. In a kaleidoscopic situation such as the one confronting these officers, where spontaneity rather than adherence to a police manual is necessarily the order of the day, the application of the exception which we recognize today should not be made to depend on *post hoc* findings at a suppression hearing concerning the subjective motivation of the arresting officer. Undoubtedly most police officers, if placed in Officer Kraft's position, would act out of a host of different, instinctive, and largely

---

[5] The dissent curiously takes us to task for "endors[ing] the introduction of coerced self-incriminating statements in criminal prosecutions," and for "sanction[ing] *sub silentio* criminal prosecutions based on compelled self-incriminating statements." Of course our decision today does nothing of the kind. As the *Miranda* Court itself recognized, the failure to provide *Miranda* warnings in and of itself does not render a confession involuntary, and respondent is certainly free on remand to argue that his statement was coerced under traditional due process standards. Today we merely reject the only argument that respondent has raised to support the exclusion of his statement, that the statement must be *presumed* compelled because of Officer Kraft's failure to read him his *Miranda* warnings.

unverifiable motives—their own safety, the safety of others, and perhaps as well the desire to obtain incriminating evidence from the suspect.

Whatever the motivation of individual officers in such a situation, we do not believe that the doctrinal underpinnings of *Miranda* require that it be applied in all its rigor to a situation in which police officers ask questions reasonably prompted by a concern for the public safety. The *Miranda* decision was based in large part on this Court's view that the warnings which it required police to give to suspects in custody would reduce the likelihood that the suspects would fall victim to constitutionally impermissible practices of police interrogation in the presumptively coercive environment of the station house. The dissenters warned that the requirement of *Miranda* warnings would have the effect of decreasing the number of suspects who respond to police questioning. The *Miranda* majority, however, apparently felt that whatever the cost to society in terms of fewer convictions of guilty suspects, that cost would simply have to be borne in the interest of enlarged protection for the Fifth Amendment privilege.

The police in this case, in the very act of apprehending a suspect, were confronted with the immediate necessity of ascertaining the whereabouts of a gun which they had every reason to believe the suspect had just removed from his empty holster and discarded in the supermarket. So long as the gun was concealed somewhere in the supermarket, with its actual whereabouts unknown, it obviously posed more than one danger to the public safety: an accomplice might make use of it, a customer or employee might later come upon it.

In such a situation, if the police are required to recite the familiar *Miranda* warnings before asking the whereabouts of the gun, suspects in Quarles' position might well be deterred from responding. Procedural safeguards which deter a suspect from responding were deemed acceptable in *Miranda* in order to protect the Fifth Amendment privilege; when the primary social cost of those added protections is the possibility of fewer convictions, the *Miranda* majority was willing to bear that cost. Here, had *Miranda* warnings deterred Quarles from responding to Officer Kraft's question about the whereabouts of the gun, the cost would have been something more than merely the failure to obtain evidence useful in convicting Quarles. Officer Kraft needed an answer to his question not simply to make his case against Quarles but to insure that further danger to the public did not result from the concealment of the gun in a public area.

We conclude that the need for answers to questions in a situation posing a threat to the public safety outweighs the need for the prophylactic rule protecting the Fifth Amendment's privilege against self-incrimination. We decline to place officers such as Officer Kraft in the untenable position of having to consider, often in a matter of seconds, whether it best serves society for them to ask the necessary questions without the *Miranda* warnings and render whatever probative evidence they uncover inadmissible, or for them to give the warnings in order to preserve the admissibility of evidence they might uncover but possibly damage or destroy their ability to obtain that evidence and neutralize the volatile situation confronting them.[7]

In recognizing a narrow exception to the *Miranda* rule in this case, we acknowledge that to some degree we lessen the desirable clarity of that rule. * * * But as we have pointed out, we believe that the exception which we recognize today lessens the necessity of that on-the-scene balancing process. The exception will not be difficult for police officers to apply because in each case it will be circumscribed by the exigency which justifies it. We think police officers can and will distinguish almost instinctively between questions necessary to secure their own safety or the safety of the public and questions designed solely to elicit testimonial evidence from a suspect.

The facts of this case clearly demonstrate that distinction and an officer's ability to recognize it. Officer Kraft asked only the question necessary to locate the missing gun before advising respondent of his rights. It was only after securing the loaded revolver and giving the warnings that he continued with investigatory questions about the ownership and place of purchase of the gun. The exception which we recognize today, far from complicating the thought processes and the on-the-scene judgments of police officers, will simply free them to follow their legitimate instincts when confronting situations presenting a danger to the public safety.

We hold that the Court of Appeals in this case erred in excluding the statement, "the gun is over there," and the gun because of the officer's failure to read respondent his *Miranda* rights before attempting to locate the weapon. Accordingly we hold that it also erred in excluding the subsequent statements as illegal fruits of a *Miranda* violation. We therefore reverse and remand for further proceedings not inconsistent with this opinion. * * *

---

[7] The dissent argues that a public safety exception to *Miranda* is unnecessary because in every case an officer can simply ask the necessary questions to protect himself or the public, and then the prosecution can decline to introduce any incriminating responses at a subsequent trial. But absent actual coercion by the officer, there is no constitutional imperative requiring the exclusion of the evidence that results from police inquiry of this kind; and we do not believe that the doctrinal underpinnings of *Miranda* require us to exclude the evidence, thus penalizing officers for asking the very questions which are the most crucial to their efforts to protect themselves and the public.

JUSTICE O'CONNOR, concurring in the judgment in part and dissenting in part.

* * * Were the Court writing from a clean slate, I could agree with its holding. But *Miranda* is now the law and, in my view, the Court has not provided sufficient justification for departing from it or for blurring its now clear strictures. Accordingly, I would require suppression of the initial statement taken from respondent in this case. [In an omitted part of her opinion, Justice O'Connor agreed that the gun was admissible and thus concurred in that part of the Court's judgment. Her view, which later formed the holding in *Oregon v. Elstad*, p. 662, was that a Miranda violation has no "fruit" beyond the statement itself.] * * *

I * * *

In my view, a "public safety" exception unnecessarily blurs the edges of the clear line heretofore established and makes *Miranda*'s requirements more difficult to understand. In some cases, police will benefit because a reviewing court will find that an exigency excused their failure to administer the required warnings. But in other cases, police will suffer because, though they thought an exigency excused their noncompliance, a reviewing court will view the "objective" circumstances differently and require exclusion of admissions thereby obtained. The end result will be a finespun new doctrine on public safety exigencies incident to custodial interrogation, complete with the hair-splitting distinctions that currently plague our Fourth Amendment jurisprudence. * * *

* * * In my view, since there is nothing about an exigency that makes custodial interrogation any less compelling, a principled application of *Miranda* requires that respondent's statement be suppressed. * * *

JUSTICE MARSHALL, with whom JUSTICE BRENNAN and JUSTICE STEVENS join, dissenting. * * *

III

* * * The majority has lost sight of the fact that *Miranda v. Arizona* and our earlier custodial-interrogation cases all implemented a constitutional privilege against self-incrimination. The rules established in these cases were designed to protect criminal defendants against prosecutions based on coerced self-incriminating statements. The majority today turns its back on these constitutional considerations, and invites the government to prosecute through the use of what necessarily are coerced statements.

A

The majority's error stems from a serious misunderstanding of *Miranda v. Arizona* and of the Fifth Amendment upon which that decision was based. The majority implies that *Miranda* consisted of no more than a judicial balancing act in which the benefits of "enlarged protection for the Fifth Amendment privilege" were weighed against "the cost to society in terms of fewer convictions of guilty suspects." Supposedly because the scales tipped in favor of the privilege against self-incrimination, the *Miranda* Court erected a prophylactic barrier around statements made during custodial interrogations. The majority now proposes to return to the scales of social utility to calculate whether *Miranda*'s prophylactic rule remains cost-effective when threats to the public's safety are added to the balance. * * *

Whether society would be better off if the police warned suspects of their rights before beginning an interrogation or whether the advantages of giving such warnings would outweigh their costs did not inform the *Miranda* decision. On the contrary, the *Miranda* Court was concerned with the proscriptions of the Fifth Amendment, and, in particular, whether the Self-Incrimination Clause permits the government to prosecute individuals based on statements made in the course of custodial interrogations. * * *

In fashioning its "public-safety" exception to *Miranda*, the majority makes no attempt to deal with the constitutional presumption established by that case. The majority does not argue that police questioning about issues of public safety is any less coercive than custodial interrogations into other matters. The majority's only contention is that police officers could more easily protect the public if *Miranda* did not apply to custodial interrogations concerning the public's safety. But *Miranda* was not a decision about public safety; it was a decision about coerced confessions. Without establishing that interrogations concerning the public's safety are less likely to be coercive than other interrogations, the majority cannot endorse the "public-safety" exception and remain faithful to the logic of *Miranda v. Arizona.*

B

The majority's avoidance of the issue of coercion may not have been inadvertent. It would strain credulity to contend that Officer Kraft's questioning of respondent Quarles was not coercive. In the middle of the night and in the back of an empty supermarket, Quarles was surrounded by four armed police officers. His hands were handcuffed behind his back. The first words out of the mouth of the arresting officer were: "Where is the gun?" In the majority's phrase, the situation was "kaleidoscopic." Police and suspect were acting on instinct. Officer Kraft's abrupt and pointed question pressured Quarles in precisely the way that the *Miranda* Court feared the custodial interrogations would coerce self-incriminating testimony.

That the application of the "public-safety" exception in this case entailed coercion is no happenstance. The majority's *ratio decidendi* is that interrogating suspects about matters of public safety *will* be coercive. In its cost-benefit analysis, the Court's strongest argument in favor of a "public-safety" exception to *Miranda* is that the police would be better able to protect the public's safety if they were not always required to give suspects their *Miranda* warnings. The crux of this argument is that, by deliberately withholding *Miranda* warnings, the police can get information out of suspects who would refuse to respond to police questioning were they advised of their constitutional rights. The "public-safety" exception is efficacious precisely because it permits police officers to coerce criminal defendants into making involuntary statements.

* * * Though the majority's opinion is cloaked in the beguiling language of utilitarianism, the Court has sanctioned *sub silentio* criminal prosecutions based on compelled self-incriminating statements. I find this result in direct conflict with the Fifth Amendment's dictate that "[n]o person * * * shall be compelled in any criminal case to be a witness against himself."

The irony of the majority's decision is that the public's safety can be perfectly well protected without abridging the Fifth Amendment. If a bomb is about to explode or the public is otherwise imminently imperiled, the police are free to interrogate suspects without advising them of their constitutional rights. Such unconsented questioning may take place not only when police officers act on instinct but also when higher faculties lead them to believe that advising a suspect of his constitutional rights might decrease the likelihood that the suspect would reveal life-saving information. If trickery is necessary to protect the public, then the police may trick a suspect into confessing. While the Fourteenth Amendment sets limits on such behavior, nothing in the Fifth Amendment or our decision in *Miranda v. Arizona* proscribes this sort of emergency questioning. All the Fifth Amendment forbids is the introduction of coerced statements at trial. * * *

NOTES AND QUESTIONS

1.   Justice Marshall, in an omitted part of his dissent, took issue with the majority's conclusion that there was a legitimate threat to public safety on these facts. What do you think? How would you phrase that threat? Would the case come out differently if a sole suspect was handcuffed in a motel room when the officer asked the location of the gun? See State v. Stephenson, 350 N.J.Super. 517, 796 A.2d 274 (App. Div. 2002).

2.   Is the majority or Justice Marshall right about whether *Quarles* can be decided within the conceptual framework of the *Miranda* opinion?

3.   Broadly construed, a "public safety" exception might swallow up much of the *Miranda* rule. One might think that in every arrest for a drug or violent crime, the police officer would ask whether the suspect was armed

and lots of suspects would say something against their interest. But when author Thomas in 2002 drew a sample of 216 state and federal cases that discuss *Miranda*, he found that only four cases presented the public safety issue. See George C. Thomas III, *Stories About* Miranda, 102 Mich. L. Rev. 1959 (2004). Three courts applied it to admit the statements and one found that the case did not fit *Quarles*.

4.   *Quarles and terror suspects.* F.B.I. agents did not provide *Miranda* warnings to Faisal Shahzad before questioning him "extensively" about the attempted Times Square car bombing in 2010. Mark Hosenball, *Obama Officials on Shahzad Case: We Did It Right*, Newsweek, May 6, 2010. Agents did not warn Shahzad until he had "provided what the F.B.I. called 'valuable intelligence and evidence.'" Peter Baker, *A Renewed Debate Over Suspect Rights*, The New York Times, May 4, 2010. Once the agents had "determined there was no imminent threat to be headed off," they read Mr. Shahzad his rights, "but he waived them and continued talking."

The Court said in *Quarles*: "We conclude that the need for answers to questions in a situation posing a threat to the public safety outweighs the need for the prophylactic rule protecting the Fifth Amendment's privilege against self-incrimination." Would the need to determine whether there were other bombs about to go off in a crowded city outweigh the need to protect the privilege of a suspect believed to be connected to at least one bomb?

Does *Quarles* justify what the agents did? Can you point to language or reasoning in the case that would support the defense assertion that the agents went too far under *Quarles*?

Attorney General Eric Holder explicitly relied on *Quarles* to justify withholding *Miranda* warnings in Shahzad's case, though he said that it was time that *Quarles* was "updated. That's one of the things that I think we're going to be reaching out to Congress to do, to come up with a proposal that is both constitutional, but that is also relevant to our time and the threat that we now face." Anne E. Kornblut, *Obama Administration Looks into Modifying Miranda Law in the Age of Terrorism*, The Washington Post, May 10, 2010.

5.   *911 calls and Quarles.* Police responded to a 911 call reporting that Ms. B had attempted suicide. The officers who answered the call were aware that Ms. B had obtained a restraining order against her estranged husband, who opened the door and admitted the police. He attempted to hand his cell phone to the officer, stating, "Can you speak to my attorney?" The officer ignored the phone and tried to assist Ms. B who was bleeding and motionless on the couch. After calling for assistance, the officer asked Mr. B when he had last heard from his wife. He said he had seen or talked to her around four o'clock. He then asked again "can you please talk to my attorney?" Two other officers arrived and Mr. B asked them to please talk to his attorney. Police ignored the request because they were attending to Ms. B. At one point, an officer took the phone and threw it across the room.

Does *Miranda* bar admission in Mr. B's murder trial of his answer to the question of when had he last heard from his wife? See State v. Boretsky, 186 N.J. 271, 894 A.2d 659 (2006).

6.   *Miranda as due process?* It is odd to think that *Miranda* sometimes offers less protection from police-coerced statements than the due process clause, but that is the necessary implication of footnote 5 in the *Quarles* majority opinion. Can you offer a theory that would explain this? For one theory, see George C. Thomas III, *Separated at Birth but Siblings Nonetheless: Miranda and the Due Process Notice Cases*, 99 Mich. L. Rev. 1081 (2001).

7.   *Problems.* Assume that no *Miranda* warnings were given in the following Problems, and concern yourself only with whether the statements would be admissible under the "public safety" exception.

A.   *L* walks into the police station and cries out, "I killed her, I killed her, I killed her." The police officer knew that *L*'s wife was missing. "Are you *L*?" "Yes." "Where is Mrs. *L*?" "At the boathouse." "Where exactly at the boathouse?" "In the last bay, in the van." Police take *L* to the boathouse. They inspect the van and find a large fiberglass box but no other sign of the victim. Police ask *L*, "Is she in the box?" "Yes." See State v. Lockhart, 830 A.2d 433 (Me. 2003).

B.   A bank robber, *F*, is shot by the bank security guard but manages to flee a Dallas bank. As he runs from the bank, a salesman from a nearby car dealership chases him. When *F* collapses in a field near the bank, the car salesman draws his gun and covers the wounded *F*. Two police officers arrive and draw their guns on the car salesman until they are persuaded that *F* is the suspect. The officers then aim their guns at *F* and tell him to put his hands over his head. He responds that he is wounded and cannot raise his arms. After frisking *F*, the police officers ascertain that he is wounded, yet keep their guns pointed at him. The officers ask the following questions: "Who shot you?", "Who was with you?", and "Where is the gun?" Are the answers admissible? See Fleming v. Collins, 954 F.2d 1109 (5th Cir. 1992) (*en banc*).

C.   After police arrest *L* on outstanding warrants, the officer notices that he is chewing and swallowing plastic bags. When she asks what is in the bags, the "savvy" suspect replies, "Methamphetamine." The State seeks to introduce the statement on the ground that the officer was concerned about the suspect's health and needed to know what he was ingesting. Which way do you rule as judge? See United States v. Lutz, 207 F.Supp.2d 1247 (D. Kan. 2002).

D.   *C* was arrested for conspiracy to distribute a large quantity of cocaine. Before searching *C* prior to placing him in detention at the station, the officer asked whether he had any drugs or needles on his person. He responded, "I don't use drugs. I sell them." Admissible? Would it matter if the officer testified that he asked the same question of every person arrested for a drug offense? See United States v. Carrillo, 16 F.3d 1046 (9th Cir. 1994).

8.   *Quarles* recognized a "public safety" exception to *Miranda*. It did so by distinguishing between compulsion—a pure violation of the Fifth Amendment—and a violation of the mere "prophylactic *Miranda* warnings." In the next case, we see this distinction made more explicit, and the Supreme Court again finds that the implications of a *Miranda* violation are not the same as a violation of the Fifth Amendment in its pristine form.

OREGON V. ELSTAD
Supreme Court of the United States, 1985.
470 U.S. 298, 105 S.Ct. 1285, 84 L.Ed.2d 222.

JUSTICE O'CONNOR delivered the opinion of the Court [joined by CHIEF JUSTICE BURGER, and JUSTICES WHITE, BLACKMUN, POWELL, and REHNQUIST].

This case requires us to decide whether an initial failure of law enforcement officers to administer the warnings required by *Miranda v. Arizona*, without more, "taints" subsequent admissions made after a suspect has been fully advised of and has waived his *Miranda* rights. Respondent, Michael James Elstad, was convicted of burglary by an Oregon trial court. The Oregon Court of Appeals reversed, holding that respondent's signed confession, although voluntary, was rendered inadmissible by a prior remark made in response to questioning without benefit of *Miranda* warnings. * * *

I

In December 1981, the home of Mr. and Mrs. Gilbert Gross, in the town of Salem, Polk County, Ore., was burglarized. Missing were art objects and furnishings valued at $150,000. A witness to the burglary contacted the Polk County Sheriff's office, implicating respondent Michael Elstad, an 18-year-old neighbor and friend of the Grosses' teenage son. Thereupon, Officers Burke and McAllister went to the home of respondent Elstad, with a warrant for his arrest. Elstad's mother answered the door. She led the officers to her son's room where he lay on his bed, clad in shorts and listening to his stereo. The officers asked him to get dressed and to accompany them into the living room. Officer McAllister asked respondent's mother to step into the kitchen, where he explained that they had a warrant for her son's arrest for the burglary of a neighbor's residence. Officer Burke remained with Elstad in the living room. He later testified:

"I sat down with Mr. Elstad and I asked him if he was aware of why Detective McAllister and myself were there to talk with him. He stated no, he had no idea why we were there. I then asked him if he knew a person by the name of Gross, and he said yes, he did, and also added that he heard that there was a robbery at the Gross house. And at that point I told Mr. Elstad that I felt he was involved in that, and he looked at me and stated, 'Yes, I was there.' "

The officers then escorted Elstad to the back of the patrol car. As they were about to leave for the Polk County Sheriff's office, Elstad's father arrived home and came to the rear of the patrol car. The officers advised him that his son was a suspect in the burglary. Officer Burke testified that Mr. Elstad became quite agitated, opened the rear door of the car and admonished his son: "I told you that you were going to get into trouble. You wouldn't listen to me. You never learn."

Elstad was transported to the Sheriff's headquarters and approximately one hour later, Officers Burke and McAllister joined him in McAllister's office. McAllister then advised respondent for the first time of his *Miranda* rights, reading from a standard card. Respondent indicated he understood his rights, and, having these rights in mind, wished to speak with the officers. Elstad gave a full statement, explaining that he had known that the Gross family was out of town and had been paid to lead several acquaintances to the Gross residence and show them how to gain entry through a defective sliding glass door. The statement was typed, reviewed by respondent, read back to him for correction, initialed and signed by Elstad and both officers. As an afterthought, Elstad added and initialed the sentence, "After leaving the house Robby & I went back to [the] van & Robby handed me a small bag of grass." Respondent concedes that the officers made no threats or promises either at his residence or at the Sheriff's office. * * *

* * * The State conceded that Elstad had been in custody when he made his statement, "I was there," and accordingly agreed that this statement was inadmissible as having been given without the prescribed *Miranda* warnings. But the State maintained that any conceivable "taint" had been dissipated prior to the respondent's written confession by McAllister's careful administration of the requisite warnings. * * *

II

The arguments advanced in favor of suppression of respondent's written confession rely heavily on metaphor. One metaphor, familiar from the Fourth Amendment context, would require that respondent's confession, regardless of its integrity, voluntariness, and probative value, be suppressed as the "tainted fruit of the poisonous tree" of the *Miranda* violation. A second metaphor questions whether a confession can be truly voluntary once the "cat is out of the bag." Taken out of context, each of these metaphors can be misleading. They should not be used to obscure fundamental differences between the role of the Fourth Amendment exclusionary rule and the function of *Miranda* in guarding against the prosecutorial use of compelled statements as prohibited by the Fifth Amendment. The Oregon court assumed and respondent here contends that a failure to administer *Miranda* warnings necessarily breeds the same consequences as police infringement of a constitutional right, so that evidence uncovered following an unwarned statement must be suppressed as "fruit of the poisonous tree." We believe this view misconstrues the nature of the protections afforded by *Miranda* warnings and therefore misreads the consequences of police failure to supply them.

A * * *

Respondent's contention that his confession was tainted by the earlier failure of the police to provide *Miranda* warnings and must be excluded as "fruit of the poisonous tree" assumes the existence of a constitutional violation. This figure of speech is drawn from *Wong Sun v. United States*, [p. 530], in which the Court held that evidence and witnesses discovered as a result of a search in violation of the Fourth Amendment must be excluded from evidence. The *Wong Sun* doctrine applies as well when the fruit of the Fourth Amendment violation is a confession. It is settled law that "a confession obtained through custodial interrogation after an illegal arrest should be excluded unless intervening events break the causal connection between the illegal arrest and the confession so that the confession is 'sufficiently an act of free will to purge the primary taint.' "

But as we explained in *Quarles* [p. 652] and *Tucker* [p. 651], a procedural *Miranda* violation differs in significant respects from violations of the Fourth Amendment, which have traditionally mandated a broad application of the "fruits" doctrine. The purpose of the Fourth Amendment exclusionary rule is to deter unreasonable searches, no matter how probative their fruits. * * * Where a Fourth Amendment violation "taints" the confession, a finding of voluntariness for the purposes of the Fifth Amendment is merely a threshold requirement in determining whether the confession may be admitted in evidence. Beyond this, the prosecution must show a sufficient break in events to undermine the inference that the confession was caused by the Fourth Amendment violation.

The *Miranda* exclusionary rule, however, serves the Fifth Amendment and sweeps more broadly than the Fifth Amendment itself. It may be triggered even in the absence of a Fifth Amendment violation. The Fifth Amendment prohibits use by the prosecution in its case in chief only of *compelled* testimony. Failure to administer *Miranda* warnings creates a presumption of compulsion. Consequently, unwarned statements that are otherwise voluntary within the meaning of the Fifth Amendment must nevertheless be excluded from evidence under *Miranda*. Thus, in the individual case, *Miranda*'s preventive medicine provides a remedy even to the defendant who has suffered no identifiable constitutional harm.

But the *Miranda* presumption, though irrebuttable for purposes of the prosecution's case in chief, does not require that the statements and their fruits be discarded as inherently tainted. Despite the fact that patently *voluntary* statements taken in violation of *Miranda* must be excluded from the prosecution's case, the presumption of coercion does not bar their use for impeachment purposes on cross-examination. * * * Where an unwarned statement is preserved for use in situations that fall outside the sweep of the *Miranda* presumption, "the primary criterion of admissibility [remains] the 'old' due process voluntariness test."

* * * In deciding "how sweeping the judicially imposed consequences" of a failure to administer *Miranda* warnings should be, the *Tucker* Court noted that neither the general goal of deterring improper police conduct nor the Fifth Amendment goal of assuring trustworthy evidence would be served by suppression of the witness' testimony. [As noted on p. 651, the police learned the name of a witness from Tucker without giving him *Miranda* warnings. Eds.] The unwarned confession must, of course, be suppressed, but the Court ruled that introduction of the third-party witness' testimony did not violate Tucker's Fifth Amendment rights.

We believe that this reasoning applies with equal force when the alleged "fruit" of a noncoercive *Miranda* violation is neither a witness nor an article of evidence but the accused's own voluntary testimony. As in *Tucker*, the absence of any coercion or improper tactics undercuts the twin rationales—trustworthiness and deterrence—for a broader rule. Once warned, the suspect is free to exercise his own volition in deciding whether or not to make a statement to the authorities. The Court has often noted: " '[A] living witness is not to be mechanically equated with the proffer of inanimate evidentiary objects illegally seized. * * * [T]he living witness is an individual human personality whose attributes of will, perception, memory and *volition* interact to determine what testimony he will give.' " * * *

* * * If errors are made by law enforcement officers in administering the prophylactic *Miranda* procedures, they should not breed the same irremediable consequences as police infringement of the Fifth Amendment itself. It is an unwarranted extension of *Miranda* to hold that a simple failure to administer the warnings, unaccompanied by any actual coercion or other circumstances calculated to undermine the suspect's ability to exercise his free will, so taints the investigatory process that a subsequent voluntary and informed waiver is ineffective for some indeterminate period. Though *Miranda* requires that the unwarned admission must be suppressed, the admissibility of any subsequent statement should turn in these circumstances solely on whether it is knowingly and voluntarily made.

B

The Oregon court, however, believed that the unwarned remark compromised the voluntariness of respondent's later confession. It was the court's view that the prior *answer* and not the unwarned questioning impaired respondent's ability to give a valid waiver and that only lapse of time and change of place could dissipate what it termed the "coercive impact" of the inadmissible statement. When a prior statement is actually coerced, the time that passes between confessions, the change in place of interrogations, and the change in identity of the interrogators all bear on whether that coercion has carried over into the second confession. The failure of police to administer *Miranda* warnings does not mean that the statements received have actually been coerced, but only that courts will presume the privilege against compulsory self-incrimination has not been intelligently exercised. * * * In these circumstances, a careful and thorough administration of *Miranda* warnings serves to cure the condition that rendered the unwarned statement inadmissible. The warning conveys the relevant information and thereafter the suspect's choice whether to exercise his privilege to remain silent should ordinarily be viewed as an "act of free will." * * *

* * * We must conclude that, absent deliberately coercive or improper tactics in obtaining the initial statement, the mere fact that a suspect has made an unwarned admission does not warrant a presumption of compulsion. A subsequent administration of *Miranda* warnings to a suspect who has given a voluntary but unwarned statement ordinarily should suffice to remove the conditions that precluded admission of the earlier statement. In such circumstances, the finder of fact may reasonably conclude that the suspect made a rational and intelligent choice whether to waive or invoke his rights.

III

Though belated, the reading of respondent's rights was undeniably complete. McAllister testified that he read the *Miranda* warnings aloud from a printed card and recorded Elstad's responses. There is no question that respondent knowingly and voluntarily waived his right to remain silent before he described his participation in the burglary. It is also beyond dispute that respondent's earlier remark was voluntary, within the meaning of the Fifth Amendment. Neither the environment nor the manner of either "interrogation" was coercive. The initial conversation took place at midday, in the living room area of respondent's own home, with his mother in the kitchen area, a few steps away. Although in retrospect the officers testified that respondent was then in custody [and thus warnings were required, eds.], at the time he made his statement he had not been informed that he was under arrest. The arresting officers' testimony indicates that the brief stop in the living room before proceeding to the station house was not to interrogate the suspect but to notify his mother of the reason for his arrest.

The State has conceded the issue of custody and thus we must assume that Burke breached *Miranda* procedures in failing to administer *Miranda* warnings before initiating the discussion in the living room. This breach may have been the result of confusion as to whether the brief exchange qualified as "custodial interrogation" or it may simply have reflected Burke's reluctance to initiate an alarming police procedure before McAllister had spoken with respondent's mother. Whatever the reason for Burke's oversight, the incident had none of the earmarks of coercion. Nor did the officers exploit the unwarned admission to pressure respondent into waiving his right to remain silent.

Respondent, however, has argued that he was unable to give a fully *informed* waiver of his rights because he was unaware that his prior statement could not be used against him. Respondent suggests that Officer McAllister, to cure this deficiency, should have added an additional warning to those given him at the Sheriff's office. Such a requirement is neither practicable nor constitutionally necessary. In many cases, a breach of *Miranda* procedures may not be identified as such until long after full *Miranda* warnings are administered and a valid confession obtained. The standard *Miranda* warnings explicitly inform the suspect of his right to consult a lawyer before speaking. Police officers are ill-equipped to pinch-hit for counsel, construing the murky and difficult questions of when "custody" begins or whether a given unwarned statement will ultimately be held admissible. * * *

JUSTICE BRENNAN, with whom JUSTICE MARSHALL joins, dissenting. * * *

Even while purporting to reaffirm [*Miranda's*] constitutional guarantees, the Court has engaged of late in a studied campaign to strip the *Miranda* decision piecemeal and to undermine the rights *Miranda* sought to secure. Today's decision not only extends this effort a further step, but delivers a potentially crippling blow to *Miranda* and the ability of courts to safeguard the rights of persons accused of crime. For at least with respect to successive confessions, the Court today appears to strip remedies for *Miranda* violations of the "fruit of the poisonous tree" doctrine prohibiting the use of evidence presumptively derived from official illegality.[2] * * *

---

[2] The Court repeatedly casts its analysis in terms of the "fruits" of a *Miranda* violation, but its dicta nevertheless surely should not be read as necessarily foreclosing application of derivative-evidence rules where the *Miranda* violation produces evidence other than a subsequent confession by the accused.

Today's decision, in short, threatens disastrous consequences far beyond the outcome in this case. * * *

I * * *

The Court today * * * [adopts] a rule that "the psychological impact of *voluntary* disclosure of a guilty secret" neither "qualifies as state compulsion" nor "compromises the voluntariness" of subsequent confessions. So long as a suspect receives the usual *Miranda* warnings before further interrogation, the Court reasons, the fact that he "is free to exercise his own volition in deciding whether or not to make" further confessions "ordinarily" is a sufficient "cure" and serves to break any causal connection between the illegal confession and subsequent statements.

The Court's marble-palace psychoanalysis is tidy, but it flies in the face of our own precedents, demonstrates a startling unawareness of the realities of police interrogation, and is completely out of tune with the experience of state and federal courts over the last 20 years. Perhaps the Court has grasped some psychological truth that has eluded persons far more experienced in these matters; if so, the Court owes an explanation of how so many could have been so wrong for so many years. * * *

[The opinion of JUSTICE STEVENS, dissenting, is omitted.]

NOTES AND QUESTIONS

1.   *Custody.* When you get to the custody materials, beginning on p. 691, decide whether the State might have won the custody issue.

2.   Do you think the Court is saying that *Miranda* is not required by the Constitution?

3.   Does the Court hold that no second statement would ever be suppressed if it followed an un-warned incriminating statement or only that *in this case* the statement was admissible? Or is there a third way to read *Elstad*?

4.   *Problem.* Police question a 17-year-old suspect held in custody without providing *Miranda* warnings. He admits his involvement in a burglary. One officer turns to the other and, in ear-shot of the suspect, asks him to let the suspect "know about his rights" because he has "already told us about going into the house [and] I don't think that's going to change [his] desire to cooperate with us." Police give *Miranda* warnings. He asks whether he is under arrest and the police tell him he is not. He later confesses to a murder as well as the burglary. Argue for suppression of this confession. Ramirez v. State, 739 So.2d 568 (Fla. 1999).

5.   Justice Brennan believed that the *Elstad* Court was engaging in a "fruits" analysis—see footnote 2 in his opinion. The Oregon Court of Appeals had used a fruits analysis. Look carefully at the majority opinion. Is the

Court talking about fruit of the poisoned tree, and finding no poisoned tree, or is it plausible to argue that *Elstad* is really holding something else?

After a brief detour to (finally?) settle *Miranda*'s constitutional status, we will return to the "fruits" issue.

6.   We saw earlier that Congress in 1968 railed against *Miranda* and enacted the 1968 Omnibus Crime Control and Safe Streets Act. Two of its provisions follow.

§ 3501. Admissibility of confessions

(a) In any criminal prosecution brought by the United States or by the District of Columbia, a confession, as defined in subsection (e) hereof, shall be admissible in evidence if it is voluntarily given. Before such confession is received in evidence, the trial judge shall, out of the presence of the jury, determine any issue as to voluntariness. If the trial judge determines that the confession was voluntarily made it shall be admitted in evidence and the trial judge shall permit the jury to hear relevant evidence on the issue of voluntariness and shall instruct the jury to give such weight to the confession as the jury feels it deserves under all the circumstances.

(b) The trial judge in determining the issue of voluntariness shall take into consideration all the circumstances surrounding the giving of the confession, including (1) the time elapsing between arrest and arraignment of the defendant making the confession, if it was made after arrest and before arraignment, (2) whether such defendant knew the nature of the offense with which he was charged or of which he was suspected at the time of making the confession, (3) whether or not such defendant was advised or knew that he was not required to make any statement and that any such statement could be used against him, (4) whether or not such defendant had been advised prior to questioning of his right to the assistance of counsel, and (5) whether or not such defendant was without the assistance of counsel when questioned and when giving such confession.

Do you think, in light of the cases you have read so far, that this part of the statute is constitutional?

7.   *Quarles* held that *Miranda* warnings are not always required. *Elstad* pointedly said that the *Miranda* exclusionary rule "serves the Fifth Amendment and sweeps more broadly than the Fifth Amendment itself." So in 2000, the Court found itself at a cross-roads: Was *Miranda* "fully" constitutional, "partly" constitutional, or not constitutional at all? Notice what the answer to this question could mean. If *Miranda* really isn't a constitutional rule, why couldn't Congress legislate a different solution to the interrogation problem, as it attempted in § 3501, above? And, for that matter, why couldn't the states ignore *Miranda* if it is not a constitutional rule? In the next case, the Supreme Court answered these questions. Or, did it?

DICKERSON V. UNITED STATES

Supreme Court of the United States, 2000.
530 U.S. 428, 120 S.Ct. 2326, 147 L.Ed.2d 405.

CHIEF JUSTICE REHNQUIST delivered the opinion of the Court [joined by JUSTICES STEVENS, O'CONNOR, KENNEDY, SOUTER, GINSBERG, and BREYER].

In *Miranda v. Arizona*, we held that certain warnings must be given before a suspect's statement made during custodial interrogation could be admitted in evidence. In the wake of that decision, Congress enacted 18 U.S.C. § 3501, which in essence laid down a rule that the admissibility of such statements should turn only on whether or not they were voluntarily made. We hold that *Miranda*, being a constitutional decision of this Court, may not be in effect overruled by an Act of Congress, and we decline to overrule *Miranda* ourselves. We therefore hold that *Miranda* and its progeny in this Court govern the admissibility of statements made during custodial interrogation in both state and federal courts.

Petitioner Dickerson was indicted for bank robbery, conspiracy to commit bank robbery, and using a firearm in the course of committing a crime of violence * * *. Before trial, Dickerson moved to suppress a statement he had made at a Federal Bureau of Investigation field office, on the grounds that he had not received "*Miranda* warnings" before being interrogated. [The Fourth Circuit held] that petitioner had not received *Miranda* warnings before making his statement. But it went on to hold that § 3501, which in effect makes the admissibility of statements such as Dickerson's turn solely on whether they were made voluntarily, was satisfied in this case. It then concluded that our decision in *Miranda* was not a constitutional holding, and that therefore Congress could by statute have the final say on the question of admissibility. * * *

In *Miranda*, we noted that the advent of modern custodial police interrogation brought with it an increased concern about confessions obtained by coercion. Because custodial police interrogation, by its very nature, isolates and pressures the individual, we stated that "even without employing brutality, the 'third degree' or [other] specific stratagems, * * * custodial interrogation exacts a heavy toll on individual liberty and trades on the weakness of individuals." We concluded that the coercion inherent in custodial interrogation blurs the line between voluntary and involuntary statements, and thus heightens the risk that an individual will not be "accorded his privilege under the Fifth Amendment * * * not to be compelled to incriminate himself." Accordingly, we laid down "concrete constitutional guidelines for law enforcement agencies and courts to follow." Those guidelines established that the admissibility in evidence of any statement given during custodial interrogation of a suspect would depend on whether the police provided the suspect with four warnings. * * *

Given § 3501's express designation of voluntariness as the touchstone of admissibility, its omission of any warning requirement, and the instruction for trial courts to consider a nonexclusive list of factors relevant to the circumstances of a confession, we agree with the Court of Appeals that Congress intended by its enactment to overrule *Miranda*. Because of the obvious conflict between our decision in *Miranda* and § 3501, we must address whether Congress has constitutional authority to thus supersede *Miranda*. If Congress has such authority, § 3501's totality-of-the-circumstances approach must prevail over *Miranda*'s requirement of warnings; if not, that section must yield to *Miranda*'s more specific requirements.

The law in this area is clear. This Court has supervisory authority over the federal courts, and we may use that authority to prescribe rules of evidence and procedure that are binding in those tribunals. However, the power to judicially create and enforce nonconstitutional "rules of procedure and evidence for the federal courts exists only in the absence of a relevant Act of Congress." Congress retains the ultimate authority to modify or set aside any judicially created rules of evidence and procedure that are not required by the Constitution.

But Congress may not legislatively supersede our decisions interpreting and applying the Constitution. This case therefore turns on whether the *Miranda* Court announced a constitutional rule or merely exercised its supervisory authority to regulate evidence in the absence of congressional direction. * * * Relying on the fact that we have created several exceptions to *Miranda*'s warnings requirement and that we have repeatedly referred to the *Miranda* warnings as "prophylactic," the Court of Appeals concluded that the protections announced in *Miranda* are not constitutionally required.

We disagree with the Court of Appeals' conclusion, although we concede that there is language in some of our opinions that supports the view taken by that court. But first and foremost of the factors on the other side—that *Miranda* is a constitutional decision—is that both *Miranda* and two of its companion cases applied the rule to proceedings in state courts—to wit, Arizona, California, and New York. Since that time, we have consistently applied Miranda's rule to prosecutions arising in state courts. It is beyond dispute that we do not hold a supervisory power over the courts of the several States. * * *

The *Miranda* opinion itself begins by stating that the Court granted certiorari "to explore some facets of the problems * * * of applying the privilege against self-incrimination to in-custody interrogation, *and to* *give concrete constitutional guidelines for law enforcement agencies and courts to follow.*" (emphasis added). * * *

Additional support for our conclusion that *Miranda* is constitutionally based is found in the *Miranda* Court's invitation for legislative action to protect the constitutional right against coerced self-incrimination. After discussing the "compelling pressures" inherent in custodial police interrogation, the *Miranda* Court concluded that, "in order to combat these pressures and to permit a full opportunity to exercise the privilege against self-incrimination, the accused must be adequately and effectively appraised of his rights and the exercise of those rights must be fully honored." However, the Court emphasized that it could not foresee "the potential alternatives for protecting the privilege which might be devised by Congress or the States," and it accordingly opined that the Constitution would not preclude legislative solutions that differed from the prescribed *Miranda* warnings but which were "at least as effective in apprising accused persons of their right of silence and in assuring a continuous opportunity to exercise it."

The Court of Appeals also relied on the fact that we have, after our *Miranda* decision, made exceptions from its rule in cases such as *New York v. Quarles* [p. 652], and *Harris v. New York* [p. 650]. But we have also broadened the application of the *Miranda* doctrine * * * . These decisions illustrate the principle—not that *Miranda* is not a constitutional rule—but that no constitutional rule is immutable. No court laying down a general rule can possibly foresee the various circumstances in which counsel will seek to apply it, and the sort of modifications represented by these cases are as much a normal part of constitutional law as the original decision.

The Court of Appeals also noted that in *Oregon v. Elstad*, [p. 662], we stated that "'the *Miranda* exclusionary rule * * * serves the Fifth Amendment and sweeps more broadly than the Fifth Amendment itself.'" Our decision in that case—refusing to apply the traditional "fruits" doctrine developed in Fourth Amendment cases—does not prove that *Miranda* is a nonconstitutional decision, but simply recognizes the fact that unreasonable searches under the Fourth Amendment are different from unwarned interrogation under the Fifth Amendment. * * *

The dissent argues that it is judicial overreaching for this Court to hold § 3501 unconstitutional unless we hold that the *Miranda* warnings are required by the Constitution, in the sense that nothing else will suffice to satisfy constitutional requirements. But we need not go farther than *Miranda* to decide this case. In *Miranda*, the Court noted that reliance on the traditional totality-of-the-circumstances test raised a risk of overlooking an involuntary custodial confession, a risk that the Court found unacceptably great when the confession is offered in the case in chief to prove guilt. The Court therefore concluded that something more than the totality test was necessary. As discussed above, § 3501 reinstates the totality test as sufficient. Section 3501 therefore cannot be sustained if *Miranda* is to remain the law.

Whether or not we would agree with *Miranda*'s reasoning and its resulting rule, were we addressing the issue in the first instance, the principles of *stare decisis* weigh heavily against overruling it now. While " '*stare decisis* is not an inexorable command,' " particularly when we are interpreting the Constitution, "even in constitutional cases, the doctrine carries such persuasive force that we have always required a departure from precedent to be supported by some 'special justification.' "

We do not think there is such justification for overruling *Miranda*. *Miranda* has become embedded in routine police practice to the point where the warnings have become part of our national culture. While we have overruled our precedents when subsequent cases have undermined their doctrinal underpinnings, we do not believe that this has happened to the *Miranda* decision. If anything, our subsequent cases have reduced the impact of the *Miranda* rule on legitimate law enforcement while reaffirming the decision's core ruling that unwarned statements may not be used as evidence in the prosecution's case in chief.

The disadvantage of the *Miranda* rule is that statements which may be by no means involuntary, made by a defendant who is aware of his "rights," may nonetheless be excluded and a guilty defendant go free as a result. But experience suggests that the totality-of-the-circumstances test which § 3501 seeks to revive is more difficult than *Miranda* for law enforcement officers to conform to, and for courts to apply in a consistent manner. The requirement that *Miranda* warnings be given does not, of course, dispense with the voluntariness inquiry. But as we said in *Berkemer v. McCarty* [p. 691], "cases in which a defendant can make a colorable argument that a self-incriminating statement was 'compelled' despite the fact that the law enforcement authorities adhered to the dictates of *Miranda* are rare."

In sum, we conclude that *Miranda* announced a constitutional rule that Congress may not supersede legislatively. Following the rule of *stare decisis*, we decline to overrule *Miranda* ourselves. * * *

JUSTICE SCALIA, with whom JUSTICE THOMAS joins, dissenting.

Those to whom judicial decisions are an unconnected series of judgments that produce either favored or disfavored results will doubtless greet today's decision as a paragon of moderation, since it declines to overrule *Miranda*. Those who understand the judicial process will appreciate that today's decision is not a reaffirmation of *Miranda*, but a radical revision of the most significant element of *Miranda* (as of all cases): the rationale that gives it a permanent place in our jurisprudence.

Marbury v. Madison, 1 Cranch 137 (1803), held that an Act of Congress will not be enforced by the courts if what it prescribes violates the Constitution of the United States. That was the basis on which *Miranda* was decided. One will search today's opinion in vain, however, for a statement (surely simple enough to make) that what 18 U.S.C. § 3501 prescribes—the use at trial of a voluntary confession, even when a *Miranda* warning or its equivalent has failed to be given—violates the Constitution. The reason the statement does not appear is not only (and perhaps not so much) that it would be absurd, inasmuch as § 3501 excludes from trial precisely what the Constitution excludes from trial, viz., compelled confessions; but also that Justices whose votes are needed to compose today's majority are on record as believing that a violation of *Miranda* is *not* a violation of the Constitution. And so, to justify today's agreed-upon result, the Court must adopt a significant *new*, if not entirely comprehensible, principle of constitutional law. As the Court chooses to describe that principle, statutes of Congress can be disregarded, not only when what they prescribe violates the Constitution, but when what they prescribe contradicts a decision of this Court that "announced a constitutional rule." As I shall discuss in some detail, the only thing that can possibly mean in the context of this case is that this Court has the power, not merely to apply the Constitution but to expand it, imposing what it regards as useful "prophylactic" restrictions upon Congress and the States. That is an immense and frightening antidemocratic power, and it does not exist.

It takes only a small step to bring today's opinion out of the realm of power-judging and into the mainstream of legal reasoning: The Court need only go beyond its carefully couched iterations that "*Miranda* is a constitutional decision," that "*Miranda* is constitutionally based," that *Miranda* has "constitutional underpinnings," and come out and say quite clearly: "We reaffirm today that custodial interrogation that is not preceded by *Miranda* warnings or their equivalent violates the Constitution of the United States." It cannot say that, because a majority of the Court does not believe it. The Court therefore acts in plain violation of the Constitution when it denies effect to this Act of Congress.

I * * *

It was once possible to characterize the so-called *Miranda* rule as resting (however implausibly) upon the proposition that what the statute here before us permits—the admission at trial of un-*Mirandized* confessions—violates the Constitution. That is the fairest reading of the *Miranda* case itself. * * *

So understood, *Miranda* was objectionable for innumerable reasons, not least the fact that cases spanning more than 70 years had rejected its core premise that, absent the warnings and an effective waiver of the right to remain silent and of the (thitherto unknown) right to have an attorney present, a statement obtained pursuant to custodial interrogation was necessarily the product of compulsion. Moreover, history and precedent aside, the decision in *Miranda*, if read as an explication of what the Constitution *requires*, is preposterous. There is, for example, simply no basis in reason for concluding that a response to the very first question asked, by a suspect who already *knows* all of the rights described in the *Miranda* warning, is anything other than a volitional act. And even if one assumes that the elimination of compulsion absolutely requires informing even the most knowledgeable suspect of his right to remain silent, it cannot conceivably require the right to have *counsel* present. There is a world of difference, which the Court recognized under the traditional voluntariness test but ignored in *Miranda*, between compelling a suspect to incriminate himself and preventing him from foolishly doing so of his own accord. Only the latter (which is *not* required by the Constitution) could explain the Court's inclusion of a right to counsel and the requirement that it, too, be knowingly and intelligently waived. Counsel's presence is not required to tell the suspect that he *need* not speak; the interrogators can do that. The only good reason for having counsel there is that he can be counted on to advise the suspect that he *should* not speak. * * *

For these reasons, and others more than adequately developed in the *Miranda* dissents and in the subsequent works of the decision's many critics, any conclusion that a violation of the *Miranda* rules *necessarily* amounts to a violation of the privilege against compelled self-incrimination can claim no support in history, precedent, or common sense, and as a result would at least presumptively be worth reconsidering even at this late date. But that is unnecessary, since the Court has (thankfully) long since abandoned the notion that failure to comply with *Miranda*'s rules is itself a violation of the Constitution.

II

As the Court today acknowledges, since *Miranda* we have explicitly, and repeatedly, interpreted that decision as having announced, not the circumstances in which custodial interrogation runs afoul of the Fifth or Fourteenth Amendment, but rather only "prophylactic" rules that go beyond the right against compelled self-incrimination. * * *

In light of these cases, and our statements to the same effect in others, it is simply no longer possible for the Court to conclude, even if it wanted to, that a violation of *Miranda*'s rules is a violation of the Constitution. But as I explained at the outset, that is what is required before the Court may disregard a law of Congress governing the admissibility of evidence in federal court. The Court today insists that the *decision* in *Miranda* is a "constitutional" one; that it has "constitutional underpinnings"; a "constitutional basis" and a "constitutional origin"; that it was "constitutionally based"; and that it announced a "constitutional rule." It is fine to play these word games; but what makes a decision "constitutional" in the only sense relevant here—in the sense that renders it impervious to supersession by congressional legislation such as § 3501—is the determination that the Constitution *requires* the result that the decision announces and the statute ignores. By disregarding congressional action that concededly does not violate the Constitution, the Court flagrantly offends fundamental principles of separation of powers, and arrogates to itself prerogatives reserved to the representatives of the people. * * *

III

There was available to the Court a means of reconciling the established proposition that a violation of *Miranda* does not itself offend the Fifth Amendment with the Court's assertion of a right to ignore the present statute. That means of reconciliation was argued strenuously by both petitioner and the United States, who were evidently more concerned than the Court is with maintaining the coherence of our jurisprudence. It is not mentioned in the Court's opinion because, I assume, a majority of the Justices intent on reversing believes that incoherence is the lesser evil. They may be right.

Petitioner and the United States contend that there is nothing at all exceptional, much less unconstitutional, about the Court's adopting prophylactic rules to buttress constitutional rights, and enforcing them against Congress and the States. * * *

I applaud * * * the refusal of the Justices in the majority to enunciate this boundless doctrine of judicial empowerment as a means of rendering today's decision rational. In nonetheless joining the Court's judgment, however, they overlook two truisms: that actions speak louder than silence, and that (in judge-made law at least) logic will out. Since there is in fact no other principle that can reconcile today's judgment with the post-*Miranda* cases that the Court refuses to abandon, what today's decision will stand for, whether the Justices can bring themselves to say it or not, is the power of the Supreme Court to write a prophylactic, extraconstitutional Constitution, binding on Congress and the States.

IV * * *

Today's judgment converts *Miranda* from a milestone of judicial overreaching into the very Cheops' Pyramid (or perhaps the Sphinx would be a better analogue) of judicial arrogance. In imposing its Court-made code upon the States, the original opinion at least *asserted* that it was demanded by the Constitution. Today's decision does not pretend that it is—and yet *still* asserts the right to impose it against the will of the people's representatives in Congress. * * * This is not the system that was established by the Framers, or that would be established by any sane supporter of government by the people.

I dissent from today's decision, and, until § 3501 is repealed, will continue to apply it in all cases where there has been a sustainable finding that the defendant's confession was voluntary.

NOTES AND QUESTIONS

1.   The Court claims that *Miranda* is "a constitutional decision of this Court" that "may not be in effect overruled by an Act of Congress." Justice Scalia in dissent claims that *Miranda* is not constitutional in the relevant sense. Can you articulate the difference in the way the majority and the dissent are using the characterization "constitutional"?

2.   Return to Note 4, p. 660. Assuming that *Quarles* does not contemplate as broad a public safety exception as the FBI relied on in the Times Square bomber case, do you think that the modification of *Miranda* rules suggested by Attorney General Holder would be constitutional in light of *Dickerson*?

3.   Do you think it is appropriate for a justice to promise (threaten) to apply a statute that the Court has held is unconstitutional? Is Justice Scalia right that "logic will out," that the only way to reconcile *Dickerson* "with the post-*Miranda* cases that the Court refuses to abandon" is "the power of the Supreme Court to write a prophylactic, extra-constitutional Constitution, binding on Congress and the States?"

4.   Which of the prophylactic cases is most inconsistent with the notion that *Miranda* is based on the Constitution?

5.   *Miranda death grip*. William Pizzi and Morris Hoffman argue that the members of the Court "remain locked in an increasingly bizarre kind of *Miranda* death grip"—unwilling to treat a violation of *Miranda* as a violation of the "pristine" self-incrimination clause and yet unwilling to live without *Miranda*. In their view, the Court should either overrule most of the exceptions that resulted from *Miranda*'s prophylactic status or overrule *Miranda* itself. See William T. Pizzi & Morris B. Hoffman, Taking *Miranda*'s Pulse, 58 Vand. L. Rev. 813, 848–49 (2005).

6.   *What a web Miranda weaves. Dickerson* said that *Miranda* "has become embedded in routine police practice to the point where the warnings have become part of our national culture." Indeed, the warnings may be "embedded" beyond our national culture even if the underlying right is not. One of the casebook authors saw a detective comedy/drama show on a Canadian TV station. A Canadian officer arrests a suspect, who says, "Aren't you going to read me my *Miranda* rights?" Cop: "This is Canada, not the U.S. You don't have any rights here."

7.   Now that we have, ahem, settled the question of *Miranda's* constitutionality, we return to the fruits issue.

MISSOURI V. SEIBERT

Supreme Court of the United States, 2004.
542 U.S. 600, 124 S.Ct. 2601, 159 L.Ed.2d 643.

JUSTICE SOUTER announced the judgment of the Court and delivered an opinion, in which JUSTICE STEVENS, JUSTICE GINSBURG, and JUSTICE BREYER join.

This case tests a police protocol for custodial interrogation that calls for giving no warnings of the rights to silence and counsel until interrogation has produced a confession. Although such a statement is generally inadmissible, since taken in violation of *Miranda v. Arizona*, the interrogating officer follows it with *Miranda* warnings and then leads the suspect to cover the same ground a second time. The question here is the admissibility of the repeated statement. Because this midstream recitation of warnings after interrogation and unwarned confession could not effectively comply with *Miranda*'s constitutional requirement, we hold that a statement repeated after a warning in such circumstances is inadmissible.

I

Respondent Patrice Seibert's 12-year-old son Jonathan had cerebral palsy, and when he died in his sleep she feared charges of neglect because of bedsores on his body. In her presence, two of her teenage sons and two of their friends devised a plan to conceal the facts surrounding Jonathan's death by incinerating his body in the course of burning the family's mobile home, in which they planned to leave Donald Rector, a mentally ill teenager living with the family, to avoid any appearance that Jonathan had been unattended. Seibert's son Darian and a friend set the fire, and Donald died.

Five days later, the police awakened Seibert at 3 a.m. at a hospital where Darian was being treated for burns. In arresting her, Officer Kevin Clinton followed instructions from Rolla, Missouri, officer Richard Hanrahan that he refrain from giving *Miranda* warnings. After Seibert had been taken to the police station and left alone in an interview room for 15 to 20 minutes, Hanrahan questioned her without *Miranda* warnings for 30 to 40 minutes, squeezing her arm and repeating "Donald was also to die in his sleep." After Seibert finally admitted she knew Donald was meant to die in the fire, she was given a 20-minute coffee and cigarette break. Officer Hanrahan then turned on a tape recorder, gave Seibert the *Miranda* warnings, and obtained a signed waiver of rights from her. He resumed the questioning with "Ok, 'trice, we've been talking for a little while about what happened on Wednesday the twelfth, haven't we?," and confronted her with her prewarning statements:

> Hanrahan: "Now, in discussion you told us, you told us that there was an understanding about Donald."

Seibert: "Yes."

Hanrahan: "Did that take place earlier that morning?"

Seibert: "Yes."

Hanrahan: "And what was the understanding about Donald?"

Seibert: "If they could get him out of the trailer, to take him out of the trailer."

Hanrahan: "And if they couldn't?"

Seibert: "I, I never even thought about it. I just figured they would."

Hanrahan: " 'Trice, didn't you tell me that he was supposed to die in his sleep?"

Seibert: "If that would happen, 'cause he was on that new medicine, you know * * * ' "

Hanrahan: "The Prozac? And it makes him sleepy. So he was supposed to die in his sleep?"

Seibert: "Yes."

* * * At the suppression hearing, Officer Hanrahan testified that he made a "conscious decision" to withhold *Miranda* warnings, thus resorting to an interrogation technique he had been taught: question first, then give the warnings, and then repeat the question "until I get the answer that she's already provided once." He acknowledged that Seibert's ultimate statement was "largely a repeat of information * * * obtained" prior to the warning.

* * * On appeal, the Missouri Court of Appeals affirmed, treating this case as indistinguishable from *Oregon v. Elstad* [p. 662]. The Supreme Court of Missouri reversed, holding that "in the circumstances here, where the interrogation was nearly continuous, * * * the second statement, clearly the product of the invalid first statement, should have been suppressed." * * *

We granted certiorari to resolve a split in the Courts of Appeals. We now affirm.

II * * *

In *Miranda*, we explained that the "voluntariness doctrine in the state cases * * * encompasses all interrogation practices which are likely to exert such pressure upon an individual as to disable him from making a free and rational choice." We appreciated the difficulty of judicial enquiry *post hoc* into the circumstances of a police interrogation and recognized that "the coercion inherent in custodial interrogation blurs the line between voluntary and involuntary statements, and thus heightens the risk" that the privilege against self-incrimination will not be observed. Hence our concern that the "traditional totality-of-the-circumstances" test posed an "unacceptably great" risk that involuntary custodial confessions would escape detection.

Accordingly, "to reduce the risk of a coerced confession and to implement the Self-Incrimination Clause," this Court in *Miranda* concluded that "the accused must be adequately and effectively apprised of his rights and the exercise of those rights must be fully honored." *Miranda* conditioned the admissibility at trial of any custodial confession on warning a suspect of his rights: failure to give the prescribed warnings and obtain a waiver of rights before custodial questioning generally requires exclusion of any statements obtained. Conversely, giving the warnings and getting a waiver has generally produced a virtual ticket of admissibility; maintaining that a statement is involuntary even though given after warnings and voluntary waiver of rights requires unusual stamina, and litigation over voluntariness tends to end with the finding of a valid waiver. To point out the obvious, this common consequence would not be common at all were it not that *Miranda* warnings are customarily given under circumstances allowing for a real choice between talking and remaining silent.

III * * *

The technique of interrogating in successive, unwarned and warned phases raises a new challenge to *Miranda*. Although we have no statistics on the frequency of this practice, it is not confined to Rolla, Missouri. An officer of that police department testified that the strategy of withholding *Miranda* warnings until after interrogating and drawing out a confession was promoted not only by his own department, but by a national police training organization and other departments in which he had worked. Consistently with the officer's testimony, the Police Law Institute, for example, instructs that "officers may conduct a two-stage interrogation * * * . At any point during the pre-*Miranda* interrogation, usually after arrestees have confessed, officers may then read the *Miranda* warnings and ask for a waiver. If the arrestees waive their *Miranda* rights, officers will be able to repeat any *subsequent* incriminating statements later in court" (emphasis in original).[2] The upshot of all this advice is a question-

---

[2] Emphasizing the impeachment exception to the *Miranda* rule approved by this Court, some training programs advise officers to omit *Miranda* warnings altogether or to continue questioning after the suspect invokes his rights. [See] Weisselberg, Saving *Miranda,* 84 Cornell L. Rev. 109, 110, 132–139 (1998) (collecting California training materials encouraging questioning "outside *Miranda*"). This training is reflected in the reported cases involving deliberate questioning after invocation of *Miranda* rights. Scholars have noted the growing trend of such practices. See, *e.g.,* Leo, Questioning the Relevance of *Miranda* in the Twenty-First Century, 99 Mich. L. Rev. 1000, 1010 (2001); Weisselberg, In the Stationhouse After *Dickerson,* 99 Mich. L. Rev. 1121, 1123–1154 (2001). * * *

first practice of some popularity, as one can see from the reported cases describing its use, sometimes in obedience to departmental policy.

IV

* * * The object of [the] question-first [interrogation method] is to render *Miranda* warnings ineffective by waiting for a particularly opportune time to give them, after the suspect has already confessed.

Just as "no talismanic incantation [is] required to satisfy [*Miranda*'s] strictures," it would be absurd to think that mere recitation of the litany suffices to satisfy *Miranda* in every conceivable circumstance. "The inquiry is simply whether the warnings reasonably 'convey to [a suspect] his rights as required by *Miranda*.' " The threshold issue when interrogators question first and warn later is thus whether it would be reasonable to find that in these circumstances the warnings could function "effectively" as *Miranda* requires. Could the warnings effectively advise the suspect that he had a real choice about giving an admissible statement at that juncture? Could they reasonably convey that he could choose to stop talking even if he had talked earlier? For unless the warnings could place a suspect who has just been interrogated in a position to make such an informed choice, there is no practical justification for accepting the formal warnings as compliance with *Miranda*, or for treating the second stage of interrogation as distinct from the first, unwarned and inadmissible segment.

There is no doubt about the answer that proponents of question-first give to this question about the effectiveness of warnings given only after successful interrogation, and we think their answer is correct. By any objective measure, applied to circumstances exemplified here, it is likely that if the interrogators employ the technique of withholding warnings until after interrogation succeeds in eliciting a confession, the warnings will be ineffective in preparing the suspect for successive interrogation, close in time and similar in content. After all, the reason that question-first is catching on is as obvious as its manifest purpose, which is to get a confession the suspect would not make if he understood his rights at the outset; the sensible underlying assumption is that with one confession in hand before the warnings, the interrogator can count on getting its duplicate, with trifling additional trouble. Upon hearing warnings only in the aftermath of interrogation and just after making a confession, a suspect would hardly think he had a genuine right to remain silent, let alone persist in so believing once the police began to lead him over the same ground again. A more likely reaction on a suspect's part would be perplexity about the reason for discussing rights at that point, bewilderment being an unpromising frame of mind for knowledgeable decision. What is worse, telling a suspect that "anything you say can and will be used against you," without expressly excepting the statement just given, could lead to an entirely reasonable inference that what he has just said will be used, with subsequent silence being of no avail. Thus, when *Miranda* warnings are inserted in the midst of coordinated and continuing interrogation, they are likely to mislead and "deprive a defendant of knowledge essential to his ability to understand the nature of his rights and the consequences of abandoning them." * * *

V

Missouri argues that a confession repeated at the end of an interrogation sequence envisioned in a question-first strategy is admissible on the authority of *Oregon v. Elstad*, but the argument disfigures that case. * * *

The contrast between *Elstad* and this case reveals a series of relevant facts that bear on whether *Miranda* warnings delivered midstream could be effective enough to accomplish their object: the completeness and detail of the questions and answers in the first round of interrogation, the overlapping content of the two statements, the timing and setting of the first and the second, the continuity of police personnel, and the degree to which the interrogator's questions treated the second round as continuous with the first. In *Elstad*, it was not unreasonable to see the occasion for questioning at the station house as presenting a markedly different experience from the short conversation at home; since a reasonable person in the suspect's shoes could have seen the station house questioning as a new and distinct experience, the *Miranda* warnings could have made sense as presenting a genuine choice whether to follow up on the earlier admission.

At the opposite extreme are the facts here, which by any objective measure reveal a police strategy adapted to undermine the *Miranda* warnings.[6] The unwarned interrogation was conducted in the station house, and the questioning was systematic, exhaustive, and managed with psychological skill. When the police were finished there was little, if anything, of incriminating potential left unsaid. The warned phase of questioning proceeded after a pause of only 15 to 20 minutes, in the same place as the unwarned segment. When the same officer who had conducted the first phase recited the *Miranda* warnings, he said nothing to counter the probable misimpression that the advice that anything Seibert said could be used against her also applied to the details of the inculpatory statement previously elicited. In particular, the police did not advise that her prior statement could not be used.[7] Nothing was said or

---

[6] Because the intent of the officer will rarely be as candidly admitted as it was here (even as it is likely to determine the conduct of the interrogation), the focus is on facts apart from intent that show the question-first tactic at work.

[7] We do not hold that a formal addendum warning that a previous statement could not be used would be sufficient to change the character of the question-first procedure to the point of

done to dispel the oddity of warning about legal rights to silence and counsel right after the police had led her through a systematic interrogation, and any uncertainty on her part about a right to stop talking about matters previously discussed would only have been aggravated by the way Officer Hanrahan set the scene by saying "we've been talking for a little while about what happened on Wednesday the twelfth, haven't we?" The impression that the further questioning was a mere continuation of the earlier questions and responses was fostered by references back to the confession already given. It would have been reasonable to regard the two sessions as parts of a continuum, in which it would have been unnatural to refuse to repeat at the second stage what had been said before. These circumstances must be seen as challenging the comprehensibility and efficacy of the *Miranda* warnings to the point that a reasonable person in the suspect's shoes would not have understood them to convey a message that she retained a choice about continuing to talk.[8]

VI

* * * Because the question-first tactic effectively threatens to thwart *Miranda*'s purpose of reducing the risk that a coerced confession would be admitted, and because the facts here do not reasonably support a conclusion that the warnings given could have served their purpose, Seibert's postwarning statements are inadmissible. * * *

JUSTICE BREYER, concurring.

In my view, the following simple rule should apply to the two-stage interrogation technique: Courts should exclude the "fruits" of the initial unwarned questioning unless the failure to warn was in good faith. I believe this is a sound and workable approach to the problem this case presents. Prosecutors and judges have long understood how to apply the "fruits" approach, which they use in other areas of law. And in the workaday world of criminal law enforcement the administrative simplicity of the familiar has significant advantages over a more complex exclusionary rule.

I believe the plurality's approach in practice will function as a "fruits" test. The truly "effective" *Miranda* warnings on which the plurality insists will occur only when certain circumstances—a lapse in time, a change in location or interrogating officer, or a shift in the focus of the questioning—intervene between the unwarned questioning and any postwarning statement.

---

rendering an ensuing statement admissible, but its absence is clearly a factor that blunts the efficacy of the warnings and points to a continuing, not a new, interrogation.

8 Because we find that the warnings were inadequate, there is no need to assess the actual voluntariness of the statement.

I consequently join the plurality's opinion in full. I also agree with Justice Kennedy's opinion insofar as it is consistent with this approach and makes clear that a good-faith exception applies.

JUSTICE KENNEDY, concurring in the judgment.

The interrogation technique used in this case is designed to circumvent *Miranda*. It undermines the *Miranda* warning and obscures its meaning. The plurality opinion is correct to conclude that statements obtained through the use of this technique are inadmissible. Although I agree with much in the careful and convincing opinion for the plurality, my approach does differ in some respects, requiring this separate statement. * * *

In my view, *Elstad* was correct in its reasoning and its result. *Elstad* reflects a balanced and pragmatic approach to enforcement of the *Miranda* warning. An officer may not realize that a suspect is in custody and warnings are required. The officer may not plan to question the suspect or may be waiting for a more appropriate time. Skilled investigators often interview suspects multiple times, and good police work may involve referring to prior statements to test their veracity or to refresh recollection. In light of these realities it would be extravagant to treat the presence of one statement that cannot be admitted under *Miranda* as sufficient reason to prohibit subsequent statements preceded by a proper warning. That approach would serve "neither the general goal of deterring improper police conduct nor the Fifth Amendment goal of assuring trustworthy evidence would be served by suppression of the * * * testimony."

This case presents different considerations. The police used a two-step questioning technique based on a deliberate violation of *Miranda*. The *Miranda* warning was withheld to obscure both the practical and legal significance of the admonition when finally given. * * *

* * * When an interrogator uses this deliberate, two-step strategy, predicated upon violating *Miranda* during an extended interview, postwarning statements that are related to the substance of prewarning statements must be excluded absent specific, curative steps.

The plurality concludes that whenever a two-stage interview occurs, admissibility of the postwarning statement should depend on "whether the *Miranda* warnings delivered midstream could have been effective enough to accomplish their object" given the specific facts of the case. This test envisions an objective inquiry from the perspective of the suspect, and applies in the case of both intentional and unintentional two-stage interrogations. In my view, this test cuts too broadly. *Miranda*'s clarity is one of its strengths, and a multifactor test that applies to every two-stage interrogation may serve to undermine that clarity. I would apply a narrower test applicable only in the infrequent case, such as we have here, in which the two-step interrogation technique was used in a calculated way to undermine the *Miranda* warning.

The admissibility of postwarning statements should continue to be governed by the principles of *Elstad* unless the deliberate two-step strategy was employed. If the deliberate two-step strategy has been used, postwarning statements that are related to the substance of prewarning statements must be excluded unless curative measures are taken before the postwarning statement is made. Curative measures should be designed to ensure that a reasonable person in the suspect's situation would understand the import and effect of the *Miranda* warning and of the *Miranda* waiver. For example, a substantial break in time and circumstances between the prewarning statement and the *Miranda* warning may suffice in most circumstances, as it allows the accused to distinguish the two contexts and appreciate that the interrogation has taken a new turn. Alternatively, an additional warning that explains the likely inadmissibility of the prewarning custodial statement may be sufficient. No curative steps were taken in this case, however, so the postwarning statements are inadmissible and the conviction cannot stand.

For these reasons, I concur in the judgment of the Court.

JUSTICE O'CONNOR, with whom THE CHIEF JUSTICE [REHNQUIST], JUSTICE SCALIA, and JUSTICE THOMAS join, dissenting.

The plurality devours *Oregon v. Elstad* even as it accuses petitioner's argument of "disfiguring" that decision. I believe that we are bound by *Elstad* to reach a different result, and I would vacate the judgment of the Supreme Court of Missouri.

I

On two preliminary questions I am in full agreement with the plurality. First, the plurality appropriately follows *Elstad* in concluding that Seibert's statement cannot be held inadmissible under a "fruit of the poisonous tree" theory. Second, the plurality correctly declines to focus its analysis on the subjective intent of the interrogating officer.

A * * *

Although the analysis the plurality ultimately espouses examines the same facts and circumstances that a "fruits" analysis would consider (such as the lapse of time between the two interrogations and change of questioner or location), it does so for entirely different reasons. The fruits analysis would examine those factors because they are relevant to the balance of deterrence value versus the "drastic and socially costly course" of excluding reliable evidence. The plurality, by contrast, looks to those factors to inform the *psychological* judgment regarding whether the suspect has been informed effectively of her right to remain silent. The analytical underpinnings of the two approaches are thus entirely distinct, and they should not be conflated just because they function similarly in practice.

B

The plurality's rejection of an intent-based test is also, in my view, correct. Freedom from compulsion lies at the heart of the Fifth Amendment, and requires us to assess whether a suspect's decision to speak truly was voluntary. Because voluntariness is a matter of the suspect's state of mind, we focus our analysis on the way in which suspects experience interrogation.

Thoughts kept inside a police officer's head cannot affect that experience. * * * A suspect who experienced the exact same interrogation as Seibert, save for a difference in the undivulged, subjective intent of the interrogating officer when he failed to give *Miranda* warnings, would not experience the interrogation any differently. * * * "Although highly inappropriate, even deliberate deception of an attorney could not possibly affect a suspect's decision to waive his *Miranda* rights unless he were at least aware of the incident."

* * * Moreover, recognizing an exception to *Elstad* for intentional violations would require focusing constitutional analysis on a police officer's subjective intent, an unattractive proposition that we all but uniformly avoid. In general, "we believe that 'sending state and federal courts on an expedition into the minds of police officers would produce a grave and fruitless misallocation of judicial resources.'" * * *

For these reasons, I believe that the approach espoused by Justice Kennedy is ill advised. Justice Kennedy would extend *Miranda*'s exclusionary rule to any case in which the use of the "two-step interrogation technique" was "deliberate" or "calculated." This approach untethers the analysis from facts knowable to, and therefore having any potential directly to affect, the suspect. * * *

II

The plurality's adherence to *Elstad*, and mine to the plurality, end there. * * *

* * * The plurality might very well think that we struck the balance between Fifth Amendment rights and law enforcement interests incorrectly in *Elstad*; but that is not normally a sufficient reason for ignoring the dictates of *stare decisis*.

I would analyze the two-step interrogation procedure under the voluntariness standards central to the Fifth Amendment and reiterated in *Elstad*. *Elstad* commands that if Seibert's first statement is shown to have been involuntary, the court must examine whether the taint dissipated through the passing of time or a change in circumstances: "When a prior statement is actually coerced, the time that passes between confessions, the change in place of interrogations, and the change in identity of the interrogators all bear on whether that coercion has carried over into the second confession." In addition, Seibert's second statement should be suppressed if she showed that it was involuntary despite the *Miranda* warnings. Although I would leave this analysis for the Missouri courts to conduct on remand, I note that, unlike the officers in *Elstad*, Officer Hanrahan referred to Seibert's unwarned statement during the second part of the interrogation when she made a statement at odds with her unwarned confession. Such a tactic may bear on the voluntariness inquiry.

* * *

Because I believe that the plurality gives insufficient deference to *Elstad* and that Justice Kennedy places improper weight on subjective intent, I respectfully dissent.

NOTES AND QUESTIONS

1.   *Counting votes.* It is time to count votes in *Seibert* to determine where *Elstad-Seibert* puts us now. Justice O'Connor, who wrote *Elstad*, sharply disputes the plurality's interpretation of what the Court did in *Elstad*. Who gets the better of that argument? What do you think of Justice Kennedy's opinion?

2.   Given that no opinion attracted five votes in *Seibert*, what is the narrow holding in *Seibert*? See Marks v. United States, 430 U.S. 188, 97 S.Ct. 990, 51 L.Ed.2d 260 (1977).

3.   The Court cites three articles that discuss what it calls a "growing trend" toward not giving *Miranda* warnings as part of a plan to use incriminating statements to impeach. See Richard A. Leo, *Questioning the Relevance of Miranda in the Twenty-First Century*, 99 Mich. L. Rev. 1000, 1010 (2001); Charles D. Weisselberg, *In the Stationhouse After Dickerson*, 99 Mich. L. Rev. 1121, 1123–1154 (2001); Charles D. Weisselberg, *Saving Miranda,* 84 Cornell L. Rev. 109, 110, 132–139 (1998). In light of *Seibert*, what do you think about the constitutionality of this practice?

Charles Weisselberg researched police training methods in California in the wake of *Seibert* and found that the training generally emphasized "the deliberate conduct of the officers in *Seibert*, distinguishing *Elstad* as a good-faith mistake." Charles D. Weisselberg, *Mourning Miranda*, 96 Cal. L. Rev. 1519, 1553 (2008). For example, the California Peace Officers Legal Sourcebook "says unequivocally that [o]fficers should not attempt to exploit the *Elstad* rule."

4.   *The three step, five factor Seibert shuffle. Seibert* is an attempt to limit calculated police avoidance of *Miranda*, but it is far from easy to apply

either the plurality's test or that of Justice Kennedy. A Westlaw search of all state and federal cases for "Missouri v. Seibert" on January 4, 2009 produced a universe of 528 cases. A random sample of twenty state cases showed six that found a *Seibert* violation, usually on facts not as extreme as *Seibert*, and fourteen that found no violation. One court has identified five factors critical to the plurality in *Seibert* and then synthesized Souter's and Kennedy's opinions. According to this district judge, a court should consider

> (1) the completeness and detail of the questions and answers in the first round of interrogation, (2) the overlapping content of the two statements, (3) the timing and setting of the first and second, (4) the continuity of police personnel, and (5) the degree to which the interrogator's questions treated the second round as continuous with the first. * * *

> [A] court applying *Seibert* should follow three steps. First, the court should determine whether law enforcement personnel deliberately employed the two-round interrogation strategy for the purpose of sidestepping *Miranda*. Justice Kennedy's concurrence requires this. [If not, then the inquiry is at an end and no *Miranda* violation occurs. If the procedure was deliberately employed to sidestep *Miranda*, then] to determine whether a given situation is more like that in *Elstad* or *Seibert*, the court should apply the five factors the *Seibert* plurality enunciated. Finally, if after applying these factors, the court concludes that the facts are more like those in *Seibert* than *Elstad*, it should follow a third, final step: determining whether the interrogator took any curative measures. Assuming that he or she did not, the confession is inadmissible.

United States v. Long Tong Kiam, 343 F.Supp.2d 398, 407, 409 (E.D. Pa. 2004).

Question: Does law *have* to be this hard?

5.   *Problems.*

A.   *Imperfect warnings.* What if the *Miranda* violation in the first interrogation was the result of the arresting officer giving incomplete warnings? The detectives who interrogated the suspect did not know that the initial warnings had been defective, and they did not give a fresh set of warnings until the suspect admitted committing the robbery. He then signed a waiver form and repeated his confession. Cf. State v. Yohnnson, 6 A.3d 963 (N.J. 2010).

B.   *Ninety-five minute first stage.* Without giving warnings, two police officers interrogated *O* first in his cell and then in the patrol commander's office. During this 95-minute interrogation, the officers insisted that *O* had to give an account of his whereabouts during the time a taxi driver was killed. Police gave him warnings only after he admitted that two acquaintances of his planned to rob a taxi driver after *O* lured him to a particular intersection. He then waived *Miranda* and "completed his account of the 'planned robbery' of the cab driver." Can you think of any argument that might permit the State to admit the confession made after the "waiver"? State v. O'Neill, 936 A.2d 438 (N.J. 2007).

C. *The silent treatment.* L was arrested for the abduction of two victims. At the police station, one agent sat with the suspect while other agents looked for a tape recorder so that the defendant's interview could be recorded if the defendant agreed to speak with them. The agent sitting with L knew that no *Miranda* warnings had been given to him. The agent said nothing to L. After several minutes sitting in silence, L's demeanor changed and he began to cry. The agent said, "I hope you know what kind of trouble you are in." L replied, "Yes, I know. I killed her." He said that he told her to get down on her knees and that the gun did not go off until the third time he pulled the trigger. After L said this, the agent left the room to report this information to other agents because, up until that moment, the law enforcement agencies had hoped that the victim was still alive. The defendant said nothing further at that time and was not asked any additional questions. When the officers located a tape recorder, they administered *Miranda* warnings. L signed the waiver form and gave a detailed confession that included the abduction of both victims, the theft of the victims' jewelry, credit cards, bank cards, and property, the sexual assault and murder of one victim, and the attempted murder of a second victim. Is the post-warnings confession admissible? See State v. Lebron, 979 So.2d 1093 (Fla. App. 2008).

6. *Physical fruits: What Elstad did not decide. Elstad* left one fruits issue undecided. Can physical evidence, as distinguished from a statement made by a third party (as in *Tucker*, p. 651) or another confession of the defendant (as in *Elstad*), be used in evidence if discovered because of a violation of *Miranda*? We know from Chapter 5 that the Fourth Amendment rule, though subject to exceptions, is that physical evidence found by means of the violation is inadmissible.

The Court decided the *Miranda* physical fruits issue the same day it decided *Seibert*. In United States v. Patane, 542 U.S. 630, 124 S.Ct. 2620, 159 L.Ed.2d 667 (2004), officers arrested Patane for violating a restraining order and one officer began to recite the *Miranda* warnings. Patane stopped him after the "right to remain silent" and said that he knew his rights. The officers did not attempt to finish the warnings. The government conceded in the Supreme Court that Patane's responses to later questions were inadmissible at trial under *Miranda*, "despite the partial warning and respondent's assertions that he knew his rights."

A detective then asked about a .40 Glock pistol that he believed Patane possessed. Though initially "reluctant to discuss the matter," Patane finally told the detective "that the pistol was in his bedroom. [Patane] then gave Detective Benner permission to retrieve the pistol. Detective Benner found the pistol and seized it."

As the government conceded a failure to comply with *Miranda*, the issue was whether the *Miranda* violation made the gun inadmissible at Patane's trial for unlawful possession of the firearm. Five members of the Court agreed it was admissible, but it took two theories to produce a judgment affirming Patane's conviction.

Justice Thomas, joined by Chief Justice Rehnquist and Justice Scalia, delivered the Court's judgment in an opinion that re-iterated *Miranda*'s prophylactic status. As *Miranda* exists to protect against violations of the self-incrimination clause, it is "not implicated by the admission into evidence of the physical fruit of a voluntary statement." In Thomas's words: "Potential violations occur, if at all, only upon the admission of unwarned statements into evidence at trial. And, at that point, 'the exclusion of unwarned statements * * * is a complete and sufficient remedy' for any perceived *Miranda* violation."

Justice Kennedy, joined by Justice O'Connor, concurred in the judgment. To their way of thinking, a simple cost-benefit balance produced a decision to admit physical evidence discovered through unwarned statements. "In light of the important probative value of reliable physical evidence, it is doubtful that exclusion can be justified by a deterrence rationale sensitive to both law enforcement interests and a suspect's rights during an in-custody interrogation."

Justice Souter, joined by Justices Stevens and Ginsburg, dissented, predicting a loss of deterrence: "There is no way to read this case except as an unjustifiable invitation to law enforcement officers to flout *Miranda* when there may be physical evidence to be gained." Justice Breyer also dissented.

7.   Despite the lack of a majority opinion, does *Patane* settle the physical fruits issue?

8.   *Dickerson fall-out.* The debate about the constitutional nature of *Miranda* continues in a post-*Dickerson* world. The key to Souter's dissent in *Patane* was the Court's failure to credit *Miranda*'s presumption of coercion. No one doubts that "the Fifth Amendment privilege against compelled self-incrimination extends to the exclusion of derivative evidence." In Souter's view, it was only by denying *Miranda* "full constitutional stature" that the Court could find five votes to admit the pistol.

But not a single justice in *Seibert* suggested that *Dickerson* somehow undermined *Elstad*. *Seibert* is thus good evidence that the Court "can have its cake and eat it, too"—that it can have a constitutional *Miranda* that has numerous exceptions and special rules. It appears that *Miranda* will co-exist indefinitely with police interrogation—the spider and its prey.

We turn now to the doctrinal web that the spider has spun. One reason to adopt rules to govern police interrogation, rather than relying on the norm of suppressing involuntary confessions, was to achieve greater clarity in the doctrine. Ask yourself, as you reflect on the chapter, whether that goal has been achieved.

D. *MIRANDA* CUSTODY

BERKEMER V. MCCARTY

Supreme Court of the United States, 1984.
468 U.S. 420, 104 S.Ct. 3138, 82 L.Ed.2d 317.

JUSTICE MARSHALL delivered the opinion of the Court [joined by CHIEF JUSTICE BURGER, and JUSTICES BRENNAN, WHITE, BLACKMUN, POWELL, REHNQUIST, and O'CONNOR].

This case presents two related questions: First, does our decision in *Miranda v. Arizona* govern the admissibility of statements made during custodial interrogation by a suspect accused of a misdemeanor traffic offense? Second, does the roadside questioning of a motorist detained pursuant to a traffic stop constitute custodial interrogation for the purposes of the doctrine enunciated in *Miranda*?

I

A

The parties have stipulated to the essential facts. On the evening of March 31, 1980, Trooper Williams of the Ohio State Highway Patrol observed respondent's car weaving in and out of a lane on Interstate Highway 270. After following the car for two miles, Williams forced respondent to stop and asked him to get out of the vehicle. When respondent complied, Williams noticed that he was having difficulty standing. At that point, "Williams concluded that [respondent] would be charged with a traffic offense and, therefore, his freedom to leave the scene was terminated." However, respondent was not told that he would be taken into custody. Williams then asked respondent to perform a field sobriety test, commonly known as a "balancing test." Respondent could not do so without falling.

While still at the scene of the traffic stop, Williams asked respondent whether he had been using intoxicants. Respondent replied that "he had consumed two beers and had smoked several joints of marijuana a short time before." Respondent's speech was slurred, and Williams had difficulty understanding him. Williams thereupon formally placed respondent under arrest and transported him in the patrol car to the Franklin County Jail.

At the jail, respondent was given an intoxilyzer test to determine the concentration of alcohol in his blood. The test did not detect any alcohol whatsoever in respondent's system. Williams then resumed questioning respondent in order to obtain information for inclusion in the State Highway Patrol Alcohol Influence Report. Respondent answered affirmatively a question whether he had been drinking. When then asked if he was under the influence of alcohol, he said, "I guess, barely."

Williams next asked respondent to indicate on the form whether the marihuana he had smoked had been treated with any chemicals. In the section of the report headed "Remarks," respondent wrote, "No ang[el] dust or PCP in the pot. Rick McCarty."

At no point in this sequence of events did Williams or anyone else tell respondent that he had a right to remain silent, to consult with an attorney, and to have an attorney appointed for him if he could not afford one.

B

Respondent was charged with operating a motor vehicle while under the influence of alcohol and/or drugs * * * .

Respondent moved to exclude the various incriminating statements he had made to Trooper Williams on the ground that introduction into evidence of those statements would violate the Fifth Amendment insofar as he had not been informed of his constitutional rights prior to his interrogation. * * *

II * * *

In the years since the decision in *Miranda*, we have frequently reaffirmed the central principle established by that case: if the police take a suspect into custody and then ask him questions without informing him of the rights enumerated [in *Miranda*], his responses cannot be introduced into evidence to establish his guilt.

Petitioner asks us to carve an exception out of the foregoing principle. When the police arrest a person for allegedly committing a misdemeanor traffic offense and then ask him questions without telling him his constitutional rights, petitioner argues, his responses should be admissible against him. We cannot agree.

One of the principal advantages of the doctrine that suspects must be given warnings before being interrogated while in custody is the clarity of that rule. * * *

The exception to *Miranda* proposed by petitioner would substantially undermine this crucial advantage of the doctrine. The police often are unaware when they arrest a person whether he may have committed a misdemeanor or a felony. Consider, for example, the reasonably common situation in which the driver of a car involved in an accident is taken into custody. Under Ohio law, both driving while under the influence of intoxicants and negligent vehicular homicide are misdemeanors, while reckless vehicular homicide is a felony. When arresting a person for causing a collision, the police may not know which of these offenses he may have committed. Indeed, the nature of his offense may depend upon circumstances unknowable to the police, such as whether the suspect has previously committed a similar offense or has a criminal record of some other kind. It may even turn upon events yet to happen, such as whether a victim of the accident dies. It would be unreasonable to expect the police to make guesses as to the nature of the criminal conduct at issue before deciding how they may interrogate the suspect.

Equally importantly, the doctrinal complexities that would confront the courts if we accepted petitioner's proposal would be Byzantine. Difficult questions quickly spring to mind: For instance, investigations into seemingly minor offenses sometimes escalate gradually into investigations into more serious matters; at what point in the evolution of an affair of this sort would the police be obliged to give *Miranda* warnings to a suspect in custody? What evidence would be necessary to establish that an arrest for a misdemeanor offense was merely a pretext to enable the police to interrogate the suspect (in hopes of obtaining information about a felony) without providing him the safeguards prescribed by *Miranda*? The litigation necessary to resolve such matters would be time-consuming and disruptive of law enforcement. And the end result would be an elaborate set of rules, interlaced with exceptions and subtle distinctions, discriminating between different kinds of custodial interrogations. Neither the police nor criminal defendants would benefit from such a development.

Absent a compelling justification we surely would be unwilling so seriously to impair the simplicity and clarity of the holding of *Miranda*. Neither of the two arguments proffered by petitioner constitutes such a justification. Petitioner first contends that *Miranda* warnings are unnecessary when a suspect is questioned about a misdemeanor traffic offense, because the police have no reason to subject such a suspect to the sort of interrogation that most troubled the Court in *Miranda*. We cannot agree that the dangers of police abuse are so slight in this context. For example, the offense of driving while intoxicated is increasingly regarded in many jurisdictions as a very serious matter. Especially when the intoxicant at issue is a narcotic drug rather than alcohol, the police sometimes have difficulty obtaining evidence of this crime. Under such circumstances, the incentive for the police to try to induce the defendant to incriminate himself may well be substantial. Similar incentives are likely to be present when a person is arrested for a minor offense but the police suspect that a more serious crime may have been committed. * * *

Petitioner's second argument is that law enforcement would be more expeditious and effective in the absence of a requirement that persons arrested for traffic offenses be informed of their rights. Again, we are unpersuaded. The occasions on which the police arrest and then interrogate someone suspected only of a misdemeanor traffic offense are rare. The police are already well accustomed to giving *Miranda* warnings to persons taken into custody. Adherence to the principle that *all* suspects must be given such warnings will not significantly hamper the efforts of the police to investigate crimes.

We hold therefore that a person subjected to custodial interrogation is entitled to the benefit of the procedural safeguards enunciated in *Miranda*, regardless of the nature or severity of the offense of which he is suspected or for which he was arrested.

The implication of this holding is that * * * the statements made by respondent at the County Jail were inadmissible. There can be no question that respondent was "in custody" at least as of the moment he was formally placed under arrest and instructed to get into the police car. Because he was not informed of his constitutional rights at that juncture, respondent's subsequent admissions should not have been used against him.

III

To assess the admissibility of the self-incriminating statements made by respondent prior to his formal arrest, we are obliged to address a second issue concerning the scope of our decision in *Miranda*: whether the roadside questioning of a motorist detained pursuant to a routine traffic stop should be considered "custodial interrogation." Respondent urges that it should, on the ground that *Miranda* by its terms applies whenever "a person has been taken into custody *or otherwise deprived of his freedom of action in any significant way*." Petitioner contends that a holding that every detained motorist must be advised of his rights before being questioned would constitute an unwarranted extension of the *Miranda* doctrine.

It must be acknowledged at the outset that a traffic stop significantly curtails the "freedom of action" of the driver and the passengers, if any, of the detained vehicle. Under the law of most States, it is a crime either to ignore a policeman's signal to stop one's car or, once having stopped, to drive away without permission. Certainly few motorists would feel free either to disobey a directive to pull over or to leave the scene of a traffic stop without being told they might do so. Partly for these reasons, we have long acknowledged that "stopping an automobile and detaining its occupants constitute a 'seizure' within the meaning of [the Fourth] Amendmen[t], even though the purpose of the stop is limited and the resulting detention quite brief."

However, we decline to accord talismanic power to the phrase in the *Miranda* opinion emphasized by respondent. Fidelity to the doctrine announced in *Miranda* requires that it be enforced strictly, but only in those types of situations in which the concerns that powered the decision are implicated. Thus, we must decide whether a traffic stop exerts upon a detained person pressures that sufficiently impair his free exercise of his privilege against self-incrimination to require that he be warned of his constitutional rights.

Two features of an ordinary traffic stop mitigate the danger that a person questioned will be induced "to speak where he would not otherwise do so freely." First, detention of a motorist pursuant to a traffic stop is presumptively temporary and brief. The vast majority of roadside detentions last only a few minutes. A motorist's expectations, when he sees a policeman's light flashing behind him, are that he will be obliged to spend a short period of time answering questions and waiting while the officer checks his license and registration, that he may then be given a citation, but that in the end he most likely will be allowed to continue on his way. In this respect, questioning incident to an ordinary traffic stop is quite different from stationhouse interrogation, which frequently is prolonged, and in which the detainee often is aware that questioning will continue until he provides his interrogators the answers they seek.

Second, circumstances associated with the typical traffic stop are not such that the motorist feels completely at the mercy of the police. To be sure, the aura of authority surrounding an armed, uniformed officer and the knowledge that the officer has some discretion in deciding whether to issue a citation, in combination, exert some pressure on the detainee to respond to questions. But other aspects of the situation substantially offset these forces. Perhaps most importantly, the typical traffic stop is public, at least to some degree. Passersby, on foot or in other cars, witness the interaction of officer and motorist. This exposure to public view both reduces the ability of an unscrupulous policeman to use illegitimate means to elicit self-incriminating statements and diminishes the motorist's fear that, if he does not cooperate, he will be subjected to abuse. The fact that the detained motorist typically is confronted by only one or at most two policemen further mutes his sense of vulnerability. In short, the atmosphere surrounding an ordinary traffic stop is substantially less "police dominated" than that surrounding the kinds of interrogation at issue in *Miranda* itself, and in the subsequent cases in which we have applied *Miranda*.

In both of these respects, the usual traffic stop is more analogous to a so-called *"Terry* stop," than to a formal arrest. Under the Fourth Amendment, we have held, a policeman who lacks probable cause but whose "observations lead him reasonably to suspect" that a particular person has committed, is committing, or is about to commit a crime, may detain that person briefly in order to "investigate the circumstances that provoke suspicion." "[T]he stop and inquiry must be 'reasonably related in scope to the justification for their initiation.'" Typically, this means that the officer may ask the detainee a moderate number of questions to determine his identity and to try to obtain information confirming or dispelling the officer's suspicions. But the detainee is not obliged to respond. And, unless the detainee's answers provide the officer with probable cause to arrest him, he must then be released. The comparatively nonthreatening character of detentions of this sort explains the absence of any suggestion in our opinions that *Terry* stops are subject to the dictates of *Miranda.* The similarly noncoercive aspect of ordinary traffic stops prompts us to hold that persons temporarily detained pursuant to such stops are not "in custody" for the purposes of *Miranda.*

Respondent contends that to "exempt" traffic stops from the coverage of *Miranda* will open the way to widespread abuse. Policemen will simply delay formally arresting detained motorists, and will subject them to sustained and intimidating interrogation at the scene of their initial detention. The net result, respondent contends, will be a serious threat to the rights that the *Miranda* doctrine is designed to protect.

We are confident that the state of affairs projected by respondent will not come to pass. It is settled that the safeguards prescribed by *Miranda* become applicable as soon as a suspect's freedom of action is curtailed to a "degree associated with formal arrest." If a motorist who has been detained pursuant to a traffic stop thereafter is subjected to treatment that renders him "in custody" for practical purposes, he will be entitled to the full panoply of protections prescribed by *Miranda.*

Admittedly, our adherence to the doctrine just recounted will mean that the police and lower courts will continue occasionally to have difficulty deciding exactly when a suspect has been taken into custody. Either a rule that *Miranda* applies to all traffic stops or a rule that a suspect need not be advised of his rights until he is formally placed under arrest would provide a clearer, more easily administered line. However, each of these two alternatives has drawbacks that make it unacceptable. The first would substantially impede the enforcement of the Nation's traffic laws—by compelling the police either to take the time to warn all detained motorists of their constitutional rights or to forgo use of self-incriminating statements made by those motorists—while doing little to protect citizens' Fifth Amendment rights. The second would enable the police to circumvent the constraints on custodial interrogations established by *Miranda.*

Turning to the case before us, we find nothing in the record that indicates that respondent should have been given *Miranda* warnings at any point prior to the time Trooper Williams placed him under arrest. For the reasons indicated above, we reject the contention that the initial stop of respondent's car, by itself, rendered him "in custody." And respondent has failed to demonstrate that, at any time between the initial stop and the arrest, he was subjected to restraints comparable to those associated with a formal arrest. Only a short period of time elapsed between the stop and the arrest. At no point during that interval was respondent informed that his detention would not be temporary. Although Trooper Williams apparently decided as soon as respondent stepped out of his car that respondent would be taken into custody and charged with a traffic offense, Williams never communicated his intention to respondent. A policeman's unarticulated plan has no bearing on the question whether a suspect was "in custody" at a particular time; the only relevant inquiry is how a reasonable man in the suspect's position would have understood his situation. Nor do other aspects of the interaction of Williams and respondent support the contention that respondent was exposed to "custodial interrogation" at the scene of the stop. From aught that appears in the stipulation of facts, a single police officer asked respondent a modest number of questions and requested him to perform a simple balancing test at a location visible to passing motorists. Treatment of this sort cannot fairly be characterized as the functional equivalent of formal arrest.

We conclude, in short, that respondent was not taken into custody for the purposes of *Miranda* until Williams arrested him. Consequently, the statements respondent made prior to that point were admissible against him. * * *

[The opinion of JUSTICE STEVENS, concurring in part and concurring in the judgment is omitted].

NOTES AND QUESTIONS

1.   The State argued for a blanket *Miranda* exception for traffic stops on the ground that they are generically different from other kinds of police interference with freedom to depart, and that *Miranda* would interfere with the efficient prosecution of traffic offenders. The Court rather casually rejected that argument. Yet in the part of the opinion holding that traffic stops do not *always* constitute custody, the Court embraced the argument that traffic stops are different from the custody that *Miranda* had in mind. How can the Court have it both ways?

2.   A.   Consider the *Berkemer* fact pattern with the following change: Before the officer administers the sobriety test, Rick says, "My house is right over there. My mother is expecting me home. Can I go tell her what's happening?" The officer says, "No." Custody? What if Rick tries to leave and the officer physically stops him? Would it matter if Rick were sixteen and driving on a learner's permit? What if the officer handcuffs him? See Stone v. City of Huntsville, 656 So.2d 404 (Ala.Crim.App.1994).

B.   A fight breaks out between rivial franternities late at night and several college students are running from the melee when police officers intercept them. With guns drawn, police order them to lie face down on the ground "and do not move." Custody?

C.   Six law enforcement officers (three uniformed officers and three parole officers) knocked on *N*'s door. He opened the door dressed only in his underwear. One of the officers asked him to step into the hallway, which he did. The officer then handcuffed *N*, telling him that he was not under arrest but was being restrained for his owns safety and that of the officers. Police let him into his apartment, where they discovered three other adults present. They asked *N* whether there was a gun in the apartment (a bullet had been shot through the wall of *N*'s apartment into the apartment next door). *Miranda* warnings were never given. Custody? Assuming custody, might the answers be admissible in any event? See United States v. Newton, 369 F.3d 659 (2d. Cir. 2004).

3.   *Is the custody test wholly objective?* Put yourself in Rick McCarty's place after the officer orders him to perform a "simple balancing test," and he falls down. Would you expect the officer to let you climb to your feet, get into your car, and drive away? Suppose that, while prone on the ground, Rick McCarty had said, "I guess I'm in a whole lot of trouble," and the officer did not respond. Custody? What if the officer had answered, "Yes"?

But if the test is wholly objective, perhaps courts cannot take into account that Rick flunked the balancing test; instead, the question is whether a motorist pulled over and asked to take a balancing test would feel that he was subject to restraints comparable to an arrest. The Court's sharply divided opinion in J.D.B. v. North Carolina, 564 U.S. 261, 131 S.Ct. 2394, 180 L.Ed.2d 310 (2011), suggests that the test *is almost* wholly objective. The issue in *J.D.B.* was whether to take into account that the suspect was thirteen years old when determining whether he was in custody. The Court, 5–4, held that "so long as the child's age was known to the officer at the time of police questioning, or would have been objectively apparent to a reasonable officer, its inclusion in the custody analysis is consistent with the objective nature of that test." Reasoning that a child's age is "a fact that 'generates commonsense conclusions about behavior and perception,'" the Court concluded:

> In some circumstances, a child's age "would have affected how a reasonable person" in the suspect's position "would perceive his or her freedom to leave." That is, a reasonable child subjected to police questioning will sometimes feel pressured to submit when a reasonable adult would feel free to go. We think it clear that courts can account for that reality without doing any damage to the objective nature of the custody analysis.

Only five votes could be mustered to take account of the fact that the suspect was thirteen, and the holding is narrowly stated. This suggests that other arguments to consider a particular characteristic of a suspect will fall on deaf ears.

4.   *In prison but not in custody?* Police came to prison to interrogate Shatzer about a crime other than the one for which he was serving time. When he requested counsel, police terminated the interrogation and Shatzer

returned to the general population. Was this a break in *Miranda* custody? Can a prisoner be said not to be in custody when he is incarcerated? Yes, the Court held in Maryland v. Shatzer, 559 U.S 98, 130 S.Ct. 1213, 175 L.Ed.2d 1045 (2010).

The Court acknowledged that being in prison met the *Berkemer* test whether "there is a 'formal arrest or restraint on freedom of movement' of the degree associated with a formal arrest." But the Court said "that the freedom-of-movement test identifies only a necessary and not a sufficient condition for *Miranda* custody." It is not a sufficient condition because "*Miranda* is to be enforced 'only in those types of situations in which the concerns that powered the decision are implicated.'"

> Interrogated suspects who have previously been convicted of crime live in prison. When they are released back into the general prison population, they return to their accustomed surroundings and daily routine-they regain the degree of control they had over their lives prior to the interrogation. Sentenced prisoners, in contrast to the *Miranda* paradigm, are not isolated with their accusers. They live among other inmates, guards, and workers, and often can receive visitors and communicate with people on the outside by mail or telephone.

In sum, "[t]The "'inherently compelling pressures'" of custodial interrogation ended when he returned to his normal life."

5. In the Court's first custody case, a police officer telephoned a parolee named Mathiason to ask where it would be convenient to meet. Mathiason said he had no preference, and the officer asked him to come to the station. When he arrived, the officer told him he was not under arrest and took him into an officer where he told him he was a suspect in a burglary and told him (falsely) that his fingerprints had been found at the scene of the burglary. He confessed and then was allowed to leave the police station. Finding the atmosphere a coercive one, the state court held that the suspect had been in custody. By a 7–2 vote, in a per curiam opinion, the Court held that in the absence of any "restraint on freedom of movement," there could be no custody. See Oregon v. Mathiason, 429 U.S. 492, 97 S.Ct. 711, 50 L.Ed.2d 714 (1977) (per curiam).

Apply *Mathiason* to the following facts. *D* threatens his wife when she moves out, and a week later her daughter and grandchildren are murdered in her new apartment. The police approach *D* at work and tell him that he is not a suspect but they need to ask him some questions in light of his prior threats. He agrees to accompany them to the police station. They inform him that department policy requires them to handcuff him and put him in the back of the car for the ride to the station. Police remove the handcuffs as soon as they reach the station and take him to an interview room. There he is interrogated, makes incriminating statements, and is released, just as Mathiason was. Custody? Dye v. State, 717 N.E.2d 5 (Ind.1999).

6. *Problems.*

A. *R* is a non-commissioned officer in the Air Force. Suspecting *R* of having downloaded child pornography on his computer, civilian authorities ask his commanding officer to order him to meet with them. As a result of this order, *R* meets the police in his home, where he is assured that he is "not about to be arrested" and "that the police were concerned not with the mere presence of child pornography on the computer but its production." Questioned by the police, *R* eventually admitted downloading the material. No *Miranda* warnings were given. Was he in custody? See United States v. Rogers, 659 F.3d 74 (1st Cir. 2011).

B. *D* has "hired" an undercover officer to kill his wife. Six police cars surround *D*'s house where he is having a pool party to provide himself an alibi. Trees prevent anyone at the party from observing the cars. A single officer (with arrest warrant in back pocket) goes to the pool area and tells *D* that someone just shot his wife. Feigning shock and dismay, *D* answers questions the officer asks (without giving *Miranda* warnings). This exchange takes place in front of fourteen of *D*'s closest friends. After the questioning, officer pulls out an arrest warrant and arrests *D*. Are the answers to the questions admissible under *Berkemer*?

C. A prostitute is found murdered and police interview her former high-school boyfriend, *D*, on three separate occasions. He was told each time that he was not under arrest; each time he voluntarily appeared at the police station. The third interview lasted eleven hours, with bathroom breaks and three other brief breaks where *D* was left alone. His car keys were taken from him to perform a consensual search of his car and never returned. Roughly ten hours into the interview, *D* asked if he could leave and return the next day to continue and the police said, "No, you're here now. Why don't we go ahead and get this all wrapped up." An hour later, he confessed. Only after the confession was reduced to writing did the police give him *Miranda* warnings. The trial court held the confession admissible because, like Mathiason, *D* was told he was not under arrest and showed up voluntarily for the interview. Do you agree? Do you believe this outcome is consistent with the rationale of *Miranda*? See Commonwealth v. DiStefano, 782 A.2d 574 (Pa.Super.2001).

E. *MIRANDA* INTERROGATION

RHODE ISLAND V. INNIS

Supreme Court of the United States, 1980.
446 U.S. 291, 100 S.Ct. 1682, 64 L.Ed.2d 297.

MR. JUSTICE STEWART delivered the opinion of the Court joined by JUSTICES WHITE, BLACKMUN, POWELL, and REHNQUIST]. * * *

I

On the night of January 12, 1975, John Mulvaney, a Providence, R.I., taxicab driver, disappeared after being dispatched to pick up a customer. His body was discovered four days later buried in a shallow grave in Coventry, R.I. He had died from a shotgun blast aimed at the back of his head.

On January 17, 1975, shortly after midnight, the Providence police received a telephone call from Gerald Aubin, also a taxicab driver, who reported that he had just been robbed by a man wielding a sawed-off shotgun. Aubin further reported that he had dropped off his assailant near Rhode Island College in a section of Providence known as Mount Pleasant. [Aubin later identified a photo of respondent. Eds.] * * *

At approximately 4:30 a. m. on the same date, Patrolman Lovell, while cruising the streets of Mount Pleasant in a patrol car, spotted the respondent standing in the street facing him. When Patrolman Lovell stopped his car, the respondent walked towards it. Patrolman Lovell then arrested the respondent, who was unarmed, and advised him of his so-called *Miranda* rights. While the two men waited in the patrol car for other police officers to arrive, Patrolman Lovell did not converse with the respondent other than to respond to the latter's request for a cigarette.

Within minutes, Sergeant Sears arrived at the scene of the arrest, and he also gave the respondent the *Miranda* warnings. Immediately thereafter, Captain Leyden and other police officers arrived. Captain Leyden advised the respondent of his *Miranda* rights. The respondent stated that he understood those rights and wanted to speak with a lawyer. Captain Leyden then directed that the respondent be placed in a "caged wagon," a four-door police car with a wire screen mesh between the front and rear seats, and be driven to the central police station. Three officers, Patrolmen Gleckman, Williams, and McKenna, were assigned to accompany the respondent to the central station. They placed the respondent in the vehicle and shut the doors. Captain Leyden then instructed the officers not to question the respondent or intimidate or coerce him in any way. The three officers then entered the vehicle, and it departed.

While en route to the central station, Patrolman Gleckman initiated a conversation with Patrolman McKenna concerning the missing shotgun. As Patrolman Gleckman later testified:

"A. At this point, I was talking back and forth with Patrolman McKenna stating that I frequent this area while on patrol and [that because a school for handicapped children is located nearby,] there's a lot of handicapped children running around in this area, and God forbid one of them might find a weapon with shells and they might hurt themselves."

Patrolman McKenna apparently shared his fellow officer's concern:

"A. I more or less concurred with him [Gleckman] that it was a safety factor and that we should, you know, continue to search for the weapon and try to find it."

While Patrolman Williams said nothing, he overheard the conversation between the two officers:

"A. He [Gleckman] said it would be too bad if the little—I believe he said a girl—would pick up the gun, maybe kill herself."

The respondent then interrupted the conversation, stating that the officers should turn the car around so he could show them where the gun was located. At this point, Patrolman McKenna radioed back to Captain Leyden that they were returning to the scene of the arrest and that the respondent would inform them of the location of the gun. At the time the respondent indicated that the officers should turn back, they had traveled no more than a mile, a trip encompassing only a few minutes.

The police vehicle then returned to the scene of the arrest where a search for the shotgun was in progress. There, Captain Leyden again advised the respondent of his *Miranda* rights. The respondent replied that he understood those rights but that he "wanted to get the gun out of the way because of the kids in the area in the school." The respondent then led the police to a nearby field, where he pointed out the shotgun under some rocks by the side of the road.

On March 20, 1975, a grand jury returned an indictment charging the respondent with the kidnaping, robbery, and murder of John Mulvaney. Before trial, the respondent moved to suppress the shotgun and the statements he had made to the police regarding it. After an evidentiary hearing at which the respondent elected not to testify, the trial judge found that the respondent had been "repeatedly and completely advised of his *Miranda* rights." He further found that it was "entirely understandable that [the officers in the police vehicle] would voice their concern [for the safety of the handicapped children] to each other." The judge then concluded that the respondent's decision to inform the police of the location of the shotgun was "a waiver, clearly, and on the basis of the evidence that I have heard, and [*sic*] intelligent waiver, of his [*Miranda*] right to remain silent." Thus, without passing on whether the police officers had in fact "interrogated" the respondent, the trial court sustained the admissibility of the shotgun and testimony related to its discovery. That evidence was later introduced at the respondent's trial, and the jury returned a verdict of guilty on all counts. * * *

II * * *

In the present case, the parties are in agreement that the respondent was fully informed of his *Miranda* rights and that he invoked his *Miranda* right to counsel when he told Captain Leyden that he wished to consult with a lawyer. It is also uncontested that the respondent was "in custody" while being transported to the police station.

The issue, therefore, is whether the respondent was "interrogated" by the police officers in violation of the respondent's undisputed right under *Miranda* to remain silent until he had consulted with a lawyer.[2] In resolving this issue, we first define the term "interrogation" under *Miranda* before turning to a consideration of the facts of this case.

A

The starting point for defining "interrogation" in this context is, of course, the Court's *Miranda* opinion. There the Court observed that "[b]y custodial interrogation, we mean *questioning* initiated by law enforcement officers after a person has been taken into custody or otherwise deprived of his freedom of action in any significant way." This passage and other references throughout the opinion to "questioning" might suggest that the *Miranda* rules were to apply only to those police interrogation practices that involve express questioning of a defendant while in custody.

We do not, however, construe the *Miranda* opinion so narrowly. The concern of the Court in *Miranda* was that the "interrogation environment" created by the interplay of interrogation and custody would "subjugate the individual to the will of his examiner" and thereby undermine the privilege against compulsory self-incrimination. The police practices that evoked this concern included several that did not involve express questioning. For example, one of the practices discussed in *Miranda* was the use of line-ups in which a coached witness would pick the defendant as the perpetrator. This was designed to establish that the defendant was in fact guilty as a predicate for further interrogation. A variation on this theme discussed in *Miranda* was the so-called "reverse line-up" in which a defendant would be identified by coached witnesses as

---

[2] Since we conclude that the respondent was not "interrogated" for *Miranda* purposes, we do not reach the question whether the respondent waived his right under *Miranda* to be free from interrogation until counsel was present.

the perpetrator of a fictitious crime, with the object of inducing him to confess to the actual crime of which he was suspected in order to escape the false prosecution. The Court in *Miranda* also included in its survey of interrogation practices the use of psychological ploys, such as to "posi[t]" "the guilt of the subject," to "minimize the moral seriousness of the offense," and "to cast blame on the victim or on society." It is clear that these techniques of persuasion, no less than express questioning, were thought, in a custodial setting, to amount to interrogation.[3]

This is not to say, however, that all statements obtained by the police after a person has been taken into custody are to be considered the product of interrogation. * * * [T]he special procedural safeguards outlined in *Miranda* are required not where a suspect is simply taken into custody, but rather where a suspect in custody is subjected to interrogation. "Interrogation," as conceptualized in the *Miranda* opinion, must reflect a measure of compulsion above and beyond that inherent in custody itself.

We conclude that the *Miranda* safeguards come into play whenever a person in custody is subjected to either express questioning or its functional equivalent. That is to say, the term "interrogation" under *Miranda* refers not only to express questioning, but also to any words or actions on the part of the police (other than those normally attendant to arrest and custody) that the police should know are reasonably likely to elicit an incriminating response from the suspect. The latter portion of this definition focuses primarily upon the perceptions of the suspect, rather than the intent of the police. This focus reflects the fact that the *Miranda* safeguards were designed to vest a suspect in custody with an added measure of protection against coercive police practices, without regard to objective proof of the underlying intent of the police. A practice that the police should know is reasonably likely to evoke an incriminating response from a suspect thus amounts to interrogation.[7] But, since the police surely cannot be held accountable for the unforeseeable results of their words or actions, the definition of interrogation can extend only to words or actions on the part of police officers that they *should have known* were reasonably likely to elicit an incriminating response.[8]

---

[3] To limit the ambit of *Miranda* to express questioning would "place a premium on the ingenuity of police to devise methods of indirect interrogation, rather than to implement the plain mandate of *Miranda*."

[7] This is not to say that the intent of the police is irrelevant, for it may well have a bearing on whether the police should have known that their words or actions were reasonably likely to evoke an incriminating response. In particular, where a police practice is designed to elicit an incriminating response from the accused, it is unlikely that the practice will not also be one which the police should have known was reasonably likely to have that effect.

[8] Any knowledge the police may have had concerning the unusual susceptibility of a defendant to a particular form of persuasion might be an important factor in determining whether the police should have known that their words or actions were reasonably likely to elicit an incriminating response from the suspect.

B

Turning to the facts of the present case, we conclude that the respondent was not "interrogated" within the meaning of *Miranda*. It is undisputed that the first prong of the definition of "interrogation" was not satisfied, for the conversation between Patrolmen Gleckman and McKenna included no express questioning of the respondent. Rather, that conversation was, at least in form, nothing more than a dialogue between the two officers to which no response from the respondent was invited.

Moreover, it cannot be fairly concluded that the respondent was subjected to the "functional equivalent" of questioning. It cannot be said, in short, that Patrolmen Gleckman and McKenna should have known that their conversation was reasonably likely to elicit an incriminating response from the respondent. There is nothing in the record to suggest that the officers were aware that the respondent was peculiarly susceptible to an appeal to his conscience concerning the safety of handicapped children. Nor is there anything in the record to suggest that the police knew that the respondent was unusually disoriented or upset at the time of his arrest.[9]

The case thus boils down to whether, in the context of a brief conversation, the officers should have known that the respondent would suddenly be moved to make a self-incriminating response. Given the fact that the entire conversation appears to have consisted of no more than a few off hand remarks, we cannot say that the officers should have known that it was reasonably likely that Innis would so respond. This is not a case where the police carried on a lengthy harangue in the presence of the suspect. Nor does the record support the respondent's contention that, under the circumstances, the officers' comments were particularly "evocative." It is our view, therefore, that the respondent was not subjected by the police to words or actions that the police should have known were reasonably likely to elicit an incriminating response from him.

The Rhode Island Supreme Court erred, in short, in equating "subtle compulsion" with interrogation. That the officers' comments struck a responsive chord is readily apparent. Thus, it may be said, as the Rhode Island Supreme Court did say, that the respondent was subjected to "subtle compulsion." But that is not the end of the inquiry. It must also be established that a suspect's incriminating response was the product of words or actions on the part of the police that they should have known

---

[9] The record in no way suggests that the officers' remarks were designed to elicit a response. It is significant that the trial judge, after hearing the officers' testimony, concluded that it was "entirely understandable that [the officers] would voice their concern [for the safety of the handicapped children] to each other."

were reasonably likely to elicit an incriminating response.[10] This was not established in the present case. * * *

[The opinion of JUSTICE WHITE, concurring, is omitted.]

MR. CHIEF JUSTICE BURGER, concurring in the judgment. * * *

The meaning of *Miranda* has become reasonably clear and law enforcement practices have adjusted to its strictures; I would neither overrule *Miranda*, disparage it, nor extend it at this late date. * * *

MR. JUSTICE MARSHALL, with whom MR. JUSTICE BRENNAN joins, dissenting.

I am substantially in agreement with the Court's definition of "interrogation" within the meaning of *Miranda*. In my view, the *Miranda* safeguards apply whenever police conduct is intended or likely to produce a response from a suspect in custody. As I read the Court's opinion, its definition of "interrogation" for *Miranda* purposes is equivalent, for practical purposes, to my formulation, since it contemplates that "where a police practice is designed to elicit an incriminating response from the accused, it is unlikely that the practice will not also be one which the police should have known was reasonably likely to have that effect." Thus, the Court requires an objective inquiry into the likely effect of police conduct on a typical individual, taking into account any special susceptibility of the suspect to certain kinds of pressure of which the police know or have reason to know.

I am utterly at a loss, however, to understand how this objective standard as applied to the facts before us can rationally lead to the conclusion that there was no interrogation. * * *

One can scarcely imagine a stronger appeal to the conscience of a suspect—*any* suspect—than the assertion that if the weapon is not found an innocent person will be hurt or killed. And not just any innocent person, but an innocent child—a little girl—a helpless, handicapped little girl on her way to school. The notion that such an appeal could not be expected to have any effect unless the suspect were known to have some special interest in handicapped children verges on the ludicrous. As a matter of fact, the appeal to a suspect to confess for the sake of others, to "display some evidence of decency and honor," is a classic interrogation technique. * * *

---

[10] By way of example, if the police had done no more than to drive past the site of the concealed weapon while taking the most direct route to the police station, and if the respondent, upon noticing for the first time the proximity of the school for handicapped children, had blurted out that he would show the officers where the gun was located, it could not seriously be argued that this "subtle compulsion" would have constituted "interrogation" within the meaning of the *Miranda* opinion.

I firmly believe that this case is simply an aberration, and that in future cases the Court will apply the standard adopted today in accordance with its plain meaning.

MR. JUSTICE STEVENS, dissenting. * * *

I * * *

In * * * order to give full protection to a suspect's right to be free from any interrogation at all, the definition of "interrogation" must include any police statement or conduct that has the same purpose or effect as a direct question. Statements that appear to call for a response from the suspect, as well as those that are designed to do so, should be considered interrogation. By prohibiting only those relatively few statements or actions that a police officer should know are likely to elicit an incriminating response, the Court today accords a suspect considerably less protection. Indeed, since I suppose most suspects are unlikely to incriminate themselves even when questioned directly, this new definition will almost certainly exclude every statement that is not punctuated with a question mark from the concept of "interrogation."

The difference between the approach required by a faithful adherence to *Miranda* and the stinted test applied by the Court today can be illustrated by comparing three different ways in which Officer Gleckman could have communicated his fears about the possible dangers posed by the shotgun to handicapped children. He could have:

(1) directly asked Innis:

Will you please tell me where the shotgun is so we can protect handicapped school children from danger?

(2) announced to the other officers in the wagon:

If the man sitting in the back seat with me should decide to tell us where the gun is, we can protect handicapped children from danger.

or (3) stated to the other officers:

It would be too bad if a little handicapped girl would pick up the gun that this man left in the area and maybe kill herself.

In my opinion, all three of these statements should be considered interrogation because all three appear to be designed to elicit a response from anyone who in fact knew where the gun was located.[12] Under the

---

[12] See White, *Rhode Island v. Innis*: The Significance of a Suspect's Assertion of His Right to Counsel, 17 Am.Crim.L.Rev. 53, 68 (1979), where the author proposes the same test and applies it to the facts of this case, stating:

"Under the proposed objective standard, the result is obvious. Since the conversation indicates a strong desire to know the location of the shotgun, any person with

Court's test, on the other hand, the form of the statements would be critical. The third statement would not be interrogation because in the Court's view there was no reason for Officer Gleckman to believe that Innis was susceptible to this type of an implied appeal; therefore, the statement would not be reasonably likely to elicit an incriminating response. Assuming that this is true, then it seems to me that the first two statements, which would be just as unlikely to elicit such a response, should also not be considered interrogation. But, because the first statement is clearly an express question, it *would* be considered interrogation under the Court's test. The second statement, although just as clearly a deliberate appeal to Innis to reveal the location of the gun, would presumably not be interrogation because (a) it was not in form a direct question and (b) it does not fit within the "reasonably likely to elicit an incriminating response" category that applies to indirect interrogation.

As this example illustrates, the Court's test creates an incentive for police to ignore a suspect's invocation of his rights in order to make continued attempts to extract information from him. If a suspect does not appear to be susceptible to a particular type of psychological pressure, the police are apparently free to exert that pressure on him despite his request for counsel, so long as they are careful not to punctuate their statements with question marks. And if, contrary to all reasonable expectations, the suspect makes an incriminating statement, that statement can be used against him at trial. The Court thus turns *Miranda*'s unequivocal rule against any interrogation at all into a trap in which unwary suspects may be caught by police deception. * * *

NOTES AND QUESTIONS

1.   Do you think Chief Justice Burger concurs in the judgment out of respect for *stare decisis* or for some other reason?

2.   Is the test for interrogation objective or subjective? Some of both? Why should the officer's intent make any difference? Indeed, why should the test focus on the *officer* at all?

3.   *The question-mark rule. J* found one of two men in the drunk tank lying in a pool of blood. The other inmate was asleep on his bunk. As *J* was unlocking the door, she yelled to the sleeping inmate: "What happened?" The inmate awoke and said, "I killed the son of a bitch last night; he would not shut up." State v. Bennett, 30 Utah 2d 343, 517 P.2d 1029 (1973). This case implies a common-sense rule that one should not irritate cell-mates, but does it fit the *Innis* doctrinal rule about express questioning? What two arguments can you make to have the answer introduced even if a court were to hold that the jailer interrogated the prisoner?

---

knowledge of the weapon's location would be likely to believe that the officers wanted him to disclose its location. Thus, a reasonable person in Innis's position would believe that the officers were seeking to solicit precisely the type of response that was given."

4.   *The functional equivalent of questioning.* The second half of the *Innis* test is designed to cover situations in which the police create a situation that produces the same kind of pressure on the suspect that a direct question would. Given that the pressure in *Innis* itself was held insufficient to constitute the functional equivalent of questioning, consider the following cases:

A.   *F* was arrested for murdering a woman during a robbery in which furs were stolen. *F* declined to answer questions. Later, the detective placed some of the stolen furs (recovered from the apartment of a co-defendant) in front of the cell, about a foot away from *F. F* immediately grabbed the wire mesh and asked to speak to the district attorney. Told that the D.A. could not do anything for him, he said, "I can't afford to do a lot of time. What can I tell you?" Was this statement obtained through interrogation? See People v. Ferro, 63 N.Y.2d 316, 472 N.E.2d 13, 482 N.Y.S.2d 237 (1984).

B.   Police took *J* into custody for the murder of his baby. They gave him *Miranda* warnings, and he said he understood his rights and would talk to them "but I want my lawyer present when I talk." The police said no lawyer was then available, but one would be appointed for him when he was transferred to the jail. *J* said, "Well, I want to tell you about it." One detective then said to *J*, "God takes care of little babies. The baby is already in heaven." *J* asked the detective: "Are you a religious man?" The detective responded, "Not as religious as I should be." *J* then began telling police how he had hit the baby and thrown it into the back yard. Interrogation? See State v. Jones, 386 So.2d 1363 (La.1980).

C.   *H* was a suspect in the burglary and sexual assault of *V. H* permitted two police officers to take his picture and agreed to accompany them to *V*'s home. En route, *H* told the officers that he knew nothing about the crime. Upon arrival, one officer remained with *H* in the squad car and the other officer entered *V*'s home, where *V* identified *H* from a photograph array. The officer returned to the squad car and said to *H*, "You're a liar." *H* responded, "You're right. I did it." Was *H* subject to interrogation? Was he in custody? See People v. Huffman, 61 N.Y.2d 795, 473 N.Y.S.2d 945, 462 N.E.2d 122 (1984).

D.   Police arrested *Y* for robbery and took him to the station, where he waived his *Miranda* rights. Agent *S* interrogated *Y*, who continually denied his involvement. When *Y*'s accomplice confessed in another room, *S* told *Y*, who then invoked his right to counsel. *S* terminated the interview and got up to leave the room. As he reached the door, however, he turned around and said, "I want you to remember me, and I want you to remember my face, and I want you to remember that I gave you a chance." Did this constitute interrogation? See United States v. Young, 46 M.J. 768 (Army Crim.App.1997).

5.   *S* walks into the sheriff's office and states, "I done it; I done it; arrest me; arrest me." A deputy asks, "What did you do?" He replies, "I killed my wife." "What did you kill her with?" asks the deputy. "With an axe, that's

all I had." Are any of these statements admissible under *Miranda*? People v. Savage, 102 Ill.App.2d 477, 242 N.E.2d 446 (1968). What if the deputy's second response is "calm down; you're no murderer"? Interrogation? Custody?

6.   *A doctrinal exception to Miranda.* Police order *M*, suspected of drunk driving, to perform three field sobriety tests. He performs poorly because, he tells the officer, he had "been drinking." Police arrest *M* and take him to a booking center where it is routine procedure to videotape all conversations with arrestees. The officer asks *M* his name, address, height, weight, eye color, date of birth, and current age. He answers all questions but "stumbl[es] over his address and age." He is then ordered to perform the three sobriety tests that he had performed earlier. No *Miranda* warnings are given. Can the videotape be introduced to show that he (a) slurred his words and (b) performed the sobriety tests badly?

One answer to that question is to announce a "routine booking question exception" to *Miranda*, and four members of the Court embraced that answer in Pennsylvania v. Muniz, 496 U.S. 582, 110 S.Ct. 2638, 110 L.Ed.2d 528 (1990). The theory here is that routine questions do not seek incriminating answers. A majority of the Court would later embrace this theory when the answer sought was a suspect's identity. In Hiibel v. Sixth Judicial District Court of Nevada, Humboldt County, 542 U.S. 177, 124 S.Ct. 2451, 159 L.Ed.2d 292 (2004), the Court held that providing one's name to the police is not incriminating.

> In this case petitioner's refusal to disclose his name was not based on any articulated real and appreciable fear that his name would be used to incriminate him, or that it 'would furnish a link in the chain of evidence needed to prosecute' him. As best we can tell, petitioner refused to identify himself only because he thought his name was none of the officer's business. Even today, petitioner does not explain how the disclosure of his name could have been used against him in a criminal case. While we recognize petitioner's strong belief that he should not have to disclose his identity, the Fifth Amendment does not override the Nevada Legislature's judgment to the contrary absent a reasonable belief that the disclosure would tend to incriminate him.

7.   *A foundational exception to Miranda.* Four members of the *Muniz* Court embraced a very different theory that focused on the *answers* rather than the *questions*. In *Schmerber v. California*, p. 620, the Court held that blood is not testimonial and thus compelling a suspect to provide blood is not making him be a witness against himself. Drawing on *Schmerber* four members of the *Muniz* Court would have held that the answers to booking questions are not testimonial. For another four justices, booking questions are a categorical exception to *Miranda*. Only Justice Marshall would have suppressed the answers to the booking questions.

8.   *Synergy between custody and interrogation.* One goal of the *Miranda* Court was to cut through the formalistic doctrines that made the Fifth

Amendment privilege beyond the reach of many suspects. But the Court's rather rigid application of the custody and interrogation requirements has led to a new type of formalism in the current *Miranda* doctrine. For example, the Court often seems to view "custody" and "interrogation" as separate requirements, deciding the "custody" issue first and then, only if the suspect was in custody, addressing the interrogation issue. For an argument that this *Miranda* formalism should be rejected in favor of a model that views custody and interrogation as "augmenting the other, rather than merely being added to the other," see Daniel Yeager, *Rethinking Custodial Interrogation*, 28 Am. Crim. L. Rev. 1, 50 (1990). In Yeager's model, high "levels" of either interrogation or custody have a synergistic multiplier effect on low "levels" of the other variable to create coercive interrogation sooner than it would under the Court's doctrine.

F. WAIVER AND INVOCATION OF THE *MIRANDA* RIGHTS

The *Miranda* Court was careful to emphasize that suspects could waive the rights that the Court found implicit in the privilege against self-incrimination. Once a court determines that the suspect made statements in response to custodial police interrogation, the next issue is whether police gave the Miranda warnings and whether the suspect waived those rights.

NORTH CAROLINA V. BUTLER

Supreme Court of the United States, 1979.
441 U.S. 369, 99 S.Ct. 1755, 60 L.Ed.2d 286.

MR. JUSTICE STEWART delivered the opinion of the Court [joined by CHIEF JUSTICE BURGER, and JUSTICES WHITE, BLACKMUN, and REHNQUIST]. * * *

[Butler was arrested by an FBI agent and subsequently] convicted in a North Carolina trial court of kidnaping, armed robbery, and felonious assault. * * *

* * * FBI Agent Martinez testified that at the time of the arrest he fully advised the respondent of the rights delineated in the *Miranda* case. * * * [A]fter the agents determined that the respondent had an 11th grade education and was literate, he was given the Bureau's "Advice of Rights" form which he read. When asked if he understood his rights, he replied that he did. The respondent refused to sign the waiver at the bottom of the form. He was told that he need neither speak nor sign the form, but that the agents would like him to talk to them. The respondent replied: "I will talk to you but I am not signing any form." He then made inculpatory statements. Agent Martinez testified that the respondent said nothing when advised of his right to the assistance of a lawyer. At no time did the

respondent request counsel or attempt to terminate the agents' questioning.

At the conclusion of this testimony the respondent moved to suppress the evidence of his incriminating statements on the ground that he had not waived his right to the assistance of counsel at the time the statements were made. The court denied the motion, finding that

> "the statement made by the defendant, William Thomas Butler, to Agent David C. Martinez, was made freely and voluntarily to said agent after having been advised of his rights as required by the *Miranda* ruling, including his right to an attorney being present at the time of the inquiry and that the defendant, Butler, understood his rights; [and] that he effectively waived his rights, including the right to have an attorney present during the questioning by his indication that he was willing to answer questions, having read the rights form together with the Waiver of Rights * * * ."

The respondent's statements were then admitted into evidence, and the jury ultimately found the respondent guilty of each offense charged.

On appeal, the North Carolina Supreme Court reversed the convictions and ordered a new trial. It found that the statements had been admitted in violation of the requirements of the *Miranda* decision, noting that the respondent had refused to waive in writing his right to have counsel present and that there had not been a *specific* oral waiver. As it had in at least two earlier cases, the court read the *Miranda* opinion as

> "provid[ing] in plain language that waiver of the right to counsel during interrogation will not be recognized unless such waiver is 'specifically made' after the *Miranda* warnings have been given."

We conclude that the North Carolina Supreme Court erred in its reading of the *Miranda* opinion. There, this Court said:

> "If the interrogation continues without the presence of an attorney and a statement is taken, a heavy burden rests on the government to demonstrate that the defendant knowingly and intelligently waived his privilege against self-incrimination and his right to retained or appointed counsel."

The Court's opinion went on to say:

> "An express statement that the individual is willing to make a statement and does not want an attorney followed closely by a statement could constitute a waiver. But a valid waiver will not be presumed simply from the silence of the accused after

warnings are given or simply from the fact that a confession was in fact eventually obtained."

Thus, the Court held that an express statement can constitute a waiver, and that silence alone after such warnings cannot do so. But the Court did not hold that such an express statement is indispensable to a finding of waiver.

An express written or oral statement of waiver of the right to remain silent or of the right to counsel is usually strong proof of the validity of that waiver, but is not inevitably either necessary or sufficient to establish waiver. The question is not one of form, but rather whether the defendant in fact knowingly and voluntarily waived the rights delineated in the *Miranda* case. As was unequivocally said in *Miranda*, mere silence is not enough. That does not mean that the defendant's silence, coupled with an understanding of his rights and a course of conduct indicating waiver, may never support a conclusion that a defendant has waived his rights. The courts must presume that a defendant did not waive his rights; the prosecution's burden is great; but in at least some cases waiver can be clearly inferred from the actions and words of the person interrogated. * * *

* * * By creating an inflexible rule that no implicit waiver can ever suffice, the North Carolina Supreme Court has gone beyond the requirements of federal organic law. It follows that its judgment cannot stand, since a state court can neither add to nor subtract from the mandates of the United States Constitution. * * *

MR. JUSTICE POWELL took no part in the consideration or decision of this case.

[The opinion of JUSTICE BLACKMUN, concurring, is omitted.]

MR. JUSTICE BRENNAN, with whom MR. JUSTICE MARSHALL and MR. JUSTICE STEVENS joins, dissenting. * * *

The rule announced by the Court today allows a finding of waiver based upon "infer[ence] from the actions and words of the person interrogated." The Court thus shrouds in half-light the question of waiver, allowing courts to construct inferences from ambiguous words and gestures. But the very premise of *Miranda* requires that ambiguity be interpreted against the interrogator. That premise is the recognition of the "compulsion inherent in custodial" interrogation, and of its purpose "to subjugate the individual to the will of [his] examiner." Under such conditions, only the most explicit waivers of rights can be considered knowingly and freely given. * * *

NOTES AND QUESTIONS

1. *The eighty percent solution.* Studies show that roughly eighty percent of suspects waive their *Miranda* rights. See Paul G. Cassell & Bret S. Hayman, *Police Interrogation in the 1990s: An Empirical Study of the Effects of Miranda*, 43 UCLA L. Rev. 839 (1996); Richard A. Leo, *Inside the Interrogation Room*, 86 J. Crim. L. & Criminology 266, 282–83 (1996). George C. Thomas III, *Stories About Miranda*, 102 Mich. L. Rev. 1959 (2004).

Does this mean *Miranda* is ineffective or only that most suspects want to tell their side of the story? For an argument that the latter character trait explains more of the waiver rate than most scholars believe, see George C. Thomas III, *Miranda's Illusion: Telling Stories in the Police Interrogation Room*, 81 Texas L. Rev. 1091 (2003) (essay on Welsh S. White, *Miranda's* Waning Protections (2001)).

2. *Elements of a valid waiver.* The *Miranda* Court drew the waiver requirements from the law of the waiver of the right to counsel. See Johnson v. Zerbst, 304 U.S. 458, 58 S.Ct. 1019, 82 L.Ed. 1461 (1938). Thus, the waiver must be a voluntary, knowing, and intelligent relinquishment of the *Miranda* rights.

Prior to *Butler*, and notwithstanding the *Miranda* Court's warning that "a heavy burden rest on the government" to prove a valid waiver, the Court held that the standard for *Miranda* waiver was preponderance of the evidence. Lego v. Twomey, 404 U.S. 477, 92 S.Ct. 619, 30 L.Ed.2d 618 (1972). Putting *Butler* and *Lego* together creates "an historical irony. *Miranda* was intended as a bright-line alternative to the much-criticized, totality-of-the-circumstances 'voluntariness' standard that preceded it. Yet, through the vehicle of *Miranda* waiver law, 'voluntariness' jurisprudence has returned." 1 Joshua Dressler & Alan C. Michaels, Understanding Criminal Procedure § 24.10[A][3][b] (5th ed. 2010).

If a suspect understands the warnings, then she presumably has the single most important piece of information that would make her waiver knowing and intelligent. But are suspects entitled to other information? We know that they are not entitled to know what crime the police are questioning them about.

In Colorado v. Spring, 479 U.S. 564, 107 S.Ct. 851, 93 L.Ed.2d 954 (1987), *S* was arrested for interstate possession of stolen firearms. He waived his *Miranda* rights, and the police questioned him not about the stolen firearms but about a murder with which *S* had not been charged. The Court held that a waiver of *Miranda* is to interrogation in general and not to interrogation about a particular crime. Thus—using language that will become important in the next chapter—*Miranda* is *not* "crime-specific."

3. *Waiver is personal.* *B* was arrested for murder. As a result of the efforts of *B*'s sister, a lawyer called the police station and informed a detective that she would act as *B*'s lawyer in the event police intended to question him. The detective told the lawyer that *B* would not be interrogated

that night. Less than an hour later, however, police began a series of interrogations of *B*. Prior to each session, police informed *B* of his *Miranda* rights, and he signed written forms waiving the right to counsel. At no time did the police inform *B* that a lawyer had offered to represent him during interrogation. *B* ultimately signed three written statements fully admitting the murder. In Moran v. Burbine, 475 U.S. 412, 106 S.Ct. 1135, 89 L.Ed.2d 410 (1986), the Court held that these were valid *Miranda* waivers even though he did not know his lawyer was trying to reach him.

Events occurring outside of the presence of the suspect and entirely unknown to him surely can have no bearing on the capacity to comprehend and knowingly relinquish a constitutional right. Under the analysis of the Court of Appeals, the same defendant, armed with the same information and confronted with precisely the same police conduct, would have knowingly waived his *Miranda* rights had a lawyer not telephoned the police station to inquire about his status. Nothing in any of our waiver decisions or in our understanding of the essential components of a valid waiver requires so incongruous a result. No doubt the additional information would have been useful to respondent; perhaps even it might have affected his decision to confess. But we have never read the Constitution to require that the police supply a suspect with a flow of information to help him calibrate his self-interest in deciding whether to speak or stand by his rights. Once it is determined that a suspect's decision not to rely on his rights was uncoerced, that he at all times knew he could stand mute and request a lawyer, and that he was aware of the State's intention to use his statements to secure a conviction, the analysis is complete and the waiver is valid as a matter of law.

4.   *J* is fifteen years old and a suspect in a murder. His mother is with him at the police station. When police give him warnings and ask whether he wishes to answer questions, *J* answers "no." His mother turns to him and says, "No, we need to get this straightened out. We'll talk with him anyway." *J* looks at his mother for a time and then nods his head. The detective asks if he wishes to answer without a lawyer being present and this time he answers "yes." Is this a valid waiver? See State v. Johnson, 136 N.C.App. 683, 525 S.E.2d 830 (2000).

5.   *Voluntariness problems persist*. Voluntariness remains part of confession law not just in the guise of *Miranda* waiver, but also in measuring the effect of interrogation techniques that follow a valid waiver.

A.   *Shackles?* Police arrested *H* for murder and provided *Miranda* warnings. He agreed to talk to the police and denied involvement. He was taken to the police station, "placed in a 10 foot by 10 foot interview room" where "the handcuffs were removed, and he was shackled to the floor." He was "allowed to take bathroom breaks as needed," but otherwise remained shackled to the floor for seven hours. Police interrogated him for about two and one-half hours while he was shackled. Police falsely implied that the victim's blood was on the suspect's coat, that several people saw him at the scene of the murder, and that people were picking his photo out of photo arrays. Indeed, four witnesses had in fact picked a different man's picture out of the photo array but the police did not disclose this fact. Are his statements admissible? See State v. Harris, 279 Kan. 163, 105 P.3d 1258 (2005).

B. *We are brothers.* Detective Boyce questioned suspect Miller about the brutal murder of a seventeen-year-old girl after Miller waived his *Miranda* rights. Audio tapes of the interview showed that Detective Boyce made no threats while questioning Miller. Instead, Boyce assumed a friendly, understanding manner and spoke in a soft tone of voice. Boyce's major theme throughout the interrogation was that whoever had committed such a heinous crime had mental problems and was desperately in need of psychological treatment. The New Jersey court described the facts as follows:

> Deborah's body was found face down in a stream. Her throat had been slashed, severing her windpipe and jugular vein. The girl was nude except for a part of her bathing suit around her waist. Stab and cutting wounds had been inflicted in her pelvic area and vagina. Her right breast had been cut.

State v. Miller, 76 N.J. 392, 388 A.2d 218, 220 (1978).

Boyce: You can see it, Frank, you can feel it, you can feel it but you are not responsible. This is what I'm trying to tell you, but you've got to come forward and tell me. Don't, don't, don't let it eat you up, don't, don't fight it. You've got to rectify it, Frank. We've got to get together on this thing, or I, I mean really, you need help, you need proper help, and you know it, my God, you know, in God's name, you, you, you know it. You are not a criminal, you are not a criminal. * * * Frank, listen to me, honest to God, I'm, I'm telling you, Frank (inaudible). I know, it's going to bother you, Frank, it's going to bother you. It's there, it's not going to go away, it's there. It's right in front of you, Frank. Am I right or wrong?

Miller: Yeah. * * *

Boyce: First thing we have to do is let it all come out. Don't fight it because it's worse, Frank, it's worse. It's hurting me because I feel it. I feel it wanting to come out, but it's hurting me, Frank. * * * Let it come out, Frank. I'm here, I'm here with you now. I'm on your side, I'm on your side, Frank. I'm your brother, you and I are brothers, Frank. We are brothers, and I want to help my brother. * * * We have, we have a relationship, don't we? Have I been sincere with you, Frank? * * * No, listen to me, Frank, please listen to me. The issue now is what happened. The issue now is truth. Truth is the issue now. You've got to believe this, and the truth prevails in the end, Frank. You have to believe that and I'm sincere when I'm saying it to you.

You've got to be truthful with yourself. * * * That's the most important thing, not, not what has happened, Frank. The fact that you were truthful, you came forward and you said, look I have a problem. I didn't mean to do what I did. I have a problem, this is what's important, Frank. This is very important, I got, I, I got to get closer to you, Frank, I got to make you believe this and I'm, and I'm sincere when I tell you this. You got to tell me exactly what happened, Frank. That's very important. I know how you feel inside, Frank, it's eating you up, am I right? It's eating you up, Frank. You've got to come forward. You've got to do it for yourself, for your family, for your father, this is what's important, the truth, Frank.

The interview lasted less than an hour. After Miller confessed, he collapsed in a state of shock. He slid off his chair and onto the floor with a blank stare on his face. The police officers sent for a first-aid squad that took him to the hospital. Is the confession voluntary? Does *Miranda* help in any way with this kind of issue? See Miller v. Fenton, 796 F.2d 598 (3d Cir. 1986).

6.   *How often do police use coercion in post-waiver interrogations?* Professor Richard Leo's field work has found very few examples of coercive police techniques following waiver. As he observed 182 interrogations, Leo looked for any coercive tactic from a list of ten tactics—a list comprehensive enough to "generally resolve any doubts in favor of the suspect, not the police." Despite his broad definition of coercion, Leo found evidence of coercive tactics in only four (or 2%) of the cases. Richard A. Leo, *Inside the Interrogation Room*, 86 J. Crim. L. & Criminology 266, 282–83 (1996).

7.   Complicating waiver matters further is the issue of how to analyze invocations of the twin *Miranda* rights—the right to remain silent and the right to counsel. In a way, the invocation issue is the other side of the coin of the waiver issue. By definition, a suspect who is invoking her rights cannot be waiving her rights. But invocation means more than lack of waiver, of course. Invocation requires conduct on the part of the suspect. Invocation also prevents conduct on the part of the police. As we will make plain later in the chapter, a suspect invoking the right to counsel has different consequences for police than invoking the right to remain silent. For present purposes, however, it is necessary only to understand the outlines of the rule about invoking the right to counsel.

In Edwards v. Arizona (p. 733), the Court held that a custodial suspect's invocation of the right to counsel requires police to cease interrogation. Davis v. United States, 512 U.S. 452, 114 S.Ct. 2350, 129 L.Ed.2d 362 (1994), presented the question of what constitutes an invocation. Davis initially waived his rights to remain silent and to a lawyer, both orally and in writing.

About an hour and a half into the interview, petitioner said, "Maybe I should talk to a lawyer." According to the uncontradicted testimony of one of the interviewing agents, the interview then proceeded as follows:

> "[We m]ade it very clear that we're not here to violate his rights, that if he wants a lawyer, then we will stop any kind of questioning with him, that we weren't going to pursue the matter unless we have it clarified is he asking for a lawyer or is he just making a comment about a lawyer, and he said, [']No, I'm not asking for a lawyer,' and then he continued on, and said, 'No, I don't want a lawyer.'"

After a short break, the agents reminded petitioner of his rights to remain silent and to counsel. The interview then continued for another hour, until petitioner said, "I think I want a lawyer before I say anything else." At that point, questioning ceased.

The Court characterized Davis's argument that his statements be suppressed as an "invitation to extend *Edwards* and require law enforcement officers to cease questioning immediately upon the making of an ambiguous or equivocal reference to an attorney." It declined to accept the argument, holding instead that

> the suspect must unambiguously request counsel. As we have observed, "a statement either is such an assertion of the right to counsel or it is not." Although a suspect need not "speak with the discrimination of an Oxford don," he must articulate his desire to have counsel present sufficiently clearly that a reasonable police officer in the circumstances would understand the statement to be a request for an attorney. If the statement fails to meet the requisite level of clarity, *Edwards* does not require that the officers stop questioning the suspect.

Four members of the *Davis* Court concurred in the judgment in an opinion by Justice Souter, agreeing that on the facts of the case no violation of *Edwards* occurred, but challenging the majority's assertion that *Edwards* did not require clarifying questions when officers are faced with an ambiguous request for counsel.

> Indeed, it is easy, amidst the discussion of layers of protection, to lose sight of a real risk in the majority's approach, going close to the core of what the Court has held that the Fifth Amendment requires. * * * When a suspect understands his (expressed) wishes to have been ignored (and by hypothesis, he has said something that an objective listener could "reasonably," although not necessarily, take to be a request), in contravention of the "rights" just read to him by his interrogator, he may well see further objection as futile and confession (true or not) as the only way to end his interrogation. * * *

> The other justifications offered for the "requisite level of clarity" rule, are that, whatever its costs, it will further society's

strong interest in "effective law enforcement," and maintain the "ease of application" that has long been a concern of our *Miranda* jurisprudence. With respect to the first point, the margin of difference between the clarification approach advocated here and the one the Court adopts is defined by the class of cases in which a suspect, if asked, would make it plain that he meant to request counsel (at which point questioning would cease). While these lost confessions do exact a real price from society, it is one that *Miranda* itself determined should be borne.

8.   *The "woman" question.* Professor Janet Ainsworth wrote on the *Davis* (Note 7) issue prior to the Court's opinion, based on what the lower courts had done. In developing her critique of the soon-to-be *Davis* approach, she first noted that "incorporation of unconscious androcentric assumptions into legal doctrine" is a "general phenomenon within the law."

> * * * [S]ociolinguistic research on typical male and female speech patterns indicates that men tend to use direct and assertive language, whereas women more often adopt indirect and deferential speech patterns. Because majority legal doctrine governing a person's rights during police interrogation favors linguistic behavior more typical of men than of women, asking the "woman question" reveals a hidden bias in this ostensibly gender-neutral doctrine.

> The sociolinguistic evidence that women disproportionately adopt indirect speech patterns predicts that legal rules requiring the use of direct and unqualified language will adversely affect female defendants more often than male defendants. * * *

> The detrimental consequences of interrogation law, however, are not limited to female defendants. Asking the "woman question" provokes related inquiry into whether legal doctrine may similarly fail to incorporate the experiences and perspectives of other marginalized groups. * * * [T]he available evidence demonstrates that there are a number of ethnic speech communities whose members habitually adopt a speech register including indirect and qualified modes of expression very much like those observed in typical female language use.

> Even within communities whose speech is not characterized by indirect modes of expression, individual speakers who are socially or situationally powerless frequently adopt an indirect speech register. In fact, several prominent researchers have concluded that the use of this characteristically "female" speech style correlates better with powerlessness than with gender. The psychosocial dynamics of the police interrogation setting inherently involve an imbalance of power between the suspect, who is situationally powerless, and the interrogator, whose role entails the exercise of power. Such asymmetries of power in the interrogation session increase the likelihood that a particular suspect will adopt an indirect, and thus

seemingly equivocal, mode of expression. This study, which begins by focusing on the disadvantages to women defendants of current invocation doctrine, ultimately has far-reaching implications for various other classes of speakers that do not share the linguistic norm of assertive and direct expression.

Janet E. Ainsworth, *The Pragmatics of Powerlessness in Police Interrogation*, 103 Yale L.J. 259, 262–264 (1993).

Which position on the *Davis* issue do you find persuasive?

9.   So you have seen *Butler* on waiver and *Davis* on the requirement that any invocation of the *Miranda* right to counsel be unambiguous. Now see how the Court puts these together in 2010. Recall that the Miranda Court seemed to set a high bar for waiver:

> If the interrogation continues without the presence of an attorney and a statement is taken, a heavy burden rests on the government to demonstrate that the defendant knowingly and intelligently waived his privilege against self-incrimination and his right to retained or appointed counsel. This Court has always set high standards of proof for the waiver of constitutional rights, and we re-assert these standards as applied to in-custody interrogation.

By the time we get to 2010, however, those statements (dicta, really) did not carry much weight with five members of the Court.

BERGHUIS V. THOMPKINS

Supreme Court of the United States, 2010.
560 U.S. 370, 130 S.Ct. 2250, 176 L.Ed.2d 1098.

JUSTICE KENNEDY delivered the opinion of the Court [joined by CHIEF JUSTICE ROBERTS, and JUSTICES SCALIA, THOMAS, and ALITO]. * * *

I

A

On January 10, 2000, a shooting occurred outside a mall in Southfield, Michigan. Among the victims was Samuel Morris, who died from multiple gunshot wounds. The other victim, Frederick France, recovered from his injuries and later testified. Thompkins, who was a suspect, fled. About one year later he was found in Ohio and arrested there.

Two Southfield police officers traveled to Ohio to interrogate Thompkins, then awaiting transfer to Michigan. The interrogation began around 1:30 p.m. and lasted about three hours. The interrogation was conducted in a room that was 8 by 10 feet, and Thompkins sat in a chair that resembled a school desk (it had an arm on it that swings around to provide a surface to write on). At the beginning of the interrogation, one of the officers, Detective Helgert, presented Thompkins with a form derived from the *Miranda* rule. It stated:

"NOTIFICATION OF CONSTITUTIONAL RIGHTS AND STATEMENT

"1. You have the right to remain silent.

"2. Anything you say can and will be used against you in a court of law.

"3. You have a right to talk to a lawyer before answering any questions and you have the right to have a lawyer present with you while you are answering any questions.

"4. If you cannot afford to hire a lawyer, one will be appointed to represent you before any questioning, if you wish one.

"5. You have the right to decide at any time before or during questioning to use your right to remain silent and your right to talk with a lawyer while you are being questioned."

Helgert asked Thompkins to read the fifth warning out loud. Thompkins complied. Helgert later said this was to ensure that Thompkins could read, and Helgert concluded that Thompkins understood English. Helgert then read the other four *Miranda* warnings out loud and asked Thompkins to sign the form to demonstrate that he understood his rights. Thompkins declined to sign the form. The record contains conflicting evidence about whether Thompkins then verbally confirmed that he understood the rights listed on the form.

Officers began an interrogation. At no point during the interrogation did Thompkins say that he wanted to remain silent, that he did not want to talk with the police, or that he wanted an attorney. Thompkins was "[l]argely" silent during the interrogation, which lasted about three hours. He did give a few limited verbal responses, however, such as "yeah," "no," or "I don't know." And on occasion he communicated by nodding his head. Thompkins also said that he "didn't want a peppermint" that was offered to him by the police and that the chair he was "sitting in was hard."

About 2 hours and 45 minutes into the interrogation, Helgert asked Thompkins, "Do you believe in God?" Thompkins made eye contact with Helgert and said "Yes," as his eyes "well[ed] up with tears." Helgert asked, "Do you pray to God?" Thompkins said "Yes." Helgert asked, "Do you pray to God to forgive you for shooting that boy down?" Thompkins answered "Yes" and looked away. Thompkins refused to make a written confession, and the interrogation ended about 15 minutes later.

Thompkins was charged with first-degree murder, assault with intent to commit murder, and certain firearms-related offenses. He moved to suppress the statements made during the interrogation. He argued that he had invoked his Fifth Amendment right to remain silent, requiring police to end the interrogation at once, that he had not waived his right to remain silent, and that his inculpatory statements were involuntary. The trial court denied the motion. * * *

* * * The [Sixth Circuit] Court of Appeals ruled that the state court, in rejecting Thompkins's *Miranda* claim, unreasonably applied clearly established federal law and based its decision on an unreasonable determination of the facts. The Court of Appeals acknowledged that a waiver of the right to remain silent need not be express, as it can be " 'inferred from the actions and words of the person interrogated.' " The panel held, nevertheless, that the state court was unreasonable in finding an implied waiver in the circumstances here. The Court of Appeals found that the state court unreasonably determined the facts because "the evidence demonstrates that Thompkins was silent for two hours and forty-five minutes." According to the Court of Appeals, Thompkins's "persistent silence for nearly three hours in response to questioning and repeated invitations to tell his side of the story offered a clear and unequivocal message to the officers: Thompkins did not wish to waive his rights." * * *

III * * *

Thompkins makes various arguments that his answers to questions from the detectives were inadmissible. He first contends that he "invoke[d] his privilege" to remain silent by not saying anything for a sufficient period of time, so the interrogation should have "cease[d]" before he made his inculpatory statements.

This argument is unpersuasive. In the context of invoking the *Miranda* right to counsel, the Court in *Davis v. United States*, [p. 717, Note 7], held that a suspect must do so "unambiguously." If an accused makes a statement concerning the right to counsel "that is ambiguous or equivocal" or makes no statement, the police are not required to end the interrogation or ask questions to clarify whether the accused wants to invoke his or her *Miranda* rights.

The Court has not yet stated whether an invocation of the right to remain silent can be ambiguous or equivocal, but there is no principled reason to adopt different standards for determining when an accused has invoked the *Miranda* right to remain silent and the *Miranda* right to counsel at issue in *Davis*. Both protect the privilege against compulsory self-incrimination by requiring an interrogation to cease when either right is invoked.

There is good reason to require an accused who wants to invoke his or her right to remain silent to do so unambiguously. A requirement of an unambiguous invocation of *Miranda* rights results in an objective inquiry that "avoid[s] difficulties of proof and * * * provide[s] guidance to officers" on how to proceed in the face of ambiguity. If an ambiguous act, omission, or statement could require police to end the interrogation, police would be required to make difficult decisions about an accused's unclear intent and face the consequence of suppression "if they guess wrong." Suppression of a voluntary confession in these circumstances would place a significant burden on society's interest in prosecuting criminal activity. Treating an ambiguous or equivocal act, omission, or statement as an invocation of *Miranda* rights "might add marginally to *Miranda*'s goal of dispelling the compulsion inherent in custodial interrogation." But "as *Miranda* holds, full comprehension of the rights to remain silent and request an attorney are sufficient to dispel whatever coercion is inherent in the interrogation process."

Thompkins did not say that he wanted to remain silent or that he did not want to talk with the police. Had he made either of these simple, unambiguous statements, he would have invoked his " 'right to cut off questioning.' " Here he did neither, so he did not invoke his right to remain silent.

B

We next consider whether Thompkins waived his right to remain silent. Even absent the accused's invocation of the right to remain silent, the accused's statement during a custodial interrogation is inadmissible at trial unless the prosecution can establish that the accused "in fact knowingly and voluntarily waived [*Miranda*] rights" when making the statement. The waiver inquiry "has two distinct dimensions": waiver must be "voluntary in the sense that it was the product of a free and deliberate choice rather than intimidation, coercion, or deception," and "made with a full awareness of both the nature of the right being abandoned and the consequences of the decision to abandon it."

Some language in *Miranda* could be read to indicate that waivers are difficult to establish absent an explicit written waiver or a formal, express oral statement. *Miranda* said "a valid waiver will not be presumed simply from the silence of the accused after warnings are given or simply from the fact that a confession was in fact eventually obtained." In addition, the *Miranda* Court stated that "a heavy burden rests on the government to demonstrate that the defendant knowingly and intelligently waived his privilege against self-incrimination and his right to retained or appointed counsel."

The course of decisions since *Miranda,* informed by the application of *Miranda* warnings in the whole course of law enforcement, demonstrates that waivers can be established even absent formal or express statements of waiver that would be expected in, say, a judicial hearing to determine if a guilty plea has been properly entered. The main purpose of *Miranda* is to ensure that an accused is advised of and understands the right to remain silent and the right to counsel. Thus, "[i]f anything, our subsequent cases have reduced the impact of the *Miranda* rule on legitimate law enforcement while reaffirming the decision's core ruling that unwarned statements may not be used as evidence in the prosecution's case in chief."

One of the first cases to decide the meaning and import of *Miranda* with respect to the question of waiver was *North Carolina v. Butler*, [p. 711]. The *Butler* Court, after discussing some of the problems created by the language in *Miranda,* established certain important propositions. *Butler* interpreted the *Miranda* language concerning the "heavy burden" to show waiver in accord with usual principles of determining waiver, which can include waiver implied from all the circumstances. And in a later case, the Court stated that this "heavy burden" is not more than the burden to establish waiver by a preponderance of the evidence.

The prosecution therefore does not need to show that a waiver of *Miranda* rights was express. An "implicit waiver" of the "right to remain silent" is sufficient to admit a suspect's statement into evidence. *Butler* made clear that a waiver of *Miranda* rights may be implied through "the defendant's silence, coupled with an understanding of his rights and a course of conduct indicating waiver." The Court in *Butler* therefore "retreated" from the "language and tenor of the *Miranda* opinion," which "suggested that the Court would require that a waiver * * * be 'specifically made.'"

If the State establishes that a *Miranda* warning was given and the accused made an uncoerced statement, this showing, standing alone, is insufficient to demonstrate "a valid waiver" of *Miranda* rights. The prosecution must make the additional showing that the accused understood these rights. Where the prosecution shows that a *Miranda* warning was given and that it was understood by the accused, an accused's uncoerced statement establishes an implied waiver of the right to remain silent.

Although *Miranda* imposes on the police a rule that is both formalistic and practical when it prevents them from interrogating suspects without first providing them with a *Miranda* warning, it does not impose a formalistic waiver procedure that a suspect must follow to relinquish those rights. As a general proposition, the law can presume that an individual who, with a full understanding of his or her rights, acts in a manner inconsistent with their exercise has made a deliberate choice to relinquish the protection those rights afford. * * *

The record in this case shows that Thompkins waived his right to remain silent. There is no basis in this case to conclude that he did not understand his rights; and on these facts it follows that he chose not to invoke or rely on those rights when he did speak. First, there is no contention that Thompkins did not understand his rights; and from this it follows that he knew what he gave up when he spoke. There was more than enough evidence in the record to conclude that Thompkins understood his *Miranda* rights. Thompkins received a written copy of the *Miranda* warnings; Detective Helgert determined that Thompkins could read and understand English; and Thompkins was given time to read the warnings. Thompkins, furthermore, read aloud the fifth warning, which stated that "you have the right to decide at any time before or during questioning to use your right to remain silent and your right to talk with a lawyer while you are being questioned." He was thus aware that his right to remain silent would not dissipate after a certain amount of time and that police would have to honor his right to be silent and his right to counsel during the whole course of interrogation. Those rights, the warning made clear, could be asserted at any time. Helgert, moreover, read the warnings aloud.

Second, Thompkins's answer to Detective Helgert's question about whether Thompkins prayed to God for forgiveness for shooting the victim is a "course of conduct indicating waiver" of the right to remain silent. If Thompkins wanted to remain silent, he could have said nothing in response to Helgert's questions, or he could have unambiguously invoked his *Miranda* rights and ended the interrogation. The fact that Thompkins made a statement about three hours after receiving a *Miranda* warning does not overcome the fact that he engaged in a course of conduct indicating waiver. Police are not required to rewarn suspects from time to time. Thompkins's answer to Helgert's question about praying to God for forgiveness for shooting the victim was sufficient to show a course of conduct indicating waiver. This is confirmed by the fact that before then Thompkins had given sporadic answers to questions throughout the interrogation.

Third, there is no evidence that Thompkins's statement was coerced. Thompkins does not claim that police threatened or injured him during the interrogation or that he was in any way fearful. * * * It is true that apparently he was in a straight-backed chair for three hours, but there is no authority for the proposition that an interrogation of this length is inherently coercive. Indeed, even where interrogations of greater duration were held to be improper, they were accompanied, as this one was not, by other facts indicating coercion, such as an incapacitated and sedated suspect, sleep and food deprivation, and threats. The fact that Helgert's question referred to Thompkins's religious beliefs also did not render Thompkins's statement involuntary. "[T]he Fifth Amendment privilege is not concerned 'with moral and psychological pressures to confess emanating from sources other than official coercion.'" In these circumstances, Thompkins knowingly and voluntarily made a statement to police, so he waived his right to remain silent.

C

Thompkins next argues that, even if his answer to Detective Helgert could constitute a waiver of his right to remain silent, the police were not allowed to question him until they obtained a waiver first. *Butler* forecloses this argument. The *Butler* Court held that courts can infer a waiver of *Miranda* rights "from the actions and words of the person interrogated." This principle would be inconsistent with a rule that requires a waiver at the outset. * * * This holding also makes sense given that "the primary protection afforded suspects subject[ed] to custodial interrogation is the *Miranda* warnings themselves." The *Miranda* rule and its requirements are met if a suspect receives adequate *Miranda* warnings, understands them, and has an opportunity to invoke the rights before giving any answers or admissions. Any waiver, express or implied, may be contradicted by an invocation at any time. If the right to counsel or the right to remain silent is invoked at any point during questioning, further interrogation must cease.

Interrogation provides the suspect with additional information that can put his or her decision to waive, or not to invoke, into perspective. As questioning commences and then continues, the suspect has the opportunity to consider the choices he or she faces and to make a more informed decision, either to insist on silence or to cooperate. When the suspect knows that *Miranda* rights can be invoked at any time, he or she has the opportunity to reassess his or her immediate and long-term interests. Cooperation with the police may result in more favorable treatment for the suspect; the apprehension of accomplices; the prevention of continuing injury and fear; beginning steps towards relief or solace for the victims; and the beginning of the suspect's own return to the law and the social order it seeks to protect.

In order for an accused's statement to be admissible at trial, police must have given the accused a *Miranda* warning. If that condition is established, the court can proceed to consider whether there has been an express or implied waiver of *Miranda* rights. In making its ruling on the admissibility of a statement made during custodial questioning, the trial court, of course, considers whether there is evidence to support the conclusion that, from the whole course of questioning, an express or implied waiver has been established. Thus, after giving a *Miranda* warning, police may interrogate a suspect who has neither invoked nor waived his or her *Miranda* rights. On these premises, it follows the police were not required to obtain a waiver of Thompkins's *Miranda* rights before commencing the interrogation.

D

In sum, a suspect who has received and understood the *Miranda* warnings, and has not invoked his *Miranda* rights, waives the right to remain silent by making an uncoerced statement to the police. Thompkins did not invoke his right to remain silent and stop the questioning. Understanding his rights in full, he waived his right to remain silent by making a voluntary statement to the police. The police, moreover, were not required to obtain a waiver of Thompkins's right to remain silent before interrogating him. The state court's decision rejecting Thompkins's *Miranda* claim was thus correct under *de novo* review and therefore necessarily reasonable under the more deferential AEDPA standard of review. [This is the federal habeas corpus standard of review; see casebook, p. 1586, Note 2.—Eds.]. * * *

JUSTICE SOTOMAYOR, with whom JUSTICE STEVENS, JUSTICE GINSBURG, and JUSTICE BREYER join, dissenting.

The Court concludes today that a criminal suspect waives his right to remain silent if, after sitting tacit and uncommunicative through nearly three hours of police interrogation, he utters a few one-word responses. The Court also concludes that a suspect who wishes to guard his right to remain silent against such a finding of "waiver" must, counterintuitively, speak—and must do so with sufficient precision to satisfy a clear-statement rule that construes ambiguity in favor of the police. Both propositions mark a substantial retreat from the protection against compelled self-incrimination that *Miranda v. Arizona* has long provided during custodial interrogation. * * *

The strength of Thompkins' *Miranda* claims depends in large part on the circumstances of the 3-hour interrogation, at the end of which he made inculpatory statements later introduced at trial. The Court's opinion downplays record evidence that Thompkins remained almost completely silent and unresponsive throughout that session. * * * Thompkins expressly declined to sign a written acknowledgment that he had been advised of and understood his rights. * * *

Even when warnings have been administered and a suspect has not affirmatively invoked his rights, statements made in custodial interrogation may not be admitted as part of the prosecution's case in chief "unless and until" the prosecution demonstrates that an individual "knowingly and intelligently waive[d] [his] rights." [*Miranda* said that a] "heavy burden rests on the government to demonstrate that the defendant knowingly and intelligently waived his privilege against self-incrimination and his right to retained or appointed counsel." The government must satisfy the "high standar[d] of proof for the waiver of constitutional rights [set forth in] Johnson v. Zerbst, 304 U.S. 458, 58 S.Ct. 1019, 82 L.Ed. 1461 (1938)."

The question whether a suspect has validly waived his right is "entirely distinct" as a matter of law from whether he invoked that right. The questions are related, however, in terms of the practical effect on the exercise of a suspect's rights. A suspect may at any time revoke his prior waiver of rights—or, closer to the facts of this case, guard against the possibility of a future finding that he implicitly waived his rights—by invoking the rights and thereby requiring the police to cease questioning.

II

A

Like the Sixth Circuit, I begin with the question whether Thompkins waived his right to remain silent. Even if Thompkins did not invoke that right, he is entitled to relief because Michigan did not satisfy its burden of establishing waiver. * * *

Even in concluding that *Miranda* does not invariably require an express waiver of the right to silence or the right to counsel, this Court in *Butler* made clear that the prosecution bears a substantial burden in establishing an implied waiver. * * *

Although this Court reversed the state-court judgment [in *Butler*] concluding that the statements were inadmissible, we quoted at length portions of the *Miranda* opinion * * *. We cautioned that even an "express written or oral statement of waiver of the right to remain silent or of the right to counsel" is not "inevitably * * * sufficient to establish waiver," emphasizing that "[t]he question is * * * whether the defendant in fact knowingly and voluntarily waived the rights delineated in the *Miranda* case." *Miranda,* we observed, "unequivocally said * * * mere silence is not enough." While we stopped short in *Butler* of announcing a *per se* rule that "the defendant's silence, coupled with an understanding of his rights and a course of conduct indicating waiver, may never support a conclusion that a defendant has waived his rights," we reiterated that "courts must presume that a defendant did not waive his rights; the prosecution's burden is great."

Rarely do this Court's precedents provide clearly established law so closely on point with the facts of a particular case. Together, *Miranda* and *Butler* establish that a court "must presume that a defendant did not waive his right[s]"; the prosecution bears a "heavy burden" in attempting to demonstrate waiver; the fact of a "lengthy interrogation" prior to obtaining statements is "strong evidence" against a finding of valid waiver; "mere silence" in response to questioning is "not enough"; and waiver may not be presumed "simply from the fact that a confession was in fact eventually obtained."

It is undisputed here that Thompkins never expressly waived his right to remain silent. His refusal to sign even an acknowledgment that he understood his *Miranda* rights evinces, if anything, an intent not to waive those rights. That Thompkins did not make the inculpatory statements at issue until after approximately 2 hours and 45 minutes of interrogation serves as "strong evidence" against waiver. *Miranda* and *Butler* expressly preclude the possibility that the inculpatory statements themselves are sufficient to establish waiver.

In these circumstances, Thompkins' "actions and words" preceding the inculpatory statements simply do not evidence a "course of conduct indicating waiver" sufficient to carry the prosecution's burden. Although the Michigan court stated that Thompkins "sporadically" participated in the interview, that court's opinion and the record before us are silent as to the subject matter or context of even a single question to which Thompkins purportedly responded, other than the exchange about God and the statements respecting the peppermint and the chair. Unlike in *Butler,* Thompkins made no initial declaration akin to "I will talk to you." Indeed, Michigan and the United States concede that no waiver occurred in this case until Thompkins responded "yes" to the questions about God. I believe it is objectively unreasonable under our clearly established precedents to conclude the prosecution met its "heavy burden" of proof on a record consisting of three one-word answers, following 2 hours and 45 minutes of silence punctuated by a few largely nonverbal responses to unidentified questions. * * *

B * * *

The Court concludes that when *Miranda* warnings have been given and understood, "an accused's uncoerced statement establishes an implied waiver of the right to remain silent." More broadly still, the Court states that, "[a]s a general proposition, the law can presume that an individual who, with a full understanding of his or her rights, acts in a manner inconsistent with their exercise has made a deliberate choice to relinquish the protection those rights afford."

These principles flatly contradict our longstanding views that "a valid waiver will not be presumed * * * simply from the fact that a confession was in fact eventually obtained," and that "[t]he courts must presume that a defendant did not waive his rights," * * * At best, the Court today creates an unworkable and conflicting set of presumptions that will undermine *Miranda*'s goal of providing "concrete constitutional guidelines for law enforcement agencies and courts to follow." At worst, it overrules *sub silentio* an essential aspect of the protections *Miranda* has long provided for the constitutional guarantee against self-incrimination. * * *

Today's dilution of the prosecution's burden of proof to the bare fact that a suspect made inculpatory statements after *Miranda* warnings were given and understood takes an unprecedented step away from the "high standards of proof for the waiver of constitutional rights" this Court has long demanded. When waiver is to be inferred during a custodial interrogation, there are sound reasons to require evidence beyond inculpatory statements themselves. *Miranda* and our subsequent cases are premised on the idea that custodial interrogation is inherently coercive. Requiring proof of a course of conduct beyond the inculpatory statements themselves is critical to ensuring that those statements are voluntary admissions and not the dubious product of an overborne will.

Today's decision thus ignores the important interests *Miranda* safeguards. The underlying constitutional guarantee against self-incrimination reflects "many of our fundamental values and most noble aspirations," our society's "preference for an accusatorial rather than an inquisitorial system of criminal justice"; a "fear that self-incriminating statements will be elicited by inhumane treatment and abuses" and a resulting "distrust of self-deprecatory statements"; and a realization that while the privilege is "sometimes a shelter to the guilty, [it] is often a protection to the innocent." For these reasons, we have observed, a criminal law system "which comes to depend on the 'confession' will, in the long run, be less reliable and more subject to abuses than a system relying on independent investigation." "By bracing against 'the possibility of unreliable statements in every instance of in-custody interrogation,'" *Miranda*'s prophylactic rules serve to "'protect the fairness of the trial itself.'" Today's decision bodes poorly for the fundamental principles that *Miranda* protects.

III

Thompkins separately argues that his conduct during the interrogation invoked his right to remain silent, requiring police to terminate questioning. Like the Sixth Circuit, I would not reach this question because Thompkins is in any case entitled to relief as to waiver. But * * * I cannot agree with the Court's much broader ruling that a suspect must clearly invoke his right to silence by speaking. Taken together with the Court's reformulation of the prosecution's burden of proof as to waiver, today's novel clear-statement rule for invocation invites police to question a suspect at length—notwithstanding his persistent refusal to answer questions—in the hope of eventually obtaining a single inculpatory response which will suffice to prove waiver of rights. Such a result bears little semblance to the "fully effective" prophylaxis that *Miranda* requires.

A * * *

Thompkins contends that in refusing to respond to questions he effectively invoked his right to remain silent, such that police were required to terminate the interrogation prior to his inculpatory statements. * * * Notwithstanding *Miranda*'s statement that "there can be no questioning" if a suspect "indicates in any manner * * * that he wishes to consult with an attorney," the Court in *Davis v. United States*, [casebook, p. 681, Note 4], established a clear-statement rule for invoking the right to counsel. * * *

B

The Court [today extends] *Davis* to hold that police may continue questioning a suspect until he unambiguously invokes his right to remain silent. Because Thompkins neither said "he wanted to remain silent" nor said "he did not want to talk with the police," the Court concludes, he did not clearly invoke his right to silence.

I disagree with this novel application of *Davis*. Neither the rationale nor holding of that case compels today's result. *Davis* involved the right to counsel, not the right to silence. * * * The different effects of invoking the rights are consistent with distinct standards for invocation. * * *

In addition, the suspect's equivocal reference to a lawyer in *Davis* occurred only *after* he had given express oral and written waivers of his rights. *Davis'* holding is explicitly predicated on that fact. The Court ignores this aspect of *Davis,* as well as the decisions of numerous federal and state courts declining to apply a clear-statement rule when a suspect has not previously given an express waiver of rights.

In my mind, a more appropriate standard for addressing a suspect's ambiguous invocation of the right to remain silent is the constraint *Mosley* places on questioning a suspect who has invoked that right: The suspect's "'right to cut off questioning'" must be "'scrupulously honored.'" Such a standard is necessarily precautionary and fact specific. The rule would acknowledge that some statements or conduct are so equivocal that police may scrupulously honor a suspect's rights without terminating questioning—for instance, if a suspect's actions are reasonably understood to indicate a willingness to listen before deciding whether to respond. But other statements or actions—in particular, when a suspect sits silent throughout prolonged interrogation, long past the point when he could be deciding whether to respond—cannot reasonably be understood other than as an invocation of the right to remain silent. Under such circumstances, "scrupulous" respect for the suspect's rights will require police to terminate questioning under *Mosley*.

To be sure, such a standard does not provide police with a bright-line rule. But, as we have previously recognized, *Mosley* itself does not offer clear guidance to police about when and how interrogation may continue after a suspect invokes his rights. * * *

Davis' clear-statement rule is also a poor fit for the right to silence. Advising a suspect that he has a "right to remain silent" is unlikely to convey that he must speak (and must do so in some particular fashion) to ensure the right will be protected. By contrast, telling a suspect "he has the right to the presence of an attorney, and that if he cannot afford an attorney one will be appointed for him prior to any questioning if he so desires" implies the need for speech to exercise that right. *Davis'* requirement that a suspect must "clearly reques[t] an attorney" to terminate questioning thus aligns with a suspect's likely understanding of the *Miranda* warnings in a way today's rule does not. The Court suggests Thompkins could have employed the "simple, unambiguous" means of saying "he wanted to remain silent" or "did not want to talk with the police." But the *Miranda* warnings give no hint that a suspect should use those magic words, and there is little reason to believe police— who have ample incentives to avoid invocation—will provide such guidance. * * *

For these reasons, I believe a precautionary requirement that police "scrupulously hono[r]" a suspect's right to cut off questioning is a more faithful application of our precedents [in the right to silence context] than the Court's awkward and needless extension of *Davis*.

* * *

Today's decision turns *Miranda* upside down. Criminal suspects must now unambiguously invoke their right to remain silent—which, counterintuitively, requires them to speak. At the same time, suspects will be legally presumed to have waived their rights even if they have given no clear expression of their intent to do so. Those results, in my view, find no basis in *Miranda* or our subsequent cases and are inconsistent with the fair-trial principles on which those precedents are grounded. * * * I respectfully dissent.

NOTES AND QUESTIONS

1.   Which opinion would you have joined? What is the weakest part of Justice Kennedy's majority opinion? Of Justice Sotomayor's dissent? Is her reading of *Butler* better than the majority's? Is she right that *Berghuis* turns the *Miranda* opinion "upside down"? Is she right that the majority ignored one of the key elements in *Davis* when applying it to these facts?

2.   What is the evidence that Thompkins understood his rights?

3.   Reading from a waiver card, an officer concludes by saying, "With these warnings in mind, do you waive your rights as I have described them to you and agree to talk to me?" The suspect said "No," at the same time smiling and nodding. With no further discussion of waiver, the officer proceeds with questioning, and the suspect makes incriminating responses. Is this a waiver?

4.   Notice that warning #5, the one the detective had Thompkins read aloud, is not required by *Miranda*. How important was that warning to the Court's theory that Thompkins waived his rights when he answered questions almost three hours later? Do you think the case would have come out differently if the warnings to Thompkins had stopped with warning #4?

5.   In a largely-omitted (because highly technical) part of the case, the majority admitted that it could have decided against Thompkins without reaching the merits of the *Miranda* issues. It could have simply held that the standard was not met for reversing a state court in a federal habeas corpus case. This highly deferential standard permits federal courts to affirm state convictions in habeas cases if they find that the state court decision was not an unreasonable application of clearly-established federal law. Why do you think that the Court went out of its way to reach the merits of the *Miranda* issues?

6.   And now for the rest of the invocation of counsel story

EDWARDS V. ARIZONA
Supreme Court of the United States, 1981.
451 U.S. 477, 101 S.Ct. 1880, 68 L.Ed.2d 378.

JUSTICE WHITE delivered the opinion of the Court [joined by JUSTICES BRENNAN, STEWART, MARSHALL, BLACKMUN, and STEVENS]. * * *

I

On January 19, 1976, a sworn complaint was filed against Edwards in Arizona state court charging him with robbery, burglary, and first-degree murder. An arrest warrant was issued pursuant to the complaint, and Edwards was arrested at his home later that same day. At the police station, he was informed of his rights as required by *Miranda v. Arizona.* Petitioner stated that he understood his rights, and was willing to submit to questioning. After being told that another suspect already in custody had implicated him in the crime, Edwards denied involvement and gave a taped statement presenting an alibi defense. He then sought to "make a deal." The interrogating officer told him that he wanted a statement, but that he did not have the authority to negotiate a deal. The officer provided Edwards with the telephone number of a county attorney. Petitioner made the call, but hung up after a few moments. Edwards then said: "I want an attorney before making a deal." At that point, questioning ceased and Edwards was taken to county jail.

At 9:15 the next morning, two detectives, colleagues of the officer who had interrogated Edwards the previous night, came to the jail and asked to see Edwards. When the detention officer informed Edwards that the detectives wished to speak with him, he replied that he did not want to talk to anyone. The guard told him that "he had" to talk and then took him to meet with the detectives. The officers identified themselves, stated they wanted to talk to him, and informed him of his *Miranda* rights. Edwards was willing to talk, but he first wanted to hear the taped statement of the alleged accomplice who had implicated him. After listening to the tape for several minutes, petitioner said that he would make a statement so long as it was not tape-recorded. The detectives informed him that the recording was irrelevant since they could testify in court concerning whatever he said. Edwards replied: "I'll tell you anything you want to know, but I don't want it on tape." He thereupon implicated himself in the crime.

Prior to trial, Edwards moved to suppress his confession on the ground that his *Miranda* rights had been violated when the officers returned to question him after he had invoked his right to counsel. * * * The [trial] court stated without explanation that it found Edwards' statement to be voluntary. Edwards was tried twice and convicted. Evidence concerning his confession was admitted at both trials.

On appeal, the Arizona Supreme Court held that Edwards had invoked both his right to remain silent and his right to counsel during the interrogation conducted on the night of January 19. The court then went on to determine, however, that Edwards had waived both rights during the January 20 meeting when he voluntarily gave his statement to the detectives after again being informed that he need not answer questions and that he need not answer without the advice of counsel. * * *

II

In *Miranda v. Arizona*, the Court determined that the Fifth and Fourteenth Amendments' prohibition against compelled self-incrimination required that custodial interrogation be preceded by advice to the putative defendant that he has the right to remain silent and also the right to the presence of an attorney. The Court also indicated the procedures to be followed subsequent to the warnings. If the accused indicates that he wishes to remain silent, "the interrogation must cease." If he requests counsel, "the interrogation must cease until an attorney is present."

Miranda thus declared that an accused has a Fifth and Fourteenth Amendment right to have counsel present during custodial interrogation. Here, the critical facts as found by the Arizona Supreme Court are that Edwards asserted his right to counsel and his right to remain silent on January 19, but that the police, without furnishing him counsel, returned the next morning to confront him and as a result of the meeting secured incriminating oral admissions. Contrary to the holdings of the state courts, Edwards insists that having exercised his right on the 19th to have counsel present during interrogation, he did not validly waive that right on the 20th. For the following reasons, we agree.

First, the Arizona Supreme Court applied an erroneous standard for determining waiver where the accused has specifically invoked his right to counsel. It is reasonably clear under our cases that waivers of counsel must not only be voluntary, but must also constitute a knowing and intelligent relinquishment or abandonment of a known right or privilege, a matter which depends in each case "upon the particular facts and circumstances surrounding that case, including the background, experience, and conduct of the accused." * * *

* * * Here, however sound the conclusion of the state courts as to the voluntariness of Edwards' admission may be, neither the trial court nor the Arizona Supreme Court undertook to focus on whether Edwards understood his right to counsel and intelligently and knowingly relinquished it. It is thus apparent that the decision below misunderstood the requirement for finding a valid waiver of the right to counsel, once invoked.

Second, although we have held that after initially being advised of his *Miranda* rights, the accused may himself validly waive his rights and respond to interrogation, the Court has strongly indicated that additional safeguards are necessary when the accused asks for counsel; and we now hold that when an accused has invoked his right to have counsel present during custodial interrogation, a valid waiver of that right cannot be established by showing only that he responded to further police-initiated custodial interrogation even if he has been advised of his rights. We further hold that an accused, such as Edwards, having expressed his desire to deal with the police only through counsel, is not subject to further interrogation by the authorities until counsel has been made available to him, unless the accused himself initiates further communication, exchanges, or conversations with the police.

Miranda itself indicated that the assertion of the right to counsel was a significant event and that once exercised by the accused, "the interrogation must cease until an attorney is present." Our later cases have not abandoned that view. * * * We reconfirm these [cases] and, to lend them substance, emphasize that it is inconsistent with *Miranda* and its progeny for the authorities, at their instance, to reinterrogate an accused in custody if he has clearly asserted his right to counsel.

In concluding that the fruits of the interrogation initiated by the police on January 20 could not be used against Edwards, we do not hold or imply that Edwards was powerless to countermand his election or that the authorities could in no event use any incriminating statements made by Edwards prior to his having access to counsel. Had Edwards initiated the meeting on January 20, nothing in the Fifth and Fourteenth Amendments would prohibit the police from merely listening to his voluntary, volunteered statements and using them against him at the trial. The Fifth Amendment right identified in *Miranda* is the right to have counsel present at any custodial interrogation. Absent such interrogation, there would have been no infringement of the right that Edwards invoked and there would be no occasion to determine whether there had been a valid waiver. *Rhode Island v. Innis* [p. 701] makes this sufficiently clear.[9]

But this is not what the facts of this case show. Here, the officers conducting the interrogation on the evening of January 19 ceased interrogation when Edwards requested counsel as he had been advised he had the right to do. The Arizona Supreme Court was of the opinion that this was a sufficient invocation of his *Miranda* rights, and we are in accord. It is also clear that without making counsel available to Edwards, the police returned to him the next day. This was not at his suggestion or request. Indeed, Edwards informed the detention officer that he did not want to talk to anyone. At the meeting, the detectives told Edwards that they wanted to talk to him and again advised him of his *Miranda* rights. Edwards stated that he would talk, but what prompted this action does not appear. He listened at his own request to part of the taped statement made by one of his alleged accomplices and then made an incriminating statement, which was used against him at his trial. We think it is clear that Edwards was subjected to custodial interrogation on January 20 within the meaning of *Rhode Island v. Innis*, and that this occurred at the instance of the authorities. His statement made without having had access to counsel, did not amount to a valid waiver and hence was inadmissible.

Accordingly, the holding of the Arizona Supreme Court that Edwards had waived his right to counsel was infirm, and the judgment of that court is reversed. * * *

[The opinion of CHIEF JUSTICE BURGER, concurring in the judgment, is omitted.]

JUSTICE POWELL, with whom JUSTICE REHNQUIST joins, concurring in the result.

Although I agree that the judgment of the Arizona Supreme Court must be reversed, I do not join the Court's opinion because I am not sure what it means. * * *

* * * [T]he Court—after reiterating the familiar principles of waiver—goes on to say:

"We further hold that an accused, such as Edwards, having expressed his desire to deal with the police only through counsel, is not subject to further interrogation by the authorities until

---

[9] If, as frequently would occur in the course of a meeting initiated by the accused, the conversation is not wholly one-sided, it is likely that the officers will say or do something that clearly would be "interrogation." In that event, the question would be whether a valid waiver of the right to counsel and the right to silence had occurred, that is, whether the purported waiver was knowing and intelligent and found to be so under the totality of the circumstances, including the necessary fact that the accused, not the police, reopened the dialogue with the authorities. * * *

> counsel has been made available to him, *unless the accused [has] himself initiate[d] further communication, exchanges, or conversations with the police.*"

In view of the emphasis placed on "initiation," I find the Court's opinion unclear. If read to create a new *per se* rule, requiring a threshold inquiry as to precisely who opened any conversation between an accused and state officials, I cannot agree. I would not superimpose a new element of proof on the established doctrine of waiver of counsel. * * *

In sum, once warnings have been given and the right to counsel has been invoked, the relevant inquiry—whether the suspect now desires to talk to police without counsel—is a question of fact to be determined in light of all of the circumstances. Who "initiated" a conversation may be relevant to the question of waiver, but it is not the *sine qua non* to the inquiry. The ultimate question is whether there was a free and knowing waiver of counsel before interrogation commenced.

If the Court's opinion does nothing more than restate these principles, I am in agreement with it. I hesitate to join the opinion only because of what appears to be an undue and undefined, emphasis on a single element: "initiation." * * * My concern is that the Court's opinion today may be read as "constitutionalizing" not the generalized *Zerbst* [waiver] standard but a *single element of fact* among the various facts that may be relevant to determining whether there has been a valid waiver.

NOTES AND QUESTIONS

1.   *How does an invocation of the right to remain silent compare to Edwards?* A single standard could measure the effect of all invocations of *Miranda*. The *Edwards* rule could apply to invocations of the right to remain silent as well as the right to counsel; the police would not then be permitted to attempt to question the suspect who invoked either right unless the suspect initiated the exchange. But the Court has not seen fit to apply the same broad rule to requests to remain silent.

In Michigan v. Mosley, 423 U.S. 96, 96 S.Ct. 321, 46 L.Ed.2d 313 (1975), decided five years before *Edwards*, Mosley was questioned by a detective of the armed robbery section of the detective bureau. The interrogation ended as soon as Mosley "said he did not want to answer any questions about the robberies." A few hours later, a detective from the homicide bureau questioned Mosley about a fatal shooting during a holdup attempt (not the same robbery that was the subject of the earlier interrogation).

> Before questioning Mosley about this homicide, Detective Hill carefully advised him of his "*Miranda* rights." Mosley read the notification form both silently and aloud, and Detective Hill then read and explained the warnings to him and had him sign the form.

Mosley at first denied any involvement in the Williams murder, but after the officer told him that Anthony Smith had confessed to participating in the slaying and had named him as the "shooter," Mosley made a statement implicating himself in the homicide. The interrogation by Detective Hill lasted approximately 15 minutes, and at no time during its course did Mosley ask to consult with a lawyer or indicate that he did not want to discuss the homicide. In short, there is no claim that the procedures followed during Detective Hill's interrogation of Mosley, standing alone, did not fully comply with the strictures of the *Miranda* opinion.

The Court considered the various meanings that the *Miranda* Court could have intended when it stated that "interrogation must cease" when the person in custody indicates that "he wishes to remain silent."

> A reasonable and faithful interpretation of the *Miranda* opinion must rest on the intention of the Court in that case to adopt "fully effective means * * * to notify the person of his right of silence and to assure that the exercise of the right will be scrupulously honored * * * ." The critical safeguard identified in the passage at issue is a person's "right to cut off questioning." Through the exercise of his option to terminate questioning he can control the time at which questioning occurs, the subjects discussed, and the duration of the interrogation. The requirement that law enforcement authorities must respect a person's exercise of that option counteracts the coercive pressures of the custodial setting. We therefore conclude that the admissibility of statements obtained after the person in custody has decided to remain silent depends under *Miranda* on whether his "right to cut off questioning" was "scrupulously honored."

The Court held that, under the facts of the case, the previous request not to talk to a different detective, from a different police bureau, about a different crime, did not extend to a second interrogation that was also preceded by warnings. Thus, the suspect who requests her right to silence is protected differently from the one who demands her right to counsel.

Does *Mosley* make sense now that the Court has decided *Edwards*? Mosley invoked a right of silence that the *Miranda* Court created as a prophylactic rule to protect the Fifth Amendment privilege. Edwards, on the other hand, invoked the *Miranda* right to counsel designed to protect the right to silence designed to protect the privilege, in essence a prophylaxis to protect a prophylaxis. Why is the *Edwards* double prophylaxis entitled to greater protection than the prophylaxis it was designed to protect? Professor Yale Kamisar has concluded that "either *Mosley* was wrongly decided or *Edwards* was." Yale Kamisar, *The Edwards and Bradshaw Cases: The Court Giveth and the Court Taketh Away*, in 5 The Supreme Court: Trends and Developments 153, 157 (J. Choper, Y. Kamisar, & L. Tribe, eds. 1984). Is Professor Kamisar right?

2.   *Problems of initiation/waiver.* A plurality of the Court sought to explain "initiation" two years after *Edwards* in Oregon v. Bradshaw, 462 U.S. 1039, 103 S.Ct. 2830, 77 L.Ed.2d 405 (1983). Initiation occurs only when an inquiry from the suspect can "be fairly said to represent a desire on the part of an accused to open up a more generalized discussion relating directly or indirectly to the investigation." Asking for a drink of water or to use a telephone would not constitute initiation because they are "routine incidents of the custodial relationship."

A.   Police arrested *B* for a misdemeanor after *B* admitted minor involvement in an offense. At that point, *B* requested counsel, and the police terminated the conversation. Later, when *B* was being transferred from the police station to the jail, *B* asked, "Well, what is going to happen to me now?" The officer responded, "You do not have to talk to me. You have requested an attorney, and I don't want you talking to me unless you so desire because anything you say—because—since you have requested an attorney, you know, it has to be at your own free will." *B* said he understood. During the following conversation, the officer suggested that *B* might "help himself" by taking a polygraph examination. *B* agreed, took the test, was told that the test revealed he was not telling the truth, and he then confessed. What are the issues under *Edwards*, and how would you resolve them?

B.   What if the officer had replied to *B*'s initial question by saying, "That's up to you. If you pass a polygraph test, it'll help your case." Then *B* agrees to take the polygraph and everything happens as above. How is this case different?

C.   A uniformed police officer arrested *C* and provided warnings, to which he responded by clearly requesting counsel. Later, at the station and after the complaining witness identified *C*, a detective said that he needed to ask *C* some questions for the booking process. The detective said that he was not going to ask *C* about the crime because he knew *C* had invoked his right to counsel. *C* became upset and said he wasn't about to talk to a patrol officer about the crime but that he wanted to talk to a detective. The detective read *C* his rights again, and *C* waived and made a statement. Admissible? See Cross v. State, 144 S.W.3d 521 (Tex. Crim. App. 2004).

3.   *How broad is the Edwards rule?* In their separate *Edwards* opinions, Chief Justice Burger and Justice Powell expressed concern that the majority opinion could be read to require a rigid prophylactic rule as a way of protecting the prophylactic rule of *Miranda*. They were quite the prophets. In Minnick v. Mississippi, 498 U.S. 146, 111 S.Ct. 486, 112 L.Ed.2d 489 (1990), Minnick answered a few questions posed by FBI agents and then said, "Come back Monday when I have a lawyer." The agents ceased interrogation, and Minnick consulted with his lawyer on at least two occasions before Monday when Mississippi police re-advised him of his rights and secured incriminating statements. The Court held that Minnick's statements were inadmissible even though he had consulted with counsel. As Justice Scalia put it in dissent, Minnick's

confession must be suppressed, not because it was "compelled," nor even because it was obtained from an individual who could realistically be assumed to be unaware of his rights, but simply because this Court sees fit to prescribe as a "systemic assuranc[e]," that a person in custody who has once asked for counsel cannot thereafter be approached by the police unless counsel is present. Of course the Constitution's proscription of compelled testimony does not remotely authorize this incursion upon state practices; and even our recent precedents are not a valid excuse. * * *

Today's extension of the *Edwards* prohibition is the latest stage of prophylaxis built upon prophylaxis, producing a veritable fairyland castle of imagined constitutional restriction upon law enforcement. This newest tower, according to the Court, is needed to avoid "inconsisten[cy] with [the] purpose" of *Edwards'* prophylactic rule, which was needed to protect *Miranda*'s prophylactic right to have counsel present, which was needed to protect the right against *compelled self-incrimination* found (at last!) in the Constitution.

It seems obvious to me that, even in *Edwards* itself but surely in today's decision, we have gone far beyond any genuine concern about suspects who do not *know* their right to remain silent, or who have been *coerced* to abandon it. Both holdings are explicable, in my view, only as an effort to protect suspects against what is regarded as their own folly. The sharp-witted criminal would know better than to confess; why should the dull-witted suffer for his lack of mental endowment? Providing him an attorney at every stage where he might be induced or persuaded (though not coerced) to incriminate himself will even the odds. Apart from the fact that this protective enterprise is beyond our authority under the Fifth Amendment or any other provision of the Constitution, it is unwise. The procedural protections of the Constitution protect the guilty as well as the innocent, but it is not their objective to set the guilty free. That some clever criminals may employ those protections to their advantage is poor reason to allow criminals who have not done so to escape justice.

Do you agree with Justice Scalia? What is the purpose of counsel in the *Miranda* context, as contrasted with the Sixth Amendment?

Scalia in the first sentence of his *Minnick* dissent accused the majority of establishing "an irrebuttable presumption that a criminal suspect, after invoking his *Miranda* right to counsel, can *never* validly waive that right during any police-initiated encounter, even after the suspect has been provided multiple *Miranda* warnings and has actually consulted his attorney."

This turned out to be an overstatement. In 2010, in an opinion by Justice Scalia himself, the Court held that suspects who invoke their right to counsel and then are released from custody can, at some point, be asked again if they wish to waive their rights. In Maryland v. Shatzer, 559 U.S. 98, 130 S.Ct. 1213, 175 L.Ed.2d 1045 (2010), two and a half years elapsed between the *Edwards* invocation and the second waiver request, and the Court unanimously agreed that his waiver was valid. What split the Court was the dicta intended to provide "certainty" about "when renewed interrogation is lawful." The majority chose two weeks as the "cleansing period" because that "provides plenty of time for the suspect to get reacclimated to his [non-custodial] normal life, to consult with friends and counsel, and to shake off any residual coercive effects of his prior custody." Rejecting fourteen days as "arbitrary," Justice Thomas wrote: "This *ipse dixit* does not explain why extending the *Edwards* presumption for 14 days following a break in custody—as opposed to 0, 10, or 100 days—provides the 'closest possible fit' with the Self-Incrimination Clause." Justice Stevens concurred in the judgment, arguing that a two-week period between attempted interrogations was not long enough if the police did not provide a lawyer as requested. The suspect who is approached fourteen days later, Stevens wrote, "is likely to feel that the police lied to him or are ignoring his rights."

4.   *Problems of invocation and waiver of the right to counsel or silence.*

Here are some Problems with which to wrestle. Do not forget in working on them that *Davis* and *Berghuis* created a rule that invocation of the right to counsel and to silence must be unambiguous.

A.   Officers arrest a suspect and place him in a squad car. An officer reads him his *Miranda* rights and asks if he understands them. He says that he does. The officer then reads a waiver form and asks him if he is willing to waive his rights. He responds: "Get the f— out of my face. I don't have nothing to say. I refuse to sign [the waiver form]." Is this invocation? See United States v. Banks, 78 F.3d 1190, 1196–98 (7th Cir. 1996).

B.   Police ask *B* to come to the station to discuss a "police matter." When he arrives, police tell him he is not under arrest and is free to leave at any time. "Great," he says. "But I want a lawyer anyway, and I want a lawyer now." Police ignore the request and ask *B* questions. He quickly answers in an incriminating way. Police allow him to leave but, of course, arrest him later. Are his answers admissible? See Burket v. Angelone, 208 F.3d 172, 198 (4th Cir. 2000).

C.   Police want to question *H* about a forgery charge. Police provide *Miranda* warnings, and *H* executes a standard waiver form. Over the course of approximately three hours, *H* freely answers questions about the forgeries. Sometime during the interrogation, the detectives begin questioning *H* about a murder that had not until then been mentioned. At this point, he says: "I think I need a lawyer because if I tell everything I know, how do I know I'm not going to wind up with a complicity charge?" Invocation? See State v. Henness, 79 Ohio St.3d 53, 679 N.E.2d 686 (1997).

D.   *A* is in police custody. Before police ask any questions, or provide warnings, *A* says, "maybe I should talk to an attorney by the name of William

Evans." He showed the police Evans's business card. The police officer left the room. When he returned, he made no mention of Evans but gave *Miranda* warnings to *A*, who signed a written waiver and gave a statement. Admissible? See Abela v. Martin, 380 F.3d 915 (6th Cir. 2004).

E.   Federal agents give *D* his *Miranda* warnings and he first signs a waiver but then requests counsel. At this point, the agents ask booking questions—age, birth date and place, address, height, weight, Social Security number. They also request a hair sample, telling him that if he refuses, they will get a court order. He agrees to permit the agents to take a hair sample at the local hospital. He then begins to talk about the crime and signs a second waiver. He talks more after which he requests a lawyer and falls silent. The agents sit in silence for a time. *D* begins to talk again and then confesses. Is any of what *D* said admissible? See United States v. Dougall, 919 F.2d 932 (5th Cir. 1990). Hint: Don't forget that some evidence is not testimonial.

5.   *A final problem: pulling together, Edwards, Davis, Mosley,* and *Berghuis.* Police arrest *H* for a fire in the apartment of his girlfriend, Deb. She is dead but police do not initially reveal this fact. They give him warnings and he signs a waiver form. He admits seeing her the evening of the fire. The officers tell him that others in the apartment complex heard *H* and Deb in a heated argument that afternoon. *H* repeatedly tells police he does not know what they are talking to him about. After the officers finally tell *H* that Deb is dead, the following exchange occurs:

H: What are you saying here?

Detective: What are we saying? We're saying that you took Deb's life.

H: You're saying I killed Deb?

Detective: Absolutely. There's no doubt about that. OK? We know that. * * * We just need to know why you did that, OK? We know you did that. That's not even a question here, Kevin. Understand that? We know that. We talked to a bunch of people here and—and we—we put the evidence together at the scene and it clearly points to you. OK? So, we need to know why. What was your—?

H: You think I killed her?

Detective: Did you—did you kill her because you were upset with her? Did you kill her because—

H: You think I killed—

Detective: Kevin, it's not that we think that, we know that. We need to know why you did that. That's all, OK? Tha—it's no question as to did you do that. That's not a question here, Kevin, OK? So—

H: Can I have a drink of water and then lock me up—I think we really should have an attorney.

Detective: We'll get you a drink of water.

H: I don't want to talk anymore please. (Pause). This is—this is really wrong. This woman has scars all over her from this [other man.] He's callin' her 50 times a week.

Detective: 'Kay. If you want to talk to an attorney, you understand that we have to stop talking to you. OK? And—and then your side of this story will never be known. That's your choice. That's a choice you're making.

H: So, that means what?

Detective: That means we're gonna put this thing together and we're gonna convict you of murder.

H: Of murder?

Detective: Absolutely. Yup.

H: Convict me of murdering her?

The interrogation continued and *H* made numerous statements regarding his involvement in Deb's death.

Did *H* invoke the right to counsel? To silence? Did the police violate any aspect of *Miranda* or did the original waiver solve any *Miranda* problems? See State v. Hannon, 636 N.W.2d 796 (Minn. 2001).

G. A YEAR ON THE KILLING STREETS: THE BITTER FRUIT OF WAIVER

Journalist David Simon observed the Baltimore Homicide Division for a year (1988). In the excerpt that follows, Simon describes the interrogation practices and strategies that he saw. Be warned: what follows is "street real," including vulgar and obscene language.

DAVID SIMON—HOMICIDE, A YEAR ON THE KILLING STREETS
(1991) 193–207.

You are a citizen of a free nation, having lived your adult life in a land of guaranteed civil liberties, and you commit a crime of violence, whereupon you are jacked up, hauled down to a police station and deposited in a claustrophobic anteroom with three chairs, a table and no windows. There you sit for a half hour or so until a police detective—a man you have never met before, a man who can in no way be mistaken for a friend—enters the room with a thin stack of lined notepaper and a ballpoint pen.

The detective offers a cigarette, not your brand, and begins an uninterrupted monologue that wanders back and forth for a half hour more, eventually coming to rest in a familiar place: *"You have the absolute right to remain silent."*

Of course you do. You're a criminal. Criminals always have the right to remain silent. At least once in your miserable life, you spent an hour in front of a television set, listening to this book-'em-Danno routine. You think Joe Friday was lying to you? You think Kojak was making this horseshit up? No way, bunk, we're talking sacred freedoms here, notably your Fifth Fucking Amendment protection against self-incrimination, and hey, it was good enough for Ollie North, so who are you to go incriminating yourself at the first opportunity? Get it straight: A police detective, a man who gets paid government money to put you in prison, is explaining your absolute right to shut up before you say something stupid.

"Anything you say or write may be used against you in a court of law."

Yo, bunky, wake the fuck up. You're now being told that talking to a police detective in an interrogation room can only hurt you. If it could help you, they would probably be pretty quick to say that, wouldn't they? They'd stand up and say you have the right not to worry because what you say or write in this godforsaken cubicle is gonna be used to your benefit in a court of law. No, your best bet is to shut up. Shut up now.

"You have the right to talk with a lawyer at any time—before any questioning, before answering any questions, or during any questions."

Talk about helpful. Now the man who wants to arrest you for violating the peace and dignity of the state is saying you can talk to a trained professional, an attorney who has read the relevant portions of the Maryland Annotated Code or can at least get his hands on some Cliffs Notes. And let's face it, pal, you just carved up a drunk in a Dundalk Avenue bar, but that don't make you a neurosurgeon. Take whatever help you can get.

"If you want a lawyer and cannot afford to hire one, you will not be asked any questions, and the court will be requested to appoint a lawyer for you."

Translation: You're a derelict. No charge for derelicts.

At this point, if all lobes are working, you ought to have seen enough of this Double Jeopardy category to know that it ain't where you want to be. How about a little something from Criminal Lawyers and Their Clients for $50, Alex?

Whoa, bunk, not so fast.

"Before we get started, lemme just get through the paperwork," says the detective, who now produces an Explanation of Rights sheet, BPD Form 69, and passes it across the table.

"EXPLANATION OF RIGHTS," declares the top line in bold block letters. The detective asks you to fill in your name, address, age, and education, then the date and time. That much accomplished, he asks you to read the next section. It begins, "YOU ARE HEREBY ADVISED THAT:"

> Read number one, the detective says. Do you understand number one?

> *"You have the absolute right to remain silent."*

> Yeah, you understand. We did this already.

> "Then write your initials next to number one. Now read number two."

And so forth, until you have initialed each component of the Miranda warning. That done, the detective tells you to write your signature on the next line, the one just below the sentence that says, "I HAVE READ THE ABOVE EXPLANATION OF MY RIGHTS AND FULLY UNDERSTAND IT."

You sign your name and the monologue resumes. The detective assures you that he has informed you of these rights because he wants you to be protected, because there is nothing that concerns him more than giving you every possible assistance in this very confusing and stressful moment in your life. If you don't want to talk, he tells you, that's fine. And if you want a lawyer, that's fine, too, because first of all, he's no relation to the guy you cut up, and second, he's gonna get six hours overtime no matter what you do. But he wants you to know—and he's been doing this a lot longer than you, so take his word for it—that your rights to remain silent and obtain qualified counsel aren't all they're cracked up to be.

Look at it this way, he says, leaning back in his chair. Once you up and call for that lawyer, son, we can't do a damn thing for you. No sir, your friends in the city homicide unit are going to have to leave you locked in this room all alone and the next authority figure to scan your case will be a tie-wearing, three-piece bloodsucker—a no-nonsense prosecutor from the Violent Crimes Unit with the official title of assistant state's attorney for the city of Baltimore. And God help you then, son, because a ruthless fucker like that will have an O'Donnell Heights motorhead like yourself halfway to the gas chamber before you get three words out. Now's the time to speak up, right now when I got my pen and paper here on the table, because once I walk out of this room any chance you have of telling your side of the story is gone and I gotta write it up the way it looks. And the way it looks right now is first-fucking-degree murder. Felony murder, mister, which when shoved up a man's asshole is a helluva lot more painful than second-degree or maybe even manslaughter. What you say right here and now could make the difference, bunk. Did I mention that Maryland has a gas chamber? Big, ugly sumbitch at the penitentiary on Eager Street, not twenty blocks from here. You don't wanna get too close to that bad boy, lemme tell you.

A small, wavering sound of protest passes your lips and the detective leans back in his chair, shaking his head sadly.

What the hell is wrong with you, son? You think I'm fucking with you? Hey, I don't even need to bother with your weak shit. I got three witnesses in three other rooms who say you're my man. I got a knife from the scene that's going downstairs to the lab for latent prints. I got blood spatter on them Air Jordans we took off you ten minutes ago. Why the fuck do you think we took 'em? Do I look like I wear high-top tennis? Fuck no. You got spatter all over 'em, and I think we both know whose blood type it's gonna be. Hey, bunk, I'm only in here to make sure that there ain't nothing you can say for yourself before I write it all up.

You hesitate.

Oh, says the detective. You want to think about it. Hey, you think about it all you want, pal. My captain's right outside in the hallway, and he already told me to charge your ass in the first fuckin' degree. For once in your beshitted little life someone is giving you a chance and you're too fucking dumb to take it. What the fuck, you go ahead and think about it and I'll tell my captain to cool his heels for ten minutes. I can do that much for you. How 'bout some coffee? Another cigarette?

The detective leaves you alone in that cramped, windowless room. Just you and the blank notepaper and the Form 69 and * * * first-degree murder. First-degree murder with witnesses and fingerprints and blood on your Air Jordans. Christ, you didn't even notice the blood on your own fucking shoes. Felony murder, mister. First-fucking-degree. How many years, you begin to wonder, how many years do I get for involuntary manslaughter?

Whereupon the man who wants to put you in prison, the man who is not your friend, comes back in the room, asking if the coffee's okay.

Yeah, you say, the coffee's fine, but what happens if I want a lawyer?

The detective shrugs. Then we get you a lawyer, he says. And I walk out of the room and type up the charging documents for first-degree murder and you can't say a fucking thing about it. Look, bunk, I'm giving you a chance. He came at you, right? You were scared. It was self-defense.

Your mouth opens to speak.

He came at you, didn't he?

"Yeah," you venture cautiously, "he came at me."

Whoa, says the detective, holding up his hands. Wait a minute. If we're gonna do this, I gotta find your rights form. Where's the fucking form? Damn things are like cops, never around when you need 'em. Here it is, he says, pushing the explanation-of-rights sheet across the table and pointing to the bottom. Read that, he says.

"I am willing to answer questions and I do not want any attorney at this time. My decision to answer questions without having an attorney present is free and voluntary on my part."

As you read, he leaves the room and returns a moment later with a second detective as a witness. You sign the bottom of the form, as do both detectives.

The first detective looks up from the form, his eyes soaked with innocence. "He came at you, huh?"

"Yeah, he came at me."

Get used to small rooms, bunk, because you are about to be drop-kicked into the lost land of pretrial detention. Because it's one thing to be a murdering little asshole from Southeast Baltimore, and it's another to be stupid about it, and with five little words you have just elevated yourself to the ranks of the truly witless.

End of the road, pal. It's over. It's history. And if that police detective wasn't so busy committing your weak bullshit to paper, he'd probably look you in the eye and tell you so. He'd give you another cigarette and say, son, you are ignorance personified and you just put yourself in for the fatal stabbing of a human being. He might even tell you that the other witnesses in the other rooms are too drunk to identify their own reflections, much less the kid who had the knife, or that it's always a long shot for the lab to pull a latent off a knife hilt, or that your $95 sneakers are as clean as the day you bought them. If he was feeling particularly expansive, he might tell you that everyone who leaves the homicide unit in handcuffs does so charged with first-degree murder, that it's for the lawyers to decide what kind of deal will be cut. He might go on to say that even after all these years working homicides, there is still a small part of him that finds it completely mystifying that anyone ever utters a single word in a police interrogation. To illustrate the point, he could hold up your Form 69, on which you waived away every last one of your rights, and say, "Lookit here, pistonhead, I told you twice that you were deep in the shit and that whatever you said could put you in deeper." And if his message was still somehow beyond your understanding, he could drag your carcass back down the sixth-floor hallway, back toward the sign that says Homicide Unit in white block letters, the sign you saw when you walked off the elevator.

Now think hard: Who lives in a homicide unit? Yeah, right. And what do homicide detectives do for a living? Yeah, you got it, bunk. And what did you do tonight? You murdered someone.

So when you opened that mouth of yours, what the fuck were you thinking?

Homicide detectives in Baltimore like to imagine a small, open window at the top of the long wall in the large interrogation room. More to the point, they like to imagine their suspects imagining a small, open window at the top of the long wall. The open window is the escape hatch, the Out. It is the perfect representation of what every suspect believes when he opens his mouth during an interrogation. Every last one envisions himself parrying questions with the right combination of alibi and excuse; every last one sees himself coming up with the right words, then crawling out the window to go home and sleep in his own bed. More often than not, a guilty man is looking for the Out from his first moments in the interrogation room; in that sense, the window is as much the suspect's fantasy as the detective's mirage.

The effect of the illusion is profound, distorting as it does the natural hostility between hunter and hunted, transforming it until it resembles a relationship more symbiotic than adversarial. That is the lie, and when the roles are perfectly performed, deceit surpasses itself, becoming manipulation on a grand scale and ultimately an act of betrayal. Because what occurs in an interrogation room is indeed little more than a carefully staged drama, a choreographed performance that allows a detective and his suspect to find common ground where none exists. There, in a carefully controlled purgatory, the guilty proclaim their malefactions, though rarely in any form that allows for contrition or resembles an unequivocal admission. * * *

Once the minefield that is Miranda has been successfully negotiated, the detective must let the suspect know that his guilt is certain and easily established by the existing evidence. He must then offer the Out.

This, too, is role playing, and it requires a seasoned actor. If a witness or suspect is belligerent, you wear him down with greater belligerence. If the man shows fear, you offer calm and comfort. When he looks weak, you appear strong. When he wants a friend, you crack a joke and offer to buy him a soda. If he's confident, you are more so, assuring him that you are certain of his guilt and are curious only about a few select details of the crime. And if he's arrogant, if he wants nothing to do with the process, you intimidate him, threaten him, make him believe that making you happy may be the only thing between his ass and the Baltimore City Jail.

Kill your woman and a good detective will come to real tears as he touches your shoulder and tells you how he knows that you must have loved her, that it wouldn't be so hard for you to talk about if you didn't. Beat your child to death and a police detective will wrap his arm around you in the interrogation room, telling you about how he beats his own children all the time, how it wasn't your fault if the kid up and died on you. Shoot a friend over a poker hand and that same detective will lie about your dead buddy's condition, telling you that the victim is in stable condition at Hopkins and probably won't press charges, which wouldn't amount to more than assault with intent even if he does. Murder a man with an accomplice and the detective will walk your co-conspirator past the open door of your interrogation room, then say your bunky's going home tonight because he gave a statement making you the triggerman. And if that same detective thinks you can be bluffed, he might tell you that they've got your prints on the weapon, or that there are two eyewitnesses who have picked your photo from an array, or that the victim made a dying declaration in which he named you as his assailant.

All of which is street legal. Reasonable deception, the courts call it. After all, what could be more reasonable than deceiving someone who has taken a human life and is now lying about it?

The deception sometimes goes too far, or at least it sometimes seems that way to those unfamiliar with the process. Not long ago, several veteran homicide detectives in Detroit were publicly upbraided and disciplined by their superiors for using the office Xerox machine as a polygraph device. It seems that the detectives, when confronted with a statement of dubious veracity, would sometimes adjourn to the Xerox room and load three sheets of paper into the feeder.

"Truth," said the first.

"Truth," said the second.

"Lie," said the third.

Then the suspect would be led into the room and told to put his hand against the side of the machine. The detectives would ask the man's name, listen to the answer, then hit the copy button.

Truth.

And where do you live?

Truth again.

And did you or did you not kill Tater, shooting him down like a dog in the 1200 block of North Durham Street?

Lie. Well, well: You lying motherfucker.

In Baltimore, the homicide detectives read newspaper accounts of the Detroit controversy and wondered why anyone had a problem. Polygraph by copier was an old trick; it had been attempted on more than one occasion in the sixth-floor Xerox room. * * *

Variations on the theme are limited only by a detective's imagination and his ability to sustain the fraud. But every bluff carries a corresponding risk, and a detective who tells a suspect his fingerprints are all over a crime scene loses all hope if the man knows he was wearing gloves. An interrogation room fraud is only as good as the material from which it was constructed—or, for that matter, as good as the suspect is witless—and a detective who underestimates his prey or overestimates his knowledge of the crime will lose precious credibility. Once a detective claims knowledge of a fact that the suspect knows to be untrue, the veil has been lifted, and the investigator is instead revealed as the liar. * * *

* * * [T]here can be no mistaking that critical moment, that light that shines from the other end of the tunnel when a guilty man is about to give it up. Later, after he's initialed each page and is alone again in the cubicle, there will be only exhaustion and, in some cases, depression. If he gets to brooding, there might even be a suicide attempt.

But that is epilogue. The emotive crest of a guilty man's performance comes in those cold moments before he opens his mouth and reaches for the Out. Just before a man gives up life and liberty in an interrogation room, his body acknowledges the defeat: His eyes are glazed, his jaw is slack, his body lists against the nearest wall or table edge. Some put their heads against the tabletop to steady themselves. Some become physically sick, holding their stomachs as if the problem were digestive: a few actually vomit.

At that critical moment, the detectives tell their suspects that they really are sick—sick of lying, sick of hiding. They tell them it's time to turn over a new leaf, that they'll only begin to feel better when they start to tell the truth. Amazingly enough, many of them actually believe it. As they reach for the ledge of that high window, they believe every last word of it.

"He came at you, right?"

"Yeah, he came at me."

The Out leads in.

NOTES AND QUESTIONS

1.   Simon's book gave rise to a television show named Homicide. For a riveting fictional account of a police interrogation, see the episode from the show's first season called "Three Men and Adena." Unlike the case in most TV police shows, the viewer *never knows* whether the suspect is guilty. Thus, the viewer is placed in the position of the interrogating officers, which makes the characters seem more real and less like actors.

Was the suspect in the Simon excerpt treated fairly by the Baltimore detectives? Does it matter? Are you sympathetic to the suspect or did you find yourself hoping that the police would obtain a confession? Is the outcome just?

2.   Assuming the facts in the Simon excerpt can be proved, do you see a *Miranda* violation? How often do you think detectives engage in conduct described in the excerpt? 2. *Suspects as thermometers?* The *Miranda* Court said that a suspect can invoke either the right to counsel or the right to remain silent at any time during interrogation. It seems likely that the Court thought a fair number of suspects would serve as "thermometers"—willing to talk until the discussion got too hot, at which point they would invoke and shut down the interrogation. A self-regulating procedure might have appealed to a Court that had struggled for decades trying to find a way to regulate police interrogation through judicial doctrine.

But as Professor William Stuntz has pointed out, if *Miranda* is to succeed as a self-regulating procedure, suspects must be generally willing to cut off questioning when it becomes too oppressive. William J. Stuntz, *Miranda's Mistake*, 99 Mich. L. Rev. 975 (2001). Two studies of police interrogation in the 1990s failed to find an appreciable number of that kind of suspect. A few suspects invoke their rights at the beginning, and many more waive their rights, but almost no one invokes in the midst of the interrogation. See Paul G. Cassell & Bret S. Hayman, *Police Interrogation in the 1990s: An Empirical Study of the Effects of Miranda*, 43 UCLA L. Rev. 839 (1996); Richard A. Leo, *Inside the Interrogation Room*, 86 J. Crim. L. & Criminology 266 (1996).

As Stuntz puts it at 991–92:

> One of two things is true: Either there is a significant amount of abusive police questioning, or there isn't. If there is, *Miranda* is a failure; it does not protect the suspects who need protecting. If there isn't, *Miranda* is pointless—it gives a few Silent Types [those who invoke prior to interrogation] a very valuable entitlement, but to no good end. Either way, *Miranda* accomplishes nothing save distributive perversity. After thirty-five years, we can be reasonably confident of this much: Suspects cannot regulate police interrogation. The law of police interrogation is broken, and needs fixing.

But perhaps the Court did not care whether *Miranda* regulated interrogation. Perhaps, as Professor Lawrence Rosenthal provocatively argues, all "that *Miranda* expects of suspects is that they will knowingly and intelligently decide whether to waive their Fifth Amendment rights, and under settled waiver principles, suspects facing interrogation are perfectly competent to engage in such 'sorting.' " After all, the due process clause is still available to regulate abusive interrogation. See Lawrence Rosenthal, *Against Orthodoxy Miranda Is Not Prophylactic and the Constitution Is Not Perfect,* 10 Chapman L. Rev. 579, 604 (2007).

3.   *Problems.*

A.   *P*, a murder suspect, was arrested and held for nineteen hours before police questioned him. During this period, police obtained information about the victim and the crime scene. Ten minutes into the interrogation, *P* waived his *Miranda* rights in writing. When told that he was suspected of the murder, he gave an alibi. Police then told him that they had spoken to an eyewitness. When *P* said nothing, police played an audiotape in which one police officer pretended to be an eyewitness being questioned by an officer. At one point the "eyewitness" identifies a picture of *P*. "Immediately after the investigators played the audiotape, defendant asked: 'Who was that motherfucker?' Defendant then confessed and agreed to give a taped statement." Admissible? See State v. Patton, 362 N.J.Super. 16, 826 A.2d 783 (2003). See also Commonwealth v. DiGiambattista, 442 Mass. 423, 813 N.E.2d 516 (Sup. Jud. Ct. 2004).

B.   Police question *W* about her husband's murder. She waives her *Miranda* rights in writing, using a pen police provide. The pen has a powder on it that makes her hands glow under a certain light. They then tell her that the glow is gunpowder residue from killing her husband. After interviewing her off and on over the next eighteen hours, police secure two incriminating statements. Admissible? See Whittington v. State, 147 Md.App. 496, 809 A.2d 721 (2002). See also Sheriff v. Bessey, 112 Nev. 322, 914 P.2d 618 (1996); Arthur v. Commonwealth, 24 Va.App. 102, 480 S.E.2d 749 (1997).

C.   The police suspect *C* of sexually assaulting and smothering his five-year-old niece. After an "extensive interview," police did not think that they had sufficient evidence with which to charge him. With the knowledge of the state attorney's office, the police fabricated two scientific reports that they used as ploys in interrogating the defendant. One false report was prepared on stationery of the Florida Department of Criminal Law Enforcement; another was prepared on stationery of Life Codes, Inc., a testing organization. These false reports indicated that a scientific test established that the semen stains on the victim's underwear came from the defendant. The police showed the reports to the defendant after he had formally waived his *Miranda* rights. He confessed. Admissible? See State v. Cayward, 552 So.2d 971 (Fla. App. 1989).

D.   *J*, a murder suspect, waived *Miranda* and was interviewed for three hours and released; the next day, again waiving *Miranda*, he was questioned and told that the clothes he wore the day of the murder were stained with blood, and that tracks made by his tennis shoes were found at the scene of the crime. Both statements were false. *J* did not confess. Ten days later, *J* voluntarily came to the police station and waived *Miranda*; he was shown a bloody fingerprint on a knife. The police said that the print on the knife was *J*'s and that an eyewitness could identify *J* leaving the murdered woman's apartment carrying a knife. Both statements were false. In addition, the officers said that if *J* denied what he had done, they would "go into court and testify that he was a black man out there viciously raping and killing white women." *J* confessed. Is it admissible under *Miranda*? Was it coerced under the due process clause? Should it matter that the case occurs in a Southern state? See State v. Jackson, 308 N.C. 549, 304 S.E.2d 134 (1983).

4. *Does Miranda help the police?* Is it possible that *Miranda* has helped police and prosecutors in obtaining statements? Empirical evidence indicates that the police almost always provide *Miranda* warnings. This suggests that police do not view *Miranda* as a particularly difficult burden. Moreover, because the police almost always obtain waivers in cases where suspects incriminate themselves, the prosecutor comes to court with an oral or written waiver of the right not to be interrogated. This creates a pretty strong presumption that the suspect *wanted* to talk to the police. The waiver not only virtually guarantees that a court will find no *Miranda* violation, but also may reduce the willingness of courts to inquire into the coerciveness of the police interrogation that follows waiver. If *Miranda* has helped police and prosecutors more than defendants, it would be a remarkable irony.

Charles Weisselberg presses deeper than irony, noting that

> if *Miranda*'s system of warnings and waivers is not effective in protecting the Fifth Amendment privilege for many suspects, this wholesale displacement of the voluntariness doctrine is a sleight-of-hand; it is bottomed on a falsehood. I am not against warnings and waivers per se, just the assumed effect of them. For me, the main problem with *Miranda* is the judiciary's unjustified confidence in *Miranda*'s safeguards. There is an almost religious belief that the warnings and waivers actually work, and an apparent deafness to claims that they do not. I am not the first to observe that *Miranda* can be an obstacle to the more important assessment of voluntariness; Professor Alfredo Garcia has made the point with particular force. I once was a proponent of *Miranda*, but I now believe that its critics are right.

Charles D. Weisselberg, *Mourning Miranda*, 96 Cal. L. Rev. 1519, 1595–96 (2008). The provocative Garcia article to which Weisselberg refers is Alfredo Garcia, *Is Miranda Dead, Was It Overruled, or Is It Irrelevant?*, 10 St. Thomas L. Rev. 461 (1988).

5. *Hoax?* One scholar puts his criticism of *Miranda* more simply: "*Miranda v. Arizona* is a hoax." Christopher Slobogin, *Toward Taping*, 1 Ohio St. J. Crim. L. 309, 309 (2003).

6. *Mourning Miranda.* Charles Weisselberg offers the following sad farewell to *Miranda*:

> *Miranda* launched a forty-year experiment in reforming police practices. I think the Court was right to try; sometimes there can be no progress without experimentation. Now, four decades later, we know that a set of bright-line rules is not a panacea for the issues endemic in police interrogation. I mourn the passing of *Miranda*. I deeply regret that the justices' ambitions and expectations were not

met. However, I think that the best way to mourn the loss is to learn from the experiment called *Miranda*, acknowledge its failures, and move forward.

Weisselberg, supra Note 4, at 1599–1600.

CHAPTER 8

POLICE INTERROGATION: THE SIXTH AMENDMENT RIGHT TO COUNSEL

■ ■ ■

A. ELICITING STATEMENTS IN THE ABSENCE OF COUNSEL

MASSIAH V. UNITED STATES

Supreme Court of the United States, 1964.
377 U.S. 201, 84 S.Ct. 1199, 12 L.Ed.2d 246.

MR. JUSTICE STEWART delivered the opinion of the Court [joined by CHIEF JUSTICE WARREN, and JUSTICES BLACK, DOUGLAS, CLARK, and GOLDBERG].

The petitioner was indicted for violating the federal narcotics laws. He retained a lawyer, pleaded not guilty, and was released on bail. * * *

A few days later, and quite without the petitioner's knowledge, [co-defendant] Colson decided to cooperate with the government agents in their continuing investigation of the narcotics activities in which the petitioner, Colson, and others had allegedly been engaged. Colson permitted an agent named Murphy to install a Schmidt radio transmitter under the front seat of Colson's automobile, by means of which Murphy, equipped with an appropriate receiving device, could overhear from some distance away conversations carried on in Colson's car.

On the evening of November 19, 1959, Colson and the petitioner held a lengthy conversation while sitting in Colson's automobile, parked on a New York street. By prearrangement with Colson, and totally unbeknown to the petitioner, the agent Murphy sat in a car parked out of sight down the street and listened over the radio to the entire conversation. The petitioner made several incriminating statements during the course of this conversation. At the petitioner's trial these incriminating statements were brought before the jury through Murphy's testimony, despite the insistent objection of defense counsel. The jury convicted the petitioner of several related narcotics offenses, and the convictions were affirmed by the Court of Appeals.

The petitioner argues that it was an error of constitutional dimensions to permit the agent Murphy at the trial to testify to the petitioner's incriminating statements which Murphy had overheard under the circumstances disclosed by this record. This argument is based upon two distinct and independent grounds. [The Court did not reach the Fourth Amendment argument.] Secondly, it is said that the petitioner's Fifth and Sixth Amendment rights were violated by the use in evidence against him of incriminating statements which government agents had deliberately elicited from him after he had been indicted and in the absence of his retained counsel. * * *

In *Spano v. New York* [p. 603], this Court reversed a state criminal conviction because a confession had been wrongly admitted into evidence against the defendant at his trial. In that case the defendant had already been indicted for first-degree murder at the time he confessed. The Court held that the defendant's conviction could not stand under the Fourteenth Amendment. While the Court's opinion relied upon the totality of the circumstances under which the confession had been obtained, four concurring Justices pointed out that the Constitution required reversal of the conviction upon the sole and specific ground that the confession had been deliberately elicited by the police after the defendant had been indicted, and therefore at a time when he was clearly entitled to a lawyer's help. It was pointed out that under our system of justice the most elemental concepts of due process of law contemplate that an indictment be followed by a trial, "in an orderly courtroom, presided over by a judge, open to the public, and protected by all the procedural safeguards of the law." It was said that a Constitution which guarantees a defendant the aid of counsel at such a trial could surely vouchsafe no less to an indicted defendant under interrogation by the police in a completely extrajudicial proceeding. Anything less, it was said, might deny a defendant "effective representation by counsel at the only stage when legal aid and advice would help him." * * *

This view no more than reflects a constitutional principle established as long ago as *Powell v. Alabama* [p. 25] where the Court noted that " * * * during perhaps the most critical period of the proceedings * * * that is to say, from the time of their arraignment until the beginning of their trial, when consultation, thorough-going investigation and preparation [are] vitally important, the defendants * * * [are] as much entitled to such aid [of counsel] during that period as at the trial itself." * * *

Here we deal not with a state court conviction, but with a federal case, where the specific guarantee of the Sixth Amendment directly applies. We hold that the petitioner was denied the basic protections of that guarantee when there was used against him at his trial evidence of his own incriminating words, which federal agents had deliberately elicited from him after he had been indicted and in the absence of his counsel. It is true that in the *Spano* case the defendant was interrogated in a police station, while here the damaging testimony was elicited from the defendant without his knowledge while he was free on bail. But, as Judge Hays pointed out in his dissent in the Court of Appeals, "if such a rule is to have any efficacy it must apply to indirect and surreptitious interrogations as well as those conducted in the jailhouse. In this case, Massiah was more seriously imposed upon * * * because he did not even know that he was under interrogation by a government agent."

* * * We do not question that in this case, as in many cases, it was entirely proper to continue an investigation of the suspected criminal activities of the defendant and his alleged confederates, even though the defendant had already been indicted. All that we hold is that the defendant's own incriminating statements, obtained by federal agents under the circumstances here disclosed, could not constitutionally be used by the prosecution as evidence against *him* at his trial. * * *

MR. JUSTICE WHITE, with whom MR. JUSTICE CLARK and MR. JUSTICE HARLAN join, dissenting. * * *

It is * * * a rather portentous occasion when a constitutional rule is established barring the use of evidence which is relevant, reliable and highly probative of the issue which the trial court has before it—whether the accused committed the act with which he is charged. Without the evidence, the quest for truth may be seriously impeded and in many cases the trial court, although aware of proof showing defendant's guilt, must nevertheless release him because the crucial evidence is deemed inadmissible. This result is entirely justified in some circumstances because exclusion serves other policies of overriding importance, as where evidence seized in an illegal search is excluded, not because of the quality of the proof, but to secure meaningful enforcement of the Fourth Amendment. But this only emphasizes that the soundest of reasons is necessary to warrant the exclusion of evidence otherwise admissible and the creation of another area of privileged testimony. With all due deference, I am not at all convinced that the additional barriers to the pursuit of truth which the Court today erects rest on anything like the solid foundations which decisions of this gravity should require. * * *

Whatever the content or scope of the rule may prove to be, I am unable to see how this case presents an unconstitutional interference with Massiah's right to counsel. Massiah was not prevented from consulting with counsel as often as he wished. No meetings with counsel were disturbed or spied upon. Preparation for trial was in no way obstructed. It is only a sterile syllogism—an unsound one, besides—to say that because Massiah had a right to counsel's aid before and during the trial, his out-of-court conversations and admissions must be excluded if obtained without counsel's consent or presence. The right to counsel has never meant as much before, and its extension in this case requires some further explanation, so far unarticulated by the Court. * * *

Applying the new exclusionary rule is peculiarly inappropriate in this case. At the time of the conversation in question, petitioner was not in custody but free on bail. He was not questioned in what anyone could call an atmosphere of official coercion. What he said was said to his partner in crime who had also been indicted. There was no suggestion or any possibility of coercion. What petitioner did not know was that Colson had decided to report the conversation to the police. Had there been no prior arrangements between Colson and the police, had Colson simply gone to the police after the conversation had occurred, his testimony relating Massiah's statements would be readily admissible at the trial, as would a recording which he might have made of the conversation. In such event, it would simply be said that Massiah risked talking to a friend who decided to disclose what he knew of Massiah's criminal activities. But if, as occurred here, Colson had been cooperating with the police prior to his meeting with Massiah, both his evidence and the recorded conversation are somehow transformed into inadmissible evidence despite the fact that the hazard to Massiah remains precisely the same—the defection of a confederate in crime. * * *

* * * It is one thing to establish safeguards against procedures fraught with the potentiality of coercion and to outlaw "easy but self-defeating ways in which brutality is substituted for brains as an instrument of crime detection." But here there was no substitution of brutality for brains, no inherent danger of police coercion justifying the prophylactic effect of another exclusionary rule. Massiah was not being interrogated in a police station, was not surrounded by numerous officers or questioned in relays, and was not forbidden access to others. Law enforcement may have the elements of a contest about it, but it is not a game. Massiah and those like him receive ample protection from the long line of precedents in this Court holding that confessions may not be introduced unless they are voluntary. In making these determinations the courts must consider the absence of counsel as one of several factors by which voluntariness is to be judged. This is a wiser rule than the automatic rule announced by the Court, which requires courts and juries to disregard voluntary admissions which they might well find to be the best possible evidence in discharging their responsibility for ascertaining truth.

NOTES AND QUESTIONS

1.   Notice that *Massiah* predates *Miranda* by two years. Justice White's dissent characterized the *Massiah* rationale as a "thinly disguised constitutional policy of minimizing or entirely prohibiting the use in evidence of voluntary out-of-court admissions and confessions made by the accused." As we have seen, the Court would soon apply this policy with a vengeance in

Miranda by giving all suspects the right to remain silent and the right to counsel. Predictably, Justice White dissented in *Miranda* as well.

2.   In the mid-eighteenth century, the role of defense counsel was minimal. In one sample of New Jersey cases from 1749–57, roughly half of the defendants represented themselves, presenting evidence as best they could. But even when lawyers appeared for defendants, their role appeared to be summing up at the end of the trial by making any points of law that might be helpful. This is consistent with English law that prohibited lawyers in felony cases from presenting the defendant's case, though lawyers could argue "points of law." In one New Jersey case, the judge appointed counsel but apparently not until after the defendant had already presented her case; the lawyer's job presumably was to sum up the case and argue points of law (she lost and was sentenced to hang). See George C. Thomas III, *Colonial Criminal Law and Procedure: The Royal Colony of New Jersey 1749–57*, 1 N.Y.U. J. L. & Liberty 671, 687–88 (2005).

Assuming that this was the model the Framers had in mind when they guaranteed the "assistance of counsel" for defendants, was it illegitimate for the *Massiah* Court to radically expand the meaning of assistance of counsel? Inappropriate? The wrong road taken?

3.   Think back to what constituted a valid waiver of *Miranda*. Using that test, do you think Massiah could have waived his right to counsel? Turning the question around, what purpose would Massiah's lawyer have served if he had been in the car with Massiah and Colson? If you don't like what the Government did in this case, what *precisely* is it that you think was improper?

4.   *Rights and remedies.* Can a statement taken in violation of Massiah be used to impeach a defendant's testimony? Yes, the Court held in Kansas v. Ventris, 556 U.S. 586, 129 S.Ct. 1841, 173 L.Ed.2d 801 (2009):

> Whether otherwise excluded evidence [statements made by Ventris suppressed in State's case] can be admitted for purposes of impeachment depends upon the nature of the constitutional guarantee that is violated. Sometimes that explicitly mandates exclusion from trial, and sometimes it does not. The Fifth Amendment guarantees that no person shall be compelled to give evidence against himself, and so is violated whenever a truly coerced confession is introduced at trial, whether by way of impeachment or otherwise. The Fourth Amendment, on the other hand, guarantees that no person shall be subjected to unreasonable searches or seizures, and says nothing about excluding their fruits from evidence; exclusion comes by way of deterrent sanction rather than to avoid violation of the substantive guarantee. Inadmissibility has not been automatic, therefore, but we have instead applied an exclusionary-rule balancing test. The same is true for violations of the Fifth and Sixth Amendment prophylactic rules forbidding certain pretrial police conduct.

Respondent argues that the Sixth Amendment's right to counsel is a "right an accused is to enjoy a[t] trial." The core of the right to counsel is indeed a trial right, ensuring that the prosecution's case is subjected to "the crucible of meaningful adversarial testing." But our opinions under the Sixth Amendment, as under the Fifth, have held that the right covers pretrial interrogations to ensure that police manipulation does not render counsel entirely impotent—depriving the defendant of " 'effective representation by counsel at the only stage when legal aid and advice would help him.' "

The Court thus held that the Massiah right is violated at the moment police deliberately elicit statements in the absence of counsel and without waiver. When the statements are introduced at trial, no new violation occurs, just like in the Fourth Amendment context. This is to be contrasted with the right against compelled self-incrimination, which is not violated until the statements are introduced at trial. The question, then, was remedy.

Our precedents make clear that the game of excluding tainted evidence for impeachment purposes is not worth the candle. The interests safeguarded by such exclusion are "outweighed by the need to prevent perjury and to assure the integrity of the trial process." "It is one thing to say that the Government cannot make an affirmative use of evidence unlawfully obtained. It is quite another to say that the defendant can * * * provide himself with a shield against contradiction of his untruths." Once the defendant testifies in a way that contradicts prior statements, denying the prosecution use of "the traditional truth-testing devices of the adversary process," is a high price to pay for vindication of the right to counsel at the prior stage. * * *

We hold that the informant's testimony, concededly elicited in violation of the Sixth Amendment, was admissible to challenge Ventris's inconsistent testimony at trial. The judgment of the Kansas Supreme Court is reversed, and the case is remanded for further proceedings not inconsistent with this opinion.

Justice Stevens dissented, joined by Justice Ginsburg.

Treating the State's actions in this case as a violation of a prophylactic right, the Court concludes that introducing the illegally obtained evidence at trial does not itself violate the Constitution. I strongly disagree. While the constitutional breach began at the time of interrogation, the State's use of that evidence at trial compounded the violation. * * * The use of ill-gotten evidence during any phase of criminal prosecution does damage to the adversarial process—the fairness of which the Sixth Amendment was designed to protect.

When counsel is excluded from a critical pretrial interaction between the defendant and the State, she may be unable to effectively counter the potentially devastating, and potentially false, evidence subsequently introduced at trial. Inexplicably, today's Court refuses to recognize that this is a constitutional harm. Yet in *Massiah,* the Court forcefully explained that a defendant is "denied the basic protections of the [Sixth Amendment] guarantee when there [is] used against him at his trial evidence of his own incriminating words" that were "deliberately elicited from him after he had been indicted and in the absence of counsel." Sadly, the majority has retreated from this robust understanding of the right to counsel.

Today's decision is lamentable not only because of its flawed underpinnings, but also because it is another occasion in which the Court has privileged the prosecution at the expense of the Constitution. Permitting the State to cut corners in criminal proceedings taxes the legitimacy of the entire criminal process. "The State's interest in truthseeking is congruent with the defendant's interest in representation by counsel, for it is an elementary premise of our system of criminal justice 'that partisan advocacy on both sides of a case will best promote the ultimate objective that the guilty be convicted and the innocent go free.'" Although the Court may not be concerned with the use of ill-gotten evidence in derogation of the right to counsel, I remain convinced that such shabby tactics are intolerable in all cases. I respectfully dissent.

Deliberate Elicitation: The Doctrine Evolves

In *Massiah,* the Government was actively seeking to elicit statements from the accused in the absence of counsel. But the Court has decided two cases in which this was not so clear. In United States v. Henry, 447 U.S. 264, 100 S.Ct. 2183, 65 L.Ed.2d 115 (1980), Henry was indicted for bank robbery and held in jail. The government agents working on the robbery contacted Nichols, an inmate at the same jail as Henry, who "had been engaged to provide confidential information to the Federal Bureau of Investigation as a paid informant. * * * Nichols informed the agent that he was housed in the same cellblock with several federal prisoners awaiting trial, including Henry." Nichols testified at trial that Henry told him about the robbery.

As Henry had been indicted, he was in the same position as Massiah with regard to his right to counsel. But had Nichols deliberately elicited the admissions from Henry? Here is what the government agent said in his affidavit concerning the instructions given Nichols:

"I recall telling Nichols at this time to be alert to any statements made by these individuals [the federal prisoners] regarding the charges against them. I specifically recall telling Nichols that he was not to question Henry or these individuals about the charges against them, however, if they engaged him in conversation or talked in front of him, he was requested to pay attention to their statements. I recall telling Nichols not to initiate any conversations with Henry regarding the bank robbery charges against Henry, but that if Henry initiated the conversations with Nichols, I requested Nichols to pay attention to the information furnished by Henry."

Was this "deliberate elicitation"? In an opinion by Chief Justice Burger, the Court held that it was. The Court reasoned that "[e]ven if the agent's statement that he did not intend that Nichols would take affirmative steps to secure incriminating information is accepted, he must have known that such propinquity likely would lead to that result." Moreover, the Court noted that "[i]n *Massiah*, no inquiry was made as to whether Massiah or his codefendant first raised the subject of the crime under investigation."

True enough but the *Massiah* Court concluded that the agents had "deliberately elicited" statements from Massiah. Could the same be said in *Henry*? It seems that the Court in *Henry* was rejecting a narrow meaning of "deliberate elicitation." *Henry* seems to stand for the proposition that "deliberate elicitation" means "deliberately put an agent in a situation where it is likely that he will hear incriminating statements." Perhaps there is no Sixth Amendment distinction between intending to elicit statements and intending to put an agent in a position where he was likely to obtain statements.

The reason to treat those two situations alike, as *Massiah* noted, is that suspects like Henry and Massiah are "more seriously imposed upon because he did not know that his codefendant was a Government agent." This, of course, is because "[a]n accused speaking to a known Government agent is typically aware that his statements may be used against him," but not when "the accused is in the company of a fellow inmate who is acting by prearrangement as a Government agent."

But Kuhlmann v. Wilson, 477 U.S. 436, 106 S.Ct. 2616, 91 L.Ed.2d 364 (1986), makes clear that the informant must do more than merely listen. The Court accepted as true for purposes of federal habeas review of a state conviction that the informant placed in the cell functioned only as an "ear" to listen to his cell mate. The Court then stressed that

the primary concern of the *Massiah* line of decisions is secret interrogation by investigatory techniques that are the equivalent of direct police interrogation. Since "the Sixth Amendment is not violated whenever—by luck or happenstance—the State obtains incriminating statements from the accused after the right to counsel has attached," a defendant does not make out a violation of that right simply by showing that an informant, either through prior arrangement or voluntarily, reported his incriminating statements to the police. Rather, the defendant must demonstrate that the police and their informant took some action, beyond merely listening, that was designed deliberately to elicit incriminating remarks.

NOTES AND QUESTIONS

1.   In Maine v. Moulton, 474 US 159, 106 S. Ct. 477, 88 L. Ed. 2d 481 (1985), Moulton and Colson were indicted for four thefts. When police learned that Moulton had talked of killing one of the State's witnesses, they arranged with Colson to record telephone calls from Moulton and to wear a body wire in a face-to-face meeting. After the recordings, the State brought new indictments for burglary, arson, and three additional thefts based on incriminating statements made by Moulton to Colson.

The State claimed it was not attempting to elicit incriminating statements from Moulton about the indicted crimes; the purpose, instead, was to elicit statements about the plan to kill one of the State's witnesses and, in the case of the body wire, to protect Colson in case Moulton suspected he was wired.

The Court held that what happened was deliberate elicitation under *Henry* and that the State's asserted legitimate investigative purpose did not provide an exception to *Massiah*'s protection.

> The Sixth Amendment guarantees the accused, at least after the initiation of formal charges, the right to rely on counsel as a "medium" between him and the State. * * * [T]his guarantee includes the State's affirmative obligation not to act in a manner that circumvents the protections accorded the accused [even when it has a legitimate investigative purpose.]. * * * [To hold otherwise] invites abuse by law enforcement personnel in the form of fabricated investigations and risks the evisceration of the Sixth Amendment right recognized in *Massiah*.

But the Court noted that the statements pertaining to the burglary, arson, and three additional thefts were not barred by the Sixth Amendment because there were no pending indictments on those charges at the time the statements were recorded. The Court said it did not want to "unnecessarily frustrate the public's interest in the investigation of criminal activities." Chief Justice Burger and Justices White, Rehnquist, and O'Connor dissented; they would have admitted all the statements as a kind of good-faith exception to *Massiah*.

2.   The cases so far have involved covert police interrogation. But what about overt police interrogation. *Massiah* was decided two years before *Miranda*. It might seem (it seemed to one of the authors of the casebook) that

Miranda rendered *Massiah* superfluous in the context of overt police interrogation. *Miranda*, after all, created its own right to counsel that protected suspects from having to face police interrogation without the aid of counsel. Why wouldn't a violation of *Massiah* in the context of police interrogation always be a violation of *Miranda*? The next case raises, but does not dispose of, this question.

B. *MASSIAH* WAIVER

BREWER V. WILLIAMS
Supreme Court of the United States, 1977.
430 U.S. 387, 97 S.Ct. 1232, 51 L.Ed.2d 424.

MR. JUSTICE STEWART delivered the opinion of the Court [joined by JUSTICES BRENNAN, MARSHALL, POWELL, and STEVENS]. * * *

I

On the afternoon of December 24, 1968, a 10-year-old girl named Pamela Powers went with her family to the YMCA in Des Moines, Iowa, to watch a wrestling tournament in which her brother was participating. When she failed to return from a trip to the washroom, a search for her began. The search was unsuccessful.

Robert Williams, who had recently escaped from a mental hospital, was a resident of the YMCA. Soon after the girl's disappearance Williams was seen in the YMCA lobby carrying some clothing and a large bundle wrapped in a blanket. He obtained help from a 14-year-old boy in opening the street door of the YMCA and the door to his automobile parked outside. When Williams placed the bundle in the front seat of his car the boy "saw two legs in it and they were skinny and white." Before anyone could see what was in the bundle Williams drove away. His abandoned car was found the following day in Davenport, Iowa, roughly 160 miles east of Des Moines. A warrant was then issued in Des Moines for his arrest on a charge of abduction.

On the morning of December 26, a Des Moines lawyer named Henry McKnight went to the Des Moines police station and informed the officers present that he had just received a long-distance call from Williams, and that he had advised Williams to turn himself in to the Davenport police. Williams did surrender that morning to the police in Davenport, and they booked him on the charge specified in the arrest warrant and gave him the warnings required by *Miranda v. Arizona*. The Davenport police then telephoned their counterparts in Des Moines to inform them that Williams had surrendered. McKnight, the lawyer, was still at the Des Moines police headquarters, and Williams conversed with McKnight on the telephone. In the presence of the Des Moines chief of police and a police detective named Leaming, McKnight advised Williams that Des

Moines police officers would be driving to Davenport to pick him up, that the officers would not interrogate him or mistreat him, and that Williams was not to talk to the officers about Pamela Powers until after consulting with McKnight upon his return to Des Moines. As a result of these conversations, it was agreed between McKnight and the Des Moines police officials that Detective Leaming and a fellow officer would drive to Davenport to pick up Williams, that they would bring him directly back to Des Moines, and that they would not question him during the trip.

In the meantime Williams was arraigned before a judge in Davenport on the outstanding arrest warrant. The judge advised him of his *Miranda* rights and committed him to jail. Before leaving the courtroom, Williams conferred with a lawyer named Kelly, who advised him not to make any statements until consulting with McKnight back in Des Moines.

Detective Leaming and his fellow officer arrived in Davenport about noon to pick up Williams and return him to Des Moines. Soon after their arrival they met with Williams and Kelly, who, they understood, was acting as Williams' lawyer. Detective Leaming repeated the *Miranda* warnings, and told Williams:

> "[W]e both know that you're being represented here by Mr. Kelly and you're being represented by Mr. McKnight in Des Moines, and * * * I want you to remember this because we'll be visiting between here and Des Moines."

Williams then conferred again with Kelly alone, and after this conference Kelly reiterated to Detective Leaming that Williams was not to be questioned about the disappearance of Pamela Powers until after he had consulted with McKnight back in Des Moines. When Leaming expressed some reservations, Kelly firmly stated that the agreement with McKnight was to be carried out—that there was to be no interrogation of Williams during the automobile journey to Des Moines. Kelly was denied permission to ride in the police car back to Des Moines with Williams and the two officers.

The two detectives, with Williams in their charge, then set out on the 160-mile drive. At no time during the trip did Williams express a willingness to be interrogated in the absence of an attorney. Instead, he stated several times that "[w]hen I get to Des Moines and see Mr. McKnight, I am going to tell you the whole story." Detective Leaming knew that Williams was a former mental patient, and knew also that he was deeply religious.

The detective and his prisoner soon embarked on a wide-ranging conversation covering a variety of topics, including the subject of religion. Then, not long after leaving Davenport and reaching the interstate highway, Detective Leaming delivered what has been referred to in the briefs and oral arguments as the "Christian burial speech." Addressing Williams as "Reverend," the detective said:

> "I want to give you something to think about while we're traveling down the road. * * * Number one, I want you to observe the weather conditions, it's raining, it's sleeting, it's freezing, driving is very treacherous, visibility is poor, it's going to be dark early this evening. They are predicting several inches of snow for tonight, and I feel that you yourself are the only person that knows where this little girl's body is, that you yourself have only been there once, and if you get a snow on top of it you yourself may be unable to find it. And, since we will be going right past the area on the way into Des Moines, I feel that we could stop and locate the body, that the parents of this little girl should be entitled to a Christian burial for the little girl who was snatched away from them on Christmas [E]ve and murdered. And I feel we should stop and locate it on the way in rather than waiting until morning and trying to come back out after a snow storm and possibly not being able to find it at all."

Williams asked Detective Leaming why he thought their route to Des Moines would be taking them past the girl's body, and Leaming responded that he knew the body was in the area of Mitchellville—a town they would be passing on the way to Des Moines.[1] Leaming then stated: "I do not want you to answer me. I don't want to discuss it any further. Just think about it as we're riding down the road."

As the car approached Grinnell, a town approximately 100 miles west of Davenport, Williams asked whether the police had found the victim's shoes. When Detective Leaming replied that he was unsure, Williams directed the officers to a service station where he said he had left the shoes; a search for them proved unsuccessful. As they continued towards Des Moines, Williams asked whether the police had found the blanket, and directed the officers to a rest area where he said he had disposed of the blanket. Nothing was found. The car continued towards Des Moines, and as it approached Mitchellville, Williams said that he would show the officers where the body was. He then directed the police to the body of Pamela Powers.

Williams was indicted for first-degree murder. Before trial, his counsel moved to suppress all evidence relating to or resulting from any statements Williams had made during the automobile ride from Davenport to Des Moines. After an evidentiary hearing the trial judge denied the motion. He found that "an agreement was made between defense counsel and the police officials to the effect that the Defendant

---

[1] The fact of the matter, of course, was that Detective Leaming possessed no such knowledge.

was not to be questioned on the return trip to Des Moines," and that the evidence in question had been elicited from Williams during "a critical stage in the proceedings requiring the presence of counsel on his request." The judge ruled, however, that Williams had "waived his right to have an attorney present during the giving of such information."

The evidence in question was introduced over counsel's continuing objection at the subsequent trial. The jury found Williams guilty of murder [and the Iowa Supreme Court affirmed]. * * *

[The federal district court granted a petition for a writ of habeas corpus, concluding] as a matter of law that the evidence in question had been wrongly admitted at Williams' trial. This conclusion was based on three alternative and independent grounds: (1) that Williams had been denied his constitutional right to the assistance of counsel; (2) that he had been denied the constitutional protections defined by this Court's decisions in *Escobedo v. Illinois* [p. 623, Note 2] and *Miranda v. Arizona* [p. 625]; and (3) that in any event, his self-incriminatory statements on the automobile trip from Davenport to Des Moines had been involuntarily made. Further, the District Court ruled that there had been no waiver by Williams of the constitutional protections in question. * * *

II * * *

B

As stated above, the District Court based its judgment in this case on three independent grounds. The Court of Appeals appears to have affirmed the judgment on two of those grounds. We have concluded that only one of them need be considered here.

Specifically, there is no need to review in this case the doctrine of *Miranda v. Arizona*, a doctrine designed to secure the constitutional privilege against compulsory self-incrimination. It is equally unnecessary to evaluate the ruling of the District Court that Williams' self-incriminating statements were, indeed, involuntarily made. For it is clear that the judgment before us must in any event be affirmed upon the ground that Williams was deprived of a different constitutional right—the right to the assistance of counsel. * * *

There has occasionally been a difference of opinion within the Court as to the peripheral scope of this constitutional right. * * * Whatever else it may mean, the right to counsel granted by the Sixth and Fourteenth Amendments means at least that a person is entitled to the help of a lawyer at or after the time that judicial proceedings have been initiated against him "whether by way of formal charge, preliminary hearing, indictment, information, or arraignment."

There can be no doubt in the present case that judicial proceedings had been initiated against Williams before the start of the automobile ride from Davenport to Des Moines. A warrant had been issued for his arrest, he had been arraigned on that warrant before a judge in a Davenport courtroom, and he had been committed by the court to confinement in jail. The State does not contend otherwise.

There can be no serious doubt, either, that Detective Leaming deliberately and designedly set out to elicit information from Williams just as surely as—and perhaps more effectively than—if he had formally interrogated him. Detective Leaming was fully aware before departing for Des Moines that Williams was being represented in Davenport by Kelly and in Des Moines by McKnight. Yet he purposely sought during Williams' isolation from his lawyers to obtain as much incriminating information as possible. Indeed, Detective Leaming conceded as much when he testified at Williams' trial:

> "Q. In fact, Captain, whether he was a mental patient or not, you were trying to get all the information you could before he got to his lawyer, weren't you?

> "A. I was sure hoping to find out where that little girl was, yes, sir. * * *

> "Q. Well, I'll put it this way: You was [sic] hoping to get all the information you could before Williams got back to McKnight, weren't you?

> "A. Yes, sir."

The state courts clearly proceeded upon the hypothesis that Detective Leaming's "Christian burial speech" had been tantamount to interrogation. * * *

The circumstances of this case are thus constitutionally indistinguishable from those presented in *Massiah v. United States*. * * *

That the incriminating statements were elicited surreptitiously in the *Massiah* case, and otherwise here, is constitutionally irrelevant. Rather, the clear rule of *Massiah* is that once adversary proceedings have commenced against an individual, he has a right to legal representation when the government interrogates him.[8] It thus requires no wooden or technical application of the *Massiah* doctrine to conclude that Williams was entitled to the assistance of counsel guaranteed to him by the Sixth and Fourteenth Amendments.

---

[8] The only other significant factual difference between the present case and *Massiah* is that here the police had agreed that they would not interrogate Williams in the absence of his counsel. This circumstance plainly provides petitioner with no argument for distinguishing away the protection afforded by *Massiah*. * * *

III

The Iowa courts recognized that Williams had been denied the constitutional right to the assistance of counsel. They held, however, that he had waived that right during the course of the automobile trip from Davenport to Des Moines. * * *

In its lengthy opinion affirming this determination, the Iowa Supreme Court applied "the totality-of-circumstances test for a showing of waiver of constitutionally-protected rights in the absence of an express waiver," and concluded that "evidence of the time element involved on the trip, the general circumstances of it, and the absence of any request or expressed desire for the aid of counsel before or at the time of giving information, were sufficient to sustain a conclusion that defendant did waive his constitutional rights as alleged."

In the federal habeas corpus proceeding the District Court, believing that the issue of waiver was not one of fact but of federal law, held that the Iowa courts had "applied the wrong constitutional standards" in ruling that Williams had waived the protections that were his under the Constitution. * * *

The District Court and the Court of Appeals were * * * correct in their understanding of the proper standard to be applied in determining the question of waiver as a matter of federal constitutional law—that it was incumbent upon the State to prove "an intentional relinquishment or abandonment of a known right or privilege." *Johnson v. Zerbst*, [304 U.S. 458, 464, 58 S.Ct. 1019, 1023, 82 L.Ed. 1461 (1938)]. That standard has been reiterated in many cases. We have said that the right to counsel does not depend upon a request by the defendant, and that courts indulge in every reasonable presumption against waiver. This strict standard applies equally to an alleged waiver of the right to counsel whether at trial or at a critical stage of pretrial proceedings.

We conclude, finally, that the Court of Appeals was correct in holding that, judged by these standards, the record in this case falls far short of sustaining petitioner's burden. It is true that Williams had been informed of and appeared to understand his right to counsel. But waiver requires not merely comprehension but relinquishment, and Williams' consistent reliance upon the advice of counsel in dealing with the authorities refutes any suggestion that he waived that right. He consulted McKnight by long-distance telephone before turning himself in. He spoke with McKnight by telephone again shortly after being booked. After he was arraigned, Williams sought out and obtained legal advice from Kelly. Williams again consulted with Kelly after Detective Leaming and his fellow officer arrived in Davenport. Throughout, Williams was advised not to make any statements before seeing McKnight in Des Moines, and was assured that the police had agreed not to question him. His statements while in the car that he would tell the whole story *after* seeing McKnight in Des Moines were the clearest expressions by Williams himself that he desired the presence of an attorney before any interrogation took place. But even before making these statements, Williams had effectively asserted his right to counsel by having secured attorneys at both ends of the automobile trip, both of whom, acting as his agents, had made clear to the police that no interrogation was to occur during the journey. Williams knew of that agreement and, particularly in view of his consistent reliance on counsel, there is no basis for concluding that he disavowed it.

Despite Williams' express and implicit assertions of his right to counsel, Detective Leaming proceeded to elicit incriminating statements from Williams. Leaming did not preface this effort by telling Williams that he had a right to the presence of a lawyer, and made no effort at all to ascertain whether Williams wished to relinquish that right. The circumstances of record in this case thus provide no reasonable basis for finding that Williams waived his right to the assistance of counsel.

The Court of Appeals did not hold, nor do we, that under the circumstances of this case Williams *could not*, without notice to counsel, have waived his rights under the Sixth and Fourteenth Amendments. It only held, as do we, that he did not.

IV

The crime of which Williams was convicted was senseless and brutal, calling for swift and energetic action by the police to apprehend the perpetrator and gather evidence with which he could be convicted. No mission of law enforcement officials is more important. Yet "[d]isinterested zeal for the public good does not assure either wisdom or right in the methods it pursues." Although we do not lightly affirm the issuance of a writ of habeas corpus in this case, so clear a violation of the Sixth and Fourteenth Amendments as here occurred cannot be condoned. The pressures on state executive and judicial officers charged with the administration of the criminal law are great, especially when the crime is murder and the victim a small child. But it is precisely the predictability of those pressures that makes imperative a resolute loyalty to the guarantees that the Constitution extends to us all. * * *

MR. JUSTICE MARSHALL, concurring.

I concur wholeheartedly in my Brother Stewart's opinion for the Court, but add these words in light of the dissenting opinions filed today. The dissenters have, I believe, lost sight of the fundamental constitutional backbone of our criminal law. They seem to think that Detective Leaming's actions were perfectly proper, indeed laudable, examples of "good police work." In my view, good police work is something far different from catching the criminal at any price. It is equally important that the police, as guardians of the law, fulfill their responsibility to obey its commands scrupulously. For "in the end life and liberty can be as much endangered from illegal methods used to convict those thought to be criminals as from the actual criminals themselves."

In this case, there can be no doubt that Detective Leaming consciously and knowingly set out to violate Williams' Sixth Amendment right to counsel and his Fifth Amendment privilege against self-incrimination, as Leaming himself understood those rights. * * *

Leaming knowingly isolated Williams from the protection of his lawyers and during that period he intentionally "persuaded" him to give incriminating evidence. It is this intentional police misconduct—not good police practice—that the Court rightly condemns. The heinous nature of the crime is no excuse, as the dissenters would have it, for condoning knowing and intentional police transgression of the constitutional rights of a defendant. If Williams is to go free—and given the ingenuity of Iowa prosecutors on retrial or in a civil commitment proceeding, I doubt very much that there is any chance a dangerous criminal will be loosed on the streets, the bloodcurdling cries of the dissents notwithstanding—it will hardly be because he deserves it. It will be because Detective Leaming, knowing full well that he risked reversal of Williams' conviction, intentionally denied Williams the right of *every* American under the Sixth Amendment to have the protective shield of a lawyer between himself and the awesome power of the State. * * *

MR. JUSTICE POWELL, concurring. * * *

I * * *

* * * It is clear from the record, as both of the federal courts below found, that there was no evidence of a knowing and voluntary waiver of the right to have counsel present beyond the fact that Williams ultimately confessed. It is settled law that an inferred waiver of a constitutional right is disfavored. I find no basis in the record of this case—or in the dissenting opinions—for disagreeing with the conclusion of the District Court that "the State has produced no affirmative evidence whatsoever to support its claim of waiver."

The dissenting opinion of the Chief Justice states that the Court's holding today "conclusively presumes a suspect is legally incompetent to change his mind and tell the truth until an attorney is present." I find no justification for this view. On the contrary, the opinion of the Court is explicitly clear that the right to assistance of counsel may be waived, after it has attached, without notice to or consultation with counsel. We would have such a case here if petitioner had proved that the police refrained from coercion and interrogation, as they had agreed, and that Williams freely on his own initiative had confessed the crime. * * *

MR. JUSTICE STEVENS, concurring. * * *

Nothing that we write, no matter how well reasoned or forcefully expressed, can bring back the victim of this tragedy or undo the consequences of the official neglect which led to the respondent's escape from a state mental institution. The emotional aspects of the case make it difficult to decide dispassionately, but do not qualify our obligation to apply the law with an eye to the future as well as with concern for the result in the particular case before us. * * *

MR. CHIEF JUSTICE BURGER, dissenting.

The result in this case ought to be intolerable in any society which purports to call itself an organized society. It continues the Court—by the narrowest margin—on the much-criticized course of punishing the public for the mistakes and misdeeds of law enforcement officers, instead of punishing the officer directly, if in fact he is guilty of wrongdoing. It mechanically and blindly keeps reliable evidence from juries whether the claimed constitutional violation involves gross police misconduct or honest human error.

Williams is guilty of the savage murder of a small child; no member of the Court contends he is not. While in custody, and after no fewer than *five* warnings of his rights to silence and to counsel, he led police to the concealed body of his victim. The Court concedes Williams was not threatened or coerced and that he spoke and acted voluntarily and with full awareness of his constitutional rights. In the face of all this, the Court now holds that because Williams was prompted by the detective's statement—not interrogation but a statement—the jury must not be told how the police found the body.

Today's holding fulfills Judge (later Mr. Justice) Cardozo's grim prophecy that someday some court might carry the exclusionary rule to the absurd extent that its operative effect would exclude evidence relating to the body of a murder victim because of the means by which it was found. In so ruling the Court regresses to playing a grisly game of "hide and seek," once more exalting the sporting theory of criminal justice which has been experiencing a decline in our jurisprudence. With Justices White, Blackmun, and Rehnquist, I categorically reject the remarkable notion that the police in this case were guilty of unconstitutional misconduct, or any conduct justifying the bizarre result reached by the Court. * * *

Under well-settled precedents which the Court freely acknowledges, it is very clear that Williams had made a valid waiver of his Fifth Amendment right to silence and his Sixth Amendment right to counsel when he led police to the child's body. Indeed, even under the Court's analysis I do not understand how a contrary conclusion is possible. * * *

The evidence is uncontradicted that Williams had abundant knowledge of his right to have counsel present and of his right to silence. Since the Court does not question his mental competence, it boggles the mind to suggest that Williams could not understand that leading police to the child's body would have other than the most serious consequences. All of the elements necessary to make out a valid waiver are shown by the record and acknowledged by the Court; we thus are left to guess how the Court reached its holding.

One plausible but unarticulated basis for the result reached is that once a suspect has asserted his right not to talk without the presence of an attorney, it becomes legally impossible for him to waive that right until he has seen an attorney. But constitutional rights are *personal*, and an otherwise valid waiver should not be brushed aside by judges simply because an attorney was not present. The Court's holding operates to "imprison a man in his privileges"; it conclusively presumes a suspect is legally incompetent to change his mind and tell the truth until an attorney is present. It denigrates an individual to a nonperson whose free will has become hostage to a lawyer so that until the lawyer consents, the suspect is deprived of any legal right or power to decide for himself that he wishes to make a disclosure. * * *

MR. JUSTICE WHITE, with whom MR. JUSTICE BLACKMUN and MR. JUSTICE REHNQUIST join, dissenting.

The respondent in this case killed a 10-year-old child. * * *

I

[During his recitation of the facts, Justice White noted that Williams began directing the police in search of incriminating evidence "[s]ome considerable time" after Leaming's "Christian burial speech." In footnote 3, White observed: "The trip was 160 miles long and was made in bad weather. Leaming's statement was made shortly after leaving Davenport. Respondent's statements about the victim's clothes were made shortly before arriving in Mitchellville, a near suburb of Des Moines." Eds.]

II

The strictest test of waiver which might be applied to this case is that set forth in *Johnson v. Zerbst*, and quoted by the majority. In order to show that a right has been waived under this test, the State must prove "an intentional relinquishment or abandonment of a known right or privilege." The majority creates no new rule preventing an accused who has retained a lawyer from waiving his right to the lawyer's presence during questioning. The majority simply finds that no waiver was *proved* in this case. I disagree. That respondent knew of his right not to say anything to the officers without advice and presence of counsel is established on this record to a moral certainty. He was advised of the right by three officials of the State—telling at least one that he understood the right—and by two lawyers. Finally, he further demonstrated his knowledge of the right by informing the police that he would tell them the story in the presence of McKnight when they arrived in Des Moines. The issue in this case, then, is whether respondent relinquished that right intentionally.

Respondent relinquished his right not to talk to the police about his crime when the car approached the place where he had hidden the victim's clothes. Men usually intend to do what they do, and there is nothing in the record to support the proposition that respondent's decision to talk was anything but an exercise of his own free will. Apparently, without any prodding from the officers, respondent—who had earlier said that he would tell the whole story when he arrived in Des Moines—spontaneously changed his mind about the timing of his disclosures when the car approached the places where he had hidden the evidence. However, even if his statements were influenced by Detective Leaming's above-quoted statement, respondent's decision to talk in the absence of counsel can hardly be viewed as the product of an overborne will. The statement by Leaming was not coercive; it was accompanied by a request that respondent not respond to it; and it was delivered hours before respondent decided to make any statement. Respondent's waiver was thus knowing and intentional.

The majority's contrary conclusion seems to rest on the fact that respondent "asserted" his right to counsel by retaining and consulting with one lawyer and by consulting with another. How this supports the conclusion that respondent's later relinquishment of his right not to talk in the absence of counsel was unintentional is a mystery. The fact that respondent consulted with counsel on the question whether he should talk to the police in counsel's absence makes his later decision to talk in counsel's absence *better* informed and, if anything, more intelligent.

The majority recognizes that even after this "assertion" of his right to counsel, it would have found that respondent waived his right not to talk in counsel's absence if his waiver had been express—*i.e.*, if the officers had asked him in the car whether he would be willing to answer questions in counsel's absence and if he had answered "yes." But waiver is not a formalistic concept. Waiver is shown whenever the facts establish that an accused knew of a right and intended to relinquish it. Such waiver, even if not express,[5] was plainly shown here. The only other conceivable basis for the majority's holding is the implicit suggestion that

---

[5]   * * * [T]he issue is, as the majority recognizes, one of the proof necessary to establish waiver. If an intentional relinquishment of the right to counsel under *Miranda* is established by proof that the accused was informed of his right and then voluntarily answered questions in counsel's absence, then similar proof establishes an intentional relinquishment of the *Massiah* right to counsel.

the right involved in *Massiah v. United States*, as distinguished from the right involved in *Miranda v. Arizona*, is a right not to be *asked* any questions in counsel's absence rather than a right not to *answer* any questions in counsel's absence, and that the right not to be *asked* questions must be waived *before* the questions are asked. Such wafer-thin distinctions cannot determine whether a guilty murderer should go free. The only conceivable purpose for the presence of counsel during questioning is to protect an accused from making incriminating *answers*. Questions, unanswered, have no significance at all. Absent coercion—no matter how the right involved is defined—an accused is amply protected by a rule requiring waiver before or simultaneously with the giving by him of an answer or the making by him of a statement.

III

The consequence of the majority's decision is, as the majority recognizes, extremely serious. A mentally disturbed killer whose guilt is not in question may be released. Why? Apparently the answer is that the majority believes that the law enforcement officers acted in a way which involves some risk of injury to society and that such conduct should be deterred. However, the officers' conduct did not, and was not likely to, jeopardize the fairness of respondent's trial or in any way risk the conviction of an innocent man—the risk against which the Sixth Amendment guarantee of assistance of counsel is designed to protect. The police did nothing "wrong," let alone anything "unconstitutional." To anyone not lost in the intricacies of the prophylactic rules of *Miranda v. Arizona*, the result in this case seems utterly senseless; and for the reasons stated in Part II, even applying those rules as well as the rule of *Massiah v. United States*, the statements made by respondent were properly admitted. In light of these considerations, the majority's protest that the result in this case is justified by a "clear violation" of the Sixth and Fourteenth Amendments has a distressing hollow ring. I respectfully dissent.

[The dissenting opinion of JUSTICE BLACKMUN, joined by JUSTICES WHITE and REHNQUIST, is omitted].

NOTES AND QUESTIONS

1.   While a law student, one of the authors of the casebook worked on *Brewer* when it was on appeal to the Eighth Circuit; his view was that the issue was better analyzed under *Miranda*. Others thought so, too. *Brewer* was widely viewed as the case the Court would use to overrule *Miranda*. Justice Blackmun noted in his *Brewer* dissent that twenty-two states "and others, as *amicus curiae*, strongly urge that" *Miranda* "be re-examined and overruled." Perhaps sensing *Miranda*'s vulnerability, the University of Iowa law professor in charge of the case—Robert Bartels—insisted that the Sixth Amendment argument was the defendant's best hope. As usual, the teacher

was wiser than the student. But the key question is *why* the Court was more comfortable deciding the case under *Massiah*. What do you think?

2.   The bitter dispute in *Brewer* is framed in terms of waiver, not whether Leaming deliberately elicited Williams's statements. Are these different inquiries or just two sides of the same coin?

3.   What did Officer Leaming do wrong? Is the problem the "Christian burial speech" or the "waiver" after the speech? If you think it is the latter, did the Court conclude that this was an involuntary waiver? An unintelligent one? Or is there another basis? The classic treatment of this question is Yale Kamisar, *Brewer v. Williams, Massiah and Miranda: What is "Interrogation"? When Does It Matter?*, 67 Geo. L.J. 1 (1978).

Other valuable perspectives on the *Brewer* interrogation issue can be found in Joseph D. Grano, *Rhode Island v. Innis: A Need to Reconsider the Constitutional Premises Underlying the Law of Confessions*, 17 Am. Crim. L. Rev. 1 (1979); and Stephen J. Schulhofer, *Confessions and the Court*, 79 Mich. L. Rev. 865 (1980) (reviewing Yale Kamisar, *Police Interrogation and Confessions* (1980)).

4.   Chief Justice Burger stated in his dissent that, following the majority's reasoning, "[I]t becomes legally impossible for [Williams] to waive that right until he has seen an attorney." Is this what the majority says? Would that be a sensible outcome? Could Officer Leaming have done something differently that would have permitted Williams to waive before seeing McKnight?

Assume Officer Leaming gave the Christian burial speech, three hours passed, and Williams asked to telephone his boyhood minister. After a lengthy telephone call in private, Williams told the police: "I am a religious man. Having thought of nothing these last three hours except the nature of sin and forgiveness, I decided to call my minister, who said that my religious duty is to direct you to where I hid the body." A violation of *Massiah*, as amplified by *Brewer*? What if, instead, Williams tells police he is going to call his lawyer and returns after the call to say he is ready to talk? Does it matter what the lawyer advised him?

Alternatively, assume the police persuade a local radio weatherman to give the speech and leave the radio on for Williams to hear. Does this change anything in the *Massiah* analysis? Does it change the *Miranda* analysis? (The hypothetical is Professor Kamisar's; see Kamisar, Note 3.)

5.   *Massiah "fruit."* What evidence is rendered inadmissible by the Sixth Amendment violation in *Brewer*? The Court held that the statements Williams made leading the police to the body were inadmissible, of course, but what about the body itself? This is one way to ask whether a *Massiah* violation has poisoned fruit, as in the case of a Fourth Amendment violation. You will recall that *Miranda* is "fruitless." Is a *Massiah* violation more like a Fourth Amendment violation or more like a *Miranda* violation?

The Court in *Brewer* suggested in a footnote that the body might be admissible if it would have been discovered in any event. As you saw in *Nix v. Williams*, p. 528, Note 4, the Court later made a holding of this dicta. Notice, however, that this "inevitable discovery" exception is precisely that—an exception to a general rule that the fruit of a violation of *Massiah* must be suppressed. Do you see why *Massiah*, but not *Miranda*, generally requires suppression of evidence found by means of the violation?

6. *Brewer v. Williams: the rest of the story.* The State of Iowa retried Williams. For details on the retrial, including the defense theory of how Williams was factually innocent, see Phillip E. Johnson, *The Return of the "Christian Burial Speech" Case*, 32 Emory L.J. 349 (1983). In brief, the theory was that the victim was killed by a janitor at the YMCA who then hid the body in Williams's room. Upon discovering the body, and fearing the inevitable inference, Williams panicked, fled, and hid the body where it was ultimately found. According to the Eighth Circuit, the defense theory of innocence "is not so far-fetched as it sounds." Williams v. Nix, 700 F.2d 1164, 1168 (8th Cir. 1983). Some evidence in Williams's favor: A witness heard the sounds of a struggle coming from the janitor's room shortly after the victim's disappearance, and the janitor made what one witness called "furtive preparations to depart" shortly after the crime occurred. Moreover, according to defense lawyers, the janitor had a history of child molestation. He could not be located for the first trial; by the time of the second trial, he had been killed in an auto accident.

As you saw in Chapter 5, in the inevitable discovery materials, Williams was again convicted, mostly on the testimony of the person who saw skinny white legs sticking out of the bundle that Williams put in his car. Iowa does not have the death penalty. Williams is still serving a life sentence at the Fort Madison, Iowa prison.

7. To appreciate the significance of the next case, you should know a little about Michigan v. Jackson, 475 U.S. 625, 106 S.Ct. 1404, 89 L.Ed.2d 631 (1986). When Jackson (who was indigent) was arraigned, he requested that counsel be appointed. The Court in *Jackson* held that this request created a Sixth Amendment version of the *Edwards v. Arizona* (p. 733) rule forbidding the initiation of further interrogation by the police. Thus, even though Jackson never invoked his *Miranda* right to counsel, and therefore could not benefit from *Edwards*, *Jackson* held that the Sixth Amendment protected him from subsequent post-arraignment police attempts to get him to answer questions. Stated differently, even though police read Jackson his *Miranda* warnings, and he waived them, he did not waive his Sixth Amendment right to counsel. But what if a defendant does *not* request counsel after indictment? Is that a distinction with constitutional significance?

PATTERSON V. ILLINOIS

Supreme Court of the United States, 1988.
487 U.S. 285, 108 S.Ct. 2389, 101 L.Ed.2d 261 (1988).

JUSTICE WHITE delivered the opinion of the Court [joined by CHIEF JUSTICE REHNQUIST, and JUSTICES O'CONNOR, SCALIA, and KENNEDY].

In this case, we are called on to determine whether the interrogation of petitioner after his indictment violated his Sixth Amendment right to counsel.

I * * *

On August 23, a Cook County grand jury indicted petitioner and two other gang members for the murder of James Jackson. Police Officer Michael Gresham, who had questioned petitioner earlier, removed him from the lockup where he was being held, and told petitioner that because he had been indicted he was being transferred to the Cook County jail. Petitioner asked Gresham which of the gang members had been charged with Jackson's murder, and upon learning that one particular Vice Lord had been omitted from the indictments, asked: "[W]hy wasn't he indicted, he did everything." Petitioner also began to explain that there was a witness who would support his account of the crime.

At this point, Gresham interrupted petitioner, and handed him a *Miranda* waiver form. The form contained five specific warnings, as suggested by this Court's *Miranda* decision, to make petitioner aware of his right to counsel and of the consequences of any statement he might make to police. Gresham read the warnings aloud, as petitioner read along with him. Petitioner initialed each of the five warnings, and signed the waiver form. Petitioner then gave a lengthy statement to police officers concerning the Jackson murder; petitioner's statement described in detail the role of each of the Vice Lords—including himself—in the murder of James Jackson.

Later that day, petitioner confessed involvement in the murder for a second time. This confession came in an interview with Assistant State's Attorney (ASA) George Smith. At the outset of the interview, Smith reviewed with petitioner the *Miranda* waiver he had previously signed, and petitioner confirmed that he had signed the waiver and understood his rights. Smith went through the waiver procedure once again: reading petitioner his rights, having petitioner initial each one, and sign a waiver form. In addition, Smith informed petitioner that he was a lawyer working with the police investigating the Jackson case. Petitioner then gave another inculpatory statement concerning the crime. * * *

On appeal, petitioner argued that he had not "knowingly and intelligently" waived his Sixth Amendment right to counsel before he gave his uncounseled postindictment confessions. Petitioner contended that the warnings he received, while adequate for the purposes of protecting his *Fifth* Amendment rights as guaranteed by *Miranda,* did not adequately inform him of his *Sixth* Amendment right to counsel. The Illinois Supreme Court, however, rejected this theory, applying its previous decision * * * which had held that *Miranda* warnings were sufficient to make a defendant aware of his Sixth Amendment right to counsel during postindictment questioning.

In reaching this conclusion, the Illinois Supreme Court noted that this Court had reserved decision on this question on several previous occasions and that the lower courts are divided on the issue. We granted this petition for certiorari to resolve this split of authority and to address the issues we had previously left open.

II

There can be no doubt that petitioner had the right to have the assistance of counsel at his postindictment interviews with law enforcement authorities. Our cases make it plain that the Sixth Amendment guarantees this right to criminal defendants. Michigan v. Jackson, 475 U.S. 625, 629–630, 106 S.Ct. 1404, 1407–1408, 89 L.Ed.2d 631 (1986); *Brewer v. Williams*; *Massiah v. United States*.[3] Petitioner asserts that the questioning that produced his incriminating statements violated his Sixth Amendment right to counsel in two ways.

A

Petitioner's first claim is that because his Sixth Amendment right to counsel arose with his indictment, the police were thereafter barred from initiating a meeting with him. He equates himself with a preindictment suspect who, while being interrogated, asserts his Fifth Amendment right to counsel; under *Edwards v. Arizona,* [p. 733], such a suspect may not be questioned again unless he initiates the meeting. * * *

At bottom, petitioner's theory cannot be squared with our rationale in *Edwards,* the case he relies on for support. *Edwards* rested on the view that once "an accused * * * ha[s] expressed his desire to deal with the police only through counsel" he should "not [be] subject to further interrogation by the authorities until counsel has been made available to him, unless the accused himself initiates further communication." Preserving the integrity of an accused's choice to communicate with police only through counsel is the essence of *Edwards* and its progeny—not barring an accused from making an *initial* election as to whether he will

---

[3] We note as a matter of some significance that petitioner had not retained, or accepted by appointment, a lawyer to represent him at the time he was questioned by authorities. Once an accused has a lawyer, a distinct set of constitutional safeguards aimed at preserving the sanctity of the attorney-client relationship takes effect. The State conceded as much at argument.

Indeed, the analysis changes markedly once an accused even *requests* the assistance of counsel. See *Michigan v. Jackson, supra.*

face the State's officers during questioning with the aid of counsel, or go it alone. If an accused "knowingly and intelligently" pursues the latter course, we see no reason why the uncounseled statements he then makes must be excluded at his trial.

B

Petitioner's principal and more substantial claim is that questioning him without counsel present violated the Sixth Amendment because he did not validly waive his right to have counsel present during the interviews. Since it is clear that after the *Miranda* warnings were given to petitioner, he not only voluntarily answered questions without claiming his right to silence or his right to have a lawyer present to advise him but also executed a written waiver of his right to counsel during questioning, the specific issue posed here is whether this waiver was a "knowing and intelligent" waiver of his Sixth Amendment right.

In the past, this Court has held that a waiver of the Sixth Amendment right to counsel is valid only when it reflects "an intentional relinquishment or abandonment of a known right or privilege." In other words, the accused must "kno[w] what he is doing" so that "his choice is made with eyes open." In a case arising under the Fifth Amendment, we described this requirement as "a full awareness of both the nature of the right being abandoned and the consequences of the decision to abandon it." Whichever of these formulations is used, the key inquiry in a case such as this one must be: Was the accused, who waived his Sixth Amendment rights during postindictment questioning, made sufficiently aware of his right to have counsel present during the questioning, and of the possible consequences of a decision to forgo the aid of counsel? In this case, we are convinced that by admonishing petitioner with the *Miranda* warnings, respondent has met this burden and that petitioner's waiver of his right to counsel at the questioning was valid.[4]

First, the *Miranda* warnings given petitioner made him aware of his right to have counsel present during the questioning. By telling petitioner that he had a right to consult with an attorney, to have a lawyer present while he was questioned, and even to have a lawyer appointed for him if he could not afford to retain one on his own, Officer Gresham and ASA Smith conveyed to petitioner the sum and substance of the rights that the Sixth Amendment provided him. "Indeed, it seems self-evident that one who is told he" has such rights to counsel "is in a curious posture to later

---

[4] We emphasize the significance of the fact that petitioner's waiver of counsel was only for this limited aspect of the criminal proceedings against him—only for postindictment questioning. Our decision on the validity of petitioner's waiver extends only so far.

Moreover, even within this limited context, we note that petitioner's waiver was binding on him *only* so long as he wished it to be. Under this Court's precedents, at any time during the questioning petitioner could have changed his mind, elected to have the assistance of counsel, and immediately dissolve the effectiveness of his waiver with respect to any subsequent statements. Our decision today does nothing to change this rule.

complain" that his waiver of these rights was unknowing. There is little more petitioner could have possibly been told in an effort to satisfy this portion of the waiver inquiry.

Second, the *Miranda* warnings also served to make petitioner aware of the consequences of a decision by him to waive his Sixth Amendment rights during postindictment questioning. Petitioner knew that any statement that he made could be used against him in subsequent criminal proceedings. This is the ultimate adverse consequence petitioner could have suffered by virtue of his choice to make uncounseled admissions to the authorities. This warning also sufficed—contrary to petitioner's claim here—to let petitioner know what a lawyer could "do for him" during the postindictment questioning: namely, advise petitioner to refrain from making any such statements. By knowing what could be done with any statements he might make, and therefore, what benefit could be obtained by having the aid of counsel while making such statements, petitioner was essentially informed of the possible consequences of going without counsel during questioning. If petitioner nonetheless lacked "a full and complete appreciation of all of the consequences flowing" from his waiver, it does not defeat the State's showing that the information it provided to him satisfied the constitutional minimum.

Our conclusion is supported by petitioner's inability, in the proceedings before this Court, to articulate with precision what additional information should have been provided to him before he would have been competent to waive his right to counsel. All that petitioner's brief and reply brief suggest is petitioner should have been made aware of his "right under the Sixth Amendment to the broad protection of counsel"—a rather nebulous suggestion—and the "gravity of [his] situation." But surely this latter "requirement" (if it is one) was met when Officer Gresham informed petitioner that he had been formally charged with the murder of James Jackson. Under close questioning on this same point at argument, petitioner likewise failed to suggest any meaningful additional information that he should have been, but was not, provided in advance of his decision to waive his right to counsel.[7] The discussions found in

---

[7]   Representative excerpts from the relevant portions of argument include the following:

"QUESTION: [Petitioner] * * * was told that he had a right to counsel.

"MR. HONCHELL [petitioner's counsel]: He was told-the word 'counsel' was used. He was told he had a right to counsel. But not through information by which it would become meaningful to him, because the method that was used was not designed to alert the accused to the Sixth Amendment rights to counsel * * * .

"QUESTION: * * * You mean they should have said you have a Sixth Amendment right to counsel instead of just, you have a right to counsel?

"He knew he had a right to have counsel present before [he] made the confession. Now, what in addition did he have to know to make the waiver an intelligent one?

"MR. HONCHELL: He had to meaningfully know he had a Sixth Amendment right to counsel present because—

"QUESTION: What is the difference between meaningfully knowing and knowing?

favorable court decisions, on which petitioner relies, are similarly lacking.[8]

As a general matter, then, an accused who is admonished with the warnings prescribed by this Court in *Miranda* has been sufficiently apprised of the nature of his Sixth Amendment rights, and of the consequences of abandoning those rights, so that his waiver on this basis will be considered a knowing and intelligent one. We feel that our conclusion in a recent Fifth Amendment case is equally apposite here: "Once it is determined that a suspect's decision not to rely on his rights was uncoerced, that he at all times knew he could stand mute and request a lawyer, and that he was aware of the State's intention to use his statements to secure a conviction, the analysis is complete and the waiver is valid as a matter of law."

C

We consequently reject petitioner's argument, which has some acceptance from courts and commentators, that since "the sixth amendment right [to counsel] is far superior to that of the fifth amendment right" and since "[t]he greater the right the greater the loss from a waiver of that right," waiver of an accused's Sixth Amendment right to counsel should be "more difficult" to effectuate than waiver of a suspect's Fifth Amendment rights. While our cases have recognized a "difference" between the Fifth Amendment and Sixth Amendment rights to counsel, and the "policies" behind these constitutional guarantees, we have never suggested that one right is "superior" or "greater" than the other, nor is there any support in our cases for the notion that because a Sixth Amendment right may be involved, it is more difficult to waive than the Fifth Amendment counterpart. Instead, we have taken a more pragmatic approach to the waiver question—asking what purposes a lawyer can serve at the particular stage of the proceedings in question, and what assistance he could provide to an accused at that stage—to determine the scope of the Sixth Amendment right to counsel, and the

---

"MR. HONCHELL: Because the warning here used did not convey or express what counsel was intended to do for him after indictment. * * * That there is a right to counsel who would act on his behalf and represent him.

"QUESTION: Well, okay. So it should have said, in addition to saying counsel, counsel who would act on your behalf and represent you? That would have been the magic solution?

"MR. HONCHELL: That is a possible method, yes."

We do not believe that adding the words "who would act on your behalf and represent you" in Sixth Amendment cases would provide any meaningful improvement in the *Miranda* warnings.

[8] * * * An exception to this is the occasional suggestion that, in addition to the *Miranda* warnings, an accused should be informed that he has been indicted before a postindictment waiver is sought. Because, in this case, petitioner concedes that he was so informed, we do not address the question whether or not an accused must be told that he has been indicted before a postindictment Sixth Amendment waiver will be valid. Nor do we even pass on the desirability of so informing the accused—a matter that can be reasonably debated. * * *

type of warnings and procedures that should be required before a waiver of that right will be recognized.

At one end of the spectrum, we have concluded there is no Sixth Amendment right to counsel whatsoever at a postindictment photographic display identification, because this procedure is not one at which the accused "require [s] aid in coping with legal problems or assistance in meeting his adversary." At the other extreme, recognizing the enormous importance and role that an attorney plays at a criminal trial, we have imposed the most rigorous restrictions on the information that must be conveyed to a defendant, and the procedures that must be observed, before permitting him to waive his right to counsel at trial. In these extreme cases, and in others that fall between these two poles, we have defined the scope of the right to counsel by a pragmatic assessment of the usefulness of counsel to the accused at the particular proceeding, and the dangers to the accused of proceeding without counsel. An accused's waiver of his right to counsel is knowing when he is made aware of these basic facts.

Applying this approach, it is our view that whatever warnings suffice for *Miranda*'s purposes will also be sufficient in the context of postindictment questioning. The State's decision to take an additional step and commence formal adversarial proceedings against the accused does not substantially increase the value of counsel to the accused at questioning, or expand the limited purpose that an attorney serves when the accused is questioned by authorities. With respect to this inquiry, we do not discern a substantial difference between the usefulness of a lawyer to a suspect during custodial interrogation, and his value to an accused at postindictment questioning.

Thus, we require a more searching or formal inquiry before permitting an accused to waive his right to counsel at trial than we require for a Sixth Amendment waiver during postindictment questioning—*not* because postindictment questioning is less important than a trial (the analysis that petitioner's "hierarchical" approach would suggest)—but because the full "dangers and disadvantages of self-representation," during questioning are less substantial and more obvious to an accused than they are at trial.[13] Because the role of counsel at questioning is relatively simple and limited, we see no problem in having a waiver procedure at that stage which is likewise simple and limited. So long as the accused is made aware of the "dangers and disadvantages of self-representation" during postindictment questioning, by use of the

---

[13] [A]n attorney's role at questioning is relatively limited. But at trial, counsel is required to help even the most gifted layman adhere to the rules of procedure and evidence, comprehend the subtleties of *voir dire,* examine and cross-examine witnesses effectively (including the accused), object to improper prosecution questions, and much more.

Miranda warnings, his waiver of his Sixth Amendment right to counsel at such questioning is "knowing and intelligent."

III

Before confessing to the murder of James Jackson, petitioner was meticulously informed by authorities of his right to counsel, and of the consequences of any choice not to exercise that right. On two separate occasions, petitioner elected to forgo the assistance of counsel, and speak directly to officials concerning his role in the murder. Because we believe that petitioner's waiver of his Sixth Amendment rights was "knowing and intelligent," we find no error in the decision of the trial court to permit petitioner's confessions to be used against him. Consequently, the judgment of the Illinois Supreme Court is

Affirmed.

JUSTICE BLACKMUN, dissenting.

I agree with most of what Justice STEVENS says in his dissenting opinion. I, however, merely would hold that after formal adversary proceedings against a defendant have been commenced, the Sixth Amendment mandates that the defendant not be "subject to further interrogation by the authorities until counsel has been made available to him, unless the accused himself initiates further communication, exchanges, or conversations with the police." *Michigan v. Jackson.* * * *

JUSTICE STEVENS, with whom JUSTICE BRENNAN and JUSTICE MARSHALL join, dissenting.

The Court should not condone unethical forms of trial preparation by prosecutors or their investigators. In civil litigation it is improper for a lawyer to communicate with his or her adversary's client without either notice to opposing counsel or the permission of the court. An attempt to obtain evidence for use at trial by going behind the back of one's adversary would be not only a serious breach of professional ethics but also a manifestly unfair form of trial practice. In the criminal context, the same ethical rules apply and, in my opinion, notions of fairness that are at least as demanding should also be enforced.

After a jury has been empaneled and a criminal trial is in progress, it would obviously be improper for the prosecutor to conduct a private interview with the defendant for the purpose of obtaining evidence to be used against him at trial. By "private interview" I mean, of course, an interview initiated by the prosecutor, or his or her agents, without notice to the defendant's lawyer and without the permission of the court. Even if such an interview were to be commenced by giving the defendant the five items of legal advice that are mandated by *Miranda,* I have no doubt that this Court would promptly and unanimously condemn such a shabby practice. As our holding in *Michigan v. Jackson* suggests, such a practice would not simply constitute a serious ethical violation, but would rise to the level of an impairment of the Sixth Amendment right to counsel.

The question that this case raises, therefore, is at what point in the adversary process does it become impermissible for the prosecutor, or his or her agents, to conduct such private interviews with the opposing party? Several alternatives are conceivable: when the trial commences, when the defendant has actually met and accepted representation by his or her appointed counsel, when counsel is appointed, or when the adversary process commences. In my opinion, the Sixth Amendment right to counsel demands that a firm and unequivocal line be drawn at the point at which adversary proceedings commence. * * *

Today, however, * * * the Court backs away from the significance previously attributed to the initiation of formal proceedings. In the majority's view, the purported waiver of counsel in this case is properly equated with that of an unindicted suspect. Yet, as recognized in [earlier cases], important differences separate the two. The return of an indictment, or like instrument, substantially alters the relationship between the state and the accused. Only after a formal accusation has "the government * * * committed itself to prosecute, and only then [have] the adverse positions of government and defendant * * * solidified." Moreover, the return of an indictment also presumably signals the government's conclusion that it has sufficient evidence to establish a prima facie case. As a result, any further interrogation can only be designed to buttress the government's case; authorities are no longer simply attempting "'to solve a crime.'" Given the significance of the initiation of formal proceedings and the concomitant shift in the relationship between the state and the accused, I think it quite wrong to suggest that *Miranda* warnings—or for that matter, any warnings offered by an adverse party—provide a sufficient basis for permitting the undoubtedly prejudicial—and, in my view, unfair—practice of permitting trained law enforcement personnel and prosecuting attorneys to communicate with as-of-yet unrepresented criminal defendants.

It is well settled that there is a strong presumption against waiver of Sixth Amendment protections, and that a waiver may only be accepted if made with full awareness of "the dangers and disadvantages of self-representation," Warnings offered by an opposing party, whether detailed or cursory, simply cannot satisfy this high standard.

The majority premises its conclusion that *Miranda* warnings lay a sufficient basis for accepting a waiver of the right to counsel on the assumption that those warnings make clear to an accused "what a lawyer could 'do for him' during the postindictment questioning: namely, advise [him] to refrain from making any [incriminating] statements." Yet, this is surely a gross understatement of the disadvantage of proceeding without a lawyer and an understatement of what a defendant must understand to make a knowing waiver. The *Miranda* warnings do not, for example, inform the accused that a lawyer might examine the indictment for legal sufficiency before submitting his or her client to interrogation or that a lawyer is likely to be considerably more skillful at negotiating a plea bargain and that such negotiations may be most fruitful if initiated prior to any interrogation. Rather, the warnings do not even go so far as to explain to the accused the nature of the charges pending against him—advice that a court would insist upon before allowing a defendant to enter a guilty plea with or without the presence of an attorney. Without defining precisely the nature of the inquiry required to establish a valid waiver of the Sixth Amendment right to counsel, it must be conceded that at least minimal advice is necessary—the accused must be told of the "dangers and disadvantages of self-representation."

Yet, once it is conceded that certain advice is required and that after indictment the adversary relationship between the state and the accused has solidified, it inescapably follows that a prosecutor may not conduct private interviews with a charged defendant. As at least one Court of Appeals has recognized, there are ethical constraints that prevent a prosecutor from giving legal advice to an uncounseled adversary. Thus, neither the prosecutor nor his or her agents can ethically provide the unrepresented defendant with the kind of advice that should precede an evidence-gathering interview after formal proceedings have been commenced. Indeed, in my opinion even the *Miranda* warnings themselves are a species of legal advice that is improper when given by the prosecutor after indictment.

Moreover, there are good reasons why such advice is deemed unethical, reasons that extend to the custodial, postindictment setting with unequaled strength. First, the offering of legal advice may lead an accused to underestimate the prosecuting authorities' true adversary posture. For an incarcerated defendant—in this case, a 17-year-old who had been in custody for 44 hours at the time he was told of the indictment—the assistance of someone to explain why he is being held, the nature of the charges against him, and the extent of his legal rights, may be of such importance as to overcome what is perhaps obvious to most, that the prosecutor is a foe and not a friend. Second, the adversary posture of the parties, which is not fully solidified until formal charges are brought, will inevitably tend to color the advice offered. As hard as a prosecutor might try, I doubt that it is possible for one to wear the hat of an effective adviser to a criminal defendant while at the same time wearing the hat of a law enforcement authority. Finally, regardless of whether or not the accused actually understands the legal and factual issues involved and the state's role as an adversary party, advice offered by a lawyer (or his or her agents) with such an evident conflict of interest cannot help but create a public perception of unfairness and unethical conduct. * * *

In sum, without a careful discussion of the pitfalls of proceeding without counsel, the Sixth Amendment right cannot properly be waived. An adversary party, moreover, cannot adequately provide such advice. As a result, once the right to counsel attaches and the adversary relationship between the state and the accused solidifies, a prosecutor cannot conduct a private interview with an accused party without "dilut[ing] the protection afforded by the right to counsel." * * *

I therefore respectfully dissent.

NOTES AND QUESTIONS

1.   The approaches of the majority and the dissent to the waiver issue in this case are fundamentally at odds, on different planets as it were. Can you articulate the theory of the right to counsel that underlies the majority and the two dissents? Which view of the right to counsel do you prefer?

2.   Look again at footnote 8 in the majority opinion. Do you think the Court would find a valid waiver of a defendant's Sixth Amendment right to counsel if he waived *Miranda* without knowing that he was under indictment?

3.   Justice White dissented in *Massiah* and *Brewer*, and wrote the majority opinion in *Patterson*. Can you articulate his theory of the Sixth Amendment right to counsel when police are deliberately eliciting statements from an accused?

4.   *Michigan v. Jackson redux.* Notice that the *Patterson* Court and both dissents cite *Michigan v. Jackson*, where, as we saw, p. 777, Note7, the Court held that a request for counsel at a judicial proceeding created an *Edwards v. Arizona* rule that barred police from approaching the accused and seeking a waiver of *Miranda*. The *Patterson* majority distinguished *Jackson* on the ground that Patterson, unlike Jackson, did not request counsel after adversary proceedings had begun. See, *e.g.*, footnote 3 in the majority opinion. Thus, following *Patterson*, defendants who were not yet represented by counsel were treated differently for purposes of waiver of the Sixth Amendment right to counsel during interrogation depending on whether they had requested counsel at a judicial proceeding. The *Patterson* dissenters argued that a request for counsel is not necessary once adversary proceedings have begun and, therefore, that Jackson and Patterson should be treated the same way.

The logic of the *Patterson* dissenters won the day, at least rhetorically, as the next case makes plain, but not in the way the *Patterson* dissenters wanted!

MONTEJO V. LOUISIANA

Supreme Court of the United States, 2009.
556 U.S. 778, 129 S.Ct. 2079, 173 L.Ed.2d 955.

JUSTICE SCALIA delivered the opinion of the Court [joined by CHIEF JUSTICE ROBERTS, and JUSTICES KENNEDY, THOMAS, and ALITO].

We consider in this case the scope and continued viability of the rule announced by this Court in *Michigan v. Jackson* forbidding police to initiate interrogation of a criminal defendant once he has requested counsel at an arraignment or similar proceeding.

I

Petitioner Jesse Montejo was arrested on September 6, 2002, in connection with the robbery and murder of Lewis Ferrari, who had been found dead in his own home one day earlier. Suspicion quickly focused on Jerry Moore, a disgruntled former employee of Ferrari's dry cleaning business. Police sought to question Montejo, who was a known associate of Moore.

Montejo waived his rights under *Miranda v. Arizona* and was interrogated at the sheriff's office by police detectives through the late afternoon and evening of September 6 and the early morning of September 7. During the interrogation, Montejo repeatedly changed his account of the crime, at first claiming that he had only driven Moore to the victim's home, and ultimately admitting that he had shot and killed Ferrari in the course of a botched burglary. These police interrogations were videotaped.

On September 10, Montejo was brought before a judge for what is known in Louisiana as a "72-hour hearing"—a preliminary hearing required under state law. Although the proceedings were not transcribed, the minute record indicates what transpired: "The defendant being charged with First Degree Murder, Court ordered N[o] Bond set in this matter. Further, Court ordered the Office of Indigent Defender be appointed to represent the defendant."

Later that same day, two police detectives visited Montejo back at the prison and requested that he accompany them on an excursion to locate the murder weapon (which Montejo had earlier indicated he had thrown into a lake). After some back-and-forth, the substance of which remains in dispute, Montejo was again read his *Miranda* rights and agreed to go along; during the excursion, he wrote an inculpatory letter of apology to the victim's widow. Only upon their return did Montejo finally meet his court-appointed attorney, who was quite upset that the detectives had interrogated his client in his absence.

At trial, the letter of apology was admitted over defense objection. The jury convicted Montejo of first-degree murder, and he was sentenced to death.

The Louisiana Supreme Court affirmed the conviction and sentence. As relevant here, the court rejected Montejo's argument that under the rule of *Jackson*, the letter should have been suppressed. *Jackson* held that "if police initiate interrogation after a defendant's assertion, at an arraignment or similar proceeding, of his right to counsel, any waiver of the defendant's right to counsel for that police-initiated interrogation is invalid."

Citing a decision of the United States Court of Appeals for the Fifth Circuit, the Louisiana Supreme Court reasoned that the prophylactic protection of *Jackson* is not triggered unless and until the defendant has actually requested a lawyer or has otherwise asserted his Sixth Amendment right to counsel. Because Montejo simply stood mute at his 72-hour hearing while the judge ordered the appointment of counsel, he had made no such request or assertion. So the proper inquiry, the court ruled, was only whether he had knowingly, intelligently, and voluntarily waived his right to have counsel present during the interaction with the police. And because Montejo had been read his *Miranda* rights and agreed to waive them, the Court answered that question in the affirmative, and upheld the conviction.

We granted certiorari.

II

Montejo and his amici raise a number of pragmatic objections to the Louisiana Supreme Court's interpretation of *Jackson*. We agree that the approach taken below would lead either to an unworkable standard, or to arbitrary and anomalous distinctions between defendants in different States. Neither would be acceptable.

Under the rule adopted by the Louisiana Supreme Court, a criminal defendant must request counsel, or otherwise "assert" his Sixth Amendment right at the preliminary hearing, before the *Jackson* protections are triggered. If he does so, the police may not initiate further interrogation in the absence of counsel. But if the court on its own appoints counsel, with the defendant taking no affirmative action to invoke his right to counsel, then police are free to initiate further interrogations provided that they first obtain an otherwise valid waiver by the defendant of his right to have counsel present.

This rule would apply well enough in States that require the indigent defendant formally to request counsel before any appointment is made, which usually occurs after the court has informed him that he will receive counsel if he asks for it. That is how the system works in Michigan, for example, whose scheme produced the factual background for this Court's decision in *Michigan v. Jackson*. Jackson, like all other represented indigent defendants in the State, had requested counsel in accordance with the applicable state law.

But many States follow other practices. In some two dozen, the appointment of counsel is automatic upon a finding of indigency, and in a number of others, appointment can be made either upon the defendant's request or sua sponte by the court. Nothing in our *Jackson* opinion indicates whether we were then aware that not all States require that a defendant affirmatively request counsel before one is appointed; and of course we had no occasion there to decide how the rule we announced would apply to these other States.

The Louisiana Supreme Court's answer to that unresolved question is troublesome. The central distinction it draws—between defendants who "assert" their right to counsel and those who do not—is exceedingly hazy when applied to States that appoint counsel absent request from the defendant. How to categorize a defendant who merely asks, prior to appointment, whether he will be appointed counsel? Or who inquires, after the fact, whether he has been? What treatment for one who thanks the court after the appointment is made? And if the court asks a defendant whether he would object to appointment, will a quick shake of his head count as an assertion of his right?

To the extent that the Louisiana Supreme Court's rule also permits a defendant to trigger *Jackson* through the "acceptance" of counsel, that notion is even more mysterious: How does one affirmatively accept counsel appointed by court order? An indigent defendant has no right to choose his counsel, so it is hard to imagine what his "acceptance" would look like, beyond the passive silence that Montejo exhibited.

In practice, judicial application of the Louisiana rule in States that do not require a defendant to make a request for counsel could take either of two paths. Courts might ask on a case-by-case basis whether a defendant has somehow invoked his right to counsel, looking to his conduct at the preliminary hearing—his statements and gestures—and the totality of the circumstances. Or, courts might simply determine as a categorical matter that defendants in these States—over half of those in the Union—simply have no opportunity to assert their right to counsel at the hearing and are therefore out of luck.

Neither approach is desirable. The former would be particularly impractical in light of the fact that, as amici describe, preliminary hearings are often rushed, and are frequently not recorded or transcribed. The sheer volume of indigent defendants, would render the monitoring of each particular defendant's reaction to the appointment of counsel almost impossible. And sometimes the defendant is not even present. Police who did not attend the hearing would have no way to know whether they could approach a particular defendant; and for a court to adjudicate that question ex post would be a fact-intensive and burdensome task, even if monitoring were possible and transcription available. Because "clarity of * * * command" and "certainty of * * * application" are crucial in rules that govern law enforcement, this would be an unfortunate way to proceed.

The second possible course fares no better, for it would achieve clarity and certainty only at the expense of introducing arbitrary distinctions: Defendants in States that automatically appoint counsel would have no opportunity to invoke their rights and trigger *Jackson*, while those in other States, effectively instructed by the court to request counsel, would be lucky winners. That sort of hollow formalism is out of place in a doctrine that purports to serve as a practical safeguard for defendants' rights.

III

But if the Louisiana Supreme Court's application of *Jackson* is unsound as a practical matter, then Montejo's solution is untenable as a theoretical and doctrinal matter. Under his approach, once a defendant is represented by counsel, police may not initiate any further interrogation. Such a rule would be entirely untethered from the original rationale of *Jackson*.

A

It is worth emphasizing first what is not in dispute or at stake here. Under our precedents, once the adversary judicial process has been initiated, the Sixth Amendment guarantees a defendant the right to have counsel present at all "critical" stages of the criminal proceedings. *Powell v. Alabama*, p. 25. Interrogation by the State is such a stage. *Massiah v. United States*.

Our precedents also place beyond doubt that the Sixth Amendment right to counsel may be waived by a defendant, so long as relinquishment of the right is voluntary, knowing, and intelligent. The defendant may waive the right whether or not he is already represented by counsel; the decision to waive need not itself be counseled. And when a defendant is read his *Miranda* rights (which include the right to have counsel present during interrogation) and agrees to waive those rights, that typically does the trick, even though the *Miranda* rights purportedly have their source in the Fifth Amendment:

> "As a general matter * * * an accused who is admonished with the warnings prescribed by this Court in Miranda * * * has been sufficiently apprised of the nature of his Sixth Amendment rights, and of the consequences of abandoning those rights, so

that his waiver on this basis will be considered a knowing and intelligent one." *Patterson.*

The only question raised by this case, and the only one addressed by the *Jackson* rule, is whether courts must presume that such a waiver is invalid under certain circumstances. We created such a presumption in *Jackson* by analogy to a similar prophylactic rule established to protect the Fifth Amendment based *Miranda* right to have counsel present at any custodial interrogation. *Edwards v. Arizona*, p. 733, decided that once "an accused has invoked his right to have counsel present during custodial interrogation * * * [he] is not subject to further interrogation by the authorities until counsel has been made available," unless he initiates the contact.

The *Edwards* rule is "designed to prevent police from badgering a defendant into waiving his previously asserted Miranda rights." It does this by presuming his postassertion statements to be involuntary, "even where the suspect executes a waiver and his statements would be considered voluntary under traditional standards." This prophylactic rule thus "protect[s] a suspect's voluntary choice not to speak outside his lawyer's presence."

Jackson represented a "wholesale importation of the *Edwards* rule into the Sixth Amendment." The *Jackson* Court decided that a request for counsel at an arraignment should be treated as an invocation of the Sixth Amendment right to counsel "at every critical stage of the prosecution," despite doubt that defendants "actually inten[d] their request for counsel to encompass representation during any further questioning," because doubts must be "resolved in favor of protecting the constitutional claim." Citing *Edwards,* the Court held that any subsequent waiver would thus be "insufficient to justify police-initiated interrogation." In other words, we presume such waivers involuntary "based on the supposition that suspects who assert their right to counsel are unlikely to waive that right voluntarily" in subsequent interactions with police.

The dissent presents us with a revisionist view of *Jackson.* The defendants' request for counsel, it contends, was important only because it proved that counsel had been appointed. Such a non sequitur (nowhere alluded to in the case) hardly needs rebuttal. Proceeding from this fanciful premise, the dissent claims that the decision actually established "a rule designed to safeguard a defendant's right to rely on the assistance of counsel," not one "designed to prevent police badgering." To safeguard the right to assistance of counsel from what? From a knowing and voluntary waiver by the defendant himself? Unless the dissent seeks to prevent a defendant altogether from waiving his Sixth Amendment rights, i.e., to "imprison a man in his privileges and call it the Constitution"—a view with zero support in reason, history or case law—

the answer must be: from police pressure, i.e., badgering. The antibadgering rationale is the only way to make sense of *Jackson's* repeated citations of *Edwards*, and the only way to reconcile the opinion with our waiver jurisprudence.

B

With this understanding of what *Jackson* stands for and whence it came, it should be clear that Montejo's interpretation of that decision— that no represented defendant can ever be approached by the State and asked to consent to interrogation—is off the mark. When a court appoints counsel for an indigent defendant in the absence of any request on his part, there is no basis for a presumption that any subsequent waiver of the right to counsel will be involuntary. There is no "initial election" to exercise the right that must be preserved through a prophylactic rule against later waivers. No reason exists to assume that a defendant like Montejo, who has done nothing at all to express his intentions with respect to his Sixth Amendment rights, would not be perfectly amenable to speaking with the police without having counsel present. And no reason exists to prohibit the police from inquiring. *Edwards* and *Jackson* are meant to prevent police from badgering defendants into changing their minds about their rights, but a defendant who never asked for counsel has not yet made up his mind in the first instance.

The dissent's argument to the contrary rests on a flawed a fortiori: "If a defendant is entitled to protection from police-initiated interrogation under the Sixth Amendment when he merely requests a lawyer, he is even more obviously entitled to such protection when he has secured a lawyer." The question in *Jackson*, however, was not whether respondents were entitled to counsel (they unquestionably were), but "whether respondents validly waived their right to counsel"; and even if it is reasonable to presume from a defendant's request for counsel that any subsequent waiver of the right was coerced, no such presumption can seriously be entertained when a lawyer was merely "secured" on the defendant's behalf, by the State itself, as a matter of course. Of course, reading the dissent's analysis, one would have no idea that Montejo executed any waiver at all.

In practice, Montejo's rule would prevent police-initiated interrogation entirely once the Sixth Amendment right attaches, at least in those States that appoint counsel promptly without request from the defendant. * * * That would have constituted a "shockingly dramatic restructuring of the balance this Court has traditionally struck between the rights of the defendant and those of the larger society."

Montejo's rule appears to have its theoretical roots in codes of legal ethics, not the Sixth Amendment. The American Bar Association's Model Rules of Professional Conduct (which nearly all States have adopted into law in whole or in part) mandate that "a lawyer shall not communicate about the subject of [a] representation with a party the lawyer knows to be represented by another lawyer in the matter, unless the lawyer has the consent of the other lawyer or is authorized to do so by law or a court order." But the Constitution does not codify the ABA's Model Rules, and does not make investigating police officers lawyers. Montejo's proposed rule is both broader and narrower than the Model Rule. Broader, because Montejo would apply it to all agents of the State, including the detectives who interrogated him, while the ethical rule governs only lawyers. And narrower, because he agrees that if a defendant initiates contact with the police, they may talk freely—whereas a lawyer could be sanctioned for interviewing a represented party even if that party "initiates" the communication and consents to the interview. * * *

The upshot is that even on *Jackson*'s own terms, it would be completely unjustified to presume that a defendant's consent to police-initiated interrogation was involuntary or coerced simply because he had previously been appointed a lawyer.

IV

So on the one hand, requiring an initial "invocation" of the right to counsel in order to trigger the *Jackson* presumption is consistent with the theory of that decision, but (as Montejo and his amici argue, see Part II, supra) would be unworkable in more than half the States of the Union. On the other hand, eliminating the invocation requirement would render the rule easy to apply but depart fundamentally from the *Jackson* rationale.

We do not think that stare decisis requires us to expand significantly the holding of a prior decision—fundamentally revising its theoretical basis in the process—in order to cure its practical deficiencies. To the contrary, the fact that a decision has proved "unworkable" is a traditional ground for overruling it. Accordingly, we called for supplemental briefing addressed to the question whether *Michigan v. Jackson* should be overruled.

Beyond workability, the relevant factors in deciding whether to adhere to the principle of stare decisis include the antiquity of the precedent, the reliance interests at stake, and of course whether the decision was well reasoned. The first two cut in favor of abandoning *Jackson*: the opinion is only two decades old, and eliminating it would not upset expectations. Any criminal defendant learned enough to order his affairs based on the rule announced in *Jackson* would also be perfectly capable of interacting with the police on his own. Of course it is likely true that police and prosecutors have been trained to comply with *Jackson*, but that is hardly a basis for retaining it as a constitutional requirement. If a State wishes to abstain from requesting interviews with represented defendants when counsel is not present, it obviously may continue to do so.

Which brings us to the strength of *Jackson*'s reasoning. When this Court creates a prophylactic rule in order to protect a constitutional right, the relevant "reasoning" is the weighing of the rule's benefits against its costs. "The value of any prophylactic rule * * * must be assessed not only on the basis of what is gained, but also on the basis of what is lost." We think that the marginal benefits of *Jackson* (viz., the number of confessions obtained coercively that are suppressed by its bright-line rule and would otherwise have been admitted) are dwarfed by its substantial costs (viz., hindering "society's compelling interest in finding, convicting, and punishing those who violate the law").

What does the *Jackson* rule actually achieve by way of preventing unconstitutional conduct? Recall that the purpose of the rule is to preclude the State from badgering defendants into waiving their previously asserted rights. The effect of this badgering might be to coerce a waiver, which would render the subsequent interrogation a violation of the Sixth Amendment. Even though involuntary waivers are invalid even apart from *Jackson*, mistakes are of course possible when courts conduct case-by-case voluntariness review. A bright-line rule like that adopted in *Jackson* ensures that no fruits of interrogations made possible by badgering-induced involuntary waivers are ever erroneously admitted at trial.

But without *Jackson*, how many would be? The answer is few if any. The principal reason is that the Court has already taken substantial other, overlapping measures toward the same end. Under *Miranda*'s prophylactic protection of the right against compelled self-incrimination, any suspect subject to custodial interrogation has the right to have a lawyer present if he so requests, and to be advised of that right. Under *Edwards*' prophylactic protection of the *Miranda* right, once such a defendant "has invoked his right to have counsel present," interrogation must stop. And under *Minnick*'s [*Minnick v. Mississippi*, 498 U.S. 146, 111 S. Ct. 486, 112 L. Ed. 2d 489 (1990)] prophylactic protection of the *Edwards* right, no subsequent interrogation may take place until counsel is present, "whether or not the accused has consulted with his attorney."

These three layers of prophylaxis are sufficient. Under the *Miranda-Edwards-Minnick* line of cases (which is not in doubt), a defendant who does not want to speak to the police without counsel present need only say as much when he is first approached and given the *Miranda* warnings. At that point, not only must the immediate contact end, but "badgering" by later requests is prohibited. If that regime suffices to protect the integrity of "a suspect's voluntary choice not to speak outside his lawyer's presence" before his arraignment, it is hard to see why it would not also suffice to protect that same choice after arraignment, when Sixth Amendment rights have attached. And if so, then *Jackson* is simply superfluous.

It is true, as Montejo points out in his supplemental brief, that the doctrine established by *Miranda* and *Edwards* is designed to protect Fifth Amendment, not Sixth Amendment, rights. But that is irrelevant. What matters is that these cases, like *Jackson*, protect the right to have counsel during custodial interrogation—which right happens to be guaranteed (once the adversary judicial process has begun) by two sources of law. Since the right under both sources is waived using the same procedure, *Patterson*, doctrines ensuring voluntariness of the Fifth Amendment waiver simultaneously ensure the voluntariness of the Sixth Amendment waiver.

Montejo also correctly observes that the *Miranda-Edwards* regime is narrower than *Jackson* in one respect: The former applies only in the context of custodial interrogation. If the defendant is not in custody then those decisions do not apply; nor do they govern other, noninterrogative types of interactions between the defendant and the State (like pretrial lineups). However, those uncovered situations are the least likely to pose a risk of coerced waivers. When a defendant is not in custody, he is in control, and need only shut his door or walk away to avoid police badgering. And noninterrogative interactions with the State do not involve the "inherently compelling pressures" that one might reasonably fear could lead to involuntary waivers.

Jackson was policy driven, and if that policy is being adequately served through other means, there is no reason to retain its rule. *Miranda* and the cases that elaborate upon it already guarantee not simply noncoercion in the traditional sense, but what Justice Harlan referred to as "voluntariness with a vengeance." There is no need to take *Jackson*'s further step of requiring voluntariness on stilts.

On the other side of the equation are the costs of adding the bright-line *Jackson* rule on top of *Edwards* and other extant protections. The principal cost of applying any exclusionary rule "is, of course, letting guilty and possibly dangerous criminals go free * * * ." *Herring v. United States*, p. 568. *Jackson* not only "operates to invalidate a confession given by the free choice of suspects who have received proper advice of their *Miranda* rights but waived them nonetheless," but also deters law enforcement officers from even trying to obtain voluntary confessions. The "ready ability to obtain uncoerced confessions is not an evil but an unmitigated good." Without these confessions, crimes go unsolved and criminals unpunished. These are not negligible costs, and in our view the *Jackson* Court gave them too short shrift. * * *

* * * Montejo expresses concern that courts will have to determine whether statements made at preliminary hearings constitute *Edwards* invocations—thus implicating all the practical problems of the Louisiana rule we discussed above, see Part II, supra. That concern is misguided. "We have in fact never held that a person can invoke his *Miranda* rights anticipatorily, in a context other than 'custodial interrogation' * * * ." What matters for *Miranda* and *Edwards* is what happens when the defendant is approached for interrogation, and (if he consents) what happens during the interrogation—not what happened at any preliminary hearing.

In sum, when the marginal benefits of the *Jackson* rule are weighed against its substantial costs to the truth-seeking process and the criminal justice system, we readily conclude that the rule does not "pay its way." *Michigan v. Jackson* should be and now is overruled.

V

Although our holding means that the Louisiana Supreme Court correctly rejected Montejo's claim under *Jackson*, we think that Montejo should be given an opportunity to contend that his letter of apology should still have been suppressed under the rule of *Edwards*. If Montejo made a clear assertion of the right to counsel when the officers approached him about accompanying them on the excursion for the murder weapon, then no interrogation should have taken place unless Montejo initiated it. Even if Montejo subsequently agreed to waive his rights, that waiver would have been invalid had it followed an "unequivocal election of the right." * * *

We do reject, however, the dissent's revisionist legal analysis of the "knowing and voluntary" issue. In determining whether a Sixth Amendment waiver was knowing and voluntary, there is no reason categorically to distinguish an unrepresented defendant from a represented one. It is equally true for each that, as we held in *Patterson*, the *Miranda* warnings adequately inform him "of his right to have counsel present during the questioning," and make him "aware of the consequences of a decision by him to waive his Sixth Amendment rights," Somewhat surprisingly for an opinion that extols the virtues of stare decisis, the dissent complains that our "treatment of the waiver question rests entirely on the dubious decision in *Patterson*." The Court in *Patterson* did not consider the result dubious, nor does the Court today.

* * *

This case is an exemplar of Justice Jackson's oft quoted warning that this Court "is forever adding new stories to the temples of constitutional law, and the temples have a way of collapsing when one story too many is added." We today remove *Michigan v. Jackson*'s fourth story of prophylaxis. * * *

JUSTICE ALITO, with whom JUSTICE KENNEDY joins, concurring. [omitted]

JUSTICE STEVENS, with whom JUSTICE SOUTER and JUSTICE GINSBURG join, and with whom JUSTICE BREYER joins, except for [omitted] footnote 5, dissenting.

Today the Court properly concludes that the Louisiana Supreme Court's parsimonious reading of our decision in *Michigan v. Jackson* is indefensible. Yet the Court does not reverse. Rather, on its own initiative and without any evidence that the longstanding Sixth Amendment protections established in *Jackson* have caused any harm to the workings of the criminal justice system, the Court rejects *Jackson* outright on the ground that it is "untenable as a theoretical and doctrinal matter." That conclusion rests on a misinterpretation of *Jackson*'s rationale and a gross undervaluation of the rule of stare decisis. The police interrogation in this case clearly violated petitioner's Sixth Amendment right to counsel. * * *

II * * *

The majority's decision to overrule *Jackson* rests on its assumption that *Jackson*'s protective rule was intended to "prevent police from badgering defendants into changing their minds about their rights" just as the rule adopted in *Edwards v. Arizona* was designed to prevent police from coercing unindicted suspects into revoking their requests for counsel at interrogation. Operating on that limited understanding of the purpose behind *Jackson*'s protective rule, the Court concludes that *Jackson* provides no safeguard not already secured by this Court's Fifth Amendment jurisprudence.

The majority's analysis flagrantly misrepresents *Jackson*'s underlying rationale and the constitutional interests the decision sought to protect. While it is true that the rule adopted in *Jackson* was patterned after the rule in *Edwards*, the *Jackson* opinion does not even mention the anti-badgering considerations that provide the basis for the Court's decision today. Instead, *Jackson* relied primarily on cases discussing the broad protections guaranteed by the Sixth Amendment right to counsel—not its Fifth Amendment counterpart. *Jackson* emphasized that the purpose of the Sixth Amendment is to " 'protec[t] the unaided layman at critical confrontations with his adversary,' " by giving him " 'the right to rely on counsel as a 'medium' between him[self] and the State.' " Underscoring that the commencement of criminal proceedings is a decisive event that transforms a suspect into an accused within the meaning of the Sixth Amendment, we concluded that arraigned defendants are entitled to "at least as much protection" during interrogation as the Fifth Amendment affords unindicted suspects. Thus, although the rules adopted in *Edwards* and *Jackson* are similar, *Jackson* did not rely on the reasoning of *Edwards* but remained firmly rooted in the unique protections afforded to the attorney-client relationship by the Sixth Amendment.

Once *Jackson* is placed in its proper Sixth Amendment context, the majority's justifications for overruling the decision crumble. * * *

III

Even if *Jackson* had never been decided, it would be clear that Montejo's Sixth Amendment rights were violated. Today's decision eliminates the rule that "any waiver of Sixth Amendment rights given in a discussion initiated by police is presumed invalid" once a defendant has invoked his right to counsel. Nevertheless, under the undisputed facts of this case, there is no sound basis for concluding that Montejo made a knowing and valid waiver of his Sixth Amendment right to counsel before acquiescing in police interrogation following his 72-hour hearing. Because police questioned Montejo without notice to, and outside the presence of, his lawyer, the interrogation violated Montejo's right to counsel even under pre-*Jackson* precedent. * * *

The Court avoids confronting the serious Sixth Amendment concerns raised by the police interrogation in this case by assuming that Montejo validly waived his Sixth Amendment rights before submitting to interrogation. It does so by summarily concluding that "doctrines ensuring voluntariness of the Fifth Amendment waiver simultaneously ensure the voluntariness of the Sixth Amendment waiver"; thus, because Montejo was given *Miranda* warnings prior to interrogation, his waiver was presumptively valid. Ironically, while the Court faults *Jackson* for blurring the line between this Court's Fifth and Sixth Amendment jurisprudence, it commits the same error by assuming that the *Miranda* warnings given in this case, designed purely to safeguard the Fifth Amendment right against self-incrimination, were somehow adequate to protect Montejo's more robust Sixth Amendment right to counsel.

The majority's cursory treatment of the waiver question rests entirely on the dubious decision in *Patterson*, in which we addressed whether, by providing *Miranda* warnings, police had adequately advised an indicted but unrepresented defendant of his Sixth Amendment right to counsel. The majority held that "[a]s a general matter * * * an accused who is admonished with the warnings prescribed * * * in *Miranda*, * * * has been sufficiently apprised of the nature of his Sixth Amendment rights, and of the consequences of abandoning those rights." The Court recognized, however, that "because the Sixth Amendment's protection of the attorney-client relationship * * * extends beyond *Miranda*'s protection of the Fifth Amendment right to counsel, . . . there will be cases where a waiver which would be valid under *Miranda* will not suffice for Sixth Amendment purposes." This is such a case. * * *

A defendant's decision to forgo counsel's assistance and speak openly with police is a momentous one. Given the high stakes of making such a choice and the potential value of counsel's advice and mediation at that critical stage of the criminal proceedings, it is imperative that a defendant possess "a full awareness of both the nature of the right being abandoned and the consequences of the decision to abandon it." Because the administration of *Miranda* warnings was insufficient to ensure Montejo understood the Sixth Amendment right he was being asked to surrender, the record in this case provides no basis for concluding that Montejo validly waived his right to counsel, even in the absence of *Jackson*'s enhanced protections.

IV

The Court's decision to overrule *Jackson* is unwarranted. Not only does it rests on a flawed doctrinal premise, but the dubious benefits it hopes to achieve are far outweighed by the damage it does to the rule of law and the integrity of the Sixth Amendment right to counsel. Moreover, even apart from the protections afforded by *Jackson*, the police interrogation in this case violated Jesse Montejo's Sixth Amendment right to counsel.

I respectfully dissent.

JUSTICE BREYER, dissenting. [omitted].

NOTES AND QUESTIONS

1. *Montejo* is a 5–4 case that overrules a precedent, *Michigan v. Jackson*, on the strength of a 5–4 case, *Patterson*, p. 777. Compare Justice Stevens's dissent in *Montejo* with his dissent in *Patterson*. Can you explain how his theory of *Massiah* differs from the majority in *Montejo*? Which view do you prefer? Which is closest to the *Massiah* opinion?

2. How far does *Montejo* extend? In *Michigan v. Jackson*, the defendant had requested counsel but had yet to consult with his lawyer. Defendants like Jackson will be in the same position when being questioned by police or prosecutors as suspects who are interrogated early in a police investigation. But what if an indicted defendant who is in jail consults with counsel and then, after the lawyer leaves, police secure a *Miranda* waiver? Can this defendant successfully argue that his *Miranda* waiver does not also waive his *Massiah* right to counsel?

3. Sherry Colb has pointed out that, at its core, *Massiah* is an empty formalism. *Massiah* treats similarly situated defendants differently depending on whether charges have been filed. But, Colb argues, indictment is a meaningless threshold when the issue is whether defendants need legal

advice about how to respond to police who are seeking statements from them. Why doesn't a defendant need advice of counsel the day before indictment just as much as he needs advice the day after indictment? See Sherry F. Colb, *Why the Supreme Court Should Overrule the Massiah Doctrine and Permit Miranda Alone to Govern Interrogations*, at http://writ.news.findlaw.com/colb/20010509.html.

4. *Miranda and Massiah: two peas in a pod?* Now that *Jackson* has been overruled, is *Massiah*'s protection different from *Miranda*'s when the defendant is being questioned by police or prosecutors? One way to read *Brewer*, p. 764, is that waiver by action might be more difficult for the State to show under *Massiah* than under *Miranda*. Compare *Berghuis v. Thompkins*, p. 720, with the facts of *Brewer*. But *Brewer* is now 35 years old, and the strength of its reasoning can be doubted. However that issue comes out, *Montejo* tells us that formal waivers of *Miranda* suffice to waive *Massiah* even if the defendant has been appointed counsel at an earlier judicial proceeding.

It may turn out that *Massiah* offers greater protection than *Miranda* along only one dimension: the facts of *Massiah* itself. *Massiah*, but not *Miranda*, applies when the police are trying to obtain information and the suspect is unaware that he is talking to the police. This principle explains not only *Massiah* but also *Henry*, p. 761, and *Maine v. Moulton*, p. 763, Note 1.

And, as we will see in the next case, *Massiah* also provides *less* protection along one dimension.

C. *MASSIAH* AND *MIRANDA*: A DIVERGENCE

McNEIL v. WISCONSIN
Supreme Court of the United States, 1991.
501 U.S. 171, 111 S.Ct. 2204, 115 L.Ed.2d 158.

JUSTICE SCALIA delivered the opinion of the Court [joined by CHIEF JUSTICE REHNQUIST, and JUSTICES WHITE, O'CONNOR, KENNEDY, and SOUTER].

This case presents the question whether an accused's invocation of his Sixth Amendment right to counsel during a judicial proceeding constitutes an invocation of his *Miranda* right to counsel.

I

Petitioner Paul McNeil was arrested in Omaha, Nebraska, in May 1987, pursuant to a warrant charging him with an armed robbery in West Allis, Wisconsin, a suburb of Milwaukee. Shortly after his arrest, two Milwaukee County deputy sheriffs arrived in Omaha to retrieve him. After advising him of his *Miranda* rights, the deputies sought to question him. He refused to answer any questions, but did not request an attorney. The deputies promptly ended the interview.

Once back in Wisconsin, petitioner was brought before a Milwaukee County Court Commissioner on the armed robbery charge. The Commissioner set bail and scheduled a preliminary examination. An attorney from the Wisconsin Public Defender's Office represented petitioner at this initial appearance.

Later that evening, Detective Joseph Butts of the Milwaukee County Sheriff's Department visited petitioner in jail. Butts had been assisting the Racine County, Wisconsin, police in their investigation of a murder, attempted murder, and armed burglary in the town of Caledonia; petitioner was a suspect. Butts advised petitioner of his *Miranda* rights, and petitioner signed a form waiving them. In this first interview, petitioner did not deny knowledge of the Caledonia crimes, but said that he had not been involved.

Butts returned two days later with detectives from Caledonia. He again began the encounter by advising petitioner of his *Miranda* rights and providing a waiver form. Petitioner placed his initials next to each of the warnings and signed the form. This time, petitioner admitted that he had been involved in the Caledonia crimes, which he described in detail. He also implicated two other men, Willie Pope and Lloyd Crowley. The statement was typed up by a detective and given to petitioner to review. Petitioner placed his initials next to every reference to himself and signed every page.

Butts and the Caledonia Police returned two days later, having in the meantime found and questioned Pope, who convinced them that he had not been involved in the Caledonia crimes. They again began the interview by administering the *Miranda* warnings and obtaining petitioner's signature and initials on the waiver form. Petitioner acknowledged that he had lied about Pope's involvement to minimize his own role in the Caledonia crimes and provided another statement recounting the events, which was transcribed, signed, and initialed as before. * * *

II

The Sixth Amendment provides that "[i]n all criminal prosecutions, the accused shall enjoy the right * * * to have the Assistance of Counsel for his defence." In *Michigan v. Jackson*, 475 U.S. 625, 106 S.Ct. 1404, 89 L.Ed.2d 631 (1986), we held that once this right to counsel has attached and has been invoked, any subsequent waiver during a police-initiated custodial interview is ineffective. It is undisputed, and we accept for purposes of the present case, that at the time petitioner provided the incriminating statements at issue, his Sixth Amendment right had attached and had been invoked with respect to the *West Allis armed robbery*, for which he had been formally charged.

The Sixth Amendment right, however, is offense specific. It cannot be invoked once for all future prosecutions, for it does not attach until a prosecution is commenced, that is, " 'at or after the initiation of adversary judicial criminal proceedings—whether by way of formal charge, preliminary hearing, indictment, information, or arraignment.' " And just as the right is offense specific, so also its *Michigan v. Jackson* effect of invalidating subsequent waivers in police-initiated interviews is offense specific. * * * Because petitioner provided the statements at issue here before his Sixth Amendment right to counsel with respect to the *Caledonia offenses* had been (or even could have been) invoked, that right poses no bar to the admission of the statements in this case.

Petitioner relies, however, upon a different "right to counsel," found not in the text of the Sixth Amendment, but in this Court's jurisprudence relating to the Fifth Amendment [*Miranda* prophylactic rights]. * * *

In *Edwards v. Arizona* [p. 733], we established a second layer of prophylaxis for the *Miranda* right to counsel: Once a suspect asserts the right, not only must the current interrogation cease, but he may not be approached for further interrogation "until counsel has been made available to him,"—which means, we have most recently held, that counsel must be present, *Minnick v. Mississippi*, 498 U.S. 146, 111 S.Ct. 486, 112 L.Ed.2d 489 (1990). If the police do subsequently initiate an encounter in the absence of counsel (assuming there has been no break in custody), the suspect's statements are presumed involuntary and therefore inadmissible as substantive evidence at trial, even where the suspect executes a waiver and his statements would be considered voluntary under traditional standards. This is "designed to prevent police from badgering a defendant into waiving his previously asserted *Miranda* rights." The *Edwards* rule, moreover, is *not* offense specific: Once a suspect invokes the *Miranda* right to counsel for interrogation regarding one offense, he may not be reapproached regarding *any* offense unless counsel is present.

Having described the nature and effects of both the Sixth Amendment right to counsel and the *Miranda-Edwards* "Fifth Amendment" right to counsel, we come at last to the issue here: Petitioner seeks to prevail by combining the two of them. He contends that, although he expressly waived his *Miranda* right to counsel on every occasion he was interrogated, those waivers were the invalid product of impermissible approaches, because his prior invocation of the offense specific Sixth Amendment right with regard to the West Allis burglary was also an invocation of the nonoffense-specific *Miranda-Edwards* right. We think that is false as a matter of fact and inadvisable (if even permissible) as a contrary-to-fact presumption of policy.

As to the former: The purpose of the Sixth Amendment counsel guarantee—and hence the purpose of invoking it—is to "protec[t] the unaided layman at critical confrontations" with his "expert adversary," the government, *after* "the adverse positions of government and defendant have solidified" with respect to a particular alleged crime. The purpose of the *Miranda-Edwards* guarantee, on the other hand—and hence the purpose of invoking it—is to protect a quite different interest: the suspect's "desire to deal with the police only through counsel." This is in one respect narrower than the interest protected by the Sixth Amendment guarantee (because it relates only to custodial interrogation) and in another respect broader (because it relates to interrogation regarding *any* suspected crime and attaches whether or not the "adversarial relationship" produced by a pending prosecution has yet arisen). To invoke the Sixth Amendment interest is, as a matter of *fact*, *not* to invoke the *Miranda-Edwards* interest. One might be quite willing to speak to the police without counsel present concerning many matters, but not the matter under prosecution. It can be said, perhaps, that it is *likely* that one who has asked for counsel's assistance in defending against a prosecution would want counsel present for all custodial interrogation, even interrogation unrelated to the charge. That is not necessarily true, since suspects often believe that they can avoid the laying of charges by demonstrating an assurance of innocence through frank and unassisted answers to questions. But even if it were true, the *likelihood* that a suspect would wish counsel to be present is not the test for applicability of *Edwards*. The rule of that case applies only when the suspect "ha[s] *expressed*" his wish for the particular sort of lawyerly assistance that is the subject of *Miranda*. It requires, at a minimum, some statement that can reasonably be construed to be an expression of a desire for the assistance of an attorney *in dealing with custodial interrogation by the police*. Requesting the assistance of an attorney at a bail hearing does not bear that construction. * * *

There remains to be considered the possibility that, even though the assertion of the Sixth Amendment right to counsel does not *in fact* imply an assertion of the *Miranda* "Fifth Amendment" right, we should declare it to be such as a matter of sound policy. Assuming we have such an expansive power under the Constitution, it would not wisely be exercised. Petitioner's proposed rule has only insignificant advantages. If a suspect does not wish to communicate with the police except through an attorney, he can simply tell them that when they give him the *Miranda* warnings. There is not the remotest chance that he will feel "badgered" by their asking to talk to him without counsel present, since the subject will not be the charge on which he has already requested counsel's assistance (for in that event *Jackson* would preclude initiation of the interview) and he will not have rejected uncounseled interrogation on *any* subject before (for in that event *Edwards* would preclude initiation of the interview). The proposed rule would, however, seriously impede effective law enforcement. The Sixth Amendment right to counsel attaches at the first formal proceeding against an accused, and in most States, at least with respect to serious offenses, free counsel is made available at that time and ordinarily requested. Thus, if we were to adopt petitioner's rule, most persons in pretrial custody for serious offenses would be *unapproachable* by police officers suspecting them of involvement in other crimes, *even though they have never expressed any unwillingness to be questioned.* Since the ready ability to obtain uncoerced confessions is not an evil but an unmitigated good, society would be the loser. Admissions of guilt resulting from valid *Miranda* waivers "are more than merely 'desirable'; they are essential to society's compelling interest in finding, convicting, and punishing those who violate the law."[2]

Petitioner urges upon us the desirability of providing a "clear and unequivocal" guideline for the police: no police-initiated questioning of any person in custody who has requested counsel to assist him in defense or in interrogation. But the police do not need our assistance to establish such a guideline; they are free, if they wish, to adopt it on their own. Of course it is our task to establish guidelines for judicial review. We like *them* to be "clear and unequivocal," but only when they guide sensibly and in a direction we are authorized to go. Petitioner's proposal would in our view do much more harm than good, and is not contained within, or even in furtherance of, the Sixth Amendment's right to counsel or the Fifth Amendment's right against compelled self-incrimination.[3] * * *

---

[2] The dissent condemns these sentiments as "revealing a preference for an inquisitorial system of justice." We cannot imagine what this means. What makes a system adversarial rather than inquisitorial is not the presence of counsel, much less the presence of counsel where the defendant has not requested it; but rather, the presence of a judge who does not (as an inquisitor does) conduct the factual and legal investigation himself, but instead decides on the basis of facts and arguments pro and con adduced by the parties. In the inquisitorial criminal process of the civil law, the defendant ordinarily has counsel; and in the adversarial criminal process of the common law, he sometimes does not. Our system of justice is, and has always been, an inquisitorial one at the investigatory stage (even the grand jury is an inquisitorial body), and no other disposition is conceivable. Even if detectives were to bring impartial magistrates around with them to all interrogations, there would be no decision for the impartial magistrate to umpire. If all the dissent means by a "preference for an inquisitorial system" is a preference not to require the presence of counsel during an investigatory interview where the interviewee has not requested it—that is a strange way to put it, but we are guilty.

[3] The dissent predicts that the result in this case will routinely be circumvented when, "[i]n future preliminary hearings, competent counsel * * * make sure that they, or their clients, make a statement on the record" invoking the *Miranda* right to counsel. We have in fact never held that a person can invoke his *Miranda* rights anticipatorily, in a context other than "custodial interrogation"—which a preliminary hearing will not always, or even usually, involve. If the *Miranda* right to counsel can be invoked at a preliminary hearing, it could be argued, there is no logical reason why it could not be invoked by a letter prior to arrest, or indeed even prior to identification as a suspect. Most rights must be asserted when the government seeks to take the action they protect against. The fact that we have allowed the *Miranda* right to counsel, once asserted, to be effective with respect to future custodial interrogation does not necessarily mean that we will allow it to be asserted initially outside the context of custodial interrogation, with similar future effect. * * *

"This Court is forever adding new stories to the temples of constitutional law, and the temples have a way of collapsing when one story too many is added." We decline to add yet another story to *Miranda*. * * *

[The opinion of JUSTICE KENNEDY, concurring, is omitted.]

JUSTICE STEVENS, with whom JUSTICE MARSHALL and JUSTICE BLACKMUN join, dissenting.

The Court's opinion demeans the importance of the right to counsel. As a practical matter, the opinion probably will have only a slight impact on current custodial interrogation procedures. As a theoretical matter, the Court's innovative development of an "offense-specific" limitation on the scope of the attorney-client relationship can only generate confusion in the law and undermine the protections that undergird our adversarial system of justice. As a symbolic matter, today's decision is ominous because it reflects a preference for an inquisitorial system that regards the defense lawyer as an impediment rather than a servant to the cause of justice. * * *

NOTES AND QUESTIONS

1.   Is it fair to say that Justice Scalia's opinion is truer to the constitutional text, while McNeil's argument is more concerned with the pragmatic effect of not having a bright-line rule? Which position do you prefer?

2.   In footnote 3, Justice Scalia is skeptical that the Fifth Amendment right to counsel can be invoked at the preliminary hearing or in a letter to the police. The Court re-affirmed this skepticism in Bobby v. Dixon, 565 U.S. ___, 132 S.Ct. 26, 181 L.Ed.2d 328 (2011) (per curiam).

3.   Notice that *McNeil* is an earlier case than *Montejo* (p. 788). Does the overruling of *Michigan v. Jackson* undermine the reasoning in *McNeil*?

4.   In Texas v. Cobb, 532 U.S. 162, 121 S.Ct. 1335, 149 L.Ed.2d 321 (2001), the Court emphasized that *McNeil* had held the Sixth Amendment right to counsel to be "offense specific." But what does it mean to say that the right is *"offense* specific"? Blackstone told us that murder is the same offense as manslaughter, for purposes of the common law prohibition of double jeopardy, but is murder the same double jeopardy offense as a burglary that led to a murder? If not, are these different *Sixth Amendment* offenses? The Court answered these questions in *Cobb*. The initial report to the sheriff was of a burglary and the disappearance of a woman and her sixteen-month-old daughter from the home. Cobb later confessed to the burglary but denied involvement in the disappearances. The state indicted Cobb for burglary, and the judge appointed counsel to represent him. The lawyer gave police permission to talk to his client, who continued to deny that he knew anything about the woman and child.

Later, free on bond, Cobb told his father that he had killed the woman when she confronted him during the burglary. The father reported this information to the authorities, who arrested Cobb. He waived his *Miranda* rights and confessed to killing and burying both the mother and her infant. The details of the death of the infant were particularly gruesome. The Texas Court of Criminal Appeals reversed Cobb's conviction on the ground that the confession was inadmissible. Cobb's Sixth Amendment right to counsel protected him from any questioning about the burglary, the state court held, and the murders were the same Sixth Amendment "offense" because they were "factually interwoven with the burglary."

The Supreme Court rejected the state court's test of "factual relation" and held that the test for "same offense" in the Sixth Amendment context is the same as in the Fifth Amendment double jeopardy clause, namely the so-called *"Blockburger"* test from Blockburger v. United States, 284 U.S. 299, 304, 52 S.Ct. 180, 182, 76 L.Ed. 306 (1932). See Chapter 18. This test finds different statutory offenses to be the same *only* when the elements of one offense are *necessarily* included in the elements of the other offense. One way to express this principle is to say that offenses are the same only when proving the elements of the greater will *always* prove the elements of the lesser.

For example, offense *A* with elements 1, 2, and 3 is the same double jeopardy offense as offense *B* with elements 1 and 2, but *A* is *not* the same offense as offense *C* with elements 1, 2, and 4. To use real life examples, if proving auto theft always proves joyriding, they are the same offense. This, of course, explains why murder is typically the same offense as manslaughter. But murder is not the same offense as burglary. Murder requires proof of a killing while burglary requires proof of breaking and entering. That the murders occurred during the course of the burglary is, according to the Court, insufficient to make the offenses the same for Sixth Amendment purposes. Thus, the Sixth Amendment did not prohibit questioning Cobb about the murders after he had been indicted for the burglary.

Justice Breyer dissented, joined by Justices Stevens, Souter, and Ginsburg, pointing out that criminal codes have overlapping statutory offenses that permit prosecutors to "spin out a startlingly numerous series of offenses from a single * * * criminal transaction." Thus, the dissent argued, the majority's rule will "significantly diminish[ ] the Sixth Amendment protections" found in earlier cases:

> In fact, under the rule today announced by the majority, [Brewer v. Williams would have been decided differently.] Because first-degree murder and child abduction each required proof of a fact not required by the other, and because at the time of the impermissible interrogation Williams had been charged only with abduction of a child, Williams' murder conviction should have remained undisturbed. This is not to suggest that this Court has previously addressed and decided the question presented by this

case. Rather, it is to point out that the Court's conception of the Sixth Amendment right at the time that *Moulton* and *Brewer* were decided naturally presumed that it extended to factually related but uncharged offenses.

Given the values that underlie the *Massiah* right to counsel, who gets the better of the argument here? Should "offense" be defined more broadly than for Fifth Amendment double jeopardy purposes? The Texas Court of Criminal Appeals used a test of "close factual relation." Is this a better test than *Blockburger*?

5.   When does *offense-specific matter*? How would *Cobb* be decided today?

6.   As the *Cobb* dissent concluded, *Brewer v. Williams* would have been decided differently if the Cobb definition of "offense" had been applied. The Court, however, did not discuss the definition of "offense" in *Brewer*. If the Court rules in favor of a defendant, without mentioning a particular issue but necessarily resolving that issue in the defendant's favor, is the question settled for purposes of *stare decisis*? Was *Cobb* wrong in treating the "offense" issue as "previously undecided?"

7.   Now that you have reached the end of the Massiah journey, can you summarize the differences between the Fifth Amendment right to counsel and the Sixth Amendment right to counsel during interrogation? For one effort to do so, see 1 Joshua Dressler & Alan C. Michaels, Understanding Criminal Procedure § 25.08 (6th ed. 2013).

CHAPTER 9

ENTRAPMENT

■ ■ ■

Introductory Comment

Entrapment is a criminal law defense. As with other defenses, a defendant who proves "entrapment" is entitled to be acquitted of an offense or to have the charge against her dismissed. Put another way, a finding of entrapment does more than result in exclusion of evidence at trial: It bars the successful prosecution of the defendant.

Entrapment is not a constitutional doctrine. That is, when a police officer "entraps" a person, she does not, *by that fact alone*, violate any provision of the Constitution. Therefore, no jurisdiction is required to recognize the entrapment defense. Nonetheless, every state and the federal courts recognize the claim in some form. And, as you will see at the end of this chapter, there remains a lingering question of whether entrapment-like techniques can become so outrageous that, at some point, the Constitution *is* offended.

Generally speaking, there are two approaches to entrapment, termed the "subjective" and "objective" tests of entrapment. In *Sherman v. United States*, the first case in this chapter, the majority opinion adopts the subjective test; the concurring justices prefer the objective standard. The subjective standard is followed in the federal courts and some states; other states apply an objective test.

SHERMAN V. UNITED STATES
Supreme Court of the United States, 1958.
356 U.S. 369, 78 S.Ct. 819, 2 L.Ed.2d 848.

MR. CHIEF JUSTICE WARREN delivered the opinion of the Court [joined by JUSTICES BLACK, BURTON, CLARK, and WHITTAKER].

The issue before us is whether petitioner's conviction should be set aside on the ground that as a matter of law the defense of entrapment was established. Petitioner was convicted under an indictment charging three sales of narcotics in violation of 21 U. S. C. § 174. * * *

In late August 1951, Kalchinian, a government informer, first met petitioner at a doctor's office where apparently both were being treated to be cured of narcotics addiction. Several accidental meetings followed, either at the doctor's office or at the pharmacy where both filled their prescriptions from the doctor. From mere greetings, conversation progressed to a discussion of mutual experiences and problems, including their attempts to overcome addiction to narcotics. Finally Kalchinian asked petitioner if he knew of a good source of narcotics. He asked petitioner to supply him with a source because he was not responding to treatment. From the first, petitioner tried to avoid the issue. Not until after a number of repetitions of the request, predicated on Kalchinian's presumed suffering, did petitioner finally acquiesce. Several times thereafter he obtained a quantity of narcotics which he shared with Kalchinian. Each time petitioner told Kalchinian that the total cost of narcotics he obtained was twenty-five dollars and that Kalchinian owed him fifteen dollars. The informer thus bore the cost of his share of the narcotics plus the taxi and other expenses necessary to obtain the drug. After several such sales Kalchinian informed agents of the Bureau of Narcotics that he had another seller for them. On three occasions during November 1951, government agents observed petitioner give narcotics to Kalchinian in return for money supplied by the Government.

At the trial the factual issue was whether the informer had convinced an otherwise unwilling person to commit a criminal act or whether petitioner was already predisposed to commit the act and exhibited only the natural hesitancy of one acquainted with the narcotics trade. The issue of entrapment went to the jury, and a conviction resulted. Petitioner was sentenced to imprisonment for ten years. * * *

In *Sorrells v. United States*, 287 U.S. 435, 53 S.Ct. 210, 77 L.Ed. 413 [(1932)], this Court firmly recognized the defense of entrapment in the federal courts. The intervening years have in no way detracted from the principles underlying that decision. The function of law enforcement is the prevention of crime and the apprehension of criminals. Manifestly, that function does not include the manufacturing of crime. Criminal activity is such that stealth and strategy are necessary weapons in the arsenal of the police officer. However, "[a] different question is presented when the criminal design originates with the officials of the Government, and they implant in the mind of an innocent person the disposition to commit the alleged offense and induce its commission in order that they may prosecute." Then stealth and strategy become as objectionable police methods as the coerced confession and the unlawful search. Congress could not have intended that its statutes were to be enforced by tempting innocent persons into violations.

However, the fact that government agents "merely afford opportunities or facilities for the commission of the offense does not" constitute entrapment. Entrapment occurs only when the criminal conduct was "the product of the *creative* activity" of law-enforcement officials. To determine whether entrapment has been established, a line must be drawn between the trap for the unwary innocent and the trap for the unwary criminal. The principles by which the courts are to make this determination were outlined in *Sorrells*. On the one hand, at trial the accused may examine the conduct of the government agent; and on the other hand, the accused will be subjected to an "appropriate and searching inquiry into his own conduct and predisposition" as bearing on his claim of innocence.

We conclude from the evidence that entrapment was established as a matter of law. * * * We reach our conclusion from the undisputed testimony of the prosecution's witnesses.

It is patently clear that petitioner was induced by Kalchinian. The informer himself testified that, believing petitioner to be undergoing a cure for narcotics addiction, he nonetheless sought to persuade petitioner to obtain for him a source of narcotics. In Kalchinian's own words we are told of the accidental, yet recurring, meetings, the ensuing conversations concerning mutual experiences in regard to narcotics addiction, and then of Kalchinian's resort to sympathy. One request was not enough, for Kalchinian tells us that additional ones were necessary to overcome, first, petitioner's refusal, then his evasiveness, and then his hesitancy in order to achieve capitulation. Kalchinian not only procured a source of narcotics but apparently also induced petitioner to return to the habit. Finally, assured of a catch, Kalchinian informed the authorities so that they could close the net. The Government cannot disown Kalchinian and insist it is not responsible for his actions. Although he was not being paid, Kalchinian was an active government informer who had but recently been the instigator of at least two other prosecutions. * * * It makes no difference that the sales for which petitioner was convicted occurred after a series of sales. They were not independent acts subsequent to the inducement but part of a course of conduct which was the product of the inducement. * * *

The Government sought to overcome the defense of entrapment by claiming that petitioner evinced a "ready complaisance" to accede to Kalchinian's request. Aside from a record of past convictions, which we discuss in the following paragraph, the Government's case is unsupported. There is no evidence that petitioner himself was in the trade. When his apartment was searched after arrest, no narcotics were found. There is no significant evidence that petitioner even made a profit on any sale to Kalchinian. The Government's characterization of petitioner's hesitancy to Kalchinian's request as the natural wariness of the criminal cannot fill the evidentiary void.

The Government's additional evidence * * * that petitioner was ready and willing to sell narcotics should the opportunity present itself was petitioner's record of two past narcotics convictions. In 1942 petitioner was convicted of illegally selling narcotics; in 1946 he was convicted of illegally possessing them. However, a nine-year-old sales conviction and a five-year-old possession conviction are insufficient to prove petitioner had a readiness to sell narcotics at the time Kalchinian approached him, particularly when we must assume from the record he was trying to overcome the narcotics habit at the time.

The case at bar illustrates an evil which the defense of entrapment is designed to overcome. The government informer entices someone attempting to avoid narcotics not only into carrying out an illegal sale but also into returning to the habit of use. Selecting the proper time, the informer then tells the government agent. The set-up is accepted by the agent without even a question as to the manner in which the informer encountered the seller. Thus the Government plays on the weaknesses of an innocent party and beguiles him into committing crimes which he otherwise would not have attempted. Law enforcement does not require methods such as this. * * *

MR. JUSTICE FRANKFURTER, whom MR. JUSTICE DOUGLAS, MR. JUSTICE HARLAN, and MR. JUSTICE BRENNAN join, concurring in the result.

Although agreeing with the Court that the undisputed facts show entrapment as a matter of law, I reach this result by a route different from the Court's. * * *

It is surely sheer fiction to suggest that a conviction cannot be had when a defendant has been entrapped by government officers or informers because "Congress could not have intended that its statutes were to be enforced by tempting innocent persons into violations." In these cases raising claims of entrapment, the only legislative intention that can with any show of reason be extracted from the statute is the intention to make criminal precisely the conduct in which the defendant has engaged. That conduct includes all the elements necessary to constitute criminality. * * * [T]he defendant has violated the statutory command. * * * In these circumstances, conduct is not less criminal because the result of temptation, whether the tempter is a private person or a government agent or informer.

The courts refuse to convict an entrapped defendant, not because his conduct falls outside the proscription of the statute, but because, even if his guilt be admitted, the methods employed on behalf of the Government to bring about conviction cannot be countenanced. As Mr. Justice Holmes said in *Olmstead v. United States*, 277 U.S. 438, 470, 48 S.Ct. 564, 575, 72 L.Ed. 944, (dissenting), in another connection, "[* * *] [F]or my part I think it a less evil that some criminals should escape than that the Government should play an ignoble part." Insofar as they are used as instrumentalities in the administration of criminal justice, the federal courts have an obligation to set their face against enforcement of the law by lawless means or means that violate rationally vindicated standards of justice, and to refuse to sustain such methods by effectuating them. * * * Public confidence in the fair and honorable administration of justice, upon which ultimately depends the rule of law, is the transcending value at stake. * * *

The crucial question, not easy of answer, to which the court must direct itself is whether the police conduct revealed in the particular case falls below standards, to which common feelings respond, for the proper use of governmental power. For answer it is wholly irrelevant to ask if the "intention" to commit the crime originated with the defendant or government officers, or if the criminal conduct was the product of "the creative activity" of law-enforcement officials. Yet in the present case the Court repeats and purports to apply these unrevealing tests. Of course in every case of this kind the intention that the particular crime be committed originates with the police, and without their inducement the crime would not have occurred. But it is perfectly clear [that] * * * where the police in effect simply furnished the opportunity for the commission of the crime, that this is not enough to enable the defendant to escape conviction.

The intention referred to, therefore, must be a general intention or predisposition to commit, whenever the opportunity should arise, crimes of the kind solicited, and in proof of such a predisposition evidence has often been admitted to show the defendant's reputation, criminal activities, and prior disposition. The danger of prejudice in such a situation, particularly if the issue of entrapment must be submitted to the jury and disposed of by a general verdict of guilty or innocent, is evident. The defendant must either forego the claim of entrapment or run the substantial risk that, in spite of instructions, the jury will allow a criminal record or bad reputation to weigh in its determination of guilt of the specific offense of which he stands charged. Furthermore, a test that looks to the character and predisposition of the defendant rather than the conduct of the police loses sight of the underlying reason for the defense of entrapment. No matter what the defendant's past record and present inclinations to criminality, or the depths to which he has sunk in the estimation of society, certain police conduct to ensnare him into further crime is not to be tolerated by an advanced society. * * * Permissible police activity does not vary according to the particular defendant concerned; surely if two suspects have been solicited at the same time in the same manner, one should not go to jail simply because he has been convicted before and is said to have a criminal disposition. * * * Appeals to sympathy, friendship, the possibility of exorbitant gain, and so forth, can no more be tolerated when directed against a past offender than against an ordinary law-abiding citizen. A contrary view runs afoul of fundamental principles of equality under law, and would espouse the notion that when dealing with the criminal classes anything goes. * * * Past crimes do not forever outlaw the criminal and open him to police practices, aimed at securing his repeated conviction, from which the ordinary citizen is protected. * * *

This does not mean that the police may not act so as to detect those engaged in criminal conduct and ready and willing to commit further crimes should the occasion arise. Such indeed is their obligation. It does mean that in holding out inducements they should act in such a manner as is likely to induce to the commission of crime only these persons and not others who would normally avoid crime and through self-struggle resist ordinary temptations. This test shifts attention from the record and predisposition of the particular defendant to the conduct of the police and the likelihood, objectively considered, that it would entrap only those ready and willing to commit crime. It is as objective a test as the subject matter permits, and will give guidance in regulating police conduct that is lacking when the reasonableness of police suspicions must be judged or the criminal disposition of the defendant retrospectively appraised. * * *

What police conduct is to be condemned, because likely to induce those not otherwise ready and willing to commit crime, must be picked out from case to case as new situations arise involving different crimes and new methods of detection. * * * Particularly reprehensible in the present case was the use of repeated requests to overcome petitioner's hesitancy, coupled with appeals to sympathy based on mutual experiences with narcotics addiction. Evidence of the setting in which the inducement took place is of course highly relevant in judging its likely effect, and the court should also consider the nature of the crime involved, its secrecy and difficulty of detection, and the manner in which the particular criminal business is usually carried out.

As Mr. Justice Roberts convincingly urged in the *Sorrells* case, * * * "[t]he protection of its own functions and the preservation of the purity of its own temple belongs only to the court. It is the province of the court and of the court alone to protect itself and the government from such prostitution of the criminal law. The violation of the principles of justice by the entrapment of the unwary into crime should be dealt with by the court no matter by whom or at what stage of the proceedings the facts are brought to its attention." Equally important is the consideration that a jury verdict, although it may settle the issue of entrapment in the particular case, cannot give significant guidance for official conduct for the future. Only the court, through the gradual evolution of explicit standards in accumulated precedents, can do this with the degree of certainty that the wise administration of criminal justice demands.

NOTES AND QUESTIONS

1. Chief Justice Warren observed that no narcotics were found in Sherman's residence during the post-arrest search. Why is this relevant to the entrapment defense?

2. The majority opinion espoused a "subjective" test of entrapment. Justice Frankfurter advocated an "objective" test. What are the elements of each test? What are the procedural differences between the two versions of entrapment? Which test do *you* prefer?

3. What is the underlying theory of the entrapment defense? Is it that no offense occurs when the police entrap an actor? Or, is it that an offense occurs, but we do not blame the actor for committing it because of police entrapment? Or, does an offense occur *and* the actor is culpable for committing it, but we still release him from liability because of police overreaching? Which of these explanations is the soundest basis of the defense? If you favor the second answer—the actor is not culpable—why is someone like Sherman excused for his actions? Is there any traditional criminal law defense analogous to entrapment?

4. *Problem.* In order to apprehend women pickpockets who were posing as prostitutes, a Minneapolis police officer pinned two $20 bills inside the front pocket of his coat so as to make portions of the bills visible. He then went into an alley at midnight and removed his penis from his pants as if to urinate. A woman drove by in a car, stopped, stuck her head out of the vehicle window, and propositioned him for sex. The officer answered, "OK with me," after which the woman (now out of the car) grabbed his penis, asked him what he wanted and how much he wanted to spend. While negotiating, the woman grabbed the $20 bills and fled. She was arrested on charges relating to prostitution and theft. R.T. Nybak, *Officer Nabs Prostitute Suspect with "Unbecoming" Technique*, Minneapolis Tribune, August 30, 1980, at 3A. Does the woman have a valid entrapment defense under the subjective test? Objective test?

JACOBSON V. UNITED STATES

Supreme Court of the United States, 1992.
503 U.S. 540, 112 S.Ct. 1535, 118 L.Ed.2d 174.

JUSTICE WHITE delivered the opinion of the Court [joined by JUSTICES BLACKMUN, STEVENS, SOUTER, and THOMAS]. * * *

I

In February 1984, petitioner, a 56-year-old veteran-turned-farmer who supported his elderly father in Nebraska, ordered two magazines and a brochure from a California adult bookstore. The magazines, entitled Bare Boys I and Bare Boys II, contained photographs of nude preteen and teenage boys. The contents of the magazines startled petitioner, who testified that he had expected to receive photographs of "young men 18 years or older." * * *

The young men depicted in the magazines were not engaged in sexual activity, and petitioner's receipt of the magazines was legal under both federal and Nebraska law. Within three months, the law with respect to child pornography changed; Congress passed the [Child Protection Act of 1984] illegalizing the receipt through the mails of sexually explicit depictions of children. In the very month that the new provision became law, postal inspectors found petitioner's name on the mailing list of the California bookstore that had mailed him Bare Boys I and II. There followed over the next 2½ years repeated efforts by two Government agencies, through five fictitious organizations and a bogus pen pal, to explore petitioner's willingness to break the new law by ordering sexually explicit photographs of children through the mail.

The Government began its efforts in January 1985 when a postal inspector sent petitioner a letter supposedly from the American Hedonist Society, which in fact was a fictitious organization. The letter included a membership application and stated the Society's doctrine: that members had the "right to read what we desire, the right to discuss similar interests with those who share our philosophy, and finally that we have the right to seek pleasure without restrictions being placed on us by outdated puritan morality." Petitioner enrolled in the organization and returned a sexual attitude questionnaire that asked him to rank on a scale of one to four his enjoyment of various sexual materials, with one being "really enjoy," two being "enjoy," three being "somewhat enjoy," and four being "do not enjoy." Petitioner ranked the entry "[p]re-teen sex" as a two, but indicated that he was opposed to pedophilia.

For a time, the Government left petitioner alone. But then a new "prohibited mailing specialist" in the Postal Service found petitioner's name in a file, and in May 1986, petitioner received a solicitation from a second fictitious consumer research company, "Midlands Data Research," seeking a response from those who "believe in the joys of sex and the complete awareness of those lusty and youthful lads and lasses of the neophite [sic] age." The letter never explained whether "neophite" referred to minors or young adults. Petitioner responded: "Please feel free to send me more information, I am interested in teenage sexuality. Please keep my name confidential."

Petitioner then heard from yet another Government creation, "Heartland Institute for a New Tomorrow" (HINT), which proclaimed that it was "an organization founded to protect and promote sexual freedom and freedom of choice. We believe that arbitrarily imposed legislative sanctions restricting *your* sexual freedom should be rescinded through the legislative process." The letter also enclosed a second survey. Petitioner indicated that his interest in "[p]reteen sex-homosexual" material was above average, but not high. In response to another question, petitioner wrote: "Not only sexual expression but freedom of the press is under attack. We must be ever vigilant to counter attack right wing fundamentalists who are determined to curtail our freedoms."

HINT replied, portraying itself as a lobbying organization seeking to repeal "all statutes which regulate sexual activities, except those laws which deal with violent behavior, such as rape. HINT is also lobbying to eliminate any legal definition of 'the age of consent'." These lobbying efforts were to be funded by sales from a catalog to be published in the future "offering the sale of various items which we believe you will find to be both interesting and stimulating." HINT also provided computer matching of group members with similar survey responses; and, although petitioner was supplied with a list of potential "pen pals," he did not initiate any correspondence.

Nevertheless, the Government's "prohibited mailing specialist" began writing to petitioner, using the pseudonym "Carl Long." The letters employed a tactic known as "mirroring," which the inspector described as "reflect[ing] whatever the interests are of the person we are writing to." Petitioner responded at first, indicating that his interest was primarily in "male-male items." Inspector "Long" wrote back:

> "My interests too are primarily male-male items. Are you satisfied with the type of VCR tapes available? Personally, I like the amateur stuff better if its [sic] well produced as it can get more kinky and also seems more real. I think the actors enjoy it more."

Petitioner responded:

> "As far as my likes are concerned, I like good looking young guys (in their late teens and early 20's) doing their thing together."

Petitioner's letters to "Long" made no reference to child pornography. After writing two letters, petitioner discontinued the correspondence.

By March 1987, 34 months had passed since the Government obtained petitioner's name from the mailing list of the California bookstore, and 26 months had passed since the Postal Service had commenced its mailings to petitioner. Although petitioner had responded to surveys and letters, the Government had no evidence that petitioner had ever intentionally possessed or been exposed to child pornography. The Postal Service had not checked petitioner's mail to determine whether he was receiving questionable mailings from persons—other than the Government—involved in the child pornography industry.

At this point, a second Government agency, the Customs Service, included petitioner in its own child pornography sting, "Operation

Borderline," after receiving his name on lists submitted by the Postal Service. Using the name of a fictitious Canadian company called "Produit Outaouais," the Customs Service mailed petitioner a brochure advertising photographs of young boys engaging in sex. Petitioner placed an order that was never filled.

The Postal Service also continued its efforts in the Jacobson case, writing to petitioner as the "Far Eastern Trading Company Ltd." The letter began:

"As many of you know, much hysterical nonsense has appeared in the American media concerning 'pornography' and what must be done to stop it from coming across your borders. This brief letter does not allow us to give much comments; however, why is your government spending millions of dollars to exercise international censorship while tons of drugs, which makes yours the world's most crime ridden country are passed through easily."

The letter went on to say:

"[W]e have devised a method of getting these to you without prying eyes of U.S. Customs seizing your mail. * * * After consultations with American solicitors, we have been advised that once we have posted our material through your system, it cannot be opened for any inspection without authorization of a judge."

The letter invited petitioner to send for more information. It also asked petitioner to sign an affirmation that he was "not a law enforcement officer or agent of the U.S. Government acting in an undercover capacity for the purpose of entrapping Far Eastern Trading Company, its agents or customers." Petitioner responded. A catalog was sent, and petitioner ordered Boys Who Love Boys, a pornographic magazine depicting young boys engaged in various sexual activities. Petitioner was arrested after a controlled delivery of a photocopy of the magazine.

When petitioner was asked at trial why he placed such an order, he explained that the Government had succeeded in piquing his curiosity:

"Well, the statement was made of all the trouble and the hysteria over pornography and I wanted to see what the material was. It didn't describe the—I didn't know for sure what kind of sexual action they were referring to in the Canadian letter."

In petitioner's home, the Government found the Bare Boys magazines and materials that the Government had sent to him in the course of its protracted investigation, but no other materials that would indicate that petitioner collected, or was actively interested in, child pornography.

Petitioner was indicted for violating [the federal child pornography statute]. The trial court instructed the jury on the petitioner's entrapment defense, petitioner was convicted * * * . * * *

II

There can be no dispute about the evils of child pornography or the difficulties that laws and law enforcement have encountered in eliminating it. Likewise, there can be no dispute that the Government may use undercover agents to enforce the law. * * *

In their zeal to enforce the law, however, Government agents may not originate a criminal design, implant in an innocent person's mind the disposition to commit a criminal act, and then induce commission of the crime so that the Government may prosecute. Where the Government has induced an individual to break the law and the defense of entrapment is at issue, as it was in this case, the prosecution must prove beyond reasonable doubt that the defendant was disposed to commit the criminal act prior to first being approached by Government agents.[2]

Thus, an agent deployed to stop the traffic in illegal drugs may offer the opportunity to buy or sell drugs and, if the offer is accepted, make an arrest on the spot or later. In such a typical case, or in a more elaborate "sting" operation involving government-sponsored fencing where the defendant is simply provided with the opportunity to commit a crime, the entrapment defense is of little use because the ready commission of the criminal act amply demonstrates the defendant's predisposition. Had the agents in this case simply offered petitioner the opportunity to order child pornography through the mails, and petitioner—who must be presumed to know the law—had promptly availed himself of this criminal opportunity, it is unlikely that his entrapment defense would have warranted a jury instruction.

---

[2] Inducement is not at issue in this case. The Government does not dispute that it induced petitioner to commit the crime. The sole issue is whether the Government carried its burden of proving that petitioner was predisposed to violate the law *before* the Government intervened. The dissent is mistaken in claiming that this is an innovation in entrapment law and in suggesting that the Government's conduct prior to the moment of solicitation is irrelevant. * * * Indeed, the proposition that the accused must be predisposed prior to contact with law enforcement officers is so firmly established that the Government conceded the point at oral argument, submitting that the evidence it developed during the course of its investigation was probative because it indicated petitioner's state of mind *prior* to the commencement of the Government's investigation.

This long-established standard in no way encroaches upon Government investigatory activities. Indeed, the Government's internal guidelines for undercover operations provide that an inducement to commit a crime should not be offered unless:

"(a) [T]here is a reasonable indication, based on information developed through informants or other means, that the subject is engaging, has engaged, or is likely to engage in illegal activity of a similar type; *or*

"(b) The opportunity for illegal activity has been structured so that there is reason for believing that persons drawn to the opportunity, or brought to it, are predisposed to engage in the contemplated illegal activity." Attorney General's Guidelines on FBI Undercover Operations (Dec. 31, 1980), reprinted in S. Rep. No. 97–682, p. 551 (1982).

But that is not what happened here. By the time petitioner finally placed his order, he had already been the target of 26 months of repeated mailings and communications from Government agents and fictitious organizations. Therefore, although he had become predisposed to break the law by May 1987, it is our view that the Government did not prove that this predisposition was independent and not the product of the attention that the Government had directed at petitioner since January 1985.

The prosecution's evidence of predisposition falls into two categories: evidence developed prior to the Postal Service's mail campaign, and that developed during the course of the investigation. The sole piece of preinvestigation evidence is petitioner's 1984 order and receipt of the Bare Boys magazines. But this is scant if any proof of petitioner's predisposition to commit an illegal act, the criminal character of which a defendant is presumed to know. It may indicate a predisposition to view sexually-oriented photographs that are responsive to his sexual tastes; but evidence that merely indicates a generic inclination to act within a broad range, not all of which is criminal, is of little probative value in establishing predisposition.

Furthermore, petitioner was acting within the law at the time he received these magazines. Receipt through the mails of sexually explicit depictions of children for noncommercial use did not become illegal under federal law until May 1984, and Nebraska had no law that forbade petitioner's possession of such material until 1988. Evidence of predisposition to do what once was lawful is not, by itself, sufficient to show predisposition to do what is now illegal, for there is a common understanding that most people obey the law even when they disapprove of it. * * * Hence, the fact that petitioner legally ordered and received the Bare Boys magazines does little to further the Government's burden of proving that petitioner was predisposed to commit a criminal act. This is particularly true given petitioner's unchallenged testimony was that he did not know until they arrived that the magazines would depict minors.

The prosecution's evidence gathered during the investigation also fails to carry the Government's burden. Petitioner's responses to the many communications prior to the ultimate criminal act were at most indicative of certain personal inclinations, including a predisposition to view photographs of preteen sex and a willingness to promote a given agenda by supporting lobbying organizations. Even so, petitioner's responses hardly support an inference that he would commit the crime of receiving child pornography through the mails.[3] Furthermore, a person's

---

[3] We do not hold, as the dissent suggests, that the Government was required to prove that petitioner knowingly violated the law. We simply conclude that proof that petitioner engaged in legal conduct and possessed certain generalized personal inclinations is not sufficient evidence to

inclinations and "fantasies * * * are his own and beyond the reach of government * * * ."

On the other hand, the strong arguable inference is that, by waving the banner of individual rights and disparaging the legitimacy and constitutionality of efforts to restrict the availability of sexually explicit materials, the Government not only excited petitioner's interest in sexually explicit materials banned by law but also exerted substantial pressure on petitioner to obtain and read such material as part of a fight against censorship and the infringement of individual rights. * * *

Petitioner's ready response to these [anti-censorship] solicitations cannot be enough to establish beyond reasonable doubt that he was predisposed, prior to the Government acts intended to create predisposition, to commit the crime of receiving child pornography through the mails. The evidence that petitioner was ready and willing to commit the offense came only after the Government had devoted 2½ years to convincing him that he had or should have the right to engage in the very behavior proscribed by law. Rational jurors could not say beyond a reasonable doubt that petitioner possessed the requisite predisposition prior to the Government's investigation and that it existed independent of the Government's many and varied approaches to petitioner. * * *

JUSTICE O'CONNOR, with whom THE CHIEF JUSTICE REHNQUIST and JUSTICE KENNEDY join, and with whom JUSTICE SCALIA joins except as to Part II, dissenting.

Keith Jacobson was offered only two opportunities to buy child pornography through the mail. Both times, he ordered. Both times, he asked for opportunities to buy more. He needed no Government agent to coax, threaten, or persuade him; no one played on his sympathies, friendship, or suggested that his committing the crime would further a greater good. In fact, no Government agent even contacted him face to face. The Government contends that from the enthusiasm with which Mr. Jacobson responded to the chance to commit a crime, a reasonable jury could permissibly infer beyond a reasonable doubt that he was predisposed to commit the crime. I agree.

The first time the Government sent Mr. Jacobson a catalog of illegal materials, he ordered a set of photographs advertised as picturing "young boys in sex action fun." He enclosed the following note with his order: "I received your brochure and decided to place an order. If I like your product, I will order more later." For reasons undisclosed in the record, Mr. Jacobson's order was never delivered.

---

prove beyond a reasonable doubt that he would have been predisposed to commit the crime charged independent of the Government's coaxing.

The second time the Government sent a catalog of illegal materials, Mr. Jacobson ordered a magazine called "Boys Who Love Boys," described as: "11 year old and 14 year old boys get it on in every way possible. Oral, anal sex and heavy masturbation. If you love boys, you will be delighted with this." Along with his order, Mr. Jacobson sent the following note: "Will order other items later. I want to be discreet in order to protect you and me."

Government agents admittedly did not offer Mr. Jacobson the chance to buy child pornography right away. Instead, they first sent questionnaires in order to make sure that he was generally interested in the subject matter. Indeed, a "cold call" in such a business would not only risk rebuff and suspicion, but might also shock and offend the uninitiated, or expose minors to suggestive materials. Mr. Jacobson's responses to the questionnaires gave the investigators reason to think he would be interested in photographs depicting preteen sex.

The Court, however, concludes that a reasonable jury could not have found Mr. Jacobson to be predisposed beyond a reasonable doubt on the basis of his responses to the Government's catalogs, even though it admits that, by that time, he was predisposed to commit the crime. The Government, the Court holds, failed to provide evidence that Mr. Jacobson's obvious predisposition at the time of the crime "was independent and not the product of the attention that the Government had directed at petitioner." In so holding, I believe the Court fails to acknowledge the reasonableness of the jury's inference from the evidence, redefines "predisposition," and introduces a new requirement that Government sting operations have a reasonable suspicion of illegal activity before contacting a suspect.

I

* * * [A] defendant's predisposition is to be assessed as of the time the Government agent first suggested the crime, not when the Government agent first became involved. Until the Government actually makes a suggestion of criminal conduct, it could not be said to have "implant[ed] in the mind of an innocent person the disposition to commit the alleged offense and induce its commission * * * ." Even in *Sherman v. United States*, [p. 809], in which the Court held that the defendant had been entrapped as a matter of law, the Government agent had repeatedly and unsuccessfully coaxed the defendant to buy drugs, ultimately succeeding only by playing on the defendant's sympathy. The Court found lack of predisposition based on the Government's numerous unsuccessful attempts to induce the crime, not on the basis of preliminary contacts with the defendant.

Today, the Court holds that Government conduct may be considered to create a predisposition to commit a crime, even before any Government action to induce the commission of the crime. In my view, this holding changes entrapment doctrine. Generally, the inquiry is whether a suspect is predisposed before the Government induces the commission of the crime, not before the Government makes initial contact with him. There is no dispute here that the Government's questionnaires and letters were not sufficient to establish inducement; they did not even suggest that Mr. Jacobson should engage in any illegal activity. If all the Government had done was to send these materials, Mr. Jacobson's entrapment defense would fail. Yet the Court holds that the Government must prove not only that a suspect was predisposed to commit the crime before the opportunity to commit it arose, but also before the Government came on the scene.

The rule that preliminary Government contact can create a predisposition has the potential to be misread by lower courts as well as criminal investigators as requiring that the Government must have sufficient evidence of a defendant's predisposition *before it ever seeks to contact him*. Surely the Court cannot intend to impose such a requirement, for it would mean that the Government must have a reasonable suspicion of criminal activity before it begins an investigation, a condition that we have never before imposed. The Court denies that its new rule will affect run-of-the-mill sting operations, and one hopes that it means what it says. Nonetheless, after this case, every defendant will claim that something the Government agent did before soliciting the crime "created" a predisposition that was not there before. For example, a bribetaker will claim that the description of the amount of money available was so enticing that it implanted a disposition to accept the bribe later offered. A drug buyer will claim that the description of the drug's purity and effects was so tempting that it created the urge to try it for the first time. In short, the Court's opinion could be read to prohibit the Government from advertising the seductions of criminal activity as part of its sting operation, for fear of creating a predisposition in its suspects. That limitation would be especially likely to hamper sting operations such as this one, which mimic the advertising done by genuine purveyors of pornography. No doubt the Court would protest that its opinion does not stand for so broad a proposition, but the apparent lack of a principled basis for distinguishing these scenarios exposes a flaw in the more limited rule the Court today adopts.

The Court's rule is all the more troubling because it does not distinguish between Government conduct that merely highlights the temptation of the crime itself, and Government conduct that threatens, coerces, or leads a suspect to commit a crime in order to fulfill some other obligation. * * *

* * * While the Court states that the Government "exerted substantial pressure on petitioner to obtain and read such material as

part of a fight against censorship and the infringement of individual rights," one looks at the record in vain for evidence of such "substantial pressure." The most one finds is letters advocating legislative action to liberalize obscenity laws, letters which could easily be ignored or thrown away. * * * Mr. Jacobson's curiosity to see what " 'all the trouble and the hysteria' " was about, is certainly susceptible of more than one interpretation. And it is the jury that is charged with the obligation of interpreting it. In sum, the Court fails to construe the evidence in the light most favorable to the Government, and fails to draw all reasonable inferences in the Government's favor. It was surely reasonable for the jury to infer that Mr. Jacobson was predisposed beyond a reasonable doubt, even if other inferences from the evidence were also possible.

II

The second puzzling thing about the Court's opinion is its redefinition of predisposition. The Court acknowledges that "[p]etitioner's responses to the many communications prior to the ultimate criminal act were * * * indicative of certain personal inclinations, including a predisposition to view photographs of preteen sex * * * ." If true, this should have settled the matter; Mr. Jacobson was predisposed to engage in the illegal conduct. Yet, the Court concludes, "petitioner's responses hardly support an inference that he would commit the crime of receiving child pornography through the mails."

The Court seems to add something new to the burden of proving predisposition. Not only must the Government show that a defendant was predisposed to engage in the illegal conduct, here, receiving photographs of minors engaged in sex, but also that the defendant was predisposed to break the law knowingly in order to do so. The statute violated here, however, does not require proof of specific intent to break the law; it requires only knowing receipt of visual depictions produced by using minors engaged in sexually explicit conduct. * * *

The crux of the Court's concern in this case is that the Government went too far and "abused" the " 'processes of detection and enforcement' " by luring an innocent person to violate the law. * * * It was, however, the jury's task, as the conscience of the community, to decide whether or not Mr. Jacobson was a willing participant in the criminal activity here or an innocent dupe. * * * There is no dispute that the jury in this case was fully and accurately instructed on the law of entrapment, and nonetheless found Mr. Jacobson guilty. Because I believe there was sufficient evidence to uphold the jury's verdict, I respectfully dissent.

NOTES AND QUESTIONS

1.   Is Justice White correct in concluding that *no* reasonable juror could say "beyond a reasonable doubt that petitioner possessed the requisite predisposition"?

2.   According to Dru Stevenson, *Entrapment by Numbers*, 16 U. Fla. J. L. & Pub. Pol'y 1, 2–3 (2005), entrapment claims decreased in almost every state and in the federal courts from the peak years in the 1980s and early 1990s. Do you have any thoughts as to why entrapment claims peaked in the 1980s and have fallen off since then?

3.   *"Outrageous conduct" defense and due process.* Can entrapment-like conduct ever violate the Constitution? In United States v. Russell, 411 U.S. 423, 93 S.Ct. 1637, 36 L.Ed.2d 366 (1973), the defendant was convicted of multiple counts of unlawful manufacture of methamphetamine ("speed"). An undercover federal agent, claiming to represent an organization interested in controlling drug manufacturing in the Pacific Northwest, offered to supply the defendant with a lawful, but difficult-to-obtain, chemical necessary for the production of speed, in exchange for one-half of the drugs produced. The defendant agreed to the arrangement.

The defendant's predisposition to commit the offense undermined his entrapment claim. He argued, however, that "a defense to a criminal charge may be founded upon an intolerable degree of governmental participation in the criminal enterprise." However, Justice Rehnquist, for five members of the Court, stated: "While we may some day be presented with a situation in which the conduct of law enforcement agents is so outrageous that due process principles would absolutely bar the government from invoking judicial processes to obtain a conviction, the instant case is distinctly not of that breed."

In Hampton v. United States, 425 U.S. 484, 489, 96 S.Ct. 1646, 48 L.Ed.2d 113 (1976), Chief Justice Rehnquist, writing now only for himself and two others, recanted his "maybe someday" dicta. In *Hampton*, a federal informant supplied heroin to the defendant and then brought him to another agent to whom the defendant sold the drug. As dissenting Justice Brennan put it, "[t]he Government [was] doing nothing less than buying contraband from itself through an intermediary and jailing the intermediary." Nonetheless, the Chief Justice stated that "[t]he limitations of the Due Process Clause of the Fifth Amendment come into play only when the Government activity in question violates some protected right of the *defendant.*"

Five justices, however—two in concurrence and three in dissent—rejected Rehnquist's categorical rejection of a due process defense. As a result, an "outrageous conduct" due process defense has developed in lower courts. Nearly every federal circuit court and many state courts now recognize, at least in dictum, a constitutional defense. One court has explained the defense this way:

In evaluating whether the State's conduct violated due process, we focus on the State's behavior and not the Defendant's predisposition. There are several factors which courts consider when determining whether police conduct offends due process: whether the police conduct instigated a crime or merely infiltrated ongoing criminal activity; whether the defendant's reluctance to commit a crime was overcome by pleas of sympathy, promises of excessive profits, or persistent solicitation; whether the government controls the criminal activity or simply allows for the criminal activity to occur; whether the police motive was to prevent crime or protect the public; and whether the government conduct itself amounted to criminal activity or conduct "repugnant to a sense of justice."

State v. Lively, 130 Wash.2d 1, 921 P.2d 1035 (1996).

Is the due process defense simply the Supreme Court-rejected objective standard of entrapment in disguise?

CHAPTER 10

EYEWITNESS IDENTIFICATION PROCEDURES

■ ■ ■

Introduction: The Problem

On January 3, 2008, Charles Chatman walked out of a Texas prison a free man. By then he had served twenty-seven years of a ninety-nine year prison sentence for a rape someone else had committed. Eyewitness misidentification was a major factor in Chatman's wrongful conviction. He was exonerated thanks to DNA testing.

Chatman's experience is hardly unique. He was the fifteenth wrongfully convicted prisoner exonerated in Dallas County, Texas in the first seven years of DNA testing. Ralph Blumenthal, *15th Dallas County Inmate Since '01 Is Freed by DNA*, N.Y. Times, Jan. 4, 2008, at A11. And, what is more significant at this point in the casebook is that *eyewitness misidentification is the single most common factor in wrongful convictions throughout the United States*. In a study of 200 DNA exonerations, faulty eyewitness identifications contributed to nearly eighty percent of the improper convictions. Brandon L. Garrett, *Judging Innocence*, 108 Colum. L. Rev. 55, 60 (2008); see also Samuel R. Gross et al., *Exonerations in the United States 1989 Through 2003*, 95 J. Crim. L. & Criminology 523, 542 (2005) (of 340 exonerations between 1980 and 2003, at least one eyewitness misidentified the defendant in sixty-four percent of the trials overall, ninety percent of the wrongful rape convictions, and about half of the homicides). Additional data are set out by Justice Sotomayor, pp. 856–857, in a recent case.

Although the recent advent of DNA testing has demonstrated that wrongful convictions are more common than previously believed (and, at that, we cannot know how many innocent persons are being convicted because DNA evidence is not left at most crime scenes), social scientists and lawyers have known for a very long time that eyewitness identifications are unreliable.

Why *are* misidentifications such a problem in the criminal justice system? What has the Supreme Court done to reduce the risk of misidentifications? The materials that follow respond to these questions. As you will see, the Supreme Court has done relatively little in the "eyewitness identification" area; however, some state courts and officials—perhaps stung by the high number of DNA exonerations that have occurred—have recently begun to look for means to reform the identification process. And yet, according to one review of appellate court decisions, it appears that "the overwhelming majority of police departments in the cases surveyed followed the same procedures that have contributed to misidentifications and wrongful convictions." Sandra Guerra Thompson, *Judicial Blindness to Eyewitness Misidentification*, 93 Marq. L. Rev. 639, 641 (2009).

In reading the case law in this chapter, you will find it helpful to ask yourself four questions: (1) What constitutional right is implicated?; (2) Did the identification procedure at issue occur before or after formal adversary proceedings commenced?; (3) Was the identification procedure corporeal (*i.e.*, the suspect was personally displayed to the witness) or noncorporeal (*e.g.*, a photograph of the suspect was displayed)?; and (4) Is the prosecutor trying to introduce the witness's *pretrial* identification into evidence at trial, or does she want the witness to conduct an *in*-court identification of the defendant, or both?

A. RIGHT TO COUNSEL

UNITED STATES V. WADE
Supreme Court of the United States, 1967.
388 U.S. 218, 87 S.Ct. 1926, 18 L.Ed.2d 1149.

MR. JUSTICE BRENNAN delivered the opinion of the Court [joined by CHIEF JUSTICE WARREN (except as to Part I), JUSTICE BLACK (except as to Parts I and V), JUSTICE DOUGLAS (except as to Part I), and JUSTICES CLARK and FORTAS (except as to Part I)].[a]

The question here is whether courtroom identifications of an accused at trial are to be excluded from evidence because the accused was exhibited to the witnesses before trial at a post-indictment lineup conducted for identification purposes without notice to and in the absence of the accused's appointed counsel.

The federally insured bank in Eustace, Texas, was robbed on September 21, 1964. A man with a small strip of tape on each side of his face entered the bank, pointed a pistol at the female cashier and the vice president, the only persons in the bank at the time, and forced them to fill a pillowcase with the bank's money. The man then drove away with an accomplice who had been waiting in a stolen car outside the bank. On

---

[a]   The Court held in Part I of the opinion, which is omitted, that requiring a person to participate in a lineup does not violate the Fifth Amendment privilege against compulsory self-incrimination, which provision only bars "evidence of a testimonial or communicative nature." (See generally p. 620.) The concurring opinion of Justice Clark is omitted, as are the opinions of Justice Black (who concurred in Parts II-IV, but dissented as to Parts I and V), and Justice Fortas (who dissented in part as to Part I).

March 23, 1965, an indictment was returned against respondent, Wade, and two others for conspiring to rob the bank, and against Wade and the accomplice for the robbery itself. Wade was arrested on April 2, and counsel was appointed to represent him on April 26. Fifteen days later an FBI agent, without notice to Wade's lawyer, arranged to have the two bank employees observe a lineup made up of Wade and five or six other prisoners and conducted in a courtroom of the local county courthouse. Each person in the line wore strips of tape such as allegedly worn by the robber and upon direction each said something like "put the money in the bag," the words allegedly uttered by the robber. Both bank employees identified Wade in the lineup as the bank robber.

At trial, the two employees, when asked on direct examination if the robber was in the courtroom, pointed to Wade. The prior lineup identification was then elicited from both employees on cross-examination. At the close of testimony, Wade's counsel moved * * * to strike the bank officials' courtroom identifications on the ground that conduct of the lineup, without notice to and in the absence of his appointed counsel, violated his Fifth Amendment privilege against self-incrimination and his Sixth Amendment right to the assistance of counsel. The motion was denied, and Wade was convicted. * * * We granted certiorari, and set the case for oral argument with No. 223, *Gilbert v. California, post*, and No. 254, *Stovall v. Denno*, [388 U.S. 293, 87 S.Ct. 1967, 18 L.Ed.2d 1199 (1967)], which present similar questions. * * *

· II. * * *

* * * [I]n this case it is urged that the assistance of counsel at the lineup was indispensable to protect Wade's most basic right as a criminal defendant—his right to a fair trial at which the witnesses against him might be meaningfully cross-examined. * * *

As early as *Powell v. Alabama* [p. 25], we recognized that the period from arraignment to trial was "perhaps the most critical period of the proceedings * * * ," during which the accused "requires the guiding hand of counsel * * * ," if the guarantee is not to prove an empty right. * * *

* * * It is central to that principle that in addition to counsel's presence at trial, the accused is guaranteed that he need not stand alone against the State at any stage of the prosecution, formal or informal, in court or out, where counsel's absence might derogate from the accused's right to a fair trial. * * *

In sum, the principle of *Powell v. Alabama* and succeeding cases requires that we scrutinize *any* pretrial confrontation of the accused to determine whether the presence of his counsel is necessary to preserve the defendant's basic right to a fair trial as affected by his right meaningfully to cross-examine the witnesses against him and to have effective assistance of counsel at the trial itself. It calls upon us to analyze whether potential substantial prejudice to defendant's rights inheres in the particular confrontation and the ability of counsel to help avoid that prejudice.

III.

The Government characterizes the lineup as a mere preparatory step in the gathering of the prosecution's evidence, not different—for Sixth Amendment purposes—from various other preparatory steps, such as systematized or scientific analyzing of the accused's fingerprints, blood sample, clothing, hair, and the like. We think there are differences which preclude such stages being characterized as critical stages at which the accused has the right to the presence of his counsel. Knowledge of the techniques of science and technology is sufficiently available, and the variables in techniques few enough, that the accused has the opportunity for a meaningful confrontation of the Government's case at trial through the ordinary processes of cross-examination of the Government's expert witnesses and the presentation of the evidence of his own experts. The denial of a right to have his counsel present at such analyses does not therefore violate the Sixth Amendment; they are not critical stages since there is minimal risk that his counsel's absence at such stages might derogate from his right to a fair trial.

IV.

But the confrontation compelled by the State between the accused and the victim or witnesses to a crime to elicit identification evidence is peculiarly riddled with innumerable dangers and variable factors which might seriously, even crucially, derogate from a fair trial. The vagaries of eyewitness identification are well-known; the annals of criminal law are rife with instances of mistaken identification. Mr. Justice Frankfurter once said: "What is the worth of identification testimony even when uncontradicted? The identification of strangers is proverbially untrustworthy. The hazards of such testimony are established by a formidable number of instances in the records of English and American trials. These instances are recent—not due to the brutalities of ancient criminal procedure." A major factor contributing to the high incidence of miscarriage of justice from mistaken identification has been the degree of suggestion inherent in the manner in which the prosecution presents the suspect to witnesses for pretrial identification. A commentator has observed that "[t]he influence of improper suggestion upon identifying witnesses probably accounts for more miscarriages of justice than any other single factor—perhaps it is responsible for more such errors than all other factors combined." Wall, EYE-WITNESS IDENTIFICATION IN CRIMINAL CASES 26. Suggestion can be created intentionally or unintentionally in many subtle ways. And the dangers for the suspect are particularly grave when the witness' opportunity for observation was insubstantial, and thus his susceptibility to suggestion the greatest.

Moreover, "[i]t is a matter of common experience that, once a witness has picked out the accused at the line-up, he is not likely to go back on his word later on, so that in practice the issue of identity may (in the absence of other relevant evidence) for all practical purposes be determined there and then, before the trial."

The pretrial confrontation for purpose of identification may take the form of a lineup, also known as an "identification parade" or "showup," as in the present case, or presentation of the suspect alone to the witness, as in *Stovall v. Denno, supra.* It is obvious that risks of suggestion attend either form of confrontation and increase the dangers inhering in eyewitness identification. But as is the case with secret interrogations, there is serious difficulty in depicting what transpires at lineups and other forms of identification confrontations. "Privacy results in secrecy and this in turn results in a gap in our knowledge as to what in fact goes on * * * ." For the same reasons, the defense can seldom reconstruct the manner and mode of lineup identification for judge or jury at trial. Those participating in a lineup with the accused may often be police officers; in any event, the participants' names are rarely recorded or divulged at trial. The impediments to an objective observation are increased when the victim is the witness. Lineups are prevalent in rape and robbery prosecutions and present a particular hazard that a victim's understandable outrage may excite vengeful or spiteful motives. In any event, neither witnesses nor lineup participants are apt to be alert for conditions prejudicial to the suspect. And if they were, it would likely be of scant benefit to the suspect since neither witnesses nor lineup participants are likely to be schooled in the detection of suggestive influences.[13] Improper influences may go undetected by a suspect, guilty or not, who experiences the emotional tension which we might expect in one being confronted with potential accusers. Even when he does observe abuse, if he has a criminal record he may be reluctant to take the stand and open up the admission of prior convictions. Moreover, any protestations by the suspect of the fairness of the lineup made at trial are likely to be in vain; the jury's choice is between the accused's unsupported version and that of the police officers present. In short, the accused's inability effectively to reconstruct at trial any unfairness that occurred at the lineup may deprive him of his only opportunity meaningfully to attack the credibility of the witness' courtroom identification. * * *

---

[13] An additional impediment to the detection of such influences by participants, including the suspect, is the physical conditions often surrounding the conduct of the lineup. In many, lights shine on the stage in such a way that the suspect cannot see the witness. In some a one-way mirror is used and what is said on the witness' side cannot be heard.

The potential for improper influence is illustrated by the circumstances, insofar as they appear, surrounding the prior identifications in the three cases we decide today. In the present case, the testimony of the identifying witnesses elicited on cross-examination revealed that those witnesses were taken to the courthouse and seated in the courtroom to await assembly of the lineup. The courtroom faced on a hallway observable to the witnesses through an open door. The cashier testified that she saw Wade "standing in the hall" within sight of an FBI agent. Five or six other prisoners later appeared in the hall. The vice president testified that he saw a person in the hall in the custody of the agent who "resembled the person that we identified as the one that had entered the bank."

The lineup in *Gilbert*, [388 U.S. 263, 87 S.Ct. 1951, 18 L.Ed.2d 1178 (1967)], was conducted in an auditorium in which some 100 witnesses to several alleged state and federal robberies charged to Gilbert made wholesale identifications of Gilbert as the robber in each other's presence, a procedure said to be fraught with dangers of suggestion. And the vice of suggestion created by the identification in *Stovall* was the presentation to the witness of the suspect alone handcuffed to police officers. It is hard to imagine a situation more clearly conveying the suggestion to the witness that the one presented is believed guilty by the police.

The few cases that have surfaced therefore reveal the existence of a process attended with hazards of serious unfairness to the criminal accused and strongly suggest the plight of the more numerous defendants who are unable to ferret out suggestive influences in the secrecy of the confrontation. We do not assume that these risks are the result of police procedures intentionally designed to prejudice an accused. Rather we assume they derive from the dangers inherent in eyewitness identification and the suggestibility inherent in the context of the pretrial identification. Williams & Hammelmann, in one of the most comprehensive studies of such forms of identification, said, "[T]he fact that the police themselves have, in a given case, little or no doubt that the man put up for identification has committed the offense, and that their chief pre-occupation is with the problem of getting sufficient proof, because he has not 'come clean,' involves a danger that this persuasion may communicate itself even in a doubtful case to the witness in some way * * *." Identification Parades, Part I, [1963] Crim. L. Rev. 479, 483.

Insofar as the accused's conviction may rest on a courtroom identification in fact the fruit of a suspect pretrial identification which the accused is helpless to subject to effective scrutiny at trial, the accused is deprived of that right of cross-examination which is an essential safeguard to his right to confront the witnesses against him. And even though cross-examination is a precious safeguard to a fair trial, it cannot be viewed as an absolute assurance of accuracy and reliability. Thus in the present context, where so many variables and pitfalls exist, the first line of defense must be the prevention of unfairness and the lessening of the hazards of eyewitness identification at the lineup itself. The trial which might determine the accused's fate may well not be that in the courtroom but that at the pretrial confrontation, with the State aligned against the accused, the witness the sole jury, and the accused unprotected against the overreaching, intentional or unintentional, and with little or no effective appeal from the judgment there rendered by the witness—"that's the man."

Since it appears that there is grave potential for prejudice, intentional or not, in the pretrial lineup, which may not be capable of reconstruction at trial, and since presence of counsel itself can often avert prejudice and assure a meaningful confrontation at trial,[26] there can be little doubt that for Wade the post-indictment lineup was a critical stage of the prosecution at which he was "as much entitled to such aid [of counsel] * * * as at the trial itself." Thus both Wade and his counsel should have been notified of the impending lineup, and counsel's presence should have been a requisite to conduct of the lineup, absent an "intelligent waiver." No substantial countervailing policy considerations have been advanced against the requirement of the presence of counsel. Concern is expressed that the requirement will forestall prompt

---

[26] One commentator proposes a model statute providing not only for counsel, but other safeguards as well:

"Most, if not all, of the attacks on the lineup process could be averted by a uniform statute modeled upon the best features of the civilian codes. Any proposed statute should provide for the right to counsel during any lineup or during any confrontation. Provision should be made that any person, whether a victim or a witness, must give a description of the suspect before he views any arrested person. A written record of this description should be required, and the witness should be made to sign it. This written record would be available for inspection by defense counsel for copying before the trial and for use at the trial in testing the accuracy of the identification made during the lineup and during the trial.

"This ideal statute would require at least six persons in addition to the accused in a lineup, and these persons would have to be of approximately the same height, weight, coloration of hair and skin, and bodily types as the suspect. In addition, all of these men should, as nearly as possible, be dressed alike. If distinctive garb was used during the crime, the suspect should not be forced to wear similar clothing in the lineup unless all of the other persons are similarly garbed. A complete written report of the names, addresses, descriptive details of the other persons in the lineup, and of everything which transpired during the identification would be mandatory. This report would include everything stated by the identifying witness during this step, including any reasons given by him as to what features, etc., have sparked his recognition.

"This statute should permit voice identification tests by having each person in the lineup repeat identical innocuous phrases, and it would be impermissible to force the use of words allegedly used during a criminal act.

"The statute would enjoin the police from suggesting to any viewer that one or more persons in the lineup had been arrested as a suspect. If more than one witness is to make an identification, each witness should be required to do so separately and should be forbidden to speak to another witness until all of them have completed the process.

"The statute could require the use of movie cameras and tape recorders to record the lineup process in those states which are financially able to afford these devices. Finally, the statute should provide that any evidence obtained as the result of a violation of this statute would be inadmissible." Murray, The Criminal Lineup at Home and Abroad, 1966 Utah L. Rev. 610, 627–628.

identifications and result in obstruction of the confrontations. As for the first, we note that in the two cases in which the right to counsel is today held to apply, counsel had already been appointed and no argument is made in either case that notice to counsel would have prejudicially delayed the confrontations. Moreover, we leave open the question whether the presence of substitute counsel might not suffice where notification and presence of the suspect's own counsel would result in prejudicial delay. And to refuse to recognize the right to counsel for fear that counsel will obstruct the course of justice is contrary to the basic assumptions upon which this Court has operated in Sixth Amendment cases. We rejected similar logic in *Miranda v. Arizona* concerning presence of counsel during custodial interrogation * * * . In our view counsel can hardly impede legitimate law enforcement; on the contrary, for the reasons expressed, law enforcement may be assisted by preventing the infiltration of taint in the prosecution's identification evidence. That result cannot help the guilty avoid conviction but can only help assure that the right man has been brought to justice.[29]

Legislative or other regulations, such as those of local police departments, which eliminate the risks of abuse and unintentional suggestion at lineup proceedings and the impediments to meaningful confrontation at trial may also remove the basis for regarding the stage as "critical." But neither Congress nor the federal authorities have seen fit to provide a solution. What we hold today "in no way creates a constitutional straitjacket which will handicap sound efforts at reform, nor is it intended to have this effect."

V.

We come now to the question whether the denial of Wade's motion to strike the courtroom identification by the bank witnesses at trial because of the absence of his counsel at the lineup required, as the Court of Appeals held, the grant of a new trial at which such evidence is to be excluded. We do not think this disposition can be justified without first giving the Government the opportunity to establish by clear and convincing evidence that the in-court identifications were based upon observations of the suspect other than the lineup identification. Where, as here, the admissibility of evidence of the lineup identification itself is not involved, a *per se* rule of exclusion of courtroom identification would be unjustified. A rule limited solely to the exclusion of testimony concerning identification at the lineup itself, without regard to admissibility of the

---

[29] Many other nations surround the lineup with safeguards against prejudice to the suspect. In England the suspect must be allowed the presence of his solicitor or a friend; Germany requires the presence of retained counsel; France forbids the confrontation of the suspect in the absence of his counsel; Spain, Mexico, and Italy provide detailed procedures prescribing the conditions under which confrontation must occur under the supervision of a judicial officer who sees to it that the proceedings are officially recorded to assure adequate scrutiny at trial.

courtroom identification, would render the right to counsel an empty one. The lineup is most often used, as in the present case, to crystallize the witnesses' identification of the defendant for future reference. We have already noted that the lineup identification will have that effect. The State may then rest upon the witnesses' unequivocal courtroom identification, and not mention the pretrial identification as part of the State's case at trial. Counsel is then in the predicament in which Wade's counsel found himself—realizing that possible unfairness at the lineup may be the sole means of attack upon the unequivocal courtroom identification, and having to probe in the dark in an attempt to discover and reveal unfairness, while bolstering the government witness' courtroom identification by bringing out and dwelling upon his prior identification. Since counsel's presence at the lineup would equip him to attack not only the lineup identification but the courtroom identification as well, limiting the impact of violation of the right to counsel to exclusion of evidence only of identification at the lineup itself disregards a critical element of that right.

We think it follows that the proper test to be applied in these situations is that quoted in *Wong Sun v. United States*, [p. 530], " '[W]hether, granting establishment of the primary illegality, the evidence to which instant objection is made has been come at by exploitation of that illegality or instead by means sufficiently distinguishable to be purged of the primary taint.' Maguire, Evidence of Guilt 221 (1959)." Application of this test in the present context requires consideration of various factors; for example, the prior opportunity to observe the alleged criminal act, the existence of any discrepancy between any pre-lineup description and the defendant's actual description, any identification prior to lineup of another person, the identification by picture of the defendant prior to the lineup, failure to identify the defendant on a prior occasion, and the lapse of time between the alleged act and the lineup identification. It is also relevant to consider those facts which, despite the absence of counsel, are disclosed concerning the conduct of the lineup.[33] * * *

On the record now before us we cannot make the determination whether the in-court identifications had an independent origin. * * * We * * * think the appropriate procedure to be followed is to vacate the conviction pending a hearing to determine whether the in-court

---

[33] Thus it is not the case that [as the dissent asserts] "[i]t matters not how well the witness knows the suspect, whether the witness is the suspect's mother, brother, or long-time associate, and no matter how long or well the witness observed the perpetrator at the scene of the crime." Such factors will have an important bearing upon the true basis of the witness' in-court identification. Moreover, the State's inability to bolster the witness' courtroom identification by introduction of the lineup identification itself, will become less significant the more the evidence of other opportunities of the witness to observe the defendant. Thus where the witness is a "kidnap victim who has lived for days with his abductor" the value to the State of admission of the lineup identification is indeed marginal, and such identification would be a mere formality.

identifications had an independent source, * * * and for the District Court to reinstate the conviction or order a new trial, as may be proper. * * *

MR. JUSTICE WHITE, whom MR. JUSTICE HARLAN and MR. JUSTICE STEWART join, dissenting [on the Sixth Amendment issue].

The Court has again propounded a broad constitutional rule barring use of a wide spectrum of relevant and probative evidence, solely because a step in its ascertainment or discovery occurs outside the presence of defense counsel. * * *

The Court's opinion is far-reaching. It proceeds first by creating a new *per se* rule of constitutional law: a criminal suspect cannot be subjected to a pretrial identification process in the absence of his counsel without violating the Sixth Amendment. If he is, the State may not buttress a later courtroom identification of the witness by any reference to the previous identification. Furthermore, the courtroom identification is not admissible at all unless the State can establish by clear and convincing proof that the testimony is not the fruit of the earlier identification made in the absence of defendant's counsel—admittedly a heavy burden for the State and probably an impossible one. To all intents and purposes, courtroom identifications are barred if pretrial identifications have occurred without counsel being present.

The rule applies to any lineup, to any other techniques employed to produce an identification and *a fortiori* to a face-to-face encounter between the witness and the suspect alone, regardless of when the identification occurs, in time or place, and whether before or after indictment or information. It matters not how well the witness knows the suspect, whether the witness is the suspect's mother, brother, or long-time associate, and no matter how long or well the witness observed the perpetrator at the scene of the crime. The kidnap victim who has lived for days with his abductor is in the same category as the witness who has had only a fleeting glimpse of the criminal. Neither may identify the suspect without defendant's counsel being present. The same strictures apply regardless of the number of other witnesses who positively identify the defendant and regardless of the corroborative evidence showing that it was the defendant who had committed the crime.

The premise for the Court's rule is not the general unreliability of eyewitness identifications nor the difficulties inherent in observation, recall, and recognition. The Court assumes a narrower evil as the basis for its rule—improper police suggestion which contributes to erroneous identifications. The Court apparently believes that improper police procedures are so widespread that a broad prophylactic rule must be laid down, requiring the presence of counsel at all pretrial identifications, in order to detect recurring instances of police misconduct. I do not share this pervasive distrust of all official investigations. None of the materials the Court relies upon supports it. Certainly, I would bow to solid fact, but the Court quite obviously does not have before it any reliable, comprehensive survey of current police practices on which to base its new rule. Until it does, the Court should avoid excluding relevant evidence from state criminal trials. * * *

I share the Court's view that the criminal trial, at the very least, should aim at truthful factfinding, including accurate eyewitness identifications. I doubt, however, on the basis of our present information, that the tragic mistakes which have occurred in criminal trials are as much the product of improper police conduct as they are the consequence of the difficulties inherent in eyewitness testimony and in resolving evidentiary conflicts by court or jury. I doubt that the Court's new rule will obviate these difficulties, or that the situation will be measurably improved by inserting defense counsel into the investigative processes of police departments everywhere.

But, it may be asked, what possible state interest militates against requiring the presence of defense counsel at lineups? After all, the argument goes, he *may* do some good, he *may* upgrade the quality of identification evidence in state courts and he can scarcely do any harm. Even if true, this is a feeble foundation for fastening an ironclad constitutional rule upon state criminal procedures. Absent some reliably established constitutional violation, the processes by which the States enforce their criminal laws are their own prerogative. * * *

Beyond this, however, requiring counsel at pretrial identifications as an invariable rule trenches on other valid state interests. One of them is its concern with the prompt and efficient enforcement of its criminal laws. Identifications frequently take place after arrest but before an indictment is returned or an information is filed. The police may have arrested a suspect on probable cause but may still have the wrong man. Both the suspect and the State have every interest in a prompt identification at that stage, the suspect in order to secure his immediate release and the State because prompt and early identification enhances *accurate* identification and because it must know whether it is on the right investigative track. Unavoidably, however, the absolute rule requiring the presence of counsel will cause significant delay and it may very well result in no pretrial identification at all. Counsel must be appointed and a time arranged convenient for him and the witnesses. Meanwhile, it may be necessary to file charges against the suspect who may then be released on bail, in the federal system very often on his own recognizance, with neither the State nor the defendant having the benefit of a properly conducted identification procedure.

Nor do I think the witnesses themselves can be ignored. They will now be required to be present at the convenience of counsel rather than their own. Many may be much less willing to participate if the identification stage is transformed into an adversary proceeding not under the control of a judge. Others may fear for their own safety if their identity is known at an early date, especially when there is no way of knowing until the lineup occurs whether or not the police really have the right man.

Finally, I think the Court's new rule is vulnerable in terms of its own unimpeachable purpose of increasing the reliability of identification testimony.

Law enforcement officers have the obligation to convict the guilty and to make sure they do not convict the innocent. They must be dedicated to making the criminal trial a procedure for the ascertainment of the true facts surrounding the commission of the crime.[5] To this extent, our so-called adversary system is not adversary at all; nor should it be. But defense counsel has no comparable obligation to ascertain or present the truth. Our system assigns him a different mission. He must be and is interested in preventing the conviction of the innocent, but, absent a voluntary plea of guilty, we also insist that he defend his client whether he is innocent or guilty. The State has the obligation to present the evidence. Defense counsel need present nothing, even if he knows what the truth is. He need not furnish any witnesses to the police, or reveal any confidences of his client, or furnish any other information to help the prosecution's case. If he can confuse a witness, even a truthful one, or make him appear at a disadvantage, unsure or indecisive, that will be his normal course. Our interest in not convicting the innocent permits counsel to put the State to its proof, to put the State's case in the worst possible light, regardless of what he thinks or knows to be the truth. Undoubtedly there are some limits which defense counsel must observe but more often than not, defense counsel will cross-examine a prosecution witness, and impeach him if he can, even if he thinks the witness is telling the truth, just as he will attempt to destroy a witness who he thinks is lying. In this respect, as part of our modified adversary system and as part of the duty imposed on the most honorable defense counsel, we countenance or require conduct which in many instances has little, if any, relation to the search for truth.

---

[5] "The United States Attorney is the representative not of an ordinary party to a controversy, but of a sovereignty whose obligation to govern impartially is as compelling as its obligation to govern at all; and whose interest, therefore, in a criminal prosecution is not that it shall win a case, but that justice shall be done. As such, he is in a peculiar and very definite sense the servant of the law, the twofold aim of which is that guilt shall not escape or innocence suffer. He may prosecute with earnestness and vigor—indeed, he should do so. But, while he may strike hard blows, he is not at liberty to strike foul ones. It is as much his duty to refrain from improper methods calculated to produce a wrongful conviction as it is to use every legitimate means to bring about a just one." *Berger v. United States*, 295 U.S. 78, 88, 55 S.Ct. 629, 633, 79 L.Ed. 1314.

I would not extend this system, at least as it presently operates, to police investigations and would not require counsel's presence at pretrial identification procedures. Counsel's interest is in not having his client placed at the scene of the crime, regardless of his whereabouts. Some counsel may advise their clients to refuse to make any movements or to speak any words in a lineup or even to appear in one. To that extent the impact on truthful factfinding is quite obvious. Others will not only observe what occurs and develop possibilities for later cross-examination but will hover over witnesses and begin their cross-examination then, menacing truthful factfinding as thoroughly as the Court fears the police now do. Certainly there is an implicit invitation to counsel to suggest rules for the lineup and to manage and produce it as best he can. I therefore doubt that the Court's new rule, at least absent some clearly defined limits on counsel's role, will measurably contribute to more reliable pretrial identifications. My fears are that it will have precisely the opposite result. * * *

NOTES AND QUESTIONS

1.   *Introducing evidence of the pretrial identification procedure.* In *Wade*, the prosecution did not seek to introduce evidence relating to the lineup. The only issue was the admissibility of the witness's *in*-court identification of Wade. However, in companion case *Gilbert v. California,* cited in *Wade*, the prosecutor elicited testimony at trial of the fact that witnesses had identified the defendant at a post-indictment pretrial lineup at which Gilbert was not represented by counsel. The Court held that

> [t]he State is * * * not entitled to an opportunity to show that that testimony had an independent source. Only a *per se* exclusionary rule as to such testimony can be an effective sanction to assure that law enforcement authorities will respect the accused's constitutional right to the presence of his counsel at the critical lineup.

How would you summarize the *"Wade-Gilbert* rule"? Specifically, under what circumstances does a defendant have a right to counsel at a lineup or other corporeal identification procedure? Does the rule apply to an identification that occurs *before* indictment? Before arrest? And, what are the evidentiary implications if the defendant's counsel right is violated?

2.   Reconsider the second and third paragraphs of Justice White's dissent. Has he correctly stated the *Wade* rule, as you understand it from Note 1? Reconsider the fourth paragraph of his dissent. Do you believe that he accurately states the "premise for the Court's rule"?

3.   *The problems with eyewitness identifications.* The *Wade* Court noted that "identification evidence is peculiarly riddled with innumerable dangers * * * which might seriously, even crucially, derogate from a fair trial." As two social scientists long ago put it, "people quite often do not see or hear things which are presented clearly to their senses, see or hear things which are not

there, do not remember things which have happened to them, and remember things which did not happen." Felice J. Levine & June Louin Tapp, *The Psychology of Criminal Identification: The Gap from Wade to Kirby*, 121 U. Pa. L. Rev. 1079, 1087–88 (1973).

Why and under what circumstances is eyewitness testimony particularly unreliable? Social scientists who have studied the subject provide various answers. (For cites to relevant literature and greater detail on the subject, see 1 Joshua Dressler & Alan C. Michaels, Understanding Criminal Procedure § 26.01 (6th ed. 2013).) First, people tend to see what they expect to see. A hunter looking for a deer in the forest may "see" a deer in the brush that turns out to be a human being. If a witness to a crime has an expectation of what a criminal should look like—the person's age, race, size, gender—she may unconsciously "see" the offender in a way that fits her preconception. Second, there is substantial evidence of unreliability in cross-racial identification cases, *i.e.*, when a person of one racial group attempts to identify a crime perpetrator of a different racial category.

Third, memory decays over time. Worse, memory is an "active, constructive process." Frederic D. Woocher, Note, *Did Your Eyes Deceive You? Expert Psychological Testimony on the Unreliability of Eyewitness Identification*, 29 Stan. L. Rev. 969, 983 (1977). That is, people dislike uncertainty; therefore, when a person experiences a memory gap, the individual unconsciously tries to fill in the memory holes with details that often are inaccurate.

Fourth, post-crime identification police procedures can aggravate the situation. For example, a lineup typically functions as a multiple-choice test in which eyewitness-participants believe—or are led to believe by the police— that "none of the above" is an unacceptable answer. Therefore, witnesses often give the "most correct" answer (pick the person whom they believe most resembles the culprit), rather than indicate that they do not recognize anyone in the lineup. And, once a witness identifies—correctly or incorrectly— someone from a lineup, she becomes psychologically committed to her identification. Her mind may even play tricks on her: when she thinks back to the crime, her "mind's eye" may now "remember" the person she selected from the lineup. It substitutes for her initial memory of the culprit.

4.   *Remedies.* Jurors tend to place a high value on eyewitness testimony. They do not distinguish between high-risk and low-risk identifications. They tend to overestimate the accuracy of eyewitness testimony. What can be done, therefore, to reduce the inherent risks in eyewitness identification procedures? The *Wade* Court invited legislatures and police departments to reform their procedures and even quoted (footnote 26) from a scholarly article recommending a model statute to deal with the problem.

For many years, social scientists have urged changes in police procedures in order to enhance the reliability of the identification process. Until recently, their recommendations were largely ignored. In 2008, however, North Carolina enacted a statute that implemented several reform ideas. Lineups there must be conducted by an independent administrator who does not know which person in the lineup is the suspect (or by a similarly "blind" procedure). The eyewitness must be instructed that the perpetrator might not be in the lineup, that it is as important to exclude innocent persons as it is to identify the perpetrator, and that the investigation will continue whether or not an identification is made. A video recording must be made of the lineup procedure unless it is "not practical." The eyewitness who identifies a person or a photo must be asked to give a statement, in the eyewitness's own words, of his confidence level that the person identified is the perpetrator. The videotape and the eyewitness' statement must be turned over to the defense. Other reform ideas are contained in this comprehensive statute. See George C. Thomas III, *Two Windows Into Innocence*, 7 Ohio State J. Crim. L. 575 (2010).

Other states have sought to reform procedures judicially. See State v. Ledbetter, 275 Conn. 534, 881 A.2d 290 (2005) (ruling that officers administering identification procedures should advise the witness that the perpetrator may or may not be present in the procedure, or else evidence at trial of the identification must be accompanied by a jury instruction stating that "psychological studies have shown" that failure to so admonish eyewitnesses "increases the likelihood that the witness will select one of the individuals in the procedure, even when the perpetrator is not present"); and State v. Guilbert, 49 A.3d 705 (Conn. 2012); Johnson v. State, 526 S.E.2d 549 (Ga. 2000); People v. Lee, 750 N.E.2d 63 (N.Y. 2001); State v. Copeland, 226 S.W.3d 287 (Tenn. 2007) (all holding that expert testimony is generally admissible in criminal trials to demonstrate the potential weaknesses of eyewitness testimony).

5.   Suppose that a police department routinely videotapes its lineups and furnishes the defense with an unedited copy of the procedure. Should the accused still have a constitutional right to the presence of counsel?

6.   *The role of counsel at the lineup.* Reconsider Justice Brennan's opinion in *Wade*. What does he envision a lawyer doing during the identification process? What is Justice White's understanding in this regard?

What *should* be the role of a lawyer at a lineup? Should she serve simply as a passive observer who can help reconstruct for the judge and jury the events of the lineup, point to alleged abuses, and thereby minimize the incriminating force of the identification? Or should she be permitted to make objections at the time of the lineup and suggest ways to improve the process? If the lawyer's role is passive, is *Wade* an adequate solution to the unreliability problem? If the lawyer's role is active, is Justice White correct in fearing that defense lawyers may make the process less efficient and, ultimately, less accurate?

For a moment, imagine that you are a Public Defender and are called to the police station to represent a person in a lineup. You look at the lineup and you believe that it is unduly suggestive (perhaps the others in the confrontation do not look like your client). What would you do? Would you complain to the police and urge them to find persons who look more like your client? Would you say nothing? What are the risks of being vocal? Of being passive?

7.   *When is the right to counsel triggered?: the Kirby "clarification."* Look again at your answers to the questions asked at the end of Note 1. (You did answer them, right?) Specifically, as you understand the majority opinion in *Wade, when* is the right to counsel triggered? Does it apply to an identification that occurs *before* indictment? Before arrest? What is dissenting Justice White's answer?

As it turns out, the answer to the timing question may not have been what some of the *Wade* justices hoped (or feared). In Kirby v. Illinois, 406 U.S. 682, 92 S.Ct. 1877, 32 L.Ed.2d 411 (1972), a case involving a corporeal identification that occurred *after* arrest but *before* indictment or arraignment, a plurality of the Court announced:

> In a line of constitutional cases in this Court stemming back to the Court's landmark opinion in *Powell v. Alabama* [p. 25], it has been firmly established that a person's Sixth and Fourteenth Amendment right to counsel attaches only at or after the time that adversary judicial proceedings have been initiated against him.

> This is not to say that a defendant in a criminal case has a constitutional right to counsel only at the trial itself. The *Powell* case makes clear that the right attaches at the time of arraignment, and the Court has recently held that it exists also at the time of a preliminary hearing. But the point is that, while members of the Court have differed as to the existence of the right to counsel in the contexts of some of the above cases, *all* of those cases have involved points of time at or after the initiation of adversary judicial criminal proceedings—whether by way of formal charge, preliminary hearing, indictment, information, or arraignment.[b] * * *

> The initiation of judicial criminal proceedings is far from a mere formalism. It is the starting point of our whole system of adversary criminal justice. For it is only then that the government has committed itself to prosecute, and only then that the adverse positions of government and defendant have solidified. It is then that a defendant finds himself faced with the prosecutorial forces of organized society, and immersed in the intricacies of substantive and procedural criminal law. It is this point, therefore, that marks the commencement of the "criminal prosecutions" to which alone the explicit guarantees of the Sixth Amendment are applicable. * * *

---

[b]   Although *Kirby* was a plurality opinion, the majority opinion in Moore v. Illinois, 434 U.S. 220, 98 S.Ct. 458, 54 L.Ed.2d 424 (1977), confirmed the line drawn here—initiation of adversary judicial proceedings—as the critical one in corporal identification cases.

What has been said is not to suggest that there may not be occasions during the course of a criminal investigation when the police do abuse identification procedures. Such abuses are not beyond the reach of the Constitution. As the Court pointed out in *Wade* itself, it is always necessary to "scrutinize *any* pretrial confrontation * * * ."c The Due Process Clause of the Fifth and Fourteenth Amendments forbids a lineup that is unnecessarily suggestive and conducive to irreparable mistaken identification. When a person has not been formally charged with a criminal offense, [the Due Process Clause rule] strikes the appropriate constitutional balance between the right of a suspect to be protected from prejudicial procedures and the interest of society in the prompt and purposeful investigation of an unsolved crime.

Is *Kirby* consistent with the underlying rationale of *Wade*? Justice White did not think so. He dissented again, in *Kirby*, stating simply that "*United States v. Wade* and *Gilbert v. California* govern this case and compel reversal of the judgment below."

8.   What is the practical effect of *Kirby* (Note 7)?

9.   *Post-indictment noncorporeal identifications.* In United States v. Ash, 413 U.S. 300, 93 S.Ct. 2568, 37 L.Ed.2d 619 (1973), the Supreme Court held that the *Wade-Gilbert* rule does *not* apply to photographic displays, even if such a procedure occurs after formal criminal proceedings have commenced.

In *Ash*, four witnesses identified Ash from a single black-and-white photograph. Then they were shown five color photographs, one of which included Ash. Three of the witnesses selected Ash, but the other was unable to make any selection. This occurred after Ash had been indicted, and in the absence of defense counsel. In light of *Wade*, can you think of any good reason for the no-right-to-counsel holding in *Ash*?

B. DUE PROCESS OF LAW

PERRY V. NEW HAMPSHIRE

Supreme Court of the United States, 2012.
565 U.S. ___, 132 S.Ct. 716, 181 L.Ed.2d 694.

JUSTICE GINSBURG delivered the opinion of the Court [joined by CHIEF JUSTICE ROBERTS, and JUSTICES SCALIA, KENNEDY, THOMAS, BREYER, ALITO, and KAGAN].

In our system of justice, fair trial for persons charged with criminal offenses is secured by the Sixth Amendment, which guarantees to defendants the right to counsel, compulsory process to obtain defense witnesses, and the opportunity to cross-examine witnesses for the

---

c   Is *Kirby* properly using this quote from *Wade*? Look back at the full quote on p. 829.

prosecution. Those safeguards apart, admission of evidence in state trials is ordinarily governed by state law, and the reliability of relevant testimony typically falls within the province of the jury to determine. This Court has recognized, in addition, a due process check on the admission of eyewitness identification, applicable when the police have arranged suggestive circumstances leading the witness to identify a particular person as the perpetrator of a crime.

An identification infected by improper police influence, our case law holds, is not automatically excluded. Instead, the trial judge must screen the evidence for reliability pretrial. If there is "a very substantial likelihood of irreparable misidentification," the judge must disallow presentation of the evidence at trial. But if the indicia of reliability are strong enough to outweigh the corrupting effect of the police-arranged suggestive circumstances, the identification evidence ordinarily will be admitted, and the jury will ultimately determine its worth.

We have not extended pretrial screening for reliability to cases in which the suggestive circumstances were not arranged by law enforcement officers. Petitioner requests that we do so because of the grave risk that mistaken identification will yield a miscarriage of justice.[1] Our decisions, however, turn on the presence of state action and aim to deter police from rigging identification procedures, for example, at a lineup, showup, or photograph array. When no improper law enforcement activity is involved, we hold, it suffices to test reliability through the rights and opportunities generally designed for that purpose, notably, the presence of counsel at postindictment lineups, vigorous cross-examination, protective rules of evidence, and jury instructions on both the fallibility of eyewitness identification and the requirement that guilt be proved beyond a reasonable doubt.

I

A

Around 3 a.m. on August 15, 2008, Joffre Ullon called the Nashua, New Hampshire, Police Department and reported that an African-American male was trying to break into cars parked in the lot of Ullon's apartment building. Officer Nicole Clay responded to the call. Upon arriving at the parking lot, Clay heard what "sounded like a metal bat hitting the ground." She then saw petitioner Barion Perry standing

---

[1] The dissent, too, appears to urge that all suggestive circumstances raise due process concerns warranting a pretrial ruling. Neither Perry nor the dissent, however, points to a single case in which we have required pretrial screening absent a police-arranged identification procedure. Understandably so, for there are no such cases. Instead, the dissent surveys our decisions, heedless of the police arrangement that underlies every one of them, and inventing a "longstanding rule" that never existed. Nor are we, as the dissent suggests, imposing a *mens rea* requirement, or otherwise altering our precedent in any way. As our case law makes clear, what triggers due process concerns is police use of an unnecessarily suggestive identification procedure, whether or not they intended the arranged procedure to be suggestive.

between two cars. Perry walked toward Clay, holding two car-stereo amplifiers in his hands. A metal bat lay on the ground behind him. Clay asked Perry where the amplifiers came from. "[I] found them on the ground," Perry responded.

Meanwhile, Ullon's wife, Nubia Blandon, woke her neighbor, Alex Clavijo, and told him she had just seen someone break into his car. Clavijo immediately went downstairs to the parking lot to inspect the car. He first observed that one of the rear windows had been shattered. On further inspection, he discovered that the speakers and amplifiers from his car stereo were missing, as were his bat and wrench. Clavijo then approached Clay and told her about Blandon's alert and his own subsequent observations.

By this time, another officer had arrived at the scene. Clay asked Perry to stay in the parking lot with that officer, while she and Clavijo went to talk to Blandon. Clay and Clavijo then entered the apartment building and took the stairs to the fourth floor, where Blandon's and Clavijo's apartments were located. They met Blandon in the hallway just outside the open door to her apartment.

Asked to describe what she had seen, Blandon stated that, around 2:30 a.m., she saw from her kitchen window a tall, African-American man roaming the parking lot and looking into cars. Eventually, the man circled Clavijo's car, opened the trunk, and removed a large box.

Clay asked Blandon for a more specific description of the man. Blandon pointed to her kitchen window and said the person she saw breaking into Clavijo's car was standing in the parking lot, next to the police officer. Perry's arrest followed this identification.

About a month later, the police showed Blandon a photographic array that included a picture of Perry and asked her to point out the man who had broken into Clavijo's car. Blandon was unable to identify Perry.

B

Perry was charged in New Hampshire state court with one count of theft by unauthorized taking and one count of criminal mischief. Before trial, he moved to suppress Blandon's identification on the ground that admitting it at trial would violate due process. Blandon witnessed what amounted to a one-person showup in the parking lot, Perry asserted, which all but guaranteed that she would identify him as the culprit.

The New Hampshire Superior Court denied the motion. To determine whether due process prohibits the introduction of an out-of-court identification at trial, the Superior Court said, this Court's decisions instruct a two-step inquiry. First, the trial court must decide whether the police used an unnecessarily suggestive identification procedure. If they did, the court must next consider whether the improper identification procedure so tainted the resulting identification as to render it unreliable and therefore inadmissible.

Perry's challenge, the Superior Court concluded, failed at step one: Blandon's identification of Perry on the night of the crime did not result from an unnecessarily suggestive procedure "manufacture[d] * * * by the police." Blandon pointed to Perry "spontaneously," the court noted, "without any inducement from the police." Clay did not ask Blandon whether the man standing in the parking lot was the man Blandon had seen breaking into Clavijo's car. Nor did Clay ask Blandon to move to the window from which she had observed the break-in.

The Superior Court recognized that there were reasons to question the accuracy of Blandon's identification: the parking lot was dark in some locations; Perry was standing next to a police officer; Perry was the only African-American man in the vicinity; and Blandon was unable, later, to pick Perry out of a photographic array. But "[b]ecause the police procedures were not unnecessarily suggestive," the court ruled that the reliability of Blandon's testimony was for the jury to consider.

At the ensuing trial, Blandon and Clay testified to Blandon's out-of-court identification. The jury found Perry guilty of theft and not guilty of criminal mischief.

On appeal, Perry repeated his challenge to the admissibility of Blandon's out-of-court identification. The trial court erred, Perry contended, in requiring an initial showing that the police arranged the suggestive identification procedure. Suggestive circumstances alone, Perry argued, suffice to trigger the court's duty to evaluate the reliability of the resulting identification before allowing presentation of the evidence to the jury.

The New Hampshire Supreme Court rejected Perry's argument and affirmed his conviction. * * *

We granted certiorari to resolve a division of opinion on the question whether the Due Process Clause requires a trial judge to conduct a preliminary assessment of the reliability of an eyewitness identification made under suggestive circumstances not arranged by the police.

II

A

The Constitution, our decisions indicate, protects a defendant against a conviction based on evidence of questionable reliability, not by prohibiting introduction of the evidence, but by affording the defendant means to persuade the jury that the evidence should be discounted as unworthy of credit. Constitutional safeguards available to defendants to counter the State's evidence include the Sixth Amendment rights to counsel; compulsory process; and confrontation plus cross-examination of witnesses. Apart from these guarantees, we have recognized, state and federal statutes and rules ordinarily govern the admissibility of evidence, and juries are assigned the task of determining the reliability of the evidence presented at trial. Only when evidence "is so extremely unfair that its admission violates fundamental conceptions of justice" have we imposed a constraint tied to the Due Process Clause.

Contending that the Due Process Clause is implicated here, Perry relies on a series of decisions involving police-arranged identification procedures. In *Stovall* v. *Denno*, 388 U. S. 293[, 87 S.Ct. 1967, 18 L.Ed.2d 1199] (1967), first of those decisions, a witness identified the defendant as her assailant after police officers brought the defendant to the witness' hospital room. At the time the witness made the identification, the defendant—the only African-American in the room—was handcuffed and surrounded by police officers. Although the police-arranged showup was undeniably suggestive, the Court held that no due process violation occurred. Crucial to the Court's decision was the procedure's necessity: The witness was the only person who could identify or exonerate the defendant; the witness could not leave her hospital room; and it was uncertain whether she would live to identify the defendant in more neutral circumstances.

A year later, in *Simmons* v. *United States*, 390 U. S. 377[, 88 S.Ct. 967, 19 L.Ed.2d 1247] (1968), the Court addressed a due process challenge to police use of a photographic array. When a witness identifies the defendant in a police-organized photo lineup, the Court ruled, the identification should be suppressed only where "the photographic identification procedure was so [unnecessarily] suggestive as to give rise to a very substantial likelihood of irreparable misidentification." Satisfied that the photo array used by Federal Bureau of Investigation agents in *Simmons* was both necessary and unlikely to have led to a mistaken identification, the Court rejected the defendant's due process challenge to admission of the identification. * * *

Synthesizing previous decisions, we set forth in *Neil* v. *Biggers*, 409 U. S. 188[, 93 S.Ct. 375, 34 L.Ed.2d 401] (1972), and reiterated in *Manson* v. *Brathwaite*, 432 U. S. 98[, 97 S.Ct. 2243, 53 L.Ed.2d 140](1977), the approach appropriately used to determine whether the Due Process Clause requires suppression of an eyewitness identification tainted by police arrangement. The Court emphasized, first, that due process concerns arise only when law enforcement officers use an identification procedure that is both suggestive and unnecessary. Even when the police use such a procedure, the Court next said, suppression of the resulting identification is not the inevitable consequence.

A rule requiring automatic exclusion, the Court reasoned, would "g[o] too far," for it would "kee[p] evidence from the jury that is reliable and relevant," and "may result, on occasion, in the guilty going free."

Instead of mandating a *per se* exclusionary rule, the Court held that the Due Process Clause requires courts to assess, on a case-by-case basis, whether improper police conduct created a "substantial likelihood of misidentification." "[R]eliability [of the eyewitness identification] is the linchpin" of that evaluation, the Court stated in *Brathwaite*. Where the "indicators of [a witness'] ability to make an accurate identification" are "outweighed by the corrupting effect" of law enforcement suggestion, the identification should be suppressed. Otherwise, the evidence (if admissible in all other respects) should be submitted to the jury.[5]

Applying this "totality of the circumstances" approach, the Court held in *Biggers* that law enforcement's use of an unnecessarily suggestive showup did not require suppression of the victim's identification of her assailant. Notwithstanding the improper procedure, the victim's identification was reliable: She saw her assailant for a considerable period of time under adequate light, provided police with a detailed description of her attacker long before the showup, and had "no doubt" that the defendant was the person she had seen. Similarly, the Court concluded in *Brathwaite* that police use of an unnecessarily suggestive photo array did not require exclusion of the resulting identification. The witness, an undercover police officer, viewed the defendant in good light for several minutes, provided a thorough description of the suspect, and was certain of his identification. Hence, the "indicators of [the witness'] ability to make an accurate identification [were] hardly outweighed by the corrupting effect of the challenged identification."

B

Perry concedes that, in contrast to every case in the *Stovall* line, law enforcement officials did not arrange the suggestive circumstances surrounding Blandon's identification. He contends, however, that it was mere happenstance that each of the *Stovall* cases involved improper police action. The rationale underlying our decisions, Perry asserts, supports a rule requiring trial judges to prescreen eyewitness evidence for reliability any time an identification is made under suggestive circumstances. We disagree.

Perry's argument depends, in large part, on the Court's statement in *Brathwaite* that "reliability is the linchpin in determining the admissibility of identification testimony." If reliability is the linchpin of

---

[5] Among "factors to be considered" in evaluating a witness' "ability to make an accurate identification," the Court listed: "the opportunity of the witness to view the criminal at the time of the crime, the witness' degree of attention, the accuracy of his prior description of the criminal, the level of certainty demonstrated at the confrontation, and the time between the crime and the confrontation."

admissibility under the Due Process Clause, Perry maintains, it should make no difference whether law enforcement was responsible for creating the suggestive circumstances that marred the identification.

Perry has removed our statement in *Brathwaite* from its mooring, and thereby attributes to the statement a meaning a fair reading of our opinion does not bear. * * * *Brathwaite* Court's reference to reliability appears in a portion of the opinion concerning the appropriate remedy *when the police use an unnecessarily suggestive identification procedure.* * * * The due process check for reliability, *Brathwaite* made plain, comes into play only after the defendant establishes improper police conduct. The very purpose of the check, the Court noted, was to avoid depriving the jury of identification evidence that is reliable, *notwithstanding* improper police conduct.

Perry's contention that improper police action was not essential to the reliability check *Brathwaite* required is echoed by the dissent. Both ignore a key premise of the *Brathwaite* decision: A primary aim of excluding identification evidence obtained under unnecessarily suggestive circumstances, the Court said, is to deter law enforcement use of improper lineups, showups, and photo arrays in the first place. Alerted to the prospect that identification evidence improperly obtained may be excluded, the Court reasoned, police officers will "guard against unnecessarily suggestive procedures." This deterrence rationale is inapposite in cases, like Perry's, in which the police engaged in no improper conduct. * * *

Perry and the dissent place significant weight on *United States* v. *Wade,* [p. 828, supra], describing it as a decision not anchored to improper police conduct. In fact, the risk of police rigging was the very danger to which the Court responded in *Wade* when it recognized a defendant's right to counsel at postindictment, police-organized identification procedures. "[T]he confrontation *compelled by the State* between the accused and the victim or witnesses," the Court began, "is peculiarly riddled with innumerable dangers and variable factors which might seriously, even crucially, derogate from a fair trial." "A major factor contributing to the high incidence of miscarriage of justice from mistaken identification," the Court continued, "has been the degree of suggestion inherent in the manner in which *the prosecution* presents the suspect to witnesses for pretrial identification." To illustrate the improper suggestion it was concerned about, the Court pointed to police-designed lineups where "all in the lineup but the suspect were known to the identifying witness, * * * the other participants in [the] lineup were grossly dissimilar in appearance to the suspect, * * * only the suspect was required to wear distinctive clothing which the culprit allegedly wore, * * * the witness is told by the police that they have caught the culprit after which the defendant is brought before the witness alone or is viewed in jail, * * * the suspect is pointed out before or during a lineup, * * * the participants in the lineup are asked to try on an article of clothing which fits only the suspect." Beyond genuine debate, then, prevention of unfair police practices prompted the Court to extend a defendant's right to counsel to cover postindictment lineups and showups.

Perry's argument, reiterated by the dissent, thus lacks support in the case law he cites. Moreover, his position would open the door to judicial preview, under the banner of due process, of most, if not all, eyewitness identifications. External suggestion is hardly the only factor that casts doubt on the trustworthiness of an eyewitness' testimony. As one of Perry's *amici* points out, many other factors bear on "the likelihood of misidentification"—for example, the passage of time between exposure to and identification of the defendant, whether the witness was under stress when he first encountered the suspect, how much time the witness had to observe the suspect, how far the witness was from the suspect, whether the suspect carried a weapon, and the race of the suspect and the witness. There is no reason why an identification made by an eyewitness with poor vision, for example, or one who harbors a grudge against the defendant, should be regarded as inherently more reliable, less of a "threat to the fairness of trial," than the identification Blandon made in this case. To embrace Perry's view would thus entail a vast enlargement of the reach of due process as a constraint on the admission of evidence.

Perry maintains that the Court can limit the due process check he proposes to identifications made under "suggestive circumstances." Even if we could rationally distinguish suggestiveness from other factors bearing on the reliability of eyewitness evidence, Perry's limitation would still involve trial courts, routinely, in preliminary examinations. Most eyewitness identifications involve some element of suggestion. Indeed, all in-court identifications do. Out-of-court identifications volunteered by witnesses are also likely to involve suggestive circumstances. For example, suppose a witness identifies the defendant to police officers after seeing a photograph of the defendant in the press captioned "theft suspect," or hearing a radio report implicating the defendant in the crime. Or suppose the witness knew that the defendant ran with the wrong crowd and saw him on the day and in the vicinity of the crime. Any of these circumstances might have "suggested" to the witness that the defendant was the person the witness observed committing the crime.

C

In urging a broadly applicable due process check on eyewitness identifications, Perry maintains that eyewitness identifications are a uniquely unreliable form of evidence. See Brief for Petitioner 17–22 (citing studies showing that eyewitness misidentifications are the leading cause of wrongful convictions); Brief for American Psychological

Association as *Amicus Curiae* 14–17 (describing research indicating that as many as one in three eyewitness identifications is inaccurate). We do not doubt either the importance or the fallibility of eyewitness identifications. Indeed, in recognizing that defendants have a constitutional right to counsel at postindictment police lineups, we observed [in *Wade*] that "the annals of criminal law are rife with instances of mistaken identification."

We have concluded in other contexts, however, that the potential unreliability of a type of evidence does not alone render its introduction at the defendant's trial fundamentally unfair. We reach a similar conclusion here: The fallibility of eyewitness evidence does not, without the taint of improper state conduct, warrant a due process rule requiring a trial court to screen such evidence for reliability before allowing the jury to assess its creditworthiness.

Our unwillingness to enlarge the domain of due process as Perry and the dissent urge rests, in large part, on our recognition that the jury, not the judge, traditionally determines the reliability of evidence. We also take account of other safeguards built into our adversary system that caution juries against placing undue weight on eyewitness testimony of questionable reliability. Another is the defendant's right to the effective assistance of an attorney, who can expose the flaws in the eyewitness' testimony during cross-examination and focus the jury's attention on the fallibility of such testimony during opening and closing arguments. Eyewitness-specific jury instructions, which many federal and state courts have adopted, likewise warn the jury to take care in appraising identification evidence. The constitutional requirement that the government prove the defendant's guilt beyond a reasonable doubt also impedes convictions based on dubious identification evidence.

State and federal rules of evidence, moreover, permit trial judges to exclude relevant evidence if its probative value is substantially outweighed by its prejudicial impact or potential for misleading the jury. In appropriate cases, some States also permit defendants to present expert testimony on the hazards of eyewitness identification evidence.
* * *

Given the safeguards generally applicable in criminal trials, protections availed of by the defense in Perry's case, we hold that the introduction of Blandon's eyewitness testimony, without a preliminary judicial assessment of its reliability, did not render Perry's trial fundamentally unfair.

* * *

For the foregoing reasons, * * * we hold that the Due Process Clause does not require a preliminary judicial inquiry into the reliability of an eyewitness identification when the identification was not procured under unnecessarily suggestive circumstances arranged by law enforcement. Accordingly, the judgment of the New Hampshire Supreme Court is

Affirmed.

[The concurring opinion of JUSTICE THOMAS is omitted.]

JUSTICE SOTOMAYOR, dissenting.

This Court has long recognized that eyewitness identifications' unique confluence of features—their unreliability, susceptibility to suggestion, powerful impact on the jury, and resistance to the ordinary tests of the adversarial process—can undermine the fairness of a trial. Our cases thus establish a clear rule: The admission at trial of out-of-court eyewitness identifications derived from impermissibly suggestive circumstances that pose a very substantial likelihood of misidentification violates due process. The Court today announces that that rule does not even "com[e] into play" unless the suggestive circumstances are improperly "police-arranged."

Our due process concern, however, arises not from the act of suggestion, but rather from the corrosive effects of suggestion on the reliability of the resulting identification. By rendering protection contingent on improper police arrangement of the suggestive circumstances, the Court effectively grafts a *mens rea* inquiry onto our rule. The Court's holding enshrines a murky distinction—between suggestive confrontations intentionally orchestrated by the police and, as here, those inadvertently caused by police actions—that will sow confusion. It ignores our precedents' acute sensitivity to the hazards of intentional and unintentional suggestion alike and unmoors our rule from the very interest it protects, inviting arbitrary results. And it recasts the driving force of our decisions as an interest in police deterrence, rather than reliability. Because I see no warrant for declining to assess the circumstances of this case under our ordinary approach, I respectfully dissent.[1]

I

The "driving force" behind *United States* v. *Wade, Gilbert* v. *California*, 388 U. S. 263 [, 87 S.Ct. 1951, 18 L.Ed.2d 1178] (1967), and *Stovall* v. *Denno*, was "the Court's concern with the problems of eyewitness identification"—specifically, "the concern that the jury not hear eyewitness testimony unless that evidence has aspects of reliability." We have pointed to the "'formidable'" number of "miscarriage[s] of justice from mistaken identification" in the annals of criminal law. We have warned of the "vagaries" and "'proverbially untrustworthy'" nature

---

[1]   Because the facts of this case involve police action, I do not reach the question whether due process is triggered in situations involving no police action whatsoever.

of eyewitness identifications. And we have singled out a "major factor contributing" to that proverbial unreliability: "the suggestibility inherent in the context of the pretrial identification."

Our precedents make no distinction between intentional and unintentional suggestion. To the contrary, they explicitly state that "[s]uggestion can be created intentionally or unintentionally in many subtle ways." Rather than equate suggestive conduct with misconduct, we specifically have disavowed the assumption that suggestive influences may only be "the result of police procedures intentionally designed to prejudice an accused." * * * The implication is that even police acting with the best of intentions can inadvertently signal " 'that's the man.' " * * *

More generally, our precedents focus not on the act of suggestion, but on suggestion's "corrupting effect" on reliability. Eyewitness evidence derived from suggestive circumstances, we have explained, is uniquely resistant to the ordinary tests of the adversary process. An eyewitness who has made an identification often becomes convinced of its accuracy. "*Regardless of how the initial misidentification comes about*, the witness thereafter is apt to retain in his memory the image of the photograph rather than of the person actually seen, reducing the trustworthiness of subsequent * * * courtroom identification." *Simmons v. United States* (emphasis added). Suggestion bolsters that confidence.

At trial, an eyewitness' artificially inflated confidence in an identification's accuracy complicates the jury's task of assessing witness credibility and reliability. It also impairs the defendant's ability to attack the eyewitness' credibility. That in turn jeopardizes the defendant's basic right to subject his accuser to meaningful cross-examination. The end result of suggestion, whether intentional or unintentional, is to fortify testimony bearing directly on guilt that juries find extremely convincing and are hesitant to discredit.

Consistent with our focus on reliability, we have declined to adopt a *per se* rule excluding all suggestive identifications. Instead, "reliability is the linchpin" in deciding admissibility. We have explained that a suggestive identification procedure "does not in itself intrude upon a constitutionally protected interest." "Suggestive confrontations are disapproved because they increase the likelihood of misidentification"— and "[i]t is the likelihood of misidentification which violates a defendant's right to due process."

To protect that evidentiary interest, we have applied a two-step inquiry: First, the defendant has the burden of showing that the eyewitness identification was derived through "impermissibly suggestive" means. Second, if the defendant meets that burden, courts consider whether the identification was reliable under the totality of the circumstances. That step entails considering the witness' opportunity to view the perpetrator, degree of attention, accuracy of description, level of certainty, and the time between the crime and pretrial confrontation, then weighing such factors against the "corrupting effect of the suggestive identification." Most identifications will be admissible. The standard of "fairness as required by the Due Process Clause," however, demands that a subset of the most unreliable identifications—those carrying a " 'very substantial likelihood of * * * misidentification' "—will be excluded.

II

A

The majority today creates a novel and significant limitation on our longstanding rule. * * * Absent "improper police arrangement," "improper police conduct," or "rigging," the majority holds, our two-step inquiry does not even "com[e] into play." I cannot agree.

* * * Those terms connote a degree of intentional orchestration or manipulation. * * * The majority thus appears to graft a *mens rea* requirement onto our existing rule.[4] * * *

I note, however, that the majority leaves what is required by its arrangement-focused inquiry less than clear. In parts, the opinion suggests that the police must arrange an identification "procedure," regardless of whether they "inten[d] the arranged procedure to be suggestive." Elsewhere, it indicates that the police must arrange the "suggestive circumstances" that lead the witness to identify the accused. Still elsewhere it refers to "improper" police conduct, connoting bad faith. Does police "arrangement" relate to the procedure, the suggestiveness, or both? If it relates to the procedure, do suggestive preprocedure encounters no longer raise the same concerns? If the police need not "inten[d] the arranged procedure to be suggestive," what makes the police action "improper"? And does that mean that good-faith, unintentional police suggestiveness in a police-arranged lineup can be "impermissibly suggestive"? * * *

The arrangement-focused inquiry will sow needless confusion. If the police had called Perry and Blandon to the police station for interviews, and Blandon saw Perry being questioned, would that be sufficiently "improper police arrangement"? If Perry had voluntarily come to the police station, would that change the result? Today's opinion renders the applicability of our ordinary inquiry contingent on a murky line-drawing exercise. Whereas our two-step inquiry focuses on overall reliability—and could account for the spontaneity of the witness' identification and degree

---

4   The majority denies that it has imposed a *mens rea* requirement, but by confining our due process concerns to police-arranged identification procedures, that is just what it has done. The majority acknowledges that "whether or not [the police] intended the arranged procedure to be suggestive" is irrelevant under our precedents, but still places dispositive weight on whether or not the police intended the procedure itself.

of police manipulation under the totality of the circumstances—today's opinion forecloses that assessment by establishing a new and inflexible step zero. * * *

C

The majority gives several additional reasons for why applying our due process rule beyond improperly police-arranged circumstances is unwarranted. In my view, none withstands close inspection.

First, the majority insists that our precedents "aim to deter police from rigging identification procedures," so our rule should be limited to applications that advance that "primary aim" and "key premise." That mischaracterizes our cases. We discussed deterrence in *Brathwaite* because Brathwaite challenged our two-step inquiry as *lacking* deterrence value. Brathwaite argued that deterrence demanded a *per se* rule excluding all suggestive identifications. He said that our rule, which probes the reliability of suggestive identifications under the totality of the circumstances, "cannot be expected to have a significant deterrent impact."

We rebutted Brathwaite's criticism in language the majority now wrenches from context: Upon summarizing Brathwaite's argument, we acknowledged "several interests to be considered." * * * First, we noted the "driving force" behind *Wade* and its companion cases—"the concern that the jury not hear eyewitness testimony unless that evidence has aspects of reliability" * * * . We noted a "second factor"—deterrence—conceding that the *per se* rule had "more significant deterrent effect," but noting that our rule "also has an influence on police behavior." Finally, we noted a "third factor"—"the effect on the administration of justice"—describing the *per se* rule as having serious drawbacks on this front. That was no list of "primary aim[s]." Nor was it a ringing endorsement of the primacy of deterrence. We simply underscored, in responding to Brathwaite, that our rule was not without deterrence benefits. To the contrary, we clarified that deterrence was a subsidiary concern to reliability, the "driving force" of our doctrine. It is a stretch to claim that our rule cannot apply wherever "[t]his deterrence rationale is inapposite." * * *

[Second,] the majority emphasizes that we should rely on the jury to determine the reliability of evidence. But our cases are rooted in the assumption that eyewitness identifications upend the ordinary expectation that it is "the province of the jury to weigh the credibility of competing witnesses." As noted, jurors find eyewitness evidence unusually powerful and their ability to assess credibility is hindered by a witness' false confidence in the accuracy of his or her identification. That disability in no way depends on the intent behind the suggestive circumstances. * * *

[Third,] the majority suggests that applying our rule beyond police-arranged suggestive circumstances would entail a heavy practical burden, requiring courts to engage in "preliminary judicial inquiry" into "most, if not all, eyewitness identifications." But that is inaccurate. The burden of showing "impermissibly suggestive" circumstances is the defendant's, so the objection falls to the defendant to raise. And as is implicit in the majority's reassurance that Perry may resort to the rules of evidence in lieu of our due process precedents, trial courts will be entertaining defendants' objections, pretrial or at trial, to unreliable eyewitness evidence in any event. The relevant question, then, is what the standard of admissibility governing such objections should be. I see no reason to water down the standard for an equally suggestive and unreliable identification simply because the suggestive confrontation was unplanned.

It bears reminding, moreover, that we set a high bar for suppression. The vast majority of eyewitnesses proceed to testify before a jury. * * *

Finally, the majority questions how to "rationally distinguish suggestiveness from other factors bearing on the reliability of eyewitness evidence," such as "poor vision" or a prior "grudge," and more broadly, how to distinguish eyewitness evidence from other kinds of arguably unreliable evidence. Our precedents, however, did just that. We emphasized the " 'formidable number of instances in the records of English and American trials' " of "miscarriage[s] of justice from mistaken identification." We then observed that " 'the influence of improper suggestion upon identifying witnesses probably accounts for more miscarriages of justice than any other single factor.' " Moreover, the majority points to no other type of evidence that shares the rare confluence of characteristics that makes eyewitness evidence a unique threat to the fairness of trial. * * *

It would be one thing if the passage of time had cast doubt on the empirical premises of our precedents. But just the opposite has happened. A vast body of scientific literature has reinforced every concern our precedents articulated nearly a half-century ago, though it merits barely a parenthetical mention in the majority opinion. Over the past three decades, more than two thousand studies related to eyewitness identification have been published. One state supreme court recently appointed a special master to conduct an exhaustive survey of the current state of the scientific evidence and concluded that "[t]he research * * * is not only extensive," but "it represents the 'gold standard in terms of the applicability of social science research to law.' " *State* v. *Henderson,* 208 N. J. 208, 283, 27 A. 3d 872, 916 (2011). "Experimental methods and findings have been tested and retested, subjected to scientific scrutiny through peer-reviewed journals, evaluated through the lens of meta-analyses, and replicated at times in real-world settings." *Ibid.;* see also

Schmechel, O'Toole, Easterly, & Loftus, Beyond the Ken? Testing Jurors' Understanding of Eyewitness Reliability Evidence, 46 Jurimetrics 177, 180 (2006) (noting "nearly unanimous consensus among researchers about the [eyewitness reliability] field's core findings").

The empirical evidence demonstrates that eyewitness misidentification is " 'the single greatest cause of wrongful convictions in this country.' " Researchers have found that a staggering 76% of the first 250 convictions overturned due to DNA evidence since 1989 involved eyewitness misidentification. Study after study demonstrates that eyewitness recollections are highly susceptible to distortion by postevent information or social cues; that jurors routinely overestimate the accuracy of eyewitness identifications; that jurors place the greatest weight on eyewitness confidence in assessing identifications even though confidence is a poor gauge of accuracy; and that suggestiveness can stem from sources beyond police-orchestrated procedures. The majority today nevertheless adopts an artificially narrow conception of the dangers of suggestive identifications at a time when our concerns should have deepened.

III

There are many reasons why Perry's particular situation might not violate due process. The trial court found that the circumstances surrounding Blandon's identification did not rise to an impermissibly suggestive level. It is not at all clear, moreover, that there was a very substantial likelihood of misidentification, given Blandon's lack of equivocation on the scene, the short time between crime and confrontation, and the "fairly well lit" parking lot. The New Hampshire Supreme Court, however, never made findings on either point and, under the majority's decision today, never will. * * *

Because the New Hampshire Supreme Court truncated its inquiry at the threshold, I would vacate the judgment and remand for a proper analysis. I respectfully dissent.

NOTES AND QUESTIONS

1. Answer these questions posed by Sotomayor in her dissent: "If the police had called Perry and Blandon to the police station for interviews, and Blandon saw Perry being questioned, would that be sufficiently 'improper police arrangement'? If Perry had voluntarily come to the police station, would that change the result?"

2. Suppose we are privileged to peek into the Supreme Court chambers when the justices are discussing *Perry*. Imagine Justice Sotomayor asking Justice Ginsburg, "What is the harm in giving defendants a chance to demonstrate to a judge that the identification might be unreliable even if the

police are not guilty of misconduct?" How do you imagine Ginsburg might respond?

3. *Problem.* During a murder investigation, the police show witness *R* photographs of six persons. *R* identifies *N* as the murderer, resulting in *N*'s arrest. Months later, as *N*'s trial approaches, the prosecutor meets with *R* to go over her trial testimony. *S*, who had not come forward as a witness, attends the meeting "to provide emotional support for her friend." During the meeting, the prosecutor hands *R* the photo of *N* she had previously identified as the murderer. *S* sees the photo and exclaims, "Oh my God, that's him. That's who I ran up to after the shooting." Would it violate due process to permit evidence at trial of *S*'s identification in the prosecutor's office? See State v. Nolan, 807 N.W.2d 520 (Neb. 2012).

4. For an argument that the Warren Court failed to come to grips with the problem of unreliable eyewitness identifications, in part because of the apparent ease of the right-to-counsel solution, see George C. Thomas III, *The Criminal Procedure Road Not Taken: Due Process and the Protection of Innocence*, 3 Ohio St. J. Crim. L. 169 (2005).

5. *A final thought.* As the *Perry* majority notes, *Neil v. Biggers* held that the identification was reliable despite an "improper procedure" because the rape victim "saw her assailant for a considerable period of time under adequate light, provided police with a detailed description of her attacker long before the showup, and had 'no doubt' that the defendant was the person she had seen."

However, Jennifer Thompson, a rape victim in 1984, was equally sure that she could identify the man who raped her. She had made a conscious decision to study "every single detail on the rapist's face." She gave police a detailed description. She picked a man out of a photo array and later the same man out of a lineup. She said, "I was sure. I knew it." When told that another man had claimed to have raped her, she looked at him and said she had never seen him before and had "no idea who he is." The other man, the one she identified twice, served 11 years in prison before he was exonerated by DNA. The man Thompson had never seen before was the man who had raped her.

> The man I was so sure I had never seen in my life was the man who was inches from my throat, who raped me, who hurt me, who took my spirit away, who robbed me of my soul. And the man I had identified so emphatically on so many occasions was absolutely innocent.

Jennifer Thompson, *I Was Certain But I Was Wrong*, The New York Times, June 18, 2000.

CHAPTER 11

PRETRIAL RELEASE

. . .

Once a suspect is arrested, taken into custody, and booked, the police or prosecutor must prepare and file a complaint, which sets out the charges against the defendant. After the complaint is filed, a determination is made whether the defendant will be held in custody or released pending trial. With minor offenses (misdemeanors) police departments often have authority to release the individual immediately if she can post a cash security deposit in an amount specified on a bail schedule, based on the offense charged. With felonies (and with misdemeanors, if the arrestee is unable to post the requisite deposit), the individual remains in custody until she can be brought before a magistrate.

In the federal courts, an arrested individual must be brought before the nearest available magistrate "without unnecessary delay." Fed. R. Crim. P. 5(a)(1)(B). (The arrest may follow the issuance of a grand jury indictment, a topic raised in Chapter 12. More often, the arrest precedes the indictment.) Similar rules exist in each state. Typically, the proceeding—variously described as the "initial arraignment," "preliminary arraignment," "initial presentment," or, simply, "first appearance"—occurs within forty-eight hours of arrest.

At the first appearance, the defendant is informed of the charges filed against her. The magistrate also informs her of various rights she possesses, such as the right to retain counsel or request that counsel be appointed if she is indigent. But, the most significant feature of the initial arraignment is that the magistrate determines whether the defendant may be released pending trial and, if so, under what conditions. It is the release decision that concerns us in this chapter.

A. INTERESTS AT STAKE IN THE RELEASE DECISION

A defendant's interest in pretrial release is a weighty one. First, the "decision affects the detainee's liberty, a fundamental interest second only to life itself in terms of constitutional importance." Van Atta v. Scott, 27 Cal.3d 424, 166 Cal.Rptr. 149, 613 P.2d 210 (1980). In the 12-month period ending September 30, 2014,, the average time from the filing of charges to the disposition of a criminal case in federal court was 7 months, but it was 10.1 months if the defendant pleaded not guilty and sought a bench trial, and it was even longer (16.6 months) for a jury trial. http://www.uscourts.gov/statistics/table/d-6/judicial-business/2014/09/30. At the state level, in the nation's seventy-five most populous counties, the median time between felony arrest and adjudication in 2009 was more than one year for murder, 247 days for rape, and 111 days overall for all offenses. U.S. Dep't of Justice, Felony Defendants in Large Urban Counties, 2009—Statistical Tables (NCJ 243777, December 2013). Thus, unless he is released pending trial, a defendant—not yet convicted of any offense—may suffer a significant period of lost liberty.

Second, the still presumed-innocent person may suffer far more than "mere" loss of liberty in jail. As Supreme Court Justice Harry Blackmun has observed:

> [W]e do not live in an ideal world * * * so far as jail and prison conditions are concerned. The complaints that this Court, and every other appellate court, receives almost daily * * * about conditions of incarceration, about filth, about * * * rape [by fellow inmates], and about brutality[a] are not always the mouthings of the purely malcontent.

United States v. Bailey, 444 U.S. 394, 100 S.Ct. 624, 62 L.Ed.2d 575 (1980) (dissenting opinion). Indeed, the unconvicted *jail* inmate suicide rate is three times the rate in state *prisons* among convicted defendants. U.S. Dep't of Justice, Suicide and Homicide in State Prisons and Local Jails (NCJ 210036, Aug. 2005). In 2013, 967 persons in local jails died, 327 by their own hands. Bureau of Justice Statistics, Morality in Local Jails and State Prisons, 2000–2013—Statistical Tables (NCJ 248756 Aug. 4, 2015).

Third, a jail detainee's ability to prepare adequately for trial is restricted. His attorney must come to the jail, an inconvenience to the lawyer (and an additional expense that must be borne by a non-indigent defendant) that is likely to result in fewer consultations. Also, incarceration hinders the detainee's ability to assist counsel by gathering evidence and speaking to witnesses who might otherwise be disinclined to talk to an attorney.

Fourth, a detained defendant, unable to return to work, is likely to lose her job and, often, her only source of income. Detention also puts considerable strain on existing family relationships.

---

[a] *E.g.*, Michael Winerip & Michael Schwirtz, *Rikers: Where Mental Illness Meets Brutality in Jail*, N.Y. Times, July 14, 2014 (describing a report by New York investigators regarding the beating by guards of a misdemeanant jailee; "[b]rutal attacks by correction officers of inmates—particularly those with mental health issues—are common occurrences inside Rikers, the country's second-largest jail").

Fifth, the state conviction rate for detained felony defendants is higher (78%) than for those released prior to trial (60%). U.S. Dep't of Justice, Pretrial Release of Felony Defendants in State Courts (NCJ 214994, Nov. 2007). And, there is a body of evidence, albeit very dated, that suggests that "some defendants unable to make bail are, *for that reason alone,* more likely to be convicted and, if convicted, more likely to be sentenced to jail." Hans Zeisel, *Bail Revisited,* 1979 Am. B. Found. Res. J. 769, 769 (emphasis added). The first proposition (higher *conviction* rate) is true, even taking into consideration the strength of the evidence against the defendant, except, perhaps, for the most serious offenses. The second finding (higher *incarceration* rate) applies regardless of the seriousness of the offense. The reasons for the higher conviction rate remain a bit of a puzzle. Various explanations might be offered for this phenomenon: (1) the curtailment of the attorney-client relationship noted above; (2) due to loss of income, a detainee may be required to rely on the services of an overworked public defender rather than a private attorney of choice; and (3) a detainee is often pressured by jail conditions to accept a disadvantageous plea offer.

The public, of course, also has a significant stake in the pretrial release decision made by the magistrate. First and foremost is the risk that a defendant may flee or hide if he is released prior to trial. The integrity of the justice system is undermined, and the retributive and deterrent purposes of punishment are frustrated, if the defendant avoids trial by flight. Left unsatisfied, as well, are the needs of crime victims, who seek official closure of the criminal case as one step toward possible emotional closure. Second, if a defendant is released, he may destroy incriminating evidence not yet discovered, intimidate or harm witnesses, or commit other crimes while free.

Although more honored in the breach than the observance, "[t]he fundamental tradition in this country is that one charged with a crime is not, in ordinary circumstances, imprisoned until after a judgment of guilt." Bandy v. United States, 81 S.Ct. 197, 5 L.Ed.2d 218 (1960). In view of the risk of flight, however, a magistrate may determine that bail or other pretrial release conditions should be imposed (see Section B.). Less frequently, but much more often than in the distant past, a magistrate may detain the defendant because she fears witness intimidation or other criminal activity by the defendant. So-called "preventive detention" is the subject of Section C.

B. BAIL AND OTHER RELEASE MECHANISMS

BRIAN MAHONEY, ET AL.—PRETRIAL SERVICES PROGRAMS: RESPONSIBILITIES AND POTENTIAL

(National Institute of Justice, NCJ 181939, March 2001), 7–8.

* * * Although specifics of the money bail system vary from one jurisdiction to another, the basic principle is the same: Courts will release a defendant if he or she can arrange to have bail bond posted in the amount of money set by the judicial officer. Courts assume that defendants released on bond will return for future court appearances rather than lose their money or pledged collateral.

In the 17th and 18th centuries, the person who posted bail and guaranteed the appearance of the defendant at trial was a private individual—usually a friend, relative, or employer of the accused. The personal association between the defendant and surety was at least as important as the monetary stake of the surety in ensuring the defendant's appearance for trial. As the population grew more mobile in the 19th century, commercial bondsmen gradually replaced private sureties.

For a fee, the bondsman would post the amount of the bail bond. Since the commercial bondsman would at least theoretically be liable if the defendant fled, the bondsman would require defendants, or their friends and relatives, to post collateral or agree to indemnify the bondsman if the bond were forfeited for nonappearance. This practice became well established by the end of the 19th century and was upheld by the U.S. Supreme Court in 1912 against claims that it was contrary to public policy. Since the late 19th century, money bail had been the principal method used in the United States to resolve the question of whether a defendant in a criminal case should be released before trial.

The transition to commercial bondsmen largely moved the pretrial release decision out of court control and into the hands of the bondsmen. In a jurisdiction that relies on money bail, a judicial officer sets bail in a specific amount or, alternatively, sets bail mechanically by reference to a "bail schedule" that fixes bond amounts in accordance with the seriousness of the charge. To obtain release on surety bond, the defendant has to be able and willing to pay the bondsman a nonrefundable fee, typically 10 percent of the bond. The defendant may also need to be able to provide collateral equal to or greater than the bond. Even then, the bondsman may decline to do business with defendants deemed to be bad risks. As a result, the judicial officer who sets a money bond cannot know whether a defendant will be able to get out of jail. This system is still the primary method of addressing release/detention decisions in many jurisdictions today.

The consequence of relying on the money bail system is that the defendant's freedom hinges largely on one factor—the ability to raise money. If the defendant can raise the money, even if the charges are serious and there is a risk of flight or potential danger to the community, the defendant will be released. Conversely, a defendant unable to raise the money languishes in jail even when the charges are minor, the person's roots in the community reduce the likelihood of flight, and release poses little threat to community safety.

Recurrent criticism of this system, based on studies in Chicago, Cleveland, and the State of Missouri during the first quarter of the 20th century, had scant impact. Not until the early 1960s were significant efforts made to develop viable alternatives. The Manhattan Bail Project used a control group research design to test the hypothesis that courts could release more defendants successfully on their own recognizance if judges were given verified information at arraignment about the individual's character and roots in the community.

Once the results confirmed the hypothesis, judges in Manhattan began releasing many more defendants on their own recognizance. Moreover, these released defendants had considerably lower failure-to-appear rates than did defendants released on bail. Acclaimed a success, the project was emulated rapidly across the country. Pretrial release projects were implemented in dozens of other jurisdictions, and significant bail reform legislation was passed by Congress and several States.

The initial reforms focused primarily on providing alternatives to the traditional surety bail system. The alternatives fall into two main categories: (1) release on nonfinancial conditions [sometimes characterized as "own recognizance" (O.R.)—Eds.] that restrict the liberty of the accused in various ways [e.g., require the defendant to appear at all relevant court proceedings; periodically check-in with the pretrial release program; reside within the area until trial, etc.[b]—Eds.] and (2) release under "deposit bail" procedures that bypass the professional bondsman and provide for money bond (or a percentage of the bond amount, typically 10 percent) to be posted directly with the court [nearly all of which is refunded if the defendant satisfies all pre-trial release conditions—Eds.].

---

[b] Some release conditions can be unusual. *E.g.*, one person indicted for allegedly trying to sell a grenade launcher was released on various ordinary conditions as well as the requirement that he spend one hour each day reading books and thirty minutes completing a book report to be delivered to the judge, http://www.sfgate.com/crime/article/Reading-a-condition-of-Richmond-defendant-s-3558234.php, In another case involving a domestic dispute, a judge ordered a husband to "treat his spouse to dinner, a bowling date and then to undergo marriage counseling." Danielle A. Alvarez, *Flowers, Dinner, Bowling—and Counseling—Ordered by Broward Judge in Domestic Case*, Sun—Sentinel, Feb. 7, 2012.

During the 1970s and 1980s, legislation involving the release/detention decision began to focus increasingly on the issue of potential danger to the community. At the Federal level, the Bail Reform Act was amended in 1984 to allow consideration of danger and to allow preventive detention in limited circumstances. Most States and the District of Columbia now address danger in their bail laws and allow—at least implicitly—preventive detention and denial of bail or severely restricted release options under some circumstances.

NOTES AND QUESTIONS

1. *Pretrial release and release-violation statistics.* Despite the reforms described above, in 2011–2012 only 33.4% of all federal felony defendants were released at any time prior to case disposition. Among released defendants, 17% violated their release conditions at least once, although nearly all of them were technical violations; 1.6% of those released, however, were charged with a new felony offense while free. U.S. Dep't of Justice, Federal Justice Statistics, 2012 (NCJ 248470, Jan. 2015).

A survey of defendants who had state felony charges filed against them in 2006 in one of the 75 most populous counties reported that 58% of them were released before case disposition. The release figure was 52% for violent offenses, but only 8% for murder defendants. Among those released, the most common form of release was by a surety bond from a commercial bail bond agent (42%). A third of released defendants committed some type of misconduct before case disposition; 11% of the released defendants were charged with a new felony. U.S. Dep't of Justice, Felony Defendants in Large Urban Counties, 2006 (NCJ 228944, May. 2010).

STACK V. BOYLE

Supreme Court of the United States, 1951.
342 U.S. 1, 72 S.Ct. 1, 96 L.Ed. 3.

MR. CHIEF JUSTICE VINSON delivered the opinion of the Court [joined by JUSTICES BLACK, REED, FRANKFURTER, DOUGLAS, JACKSON, BURTON, and CLARK].

Indictments have been returned in the Southern District of California charging the twelve petitioners with conspiring to violate the Smith Act, 18 U.S.C. (Supp. IV) §§ 371, 2385.c Upon their arrest, bail was fixed for each petitioner in the widely varying amounts of $2,500, $7,500, $75,000 and $100,000. On motion of petitioner Schneiderman following arrest in the Southern District of New York, his bail was reduced to $50,000 before his removal to California. On motion of the Government to increase bail in the case of other petitioners, * * * bail was fixed in the

---

c The Smith Act prohibited advocacy of the overthrow of the Federal Government by violence or destruction. The defendants belonged to the Communist Party U.S.A.

District Court for the Southern District of California in the uniform amount of $50,000 for each petitioner.

Petitioners moved to reduce bail on the ground that bail as fixed was excessive under the Eighth Amendment. In support of their motion, petitioners submitted statements as to their financial resources, family relationships, health, prior criminal records, and other information. The only evidence offered by the Government was a certified record showing that four persons previously convicted under the Smith Act in the Southern District of New York had forfeited bail. No evidence was produced relating those four persons to the petitioners in this case. * * *

First. From the passage of the Judiciary Act of 1789, to the present Federal Rules of Criminal Procedure, * * * federal law has unequivocally provided that a person arrested for a non-capital offense *shall* be admitted to bail. This traditional right to freedom before conviction permits the unhampered preparation of a defense, and serves to prevent the infliction of punishment prior to conviction. Unless this right to bail before trial is preserved, the presumption of innocence, secured only after centuries of struggle, would lose its meaning.

The right to release before trial is conditioned upon the accused's giving adequate assurance that he will stand trial and submit to sentence if found guilty. Like the ancient practice of securing the oaths of responsible persons to stand as sureties for the accused, the modern practice of requiring a bail bond or the deposit of a sum of money subject to forfeiture serves as additional assurance of the presence of an accused. Bail set at a figure higher than an amount reasonably calculated to fulfill this purpose is "excessive" under the Eighth Amendment.

Since the function of bail is limited, the fixing of bail for any individual defendant must be based upon standards relevant to the purpose of assuring the presence of that defendant. The traditional standards as expressed in the Federal Rules of Criminal Procedure[3] are to be applied in each case to each defendant. In this case petitioners are charged with offenses under the Smith Act and, if found guilty, their convictions are subject to review with the scrupulous care demanded by our Constitution. Upon final judgment of conviction, petitioners face imprisonment of not more than five years and a fine of not more than $10,000. It is not denied that bail for each petitioner has been fixed in a sum much higher than that usually imposed for offenses with like penalties and yet there has been no factual showing to justify such action in this case. The Government asks the courts to depart from the norm by

---

[3]   Rule 46(c). "AMOUNT. If the defendant is admitted to bail, the amount thereof shall be such as in the judgment of the commissioner or court or judge or justice will insure the presence of the defendant, having regard to the nature and circumstances of the offense charged, the weight of the evidence against him, the financial ability of the defendant to give bail and the character of the defendant."

assuming, without the introduction of evidence, that each petitioner is a pawn in a conspiracy and will, in obedience to a superior, flee the jurisdiction. To infer from the fact of indictment alone a need for bail in an unusually high amount is an arbitrary act. Such conduct would inject into our own system of government the very principles of totalitarianism which Congress was seeking to guard against in passing the statute under which petitioners have been indicted.

If bail in an amount greater than that usually fixed for serious charges of crimes is required in the case of any of the petitioners, that is a matter to which evidence should be directed in a hearing so that the constitutional rights of each petitioner may be preserved. In the absence of such a showing, we are of the opinion that the fixing of bail before trial in these cases cannot be squared with the statutory and constitutional standards for admission to bail. * * *

* * * Petitioners may move for reduction of bail in the criminal proceeding so that a hearing may be held for the purpose of fixing reasonable bail for each petitioner.

It is so ordered.

MR. JUSTICE MINTON took no part in the consideration or decision of this case.

By MR. JUSTICE JACKSON, whom MR. JUSTICE FRANKFURTER joins. * * *

It is complained that the District Court fixed a uniform blanket bail chiefly by consideration of the nature of the accusation and did not take into account the difference in circumstances between different defendants. If this occurred, it is a clear violation of Rule 46(c). Each defendant stands before the bar of justice as an individual. Even on a conspiracy charge defendants do not lose their separateness or identity. While it might be possible that these defendants are identical in financial ability, character and relation to the charge—elements Congress has directed to be regarded in fixing bail—I think it violates the law of probabilities. Each accused is entitled to any benefits due to his good record, and misdeeds or a bad record should prejudice only those who are guilty of them. The question when application for bail is made relates to each one's trustworthiness to appear for trial and what security will supply reasonable assurance of his appearance. * * *

NOTES AND QUESTIONS

1. Like all other Bill of Rights provisions, the "no excessive bail" clause of the Eighth Amendment only applies in the federal system. The Supreme Court has not determined whether the right to non-excessive bail is fundamental and, therefore, incorporated to the states through the

Fourteenth Amendment due process clause. However, state constitutions typically contain a similar bail provision.

2.   *Federal Bail Reform Act of 1984. Stack* quotes from then-existing Rule 46 of the Federal Rules of Criminal Procedure regarding release from custody. The current version of the rule differs significantly in that it no longer sets out the eligibility factors for release. They are now listed in detail in 18 U.S.C. §§ 3142 and 3144, as part of the Federal Bail Reform Act of 1984. The latter Act, set out in Appendix A in the Supplement to this casebook, is complicated. Look at it now and see if you can answer the following questions:

A.   Under federal law, is the statutory presumption that an arrestee should be released pending trial or held in custody? In release cases, is the statutory presumption that a defendant should be released on her own recognizance or that bail should be set?

B.   What factor other than "appearance in court" may a federal magistrate consider in determining whether to release a defendant?

C.   What factors does the judicial officer consider in determining whether and what conditions of release will reasonably assure the appearance of a defendant at subsequent court proceedings?

3.   Look again at your answer to Note 2.C. Do you think that the factors set out in the Bail Reform Act are sensible ones? Are any left out? If you were a magistrate, which of these factors would *you* consider most significant in deciding whether a defendant is a flight or safety risk?

In overcrowded urban courtrooms, most magistrates make release determinations rapidly—in a manner of minutes—based on the limited information provided them by the prosecutor. (Many indigents are not even represented by counsel at this stage. See Note 7, *infra*.) Do you think you would feel qualified to reliably measure flight risk in this manner?

4.   *Excessive bail versus no bail.* In 2005, a Boston judge set bail at $250,000 for a twelve-year-old boy arrested for possession of a loaded gun. The boy, a special education student, had no criminal record. His single mother, a nursing assistant, could not afford the bail. The judge explained that "[m]y intention is to send a message to the general public that their safety is a concern of mine * * * ." Katie Zezima, *$250,000 Bail Set in Boston For Boy, 12, Found With Gun,* N.Y. Times, Aug. 25, 2005, at A12. Based on *Stack*, was this unconstitutionally excessive bail?

Assuming that the quarter-a-million-dollar figure constituted excessive bail, could the judge have reached the same outcome by simply refusing to set *any* bail? Would *that* have been constitutional? Does *Stack* say anything relevant in this regard? If the boy does *not* have a constitutional right to pretrial release, how was he prejudiced if he was told that he will be released if his mother can pay the 10% deposit fee necessary to obtain bail surety?

5. *Bail for capital offenses.* Chief Justice Vinson stated in *Stack* that federal law has "unequivocally provided that a person arrested for a *non-capital* offense shall be admitted to bail." Approximately forty states by constitutional or statutory provision treat capital offenses differently. For example, New Jersey's constitution provides that "[a]ll persons shall, before conviction, be bailable by sufficient sureties, except for capital offenses, when the proof is evident or presumption great." N.J.Const. of 1947, art I, para. 11.

The phrase "proof is evident or presumption is great" is rarely defined. One court stated that it "denote[s] that the evidence that is produced at the bail hearing pointing to the commission of the crime of capital murder must be cogent and persuasive." State v. Engel, 99 N.J. 453, 493 A.2d 1217 (1985). Why would capital offenses be treated differently than other crimes?

6. *Problem.* In 1983, seven men were indicted in an alleged billion-dollar multi-count federal drug conspiracy. The defendants faced more than eighty years' imprisonment each if convicted of the various charges. Bail was set at $1 million each, which the defendants promptly paid and were released. A few months later, six of the men simultaneously fled the country. A federal prosecutor moved to have bail withdrawn for the seventh defendant. If you were the federal magistrate, would you grant the motion? If not, would you impose more stringent release conditions and, if so, what would they be? How high might you set bail?

7. *The right to counsel.* The Supreme Court held, 8–1, in Rothgery v. Gillespie County, 554 U.S. 191, 128 S.Ct. 2578, 171 L.Ed.2d 366 (2008), that the Sixth Amendment right to counsel, which attaches to the "accused" once a criminal prosecution commences, attaches at the initial appearance of a defendant before a judicial officer, when conditions for pretrial release are determined. This right, *Rothgery* holds, attaches even if the prosecutor is not present at the proceeding or aware that it is occurring.

Although the Sixth Amendment right "attaches" at this initial arraignment, the Court did *not* decide whether Rothgery's Sixth Amendment rights were denied when Gillespie County, Texas failed to provide him with a lawyer at the initial arraignment. How can this be, if the right attaches at this proceeding? The Court explained:

> Attachment occurs when the government has used the judicial machinery to signal commitment to prosecute * * *. Once attachment occurs, the accused is at least entitled to the presence of appointed counsel during any "critical stage" of the postattachment proceedings; what makes a stage critical is what shows the need for counsel's presence. *Thus counsel must be appointed within a reasonable time after attachment to allow for adequate representation at any critical stage before trial, as well as at trial itself.*

(Emphasis added.)

The Court warned against the "analytical mistake" of thinking that the attachment of the Sixth Amendment right to counsel necessarily implies the "occurrence or imminence of a critical stage." Indeed, without evident criticism, the Court observed that the Federal Government and forty-three states "take the first step toward appointing counsel 'before, at, or just after initial appearance,'" which would seem to suggest that the initial appearance itself is *not* a critical stage of the prosecution. (Indeed, as recently as fifteen years ago, only eight states and the District of Columbia uniformly furnished legal counsel to indigents at the bail-setting stage itself. Douglas L. Colbert, *Thirty-Five Years After Gideon: The Illusory Right to Counsel at Bail Proceedings*, 1998 U. Ill. L. Rev. 1, 8–11. As for the federal courts, see Fed. R. Crim. P. 5(d)(1)–(2).)

If it is sufficient that a lawyer be appointed within a "reasonable time after attachment"—and, thus, no lawyer must be provided at the initial appearance itself—this means that an indigent may find that bail is set before counsel is available to argue for less restrictive release conditions. This may be significant. Based on one controlled experiment in Baltimore, Maryland, an indigent represented by counsel was found to be "considerably more likely to be released, * * *, to keep his job, and to help prepare a meaningful defense" than an uncounseled indigent. Douglas L. Colbert et al., *Do Attorneys Really Matter? The Empirical and Legal Case for the Right to Counsel at Bail,* 23 Cardozo L. Rev. 1719, 1783 (2002).

8.   The Federal Bail Reform Act of 1984 provides that a "judicial officer may not impose a financial condition that results in the pretrial detention of the person." 18 U.S.C. § 3142(c)(2). The purpose of this provision is to compel a magistrate who opposes release of a defendant to use the Act's preventive detention provisions (see Part C., *infra*) rather than to set bail at an unrealistically high figure to accomplish the same result *sub rosa.* Nonetheless, in 2004, among federal defendants detained at any time before case disposition, 11.1% were held for the entire period, although bail was set, because they could not secure the requisite funds for release, and another 18.2% were detained for a part of the pretrial period for the same reason. U.S. Dep't of Justice, Sourcebook of Criminal Justice Statistics Online, at http://www.albany.edu/sourcebook/pdf/t5132004.pdf.

If a defendant charged with a serious felony can demonstrate that even a very low bail figure is beyond her reach, is the effect of § 3142(c)(2) that the magistrate must release her, subject only to nonfinancial conditions? Indeed, would *any* bail figure set, no matter how small, be *unconstitutionally* excessive in regard to an indigent? In Bandy v. United States, 81 S.Ct. 197, 5 L.Ed.2d 218 (1960), in an application for reduction of bail, Justice Douglas expressed his views on the subject:

> The fundamental tradition in this country is that one charged with a crime is not, in ordinary circumstances, imprisoned until after a judgment of guilt. * * *

This traditional right to freedom during trial and pending judicial review has to be squared with the possibility that the defendant may flee or hide himself. Bail is the device which we have borrowed to reconcile these conflicting interests. * * * It is assumed that the threat of forfeiture of one's goods will be an effective deterrent to the temptation to break the conditions of one's release.

But this theory is based on the assumption that a defendant has property. To continue to demand a substantial bond which the defendant is unable to secure raises considerable problems for the equal administration of the law. We have held that an indigent defendant is denied equal protection of the law if he is denied an appeal on equal terms with other defendants, solely because of his indigence. *Griffin v. Illinois*, 351 U.S. 12, 76 S.Ct. 585, 100 L.Ed. 891. Can an indigent be denied freedom, where a wealthy man would not, because he does not happen to have enough property to pledge for his freedom?

It would be unconstitutional to fix excessive bail to assure that a defendant will not gain his freedom. *Stack v. Boyle*. Yet in the case of an indigent defendant, the fixing of bail in even a modest amount may have the practical effect of denying him release.

Notwithstanding Justice Douglas's observations, no pretrial release system has ever been invalidated on the ground that, practically speaking, non-indigents can pay for their freedom but indigents cannot.

C. PREVENTIVE DETENTION

UNITED STATES V. SALERNO
Supreme Court of the United States, 1987.
481 U.S. 739, 107 S.Ct. 2095, 95 L.Ed.2d 697.

CHIEF JUSTICE REHNQUIST delivered the opinion of the Court [joined by JUSTICES WHITE, BLACKMUN, POWELL, O'CONNOR, and SCALIA].

The Bail Reform Act of 1984 (Act) allows a federal court to detain an arrestee pending trial if the Government demonstrates by clear and convincing evidence after an adversary hearing that no release conditions "will reasonably assure * * * the safety of any other person and the community." The United States Court of Appeals for the Second Circuit struck down this provision of the Act as facially unconstitutional, because, in that court's words, this type of pretrial detention violates "substantive due process." * * * We hold that, as against the facial attack mounted by these respondents, the Act fully comports with constitutional requirements. We therefore reverse.

I

Responding to "the alarming problem of crimes committed by persons on release," Congress formulated the Bail Reform Act of 1984 [see Supp. App. A], as the solution to a bail crisis in the federal courts. The Act represents the National Legislature's considered response to numerous perceived deficiencies in the federal bail process. By providing for sweeping changes in both the way federal courts consider bail applications and the circumstances under which bail is granted, Congress hoped to "give the courts adequate authority to make release decisions that give appropriate recognition to the danger a person may pose to others if released."

To this end, § 3141(a) of the Act requires a judicial officer to determine whether an arrestee shall be detained. Section 3142(e) provides that "[i]f, after a hearing pursuant to the provisions of subsection (f), the judicial officer finds that no condition or combination of conditions will reasonably assure the appearance of the person as required and the safety of any other person and the community, he shall order the detention of the person prior to trial." Section 3142(f) provides the arrestee with a number of procedural safeguards. He may request the presence of counsel at the detention hearing, he may testify and present witnesses in his behalf, as well as proffer evidence, and he may cross-examine other witnesses appearing at the hearing. If the judicial officer finds that no conditions of pretrial release can reasonably assure the safety of other persons and the community, he must state his findings of fact in writing, § 3142(i), and support his conclusion with "clear and convincing evidence," § 3142(f).

The judicial officer is not given unbridled discretion in making the detention determination. Congress has specified the considerations relevant to that decision. These factors include the nature and seriousness of the charges, the substantiality of the Government's evidence against the arrestee, the arrestee's background and characteristics, and the nature and seriousness of the danger posed by the suspect's release. § 3142(g). Should a judicial officer order detention, the detainee is entitled to expedited appellate review of the detention order. §§ 3145(b), (c). *[margin note: relevant considerations from Congress]*

Respondents Anthony Salerno and Vincent Cafaro were arrested on March 21, 1986, after being charged in a 29-count indictment alleging various Racketeer Influenced and Corrupt Organizations Act (RICO) violations, mail and wire fraud offenses, extortion, and various criminal gambling violations. The RICO counts alleged 35 acts of racketeering activity, including fraud, extortion, gambling, and conspiracy to commit murder. At respondents' arraignment, the Government moved to have Salerno and Cafaro detained pursuant to § 3142(e), on the ground that no condition of release would assure the safety of the community or any person. The District Court held a hearing at which the Government made a detailed proffer of evidence. The Government's case showed that Salerno was the "boss" of the Genovese crime family of La Cosa Nostra and that Cafaro was a "captain" in the Genovese family. According to the Government's proffer, based in large part on conversations intercepted by a court-ordered wiretap, the two respondents had participated in wide-ranging conspiracies to aid their illegitimate enterprises through violent means. The Government also offered the testimony of two of its trial witnesses, who would assert that Salerno personally participated in two murder conspiracies. Salerno opposed the motion for detention, challenging the credibility of the Government's witnesses. He offered the testimony of several character witnesses as well as a letter from his doctor stating that he was suffering from a serious medical condition. Cafaro presented no evidence at the hearing, but instead characterized the wiretap conversations as merely "tough talk."

The District Court granted the Government's detention motion, concluding that the Government had established by clear and convincing evidence that no condition or combination of conditions of release would ensure the safety of the community or any person * * * . * * *

Respondents appealed, contending that to the extent that the Bail Reform Act permits pretrial detention on the ground that the arrestee is likely to commit future crimes, it is unconstitutional on its face. Over a dissent, the United States Court of Appeals for the Second Circuit agreed. Although the court agreed that pretrial detention could be imposed if the defendants were likely to intimidate witnesses or otherwise jeopardize the trial process, it found "§ 3142(e)'s authorization of pretrial detention [on the ground of future dangerousness] repugnant to the concept of substantive due process, which we believe prohibits the total deprivation of liberty simply as a means of preventing future crimes." The court concluded that the Government could not, consistent with due process, detain persons who had not been accused of any crime merely because they were thought to present a danger to the community. It reasoned that our criminal law system holds persons accountable for past actions, not anticipated future actions. Although a court could detain an arrestee who threatened to flee before trial, such detention would be permissible because it would serve the basic objective of a criminal system—bringing the accused to trial. The court * * * found our decision in *Schall v. Martin*, 467 U.S. 253, 104 S.Ct. 2403, 81 L.Ed.2d 207 (1984), upholding postarrest, pretrial detention of juveniles, inapposite because juveniles have a lesser interest in liberty than do adults. * * *

II

A facial challenge to a legislative Act is, of course, the most difficult challenge to mount successfully, since the challenger must establish that no set of circumstances exists under which the Act would be valid. The fact that the Bail Reform Act might operate unconstitutionally under some conceivable set of circumstances is insufficient to render it wholly invalid * * *. We think respondents have failed to shoulder their heavy burden to demonstrate that the Act is "facially" unconstitutional.[3]

Respondents present two grounds for invalidating the Bail Reform Act's provisions permitting pretrial detention on the basis of future dangerousness. First, they rely upon the Court of Appeals' conclusion that the Act exceeds the limitations placed upon the Federal Government by the Due Process Clause of the Fifth Amendment. Second, they contend that the Act contravenes the Eighth Amendment's proscription against excessive bail. We treat these contentions in turn.

A

* * * This Court has held that the Due Process Clause protects individuals against two types of government action. So-called "substantive due process" prevents the government from engaging in conduct that "shocks the conscience," or interferes with rights "implicit in the concept of ordered liberty." When government action depriving a person of life, liberty, or property survives substantive due process scrutiny, it must still be implemented in a fair manner. This requirement has traditionally been referred to as "procedural" due process.

Respondents first argue that the Act violates substantive due process because the pretrial detention it authorizes constitutes impermissible punishment before trial. The Government, however, has never argued that pretrial detention could be upheld if it were "punishment." The Court of Appeals assumed that pretrial detention under the Bail Reform Act is regulatory, not penal, and we agree that it is.

As an initial matter, the mere fact that a person is detained does not inexorably lead to the conclusion that the government has imposed punishment. To determine whether a restriction on liberty constitutes impermissible punishment or permissible regulation, we first look to legislative intent. Unless Congress expressly intended to impose punitive restrictions, the punitive/regulatory distinction turns on " 'whether an alternative purpose to which [the restriction] may rationally be connected is assignable for it, and whether it appears excessive in relation to the alternative purpose assigned [to it].' "

---

[3] We intimate no view on the validity of any aspects of the Act that are not relevant to respondents' case. Nor have respondents claimed that the Act is unconstitutional because of the way it was applied to the particular facts of their case.

We conclude that the detention imposed by the Act falls on the regulatory side of the dichotomy. The legislative history of the Bail Reform Act clearly indicates that Congress did not formulate the pretrial detention provisions as punishment for dangerous individuals. Congress instead perceived pretrial detention as a potential solution to a pressing societal problem. There is no doubt that preventing danger to the community is a legitimate regulatory goal.

Nor are the incidents of pretrial detention excessive in relation to the regulatory goal Congress sought to achieve. The Bail Reform Act carefully limits the circumstances under which detention may be sought to the most serious of crimes. See § 3142(f) (detention hearings available if case involves crimes of violence, offenses for which the sentence is life imprisonment or death, serious drug offenses, or certain repeat offenders). The arrestee is entitled to a prompt detention hearing, and the maximum length of pretrial detention is limited by the stringent time limitations of the Speedy Trial Act.[4] See 18 U.S.C. § 3161 *et seq*. Moreover, as in *Schall v. Martin*, the conditions of confinement envisioned by the Act "appear to reflect the regulatory purposes relied upon by the" Government. As in *Schall*, the statute at issue here requires that detainees be housed in a "facility separate, to the extent practicable, from persons awaiting or serving sentences or being held in custody pending appeal." § 3142(i)(2). We conclude, therefore, that the pretrial detention contemplated by the Bail Reform Act is regulatory in nature, and does not constitute punishment before trial in violation of the Due Process Clause.

* * * Respondents characterize the Due Process Clause as erecting an impenetrable "wall" in this area that "no governmental interest—rational, important, compelling or otherwise—may surmount."

We do not think the Clause lays down any such categorical imperative. We have repeatedly held that the Government's regulatory interest in community safety can, in appropriate circumstances, outweigh an individual's liberty interest. For example, in times of war or insurrection, when society's interest is at its peak, the Government may detain individuals whom the Government believes to be dangerous. Even outside the exigencies of war, we have found that sufficiently compelling governmental interests can justify detention of dangerous persons. Thus, we have found no absolute constitutional barrier to detention of potentially dangerous resident aliens pending deportation proceedings. We have also held that the government may detain mentally unstable individuals who present a danger to the public, and dangerous defendants who become incompetent to stand trial. We have approved of postarrest

---

[4] We intimate no view as to the point at which detention in a particular case might become excessively prolonged, and therefore punitive, in relation to Congress' regulatory goal.

regulatory detention of juveniles when they present a continuing danger to the community. *Schall v. Martin*. Even competent adults may face substantial liberty restrictions as a result of the operation of our criminal justice system. If the police suspect an individual of a crime, they may arrest and hold him until a neutral magistrate determines whether probable cause exists. Finally, respondents concede and the Court of Appeals noted that an arrestee may be incarcerated until trial if he presents a risk of flight, or a danger to witnesses.

Respondents characterize all of these cases as exceptions to the "general rule" of substantive due process that the government may not detain a person prior to a judgment of guilt in a criminal trial. Such a "general rule" may freely be conceded, but we think that these cases show a sufficient number of exceptions to the rule that the congressional action challenged here can hardly be characterized as totally novel. Given the well-established authority of the government, in special circumstances, to restrain individuals' liberty prior to or even without criminal trial and conviction, we think that the present statute providing for pretrial detention on the basis of dangerousness must be evaluated in precisely the same manner that we evaluated the laws in the cases discussed above.

The government's interest in preventing crime by arrestees is both legitimate and compelling. In *Schall*, we recognized the strength of the State's interest in preventing juvenile crime. This general concern with crime prevention is no less compelling when the suspects are adults. Indeed, "[t]he harm suffered by the victim of a crime is not dependent upon the age of the perpetrator." The Bail Reform Act of 1984 responds to an even more particularized governmental interest than the interest we sustained in *Schall*. The statute we upheld in *Schall* permitted pretrial detention of any juvenile arrested on any charge after a showing that the individual might commit some undefined further crimes. The Bail Reform Act, in contrast, narrowly focuses on a particularly acute problem in which the Government interests are overwhelming. The Act operates only on individuals who have been arrested for a specific category of extremely serious offenses. § 3142(f). Congress specifically found that these individuals are far more likely to be responsible for dangerous acts in the community after arrest. Nor is the Act by any means a scattershot attempt to incapacitate those who are merely suspected of these serious crimes. The Government must first of all demonstrate probable cause to believe that the charged crime has been committed by the arrestee, but that is not enough. In a full-blown adversary hearing, the Government must convince a neutral decisionmaker by clear and convincing evidence that no conditions of release can reasonably assure the safety of the community or any person. § 3142(f). While the Government's general interest in preventing crime is compelling, even this interest is heightened when the Government musters convincing proof that the arrestee, already indicted or held to answer for a serious crime, presents a demonstrable danger to the community. Under these narrow circumstances, society's interest in crime prevention is at its greatest.

On the other side of the scale, of course, is the individual's strong interest in liberty. We do not minimize the importance and fundamental nature of this right. But, as our cases hold, this right may, in circumstances where the government's interest is sufficiently weighty, be subordinated to the greater needs of society. We think that Congress' careful delineation of the circumstances under which detention will be permitted satisfies this standard. When the Government proves by clear and convincing evidence that an arrestee presents an identified and articulable threat to an individual or the community, we believe that, consistent with the Due Process Clause, a court may disable the arrestee from executing that threat. Under these circumstances, we cannot categorically state that pretrial detention "offends some principle of justice so rooted in the traditions and conscience of our people as to be ranked as fundamental."

Finally, we may dispose briefly of respondents' facial challenge to the procedures of the Bail Reform Act. To sustain them against such a challenge, we need only find them "adequate to authorize the pretrial detention of at least some [persons] charged with crimes," whether or not they might be insufficient in some particular circumstances. We think they pass that test. As we stated in *Schall*, "there is nothing inherently unattainable about a prediction of future criminal conduct."

Under the Bail Reform Act, the procedures by which a judicial officer evaluates the likelihood of future dangerousness are specifically designed to further the accuracy of that determination. Detainees have a right to counsel at the detention hearing. § 3142(f). They may testify in their own behalf, present information by proffer or otherwise, and cross-examine witnesses who appear at the hearing. The judicial officer charged with the responsibility of determining the appropriateness of detention is guided by statutorily enumerated factors, which include the nature and the circumstances of the charges, the weight of the evidence, the history and characteristics of the putative offender, and the danger to the community. § 3142(g). The Government must prove its case by clear and convincing evidence. § 3142(f). Finally, the judicial officer must include written findings of fact and a written statement of reasons for a decision to detain. § 3142(i). The Act's review provisions, § 3145(c), provide for immediate appellate review of the detention decision.

We think these extensive safeguards suffice to repel a facial challenge. * * * Given the legitimate and compelling regulatory purpose of the Act and the procedural protections it offers, we conclude that the Act

Procedural Safeguards

is not facially invalid under the Due Process Clause o~~f~~
Amendment.

B

Respondents also contend that the Bail Reform Act violates t~~he~~
Excessive Bail Clause of the Eighth Amendment. * * * We think that the
Act survives a challenge founded upon the Eighth Amendment.

The Eighth Amendment addresses pretrial release by providing
merely that "[e]xcessive bail shall not be required." This Clause, of course,
says nothing about whether bail shall be available at all. Respondents
nevertheless contend that this Clause grants them a right to bail
calculated solely upon considerations of flight. They rely on *Stack v.
Boyle*, [p. 864], in which the Court stated that "[b]ail set at a figure higher
than an amount reasonably calculated [to ensure the defendant's
presence at trial] is 'excessive' under the Eighth Amendment." In
respondents' view, since the Bail Reform Act allows a court essentially to
set bail at an infinite amount for reasons not related to the risk of flight,
it violates the Excessive Bail Clause. Respondents concede that the right
to bail they have discovered in the Eighth Amendment is not absolute. A
court may, for example, refuse bail in capital cases. And, as the Court of
Appeals noted and respondents admit, a court may refuse bail when the
defendant presents a threat to the judicial process by intimidating
witnesses. Respondents characterize these exceptions as consistent with
what they claim to be the sole purpose of bail—to ensure the integrity of
the judicial process.

While we agree that a primary function of bail is to safeguard the
courts' role in adjudicating the guilt or innocence of defendants, we reject
the proposition that the Eighth Amendment categorically prohibits the
government from pursuing other admittedly compelling interests through
regulation of pretrial release. The above-quoted dictum in *Stack v. Boyle*
is far too slender a reed on which to rest this argument. The Court in
Stack had no occasion to consider whether the Excessive Bail Clause
requires courts to admit all defendants to bail, because the statute before
the Court in that case in fact allowed the defendants to be bailed. Thus,
the Court had to determine only whether bail, admittedly available in
that case, was excessive if set at a sum greater than that necessary to
ensure the arrestees' presence at trial.

The holding of *Stack* is illuminated by the Court's holding just four
months later in *Carlson v. Landon*, 342 U.S. 524, 72 S.Ct. 525, 96 L.Ed.
547 (1952). In that case, remarkably similar to the present action, the
detainees had been arrested and held without bail pending a
determination of deportability. The Attorney General refused to release
the individuals, "on the ground that there was reasonable cause to believe
that [their] release would be prejudicial to the public interest and *would*

safety of the United States." The detainees
...e that respondents bring to us today: the
...d them to be admitted to bail. The Court
...ition:

...as lifted with slight changes from the
...t. In England that clause has never been
...ght to bail in all cases, but merely to
...ot be excessive in those cases where it is
...en this clause was carried over into our
...was said that indicated any different
...nendment has not prevented Congress
...uciining the classes of cases in which bail shall be allowed
in this country. Thus, in criminal cases bail is not compulsory
where the punishment may be death. Indeed, the very language
of the Amendment fails to say all arrests must be bailable."

Carlson v. Landon was a civil case, and we need not decide today
whether the Excessive Bail Clause speaks at all to Congress' power to
define the classes of criminal arrestees who shall be admitted to bail. For
even if we were to conclude that the Eighth Amendment imposes some
substantive limitations on the National Legislature's powers in this area,
we would still hold that the Bail Reform Act is valid. Nothing in the text
of the Bail Clause limits permissible Government considerations solely to
questions of flight. The only arguable substantive limitation of the Bail
Clause is that the Government's proposed conditions of release or
detention not be "excessive" in light of the perceived evil. Of course, to
determine whether the Government's response is excessive, we must
compare that response against the interest the Government seeks to
protect by means of that response. Thus, when the Government has
admitted that its only interest is in preventing flight, bail must be set by
a court at a sum designed to ensure that goal, and no more. We believe
that when Congress has mandated detention on the basis of a compelling
interest other than prevention of flight, as it has here, the Eighth
Amendment does not require release on bail.

III

In our society liberty is the norm, and detention prior to trial or
without trial is the carefully limited exception. We hold that the
provisions for pretrial detention in the Bail Reform Act of 1984 fall within
that carefully limited exception. * * * We are unwilling to say that this
congressional determination, based as it is upon that primary concern of
every government—a concern for the safety and indeed the lives of its
citizens—on its face violates either the Due Process Clause of the Fifth
Amendment or the Excessive Bail Clause of the Eighth Amendment.

JUSTICE MARSHALL, with whom JUSTICE BRENNAN joins, dissenting.

This case brings before the Court for the first time a statute in which Congress declares that a person innocent of any crime may be jailed indefinitely, pending the trial of allegations which are legally presumed to be untrue, if the Government shows to the satisfaction of a judge that the accused is likely to commit crimes, unrelated to the pending charges, at any time in the future. Such statutes, consistent with the usages of tyranny and the excesses of what bitter experience teaches us to call the police state, have long been thought incompatible with the fundamental human rights protected by our Constitution. Today a majority of this Court holds otherwise. Its decision disregards basic principles of justice established centuries ago and enshrined beyond the reach of governmental interference in the Bill of Rights. * * *

II

The majority approaches respondents' challenge to the Act by dividing the discussion into two sections, one concerned with the substantive guarantees implicit in the Due Process Clause, and the other concerned with the protection afforded by the Excessive Bail Clause of the Eighth Amendment. This is a sterile formalism, which divides a unitary argument into two independent parts and then professes to demonstrate that the parts are individually inadequate.

On the due process side of this false dichotomy appears an argument concerning the distinction between regulatory and punitive legislation. The majority concludes that the Act is a regulatory rather than a punitive measure. The ease with which the conclusion is reached suggests the worthlessness of the achievement. * * * The majority finds that "Congress did not formulate the pretrial detention provisions as punishment for dangerous individuals," but instead was pursuing the "legitimate regulatory goal" of "preventing danger to the community." Concluding that pretrial detention is not an excessive solution to the problem of preventing danger to the community, the majority thus finds that no substantive element of the guarantee of due process invalidates the statute.

This argument does not demonstrate the conclusion it purports to justify. Let us apply the majority's reasoning to a similar, hypothetical case. After investigation, Congress determines (not unrealistically) that a large proportion of violent crime is perpetrated by persons who are unemployed. It also determines, equally reasonably, that much violent crime is committed at night. From amongst the panoply of "potential solutions," Congress chooses a statute which permits, after judicial proceedings, the imposition of a dusk-to-dawn curfew on anyone who is unemployed. Since this is not a measure enacted for the purpose of punishing the unemployed, and since the majority finds that preventing danger to the community is a legitimate regulatory goal, the curfew statute would, according to the majority's analysis, be a mere "regulatory" detention statute, entirely compatible with the substantive components of the Due Process Clause.

The absurdity of this conclusion arises, of course, from the majority's cramped concept of substantive due process. The majority proceeds as though the only substantive right protected by the Due Process Clause is a right to be free from punishment before conviction. The majority's technique for infringing this right is simple: merely redefine any measure which is claimed to be punishment as "regulation," and, magically, the Constitution no longer prohibits its imposition. Because, as I discuss in Part III, *infra*, the Due Process Clause protects other substantive rights which are infringed by this legislation, the majority's argument is merely an exercise in obfuscation.

The logic of the majority's Eighth Amendment analysis is equally unsatisfactory. The Eighth Amendment, as the majority notes, states that "[e]xcessive bail shall not be required." The majority then declares, as if it were undeniable, that: "[t]his Clause, of course, says nothing about whether bail shall be available at all." If excessive bail is imposed the defendant stays in jail. The same result is achieved if bail is denied altogether. Whether the magistrate sets bail at $1 billion or refuses to set bail at all, the consequences are indistinguishable. It would be mere sophistry to suggest that the Eighth Amendment protects against the former decision, and not the latter. Indeed, such a result would lead to the conclusion that there was no need for Congress to pass a preventive detention measure of any kind; every federal magistrate and district judge could simply refuse, despite the absence of any evidence of risk of flight or danger to the community, to set bail. This would be entirely constitutional, since, according to the majority, the Eighth Amendment "says nothing about whether bail shall be available at all."

But perhaps, the majority says, this manifest absurdity can be avoided. Perhaps the Bail Clause is addressed only to the Judiciary. "[W]e need not decide today," the majority says, "whether the Excessive Bail Clause speaks at all to Congress' power to define the classes of criminal arrestees who shall be admitted to bail." The majority is correct that this question need not be decided today; it was decided long ago. Federal and state statutes which purport to accomplish what the Eighth Amendment forbids, such as imposing cruel and unusual punishments, may not stand. The text of the Amendment, which provides simply that "[e]xcessive bail shall not be required, nor excessive fines imposed, nor cruel and unusual punishments inflicted," provides absolutely no support for the majority's speculation that both courts and Congress are forbidden to inflict cruel and unusual punishments, while only the courts are forbidden to require excessive bail.[5]

The majority's attempts to deny the relevance of the Bail Clause to this case are unavailing, but the majority is nonetheless correct that the prohibition of excessive bail means that in order "to determine whether the Government's response is excessive, we must compare that response against the interest the Government seeks to protect by means of that response." The majority concedes, as it must, that "when the Government has admitted that its only interest is in preventing flight, bail must be set by a court at a sum designed to ensure that goal, and no more." But, the majority says, "when Congress has mandated detention on the basis of a compelling interest other than prevention of flight, as it has here, the Eighth Amendment does not require release on bail." This conclusion follows only if the "compelling" interest upon which Congress acted is an interest which the Constitution permits Congress to further through the denial of bail. The majority does not ask, as a result of its disingenuous division of the analysis, if there are any substantive limits contained in both the Eighth Amendment and the Due Process Clause which render this system of preventive detention unconstitutional. The majority does not ask because the answer is apparent and, to the majority, inconvenient.

III

The essence of this case may be found, ironically enough, in a provision of the Act to which the majority does not refer. Title 18 U.S.C. § 3142(j) provides that "[n]othing in this section shall be construed as modifying or limiting the presumption of innocence." But the very pith and purpose of this statute is an abhorrent limitation of the presumption of innocence. The majority's untenable conclusion that the present Act is constitutional arises from a specious denial of the role of the Bail Clause and the Due Process Clause in protecting the invaluable guarantee afforded by the presumption of innocence.

"The principle that there is a presumption of innocence in favor of the accused is the undoubted law, axiomatic and elementary, and its enforcement lies at the foundation of the administration of our criminal law." Our society's belief, reinforced over the centuries, that all are innocent until the state has proved them to be guilty, like the companion principle that guilt must be proved beyond a reasonable doubt, is "implicit in the concept of ordered liberty," and is established beyond legislative contravention in the Due Process Clause.

---

[5] The majority refers to the statement in *Carlson v. Landon* that the Bail Clause was adopted by Congress from the English Bill of Rights Act of 1689 * * * . A sufficient answer to this meager argument was made at the time by Justice Black: "The Eighth Amendment is in the American Bill of Rights of 1789, not the English Bill of Rights of 1689." *Carlson v. Landon, supra* (dissenting opinion). * * *

The statute now before us declares that persons who have been indicted may be detained if a judicial officer finds clear and convincing evidence that they pose a danger to individuals or to the community. The statute does not authorize the Government to imprison anyone it has evidence is dangerous; indictment is necessary. But let us suppose that a defendant is indicted and the Government shows by clear and convincing evidence that he is dangerous and should be detained pending a trial, at which trial the defendant is acquitted. May the Government continue to hold the defendant in detention based upon its showing that he is dangerous? The answer cannot be yes, for that would allow the Government to imprison someone for uncommitted crimes based upon "proof" not beyond a reasonable doubt. The result must therefore be that once the indictment has failed, detention cannot continue. But our fundamental principles of justice declare that the defendant is as innocent on the day before his trial as he is on the morning after his acquittal. Under this statute an untried indictment somehow acts to permit a detention, based on other charges, which after an acquittal would be unconstitutional. The conclusion is inescapable that the indictment has been turned into evidence, if not that the defendant is guilty of the crime charged, then that left to his own devices he will soon be guilty of something else. " 'If it suffices to accuse, what will become of the innocent?' "

To be sure, an indictment is not without legal consequences. It establishes that there is probable cause to believe that an offense was committed, and that the defendant committed it. Upon probable cause a warrant for the defendant's arrest may issue; a period of administrative detention may occur before the evidence of probable cause is presented to a neutral magistrate. Once a defendant has been committed for trial he may be detained in custody if the magistrate finds that no conditions of release will prevent him from becoming a fugitive. But in this connection the charging instrument is evidence of nothing more than the fact that there will be a trial * * * .[6] * * * The finding of probable cause conveys power to try, and the power to try imports of necessity the power to assure that the processes of justice will not be evaded or obstructed. "Pretrial detention to prevent future crimes against society at large, however, is not justified by any concern for holding a trial on the charges for which a defendant has been arrested." The detention purportedly authorized by this statute bears no relation to the Government's power to try charges supported by a finding of probable cause, and thus the

---

[6] The majority states that denial of bail in capital cases has traditionally been the rule rather than the exception. And this of course is so, for it has been the considered presumption of generations of judges that a defendant in danger of execution has an extremely strong incentive to flee. If in any particular case the presumed likelihood of flight should be made irrebuttable, it would in all probability violate the Due Process Clause. Thus what the majority perceives as an exception is nothing more than an example of the traditional operation of our system of bail.

interests it serves are outside the scope of interests which may be considered in weighing the excessiveness of bail under the Eighth Amendment.

It is not a novel proposition that the Bail Clause plays a vital role in protecting the presumption of innocence. Reviewing the application for bail pending appeal by members of the American Communist Party convicted under the Smith Act, 18 U.S.C. § 2385, Justice Jackson wrote:

> "Grave public danger is said to result from what [the defendants] may be expected to do, in addition to what they have done since their conviction. If I assume that defendants are disposed to commit every opportune disloyal act helpful to Communist countries, it is still difficult to reconcile with traditional American law the jailing of persons by the courts because of anticipated but as yet uncommitted crimes. Imprisonment to protect society from predicted but unconsummated offenses is * * * unprecedented in this country and * * * fraught with danger of excesses and injustice * * * ." *Williamson v. United States*, 95 L. Ed. 1379, 1382 (1950) (opinion in chambers).

As Chief Justice Vinson wrote for the Court in *Stack v. Boyle*: "Unless th[e] right to bail before trial is preserved, the presumption of innocence, secured only after centuries of struggle, would lose its meaning."

IV * * *

Throughout the world today there are men, women, and children interned indefinitely, awaiting trials which may never come or which may be a mockery of the word, because their governments believe them to be "dangerous." Our Constitution, whose construction began two centuries ago, can shelter us forever from the evils of such unchecked power. Over 200 years it has slowly, through our efforts, grown more durable, more expansive, and more just. But it cannot protect us if we lack the courage, and the self-restraint, to protect ourselves. Today a majority of the Court applies itself to an ominous exercise in demolition. Theirs is truly a decision which will go forth without authority, and come back without respect.

JUSTICE STEVENS, dissenting.

There may be times when the Government's interest in protecting the safety of the community will justify the brief detention of a person who has not committed any crime. To use Judge Feinberg's example, it is indeed difficult to accept the proposition that the Government is without power to detain a person when it is a virtual certainty that he or she would otherwise kill a group of innocent people in the immediate future. *United States v. Salerno*, 794 F.2d 64, 77 (C.A.2 1986) (dissenting opinion). Similarly, I am unwilling to decide today that the police may never impose a limited curfew during a time of crisis. These questions are obviously not presented in this case, but they lurk in the background and preclude me from answering the question that is presented in as broad a manner as Justice Marshall has. Nonetheless, I firmly agree with Justice Marshall that the provision of the Bail Reform Act allowing pretrial detention on the basis of future dangerousness is unconstitutional. Whatever the answers are to the questions I have mentioned, it is clear to me that a pending indictment may not be given any weight in evaluating an individual's risk to the community or the need for immediate detention.

If the evidence of imminent danger is strong enough to warrant emergency detention, it should support that preventive measure regardless of whether the person has been charged, convicted, or acquitted of some other offense. In this case, for example, it is unrealistic to assume that the danger to the community that was present when respondents were at large did not justify their detention before they were indicted, but did require that measure the moment that the grand jury found probable cause to believe they had committed crimes in the past. It is equally unrealistic to assume that the danger will vanish if a jury happens to acquit them. Justice Marshall has demonstrated that the fact of indictment cannot, consistent with the presumption of innocence and the Eighth Amendment's Excessive Bail Clause, be used to create a special class, the members of which are, alone, eligible for detention because of future dangerousness. * * *

NOTES AND QUESTIONS

1. *Data.* The percentage of federal defendants detained without bail rose from 1.7% in 1983, the year before enactment of the Federal Bail Reform Act, to 18.8% in 1985, the first full year of the new law's implementation. U.S. Dep't of Justice, Pretrial Release and Detention: The Bail Reform Act of 1984 (Bureau of Justice Statistics, Feb. 1988), at 2.

Pretrial detention hearings are now common. In 2004, hearings were held for 56.1% of all federal defendants. Of the hearings held, detentions were ordered in 78.8% of the cases. U.S. Dep't of Justice, Sourcebook of Criminal Justice Statistics Online, at http://www.albany.edu/sourcebook/pdf/t 5142004.pdf.

Some states following the lead of Congress have enacted preventive detention laws. Nonetheless, the state preventive detention rate in large urban counties is only four percent. U.S. Dep't of Justice, Felony Defendants in Large Urban Counties 2009—Statistical Tables (NCJ 243777, Dec. 2013).

2. The *Salerno* Court stated that "Congress * * * perceived pretrial detention as a potential solution to a pressing societal problem. There is no doubt that preventing danger to the community is a legitimate regulatory goal." But, isn't "preventing danger to the community"—crime deterrence—

the goal of the *criminal* law? If so, how do we distinguish criminal from civil commitment?

3.   As a matter of constitutional law, who do you believe has the better side of the argument, the majority or the dissenters in *Salerno*? For the constitutional argument that the due process clause "is the constitutional basis for the presumption of innocence and * * * that presumption secures the right against pretrial detention, absent serious flight risk," see Shima Baradaran, *Restoring the Presumption of Innocence*, 72 Ohio St. L.J. 723 (2011). Who is right as a matter of public policy? The following Notes primarily focus on the latter question.

4.   *For those of you who believe that preventive detention should be permitted: predicting dangerousness.* Although preventive detention can be based on future flight risk, advocates of preventive detention concede that the justifiability of the practice depends in considerable part on the assumption that magistrates can determine which defendants represent a danger to the community during the period of time from release until case disposition. The *Salerno* Court, quoting *Schall v. Martin*, stated that "there is nothing inherently unattainable about a prediction of future criminal conduct." Is that so? Even if reliable dangerousness predictions are not inherently unattainable, have we *in fact* attained that ability? And, are magistrates, based on the information provided them at bail hearings, qualified to make such predictions?

According to one expert, "the level of predictive validity revealed in the [social science] research has at least in the case of violent crime been rather modest * * * ." John Monahan, *Prediction of Crime and Recidivism* in 3 Encyclopedia of Crime and Justice 1125, 1129 (Joshua Dressler, ed., 2d. ed. 2002). And, a recent study of 100,000 defendants over a fifteen-year period concluded that "judges often detain the wrong people." The study demonstrated that using the authors' model for predicting future violence, "[j]udges would be able to release 25% more defendants while decreasing both violent crime and total pretrial crime rates." Shima Baradaran & Frank L. McIntyre, *Predicting Violence*, 90 Texas L. Rev. 497, 497 (2012).

This rather discouraging picture applies in particular to false positive predictions (incorrect predictions of dangerousness) and less so to false negatives (wrong predictions that a person will not commit a crime). At least among mental health professionals, predictions that a person may safely be released are, on the whole, accurate. In one important study, for example, "[n]inety-two-percent of the patients released by the court with the professionals' approval were not arrested for serious assaults within the study period." Albert W. Alschuler, *Preventive Pretrial Detention and the Failure of Interest-Balancing Approaches to Due Process*, 85 Mich. L. Rev. 510, 540 (1986) (summarizing the results of a study published in Kozol et al., *The Diagnosis and Treatment of Dangerousness*, 18 Crime & Delinq. 371 (1972)).

In evaluating preventive detention laws, however, the positive predictions are the key. A Harvard study of the predictive mechanisms of a pre-1984 District of Columbia preventive detention statute suggests that false positives may be a serious concern. United States Senator Sam Ervin summarized the findings this way:

> The Harvard researchers have applied the ten factors of the preventive detention bill in an effort to measure their reliability. They have constructed two point systems * * * . In the first test, they assign weights to the factors on a "hunch" basis—that is, they use a system which is very much like that which judges and magistrates will use in implementing the law, relying on their experience with criminal types and their characteristics. Needless to say, this is a very "unscientific" approach, but it is the one which actually will be used when preventive detention [is] applied in the courtroom. * * *

> It should not be too surprising to discover * * * that the first system, the hunch system, fails as a reliable prediction method. Charting the persons labeled dangerous and violent and thus subject to possible detention, the Harvard project discloses that at no point on the scale does the point system include more actual recidivists than nonrecidivists. Wrong answers, improper detentions, occur more often than right answers wherever the cut-off point is placed. What is worse, the ratio of wrong to right answers is never less than about five to two. * * * At its best, it appears that the hunch system is accurate about 30% of the time. * * *

> The second, or statistical analysis employed in the study shows the bill's predictive system at its theoretical best. The researchers measured nine of the ten factors to determine the actual correlation of each to recidivism, and then gave each factor a weight which corresponded to the relationship it had to further crime. By this means, they obtained the most accurate measure of the predictive value of the bill's mechanism. * * *

> Under the second system, the optimum point on the scale produces 40% accuracy. That is, four out of every ten detained were actually recidivists.

Sam J. Ervin, Jr., *Foreword: Preventive Detention—A Step Backward for Criminal Justice*, 6 Harv. Civ. Rts.-Civ. Lib. L. Rev. 291, 296–97 (1971).

One hundred percent predictive accuracy, of course, is unattainable. What rate of false positives do you believe society should be prepared to accept in order to keep apparently dangerous persons—but ones who have not yet been convicted of the charged offense—off the street? Or, are there other values, unrelated to cost-benefit analysis, that should take precedence?

5. *For those of you who believe that preventive detention should not be permitted: can you really defend your opposition?* Why do you categorically reject preventive detention? Is it a matter of cost-benefit analysis, or does some other value explain your position? If you oppose preventive detention, what should a court do if a person charged with murder, screams at the judge at the bail hearing, "Let me tell you something, judge. If you release me, the first thing I am going to do is kill the [expletive deleted] prosecutor. Then I am going to come after you, and shoot your [expletive deleted] brains out, and then I am going to kill [the witness against him]." No preventive detention here? If you are prepared to justify detention in *this* case, haven't you essentially come over to the other side, and now the only issue is *when*—not *whether*—we should permit preventive detention?

Professor Albert Alschuler has observed, "[a]lthough predicting the weather is a difficult task, almost anyone can do it when a funnel cloud is headed in his direction. * * * These funnel clouds * * * should not merely be acknowledged and forgotten." Albert W. Alschuler, *Preventive Pretrial Detention and the Failure of Interest-Balancing Approaches to Due Process*, 85 Mich. L. Rev. 510, 544–545 (1986). Preventive detention, of course, focuses on "human funnel clouds." Do you have any successful riposte for Professor Alschuler's observation?

6. *Problem: Watching out for your MMDI score.* Albert W. Alschuler, *Preventive Pretrial Detention and the Failure of Interest-Balancing Approaches to Due Process*, 85 Mich. L. Rev. 510, 534 (1986), asks us to consider the following imaginary case:

> [P]sychologists at Menninger University have developed a written test, the Menninger Multiphasic Dangerousness Inventory or MMDI. The test asks subjects to record the extent of their agreement or disagreement with statements like: "My mother is insecure," "My father obtained a better-paying job at least once during my childhood," "I prefer western movies to situation comedies," "I sometimes wet my bed as a child," and "I am fascinated by fire." After pretesting and refining the MMDI, the psychologists have administered it to a large random sample of the population. Careful follow-up studies have revealed that although only 0.7 percent of the population scored 140 points or higher on the test, 69.2 percent of the subjects with these high scores were convicted of serious crimes within the next two years.

> Impressed by this evidence, a state legislature has required everyone to take the MMDI. It has provided for the administrative detention in secure but nonpunitive facilities of people who score 140 points or higher. Prior to detention, these people are to be afforded hearings with full procedural safeguards on the single determinative issue—whether they failed the test. They are to be detained only until they reduce their scores to an acceptable level.

Is the statute constitutional? Even if it is, would you have voted for its passage? In what ways does this detention scheme differ from the Federal Bail Reform Act? In what ways is it preferable? In what ways is it more troubling? How would you feel about the law if the MMDI had a 100% accuracy rate, *i.e.* no false positives?

7. *Problem: the suicidal defendant.* We were told of this interesting case: A formerly reputable member of the community, released on bail for a child sex charge, swallowed a bottle of Excedrin. The defense characterized this as a suicide attempt; the prosecutor disagreed, but in any case, a mental health expert accepted by both the defense and prosecution testified that the defendant was no longer a suicide risk. The judge substantially increased the man's bail, the defendant paid it, and two days later he killed himself.

Here are the questions. First, did the judge have a legitimate basis for increasing the bail figure? What would be the theory? Second, if this had been a federal case, would there have been any statutory basis for preventively detaining the defendant (and then placing him in a "suicide watch" facility)?

CHAPTER 12

CASE SCREENING

▪ ▪ ▪

So You Want to Be a Prosecutor?

You are the chief prosecutor in a fairly small Midwestern city that has seen its problems with poverty, crime, and race relations. This afternoon, about 4:30 p.m., you are getting ready to go home early to go out to dinner with your husband. Then comes an emergency call from the assistant police chief. One of his officers has shot and killed a 12-year old African-American male. An investigation is already under way but what is known so far is that there was a 911 call about a young man waving a gun around in a park, pointing it at others. Near the end of the 911 call, the caller said the pistol might be a fake and that the male is probably a juvenile but, for reasons that are not yet clear, the 911 dispatcher did not communicate that information to the officers sent to the scene. When they arrived, according to their report, they saw the male walking toward their car and appearing to reach into his pocket. That was when one of the officers shot and killed him.[a]

To make matters worse, this killing has occurred within one year of police killings of several unarmed African-American young men. You will ultimately have to decide whether to bring criminal charges against the officer who fired the fatal shot. What factors will you consider? Can you be fair to him? Can you deliver justice to the family of the young boy? Will the city be torn apart by riots depending on what decision you make? You might still decide to go home early but your dinner will not be as much fun as it would have been yesterday. We will follow this case throughout this chapter and the next one for what it can teach us about the process of case screening and preparing for trial. Case screening, in the broadest sense, occurs at every point in the criminal process and all the time. Police decide whether to stop a suspicious person in an alley; if they stop him, they must decide whether to question or search; if they question or search, they must decide whether any statements made or items found create sufficient indicia of serious criminal activity to justify a full-fledged arrest. If a search reveals a very small quantity of marijuana, for example, many police in urban areas will decide to ignore the evidence.

---

[a] Though these facts are drawn, roughly, from the police shooting of Tamir Rice in Cleveland, Ohio, in 2014, we have changed or made up facts for the purpose of sharpening the issues we wish to illustrate.

When police ignore evidence of a relatively minor crime, they are, of course, engaged in "case screening." They are making an assessment that in their city or precinct, the resources of the police, the prosecutors, and the courts are better used in other cases. You may believe that police should not take it upon themselves to make this decision, but it remains true that no one can stop police from informal case screening. It is human nature to weigh the costs and benefits of our actions.

But this chapter is about the more formal screening that typically occurs after arrest. At this stage, the prosecutor almost always becomes involved in the case, sometimes making the initial charging decision herself, sometimes reviewing a charging decision made by the police. Some states permit the prosecutor to begin the criminal proceeding by filing a sworn information setting out the basis for the charge. In these states, the prosecutor alone conducts the initial formal screening. Once the police "have done their winnowing, the scope of prosecutorial discretion remains immense." Daniel C. Richman, *Old Chief v. United States: Stipulating Away Prosecutorial Accountability?*, 83 Va. L. Rev. 939 (1997). The chapter begins, in Part A., with a study of that "immense" prosecutorial discretion.

Part B. involves the judicial role in screening cases. The federal system and most states require a preliminary hearing shortly after arrest, which provides an opportunity for the accused to test the prosecution's case. Part C. considers yet another screening device: the grand jury. Grand jury screening differs from prosecutorial and judicial screening (in theory at least) because it represents the judgment of the community about whether cause exists to proceed to trial. The grand jury stage is the last one in most judicial systems; if the grand jury votes an indictment, the screening process is done and the accused will be formally arraigned (which includes setting a date for trial).

We note that prosecutorial discretion continues after indictment throughout the criminal process, featured most prominently in plea bargaining but also appearing in jury selection and sentencing, but this chapter involves only the initial discretion involved in screening cases to decide which ones to pursue.

A. PROSECUTORIAL DISCRETION IN CHARGING

The prosecutor has more control over life, liberty, and reputation than any other person in America. His discretion is tremendous. * * * If the prosecutor is obliged to choose his cases, it follows that he can choose his defendants. * * * It is in this realm—in which the prosecutor picks some person whom he likes or dislikes or desires to embarrass, or selects some group of unpopular persons and then looks for an offense, that the greatest danger of abuse in prosecutorial power lies. It is there that law enforcement becomes * * * personal.

Robert H. Jackson, 24 J. Am. Judicature Soc'y 18, 18–19 (1940).

Every prosecuting office—and every prosecutor, to some extent—faces a daunting range of targets against which to deploy relatively scarce resources. Some of the decisions are quite general: White collar criminals or violent offenders? Higher level drug traffickers or street peddlers? With a broadly defined policy agenda set, the finer-grained questions will emerge: Which street robbers are most deserving of punishment? Which illegal gun cases? The response to a particular case need not be binary. Prosecution can be declined. Prosecution might be initiated, but with little commitment of investigative or adjudicative resources. Or the maximum penalty can be pursued hotly. * * * [Once law enforcement] entities have done their winnowing, the scope of prosecutorial discretion remains immense.

Daniel C. Richman, *Old Chief v. United States: Stipulating Away Prosecutorial Accountability?*, 83 Va. L. Rev. 939 (1997).

1.   CASE STUDY: 235 COUNTS VERSUS 0 COUNTS

Prosecutors suspect that a day care worker, Kelly Michaels, is sexually abusing the four-year-old children under her supervision. They interrogate Michaels for nine hours. She denies any wrongdoing and passes a lie detector test. Yet the prosecutors remain convinced that she is guilty and proceed to build a case against her by interviewing the children. Grand juries return three indictments that contain a total of 235 counts. Prior to trial, the prosecutors dismiss 72 counts and proceed to trial on the remaining 163 counts.

The trial lasts nine months. At its conclusion, 32 counts had been dismissed, leaving 131 counts. After twelve days of deliberation, the jury convicts on 115 counts. The judge sentences Michaels to an aggregate term of forty-seven years with fourteen years of parole ineligibility. A college senior when the investigation began, Michaels faces the prospect of spending most of her life in prison as a result of a process that has no limit on the number of counts that a prosecutor can bring or any judicial review of the prosecutor's decision to charge.

Six years later, the New Jersey Supreme Court holds that the investigative techniques were flawed because "a substantial likelihood exists that the children's recollection of past events was both stimulated and materially influenced" by the questions that the investigators asked. State v. Michaels, 136 N.J. 299, 642 A.2d 1372, 1380 (1994). The court holds that all 115 convictions must be reversed and a hearing held to determine whether the children's testimony was sufficiently reliable to be admissible in any new trial. The State chooses not to re-prosecute. We will never know whether Michaels was guilty of some, all, or none of the charges against her. But we do know that the process of deciding what and how many charges to bring was completely within the discretion of the prosecutor. We know that enormous prosecutorial resources were committed to this ultimately futile gesture.

The "discretion coin" has two sides, of course. If a prosecutor is free to bring 235 counts, she is free to bring zero counts even if the suspect is guilty. After spending seventy million dollars and seven years investigating President Clinton, the special prosecutor's office in late 2001 filed a report claiming that sufficient evidence existed "to obtain and sustain a conviction" of Clinton for obstruction of justice and perjury. This judgment, the report noted, was "confirmed by President Clinton's admissions" that he "knowingly gave evasive and misleading answers" about his relationship with Monica Lewinsky.[b] The report concluded that "President Clinton's offenses had a significant adverse impact on the community, substantially affecting the public's view of the integrity of our legal system." Neil A. Lewis, *Special Counsel Puts Lewinsky Case to Rest*, New York Times, March 7, 2002, A18.

But special prosecutor Robert Ray "invoked his discretion as a prosecutor to decline to bring those charges," on the ground that Clinton "had already paid a sufficient penalty for having lied before a federal judge in 1998 when he denied ever being alone with Ms. Lewinsky and engaging in intimate relations with her." *Id.* That the president had "suffered enough" was of course the same ground that Gerald Ford used when he pardoned Richard Nixon for his involvement in Watergate. One question raised by the Michaels case and the Clinton case is whether this kind of unreviewable discretion is an inevitable part of a justice system and, if not, whether it is an aspect that should be changed.

NOTES AND QUESTIONS

1.   Assuming that Special Prosecutor Robert Ray was correct in his assessment of the evidence and of the harm done to the "integrity of our legal system," do you think declining to prosecute President Clinton was appropriate?

2.   Is the "immense" discretion exemplified by the Michaels case, a good idea or should there be some sort of routine review of the prosecutor's decision to file charges? Who would conduct that review?

3.   *Discretion not to prosecute federal crimes.* The discretion not to prosecute is explicitly recognized in the manual governing federal

---

[b]   If you're too young to remember the relationship, Google was invented for just this purpose. Enjoy (or not).

prosecutors: a "United States Attorney is authorized to decline prosecution in any case referred directly to him/her by an agency unless a statute provides otherwise." Exec. Office for U.S. Attorneys, U.S. Dep't of Justice, United States Attorneys' Manual 9–2.020.

Federal prosecutors are authorized not to prosecute a federal crime if they believe that (1) "no substantial Federal interest would be served by [the] prosecution," (2) the defendant "is subject to effective prosecution in another jurisdiction," or (3) "there exists an adequate non-criminal alternative to prosecution." *Id.* at 9–27.220, 642 A.2d 1372.

4.   *What the data show.* Professor O'Neill's careful study of federal prosecutions from 1994–2000 showed that federal prosecutors decline roughly a quarter of all cases referred to them by federal agencies. Michael Edmund O'Neill, *When Prosecutors Don't: Trends in Federal Prosecutorial Declinations*, 79 Notre Dame L. Rev. 221, 271 (2003). As greater resources were given to federal prosecutors and investigators during this period, however, the rate of declination went down in each year of the study. Drug offenses are the least likely category to be declined, suggesting, at least in these pre-9/11 days, that "federal resources are being spent chiefly upon crimes involving the use or trafficking of illegal drugs." *Id.* at 272.

5.   *Prison overcrowding as a factor in discretion not to prosecute?* To Adam Gershowitz, "The overwhelming majority of prosecutors are reasonable and exercise their discretion soundly. * * * Yet, incarceration rates are at record levels and continue to climb." This is so, he believes, because prosecutors do not take into account prison overcrowding when they exercise their discretion to prosecute. Should they? For an argument that prosecutors should be "more cognizant about the funding of the rest of the criminal justice system," and that this knowledge will in the general run of cases cause prosecutors to offer "marginally lower plea bargains," see Adam M. Gershowitz, *An Informational Approach to the Mass Imprisonment Problem*, 40 Ariz. St. L. J. 47 (2008).

6.   *Inevitability of prosecutorial discretion.* Prosecutorial discretion is, of course, inevitable. "Scarce resources * * * dictate that prosecutors will be unable to pursue each matter that is placed upon their desk for consideration." O'Neill, 79 Notre Dame L. Rev. at 224. And, as Professor O'Neill observes, the decision not to prosecute "is difficult to monitor because it is largely hidden from public scrutiny. * * * Indeed, with perhaps the sole exception of the putative victim (if an identifiable victim exists), other defendants and the general public seldom have any idea about individuals not prosecuted." *Id.*

But to say that prosecutorial discretion is inevitable is not to say that it cannot be reviewed. Kenneth Culp Davis asks why a prosecutor should have discretionary power to refuse to prosecute "when the evidence of guilt is clear * * * without ever having to state to anyone what evidence was brought to light by his investigation and without having to explain to anyone why he interprets a statute as he does or why he chooses a particular position on a difficult question of policy?" Kenneth Culp Davis, Discretionary Justice: A Preliminary Inquiry 189 (1969). Davis gives a hypothetical case in which six defendants are equally guilty but the prosecutor decides, perhaps for idiosyncratic reasons, to throw the book at one and dismiss the charges against the others. Can this be fair or just?

To the pragmatic charge that prosecutors simply must have this discretion because not every criminal violation can be enforced, and some actor must have discretion, Davis gives Germany as a counter example. In Germany, "Every prosecutor is supervised by a superior in a hierarchical system headed by the Minister of Justice, who is himself responsible to the cabinet." *Id.* at 194–95. Moreover, the German

> prosecutor is obliged by law to file charges whenever there is "sufficient" suspicion that the suspect has committed a crime. The standard of sufficiency to be applied in this context is likelihood that the suspect will be convicted after trial. The required prognosis leaves some leeway to individual prosecutors' appraisal of the strength of the evidence. German prosecutors tend to err in favor of bringing charges because a non-conviction is not regarded as a personal (or institutional) defeat to the extent it would be in a partisan system of justice.

Thomas Weigend, *Germany*, in Criminal Procedure: A Worldwide View 205 (Craig Bradley ed. 1998).

And, unlike American law, there is a structural role for victims to play in those cases where prosecutors think the evidence insufficient to prosecute.

> The victim of an offense can challenge a prosecutor's refusal to bring charges for lack of sufficient evidence. If an intra-office review of the matter does not lead to a reversal of the decision not to bring charges, the victim can present the issue to the State Court of Appeals, which can direct the prosecutor's office to file an accusation. Although victims' efforts to force an accusation are seldom successful in practice, the mere existence of the possibility of judicial review provides a check on arbitrary dismissals by prosecutors.

Id. at 206.

7. The issue ultimately is political accountability for prosecutor decisions. As Ron Wright and Marc Miller put it: "Prosecutors the world over must cope with an accountability deficit. Scholars have noted this deficit for years, but their proposals to confront the problem have either been too modest, or else they have been too unrealistic and thus have gone unheeded." Ronald F. Wright & Marc L. Miller, *Prosecutorial Power: A Transnational Symposium: The Worldwide Accountability Deficit for Prosecutors*, 67 Wash. & Lee L. Rev. 1587, 1588 (2010).

Prosecutors are politically accountable in the United States. United States Attorneys are selected by, and serve at the pleasure of, the president.

In many states, prosecutors are elected officials. Do you prefer the German way of dealing with prosecutorial accountability over the much more laissez-faire approach in the United States? Would you prefer that prosecutors be elected or appointed by the governor or the president?

2. THE STANDARDS OF THE BAR

Three points can be made here. First, the ABA Standards make explicit the discretion of the prosecutor to decide whether to bring charges: "In order to fully implement the prosecutor's functions and duties, including the obligation to enforce the law while exercising sound discretion, the prosecutor is not obliged to file or maintain all criminal charges which the evidence might support." The Standards list sixteen factors that can be considered when deciding which crimes to prosecute, including "the views and motives of the victim," "the background and characteristics of the offender," "any improper conduct by law enforcement," and "the fair and efficient distribution of limited prosecutorial resources." American Bar Association, Criminal Justice Standards for the Prosecution Function, Fourth Edition, 3–4.4(a), Discretion in Filing, Declining, Maintaining, and Dismissing Criminal Charges (2015). Second, as to quantum of evidence, the ABA Standards provide: "A prosecutor should seek or file criminal charges only if the prosecutor reasonably believes that the charges are supported by probable cause, that admissible evidence will be sufficient to support conviction beyond a reasonable doubt, and that the decision to charge is in the interests of justice." Id. at 3–4.3(a), Discretion in Filing, Declining, Maintaining, and Dismissing Criminal Charges. Third, as to the appropriate *number* of charges, the standards provide: "The prosecutor should not file or maintain charges greater in number or degree than can reasonably be supported with evidence at trial and are necessary to fairly reflect the gravity of the offense or deter similar conduct." Id. at 3–4.4(d).

NOTES AND QUESTIONS

1.   *The zealous prosecutor.* A police officer searches a man sitting on a park bench across the street from a school playground based purely on a hunch. You are the prosecutor assigned for the case. When you question the officer, he says that the only ground for the search was that he hadn't seen the man before. The search turns up narcotics and further evidence that the man was selling to children. You charge him with possession with intent to sell to children, a Class 2 felony punishable by up to twenty years in prison. The town has been vocal lately in its concern about drug sales to children and you want to bring this case to trial, even if you lose it. You are almost certain, however, that the defense will win a motion to suppress the evidence found by the officer and you will lose the only evidence you have. What should you do?

2. *The super zealous prosecutor.* Using the ABA Standards discussed above, what is your view of the New Jersey prosecutors in the Michaels case?

3. *The forgiving victim.* A husband-wife assault case has the following facts. (1) *H* is a loving husband, distraught at the loss of his job of twenty years; (2) *H* had never before physically abused *W*; (3) *H* feels tremendous guilt about what he has done, and has offered to plead guilty "and take my medicine"; (4) the abuse took place in front of three acquaintances, all of whom are willing to testify; (5) *W* has asked you not to prosecute. You have witnesses; there is no doubt that a crime occurred. Assault is a misdemeanor, punishable by up to one year. Would you prosecute?

4. *The recalcitrant victim/witness.* Police answer a family disturbance call to discover husband and wife screaming and threatening each other. *W* has a bruise on her cheek. Police separate the combatants; one of the officers calls in the address and learns that this is the fourth disturbance call in the last six months (all the calls came from neighbors, not from *W*).

W tells the police to leave, that she can handle the situation without them. The officers instead arrest *H* and charge him with assault. When the prosecutor contacts *W* asking her to testify against *H*, she refuses. "Are you afraid of him?" asks the prosecutor. "Of course, I'm afraid of him. I'm no fool. But he's a good man, and a criminal record will ruin his life."

"Will he retaliate against you if you testify against him?" asks the prosecutor. "I won't testify," says *W*. "I'll subpoena you." "I'll deny everything," she says. "The police will testify," says the prosecutor. "They never saw him lay a hand on me. I'll say I got the bruise falling down the stairs." "I'm trying to help," pleads the prosecutor. "You don't know how to start," she says and walks out of the office.

If you were the prosecutor, would you dismiss the charges? Reduce them to disturbing the peace? Require counseling?

For an analysis of the prosecution of domestic violence cases, with and without victim testimony, see Kimberly D. Bailey, *The Aftermath of Crawford and Davis: Deconstructing the Sound of Silence*, 2009 Brigham Young U. L. Rev. 1.

5. *Domestic violence.* Cases like Note 4 pose multiple risks to the victims. Consider the case of New York Giants safety Tito Wooten and his girlfriend, Akina Wilson. They appeared in a New York court together on December 17, 1997. Wooten was charged with pushing her to the floor, punching her in the face, and choking her. She was pregnant. In a development prosecutors later characterized as "unusual," the lawyer for Wooten spoke for Wilson, telling the judge that Wilson wanted the charges dropped. The prosecutor "spoke briefly with Wilson and then agreed that the charges be dismissed. There was no mention of the fact that Wooten had twice before been arrested on charges of assaulting women. The idea of counseling was not brought up." The judge's final remark was directed to

Wooten in his role as football player: "Have a good game." Five weeks later, Wilson committed suicide. New York Times, February 27, 1998, at C1.

The next summer, the Giants released Wooten. He played a little over a season with the Indianapolis Colts. He was suspended for missing bed check mid-way through the 1999 season and never returned to the team.

6.   *Prosecuting mothers.* It is a crime to give birth to a crack-addicted baby, punishable by up to one year in jail. See Rosa Goldensohn & Rachael Levy, "The State Where Giving Birth Can Be Criminal," The Nation, December 14, 2014, https://www.thenation.com/article/state-where-giving-birth-can-be-criminal/. The statute requires hospitals to notify the local prosecutor when a baby tests positive for crack addiction. Would you (1) routinely prosecute every mother; (2) investigate each case before deciding whether to prosecute; or (3) adopt a "no-prosecution" policy? If (2), what would you want to know about the individual cases? What are the strongest arguments in favor of outcome (1)? Does this Problem make you more favorably disposed toward the U.S. model of prosecutorial discretion when compared to the German model?

7.   Back to you, our Midwestern prosecutor with the police shooting on her hands. A surveillance video shows the shooting. Enhanced images of that video show a boy walking toward the police cruiser, reaching for his waist and lifting his arm and shoulder in the split-second before the officer shot him. Three experts on police shootings, including a retired FBI agent, give you a report that concludes the officer acted reasonably under the circumstances. The dead boy's family has come to your office to ask why the police officer could not tell that the "shooter" was a very young person. Your expert reports include the fact that the victim was five feet seven inches tall and weighed 195 pounds. You have just learned that the United States Justice Department will be investigating the Chicago police department (not your city) and that one Chicago police officer has been indicted for first degree murder for killing a young black man, Do you seek an indictment?

8.   We have seen that there are no formal limits on the discretion of the prosecutor *not* to bring charges. We turn next to whether there are limits on the decision *to bring* charges.

3. CONSTITUTIONAL LIMITS ON DISCRETION IN CHARGING

UNITED STATES V. ARMSTRONG

Supreme Court of the United States, 1996.
517 U.S. 456, 116 S.Ct. 1480, 134 L.Ed.2d 687.

CHIEF JUSTICE REHNQUIST delivered the opinion of the Court [joined by JUSTICES O'CONNOR, SCALIA, KENNEDY, SOUTER, THOMAS, and GINSBURG, and joined in part by JUSTICE BREYER].

In this case, we consider the showing necessary for a defendant to be entitled to discovery on a claim that the prosecuting attorney singled him out for prosecution on the basis of his race. We conclude that respondents failed to satisfy the threshold showing: They failed to show that the Government declined to prosecute similarly situated suspects of other races.

In April 1992, respondents were indicted in the United States District Court for the Central District of California on charges of conspiring to possess with intent to distribute more than 50 grams of cocaine base (crack) and conspiring to distribute the same, in violation of 21 U.S.C. §§ 841 and 846, and federal firearms offenses. For three months prior to the indictment, agents of the Federal Bureau of Alcohol, Tobacco, and Firearms and the Narcotics Division of the Inglewood, California, Police Department had infiltrated a suspected crack distribution ring by using three confidential informants. On seven separate occasions during this period, the informants had bought a total of 124.3 grams of crack from respondents and witnessed respondents carrying firearms during the sales. The agents searched the hotel room in which the sales were transacted, arrested respondents Armstrong and Hampton in the room, and found more crack and a loaded gun. The agents later arrested the other respondents as part of the ring.

In response to the indictment, respondents filed a motion for discovery or for dismissal of the indictment, alleging that they were selected for federal prosecution because they are black. In support of their motion, they offered only an affidavit by a "Paralegal Specialist," employed by the Office of the Federal Public Defender representing one of the respondents. The only allegation in the affidavit was that, in every one of the 24 § 841 or 846 cases closed by the office during 1991, the defendant was black. Accompanying the affidavit was a "study" listing the 24 defendants, their race, whether they were prosecuted for dealing cocaine as well as crack, and the status of each case.

The Government opposed the discovery motion, arguing, among other things, that there was no evidence or allegation "that the Government has acted unfairly or has prosecuted non-black defendants or failed to prosecute them." The District Court granted the motion. It ordered the Government (1) to provide a list of all cases from the last three years in which the Government charged both cocaine and firearms offenses, (2) to identify the race of the defendants in those cases, (3) to identify what levels of law enforcement were involved in the investigations of those cases, and (4) to explain its criteria for deciding to prosecute those defendants for federal cocaine offenses.

The Government moved for reconsideration of the District Court's discovery order. With this motion it submitted affidavits and other evidence to explain why it had chosen to prosecute respondents and why respondents' study did not support the inference that the Government was singling out blacks for cocaine prosecution. The federal and local agents participating in the case alleged in affidavits that race played no role in their investigation. An Assistant United States Attorney explained in an affidavit that the decision to prosecute met the general criteria for prosecution, because

> "there was over 100 grams of cocaine base involved, over twice the threshold necessary for a ten year mandatory minimum sentence; there were multiple sales involving multiple defendants, thereby indicating a fairly substantial crack cocaine ring; * * * there were multiple federal firearms violations intertwined with the narcotics trafficking; the overall evidence in the case was extremely strong, including audio and videotapes of defendants; * * * and several of the defendants had criminal histories including narcotics and firearms violations."

The Government also submitted sections of a published 1989 Drug Enforcement Administration report which concluded that "[l]arge-scale, interstate trafficking networks controlled by Jamaicans, Haitians and Black street gangs dominate the manufacture and distribution of crack."

In response, one of respondents' attorneys submitted an affidavit alleging that an intake coordinator at a drug treatment center had told her that there are "an equal number of caucasian users and dealers to minority users and dealers." Respondents also submitted an affidavit from a criminal defense attorney alleging that in his experience many nonblacks are prosecuted in state court for crack offenses, and a newspaper article reporting that Federal "crack criminals * * * are being punished far more severely than if they had been caught with powder cocaine, and almost every single one of them is black."

The District Court denied the motion for reconsideration. When the Government indicated it would not comply with the court's discovery order, the court dismissed the case.

A divided three-judge panel of the Court of Appeals for the Ninth Circuit reversed, holding that, because of the proof requirements for a selective-prosecution claim, defendants must "provide a colorable basis for believing that 'others similarly situated have not been prosecuted'" to obtain discovery.

A selective-prosecution claim is not a defense on the merits to the criminal charge itself, but an independent assertion that the prosecutor has brought the charge for reasons forbidden by the Constitution. Our cases delineating the necessary elements to prove a claim of selective prosecution have taken great pains to explain that the standard is a demanding one. These cases afford a "background presumption" that the showing necessary to obtain discovery should itself be a significant barrier to the litigation of insubstantial claims.

A selective-prosecution claim asks a court to exercise judicial power over a "special province" of the Executive. The Attorney General and United States Attorneys retain "'broad discretion'" to enforce the Nation's criminal laws. They have this latitude because they are designated by statute as the President's delegates to help him discharge his constitutional responsibility to "take Care that the Laws be faithfully executed." U.S. Const., Art. II, § 3. As a result, "[t]he presumption of regularity supports" their prosecutorial decisions and "in the absence of clear evidence to the contrary, courts presume that they have properly discharged their official duties." In the ordinary case, "so long as the prosecutor has probable cause to believe that the accused committed an offense defined by statute, the decision whether or not to prosecute, and what charge to file or bring before a grand jury, generally rests entirely in his discretion."

Of course, a prosecutor's discretion is "subject to constitutional constraints." One of these constraints, imposed by the equal protection component of the Due Process Clause of the Fifth Amendment, is that the decision whether to prosecute may not be based on "an unjustifiable standard such as race, religion, or other arbitrary classification." A defendant may demonstrate that the administration of a criminal law is "directed so exclusively against a particular class of persons * * * with a mind so unequal and oppressive" that the system of prosecution amounts to "a practical denial" of equal protection of the law.

In order to dispel the presumption that a prosecutor has not violated equal protection, a criminal defendant must present "clear evidence to the contrary." We explained in *Wayte* [*v. United States*, 470 U.S. 598, 105 S.Ct. 1524, 84 L.Ed.2d 547 (1985)] why courts are "properly hesitant to examine the decision whether to prosecute." Judicial deference to the decisions of these executive officers rests in part on an assessment of the relative competence of prosecutors and courts. "Such factors as the strength of the case, the prosecution's general deterrence value, the Government's enforcement priorities, and the case's relationship to the Government's overall enforcement plan are not readily susceptible to the kind of analysis the courts are competent to undertake." It also stems from a concern not to unnecessarily impair the performance of a core executive constitutional function. "Examining the basis of a prosecution delays the criminal proceeding, threatens to chill law enforcement by subjecting the prosecutor's motives and decisionmaking to outside inquiry, and may undermine prosecutorial effectiveness by revealing the Government's enforcement policy."

The requirements for a selective-prosecution claim draw on "ordinary equal protection standards." The claimant must demonstrate that the federal prosecutorial policy "had a discriminatory effect and that it was motivated by a discriminatory purpose." To establish a discriminatory effect in a race case, the claimant must show that similarly situated individuals of a different race were not prosecuted. * * *

The similarly situated requirement does not make a selective-prosecution claim impossible to prove. * * * [In *Yick Wo v. Hopkins*, 118 U.S. 356, 373, 6 S.Ct. 1064, 1073, 30 L.Ed. 220 (1886)], we invalidated an ordinance * * * that prohibited the operation of laundries in wooden buildings. The plaintiff in error successfully demonstrated that the ordinance was applied against Chinese nationals but not against other laundry-shop operators. The authorities had denied the applications of 200 Chinese subjects for permits to operate shops in wooden buildings, but granted the applications of 80 individuals who were not Chinese subjects to operate laundries in wooden buildings "under similar conditions." * * *

Having reviewed the requirements to prove a selective-prosecution claim, we turn to the showing necessary to obtain discovery in support of such a claim. If discovery is ordered, the Government must assemble from its own files documents which might corroborate or refute the defendant's claim. Discovery thus imposes many of the costs present when the Government must respond to a prima facie case of selective prosecution. It will divert prosecutors' resources and may disclose the Government's prosecutorial strategy. The justifications for a rigorous standard for the elements of a selective-prosecution claim thus require a correspondingly rigorous standard for discovery in aid of such a claim.

[The Court agreed with the lower courts that the threshold showing required to compel discovery was] "some evidence tending to show the existence of the essential elements of the defense," discriminatory effect and discriminatory intent.

In this case we consider what evidence constitutes "some evidence tending to show the existence" of the discriminatory effect element. The

Court of Appeals held that a defendant may establish a colorable basis for discriminatory effect without evidence that the Government has failed to prosecute others who are similarly situated to the defendant. We think it was mistaken in this view. The vast majority of the Courts of Appeals require the defendant to produce some evidence that similarly situated defendants of other races could have been prosecuted, but were not, and this requirement is consistent with our equal protection case law. As the three-judge panel explained, " '[s]elective prosecution' implies that a selection has taken place."

The Court of Appeals reached its decision in part because it started "with the presumption that people of *all* races commit *all* types of crimes—not with the premise that any type of crime is the exclusive province of any particular racial or ethnic group." It cited no authority for this proposition, which seems contradicted by the most recent statistics of the United States Sentencing Commission. Those statistics show that: More than 90% of the persons sentenced in 1994 for crack cocaine trafficking were black; 93.4% of convicted LSD dealers were white; and 91% of those convicted for pornography or prostitution were white. Presumptions at war with presumably reliable statistics have no proper place in the analysis of this issue.

The Court of Appeals also expressed concern about the "evidentiary obstacles defendants face." But all of its sister Circuits that have confronted the issue have required that defendants produce some evidence of differential treatment of similarly situated members of other races or protected classes. In the present case, if the claim of selective prosecution were well founded, it should not have been an insuperable task to prove that persons of other races were being treated differently than respondents. For instance, respondents could have investigated whether similarly situated persons of other races were prosecuted by the State of California, were known to federal law enforcement officers, but were not prosecuted in federal court. We think the required threshold—a credible showing of different treatment of similarly situated persons—adequately balances the Government's interest in vigorous prosecution and the defendant's interest in avoiding selective prosecution.

In the case before us, respondents' "study" did not constitute "some evidence tending to show the existence of the essential elements of" a selective-prosecution claim. The study failed to identify individuals who were not black, could have been prosecuted for the offenses for which respondents were charged, but were not so prosecuted. This omission was not remedied by respondents' evidence in opposition to the Government's motion for reconsideration. The newspaper article, which discussed the discriminatory effect of federal drug sentencing laws, was not relevant to an allegation of discrimination in decisions to prosecute. Respondents' affidavits, which recounted one attorney's conversation with a drug treatment center employee and the experience of another attorney defending drug prosecutions in state court, recounted hearsay and reported personal conclusions based on anecdotal evidence. The judgment of the Court of Appeals is therefore reversed, and the case is remanded for proceedings consistent with this opinion. * * *

[The opinions of JUSTICE SOUTER, concurring; JUSTICE GINSBURG, concurring; and JUSTICE BREYER, concurring in part and concurring in the judgment, are omitted.]

JUSTICE STEVENS, dissenting.

Federal prosecutors are respected members of a respected profession. Despite an occasional misstep, the excellence of their work abundantly justifies the presumption that "they have properly discharged their official duties." Nevertheless, the possibility that political or racial animosity may infect a decision to institute criminal proceedings cannot be ignored. For that reason, it has long been settled that the prosecutor's broad discretion to determine when criminal charges should be filed is not completely unbridled. * * *

The Court correctly concludes that in this case the facts presented to the District Court in support of respondents' claim that they had been singled out for prosecution because of their race were not sufficient to prove that defense. Moreover, I agree with the Court that their showing was not strong enough to give them a *right* to discovery, either under Rule 16 or under the District Court's inherent power to order discovery in appropriate circumstances. Like Chief Judge Wallace of the Court of Appeals, however, I am persuaded that the District Judge did not abuse her discretion when she concluded that the factual showing was sufficiently disturbing to require some response from the United States Attorney's Office. Perhaps the discovery order was broader than necessary, but I cannot agree with the Court's apparent conclusion that no inquiry was permissible.

The District Judge's order should be evaluated in light of three circumstances that underscore the need for judicial vigilance over certain types of drug prosecutions. First, the Anti-Drug Abuse Act of 1986 and subsequent legislation established a regime of extremely high penalties for the possession and distribution of so-called "crack" cocaine. Those provisions treat one gram of crack as the equivalent of 100 grams of powder cocaine. * * * These penalties result in sentences for crack offenders that average three to eight times longer than sentences for comparable powder offenders.

Second, the disparity between the treatment of crack cocaine and powder cocaine is matched by the disparity between the severity of the punishment imposed by federal law and that imposed by state law for the same conduct. * * * For example, if respondent Hampton is found guilty, his federal sentence might be as long as a mandatory life term. Had he been tried in state court, his sentence could have been as short as 12 years, less worktime credits of half that amount.

Finally, it is undisputed that the brunt of the elevated federal penalties falls heavily on blacks. While 65% of the persons who have used crack are white, in 1993 they represented only 4% of the federal offenders convicted of trafficking in crack. Eighty-eight percent of such defendants were black. During the first 18 months of full guideline implementation, the sentencing disparity between black and white defendants grew from preguideline levels: blacks on average received sentences over 40% longer than whites. Those figures represent a major threat to the integrity of federal sentencing reform, whose main purpose was the elimination of disparity (especially racial) in sentencing. The Sentencing Commission acknowledges that the heightened crack penalties are a "primary cause of the growing disparity between sentences for Black and White federal defendants."

The extraordinary severity of the imposed penalties and the troubling racial patterns of enforcement give rise to a special concern about the fairness of charging practices for crack offenses. Evidence tending to prove that black defendants charged with distribution of crack in the Central District of California are prosecuted in federal court, whereas members of other races charged with similar offenses are prosecuted in state court, warrants close scrutiny by the federal judges in that District. In my view, the District Judge, who has sat on both the federal and the state benches in Los Angeles, acted well within her discretion to call for the development of facts that would demonstrate what standards, if any, governed the choice of forum where similarly situated offenders are prosecuted. * * *

Even if respondents failed to carry their burden of showing that there were individuals who were not black but who could have been prosecuted in federal court for the same offenses, it does not follow that the District Court abused its discretion in ordering discovery. There can be no doubt that such individuals exist, and indeed the Government has never denied the same. In those circumstances, I fail to see why the District Court was unable to take judicial notice of this obvious fact and demand information from the Government's files to support or refute respondents' evidence. The presumption that some whites are prosecuted in state court is not "contradicted" by the statistics the majority cites, which show only that high percentages of blacks are *convicted* of certain federal crimes, while high percentages of whites are convicted of other federal crimes. Those figures are entirely consistent with the allegation of selective prosecution. The relevant comparison, rather, would be with the percentages of blacks and whites who *commit* those crimes. But, as discussed above, in the case of crack far greater numbers of whites are believed guilty of using the substance. The District Court, therefore, was entitled to find the evidence before her significant and to require some explanation from the Government. * * *

NOTES AND QUESTIONS

1.   Does the dissent or majority get the better of the statistical argument—*i.e.*, determining the proper inference to draw from statistics about the racial composition of defendants convicted of various federal crimes?

2.   *The Berk study*. Both the majority and the dissent appear to assume that no study had compared California state prosecution of crack cocaine offenses with federal prosecution, but that assumption turns out to be false. In 1993, three years prior to *Armstrong*, UCLA professor Richard Berk conducted, with Alec Campbell, a study of 8,000 state cases involving crack cocaine and then compared those prosecutions to forty-three federal cases prosecuted in the Central District of California. Because the state offenses are similar to 21 U.S. §§ 841 and 846, Berk assumed that the race of defendants in the state system should mirror that in the federal system. But the data showed a statistically significant higher percentage of black defendants in federal (83%) than in state (53%) cases. The balance of the state defendants were largely Hispanic. In a stark contrast, only 3% of the defendants in state cases, and zero in federal cases, were white. Richard Berk & Alec Campbell, *Preliminary Data on Race and Crack Charging Practices in Los Angeles*, 6 Federal Sentencing Reporter, Number 1, July/August 1993.

A federal district judge found the Berk study sufficient evidence to compel discovery in United States v. Turner, 901 F.Supp. 1491 (C.D. Ca. 1995) (decided the year before the Supreme Court decided *Armstrong*). As in *Armstrong*, the government refused to comply, and the judge dismissed the indictments. But the Ninth Circuit reversed and reinstated the indictments in a case decided after *Armstrong*. United States v. Turner, 104 F.3d 1180 (9th Cir. 1997).

The Berk study suffers from three methodological problems. First, the federal sample was only forty-three cases. Second, the number of whites prosecuted in state cases, 3%, was so low that a pattern of discrimination between state and federal prosecutions is not obvious. While the difference between 3% and 0% could be statistically significant (and Berk concluded that it was), to a non-statistician it might seem that the state numbers actually support the majority's speculation in *Armstrong* that perhaps whites just don't commit this particular crime often enough to matter when looking for patterns of prosecution. Third, regardless of how similar are the state and federal statutory offenses, *violators* are not necessarily the same. The government claimed in *Turner* that the sellers it pursued were those in gangs who sold large quantities of crack. The Berk study did not control for this variable. The Ninth Circuit seemed to find this failing the most serious as it applied the *Armstrong* requirement of "some evidence that similarly situated defendants of other races could have been prosecuted, but were not":

> The defendants have shown no more than the consequences of the investigation of violent street gangs, not that they were targeted because of race. That such gangs should be targeted is a neutral, nonracial law enforcement decision; the distribution of cocaine by gang members inclined to violence makes the distribution more heinous and more dangerous than the single sale of cocaine by individuals.

3.　　Think back to the Chapter 1 discussion of the norms that animate the criminal process—accuracy of outcomes, efficiency in reaching large numbers of outcomes, fairness to defendants as the process unfolds, and limiting the power of government to intrude on particular spheres of our privacy or autonomy. Which of these norms best explains the majority in *Armstrong*? Which best explains the dissent?

4.　　*The Court unanimously affirms Armstrong.* The broad discretion given prosecutors is not limitless, of course. Even *Armstrong* concedes that, with the right empirical evidence, a claim of discriminatory prosecution can prevail. Indeed, the Sixth Circuit held that a defendant presented sufficient evidence of racial discrimination in whether to seek the death penalty to require discovery on that issue. In United States v. Bass, 266 F.3d 532 (6th Cir. 2001), the Court of Appeals concluded that

> the evidence shows that although whites make up the majority of all federal prisoners, they are only one-fifth of those charged by the United States with death-eligible offenses. The United States charges blacks with a death-eligible offense more than twice as often as it charges whites. * * * Among death penalty defendants, the United States enters plea bargains with whites almost twice as often as it does with blacks. * * * [T]he statistics presented by Bass constitute sufficient evidence of a discriminatory effect to warrant further discovery as a matter of law.

In a per curiam opinion, a unanimous Supreme Court reversed the Sixth Circuit. "[B]ecause respondent failed to submit relevant evidence that similarly situated persons were treated differently, he was not entitled to discovery." United States v. Bass, 536 U.S. 862, 122 S.Ct. 2389, 153 L.Ed.2d 769 (2002). The Court concluded that "raw statistics regarding overall charges say nothing about charges brought against *similarly situated defendants.*"

BLACKLEDGE V. PERRY

Supreme Court of the United States, 1974.
417 U.S. 21, 94 S.Ct. 2098, 40 L.Ed.2d 628.

MR. JUSTICE STEWART delivered the opinion of the Court [joined by CHIEF JUSTICE BURGER, and JUSTICES DOUGLAS, BRENNAN, WHITE, MARSHALL, and BLACKMUN].

While serving a term of imprisonment in a North Carolina penitentiary, the respondent Perry became involved in an altercation with another inmate. A warrant issued, charging Perry with the misdemeanor of assault with a deadly weapon. Under North Carolina law, the District Court Division of the General Court of Justice has exclusive jurisdiction for the trial of misdemeanors. Following a trial without a jury in the District Court of Northampton County, Perry was convicted of this misdemeanor and given a six-month sentence, to be served after completion of the prison term he was then serving.

Perry then filed a notice of appeal to the Northampton County Superior Court. Under North Carolina law, a person convicted in the District Court has a right to a trial *de novo* in the Superior Court. The right to trial *de novo* is absolute, there being no need for the appellant to allege error in the original proceeding. When an appeal is taken, the statutory scheme provides that the slate is wiped clean; the prior conviction is annulled, and the prosecution and the defense begin anew in the Superior Court.

After the filing of the notice of appeal, but prior to the respondent's appearance for trial *de novo* in the Superior Court, the prosecutor obtained an indictment from a grand jury, charging Perry with the felony of assault with a deadly weapon with intent to kill and inflict serious bodily injury. The indictment covered the same conduct for which Perry had been tried and convicted in the District Court. Perry entered a plea of guilty to the indictment in the Superior Court, and was sentenced to a term of five to seven years in the penitentiary, to be served concurrently with the identical prison sentence he was then serving. * * *

I

* * * Perry * * * urges that the indictment on the felony charge constituted a penalty for his exercising his statutory right to appeal, and thus contravened the Due Process Clause of the Fourteenth Amendment. * * *

Perry's due process arguments are derived substantially from *North Carolina v. Pearce*, [p. 1464], and its progeny. In *Pearce*, the Court considered the constitutional problems presented when, following a successful appeal and reconviction, a criminal defendant was subjected to a greater punishment than that imposed at the first trial. While we concluded that such a harsher sentence was not absolutely precluded by either the Double Jeopardy or Due Process Clause, we emphasized that "imposition of a penalty upon the defendant for having successfully pursued a statutory right of appeal or collateral remedy would be * * * a violation of due process of law." * * *

The lesson that emerges from *Pearce* [and its progeny] is that the Due Process Clause is not offended by all possibilities of increased punishment upon retrial after appeal, but only by those that pose a realistic likelihood of "vindictiveness." Unlike the circumstances presented by those cases, however, in the situation here the central figure is not the judge or the jury, but the prosecutor. The question is whether the opportunities for vindictiveness in this situation are such as to impel the conclusion that due process of law requires a rule analogous to that of the *Pearce* case. We conclude that the answer must be in the affirmative.

A prosecutor clearly has a considerable stake in discouraging convicted misdemeanants from appealing and thus obtaining a trial *de novo* in the Superior Court, since such an appeal will clearly require increased expenditures of prosecutorial resources before the defendant's conviction becomes final, and may even result in a formerly convicted defendant's going free. And, if the prosecutor has the means readily at hand to discourage such appeals—by "upping the ante" through a felony indictment whenever a convicted misdemeanant pursues his statutory appellate remedy—the State can insure that only the most hardy defendants will brave the hazards of a *de novo* trial.

There is, of course, no evidence that the prosecutor in this case acted in bad faith or maliciously in seeking a felony indictment against Perry. The rationale of our judgment in the *Pearce* case, however, was not grounded upon the proposition that actual retaliatory motivation must inevitably exist. Rather, we emphasized that "since the fear of such vindictiveness may unconstitutionally deter a defendant's exercise of the right to appeal or collaterally attack his first conviction, due process also requires that a defendant be freed of apprehension of such a retaliatory motivation on the part of the sentencing judge." We think it clear that the same considerations apply here. A person convicted of an offense is entitled to pursue his statutory right to a trial *de novo*, without apprehension that the State will retaliate by substituting a more serious charge for the original one, thus subjecting him to a significantly increased potential period of incarceration.

Due process of law requires that such a potential for vindictiveness must not enter into North Carolina's two-tiered appellate process. We hold, therefore, that it was not constitutionally permissible for the State to respond to Perry's invocation of his statutory right to appeal by

bringing a more serious charge against him prior to the trial *de novo*.[7]
* * *

MR. JUSTICE REHNQUIST, dissenting [joined in part by Justice POWELL].

I would find it more difficult than the Court apparently does in Part I of its opinion to conclude that the very bringing of more serious charges against respondent following his request for a trial de novo violated due process as defined in *North Carolina v. Pearce*. Still more importantly, I believe the Court's conclusion that respondent may assert the Court's new-found *Pearce* claim in this federal habeas action, despite his plea of guilty to the charges brought after his invocation of his statutory right to a trial de novo, marks an unwarranted departure from the principles we have recently enunciated [about the various rights that a guilty plea waives; see p. 1195, Note 2, Eds.]. * * *

NOTES AND QUESTIONS

1. *What prosecutorial conduct triggers the Perry presumption of vindictiveness?* The presumption might apply every time prosecutors increase a charge previously made after a defendant exercises a right that burdens the prosecution. But the Court rejected that reading in United States v. Goodwin, 457 U.S. 368, 102 S.Ct. 2485, 73 L.Ed.2d 74 (1982), concluding that pre-trial decisions to increase charges are qualitatively different from post-conviction decisions. The Court reasoned:

> In the course of preparing a case for trial, the prosecutor may uncover additional information that suggests a basis for further prosecution or he simply may come to realize that information possessed by the State has a broader significance. At this stage of the proceedings, the prosecutor's assessment of the proper extent of prosecution may not have crystallized. In contrast, once a trial begins—and certainly by the time a conviction has been obtained— it is much more likely that the State has discovered and assessed all of the information against an accused and has made a determination, on the basis of that information, of the extent to which he should be prosecuted. Thus, a change in the charging decision made after an initial trial is completed is much more likely to be improperly motivated than is a pretrial decision.

The Court concluded that a "prosecutor should remain free before trial to exercise the broad discretion entrusted to him to determine the extent of the societal interest in prosecution. An initial decision should not freeze future conduct." The Court thus declined to apply the *Pearce* presumption in

---

[7] This would clearly be a different case if the State had shown that it was impossible to proceed on the more serious charge at the outset, as in *Diaz v. United States*, 223 U.S. 442, 32 S.Ct. 250, 56 L.Ed. 500 (1912). In that case the defendant was originally tried and convicted of assault and battery. Subsequent to the original trial, the assault victim died, and the defendant was then tried and convicted for homicide. Obviously, it would not have been possible for the authorities in *Diaz* to have originally proceeded against the defendant on the more serious charge, since the crime of homicide was not complete until after the victim's death.

Goodwin's case. *Goodwin* makes clear that a prosecutor's decision to increase charges will stand except when (1) there is proof of actual vindictiveness, or (2) the increase occurs after a defendant has acted to reverse a conviction.

2.   *And why would prosecutors act in vindictive ways?* Despite the ethical injunction to "seek justice," prosecutors are of course trained advocates who wish to win convictions against defendants they believe to be guilty. But why be vindictive when a defendant exercises a right? One commentator uses game theory to seek to understand this phenomenon. Prosecutors and defense counsel alike are better served by a cooperative approach. One way to seek to enforce cooperation in future cases is for prosecutors to act vindictively when defense counsel "defect" from the game by not cooperating. But "the prosecutor can ensure the credibility of his threat only by defecting whenever the defense attorney defects—and this result is a paradigmatic case of prosecutorial vindictiveness, of 'punishing a person because he has done what the law plainly allows him to do.'" Note, *Breathing New Life Into Prosecutorial Vindictiveness Doctrine*, 114 Harv. L. Rev. 2074, 2082–84 (2001).

B. JUDICIAL SCREENING OF CASES: THE PRELIMINARY HEARING

States vary widely in structuring the case screening process. As we saw in the last chapter, states provide various mechanisms for determining whether to hold a defendant in jail pending trial. If a defendant is held in jail more than forty-eight hours, the Fourth Amendment requires a judicial finding of probable cause to believe that the defendant committed the crime. County of Riverside v. McLaughlin, 500 U.S. 44, 111 S.Ct. 1661, 114 L.Ed.2d 49 (1991); Gerstein v. Pugh, 420 U.S. 103, 95 S.Ct. 854, 43 L.Ed.2d 54 (1975) (see p. 213, Note 4). This determination is sometimes described as a "*Gerstein* hearing," though the terminology is misleading. All the Fourth Amendment requires is a judicial determination of probable cause, which can be *ex parte*, like the magistrate's decision to issue search or arrest warrants.

The processing of federal cases is governed by the Federal Rules of Criminal Procedure. The first adversarial testing of the federal government's case is the preliminary hearing; see Fed. R. Crim. P. 5.1. Many states also require a preliminary hearing.

COLEMAN V. ALABAMA
Supreme Court of the United States, 1970.
399 U.S. 1, 90 S.Ct. 1999, 26 L.Ed.2d 387.

MR. JUSTICE BRENNAN announced the judgment of the Court and delivered the following opinion [joined in whole or in part by JUSTICES BLACK, DOUGLAS, HARLAN, WHITE, and MARSHALL]

Petitioners were convicted in an Alabama Circuit Court of assault with intent to murder in the shooting of one Reynolds after he and his wife parked their car on an Alabama highway to change a flat tire. * * *

Petitioners * * * argue that the preliminary hearing prior to their indictment was a "critical stage" of the prosecution and that Alabama's failure to provide them with appointed counsel at the hearing therefore unconstitutionally denied them the assistance of counsel. * * *

II

This Court has held that a person accused of crime "requires the guiding hand of counsel at every step in the proceedings against him," and that that constitutional principle is not limited to the presence of counsel at trial. "It is central to that principle that in addition to counsel's presence at trial, the accused is guaranteed that he need not stand alone against the State at any stage of the prosecution, formal or informal, in court or out, where counsel's absence might derogate from the accused's right to a fair trial." Accordingly, "the principle of *Powell v. Alabama* [p. 25] and succeeding cases requires that we scrutinize *any* pretrial confrontation of the accused to determine whether the presence of his counsel is necessary to preserve the defendant's basic right to a fair trial as affected by his right meaningfully to cross-examine the witnesses against him and to have effective assistance of counsel at the trial itself. It calls upon us to analyze whether potential substantial prejudice to defendant's rights inheres in the particular confrontation and the ability of counsel to help avoid that prejudice." Applying this test, the Court has held that "critical stages" include the pretrial type of arraignment where certain rights may be sacrificed or lost, and the pretrial lineup * * * .

The preliminary hearing is not a required step in an Alabama prosecution. The prosecutor may seek an indictment directly from the grand jury without a preliminary hearing. The opinion of the Alabama Court of Appeals in this case instructs us that under Alabama law the sole purposes of a preliminary hearing are to determine whether there is sufficient evidence against the accused to warrant presenting his case to the grand jury and, if so, to fix bail if the offense is bailable. The court continued:

> "At the preliminary hearing * * * the accused is not required to advance any defenses, and failure to do so does not preclude him from availing himself of every defense he may have upon the trial of the case. Also *Pointer v. State of Texas* [380 U.S. 400, 85 S.Ct. 1065, 13 L.Ed.2d 923 (1965)] bars the admission of testimony given at a pretrial proceeding where the accused did not have the benefit of cross-examination by and through counsel. Thus, nothing occurring at the preliminary hearing in

absence of counsel can substantially prejudice the rights of the accused on trial."

This Court is of course bound by this construction of the governing Alabama law. However, from the fact that in cases where the accused has no lawyer at the hearing the Alabama courts prohibit the State's use at trial of anything that occurred at the hearing, it does not follow that the Alabama preliminary hearing is not a "critical stage" of the State's criminal process. The determination whether the hearing is a "critical stage" requiring the provision of counsel depends, as noted, upon an analysis "whether potential substantial prejudice to defendant's rights inheres in the * * * confrontation and the ability of counsel to help avoid that prejudice." Plainly the guiding hand of counsel at the preliminary hearing is essential to protect the indigent accused against an erroneous or improper prosecution. First, the lawyer's skilled examination and cross-examination of witnesses may expose fatal weaknesses in the State's case that may lead the magistrate to refuse to bind the accused over. Second, in any event, the skilled interrogation of witnesses by an experienced lawyer can fashion a vital impeachment tool for use in cross-examination of the State's witnesses at the trial, or preserve testimony favorable to the accused of a witness who does not appear at the trial. Third, trained counsel can more effectively discover the case the State has against his client and make possible the preparation of a proper defense to meet that case at the trial. Fourth, counsel can also be influential at the preliminary hearing in making effective arguments for the accused on such matters as the necessity for an early psychiatric examination or bail.

The inability of the indigent accused on his own to realize these advantages of a lawyer's assistance compels the conclusion that the Alabama preliminary hearing is a "critical stage" of the State's criminal process at which the accused is "as much entitled to such aid [of counsel] * * * as at the trial itself."

III

There remains, then, the question of the relief to which petitioners are entitled. The trial transcript indicates that the prohibition against use by the State at trial of anything that occurred at the preliminary hearing was scrupulously observed. But on the record it cannot be said whether or not petitioners were otherwise prejudiced by the absence of counsel at the preliminary hearing. That inquiry in the first instance should more properly be made by the Alabama courts. The test to be applied is whether the denial of counsel at the preliminary hearing was harmless error under *Chapman v. California*, 386 U.S. 18, 87 S.Ct. 824, 17 L.Ed.2d 705 (1967).

We accordingly vacate the petitioners' convictions and remand the case to the Alabama courts for such proceedings not inconsistent with this opinion as they may deem appropriate to determine whether such denial of counsel was harmless error, and therefore whether the convictions should be reinstated or a new trial ordered. * * *

MR. JUSTICE BLACKMUN took no part in the consideration or decision of this case.

MR. JUSTICE BLACK, concurring.

I wholeheartedly agree * * * that an accused has a constitutional right to the assistance of counsel at the preliminary hearing which Alabama grants criminal defendants. The purpose of the preliminary hearing in Alabama is to determine whether an offense has been committed and, if so, whether there is probable cause for charging the defendant with that offense. If the magistrate finds that there is probable cause for charging the defendant with the offense, the defendant must, under Alabama law, be either incarcerated or admitted to bail. In the absence of such a finding of probable cause, the defendant must be released from custody. The preliminary hearing is therefore a definite part or stage of a criminal prosecution in Alabama, and the plain language of the Sixth Amendment requires that "[i]n all criminal prosecutions, the accused shall enjoy the right * * * to have the Assistance of Counsel for his defence." Moreover, every attorney with experience in representing criminal defendants in a State which has a preliminary hearing similar to Alabama's knows—sometimes from sad experience—that adequate representation requires that counsel be present at the preliminary hearing to protect the interests of his client. * * *

[Omitted are the opinions of JUSTICE DOUGLAS, concurring; JUSTICE WHITE, concurring; JUSTICE HARLAN, concurring in part and dissenting in part; and CHIEF JUSTICE BURGER, dissenting.]

MR. JUSTICE STEWART, with whom THE CHIEF JUSTICE [BURGER] joins, dissenting. * * *

* * * [T]he prevailing opinion holds today that the Constitution required Alabama to provide a lawyer for the petitioners at their preliminary hearing, not so much, it seems, to assure a fair trial as to assure a fair preliminary hearing. A lawyer at the preliminary hearing, the opinion says, might have led the magistrate to "refuse to bind the accused over." Or a lawyer might have made "effective arguments for the accused on such matters as the necessity for an early psychiatric examination or bail."

If *those* are the reasons a lawyer must be provided, then the most elementary logic requires that a new preliminary hearing must now be held, with counsel made available to the petitioners. In order to provide such relief, it would, of course, be necessary not only to set aside these convictions, but also to set aside the grand jury indictments, and the magistrate's orders fixing bail and binding over the petitioners. Since the petitioners have now been found by a jury in a constitutional trial to be guilty beyond a reasonable doubt, the prevailing opinion understandably boggles at these logical consequences of the reasoning therein. It refrains, in short, from now turning back the clock by ordering a new preliminary hearing to determine all over again whether there is sufficient evidence against the accused to present their case to a grand jury. Instead, the Court sets aside these convictions and remands the case for determination "whether the convictions should be reinstated or a new trial ordered," and this action seems to me * * * quixotic. * * *

NOTES AND QUESTIONS

1. *Remedy.* The majority opinion certainly seems compelling, yet it does have a weak spot. Isn't Justice Stewart right in dissent that the majority undermines its own logic by refusing to order the State to start Coleman's case over again? Instead, the Court ordered a rehearing to determine whether the lack of counsel at the preliminary hearing was harmless beyond a reasonable doubt. (We will study the harmless error doctrine in Chapter 19.) In *Coleman*, the error is the absence of a lawyer who might have learned something about the case that would have proven helpful. This kind of counterfactual, in which a court must decide what a lawyer might have done, may be almost impossible to perform without an implicit presumption about the value of lawyers at the preliminary hearing. Are there hints in the majority opinion about the appropriate presumption in the *Coleman* context? The remedy part of *Coleman* attracted only five votes.

After the case came back to it on remand, the Alabama Court of Criminal Appeals remanded to the trial court for "proceedings consistent with the opinion of" the Supreme Court. Coleman v. State, 46 Ala. App. 737 (Ala. Ct. Crim. App. 1970) (per curiam). One judge dissented on the ground "that the object of remand as stated by the opinion of Brennan, J., is infeasible."

2. Once again, the debate between majority and dissent can be framed in terms of fairness, accuracy, and efficiency, though the matter is more complex in *Coleman* than when the right to counsel at trial is the issue. Do you see the difference?

The Court ruled in 1913 that states are not constitutionally required to provide either a preliminary hearing or a grand jury indictment. Lem Woon v. Oregon, 229 U.S. 586, 33 S.Ct. 783, 57 L.Ed. 1340 (1913). Thus, states may authorize a procedure in which defendants are brought to trial on nothing more than the prosecutor's official oath that probable cause exists. Does *Lem Woon* help illuminate how the Court views the structural role of the preliminary hearing?

Few *Coleman* cases exist, which indicates that states routinely provide indigent defendants with counsel for preliminary hearings. This may manifest (1) general agreement that defendants should be represented by counsel at preliminary hearings; (2) fear that courts would routinely overturn convictions tainted by a *Coleman* violation; or (3) realization that some adversarial testing of the prosecution case can be helpful to the State. With regard to the latter point, prosecutors can get an early indication of how effectively their witnesses will testify. This knowledge makes the prosecutor a more savvy bargainer during plea negotiations.

3.   You decide to proceed with charges against the police officer who shot the twelve-year-old (p. 889). How would you proceed to prove probable cause at a preliminary hearing? What witnesses would you call? Would you show the surveillance video of the shooting?

4.   *Uses of preliminary hearing testimony.* Do you see the advantage of having a lawyer at the preliminary hearing to fashion a potential impeachment tool and preserve "testimony favorable to the accused of a witness who does not appear at the trial"? It takes careful, exacting cross-examination in most cases to develop testimony that can be helpful to the defendant at trial.

5.   Suppose you represent a rape defendant whose defense is consent. At the preliminary hearing, the victim testifies to the intercourse and her lack of consent. She resists your initial efforts to undermine her testimony on the consent point. You then ask, "Isn't it true that you believe in witches and that you practice witchcraft?" The prosecutor objects. The judge refuses to rule on the objection, instead declaring that the State has already shown probable cause to believe that a rape occurred. Do you see why this is a plausible ruling? Should the judge be permitted to terminate the hearing in this fashion? See Myers v. Commonwealth, 363 Mass. 843, 298 N.E.2d 819 (1973).

Same hypothetical but this time the judge listens to the witchcraft testimony and finds a lack of probable cause because he finds the victim not to be a credible witness. Is this an appropriate task for the preliminary hearing judge? Why or why not? See Hunter v. District Court, 190 Colo. 48, 543 P.2d 1265 (1975).

6.   The prosecutor is extremely unlikely to lose a preliminary hearing. An experienced defense lawyer calculated "the odds of a magistrate throwing a case out are like 1,000 to 1." Roy B. Flemming, *Elements of the Defense Attorney's Craft: An Adaptive Expectations Model of the Preliminary Hearing Decision*, 8 Law & Policy 33, 40 (1986). Thus, there is little to gain in most cases from presenting a defense which gives the prosecutor a preview of the defense strategy. But the prosecutor is forced to put on enough witnesses to demonstrate probable cause, and these witnesses can be extensively cross-examined, both about their personal knowledge of the case, and about the existence of other evidence (other witnesses and physical evidence). For example, a police officer who testifies about something the defendant said can be questioned about witnesses to whom the officer spoke, or even about the existence of witnesses or evidence that she has not directly seen. Preliminary

hearing judges vary greatly in how much cross-examination they will permit, but a defense lawyer gave the following advice to a researcher about examining witnesses at a preliminary hearing:

> Prepare every possible kind of question you can ask, and get it all down in black and white. Because what happens at a preliminary hearing is people go and it's not a big pressure situation. And they relax and they slip. * * * [Y]ou get them to admit certain things at a hearing that would never generally come out in the courtroom. * * * I can tell you right now, that has worked so many times to my clients' advantage, it's not funny.

Flemming, *supra*, at 43.

7. *Losing but not really.* In federal court, the prosecutor who loses the 1 in 1,000 preliminary hearing can simply file another charge and begin again. See Fed. R. Crim. P. 5.1(f). This is true as well in most states. And it is also true for the rare prosecutor who cannot obtain an indictment from a grand jury. As a practical matter, of course, few prosecutors will begin again in the face of a finding of no probable cause, unless they uncover additional evidence.

8. As we have seen, one value of a preliminary hearing is informal discovery of the state's case. In states that do not provide a preliminary hearing, this informal discovery is simply unavailable. And even in states that offer a preliminary hearing, defendants in some jurisdictions often waive the preliminary hearing. Flemming, Note 7, at 38, tbl. 2 (showing 61% waiver in one county, between 27% and 39% in four counties, and from 0.7% to 7.3% in four counties). Can you think of any explanation for this finding? Professor Anthony Amsterdam has cogently noted that defense counsel may frequently "find that s/he is working at cross-purposes in seeking to discover and to lay a foundation for impeachment simultaneously." Anthony Amsterdam, Trial Manual for the Defense of Criminal Cases § 139 (5th ed. 1989). For example, a good discovery cross-examination might be "then what did you see?" A good impeachment foundation might be "When you looked up, it was too dark to see clearly, wasn't it?" While this observation highlights the difficulty of conducting a good defense at a preliminary hearing, it does not suggest waiving the entire hearing.

One defense lawyer counsels: "Absolutely never waive a preliminary hearing unless there's some extreme circumstances, where the writing is on the wall, open and shut. [A preliminary hearing is] only to your client's benefit because you've got everything to gain and nothing to lose." Flemming, Note 7, at 40.

C. GRAND JURY SCREENING OF CASES

Welcome to the Grand Jury Venire

It is a pleasure to welcome you on behalf of the judges of the United States District Court for New Jersey as potential members of the grand jury for the period August 3, 2009 to February 3, 2011.

Although my welcoming remarks are intended for all, only twenty-three of you, plus ten alternates, will be selected to form this new grand jury. Also, although your term will be for the next eighteen months, you will sit as a jury from time to time only when called on by the office of the U.S. attorney. I cannot tell you in advance how much time will be involved, but normally you can expect to be called an average of four days a month during your term of office. * * *

Just as the English grand jury was independent of the king, the federal grand jury under the United States Constitution is independent of the U.S. attorney, as well as other government lawyers. The grand jury is not an arm of the Federal Bureau of Investigation; it is not an arm of the Internal Revenue Service; it is not an arm of the U.S. attorney's office. While you would perform a disservice if you did not indict where the evidence justifies an indictment, you would violate your oath if you merely "rubber-stamped" indictments brought before you by the government representatives.

Grand jury selection and instructions, Federal Judge's Benchbook, Chapter 7.04 (1996 with March 2000 revisions) (Venue and dates added by eds.).

Introductory Comment

We divide the study of the grand jury into two parts because it has two very different functions. In the next chapter, we will examine the "sword" function of the grand jury—how prosecutors use grand juries to gather evidence and to investigate crime. When the grand jury is operating as a "sword," it is effectively an adjunct to the prosecutor and serves the interests of the executive branch. This was the historical origin of the grand jury. In 1166 Henry II ordered that grand juries be assembled in the local villages for the purpose of ferreting out crime, to report whether "there be any man who is accused or generally suspected of being a robber or murderer or thief." Assize of Clarendon § 1.

As the grand jury evolved, however, it occasionally took on another function, that of a "shield" to keep the executive from harassing citizens with ill-founded prosecutions. The grand jury performed this function perhaps most notably prior to the Revolutionary War. As the colonists grew weary of British rule, they began to challenge the authority of the royal governors. In 1734, John Peter Zenger published a newspaper critical of New York Governor William Cosby. The governor charged him with the common law crime of "seditious libel"—publishing untrue material that might lead to revolution. Three grand juries heard the case put forth by the king's prosecutors. Each refused to indict. Ultimately, the governor filed a charge without getting an indictment. The trial jury acquitted Zenger. The governor's end run around the grand jury in Zenger's case was "a controversial move that further eroded popular support for the Governor's actions." Andrew D. Leipold, *Why Grand Juries Do Not (and Cannot) Protect the Accused*, 80 Cornell L. Rev. 260, 284 (1995).

The closer we got to the Revolution, the more the colonists violated British laws, particularly those involving taxes and customs duties. When royal prosecutors brought criminal charges against the colonists, the grand juries often refused to indict. For these relatively few years, the grand jury was viewed as a shield against the enforcement of arbitrary and oppressive laws that had been forced on the colonists. Little wonder, then, that the Framers included the grand jury right in the Fifth Amendment to our Constitution.

The rest of this chapter concerns the "shield" or screening function. Federal felony defendants have their cases screened by two quite different mechanisms—the magistrate who hears the preliminary hearing and the grand jury. See Fed. R. Crim. P. 5 & 6. The conceptual relationship between these screening mechanisms is unclear. Both require the government to make a threshold showing of probable cause that a crime has been committed and that the defendant is the one who committed the crime. Conceptually, the grand jury seems to add nothing. Indeed, it is one of only two criminal procedure rights not to have been made applicable to the states via incorporation in the due process clause. (The other is the right to bail.) The refusal of the Court to apply the right to a grand jury to the states may say much about the modern view of the relative unimportance of the grand jury as a screening mechanism.

The most colorful description of the lack of importance of the grand jury in screening cases was attributed to Sol Wachtler, former Chief Judge of the New York Court of Appeals. According to Wachtler, a grand jury would "indict a ham sandwich" if that's what a prosecutor wanted. Tom Wolfe, Bonfire of the Vanities 629 (Bantam ed., 1987). Or as a former prosecutor put it, "If you gave [grand jurors] a napkin, they'd sign it." Richard L. Braun, *The Grand Jury—Spirit of the Community?*, 15 Ariz. L. Rev. 893, 914–15 n.144 (1974). As you will see, federal prosecutors obtain indictments in 99.6% of their cases.

The other side of the coin is that grand juries are a convenient way to avoid having to proceed in cases where the prosecutor does not want to proceed but also does not want to explain his reasons to the victim or the victim's family. One of the casebook authors witnessed a preliminary hearing in which a thirty-year-old woman was charged with statutory rape of a sixteen-year-old male. The parents of the victim returned home early and caught the two in an act of consensual intercourse. The parents insisted that the prosecutor bring charges under the state sex-neutral rape law. Because the law was clear that it was a felony for an adult woman to have sex with a sixteen-year-old male, the preliminary hearing judge, with obvious reluctance, bound the defendant over to the grand jury. The grand jury failed to indict. So perhaps Wachtler's old saw should be amended: the prosecutor can get a grand jury to indict a ham sandwich, or *not* to indict a felon, whichever the prosecutor wishes. The point here is that the modern grand jury rarely serves as the shield that the Framers intended. It appears to function today largely as a tool for the prosecutor to screen cases as she wishes.

Grand juries recently failed to indict in cases where African-American suspects were shot and killed by white police officers. The deaths provoked outrage and, in the Michael Brown case in Baltimore, Maryland, riots and civil unrest that made order difficult to restore. Another high-profile case involved the chokehold death of Eric Garner, an African-American, at the hands of a New York City white police officer. The officers initially accosted Garner because they suspected him of selling loose cigarettes from packs without tax stamps. The failure of the grand juries to indict in these cases, despite intense public pressure, was itself controversial.

Finally, in the Tamir Rice case, from which we drew the hypothetical case that begins this chapter, the grand jury failed to indict. The prosecutors candidly admitted that they had recommended a no-true bill. In their view, the evidence was "indisputable" that the victim was reaching into his waistband for what appeared to be a real gun when the officer shot him. Patrick Cooley, "McGinty to meet with Cleveland area clergy following Tamir Rice grand jury decision," *cleveland.com*, January 3, 2016.

Many commentators have called for the abolition of the grand jury. No other country in the world uses grand juries. England, the country of origin, abolished it by Act of Parliament in 1933.

SUSAN W. BRENNER—THE VOICE OF THE COMMUNITY: A CASE FOR GRAND JURY INDEPENDENCE

3 Virginia Journal of Social Policy & Law 67 (1995), 83–85, 101–02, 121, 124, 130.

Except for the law governing privileges, federal grand juries operate unconstrained by the Federal Rules of Evidence. The states diverge over whether evidentiary constraints should apply in grand jury proceedings. A few apply certain rules of evidence, most often prohibiting prosecutors from presenting inadmissible hearsay in grand jury proceedings. Most states, however, impose few, if any, evidentiary restraints on grand jury proceedings, following federal practice. [Moreover,] federal grand juries can hear evidence that was obtained in violation of the Fourth Amendment's prohibition on unreasonable searches and seizures. Most states also allow their grand juries to consider evidence that was illegally obtained, but a few apply their own versions of the exclusionary rule to grand jury proceedings. * * *

Most states and the District of Columbia use grand juries to indict. Twenty-three states and the District of Columbia require an indictment to charge at least certain offenses. Like the federal system, these states generally require that an indictment be used to charge capital crimes and/or serious felonies, reserving other charging instruments, such as informations and complaints, for misdemeanors and minor felonies. Of the many states that make use of indictments optional, most permit charges for any offense to be brought either by indictment or information. As in the federal system, states that use an information instead of an indictment must provide an independent determination of probable cause made by a magistrate at a preliminary hearing. * * *

Although the federal system is constitutionally obliged to employ the indicting grand jury, the states are not. It is remarkable, therefore, that forty-eight states have retained the indicting grand jury despite concerted efforts to eliminate it in the nineteenth century. This persistence suggests that the institution contributes, or can contribute, something important to the criminal justice system. * * *

* * * [T]he major threat to a federal indicting grand jury's ability to exercise its own judgment comes from the control prosecutors exert over jurors. The best way to restore grand jurors' independence is, therefore, to diminish prosecutors' influence. Abolishing a federal prosecutor's role as the grand jury's legal advisor would go a long way toward accomplishing this goal, though it would also deprive grand jurors of necessary legal advice unless an alternative source is established. The ideal solution is to follow Hawaii's lead and provide federal grand juries with their own counsel. Statutes could create the office of "grand jury counsel" and specify the qualifications required of those who would fill this position.

The district court impaneling a grand jury could appoint counsel at the time the jurors are sworn. * * *

Without intervention, the federal indicting grand jury will become an ever more powerful tool of the prosecutors who dominate it. The history of the federal grand jury is the history of the voice of the prosecutor subtly but surely overwhelming the voice of the community. As the federal grand jury becomes the prosecutor's pawn, it moves further away from its intended function of injecting the community's notions of morality and justice into the charging process.

ANDREW D. LEIPOLD—WHY GRAND JURIES DO NOT (AND CANNOT) PROTECT THE ACCUSED

80 Cornell Law Review 260 (1995), 274–75, 294–95, 321–23.

Those who claim that grand juries fail to screen effectively often point to statistics to support this view. Most commonly, they note that an extremely high percentage of cases submitted to grand juries result in indictments. The numbers are impressive: during fiscal 1984, for example, federal grand juries returned 17,419 indictments and only sixty-eight no bills, an astounding 99.6% success rate. Statistics from other years are in accord. Even in the rare instances when the grand jury refused to indict, it is not clear that the jurors were rejecting the prosecutor's recommendation; in some of these cases even the prosecutor apparently agreed that a true bill should not be returned. For some critics these numbers are persuasive evidence of the grand jury's ineffectiveness.

Yet even brief reflection shows how unhelpful these figures are. That grand juries nearly always return true bills may indeed demonstrate that jurors simply approve whatever charges the government submits, but it could also show that grand juries are a great success. A review of the prosecutor's decisionmaking leading up to the request for an indictment shows why.

Federal prosecutors know that virtually all of their charging decisions must be approved by the grand jury. Thus, in deciding which charges to bring, the prosecutor must determine not only which accusations can be proven at trial, but also which accusations will result in an indictment. If we assume that prosecutors as a group will normally decline to present charges to a grand jury that they think will be rejected, we would expect that prosecutors would submit only those cases that are sufficiently strong to survive a grand jury's review. Thus, *regardless* of whether the grand jury is serving as an effective screen, we would expect a high percentage of the cases presented to lead to indictments. * * *

The barriers to a grand jury's ability to screen are not obvious, because its task seems so simple. Jurors listen to the prosecutor's case and then are asked to answer a single question: is there probable cause to believe that the suspect committed the specified crime?

Stated simply, grand jurors are not qualified to answer this question. Whether probable cause exists is ultimately a legal determination about the sufficiency of the evidence: whether the prosecutor put forth enough information to surpass the legal threshold established by the probable cause standard. In submitting a case to the grand jury we are asking nonlawyers with no experience in weighing evidence to decide whether a legal test is satisfied, and to do so after the only lawyer in the room, the prosecutor, has concluded that it has. Because jurors lack any experience or expertise in deciding whether probable cause exists, it becomes not only predictable but also logical that the jurors will return a true bill. This is not because they are a rubber stamp, but because they have no benchmark against which to weigh the evidence, and thus no rational basis for rejecting the prosecutor's recommendation to indict. * * *

The best reason for retaining the grand jury requirement has nothing to do with the desirability of the institution itself. The Bill of Rights has never been amended, with good reason. The principles and protections contained in the first ten amendments reflect many of our core beliefs about the relationship between state and citizen, beliefs that remain even when a particular amendment no longer seems as important. To change the Fifth Amendment would be to remove not only the grand jury requirement, but also the *idea* that pretrial screening of criminal charges is sufficiently important to warrant constitutional protection. Losing the idea of pretrial screening is more serious than losing the illusory protection of the grand jury, but the latter cannot be removed without undermining the former. * * *

This solution—the replacement of the grand jury with a preliminary hearing—is occasionally proposed, but it creates two problems. First, it fails to satisfy the Fifth Amendment. Second, it fails to achieve the goal of having a nongovernment actor review the charging decisions. * * *

The natural, but radical, implication of the desire for a decisionmaker with both expertise and independence from the government is to replace the grand jurors with lawyers who are randomly selected from the community. Lawyers generally have the expertise to assess the sufficiency of the evidence, thus making them qualified to screen the prosecutor's charging decisions. They also would not have ties to the government, and because they would hear only a limited number of cases, they would be less prone to treat cases as if they were on an assembly line. Moreover, there would be a decreased chance of prosecutor domination of the grand jury hearing, since lawyers as a group are normally less deferential to the judgment of others, particularly (although not exclusively) on legal matters.

The impediments to such a reform are large and obvious. Prosecutors would not like it because it would create a new barrier to obtaining a conviction. Lawyers would not like it because serving on grand juries would be burdensome and expensive. And citizens would almost certainly dislike the idea of replacing members of the community with members of the bar. The view, correct or not, that the criminal justice system was becoming further removed from the people it serves would strongly militate against such a change.

But while such a change is highly unlikely, it seems no more unlikely than any other significant reform that would allow the grand jury to effectively monitor the prosecutor's decisions. Nearly all reform proposals come at a high cost, either by making the grand jury process more closely resemble a trial—with the associated resource requirements—or by requiring a constitutional amendment, a move fraught with political and philosophical difficulties.

NOTES AND QUESTIONS

1.   Which writer, Professor Brenner or Professor Leipold, has a higher regard for what grand juries do? Do you favor any of the reforms discussed in these excerpts?

Hawaii's "independent counsel" rule is found it its state constitution:

Whenever a grand jury is impaneled, there shall be an independent counsel appointed as provided by law to advise the members of the grand jury regarding matters brought before it. Independent counsel shall be selected from among those persons licensed to practice law by the supreme court of the State and shall not be a public employee. The term and compensation for independent counsel shall be as provided by law. Haw. Const. art. I, § 11

2.   *What numbers tell us (or don't tell us).* Are you persuaded by Professor Leipold that the 99.6% success rate of federal prosecutors at the grand jury level is indicative of the care and attention they give their cases? Are you persuaded by Professor Brenner that the presence of the indicting grand jury in forty-eight states is evidence of its potential contribution to our criminal justice system?

3.   Professor Roger Fairfax rejects the idea that the grand jury should be taken away from the community, as recommended by Leipold:

The grand jury, by design, serves a structural role in our constitutional system as a check on the three branches of government and moderator of criminal law federalism. Given its characteristics, the grand jury is uniquely equipped to serve as a conduit for communication between the people and the governmental structure, as well as between the national government and local communities, on issues of criminal justice policy. The grand jury's robust discretion—its ability to determine the propriety of indictments on bases beyond sufficiency of the evidence—enhances this communicative function.

Roger A. Fairfax, Jr., *Grand Jury Discretion and Constitutional Design*, 93 Cornell L. Rev. 703, 762 (2008).

4.   *Selection of grand jurors.* Federal grand jurors are selected from the same lists that are used to generate the venire for trial juries: voter registration lists, property tax rolls, and lists of drivers' licenses. In a typical district, the court calls ninety prospective grand jurors and from that group selects a panel of twenty-three jurors and ten alternates. The alternates sit only if members of the grand jury are excused permanently. Because grand juries can continue for twenty-four months—see Fed. R. Crim. Pro. 6(g)—judges are more generous in dismissing jurors on grounds of inconvenience, though this, like all else, depends on the particular judge.

5.   *Functioning of grand juries.* Because grand jury proceedings are held in secret and the records are sealed, we know far less about grand juries than just about any other institution in the criminal process. To lessen the strain on the grand jurors, federal grand jurors generally meet only one day a week and require only 16 jurors to conduct business. By empaneling 23, the prosecutor protects against the grand jury not having sufficient numbers; up to seven can be absent and the grand jury can still continue its work. Nonetheless, given the length of service of some grand juries, the number of jurors present occasionally falls below 16, and the grand jury cannot conduct business on those days.[c]

6.   Assume you decide to seek a grand jury indictment in the police shooting of the 12-year-old black male. How would you present the case before the grand jury? What witnesses would you call? How might this presentation differ from your approach at the preliminary hearing?

7.   *Structural role.* What is the proper role of the grand jury in a structure that has a legislative branch that makes law, an executive branch that seeks to enforce those laws, and a judicial branch that hears cases? Does the grand jury exist to advance accuracy? Fairness? To limit government? Is it part of the judiciary? The executive? Who makes rules that govern grand jury procedures? Controversial answers can be found in the next case.

---

[c]   For the general information contained in Notes 4 & 5, we thank former Assistant United States Attorney Barry S. Pollack.

UNITED STATES V. WILLIAMS
Supreme Court of the United States, 1992.
504 U.S. 36, 112 S.Ct. 1735, 118 L.Ed.2d 352.

JUSTICE SCALIA delivered the opinion of the Court [joined by CHIEF JUSTICE REHNQUIST, and JUSTICES WHITE, KENNEDY, and SOUTER].

The question presented in this case is whether a district court may dismiss an otherwise valid indictment because the Government failed to disclose to the grand jury "substantial exculpatory evidence" in its possession.

I

On May 4, 1988, respondent John H. Williams, Jr., a Tulsa, Oklahoma, investor, was indicted by a federal grand jury on seven counts of "knowingly mak[ing] [a] false statement or report * * * for the purpose of influencing * * * the action [of a federally insured financial institution]," in violation of 18 U.S.C. § 1014. * * *

Shortly after arraignment, the District Court granted Williams' motion for disclosure of all exculpatory portions of the grand jury transcripts. Upon reviewing this material, Williams demanded that the District Court dismiss the indictment, alleging that the Government had failed to fulfill its obligation * * *, to present "substantial exculpatory evidence" to the grand jury. * * * This [evidence], he contended, belied an intent to mislead the banks, and thus directly negated an essential element of the charged offense.

[The District Court found] that the withheld evidence was "relevant to an essential element of the crime charged," created " 'a reasonable doubt about [respondent's] guilt,' " and thus "render[ed] the grand jury's decision to indict gravely suspect." [The Court of Appeals affirmed, finding] that the Government's behavior " 'substantially influence[d]' " the grand jury's decision to indict, or at the very least raised a " 'grave doubt that the decision to indict was free from such substantial influence.' " * * *

III

Respondent does not contend that the Fifth Amendment itself obliges the prosecutor to disclose substantial exculpatory evidence in his possession to the grand jury. Instead, building on our statement that the federal courts "may, within limits, formulate procedural rules not specifically required by the Constitution or the Congress," he argues that imposition of the Tenth Circuit's disclosure rule is supported by the courts' "supervisory power." We think not. [The supervisory power cases] deal strictly with the courts' power to control their *own* procedures. * * * Thus, *Bank of Nova Scotia v. United States*, 487 U.S. 250, 108 S.Ct. 2369, 101 L.Ed.2d 228 (1988), makes clear that the supervisory power can be used to dismiss an indictment because of misconduct before the grand jury, at least where that misconduct amounts to a violation of one of those "few, clear rules which were carefully drafted and approved by this Court and by Congress to ensure the integrity of the grand jury's functions."[d]

We did not hold in *Bank of Nova Scotia*, however, that the courts' supervisory power could be used, not merely as a means of enforcing or vindicating legally compelled standards of prosecutorial conduct before the grand jury, but as a means of *prescribing* those standards of prosecutorial conduct in the first instance—just as it may be used as a means of establishing standards of prosecutorial conduct before the courts themselves. It is this latter exercise that respondent demands. Because the grand jury is an institution separate from the courts, over whose functioning the courts do not preside, we think it clear that, as a general matter at least, no such "supervisory" judicial authority exists, and that the disclosure rule applied here exceeded the Tenth Circuit's authority.

A

"[R]ooted in long centuries of Anglo-American history," the grand jury is mentioned in the Bill of Rights, but not in the body of the Constitution. It has not been textually assigned, therefore, to any of the branches described in the first three Articles. It " 'is a constitutional fixture in its own right.' " In fact the whole theory of its function is that it belongs to no branch of the institutional Government, serving as a kind of buffer or referee between the Government and the people. Although the grand jury normally operates, of course, in the courthouse and under judicial auspices, its institutional relationship with the Judicial Branch has traditionally been, so to speak, at arm's length. Judges' direct involvement in the functioning of the grand jury has generally been confined to the constitutive one of calling the grand jurors together and administering their oaths of office.

The grand jury's functional independence from the Judicial Branch is evident both in the scope of its power to investigate criminal wrongdoing and in the manner in which that power is exercised. "Unlike [a] [c]ourt, whose jurisdiction is predicated upon a specific case or controversy, the grand jury 'can investigate merely on suspicion that the law is being violated, or even because it wants assurance that it is not.' " It need not identify the offender it suspects, or even "the precise nature of the offense" it is investigating. The grand jury requires no authorization from its constituting court to initiate an investigation, nor does the prosecutor require leave of court to seek a grand jury indictment. And in its day-to-day functioning, the grand jury generally operates without the

---

[d] One rule in question in *Bank of Nova Scotia* was Fed. R. Crim. P. 6. The Court indicated that federal courts had supervisory power to dismiss an indictment obtained in violation of Rule 6 if that violation prejudiced the case before the grand jury. On the facts before it, the Court did not find sufficient prejudice. Eds.

interference of a presiding judge. It swears in its own witnesses, and deliberates in total secrecy.

True, the grand jury cannot compel the appearance of witnesses and the production of evidence, and must appeal to the court when such compulsion is required. And the court will refuse to lend its assistance when the compulsion the grand jury seeks would override rights accorded by the Constitution, or even testimonial privileges recognized by the common law. Even in this setting, however, we have insisted that the grand jury remain "free to pursue its investigations unhindered by external influence or supervision so long as it does not trench upon the legitimate rights of any witness called before it." Recognizing this tradition of independence, we have said that the Fifth Amendment's "constitutional guarantee *presupposes* an investigative body 'acting independently of either prosecuting attorney *or judge*' * * * ."

No doubt in view of the grand jury proceeding's status as other than a constituent element of a "criminal prosecutio[n]," we have said that certain constitutional protections afforded defendants in criminal proceedings have no application before that body. The Double Jeopardy Clause of the Fifth Amendment does not bar a grand jury from returning an indictment when a prior grand jury has refused to do so. We have twice suggested, though not held, that the Sixth Amendment right to counsel does not attach when an individual is summoned to appear before a grand jury, even if he is the subject of the investigation. And although "the grand jury may not force a witness to answer questions in violation of [the Fifth Amendment's] constitutional guarantee" against self-incrimination, our cases suggest that an indictment obtained through the use of evidence previously obtained in violation of the privilege against self-incrimination "is nevertheless valid."

Given the grand jury's operational separateness from its constituting court, it should come as no surprise that we have been reluctant to invoke the judicial supervisory power as a basis for prescribing modes of grand jury procedure. Over the years, we have received many requests to exercise supervision over the grand jury's evidence-taking process, but we have refused them all, including some more appealing than the one presented today. In *United States v. Calandra*, [414 U.S. 338, 94 S.Ct. 613, 38 L.Ed.2d 561 (1974)], a grand jury witness faced questions that were allegedly based upon physical evidence the Government had obtained through a violation of the Fourth Amendment; we rejected the proposal that the exclusionary rule be extended to grand jury proceedings, because of "the potential injury to the historic role and functions of the grand jury." In *Costello v. United States*, 350 U.S. 359, 76 S.Ct. 406, 100 L.Ed. 397 (1956), we declined to enforce the hearsay rule in grand jury proceedings, since that "would run counter to the whole history of the grand jury institution, in which laymen conduct their inquiries unfettered by technical rules."

These authorities suggest that any power federal courts may have to fashion, on their own initiative, rules of grand jury procedure is a very limited one, not remotely comparable to the power they maintain over their own proceedings. It certainly would not permit judicial reshaping of the grand jury institution, substantially altering the traditional relationships between the prosecutor, the constituting court, and the grand jury itself. As we proceed to discuss, that would be the consequence of the proposed rule here.

B

Respondent argues that the Court of Appeals' rule can be justified as a sort of Fifth Amendment "common law," a necessary means of assuring the constitutional right to the judgment "of an independent and informed grand jury." Respondent makes a generalized appeal to functional notions: Judicial supervision of the quantity and quality of the evidence relied upon by the grand jury plainly facilitates, he says, the grand jury's performance of its twin historical responsibilities, *i.e.*, bringing to trial those who may be justly accused and shielding the innocent from unfounded accusation and prosecution. We do not agree. The rule would neither preserve nor enhance the traditional functioning of the institution that the Fifth Amendment demands. To the contrary, requiring the prosecutor to present exculpatory as well as inculpatory evidence would alter the grand jury's historical role, transforming it from an accusatory to an adjudicatory body.

It is axiomatic that the grand jury sits not to determine guilt or innocence, but to assess whether there is adequate basis for bringing a criminal charge. That has always been so; and to make the assessment it has always been thought sufficient to hear only the prosecutor's side. As Blackstone described the prevailing practice in 18th-century England, the grand jury was "only to hear evidence on behalf of the prosecution[,] for the finding of an indictment is only in the nature of an enquiry or accusation, which is afterwards to be tried and determined." So also in the United States. According to the description of an early American court, three years before the Fifth Amendment was ratified, it is the grand jury's function not "to enquire * * * upon what foundation [the charge may be] denied," or otherwise to try the suspect's defenses, but only to examine "upon what foundation [the charge] is made" by the prosecutor. As a consequence, neither in this country nor in England has the suspect under investigation by the grand jury ever been thought to have a right to testify or to have exculpatory evidence presented.

Imposing upon the prosecutor a legal obligation to present exculpatory evidence in his possession would be incompatible with this system. If a "balanced" assessment of the entire matter is the objective, surely the first thing to be done—rather than requiring the prosecutor to say what he knows in defense of the target of the investigation—is to entitle the target to tender his own defense. To require the former while denying (as we do) the latter would be quite absurd. It would also be quite pointless, since it would merely invite the target to circumnavigate the system by delivering his exculpatory evidence to the prosecutor, whereupon it would *have* to be passed on to the grand jury—unless the prosecutor is willing to take the chance that a court will not deem the evidence important enough to qualify for mandatory disclosure.

Respondent acknowledges (as he must) that the "common law" of the grand jury is not violated if the *grand jury itself* chooses to hear no more evidence than that which suffices to convince it an indictment is proper. Thus, had the Government offered to familiarize the grand jury in this case with the five boxes of financial statements and deposition testimony alleged to contain exculpatory information, and had the grand jury rejected the offer as pointless, respondent would presumably agree that the resulting indictment would have been valid. Respondent insists, however, that courts must require the modern prosecutor to alert the grand jury to the nature and extent of the available exculpatory evidence, because otherwise the grand jury "merely functions as an arm of the prosecution." We reject the attempt to convert a nonexistent duty of the grand jury itself into an obligation of the prosecutor. The authority of the prosecutor to seek an indictment has long been understood to be "coterminous with the authority of the grand jury to entertain [the prosecutor's] charges." If the grand jury has no obligation to consider all "substantial exculpatory" evidence, we do not understand how the prosecutor can be said to have a binding obligation to present it. * * *

* * * [R]espondent argues that a rule requiring the prosecutor to disclose exculpatory evidence to the grand jury would, by removing from the docket unjustified prosecutions, save valuable judicial time. That depends, we suppose, upon what the ratio would turn out to be between unjustified prosecutions eliminated and grand jury indictments challenged—for the latter as well as the former consume "valuable judicial time." We need not pursue the matter; if there is an advantage to the proposal, Congress is free to prescribe it. For the reasons set forth above, however, we conclude that courts have no authority to prescribe such a duty pursuant to their inherent supervisory authority over their own proceedings. The judgment of the Court of Appeals is accordingly reversed, and the cause is remanded for further proceedings consistent with this opinion. * * *

JUSTICE STEVENS, with whom JUSTICE BLACKMUN and JUSTICE O'CONNOR join, and with whom JUSTICE THOMAS joins as to Parts II and III, dissenting. * * *

II

Like the Hydra slain by Hercules, prosecutorial misconduct has many heads. * * *

Justice Sutherland's identification [for the Court in *Berger v. United States*, 295 U.S. 78, 55 S.Ct. 629, 79 L.Ed. 1314 (1935)] of the basic reason why that sort of misconduct is intolerable merits repetition:

> "The United States Attorney is the representative not of an ordinary party to a controversy, but of a sovereignty whose obligation to govern impartially is as compelling as its obligation to govern at all; and whose interest, therefore, in a criminal prosecution is not that it shall win a case, but that justice shall be done. As such, he is in a peculiar and very definite sense the servant of the law, the twofold aim of which is that guilt shall not escape or innocence suffer. He may prosecute with earnestness and vigor—indeed, he should do so. But, while he may strike hard blows, he is not at liberty to strike foul ones. It is as much his duty to refrain from improper methods calculated to produce a wrongful conviction as it is to use every legitimate means to bring about a just one."

It is equally clear that the prosecutor has the same duty to refrain from improper methods calculated to produce a wrongful indictment. Indeed, the prosecutor's duty to protect the fundamental fairness of judicial proceedings assumes special importance when he is presenting evidence to a grand jury. As the Court of Appeals for the Third Circuit recognized, "the costs of continued unchecked prosecutorial misconduct" before the grand jury are particularly substantial because there

> "the prosecutor operates without the check of a judge or a trained legal adversary, and virtually immune from public scrutiny. The prosecutor's abuse of his special relationship to the grand jury poses an enormous risk to defendants as well. For while in theory a trial provides the defendant with a full opportunity to contest and disprove the charges against him, in practice, the handing up of an indictment will often have a devastating personal and professional impact that a later dismissal or acquittal can never undo. Where the potential for abuse is so great, and the consequences of a mistaken indictment so serious, the ethical responsibilities of the prosecutor, and the obligation of the judiciary to protect against even the appearance of unfairness, are correspondingly heightened." * * *

In an opinion that I find difficult to comprehend, the Court today repudiates the assumptions underlying [*Bank of Nova Scotia, supra,* and other supervisory powers] cases and seems to suggest that the court has no authority to supervise the conduct of the prosecutor in grand jury proceedings so long as he follows the dictates of the Constitution, applicable statutes, and Rule 6 of the Federal Rules of Criminal Procedure. The Court purports to support this conclusion by invoking the doctrine of separation of powers and citing a string of cases in which we have declined to impose categorical restraints on the grand jury. Needless to say, the Court's reasoning is unpersuasive.

Although the grand jury has not been "textually assigned" to "any of the branches described in the first three Articles" of the Constitution, it is not an autonomous body completely beyond the reach of the other branches. Throughout its life, from the moment it is convened until it is discharged, the grand jury is subject to the control of the court. As Judge Learned Hand recognized over 60 years ago, "a grand jury is neither an officer nor an agent of the United States, but a part of the court." * * *

This Court has, of course, long recognized that the grand jury has wide latitude to investigate violations of federal law as it deems appropriate and need not obtain permission from either the court or the prosecutor. Correspondingly, we have acknowledged that "its operation generally is unrestrained by the technical procedural and evidentiary rules governing the conduct of criminal trials." But this is because Congress and the Court have generally thought it best not to impose procedural restraints on the grand jury; it is not because they lack all power to do so. * * *

Although the Court recognizes that it may invoke its supervisory authority to fashion and enforce privilege rules applicable in grand jury proceedings, and suggests that it may also invoke its supervisory authority to fashion other limited rules of grand jury procedure, it concludes that it has no authority to *prescribe* "standards of prosecutorial conduct before the grand jury," because that would alter the grand jury's historic role as an independent, inquisitorial institution. I disagree. * * *

Unlike the Court, I am unwilling to hold that countless forms of prosecutorial misconduct must be tolerated—no matter how prejudicial they may be, or how seriously they may distort the legitimate function of the grand jury—simply because they are not proscribed by Rule 6 of the Federal Rules of Criminal Procedure or a statute that is applicable in grand jury proceedings. Such a sharp break with the traditional role of the federal judiciary is unprecedented, unwarranted, and unwise. Unrestrained prosecutorial misconduct in grand jury proceedings is inconsistent with the administration of justice in the federal courts and should be redressed in appropriate cases by the dismissal of indictments obtained by improper methods.

III

What, then, is the proper disposition of this case? I agree with the Government that the prosecutor is not required to place all exculpatory evidence before the grand jury. A grand jury proceeding is an *ex parte* investigatory proceeding to determine whether there is probable cause to believe a violation of the criminal laws has occurred, not a trial. Requiring the prosecutor to ferret out and present all evidence that could be used at trial to create a reasonable doubt as to the defendant's guilt would be inconsistent with the purpose of the grand jury proceeding and would place significant burdens on the investigation. But that does not mean that the prosecutor may mislead the grand jury into believing that there is probable cause to indict by withholding clear evidence to the contrary. I thus agree with the Department of Justice that "when a prosecutor conducting a grand jury inquiry is personally aware of substantial evidence which directly negates the guilt of a subject of the investigation, the prosecutor must present or otherwise disclose such evidence to the grand jury before seeking an indictment against such a person." * * *

NOTES AND QUESTIONS

1.   The split on the Court in *Williams* is unusual: Centrists Souter, White, and Kennedy joined conservatives Scalia and Rehnquist to forge a majority, while liberals Stevens and Blackmun were joined by centrist O'Connor and conservative Thomas in dissent. Is there something about the issue in *Williams* that would produce this kind of division?

2.   *The instrumental explanation for doctrine.* In the nineteenth century, judges rarely spoke about policy reasons for constructing doctrine in a particular way. Judicial opinions often seemed instead to justify the outcome as an inevitably pre-determined application of principles drawn from a fundamental and unchanging source—the common law or the Constitution. This ignored what might be called the "instrumental explanation" for doctrine, the idea that judges construct doctrine hoping to move relevant actors toward what is perceived to be more beneficial outcomes. One does not have to be too much of a cynic to assume that instrumental reasons moved the Warren Court to fix the exclusionary rule on the states via *Mapp v. Ohio*, 367 U.S. 643, 81 S.Ct. 1684, 6 L.Ed.2d 1081 (1961), and to create the interrogation rules spelled out in *Miranda v. Arizona*, 384 U.S. 436, 86 S.Ct. 1602, 16 L.Ed.2d 694 (1966). Perhaps *Williams* has an instrumental explanation as well.

Recall from the Introductory Comment to this section that the grand jury has "sword" and "shield" roles that are in tension. Perhaps the Court favors one role over the other. Consider what Professor Peter Henning has to say on this point:

> My thesis is that the Supreme Court has made the grand jury, and the prosecutors that guide its proceedings, free from judicial oversight in order to protect the investigative function from outside interference. That function, more than the accusatory function, defines the importance of the grand jury in the criminal justice system. * * * The grand jury serves a special role in the investigation of crime, especially white collar crimes in which the authority and presence of a grand jury are the best means of ferreting out information. Because of the grand jury's broad authority to investigate crime, the Court does not want judges interfering with, and possibly exerting control over, the investigative process. Absent congressional action to expand the rights of individuals in a grand jury investigation, the Court has refused to permit judges to exercise what it has termed a "chancellor's foot veto" that would allow second-guessing of the methods prosecutors use to gather evidence and examine witnesses appearing before grand jurors. The Court's approach has been to prohibit defendants from challenging the prosecutor's conduct of the grand jury investigation because such challenges would provide a means to delay criminal proceedings by tying up the government's resources in defending its investigation. The Court relies on the criminal trial to vindicate a defendant's rights; thus a decision on the core issue of the defendant's guilt or innocence should be the focus of the criminal process, not the prosecutor's conduct.

Peter J. Henning, *Prosecutorial Misconduct in Grand Jury Investigations*, 51 S. Car. L. Rev. 1, 7–8 (1999).

3.   *More evidence of instrumental motives in grand jury doctrine.* As you saw in *Williams, Costello* involved an indictment obtained solely on the basis of hearsay evidence. At trial, the government "called and examined 144 witnesses and introduced 368 exhibits." None of these witnesses had testified before the grand jury; the only grand jury witnesses had been three government agents, none of whom had any firsthand knowledge of the evidence. Based on this revelation at trial, defendant moved to dismiss the indictment. The Supreme Court affirmed the district court's action in overruling the motion. Comparing our grand jury with its historical antecedent in England, Justice Black wrote for the Court:

> Grand jurors were selected from the body of the people and their work was not hampered by rigid procedural or evidential rules. In fact, grand jurors could act on their own knowledge and were free to make their presentments or indictments on such information as they deemed satisfactory. Despite its broad power to institute criminal proceedings the grand jury grew in popular favor with the years. It acquired an independence in England free from control by

the Crown or judges. Its adoption in our Constitution as the sole method for preferring charges in serious criminal cases shows the high place it held as an instrument of justice. And in this country as in England of old the grand jury was convened as a body of laymen, free from technical rules, acting in secret, pledged to indict no one because of prejudice and to free no one because of special favor.

The Court held in *Costello*: "An indictment returned by a legally constituted and unbiased grand jury, * * * if valid on its face, is enough to call for trial of the charge on the merits. The Fifth Amendment requires nothing more."

4.   How are the norms of fairness, accuracy, and efficiency manifested in *Costello*'s holding? What about *Williams*? In *Williams*, do the norms of fairness and accuracy work at cross purposes, one norm explaining the majority's approach and the other explaining the dissent? What is the role for the limited-government norm in the debate?

5.   Justice Stevens in dissent quotes extensively from Justice Sutherland's opinion for a unanimous Court in *Berger*. The Court reversed Berger's conviction on the ground of prosecutorial misconduct, but the misconduct occurred during the trial itself, and the expressed concern was the effect on the jury. Does this distinction undermine the dissent's point?

6.   Which *Williams* opinion do you prefer as a means of regulating the conduct of the prosecutor in obtaining a grand jury indictment? Is there a pragmatic dimension that makes the incidence of prosecutorial misconduct in obtaining indictments tolerably low even after *Williams*?

7.   Even before *Williams* it was difficult to challenge the prosecutor's motives or conduct. In United States v. Mechanik, 475 U.S. 66, 106 S.Ct. 938, 89 L.Ed.2d 50 (1986), the Court held that a conviction made any error before the grand jury harmless beyond a reasonable doubt. In Bank of Nova Scotia v. United States, 487 U.S. 250, 108 S.Ct. 2369, 101 L.Ed.2d 228 (1988), the Court held that in pre-verdict cases, the supervisory-powers doctrine could not result in dismissal unless the defendant showed prejudice. How does *Williams* limit *Nova Scotia?*

8.   *Should the law be different?* For a different approach to the *Williams* problem, see Herrell v. Sargeant, 189 Ariz. 627, 944 P.2d 1241 (1997). In a case that, remarkably, does not even cite *Williams*, the state court noted the "devastating personal and professional impact that a later dismissal or acquittal can never undo" and held that the failure of the prosecutor to present exculpatory evidence denied defendant's "right to due process and a fair and impartial presentation of the evidence." The opinion can, perhaps, be read as based on state law. That it does not even cite *Williams*, however, suggests that neither party knew of the case.

To vacate the earlier indictment, *Herrell* goes into considerable detail discussing the evidence presented to the grand jury and the facts and procedural history of the case. Is this the best use of appellate courts? Perhaps. Holding New York state up as a model, Professor Ric Simmons concludes that "[m]any critics of the institution focus exclusively on the anemic federal grand jury without examining the functions and influence of grand juries at the state level." Ric Simmons, *Re-examining the Grand Jury: Is There Room for Democracy in the Criminal Justice System?*, 82 B.U. L. Rev. 1, 2 (2002). New York is different from the federal grand jury model that we have studied in two ways. First, New York requires judicial review of the grand jury minutes, upon defense motion, "unless good cause exists to deny the motion." *Id.* at 27. That review ensures that the minutes

> contain sufficient evidence to support the charges in the indictment. Motions to inspect the minutes are routinely made and granted, and although the judge may only spend a few minutes reviewing a transcript, especially in simple cases, this process provides a critical check on the legitimacy of the grand jury presentation. A prosecutor must present a more detailed case and exercise additional care to establish all of the essential elements of the crime if she is certain that the transcript will be reviewed by a judge. The Court of Appeals of New York reiterated the courts' commitment to this duty in People v. Huston, [668 N.E.2d 1362 (N.Y.1996),] in which the court overturned a murder conviction because of improprieties in the grand jury.

Id.

A second difference, according to Professor Simmons, is that New York rejects the *Mechanik* rule, set out in Note 7.

> New York state law allows a defendant to challenge the indictment even after the defendant has been convicted. * * * On the federal level, the grand jury is merely a means to an end—a procedural hoop for the prosecutor to jump through however she can in order to advance the case towards trial. As long as the defendant is convicted at trial, he could not possibly have been harmed by any irregularity in the grand jury, since his guilt has been established beyond a reasonable doubt at trial. This laissez-faire philosophy stands in stark contrast to the consequences that federal courts attach to other pre-trial prosecutorial errors. For example, if the government acquires evidence illegally, obtains an improper confession, uses an overly suggestive identification procedure, fails to turn over exculpatory evidence, or even fails to comply with discovery rules, there is at least a possibility of sanction against the government even if the actions were deemed improper only after conviction. The Supreme Court has thus placed the grand jury on the lowest tier of the procedural safeguards in the federal system. * * *

> [In 1996, the New York Court of Appeals] reasoned that the only way to keep the grand jury proceeding fair is to overturn the conviction as a sanction, even if the defendant has been found guilty

at trial. Thus the grand jury in New York State has an important value in itself, not merely as a means to an end. * * *

[G]iven the scarcity of criminal trials, the criminal justice system needs a more consistent contact point with the community that it serves. Grand juries that exercise their discretion to reduce or dismiss cases do not only provide a more democratic sense of justice in that particular case, they send a message to the prosecutor and to the police about how law enforcement is viewed in their community. If the community believes that a bribery statute, a drug possession statute, or even an anti-abortion law should not be applied in a certain way, it is important that a prosecutor's office take notice. Similarly, if the community is dissatisfied with the conduct of the police in general, the grand jury gives them a meaningful method of demonstrating that dissatisfaction. * * *

Throughout the centuries, the grand jury has always reinvented itself to perform a necessary role in our justice system, but only if it was given the procedural and structural framework in which do so. The mere phantom of a grand jury that is found in the federal system may satisfy the bare constitutional language of the Fifth Amendment, but there is no reason why professionals on both sides of the debate should not aspire to build a system that performs the valuable functions of democratizing the justice system, giving voice to the community's political sentiments, and enhancing the legitimacy of the system as a whole.

Id. at 29, 44, 75–76.

Which approach to these issues, that of New York or *Williams*, do you think makes the most sense?

9. Whatever may be true of New York grand juries, the Leipold excerpt, p. 921, demonstrates that the federal grand jury contributes almost nothing to the screening function already performed by the United States Attorneys. Having seen this feeble "shield" effort, you may be surprised to learn in the next chapter that a federal grand has a powerful "sword" function.

10. So what did you decide about whether to prosecute the police officer who shot the 12-year-old? You do not, of course, have to defer to the real-life prosecutor who guided the grand jury to return a no-true bill.

CHAPTER 13

PREPARING FOR ADJUDICATION

■ ■ ■

A. INTRODUCTION TO CASE PROCESSING

Professor Alan Dershowitz has "discerned a series of 'rules' that seem—in practice—to govern" the criminal justice system. He lists thirteen rules, but the first two are pertinent here. "Rule I: Almost all criminal defendants are, in fact, guilty. Rule II: All criminal defense lawyers, prosecutors and judges understand and believe Rule I." Alan M. Dershowitz, The Best Defense xxi (1982). But the cynicism that undergirds these "rules" should be resisted. As we saw at p. 65, Note 1, police arrest many innocent suspects.

Getting the client's version of what happened, and conducting a rigorous fact investigation, are obviously crucial in providing an effective defense to an innocent client. But they are just as important when the client is guilty of what the state charged or some lesser offense. While you might feel more noble representing innocent clients, *you have the same duty to represent zealously the guilty as well as the innocent.* As we saw in Chapter 12, prosecutors have almost unlimited charging discretion, and they sometimes charge a more serious offense than the facts will sustain. Perhaps, as well, there are errors in the investigation that can lead to suppression of evidence and a more favorable plea offer..

Representing a guilty client is usually easier if the defense lawyer knows the truth about what happened. Persuading guilty clients to tell the unvarnished truth, however, is far from easy. Even recidivist criminals might feel social opprobrium in admitting to a crime, particularly a sexual crime or crime of violence against a child or other vulnerable person. Clients who have not committed crimes in the past might deny to themselves that they are guilty, particularly in rape or homicide cases where the client will offer some kind of consent or self-defense claim. Some clients, because of drug use or psychological problems, do not know what really happened. Many clients view the lawyer as part of the middle-class establishment that is trying to put them in prison. More globally, some people seem incapable of telling the truth when it reflects negatively on them or, perhaps, at any time.

Another reason clients do not tell their lawyer the truth is that the client might not know the "legal truth" that the lawyer would recognize.

One of our students who worked as an investigator in a public defender's office called this the "life is a mystery" phenomenon. Clients who drift into drug use and street crime tend to have a looser understanding of cause and effect than you have. They are surprised to have been arrested and may not see any connection with the conduct that the prosecutor will charge. They have been in prison before and view their life in prison as somehow unconnected to what they did that led them to be convicted. They will talk to the lawyer about their life experiences in a sort of random way and may simply omit some aspect that the State thinks crucial.

An additional truth-difficulty arises when the defense lawyer is interviewing her client. The client might want to take the witness stand and tell a version of what happened that does not match the story the client initially tells the lawyer. You will see a good example of this dilemma in *Nix v. Whiteside* in Chapter 14. Whether the defense lawyer should protect her client's strategy to tell a different story at trial by not questioning the client about what happened presents an ethical problem that is beyond the scope of this introduction. The Notes and Questions following *Nix* raise some of these ethical issues.

All of these difficulties suggest that interviewing and fact investigation are probably the most important skills that a good defense lawyer can offer her client. Unfortunately, we can do little to advance those skills in this casebook, beyond pointing out their importance and suggesting that you take courses or clinics that will improve your ability to represent clients. This would be a very short chapter, then, except that case preparation for the defense can involve more than fact investigation.

Several strategic decisions must be made in the course of preparing the defense, including (a) which motions to suppress evidence should be made; (b) whether to move for a change of venue; (c) how best to keep your client from facing one trial with multiple counts and multiple defendants (this usually involves moving to sever counts and defendants); and (d) whether to move for a speedy trial.

The prosecutor prepares more or less the same way as the defense. Fact investigation is just as important to the prosecutor as to the defense. As prosecutor, you have no "client" who has to be persuaded to tell the truth. A somewhat similar problem, however, is the possibility that some of the police officers may be shading the truth, or lying, about the conditions under which they discovered evidence or obtained a confession. Sometimes called "testilying," this is a problem of unknown scope in the criminal justice system. See p. 956. Generally, the prosecutor has more resources than the defense—more investigators and laboratories as well as better access to victims and other witnesses—and can work up the facts more easily and more thoroughly.

The prosecutor has both broader and narrower discovery rights than the defendant. The prosecutor's discovery rights are narrower because the Fifth Amendment privilege protects the defendant from being forced to disclose certain kinds of information. But the prosecutor has another tool at her disposal that more than compensates for Fifth Amendment problems—the grand jury can be used as a powerful investigative tool. We saw the grand jury screening or "shield" function in the last chapter. Now we examine the "sword" function.

Thumbnail Guide to Case Processing

There are, of course, fifty states, and each one is permitted to craft its own process for criminal cases, as long as it meets minimum federal constitutional standards. In addition, states are free to create a different procedure for less serious offenses, including municipal violations. Thus, in theory, there could be over one hundred different paths from the beginning of a case to its end. Nonetheless, it is useful to sketch what is probably the most common path a felony case takes, drawing largely on the Federal Rules of Criminal Procedure (see Supplement, Appendix B). Some of these stages you saw in Chapter 12.

Rule 4. Arrest. Most criminal cases begin with an arrest, typically made without an arrest warrant.

Rule 5. Initial Appearance. The magistrate will inform the defendant of the charge against him, the defendant's right to retained or appointed counsel, how he might secure pretrial release, his right to a preliminary hearing, and his right not to make a statement and that any statement made may be used against the defendant.

Bail is governed by a statute (see 18 U.S.C. § 3142, Supplement, Appendix A). A bail hearing can be held at any point after the defendant is in custody. The magistrate's choices are generally to release the defendant subject to certain conditions or to order him held because he represents a danger to the community.

Rule 5.1. Preliminary Hearing. In most jurisdictions, the grand jury follows the preliminary hearing, which is held shortly after the initial appearance. At the preliminary hearing, the government must demonstrate both that an offense has been committed and that the defendant committed it. The defendant has a right to counsel who can put on evidence and who can cross-examine the government's witnesses.

In the rare case where the magistrate finds no probable cause, he must discharge the defendant; this action does not preclude filing the same charge at a later date. If the magistrate judge finds probable cause to believe that the defendant committed the crime charged, the case proceeds to the next stage, typically a grand jury hearing.

Rule 6. The Grand Jury. Left over from the days of Henry II (1166), the grand jury process is complex and shrouded in secrecy. Only the government attorneys, the witness being questioned, and a court reporter are permitted in the grand jury room. Participants are generally forbidden to disclose what transpired in the grand jury room. The grand jury's function essentially duplicates that of the magistrate judge in the preliminary hearing—to determine whether there is probable cause to believe the defendant committed the crime with which he is charged.

If the grand jury finds probable cause—this requires a vote of 12 grand jurors in the federal system—it issues an indictment. This is a document that justifies bringing the defendant to trial.

Rule 10. Arraignment. In open court, the judge ensures that the defendant is aware of the charge of which he has been indicted. The defendant then must plead to the indictment.

The case will then be put on the judge's trial docket, paving the way for the various pre-trial motions, some of which are the subject of this chapter.

B. THE FIFTH AMENDMENT PRIVILEGE AND THE GRAND JURY INVESTIGATIVE FUNCTION

Introductory Comment

Henry II in the Assize of Clarendon (1166) created a body that would become the English and then the American grand jury. Its purpose was to uncover crimes that had been committed, and not prosecuted, since Henry became king twelve years earlier. In the remarkably modern language of the assize: "[A]n inquest shall be made * * * through twelve of the more lawful men of the [village], and through four of the more lawful men of each township, upon oath that they will speak the truth: whether in their [village] or in their township there be any man who, since the lord king has been king, has been charged or published as being a robber or murderer or thief; or any one who is a harbourer of robbers or murderers or thieves." We see that the number of this early grand jury was set at sixteen, which is still the minimum size of the federal grand jury.

This is a course in criminal procedure and not evidence. Yet to understand the awesome power of the grand jury, it is useful to reflect on Lord Bacon's observation in 1612 that all subjects owed the king their "knowledge and discovery." While this was true when Henry II created the grand jury to uncover crimes in the villages and was perhaps still true in 1612, it is no longer strictly true because certain privileges can be asserted. Outside of those privileges, however, Bacon's remark remains accurate. If your daughter confesses to you that she killed someone, and you are called before the grand jury, you have only two choices: disclose what she told you or lie and face perjury charges (ask Barry Bonds about that). There is no parent-child privilege under the federal rules of evidence.

Consider the case of Monica Lewinsky's mother. Because Lewinsky had apparently told her mother details about her sexual relationship with President Clinton, a grand jury called her mother to testify in the perjury investigation of Clinton. This all occurred, of course, in the midst of the House impeachment of Clinton and his trial in the Senate. The lack of a relevant privilege probably explains why when Lewinsky's mother left the courthouse, she "appeared very upset" and was "[n]ear tears * * * with nose red and eyes downcast." Thomas Galvin & Tara George, *Long Grilling Leaves Monica Mom Teary*, N.Y. Daily News, February 12, 1998, at 5. Her lawyer said, "No mother should ever be forced by federal prosecutors to testify against their [sic] child." But, presumably, she *was* forced to testify.

Federal Rule of Evidence 501 provides that the privileges of witnesses not to testify "shall be governed by the principles of the common law as they may be interpreted by the courts of the United States in the light of reason and experience." Some long-standing common-law privileges include communications made between lawyer and client, wife and husband, physician and patient, and priest and penitent. If a grand jury witness asserts one of these privileges (or another), the prosecutor will ask the judge who called the grand jury into session to decide whether the privilege protects the witness.

The Court has told us that the "most important" privilege

is the Fifth Amendment privilege against compulsory self-incrimination. The privilege reflects a complex of our fundamental values and aspirations, and marks an important advance in the development of our liberty. It can be asserted in any proceeding, civil or criminal, administrative or judicial, investigatory or adjudicatory; and it protects against any disclosures which the witness reasonably believes could be used in a criminal prosecution or could lead to other evidence that might be so used. This Court has been zealous to safeguard the values which underlie the privilege.

Kastigar v. United States, 406 U.S. 441, 92 S.Ct. 1653, 32 L.Ed.2d 212 (1972).

We examine the Fifth Amendment privilege first and then explore how immunity affects the equation.

HOFFMAN V. UNITED STATES

Supreme Court of the United States, 1951.
341 U.S. 479, 71 S.Ct. 814, 95 L.Ed. 1118.

MR. JUSTICE CLARK delivered the opinion of the Court [joined by CHIEF JUSTICE VINSON and JUSTICES BLACK, FRANKFURTER, DOUGLAS, JACKSON, BURTON, and MINTON].

Petitioner has been convicted of criminal contempt for refusing to obey a federal court order requiring him to answer certain questions asked in a grand jury investigation. He raises here important issues as to the application of the privilege against self-incrimination under the Fifth Amendment, claimed to justify his refusal.

A special federal grand jury was convened at Philadelphia on September 14, 1950, to investigate frauds upon the Federal Government, including violations of the customs, narcotics and internal revenue liquor laws of the United States, the White Slave Traffic Act, perjury, bribery, and other federal criminal laws, and conspiracy to commit all such offenses. In response to subpoena petitioner appeared to testify on the day the grand jury was empaneled, and was examined on October 3. The pertinent interrogation, in which he refused to answer, follows:

"Q. What do you do now, Mr. Hoffman?

"A. I refuse to answer.

"Q. Have you been in the same undertaking since the first of the year?

"A. I don't understand the question.

"Q. Have you been doing the same thing you are doing now since the first of the year?

"A. I refuse to answer.

"Q. Do you know Mr. William Weisberg?

"A. I do.

"Q. How long have you known him?

"A. Practically twenty years, I guess.

"Q. When did you last see him?

"A. I refuse to answer.

"Q. Have you seen him this week?

"A. I refuse to answer.

"Q. Do you know that a subpoena has been issued for Mr. Weisberg?

"A. I heard about it in Court.

"Q. Have you talked with him on the telephone this week?

"A. I refuse to answer.

"Q. Do you know where Mr. William Weisberg is now?

"A. I refuse to answer."

It was stipulated that petitioner declined to answer on the ground
that his answers might tend to incriminate him of a federal offense.

Petitioner's claim of privilege was challenged by the Government in
the Federal District Court for the Eastern District of Pennsylvania, which
found no real and substantial danger of incrimination to petitioner and
ordered him to return to the grand jury and answer. Petitioner stated in
open court that he would not obey the order, and on October 5 was
adjudged in criminal contempt and sentenced to five months
imprisonment.

The Court of Appeals * * * affirmed the conviction. With respect to
the questions regarding Weisberg, the court held unanimously that "the
relationship between possible admissions in answer to the questions * * *
and the proscription of [pertinent federal criminal statutes] would need to
be much closer for us to conclude that there was real danger in
answering." * * * [W]ith respect to the business questions, * * * "the
witness here failed to give the judge any information which would allow
the latter to rule intelligently on the claim of privilege for the witness
simply refused to say anything and gave no facts to show why he refused
to say anything." One judge dissented, concluding that the District Court
knew that "the setting of the controversy" was "a grand jury investigation
of racketeering and federal crime in the vicinity" and "should have
adverted to the fact of common knowledge that there exists a class of
persons who live by activity prohibited by federal criminal laws and that
some of these persons would be summoned as witnesses in this grand jury
investigation." * * *

This is another of five proceedings before this Court during the
present Term in each of which the privilege against self-incrimination has
been asserted in the course of federal grand-jury investigations. A
number of similar cases have been considered recently by the lower
courts. The signal increase in such litigation emphasizes the continuing
necessity that prosecutors and courts alike be "alert to repress" any
abuses of the investigatory power invoked * * *. Enforcement officials
taking the initiative in grand-jury proceedings and courts charged with
their superintendence should be sensitive to the considerations making
for wise exercise of such investigatory power, not only where
constitutional issues may be involved but also where the noncoercive

assistance of other federal agencies may render it unnecessary to invoke the compulsive process of the grand jury.

The Fifth Amendment declares in part that "No person * * * shall be compelled in any criminal case to be a witness against himself." This guarantee against testimonial compulsion, like other provisions of the Bill of Rights, "was added to the original Constitution in the conviction that too high a price may be paid even for the unhampered enforcement of the criminal law and that, in its attainment, other social objects of a free society should not be sacrificed." This provision of the Amendment must be accorded liberal construction in favor of the right it was intended to secure.

The privilege afforded not only extends to answers that would in themselves support a conviction under a federal criminal statute but likewise embraces those which would furnish a link in the chain of evidence needed to prosecute the claimant for a federal crime. But this protection must be confined to instances where the witness has reasonable cause to apprehend danger from a direct answer. The witness is not exonerated from answering merely because he declares that in so doing he would incriminate himself—his say-so does not of itself establish the hazard of incrimination. It is for the court to say whether his silence is justified, and to require him to answer if "it clearly appears to the court that he is mistaken." However, if the witness, upon interposing his claim, were required to prove the hazard in the sense in which a claim is usually required to be established in court, he would be compelled to surrender the very protection which the privilege is designed to guarantee. To sustain the privilege, it need only be evident from the implications of the question, in the setting in which it is asked, that a responsive answer to the question or an explanation of why it cannot be answered might be dangerous because injurious disclosure could result. The trial judge in appraising the claim "must be governed as much by his personal perception of the peculiarities of the case as by the facts actually in evidence."

What were the circumstances which the District Court should have considered in ruling upon petitioner's claim of privilege? This is the background as indicated by the record:

The judge who ruled on the privilege had himself impaneled the special grand jury to investigate "rackets" in the district. He had explained to the jury that "the Attorney General's office has come into this district to conduct an investigation * * * [that] will run the gamut of all crimes covered by federal statute." "If rackets infest or encrust our system of government," he instructed, "just as any blight attacks any other growth, it withers and dies * * *." Subpoenas had issued for some twenty witnesses, but only eleven had been served; as the prosecutor put it, he was "having trouble finding some big shots." Several of those who did appear and were called into the grand-jury room before petitioner had refused to answer questions until ordered to do so by the court. The prosecutor had requested bench warrants for eight of the nine who had not appeared the first day of the session, one of whom was William Weisberg. Petitioner had admitted having known Weisberg for about twenty years. In addition, counsel for petitioner had advised the court that "It has been broadly published that [petitioner] has a police record."

The court should have considered, in connection with the business questions, that the chief occupation of some persons involves evasion of federal criminal laws, and that truthful answers by petitioner to these questions might have disclosed that he was engaged in such proscribed activity.

Also, the court should have recognized, in considering the Weisberg questions, that one person with a police record summoned to testify before a grand jury investigating the rackets might be hiding or helping to hide another person of questionable repute sought as a witness. To be sure, the Government may inquire of witnesses before the grand jury as to the whereabouts of unlocated witnesses; ordinarily the answers to such questions are harmless if not fruitless. But of the seven questions relating to Weisberg (of which three were answered), three were designed to draw information as to petitioner's contacts and connection with the fugitive witness; and the final question, perhaps an afterthought of the prosecutor, inquired of Weisberg's whereabouts at the time. All of them could easily have required answers that would forge links in a chain of facts imperiling petitioner with conviction of a federal crime. The three questions, if answered affirmatively, would establish contacts between petitioner and Weisberg during the crucial period when the latter was eluding the grand jury; and in the context of these inquiries the last question might well have called for disclosure that Weisberg was hiding away on petitioner's premises or with his assistance. Petitioner could reasonably have sensed the peril of prosecution for federal offenses ranging from obstruction to conspiracy.

In this setting it was not "*perfectly clear*, from a careful consideration of all the circumstances in the case, that the witness is mistaken, and that the answer[s] *cannot possibly* have such tendency" to incriminate [which is the constitutional standard; eds.]. * * *

For these reasons we cannot agree with the judgments below. If this result adds to the burden of diligence and efficiency resting on enforcement authorities, any other conclusion would seriously compromise an important constitutional liberty. "The immediate and potential evils of compulsory self-disclosure transcend any difficulties that the exercise of the privilege may impose on society in the detection and prosecution of crime." Pertinent here is the observation of Mr. Justice Brandeis for this Court: "If Congress should hereafter conclude that a full disclosure * * * by the witnesses is of greater importance than the possibility of punishing them for some crime in the past, it can, as in other cases, confer the power of unrestricted examination by providing complete immunity."

Reversed.

Mr. Justice REED dissents. He agrees with the conclusions reached by Judges Goodrich and Kalodner as expressed in the opinion below.

NOTES AND QUESTIONS

1. *The Smith Act.* In 1940, Congress enacted a law that came to be known as the Smith Act: "Whoever knowingly or willfully advocates, abets, advises, or teaches the duty, necessity, desirability, or propriety of overthrowing or destroying the government of the United States or the government of any State, Territory, District or Possession thereof, or the government of any political subdivision therein, by force or violence, or by the assassination of any officer of any such government" commits a federal felony, punishable by up to twenty years in prison. In the late 1940s and early 1950s, federal prosecutors sometimes used the Smith Act to investigate what some perceived as a Communist conspiracy capable of overthrowing the United States government.

Notice the Court's remark about *Hoffman* being "another of five proceedings before this Court during the present Term" where the Fifth Amendment privilege was asserted before a grand jury. Three of those cases involved investigations into suspected Communist activities. Given the ultimate failure of the Soviet version of Communism, the fear that Communists would infiltrate, and overthrow, the United States government may seem quaint today, but it was very real in 1950. The very word "red" became identified with the feared Communist Party. For example, the New York Times reported on one of the Court's Smith Act cases with the headline: "High Court Upholds Self-Incrimination as Plea in Red Case." Lewis Wood, N.Y. Times, December 12, 1950, at p.1.

The word "red" became so controversial that the oldest major league baseball team, the Cincinnati Reds, changed its name to the Red Legs in 1953. When it became apparent that the Communist Party was not going to overthrow the United States by force, the Red Legs changed their name back to Reds in 1960.

In two of the cases involving suspected Communist activities, witnesses were called before federal grand juries and asked about their employment by, or activities of, the Communist Party of Colorado. Both witnesses claimed a Fifth Amendment privilege not to answer, which was rejected by the lower courts. The Supreme Court reversed, stating in one of the cases:

Answers to the questions asked by the grand jury would have furnished a link in the chain of evidence needed in a prosecution of petitioner for violation of (or conspiracy to violate) the Smith Act. Prior decisions of this Court have clearly established that under such circumstances, the Constitution gives a witness the privilege of remaining silent. The attempt by the courts below to compel petitioner to testify runs counter to the Fifth Amendment as it has been interpreted from the beginning.

(Patricia) Blau v. United States, 340 U.S. 159, 71 S.Ct. 223, 95 L.Ed. 170 (1950).

In the third case, the witness admitted that she had been the treasurer of the Communist Party of Denver. When asked to produce the membership lists and dues records, she said she had turned them over to another member of the party. When asked to name that person, she replied, "I don't feel that I should subject a person or persons to the same thing that I'm going through." Held in contempt by the district court, she lost in the Supreme Court. The issue was whether naming the holder of the records created a risk of incrimination beyond what she had freely chosen by admitting to having been the treasurer. The Court held that "disclosure of acquaintance with her successor presents no more than a 'mere imaginary possibility' of increasing the danger of prosecution." Thus, the contempt order was affirmed. Rogers v. United States, 340 U.S. 367, 71 S.Ct. 438, 95 L.Ed. 344 (1951). Justices Black, Frankfurter, and Douglas dissented.

2. *The privilege and the innocent.* You might think from the readings so far that the Fifth Amendment privilege is solely a sanctuary for the guilty. The Ohio Supreme Court made that mistake in 2000, holding that a witness who claims to be innocent cannot assert the Fifth Amendment privilege. Reversing the state court in a unanimous per curiam opinion, the United States Supreme Court said that

we have never held, as the Supreme Court of Ohio did, that the privilege is unavailable to those who claim innocence. To the contrary, we have emphasized that one of the Fifth Amendment's "basic functions * * * is to protect *innocent* men * * * 'who otherwise might be ensnared by ambiguous circumstances.'" In *Grunewald* [*v. United States*, 353 U.S. 391, 421, 77 S.Ct. 963, 1 L.Ed.2d 931 (1957)], we recognized that truthful responses of an innocent witness, as well as those of a wrongdoer, may provide the government with incriminating evidence from the speaker's own mouth.

Ohio v. Reiner, 532 U.S. 17, 121 S.Ct. 1252, 149 L.Ed.2d 158 (2001) (per curiam).

Comment on the Investigative Grand Jury

Despite the grand jury's historic independence, noted in *United States v. Williams*, p. 925, the investigative grand jury cannot function without the careful guidance of the prosecutor. The grand jury deliberates in total secrecy, but the prosecutor advises the grand jury on which witnesses to call, and then examines the witnesses for the benefit of the grand jury. She also instructs the grand jury on the relevant law. While judges do not sit with the grand jury, they too are major players in its investigative role because their office issues the subpoenas, and the judge will decide whether witnesses are privileged not to answer.

What is a subpoena? A subpoena is a judicial order. The most common type of subpoena compels attendance before a grand jury, sometimes requiring the subpoenaed individual to produce documents as well as herself (a subpoena *duces tecum*). The documents may be subject to a privilege that protects them from disclosure, as we will see soon.

Persons subpoenaed to appear before a grand jury must appear or face contempt of court. As the Court has noted:

> While it is not clear when grand juries first resorted to compulsory process to secure the attendance and testimony of witnesses, the general common-law principle that "the public has a right to every man's evidence" was considered an "indubitable certainty" that "cannot be denied" by 1742. * * * The first Congress recognized the testimonial duty in the Judiciary Act of 1789, which provided for compulsory attendance of witnesses in the federal courts.

Kastigar v. United States, 406 U.S. 441, 92 S.Ct. 1653, 32 L.Ed.2d 212 (1972).

The prosecutor can comply with the Fifth Amendment and still compel the testimony by giving immunity to the witness. For almost eighty years, federal law provided for "transactional immunity"— immunity from prosecution for all offenses to which the compelled testimony relates—as the only way to satisfy the Fifth Amendment. Then, in 1970, Attorney General John Mitchell and President Richard Nixon persuaded Congress to enact a new immunity statute that replaced transactional immunity with what is known as "use and derivative-use" immunity or, often, simply "use" immunity. The Court upheld its constitutionality in *Kastigar, supra.*

> Immunity statutes, which have historical roots deep in Anglo-American jurisprudence, are not incompatible with [Fifth Amendment] values. Rather, they seek a rational accommodation between the imperatives of the privilege and the legitimate demands of government to compel citizens to testify.

The existence of these statutes reflects the importance of testimony, and the fact that many offenses are of such a character that the only persons capable of giving useful testimony are those implicated in the crime. * * *

Petitioners draw a distinction between statutes that provide transactional immunity and those that provide, as does the statute before us, immunity from use and derivative use. They contend that a statute must at a minimum grant full transactional immunity in order to be coextensive with the scope of the privilege. * * *

The statute's explicit proscription of the use in any criminal case of "testimony or other information compelled under the order (or any information directly or indirectly derived from such testimony or other information)" is consonant with Fifth Amendment standards. We hold that such immunity from use and derivative use is coextensive with the scope of the privilege against self-incrimination, and therefore is sufficient to compel testimony over a claim of the privilege. While a grant of immunity must afford protection commensurate with that afforded by the privilege, it need not be broader. Transactional immunity, which accords full immunity from prosecution for the offense to which the compelled testimony relates, affords the witness considerably broader protection than does the Fifth Amendment privilege. The privilege has never been construed to mean that one who invokes it cannot subsequently be prosecuted. Its sole concern is to afford protection against being "forced to give testimony" leading to the infliction of "penalties affixed to * * * criminal acts." Immunity from the use of compelled testimony, as well as evidence derived directly and indirectly therefrom, affords this protection. It prohibits the prosecutorial authorities from using the compelled testimony in any respect, and it therefore insures that the testimony cannot lead to the infliction of criminal penalties on the witness. * * *

Justice Douglas in his dissent in *Kastigar* argued that use and derivative-use immunity fails to provide sufficient protection to those compelled to testify because the derivative use will be impossible to enforce.

My view is that the framers put it beyond the power of Congress to *compel* anyone to confess his crimes. The Self-Incrimination Clause creates, as I have said before, "the federally protected right of silence," making it unconstitutional to use a law "to pry open one's lips and make him a witness against himself." That is indeed one of the chief procedural guarantees in our accusatorial system. Government acts in an ignoble way when it stoops to the end which we authorize today. * * *

The majority responded that the "total prohibition on use provides a comprehensive safeguard."

> A person accorded this immunity * * * and subsequently prosecuted, is not dependent for the preservation of his rights upon the integrity and good faith of the prosecuting authorities. As [we have] stated:
>
>> Once a defendant demonstrates that he has testified, under a state grant of immunity, to matters related to the federal prosecution, the federal authorities have the burden of showing that their evidence is not tainted by establishing that they had an independent, legitimate source for the disputed evidence.
>
>> This burden of proof, which we reaffirm as appropriate, is not limited to a negation of taint; rather, it imposes on the prosecution the affirmative duty to prove that the evidence it proposes to use is derived from a legitimate source wholly independent of the compelled testimony.

NOTES AND QUESTIONS

1. *Maybe the Kastigar majority was correct.* Satisfying the use-derivative use immunity proved impossible in the Oliver North, case. North was prosecuted for his role in funneling money to Iran-Contra rebels when he was a White House aide to President Ronald Reagan. North was first subpoenaed to testify before Congress, where he invoked his Fifth Amendment privilege not to testify. After receiving "use immunity" pursuant to federal law, North testified for six days before Congress. The testimony was carried live on national television and radio. The issue in his later prosecution was whether the Independent Counsel (Lawrence E. Walsh) had used the congressional testimony to uncover evidence against North.

The District Court found no forbidden use of the immunized testimony. The D.C. Circuit Court of Appeals held that the district court had not held a "full hearing as required by *Kastigar* to ensure that the [government] made no use of North's immunized congressional testimony." The Court of Appeals stressed *Kastigar's* language about the government's "heavy burden" to establish independent sources for all of its evidence. United States v. North, 910 F.2d 843 (D.C. Cir. 1990). The case was remanded to the district court, and the Independent Counsel told his staff to go through the voluminous trial record line by line and document the independent source of each statement. After a week or two, it became apparent that the task required far more resources than could be marshaled, and Walsh dismissed the indictment against North.

Assuming a state also had criminal jurisdiction over some of North's activities that were covered by the grant of immunity, should state officials be permitted to use the immunized testimony against North in a state criminal trial?

2.   Grand jury subpoenas raise Fifth Amendment self-incrimination issues other than the required scope of immunity. The Fifth Amendment is violated *only* if the grand jury order will (1) compel the witness to (2) testify (3) in a way that might incriminate herself. If the grand jury order in a particular case will not satisfy *all* of these conditions, there is no constitutional self-incrimination problem, and the witness can be compelled to comply with the order without receiving immunity.

We saw, in *Hoffman*, the low threshold needed to show that the answers might be incriminating. Most witnesses can make that showing. Now we discuss the other two elements of a claim of privilege—that what is *compelled* is *testimony*. The next four Notes develop these concepts.

3.   *The testimonial requirement.* "Testimonial" evidence requires a communicative act. Compelling a suspect to stand in a lineup or wear an item of clothing does not compel a communicative act, as Justice Holmes recognized in Holt v. United States, 218 U.S. 245, 31 S.Ct. 2, 54 L.Ed. 1021 (1910). Similarly, a blood test is not testimonial, because no communication from the mind is manifested in the contents of blood; the government may therefore compel a suspect to submit to a blood test without violating the Fifth Amendment. Schmerber v. California, 384 U.S. 757, 86 S.Ct. 1826, 16 L.Ed.2d 908 (1966). Though "communicative act" defies a precise definition, it must be an act that expresses something about the thought process of the suspect/defendant.

Which of the following would you expect to be communicative acts that will be included within the ambit of the Fifth Amendment privilege?

a) The suspect's slurred speech and lack of physical coordination (contained on a videotape that will be introduced to prove intoxication in a drunk driving prosecution).

b) The answer to the question, "Do you know the date of your sixth birthday?" The suspect responded, "I don't know." It was the same suspect as in prior question!

c) Providing a voice or handwriting sample (the suspect is told what to say or write).

d) The results of a lie detector test.

4.   *The compulsion requirement (warning—this is hard).* When someone is subpoenaed to testify before a grand jury or other judicial body, the subpoena compels attendance and the threat of a contempt order compels testimony. These are the easy cases. The hard cases are orders to produce documents. Simplifying the facts in Fisher v. United States, 425 U.S. 391, 96 S.Ct. 1569, 48 L.Ed.2d 39 (1976), and making it a hypothetical, suppose the

government summoned tax records and documents from a taxpayer-defendant. Further, assume the documents were potentially incriminating.

The Court in *Fisher* noted that the *creation* of the records here was not compelled. What *was* compelled was the *production*. Which act, therefore, implicates the Fifth Amendment prohibition against compelling someone "to be a witness against himself"? At what point, in other words, is the taxpayer being a witness against himself? Though the matter is not completely free from doubt, the Court concluded in *Fisher* that, for the words or numbers on a page, the key moment is the creation of the records. This is when the taxpayer is creating evidence (testifying) against himself. Whatever interest he has in the contents of the documents after that is a *privacy* interest, not an interest in being free from compulsion. Thus, a taxpayer cannot claim a Fifth Amendment interest in the *contents* of documents that she had voluntarily created.

It gets harder. Can the *production itself* ever be both incriminating and testimonial? Yes, but not in *Fisher*. The Court explained:

> The act of producing evidence in response to a subpoena nevertheless has communicative aspects of its own, wholly aside from the contents of the papers produced. Compliance with the subpoena tacitly concedes the existence of the papers demanded and their possession or control by the taxpayer. It also would indicate the taxpayer's belief that the papers are those described in the subpoena. The elements of compulsion are clearly present [in this case], but the more difficult issues are whether the tacit averments of the taxpayer are both "testimonial" and "incriminating" for purposes of applying the Fifth Amendment. These questions perhaps do not lend themselves to categorical answers; their resolution may instead depend on the facts and circumstances of particular cases or classes thereof.

In *Fisher*, the Court identified three implicit communicative acts that can be entailed in production: existence, possession, and authentication of the evidence subpoenaed. But in *Fisher*, the State knew of the evidence and its location. As for authentication, producing records expresses a belief that these are the records that are the subject of the subpoena but does not vouch for their accuracy. Thus, Fisher had no Fifth Amendment right to resist the subpoena!

5. *Doctor Jekyll's case.* Let's take the next step, based on the preceding Note. Assume Dr. Jekyll keeps a handwritten diary describing the murder he committed as Mr. Hyde. Now the grand jury subpoenas the Jekyll diary. The words in the diary, of course, were voluntarily written. His *production* of the diary is compelled, of course, but the act of production must be *testimonial* before Dr. Jekyll is protected by the Fifth Amendment. Suppose, for example, that the subpoena requires Jekyll to bring "the diary Robert Louis Stevenson used to write the book, Dr. Jekyll and Mr. Hyde." Jekyll's act of producing a particular diary is a testimonial act because it states Jekyll's opinion that the

produced diary is the one Stevenson used to write the book. (Note that Jekyll may be wrong about this fact, but accuracy is not the issue. If Jekyll is implicitly stating his opinion, that is a form of testimony.)

Now a more subtle point. If the subpoena requires production of "all diaries of Dr. Jekyll," the act of producing a diary may still be considered testimonial because it admits that there *is* a diary of Dr. Jekyll. The prosecution can avoid the Fifth Amendment claim here by producing evidence that independently establishes the existence of a Jekyll diary. In that event, the production seems unlikely to be testimonial. Although Jekyll is implicitly testifying to the authenticity of the diary he produces (in effect, saying that *this* is a Jekyll diary), the State will likely be able to establish its authenticity with handwriting experts. Does this mean, as one of our students once asked in frustration, that the prosecutor can avoid the Fifth Amendment privilege by careful wording of a subpoena? Well, yes; surely you knew that law is often a matter of choosing the right words.

In United States v. Hubbell, 530 U.S. 27, 120 S.Ct. 2037, 147 L.Ed.2d 24 (2000), the Court elaborated on the idea first enunciated in *Fisher* that the act of production can be testimonial. In *Hubbell*, the government issued a subpoena requesting documents in eleven broad categories. The Court unanimously held that Hubbell's act in providing 13,120 pages of material in response to the subpoena was a testimonial act. The subpoena required Hubbell to make extensive use of his mind in deciding what documents belonged in each of the categories. As the Court put it: "The assembly of those documents was like telling an inquisitor the combination to a wall safe * * * ." This "catalog of existing documents" fitting within the categories provided the prosecutor with a link in the chain of evidence needed to prosecute. The Court thus affirmed the Court of Appeals order requiring, on remand, that the prosecutor "demonstrat[e] with reasonable particularity a prior awareness that the exhaustive litany of documents sought in the subpoena existed and were in Hubbell's possession * * * ." Because the prosecutor had already indicated that he could not demonstrate with "reasonable particularity" the requisite prior awareness, the effect of *Hubbell* was to affirm a conditional guilty plea that the parties entered into after the Court of Appeals decision.

The following "quiz" seeks to illuminate how these issues might arise and be decided. Have fun.

6. *Compelled production as testimony: a quiz.* Apply the *Fisher-Hubbell* concepts to the following subpoenas, both of which are drawn from Robert P. Mosteller, *Cowboy Prosecutors and Subpoenas for Incriminating Evidence: The Consequences and Correction of Excess*, 58 Wash. & Lee L. Rev. 487 (2001):

> 1) The prosecutor knows that *D* purchased a .38 caliber gun because of the state handgun registration law. As the State has the .38 caliber bullet that killed the victim, it wishes to have the gun so that forensics can attempt to match the bullet to the gun. The

prosecution subpoenas "the gun *D* purchased" on the particular day she bought the .38. Objectionable?

    2) Same as 1) except the particular state does *not* have a gun registration law but the prosecutor can prove through various witnesses that *D* has a large number of guns in her house, including at least one .38 caliber gun. Now the prosecutor subpoenas "all .38 guns in *D*'s possession." Is this constitutionally different from 1)?

    7.   *Post-graduate work.* This is the hardest self-incrimination question yet. A prosecutor subpoenas your client to appear before a grand jury investigating possible federal offenses arising from suspected fraudulent manipulation of oil cargoes and receipt of unreported income. Client appears and testifies about some bank records. When questioned about the existence or location of additional records, Client invokes the Fifth Amendment privilege against self-incrimination. The Government then files a motion that the court order Client to sign twelve forms consenting to disclosure of any bank records respectively relating to twelve foreign bank accounts over which the Government knew or suspected that Client had control. Here is part of the form:

> "I, [client], of the State of Texas in the United States of America, do hereby direct any bank or trust company at which I may have a bank account of any kind, and its officers, employees and agents, to disclose all information and deliver copies of all documents of every nature in your possession or control which relate to said bank account to Grand Jury 84–2, and this shall be irrevocable authority for so doing.

The form also states that the directive "shall be construed as consent" with respect to relevant bank-secrecy laws. Limiting your consideration only to the Fifth Amendment privilege against compelled self-incrimination, can your client be forced to sign this form? We give you the answer—yes—and leave the analysis up to you. See Doe v. United States, 487 U.S. 201, 108 S.Ct. 2341, 101 L.Ed.2d 184 (1988).

    8.   *Fourth Amendment issues.* One could construct a theory of the Fourth Amendment that would make grand jury subpoenas a "seizure," which would then be subject to the Fourth Amendment's requirement of reasonableness. Indeed, the Court began its Fourth Amendment journey with that conception, holding in Boyd v. United States, 116 U.S. 616, 6 S.Ct. 524, 29 L.Ed. 746 (1886), that a subpoena requiring the production of documents implicated both the Fourth and Fifth Amendments, and could not be justified if it required the production of private books and records that would be incriminating.

    The modern Court has abandoned the *Boyd* conception of the Fourth Amendment, holding that a subpoena is an unreasonable Fourth Amendment "seizure" of effects only if "too sweeping in its terms 'to be regarded as reasonable.'" United States v. Dionisio, 410 U.S. 1, 93 S.Ct. 764, 35 L.Ed.2d

67 (1973). The internal quote is from *Hale v. Henkel*, 201 U.S. 43, 26 S.Ct. 370, 50 L.Ed. 652 (1906). In *Hale*, the Court rejected as unreasonable a subpoena that required all documents, accounts, reports and correspondence involving the target company and six other companies, "as well as all letters received by that company since its organization from more than a dozen different companies, situated in seven different states in the Union." The Court conceded that many, if not all, of the documents might ultimately be subject to subpoena but held that the government had to make a showing of "necessity" and "materiality." The Court concluded that a "general subpoena of this description is equally indefensible as a search warrant would be if couched in similar terms."

Hale stands for the proposition that the government must show a connection between the items sought by subpoena and the pending criminal case. This is surely a lower standard than probable cause, though there is little case law on point. For an argument that the *Boyd* approach to subpoenas is preferable to the current approach, see Morgan Cloud, *The Fourth Amendment During the Lochner Era: Privacy, Property, and Liberty in Constitutional Theory*, 48 Stan. L. Rev. 555 (1996).

C. PRETRIAL MOTION PRACTICE

Despite what you might think from watching TV shows and movies about lawyers, many of the difficult evidentiary issues are resolved well in advance of trial. Pre-trial resolution of issues accomplishes three important goals: (1) it makes the trial go more smoothly and efficiently; (2) it makes it easier to keep the jury from being prejudiced by testimony that the judge ultimately rules inadmissible; (3) it facilitates plea bargaining by forcing both sides to take a realistic look at the flaws in their cases.

Consider Federal Rule of Criminal Procedure 12. It contains both mandatory and permissive rules about raising issues prior to trial. It requires motions to suppress evidence be made prior to trial. It requires pre-trial motions in four other categories, which include motions to discover under Rule 16 and for severance of charges or defendants under Rule 14. See Supp. App. B. for these rules. It permits pre-trial motions to dismiss on speedy trial grounds. These substantive topics are covered later in this Chapter.

One frequent pre-trial motion is a motion *in limine*, which requests a ruling in advance of trial on the admissibility of a particular category of evidence. For example, in a case involving child sexual abuse, the defense by motion *in limine* might ask the trial court to rule inadmissible any evidence that the defendant committed adultery and read pornography because neither activity bears sufficient relevance to child sex abuse to justify its prejudicial effect. The advantage of this procedure, of course, is that both parties can plan their presentation of evidence more effectively, and the judge will presumably have fewer objections to consider during trial.

1.   MOTIONS TO SUPPRESS EVIDENCE

Probably the most common use of federal Rule 12 is to file motions to suppress evidence. If you have studied the investigatory phase of the criminal justice process, you know that the Supreme Court has created numerous doctrines that permit a defendant to move to suppress evidence. Many pre-trial hearings are consumed with these issues. One controversial aspect of pre-trial practice is the possibility of police perjury when the motion seeks to suppress evidence.

Police Perjury

A provocative approach to this issue is that of Professor Alan Dershowitz, who claims: "Almost all police lie about whether they violated the Constitution in order to convict guilty defendants." Alan M. Dershowitz, The Best Defense xxi (1982). A more moderate view follows:

> Police perjury occurs. No one can know with certainty the extent of the problem, but no one familiar with the criminal justice system would deny its existence. The problem persists for a number of reasons. Most notably, it can be hard to detect a lie, especially when the testimony is offered by an experienced witness like a veteran police detective. The problem persists, as well, because of attitudes shared by many participants in the justice system about the veracity and guilt of defendants, the undesirability of calling police officers liars, and the costs of the exclusionary rule. When combined with so-called objective tests used for determining whether police officers have violated the Fourth Amendment, these * * * reasons implement a functional presumption favoring the government.

Morgan Cloud, *The Dirty Little Secret*, 43 Emory L.J. 1311, 1348 (1994).

Justice Marshall described the problem of police perjury as follows (but it is a dissent):

> A police officer comes to the witness stand clothed with the authority of the State. His official status gives him credibility and creates a far greater potential for harm than exists when the average citizen testifies. The situation is aggravated when the official draws on special expertise. A policeman testifying about a fingerprint identification or a medical examiner testifying as to the cause of a death can have a critical impact on a defendant's trial. At the same time, the threat of a criminal perjury prosecution, which serves as an important constraint on the average witness' testimony, is virtually nonexistent in the police-

witness context. Despite the apparent prevalence of police perjury, prosecutors exhibit extreme reluctance in charging police officials with criminal conduct because of their need to maintain close working relationships with law enforcement agencies.

Briscoe v. LaHue, 460 U.S. 325, 365–66 (1983) (Marshall, J., dissenting).

But, as Bob Dylan would say, the times they may be a-changing. The existence of body-cams and dash-cams, as well as smart phones, can make a video record that will preclude testilying or unmask it when it happens. For example, Chicago police described a stop of a car after which they smelled marijuana while obtaining the driver's license and proof of insurance; now based on probable cause, police searched the car and found a pound of marijuana. Unfortunately for the police, the dash-cam told a different story. "It showed [the officer] approaching the car, reaching in the window to unlock the door and ordering the driver to step out. [The driver] was frisked, handcuffed and escorted to a cruiser before his car was searched. Editorial: "Police perjury: It's called 'testilying,' " *Chicago Tribune*, July 5, 2015.

Five police officers, three from Chicago and two from Glenview, obviously had reason to suspect the driver of possession contraband. But the dash-cam story left no time for the police to smell the marijuana and thus develop probable cause. The "judge threw out the evidence after the video was played in court. Prosecutors dropped the charges. Sperling not only went free—he filed a federal lawsuit and got a $195,000 settlement from Chicago and Glenview." Four of the officers were charged with perjury, obstruction of justice, and official misconduct.

Frequency of Motions to Suppress

How often are pre-trial motions to suppress filed? How often are they successful? Professor Peter J. Nardulli has published two classic empirical studies of pre-trial motion practice. In one, he analyzed 7,767 cases drawn from nine middle-sized counties in Illinois, Michigan, and Pennsylvania. He discovered one county in which the public defender's office had a policy of automatically filing "motions to suppress an identification or confession along with standard discovery motions—even in cases with no identification or confession." Peter J. Nardulli, *The Societal Cost of the Exclusionary Rule: An Empirical Reassessment*, 1983 Am. Bar Found. Research J. 585, 594. Removing these largely pro forma motions from the sample, Nardulli found that motions to suppress physical evidence, a confession, or an identification occurred in only 7.6% of all cases. *Id.*

In the relatively small universe of cases in which a motion to suppress was made, the rates of success were 16.9% for motions to suppress physical evidence, 2.5% for motions to suppress a confession, and 1.7% for motions to suppress an identification. Restated as a percentage of all cases, successful motions to suppress occurred in 0.69% of cases involving physical evidence, 0.16% of the cases involving confessions, and 0.08% of the cases involving an identification (eight one-hundredths of one percent). It seems clear that criminal lawyers should not expect too many victories when they file motions to suppress! These data are over twenty years old now, and the chances of winning a motion to suppress physical evidence are probably lower today than in the early 1980s. The combined effect of several Supreme Court doctrines—good faith exceptions to the exclusionary rule, the public safety exception to *Miranda*, continued expansion of the "stop and frisk" rule, elaborations on standing, and greater ease of showing consent—provide judges with more grounds to rule against a defendant in 2017 than in 1983.

A later study of motion practice in Chicago revealed a much higher success rate for motions to suppress physical evidence (64%), but roughly the same low rate of filing motions to suppress (in 9.7% of cases for all kinds of motions to suppress, and 8.3% for motions to suppress physical evidence). Peter J. Nardulli, *The Societal Costs of the Exclusionary Rule Revisited*, 1987 U. Ill. L. Rev. 223, 229–30. The reasons why a big city would have a higher success rate than middle-sized counties are probably both fascinating and complex, perhaps having to do with more aggressive policing and less pliant judges in big cities. Even in Chicago, however, motions to suppress physical evidence were granted in only 5% of all criminal cases (64% times 8.3%)—not rare but not frequent either.

While these data might be read to suggest the futility of an aggressive pre-trial motion practice, most experienced lawyers would disagree with that inference. G. Robert Radford, an excellent defense lawyer who retired as a District Attorney in Tennessee, provided the following advice to one of the casebook authors: File every motion for which a colorable argument exists—suppression, discovery, severance, change of venue, etc. "When the DA hears that Radford is the defense lawyer, I want him to slap his head and go, 'Aw, hell, not that Radford guy. I don't have time for him.'"

NOTES AND QUESTIONS

1. *Reality of criminal defense work.* Why do you think motions to suppress are filed in fewer than 10% of the cases? What does this tell you about routine criminal defense practice?

2. *Use of pre-trial testimony.* Suppose you represent S, who is charged with armed robbery. The police seized a suitcase in the basement of a home belonging to M. It contained a gun holster, a sack similar to the one used in the robbery, and bill wrappers from the bank that had been robbed. You move to suppress the contents of the suitcase on the ground that the police did not have a warrant to search the basement of M's house. S did not live in M's

house. Under Fourth Amendment doctrine, *S* must show that he has standing in the area searched before he can argue the merits of the Fourth Amendment claim. To do that, *S* can testify at the motion to suppress that he was a visitor in *M*'s house, that he had access to the basement, and that he stored items there, including the suitcase. Suppose you elicit that testimony from *S* and then lose the motion to suppress. This could be the worst of all worlds—the suitcase and holster admitted, together with *S*'s statements that the suitcase was his. The lower courts in the case from which this Note was drawn had so held. The Supreme Court reversed.

> The rule adopted by the courts below does not merely impose upon a defendant a condition which may deter him from asserting a Fourth Amendment objection—it imposes a condition of a kind to which this Court has always been peculiarly sensitive. For a defendant who wishes to establish standing must do so at the risk that the words which he utters may later be used to incriminate him. * * * Thus, in this case [*S*] was obliged either to give up what he believed, with advice of counsel, to be a valid Fourth Amendment claim or, in legal effect, to waive his Fifth Amendment privilege against self-incrimination. In these circumstances, we find it intolerable that one constitutional right should have to be surrendered in order to assert another. We therefore hold that when a defendant testifies in support of a motion to suppress evidence on Fourth Amendment grounds, his testimony may not thereafter be admitted against him at trial on the issue of guilt unless he makes no objection.

Simmons v. United States, 390 U.S. 377, 88 S.Ct. 967, 19 L.Ed.2d 1247 (1968).

2.   MOTIONS TO CHANGE VENUE

Defendants have a right to be tried "[1] by an impartial jury [2] of the State and district wherein the crime shall have been committed." U.S. Const. amend. VI. See also Fed. R. Crim. P. 18 (Supp. App. B.). Venue was of critical importance to the anti-Federalists who demanded a Bill of Rights as a restraint on the new central government. More ink was spilled, and more energy expended, in favor of a right to venue in the county or vicinage where the crime occurred than on any other right now found in the Bill of Rights. Many argued that the right to a jury trial contained in Article III of the United States Constitution (see p. 1) was inadequate to protect the common law right to a jury trial because it required only that the trial take place in the *state* where the crime was committed. The following excerpt captures the flavor of the debate:

> It is a maxim universally admitted, that the safety of the subject consists in having a right to a trial as free and impartial as the lot of humanity will admit of. Does the Constitution [in Article III] make provision for such a trial? I think not; for in a criminal

process, a person shall not have a right to insist on a trial in the vicinity where the fact was committed, where a jury of the peers would, from their local situation, have an opportunity to form a judgment of the *character* of the person charged with the crime, and also to judge of the *credibility* of the witnesses. There a person must be tried by a jury of strangers; a jury who *may be* interested in his conviction; and where he *may*, by reason of the distance of his residence from the place of the trial, be incapable of making such a defence, as he is, in justice, entitled to, and which he could avail himself of, if his trial was in the same county where the crime is said to have been committed.

Neil H. Cogan, The Complete Bill of Rights 419–20 (1997) (quoting from the proceedings in the Massachusetts State Convention, January 30, 1788).

As this excerpt suggests, some Framers considered an "impartial jury" to be one that was familiar with the defendant and the witnesses. This understanding of "impartial jury" dates back to the thirteenth century when the defendant had to choose to "put himself upon the country" and receive a verdict that was the voice of the community. See 2 Frederick Pollock & Frederick William Maitland, The History of English Law 598–600 (2d ed. 1899). The verdict of the community was a more inclusive judgment than whether the defendant had engaged in particular conduct. It was, in a real sense, designed to determine whether the defendant remained part of the community or became an "outlaw"— literally found to be outside the law that protected those in the community. Over time trials became more focused on the culpability of conduct, and less on whether the defendant should remain as part of the community, causing the function of the jury also to change. Rules of evidence would later restrict inquiry into the character of the defendant.

The concept of a verdict as a broad judgment of the defendant's fitness to be part of the community was in flux in the late eighteenth century. Indeed, the defenders of the Article III jury trial right made the opposite modern argument that impartiality is served, not hindered, by lack of knowledge of the case and the litigants. The Sixth Amendment reflects a compromise between those satisfied with trial in the state where the crime was committed and those who wanted trial within the county. The compromise was to require trial in "the district," an area typically larger than a county and smaller than the entire state.

But the Framers' rather tidy solution to the venue problem fails to keep venue "close to home" when some modern crimes are committed. Many crimes today are defined to include conduct that can occur over days, months, or even years and in many jurisdictions. In United States v. Rodriguez-Moreno, 526 U.S. 275, 119 S.Ct. 1239, 143 L.Ed.2d 388

(1999), the issue was the proper venue for using or carrying a firearm "during and in relation to any crime of violence," in violation of 18 U.S.C. § 924(c)(1). The underlying crimes were conspiracy to kidnap and kidnaping, which spanned all the states from Texas to New York, but the defendant used a gun only in Maryland. Could the 924(c)(1) charge be brought in New Jersey? The Court, in an opinion by Justice Thomas, held that it could. The defendant argued that the New Jersey kidnaping is "completely irrelevant to the firearm crime" because he "did not *use* or *carry* a gun *during* the New Jersey crime."

The Court rejected that argument on the ground that kidnaping "is a unitary crime" that "does not end until the victim is free. * * * It does not matter that respondent used the .357 magnum revolver, as the Government concedes, only in Maryland because he did so 'during and in relation to' a kidnaping that was begun in Texas and continued in New York, New Jersey, and Maryland."

Justice Scalia, in an opinion joined only by Justice Stevens, found the majority's approach almost incomprehensible.

> To answer the question before us we need only ask where the defendant's alleged act of using a firearm during (and in relation to) a kidnaping occurred. Since it occurred only in Maryland, venue will lie only there. * * *
>
> The short of the matter is that this defendant, who has a constitutional right to be tried in the State and district where his alleged crime was "committed," has been prosecuted for using a gun during a kidnaping in a State and district where all agree he did not use a gun during a kidnaping. If to state this case is not to decide it, the law has departed further from the meaning of language than is appropriate for a government that is supposed to rule (and to be restrained) through the written word.

NOTES AND QUESTIONS

1. Is the statutory interpretation question as clear as Justice Scalia claims? If so, how could seven members of the Court reach the contrary result?

2. Rodriguez-Moreno did not make a motion to change venue. Why was this not a waiver of the venue argument? Hint: Look at Fed. R. Crim. Pro. 18.

3. Of course, sometimes the right to an impartial jury and the right to be tried in the local venue can conflict. Sometimes defendants want venue to be other than in the district where the crime occurred because of a belief that it will be difficult or impossible to empanel an impartial jury. In these cases, defendants file a motion to change venue and seek to prove that any jury drawn from the venire will have prejudged the case. This proof typically

consists of evidence about the quantity and nature of pretrial publicity and perhaps opinion surveys drawn from random samples of the local population.

Motions to change venue are made infrequently and granted rarely. Most crime is routine and not all that newsworthy. The Court's test for when venue must be changed manifests an abiding faith in jurors and in the jury system. In the typical case, the Court has held, jurors are impartial if they can lay aside any impressions they had formed "and render a verdict based on the evidence in court." Irvin v. Dowd, 366 U.S. 717, 81 S.Ct. 1639, 6 L.Ed.2d 751 (1961). Deciding when a juror can truly "lay aside" any prior impression or opinion is not always easy, of course. *Voir dire* questions about the influence of what the juror has read or heard about the case will test the sincerity of each juror's assurance of impartiality. But as long as enough jurors state categorically that they can decide the case based only on the evidence presented in court, the trial judge is unlikely to grant a change of venue. And if the trial court does not grant a change of venue, the appellate courts are unlikely to reverse that decision. After all, the trial judge is in the best position to determine, based on observing demeanor, tone, and inflection, whether a juror's protestation of impartiality is sincere.

About the only time appellate courts will reverse a trial court finding that a jury was impartial despite the pre-trial publicity is when a court is willing to find that prejudice is presumed. The Court presumed prejudice in Irvin v. Dowd, 366 U.S. 717, 81 S.Ct. 1639, 6 L.Ed.2d 751 (1961), Rideau v. Louisiana, 373 U.S. 723, 83 S.Ct. 1417, 10 L.Ed.2d 663 (1963), Estes v. Texas, 381 U.S. 532, 85 S.Ct. 1628, 14 L.Ed.2d 543 (1965), and Sheppard v. Maxwell, 384 U.S. 333, 86 S.Ct. 1507, 16 L.Ed.2d 600 (1966).

In those cases the influence of the news media, either in the community at large or in the courtroom itself, pervaded the proceedings. In *Rideau* the defendant had "confessed" under police interrogation to the murder of which he stood convicted. A 20-minute film of his confession was broadcast three times by a television station in the community where the crime and the trial took place. In reversing, the Court did not examine the *voir dire* for evidence of actual prejudice because it considered the trial under review "but a hollow formality"—the real trial had occurred when tens of thousands of people, in a community of 150,000, had seen and heard the defendant admit his guilt before the cameras.

The trial in *Estes* had been conducted in a circus atmosphere, due in large part to the intrusions of the press, which was allowed to sit within the bar of the court and to overrun it with television equipment. Similarly, *Sheppard* arose from a trial infected not only by a background of extremely inflammatory publicity but also by a courthouse given over to accommodate the public appetite for carnival. The proceedings in these cases were entirely lacking in the solemnity and sobriety to which a defendant is entitled in a system that subscribes to any notion of fairness and rejects the verdict of a mob. Murphy v. Florida, 421 U.S. 794, 95 S.Ct. 2031, 44 L.Ed.2d 589 (1975).

4.   *Murph the Surf.* In cases that do not involve a circus atmosphere, judges are likely to find an impartial jury if the jurors are willing to state that they will decide the case on the facts and law presented in court. In *Murphy*, last Note, the media referred to the notorious criminal defendant as "Murph the Surf." Noting that "one juror freely admitted that he was predisposed to convict [Murphy]," Justice Brennan's description in dissent of the case continues:

> [One] juror testified that she knew from several sources that petitioner was a convicted murderer, and was aware that the community regarded petitioner as a criminal who "should be put away." She disclaimed having a fixed opinion about the result she would reach, but acknowledged that the fact that petitioner was a convicted criminal would probably influence her verdict. * * *

> Still another juror testified that the comments of venire members in discussing the case had made him "sick to [his] stomach." He testified that one venireman had said that petitioner was "thoroughly rotten," and that another had said, "Hang him, he's guilty."

Faced with this record, the Court nonetheless affirmed the trial court's refusal to grant a change of venue. Justice Brennan was the only dissenter. Justice Marshall wrote the Court's opinion. *Murphy* makes clear the extent to which trial judges defer to the juror's assurance of impartiality and the extent to which federal courts defer to the decisions of trial judges not to grant motions to change venue

5.   *A tidbit about Sheppard.* The defendant in *Sheppard*, Note 3, was Sam Sheppard, a physician who was convicted of murdering his wife—falsely, he claimed. This was the case on which the television series and later the movie, "The Fugitive," were based. Dr. Sheppard served ten years in prison before the Supreme Court reversed his conviction in 1966; he was acquitted following a second trial later that same year and died in 1970. The state's theory of the case was that he had bludgeoned his wife to death and left a trail of blood. Dr. Sheppard claimed that the blood must have come from a third person "because Mrs. Sheppard had bitten her killer, breaking two teeth, and [Dr. Sheppard] had not been cut." Fox Butterfield, *"The Fugitive" Didn't Do It*, N.Y. Times, February 9, 1998, Section 4, p. 2. "The DNA, taken from two specks from the trail of blood preserved in the county coroner's office, proved that it was not Mrs. Sheppard's blood." *Id.* The current local prosecutor said that he believed Dr. Sheppard had been innocent and that a former part-time employee of the Sheppard's, now in prison for another murder, was probably a serial killer.

D. DISCOVERY

1. NON-CONSTITUTIONAL DISCOVERY

Introductory Comment

The trend for many years in civil cases has been toward almost unlimited discovery. The arguments sound in efficiency, fairness, and accuracy. Cases will settle more quickly, more fairly, and come closer to manifesting the factual and legal truth of what happened if each side has access to the evidence that the other has uncovered. Though the trend in criminal cases has been toward more liberal discovery, two major differences between civil and criminal cases have resulted in significant restrictions on discovery. First, the Fifth Amendment privilege against compelled self-incrimination produces restrictions on discovery requests directed to defendants.

The second difference is that Congress considers criminal defendants as a class more likely to attempt to influence witnesses to change their testimony, or not to testify, than civil litigants. Moreover, as an early and passionate advocate of broad discovery conceded, "many witnesses, if they know that the defendant will have knowledge of their names prior to trial, will be reluctant to come forward with information during the investigation of the crime." State v. Tune, 13 N.J. 203, 98 A.2d 881 (1953) (majority opinion of Chief Justice Arthur T. Vanderbilt).

One can see the power of this argument in the reaction of Congress when the Supreme Court recommended changing Federal Rule of Criminal Procedure 16, the discovery rule, to give defendants the right to demand a witness list from the government. The Department of Justice opposed the witness list provision passionately, quoting many United States Attorneys who called it "dangerous" and "frightening"—an invitation to "bribery and obstruction of justice" and the "manufacturing of defenses." *Hearing before the Subcommittee on Criminal Justice of the Committee on the Judiciary*, House of Representatives, 93d Cong., 2d Sess., September 17, 1974, at 49. In rejecting this amendment to Rule 16, the House-Senate conference committee cited as "paramount concerns" the "[d]iscouragement of witnesses and improper contact directed at influencing their testimony."

The reluctance to compel discovery of a witness list is understandable, but it is unfortunate in the vast majority of cases where the defendant will not tamper with the witnesses. It means that federal defendants can face trial without knowing how best to respond to the prosecution's case because the defendant does not know the source of testimony that will be offered against him. And there is an irony here: Civil litigants, for whom the stakes are so very much lower than criminal defendants, have far broader discovery rights. If broader criminal discovery could prevent even a small number of unjust convictions, it would be worth some level of anxiety about witness tampering. Whether it would be worth a certain number of actual cases of obstruction of justice, or physical harm to witnesses, is a more difficult question, one that Congress has so far resolved against broader discovery.

In 2012, the Chief Judge of the United States District Court for the District of Vermont called for revisions to Rule 16 that would at least require the prosecution to disclose all statements of the defendant in the government's possession, custody, or control. Judge Reiss argues that this rule is easy to enforce and "provides a criminal defendant with the information necessary to engage in effective plea negotiations or prepare for trial." She concludes that permitting the government sometimes not to disclose the defendant's own statements is neither fair nor just. "It is time to eliminate [those exceptions] in order to achieve a more fair, efficient, and uniform administration of justice." Christina Reiss, *Closing Fed. R. Crim. P. 16(a)'s Loopholes: Why Criminal Defendants Are Entitled to Discovery of All of Their Statements*, Criminal Law Brief, Spring 2012, 4, 13. Rule 16(a) has not been amended to take account of these criticisms.

Perhaps because of the potential unfairness in the federal approach to this issue, there seems to be a fairly high level of voluntary disclosure. Seventy-six percent of U.S. Attorneys who responded to a 1984 ABA survey said that they provided "extensive informal discovery beyond the dictates of Rule 16." Wm. Bradford Middlekauf, *What Practitioners Say About Broad Criminal Discovery*, Criminal Justice, Spring 1994, at 55 (quoting 99 Cong., 1st Sess. 156 (1985)). Of the responding U.S. Attorneys, 60 percent "noted that they disclosed witness names and statements, and 42 percent said that they followed an open-file discovery policy." *Id.* But most U.S. Attorneys "did not grant additional discovery in cases in which they felt it would compromise the system—for example, serious drug cases or cases in which there was a considerable risk of witness intimidation." *Id.*

Most states have followed a different path, providing more formal rights of discovery of witness information. A 2008 survey of state practices disclosed that thirty states, and the military courts, granted defendants the right to discover "all prosecution witnesses," "all witnesses," or "all persons having knowledge of relevant facts who may be called by the state as witnesses at the trial." Stephen D. Easton & Kaitlin A. Bridges, *Peeking Behind the Wizard's Curtain: Expert Discovery and Disclosure in Criminal Cases*, 32 AMER. J. TRIAL ADVOC. 1, 35 (2008). The latter, remarkably broad, provision is Idaho's. "Of the ten most populous American cities, only New York City is located in a state that does not require pretrial disclosure of witness lists." Middlekauf, *supra*, at 16. That a total of thirty states, which include nine of the ten largest cities, require disclosure of at least some of the state's witnesses is strong evidence that, in typical cases, the risk of witness intimidation is outweighed by the fairness interest in the defendant having a witness list.

A mere list of potential witnesses, while helpful to defendants, is obviously not as useful as being able to depose those witnesses. Six states permit defendants to depose all prosecution witnesses and five others permit discovery upon leave of the court. See George C. Thomas III, *Two Windows Into Innocence*, 7 Ohio St. J. Crim. L. 575 (2009). Thomas concluded that for defendants "deposing prosecution witnesses is far preferable to preliminary hearings. The scope of questioning can be much broader in a deposition than in a preliminary hearing" and "the defense lawyer is the party who decides what witnesses to question; the prosecutor cannot hide weak witnesses." *Id.* at 593.

Even though there is no right to routine discovery of witnesses in federal court, defendants do have a rule of procedure right to discover various items of evidence. See Fed. R. Crim. P. 16. Moreover, as explained in subsection 1, defendants have a due process right to discover all exculpatory evidence in the hands of the prosecutor. Vigorous cross-examination of the prosecution witnesses at a preliminary hearing, as we have seen, can also be an effective discovery tool. Discovery of as much evidence as possible prepares the defense lawyer to cross-examine the state's witnesses. This discovery also permits the defendant to learn if there are witnesses who might provide favorable testimony; the defendant can subpoena these witnesses by using the Sixth Amendment right of "compulsory process" (see Chapter 16) if the State does not call them as witnesses. Thus, although discovery occurs in the pretrial stages of a criminal prosecution, its real significance is for the trial and the plea bargaining that is a surrogate for trial—defendants get much better bargains if they have a reasonably strong defense. If you visualize discovery requests as a way of preparing the best defense for trial, rather than a routine pretrial practice, you will have a better idea of the way good lawyers approach discovery.

If informal discovery fails, the recourse is to state or federal rules of procedure. Fed. R. Crim. P. 16 is a good example. Read it carefully and apply it to the following Problem. Also note that discovery is not limited to the pre-trial context. Consider Rule 26.2, which is based on the constitutional rule established in *Jencks v. United States*, 353 U.S. 657, 77 S.Ct. 1007, 1 L.Ed.2d 1103 (1957).

NOTES AND QUESTIONS

1.   *Problem.* In a federal prosecution for a conspiracy to bomb a government building, one of the defendants files a pretrial request under Rule 16 for the following items from the prosecution:

A.   All written or recorded statements, and oral statements or confessions or admissions subsequently reduced to writing, or summarized in F.B.I., police, or other federal or state governmental reports, made or adopted by any defendant or defendants, or copies thereof, within the possession, custody or control of the government, the existence of which is known or by the exercise of due diligence could become known to the attorney for the government. [This request includes statements made to persons other than government agents at any time, provided the substance of such statements has been recorded or summarized in written form.]

yes an

B.   All results or reports of physical or mental examinations and of scientific tests or experiments arguably relevant to this case, including handwriting analyses and fingerprint comparisons. *yes*

C.   Recorded testimony of any named or unnamed alleged co-conspirator before the grand jury in this case.   *no*

D.   Names and addresses of all persons who have knowledge pertaining to the case, or who have been interviewed by government agents in connection with the case.   *no*

E.   Written or recorded or summarized statements of all persons the government plans to call as witnesses. *no*

What result under Federal Rule 16? See United States v. Ahmad, 53 F.R.D. 186 (M.D.Pa.1971). Does the defendant have a right to discover any of these items later, at trial? (Hint: look at Rule 26.2.)

2.   *Oral statements.* You are a federal prosecutor. Your case file contains a summary of a statement *D* volunteered to police before they arrested him. The arresting officer wrote the summary a few hours after the arrest while preparing the arrest report (it is not part of the arrest report). If the defendant makes a Rule 16 request for all of *D's* statements, are you required to disclose this statement? *yes*

3.   *Statements made to undercover officer.* Suppose an undercover officer questions *D* who responds with incriminating statements. If the officer later writes down these statements, can *D* discover them under Rule 16? *no if didnt know*

4.   *Statements of government witnesses.* *W* writes a letter relating to a crime. The prosecution has the letter and intends to call *W* as a witness to testify to the same information contained in the letter. After *W* testifies, can the defense lawyer compel production of the letter? Can the defense compel production prior to trial under Rule 16?

5. *Informal discovery—"My Cousin Vinny."* In the 20th Century Fox movie "My Cousin Vinny," Vinny is a 40ish but newly-licensed lawyer (after six tries at the New York bar exam) who defends his cousin in a small town in rural Alabama. Vinny and his girlfriend, Mona Lisa Vito, arrive looking very much like New Yorkers. She surveys the handful of aging buildings on the isolated Southern court square, and proclaims, "I bet the Chinese food here is terrible." At one point, Vinny wants to know what evidence the prosecutor has against his client (who is wrongfully accused, of course). Lisa helps him understand the Alabama Rules of Criminal Procedure on the subject of disclosure, but when Vinny goes hunting with the prosecutor, he employs a more direct, New York strategy, saying that he'd sure like to get a look at the prosecutor's files. The prosecutor says, "You got a Xerox machine over there?" "No," Vinny says (the hotel rooms are part of the charm of the movie). "Never mind," says the prosecutor. "I'll take care of it." As you might expect, Vinny wins the case, with a huge assist from Lisa. If you haven't seen the movie, it's worth renting.

Why would a prosecutor be so willing to turn the file over to the defense? Whatever explains the generosity of a prosecutor in individual cases, it is a good idea always to pursue informal discovery before resorting to the formal variety.

6. *Informal discovery—a real case.* L was appointed to represent D, charged with second degree murder for the death of his passenger in a car accident. D's blood alcohol, taken at the hospital where he was treated, was three times the limit that presumed intoxication. L made a motion to suppress the blood alcohol test, on state law grounds, based on the failure to obtain D's consent. A serious pragmatic problem for the defense was that D remembered nothing about the accident, the trip to the hospital, or his treatment at the hospital. L, in his first year of practice, prepared a proof of non-consent based on D's subjective state of unconsciousness. It did not occur to L until the morning of the hearing that a single phone call to the emergency room treating physician could make D's testimony unnecessary. The doctor testified that D was incapable of consenting to anything, and the judge granted the motion to suppress.

2. CONSTITUTIONAL DISCOVERY

Introductory Comment

The Court's first constitutional discovery case was a "shot heard 'round the world,'" if the world is limited to lawyers who try criminal cases, and particularly if limited to the defense bar. Scott Sundby, *Fallen Superheroes and Constitutional Mirages: The Tale of Brady v. Maryland,* 33 McGeorge L. Rev. 643 (2002) (manuscript version). The case was *Brady v. Maryland,* 373 U.S. 83, 83 S.Ct. 1194, 10 L.Ed.2d 215 (1963).

Brady announced a broad rule of constitutional criminal discovery: "[T]he suppression by the prosecution of evidence favorable to an accused upon request violates due process where the evidence is material either to guilt or to punishment, irrespective of the good faith or bad faith of the prosecution." Brady had specifically requested his co-defendant's extrajudicial statements. "Several of those statements were shown to him; but one dated July 9, 1958, in which [the co-defendant] admitted the actual homicide, was withheld by the prosecution * * * ."

Brady compared the failure to disclose the exculpatory statement to the prosecutor's knowing use of perjured evidence in *Mooney v. Holohan*, 294 U.S. 103, 112, 55 S.Ct. 340, 342, 79 L.Ed. 791 (1935):

> The principle of *Mooney v. Holohan* is not punishment of society for misdeeds of a prosecutor but avoidance of an unfair trial to the accused. Society wins not only when the guilty are convicted but when criminal trials are fair; our system of the administration of justice suffers when any accused is treated unfairly. An inscription on the walls of the Department of Justice states the proposition candidly for the federal domain: "The United States wins its point whenever justice is done its citizens in the courts." A prosecution that withholds evidence on demand of an accused which, if made available, would tend to exculpate him or reduce the penalty helps shape a trial that bears heavily on the defendant. That casts the prosecutor in the role of an architect of a proceeding that does not comport with standards of justice * * * .

The closest the Court in *Brady* came to defining the class of "material" evidence that had to be disclosed on request was evidence "which, if made available, would tend to exculpate him or reduce the penalty." The Court also said nothing about cases in which prosecutors possessed material evidence but the defendant either failed to request it or made a general request that failed to put the prosecution on notice of the particular evidence that was sought. Both of those issues were before the Court in the next case.

UNITED STATES V. AGURS

Supreme Court of the United States, 1976.
427 U.S. 97, 96 S.Ct. 2392, 49 L.Ed.2d 342.

MR. JUSTICE STEVENS delivered the opinion of the Court [joined by CHIEF JUSTICE BURGER and JUSTICES STEWART, WHITE, BLACKMUN, POWELL, and REHNQUIST].

After a brief interlude in an inexpensive motel room, respondent repeatedly stabbed James Sewell, causing his death. She was convicted of second-degree murder. The question before us is whether the prosecutor's failure to provide defense counsel with certain background information about Sewell, which would have tended to support the argument that respondent acted in self-defense, deprived her of a fair trial under the rule of *Brady v. Maryland*. * * *

I

At about 4:30 p.m. on September 24, 1971, respondent, who had been there before, and Sewell, registered in a motel as man and wife. They were assigned a room without a bath. Sewell was wearing a bowie knife in a sheath, and carried another knife in his pocket. Less than two hours earlier, according to the testimony of his estranged wife, he had had $360 in cash on his person.

About 15 minutes later three motel employees heard respondent screaming for help. A forced entry into their room disclosed Sewell on top of respondent struggling for possession of the bowie knife. She was holding the knife; his bleeding hand grasped the blade; according to one witness he was trying to jam the blade into her chest. The employees separated the two and summoned the authorities. Respondent departed without comment before they arrived. Sewell was dead on arrival at the hospital.

Circumstantial evidence indicated that the parties had completed an act of intercourse, that Sewell had then gone to the bathroom down the hall, and that the struggle occurred upon his return. The contents of his pockets were in disarray on the dresser and no money was found; the jury may have inferred that respondent took Sewell's money and that the fight started when Sewell re-entered the room and saw what she was doing.

On the following morning respondent surrendered to the police. She was given a physical examination which revealed no cuts or bruises of any kind, except needle marks on her upper arm. An autopsy of Sewell disclosed that he had several deep stab wounds in his chest and abdomen, and a number of slashes on his arms and hands, characterized by the pathologist as "defensive wounds."

Respondent offered no evidence. Her sole defense was the argument made by her attorney that Sewell had initially attacked her with the knife, and that her actions had all been directed toward saving her own life. The support for this self-defense theory was based on the fact that she had screamed for help. Sewell was on top of her when help arrived, and his possession of two knives indicated that he was a violence-prone person. It took the jury about 25 minutes to elect a foreman and return a verdict.

Three months later defense counsel filed a motion for a new trial asserting that he had discovered (1) that Sewell had a prior criminal record that would have further evidenced his violent character; (2) that the prosecutor had failed to disclose this information to the defense; and (3) that a recent opinion of the United States Court of Appeals for the District of Columbia Circuit made it clear that such evidence was admissible even if not known to the defendant. Sewell's prior record included a plea of guilty to a charge of assault and carrying a deadly weapon in 1963, and another guilty plea to a charge of carrying a deadly weapon in 1971. Apparently both weapons were knives.

The Government opposed the motion, arguing that there was no duty to tender Sewell's prior record to the defense in the absence of an appropriate request; that the evidence was readily discoverable in advance of trial and hence was not the kind of "newly discovered" evidence justifying a new trial; and that, in all events, it was not material.

The District Court denied the motion. It rejected the Government's argument that there was no duty to disclose material evidence unless requested to do so, assumed that the evidence was admissible, but held that it was not sufficiently material. The District Court expressed the opinion that the prior conviction shed no light on Sewell's character that was not already apparent from the uncontradicted evidence, particularly the fact that he carried two knives; the court stressed the inconsistency between the claim of self-defense and the fact that Sewell had been stabbed repeatedly while respondent was unscathed.

The Court of Appeals reversed. The court found no lack of diligence on the part of the defense and no misconduct by the prosecutor in this case. It held, however, that the evidence was material, and that its nondisclosure required a new trial because the jury might have returned a different verdict if the evidence had been received.

The decision of the Court of Appeals represents a significant departure from this Court's prior holding; because we believe that that court has incorrectly interpreted the constitutional requirement of due process, we reverse.

II

The rule of *Brady* arguably applies in three quite different situations. Each involves the discovery, after trial of information which had been known to the prosecution but unknown to the defense.

In the first situation, typified by *Mooney v. Holohan*, 294 U.S. 103, 55 S.Ct. 340, 79 L.Ed. 791 [(1935)], the undisclosed evidence demonstrates that the prosecution's case includes perjured testimony and that the prosecution knew, or should have known, of the perjury. In a series of subsequent cases, the Court has consistently held that a conviction obtained by the knowing use of perjured testimony is fundamentally unfair, and must be set aside if there is any reasonable likelihood that the false testimony could have affected the judgment of the jury. It is this line of cases on which the Court of Appeals placed primary reliance. In those cases the Court has applied a strict standard of materiality, not just because they involve prosecutorial misconduct, but more importantly because they involve a corruption of the truth-seeking function of the trial process. Since this case involves no misconduct, and since there is no reason to question the veracity of any of the prosecution witnesses, the test of materiality followed in the *Mooney* line of cases is not necessarily applicable to this case.

The second situation, illustrated by the *Brady* case itself, is characterized by a pretrial request for specific evidence. In that case defense counsel had requested the extrajudicial statements made by Brady's accomplice, one Boblit. This Court held that the suppression of one of Boblit's statements deprived Brady of due process, noting specifically that the statement had been requested and that it was "material." A fair analysis of the holding in *Brady* indicates that implicit in the requirement of materiality is a concern that the suppressed evidence might have affected the outcome of the trial.

* * * At his trial Brady did not deny his involvement in the deliberate killing, but testified that it was his accomplice, Boblit, rather than he, who had actually strangled the decedent. This version of the event was corroborated by one of several confessions made by Boblit but not given to Brady's counsel despite an admittedly adequate request. * * *

The test of materiality in a case like *Brady* in which specific information has been requested by the defense is not necessarily the same as in a case in which no such request has been made. Indeed, this Court has not yet decided whether the prosecutor has any obligation to provide defense counsel with exculpatory information when no request has been made. Before addressing that question, a brief comment on the function of the request is appropriate.

In *Brady* the request was specific. It gave the prosecutor notice of exactly what the defense desired. Although there is, of course, no duty to provide defense counsel with unlimited discovery of everything known by the prosecutor, if the subject matter of such a request is material, or indeed if a substantial basis for claiming materiality exists, it is reasonable to require the prosecutor to respond either by furnishing the information or by submitting the problem to the trial judge. When the prosecutor receives a specific and relevant request, the failure to make any response is seldom, if ever, excusable.

In many cases, however, exculpatory information in the possession of the prosecutor may be unknown to defense counsel. In such a situation he may make no request at all, or possibly ask for "all *Brady* material" or for "anything exculpatory." Such a request really gives the prosecutor no better notice than if no request is made. If there is a duty to respond to a general request of that kind, it must derive from the obviously exculpatory character of certain evidence in the hands of the prosecutor. But if the evidence is so clearly supportive of a claim of innocence that it gives the prosecution notice of a duty to produce, that duty should equally arise even if no request is made. Whether we focus on the desirability of a precise definition of the prosecutor's duty or on the potential harm to the defendant, we conclude that there is no significant difference between cases in which there has been merely a general request for exculpatory matter and cases, like the one we must now decide, in which there has been no request at all. The third situation in which the *Brady* rule arguably applies, typified by this case, therefore embraces the case in which only a general request for "*Brady* material" has been made.

We now consider whether the prosecutor has any constitutional duty to volunteer exculpatory matter to the defense, and if so, what standard of materiality gives rise to that duty.

III

We are not considering the scope of discovery authorized by the Federal Rules of Criminal Procedure, or the wisdom of amending those Rules to enlarge the defendant's discovery rights. We are dealing with the defendant's right to a fair trial mandated by the Due Process Clause of the Fifth Amendment to the Constitution. Our construction of that Clause will apply equally to the comparable Clause in the Fourteenth Amendment applicable to trials in state courts.

The problem arises in two principal contexts. First, in advance of trial, and perhaps during the course of a trial as well, the prosecutor must decide what, if anything, he should voluntarily submit to defense counsel. Second, after trial a judge may be required to decide whether a nondisclosure deprived the defendant of his right to due process. Logically the same standard must apply at both times. For unless the omission deprived the defendant of a fair trial, there was no constitutional violation requiring that the verdict be set aside; and absent a constitutional violation, there was no breach of the prosecutor's constitutional duty to disclose.

Nevertheless, there is a significant practical difference between the pretrial decision of the prosecutor and the post-trial decision of the judge. Because we are dealing with an inevitably imprecise standard, and because the significance of an item of evidence can seldom be predicted accurately until the entire record is complete, the prudent prosecutor will resolve doubtful questions in favor of disclosure. But to reiterate a critical point, the prosecutor will not have violated his constitutional duty of disclosure unless his omission is of sufficient significance to result in the denial of the defendant's right to a fair trial.

The Court of Appeals appears to have assumed that the prosecutor has a constitutional obligation to disclose any information that might affect the jury's verdict. That statement of a constitutional standard of materiality approaches the "sporting theory of justice" which the Court expressly rejected in *Brady*. For a jury's appraisal of a case "might" be affected by an improper or trivial consideration as well as by evidence giving rise to a legitimate doubt on the issue of guilt. If everything that might influence a jury must be disclosed, the only way a prosecutor could discharge his constitutional duty would be to allow complete discovery of his files as a matter of routine practice.

Whether or not procedural rules authorizing such broad discovery might be desirable, the Constitution surely does not demand that much. * * *

Nor do we believe the constitutional obligation is measured by the moral culpability, or the willfulness, of the prosecutor. If evidence highly probative of innocence is in his file, he should be presumed to recognize its significance even if he has actually overlooked it. Conversely, if evidence actually has no probative significance at all, no purpose would be served by requiring a new trial simply because an inept prosecutor incorrectly believed he was suppressing a fact that would be vital to the defense. If the suppression of evidence results in constitutional error, it is because of the character of the evidence, not the character of the prosecutor.

As the District Court recognized in this case, there are situations in which evidence is obviously of such substantial value to the defense that elementary fairness requires it to be disclosed even without a specific request. For though the attorney for the sovereign must prosecute the accused with earnestness and vigor, he must always be faithful to his client's overriding interest that "justice shall be done." He is the "servant of the law, the twofold aim of which is that guilt shall not escape or innocence suffer." This description of the prosecutor's duty illuminates the standard of materiality that governs his obligation to disclose exculpatory evidence. * * *

On the other hand, since we have rejected the suggestion that the prosecutor has a constitutional duty routinely to deliver his entire file to defense counsel, we cannot consistently treat every nondisclosure as though it were error. It necessarily follows that the judge should not order a new trial every time he is unable to characterize a nondisclosure as harmless under the customary harmless-error standard. Under that standard when error is present in the record, the reviewing judge must set aside the verdict and judgment unless his "conviction is sure that the error did not influence the jury, or had but very slight effect." Unless every nondisclosure is regarded as automatic error, the constitutional standard of materiality must impose a higher burden on the defendant.

The proper standard of materiality must reflect our overriding concern with the justice of the finding of guilt. Such a finding is permissible only if supported by evidence establishing guilt beyond a reasonable doubt. It necessarily follows that if the omitted evidence creates a reasonable doubt that did not otherwise exist, constitutional error has been committed. This means that the omission must be evaluated in the context of the entire record.[21] If there is no reasonable doubt about guilt whether or not the additional evidence is considered, there is no justification for a new trial. On the other hand, if the verdict is already of questionable validity, additional evidence of relatively minor importance might be sufficient to create a reasonable doubt.

This statement of the standard of materiality describes the test which courts appear to have applied in actual cases although the standard has been phrased in different language. It is also the standard which the trial judge applied in this case. He evaluated the significance of Sewell's prior criminal record in the context of the full trial which he recalled in detail. Stressing in particular the incongruity of a claim that Sewell was the aggressor with the evidence of his multiple wounds and respondent's unscathed condition, the trial judge indicated his unqualified opinion that respondent was guilty. He noted that Sewell's prior record did not contradict any evidence offered by the prosecutor, and was largely cumulative of the evidence that Sewell was wearing a bowie knife in a sheath and carrying a second knife in his pocket when he registered at the motel.

Since the arrest record was not requested and did not even arguably give rise to any inference of perjury, since after considering it in the context of the entire record the trial judge remained convinced of respondent's guilt beyond a reasonable doubt, and since we are satisfied that his firsthand appraisal of the record was thorough and entirely reasonable, we hold that the prosecutor's failure to tender Sewell's record to the defense did not deprive respondent of a fair trial as guaranteed by the Due Process Clause of the Fifth Amendment. Accordingly, the judgment of the Court of Appeals is

Reversed.

---

[21] "If, for example, one of only two eyewitnesses to a crime had told the prosecutor that the defendant was definitely not its perpetrator and if this statement was not disclosed to the defense, no court would hesitate to reverse a conviction resting on the testimony of the other eyewitness. But if there were fifty eyewitnesses, forty-nine of whom identified the defendant, and the prosecutor neglected to reveal that the other, who was without his badly needed glasses on the misty evening of the crime, had said that the criminal looked something like the defendant but he could not be sure as he had only had a brief glimpse, the result might well be different." Comment, [*Brady v. Maryland and The Prosecutor's Duty to Disclose,*] 40 U.Chi.L.Rev. [112], n.10, at 125 [(1972)].

Mr. Justice Marshall, with whom Mr. Justice Brennan joins, dissenting.

The Court today holds that the prosecutor's constitutional duty to provide exculpatory evidence to the defense is not limited to cases in which the defense makes a request for such evidence. But once having recognized the existence of a duty to volunteer exculpatory evidence, the Court so narrowly defines the category of "material" evidence embraced by the duty as to deprive it of all meaningful content. * * *

Our overriding concern in cases such as the one before us is the defendant's right to a fair trial. One of the most basic elements of fairness in a criminal trial is that available evidence tending to show innocence, as well as that tending to show guilt, be fully aired before the jury; more particularly, it is that the State in its zeal to convict a defendant not suppress evidence that might exonerate him. This fundamental notion of fairness does not pose any irreconcilable conflict for the prosecutor, for as the Court reminds us, the prosecutor "must always be faithful to his client's overriding interest that 'justice shall be done.'" No interest of the State is served, and no duty of the prosecutor advanced, by the suppression of evidence favorable to the defendant. On the contrary, the prosecutor fulfills his most basic responsibility when he fully airs all the relevant evidence at his command. * * *

Under today's ruling, if the prosecution has not made knowing use of perjury, and if the defense has not made a specific request for an item of information, the defendant is entitled to a new trial only if the withheld evidence actually creates a reasonable doubt as to guilt in the judge's mind. With all respect, this rule is completely at odds with the overriding interest in assuring that evidence tending to show innocence is brought to the jury's attention. The rule creates little, if any, incentive for the prosecutor conscientiously to determine whether his files contain evidence helpful to the defense. Indeed, the rule reinforces the natural tendency of the prosecutor to overlook evidence favorable to the defense, and creates an incentive for the prosecutor to resolve close questions of disclosure in favor of concealment. * * *

* * * Leaving open the question whether a different rule might appropriately be applied in cases involving deliberate misconduct, I would hold that the defendant in this case had the burden of demonstrating that there is a significant chance that the withheld evidence, developed by skilled counsel, would have induced a reasonable doubt in the minds of enough jurors to avoid a conviction. This is essentially the standard applied by the Court of Appeals, and I would affirm its judgment.

NOTES AND QUESTIONS

1. The Court compares the *Mooney*/perjured testimony doctrine with the due process right to have the prosecutor disclose exculpatory evidence. In *Mooney*, the prosecutor presented evidence that he knew, or should have known, was perjured. In that context, a conviction "must be set aside if there is any reasonable likelihood that the false testimony could have affected the judgment of the jury." This is an easy standard to meet, surely met on facts like those in *Agurs*, designed to ensure that no conviction rests on perjured testimony. It may also be designed to punish the prosecutor's bad faith.

But what does the prosecutor's good or bad faith have to do with the due process right to an accurate verdict? Should it matter if the prosecutor did (or did not) consider the evidence exculpatory? *Agurs* reaffirms that it is easier for a defendant to get relief if the prosecutor uses perjured evidence than if the prosecutor fails to disclose exculpatory evidence. Is there any justification for this distinction? If the concern is the accuracy of the outcome—rather than the culpability of the prosecutor—is there any reason to think that the use of perjured evidence is always more damaging to accuracy than the failure to disclose exculpatory evidence?

2. *Bagley modifies Agurs?* In United States v. Bagley, 473 U.S. 667, 105 S.Ct. 3375, 87 L.Ed.2d 481 (1985), five members of the Court (in two separate opinions) agreed with the following reformulation of *Agurs*: "[E]vidence is material only if there is a reasonable probability that, had the evidence been disclosed to the defense, the result of the proceeding would have been different." The same five members of the Court also seemed to agree that this standard is adequate "to cover the 'no request,' 'general request,' and 'specific request' cases of prosecutorial failure to disclose evidence favorable to the accused." Notice this would not include the *Mooney v. Holohan* category where the prosecution used perjured evidence; in that category, it is easier for defendants to obtain a reversal of the resulting conviction. See Note 1.

Two members of the *Bagley* majority sought to keep alive the distinction that favors defendants who make a specific request. On their view, the specificity of the request (as in *Brady*) should make it easier to meet the materiality standard, because the defense would naturally assume from the state's failure to disclose that the specific evidence did not exist and would thus "make pretrial and trial decisions based on that assumption."

3. *Some states go a different route.* In People v. Vilardi, 76 N.Y.2d 67, 555 N.E.2d 915, 556 N.Y.S.2d 518 (1990), New York's highest court rejected the *Bagley* test. The "discovery" question in New York is not whether the non-disclosed evidence *would have* made a difference but, rather, whether the evidence *might have* affected the outcome. The state court noted that this standard should create more incentive for prosecutors to turn over evidence that might be exculpatory. For other states that have rejected the *Bagley* plurality's formulation in specific request cases, see, *e.g.*, State v. Engel, 249 N.J.Super. 336, 592 A.2d 572 (App.Div.1991); Commonwealth v. Gallarelli,

399 Mass. 17, 502 N.E.2d 516 (1987); State v. Kaiser, 486 N.W.2d 384 (Minn.1992).

Vilardi's "might have" standard probably requires a less laborious review of the entire trial transcript than the *Bagley* "would have" standard. In Kyles v. Whitley, 514 U.S. 419, 115 S.Ct. 1555, 131 L.Ed.2d 490 (1995), for example, the Court ruled in favor of the defendant after an exhaustive thirty-page review of the evidence and trials—the first jury deadlocked, resulting in a mistrial. The exhaustive nature of the Court's opinion, and the decision to grant certiorari in such a fact-dependent case, provoked Justice Scalia to write in dissent:

> In a sensible system of criminal justice, wrongful conviction is avoided by establishing, at the trial level, lines of procedural legality that leave ample margins of safety (for example, the requirement that guilt be proved beyond a reasonable doubt)—not by providing recurrent and repetitive appellate review of whether the facts in the record show those lines to have been narrowly crossed.

4.   *Change is a-coming?* Justice Marshall dissented in *Bagley*, arguing for a more rigorous *Brady* standard. Part of his evidence was an article by a federal judge recounting a meeting when he was a U.S. Attorney:

> "I recently had occasion to discuss [*Brady*] at a PLI Conference in New York City before a large group of State prosecutors * * * . I put to them this case: You are prosecuting a bank robbery. You have talked to two or three of the tellers and one or two of the customers at the time of the robbery. They have all taken a look at your defendant in a line-up, and they have said, 'This is the man.' In the course of your investigation you also have found another customer who was in the bank that day, who viewed the suspect, and came back and said, 'This is *not* the man.'

> "The question I put to these prosecutors was, do you believe you should disclose to the defense the name of the witness who, when he viewed the suspect, said 'that is not the man'? In a room of prosecutors * * * , only two hands went up. There were only two prosecutors in that group who felt they should disclose or would disclose that information. Yet I was putting to them what I thought was the easiest case—the clearest case for disclosure of exculpatory information!"

Two members of the *Bagley* majority phrased the test as whether the non-disclosed evidence was "sufficient to undermine confidence in the outcome." A majority of the Court in *Kyles*, Note 3, and Strickler v. Greene, 527 U.S. 263, 119 S.Ct. 1936, 144 L.Ed.2d 286 (1999), embraced the "undermined confidence" standard. Perhaps that is easier for a defendant to meet than the "would have been different" standard.

One problem with the "undermined confidence" standard is that it potentially creates a dilemma for prosecutors. As Scott Sundby has pointed out, "It will be—and perhaps ethically should be—a rare case where a prosecutor will possess evidence that she believes objectively raises serious questions about the defendant's guilt and yet decides to still pursue a conviction." Scott Sundby, *Fallen Superheroes and Constitutional Mirages: The Tale of Brady v. Maryland*, 33 McGeorge L. Rev. 643, 659 (2002).

Imagine that the prosecutor has evidence that she believes satisfies the materiality standard from *Agurs* and *Bagley*. For the constitutional duty to disclose the evidence to be triggered, she would have to think, *id.* at 651:

> This piece of evidence is so exculpatory in nature that it actually undermines my belief that a guilty verdict would be worthy of confidence. Under *Brady*, therefore, I need to turn this evidence over to the defense. Then, once I turn the evidence over and satisfy my constitutional obligation, I can resume my zealous efforts to obtain a guilty verdict that I have just concluded will not be worthy of confidence.

Keep Sundby's dilemma in mind as you read the Court's most recent pronouncement on the discovery issue.

SMITH V. CAIN

Supreme Court of the United States, 2012.
565 U.S. ___, 132 S.Ct. 627, 181 L.Ed.2d 571.

CHIEF JUSTICE ROBERTS delivered the opinion of the Court [joined by JUSTICES SCALIA, KENNEDY, GINSBURG, BREYER, ALITO, SOTOMAYOR, and KAGAN].

The State of Louisiana charged petitioner Juan Smith with killing five people during an armed robbery. At Smith's trial a single witness, Larry Boatner, linked Smith to the crime. Boatner testified that he was socializing at a friend's house when Smith and two other gunmen entered the home, demanded money and drugs, and shortly thereafter began shooting, resulting in the death of five of Boatner's friends. In court Boatner identified Smith as the first gunman to come through the door. He claimed that he had been face to face with Smith during the initial moments of the robbery. No other witnesses and no physical evidence implicated Smith in the crime.

The jury convicted Smith of five counts of first-degree murder. The Louisiana Court of Appeal affirmed Smith's conviction. The Louisiana Supreme Court denied review, as did this Court.

Smith then sought postconviction relief in the state courts. As part of his effort, Smith obtained files from the police investigation of his case, including those of the lead investigator, Detective John Ronquillo. Ronquillo's notes contain statements by Boatner that conflict with his testimony identifying Smith as a perpetrator. The notes from the night of the murder state that Boatner "could not * * * supply a description of the perpetrators other then [sic] they were black males." Ronquillo also made a handwritten account of a conversation he had with Boatner five days after the crime, in which Boatner said he "could not ID anyone because [he] couldn't see faces" and "would not know them if [he] saw them." And Ronquillo's typewritten report of that conversation states that Boatner told Ronquillo he "could not identify any of the perpetrators of the murder."

Smith requested that his conviction be vacated, arguing, inter alia, that the prosecution's failure to disclose Ronquillo's notes violated this Court's decision in *Brady v. Maryland*. The state trial court rejected Smith's *Brady* claim, and the Louisiana Court of Appeal and Louisiana Supreme Court denied review. We granted certiorari, and now reverse.

Under *Brady*, the State violates a defendant's right to due process if it withholds evidence that is favorable to the defense and material to the defendant's guilt or punishment. The State does not dispute that Boatner's statements in Ronquillo's notes were favorable to Smith and that those statements were not disclosed to him. The sole question before us is thus whether Boatner's statements were material to the determination of Smith's guilt. We have explained that "evidence is 'material' within the meaning of Brady when there is a reasonable probability that, had the evidence been disclosed, the result of the proceeding would have been different." A reasonable probability does not mean that the defendant "would more likely than not have received a different verdict with the evidence," only that the likelihood of a different result is great enough to "undermine[ ] confidence in the outcome of the trial." *Kyles v. Whitley*.

We have observed that evidence impeaching an eyewitness may not be material if the State's other evidence is strong enough to sustain confidence in the verdict. See *Agurs*. That is not the case here. Boatner's testimony was the only evidence linking Smith to the crime. And Boatner's undisclosed statements directly contradict his testimony: Boatner told the jury that he had "[n]o doubt" that Smith was the gunman he stood "face to face" with on the night of the crime, but Ronquillo's notes show Boatner saying that he "could not ID anyone because [he] couldn't see faces" and "would not know them if [he] saw them." Boatner's undisclosed statements were plainly material.

The State and the dissent advance various reasons why the jury might have discounted Boatner's undisclosed statements. They stress, for example, that Boatner made other remarks on the night of the murder indicating that he could identify the first gunman to enter the house, but not the others. That merely leaves us to speculate about which of

Boatner's contradictory declarations the jury would have believed. The State also contends that Boatner's statements made five days after the crime can be explained by fear of retaliation. Smith responds that the record contains no evidence of any such fear. Again, the State's argument offers a reason that the jury could have disbelieved Boatner's undisclosed statements, but gives us no confidence that it would have done so.

The police files that Smith obtained in state postconviction proceedings contain other evidence that Smith contends is both favorable to him and material to the verdict. Because we hold that Boatner's undisclosed statements alone suffice to undermine confidence in Smith's conviction, we have no need to consider his arguments that the other undisclosed evidence also requires reversal under Brady.

The judgment of the Orleans Parish Criminal District Court of Louisiana is reversed, and the case is remanded for further proceedings not inconsistent with this opinion. * * *

JUSTICE THOMAS, dissenting.

The Court holds that Juan Smith is entitled to a new murder trial because the State, in violation of *Brady v. Maryland*, did not disclose that the eyewitness who identified Smith at trial stated shortly after the murders that he could not identify any of the perpetrators. I respectfully dissent. In my view, Smith has not shown a "reasonable probability" that the jury would have been persuaded by the undisclosed evidence. That materiality determination must be made "in the context of the entire record," *Agurs*, and "turns on the cumulative effect of all such evidence suppressed by the government," *Kyles v. Whitley*. Applying these principles, I would affirm the judgment of the Louisiana trial court.

I * * *

Like the postconviction court below, I conclude that Smith is not entitled to a new trial under *Brady*. In my view, Smith has not established a reasonable probability that the cumulative effect of this evidence would have caused the jury to change its verdict. * * *

The question presented here is not whether a prudent prosecutor should have disclosed the information that Smith identifies. Rather, the question is whether the cumulative effect of the disclosed and undisclosed evidence in Smith's case "put[s] the whole case in such a different light as to undermine confidence in the verdict." *Kyles*. When, as in this case, the Court departs from its usual practice of declining to review alleged misapplications of settled law to particular facts, the Court should at least consider all of the facts. And, the Court certainly should not decline to review all of the facts on the assumption that the remainder of the record would only further support Smith's claims, as the Court appears to have done here.

Such an assumption is incorrect. Here, much of the record evidence confirms that, from the night of the murders through trial, Boatner consistently described—with one understandable exception—the first perpetrator through the door, that Boatner's description matched Smith, and that Boatner made strong out-of-court and in-court identifications implicating Smith. Some of the undisclosed evidence cited by Smith is not favorable to him at all, either because it is of no impeachment or exculpatory value or because it actually inculpates him. Because what remains is evidence of such minimal impeachment and exculpatory value as to be immaterial in light of the whole record, I must dissent from the Court's holding that the State violated *Brady*.

NOTES AND QUESTIONS

1. *Orleans Parish.* The case you just read was on certiorari to the criminal district court in the Louisiana Orleans Parish. In the 2010–11 Term, the Court decided another case from that parish, also involving a failure to disclose. In Connick v. Thompson, 563 U.S. 51, 131 S.Ct. 1350, 179 L.Ed.2d 417 (2011), an Orleans Parish prosecutor intentionally withheld from the defense a crime lab report that the perpetrator had type B blood. Moreover, the prosecutor removed a cloth stained with the perpetrator's blood from the evidence room, presumably so that it could not be tested by the defense. Eighteen years after Thompson was convicted and sentenced to death, and only a month before he was to be electrocuted, a defense investigator found the lab report in the crime lab's records. When Thompson's blood type was determined to be type O, all his convictions were vacated. He then sued Harry Connick, the New Orleans district attorney, for failing to train prosecutors "adequately about their duty to produce exculpatory evidence and that the lack of training had caused the nondisclosure" in his case.

One way Thompson could win his suit against Connick in his official capacity, the Court said, was to show that Connick "was aware of a pattern of similar *Brady* violations." Though there were four other New Orleans cases reversed for *Brady* violations in the ten years preceding Thompson's case, the Court held that they were not sufficiently similar to constitute a pattern. *Smith* makes six cases of *Brady* violations out of the Orleans Parish that have come to the attention of the Supreme Court.

2. *"Ample margins of safety."* We mercifully omitted almost all of Justice Thomas's 17-page discussion of the facts that he believes requires the Court to affirm the state court in *Smith*. Assuming the accuracy of Thomas's characterization of the facts, does that tell you something about the way the current Court is going to apply *Brady* and *Bagley*? See also Banks v. Dretke, 540 U.S. 668, 124 S.Ct. 1256, 157 L.Ed.2d 1166 (2004) (suggesting that withholding a single piece of evidence could violate *Brady*). Recall Justice Scalia's concern with "ample margins" of safety that he believes are established by "lines of procedural legality * * * (for example, the requirement that guilt be proved beyond a reasonable doubt)." Note 3, p. 978.

Perhaps the Court is worried about "ample margins of safety" and the dilemma for prosecutors who are required to examine the entire case, *prior to trial*, to ascertain whether one piece of evidence would have created a reasonable doubt.

To Craig Bradley, *Smith* and *Banks* suggest at least that "if the defendant can show that police/prosecutors purposely or recklessly suppressed important evidence favorable to the defense, the Court is not going to be too finicky about the 'reasonable probability of a different result' prong of the *Brady* test." See Craig M. Bradley, *Smith v. Cain*: Taking *Brady* Seriously, 48 Trial (April 2012).

3.　*Jailhouse "snitches."* Convictions of innocent defendants often result from jailhouse informants who offer false information to gain an advantage with the prosecutor. In Wearry v. Cain, 577 U.S. ___, 136 S.Ct. 1002, 194 L.Ed.2d 78 (2016) (per curiam), Sam Scott contacted authorities from jail in order to implicate Michael Wearry in a murder. Scott told at least six different stories about Wearry's involvement in the murder. As the Court dryly pointed out, "By the time Scott testified as the State's star witness at Wearry's trial, his story bore little resemblance to his original account."

The Court reversed Wearry's conviction in a 7–2 per curiam opinion on the ground that the prosecutor did not turn over material exculpatory evidence (including that another prosecution witness told investigators that "Scott had told [me] what to say"). The Court stressed what it said in *Smith v. Cain* about the standard for materiality: "Wearry need not show that he 'more likely than not' would have been acquitted had the new evidence been admitted [but] only that the new evidence is sufficient to 'undermine confidence' in the verdict." That Scott was a jailhouse snitch could not, however, have escaped the Court's attention.

4.　*And speaking of innocence.* One value of discovery is that it helps protect innocent defendants from wrongful convictions. A 2015 sample of cases from the National Registry of Exonerations showed that 13% of the exonerations involved a violation of the constitutional requirement that the State disclose exculpatory evidence, See George C. Thomas III, "Prosecutors: The Thin Last Line Protecting the Innocent," in Wrongful Convictions and the DNA Revolution: Reflections on 25 Years of Freeing the Innocent (Medwed ed. 2016). The Thomas study also uncovered 43 cases where innocent defendants pleaded guilty to drug possession when the object they possessed was not contraband, contrary to faulty field drug tests. See generally, National Registry of Exonerations, http://www.law.umich.edu/special/exoneration/Pages/about.aspx (as of May 1, 2016, total of 1,778 exonerations).

ARIZONA V. YOUNGBLOOD

Supreme Court of the United States, 1988.
488 U.S. 51, 109 S.Ct. 333, 102 L.Ed.2d 281.

CHIEF JUSTICE REHNQUIST delivered the opinion of the Court [joined by JUSTICES WHITE, O'CONNOR, SCALIA, and KENNEDY.

Respondent Larry Youngblood was convicted by a Pima County, Arizona, jury of child molestation, sexual assault, and kidnaping. The Arizona Court of Appeals reversed his conviction on the ground that the State had failed to preserve semen samples from the victim's body and clothing. We granted certiorari to consider the extent to which the Due Process Clause of the Fourteenth Amendment requires the State to preserve evidentiary material that might be useful to a criminal defendant.

On October 29, 1983, David L., a 10-year-old boy, attended a church service with his mother. After he left the service at about 9:30 p.m., the boy went to a carnival behind the church, where he was abducted by a middle-aged man of medium height and weight. The assailant drove the boy to a secluded area near a ravine and molested him. He then took the boy to an unidentified, sparsely furnished house where he sodomized the boy four times. Afterwards, the assailant tied the boy up while he went outside to start his car. Once the assailant started the car, albeit with some difficulty, he returned to the house and again sodomized the boy. The assailant then sent the boy to the bathroom to wash up before he returned him to the carnival. He threatened to kill the boy if he told anyone about the attack. The entire ordeal lasted about 1 1/2 hours.

After the boy made his way home, his mother took him to Kino Hospital. At the hospital, a physician treated the boy for rectal injuries. The physician also used a "sexual assault kit" to collect evidence of the attack. The Tucson Police Department provided such kits to all hospitals in Pima County for use in sexual assault cases. Under standard procedure, the victim of a sexual assault was taken to a hospital, where a physician used the kit to collect evidence. The kit included paper to collect saliva samples, a tube for obtaining a blood sample, microscopic slides for making smears, a set of Q-Tip-like swabs, and a medical examination report. Here, the physician used the swab to collect samples from the boy's rectum and mouth. He then made a microscopic slide of the samples. The doctor also obtained samples of the boy's saliva, blood, and hair. The physician did not examine the samples at any time. The police placed the kit in a secure refrigerator at the police station. At the hospital, the police also collected the boy's underwear and T-shirt. This clothing was not refrigerated or frozen.

Nine days after the attack, on November 7, 1983, the police asked the boy to pick out his assailant from a photographic lineup. The boy identified respondent as the assailant. Respondent was not located by the police until four weeks later; he was arrested on December 9, 1983.

On November 8, 1983, Edward Heller, a police criminologist, examined the sexual assault kit. He testified that he followed standard department procedure, which was to examine the slides and determine whether sexual contact had occurred. After he determined that such contact had occurred, the criminologist did not perform any other tests, although he placed the assault kit back in the refrigerator. He testified that tests to identify blood group substances were not routinely conducted during the initial examination of an assault kit and in only about half of all cases in any event. He did not test the clothing at this time.

Respondent was indicted on charges of child molestation, sexual assault, and kidnaping. The State moved to compel respondent to provide blood and saliva samples for comparison with the material gathered through the use of the sexual assault kit, but the trial court denied the motion on the ground that the State had not obtained a sufficiently large semen sample to make a valid comparison. The prosecutor then asked the State's criminologist to perform an ABO blood group test on the rectal swab sample in an attempt to ascertain the blood type of the boy's assailant. This test failed to detect any blood group substances in the sample.

In January 1985, the police criminologist examined the boy's clothing for the first time. He found one semen stain on the boy's underwear and another on the rear of his T-shirt. The criminologist tried to obtain blood group substances from both stains using the ABO technique, but was unsuccessful. He also performed a P-30 protein molecule test on the stains, which indicated that only a small quantity of semen was present on the clothing; it was inconclusive as to the assailant's identity. The Tucson Police Department had just begun using this test, which was then used in slightly more than half of the crime laboratories in the country.

Respondent's principal defense at trial was that the boy had erred in identifying him as the perpetrator of the crime. In this connection, both a criminologist for the State and an expert witness for respondent testified as to what might have been shown by tests performed on the samples shortly after they were gathered, or by later tests performed on the samples from the boy's clothing had the clothing been properly refrigerated. The court instructed the jury that if they found the State had destroyed or lost evidence, they might "infer that the true fact is against the State's interest."

The jury found respondent guilty as charged, but the Arizona Court of Appeals reversed the judgment of conviction. It stated that " 'when identity is an issue at trial and the police permit the destruction of evidence that could eliminate the defendant as the perpetrator, such loss is material to the defense and is a denial of due process.' " The Court of Appeals concluded on the basis of the expert testimony at trial that timely performance of tests with properly preserved semen samples could have produced results that might have completely exonerated respondent. The Court of Appeals reached this conclusion even though it did "not imply any bad faith on the part of the State." The Supreme Court of Arizona denied the State's petition for review, and we granted certiorari. We now reverse. * * *

There is no question but that the State complied with *Brady* [373 U.S. 83, 83 S.Ct. 1194, 10 L.Ed.2d 215 (1963)] and *Agurs* [p. 969] here. The State disclosed relevant police reports to respondent, which contained information about the existence of the swab and the clothing, and the boy's examination at the hospital. The State provided respondent's expert with the laboratory reports and notes prepared by the police criminologist, and respondent's expert had access to the swab and to the clothing.

If respondent is to prevail on federal constitutional grounds, then, it must be because of some constitutional duty over and above that imposed by cases such as *Brady* and *Agurs*. Our most recent decision in this area of the law, *California v. Trombetta*, 467 U.S. 479, 104 S.Ct. 2528, 81 L.Ed.2d 413 (1984), arose out of a drunk-driving prosecution in which the State had introduced test results indicating the concentration of alcohol in the blood of two motorists. The defendants sought to suppress the test results on the ground that the State had failed to preserve the breath samples used in the test. We rejected this argument for several reasons: first, "the officers here were acting in 'good faith and in accord with their normal practice,' "; second, in the light of the procedures actually used the chances that preserved samples would have exculpated the defendants were slim; and, third, even if the samples might have shown inaccuracy in the tests, the defendants had "alternative means of demonstrating their innocence." In the present case, the likelihood that the preserved materials would have enabled the defendant to exonerate himself appears to be greater than it was in *Trombetta*, but here, unlike in *Trombetta*, the State did not attempt to make any use of the materials in its own case in chief.

Our decisions in related areas have stressed the importance for constitutional purposes of good or bad faith on the part of the Government when the claim is based on loss of evidence attributable to the Government. In *United States v. Marion*, 404 U.S. 307, 92 S.Ct. 455, 30 L.Ed.2d 468 (1971), we said that "[n]o actual prejudice to the conduct of the defense is alleged or proved, and there is no showing that the Government intentionally delayed to gain some tactical advantage over appellees or to harass them." Similarly, in *United States v. Valenzuela-Bernal*, [458 U.S. 858, 102 S.Ct. 3440, 73 L.Ed.2d 1193 (1982)], we considered whether the Government's deportation of two witnesses who were illegal aliens violated due process. We held that the prompt deportation of the witnesses was justified "upon the Executive's good-faith determination that they possess no evidence favorable to the defendant in a criminal prosecution."

The Due Process Clause of the Fourteenth Amendment, as interpreted in *Brady*, makes the good or bad faith of the State irrelevant when the State fails to disclose to the defendant material exculpatory evidence. But we think the Due Process Clause requires a different result when we deal with the failure of the State to preserve evidentiary material of which no more can be said than that it could have been subjected to tests, the results of which might have exonerated the defendant. Part of the reason for the difference in treatment is found in the observation made by the Court in *Trombetta* that "[w]henever potentially exculpatory evidence is permanently lost, courts face the treacherous task of divining the import of materials whose contents are unknown and, very often, disputed." Part of it stems from our unwillingness to read the "fundamental fairness" requirement of the Due Process Clause as imposing on the police an undifferentiated and absolute duty to retain and to preserve all material that might be of conceivable evidentiary significance in a particular prosecution. We think that requiring a defendant to show bad faith on the part of the police both limits the extent of the police's obligation to preserve evidence to reasonable bounds and confines it to that class of cases where the interests of justice most clearly require it, *i.e.*, those cases in which the police themselves by their conduct indicate that the evidence could form a basis for exonerating the defendant. We therefore hold that unless a criminal defendant can show bad faith on the part of the police, failure to preserve potentially useful evidence does not constitute a denial of due process of law.

In this case, the police collected the rectal swab and clothing on the night of the crime; respondent was not taken into custody until six weeks later. The failure of the police to refrigerate the clothing and to perform tests on the semen samples can at worst be described as negligent. None of this information was concealed from respondent at trial, and the evidence—such as it was—was made available to respondent's expert who declined to perform any tests on the samples. The Arizona Court of Appeals noted in its opinion—and we agree—that there was no suggestion of bad faith on the part of the police. It follows, therefore, from what we have said, that there was no violation of the Due Process Clause.

The Arizona Court of Appeals also referred somewhat obliquely to the State's "inability to quantitatively test" certain semen samples with the newer P-30 test. If the court meant by this statement that the Due Process Clause is violated when the police fail to use a particular investigatory tool, we strongly disagree. The situation here is no different than a prosecution for drunken driving that rests on police observation alone; the defendant is free to argue to the finder of fact that a breathalyzer test might have been exculpatory, but the police do not have a constitutional duty to perform any particular tests.

The judgment of the Arizona Court of Appeals is reversed, and the case is remanded for further proceedings not inconsistent with this opinion. * * *

JUSTICE STEVENS, concurring in the judgment.

Three factors are of critical importance to my evaluation of this case. First, at the time the police failed to refrigerate the victim's clothing, and thus negligently lost potentially valuable evidence, they had at least as great an interest in preserving the evidence as did the person later accused of the crime. Indeed, at that time it was more likely that the evidence would have been useful to the police—who were still conducting an investigation—and to the prosecutor—who would later bear the burden of establishing guilt beyond a reasonable doubt—than to the defendant. In cases such as this, even without a prophylactic sanction such as dismissal of the indictment, the State has a strong incentive to preserve the evidence.

Second, although it is not possible to know whether the lost evidence would have revealed any relevant information, it is unlikely that the defendant was prejudiced by the State's omission. In examining witnesses and in her summation, defense counsel impressed upon the jury the fact that the State failed to preserve the evidence and that the State could have conducted tests that might well have exonerated the defendant. More significantly, the trial judge instructed the jury: "If you find that the State has * * * allowed to be destroyed or lost any evidence whose content or quality are in issue, you may infer that the true fact is against the State's interest." As a result, the uncertainty as to what the evidence might have proved was turned to the defendant's advantage.

Third, the fact that no juror chose to draw the permissive inference that proper preservation of the evidence would have demonstrated that the defendant was not the assailant suggests that the lost evidence was "immaterial." Our cases make clear that "[t]he proper standard of materiality must reflect our overriding concern with the justice of the finding of guilt," and that a State's failure to turn over (or preserve) potentially exculpatory evidence therefore "must be evaluated in the context of the entire record." In declining defense counsel's and the court's invitations to draw the permissive inference, the jurors in effect indicated that, in their view, the other evidence at trial was so overwhelming that it was highly improbable that the lost evidence was exculpatory. In *Trombetta*, this Court found no due process violation because "the chances [were] extremely low that preserved [breath] samples would have been exculpatory." In this case, the jury has already performed this calculus based on its understanding of the evidence introduced at trial. Presumably, in a case involving a closer question as to guilt or innocence, the jurors would have been more ready to infer that the lost evidence was exculpatory.

With these factors in mind, I concur in the Court's judgment. I do not, however, join the Court's opinion because it announces a proposition of law that is much broader than necessary to decide this case. It states that "unless a criminal defendant can show bad faith on the part of the police, failure to preserve potentially useful evidence does not constitute a denial of due process of law." In my opinion, there may well be cases in which the defendant is unable to prove that the State acted in bad faith but in which the loss or destruction of evidence is nonetheless so critical to the defense as to make a criminal trial fundamentally unfair. This, however, is not such a case. Accordingly, I concur in the judgment.

JUSTICE BLACKMUN, with whom JUSTICE BRENNAN and JUSTICE MARSHALL join, dissenting.

The Constitution requires that criminal defendants be provided with a fair trial, not merely a "good faith" try at a fair trial. Respondent here, by what may have been nothing more than police ineptitude, was denied the opportunity to present a full defense. That ineptitude, however, deprived respondent of his guaranteed right to due process of law. In reversing the judgment of the Arizona Court of Appeals, this Court, in my view, misreads the import of its prior cases and unduly restricts the protections of the Due Process Clause. * * *

I * * *

Brady and *Agurs* could not be more clear in their holdings that a prosecutor's bad faith in interfering with a defendant's access to material evidence is not an essential part of a due process violation. Nor did *Trombetta* create such a requirement. *Trombetta*'s initial discussion focused on the due process requirement "that criminal defendants be afforded a meaningful opportunity to present a complete defense," and then noted that the delivery of exculpatory evidence to the defendant "protect[s] the innocent from erroneous conviction and ensur[es] the integrity of our criminal justice system." * * *

The cases in this area clearly establish that police actions taken in bad faith are not the only species of police conduct that can result in a violation of due process. As *Agurs* points out, it makes no sense to overturn a conviction because a malicious prosecutor withholds information that he mistakenly believes to be material, but which actually would have been of no help to the defense. In the same way, it makes no sense to ignore the fact that a defendant has been denied a fair trial because the State allowed evidence that was material to the defense to deteriorate beyond the point of usefulness, simply because the police were inept rather than malicious.

I also doubt that the "bad faith" standard creates the bright-line rule sought by the majority. Apart from the inherent difficulty a defendant would have in obtaining evidence to show a lack of good faith, the line between "good faith" and "bad faith" is anything but bright, and the majority's formulation may well create more questions than it answers. What constitutes bad faith for these purposes? Does a defendant have to show actual malice, or would recklessness, or the deliberate failure to establish standards for maintaining and preserving evidence, be sufficient? Does "good faith police work" require a certain minimum of diligence, or will a lazy officer, who does not walk the few extra steps to the evidence refrigerator, be considered to be acting in good faith? While the majority leaves these questions for another day, its quick embrace of a "bad faith" standard has not brightened the line; it only has moved the line so as to provide fewer protections for criminal defendants.

II * * *

I recognize the difficulties presented by such a situation. The societal interest in seeing criminals punished rightly requires that indictments be dismissed only when the unavailability of the evidence prevents the defendant from receiving a fair trial. In a situation where the substance of the lost evidence is known, the materiality analysis laid out in *Trombetta* is adequate. But in a situation like the present one, due process requires something more. Rather than allow a State's ineptitude to saddle a defendant with an impossible burden, a court should focus on the type of evidence, the possibility it might prove exculpatory, and the existence of other evidence going to the same point of contention in determining whether the failure to preserve the evidence in question violated due process. To put it succinctly, where no comparable evidence is likely to be available to the defendant, police must preserve physical evidence of a type that they reasonably should know has the potential, if tested, to reveal immutable characteristics of the criminal, and hence to exculpate a defendant charged with the crime.

The first inquiry under this standard concerns the particular evidence itself. It must be of a type which is clearly relevant, a requirement satisfied, in a case where identity is at issue, by physical evidence which has come from the assailant. Samples of blood and other body fluids, fingerprints, and hair and tissue samples have been used to implicate guilty defendants, and to exonerate innocent suspects. This is not to say that all physical evidence of this type must be preserved. For example, in a case where a blood sample is found, but the circumstances make it unclear whether the sample came from the assailant, the dictates of due process might not compel preservation (although principles of sound investigation might certainly do so). But in a case where there is no doubt that the sample came from the assailant, the presumption must be that it be preserved.

A corollary, particularly applicable to this case, is that the evidence embody some immutable characteristic of the assailant which can be determined by available testing methods. So, for example, a clear fingerprint can be compared to the defendant's fingerprints to yield a conclusive result; a blood sample, or a sample of body fluid which contains blood markers, can either completely exonerate or strongly implicate a defendant. As technology develops, the potential for this type of evidence to provide conclusive results on any number of questions will increase. Current genetic testing measures, frequently used in civil paternity suits, are extraordinarily precise. The importance of these types of evidence is indisputable, and requiring police to recognize their importance is not unreasonable.

The next inquiry is whether the evidence, which was obviously relevant and indicates an immutable characteristic of the actual assailant, is of a type likely to be independently exculpatory. Requiring the defendant to prove that the particular piece of evidence probably would be independently exculpatory would require the defendant to prove the content of something he does not have because of the State's misconduct. Focusing on the *type* of evidence solves this problem. A court will be able to consider the type of evidence and the available technology, as well as the circumstances of the case, to determine the likelihood that the evidence might have proved to be exculpatory. The evidence must also be without equivalent in the particular case. It must not be cumulative or collateral, and must bear directly on the question of innocence or guilt.

Due process must also take into account the burdens that the preservation of evidence places on the police. Law enforcement officers must be provided the option, as is implicit in *Trombetta*, of performing the proper tests on physical evidence and then discarding it. Once a suspect has been arrested the police, after a reasonable time, may inform defense counsel of plans to discard the evidence. When the defense has been informed of the existence of the evidence, after a reasonable time the burden of preservation may shift to the defense. There should also be flexibility to deal with evidence that is unusually dangerous or difficult to store.

III

Applying this standard to the facts of this case, I conclude that the Arizona Court of Appeals was correct in overturning respondent's conviction. The clothing worn by the victim contained samples of his assailant's semen. The appeals court found that these samples would probably be larger, less contaminated, and more likely to yield conclusive test results than would the samples collected by use of the assault kit. The clothing and the semen stains on the clothing therefore obviously were material.

Because semen is a body fluid which could have been tested by available methods to show an immutable characteristic of the assailant, there was a genuine possibility that the results of such testing might have exonerated respondent. The only evidence implicating respondent was the testimony of the victim.[8] There was no other eyewitness, and the only other significant physical evidence, respondent's car, was seized by police, examined, turned over to a wrecking company, and then dismantled without the victim's having viewed it. The police also failed to check the car to confirm or refute elements of the victim's testimony.[9]

Although a closer question, there was no equivalent evidence available to respondent. The swab contained a semen sample, but it was not sufficient to allow proper testing. Respondent had access to other evidence tending to show that he was not the assailant, but there was no other evidence that would have shown that it was physically impossible for respondent to have been the assailant. Nor would the preservation of the evidence here have been a burden upon the police. There obviously was refrigeration available, as the preservation of the swab indicates, and the items of clothing likely would not tax available storage space.

Considered in the context of the entire trial, the failure of the prosecution to preserve this evidence deprived respondent of a fair trial. It still remains "a fundamental value determination of our society that it is far worse to convict an innocent man than to let a guilty man go free." The evidence in this case was far from conclusive, and the possibility that the evidence denied to respondent would have exonerated him was not remote. The result is that he was denied a fair trial by the actions of the State, and consequently was denied due process of law. Because the Court's opinion improperly limits the scope of due process, and ignores its proper focus in a futile pursuit of a bright-line rule, I dissent.

---

[8] This Court "has recognized the inherently suspect qualities of eyewitness identification evidence." * * *

Studies show that children are more likely to make mistaken identifications than are adults, especially when they have been encouraged by adults. Other studies show another element of possible relevance in this case: "Cross-racial identifications are much less likely to be accurate than same race identifications." These authorities suggest that eyewitness testimony alone, in the absence of corroboration, is to be viewed with some suspicion.

[9] The victim testified that the car had a loud muffler, that country music was playing on its radio, and that the car was started using a key. Respondent and others testified that his car was inoperative on the night of the incident, that when it was working it ran quietly, that the radio did not work, and that the car could be started only by using a screwdriver. The police did not check any of this before disposing of the car.

NOTES AND QUESTIONS

1. The majority and dissent in *Youngblood* make different assumptions about the evil to be guarded against in these "failure to preserve" cases, and about the appropriate standard to apply. Given the potential for the DNA analysis of blood and semen to point conclusively toward (or away) from a defendant, which approach do you prefer?

2. *Bad faith redux.* Recall that prosecutorial bad faith is critical when the prosecutor fails to disclose that perjury contributed to the conviction. Now we see that it is also critical when the State fails to preserve evidence. Why would these contexts require bad faith even though the more typical *Brady-Bagley* context does not?

3. Do you doubt that Youngblood was guilty?

4. What remedy would be necessary if the Court had ruled in Youngblood's favor? Given that remedy, which opinion would you have joined? *Please answer this question before reading further.*

5. What would be the best course of action today on the *Youngblood* facts if you were appointed to represent Youngblood shortly after his arrest?

6. *The rest of the story.* Youngblood served his sentence and was released. He had to register as a sex offender and landed back in jail when he failed to notify authorities of his new address. In 2000, lawyers for Youngblood persuaded the state court to order testing of a cotton swab that, unlike the clothing, had been refrigerated. The swab was then 17 years old but the newer, more sophisticated DNA test proved that Youngblood was not the man who raped the boy. Barry Scheck, Peter Neufeld, & Jim Dwyer, Actual Innocence 335 (2001).

7. If you are troubled by the revelation that Youngblood was innocent, does this mean that the Court should change course and adopt Justice Blackmun's approach? Or is it simply inevitable that some innocent defendants will be convicted and what we want to avoid is the wholesale release of guilty ones? Would Blackmun's approach lead to wholesale reversals?

8. So far, we have dealt only with the prosecutor's duty to disclose. What sort of duty does the defense have? Unlike civil litigation, where discovery is a broad two-way street, the defense is under no general obligation to turn over inculpatory evidence. Moreover, there are constitutional implications to attempts to discover the defendant's case, as the next case discusses.

WILLIAMS V. FLORIDA

Supreme Court of the United States, 1970.
399 U.S. 78, 90 S.Ct. 1893, 26 L.Ed.2d 446.

MR. JUSTICE WHITE delivered the opinion of the Court [joined by CHIEF JUSTICE BURGER, and JUSTICES HARLAN, BRENNAN, and STEWART].
* * *

I

Florida's notice-of-alibi rule is in essence a requirement that a defendant submit to a limited form of pretrial discovery by the State whenever he intends to rely at trial on the defense of alibi.[a] In exchange for the defendant's disclosure of the witnesses he proposes to use to establish that defense, the State in turn is required to notify the defendant of any witnesses it proposes to offer in rebuttal to that defense. Both sides are under a continuing duty promptly to disclose the names and addresses of additional witnesses bearing on the alibi as they become available. The threatened sanction for failure to comply is the exclusion at trial of the defendant's alibi evidence—except for his own testimony— or, in the case of the State, the exclusion of the State's evidence offered in rebuttal of the alibi.

In this case, following the denial of his Motion for a Protective Order, petitioner complied with the alibi rule and gave the State the name and address of one Mary Scotty. Mrs. Scotty was summoned to the office of the State Attorney on the morning of the trial, where she gave pretrial testimony. At the trial itself, Mrs. Scotty, petitioner, and petitioner's wife all testified that the three of them had been in Mrs. Scotty's apartment during the time of the robbery. On two occasions during cross-examination of Mrs. Scotty, the prosecuting attorney confronted her with her earlier deposition in which she had given dates and times that in some respects did not correspond with the dates and times given at trial. Mrs. Scotty adhered to her trial story, insisting that she had been mistaken in her earlier testimony. The State also offered in rebuttal the testimony of one of the officers investigating the robbery who claimed that Mrs. Scotty had asked him for directions on the afternoon in

---

[a] The rule provides, in pertinent part: "Upon the written demand of the prosecuting attorney, specifying as particularly as is known to such prosecuting attorney, the place, date and time of the commission of the crime charged, a defendant in a criminal case who intends to offer evidence of an alibi in his defense shall, not less than ten days before trial or such other time as the court may direct, file and serve upon such prosecuting attorney a notice in writing of his intention to claim such alibi, which notice shall contain specific information as to the place at which the defendant claims to have been at the time of the alleged offense and, as particularly as is known to defendant or his attorney, the names and addresses of the witnesses by whom he proposes to establish such alibi. Not less than five days after receipt of defendant's witness list, or such other times as the court may direct, the prosecuting attorney shall file and serve upon the defendant the names and addresses (as particularly as are known to the prosecuting attorney) of the witnesses the State proposes to offer in rebuttal to discredit the defendant's alibi at the trial of the cause." Eds.

question during the time when she claimed to have been in her apartment with petitioner and his wife.

We need not linger over the suggestion that the discovery permitted the State against petitioner in this case deprived him of "due process" or a "fair trial." Florida law provides for liberal discovery by the defendant against the State, and the notice-of-alibi rule is itself carefully hedged with reciprocal duties requiring state disclosure to the defendant. Given the ease with which an alibi can be fabricated, the State's interest in protecting itself against an eleventh-hour defense is both obvious and legitimate. Reflecting this interest, notice-of-alibi provisions, dating at least from 1927, are now in existence in a substantial number of States. The adversary system of trial is hardly an end in itself; it is not yet a poker game in which players enjoy an absolute right always to conceal their cards until played. We find ample room in that system, at least as far as "due process" is concerned, for the instant Florida rule, which is designed to enhance the search for truth in the criminal trial by insuring both the defendant and the State ample opportunity to investigate certain facts crucial to the determination of guilt or innocence.

Petitioner's major contention is that he was "compelled * * * to be a witness against himself" contrary to the commands of the Fifth and Fourteenth Amendments because the notice-of-alibi rule required him to give the State the name and address of Mrs. Scotty in advance of trial and thus to furnish the State with information useful in convicting him. No pretrial statement of petitioner was introduced at trial; but armed with Mrs. Scotty's name and address and the knowledge that she was to be petitioner's alibi witness, the State was able to take her deposition in advance of trial and to find rebuttal testimony. Also, requiring him to reveal the elements of his defense is claimed to have interfered with his right to wait until after the State had presented its case to decide how to defend against it. We conclude, however, as has apparently every other court that has considered the issue, that the privilege against self-incrimination is not violated by a requirement that the defendant give notice of an alibi defense and disclose his alibi witnesses.

The defendant in a criminal trial is frequently forced to testify himself and to call other witnesses in an effort to reduce the risk of conviction. When he presents his witnesses, he must reveal their identity and submit them to cross-examination which in itself may prove incriminating or which may furnish the State with leads to incriminating rebuttal evidence. That the defendant faces such a dilemma demanding a choice between complete silence and presenting a defense has never been thought an invasion of the privilege against compelled self-incrimination. The pressures generated by the State's evidence may be severe but they do not vitiate the defendant's choice to present an alibi defense and witnesses to prove it, even though the attempted defense ends in catastrophe for the defendant. However "testimonial" or "incriminating" the alibi defense proves to be, it cannot be considered "compelled" within the meaning of the Fifth and Fourteenth Amendments.

Very similar constraints operate on the defendant when the State requires pretrial notice of alibi and the naming of alibi witnesses. Nothing in such a rule requires the defendant to rely on an alibi or prevents him from abandoning the defense; these matters are left to his unfettered choice. That choice must be made, but the pressures that bear on his pretrial decision are of the same nature as those that would induce him to call alibi witnesses at the trial: the force of historical fact beyond both his and the State's control and the strength of the State's case built on these facts. Response to that kind of pressure by offering evidence or testimony is not compelled self-incrimination transgressing the Fifth and Fourteenth Amendments.

In the case before us, the notice-of-alibi rule by itself in no way affected petitioner's crucial decision to call alibi witnesses or added to the legitimate pressures leading to that course of action. At most, the rule only compelled petitioner to accelerate the timing of his disclosure, forcing him to divulge at an earlier date information that the petitioner from the beginning planned to divulge at trial. Nothing in the Fifth Amendment privilege entitles a defendant as a matter of constitutional right to await the end of the State's case before announcing the nature of his defense, any more than it entitles him to await the jury's verdict on the State's case-in-chief before deciding whether or not to take the stand himself.

Petitioner concedes that absent the notice-of-alibi rule the Constitution would raise no bar to the court's granting the State a continuance at trial on the ground of surprise as soon as the alibi witness is called. Nor would there be self-incrimination problems if, during that continuance, the State was permitted to do precisely what it did here prior to trial: take the deposition of the witness and find rebuttal evidence. But if so utilizing a continuance is permissible under the Fifth and Fourteenth Amendments, then surely the same result may be accomplished through pretrial discovery, as it was here, avoiding the necessity of a disrupted trial.[17] We decline to hold that the privilege against compulsory self-incrimination guarantees the defendant the right to surprise the State with an alibi defense. * * *

MR. JUSTICE BLACKMUN took no part in the consideration or decision of this case.

[The concurring opinion of CHIEF JUSTICE BURGER is omitted.]

---

[17] It might also be argued that the "testimonial" disclosures protected by the Fifth Amendment include only statements relating to the historical facts of the crime, not statements relating solely to what a defendant proposes to do at trial.

MR. JUSTICE BLACK, with whom MR. JUSTICE DOUGLAS joins, concurring in part and dissenting in part. * * *

The Court * * * holds that a State can require a defendant in a criminal case to disclose in advance of trial the nature of his alibi defense and give the names and addresses of witnesses he will call to support that defense. This requirement, the majority says, does not violate the Fifth Amendment prohibition against compelling a criminal defendant to be a witness against himself. Although this case itself involves only a notice-of-alibi provision, it is clear that the decision means that a State can require a defendant to disclose in advance of trial any and all information he might possibly use to defend himself at trial. This decision, in my view, is a radical and dangerous departure from the historical and constitutionally guaranteed right of a defendant in a criminal case to remain completely silent, requiring the State to prove its case without any assistance of any kind from the defendant himself.

I

The core of the majority's decision is an assumption that compelling a defendant to give notice of an alibi defense before a trial is no different from requiring a defendant, after the State has produced the evidence against him at trial, to plead alibi before the jury retires to consider the case. This assumption is clearly revealed by the statement that "the pressures that bear on [a defendant's] pre-trial decision are of the same nature as those that would induce him to call alibi witnesses at the trial: the force of historical fact beyond both his and the State's control and the strength of the State's case built on these facts." That statement is plainly and simply wrong as a matter of fact and law, and the Court's holding based on that statement is a complete misunderstanding of the protections provided for criminal defendants by the Fifth Amendment and other provisions of the Bill of Rights.

A * * *

The Court apparently * * * assumes that a defendant who has given the required notice can abandon his alibi without hurting himself. Such an assumption is implicit in and necessary for the majority's argument that the pretrial decision is no different from that at the trial itself. I, however, cannot so lightly assume that pretrial notice will have no adverse effects on a defendant who later decides to forgo such a defense. Necessarily the defendant will have given the prosecutor the names of persons who may have some knowledge about the defendant himself or his activities. Necessarily the prosecutor will have every incentive to question these persons fully, and in doing so he may discover new leads or evidence. Undoubtedly there will be situations in which the State will seek to use such information—information it would probably never have obtained but for the defendant's coerced cooperation.

B

It is unnecessary for me, however, to engage in any such intellectual gymnastics concerning the practical effects of the notice-of-alibi procedure, because the Fifth Amendment itself clearly provides that "[n]o person * * * shall be compelled in any criminal case to be a witness against himself." If words are to be given their plain and obvious meaning, that provision, in my opinion, states that a criminal defendant cannot be required to give evidence, testimony, or any other assistance to the State to aid it in convicting him of crime. The Florida notice-of-alibi rule in my opinion is a patent violation of that constitutional provision because it requires a defendant to disclose information to the State so that the State can use that information to destroy him. * * *

It is no answer to this argument to suggest that the Fifth Amendment as so interpreted would give the defendant an unfair element of surprise, turning a trial into a "poker game" or "sporting contest," for that tactical advantage to the defendant is inherent in the type of trial required by our Bill of Rights. The Framers were well aware of the awesome investigative and prosecutorial powers of government and it was in order to limit those powers that they spelled out in detail in the Constitution the procedure to be followed in criminal trials. A defendant, they said, is entitled to notice of the charges against him, trial by jury, the right to counsel for his defense, the right to confront and cross-examine witnesses, the right to call witnesses in his own behalf, and the right not to be a witness against himself. All of these rights are designed to shield the defendant against state power. None are designed to make convictions easier and taken together they clearly indicate that in our system the entire burden of proving criminal activity rests on the State. The defendant, under our Constitution, need not do anything at all to defend himself, and certainly he cannot be required to help convict himself. Rather he has an absolute, unqualified right to compel the State to investigate its own case, find its own witnesses, prove its own facts, and convince the jury through its own resources. Throughout the process the defendant has a fundamental right to remain silent, in effect challenging the State at every point to: "Prove it!"

The Bill of Rights thus sets out the type of constitutionally required system that the State must follow in order to convict individuals of crime. That system requires that the State itself must bear the entire burden without any assistance from the defendant. This requirement is clearly indicated in the Fifth Amendment itself, but it is equally apparent when all the specific provisions of the Bill of Rights relating to criminal prosecutions are considered together. And when a question concerning the constitutionality of some aspect of criminal procedure arises, this Court must consider all those provisions and interpret them together. The Fifth Amendment prohibition against compelling a defendant to be a witness against himself is not an isolated, distinct provision. It is part of a system of constitutionally required procedures, and its true meaning can be seen only in light of all those provisions. * * *

This constitutional right to remain absolutely silent cannot be avoided by superficially attractive analogies to any so-called "compulsion" inherent in the trial itself that may lead a defendant to put on evidence in his own defense. Obviously the Constitution contemplates that a defendant can be "compelled" to stand trial, and obviously there will be times when the trial process itself will require the defendant to do something in order to try to avoid a conviction. But nothing in the Constitution permits the State to add to the natural consequences of a trial and compel the defendant in advance of trial to participate in any way in the State's attempt to condemn him.

A criminal trial is in part a search for truth. But it is also a system designed to protect "freedom" by insuring that no one is criminally punished unless the State has first succeeded in the admittedly difficult task of convincing a jury that the defendant is guilty. That task is made more difficult by the Bill of Rights, and the Fifth Amendment may be one of the most difficult of the barriers to surmount. The Framers decided that the benefits to be derived from the kind of trial required by the Bill of Rights were well worth any loss in "efficiency" that resulted. Their decision constitutes the final word on the subject, absent some constitutional amendment. That decision should not be set aside as the Court does today.

II

On the surface this case involves only a notice-of-alibi provisions, but in effect the decision opens the way for a profound change in one of the most important traditional safeguards of a criminal defendant. The rationale of today's decision is in no way limited to alibi defenses, or any other type or classification of evidence. The theory advanced goes at least so far as to permit the State to obtain under threat of sanction complete disclosure by the defendant in advance of trial of all evidence, testimony, and tactics he plans to use at that trial. In each case the justification will be that the rule affects only the "timing" of the disclosure, and not the substantive decision itself. * * *

There is a hint in the State's brief in this case—as well as, I fear, in the Court's opinion—of the ever-recurring suggestion that the test of constitutionality is the test of "fairness," "decency", or in short the Court's own views of what is "best." Occasionally this test emerges in disguise as an intellectually satisfying "distinction" or "analogy" designed to cover up a decision based on the wisdom of a proposed procedure rather than its conformity with the commands of the Constitution. * * * [Today's] decision is one more step away from the written Constitution and a radical departure from the system of criminal justice that has prevailed in this country. Compelling a defendant in a criminal case to be a witness against himself in any way, including the use of the system of pretrial discovery approved today, was unknown in English law, except for the un-lamented proceedings in the Star Chamber courts—the type of proceedings the Fifth Amendment was designed to prevent. For practically the first 150 years of this Nation's history no State considered adopting such procedures compelling a criminal defendant to help convict himself, although history does not indicate that our ancestors were any less intelligent or solicitous of having a fair and efficient system of criminal justice than we are. History does indicate that persons well familiar with the dangers of arbitrary and oppressive use of the criminal process were determined to limit such dangers for the protection of each and every inhabitant of this country. They were well aware that any individual might some day be subjected to criminal prosecution, and it was in order to protect the freedom of *each* of us that they restricted the Government's ability to punish or imprison *any* of us. Yet in spite of the history of oppression that produced the Bill of Rights and the strong reluctance of our governments to compel a criminal defendant to assist in his own conviction, the Court today reaches out to embrace and sanctify at the first opportunity a most dangerous departure from the Constitution and the traditional safeguards afforded persons accused of crime. I cannot accept such a result and must express my most emphatic disagreement and dissent.

[The opinion of JUSTICE MARSHALL, dissenting in part, is omitted.]

NOTES AND QUESTIONS

1. Refer back to p. 951, Note 3, for some thoughts on what is "testimonial" evidence under the Fifth Amendment. Does the Florida notice-of-alibi rule require testimonial evidence? Does the Court uphold the rule because producing alibi witnesses is not a testimonial act? Or does the Court find an absence of compulsion?

2. Do you prefer the Court's analysis to Justice Black's? What role does the Fifth Amendment privilege play in the criminal justice system, according to Justice Black?

3. Professor Akhil Reed Amar disagrees with Justice Black's plain meaning interpretation of the Fifth Amendment. For Amar, the plain meaning of being compelled to be a witness means testimony given by the defendant in the courtroom, not a list of alibi witnesses or other evidence learned from pre-trial testimony. Akhil Reed Amar, The Constitution and Criminal Procedure 70 (1997). Here we have two constitutional scholars, both of whom believe in plain meaning. Yet one concludes that it is a "remarkably clean" plain meaning argument to say that the only way to "be a witness" is to testify (Amar). The other (Black) views "being a witness" to have a much

broader plain meaning. Perhaps this is why the Court has rarely relied on "plain meaning" theories of interpretation.

4.   *Reciprocity.* The Court was careful to note that the Florida notice-of-alibi rule is "carefully hedged with reciprocal duties requiring state disclosure to the defendant." Thus, after the defendant discloses the names of alibi witnesses, the State must disclose the names of any witnesses it will call to testify on the alibi issue. What if these reciprocal duties were absent? Would such a statute violate the self-incrimination clause? Any other part of the Constitution? See Wardius v. Oregon, 412 U.S. 470, 93 S.Ct. 2208, 37 L.Ed.2d 82 (1973).

5.   Is Justice Black right that the Court's holding will permit the State to require disclosure "in advance of trial of all evidence, testimony, and tactics [defendant] plans to use at trial"? If not, on what Fifth Amendment ground can *Williams* be limited to alibi? What result if the state rule of procedure required the defendant to turn over to the prosecutor "all exculpatory evidence in the defendant's possession"?

Massachusetts authorizes the judge to require that, as part of reciprocal discovery, the defendant disclose "names, addresses, and statements of those persons whom the defendant intends to use as witnesses at trial." In Massachusetts v. Durham, 446 Mass. 212, 843 N.E.2d 1035 (2006), the defendant's investigator interviewed some of the Commonwealth's witnesses. This of course would give Durham ammunition to cross-examine the witnesses if they testified differently at trial. The prosecutor asked for copies of statements of *its own witnesses* in possession of the defendant, and the judge granted the request. Leaving aside whether this is the best reading of the discovery rule (the state supreme judicial court split 4–3 on that question), is there any constitutional problem given the Supreme Court's holding in *Williams*?

6.   *Remedy.* Suppose a defendant does not comply with a mandatory disclosure requirement. What should the remedy be? If the remedy is not substantial, of course, few defendants will comply. On the other hand, if the sanction is to preclude a defense witness from testifying, the Sixth Amendment right "to have compulsory process for obtaining witnesses in his favor" is implicated. See *Taylor v. Illinois*, p. 1359.

E. JOINDER AND SEVERANCE

Read Federal Rules of Criminal Procedure 8 and 14.

NOTES AND QUESTIONS

1.   Compare Rule 8(a) and Rule 8(b). Is it easier to join defendants or counts? Which should be easier? For example, may the prosecution join two unrelated murders allegedly committed by the same defendant on different occasions? May the prosecution join two defendants who coincidentally committed unrelated murders at the same site at the same time? Is there a

valid reason under the federal rules for permitting joinder in one, but not the other, case?

2. *Problem.* A three-count indictment alleges (1) Maria, Nell, and Olivia committed conspiracy to commit false pretenses by selling cars with phony mileage statements and "doctored" odometers; (2) pursuant to the conspiracy, Maria committed false pretenses based on actually selling cars with phony mileage statements and doctored odometers; (3) Nell committed auto theft (no mention is made of these cars being used in the conspiracy). Is the joinder of defendants permissible under Rule 8(b)? See Cupo v. United States, 359 F.2d 990 (D.C. Cir. 1966).

3. *Joinder as source of bias.* Do you think joinder of offenses or defendants is likely to be prejudicial to defendants? One possible source of bias is that the jury might confuse evidence in a way that is harmful to defendants when the evidence supporting some counts is weaker than others. Another possible source of bias is an inference based on the old saying "where there's smoke there's fire"—and the more smoke, the more likely everything is on fire.

One commentator examined seven published studies on the joinder of offenses. The studies used mock jurors to test for the effect of joinder and to explore the reasons why joinder might create bias. "[T]he studies are unanimous in finding that defendants do face a greater likelihood of conviction if offenses are tried jointly rather that separately. Furthermore, the effect of joinder increases with the number of offenses charged." Note, *Rethinking Criminal Joinder: An Analysis of the Empirical Research and Its Implications for Justice*, 52 Law & Contemp. Probs. 325, 330–31 (1989). Two studies "found that the joinder effect was greater when cases are weak." *Id.* at 331. Two studies found a greater joinder effect when the cases joined were similar—in other words, joinder of two rape charges because they are similar offenses caused greater bias than joinder of a robbery and rape because they occurred during the same transaction. *Id.* at 332.

Given these data, one could speculate that the prejudicial effect of joinder is greatest when the jury is presented with multiple similar offenses, the case is weak, and the defendant *more likely to be innocent.* The commentator who examined the studies concluded that Rule 8(a) should be "revised to protect defendants against prejudices involved in similar-offense joinder." *Id.* at 333.

Andrew Leipold agrees that joinder likely causes a "prejudicial overlay" that threatens innocent defendants. "By allowing governmental interest in [the efficiency of] a single trial to swamp the defendant's interest in being tried on untainted evidence, a clear choice is being made about the risks of wrongful convictions." Andrew D. Leipold, *How the Pretrial Process Contributes to Wrongful Convictions*, 42 Am. Crim. L. Rev. 1123, 1147 (2005).

4. Rule 8 is permissive in scope, giving permission to proceed with joinder in certain categories of cases but not *requiring* joinder (offenses "may

be charged"; defendants "may be joined"). Because Rule 8 potentially encompasses a broad range of cases, however, Rule 14 requires severance of counts or defendants when prejudice exists. Of course, trying to figure out when prejudice exists—the issue in the next case—is not always easy. As the New Jersey rules about joinder and severance are similar to the federal rules, the next case in effect explores Rule 14 prejudice.

STATE V. RELDAN

Superior Court of New Jersey, Law Division, 1979.
167 N.J.Super. 595, 401 A.2d 563.

MADDEN, J. S. C.

This matter comes before the court on a motion, pursuant to *R.* 3:15–2(b), to order separate trials of counts 1 and 2 of indictment S-63-77. That indictment charges defendant in count 1 with the first degree murder of Susan Heynes and in count 2 with the first degree murder of Susan Reeves. Susan Heynes was reported missing from her home in Haworth, New Jersey, on October 6, 1975, and her nude body was subsequently found in the Valley Cottage area of Clarkstown, in Rockland County, New York, on October 27, 1975. Susan Reeves was reported missing from her home in Demarest, New Jersey, on October 14, 1975, and her nude body was subsequently found in Tallman State Park, Bear Mountain, in Rockland County, New York, on October 28, 1975. The Medical Examiner of Rockland County examined the two bodies and found that the cause of death in both cases was strangulation due to a ligature of pantyhose found around the necks of the victims.

Defendant was charged with both murders in separate counts of a single indictment on January 20, 1977. The State maintains that the joinder of the two murders was proper under *R.* 3:7–6 which permits the specification of two or more offenses in the same indictment if the offenses charged are of the same or similar character. The defendant contends that the joinder is prejudicial and seeks separate trials on each count under *R.* 3:15–2(b).

In discussing these two rules our courts have stated that although separate and distinct crimes which are the same or similar in character may be joined together in a single trial in the interests of judicial economy and efficiency, where there exists a possibility of prejudice to defendant, a trial severance of the offenses should be granted.

It should also be noted that the mere claim that prejudice attaches to a consolidated trial of multiple charges is insufficient to justify a severance. More than a cavil allegation of prejudice must be offered to warrant an order for separate trials of properly joined offenses. If separate crimes were required to be tried separately in all circumstances, the multiplicity of trials would disserve the State and defendants alike.

In order to practically and properly evaluate a claim of prejudice, several basic categories have been formulated which contain the potential harm accruing to a defendant by a joinder of separate offenses:

> 1. he may become embarrassed or confounded in presenting separate defenses; 2. the jury may use the evidence of one of the crimes charged to infer a criminal disposition on the part of the defendant from which is found his guilt of the other crime or crimes charged; or 3. the jury may cumulate the evidence of the various crimes charged and find guilt when, if considered separately, it would not so find. A less tangible, but perhaps equally persuasive, element of prejudice may reside in a latent feeling of hostility engendered by the charging of several crimes as distinct from only one.

This formulation has gained widespread acceptance, for (as will be seen) cases discussing prejudicial joinder do so in contexts that fall into one of these categories.

Defendant in the present case has claimed that each of these elements of prejudice is extant, and so I will consider them individually.

Defendant claims that he will be confounded or embarrassed in his defense by the consolidation in the event he wishes to take the stand and testify as to only one count of the indictment. It is true that it is potentially prejudicial to put a defendant in a position where, if he chooses to testify as to one charge, he opens himself to cross-examination or, alternatively, to the possibly damaging effect of remaining silent as to another charge.[4]

Defendant does not, however, proffer that he wishes to take the stand and testify as to only one count. Even if he were to so indicate, that fact alone is not dispositive of a motion to sever so as to divest a court of all control over the matter. * * * "[N]o need for a severance exists until the defendant makes a convincing showing that he has both important testimony to give concerning one count and strong need to refrain from testifying on the other." Only in this way can a court determine whether a claim of prejudice of this type is genuine. Should such a proffer be made during trial, I am empowered to determine at that point whether a severance should be granted. There has therefore been an insufficient showing of prejudice on that basis to justify a severance.

Turning to the second claim of prejudice, defendant argues that a joint trial will result in the jury using evidence of one of the crimes to

---

[4] *Evid.R.* 25(d), N.J.S.A. 2A:84A–(d) provides that where a defendant voluntarily testifies in a criminal case, he may be cross-examined on any matter relevant to the issues therein. In light of my resolution of the question of criminal disposition prejudice and other crimes evidence, it is apparent that were defendant to testify as to one count of the indictment, he could be cross-examined on the other.

infer a criminal disposition on the part of defendant to commit the other crime, in violation of *Evid.R.* 55. The reason for this rule is the belief that the potential for prejudice to a defendant in the eyes of a jury outweighs any probative value such evidence may have. This same principle operates to militate against the joining of separate offenses in a single trial, since one trial of multiple charges means by its very nature that the jury will hear other crimes evidence.

Other crimes evidence, however, is admissible to prove a relevant fact in issue, such as motive, intent, common scheme or plan, knowledge, absence of mistake, or identity. Thus, where evidence of one crime would be admissible at a separate trial of another crime under one of the above exceptions, it follows that a defendant will not suffer any additional prejudice if the two offenses are tried together. As [one federal court] stated * * * :

> In *Drew* [*v. United States*, 331 F.2d 85 (D.C. Cir. 1964)], we recognized that the principal elements of prejudice from a joint trial are largely absent in a situation where evidence of each of the joined offenses would be admissible in a separate trial for the other, under the rules governing admissibility of "other crimes" evidence. The standard we there laid down requires a severance unless evidence of the joined offenses would be mutually admissible, or if not, the evidence is sufficiently "simple and distinct" to mitigate the danger of cumulation.

Our own State has followed this logic when dealing with, for example, separate crimes found to be part of a common scheme, and has denied motions to sever accordingly.

The State here contends that evidence of one homicide would be admissible in the trial of the other in order to show the identity of the murderer, and for that reason it would not prejudice defendant to try the two offenses together. In examining this contention, I must determine first whether such evidence is sufficiently probative to warrant admission under *Evid.R.* 55 and, if so, whether it is so prejudicial as to bar its admission under *Evid.R.* 4.

In support of its argument, the State has indicated that it will attempt to show that both victims were murdered by the same person, and that therefore evidence tending to show that this defendant killed one victim is probative as to the identity of the murderer of the other victim, and would be admissible as such. The State points to the following evidence which it claims shows a single perpetrator of both crimes.

Both victims were women in their twenties and of the same approximate height and weight; they were both abducted from the same general geographic area; they were both found nude, in relatively isolated areas of New York State not far from one another, and, most significantly, both died from strangulation caused by a ligature of pantyhose which resulted in fractured hyoid bones in their necks. The State relies heavily on this last point, pointing out that Dr. Frederick Zugibe, Chief Medical Examiner of Rockland County, who examined the bodies, was of the opinion that less than 1% of strangulations resulted in the fracture of cartilages of the Hyoid bone. Dr. Zugibe testified before the grand jury that in his opinion both girls were murdered by the same person. The State also points out that since 1966 no other homicides in this county resulted in strangulation by ligatures using pantyhose, and that of the six unsolved homicides by strangulation in this county in the last 12 years, only these two involved injuries of the type sustained here.

The State also relies on the statements given by two co-inmates of defendant while he was incarcerated at Rahway State Prison in December 1976. Both statements contain the allegation that defendant confided to the two inmates that it was a mistake on his part to place the two bodies so close together in New York State.[5]

The State concedes that its case is largely circumstantial and that the identity of the murderer of two victims is at issue. The State argues, however, that if a severance were ordered, the above facts show that the identity of the perpetrator in each case is the same, and that therefore evidence showing defendant's guilt of one crime would be probative at his trial on the other. It is true that:

> Evidence of an independent and separate crime is admissible when such evidence tends to aid in identifying the accused as the person who committed the particular crime under investigation.
> * * *
>
> In order, however, for evidence of another crime to be admissible to prove the identity of the accused, there must be such a logical connection between the crimes that the proof of one will naturally tend to show that the accused is the person who committed the other.

I find that the facts here demonstrate sufficient similarity in the details of both murders to permit evidence of one murder to be introduced into evidence in the trial of the other to show identity.[6] That the details of the two crimes are novel and unusual enough to warrant this conclusion finds support by analogy to a variety of cases where a similar result was reached. * * *

---

[5]   No opinion is offered here as to the admissibility of these statements at trial.

[6]   It should be noted that all the evidence relating to one offense need not be admissible in a separate trial for the other in order to justify the consolidation for trial of two offenses under the other crimes evidence theory, so long as those portions of the evidence which would be admitted are significant and link the two offenses together.

Moreover, I find the evidence not to be so prejudicial to defendant as to outweigh its probative value. The prejudice to be here considered is essentially the intangible fourth element of prejudice * * * *viz*, that a jury will engender a feeling of hostility towards the defendant by the charging of several crimes together, or by the joining of particularly heinous offenses in one trial. To quote former Chief Justice Weintraub:

> That evidence is shrouded with unsavory implications is no reason for exclusion when it is a significant part of the proof. The unwholesome aspects, authored by defendant himself, if the evidence is believed, were inextricably entwined with the material facts.

I therefore conclude that the evidence of one homicide would be admissible in the trial of the other, thereby rendering it unnecessary to sever on the theory that a jury would be improperly hearing other crimes evidence in a single trial.

The final argument to be considered is that a single trial would result in the cumulation of the evidence by the jury, with the result that a conviction might be obtained where, if the charges were considered separately, this would not be the case. Where such an argument is made the court must consider whether the evidence is sufficiently separate and distinct to permit a jury to consider the charges individually, without undue confusion. As to those proofs going to the question of identity, such evidence will be before a jury whether or not separate trials are ordered, and the objection that a jury would cumulate such evidence is therefore moot. Defendant has not offered any other potential evidence which could be said to be likely to mislead or confuse a jury, and I find nothing inherently unclear or indistinct about the charges here. I am therefore confident that the jury can be properly instructed to accord the appropriate weight to evidence admitted under *Evid.R.* 55, as well as to consider separately each count of the indictment.

The proofs here are distinguishable from those in *State v. Orlando*, 101 N.J. Super. 390 (App.Div.1968). There, defendant was charged with impairing the morals of two different minors on two different occasions, and the only evidence was the testimony of the two victims. The effect of a joinder in that case would have necessarily given the State two witnesses instead of one to overcome defendant's denial of either offense. Here, each charge rests on differing circumstantial evidence, without the cumulative possibilities of *Orlando*. Accordingly, defendant's motion to sever on this basis must also be denied.

I, therefore, conclude that defendant will not be unduly prejudiced by a joinder of the two counts in Indictment S-63-77, and his motion to sever is denied. [The state appellate division affirmed "substantially for the reasons expressed by Judge Madden." State v. Reldan, 185 N.J.Super. 494, 449 A.2d 1317 (App.Div.1982). Eds.]

NOTES AND QUESTIONS

1. What is the relevance of deciding whether evidence of one count would be admissible in a trial for the other count?

2. Is the presumption of prejudice conclusive when an appellate court holds that evidence of one count was inadmissible on the other count and thus should not have been admitted in the joint trial? What would the State argue to rebut the presumption of prejudice?

3. *The Reldan story continues.* Prior to the trial for the two murders, Reldan filed a motion to suppress evidence found in an automobile search. The trial court granted the motion.

> The ensuing trial lasted from May 21 through June 16, 1979, when it ended in the declaration of a mistrial because the jury was unable to agree on a verdict. A second trial, which lasted from September 19 through October 17, 1979, resulted in convictions for first-degree and second-degree murder, but the judgments were reversed by the Appellate Division in May 1982 [on the ground that evidence of prior convictions was erroneously admitted] and the matter remanded for yet a third trial.

State v. Reldan, 100 N.J. 187, 495 A.2d 76, 78–79 (1985). Prior to the third trial, however, the State moved for reconsideration of the motion to suppress, and the state courts this time held the evidence admissible. *Id.* The case ultimately ended in 1986 in convictions of first-degree and second-degree murder, with sentences of life and thirty years.

4. *Bruton prejudice. Reldan* involved joinder of counts. The issue of joinder of defendants, though similar, has a somewhat different solution under the Federal Rules. The usual prejudice associated with joinder of defendants is that the jury would transfer evidence (consciously or unconsciously) from one defendant to another, making it easier to convict co-defendants than defendants tried separately. The judge who has a motion to sever defendants before her must decide the extent of this "birds-of-a-feather" prejudice in a particular case.

Joinder of defendants can also create a Sixth Amendment problem. In Bruton v. United States, 391 U.S. 123, 88 S.Ct. 1620, 20 L.Ed.2d 476 (1968), the Court discovered a specific kind of prejudice from joinder of defendants when a confession is offered into evidence against only one defendant, but also incriminates other defendants. Normally, when evidence is offered against one defendant but not another, the judge instructs the jury not to consider that evidence against the other defendant. But the Court found that special considerations governed the confession issue, noting that it is very difficult to ignore testimony in which one co-defendant essentially says: "The other guy sitting here in the courtroom? He did it."

To the extent jurors cannot ignore that testimony, its admission into evidence potentially violates the Sixth Amendment confrontation clause, which gives defendants the right to confront witnesses against them. We will study the confrontation clause in Chapter 16, including the *Bruton* problem, but for present you should know that *Bruton* often requires prosecutors to sever co-defendants when a confession is part of the state's evidence. To have the confession considered against the non-confessing defendant is not only prejudice, in the Rule 14 sense, but also a constitutional violation.

F. SPEEDY TRIAL

The Sixth Amendment contains a series of rights that attend the trial process and mostly have to do with producing and evaluating evidence (*e.g.*, right to counsel; right to jury trial; right to confront prosecution witnesses; right to subpoena witnesses). One Sixth Amendment right is out of place on a functional view of the Sixth Amendment because it has nothing to do with the mechanism of trial but, rather, the timeliness of it. Defendants have a right to a speedy trial, the Amendment tells us. By what standard would courts determine whether a trial is speedy? Does it matter whether a defendant *wants* a speedy trial? Why do you think the Framers included "speedy" along with "public" when guaranteeing the right to trial in the Sixth Amendment?

Though the history is less than clear, the existence of a right to a speedy trial is not fully explained by the norm of truth/reliability that explains the rest of the Sixth Amendment. It seems clear that a speedy trial is more likely to be reliable than a trial years later, but the Framers had other goals in mind. The ability of the monarch to detain political prisoners for long periods in the Tower of London led to distress in England, ultimately producing the English Habeas Corpus Act of 1679. It thus "seems likely that the Framers intended the speedy trial right to permit defendants to demand that they be released or tried, an action which would be in substance, and perhaps in form, a petition for a writ of habeas corpus." George C. Thomas III, *Remapping the Criminal Procedure Universe*, 83 Va. L.Rev. 1845 (1997).

[handwritten margin note: Parallel to habeas corpus motivation]

But the remedy of demanding a speedy trial is of little practical utility today. Many defendants are out on bail and the last thing they want is a speedy trial. Over ninety percent of felony charges result in plea bargains, thus avoiding trial altogether. Most trials are reasonably speedy, at least compared to seventeenth century Tower of London cases. Thus, the speedy trial issue today almost always comes up after a conviction as a grounds for setting aside the conviction. But the remedy issue is very difficult. How does a court cure the failure to grant a speedy trial? By reversing and remanding for another, even less speedy, trial? Surely not. Thus, a speedy trial violation, alone among the various criminal procedure rights, requires in every case a dismissal of the indictment with prejudice and the freeing of a defendant found guilty of a crime. You will see the pressure this puts on the Court as it struggles to formulate a speedy trial analysis in the next case.

BARKER V. WINGO

Supreme Court of the United States, 1972.
407 U.S. 514, 92 S.Ct. 2182, 33 L.Ed.2d 101.

MR. JUSTICE POWELL delivered the opinion of the Court [joined by CHIEF JUSTICE BURGER and JUSTICES DOUGLAS, BRENNAN, STEWART, WHITE, MARSHALL, BLACKMUN, and REHNQUIST]. * * *

I

On July 20, 1958, in Christian County, Kentucky, an elderly couple was beaten to death by intruders wielding an iron tire tool. Two suspects, Silas Manning and Willie Barker, the petitioner, were arrested shortly thereafter. The grand jury indicted them on September 15. Counsel was appointed on September 17, and Barker's trial was set for October 21. The Commonwealth had a stronger case against Manning, and it believed that Barker could not be convicted unless Manning testified against him. Manning was naturally unwilling to incriminate himself. Accordingly, on October 23, the day Silas Manning was brought to trial, the Commonwealth sought and obtained the first of what was to be a series of 16 continuances of Barker's trial. Barker made no objection. By first convicting Manning, the Commonwealth would remove possible problems of self-incrimination and would be able to assure his testimony against Barker.

The Commonwealth encountered more than a few difficulties in its prosecution of Manning. The first trial ended in a hung jury. A second trial resulted in a conviction, but the Kentucky Court of Appeals reversed because of the admission of evidence obtained by an illegal search. At his third trial, Manning was again convicted, and the Court of Appeals again reversed because the trial court had not granted a change of venue. A fourth trial resulted in a hung jury. Finally, after five trials, Manning was convicted, in March 1962, of murdering one victim, and after a sixth trial, in December 1962, he was convicted of murdering the other.[4]

The Christian County Circuit Court holds three terms each year—in February, June, and September. Barker's initial trial was to take place in the September term of 1958. The first continuance postponed it until the February 1959 term. The second continuance was granted for one month only. Every term thereafter for as long as the Manning prosecutions were in process, the Commonwealth routinely moved to continue Barker's case to the next term. When the case was continued from the June 1959 term

---

[4] Apparently Manning chose not to appeal these final two convictions.

until the following September, Barker, having spent 10 months in jail, obtained his release by posting a $5,000 bond. He thereafter remained free in the community until his trial. Barker made no objection, through his counsel, to the first 11 continuances.

When on February 12, 1962, the Commonwealth moved for the twelfth time to continue the case until the following term, Barker's counsel filed a motion to dismiss the indictment. The motion to dismiss was denied two weeks later, and the Commonwealth's motion for a continuance was granted. The Commonwealth was granted further continuances in June 1962 and September 1962, to which Barker did not object.

In February 1963, the first term of court following Manning's final conviction, the Commonwealth moved to set Barker's trial for March 19. But on the day scheduled for trial, it again moved for a continuance until the June term. It gave as its reason the illness of the ex-sheriff who was the chief investigating officer in the case. To this continuance, Barker objected unsuccessfully.

The witness was still unable to testify in June, and the trial, which had been set for June 19, was continued again until the September term over Barker's objection. This time the court announced that the case would be dismissed for lack of prosecution if it were not tried during the next term. The final trial date was set for October 9, 1963. On that date, Barker again moved to dismiss the indictment, and this time specified that his right to a speedy trial had been violated. The motion was denied; the trial commenced with Manning as the chief prosecution witness; Barker was convicted and given a life sentence.[5]

Barker appealed his conviction to the Kentucky Court of Appeals, relying in part on his speedy trial claim. The court affirmed. In February 1970 Barker petitioned for habeas corpus * * * [and] the Court of Appeals for the Sixth Circuit * * * ruled that Barker had waived his speedy trial claim for the entire period before February 1963, the date on which the court believed he had first objected to the delay by filing a motion to dismiss. In this belief the court was mistaken, for the record reveals that the motion was filed in February 1962. The Commonwealth so conceded at oral argument before this Court. The court held further that the remaining period after the date on which Barker first raised his claim and before his trial—which it thought was only eight months but which was actually 20 months—was not unduly long. In addition, the court held that Barker had shown no resulting prejudice, and that the illness of the

---

[5]   The written motion Barker filed alleged that he had objected to every continuance since February 1959. The record does not reflect any objections until the motion to dismiss, filed in February 1962, and the objections to the continuances sought by the Commonwealth in March 1963 and June 1963.

ex-sheriff was a valid justification for the delay. We granted Barker's petition for certiorari.

II

The right to a speedy trial is generically different from any of the other rights enshrined in the Constitution for the protection of the accused. In addition to the general concern that all accused persons be treated according to decent and fair procedures, there is a societal interest in providing a speedy trial which exists separate from, and at times in opposition to, the interests of the accused. The inability of courts to provide a prompt trial has contributed to a large backlog of cases in urban courts which, among other things, enables defendants to negotiate more effectively for pleas of guilty to lesser offenses and otherwise manipulate the system. In addition, persons released on bond for lengthy periods awaiting trial have an opportunity to commit other crimes. It must be of little comfort to the residents of Christian County, Kentucky, to know that Barker was at large on bail for over four years while accused of a vicious and brutal murder of which he was ultimately convicted. Moreover, the longer an accused is free awaiting trial, the more tempting becomes his opportunity to jump bail and escape. Finally, delay between arrest and punishment may have a detrimental effect on rehabilitation.

If an accused cannot make bail, he is generally confined, as was Barker for 10 months, in a local jail. This contributes to the overcrowding and generally deplorable state of those institutions. Lengthy exposure to these conditions "has a destructive effect on human character and makes the rehabilitation of the individual offender much more difficult." At times the result may even be violent rioting. Finally, lengthy pretrial detention is costly. The cost of maintaining a prisoner in jail varies from $3 to $9 per day, and this amounts to millions across the Nation. In addition, society loses wages which might have been earned, and it must often support families of incarcerated breadwinners.

A second difference between the right to speedy trial and the accused's other constitutional rights is that deprivation of the right may work to the accused's advantage. Delay is not an uncommon defense tactic. As the time between the commission of the crime and trial lengthens, witnesses may become unavailable or their memories may fade. If the witnesses support the prosecution, its case will be weakened, sometimes seriously so. And it is the prosecution which carries the burden of proof. Thus, unlike the right to counsel or the right to be free from compelled self-incrimination, deprivation of the right to speedy trial does not *per se* prejudice the accused's ability to defend himself.

Finally, and perhaps most importantly, the right to speedy trial is a more vague concept than other procedural rights. It is, for example, impossible to determine with precision when the right has been denied.

We cannot definitely say how long is too long in a system where justice is supposed to be swift but deliberate. As a consequence, there is no fixed point in the criminal process when the State can put the defendant to the choice of either exercising or waiving the right to a speedy trial. If, for example, the State moves for a 60-day continuance, granting that continuance is not a violation of the right to speedy trial unless the circumstances of the case are such that further delay would endanger the values the right protects. It is impossible to do more than generalize about when those circumstances exist. There is nothing comparable to the point in the process when a defendant exercises or waives his right to counsel or his right to a jury trial. * * *

The amorphous quality of the right also leads to the unsatisfactorily severe remedy of dismissal of the indictment when the right has been deprived. This is indeed a serious consequence because it means that a defendant who may be guilty of a serious crime will go free, without having been tried. Such a remedy is more serious than an exclusionary rule or a reversal for a new trial, but it is the only possible remedy.

III

Perhaps because the speedy trial right is so slippery, two rigid approaches are urged upon us as ways of eliminating some of the uncertainty which courts experience in protecting the right. The first suggestion is that we hold that the Constitution requires a criminal defendant to be offered a trial within a specified time period. The result of such a ruling would have the virtue of clarifying when the right is infringed and of simplifying courts' application of it. Recognizing this, some legislatures have enacted laws, and some courts have adopted procedural rules which more narrowly define the right. The United States Court of Appeals for the Second Circuit has promulgated rules for the district courts in that Circuit establishing that the government must be ready for trial within six months of the date of arrest, except in unusual circumstances, or the charge will be dismissed. This type of rule is also recommended by the American Bar Association.

But such a result would require this Court to engage in legislative or rulemaking activity, rather than in the adjudicative process to which we should confine our efforts. We do not establish procedural rules for the States, except when mandated by the Constitution. We find no constitutional basis for holding that the speedy trial right can be quantified into a specified number of days or months. The States, of course, are free to prescribe a reasonable period consistent with constitutional standards, but our approach must be less precise.

The second suggested alternative would restrict consideration of the right to those cases in which the accused has demanded a speedy trial. Most States have recognized what is loosely referred to as the "demand rule," although eight States reject it. It is not clear, however, precisely what is meant by that term. Although every federal court of appeals that has considered the question has endorsed some kind of demand rule, some have regarded the rule within the concept of waiver, whereas others have viewed it as a factor to be weighed in assessing whether there has been a deprivation of the speedy trial right. We shall refer to the former approach as the demand-waiver doctrine. The demand-waiver doctrine provides that a defendant waives any consideration of his right to speedy trial for any period prior to which he has not demanded a trial. Under this rigid approach, a prior demand is a necessary condition to the consideration of the speedy trial right. This essentially was the approach the Sixth Circuit took below.

Such an approach, by presuming waiver of a fundamental right from inaction, is inconsistent with this Court's pronouncements on waiver of constitutional rights. The Court has defined waiver as "an intentional relinquishment or abandonment of a known right or privilege." *Johnson v. Zerbst*, 304 U.S. 458, 464, 58 S.Ct. 1019, 1023, 82 L.Ed. 1461 (1938). * * *

In excepting the right to speedy trial from the rule of waiver we have applied to other fundamental rights, courts that have applied the demand-waiver rule have relied on the assumption that delay usually works for the benefit of the accused and on the absence of any readily ascertainable time in the criminal process for a defendant to be given the choice of exercising or waiving his right. But it is not necessarily true that delay benefits the defendant. There are cases in which delay appreciably harms the defendant's ability to defend himself. Moreover, a defendant confined to jail prior to trial is obviously disadvantaged by delay as is a defendant released on bail but unable to lead a normal life because of community suspicion and his own anxiety.

The nature of the speedy trial right does make it impossible to pinpoint a precise time in the process when the right must be asserted or waived, but that fact does not argue for placing the burden of protecting the right solely on defendants. A defendant has no duty to bring himself to trial; the State has that duty as well as the duty of insuring that the trial is consistent with due process. Moreover, for the reasons earlier expressed, society has a particular interest in bringing swift prosecutions, and society's representatives are the ones who should protect that interest.

It is also noteworthy that such a rigid view of the demand-waiver rule places defense counsel in an awkward position. Unless he demands a trial early and often, he is in danger of frustrating his client's right. If counsel is willing to tolerate some delay because he finds it reasonable and helpful in preparing his own case, he may be unable to obtain a speedy trial for his client at the end of that time. Since under the demand-waiver rule no time runs until the demand is made, the government will have whatever time is otherwise reasonable to bring the defendant to trial after a demand has been made. Thus, if the first demand is made three months after arrest in a jurisdiction which prescribes a six-month rule, the prosecution will have a total of nine months—which may be wholly unreasonable under the circumstances. The result in practice is likely to be either an automatic, *pro forma* demand made immediately after appointment of counsel or delays which, but for the demand-waiver rule, would not be tolerated. Such a result is not consistent with the interests of defendants, society, or the Constitution.

We reject, therefore, the rule that a defendant who fails to demand a speedy trial forever waives his right. This does not mean, however, that the defendant has no responsibility to assert his right. We think the better rule is that the defendant's assertion of or failure to assert his right to a speedy trial is one of the factors to be considered in an inquiry into the deprivation of the right. Such a formulation avoids the rigidities of the demand-waiver rule and the resulting possible unfairness in its application. It allows the trial court to exercise a judicial discretion based on the circumstances, including due consideration of any applicable formal procedural rule. It would permit, for example, a court to attach a different weight to a situation in which the defendant knowingly fails to object from a situation in which his attorney acquiesces in long delay without adequately informing his client, or from a situation in which no counsel is appointed. It would also allow a court to weigh the frequency and force of the objections as opposed to attaching significant weight to a purely *pro forma* objection.

In ruling that a defendant has some responsibility to assert a speedy trial claim, we do not depart from our holdings in other cases concerning the waiver of fundamental rights, in which we have placed the entire responsibility on the prosecution to show that the claimed waiver was knowingly and voluntarily made. Such cases have involved rights which must be exercised or waived at a specific time or under clearly identifiable circumstances, such as the rights to plead not guilty, to demand a jury trial, to exercise the privilege against self-incrimination, and to have the assistance of counsel. We have shown above that the right to a speedy trial is unique in its uncertainty as to when and under what circumstances it must be asserted or may be deemed waived. But the rule we announce today, which comports with constitutional principles, places the primary burden on the courts and the prosecutors to assure that cases are brought to trial. We hardly need add that if delay is attributable to the defendant, then his waiver may be given effect under standard waiver doctrine, the demand rule aside.

We, therefore, reject both of the inflexible approaches—the fixed-time period because it goes further than the Constitution requires; the demand-waiver rule because it is insensitive to a right which we have deemed fundamental. The approach we accept is a balancing test, in which the conduct of both the prosecution and the defendant are weighed.

IV

A balancing test necessarily compels courts to approach speedy trial cases on an *ad hoc* basis. We can do little more than identify some of the factors which courts should assess in determining whether a particular defendant has been deprived of his right. Though some might express them in different ways, we identify four such factors: Length of delay, the reason for the delay, the defendant's assertion of his right, and prejudice to the defendant.

The length of the delay is to some extent a triggering mechanism. Until there is some delay which is presumptively prejudicial, there is no necessity for inquiry into the other factors that go into the balance. Nevertheless, because of the imprecision of the right to speedy trial, the length of delay that will provoke such an inquiry is necessarily dependent upon the peculiar circumstances of the case. To take but one example, the delay that can be tolerated for an ordinary street crime is considerably less than for a serious, complex conspiracy charge.

Closely related to length of delay is the reason the government assigns to justify the delay. Here, too, different weights should be assigned to different reasons. A deliberate attempt to delay the trial in order to hamper the defense should be weighted heavily against the government. A more neutral reason such as negligence or overcrowded courts should be weighted less heavily but nevertheless should be considered since the ultimate responsibility for such circumstances must rest with the government rather than with the defendant. Finally, a valid reason, such as a missing witness, should serve to justify appropriate delay.

We have already discussed the third factor, the defendant's responsibility to assert his right. Whether and how a defendant asserts his right is closely related to the other factors we have mentioned. The strength of his efforts will be affected by the length of the delay, to some extent by the reason for the delay, and most particularly by the personal prejudice, which is not always readily identifiable, that he experiences. The more serious the deprivation, the more likely a defendant is to complain. The defendant's assertion of his speedy trial right, then, is entitled to strong evidentiary weight in determining whether the defendant is being deprived of the right. We emphasize that failure to assert the right will make it difficult for a defendant to prove that he was denied a speedy trial.

A fourth factor is prejudice to the defendant. Prejudice, of course, should be assessed in the light of the interests of defendants which the speedy trial right was designed to protect. This Court has identified three such interests: (i) to prevent oppressive pretrial incarceration; (ii) to minimize anxiety and concern of the accused; and (iii) to limit the possibility that the defense will be impaired. Of these, the most serious is the last, because the inability of a defendant adequately to prepare his case skews the fairness of the entire system. If witnesses die or disappear during a delay, the prejudice is obvious. There is also prejudice if defense witnesses are unable to recall accurately events of the distant past. Loss of memory, however, is not always reflected in the record because what has been forgotten can rarely be shown.

We have discussed previously the societal disadvantages of lengthy pretrial incarceration, but obviously the disadvantages for the accused who cannot obtain his release are even more serious. The time spent in jail awaiting trial has a detrimental impact on the individual. It often means loss of a job; it disrupts family life; and it enforces idleness. Most jails offer little or no recreational or rehabilitative programs. The time spent in jail is simply dead time. Moreover, if a defendant is locked up, he is hindered in his ability to gather evidence, contact witnesses, or otherwise prepare his defense. Imposing those consequences on anyone who has not yet been convicted is serious. It is especially unfortunate to impose them on those persons who are ultimately found to be innocent. Finally, even if an accused is not incarcerated prior to trial, he is still disadvantaged by restraints on his liberty and by living under a cloud of anxiety, suspicion, and often hostility.

We regard none of the four factors identified above as either a necessary or sufficient condition to the finding of a deprivation of the right of speedy trial. Rather, they are related factors and must be considered together with such other circumstances as may be relevant. In sum, these factors have no talismanic qualities; courts must still engage in a difficult and sensitive balancing process. But, because we are dealing with a fundamental right of the accused, this process must be carried out with full recognition that the accused's interest in a speedy trial is specifically affirmed in the Constitution.

V

The difficulty of the task of balancing these factors is illustrated by this case, which we consider to be close. It is clear that the length of delay between arrest and trial—well over five years—was extraordinary. Only seven months of that period can be attributed to a strong excuse, the illness of the ex-sheriff who was in charge of the investigation. Perhaps some delay would have been permissible under ordinary circumstances, so that Manning could be utilized as a witness in Barker's trial, but more than four years was too long a period, particularly since a good part of that period was attributable to the Commonwealth's failure or inability to try Manning under circumstances that comported with due process.

Two counterbalancing factors, however, outweigh these deficiencies. The first is that prejudice was minimal. Of course, Barker was prejudiced to some extent by living for over four years under a cloud of suspicion and anxiety. Moreover, although he was released on bond for most of the period, he did spend 10 months in jail before trial. But there is no claim that any of Barker's witnesses died or otherwise became unavailable owing to the delay. The trial transcript indicates only two very minor lapses of memory—one on the part of a prosecution witness—which were in no way significant to the outcome.

More important than the absence of serious prejudice, is the fact that Barker did not want a speedy trial. Counsel was appointed for Barker immediately after his indictment and represented him throughout the period. No question is raised as to the competency of such counsel. Despite the fact that counsel had notice of the motions for continuances, the record shows no action whatever taken between October 21, 1958, and February 12, 1962, that could be construed as the assertion of the speedy trial right. On the latter date, in response to another motion for continuance, Barker moved to dismiss the indictment. The record does not show on what ground this motion was based, although it is clear that no alternative motion was made for an immediate trial. Instead the record strongly suggests that while he hoped to take advantage of the delay in which he had acquiesced, and thereby obtain a dismissal of the charges, he definitely did not want to be tried. Counsel conceded as much at oral argument:

> "Your honor, I would concede that Willie Mae Barker probably—
> I don't know this for a fact—probably did not want to be tried. I
> don't think any man wants to be tried. And I don't consider this
> a liability on his behalf. I don't blame him."

The probable reason for Barker's attitude was that he was gambling on Manning's acquittal. The evidence was not very strong against Manning, as the reversals and hung juries suggest, and Barker undoubtedly thought that if Manning were acquitted, he would never be tried. Counsel also conceded this:

> "Now, it's true that the reason for this delay was the
> Commonwealth of Kentucky's desire to secure the testimony of
> the accomplice, Silas Manning. And it's true that if Silas

Manning were never convicted, Willie Mae Barker would never have been convicted. We concede this."[39]

That Barker was gambling on Manning's acquittal is also suggested by his failure, following the *pro forma* motion to dismiss filed in February 1962, to object to the Commonwealth's next two motions for continuances. Indeed, it was not until March 1963, after Manning's convictions were final, that Barker, having lost his gamble, began to object to further continuances. At that time, the Commonwealth's excuse was the illness of the ex-sheriff, which Barker has conceded justified the further delay.

We do not hold that there may never be a situation in which an indictment may be dismissed on speedy trial grounds where the defendant has failed to object to continuances. There may be a situation in which the defendant was represented by incompetent counsel, was severely prejudiced, or even cases in which the continuances were granted *ex parte*. But barring extraordinary circumstances, we would be reluctant indeed to rule that a defendant was denied this constitutional right on a record that strongly indicates, as does this one, that the defendant did not want a speedy trial. We hold, therefore, that Barker was not deprived of his due process right to a speedy trial. * * *

MR. JUSTICE WHITE, with whom MR. JUSTICE BRENNAN joins, concurring.

Although the Court rejects petitioner's speedy trial claim and affirms denial of his petition for habeas corpus, it is apparent that had Barker not so clearly acquiesced in the major delays involved in this case, the result would have been otherwise. From the Commonwealth's point of view, it is fortunate that the case was set for early trial and that postponements took place only upon formal requests to which Barker had opportunity to object.

Because the Court broadly assays the factors going into constitutional judgments under the speedy trial provision, it is appropriate to emphasize that one of the major purposes of the provision is to guard against inordinate delay between public charge and trial, which, wholly aside from possible prejudice to a defense on the merits, may "seriously interfere with the defendant's liberty, whether he is free on bail or not, and that may disrupt his employment, drain his financial resources, curtail his associations, subject him to public obloquy, and create anxiety in him, his family and his friends." *United States v. Marion*, 404 U.S. 307, 320, 92 S.Ct. 455, 463, 30 L.Ed.2d 468 (1971).

---

[39] Hindsight is, of course, 20/20, but we cannot help noting that if Barker had moved immediately and persistently for a speedy trial following indictment, and if he had been successful, he would have undoubtedly been acquitted since Manning's testimony was crucial to the Commonwealth's case. It could not have been anticipated at the outset, however, that Manning would have been tried six times over a four-year period. Thus, the decision to gamble on Manning's acquittal may have been a prudent choice at the time it was made.

These factors are more serious for some than for others, but they are inevitably present in every case to some extent, for every defendant will either be incarcerated pending trial or on bail subject to substantial restrictions on his liberty. * * *

NOTES AND QUESTIONS

1. *Practice pointer*. Notice footnote 5. Barker claims to have objected to every continuance since February 1959, but the earliest written objection was in February 1962, three years later. It is possible, of course, that in the easy-going rural style, Barker's lawyer did object orally at the various docket calls, but failed to file a written motion to dismiss. Also note that all the motions to dismiss failed to specify the grounds for dismissal until the motion to dismiss filed the day the trial began in October 1963. The practice pointer here is obvious.

2. The Court carefully identifies four factors to be balanced in deciding speedy trial cases. From the outcome in *Barker* itself, does it seem that one or two of the factors weigh more heavily in the balance than the others?

3. *Barker factors*.

A. *Length of delay and responsibility to assert the right*. The length of the delay is an obvious and textually-linked factor. The Court also argues persuasively that whether and how vigorously a particular defendant asserts the right is a good proxy for how much injury is being done to that defendant. Both of these factors are thus markers for speedy trial violations, without regard to questions of fairness and accuracy. But the other two factors (the government's reason for the delay, and the prejudice to the defense) are less easily defended.

B. *Reason for delay*. Though the Court is right that "speedy" is a vague concept, it is unclear why vagueness makes relevant the government's reasons for delay. The Sixth Amendment does not say "speedy unless the government has a good reason to justify delay." If "speedy" has some kind of core meaning, why change that meaning because the government had a good reason for a long delay? Assuming the government's reason could never justify an extreme delay—let's say twenty years—why should it justify a lesser delay, as in *Barker*? The Court notes that a "deliberate attempt to delay the trial in order to hamper the defense should be weighted heavily against the government." Really? Why should the speedy trial guarantee be seen as a way of preventing prosecutorial bad faith? The Court seems to be creating a speedy trial factor out of a general concern about fairness. Justice Black left the Court about a year before *Barker*. What do you think he would have had to say about the *Barker* balancing test? See Black's dissent in *Williams v. Florida*, p. 994.

C. *Prejudice*. The Court notes three kinds of prejudice. The "anxiety and concern" of the accused is present in almost every case, and can be viewed as an inevitable, textually-linked concomitant of delay. A second kind of prejudice is "oppressive pretrial incarceration." Though this is not present in all cases, it is an obvious factor that the Framers would have had in their minds and that should be weighed heavily when it is present.

Somewhat less obvious is the relevance of the third kind of prejudice: "to limit the possibility that the defense will be impaired." If the relevance of the reason for the delay is created out of fairness cloth, the prejudice-to-the-defense factor is created out of accuracy cloth. One could be a textualist here. If a defendant receives a speedy trial, what difference does it make if all of his witnesses died and the outcome is thus made less accurate? Conversely, if a defendant does not receive a speedy trial, why should it matter that the defense was not impaired? Justice White's concurrence appears to weigh prejudice to the defense less and to put more weight on the more typical and obvious consequences associated with delay (anxiety and disruptions in a defendant's life).

4.   How do you think Justice Powell would have responded to the criticism in Note 3 that the prejudice to the defense and the reason for delay have nothing to do with whether the trial is speedy?

5.   *Remedy*. The Court was clear in *Barker* that "the only possible remedy" is dismissal of the indictment with prejudice. How can providing the defendant a new, and later, trial be a remedy? One creative Court of Appeals deviated from the *Barker* dictum by ordering the district judge to affirm the conviction but to credit against the defendant's sentence the number of days of unjustified delay (259 days, according to the Court of Appeals). This remedy has appeal along two dimensions: it is less drastic than dismissal with prejudice and might encourage courts to be more willing to find speedy trial violations; moreover, there is a certain rough justice in that the defendant is given days in freedom at the other end of his sentence to compensate for the days that the State delayed his trial. Do you see any problems with this remedy?

The Supreme Court unanimously reversed the lower court, holding what it had suggested in dictum in *Barker*: the only remedy is dismissal with prejudice. Strunk v. United States, 412 U.S. 434, 93 S.Ct. 2260, 37 L.Ed.2d 56 (1973).

6.   *Federal Speedy Trial Act*. Two years after *Barker*, Congress passed the Speedy Trial Act (its two principal provisions, 18 U.S.C. § 3161 and § 3162, appear in Supp. App. A). This Act imposes much more stringent time limits (in most cases) than courts have found in the Sixth Amendment. Though the Act is complex, and many exceptions exist, the basic time limits are (1) indictment must be presented within thirty days of arrest or issuance of summons (a thirty-day extension can be granted if no grand jury is in session); and (2) trial must occur within seventy days from the indictment or appearance before "a judicial officer of the court in which such charge is pending," whichever last occurs.

Another way the Speedy Trial Act differs from the Court's speedy trial jurisprudence is that violations do not require dismissal with prejudice. Instead, the Act gives judges wide discretion to dismiss without prejudice if the government fails to provide a trial in time.

A federal district judge confided in us that prosecutors and defense lawyers in his district had developed a routine way around the Speedy Trial Act. This should not surprise. As long as the advocates on both sides have a common interest, it is difficult to invent rules that prevent the parties from achieving their shared goal. This is why courts prohibit "friendly" lawsuits and is one reason plea bargaining is difficult to regulate or ban. Take a look at the Speedy Trial Act, Supp.App.A. Do you see a way around the time limits in (c)(1)? Hint: what might be one way to construe "appeared before a judicial officer of the court in which such charge is pending"?

Federal case processing data suggest that prosecutors and defense lawyers are finding modest loopholes. Rather than roughly two to four months, as envisioned by the Speedy Trial Act, the average case is terminated in 6.5 months with an average of 15 months for cases tried to a conviction. U.S. Department of Justice, Bureau of Justice Statistics, Federal Justice Statistics, 2009, p. 12, tbl. 9.

7.   *And the states?* States are of course free to adopt their own statutory or constitutional approaches to speedy trial as long as they provide at least as much protection as the Sixth Amendment. A Montana statute, for example, requires that "a prosecution on a misdemeanor charge must be dismissed, with prejudice, if the defendant is not brought to trial within six months after entering his plea, unless (1) the trial has been postponed upon the defendant's motion or (2) the State has shown 'good cause' for the delay." State v. Hodge, 339 P.3d 8, 13 (Mont. 2014). For purposes of the Montana Constitution, the state supreme court has held that a 200-day delay creates a presumption of prejudice that requires the State to demonstrate that the defendant was not prejudiced by the delay and that there is a reasonable excuse for the delay. City of Billings v. Bruce, 965 P.2d 866 (Mont. 1998).

8.   *The disappearing suspect.* In 1980, a grand jury indicted *D* for conspiracy to import and distribute cocaine. Before the arrest warrant could be served on *D*, he left the country for Colombia. His leaving at that moment was purely a coincidence; a federal court found later that *D* did not know of his indictment then and never learned of it until he was arrested eight years later. Though he was placed on a customs list to be apprehended should he attempt to reenter the country, the entry was inexplicably purged from the computer, and *D* entered the United States without incident in 1982. Once here, he married, earned a college degree, found a steady job as a computer operations manager, lived openly under his own name, and stayed within the law. In 1988, the government discovered his whereabouts during a routine credit check and arrested him on the outstanding eight-year-old warrant. He raised a speedy trial objection to his trial.

In *Doggett v. United States*, 505 U.S. 647, 112 S.Ct. 2686, 120 L.Ed.2d 520 (1992), the Court began by noting that the lower courts had developed a sort of rule of thumb that delay of a year or more required inquiry into the government's reasons for the delay, prejudice resulting from the delay, and the failure to assert the right. Given the odd facts of the case, Doggett had no opportunity to assert his right to a speedy trial and that factor drops out of the mix. As for the government's reasons for the delay, the Court reaffirmed *Barker*'s notion that good faith excuses delay and bad faith counts strongly against the government in speedy trial cases, noting that "if the Government had pursued Doggett with reasonable diligence from his indictment to his arrest, his speedy trial claim would fail."

Thus, the government could not show good faith in *Doggett*. As demand was out of the equation, and the government could not show good faith, that left only the issue of prejudice. Though Doggett did not show specific prejudice to his case, the Court seemed to say that extraordinary, unjustified periods of delay need not be accompanied by a specific showing of prejudice. Concluding that six years of the delay were attributed to "the Government's inexcusable oversights," the Court observed that "the Government's negligence" had caused "delay six times as long as that generally sufficient to trigger judicial review." Moreover, "the presumption of prejudice" was "neither extenuated, as by the defendant's acquiescence, nor persuasively rebutted." Thus, Doggett had shown a violation of the right to a speedy trial.

9. *A due process right against delayed prosecution.* Suppose a prosecutor reviews a case file and decides not to bring charges. The suspect is released from jail. Then, years later, the prosecutor obtains an indictment. What is the state's argument against a Sixth Amendment speedy trial claim? Would you expect it to succeed?

The answer to the last question is that the government will win the speedy trial argument. (You figure out the best argument to support the prosecutor here. Hint: look at the text of the Sixth Amendment.) Yet the Court has suggested that a due process violation would exist "if it were shown at trial that the pre-indictment delay * * * caused substantial prejudice to [defendant's] rights to a fair trial and that the delay was an intentional device to gain tactical advantage over the accused." *United States v. Marion*, 404 U.S. 307, 92 S.Ct. 455, 30 L.Ed.2d 468 (1971).

Notice that the due process protection encompasses two of the factors in *Barker*: prejudice to the defense case, and the reason for the delay.

CHAPTER 14

THE ROLE OF DEFENSE COUNSEL

■ ■ ■

In all criminal prosecutions, the accused shall enjoy the right
* * * to have the Assistance of Counsel for his defence. U.S.
Const. amend. VI.

* * *

"How can you defend those people?" is a question frequently put
to criminal defense attorneys, often in a tone suggesting that it
is not so much a question as a demand for an apology, as though
a defense attorney needs to justify his work, in a way that a
prosecutor doesn't. Because the question presumes that "those
people" accused of crime are guilty, and that people who are
guilty of crimes ought not to be defended, it reflects a profound
misunderstanding of our criminal justice system and the defense
attorney's role in it. James S. Kunen, How Can You Defend
Those People?: The Making of a Criminal Lawyer xi (1983).

* * *

In the Laws of Henry I, collected around 1115, "counsel" was meant
quite literally:

> In [most] cases an accused person may seek counsel and
> obtain it from his friends and relatives (no law should forbid
> this), in particular the advice of those whom he brings with him
> or invites to attend his [case]; and in taking counsel he shall
> faithfully state the truth of the matter so that circumstances
> may appear to the best advantage with respect to the [case] or its
> peaceful settlement. * * *

> For it is often the case that a person sees less in his own
> cause than in someone else's and it is generally possible to
> amend in another person's mouth what may not be amended in
> his own.

Leges Henrici Primi, laws 46.4 & 46.6

Notice that even in the twelfth century, scribes recognized that to
take maximum advantage of counsel, the accused should "faithfully state
the truth of the matter." Beyond that, it is clear that the principal role of

counsel was to provide advice about how to proceed in a case. That is still true today.

It is difficult to exaggerate the importance of the lawyer to the criminal process. The norms that we identified in Chapter 1 as underlying the process—accuracy, efficiency, fairness, and limiting the power of government—simply cannot be achieved if the lawyer for the defense or the prosecution is inept, incompetent, indifferent, or corrupt. Consider a hypothetical based on a real case. *D* is charged with a rape-murder. He denies guilt, claiming he wasn't there that night. While preparing for trial, the lawyer learns that the rapist was sterile *but the lawyer never asks D whether he was sterile and does not even tell D this fact about the case.* Thus, the client never had a chance to offer his thoughts on whether he should take a sperm test. Without evidence that he was not sterile, *D* is convicted and given a long sentence. On appeal, a different lawyer discovered the sterility issue, has *D* tested, and (guess what?) *D* is not sterile. Whether the original lawyer was guilty of ineffective assistance of counsel is an issue for Part D. For present purposes, it is easy to see that had the lawyer performed at a higher level, *D* would have been acquitted in the first place, an outcome that serves the norms of accuracy, fairness, and efficiency.

The ethics of representing criminal defendants thus include zealous and competent representation. The ethics of lawyering also include duties owed to the court. Prosecutors, of course, also have ethical duties to provide competent representation and, above that, to seek justice rather than merely to be an advocate. The prosecutor's duties were explored in connection with prosecutorial discretion and pre-trial discovery in Chapters 12 and 13. In this chapter, we consider the role, duties, and ethics of defense counsel.

The problem of representing *indigent* defendants is particularly complicated because of funding problems. While we lack data on the provision of counsel to indigent defendants in all state courts, the Bureau of Justice Statistics determined that, in 1996, 82% of indigent felony defendants in the 75 most populous counties were represented by counsel paid for by the State; 66% of federal felony defendants in the same year were represented by publicly-financed counsel. Bureau of Justice Statistics, "Two of Three Felony Defendants Represented by Publicly-FinancedCounsel," http://www.bjs.gov/content/pub/press/iddcpr.cfm. Case loads for public defenders vary widely but in some states are astronomical: 340 in Colorado (229 of which were felonies), 367 in Wisconsin (122 felonies), and 374 in Delaware (83 felonies). We will return to this problem in Part B, where we examine one state public defender system on the verge of collapse.

A. THE ETHICS OF DEFENDING "THOSE" PEOPLE

1. A CASE STUDY: DEFENDING THE DEFENSELESS CLIENT

What follows is based on the New York City police treatment of suspect named Abner Louima in 1997. The worst of the abuse, allegedly committed by Officer Justin Volpe, was shoving a broom handle into Louima's rectum so violently that it caused serious internal injuries. Volpe was charged, along with three other officers, with violating the civil rights of Louima. Volpe faced life in prison for his part in the brutal treatment. For the facts of the case, as well as the commentary on the duties of defense counsel representing Volpe, we draw heavily from Abbe Smith, *Defending Defending: The Case for Unmitigated Zeal on Behalf of People Who Do Terrible Things*, 28 Hofstra L. Rev. 925 (2000).

First, let us assume you are a lawyer specializing in criminal defense work and Officer Volpe asks you to represent him. Does it matter to you whether Volpe is guilty? Should it? If he admits that he is guilty, you might decide you do not want to represent him. If so, do you have any obligation to provide him a defense?

Suppose Volpe denies any role in the abuse, but you do not believe him. You think you have before you "a sadistic, racist cop who, in some sort of monstrous rage, had brutalized an innocent, hard-working immigrant who had the misfortune to cross Volpe's path." Smith, *supra*, at 927. Now assume that you decide to represent Volpe. You have a sign on your desk that says "Presumption of Innocence Commences With Payment of Retainer." *Id.* Volpe pays. You are his lawyer. You have suspended your judgment about Volpe's moral culpability and your job is to minimize the legal consequences of what he did. Now should your belief about his guilt or innocence make any difference in how you approach your job?

Do you think the prosecutor will offer a favorable plea bargain in Volpe's case? Suppose a hard but fair plea offer is made and you suspect, the well-known "blue wall of silence" notwithstanding, that some of the police officers involved in the incident will testify against Volpe. You decide that it is in the best interests of your client to plead guilty. Should you simply provide advice and leave it up to Volpe or should you advocate for a guilty plea? If the latter, how intensely should you advocate?

> Although much has been written about lawyer-client counseling and the proper allocation of power in decision-making, nothing can prepare a criminal lawyer for the intensity of counseling clients about the decision to plead guilty or go to trial, especially where the stakes are high. The timing of this conversation is crucial and can sorely test even a good lawyer-

client relationship. Sometimes the moment of reckoning is early on, and sometimes not until the eve of trial.

Most experienced criminal defense lawyers have had grueling sessions during which they urge recalcitrant clients to plead guilty. These intense and often unpleasant encounters can ultimately be enlightening and even redemptive for the client. Sometimes there is enormous relief in accepting the reality of a situation, putting an end to the uncertainty, and admitting guilt. Of course, sometimes the client simply sees the writing on the wall and wishes to cut his or her losses.

Smith, *supra*, at 946–47.

If no plausible plea bargain is forthcoming, or Volpe simply refuses to accept, you must prepare a defense. Whether other police officers will incriminate Volpe is not certain, but you have one very real problem. Mr. Louima suffered a torn colon, lacerated bladder, and ruptured intestine, all of which is documented in the medical evidence. How to explain these injuries without admitting that *someone* put a broom stick violently into his rectum? And if someone did that, and if the other officers point the finger at Volpe, his case is hopeless.

One way to explain the terrible injuries—the way Volpe's lawyer chose in real life—is to suggest that "Louima's injuries were not the result of police brutality, but of consensual anal sex with another man." Smith, *supra*, at 930. Would you choose this path? Is there any ethical reason not to? Turning the question around, if this is the *only* half-way plausible alternative explanation, are you ethically obligated to present the explanation?

Perhaps. Alan Dershowitz has argued, "What a defense attorney 'may' do, he must do, if it is necessary to defend his client. A zealous defense attorney has a professional obligation to take every legal and ethically permissible step that will serve the client's best interest—even if the attorney finds the step personally distasteful." Smith, *supra*, at 958, quoting Alan M. Dershowitz, Reasonable Doubts: The O.J. Simpson Case and the Criminal Justice System 145 (1996).

But we have yet to answer the question of *whether* this is permissible defense conduct. Many commentators were harshly condemning of the "rough sex" defense, denouncing it as a "vile insinuation," a "vile fantasy," and as "a second rape." Smith, *supra*, at 930–31. Does it matter if you believe that Volpe is guilty and thus that your story cannot be true? What if you are not certain of Volpe's guilt, but you have no evidence to support the allegation of homosexual conduct? Even if you believe Volpe is innocent, can you allege "rough sex" without *any* evidence? Does it matter that Abner Louima is married and has two children?

To Lord Brougham in the early nineteenth century, the answer was that you can present the explanation without regard to your belief in your client's innocence or the truth of the story. Here is how Brougham put it:

> [A]n advocate, in the discharge of his duty, knows but one person in all the world, and that person is his client. To save that client by all means and expedients, and at all hazards and costs to other persons, and, amongst them to himself, is his first and only duty; and in performing this duty he must not regard the alarm, the torments, the destruction which he may bring upon others. Separating the duty of a patriot from that of an advocate, he must go on reckless of consequences, though it should be his unhappy fate to involve his country in confusion.

Smith, *supra*, at 928 n.23, citing 2 Trial of Queen Caroline 8 (London, Shackell & Arrowsmith 1820–21).

Justice White contrasted the role of defense counsel with that of the prosecutor in *United States v. Wade*, 388 U.S. 218, 87 S.Ct. 1926, 18 L.Ed.2d 1149 (1967) (White, J., dissenting in part):

> [D]efense counsel has no comparable obligation to ascertain or present the truth. Our system assigns him a different mission. * * * Defense counsel need present nothing, even if he knows what the truth is. He need not furnish any witnesses to the police, or reveal any confidences of his client, or furnish any other information to help the prosecution's case. If he can confuse a witness, even a truthful one, or make him appear at a disadvantage, unsure or indecisive, that will be his normal course. Our interest in not convicting the innocent permits counsel to put the State to its proof, to put the State's case in the worst possible light, regardless of what he thinks or knows to be the truth. Undoubtedly there are some limits which defense counsel must observe but more often than not, defense counsel will cross-examine a prosecution witness, and impeach him if he can, even if he thinks the witness is telling the truth, just as he will attempt to destroy a witness who he thinks is lying. In this respect, as part of our modified adversary system and as part of the duty imposed on the most honorable defense counsel, we countenance or require conduct which in many instances has little, if any, relation to the search for truth.

Now return to the Volpe case. What if part of your calculation is not just to create doubt among the jury by offering an alternative explanation of the facts in evidence but, rather, to invoke jury antipathy toward homosexuals, to invite homophobia to cloud the minds of the jurors? Does this take the case out of Lord Brougham's prescription for defending defenseless clients?

Some argue yes, that it crosses an ethical line when a criminal defense lawyer exploits racism, sexism, homophobia, or ethnic bias. But why would it be ethically improper to exploit homophobia if it is ethically desirable (or at least ethically neutral) for a defense lawyer to suggest through cross-examination that the eyewitness is lying when the lawyer knows she is telling the truth? To answer that challenge, some have argued that criminal defense lawyers sometimes have a duty to the community that is at least as important as the duty to the client. Exploiting various nefarious attitudes that exist in society would presumably be more injurious than suggesting that eyewitnesses are lying. But Professor Abbe Smith is unpersuaded by this "progressive" scholarship.

Anthony Alfieri, the most prominent progressive scholar on this subject, wants to have it both ways: He would like criminal defense lawyers to be more "community-centered," and to embrace a "color-conscious, pluralist approach to advocacy that honors the integrity of diverse individual and collective * * * identities *without sacrificing effective representation*." This is both untenable and disingenuous. In truth, he wants to transform criminal defense lawyers from defenders of individuals accused of crime to defenders of the community and of certain values he holds dear.

It is difficult, if not impossible, to zealously represent the criminally accused and simultaneously tend to the feelings of others. This is so in any political climate, but even more so in a time when criminal punishment is regarded as the answer to almost all of our social problems. We cannot seem to build prisons fast enough, and we are on the road to the virtual banishment of young African American men from society. It is simply wrong to place an additional burden on criminal defense lawyers to make the world a better place as they labor to represent individuals facing loss of liberty or life. * * *

There is nothing unethical about using racial, gender, ethnic, or sexual stereotypes in criminal defense. It is simply an aspect of zealous advocacy. Prejudice exists in the community and in the courthouse, and criminal defense lawyers would be foolhardy not to recognize this as a fact of life. Of course, most bias and prejudice works against the accused, disproportionate numbers of whom are poor and nonwhite. Defense lawyers must incorporate this knowledge, as well as knowledge about the stereotypes that might apply, to the prosecution and defense witnesses in all their trial decisions.

> A trial is theater. Defense lawyers cannot afford to be color-blind, gender-blind, or even slightly near-sighted when it comes to race, gender, sexual orientation, and ethnicity, because jurors will be paying close attention and they have come to the trial with their own feelings about these issues. Many stereotypes arise in a criminal trial, whether or not they are actively exploited by either party. Sometimes the exploitation of stereotypes is unavoidable.

Smith, *supra*, at 951–52, 954–55, citing Anthony V. Alfieri, Defending Racial Violence, 95 Colum. L. Rev. 1301, 1320–21 (1995); Anthony V. Alfieri, *Race Trials*, 76 Tex. L. Rev. 1293, 1305–23 (1998).

For Professor Smith, defending the defenseless with vigorous arguments, even those designed to appeal to prejudices, poses no ethical problems.

> Justin Volpe did a terrible thing, and he will pay the price for his brutal crime for a long time. Given his client's insistence on going to trial, Volpe's lawyer had no choice but to try to mount a vigorous defense, however ill fated. This was the right thing for Volpe's lawyer to do—for his client and for the rest of us.

Smith, *supra*, at 961.

NOTES AND QUESTIONS

1.   A.   Would you represent Volpe and, if so, under what conditions concerning your belief as to his guilt?

B.   If you say you would not represent Volpe under any circumstances as a retained lawyer, assume that you are a public defender, the case has been assigned to you, and all your efforts to get it assigned elsewhere have failed. Given the Sixth Amendment, Volpe has the right to have *somebody* represent him. Do you think you could provide zealous representation? For an example of an appointed lawyer who might have faced an even more hopeless case, see Messer v. Kemp, 760 F.2d 1080 (11th Cir. 1985), where two appointed lawyers had asked to be "relieved," citing "community pressure," but the third lawyer had to try the death penalty case all the way to the gruesome end.

C.   If a hard, but fair, guilty plea were offered, how strongly would you urge Volpe to take it?

D.   If the case goes to trial, would you (should you) raise the "rough sex" defense if you have no evidence that it is true? Would your degree of certainty of Volpe's guilt or innocence make any difference to your thinking on this issue?

In this regard, consider American Bar Association, Criminal Justice Standards for the Defense Function (4th ed. 2015), Standard 4–7.7 (d): "Defense counsel should not ask a question which implies the existence of a factual predicate for which a good faith belief is lacking." Does this mean that, in the absence of proof, you cannot ask Louima whether anal sex caused his injuries?

2.   Do you agree with Professor Alfieri (quoted in the Smith excerpt) that a criminal defense lawyer can adopt a "community-centered" approach and provide zealous defense at the same time?

3.   Midway through his federal trial for violating Louima's civil rights, Volpe changed his plea to guilty. He was sentenced to 30 years in federal prison. In 2012, he married Caroline Rose DeMaso in a ceremony in a federal correctional facility in Florida, officiated by a priest. "While it's unclear if the bride wore white, prison policy barred Volpe from wearing a suit. Inmate No. 49477–053 likely sported a prison-issued wedding ensemble of khaki pants and matching shirt with sneakers." Federal prisoners are not permitted conjugal visits. The earliest date for his release is August 3, 2025. Rocco Parascandola, Kerry Burke, Barry Paddock, Larry McShane, "Justin Volpe, cop who sodomized Abner Louima with broomstick inside Brooklyn police station, marries Staten Island woman in Florida prison," New York Daily News, December 5, 2012, http://www.nydailynews.com/new-york/sodomized-abner-louima-marries-staten-island-woman-article-1.1213532.

4.   Of course, Justin Volpe is not the only high-profile defendant who would prove difficult to represent. How would you like to being assigned to represent the surviving Boston Marathon bomber, Dzhokhar Tsarnaev? His lawyers argued "that he was pulled into the plot by his radicalized Muslim older brother." Massachusetts has no state death penalty, reflecting the anti-death penalty of many residents. Despite this aversion, the federal jury imposed the death penalty; when it was announced in court, some of the jurors wept. Tom Winter, Andy Thibault and Jon Schuppe, "Tsarnaev Sentenced to Death in Boston Bombing Trial, NBC News, May 15, 2015.

Or consider representing Jerry Sandusky who was tried for 48 counts of child sexual abuse that occurred while he was an assistant football coach at Penn State University. At trial, eight witnesses testified to the details of the sexual acts that Sandusky performed on them. The jury deliberated for two days before convicting on 45 of the 48 charges. Sandusky did not testify. The judge sentenced him to 30–60 years and declared him a "dangerous" child molester who should never be allowed to be free again. As his lawyer, your job would be to cross-examine these men, seeking to discredit their testimony; you could ask why they waited so long to report the alleged abuse and whether they were motivated to lie by the financial gain and publicity. Sandusky made similar allegations in public statements about the case. "Jerry Sandusky," https://en.wikipedia.org/wiki/Jerry_Sandusky (and sources cited by Wikipedia). In sum, you would be putting the victims on trial.

Your client would deny guilt to the end. Sandusky's case ended after the verdict, "as it began: in denial and delusion. 'In my heart, I know I did not do these alleged disgusting acts,' Mr. Sandusky said in a call from the jailhouse * * * . 'My wife has been my only sex partner, and that was after marriage.' " Editorial, "The Sandusky Rape Trial," *New York Times*, October 9, 2012.

2. ETHICS AND DUTIES OF DEFENSE COUNSEL

GERALD B. LEFCOURT—RESPONSIBILITIES OF A CRIMINAL DEFENSE ATTORNEY
30 Loyola of Los Angeles Law Review 59 (1996), 59–63.

Re-read the part of the Lefcourt excerpt at p. 36. It continues:

In twenty-five years of practice, I have seen all sides of the criminal defense bar. I have represented indigent defendants accused of killing police officers, college protesters accused of violating student codes, politicians accused of corruption, and wealthy professionals accused of sophisticated financial crimes. The fact is, in some ways, it is always the same. I truly believe that my responsibility as a lawyer to a client is the same no matter who the defendant and no matter what the crime, and I endeavor to discharge that responsibility as zealously as possible for all.

Society expects a lot from us, all the while bashing us in every possible way. Under the Sixth Amendment we are expected to provide the criminal defendant with a rigorous defense undivided by conflicts. At the same time, in many cases we must fight with judges and prosecutors just to get paid out of frozen funds. We have to worry about whether we will be subpoenaed or have our law offices searched. We have to worry about whether the government is secretly courting our clients to turn against us. And we are told by our friends and by the media that we should not be representing guilty defendants.

These are all situations that drive wedges between our clients and our solemn responsibilities. How do we handle this? What are our fundamental obligations?

I. RESPONSIBILITIES TO THE CLIENT

First and foremost, defense attorneys must zealously and uncompromisingly represent the client. They must do so with all their ability and creativity, within the bounds of law. Defense attorneys must accept this duty as sacrosanct and be prepared to do whatever it takes to improve the client's position. That means they may have to offend. They may have to do the uncomfortable thing. They may have to have prosecutors and judges think of them as "the other," not one of them.

Of course, paramount is making use of one's own good judgment. While defense attorneys must take into consideration what the client wants, it is the lawyer's judgment that is being offered to the client, and the lawyer must not be afraid to use it. Defense counsel must be both an advisor and an advocate with courage and devotion. Indeed, some have described the role as a "learned friend," often the only one to whom a criminal defendant may turn in total confidence. The defendant needs counsel to evaluate the risks and advantages of alternative courses of action. But the defendant also needs a broad and comprehensive approach to the predicament.

Devoted service to the client does raise the issue of whether the attorney must do whatever the client wants. I believe that we must allow the client to make informed decisions about all matters, including strategy. An informed and participating client is a critical component of discharging our responsibilities. That is not the same thing as doing something illegal, and a lawyer should leave a case if a serious conflict arises. If defense counsel is truly repulsed by the client, the lawyer should not represent the individual. Lawyers are not busses, and they are not obligated to stop at every stop. * * *

Representing an innocent client is an easy situation for the public to support. In practice it is the hardest because of the overwhelming fear of loss. A factually guilty client, where guilt is apparent, raises society's challenge to the defense attorney: "How can you go into court knowing your client is guilty and try to get him or her off?" If this is a problem for you, you should not be a defense attorney. The committed defense attorney must be prepared to ensure that before the government takes away the client's liberty, the process of doing so is fair and true. Defense attorneys are not advocates for crime. They are as interested as anyone in a safe environment in which to live and raise their families. But they are, or should be, overwhelmingly interested in making sure that the government deprives no one of liberty without doing so consistent with the law. Otherwise, the government is just another thug interfering with a citizen's freedom.

NOTES AND QUESTIONS

1.   In the Volpe case study, you considered how it might feel to represent someone who is guilty of a horrific crime. Yet, as Lefcourt suggests, it might be worse to represent an innocent defendant. How would you feel if your innocent client were sentenced to a long prison sentence? To die?

2.   Does the Lefcourt excerpt make you more or less likely to make criminal defense work part of your career? More or less likely to go to work for a public defender's office?

3.   For those who are thinking about becoming prosecutors, what is your reaction to the picture drawn by Lefcourt?

4.   If you had to name one personality aspect that Lefcourt might say was crucial to providing consistent, competent representation of "those people," what would it be?

5.   *American Bar Association standards.* The overarching function of defense counsel is "to serve as their clients' counselor and advocate with courage and devotion; to ensure that constitutional and other legal rights of their clients are protected; and to render effective, high-quality legal representation with integrity." American Bar Association, Criminal Justice Standards for the Defense Function (4th ed. 2015). Beyond interviewing the client, there is of course a duty to investigate the case, put this way in Standard 4–4.1:

> Defense counsel's investigation of the merits of the criminal charges should include efforts to secure relevant information in the possession of the prosecution, law enforcement authorities, and others, as well as independent investigation. Counsel's investigation should also include evaluation of the prosecution's evidence (including possible re-testing or re-evaluation of physical, forensic, and expert evidence) and consideration of inconsistencies, potential avenues of impeachment of prosecution witnesses, and other possible suspects and alternative theories that the evidence may raise

For over seven hundred years, counsel in England provided advice but the accused actually pled the case. Though lawyers today do much of the pleading of the case, in some ways the client is still the principal and the lawyer merely the agent or the specialized assistant. For example, Standard 4–5.2. sets out eight categories of decisions belonging to the client:

(i)   whether to proceed without counsel;

(ii)   what pleas to enter;

(iii)   whether to accept a plea offer;

(iv)   whether to cooperate with or provide substantial assistance to the government;

(v)   whether to waive jury trial;

(vi)   whether to testify in his or her own behalf;

(vii)   whether to speak at sentencing; and

(viii)   whether to appeal.

Other decisions in trial strategy and tactics "should be made by defense counsel, after consultation with the client where feasible and appropriate. Such decisions include how to pursue plea negotiations, how to craft and respond to motions and, at hearing or trial, what witnesses to call, whether and how to conduct cross-examination, what jurors to accept or strike, what motions and objections should be made, and what and how evidence should be introduced." Standard 4–5.2(d).

6. Suppose your client insists on calling his girlfriend as an alibi witness. Having interviewed her, you think the prosecutor will destroy her on cross examination because you believe she is lying about the alibi. Must you call her? Apply Note 5.

7. *Dealing with pain.* Writing about defense counsel, Susan Bandes concludes that "[t]here may be no other profession whose practitioners are required to deal with so much pain with so little support and guidance." Susan Bandes, *Repression and Denial in Criminal Lawyering*, 9 Buffalo Crim. L. Rev. 339, 342 (2006). As a result, defense lawyers adopt mechanisms to minimize the pain, "including avoidance, denial, suppression, repression," and splitting one's personal and professional life. *Id.* at 366. While some of these mechanisms are healthy in moderation, "the danger is that they will be used to excess, leading to burnout and other forms of distress—both personal and professional." *Id.* at 380.

NIX V. WHITESIDE

Supreme Court of the United States, 1986.
475 U.S. 157, 106 S.Ct. 988, 89 L.Ed.2d 123.

CHIEF JUSTICE BURGER delivered the opinion of the Court [joined by JUSTICES WHITE, POWELL, REHNQUIST, and O'CONNOR]. * * *

Whiteside was convicted of second-degree murder by a jury verdict which was affirmed by the Iowa courts. The killing took place on February 8, 1977, in Cedar Rapids, Iowa. Whiteside and two others went to one Calvin Love's apartment late that night, seeking marihuana. Love was in bed when Whiteside and his companions arrived; an argument between Whiteside and Love over the marihuana ensued. At one point, Love directed his girlfriend to get his "piece," and at another point got up, then returned to his bed. According to Whiteside's testimony, Love then started to reach under his pillow and moved toward Whiteside. Whiteside stabbed Love in the chest, inflicting a fatal wound.

Whiteside was charged with murder, and when counsel was appointed he objected to the lawyer initially appointed, claiming that he felt uncomfortable with a lawyer who had formerly been a prosecutor. Gary L. Robinson was then appointed and immediately began an investigation. Whiteside gave him a statement that he had stabbed Love as the latter "was pulling a pistol from underneath the pillow on the bed." Upon questioning by Robinson, however, Whiteside indicated that he had not actually seen a gun, but that he was convinced that Love had a gun. No pistol was found on the premises; shortly after the police search following the stabbing, which had revealed no weapon, the victim's family had removed all of the victim's possessions from the apartment. Robinson interviewed Whiteside's companions who were present during the stabbing, and none had seen a gun during the incident. Robinson advised Whiteside that the existence of a gun was not necessary to establish the claim of self-defense, and that only a reasonable belief that the victim had a gun nearby was necessary even though no gun was actually present.

Until shortly before trial, Whiteside consistently stated to Robinson that he had not actually seen a gun, but that he was convinced that Love had a gun in his hand. About a week before trial, during preparation for direct examination, Whiteside for the first time told Robinson and his associate Donna Paulsen that he had seen something "metallic" in Love's hand. When asked about this, Whiteside responded:

> "[I]n Howard Cook's case there was a gun. If I don't say I saw a gun, I'm dead."

Robinson told Whiteside that such testimony would be perjury and repeated that it was not necessary to prove that a gun was available but only that Whiteside reasonably believed that he was in danger. On Whiteside's insisting that he would testify that he saw "something metallic" Robinson told him, according to Robinson's testimony:

> "[W]e could not allow him to [testify falsely] because that would be perjury, and as officers of the court we would be suborning perjury if we allowed him to do it; * * * I advised him that if he did do that it would be my duty to advise the Court of what he was doing and that I felt he was committing perjury; also, that I probably would be allowed to attempt to impeach that particular testimony."

Robinson also indicated he would seek to withdraw from the representation if Whiteside insisted on committing perjury.[2]

Whiteside testified in his own defense at trial and stated that he "knew" that Love had a gun and that he believed Love was reaching for a gun and he had acted swiftly in self-defense. On cross-examination, he admitted that he had not actually seen a gun in Love's hand. Robinson presented evidence that Love had been seen with a sawed-off shotgun on other occasions, that the police search of the apartment may have been careless, and that the victim's family had removed everything from the apartment shortly after the crime. Robinson presented this evidence to show a basis for Whiteside's asserted fear that Love had a gun.

The jury returned a verdict of second-degree murder, and Whiteside moved for a new trial, claiming that he had been deprived of a fair trial by Robinson's admonitions not to state that he saw a gun or "something metallic." The trial court held a hearing, heard testimony by Whiteside

---

[2]   Whiteside's version of the events at this pretrial meeting is considerably more cryptic:

"Q. And as you went over the questions, did the two of you come into conflict with regard to whether or not there was a weapon?

"A. I couldn't—I couldn't say a conflict. But I got the impression at one time that maybe if I didn't go along with—with what was happening, that it was no gun being involved, maybe that he will pull out of my trial."

and Robinson, and denied the motion. The trial court made specific findings that the facts were as related by Robinson. * * *

B * * *

The [Eighth Circuit] Court of Appeals accepted the findings of the trial judge, affirmed by the Iowa Supreme Court, that trial counsel believed with good cause that Whiteside would testify falsely and acknowledged that under *Harris v. New York*, 401 U.S. 222, 91 S.Ct. 643, 28 L.Ed.2d 1 (1971), a criminal defendant's privilege to testify in his own behalf does not include a right to commit perjury. Nevertheless, the court reasoned that an intent to commit perjury, communicated to counsel, does not alter a defendant's right to effective assistance of counsel and that Robinson's admonition to Whiteside that he would inform the court of Whiteside's perjury constituted a threat to violate the attorney's duty to preserve client confidences. According to the Court of Appeals, this threatened violation of client confidences breached the standards of effective representation set down in *Strickland v. Washington* [holding, p. 1088, that the Sixth Amendment requires "reasonably effective" representation.] * * *

II * * *

C

* * * We must determine whether, in this setting, Robinson's conduct fell within the wide range of professional responses to threatened client perjury acceptable under the Sixth Amendment.

In *Strickland*, we recognized counsel's duty of loyalty and his "overarching duty to advocate the defendant's cause." Plainly, that duty is limited to legitimate, lawful conduct compatible with the very nature of a trial as a search for truth. Although counsel must take all reasonable lawful means to attain the objectives of the client, counsel is precluded from taking steps or in any way assisting the client in presenting false evidence or otherwise violating the law. This principle has consistently been recognized in most unequivocal terms by expositors of the norms of professional conduct since the first Canons of Professional Ethics were adopted by the American Bar Association in 1908. * * *

These principles have been carried through to contemporary codifications of an attorney's professional responsibility. Disciplinary Rule 7–102 of the Model Code of Professional Responsibility (1980), entitled "Representing a Client Within the Bounds of the Law," provides:

> "(A) In his representation of a client, a lawyer shall not: * * * (4) Knowingly use perjured testimony or false evidence. * * * (7) Counsel or assist his client in conduct that the lawyer knows to be illegal or fraudulent."

This provision has been adopted by Iowa, and is binding on all lawyers who appear in its courts. The more recent Model Rules of Professional Conduct (1983) similarly admonish attorneys to obey all laws in the course of representing a client. * * *

Both the Model Code of Professional Responsibility and the Model Rules of Professional Conduct also adopt the specific exception from the attorney-client privilege for disclosure of perjury that his client intends to commit or has committed. DR 4–101(C)(3) (intention of client to commit a crime); Rule 3.3 (lawyer has duty to disclose falsity of evidence even if disclosure compromises client confidences). Indeed, both the Model Code and the Model Rules do not merely *authorize* disclosure by counsel of client perjury; they *require* such disclosure.

These standards confirm that the legal profession has accepted that an attorney's ethical duty to advance the interests of his client is limited by an equally solemn duty to comply with the law and standards of professional conduct; it specifically ensures that the client may not use false evidence. This special duty of an attorney to prevent and disclose frauds upon the court derives from the recognition that perjury is as much a crime as tampering with witnesses or jurors by way of promises and threats, and undermines the administration of justice. * * *

* * * [A]n attorney's revelation of his client's perjury to the court is a professionally responsible and acceptable response to the conduct of a client who has actually given perjured testimony. Similarly, the Model Rules and the commentary, as well as the Code of Professional Responsibility adopted in Iowa, expressly permit withdrawal from representation as an appropriate response of an attorney when the client threatens to commit perjury. Withdrawal of counsel when this situation arises at trial gives rise to many difficult questions including possible mistrial and claims of double jeopardy.[6]

The essence of the brief *amicus* of the American Bar Association reviewing practices long accepted by ethical lawyers is that under no circumstance may a lawyer either advocate or passively tolerate a client's

---

[6] In the evolution of the contemporary standards promulgated by the American Bar Association, an early draft reflects a compromise suggesting that when the disclosure of intended perjury is made during the course of trial, when withdrawal of counsel would raise difficult questions of a mistrial holding, counsel had the option to let the defendant take the stand but decline to affirmatively assist the presentation of perjury by traditional direct examination. Instead, counsel would stand mute while the defendant undertook to present the false version in narrative form in his own words unaided by any direct examination. This conduct was thought to be a signal at least to the presiding judge that the attorney considered the testimony to be false and was seeking to disassociate himself from that course. Additionally, counsel would not be permitted to discuss the known false testimony in closing arguments. Most courts treating the subject rejected this approach and insisted on a more rigorous standard. The Eighth Circuit in this case and the Ninth Circuit have expressed approval of the "free narrative" standards.

The Rule finally promulgated in the current Model Rules of Professional Conduct rejects any participation or passive role whatever by counsel in allowing perjury to be presented without challenge.

giving false testimony. This, of course, is consistent with the governance of trial conduct in what we have long called "a search for truth." The suggestion sometimes made that "a lawyer must believe his client, not judge him" in no sense means a lawyer can honorably be a party to or in any way give aid to presenting known perjury.

D

Considering Robinson's representation of respondent in light of these accepted norms of professional conduct, we discern no failure to adhere to reasonable professional standards that would in any sense make out a deprivation of the Sixth Amendment right to counsel. Whether Robinson's conduct is seen as a successful attempt to dissuade his client from committing the crime of perjury, or whether seen as a "threat" to withdraw from representation and disclose the illegal scheme, Robinson's representation of Whiteside falls well within accepted standards of professional conduct and the range of reasonable professional conduct acceptable under *Strickland*. * * *

The Court of Appeals' holding that Robinson's "action deprived [Whiteside] of due process and effective assistance of counsel" is not supported by the record since Robinson's action, at most, deprived Whiteside of his contemplated perjury. Nothing counsel did in any way undermined Whiteside's claim that he believed the victim was reaching for a gun. Similarly, the record gives no support for holding that Robinson's action "also impermissibly compromised [Whiteside's] right to testify in his own defense by conditioning continued representation * * * and confidentiality upon [Whiteside's] *restricted* testimony." The record in fact shows the contrary: (a) that Whiteside did testify, and (b) he was "restricted" or restrained only from testifying falsely and was aided by Robinson in developing the basis for the fear that Love was reaching for a gun. Robinson divulged no client communications until he was compelled to do so in response to Whiteside's post-trial challenge to the quality of his performance. We see this as a case in which the attorney successfully dissuaded the client from committing the crime of perjury. * * *

The rule adopted by the Court of Appeals, which seemingly would require an attorney to remain silent while his client committed perjury, is wholly incompatible with the established standards of ethical conduct and the laws of Iowa and contrary to professional standards promulgated by that State. The position advocated by petitioner, on the contrary, is wholly consistent with the Iowa standards of professional conduct and law, with the overwhelming majority of courts, and with codes of professional ethics. Since there has been no breach of any recognized professional duty, it follows that there can be no deprivation of the right to assistance of counsel under the *Strickland* standard. * * *

JUSTICE BRENNAN, concurring in the judgment.

This Court has no constitutional authority to establish rules of ethical conduct for lawyers practicing in the state courts. Nor does the Court enjoy any statutory grant of jurisdiction over legal ethics. * * *

Unfortunately, the Court seems unable to resist the temptation of sharing with the legal community its vision of ethical conduct. But let there be no mistake: the Court's essay regarding what constitutes the correct response to a criminal client's suggestion that he will perjure himself is pure discourse without force of law. * * * [T]hat issue is a thorny one, but it is not an issue presented by this case. Lawyers, judges, bar associations, students, and others should understand that the problem has not now been "decided." * * *

JUSTICE BLACKMUN, with whom JUSTICE BRENNAN, JUSTICE MARSHALL, and JUSTICE STEVENS join, concurring in the judgment [omitted].

JUSTICE STEVENS, concurring in the judgment.

Justice Holmes taught us that a word is but the skin of a living thought. A "fact" may also have a life of its own. From the perspective of an appellate judge, after a case has been tried and the evidence has been sifted by another judge, a particular fact may be as clear and certain as a piece of crystal or a small diamond. A trial lawyer, however, must often deal with mixtures of sand and clay. Even a pebble that seems clear enough at first glance may take on a different hue in a handful of gravel.

As we view this case, it appears perfectly clear that respondent intended to commit perjury, that his lawyer knew it, and that the lawyer had a duty—both to the court and to his client, for perjured testimony can ruin an otherwise meritorious case—to take extreme measures to prevent the perjury from occurring. The lawyer was successful and, from our unanimous and remote perspective, it is now pellucidly clear that the client suffered no "legally cognizable prejudice."

Nevertheless, beneath the surface of this case there are areas of uncertainty that cannot be resolved today. A lawyer's certainty that a change in his client's recollection is a harbinger of intended perjury—as well as judicial review of such apparent certainty—should be tempered by the realization that, after reflection, the most honest witness may recall (or sincerely believe he recalls) details that he previously overlooked. Similarly, the post-trial review of a lawyer's pretrial threat to expose perjury that had not yet been committed—and, indeed, may have been prevented by the threat—is by no means the same as review of the way in which such a threat may actually have been carried out. Thus, one can be convinced—as I am—that this lawyer's actions were a proper way to provide his client with effective representation without confronting the much more difficult questions of what a lawyer must, should, or may do after his client has given testimony that the lawyer does not believe. The answer to such questions may well be colored by the particular circumstances attending the actual event and its aftermath. * * *

NOTES AND QUESTIONS

1.   If you had been Robinson, what would you have done?

2.   Suppose your client said, "I recently underwent hypnosis and it refreshed my recollection of what I saw that night." You call the hypnotist, and she confirms the client's story and is willing to testify to the general reliability of hypnotically refreshed recollection. What do you do in this case?

3.   Suppose your client said, "I saw something metallic in Love's hand that night, which is why I told you I thought he had a gun. I never told you I didn't see something metallic. I told you I wasn't sure what I saw was a gun. If you thought I said otherwise, you were mistaken." Does Justice Steven's concurring opinion help here?

4.   *Standard to apply.* How certain should a defense lawyer be before she takes some kind of action, such as having the client testify in a narrative fashion? The Wisconsin Supreme Court recently considered two standards that might govern here. The State argued that defense counsel should be permitted to assume the client is going to testify falsely if the lawyer has "a firm factual basis" for her belief. The defendant urged that the right standard was whether the defense lawyer *knew* the defendant was going to testify falsely. The state court adopted the latter standard, elaborating: "Absent the most extraordinary circumstances, such knowledge must be based on the client's expressed admission of intent to testify untruthfully. While we recognize that the defendant's admission need not be phrased in 'magic words,' it must be unambiguous and directly made to the attorney." State v. McDowell, 272 Wis.2d 488, 681 N.W.2d 500 (2004). See also People v. Johnson, 62 Cal.App.4th 608, 72 Cal.Rptr.2d 805 (1998). Do you agree? Did the lawyer in *Nix* have that level of certainty?

5.   *Conflicting duties.* The ethical dilemma in *Nix* arises from the easy assumption that the lawyer has co-equal duties to her client and to the court. One does not have to accept this premise. Professor Monroe Freedman argues forcefully that the lawyer's first duty is to the client, which requires the lawyer to facilitate and argue the client's perjured testimony if the client cannot be persuaded not to commit perjury. See Monroe Freedman, *Professional Responsibility of the Criminal Defense Lawyer: The Three Hardest Questions*, 64 Mich. L. Rev. 1469 (1966). Does this appeal to you as a solution to the perjury dilemma?

B. THE RIGHT TO HAVE APPOINTED COUNSEL

The first case in which the Court required a state to provide counsel for indigent defendants was *Powell v. Alabama*, p. 25, holding that "in a capital case, where the defendant is unable to employ counsel, and is incapable adequately of making his own defense because of ignorance, feeble-mindedness, illiteracy, or the like, it is the duty of the court, whether requested or not, to assign counsel for him as a necessary requisite of due process of law * * * ." The inevitable question after *Powell* was whether its counsel rule would be limited to the narrow set of circumstances set out in the holding or expanded to include most or all indigent defendants.

In Betts v. Brady, 316 U.S. 455, 62 S.Ct. 1252, 86 L.Ed. 1595 (1942), the Court held that there was a due process right to appointed counsel at state expense only when the failure to appoint counsel would be "offensive to the common and fundamental ideas of fairness." This required a case by case determination, with much discretion in trial judges. At least viewed in light of present-day attitudes about fairness, *Betts* was highly unstable. Could courts continue to say that it is fair to convict indigent defendants of felonies without providing counsel? If not, then why not have a rule requiring appointment? Enter Clarence Gideon, a drifter convicted of breaking and entering a poolroom in Florida. He would provide the Court with a vehicle to change the law.

GIDEON V. WAINWRIGHT
Supreme Court of the United States, 1963.
372 U.S. 335, 83 S.Ct. 792, 9 L.Ed.2d 799.

MR. JUSTICE BLACK delivered the opinion of the Court [joined by CHIEF JUSTICE WARREN, and JUSTICES DOUGLAS, HARLAN, BRENNEN, STEWART, WHITE, and GOLDBERG].

Petitioner was charged in a Florida state court with having broken and entered a poolroom with intent to commit a misdemeanor. This offense is a felony under Florida law. Appearing in court without funds and without a lawyer, petitioner asked the court to appoint counsel for him, whereupon the following colloquy took place:

"The COURT: Mr. Gideon, I am sorry, but I cannot appoint Counsel to represent you in this case. Under the laws of the State of Florida, the only time the Court can appoint Counsel to represent a Defendant is when that person is charged with a capital offense. I am sorry, but I will have to deny your request to appoint Counsel to defend you in this case.

"The DEFENDANT: The United States Supreme Court says I am entitled to be represented by Counsel."

Put to trial before a jury, Gideon conducted his defense about as well as could be expected from a layman. He made an opening statement to the jury, cross-examined the State's witnesses, presented witnesses in his own defense, declined to testify himself, and made a short argument "emphasizing his innocence to the charge contained in the Information filed in this case." The jury returned a verdict of guilty, and petitioner was sentenced to serve five years in the state prison. * * * Since 1942, when *Betts v. Brady* was decided by a divided Court, the problem of a defendant's federal constitutional right to counsel in a state court has been a continuing source of controversy and litigation in both state and federal courts. To give this problem another review here, we granted certiorari. Since Gideon was proceeding *in forma pauperis*, we appointed counsel to represent him and requested both sides to discuss in their briefs and oral arguments the following: "Should this Court's holding in *Betts v. Brady* be reconsidered?"

I

The facts upon which Betts claimed that he had been unconstitutionally denied the right to have counsel appointed to assist him are strikingly like the facts upon which Gideon here bases his federal constitutional claim. Betts was indicted for robbery in a Maryland state court. On arraignment, he told the trial judge of his lack of funds to hire a lawyer and asked the court to appoint one for him. Betts was advised that it was not the practice in that county to appoint counsel for indigent defendants except in murder and rape cases. He then pleaded not guilty, had witnesses summoned, cross-examined the State's witnesses, examined his own, and chose not to testify himself. He was found guilty by the judge, sitting without a jury, and sentenced to eight years in prison. Like Gideon, Betts sought release by habeas corpus, alleging that he had been denied the right to assistance of counsel in violation of the Fourteenth Amendment. Betts was denied any relief, and on review this Court affirmed. It was held that a refusal to appoint counsel for an indigent defendant charged with a felony did not necessarily violate the Due Process Clause of the Fourteenth Amendment, which for reasons given the Court deemed to be the only applicable federal constitutional provision. The Court said:

> "Asserted denial [of due process] is to be tested by an appraisal of the totality of facts in a given case. That which may, in one setting, constitute a denial of fundamental fairness, shocking to the universal sense of justice, may, in other circumstances, and in the light of other considerations, fall short of such denial."

Treating due process as "a concept less rigid and more fluid than those envisaged in other specific and particular provisions of the Bill of Rights," the Court held that refusal to appoint counsel under the particular facts and circumstances in the *Betts* case was not so "offensive to the common and fundamental ideas of fairness" as to amount to a denial of due process. Since the facts and circumstances of the two cases are so nearly indistinguishable, we think the *Betts v. Brady* holding if left standing would require us to reject Gideon's claim that the Constitution guarantees him the assistance of counsel. Upon full reconsideration we conclude that *Betts v. Brady* should be overruled.

II

The Sixth Amendment provides, "In all criminal prosecutions, the accused shall enjoy the right * * * to have the Assistance of Counsel for his defence." We have construed this to mean that in federal courts counsel must be provided for defendants unable to employ counsel unless the right is competently and intelligently waived. Betts argued that this right is extended to indigent defendants in state courts by the Fourteenth Amendment. * * * In order to decide whether the Sixth Amendment's guarantee of counsel is of this fundamental nature, the Court in *Betts* set out and considered "[r]elevant data on the subject * * * afforded by constitutional and statutory provisions subsisting in the colonies and the states prior to the inclusion of the Bill of Rights in the national Constitution, and in the constitutional, legislative, and judicial history of the states to the present date." On the basis of this historical data the Court concluded that "appointment of counsel is not a fundamental right, essential to a fair trial." It was for this reason the *Betts* Court refused to accept the contention that the Sixth Amendment's guarantee of counsel for indigent federal defendants was extended to or, in the words of that Court, "made obligatory upon the states by the Fourteenth Amendment." Plainly, had the Court concluded that appointment of counsel for an indigent criminal defendant was "a fundamental right, essential to a fair trial," it would have held that the Fourteenth Amendment requires appointment of counsel in a state court, just as the Sixth Amendment requires in a federal court. * * *

We accept *Betts v. Brady*'s assumption, based as it was on our prior cases, that a provision of the Bill of Rights which is "fundamental and essential to a fair trial" is made obligatory upon the States by the Fourteenth Amendment. We think the Court in *Betts* was wrong, however, in concluding that the Sixth Amendment's guarantee of counsel is not one of these fundamental rights. Ten years before *Betts v. Brady*, this Court, after full consideration of all the historical data examined in *Betts*, had unequivocally declared that "the right to the aid of counsel is of this fundamental character." *Powell v. Alabama*. While the Court at the close of its *Powell* opinion did by its language, as this Court frequently does, limit its holding to the particular facts and circumstances of that case, its conclusions about the fundamental nature of the right to counsel are unmistakable. * * *

* * * The fact is that in deciding as it did—that "appointment of counsel is not a fundamental right, essential to a fair trial"—the Court in

Betts v. Brady made an abrupt break with its own well-considered precedents. In returning to these old precedents, sounder we believe than the new, we but restore constitutional principles established to achieve a fair system of justice. Not only these precedents but also reason and reflection require us to recognize that in our adversary system of criminal justice, any person haled into court, who is too poor to hire a lawyer, cannot be assured a fair trial unless counsel is provided for him. This seems to us to be an obvious truth. Governments, both state and federal, quite properly spend vast sums of money to establish machinery to try defendants accused of crime. Lawyers to prosecute are everywhere deemed essential to protect the public's interest in an orderly society. Similarly, there are few defendants charged with crime, few indeed, who fail to hire the best lawyers they can get to prepare and present their defenses. That government hires lawyers to prosecute and defendants who have the money hire lawyers to defend are the strongest indications of the wide-spread belief that lawyers in criminal courts are necessities, not luxuries. The right of one charged with crime to counsel may not be deemed fundamental and essential to fair trials in some countries, but it is in ours. From the very beginning, our state and national constitutions and laws have laid great emphasis on procedural and substantive safeguards designed to assure fair trials before impartial tribunals in which every defendant stands equal before the law. This noble ideal cannot be realized if the poor man charged with crime has to face his accusers without a lawyer to assist him. * * *

The Court in *Betts v. Brady* departed from the sound wisdom upon which the Court's holding in *Powell v. Alabama* rested. Florida, supported by two other States, has asked that *Betts v. Brady* be left intact. Twenty-two States, as friends of the Court, argue that *Betts* was "an anachronism when handed down" and that it should now be overruled. We agree.

[The separate opinion of JUSTICE DOUGLAS, and the opinion of JUSTICE CLARK, concurring in the result, are omitted.]

MR. JUSTICE HARLAN, concurring.

I agree that *Betts v. Brady* should be overruled, but consider it entitled to a more respectful burial than has been accorded, at least on the part of those of us who were not on the Court when that case was decided.

I cannot subscribe to the view that *Betts v. Brady* represented "an abrupt break with its own well-considered precedents." In 1932, in *Powell v. Alabama*, a capital case, this Court declared that under the particular facts there presented—"the ignorance and illiteracy of the defendants, their youth, the circumstances of public hostility * * * and above all that they stood in deadly peril of their lives"—the state court had a duty to assign counsel for the trial as a necessary requisite of due process of law.

It is evident that these limiting facts were not added to the opinion as an after-thought; they were repeatedly emphasized, and were clearly regarded as important to the result.

Thus when this Court, a decade later, decided *Betts v. Brady*, it did no more than to admit of the possible existence of special circumstances in noncapital as well as capital trials, while at the same time insisting that such circumstances be shown in order to establish a denial of due process. The right to appointed counsel had been recognized as being considerably broader in federal prosecutions, see *Johnson v. Zerbst*, 304 U.S. 458, 58 S.Ct. 1019, 82 L.Ed. 1461, but to have imposed these requirements on the States would indeed have been "an abrupt break" with the almost immediate past. The declaration that the right to appointed counsel in state prosecutions, as established in *Powell v. Alabama*, was not limited to capital cases was in truth not a departure from, but an extension of, existing precedent. * * *

The special circumstances rule has been formally abandoned in capital cases, and the time has now come when it should be similarly abandoned in noncapital cases, at least as to offenses which, as the one involved here, carry the possibility of a substantial prison sentence. (Whether the rule should extend to all criminal cases need not now be decided.) This indeed does no more than to make explicit something that has long since been foreshadowed in our decisions. * * *

NOTES AND QUESTIONS

1.   In considering whether *Betts* was a "break" with precedent, Black reads *Powell* broadly while Harlan reads it narrowly. Just based on what these two opinions tell us about *Powell*, which do you think is the better reading of *Powell*?

2.   Look again at the language of the Sixth Amendment. Does the "right to the Assistance of Counsel" carry with it the correlative duty on the part of state governments to appoint and compensate counsel for indigent defendants?

Not according to *Betts*, which noted the English rule that denied representation by counsel in felony cases (oddly enough, counsel could represent misdemeanor, but not felony, defendants in England at that time). *Betts* read the eighteenth century state constitutional provisions as abrogating the English rule and thus *permitting* the assistance of counsel but not *compelling* appointment of counsel at state expense. The two ideas are conceptually very different. To have the right to do something (own property, for example) is not always the same as having the means to that right guaranteed. But some rights create a correlative duty on the part of government. The right to vote, for example, creates a duty on government to make available the means to vote (voting booths, ballots, etc.), and a duty to ensure that every vote is weighted roughly the same.

Betts accepted that the Sixth Amendment right to counsel creates a correlative duty on the *federal* government to provide counsel to all indigent federal defendants. But it did not find that duty in the due process clause of the Fourteenth Amendment and thus did not find any similar duty on States. *Betts* can thus be explained by the historic importance of federalism in the United States, but it does seem anachronistic in light of the crucial role that lawyers play in trials.

3.   *Gideon's Trumpet.* When Clarence Earl Gideon's case was called for trial, the judge asked if he was ready. He responded: "I am not ready, your Honor." After more questioning from the judge, Gideon asked for counsel and the colloquy followed that you saw in *Gideon*. Anthony Lewis, Gideon's Trumpet 9–10 (1964). From prison, he filed a handwritten habeas petition in the Florida Supreme Court and, when he lost there, a handwritten petition for certiorari in the United States Supreme Court. *Id.* at 34–35. Perhaps signaling that the Supreme Court was ready to change its mind about the rule of *Betts*, the Court appointed Abe Fortas to represent Gideon. Fortas, who, of course, went on to become a justice, was in 1962, "a high-powered example of that high-powered species, the Washington lawyer." *Id.* at 48.

After preparing a brief on Gideon's behalf, Fortas sent a copy to Gideon at the state prison. He responded by thanking Fortas for the copy and added: "Everone [sic] and myself thinks it is a very wonderful and brilliant document. I do not know how you have enticed the general public to take such a [sic] interest in this cause. But I must say it makes me feel very good." *Id.* at 138.

During oral argument Fortas sought rather ingeniously to make the federalism argument work for, rather than against, Gideon. He responded to Justice Harlan's argumentative question about federalism by stating that it was "a fundamental principle for which I personally have the highest regard and concern." Then he added the *tour de force*: "Betts against Brady does not incorporate a proper regard for federalism. It requires a case-by-case supervision by this Court of state criminal proceedings, and that cannot be wholesome. * * * Intervention should be in the least abrasive, the least corrosive way possible." *Id.* at 171–72. For Fortas, the "least abrasive" intervention was a bright-line rule that state judges could apply without having federal judges looking over their shoulder.

Justice Black dissented in *Betts*. He said to a friend shortly after *Gideon* was announced, "When *Betts v. Brady* was decided, I never thought I'd live to see it overruled." Lewis, *supra* at 192.

And what of Clarence Earl Gideon? Facing a second prosecution after remand, he rejected the trial lawyer the ACLU provided; after interviewing Gideon, this lawyer characterized him as "an irascible but spunky" man. *Id.* at 224. The trial judge then appointed a lawyer whom Gideon grudgingly accepted, the case proceeded to trial, and the jury acquitted. "After nearly two years in the state penitentiary Gideon was a free man. There were tears in his eyes, and he trembled even more than usual * * *." A newspaper reporter asked, "Do you feel like you accomplished something?" Gideon replied: "Well I did." *Id.* at 238.

4.   The *Gideon* Court was unanimous that *Betts* should be overruled, and that the right to counsel should extend at least to indigent state defendants like Gideon, who face felony charges. Can you determine from Justice Black's opinion whether *Gideon* applies more broadly than to felonies?

5.   Suppose the judge told *Gideon* prior to trial, "If you are convicted, I won't send you to prison, so I'm not going to give you a lawyer." Would that violate the Constitution as interpreted by *Gideon*?

6.   *Is the state prosecuting and defending?* As should be obvious, and we will see in the next Comment, the only way to provide counsel to indigent defendants is some form of public financing. The net effect is that the State is paying the lawyers on both sides. While this fact could hardly be characterized as a formal conflict of interest, it might lead to a more subtle problem. As long as the only client is the State, doesn't this create an incentive for everyone involved to process the cases as smoothly as possible? To plea bargain rather than engage in pre-trial discovery, investigation, and motion practice?

What would you say, as public defender, if your client said to you, "Who's paying your salary, dude? The same dudes as for the [bleeping] DA, right?"

In this context, Justice Blackmun once observed:

> The right to privately chosen and compensated counsel * * * serves broader institutional interests. The "virtual socialization of criminal defense work in this country that would be the result of a widespread abandonment of the right to retain chosen counsel too readily would standardize the provision of criminal-defense services and diminish defense counsel's independence. There is a place in our system of criminal justice for the maverick and the risk taker and for approaches that might not fit into the structured environment of a public defender's office, or that might displease a judge whose preference for nonconfrontational styles of advocacy might influence the judge's appointment decisions.

Caplin & Drysdale, Chartered v. United States, 491 U.S. 617, 109 S.Ct. 2646, 105 L.Ed.2d 528 (1989) (Blackmun, J., dissenting).

Perhaps the public financed "system is designed to institutionalize cost-efficient lawyering arrangements that depend on routinized case processing and discourage individual lawyers assigned to the poor from providing them with adversarial advocacy." Perhaps the "principal effects" of public financed criminal defense "have been to strengthen the private bar's monopoly over fee-paying cases and to enable the state to discipline the poor through the implementation of the criminal sanction." Perhaps the system is "in reality a triumph of the alliance between the organized bar and the state." That, at least, is the view of two scholars. *See* Michael McConville & Chester L.

Mirsky, *Understanding Defense of the Poor in State Courts*, 10 Studies in Law, Politics, and Society 217 (1990).

And How Is That Working Out for You? A Gathering Storm

Comment on *Gideon's* Legacy

None of the Justices in *Gideon* mentioned the problem of funding the new right to counsel in state courts. In 1963, relatively few federal crimes existed. The problem of paying for lawyers to represent indigent federal defendants was minuscule by comparison to indigent criminal defendants in state court. Three basic forms of public financing have evolved: public-defender programs, contract-attorney representation; and assigned-lawyer programs.

A public-defender system is an organization of lawyers designated by a jurisdiction to provide representation to indigents in criminal cases. The attorneys who work in a public defender office are full-time salaried government employees working together under a single head defender who has responsibility for indigent representation in a particular jurisdiction—just as prosecutors are typically salaried government employees working under a single district attorney for a jurisdiction. Virtually all states have at least a minority of counties with such defender programs.

Many counties have an assigned-counsel program. Under this approach, often inexperienced or underemployed private practitioners are placed on a list to provide representation to poor defendants on a case-by-case basis. They are paid by the hour (usually well below ordinary rates for attorneys in the community) or receive a flat fee per case. * * *

A contract-attorney program is one in which a jurisdiction enters into an agreement with private attorneys, law firms, or bar associations to represent indigents in the community. Attorneys in such a system often maintain a substantial private practice apart from their contract work. They are paid either on a fixed-price basis (they agree to accept an undetermined number of cases for a determined flat fee) or on a fixed-fee-per-case basis. Frequently, the fees are so low that quality representation, particularly in capital cases, is difficult to obtain.

Today, most large counties employ some combination of these programs.

1 Joshua Dressler & Alan C. Michaels, Understanding Criminal Procedure § 28.03 [B][5] (6th ed. 2013). And sometimes the combination is

not the result of a choice made by the legislature! In March, 2016, the Louisiana public defender system faced an existential crisis.

> The constitutional obligation to provide criminal defense for the poor has been endangered by funding problems across the country, but nowhere else is a system in statewide free fall like Louisiana's, where public defenders represent more than eight out of 10 criminal defendants. Offices throughout the state have been forced to lay off lawyers, leaving those who remain with caseloads well into the hundreds. In seven of the state's 42 judicial districts, poor defendants are already being put on wait lists; here in the 15th, the list is over 2,300 names long and growing.

> A system that less than a decade ago was set on a course of long-needed improvement is succumbing to years of draining resources, just as the state is facing a fiscal crisis that could make things much worse. Judges throughout the state have ordered private lawyers to represent people for free, prompting objections from members of the private bar. Some lawyers being conscripted are tax and real estate lawyers without any background in courtrooms or criminal law: "No prior experience is necessary," wrote a district judge in Lafayette in a recent plea for volunteers.

> Here in the state with the country's highest incarceration rate, hundreds of those without counsel are sitting in prison, including more than 60 people in New Orleans whose cases have either been put on a wait list or refused altogether by the local public defender's office.

> With felony caseloads already far above the professional standard, the public defender concluded that turning down cases was the only ethical option. In January, the American Civil Liberties Union sued over this in federal court.

> With the state in deep fiscal distress, and with higher education and health care funding already slashed, further cuts to the public defenders are possible, and perhaps likely.

> "Obviously, it's an obligation that they have to be adequately funded," said E. Pete Adams, the executive director of the Louisiana District Attorneys Association. "But it's also an obligation to fund a lot of other things in this state that are right now in jeopardy."

Campbell Robertson, "In Louisiana, the Poor Lack Legal Defense," *New York Times*, March 16, 2016. In the words of Jay Dixon, the chief executive of the Louisiana Public Defender Board, "We have essentially been managing a financial collapse."

In Vermilion Parish, Louisiana, a public defender office of ten lawyers was, in March, 2016, reduced to a single lawyer, Natasha George. Ms. George handed out applications for defense counsel, telling them they would be put on a "wait list," a list "that is over 2,300 names long and growing." For those denied bail, the waiting would be done in jail.

The problem of underfunded public defense is not, of course, limited to Louisiana. As Professor John Pfaff notes:

> [S]ince 1995, real spending on indigent defense has fallen, by 2 percent, even as the number of felony cases has risen by approximately 40 percent.
>
> Not surprisingly, public defense finds itself starved of resources while facing impossible caseloads that mock the idea of justice for the poor.
>
> In Fresno, Calif., for instance, public defenders have caseloads that are four times the recommended maximum of around 150. In Minnesota, one public defender followed by a reporter estimated that he had about 12 minutes to devote to each client that day. There is no way these lawyers can manage the cases being thrown at them. * * *
>
> To make things worse, 43 states now require indigent defendants to pay at least a portion of their lawyers' fees, even though these defendants are by definition indisputably poor. [And in at least one state, failure] to pay is a crime. Someone who qualifies as indigent may be acquitted, only to be convicted of being too poor to pay for the legal services the Constitution requires the state to provide.

John Pfaff, "A Mockery of Justice for the Poor," *New York Times*, April 29, 2016.

SCOTT V. ILLINOIS

Supreme Court of the United States, 1979.
440 U.S. 367, 99 S.Ct. 1158, 59 L.Ed.2d 383.

MR. JUSTICE REHNQUIST delivered the opinion of the Court [joined by CHIEF JUSTICE BURGER and JUSTICES STEWART, WHITE, and POWELL].

We granted certiorari in this case to resolve a conflict among state and lower federal courts regarding the proper application of our decision in *Argersinger v. Hamlin,* 407 U.S. 25, 92 S.Ct. 2006, 32 L.Ed.2d 530 (1972). Petitioner Scott was convicted of theft and fined $50 after a bench trial in the Circuit Court of Cook County, Ill. His conviction was affirmed by the state intermediate appellate court and then by the Supreme Court of Illinois, over Scott's contention that the Sixth and Fourteenth Amendments to the United States Constitution required that Illinois provide trial counsel to him at its expense.

Petitioner Scott was convicted of shoplifting merchandise valued at less than $150. The applicable Illinois statute set the maximum penalty for such an offense at a $500 fine or one year in jail, or both. The petitioner argues that a line of this Court's cases culminating in *Argersinger v. Hamlin*, requires state provision of counsel whenever imprisonment is an authorized penalty.

The Supreme Court of Illinois rejected this contention, quoting the following language from *Argersinger*:

> "We hold, therefore, that absent a knowing and intelligent waiver, no person may be imprisoned for any offense, whether classified as petty, misdemeanor, or felony, unless he was represented by counsel at his trial."

> "Under the rule we announce today, every judge will know when the trial of a misdemeanor starts that no imprisonment may be imposed, even though local law permits it, unless the accused is represented by counsel. He will have a measure of the seriousness and gravity of the offense and therefore know when to name a lawyer to represent the accused before the trial starts."

The Supreme Court of Illinois went on to state that it was "not inclined to extend *Argersinger*" to the case where a defendant is charged with a statutory offense for which imprisonment upon conviction is authorized but not actually imposed upon the defendant. We agree with the Supreme Court of Illinois that the Federal Constitution does not require a state trial court to appoint counsel for a criminal defendant such as petitioner, and we therefore affirm its judgment. * * *

There is considerable doubt that the Sixth Amendment itself, as originally drafted by the Framers of the Bill of Rights, contemplated any guarantee other than the right of an accused in a criminal prosecution in a federal court to employ a lawyer to assist in his defense. * * *

[We] held in *Duncan v. Louisiana*, p. 39, that the right to jury trial in federal court guaranteed by the Sixth Amendment was applicable to the States by virtue of the Fourteenth Amendment. The Court held, however: "It is doubtless true that there is a category of petty crimes or offenses which is not subject to the Sixth Amendment jury trial provision and should not be subject to the Fourteenth Amendment jury trial requirement here applied to the States. Crimes carrying possible penalties up to six months do not require a jury trial if they otherwise qualify as petty offenses * * * ." In *Baldwin v. New York*, 399 U.S. 66, 69, 90 S.Ct. 1886, 1888, 26 L.Ed.2d 437 (1970), the controlling opinion of Mr. Justice White concluded that "no offense can be deemed 'petty' for purposes of the right to trial by jury where imprisonment for more than six months is authorized."

In *Argersinger* the State of Florida urged that a similar dichotomy be employed in the right-to-counsel area: Any offense punishable by less than six months in jail should not require appointment of counsel for an indigent defendant. The *Argersinger* Court rejected this analogy, however, observing that "the right to trial by jury has a different genealogy and is brigaded with a system of trial to a judge alone."

The number of separate opinions in *Gideon, Duncan, Baldwin*, and *Argersinger*, suggests that constitutional line drawing becomes more difficult as the reach of the Constitution is extended further, and as efforts are made to transpose lines from one area of Sixth Amendment jurisprudence to another. The process of incorporation creates special difficulties, for the state and federal contexts are often different and application of the same principle may have ramifications distinct in degree and kind. The range of human conduct regulated by state criminal laws is much broader than that of the federal criminal laws, particularly on the "petty" offense part of the spectrum. As a matter of constitutional adjudication, we are, therefore, less willing to extrapolate an already extended line when, although the general nature of the principle sought to be applied is clear, its precise limits and their ramifications become less so. We have now in our decided cases departed from the literal meaning of the Sixth Amendment. And we cannot fall back on the common law as it existed prior to the enactment of that Amendment, since it perversely gave less in the way of right to counsel to accused felons than to those accused of misdemeanors. * * *

Although the intentions of the *Argersinger* Court are not unmistakably clear from its opinion, we conclude today that *Argersinger* did indeed delimit the constitutional right to appointed counsel in state criminal proceedings. Even were the matter *res nova*, we believe that the central premise of *Argersinger*—that actual imprisonment is a penalty different in kind from fines or the mere threat of imprisonment—is eminently sound and warrants adoption of actual imprisonment as the line defining the constitutional right to appointment of counsel. *Argersinger* has proved reasonably workable, whereas any extension would create confusion and impose unpredictable, but necessarily substantial, costs on 50 quite diverse States. We therefore hold that the Sixth and Fourteenth Amendments to the United States Constitution require only that no indigent criminal defendant be sentenced to a term of imprisonment unless the State has afforded him the right to assistance of appointed counsel in his defense. * * *

MR. JUSTICE POWELL, concurring.

For the reasons stated in my opinion in *Argersinger v. Hamlin*, I do not think the rule adopted by the Court in that case is required by the Constitution. Moreover, the drawing of a line based on whether there is imprisonment (even for overnight) can have the practical effect of precluding provision of counsel in other types of cases in which conviction can have more serious consequences. The *Argersinger* rule also tends to impair the proper functioning of the criminal justice system in that trial judges, in advance of hearing any evidence and before knowing anything about the case except the charge, all too often will be compelled to forgo the legislatively granted option to impose a sentence of imprisonment upon conviction. Preserving this option by providing counsel often will be impossible or impracticable—particularly in congested urban courts where scores of cases are heard in a single sitting, and in small and rural communities where lawyers may not be available.

Despite my continuing reservations about the *Argersinger* rule, it was approved by the Court in the 1972 opinion and four Justices have reaffirmed it today. It is important that this Court provide clear guidance to the hundreds of courts across the country that confront this problem daily. Accordingly, and mindful of *stare decisis*, I join the opinion of the Court. I do so, however, with the hope that in due time a majority will recognize that a more flexible rule is consistent with due process and will better serve the cause of justice.

MR. JUSTICE BRENNAN, with whom MR. JUSTICE MARSHALL and MR. JUSTICE STEVENS join, dissenting. * * *

II

In my view petitioner could prevail in this case without extending the right to counsel beyond what was assumed to exist in *Argersinger*. Neither party in that case questioned the existence of the right to counsel in trials involving "non-petty" offenses punishable by more than six months in jail. The question the Court addressed was whether the right applied to some "petty" offenses to which the right to jury trial did not extend. The Court's reasoning in applying the right to counsel in the case before it—that the right to counsel is more fundamental to a fair proceeding than the right to jury trial and that the historical limitations on the jury trial right are irrelevant to the right to counsel—certainly cannot support a standard for the right to counsel that is more restrictive than the standard for granting a right to jury trial. * * * *Argersinger* thus established a "two dimensional" test for the right to counsel: the right attaches to any "nonpetty" offense punishable by more than six months in jail and in addition to any offense where actual incarceration is likely regardless of the maximum authorized penalty.

The offense of "theft" with which Scott was charged is certainly not a "petty" one. It is punishable by a sentence of up to one year in jail. Unlike many traffic or other "regulatory" offenses, it carries the moral stigma associated with common-law crimes traditionally recognized as indicative of moral depravity. The State indicated at oral argument that the services of a professional prosecutor were considered essential to the prosecution of this offense. Likewise, nonindigent defendants charged with this offense would be well advised to hire the "best lawyers they can get." Scott's right to the assistance of appointed counsel is thus plainly mandated by the logic of the Court's prior cases, including *Argersinger* itself.

III

But rather than decide consonant with the assumption in regard to nonpetty offenses that was both implicit and explicit in *Argersinger*, the Court today retreats to the indefensible position that the *Argersinger* "actual imprisonment" standard is the *only* test for determining the boundary of the Sixth Amendment right to appointed counsel in state misdemeanor cases, thus necessarily deciding that in many cases (such as this one) a defendant will have no right to appointed counsel even when he has a constitutional right to a jury trial. This is simply an intolerable result. Not only is the "actual imprisonment" standard unprecedented as the exclusive test, but also the problems inherent in its application demonstrate the superiority of an "authorized imprisonment" standard that would require the appointment of counsel for indigents accused of any offense for which imprisonment for any time is authorized.

First, the "authorized imprisonment" standard more faithfully implements the principles of the Sixth Amendment identified in *Gideon*. The procedural rules established by state statutes are geared to the nature of the potential penalty for an offense, not to the actual penalty imposed in particular cases. The authorized penalty is also a better predictor of the stigma and other collateral consequences that attach to conviction of an offense. * * *

Second, the "authorized imprisonment" test presents no problems of administration. It avoids the necessity for time-consuming consideration of the likely sentence in each individual case before trial and the attendant problems of inaccurate predictions, unequal treatment, and apparent and actual bias. These problems with the "actual imprisonment" standard were suggested in my Brother Powell's concurrence in *Argersinger*, which was echoed in scholarly criticism of that decision. * * *

Perhaps the strongest refutation of respondent's alarmist prophecies that an "authorized imprisonment" standard would wreak havoc on the States is that the standard has not produced that result in the substantial number of States that already provide counsel in all cases where imprisonment is authorized—States that include a large majority of the country's population and a great diversity of urban and rural environments. Moreover, of those States that do not yet provide counsel in all cases where *any* imprisonment is authorized, many provide counsel when periods of imprisonment longer than 30 days, 3 months, or 6 months are authorized. In fact, Scott would be entitled to appointed counsel under the current laws of at least 33 States. * * *

IV

The Court's opinion turns the reasoning of *Argersinger* on its head. It restricts the right to counsel, perhaps the most fundamental Sixth Amendment right, more narrowly than the admittedly less fundamental right to jury trial. The abstract pretext that "constitutional line drawing becomes more difficult as the reach of the Constitution is extended further, and as efforts are made to transpose lines from one area of Sixth Amendment jurisprudence to another," cannot camouflage the anomalous result the Court reaches. Today's decision reminds one of Mr. Justice Black's description of *Betts v. Brady*: "an anachronism when handed down" that "ma[kes] an abrupt break with its own well-considered precedents."

MR. JUSTICE BLACKMUN, dissenting.

For substantially the reasons stated by Mr. Justice BRENNAN in Parts I and II of his dissenting opinion, I would hold that the right to counsel secured by the Sixth and Fourteenth Amendments extends at least as far as the right to jury trial secured by those Amendments. * * *

This resolution, I feel, would provide the "bright line" that defendants, prosecutors, and trial and appellate courts all deserve and, at the same time, would reconcile on a principled basis the important considerations that led to the decisions in *Duncan*, *Baldwin*, and *Argersinger*. * * *

NOTES AND QUESTIONS

1.   Does the *Scott* rule apply to felonies?

2.   As you will see in Chapter 16, Scott had a constitutional right to a jury trial. Consider the spectacle of a *pro se* defendant selecting a jury through the *voir dire* process and trying his case before that jury.

3.   The "backward-looking" nature of *Argersinger* is in stark contrast to most rules of constitutional criminal procedure. Absent *Argersinger*, a judge in a misdemeanor or traffic court would not be called upon to make a prediction about the sanction to be imposed if the defendant is found guilty. *Argersinger* requires precisely that prediction. Is this a reason to reject the imprisonment test? See Sherry F. Colb, *Freedom From Incarceration: Why Is This Right Different From All Other Rights?*, 69 N.Y.U. L. Rev. 781 (1994)

(arguing that freedom from incarceration is a separate due process right and using *Argersinger* to demonstrate the Court's commitment to that right).

4.   Justice Rehnquist seems to concede that *Argersinger* did not compel a rejection of Scott's claim. Thus, the Court had a chance to examine the issue left open by *Argersinger*. What seems to be the key factor in ruling against Scott?

5.   Justice Brennan notes that Scott would have had a right to counsel under state law in thirty-three states (but not Illinois). To what extent should this be relevant in interpreting the due process clause?

6.   What does Justice Rehnquist mean when he claims that the Court has now "departed from the literal meaning of the Sixth Amendment"? Do you agree?

7.   *Another prophylactic rule*? Many states require restitution from those convicted of crimes. One way to create incentives for defendants to pay these sums is to impose a jail sentence and suspend it on the condition that the defendant pay restitution plus any fines and court costs that might also be imposed. If the defendant does not pay, within whatever time period the court sets, the jail sentence can be "activated" by a showing of non-payment. Do indigent defendants facing that sentencing structure have a right to counsel under *Argersinger*?

Yes, the Court held by a 5–4 margin in Alabama v. Shelton, 535 U.S. 654, 122 S.Ct. 1764, 152 L.Ed.2d 888 (2002). Focusing on the fact that the Alabama probation revocation hearing would not permit the defendant to inquire into the basis of his conviction, the Court adopted what amounts to a prophylactic rule. Because defendants might later face incarceration without having had counsel at the trial where guilt was determined, the Court held that courts cannot impose suspended sentences on indigent defendants without providing counsel at trial or finding waiver.

8.   *Right to counsel in bail hearings*. Do indigent defendants have a right to counsel at bail hearings? The answer is "sort of." See p. 868, Note 7.

9.   To what extent is the *Powell-Gideon-Scott* line of cases based on a concern about inaccurate outcomes if defendants do not have lawyers (innocent defendants being convicted) and to what extent is it based on fairness (even guilty defendants deserve a fair procedure to determine their guilt)? These norms are discussed in Chapter 1. Though these norms overlap substantially in the cases we have read so far, a tension between them appears when the issue is the right to appointed counsel on appeal, as the next two cases demonstrate.

DOUGLAS V. CALIFORNIA

Supreme Court of the United States, 1963.
372 U.S. 353, 83 S.Ct. 814, 9 L.Ed.2d 811.

MR. JUSTICE DOUGLAS delivered the opinion of the Court [joined by CHIEF JUSTICE WARREN, and JUSTICES BLACK, BRENNAN, STEWART, WHITE, and GOLDBERG].

Petitioners, Bennie Will Meyes and William Douglas, were jointly tried and convicted in a California court on an information charging them with 13 felonies. A single public defender was appointed to represent them. At the commencement of the trial, the defender moved for a continuance, stating that the case was very complicated, that he was not as prepared as he felt he should be because he was handling a different defense every day, and that there was a conflict of interest between the petitioners requiring the appointment of separate counsel for each of them. This motion was denied. Thereafter, petitioners dismissed the defender, claiming he was unprepared, and again renewed motions for separate counsel and for a continuance. These motions also were denied, and petitioners were ultimately convicted by a jury of all 13 felonies, which included robbery, assault with a deadly weapon, and assault with intent to commit murder. Both were given prison terms. Both appealed as of right to the California District Court of Appeal. That court affirmed their convictions. Both Meyes and Douglas then petitioned for further discretionary review in the California Supreme Court, but their petitions were denied without a hearing.

Although several questions are presented in the petition for certiorari, we address ourselves to only one of them. The record shows that petitioners requested, and were denied, the assistance of counsel on appeal, even though it plainly appeared they were indigents. In denying petitioners' requests, the California District Court of Appeal stated that it had "gone through" the record and had come to the conclusion that "no good whatever could be served by appointment of counsel." The District Court of Appeal was acting in accordance with a California rule of criminal procedure which provides that state appellate courts, upon the request of an indigent for counsel, may make "an independent investigation of the record and determine whether it would be of advantage to the defendant or helpful to the appellate court to have counsel appointed. * * * After such investigation, appellate courts should appoint counsel if in their opinion it would be helpful to the defendant or the court, and should deny the appointment of counsel only if in their judgment such appointment would be of no value to either the defendant or the court."

We agree, however, with Justice Traynor of the California Supreme Court, who said that the "[d]enial of counsel on appeal [to an indigent] would seem to be a discrimination at least as invidious as that condemned in *Griffin v. Illinois* * * * ." In *Griffin v. Illinois,* 351 U.S. 12, 76 S.Ct. 585, 100 L.Ed. 891, we held that a State may not grant appellate review in such a way as to discriminate against some convicted defendants on account of their poverty. There * * * , the right to a free transcript on appeal was in issue. Here the issue is whether or not an indigent shall be denied the assistance of counsel on appeal. In either case the evil is the same: discrimination against the indigent. For there can be no equal justice where the kind of an appeal a man enjoys "depends on the amount of money he has."

In spite of California's forward treatment of indigents, under its present practice the type of an appeal a person is afforded in the District Court of Appeal hinges upon whether or not he can pay for the assistance of counsel. If he can the appellate court passes on the merits of his case only after having the full benefit of written briefs and oral argument by counsel. If he cannot the appellate court is forced to prejudge the merits before it can even determine whether counsel should be provided. At this stage in the proceedings only the barren record speaks for the indigent, and, unless the printed pages show that an injustice has been committed, he is forced to go without a champion on appeal. Any real chance he may have had of showing that his appeal has hidden merit is deprived him when the court decides on an *ex parte* examination of the record that the assistance of counsel is not required.

We are not here concerned with problems that might arise from the denial of counsel for the preparation of a petition for discretionary or mandatory review beyond the stage in the appellate process at which the claims have once been presented by a lawyer and passed upon by an appellate court. We are dealing only with the *first appeal*, granted as a matter of right to rich and poor alike, from a criminal conviction. We need not now decide whether California would have to provide counsel for an indigent seeking a discretionary hearing from the California Supreme Court after the District Court of Appeal had sustained his conviction, or whether counsel must be appointed for an indigent seeking review of an appellate affirmance of his conviction in this Court by appeal as of right or by petition for a writ of certiorari which lies within the Court's discretion. But it is appropriate to observe that a State can, consistently with the Fourteenth Amendment, provide for differences so long as the result does not amount to a denial of due process or an "invidious discrimination." Absolute equality is not required; lines can be and are drawn and we often sustain them. But where the merits of the one and only appeal an indigent has as of right are decided without benefit of counsel, we think an unconstitutional line has been drawn between rich and poor.

When an indigent is forced to run this gantlet of a preliminary showing of merit, the right to appeal does not comport with fair procedure. * * * The present case, where counsel was denied petitioners on appeal, shows that the discrimination is not between "possibly good and obviously bad cases," but between cases where the rich man can require the court to listen to argument of counsel before deciding on the merits, but a poor man cannot. There is lacking that equality demanded by the Fourteenth Amendment where the rich man, who appeals as of right, enjoys the benefit of counsel's examination into the record, research of the law, and marshalling of arguments on his behalf, while the indigent, already burdened by a preliminary determination that his case is without merit, is forced to shift for himself. The indigent, where the record is unclear or the errors are hidden, has only the right to a meaningless ritual, while the rich man has a meaningful appeal. * * *

[The opinion of JUSTICE CLARK, dissenting, is omitted.]

MR. JUSTICE HARLAN, whom MR. JUSTICE STEWART joins, dissenting.

In holding that an indigent has an absolute right to appointed counsel on appeal of a state criminal conviction, the Court appears to rely both on the Equal Protection Clause and on the guarantees of fair procedure inherent in the Due Process Clause of the Fourteenth Amendment, with obvious emphasis on "equal protection." In my view the Equal Protection Clause is not apposite, and its application to cases like the present one can lead only to mischievous results. This case should be judged solely under the Due Process Clause, and I do not believe that the California procedure violates that provision.

EQUAL PROTECTION

To approach the present problem in terms of the Equal Protection Clause is, I submit, but to substitute resounding phrases for analysis. I dissented from this approach in *Griffin v. Illinois*, and I am constrained to dissent from the implicit extension of the equal protection approach here—to a case in which the State denies no one an appeal, but seeks only to keep within reasonable bounds the instances in which appellate counsel will be assigned to indigents.

The States, of course, are prohibited by the Equal Protection Clause from discriminating between "rich" and "poor" *as such* in the formulation and application of their laws. But it is a far different thing to suggest that this provision prevents the State from adopting a law of general applicability that may affect the poor more harshly than it does the rich, or, on the other hand, from making some effort to redress economic imbalances while not eliminating them entirely.

Every financial exaction which the State imposes on a uniform basis is more easily satisfied by the well-to-do than by the indigent. Yet I take it that no one would dispute the constitutional power of the State to levy a uniform sales tax, to charge tuition at a state university, to fix rates for the purchase of water from a municipal corporation, to impose a standard fine for criminal violations, or to establish minimum bail for various categories of offenses. Nor could it be contended that the State may not classify as crimes acts which the poor are more likely to commit than are the rich. And surely, there would be no basis for attacking a state law which provided benefits for the needy simply because those benefits fell short of the goods or services that others could purchase for themselves.

Laws such as these do not deny equal protection to the less fortunate for one essential reason: the Equal Protection Clause does not impose on the States "an affirmative duty to lift the handicaps flowing from differences in economic circumstances." To so construe it would be to read into the Constitution a philosophy of leveling that would be foreign to many of our basic concepts of the proper relations between government and society. The State may have a moral obligation to eliminate the evils of poverty, but it is not required by the Equal Protection Clause to give to some whatever others can afford.

* * * California does not discriminate between rich and poor in having a uniform policy permitting everyone to appeal and to retain counsel, and in having a separate rule dealing *only* with the standards for the appointment of counsel for those unable to retain their own attorneys. The sole classification established by this rule is between those cases that are believed to have merit and those regarded as frivolous. And, of course, no matter how far the state rule might go in providing counsel for indigents, it could never be expected to satisfy an affirmative duty—if one existed—to place the poor on the same level as those who can afford the best legal talent available.

Parenthetically, it should be noted that if the present problem may be viewed as one of equal protection, so may the question of the right to appointed counsel at trial, and the Court's analysis of that right in *Gideon v. Wainwright* is wholly unnecessary. The short way to dispose of *Gideon v. Wainwright*, in other words, would be simply to say that the State deprives the indigent of equal protection whenever it fails to furnish him with legal services, and perhaps with other services as well, equivalent to those that the affluent defendant can obtain.

The real question in this case, I submit, and the only one that permits of satisfactory analysis, is whether or not the state rule, as applied in this case, is consistent with the requirements of fair procedure guaranteed by the Due Process Clause. Of course, in considering this question, it must not be lost sight of that the State's responsibility under the Due Process Clause is to provide justice for all. Refusal to furnish criminal indigents with some things that others can afford may fall short of constitutional standards of fairness. The problem before us is whether this is such a case.

DUE PROCESS * * *

It was precisely towards providing adequate appellate review—as part of what the Court concedes to be "California's forward treatment of indigents"—that the State formulated the system which the Court today strikes down. That system requires the state appellate courts to appoint counsel on appeal for any indigent defendant except "if in their judgment such appointment would be of no value to either the defendant or the court." This judgment can be reached only after an independent investigation of the trial record by the reviewing court. And even if counsel is denied, a full appeal on the merits is accorded to the indigent appellant, together with a statement of the reasons why counsel was not assigned. There is nothing in the present case, or in any other case that has been cited to us, to indicate that the system has resulted in injustice. Quite the contrary, there is every reason to believe that California appellate courts have made a painstaking effort to apply the rule fairly and to live up to the State Supreme Court's mandate.

We have today held that in a case such as the one before us, there is an absolute right to the services of counsel at trial. *Gideon v. Wainwright.* But the appellate procedures involved here stand on an entirely different constitutional footing. *First*, appellate review is in itself not required by the Fourteenth Amendment, and thus the question presented is the narrow one whether the State's rules with respect to the appointment of counsel are so arbitrary or unreasonable, *in the context of the particular appellate procedure that it has established*, as to require their invalidation. *Second*, the kinds of questions that may arise on appeal are circumscribed by the record of the proceedings that led to the conviction; they do not encompass the large variety of tactical and strategic problems that must be resolved at the trial. *Third*, as California applies its rule, the indigent appellant receives the benefit of expert and conscientious legal appraisal of the merits of his case on the basis of the trial record, and whether or not he is assigned counsel, is guaranteed full consideration of his appeal. It would be painting with too broad a brush to conclude that under these circumstances an appeal is just like a trial. * * *

I cannot agree that the Constitution prohibits a State in seeking to redress economic imbalances at its bar of justice and to provide indigents with full review, from taking reasonable steps to guard against needless expense. This is all that California has done. Accordingly, I would affirm the state judgment.

NOTES AND QUESTIONS

1.   What is the constitutional basis for the majority opinion? Sixth Amendment? Due process? Equal protection?

2.   *Free transcripts.* As the Court noted in *Douglas*, Griffin v. Illinois, 351 U.S. 12, 76 S.Ct. 585, 100 L.Ed. 891 (1956), held that a state must provide a transcript free of charge to indigent defendants when it is necessary for them to obtain "adequate appellate review of their alleged trial errors." Can you distinguish *Griffin* from *Douglas*? Justice Harlan dissented in both, but could you have joined the majority in *Griffin* and the dissent in *Douglas*?

3.   *Justice for sale.* The plurality opinion in *Griffin*, authored by Justice Black, contained stirring words about equal justice.

> Providing equal justice for poor and rich, weak and powerful alike is an age-old problem. People have never ceased to hope and strive to move closer to that goal. This hope, at least in part, brought about in 1215 the royal concessions of Magna Charta: "To no one will we sell, to no one will we refuse, or delay, right or justice. * * * No free man shall be taken or imprisoned, or disseised, or outlawed, or exiled, or anywise destroyed; nor shall we go upon him nor send upon him, but by the lawful judgement of his peers or by the law of the land." These pledges were unquestionably steps toward a fairer and more nearly equal application of criminal justice. In this tradition, our own constitutional guaranties of due process and equal protection both call for procedures in criminal trials which allow no invidious discriminations between persons and different groups of persons. Both equal protection and due process emphasize the central aim of our entire judicial system—all people charged with crime must, so far as the law is concerned, "stand on an equality before the bar of justice in every American court."

Black's rhetoric expresses noble goals. Does it tell us anything about how to apply the equality principle in a case like *Douglas*?

4.   Chapter 1 noted that fairness sometimes requires at least rough equality of treatment. How does Justice Harlan, in his dissent, find California's procedure consistent with due process fairness?

5.   Justice Harlan turned out to be quite a prophet. The equal protection clause could not bear the weight that Justice Douglas put on it in the majority opinion in *Douglas*.

ROSS V. MOFFITT

Supreme Court of the United States, 1974.
417 U.S. 600, 94 S.Ct. 2437, 41 L.Ed.2d 341.

MR. JUSTICE REHNQUIST delivered the opinion of the Court [joined by CHIEF JUSTICE BURGER and JUSTICES STEWART, WHITE, BLACKMUN, and POWELL].

We are asked in this case to decide whether *Douglas v. California*, which requires appointment of counsel for indigent state defendants on their first appeal as of right, should be extended to require counsel for discretionary state appeals and for applications for review in this Court. * * *

II * * *

The precise rationale for the *Griffin* and *Douglas* lines of cases has never been explicitly stated, some support being derived from the Equal Protection Clause of the Fourteenth Amendment, and some from the Due Process Clause of that Amendment. Neither Clause by itself provides an entirely satisfactory basis for the result reached, each depending on a different inquiry which emphasizes different factors. "Due process" emphasizes fairness between the State and the individual dealing with the State, regardless of how other individuals in the same situation may be treated. "Equal protection," on the other hand, emphasizes disparity in treatment by a State between classes of individuals whose situations are arguably indistinguishable. * * *

III * * *

We do not believe that the Due Process Clause requires North Carolina to provide respondent with counsel on his discretionary appeal to the State Supreme Court. At the trial stage of a criminal proceeding, the right of an indigent defendant to counsel is fundamental and binding upon the States by virtue of the Sixth and Fourteenth Amendments. But there are significant differences between the trial and appellate stages of a criminal proceeding. The purpose of the trial stage from the State's point of view is to convert a criminal defendant from a person presumed innocent to one found guilty beyond a reasonable doubt. To accomplish this purpose, the State employs a prosecuting attorney who presents evidence to the court, challenges any witnesses offered by the defendant, argues rulings of the court, and makes direct arguments to the court and jury seeking to persuade them of the defendant's guilt. Under these circumstances "reason and reflection require us to recognize that in our adversary system of criminal justice, any person haled into court, who is too poor to hire a lawyer, cannot be assured a fair trial unless counsel is provided for him."

By contrast, it is ordinarily the defendant, rather than the State, who initiates the appellate process, seeking not to fend off the efforts of the State's prosecutor but rather to overturn a finding of guilt made by a judge or a jury below. The defendant needs an attorney on appeal not as a shield to protect him against being "haled into court" by the State and stripped of his presumption of innocence, but rather as a sword to upset the prior determination of guilt. This difference is significant for, while no one would agree that the State may simply dispense with the trial stage of proceedings without a criminal defendant's consent, it is clear that the State need not provide any appeal at all. The fact that an appeal *has* been provided does not automatically mean that a State then acts unfairly by refusing to provide counsel to indigent defendants at every stage of the way. Unfairness results only if indigents are singled out by the State and denied meaningful access to the appellate system because of their poverty. That question is more profitably considered under an equal protection analysis.

IV * * *

Despite the tendency of all rights "to declare themselves absolute to their logical extreme," there are obviously limits beyond which the equal protection analysis may not be pressed without doing violence to principles recognized in other decisions of this Court. * * * The question is not one of absolutes, but one of degrees. In this case we do not believe that the Equal Protection Clause, when interpreted in the context of these cases, requires North Carolina to provide free counsel for indigent defendants seeking to take discretionary appeals to the North Carolina Supreme Court, or to file petitions for certiorari in this Court. * * *

The facts show that respondent, in connection with his Mecklenburg County conviction, received the benefit of counsel in examining the record of his trial and in preparing an appellate brief on his behalf for the state Court of Appeals. Thus, prior to his seeking discretionary review in the State Supreme Court, his claims had "once been presented by a lawyer and passed upon by an appellate court." We do not believe that it can be said, therefore, that a defendant in respondent's circumstances is denied meaningful access to the North Carolina Supreme Court simply because the State does not appoint counsel to aid him in seeking review in that court. At that stage he will have, at the very least, a transcript or other record of trial proceedings, a brief on his behalf in the Court of Appeals setting forth his claims of error, and in many cases an opinion by the Court of Appeals disposing of his case. These materials, supplemented by whatever submission respondent may make *pro se*, would appear to provide the Supreme Court of North Carolina with an adequate basis for its decision to grant or deny review.

We are fortified in this conclusion by our understanding of the function served by discretionary review in the North Carolina Supreme Court. The critical issue in that court, as we perceive it, is not whether there has been "a correct adjudication of guilt" in every individual case, see *Griffin v. Illinois*, but rather whether "the subject matter of the appeal has significant public interest," whether "the cause involves legal principles of major significance to the jurisprudence of the State," or whether the decision below is in probable conflict with a decision of the Supreme Court. The Supreme Court may deny certiorari even though it believes that the decision of the Court of Appeals was incorrect, since a decision which appears incorrect may nevertheless fail to satisfy any of the criteria discussed above. Once a defendant's claims of error are organized and presented in a lawyerlike fashion to the Court of Appeals, the justices of the Supreme Court of North Carolina who make the decision to grant or deny discretionary review should be able to ascertain whether his case satisfies the standards established by the legislature for such review.

This is not to say, of course, that a skilled lawyer, particularly one trained in the somewhat arcane art of preparing petitions for discretionary review, would not prove helpful to any litigant able to employ him. An indigent defendant seeking review in the Supreme Court of North Carolina is therefore somewhat handicapped in comparison with a wealthy defendant who has counsel assisting him in every conceivable manner at every stage in the proceeding. But both the opportunity to have counsel prepare an initial brief in the Court of Appeals and the nature of discretionary review in the Supreme Court of North Carolina make this relative handicap far less than the handicap borne by the indigent defendant denied counsel on his initial appeal as of right in *Douglas*. And the fact that a particular service might be of benefit to an indigent defendant does not mean that the service is constitutionally required. The duty of the State under our cases is not to duplicate the legal arsenal that may be privately retained by a criminal defendant in a continuing effort to reverse his conviction, but only to assure the indigent defendant an adequate opportunity to present his claims fairly in the context of the State's appellate process. We think respondent was given that opportunity under the existing North Carolina system.

V

Much of the discussion in the preceding section is equally relevant to the question of whether a State must provide counsel for a defendant seeking review of his conviction in this Court. North Carolina will have provided counsel for a convicted defendant's only appeal as of right, and the brief prepared by that counsel together with one and perhaps two North Carolina appellate opinions will be available to this Court in order that it may decide whether or not to grant certiorari. This Court's review, much like that of the Supreme Court of North Carolina, is discretionary and depends on numerous factors other than the perceived correctness of the judgment we are asked to review. * * *

MR. JUSTICE DOUGLAS, with whom MR. JUSTICE BRENNAN and MR. JUSTICE MARSHALL concur, dissenting.

I would affirm the judgment below because I am in agreement with the opinion of Chief Judge Haynsworth for a unanimous panel in the Court of Appeals. * * *

Chief Judge Haynsworth could find "no logical basis for differentiation between appeals of right and permissive review procedures in the context of the Constitution and the right to counsel." * * *

Douglas v. California was grounded on concepts of fairness and equality. The right to seek discretionary review is a substantial one, and one where a lawyer can be of significant assistance to an indigent defendant. It was correctly perceived below that the "same concepts of fairness and equality, which require counsel in a first appeal of right, require counsel in other and subsequent discretionary appeals."

NOTES AND QUESTIONS

1. *And who is Judge Haynsworth?* Justice Douglas twice refers, with respect, to Chief Judge Haynsworth. A trivia prize to the students who know the role Judge Haynsworth played in the Supreme Court nomination process. No fair looking it up on the internet.

2. *Another (losing) war story.* You may be cynical about the value of having had a lawyer prepare the first appeal if the defendant has to face the second level of appeal without a lawyer. We invite the cynics to read Tansil v. Tansil, 673 S.W.2d 131 (Tenn.1984), a case in which a civil appellant discharged the lawyer who had represented him at trial and in the intermediate appellate court. The appellant represented himself for the rest of the process. He filed a handwritten petition for discretionary review in the state supreme court, which was granted, and then a badly-typed and poorly-organized brief roughly based on his lawyer's brief in the court of appeals. He also argued the case before the Tennessee Supreme Court, at one point rising from his seat among the spectators to yell that appellee's lawyer was a liar. The Chief Justice threatened appellant with expulsion, and no more outbursts occurred. The *pro se* appellant won 5–0. (One of the authors of the present casebook represented appellee; how do you explain to your client that you lost to a *pro se* appellant?).

3. One way to read *Ross* is that indigents have a right to counsel for appeals as of right but not for permissive appeals. The next case shows that this is not the best reading.

4. *The Court clarifies the Douglas-Ross rationale.* The state system in Halbert v. Michigan, 545 U.S. 605, 125 S.Ct. 2582, 162 L.Ed.2d 552 (2005), is

complex but, in essence, Michigan did not allow automatic appeal from a conviction resulting from a guilty plea or a plea of nolo contendere. Instead, the state court of appeals could *permit* an appeal in those cases, depending on the merits of the application. The state in *Halbert* argued that the discretionary nature of the appeal meant that the case was governed by *Ross*, while the defendant argued that the lack of a lawyer to brief and file the first appeal moved the case within the ambit of *Douglas*. The Court agreed with the defendant, noting the emphasis in *Ross* on the fact that, under the state system there, a lawyer had already prepared one appeal and thus

> will have reviewed the trial court record, researched the legal issues, and prepared a brief reflecting that review and research. The defendant seeking second-tier review may also be armed with an opinion of the intermediate appellate court addressing the issues counsel raised. A first-tier review applicant, forced to act *pro se*, will face a record unreviewed by appellate counsel, and will be equipped with no attorney's brief prepared for, or reasoned opinion by, a court of review.

In Michigan, the court of appeals ruling on the application from a plea-convicted defendant "provides the first, and likely the only, direct review the defendant's conviction and sentence will receive." The Court then noted: "Navigating the appellate process without a lawyer's assistance is a perilous endeavor for a layperson, and well beyond the competence of individuals, like Halbert, who have little education, learning disabilities, and mental impairments." Michigan's system was thus unconstitutional under the authority of *Douglas* because it did not require lawyers for all defendants who wish to appeal their convictions to the first appellate court.

Justice Thomas's dissent, joined by Justice Scalia and, in large part by Chief Justice Rehnquist, argued that the risk to the innocent is less significant in *Halbert* than in *Douglas* because defendants who accept a conviction are less likely to be innocent. Moreover, "When a defendant pleads in open court, there is less need for counsel to develop the record and refine claims to present to an appellate court." Thus, because lawyers are less necessary, and the risk to the innocent, lower, the dissent did not find a violation of due process.

Which view of the right to counsel in the Michigan appellate system do you prefer?

5.   We saw in Chapter 12 that defendants have a constitutional right to counsel during preliminary hearings, p. 911, even though no judgment on the merits of the case can be entered. What theory requires counsel during a preliminary hearing, but not on appeal to the state supreme court?

C. THE RIGHT TO DECIDE WHETHER TO HAVE COUNSEL

Does the right "to have the Assistance of Counsel for his defence" imply the right *not* to have a lawyer—that is the right to represent oneself?

FARETTA V. CALIFORNIA

Supreme Court of the United States, 1975.
422 U.S. 806, 95 S.Ct. 2525, 45 L.Ed.2d 562.

MR. JUSTICE STEWART delivered the opinion of the Court [joined by JUSTICES DOUGLAS, BRENNAN, WHITE, MARSHALL, and POWELL].

The Sixth and Fourteenth Amendments of our Constitution guarantee that a person brought to trial in any state or federal court must be afforded the right to the assistance of counsel before he can be validly convicted and punished by imprisonment. This clear constitutional rule has emerged from a series of cases decided here over the last 50 years. The question before us now is whether a defendant in a state criminal trial has a constitutional right to proceed *without* counsel when he voluntarily and intelligently elects to do so. Stated another way, the question is whether a State may constitutionally hale a person into its criminal courts and there force a lawyer upon him, even when he insists that he wants to conduct his own defense. It is not an easy question, but we have concluded that a State may not constitutionally do so. *Rule*

Issue

I

Anthony Faretta was charged with grand theft in an information filed in the Superior Court of Los Angeles County, Cal. At the arraignment, the Superior Court Judge assigned to preside at the trial appointed the public defender to represent Faretta. Well before the date of trial, however, Faretta requested that he be permitted to represent himself. Questioning by the judge revealed that Faretta had once represented himself in a criminal prosecution, that he had a high school education, and that he did not want to be represented by the public defender because he believed that that office was "very loaded down with * * * a heavy case load." The judge responded that he believed Faretta was "making a mistake" and emphasized that in further proceedings Faretta would receive no special favors. Nevertheless, after establishing that Faretta wanted to represent himself and did not want a lawyer, the judge, in a "preliminary ruling," accepted Faretta's waiver of the assistance of counsel. The judge indicated, however, that he might reverse this ruling if it later appeared that Faretta was unable adequately to represent himself.

Several weeks thereafter, but still prior to trial, the judge *sua sponte* held a hearing to inquire into Faretta's ability to conduct his own defense, and questioned him specifically about both the hearsay rule and the state law governing the challenge of potential jurors.[3] After consideration of

---

[3]   The colloquy was as follows:

"THE COURT: In the Faretta matter, I brought you back down here to do some reconsideration as to whether or not you should continue to represent yourself.

"How have you been getting along on your research?

"THE DEFENDANT: Not bad, your Honor.

"Last night I put in the mail a 995 motion and it should be with the Clerk within the next day or two.

"THE COURT: Have you been preparing yourself for the intricacies of the trial of the matter?

"THE DEFENDANT: Well, your Honor, I was hoping that the case could possibly be disposed of on the 995.

"Mrs. Ayers informed me yesterday that it was the Court's policy to hear the pretrial motions at the time of trial. If possible, your Honor, I would like a date set as soon as the Court deems adequate after they receive the motion, sometime before trial.

"THE COURT: Let's see how you have been doing on your research.

"How many exceptions are there to the hearsay rule?

"THE DEFENDANT: Well, the hearsay rule would, I guess, be called the best evidence rule, your Honor. And there are several exceptions in case law, but in actual statutory law, I don't feel there is none.

"THE COURT: What are the challenges to the jury for cause?

"THE DEFENDANT: Well, there is twelve peremptory challenges.

"THE COURT: And how many for cause?

"THE DEFENDANT: Well, as many as the Court deems valid.

"THE COURT: And what are they? What are the grounds for challenging a juror for cause?

"THE DEFENDANT: Well, numerous grounds to challenge a witness—I mean, a juror, your Honor, one being the juror is perhaps suffered, was a victim of the same type of offense, might be prejudiced toward the defendant. Any substantial ground that might make the juror prejudice[d] toward the defendant.

"THE COURT: Anything else?

"THE DEFENDANT: Well, a relative perhaps of the victim.

"THE COURT: Have you taken a look at that code section to see what it is?

"THE DEFENDANT: Challenge a juror?

"THE COURT: Yes.

"THE DEFENDANT: Yes, your Honor. I have done—

"THE COURT: What is the code section?

"THE DEFENDANT: On voir diring a jury, your Honor?

"THE COURT: Yes.

"THE DEFENDANT: I am not aware of the section right offhand.

"THE COURT: What code is it in?

"THE DEFENDANT: Well, the research I have done on challenging would be in Witkins Jurisprudence.

"THE COURT: Have you looked at any of the codes to see where these various things are taken up?

"THE DEFENDANT: No, your Honor, I haven't.

"THE COURT: Have you looked in any of the California Codes with reference to trial procedure?

"THE DEFENDANT: Yes, your Honor.

"THE COURT: What codes?

consideration of Faretta's answers, and observation of his demeanor, the judge ruled that Faretta had not made an intelligent and knowing waiver of his right to the assistance of counsel, and also ruled that Faretta had no constitutional right to conduct his own defense. The judge, accordingly, reversed his earlier ruling permitting self-representation and again appointed the public defender to represent Faretta. Faretta's subsequent request for leave to act as co-counsel was rejected, as were his efforts to make certain motions on his own behalf.[5] Throughout the subsequent trial, the judge required that Faretta's defense be conducted only through the appointed lawyer from the public defender's office. At the conclusion of the trial, the jury found Faretta guilty as charged, and the judge sentenced him to prison. * * *

II

In the federal courts, the right of self-representation has been protected by statute since the beginnings of our Nation. Section 35 of the Judiciary Act of 1789, 1 Stat. 73, 92, enacted by the First Congress and signed by President Washington one day before the Sixth Amendment was proposed, provided that "in all the courts of the United States, the parties may plead and manage their own causes personally or by the assistance of * * * counsel * * *." The right is currently codified in 28 U.S.C. § 1654.

With few exceptions, each of the several States also accords a defendant the right to represent himself in any criminal case. The constitutions of 36 States explicitly confer that right. Moreover, many state courts have expressed the view that the right is also supported by the Constitution of the United States. * * *

III

This consensus is soundly premised. The right of self-representation finds support in the structure of the Sixth Amendment, as well as in the English and colonial jurisprudence from which the Amendment emerged.

"THE DEFENDANT: I have done extensive research in the Penal Code, your Honor, and the Civil Code.

"THE COURT: If you have done extensive research into it, then tell me about it.

"THE DEFENDANT: On empaneling a jury, your Honor?

"THE COURT: Yes.

"THE DEFENDANT: Well, the District Attorney and the defendant, defense counsel, has both the right to 12 peremptory challenges of a jury. These 12 challenges are undisputable. Any reason that the defense or prosecution should feel that a juror would be inadequate to try the case or to rule on a case, they may then discharge that juror.

"But if there is a valid challenge due to grounds of prejudice or some other grounds, that these aren't considered in the 12 peremptory challenges. There are numerous and the defendant, the defense and the prosecution both have the right to make any inquiry to the jury as to their feelings toward the case."

[5]   Faretta also urged without success that he was entitled to counsel of his choice, and three times moved for the appointment of a lawyer other than the public defender. These motions, too, were denied.

A

The Sixth Amendment includes a compact statement of the rights necessary to a full defense:

> "In all criminal prosecutions, the accused shall enjoy the right * * * to be informed of the nature and cause of the accusation; to be confronted with the witnesses against him; to have compulsory process for obtaining witnesses in his favor, and to have the Assistance of Counsel for his defence."

Because these rights are basic to our adversary system of criminal justice, they are part of the "due process of law" that is guaranteed by the Fourteenth Amendment to defendants in the criminal courts of the States. The rights to notice, confrontation, and compulsory process, when taken together, guarantee that a criminal charge may be answered in a manner now considered fundamental to the fair administration of American justice—through the calling and interrogation of favorable witnesses, the cross-examination of adverse witnesses, and the orderly introduction of evidence. In short, the Amendment constitutionalizes the right in an adversary criminal trial to make a defense as we know it.

The Sixth Amendment does not provide merely that a defense shall be made for the accused; it grants to the accused personally the right to make his defense. It is the accused, not counsel, who must be "informed of the nature and cause of the accusation," who must be "confronted with the witnesses against him," and who must be accorded "compulsory process for obtaining witnesses in his favor." Although not stated in the Amendment in so many words, the right to self-representation—to make one's own defense personally—is thus necessarily implied by the structure of the Amendment. The right to defend is given directly to the accused; for it is he who suffers the consequences if the defense fails.

The counsel provision supplements this design. It speaks of the "assistance" of counsel, and an assistant, however expert, is still an assistant. The language and spirit of the Sixth Amendment contemplate that counsel, like the other defense tools guaranteed by the Amendment, shall be an aid to a willing defendant—not an organ of the State interposed between an unwilling defendant and his right to defend himself personally. To thrust counsel upon the accused, against his considered wish, thus violates the logic of the Amendment. In such a case, counsel is not an assistant, but a master;[16] and the right to make a defense is stripped of the personal character upon which the Amendment

---

[16] Such a result would sever the concept of counsel from its historic roots. The first lawyers were personal friends of the litigant, brought into court by him so that he might "take 'counsel' with them" before pleading. 1 F. Pollock & F. Maitland, The History of English Law 211 (2d ed. 1909). Similarly, the first "attorneys" were personal agents, often lacking any professional training, who were appointed by those litigants who had secured royal permission to carry on their affairs through a representative, rather than personally. *Id.*, at 212–213.

insists. It is true that when a defendant chooses to have a lawyer manage and present his case, law and tradition may allocate to the counsel the power to make binding decisions of trial strategy in many areas. This allocation can only be justified, however, by the defendant's consent, at the outset, to accept counsel as his representative. An unwanted counsel "represents" the defendant only through a tenuous and unacceptable legal fiction. Unless the accused has acquiesced in such representation, the defense presented is not the defense guaranteed him by the Constitution, for, in a very real sense, it is not *his* defense.

B

The Sixth Amendment, when naturally read, thus implies a right of self-representation. This reading is reinforced by the Amendment's roots in English legal history. * * *

By the common law of [the 17th century], it was not representation by counsel but self-representation that was the practice in prosecutions for serious crime. At one time, every litigant was required to "appear before the court in his own person and conduct his own cause in his own words." While a right to counsel developed early in civil cases and in cases of misdemeanor, a prohibition against the assistance of counsel continued for centuries in prosecutions for felony or treason. Thus, in the 16th and 17th centuries the accused felon or traitor stood alone, with neither counsel nor the benefit of other rights—to notice, confrontation, and compulsory process—that we now associate with a genuinely fair adversary proceeding. The trial was merely a "long argument between the prisoner and the counsel for the Crown." As harsh as this now seems, at least "the prisoner was allowed to make what statements he liked. * * * Obviously this public oral trial presented many more opportunities to a prisoner than the secret enquiry based on written depositions, which, on the continent, had taken the place of a trial * * * ." * * *

C

In the American Colonies the insistence upon a right of self-representation was, if anything, more fervent than in England.

The colonists brought with them an appreciation of the virtues of self-reliance and a traditional distrust of lawyers. When the Colonies were first settled, "the lawyer was synonymous with the cringing Attorneys-General and Solicitors-General of the Crown and the arbitrary Justices of the King's Court, all bent on the conviction of those who opposed the King's prerogatives, and twisting the law to secure convictions." This prejudice gained strength in the Colonies where "distrust of lawyers became an institution." Several Colonies prohibited pleading for hire in the 17th century. The prejudice persisted into the 18th century as "the lower classes came to identify lawyers with the upper class." The years of Revolution and Confederation saw an upsurge of antilawyer sentiment, a "sudden revival, after the War of the Revolution, of the old dislike and distrust of lawyers as a class." In the heat of these sentiments the Constitution was forged.

This is not to say that the Colonies were slow to recognize the value of counsel in criminal cases. Colonial judges soon departed from ancient English practice and allowed accused felons the aid of counsel for their defense. At the same time, however, the basic right of self-representation was never questioned. We have found no instance where a colonial court required a defendant in a criminal case to accept as his representative an unwanted lawyer. Indeed, even where counsel was permitted, the general practice continued to be self-representation.

The right of self-representation was guaranteed in many colonial charters and declarations of rights. These early documents establish that the "right to counsel" meant to the colonists a right to choose between pleading through a lawyer and representing oneself. After the Declaration of Independence, the right of self-representation, along with other rights basic to the making of a defense, entered the new state constitutions in wholesale fashion. The right to counsel was clearly thought to supplement the primary right of the accused to defend himself, utilizing his personal rights to notice, confrontation, and compulsory process. And when the Colonies or newly independent States provided by statute rather than by constitution for court appointment of counsel in criminal cases, they also meticulously preserved the right of the accused to defend himself personally. * * *

In sum, there is no evidence that the colonists and the Framers ever doubted the right of self-representation, or imagined that this right might be considered inferior to the right of assistance of counsel. To the contrary, the colonists and the Framers, as well as their English ancestors, always conceived of the right to counsel as an "assistance" for the accused, to be used at his option, in defending himself. The Framers selected in the Sixth Amendment a form of words that necessarily implies the right of self-representation. That conclusion is supported by centuries of consistent history.

IV

There can be no blinking the fact that the right of an accused to conduct his own defense seems to cut against the grain of this Court's decisions holding that the Constitution requires that no accused can be convicted and imprisoned unless he has been accorded the right to the assistance of counsel. For it is surely true that the basic thesis of those decisions is that the help of a lawyer is essential to assure the defendant a fair trial. And a strong argument can surely be made that the whole thrust of those decisions most inevitably lead to the conclusion that a

State may constitutionally impose a lawyer upon even an unwilling defendant.

But it is one thing to hold that every defendant, rich or poor, has the right to the assistance of counsel, and quite another to say that a State may compel a defendant to accept a lawyer he does not want. The value of state-appointed counsel was not unappreciated by the Founders, yet the notion of compulsory counsel was utterly foreign to them. And whatever else may be said of those who wrote the Bill of Rights, surely there can be no doubt that they understood the inestimable worth of free choice.

It is undeniable that in most criminal prosecutions defendants could better defend with counsel's guidance than by their own unskilled efforts. But where the defendant will not voluntarily accept representation by counsel, the potential advantage of a lawyer's training and experience can be realized, if at all, only imperfectly. To force a lawyer on a defendant can only lead him to believe that the law contrives against him. Moreover, it is not inconceivable that in some rare instances, the defendant might in fact present his case more effectively by conducting his own defense. Personal liberties are not rooted in the law of averages. The right to defend is personal. The defendant, and not his lawyer or the State, will bear the personal consequences of a conviction. It is the defendant, therefore, who must be free personally to decide whether in his particular case counsel is to his advantage. And although he may conduct his own defense ultimately to his own detriment, his choice must be honored out of "that respect for the individual which is the lifeblood of the law."[46]

V

When an accused manages his own defense, he relinquishes, as a purely factual matter, many of the traditional benefits associated with the right to counsel. For this reason, in order to represent himself, the accused must "knowingly and intelligently" forgo those relinquished benefits. Although a defendant need not himself have the skill and experience of a lawyer in order competently and intelligently to choose self-representation, he should be made aware of the dangers and

---

[46] We are told that many criminal defendants representing themselves may use the courtroom for deliberate disruption of their trials. But the right of self-representation has been recognized from our beginnings by federal law and by most of the States, and no such result has thereby occurred. Moreover, the trial judge may terminate self-representation by a defendant who deliberately engages in serious and obstructionist misconduct. Of course, a State may—even over objection by the accused—appoint a "standby counsel" to aid the accused if and when the accused requests help, and to be available to represent the accused in the event that termination of the defendant's self-representation is necessary.

The right of self-representation is not a license to abuse the dignity of the courtroom. Neither is it a license not to comply with relevant rules of procedural and substantive law. Thus, whatever else may or may not be open to him on appeal, a defendant who elects to represent himself cannot thereafter complain that the quality of his own defense amounted to a denial of "effective assistance of counsel."

disadvantages of self-representation, so that the record will establish that "he knows what he is doing and his choice is made with eyes open."

Here, weeks before trial, Faretta clearly and unequivocally declared to the trial judge that he wanted to represent himself and did not want counsel. The record affirmatively shows that Faretta was literate, competent, and understanding, and that he was voluntarily exercising his informed free will. The trial judge had warned Faretta that he thought it was a mistake not to accept the assistance of counsel, and that Faretta would be required to follow all the "ground rules" of trial procedure. We need make no assessment of how well or poorly Faretta had mastered the intricacies of the hearsay rule and the California code provisions that govern challenges of potential jurors on *voir dire*. For his technical legal knowledge, as such, was not relevant to an assessment of his knowing exercise of the right to defend himself.

In forcing Faretta, under these circumstances, to accept against his will a state-appointed public defender, the California courts deprived him of his constitutional right to conduct his own defense. * * *

MR. CHIEF JUSTICE BURGER, with whom MR. JUSTICE BLACKMUN and MR. JUSTICE REHNQUIST join, dissenting. * * *

I

The most striking feature of the Court's opinion is that it devotes so little discussion to the matter which it concedes is the core of the decision, that is, discerning an independent basis in the Constitution for the supposed right to represent oneself in a criminal trial. Its ultimate assertion that such a right is tucked between the lines of the Sixth Amendment is contradicted by the Amendment's language and its consistent judicial interpretation.

As the Court seems to recognize, the conclusion that the rights guaranteed by the Sixth Amendment are "personal" to an accused reflects nothing more than the obvious fact that it is he who is on trial and therefore has need of a defense. But neither that nearly trivial proposition nor the language of the Amendment, which speaks in uniformly mandatory terms, leads to the further conclusion that the right to counsel is merely supplementary and may be dispensed with at the whim of the accused. Rather, this Court's decisions have consistently included the right to counsel as an integral part of the bundle making up the larger "right to a defense as we know it." * * *

In short, both the "spirit and the logic" of the Sixth Amendment are that every person accused of crime shall receive the fullest possible defense; in the vast majority of cases this command can be honored only by means of the expressly guaranteed right to counsel, and the trial judge is in the best position to determine whether the accused is capable of conducting his defense. True freedom of choice and society's interest in seeing that justice is achieved can be vindicated only if the trial court retains discretion to reject any attempted waiver of counsel and insist that the accused be tried according to the Constitution. This discretion is as critical an element of basic fairness as a trial judge's discretion to decline to accept a plea of guilty. * * *

III

* * * I hesitate to participate in the Court's attempt to use history to take it where legal analysis cannot. Piecing together shreds of English legal history and early state constitutional and statutory provisions, without a full elaboration of the context in which they occurred or any evidence that they were relied upon by the drafters of our Federal Constitution, creates more questions than it answers and hardly provides the firm foundation upon which the creation of new constitutional rights should rest. We are well reminded that this Court once employed an exhaustive analysis of English and colonial practices regarding the right to counsel to justify the conclusion that it was fundamental to a fair trial and, less than 10 years later, used essentially the same material to conclude that it was not.

As if to illustrate this point, the single historical fact cited by the Court which would appear truly relevant to ascertaining the meaning of the Sixth Amendment proves too much. As the Court points out, § 35 of the Judiciary Act of 1789 provided a statutory right to self-representation in federal criminal trials. The text of the Sixth Amendment, which expressly provides only for a right to counsel, was proposed the day after the Judiciary Act was signed. It can hardly be suggested that the Members of the Congress of 1789, then few in number, were unfamiliar with the Amendment's carefully structured language, which had been under discussion since the 1787 Constitutional Convention. And it would be most remarkable to suggest, had the right to conduct one's own defense been considered so critical as to require constitutional protection, that it would have been left to implication. Rather, under traditional canons of construction, *inclusion* of the right in the Judiciary Act and its *omission* from the constitutional amendment drafted at the same time by many of the same men, supports the conclusion that the omission was intentional.

There is no way to reconcile the idea that the Sixth Amendment impliedly guaranteed the right of an accused to conduct his own defense with the contemporaneous action of the Congress in passing a statute explicitly giving that right. If the Sixth Amendment created a right to self-representation it was unnecessary for Congress to enact any statute on the subject at all. In this case, therefore, history ought to lead judges to conclude that the Constitution leaves to the judgment of legislatures, and the flexible process of statutory amendment, the question whether criminal defendants should be permitted to conduct their trials *pro se.* And the fact that we have not hinted at a contrary view for 185 years is surely entitled to some weight in the scales. * * *

MR. JUSTICE BLACKMUN, with whom THE CHIEF JUSTICE [BURGER] and MR. JUSTICE REHNQUIST join, dissenting.

III

* * * I note briefly the procedural problems that, I suspect, today's decision will visit upon trial courts in the future. Although the Court indicates that a *pro se* defendant necessarily waives any claim he might otherwise make of ineffective assistance of counsel, the opinion leaves open a host of other procedural questions. Must every defendant be advised of his right to proceed *pro se?* If so, when must that notice be given? Since the right to assistance of counsel and the right to self-representation are mutually exclusive, how is the waiver of each right to be measured? If a defendant has elected to exercise his right to proceed *pro se,* does he still have a constitutional right to assistance of standby counsel? How soon in the criminal proceeding must a defendant decide between proceeding by counsel or *pro se?* Must he be allowed to switch in midtrial? May a violation of the right to self-representation ever be harmless error? Must the trial court treat the *pro se* defendant differently than it would professional counsel? I assume that many of these questions will be answered with finality in due course. Many of them, however, such as the standards of waiver and the treatment of the *pro se* defendant, will haunt the trial of every defendant who elects to exercise his right to self-representation. * * *

If there is any truth to the old proverb that "one who is his own lawyer has a fool for a client," the Court by its opinion today now bestows a *constitutional* right on one to make a fool of himself.

NOTES AND QUESTIONS

1.   Recall from p. 1035, Note 5, that a defense lawyer makes countless strategic and tactical decisions about how to present a defense, how to challenge the prosecution's case, and how best to argue to the judge and jury. When a criminal defendant exercises his *Faretta* right to represent himself, he must make all those decisions. Which *Faretta* position, majority or dissent, do you prefer as a matter of policy? Does it seem at all odd to you that the eloquent defenders of *Gideon* in this case are the "conservative" justices?

2.   Who gets the better of the argument from history? Perhaps more importantly, *why* does history seem to count so much on this issue?

3.   The Court says that "even where counsel was permitted, the general practice continued to be self-representation" during the colonial era. Author Thomas reviewed the records of forty-eight trials in the New Jersey criminal

courts from 1749 to 1757. In those records, defendants were represented by counsel in twenty-six cases. See George C. Thomas III, *Colonial Criminal Law and Procedure: The Royal Colony of New Jersey, 1749–57*, 1 N.Y.U. J. L. & Liberty 671, 689 (2005). These data suggest that the colonial cases were roughly evenly split between counseled and un-counseled criminal defendants. The acquittal rate was much higher (77%) in cases where the defendant was represented by counsel than in *pro se* cases (18%). Id. at 691. Before we feel too smug about those data, it is possible that a good deal of the difference is explained by self-selection. Defendants whose guilt was obvious, or who had worked out some kind of sentence deal with the prosecutor, would be less likely to spend money or try to persuade a friend to represent them.

4.   Should the *Faretta* arguments, sounding in autonomy, history, and the text of the Sixth Amendment, apply equally to defendants who want to represent themselves on appeal? In Martinez v. Court of Appeal of California, 528 U.S. 152, 120 S.Ct. 684, 145 L.Ed.2d 597 (2000), the Court concluded that these concerns were less weighty. There was no right to appeal at common law, and no statutory right to appeal in federal court or state court until, at the earliest, the late nineteenth century. As to the textual argument, the Court reiterated that the Sixth Amendment applies only to rights "that are available in preparation for trial and at the trial itself. The Sixth Amendment does not include any right to appeal."

There remain the *Faretta* autonomy interests but, given that there is no Sixth Amendment right at stake, the Court found that the autonomy question had to be analyzed under the due process clause. One autonomy interest is the value of not forcing a lawyer on an appellant, who might "be skeptical of whether a lawyer, who is employed by the same government that is prosecuting him, will serve his cause with undivided loyalty." The other autonomy interest is that it is the appellant, just like the defendant in *Faretta*, who personally will bear the consequences of the proceeding. But there are costs associated with the exercise of autonomy in this context. As the Court noted, no one argues that *pro se* representation "is wise, desirable or efficient." Rather, it is usually a "bad defense, particularly when compared to a defense provided by an experienced criminal defense attorney."

Martinez concluded that the autonomy interests weigh less in the appellate context. "The status of the accused defendant, who retains a presumption of innocence throughout the trial process, changes dramatically when a jury returns a guilty verdict." Any autonomy interests "that survive a felony conviction are less compelling than those motivating the decision in *Faretta*. Yet the overriding state interest in the fair and efficient administration of justice remains as strong as at the trial level. Thus, the States are clearly within their discretion to conclude that the government's interests outweigh an invasion of the appellant's interest in self-representation."

Do you agree that the existence of a conviction impairs the autonomy interest implicit in deciding whether to represent oneself in an appellate procedure?

5.   Does the *Faretta* Court find that the Sixth Amendment entails a right to waive counsel or that the Sixth Amendment contains a positive right of self-representation?

6.   How many peremptory challenges do criminal defendants get in non-capital cases under your state law? If you don't know, perhaps Faretta is in better shape to defend himself than it might first appear. Why do you think the Court included footnote 3?

7.   *Standby counsel.* In footnote 46 of *Faretta*, the Court anticipated the desire of trial courts to appoint standby counsel. In McKaskle v. Wiggins, 465 U.S. 168, 104 S.Ct. 944, 79 L.Ed.2d 122 (1984), the issue was whether unwanted intervention by standby counsel was an unconstitutional erosion of the *pro se* defendant's right of self-representation.

The Court approached this difficult inquiry by keeping its focus on the autonomy dimension of the *Faretta* doctrine:

> First, the *pro se* defendant is entitled to preserve actual control over the case he chooses to present to the jury. This is the core of the *Faretta* right. If standby counsel's participation over the defendant's objection effectively allows counsel to make or substantially interfere with any significant tactical decision, or to control the questioning of witnesses, or to speak instead of the defendant on any matter of importance, the *Faretta* right is eroded.
>
> Second, participation by standby counsel without the defendant's consent should not be allowed to destroy the jury's perception that the defendant is representing himself. The defendant's appearance in the status of one conducting his own defense is important in a criminal trial, since the right to appear *pro se* exists to affirm the accused's individual dignity and autonomy.

Is this statement inconsistent with at least the surface meaning of *Faretta* footnote 46? Can you reconcile the two?

Professor Anne Bowen Poulin offers insight into why the relationship between the *pro se* defendant and standby counsel might be fractious. Anne Bowen Poulin, *The Role of Standby Counsel in Criminal Cases: In the Twilight Zone of the Criminal Justice System*, 75 N.Y.U. L. Rev. 676 (2000). Many requests to proceed *pro se* result from a trial judge's refusal to appoint substitute counsel when the defendant has concluded that a fair trial is not possible with current counsel. If the judge grants the *pro se* request somewhat late in the process, which is when the motion is usually made, efficiency suggests not appointing a different lawyer to act as standby counsel. But to appoint the lawyer that the defendant has already rejected is only asking for trouble.

8.   *Professor Poulin on the role of standby counsel.* Professor Poulin's comprehensive examination of the proper role for standby counsel, Note 7, concludes that the role varies substantially by the stage of the proceedings at issue. The threat to the jury's "perception that the defendant is representing himself" is a problem only at the trial stage. But even at trial, Professor Poulin argues that standby counsel should do more than merely sit passively and wait for a plea for help. Instead, standby counsel "should actively guide the defendant through the procedures of the trial" and should "identify hurdles, inform the defendant, and help the defendant surmount them." *Id.* at 718.

Do you think this a sound idea? Is it consistent with *Faretta* and *McKaskle*, Note 7?

According to Poulin, at the pre-trial, evidence-gathering stage, the standby lawyer should be as active as possible. "Only if the defendant rejects standby counsel's offer of assistance has the professional obligation of standby counsel been satisfied." *Id.* at 716. Under this conception of the role of standby counsel, the lawyer would be the client's specialized assistant, much as serjeants assisted clients in English courts in the sixteenth and seventeenth centuries.

9.   *Competency to waive counsel.* In Godinez v. Moran, 509 U.S. 389, 113 S.Ct. 2680, 125 L.Ed.2d 321 (1993), the defendant had committed three cold blooded murders, including that of his ex-wife. He was evaluated by two psychiatrists, "both of whom concluded that he was competent to stand trial." The doctors prescribed medications because he was depressed and suicidal. While being treated for his depression, he sought to discharge his public defender and represent himself, with the plan of pleading guilty and not resisting the State's attempt to impose the death penalty.

The issue in *Godinez* was whether defendants who are competent to stand trial are also competent to waive counsel and plead guilty. The standard for competence to stand trial is whether the defendant has both a "sufficient present ability to consult with his lawyer with a reasonable degree of rational understanding" and "a rational as well as factual understanding of the proceedings against him." *Godinez* reasoned that while defendants who plead guilty have to make many decisions and waive several rights, the defendant who stands trial has additional decisions to make about how to present a defense. Thus, the Court held that if the competence standard "is adequate for defendants who plead not guilty, it is necessarily adequate for those who plead guilty." The Court also held that a defendant who is competent to stand trial is competent to waive counsel en route to a guilty plea.

The Court then explained why the waiver of right to counsel does not require a greater capacity:

> Nor do we think that a defendant who waives his right to the assistance of counsel must be more competent than a defendant who

does not, since there is no reason to believe that the decision to waive counsel requires an appreciably higher level of mental functioning than the decision to waive other constitutional rights. [Moran] suggests that a higher competency standard is necessary because a defendant who represents himself " 'must have greater powers of comprehension, judgment, and reason than would be necessary to stand trial with the aid of an attorney.' " But this argument has a flawed premise; the competence that is required of a defendant seeking to waive his right to counsel is the competence to *waive the right*, not the competence to represent himself. In *Faretta v. California*, we held that a defendant choosing self-representation must do so "competently and intelligently," but we made it clear that the defendant's "technical legal knowledge" is "not relevant" to the determination whether he is competent to waive his right to counsel, and we emphasized that although the defendant "may conduct his own defense ultimately to his own detriment, his choice must be honored."

The Court stressed that the validity of the guilty plea or the waiver of the right to counsel requires more than competence or capacity. It requires a finding that the plea or the waiver "is knowing and voluntary. In this sense there is a 'heightened' standard for pleading guilty and for waiving the right to counsel, but it is not a heightened standard of *competence*."

Justice Blackmun, joined by Justice Stevens, dissented on the ground that the trial judge was on notice of Moran's "self-destructive behavior" and "his deep depression" and should therefore "have conducted another competency evaluation to determine Moran's capacity to waive the right to counsel and represent himself, instead of relying upon the psychiatrists' reports that he was able to stand trial with the assistance of counsel."

On March 30, 1996, Moran was executed. *Nevada Executes Man Who Killed 3 People*, New York Times, March 31, 1996, Sect. 1, at 27.

Faretta Hell
Do Judges Look Like Grapefruits?

Colin Ferguson was charged with killing six railroad commuters and wounding nineteen others in a 1993 shooting rampage on the Long Island Railroad. Ferguson chose this location, rather than the New York City subways, because he did not want to embarrass African-American Mayor David Dinkins. *Gunman's Shooting Spree on Commuter Train Racially Motivated: Police Say*, Agence France-Presse (France), December 8, 1993, at 1. He entered the train with more than 100 rounds of ammunition already loaded in magazine clips. James Barron, *Suspect's Notes Suggest Motive*, The Patriot Ledger (Quincy, Mass.), December 9, 1993, at 17. He fired thirty to fifty rounds in the train, hitting the twenty-five victims. Pat Milton, *Race-Obsessed Loner Blamed in Train Tragedy*, Associated

Press, December 8, 1993. All of his victims were either Caucasian or Asian, and these individuals were deliberately targeted as evidenced by four pages of handwritten notes. The notes listed racism by these groups as his primary motivation. Two examples: "That Chinese fascist will never put me to shame again without cause"; and "The sloppy running of the No. 2 train. It is racism by Caucasians and Uncle Tom Negroes." *Id.*

While in jail awaiting trial, Ferguson accused guards of throwing a fire extinguisher and a milk crate at him. *Train Suspect Claims Abuse From Jailers*, The New Orleans Times-Picayune, December 18, 1993, at A10. He also claimed that the light in his cell was kept on twenty-four hours a day to prevent him from sleeping, and that guards were plotting to poison his food. *Id.* Nassau County Sheriff officials investigated these allegations and found no evidence of mistreatment. *Id.* Despite Ferguson's mental state while in jail, two court-appointed experts found him to be competent to stand trial. *Court Psychiatrist Says Ferguson is Competent to Stand Trial*, Associated Press, January 4, 1994.

His lawyers claimed he was paranoid and delusional. He accused the lawyers of plotting against him, fired them, and requested his right to represent himself. The trial judge found him fit to stand trial and, therefore, under *Godinez*, capable of representing himself. John T. McQuiston, *Accused Killer Asks Search for "Real Killer,"* N.Y. Times, December 15, 1994, at 12. While representing himself, Ferguson asked the court to allow him to hire a private investigator so he could find the real killer. *Id.*

During the ten-day trial, he attempted to subpoena President Clinton and former New York Governor Mario Cuomo because they met with some of the survivors of the shooting. Pat Milton, *Man Convicted of Murdering Six in Train Massacre*, Associated Press, February 17, 1995. He claimed that the only reason the indictment against him had ninety-three counts was that the shootings occurred in 1993. He also claimed that he was a victim of a government conspiracy. *Id.*

His claim that he was not the killer prompted ridicule throughout the trial. On cross-examination of a detective, Ferguson asked if the suspect was ever searched. The detective replied, "Did I ever search you, no." *Id.* Ferguson cross-examined the victims he was accused of wounding. One victim, Maryanne Phillips, responded to his cross-examination by stating, "I saw you shoot me." *Id.* When he made a reference to "the gunman," the witnesses would correct him by responding with the pronoun "you." Janet Cawley, *In Bizarre Trial, Accused Gunman Defends Self; "You Shot Us," Train Survivors Testify*, Chicago Tribune, February 16, 1995, at 4. Ferguson changed his mind at least once but finally decided not to testify. In a twenty-minute monologue to the judge, with the jury out of the room, Ferguson alleged that he was the victim of a conspiracy that was somehow connected to the slaying in prison of mass murderer Jeffrey Dahmer. Pat Milton, *Ferguson Decides Not to Testify in Train-Massacre Trial*, Associated Press, February 16, 1995. He claimed the Dahmer murder was "a prelude against me. There's a conspiracy to murder me if I'm convicted." *Id.*

After ten hours of deliberation, the jury found Ferguson guilty of six counts of murder, nineteen counts of attempted murder, and three other counts. The sentencing hearing for Ferguson took three days because so many victims and family members wanted to speak. "In those three days, I don't think I was ever so moved in 30 years of being a judge," the trial judge said. The judge sentenced him to 200 years. Ferguson, now 55, is serving his sentence at the Upstate Correctional Facility in Malone, N.Y He is eligible for parole in 2309 (and that is not a typo error). "20 years later: Long Island Rail Road shooting remembered as day killer Colin Ferguson went off the rails," Associated Press, *New York Daily News*, December 6, 2013.

On appeal, his lawyer, Richard Barbuto, asked the New York courts to require a higher standard of competency for self-representation than the federal standard in *Godinez*. The Ferguson case, argued Barbuto, "resulted in a perversion of the criminal justice system process." The standard for self-representation "has to be more than being able to tell the difference between a judge and a grapefruit." Robin Topping, *LIRR Gunman Didn't Have a Clue in Court*, Newsday, June 25, 1996, at A29.

These antics might appear a "perversion" of the process to Ferguson's appellate lawyer, or to you, or to the editors of this casebook. But the New York Appellate Division devoted exactly one sentence to the argument that Ferguson was not competent to represent himself: "The [trial] court properly permitted the defendant to appear *pro se,* since a defendant who is competent to stand trial is necessarily competent to waive his right to counsel and proceed *pro se.*" People v. Ferguson, 670 N.Y.S.2d 327, 248 A.D.2d 725 (1998). The highest New York court denied leave to appeal.

NOTES AND QUESTIONS

1.   *A third way.* The Court in *Godinez*—Note 9, p. 1082—held that a defendant who is competent to stand trial is competent to waive counsel and plead guilty. But as the Court realized in Indiana v. Edwards, 554 U.S. 164, 128 S.Ct. 2379, 171 L.Ed.2d 345 (2008), the competence to waive counsel and plead guilty is not necessarily the same as the competence to waive counsel and represent oneself at trial. Edwards had been found to be schizophrenic but, after a stay in the state mental hospital, competent to stand trial. The trial judge, however, drew a distinction between competence to stand trial and competence to be his own lawyer: "With these findings, he's competent to stand trial but I'm not going to find he's competent to defend himself."

Edwards proceeded to trial represented by appointed counsel, was convicted of attempted murder, and claimed on appeal that his Sixth Amendment self-representation rights were violated. The Indiana Supreme Court agreed, concluding that *Faretta* and *Godinez* stood for the proposition that a defendant has a right to represent himself at trial if he is competent to stand trial. The Court disagreed, 7–2, finding nothing in the Sixth Amendment or the Court's precedents that would deny the state the right to force counsel on a defendant who is not mentally competent to represent himself:

> [T]he Constitution permits judges to take realistic account of the particular defendant's mental capacities by asking whether a defendant who seeks to conduct his own defense at trial is mentally competent to do so. That is to say, the Constitution permits States to insist upon representation by counsel for those competent enough to stand trial * * * but who still suffer from severe mental illness to the point where they are not competent to conduct trial proceedings by themselves.

Notably, the Court in *Edwards* did not elaborate on its standard of "not competent to conduct trial proceedings." Presumably, Colin Ferguson would not meet whatever standard is finally adopted.

After *Edwards*, three levels of defendant competence seem to exist. A defendant might be incompetent to stand trial and thus must be released or made the subject of civil commitment proceedings. See Jackson v. Indiana, 406 U.S. 715, 92 S.Ct. 1845, 32 L.Ed.2d 435 (1972). If competent to stand trial, a defendant might be competent to waive counsel and plead guilty but not competent to represent himself at trial. Finally, a defendant might be competent to waive counsel and represent himself at trial, in which case *Faretta* gives him the absolute right to do so.

(handwritten margin note: 3 levels of △ competence)

2. *What Edwards fails to answer.* *Edwards* held that a state is *permitted* to require counsel when defendants fall below the standard of "not competent to conduct trial proceedings." Is the converse of this holding also implied—is a state *required* to appoint counsel for all defendants who wish to represent themselves but are not mentally competent to do so?

Though *Edwards* does not decide this issue, the Court offered a comment on the perception of fairness, noting that "proceedings must not only be fair, they must 'appear fair to all who observe them.'" The majority referred to an *amicus* brief in which a psychiatrist observed his patient represent himself at trial and asked "how in the world can our legal system allow an insane man to defend himself?" Taken to its logical conclusion, this comment suggests that there may be a constitutional requirement for counsel when defendants who are "not competent to conduct trial proceedings" seek to represent themselves at trial. The possibility that this issue might be raised on appeal will probably encourage trial judges to err on the side of appointing counsel in close cases.

3.   *The Unabomber client.* Suppose you were appointed to represent "Unabomber" Ted Kaczynski, charged with several bombings and killings. The Government has asked for the death penalty, and the prosecutors have overwhelming evidence of guilt—*e.g.*, a fully-armed bomb found in his tiny cabin, bomb-making parts and chemicals, carbon copies of the Unabomber's manifesto and taunting letters to victims and the news media, thousands of pages of diaries and journals that Kaczynski kept over a twenty-year period. The journals are filled with observations of a man who wanted only to kill his enemies by building a perfect bomb. All of this evidence, and more, will almost certainly be presented to the jury.

You believe your client is mentally ill. If his mental illness is insufficient to qualify for an insanity defense, at the very least it will be his best argument to the jury to impose life without parole rather than the death penalty. You have repeatedly given your client the benefit of your advice on this point, but he refuses to cooperate in the mental illness defense, and orders you not to raise it at trial or at the penalty phase. He tells you that if you raise the issue in court, even indirectly, he will fire you on the spot and represent himself.

What do you do? Let us assume that you are convinced that, without a mental illness defense, your client will be given the death penalty. Can you ignore his orders? What if you also believe that his decision not to plead mental illness is itself caused by his mental illness? Can you proceed with the defense without his permission?

For an argument that "the criminal process failed Kaczynski, his counsel, and the public," see Martin Sabelli & Stacey Leyton, *Train Wrecks and Freeway Crashes: An Argument For Fairness and Against Self Representation in the Criminal Justice System*, 91 J. Crim. L. & Criminology 161, 164 (2000). The authors conclude that to help avoid this kind of failure in the future, "the ethical rules must be modified to clearly allocate the authority to present evidence of mental illness to defense counsel, regardless of the defendant's wishes." *Id.* at 217. What do you think of that solution?

D.   THE RIGHT TO EFFECTIVE ASSISTANCE OF COUNSEL

The right to counsel cases considered so far, from *Powell* to *Faretta*, can be described as the "structural" right to counsel. The Court in these cases decided *when* defendants have a right to counsel at state expense (or the right to proceed without counsel), but not *what* constitutes the "Assistance of Counsel." But there must also be a substantive component to the right to counsel. If the defense lawyer were in a coma during the trial, it could not be said that the accused had received the "Assistance of Counsel." From there, it is merely a matter of degree to questions about lawyers who are drunk, incompetent, depressed, asleep part of the time, or representing a co-defendant with conflicting interests. These questions of substance are not easy, and many commentators think the Supreme Court has failed to grapple meaningfully with them.

STRICKLAND V. WASHINGTON

Supreme Court of the United States, 1984.
466 U.S. 668, 104 S.Ct. 2052, 80 L.Ed.2d 674.

JUSTICE O'CONNOR delivered the opinion of the Court [joined by CHIEF JUSTICE BURGER and JUSTICES WHITE, BLACKMUN, POWELL, REHNQUIST, and STEVENS].

This case requires us to consider the proper standards for judging a criminal defendant's contention that the Constitution requires a conviction or death sentence to be set aside because counsel's assistance at the trial or sentencing was ineffective.

I

A

During a 10-day period in September 1976, respondent planned and committed three groups of crimes, which included three brutal stabbing murders, torture, kidnaping, severe assaults, attempted murders, attempted extortion, and theft. After his two accomplices were arrested, respondent surrendered to police and voluntarily gave a lengthy statement confessing to the third of the criminal episodes. The State of Florida indicted respondent for kidnaping and murder and appointed an experienced criminal lawyer to represent him.

Counsel actively pursued pretrial motions and discovery. He cut his efforts short, however, and he experienced a sense of hopelessness about the case, when he learned that, against his specific advice, respondent had also confessed to the first two murders. By the date set for trial, respondent was subject to indictment for three counts of first-degree murder and multiple counts of robbery, kidnaping for ransom, breaking and entering and assault, attempted murder, and conspiracy to commit robbery. Respondent waived his right to a jury trial, again acting against counsel's advice, and pleaded guilty to all charges, including the three capital murder charges.

In the plea colloquy, respondent told the trial judge that, although he had committed a string of burglaries, he had no significant prior criminal record and that at the time of his criminal spree he was under extreme stress caused by his inability to support his family. He also stated, however, that he accepted responsibility for the crimes. The trial judge told respondent that he had "a great deal of respect for people who are willing to step forward and admit their responsibility" but that he was making no statement at all about his likely sentencing decision.

Counsel advised respondent to invoke his right under Florida law to an advisory jury at his capital sentencing hearing. Respondent rejected the advice and waived the right. He chose instead to be sentenced by the trial judge without a jury recommendation.

In preparing for the sentencing hearing, counsel spoke with respondent about his background. He also spoke on the telephone with respondent's wife and mother, though he did not follow up on the one unsuccessful effort to meet with them. He did not otherwise seek out character witnesses for respondent. Nor did he request a psychiatric examination, since his conversations with his client gave no indication that respondent had psychological problems.

Counsel decided not to present and hence not to look further for evidence concerning respondent's character and emotional state. That decision reflected trial counsel's sense of hopelessness about overcoming the evidentiary effect of respondent's confessions to the gruesome crimes. It also reflected the judgment that it was advisable to rely on the plea colloquy for evidence about respondent's background and about his claim of emotional stress: the plea colloquy communicated sufficient information about these subjects, and by forgoing the opportunity to present new evidence on these subjects, counsel prevented the State from cross-examining respondent on his claim and from putting on psychiatric evidence of its own.

Counsel also excluded from the sentencing hearing other evidence he thought was potentially damaging. He successfully moved to exclude respondent's "rap sheet." Because he judged that a presentence report might prove more detrimental than helpful, as it would have included respondent's criminal history and thereby would have undermined the claim of no significant history of criminal activity, he did not request that one be prepared.

At the sentencing hearing, counsel's strategy was based primarily on the trial judge's remarks at the plea colloquy as well as on his reputation as a sentencing judge who thought it important for a convicted defendant to own up to his crime. Counsel argued that respondent's remorse and acceptance of responsibility justified sparing him from the death penalty. Counsel also argued that respondent had no history of criminal activity and that respondent committed the crimes under extreme mental or emotional disturbance, thus coming within the statutory list of mitigating circumstances. He further argued that respondent should be spared death because he had surrendered, confessed, and offered to testify against a codefendant and because respondent was fundamentally a good person who had briefly gone badly wrong in extremely stressful circumstances. The State put on evidence and witnesses largely for the purpose of describing the details of the crimes. Counsel did not cross-examine the medical experts who testified about the manner of death of respondent's victims.

The trial judge found several aggravating circumstances with respect to each of the three murders. He found that all three murders were especially heinous, atrocious, and cruel, all involving repeated stabbings. All three murders were committed in the course of at least one other dangerous and violent felony, and since all involved robbery, the murders were for pecuniary gain. All three murders were committed to avoid arrest for the accompanying crimes and to hinder law enforcement. In the course of one of the murders, respondent knowingly subjected numerous persons to a grave risk of death by deliberately stabbing and shooting the murder victim's sisters-in-law, who sustained severe—in one case, ultimately fatal—injuries.

With respect to mitigating circumstances, the trial judge made the same findings for all three capital murders. First, although there was no admitted evidence of prior convictions, respondent had stated that he had engaged in a course of stealing. In any case, even if respondent had no significant history of criminal activity, the aggravating circumstances "would still clearly far outweigh" that mitigating factor. Second, the judge found that, during all three crimes, respondent was not suffering from extreme mental or emotional disturbance and could appreciate the criminality of his acts. Third, none of the victims was a participant in, or consented to, respondent's conduct. Fourth, respondent's participation in the crimes was neither minor nor the result of duress or domination by an accomplice. Finally, respondent's age (26) could not be considered a factor in mitigation, especially when viewed in light of respondent's planning of the crimes and disposition of the proceeds of the various accompanying thefts.

In short, the trial judge found numerous aggravating circumstances and no (or a single comparatively insignificant) mitigating circumstance. With respect to each of the three convictions for capital murder, the trial judge concluded: "A careful consideration of all matters presented to the court impels the conclusion that there are insufficient mitigating circumstances * * * to outweigh the aggravating circumstances." He therefore sentenced respondent to death on each of the three counts of murder and to prison terms for the other crimes. The Florida Supreme Court upheld the convictions and sentences on direct appeal.

B

Respondent subsequently sought collateral relief in state court on numerous grounds, among them that counsel had rendered ineffective assistance at the sentencing proceeding. Respondent challenged counsel's assistance in six respects. He asserted that counsel was ineffective because he failed to move for a continuance to prepare for sentencing, to request a psychiatric report, to investigate and present character witnesses, to seek a presentence investigation report, to present meaningful arguments to the sentencing judge, and to investigate the medical examiner's reports or cross-examine the medical experts. In support of the claim, respondent submitted 14 affidavits from friends, neighbors, and relatives stating that they would have testified if asked to do so. He also submitted one psychiatric report and one psychological report stating that respondent, though not under the influence of extreme mental or emotional disturbance, was "chronically frustrated and depressed because of his economic dilemma" at the time of his crimes.

The trial court denied relief without an evidentiary hearing, finding that the record evidence conclusively showed that the ineffectiveness claim was meritless. Four of the assertedly prejudicial errors required little discussion. First, there were no grounds to request a continuance, so there was no error in not requesting one when respondent pleaded guilty. Second, failure to request a presentence investigation was not a serious error because the trial judge had discretion not to grant such a request and because any presentence investigation would have resulted in admission of respondent's "rap sheet" and thus would have undermined his assertion of no significant history of criminal activity. Third, the argument and memorandum given to the sentencing judge were "admirable" in light of the overwhelming aggravating circumstances and absence of mitigating circumstances. Fourth, there was no error in failure to examine the medical examiner's reports or to cross-examine the medical witnesses testifying on the manner of death of respondent's victims, since respondent admitted that the victims died in the ways shown by the unchallenged medical evidence.

The trial court dealt at greater length with the two other bases for the ineffectiveness claim. The court pointed out that a psychiatric examination of respondent was conducted by state order soon after respondent's initial arraignment. That report states that there was no indication of major mental illness at the time of the crimes. Moreover, both the reports submitted in the collateral proceeding state that, although respondent was "chronically frustrated and depressed because of his economic dilemma," he was not under the influence of extreme mental or emotional disturbance. All three reports thus directly undermine the contention made at the sentencing hearing that respondent was suffering from extreme mental or emotional disturbance during his crime spree. Accordingly, counsel could reasonably decide not to seek psychiatric reports; indeed, by relying solely on the plea colloquy to support the emotional disturbance contention, counsel denied the State an opportunity to rebut his claim with psychiatric testimony. In any event, the aggravating circumstances were so overwhelming that no substantial prejudice resulted from the absence at sentencing of the psychiatric evidence offered in the collateral attack.

The court rejected the challenge to counsel's failure to develop and to present character evidence for much the same reasons. The affidavits submitted in the collateral proceeding showed nothing more than that certain persons would have testified that respondent was basically a good person who was worried about his family's financial problems. Respondent himself had already testified along those lines at the plea colloquy. Moreover, respondent's admission of a course of stealing rebutted many of the factual allegations in the affidavits. For those reasons, and because the sentencing judge had stated that the death sentence would be appropriate even if respondent had no significant prior criminal history, no substantial prejudice resulted from the absence at sentencing of the character evidence offered in the collateral attack. * * *

C

Respondent * * * filed a petition for a writ of habeas corpus in the United States District Court for the Southern District of Florida. He advanced numerous grounds for relief, among them ineffective assistance of counsel based on the same errors, except for the failure to move for a continuance, as those he had identified in state court. The District Court held an evidentiary hearing to inquire into trial counsel's efforts to investigate and to present mitigating circumstances. Respondent offered the affidavits and reports he had submitted in the state collateral proceedings; he also called his trial counsel to testify. The State of Florida, over respondent's objection, called the trial judge to testify.

* * * On the legal issue of ineffectiveness, the District Court concluded that, although trial counsel made errors in judgment in failing to investigate nonstatutory mitigating evidence further than he did, no prejudice to respondent's sentence resulted from any such error in judgment. Relying in part on the trial judge's testimony but also on the same factors that led the state courts to find no prejudice, the District Court concluded that "there does not appear to be a likelihood, or even a significant possibility," that any errors of trial counsel had affected the outcome of the sentencing proceeding. * * *

[The Court of Appeals reversed and remanded for a new factfinding hearing.]

D

* * * [This case] presents a type of Sixth Amendment claim that this Court has not previously considered in any generality. The Court has considered Sixth Amendment claims based on actual or constructive denial of the assistance of counsel altogether, as well as claims based on state interference with the ability of counsel to render effective assistance

to the accused. With the exception of *Cuyler v. Sullivan*, 446 U.S. 335, 100 S.Ct. 1708, 64 L.Ed.2d 333 (1980), however, which involved a claim that counsel's assistance was rendered ineffective by a conflict of interest, the Court has never directly and fully addressed a claim of "actual ineffectiveness" of counsel's assistance in a case going to trial. * * *

II

In a long line of cases that includes *Powell v. Alabama* [p. 25], *Johnson v. Zerbst*, 304 U.S. 458, 58 S.Ct. 1019, 82 L.Ed. 1461 (1938), and *Gideon v. Wainwright*, [p. 1043], this Court has recognized that the Sixth Amendment right to counsel exists, and is needed, in order to protect the fundamental right to a fair trial. The Constitution guarantees a fair trial through the Due Process Clauses, but it defines the basic elements of a fair trial largely through the several provisions of the Sixth Amendment, including the Counsel Clause * * * .

[Using the Sixth Amendment as a guide], a fair trial is one in which evidence subject to adversarial testing is presented to an impartial tribunal for resolution of issues defined in advance of the proceeding. The right to counsel plays a crucial role in the adversarial system embodied in the Sixth Amendment, since access to counsel's skill and knowledge is necessary to accord defendants the "ample opportunity to meet the case of the prosecution" to which they are entitled.

Because of the vital importance of counsel's assistance, this Court has held that, with certain exceptions, a person accused of a federal or state crime has the right to have counsel appointed if retained counsel cannot be obtained. That a person who happens to be a lawyer is present at trial alongside the accused, however, is not enough to satisfy the constitutional command. The Sixth Amendment recognizes the right to the assistance of counsel because it envisions counsel's playing a role that is critical to the ability of the adversarial system to produce just results. An accused is entitled to be assisted by an attorney, whether retained or appointed, who plays the role necessary to ensure that the trial is fair.

For that reason, the Court has recognized that "the right to counsel is the right to the effective assistance of counsel." * * *

The Court has not elaborated on the meaning of the constitutional requirement of effective assistance in the latter class of cases—that is, those presenting claims of "actual ineffectiveness." In giving meaning to the requirement, however, we must take its purpose—to ensure a fair trial—as the guide. The benchmark for judging any claim of ineffectiveness must be whether counsel's conduct so undermined the proper functioning of the adversarial process that the trial cannot be relied on as having produced a just result.

The same principle applies to a capital sentencing proceeding such as that provided by Florida law. * * *

III

A convicted defendant's claim that counsel's assistance was so defective as to require reversal of a conviction or death sentence has two components. First, the defendant must show that counsel's performance was deficient. This requires showing that counsel made errors so serious that counsel was not functioning as the "counsel" guaranteed the defendant by the Sixth Amendment. Second, the defendant must show that the deficient performance prejudiced the defense. This requires showing that counsel's errors were so serious as to deprive the defendant of a fair trial, a trial whose result is reliable. Unless a defendant makes both showings, it cannot be said that the conviction or death sentence resulted from a breakdown in the adversary process that renders the result unreliable.

A

As all the Federal Courts of Appeals have now held, the proper standard for attorney performance is that of reasonably effective assistance. * * * When a convicted defendant complains of the ineffectiveness of counsel's assistance, the defendant must show that counsel's representation fell below an objective standard of reasonableness.

More specific guidelines are not appropriate. The Sixth Amendment refers simply to "counsel," not specifying particular requirements of effective assistance. It relies instead on the legal profession's maintenance of standards sufficient to justify the law's presumption that counsel will fulfill the role in the adversary process that the Amendment envisions. The proper measure of attorney performance remains simply reasonableness under prevailing professional norms.

Representation of a criminal defendant entails certain basic duties. Counsel's function is to assist the defendant, and hence counsel owes the client a duty of loyalty, a duty to avoid conflicts of interest. From counsel's function as assistant to the defendant derive the overarching duty to advocate the defendant's cause and the more particular duties to consult with the defendant on important decisions and to keep the defendant informed of important developments in the course of the prosecution. Counsel also has a duty to bring to bear such skill and knowledge as will render the trial a reliable adversarial testing process.

These basic duties neither exhaustively define the obligations of counsel nor form a checklist for judicial evaluation of attorney performance. In any case presenting an ineffectiveness claim, the performance inquiry must be whether counsel's assistance was reasonable considering all the circumstances. Prevailing norms of practice as reflected in American Bar Association standards and the like are guides to determining what is reasonable, but they are only guides. No particular set of detailed rules for counsel's conduct can satisfactorily take account of the variety of circumstances faced by defense counsel or the range of legitimate decisions regarding how best to represent a criminal defendant. Any such set of rules would interfere with the constitutionally protected independence of counsel and restrict the wide latitude counsel must have in making tactical decisions. Indeed, the existence of detailed guidelines for representation could distract counsel from the overriding mission of vigorous advocacy of the defendant's cause. Moreover, the purpose of the effective assistance guarantee of the Sixth Amendment is not to improve the quality of legal representation, although that is a goal of considerable importance to the legal system. The purpose is simply to ensure that criminal defendants receive a fair trial.

Judicial scrutiny of counsel's performance must be highly deferential. It is all too tempting for a defendant to second-guess counsel's assistance after conviction or adverse sentence, and it is all too easy for a court, examining counsel's defense after it has proved unsuccessful, to conclude that a particular act or omission of counsel was unreasonable. A fair assessment of attorney performance requires that every effort be made to eliminate the distorting effects of hindsight, to reconstruct the circumstances of counsel's challenged conduct, and to evaluate the conduct from counsel's perspective at the time. Because of the difficulties inherent in making the evaluation, a court must indulge a strong presumption that counsel's conduct falls within the wide range of reasonable professional assistance; that is, the defendant must overcome the presumption that, under the circumstances, the challenged action "might be considered sound trial strategy." There are countless ways to provide effective assistance in any given case. Even the best criminal defense attorneys would not defend a particular client in the same way.

The availability of intrusive post-trial inquiry into attorney performance or of detailed guidelines for its evaluation would encourage the proliferation of ineffectiveness challenges. Criminal trials resolved unfavorably to the defendant would increasingly come to be followed by a second trial, this one of counsel's unsuccessful defense. Counsel's performance and even willingness to serve could be adversely affected. Intensive scrutiny of counsel and rigid requirements for acceptable assistance could dampen the ardor and impair the independence of defense counsel, discourage the acceptance of assigned cases, and undermine the trust between attorney and client.

Thus, a court deciding an actual ineffectiveness claim must judge the reasonableness of counsel's challenged conduct on the facts of the particular case, viewed as of the time of counsel's conduct. A convicted defendant making a claim of ineffective assistance must identify the acts or omissions of counsel that are alleged not to have been the result of reasonable professional judgment. The court must then determine whether, in light of all the circumstances, the identified acts or omissions were outside the wide range of professionally competent assistance. In making that determination, the court should keep in mind that counsel's function, as elaborated in prevailing professional norms, is to make the adversarial testing process work in the particular case. At the same time, the court should recognize that counsel is strongly presumed to have rendered adequate assistance and made all significant decisions in the exercise of reasonable professional judgment.

These standards require no special amplification in order to define counsel's duty to investigate, the duty at issue in this case. * * * [S]trategic choices made after thorough investigation of law and facts relevant to plausible options are virtually unchallengeable; and strategic choices made after less than complete investigation are reasonable precisely to the extent that reasonable professional judgments support the limitations on investigation. In other words, counsel has a duty to make reasonable investigations or to make a reasonable decision that makes particular investigations unnecessary. In any ineffectiveness case, a particular decision not to investigate must be directly assessed for reasonableness in all the circumstances, applying a heavy measure of deference to counsel's judgments.

The reasonableness of counsel's actions may be determined or substantially influenced by the defendant's own statements or actions. Counsel's actions are usually based, quite properly, on informed strategic choices made by the defendant and on information supplied by the defendant. In particular, what investigation decisions are reasonable depends critically on such information. For example, when the facts that support a certain potential line of defense are generally known to counsel because of what the defendant has said, the need for further investigation may be considerably diminished or eliminated altogether. And when a defendant has given counsel reason to believe that pursuing certain investigations would be fruitless or even harmful, counsel's failure to pursue those investigations may not later be challenged as unreasonable. In short, inquiry into counsel's conversations with the defendant may be critical to a proper assessment of counsel's investigation decisions, just as it may be critical to a proper assessment of counsel's other litigation decisions.

B

An error by counsel, even if professionally unreasonable, does not warrant setting aside the judgment of a criminal proceeding if the error had no effect on the judgment. The purpose of the Sixth Amendment guarantee of counsel is to ensure that a defendant has the assistance necessary to justify reliance on the outcome of the proceeding. Accordingly, any deficiencies in counsel's performance must be prejudicial to the defense in order to constitute ineffective assistance under the Constitution.

In certain Sixth Amendment contexts, prejudice is presumed. Actual or constructive denial of the assistance of counsel altogether is legally presumed to result in prejudice. So are various kinds of state interference with counsel's assistance. Prejudice in these circumstances is so likely that case-by-case inquiry into prejudice is not worth the cost. Moreover, such circumstances involve impairments of the Sixth Amendment right that are easy to identify and, for that reason and because the prosecution is directly responsible, easy for the government to prevent.

One type of actual ineffectiveness claim warrants a similar, though more limited, presumption of prejudice. In *Cuyler v. Sullivan*, the Court held that prejudice is presumed when counsel is burdened by an actual conflict of interest. In those circumstances, counsel breaches the duty of loyalty, perhaps the most basic of counsel's duties. Moreover, it is difficult to measure the precise effect on the defense of representation corrupted by conflicting interests. Given the obligation of counsel to avoid conflicts of interest and the ability of trial courts to make early inquiry in certain situations likely to give rise to conflicts, it is reasonable for the criminal justice system to maintain a fairly rigid rule of presumed prejudice for conflicts of interest. Even so, the rule is not quite the *per se* rule of prejudice that exists for the Sixth Amendment claims mentioned above. Prejudice is presumed only if the defendant demonstrates that counsel "actively represented conflicting interests" and that "an actual conflict of interest adversely affected his lawyer's performance."

Conflict of interest claims aside, actual ineffectiveness claims alleging a deficiency in attorney performance are subject to a general requirement that the defendant affirmatively prove prejudice. The government is not responsible for, and hence not able to prevent, attorney errors that will result in reversal of a conviction or sentence. Attorney errors come in an infinite variety and are as likely to be utterly harmless in a particular case as they are to be prejudicial. They cannot be classified according to likelihood of causing prejudice. Nor can they be defined with sufficient precision to inform defense attorneys correctly just what conduct to avoid. Representation is an art, and an act or omission that is unprofessional in one case may be sound or even brilliant in another. Even if a defendant shows that particular errors of counsel were unreasonable, therefore, the defendant must show that they actually had an adverse effect on the defense.

It is not enough for the defendant to show that the errors had some conceivable effect on the outcome of the proceeding. Virtually every act or omission of counsel would meet that test, and not every error that conceivably could have influenced the outcome undermines the reliability of the result of the proceeding. Respondent suggests requiring a showing that the errors "impaired the presentation of the defense." That standard, however, provides no workable principle. Since any error, if it is indeed an error, "impairs" the presentation of the defense, the proposed standard is inadequate because it provides no way of deciding what impairments are sufficiently serious to warrant setting aside the outcome of the proceeding.

On the other hand, we believe that a defendant need not show that counsel's deficient conduct more likely than not altered the outcome in the case. This outcome-determinative standard has several strengths. It defines the relevant inquiry in a way familiar to courts, though the inquiry, as is inevitable, is anything but precise. The standard also reflects the profound importance of finality in criminal proceedings. Moreover, it comports with the widely used standard for assessing motions for new trial based on newly discovered evidence. Nevertheless, the standard is not quite appropriate.

Even when the specified attorney error results in the omission of certain evidence, the newly discovered evidence standard is not an apt source from which to draw a prejudice standard for ineffectiveness claims. The high standard for newly discovered evidence claims presupposes that all the essential elements of a presumptively accurate and fair proceeding were present in the proceeding whose result is challenged. An ineffective assistance claim asserts the absence of one of the crucial assurances that the result of the proceeding is reliable, so finality concerns are somewhat weaker and the appropriate standard of prejudice should be somewhat lower. The result of a proceeding can be rendered unreliable, and hence the proceeding itself unfair, even if the errors of counsel cannot be shown by a preponderance of the evidence to have determined the outcome.

Accordingly, the appropriate test for prejudice finds its roots in the test for materiality of exculpatory information not disclosed to the defense by the prosecution, [Chapter 13, C. 2], and in the test for materiality of testimony made unavailable to the defense by Government deportation of a witness, *United States v. Valenzuela-Bernal*, [458 U.S. 858, 102 S.Ct. 3440, 73 L.Ed.2d 1193 (1982)]. The defendant must show that there is a reasonable probability that, but for counsel's unprofessional errors, the result of the proceeding would have been different. A reasonable probability is a probability sufficient to undermine confidence in the outcome.

In making the determination whether the specified errors resulted in the required prejudice, a court should presume, absent challenge to the judgment on grounds of evidentiary insufficiency, that the judge or jury acted according to law. An assessment of the likelihood of a result more favorable to the defendant must exclude the possibility of arbitrariness, whimsy, caprice, "nullification," and the like. A defendant has no entitlement to the luck of a lawless decisionmaker, even if a lawless decision cannot be reviewed. The assessment of prejudice should proceed on the assumption that the decisionmaker is reasonably, conscientiously, and impartially applying the standards that govern the decision. It should not depend on the idiosyncracies of the particular decisionmaker, such as unusual propensities toward harshness or leniency. Although these factors may actually have entered into counsel's selection of strategies and, to that limited extent, may thus affect the performance inquiry, they are irrelevant to the prejudice inquiry. Thus, evidence about the actual process of decision, if not part of the record of the proceeding under review, and evidence about, for example, a particular judge's sentencing practices, should not be considered in the prejudice determination.

The governing legal standard plays a critical role in defining the question to be asked in assessing the prejudice from counsel's errors. When a defendant challenges a conviction, the question is whether there is a reasonable probability that, absent the errors, the factfinder would have had a reasonable doubt respecting guilt. When a defendant challenges a death sentence such as the one at issue in this case, the question is whether there is a reasonable probability that, absent the errors, the sentencer—including an appellate court, to the extent it independently reweighs the evidence—would have concluded that the balance of aggravating and mitigating circumstances did not warrant death.

In making this determination, a court hearing an ineffectiveness claim must consider the totality of the evidence before the judge or jury. Some of the factual findings will have been unaffected by the errors, and factual findings that were affected will have been affected in different ways. Some errors will have had a pervasive effect on the inferences to be drawn from the evidence, altering the entire evidentiary picture, and some will have had an isolated, trivial effect. Moreover, a verdict or conclusion only weakly supported by the record is more likely to have been affected by errors than one with overwhelming record support. Taking the unaffected findings as a given, and taking due account of the effect of the errors on the remaining findings, a court making the prejudice inquiry must ask if the defendant has met the burden of showing that the decision reached would reasonably likely have been different absent the errors.

IV

A number of practical considerations are important for the application of the standards we have outlined. Most important, in adjudicating a claim of actual ineffectiveness of counsel, a court should keep in mind that the principles we have stated do not establish mechanical rules. Although those principles should guide the process of decision, the ultimate focus of inquiry must be on the fundamental fairness of the proceeding whose result is being challenged. In every case the court should be concerned with whether, despite the strong presumption of reliability, the result of the particular proceeding is unreliable because of a breakdown in the adversarial process that our system counts on to produce just results. * * *

Although we have discussed the performance component of an ineffectiveness claim prior to the prejudice component, there is no reason for a court deciding an ineffective assistance claim to approach the inquiry in the same order or even to address both components of the inquiry if the defendant makes an insufficient showing on one. In particular, a court need not determine whether counsel's performance was deficient before examining the prejudice suffered by the defendant as a result of the alleged deficiencies. The object of an ineffectiveness claim is not to grade counsel's performance. If it is easier to dispose of an ineffectiveness claim on the ground of lack of sufficient prejudice, which we expect will often be so, that course should be followed. Courts should strive to ensure that ineffectiveness claims not become so burdensome to defense counsel that the entire criminal justice system suffers as a result. * * *

V

Having articulated general standards for judging ineffectiveness claims, we think it useful to apply those standards to the facts of this case in order to illustrate the meaning of the general principles. The record makes it possible to do so. There are no conflicts between the state and federal courts over findings of fact, and the principles we have articulated are sufficiently close to the principles applied both in the Florida courts and in the District Court that it is clear that the factfinding was not affected by erroneous legal principles.

Application of the governing principles is not difficult in this case. The facts as described above make clear that the conduct of respondent's counsel at and before respondent's sentencing proceeding cannot be found unreasonable. They also make clear that, even assuming the challenged conduct of counsel was unreasonable, respondent suffered insufficient prejudice to warrant setting aside his death sentence.

With respect to the performance component, the record shows that respondent's counsel made a strategic choice to argue for the extreme emotional distress mitigating circumstance and to rely as fully as possible on respondent's acceptance of responsibility for his crimes. Although counsel understandably felt hopeless about respondent's prospects, nothing in the record indicates, as one possible reading of the District Court's opinion suggests, that counsel's sense of hopelessness distorted his professional judgment. Counsel's strategy choice was well within the range of professionally reasonable judgments, and the decision not to seek more character or psychological evidence than was already in hand was likewise reasonable.

The trial judge's views on the importance of owning up to one's crimes were well known to counsel. The aggravating circumstances were utterly overwhelming. Trial counsel could reasonably surmise from his conversations with respondent that character and psychological evidence would be of little help. Respondent had already been able to mention at the plea colloquy the substance of what there was to know about his financial and emotional troubles. Restricting testimony on respondent's character to what had come in at the plea colloquy ensured that contrary character and psychological evidence and respondent's criminal history, which counsel had successfully moved to exclude, would not come in. On these facts, there can be little question, even without application of the presumption of adequate performance, that trial counsel's defense, though unsuccessful, was the result of reasonable professional judgment.

With respect to the prejudice component, the lack of merit of respondent's claim is even more stark. The evidence that respondent says his trial counsel should have offered at the sentencing hearing would barely have altered the sentencing profile presented to the sentencing judge. As the state courts and District Court found, at most this evidence shows that numerous people who knew respondent thought he was generally a good person and that a psychiatrist and a psychologist believed he was under considerable emotional stress that did not rise to the level of extreme disturbance. Given the overwhelming aggravating factors, there is no reasonable probability that the omitted evidence would have changed the conclusion that the aggravating circumstances outweighed the mitigating circumstances and, hence, the sentence imposed. Indeed, admission of the evidence respondent now offers might even have been harmful to his case: his "rap sheet" would probably have been admitted into evidence, and the psychological reports would have directly contradicted respondent's claim that the mitigating circumstance of extreme emotional disturbance applied to his case. * * *

Failure to make the required showing of either deficient performance or sufficient prejudice defeats the ineffectiveness claim. Here there is a double failure. More generally, respondent has made no showing that the justice of his sentence was rendered unreliable by a breakdown in the adversary process caused by deficiencies in counsel's assistance. Respondent's sentencing proceeding was not fundamentally unfair. * * *

JUSTICE BRENNAN, concurring in part and dissenting in part.

I join the Court's opinion but dissent from its judgment. Adhering to my view that the death penalty is in all circumstances cruel and unusual punishment forbidden by the Eighth and Fourteenth Amendments, I would vacate respondent's death sentence and remand the case for further proceedings. * * *

I join the Court's opinion because I believe that the standards it sets out today will both provide helpful guidance to courts considering claims of actual ineffectiveness of counsel and also permit those courts to continue their efforts to achieve progressive development of this area of the law. * * *

JUSTICE MARSHALL, dissenting. * * *

I * * *

A

My objection to the performance standard adopted by the Court is that it is so malleable that, in practice, it will either have no grip at all or will yield excessive variation in the manner in which the Sixth Amendment is interpreted and applied by different courts. To tell lawyers and the lower courts that counsel for a criminal defendant must behave "reasonably" and must act like "a reasonably competent attorney," is to tell them almost nothing. In essence, the majority has instructed judges called upon to assess claims of ineffective assistance of counsel to advert to their own intuitions regarding what constitutes "professional" representation, and has discouraged them from trying to develop more detailed standards governing the performance of defense counsel. In my view, the Court has thereby not only abdicated its own responsibility to interpret the Constitution, but also impaired the ability of the lower courts to exercise theirs. * * *

The majority defends its refusal to adopt more specific standards primarily on the ground that "[n]o particular set of detailed rules for counsel's conduct can satisfactorily take account of the variety of circumstances faced by defense counsel or the range of legitimate decisions regarding how best to represent a criminal defendant." I agree that counsel must be afforded "wide latitude" when making "tactical decisions" regarding trial strategy, but many aspects of the job of a criminal defense attorney are more amenable to judicial oversight. For example, much of the work involved in preparing for a trial, applying for bail, conferring with one's client, making timely objections to significant, arguably erroneous rulings of the trial judge, and filing a notice of appeal if there are colorable grounds therefor could profitably be made the subject of uniform standards. * * *

B

I object to the prejudice standard adopted by the Court for two independent reasons. First, it is often very difficult to tell whether a defendant convicted after a trial in which he was ineffectively represented would have fared better if his lawyer had been competent. Seemingly impregnable cases can sometimes be dismantled by good defense counsel. On the basis of a cold record, it may be impossible for a reviewing court confidently to ascertain how the government's evidence and arguments would have stood up against rebuttal and cross-examination by a shrewd, well-prepared lawyer. The difficulties of estimating prejudice after the fact are exacerbated by the possibility that evidence of injury to the defendant may be missing from the record precisely because of the incompetence of defense counsel. In view of all these impediments to a fair evaluation of the probability that the outcome of a trial was affected by ineffectiveness of counsel, it seems to me senseless to impose on a defendant whose lawyer has been shown to have been incompetent the burden of demonstrating prejudice.

Second and more fundamentally, the assumption on which the Court's holding rests is that the only purpose of the constitutional guarantee of effective assistance of counsel is to reduce the chance that innocent persons will be convicted. In my view, the guarantee also functions to ensure that convictions are obtained only through fundamentally fair procedures. The majority contends that the Sixth Amendment is not violated when a manifestly guilty defendant is convicted after a trial in which he was represented by a manifestly ineffective attorney. I cannot agree. Every defendant is entitled to a trial in which his interests are vigorously and conscientiously advocated by an able lawyer. A proceeding in which the defendant does not receive meaningful assistance in meeting the forces of the State does not, in my opinion, constitute due process. * * *

II

Even if I were inclined to join the majority's two central holdings, I could not abide the manner in which the majority elaborates upon its rulings. * * *

A

In defining the standard of attorney performance required by the Constitution, the majority appropriately notes that many problems confronting criminal defense attorneys admit of "a range of legitimate" responses. And the majority properly cautions courts, when reviewing a lawyer's selection amongst a set of options, to avoid the hubris of hindsight. The majority goes on, however, to suggest that reviewing courts should "indulge a strong presumption that counsel's conduct" was constitutionally acceptable, and should "appl[y] a heavy measure of deference to counsel's judgments."

I am not sure what these phrases mean, and I doubt that they will be self-explanatory to lower courts. If they denote nothing more than that a defendant claiming he was denied effective assistance of counsel has the burden of proof, I would agree. But the adjectives "strong" and "heavy" might be read as imposing upon defendants an unusually weighty burden of persuasion. If that is the majority's intent, I must respectfully dissent. The range of acceptable behavior defined by "prevailing professional norms" seems to me sufficiently broad to allow defense counsel the flexibility they need in responding to novel problems of trial strategy. To afford attorneys more latitude, by "strongly presuming" that their behavior will fall within the zone of reasonableness, is covertly to legitimate convictions and sentences obtained on the basis of incompetent conduct by defense counsel. * * *

IV

The views expressed in the preceding section oblige me to dissent from the majority's disposition of the case before us. It is undisputed that respondent's trial counsel made virtually no investigation of the possibility of obtaining testimony from respondent's relatives, friends, or former employers pertaining to respondent's character or background. Had counsel done so, he would have found several persons willing and able to testify that, in their experience, respondent was a responsible, non-violent man, devoted to his family, and active in the affairs of his church. Respondent contends that his lawyer could have and should have used that testimony to "humanize" respondent, to counteract the impression conveyed by the trial that he was little more than a cold-blooded killer. Had this evidence been admitted, respondent argues, his chances of obtaining a life sentence would have been significantly better.

Measured against the standards outlined above, respondent's contentions are substantial. Experienced members of the death-penalty bar have long recognized the crucial importance of adducing evidence at a sentencing proceeding that establishes the defendant's social and familial connections. See Goodpaster, The Trial for Life: Effective Assistance of Counsel in Death Penalty Cases, 58 N.Y.U. L.Rev. 299, 300–303, 334–335 (1983). The State makes a colorable—though in my view not compelling— argument that defense counsel in this case might have made a reasonable "strategic" decision not to present such evidence at the sentencing hearing on the assumption that an unadorned acknowledgment of respondent's responsibility for his crimes would be more likely to appeal to the trial judge, who was reputed to respect persons who accepted responsibility for their actions. But however justifiable such a choice might have been after counsel had fairly assessed the potential strength of the mitigating evidence available to him, counsel's failure to make any significant effort to find out what evidence might be garnered from respondent's relatives and acquaintances surely cannot be described as "reasonable." Counsel's failure to investigate is particularly suspicious in light of his candid admission that respondent's confessions and conduct in the course of the trial gave him a feeling of "hopelessness" regarding the possibility of saving respondent's life.

That the aggravating circumstances implicated by respondent's criminal conduct were substantial does not vitiate respondent's constitutional claim; judges and juries in cases involving behavior at least as egregious have shown mercy, particularly when afforded an opportunity to see other facets of the defendant's personality and life. Nor is respondent's contention defeated by the possibility that the material his counsel turned up might not have been sufficient to establish a statutory mitigating circumstance under Florida law; Florida sentencing judges and the Florida Supreme Court sometimes refuse to impose death sentences in cases "in which, even though *statutory* mitigating circumstances do not outweigh statutory aggravating circumstances, the addition of nonstatutory mitigating circumstances tips the scales in favor of life imprisonment."

If counsel had investigated the availability of mitigating evidence, he might well have decided to present some such material at the hearing. If he had done so, there is a significant chance that respondent would have been given a life sentence. In my view, those possibilities, conjoined with the unreasonableness of counsel's failure to investigate, are more than sufficient to establish a violation of the Sixth Amendment and to entitle respondent to a new sentencing proceeding. * * *

NOTES AND QUESTIONS

1.   It is important, when representing clients who committed gruesome crimes, to attempt to see the defendant as a person. There are few individuals who are truly evil, who commit crimes for no reason or for reasons that are unfathomable to those of us who do not commit crimes. According to David von Drehle, David Washington, the defendant in *Strickland v. Washington*, "could often be heard weeping in his cell" on death row. Most of the men on death row "have nothing but empty space where their conscience should be," but observers thought that Washington's "remorse was real and gut-wrenching." David von Drehle, Among the Lowest of the Dead 134 (1995).

And how did someone who felt real remorse do the awful deeds that he did? Out of work, depressed, and worried about supporting his family, he was in a laundromat when a man identified himself as a minister and made a proposition—if Washington came to the minister's home, there might be money in it for him. What he did not know until later was that the proposition was sexual in nature; it included "that Washington strip and straddle his face." Washington would later explain: "I stabbed him about five times. The only thing going through my mind, I said, 'Here I am out here trying to get some money to feed my family, and here go a minister supposed to be a minister in the church, running around doing stuff like this.'" *Id.*

2.   With this knowledge of David Washington, and attempting to put out of your mind that the evidence against him was overwhelming, how would you grade counsel's performance in handling the case? Consider yourself a professor who teaches a course in representing criminal defendants, forget about the crime committed, focus on the details of what counsel did and did not do, and give the lawyer in this case a grade from the following list: C (competent); D (less than competent but within the range of reasonable); D- (barely above the line of incompetence); F (incompetent). (If you think a grade of A or B is justified, see us after class!)

Put another way, imagine you were the lawyer in *Strickland* and you are later describing your performance to your spouse, your parents, or your children. Would you be proud of your accomplishment? Satisfied? Embarrassed?

(We do not minimize the harm that David Washington caused or his blameworthiness for that harm. According to von Drehle, one of Washington's crimes was to kidnap a student from the University of Miami, rob him, and stab him to death "as the young man recited the Lord's prayer." *Id.* at 134.)

3.   The Court in Strickland said that "[p]revailing norms of practice as reflected in the American Bar Association standards and the like are guidelines to determining what is reasonable [representation]. . . ." The 2015 standards about the duty to investigate the case have been substantially revised since the 1994 version. Standard 4–4.1 (b) now states: "The duty to investigate is not terminated by factors such as the apparent force of the prosecution's evidence, a client's alleged admissions to others of facts suggesting guilt, a client's expressed desire to plead guilty or that there should be no investigation, or statements to defense counsel supporting guilt."

It's almost as if the writer had the *Strickland* facts in front of her when she crafted the 2015 standard about the duty to investigate. Using the 2015 standard, would you find the lawyer's representation reasonable?

4.   *Categories of denial of counsel.* The Court in *Strickland* draws a distinction between "actual or constructive denial of the assistance of counsel altogether," and the denial through "actual ineffectiveness." The difference is between not having a lawyer at all (or having one that the State has disabled in some significant way), and having one that is free to provide assistance of counsel but fails to do so. The former category is exemplified by *Gideon v. Wainwright*, p. 1043, where the State refused to provide a lawyer to an indigent defendant, and Geders v. United States, 425 U.S. 80, 96 S.Ct. 1330,

47 L.Ed.2d 592 (1976), where the trial judge prohibited the defendant from consulting with his lawyer during an overnight recess. These cases are relatively easy; one merely has to decide whether the defendant had a right to have a lawyer (*Gideon*) or whether the restraints on the lawyer were an unjustifiable interference with the lawyer-client relationship (*Geders*).

The second category—no state interference but ineffective representation—is *Strickland*. These cases are much more difficult than the structural denial.

Insight in how to approach *Strickland* cases can be gained from a hybrid doctrine that bridges the gap between the categories—the conflict-of-interest cases. In Holloway v. Arkansas, 435 U.S. 475, 98 S.Ct. 1173, 55 L.Ed.2d 426 (1978), the trial judge refused to appoint separate counsel for defendants being tried jointly even though the single public defender stated that he was operating with a conflict of interest. The trial judge refused even to have a hearing on the conflict question. Here, because the State (through the judge) was directly interfering with the ability of the lawyer to provide zealous and loyal representation, the Court reversed without regard to whether the defendant could show actual prejudice. The Court held that when the trial judge is apprised of a potential conflict from joint representation, he must hold a hearing; the failure to hold a hearing requires automatic reversal on Sixth Amendment grounds.

Cuyler v. Sullivan, 446 U.S. 335, 347, 100 S.Ct. 1708, 64 L.Ed.2d 333 (1980), on the other hand, involved a retained lawyer, who did nothing to put the judge on notice that he was laboring under a conflict of interest. The Court rejected the facile distinction between retained and appointed lawyers, finding that ineffective assistance by retained lawyers is just as much a violation of the Sixth Amendment as if the lawyer is appointed. But the Court did find a major difference between *Cuyler* and *Holloway*—the lack of actual notice to the judge in *Cuyler* that a conflict might exist. In *Cuyler* the State did not directly abridge the lawyer's ability to defend the client by failing to inquire into the potential conflict, and no rule of automatic reversal thus applies. *Cuyler* is more like *Strickland*, requiring proof that an actual conflict existed (a form of ineffective assistance) and that the conflict "adversely affected" the lawyer's performance (a form of prejudice). *Holloway*, on the other hand, is more like *Gideon*—if the trial judge fails to inquire when put on notice, both lack of assistance and prejudice will be presumed.

In Mickens v. Taylor, 535 U.S. 162, 122 S.Ct. 1237, 152 L.Ed.2d 291 (2002), the Court made clear that *Holloway* mandates a hearing only when trial counsel objects to the dual representation. Thus, even when the trial judge *in fact* knows of the conflict, only an objection from counsel triggers the right to a hearing and an automatic reversal if no hearing is held. *Mickens* stressed, however, that if there is no objection, and the defendant demonstrates a conflict that "adversely affected the lawyer's performance," the defendant need not show "prejudice" in the *Strickland* sense—that the result would have been different. Prejudice is, in effect, presumed when defendant shows a conflict that adversely affected counsel's performance.

5. *Criticisms of lawyers.* After an exhaustive study of the American indigent defense system, the Reporters for the National Committee on the Right to Counsel concluded in 2006 that a national crisis existed.

> By every measure in every report analyzing the U.S. criminal justice system, the defense function for poor people is drastically underfinanced. This lack of money is reflected in a wide range of problems, including poor people's limited access to attorneys and the resulting ineffective assistance of counsel, * * * excessive public defender caseloads and insufficient salaries and compensation for defense lawyers.

Mary Sue Backus & Paul Marcus, *The Right to Counsel in Criminal Cases, A National Crisis*, 57 Hastings L. J. 1031, 1045–46 (2006).

Backus and Marcus offered many examples of the crisis in indigent representation. For example:

> Poor people account for more than 80% of individuals prosecuted. These criminal defendants plead guilty approximately 90% of the time. In those cases, more than half the lawyers entered pleas for their clients without spending any significant time on the cases, without interviewing witnesses or filing motions. Sometimes they barely spoke with their clients.

> An attorney was found to have entered pleas of guilty for more than 300 defendants without ever taking a matter to trial. In one case from Mississippi, a woman accused of a minor shoplifting offense spent a year in jail, before any trial, without even speaking to her appointed counsel. In some places, one lawyer may handle more than twenty criminal cases in a single day, with a flat rate of $50 per case. In others, some defense lawyers providing counsel to indigent defendants under a state contract system can be responsible for more than 1000 cases per year. In one major metropolitan area, San Jose, California, numerous defense attorneys failed to take simple steps to investigate and prepare their cases for trial. Some attorneys went to trial without ever meeting their clients outside the courtroom. Some neglected to interview obvious alibi witnesses. Some accepted without question reports from prosecutors' medical and forensic experts that were ripe for challenge.

Id. at 1034–35.

The National Committee on the Right to Counsel included prosecutors, judges, defense lawyers, and academics. The honorary co-chairs were Walter Mondale, Democratic candidate for president in 1984, and William Sessions, former director of the FBI. In 2009, the committee issued a report entitled *Justice Denied: America's Continuing Neglect of our Constitutional Right to*

Counsel. The report details systemic and endemic failures of indigent defense in this country. It found "overwhelming" evidence that, in most of the country, "quality defense work is simply impossible because of inadequate funding, excessive caseloads, a lack of genuine independence, and insufficient availability of other essential resources."

The report provides twenty-two recommendations for improvement and can be found at http://tcpjusticedenied.org/.

6.   *Criticisms of Strickland.* The Court's opinion in *Strickland* has not met with favor among the commentators. "Scholars have concluded that the *Strickland* approach is a cynical dead end, designed to affirm all but the most deeply flawed convictions." George C. Thomas III, *History's Lesson for the Right to Counsel*, 2004 U. Ill. L. Rev. 543, 547. One problem, identified by Professor Donald Dripps, is that the appellate review is of a record made by the lawyer charged with incompetence: "It is all but ludicrous to ask a reviewing court to assess a record made by counsel to determine how counsel erred. As one might expect, this inquiry has done little to improve the quality of defense representation." Donald A. Dripps, *Ineffective Assistance of Counsel: The Case for an Ex Ante Parity Standard*, 88 J. Crim. L. & Criminology 242, 243 (1997). As the title of this article implies, Professor Dripps would replace the *Strickland* after-the-fact inquiry with an ex ante standard that requires the judge to determine, prior to the trial, "whether the defendant's lawyer can effectively represent him. Because the effectiveness of counsel is relative to the opposition, the test should be whether the defendant is represented by a lawyer roughly as good and roughly as well-prepared as counsel for the prosecution." *Id.* at 244.

7.   *Why did Justice Brennan concur in Strickland?* Professor Vivian Berger, in the excerpt that follows, calls Brennan's concurrence "puzzling." We agree.

VIVIAN O. BERGER—THE SUPREME COURT AND DEFENSE COUNSEL: OLD ROADS, NEW PATHS—A DEAD END?

86 Columbia Law Review 9 (1986), 112–116.

The "moral bases of attribution in the counsel/client relationship" * * * are most tenuous in criminal proceedings. The bulk of clients do not choose their own lawyers and the stakes are liberty and, at times, even life. Yet in our complex, adversarial system, practical responsibility for the accused's cause will inevitably fall upon his professional representative unless he forgoes a lawyer entirely. * * *

Given this fact, the Court's long-awaited treatment of the subject was disappointing. The *Strickland* majority's weighty presumption of lawyer competence (despite an otherwise acceptable test of "reasonable" performance) appeared to abolish the problem by fiat. If the language of presumption and deference can be relegated to some extent to the realm of rhetoric, the burden that the Court imposed on defendants to demonstrate actual prejudice cannot. Altogether, the justices signaled an intent to shield at least appellate courts from more than minimal involvement with claims of inadequate representation, leaving it to defendants themselves and conscientious trial court judges to deal with the problem as best they can.

But if the Court paid mere lip service to the importance of effective assistance by defense counsel while offering little by way of concrete vindication of the right, one must ask, nonetheless, how much difference it would have made had a better opinion been written in *Strickland.* Few people would disagree that upsetting convictions is an inefficient way to guarantee effective assistance—not to mention the systemic costs that vacating judgments invariably inflicts. One can only speculate whether reversals of judgments or grants of the writ [of habeas corpus] educate the target population of lawyers. Very likely, these decisions have greater impact on the judiciary, teaching courts what types of conduct by attorneys will not pass constitutional muster.

I believe that the justices might have at least increased the probability of such beneficial fallout by declining to make the element of prejudice the centerpiece of their analysis. However, reformers attempting to enhance the quality of counsel's representation have fielded much more ambitious programs than simply varying the legal standards used to evaluate lawyer performance after the fact. Suggestions range from exhortations to trial judges to monitor attorneys in pending cases— by inquiring into counsel preparation and client satisfaction—to calls for broad systemic improvements. The latter include continuing legal education, professional certification or specialization requirements for practice in certain courts or subjects, more clinically oriented law school training, higher pay and greater auxiliary resources for assigned counsel, and structural changes in the delivery of defense services.

* * * Not surprisingly, none [of these proposals] promises to yield a ready panacea for the problem of ineffective assistance, and a number pose difficulties of their own; yet some merit further exploration. For present purposes, I wish to make only one point concerning such ideas: individually and as a group, they largely resist constitutionalization. In *Strickland*—which involved a state conviction—the Court was, of course, necessarily expounding the Constitution.

* * * [I]t is hard to find power in the federal courts to order expansive structural remedies addressed to the qualifications of counsel or the organization or funding of defender associations. The most generous conception of the Court's authority to mold constitutional "common law" could hardly sustain many needed forms of systemic relief, although it might conceivably permit some form of mandated trial court procedures designed to smoke out lawyer incompetence before irremediable damage

occurs. * * * I believe that there is little in a practical vein the Court could have done, or can do in the future, to promote competent performance by counsel. If I am correct, perhaps Justice Brennan's puzzling concurrence with the *Strickland* majority stems from understandable reluctance to face that extremely discomfiting fact. * * *

In short, the Court's visions of the right to counsel and the role of counsel are incoherent, or downright cynical. In this area, most of the justices have failed to speak thoughtfully and candidly about the issues, an obligation that the Court as teacher owes us always. With regard to inadequate representation, even an honest acknowledgment of the Court's limitations might have encouraged further thought about solutions transcending the factual and legal bounds of particular cases as well as the jurisdictional constraints of a Court construing the Constitution. Thus, the road mapped in *Powell*, *Gideon*, and *Douglas* has petered out in a dead end, at least for now. Signposts for new directions for counsel will have to come from a different source.

NOTES AND QUESTIONS

1.   *The end of the David Washington story.*

> He was ashamed and remorseful to the very end; he had that small credit. As his twelve-year-old daughter sobbed through their final visit, he cupped her trembling chin in his hand and said: "I want you to look at me, and I want you to see where I am * * * and I want you to do better."

David von Drehle, Among the Lowest of the Dead 254 (1995).

2.   *Startling ignorance.* In Kimmelman v. Morrison, 477 U.S. 365, 106 S.Ct. 2574, 91 L.Ed.2d 305 (1986), the charge was rape, the defense was that it never happened, and an important piece of evidence was a bedsheet taken without a warrant from defendant's apartment. Here is how Justice Powell, concurring in the judgment, characterized the performance issue:

> [Defendant]'s ineffective-assistance claim is uncomplicated. [Defendant] argues that his trial counsel incompetently failed to conduct any pretrial discovery. Had counsel conducted discovery, he would have known that the police had seized a bedsheet from [defendant]'s apartment without a warrant. The bedsheet contained hair samples matching hair of both [defendant] and the rape victim. The sheet also contained semen stains matching those found in the victim's underpants. The State introduced the bedsheet and accompanying expert analysis at trial, and the trial judge denied [defendant]'s belated motion to suppress on the ground that it was untimely. [Defendant] contends that the sheet would have been excluded on Fourth Amendment grounds had the suppression motion been timely filed. Thus, [defendant] argues, counsel's failure

to conduct discovery led to the admission of evidence that was both damning and excludible.

Counsel's "explanation" for his failure to conduct discovery was two-fold. First, he "asserted that it was the State's obligation to inform him of its case against his client, even though he made no request for discovery." Second, counsel said "he had not expected to go to trial because he had been told that the victim did not wish to proceed." The Supreme Court unanimously held that these explanations were not sufficient to bring the case under the *Strickland* rule that trial strategy is generally not to be second-guessed. As the Court put it: "The justifications [defendant]'s attorney offered for his omission betray a startling ignorance of the law—or a weak attempt to shift blame for inadequate preparation." The Court remanded for a hearing on prejudice.

3. *Another failure to know the relevant law.* The critical aspect of *Kimmelman*, Note 2, seems to be defense counsel's "ignorance" of law that was easily known. Continuing in that vein is Padilla v. Kentucky, 559 U.S. 356, 130 S.Ct. 1473, 176 L.Ed.2d 284 (2010), where counsel did not advise his client that a state narcotics conviction would make him subject to automatic deportation under federal law. Padilla had been "a lawful permanent resident of the United States for more than 40 years" and had "served this Nation with honor as a member of the U.S. Armed Forces during the Vietnam War." His lawyer not only failed to advise him of the automatic deportation but also affirmatively misled him by telling him that he " 'did not have to worry about immigration status since he had been in the country so long.' " Thus unaware of his situation, Padilla pled guilty to drug transportation charges.

The Court held that counsel's failure to warn Padilla of the consequences of his guilty plea (automatic deportation) "fell below" *Strickland*'s "objective standard of reasonableness." and thus constituted constitutionally deficient performance. "[W]hen the deportation consequence is truly clear, as it was in this case, the duty to give correct advice is equally clear." Justice Scalia, joined by Justice Thomas, dissented.

Justice Alito, concurring in the judgment, would have accepted the Solicitor General's request to limit the holding to "affirmative misadvice," but the majority refused to do so. "It is quintessentially the duty of counsel to provide her client with available advice about an issue like deportation and the failure to do so 'clearly satisfies the first prong of the *Strickland* analysis.' "

Notice that the deportation law in *Padilla* was "not within the sentencing authority of the state trial court." As the Court conceded, many courts had taken the position that failure to advise a client about "collateral consequences" of a conviction could never be constitutionally deficient performance. That is no longer true, though the full scope of *Padilla* is unknown. Will it be limited to collateral consequences spelled out in a statute that is, in the Court's words, "succinct, clear, and explicit"? Will it also be limited to the consequence of deportation, which the Court noted it had "long recognized" as a "particularly severe" penalty?

Finally, the Court did not reach *Strickland*'s second prong—whether the constitutionally deficient performance resulted in constitutionally recognized prejudice, which is likely to prove a particularly daunting challenge for most defendants. In Hill v. Lockhart, 474 U.S. 52, 58, 106 S.Ct. 366, 88 L.Ed.2d 203 (1985) (see p. 1154), the Court suggested that proving prejudice when ineffective assistance led to a guilty plea entails more than merely proving that the client would have insisted on pleading not guilty. At one point, *Hill* phrased the prejudice inquiry as whether the outcome of the *trial* "would have been different" had the defendant pled not guilty. In *Padilla*, the Court phrased the issue as "whether 'there is a reasonable probability that, but for counsel's unprofessional errors, the result of the *proceeding* would have been different.'" (Emphasis added.) And in a footnote, the Court ominously noted "that it is often quite difficult for petitioners who have acknowledged their guilt to satisfy *Strickland*'s prejudice prong."

Padilla pled guilty to three drug-related charges and agreed to serve five years in prison and be on probation for five years after his release from prison. See Commonwealth v. Padilla, 253 S.W.3d 482 (Ky. 2008). Presumably, he made that decision because the State had a strong case. So, even if he persuades a reviewing court that he would have gone to trial, the State can seek to show that a conviction was likely and thus would have resulted in the same deportation order. How likely a conviction would have to be to avoid a finding of prejudice is yet one more unknown left in the wake of *Padilla*.

4.   *Yet one more failure to know the relevant law.* In Hinton v. Alabama, 571 U.S. ___, 134 S.Ct. 1081, 188 L.Ed.2d 1 (2014) (per curiam), the defendant was tried in 1985 for two murders. The critical—and essentially the only—evidence against defendant was the testimony of the state forensics experts that the bullets that killed the victims came from defendant's gun. Thus, the testimony of a defense expert was central to the defense. Both the trial judge and the defense lawyer believed that the State only allowed $1,000 to pay an expert witness. The judge invited the defense lawyer to request more if needed and he would check to see whether more money could be awarded. The lawyer, however, did not request additional funding. Had he done so, the judge would presumably have discovered that Alabama had removed the limit on reimbursing defense experts in capital cases more than a year before Hinton's trial.

The lawyer made an "extensive search for a well-regarded expert," but could find only one expert, Andrew Payne, willing to testify for $1,000. Hinton's lawyer "testified that Payne did not have the expertise he thought he needed and that he did not consider Payne's testimony to be effective." Indeed, that might be an understatement. Here is how the Court characterized Payne's effectiveness:

On cross-examination, the prosecutor badly discredited Payne. Payne admitted that he'd testified as an expert on firearms and toolmark identification just twice in the preceding eight years and that one of the two cases involved a shotgun rather than a handgun. Payne also conceded that he had had difficulty operating the microscope at the state forensic laboratory and had asked for help from one of the state experts. The prosecutor ended the cross-examination with this colloquy:

"Q. Mr. Payne, do you have some problem with your vision?

"A. Why, yes.

"Q. How many eyes do you have?

"A. One."

The jury convicted, and Hinton was sentenced to die. Both on direct appeal and in post-conviction review, the Alabama courts held that Payne was qualified as an expert witness under the Alabama standard, which required only that the witness have "knowledge of firearms and toolmarks examination beyond that of an average layperson."

The Supreme Court unanimously reversed the state courts, holding that the defense lawyer's "failure to request additional funding in order to replace an expert he knew to be inadequate because he mistakenly believed that he had received all he could get under Alabama law constituted deficient performance." The Court stressed that the deficient performance was not hiring the wrong expert: "We do not today launch federal courts into examination of the relative qualifications of experts hired and experts that might have been hired." Instead, the "inadequate assistance of counsel here was the inexcusable mistake of law—the unreasonable failure to understand the resources that state law made available to him—that caused counsel to employ an expert that he *himself* deemed inadequate." (Emphasis in original).

Holding that "no court has yet evaluated the prejudice question by applying the proper inquiry to the facts of this case," the Court remanded on that issue. But the Court seemed to be sending a broad hint that it considered prejudicial the failure to hire a competent expert. Notice the emphasis on the possibility that Hinton might be innocent:

That the State presented testimony from two experienced expert witnesses that tended to inculpate Hinton does not, taken alone, demonstrate that Hinton is guilty. Prosecution experts, of course, can sometimes make mistakes. * * * This threat is minimized when the defense retains a competent expert to counter the testimony of the prosecution's expert witnesses; it is maximized when the defense instead fails to understand the resources available to it by law.

5.   *Hinton, the man, and the rest of the story.* On remand, the Alabama trial court held "that counsel, in fact, would have hired a different and more qualified expert had counsel known that the statutory-funding limit had been lifted and that there was a reasonable probability that the testimony of a different and more qualified expert would have instilled in the jury a reasonable doubt as to Hinton's guilt." Hinton v. State, 172 So.3d 355 (Ct. Crim. App. Ala. 2014). The trial judge thus granted Hinton's petition to vacate his two convictions.

Faced with the prospect of retrying Hinton, state prosecutors conceded that his guilt "depends upon an absolute, conclusive determination that the bullets recovered from their bodies were in fact fired through the barrel of the firearm taken from the defendant's home." After new tests, the State's own experts "found that they could not conclusively determine that any of the six bullets were or were not fired through the same firearm or that they were fired through the firearm recovered from the defendant's home." Prosecutors moved to dismiss the case against Hinton. Alan Blinder, "Alabama Man Freed After Decades on Death Row," *New York Times*, April 3, 2015.

Hinton "spoke of unjustly losing three decades of his life, under fear of execution, for something he didn't do. 'All they had to do was to test the gun, but when you think you're high and mighty and you're above the law, you don't have to answer to nobody,' " Hinton told reporters.

"But I've got news for you—everybody that played a part in sending me to death row, you will answer to God." Jason Hanna and Ed Payne, "Alabama Inmate Freed After Nearly 30 Years on Death Row," *CNN*, April 3, 2015.

"And, haltingly, he began to talk about mercy. 'I've got to forgive,' he said. 'I lived in hell for 30 years, so I don't want to die and go to hell. So I've got to forgive. I don't have a choice.' " Blinder, *New York Times*.

6.   *And more about Alabama indigent defense.* In Maples v. Thomas, 565 U.S. ___, 132 S.Ct. 912, 181 L.Ed.2d 807 (2012), the defendant procedurally defaulted his state post-conviction proceedings by missing a filing deadline. Normally, defaulting state remedies precludes federal habeas corpus relief. See Chapter 19. The Court held, however, that there was "cause" for his failure to meet the deadline.

The Court began its opinion in *Maples* by describing the Alabama procedure for appointing counsel in capital cases:

> Alabama sets low eligibility requirements for lawyers appointed to represent indigent capital defendants at trial. Appointed counsel need only be a member of the Alabama bar and have "five years' prior experience in the active practice of criminal law." Experience with capital cases is not required. Nor does the State provide, or require appointed counsel to gain, any capital-case-specific professional education or training.

> Appointed counsel in death penalty cases are also undercompensated. Until 1999, the State paid appointed capital

defense attorneys just "$40.00 per hour for time expended in court and $20.00 per hour for time reasonably expended out of court in the preparation of [the defendant's] case." Although death penalty litigation is plainly time intensive, the State capped at $1,000 fees recoverable by capital defense attorneys for out-of-court work. Even today, court-appointed attorneys receive only $70 per hour.

Nearly alone among the States, Alabama does not guarantee representation to indigent capital defendants in postconviction proceedings. The State has elected, instead, "to rely on the efforts of typically well-funded [out-of-state] volunteers." Thus, as of 2006, 86% of the attorneys representing Alabama's death row inmates in state collateral review proceedings "either worked for the Equal Justice Initiative (headed by NYU Law professor Bryan Stevenson), out-of-state public interest groups like the Innocence Project, or an out-of-state mega-firm." On occasion, some prisoners sentenced to death receive no postconviction representation at all. See ABA Report 112 ("[A]s of April 2006, approximately fifteen of Alabama's death row inmates in the final rounds of state appeals had no lawyer to represent them.").

For a biting critique of the representation of counsel in death cases, see Vivian O. Berger, *The Chiropractor as Brain Surgeon: Defense Lawyering in Capital Cases*, 18 N.Y.U. Rev. L. & Social Change 245 (1990); Stephen B. Bright, *Death By Lottery—Procedural Bar of Constitutional Claims in Capital Cases Due to Inadequate Representation of Indigent Defendants*, 92 W. Va. L. Rev. 679 (1990).

BRUCE A. GREEN—LETHAL FICTION: THE MEANING OF "COUNSEL" IN THE SIXTH AMENDMENT
78 Iowa Law Review 433, 433, 437 (1993).

Charles Bell, Donald Paradis, and Shirley Tyler were tried in different states for murder. Each was convicted and sentenced to death. Charles Bell was represented at trial by a recent law school graduate who had never before tried a criminal case to completion. Donald Paradis's lawyer had passed the bar exam six months earlier, had never previously represented a criminal accused, and had not elected courses in criminal law, criminal procedure, or trial advocacy while in law school. Shirley Tyler's trial lawyer was also a member of the bar for only a few months. He had defended one previous assault case and one previous robbery case, each lasting half a day. Each condemned prisoner later asserted that he or she had been denied the Sixth Amendment right of a criminal accused "to have the assistance of counsel for his defence" on the ground that the defense attorney had rendered ineffective legal assistance. In asserting this claim, each undertook the difficult burden of demonstrating the likelihood that he or she had received a sentence of death only because of the attorney's unreasonably poor performance.

Not surprisingly, none of the three death-row defendants claimed to have been deprived of "counsel" altogether, since courts unwaveringly adhere to the view that "counsel" under the Sixth Amendment includes any duly licensed attorney. This Article argues, however, that a narrower construction of the constitutional term is warranted: "counsel" should include only those attorneys who are qualified to render legal assistance to a person accused of a crime. By that standard, these three defendants, and many others who similarly have been tried, convicted, and sentenced to death with an unqualified attorney by their side, have been deprived of their right to "counsel." * * *

[This Article] describes what redefining "counsel" would mean for the criminal justice system. To be regarded as "counsel" for constitutional purposes, a member of the bar should possess the skill and knowledge understood within the profession as prerequisites to defending criminal cases adequately. The right to "counsel," meaning a qualified advocate, would not supplant the presently recognized right to effective assistance of counsel, but would supplement it. Criminal defendants would be entitled, at the threshold, to a qualified attorney. In individual cases in which a seemingly capable lawyer provided substandard representation, a convicted defendant could claim that he was denied the right to effective assistance of counsel.

Because most lawyers do not possess the requisite skill and knowledge to be qualified to defend a criminal case, some mechanism to train and certify those lawyers must be established. Courts are undoubtedly capable of establishing such a mechanism. The judiciary is, after all, responsible for the existing licensing process, and some courts already have established processes either for certifying criminal lawyers as specialists or for determining which lawyers are qualified to serve by assignment in criminal cases. Moreover, legislatures are equally capable of devising a process for upgrading the quality of criminal defense lawyers. Congress, for one, recently considered legislation designed in part to improve the quality of defense lawyers in death penalty cases.

NOTES AND QUESTIONS

1.   *Sleeping beauty.* According to a court clerk assigned to the trial judge, Calvin Burdine's lawyer slept "a lot" and "for long periods of time" during the prosecution's questioning of witnesses in a death penalty trial. Yet a Fifth Circuit panel held that this fact, by itself, did not automatically require a finding that the counsel was ineffective. Burdine v. Johnson, 231 F.3d 950 (5th Cir. 2000). To be sure, an en banc decision overturned the panel, by a vote of nine to five—see Burdine v. Johnson, 262 F.3d 336 (5th

Cir. 2001)—but it might give one pause that five members of the Fifth Circuit did not believe that a sleeping lawyer is necessarily an ineffective one.

2. *Awake but little more.* Prior to jury selection in a capital murder trial, defense counsel files a motion for continuance, stating that he is "totally unprepared to begin with this case." The judge denied the motion. Defense counsel questions the jury but at the close of *voir dire* refuses to exercise any of his client's peremptory challenges (available to exclude potential jurors if a challenge for cause fails). He renews his motion for a continuance and when the judge again denies it, states: "[I]f we are going ahead with this trial, * * * I will be physically present because I am sure the Court would require that, but I do not in any way intend to participate in the trial of this matter." He again asserts that he is unprepared and physically exhausted. He attends the trial but does not participate in any way. The jury convicted and, after a sentencing hearing, the judge sentenced *H* to die. State v. Harvey, 692 S.W.2d 290 (Mo.1985).

This is either the most fundamental failure imaginable or a clever strategy. Do you see how it could be a strategy? Is there a way for the judge to defeat the strategy short of having to grant the continuance?

3. *Does this sound like effective assistance to you?* Cronic was "indicted on mail fraud charges involving the transfer of over $9,400,000 in checks." About a month before the scheduled trial date, respondent's retained counsel withdrew. (Dressler and Thomas speculate that the fee was not paid).

> The court appointed a young lawyer with a real estate practice to represent respondent, but allowed him only 25 days for pretrial preparation, even though it had taken the Government over four and one-half years to investigate the case and it had reviewed thousands of documents during that investigation. The two codefendants agreed to testify for the Government; respondent was convicted on 11 of the 13 counts in the indictment and received a 25-year sentence.

The Court unanimously held that these facts, standing alone, did not justify a finding of ineffective assistance of counsel (Justice Marshall concurred in the judgment). See United States v. Cronic, 466 U.S. 648, 104 S. Ct. 2039, 80 L. Ed. 2d 657 (1984). On the assumption that the Court did not temporarily lose its mind, explain the narrow holding.

4. *The simple closing argument.* Death penalty cases require a separate sentencing phase, as you saw in *Strickland*. What if the defense lawyer failed to present *any* mitigating evidence in the sentencing phase and a court later found "sufficient grounds" to argue several mitigating factors, including "youth, intoxication, and family background"? The only defense at sentencing consisted of the following closing argument:

> Defense Counsel: Ladies and Gentlemen, I appreciate the time you took deliberating and the thought you put into this. I'm going to be extremely brief. I have a reputation for not being brief.

Jesse, stand up. Jesse?

The Defendant: Sir?

Defense Counsel: Stand up.

> You are an extremely intelligent jury. You've got that man's life in your hands. You can take it or not. That's all I have to say.

Is this effective assistance under *Strickland*? See Romero v. Lynaugh, 884 F.2d 871 (5th Cir. 1989).

5.   *Thank God it's over.* In another capital case, the crime was a brutal rape and murder of an eight-year-old girl; she suffered six stab wounds to the body and five knife slashes traversing her abdomen, along with numerous lacerations and abrasions on her face, neck, and upper chest. At the close of the *guilt* phase, defense counsel argued as follows:

> I would be [dishonest] with each and every one of you if I tried to tell you the evidence said something other than what [the prosecutor] indicates occurred on that day so I'm not going to. * * * I don't think in a situation like this there's anything that I can say except to say thank God this is over. * * * I pray to God that none of you or myself, or the other people in this court room, will ever see anything like this again. I'm not going to be dishonest to y'all and say something to change what is, the evidence is, what the evidence is, the law the judge gives you as to how to consider this evidence. That's all I have. Thank you.

Assuming the evidence of guilt was overwhelming, does this closing argument at the guilt phase meet the *Strickland* standard? See Messer v. Kemp, 760 F.2d 1080 (11th Cir. 1985).

6.   *Forgiveness from heaven.* Same case as Note 5. The jury convicts. At the sentencing phase, the lawyer presents a single witness, the defendant's mother, and elicits from her that she and the defendant both expected the death penalty. She also testified that the defendant "has got saved, he's confessed his sins to Christ, and he told me, he said 'mama, the Lord has forgiven me * * * .' "

In the closing argument in the sentencing phase, the lawyer said to the jury, "[Your decision] is an awesome responsibility and I dare say I would rather be over here than in y'all's seats, because as a parent under these circumstances"—here he paused before continuing—"but that's for y'all to decide." Is this effective representation under *Strickland*?

7.   *Is the Court quietly requiring more competent lawyering in death cases?* Two of the Court's recent death cases suggest that *Strickland*'s refusal to engage in "Monday-morning quarter-backing" seems to be receding a bit. To be sure, *Strickland* claims in death cases are even more fact-sensitive and complex than in ordinary run-of-the mill cases, and it is difficult to generalize.

The defendant in Wiggins v. Smith, 539 U.S. 510, 123 S.Ct. 2527, 156 L.Ed.2d 471 (2003), convinced the Court that his lawyer was ineffective because he did not investigate the severe physical and sexual abuse at the hands of his mother and under the care of a series of foster parents. Notably, the Court was willing to rely on the standards for capital defense work articulated by the American Bar Association, which require "efforts to discover *all reasonably available* mitigating evidence and evidence to rebut any aggravating evidence that may be introduced by the prosecutor." ABA Guidelines for the Appointment and Performance of Counsel in Death Penalty Cases 11.4.1(C), p. 93 (1989) (emphasis added). Might Washington have proven lack of competence of his counsel if the *Strickland* Court had applied that standard? To be sure, the ABA Guidelines appeared five years after *Strickland* was decided, but evolving guidelines can be viewed as part of a partial retreat from *Strickland*.

In Rompilla v. Beard, 545 U.S. 374, 125 S.Ct. 2456, 162 L.Ed.2d 360 (2005), the defendant's trial lawyers worked harder than did Wiggins's lawyers to find mitigating evidence. They interviewed five family members in a "detailed manner" and reviewed the reports of three mental health experts who examined Rompilla. But the lawyers did not review a court file, readily available in the courthouse, containing material about one of Rompilla's prior convictions. The prosecutor had told defense counsel that he was going to use the rape victim's testimony in the prior case to prove Rompilla's violent character, which was relevant to an aggravating circumstance under the state death penalty law. Defense lawyers read the victim's testimony in the court file but did not examine the rest of the file. If defense lawyers had examined the file completely, they would have found mitigating evidence. The Court held that this constituted deficient defense. Is this really more deficient than the utter failure of the lawyer in *Strickland* to investigate his client's possible emotional disturbance? Perhaps. Justice O'Connor, the author of *Strickland*, joined the *Rompilla* majority.

8. *Foggy mirrors.* Perhaps the pithiest criticism of the *Strickland* test is that some defense counsel call it the "foggy mirror" test. "If you place a mirror in front of defense counsel during trial and it fogs, counsel is in fact effective." Randall Coyne, Capital Punishment and the Judicial Process, Teacher's Manual 148 (1995).

9. *Can an indigent defendant sue his foggy mirror for malpractice?* The answer, in Minnesota at least, is no. See Dziubak v. Mott, 503 N.W.2d 771 (Minn. 1993). But, wait, you say: privately-retained lawyers can be sued by criminal clients for malpractice so why not publicly-financed lawyers? The court offered two reasons: first, unlike private counsel, public defenders have no choice about which clients to accept: the defender "is obligated to represent whomever is assigned to her or him, regardless of her or his current caseload or the degree of difficulty the case presents." Second, public defenders are grossly underfunded. "It would be an unfair burden to subject the public defender to possible malpractice for acts or omissions due to impossible

caseloads and an under-funded office: something completely out of the defender's control."

10. *Chances of winning an ineffective assistance claim.* The Center for Capital Litigators in Columbia, South Carolina has collected citations and summaries of all published successful ineffective assistance of counsel claims since *Strickland.* As of December, 2001, the list contained roughly 1,200 state and federal cases. Running *Strickland* in Westlaw for the same time period produced about 37,000 entries. Thus, as the lower courts have understood and applied *Strickland,* lawyers provided constitutionally competent assistance in roughly 97% of the cases where their performance was challenged. Perhaps Justice O'Connor would say that this demonstrates the basic soundness of lawyering in criminal cases. Perhaps it does.

CHAPTER 15

PLEA BARGAINING AND GUILTY PLEAS

■ ■ ■

"During most of the history of the common law, pleas of guilty were actively discouraged by English and American courts. For centuries, litigation was thought 'the safest test of justice.' The past one hundred years have, however, seen a revolution in methods of criminal procedure." Albert W. Alschuler, *The Prosecutor's Role in Plea Bargaining*, 36 U. Chi. L. Rev. 50, 50 (1968).

Indeed, today, the supposed "safest test of justice"—a criminal trial— is an endangered—in fact, nearly extinct—species. According to recent data, 97.47% of federal felony convictions in 2011–2012, and 94% or more of state convictions are the result of guilty pleas. Dept. of Justice, Federal Justice Statistics, 2012—Statistical Table (NCJ 248870, Jan. 2015); Dept. of Justice, Bureau of Justice Statistics, S. Rosenmerkel, M. Durose, & D. Farole, Felony Sentences in State Courts, 2006-Statistical Tables, p. 1 (NCJ226846, rev. Nov. 2010). (Cited in Missouri v. Frye, 566 U.S. ___, 132 S.Ct. 1399, 182 L.Ed.2d 379 (2012).) In short, in the overwhelming majority of criminal prosecutions, defendants waive the constitutional procedural protections of a criminal trial, including the presumption of innocence, the privilege against compulsory self-incrimination, the right to confront and cross-examine accusers, the right to call witness on one's own behalf, and the right to a public and speedy trial by jury. As the Supreme Court recently put it, "the reality [is] that criminal justice today is for the most part a system of pleas, not a system of trials." Lafler v. Cooper, 566 U.S. ___, 132 S.Ct. 1376, 182 L.Ed.2d 398 (2012).

What should we make of this data? Should we worry that defendants are pleading guilty to crimes they did not commit or, even if they are guilty, that their pleas are involuntary or uninformed? Or, should we rejoice at the fact that the criminal justice system has developed speedier, less costly procedures for reliable and fair resolution of criminal charges? As you read the materials in this chapter, consider these questions.

A. PLEA BARGAINING

1. THE BACKGROUND

Look again at the remarkable data set out above on the frequency of guilty pleas. In nearly every case, the guilty plea was the result of plea bargaining, *i.e.*, "the exchange of official concessions for a defendant's act of self-conviction." Albert W. Alschuler, *Plea Bargaining And Its History*, 79 Colum. L. Rev. 1, 3 (1979).

Though informal bargaining between parties to legal disputes has likely occurred from the beginning of law itself, formal plea bargaining was "essentially unknown during most of the history of the common law," Alschuler, *supra*, at 4. However, by the 1920s or even sooner, trial-by-jury had lost out to the plea bargaining process in the United States. George Fisher, *Plea Bargaining's Triumph*, 109 Yale L.J. 857, 859 (2000). In the early years, most bargaining occurred under the table—the court and parties would deny on the record that the guilty plea was the result of any deal—because the constitutionality of the process was in doubt. In 1970, however, the Supreme Court resolved the constitutional question in Brady v. United States, 397 U.S. 742, 90 S.Ct. 1463, 25 L.Ed.2d 747 (1970):

> [W]e cannot hold that it is unconstitutional for the State to extend a benefit to a defendant who in turn extends a substantial benefit to the State and who demonstrates by his plea that he is ready and willing to admit his crime and to enter the correctional system in a frame of mind that affords hope for success in rehabilitation over a shorter period of time than might otherwise be necessary.

With the constitutionality of plea bargaining resolved, jurisdictions implemented written procedures regulating the process. (Federal Rule 11 is the federal version.) Generally speaking plea agreements in state and federal courts involve one or more of three types of deals. First, in a dismissal agreement, "[i]f the defendant pleads guilty or nolo contendere to either a charged offense or a lesser or related offense, the plea agreement may specify that an attorney for the government will not bring, or will move to dismiss, other charges." Fed. R. Crim. P. 11(c)(1)(A).

Second, in sentencing agreements, the parties agree that, in exchange for a plea of guilty or *nolo contendere*, a specific sentence or sentencing range will be imposed. Fed. R. Crim. P. 11(c)(1)(C). The court, upon acceptance of the plea, is bound to the agreement.

Third, in sentencing recommendation agreements, the prosecutor only agrees to make a sentencing recommendation or agrees "not to oppose the defendant's request that a particular sentence or sentencing range is appropriate." Fed. R. Crim. P. 11(c)(1)(B). This agreement offers the defendant the least benefit: The recommendation is not binding upon the court; and the defendant has no right to withdraw her plea if the court rejects the sentencing recommendation. The court must advise the defendant to this effect prior to accepting a plea based on a sentencing recommendation agreement. Fed. R. Crim. P. 11(c)(3)(B).

Professor George Fisher has written that "plea bargaining has triumphed. Bloodlessly and clandestinely, it has swept across the penal landscape and driven our vanquished jury into small pockets of resistance." Fisher, *supra*, at 859. Perhaps so. But, some "victories," such as plea bargaining, are controversial, as seen immediately below.

2. THE DEBATE

JOSHUA DRESSLER & ALAN C. MICHAELS— UNDERSTANDING CRIMINAL PROCEDURE
(Volume 2) (Fourth edition 2006), 197–203.

§ 9.06   Plea Bargaining: Policy Debate

[A]   Is Plea Bargaining Inevitable?

One scholar of plea bargaining recently wrote, "[* * *] Plea bargaining may be, as some chroniclers claim, the invading barbarian. But it has won all the same."[124]

If this is so, was this outcome inevitable? Or, perhaps as importantly, must critics of plea bargaining consider the battle over for good? The conventional wisdom is that plea bargaining is inevitable. The thesis is that if bargaining were not permitted, the guilty-plea rate * * * would drop substantially, the resulting number of trials would increase dramatically (even a one-third reduction in plea bargains could result in a 400 percent increase in the number of trials), and this would overwhelm an already beleaguered criminal justice system, causing socially unacceptable and, perhaps, even unconstitutional, delays in the distribution of justice. Consequently, plea bargaining would either be reinstituted or participants in the system would return to the days when bargaining was an under-the-table, and, therefore, unregulated, phenomenon.

Some studies support the inevitability thesis, particularly the claim that plea bargaining will be forced underground where it is not expressly permitted. * * *

On the other hand, two studies of the Philadelphia criminal justice system, one in which guilty pleas were obtained in considerably fewer cases than is the national norm, suggest that an urban criminal justice system can make trials available in most cases without insurmountable difficulties. * * *

Obviously, if plea bargaining is not inevitable, advocates of the process ought to be able to offer principled reasons why the justice system should not abolish or limit plea bargaining. Even if plea bargaining *is*

---

[124] [George Fisher, *Plea Bargaining's Triumph*, 109 Yale L.J. 857, 859 (2000).]

inevitable, this does not render policy analysis irrelevant. If bargaining is undesirable, albeit inevitable, plea negotiations should be reduced to the extent possible, and the process that remains should be more carefully regulated. If bargaining is desirable, the law should recognize this fact and allow the process to proceed in a comparatively unfettered manner. Therefore, it is still appropriate to ask whether bargaining is good in principle.

[B] Is Plea Bargaining Good in Principle?

[1] In Support of Plea Bargaining

The Supreme Court has described plea bargaining as "not only an essential part of the [criminal justice] process but a highly desirable part." Indeed, although many legal scholars are critical of plea bargaining, most of the major participants in the system—prosecutors, defense attorneys, and judges—are either "remarkably untroubled" by the process or advocates of it.

First, from the defense perspective, advocates of plea bargaining contend that the negotiation process permits the accused, presumably with the assistance of counsel, to determine rationally whether "the contemplated punishment [arising from a guilty plea] is lower than the anticipated posttrial sentence, discounted by the possibility of acquittal." Particularly if the risk of conviction is great, plea bargaining provides the defendant with an opportunity for minimizing her punishment, legal expenses, and anxiety.

Second, plea bargaining is beneficial to the prosecutor. A prosecutor seeks to obtain the optimum level of punishment—punishment that is retributively just, provides the best deterrent bite, and/or is tailored to the rehabilitative needs of the offender—at the least cost in terms of allocation of resources. In a system in which plea negotiations are permitted, she can determine the foreseeable costs of a trial, the likelihood of conviction, and the probable sentence disposition, and then use the negotiation process to "fit the crime to the punishment."

Third, as a result of plea negotiations, society more efficiently attains the objectives of criminal punishment, by ensuring that it is more promptly imposed. And, the Supreme Court has suggested, by "the avoidance of trial, scarce judicial and prosecutorial resources are conserved for those cases in which there is a substantial issue of the defendant's guilt or in which there is substantial doubt that the State can sustain its burden of proof." In short, those whose guilt is clearest are bargained out of the trial process, allowing time and energy to go to the more troubling cases. The consequence, advocates of plea bargaining assert, is that the justice system is more reliable.

Defenders of plea bargaining would have us imagine a justice system without it. There would be a huge increase in trials. Very likely, the quality of those trials would decrease dramatically, as over-burdened lawyers and judges seek to keep up with the flood of cases. As a consequence, the trial process would be less reliable than it is today. One can readily expect that, in view of the pressures such a system would place on harried defense lawyers, the higher error rate would result in the conviction of more innocent persons, especially defendants who are compelled by poverty to rely on appointed counsel, even as the overall conviction rate dropped!

[2] In Opposition to Plea Bargaining

[a] Overview: Serving the Interests of the Powerful?

According to Professor George Fisher, "[ ]like most of history's victors, plea bargaining won in great part because it served the interests of the powerful."[142] Another observer of plea bargaining has put it differently, although it may add up to much the same point: principled support for plea bargaining consists of little more than the "jurisprudence of joy," in that bargaining is deemed good simply because the process pleases the participants. But, as anti-bargaining scholars point out, the real parties in interest are the defendant and the public (including the crime victim); but their agents—defense lawyers and prosecutors—have goals that are often "far from congruent with those of their principals."

What makes the criticisms of plea bargaining especially interesting is that they come from divergent political and philosophical camps. The "hawks" oppose the process because they believe that it prejudices the crime control interests of the community. The "doves" are concerned with the effects of plea bargaining on the accused's ability to retain her constitutional trial rights.

[b] Sentencing Differential

The hawks oppose plea bargaining because, in their view, it results in undue leniency to criminals. The evidence of leniency is overwhelming in this regard: according to the United States Sentencing Commission, in the absence of sentencing guidelines that severely reduce judicial discretion, those who plead guilty are likely to receive a sentence from 30 to 40 percent below that which they would have received had they pleaded not guilty and been convicted at trial of the same offense. * * * Therefore, the hawks suggest, many wrongdoers receive a penalty far below that which is retributively justified. Reduced penalties also weaken the deterrent value of punishment.

---

[142] Fisher, * * * *supra*, at 859.

Dovish critics of plea bargaining also attack the leniency shown defendants, but their sympathies lie with those who do *not* plead guilty. As they view it, plea bargaining unfairly burdens a defendant who chooses to assert her constitutional right to a trial. In essence, the unusual defendant who forces the state to prove its case against her is penalized for her actions.

[c] Prosecutorial Overcharging

Many critics maintain that prosecutors overcharge defendants. As a result, the deal that a defendant receives during plea negotiations is largely illusory. According to some observers, prosecutors treat the charging process "like horse trading," in which "both sides start out asking for more than they expect to get." They claim that prosecutors typically divide a criminal transaction into as many offenses as they can and charge them all ("horizontal overcharging"), charge the highest degree of an offense that the evidence could even remotely permit ("vertical overcharging"), or both.

If the evidence does not support the charges filed, it is genuine overcharging. But even if there is sufficient evidence to support the charges, critics of plea bargaining reason that the purpose of the extra or heightened charges is to compel the defendant to participate in the horse trading. Ultimately, if the prosecutor succeeds, the defendant will plead guilty to an offense (or offenses) at least as serious as a jury would have convicted her at trial in a no-bargaining system. Thus, the bargain is illusory: the prosecutor ends up where she should have started or, perhaps, even better off; meanwhile, the defendant has waived her trial rights. * * *

[d] Inadequate Representation

Defense lawyers are supposed to be equalizers. They zealously and loyally defend their clients against the State, supposedly serving as "an antidote to the fear, ignorance, and bewilderment of the impoverished and uneducated defendant." * * *

Some critics of plea bargaining question whether the quality of representation of defendants in the bargaining process merits this optimistic, even romantic, view. They suggest that defense attorneys, like other people, desire money. For a private defense attorney, there are two ways to become financially successful: develop a reputation as a high-quality trial attorney; or do a high-volume business. The latter approach is the path of least resistance. But, to handle large quantities of cases, a defense lawyer must try very few of them. In short, private defense attorneys too often become "pleaders." The result is that defendants receive misleading advice, or they are unduly influenced to plead guilty by their own attorneys.

Second, even the most ethical but fatigued and overwhelmed public defender, forced to deal with huge caseloads, is apt to rely too heavily on plea bargaining. Third, public defenders have an incentive to cooperate with the prosecutors with whom they deal on a daily basis; the result is that bargaining is not always in the best interests of an individual client.

Finally, lawyers, like others, do not like to be wrong, and the decision to plead guilty is never wrong, in the sense that there is no way to determine whether the client would have been acquitted or received a more lenient penalty had she proceeded to trial. In contrast, a lawyer's recommendation *not* to plead guilty can prove to be wrong, if the defendant is convicted and receives a more severe sentence than was offered by the prosecutor. Therefore, a bias exists to accept a guilty plea.

[e] Conviction of the Innocent

* * * [C]ritics believe that lawful plea bargaining * * * often places too much pressure on defendants—even those competently represented—especially those who are risk-averse. As a result, there is an enhanced possibility that innocent persons will plead guilty.

Consider this anecdote: *D* was charged with kidnapping and forcible rape, punishable by life imprisonment. *D* continually asserted his innocence to his lawyer, and the case against him was so weak that his counsel was confident of acquittal at trial. However, the prosecutor (aware of the weakness of the case) offered *D* a deal: he would drop the rape and kidnapping charges in exchange for a guilty plea to simple battery, a thirty-day misdemeanor. Over the lawyer's objections, the defendant pleaded guilty, saying "I can't take the chance." Whether or not this story, reported as accurate, is true, the critics' point is made: a defendant who is innocent can be lawfully pressured to plead guilty as a result of hard bargaining by a prosecutor.

NOTES AND QUESTIONS

1.   *The inevitability thesis.* Most proponents of plea bargaining, and even some of its opponents, believe that if bargaining were abolished there would be a massive increase in the trial rate and, with it, "the error rate of trials would rise * * * at least as long as one assumes a constant level of expenditures on the system." Robert E. Scott & William J. Stuntz, *Plea Bargaining as Contract*, 101 Yale L.J. 1909, 1932 (1992). Therefore, the reasoning goes, bargaining would return overtly or covertly anyway.

According to Stephen Schulhofer, this may overstate the case. Based on his studies of the Philadelphia court system mentioned in the preceding excerpt, Schulhofer concluded that "[p]lea bargaining is not inevitable. In most American cities, attorneys have *chosen* to process cases that way." Stephen J. Schulhofer, *Is Plea Bargaining Inevitable?*, 97 Harv. L. Rev. 1037, 1107 (1984). His study found no serious disruption of the justice system, in American's fourth-largest city, [even though] no concessions of any kind * * * [were] offered for guilty pleas in the great majority of felony cases. In the absence of concessions, most felony defendants * * * [did] in fact demand a trial, and their cases * * * [were] resolved in genuinely contested adversary proceedings. * * * [M]any defendants [won] * * * acquittal or substantial charge reduction— results that in nearly all cases reflect[ed] not intuitive or off-the-cuff compromise, but the considered application of law to facts proved in open court.

Id., at 1106.

According to two scholars, the "dilemma about plea bargaining—take it or leave it—is a false one. It is based on a false dichotomy." Ronald Wright & Marc Miller, *The Screening/Bargaining Tradeoff*, 55 Stan. L. Rev. 29, 31 (2002). They contend that if the prosecutorial screening system were improved through "training, oversight and other internal enforcement mechanisms," plea bargaining could be substantially reduced without a proportional increase in trials. They recommend that prosecutors "make an early and careful assessment of each case, and demand that police and investigators provide sufficient information before the initial charge is filed." Moreover, to avoid overcharging, they would require prosecutors to file only charges that the "office would generally want to result * * * in conviction and sanction." These charges would need to "reflect reasonably accurately what actually occurred," and be limited to those charges that the prosecutor "can very likely" prove in court. If these conditions are met, they reason, a prosecutor could—and should—"severely restrict all plea bargaining, * * * most especially charge bargains." *Id.* at 32.

2.   *Moving from inevitability to principle.* Are there principled reasons to favor a system heavily weighted in favor of guilty pleas through plea negotiation? Yes, according to Judge Frank Easterbrook because, as he puts it, "compromise is better than conflict." In his view, both sides in the would-be adversarial conflict benefit from plea agreements:

> Defendants can use or exchange their [constitutional trial] rights, whichever makes them better off. So plea bargaining helps defendants. Forcing them to use their rights at trial means compelling them to take the risk of conviction or acquittal; risk-averse persons prefer a certain but small punishment to a chancy but large one. Defendants also get the process over sooner, and solvent ones can save the expense of trial. Compromise also benefits prosecutors and society at large. In purchasing procedural entitlements with lower sentences, prosecutors buy that most valuable commodity, *time*. With time they can prosecute more criminals.

Frank H. Easterbrook, *Plea Bargaining as Compromise*, 101 Yale L.J. 1969, 1975 (1992).

Do you agree? Professor Easterbrook states in this excerpt that risk-averse defendants will prefer to choose "a certain but small punishment to a chancy but large one." However, is it possible that innocent persons, as a group, are more apt to be risk-averse than guilty ones, thereby increasing the chances that innocent persons will disproportionately plead guilty to crimes they did not commit? Consider:

> [O]ne's personality powerfully shapes one's risk preferences, so that impulsive gamblers will be more likely to take risks. Those who are cautious or anxious will be more amenable to plea bargains than gambling types and so will demand smaller discounts and be less likely to go to trial. Most criminals are less risk averse (at least with regard to imprisonment) than law-abiding citizens. This understanding fits with the view of criminals as reckless thrill-seekers who fail to exercise self-control over their impulses to commit crime.

Stephanos Bibas, *Plea Bargaining Outside the Shadow of Trial*, 117 Harv. L. Rev. 2463, 2509–2510 (2004). (There is more to be said about the risk of innocent persons pleading guilty in subsequent Notes.)

Judge Easterbrook's view of the system also assumes that defendants are reasonably informed of their options before they choose to plead guilty. There is more to be said about this in coming pages, but consider the comments of Professor Bibas, who has written of what he calls "the myth of the fully informed rational actor":

> Most defendants do indeed know whether they are guilty of something and whether they have an obvious defense * * * . But criminal cases are much more complex than binary judgments of guilt or innocence. Often, there is a range of criminal charges that can fit a criminal transaction, and prosecutors start out stacking multiple charges only to bargain some away. There also is usually a range of criminal sentences that can fit a particular charge.

Stephanos Bibas, *The Myth of the Fully Informed Rational Actor,* 31 St. Louis U. Pub. L. Rev. 79, 80 (2011). In order, therefore, for the defendant to determine what she should do, she must rely heavily on her attorney. But, as Bibas points out, public defenders are "often underpaid and overworked," so they have a strong incentive to plead their clients guilty quickly. And, they lack the resources "to turn over every stone," thus often leaving the lawyer without enough information to provide accurate advice of her client's chances of success at trial.

3. *The sentencing differential.* Albert Alschuler writes:

> Criminal defendants today plead guilty in overwhelming numbers primarily because they perceive that this action is likely to lead to more lenient treatment than would follow conviction at trial. A number of studies suggest that this perception is justified. * * * Some empirical studies have concluded that a federal defendant's

choice of guilty plea, bench trial, or jury trial is likely to have a greater impact on his sentence than even his prior criminal record. In addition, Professor Hans Zeisel found that the sentences of New York City defendants convicted at trial were * * * [more than double] those proposed by prosecutors in pretrial offers to the same defendants. * * * Although the empirical evidence is not of one piece, the best conclusion probably is that in a great many cases the sentence differential in America assumes shocking proportions.[a]
* * *

* * * One mark of a just legal system is that it minimizes the effect of tactical choices upon the outcome of its processes. In criminal cases, the extent of an offender's punishment ought to turn primarily upon what he did and, perhaps, upon his personal characteristics rather than upon a postcrime, postarrest decision to exercise or not to exercise some procedural options. As an initial matter, it seems unjust that when two virtually identical defendants have committed virtually identical crimes, one should receive a more severe sentence than the other only because he has exercised his right to trial. * * *

Nevertheless, in resisting this conclusion about a decade ago, some prominent advocates of plea bargaining articulated a series of penological rationales for extending special consideration to defendants who plead guilty. These rationales usually were designed to show that, although it is improper to penalize a defendant for exercising the right to trial, it is appropriate to reward a defendant for pleading guilty.

Albert W. Alschuler, *The Changing Plea Bargaining Debate*, 69 Calif. L. Rev. 652, 652–58 (1981).

What *is* the penological justification for "rewarding" those who plead guilty?

4. *Innocent defendants.* As the Dressler/Michaels excerpt suggests, some critics maintain that plea bargaining jeopardizes innocent defendants. Consider this:

In an ideal world, factually innocent defendants would not be charged with crimes they did not commit. In that same world, innocent defendants who were wrongly charged would never plead guilty, but would go to trial and be acquitted by a jury of their peers. But this is not the world we live in. We now know, for example, due

---

[a]   See Nancy J. King et al., *When Process Affects Punishment: Differences in Sentences After Guilty Plea, Bench Trial, and Jury Trial in Five Guideline States*, 105 Colum. L. Rev. 959, 962 (2005) (reporting results of a survey of five state sentencing guideline systems: Although the guidelines did not expressly recognize a plea agreement as a valid basis for a reduced sentence, the authors found "a significant plea discount—the difference between the average sentence given after a guilty verdict and the average sentence given after a guilty plea for the same offense—is evident for most offenses in all five states.").

to the availability of DNA testing, that at least twenty-nine individuals who pled guilty to crimes they did not commit served a combined total of more than one hundred fifty years in prison before their exonerations, and the National Registry of Exonerations now lists 151 defendants who pled guilty and were subsequently exonerated.

John H. Blume & Rebecca K. Helm, *The Unexonerated: Factually Innocent Defendants Who Plead Guilty*, 100 Cornell L. Rev. 157, 172–73 (2014).

Why would this happen, and presumably happen in far greater numbers than the 151 cases mentioned above? The authors offer three reasons why innocent defendants plead guilty. First, if they are charged with a relatively low-level offense, they will plead guilty "in order to get out of jail, to avoid the hassle of having criminal charges hanging over their heads, or to avoid being punished for exercising their right to trial." Id. at 173. Second, some defendants go to trial, are wrongly convicted, have their conviction overturned on appeal, and then plead guilty to a sentence of "time already served" rather than risk another trial. And, third, some innocent persons accept a plea deal out of fear of the likely harsher punishment that would be imposed if they go to trial and are wrongly convicted. This third reason is particularly a problem:

> Trial-distorting plea bargains are more likely to occur in cases where the government has weak evidence to support the charges as filed. In these cases, the discount that a prosecutor offers might grow quite large, because a lucrative offer is needed to convince a defendant to give up a strong chance of outright acquittal.

Ronald F. Wright, *Trial Distortion and the End of Innocence in Federal Criminal Justice*, 154 U. Pa. L. Rev. 79, 109 (2005).

As for this latter point, look at the matter for a moment from a prosecutor's perspective. Suppose that you are prosecuting two rape cases. Your case against Defendant *A*, who has no criminal record, is very strong. The evidence against Defendant *B*, who also has no criminal history, is much weaker, although you believe he is guilty. You estimate that you have a 95% chance of convicting *A*, but only a 25% chance in the prosecution of *B*. How would these facts affect your bargaining position in the two cases?

In this context, reconsider the kidnapping/rape anecdote mentioned in the Dressler/Michaels excerpt (p. 1129). Was it wrong for the prosecutor to tender the offer? Professor Alschuler, who recounted the story, wrote that he "assumed that most readers, and even most defenders of plea bargaining, would share the view that a prosecutor who recognized his inability to prove a serious charge at trial ought not use that charge as leverage to obtain a minor conviction." Alschuler, Note 3, *supra*, at 685. Do *you* share that view? What should a prosecutor do if she believes that a defendant *is* guilty of a serious offense, but she worries that she has insufficient admissible evidence to prove the charge? Should she seek dismissal of the charges, or do exactly what happened here—make an offer "too good to refuse"?

5. *But do we worry too much about guilty pleas from innocent defendants?* Professor Josh Bowers has argued that while many parts of our justice system fail innocent defendants, the plea bargaining process is not a significant part of that failure. Josh Bowers, *Punishing the Innocent*, 156 U. Pa. L. Rev. 1117 (2008). He provocatively argues that almost all guilty pleas by innocent defendants are pleas to misdemeanor charges by repeat players who already have criminal records. When faced with the choice of a trial, with its inconvenience and risk of a longer sentence, the recidivist who falsely pleads guilty in exchange for time served or a very short sentence is engaging in supremely rational behavior. And it is behavior, Bowers argues, that the system should do nothing to discourage.

George Thomas in 2015 examined a sample of cases from the National Registry of Exonerations, which led him to discover that the Houston police department had a serious problem with field testing of suspected contraband in 2013 and 2014. In forty-three cases in the registry, defendants pleaded guilty to drug possession based on field tests only to be exonerated when the tardy lab tests found no evidence of contraband drugs. One possibility, mentioned earlier, is that the defendant already had a record, did not make bail, and chose to plead guilty in exchange for a light sentence, usually time served. A second possibility is that the defendant believed what he possessed was contraband, that he had been suckered by the seller. A darker possibility is that the defendant thought the police were willing to fabricate the results so he might as well take a few days in jail or probation to avoid the greater harm.

6. *Federal sentencing guidelines.* Due to widespread sentencing disparity in the federal courts, Congress in 1984 passed the Sentencing Reform Act. The Act created the United States Sentencing Commission, which drafted sentencing guidelines that today are advisory in nature, but which were and are intended to substantially reduce sentencing disparity. The primary features of the Federal Sentencing Guidelines (FSG) are considered in Chapter 17.

A few aspects of the FSG as they relate to the guilty plea process deserve note. First, Guideline § 6B1.2(a) recommends that a court not accept a plea agreement that includes dismissal of charges or an agreement not to pursue potential charges, unless "the court determines, for reasons stated on the record, that the remaining charges adequately reflect the seriousness of the actual offense behavior and that accepting the agreement will not undermine the statutory purpose of sentencing or the sentencing guidelines."

Second, certain FSG features can frustrate the parties' efforts to reach an accommodation. Guideline § 1B1.3 authorizes the judge to consider "all acts and omissions committed, aided, abetted, counseled, commanded, induced, procured, or willfully caused by the defendant * * * that occurred during the commission of the offense of conviction, in preparation for that offense, or in the course of attempting to avoid detection or responsibility for that offense * * * .'' Most courts have interpreted this language to mean that the sentencing judge may take into consideration charges dismissed as the result of a plea agreement, if they are "sufficiently related to the offense of conviction * * * to be available for consideration as a basis for departure." United States v. Kim, 896 F.2d 678, 685 (2d Cir. 1990). Thus, the benefit of the bargain—dismissal of charges—may prove to be illusory at the sentencing phase, unless a binding sentencing agreement is also a part of the bargain.

Third, to the extent that a judge follows the advisory guidelines, a guilty plea only indirectly serves as a justification for a more lenient sentence. Section 3E1.1 of the FSG provides that if a "defendant clearly demonstrates acceptance of responsibility for his offense," the judge may decrease the sentence within applicable guidelines. However, Application Note 3 of the Commentary to the § 3E1.1 states that "[a] defendant who enters a guilty plea is not entitled to an adjustment under this section as a matter of right." However, it goes on,

> [e]ntry of a plea of guilty prior to the commencement of trial combined with truthfully admitting the conduct comprising the offense of conviction, and truthfully admitting or not falsely denying any additional relevant conduct for which he is accountable * * * will constitute significant evidence of acceptance of responsibility * * * .

Finally, under Section 5K1.1, a defendant is entitled to a reduction in his sentence "[u]pon motion of the government stating that the defendant has provided substantial assistance in the investigation or prosecution of another person who has committed an offense." Thus, for example, a defendant who pleads guilty and assists in the prosecution of co-conspirators by testifying against them may receive a reduced sentence.

7. *A final thought.* Consider the observation of Professor David A. Moran, Clinical Professor of Law, at the University of Michigan Law School:

> After teaching a class this morning about plea bargaining, I was suddenly struck by the thought that for many defendants, the plea bargaining process is very much like the game show, "Deal or No deal." (If you haven't seen the show, you can stop reading.)[b] Like a contestant on the show, the defendant begins with a case with a highly uncertain value. As pretrial motions and discovery unfold, the defendant learns information that changes the expected value of her case. As the value of her case changes, the prosecutor makes offers whose values reflect those changes, and the defendant receives advice about whether to accept those offers from her family and friend (and that advice is often really, really bad). Ultimately,

---

[b] No, don't. But, if you have never seen the program (it still shows on Game Show Network), here is your chance: https://www.youtube.com/watch?v=QO_gpyrI0lc. Who says that silly game shows can't help you in law school?

she almost always accepts an offer instead of going all the way and opening her case (going to trial).

B. CHARACTERISTICS OF A VALID GUILTY PLEA

1. "VOLUNTARY, KNOWING, AND INTELLIGENT"

BRADY V. UNITED STATES
Supreme Court of the United States, 1970.
397 U.S. 742, 90 S.Ct. 1463, 25 L.Ed.2d 747.

MR. JUSTICE WHITE delivered the opinion of the Court [joined by CHIEF JUSTICE BURGER, and JUSTICES HARLAN, STEWART, and BLACKMUN].

In 1959, petitioner was charged with kidnaping in violation of 18 U.S.C. § 1201(a).[1] Since the indictment charged that the victim of the kidnaping was not liberated unharmed, petitioner faced a maximum penalty of death if the verdict of the jury should so recommend. Petitioner, represented by competent counsel throughout, first elected to plead not guilty. * * * Upon learning that his codefendant, who had confessed to the authorities, would plead guilty and be available to testify against him, petitioner changed his plea to guilty. His plea was accepted after the trial judge twice questioned him as to the voluntariness of his plea. Petitioner was sentenced to 50 years' imprisonment, later reduced to 30.

In 1967, petitioner sought relief [by writ of habeas corpus] under 28 U.S.C. § 2255, claiming that his plea of guilty was not voluntarily given because § 1201(a) operated to coerce his plea * * * . * * *

After a hearing, the District Court for the District of New Mexico denied relief. * * * The court * * * found that petitioner decided to plead guilty when he learned that his codefendant was going to plead guilty: petitioner pleaded guilty "by reason of other matters and not by reason of the statute" or because of any acts of the trial judge. The court concluded that "the plea was voluntarily and knowingly made."

The Court of Appeals for the Tenth Circuit affirmed, determining that the District Court's findings were supported by substantial evidence and specifically approving the finding that petitioner's plea of guilty was voluntary. * * *

---

[1] "Whoever knowingly transports in interstate or foreign commerce, any person who has been unlawfully seized, confined, inveigled, decoyed, kidnaped, abducted, or carried away and held for ransom or reward or otherwise, except, in the case of a minor, by a parent thereof, shall be punished (1) by death if the kidnaped person has not been liberated unharmed, and if the verdict of the jury shall so recommend, or (2) by imprisonment for any term of years or for life, if the death penalty is not imposed."

I

In *United States v. Jackson,* [390 U.S. 570, 88 S.Ct. 1209, 20 L.Ed.2d 138 (1968)], the defendants were indicted under § 1201(a). The District Court dismissed the § 1201(a) count of the indictment, holding the statute unconstitutional because it permitted imposition of the death sentence only upon a jury's recommendation and thereby made the risk of death the price of a jury trial. This Court held the statute valid, except for the death penalty provision; with respect to the latter, the Court agreed with the trial court "that the death penalty provision * * * imposes an impermissible burden upon the exercise of a constitutional right * * * ." * * * The inevitable effect of the provision was said to be to discourage assertion of the Fifth Amendment right not to plead guilty and to deter exercise of the Sixth Amendment right to demand a jury trial. * * *

Since the "inevitable effect" of the death penalty provision of § 1201(a) was said by the Court to be the needless encouragement of pleas of guilty and waivers of jury trial, Brady contends that *Jackson* requires the invalidation of every plea of guilty entered under that section, at least when the fear of death is shown to have been a factor in the plea. Petitioner, however, has read far too much into the *Jackson* opinion.

The Court made it clear in *Jackson* that it was not holding § 1201(a) inherently coercive of guilty pleas: "the fact that the Federal Kidnaping Act tends to discourage defendants from insisting upon their innocence and demanding trial by jury hardly implies that every defendant who enters a guilty plea to a charge under the Act does so involuntarily." * * *

Plainly, it seems to us, *Jackson* ruled neither that all pleas of guilty encouraged by the fear of a possible death sentence are involuntary pleas nor that such encouraged pleas are invalid whether involuntary or not. *Jackson* prohibits the imposition of the death penalty under § 1201(a), but that decision neither fashioned a new standard for judging the validity of guilty pleas nor mandated a new application of the test theretofore fashioned by courts and since reiterated that guilty pleas are valid if both "voluntary" and "intelligent."

That a guilty plea is a grave and solemn act to be accepted only with care and discernment has long been recognized. Central to the plea and the foundation for entering judgment against the defendant is the defendant's admission in open court that he committed the acts charged in the indictment. He thus stands as a witness against himself and he is shielded by the Fifth Amendment from being compelled to do so—hence the minimum requirement that his plea be the voluntary expression of his own choice. But the plea is more than an admission of past conduct; it is the defendant's consent that judgment of conviction may be entered without a trial—a waiver of his right to trial before a jury or a judge. Waivers of constitutional rights not only must be voluntary but must be knowing, intelligent acts done with sufficient awareness of the relevant circumstances and likely consequences.[6] On neither score was Brady's plea of guilty invalid.

II

The trial judge in 1959 found the plea voluntary before accepting it; the District Court in 1968, after an evidentiary hearing, found that the plea was voluntarily made; the Court of Appeals specifically approved the finding of voluntariness. We see no reason on this record to disturb the judgment of those courts. Petitioner, advised by competent counsel, tendered his plea after his codefendant, who had already given a confession, determined to plead guilty and became available to testify against petitioner. It was this development that the District Court found to have triggered Brady's guilty plea.

The voluntariness of Brady's plea can be determined only by considering all of the relevant circumstances surrounding it. One of these circumstances was the possibility of a heavier sentence following a guilty verdict after a trial. It may be that Brady, faced with a strong case against him and recognizing that his chances for acquittal were slight, preferred to plead guilty and thus limit the penalty to life imprisonment rather than to elect a jury trial which could result in a death penalty. But even if we assume that Brady would not have pleaded guilty except for the death penalty provision of § 1201(a), this assumption merely identifies the penalty provision as a "but for" cause of his plea. That the statute caused the plea in this sense does not necessarily prove that the plea was coerced and invalid as an involuntary act.

The State to some degree encourages pleas of guilty at every important step in the criminal process. For some people, their breach of a State's law is alone sufficient reason for surrendering themselves and accepting punishment. For others, apprehension and charge, both threatening acts by the Government, jar them into admitting their guilt. In still other cases, the post-indictment accumulation of evidence may convince the defendant and his counsel that a trial is not worth the agony and expense to the defendant and his family. All these pleas of guilty are valid in spite of the State's responsibility for some of the factors motivating the pleas; the pleas are no more improperly compelled than is the decision by a defendant at the close of the State's evidence at trial that he must take the stand or face certain conviction.

---

[6] Since an intelligent assessment of the relative advantages of pleading guilty is frequently impossible without the assistance of an attorney, this Court has scrutinized with special care pleas of guilty entered by defendants without the assistance of counsel and without a valid waiver of the right to counsel. Since *Gideon v. Wainwright*, [p. 1043], it has been clear that a guilty plea to a felony charge entered without counsel and without a waiver of counsel is invalid. * * *

Of course, the agents of the State may not produce a plea by actual or threatened physical harm or by mental coercion overbearing the will of the defendant. But nothing of the sort is claimed in this case; nor is there evidence that Brady was so gripped by fear of the death penalty or hope of leniency that he did not or could not, with the help of counsel, rationally weigh the advantages of going to trial against the advantages of pleading guilty. Brady's claim is of a different sort: that it violates the Fifth Amendment to influence or encourage a guilty plea by opportunity or promise of leniency and that a guilty plea is coerced and invalid if influenced by the fear of a possibly higher penalty for the crime charged if a conviction is obtained after the State is put to its proof.

* * * We decline to hold * * * that a guilty plea is compelled and invalid under the Fifth Amendment whenever motivated by the defendant's desire to accept the certainty or probability of a lesser penalty rather than face a wider range of possibilities extending from acquittal to conviction and a higher penalty authorized by law for the crime charged. * * *

The standard as to the voluntariness of guilty pleas must be essentially that defined by Judge Tuttle of the Court of Appeals for the Fifth Circuit:

> "[A] plea of guilty entered by one fully aware of the direct consequences, including the actual value of any commitments made to him by the court, prosecutor, or his own counsel, must stand unless induced by threats (or promises to discontinue improper harassment), misrepresentation (including unfulfilled or unfulfillable promises), or perhaps by promises that are by their nature improper as having no proper relationship to the prosecutor's business (*e.g.* bribes)."[13]

Under this standard, a plea of guilty is not invalid merely because entered to avoid the possibility of a death penalty.

III

The record before us also supports the conclusion that Brady's plea was intelligently made. He was advised by competent counsel, he was made aware of the nature of the charge against him, and there was nothing to indicate that he was incompetent or otherwise not in control of his mental faculties; once his confederate had pleaded guilty and became available to testify, he chose to plead guilty, perhaps to ensure that he would face no more than life imprisonment or a term of years. Brady was aware of precisely what he was doing when he admitted that he had kidnaped the victim and had not released her unharmed.

---

[13] *Shelton v. United States*, 246 F.2d 571, 572 n. 2 (5th Cir. 1957) (en banc), rev'd on confession of error on other grounds, 356 U.S. 26, 78 S.Ct. 563, 2 L.Ed.2d 579 (1958).

It is true that Brady's counsel advised him that § 1201(a) empowered the jury to impose the death penalty and that nine years later in *United States v. Jackson, supra,* the Court held that the jury had no such power as long as the judge could impose only a lesser penalty if trial was to the court or there was a plea of guilty. But these facts do not require us to set aside Brady's conviction.

Often the decision to plead guilty is heavily influenced by the defendant's appraisal of the prosecution's case against him and by the apparent likelihood of securing leniency should a guilty plea be offered and accepted. Considerations like these frequently present imponderable questions for which there are no certain answers; judgments may be made that in the light of later events seem improvident, although they were perfectly sensible at the time. The rule that a plea must be intelligently made to be valid does not require that a plea be vulnerable to later attack if the defendant did not correctly assess every relevant factor entering into his decision. A defendant is not entitled to withdraw his plea merely because he discovers long after the plea has been accepted that his calculus misapprehended the quality of the State's case or the likely penalties attached to alternative courses of action. More particularly, absent misrepresentation or other impermissible conduct by state agents, a voluntary plea of guilty intelligently made in the light of the then applicable law does not become vulnerable because later judicial decisions indicate that the plea rested on a faulty premise. A plea of guilty triggered by the expectations of a competently counseled defendant that the State will have a strong case against him is not subject to later attack because the defendant's lawyer correctly advised him with respect to the then existing law as to possible penalties but later pronouncements of the courts, as in this case, hold that the maximum penalty for the crime in question was less than was reasonably assumed at the time the plea was entered. * * *

This is not to say that guilty plea convictions hold no hazards for the innocent or that the methods of taking guilty pleas presently employed in this country are necessarily valid in all respects. This mode of conviction is no more foolproof than full trials to the court or to the jury. Accordingly, we take great precautions against unsound results, and we should continue to do so, whether conviction is by plea or by trial. We would have serious doubts about this case if the encouragement of guilty pleas by offers of leniency substantially increased the likelihood that defendants, advised by competent counsel, would falsely condemn themselves. But our view is to the contrary and is based on our expectations that courts will satisfy themselves that pleas of guilty are voluntarily and intelligently made by competent defendants with adequate advice of counsel and that there is nothing to question the accuracy and reliability of the defendants' admissions that they committed the crimes with which they are charged. In the case before us, nothing in the record impeaches Brady's plea or suggests that his admissions in open court were anything but the truth. * * *

[JUSTICE BRENNAN, with whom JUSTICES DOUGLAS and MARSHALL joined, concurred in the result. JUSTICE BLACK concurred in the judgment "and in substantially all of the opinion."]

NOTES AND QUESTIONS

1.   *Competency.* As *Brady* states, "Waivers of constitutional rights not only must be voluntary but must be knowing, intelligent acts done with sufficient awareness of the relevant circumstances and likely consequences." In shorthand, a guilty plea must be "voluntarily, knowingly, and intelligently" made. It follows from this that it is essential that the defendant possesses the *mental capacity* to make the decision to plead guilty, i.e., that he is *competent* to plead guilty. For more on this subject, see p. 1082, Note 9.

2.   Justice White characterized Brady's claim this way: "[A] guilty plea is coerced and invalid if influenced by the fear of a possibly higher penalty." Not surprisingly, stated this way, the involuntariness claim was rejected. If you had represented Brady, how might you have articulated the claim that the plea was involuntary in light of *Jackson*?

3.   "Five months after the district attorney here made the controversial decision to pursue the death penalty against Andrea Yates, the mother charged with drowning her five young children in a bathtub, a prosecutor suggested today that he would agree to a life sentence if Mrs. Yates pleaded guilty to the murders." Jim Yardley, *Prosecutor Willing to Deal in Child Drownings Case*, New York Times, Jan. 9, 2002, at A14. Yates did not plead guilty, the prosecutor pursued the death penalty, Yates was convicted of the murders, but the jury recommended against the death penalty. (Her conviction subsequently was overturned; on retrial she was found not guilty by reason of insanity.) If Yates *had* received the death penalty, could she have successfully challenged it on *Jackson* grounds? How is this case similar to *Jackson* and *Brady*? How is this situation different?

4.   *Voluntariness and judicial participation in plea bargaining.* Federal Rule 11(c)(1) provides that the court must not participate in discussions between the parties concerning any plea agreement. Some states, however, permit a judge to participate. *Should* judges be permitted to participate in plea negotiations? What risks are there in judicial participation? What are the benefits?

In this regard consider United States v. Barrett, 982 F.2d 193 (6th Cir. 1992), in which the defendant was indicted for kidnaping a five-year-old girl in Ohio, whom he allegedly sexually abused and abandoned beneath a highway underpass in North Carolina.

> Prior to trial, the District Court judge arranged a conference call between himself, the prosecutor and the defense counsel. The

purpose of the call was to facilitate a plea by helping the parties work through a dispute regarding the proper application of the sentencing guidelines. The judge began the conversation by stating that he was "not soliciting the defendant to do anything." Throughout the conversation he repeated that he was not urging the defendant to plead guilty, and would not punish him for going to trial.

    * * * The judge first proposed that the parties consider a plea with a right of appeal from the sentence. He then suggested that it did not much matter what guidelines interpretation the parties agreed to, because he would likely exceed the guidelines in any event. The judge solicited and received information about the range of sentences being discussed. He rejected a defense suggestion that the minimum sentence might be seven years, saying "there is no way on God's green Earth I'm going to sentence him to only seven years, and I think the likelihood is I'm going to exceed the guidelines." The prosecutor's assertion that 150 to 170 months would be more appropriate was likewise rejected: "Don't put any money on it * * * . Don't bet your nest egg on it."

    * * * Six days after this conversation, Barrett entered a plea of guilty and was sentenced to life imprisonment.

The defendant later sought to have his conviction by guilty plea overturned on the ground that the judge violated Federal Rule 11. Is there any basis for arguing that Rule 11 was *not* violated? Irrespective of Rule 11—assume for a moment that the events had occurred in a state in which judicial participation is not barred—do you find the judge's involvement here objectionable? If so, in what way? Returning to the questions raised at the start of this Note, why do you think some states *permit* judicial involvement in plea negotiations?

    5.   *"Knowing and intelligent": waiving legal assistance.* Although a defendant is entitled to representation by counsel during the plea process, she is permitted to forego representation as long as her waiver of counsel is knowingly and intelligently made. In Iowa v. Tovar, 541 U.S. 77, 124 S.Ct. 1379, 158 L.Ed.2d 209 (2004), the Supreme Court acknowledged that it has never "prescribed any formula or script to be read to a defendant who states that he elects to proceed without counsel."

In *Tovar*, the Iowa Supreme Court ruled that when a defendant seeks to plead guilty without representation of counsel, the trial court must not only inform the defendant of his right to the assistance of counsel in entering a plea, but must also inform the defendant "that there are defenses to criminal charges that may not be known by laypersons and that the danger in waiving the assistance of counsel in deciding whether to plead guilty is the risk that a viable defense will be overlooked," and "that by waiving his right to an attorney, he will lose the opportunity to obtain an independent opinion on whether, under the facts and applicable law, it is wise to plead guilty."

The Supreme Court unanimously held that the Sixth Amendment does not compel a trial judge to provide these two "scripted admonitions" devised by the Iowa court. Justice Ginsburg reiterated the Court's prior admonition that "the information a defendant must have to waive counsel intelligently will 'depend, in each case, upon the particular facts and circumstances surrounding that case.' " The Court noted, however, "that States are free to adopt by statute, rule, or decision any guides to the acceptance of an uncounseled plead they deem useful. We hold only that the admonitions the Iowa Supreme Court ordered are not required by the Federal Constitution."

6. *"Knowing and intelligent": knowing what you are giving up.* A plea is invalid if an accused is unaware of the constitutional protections that she is waiving by pleading guilty. As the Court emphasized in Boykin v. Alabama, 395 U.S. 238, 89 S.Ct. 1709, 23 L.Ed.2d 274 (1969), a guilty plea involves the waiver of "[s]everal federal constitutional rights * * * . The first right is the privilege against compulsory self-incrimination guaranteed by the Fifth Amendment and applicable to the States by reason of the Fourteenth. Second, is the right to trial by jury. Third, is the right to confront one's accusers." (Of course, there are other rights waived, including the presumption of innocence and the right to compulsory process.)

The Court stated in *Boykin* that, on the facts of that case, "[i]t was error, plain on the face of the record, for the trial judge to accept petitioner's guilty plea without an affirmative showing" that the waiver was voluntary, knowing and intelligent; in particular, a court "cannot presume a waiver of these three important federal rights from a silent record." To satisfy *Boykin*, Federal Rule 11(b)(1) and state rules typically require the trial judge to inform the defendant in open court of the various rights she is giving up by pleading guilty.

7. *Knowing and intelligent": knowing to what you are pleading guilty.* In Henderson v. Morgan, 426 U.S. 637, 96 S.Ct. 2253, 49 L.Ed.2d 108 (1976), a nineteen-year-old defendant, with an I.Q. between 68 and 72, pleaded guilty to second-degree murder in the stabbing death of the victim. The defendant had been indicted for first-degree murder, but he agreed to the guilty plea in exchange for the reduced charge and a lesser sentence. At his sentencing, the defendant explained that he "meant no harm" to the victim. Subsequently, he sought to have his plea vacated on the ground that he did not realize when he pled guilty that an element of second-degree murder was an intention to kill the victim.

The Supreme Court held that a guilty plea is invalid unless the defendant "received 'real notice of the true nature of the charge against him, the first and most universally recognized requirement of due process.' " The Court's ruling, however, was exceptionally narrow. First, the Court assumed, without deciding, that "notice of the true nature, or substance, of a charge [does not] always requires a description of every element of the offense," but rather only requires notice of "critical elements" of the offense, such as intent-to-kill. Second, the Court noted:

> Normally the record contains either an explanation of the charge by the trial judge, or at least a representation by defense counsel that the nature of the offense has been explained to the accused. Moreover, even without such an express representation, it may be appropriate to presume that in most cases defense counsel routinely explain the nature of the offense in sufficient detail to give the accused notice of what he is being asked to admit. This case is unique because the trial judge found as a fact that the element of intent was not explained to respondent. Moreover, respondent's unusually low mental capacity provides a reasonable explanation for counsel's oversight * * * .

That limiting language proved critical in *Bradshaw v. Stumpf*, 545 U.S. 175, 125 S.Ct. 2398, 162 L.Ed.2d 143 (2005), in which the defendant sought to withdraw his guilty plea to aggravated murder, in part because he claimed he did not know that aggravated murder required a specific intent to kill. Unlike in *Henderson*, however, this defendant's lawyers informed the trial judge in the guilty plea hearing that they had explained the elements of the charge of aggravated murder to their client, a representation that the client confirmed on the record. On that basis, the Court unanimously rejected the claim that the guilty plea was invalid.

Indeed, even in the absence of such explicit representations as existed in *Bradshaw*, a court may—as the Supreme Court did in *Marshall v. Lonberger*, 459 U.S. 422, 103 S.Ct. 843, 74 L.Ed.2d 646 (1983)—rely on the general presumption set out in *Henderson* that a competent defense lawyer will inform her client of the critical elements of the offense to which the defendant is pleading guilty.

8. *"Knowing and intelligent": the consequences of the plea.* Courts generally hold that neither the trial judge nor defense counsel is constitutionally required to explain the "collateral consequences" of a guilty plea to a defendant before a plea is taken. The distinction between a "direct consequence" of a guilty plea, which must be disclosed to the defendant, and a "collateral consequence," which does not need to be, is "obvious at the extreme and often subtle at the margin." *United States v. Russell*, 686 F.2d 35 (D.C. Cir. 1982). However, most courts treat as collateral such matters as: ineligibility for parole; higher penalties for subsequent offenses due to recidivist laws; registration requirements for sex offenders; and lifetime disenfranchisement. On the other hand, the United States Supreme Court stated in *Padilla v. Kentucky*, 559 U.S. 356, 130 S.Ct. 1473, 176 L.Ed.2d 284 (2010), that defense counsel *is* required, at a minimum, to "advise a noncitizen client that pending criminal charges may carry a risk of adverse immigration consequences." And, where deportation consequences are clear— where deportation law is "succinct and straightforward"—defense counsel has a duty to give correct advice.

For an idea of what information a federal judge must generally provide to a defendant prior to accepting a guilty plea, see Fed. R. Crim. P. 11(b)(1).

9.   *Problem.* Thomas Creech, an inmate of the Idaho State Correctional Institution where he was serving a life sentence for first-degree murder, engaged in an argument with Dale Jensen, another inmate. At some point in the altercation, Jensen approached Creech and

> swung a weapon at him which consisted of a sock containing batteries. Creech took the weapon away from Jensen, who returned to his cell but emerged with a toothbrush in which had been taped a razor blade. * * * Jensen made some movement toward Creech, who then struck Jensen between the eyes with the battery laden sock, knocking Jensen to the floor. The fight continued * * * with Jensen swinging the razor blade at Creech and Creech hitting Jensen with the battery filled sock.

The latter blows left Jensen helpless on the floor, at which time Creech kicked the victim about the throat and head, ultimately resulting in Jensen's death.

Creech was charged with first-degree murder. After originally pleading not guilty, Creech sent a letter to the trial judge stating that he wanted to change his plea to guilty, which he did against the wishes of his lawyer. Creech was later sentenced to death.

At a post-conviction hearing, Creech explained why he had thought himself guilty of first degree murder:

Q. Why did you write that letter to Judge Newhouse?

A. Because that's the way I felt.

Q. Okay. I want you to piece by piece put together for these people and Judge Newhouse why you felt that way. * * *

A. Well, first of all, I thought that I was charged with first degree murder, which I had been told when that new law passed, that anybody that killed another inmate in prison that was already doing time for murder, that it was automatic first degree murder.

Q. Okay.

A. And that was the main reason. Because I felt that, you know, it is obvious that he did die and I killed him. So I felt that I was guilty of it. * * *

Q. So there was no defense. You felt there was no defense to the charge?

A. That is the way I understood it to be.

Q. By the time you wrote that letter, had you and any attorneys talked about the difference between manslaughter and first degree murder surrounding the case?

A. No. * * *

Q. Mr. Creech, did you intend to kill Mr. Jensen? * * *

A. Yes, sir.

State v. Creech, 109 Idaho 592, 710 P.2d 502 (1985).

Idaho law provided that "any murder committed by a person under a sentence for murder * * * shall be murder in the first degree." "Murder" is "the unlawful killing of a human being with malice aforethought." If you represented Creech in a subsequent appeal to overturn the guilty plea, can you make a plausible argument that your client did not knowingly and intelligently plead guilty? Consider Note 7 in this regard.

10. *Discovery and guilty pleas.* "If due process forbids a prosecutor to sit silent through trial without disclosing [material] exculpatory information to the defense [see pp. 968–969—Eds.], then surely she cannot induce the defendant to forego his right to trial by withholding the same information." John G. Douglass, *Fatal Attraction? The Uneasy Courtship of Brady and Plea Bargaining,* 50 Emory L.J. 437, 439 (2001). Or, so it might seem.

In United States v. Ruiz, 536 U.S. 622, 122 S.Ct. 2450, 153 L.Ed.2d 586 (2002), after immigration agents discovered a large quantity of marijuana in Angela Ruiz's luggage, federal prosecutors offered her what was known in the Southern District of California as a "fast track" plea bargain: If she waived indictment, trial, and appeal, the prosecutor would recommend a reduced sentence under the Federal Sentencing Guidelines. But, the "fast track" deal involved more, as the Court, per Justice Breyer, explained:

> The prosecutors' proposed plea agreement contains a set of detailed terms. Among other things, it specifies that "any [known] information establishing the factual innocence of the defendant" "has been turned over to the defendant," and it acknowledges the Government's "continuing duty to provide such information." At the same time it requires that the defendant "waiv[e] the right" to receive "impeachment information relating to any informants or other witnesses" as well as the right to receive information supporting any affirmative defense the defendant raises if the case goes to trial.

Ruiz refused to agree to the preceding waivers, so the prosecutor withdrew the offer and indicted her for unlawful drug possession. Later, despite the absence of any new agreement, Ruiz pleaded guilty. At sentencing, however, she asked the judge to sentence her as the prosecutor would have recommended had she accepted the "fast track" agreement. The judge refused, and Ruiz appealed to the Ninth Circuit, which held that the "fast track" waiver was unlawful. The Supreme Court, with no dissenters, reversed the Ninth Circuit:

> The constitutional question concerns a federal criminal defendant's waiver of the right to receive from prosecutors exculpatory impeachment material—a right that the Constitution provides as part of its basic "fair trial" guarantee. *Brady v. Maryland,* [pp. 968–969]. * * *

In this case, the Ninth Circuit in effect held that a guilty plea is not "voluntary" (and that the defendant could not, by pleading guilty, waive her right to a fair trial) unless the prosecutors first made the same disclosure of material impeachment information that the prosecutors would have had to make had the defendant insisted upon a trial. We must decide whether the Constitution requires that preguilty plea disclosure of impeachment information. We conclude that it does not.

First, impeachment information is special in relation to the *fairness of a trial,* not in respect to whether a plea is *voluntary* ("knowing," "intelligent," and "sufficient[ly] aware"). Of course, the more information the defendant has, the more aware he is of the likely consequences of a plea, waiver, or decision, and the wiser that decision will likely be. But the Constitution does not require the prosecutor to share all useful information with the defendant. And the law ordinarily considers a waiver knowing, intelligent, and sufficiently aware if the defendant fully understands the nature of the right and how it would likely apply *in general* in the circumstances—even though the defendant may not know the *specific detailed* consequences of invoking it. * * *

It is particularly difficult to characterize impeachment information as critical information of which the defendant must always be aware prior to pleading guilty given the random way in which such information may, or may not, help a particular defendant. The degree of help that impeachment information can provide will depend upon the defendant's own independent knowledge of the prosecution's potential case—a matter that the Constitution does not require prosecutors to disclose.

Second, * * * this Court has found that the Constitution, in respect to a defendant's awareness of relevant circumstances, does not require complete knowledge of the relevant circumstances, but permits a court to accept a guilty plea, with its accompanying waiver of various constitutional rights, despite various forms of misapprehension under which a defendant might labor. [The Court cited a number of cases, including *Brady v. United States*, in which the defendant "misapprehended the quality of the State's case."] It is difficult to distinguish, in terms of importance, (1) a defendant's ignorance of grounds for impeachment of potential witnesses at a possible future trial from (2) the varying forms of ignorance at issue in [*Brady* and other cases cited by the Court].

Third, due process considerations, the very considerations that led this Court to find trial-related rights to exculpatory and impeachment information in *Brady* and [related cases] argue against the existence of the "right" that the Ninth Circuit found here. This Court has said that due process considerations include not only (1) the nature of the private interest at stake, but also (2) the value of the additional safeguard, and (3) the adverse impact of the requirement upon the Government's interests. Here, as we have just pointed out, the added value of the Ninth Circuit's "right" to a defendant is often limited, for it depends upon the defendant's independent awareness of the details of the Government's case. And in any case, as the proposed plea agreement at issue here specifies, the Government will provide "any information establishing the factual innocence of the defendant" regardless. That fact, along with other guilty-plea safeguards, diminishes the force of Ruiz's concern that, in the absence of impeachment information, innocent individuals, accused of crimes, will plead guilty.

At the same time, a constitutional obligation to provide impeachment information during plea bargaining, prior to entry of a guilty plea, could seriously interfere with the Government's interest in securing those guilty pleas that are factually justified, desired by defendants, and help to secure the efficient administration of justice. The Ninth Circuit's rule risks premature disclosure of Government witness information, which, the Government tells us, could "disrupt ongoing investigations" and expose prospective witnesses to serious harm. * * *

These considerations, taken together, lead us to conclude that the Constitution does not require the Government to disclose material impeachment evidence prior to entering a plea agreement with a criminal defendant.

In dictum, the Court also stated that a guilty plea is not invalid merely because the prosecutor failed to disclose information relevant to any affirmative defense that the defendant might have raised at trial.

2.   "FACTUAL BASIS" FOR THE PLEA

NORTH CAROLINA V. ALFORD
Supreme Court of the United States, 1970.
400 U.S. 25, 91 S.Ct. 160, 27 L.Ed.2d 162.

MR. JUSTICE WHITE delivered the opinion of the Court [joined by CHIEF JUSTICE BURGER, and JUSTICES HARLAN, STEWART, and BLACKMUN].

On December 2, 1963, Alford was indicted for first-degree murder, a capital offense under North Carolina law. The court appointed an attorney to represent him, and this attorney questioned all but one of the various witnesses who appellee said would substantiate his claim of innocence. The witnesses, however, did not support Alford's story but gave statements that strongly indicated his guilt. Faced with strong evidence of guilt and no substantial evidentiary support for the claim of

innocence, Alford's attorney recommended that he pl[ ]
the ultimate decision to Alford himself. The prosecuto[ ]
plea of guilty to a charge of second-degree murder, ar[ ]
1963, Alford pleaded guilty to the reduced charge.

Before the plea was finally accepted by the tri[ ]
heard the sworn testimony of a police officer who sum[ ]
case. Two other witnesses besides Alford were also he[ ]
was no eyewitness to the crime, the testimony ind[ ]
before the killing Alford took his gun from his house, stated his intention
to kill the victim, and returned home with the declaration that he had
carried out the killing. After the summary presentation of the State's
case, Alford took the stand and testified that he had not committed the
murder but that he was pleading guilty because he faced the threat of the
death penalty if he did not do so.[2] * * * The trial court then asked
appellee if, in light of his denial of guilt, he still desired to plead guilty to
second-degree murder and appellee answered, "Yes, sir. I plead guilty
on—from the circumstances that he (Alford's attorney) told me." After
eliciting information about Alford's prior criminal record, which was a
long one, the trial court sentenced him to 30 years' imprisonment, the
maximum penalty for second-degree murder. * * *

Alford sought post-conviction relief * * * . * * *

As previously recounted, after Alford's plea of guilty was offered and
the State's case was placed before the judge, Alford denied that he had
committed the murder but reaffirmed his desire to plead guilty to avoid a
possible death sentence and to limit the penalty to the 30-year maximum
provided for second-degree murder. Ordinarily, a judgment of conviction
resting on a plea of guilty is justified by the defendant's admission that he
committed the crime charged against him and his consent that judgment
be entered without a trial of any kind. The plea usually subsumes both
elements, and justifiably so, even though there is no separate, express
admission by the defendant that he committed the particular acts claimed
to constitute the crime charged in the indictment. Here Alford entered his
plea but accompanied it with the statement that he had not shot the
victim. * * *

In addition to Alford's statement, however, the court had heard an
account of the events on the night of the murder, including information
from Alford's acquaintances that he had departed from his home with his
gun stating his intention to kill and that he had later declared that he
had carried out his intention. * * * Although denying the charge against

---

[2]   After giving his version of the events of the night of the murder, Alford stated:

"I pleaded guilty on second degree murder because they said there is too much
evidence, but I ain't shot no man, but I take the fault for the other man. We never had
an argument in our life and I just pleaded guilty because they said if I didn't they would
gas me for it, and that is all." * * *

, he nevertheless preferred the dispute between him and the State to e settled by the judge in the context of a guilty plea proceeding rather than by a formal trial. Thereupon, with the State's telling evidence and Alford's denial before it, the trial court proceeded to convict and sentence Alford for second-degree murder.

State and lower federal courts are divided upon whether a guilty plea can be accepted when it is accompanied by protestations of innocence and hence contains only a waiver of trial but no admission of guilt. Some courts, giving expression to the principle that "[o]ur law only authorizes a conviction where guilt is shown," require that trial judges reject such pleas. But others have concluded that they should not "force any defense on a defendant in a criminal case," particularly when advancement of the defense might "end in disaster * * * ." They have argued that, since "guilt, or the degree of guilt, is at times uncertain and elusive," "[a]n accused, though believing in or entertaining doubts respecting his innocence, might reasonably conclude a jury would be convinced of his guilt and that he would fare better in the sentence by pleading guilty * * * ." As one state court observed nearly a century ago, "[r]easons other than the fact that he is guilty may induce a defendant to so plead, * * * [and] [h]e must be permitted to judge for himself in this respect."[7]

This Court has not confronted this precise issue, but prior decisions do yield relevant principles. In *Lynch v. Overholser*, 369 U.S. 705, 82 S.Ct. 1063, 8 L.Ed.2d 211 (1962), Lynch, who had been charged in the Municipal Court of the District of Columbia with drawing and negotiating bad checks, a misdemeanor punishable by a maximum of one year in jail, sought to enter a plea of guilty, but the trial judge refused to accept the plea since a psychiatric report in the judge's possession indicated that Lynch had been suffering from "a manic depressive psychosis, at the time of the crime charged," and hence might have been not guilty by reason of insanity. Although at the subsequent trial Lynch did not rely on the insanity defense, he was found not guilty by reason of insanity and committed for an indeterminate period to a mental institution. On habeas corpus, the Court ordered his release, construing the congressional legislation seemingly authorizing the commitment as not reaching a case where the accused preferred a guilty plea to a plea of insanity. The Court expressly refused to rule that Lynch had an absolute right to have his guilty plea accepted, but implied that there would have been no constitutional error had his plea been accepted even though evidence before the judge indicated that there was a valid defense.

The issue in *Hudson v. United States*, 272 U.S. 451, 47 S.Ct. 127, 71 L.Ed. 347 (1926), was whether a federal court has power to impose a

---

[7]   A third approach has been to decline to rule definitively that a trial judge must either accept or reject an otherwise valid plea containing a protestation of innocence, but to leave that decision to his sound discretion.

prison sentence after accepting a plea of *nolo contendere*, a plea by which a defendant does not expressly admit his guilt, but nonetheless waives his right to a trial and authorizes the court for purposes of the case to treat him as if he were guilty.[8] The Court held that a trial court does have such power, and except for the cases which were rejected in *Hudson*, the federal courts have uniformly followed this rule * * * . Implicit in the *nolo contendere* cases is a recognition that the Constitution does not bar imposition of a prison sentence upon an accused who is unwilling expressly to admit his guilt but who, faced with grim alternatives, is willing to waive his trial and accept the sentence.

These cases would be directly in point if Alford had simply insisted on his plea but refused to admit the crime. The fact that his plea was denominated a plea of guilty rather than a plea of *nolo contendere* is of no constitutional significance with respect to the issue now before us, for the Constitution is concerned with the practical consequences, not the formal categorizations, of state law. Thus, while most pleas of guilty consist of both a waiver of trial and an express admission of guilt, the latter element is not a constitutional requisite to the imposition of criminal penalty. An individual accused of crime may voluntarily, knowingly, and understandingly consent to the imposition of a prison sentence even if he is unwilling or unable to admit his participation in the acts constituting the crime.

Nor can we perceive any material difference between a plea that refuses to admit commission of the criminal act and a plea containing a protestation of innocence when, as in the instant case, a defendant intelligently concludes that his interests require entry of a guilty plea and the record before the judge contains strong evidence of actual guilt. Here the State had a strong case of first-degree murder against Alford. Whether he realized or disbelieved his guilt, he insisted on his plea because in his view he had absolutely nothing to gain by a trial and much to gain by pleading. Because of the overwhelming evidence against him, a trial was precisely what neither Alford nor his attorney desired. Confronted with the choice between a trial for first-degree murder, on the one hand, and a plea of guilty to second-degree murder, on the other, Alford quite reasonably chose the latter and thereby limited the maximum penalty to a 30-year term. When his plea is viewed in light of

---

[8] Courts have defined the plea of *nolo contendere* in a variety of different ways, describing it, on the one hand, as "in effect, a plea of guilty," and on the other, as a query directed to the court to determine the defendant's guilt. * * *

Throughout its [common law] history, * * * the plea of *nolo contendere* has been viewed not as an express admission of guilt but as a consent by the defendant that he may be punished as if he were guilty and a prayer for leniency. Fed. Rule Crim. Proc. 11 preserves this distinction in its requirement that a court cannot accept a guilty plea "unless it is satisfied that there is a factual basis for the plea"; there is no similar requirement for pleas of *nolo contendere*, since it was thought desirable to permit defendants to plead *nolo* without making any inquiry into their actual guilt.

the evidence against him, which substantially negated his claim of innocence and which further provided a means by which the judge could test whether the plea was being intelligently entered,[10] its validity cannot be seriously questioned. In view of the strong factual basis for the plea demonstrated by the State and Alford's clearly expressed desire to enter it despite his professed belief in his innocence, we hold that the trial judge did not commit constitutional error in accepting it.[11]

* * * Alford now argues in effect that the State should not have allowed him this choice but should have insisted on proving him guilty of murder in the first degree. The States in their wisdom may take this course by statute or otherwise and may prohibit the practice of accepting pleas to lesser included offenses under any circumstances. But this is not the mandate of the Fourteenth Amendment and the Bill of Rights. The prohibitions against involuntary or unintelligent pleas should not be relaxed, but neither should an exercise in arid logic render those constitutional guarantees counterproductive and put in jeopardy the very human values they were meant to preserve. * * *

MR. JUSTICE BLACK * * * concurs in the judgment and in substantially all of the opinion in this case.

[The dissenting opinion of JUSTICE BRENNAN, with whom JUSTICES DOUGLAS and MARSHALL joined, is omitted.]

NOTES AND QUESTIONS

1.   What is a "factual basis" for a plea? Does it mean that there is proof beyond a reasonable doubt that the defendant is guilty? That the judge subjectively believes that the defendant is guilty? What does Fed. R. Crim. P. 11 suggest in regard to these questions? What insight does *Alford* provide?

2.   What does *Alford* teach us as a matter of constitutional law? Is a guilty plea constitutionally valid if it is voluntarily, knowingly, and intelligently made, even if the judge does not seek to determine whether there is factual basis for the plea? Does your answer change if the defendant

---

[10] Because of the importance of protecting the innocent and of insuring that guilty pleas are a product of free and intelligent choice, various state and federal court decisions properly caution that pleas coupled with claims of innocence should not be accepted unless there is a factual basis for the plea; and until the judge taking the plea has inquired into and sought to resolve the conflict between the waiver of trial and the claim of innocence.

In the federal courts, Fed. Rule Crim. Proc. 11 expressly provides that a court "shall not enter a judgment upon a plea of guilty unless it is satisfied that there is a factual basis for the plea."

[11] Our holding does not mean that a trial judge must accept every constitutionally valid guilty plea merely because a defendant wishes so to plead. A criminal defendant does not have an absolute right under the Constitution to have his guilty plea accepted by the court, although the States may by statute or otherwise confer such a right. Likewise, the States may bar their courts from accepting guilty pleas from any defendants who assert their innocence. Cf. Fed. Rule Crim. Proc. 11 [since amended, eds.], which gives a trial judge discretion to "refuse to accept a plea of guilty * * * ." We need not now delineate the scope of that discretion.

affirmatively asserts her innocence? Suppose that the judge *does* inquire as to the factual basis for a plea, determines that there *isn't* one, but she accepts the plea anyway. May she do this? If a judge determines that there *is* a factual basis for a plea, must that factual basis be placed on the record? See Meyers v. Gillis, 93 F.3d 1147 (3d Cir. 1996).

3.   Reconsider footnote 11. Constitutional law aside, should a judge have authority to reject a voluntary and informed guilty plea, if she believes that there is no factual basis for it? Should a counseled defendant, *even an innocent one*, be permitted to plead guilty if she rationally determines that a plea bargain is in her best interests? Do you agree with the state court quoted in *Alford* that "reasons other than the fact [a defendant] is guilty may induce a defendant to so plead * * * [and] * * * must be permitted to judge for himself" what is in his own best interests?

4.   Is *Alford* bad law from a *substantive* criminal law perspective? Are *nolo contendere* pleas also inadvisable? Consider:

> Criminal procedure has for too long treated itself as a subset of constitutional law, * * * distancing itself from substantive criminal law. Although substantive criminal law * * * discusses how well rules deter, rehabilitate, or exact retribution, these substantive values are largely absent from criminal procedure * * * [which] seems to care only about whether procedures are efficient, constitutional, fair, and accurate.

Stephanos Bibas, *Harmonizing Substantive-Criminal-Law Values and Criminal Procedure: The Case of Alford and Nolo Contendere Pleas*, 88 Cornell L. Rev. 1361, 1362 (2003).

Among Professor Bibas's criticisms are that "*Alford*-type and nolo contendere pleas, in the name of efficiency and autonomy [of the defendant], subvert the substantive moral messages that unambiguous trial verdicts send. * * * Guilty-but-not-guilty pleas muddy the moral message by implying that the law does not care enough to insist on clear, honest resolutions and vindications." *Id.* at 1402–03. Bibas also contends that such pleas undermine the offenders' rehabilitation, deny victims their deserved unambiguous vindication, and undercut deterrence by allowing wrongdoers, who dislike admitting guilt, to avoid that additional hardship and, in the case of nolo pleas, permit wrongdoers to make it more difficult for victims to collect compensation and restitution by requiring them to litigate guilt in a civil proceeding. *Id.* at 1406–07. Do any of these arguments convince you that *Alford* and nolo contendere pleas should be abolished?

5.   *Withdrawal of guilty pleas.* A defendant does not have a constitutional right to withdraw her plea once it has been accepted, even before sentencing. Judges typically have discretion, however, to permit withdrawal. The federal rule is that if a defendant seeks to withdraw her plea after it has been accepted but before sentence is imposed, the court may

permit the plea to be withdrawn if the defendant shows "a fair and just reason for requesting the withdrawal." Fed. R. Crim. P. 11(d)(2)(B).

C. DEFENSE ATTORNEY COMPETENCY IN PLEA NEGOTIATIONS

Introduction

In *Strickland v. Washington*, p. 1088, the Supreme Court held that a defendant's Sixth Amendment constitutional right to counsel includes the right to *effective* assistance of counsel. The *Strickland* Court held that this right is violated if the defendant can show that: (1) counsel's performance was deficient; and (2) the deficient performance prejudiced the defendant, i.e., "counsel's errors were so serious as to deprive the defendant of a fair trial, a trial whose result is reliable."

In Hill v. Lockhart, 474 U.S. 52, 106 S.Ct. 366, 88 L.Ed.2d 203 (1985), the Supreme Court applied the right to effective assistance of counsel in a plea bargaining context. In *Hill*, the defendant, who pled guilty, claimed on appeal that his counsel misinformed him of the length of time he would be required to serve before he would become eligible for parole. The Court's focus in *Hill* was on the prejudice prong, stated this way: "The second, or 'prejudice,' requirement * * * focuses on whether counsel's constitutionally ineffective performance affected the outcome of the plea process. In other words, in order to satisfy the 'prejudice' requirement, the defendant must show that there is a reasonable probability that, but for counsel's errors, he would not have pleaded guilty and would have insisted on going to trial." The Court proceeded:

> In many guilty plea cases, the "prejudice" inquiry will closely resemble the inquiry engaged in by courts reviewing ineffective-assistance challenges to convictions obtained through a trial. For example, where the alleged error of counsel is a failure to investigate or discover potentially exculpatory evidence, the determination whether the error "prejudiced" the defendant by causing him to plead guilty rather than go to trial will depend on the likelihood that discovery of the evidence would have led counsel to change his recommendation as to the plea. This assessment, in turn, will depend in large part on a prediction whether the evidence likely would have changed the outcome of a trial. Similarly, where the alleged error of counsel is a failure to advise the defendant of a potential affirmative defense to the crime charged, the resolution of the "prejudice" inquiry will depend largely on whether the affirmative defense likely would have succeeded at trial.

In *Hill*, the Court found that the prejudice prong was not satisfied because the defendant had not alleged that, even if he had received competent advice, he would have chosen to go to trial rather than plead guilty.

In 2012, the Supreme Court decided two more *Strickland* cases involving plea bargaining. In the first one, the defendant pled guilty to a felony unaware (due to deficient performance of his lawyer) that the prosecutor had made an expiring offer to reduce the offense to a misdemeanor in exchange for a guilty plea. The defendant, not surprisingly, alleged that had his lawyer informed him of this offer, he would have accepted it.

In the second case, due to a lawyer's faulty advice, the defendant rejected a guilty plea and stood trial. (Notice, this is the opposite of *Hill*, where the faulty advice caused the defendant to *accept* the guilty plea rather than, perhaps, go to trial.) The trial itself was fair, but the sentence the defendant received was more severe than what was offered to him by the prosecutor during plea negotiations.

In both cases, the first prong of *Strickland* was proven (or assumed on appeal). The issue focused on the prejudice prong and, even more importantly, on the remedy that should be enforced if prejudice is proven. We look at those two cases now.

MISSOURI V. FRYE

Supreme Court of the United States, 2012.
566 U.S. ___, 132 S.Ct. 1399, 182 L.Ed.2d 379.

JUSTICE KENNEDY delivered the opinion of the Court [joined by JUSTICES GINSBURG, BREYER, SOTOMAYOR, and KAGAN].

* * * This case arises in the context of claimed ineffective assistance that led to the lapse of a prosecution offer of a plea bargain, a proposal that offered terms more lenient than the terms of the guilty plea entered later. The initial question is whether the constitutional right to counsel extends to the negotiation and consideration of plea offers that lapse or are rejected. If there is a right to effective assistance with respect to those offers, a further question is what a defendant must demonstrate in order to show that prejudice resulted from counsel's deficient performance. * * *

I

In August 2007, respondent Galin Frye was charged with driving with a revoked license. Frye had been convicted for that offense on three other occasions, so the State of Missouri charged him with a class D felony, which carries a maximum term of imprisonment of four years. * * *

On November 15, the prosecutor sent a letter to Frye's counsel offering a choice of two plea bargains. The prosecutor first offered to recommend a 3-year sentence if there was a guilty plea to the felony charge, without a recommendation regarding probation but with a recommendation that Frye serve 10 days in jail as so-called "shock" time. The second offer was to reduce the charge to a misdemeanor and, if Frye pleaded guilty to it, to recommend a 90-day sentence. The misdemeanor charge of driving with a revoked license carries a maximum term of imprisonment of one year. The letter stated both offers would expire on December 28. Frye's attorney did not advise Frye that the offers had been made. The offers expired.

Frye's preliminary hearing was scheduled for January 4, 2008. On December 30, 2007, less than a week before the hearing, Frye was again arrested for driving with a revoked license. At the January 4 hearing, Frye waived his right to a preliminary hearing on the charge arising from the August 2007 arrest. He pleaded not guilty at a subsequent arraignment but then changed his plea to guilty. There was no underlying plea agreement. The state trial court accepted Frye's guilty plea. The prosecutor recommended a 3-year sentence, made no recommendation regarding probation, and requested 10 days shock time in jail. The trial judge sentenced Frye to three years in prison.

Frye filed for postconviction relief in state court. He alleged his counsel's failure to inform him of the prosecution's plea offer denied him the effective assistance of counsel. At an evidentiary hearing, Frye testified he would have entered a guilty plea to the misdemeanor had he known about the offer.

A state court denied the postconviction motion, but the Missouri Court of Appeals reversed. It determined that Frye met both of the requirements for showing a Sixth Amendment violation under *Strickland*. First, the court determined Frye's counsel's performance was deficient because the "record is void of any evidence of any effort by trial counsel to communicate the Offer to Frye during the Offer window." The court next concluded Frye had shown his counsel's deficient performance caused him prejudice because "Frye pled guilty to a felony instead of a misdemeanor and was subject to a maximum sentence of four years instead of one year."

To implement a remedy for the violation, the court deemed Frye's guilty plea withdrawn and remanded to allow Frye either to insist on a trial or to plead guilty to any offense the prosecutor deemed it appropriate to charge. * * *

II

A * * *

With respect to the right to effective counsel in plea negotiations, a proper beginning point is to discuss two cases from this Court considering the role of counsel in advising a client about a plea offer and an ensuing guilty plea: *Hill* v. *Lockhart*, and *Padilla* v. *Kentucky*, [p. 1144, Note 8].

Hill established that claims of ineffective assistance of counsel in the plea bargain context are governed by the two-part test set forth in *Strickland.* * * *

In *Padilla*, the Court again discussed the duties of counsel in advising a client with respect to a plea offer that leads to a guilty plea. *Padilla* held that a guilty plea, based on a plea offer, should be set aside because counsel misinformed the defendant of the immigration consequences of the conviction. The Court made clear that "the negotiation of a plea bargain is a critical phase of litigation for purposes of the Sixth Amendment right to effective assistance of counsel." It also rejected the argument made by petitioner in this case that a knowing and voluntary plea supersedes errors by defense counsel.

In the case now before the Court the State, as petitioner, points out that the legal question presented is different from that in *Hill* and *Padilla*. In those cases the claim was that the prisoner's plea of guilty was invalid because counsel had provided incorrect advice pertinent to the plea. In the instant case, by contrast, the guilty plea that was accepted, and the plea proceeding concerning it in court, were all based on accurate advice and information from counsel. The challenge is not to the advice pertaining to the plea that was accepted but rather to the course of legal representation that preceded it with respect to other potential pleas and plea offers.

To give further support to its contention that the instant case is in a category different from what the Court considered in *Hill* and *Padilla*, the State urges that there is no right to a plea offer or a plea bargain in any event. See *Weatherford* v. *Bursey*, 429 U. S. 545, 561 (1977). It claims Frye therefore was not deprived of any legal benefit to which he was entitled. Under this view, any wrongful or mistaken action of counsel with respect to earlier plea offers is beside the point. * * *

The State's contentions are neither illogical nor without some persuasive force, yet they do not suffice to overcome a simple reality. Ninety-seven percent of federal convictions and ninety-four percent of state convictions are the result of guilty pleas. The reality is that plea bargains have become so central to the administration of the criminal justice system that defense counsel have responsibilities in the plea bargain process, responsibilities that must be met to render the adequate assistance of counsel that the Sixth Amendment requires in the criminal process at critical stages. Because ours "is for the most part a system of pleas, not a system of trials," it is insufficient simply to point to the guarantee of a fair trial as a backstop that inoculates any errors in the pretrial process. "To a large extent * * * horse trading [between prosecutor and defense counsel] determines who goes to jail and for how long. That is what plea bargaining is. It is not some adjunct to the criminal justice system; it *is* the criminal justice system." Scott & Stuntz, Plea Bargaining as Contract, 101 Yale L. J. 1909, 1912 (1992). See also Barkow, Separation of Powers and the Criminal Law, 58 Stan. L. Rev. 989, 1034 (2006) ("[Defendants] who do take their case to trial and lose receive longer sentences than even Congress or the prosecutor might think appropriate, because the longer sentences exist on the books largely for bargaining purposes. This often results in individuals who accept a plea bargain receiving shorter sentences than other individuals who are less morally culpable but take a chance and go to trial" (footnote omitted)). In today's criminal justice system, therefore, the negotiation of a plea bargain, rather than the unfolding of a trial, is almost always the critical point for a defendant.

To note the prevalence of plea bargaining is not to criticize it. The potential to conserve valuable prosecutorial resources and for defendants to admit their crimes and receive more favorable terms at sentencing means that a plea agreement can benefit both parties. In order that these benefits can be realized, however, criminal defendants require effective counsel during plea negotiations. "Anything less * * * might deny a defendant 'effective representation by counsel at the only stage when legal aid and advice would help him.' "

B

The inquiry then becomes how to define the duty and responsibilities of defense counsel in the plea bargain process. This is a difficult question. "The art of negotiation is at least as nuanced as the art of trial advocacy and it presents questions farther removed from immediate judicial supervision." Bargaining is, by its nature, defined to a substantial degree by personal style. The alternative courses and tactics in negotiation are so individual that it may be neither prudent nor practicable to try to elaborate or define detailed standards for the proper discharge of defense counsel's participation in the process.

This case presents neither the necessity nor the occasion to define the duties of defense counsel in those respects, however. Here the question is whether defense counsel has the duty to communicate the terms of a formal offer to accept a plea on terms and conditions that may result in a lesser sentence, a conviction on lesser charges, or both.

This Court now holds that, as a general rule, defense counsel has the duty to communicate formal offers from the prosecution to accept a plea on terms and conditions that may be favorable to the accused. Any exceptions to that rule need not be explored here, for the offer was a formal one with a fixed expiration date. When defense counsel allowed the offer to expire without advising the defendant or allowing him to consider it, defense counsel did not render the effective assistance the Constitution requires.

Though the standard for counsel's performance is not determined solely by reference to codified standards of professional practice, these standards can be important guides. The American Bar Association recommends defense counsel "promptly communicate and explain to the defendant all plea offers made by the prosecuting attorney," and this standard has been adopted by numerous state and federal courts over the last 30 years. The standard for prompt communication and consultation is also set out in state bar professional standards for attorneys. * * *

Here defense counsel did not communicate the formal offers to the defendant. As a result of that deficient performance, the offers lapsed. Under *Strickland*, the question then becomes what, if any, prejudice resulted from the breach of duty.

C

To show prejudice from ineffective assistance of counsel where a plea offer has lapsed or been rejected because of counsel's deficient performance, defendants must demonstrate a reasonable probability they would have accepted the earlier plea offer had they been afforded effective assistance of counsel. Defendants must also demonstrate a reasonable probability the plea would have been entered without the prosecution canceling it or the trial court refusing to accept it, if they had the authority to exercise that discretion under state law. To establish prejudice in this instance, it is necessary to show a reasonable probability that the end result of the criminal process would have been more favorable by reason of a plea to a lesser charge or a sentence of less prison time.

This application of *Strickland* to the instances of an uncommunicated, lapsed plea does nothing to alter the standard laid out in *Hill*. In cases where a defendant complains that ineffective assistance led him to accept a plea offer as opposed to proceeding to trial, the defendant will have to show "a reasonable probability that, but for counsel's errors, he would not have pleaded guilty and would have insisted on going to trial." *Hill* was correctly decided and applies in the context in which it arose. *Hill* does not, however, provide the sole means for demonstrating prejudice arising from the deficient performance of counsel during plea negotiations. Unlike the defendant in *Hill*, Frye argues that with effective assistance he would have accepted an earlier plea offer (limiting his sentence to one year in prison) as opposed to entering an open plea (exposing him to a maximum sentence of four years' imprisonment). In a case, such as this, where a defendant pleads guilty to less favorable terms and claims that ineffective assistance of counsel caused him to miss out on a more favorable earlier plea offer, *Strickland*'s inquiry into whether "the result of the proceeding would have been different," requires looking not at whether the defendant would have proceeded to trial absent ineffective assistance but whether he would have accepted the offer to plead pursuant to the terms earlier proposed.

In order to complete a showing of *Strickland* prejudice, defendants who have shown a reasonable probability they would have accepted the earlier plea offer must also show that, if the prosecution had the discretion to cancel it or if the trial court had the discretion to refuse to accept it, there is a reasonable probability neither the prosecution nor the trial court would have prevented the offer from being accepted or implemented. This further showing is of particular importance because a defendant has no right to be offered a plea, nor a federal right that the judge accept it. In at least some States, including Missouri, it appears the prosecution has some discretion to cancel a plea agreement to which the defendant has agreed. The Federal Rules, some state rules including in Missouri, and this Court's precedents give trial courts some leeway to accept or reject plea agreements, see Fed. Rule Crim. Proc. 11(c)(3). It can be assumed that in most jurisdictions prosecutors and judges are familiar with the boundaries of acceptable plea bargains and sentences. So in most instances it should not be difficult to make an objective assessment as to whether or not a particular fact or intervening circumstance would suffice, in the normal course, to cause prosecutorial withdrawal or judicial nonapproval of a plea bargain. The determination that there is or is not a reasonable probability that the outcome of the proceeding would have been different absent counsel's errors can be conducted within that framework.

III

These standards must be applied to the instant case. * * * The Missouri Court of Appeals was correct that "counsel's representation fell below an objective standard of reasonableness."

The Court of Appeals erred, however, in articulating the precise standard for prejudice in this context. As noted, a defendant in Frye's position must show not only a reasonable probability that he would have accepted the lapsed plea but also a reasonable probability that the prosecution would have adhered to the agreement and that it would have been accepted by the trial court. Frye can show he would have accepted the offer, but there is strong reason to doubt the prosecution and the trial court would have permitted the plea bargain to become final.

There appears to be a reasonable probability Frye would have accepted the prosecutor's original offer of a plea bargain if the offer had been communicated to him, because he pleaded guilty to a more serious charge, with no promise of a sentencing recommendation from the prosecutor. It may be that in some cases defendants must show more than just a guilty plea to a charge or sentence harsher than the original offer. For example, revelations between plea offers about the strength of the prosecution's case may make a late decision to plead guilty insufficient to demonstrate, without further evidence, that the defendant would have pleaded guilty to an earlier, more generous plea offer if his counsel had reported it to him. Here, however, that is not the case. The Court of Appeals did not err in finding Frye's acceptance of the less favorable plea offer indicated that he would have accepted the earlier (and more favorable) offer had he been apprised of it; and there is no need to address here the showings that might be required in other cases.

The Court of Appeals failed, however, to require Frye to show that the first plea offer, if accepted by Frye, would have been adhered to by the prosecution and accepted by the trial court. Whether the prosecution and trial court are required to do so is a matter of state law, and it is not the place of this Court to settle those matters. * * * In Missouri, it appears "a plea offer once accepted by the defendant can be withdrawn without recourse" by the prosecution. The extent of the trial court's discretion in Missouri to reject a plea agreement appears to be in some doubt.

We remand for the Missouri Court of Appeals to consider these state-law questions, because they bear on the federal question of *Strickland* prejudice. If, as the Missouri court stated here, the prosecutor could have canceled the plea agreement, and if Frye fails to show a reasonable probability the prosecutor would have adhered to the agreement, there is no *Strickland* prejudice. Likewise, if the trial court could have refused to accept the plea agreement, and if Frye fails to show a reasonable probability the trial court would have accepted the plea, there is no *Strickland* prejudice. In this case, given Frye's new offense for driving without a license on December 30, 2007, there is reason to doubt that the prosecution would have adhered to the agreement or that the trial court would have accepted it at the January 4, 2008, hearing, unless they were required by state law to do so.

It is appropriate to allow the Missouri Court of Appeals to address this question in the first instance. The judgment of the Missouri Court of Appeals is vacated, and the case is remanded for further proceedings not inconsistent with this opinion. * * *

JUSTICE SCALIA, with whom THE CHIEF JUSTICE [ROBERTS], JUSTICE THOMAS, and JUSTICE ALITO join, dissenting.

* * * Frye's conviction here was established by his own admission of guilt, received by the court after the usual colloquy that assured it was voluntary and truthful. * * * Here it can be said not only that the process was fair, but that the defendant acknowledged the correctness of his conviction. * * *

* * *

Galin Frye's attorney failed to inform him about a plea offer, and Frye ultimately pleaded guilty without the benefit of a deal. Counsel's mistake did not deprive Frye of any substantive or procedural right; only of the opportunity to accept a plea bargain to which he had no entitlement in the first place. So little entitlement that, had he known of and accepted the bargain, the prosecution would have been able to withdraw it right up to the point that his guilty plea pursuant to the bargain was accepted.

The Court acknowledges, moreover, that Frye's conviction was untainted by attorney error: "[T]he guilty plea that was accepted, and the plea proceedings concerning it in court, were all based on accurate advice and information from counsel." Given the "ultimate focus" of our ineffective-assistance cases on "the fundamental fairness of the proceeding whose result is being challenged," *Strickland* v. *Washington*, that should be the end of the matter. Instead, * * * the Court mechanically applies an outcome-based test for prejudice, and mistakes the possibility of a different result for constitutional injustice. * * * [T]hat approach is contrary to our precedents on the right to effective counsel, and for good reason.

The Court announces its holding that "as a general rule, defense counsel has the duty to communicate formal offers from the prosecution" as though that resolves a disputed point; in reality, however, neither the State nor the Solicitor General argued that counsel's performance here was adequate. * * * In other cases, however, it will not be so clear that counsel's plea-bargaining skills, which must now meet a constitutional minimum, are adequate. "[H]ow to define the duty and responsibilities of defense counsel in the plea bargain process," the Court acknowledges, "is a difficult question," since "[b]argaining is, by its nature, defined to a substantial degree by personal style." Indeed. * * * The Court ignores such difficulties, however, since "[t]his case presents neither the necessity nor the occasion to define the duties of defense counsel in those respects." Perhaps not. But it does present the necessity of confronting the serious difficulties that will be created by constitutionalization of the plea-bargaining process. It will not do simply to announce that they will be solved in the sweet by-and-by.

While the inadequacy of counsel's performance in this case is clear enough, whether it was prejudicial (in the sense that the Court's new version of *Strickland* requires) is not. The Court's description of how that question is to be answered on remand is alone enough to show how unwise it is to constitutionalize the plea-bargaining process. Prejudice is to be determined, the Court tells us, by a process of retrospective crystal-ball gazing posing as legal analysis. First of all, of course, we must estimate whether the defendant *would have accepted* the earlier plea bargain. Here that seems an easy question, but as the Court acknowledges, it will not always be. Next, since Missouri, like other States, permits accepted plea offers to be withdrawn by the prosecution (a reality which alone should suffice, one would think, to demonstrate that Frye had no entitlement to the plea bargain), we must estimate whether the prosecution *would have withdrawn* the plea offer. And finally, we must estimate whether the trial court *would have approved* the plea agreement. These last two estimations may seem easy in the present case, since Frye committed a new infraction before the hearing at which the agreement would have been presented; but they assuredly will not be easy in the mine run of cases.

The Court says "[i]t can be assumed that in most jurisdictions prosecutors and judges are familiar with the boundaries of acceptable plea bargains and sentences." Assuredly it can, just as it can be assumed that the sun rises in the west; but I know of no basis for the assumption. Virtually no cases deal with the standards for a prosecutor's withdrawal from a plea agreement beyond stating the general rule that a prosecutor may withdraw any time prior to, but not after, the entry of a guilty plea or other action constituting detrimental reliance on the defendant's part. And cases addressing trial courts' authority to accept or reject plea agreements almost universally observe that a trial court enjoys broad discretion in this regard. Of course after today's opinions there will be cases galore, so the Court's *assumption* would better be cast as an optimistic *prediction* of the certainty that will emerge, many years hence, from our newly created constitutional field of plea-bargaining law. Whatever the "boundaries" ultimately devised (if that were possible), a vast amount of discretion will still remain, and it is extraordinary to make a defendant's constitutional rights depend upon a series of retrospective mind-readings as to how that discretion, in prosecutors and trial judges, *would have been* exercised.

The plea-bargaining process is a subject worthy of regulation, since it is the means by which most criminal convictions are obtained. It happens not to be, however, a subject covered by the Sixth Amendment, which is concerned not with the fairness of bargaining but with the fairness of conviction. * * * In this case * * *, the Court's sledge may require the reversal of perfectly valid, eminently just, convictions. A legislature could solve the problems presented by these cases in a much more precise and efficient manner. It might begin, for example, by penalizing the attorneys who made such grievous errors. That type of sub-constitutional remedy is not available to the Court, which is limited to penalizing (almost) everyone else by reversing valid convictions or sentences. Because that result is inconsistent with the Sixth Amendment and decades of our precedent, I respectfully dissent.

LAFLER V. COOPER

Supreme Court of the United States, 2012.
566 U.S. ___, 132 S.Ct. 1376, 182 L.Ed.2d 398.

JUSTICE KENNEDY delivered the opinion of the Court [joined by JUSTICES GINSBURG, BREYER, SOTOMAYOR, and KAGAN].

In this case, as in *Missouri* v. *Frye,* * * * a criminal defendant seeks a remedy when inadequate assistance of counsel caused nonacceptance of a plea offer and further proceedings led to a less favorable outcome. * * * The instant case comes to the Court with the concession that counsel's advice with respect to the plea offer fell below the standard of adequate assistance of counsel guaranteed by the Sixth Amendment, applicable to the States through the Fourteenth Amendment.

I

On the evening of March 25, 2003, respondent pointed a gun toward Kali Mundy's head and fired. From the record, it is unclear why respondent did this, and at trial it was suggested that he might have acted either in self-defense or in defense of another person. In any event the shot missed and Mundy fled. Respondent followed in pursuit, firing repeatedly. Mundy was shot in her buttock, hip, and abdomen but survived the assault.

Respondent was charged under Michigan law with assault with intent to murder, possession of a firearm by a felon, possession of a firearm in the commission of a felony, misdemeanor possession of marijuana, and for being a habitual offender. On two occasions, the prosecution offered to dismiss two of the charges and to recommend a sentence of 51 to 85 months for the other two, in exchange for a guilty plea. In a communication with the court respondent admitted guilt and expressed a willingness to accept the offer. Respondent, however, later rejected the offer on both occasions, allegedly after his attorney convinced him that the prosecution would be unable to establish his intent to murder Mundy because she had been shot below the waist. On the first day of trial the prosecution offered a significantly less favorable plea deal, which respondent again rejected. After trial, respondent was convicted on all counts and received a mandatory minimum sentence of 185 to 360 months' imprisonment.

In a * * * hearing before the state trial court, respondent argued his attorney's advice to reject the plea constituted ineffective assistance. The trial judge rejected the claim, and the Michigan Court of Appeals affirmed. * * *

Respondent then filed a petition for federal habeas relief under 28 U. S. C. § 2254, renewing his ineffective-assistance-of-counsel claim. * * * [T]he District Court granted a conditional writ. To remedy the violation, the District Court ordered "specific performance of [respondent's] original plea agreement, for a minimum sentence in the range of fifty-one to eighty-five months."

The United States Court of Appeals for the Sixth Circuit affirmed * * * . * * *

II

A

* * * In this case all parties agree the performance of respondent's counsel was deficient when he advised respondent to reject the plea offer on the grounds he could not be convicted at trial. In light of this concession, it is unnecessary for this Court to explore the issue.

The question for this Court is how to apply *Strickland*'s prejudice test where ineffective assistance results in a rejection of the plea offer and the defendant is convicted at the ensuing trial.

B

To establish *Strickland* prejudice a defendant must "show that there is a reasonable probability that, but for counsel's unprofessional errors, the result of the proceeding would have been different." In the context of pleas a defendant must show the outcome of the plea process would have been different with competent advice. In *Hill*, when evaluating the petitioner's claim that ineffective assistance led to the improvident acceptance of a guilty plea, the Court required the petitioner to show "that there is a reasonable probability that, but for counsel's errors, [the defendant] would not have pleaded guilty and would have insisted on going to trial."

In contrast to *Hill*, here the ineffective advice led not to an offer's acceptance but to its rejection. Having to stand trial, not choosing to waive it, is the prejudice alleged. In these circumstances a defendant must show that but for the ineffective advice of counsel there is a reasonable probability that the plea offer would have been presented to the court (*i.e.*, that the defendant would have accepted the plea and the prosecution would not have withdrawn it in light of intervening circumstances), that the court would have accepted its terms, and that the conviction or sentence, or both, under the offer's terms would have been less severe than under the judgment and sentence that in fact were imposed. * * *

Petitioner and the Solicitor General propose a different, far more narrow, view of the Sixth Amendment. They contend there can be no finding of *Strickland* prejudice arising from plea bargaining if the defendant is later convicted at a fair trial. The * * * reasons petitioner and the Solicitor General offer for their approach are unpersuasive.

First, [they] claim that the sole purpose of the Sixth Amendment is to protect the right to a fair trial. Errors before trial, they argue, are not cognizable under the Sixth Amendment unless they affect the fairness of the trial itself. The Sixth Amendment, however, is not so narrow in its reach. The Sixth Amendment requires effective assistance of counsel at critical stages of a criminal proceeding. Its protections are not designed simply to protect the trial * * *. The constitutional guarantee applies to pretrial critical stages that are part of the whole course of a criminal proceeding, a proceeding in which defendants cannot be presumed to make critical decisions without counsel's advice. This is consistent, too, with the rule that defendants have a right to effective assistance of counsel on appeal, even though that cannot in any way be characterized as part of the trial. The precedents also establish that there exists a right to counsel during sentencing in both noncapital and capital cases. * * *

The Court, moreover, has not followed a rigid rule that an otherwise fair trial remedies errors not occurring at the trial itself. It has inquired instead whether the trial cured the particular error at issue. Thus, in *Vasquez* v. *Hillery*, 474 U. S. 254 (1986), the deliberate exclusion of all African-Americans from a grand jury was prejudicial because a defendant may have been tried on charges that would not have been brought at all by a properly constituted grand jury. * * *

[Second], petitioner seeks to preserve the conviction obtained by the State by arguing that the purpose of the Sixth Amendment is to ensure "the reliability of [a] conviction following trial." This argument, too, fails to comprehend the full scope of the Sixth Amendment's protections; and it is refuted by precedent. *Strickland* recognized "[t]he benchmark for judging any claim of ineffectiveness must be whether counsel's conduct so undermined the proper functioning of the adversarial process that the trial cannot be relied on as having produced a just result." The goal of a just result is not divorced from the reliability of a conviction; but here the question is not the fairness or reliability of the trial but the fairness and regularity of the processes that preceded it, which caused the defendant to lose benefits he would have received in the ordinary course but for counsel's ineffective assistance.

There are instances, furthermore, where a reliable trial does not foreclose relief when counsel has failed to assert rights that may have altered the outcome. In *Kimmelman* v. *Morrison*, [p. 1111, Note 2], the Court held that an attorney's failure to timely move to suppress evidence during trial could be grounds for federal habeas relief. The Court rejected the suggestion that the "failure to make a timely request for the exclusion of illegally seized evidence" could not be the basis for a Sixth Amendment violation because the evidence "is 'typically reliable and often the most probative information bearing on the guilt or innocence of the defendant.' " "The constitutional rights of criminal defendants," the Court observed, "are granted to the innocent and the guilty alike. Consequently, we decline to hold either that the guarantee of effective assistance of counsel belongs solely to the innocent or that it attaches only to matters affecting the determination of actual guilt." The same logic applies here. The fact that respondent is guilty does not mean he was not entitled by the Sixth Amendment to effective assistance or that he suffered no prejudice from his attorney's deficient performance during plea bargaining.

In the end, petitioner's * * * arguments amount to one general contention: A fair trial wipes clean any deficient performance by defense counsel during plea bargaining. * * * As explained in *Frye*, the right to adequate assistance of counsel cannot be defined or enforced without taking account of the central role plea bargaining plays in securing convictions and determining sentences.

C

Even if a defendant shows ineffective assistance of counsel has caused the rejection of a plea leading to a trial and a more severe sentence, there is the question of what constitutes an appropriate remedy. That question must now be addressed.

Sixth Amendment remedies should be "tailored to the injury suffered from the constitutional violation and should not unnecessarily infringe on competing interests." Thus, a remedy must "neutralize the taint" of a constitutional violation, while at the same time not grant a windfall to the defendant or needlessly squander the considerable resources the State properly invested in the criminal prosecution.

The specific injury suffered by defendants who decline a plea offer as a result of ineffective assistance of counsel and then receive a greater sentence as a result of trial can come in at least one of two forms. In some cases, the sole advantage a defendant would have received under the plea is a lesser sentence. This is typically the case when the charges that would have been admitted as part of the plea bargain are the same as the charges the defendant was convicted of after trial. In this situation the court may conduct an evidentiary hearing to determine whether the defendant has shown a reasonable probability that but for counsel's errors he would have accepted the plea. If the showing is made, the court may exercise discretion in determining whether the defendant should receive the term of imprisonment the government offered in the plea, the sentence he received at trial, or something in between.

In some situations it may be that resentencing alone will not be full redress for the constitutional injury. If, for example, an offer was for a guilty plea to a count or counts less serious than the ones for which a defendant was convicted after trial, or if a mandatory sentence confines a judge's sentencing discretion after trial, a resentencing based on the conviction at trial may not suffice. In these circumstances, the proper exercise of discretion to remedy the constitutional injury may be to require the prosecution to reoffer the plea proposal. Once this has occurred, the judge can then exercise discretion in deciding whether to vacate the conviction from trial and accept the plea or leave the conviction undisturbed.

In implementing a remedy in both of these situations, the trial court must weigh various factors; and the boundaries of proper discretion need not be defined here. Principles elaborated over time in decisions of state and federal courts, and in statutes and rules, will serve to give more complete guidance as to the factors that should bear upon the exercise of the judge's discretion. At this point, however, it suffices to note two considerations that are of relevance.

First, a court may take account of a defendant's earlier expressed willingness, or unwillingness, to accept responsibility for his or her actions. Second, it is not necessary here to decide as a constitutional rule that a judge is required to prescind (that is to say disregard) any information concerning the crime that was discovered after the plea offer was made. The time continuum makes it difficult to restore the defendant and the prosecution to the precise positions they occupied prior to the rejection of the plea offer, but that baseline can be consulted in finding a remedy that does not require the prosecution to incur the expense of conducting a new trial. * * *

III

The standards for ineffective assistance of counsel when a defendant rejects a plea offer and goes to trial must now be applied to this case. * * *

Respondent has satisfied *Strickland*'s two-part test. * * * Here, * * * the fact of deficient performance has been conceded by all parties. The case comes to us on that assumption, so there is no need to address this question.

As to prejudice, respondent has shown that but for counsel's deficient performance there is a reasonable probability he and the trial court would have accepted the guilty plea. In addition, as a result of not accepting the plea and being convicted at trial, respondent received a minimum sentence 3 times greater than he would have received under the plea. The standard for ineffective assistance under *Strickland* has thus been satisfied.

As a remedy, the District Court ordered specific performance of the original plea agreement. The correct remedy in these circumstances, however, is to order the State to reoffer the plea agreement. Presuming respondent accepts the offer, the state trial court can then exercise its discretion in determining whether to vacate the convictions and resentence respondent pursuant to the plea agreement, to vacate only some of the convictions and resentence respondent accordingly, or to leave the convictions and sentence from trial undisturbed. Today's decision leaves open to the trial court how best to exercise that discretion in all the circumstances of the case. * * *

JUSTICE SCALIA, with whom JUSTICE THOMAS joins, and with whom THE CHIEF JUSTICE ROBERTS joins as to all but Part IV, dissenting. * * *

Anthony Cooper received a full and fair trial, was found guilty of all charges by a unanimous jury, and was given the sentence that the law prescribed. The Court nonetheless concludes that Cooper is entitled to some sort of habeas corpus relief (perhaps) because his attorney's allegedly incompetent advice regarding a plea offer *caused* him to receive a full and fair trial. That conclusion is foreclosed by our precedents. * * * And the remedy the Court announces—namely, whatever the state trial court in its discretion prescribes, down to and including no remedy at all—is unheard-of and quite absurd for violation of a constitutional right. I respectfully dissent.

I

This case and its companion, *Missouri* v. *Frye*, raise relatively straightforward questions about the scope of the right to effective assistance of counsel. * * * As the Court notes, the right to counsel does not begin at trial. It extends to "any stage of the prosecution, formal or informal, in court or out, where counsel's absence might derogate from the accused's right to a fair trial." Applying that principle, we held that the "entry of a guilty plea, whether to a misdemeanor or a felony charge, ranks as a 'critical stage' at which the right to counsel adheres." And it follows from this that *acceptance* of a plea offer is a critical stage. That, and nothing more, is the point of the Court's observation in *Padilla* v. *Kentucky* that "the negotiation of a plea bargain is a critical phase of litigation for purposes of the Sixth Amendment right to effective assistance of counsel." The defendant in *Padilla* had accepted the plea bargain and pleaded guilty, abandoning his right to a fair trial; he was entitled to advice of competent counsel before he did so. The Court has never held that the rule articulated in *Padilla* * * * and *Hill* extends to all aspects of plea negotiations, requiring not just advice of competent counsel before the defendant accepts a plea bargain and pleads guilty, but also the advice of competent counsel before the defendant rejects a plea bargain and stands on his constitutional right to a fair trial. The latter is a vast departure from our past cases, protecting not just the constitutionally prescribed right to a fair adjudication of guilt and punishment, but a judicially invented right to effective plea bargaining.

It is also apparent from *Strickland* that bad plea bargaining has nothing to do with ineffective assistance of counsel in the constitutional sense. *Strickland* explained that "[i]n giving meaning to the requirement [of effective assistance], . . . we must take its purpose—to ensure a fair trial—as the guide." Since "the right to the effective assistance of counsel is recognized not for its own sake, but because of the effect it has on the ability of the accused to receive a fair trial," the "benchmark" inquiry in evaluating any claim of ineffective assistance is whether counsel's performance "so undermined the proper functioning of the adversarial process" that it failed to produce a reliably "just result." That is what *Strickland*'s requirement of "prejudice" consists of: Because the right to effective assistance has as its purpose the assurance of a fair trial, the right is not infringed unless counsel's mistakes call into question the basic justice of a defendant's conviction or sentence. That has been, until today, entirely clear. A defendant must show "that counsel's errors were so serious as to deprive the defendant of a fair trial, a trial whose result is reliable." Impairment of fair trial is how we distinguish between unfortunate attorney error and error of constitutional significance.

To be sure, *Strickland* stated a rule of thumb for measuring prejudice which, applied blindly and out of context, could support the Court's holding today: "The defendant must show that there is a reasonable probability that, but for counsel's unprofessional errors, the result of the proceeding would have been different." *Strickland* itself cautioned, however, that its test was not to be applied in a mechanical fashion, and that courts were not to divert their "ultimate focus" from "the fundamental fairness of the proceeding whose result is being challenged." And until today we have followed that course. * * *[2]

* * * In ignoring *Strickland*'s "ultimate focus . . . on the fundamental fairness of the proceeding whose result is being challenged," the Court has lost the forest for the trees, leading it to accept what we have previously rejected, the "novel argument that constitutional rights are

---

[2] *Kimmelman* v. *Morrison*, cited by the Court, does not contradict this principle. * * * The parties in *Kimmelman* had not raised the question "whether the admission of illegally seized but reliable evidence can ever constitute 'prejudice' under *Strickland*" * * * and the Court therefore did not address it. *Kimmelman* made clear, however, how the answer to that question is to be determined: "The essence of an ineffective-assistance claim is that counsel's unprofessional errors so upset the adversarial balance between defense and prosecution *that the trial was rendered unfair and the verdict rendered suspect.*" In short, *Kimmelman*'s only relevance is to prove the Court's opinion wrong.

infringed by trying the defendant rather than accepting his plea of guilty." * * *

III

It is impossible to conclude discussion of today's extraordinary opinion without commenting upon the remedy it provides for the unconstitutional conviction. It is a remedy unheard-of in American jurisprudence—and, I would be willing to bet, in the jurisprudence of any other country.

The Court requires Michigan to "reoffer the plea agreement" that was rejected because of bad advice from counsel. That would indeed be a powerful remedy—but for the fact that Cooper's acceptance of that re-offered agreement is not conclusive. Astoundingly, "the state trial court can then *exercise its discretion* in determining whether to vacate the convictions and resentence respondent pursuant to the plea agreement, to vacate only some of the convictions and resentence respondent accordingly, *or to leave the convictions and sentence from trial undisturbed.*"

Why, one might ask, require a "reoffer" of the plea agreement, and its acceptance by the defendant? If the district court finds (as a necessary element, supposedly, of *Strickland* prejudice) that Cooper *would have accepted* the original offer, and would thereby have avoided trial and conviction, why not skip the reoffer-and-reacceptance minuet and simply leave it to the discretion of the state trial court what the remedy shall be? The answer, of course, is camouflage. Trial courts, after all, *regularly* accept or reject plea agreements, so there seems to be nothing extraordinary about their accepting or rejecting the new one mandated by today's decision. But the acceptance or rejection of a plea agreement that has no status whatever under the United States Constitution is worlds apart from what this is: "discretionary" specification of a remedy for an unconstitutional criminal conviction.

To be sure, the Court asserts that there are "factors" which bear upon (and presumably limit) exercise of this discretion—factors that it is not prepared to specify in full, much less assign some determinative weight. "Principles elaborated over time in decisions of state and federal courts, and in statutes and rules" will (in the Court's rosy view) sort all that out. I find it extraordinary that "statutes and rules" can specify the remedy for a criminal defendant's unconstitutional conviction. Or that the remedy for an unconstitutional conviction should *ever* be subject *at all* to a trial judge's discretion. Or, finally, that the remedy could *ever* include no remedy at all.

I suspect that the Court's squeamishness in fashioning a remedy, and the incoherence of what it comes up with, is attributable to its realization, deep down, that there is no real constitutional violation here anyway. The defendant has been fairly tried, lawfully convicted, and properly sentenced, and *any* "remedy" provided for this will do nothing but undo the just results of a fair adversarial process.

IV

In many—perhaps most—countries of the world, American-style plea bargaining is forbidden in cases as serious as this one, even for the purpose of obtaining testimony that enables conviction of a greater malefactor, much less for the purpose of sparing the expense of trial. In Europe, many countries adhere to what they aptly call the "legality principle" by requiring prosecutors to charge all prosecutable offenses, which is typically incompatible with the practice of charge-bargaining. Such a system reflects an admirable belief that the law is the law, and those who break it should pay the penalty provided.

In the United States, we have plea bargaining a-plenty, but until today it has been regarded as a necessary evil. It presents grave risks of prosecutorial overcharging that effectively compels an innocent defendant to avoid massive risk by pleading guilty to a lesser offense; and for guilty defendants it often—perhaps usually—results in a sentence well below what the law prescribes for the actual crime. But even so, we accept plea bargaining because many believe that without it our long and expensive process of criminal trial could not sustain the burden imposed on it, and our system of criminal justice would grind to a halt.

Today, however, the Supreme Court of the United States elevates plea bargaining from a necessary evil to a constitutional entitlement. It is no longer a somewhat embarrassing adjunct to our criminal justice system; rather, as the Court announces in the companion case to this one, " 'it *is* the criminal justice system.' " Thus, even though there is no doubt that the respondent here is guilty of the offense with which he was charged; even though he has received the exorbitant gold standard of American justice—a full-dress criminal trial with its innumerable constitutional and statutory limitations upon the evidence that the prosecution can bring forward, and (in Michigan as in most States) the requirement of a unanimous guilty verdict by impartial jurors; the Court says that his conviction is invalid because he was deprived of his *constitutional entitlement* to plea-bargain.

I am less saddened by the outcome of this case than I am by what it says about this Court's attitude toward criminal justice. The Court today embraces the sporting-chance theory of criminal law, in which the State functions like a conscientious casino-operator, giving each player a fair chance to beat the house, that is, to serve less time than the law says he deserves. And when a player is excluded from the tables, his *constitutional rights* have been violated. I do not subscribe to that theory. No one should, least of all the Justices of the Supreme Court. * * *

[JUSTICE ALITO'S dissent is omitted.]

NOTES AND QUESTIONS

1.   One scholar has suggested that "[t]he majority and dissenting opinions [in *Frye* and *Lafler*] almost talked past each other, reaching starkly different conclusions because they started from opposite premises: contemporary and pragmatic versus historical and formalist." Stephanos Bibas, *Incompetent Plea Bargaining and Extrajudicial Reforms*, 126 Harv. L. Rev. 150, 151 (2012). What is Professor Bibas getting at?

2.   Is Justice Scalia right that applying *Strickland* in the plea bargaining context will create "serious difficulties" in the "sweet by-and-by" as the Court is forced to confront the protean, shadowy plea bargaining process? Not according to Professor Bibas, supra. He says that courts have been applying the *Strickland* standard for years "without evident problems," so it should be able to do so in this new context satisfactorily. But, will these cases result in significant change? No, according to Bibas, at 159:

> [F]ew defendants will muster the necessary proof to demonstrate ineffective [and prejudicial] plea-bargaining assistance, judges are naturally disinclined to overturn convictions, and judges are unlikely to dispense overly generous remedies. Defendants must hope not so much for judicial redress after the fact as for other actors' proactive reforms to ensure competent advice in the first place.

3.   *The regulation of plea bargaining going forward.* How will these cases affect future plea bargaining? What changes would you expect?

D. MAKING AND BREAKING DEALS

1. MAKING THE DEAL

With plea bargaining legitimized, the Supreme Court has had to advise lower courts on how to distinguish between coercive and, simply, hard, plea negotiations. In essence, the question is: How much pressure may a prosecutor impose in order to make a deal? The next case provides some insight.

BORDENKIRCHER V. HAYES

Supreme Court of the United States, 1978.
434 U.S. 357, 98 S.Ct. 663, 54 L.Ed.2d 604.

MR. JUSTICE STEWART delivered the opinion of the Court [joined by CHIEF JUSTICE BURGER, and JUSTICES WHITE, REHNQUIST, and STEVENS].

The question in this case is whether the Due Process Clause of the Fourteenth Amendment is violated when a state prosecutor carries out a threat made during plea negotiations to reindict the accused on more serious charges if he does not plead guilty to the offense with which he was originally charged.

I

The respondent, Paul Lewis Hayes, was indicted by a Fayette County, Ky., grand jury on a charge of uttering a forged instrument in the amount of $88.30, an offense then punishable by a term of 2 to 10 years in prison. After arraignment, Hayes, his retained counsel, and the Commonwealth's Attorney met in the presence of the Clerk of the Court to discuss a possible plea agreement. During these conferences the prosecutor offered to recommend a sentence of five years in prison if Hayes would plead guilty to the indictment. He also said that if Hayes did not plead guilty and "saved the court the inconvenience and necessity of a trial," he would return to the grand jury to seek an indictment under the Kentucky Habitual Criminal Act, * * * which would subject Hayes to a mandatory sentence of life imprisonment by reason of his two prior felony convictions. Hayes chose not to plead guilty, and the prosecutor did obtain an indictment charging him under the Habitual Criminal Act. It is not disputed that the recidivist charge was fully justified by the evidence, that the prosecutor was in possession of this evidence at the time of the original indictment, and that Hayes' refusal to plead guilty to the original charge was what led to his indictment under the habitual criminal statute.

A jury found Hayes guilty on the principal charge of uttering a forged instrument and, in a separate proceeding, further found that he had twice before been convicted of felonies. As required by the habitual offender statute, he was sentenced to a life term in the penitentiary. The Kentucky Court of Appeals [held] * * * that the prosecutor's decision to indict him as a habitual offender was a legitimate use of available leverage in the plea-bargaining process.

On Hayes' petition for a federal writ of habeas corpus, the United States District Court for the Eastern District of Kentucky agreed that there had been no constitutional violation in the * * * indictment procedure, and denied the writ. The Court of Appeals for the Sixth Circuit reversed the District Court's judgment. While recognizing "that plea bargaining now plays an important role in our criminal justice system," the appellate court thought that the prosecutor's conduct during the bargaining negotiations had violated the principles of *Blackledge v. Perry* [p. 907], which "protect[ed] defendants from the vindictive exercise of a prosecutor's discretion." * * *

II

It may be helpful to clarify at the outset the nature of the issue in this case. While the prosecutor did not actually obtain the recidivist indictment until after the plea conferences had ended, his intention to do so was clearly expressed at the outset of the plea negotiations. Hayes was thus fully informed of the true terms of the offer when he made his decision to plead not guilty. This is not a situation, therefore, where the prosecutor without notice brought an additional and more serious charge after plea negotiations relating only to the original indictment had ended with the defendant's insistence on pleading not guilty. As a practical matter, in short, this case would be no different if the grand jury had indicted Hayes as a recidivist from the outset, and the prosecutor had offered to drop that charge as part of the plea bargain.

The Court of Appeals nonetheless drew a distinction between "concessions relating to prosecution under an existing indictment," and threats to bring more severe charges not contained in the original indictment—a line it thought necessary in order to establish a prophylactic rule to guard against the evil of prosecutorial vindictiveness. Quite apart from this chronological distinction, however, the Court of Appeals found that the prosecutor had acted vindictively in the present case since he had conceded that the indictment was influenced by his desire to induce a guilty plea. The ultimate conclusion of the Court of Appeals thus seems to have been that a prosecutor acts vindictively and in violation of due process of law whenever his charging decision is influenced by what he hopes to gain in the course of plea bargaining negotiations. * * *

IV

This Court held in *North Carolina v. Pearce* [p. 1464] that the Due Process Clause of the Fourteenth Amendment "requires that vindictiveness against a defendant for having successfully attacked his first conviction must play no part in the sentence he receives after a new trial." The same principle was later applied to prohibit a prosecutor from reindicting a convicted misdemeanant on a felony charge after the defendant had invoked an appellate remedy, since in this situation there was also a "realistic likelihood of 'vindictiveness.' " *Blackledge v. Perry.*

In those cases the Court was dealing with the State's unilateral imposition of a penalty upon a defendant who had chosen to exercise a legal right to attack his original conviction—a situation "very different from the give-and-take negotiation common in plea bargaining between the prosecution and defense, which arguably possess relatively equal bargaining power." The Court has emphasized that the due process violation in cases such as *Pearce* and *Perry* lay not in the possibility that a defendant might be deterred from the exercise of a legal right, but rather in the danger that the State might be retaliating against the accused for lawfully attacking his conviction.

To punish a person because he has done what the law plainly allows him to do is a due process violation of the most basic sort, and for an agent of the State to pursue a course of action whose objective is to penalize a person's reliance on his legal rights is "patently unconstitutional." But in the "give-and-take" of plea bargaining, there is no such element of punishment or retaliation so long as the accused is free to accept or reject the prosecution's offer.

Plea bargaining flows from "the mutuality of advantage" to defendants and prosecutors, each with his own reasons for wanting to avoid trial. Defendants advised by competent counsel and protected by other procedural safeguards are presumptively capable of intelligent choice in response to prosecutorial persuasion, and unlikely to be driven to false self-condemnation. Indeed, acceptance of the basic legitimacy of plea bargaining necessarily implies rejection of any notion that a guilty plea is involuntary in a constitutional sense simply because it is the end result of the bargaining process. By hypothesis, the plea may have been induced by promises of a recommendation of a lenient sentence or a reduction of charges, and thus by fear of the possibility of a greater penalty upon conviction after a trial.

While confronting a defendant with the risk of more severe punishment clearly may have a "discouraging effect on the defendant's assertion of his trial rights, the imposition of these difficult choices [is] an inevitable"—and permissible—"attribute of any legitimate system which tolerates and encourages the negotiation of pleas." It follows that, by tolerating and encouraging the negotiation of pleas, this Court has necessarily accepted as constitutionally legitimate the simple reality that the prosecutor's interest at the bargaining table is to persuade the defendant to forgo his right to plead not guilty.

* * * Moreover, a rigid constitutional rule that would prohibit a prosecutor from acting forthrightly in his dealings with the defense could only invite unhealthy subterfuge that would drive the practice of plea bargaining back into the shadows from which it has so recently emerged.

There is no doubt that the breadth of discretion that our country's legal system vests in prosecuting attorneys carries with it the potential for both individual and institutional abuse. And broad though that discretion may be, there are undoubtedly constitutional limits upon its exercise. We hold only that the course of conduct engaged in by the prosecutor in this case, which no more than openly presented the defendant with the unpleasant alternatives of forgoing trial or facing charges on which he was plainly subject to prosecution, did not violate the Due Process Clause of the Fourteenth Amendment.

MR. JUSTICE BLACKMUN, with whom MR. JUSTICE BRENNAN and MR. JUSTICE MARSHALL join, dissenting.

I feel that the Court, although purporting to rule narrowly * * * is departing from, or at least restricting, the principles established in *North Carolina v. Pearce* and in *Blackledge v. Perry*. * * *

In *Pearce*, as indeed the Court notes, it was held that "vindictiveness against a defendant for having successfully attacked his first conviction must play no part in the sentence he receives after a new trial." Accordingly, if on the new trial, the sentence the defendant receives from the court is greater than that imposed after the first trial, it must be explained by reasons "based upon objective information concerning identifiable conduct on the part of the defendant occurring after the time of the original sentencing proceeding," other than his having pursued the appeal or collateral remedy. * * *

Then later, in *Perry*, the Court applied the same principle to prosecutorial conduct where there was a "realistic likelihood of 'vindictiveness.' " It held that the requirement of Fourteenth Amendment due process prevented a prosecutor's reindictment of a convicted misdemeanant on a felony charge after the defendant had exercised his right to appeal the misdemeanor conviction and thus to obtain a trial *de novo*. It noted the prosecution's "considerable stake" in discouraging the appeal.

* * * [I]n this case vindictiveness is present to the same extent as it was thought to be in *Pearce* and in *Perry*; the prosecutor here admitted that the sole reason for the new indictment was to discourage the respondent from exercising his right to a trial. Even had such an admission not been made, when plea negotiations, conducted in the face of the less serious charge under the first indictment, fail, charging by a second indictment a more serious crime for the same conduct creates "a strong inference" of vindictiveness. * * * I therefore do not understand why, as in *Pearce*, due process does not require that the prosecution justify its action on some basis other than discouraging respondent from the exercise of his right to a trial. * * *

It might be argued that it really makes little difference how this case, now that it is here, is decided. The Court's holding gives plea bargaining full sway despite vindictiveness. A contrary result, however, merely would prompt the aggressive prosecutor to bring the greater charge initially in every case, and only thereafter to bargain. The consequences to the accused would still be adverse, for then he would bargain against a greater charge, face the likelihood of increased bail, and run the risk that the court would be less inclined to accept a bargained plea. Nonetheless, it is far preferable to hold the prosecution to the charge it was originally content to bring and to justify in the eyes of its public.[12]

MR. JUSTICE POWELL, dissenting. * * *

Although I agree with much of the Court's opinion, I am not satisfied that the result in this case is just or that the conduct of the plea bargaining met the requirements of due process. * * *

The prosecutor's initial assessment of respondent's case led him to forgo an indictment under the habitual criminal statute. The circumstances of respondent's prior convictions are relevant to this assessment and to my view of the case. Respondent was 17 years old when he committed his first offense. * * * Although respondent's prior convictions brought him within the terms of the Habitual Criminal Act, the offenses themselves did not result in imprisonment; yet the addition of a conviction on a charge involving $88.30 subjected respondent to a mandatory sentence of imprisonment for life. Persons convicted of rape and murder often are not punished so severely.

No explanation appears in the record for the prosecutor's decision to escalate the charge against respondent other than respondent's refusal to plead guilty. The prosecutor has conceded that his purpose was to discourage respondent's assertion of constitutional rights, and the majority accepts this characterization of events.

---

[12] That prosecutors, without saying so, may sometimes bring charges more serious than they think appropriate for the ultimate disposition of a case, in order to gain bargaining leverage with a defendant, does not add support to today's decision, for this Court, in its approval of the advantages to be gained from plea negotiations, has never openly sanctioned such deliberate overcharging or taken such a cynical view of the bargaining process. Normally, of course, it is impossible to show that this is what the prosecutor is doing, and the courts necessarily have deferred to the prosecutor's exercise of discretion in initial charging decisions.

Even if overcharging is to be sanctioned, there are strong reasons of fairness why the charges should be presented at the beginning of the bargaining process, rather than as a filliped threat at the end. First, it means that a prosecutor is required to reach a charging decision without any knowledge of the particular defendant's willingness to plead guilty; hence the defendant who truly believes himself to be innocent, and wishes for that reason to go to trial, is not likely to be subject to quite such a devastating gamble since the prosecutor has fixed the incentives for the average case.

Second, it is healthful to keep charging practices visible to the general public, so that political bodies can judge whether the policy being followed is a fair one. Visibility is enhanced if the prosecutor is required to lay his cards on the table with an indictment of public record at the beginning of the bargaining process, rather than making use of unrecorded verbal warnings of more serious indictments yet to come.

Finally, I would question whether it is fair to pressure defendants to plead guilty by threat of reindictment on an enhanced charge for the same conduct when the defendant has no way of knowing whether the prosecutor would indeed be entitled to bring him to trial on the enhanced charge. Here, though there is no dispute that respondent met the then-current definition of a habitual offender under Kentucky law, it is conceivable that a properly instructed Kentucky grand jury, in response to the same considerations that ultimately moved the Kentucky Legislature to amend the habitual offender statute, would have refused to subject respondent to such an onerous penalty for his forgery charge. * * *

It seems to me that the question to be asked under the circumstances is whether the prosecutor reasonably might have charged respondent under the Habitual Criminal Act in the first place. The deference that courts properly accord the exercise of a prosecutor's discretion perhaps would foreclose judicial criticism if the prosecutor originally had sought an indictment under that Act, as unreasonable as it would have seemed.[2] But here the prosecutor evidently made a reasonable, responsible judgment not to subject an individual to a mandatory life sentence when his only new offense had societal implications as limited as those accompanying the uttering of a single $88 forged check and when the circumstances of his prior convictions confirmed the inappropriateness of applying the habitual criminal statute. I think it may be inferred that the prosecutor himself deemed it unreasonable and not in the public interest to put this defendant in jeopardy of a sentence of life imprisonment.

There may be situations in which a prosecutor would be fully justified in seeking a fresh indictment for a more serious offense. * * *

But this is not such a case. Here, any inquiry into the prosecutor's purpose is made unnecessary by his candid acknowledgment that he threatened to procure and in fact procured the habitual criminal indictment because of respondent's insistence on exercising his constitutional rights. * * *

The plea-bargaining process, as recognized by this Court, is essential to the functioning of the criminal-justice system. It normally affords genuine benefits to defendants as well as to society. * * * Only in the most exceptional case should a court conclude that the scales of the bargaining are so unevenly balanced as to arouse suspicion. In this case, the prosecutor's actions denied respondent due process because their admitted purpose was to discourage and then to penalize with unique severity his exercise of constitutional rights. Implementation of a strategy calculated solely to deter the exercise of constitutional rights is not a constitutionally permissible exercise of discretion. I would affirm the opinion of the Court of Appeals on the facts of this case.

NOTES AND QUESTIONS

1.   The purpose of the rules announced in *Blackledge v. Perry* and *North Carolina v. Pearce* is to deter vindictiveness by prosecutors and judges,

---

[2]   The majority suggests that this case cannot be distinguished from the case where the prosecutor initially obtains an indictment under an enhancement statute and later agrees to drop the enhancement charge in exchange for a guilty plea. I would agree that these two situations would be alike *only if* it were assumed that the hypothetical prosecutor's decision to charge under the enhancement statute was occasioned not by consideration of the public interest but by a strategy to discourage the defendant from exercising his constitutional rights. In theory, I would condemn both practices. In practice, the hypothetical situation is largely unreviewable. The majority's view confuses the propriety of a particular exercise of prosecutorial discretion with its unreviewability. In the instant case, however, we have no problem of proof.

respectively. Would you characterize the prosecutor's actions here as vindictive? Why, or why not?

2.   Are you satisfied with Justice Stewart's efforts to distinguish *Blackledge* and *Pearce* from the present case? Is it accurate to suggest that the Court bent "vindictive prosecution doctrine to meet the needs of plea bargaining"? Doug Lieb, *Vindicating Vindictiveness: Prosecutorial Discretion and Plea Bargaining, Past and Future*, 123 Yale L.J. 1014, 1037 (2014). Is it fair to suggest that, if plea bargaining is legitimate, the prosecutor's conduct in this case was well within an acceptable range? If you are bothered by what the prosecutor did here, can you suggest a method to bar such tactics without undermining plea bargaining? Does either dissent in *Bordenkircher* offer a practical solution?

3.   Suppose that a prosecutor obtains a valid indictment of a defendant for capital murder, and then offers to reduce the offense to misdemeanor battery in exchange for a guilty plea. Is such a plea valid after *Bordenkircher*? Should it be? What if the prosecutor's deal consists of reducing the charge to battery and requiring the defendant to testify against an alleged co-defendant?

4.   *Problem.* P, a police officer, stopped automobile driver, M, and arrested him for driving under the influence of an intoxicant (DUI), a misdemeanor offense. M pled not guilty. The prosecutor determined that the DUI charge was weak, so he offered to dismiss the charge on condition that M stipulate that there was probable cause for the arrest. The prosecutor acknowledged that the only purpose for requesting this stipulation was that he wanted to block a likely future civil rights action against the city based on M's allegation that P beat him after the arrest. As a result of M's refusal to accept the stipulation, the prosecutor revoked the offer to dismiss the DUI charge and filed an amended complaint adding an additional misdemeanor charge of resisting arrest, a charge he had not previously intended to bring. MacDonald v. Musick, 425 F.2d 373 (9th Cir. 1970).

Assume the prosecutor now offers to dismiss the resisting arrest charge in exchange for a guilty plea to the original DUI charge. M accepts the offer. In light of *Blackledge* and *Bordenkircher*, is the plea valid or invalid? Hint: In thinking about this question, read the Supreme Court's remarks in *Wasman v. United States* (p. 1467, Note 1). (Go ahead, read ahead. It won't kill you!)

2. BREAKING THE DEAL

SANTOBELLO V. NEW YORK
Supreme Court of the United States, 1971.
404 U.S. 257, 92 S.Ct. 495, 30 L.Ed.2d 427.

MR. CHIEF JUSTICE BURGER delivered the opinion of the Court [joined by JUSTICES DOUGLAS, WHITE, and BLACKMUN].c * * *

The facts are not in dispute. The State of New York indicted petitioner in 1969 on two felony counts, Promoting Gambling in the First Degree, and Possession of Gambling Records in the First Degree. Petitioner first entered a plea of not guilty to both counts. After negotiations, the Assistant District Attorney in charge of the case agreed to permit petitioner to plead guilty to a lesser-included offense, Possession of Gambling Records in the Second Degree, conviction of which would carry a maximum prison sentence of one year. The prosecutor agreed to make no recommendation as to the sentence.

On June 16, 1969, petitioner accordingly withdrew his plea of not guilty and entered a plea of guilty to the lesser charge. Petitioner represented to the sentencing judge that the plea was voluntary and that the facts of the case, as described by the Assistant District Attorney, were true. The court accepted the plea and set a date for sentencing. * * *

[At the sentencing hearing,] another prosecutor had replaced the prosecutor who had negotiated the plea. The new prosecutor recommended the maximum one-year sentence. In making this recommendation, he cited petitioner's criminal record and alleged links with organized crime. Defense counsel immediately objected on the ground that the State had promised petitioner before the plea was entered that there would be no sentence recommendation by the prosecution. He sought to adjourn the sentence hearing in order to have time to prepare proof of the first prosecutor's promise. The second prosecutor, apparently ignorant of his colleague's commitment, argued that there was nothing in the record to support petitioner's claim of a promise, but the State, in subsequent proceedings, has not contested that such a promise was made.

The sentencing judge ended discussion, with the following statement, quoting extensively from the pre-sentence report:

> "Mr. Aronstein (Defense Counsel), I am not at all influenced by what the District Attorney says, so that there is no need to adjourn the sentence, and there is no need to have any testimony. It doesn't make a particle of difference what the District Attorney says he will do, or what he doesn't do.

---

c   There were two vacancies on the Court at the time of *Santobello*.

"I have here, Mr. Aronstein, a probation report. I have here a history of a long, long serious criminal record. I have here a picture of the life history of this man. * * * "

The judge then imposed the maximum sentence of one year. * * *

This record represents another example of an unfortunate lapse in orderly prosecutorial procedures, in part, no doubt, because of the enormous increase in the workload of the often understaffed prosecutor's offices. The heavy workload may well explain these episodes, but it does not excuse them. The disposition of criminal charges by agreement between the prosecutor and the accused, sometimes loosely called "plea bargaining," is an essential component of the administration of justice. Properly administered, it is to be encouraged. If every criminal charge were subjected to a full-scale trial, the States and the Federal Government would need to multiply by many times the number of judges and court facilities.

Disposition of charges after plea discussions is not only an essential part of the process but a highly desirable part for many reasons. It leads to prompt and largely final disposition of most criminal cases; it avoids much of the corrosive impact of enforced idleness during pre-trial confinement for those who are denied release pending trial; it protects the public from those accused persons who are prone to continue criminal conduct even while on pretrial release; and, by shortening the time between charge and disposition, it enhances whatever may be the rehabilitative prospects of the guilty when they are ultimately imprisoned.

However, all of these considerations presuppose fairness in securing agreement between an accused and a prosecutor. * * * The plea must, of course, be voluntary and knowing and if it was induced by promises, the essence of those promises must in some way be made known. * * *

This phase of the process of criminal justice, and the adjudicative element inherent in accepting a plea of guilty, must be attended by safeguards to insure the defendant what is reasonably due in the circumstances. Those circumstances will vary, but a constant factor is that when a plea rests in any significant degree on a promise or agreement of the prosecutor, so that it can be said to be part of the inducement or consideration, such promise must be fulfilled.

On this record, petitioner "bargained" and negotiated for a particular plea in order to secure dismissal of more serious charges, but also on condition that no sentence recommendation would be made by the prosecutor. It is now conceded that the promise to abstain from a recommendation was made, and at this stage the prosecution is not in a good position to argue that its inadvertent breach of agreement is immaterial. The staff lawyers in a prosecutor's office have the burden of "letting the left hand know what the right hand is doing" or has done. That the breach of agreement was inadvertent does not lessen its impact.

We need not reach the question whether the sentencing judge would or would not have been influenced had he known all the details of the negotiations for the plea. He stated that the prosecutor's recommendation did not influence him and we have no reason to doubt that. Nevertheless, we conclude that the interests of justice and appropriate recognition of the duties of the prosecution in relation to promises made in the negotiation of pleas of guilty will be best served by remanding the case to the state courts for further consideration. The ultimate relief to which petitioner is entitled we leave to the discretion of the state court, which is in a better position to decide whether the circumstances of this case require only that there be specific performance of the agreement on the plea, in which case petitioner should be resentenced by a different judge, or whether, in the view of the state court, the circumstances require granting the relief sought by petitioner, *i.e.*, the opportunity to withdraw his plea of guilty.[2] We emphasize that this is in no sense to question the fairness of the sentencing judge; the fault here rests on the prosecutor, not on the sentencing judge.

The judgment is vacated and the case is remanded for reconsideration not inconsistent with this opinion.

MR. JUSTICE DOUGLAS, concurring.

I join the opinion of the Court and add only a word. * * *

This is a state case over which we have no "supervisory" jurisdiction; and Rule 11 of the Federal Rules of Criminal Procedure obviously has no relevancy to the problem.

I join the opinion of the Court and favor a constitutional rule for this as well as for other pending or oncoming cases. Where the "plea bargain" is not kept by the prosecutor, the sentence must be vacated and the state court will decide in light of the circumstances of each case whether due process requires (a) that there be specific performance of the plea bargain or (b) that the defendant be given the option to go to trial on the original charges. One alternative may do justice in one case, and the other in a different case. In choosing a remedy, however, a court ought to accord a defendant's preference considerable, if not controlling, weight inasmuch as the fundamental rights flouted by a prosecutor's breach of a plea bargain are those of the defendant, not of the State.

---

[2]   If the state court decides to allow withdrawal of the plea, the petitioner will, of course, plead anew to the original charge on two felony counts.

MR. JUSTICE MARSHALL, with whom MR. JUSTICE BRENNAN and MR. JUSTICE STEWART join, concurring in part and dissenting in part.

I agree with much of the majority's opinion, but conclude that petitioner must be permitted to withdraw his guilty plea. This is the relief petitioner requested and, on the facts set out by the majority, it is a form of relief to which he is entitled. * * *

Here, petitioner never claimed any automatic right to withdraw a guilty plea before sentencing. Rather, he tendered a specific reason why, in his case, the plea should be vacated. His reason was that the prosecutor had broken a promise made in return for the agreement to plead guilty. When a prosecutor breaks the bargain, he undercuts the basis for the waiver of constitutional rights implicit in the plea. This, it seems to me, provides the defendant ample justification for rescinding the plea. * * * Of course, where the prosecutor has broken the plea agreement, it may be appropriate to permit the defendant to enforce the plea bargain. But that is not the remedy sought here.*

It is worth noting that in the ordinary case where a motion to vacate is made prior to sentencing, the government has taken no action in reliance on the previously entered guilty plea and would suffer no harm from the plea's withdrawal. More pointedly, here the State claims no such harm beyond disappointed expectations about the plea itself. At least where the government itself has broken the plea bargain, this disappointment cannot bar petitioner from withdrawing his guilty plea and reclaiming his right to a trial.

I would remand the case with instructions that the plea be vacated and petitioner given an opportunity to replead to the original charges in the indictment.

NOTES AND QUESTIONS

1. *A lesson for lawyers in the trenches.* The second prosecutor apparently was unaware of the promise made by his predecessor because there was nothing in the record to support Santobello's claim of a "no sentencing recommendation" promise. One lesson of this case is that plea agreements ought to be reduced to writing. One Circuit Court has stated that "[w]hen a defendant's fundamental and constitutional rights hang in the balance, * * * justice requires and common sense dictates memorializing the terms of the plea agreement." United States v. McQueen, 108 F.3d 64 (4th Cir. 1997). This point was recently made, as well, by the Supreme Court in *Missouri v. Frye* (p. 1155), when it suggested that "States may elect to follow

---

* Mr. Justice Douglas, although joining the Court's opinion (apparently because he thinks the remedy should be chosen by the state court), concludes that the state court "ought to accord a defendant's preference considerable, if not controlling, weight." Thus, a majority of the Court appears to believe that in cases like these, when the defendant seeks to vacate the plea, that relief should generally be granted.

rules that all offers must be in writing, again to ensure against later misunderstandings or fabricated charges."

2.   Look again carefully at the various *Santobello* opinions to see if they answer the following questions. First, what provision of the Constitution, if any, was violated by the prosecutor's breach of the plea agreement?

Second, what is the underlying basis of the violation? That is, were Santobello's constitutional rights violated because his plea was coerced? Is it that the plea was unintelligently made? Or, does the Constitution protect "the personal expectations created in defendants by plea agreements, on the notion that it is fundamentally unfair for the state to create and then destroy a defendant's expectations"? Or, is something else involved? Wayne R. LaFave, et al., Criminal Procedure 1022–23 (5th ed. 2009).

Finally, what is the proper remedy for a prosecutorial breach? Vacate the plea and allow the defendant to plead anew? Specific performance of the deal? Whichever remedy the defendant requests? What answer do we get from *Santobello*? In your view, what *should* the answer be?

3.   *Determining if a breach occurred.* The Government admitted that it breached the plea agreement in *Santobello*, but sometimes it does not concede this in ambiguous circumstances. For example, in United States v. Benchimol, 471 U.S. 453, 105 S.Ct. 2103, 85 L.Ed.2d 462 (1985), the defendant agreed to plead guilty to mail fraud; in exchange, the Assistant United States Attorney (AUSA) promised to recommend probation on condition that restitution be made. At the sentencing hearing, the presentence report incorrectly asserted that the prosecutor took no position on sentencing. The defendant's lawyer corrected the record by informing the court that the government recommended probation with restitution. The AUSA responded only, "That is an accurate representation." Nonetheless, the court sentenced the defendant to six years' commitment.

Subsequently, the District Court denied a motion to vacate the plea, ruling that the AUSA had not breached the agreement. The Court of Appeals reversed the judgment, holding that "when the government undertakes to recommend a sentence pursuant to a plea bargain, it has the duty to state its recommendation clearly to the sentencing judge and to express the justification for it." The Supreme Court disagreed:

> It may well be that the Government in a particular case might commit itself to "enthusiastically" make a particular recommendation to the court, and it may be that the Government in a particular case might agree to explain to the court the reasons for the Government's making a particular recommendation. But respondent does not contend, nor did the Court of Appeals find, that the Government had in fact undertaken to do either of these things here. The Court of Appeals simply held that as a matter of law such an undertaking was to be implied from the Government's agreement to recommend a particular sentence. But our view of [Federal] Rule

11(e) is that it speaks in terms of what the parties in fact agree to, and does not suggest that such implied-in-law terms as were read into this agreement by the Court of Appeals have any place under the Rule.

What lesson should defense attorneys learn from *Benchimol*?

4.   *Problems*. Prosecutorial breaches in the following cases? Why or why not?

A.   *E* pleaded guilty to a charge of lewdness with a child under fourteen years of age, in exchange for the prosecutor's promise to recommend probation. At sentencing, however, the prosecutor argued that *E* was not eligible for probation. The judge, while observing that the prosecutor had promised *E* to recommend probation, stated that this did not matter as the decision was his own and that *E*'s history of alcohol abuse and other factors warranted a life sentence. Echeverria v. State, 119 Nev. 41, 62 P.3d 743 (2003).

B.   *H* was charged with illegal entry of the country. As part of a plea deal, H agreed to plead guilty to this offense. In exchange, the prosecutor agreed to a prison term at the low end of the applicable Federal Sentencing Guidelines, and further agreed not to "seek, argue, or suggest in any way, either orally or in writing, that * * * the Court impose a sentence other than what has been stipulated to the parties herein." Under the agreement, if the trial court rejected the agreement and indicated that it might impose a more severe sentence, *H* would have a right to withdraw his guilty plea. Based on this arrangement, *H* pled guilty. Prior to sentencing, the Probation Office prepared a pre-sentence report that set out *H*'s long criminal record in the country. At the sentencing hearing, the prosecutor argued that the low-level sentence to which the parties has agreed was reasonable, but he also noted to the court *H*'s long criminal record set out in the sentencing report. The judge informed the parties that he would not accept the agreed-upon lenient sentence. Prosecutorial breach? If so, what should be the remedy to which *H* is entitled? United States v. Heredia, 768 F.3d 1220 (9th Cir. 2014).

C.   *S* pleaded guilty to second-degree murder in exchange for a prosecutorial promise not to recommend a sentence of life imprisonment. At sentencing, the prosecutor recommended a prison term of 70 to 100 years. Smith v. Stegall, 385 F.3d 993 (6th Cir. 2004).

D.   Whitehurst v. Kavanagh, 167 Misc.2d 86, 636 N.Y.S.2d 591 (1995):

Seven year old Rickel Knox was reported missing from her home in Kingston, New York, at approximately 4:30 p.m. on September 21, 1995. At approximately 6:30 p.m., Kingston police officers took petitioner Whitehurst to the Kingston Police Station and interrogated him concerning the child's disappearance. * * * On September 24, 1995 a felony complaint charging petitioner with first-degree kidnapping was signed and filed. Between 10:30 p.m. on September 24 and 1:00 a.m. on September 25, Ulster County

Assistant District Attorney John Prizzia interrogated petitioner and requested his assistance in locating the missing girl. At that point in time, the District Attorney did not know whether or not the victim was alive. Without assistance of counsel, petitioner negotiated a cooperation agreement with Assistant District Attorney Prizzia which provides:

"This contract is to set forth in writing the agreement between the Ulster County District Attorney's Office and the defendant, Larry Whitehurst. The agreement is as follows:

"1. It is agreed and understood that Larry Whitehurst currently stands charged with Kidnapping in the First Degree.

"2. It is further understood that Larry Whitehurst has indicated to the City of Kingston Police Department that he knows the location of Rickel Knox, and has indicated there is a possibility that she is still alive.

"3. In exchange for information as to the location of Rickel Knox, is agreed as follows:

"a. Larry Whitehurst must plead guilty to Kidnapping.

"b. There will be no Murder charge.

"c. If Rickel Knox is found alive, Larry Whitehurst will receive a minimum sentence of ten years.

"d. If she is found dead, Larry Whitehurst will receive a minimum sentence of between ten and fifteen years, depending on the surrounding facts and circumstances. * * *

"4. Should Rickel Knox or her remains not be found, this agreement will be void and will have no force or effect, I have the right to go to trial and if so this contract is void."

On September 25, 1995, petitioner Whitehurst led Mr. Prizzia and police officers to the victim's body. Thereafter, District Attorney Kavanagh announced that he did not consider himself bound by the cooperation agreement, and that he would prosecute Mr. Whitehurst for first degree murder and seek the death penalty.

The defendant sought a judgment prohibiting the District Attorney from prosecuting him for first- or second-degree murder in the death of Rickel Knox. Does the defendant have an actionable claim? *Should* he have an actionable claim? Is this case even controlled by *Santobello*? Why might a court conclude that it is not?

5. *Thinking about—and rethinking—a "Santobello violation."* In Mabry v. Johnson, 467 U.S. 504, 104 S.Ct. 2543, 81 L.Ed.2d 437 (1984), the Supreme Court suggested in dictum that the reason why a defendant is entitled to a remedy when a prosecutor breaches a plea agreement is that, as a result of the breach, the guilty plea was not knowingly or voluntarily made.

In Puckett v. United States, 556 U.S. 129, 129 S.Ct. 1423, 173 L.Ed.2d 266 (2009), however, the Court backed away from that reasoning:

> [T]here is nothing to support the proposition that the Government's breach of a plea agreement retroactively causes the defendant's agreement to have been unknowing or involuntary. Any more than there is anything to support the proposition that a mere breach of contract retroactively causes the other party's promise to have been coerced or induced by fraud. Although the analogy may not hold in all respects, plea bargains are essentially contracts. When the consideration for a contract fails—that is, when one of the exchanged promises is not kept—we do not say that the voluntary bilateral consent to the contract never existed * * * ; we say that the contract was broken. The party injured by the breach will generally be entitled to some remedy, which might include the right to rescind the contract entirely, but that is not the same thing as saying the contract was never validly concluded.
>
>   So too here. When a defendant agrees to a plea bargain, the Government takes on certain obligations. If those obligations are not met, the defendant is entitled to seek a remedy, which might in some cases be rescission of the agreement, allowing him to take back the consideration he has furnished, i.e., to withdraw his plea. But rescission is not the only remedy; in Santobello we allowed for a resentencing at which the Government would fully comply with the agreement—in effect, specific performance of the contract. In any case, it is entirely clear that a breach does not cause the guilty plea, when entered, to have become unknowing or involuntary.

Should there be any doubt, the *Puckett* Court stated, in footnote, "[w]e disavow any aspect of the *Mabry* dictum that contradicts our holding today."

So, we return to some of the questions raised in Note 2: Does *Santobello* announce a constitutional principle, or is it nothing more than a contract breach? And, if the Constitution *is* implicated, what is the underlying basis of the constitutional violation?

6. *Breach by the defendant.* Typically, *Santobello* motions are made by defendants, but sometimes the prosecution will claim that the defendant has breached a deal. The next case deals with this situation.

UNITED STATES V. BRECHNER

United States Court of Appeals, Second Circuit, 1996.
99 F.3d 96.

LEVAL, CIRCUIT JUDGE: * * *

Brechner was president of a company that manufactured stuffed toy animals for sale to carnivals. In January 1992, shortly after the government began investigating him, Brechner offered to plead guilty to four counts of income tax evasion. In exchange for his plea, the government agreed not to prosecute Brechner's company, its affiliates, or his wife or son for their involvement in Brechner's tax fraud schemes. As was later determined, those schemes included at least three sources of unreported income. Most of the unreported income came from payments from one of Brechner's main customers, the Fred Silber Company. Two other sources were Brechner's Asian supplier, Manley Company, and the company that transported Manley's goods to Brechner, Zim Israel Navigation Company. Both of these companies issued inflated invoices to Brechner's company and then kicked back the difference to Brechner.

In May 1992, seeking a downward departure on his sentence, Brechner, through counsel, contacted the Assistant U.S. Attorney in charge of the investigation and offered to provide information about bribes he had paid to a corrupt bank officer. The Assistant expressed interest and arranged a formal proffer session on June 12, 1992, at which Brechner gave government representatives the details of his payments to the bank officer and the tax evasion scheme involving Fred Silber. Brechner's lawyer also advised the government that Brechner had received approximately $500,000 in unreported income from his overseas supplier, Manley. The payments from Zim Israel, however, were never mentioned. The district court later found that Brechner received almost $5 million dollars in income from Fred Silber, $50,000–$100,000 from Manley and about $200,000 from Zim Israel.

On August 12, 1992, Brechner and the Assistant executed a written cooperation agreement, which provided that "Milton Brechner will provide truthful, complete, and accurate information, and will cooperate fully with the [U.S. Attorney's] Office." According to the agreement, this cooperation would include debriefings "concerning his involvement in and knowledge of all criminal activities," participating in undercover work, and testifying at proceedings upon request.

In exchange for Brechner's cooperation, the government agreed to move for a downward sentencing departure under § 5K1.1 of the United States Sentencing Guidelines "[i]f the [U.S. Attorney's] Office determines that the defendant has cooperated fully, provided substantial assistance to law enforcement authorities, and otherwise complied with the terms of this agreement." The agreement further provided that, in connection with the sentencing departure, "it is understood that the [U.S. Attorney's] Office's assessment of the value, truthfulness, completeness, and accuracy of the cooperation shall be binding upon [Brechner]."

In the following paragraph, the agreement cautioned that

Milton Brechner must at all times give complete, truthful, and accurate information and testimony. * * * Should it be judged by the [U.S. Attorney's] Office that the defendant has failed to cooperate fully, has intentionally given false, misleading, or incomplete information or testimony * * * or has otherwise violated any provision of this agreement, the defendant will not be released from his plea of guilty but this Office will be released from its obligation under this agreement * * * to file the motion [for downward departure].

After signing the agreement, Brechner participated actively in the government's bribery investigation of the bank officer, who by this time had retired from the bank and apparently was employed as a consultant by Brechner. For over a year, Brechner arranged meetings with him about once a month, under audiotape and videotape surveillance, at which Brechner attempted, with limited success, to elicit incriminating statements from the bank officer about the bribes he had taken. In September 1993, the Assistant informed Brechner's attorney that the bank officer would be arrested.

Two months later, in November 1993, the Assistant scheduled a debriefing session with Brechner. At the debriefing, Brechner was asked whether he had received kickbacks from Manley and Zim. He denied receiving any such payments. Brechner's lawyer then asked to interrupt the session so that he could speak with his client in private. After a break, Brechner acknowledged his receipt of payments from both Manley and Zim. The Assistant said he would give Brechner a "fresh start," and Brechner proceeded to provide details of the Manley and Zim kickbacks. This was Brechner's last meeting with government representatives.

In April 1994, the Assistant informed Brechner's counsel that he was not inclined to move for a downward departure because of Brechner's misrepresentations and the fact that it would be difficult to prosecute the bank officer with Brechner as the sole witness in the case.

At sentencing, the government declined to move for a downward departure; Brechner moved to compel the § 5K1.1 motion, alleging prosecutorial bad faith. The district court held a hearing after which Judge Mishler found that Brechner "cooperated fully and completely" and that his "substantial assistance to the investigation was sufficient to warrant a § 5K1.1 motion" despite his false statements. * * *

Brechner contends he did not receive the benefit of his bargain essentially because he was promised a § 5K1.1 letter if he cooperated satisfactorily, which he did, but was denied the letter. We find no merit in Brechner's claim.

Under the agreement Brechner signed, the government's § 5K1.1 motion was contingent on Brechner's having "cooperated fully, provided substantial assistance to law enforcement authorities, and otherwise complied with the terms of this agreement." Those terms included that Brechner "provide truthful, complete, and accurate information."

Furthermore, the agreement expressly stated that the government would be released from its obligation to file the § 5K1.1 motion if Brechner had "intentionally given false, misleading, or incomplete information." By falsely denying his receipt of kickbacks from Zim and Manley, Brechner breached his obligations under the agreement. According to the terms of the agreement, the government was expressly entitled to withhold the letter in those circumstances.

The district court found that, because Brechner "corrected his misstatements" when he subsequently admitted the kickbacks, the breach was not material. The court characterized Brechner's initial lies as "trivial defects" that did not prejudice the government, and thus held that they could not constitute a good faith basis for refusing to make the § 5K1.1 motion. We disagree.

These lies, although swiftly corrected, seriously undermined Brechner's credibility as a potential government witness. As we have previously explained, a cooperating defendant's truthfulness about his own past conduct is highly relevant to the quality of his cooperation. By lying to the prosecutor *during the period of his cooperation* about his own criminal involvement, Brechner made it impossible for the government to argue at any future trial that, despite his past sins, Brechner had acknowledged his guilt, turned over a new leaf and cooperated in a truthful and trustworthy manner. The disclosure of Brechner's lies to the bank officer's defense counsel * * * would have brought on harsh cross-examination and a powerful argument that Brechner was no more trustworthy as a cooperating witness than he had been as a crook. Brechner's swift correction would not cure the problem, as it was obviously due not to honesty but to his attorney's warning about Brechner's self-interest. Because Brechner would be the sole witness, his lies created a serious problem for the government's contemplated prosecution of the bank officer and provided good faith grounds for refusing to move for a downward departure. * * *

We vacate the sentence of the district court and remand for resentencing.

NOTES AND QUESTIONS

1. The court suggests that Brechner's lies would have destroyed his credibility as a witness in later prosecutions. How would defense lawyers in *those* trials know about Brechner's lies? Do you think the prosecution would be required, on its own, to inform the defendant of Brechner's brief and quickly corrected lie? What if the defense expressly sought discovery of "any and all information relating to Brechner's credibility"?

E. THE PROCEDURAL EFFECT OF A GUILTY PLEA

McMANN v. RICHARDSON

Supreme Court of the United States, 1970.
397 U.S. 759, 90 S.Ct. 1441, 25 L.Ed.2d 763.

MR. JUSTICE WHITE delivered the opinion of the Court [joined by CHIEF JUSTICE BURGER, and JUSTICES BLACK, HARLAN, STEWART, and WHITE].

The petition for certiorari, which we granted, seeks reversal of three separate judgments of the Court of Appeals for the Second Circuit ordering hearings on petitions for habeas corpus filed by the respondents in this case. The principal issue before us is whether and to what extent an otherwise valid guilty plea may be impeached in collateral proceedings by assertions or proof that the plea was motivated by a prior coerced confession. We find ourselves in substantial disagreement with the Court of Appeals. * * *

II

The core of the Court of Appeals' holding is the proposition that if in a collateral proceeding a guilty plea is shown to have been triggered by a coerced confession—if there would have been no plea had there been no confession—the plea is vulnerable * * *. We are unable to agree with the Court of Appeals on this proposition.

A conviction after a plea of guilty normally rests on the defendant's own admission in open court that he committed the acts with which he is charged. That admission may not be compelled, and since the plea is also a waiver of trial—and unless the applicable law otherwise provides, a waiver of the right to contest the admissibility of any evidence the State might have offered against the defendant—it must be an intelligent act "done with sufficient awareness of the relevant circumstances and likely consequences."

For present purposes, we put aside those cases where the defendant has his own reasons for pleading guilty wholly aside from the strength of the case against him as well as those cases where the defendant, although he would have gone to trial had he thought the State could not prove its case, is motivated by evidence against him independent of the confession. In these cases, as the Court of Appeals recognized, the confession, even if coerced, is not a sufficient factor in the plea to justify relief. Neither do we have before us the uncounseled defendant, nor the situation where the circumstances that coerced the confession have abiding impact and also taint the plea. It is not disputed that in such cases a guilty plea is properly open to challenge.

The issue on which we differ with the Court of Appeals arises in those situations involving the counseled defendant who allegedly would put the State to its proof if there was a substantial enough chance of acquittal, who would do so except for a prior confession that might be offered against him, and who because of the confession decides to plead guilty to save himself the expense and agony of a trial and perhaps also to minimize the penalty that might be imposed. After conviction on such a plea, is a defendant entitled to a hearing, and to relief if his factual claims are accepted, when his petition for habeas corpus alleges that his confession was in fact coerced and that it motivated his plea? We think not if he alleges and proves no more than this.

III

Since we are dealing with a defendant who deems his confession crucial to the State's case against him and who would go to trial if he thought his chances of acquittal were good, his decision to plead guilty or not turns on whether he thinks the law will allow his confession to be used against him. For the defendant who considers his confession involuntary and hence unusable against him at a trial, tendering a plea of guilty would seem a most improbable alternative. The sensible course would be to contest his guilt, prevail on his confession claim at trial, on appeal, or, if necessary, in a collateral proceeding, and win acquittal, however guilty he might be. The books are full of cases * * * where the defendant has made this choice and has prevailed. If he nevertheless pleads guilty the plea can hardly be blamed on the confession which in his view was inadmissible evidence and no proper part of the State's case. Since by hypothesis the evidence aside from the confession is weak and the defendant has no reasons of his own to plead, a guilty plea in such circumstances is nothing less than a refusal to present his federal claims to the state court in the first instance—a choice by the defendant to take the benefits, if any, of a plea of guilty and then to pursue his coerced-confession claim in collateral proceedings. Surely later allegations that the confession rendered his plea involuntary would appear incredible, and whether his plain bypass of state remedies was an intelligent act depends on whether he was so incompetently advised by counsel concerning the forum in which he should first present his federal claim that the Constitution will afford him another chance to plead.

A more credible explanation for a plea of guilty by a defendant who would go to trial except for his prior confession is his prediction that the law will permit his admissions to be used against him by the trier of fact. At least the probability of the State's being permitted to use the confession as evidence is sufficient to convince him that the State's case is too strong to contest and that a plea of guilty is the most advantageous course. Nothing in this train of events suggests that the defendant's plea, as distinguished from his confession, is an involuntary act. His later petition for collateral relief asserting that a *coerced* confession induced his plea is at most a claim that the admissibility of his confession was mistakenly assessed and that since he was erroneously advised, either under the then applicable law or under the law later announced, his plea was an unintelligent and voidable act. The Constitution, however, does not render pleas of guilty so vulnerable.

As we said in *Brady v. United States* [p. 1136], the decision to plead guilty before the evidence is in frequently involves the making of difficult judgments. All the pertinent facts normally cannot be known unless witnesses are examined and cross-examined in court. Even then the truth will often be in dispute. In the face of unavoidable uncertainty, the defendant and his counsel must make their best judgment as to the weight of the State's case. Counsel must predict how the facts, as he understands them, would be viewed by a court. If proved, would those facts convince a judge or jury of the defendant's guilt? On those facts would evidence seized without a warrant be admissible? Would the trier of fact on those facts find a confession voluntary and admissible? Questions like these cannot be answered with certitude; yet a decision to plead guilty must necessarily rest upon counsel's answers, uncertain as they may be. Waiving trial entails the inherent risk that the good-faith evaluations of a reasonably competent attorney will turn out to be mistaken either as to the facts or as to what a court's judgment might be on given facts.

That a guilty plea must be intelligently made is not a requirement that all advice offered by the defendant's lawyer withstand retrospective examination in a post-conviction hearing. * * *

In our view a defendant's plea of guilty based on reasonably competent advice is an intelligent plea not open to attack on the ground that counsel may have misjudged the admissibility of the defendant's confession. Whether a plea of guilty is unintelligent and therefore vulnerable when motivated by a confession erroneously thought admissible in evidence depends as an initial matter, not on whether a court would retrospectively consider counsel's advice to be right or wrong, but on whether that advice was within the range of competence demanded of attorneys in criminal cases. * * *

IV

We hold, therefore, that a defendant who alleges that he pleaded guilty because of a prior coerced confession is not, without more, entitled to a hearing on his petition for habeas corpus. * * *

[JUSTICE BRENNAN, joined by JUSTICES DOUGLAS and MARSHALL, dissented.]

NOTES AND QUESTIONS

1. Notice that the law announced in *McMann* assumes that the defendant's guilty plea was based on "the good-faith evaluations of a reasonably competent attorney." For more on what satisfies this standard, see *Strickland v. Washington* (p. 1088). In the specific context of plea bargaining, see the materials beginning on page 1154.

2. Assuming that a defendant is represented by competent counsel, under what circumstances may she attack her guilty plea on the ground of a constitutional violation unrelated to the guilty plea itself? *McMann* is not the final word on the subject.

In Tollett v. Henderson, 411 U.S. 258, 93 S.Ct. 1602, 36 L.Ed.2d 235 (1973), the Supreme Court stated that a "guilty plea represents a break in the chain of events which has preceded it in the criminal process." Therefore, a criminal defendant who pleads guilty to murder on the advice of competent counsel is not entitled to federal collateral relief on proof that the indicting grand jury was unconstitutionally selected.

However, just one year later came *Blackledge v. Perry* (p. 907), in which a state defendant was convicted of misdemeanor assault in a district court, and then asserted his statutory right to a *de novo* trial in superior court. The prosecutor, with no new evidence in the case, escalated the charge to felony assault. The Supreme Court ruled that Perry, who pled guilty to felony assault, was *not* barred in a federal habeas corpus proceeding from raising his constitutional claim that the due process clause prohibited the prosecutor's conduct. The Court explained:

> While [the government's] reliance upon the *Tollett* opinion is understandable, there is a fundamental distinction between this case and that one. Although the underlying claims presented in *Tollett* and * * * [*McMann*] were of constitutional dimensions, none went to the very power of the State to bring the defendant into court to answer the charge brought against him. The defendants in *McMann v. Richardson*, for example, could surely have been brought to trial without the use of the allegedly coerced confessions, and even a tainted indictment of the sort alleged in *Tollett* could have been "cured" through a new indictment by a properly selected grand jury. In the case at hand, by contrast, the nature of the underlying constitutional infirmity is markedly different. Having chosen originally to proceed on the misdemeanor charge in the District Court, the State of North Carolina was, under the facts of this case, simply precluded by the Due Process Clause from calling upon the respondent to answer to the more serious charge in the Superior Court. Unlike the defendant in *Tollett*, Perry is not complaining of "antecedent constitutional violations" or of a "deprivation of constitutional rights that occurred prior to the entry of the guilty plea." Rather, the right that he asserts and that we today accept is the right not to be haled into court at all upon the

felony charge. The very initiation of the proceedings against him in the Superior Court thus operated to deny him due process of law.

One year later, the Court ruled in Menna v. New York, 423 U.S. 61, 96 S.Ct. 241, 46 L.Ed.2d 195 (1975) that an indicted defendant's guilty plea did not constitute a forfeiture of his right to claim that the double jeopardy clause barred his prosecution on the indictment. Citing *Blackledge*, the Court explained that "[w]here the State is precluded by the United States Constitution from haling a defendant into court on a charge, federal law requires that a conviction on that charge be set aside even if the conviction was entered pursuant to a counseled plea of guilty * * * ."

What does this all add up to? One scholar explains the law this way:

> [A] defendant who has been convicted on a plea of guilty may challenge his conviction on any constitutional ground that, if asserted before trial, would forever preclude the state from obtaining a valid conviction against him, regardless of how much the state might endeavor to correct the defect. In other words, a plea of guilty may operate as a forfeiture of all defenses except those that, once raised, cannot be "cured."

Peter Westen, *Away from Waiver: A Rationale for the Forfeiture of Constitutional Rights in Criminal Procedure*, 75 Mich. L. Rev. 1214, 1226 (1977).

Notice how this explanation fits the cases described above. In *Tollett*, the defect was curable: Had the defendant, prior to trial, moved to have his indictment quashed on the ground that there was a defect in the grand jury selection process, a proper grand jury could have been empaneled and a new indictment issued, so this claim is forfeited as a result of the guilty plea. This cannot be said about the *Blackledge* prosecution or the double jeopardy claim in *Menna*: those defects, had they been raised prior to the respective second trials, were incurable—the state could not constitutionally bring the greater charge (*Blackledge*) or reprosecute for the same offense (*Menna*).

There is at least one limitation on the "rule" described above. In United States v. Broce, 488 U.S. 563, 109 S.Ct. 757, 102 L.Ed.2d 927 (1989), the defendants pleaded guilty to two conspiracy indictments: one indictment charged them with entering into an agreement to fix bids on a specific highway contract; the second indictment charged them with entering into a separate agreement to fix bids on a different highway project. After the defendants pled guilty, other alleged co-conspirators who did not plead guilty successfully convinced a court that the two agreements were in fact, smaller parts of a single conspiracy. Based on that ruling, the *Broce* defendants sought to raise a double jeopardy claim, i.e., that they had been convicted twice of what was, in fact, a single offense.

The *Broce* Court did *not* permit the defendants to raise the double jeopardy claim, notwithstanding *Menna*:

Respondents had the opportunity, instead of entering their guilty pleas, to challenge the theory of the indictments and to attempt to show the existence of only one conspiracy in a trial-type proceeding. They chose not to, and hence relinquished that entitlement. * * * [R]espondents may believe that they made a strategic miscalculation. Our precedents demonstrate, however, that such grounds do not justify setting aside an otherwise valid guilty plea. * * *

* * * [W]e held in *McMann v. Richardson* that a counseled defendant may not make a collateral attack on a guilty plea on the allegation that he misjudged the admissibility of his confession. "Waiving trial entails the inherent risk that the good-faith evaluations of a reasonably competent attorney will turn out to be mistaken either as to the facts or as to what a court's judgment might be on given facts." * * *

An exception to the rule barring collateral attack on a guilty plea was established by our decisions in *Blackledge v. Perry* and *Menna v. New York*, but it has no application to the case at bar. * * *

In neither *Blackledge* nor *Menna* did the defendants seek further proceedings at which to expand the record with new evidence. In those cases, the determination that the second indictment could not go forward should have been made by the presiding judge at the time the plea was entered on the basis of the existing record. Both *Blackledge* and *Menna* could be (and ultimately were) resolved without any need to venture beyond that record. In *Blackledge*, the concessions implicit in the defendant's guilty plea were simply irrelevant, because the constitutional infirmity in the proceedings lay in the State's power to bring any indictment at all. In *Menna*, the indictment was facially duplicative of the earlier offense of which the defendant had been convicted and sentenced so that the admissions made by Menna's guilty plea could not conceivably be construed to extend beyond a redundant confession to the earlier offense.

Respondents here, in contrast, pleaded guilty to indictments that on their face described separate conspiracies. They cannot prove their claim by relying on those indictments and the existing record. Indeed, as noted earlier, they cannot prove their claim without contradicting those indictments, and that opportunity is foreclosed by the admissions inherent in their guilty pleas.

3.   One practical effect of *McMann* is that some defendants do not plead guilty, even when it would otherwise be in their interests, because they are fearful of forfeiting their right to assert a constitutional claim in the appellate courts. For example, suppose that nearly all of the evidence against a defendant is seized without a warrant from her home. Prior to trial, she

moves to suppress the evidence, but her motion is denied. If the defendant now pleads guilty, she can no longer contest the search. Therefore, if her lawyer believes that there is a reasonable possibility that an appellate court might overturn the trial court's suppression ruling, the only way the defendant can preserve her claim is to plead not guilty, go to trial, presumably be convicted, and then appeal on Fourth Amendment grounds. Thus, a trial that neither the prosecutor nor the defendant wants is conducted, simply so that a constitutional claim can be preserved.

Look at Federal Rule 11. How did the drafters get around this problem?

CHAPTER 16

THE TRIAL PROCESS

■ ■ ■

In all criminal prosecutions, the accused shall enjoy the right to a speedy and public trial, by an impartial jury of the State and district wherein the crime shall have been committed, which district shall have been previously ascertained by law, and to be informed of the nature and cause of the accusation; to be confronted with the witnesses against him; to have compulsory process for obtaining witnesses in his favor, and to have the Assistance of Counsel for his defence. U.S. Const. amend. VI.

A. RIGHT TO TRIAL BY IMPARTIAL JURY

The Sixth Amendment provides that the accused "shall enjoy" a series of rights that seem designed mostly to enhance the accuracy of the trial outcome. To be sure, fairness is also achieved by placing the accused in a position of rough equality with the prosecution, and the voice of the community is included through the right to trial by jury, but the thrust of the Sixth Amendment is to avoid inaccurate convictions. The right to counsel is the right most important to the accuracy goal, and it is, therefore, the glue that holds the criminal process together. It crucially affects all stages of the process, from arrest and interrogation to arraignment and plea bargaining, from motion practice to trial, sentencing, and appeal. We examine the right to counsel in several places in the book, most prominently in Chapter 14. This chapter examines the rest of the Sixth Amendment. *These trial rights require—indeed, presuppose—effective assistance of counsel.* We begin with the right that was the most important to the Framers, trial by jury.

The Framers' experience with English judges led them to fear arbitrary judges. They saw the judgment of their peers as an invaluable ally if the distant federal Congress should pass oppressive laws or if federal prosecutors should seek to harass citizens by the "great instrument of arbitrary power" that a criminal prosecution can become. Neil H. Cogan, The Complete Bill of Rights 426 (1998). These concerns are summarized, in a fiery fashion, in remarks of Patrick Henry made in the Virginia convention considering whether to ratify the Constitution, which at that time lacked a Bill of Rights:

Why do we love this trial by jury? Because it prevents the hand of oppression from cutting you off. They may call any thing rebellion, and deprive you of a fair trial by an impartial jury of your neighbors. Has not your mother country magnanimously preserved this noble privilege upwards of a thousand years? * * * That country had juries of hundredoers [local citizens] for many generations. And shall America give up that which nothing could induce the English people to relinquish? The idea is abhorrent to my mind. There was a time when we should have spurned it. This gives me comfort—that as long as I have existence, my neighbors will protect me. Old as I am, it is probable that I may yet have the appellation of *rebel*. I trust that I shall see congressional oppression crushed in embryo. As this government stands [without a Bill of Rights], I despise and abhor it.

Id. at 438.

1. TRIAL-BY-JURY: NATURE OF THE CONSTITUTIONAL RIGHT

In *Duncan v. Louisiana*, the Supreme Court held that the Fourteenth Amendment due process clause "guarantees a right to jury trial in all criminal cases which—were they to be tried in a federal court—would come within the Sixth Amendment guarantee." What follows are some observations about juries by Justice White (for the majority), and by Justices Harlan and Stewart, dissenters. (For more of *Duncan*, see p. 53.)

DUNCAN V. LOUISIANA
Supreme Court of the United States, 1968.
391 U.S. 145, 88 S.Ct. 1444, 20 L.Ed.2d 491.

MR. JUSTICE WHITE delivered the opinion of the Court [joined by CHIEF JUSTICE WARREN, and JUSTICES BLACK, DOUGLAS, BRENNAN, FORTAS, and MARSHALL].

Appellant, Gary Duncan, was convicted of simple battery * * *. Under Louisiana law simple battery is a misdemeanor, punishable by a maximum of two years' imprisonment and a $300 fine. Appellant sought trial by jury, but because the Louisiana Constitution grants jury trials only in cases in which capital punishment or imprisonment at hard labor may be imposed, the trial judge denied the request. Appellant was convicted and sentenced to serve 60 days in the parish prison and pay a fine of $150. * * *

I. * * *

The guarantees of jury trial in the Federal and State Constitutions reflect a profound judgment about the way in which law should be enforced and justice administered. A right to jury trial is granted to criminal defendants in order to prevent oppression by the Government. Those who wrote our constitutions knew from history and experience that it was necessary to protect against unfounded criminal charges brought to eliminate enemies and against judges too responsive to the voice of higher authority. The framers of the constitutions strove to create an independent judiciary but insisted upon further protection against arbitrary action. Providing an accused with the right to be tried by a jury of his peers gave him an inestimable safeguard against the corrupt or overzealous prosecutor and against the compliant, biased, or eccentric judge. If the defendant preferred the common-sense judgment of a jury to the more tutored but perhaps less sympathetic reaction of the single judge, he was to have it. Beyond this, the jury trial provisions in the Federal and State Constitutions reflect a fundamental decision about the exercise of official power—a reluctance to entrust plenary powers over the life and liberty of the citizen to one judge or to a group of judges. Fear of unchecked power, so typical of our State and Federal Governments in other respects, found expression in the criminal law in this insistence upon community participation in the determination of guilt or innocence. The deep commitment of the Nation to the right of jury trial in serious criminal cases as a defense against arbitrary law enforcement qualifies for protection under the Due Process Clause of the Fourteenth Amendment, and must therefore be respected by the States.

Of course jury trial has "its weaknesses and the potential for misuse." We are aware of the long debate, especially in this century, among those who write about the administration of justice, as to the wisdom of permitting untrained laymen to determine the facts in civil and criminal proceedings. Although the debate has been intense, with powerful voices on either side, most of the controversy has centered on the jury in civil cases. Indeed, some of the severest critics of civil juries acknowledge that the arguments for criminal juries are much stronger. In addition, at the heart of the dispute have been express or implicit assertions that juries are incapable of adequately understanding evidence or determining issues of fact, and that they are unpredictable, quixotic, and little better than a roll of dice. Yet, the most recent and exhaustive study of the jury in criminal cases concluded that juries do understand the evidence and come to sound conclusions in most of the cases presented to them and that when juries differ with the result at which the judge would have arrived, it is usually because they are serving some of the very purposes for which they were created and for which they are now employed. * * *

II.

Louisiana's final contention is that even if it must grant jury trials in serious criminal cases, the conviction before us is valid and constitutional because here the petitioner was tried for simple battery and was sentenced to only 60 days in the parish prison. We are not persuaded. It is doubtless true that there is a category of petty crimes or offenses which is not subject to the Sixth Amendment jury trial provision and should not be subject to the Fourteenth Amendment jury trial requirement here applied to the States. Crimes carrying possible penalties up to six months do not require a jury trial if they otherwise qualify as petty offenses. But the penalty authorized for a particular crime is of major relevance in determining whether it is serious or not and may in itself, if severe enough, subject the trial to the mandates of the Sixth Amendment. The penalty authorized by the law of the locality may be taken "as a gauge of its social and ethical judgments" of the crime in question. * * * In the case before us the Legislature of Louisiana has made simple battery a criminal offense punishable by imprisonment for up to two years and a fine. The question, then, is whether a crime carrying such a penalty is an offense which Louisiana may insist on trying without a jury.

We think not. So-called petty offenses were tried without juries both in England and in the Colonies and have always been held to be exempt from the otherwise comprehensive language of the Sixth Amendment's jury trial provisions. There is no substantial evidence that the Framers intended to depart from this established common-law practice, and the possible consequences to defendants from convictions for petty offenses have been thought insufficient to outweigh the benefits to efficient law enforcement and simplified judicial administration resulting from the availability of speedy and inexpensive nonjury adjudications. These same considerations compel the same result under the Fourteenth Amendment. Of course the boundaries of the petty offense category have always been ill-defined, if not ambulatory. In the absence of an explicit constitutional provision, the definitional task necessarily falls on the courts, which must either pass upon the validity of legislative attempts to identify those petty offenses which are exempt from jury trial or, where the legislature has not addressed itself to the problem, themselves face the question in the first instance. In either case it is necessary to draw a line in the spectrum of crime, separating petty from serious infractions. This process, although essential, cannot be wholly satisfactory, for it requires attaching different consequences to events which, when they lie near the line, actually differ very little.

In determining whether the length of the authorized prison term or the seriousness of other punishment is enough in itself to require a jury trial, we are counseled * * * to refer to objective criteria, chiefly the existing laws and practices in the Nation. In the federal system, petty offenses are defined as those punishable by no more than six months in prison and a $500 fine. * * * We need not, however, settle in this case the exact location of the line between petty offenses and serious crimes. It is sufficient for our purposes to hold that a crime punishable by two years in prison is, based on past and contemporary standards in this country, a serious crime and not a petty offense. Consequently, appellant was entitled to a jury trial and it was error to deny it. * * *

MR. JUSTICE HARLAN, whom MR. JUSTICE STEWART joins, dissenting. * * *

The jury is of course not without virtues. It affords ordinary citizens a valuable opportunity to participate in a process of government, an experience fostering, one hopes, a respect for law. It eases the burden on judges by enabling them to share a part of their sometimes awesome responsibility. A jury may, at times, afford a higher justice by refusing to enforce harsh laws (although it necessarily does so haphazardly, raising the questions whether arbitrary enforcement of harsh laws is better than total enforcement, and whether the jury system is to be defended on the ground that jurors sometimes disobey their oaths). And the jury may, or may not, contribute desirably to the willingness of the general public to accept criminal judgments as just. * * *

The jury system can also be said to have some inherent defects, which are multiplied by the emergence of the criminal law from the relative simplicity that existed when the jury system was devised. It is a cumbersome process, not only imposing great cost in time and money on both the State and the jurors themselves, but also contributing to delay in the machinery of justice. Untrained jurors are presumably less adept at reaching accurate conclusions of fact than judges, particularly if the issues are many or complex. And it is argued by some that trial by jury, far from increasing public respect for law, impairs it: the average man, it is said, reacts favorably neither to the notion that matters he knows to be complex are being decided by other average men, nor to the way the jury system distorts the process of adjudication. * * *

The point is not that many offenses that English-speaking communities have, at one time or another, regarded as triable without a jury are more serious, and carry more serious penalties, than the one involved here. The point is rather that until today few people would have thought the exact location of the line mattered very much. There is no obvious reason why a jury trial is a requisite of fundamental fairness when the charge is robbery, and not a requisite of fairness when the same defendant, for the same actions, is charged with assault and petty theft. The reason for the historic exception for relatively minor crimes is the obvious one: the burden of jury trial was thought to outweigh its marginal advantages. Exactly why the States should not be allowed to make continuing adjustments, based on the state of their criminal dockets and the difficulty of summoning jurors, simply escapes me. * * *

NOTES AND QUESTIONS

1. The first juries were "juries of recognition" used in land disputes. Their function was to "recognize" by memory who had received title from William the Conqueror. Thus, the older the juror the better (at least as long as he still had a working memory!). But this role gradually changed, as Pollock and Maitland explain in their monumental history of English law. By the fourteenth century, "the jury took a turn which made our jurors, not witnesses, but judges of fact." Rather than "speak only of what they have seen with their own eyes," the jurors "must collect testimony; they must weigh it and state the net result in a verdict." The verdict was considered "not just the verdict of twelve men" but that of the country. Moreover, the verdict must be unanimous. "Just as a corporation can have but one will, so a country can have but one voice. In a later age this communal principle might have led to the acceptance of the majority's verdict: *le pays vint e dyt* [the country came and spoke]. But as yet men had not accepted the dogma that the voice of a majority binds the community." 2 Frederick Pollock & Frederick William Maitland—The History of English Law (2d ed. 1899) 622–627.

2. Justice Harlan stated in *Duncan* that "[a] jury may, at times, afford a higher justice by refusing to enforce harsh laws." What do you think he had in mind by this remark?

3. *The purpose of the "jury trial" right.* Is there a *societal* interest in jury trials independent of protection of the accused? There are intimations of this in *Duncan*, which the Supreme Court, in Powers v. Ohio, 499 U.S. 400, 111 S.Ct. 1364, 113 L.Ed.2d 411 (1991), has more recently developed:

> The opportunity for ordinary citizens to participate in the administration of justice has long been recognized as one of the principal justifications for retaining the jury system. In *Balzac v. Porto Rico*, 258 U.S. 298, 42 S.Ct. 343, 66 L.Ed. 627 (1922), Chief Justice Taft wrote for the Court:
>
>> "The jury system postulates a conscious duty of participation in the machinery of justice. * * * One of its greatest benefits is in the security it gives the people that they, as jurors actual or possible, being part of the judicial system of the country can prevent its arbitrary use or abuse."

And, over 150 years ago, Alexis de Tocqueville remarked:

> "[T]he institution of the jury raises the people itself, or at least a class of citizens, to the bench of judicial authority [and] invests the people, or that class of citizens, with the direction of society. * * *
>
> " * * * The jury * * * invests each citizen with a kind of magistracy; it makes them all feel the duties which they are bound to discharge towards society; and the part which they take in the Government. By obliging men to turn their

attention to affairs which are not exclusively their own, it rubs off that individual egotism which is the rust of society. * * *

"I do not know whether the jury is useful to those who are in litigation; but I am certain it is highly beneficial to those who decide the litigation; and I look upon it as one of the most efficacious means for the education of the people which society can employ." 1 Democracy in America 334–337 (Schocken 1st ed. 1961).[a]

Jury service preserves the democratic element of the law, as it guards the rights of the parties and ensures continued acceptance of the laws by all of the people. It "affords ordinary citizens a valuable opportunity to participate in a process of government, an experience fostering, one hopes, a respect for law." Indeed, with the exception of voting, for most citizens the honor and privilege of jury duty is their most significant opportunity to participate in the democratic process.

Do you think the public's right to serve on juries might conflict with a defendant's interests? If so, whose rights—the defendant's or the community's—should prevail? Does the political-participation view of the jury system run up against a constitutional textual problem? Look again at the Sixth Amendment.

4. *"Petty" offenses versus "serious" crimes: drawing the line. Duncan* failed to settle on "the exact location of the line between petty offenses and serious crimes." In Baldwin v. New York, 399 U.S. 66, 90 S.Ct. 1886, 26 L.Ed.2d 437 (1970), however, the Court stated that "no offense can be deemed 'petty' for purposes of the right to trial by jury where imprisonment for more than six months is authorized."

As for an offense with a maximum sentence of six months' imprisonment or less, the Court "presumes for purposes of the Sixth Amendment that society views such an offense as 'petty.' " Blanton v. City of North Las Vegas, Nevada, 489 U.S. 538, 109 S.Ct. 1289, 103 L.Ed.2d 550 (1989). This presumption is rebutted "only if [the defendant] can demonstrate that any additional statutory penalties, viewed in conjunction with the maximum authorized period of incarceration, are so severe that they clearly reflect a legislative determination that the offense in question is a 'serious' one."

If a defendant is charged in a single proceeding with multiple counts of a petty offense, she is not entitled to a jury trial even if the aggregate

---

[a] Tocqueville also wrote that the jury "puts the real control of affairs into the hands of the ruled, * * * rather than into those of the rulers." And: "The jury system as understood in America seems to me as direct and extreme a consequence of the dogma of the sovereignty of the people as universal suffrage. They are both equally powerful means of making the majority prevail. * * * [T]he jury is above all a political institution * * * ." Tocqueville, Democracy in America 250–51 (J.P. Mayer & Max Lerner eds. 1966), *quoted in* Vikram David Amar, *Jury Service as Political Participation Akin to Voting*, 80 Cornell L. Rev. 203, 220 (1995).

maximum prison term exceeds six months. Lewis v. United States, 518 U.S. 322, 116 S.Ct. 2163, 135 L.Ed.2d 590 (1996).

5. *More on the Duncan case: some background and follow-up.* The Court's description of the facts in *Duncan*—the first paragraph of the opinion—is bland and unevocative. In fact, as is often the case, the real story is far more interesting than first appearances and, as is too often the case, the story here has to do with the role of racism in enforcement of the criminal law. This story, however, has a happy ending. Here are the first-person recollections of attorney Alvin J. Bronstein, who represented Duncan:

> This case arose in October of 1966. I don't know whether any of you have ever heard of Judge Leander Perez in Plaquemines Parish, Louisiana. Plaquemines Parish is that strip of land along the Mississippi Delta, below New Orleans, which empties into the Gulf. Plaquemines Parish had been run since the twenties by Judge Leander Perez, who had been a state district judge from 1920 to '24. He still used the title and was really the king or the emperor of Plaquemines Parish, which was an extraordinarily mineral-wealthy piece of land. * * * Judge Perez had put through a constitutional amendment in Louisiana to create a separate special form of government in that Parish so that everything was controlled by the Parish Council. The president of the Council was Judge Perez, the district attorney was Leander Perez Jr., and the vice president of the Council was Chalen Perez, the judge's older son. * * * Leander Perez was a close associate of Senator Bilbo and Senator Jim Eastland from Mississippi. He was a racist par excellence. He was one of the people who first began to distribute the phony Protocols of the Elders of Zion and a number of other racist, anti-Semitic publications. He's the man who bragged that if Martin Luther King ever came to Plaquemines Parish, they had bought a little island in the Mississippi that was snake-infested and that had an old Spanish prison fort on it, and that's where Dr. King would be imprisoned if he tried to do anything in Plaquemines Parish. Perez was also excommunicated by the Archbishop of New Orleans because he physically tried to prevent the integration of the Catholic schools there in 1962 and '63.
>
> In September of 1966, the Plaquemines Parish schools were finally integrated by a few young black students, and in October of that year a man by the name of Gary Duncan, a twenty-year-old black fisherman, married with an infant, who lived in Plaquemines Parish all his life, was driving home from work and passed the school and saw a bunch of kids on the sidewalk outside of the school. Two of the boys were his nephews, eleven-and twelve-year-old black kids who had been among the few to attend the previously all-white school. He saw that they were surrounded by about five or six white boys about the same age, and it looked like there was an incident or that something was going on so he pulled over, got out, and asked

what was happening. There had been a little pushing and shoving between the kids, and his nephews said the other boys were taunting and teasing and threatening them. He said, "Okay, well, get in the car and I'll take you home." He then said to one of the young white boys, touching him on the elbow, "Go run along and go on home." Just like that. Across the street was one of the members of the Parish School Board, a man by the name of Herman Landry who had resisted the school integration, and who was a pal of the Perezes. He went to the phone and called Leander, Jr., the D.A., and said, "I just saw this (using a racist term), this black man touch that boy, and I think it was an assault." Sure enough, two days later, although the police investigated and found there was no assault, Gary Duncan was arrested and charged with battery, common law battery; that is, touching without permission and without the intent necessary to commit a real assault. He was charged with this battery, a misdemeanor which carried a possible penalty of two years in prison. * * *

* * * [H]is family called our office [Lawyers' Constitutional Defense Committee] in New Orleans and asked for help. Dick Sobol and one of the black lawyers in the office, our local counsel, went down there, put up the bail money, got him out, and then looked at the statute, and saw this peculiar, bizarre thing: This man could face two years in prison and there was no right to a jury trial. They knew that trying a case like that in Plaquemines Parish before Judge Leon, who was also a crony of Judge Perez, was a futile exercise, so they demanded a jury trial. It was rejected, of course, the local court saying you're not entitled to a jury trial, this is only a misdemeanor. * * *

Duncan * * * was tried without a jury. He was convicted and rearrested;[b] indeed, they arrested him about eight times in the course of this case—at every possible opportunity. He had to put up another bond to appeal to the Louisiana Supreme Court. The appeal was rejected there. He was rearrested, and then we decided to go directly to the Supreme Court of the United States rather than go through the lower federal courts with a habeas corpus petition. * * *

* * * [T]he *Duncan* case went up to the Supreme Court of the United States * * * and it resulted in the landmark decision of *Duncan v. Louisiana.* * * *

End of story? Not quite. Bronstein continues:

The Supreme Court remanded the case to Louisiana for implementation of its decision. And, of course, what the Louisiana legislature did immediately was to amend the statute and read the

---

[b]   By "rearrested," we are unsure whether the author meant that Duncan was arrested for a different offense or arrested under the judgment of conviction.—Eds.

decision as saying, "Well, if you could only get six months you would not be entitled to a jury trial." So they amended the punishment part of the battery statute to max the punishment at six months rather than two years, and then they wanted to prosecute Duncan again without a jury trial. They arrested him again, and we went back in, got him out on bail, and then brought another action in federal court to enjoin this prosecution.

* * * We just couldn't let this guy go to jail in the Parish. We brought a new injunction action, which was tried before Judge Cassibry. I tried this case, and we proved that it was a bad-faith prosecution, that there was no crime committed, that the touching was an everyday occurrence. People touched, people said, "Run along. Go home. Do this." We proved that the only reason that he was being prosecuted was because it was to be a lesson to teach the black citizens of Plaquemines Parish that if they fool around with the white power structure, they're going to get punished. We had a lot of evidence to that effect—that it was bad faith. The Perezes were sort of falling apart at that point. Judge Cassibry enjoined the prosecution of Duncan and held that the Louisiana officials were acting in bad faith. * * *

As I think back on this case, I remember leaving the Supreme Court after the argument, and Gary Duncan, his wife, and his parents were there * * *. When we left and walked down the steps, Gary Duncan looked up at the inscription on top of the front of the courthouse—"Equal Justice Under the Law"—and he said something about how it was so great to be there. He really didn't care anymore whether he won or lost. He could go to jail and do the sixty days, which is what he was sentenced to originally, because he thought he had really won. It was clear that he had been listened to and had been heard, and that was what was important to him.

Alvin J. Bronstein, *Representing the Powerless: Lawyers Can Make a Difference*, 49 Me. L. Rev. 1, 5–7, 12–13 (1997).

6. *Judge versus jury. Duncan* teaches that the constitutional framers saw the jury as "an inestimable safeguard against . . . the complaint, biased, or eccentric judge." *Duncan* also stated that "[i]f the defendant preferred the common-sense judgment of a jury to the more tutored but perhaps less sympathetic reaction of the single judge, he was to have it." Does this suggest that the drafters of the Sixth Amendment (or, at least, the *Duncan* Court) thought juries were more likely to acquit than judges? Is that what *you* think?

If so, think again. At least in federal courts, the average conviction rate of juries between 1946 and 2002 was 75%; judges convicted at roughly the same rate (73%). In the last decade of this period, however, judges were considerably more lenient: juries convicted 86% of the time, compared to 54% of the time by judges. Andrew D. Leipold, *Why Are Federal Judges So*

Acquittal Prone?, 83 Wash. U.L.Q. 151, 164 (2005). Although some of this explanation has to do with the type of crime involved—judges were far more likely to acquit than juries in so-called "public order" cases (*e.g.*, weapons and tax offenses, obstruction of justice, racketeering) compared to other offenses, judges were more lenient in *all* categories of cases between 1989 and 2002. *Id.* at 171–175.

What explains the changing judicial conviction rates? Professor Leipold offers a "provocative inference drawn by the study" that he admits is not yet provable: The years in which judicial conviction patterns changed dramatically (in the direction of leniency) followed Congressional legislation decreasing judicial sentencing discretion. (We cover this change in federal sentencing rules in the next chapter.) In other words, perhaps a judge is more prone to acquit a defendant in a case in which she knows she will have to impose a sentence more severe than she believes is appropriate. In contrast, jurors do not generally know during the guilt phase of a trial what sentence may or must be imposed if they convict.

7. *Waiver.* Federal Rule of Criminal Procedure 23(a) provides that a defendant may waive a jury trial, but only with the approval of the court and consent of the government. Does that seem proper? Why should the prosecutor have to consent to a defendant's waiver of her constitutional right to a jury trial? In Singer v. United States, 380 U.S. 24, 85 S.Ct. 783, 13 L.Ed.2d 630 (1965), Chief Justice Warren answered the question:

> The ability to waive a constitutional right does not ordinarily carry with it the right to insist upon the opposite of that right. For example, although a defendant can, under some circumstances, waive his constitutional right to a public trial, he has no absolute right to compel a private trial; although he can waive his right to be tried in the State and district where the crime was committed, he cannot in all cases compel transfer of the case to another district; and although he can waive his right to be confronted by the witnesses against him, it has never been seriously suggested that he can thereby compel the Government to try the case by stipulation. * * *

> Trial by jury has been established by the Constitution as the "normal and * * * preferable mode of disposing of issues of fact in criminal cases." As with any mode that might be devised to determine guilt, trial by jury has it weaknesses and the potential for misuse. However, the mode itself has been surrounded with safeguards to make it as fair as possible * * * . * * *

> In light of the Constitution's emphasis on jury trial, we find it difficult to understand how the petitioner can submit the bald proposition that to compel a defendant in a criminal case to undergo a jury trial against his will is contrary to his right to a fair trial or to due process. A defendant's only constitutional right concerning the method of trial is to an impartial trial by jury. We find no

constitutional impediment to conditioning a waiver of this right on the consent of the prosecuting attorney and the trial judge when, if either refuses to consent, the result is simply that the defendant is subject to an impartial trial by jury—the very thing that the Constitution guarantees him. The Constitution recognizes an adversary system as the proper method of determining guilt, and the Government, as a litigant, has a legitimate interest in seeing that cases in which it believes a conviction is warranted are tried before the tribunal which the Constitution regards as most likely to produce a fair result.

8. *Jury size: fewer than twelve?* Historically, Anglo-American criminal juries have been composed of twelve persons. But, it turns out, this jury size is not constitutionally compelled. In Williams v. Florida, 399 U.S. 78, 90 S.Ct. 1893, 26 L.Ed.2d 446 (1970), the Supreme Court upheld the constitutionality of a Florida statute that provided for six-person juries in non-capital cases. Justice White surveyed common law history and concluded that there was "absolutely no indication in 'the intent of the Framers' of an explicit decision to equate the constitutional and common-law characteristics of the jury." Therefore, he concluded, the "relevant inquiry, as we see it, must be the function that the particular feature performs and its relation to the purposes of the jury trial. Measured by this standard, the 12-man requirement cannot be regarded as an indispensable component of the Sixth Amendment." The Court explained:

> The purpose of the jury trial, as we noted in *Duncan*, is to prevent oppression by the Government. * * * Given this purpose, the essential feature of a jury obviously lies in the interposition between the accused and his accuser of the commonsense judgment of a group of laymen, and in the community participation and shared responsibility that results from that group's determination of guilt or innocence. The performance of this role is not a function of the particular number of the body that makes up the jury. To be sure, the number should probably be large enough to promote group deliberation, free from outside attempts at intimidation, and to provide a fair possibility for obtaining a representative cross-section of the community. But we find little reason to think that these goals are in any meaningful sense less likely to be achieved when the jury numbers six, than when it numbers 12—particularly if the requirement of unanimity is retained. And, certainly the reliability of the jury as a factfinder hardly seems likely to be a function of its size.

Six states authorize criminal juries of fewer than twelve persons. *12-member Juries and Unanimous Verdicts,* 88 Judicature 300 (2005).

9. *How small is too small?* The *Williams* Court did not fear that a reduction in jury size from 12 to 6 would impair the reliability of jury verdicts. Of course, there is no foolproof way to evaluate this claim. However,

one study using complicated probabilistic models, taken in conjunction with available empirical data, approximated that the probability of a jury "wrongly" acquitting a guilty person more than doubles from 6.15% to 13.95% when the jury size is reduced from 12 to 6. The probability of convicting an innocent person purportedly rises nearly in half, from 2.21% to 3.25%, with a similar jury-size reduction. Alan E. Gelfand & Herbert Solomon, *Considerations in Building Jury Behavior Models and In Comparing Jury Schemes: An Argument in Favor of 12-Member Juries*, 17 Jurimetrics J. 292, 310–11 (1977).

In Ballew v. Georgia, 435 U.S. 223, 98 S.Ct. 1029, 55 L.Ed.2d 234 (1978), the Supreme Court unanimously declared five-person juries unconstitutional. It stated that "recent empirical data suggest that progressively smaller juries are less likely to foster effective group deliberation. At some point, this decline leads to inaccurate fact-finding and incorrect application of the common sense of the community to the facts."

10. *Unanimous jury verdicts.* "For over six hundred years, the unanimous verdict has stood as a distinctive and defining feature of jury trials. The first recorded instance of a unanimous verdict occurred in 1367, when an English Court refused to accept an 11–1 guilty vote * * * ." Jeffrey Abramson, We, the Jury: The Jury System and the Ideal of Democracy 179 (1994).

Today, federal law (Fed. R. Crim. P. 31(a)) and all but two states require unanimous jury verdicts in criminal trials. When the legislatures of Louisiana and Oregon abandoned the unanimity requirement, however, their statutes were attacked on two grounds: (1) the Sixth Amendment right to trial by jury, incorporated to the states through the Fourteenth Amendment, implicitly requires unanimous jury verdicts; and (2) the proof-beyond-a-reasonable-doubt requirement of due process is violated by nonunanimous verdicts. These arguments ultimately failed.

In Apodaca v. Oregon, 406 U.S. 404, 92 S.Ct. 1628, 32 L.Ed.2d 184 (1972), a four-justice plurality stated that the Sixth Amendment is not violated by convictions based on 11–1 and 10–2 verdicts. A fifth member of the Court, Justice Powell, concurred in the judgment. He concluded, however, that the *Sixth Amendment* mandates unanimity—and, thus, unanimous verdicts are required in the *federal* system—but that the Fourteenth Amendment due process clause does not incorporate this feature of jury trials to the states.

In a companion case, Johnson v. Louisiana, 406 U.S. 356, 92 S.Ct. 1620, 32 L.Ed.2d 152 (1972), the majority held that a conviction based on a vote of nine of twelve jurors—what the majority described as "a substantial majority of the jury"—does not violate the proof-beyond-a-reasonable-doubt standard of the due process clause. Justice Blackmun, who joined the majority, warned that "a system employing a 7–5 standard, rather than a 9–3 or 75% minimum, would afford me great difficulty." On the matter of the presumption of innocence, the majority explained:

Appellant, in effect, asks us to assume that, when minority jurors express sincere doubts about guilt, their fellow jurors will nevertheless ignore them and vote to convict even if deliberation has not been exhausted and minority jurors have grounds for acquittal which, if pursued, might persuade members of the majority to acquit. * * * We have no grounds for believing that majority jurors, aware of their responsibility and power over the liberty of the defendant, would simply refuse to listen to arguments presented to them in favor of acquittal, terminate discussion, and render a verdict. On the contrary it is far more likely that a juror presenting reasoned argument in favor of acquittal would either have his arguments answered or would carry enough other jurors with him to prevent conviction. A majority will cease discussion and outvote a minority only after reasoned discussion has ceased to have persuasive effect or to serve any other purpose—when a minority, that is, continues to insist upon acquittal without having persuasive reasons in support of its position. At that juncture there is no basis for denigrating the vote of so large a majority of the jury or for refusing to accept their decision as being, at least in their minds, beyond a reasonable doubt.

Do you find these arguments persuasive? If the government can only convince nine of twelve jurors of the defendant's guilt, isn't that a lesser burden of proof than if it must convince everyone? Justices Marshall and Brennan dissented:

The [majority's] argument seems to be that since, under *Williams*, nine jurors are enough to convict, the three dissenters are mere surplusage. But there is all the difference in the world between three jurors who are not there, and three jurors who entertain doubts after hearing all the evidence. In the first case we can never know, and it is senseless to ask, whether the prosecutor might have persuaded additional jurors had they been present. But in the second case we know what has happened: the prosecutor has tried and failed to persuade those jurors of the defendant's guilt. In such circumstances, it does violence to language and to logic to say that the government has proved the defendant's guilt beyond a reasonable doubt.

What about the majority's expectation that jurors will continue to deliberate even after there are enough votes to render a verdict. Does that seem likely to you?

The Court's rulings sparked considerable social science research with mock juries. The data indicate that the ratio of convictions to acquittals does not change markedly with nonunanimous jury verdicts, as long as verdicts require a two-thirds majority or more. Predictably, the hung-jury rate is higher with unanimous verdicts. Abramson, *supra*, at 198.

What changes markedly is the deliberative process. Contrary to the Court's assumptions, in one simulation study, juries allowed to return 8–4 verdicts deliberated, on average, less than five minutes after the 8–4 point was reached. Another study showed that juries that must reach unanimity deliberate 138 minutes on average; when a vote of 10–2 is permitted the time is reduced to 103 minutes; and with an 8–4 vote, the time is cut to 75 minutes. Finally, and arguably most critically, studies report that jurors returning nonunanimous verdicts—even those in the majority—felt less certain of their conclusions than jurors who sat on juries that reached unanimous verdicts. *Id.* at 199–200.

11. *Smaller juries versus nonunanimous ones.* In terms of the reliability of jury verdicts, which change in the jury system—reducing its size or nonunanimous verdicts—would you expect to be more risky? See George C. Thomas III & Barry S. Pollack, *Rethinking Guilt, Juries, and Jeopardy*, 91 Mich. L. Rev. 1, 24 (1992). If you were a defense attorney and had to choose to give up either 12-person juries or unanimous jury verdicts, which would you choose?

12. Given Supreme Court case law, as described in the previous Notes, how would you expect it to rule if a state legislature enacted a law that combined nonunanimity with smaller juries, specifically by permitting a jury verdict of 5–1? See Burch v. Louisiana, 441 U.S. 130, 99 S.Ct. 1623, 60 L.Ed.2d 96 (1979).

2. JURY SELECTION

a. "Fair Cross-Section" Requirement

TAYLOR V. LOUISIANA
Supreme Court of the United States, 1975.
419 U.S. 522, 95 S.Ct. 692, 42 L.Ed.2d 690.

MR. JUSTICE WHITE delivered the opinion of the Court [joined by JUSTICES DOUGLAS, BRENNAN, STEWART, MARSHALL, BLACKMUN, and POWELL].

When this case was tried, Art. VII, § 41 of the Louisiana Constitution, and Art. 402 of the Louisiana Code of Criminal Procedure provided that a woman should not be selected for jury service unless she had previously filed a written declaration of her desire to be subject to jury service. The constitutionality of these provisions is the issue in this case.

I

Appellant, Billy J. Taylor, was indicted by the grand jury of St. Tammany Parish, in the Twenty-second Judicial District of Louisiana, for aggravated kidnaping. On April 12, 1972, appellant moved the trial court to quash the petit jury venire drawn for the special criminal term beginning with his trial the following day. Appellant alleged that women were systematically excluded from the venire and that he would therefore be deprived of what he claimed to be his federal constitutional right to "a fair trial by jury of a representative segment of the community * * * ."

The Twenty-second Judicial District comprises the parishes of St. Tammany and Washington. The appellee has stipulated that 53% of the persons eligible for jury service in these parishes were female, and that no more than 10% of the persons on the jury wheel in St. Tammany Parish were women. During the period from December 8, 1971, to November 3, 1972, 12 females were among the 1,800 persons drawn to fill petit jury venires in St. Tammany Parish. It was also stipulated that the discrepancy between females eligible for jury service and those actually included in the venire was the result of the operation of La. Const., Art. VII, § 41, and La. Code Crim. Proc., Art. 402. In the present case, a venire totaling 175 persons was drawn for jury service beginning April 13, 1972. There were no females on the venire. * * *

II

The Louisiana jury-selection system does not disqualify women from jury service, but in operation its conceded systematic impact is that only a very few women, grossly disproportionate to the number of eligible women in the community, are called for jury service. In this case, no women were on the venire from which the petit jury was drawn. The issue we have, therefore, is whether a jury-selection system which operates to exclude from jury service an identifiable class of citizens constituting 53% of eligible jurors in the community comports with the Sixth and Fourteenth Amendments.

The State first insists that Taylor, a male, has no standing to object to the exclusion of women from his jury. But Taylor's claim is that he was constitutionally entitled to a jury drawn from a venire constituting a fair cross section of the community and that the jury that tried him was not such a jury by reason of the exclusion of women. Taylor was not a member of the excluded class; but there is no rule that claims such as Taylor presents may be made only by those defendants who are members of the group excluded from jury service. * * *

III

The background against which this case must be decided includes our holding in *Duncan v. Louisiana* (p. 53) that the Sixth Amendment's provision for jury trial is made binding on the States by virtue of the Fourteenth Amendment. Our inquiry is whether the presence of a fair cross section of the community on venires, panels, or lists from which petit juries are drawn is essential to the fulfillment of the Sixth

Amendment's guarantee of an impartial jury trial in criminal prosecutions.

The Court's prior cases are instructive. Both in the course of exercising its supervisory powers over trials in federal courts and in the constitutional context, the Court has unambiguously declared that the American concept of the jury trial contemplates a jury drawn from a fair cross section of the community. * * * *Glasser v. United States*, 315 U.S. 60, 85, 86, 62 S.Ct. 457, 472, 86 L.Ed. 680 (1942), in the context of a federal criminal case and the Sixth Amendment's jury trial requirement, stated that "[o]ur notions of what a proper jury is have developed in harmony with our basic concepts of a democratic system and representative government," and repeated the Court's understanding that the jury " 'be a body truly representative of the community' * * * and not the organ of any special group or class."

A federal conviction by a jury from which women had been excluded, although eligible for service under state law, was reviewed in *Ballard v. United States*, 329 U.S. 187, 67 S.Ct. 261, 91 L.Ed. 181 (1946). Noting the federal statutory "design to make the jury 'a cross-section of the community' " and the fact that women had been excluded, the Court exercised its supervisory powers over the federal courts and reversed the conviction. * * *

The unmistakable import of this Court's opinions * * * is that the selection of a petit jury from a representative cross section of the community is an essential component of the Sixth Amendment right to a jury trial. Recent federal legislation governing jury selection within the federal court system has a similar thrust. Shortly prior to this Court's decision in *Duncan v. Louisiana*, the Federal Jury Selection and Service Act of 1968 was enacted. * * * In passing this legislation, the Committee Reports of both the House[7] and the Senate recognized that the jury plays a political function in the administration of the law and that the requirement of a jury's being chosen from a fair cross section of the community is fundamental to the American system of justice. * * *

We accept the fair-cross-section requirement as fundamental to the jury trial guaranteed by the Sixth Amendment and are convinced that the requirement has solid foundation. The purpose of a jury is to guard against the exercise of arbitrary power—to make available the commonsense judgment of the community as a hedge against the overzealous or mistaken prosecutor and in preference to the professional

---

[7]   H.R. Rep. No. 1076, 90th Cong., 2d Sess., 8 (1968):

It must be remembered that the jury is designed not only to understand the case, but also to reflect the community's sense of justice in deciding it. As long as there are significant departures from the cross-sectional goal, biased juries are the result—biased in the sense that they reflect a slanted view of the community they are supposed to represent.

or perhaps overconditioned or biased response of a judge. This prophylactic vehicle is not provided if the jury pool is made up of only special segments of the populace or if large, distinctive groups are excluded from the pool. Community participation in the administration of the criminal law, moreover, is not only consistent with our democratic heritage but is also critical to public confidence in the fairness of the criminal justice system. Restricting jury service to only special groups or excluding identifiable segments playing major roles in the community cannot be squared with the constitutional concept of jury trial. "Trial by jury presupposes a jury drawn from a pool broadly representative of the community as well as impartial in a specific case. * * * [T]he broad representative character of the jury should be maintained, partly as assurance of a diffused impartiality and partly because sharing in the administration of justice is a phase of civic responsibility."

IV

We are also persuaded that the fair-cross-section requirement is violated by the systematic exclusion of women, who in the judicial district involved here amounted to 53% of the citizens eligible for jury service. This conclusion necessarily entails the judgment that women are sufficiently numerous and distinct from men and that if they are systematically eliminated from jury panels, the Sixth Amendment's fair-cross-section requirement cannot be satisfied. This very matter was debated in *Ballard v. United States, supra.* Positing the fair-cross-section rule—there said to be a statutory one—the Court concluded that the systematic exclusion of women was unacceptable. The dissenting view that an all-male panel drawn from various groups in the community would be as truly representative as if women were included, was firmly rejected:

> "The thought is that the factors which tend to influence the action of women are the same as those which influence the action of men—personality, background, economic status—and not sex. Yet it is not enough to say that women when sitting as jurors neither act nor tend to act as a class. Men likewise do not act as a class. But, if the shoe were on the other foot, who would claim that a jury was truly representative of the community if all men were intentionally and systematically excluded from the panel? The truth is that the two sexes are not fungible; a community made up exclusively of one is different from a community composed of both; the subtle interplay of influence one on the other is among the imponderables. To insulate the courtroom from either may not in a given case make an iota of difference. Yet a flavor, a distinct quality is lost if either sex is excluded. The exclusion of one may indeed make the jury less

representative of the community than would be true if an economic or racial group were excluded."

In this respect, we agree with the Court in *Ballard*: If the fair-cross-section rule is to govern the selection of juries, as we have concluded it must, women cannot be systematically excluded from jury panels from which petit juries are drawn. * * *

V

There remains the argument that women as a class serve a distinctive role in society and that jury service would so substantially interfere with that function that the State has ample justification for excluding women from service unless they volunteer, even though the result is that almost all jurors are men. It is true that *Hoyt v. Florida*, 368 U.S. 57, 82 S.Ct. 159, 7 L.Ed.2d 118 (1961), held that such a system did not deny due process of law or equal protection of the laws because there was a sufficiently rational basis for such an exemption. But *Hoyt* did not involve a defendant's Sixth Amendment right to a jury drawn from a fair cross section of the community and the prospect of depriving him of that right if women as a class are systematically excluded. The right to a proper jury cannot be overcome on merely rational grounds. There must be weightier reasons if a distinctive class representing 53% of the eligible jurors is for all practical purposes to be excluded from jury service. No such basis has been tendered here.

The States are free to grant exemptions from jury service to individuals in case of special hardship or incapacity and to those engaged in particular occupations the uninterrupted performance of which is critical to the community's welfare. It would not appear that such exemptions would pose substantial threats that the remaining pool of jurors would not be representative of the community. A system excluding all women, however, is a wholly different matter. It is untenable to suggest these days that it would be a special hardship for each and every woman to perform jury service or that society cannot spare *any* women from their present duties. This may be the case with many, and it may be burdensome to sort out those who should be exempted from those who should serve. But that task is performed in the case of men, and the administrative convenience in dealing with women as a class is insufficient justification for diluting the quality of community judgment represented by the jury in criminal trials.

VI * * *

* * * If at one time it could be held that Sixth Amendment juries must be drawn from a fair cross section of the community but that this requirement permitted the almost total exclusion of women, this is not the case today. Communities differ at different times and places. What is a fair cross section at one time or place is not necessarily a fair cross

section at another time or a different place. Nothing persuasive has been presented to us in this case suggesting that all-male venires in the parishes involved here are fairly representative of the local population otherwise eligible for jury service.

VII

Our holding does not augur or authorize the fashioning of detailed jury-selection codes by federal courts. The fair-cross-section principle must have much leeway in application. The States remain free to prescribe relevant qualifications for their jurors and to provide reasonable exemptions so long as it may be fairly said that the jury lists or panels are representative of the community. * * *

It should also be emphasized that in holding that petit juries must be drawn from a source fairly representative of the community we impose no requirement that petit juries actually chosen must mirror the community and reflect the various distinctive groups in the population. Defendants are not entitled to a jury of any particular composition; but the jury wheels, pools of names, panels, or venires from which juries are drawn must not systematically exclude distinctive groups in the community and thereby fail to be reasonably representative thereof. * * *

MR. CHIEF JUSTICE BURGER concurs in the result.

MR. JUSTICE REHNQUIST, dissenting. * * *

I cannot conceive that today's decision is necessary to guard against oppressive or arbitrary law enforcement, or to prevent miscarriages of justice and to assure fair trials. Especially is this so when the criminal defendant involved makes no claims of prejudice or bias. The Court does accord some slight attention to justifying its ruling in terms of the basis on which the right to jury trial was read into the Fourteenth Amendment. It concludes that the jury is not effective, as a prophylaxis against arbitrary prosecutorial and judicial power, if the "jury pool is made up of only special segments of the populace or if large, distinctive groups are excluded from the pool." It fails, however, to provide any satisfactory explanation of the mechanism by which the Louisiana system undermines the prophylactic role of the jury, either in general or in this case. The best it can do is to posit "a flavor, a distinct quality," which allegedly is lost if either sex is excluded. However, this "flavor" is not of such importance that the Constitution is offended if any given petit jury is not so enriched. This smacks more of mysticism than of law. The Court does not even purport to practice its mysticism in a consistent fashion—presumably doctors, lawyers, and other groups, whose frequent exemption from jury service is endorsed by the majority, also offer qualities as distinct and important as those at issue here. * * *

NOTES AND QUESTIONS

1.   Justice Rehnquist ridiculed the majority opinion, describing it as more mysticism than law. Do you agree? If you disagree, what *is* the "flavor" or "distinct quality" that is lost if women are absent from juries? Do women, *as women*, share a common outlook on the world, or share similar attitudes and ideas?

All jurors hear the same testimony and are expected to apply the same rules of law, as instructed by the judge. Why should it matter, therefore, whether the jury pool is composed nearly exclusively of either men or women? Do women interpret testimony differently than men? Do they make witness-credibility judgments differently *because* they are women?

If you believe that there is a significant male/female dichotomy, is it as great as the difference in the way, for example, accountants and social workers look at the world, filter the testimony they hear, and make credibility judgments?

2.   The Sixth Amendment entitles an accused to trial by an "impartial jury." It says nothing about a "fair cross-section of the community." Was there any evidence that the twelve male jurors in Taylor's case were other than impartial? Is the implication of *Taylor* that a *jury* can never be impartial if the *jury pool* is composed only of men or only of women? If so, why would this be the case? If not, what interest is protected by *Taylor*?

3.   Look again at footnote 7 of *Taylor*. According to one observer, "[t]he revealing aspect of this quotation is how it connected one view of an impartial jury (the jury that understands the case) to another view (the jury that understands the community). The implication was there is not one but many ways to understand cases." Jeffrey Abramson, We, the Jury: The Jury System and the Ideal of Democracy 123 (1994). If this *is* what *Taylor* is saying, does this mean that the search for truth is nothing more than "a partisan operation, [that] justice is one thing for the hyphenated American, another for the New England Yankee"? Sam J. Ervin, Jr., *Jury Reform Needs More Thought*, 53 A.B.A. J. 132, 134 (Feb. 1967).

4.   *Applying Taylor*. In Duren v. Missouri, 439 U.S. 357, 99 S.Ct. 664, 58 L.Ed.2d 579 (1979), Ruth Bader Ginsburg and her co-counsel successfully challenged a statute that provided women, upon request, an exemption from jury service. The Court explained the Sixth Amendment requirement this way:

> In order to establish a prima facie violation of the fair-cross-section requirement, the defendant must show (1) that the group alleged to be excluded is a "distinctive" group in the community; (2) that the representation of this group in venires from which juries are selected is not fair and reasonable in relation to the number of such persons in the community; and (3) that this underrepresentation is due to systematic exclusion of the group in the jury-selection process. * * *

* * * However, once the defendant has made a prima facie showing of an infringement of his constitutional right to a jury drawn from a fair cross section of the community, it is the State that bears the burden of justifying this infringement by showing attainment of a fair cross section to be incompatible with a significant state interest.

The first element of the *Duren* test—that the excluded group is "distinctive"—is considered in the next Note. Regarding the second element, "the defendant must show that the procedure employed resulted in substantial underrepresentation" of the distinctive group. Castaneda v. Partida, 430 U.S. 482, 97 S.Ct. 1272, 51 L.Ed.2d 498 (1977). Because this is a Sixth Amendment issue and not one based on equal protection principles, it is unnecessary for the defendant to prove that the substantial underrepresentation of the distinctive group was the result of a discriminatory purpose. It is enough to show, as the third element suggests, that it was the result of "systematic" exclusion or underrepresentation—that is, the underrepresentation was not a one-time coincidence, but rather is inherent to the selection process.

How does a defendant go about showing the requisite underrepresentation of the distinctive group (second element), and that this underrepresentation was due to "systematic exclusion" (third element)? In Berghuis v. Smith, 559 U.S. 314, 130 S.Ct. 1382, 176 L.Ed.2d 249 (2010), Diapolis Smith proved that African Americans constituted 7.28% of Kent County, Michigan's jury-eligible population, and 6% of the pool from which jurors were drawn over the preceding six-month period. The trial court ruled that, based on these figures, African-Americans *were* underrepresented, but it ruled against Smith on the ground that there was insufficient evidence that the jury selection process "systematically" excluded African-Americans.

Justice Ginsburg, writing for a unanimous Court observed that courts have considered three means of measuring the extent of underrepresentation: "absolute disparity," "comparative disparity," and "standard deviation." She went on to explain:

> "Absolute disparity" is determined by subtracting the percentage of African-Americans in the jury pool (here, 6% * * *) from the percentage of African-Americans in the local, jury-eligible population (here, 7.28%). By an absolute disparity measure, therefore, African-Americans were underrepresented by 1.28%. "Comparative disparity" is determined by dividing the absolute disparity (here, 1.28%) by the group's representation in the jury-eligible population (here, 7.28%). The quotient (here, 18%), showed that * * * African-Americans were, on average, 18% less likely, when compared to the overall jury-eligible population, to be on the jury-service list.

As for "standard deviation" analysis, Justice Ginsburg explained that this approach "seeks to determine the probability that the disparity between a group's jury-eligible population and the group's percentage in the qualified jury pool is attributable to random chance."

Is one of these tests required or preferred by the Supreme Court? According to the Court, "neither *Duren* nor any other decision of this Court specifies the method or test courts must use to measure the representation of distinctive groups in jury pools." The Court went on:

> Each test is imperfect. Absolute disparity and comparative disparity measurements, courts have recognized, can be misleading when, as here, "members of the distinctive group comp[ose] [only] a small percentage of those eligible for jury service." And, to our knowledge, "[n]o court * * * has accepted [a standard deviation analysis] alone as determinative in Sixth Amendment challenges to jury selection systems." * * *

Because it was unnecessary to its ruling, the Court indicated that it would not "take sides today on the method or methods by which underrepresentation is appropriately measured."

As for the matter of "systematic exclusion," however, the Court upheld the trial court:

> To establish systematic exclusion, Smith contends, the defendant must show only that the underrepresentation is persistent and "produced by the method or 'system' used to select [jurors]," rather than by chance. In this regard, Smith catalogs a laundry list of factors * * * that, he urges, rank as "systematic" causes of underrepresentation of African-Americans in Kent County's jury pool. Smith's list includes the County's practice of excusing people who merely alleged hardship or simply failed to show up for jury service, its reliance on mail notices, its failure to follow up on nonresponses, its use of residential addresses at least 15 months old, and the refusal of Kent County police to enforce court orders for the appearance of prospective jurors.

> No "clearly established" precedent of this Court supports Smith's claim that he can make out a prima facie case merely by pointing to a host of factors that, individually or in combination, *might* contribute to a groups's underrepresentation. * * * *Duren* first and foremost required Smith himself to show that the underrepresentation complained of was "due to systematic exclusion."

> This Court, furthermore, has never "clearly established" that jury-section-process features of the kind on Smith's list can give rise to a fair-cross-section claim. In *Taylor*, we "recognized broad discretion in the States" to "prescribe relevant qualifications for their jurors and to provide reasonable exemptions." And, in *Duren*, the Court understood that hardship exemptions resembling those Smith assails might well "survive a fair-cross-section challenge."

Justice Thomas concurred. He stated in his short opinion that *Taylor's* holding "seems difficult to square with the Sixth Amendment's text and history. Accordingly, in an appropriate case, I would be willing to reconsider our precedents articulating the 'fair cross section' requirement."

5.   *"Distinctive" groups.* What is a "distinctive" group (Note 4) for purposes of the fair-cross-section requirement of the Sixth Amendment? One explanation, followed by many courts, is:

> (1) that the group is defined and limited by some factor (i.e., that the group has a definite composition such as by race or sex); (2) that a common thread or basic similarity in attitude, ideas, or experience runs through the group; and (3) that there is a community of interests among members of the group such that the group's interest cannot be adequately represented if the group is excluded from the jury selection process.

Willis v. Zant, 720 F.2d 1212 (11th Cir. 1983).

In view of this standard, are any of the following groups "distinctive" for purposes of the fair-cross-section requirement: (1) blue-collar workers, Anaya v. Hansen, 781 F.2d 1 (1st Cir. 1986); (2) Hispanics, People v. Howard, 1 Cal.4th 1132, 5 Cal.Rptr.2d 268, 824 P.2d 1315 (1992); (3) Native Americans, United States v. Black Bear, 878 F.2d 213 (8th Cir. 1989); (4) lesbians, People v. Garcia, 77 Cal.App.4th 1269, 92 Cal.Rptr.2d 339 (2000); (5) college students, Commonwealth v. Evans, 438 Mass. 142, 778 N.E.2d 885 (2002); and (6) persons over the age of 70, People v. McCoy, 40 Cal.App.4th 778, 47 Cal.Rptr.2d 599 (1995).

b.   Voir Dire

Even if a jury pool includes a fair cross-section of the community, this does not guarantee that every member of the pool is able and willing to render an impartial verdict, as the Sixth Amendment demands. Therefore, trial courts conduct an examination (*voir dire*) of prospective jurors in order to determine if they are legally qualified (*e.g.* understand English and are of legal age), and otherwise suitable to serve as jurors.

Either party may challenge any prospective juror "for cause," *i.e.*, on the ground that the person is unqualified to serve or is biased to a degree that would substantially impair her ability to render an impartial verdict. "For cause" challenges are considered below, in subsection c. As well, each party is permitted, as a matter of statutory right, to exclude a specific number of prospective jurors who were not excluded for cause, so-called "peremptory challenges." Peremptories are discussed in subsection d.

The *voir dire* plays a critical role in the jury selection process. It "provides a means of discovering actual or implied bias and a firmer basis upon which the parties may exercise their peremptory challenges intelligently." J.E.B. v. Alabama ex rel. T.B., 511 U.S. 127, 114 S.Ct.

1419, 128 L.Ed.2d 89 (1994). The process can also serve strategic goals: A defense lawyer may try to use the examination to enhance jurors' appreciation of the presumption of innocence; and both sides use the give-and-take of *voir dire* to build rapport with the jurors.

Many lawyers believe that trials are won or lost at this stage. Therefore, they want to participate actively in the *voir dire*. In most jurisdictions, including the federal courts, however, the trial judge conducts the *voir dire*. In such circumstances, the judge will typically permit the parties to ask further questions or "submit further questions that the court may ask if it considers them proper." Fed. R. Crim. P. 24(a)(2)(B). Thus, a struggle between the lawyers and the judge for effective control of the jury selection process is common.

A Special Problem: Race and Racism in Jury Selection

Professor Sheri Lynn Johnson has accused the Supreme Court, and the judiciary in general, of a "large blindspot, a blindspot that mars the reasoning of all of the recent cases involving both race and criminal procedure * * *. In that blindspot is the empirical reality of unconscious racism." Sheri Lynn Johnson, *Unconscious Racism and the Criminal Law*, 73 Cornell L. Rev. 1016, 1016–1017 (1988).

According to some social science data, "white subjects consistently display an own-race bias in guilt-attribution decisions as mock jurors in a laboratory setting, and * * * the more limited studies on minority-race subjects suggest that they display a reciprocal bias." Sheri Lynn Johnson, *Black Innocence and the White Jury*, 83 Mich. L. Rev. 1605, 1640 (1985).

As you read the materials that follow, ask yourself whether the judiciary has erected adequate safeguards against the intrusion of racism in the jury-selection and deliberative process.

HAM v. SOUTH CAROLINA
Supreme Court of the United States, 1973.
409 U.S. 524, 93 S.Ct. 848, 35 L.Ed.2d 46.

MR. JUSTICE REHNQUIST delivered the opinion of the Court [joined by CHIEF JUSTICE BURGER, and JUSTICES BRENNAN, STEWART, WHITE, BLACKMUN, and POWELL].

Petitioner was convicted in the South Carolina trial court of the possession of marihuana in violation of state law. * * * We granted certiorari limited to the question of whether the trial judge's refusal to examine jurors on *voir dire* as to possible prejudice against petitioner violated the latter's federal constitutional rights.

Petitioner is a young, bearded Negro who has lived most of his life in Florence County, South Carolina. He appears to have been well known locally for his work in such civil rights activities as the Southern Christian Leadership Conference and the Bi-racial Committee of the City of Florence. He has never previously been convicted of a crime. His basic defense at the trial was that law enforcement officers were "out to get him" because of his civil rights activities, and that he had been framed on the drug charge.

Prior to the trial judge's *voir dire* examination of prospective jurors, petitioner's counsel requested the judge to ask jurors [three] questions relating to possible prejudice against petitioner.[2] The first two questions sought to elicit any possible racial prejudice against Negroes; [and] the third question related to possible prejudice against beards * * * . The trial judge, while putting to the prospective jurors three general questions as to bias, prejudice, or partiality that are specified in the South Carolina statutes,[3] declined to ask any of the * * * questions posed by petitioner.

The dissenting justices in the Supreme Court of South Carolina thought that this Court's decision in *Aldridge v. United States*, 283 U.S. 308, 51 S.Ct. 470, 75 L.Ed. 1054 (1931), was binding on the State. There a Negro who was being tried for the murder of a white policeman requested that prospective jurors be asked whether they entertained any racial prejudice. This Court reversed the judgment of conviction because of the trial judge's refusal to make such an inquiry. Mr. Chief Justice Hughes, writing for the Court, stated that the "essential demands of fairness" required the trial judge under the circumstances of that case to interrogate the veniremen with respect to racial prejudice upon the request of counsel for a Negro criminal defendant.

The Court's opinion relied upon a number of state court holdings throughout the country to the same effect, but it was not expressly grounded upon any constitutional requirement. Since one of the purposes of the Due Process Clause of the Fourteenth Amendment is to insure these "essential demands of fairness," and since a principal purpose of the adoption of the Fourteenth Amendment was to prohibit the States from invidiously discriminating on the basis of race, we think that the

---

[2] The * * * questions sought to be asked are the following:

"1. Would you fairly try this case on the basis of the evidence and disregarding the defendant's race?

"2. You have no prejudice against negroes? Against black people? You would not be influenced by the use of the term 'black'?

"3. Would you disregard the fact that this defendant wears a beard in deciding this case? * * * "

[3] The three questions asked of all prospective jurors in this case were, in substance, the following:

"1. Have you formed or expressed any opinion as to the guilt or innocence of the defendant, Gene Ham?

"2. Are you conscious of any bias or prejudice for or against him?

"3. Can you give the State and the defendant a fair and impartial trial?"

Fourteenth Amendment required the judge in this case to interrogate the jurors upon the subject of racial prejudice. * * *

* * * [T]he trial judge was not required to put the question in any particular form, or to ask any particular number of questions on the subject, simply because requested to do so by petitioner. The Court in *Aldridge* was at pains to point out, in a context where its authority within the federal system of courts allows a good deal closer supervision than does the Fourteenth Amendment, that the trial court "had a broad discretion as to the questions to be asked." The discretion as to form and number of questions permitted by the Due Process Clause of the Fourteenth Amendment is at least as broad. In this context, either of the brief, general questions urged by the petitioner would appear sufficient to focus the attention of prospective jurors on any racial prejudice they might entertain.

The third of petitioner's proposed questions was addressed to the fact that he wore a beard. While we cannot say that prejudice against people with beards might not have been harbored by one or more of the potential jurors in this case, this is the beginning and not the end of the inquiry as to whether the Fourteenth Amendment required the trial judge to interrogate the prospective jurors about such possible prejudice. Given the traditionally broad discretion accorded to the trial judge in conducting *voir dire*, and our inability to constitutionally distinguish possible prejudice against beards from a host of other possible similar prejudices, we do not believe the petitioner's constitutional rights were violated when the trial judge refused to put this question. The inquiry as to racial prejudice derives its constitutional statute from the firmly established precedent of *Aldridge* and the numerous state cases upon which it relied, and from a principal purpose as well as from the language of those who adopted the Fourteenth Amendment. The trial judge's refusal to inquire as to particular bias against beards, after his inquiries as to bias in general, does not reach the level of a constitutional violation. * * *

Because of the trial court's refusal to make any inquiry as to racial bias of the prospective jurors after petitioner's timely request therefor, the judgment of the Supreme Court of South Carolina is reversed. * * *

MR. JUSTICE DOUGLAS, concurring in part and dissenting in part.

I concur in that portion of the majority's opinion that holds that the trial judge was constitutionally compelled to inquire into the possibility of racial prejudice on *voir dire*. I think, however, that it was an abuse of discretion for the trial judge to preclude the defendant from an inquiry by which prospective jurors' prejudice to hair growth could have been explored. * * *

[JUSTICE MARSHALL concurred in the portion of the majority opinion holding that the trial judge was constitutionally required to inquire into the possibility of racial prejudice. Along with Douglas, he would have required that the judge propound a question regarding prejudice toward people with beards.]

NOTES AND QUESTIONS

1.   Why do you think Justices Douglas and Marshall believed that the Constitution required inquiry into prejudice toward bearded persons?

2.   How demanding a rule is *Ham*? Later cases show that the constitutional rule is narrow. In Ristaino v. Ross, 424 U.S. 589, 96 S.Ct. 1017, 47 L.Ed.2d 258 (1976), Ross and a co-defendant, both African-Americans, were prosecuted for armed robbery, assault and battery by means of a dangerous weapon, and assault with intent to murder. The victim was a white security guard employed by Boston University.

The trial judge conducting the *voir dire* notified the prospective jurors: "If any of you are related to the defendants or to the victim, or if any of you have any interest in this case, or have formed an opinion or is sensible of any bias or prejudice, you should make it known to the court at this time." He refused to ask a question propounded by the defense: "Are there any of you who believe that a white person is more likely to be telling the truth than a black person?" Justice Powell held that the trial judge's refusal to ask this question did *not* violate the Constitution:

> The Constitution does not always entitle a defendant to have questions posed during *voir dire* specifically directed to matters that conceivably might prejudice veniremen against him. *Voir dire* "is conducted under the supervision of the court, and a great deal must, of necessity, be left to its sound discretion." This is so because the "determination of impartiality, in which demeanor plays such an important part, is particularly within the province of the trial judge." Thus, the State's obligation to the defendant to impanel an impartial jury generally can be satisfied by less than an inquiry into a specific prejudice feared by the defendant. * * *

> By its terms *Ham* did not announce a requirement of universal applicability. Rather, it reflected an assessment of whether under all of the circumstances presented there was a constitutionally significant likelihood that, absent questioning about racial prejudice, the jurors would not be as "indifferent as (they stand) unsworne." * * *

> The circumstances in *Ham* strongly suggested the need for *voir dire* to include specific questioning about racial prejudice. Ham's defense was that he had been framed because of his civil rights activities. His prominence in the community as a civil rights activist, if not already known to veniremen, inevitably would have been revealed to the members of the jury in the course of his presentation of that defense. Racial issues therefore were

inextricably bound up with the conduct of the trial. Further, Ham's reputation as a civil rights activist and the defense he interposed were likely to intensify any prejudice that individual members of the jury might harbor. * * *

We do not agree * * * that the need to question veniremen specifically about racial prejudice also rose to constitutional dimensions in this case. The mere fact that the victim of the crimes alleged was a white man and the defendants were Negroes was less likely to distort the trial than were the special factors involved in *Ham*. * * * The circumstances thus did not suggest a significant likelihood that racial prejudice might infect Ross' trial. This was made clear to the trial judge when Ross was unable to support his motion concerning *voir dire* by pointing to racial factors such as existed in *Ham* or others of comparable significance.

In a closing footnote, however, the Court stated: "Although we hold that *voir dire* questioning directed to racial prejudice was not constitutionally required, the wiser course generally is to propound appropriate questions designed to identify racial prejudice if requested by the defendant. Under our supervisory power we would have required as much of a federal court faced with the circumstances here. The States also are free to allow or require questions not demanded by the Constitution."

The Court considered the footnote in Rosales-Lopez v. United States, 451 U.S. 182, 101 S.Ct. 1629, 68 L.Ed.2d 22 (1981). Justice White (for a four-justice plurality) stated that "it is usually best" to permit a defendant to determine "whether or not he would prefer to have [an] inquiry into racial or ethnic prejudice pursued" in a federal criminal trial. Failure to honor a request for such an inquiry is reversible error, however, "only where the circumstances of the case indicate that there is a reasonable possibility that racial or ethnic prejudice might have influenced the jury." The plurality stated that such a "reasonable possibility" exists when a defendant is "accused of a violent crime and where the defendant and the victim are members of different racial or ethnic groups." Justice Rehnquist and Chief Justice Burger concurred in the result. They rejected the *per se* rule. They would have left the matter to the sound discretion of the trial court, subject to case-by-case review by the appellate courts.

In *Rosales-Lopez*, the Court concluded that the trial judge committed no error in refusing to inquire into racial or ethnic prejudice in the trial of a defendant of Mexican descent who was charged with bringing other Mexicans illegally into the country. No special circumstances of constitutional dimension were alleged (rendering *Ham* inapplicable); and the federal supervisory plurality rule did not apply because the defendant was not charged with a crime of violence (nor, in any case, did the case involve a victim of a different racial or ethnic group than the defendant).

3.   *Capital crimes: a special rule.* Notwithstanding *Ristaino* (Note 2), the Supreme Court held in Turner v. Murray, 476 U.S. 28, 106 S.Ct. 1683, 90

L.Ed.2d 27 (1986), that a defendant accused of an interracial *capital* crime *is* constitutionally entitled, upon request, to have prospective jurors informed of the victim's race and questioned on the matter of racial bias. Justice White reasoned that "[b]ecause of the range of discretion entrusted to a jury in a capital sentencing hearing, there is a unique opportunity for racial prejudice to operate but remain undetected."

The question that the Court approved in *Turner* was: "The defendant * * * is a member of the Negro race. The victim * * * was a white Caucasian. Will these facts prejudice you against [the defendant] or affect your ability to render a fair and impartial verdict based solely on the evidence?" What do you think of this question? Do you think it will adequately identify jurors with prejudicial views? Beyond this, is this question insulting to jurors? Do you agree with this observation:

> [N]o respectful adult would ask another adult in polite conversation, "Pardon me. Are you a bigot?" Instead, the proposed question [that the Supreme Court approved] embodied a form of instruction typically reserved for children:
>
> > We're good Americans, aren't we, boys and girls? We would never judge a person on the basis of the color of his or her skin, would we? * * *
>
> [W]e have become so accustomed to thinking of jurors as children that we may fail to recognize how patronizing the question is.

Albert W. Alschuler, *The Supreme Court and the Jury: Voir Dire, Peremptory Challenges, and the Review of Jury Verdicts*, 56 U. Chi. L. Rev. 153, 159 (1989).

4. *Problem*. United States v. Barber, 80 F.3d 964 (4th Cir. 1996): Norwood and Linda Barber, an interracial married couple, were prosecuted for illegally laundering cash proceeds from the sale of marijuana. The Barbers requested that the trial court ask whether any member of the venire would prejudge the defendants because they were partners in an interracial marriage. Although they claimed that race was not a true issue in the case, the defendants feared that "race is * * * injected by the fact that the defendants are sitting there as an interracial couple." They argued that the question "clears the air. * * * I'd like to clear [the jurors'] subconscious and agree that it is not an issue, a non-issue."

Is the judge constitutionally required to ask a race-bias question? Is the judge required on federal supervisory grounds (*Rosales-Lopez*, Note 2, *supra*) to inquire? Is it relevant that the federal trial occurred in Virginia, one of sixteen states that prohibited interracial marriages until the Supreme Court declared such laws unconstitutional? Is it relevant that in 1991, a Gallup Poll found that 42% of Americans disapproved of interracial marriages, and that the disapproval rate in Southern states was fifty-four percent?

5. *Beyond race*? Should the rule of *Ham*, as narrow as it is, be extended beyond the area of race? For example, in a capital case in which the

prosecution will claim that the defendant attacked the victim because of the latter's sexual orientation, should a judge during *voir dire* be constitutionally required to exercise the same level of scrutiny in probing potential jurors regarding their possible prejudice against gay people as would be necessary if racial bias were implicated? For one answer, see Kemp v. Ryan, 638 F.3d 1245 (9th Cir. 2011).

6.   *Intrusive voir dire.* Note 3 noted the possibility that some questions asked of jurors may insult them. There is also the issue of how courts should handle questions that arguably invade jurors' privacy. What if you were asked by a judge what websites you frequent on the Internet? Would you consider that unduly intrusive? Should you be able to refuse to answer the question? Consider United States v. Padilla-Valenzuela, 896 F.Supp. 968 (D.Ariz.1995), in which the defendant was charged with possession with intent to distribute cocaine. His attorney submitted a questionnaire to the court that he wanted venirepersons to fill out:

> The questionnaire submitted by the defendant seeks information concerning the educational background of (a) each juror, (b) each juror's spouse, and (c) the children of each prospective juror. It also inquires as to whether prospective jurors have "read or heard about the issue regarding immigrants in California" and whether any prospective juror believes "a similar situation should be promoted nationally." The questionnaire asks whether any prospective juror or the family member of any prospective juror has "ever been a member of any racially-exclusive clubs, or clubs where even though not avowedly discriminatory—there are no minority members." The questionnaire asks whether any prospective juror has "ever used derogatory language in referring to members of a minority group," "ever expressed an opinion on the 'wasted' finances used to defend immigrants charged with unlawful conduct," "ever made any statement to or about immigrants (whether legal or illegal) that would demonstrate an appearance of bias," "believed that immigrants (whether legal or illegal) dominate the welfare roles," and "believe immigrants (whether legal or illegal) are taking jobs from United States citizens."

District Judge Roll refused to authorize the questionnaire. His observations in this regard are noteworthy:

> While the trial lawyer's appetite for information concerning prospective jurors may be insatiable, the burden is borne by prospective jurors. * * *

> Certain   areas   may   be   explored   despite   potential embarrassment to prospective jurors. * * *

> Courts have determined that other sensitive areas, however, are simply beyond the scope of inquiry, regardless of available means to minimize embarrassment. See, *e.g.,* * * * *United States v.*

Taylor, 562 F.2d 1345, 1355 (2d Cir. [1977]) (educational backgrounds and whether prospective jurors had children); *United States v. Hamling*, 481 F.2d 307, 314 (9th Cir. 1973) (views towards sex and obscenity), aff'd, 418 U.S. 87, 94 S.Ct. 2887, 41 L.Ed.2d 590 (1974); *United States v. Workman*, 454 F.2d 1124, 1128 (9th Cir. [1972]) (attitudes toward drug users, political activists, and antiwar demonstrators); *Maguire v. United States*, 358 F.2d 442, 444–45 (10th Cir. [1966]) (bias against homosexuals) * * * . * * *

"[N]othing about becoming a prospective juror amounts to a willing waiver of an expectation of privacy." Prospective jurors are summoned, they do not volunteer. Jurors are not on trial. Many individuals have demonstrated a reluctance to serve by their failure to even appear for jury duty. Perhaps most distressing, prospective jurors may find that unless the trial judge monitors the scope of inquiry, no one will be concerned about their privacy. "While the parties have attorneys to champion their rights, the courts must protect the privacy rights of the prospective jurors."

Do you believe that the court was right to reject the questionnaire? Do you believe that some of the questions should have been asked?

In one survey of North Carolina jurors, 27% reported they were asked one or more questions that made them uncomfortable (*e.g.*, whether the juror had ever been a crime victim), and 27% also reported that they were asked "too private" questions (*e.g.*, whether anyone in the juror's family had ever been charged with a crime). Mary R. Rose, *Expectations of Privacy? Jurors' Views of Voir Dire Questions*, 85 Judicature 10 (July–August 2001). Do you believe these are legitimate questions to ask prospective jurors? If so, should they be asked regardless of the privacy invasion?

Voir Dire in a Highly Charged Criminal Prosecution

PEOPLE V. NEWTON

Superior Court of the State of California, In and For the County of Alameda, 1968.
Case No. 41266.

[The trial judge has primary authority to examine prospective jurors. Sometimes, however, a judge will permit the parties to participate significantly in the *voir dire*, especially if the case is one in which there has been considerable pretrial media publicity. Although a defendant is entitled to trial by an impartial jury, the Supreme Court has stated that "[i]t is not required * * * that the jurors be totally ignorant of the facts and issues involved. * * * It is sufficient if the juror can lay aside his impression or opinion and render a verdict on the evidence presented in court." Irvin v. Dowd, 366 U.S. 717, 81 S.Ct. 1639, 6 L.Ed.2d 751 (1961). With extensive *voir dire*, the parties can more accurately determine whether a prospective juror can put aside his pretrial impressions.

Consider in this context the examination of a juror, a Mr. Strauss, in the murder prosecution of Huey P. Newton, co-founder and Minister of Defense of the Black Panther Party, for the 1967 shooting of a white police officer in Oakland, California. Because of the controversial nature of the Black Panther Society—its "Ten Point Program" called for, among other things, an end to "police brutality in our Black community by organizing Black self-defense groups * * * dedicated to defending our Black community from racist police oppression and brutality"—and extensive pretrial publicity supposedly linking Newton to the killing, the defense was concerned whether it could secure an impartial jury.

What follows are excerpts from the transcript of the *voir dire* found in Minimizing Racism in Jury Trials 90–94 (Ann Fagan Ginger, ed. 1969). Newton was eventually convicted of the lesser offense of voluntary manslaughter. The conviction was reversed on grounds unrelated to the jury selection. People v. Newton, 8 Cal.App.3d 359, 87 Cal.Rptr. 394 (1970).]

BY MR. GARRY [defense counsel]: Well, let me ask you this, Mr. Strauss: You know what we are trying to arrive at, do you, sir?

A: I beg your pardon?

Q: I say, you know what * * * we are trying to ask, these questions, both Mr. Jensen [the prosecutor] and myself?

A: Yes.

Q: We are trying to give you an opportunity to speak so that we will be able to tell whether there is some hidden crevices in your mind that may be an interference in the proper evaluation of that case as the evidence unfolds. You understand that?

A: Yes.

Q: Now, it's a fact, is it not, that you already had an opinion before you came here about this case?

A: Well, to a certain extent, yes.

Q: All right. Now, is your opinion that you had about this case before you got here such that it would take the tremendous amount of evidence to overcome that opinion?

A: No. It wouldn't. If—what evidence will show, that I will evaluate and see who is right and who is wrong.

Q: It's not a question so much as to who is right and who is wrong. As you sit there, Mr. Strauss, in your opinion, right now while you are sitting there this minute, is Huey P. Newton guilty or not guilty?

A: Well, I don't know for sure whether he shot the officer or not, but the officer is dead.

Q: And by that same standard, just because the officer is dead, you are going to say that Huey Newton did it; is that right?

A: Well, that's got to be proven.

Q: Well, my question is: As you sit there right now, do you believe that Huey Newton shot and killed, stabbed, whatever it was, Officer Frey?

A: I don't know whether he shot him or not. That I can't say.

THE COURT: Mr. Strauss, you see, under our law there is a presumption of innocence to start with. When you start the case the defendant is presumed to be innocent, and it is up to the People, the prosecution, to prove to you beyond a reasonable doubt that the defendant is guilty. Do you understand that?

THE JUROR: Yes.

THE COURT: So, now, not having heard any evidence, you must start with a presumption of innocence. Do you know what I mean by presumption? You must say, 'As far as I know the man is innocent' Do you understand that?

THE JUROR: Yes.

THE COURT: 'And it is up to the prosecution to prove to me that he is guilty.' Do you understand that?

THE JUROR: Yes.

THE COURT: So, therefore, as it stands right now, do you believe he is guilty before you hear any evidence? * * *

THE JUROR: No.

THE COURT: All right. Now, before you hear any evidence, do you believe he is not guilty? And, you see, with the presumption of innocence, * * * unless you can say to yourself that as far as you are concerned before you hear any evidence that he is not guilty, that is what the law requires. [Now,] are you able to do that.

THE JUROR: I think so.

THE COURT: All right. Go ahead.

MR. GARRY: Mr. Strauss, you have been on two other criminal jury trials in the last two weeks. Isn't that right?

A: Yes.

Q: Did you actually go into deliberation and verdict?

A: Yes.

Q: And what type of cases were they?

A: Automobile theft. * * *

Q: You had heard this instruction of presumption of innocence on at least two occasions, had you not?

A: Yes.

Q: And yet when I asked you the question today, whether you believed Huey Newton killed Officer Frey, you said you didn't know.

THE COURT: Well, that's argumentative, and it is a statement, not a question. Please ask questions.

MR. GARRY: Well, do you really believe that as Huey Newton sits here right now next to me, that he is innocent of any wrongdoing of any kind?

A: No. That I don't believe.

MR. GARRY: See? There you are, Judge. I challenge this juror for cause.

THE COURT: Well, you see, I will have to explain to you again and see if you understand it, Mr. Strauss. The fact that the Grand Jury has indicted under our law, from that mere fact that he has been indicted by the Grand Jury, you are not to infer or presume in any way that the defendant is or must be guilty. Do you understand that?

THE JUROR: Yes.

THE COURT: Do you accept that rule of law? If you don't accept that rule of law, you don't understand it. Do you accept it? Do you understand what I am saying?

THE JUROR: (Juror nods head affirmatively.)

THE COURT: Now, under the rule of law, different places in the world have different rules of law, but it is the law of the United States and of the State of California that a defendant charged with a crime is presumed to be innocent until his guilt is established beyond and to the exclusion of every reasonable doubt. Do you understand what that means?

THE JUROR: (Juror nods head affirmatively.)

THE COURT: Now, if that is the case, you must—before you hear any evidence at all—you must start on the theory and believe that this man is innocent. But as soon as they produce proof which satisfies you beyond a reasonable doubt that he is guilty, then you can feel otherwise. Do you understand that?

THE JUROR: Yes.

THE COURT: Are you willing to start out with that theory? Are you willing to start out on that basis?

THE JUROR: Yes.

THE COURT: You may examine further.

MR. GARRY: But you are not willing, Mr. Strauss, as you have already stated, to accept the fact that Huey Newton is absolutely innocent as he sits right now, are you, sir?

A: Well, that's a question I can't answer before I hear the evidence.

MR. GARRY: I submit the challenge, Your Honor.

THE COURT: No. I don't think that's sufficient. I think that it is a matter of semantics. Before you hear any evidence, have you got an idea that he must be guilty or else he wouldn't be here? Is that your idea?

THE JUROR: Yes.

THE COURT: Well, that is not our law, Mr. Strauss. Under our law the fact that he is here is not any evidence at all of his guilt. You may examine further, Mr. Jensen [the prosecutor—eds.], if you wish, but otherwise—

MR. GARRY: I submit the challenge, Your Honor.

MR. JENSEN: Let me ask you this, Mr. Strauss: If you walked out of this courtroom right now with this jury and you went upstairs and they gave you two verdicts to vote on, guilty or not guilty, and all you know about the case is what you know right now, would you find him not guilty?

A: No, not alone on that, what I have heard here.

Q: So that there is no evidence at all for you to make a verdict; is that right?

A: That's correct.

Q: So there is no evidence that would justify you in finding the man guilty; is that correct?

A: (Juror nods head affirmatively.)

Q: In other words, as Mr. Newton sits there, you, as a juror, have no evidence about any of the charges in this case; is that correct?

A: Right.

Q: Now, the District Attorney, the prosecution has the burden of bringing some evidence in before you before anything can happen. Do you understand that?

A: Yes.

Q: Now, if the District Attorney does not produce any evidence at all, the man is not guilty. Isn't that correct?

A: That's right.

Q: So that if you are to deliberate right now you have no evidence; isn't that right?

A: That's right.

Q: So you would find him not guilty; isn't that right? Is there any evidence as far as you are concerned right now that Mr. Newton is guilty of anything?

A: No.

Q: The fact that there has been a charge here, that is that he is charged with murder, assault, and kidnapping, is that, as far as you are concerned, evidence that he is guilty of anything?

A: No. That isn't evidence, no.

Q: As far as you are concerned, what is evidence?

A: What I am going to hear here in Court.

Q: Is that going to come from witnesses, as far as you are concerned?

A: From witnesses, yes.

Q: Is it going to be newspapers or anything like that?

A: No.

Q: Will you decide the case just on what the witnesses say?

A: Yes.

MR. JENSEN: As Your Honor said, I think this is a semantic problem.

THE COURT: You may examine further, Mr. Garry.

BY MR. GARRY: Mr. Strauss, again I ask you that same question which you have answered three times to me now—

THE COURT: No. Please ask the question without preface.

MR. GARRY: As Huey Newton sits here next to me now, in your opinion is he absolutely innocent?

A: Yes.

Q: But you don't believe it, do you?

A: No.

THE COURT: Challenge is allowed.

NOTES AND QUESTIONS

1.　To the extent that this excerpt is typical of the examination of jurors that occurred in this case, do you believe the trial judge was wise in permitting the attorneys to conduct the *voir dire*?

2. Do you sense that defense counsel Garry had any goals—other than to determine whether Strauss could act impartially—in conducting this *voir dire*? Do you think that Garry had decided before the conclusion of the examination that he was going to exercise a peremptory challenge if he could not successfully remove Strauss for cause? If so, at what point? What do you think of prosecutor Jensen's efforts to rehabilitate Strauss, *i.e.*, to show that he had not prejudged the case?

c. "For Cause" Challenges

UNITED STATES V. SALAMONE
United States Court of Appeals, Third Circuit, 1986.
800 F.2d 1216.

A. LEON HIGGINBOTHAM, JR., CIRCUIT JUDGE.

This appeal arises from the conviction of appellant Salvatore Salamone pursuant to a multicount indictment charging him with various firearm offenses. Our opinion is restricted to one issue: whether potential jurors in an action involving charges brought under the gun control statutes may be dismissed for cause solely due to their affiliation with the National Rifle Association. For the reasons set forth below we will reverse the judgment of the district court.

I.

* * * Prior to trial, during *voir dire*, the district court excused for cause one potential juror and five potential alternates solely on the basis of their affiliation with the National Rifle Association ("NRA"). Of the jurors selected, ten had firearms in their homes. Of the six alternates selected, five had firearms in their homes. Two of the alternates ultimately served on the jury. Salamone was convicted on six of the seven counts with which he was charged. He was sentenced to a total of twenty years imprisonment and $35,000 in fines. This appeal followed. * * *

IV.

* * * [O]ur review of the record * * * leads us inexorably to the conclusion that the trial judge abused his discretion in conducting the *voir dire* proceedings.

During *voir dire* for the main jury panel the court posed the following questions to the prospective jurors:

THE COURT: * * * Are you now or have you ever been a member of or affiliated in any way with the National Rifle Association?

MR. LAUGHLIN: I've been a member of the NRA.

THE COURT: All right. Do you support the principles of that organization, Mr. Laughlin?

MR. LAUGHLIN: Yes, I do.

THE COURT: Okay. Mrs. Houtz.

MRS. HOUTZ: My husband is a member of NRA. He does support it.

THE COURT: And he does support it?

MRS. HOUTZ: Yes.

THE COURT: All right. Are you now or have you ever been a member of or affiliated in any way with a gun, marksmanship or sporting club/organization? Mr. Laughlin.

MR. LAUGHLIN: I belong to the Bucktail club and hunting club in Emporium.

THE COURT: Are you now or have you ever been a member of or affiliated in any way with a survivalist club or organization? The United States Constitution, as amended by the Bill of Rights, the first ten amendments, it states in one of those amendments, "The right of the people to keep and bear arms shall not be infringed." The United States has, in fact, laws restricting the possession and transfer of automatic weapons and machine guns; additionally, it has laws requiring, under most circumstances, buyers of firearms to supply certain information and to fill out documents at the time firearms are purchased. The Courts of the United States have consistently ruled that such laws are proper and are not in conflict with the provision of the Bill of Rights which I have just read to you about the right of the people to keep and bear arms not being infringed. Despite such Court rulings, is any juror opposed to such laws on constitutional grounds or other grounds?

(NO RESPONSE)

THE COURT: The possession and transfer of an automatic weapon or machine gun is, in most cases, illegal. If I should instruct you along those lines at the conclusion of the trial, with [*sic*] any juror have any difficulty following any such instruction for any reason? Is any juror opposed to gun control? I would assume, Mr. Laughlin, you are opposed to it?

MR. LAUGHLIN: That's correct, yes.

THE COURT: And I would assume, Mrs. Houtz, you are opposed to it?

MRS. HOUTZ: Yes. * * *

After completion of *voir dire*, the district court entertained challenges for cause. The following exchange took place:

MR. CLARK: Your Honor, the government would challenge for cause Mr. Laughlin.

THE COURT: On what ground? * * *

MR. CLARK: He stated he was a former member of the NRA and is—

THE COURT: Well, why—

MR. CLARK: He's a member and firm opponent—

THE COURT: Wait.

MR. CLARK:—of gun control.

THE COURT: Well, why is that disqualification for cause? It may be, but I need some illumination on that.

MR. CLARK: Your Honor, the government's position in respect to that would be that because the charges here deal with the regulation of the possession of automatic weapons, machine guns and because the charges also deal with the falsification of ATF Forms 4473, which are forms of gun control.

THE COURT: Well, I have got enough on it now. What is your— do you oppose that challenge?

MR. CASALE: Yes.

THE COURT: What is the basis of the opposition? * * *

MR. CASALE: The basis of the opposition is that the defense doesn't feel that any member of the NRA *automatically disqualifies* unless he says, I can't sit on this jury fairly.

THE COURT: Well, the NRA blocked a bill in the last Congress which would have prevented the importation and sale and, I believe, manufacture of armor piercing bullets. That legislation was supported by the police chiefs and police organizations throughout the nation. And *I think that somebody who is a member of that organization may well not be able to sit on this case impartially*. So I'll grant that one.

The government made no further challenges for cause.[6]

During *voir dire* for the selection of alternates, several jurors indicated some affiliation with the NRA. * * * All were challenged and

---

[6] Both Mrs. Houtz and [another juror] were eliminated from the jury on peremptory challenges. It is unclear from the record which party exercised the challenges.

excluded for cause solely on the basis of their affiliation with the NRA.
* * *

B.

* * * Federal Rule of Criminal Procedure 24 commits to the trial judge the function of conducting an appropriate *voir dire.* "Because the obligation to impanel an impartial jury lies in the first instance with the trial judge, and because he must rely largely on his immediate perceptions, federal judges have been accorded ample discretion in determining how best to conduct the *voir dire.*" This discretion extends to the determination of what questions should be asked to the potential jurors. * * *

According the full recognition to these general principles, however, it is nonetheless equally clear that the trial judge's broad discretion is not without limitation. "While impaneling a jury the trial court has a serious duty to determine the question of actual bias. * * * In exercising its discretion, the trial court must be zealous to protect the rights of the accused." * * *

In the instant appeal, Salamone's challenge to the district court's *voir dire* does not allege a failure to uncover actual bias thereby resulting in the paneling of partial jurors. Rather, Salamone's objection is to the *presumed* bias of potential jurors which occasioned the arbitrary exclusion of an entire class of otherwise qualified jurors from his panel. "In disqualifying all NRA-related jurors without particularized inquiry," Salamone argues, "the trial judge simply assumed that any person connected with that association was incapable of fairly applying existing law."

The government contends that no abuse occurs in the exclusion of jurors whose views on gun control might affect their ability to serve impartially on a jury considering implementation of gun control statutes. The government conveniently ignores, however, the total absence on this record of any indication that the excluded jurors individually possessed such views which would rightfully justify their dismissal. Instead, the government relies on a theory of "implied bias" in suggesting that "where as here, the charges involve state and federal gun registration—a subject on which the NRA's opposition is well-known—a trial judge is well within his discretion in excluding those opponents from the jury for cause." Under such circumstances, the government maintains "[i]f the judge believes, as he reasonably could, that bias against enforcing a particular statute would make it difficult for the juror to vote for conviction even if the evidence supported guilt, additional questioning would simply be superfluous."

We find the government's position untenable and potentially dangerous. To allow trial judges and prosecutors to determine juror eligibility based solely on their perceptions of the external associations of a juror threatens the heretofore guarded right of an accused to a fair trial by an impartial jury as well as the integrity of the judicial process as a whole. Taken to its illogical conclusion, the government's position would sanction, *inter alia*, the summary exclusion for cause of NAACP members from cases seeking the enforcement of civil rights statutes, * * * Catholics from cases involving abortion clinic protests, members of NOW [National Organization of Women] from sex discrimination cases, and subscribers to Consumer Reports from cases involving products liability claims.

Moreover, the government's position misconceives the grounds for juror disqualification. "Jury competence is an individual rather than a group or class matter." Challenges for cause "permit rejection of jurors on narrowly specified, provable and legally cognizable bas[e]s of partiality." The central inquiry in the determination whether a juror should be excused for cause is whether the juror holds a particular belief or opinion that will "prevent or substantially impair the performance of his duties as a juror in accordance with his instructions and his oath." Juror bias need not be established with "unmistakable clarity." Thus, the factual determination by the trial court whether a juror can in fact serve impartially is entitled to "special deference" by the reviewing court. In the instant appeal, however, at no time were the excluded jurors questioned as to their ability to faithfully and impartially apply the law. Indeed, no inquiries whatsoever were directed to the excluded jurors to determine the nature and extent of their commitment to any principles that might have impaired their ability to serve impartially. While we recognize that the scope and content of *voir dire* is committed to the sound discretion of the trial court, that discretion will "include[ ] the decision as to what questions should be asked when the court itself decides to examine the prospective jurors *so long as inquiries relevant to the discovery of actual bias are not omitted.*" Where the appropriate inquiries have been made and the district court has made a judgment on the basis of the jurors' responses, normally, that judgment will not be disturbed.[13] The usual factors cautioning restraint in appellate review, *i.e.*, credibility and demeanor evidence, however, are simply absent from this record. Thus, the "factual determination" by the district court in the instant appeal, being totally devoid of any foundation, leaves us with the single conclusion that the *voir dire* was inadequate to preserve and protect the rights of the accused. Absent the requisite nexus—that the challenged affiliation will "prevent or substantially impair" a juror's impartiality—no juror may be excluded for cause on the basis of his or her membership in an organization that adheres to a particular view. Failure to make the

---

[13] Nothing in this opinion is intended to upset settled practice in the district courts of excluding without further inquiry prospective jurors with well recognized characteristics warranting dismissal, such as blood relation to the parties or counsel.

necessary inquiry deprives the trial court of the benefit of the factual predicate that justifies an exclusion for cause. * * *

We conclude that the cursory disqualification by the district judge of all jurors with NRA affiliations constitutes an abuse of discretion and is not in accord with the "essential demands of fairness" to which the appellate was entitled. * * *

For the foregoing reasons, the judgment of the district court will be reversed * * * .

[The concurring opinion of CIRCUIT JUDGE STAPLETON is omitted.]

NOTES AND QUESTIONS

1.   A juror must be excluded for cause in two circumstances: she is statutorily unqualified to serve (*e.g.*, is not a citizen, cannot speak English, or has criminal charges pending against her); or she is biased. Bias is of two varieties: actual bias, *i.e.*, bias demonstrated during *voir dire*; and implied bias, *i.e.* bias legally presumed to exist (*e.g.* see footnote 13 of the case). Which form of bias did the prosecutor allege here?

2.   We have deleted the portion of the *Salamone* court's opinion that considers the question of what *remedy* should be afforded to the defendant in view of the judge's abuse of discretion. Notice the problem: This was not a case in which the trial judge improperly permitted a *biased* juror to serve. Instead, the judge excluded for cause prospective jurors who may have been entirely unbiased. Salamone did not claim that the jurors who were empanelled were biased, so why should he have his conviction overturned? Hasn't he received a fair trial as long as the twelve jurors empaneled were impartial? Put differently, wasn't the trial judge's error harmless in this case?

This question is discussed a bit (at least in capital cases) in the Notes that follow, but most of the discussion of harmless-versus-prejudicial error must away reaching Chapter 19 of this casebook.

3.   *Problem.* During jury selection in a sexual assault case, the prosecutor asked the jury panel whether it could convict a defendant on the basis of one eyewitness's (the alleged victim's) testimony, if they believed that witness beyond a reasonable doubt. Later, the judge explained to the panel that if it believed an eyewitness beyond a reasonable doubt, "even though there's only one and they have met your burden, * * * you're required to vote guilty." Later, however, during individual questioning, one prospective juror explained his position:

[**Prosecutor**]: Mr. Gatling, I was questioning you about whether you could believe a witness—if you believed a witness beyond a reasonable doubt and that witness established all the elements of the State's case, that one witness. And I believe it was your statement was [sic] that one witness is not enough, you were going to need more.

Gatling: That's correct. In the scenario that you laid out, if someone was walking down the street, my neighbor robbed me, in that scenario, yes. If there was nothing else, even though I probably wouldn't like it myself, but that's the situation.

[**Prosecutor**]: And what it comes down to is, even though you can believe that person beyond a reasonable doubt, what that person is saying, you still want more?

Gatling: *There's a question right there of reasonable doubt.*

[**Prosecutor**]: What the law says is that that's the standard.

Gatling: Okay.

[**Prosecutor**]: Are you saying that anytime there's only one witness, that that standard can't be reached for you, no matter what?

Gatling: Not for me, no, sir. I wouldn't—no matter who it was, if it was just one person against another person, to get to that point that you're suggesting, I wouldn't be able to do it.

[**Prosecutor**]: You couldn't do it?

Gatling: No, sir.

[**Defense Attorney**]: So what you're saying, you understand that if you were convinced beyond a reasonable doubt, your obligation would be to vote to convict someone, but what you're saying, as I understand it, is you just cannot conceive reaching proof beyond a reasonable doubt only on one witness.

Gatling: I couldn't get to that point.

The prosecutor challenged Gatling for cause. What would be the basis for this claim? Should the motion be granted? Zinger v. State, 932 S.W.2d 511 (Tex.Crim.App.1996).

4. *Death penalty opponents and challenges for cause.* In general, trials for capital crimes are bifurcated: first, the jury decides the guilt or innocence of the defendant; if it finds the defendant guilty of a capital crime, i.e., a crime for which the death penalty is an option, a sentencing hearing is conducted at which the jury determines the guilty party's punishment. In Witherspoon v. Illinois, 391 U.S. 510, 88 S.Ct. 1770, 20 L.Ed.2d 776 (1968), the Court considered the question of whether a prospective juror who is morally opposed to the death penalty may properly be excused for cause in a capital trial. In the case, the trial judge said in the *voir dire*, "Let's get these conscientious objectors [to the death penalty] out of the way, without wasting any time on them." In quick succession, forty-seven venirepersons opposed in differing degrees to the death penalty were excluded for cause.

The Supreme Court held in *Witherspoon* that a death sentence may not be carried out in a case in which jurors were excluded for cause solely because they expressed religious or moral scruples against capital punishment. In such circumstances, Justice Stewart reasoned, "the State [has] produced a jury uncommonly willing to condemn a man to die." On the other hand, prospective jurors *may* be excluded for cause—they are sometimes called "*Witherspoon*-excludables"—if they make it:

> unmistakably clear (1) that they would *automatically* vote against the imposition of capital punishment without regard to any evidence that might be developed at the trial of the case before them, or (2) that their attitude toward the death penalty would prevent them making an impartial decision as to the defendant's *guilt*.

This latter *Witherspoon* rule was narrowed in Wainwright v. Witt, 469 U.S. 412, 105 S.Ct. 844, 83 L.Ed.2d 841 (1985). According to *Witt*, challenges for cause in capital crimes should be treated no differently than challenges in non-capital cases: a juror should be excluded if the juror, simply, lacks impartiality. The stated standard is

> whether the juror's views would "prevent or substantially impair the performance of his duties as a juror in accordance with his instructions and his oath." We note that, in addition to dispensing with *Witherspoon*'s reference to "automatic" decisionmaking, this standard likewise does not require that a juror's bias be proved with "unmistakable clarity." This is because determinations of juror bias cannot be reduced to question-and-answer sessions which obtain results in the manner of a catechism. What common sense should have realized experience has proved: many veniremen simply cannot be asked enough questions to reach the point where their bias has been made "unmistakably clear"; these veniremen may not know how they will react when faced with imposing the death sentence, or may be unable to articulate, or may wish to hide their true feelings. Despite this lack of clarity in the printed record, however, there will be situations where the trial judge is left with the definite impression that a prospective juror would be unable to faithfully and impartially apply the law. * * * [T]his is why deference must be paid to the trial judge who sees and hears the juror.

In Uttect v. Brown, 551 U.S. 1, 127 S.Ct. 2218, 167 L.Ed.2d 1014 (2007), the Supreme Court summarized "four principles" of *Witherspoon* and *Witt*:

> First, a criminal defendant has a right to an impartial jury drawn from a venire that has not been tilted in favor of capital punishment by selective prosecutorial challenges for cause. Second, the State has a strong interest in having jurors who are able to apply capital punishment within the framework state law prescribes. Third, to balance these interests, a juror who is substantially impaired in his or her ability to impose the death penalty under the state-law

framework can be excused for cause; but if the juror is not substantially impaired, removal for cause is impermissible. Fourth, in determining whether the removal of a potential juror would vindicate the State's interest without violating the defendant's right, the trial court makes a judgment based on part on the demeanor of the juror, a judgment owed deference by reviewing courts.

If a prospective juror *is* improperly excluded for cause according to the preceding principles, this constitutional error requires automatic reversal of a defendant's death sentence, Gray v. Mississippi, 481 U.S. 648, 107 S.Ct. 2045, 95 L.Ed.2d 622 (1987), but it does not affect the guilty verdict.

The automatic reversal rule applies, even if the Government had an unexercised peremptory challenge that it could have used to exclude the anti-death penalty juror in question. The *Gray* Court stated that the appropriate test is whether "the composition of the jury panel as a whole could *possibly* have been affected by the trial court's error." In such circumstances, the Court reasoned, it cannot ever say that the composition of the jury could not possibly have been affected by the erroneous exclusion of the juror.

5. *Excluding death penalty opponents at the guilt phase of a criminal trial.* In *Witherspoon*, as modified by *Witt* (Note 4), the Court held that, *for sentencing purposes*, a prospective juror whose opposition to capital punishment would substantially impair her ability to impose the death penalty, regardless of the evidence, may properly be excluded for cause. But, does exclusion of such a juror at the *guilt* phase of the capital trial violate a defendant's Sixth Amendment fair-cross-section right and his more general right to an impartial jury? The Court rejected these claims in Lockhart v. McCree, 476 U.S. 162, 106 S.Ct. 1758, 90 L.Ed.2d 137 (1986).

Why *might* removal of a *Witherspoon-Witt* excludable at the guilt phase violate the Sixth Amendment? Some studies assert, in the words of the dissenters in *Lockhart*, that "[t]he perspectives on the criminal justice system of jurors who survive death qualification are systematically different from those of the excluded jurors." For example, death-qualified jurors are "more likely to believe that a defendant's failure to testify is indicative of his guilt, more hostile to the insanity defense, more distrustful of defense attorneys, and less concerned about the danger of erroneous convictions." Nonetheless, the majority in *Lockhart* ruled that these findings, even if statistically valid (which it questioned), do not state a valid Sixth Amendment claim.

The Court asserted that the "death qualification" of a jury does not violate a capital defendant's Sixth Amendment fair-cross-section right because that right applies only to the jury pool and not to the particular jury selected. Even if that requirement were extended to the jury itself, however, the Court said that it would still reject the conclusion that "death qualification" violates the requirement.

The essence of a "fair-cross-section" claim is the systematic exclusion of "a 'distinctive' group in the community." * * * [G]roups defined solely in terms of shared attitudes that would prevent or substantially impair members of the group from performing their duties as jurors, such as the *Witherspoon*-excludables" at issue here, are not "distinctive groups" for fair-cross-section purposes.

The defendant also argued that "death qualification" violated his rights to an impartial jury. In essence, he reasoned that all jurors are, to some extent, biased or predisposed to one side or the other in a criminal trial; therefore, the only way to construct an impartial jury is to balance the competing predispositions. Exclusion, therefore, of "*Witherspoon*-excludables" at the guilt phase of a trial unconstitutionally tips the scale in favor of a jury inclined to convict.

The Court described this argument as "both illogical and hopelessly impractical." It was illogical because exactly the same twelve persons "could have ended up on the jury through the 'luck of the draw' without in any way violating the constitutional guarantee of impartiality." As a practical matter, the majority stated,

> if it were true that the Constitution required a certain mix of individual viewpoints on the jury, then trial judges would be required to undertake the Sisyphean task of "balancing" juries, making sure that each contains the proper number of Democrats and Republicans, young persons and old persons, white-collar executives and blue-collar laborers, and so on. Adopting [this] concept of jury impartiality would also likely require the elimination of peremptory challenges, which are commonly used by both the State and the defendant to attempt to produce a jury favorable to the challenger.

6. *Death penalty proponents and challenges for cause.* The *Witherspoon-Witt* principle (Note 4) applies in reverse. That is, a trial court must, at the defendant's request, inquire into the venireperson's views on capital punishment and, pursuant to the Sixth Amendment guarantee of an impartial jury, exclude for cause any prospective juror who would vote *for* the death penalty without regard to mitigating evidence presented at the capital sentencing hearing. Morgan v. Illinois, 504 U.S. 719, 112 S.Ct. 2222, 119 L.Ed.2d 492 (1992).

Suppose that a judge erroneously fails to exclude a juror who will always vote for the death penalty, and the defense is required to exercise one of its limited peremptory challenges to remove that juror. Should his death sentence be reversed on this basis alone? Or is there a way to distinguish this situation—a judge's erroneous *inclusion* of a *disqualified* juror that required the defendant to use a peremptory challenge to cure the error—from that involved in *Gray v. Mississippi* (Note 4), which concerned the erroneous *exclusion* of a *qualified* juror? See Ross v. Oklahoma, 487 U.S. 81, 108 S.Ct. 2273, 101 L.Ed.2d 80 (1988) (holding that the defendant was not entitled to reversal on the ground that he was denied an impartial jury); William T. Pizzi & Morris B. Hoffman, *Jury Selection Errors on Appeal*, 38 Am. Crim. L. Rev. 1391 (2001).

d. Peremptory Challenges

When the prosecution or defense is unsuccessful in convincing the trial judge to remove a prospective juror for cause, that party may exercise one of its peremptory challenges to remove the person whom they do not wish to have sit on the jury. The number of such challenges that may be exercised at trial is limited by statute or rule but, until recently, attorneys had unfettered discretion in exercising those limited challenges they possessed. That is no longer so.

To understand what and why this has happened, consider first the Thompson and Muller excerpts, which are followed by *Batson v. Kentucky*, one of the Supreme Court's most provocative cases in the field of criminal adjudication.

> **SANDRA GUERRA THOMPSON—THE NON-DISCRIMINATION IDEAL OF *HERNANDEZ V. TEXAS* CONFRONTS A "CULTURE" OF DISCRIMINATION: THE AMAZING STORY OF *MILLER-EL V. TEXAS***
>
> 25 Chicano-Latino Law Review 97 (1996), 97–99.

The history of race discrimination in jury selection dates back to the founding of our nation, but it was not until after Reconstruction that the Supreme Court recognized the right of African-Americans to participate in the jury process. The Court struck down exclusionary statutes and disapproved of discriminatory practices. Congress also provided criminal sanctions for any person who excluded African-Americans from jury service on the basis of race. Thus, no longer can African-Americans be totally excluded from jury lists by statute, nor can they be totally excluded by the discriminatory application of facially neutral statutes.

The Supreme Court has likewise vindicated the constitutional rights of other groups who have been excluded from service on juries. * * *

Despite these successes in the Supreme Court for the principal of non-discrimination in jury selection, discrimination continues in many old and new forms. While the Court vigorously rejected total exclusion of a particular racial group from jury lists and even requires fair representation for distinct groups on jury lists, * * * the Court continues to allow the exercise of peremptory strikes during jury selection, a practice that had the potential to be used to eliminate all or virtually all of the available minority jurors, and is often used in just that way.

ERIC L. MULLER—SOLVING THE *BATSON* PARADOX: HARMLESS ERROR, JURY REPRESENTATION, AND THE SIXTH AMENDMENT
106 Yale Law Journal 93 (1996), 97–101.

In the prosecutor's office where I once worked, a supervisor always counseled new attorneys litigating drug cases to use a peremptory challenge to remove any prospective juror who came to court with a coffee mug or shoulder bag bearing the emblem of the local public broadcasting station. He reasoned that people get such merchandise in only one way— by donating money to public broadcasting. Anyone who would give money to public broadcasting, he argued, was too much of a mushy-headed liberal to give the government's case a favorable hearing.

Such rough inferences drive our system of peremptory challenges. The supervisor knew that the inference was ridiculously overbroad, but his experience told him that it was not flatly irrational. He saw enough of a correlation between a juror's television and radio preferences and her likely viewpoint on drug enforcement to make the peremptory strike worthwhile.

For many years, the Supreme Court has struggled with the similar question of whether it is rational for an attorney to draw inferences about viewpoint from a prospective juror's race or gender. This inquiry has been just one piece of a larger problem that has plagued the Court: Is it ever rational, in any context, to attribute distinctive views or beliefs to a segment of the community defined by an immutable characteristic like race or gender? * * *

In one area * * * the Court has historically been unequivocal in embracing what might be called the "theory of difference"—that is, the theory that jurors' race and gender are at least minimally rational predictors of their perspective. This area is the law of grand and petit jury composition. * * *

The Court first expressed this premise openly in *Ballard v. United States*, [329 U.S. 187, 67 S.Ct. 261, 91 L.Ed. 181 (1946),] where it exercised its supervisory power over the administration of justice in the federal courts to require the inclusion of women in the venires from which grand and petit juries were selected. While rejecting the simplistic notion that men and women act predictably as rigid classes, the Court readily embraced the subtler idea that "the two sexes are not fungible; a community made up exclusively of one is different from a community composed of both." "[A] flavor, a distinct quality is lost," the Court insisted, "if either sex is excluded" from juries.

The Court reaffirmed its commitment to this theory of difference in *Taylor v. Louisiana* [p. 1213], when it expanded *Ballard* from a supervisory to a constitutional rule. * * * Holding that "the selection of a petit jury from a representative cross section of the community is an essential component of the Sixth Amendment right to a jury trial," the Court struck down Louisiana's "opt-in" system for women. * * *

The Court has also embraced the theory of difference in the context of racial exclusion. In *Peters v. Kiff*, [407 U.S. 493, 92 S.Ct. 2163, 33 L.Ed.2d 83 (1972),] the Court granted a writ of habeas corpus to a defendant who had been indicted for, and convicted of, burglary by grand and petit juries from which blacks had been systematically excluded. The novelty in *Peters* was that the defendant was white. Seizing on this, the State argued that he had suffered no harm by the exclusion of blacks from his grand and petit juries. The Court rejected this argument. Writing for himself and two other Justices, Justice Marshall * * * refused to assume that the exclusion of black jurors has an impact only on cases touching explicitly on race:

> When any large and identifiable segment of the community is excluded from jury service, the effect is to remove from the jury room qualities of human nature and varieties of human experience, the range of which is unknown and perhaps unknowable. It is not necessary to assume that the excluded group will consistently vote as a class in order to conclude, as we do, that its exclusion deprives the jury of a perspective on human events that may have unsuspected importance in any case that may be presented.

Thus, while race may not offer hard and fast predictions on precise voting patterns in specific cases, it does produce "a perspective on human events" that cannot be excluded without subverting the representativeness of the jury.

The Court's [early] cases on grand and petit jury discrimination reflected a commitment to the view that one might rationally glean some hint of a person's perspective from his or her race or gender. Yet in 1986, when the Court began to grapple with the discriminatory use of the peremptory challenge [in *Batson v. Kentucky*], it had a change of heart. Race and gender became not just impermissible but flatly irrational predictors of juror perspective.

BATSON V. KENTUCKY

Supreme Court of the United States, 1986.
476 U.S. 79, 106 S.Ct. 1712, 90 L.Ed.2d 69.

JUSTICE POWELL delivered the opinion of the Court [joined by JUSTICES BRENNAN, WHITE, MARSHALL, BLACKMUN, STEVENS, and O'CONNOR]. * * *

I

Petitioner, a black man, was indicted in Kentucky on charges of second-degree burglary and receipt of stolen goods. On the first day of trial in Jefferson Circuit Court, the judge conducted *voir dire* examination of the venire, excused certain jurors for cause, and permitted the parties to exercise peremptory challenges. The prosecutor used his peremptory challenges to strike all four black persons on the venire, and a jury composed only of white persons was selected. Defense counsel moved to discharge the jury before it was sworn on the ground that the prosecutor's removal of the black veniremen violated petitioner's rights under the Sixth and Fourteenth Amendments to a jury drawn from a cross section of the community, and under the Fourteenth Amendment to equal protection of the laws. Counsel requested a hearing on his motion. Without expressly ruling on the request for a hearing, the trial judge observed that the parties were entitled to use their peremptory challenges to "strike anybody they want to." The judge then denied petitioner's motion, reasoning that the cross-section requirement applies only to selection of the venire and not to selection of the petit jury itself.

The jury convicted petitioner on both counts. * * *

II

In *Swain v. Alabama*, [380 U.S. 202, 85 S.Ct. 824, 13 L.Ed.2d 759 (1965),] this Court recognized that a "State's purposeful or deliberate denial to Negroes on account of race of participation as jurors in the administration of justice violates the Equal Protection Clause." This principle has been "consistently and repeatedly" reaffirmed, in numerous decisions of this Court both preceding and following *Swain*. We reaffirm the principle today.[4] * * *

Accordingly, the component of the jury selection process at issue here, the State's privilege to strike individual jurors through peremptory challenges, is subject to the commands of the Equal Protection Clause. Although a prosecutor ordinarily is entitled to exercise permitted peremptory challenges "for any reason at all, as long as that reason is related to his view concerning the outcome" of the case to be tried, the

---

[4] * * * We agree with the State that resolution of petitioner's claim properly turns on application of equal protection principles and express no view on the merits of any of petitioner's Sixth Amendment arguments.

Equal Protection Clause forbids the prosecutor to challenge potential jurors solely on account of their race or on the assumption that black jurors as a group will be unable impartially to consider the State's case against a black defendant.

III * * *

Swain required the Court to decide, among other issues, whether a black defendant was denied equal protection by the State's exercise of peremptory challenges to exclude members of his race from the petit jury. The record in *Swain* showed that the prosecutor had used the State's peremptory challenges to strike the six black persons included on the petit jury venire. While rejecting the defendant's claim for failure to prove purposeful discrimination, the Court nonetheless indicated that the Equal Protection Clause placed some limits on the State's exercise of peremptory challenges.

The Court sought to accommodate the prosecutor's historical privilege of peremptory challenge free of judicial control, and the constitutional prohibition on exclusion of persons from jury service on account of race. While the Constitution does not confer a right to peremptory challenges, those challenges traditionally have been viewed as one means of assuring the selection of a qualified and unbiased jury. To preserve the peremptory nature of the prosecutor's challenge, the Court in *Swain* declined to scrutinize his actions in a particular case by relying on a presumption that he properly exercised the State's challenges.

The Court went on to observe, however, that a State may not exercise its challenges in contravention of the Equal Protection Clause. It was impermissible for a prosecutor to use his challenges to exclude blacks from the jury "for reasons wholly unrelated to the outcome of the particular case on trial" or to deny to blacks "the same right and opportunity to participate in the administration of justice enjoyed by the white population." Accordingly, a black defendant could make out a prima facie case of purposeful discrimination on proof that the peremptory challenge system was "being perverted" in that manner. For example, an inference of purposeful discrimination would be raised on evidence that a prosecutor, "in case after case, whatever the circumstances, whatever the crime and whoever the defendant or the victim may be, is responsible for the removal of Negroes who have been selected as qualified jurors by the jury commissioners and who have survived challenges for cause, with the result that no Negroes ever serve on petit juries." Evidence offered by the defendant in *Swain* did not meet that standard. While the defendant showed that prosecutors in the jurisdiction had exercised their strikes to exclude blacks from the jury, he offered no proof of the circumstances under which prosecutors were responsible for striking black jurors beyond the facts of his own case.

A number of lower courts following the teaching of *Swain* reasoned that proof of repeated striking of blacks over a number of cases was necessary to establish a violation of the Equal Protection Clause. Since this interpretation of *Swain* has placed on defendants a crippling burden of proof,[17] prosecutors' peremptory challenges are now largely immune from constitutional scrutiny. For reasons that follow, we reject this evidentiary formulation as inconsistent with standards that have been developed since *Swain* for assessing a prima facie case under the Equal Protection Clause. * * *

The standards for assessing a prima facie case in the context of discriminatory selection of the venire have been fully articulated since *Swain*. These principles support our conclusion that a defendant may establish a prima facie case of purposeful discrimination in selection of the petit jury solely on evidence concerning the prosecutor's exercise of peremptory challenges at the defendant's trial. To establish such a case, the defendant first must show that he is a member of a cognizable racial group, and that the prosecutor has exercised peremptory challenges to remove from the venire members of the defendant's race. Second, the defendant is entitled to rely on the fact, as to which there can be no dispute, that peremptory challenges constitute a jury selection practice that permits "those to discriminate who are of a mind to discriminate." Finally, the defendant must show that these facts and any other relevant circumstances raise an inference that the prosecutor used that practice to exclude the veniremen from the petit jury on account of their race. This combination of factors in the empaneling of the petit jury, as in the selection of the venire, raises the necessary inference of purposeful discrimination.

In deciding whether the defendant has made the requisite showing, the trial court should consider all relevant circumstances. For example, a "pattern" of strikes against black jurors included in the particular venire might give rise to an inference of discrimination. Similarly, the prosecutor's questions and statements during *voir dire* examination and in exercising his challenges may support or refute an inference of discriminatory purpose. These examples are merely illustrative. We have confidence that trial judges, experienced in supervising *voir dire*, will be able to decide if the circumstances concerning the prosecutor's use of

---

[17] The lower courts have noted the practical difficulties of proving that the State systematically has exercised peremptory challenges to exclude blacks from the jury on account of race. * * * [T]he defendant would have to investigate, over a number of cases, the race of persons tried in the particular jurisdiction, the racial composition of the venire and petit jury, and the manner in which both parties exercised their peremptory challenges. * * * In jurisdictions where court records do not reflect the jurors' race and where *voir dire* proceedings are not transcribed, the burden would be insurmountable.

peremptory challenges creates a prima facie case of discrimination against black jurors.

Once the defendant makes a prima facie showing, the burden shifts to the State to come forward with a neutral explanation for challenging black jurors. Though this requirement imposes a limitation in some cases on the full peremptory character of the historic challenge, we emphasize that the prosecutor's explanation need not rise to the level justifying exercise of a challenge for cause. But the prosecutor may not rebut the defendant's prima facie case of discrimination by stating merely that he challenged jurors of the defendant's race on the assumption—or his intuitive judgment—that they would be partial to the defendant because of their shared race. Just as the Equal Protection Clause forbids the States to exclude black persons from the venire on the assumption that blacks as a group are unqualified to serve as jurors, so it forbids the States to strike black veniremen on the assumption that they will be biased in a particular case simply because the defendant is black. The core guarantee of equal protection, ensuring citizens that their State will not discriminate on account of race, would be meaningless were we to approve the exclusion of jurors on the basis of such assumptions, which arise solely from the jurors' race. Nor may the prosecutor rebut the defendant's case merely by denying that he had a discriminatory motive or "affirm[ing] [his] good faith in making individual selections." If these general assertions were accepted as rebutting a defendant's prima facie case, the Equal Protection Clause "would be but a vain and illusory requirement." The prosecutor therefore must articulate a neutral explanation related to the particular case to be tried. The trial court then will have the duty to determine if the defendant has established purposeful discrimination.

IV

The State contends that our holding will eviscerate the fair trial values served by the peremptory challenge. Conceding that the Constitution does not guarantee a right to peremptory challenges and that *Swain* did state that their use ultimately is subject to the strictures of equal protection, the State argues that the privilege of unfettered exercise of the challenge is of vital importance to the criminal justice system.

While we recognize, of course, that the peremptory challenge occupies an important position in our trial procedures, we do not agree that our decision today will undermine the contribution the challenge generally makes to the administration of justice. The reality of practice, amply reflected in many state-and federal-court opinions, shows that the challenge may be, and unfortunately at times has been, used to discriminate against black jurors. By requiring trial courts to be sensitive to the racially discriminatory use of peremptory challenges, our decision enforces the mandate of equal protection and furthers the ends of justice. In view of the heterogeneous population of our Nation, public respect for our criminal justice system and the rule of law will be strengthened if we ensure that no citizen is disqualified from jury service because of his race.

Nor are we persuaded by the State's suggestion that our holding will create serious administrative difficulties. In those States applying a version of the evidentiary standard we recognize today, courts have not experienced serious administrative burdens, and the peremptory challenge system has survived. We decline, however, to formulate particular procedures to be followed upon a defendant's timely objection to a prosecutor's challenges.[24]

V

In this case, petitioner made a timely objection to the prosecutor's removal of all black persons on the venire. Because the trial court flatly rejected the objection without requiring the prosecutor to give an explanation for his action, we remand this case for further proceedings. If the trial court decides that the facts establish, prima facie, purposeful discrimination and the prosecutor does not come forward with a neutral explanation for his action, our precedents require that petitioner's conviction be reversed.[25]

[JUSTICE WHITE'S concurring opinion is omitted.]

JUSTICE MARSHALL, concurring.

I join Justice Powell's eloquent opinion for the Court, which takes a historic step toward eliminating the shameful practice of racial discrimination in the selection of juries. * * * I nonetheless write separately to express my views. The decision today will not end the racial discrimination that peremptories inject into the jury-selection process. That goal can be accomplished only by eliminating peremptory challenges entirely. * * *

II

I wholeheartedly concur in the Court's conclusion that use of the peremptory challenge to remove blacks from juries, on the basis of their race, violates the Equal Protection Clause. I would go further, however, in fashioning a remedy adequate to eliminate that discrimination. Merely allowing defendants the opportunity to challenge the racially

---

[24] * * * [W]e express no view on whether it is more appropriate in a particular case, upon a finding of discrimination against black jurors, for the trial court to discharge the venire and select a new jury from a panel not previously associated with the case, or to disallow the discriminatory challenges and resume selection with the improperly challenged jurors reinstated on the venire.

[25] To the extent that anything in *Swain v. Alabama* is contrary to the principles we articulate today, that decision is overruled.

discriminatory use of peremptory challenges in individual cases will not end the illegitimate use of the peremptory challenge.

Evidentiary analysis similar to that set out by the Court has been adopted as a matter of state law in States including Massachusetts and California. Cases from those jurisdictions illustrate the limitations of the approach. First, defendants cannot attack the discriminatory use of peremptory challenges at all unless the challenges are so flagrant as to establish a prima facie case. This means, in those States, that where only one or two black jurors survive the challenges for cause, the prosecutor need have no compunction about striking them from the jury because of their race. Prosecutors are left free to discriminate against blacks in jury selection provided that they hold that discrimination to an "acceptable" level.

Second, when a defendant can establish a prima facie case, trial courts face the difficult burden of assessing prosecutors' motives. Any prosecutor can easily assert facially neutral reasons for striking a juror, and trial courts are ill equipped to second-guess those reasons. How is the court to treat a prosecutor's statement that he struck a juror because the juror had a son about the same age as defendant, or seemed "uncommunicative," or "never cracked a smile" and, therefore "did not possess the sensitivities necessary to realistically look at the issues and decide the facts in this case"? If such easily generated explanations are sufficient to discharge the prosecutor's obligation to justify his strikes on nonracial grounds, then the protection erected by the Court today may be illusory.

Nor is outright prevarication by prosecutors the only danger here. * * * A prosecutor's own conscious or unconscious racism may lead him easily to the conclusion that a prospective black juror is "sullen," or "distant," a characterization that would not have come to his mind if a white juror had acted identically. A judge's own conscious or unconscious racism may lead him to accept such an explanation as well supported. As Justice Rehnquist concedes, prosecutors' peremptories are based on their "seat-of-the-pants instincts" as to how particular jurors will vote. Yet "seat-of-the-pants instincts" may often be just another term for racial prejudice. Even if all parties approach the Court's mandate with the best of conscious intentions, that mandate requires them to confront and overcome their own racism on all levels—a challenge I doubt all of them can meet. * * *

III

The inherent potential of peremptory challenges to distort the jury process by permitting the exclusion of jurors on racial grounds should ideally lead the Court to ban them entirely from the criminal justice system. * * *

Some authors have suggested that the courts should ban prosecutors' peremptories entirely, but should zealously guard the defendant's peremptory as "essential to the fairness of trial by jury," and "one of the most important of the rights secured to the accused." I would not find that an acceptable solution. Our criminal justice system "requires not only freedom from any bias against the accused, but also from any prejudice against his prosecution. Between him and the state the scales are to be evenly held." We can maintain that balance, not by permitting both prosecutor and defendant to engage in racial discrimination in jury selection, but by banning the use of peremptory challenges by prosecutors and by allowing the States to eliminate the defendant's peremptories as well.

Much ink has been spilled regarding the historic importance of defendants' peremptory challenges. The * * * *Swain* Court emphasized the "very old credentials" of the peremptory challenge, and cited the "long and widely held belief that peremptory challenge is a necessary part of trial by jury." But this Court has also repeatedly stated that the right of peremptory challenge is not of constitutional magnitude, and may be withheld altogether without impairing the constitutional guarantee of impartial jury and fair trial. The potential for racial prejudice, further, inheres in the defendant's challenge as well. If the prosecutor's peremptory challenge could be eliminated only at the cost of eliminating the defendant's challenge as well, I do not think that would be too great a price to pay. * * *

[The concurring opinions of JUSTICE STEVENS, with whom JUSTICE BRENNAN joined, and JUSTICE O'CONNOR are omitted.]

[The dissenting opinion of CHIEF JUSTICE BURGER, joined by JUSTICE REHNQUIST, is omitted.]

JUSTICE REHNQUIST, with whom THE CHIEF JUSTICE joins, dissenting. * * *

I cannot subscribe to the Court's unprecedented use of the Equal Protection Clause to restrict the historic scope of the peremptory challenge, which has been described as "a necessary part of trial by jury." In my view, there is simply nothing "unequal" about the State's using its peremptory challenges to strike blacks from the jury in cases involving black defendants, so long as such challenges are also used to exclude whites in cases involving white defendants, Hispanics in cases involving Hispanic defendants, Asians in cases involving Asian defendants, and so on. This case-specific use of peremptory challenges by the State does not single out blacks, or members of any other race for that matter, for discriminatory treatment. Such use of peremptories is at best based upon seat-of-the-pants instincts, which are undoubtedly crudely stereotypical and may in many cases be hopelessly mistaken. But as long as they are applied across-the-board to jurors of all races and nationalities, I do not see—and the Court most certainly has not explained—how their use violates the Equal Protection Clause. * * *

The use of group affiliations, such as age, race, or occupation, as a "proxy" for potential juror partiality, based on the assumption or belief that members of one group are more likely to favor defendants who belong to the same group, has long been accepted as a legitimate basis for the State's exercise of peremptory challenges. Indeed, given the need for reasonable limitations on the time devoted to *voir dire*, the use of such "proxies" by both the State and the defendant may be extremely useful in eliminating from the jury persons who might be biased in one way or another. * * *

NOTES AND QUESTIONS

1. *Sixth Amendment.* According to Professor Pamela Karlan,

Batson pitched his brief almost exclusively in terms of the sixth amendment's fair cross-section requirement. That strategic decision was hardly surprising: it avoided asking the Court to overrule *Swain* [*v. Alabama*] expressly, and the general wisdom among lawyers is that it's easier to persuade the Court to sidestep or ignore precedent than to reject it outright.

Pamela S. Karlan, *Batson v. Kentucky: The Constitutional Challenges of Peremptory Challenges*, in Criminal Procedure Stories 381, 396 (Carol S. Steiker, ed. 2006).

Some of the *amici* briefs filed in support of Batson, however, called on the Supreme Court to overrule or narrow *Swain*. And, as Professor Karlan reports, *id.* at 399, Batson's lawyer "stunned" the justices in oral argument when he repeatedly declined their offer to argue for reconsideration of *Swain*. Nonetheless, as we see, that is the direction the Court took, avoiding for awhile (see footnote 4) the Sixth Amendment claim.

Subsequently, in Holland v. Illinois, 493 U.S. 474, 110 S.Ct. 803, 107 L.Ed.2d 905 (1990), the Court held, 5–4, that a prosecutor's use of peremptory strikes to exclude African-Americans from juries does *not* violate the Sixth Amendment fair-cross-section right. (Holland did not raise an equal protection claim on appeal.) Justice Scalia, for the majority, stated that this Sixth Amendment right applies exclusively to the jury pool and not to the jury selected: "The Sixth Amendment requirement of a fair cross section on the venire is a means of assuring, not a *representative* jury (which the Constitution does not demand), but an *impartial* one (which it does)."

2. *Batson versus Taylor.* Is *Batson* inconsistent with the assumptions underlying the fair-cross-section principle announced in *Taylor v. Louisiana*, p. 1213? For example, is it true that:

racial identity, though not biological race, informs cultural experience. * * * Racial identity, like gender identity, is an organizing principle of group consciousness: as long as patterns of residential and economic segregation continue to separate the races in different enclaves, blacks, whites, Latinos, and others will exhibit cultural differences in their perceptions of the world.

Tanya Coke, *Lady Justice May Be Blind, But Is She a Soul Sister? Race-Neutrality and the Ideal of Representative Juries*, 69 N.Y.U. L. Rev. 327, 359 (1994).

If this observation is accurate, aren't race-based peremptories justifiable, i.e., *Batson* is wrongly decided? If this observation is *not* accurate, does this mean that *Taylor* was wrongly decided? Or is there a way to justify both cases?

3.   *"Let's get real."* A Philadelphia prosecutor stated on a training film for new prosecutors that case law provides that the goal of jury selection "is to get a competent, fair, and impartial jury. Well, that's ridiculous. The only way you're going to do your best is to get jurors that are unfair and more likely to convict than anybody else in the room." *Former Prosecutor Accused of Bias in Election Year*, N.Y. Times, April 3, 1997, at A10.

Is his statement correct? Is it also a fair statement that "neither side"— defense nor prosecution—"really wishes an impartial jury, but rather wishes to do everything possible to find jurors more attuned to its world view"? Richard Singer, *Peremptory Holds: A Suggestion (Only Half Specious) of a Solution to the Discriminatory Use of Peremptory Challenges*, 62 U. Det. L. Rev. 275, 288 (1985). If so, does this mean that the primary purpose of peremptory challenges is to let each side get rid of those persons whom they most *dis*favor (presumably, the jurors the other side most wants)?

If you go along with the preceding analysis, does *Batson* in effect mischaracterize the motivations of most prosecutors who seek to exclude African-Americans from juries involving black defendants? For example, suppose that a prosecutor uses her peremptories to exclude black jurors in a case involving an African-American defendant and a white victim. She explains her action this way:

"I believe that both black and white jurors can fairly try cases involving defendants of their own race. But, I want to get the jury *most* supportive of my side. And, based on my experience, when a defendant is black, and especially when a victim is white, black jurors are less receptive to my case. The same applies to white jurors if the facts are reversed."

See Albert W. Alschuler, *The Supreme Court and the Jury: Voir Dire, Peremptory Challenges, and the Review of Jury Verdicts*, 56 U. Chi. L. Rev. 153, 168 (1989). Is this explanation unreasonable? Is it racist? Under *Batson*, has she provided a satisfactory explanation for eliminating black jurors from the venire?

Or, consider this: Suppose that a prosecutor needs to introduce tape recordings in which white police officers are heard uttering harsh and highly offensive racial epithets. Therefore, she uses her peremptories to exclude African-Americans in the jury pool. She explains that, notwithstanding assurances by these jurors that they could overlook the slurs and deliberate impartially, in her view "no minority juror would be able to make an unbiased decision regarding * * * guilt or innocence after hearing these awful tapes." Is her use of peremptories irrational? Racist? Has she violated the *Batson* standard? See United States v. Huey, 76 F.3d 638 (5th Cir. 1996).

4.   What constitutes a "race"-based peremptory challenge? The Supreme Court observed in Hernandez v. New York, 500 U.S. 352, 111 S.Ct. 1859, 114 L.Ed.2d 395 (1991), that it has not resolved the "difficult question of the breadth with which the concept of race should be defined for equal protection purposes." What if a prosecutor purposely exercises her peremptory challenges to exclude Spanish-speaking jurors. Does this state a prima facie violation of the equal protection clause? In response to this hypothetical, the *Hernandez* Court observed that

> [i]t may well be, for certain ethnic groups and in some communities, that proficiency in a particular language, like skin color, should be treated as a surrogate for race under an equal protection analysis. * * * [A] policy of striking all who speak a given language, without regard to the particular circumstances of the trial or the individual responses of the jurors, may be found by the trial judge to be a pretext for racial discrimination.

5.   *Proving a Batson violation: the three-step process.* In Purkett v. Elem, 514 U.S. 765, 115 S.Ct. 1769, 131 L.Ed.2d 834 (1995), Elem was prosecuted for robbery in a Missouri court. During jury selection, he objected to the prosecutor's use of peremptories to strike two African-American men from the jury panel. The prosecutor defended his strikes as follows:

> I struck [juror] number twenty-two because of his long hair. He had long curly hair. He had the longest hair of anybody on the panel by far. He appeared to me to not be a good juror for that fact, the fact that he had long hair hanging down shoulder length, curly, unkempt hair. Also, he had a mustache and a goatee type beard. And juror number twenty-four also has a mustache and goatee type beard. Those are the only two people on the jury * * * with facial hair. * * * And I don't like the way they looked, with the way the hair is cut, both of them. And the mustaches and the beards look suspicious to me.

The trial court rejected Elem's *Batson* motion, and empaneled the jury. Upon conviction, Elem renewed his *Batson* claim. After losing in his state appeals, Elem filed a habeas corpus petition. The Court of Appeals ultimately ruled in his favor, but the Supreme Court reversed the judgment of the Court of Appeals, setting out the three-step process that trial courts should follow:

Under our *Batson* jurisprudence, once the opponent of a peremptory challenge has made out a prima facie case of racial discrimination (step one), the burden of production shifts to the proponent of the strike to come forward with a race-neutral explanation (step two). If a race-neutral explanation is tendered, the trial court must then decide (step three) whether the opponent of the strike has proved purposeful racial discrimination. The second step of this process does not demand an explanation that is persuasive, or even plausible. "At this [second] step of the inquiry, the issue is the facial validity of the prosecutor's explanation. Unless a discriminatory intent is inherent in the prosecutor's explanation, the reason offered will be deemed race neutral."

The Court of Appeals erred by combining *Batson*'s second and third steps into one, requiring that the justification tendered at the second step be not just neutral but also at least minimally persuasive, *i.e.*, a "plausible" basis for believing that "the person's ability to perform his or her duties as a juror" will be affected. It is not until the *third* step that the persuasiveness of the justification becomes relevant—the step in which the trial court determines whether the opponent of the strike has carried his burden of proving purposeful discrimination. At that stage, implausible or fantastic justifications may (and probably will) be found to be pretexts for purposeful discrimination. But to say that a trial judge *may choose to disbelieve* a silly or superstitious reason at step three is quite different from saying that a trial judge *must terminate* the inquiry at step two when the race-neutral reason is silly or superstitious. The latter violates the principle that the ultimate burden of persuasion regarding racial motivation rests with, and never shifts from, the opponent of the strike. * * *

The prosecutor's proffered explanation in this case—that he struck juror number 22 because he had long, unkempt hair, a mustache, and a beard—is race neutral and satisfies the prosecution's step two burden of articulating a nondiscriminatory reason for the strike. "The wearing of beards is not a characteristic that is peculiar to any race." And neither is the growing of long, unkempt hair. Thus, the inquiry properly proceeded to step three, where the state court found that the prosecutor was not motivated by discriminatory intent.

In Johnson v. California, 545 U.S. 162, 125 S.Ct. 2410, 162 L.Ed.2d 129 (2005), the Supreme Court further clarified the "the narrow but important" issue of the first-step burden of proof in the three-step process. Justice Stevens, writing for eight justices, held that the California requirement that "the objector must show that it is more likely than not the other party's peremptory challenges, if unexplained, were based on impermissible group bias," is "an inappropriate yardstick by which to measure the sufficiency of a prima face case." Justice Stevens explained:

We did not intend the first step to be so onerous that a defendant would have to persuade the judge—on the basis of all the facts, some of which are impossible for the defendant to know with certainty—that the challenge was more likely than not the product of purposeful discrimination. Instead a defendant satisfies the requirement of *Batson*'s first step by producing evidence sufficient to permit the trial judge to draw an inference that discrimination has occurred.

Justice Stevens went on to explain that the defendant "ultimately"—as part of step three—carries the burden of persuasion to prove the existence of purposeful discrimination:

Thus, even if the State produces only a frivolous or utterly nonsensical justification for its strike [at step two], the case does not end—it merely proceeds to step three. The first two *Batson* steps govern the production of evidence that allows the trial court to determine the persuasiveness of the defendant's constitutional claim. "It is not until the *third* step that the persuasiveness of the justification becomes relevant—the step in which the trial court determines whether the opponent of the strike has carried his burden of proving purposeful discrimination."

In regard to the third step, "the defendant's practical burden [is] to make a liar out of the prosecutor," by demonstrating that the Step-Two racially-neutral explanations were not the prosecutor's true motivations. Munson v. State, 774 S.W.2d 778 (Tex. Crim. App. 1989).

6. *Step one.* How does a defendant satisfy step one of the *Batson* process? Is it enough simply for an African-American defendant to show that the prosecutor removed one African-American juror? Does it matter whether that one juror was the only African-American in the jury pool, thus resulting in an all-white jury, or whether other African-Americans were seated on the jury?

7. *Step two.* Suppose a prosecutor, in a murder trial, explains her reason for removing an African-American juror, this way: "She seemed from her answers to be indifferent toward police." State v. Taylor, 650 N.W.2d 190 (Minn. 2002). Does this satisfy step two of the *Batson* process? What if the prosecutor uses this explanation for *five* African-American jurors? What if the prosecutor's explanation for removing the five jurors is "they all have a small gap in their front teeth"? What *doesn't* satisfy step two?

8. *Step three.* Here is what Justice Alito, writing for the Court, has said about the role of the trial judge at step three:

The trial court has a pivotal role in evaluating *Batson* claims. Step three of the *Batson* inquiry involves an evaluation of the prosecutor's credibility, and "the best evidence [of discriminatory intent] often will be the demeanor of the attorney who exercises the challenge." In addition, race-neutral reasons for peremptory challenges often invoke a juror's demeanor (*e.g.*, nervousness, inattention), making the trial court's first-hand observations of even greater importance. In this situation, the trial court must evaluate not only whether the prosecutor's demeanor belies a discriminatory intent, but also whether the juror's demeanor can credibly be said to have exhibited the basis for the strike attributed to the juror by the prosecutor. We have recognized that these determinations of credibility and demeanor lie "peculiarly with a trial judge's province," and we have stated that "in the absence of exceptional circumstances, we * * * defer to [the trial court]."

Snyder v. Louisiana, 552 U.S. 472, 128 S.Ct. 1203, 170 L.Ed.2d 175 (2008).

This statement would seem to suggest that the trial judge's step three ruling is virtually unchallengeable on appeal. Indeed, one state court called the *Batson* process a "charade," observing:

The State may provide the trial court with a series of pat race-neutral reasons for exercise of peremptory challenges. Since reviewing courts examine only the record, we wonder if the reasons can be given without a smile. Surely, new prosecutors are given a manual, probably entitled, "Handy Race-Neutral Explanations" or "20 Time-Tested Race-Neutral Explanations." It might include [citing cases that upheld striking African-Americans from the jury]: too old, too young, divorced, "long, unkempt hair," free-lance writer, religion, social worker, renter, lack of family contact, attempting to make eye-contact with defendant, "lived in an area consisting predominantly of apartment complexes," single, over-educated, lack of maturity, improper demeanor, unemployed, improper attire, juror lived alone, misspelled place of employment, living with girlfriend, unemployed spouse, spouse employed as school teacher, employment as part-time barber, friendship with city council member, failure to remove hat, lack of community ties, children same "age bracket" as defendant, deceased father and prospective juror's aunt receiving psychiatric care. Recent consideration of the *Batson* issue makes us wonder if the rule would be imposed only where the prosecutor states that he does not care to have an African-American on the jury. We are reminded of the musing of Justice Cardozo, "We are not to close our eyes as judges to what we must perceive as men."

State v. Randall, 671 N.E.2d 60 (Ill. App. Ct. 1996).

Indeed, a senior Philadelphia prosecutor, training new prosecutors, instructed his staff to strike African-Americans from juries because "blacks from low-income areas are less likely to convict." To win *Batson* claims, he told them that, "when you do have a black juror, * * * question them at length. And on this little sheet that you have, mark something down that you can articulate later if something happens." He suggested possible race-neutral explanations, "Well, the woman has a kid the same age as the defendant and I thought she'd be sympathetic to him." After noting some other potential justifications, such as "she's unemployed and I just don't like unemployed people," he said that "you may want to ask more questions of these people so it gives you more ammunition to make an articulable reason as to why you are striking them, not for race." Jeffrey Bellin & Junichi P. Semitsu, *Widening Batson's Net to Ensure More Than the Unapologetically Bigoted or Painfully Unimaginative Attorney*, 96 Cornell L. Rev. 1075 (2011) (quoting from a training program videotape of Assistant District Attorney Jack McMahon).

Does all of this suggest that Justice Marshall was correct in *Batson* that the only way truly to enforce equal protection principles is to abolish all peremptory challenges? (See Note 17 in that regard.)

9. *Proving racial discrimination: one successful example.* Notwithstanding the pessimism expressed in the last Note, occasionally an appellate court—here, the United States Supreme Court!—is willing to find the requisite "exceptional circumstances" to overturn a trial court's rejection of a *Batson* claim.

In Foster v. Chatman, 578 U.S. ___, 136 S.Ct. 1737, 195 L.Ed.2d 1 (2016), the prosecutor used peremptory challenges in a capital murder case to strike all four black prospective jurors. Nonetheless, the trial court rejected the defense's *Batson* claim at the Step-3 stage. The Georgia Supreme Court affirmed. The defense then renewed its claim in a state habeas proceeding.

While that proceeding was pending, the defense obtained (by means of the Georgia Open Records Act) copies of files used by the prosecutor during the trial. The documents included: a jury venire list with black prospective jurors highlighted in bright green with a legend indicating that green "represents Blacks"; three handwritten notes in which black prospective jurors were denoted as ""B#1," "B#2," and "B#3"; a document titled "definite NO's," listing six names, the first five of which were all five qualified black prospective jurors; and a handwritten note titled "Church of Christ," with a notation on it reading "No <u>Black</u> Church." There was also a note from one of the prosecution's investigators stating, in part, that "if it comes down to having to pick one of the black jurors, [a particular black juror] might be okay."

Chief Justice Roberts, writing for the Court, first reviewed the three-step process for determining whether a peremptory strike was racially discriminatory. He then stated:

> Both parties agree that Foster has demonstrated a prima facie case [of a *Batson* violation], and that the prosecutors offered race-neutral reasons for their strikes. We therefore address only *Batson*'s third step. That step turns on factual determinations, and "in the absence of exceptional circumstances," we defer to state court factual findings unless we conclude that they are clearly erroneous.

Despite the heavy burden, the Supreme Court, by a 7–1 vote, reversed the trial judge's finding that there had been no *Batson* violation. To do so, it relied heavily on the newly discovered documents in conjunction with a careful analysis of the *voir dire* transcripts and the explanations provided by prosecutor Lanier at the *Batson* hearings.

The *Batson* claim centered on the strikes of two African-American prospective jurors, Marilyn Garrett and Eddie Hood. Regarding Garrett:

> In justifying that strike to the trial court, [the prosecutor] articulated a laundry list of reasons. Specifically, Lanier objected to Garrett because she: (1) worked with disadvantaged youth in her job as a teacher's aide; (2) kept looking at the ground during *voir dire*; (3) gave short and curt answers during *voir dire*; (4) appeared nervous; (5) was too young; (6) misrepresented her familiarity with the location of the crime; (7) failed to disclose that her cousin had been arrested on a drug charge; (8) was divorced; (9) had two children and two jobs; (10) was asked few questions by the defense; and (11) did not ask to be excused from jury service.

Chief Justice Roberts noted that these justifications on their face seemed "reasonable enough." However, the Court's "independent examination of the record * * * reveal[ed] that much of the reasoning provided by Lanier had no grounding in fact."

Why was it not grounded in fact? Lanier had reported to the trial judge that he had to choose "at the last moment" between two questionable jurors: white prospective Juror Blackmon or Juror Garrett. The prosecutor explained to the trial judge his reason for striking Garrett rather than Blackmon. In contrast to Garrett, he explained, Juror Blackmon:

> "was 46 years old, married 13 years to her husband who works at GE, buying her own home and [was recommended by a third party to] this prosecutor. She was no longer employed at Northwest Georgia Regional Hospital and she attended Catholic church on an irregular basis. She did not hesitate when answering the questions concerning the death penalty, had good eye contact with the prosecutor and gave good answers on the insanity issue. She was perceived by the prosecutor as having a stable home environment, of the right age and no association with any disadvantaged youth organizations."

Overall, Lanier concluded, "the chances of [Blackmon] returning a death sentence were greater when all these factors were considered than Juror Garrett. Consequently, Juror Garrett was excused."

The problem with the explanation of this "last moment" decision, as the Court observed, was that Garrett was listed from the start, even before *voir dire*, on a list of the ten persons whom the prosecutor intended to strike. The State tried to explain away this contradiction as merely "misspeaking" by the prosecutor. But, as Chief Justice Roberts noted, "this was not some off-the-cuff remark; it was an intricate story expounded by the prosecution in writing, laid out over three single-spaced pages in a brief filed with the trial court."

Moreover, several of Lanier's reasons for *why* he chose Garrett over Blackmon are similarly contradicted by the record. Lanier told the court, for example, that he struck Garrett because "the defense did not ask her questions about" pertinent trial issues such as her thoughts on "insanity" or "alcohol," or "much questions on publicity." But the trial transcripts reveal that the defense asked her several questions on all three topics.

Still other explanations given by the prosecution, while not explicitly contradicted by the record, are difficult to credit because the State willingly accepted white jurors with the same traits that supposedly rendered Garrett an unattractive juror.

As for the second African-American prospective juror, Hood, the reasons given for striking him from the juror were:

Hood: (1) had a son who was the same age as the defendant and who had previously been convicted of a crime; (2) had a wife who worked in food service at the local mental health institution; (3) had experienced food poisoning during *voir dire*; (4) was slow in responding to death penalty questions; (5) was a member of the Church of Christ; (6) had a brother who counseled drug offenders; (7) was not asked enough questions by the defense during *voir dire*; and (8) asked to be excused from jury service. An examination of the record, however, convinces us that many of these justifications cannot be credited.

The Chief Justice noted, however, that the prosecutor's reasons for striking Hood "shifted over time, suggesting that those reasons may be pretextual." At first, the justification centered on the fact that Hood had an 18-year-old son, about the age of the defendant, but later the prosecutor said the "key reason"—the "bottom line"—was Hood's membership in the Church of Christ, a denomination that, according to the prosecutor "may not take a formal stand against the death penalty, [but] they are very, very reluctant to vote for the death penalty." The problem was that neither of these explanations "withst[ood] closer scrutiny."

Take Hood's son. If Darrell Hood's age was the issue, why did the State accept (white) juror Billy Graves, who had a 17-year-old son? And why did the State accept (white) juror Martha Duncan, even though she had a 20-year-old son?

The comparison between Hood and Graves is particularly salient. When the prosecution asked Hood if Foster's age would be a factor for him in sentencing, he answered "None whatsoever." Graves, on the other hand, answered the same question "probably so." Yet the State struck Hood and accepted Graves.

And, as to church affiliation:

> Hood asserted no fewer than four times during *voir dire* that he could impose the death penalty. A prosecutor is entitled to disbelieve a juror's *voir dire* answers, of course. But the record persuades us that Hood's race, and not his religious affiliation, was Lanier's true motivation.
>
> The first indication to that effect is Lanier's mischaracterization of the record. On multiple occasions, Lanier asserted to the trial court that three white prospective jurors who were members of the Church of Christ had been struck for cause due to their opposition to the death penalty. [But, they were excluded for other reasons, set out by the Chief Justice.] * * *
>
> The prosecution's file fortifies our conclusion that any reliance on Hood's religion was pretextual. The file contains a handwritten document titled "Church of Christ." The document notes that the church "doesn't take a stand on [the] Death Penalty," and that the issue is "left for each individual member." The document then states: "<u>NO</u>. NO <u>Black </u>Church."

Justice Alito concurred in the judgment. He agreed with the majority "that the totality of the evidence now adduced * * * is sufficient to make out a *Batson* claim." But, he focused on procedural reasons why the Georgia court, although "bound to accept [the Court's] evaluation of the federal question," is still entitled to determine whether that conclusion justified relief.

Justice Thomas, the sole dissenter, criticized the majority for not "adequately grappling with the possibility that we lack jurisdiction" to hear the case, because the state judgment might have been based on an independent state ground, and for "distort[ing] the deferential *Batson* inquiry."

Does *Foster* realistically provide defendants who make *Batson* motions grounds for optimism?

10. Foster's success (Note 9) notwithstanding, according to a study of jury selection procedures in eight Southern states conducted by the Equal Justice Initiative, racial discrimination in jury selection remains a serious problem. Among the findings: (1) various counties have excluded nearly 80% of African-Americans qualified for jury service; (2) in some black-majority counties, African-American defendants in capital trials were tried by all-white juries; and (3) some prosecutors received instructions by their superiors to exclude jurors of color and were trained on how to conceal their race-based peremptory challenges. See Equal Justice Initiative, Illegal Racial Discrimination in Jury Selection: A Continuing Legacy (2010).

11. *Batson and the "standing" requirement.* The defendant in *Batson* was a black man who objected to the exclusion of fellow African-Americans in the jury pool. The ordinary rule in equal protection cases is that a defendant must be a member of the group that is the victim of the alleged

discrimination. In Powers v. Ohio, 499 U.S. 400, 111 S.Ct. 1364, 113 L.Ed.2d 411 (1991), however, the Court held that a criminal defendant may object to race-based peremptory challenges whether or not he and the excluded jurors share the same race.

The Court, per Justice Kennedy, provided three justifications for removing the standing requirement. First, "the discriminatory use of peremptory challenges by the prosecution causes a criminal defendant cognizable injury * * * . This * * * is because racial discrimination in the selection of jurors 'casts doubt on the integrity of the judicial process,' and places the fairness of a criminal proceeding in doubt." If the public does not trust in the judicial process, "[t]he verdict"—even an acquittal—"will not be accepted" by the public, thereby injuring the defendant, regardless of his race.

Second, the Court focused on the excluded juror: He and "the criminal defendant have a common interest in eliminating racial discrimination from the courtroom. A venireperson excluded from jury service because of race suffers a profound personal humiliation heightened by its public character. The rejected juror may lose confidence in the court and its verdicts, as may the defendant if his or her objections cannot be heard. This congruence of interests makes it necessary and appropriate for the defendant to raise the rights of the juror."

Third, and closely related to the latter point, "[t]he barriers to a suit by an excluded juror are daunting. Potential jurors are not parties to the jury selection process and have no opportunity to be heard at the time of their exclusion. Nor can excluded jurors easily obtain declaratory or injunctive relief when discrimination occurs through an individual prosecutor's exercise of peremptory challenges. * * * And, there exist considerable practical barriers to suit by the excluded juror because of the small financial stake involved and the economic burdens of litigation." Consequently, a party to the prosecution is in better position to protect the interests of jurors who may be victims of racial discrimination.

12. *Batson is extended.* The *Batson* rule no longer is limited to race-based peremptory challenges by prosecutors in criminal trials. The Supreme Court extended *Batson* to civil trials in Edmonson v. Leesville Concrete Company, Inc., 500 U.S. 614, 111 S.Ct. 2077, 114 L.Ed.2d 660 (1991). It extended *Batson* principles, as well, to gender-based peremptory challenges (discussed in Note 13). And, perhaps most controversially, it has extended *Batson* to *defense* exercise of peremptory challenges in criminal cases (Note 14).

13. *Batson and gender-based peremptory challenges.* In J.E.B. v. Alabama ex rel. T.B., 511 U.S. 127, 114 S.Ct. 1419, 128 L.Ed.2d 89 (1994), the State of Alabama used nine of its ten peremptories to remove males in a paternity and child custody action. The Supreme Court, per Justice Blackmun, extended the *Batson* rule to such gender-based peremptory challenges. Blackmun wrote that "[d]iscriminatory use of peremptory

challenges may create the impression that the judicial system has acquiesced in suppressing full participation by one gender or that the 'deck has been stacked' in favor of one side."

Although Justice O'Connor concurred in the opinion, she expressed reservations, based in part on her belief that *Batson* undermines the legitimate use of peremptories:

> Our belief that experienced lawyers will often correctly intuit which jurors are likely to be the least sympathetic, and our understanding that the lawyer will often be unable to explain the intuition, are the very reason we cherish the peremptory challenge. But, as we add, layer by layer, additional constitutional restraints on the use of the peremptory, we force lawyers to articulate what we know is often inarticulable.
>
> In so doing we make the peremptory challenge less discretionary and more like a challenge for cause. We also increase the possibility that biased jurors will be allowed onto the jury, because sometimes a lawyer will be unable to provide an acceptable gender-neutral explanation even though the lawyer is in fact correct that the juror is unsympathetic. Similarly, in jurisdictions where lawyers exercise their strikes in open court, lawyers may be deterred from using their peremptories, out of the fear that if they are unable to justify the strike the court will seat a juror who knows that the striking party thought him unfit. Because I believe the peremptory remains an important litigator's tool and a fundamental part of the process of selecting impartial juries, our increasing limitation of it gives me pause.
>
> Nor is the value of the peremptory challenge to the litigant diminished when the peremptory is exercised in a gender-based manner. We know that like race, gender matters. A plethora of studies make clear that in rape cases, for example, female jurors are somewhat more likely to vote to convict than male jurors. Moreover, though there have been no similarly definitive studies regarding, for example, sexual harassment, child custody, or spousal or child abuse, one need not be a sexist to share the intuition that in certain cases a person's gender and resulting life experience will be relevant to his or her view of the case. * * * Individuals are not expected to ignore as jurors what they know as men—or women.
>
> Today's decision severely limits a litigant's ability to act on this intuition, for the import of our holding is that any correlation between a juror's gender and attitudes is irrelevant as a matter of constitutional law. But to say that gender makes no difference as a matter of law is not to say that gender makes no difference as a matter of fact. * * * In extending *Batson* to gender we have added an additional burden to the state and federal trial process, taken a step closer to eliminating the peremptory challenge, and diminished the

ability of litigants to act on sometimes accurate gender-based assumptions about juror attitudes.

Justice Scalia, writing as well for Chief Justice Rehnquist and Justice Thomas, dissented in *J.E.B.* In part, he expressed concern about the future of peremptory challenges: "In order * * * to pay conspicuous obeisance to the equality of the sexes, the Court imperils a practice that has been considered an essential part of fair jury trial since the dawn of the common law. The Constitution of the United States neither requires nor permits this vandalizing of our people's traditions."

14. *Batson is extended to the defense in criminal trials.* In Georgia v. McCollum, 505 U.S. 42, 112 S.Ct. 2348, 120 L.Ed.2d 33 (1992), the Supreme Court extended *Batson* principles to the exercise of peremptory challenges by criminal defense attorneys. In *McCollum*, three white businesspersons were charged with aggravated assault and simple battery of two African-Americans. As the Court recounted, "[s]hortly after the events, a leaflet was widely distributed in the local African-American community reporting the assault and urging community residents not to patronize respondents' business." Before jury selection began, the prosecution moved unsuccessfully to prohibit the defense from exercising its peremptory challenges in a racially discriminatory manner. On appeal, the Supreme Court concluded that *Batson* applies with equal force to the defense. Concurring Justice Thomas, however, expressed concern:

> In [prior cases], we put the rights of defendants foremost. Today's decision, while protecting jurors, leaves defendants with less means of protecting themselves. Unless jurors actually admit prejudice during *voir dire*, defendants generally must allow them to sit and run the risk that racial animus will affect the verdict. In effect, we have exalted the right of citizens to sit on juries over the rights of the criminal defendant, even though it is the defendant, not the jurors, who faces imprisonment or even death. At a minimum, I think that this inversion of priorities should give us pause.

Does this case give *you* pause? Is there a principled basis for arguing that defense attorneys should not be held to the same standard as prosecutors?

Reconsider the facts in *United States v. Huey* (end of Note 3, *supra*) but assume instead that the *prosecutor* in that case intended to introduce taped statements in which a white *defendant* is heard uttering racial epithets. Should the *defense* be permitted to use its peremptories to exclude African-Americans for the reasons quoted in the Note?

15. *Batson and peremptories based on religion.* Since peremptory challenges based on race and gender are subject to special rules, are peremptory strikes based on religious affiliation subject to the same special scrutiny? The Supreme Court has not yet ruled on this question. Lower courts are split on the issue. *E.g.*, United States v. Brown, 352 F.3d 654 (2d

Cir. 2003) (*Batson* principles apply); State v. Purcell, 199 Ariz. 319, 18 P.3d 113 (Ct. App. 2001) (same); State v. Hodge, 248 Conn. 207, 726 A.2d 531 (1999) (same); *contra* United States v. DeJesus, 347 F.3d 500 (3d Cir. 2003); Casarez v. State, 913 S.W.2d 468 (Tex. Crim. App. 1994) (en banc); State v. Davis 504 N.W.2d 767 (Minn. 1993).

16. *Batson and peremptories based on sexual orientation.* The United States Supreme Court has not considered the question of whether the principles of *Batson* apply to peremptory challenges based on sexual orientation.

In SmithKline Beecham Corp. v. Abbott Labs., 740 F.3d 471 (9th Cir. 2014**)**, *rehearing en banc denied*, 759 F.3d 990 (2014), however, the Ninth Circuit held, 3–0, that striking a prospective male juror because of his sexual orientation (he was gay), in a civil trial about alleged price-fixing in HIV medications, violated the Equal Protection Clause as applied in *Batson*. Judge Reinhardt concluded that recent Supreme Court decisions pertaining to sexual orientation suggested that this classification is entitled to "heightened scrutiny." It unequivocally extended the scope of *Batson* to sexual orientation.

17. *Peremptories after Batson.* In light of *Batson* and its progeny, should peremptories be abolished, as called for by Justice Marshall? Or, is abolition of peremptories too great a loss to bear? In Miller-El v. Dretke, 545 U.S. 231, 125 S.Ct. 2317, 162 L.Ed.2d 196 (2005), Justice Breyer joined Justice Marshall's camp on this issue:

> In his separate opinion [in *Batson*], Justice Thurgood Marshall predicted that the Court's rule would not achieve its goal. The only way to "end the racial discrimination that peremptories inject into the jury-selection process," he concluded, was to "eliminate peremptory challenges entirely." Today's case reinforces Justice Marshall's concerns.

> To begin with, this case illustrates the practical problems of proof that Justice Marshall described. As the Court's [fact-intensive] opinion makes clear, Miller-El marshaled extensive evidence of racial bias. But despite the strength of his claim, Miller-El's challenge has resulted in 17 years of largely unsuccessful and protracted litigation—including 8 different judicial proceedings and 8 different judicial opinions, and involving 23 judges, of whom 6 found the *Batson* standard violated and 16 the contrary.

> The complexity of this process reflects the difficulty of finding a legal test that will objectively measure the inherently subjective reasons that underlie use of a peremptory challenge. * * *

> At *Batson*'s first step, litigants remain free to misuse peremptory challenges as long as the strikes fall *below* the prima facie threshold level.

At *Batson*'s second step, prosecutors need only tender a neutral reason, not a "persuasive, or even plausible" one. And most importantly, at step three, *Batson* asks judges to engage in the awkward, sometime hopeless, task of second-guessing a prosecutor's instinctive judgment—the underlying basis for which may be invisible even to the prosecutor exercising the challenge. In such circumstances, it may be impossible for trial courts to discern if a " 'seat-of-the-pants' " peremptory challenge reflects a " 'seat-of-the-pants' " racial stereotype.

Given the inevitably clumsy fit between any objectively measurable standard and the subjective decisionmaking at issue, I am not surprised to find studies and anecdotal reports suggesting that, despite *Batson*, the discriminatory use of peremptory challenges remains a problem.

Practical problems of proof to the side, peremptory challenges seem increasingly anomalous in our judicial system. On the one hand, the Court has widened and deepened *Batson*'s basic constitutional rule. It has applied *Batson*'s antidiscrimination test to the use of peremptories by criminal defendants, by private litigants in civil cases, and by prosecutors where the defendant and the excluded juror are of different races. It has recognized that the Constitution protects not just defendants, but the jurors themselves. And it has held that equal protection principles prohibit excusing jurors on account of gender.

On the other hand, the use of race-and gender-based stereotypes in the jury-selection process seems better organized and more systematized than ever before. For example, one jury-selection guide counsels attorneys to perform a "demographic analysis" that assigns numerical points to characteristics such as age, occupation, and marital status—in addition to race as well as gender. See V. Starr & A. McCormick, Jury Selection 193–200 (3d ed. 2001). Thus, in a hypothetical dispute between a white landlord and an African-American tenant, the authors suggest awarding two points to an African-American venire member while subtracting one point from her white counterpart. * * *

For example, a trial consulting firm advertises a new jury-selection technology: "Whether you are trying a civil case or a criminal case, SmartJURY TM has likely determined the exact demographics (age, race, gender, education, occupation, marital status, number of children, religion, and income) of the type of jurors you should select and the type you should strike."

These examples reflect a professional effort to fulfill the lawyer's obligation to help his or her client. Nevertheless, the outcome in terms of jury selection is the same as it would be were the motive less benign. And as long as that is so, the law's antidiscrimination command and a peremptory jury-selection system that permits or encourages the use of stereotypes work at cross-purposes.

Finally, a jury system without peremptories is no longer unthinkable. Members of the legal profession have begun serious consideration of that possibility. And England, a common-law jurisdiction that has eliminated peremptory challenges, continues to administer fair trials based largely on random jury selection.

I recognize that peremptory challenges have a long historical pedigree. They may help to reassure a party of the fairness of the jury. But long ago, Blackstone recognized the peremptory challenge as an "arbitrary and capricious species of [a] challenge." If used to express stereotypical judgments about race, gender, religion, or national origin, peremptory challenges betray the jury's democratic origins and undermine its representative function. * * *

* * * In light of the considerations I have mentioned, I believe it necessary to reconsider *Batson*'s test and the peremptory challenge system as a whole.

If peremptory challenges *were* abolished, what changes (if any) in the jury selection process would be necessary to accommodate their abolition?

3. JURY NULLIFICATION

UNITED STATES v. THOMAS
United States Court of Appeals, Second Circuit, 1997.
116 F.3d 606.

JOSE A. CABRANES, CIRCUIT JUDGE.

We consider here the propriety of the district court's dismissal of a juror allegedly engaged in "nullification"—the intentional disregard of the law as stated by the presiding judge—during the course of deliberations. We address, in turn, (1) whether such alleged misconduct constitutes "just cause" for dismissal of a deliberating juror under Rule 23(b) of the Federal Rules of Criminal Procedure ("Rule 23(b)")[1], so that a jury of only eleven persons may continue to deliberate and return a verdict, and (2)

---

[1] Fed.R.Crim.P. 23(b) [since amended in form, but not changed in substance—Eds.] provides:

> *Jury of Less Than Twelve.* Juries shall be of 12 but at any time before verdict the parties may stipulate in writing with the approval of the court that the jury shall consist of any number less than 12 or that a valid verdict may be returned by a jury of less than 12 should the court find it necessary to excuse one or more jurors for any just cause after trial commences. Even absent such stipulation, if the court finds it necessary to excuse a juror for just cause *after the jury has retired to consider its verdict,* in the discretion of the court a valid verdict may be returned by the remaining 11 jurors. (Emphasis supplied.)

what evidentiary standard must be met to support a dismissal on this ground.

The appellants are * * * defendants convicted of violations of federal narcotics laws after two separate trials in the United States District Court for the Northern District of New York (Thomas J. McAvoy, *Chief Judge*). * * *

I. * * *

During jury selection, the Government attempted to exercise a peremptory challenge to a juror who would later be empaneled as "Juror No. 5." Because the juror was black—indeed, the only black person remaining as a potential juror in a case in which, as the record indicates, all of the defendants are black—defense counsel objected to the peremptory challenge under *Batson v. Kentucky* [p. 1249], as racially motivated. The Government responded that it wished to exclude the juror based not on his race, but on the fact that he failed to make eye contact with the Government's counsel during the *voir dire*. Although the district court explicitly found that the Government's peremptory challenge was not motivated by race, the court, in a misapplication of *Batson*, nevertheless denied the challenge on the ground that the juror's failure to make eye contact was an insufficient basis for his removal. The court would later explain that Juror No. 5's status as the only black juror in a case involving black defendants had motivated its decision to deny the Government's challenge.

Problems regarding Juror No. 5 did not end with his selection for the jury, however. During the course of defense summations on Friday, February 17, 1995, following several weeks of trial, a group of six jurors approached the courtroom clerk to express their concerns about the juror. The six jurors complained that Juror No. 5 was distracting them in court by squeaking his shoe against the floor, rustling cough drop wrappers in his pocket, and showing agreement with points made by defense counsel by slapping his leg and, occasionally during the defense summations, saying "[y]eah, yes."

Chief Judge McAvoy met with counsel in chambers to discuss the complaints about Juror No. 5. The judge raised the possibility of conducting interviews with each member of the jury to determine the extent to which Juror No. 5 was distracting them from their duties. Alternatively, he considered dismissing Juror No. 5 in favor of an alternate juror pursuant to Fed.R.Crim.24(c). While the Government approved of the idea of interviewing the jurors, and dismissing Juror No. 5 if the interviews revealed that his behavior was disturbing other members of the jury, defense counsel generally opposed both options, preferring that the court permit summations to continue with only a general instruction to the jurors that they were not to form any opinions before starting their deliberations. * * *

* * * [T]he court followed the procedure recommended by the Government. Without counsel present, the court conducted *in camera*, on-the-record interviews with each juror to determine the extent of any distraction resulting from Juror No. 5's behavior in the jury box. Quite appropriately, the court began each interview with a general inquiry as to whether anything had happened during the course of trial that would interfere with the juror's ability to deliberate and decide the case properly; the court did not ask about Juror No. 5's behavior unless the interviewee first raised the issue. Although seven of the jurors indicated that Juror No. 5 was a source of some distraction, all but one, who "thought possibly" that she would experience problems during deliberations because of Juror No. 5, anticipated nothing that would interfere with their own ability to deliberate. For his part, Juror No. 5 explained to the court that he sometimes got "carried away" in listening to the attorneys' arguments, but he stated that he would have no difficulty in applying the law as set out by the court to the evidence presented at trial. He also assured the court that he would "restrain [him]self" from engaging in any further distracting behavior.

After completing his *in camera* interviews, Chief Judge McAvoy met with counsel in chambers. He * * * expressed his intention, based on these interviews, to remove Juror No. 5 in favor of one of the alternate jurors. The judge indicated that he was concerned that Juror No. 5's behavior, especially in light of the court's own inquiries of the jurors, might place him in an adversarial relationship with his fellow jurors as they began deliberations. * * * The Government agreed with the court's proposal to remove Juror No. 5, but the proposed dismissal met with unanimous opposition from defense counsel. Apparently persuaded by the defense's vigorous objections, the judge reconsidered the matter and decided to retain Juror No. 5 on the panel. Following the court's meeting with counsel, summations concluded, and the court charged the jury that same day.

The jury deliberated throughout the day on February 22. On February 23, the courtroom clerk reported to the court, and then on the record to all counsel, that she had been approached on two separate occasions earlier in the day by jurors expressing concern over the course of their deliberations. Juror No. 1 reportedly had indicated to the clerk that deliberations were likely to continue beyond February 23 because of a "problem with an unnamed juror." That same morning, Juror No. 12 had also reported to the clerk "that there was a problem * * * in the jury room [with] one of their number, and specifically * * * indicated [that] juror number five, had, at each time a vote was taken, voted not guilty and had indicated verbally that he would not change his mind." The court concluded, after hearing argument from counsel for the parties, that no action was immediately necessary; the court would "give it a little more time to see what develops."

Troubles in the jury room seemed to escalate rapidly, however. On the following morning, February 24, the court received a note from Juror No. 6, apparently written only on his own behalf. The note indicated that, due to Juror No. 5's "predisposed disposition," the jury was unable to reach a verdict. * * * [T]he court again conducted *in camera*, on-the-record interviews with each of the jurors outside the presence of counsel. This time, jurors focused their comments more directly on Juror No. 5. Several mentioned the disruptive effect he was having on the deliberations. One juror described him "hollering" at fellow jurors, another said he had called his fellow jurors racists, and two jurors told the court that Juror No. 5 had come close to striking a fellow juror. The judge was also informed by a juror that, at one point, Juror No. 5 pretended to vomit in the bathroom while other jurors were eating lunch outside the bathroom door. The jurors, however, were not unanimous in identifying Juror No. 5 as a source of disruption in the jury room. One juror informed the judge that friction among the jurors had been "pretty well ironed out," and another indicated that the other jurors were in fact "picking on" Juror No. 5.

Although the district court did not specifically inquire into any juror's position on the merits of the case, at least five of the jurors indicated that Juror No. 5 was unyieldingly in favor of acquittal for all of the defendants. The accounts differed, however, regarding the *basis* for Juror No. 5's position. On the one hand, one juror described Juror No. 5 as favoring acquittal because the defendants were his "people," another suggested that it was because Juror No. 5 thought the defendants were good people, two others stated that Juror No. 5 simply believed that drug dealing is commonplace, and another two jurors indicated that Juror No. 5 favored acquittal because he thought that the defendants had engaged in the alleged criminal activity out of economic necessity. On the other hand, several jurors recounted Juror No. 5 couching his position in terms of the evidence—one juror indicated specifically that Juror No. 5 was discussing the evidence, and four recalled him saying that the evidence, including the testimony of the prosecution's witnesses, was insufficient or unreliable. As for Juror No. 5, he said nothing in his interview with the court to suggest that he was not making a good faith effort to apply the law as instructed to the facts of the case. On the contrary, he informed the court that he needed "substantive evidence" establishing guilt "beyond a reasonable doubt" in order to convict.

After interviewing the jurors, the judge met in chambers with counsel for the parties. * * * The Government argued that the jurors' responses indicated that there was "almost a jury nullification issue pattern with [Juror No. 5]," and urged the court to order the juror's dismissal, while defense counsel unanimously opposed his removal. Having heard argument from counsel, the judge rendered his decision to remove Juror No. 5. He believed that Juror No. 5 had become a "distraction" and a "focal point" for the jury's attention, and that his removal might "allow [the jury] to deliberate in a full and a fair fashion." The court cited Juror No. 5's failure to live up to his assurances regarding proper conduct, referring in particular to the allegation that he nearly struck another juror and to his feigned vomiting. Most importantly, however, the court found that Juror No. 5 was ignoring the evidence in favor of his own, preconceived ideas about the case:

> I believe after hearing everything that [Juror No. 5's] motives are immoral, that he believes that these folks have a right to deal drugs, because they don't have any money, they are in a disadvantaged situation and probably that's the thing to do. And I don't think he would convict them no matter what the evidence was.

The court found that Juror No. 5 was refusing to convict "because of preconceived, fixed, cultural, economic, [or] social * * * reasons that are totally improper and impermissible."

The court then called Juror No. 5 into chambers to inform him of his dismissal and, that afternoon, announced the dismissal to the remaining jurors. Jurors were instructed that they were "to draw no inferences or conclusions whatsoever" from the removal and told that they were to start over in their deliberations.

On the afternoon of the following Monday, February 27, 1995, the remaining eleven jurors returned a [guilty] verdict. * * *

II. * * *

Language was added in 1983 to Rule 23(b) to provide a court with the unilateral authority to remove jurors during the course of deliberations. Prior to that time, Rule 23(b) required the consent of all parties in order for the trial court to dismiss one or more jurors, and to allow the remaining jurors to proceed to a verdict. As explained in the Note of the Advisory Committee on the Federal Rules of Criminal Procedure ("Advisory Committee"), the 1983 amendment was a response to cases in which, after a trial of significant length and involving substantial expense, a juror became "seriously incapacitated or [was] otherwise found to be unable to continue service upon the jury." The amendment provides an alternative short of mistrial in such cases, and it does so without calling for the use of alternate jurors once deliberations have begun, an option that the Advisory Committee expressly rejected. * * *

"Just cause" is not limited to instances of juror illness or unavailability, however. Courts have also found "just cause" to dismiss jurors who, although available and physically capable of serving, are nonetheless found to be unable to perform their duties properly. In particular, Rule 23(b) dismissals have been upheld repeatedly in cases where the trial court found that a juror was no longer capable of rendering an impartial verdict. These cases have involved instances of jurors who felt threatened by one of the parties, who are discovered to have a relationship with one of the parties, or whose life circumstances otherwise change during the course of deliberations in such a way that they are no longer considered capable of rendering an impartial verdict, *see United States v. Egbuniwe*, 969 F.2d 757, 762–63 (9th Cir. 1992) (juror "might not be able to be fair to both parties" after learning that girlfriend had been arrested and mistreated by police). * * *

Here, Chief Judge McAvoy identified a different form of bias as the primary ground for dismissing Juror No. 5—one arising not from an external event or from a relationship between a juror and a party, but rather, from a more general opposition to the application of the criminal narcotics laws to the defendants' conduct. * * *

We take this occasion to restate some basic principles regarding the character of our jury system. Nullification is, by definition, a violation of a juror's oath to apply the law as instructed by the court—in the words of the standard oath administered to jurors in the federal courts, to "render a true verdict *according to the law and the evidence.*" We categorically reject the idea that, in a society committed to the rule of law, jury nullification is desirable or that courts may permit it to occur when it is within their authority to prevent. Accordingly, we conclude that a juror who intends to nullify the applicable law is no less subject to dismissal than is a juror who disregards the court's instructions due to an event or relationship that renders him biased or otherwise unable to render a fair and impartial verdict.

We are mindful that the term "nullification" can cover a number of distinct, though related, phenomena, encompassing in one word conduct that takes place for a variety of different reasons; jurors may nullify, for example, because of the identity of a party, a disapprobation of the particular prosecution at issue, or a more general opposition to the applicable criminal law or laws. We recognize, too, that nullification may at times manifest itself as a form of civil disobedience that some may regard as tolerable. The case of John Peter Zenger, the publisher of the *New York Weekly Journal* acquitted of criminal libel in 1735, and the nineteenth-century acquittals in prosecutions under the fugitive slave laws, are perhaps our country's most renowned examples of "benevolent" nullification. * * *

But, * * * the power of juries to "nullify" or exercise a power of lenity is just that—a power; it is by no means a right or something that a judge

should encourage or permit if it is within his authority to prevent. * * *
As a panel of the Court of Appeals for the District of Columbia Circuit—
composed of Chief Judge Spottswood W. Robinson, III, Judge George E.
MacKinnon, and then-Judge Ruth Bader Ginsburg—explained:

> A jury has no more *"right"* to find a "guilty" defendant "not
> guilty" than it has to find a "not guilty" defendant guilty, and the
> fact that the former cannot be corrected by a court, while the
> latter can be, does not create a right out of the power to misapply
> the law. Such verdicts are lawless, a denial of due process and
> constitute an exercise of erroneously seized power.

United States v. Washington, 705 F.2d 489, 494 (D.C. Cir. 1983) (per
curiam) (emphasis in original). * * *

Moreover, although the early history of our country includes the
occasional *Zenger* trial or acquittals in fugitive slave cases, more recent
history presents numerous and notorious examples of jurors nullifying—
cases that reveal the destructive potential of a practice Professor Randall
Kennedy of the Harvard Law School has rightly termed a "sabotage of
justice." * * * Consider, for example, the two hung juries in the 1964 trials
of Byron De La Beckwith in Mississippi for the murder of NAACP field
secretary Medgar Evers, or the 1955 acquittal of J.W. Millam and Roy
Bryant for the murder of fourteen-year-old Emmett Till—shameful
examples of how nullification has been used to sanction murder and
lynching.

Inasmuch as no juror has a right to engage in nullification—and, on
the contrary, it is a violation of a juror's sworn duty to follow the law as
instructed by the court—trial courts have the duty to forestall or prevent
such conduct, whether by firm instruction or admonition or, where it does
not interfere with guaranteed rights or the need to protect the secrecy of
jury deliberations, by dismissal of an offending juror from the venire or
the jury. * * *

The extent to which a presiding judge may investigate alleged juror
bias or misconduct differs depending on when the investigation takes
place. In particular, * * * a district court's authority to investigate
allegations of juror impropriety necessarily becomes more limited once
the jury has begun to deliberate. Once a jury retires to the deliberation
room, the presiding judge's duty to dismiss jurors for misconduct comes
into conflict with a duty that is equally, if not more, important—
safeguarding the secrecy of jury deliberations. * * *

Courts face a delicate and complex task whenever they undertake to
investigate reports of juror misconduct or bias during the course of a trial.
This undertaking is particularly sensitive where, as here, the court
endeavors to investigate allegations of juror misconduct during
deliberations. As a general rule, no one—including the judge presiding at

a trial—has a "right to know" how a jury, or any individual juror, has deliberated or how a decision was reached by a jury or juror. The secrecy of deliberations is the cornerstone of the modern Anglo-American jury system. * * * Indeed, courts and commentators alike recognize that the secrecy of deliberations is essential to the proper functioning of juries. It is well understood, for example, that disclosure of the substance of jury deliberations may undermine public confidence in the jury system, and poses a threat to adjudicatory finality. Especially troublesome is the danger that such disclosure presents to the operation of the deliberative process itself. * * * "Freedom of debate," as Justice Cardozo wrote, "might be stifled and independence of thought checked if jurors were made to feel that their arguments and ballots were to be freely published to the world." * * *

Because the rule of secrecy is fundamental to the effective operation of the jury system, it is not surprising that courts have been concerned to maintain the confidentiality of the process even after a verdict has been returned and the jury has been formally discharged. * * *

Today, it is common—and entirely appropriate—for a conscientious trial judge to advise jurors against disclosing the substance of their deliberations after the end of a trial. At times, courts quite properly go further than this to protect the secrecy of deliberations, imposing strict limitations on what jurors are permitted to disclose. In addition, many federal judicial districts have enacted rules that subject post-verdict juror interviews to judicial supervision. While these rules often apply only to parties and their counsel, some federal districts have adopted rules that extend the court's supervisory authority to *any* post-verdict interviews of jurors. None of this is to suggest that we cannot do more to protect the secrecy of deliberations. One eminent authority, for example, has proposed a statute that would impose criminal sanctions on jurors who disclose information about their deliberations, as well as on anyone who seeks such disclosure, without permission of the court. * * *

Protecting the deliberative process requires not only a vigilant watch against external threats to juror secrecy, but also strict limitations on intrusions from those who participate in the trial process itself, including counsel and the presiding judge. A court must limit its own inquiries of jurors once deliberations have begun. As the district court observed in the instant case, the very act of judicial investigation can at times be expected to foment discord among jurors. In particular, a presiding judge is limited in the extent to which he may investigate the reasons underlying a juror's position on the merits of a case. *United States v. Brown*, 823 F.2d 591, 596 (D.C. Cir. 1987). The mental processes of a deliberating juror with respect to the merits of the case at hand must remain largely beyond examination and second-guessing, shielded from scrutiny by the court as much as from the eyes and ears of the parties and the public. Were a district judge permitted to conduct intrusive inquiries into—and make extensive findings of fact concerning—the reasoning behind a juror's view of the case, or the particulars of a juror's (likely imperfect) understanding or interpretation of the law as stated by the judge, this would not only seriously breach the principle of the secrecy of jury deliberations, but it would invite trial judges to second-guess and influence the work of the jury.

In many cases, a presiding judge is able to determine whether there is "just cause" to dismiss a deliberating juror without *any* inquiry into the juror's thoughts on the merits of the case. Evidence of the nature and extent of a juror's unavailability, or incapacitation, for example, is ordinarily available without inquiring into the substance of deliberations. In such instances, the judge is free to conduct a thorough examination of the basis for removal—a basis that is itself unlikely to be confused with a juror's views of the sufficiency of the evidence—and to make appropriate findings of fact, including determinations of the credibility of the juror in question.

[The court gave, as one example, *Egbuniwe, supra*, where the juror learned that his girlfriend had been arrested and mistreated by the police. In that kind of case, the court said, the source of "possible bias" was "subject to ready identification."—Eds.] * * *

Where, however, as here, a presiding judge receives reports that a deliberating juror is intent on defying the court's instructions on the law, the judge may well have no means of investigating the allegation without unduly breaching the secrecy of deliberations. There is no allegedly prejudicial event or relationship at issue, nor is the court being asked to assess whether a juror is so upset or otherwise distracted that he is unable to carry out his duties. Rather, to determine whether a juror is bent on defiant disregard of the applicable law, the court would generally need to intrude into the juror's thought processes. Such an investigation must be subject to strict limitations. Without such an inquiry, however, the court will have little evidence with which to make the often difficult distinction between the juror who favors acquittal because he is purposefully disregarding the court's instructions on the law, and the juror who is simply unpersuaded by the Government's evidence. Yet this distinction is a critical one, for to remove a juror because he is unpersuaded by the Government's case is to deny the defendant his right to a unanimous verdict. In a case involving a juror's own request to be dismissed from duty because of what the prosecution interpreted to be an unwillingness to apply the law as instructed, Judge Mikva, in an opinion joined by Judge Bork and Judge Douglas H. Ginsburg, observed:

> [A] court may not delve deeply into a juror's motivations because it may not intrude on the secrecy of the jury's deliberations.

Thus, unless the initial request for [a juror's] dismissal is transparent, the court will likely prove unable to establish conclusively the reasons underlying it. Given these circumstances, we must hold that *if the record evidence discloses any possibility that the request to discharge stems from the juror's view of the sufficiency of the government's evidence, the court must deny the request.*

[*Brown, supra*]

We adopt the *Brown* rule as an appropriate limitation on a juror's dismissal *in any case* where the juror allegedly refuses to follow the law—whether the juror himself requests to be discharged from duty or, as in the instant case, fellow jurors raise allegations of this form of misconduct. Given the necessary limitations on a court's investigatory authority in cases involving a juror's alleged refusal to follow the law, a lower evidentiary standard could lead to the removal of jurors on the basis of their view of the sufficiency of the prosecution's evidence.

Consider a case where, for example, a strong majority of the jury favors conviction, but a small set of jurors—perhaps just one—disagrees. The group of jurors favoring conviction may well come to view the "holdout" or "holdouts" not only as unreasonable, but as unwilling to follow the court's instructions on the law. The evidentiary standard that we endorse today—that "if the record evidence discloses any possibility that" a complaint about a juror's conduct "stems from the juror's view of the sufficiency of the government's evidence, the court must deny the request"—serves to protect these holdouts from fellow jurors who have come to the conclusion that the holdouts are acting lawlessly.

This evidentiary standard protects not only against the wrongful removal of jurors; it also serves to protect against overly intrusive judicial inquiries into the substance of the jury's deliberations. A presiding judge faced with anything but unambiguous evidence that a juror refuses to apply the law as instructed need go no further in his investigation of the alleged nullification; in such circumstances, the juror is not subject to dismissal on the basis of his alleged refusal to follow the court's instructions. * * *

We recognize that this standard—buttressing the core principle of the secrecy of jury deliberations—leaves open the possibility that jurors will engage in irresponsible activity that will remain outside the court's powers to investigate or correct. It is an imperfect rule, no doubt, but one fully consistent with our history and traditions, in which the judge's duty and authority to prevent nullification and the need for jury secrecy co-exist uneasily. * * *

* * * [W]e cannot uphold the dismissal [of Juror No. 5]. Juror No. 5 said nothing to the court to indicate that he was unwilling to follow the

court's instructions. On the contrary, he assured the court that his vote was based on his view of the evidence: "I want substantive evidence against them * * * and I want to know that it's clear in my mind beyond a reasonable doubt." Nor was this statement without corroboration from fellow jurors. Several of the jurors indicated in their interviews with the court that Juror No. 5 justified his position during deliberations in terms of the evidence—that he found the Government's evidence, including its witness testimony, insufficient or unreliable. On this record, we cannot say that it is beyond doubt that Juror No. 5's position during deliberations was the result of his defiant unwillingness to apply the law, as opposed to his reservations about the sufficiency of the Government's case against the defendants. * * *

We need not reach the question of whether the court's inquiries were themselves sufficiently intrusive to constitute reversible error. Moreover, we do not decide here whether it would have been within the district court's discretion to dismiss Juror No. 5 for his distracting behavior, pursuant to Rule 24(c), after the first round of *in camera* interviews but *before* the jury began its deliberations. Finally, we do not suggest, much less hold, that a juror's disruptive behavior—his reported "hollering," threatening to strike a fellow juror, or feigned vomiting—could not serve as grounds for dismissal, but we conclude that, in the circumstances presented here, the juror was removed largely for his allegedly nullifying behavior. * * *

NOTES AND QUESTIONS

1.   Consider some of the explanations given for Juror No. 5's refusal to convict: that the defendants were "his people"; that they were "good people"; that drug dealing is commonplace; that the defendants acted out of economic necessity; and that he did not believe the testimony of the prosecution's witnesses. Do any or all of these explanations constitute "juror nullification"?

Suppose that Juror No. 5 had stated, "I don't believe the Government's witnesses because they are police, and the police always lie." Is this nullification? What if he says, "The defendants had a terrible home life; therefore, they are not culpable for their actions; so I refuse to convict." Nullification? What if he says, "Sure they did it, but the Government seems to be singling out African-Americans for discriminatory conduct, and that isn't fair."

2.   *Pro-nullification.* Consider the following observations:

It is not by chance that the jury has the power to issue an unreviewable general verdict of acquittal; it is a considered decision that the people should apply laws when criminal punishment is at stake to ensure that an individual does not lose her liberty unless it would be just in a particular case. * * * Trial by jury "gives protection against laws which the ordinary man may regard as harsh and oppressive" and provides "insurance that the criminal law will conform to the ordinary man's idea of what is fair and just."

Rachel E. Barkow, *Recharging the Jury: The Criminal Jury's Constitutional Role in an Era of Mandatory Sentencing*, 152 U. Pa. L. Rev. 33, 59 (2003).

> The role of the criminal jury * * * involves even more than reliable factfinding and republican self-government. It also involves normative judgment. * * * Criminal trials are unavoidably morality plays, focusing on the defendant's moral blameworthiness or lack thereof. And the assessment of his moral culpability is, under the Sixth Amendment, a test for the community, via the jury * * * . No man who claims innocence can be condemned as guilty unless the community, via the jury, pronounces him worthy of moral condemnation.

Akhil Reed Amar, *Sixth Amendment First Principles*, 84 Geo. L.J. 641, 685 (1996).

If these observations are correct, isn't jury nullification an inherent—and desirable—feature of trial by jury?

3. *Anti-nullification.* Consider the following observations:

> If it were taken seriously by mainstream Americans, jury nullification would threaten to unravel the fabric of our democracy. The impropriety of nullification emanates from the notion that ours is "a government of laws and not of men." This means simply that no citizen is above the law, and none is free to make his own law. As Thomas Paine stated in *Common Sense*, "For as in absolute governments the king is law, so in free countries the law ought to be king; and there ought to be no other." * * *

> The notion that nullification will change the law is drivel. Those who would characterize it as a noble form of civil disobedience are deeply delusional. Under the theory of civil disobedience followed by Gandhi and Dr. Martin Luther King, Jr., it is only appropriate to disobey the law if one does so publicly, in an effort to change the law, and then accepts the punishment. As Dr. King explained in his Letter from Birmingham Jail, "In no sense do I advocate evading or defying the law. * * * That would lead to anarchy. One who breaks an unjust law must do so openly, lovingly, and with a willingness to accept the penalty." Nullifiers do not openly disobey the law in order to change it. They conspire behind closed doors and cast the law aside at their caprice. This is not civil disobedience; it is anarchy. One who engages in such a practice cannot hope to change the law, but only displace laws altogether. * * *

> Nullification frustrates the sole purpose of the jury. As this Court has instructed juries for some thirty years now, the word verdict comes from two Latin words meaning roughly "to speak the

truth." Nullifiers, however, would render verdicts without regard to the truth. Once juries begin to deviate from this core function, our justice system has no more legitimacy than a Kangaroo court.

United States v. Luisi, 568 F.Supp.2d 106 (D. Mass. 2008).

In light of these remarks and those in the preceding Note, what do *you* think about jury nullification, and why?

4.   *Race-based jury nullification.* Professor Paul Butler, a former Special Assistant United States Attorney in the District of Columbia, has proposed race-based jury nullification. Under his proposal, black jurors should *not* nullify the law in cases involving black defendants charged with violent crimes, such as murder, rape, and assault; they should "consider the case strictly on the evidence presented, and, if they have no reason to doubt that the defendant is guilty, they should convict." However,

> [f]or nonviolent * * * crimes such as theft or perjury, nullification is an option that the juror should consider, although there should be no presumption in favor of it. A jury might vote for acquittal, for example, when a poor woman steals from Tiffany's, but not when the same woman steals from her next-door neighbor. Finally, in cases involving nonviolent *malum prohibitum* offenses, including "victimless" crimes likes narcotics offenses, there should be a presumption in favor of nullification.

Paul Butler, *Racially Based Jury Nullification: Black Power in the Criminal Justice System*, 105 Yale L.J. 677, 715 (1995).

What do you think of the proposal? In a recent speech, Professor Butler explained his position this way:

> I teach criminal law. My students learned that prison is for people who are the most dangerous and the most immoral in our society. Is there anyone here who really believes that over half of the most immoral and dangerous people in the United States are African-American when they constitute only 12 percent of the population? When I look at those statistics, I think that punishment, prison, and criminal law have become the way that we treat the problems of the poor, especially poor African-American people. I think that is immoral. I am confident that one day we, as a society, will understand that, but African-American people cannot afford to wait that long. * * *
>
> Now, to prevent that kind of "just us" justice, I advocate a program of black self-help outside and inside the courtroom. Outside the courtroom self-help includes the kind of community-building efforts that many of us are already engaged in: mentoring, tutoring, after-school programs, providing legal and medical care to the poor, working with inmates, and taking better care of our families. * * * Inside the courtroom self-help includes the responsible use of prosecutorial discretion, especially by black

prosecutors. It also includes selective jury nullification for victimless crimes. * * *

Now, I am a former prosecutor. Nullification is a partial cure that I come to reluctantly and for moral reasons. To me it is not enough to say that there is a power to nullify; there also has to be some moral basis for this power. In the [*Yale*] article I make several moral claims as to the power. I am going to quickly tell you about two.

One is this phenomenon of democratic domination. * * * The reason why I believe that African-American jurors have a moral claim to selective nullification is based on this idea that they do not effectively have a say; they do not have the say that they should in the making of the law. They are the victims of the tyranny of the majority. * * *

The [other] moral claim African-Americans have to the power of jury nullification is what I call the symbolic role of black jurors. If you look at Supreme Court cases, they often have the occasion to discuss black jurors. They do so because of our country's sad history of excluding black people from juries. The Court said that is a bad thing because black jurors serve this symbolic function. Essentially they symbolize the fairness and the impartiality of the law. * * *

* * * What about an African-American juror who endorses racial critiques of the American criminal justice system? She does not hold any confidence in the integrity of the system. So if she is aware of the implicit message that the Supreme Court says her presence sends, maybe she does not want to be the vehicle for that message. * * *

Paul D. Butler, *Race-Based Jury Nullification: Case-in-Chief*, 30 J. Marshall L. Rev. 911, 912–13, 918–21 (1997).

Professor Andrew Leipold criticized Professor Butler's proposal in Andrew D. Leipold, *The Dangers of Race-Based Jury Nullification: A Response to Professor Butler*, 44 UCLA L. Rev. 109 (1996). He summarized a few of his criticisms in a response to the Butler speech excerpted above:

Let me briefly outline a few of my concerns about Professor Butler's plan. The first two are technical, lawyer-type arguments. The last two address philosophical concerns I have about his proposal.

The first technical point involves the impact of Professor Butler's proposal on the makeup of juries. * * * It is critically important to have juries that are reflective of community sentiments and community norms. Given this, we should ask ourselves what juries will look like if large numbers of African-American potential jurors were to embrace the Butler plan.

I think the answer, without a doubt, is that there would be fewer African-Americans seated on juries than there are today. This is true for a couple reasons. As most of you know, the Supreme Court has said that a lawyer may not use a peremptory strike to remove a person from a jury panel because of the juror's race or sex. If a party appears to be using peremptory challenges in this manner, the judge can require the lawyer to give a race-neutral explanation for the strikes. * * *

On the other hand, either party can have a person removed from a jury panel for cause if that juror indicates during *voir dire* that he or she will not follow the law contained in the instructions given by the judge. * * *

If potential African-American jurors were to embrace the Butler plan, and if they were honest during *voir dire*, their belief in jury nullification would at least give prosecutors a race-neutral explanation for removing these jurors with their peremptory strikes. In addition, if the jurors were candid in admitting that they came to the jury box with a very strong presumption of acquitting a defendant regardless of what the facts show, such jurors could almost certainly be removed for cause. Since there are no limits on the number of challenges for cause, every African-American juror who believed in race-based nullification might be excused in certain cases. The result would inevitably be juries that are less diverse; this surely can not be part of the solution that Professor Butler seeks.

My second technical argument is that juries are incapable of making reasoned nullification decisions, because at trial they will not be given the information they need. At the heart of Professor Butler's plan is the notion that juries should engage in a cost-benefit analysis when deciding whether to convict. Jurors are supposed to look at the defendant and ask, "Even if this defendant committed the crime charged, what are the rewards of keeping this person out of jail, and what are the risks to the community of letting this person stay free?" The problem is that juries will never hear the evidence that would help them answer this question.

Consider the problem in the context of a simple drug possession case. If we were sitting on a jury, what would we like to know about the defendant before we decided whether to nullify his conviction? We would probably want to know whether the defendant is contrite. We would want to know whether he had a criminal record, and if so, how serious were his prior crimes. We might want to know whether there was anyone else involved in the crime who is more blameworthy. We might wonder how the prosecution enforces this crime against others: are African-Americans disproportionately targeted or arrested for this type of crime? We might also want to know about the potential sentences the defendant would face if convicted; under our cost-benefit analysis, we might be more willing to nullify if the defendant faced a stiff, mandatory sentence.

The problem is that almost none of this information is admissible at trial. * * *

My philosophical concerns begin with the idea of legitimizing and institutionalizing a cost-benefit analysis as a method of jury decision-making. * * * Once we have agreed that jurors can legitimately decide the outcome of cases by a cost-benefit analysis rather than by applying the law as written to the evidence presented, we have started down a dangerous road. Is there any doubt that many other groups will also be drawn to the cost-benefit analysis? Although Professor Butler is careful to limit his plan to African-American jurors in cases where African-Americans are allegedly involved in nonviolent crimes, these are limits by fiat, not by logic.

* * * The problem with nullification is that once we tell a jury, directly or indirectly, that it is okay to engage in an uninformed cost-benefit analysis, we have no moral basis for complaining about any decision that a jury makes. * * *

The final concern I have is at the broadest philosophical level. It is a comment that makes me very sad to have to raise at all: whether you go to jail or get set free should not depend on the color of your skin. Using race as the reason for acquitting or convicting is a bad idea, and no matter how strategic the reasoning and no matter how good our intentions, it is still wrong. It is wrong because it encourages the kind of stereotyping that had led to problems in the first place. It is wrong because we are telling people that they will never get equal justice in the courts and so you should take whatever you can get, however you can get it, and be satisfied with that. In short, the plan raises the flag of surrender in the fight for equal justice under the law.

Andrew D. Leipold, *Race-Based Jury Nullification: Rebuttal (Part A)*, 30 J. Marshall L. Rev. 923, 923–26 (1997).

Professor Butler has responded to Professor Leipold's practical concern that the Butler proposal for race-based jury nullification will result in the exclusion of more African-Americans from jury panels. At least in some cases—he mentions death penalty and crack cocaine prosecutions of black defendants—Professor Butler contends that racial critics of the criminal justice system have the moral right to "lie to get on juries so that they can thwart the discriminatory application of those laws." Paul Butler, *By Any Means Necessary: Using Violence and Subversion to Change Unjust Law*, 50 UCLA L. Rev. 721, 771 (2003).

5. Since jurors have the raw power to nullify the law, and the double jeopardy clause bars reprosecution after an acquittal (Chapter 18) even if it is based on nullification, is a defendant entitled to an instruction informing the jurors of their power? Courts consistently answer this question in the negative. For example, consider *United States v. Dougherty*, 473 F.2d 1113 (D.C. Cir. 1972):

> The jury knows well enough that its prerogative is not limited to the choices articulated in the formal instructions of the court. * * * There is the informal communication from the total culture— literature * * * ; current comment (newspapers, magazines, and television); conversation; and, of course, history and tradition. The totality of input generally convey adequately enough the idea of [nullification].

Is the court's factual assumption correct? See David C. Brody and Craig Rivera, *Examining the Dougherty "All-Knowing Assumption": Do Jurors Know About Their Jury Nullification Power?*, 33 Crim. L. Bull. 151 (1997) (presenting the results of two studies that indicate that "a vast majority of individuals [do] not have an accurate knowledge of jury nullification").

Even if the jury is not informed of its power of nullification, should defendants be permitted to argue nullification to the jury in closing arguments? For example, should a lawyer in a statutory rape prosecution be permitted over objection, to say to the jury:

> Law as you know is not uniformly applied. I can see five cars speeding and the highway patrol is not likely to arrest any of the five. Mores, customs change. Times change. And the law must be applied fairly, that's why you need fair jurors. The right to jury trial is granted to criminal defendants in order to prevent oppression by the government. A jury may, at times, afford a higher justice by refusing to enforce harsh laws. Remember that.

People v. Williams, 25 Cal.4th 441, 106 Cal.Rptr.2d 295, 21 P.3d 1209 (2001).

6. In a federal prosecution of an eighteen-year-old defendant for advertising child pornography on the Internet, District Judge Gerard Lynch stated that "I don't intend to allow the defense to argue nullification. * * * I will instruct the jury, in the usual way, that if they find that the government has met its burden of proving all the elements [of the offense] beyond a reasonable doubt, then they must convict the defendant." But, he also stated that it was his intention to inform the jurors that he would be required by statute to impose a minimum ten-year prison sentence if they convicted the defendant of the charge. Should Judge Lynch be permitted to inform jurors of the lengthy sentence he would be required to impose? Why, or why not? United States v. Pabon-Cruz, 391 F.3d 86 (2d Cir. 2004).

B. RIGHT TO BE CONFRONTED WITH PROSECUTION WITNESSES

In all criminal prosecutions, the accused shall enjoy the right * * * to be confronted with the witnesses against him. U.S. Const. amend. VI.

1. FACE-TO-FACE CONFRONTATION

MARYLAND V. CRAIG

Supreme Court of the United States, 1990.
497 U.S. 836, 110 S.Ct. 3157, 111 L.Ed.2d 666.

JUSTICE O'CONNOR delivered the opinion of the Court [joined by CHIEF JUSTICE REHNQUIST and JUSTICES WHITE, BLACKMUN, and KENNEDY].

This case requires us to decide whether the Confrontation Clause of the Sixth Amendment categorically prohibits a child witness in a child abuse case from testifying against a defendant at trial, outside the defendant's physical presence, by one-way closed circuit television.

I

In October 1986, a Howard County grand jury charged respondent, Sandra Ann Craig, with child abuse, first and second degree sexual offenses, perverted sexual practice, assault, and battery. The named victim in each count was a 6-year-old girl who, from August 1984 to June 1986, had attended a kindergarten and prekindergarten center owned and operated by Craig.

In March 1987, before the case went to trial, the State sought to invoke a Maryland statutory procedure that permits a judge to receive, by one-way closed circuit television, the testimony of a child witness who is alleged to be a victim of child abuse. To invoke the procedure, the trial judge must first "determin[e] that testimony by the child victim in the courtroom will result in the child suffering serious emotional distress such that the child cannot reasonably communicate." Once the procedure is invoked, the child witness, prosecutor, and defense counsel withdraw to a separate room; the judge, jury, and defendant remain in the courtroom. The child witness is then examined and cross-examined in the separate room, while a video monitor records and displays the witness' testimony to those in the courtroom. During this time the witness cannot see the defendant. The defendant remains in electronic communication with defense counsel, and objections may be made and ruled on as if the witness were testifying in the courtroom. * * *

II

The Confrontation Clause of the Sixth Amendment, made applicable to the States through the Fourteenth Amendment, provides: "In all criminal prosecutions, the accused shall enjoy the right * * * to be confronted with the witnesses against him."

We observed in *Coy v. Iowa* [487 U.S. 1012, 108 S.Ct. 2798, 101 L.Ed.2d 857 (1988)] that "the Confrontation Clause guarantees the defendant a face-to-face meeting with witnesses appearing before the trier of fact." This interpretation derives not only from the literal text of the Clause, but also from our understanding of its historical roots.

We have never held, however, that the Confrontation Clause guarantees criminal defendants the *absolute* right to a face-to-face meeting with witnesses against them at trial. Indeed, in *Coy v. Iowa*, we expressly "le[ft] for another day * * * the question whether any exceptions exist" to the "irreducible literal meaning of the Clause: 'a right to *meet face to face* all those who appear and give evidence *at trial*.'" The procedure challenged in *Coy* involved the placement of a screen that prevented two child witnesses in a child abuse case from seeing the defendant as they testified against him at trial. In holding that the use of this procedure violated the defendant's right to confront witnesses against him, we suggested that any exception to the right "would surely be allowed only when necessary to further an important public policy"— *i.e.*, only upon a showing of something more than the generalized, "legislatively imposed presumption of trauma" underlying the statute at issue in that case. We concluded that "[s]ince there ha[d] been no individualized findings that these particular witnesses needed special protection, the judgment [in the case before us] could not be sustained by any conceivable exception." Because the trial court in this case made individualized findings that each of the child witnesses needed special protection, this case requires us to decide the question reserved in *Coy*.

The central concern of the Confrontation Clause is to ensure the reliability of the evidence against a criminal defendant by subjecting it to rigorous testing in the context of an adversary proceeding before the trier of fact. The word "confront," after all, also means a clashing of forces or ideas, thus carrying with it the notion of adversariness. As we noted in our earliest case interpreting the Clause:

> "The primary object of the constitutional provision in question was to prevent depositions or *ex parte* affidavits, such as were sometimes admitted in civil cases, being used against the prisoner in lieu of a personal examination and cross-examination of the witness in which the accused has an opportunity, not only of testing the recollection and sifting the conscience of the witness, but of compelling him to stand face to

face with the jury in order that they may look at him, and judge by his demeanor upon the stand and the manner in which he gives his testimony whether he is worthy of belief." *Mattox* [*v. United States*, 156 U.S. 237, 15 S.Ct. 337, 39 L.Ed. 409 (1895)].

As this description indicates, the right guaranteed by the Confrontation Clause includes not only a "personal examination," but also "(1) insures that the witness will give his statements under oath—thus impressing him with the seriousness of the matter and guarding against the lie by the possibility of a penalty for perjury; (2) forces the witness to submit to cross-examination, the 'greatest legal engine ever invented for the discovery of truth'; [and] (3) permits the jury that is to decide the defendant's fate to observe the demeanor of the witness in making his statement, thus aiding the jury in assessing his credibility."

The combined effect of these elements of confrontation—physical presence, oath, cross-examination, and observation of demeanor by the trier of fact—serves the purposes of the Confrontation Clause by ensuring that evidence admitted against an accused is reliable and subject to the rigorous adversarial testing that is the norm of Anglo-American criminal proceedings.

We have recognized, for example, that face-to-face confrontation enhances the accuracy of factfinding by reducing the risk that a witness will wrongfully implicate an innocent person. See *Coy* ("It is always more difficult to tell a lie about a person 'to his face' than 'behind his back.' * * * That face-to-face presence may, unfortunately, upset the truthful rape victim or abused child; but by the same token it may confound and undo the false accuser, or reveal the child coached by a malevolent adult"). We have also noted the strong symbolic purpose served by requiring adverse witnesses at trial to testify in the accused's presence. See *Coy* ("[T]here is something deep in human nature that regards face-to-face confrontation between accused and accuser as 'essential to a fair trial in a criminal prosecution' ").

Although face-to-face confrontation forms "the core of the values furthered by the Confrontation Clause," we have nevertheless recognized that it is not the *sine qua non* of the confrontation right.

For this reason, we have never insisted on an actual face-to-face encounter at trial in *every* instance in which testimony is admitted against a defendant. Instead, we have repeatedly held that the Clause permits, where necessary, the admission of certain hearsay statements against a defendant despite the defendant's inability to confront the declarant at trial. * * * We have accordingly stated that a literal reading of the Confrontation Clause would "abrogate virtually every hearsay exception, a result long rejected as unintended and too extreme." Thus, in certain narrow circumstances, "competing interests, if 'closely examined,' may warrant dispensing with confrontation at trial." We have recently held, for example, that hearsay statements of nontestifying co-conspirators may be admitted against a defendant despite the lack of any face-to-face encounter with the accused. Given our hearsay cases, the word "confronted," as used in the Confrontation Clause, cannot simply mean face-to-face confrontation, for the Clause would then, contrary to our cases, prohibit the admission of any accusatory hearsay statement made by an absent declarant—a declarant who is undoubtedly as much a "witness against" a defendant as one who actually testifies at trial.

In sum, our precedents establish that "the Confrontation Clause reflects a *preference* for face-to-face confrontation at trial," a preference that "must occasionally give way to considerations of public policy and the necessities of the case." "[W]e have attempted to harmonize the goal of the Clause—placing limits on the kind of evidence that may be received against a defendant—with a societal interest in accurate factfinding, which may require consideration of out-of-court statements." We have accordingly interpreted the Confrontation Clause in a manner sensitive to its purposes and sensitive to the necessities of trial and the adversary process. * * *

That the face-to-face confrontation requirement is not absolute does not, of course, mean that it may easily be dispensed with. As we suggested in *Coy*, our precedents confirm that a defendant's right to confront accusatory witnesses may be satisfied absent a physical, face-to-face confrontation at trial only where denial of such confrontation is necessary to further an important public policy and only where the reliability of the testimony is otherwise assured.

III

Maryland's statutory procedure, when invoked, prevents a child witness from seeing the defendant as he or she testifies against the defendant at trial. We find it significant, however, that Maryland's procedure preserves all of the other elements of the confrontation right: The child witness must be competent to testify and must testify under oath; the defendant retains full opportunity for contemporaneous cross-examination; and the judge, jury, and defendant are able to view (albeit by video monitor) the demeanor (and body) of the witness as he or she testifies. Although we are mindful of the many subtle effects face-to-face confrontation may have on an adversary criminal proceeding, the presence of these other elements of confrontation—oath, cross-examination, and observation of the witness' demeanor—adequately ensures that the testimony is both reliable and subject to rigorous adversarial testing in a manner functionally equivalent to that accorded live, in-person testimony. These safeguards of reliability and adversariness render the use of such a procedure a far cry from the undisputed prohibition of the Confrontation Clause: trial by *ex parte* affidavit or inquisition. Rather, we think these elements of effective confrontation not only permit a defendant to "confound and undo the false accuser, or reveal the child coached by a malevolent adult," but may well aid a defendant in eliciting favorable testimony from the child witness. Indeed, to the extent the child witness' testimony may be said to be technically given out of court (though we do not so hold), these assurances of reliability and adversariness are far greater than those required for admission of hearsay testimony under the Confrontation Clause. We are therefore confident that use of the one-way closed circuit television procedure, where necessary to further an important state interest, does not impinge upon the truth-seeking or symbolic purposes of the Confrontation Clause.

The critical inquiry in this case, therefore, is whether use of the procedure is necessary to further an important state interest. The State contends that it has a substantial interest in protecting children who are allegedly victims of child abuse from the trauma of testifying against the alleged perpetrator and that its statutory procedure for receiving testimony from such witnesses is necessary to further that interest. * * *

We * * * conclude today that a State's interest in the physical and psychological well-being of child abuse victims may be sufficiently important to outweigh, at least in some cases, a defendant's right to face his or her accusers in court. That a significant majority of States have enacted statutes to protect child witnesses from the trauma of giving testimony in child abuse cases attests to the widespread belief in the importance of such a public policy. Thirty-seven States, for example, permit the use of videotaped testimony of sexually abused children; 24 States have authorized the use of one-way closed circuit television testimony in child abuse cases; and 8 States authorize the use of a two-way system in which the child witness is permitted to see the courtroom and the defendant on a video monitor and in which the jury and judge are permitted to view the child during the testimony. * * *

To be sure, face-to-face confrontation may be said to cause trauma for the very purpose of eliciting truth, but we think that the use of Maryland's special procedure, where necessary to further the important state interest in preventing trauma to child witnesses in child abuse cases, adequately ensures the accuracy of the testimony and preserves the adversary nature of the trial. Indeed, where face-to-face confrontation causes significant emotional distress in a child witness, there is evidence that such confrontation would in fact *disserve* the Confrontation Clause's truth-seeking goal.

In sum, we conclude that where necessary to protect a child witness from trauma that would be caused by testifying in the physical presence of the defendant, at least where such trauma would impair the child's ability to communicate, the Confrontation Clause does not prohibit use of a procedure that, despite the absence of face-to-face confrontation, ensures the reliability of the evidence by subjecting it to rigorous adversarial testing and thereby preserves the essence of effective confrontation. Because there is no dispute that the child witnesses in this case testified under oath, were subject to full cross-examination, and were able to be observed by the judge, jury, and defendant as they testified, we conclude that, to the extent that a proper finding of necessity has been made, the admission of such testimony would be consonant with the Confrontation Clause.

[In Part IV, the Court discusses what would constitute a "case-specific finding of necessity" and then remands the case to the state court.]

JUSTICE SCALIA, with whom JUSTICE BRENNAN, JUSTICE MARSHALL, and JUSTICE STEVENS join, dissenting.

Seldom has this Court failed so conspicuously to sustain a categorical guarantee of the Constitution against the tide of prevailing current opinion. The Sixth Amendment provides, with unmistakable clarity, that "[i]n all criminal prosecutions, the accused shall enjoy the right * * * to be confronted with the witnesses against him." The purpose of enshrining this protection in the Constitution was to assure that none of the many policy interests from time to time pursued by statutory law could overcome a defendant's right to face his or her accusers in court. * * *

Because of this subordination of explicit constitutional text to currently favored public policy, the following scene can be played out in an American courtroom for the first time in two centuries: A father whose young daughter has been given over to the exclusive custody of his estranged wife, or a mother whose young son has been taken into custody by the State's child welfare department, is sentenced to prison for sexual abuse on the basis of testimony by a child the parent has not seen or spoken to for many months; and the guilty verdict is rendered without giving the parent so much as the opportunity to sit in the presence of the child, and to ask, personally or through counsel, "it is really not true, is it, that I—your father (or mother) whom you see before you—did these terrible things?" Perhaps that is a procedure today's society desires; perhaps (though I doubt it) it is even a fair procedure; but it is assuredly not a procedure permitted by the Constitution.

Because the text of the Sixth Amendment is clear, and because the Constitution is meant to protect against, rather than conform to, current "widespread belief," I respectfully dissent.

I

According to the Court, "we cannot say that [face-to-face] confrontation [with witnesses appearing at trial] is an indispensable element of the Sixth Amendment's guarantee of the right to confront one's accusers." That is rather like saying "we cannot say that being tried before a jury is an indispensable element of the Sixth Amendment's guarantee of the right to jury trial." The Court makes the impossible plausible by recharacterizing the Confrontation Clause, so that confrontation (redesignated "face-to-face confrontation") becomes only one of many "elements of confrontation." The reasoning is as follows: The Confrontation Clause guarantees not only what it explicitly provides for—"face-to-face" confrontation—but also implied and collateral rights such as cross-examination, oath, and observation of demeanor (TRUE); the purpose of this entire cluster of rights is to ensure the reliability of evidence (TRUE); the Maryland procedure preserves the implied and collateral rights (TRUE), which adequately ensure the reliability of evidence (perhaps TRUE); therefore the Confrontation Clause is not violated by denying what it explicitly provides for—"face-to-face" confrontation (unquestionably FALSE). This reasoning abstracts from the right to its purposes, and then eliminates the right. It is wrong because the Confrontation Clause does not guarantee reliable evidence; it guarantees specific trial procedures that were thought to *assure* reliable evidence, undeniably among which was "face-to-face" confrontation. Whatever else it may mean in addition, the defendant's constitutional right "to be confronted with the witnesses against him" means, always and everywhere, at least what it explicitly says: the " 'right to meet face to face all those who appear and give evidence at trial.' "

The Court supports its antitextual conclusion by cobbling together scraps of dicta from various cases that have no bearing here. It will suffice to discuss one of them, since they are all of a kind: Quoting *Ohio v. Roberts*, 448 U.S. 56, 63, 100 S.Ct. 2531, 2537, 65 L.Ed.2d 597 (1980), the Court says that "[i]n sum, our precedents establish that 'the Confrontation Clause reflects a *preference* for face-to-face confrontation at trial.' " But *Roberts*, and all the other "precedents" the Court enlists to prove the implausible, dealt with the implications of the Confrontation Clause, and not its literal, unavoidable text. When *Roberts* said that the Clause merely "reflects a preference for face-to-face confrontation at trial," what it had in mind as the nonpreferred alternative was not (as the Court implies) the appearance of a witness at trial without confronting the defendant. That has been, until today, not merely "nonpreferred" but utterly unheard-of. What *Roberts* had in mind was the receipt of *other-than-first-hand testimony* from witnesses at trial—that is, witnesses' recounting of hearsay statements by absent parties who, *since they did not appear at trial*, did not have to endure face-to-face confrontation.

Rejecting that, I agree, was merely giving effect to an evident constitutional preference; there are, after all, many exceptions to the Confrontation Clause's hearsay rule. But that the defendant should be confronted by the witnesses who appear at trial is not a preference "reflected" by the Confrontation Clause; it is a constitutional right unqualifiedly guaranteed.

The Court claims that its interpretation of the Confrontation Clause "is consistent with our cases holding that other Sixth Amendment rights must also be interpreted in the context of the necessities of trial and the adversary process." I disagree. It is true enough that the "necessities of trial and the adversary process" limit the *manner* in which Sixth Amendment rights may be exercised, and limit the *scope* of Sixth Amendment guarantees to the extent that scope is textually indeterminate. Thus (to describe the cases the Court cites): The right to confront is not the right to confront in a manner that disrupts the trial. The right "to have compulsory process for obtaining witnesses" is not the right to call witnesses in a manner that violates fair and orderly procedures. The scope of the right "to have the assistance of counsel" does not include consultation with counsel at all times during the trial. The scope of the right to cross-examine does not include access to the State's investigative files. But we are not talking here about denying expansive scope to a Sixth Amendment provision whose scope for the purpose at issue is textually unclear; "to confront" plainly means to encounter face-to-face, whatever else it may mean in addition. And we are not talking about the manner of arranging that face-to-face encounter, but about whether it shall occur at all. The "necessities of trial and the adversary process" are irrelevant here, since they cannot alter the constitutional text. * * *

III

The Court characterizes the State's interest which "outweigh[s]" the explicit text of the Constitution as an "interest in the physical and psychological well-being of child abuse victims," an "interest in protecting" such victims "from the emotional trauma of testifying." That is not so. A child who meets the Maryland statute's requirement of suffering such "serious emotional distress" from confrontation that he "cannot reasonably communicate" would seem entirely safe. Why would a prosecutor want to call a witness who cannot reasonably communicate? And if he did, it would be the State's own fault. Protection of the child's interest—as far as the Confrontation Clause is concerned—is entirely within Maryland's control. The State's interest here is in fact no more and no less than what the State's interest always is when it seeks to get a class of evidence admitted in criminal proceedings: more convictions of guilty defendants. That is not an unworthy interest, but it should not be dressed up as a humanitarian one.

And the interest on the other side is also what it usually is when the State seeks to get a new class of evidence admitted: fewer convictions of innocent defendants—specifically, in the present context, innocent defendants accused of particularly heinous crimes. The "special" reasons that exist for suspending one of the usual guarantees of reliability in the case of children's testimony are perhaps matched by "special" reasons for being particularly insistent upon it in the case of children's testimony. Some studies show that children are substantially more vulnerable to suggestion than adults, and often unable to separate recollected fantasy (or suggestion) from reality. The injustice their erroneous testimony can produce is evidenced by the tragic Scott County investigations of 1983–1984, which disrupted the lives of many (as far as we know) innocent people in the small town of Jordan, Minnesota. At one stage those investigations were pursuing allegations by at least eight children of multiple murders, but the prosecutions actually initiated charged only sexual abuse. Specifically, 24 adults were charged with molesting 37 children. In the course of the investigations, 25 children were placed in foster homes. Of the 24 indicted defendants, one pleaded guilty, two were acquitted at trial, and the charges against the remaining 21 were voluntarily dismissed. There is no doubt that some sexual abuse took place in Jordan; but there is no reason to believe it was as widespread as charged. A report by the Minnesota attorney general's office, based on inquiries conducted by the Minnesota Bureau of Criminal Apprehension and the Federal Bureau of Investigation, concluded that there was an "absence of credible testimony and [a] lack of significant corroboration" to support reinstitution of sex-abuse charges, and "no credible evidence of murders." The report describes an investigation full of well-intentioned techniques employed by the prosecution team, police, child protection workers, and foster parents, that distorted and in some cases even coerced the children's recollection. Children were interrogated repeatedly, in some cases as many as 50 times; answers were suggested by telling the children what other witnesses had said; and children (even some who did not at first complain of abuse) were separated from their parents for months. The report describes the consequences as follows:

> "As children continued to be interviewed the list of accused citizens grew. In a number of cases, it was only after weeks or months of questioning that children would 'admit' their parents abused them. * * *

> "In some instances, over a period of time, the allegations of sexual abuse turned to stories of mutilations, and eventually homicide."

The value of the confrontation right in guarding against a child's distorted or coerced recollections is dramatically evident with respect to one of the misguided investigative techniques the report cited: some children were told by their foster parents that reunion with their real parents would be hastened by "admission" of their parents' abuse. Is it difficult to imagine how unconvincing such a testimonial admission might be to a jury that witnessed the child's delight at seeing his parents in the courtroom? Or how devastating it might be if, pursuant to a psychiatric evaluation that "trauma would impair the child's ability to communicate" in front of his parents, the child were permitted to tell his story to the jury on closed-circuit television?

In the last analysis, however, this debate is not an appropriate one. I have no need to defend the value of confrontation, because the Court has no authority to question it. It is not within our charge to speculate that, "where face-to-face confrontation causes significant emotional distress in a child witness," confrontation might "in fact *disserve* the Confrontation Clause's truth-seeking goal." If so, that is a defect in the Constitution— which should be amended by the procedures provided for such an eventuality, but cannot be corrected by judicial pronouncement that it is archaic, contrary to "widespread belief," and thus null and void. For good or bad, the Sixth Amendment requires confrontation, and we are not at liberty to ignore it. To quote the document one last time (for it plainly says all that need be said): "In *all* criminal prosecutions, the accused shall enjoy the right * * * to be confronted with the witnesses against him" (emphasis added). * * *

The Court today has applied "interest-balancing" analysis where the text of the Constitution simply does not permit it. We are not free to conduct a cost-benefit analysis of clear and explicit constitutional guarantees, and then to adjust their meaning to comport with our findings. The Court has convincingly proved that the Maryland procedure serves a valid interest, and gives the defendant virtually everything the Confrontation Clause guarantees (everything, that is, except confrontation). I am persuaded, therefore, that the Maryland procedure is virtually constitutional. Since it is not, however, actually constitutional I would affirm the judgment of the Maryland Court of Appeals reversing the judgment of conviction.

NOTES AND QUESTIONS

1.   Considering the criminal process goals of fairness, accuracy, efficiency, and limiting government (pp. 38–49), which goals are manifested in the majority and dissenting opinions?

2.   *Language.* All nine members of the Court seem to agree that the "irreducible literal meaning" of the confrontation clause is the "right to a face-to-face meeting with witnesses against [criminal defendants] at trial." If this is indeed the "irreducible literal meaning" of the confrontation clause, then is Justice Scalia right that the debate on the value of the Maryland system "is

not an appropriate one" because "the Court has no authority to question" the "value of confrontation"?

3.   The majority embraces the *Roberts* substantive analysis—is the evidence presumptively reliable? The dissent, on the other hand, prefers procedure. Whether or not Maryland's system delivers a more, or less, accurate outcome is beside the point. What Maryland did not give Craig was confrontation. Which view do you prefer?

4.   Professor John Douglass noted an oddity about the Court's reliance on the *Roberts* dicta. It protected "the right of confrontation only through surrogates. Judicial determination of reliability ha[d] become the surrogate for cross-examination. And categorical, 'firmly rooted' hearsay exceptions [were] the surrogates for any real assessment of reliability." John G. Douglass, *Confronting the Reluctant Accomplice*, 101 Colum. L. Rev. 1797, 1801 (2001).

And the net effect of using surrogates was that there was precious little confrontation. Consider Lilly v. Virginia, 527 U.S. 116, 119 S.Ct. 1887, 144 L.Ed.2d 117 (1999). Lilly's brother, Mark, identified Lilly as the triggerman in a murder. "Later, having discovered the value of silence, Mark asserted his Fifth Amendment privilege and refused to testify at Lilly's trial. The trial court nevertheless allowed the prosecutor to introduce Mark's confession under the hearsay exception for statements against penal interest." Douglass, *supra*, at 1799. The Supreme Court unanimously reversed, albeit without a majority opinion. Douglass explains the irony of *Lilly* as follows:

> Somewhere in a Virginia prison, perhaps Ben Lilly appreciates the irony at the heart of his case. Lilly won a new trial because of Mark's absence from the witness stand. Yet neither prosecution nor defense really seems to have wanted Mark as a witness. At trial, and before trial, both parties passed up opportunities to confront the reluctant accomplice. In other words, the confrontation issue that perplexed the Court seems, in retrospect, easily avoidable. The pretrial choices of prosecution and defense suggest that both parties preferred a confrontation issue to a real confrontation.

> That contradiction—the parties' apparent disdain for real confrontation in the midst of a Confrontation Clause debate—may seem extraordinary. But [it] is not unusual in that respect. It is only the most recent in a line of cases that have exposed, but seldom addressed, the uncomfortable irony of a Confrontation Clause doctrine that no longer seems concerned with confrontation.

Id. at 1800.

5.   The paradox of a confrontation clause without meaningful confrontation would plague the Court's doctrine for a quarter century.

2. THE SEARCH FOR THE MEANING OF CONFRONTATION

"[T]he Confrontation Clause comes to us on faded parchment." California v. Green, 399 U.S. 149, 90 S.Ct. 1930, 26 L.Ed.2d 489 (1970) (Harlan, J., concurring).

What is the textual and historical meaning of a defendant's right "to be confronted with the witnesses against him"? The text suggests a right of the defendant to require the State's witnesses to testify at the defendant's trial, rather than have their testimony introduced by some other means, such as in an affidavit or in the form of an out-of-court statement. Out-of-court statements are often hearsay, which is defined as an out-of-court statement made by someone other than the defendant for the truth of the matter asserted. The common law developed a rule that hearsay statements are inadmissible, subject to what were at first a few exceptions. As students of evidence know, statutory iterations of the hearsay rule now have roughly thirty exceptions.

To understand the issue of hearsay, consider this example: A tells B that C killed V. The State offers B as a witness against C, and the prosecutor wishes to elicit what A said to B. This is an out-of-court statement offered to prove that C killed V. It is hearsay and is normally considered too unreliable to admit into evidence. It is unreliable because B may misremember what A said. Even if B's memory is perfect, we do not know what basis A had for making the statement. Did he see C kill V? Or was his basis of knowledge second- or third-hand? If A were on the witness stand, he could be cross-examined about what he knew and how he knew it. But B cannot be cross-examined on anything other than his memory of what A said. According to Wigmore, cross-examination "is beyond any doubt the greatest legal engine ever invented for the discovery of truth." 3 Wigmore on Evidence 2, § 1367 (1923 ed.). Without the ability to cross-examine A, however, the risk that A's information is false is too great to allow B to testify to what A said. All of this fine legal analysis goes out the window, however, if the State proves that A, B, and C were conspirators because that is one of the exceptions to the hearsay rule.

The relationship between the hearsay rule and the confrontation clause was, for many years, unclear along two dimensions. Did the confrontation clause simply constitutionalize the hearsay rule and, if so, what rule? Was it the hearsay rule that existed in 1791 or the modern rule with all of its exceptions? A second dimension, first raised by Justice Harlan in 1970, is determining what it means to be a "witness" against an accused. If you are drinking in a bar and tell someone that Z cheats on his income tax, does that constitute being a witness against Z? Harlan would have said "no" to that question, insisting that being a witness entails testifying in a legal proceeding.

Can history help here? The answer is "sort of." Though the history comes to us, as Justice Harlan said, "on faded parchment," it does set some parameters on the debate. A place to start is the trial of Sir Walter Raleigh in 1603 for conspiring to commit treason against King James I. See 2 How. St. Tr. 1 (1603). The principal evidence against Raleigh was the confession of his alleged accomplice, Lord Cobham, given before the Privy Council and reported to the trial court via an affidavit.

Raleigh repeatedly begged the judges to bring Cobham into court so that he could tell his story to the judges. Raleigh's theory was that Cobham's confession was false and that he would renounce it if allowed to tell his story in open court. The judges refused to call Cobham as a witness, and Raleigh was convicted, and sentenced to die, on evidence that he was never allowed to challenge. While Raleigh's case caused no public outcry at the time—to oppose James I publicly was to risk Raleigh's fate—later in the seventeenth century the anti-monarch Whigs seized on Raleigh's case as a reason to fear the unchecked power of the monarch. Indeed, in 1665, Parliament made clear that no one could be tried for treason unless two accusers met him "face to face" at arraignment and testified under oath what they had to say about the charge of treason. 13 Car. II, ch. 1, 5 (1665). Requiring two accusers and face-to-face confrontation was a clear response to what was then perceived as a miscarriage of justice in Raleigh's case.

What history leaves unclear, though, is whether the hearsay rule developed as a parallel *common law* solution to what happened to Raleigh. The act of Parliament, after all, applied only in treason cases while the hearsay rule applies to all trials. Perhaps Raleigh's case is a station stop on the journey of the hearsay rule. The term "hearsay" was already in use in 1603 because both Raleigh and the prosecutor referred to it in a negative way. Raleigh said that the evidence against him was not from an accuser's "own knowledge" but "by hear-say." The prosecutor argued that Cobham would not have confessed falsely when confronted with mere hearsay evidence against him. If the hearsay rule was the accepted solution to the confrontation problem, perhaps the Framers had it, and its exceptions, in mind when they wrote the Sixth Amendment. Indeed, one of the judges in Raleigh's case responded to his plea that Cobham's confession was false by saying, "The law presumes, a man will not accuse himself to accuse another." This might be an early statement of the exception to the hearsay rule for statements against penal interest.

The hearsay rule understanding of the confrontation clause, however, is not easy to square with the text, which states a categorical rule without exceptions. But the hearsay rule understanding is nonetheless attractive because the rationale of the hearsay rule bears a striking resemblance to the rationale of the confrontation clause. *Why* must the State produce its witnesses at trial? Answer: to give the defendant an opportunity to "confront" them with cross-examination. Indeed, Hale's Pleas of the Crown, written around 1670, referred to the statutory requirement of a face-to-face meeting with the accusers in treason cases and then added "to the end that [the defendant] may cross-examine them." 1 Hale, Pleas of the Crown 306. The exceptions to the hearsay rule exist because judges have found those statements sufficiently reliable that cross-examination may be safely foregone. Thus, one can argue that the hearsay rule understanding of the confrontation clause gives defendants what confrontation requires—the right not to be convicted on unreliable evidence.

The two most plausible interpretations of the confrontation clause, then, are that it (1) constitutionalized some version of the hearsay rule or (2) created some yet-to-be-defined right to force the State to present those who are witnesses against the defendant (whatever it means to be "a witness against" a defendant) at trial.. In thinking about what constitutes being a witness against a defendant, one category would be an affidavit given to a formal legal body, like Lord Cobham's affidavit against Raleigh given to the king's Privy Council; a second category would be testimony given under oath to the magistrate who, beginning in 1554, was required to take testimony from those who might know the facts about a crime alleged in a complaint.

Keep these two possible interpretations in mind as we briefly recount the Court's confrontation clause journey, which began in 1895 in Mattox v. United States, 156 U.S. 237, 15 S.Ct. 337, 39 L.Ed. 409 (1895). Mattox was convicted of murder, but the Supreme Court reversed his conviction and remanded the case. By the time of the second trial, two of the government's witnesses had died, and the prosecution sought to introduce their testimony from the first trial. Later courts have interpreted *Mattox* as resting on the exception to the hearsay rule for dying declarations, but a close study of the opinion does not bear out this reading. The Court stressed that "[t]he substance of the constitutional protection is preserved to the prisoner in the advantage he has once had of seeing the witness face to face, and of subjecting him to the ordeal of a cross-examination." *Mattox* thus stands for the unremarkable principle that the confrontation clause permits use of a trial transcript when (1) a witness is dead and (2) the defendant had the opportunity to cross-examine the witness in a prior judicial proceeding.

Notice that the witness in *Mattox* had testified in a criminal trial. Thus, he was unquestionably a witness against the accused, and there was opportunity to cross-examine him. On both dimensions of the confrontation puzzle, this was an easy case.

The next stage in the journey also involved a transcript of a prior judicial proceeding. In Ohio v. Roberts, 448 U.S. 56, 100 S.Ct. 2531, 65 L.Ed.2d 597 (1980), a *defense* witness testified at a preliminary hearing in a manner hostile to Roberts. The witness did not appear for Roberts's trial even though the state issued five separate subpoenas for her. When the fifth subpoena proved fruitless, the trial court permitted the prosecution to introduce the preliminary hearing transcript. The Court ruled that a witness who has disappeared is just as unavailable as one who, as in *Mattox*, has died. The transcript of the preliminary hearing where the defendant had the opportunity to cross-examine the witness was thus admissible under the authority of *Mattox*.

Again, the speaker was a witness in a judicial proceeding and the defendant had a chance to cross-examine. Another easy case. The next case was more difficult, though the Court did not seem to appreciate how it was different from *Mattox* and *Roberts*. In United States v. Inadi, 475 U.S. 387, 106 S.Ct. 1121, 89 L.Ed.2d 390 (1986), the issue was whether the Sixth Amendment permitted a co-conspirator's hearsay statement to be admitted. This out-of-court statement did *not* fit the classic definition of being a "witness" against the accused; it was not made as part of a formal legal proceeding or to a formal legal body. And there had *not* been an opportunity to cross-examine the person who made the statement. Yet the Court found the case an easy one because of dicta in *Roberts*.

In explaining the reasoning behind its confrontation decisions, the *Roberts* Court subtly changed the meaning of confrontation from a procedural mechanism that is designed to result in more reliable evidence in a universe of cases, to a hearsay-rule concern with the substance of the particular evidence offered in the case before the Court. *Roberts* explained that an out-of-court statement could be admitted if the State showed that the particular statement had a sufficient "indicia of reliability." This "indicia of reliability" could be shown in either of two ways: by showing that the hearsay statement "falls within a firmly rooted hearsay exception," or by showing "particularized guarantees of trustworthiness" in some other, undefined way. Thus, because the exception to the confrontation clause for statements of co-conspirators was a "firmly-rooted" exception, the *Inadi* Court held, without much analysis, that admission of the statement satisfied the confrontation clause.

In effect, later Courts seized on the *Roberts* dicta as the solution to both dimensions of the confrontation puzzle. *Any statement* sought to be introduced against the accused would be considered as coming from a witness against the accused. But the many exceptions to the hearsay rule made it easy, in most cases, for the State to win the confrontation issue. The speaker would not be produced in court to be cross-examined, but the out-of-court statement would be admitted. In effect, the *Roberts* solution made the protection of the confrontation clause very wide but only inches deep.

You saw the Court's 5–4 split *Maryland v. Craig*, p. 1288, over whether to continue to embrace the *Roberts* reliability approach or to attempt to get to the "plain meaning" of the confrontation clause. That dispute re-surfaces in the next case but this time Justice Scalia had the votes for his "plain meaning" approach.

CRAWFORD V. WASHINGTON

Supreme Court of the United States, 2004.
541 U.S. 36, 124 S.Ct. 1354, 158 L.Ed.2d 177.

JUSTICE SCALIA delivered the opinion of the Court [joined by JUSTICES STEVENS, KENNEDY, SOUTER, THOMAS, GINSBURG, and BREYER].

Petitioner Michael Crawford stabbed a man who allegedly tried to rape his wife, Sylvia. At his trial, the State played for the jury Sylvia's tape-recorded statement to the police describing the stabbing, even though he had no opportunity for cross-examination. The Washington Supreme Court upheld petitioner's conviction after determining that Sylvia's statement was reliable. The question presented is whether this procedure complied with the Sixth Amendment's guarantee that, "[i]n all criminal prosecutions, the accused shall enjoy the right * * * to be confronted with the witnesses against him."

I

On August 5, 1999, Kenneth Lee was stabbed at his apartment. Police arrested petitioner later that night. After giving petitioner and his wife *Miranda* warnings, detectives interrogated each of them twice. Petitioner eventually confessed that he and Sylvia had gone in search of Lee because he was upset over an earlier incident in which Lee had tried to rape her. The two had found Lee at his apartment, and a fight ensued in which Lee was stabbed in the torso and petitioner's hand was cut. * * *

Sylvia generally corroborated petitioner's story about the events leading up to the fight, but her account of the fight itself was arguably different—particularly with respect to whether Lee had drawn a weapon before petitioner assaulted him. * * *

The State charged petitioner with assault and attempted murder. At trial, he claimed self-defense. Sylvia did not testify because of the state marital privilege, which generally bars a spouse from testifying without the other spouse's consent. In Washington, this privilege does not extend to a spouse's out-of-court statements admissible under a hearsay exception, so the State sought to introduce Sylvia's tape-recorded statements to the police as evidence that the stabbing was not in self-defense. Noting that Sylvia had admitted she led petitioner to Lee's apartment and thus had facilitated the assault, the State invoked the hearsay exception for statements against penal interest.

Petitioner countered that, state law notwithstanding, admitting the evidence would violate his federal constitutional right to be "confronted with the witnesses against him." According to our description of that right in *Ohio v. Roberts*, 448 U.S. 56, 100 S.Ct. 2531, 65 L.Ed.2d 597 (1980), it does not bar admission of an unavailable witness's statement against a criminal defendant if the statement bears "adequate 'indicia of reliability.' " To meet that test, evidence must either fall within a "firmly rooted hearsay exception" or bear "particularized guarantees of trustworthiness." The trial court here admitted the statement on the latter ground, offering several reasons why it was trustworthy: Sylvia was not shifting blame but rather corroborating her husband's story that he acted in self-defense or "justified reprisal"; she had direct knowledge as an eyewitness; she was describing recent events; and she was being questioned by a "neutral" law enforcement officer. The prosecution played the tape for the jury and relied on it in closing, arguing that it was "damning evidence" that "completely refutes [petitioner's] claim of self-defense." The jury convicted petitioner of assault.

The Washington Court of Appeals reversed. It applied a nine-factor test to determine whether Sylvia's statement bore particularized guarantees of trustworthiness, and noted several reasons why it did not: The statement contradicted one she had previously given; it was made in response to specific questions; and at one point she admitted she had shut her eyes during the stabbing. The court considered and rejected the State's argument that Sylvia's statement was reliable because it coincided with petitioner's to such a degree that the two "interlocked." The court determined that, although the two statements agreed about the events leading up to the stabbing, they differed on the issue crucial to petitioner's self-defense claim: "[Petitioner's] version asserts that Lee may have had something in his hand when he stabbed him; but Sylvia's version has Lee grabbing for something only after he has been stabbed."

The Washington Supreme Court reinstated the conviction, unanimously concluding that, although Sylvia's statement did not fall under a firmly rooted hearsay exception, it bore guarantees of trustworthiness: " '[W]hen a codefendant's confession is virtually identical [to, *i.e.,* interlocks with,] that of a defendant, it may be deemed reliable.' " * * *

II

The Sixth Amendment's Confrontation Clause provides that, "[i]n all criminal prosecutions, the accused shall enjoy the right * * * to be confronted with the witnesses against him." We have held that this bedrock procedural guarantee applies to both federal and state prosecutions. As noted above, *Roberts* says that an unavailable witness's out-of-court statement may be admitted so long as it has adequate indicia of reliability—*i.e.,* falls within a "firmly rooted hearsay exception" or bears "particularized guarantees of trustworthiness." Petitioner argues that this test strays from the original meaning of the Confrontation Clause and urges us to reconsider it.

A

The Constitution's text does not alone resolve this case. One could plausibly read "witnesses against" a defendant to mean those who actually testify at trial, those whose statements are offered at trial, or something in-between. We must therefore turn to the historical background of the Clause to understand its meaning.

The right to confront one's accusers is a concept that dates back to Roman times. The founding generation's immediate source of the concept, however, was the common law. English common law has long differed from continental civil law in regard to the manner in which witnesses give testimony in criminal trials. The common-law tradition is one of live testimony in court subject to adversarial testing, while the civil law condones examination in private by judicial officers. * * *

The most notorious instances of civil-law examination occurred in the great political trials of the 16th and 17th centuries. One such was the 1603 trial of Sir Walter Raleigh for treason. Lord Cobham, Raleigh's alleged accomplice, had implicated him in an examination before the Privy Council and in a letter. At Raleigh's trial, these were read to the jury. Raleigh argued that Cobham had lied to save himself: "Cobham is absolutely in the King's mercy; to excuse me cannot avail him; by accusing me he may hope for favour." Suspecting that Cobham would recant, Raleigh demanded that the judges call him to appear, arguing that "[t]he Proof of the Common Law is by witness and jury: let Cobham be here, let him speak it. Call my accuser before my face * * * ." The judges refused, and, despite Raleigh's protestations that he was being tried "by the Spanish Inquisition," the jury convicted, and Raleigh was sentenced to death.

One of Raleigh's trial judges later lamented that " 'the justice of England has never been so degraded and injured as by the condemnation of Sir Walter Raleigh.' " Through a series of statutory and judicial reforms, English law developed a right of confrontation that limited these abuses. For example, treason statutes required witnesses to confront the accused "face to face" at his arraignment. * * *

One recurring question was whether the admissibility of an unavailable witness's pretrial examination depended on whether the defendant had had an opportunity to cross-examine him. In 1696, the Court of King's Bench answered this question in the affirmative, in the widely reported misdemeanor libel case of *King v. Paine*. The court ruled that, even though a witness was dead, his examination was not admissible where "the defendant not being present when [it was] taken before the mayor * * * had lost the benefit of a cross-examination." * * *

B

Controversial examination practices were also used in the Colonies. [We mercifully omit the details of the colonial history recounted by the Court—Eds.]

III

This history supports two inferences about the meaning of the Sixth Amendment.

A

First, the principal evil at which the Confrontation Clause was directed was the civil-law mode of criminal procedure, and particularly its use of *ex parte* examinations as evidence against the accused. It was these practices that the Crown deployed in notorious treason cases like Raleigh's; that the Marian statutes invited [these statutes required magistrates to examine suspects prior to trial and certify their statements to the criminal court—Eds.]; that English law's assertion of a right to confrontation was meant to prohibit; and that the founding-era rhetoric decried. The Sixth Amendment must be interpreted with this focus in mind.

Accordingly, we once again reject the view that the Confrontation Clause applies of its own force only to in-court testimony, and that its application to out-of-court statements introduced at trial depends upon "the law of Evidence for the time being." Leaving the regulation of out-of-court statements to the law of evidence would render the Confrontation Clause powerless to prevent even the most flagrant inquisitorial practices. Raleigh was, after all, perfectly free to confront those who read Cobham's confession in court.

This focus also suggests that not all hearsay implicates the Sixth Amendment's core concerns. An off-hand, overheard remark might be unreliable evidence and thus a good candidate for exclusion under hearsay rules, but it bears little resemblance to the civil-law abuses the Confrontation Clause targeted. On the other hand, *ex parte* examinations might sometimes be admissible under modern hearsay rules, but the Framers certainly would not have condoned them.

The text of the Confrontation Clause reflects this focus. It applies to "witnesses" against the accused—in other words, those who "bear testimony." "Testimony," in turn, is typically "[a] solemn declaration or affirmation made for the purpose of establishing or proving some fact." An accuser who makes a formal statement to government officers bears testimony in a sense that a person who makes a casual remark to an acquaintance does not. The constitutional text, like the history underlying the common-law right of confrontation, thus reflects an especially acute concern with a specific type of out-of-court statement.

Various formulations of this core class of "testimonial" statements exist: "*ex parte* in-court testimony or its functional equivalent—that is, material such as affidavits, custodial examinations, prior testimony that the defendant was unable to cross-examine, or similar pretrial statements that declarants would reasonably expect to be used prosecutorially,"; "extrajudicial statements * * * contained in formalized testimonial materials, such as affidavits, depositions, prior testimony, or confessions"; "statements that were made under circumstances which would lead an objective witness reasonably to believe that the statement would be available for use at a later trial." These formulations all share a common nucleus and then define the Clause's coverage at various levels of abstraction around it. Regardless of the precise articulation, some statements qualify under any definition—for example, *ex parte* testimony at a preliminary hearing.

Statements taken by police officers in the course of interrogations are also testimonial under even a narrow standard. Police interrogations bear a striking resemblance to examinations by justices of the peace in England. The statements are not *sworn* testimony, but the absence of oath was not dispositive. Cobham's examination was unsworn, yet Raleigh's trial has long been thought a paradigmatic confrontation violation. Under the Marian statutes, witnesses were typically put on oath, but suspects were not. Yet Hawkins and others went out of their way to caution that such unsworn confessions were not admissible against anyone but the confessor.

That interrogators are police officers rather than magistrates does not change the picture either. Justices of the peace conducting examinations under the Marian statutes were not magistrates as we understand that office today, but had an essentially investigative and prosecutorial function. England did not have a professional police force until the 19th century, so it is not surprising that other government officers performed the investigative functions now associated primarily with the police. The involvement of government officers in the production of testimonial evidence presents the same risk, whether the officers are police or justices of the peace.

In sum, even if the Sixth Amendment is not solely concerned with testimonial hearsay, that is its primary object, and interrogations by law enforcement officers fall squarely within that class.

B

The historical record also supports a second proposition: that the Framers would not have allowed admission of testimonial statements of a witness who did not appear at trial unless he was unavailable to testify, and the defendant had had a prior opportunity for cross-examination. The text of the Sixth Amendment does not suggest any open-ended exceptions from the confrontation requirement to be developed by the courts. Rather, the "right * * * to be confronted with the witnesses against him," is most naturally read as a reference to the right of confrontation at common law, admitting only those exceptions established at the time of the founding. As the English authorities above reveal, the common law in 1791 conditioned admissibility of an absent witness's examination on unavailability and a prior opportunity to cross-examine. The Sixth Amendment therefore incorporates those limitations. The numerous early state decisions applying the same test confirm that these principles were received as part of the common law in this country.

We do not read the historical sources to say that a prior opportunity to cross-examine was merely a sufficient, rather than a necessary, condition for admissibility of testimonial statements. They suggest that this requirement was dispositive, and not merely one of several ways to establish reliability. This is not to deny, as the Chief Justice notes, that "[t]here were always exceptions to the general rule of exclusion" of hearsay evidence. Several had become well established by 1791. But there is scant evidence that exceptions were invoked to admit *testimonial* statements against the accused in a *criminal* case. Most of the hearsay exceptions covered statements that by their nature were not testimonial—for example, business records or statements in furtherance of a conspiracy. We do not infer from these that the Framers thought exceptions would apply even to prior testimony.

IV

Our case law has been largely consistent with these two principles. Our leading early decision, for example, involved a deceased witness's prior trial testimony. *Mattox v. United States*, 156 U.S. 237, 15 S.Ct. 337, 39 L.Ed. 409 (1895). In allowing the statement to be admitted, we relied on the fact that the defendant had had, at the first trial, an adequate opportunity to confront the witness: "The substance of the constitutional protection is preserved to the prisoner in the advantage he has once had of seeing the witness face to face, and of subjecting him to the ordeal of a cross-examination. This, the law says, he shall under no circumstances be deprived of * * * ."

Our later cases conform to *Mattox's* holding that prior trial or preliminary hearing testimony is admissible only if the defendant had an adequate opportunity to cross-examine. * * * In contrast, we considered reliability factors beyond prior opportunity for cross-examination when the hearsay statement at issue was not testimonial. See *Dutton v. Evans*, 400 U.S., at 87–89, 91 S.Ct. 210 (plurality opinion).

Even our recent cases, in their outcomes, hew closely to the traditional line. *Ohio v. Roberts* admitted testimony from a preliminary hearing at which the defendant had examined the witness. *Lilly v. Virginia*, 527 U.S. 116, 119 S.Ct. 1887, 144 L.Ed.2d 117 (1999), excluded testimonial statements that the defendant had had no opportunity to test by cross-examination. And *Bourjaily v. United States*, 483 U.S. 171, 181–184, 107 S.Ct. 2775, 97 L.Ed.2d 144 (1987), admitted statements made unwittingly to an FBI informant after applying a more general test that did *not* make prior cross-examination an indispensable requirement? * * *

Our cases have thus remained faithful to the Framers' understanding: Testimonial statements of witnesses absent from trial have been admitted only where the declarant is unavailable, and only where the defendant has had a prior opportunity to cross-examine.

V

Although the results of our decisions have generally been faithful to the original meaning of the Confrontation Clause, the same cannot be said of our rationales. *Roberts* conditions the admissibility of all hearsay evidence on whether it falls under a "firmly rooted hearsay exception" or bears "particularized guarantees of trustworthiness." This test departs from the historical principles identified above in two respects. First, it is too broad: It applies the same mode of analysis whether or not the hearsay consists of *ex parte* testimony. This often results in close constitutional scrutiny in cases that are far removed from the core concerns of the Clause. At the same time, however, the test is too narrow: It admits statements that *do* consist of *ex parte* testimony upon a mere finding of reliability. This malleable standard often fails to protect against paradigmatic confrontation violations.

Members of this Court and academics have suggested that we revise our doctrine to reflect more accurately the original understanding of the Clause. They offer two proposals: First, that we apply the Confrontation Clause only to testimonial statements, leaving the remainder to regulation by hearsay law—thus eliminating the overbreadth referred to above. Second, that we impose an absolute bar to statements that are testimonial, absent a prior opportunity to cross-examine—thus eliminating the excessive narrowness referred to above.

In *White*, we considered the first proposal and rejected it. Although our analysis in this case casts doubt on that holding, we need not definitively resolve whether it survives our decision today, because Sylvia Crawford's statement is testimonial under any definition. This case does, however, squarely implicate the second proposal.

A

Where testimonial statements are involved, we do not think the Framers meant to leave the Sixth Amendment's protection to the vagaries of the rules of evidence, much less to amorphous notions of "reliability." Certainly none of the authorities discussed above acknowledges any general reliability exception to the common-law rule. Admitting statements deemed reliable by a judge is fundamentally at odds with the right of confrontation. To be sure, the Clause's ultimate goal is to ensure reliability of evidence, but it is a procedural rather than a substantive guarantee. It commands, not that evidence be reliable, but that reliability be assessed in a particular manner: by testing in the crucible of cross-examination. The Clause thus reflects a judgment, not only about the desirability of reliable evidence (a point on which there could be little dissent), but about how reliability can best be determined. Cf. * * * M. Hale, History and Analysis of the Common Law of England 258 (1713) (adversarial testing "beats and bolts out the Truth much better").

The *Roberts* test allows a jury to hear evidence, untested by the adversary process, based on a mere judicial determination of reliability. It thus replaces the constitutionally prescribed method of assessing reliability with a wholly foreign one. * * *

The Raleigh trial itself involved the very sorts of reliability determinations that *Roberts* authorizes. In the face of Raleigh's repeated demands for confrontation, the prosecution responded with many of the arguments a court applying *Roberts* might invoke today: that Cobham's statements were self-inculpatory, that they were not made in the heat of passion, and that they were not "extracted from [him] upon any hopes or promise of Pardon." It is not plausible that the Framers' only objection to the trial was that Raleigh's judges did not properly weigh these factors before sentencing him to death. Rather, the problem was that the judges refused to allow Raleigh to confront Cobham in court, where he could cross-examine him and try to expose his accusation as a lie.

Dispensing with confrontation because testimony is obviously reliable is akin to dispensing with jury trial because a defendant is obviously guilty. This is not what the Sixth Amendment prescribes.

B

The legacy of *Roberts* in other courts vindicates the Framers' wisdom in rejecting a general reliability exception. The framework is so unpredictable that it fails to provide meaningful protection from even core confrontation violations.

Reliability is an amorphous, if not entirely subjective, concept. There are countless factors bearing on whether a statement is reliable; the nine-factor balancing test applied by the Court of Appeals below is representative. Whether a statement is deemed reliable depends heavily on which factors the judge considers and how much weight he accords each of them. Some courts wind up attaching the same significance to opposite facts. For example, the Colorado Supreme Court held a statement more reliable because its inculpation of the defendant was "detailed," while the Fourth Circuit found a statement more reliable because the portion implicating another was "fleeting." The Virginia Court of Appeals found a statement more reliable because the witness was in custody and charged with a crime (thus making the statement more obviously against her penal interest), while the Wisconsin Court of Appeals found a statement more reliable because the witness was *not* in custody and *not* a suspect. Finally, the Colorado Supreme Court in one case found a statement more reliable because it was given "immediately after" the events at issue, while that same court, in another case, found a statement more reliable because two years had elapsed.

The unpardonable vice of the *Roberts* test, however, is not its unpredictability, but its demonstrated capacity to admit core testimonial statements that the Confrontation Clause plainly meant to exclude. * * *

To add insult to injury, some of the courts that admit untested testimonial statements find reliability in the very factors that *make* the statements testimonial. As noted earlier, one court relied on the fact that the witness's statement was made to police while in custody on pending charges—the theory being that this made the statement more clearly against penal interest and thus more reliable. Other courts routinely rely on the fact that a prior statement is given under oath in judicial proceedings [*e.g.*, grand jury testimony and plea allocution—Eds.]. That inculpating statements are given in a testimonial setting is not an antidote to the confrontation problem, but rather the trigger that makes the Clause's demands most urgent. It is not enough to point out that most of the usual safeguards of the adversary process attend the statement, when the single safeguard missing is the one the Confrontation Clause demands.

C

Roberts' failings were on full display in the proceedings below. Sylvia Crawford made her statement while in police custody, herself a potential suspect in the case. Indeed, she had been told that whether she would be released "depend[ed] on how the investigation continues." In response to often leading questions from police detectives, she implicated her husband in Lee's stabbing and at least arguably undermined his self-defense claim. Despite all this, the trial court admitted her statement, listing several reasons why it was reliable. In its opinion reversing, the Court of Appeals listed several *other* reasons why the statement was *not* reliable. Finally, the State Supreme Court relied exclusively on the interlocking character of the statement and disregarded every other factor the lower courts had considered. The case is thus a self-contained demonstration of *Roberts'* unpredictable and inconsistent application. * * *

* * * The trial court also buttressed its reliability finding by claiming that Sylvia was "being questioned by law enforcement, and, thus, the [questioner] is * * * neutral to her and not someone who would be inclined to advance her interests and shade her version of the truth unfavorably toward the defendant." The Framers would be astounded to learn that *ex parte* testimony could be admitted against a criminal defendant because it was elicited by "neutral" government officers. But even if the court's assessment of the officer's motives was accurate, it says nothing about Sylvia's perception of her situation. Only cross-examination could reveal that. * * *

We readily concede that we could resolve this case by simply reweighing the "reliability factors" under *Roberts* and finding that Sylvia Crawford's statement falls short. But we view this as one of those rare cases in which the result below is so improbable that it reveals a fundamental failure on our part to interpret the Constitution in a way that secures its intended constraint on judicial discretion. Moreover, to reverse the Washington Supreme Court's decision after conducting our own reliability analysis would perpetuate, not avoid, what the Sixth Amendment condemns. The Constitution prescribes a procedure for determining the reliability of testimony in criminal trials, and we, no less than the state courts, lack authority to replace it with one of our own devising.

We have no doubt that the courts below were acting in utmost good faith when they found reliability. The Framers, however, would not have been content to indulge this assumption. They knew that judges, like other government officers, could not always be trusted to safeguard the rights of the people; the likes of the dread Lord Jeffreys were not yet too distant a memory. They were loath to leave too much discretion in judicial hands. By replacing categorical constitutional guarantees with open-ended balancing tests, we do violence to their design. Vague standards are manipulable, and, while that might be a small concern in run-of-the-mill assault prosecutions like this one, the Framers had an eye toward politically charged cases like Raleigh's—great state trials where the impartiality of even those at the highest levels of the judiciary might not be so clear. It is difficult to imagine *Roberts* providing any meaningful protection in those circumstances.

* * *

Where nontestimonial hearsay is at issue, it is wholly consistent with the Framers' design to afford the States flexibility in their development of hearsay law—as does *Roberts,* and as would an approach that exempted such statements from Confrontation Clause scrutiny altogether. Where testimonial evidence is at issue, however, the Sixth Amendment demands what the common law required: unavailability and a prior opportunity for cross-examination. We leave for another day any effort to spell out a comprehensive definition of "testimonial."[10] Whatever else the term covers, it applies at a minimum to prior testimony at a preliminary hearing, before a grand jury, or at a former trial; and to police interrogations. These are the modern practices with closest kinship to the abuses at which the Confrontation Clause was directed.

In this case, the State admitted Sylvia's testimonial statement against petitioner, despite the fact that he had no opportunity to cross-examine her. That alone is sufficient to make out a violation of the Sixth Amendment. *Roberts* notwithstanding, we decline to mine the record in search of indicia of reliability. Where testimonial statements are at issue, the only indicium of reliability sufficient to satisfy constitutional demands is the one the Constitution actually prescribes: confrontation. * * *

CHIEF JUSTICE REHNQUIST, with whom JUSTICE O'CONNOR joins, concurring in the judgment.

I dissent from the Court's decision to overrule *Ohio v. Roberts.* I believe that the Court's adoption of a new interpretation of the Confrontation Clause is not backed by sufficiently persuasive reasoning to overrule long-established precedent. Its decision casts a mantle of uncertainty over future criminal trials in both federal and state courts, and is by no means necessary to decide the present case.

The Court's distinction between testimonial and nontestimonial statements, contrary to its claim, is no better rooted in history than our current doctrine. Under the common law, although the courts were far from consistent, out-of-court statements made by someone other than the accused and not taken under oath, unlike *ex parte* depositions or affidavits, were generally not considered substantive evidence upon which a conviction could be based. Testimonial statements such as accusatory statements to police officers likely would have been disapproved of in the 18th century, not necessarily because they resembled *ex parte* affidavits or depositions as the Court reasons, but more likely than not because they were not made under oath. Without an oath, one usually did not get to the second step of whether confrontation was required. * * *

Thus, while I agree that the Framers were mainly concerned about sworn affidavits and depositions, it does not follow that they were

---

[10] We acknowledge the Chief Justice's objection that our refusal to articulate a comprehensive definition in this case will cause interim uncertainty. But it can hardly be any worse than the status quo. The difference is that the *Roberts* test is *inherently,* and therefore *permanently,* unpredictable.

similarly concerned about the Court's broader category of testimonial statements. * * *

In choosing the path it does, the Court of course overrules *Ohio v. Roberts*, a case decided nearly a quarter of a century ago. *Stare decisis* is not an inexorable command in the area of constitutional law, but by and large, it "is the preferred course because it promotes the evenhanded, predictable, and consistent development of legal principles, fosters reliance on judicial decisions, and contributes to the actual and perceived integrity of the judicial process." And in making this appraisal, doubt that the new rule is indeed the "right" one should surely be weighed in the balance. Though there are no vested interests involved, unresolved questions for the future of everyday criminal trials throughout the country surely counsel the same sort of caution. The Court grandly declares that "[w]e leave for another day any effort to spell out a comprehensive definition of 'testimonial,'" But the thousands of federal prosecutors and the tens of thousands of state prosecutors need answers as to what beyond the specific kinds of "testimony" the Court lists is covered by the new rule. They need them now, not months or years from now. Rules of criminal evidence are applied every day in courts throughout the country, and parties should not be left in the dark in this manner.

To its credit, the Court's analysis of "testimony" excludes at least some hearsay exceptions, such as business records and official records. To hold otherwise would require numerous additional witnesses without any apparent gain in the truth-seeking process. Likewise to the Court's credit is its implicit recognition that the mistaken application of its new rule by courts which guess wrong as to the scope of the rule is subject to harmless-error analysis.

But these are palliatives to what I believe is a mistaken change of course. It is a change of course not in the least necessary to reverse the judgment of the Supreme Court of Washington in this case. The result the Court reaches follows inexorably from *Roberts* and its progeny without any need for overruling that line of cases. In *Idaho v. Wright*, we held that an out-of-court statement was not admissible simply because the truthfulness of that statement was corroborated by other evidence at trial. As the Court notes, the Supreme Court of Washington gave decisive weight to the "interlocking nature of the two statements." No re-weighing of the "reliability factors," which is hypothesized by the Court, is required to reverse the judgment here. A citation to *Idaho v. Wright* would suffice. For the reasons stated, I believe that this would be a far preferable course for the Court to take here.

NOTES AND QUESTIONS

1. *Precedent and history.* Justice Scalia's ability to make the Court's new rule consistent with its prior holdings—as opposed to the language used—is nothing short of a tour de force. The cases, like *Inadi*, p. 1302, that admitted hearsay statements based on "indicia of reliability" are now explained as cases not implicating the confrontation clause because the statements were not testimonial. The first two major confrontation clause cases, *Mattox* and *Roberts*, p. 1302, were correctly decided because the statements were given by now-unavailable witnesses in a prior judicial in which the defendant had the opportunity to cross-examine the speaker.

Professor Tom Davies concludes that the *Crawford* Court makes two very large historical errors. First, Davies argues, the Court misreads the cases that supposedly established a pre-Framing rule forbidding the introduction of depositions unless there had been an opportunity to cross-examine the deponent. Second, Davies agrees with Chief Justice Rehnquist's dissent that the rigid distinction between testimonial and non-testimonial statements simply did not exist in the pre-Framing era. These disagreements with the Court led Davies ultimately to conclude

> that originalism is a defective and undisciplined mode of justification for criminal procedure decisions. * * * [T]here is now so much distance between modern doctrine and the framing-era law that shaped the authentic original meaning of the criminal procedure provisions of the Bill of Rights that the authentic history rarely connects in any meaningful way with modern criminal procedure issues.

Thomas Y. Davies, *What Did the Framers Know, and When Did They Know It? Fictional Originalism in Crawford v. Washington*, 71 Brook. L. Rev. 105 (2005).

2. *The role for the hearsay rule.* The Court has left a very large role for the hearsay rule. Davis v. Washington, 547 U.S. 813, 126 S.Ct. 2266, 165 L.Ed.2d 224 (2006), held what the Court suggested in *Crawford*: The confrontation clause applies *only* to testimonial statements. "Only statements of this sort cause the declarant to be a 'witness' within the meaning of the Confrontation Clause. It is the testimonial character of the statement that separates it from other hearsay that, while subject to traditional limitations upon hearsay evidence, is not subject to the Confrontation Clause." It appeared in 2006 that the Court was done testing hearsay statements for "indicia of reliability." Either the statements are testimonial, in which case the speaker must have been subject to cross-examination (with two exceptions; see Note 4), or the case is governed by hearsay law with its rules and exceptions. Later cases, particularly Michigan v. Bryant, p. 1320, cause us to doubt that "reliability" has disappeared from confrontation clause analysis.

The *Crawford-Davis* approach to the confrontation clause is a vindication of Wigmore and Justice Harlan. Both argued that the confrontation clause was not intended to regulate hearsay law but, instead, to prescribe a method of trial procedure for testing testimonial statements—i.e., by cross-examination. See Dutton v. Evans, 400 U.S. 74, 91 S.Ct. 210, 27 L.Ed.2d 213 (1970) (Harlan, J. concurring in the judgment); 5 J. Wigmore, Evidence § 1397, at 131 (3d ed.1940). Justice Harlan wrote alone when he embraced Wigmore's view, and it is a testimonial to the power of his idea that it appears to have prevailed.

3. *And what statements are testimonial?* In *Davis*, Note 2, a caller told a 911 operator that she had just been assaulted by her former boyfriend. The Court held that the statements made to the 911 operator were not testimonial and thus not barred by the confrontation clause. Justice Scalia, for the Court, set out the beginnings of a rule.

> Without attempting to produce an exhaustive classification of all conceivable statements—or even all conceivable statements in response to police interrogation—as either testimonial or nontestimonial, it suffices to decide the present cases to hold as follows: Statements are nontestimonial when made in the course of police interrogation under circumstances objectively indicating that the primary purpose of the interrogation is to enable police assistance to meet an ongoing emergency. They are testimonial when the circumstances objectively indicate that there is no such ongoing emergency, and that the primary purpose of the interrogation is to establish or prove past events potentially relevant to later criminal prosecution.

During the call, the 911 operator asked questions about the nature of the assault, where the victim, McCottry, was located, and the name of the assailant. "The police arrived within four minutes of the 911 call and observed McCottry's shaken state, the 'fresh injuries on her forearm and her face,' and her 'frantic efforts to gather her belongings and her children so that they could leave the residence.'"

To the Court, the "difference between the interrogation in *Davis* and the one in *Crawford* is apparent on the face of things." As Justice Scalia explained,

> McCottry was speaking about events *as they were actually happening*, rather than "describing past events." Sylvia Crawford's interrogation, on the other hand, took place hours after the events she described had occurred. Moreover, any reasonable listener would recognize that McCottry (unlike Sylvia Crawford) was facing an ongoing emergency. Although one *might* call 911 to provide a narrative report of a crime absent any imminent danger, McCottry's call was plainly a call for help against bona fide physical threat. Third, the nature of what was asked and answered in *Davis*, again viewed objectively, was such that the elicited statements were

necessary to be able to *resolve* the present emergency, rather than simply to learn (as in *Crawford*) what had happened in the past. That is true even of the operator's effort to establish the identity of the assailant, so that the dispatched officers might know whether they would be encountering a violent felon. And finally, the difference in the level of formality between the two interviews is striking. Crawford was responding calmly, at the station house, to a series of questions, with the officer-interrogator taping and making notes of her answers; McCottry's frantic answers were provided over the phone, in an environment that was not tranquil, or even (as far as any reasonable 911 operator could make out) safe.

We conclude from all this that the circumstances of McCottry's interrogation objectively indicate its primary purpose was to enable police assistance to meet an ongoing emergency. She simply was not acting as a *witness;* she was not *testifying.* What she said was not "a weaker substitute for live testimony" at trial, like Lord Cobham's statements in *Raleigh's Case,* * * * or Sylvia Crawford's statement in *Crawford.* In each of those cases, the *ex parte* actors and the evidentiary products of the *ex parte* communication aligned perfectly with their courtroom analogues. McCottry's emergency statement does not. No "witness" goes into court to proclaim an emergency and seek help.

In *Hammon v. Indiana,* a companion case to *Davis,* the police arrived at the scene of the domestic disturbance and interviewed the victim in a room away from the alleged assailant. The Court held that statements made to the police here *were* testimonial under *Crawford* and thus inadmissible.

It is entirely clear from the circumstances that the interrogation was part of an investigation into possibly criminal past conduct—as, indeed, the testifying officer expressly acknowledged. There was no emergency in progress; the interrogating officer testified that he had heard no arguments or crashing and saw no one throw or break anything. When the officers first arrived, Amy told them that things were fine, and there was no immediate threat to her person. When the officer questioned Amy for the second time, and elicited the challenged statements, he was not seeking to determine (as in *Davis*) "what is happening," but rather "what happened." Objectively viewed, the primary, if not indeed the sole, purpose of the interrogation was to investigate a possible crime—which is, of course, precisely what the officer *should* have done.

For a thoughtful analysis of the effect of *Crawford* and *Davis* on the prosecution of domestic violence cases, see Kimberly D. Bailey, *The Aftermath of Crawford and Davis: Deconstructing the Sound of Silence,* 2009 Brigham Young U. L. Rev. 1.

4.   *Two exceptions to Crawford.* In Giles v. California, 554 U.S. 353, 128 S.Ct. 2678, 171 L.Ed.2d 488 (2008), the Court began its analysis by noting

two exceptions to *Crawford*, the first of which are "declarations made by a speaker who was both on the brink of death and aware that he was dying." A second exception is the rule of forfeiture by wrongful conduct. The state courts had held that Giles's intentional conduct in killing his ex-girlfriend prevented her from testifying and he had, therefore, forfeited the protection of the confrontation clause. The Court reversed the state court, holding that the common law cases and commentators were best read as applying the forfeiture exception "only when the defendant engaged in conduct *designed* to prevent the witness from testifying," an issue not reached by the state court.

5.   In Melendez-Diaz v. Massachusetts, 557 U.S. 305, 129 S.Ct. 2527, 174 L.Ed.2d 314 (2009), the Court rejected an attempt to limit *Crawford* to what the dissent called "conventional" or "ordinary" or "typical" witnesses. At issue in *Melendez-Diaz* were lab reports identifying the type and quantity of narcotics seized by police and connected to the defendant. As required by Massachusetts law, the reports were sworn to before a notary public and were submitted as prima facie evidence of what they asserted. They were admitted over the defendant's *Crawford* objection.

In an opinion by Justice Scalia, the Court found no legitimate basis to treat experts any differently from any other kind of witness. The confrontation clause "imposes a burden on the prosecution to present its witnesses" and not to rely on "a system in which the prosecution presents its evidence via *ex parte* affidavits." Indeed, the Court noted the risks of wrongful conviction because of inaccurate or fraudulent laboratory results, citing a study in which invalid forensic evidence contributed to 60% of the convictions of innocent defendants. See Brandon L. Garrett & Peter J. Neufeld, *Invalid Forensic Science Testimony and Wrongful Convictions*, 95 Va. L. Rev. 1, 14 (2009).

The dissent of Justice Kennedy, joined by Chief Justice Roberts and Justices Breyer and Alito, sought to show that the case was not controlled by *Crawford*, but the majority concluded that it "involves little more than the application of our holding in *Crawford* v. *Washington*. The Sixth Amendment does not permit the prosecution to prove its case via *ex parte* out-of-court affidavits, and the admission of such evidence against Melendez-Diaz was error." In sum, the State could use the lab reports only if it showed that the "analysts were unavailable to testify at trial *and* that petitioner had a prior opportunity to cross-examine them."

In a typical riposte, Scalia wrote: "Respondent and the dissent may be right that there are other ways—and in some cases better ways—to challenge or verify the results of a forensic test. But the Constitution guarantees one way: confrontation. We do not have license to suspend the Confrontation Clause when a preferable trial strategy is available." Notice, however, that the original seven-justice majority in *Crawford* had shrunk to a five-justice majority and that the two newest members of the Court (Roberts and Alito) dissented in *Melendez-Diaz*.

6.   The departures of Justice Souter and Justice Stevens from the narrow majority in *Melendez-Diaz* did not undermine the reach of that case. Indeed, the four dissenters in Bullcoming v. New Mexico, 564 U.S. 2, 131 S.Ct. 2705, 180 L.Ed.2d 610 (2011), accused the majority—that included Justice Sotomayor and Justice Kagan—of extending *Melendez-Diaz*. At issue in *Bullcoming* was the testimony of a lab technician about a test confirming that Bullcoming's blood alcohol was above the threshold for aggravated DWI. Caylor, the technician who performed the test, was not produced as a witness nor did the State claim that he was unavailable.

The New Mexico Supreme Court distinguished *Melendez-Diaz* on the ground that Caylor was a mere scrivener who read a number off a machine. The technician who presented the test results was qualified as an expert witness and was cross-examined about the accuracy of the machine that was used to read the blood alcohol level. He thus functioned as a surrogate for Caylor. Because Bullcoming's "true 'accuser' " was the machine, according to the state court, the defendant's right to cross-examine the surrogate satisfied the confrontation clause.

Justice Ginsburg's majority opinion rejected that reasoning:

> Caylor certified that he received Bullcoming's blood sample intact with the seal unbroken, that he checked to make sure that the forensic report number and the sample number "correspond[ed]," and that he performed on Bullcoming's sample a particular test, adhering to a precise protocol. He further represented, by leaving the "[r]emarks" section of the report blank, that no "circumstance or condition * * * affect[ed] the integrity of the sample or * * * the validity of the analysis." These representations, relating to past events and human actions not revealed in raw, machine-produced data, are [properly the subject of] cross-examination.

Moreover, the Court could not see how to limit a "scrivener" exception, if it recognized one. Defendant's counsel posited a hypothetical that the Court concluded could not be sensibly distinguished from Bullcoming's case:

> Suppose a police report recorded an objective fact—Bullcoming's counsel posited the address above the front door of a house or the read-out of a radar gun. Could an officer other than the one who saw the number on the house or gun present the information in court—so long as that officer was equipped to testify about any technology the observing officer deployed and the police department's standard operating procedures? As our precedent makes plain, the answer is emphatically "No."

Justice Sotomayor, who joined the key parts of the majority opinion, wrote separately to make clear that there are forensic evidence issues yet to be decided—*e.g.*, where the testimony is from a supervisor "with a personal, albeit limited connection to the scientific test" or is a print-out from a machine.

Justice Kennedy's dissent, joined by Chief Justice Roberts, Justice Breyer, and Justice Alito, essentially accepted the state court's surrogate argument. Kennedy noted that only the laboratory certificates were introduced in *Melendez-Diaz,* while in *Bullcoming* the report would "be assessed and explained by in-court testimony subject to full cross-examination. The only sworn statement at issue was that of the witness who was present and who testified."

Justice Kennedy's dissent also complained that a perverse effect of the *Crawford* doctrine was to treat "the reliability of evidence as a reason to exclude it." In the dissent's view, reducing the read-out to a formalized document makes it more reliable, and yet the Court's holding makes it less likely to be admitted. What would Justice Scalia, the author of *Crawford*, say in response to this attack on *Crawford*?

7. *Is the Court lurching back toward reliability instead of confrontation?* Consider the next case.

MICHIGAN V. BRYANT

Supreme Court of the United States, 2011.
562 U.S. 344, 131 S.Ct. 1143, 179 L.Ed.2d 93.

JUSTICE SOTOMAYOR delivered the opinion of the Court [joined by CHIEF JUSTICE ROBERTS, and JUSTICES KENNEDY, BREYER, and ALITO].

At respondent Richard Bryant's trial, the court admitted statements that the victim, Anthony Covington, made to police officers who discovered him mortally wounded in a gas station parking lot. A jury convicted Bryant of, *inter alia,* second-degree murder. On appeal, the Supreme Court of Michigan held that the Sixth Amendment's Confrontation Clause, as explained in our decisions in *Crawford v. Washington*, and *Davis v. Washington*, [p. 1315, Note 2], rendered Covington's statements inadmissible testimonial hearsay, and the court reversed Bryant's conviction. We granted the State's petition for a writ of certiorari to consider whether the Confrontation Clause barred the admission at trial of Covington's statements to the police. We hold that the circumstances of the interaction between Covington and the police objectively indicate that the "primary purpose of the interrogation" was "to enable police assistance to meet an ongoing emergency." Therefore, Covington's identification and description of the shooter and the location of the shooting were not testimonial statements, and their admission at Bryant's trial did not violate the Confrontation Clause. * * *

I

Around 3:25 a.m. on April 29, 2001, Detroit, Michigan police officers responded to a radio dispatch indicating that a man had been shot. At the scene, they found the victim, Anthony Covington, lying on the ground next to his car in a gas station parking lot. Covington had a gunshot wound to his abdomen, appeared to be in great pain, and spoke with difficulty.

The police asked him "what had happened, who had shot him, and where the shooting had occurred." Covington stated that "Rick" shot him at around 3 a.m. He also indicated that he had a conversation with Bryant, whom he recognized based on his voice, through the back door of Bryant's house. Covington explained that when he turned to leave, he was shot through the door and then drove to the gas station, where police found him.

Covington's conversation with the police ended within 5 to 10 minutes when emergency medical services arrived. Covington was transported to a hospital and died within hours. * * *

* * * [The Michigan Supreme Court] concluded that the circumstances "clearly indicate that the primary purpose of the questioning was to establish the facts of an event that had *already* occurred; the primary purpose was not to enable police assistance to meet an ongoing emergency." The court explained that, in its view, Covington was describing past events and as such, his "primary purpose in making these statements to the police * * * was * * * to tell the police who had committed the crime against him, where the crime had been committed, and where the police could find the criminal." Noting that the officers' actions did not suggest that they perceived an ongoing emergency at the gas station, the court held that there was in fact no ongoing emergency. The court distinguished the facts of this case from those in *Davis*, where we held a declarant's statements in a 911 call to be nontestimonial. It instead analogized this case to *Hammon v. Indiana* [p. 1317, Note 3], which we decided jointly with *Davis* and in which we found testimonial a declarant's statements to police just after an assault. Based on this analysis, the Supreme Court of Michigan held that the admission of Covington's statements constituted prejudicial plain error warranting reversal and ordered a new trial. The court did not address whether, absent a Confrontation Clause bar, the statements' admission would have been otherwise consistent with Michigan's hearsay rules or due process.[1]

II * * *

Crawford examined the common-law history of the confrontation right and explained that "the principal evil at which the Confrontation

---

[1] The Supreme Court of Michigan held that the question whether the victim's statements would have been admissible as "dying declarations" was not properly before it because at the preliminary examination, the prosecution, after first invoking both the dying declaration and excited utterance hearsay exceptions, established the factual foundation only for admission of the statements as excited utterances. The trial court ruled that the statements were admissible as excited utterances and did not address their admissibility as dying declarations.

Clause was directed was the civil-law mode of criminal procedure, and particularly its use of *ex parte* examinations as evidence against the accused." We noted that in England, pretrial examinations of suspects and witnesses by government officials "were sometimes read in court in lieu of live testimony." In light of this history, we emphasized the word "witnesses" in the Sixth Amendment, defining it as "those who bear testimony." We defined "testimony" as "[a] solemn declaration or affirmation made for the purpose of establishing or proving some fact." We noted that "[a]n accuser who makes a formal statement to government officers bears testimony in a sense that a person who makes a casual remark to an acquaintance does not." We therefore limited the Confrontation Clause's reach to testimonial statements and held that in order for testimonial evidence to be admissible, the Sixth Amendment "demands what the common law required: unavailability and a prior opportunity for cross-examination." * * *

In 2006, the Court in *Davis* and *Hammon* took a further step to "determine more precisely which police interrogations produce testimony" and therefore implicate a Confrontation Clause bar. * * *

To address the facts of both cases, we expanded upon the meaning of "testimonial" that we first employed in *Crawford* and discussed the concept of an ongoing emergency. We explained:

> "Statements are nontestimonial when made in the course of police interrogation under circumstances objectively indicating that the primary purpose of the interrogation is to enable police assistance to meet an ongoing emergency. They are testimonial when the circumstances objectively indicate that there is no such ongoing emergency, and that the primary purpose of the interrogation is to establish or prove past events potentially relevant to later criminal prosecution."

Examining the *Davis* and *Hammon* statements in light of those definitions, we held that the statements at issue in *Davis* were nontestimonial and the statements in *Hammon* were testimonial. We distinguished the statements in *Davis* from the testimonial statements in *Crawford* on several grounds, including that the victim in *Davis* was "speaking about events *as they were actually happening,* rather than 'describ[ing] past events,' " that there was an ongoing emergency, that the "elicited statements were necessary to be able to *resolve* the present emergency," and that the statements were not formal. In *Hammon,* on the other hand, we held that, "[i]t is entirely clear from the circumstances that the interrogation was part of an investigation into possibly criminal past conduct." There was "no emergency in progress." The officer questioning [the domestic abuse victim] "was not seeking to determine * * * 'what is happening,' but rather 'what happened.' " It was "formal enough" that the police interrogated [her] in a room separate from her husband where, "some time after the events described were over," she "deliberately recounted, in response to police questioning, how potentially criminal past events began and progressed." Because her statements "were neither a cry for help nor the provision of information enabling officers immediately to end a threatening situation," we held that they were testimonial.

Davis did not "attemp[t] to produce an exhaustive classification of all conceivable statements—or even all conceivable statements in response to police interrogation—as either testimonial or nontestimonial." The basic purpose of the Confrontation Clause was to "targe[t]" the sort of "abuses" exemplified at the notorious treason trial of Sir Walter Raleigh. Thus, the most important instances in which the Clause restricts the introduction of out-of-court statements are those in which state actors are involved in a formal, out-of-court interrogation of a witness to obtain evidence for trial. Even where such an interrogation is conducted with all good faith, introduction of the resulting statements at trial can be unfair to the accused if they are untested by cross-examination. Whether formal or informal, out-of-court statements can evade the basic objective of the Confrontation Clause, which is to prevent the accused from being deprived of the opportunity to cross-examine the declarant about statements taken for use at trial. When, as in *Davis,* the primary purpose of an interrogation is to respond to an "ongoing emergency," its purpose is not to create a record for trial and thus is not within the scope of the Clause. But there may be *other* circumstances, aside from ongoing emergencies, when a statement is not procured with a primary purpose of creating an out-of-court substitute for trial testimony. In making the primary purpose determination, standard rules of hearsay, designed to identify some statements as reliable, will be relevant. Where no such primary purpose exists, the admissibility of a statement is the concern of state and federal rules of evidence, not the Confrontation Clause.

Deciding this case also requires further explanation of the "ongoing emergency" circumstance addressed in *Davis*. Because *Davis* and *Hammon* arose in the domestic violence context, that was the situation "we had immediately in mind (for that was the case before us)." We now face a new context: a nondomestic dispute, involving a victim found in a public location, suffering from a fatal gunshot wound, and a perpetrator whose location was unknown at the time the police located the victim. Thus, we confront for the first time circumstances in which the "ongoing emergency" discussed in *Davis* extends beyond an initial victim to a potential threat to the responding police and the public at large. This new context requires us to provide additional clarification with regard to what *Davis* meant by "the primary purpose of the interrogation is to enable police assistance to meet an ongoing emergency."

III

To determine whether the "primary purpose" of an interrogation is "to enable police assistance to meet an ongoing emergency," which would render the resulting statements nontestimonial, we objectively evaluate the circumstances in which the encounter occurs and the statements and actions of the parties.

A * * *

An objective analysis of the circumstances of an encounter and the statements and actions of the parties to it provides the most accurate assessment of the "primary purpose of the interrogation." The circumstances in which an encounter occurs—*e.g.,* at or near the scene of the crime versus at a police station, during an ongoing emergency or afterwards—are clearly matters of objective fact. The statements and actions of the parties must also be objectively evaluated. That is, the relevant inquiry is not the subjective or actual purpose of the individuals involved in a particular encounter, but rather the purpose that reasonable participants would have had, as ascertained from the individuals' statements and actions and the circumstances in which the encounter occurred.

B

As our recent Confrontation Clause cases have explained, the existence of an "ongoing emergency" at the time of an encounter between an individual and the police is among the most important circumstances informing the "primary purpose" of an interrogation. The existence of an ongoing emergency is relevant to determining the primary purpose of the interrogation because an emergency focuses the participants on something other than "prov[ing] past events potentially relevant to later criminal prosecution." Rather, it focuses them on "end[ing] a threatening situation." Implicit in *Davis* is the idea that because the prospect of fabrication in statements given for the primary purpose of resolving that emergency is presumably significantly diminished, the Confrontation Clause does not require such statements to be subject to the crucible of cross-examination.

This logic is not unlike that justifying the excited utterance exception in hearsay law. Statements "relating to a startling event or condition made while the declarant was under the stress of excitement caused by the event or condition" are considered reliable because the declarant, in the excitement, presumably cannot form a falsehood. An ongoing emergency has a similar effect of focusing an individual's attention on responding to the emergency.[9] * * *

---

[9] Many other exceptions to the hearsay rules similarly rest on the belief that certain statements are, by their nature, made for a purpose other than use in a prosecution and

* * * [O]ur discussion of the Michigan Supreme Court's misunderstanding of what *Davis* meant by "ongoing emergency" should not be taken to imply that the existence *vel non* of an ongoing emergency is dispositive of the testimonial inquiry. As *Davis* made clear, whether an ongoing emergency exists is simply one factor—albeit an important factor—that informs the ultimate inquiry regarding the "primary purpose" of an interrogation. Another factor the Michigan Supreme Court did not sufficiently account for is the importance of *informality* in an encounter between a victim and police. Formality is not the sole touchstone of our primary purpose inquiry because, although formality suggests the absence of an emergency and therefore an increased likelihood that the purpose of the interrogation is to "establish or prove past events potentially relevant to later criminal prosecution," informality does not necessarily indicate the presence of an emergency or the lack of testimonial intent. The court below, however, too readily dismissed the informality of the circumstances in this case in a single brief footnote and in fact seems to have suggested that the encounter in this case was formal. As we explain further below, the questioning in this case occurred in an exposed, public area, prior to the arrival of emergency medical services, and in a disorganized fashion. All of those facts make this case distinguishable from the formal station-house interrogation in *Crawford*.

C

In addition to the circumstances in which an encounter occurs, the statements and actions of both the declarant and interrogators provide objective evidence of the primary purpose of the interrogation. The Michigan Supreme Court did, at least briefly, conduct this inquiry.

As the Michigan Supreme Court correctly recognized, *Davis* requires a combined inquiry that accounts for both the declarant and the interrogator. In many instances, the primary purpose of the interrogation will be most accurately ascertained by looking to the contents of both the questions and the answers. To give an extreme example, if the police say to a victim, "Tell us who did this to you so that we can arrest and

---

therefore should not be barred by hearsay prohibitions. See, *e.g.,* (statement by a co-conspirator during and in furtherance of the conspiracy); 803(4) (Statements for Purposes of Medical Diagnosis or Treatment); 803(6) (Records of Regularly Conducted Activity); 803(8) (Public Records and Reports); 803(9) (Records of Vital Statistics); 803(11) (Records of Religious Organizations); 803(12) (Marriage, Baptismal, and Similar Certificates); 803(13) (Family Records); 804(b)(3) (Statement Against Interest); see also *Melendez-Diaz v. Massachusetts*, [p. 1318, Note 5] ("Business and public records are generally admissible absent confrontation not because they qualify under an exception to the hearsay rules, but because-having been created for the administration of an entity's affairs and not for the purpose of establishing or proving some fact at trial-they are not testimonial"); *Giles v. California*, [p. 1317, Note 4] (noting in the context of domestic violence that "[s]tatements to friends and neighbors about abuse and intimidation and statements to physicians in the course of receiving treatment would be excluded, if at all, only by hearsay rules"); *Crawford* ("Most of the hearsay exceptions covered statements that by their nature were not testimonial—for example, business records or statements in furtherance of a conspiracy").

prosecute them," the victim's response that "Rick did it," appears purely accusatory because by virtue of the phrasing of the question, the victim necessarily has prosecution in mind when she answers.

The combined approach also ameliorates problems that could arise from looking solely to one participant. Predominant among these is the problem of mixed motives on the part of both interrogators and declarants. Police officers in our society function as both first responders and criminal investigators. Their dual responsibilities may mean that they act with different motives simultaneously or in quick succession.

Victims are also likely to have mixed motives when they make statements to the police. During an ongoing emergency, a victim is most likely to want the threat to her and to other potential victims to end, but that does not necessarily mean that the victim wants or envisions prosecution of the assailant. A victim may want the attacker to be incapacitated temporarily or rehabilitated. Alternatively, a severely injured victim may have no purpose at all in answering questions posed; the answers may be simply reflexive. The victim's injuries could be so debilitating as to prevent her from thinking sufficiently clearly to understand whether her statements are for the purpose of addressing an ongoing emergency or for the purpose of future prosecution. Taking into account a victim's injuries does not transform this objective inquiry into a subjective one. The inquiry is still objective because it focuses on the understanding and purpose of a reasonable victim in the circumstances of the actual victim-circumstances that prominently include the victim's physical state. * * *

IV * * *

Applying this analysis to the facts of this case is more difficult than in *Davis* because we do not have the luxury of reviewing a transcript of the conversation between the victim and the police officers. Further complicating our task is the fact that the trial in this case occurred before our decisions in *Crawford* and *Davis*. We therefore review a record that was not developed to ascertain the "primary purpose of the interrogation."

We first examine the circumstances in which the interrogation occurred. The parties disagree over whether there was an emergency when the police arrived at the gas station. Bryant argues, and the Michigan Supreme Court accepted, that there was no ongoing emergency because "there * * * was no criminal conduct occurring. No shots were being fired, no one was seen in possession of a firearm, nor were any witnesses seen cowering in fear or running from the scene." Bryant, while conceding that "a serious or life-threatening injury creates a medical emergency for a victim," further argues that a declarant's medical emergency is not relevant to the ongoing emergency determination.

In contrast, Michigan and the Solicitor General explain that when the police responded to the call that a man had been shot and found Covington bleeding on the gas station parking lot, "they did not know who Covington was, whether the shooting had occurred at the gas station or at a different location, who the assailant was, or whether the assailant posed a continuing threat to Covington or others."

* * * The officers' testimony is essentially consistent but, at the same time, not specific. The officers basically agree on what information they learned from Covington, but not on the order in which they learned it or on whether Covington's statements were in response to general or detailed questions. They all agree that the first question was "what happened?" The answer was either "I was shot" or "Rick shot me."

As explained above, the scope of an emergency in terms of its threat to individuals other than the initial assailant and victim will often depend on the type of dispute involved. Nothing Covington said to the police indicated that the cause of the shooting was a purely private dispute or that the threat from the shooter had ended. The record reveals little about the motive for the shooting. * * * What Covington did tell the officers was that he fled Bryant's back porch, indicating that he perceived an ongoing threat. The police did not know, and Covington did not tell them, whether the threat was limited to him. The potential scope of the dispute and therefore the emergency in this case thus stretches more broadly than those at issue in *Davis* and *Hammon* and encompasses a threat potentially to the police and the public.

This is also the first of our post-*Crawford* Confrontation Clause cases to involve a gun. The physical separation that was sufficient to end the emergency in *Hammon* was not necessarily sufficient to end the threat in this case; Covington was shot through the back door of Bryant's house. Bryant's argument that there was no ongoing emergency because "[n]o shots were being fired," surely construes ongoing emergency too narrowly. An emergency does not last only for the time between when the assailant pulls the trigger and the bullet hits the victim. If an out-of-sight sniper pauses between shots, no one would say that the emergency ceases during the pause. That is an extreme example and not the situation here, but it serves to highlight the implausibility, at least as to certain weapons, of construing the emergency to last only precisely as long as the violent act itself, as some have construed our opinion in *Davis*.

* * * At bottom, there was an ongoing emergency here where an armed shooter, whose motive for and location after the shooting were unknown, had mortally wounded Covington within a few blocks and a few minutes of the location where the police found Covington.

This is not to suggest that the emergency continued until Bryant was arrested in California a year after the shooting. We need not decide precisely when the emergency ended because Covington's encounter with the police and all of the statements he made during that interaction occurred within the first few minutes of the police officers' arrival and well before they secured the scene of the shooting—the shooter's last known location. * * *

For their part, the police responded to a call that a man had been shot. As discussed above, they did not know why, where, or when the shooting had occurred. Nor did they know the location of the shooter or anything else about the circumstances in which the crime occurred. The questions they asked—"what had happened, who had shot him, and where the shooting occurred,"—were the exact type of questions necessary to allow the police to " 'assess the situation, the threat to their own safety, and possible danger to the potential victim' " and to the public, including to allow them to ascertain "whether they would be encountering a violent felon," In other words, they solicited the information necessary to enable them "to meet an ongoing emergency."

Nothing in Covington's responses indicated to the police that, contrary to their expectation upon responding to a call reporting a shooting, there was no emergency or that a prior emergency had ended. Covington did indicate that he had been shot at another location about 25 minutes earlier, but he did not know the location of the shooter at the time the police arrived and, as far as we can tell from the record, he gave no indication that the shooter, having shot at him twice, would be satisfied that Covington was only wounded. In fact, Covington did not indicate any possible motive for the shooting, and thereby gave no reason to think that the shooter would not shoot again if he arrived on the scene. * * *

Finally, we consider the informality of the situation and the interrogation. This situation is more similar, though not identical, to the informal, harried 911 call in *Davis* than to the structured, station-house interview in *Crawford*. As the officers' trial testimony reflects, the situation was fluid and somewhat confused: the officers arrived at different times; apparently each, upon arrival, asked Covington "what happened?"; and, contrary to the dissent's portrayal, they did not conduct a structured interrogation. The informality suggests that the interrogators' primary purpose was simply to address what they perceived to be an ongoing emergency, and the circumstances lacked any formality that would have alerted Covington to or focused him on the possible future prosecutorial use of his statements. * * *

For the foregoing reasons, we hold that Covington's statements were not testimonial and that their admission at Bryant's trial did not violate the Confrontation Clause. * * *

JUSTICE KAGAN took no part in the consideration or decision of this case.

JUSTICE THOMAS, concurring in the judgment.

I agree with the Court that the admission of Covington's out-of-court statements did not violate the Confrontation Clause, but I reach this conclusion because Covington's questioning by police lacked sufficient formality and solemnity for his statements to be considered "testimonial."

In determining whether Covington's statements to police implicate the Confrontation Clause, the Court evaluates the "primary purpose" of the interrogation. The majority's analysis which relies on, *inter alia,* what the police knew when they arrived at the scene, the specific questions they asked, the particular information Covington conveyed, the weapon involved, and Covington's medical condition illustrates the uncertainty that this test creates for law enforcement and the lower courts. I have criticized the primary-purpose test as "an exercise in fiction" that is "disconnected from history" and "yields no predictable results."

Rather than attempting to reconstruct the "primary purpose" of the participants, I would consider the extent to which the interrogation resembles those historical practices that the Confrontation Clause addressed. As the majority notes, Covington interacted with the police under highly informal circumstances, while he bled from a fatal gunshot wound. The police questioning was not "a formalized dialogue," did not result in "formalized testimonial materials" such as a deposition or affidavit, and bore no "indicia of solemnity." Nor is there any indication that the statements were offered at trial "in order to evade confrontation." This interrogation bears little if any resemblance to the historical practices that the Confrontation Clause aimed to eliminate. Covington thus did not "bea[r] testimony" against Bryant, and the introduction of his statements at trial did not implicate the Confrontation Clause. I concur in the judgment.

JUSTICE SCALIA, dissenting.

Today's tale—a story of five officers conducting successive examinations of a dying man with the primary purpose, not of obtaining and preserving his testimony regarding his killer, but of protecting him, them, and others from a murderer somewhere on the loose—is so transparently false that professing to believe it demeans this institution. But reaching a patently incorrect conclusion on the facts is a relatively benign judicial mischief; it affects, after all, only the case at hand. In its vain attempt to make the incredible plausible, however—or perhaps as an intended second goal—today's opinion distorts our Confrontation Clause jurisprudence and leaves it in a shambles. Instead of clarifying the law, the Court makes itself the obfuscator of last resort. Because I continue to adhere to the Confrontation Clause that the People adopted, as described in *Crawford*, I dissent.

I

A * * *

Crawford and *Davis* did not address whose perspective matters—the declarant's, the interrogator's, or both—when assessing "the primary purpose of [an] interrogation." In those cases the statements were testimonial from any perspective. I think the same is true here, but because the Court picks a perspective so will I: The declarant's intent is what counts. In-court testimony is more than a narrative of past events; it is a solemn declaration made in the course of a criminal trial. For an out-of-court statement to qualify as testimonial, the declarant must intend the statement to be a solemn declaration rather than an unconsidered or offhand remark; and he must make the statement with the understanding that it may be used to invoke the coercive machinery of the State against the accused.[1] That is what distinguishes a narrative told to a friend over dinner from a statement to the police. The hidden purpose of an interrogator cannot substitute for the declarant's intentional solemnity or his understanding of how his words may be used.

A declarant-focused inquiry is also the only inquiry that would work in every fact pattern implicating the Confrontation Clause. The Clause applies to volunteered testimony as well as statements solicited through police interrogation. An inquiry into an officer's purposes would make no sense when a declarant blurts out "Rick shot me" as soon as the officer arrives on the scene. I see no reason to adopt a different test—one that accounts for an officer's intent—when the officer asks "what happened" before the declarant makes his accusation. (This does not mean the interrogator is irrelevant. The identity of an interrogator, and the content and tenor of his questions, can bear upon whether a declarant intends to make a solemn statement, and envisions its use at a criminal trial. But none of this means that the interrogator's purpose matters.)

In an unsuccessful attempt to make its finding of emergency plausible, the Court instead adopts a test that looks to the purposes of both the police and the declarant. It claims that this is demanded by necessity, fretting that a domestic-violence victim may want her abuser briefly arrested—presumably to teach him a lesson—but not desire prosecution. I do not need to probe the purposes of the police to solve that problem. Even if a victim speaks to the police "to establish or prove past events" solely for the purpose of getting her abuser arrested, she surely knows her account is "potentially relevant to later criminal prosecution" should one ensue.

---

[1] I remain agnostic about whether and when statements to nonstate actors are testimonial.

The Court also wrings its hands over the possibility that "a severely injured victim" may lack the capacity to form a purpose, and instead answer questions "reflexive[ly]." How to assess whether a declarant with diminished capacity bore testimony is a difficult question, and one I do not need to answer today. But the Court's proposed answer—to substitute the intentions of the police for the missing intentions of the declarant—cannot be the correct one. When the declarant has diminished capacity, focusing on the interrogators make less sense, not more. The inquiry under *Crawford* turns in part on the actions and statements of a declarant's audience only because they shape the declarant's perception of why his audience is listening and therefore influence *his purpose* in making the declaration. But a person who cannot perceive his own purposes certainly cannot perceive why a listener might be interested in what he has to say. * * *

The Court claims one affirmative virtue for its focus on the purposes of both the declarant and the police: It "ameliorates problems that * * * arise" when declarants have "mixed motives." I am at a loss to know how. Sorting out the primary purpose of a declarant with mixed motives is sometimes difficult. But adding in the mixed motives of the police only compounds the problem. Now courts will have to sort through two sets of mixed motives to determine the primary purpose of an interrogation. And the Court's solution creates a mixed-motive problem where (under the proper theory) it does not exist—viz., where the police and the declarant each have one motive, but those motives conflict. The Court does not provide an answer to this glaringly obvious problem, probably because it does not have one.

The only virtue of the Court's approach (if it can be misnamed [sic] a virtue) is that it leaves judges free to reach the "fairest" result under the totality of the circumstances. If the dastardly police trick a declarant into giving an incriminating statement against a sympathetic defendant, a court can focus on the police's intent and declare the statement testimonial. If the defendant "deserves" to go to jail, then a court can focus on whatever perspective is necessary to declare damning hearsay nontestimonial. And when all else fails, a court can mix-and-match perspectives to reach its desired outcome. Unfortunately, under this malleable approach "the guarantee of confrontation is no guarantee at all."

B

Looking to the declarant's purpose (as we should), this is an absurdly easy case. Roughly 25 minutes after Anthony Covington had been shot, Detroit police responded to a 911 call reporting that a gunshot victim had appeared at a neighborhood gas station. They quickly arrived at the scene, and in less than 10 minutes five different Detroit police officers questioned Covington about the shooting. Each asked him a similar battery of questions: "what happened" and when, "who shot the victim," and "where" did the shooting take place. After Covington would answer, they would ask follow-up questions, such as "how tall is" the shooter, "[h]ow much does he weigh," what is the exact address or physical description of the house where the shooting took place, and what chain of events led to the shooting. The battery relented when the paramedics arrived and began tending to Covington's wounds.

From Covington's perspective, his statements had little value except to ensure the arrest and eventual prosecution of Richard Bryant. He knew the "threatening situation" had ended six blocks away and 25 minutes earlier when he fled from Bryant's back porch. * * * Even if Bryant had pursued him (unlikely), and after seeing that Covington had ended up at the gas station was unable to confront him there before the police arrived (doubly unlikely), it was entirely beyond imagination that Bryant would again open fire while Covington was surrounded by five armed police officers. And Covington knew the shooting was the work of a drug dealer, not a spree killer who might randomly threaten others.

Covington's knowledge that he had nothing to fear differs significantly from Michelle McCottry's state of mind during her "frantic" statements to a 911 operator at issue in *Davis*. Her "call was plainly a call for help against a bona fide physical threat" describing "events *as they were actually happening*." She did not have the luxuries of police protection and of time and space separating her from immediate danger that Covington enjoyed when he made his statements.

Covington's pressing medical needs do not suggest that he was responding to an emergency, but to the contrary reinforce the testimonial character of his statements. He understood the police were focused on investigating a past crime, not his medical needs. None of the officers asked Covington how he was doing, attempted more than superficially to assess the severity of his wounds, or attempted to administer first aid. They instead primarily asked questions with little, if any, relevance to Covington's dire situation. Police, paramedics, and doctors do not need to know the address where a shooting took place, the name of the shooter, or the shooter's height and weight to provide proper medical care. Underscoring that Covington understood the officers' investigative role, he interrupted their interrogation to ask "when is EMS coming?" When, in other words, would the focus shift to his medical needs rather than Bryant's crime?

Neither Covington's statements nor the colloquy between him and the officers would have been out of place at a trial; it would have been a routine direct examination. Like a witness, Covington recounted in detail how a past criminal event began and progressed, and like a prosecutor, the police elicited that account through structured questioning. Preventing the admission of "weaker substitute[s] for live testimony at trial" such as this is precisely what motivated the Framers to adopt the Confrontation Clause and what motivated our decisions in *Crawford* and in *Hammon v. Indiana,* decided with *Davis. Ex parte* examinations raise the same constitutional concerns whether they take place in a gas-station parking lot or in a police interrogation room.

C

Worse still for the repute of today's opinion, this is an absurdly easy case even if one (erroneously) takes the interrogating officers' purpose into account. The five officers interrogated Covington primarily to investigate past criminal events. None—absolutely none—of their actions indicated that they perceived an imminent threat. They did not draw their weapons, and indeed did not immediately search the gas station for potential shooters. To the contrary, all five testified that they questioned Covington *before conducting any investigation at the scene.* Would this have made any sense if they feared the presence of a shooter? Most tellingly, none of the officers started his interrogation by asking what would have been the obvious first question if any hint of such a fear existed: Where is the shooter?

But do not rely solely on my word about the officers' primary purpose. Listen to Sergeant Wenturine, who candidly admitted that he interrogated Covington because he "ha[d] a man here that [he] believe[d] [was] dying [so he was] gonna find out who did this, period." In short, he needed to interrogate Covington to solve a crime. Wenturine never mentioned an interest in ending an ongoing emergency.

At the very least, the officers' intentions *turned* investigative during their 10-minute encounter with Covington, and the conversation "evolve[d] into testimonial statements." The fifth officer to arrive at the scene did not need to run straight to Covington and ask a battery of questions "to determine the need for emergency assistance," He could have asked his fellow officers, who presumably had a better sense of that than Covington—and a better sense of what he could do to assist. No, the value of asking the same battery of questions a fifth time was to ensure that Covington told a consistent story and to see if any new details helpful to the investigation and eventual prosecution would emerge. Having the testimony of five officers to recount Covington's consistent story undoubtedly helped obtain Bryant's conviction. (Which came, I may note, after the first jury could not reach a verdict.)

D

A final word about the Court's active imagination. The Court invents a world where an ongoing emergency exists whenever "an armed shooter, whose motive for and location after the shooting [are] unknown, * * * mortally wound[s]" one individual "within a few blocks and [25] minutes of the location where the police" ultimately find that victim. Breathlessly, it worries that a shooter could leave the scene armed and ready to pull the trigger again. Nothing suggests the five officers in this case shared the Court's dystopian[4] view of Detroit, where drug dealers hunt their shooting victim down and fire into a crowd of police officers to finish him off, or where spree killers shoot through a door and then roam the streets leaving a trail of bodies behind. Because almost 90 percent of murders involve a single victim, it is much more likely—indeed, I think it certain—that the officers viewed their encounter with Covington for what it was: an investigation into a past crime with no ongoing or immediate consequences.

The Court's distorted view creates an expansive exception to the Confrontation Clause for violent crimes. Because Bryant posed a continuing threat to public safety in the Court's imagination, the emergency persisted for confrontation purposes at least until the police learned his "motive for and location after the shooting." It may have persisted in this case until the police "secured the scene of the shooting" two-and-a-half hours later. (The relevance of securing the scene is unclear so long as the killer is still at large—especially if, as the Court speculates, he may be a spree-killer.) This is a dangerous definition of emergency. Many individuals who testify against a defendant at trial first offer their accounts to police in the hours after a violent act. If the police can plausibly claim that a "potential threat to * * * the public" persisted through those first few hours, (and if the claim is plausible here it is always plausible) a defendant will have no constitutionally protected right to exclude the uncross-examined testimony of such witnesses. His conviction could rest (as perhaps it did here) solely on the officers' recollection at trial of the witnesses' accusations. * * *

II

A

But today's decision is not only a gross distortion of the facts. It is a gross distortion of the law—a revisionist narrative in which reliability continues to guide our Confrontation Clause jurisprudence, at least where emergencies and faux emergencies are concerned. According to today's opinion, the *Davis* inquiry into whether a declarant spoke to end an ongoing emergency or rather to "prove past events potentially relevant to later criminal prosecution" is *not* aimed at answering whether the declarant acted as a witness. Instead, the *Davis* inquiry probes the *reliability* of a declarant's statements, "[i]mplicit[ly]" importing the

---

[4] The opposite of utopian. The word was coined by John Stuart Mill as a caustic description of British policy. See 190 Hansard's Parliamentary Debates, Third Series 1517 (3d Ser.1868); 5 Oxford English Dictionary 13 (2d ed.1989).

excited-utterances hearsay exception into the Constitution. A statement during an ongoing emergency is sufficiently reliable, the Court says, "because the prospect of fabrication * * * is presumably significantly diminished," so it "does not [need] to be subject to the crucible of cross-examination."

Compare that with the holding of *Crawford:* "Where testimonial statements are at issue, the only indicium of reliability sufficient to satisfy constitutional demands is the one the Constitution actually prescribes: confrontation." * * * (This is not to say that that "reliability" logic can actually justify today's result: Twenty-five minutes is plenty of time for a shooting victim to reflect and fabricate a false story.)

The Court announces that in future cases it will look to "standard rules of hearsay, designed to identify some statements as reliable," when deciding whether a statement is testimonial. *Ohio v. Roberts*, [p. 1302], said something remarkably similar: An out-of-court statement is admissible if it "falls within a firmly rooted hearsay exception" or otherwise "bears adequate 'indicia of reliability.'" We tried that approach to the Confrontation Clause for nearly 25 years before *Crawford rejected* it as an unworkable standard unmoored from the text and the historical roots of the Confrontation Clause. The arguments in Raleigh's infamous 17th-century treason trial contained full debate about the reliability of Lord Cobham's *ex parte* accusations; that case remains the canonical example of a Confrontation Clause violation, not because Raleigh should have won the debate but because he should have been allowed cross-examination.

The Court attempts to fit its resurrected interest in reliability into the *Crawford* framework, but the result is incoherent. Reliability, the Court tells us, is a good indicator of whether "a statement is * * * an out-of-court substitute for trial testimony." That is patently false. Reliability tells us *nothing* about whether a statement is testimonial. Testimonial and nontestimonial statements alike come in varying degrees of reliability. An eyewitness's statements to the police after a fender-bender, for example, are both reliable and testimonial. Statements to the police from one driver attempting to blame the other would be similarly testimonial but rarely reliable.

The Court suggests otherwise because it "misunderstands the relationship" between qualification for one of the standard hearsay exceptions and exemption from the confrontation requirement. That relationship is not a causal one. Hearsay law exempts business records, for example, because businesses have a financial incentive to keep reliable records. The Sixth Amendment also generally admits business records into evidence, but not because the records are reliable or because hearsay law says so. It admits them "because—having been created for the administration of an entity's affairs and not for the purpose of establishing or proving some fact at trial—they are not" weaker substitutes for live testimony. Moreover, the scope of the exemption from confrontation and that of the hearsay exceptions also are not always coextensive. The reliability logic of the business-record exception would extend to records maintained by neutral parties providing litigation-support services, such as evidence testing. The Confrontation Clause is not so forgiving. Business records prepared specifically for use at a criminal trial are testimonial and require confrontation.

Is it possible that the Court does not recognize the contradiction between its focus on reliable statements and *Crawford*'s focus on testimonial ones? Does it not realize that the two cannot coexist? Or does it intend, by following today's illogical roadmap, to resurrect *Roberts* by a thousand unprincipled distinctions without ever explicitly overruling *Crawford*? After all, honestly overruling *Crawford* would destroy the illusion of judicial minimalism and restraint. And it would force the Court to explain how the Justices' preference comports with the meaning of the Confrontation Clause that the People adopted—or to confess that only the Justices' preference really matters.

B

The Court recedes from *Crawford* in a second significant way. It requires judges to conduct "open-ended balancing tests" and "amorphous, if not entirely subjective," inquiries into the totality of the circumstances bearing upon reliability. Where the prosecution cries "emergency," the admissibility of a statement now turns on "a highly context-dependent inquiry" into the type of weapon the defendant wielded; the type of crime the defendant committed; the medical condition of the declarant; if the declarant is injured, whether paramedics have arrived on the scene; whether the encounter takes place in an "exposed public area"; whether the encounter appears disorganized; whether the declarant is capable of forming a purpose; whether the police have secured the scene of the crime; the formality of the statement; and finally, whether the statement strikes us as reliable. This is no better than the nine-factor balancing test we rejected in *Crawford*. I do not look forward to resolving conflicts in the future over whether knives and poison are more like guns or fists for Confrontation Clause purposes, or whether rape and armed robbery are more like murder or domestic violence. * * *

* * * [W]e did not disavow multifactor balancing for reliability in *Crawford* out of a preference for rules over standards. We did so because it "d[id] violence to" the Framers' design. It was judges' open-ended determination of what was reliable that violated the trial rights of Englishmen in the political trials of the 16th and 17th centuries. The Framers placed the Confrontation Clause in the Bill of Rights to ensure

that those abuses (and the abuses by the Admiralty courts in colonial America) would not be repeated in this country. Not even the least dangerous branch can be trusted to assess the reliability of uncross-examined testimony in politically charged trials or trials implicating threats to national security.

* * *

Judicial decisions, like the Constitution itself, are nothing more than "parchment barriers," 5 Writings of James Madison 269, 272 (G. Hunt ed.1901). Both depend on a judicial culture that understands its constitutionally assigned role, has the courage to persist in that role when it means announcing unpopular decisions, and has the modesty to persist when it produces results that go against the judges' policy preferences. Today's opinion falls far short of living up to that obligation—short on the facts, and short on the law.

For all I know, Bryant has received his just deserts. But he surely has not received them pursuant to the procedures that our Constitution requires. And what has been taken away from him has been taken away from us all.

JUSTICE GINSBURG, dissenting.

I agree with Justice Scalia that Covington's statements were testimonial and that "[t]he declarant's intent is what counts." Even if the interrogators' intent were what counts, I further agree, Covington's statements would still be testimonial. It is most likely that "the officers viewed their encounter with Covington [as] an investigation into a past crime with no ongoing or immediate consequences." Today's decision, Justice Scalia rightly notes, "creates an expansive exception to the Confrontation Clause for violent crimes." In so doing, the decision confounds our recent Confrontation Clause jurisprudence, which made it plain that "[r]eliability tells us nothing about whether a statement is testimonial."

I would add, however, this observation. In *Crawford*, this Court noted that, in the law we inherited from England, there was a well-established exception to the confrontation requirement: The cloak protecting the accused against admission of out-of-court testimonial statements was removed for dying declarations. This historic exception, we recalled in *Giles v. California*, applied to statements made by a person about to die and aware that death was imminent. Were the issue properly tendered here, I would take up the question whether the exception for dying declarations survives our recent Confrontation Clause decisions. The Michigan Supreme Court, however, held, as a matter of state law, that the prosecutor had abandoned the issue. The matter, therefore, is not one the Court can address in this case.

NOTES AND QUESTIONS

1.   Do you think the majority's approach is a faithful application of *Crawford* or are Justices Scalia and Ginsburg right that the majority "confounds our recent Confrontation Clause jurisprudence, which made it plain that '[r]eliability tells us nothing about whether a statement is testimonial' "? Faithfulness aside, do you believe that the majority's approach will be workable in the trial courts?

2.   If the intent of the police should "count" on the issue of whether Covington's statements were testimonial, do you believe that the "primary purpose" of the police questions was to deal with an "ongoing emergency"?

3.   *More Bryant fallout?* The *Bryant* majority suggested that reliability might still have a place in the confrontation clause doctrine. In Ohio v. Clark, 576 U.S. 1, 135 S.Ct. 2173, 192 L.Ed.2d 306 (2015), the issue was the admissibility of statements made to preschool teachers by a three-year-old victim of child abuse. The child did not testify at trial, but his statements were introduced. The Court unanimously agreed that the admission of the statements did not violate the confrontation clause, but Justice Scalia, concurring in the judgment, protested the Court's "shoveling of fresh dirt upon the Sixth Amendment right of confrontation so recently rescued from the grave in *Crawford v. Washington.*" Scalia accused the majority of wishing to return to "that halcyon era for prosecutors" when hearsay exceptions, based on presumed reliability, permitted the introduction of statements that had never been cross-examined.

The majority found that the primary purpose of the questioning by the teachers was not to elicit testimony for trial but, rather, to identify and end the threat to the child. Scalia and Ginsburg agreed. Thus, using the *Crawford* test, the confrontation clause permitted use of the statements. But the majority incurred Scalia's ire when it suggested that, even if the primary purpose was to elicit trial testimony, there are other conditions that must be satisfied before the confrontation clause will bar the testimony. Scalia being of a self-described "suspicious mind" worried that announcing the existence of these mysterious other conditions might be "the first step in an attempt to smuggle long-standing hearsay exceptions back into the Confrontation Clause—in other words, an attempt to return to *Ohio v. Roberts.*"

For Scalia (and Ginsburg who joined his opinion), if the primary purpose of the questioning is to elicit testimony for trial, the State bears the burden of proving a "long-established practice of introducing specific kinds of evidence, such as dying declarations, for which cross-examination was not typically necessary." A generalized finding of reliability would not suffice. For the majority, it is not clear what other conditions must be satisfied before there is a violation of the confrontation clause. What we do know is that there was no violation in *Clark.*

4.   *Crawford in chaos?* Cellmark Lab tested a vaginal swab from a rape victim and produced a DNA profile of the rapist. When Williams was

arrested, his DNA profile was produced by the Illinois State Police lab. At a bench trial, an expert from the state lab testified that the DNA profile she produced matched the profile produced by Cellmark. The State did not call the Cellmark expert who produced the DNA profile from the vaginal swab, and Williams claimed that his confrontation clause rights were violated because he could not cross-examine the expert who produced evidence against him. Williams v. Illinois, 567 U.S. ___, 132 S.Ct. 2221, 183 L.Ed.2d 89 (2012).

The Illinois courts held that the State did not have to call the Cellmark expert, and the United States Supreme Court affirmed in an opinion so badly-splintered that it is difficult to determine the holding. Justice Alito, writing also for the Chief Justice, and Justices Kennedy and Breyer, concluded that the reference to the Cellmark DNA profile was not offered for the truth of the matter asserted and thus was an exception both to the hearsay rule and the protection of the confrontation clause. Alito claimed that the Cellmark DNA profile was offered merely as a premise along the lines of a hypothetical question: "Assuming that this was the DNA profile of the rapist, does it match that of the defendant?"

But five justices flatly rejected this line of analysis. As Justice Thomas wrote, concurring in the judgment, "[T]here was no plausible reason for the introduction of Cellmark's statements other than to establish their truth." Justice Kagan's dissent, joined by Justices Scalia, Ginsburg, and Sotomayor, agreed with Thomas that the "no truth" characterization was fanciful. Thus, five justices held that, on the facts of the case, the "no-truth" exception to the hearsay rule and the confrontation clause did not permit the State to present the Cellmark DNA profile without making the expert available to testify.

Consistent with his long-standing approach to the confrontation clause, however, Justice Thomas concluded that scientific testing does not qualify for protection because it is not "testimonial." For Thomas, "testimonial" means "formalized" materials prepared for use at trial "such as depositions, affidavits, and prior testimony," as well as statements made during custodial interrogation. This of course fits the history quite well, and for Thomas that is the end of the matter. A scientific test does not fit Thomas's test of "formalized" materials because it is "neither a sworn nor a certified declaration of fact." Thus, Thomas concluded that there is no right to confront the expert who prepared the DNA profile of the rapist.

Eight members of the Court rejected Thomas's definition so the question for the rest of the Court was whether the Cellmark report qualifies as a no-truth exception to the confrontation clause. Four said yes, four said no. Since Thomas voted with the four who said yes, Williams's conviction was affirmed but the holding of the case is elusive. Indeed, Justice Breyer wrote a concurring opinion that begins, "This case raises a question that I believe neither the plurality nor the dissent answers adequately."

Justice Kagan's dissent for four members of the Court argued that the Cellmark DNA profile was no different from the scientific reports at the heart of two recent cases, *Melendez-Diaz*, p. 1318, Note 5, and *Bullcoming*, p. 1319,

Note 6. The Court in those cases held that the confrontation clause gave the defendant the right to cross-examine the expert who prepared those reports. Thus, for the dissent, "the substance of the [Cellmark] report would come into evidence only if Williams had a chance to cross-examine the responsible [Cellmark] analyst." The dissent also complained about lack of clarity engendered by the combined votes of the plurality and Justice Thomas:

> The five Justices who control the outcome of today's case agree on very little. Among them, though, they can boast of two accomplishments. First, they have approved the introduction of testimony at Williams's trial that the Confrontation Clause, rightly understood, clearly prohibits. Second, they have left significant confusion in their wake. What comes out of four Justices' desire to limit *Melendez-Diaz* and *Bullcoming* in whatever way possible, combined with one Justice's one-justice view of those holdings is—to be frank—who knows what. Those decisions apparently no longer mean all that they say. Yet no one can tell in what way or to what extent they are altered because no proposed limitation commands the support of the majority.

5. Where *Crawford* goes from here is anybody's guess, especially in light of Justice Scalia's death. One issue left unresolved in the *Crawford* line of cases was whether statements to private citizens are within the scope of the confrontation clause. Although the Court "declined to adopt" a "categorical[ ]" rule here, it concluded that "[s]tatements made to someone who is not principally charged with uncovering and prosecuting criminal behavior are significantly less likely to be testimonial than statements given to law enforcement officers."

6. *A procedural wrinkle.* We have developed the core of confrontation clause doctrine. Now for a wrinkle. Bonnie and Clyde are arrested for bank robbery. In response to police interrogation, Clyde gives a rambling, partly incoherent confession accusing Bonnie of being the brains behind the team but admitting his own involvement in the robberies. After *Crawford*, it is clear that this confession cannot be admitted against Bonnie unless Clyde testifies and is thus subject to cross-examination.

If Bonnie is tried separately, and Clyde does not testify, the solution is simple: Clyde's confession is not introduced in Bonnie's trial. If Bonnie and Clyde are tried jointly, the confrontation clause is a potential problem. If Clyde testifies, then Bonnie can confront him and the clause is satisfied. If he does not testify—certainly a strong possibility, given Clyde's constitutional right not to be a witness against himself—one potential solution would be to admit the confession against Clyde but tell the jury not to consider it against Bonnie. It is quite common for evidence to be introduced against one party, with the court instructing the jury not to consider that evidence against another party. But is that a solution for the confrontation clause problem in joint trials? The next two cases explore this procedural wrinkle.

3. RIGHT TO HAVE A CO-DEFENDANT'S CONFESSION EXCLUDED

"Once more into the breach, dear friends, once more." William Shakespeare, Henry V, Act III, Scene I (as King Henry V urges his soldiers to exploit a hole in the French fortifications).

The Supreme Court sometimes protects a constitutional right by creating a prophylactic rule that, in effect, grants rights not specifically provided in the Constitution. *Miranda v. Arizona*, p. 625, is a good example. While the Fifth Amendment right against compelled self-incrimination may very well create a "right to remain silent" during police interrogation, the right to receive a detailed set of warnings cannot be found in the words of the Fifth Amendment. In this subsection, we see the Court struggling to define the contours of a prophylactic rule designed to protect the confrontation clause.

CRUZ V. NEW YORK

Supreme Court of the United States, 1987.
481 U.S. 186, 107 S.Ct. 1714, 95 L.Ed.2d 162.

JUSTICE SCALIA delivered the opinion of the Court [joined by JUSTICES BRENNAN, MARSHALL, BLACKMUN, and STEVENS].

In *Bruton v. United States*, 391 U.S. 123, 88 S.Ct. 1620, 20 L.Ed.2d 476 (1968), we held that a defendant is deprived of his rights under the Confrontation Clause when his codefendant's incriminating confession is introduced at their joint trial, even if the jury is instructed to consider that confession only against the codefendant. In *Parker v. Randolph*, 442 U.S. 62, 99 S.Ct. 2132, 60 L.Ed.2d 713 (1979), we considered, but were unable authoritatively to resolve, the question whether *Bruton* applies where the defendant's own confession, corroborating that of his codefendant, is introduced against him. We resolve that question today.

I

Jerry Cruz was murdered on March 15, 1982. That is not the murder for which petitioner was tried and convicted, but the investigation of the one led to the solving of the other. On the day following Jerry Cruz's murder, and on several later occasions, the police talked to Jerry's brother Norberto about the killing. On April 27, Norberto for the first time informed the police of a November 29, 1981, visit by petitioner Eulogio Cruz and his brother Benjamin to the apartment Norberto shared with Jerry. (Eulogio and Benjamin Cruz were long time friends of Norberto and Jerry Cruz, but the two sets of brothers were not related.) Norberto said that at the time of the visit Eulogio was nervous and was wearing a blood stained bandage around his arm. According to Norberto, Eulogio confided that he and Benjamin had gone to a Bronx gas station the night before, intending to rob it; that Eulogio and the attendant had struggled; and that, after the attendant had grabbed a gun from behind a counter and shot Eulogio in the arm, Benjamin had killed him. Norberto claimed that Benjamin gave a similar account of the incident.

On May 3, 1982, the police questioned Benjamin about the murder of Jerry Cruz. He strongly denied any connection with that homicide and became frustrated when the police seemed unwilling to believe him. Suddenly, to prove that he would tell the truth about killing someone if he were guilty, Benjamin spontaneously confessed to the murder of the gas station attendant. Later that evening, he gave a detailed videotaped confession to an Assistant District Attorney, in which he admitted that he, Eulogio, Jerry Cruz, and a fourth man had robbed the gas station, and that he had killed the attendant after the attendant shot Eulogio. Benjamin and Eulogio were indicted for felony murder of the station attendant.

The brothers were tried jointly, over Eulogio's objection. Likewise over Eulogio's objection, the trial judge allowed the prosecutor to introduce Benjamin's videotaped confession, warning the jury that the confession was not to be used against Eulogio. The government also called Norberto, who testified about his November 29 conversation with Eulogio and Benjamin. Finally, the government introduced police testimony, forensic evidence, and photographs of the scene of the murder, all of which corroborated Benjamin's videotaped confession and the statements recounted by Norberto. At the trial's end, however, Norberto's testimony stood as the only evidence admissible against Eulogio that directly linked him to the crime. Eulogio's attorney tried to persuade the jury that Norberto had suspected Eulogio and Benjamin of killing his brother Jerry and had fabricated his testimony to gain revenge. Unconvinced, the jury convicted both defendants.

The New York Court of Appeals affirmed Eulogio's conviction, adopting the reasoning of the plurality opinion in *Parker* that *Bruton* did not require the codefendant's confession to be excluded because Eulogio had himself confessed and his confession "interlocked" with Benjamin's. We granted certiorari.

II

The Confrontation Clause of the Sixth Amendment guarantees the right of a criminal defendant "to be confronted with the witnesses against him." We have held that that guarantee, extended against the States by the Fourteenth Amendment, includes the right to cross-examine witnesses. Where two or more defendants are tried jointly, therefore, the pretrial confession of one of them that implicates the others is not admissible against the others unless the confessing defendant waives his Fifth Amendment rights so as to permit cross-examination.

Ordinarily, a witness is considered to be a witness "against" a defendant for purposes of the Confrontation Clause only if his testimony is part of the body of evidence that the jury may consider in assessing his guilt. Therefore, a witness whose testimony is introduced in a joint trial with the limiting instruction that it be used only to assess the guilt of one of the defendants will not be considered to be a witness "against" the other defendants. In *Bruton*, however, we held that this principle will not be applied to validate, under the Confrontation Clause, introduction of a nontestifying codefendant's confession implicating the defendant, with instructions that the jury should disregard the confession insofar as its consideration of the defendant's guilt is concerned. We said:

> "[T]here are some contexts in which the risk that the jury will not, or cannot, follow instructions is so great, and the consequences of failure so vital to the defendant, that the practical and human limitations of the jury system cannot be ignored. Such a context is presented here, where the powerfully incriminating extrajudicial statements of a codefendant, who stands accused side-by-side with the defendant, are deliberately spread before the jury in a joint trial. Not only are the incriminations devastating to the defendant but their credibility is inevitably suspect * * * ."

We had occasion to revisit this issue in *Parker*, which resembled *Bruton* in all major respects save one: Each of the jointly tried defendants had himself confessed, his own confession was introduced against him, and his confession recited essentially the same facts as those of his nontestifying codefendants. The plurality of four Justices found no Sixth Amendment violation. It understood *Bruton* to hold that the Confrontation Clause is violated only when introduction of a codefendant's confession is "devastating" to the defendant's case. When the defendant has himself confessed, the plurality reasoned, "[his] case has already been devastated," so that the codefendant's confession "will seldom, if ever, be of the 'devastating' character referred to in *Bruton*," and impeaching that confession on cross-examination "would likely yield small advantage." Thus, the plurality would have held *Bruton* inapplicable to cases involving interlocking confessions. The four remaining Justices participating in the case disagreed, subscribing to the view expressed by Justice Blackmun that introduction of the defendant's own interlocking confession might, in some cases, render the violation of the Confrontation Clause harmless, but could not cause introduction of the nontestifying codefendant's confession not to constitute a violation. (Justice Blackmun alone went on to find that the interlocking confession did make the error harmless in the case before the Court, thereby producing a majority for affirmance of the convictions.) We face again today the issue on which the Court was evenly divided in *Parker*.

We adopt the approach espoused by Justice Blackmun. While "devastating" practical effect was one of the factors that *Bruton* considered in assessing whether the Confrontation Clause might sometimes require departure from the general rule that jury instructions suffice to exclude improper testimony, it did not suggest that the existence of such an effect should be assessed on a case-by-case basis. Rather, that factor was one of the justifications for excepting from the general rule the entire category of codefendant confessions that implicate the defendant in the crime. It is impossible to imagine why there should be excluded from that category, as generally not "devastating," codefendant confessions that "interlock" with the defendant's own confession. "[T]he infinite variability of inculpatory statements (whether made by defendants or codefendants), and of their likely effect on juries, makes [the assumption that an interlocking confession will preclude devastation] untenable." In this case, for example, the precise content and even the existence of petitioner's own confession were open to question, since they depended upon acceptance of Norberto's testimony, whereas the incriminating confession of codefendant Benjamin was on videotape.

In fact, it seems to us that "interlocking" bears a positively inverse relationship to devastation. A codefendant's confession will be relatively harmless if the incriminating story it tells is different from that which the defendant himself is alleged to have told, but enormously damaging if it confirms, in all essential respects, the defendant's alleged confession. It might be otherwise if the defendant were *standing by* his confession, in which case it could be said that the codefendant's confession does no more than support the defendant's very own case. But in the real world of criminal litigation, the defendant is seeking to *avoid* his confession—on the ground that it was not accurately reported, or that it was not really true when made. In the present case, for example, petitioner sought to establish that Norberto had a motive for falsely reporting a confession that never in fact occurred. In such circumstances a codefendant's confession that corroborates the defendant's confession significantly harms the defendant's case, whereas one that is positively incompatible gives credence to the defendant's assertion that his own alleged confession was nonexistent or false. Quite obviously, what the "interlocking" nature of the codefendant's confession pertains to is not its *harmfulness* but rather its *reliability*: If it confirms essentially the same facts as the defendant's own confession it is more likely to be true. Its reliability, however, may be relevant to whether the confession should (despite the lack of opportunity for cross-examination) *be admitted as evidence* against the defendant, but cannot conceivably be relevant to whether, assuming it cannot be admitted, the jury is likely to obey the instruction to disregard it, or the jury's failure to obey is likely to be inconsequential. The law cannot command respect if such an inexplicable exception to a supposed constitutional imperative is adopted. Having decided *Bruton*, we must face the honest consequences of what it holds.

The dissent makes no effort to respond to these points, urging instead a rejection of our "remorseless logic" in favor of "common sense and judgment." But those qualities, even in their most remorseless form, are not separable. It seems to us illogical, and therefore contrary to common sense and good judgment, to believe that codefendant confessions are less likely to be taken into account by the jury the more they are corroborated by the defendant's own admissions; or that they are less likely to be harmful when they confirm the validity of the defendant's alleged confession. Far from carrying *Bruton* "to the outer limits of its logic," our holding here does no more than reaffirm its central proposition. This case is indistinguishable from *Bruton* with respect to those factors the Court has deemed relevant in this area: the likelihood that the instruction will be disregarded; the probability that such disregard will have a devastating effect; and the determinability of these facts in advance of trial.

We hold that, where a nontestifying codefendant's confession incriminating the defendant is not directly admissible against the defendant, the Confrontation Clause bars its admission at their joint trial, even if the jury is instructed not to consider it against the defendant, and even if the defendant's own confession is admitted against him. * * *

JUSTICE WHITE, with whom THE CHIEF JUSTICE [REHNQUIST], JUSTICE POWELL, and JUSTICE O'CONNOR join, dissenting. * * *

In *Bruton*, the defendant himself had not confessed. Here, it is otherwise: defendant Cruz had confessed and his confession was properly before the jury. Yet the Court's holding is that the codefendant's confession was inadmissible even if it completely "interlocked" with that of Cruz himself, that is, was substantially the same as and consistent with Cruz's confession with respect to all elements of the crime and did not threaten to incriminate Cruz any more than his own confession.

This makes little sense to me. "[T]he defendant's own confession is probably the most probative and damaging evidence that can be admitted against him. Though itself an out-of-court statement, it is admitted as reliable evidence because it is an admission of guilt by the defendant and constitutes direct evidence of the facts to which it relates. Even the testimony of an eyewitness may be less reliable than the defendant's own confession. An observer may not correctly perceive, understand, or remember the acts of another, but the admissions of a defendant come from the actor himself, the most knowledgeable and unimpeachable source of information about his past conduct." [*Bruton*] (White, J., dissenting). Confessions of defendants have profound impact on juries, so much that we held in *Jackson v. Denno*, 378 U.S. 368, 84 S.Ct. 1774, 12 L.Ed.2d 908 (1964), that there is justifiable doubt that juries will disregard them even if told to do so. But a codefendant's out-of-court statements implicating the defendant are not only hearsay but also have traditionally been viewed with special suspicion. And the jury may be so informed. *Bruton* held that where the defendant has not himself confessed, there is too great a chance that the jury would rely on the codefendant's confession. But here, Cruz had admitted the crime and this fact was before the jury. I disagree with the Court's proposition that in every interlocking confession case, the jury, with the defendant's confession properly before it, would be tempted to disobey its instructions and fail to understand that presumptively unreliable evidence must not be used against the defendant. Nor is it remotely possible that in every case the admission of an interlocking confession by a codefendant will have the devastating effect referred to in *Bruton*. * * *

That the error the Court finds may be harmless and the conviction saved will not comfort prosecutors and judges. I doubt that the former will seek joint trials in interlocking confession cases, and if that occurs, the judge is not likely to commit error by admitting the codefendant's confession. Of course, defendants may be tried separately and *Bruton* problems avoided. But joint trials "conserve state funds, diminish inconvenience to witnesses and public authorities, and avoid delays in bringing those accused of crime to trial," to say nothing of the possibility of inconsistent verdicts and the effect of severance on already overburdened state and federal court systems.

I thus adhere to the views expressed by the plurality in *Parker v. Randolph*. There was no constitutional error here that *Bruton* sought to avoid, and no occasion to inquire into harmless error. In announcing its prophylactic rule, *Bruton* did not address the situation where the defendant himself had confessed, and I would not extend its holding to cases where the jury has heard the defendant's own confession. * * *

NOTES AND QUESTIONS

1. Justice Scalia's majority opinion claims logic on its side ("remorseless logic" in the view of the dissent), while Justice White's dissent claims to follow "common sense." Who gets the better of this argument?

2. *Bruton solutions.* Notice that *Bruton*, unlike *Crawford*, is not a core command of the confrontation clause but, instead, a prophylactic protection of the core right. Thus, as Justice White noted in his dissent, *Bruton* is easily satisfied by severing the defendants and providing separate trials. In that case, the confession of #1 is used against him but not against #2 and vice-versa. A second solution, perhaps, is to "redact" the confession to omit reference to the non-confessing co-defendant. But this can get tricky, as the next case shows.

GRAY V. MARYLAND

Supreme Court of the United States, 1998.
523 U.S. 185, 118 S.Ct. 1151, 140 L.Ed.2d 294.

JUSTICE BREYER delivered the opinion of the Court [joined by JUSTICES STEVENS, O'CONNOR, SOUTER, and GINSBURG].

The issue in this case concerns the application of *Bruton v. United States*, 391 U.S. 123, 88 S.Ct. 1620, 20 L.Ed.2d 476 (1968). *Bruton* involved two defendants accused of participating in the same crime and tried jointly before the same jury. One of the defendants had confessed. His confession named and incriminated the other defendant. The trial judge issued a limiting instruction, telling the jury that it should consider the confession as evidence only against the codefendant who had confessed and not against the defendant named in the confession. *Bruton* held that, despite the limiting instruction, the Constitution forbids the use of such a confession in the joint trial.

The case before us differs from *Bruton* in that the prosecution here redacted the codefendant's confession by substituting for the defendant's name in the confession a blank space or the word "deleted." We must decide whether these substitutions make a significant legal difference. We hold that they do not and that *Bruton*'s protective rule applies.

I

In 1993, Stacy Williams died after a severe beating. Anthony Bell gave a confession, to the Baltimore City police, in which he said that he (Bell), Kevin Gray, and Jacquin "Tank" Vanlandingham had participated in the beating that resulted in Williams' death. Vanlandingham later died. A Maryland grand jury indicted Bell and Gray for murder. The State of Maryland tried them jointly.

The trial judge, after denying Gray's motion for a separate trial, permitted the State to introduce Bell's confession into evidence at trial. But the judge ordered the confession redacted. Consequently, the police detective who read the confession into evidence said the word "deleted" or "deletion" whenever Gray's name or Vanlandingham's name appeared. Immediately after the police detective read the redacted confession to the jury, the prosecutor asked, "after he gave you that information, you subsequently were able to arrest Mr. Kevin Gray; is that correct?" The officer responded, "That's correct." The State also introduced into evidence a written copy of the confession with those two names omitted, leaving in their place blank white spaces separated by commas. The State produced other witnesses, who said that six persons (including Bell, Gray, and Vanlandingham) participated in the beating. Gray testified and denied his participation. Bell did not testify.

When instructing the jury, the trial judge specified that the confession was evidence only against Bell; the instructions said that the jury should not use the confession as evidence against Gray. The jury convicted both Bell and Gray. * * *

II

In deciding whether *Bruton*'s protective rule applies to the redacted confession before us, we must consider both *Bruton*, and a later case, *Richardson v. Marsh*, 481 U.S. 200, 107 S.Ct. 1702, 95 L.Ed.2d 176 (1987), which limited *Bruton*'s scope. * * *

In *Richardson v. Marsh*, the Court considered a redacted confession. The case involved a joint murder trial of Marsh and Williams. The State had redacted the confession of one defendant, Williams, so as to "omit all reference" to his codefendant, Marsh—"indeed, to omit all indication that *anyone* other than * * * Williams" and a third person had "participated in the crime." The trial court also instructed the jury not to consider the confession against Marsh. As redacted, the confession indicated that Williams and the third person had discussed the murder in the front seat of a car while they traveled to the victim's house. The redacted confession contained no indication that Marsh—or any other person—was in the car. Later in the trial, however, Marsh testified that she was in the back seat of the car. For that reason, in context, the confession still could have helped convince the jury that Marsh knew about the murder in advance and therefore had participated knowingly in the crime.

The Court held that this redacted confession fell outside *Bruton*'s scope and was admissible (with appropriate limiting instructions) at the joint trial. The Court distinguished Evans' confession in *Bruton* as a confession that was "incriminating on its face," and which had "expressly implicat[ed]" Bruton. By contrast, Williams' confession amounted to "evidence requiring linkage" in that it "became" incriminating in respect to Marsh "only when linked with evidence introduced later at trial." The Court held

> "that the Confrontation Clause is not violated by the admission of a nontestifying codefendant's confession with a proper limiting instruction when, as here, the confession is redacted to eliminate not only the defendant's name, but any reference to his or her existence."

The Court added: "We express no opinion on the admissibility of a confession in which the defendant's name has been replaced with a symbol or neutral pronoun."

III

Originally, the codefendant's confession in the case before us, like that in *Bruton*, referred to, and directly implicated, another defendant.

The State, however, redacted that confession by removing the nonconfessing defendant's name. Nonetheless, unlike Richardson's redacted confession, this confession refers directly to the "existence" of the nonconfessing defendant. The State has simply replaced the nonconfessing defendant's name with a kind of symbol, namely the word "deleted" or a blank space set off by commas. The redacted confession, for example, responded to the question "Who was in the group that beat Stacey," with the phrase, "Me, _____, and a few other guys." And when the police witness read the confession in court, he said the word "deleted" or "deletion" where the blank spaces appear. We therefore must decide a question that *Richardson* left open, namely whether redaction that replaces a defendant's name with an obvious indication of deletion, such as a blank space, the word "deleted," or a similar symbol, still falls within *Bruton*'s protective rule. We hold that it does.

Bruton, as interpreted by *Richardson*, holds that certain "powerfully incriminating extrajudicial statements of a codefendant"—those naming another defendant—considered as a class, are so prejudicial that limiting instructions cannot work. Unless the prosecutor wishes to hold separate trials or to use separate juries or to abandon use of the confession, he must redact the confession to reduce significantly or to eliminate the special prejudice that the *Bruton* Court found. Redactions that simply replace a name with an obvious blank space or a word such as "deleted" or a symbol or other similarly obvious indications of alteration, however, leave statements that, considered as a class, so closely resemble Bruton's unredacted statements that, in our view, the law must require the same result.

For one thing, a jury will often react similarly to an unredacted confession and a confession redacted in this way, for the jury will often realize that the confession refers specifically to the defendant. This is true even when the State does not blatantly link the defendant to the deleted name, as it did in this case by asking whether Gray was arrested on the basis of information in Bell's confession as soon as the officer had finished reading the redacted statement. Consider a simplified but typical example, a confession that reads "I, Bob Smith, along with Sam Jones, robbed the bank." To replace the words "Sam Jones" with an obvious blank will not likely fool anyone. A juror somewhat familiar with criminal law would know immediately that the blank, in the phrase "I, Bob Smith, along with _____, robbed the bank," refers to defendant Jones. A juror who does not know the law and who therefore wonders to whom the blank might refer need only lift his eyes to Jones, sitting at counsel table, to find what will seem the obvious answer, at least if the juror hears the judge's instruction not to consider the confession as evidence against Jones, for that instruction will provide an obvious reason for the blank. A more sophisticated juror, wondering if the blank refers to someone else, might also wonder how, if it did, the prosecutor could argue the confession is reliable, for the prosecutor, after all, has been arguing that Jones, not someone else, helped Smith commit the crime.

For another thing, the obvious deletion may well call the jurors' attention specially to the removed name. By encouraging the jury to speculate about the reference, the redaction may overemphasize the importance of the confession's accusation—once the jurors work out the reference. That is why Judge Learned Hand, many years ago, wrote in a similar instance that blacking out the name of a codefendant not only "would have been futile. * * * [T]here could not have been the slightest doubt as to whose names had been blacked out," but "even if there had been, that blacking out itself would have not only laid the doubt, but underscored the answer."

Finally, *Bruton*'s protected statements and statements redacted to leave a blank or some other similarly obvious alteration, function the same way grammatically. They are directly accusatory. Evans' statement in *Bruton* used a proper name to point explicitly to an accused defendant. And *Bruton* held that the "powerfully incriminating" effect of what Justice Stewart called "an out-of-court accusation," creates a special, and vital, need for cross-examination—a need that would be immediately obvious had the codefendant pointed directly to the defendant in the courtroom itself. The blank space in an obviously redacted confession also points directly to the defendant, and it accuses the defendant in a manner similar to Evans' use of Bruton's name or to a testifying codefendant's accusatory finger. By way of contrast, the factual statement at issue in *Richardson*—a statement about what others said in the front seat of a car—differs from directly accusatory evidence in this respect, for it does not point directly to a defendant at all.

We concede certain differences between *Bruton* and this case. A confession that uses a blank or the word "delete" (or, for that matter, a first name or a nickname) less obviously refers to the defendant than a confession that uses the defendant's full and proper name. Moreover, in some instances the person to whom the blank refers may not be clear: Although the follow-up question asked by the State in this case eliminated all doubt, the reference might not be transparent in other cases in which a confession, like the present confession, uses two (or more) blanks, even though only one other defendant appears at trial, and in which the trial indicates that there are more participants than the confession has named. Nonetheless, as we have said, we believe that, considered as a class, redactions that replace a proper name with an obvious blank, the word "delete," a symbol, or similarly notify the jury that a name has been deleted are similar enough to Bruton's unredacted confessions as to warrant the same legal results.

IV

The State, in arguing for a contrary conclusion, relies heavily upon *Richardson*. But we do not believe *Richardson* controls the result here. We concede that *Richardson* placed outside the scope of *Bruton*'s rule those statements that incriminate inferentially. We also concede that the jury must use inference to connect the statement in this redacted confession with the defendant. But inference pure and simple cannot make the critical difference, for if it did, then *Richardson* would also place outside *Bruton*'s scope confessions that use shortened first names, nicknames, descriptions as unique as the "red-haired, bearded, one-eyed man-with-a-limp," and perhaps even full names of defendants who are always known by a nickname. This Court has assumed, however, that nicknames and specific descriptions fall inside, not outside, *Bruton*'s protection. See *Harrington v. California*, 395 U.S. 250, 253, 89 S.Ct. 1726, 1728, 23 L.Ed.2d 284 (1969) (assuming *Bruton* violation where confessions describe codefendant as the "white guy" and gives a description of his age, height, weight, and hair color). The Solicitor General, although supporting Maryland in this case, concedes that this is appropriate.

That being so, *Richardson* must depend in significant part upon the kind of, not the simple fact of, inference. *Richardson*'s inferences involved statements that did not refer directly to the defendant himself and which became incriminating "only when linked with evidence introduced later at trial." The inferences at issue here involve statements that, despite redaction, obviously refer directly to someone, often obviously the defendant, and which involve inferences that a jury ordinarily could make immediately, even were the confession the very first item introduced at trial. Moreover, the redacted confession with the blank prominent on its face, in *Richardson*'s words, "facially incriminat[es]" the codefendant. Like the confession in *Bruton* itself, the accusation that the redacted confession makes "is more vivid than inferential incrimination, and hence more difficult to thrust out of mind."

Nor are the policy reasons that *Richardson* provided in support of its conclusion applicable here. *Richardson* expressed concern lest application of *Bruton*'s rule apply where "redaction" of confessions, particularly "confessions incriminating by connection," would often "not [be] possible," thereby forcing prosecutors too often to abandon use either of the confession or of a joint trial. Additional redaction of a confession that uses a blank space, the word "delete," or a symbol, however, normally is possible. Consider as an example a portion of the confession before us: The witness who read the confession told the jury that the confession (among other things) said,

"Question: Who was in the group that beat Stacey?

"Answer: Me, deleted, deleted, and a few other guys."

Why could the witness not, instead, have said:

"Question: Who was in the group that beat Stacey?

"Answer: Me and a few other guys."

Richardson itself provides a similar example of this kind of redaction. The confession there at issue had been "redacted to omit all reference to respondent—indeed, to omit all indication that anyone other than Martin and Williams participated in the crime." * * *

JUSTICE SCALIA, with whom THE CHIEF JUSTICE [REHNQUIST], JUSTICE KENNEDY, and JUSTICE THOMAS join, dissenting. * * *

The almost invariable assumption of the law is that jurors follow their instructions. This rule "is a pragmatic one, rooted less in the absolute certitude that the presumption is true than in the belief that it represents a reasonable practical accommodation of the interests of the state and the defendant in the criminal justice process." We have held, for example, that the state may introduce evidence of a defendant's prior convictions for the purpose of sentencing enhancement, or statements elicited from a defendant in violation of *Miranda v. Arizona* for the purpose of impeachment, so long as the jury is instructed that such evidence may not be considered for the purpose of determining guilt. The same applies to codefendant confessions: "a witness whose testimony is introduced at a joint trial is not considered to be a witness 'against' a defendant if the jury is instructed to consider that testimony only against a codefendant." In *Bruton*, we recognized a "narrow exception" to this rule: "We held that a defendant is deprived of his Sixth Amendment right of confrontation when the facially incriminating confession of a nontestifying codefendant is introduced at their joint trial, even if the jury is instructed to consider the confession only against the codefendant."

We declined in *Richardson*, however, to extend *Bruton* to confessions that incriminate only by inference from other evidence. When incrimination is inferential, "it is a less valid generalization that the jury will not likely obey the instruction to disregard the evidence." Today the Court struggles to decide whether a confession redacted to omit the defendant's name is incriminating on its face or by inference. On the one hand, the Court "concede[s] that the jury must use inference to connect the statement in this redacted confession with the defendant," but later asserts, on the other hand, that "the redacted confession with the blank prominent on its face * * * 'facially incriminat[es]'" him. The Court should have stopped with its concession: the statement "Me, deleted, deleted, and a few other guys" does not facially incriminate anyone but the speaker. The Court's analogizing of "deleted" to a physical description that clearly identifies the defendant (which we have assumed *Bruton* covers) does not survive scrutiny. By "facially incriminating," we have meant incriminating independent of other evidence introduced at trial. Since the defendant's appearance at counsel table is not evidence, the description "red-haired, bearded, one-eyed man-with-a-limp," would be facially incriminating—unless, of course, the defendant had dyed his hair black and shaved his beard before trial, and the prosecution introduced evidence concerning his former appearance. Similarly, the statement "Me, Kevin Gray, and a few other guys" would be facially incriminating, unless the defendant's name set forth in the indictment was not Kevin Gray, and evidence was introduced to the effect that he sometimes used "Kevin Gray" as an alias. By contrast, the person to whom "deleted" refers in "Me, deleted, deleted, and a few other guys" is not apparent from anything the jury knows independent of the evidence at trial. Though the jury may speculate, the statement expressly implicates no one but the speaker.

Of course the Court is correct that confessions redacted to omit the defendant's name are more likely to incriminate than confessions redacted to omit any reference to his existence. But it is also true—and more relevant here—that confessions redacted to omit the defendant's name are less likely to incriminate than confessions that expressly state it. The latter are "powerfully incriminating" as a class; the former are not so. Here, for instance, there were two names deleted, five or more participants in the crime, and only one other defendant on trial. The jury no doubt may "speculate about the reference," as it speculates when evidence connects a defendant to a confession that does not refer to his existence. The issue, however, is not whether the confession incriminated petitioner, but whether the incrimination is so "powerful" that we must depart from the normal presumption that the jury follows its instructions. I think it is not—and I am certain that drawing the line for departing from the ordinary rule at the facial identification of the defendant makes more sense than drawing it anywhere else.

The Court's extension of *Bruton* to name-redacted confessions "as a class" will seriously compromise "society's compelling interest in finding, convicting, and punishing those who violate the law." We explained in *Richardson* that forgoing use of codefendant confessions or joint trials was "too high" a price to insure that juries never disregard their instructions. The Court minimizes the damage that it does by suggesting that "[a]dditional redaction of a confession that uses a blank space, the word 'delete,' or a symbol * * * normally is possible." In the present case, it asks, why could the police officer not have testified that Bell's answer was "Me and a few other guys"? The answer, it seems obvious to me, is because that is not what Bell said. Bell's answer was "Me, Tank, Kevin and a few other guys." Introducing the statement with full disclosure of deletions is one thing; introducing as the complete statement what was in fact only a part is something else. And of course even concealed deletions from the text will often not do the job that the Court demands. For inchoate offenses—conspiracy in particular—redaction to delete all reference to a confederate would often render the confession nonsensical. If the question was "Who agreed to beat Stacey?", and the answer was "Me and Kevin," we might redact the answer to "Me and [deleted]," or perhaps to "Me and somebody else," but surely not to just "Me"—for that would no longer be a confession to the conspiracy charge, but rather the foundation for an insanity defense. To my knowledge we have never before endorsed—and to my strong belief we ought not endorse—the redaction of a statement by some means other than the deletion of certain words, with the fact of the deletion shown. The risk to the integrity of our system (not to mention the increase in its complexity) posed by the approval of such free-lance editing seems to me infinitely greater than the risk posed by the entirely honest reproduction that the Court disapproves.

The United States Constitution guarantees, not a perfect system of criminal justice (as to which there can be considerable disagreement), but a minimum standard of fairness. Lest we lose sight of the forest for the trees, it should be borne in mind that federal and state rules of criminal procedure—which can afford to seek perfection because they can be more readily changed—exclude non-testifying-codefendant confessions even where the Sixth Amendment does not. Under the Federal Rules of Criminal Procedure (and Maryland's), a trial court may order separate trials if joinder will prejudice a defendant. * * *

NOTES AND QUESTIONS

1. Because both opinions accept *Bruton*, the division on the Court must be about something else. What is it that divides the Court?

2. When the Court discovers "new" constitutional rights hidden within the "plain meaning" of the text, it will be left to future Courts to decide how to shape those rights. Rights not found in the "plain meaning" are considerably more supple than their plain meaning kin. An interpretation of the confrontation clause that did not appear until 1968 is unlikely to be found in, and thus limited by, the text itself. So, too, with *Miranda*; because the doctrine of warnings-and-waiver cannot be found in the language of the self-incrimination clause, it took the Court dozens of cases to develop *Miranda*'s doctrinal structure. Of course, the fruit of *Bruton* could have been that a co-defendant's confession cannot be introduced in a joint trial, period. But if the Court is not willing to go that far, it must find limits that are coherent and responsive to the policy rationale behind *Bruton*. Which opinion do you prefer in *Gray*?

3. *Implications of Gray.* In a capital murder case, defendant *S* confessed that he participated in the robbery but was unarmed and did not

intend to harm anyone. He said his co-defendant, John, had the idea for the robbery and also shot the clerk. Here is a portion of his confession, bad grammar and all:

> After crossing the bridge John said lets go get some money. He meant go strong arm somebody. We drove pass a lot of gas stations, I remember we went by about six. Most of them had several people there and John kept saying lets go someplace else. Sometime between 12:00 midnight and 12:30 I saw a station that had only one guy in it. * * * I remember [John] tore the sleeves off his shirt we were going to use them for mask to cover our faces. * * * Then we went in the store. I opened the door the next thing I knew John threw up the gun and started shooting. * * * John leaned over the counter and the store clerk was trying to hide on the floor behind the counter John pointed the gun at the store clerk and he shot him in the shoulder. I was trying to get the cash register open. * * * John kept shooting the man. I heard about nine shots.

To comply with *Bruton*, the prosecutor redacted the confession rather than try each defendant separately. Here is the same portion of *S*'s confession after redaction:

> I remember crossing a draw bridge over a river. After crossing the bridge, I went past a lot of gas stations. I remember, I went by about 6. Most of them had several people there. Sometime between 12:00 midnight and 12:30 a.m., I saw a station that had only one guy in it. * * * I used the sleeves from a shirt for a mask to cover my face. * * * I tied the mask on my face and I went in the store. I opened the door and the next thing I knew, the shooting started. * * *

If you represented *S* what objection would you raise to the redacted version? Would your objection be based on the confrontation clause or another part of the Bill of Rights? See Ex parte Sneed, 783 So.2d 863 (Ala.2000).

4. *Judicial philosophy.* You have seen in the confrontation clause materials four opinions by Scalia: a majority opinion for five members of the Court in *Cruz*, a majority opinion for seven justices in *Crawford*, and two dissents, in each case for four members of the Court. Can you reconcile Scalia's positions in these cases to discern some small part of his judicial philosophy, at least in the confrontation clause context?

C. RIGHT TO COMPULSORY PROCESS

Introductory Comment

Parallel to the right to confront the "witnesses against" the accused is the right "to have compulsory process for obtaining witnesses in his favor." There have not been many cases testing this provision because defendants are routinely given full access to the subpoena power. But in

Washington v. Texas, 388 U.S. 14, 87 S.Ct. 1920, 18 L.Ed.2d 1019 (1967), the Court had to decide whether the right to compulsory process was violated by Texas statutes that prohibited testimony from persons charged or convicted as coparticipants in the same crime. The language of the Sixth Amendment and the debate among the Framers suggest that the sole purpose of the compulsory process clause was to make the subpoena power available to the accused. One of the Framers proposed amending the compulsory process language to give the accused power to obtain a continuance if he could show that the process was granted but not served. Responding to this proposal, another Framer said that if process issued, "the Government did all it could; the remainder must lie in the discretion of the court." The amendment to require continuance when the witnesses did not appear and testify failed by a vote of 41–9. 1 Annals of Cong. 756 (1789).

This language and history might have sustained the Texas statutes on the theory that no one had denied Washington the use of the subpoena power to produce witnesses; the Texas law instead prevented witnesses who were present from testifying due to presumed bias. But the Court in *Washington* chose to read the Sixth Amendment broadly here, reasoning that the Framers "did not intend to commit the futile act of giving to a defendant the right to secure the attendance of witnesses whose testimony he had no right to use." Thus, the Court treated the statutes as an infringement on the right to compulsory process, and held insufficient the State's justification that the statutory disqualification would keep codefendants from lying to exonerate each other.

The earliest case construing the compulsory process clause was high drama. While serving as Jefferson's vice-president, Burr killed Alexander Hamilton in a duel. Burr spent the next two years organizing an army with General James Wilkinson and planning a mission into what were then the western territories (what is now Louisiana). His goal is to this day shrouded in mystery but President Jefferson wrote the following in a letter to the governor of New Hampshire in 1806:

> Our Cataline [one who would overthrow the government] is at the head of an armed body, and his object is to seize New Orleans, from there attack Mexico, place himself on the throne of Montezuma, add Louisiana to his empire, and the Western States from the Allegheny, if he can. I do not believe he will attain the crown but neither am I certain the halter will get its due.

Jean Edward Smith, John Marshall: Definer of a Nation 353 (1996).

Months earlier, General Wilkinson had changed sides, sending the president a translation of a ciphered letter Burr had sent him. It was this letter that was at issue in *United States v. Burr*. For more drama, Chief

Justice John Marshall sat as one of the two trial judges in the case. The reporter noted that upon Burr's motion to compel President Jefferson to produce the Wilkinson letter, "a protracted debate arose, occupying two entire days, and extending into the third * * * . Much ability and eloquence were displayed on both sides." 25 Fed. Cas. 30, 31. For more on the criminal cases that arose from the Burr adventure, see George C. Thomas III, The Supreme Court on Trial: How the American Justice System Sacrifices Innocent Defendants 103–11 (2008).

UNITED STATES V. BURR

Circuit Court, D. Virginia, 1807.
25 Fed.Cas. 30 (No. 14,692D).

MARSHALL, CHIEF JUSTICE [sitting as trial judge].

The object of the motion now to be decided is to obtain * * * an original letter from General Wilkinson to the president in relation to the accused, with the answer of the president to that letter, which papers are supposed to be material to the defence. As the legal mode of effecting this object, a motion is made for a subpoena duces tecum, to be directed to the president of the United States. * * *

* * * The right given by [the Sixth Amendment] must be deemed sacred by the courts, and the article should be so construed as to be something more than a dead letter. * * *

Upon immemorial usage * * * and upon what is deemed a sound construction of the constitution and law of the land, the court is of the opinion that any person charged with a crime in the courts of the United States has a right * * * to the process of the court to compel the attendance of his witnesses. * * *

This point being disposed of, it remains to inquire whether a subpoena duces tecum can be directed to the president of the United States and whether it ought to be directed in this case? * * * It was at first doubted whether a subpoena could issue, in any case, to the chief magistrate of the nation; and if it could, whether that subpoena could do more than direct his personal attendance; whether it could direct him to bring with him a paper which was to constitute the gist of his testimony. * * * In the provisions of the constitution, and of the statute, which give to the accused a right to the compulsory process of the court, there is no exception whatever. The obligation, therefore, of those provisions is general; and it would seem that no person could claim an exemption from them, but one who would not be a witness. * * *

* * * If, in being summoned to give his personal attendance to testify, the law does not discriminate between the president and a private citizen, what foundation is there for the opinion that this difference is created by

the circumstance that his testimony depends on a paper in his possession, not on facts which have come to his knowledge otherwise than by writing? The court can perceive no foundation for such an opinion. * * * This court would certainly be very unwilling to say that upon fair construction the constitutional and legal right to obtain its processes, to compel the attendance of witnesses, does not extend to their bringing with them such papers as may be material in the defence. The literal distinction which exists between the cases is too much attenuated to be countenanced in the tribunals of a just and humane nation. * * * If it be apparent that the papers are irrelative to the case, or that for state reasons they cannot be introduced into the defence, the subpoena duces tecum would be useless. But, if this be not apparent, if they may be important in the defence, if they may be safely read at the trial, would it not be a blot in the page which records the judicial proceedings of this country, if, in a case of such serious import as this, the accused should be denied the use of them? * * *

NOTES AND QUESTIONS

1.   President Jefferson delivered the letter to his attorney who turned over an edited copy. When Burr insisted on seeing the unexpurgated version, Jefferson made an early claim of executive privilege. Chief Justice John Marshall, ever the clever political judge, ruled that the president possessed a qualified privilege but that the privilege was personal to the president and could not be asserted through his attorney. "Accordingly, Marshall ruled that while he would consider entering a protective order to prohibit unnecessary public disclosure of the letter, he had no choice but to halt the proceedings until the letter was produced for Burr's personal inspection." Peter Westen, *The Compulsory Process Clause*, 73 Mich. L. Rev. 71, 106 (1974). Before Jefferson's response arrived, Burr decided to proceed to trial without the full version of the letter (which he was apparently shown in confidence). The jury acquitted Burr of treason charges. Id. at 107.

2.   Burr is widely regarded as a "sweeping construction to the compulsory process clause." Id. at 101. But was it helpful to the defendant in *Washington v. Texas*, p. 1356?

3.   In Chapter 13, we saw that discovery statutes provide sanctions for noncompliance. One available sanction is to forbid the party who failed to comply to use the withheld evidence. When that party is the defendant, compulsory process issues arise, as the next case shows.

TAYLOR V. ILLINOIS

Supreme Court of the United States, 1988.
484 U.S. 400, 108 S.Ct. 646, 98 L.Ed.2d 798.

JUSTICE STEVENS delivered the opinion of the Court [joined by CHIEF JUSTICE REHNQUIST, and JUSTICES WHITE, O'CONNOR, and SCALIA].

As a sanction for failing to identify a defense witness in response to a pretrial discovery request, an Illinois trial judge refused to allow the undisclosed witness to testify. The question presented is whether that refusal violated the petitioner's constitutional right to obtain the testimony of favorable witnesses. We hold that such a sanction is not absolutely prohibited by the Compulsory Process Clause of the Sixth Amendment and find no constitutional error on the specific facts of this case.

I

A jury convicted petitioner in 1984 of attempting to murder Jack Bridges in a street fight on the south side of Chicago on August 6, 1981. The conviction was supported by the testimony of Bridges, his brother, and three other witnesses. They described a 20-minute argument between Bridges and a young man named Derrick Travis, and a violent encounter that occurred over an hour later between several friends of Travis, including petitioner, on the one hand, and Bridges, belatedly aided by his brother, on the other. The incident was witnessed by 20 or 30 bystanders. It is undisputed that at least three members of the group which included Travis and petitioner were carrying pipes and clubs that they used to beat Bridges. Prosecution witnesses also testified that petitioner had a gun, that he shot Bridges in the back as he attempted to flee, and that, after Bridges fell, petitioner pointed the gun at Bridges' head but the weapon misfired.

Two sisters, who are friends of petitioner, testified on his behalf. In many respects their version of the incident was consistent with the prosecution's case, but they testified that it was Bridges' brother, rather than petitioner, who possessed a firearm and that he had fired into the group hitting his brother by mistake. No other witnesses testified for the defense.

Well in advance of trial, the prosecutor filed a discovery motion requesting a list of defense witnesses. In his original response, petitioner's attorney identified the two sisters who later testified and two men who did not testify. On the first day of trial, defense counsel was allowed to amend his answer by adding the names of Derrick Travis and a Chicago police officer; neither of them actually testified.

On the second day of trial, after the prosecution's two principal witnesses had completed their testimony, defense counsel made an oral motion to amend his "Answer to Discovery" to include two more witnesses, Alfred Wormley and Pam Berkhalter. In support of the motion, counsel represented that he had just been informed about them and that they had probably seen the "entire incident."

In response to the court's inquiry about defendant's failure to tell him about the two witnesses earlier, counsel acknowledged that defendant had done so, but then represented that he had been unable to locate Wormley. After noting that the witnesses' names could have been supplied even if their addresses were unknown, the trial judge directed counsel to bring them in the next day, at which time he would decide whether they could testify. The judge indicated that he was concerned about the possibility "that witnesses are being found that really weren't there."

The next morning Wormley appeared in court with defense counsel.[7] After further colloquy about the consequences of a violation of discovery rules, counsel was permitted to make an offer of proof in the form of Wormley's testimony outside the presence of the jury. It developed that Wormley had not been a witness to the incident itself. He testified that prior to the incident he saw Jack Bridges and his brother with two guns in a blanket, that he heard them say "they were after Ray [petitioner] and the other people," and that on his way home he "happened to run into Ray and them" and warned them "to watch out because they got weapons." On cross-examination, Wormley acknowledged that he had first met defendant "about four months ago" (*i.e.*, over two years after the incident). He also acknowledged that defense counsel had visited him at his home on the Wednesday of the week before the trial began. Thus, his testimony rather dramatically contradicted defense counsel's representations to the trial court.

After hearing Wormley testify, the trial judge concluded that the appropriate sanction for the discovery violation was to exclude his testimony. The judge explained:

> "THE COURT: All right, I am going to deny Wormley an opportunity to testify here. He is not going to testify. I find this is a blatent [*sic*] violation of the discovery rules, willful violation of the rules. I also feel that defense attorneys have been violating discovery in this courtroom in the last three or four cases blatantly and I am going to put a stop to it and this is one way to do so.
>
> "Further, for whatever value it is, because this is a jury trial, I have a great deal of doubt in my mind as to the veracity of this young man that testified as to whether he was an

---

7   The record does not explain why Pam Berkhalter did not appear.

eyewitness on the scene, sees guns that are wrapped up. He doesn't know Ray but he stops Ray.

"At any rate, Mr. Wormley is not going to testify, be a witness in this courtroom."

The Illinois Appellate Court affirmed petitioner's conviction. * * *

II

In the State's view, no Compulsory Process Clause concerns are even raised by authorizing preclusion as a discovery sanction, or by the application of the Illinois rule in this case. The State's argument is supported by the plain language of the Clause, by the historical evidence that it was intended to provide defendants with subpoena power that they lacked at common law, by some scholarly comment, and by a brief excerpt from the legislative history of the Clause. We have, however, consistently given the Clause the broader reading reflected in contemporaneous state constitutional provisions.[13] * * *

The right of the defendant to present evidence "stands on no lesser footing than the other Sixth Amendment rights that we have previously held applicable to the States." We cannot accept the State's argument that this constitutional right may never be offended by the imposition of a discovery sanction that entirely excludes the testimony of a material defense witness.

III

Petitioner's claim that the Sixth Amendment creates an absolute bar to the preclusion of the testimony of a surprise witness is just as extreme and just as unacceptable as the State's position that the Amendment is simply irrelevant. The accused does not have an unfettered right to offer testimony that is incompetent, privileged, or otherwise inadmissible under standard rules of evidence. The Compulsory Process Clause provides him with an effective weapon, but it is a weapon that cannot be used irresponsibly. * * *

The principle that undergirds the defendant's right to present exculpatory evidence is also the source of essential limitations on the right. The adversary process could not function effectively without adherence to rules of procedure that govern the orderly presentation of facts and arguments to provide each party with a fair opportunity to assemble and submit evidence to contradict or explain the opponent's

---

[13] * * * "Some of the state provisions originated in English statutes, some in colonial enactments, and some were original. Regardless, they all reflected the principle that the defendant must have a meaningful opportunity, at least as advantageous as that possessed by the prosecution, to establish the essential elements of his case. The states pressed the principle so vigorously that the framers of the federal Bill of Rights included it in the sixth amendment in a distinctive formulation of their own." Westen, The *Compulsory Process Clause*, 73 Mich.L.Rev. 71, 94–95 (1974) (footnotes omitted).

case. The trial process would be a shambles if either party had an absolute right to control the time and content of his witnesses' testimony. Neither may insist on the right to interrupt the opposing party's case, and obviously there is no absolute right to interrupt the deliberations of the jury to present newly discovered evidence. The State's interest in the orderly conduct of a criminal trial is sufficient to justify the imposition and enforcement of firm, though not always inflexible, rules relating to the identification and presentation of evidence.

The defendant's right to compulsory process is itself designed to vindicate the principle that the "ends of criminal justice would be defeated if judgments were to be founded on a partial or speculative presentation of the facts." Rules that provide for pretrial discovery of an opponent's witnesses serve the same high purpose. Discovery, like cross-examination, minimizes the risk that a judgment will be predicated on incomplete, misleading, or even deliberately fabricated testimony. The "State's interest in protecting itself against an eleventh-hour defense" is merely one component of the broader public interest in a full and truthful disclosure of critical facts.

To vindicate that interest we have held that even the defendant may not testify without being subjected to cross-examination. * * *

Petitioner does not question the legitimacy of a rule requiring pretrial disclosure of defense witnesses, but he argues that the sanction of preclusion of the testimony of a previously undisclosed witness is so drastic that it should never be imposed. He argues, correctly, that a less drastic sanction is always available. Prejudice to the prosecution could be minimized by granting a continuance or a mistrial to provide time for further investigation; moreover, further violations can be deterred by disciplinary sanctions against the defendant or defense counsel.

It may well be true that alternative sanctions are adequate and appropriate in most cases, but it is equally clear that they would be less effective than the preclusion sanction and that there are instances in which they would perpetuate rather than limit the prejudice to the State and the harm to the adversary process. One of the purposes of the discovery rule itself is to minimize the risk that fabricated testimony will be believed. Defendants who are willing to fabricate a defense may also be willing to fabricate excuses for failing to comply with a discovery requirement. The risk of a contempt violation may seem trivial to a defendant facing the threat of imprisonment for a term of years. A dishonest client can mislead an honest attorney, and there are occasions when an attorney assumes that the duty of loyalty to the client outweighs elementary obligations to the court.

We presume that evidence that is not discovered until after the trial is over would not have affected the outcome. It is equally reasonable to

presume that there is something suspect about a defense witness who is not identified until after the 11th hour has passed. If a pattern of discovery violations is explicable only on the assumption that the violations were designed to conceal a plan to present fabricated testimony, it would be entirely appropriate to exclude the tainted evidence regardless of whether other sanctions would also be merited.
* * *

A trial judge may certainly insist on an explanation for a party's failure to comply with a request to identify his or her witnesses in advance of trial. If that explanation reveals that the omission was willful and motivated by a desire to obtain a tactical advantage that would minimize the effectiveness of cross-examination and the ability to adduce rebuttal evidence, it would be entirely consistent with the purposes of the Compulsory Process Clause simply to exclude the witness' testimony.

The simplicity of compliance with the discovery rule is also relevant. As we have noted, the Compulsory Process Clause cannot be invoked without the prior planning and affirmative conduct of the defendant. Lawyers are accustomed to meeting deadlines. Routine preparation involves location and interrogation of potential witnesses and the serving of subpoenas on those whose testimony will be offered at trial. The burden of identifying them in advance of trial adds little to these routine demands of trial preparation.

It would demean the high purpose of the Compulsory Process Clause to construe it as encompassing an absolute right to an automatic continuance or mistrial to allow presumptively perjured testimony to be presented to a jury. We reject petitioner's argument that a preclusion sanction is never appropriate no matter how serious the defendant's discovery violation may be.

IV

Petitioner argues that the preclusion sanction was unnecessarily harsh in this case because the *voir dire* examination of Wormley adequately protected the prosecution from any possible prejudice resulting from surprise. Petitioner also contends that it is unfair to visit the sins of the lawyer upon his client. Neither argument has merit.

More is at stake than possible prejudice to the prosecution. We are also concerned with the impact of this kind of conduct on the integrity of the judicial process itself. The trial judge found that the discovery violation in this case was both willful and blatant.[22] In view of the fact

---

[22] The trial judge also expressed concern about discovery violations in other trials. If those violations involved the same attorney, or otherwise contributed to a concern about the trustworthiness of Wormley's 11th-hour testimony, they were relevant. Unrelated discovery violations in other litigation would not, however, normally provide a proper basis for curtailing the defendant's constitutional right to present a complete defense.

that petitioner's counsel had actually interviewed Wormley during the week before the trial began and the further fact that he amended his Answer to Discovery on the first day of trial without identifying Wormley while he did identify two actual eyewitnesses whom he did not place on the stand, the inference that he was deliberately seeking a tactical advantage is inescapable. Regardless of whether prejudice to the prosecution could have been avoided in this particular case, it is plain that the case fits into the category of willful misconduct in which the severest sanction is appropriate. After all, the court, as well as the prosecutor, has a vital interest in protecting the trial process from the pollution of perjured testimony. Evidentiary rules which apply to categories of inadmissible evidence—ranging from hearsay to the fruits of illegal searches—may properly be enforced even though the particular testimony being offered is not prejudicial. The pretrial conduct revealed by the record in this case gives rise to a sufficiently strong inference that "witnesses are being found that really weren't there," to justify the sanction of preclusion.

The argument that the client should not be held responsible for his lawyer's misconduct strikes at the heart of the attorney-client relationship. Although there are basic rights that the attorney cannot waive without the fully informed and publicly acknowledged consent of the client, the lawyer has—and must have—full authority to manage the conduct of the trial. The adversary process could not function effectively if every tactical decision required client approval. Moreover, given the protections afforded by the attorney-client privilege and the fact that extreme cases may involve unscrupulous conduct by both the client and the lawyer, it would be highly impracticable to require an investigation into their relative responsibilities before applying the sanction of preclusion. In responding to discovery, the client has a duty to be candid and forthcoming with the lawyer, and when the lawyer responds, he or she speaks for the client. Putting to one side the exceptional cases in which counsel is ineffective, the client must accept the consequences of the lawyer's decision to forgo cross-examination, to decide not to put certain witnesses on the stand, or to decide not to disclose the identity of certain witnesses in advance of trial. In this case, petitioner has no greater right to disavow his lawyer's decision to conceal Wormley's identity until after the trial had commenced than he has to disavow the decision to refrain from adducing testimony from the eyewitnesses who were identified in the Answer to Discovery. Whenever a lawyer makes use of the sword provided by the Compulsory Process Clause, there is some risk that he may wound his own client. * * *

JUSTICE BRENNAN, with whom JUSTICE MARSHALL and JUSTICE BLACKMUN join, dissenting.

Criminal discovery is not a game. It is integral to the quest for truth and the fair adjudication of guilt or innocence. Violations of discovery rules thus cannot go uncorrected or undeterred without undermining the truthseeking process. The question in this case, however, is not whether discovery rules should be enforced but whether the need to correct and deter discovery violations requires a sanction that itself distorts the truthseeking process by excluding material evidence of innocence in a criminal case. I conclude that, at least where a criminal defendant is not personally responsible for the discovery violation, alternative sanctions are not only adequate to correct and deter discovery violations but are far superior to the arbitrary and disproportionate penalty imposed by the preclusion sanction. Because of this, and because the Court's balancing test creates a conflict of interest in every case involving a discovery violation, I would hold that, absent evidence of the defendant's personal involvement in a discovery violation, the Compulsory Process Clause *per se* bars discovery sanctions that exclude criminal defense evidence. * * *

II

A * * *

The Compulsory Process and Due Process Clauses * * * require courts to conduct a searching substantive inquiry whenever the government seeks to exclude criminal defense evidence. After all, "[f]ew rights are more fundamental than that of an accused to present witnesses in his own defense." The exclusion of criminal defense evidence undermines the central truthseeking aim of our criminal justice system because it deliberately distorts the record at the risk of misleading the jury into convicting an innocent person. Surely the paramount value our criminal justice system places on acquitting the innocent demands close scrutiny of any law preventing the jury from hearing evidence favorable to the defendant. On the other hand, the Compulsory Process Clause does not invalidate every restriction on the presentation of evidence. The Clause does not, for example, require criminal courts to admit evidence that is irrelevant, testimony by persons who are mentally infirm, or evidence that represents a half-truth. That the inquiry required under the Compulsory Process Clause is sometimes difficult does not, of course, justify abandoning the task altogether. * * *

B

The question at the heart of this case, then, is whether precluding a criminal defense witness from testifying bears an arbitrary and disproportionate relation to the purposes of discovery, at least absent any evidence that the defendant was personally responsible for the discovery violations. This question is not answered by merely pointing out that discovery, like compulsory process, serves truthseeking interests. I would be the last to deny the utility of discovery in the truthseeking process. See Brennan, The Criminal Prosecution: Sporting Event or Quest for Truth?, 1963 Wash.U.L.Q. 279. By aiding effective trial preparation, discovery helps develop a full account of the relevant facts, helps detect and expose attempts to falsify evidence, and prevents factors such as surprise from influencing the outcome at the expense of the merits of the case. But these objectives are accomplished by compliance with the discovery rules, not by the exclusion of material evidence. Discovery sanctions serve the objectives of discovery by correcting for the adverse effects of discovery violations and deterring future discovery violations from occurring. If sanctions other than excluding evidence can sufficiently correct and deter discovery violations, then there is no reason to resort to a sanction that itself constitutes "a conscious mandatory distortion of the fact-finding process whenever applied." * * *

C * * *

The Court's balancing approach, moreover, has the unfortunate effect of creating a conflict of interest in every case involving a willful discovery violation because the defense counsel is placed in a position where the best argument he can make on behalf of his client is: "Don't preclude the defense witness—punish me personally." In this very case, for example, the defense attorney became noticeably timid once the judge threatened to report his actions to the disciplinary commission. He did not argue: "Sure, bring me before the disciplinary commission; that's a much more appropriate sanction than excluding a witness who might get my client acquitted." I cannot see how we can expect defense counsel in this or any other case to act as vigorous advocates for the interests of their clients when those interests are adverse to their own. * * *

Discovery rules are important, but only as a means for helping the criminal system convict the guilty and acquit the innocent. Precluding defense witness testimony as a sanction for a defense counsel's willful discovery violation not only directly subverts criminal justice by basing convictions on a partial presentation of the facts, but is also arbitrary and disproportionate to any of the purposes served by discovery rules or discovery sanctions. The Court today thus sacrifices the paramount values of the criminal system in a misguided and unnecessary effort to preserve the sanctity of discovery. We may never know for certain whether the defendant or Bridges' brother fired the shot for which the defendant was convicted. We do know, however, that the jury that convicted the defendant was not permitted to hear evidence that would have both placed a gun in Bridges' brother's hands and contradicted the testimony of Bridges and his brother that they possessed no weapons that evening—and that, because of the defense counsel's 5-day delay in identifying a witness, an innocent man may be serving 10 years in prison. I dissent.

[The opinion of JUSTICE BLACKMUN, dissenting, is omitted. The Court was operating with only eight justices during this period.]

NOTES AND QUESTIONS

1.   Which opinion gets the better of the argument? Referring back to the norms of the criminal process (accuracy, fairness, efficiency, and limiting government), which norms seem to predominate in Justice Stevens's opinion? Justice Brennan's?

2.   Justice Stevens noted that "[l]awyers are accustomed to meeting deadlines" and that the "burden of identifying [witnesses] in advance of trial adds little to [the] routine demands of trial preparation." Perhaps. But recall the cases from the ineffective assistance portion of Chapter 14. Are you persuaded that most, or even many, failures to comply will be purposeful attempts to gain a strategic advance? What about in *Taylor* itself? How does the Court justify assuming that the failure was strategic?

3.   Chambers was charged with the 1969 murder of a police officer in Mississippi. He requested the court to order *M* to appear and to qualify *M* as an adverse witness because he had confessed to the murder (*M* repudiated the confession at Chambers's preliminary hearing). If the judge agreed that *M* was an adverse witness, Chambers's lawyer could treat him as if the State had called him, probing his story through cross-examination. If *M* was not an adverse witness, and the State did not call him—and why would the State call someone who had confessed to the murder for which it was trying Chambers?—Chambers's lawyer could only ask non-leading questions. In that case, it would be far easier for *M* to stand by his repudiation of the confession.

Chambers also called three witnesses to whom *M* admitted that he shot the officer (this would be offered to challenge *M*'s repudiation of his confession). The trial judge ruled (1) *M* is not an adverse witness; and (2) the three witnesses to whom *M* repeated his confession cannot testify because of state hearsay law. Any hope for Chambers from the right to compulsory process? The right to cross-examine witnesses?

In Chambers v. Mississippi, 410 U.S. 284, 93 S.Ct. 1038, 35 L.Ed.2d 297 (1973), the Court held, 8–1, that *C*'s constitutional rights were violated, noting that the "rights to confront and cross-examine witnesses and to call witnesses in one's own behalf have long been recognized as essential to due process." The Court was self-consciously narrow in its holding, however: "In reaching this judgment, we establish no new principles of constitutional law. * * * Rather, we hold quite simply that under the facts and circumstances of this case the rulings of the trial court deprived Chambers of a fair trial." For an excellent discussion of *Chambers*, see Peter Westen, *Confrontation and*

Compulsory Process: A Unified Theory of Evidence for Criminal Cases, 91 Harv. L. Rev. 567, 606–11 (1978).

4. What if a defendant wants to present an expert in eyewitness reliability or in the factors that might lead to a false confession? Janet C. Hoeffel, *The Sixth Amendment's Lost Clause: Unearthing Compulsory Process*, 2002 Wis. L. Rev. 1275, argues that the compulsory process clause requires courts to admit expert testimony offered by defendants as long as a reasonable jury could find the evidence reliable. What is the substantive difference between the right to present a witness to testify to the facts or the right to present a witness who can help the jury interpret the facts? In both cases, if the evidence passes a threshold relevance and reliability test, perhaps the compulsory process clause requires courts to admit it. Cf. Montana v. Egelhoff, 518 U.S. 37, 116 S.Ct. 2013, 135 L.Ed.2d 361 (1996) (holding that state legislature can construct statutes to preclude logically relevant evidence).

D. DEFENDANT'S RIGHT TO TESTIFY

Introductory Comment

Nowhere does the Constitution explicitly guarantee the accused the right to testify in his defense. The reason for that is clear: In 1792, defendants were not *permitted* to testify in their own behalf. All parties to litigation, at common law,

> were disqualified from testifying because of their interest in the outcome of the trial. The principal rationale for this rule was the possible untrustworthiness of a party's testimony. Under the common law, the practice did develop of permitting criminal defendants to tell their side of the story, but they were limited to making an unsworn statement that could not be elicited through direct examination by counsel and was not subject to cross-examination.

Rock v. Arkansas, 483 U.S. 44, 107 S.Ct. 2704, 97 L.Ed.2d 37 (1987).

Indeed, the common law disabled the testimony of the *accuser* as well as the accused, again on the ground that parties have too great an interest in the outcome to be permitted to testify. In place of evidence from the persons most likely to know the true facts of the dispute, the common law emphasized the testimony of other, presumably disinterested witnesses—the descendants of the oathhelpers from the sixth century. The rules of relevance were more relaxed in the common law world (as in the Frankish procedures from the sixth century); the ultimate issue was at least partly about the character of the accuser and the accused. In the Assize of Clarendon (1166), for example, Henry II decreed that even acquitted defendants must nonetheless depart the realm if "they have been of ill repute and openly and disgracefully spoken of by the testimony of many and that of lawful men." If they returned "except by the mercy of the lord king," they would "be seized as outlaws."

As hard as it may be to believe today, criminal defendants in Georgia as late as 1960 *were not permitted* to give sworn testimony at trial. See Ferguson v. Georgia, 365 U.S. 570, 81 S.Ct. 756, 5 L.Ed.2d 783 (1961) (holding unconstitutional, under the due process clause, the Georgia statute to the extent that it denied the accused "the right to have his counsel question him to elicit his [unsworn] statement"). The law changed more quickly in jurisdictions other than Georgia. Congress enacted a general competency statute for federal litigants in 1878 and, by the end of the nineteenth century, all states but Georgia had declared criminal defendants competent to testify. As the Court put it in *Ferguson*, "[T]he considered consensus of the English-speaking world came to be that there was no rational justification for prohibiting the sworn testimony of the accused, who above all others may be in a position to meet the prosecution's case."

NOTES AND QUESTIONS

1. *Categorical limits on the subject matter of testimony.* Rock was charged with manslaughter for shooting her husband during an argument. Because her recollection was less than complete, she underwent hypnosis to refresh her recollection as to some of the details of the shooting. After the hypnosis, she remembered details indicating that the gun was defective and had misfired; an expert corroborated her testimony that the gun was defective and could easily misfire. The trial court applied a *per se* rule that hypnotically refreshed testimony could not be admitted because "whatever probative value it may have" is always outweighed by "the dangers of admitting this kind of unscientific testimony." The trial court limited Rock's testimony to a reiteration of her statements prior to the hypnosis, and she was convicted. Stressing the categorical bar applied by the trial court, the Supreme Court held that the ruling infringed Rock's right to testify in her own defense. See Rock v. Arkansas, 483 U.S. 44, 107 S.Ct. 2704, 97 L.Ed.2d 37 (1987).

2. Since the Bill of Rights contains no explicit right for defendants to testify, the Court has had to find a conceptual home for this right. One home, obviously, is the due process clause—if an argument cannot be located anywhere else in the Bill of Rights, it can always be grounded in due process fairness. But there are more specific constitutional guarantees that, in today's criminal procedure, can be understood to imply a right to testify in one's defense. One of the rights we have studied in this chapter seems to imply a defendant's right to testify. Do you see which one?

3.   There may be something in the Sixth Amendment right to counsel that also supports a right for defendants to testify. Hint: think about *Faretta v. California*, p. 1070.

4.   Combining *Rock*, Note 1, and *Taylor v. Illinois*, p. 1359, consider the following case. A state rape shield statute permits testimony about consensual sex acts with the defendant only if the defendant gives written notice and an offer of proof within ten days after arraignment. Defendant *L* did not provide that notice, but moves to permit the introduction of evidence of consensual sex acts between the victim and him. The judge denied the motion. What argument do you make on appeal, and what result? Cf. Michigan v. Lucas, 500 U.S. 145, 111 S.Ct. 1743, 114 L.Ed.2d 205 (1991).

GRIFFIN V. CALIFORNIA
Supreme Court of the United States, 1965.
380 U.S. 609, 85 S.Ct. 1229, 14 L.Ed.2d 106.

MR. JUSTICE DOUGLAS delivered the opinion of the Court [joined by JUSTICES BLACK, CLARK, HARLAN, BRENNAN, and GOLDBERG].

Petitioner was convicted of murder in the first degree after a jury trial in a California court. He did not testify at the trial on the issue of guilt, though he did testify at the separate trial on the issue of penalty. The trial court instructed the jury on the issue of guilt, stating that a defendant has a constitutional right not to testify. But it told the jury:[2]

"As to any evidence or facts against him which the defendant can reasonably be expected to deny or explain because of facts within his knowledge, if he does not testify or if, though he does testify, he fails to deny or explain such evidence, the jury may take that failure into consideration as tending to indicate the truth of such evidence and as indicating that among the inferences that may be reasonably drawn therefrom those unfavorable to the defendant are the more probable."

It added, however, that no such inference could be drawn as to evidence respecting which he had no knowledge. It stated that failure of a defendant to deny or explain the evidence of which he had knowledge does not create a presumption of guilt nor by itself warrant an inference of guilt nor relieve the prosecution of any of its burden of proof.

Petitioner had been seen with the deceased the evening of her death, the evidence placing him with her in the alley where her body was found. The prosecutor made much of the failure of petitioner to testify:

---

[2]   Article I, § 13, of the California Constitution provides in part:

"* * * in any criminal case, whether the defendant testifies or not, his failure to explain or to deny by his testimony any evidence or facts in the case against him may be commented upon by the court and by counsel, and may be considered by the court or the jury."

"The defendant certainly knows whether Essie Mae had this beat up appearance at the time he left her apartment and went down the alley with her.

"What kind of a man is it that would want to have sex with a woman that beat up if she was beat up at the time he left?

"He would know that. He would know how she got down the alley. He would know how the blood got on the bottom of the concrete steps. He would know how long he was with her in that box. He would know how her wig got off. He would know whether he beat her or mistreated her. He would know whether he walked away from that place cool as a cucumber when he saw Mr. Villasenor because he was conscious of his own guilt and wanted to get away from that damaged or injured woman.

"These things he has not seen fit to take the stand and deny or explain.

"And in the whole world, if anybody would know, this defendant would know.

"Essie Mae is dead, she can't tell you her side of the story. The defendant won't."

The death penalty was imposed and the California Supreme Court affirmed. The case is here on a writ of certiorari which we granted to consider whether comment on the failure to testify violated the Self-Incrimination Clause of the Fifth Amendment which we made applicable to the States by the Fourteenth in *Malloy v. Hogan*, 378 U.S. 1, 84 S.Ct. 1489, 12 L.Ed.2d 653 [1964], decided after the Supreme Court of California had affirmed the present conviction.

If this were a federal trial, reversible error would have been committed. *Wilson v. United States*, 149 U.S. 60, 13 S.Ct. 765, 37 L.Ed. 650 [1893], so holds. It is said, however, that the *Wilson* decision rested not on the Fifth Amendment, but on an Act of Congress, now 18 U.S.C. § 3481. That indeed is the fact, as the opinion of the Court in the *Wilson* case states. But that is the beginning, not the end, of our inquiry. The question remains whether, statute or not, the comment rule, approved by California, violates the Fifth Amendment.

We think it does. It is in substance a rule of evidence that allows the State the privilege of tendering to the jury for its consideration the failure of the accused to testify. No formal offer of proof is made as in other situations; but the prosecutor's comment and the court's acquiescence are the equivalent of an offer of evidence and its acceptance. The Court in the *Wilson* case stated:

"* * * the act was framed with a due regard also to those who might prefer to rely upon the presumption of innocence which the law gives to every one, and not wish to be witnesses. It is not every one who can safely venture on the witness stand, though entirely innocent of the charge against him. Excessive timidity, nervousness when facing others and attempting to explain transactions of a suspicious character, and offenses charged against him, will often confuse and embarrass him to such a degree as to increase rather than remove prejudices against him. It is not every one, however, honest, who would therefore willingly be placed on the witness stand. The statute, in tenderness to the weakness of those who from the causes mentioned might refuse to ask to be witnesses, particularly when they may have been in some degree compromised by their association with others, declares that the failure of a defendant in a criminal action to request to be a witness shall not create any presumption against him."

If the words "Fifth Amendment" are substituted for "act" and for "statute," the spirit of the Self-Incrimination Clause is reflected. For comment on the refusal to testify is a remnant of the "inquisitorial system of criminal justice," which the Fifth Amendment outlaws. It is a penalty imposed by courts for exercising a constitutional privilege. It cuts down on the privilege by making its assertion costly. It is said, however, that the inference of guilt for failure to testify as to facts peculiarly within the accused's knowledge is in any event natural and irresistible, and that comment on the failure does not magnify that inference into a penalty for asserting a constitutional privilege. What the jury may infer, given no help from the court, is one thing. What it may infer when the court solemnizes the silence of the accused into evidence against him is quite another. That the inference of guilt is not always so natural or irresistible is brought out in [a state court] opinion * * * :

"Defendant contends that the reason a defendant refuses to testify is that his prior convictions will be introduced in evidence to impeach him and not that he is unable to deny the accusations. It is true that the defendant might fear that his prior convictions will prejudice the jury, and therefore another possible inference can be drawn from his refusal to take the stand."

We said in *Malloy v. Hogan* that "the same standards must determine whether an accused's silence in either a federal or state proceeding is justified." We take that in its literal sense and hold that the Fifth Amendment, in its direct application to the Federal Government and in its bearing on the States by reason of the Fourteenth Amendment, forbids either comment by the prosecution on the accused's silence or instructions by the court that such silence is evidence of guilt.[6] * * *

THE CHIEF JUSTICE [WARREN] took no part in the decision of this case.

MR. JUSTICE HARLAN, concurring.

I agree with the Court that within the federal judicial system the Fifth Amendment bars adverse comment by federal prosecutors and judges on a defendant's failure to take the stand in a criminal trial, a right accorded him by that amendment. And given last Term's decision in *Malloy v. Hogan* that the Fifth Amendment applies to the States in all its refinements, I see no legitimate escape from today's decision and therefore concur in it. I do so, however, with great reluctance, since for me the decision exemplifies the creeping paralysis with which this Court's recent adoption of the "incorporation" doctrine is infecting the operation of the federal system. * * *

Although compelled to concur in this decision, I am free to express the hope that the Court will eventually return to constitutional paths which, until recently, it has followed throughout its history.

MR. JUSTICE STEWART, with whom MR. JUSTICE WHITE joins, dissenting. * * *

With both candor and accuracy, the Court concedes that the question before us is one of first impression here. It is a question which has not arisen before, because until last year the self-incrimination provision of the Fifth Amendment had been held to apply only to federal proceedings, and in the federal judicial system the matter has been covered by a specific Act of Congress which has been in effect ever since defendants have been permitted to testify at all in federal criminal trials.

We must determine whether the petitioner has been "compelled * * * to be a witness against himself." Compulsion is the focus of the inquiry. Certainly, if any compulsion be detected in the California procedure, it is of a dramatically different and less palpable nature than that involved in the procedures which historically gave rise to the Fifth Amendment guarantee. When a suspect was brought before the Court of High Commission or the Star Chamber, he was commanded to answer whatever was asked of him, and subjected to a far-reaching and deeply probing inquiry in an effort to ferret out some unknown and frequently unsuspected crime. He declined to answer on pain of incarceration, banishment, or mutilation. And if he spoke falsely, he was subject to

---

[6] We reserve decision on whether an accused can require, as in *Bruno v. United States*, 308 U.S. 287, 60 S.Ct. 198, 84 L.Ed. 257 [1939], that the jury be instructed that his silence must be disregarded.

further punishment. Faced with this formidable array of alternatives, his decision to speak was unquestionably coerced.

Those were the lurid realities which lay behind enactment of the Fifth Amendment, a far cry from the subject matter of the case before us. I think that the Court in this case stretches the concept of compulsion beyond all reasonable bounds, and that whatever compulsion may exist derives from the defendant's choice not to testify, not from any comment by court or counsel. In support of its conclusion that the California procedure does compel the accused to testify, the Court has only this to say: "It is a penalty imposed by courts for exercising a constitutional privilege. It cuts down on the privilege by making its assertion costly." Exactly what the penalty imposed consists of is not clear. It is not, as I understand the problem, that the jury becomes aware that the defendant has chosen not to testify in his own defense, for the jury will, of course, realize this quite evident fact, even though the choice goes unmentioned. Since comment by counsel and the court does not compel testimony by creating such an awareness, the Court must be saying that the California constitutional provision places some other compulsion upon the defendant to incriminate himself, some compulsion which the Court does not describe and which I cannot readily perceive.

It is not at all apparent to me, on any realistic view of the trial process, that a defendant will be at more of a disadvantage under the California practice than he would be in a court which permitted no comment at all on his failure to take the witness stand. How can it be said that the inferences drawn by a jury will be more detrimental to a defendant under the limiting and carefully controlling language of the instruction here involved than would result if the jury were left to roam at large with only its untutored instincts to guide it, to draw from the defendant's silence broad inferences of guilt? The instructions in this case expressly cautioned the jury that the defendant's failure to testify "does not create a presumption of guilt or by itself warrant an inference of guilt"; it was further admonished that such failure does not "relieve the prosecution of its burden of providing every essential element of the crime," and finally the trial judge warned that the prosecution's burden remained that of proof "beyond a reasonable doubt." Whether the same limitations would be observed by a jury without the benefit of protective instructions shielding the defendant is certainly open to real doubt. * * *

I think the California comment rule is not a coercive device which impairs the right against self-incrimination, but rather a means of articulating and bringing into the light of rational discussion a fact inescapably impressed on the jury's consciousness. The California procedure is not only designed to protect the defendant against unwarranted inferences which might be drawn by an uninformed jury; it is also an attempt by the State to recognize and articulate what it believes to be the natural probative force of certain facts. Surely no one would deny that the State has an important interest in throwing the light of rational discussion on that which transpires in the course of a trial, both to protect the defendant from the very real dangers of silence and to shape a legal process designed to ascertain the truth. * * *

The formulation of procedural rules to govern the administration of criminal justice in the various States is properly a matter of local concern. We are charged with no general supervisory power over such matters; our only legitimate function is to prevent violations of the Constitution's commands. California has honored the constitutional command that no person shall "be compelled in any criminal case to be a witness against himself." The petitioner was not compelled to testify, and he did not do so. But whenever in a jury trial a defendant exercises this constitutional right, the members of the jury are bound to draw inferences from his silence. No constitution can prevent the operation of the human mind. Without limiting instructions, the danger exists that the inferences drawn by the jury may be unfairly broad. Some States have permitted this danger to go unchecked, by forbidding any comment at all upon the defendant's failure to take the witness stand. Other States have dealt with this danger in a variety of ways * * * . * * * But, so long as the constitutional command is obeyed, such matters of state policy are not for this Court to decide. * * *

NOTES AND QUESTIONS

1.   How was Griffin compelled to be a witness against himself in the particular case before the Court? Didn't he in fact *not* testify? Which analysis do you find more persuasive, Justice Stewart's dissent or the majority? For an excellent explanation of *Griffin*'s compulsion theory, see Stephen J. Schulhofer, *Reconsidering Miranda*, 54 U. Chic. L. Rev. 435 (1987).

2.   *Right to a "no-inference" instruction.* The issue the Court reserved in footnote 6 in *Griffin* was answered in Carter v. Kentucky, 450 U.S. 288, 101 S.Ct. 1112, 67 L.Ed.2d 241 (1981), where the Court unanimously held that defendants have a right to an instruction from the judge that the jury should draw no inference from the failure to testify. The Court's opinion was written by Justice Stewart, who wrote the dissent in *Griffin*. Does *Carter* extend *Griffin*? Does it follow that if the judge and prosecutor should not comment on a defendant's silence, that the jury is not permitted to draw a negative inference?

3.   What if the trial judge gives a no-inference instruction over the objection of the defendant? Does *this* violate *Griffin*? If *Griffin* is based on the notion that the threatened penalty of an adverse instruction might compel defendants to testify, presumably a defendant who does not want to call attention to his failure to testify might be equally compelled to testify by a no-inference instruction. But the Court has held that a no-inference

instruction does not violate the self-incrimination clause. Lakeside v. Oregon, 435 U.S. 333, 98 S.Ct. 1091, 55 L.Ed.2d 319 (1978).

4. *Extending Griffin to sentencing.* In Mitchell v. United States, 526 U.S. 314, 119 S.Ct. 1307, 143 L.Ed.2d 424 (1999), the Court held that federal judges may not draw adverse inferences about "the facts of the offense" from a defendant's silence at a sentencing hearing. Justice Scalia argued in his dissent (joined by Chief Justice Rehnquist and Justices O'Connor and Thomas) that *Griffin* should not be extended to sentencing hearings and, in any event, the bulk of the inquiry is not about the "facts of the offense." Instead, sentencing judges largely seek to determine "acceptance of responsibility, repentance, character, and future dangerousness."

Justice Thomas's *Mitchell* dissent called for *Griffin* to be overruled. While refusing to join that call, Justice Scalia's dissent noted at length that *Griffin*'s textual and historical "pedigree" were "equally dubious."

> The Fifth Amendment provides that "[n]o person * * * shall be compelled in any criminal case to be a witness against himself." As an original matter, it would seem to me that the threat of an adverse inference does not "compel" anyone to testify. It is one of the natural (and not governmentally imposed) consequences of failing to testify—as is the factfinder's increased readiness to believe the incriminating testimony that the defendant chooses not to contradict. Both of these consequences are assuredly cons rather than pros in the "to testify or not to testify" calculus, but they do not *compel* anyone to take the stand. Indeed, I imagine that in most instances, a guilty defendant would choose to remain silent *despite* the adverse inference, on the theory that it would do him less damage than his own cross-examined testimony.

> Despite the text, we held in *Griffin v. California* that it was impermissible for the prosecutor or judge to comment on a defendant's refusal to testify. We called it a "penalty" imposed on the defendant's exercise of the privilege. And we did not stop there, holding in *Carter v. Kentucky* [Note 2] that a judge must, if the defendant asks, instruct the jury that it may not *sua sponte* consider the defendant's silence as evidence of his guilt. * * *

> The majority muses that the no-adverse-inference rule has found "wide acceptance in the legal culture" and has even become "an essential feature of our legal tradition." Although the latter assertion strikes me as hyperbolic, the former may be true—which is adequate reason not to overrule these cases, a course I in no way propose. It is not adequate reason, however, to extend these cases into areas where they do not yet apply, since neither logic nor history can be marshaled in defense of them. The illogic of the *Griffin* line is plain, for it runs exactly counter to normal evidentiary inferences: If I ask my son whether he saw a movie I

had forbidden him to watch, and he remains silent, the import of his silence is clear. * * *

Whatever the merits of prohibiting adverse inferences as a legislative policy, the text and history of the Fifth Amendment give no indication that there is a federal *constitutional* prohibition on the use of the defendant's silence as demeanor evidence. Our hardy forebears, who thought of compulsion in terms of the rack and oaths forced by the power of law, would not have viewed the drawing of a commonsense inference as equivalent pressure.

5.   *Sequestration.* If you were designing a judicial system, what would you do to protect witnesses from being biased (consciously or unconsciously) by the testimony of previous witnesses? You would probably apply the same rule that the common law developed: on the motion of either party, the witnesses are sequestered out of the courtroom and ordered not to discuss the case among themselves. Then each witness testifies without knowledge of what has come before.

Sequestration keeps witnesses from influencing each other. But what about the defendant, who has a right to be present in the courtroom and confront the witnesses against him? Of all the witnesses who will testify, the defendant has the most incentive to shade his testimony (or to lie outright). Yet the defendant is not subject to the rule of sequestration. Can the prosecutor comment on the fact that the defendant gets to hear the other evidence before he testifies?

That was the issue in Portuondo v. Agard, 529 U.S. 61, 120 S.Ct. 1119, 146 L.Ed.2d 47 (2000). The defendant offered consent as a defense to charges of sodomy and assault, and the whole trial turned on the credibility of the victim, the victim's friend, and the defendant. The prosecutor in her closing argument drew the jury's attention to a "benefit" the defendant has—"he gets to sit here and listen to the testimony of all the other witnesses before he testifies." Noting that no other witness has this benefit, the prosecutor characterized it as "a big advantage." He gets to "sit here and think what am I going to say and how am I going to say it? How am I going to fit it into the evidence?"

The defendant objected to these remarks on the ground that they were an impermissible penalty on his Sixth Amendment right to be present in the courtroom and confront the witnesses against him, and on his Fifth and Sixth Amendment rights to testify in his own behalf. The defendant relied explicitly on the penalty analysis in *Griffin*. The Court rejected the analogy, noting, first, that *Griffin* prohibited the prosecutor from inviting the jury to do something that the Constitution forbids—drawing an adverse inference from a defendant's silence—while there is no similar prohibition against the jury noting that the defendant gets to hear all the witnesses testify before he testifies. More importantly, the Court said that *Griffin* prohibits the judge and prosecutor from suggesting that the jury use the defendant's silence as *evidence of guilt.* In *Portuondo*, on the other hand, the comments invited only an adverse inference about credibility, an issue that a defendant always puts into play when he takes the witness stand.

6. *Tactics.* Part of a defendant's decision in presenting a defense is whether to testify. In many cases, it is the most important decision that the defendant will make. The uncontroversial core of the privilege against self-incrimination is that the state cannot subpoena the defendant to testify. Yet his choice not to testify is hardly without cost even after *Griffin*. If the defense contests the degree or culpability of the defendant's involvement, the jury will very much want to hear from him. If he does not testify, the jury will likely draw a negative inference, even if the judge instructs the jury not to draw a negative inference.

If the defendant denies being present—if the defense is misidentification or that the state's circumstantial evidence points to the wrong person—his failure to testify will not be quite so obvious. In those cases, a rule forbidding comment on the failure to testify might lessen the negative effect of the defendant's exercise of his right not to testify.

7. *Reasons not to testify.* An obvious reason not to testify is that the defendant is guilty, the defense lawyer knows it, and the defendant thus cannot take the witness stand and lie about guilt. See *Nix v. Whiteside*, p. 1036. If the defendant is guilty, but the defense lawyer does not know for sure, the defendant can (and defendants often do) take the witness stand to tell an exaggerated or untrue version of the events. But criminal defendants often make poor witnesses, and the jury may well decide that the prosecution witnesses are more credible. Whether this inference is more damaging than the inference that the jury will probably draw from the failure to testify is one of those eternal questions that no one can ever answer.

There are other costs of testifying. Though the matter is complex, and governed by evidence law, prior convictions are often admissible to impeach the credibility of the testifying defendant, but they are not (generally) admissible if the defendant does not testify. The judge will of course instruct the jurors that they may consider the prior convictions only on the issue of credibility and not on the ultimate issue of guilt or innocence. Most defense lawyers are quite cynical about the ability of jurors to disregard prior convictions on the issue of guilt.

In addition to impeachment permitted under evidence law, constitutional exclusionary rules relax when the defendant testifies. Confessions taken in violation of *Miranda* and physical evidence seized in violation of the Fourth Amendment are admissible to impeach testimony that is inconsistent with the confession or the physical evidence. See Harris v. New York, 401 U.S. 222, 91 S.Ct. 643, 28 L.Ed.2d 1 (1971) (*Miranda* impeachment); United States v. Havens, 446 U.S. 620, 100 S.Ct. 1912, 64 L.Ed.2d 559 (1980) (Fourth Amendment impeachment). As the Court is fond of saying, a defendant may not use either of these exclusionary rules as a shield to protect perjury. Again, the judge will instruct the jury to consider the confession or the physical evidence only insofar as it impeaches the defendant's credibility, but cynicism about the ability of jurors to follow the judge's instructions seems entirely justified here. Recall the Court's cynicism in the *Bruton* line of cases about jurors following instructions to disregard a co-defendant's confession. See p. 1343. Would you be able to disregard a confession that the defendant gave or the fact that the murder weapon was found in his possession?

8. *Cross-examination of defendants.* Defendants would probably prefer to tell their side of the story through friendly questioning by the defense lawyer and then refuse to answer probing questions on cross-examination. Does the Fifth Amendment privilege against compelled self-incrimination have a role to play here? The defendant is not being compelled to take the witness stand but does face compulsion to answer particular questions. Each question might be viewed as a separate Fifth Amendment event, and the defendant could decide whether to waive or not for each question. But the law has been settled otherwise. A defendant waives the Fifth Amendment privilege by taking the witness stand and testifying on direct examination. See Brown v. United States, 356 U.S. 148, 78 S.Ct. 622, 2 L.Ed.2d 589 (1958).

E. JURY DECISION-MAKING

Bringing It All Home

To this point, the focus in the chapter has been on the presentation of evidence to the factfinder. Though the factfinder can be a judge, it is usually a jury, and in this Part we will assume the typical trial to a jury. We now turn to the role of the lawyers in addressing the jury, the judge's role in instructing the jury, and the jury's role in returning a verdict. The opening statement and closing argument are the only times during the trial when the lawyers are permitted to address the jury directly, and most lawyers believe these opportunities are critical parts of trial advocacy. In the opening statement, the prosecutors and defense tell the jury what the evidence will show, each side hoping to predispose the jury toward its theory of the case. In the closing argument, if all goes roughly as expected, the lawyers should be able to remind the jury of what evidence was promised and stress the parts of the proof that deliver on the promise (while seeking to minimize the evidence that seems inconsistent). Under the rules of most jurisdictions, the prosecution makes the first closing argument and also gets to argue in rebuttal after the defense argues. See, *e.g.*, Fed. R. Crim. P. 29.1.

In preparing for closing argument, both parties need to know how the judge will instruct the jury. To that end, the judge will request proposed jury instructions from the parties and will rule on the proposed instructions prior to closing argument. See Fed. R. Crim. P. 30. Seeking favorable instructions is an important aspect of trial strategy. Slight differences in the way a legal standard is phrased might, in close cases, spell the difference between conviction and a hung jury, or between a hung jury and an acquittal. On the other hand, if you have watched juries being instructed, you would likely be cynical about whether jurors listen carefully. Many trial lawyers believe that jurors often make up their mind by the time all the evidence has been presented and thus may view the judge's instructions as just so much noise. This criticism is, we believe, properly directed at the complex "legalese" that infuses modern jury instructions.

Because the judge will have ruled on the instruction requests prior to closing argument, each party can stress to the jury during closing argument the parts of the instructions that are favorable to its theory of the case. In a larceny case, for example, the defense lawyer might argue: "The judge will instruct you that you must find the defendant not guilty of larceny if you find that the defendant believed that the property was abandoned. The judge will further instruct you that the reasonableness of this belief is simply not important; it does not matter whether you would have had the same belief. As long as you find the defendant believed, however unreasonably, that the owner had abandoned the property, you must return a verdict of not guilty." The prosecutor will likely focus attention on the part of the instruction that requires a honestly-held belief, and ask the jury whether under the circumstances of this case, the defendant could have honestly believed that the property was abandoned.

After the judge instructs the jury, it retires to deliberate. Most jurisdictions require unanimous verdicts and deliberation can take days in close cases. Juries sometimes require clarification of the instructions, in which case the judge will usually simply read the instruction again, with little or no explanation. A frequent ground for reversal is error in jury instructions, and judges thus tend to stay with standard language, often language that has been approved in prior appellate decisions.

If the jury reports that it is deadlocked, the judge will usually ask the jury to continue deliberations. Judges are loathe to accept a mistrial, particularly when the trial has been long and costly. Judges sometimes give what is called a "dynamite" or *Allen* charge, named after the Supreme Court decision approving it. Allen v. United States, 164 U.S. 492, 17 S.Ct. 154, 41 L.Ed. 528 (1896). As the Court paraphrased the crux of the charge: "if much the larger number were for conviction, a dissenting juror should consider whether his doubt was a reasonable one * * * . If, upon the other hand, the majority were for acquittal, the minority ought to ask themselves whether they might reasonably doubt the correctness of a judgment which was not concurred in by the majority."

By the 1960s, the *Allen* charge was being challenged as too coercive and thus a violation of due process. For an argument that a simple charge of "please continue deliberations" avoids any constitutional challenge, and might be just as effective in breaking deadlocks, see George C. Thomas III & Mark Greenbaum, *Justice Story Cuts the Gordian Knot of Hung Jury Instructions*, 15 Wm. & Mary Bill Rts. J. 893 (2007).

Only three outcomes of the jury deliberation are possible: conviction, acquittal, or hung jury. Chapter 18 discusses the double jeopardy implications of each of these outcomes. In this chapter we discuss the deliberative process. Three types of jury misconduct can cause the deliberation to "fail." The first type is the most serious—jury tampering by someone seeking purposefully to influence the outcome. Few cases involve evidence of overt jury tampering. In Remmer v. United States, 347 U.S. 227, 74 S.Ct. 450, 98 L.Ed. 654 (1954), a juror was approached during trial and told that he could profit by returning a verdict favorable to defendant. The United States Attorney and Federal Bureau of Investigation checked the allegation and determined that the remark was made in jest. No one informed the defendant. After conviction, the defendant learned of the remark through newspaper accounts and appealed his conviction. The Supreme Court vacated and remanded for a determination of whether the contact was "harmful" to defendant. The Court stated a rule of presumed prejudice:

> In a criminal case, any private communication, contact, or tampering directly or indirectly, with a juror during a trial about the matter pending before the jury is, for obvious reasons, deemed presumptively prejudicial, if not made in pursuance of known rules of the court and the instructions and directions of the court made during the trial, with full knowledge of the parties. The presumption is not conclusive, but the burden rests heavily upon the Government to establish, after notice to and hearing of the defendant, that such contact with the juror was harmless to the defendant.

A second type of jury misconduct involves external influences that lack the purposeful nature of jury tampering. Typically, these influences are outside sources of information about the case. In People v. Holloway, 50 Cal.3d 1098, 269 Cal.Rptr. 530, 790 P.2d 1327 (1990), for example, the defendant was charged with two capital murder counts for killing two young women during a burglary and attempted rape. Prior to trial, the judge ruled the defendant's prior record inadmissible on the ground that it was more prejudicial than probative. The judge ordered the jury not to read the newspapers. The judge "warned the jurors about the possibility of a mistrial resulting from corruption by outside influences and urged them to do their best to avoid it."

> Despite these efforts, it was discovered shortly after the jury returned its verdicts in the guilt phase that one of the jurors,

Juror Beck, had read a newspaper article on * * * the second day
of trial, stating that defendant was on parole from prison after
having served time for assaulting a Sacramento woman with a
hammer. Juror Beck had known this information throughout the
trial and, according to him, had kept it to himself until after the
jurors had signed their guilt phase verdicts.

The California Supreme Court noted that it was well settled that it
was misconduct for a juror to read news accounts of a case on which he is
sitting.

> It is equally well settled that such juror misconduct raises a
> presumption of prejudice that may be rebutted by proof that no
> prejudice actually resulted. As early as 1896, we said, "when
> misconduct of jurors is shown, it is presumed to be injurious to
> defendant, unless the contrary appears." We have long
> recognized the reason for this rule: "A juror is not allowed to say:
> 'I acknowledge to grave misconduct. I received evidence without
> the presence of the court, but those matters had no influence
> upon my mind when casting my vote in the jury-room.' The law,
> in its wisdom, does not allow a juror to purge himself in that
> way."

Having found misconduct and presumed prejudice from that
misconduct, the California court turned to the proper standard to apply in
deciding whether the presumed prejudice had been rebutted. A prior state
supreme court case had held that a

> verdict of guilty must be reversed or vacated "whenever * * * the
> court finds a substantial likelihood that the vote of one or more
> jurors was influenced by exposure to prejudicial matter relating
> to the defendant or to the case itself that was not part of the trial
> record on which the case was submitted to the jury." * * *

> We cannot say at this point that Juror Beck's improper
> knowledge had no impact. Although we know he was not the
> foreperson of the jury, we do not know, and may not discover
> under [the state evidence law] what, if any, influence the
> improper information had on Juror Beck or what influence he in
> turn had on the other jurors.

> Under the circumstances, we are unable to conclude that the
> presumption of prejudice has been rebutted. Our conclusion
> might have been different had the misconduct been revealed in
> time for the court to have taken corrective steps to cure it
> through admonition or by other prophylactic measures. It might
> also have been different if the information improperly obtained
> by Juror Beck had been less prejudicial. * * * [Under the facts of

the case, however,] we are unable to say that the juror misconduct did not prejudicially affect the outcome of the trial.

Defendant was entitled to be tried by 12, not 11, impartial and unprejudiced jurors. * * * Accordingly, we hold that the judgment must be reversed for jury misconduct.

The third kind of jury misconduct involves prejudging the case or reaching a verdict by some means other than considering the facts of the case. The principal case, which we saw earlier in the Chapter, is an example of this type of potential jury failure.

UNITED STATES V. THOMAS
United States Court of Appeals, Second Circuit, 1997.
116 F.3d 606.

For opinion, see p. 1271.

NOTES AND QUESTIONS

1. *The secrecy of jury deliberation.* Notice the point in *Thomas* that jury deliberation requires something approaching total secrecy. Jury misconduct as alleged in *Thomas* is difficult to detect because it is almost always inextricably intertwined with the jury function of putting the State to its burden of proof beyond a reasonable doubt. The veil of secrecy that protects the deliberative process makes inquiry into the basis of the acquittal (nullification or reasonable doubt) next to impossible.

2. *You will probably think we made this one up.* A jury in Louisville, Kentucky was deadlocked 11–1 in favor of murder and 11–1 in favor of manslaughter. Ten jurors were willing to compromise on either a murder or manslaughter conviction but one insisted on a murder conviction and another insisted that manslaughter was the only conviction he could endorse. As all twelve agreed that the defendant was guilty of either murder or manslaughter, but could not agree on which offense, out came a silver dollar and a coin flip produced a murder conviction. Word got back to the prosecutor, who told the judge. The judge declared a mistrial. Kim Wessel, *Jury Flipped Coin to Convict Man of Murder*, The Courier Journal, April 25, 2000, at 1A.

What result if the coin flip produced a manslaughter conviction?

3. *The jury verdict as a "black hole."* For good or ill, our law values the autonomy of jurors and juries. We saw this in *Thomas.* One manifestation of our regard for jury verdicts is that the law treats the verdict as "opaque"—the jury's fact-finding beyond review or challenge.

A. *The last ray of light from the jury black hole.* The last glimmer of light that the system permits to emerge from jury deliberation is from polling the jury. Consider, for example, Fed. R. Crim. P. 31(d): "if the poll reveals a lack of unanimity, the court may direct the jury to deliberate further or may declare a mistrial and discharge the jury." The point to a poll is that forcing each member of the jury to say "guilty" or "not guilty" can unearth a lingering doubt or encourage a juror to give voice to the feeling that he or she was pressured by the others.

   B.   *Inside the black hole—the rule against impeaching the verdict.* If after the verdict is entered, a juror comes forward and announces that other jurors pressured him to vote for the verdict, nothing can be done. The common-law rule was that juror testimony to impeach a jury verdict was flatly prohibited, with an exception for "extraneous influences." Tanner v. United States, 483 U.S. 107, 107 S.Ct. 2739, 97 L.Ed.2d 90 (1987). As we saw earlier, these "extraneous influences" include outside sources of prejudicial information. Rule 606(b) of the Federal Rules of Evidence embodies this common-law concept, permitting juror testimony in derogation of the verdict only "on the question whether extraneous prejudicial information was improperly brought to the jury's attention or whether any outside influence was improperly brought to bear upon any juror."

   The jury verdict black hole otherwise remains dark. Consider, for example, a challenge to a jury verdict based on the testimony of three female jurors that they had been "pressured into concurring with the guilty verdicts by the jury foreman who, along with other jurors, had used gender-based insults to intimidate them." Examples of these insults included that they were "stupid female[s]," who "didn't have minds" because they were women. All three jurors testified that, but for this pressure, they would have voted for acquittal on some counts. The Third Circuit noted the "common-law rule of ancient vintage that a jury's verdict may not be impeached by the testimony of a juror concerning any influences on the jury's deliberations that emanated from within the jury room."

   The Third Circuit held that Rule 606(b) codifies that common law rule and does not permit inquiry into the jury's internal deliberations. Some of the rationales offered for Rule 606(b) are that it discourages "harassment of jurors by losing parties eager to have the verdict set aside"; that it encourages "free and open discussion among jurors"; that it promotes verdict finality; and that it maintains "the viability of the jury as a judicial decision-making body." United States v. Stansfield, 101 F.3d 909 (3d Cir. 1996). See also Warger v. Shauers, 574 U.S. ___, 135 S. Ct. 521, 190 L. Ed. 2d 422 (2014) (holding in a civil case that a litigant could not use an affidavit about what a jury said during deliberations to show that the juror lied during voir dire).

   But this rule might be changing. On April 4, 2016, the Court granted certiorari in a case presenting the following question: whether a "no impeachment" rule constitutionally may bar evidence of racial bias offered to prove a violation of the Sixth Amendment right to an impartial jury. See Pena-Rodriguez v. Colorado, U.S.S.Ct. No. 15–606.

   C.   *The black hole stays dark—verdicts permitted on alternative theories.* In Schad v. Arizona, 501 U.S. 624, 111 S.Ct. 2491, 115 L.Ed.2d 555 (1991), the defendant was charged with first-degree murder on two theories—

premeditated murder and felony murder. Both types of murder were defined in a single first-degree murder statute. When the jury returned a general verdict of guilty, the nature of the verdict was thus hidden from view. As Schad argued, six members of the jury could have found him not guilty of felony murder, and a different six could have found him not guilty of premeditated murder, and the jury as a whole could still have returned a unanimous verdict of guilty. The Court held that this possibility did not offend due process. There is nothing wrong with charging different means of commission of a crime, the Court noted, and no rule that "jurors should be required to agree upon a single means of commission." Due process thus would not be offended if half the jury thought Schad had committed first degree murder because the killing occurred during a felony and half thought him guilty of premeditated first degree murder.

D. *The black hole stays dark—inconsistent verdicts permitted.* One might have thought that jury verdicts could at least be tested for logical consistency. For example, in United States v. Powell, 469 U.S. 57, 105 S.Ct. 471, 83 L.Ed.2d 461 (1984), the jury convicted Powell of using a telephone to commit a drug conspiracy and acquitted her of the *very same drug conspiracy.* Because these verdicts are logically inconsistent, Powell sought a reversal of her conviction. The Court unanimously rejected her argument. As Professor Eric L. Muller explained the Court's reasoning, it rested on three grounds: the argument from uncertainty, the argument from equity, and the argument from remedy. Eric Muller, *The Hobgoblin of Little Minds? Our Foolish Law of Inconsistent Verdicts*, 111 Harv. L. Rev. 771 (1998).

The argument from uncertainty is that a general verdict is opaque. Beyond the fact that the jury failed to follow its instructions, "everything is conjecture. The Court seems uncomfortable with the idea of reversing convictions based on guesswork." *Id.* at 789. One possible explanation of the uncertain outcome is that the verdict is a compromise, and the Court viewed this as part of the jury's factfinding function. The argument from equity "is the simple notion of fair play." Compromise or not, there is a manifest failure to follow the judge's instructions. But we do not know in which "direction" the failure occurred—did the jury acquit against the evidence on the conspiracy charge or convict against the evidence on the telephone charge? Thus, the only fair resolution is to defer to the jury's factfinding and leave the parties where the jury put them. *Id.* at 791. The argument from remedy is that the conviction can be reviewed for sufficiency of evidence, see Chapter 19 A., and thus the Court need not create a new procedure for reviewing inconsistent verdicts. *Id.* at 791–92.

Do these arguments persuade you that courts should not review inconsistent verdicts? They do not persuade Professor Muller who, despite the unanimous Supreme Court decision in *Powell*, argues that the Court's arguments are seductive but shallow, devilishly simple but disingenuous. Muller's arguments are too detailed for presentation here, and we commend the article to you. But note, once again, the extent to which the Court views the opaqueness of the jury verdict as a value to be protected.

Chapter 17

Sentencing

■ ■ ■

A. THEORIES OF PUNISHMENT

"A major obstacle to developing acceptable approaches to sentencing is the historical disagreement over the primary purpose of punishment." Charles J. Ogletree, Jr., *The Death of Discretion? Reflections on the Federal Sentencing Guidelines*, 101 Harv. L. Rev. 1938, 1940 (1988). In general, punishment is justified on utilitarian or retributive grounds, or a combination of these two principles. A brief explanation of these competing theories is provided in the following excerpt.

JOSHUA DRESSLER—UNDERSTANDING CRIMINAL LAW
(7th ed. 2015), 14–16.

§ 2.03   Theories of Punishment * * *

[B] Utilitarianism

[1] Basic Principles * * *

[A]ccording to classical utilitarianism, * * * the purpose of all laws is to maximize the net happiness of society. Laws should be used to exclude, as far as possible, all painful or unpleasant events. To a utilitarian, both crime and punishment are unpleasant and, therefore, normally undesirable occurrences. In a perfect world, neither would exist.

As we do not live in a perfect world—some persons are disposed to commit crimes—utilitarians believe that the pain inflicted by punishment is justifiable if, but only if, it is expected to result in a reduction in the pain of crime that would otherwise occur. * * *

Classical utilitarianism is founded on the belief that the threat or imposition of punishment can reduce crime because * * * "[p]ain and pleasure are the great springs of human action," and "[i]n matters of importance every one calculates." Put slightly differently, utilitarians believe that human beings generally act hedonistically and rationally: A person will act according to his immediate desires to the extent that he believes that his conduct will augment his overall happiness. As a rational calculator, however, a person contemplating criminal activity (to augment his happiness) will balance the expected benefits of the proposed conduct against its risks, taking into account such factors as the likelihood of successful commission of the crime, the risk of detection and conviction, and the severity of the likely punishment. He will avoid criminal activity if the perceived potential pain (punishment) outweighs the expected potential pleasure (criminal rewards). * * *

[2] Forms of Utilitarianism

Utilitarianism as applied to the criminal law takes different forms. Most commonly, utilitarians stress *general deterrence*. That is, *D* is punished in order to convince the *general* community * * * to forego criminal conduct in the future. In this model, *D*'s punishment serves as an object lesson to others; *D* is used as a means to a desired end, namely, a net reduction in crime. *D*'s punishment teaches us what conduct is impermissible; it instills fear of punishment in would-be violators of the law; and, at least to some extent, it habituates us to act lawfully, even in the absence of fear of punishment.

Individual deterrence (sometimes characterized as *specific deterrence*) is a second utilitarian goal. Here, *D*'s punishment is meant to deter, specifically, *D*'s future misconduct by intimidation. By punishing *D*—by inflicting pain and suffering upon him for his criminal actions—we provide a clear reminder to him of the risks of future offending. We "scare him straight."

A third form of utilitarianism is *incapacitation*. Quite simply, *D*'s imprisonment prevents him from committing crimes in the outside society during the period of segregation.

A non-classical variety of utilitarianism is *rehabilitation* (or *reform*). Although the goal is the same—to reduce future crime—advocates of this model prefer to use the correctional system to reform the wrongdoer rather than to secure compliance through the fear or "bad taste" of punishment. The methods of reformation will vary from case to case, but could consist of, for example, psychiatric care, therapy for drug addiction, or academic or vocational training.

[C] Retributivism

[1] Basic Principles

Retributivists believe that punishment is justified when it is deserved. It is deserved when the wrongdoer freely chooses to violate society's rules. To an uncompromising retributivist, the wrongdoer should be punished, whether or not it will result in a reduction in crime. * * * According to a retributivist "[i]t is morally fitting that an offender should suffer in proportion to [his] desert of culpable wrongdoing."

Notice [that] * * * retributivism looks backward in time and justifies punishment solely on the basis of the previous, voluntary commission of a crime. In contrast, utilitarians look forward in time. They care about the past only to the extent that it helps them to predict the future. No matter how egregious the wrongdoing, utilitarians do not advocate punishment unless they believe it will provide an overall social benefit.

B. SENTENCING SYSTEMS: OVERVIEW

William J. Powell & Michael T. Cimino— Prosecutorial Discretion Under the Federal Sentencing Guidelines: Is the Fox Guarding the Hen House?
97 West Virginia Law Review 373 (1995), 374–80.

A.   Rigid Sentencing of Colonial America

At the core of the early colonial approach to sentencing was the "prevailing belief in the basic depravity of all human beings, a feeling that made any notion of an offender's possible rehabilitation absurd." Thus, colonial law enforcement swiftly attacked criminal behavior with public and often harsh punishment designed to maximize a sense of disgrace to the offender. The Capital Laws of New England, for example, prescribed the death penalty for twelve offenses including witchcraft, assault in sudden anger, and adultery. Eventually, however, the "demoralizing influence both upon the community and the convict of these public manifestations of disgrace was soon realized, and led, shortly after the adoption of our Constitution, to their discontinuance in Pennsylvania" and throughout the colonies.

This reform in colonial sentencing can be attributed in part to the 1764 work by the Italian, Cesare Beccaria, entitled *On Crimes And Punishments*. Beccaria called for the creation of legislatively determined sentences, the establishment of a clear criminal code, the restriction of pre-trial detention, the need to base a finding of guilt on certainty rather than a mere preponderance of the evidence, and the open administration of the accusation and prosecution of criminal matters before a jury. Beccaria also demanded the elimination of torture and the abolishment of capital punishment. Beccaria's work was based on the theory prevailing at the time that "the certainty of punishment, even if it be moderate, will always make a stronger impression than the fear of another which is more terrible but combined with the hope of impunity."

Beccaria's reform movement eventually reached the American colonies. * * *

In late eighteenth-century America, imprisonment of the offender, as a means of encouraging spiritual rehabilitation, was substituted for the practice of inflicting physical pain as punishment. The belief spread throughout the new American states "that if, instead of being 'punished,' the offender were incarcerated and subjected to a rigorous system of labor and religion he or she would become 'cured' of criminal tendencies." In 1787, the prominent Quaker Benjamin Rush outlined his proposals for a "House of Reform," where criminals could be kept from society and amend their deviant ways. In 1790, Pennsylvania adopted Rush's ideas of a "House of Reform" or "penitentiary," as the Quakers called it. Inmates were sentenced to the penitentiary for fixed terms, but did not know the length of their terms. * * *

B.   TOWARD INDETERMINATE SENTENCING

The growing population of the new nation, its immigrant and transient composition, the increased efficiency of the police and courts, the fixed sentence, and other factors all contributed to the rapidly increasing number of inmates, and resulted in overcrowded prisons. To relieve the overcrowding and to make room for new inmates, the use of pardons became widespread. * * * Problems with the pardon system, however, including bribery and extortion, led New York to adopt the nation's first "good time" computation law in 1817. The good time proposal was quickly adopted by the majority of states. * * *

C.   INDETERMINATE SENTENCING

The use of pardons, good time, probation and later parole all contributed to the growing indeterminacy of sentences rendered by judges of the nineteenth century, vastly different from the rigid sentencing of early colonial America. Each of these practices affected the time served under a sentence by altering the fixed term handed down by the judge at sentencing. These practices led to a refocusing of the sentencing approach toward what is now called "indeterminate sentencing." Under this approach, judges were not only encouraged to weigh the character of the individual defender when imposing a sentence, but when the offender was sentenced to prison, correctional officers were given the ultimate authority to determine when the offender was sufficiently rehabilitated to merit release or parole. The judge's role under indeterminate sentencing was "to bring to bear his accumulated experience, judgment, and, hopefully, wisdom, in order to determine what punishment was appropriate for the offense and the offender, convicted after a trial with well defined rules of evidence and procedure or after a plea of guilty." Thus, judicial decisionmaking remained the hallmark of our system of justice under this new sentencing system.

In 1870, New York became the first state to utilize an indeterminate-sentencing system. By 1922, all but four states and the federal government employed some type of indeterminate sentencing or used the parole system which functioned in the same way. By the 1960s, every state had an indeterminate-sentencing structure or some variation.

NOTES AND QUESTIONS

1. *Indeterminate sentencing systems.* A sentencing system is sometimes described as "indeterminate" if trial judges have broad sentencing authority. For example, a judge may have authority to incarcerate a robber, in the words of a hypothetical sentencing statute, to "a term of years not exceeding ten," or even to put the convicted party on probation. Thus, the judge may choose to impose a five-year prison sentence in one case, and ten in another, and order probation in a third, typically based on information provided to the judge in presentencing reports. Such a sentencing system is "indeterminate" in the sense that the judge, and not the legislature, determines the appropriate punishment for each offender.

In a pure version of indeterminate sentencing, the judge imposes an indeterminate sentence, for example, by sentencing a convicted robber to imprisonment for "six months to ten years." In this example, as she leaves for prison, the defendant does not know how long she will be incarcerated, except within the broad parameters of the indeterminate sentence imposed. The ultimate release decision is made by a parole board.

2. *The "rehabilitative ideal."* The move to indeterminate sentencing coincided with the advent of the so-called "rehabilitative ideal," which "functioned as the central organizing principle of American sentencing systems" for much of the first-half of the twentieth century. Michael M. O'Hear, *The Original Intent of Uniformity in Federal Sentencing,* 74 U. Cin. L. Rev. 749, 757 (2006). The ideal of rehabilitation is "the notion that a primary purpose of penal treatment is to effect changes in the characters, attitudes, and behavior of convicted offenders, so as to strengthen the social defense against unwanted behavior, but also to contribute to the welfare and satisfaction of offenders." Francis A. Allen, The Decline of the Rehabilitative Ideal: Penal Policy and Social Purpose 2 (1981). Can you see why indeterminate sentencing is appropriate in a rehabilitative penal system?

3. *The move to determinate sentencing.* We left off the Powell and Cimino excerpt above in the 1960s, at the peak of the rehabilitative ideal and indeterminate sentencing. But, let's continue the story.

SANFORD H. KADISH—FIFTY YEARS OF CRIMINAL LAW: AN OPINIONATED REVIEW
87 California Law Review 943 (1999), 979–981.

* * * Beginning in the early 1970s, a widespread disaffection with rehabilitation as a theory and in practice took hold, which revolutionized sentencing laws in this country. The individualization of punishment had run its course, yielding to the sentiment that those who commit crime should be punished because they deserve it, and in an amount determined by the seriousness of their crime. * * * [S]uccessful translation of this change of sentiment into a new pattern of sentencing

laws was in important measure the product of an unlikely coincidence of views between two historically antagonistic schools of thought.

On one side were those who had long-opposed policies of individualization and rehabilitation because they coddled offenders and promptly put them back on the streets to commit more crimes, failed justice in not giving the offender the punishment he deserved, and did both these things deceptively by ostensibly allowing long terms of imprisonment while at the same time authorizing behind-the-scenes bureaucrats to release offenders early on parole. On the other side were the traditional supporters of individualization and rehabilitation, those who tended to see offenders as themselves victims of social injustices and their own pathologies. But they had become disillusioned with the way the theory of individual punishment had worked out in practice. It was often invidiously exercised against minorities; it produced indefensible inequalities in punishment of people convicted of the same offense; it permitted offenders to be held for unconscionably long terms on the unreviewable judgment of correctional agencies; and it never received the financial resources needed to make it work.

The alliance of these forces produced a radical departure in sentencing laws and policies. The transition is exemplified by the change in California, which had been at the forefront of states committed to individualized and rehabilitative punishment. In 1976, the legislature replaced its elaborate system of indeterminate sentencing with a determinate sentencing law that opened with this ringing commitment:

> The Legislature finds and declares that the purpose of imprisonment for crime is punishment. This purpose is best served by terms proportionate to the seriousness of the offense with provision for uniformity in the sentences of offenders committing the same offense under similar circumstances.

The law went on to command the judge to impose a specific sentence for each major felony, permitting only a specified higher or lower sentence if the judge found aggravating or mitigating circumstances, as the case might be. It also abolished parole as inconsistent with the principles of truth in sentencing and just deserts.

Other jurisdictions, including the federal, chose to implement determinate sentencing programs through a system of sentencing guidelines rather than fixed sentences. The Federal Sentencing Guidelines have been the most consequential. In 1984, Congress created a commission to promulgate sentencing guidelines that judges would be bound to follow. [These guidelines are considered in Section C. of this chapter.—Eds.]

The supplanting of indeterminate individualized sentencing with determinate or guideline sentencing was, in a way, the product of an implicit bargain between the retributive punishers and the disillusioned reformers. It has turned out, however, to be a Faustian bargain for the reformers. They wanted more uniformity, less discretion, less imprisonment, and shorter prison terms, and embraced a desert theory of punishment thinking it would serve these purposes. But perhaps they should have seen that what is "deserved" rises with the tide of public resentment and anxiety. In the upshot, they got the greater uniformity and less discretion that they wanted, but at the cost of vastly longer terms of imprisonment, a proliferation of mandatory and repeat offender sentences (the infamous "three strikes" laws, for example), and an unprecedented explosion of the prison population, producing a "level of incarceration * * * unprecedented in this country's history and throughout the world today."

NOTES AND QUESTIONS

1. The effects of determinate and guideline sentencing, as described by Professor Kadish in the preceding excerpt, may be seen in recent data. The number of prisoners held by federal and state correctional authorities on December 31, 2014 was 1,561,500, a per capita rate of 612 persons per 100,000 population. U.S. Dep't of Justice, Prisoners in 2014 (Sept. 2015, NCJ 248955). If one includes persons under community supervision (*e.g.*, on probation or parole), the total at yearend 2013 was nearly 6.9 million, or about 2.8% of the U.S. adult population. U.S. Dep't of Justice, Correctional Population in the United States, 2013 (Dec. 2014, NCJ 248249). On a per capita basis, the United States has the highest prison population in the world. Sentencing Project, The State of Sentencing 2014: Developments in Policy and Practice 1 (2015).

2. As the preceding Kadish excerpt observes, the movement to determinate sentencing has often been linked to increasing public support for retributive theories of punishment, as well as increasing concern regarding sentencing disparity. Why is retribution inconsistent with an indeterminate sentencing system? If one believes in retribution, does it follow that two persons who have committed the same offense, *e.g.*, robbery, should *always* receive the same punishment?

3. *Mandatory minimum sentences.* An increasingly common legislative method for limiting judicial sentencing discretion is to enact mandatory minimum sentencing laws. Such statutes "generally provide that when a specified circumstance exists in connection with the commission of a crime (1) the court must sentence the defendant to prison and (2) the duration of the defendant's incarceration will be substantially longer than it would have been in the absence of the circumstance." Gary T. Lowenthal, *Mandatory Sentencing Laws: Undermining the Effectiveness of Determinate Sentencing Reform*, 81 Calif. L. Rev. 61, 64 (1993). For example, a legislature may generally provide for a sentence of from five to twenty years for commission of a drug offense; but the legislature may further provide that the judge *must*

impose a sentence of no less than ten years if the offender brandished a firearm during the commission of the offense.

Mandatory sentencing laws are controversial, even among some judges required to apply them. One federal district court judge, forced to apply a mandatory minimum statute in his first criminal case on the bench, observed: "I did not expect sentencing people to prison to feel good. But I was sorry and surprised to find that the very first sentence I imposed felt like an injustice. And not a small one." Gerard E. Lynch, *Sentencing Eddie*, 91 J. Crim. L. & Criminology 547, 566 (2001).

Similarly, District Judge Paul Cassell (a conservative-leaning former-and-again law professor) protested a federal sentencing provision that required him to impose a fifty-five year prison sentence on a 25-year-old man for selling small bags of marijuana to a police informant. The sentence—characterized by Judge Cassell as "unjust, cruel, and even irrational"—was required because the man possessed a gun during the drug sales. United States v. Angelos, 345 F.Supp.2d 1227, 1230 (D. Utah 2004). The judge further observed that this sentence was over twice as long as the one he imposed just hours earlier—nearly twenty-two years, the sentence recommended by the Government—on a defendant convicted of beating to death a 68-year-old woman.

Supreme Court Justice Stephen Breyer has commented on the effect of mandatory minimum sentencing laws:

> Mandatory minimum statutes are fundamentally inconsistent with [the] simultaneous effort to create a fair, honest, and rational sentencing system * * *. * * * [S]tatutory mandatory minimums generally deny the judge the legal power to depart downward, no matter how unusual the special circumstances that call for leniency. They rarely reflect an effort to achieve sentencing proportionality— a key element of sentencing fairness that demands that the law punish a drug "kingpin" and a "mule" differently. They transfer sentencing power to prosecutors, who can determine sentences through the charges they decide to bring, and who thereby have reintroduced much of the sentencing disparity that Congress [and many state legislatures have sought] to eliminate.

Harris v. United States, 536 U.S. 545, 122 S.Ct. 2406, 153 L.Ed.2d 524 (2002) (concurring opinion).

What are the arguments in defense of mandatory minimum sentencing laws? Why do you think such laws are popular with lawmakers? For more on the subject, including arguments for and against mandatory minimum sentencing laws and proposals for reform, see Erik Luna & Paul G. Cassell, *Mandatory Minimalism*, 32 Cardozo L. Rev. 1 (2010).

C. FEDERAL SENTENCING GUIDELINES

Introductory Comment

As explained in the last chapter section, sentencing laws underwent substantial change beginning in the 1970s. Most jurisdictions moved, in one form or another, from indeterminate to determine sentencing. Some of these jurisdictions implemented determinate sentencing through the adoption of sentencing guidelines. This was the approach taken in the federal system.

In 1984 Congress authorized the development of the Federal Sentencing Guidelines, the subject of this chapter section. As originally devised, the Guidelines were mandatory: Federal judges were required in nearly all cases to sentence a defendant within the specified "guideline range." A judge could only depart from the Guideline sentence in very limited circumstances—circumstances themselves set out in the Guidelines.

As a result of a line of complicated constitutional decisions (covered on pp. 1418–1464 of the casebook), however, the Federal Sentencing Guidelines are now advisory rather than mandatory. As you read this chapter section, therefore, you should keep in mind that when the readings describe the Guidelines as mandatory, this is no longer so.

MISTRETTA V. UNITED STATES

Supreme Court of the United States, 1989.
488 U.S. 361, 109 S.Ct. 647, 102 L.Ed.2d 714.

JUSTICE BLACKMUN delivered the opinion of the Court [joined by CHIEF JUSTICE REHNQUIST, and JUSTICES WHITE, MARSHALL, STEVENS, O'CONNOR, and KENNEDY. JUSTICE BRENNAN joined in pertinent part (all but n. 11)]. * * *

I

A

BACKGROUND

For almost a century, the Federal Government employed in criminal cases a system of indeterminate sentencing. Statutes specified the penalties for crimes but nearly always gave the sentencing judge wide discretion to decide whether the offender should be incarcerated and for how long, whether he should be fined and how much, and whether some lesser restraint, such as probation, should be imposed instead of imprisonment or fine. This indeterminate-sentencing system was supplemented by the utilization of parole, by which an offender was returned to society under the "guidance and control" of a parole officer.

Both indeterminate sentencing and parole were based on concepts of the offender's possible, indeed probable, rehabilitation, a view that it was realistic to attempt to rehabilitate the inmate and thereby to minimize the risk that he would resume criminal activity upon his return to society. It obviously required the judge and the parole officer to make their respective sentencing and release decisions upon their own assessments of the offender's amenability to rehabilitation. As a result, the court and the officer were in positions to exercise, and usually did exercise, very broad discretion. This led almost inevitably to the conclusion on the part of a reviewing court that the sentencing judge "sees more and senses more" than the appellate court; thus, the judge enjoyed the "superiority of his nether position," for that court's determination as to what sentence was appropriate met with virtually unconditional deference on appeal. The correction official possessed almost absolute discretion over the parole decision. * * *

Serious disparities in sentences, however, were common. Rehabilitation as a sound penological theory came to be questioned and, in any event, was regarded by some as an unattainable goal for most cases. In 1958, Congress authorized the creation of judicial sentencing institutes and joint councils, to formulate standards and criteria for sentencing. In 1973, the United States Parole Board adopted guidelines that established a "customary range" of confinement. Congress in 1976 endorsed this initiative through the Parole Commission and Reorganization Act, an attempt to envision for the Parole Commission a role, at least in part, "to moderate the disparities in the sentencing practices of individual judges." That Act, however, did not disturb the division of sentencing responsibility among the three Branches. The judge continued to exercise discretion and to set the sentence within the statutory range fixed by Congress, while the prisoner's actual release date generally was set by the Parole Commission.

This proved to be no more than a way station. Fundamental and widespread dissatisfaction with the uncertainties and the disparities continued to be expressed. Congress had wrestled with the problem for more than a decade when, in 1984, it enacted * * * sweeping reforms * * * . * * *

Before settling on a mandatory-guideline system, Congress considered other competing proposals for sentencing reform. It rejected strict determinate sentencing because it concluded that a guideline system would be successful in reducing sentence disparities while retaining the flexibility needed to adjust for unanticipated factors arising in a particular case. The Judiciary Committee rejected a proposal that would have made the sentencing guidelines only advisory.

B

THE ACT

The [Sentencing Reform Act of 1984], as adopted, revises the old sentencing process in several ways:

1. It rejects imprisonment as a means of promoting rehabilitation, and it states that punishment should serve retributive, educational, deterrent, and incapacitative goals.

2. It consolidates the power that had been exercised by the sentencing judge and the Parole Commission to decide what punishment an offender should suffer. This is done by creating the United States Sentencing Commission, directing that Commission to devise guidelines to be used for sentencing, and prospectively abolishing the Parole Commission.

3. It makes all sentences basically determinate. A prisoner is to be released at the completion of his sentence reduced only by any credit earned by good behavior while in custody.

4. It makes the Sentencing Commission's guidelines binding on the courts, although it preserves for the judge the discretion to depart from the guideline applicable to a particular case if the judge finds an aggravating or mitigating factor present that the Commission did not adequately consider when formulating guidelines. The Act also requires the court to state its reasons for the sentence imposed and to give "the specific reason" for imposing a sentence different from that described in the guideline.

5. It authorizes limited appellate review of the sentence. It permits a defendant to appeal a sentence that is above the defined range, and it permits the Government to appeal a sentence that is below that range. It also permits either side to appeal an incorrect application of the guideline. * * *

C

THE SENTENCING COMMISSION

The Commission is established "as an independent commission in the judicial branch of the United States." It has seven voting members (one of whom is the Chairman) appointed by the President "by and with the advice and consent of the Senate." "At least three of the members shall be Federal judges selected after considering a list of six judges recommended to the President by the Judicial Conference of the United States."[a] No more than four members of the Commission shall be members of the same political party. The Attorney General, or his designee, is an ex officio non-

---

[a] In 2003, Congress amended the law to provide that a judge need not be on the Commission, and that no more than three may serve at any one time.

voting member.[b] The Chairman and other members of the Commission are subject to removal by the President "only for neglect of duty or malfeasance in office or for other good cause shown." Except for initial staggering of terms, a voting member serves for six years and may not serve more than two full terms.

D

THE RESPONSIBILITIES OF THE COMMISSION

In addition to the duty the Commission has to promulgate determinative-sentence guidelines, it is under an obligation periodically to "review and revise" the guidelines. It is to "consult with authorities on, and individual and institutional representatives of, various aspects of the Federal criminal justice system." It must report to Congress "any amendments of the guidelines." It is to make recommendations to Congress whether the grades or maximum penalties should be modified. It must submit to Congress at least annually an analysis of the operation of the guidelines. It is to issue "general policy statements" regarding their application. And it has the power to "establish general policies * * * as are necessary to carry out the purposes" of the legislation; to "monitor the performance of probation officers" with respect to the guidelines; to "devise and conduct periodic training programs of instruction in sentencing techniques for judicial and probation personnel" and others; and to "perform such other functions as are required to permit Federal courts to meet their responsibilities" as to sentencing. * * *

[JUSTICE SCALIA's dissent is omitted.]

STEPHEN BREYER—THE FEDERAL SENTENCING GUIDELINES AND THE KEY COMPROMISES UPON WHICH THEY REST

17 Hofstra Law Review 1 (1988), 4–7, 39–40, 42–45.

Congress had two primary purposes when it enacted the new federal sentencing statute in October of 1984. The first was "honesty in sentencing." By "honesty," Congress meant to end the previous system whereby a judge might sentence an offender to twelve years, but the Parole Commission could release him after four. Since release by the Parole Commission in such circumstances was likely, but not inevitable, this system sometimes fooled the judges, sometimes disappointed the offender, and often misled the public. Congress responded by abolishing parole. Under the new law, the sentence the judge gives is the sentence the offender will serve; for example, the judge will impose a four-year sentence (not twelve), and the offender (with the exception of fifty-four

---

    [b] The law does not provide for an institutional member of the defense bar to be represented.

days of "good time" per year after the first year) must serve those four years.

Congress' second purpose was to reduce "unjustifiably wide" sentencing disparity. It relied upon statistical studies showing, for example, that in the Second Circuit, punishments for identical actual cases could range from three years to twenty years imprisonment. * * *

To remedy this problem, Congress created the United States Sentencing Commission * * * and instructed [it] to write * * * sentencing guidelines * * * . * * *

[The author then proceeded to explain how the Guidelines work:]

Imagine the case of a bank robber, with one serious prior conviction (i.e. a sentence of imprisonment exceeding thirteen months), who robs a bank of $40,000, while pointing a gun at the teller. The sentencing judge (and probation officer) would proceed through the following steps.

1.   Look up the statute of conviction in the statutory index. [For this and the following steps, see Appendix A at the end of this excerpt.—Eds.] The index will lead the judge to Guideline § 2B3.1 ("Robbery").

2.   Find the "base offense level" for "Robbery" (Level "18").

3.   Add "specific offense characteristics." In this example, add two levels for the money taken and three more levels for the gun.

4.   Determine if any "adjustments" from * * * the Guidelines apply. They include adjustments for a vulnerable victim or an official victim, abduction of the victim, [the defendant's] role in the offense, efforts to obstruct justice, [the defendant's] acceptance of responsibility, and rules for multiple counts.

5.   Calculate a criminal history score on the basis of the offender's past conviction record Here, § 4A1.1 assigns three points for one prior serious conviction.

6.   Look at the table * * * of the Guidelines to determine the sentence. Here, an offense level of "23," with three points for the prior conviction, yields a range of fifty-one to sixty-three months in prison for this armed robbery by a previously convicted felon.

7.   Impose the Guideline sentence, or, if the court finds unusual factors, depart and impose a non-Guideline sentence. The judge must then give reasons for departure, and the appellate courts may then review the "reasonableness" of the resulting sentence. * * *

If the Commission has done its job as it hopes, the resulting term of confinement—about four to five years—should strike most observers as about the typical time such an offender would have served prior to the Guidelines.

APPENDIX A

[For Steps 1–3]

§ 2B3.1. *Robbery*

(a) Base Offense Level: 18

(b) Specific Offense Characteristics

    (1) If the value of the property taken or destroyed exceeded $2,500, increase the offense level as follows:

Loss	Increase in Level
(A) $2,500 or less	no increase
(B) $2,501–$10,000	add 1
(C) $10,001–$50,000	add 2
(D) $50,001–$250,000	add 3
(E) $250,001–$1,000,000	add 4
(F) $1,000,001–$5,000,000	add 5
(G) more than $5,000,000	add 6 * * *

    (2) (A) If a firearm was discharged increase by 5 levels; (B) if a firearm or a dangerous weapon was otherwise used, increase by 4 levels; (C) if a firearm or other dangerous weapon was brandished, displayed or possessed, increase by 3 levels.

    (3) If any victim sustained bodily injury, increase the offense level according to the seriousness of the injury:

Degree of Bodily Injury	Increase in Level
(A) Bodily Injury	add 2
(B) Serious Bodily Injury	add 4
(C) Permanent or Life—Threatening Bodily Injury	add 6

Provided, however, that the cumulative adjustments from (2) and (3) shall not exceed 9 levels.

    (4) (A) If any person was abducted to facilitate commission of the offense or to facilitate escape, increase by 4 levels; or (B) if any person was physically restrained to facilitate commission of the offense or to facilitate escape, increase by 2 levels.

    (5) If obtaining a firearm, destructive device, or controlled substance was the object of the offense, increase by 1 level.

[For Step 5]

§ 4A1.1. Criminal History Category

The total points from items (a) through (e) determine the criminal history category in the Sentencing Table in Chapter Five, Part A.

(a) Add 3 points for each prior sentence of imprisonment exceeding one year and one month.

(b) Add 2 points for each prior sentence of imprisonment of at least sixty days not counted in (a).

(c) Add 1 point for each prior sentence not included in (a) or (b), up to a total of 4 points for this item.

(d) Add 2 points if the defendant committed the instant offense while under any criminal justice sentence, including probation, parole, supervised release, imprisonment, work release, or escape status.

(e) Add 2 points if the defendant committed the instant offense less than two years after release from imprisonment on a sentence counted under (a) or (b). If 2 points are added for item (d), add only 1 point for this item.

[For Step 6]

SENTENCING TABLE

Criminal History Category

Offense Level	I 0 or 1	II 2 or 3	III 4, 5, 6	IV 7, 8, 9	V 10, 11, 12	VI 13 or more
1	0–1	0–2	0–3	0–4	0–5	0–6
2	0–2	0–3	0–4	0–5	0–6	1–7
3	0–3	0–4	0–5	0–6	2–8	3–9
* * *						
17	24–30	27–33	30–37	37–46	46–57	51–63
18	27–33	30–37	33–41	41–51	51–63	57–71
19	30–37	33–41	37–46	46–57	57–71	63–78
20	33–41	37–46	41–51	51–63	63–78	70–87
21	37–46	41–51	46–57	57–71	70–87	77–96
22	41–51	46–57	51–63	63–78	77–96	84–105
23	46–57	51–63	57–71	70–87	84–105	92–115
* * *						
42	360–life	360–life	360–life	360–life	360–life	360–life
43	life	life	life	life	life	life

[For Step 7]

Departures

The * * * sentencing statute permits a court to depart from a guideline-specified sentence only when it finds "an aggravating or mitigating circumstance in kind or degree * * * that was not adequately taken into consideration by the sentencing commission * * *." 18 U.S.C. § 3553(b). Thus, in principle the Commission, by specifying that it had adequately considered a particular factor, could prevent a court from using it as grounds for departure. * * * The Commission intends the sentencing courts to treat each guideline as carving out a "heartland," a set of typical cases embodying the conduct that each guideline describes. When a court finds an atypical case, one to which a particular guideline linguistically applies but where conduct significantly differs from the norm, the court may consider whether a departure is warranted. Section 5H1.10 (Race, Sex, National Origin, Creed, Religion, Socio-Economic Status), the third sentence of § 5H1.4 [drug dependence or alcohol abuse], and the last sentence of § 5K2.12 [economic hardship], list a few factors that the court cannot take into account as grounds for departure. With those specific exceptions, however, the Commission does not intend to limit the kinds of factors (whether or not mentioned anywhere else in the guidelines) that could constitute grounds for departure in an unusual case.

NOTES AND QUESTIONS

1. *The Guidelines' complexity and, perhaps, "bloodlessness."* At a 1998 conference, Justice Stephen Breyer, one architect of the Federal Sentencing Guidelines, expressed concern that—although he was still "cautiously optimistic" about the Guidelines—they are "simply too long and too complicated. There are too many words, too many provisions, too many distinctions." Linda Greenhouse, *Federal Sentencing Guidelines Criticized by a Key Supporter*, New York Times, Nov. 21, 1998, at A10. In this regard, consider these remarks:

> The Guidelines * * * set down a sentence for every case through exhaustive rules contained in the "Guidelines Manual," a document that has ballooned to some 1,500 pages of regulations marked as "Guidelines," "Policy Statements," and "Commentary," and packed with examples, cross-references, and amendments. * * *

> * * * [P]unishment in federal courts is largely bereft of words such as "right," "wrong," "pity," and "hope," and instead is marked by a technical language—"base levels," "categories," "points," "scores," and so on—that resonates like the jargon of actuaries or tax accountants, or maybe players in a parlor game. A sentence will thus sound something like this:

> > For a violation of 18 U.S.C. 1344, USSG 2F1.1(a) calls for a base offense level of six (6). Pursuant to USSG 2F1.1(b)(1)(I)–(J), eight (8) levels are added because the loss amount was more than $200,000 but less than $350,000. Pursuant to USSG 2F1.1(b)(2)(A), two (2) levels are added because the offense

involved more than minimal planning. Pursuant to USSG 3B1.3, two (2) levels are added because Stevenson abused a position of trust (bookkeeper) that involved minimal supervision and sole responsibility for the daily finances of her employer. * * * Stevenson's adjusted offense level (subtotal) is eighteen (18). With the Government's consent to the application of USSG 3E1.1(a), the offense level is reduced by two (2) for acceptance of responsibility. Accordingly, Stevenson's total offense level is sixteen (16). Stevenson's criminal history score is ten (10). At the time of the instant offense, Stevenson was on probation for arrests of October 17, 1992 and April 5, 1993. Thus, pursuant to USSG 4A1.1(d), two (2) points are added, bringing her total criminal history score to twelve (12). For criminal history points of 10, 11 or 12, the sentencing table at USSG Chapter 5, Part A, establishes a criminal history category of V. With an offense level of 16 and criminal history score of 10, the sentencing table provides a Guideline range for imprisonment of forty-one (41) to fifty-one (51) months. [United States v. Stevenson, 325 F.Supp.2d 543, 545–46 (E.D. Pa. 2004).]

Voila! A human being has been transformed from a multidimensional being into a string of letters and numbers, cast onto the grid of Gridland for internment in a federal penitentiary. The defendant is now a two-dimensional character—* * * his vertical axis an offense level and his horizontal axis a criminal history category. There is no depth or detail, no shading or perspective, only an initial movement within the grid pursuant to points or levels duly added or subtracted, placing him within a narrow range of punishment.

Erik Luna, *Gridland: An Allegorical Critique of Federal Sentencing*, 96 J. Crim. L. & Criminology 25, 35, 38–39 (2005).

Professor Luna's remarks suggest that some critics, such as he, are concerned about more than the Guidelines' complexity. Their criticism runs deeper, as two more scholars (one of whom is also a judge) suggest:

We take it as an established truth * * * that the criminal justice system exists not only to protect society in a reasonably efficient and humane way, but also to defend, affirm, and, when necessary, clarify the moral principles embodied in our laws. In the traditional [pre-Guidelines] ritual of sentencing, the judge pronounced not only a sentence, but society's condemnation as well. The judge affirmed not only society's need to punish, but also its right to do so. Central to that venerable ritual was the presiding judge's exercise of informed discretion. The judge's power—duty—to weigh *all* of the circumstances of the particular case and all of the purposes of criminal punishment, represented an important acknowledgment of the moral personhood of the defendant, and of the moral dimension of crime and punishment. * * *

Those present at a [pre-Guidelines] sentencing proceeding * * * witnessed a ritual of undeniable moral significance. * * * [T]he judge *addressed* only one person when imposing a sentence and ordering the entry of the judgment of convictions. This solemn confrontation was predicated on the fundamental understanding that only a person can pass moral judgment, and only a person can be morally judged.

* * * By replacing the case-by-case exercise of human judgment with a mechanical calculus [such as the Federal Sentencing Guidelines], we do not judge better or more objectively, nor do we judge worse. Instead, we cease to judge at all. * * *

The federal Sentencing Guidelines retained the traditional venue of sentencing while effectively abandoning the substance of the traditional sentencing rite. The Guidelines have replaced the traditional judicial role of deliberation and moral judgment (inherently imperfect) with complex quantitative calculations that convey the impression of scientific precision and objectivity. The judge on the elevated bench remains a visible symbol of society's moral authority, but the substance and meaning of this ancient staging is gone in most cases.

Kate Stith & José Cabrenes, Fear of Judging: Sentencing Guidelines in the Federal Courts 78, 81–83 (1998).

2. *"Uniformity" in sentencing.* One goal of the Federal Sentencing Guidelines is to reduce sentencing disparities, i.e., to bring uniformity to sentencing. As one scholar has stated,

At one level, * * * the meaning of uniformity is clear enough: similarly situated defendants should get similar sentences, while differently situated defendants should get appropriately different sentences. Put differently, uniformity seeks to eliminate *unwarranted* sentencing disparities, but also to provide for *warranted* disparities. The problem lies in distinguishing the warranted from the unwarranted.

Michael M. O'Hear, *The Original Intent of Uniformity in Federal Sentencing,* 74 U. Cin. L. Rev. 749, 749–750 (2006).

How *should* we distinguish warranted from unwarranted disparities? Professor Albert Alschuler has explained:

What counts as sentencing disparity is inescapably normative. For many people, the archetype of unequal sentencing is "sentencing by lottery." In a system of punishment by lottery, however, every offender would be treated like every other who drew the same number. When we say that punishment by lottery is unequal or capricious, we mean that this practice is morally incoherent. Drawing the same number is not the kind of "likeness" we believe should matter. Equality requires the consistent application of a comprehensible normative principle or mix of principles to different cases.

Albert W. Alschuler, *Disparity: The Normative and Empirical Failure of the Federal Guidelines*, 58 Stan. L. Rev. 85, 87 (2005).

Alschuler points out that some pre-Guidelines sentencing—such as when judges imposed very different sentences for the same crime—may not have involved inappropriate disparity: "Judges in the pre-guidelines period might not have sought to treat everyone who committed the same crime alike. They might have tried to treat offenders of equal moral culpability alike or offenders of equal dangerousness alike or offenders with equal rehabilitative prospects alike." *Id.* at 88. In short, the rule that a judge ought to treat "like case alike" requires a normative judgment as to what constitutes "like" cases.

Alschuler contends that if one applies "ordinary moral sensibilities," the Federal Sentencing Guidelines have "substituted new disparities for old ones," *id.* at 89. Three examples: A person who possessed six grams of crack cocaine for personal use was assigned a higher offense level that someone who committed criminal sexual abuse of a minor; sending a single computer image of "virtual" child pornography (that is, a photo made *without* the use of actual children) faced punishment twice as severe as one who actually raped a child; and punishment for possession of a weapon was sometimes more severe than that for actually using the weapon in a violent crime. See also Mark Osler, *Indirect Harms and Proportionality: The Upside-Down World of Federal Sentencing*, 74 Miss. L.J. 1, 1–6 (2004) (providing these and other examples in existence at the time of the article).

3. *The "real offense" standard of the Guidelines.* Generally speaking, there are two types of sentencing systems—"charge" and "real" offense systems. With a "charge" offense system, the sentence imposed is based only on the offense of which the defendant has been charged and convicted. In contrast, a "real" offense system, sentencing "is driven not by the particularities of the charge, but by what the defendant 'really' did." James E. Felman, *The Fundamental Incompatibility of Real Offense Sentencing Guidelines and the Federal Criminal Code*, 7 Fed. Sent. Rep. 125, 125 (1994).

The Federal Sentencing Commission adopted a "modified real offense" system. The recommended length of a defendant's sentence under the Guidelines is based not only upon the crime or crimes for which she has been convicted, but also on the basis of crimes *related* to the offense or offenses for which she has been convicted. Guideline § 1B1.3 provides in part that, even if a defendant has *not* been found criminally liable for an offense as a principal, accomplice, or conspirator, she is held accountable in determining the applicable sentencing guideline range for:

(1)(A) all acts and omissions committed, aided, abetted, counseled, commanded, induced, procured, or willfully caused by the defendant; and (B) in the case of jointly undertaken criminal activity * * *, all reasonably foreseeable acts and omissions of others in furtherance of the jointly undertaken criminal activity, that occurred during the commission of the offense of conviction, in preparation for that offense, or in the course of attempting to avoid detection or responsibility for that offense * * *.

The impact of § 1B1.3 can prove substantial. For example, suppose that *D* is convicted of one count of fraud involving $10,000. If the sentencing judge concludes, however, that *D* or a co-conspirator actually committed other fraudulent transactions, amounting to $1 million, in the same course of conduct, *D*'s sentence will be calculated on the basis of this much higher monetary figure. This sentencing adjustment can occur even though *D* has not been convicted of the other claims of fraud—perhaps because the other charges were dismissed as a result of plea bargaining. See David Yellen, *Illusion, Illogic, and Injustice: Real-Offense Sentencing and the Federal Sentencing Guidelines*, 78 Minn. L. Rev. 403, 431 (1993).

D. IMPOSING A SENTENCE: CONSTITUTIONAL LIMITS

1. TRIAL VERSUS SENTENCING: DIFFERENT ENTERPRISES?

Consider for a moment what you have learned about criminal trials. You know, for example, that a criminal defendant is entitled to trial by jury for serious crimes, and that the factfinder—whether it be a judge or jury—must find guilt beyond a reasonable doubt. The accused is also entitled to compulsory process to call witnesses in her favor and to cross-examine her accusers. She has the right not to be compelled to be a witness against herself at the trial. All of this is constitutionally mandated. There are also many technical rules of evidence that apply at the trial, which help protect a defendant's right to a fair trial.

The question that now must be considered is whether the sentencing stage of a criminal proceeding is—and should be—treated as a different type of enterprise than the trial. To what extent should trial rules of evidence (for example, hearsay rules) apply to the sentencing process? Even more critically, to what extent do and should the constitutional rules protecting defendants at trial carry over to sentencing? Put differently, to what extent should the sentencing proceeding, itself, be considered a "trial"? The materials that follow consider these questions.

a.   The Traditional View: Sentencing as a Different (and More Informal) Enterprise

WILLIAMS V. NEW YORK
Supreme Court of the United States, 1949.
337 U.S. 241, 69 S.Ct. 1079, 93 L.Ed. 1337.

MR. JUSTICE BLACK delivered the opinion of the Court [joined by CHIEF JUSTICE VINSON, and JUSTICES REED, FRANKFURTER, DOUGLAS, JACKSON, RUTLEDGE, and BURTON].

A jury in a New York state court found appellant guilty of murder in the first degree. The jury recommended life imprisonment, but the trial judge imposed sentence of death. In giving his reasons for imposing the death sentence the judge discussed in open court the evidence upon which the jury had convicted stating that this evidence had been considered in the light of additional information obtained through the court's "Probation Department, and through other sources." Consideration of this additional information was pursuant to [state law]. * * * The Court of Appeals of New York affirmed the conviction and sentence over the contention that as construed and applied the controlling penal statutes are in violation of the due process clause of the Fourteenth Amendment of the Constitution of the United States "in that the sentence of death was based upon information supplied by witnesses with whom the accused had not been confronted and as to whom he had no opportunity for cross-examination or rebuttal * * * ." * * *

About five weeks after the verdict of guilty with recommendation of life imprisonment, and after a statutory pre-sentence investigation report to the judge, the defendant was brought to court to be sentenced. Asked what he had to say, appellant protested his innocence. After each of his three lawyers had appealed to the court to accept the jury's recommendation of a life sentence, the judge gave reasons why he felt that the death sentence should be imposed. He narrated the shocking details of the crime as shown by the trial evidence, expressing his own complete belief in appellant's guilt. He stated that the pre-sentence investigation revealed many material facts concerning appellant's background which though relevant to the question of punishment could not properly have been brought to the attention of the jury in its consideration of the question of guilt. He referred to the experience appellant "had had on thirty other burglaries in and about the same vicinity" where the murder had been committed. The appellant had not been convicted of these burglaries although the judge had information that he had confessed to some and had been identified as the perpetrator of some of the others. The judge also referred to certain activities of appellant as shown by the probation report that indicated appellant possessed "a morbid sexuality" and classified him as a "menace to society." The accuracy of the statements made by the judge as to appellant's background and past practices were not challenged by appellant or his counsel, nor was the judge asked to disregard any of them or to afford appellant a chance to refute or discredit any of them by cross-examination or otherwise.

The case presents a serious and difficult question. The question relates to the rules of evidence applicable to the manner in which a judge may obtain information to guide him in the imposition of sentence upon an already convicted defendant. Within limits fixed by statutes, New York judges are given a broad discretion to decide the type and extent of punishment for convicted defendants. Here, for example, the judge's discretion was to sentence to life imprisonment or death. To aid a judge in exercising this discretion intelligently the New York procedural policy encourages him to consider information about the convicted person's past life, health, habits, conduct, and mental and moral propensities. The sentencing judge may consider such information even though obtained outside the courtroom from persons whom a defendant has not been permitted to confront or cross-examine. * * *

Appellant urges that the New York statutory policy is in irreconcilable conflict with the underlying philosophy of a second procedural policy grounded in the due process of law clause of the Fourteenth Amendment. That policy as stated in *In re Oliver*, 333 U.S. 257, 273, 68 S.Ct. 499, 507, 508, 92 L.Ed. 682, is in part that no person shall be tried and convicted of an offense unless he is given reasonable notice of the charges against him and is afforded an opportunity to examine adverse witnesses. That the due process clause does provide these salutary and time-tested protections where the question for consideration is the guilt of a defendant seems entirely clear from the genesis and historical evolution of the clause.

Tribunals passing on the guilt of a defendant always have been hedged in by strict evidentiary procedural limitations. But both before and since the American colonies became a nation, courts in this country and in England practiced a policy under which a sentencing judge could exercise a wide discretion in the sources and types of evidence used to assist him in determining the kind the extent of punishment to be imposed within limits fixed by law. Out-of-court affidavits have been used frequently, and of course in the smaller communities sentencing judges naturally have in mind their knowledge of the personalities and backgrounds of convicted offenders. A recent manifestation of the historical latitude allowed sentencing judges appears in Rule 32 of the Federal Rules of Criminal Procedure. That rule provides for consideration by federal judges of reports made by probation officers containing information about a convicted defendant, including such information "as may be helpful in imposing sentence or in granting probation or in the correctional treatment of the defendant * * * ."

In addition to the historical basis for different evidentiary rules governing trial and sentencing procedures there are sound practical reasons for the distinction. In a trial before verdict the issue is whether a defendant is guilty of having engaged in certain criminal conduct of which he has been specifically accused. Rules of evidence have been fashioned for criminal trials which narrowly confine the trial contest to evidence that is strictly relevant to the particular offense charged. These rules rest in part on a necessity to prevent a time-consuming and confusing trial of collateral issues. They were also designed to prevent tribunals concerned solely with the issue of guilt of a particular offense from being influenced to convict for that offense by evidence that the defendant had habitually engaged in other misconduct. A sentencing judge, however, is not confined to the narrow issue of guilt. His task within fixed statutory or constitutional limits is to determine the type and extent of punishment after the issue of guilt has been determined. Highly relevant—if not essential—to his selection of an appropriate sentence is the possession of the fullest information possible concerning the defendant's life and characteristics. And modern concepts individualizing punishment have made it all the more necessary that a sentencing judge not be denied an opportunity to obtain pertinent information by a requirement of rigid adherence to restrictive rules of evidence properly applicable to the trial.

Undoubtedly the New York statutes emphasize a prevalent modern philosophy of penology that the punishment should fit the offender and not merely the crime. The belief no longer prevails that every offense in a like legal category calls for an identical punishment without regard to the past life and habits of a particular offender. * * * Today's philosophy of individualizing sentences makes sharp distinctions for example between first and repeated offenders. Indeterminate sentences the ultimate termination of which are sometimes decided by nonjudicial agencies have to a large extent taken the place of the old rigidly fixed punishments. * * * Retribution is no longer the dominant objective of the criminal law. Reformation and rehabilitation of offenders have become important goals of criminal jurisprudence.

Modern changes in the treatment of offenders make it more necessary now than a century ago for observance of the distinctions in the evidential procedure in the trial and sentencing processes. For indeterminate sentences and probation have resulted in an increase in the discretionary powers exercised in fixing punishments. In general, these modern changes have not resulted in making the lot of offenders harder. On the contrary a strong motivating force for the changes has been the belief that by careful study of the lives and personalities of convicted offenders many could be less severely punished and restored sooner to complete freedom and useful citizenship. This belief to a large extent has been justified.

Under the practice of individualizing punishments, investigation techniques have been given an important role. Probation workers making reports of their investigations have not been trained to prosecute but to aid offenders. Their reports have been given a high value by conscientious judges who want to sentence persons on the best available information rather than on guesswork and inadequate information. To deprive sentencing judges of this kind of information would undermine modern penological procedural policies that have been cautiously adopted throughout the nation after careful consideration and experimentation. We must recognize that most of the information now relied upon by judges to guide them in the intelligent imposition of sentences would be unavailable if information were restricted to that given in open court by witnesses subject to cross-examination. And the modern probation report draws on information concerning every aspect of a defendant's life. The type and extent of this information make totally impractical if not impossible open court testimony with cross-examination. Such a procedure could endlessly delay criminal administration in a retrial of collateral issues.

The considerations we have set out admonish us against treating the due process clause as a uniform command that courts throughout the Nation abandon their age-old practice of seeking information from out-of-court sources to guide their judgment toward a more enlightened and just sentence. * * * The due process clause should not be treated as a device for freezing the evidential procedure of sentencing in the mold of trial procedure. So to treat the due process clause would hinder if not preclude all courts—state and federal—from making progressive efforts to improve the administration of criminal justice.

It is urged, however, that we should draw a constitutional distinction as to the procedure for obtaining information where the death sentence is imposed. We cannot accept the contention. * * * We cannot say that the due process clause renders a sentence void merely because a judge gets additional out-of-court information to assist him in the exercise of this awesome power of imposing the death sentence. * * *

MR. JUSTICE MURPHY, dissenting.

* * * The jury which heard the trial unanimously recommended life imprisonment as a suitable punishment for the defendant. They had observed him throughout the trial, had heard all the evidence adduced against him, and in spite of the shocking character of the crime of which they found him guilty, were unwilling to decree that his life should be taken. In our criminal courts the jury sits as the representative of the community; its voice is that of the society against which the crime was

committed. A judge even though vested with statutory authority to do so, should hesitate indeed to increase the severity of such a community expression.

He should be willing to increase it, moreover, only with the most scrupulous regard for the rights of the defendant. * * *

Due process of law includes at least the idea that a person accused of crime shall be accorded a fair hearing through all the stages of the proceedings against him. I agree with the Court as to the value and humaneness of liberal use of probation reports as developed by modern penologists, but, in a capital case, against the unanimous recommendation of a jury, where the report would concededly not have been admissible at the trial, and was not subject to examination by the defendant, I am forced to conclude that the high commands of due process were not obeyed.

NOTES AND QUESTIONS

1.   Is *Williams* less persuasive in the *determinate* sentencing systems that commonly exist today?

2.   Federal Rule of Criminal Procedure 32 has undergone many amendments since *Williams* quoted it. Take a look at the current version (Supp., App. B.). How would the federal procedure differ today from those approved in *Williams*?

3.   *Williams in the death penalty context. Williams* was distinguished in Gardner v. Florida, 430 U.S. 349, 97 S.Ct. 1197, 51 L.Ed.2d 393 (1977). There, a trial judge imposed the death penalty based in part on information in a presentence report, portions of which were not disclosed to the defendant. The trial judge did not indicate what was in the undisclosed portions, nor did he indicate whether he relied on the confidential information. The Court, 7–2, vacated the death sentence.

The seven justices were divided on whether the case should be resolved on due process or Eighth Amendment cruel-and-unusual-punishment grounds. Justice Stevens, author of the plurality opinion, reached the issue on due process grounds. He distinguished *Williams* on the ground that "in *Williams* the material facts concerning the defendant's background which were contained in the presentence report were described in detail by the trial judge in open court." Second, "when the *Williams* case was decided, no significant constitutional difference between the death penalty and lesser punishments for crime had been expressly recognized by this Court." Since then, the Court has "expressly recognized that death is a different kind of punishment from any other which may be imposed"; therefore, capital-sentencing procedures now require closer due process scrutiny.

McMILLAN v. PENNSYLVANIA
Supreme Court of the United States, 1986.
477 U.S. 79, 106 S.Ct. 2411, 91 L.Ed.2d 67.

JUSTICE REHNQUIST delivered the opinion of the Court [joined by CHIEF JUSTICE BURGER, and JUSTICES WHITE, POWELL, and O'CONNOR].

We granted certiorari to consider the constitutionality, under the Due Process Clause of the Fourteenth Amendment and the jury trial guarantee of the Sixth Amendment, of Pennsylvania's Mandatory Minimum Sentencing Act, 42 Pa. Const. Stat. § 9712 (1982) (the Act).

I

The Act was adopted in 1982. It provides that anyone convicted of certain enumerated felonies is subject to a mandatory minimum sentence of five years' imprisonment if the sentencing judge finds, by a preponderance of the evidence, that the person "visibly possessed a firearm" during the commission of the offense. At the sentencing hearing, the judge is directed to consider the evidence introduced at trial and any additional evidence offered by either the defendant or the Commonwealth. § 9712(b).[1] The Act operates to divest the judge of discretion to impose any sentence of less than five years for the underlying felony; it does not authorize a sentence in excess of that otherwise allowed for that offense.

Each petitioner was convicted of, among other things, one of § 9712's enumerated felonies. * * * In each case the Commonwealth gave notice that at sentencing it would seek to proceed under the Act. No § 9712 hearing was held, however, because each of the sentencing judges before whom petitioners appeared found the Act unconstitutional; each imposed a lesser sentence than that required by the Act.

The Commonwealth appealed all four cases to the Supreme Court of Pennsylvania. That court consolidated the appeals and unanimously concluded that the Act is consistent with due process. Petitioners' principal argument was that visible possession of a firearm is an element

---

[1] Section 9712 provides * * * :

"(a) Mandatory sentence.—Any person who is convicted in any court of this Commonwealth of murder of the third degree, voluntary manslaughter, rape, involuntary deviate sexual intercourse, robbery * * * , aggravated assault * * * or kidnapping, or who is convicted of attempt to commit any of these crimes, shall, if the person visibly possessed a firearm during the commission of the offense, be sentenced to a minimum sentence of at least five years of total confinement notwithstanding any other provision of this title or other statute to the contrary.

"(b) Proof at sentencing.—Provisions of this section shall not be an element of the crime and notice thereof to the defendant shall not be required prior to conviction, but reasonable notice of the Commonwealth's intention to proceed under this section shall be provided after conviction and before sentencing. The applicability of this section shall be determined at sentencing. The court shall consider any evidence presented at trial and shall afford the Commonwealth and the defendant an opportunity to present any necessary additional evidence and shall determine, by a preponderance of the evidence, if this section is applicable. * * * "

of the crimes for which they were being sentenced and thus must be proved beyond a reasonable doubt under *In re Winship*, 397 U.S. 358, 90 S.Ct. 1068, 25 L.Ed.2d 368 (1970), and *Mullaney v. Wilbur*, 421 U.S. 684, 95 S.Ct. 1881, 44 L.Ed.2d 508 (1975).[c] After observing that the legislature had expressly provided that visible possession "shall not be an element of the crime," § 9712(b), and that the reasonable-doubt standard " 'has always been dependent on how a state defines the offense' " in question, quoting *Patterson v. New York*, 432 U.S. 197, 211, n. 12, 97 S.Ct. 2319, 2327, n. 12, 53 L.Ed.2d 281 (1977), the court rejected the claim that the Act effectively creates a new set of upgraded felonies of which visible possession is an "element." Section 9712, which comes into play only after the defendant has been convicted of an enumerated felony, neither provides for an increase in the maximum sentence for such felony nor authorizes a separate sentence; it merely requires a minimum sentence of five years, which may be more or less than the minimum sentence that might otherwise have been imposed. And consistent with *Winship*, *Mullaney*, and *Patterson*, the Act "creates no presumption as to any essential fact and places no burden on the defendant"; it "in no way relieve[s] the prosecution of its burden of proving guilt." * * *

II

Petitioners argue that under the Due Process Clause as interpreted in *Winship* and *Mullaney*, if a State wants to punish visible possession of a firearm it must undertake the burden of proving that fact beyond a reasonable doubt. We disagree. *Winship* held that "the Due Process Clause protects the accused against conviction except upon proof beyond a reasonable doubt of every fact necessary to constitute the crime with which he is charged." * * * [I]n *Patterson* we rejected the claim that whenever a State links the "severity of punishment" to "the presence or absence of an identified fact" the State must prove that fact beyond a reasonable doubt. * * *

Patterson stressed that in determining what facts must be proved beyond a reasonable doubt the state legislature's definition of the elements of the offense is usually dispositive: "[T]he Due Process Clause requires the prosecution to prove beyond a reasonable doubt all of the elements *included in the definition of the offense* of which the defendant is charged." While "there are obviously constitutional limits beyond which the States may not go in this regard," "[t]he applicability of the reasonable-doubt standard * * * has always been dependent on how a State defines the offense that is charged in any given case." * * *

We believe that the present case is controlled by *Patterson*, our most recent pronouncement on this subject, rather than by *Mullaney*. As the Supreme Court of Pennsylvania observed, the Pennsylvania Legislature

---

c   It may be worth your time to read Note 1, p. 1416, now to better understand *Mullaney*.

has expressly provided that visible possession of a firearm is not an element of the crimes enumerated in the mandatory sentencing statute, § 9712(b), but instead is a sentencing factor that comes into play only after the defendant has been found guilty of one of those crimes beyond a reasonable doubt. Indeed, the elements of the enumerated offenses, like the maximum permissible penalties for those offenses, were established long before the Mandatory Minimum Sentencing Act was passed. While visible possession might well have been included as an element of the enumerated offenses, Pennsylvania chose not to redefine those offenses in order to so include it, and *Patterson* teaches that we should hesitate to conclude that due process bars the State from pursuing its chosen course in the area of defining crimes and prescribing penalties. * * *

* * * Section 9712 neither alters the maximum penalty for the crime committed nor creates a separate offense calling for a separate penalty; it operates solely to limit the sentencing court's discretion in selecting a penalty within the range already available to it without the special finding of visible possession of a firearm. Section 9712 "ups the ante" for the defendant only by raising to five years the minimum sentence which may be imposed within the statutory plan. The statute gives no impression of having been tailored to permit the visible possession finding to be a tail which wags the dog of the substantive offense. Petitioners' claim that visible possession under the Pennsylvania statute is "really" an element of the offenses for which they are being punished—that Pennsylvania has in effect defined a new set of upgraded felonies—would have at least more superficial appeal if a finding of visible possession exposed them to greater or additional punishment, but it does not. * * *

Finally, we note that the specter raised by petitioners of States restructuring existing crimes in order to "evade" the commands of *Winship* just does not appear in this case. As noted above, § 9712's enumerated felonies retain the same elements they had before the Mandatory Minimum Sentencing Act was passed. The Pennsylvania Legislature did not change the definition of any existing offense. It simply took one factor that has always been considered by sentencing courts to bear on punishment—the instrumentality used in committing a violent felony—and dictated the precise weight to be given that factor if the instrumentality is a firearm. Pennsylvania's decision to do so has not transformed against its will a sentencing factor into an "element" of some hypothetical "offense." * * *

IV

In light of the foregoing, petitioners' final claim—that the Act denies them their Sixth Amendment right to a trial by jury—merits little discussion. Petitioners again argue that the jury must determine all ultimate facts concerning the offense committed. Having concluded that

Pennsylvania may properly treat visible possession as a sentencing consideration and not an element of any offense, we need only note that there is no Sixth Amendment right to jury sentencing, even where the sentence turns on specific findings of fact. * * *

[The dissenting opinion of JUSTICE MARSHALL, joined by JUSTICES BRENNAN and BLACKMUN, is omitted.]

JUSTICE STEVENS, dissenting. * * *

* * * In my view, a state legislature may not dispense with the requirement of proof beyond a reasonable doubt for conduct that it targets for severe criminal penalties. Because the Pennsylvania statute challenged in this case describes conduct that the Pennsylvania Legislature obviously intended to prohibit, and because it mandates lengthy incarceration for the same, I believe that the conduct so described is an element of the criminal offense to which the proof beyond a reasonable doubt requirement applies. * * *

* * * *Patterson* * * * requires proof beyond a reasonable doubt of conduct which exposes a criminal defendant to greater stigma or punishment, but does not likewise constrain state reductions of criminal penalties—even if such reductions are conditioned on a prosecutor's failure to prove a fact by a preponderance of the evidence or on proof supplied by the criminal defendant.

The distinction between aggravating and mitigating facts has been criticized as formalistic. But its ability to identify genuine constitutional threats depends on nothing more than the continued functioning of the democratic process. To appreciate the difference between aggravating and mitigating circumstances, it is important to remember that although States may reach the same destination either by criminalizing conduct and allowing an affirmative defense, or by prohibiting lesser conduct and enhancing the penalty, legislation proceeding along these two paths is very different even if it might theoretically achieve the same result. Consider, for example, a statute making presence "in any private or public place" a "felony punishable by up to five years imprisonment" and yet allowing "an affirmative defense for the defendant to prove, to a preponderance of the evidence, that he was not robbing a bank." No democratically elected legislature would enact such a law, and if it did, a broad-based coalition of bankers and bank customers would soon see the legislation repealed. Nor is there a serious danger that a State will soon define murder to be the "mere physical contact between the defendant and the victim leading to the victim's death, but then set up an affirmative defense leaving it to the defendant to prove that he acted without culpable *mens rea*." No legislator would be willing to expose himself to the severe opprobrium and punishment meted out to murderers for an accidental stumble on the subway. * * * The very inconceivability of the hypothesized legislation * * * is reason enough to feel secure that it will not command a majority of the electorate.

It is not at all inconceivable, however, to fear that a State might subject those individuals convicted of engaging in antisocial conduct to further punishment for aggravating conduct not proved beyond a reasonable doubt. As this case demonstrates, a State may seek to enhance the deterrent effect of its law forbidding the use of firearms in the course of felonies by mandating a minimum sentence of imprisonment upon proof by a preponderance against those already convicted of specified crimes. But *In re Winship* and *Patterson* teach that a State may not advance the objectives of its criminal laws at the expense of the accurate factfinding owed to the criminally accused who suffer the risk of nonpersuasion. * * *

Appropriate respect for the rule of *In re Winship* requires that there be some constitutional limits on the power of a State to define the elements of criminal offenses. The high standard of proof is required because of the immense importance of the individual interest in avoiding both the loss of liberty and the stigma that results from a criminal conviction. It follows, I submit, that if a State provides that a specific component of a prohibited transaction shall give rise both to a special stigma and to a special punishment, that component must be treated as a "fact necessary to constitute the crime" within the meaning of our holding in *In re Winship*.

Pennsylvania's Mandatory Minimum Sentencing Act reflects a legislative determination that a defendant who "visibly possessed a firearm" during the commission of an aggravated assault is more blameworthy than a defendant who did not. * * *

* * * In my opinion the constitutional significance of the special sanction cannot be avoided by the cavalier observation that it merely "ups the ante" for the defendant. * * *

NOTES AND QUESTIONS

1. *Patterson and Mullaney*. The majority in *McMillan* stated that the present case was "controlled by *Patterson*, our most recent pronouncement on the subject, rather than by *Mullaney*." Perhaps so, but to understand the law here one must start with *Mullaney v. Wilbur*. (Try to follow this carefully!) In *Mullaney*, the defendant was charged with murder. The evidence at trial tended to show that the accused had intentionally killed the victim, but that he may have committed the crime "in the heat of passion on sudden provocation," the language for the offense of manslaughter. The due process issue was whether the State of Maine could impose on the defendant the burden of proving (by preponderance of the evidence) that the killing was committed in the heat of passion. The Court, in an opinion authored by

Justice Powell, held that the State could not do so. It ruled that the due process clause required the government not only to prove that the defendant was guilty of criminal homicide, but also to persuade the jury beyond a reasonable doubt regarding the critical fact (whether the killing was or was not in sudden heat of passion) relating to the defendant's "degree of criminal culpability."

Just two years later, *Patterson* came along. Superficially, at least, the statutory scheme in question looked similar to the one rejected in *Mullaney*: New York explicitly allocated to the defendant the burden of proving "extreme emotional disturbance" (that state's version of "heat of passion") in order to reduce the offense of murder to manslaughter. This time, however, the Court held, 5–3, that due process was *not* violated. The Court conceded that there was "language in *Mullaney* that has been understood as perhaps construing the Due Process Clause to require the prosecution to prove * * * any fact affecting 'the [defendant's] degree of criminal culpability.'" Nonetheless, *Patterson* rejected that reading of *Mullaney* and basically held that, subject to largely unstated limits, a legislature could define an offense however it wished, and that the due process clause only required that the Government carry the burden of proof, beyond a reasonable doubt, as to each "ingredient"—that is, element—of the offense, as legislatively defined. Because the New York murder statute under review in *Patterson* did not require the State to prove a lack of extreme emotional disturbance, the defendant could be required to prove its existence. Although *Patterson* purported to apply *Mullaney*, the author of *Mullaney* (Justice Powell) dissented in *Patterson*. He stated that the majority's explanation of *Mullaney* bore "little resemblance to the basic rationale of that decision."

Thus, it would seem that the majority in *McMillan* had the better side of the argument as to the essence of *Patterson*. *Patterson* largely accepted a formalistic approach to the due process clause: Let the legislature define an offense as it wishes, and only require the Government to prove (beyond a reasonable doubt) the expressed or implied elements in the definition of the crime. The majority seems on strong footing in its claim that the Pennsylvania legislature intended to treat "visible possession of a firearm" as a sentencing factor and not as an element of any underlying crime.

2.   The *McMillan* Court gave short shrift to the petitioners' Sixth Amendment claim. Should it have done so? However you feel about the burden-of-proof issue, why shouldn't criminal defendants have the right, as with facts relating to the issue of guilt or innocence, to a jury determination of sentencing facts? We will return to this question shortly.

3.   *Almendarez-Torres v. United States.* Notice where we are. In *Williams*, p. 1407, the Supreme Court found no constitutional problem with a judge sentencing a defendant to death, thereby overriding a jury's recommendation that the defendant's life be spared, based on information in a report never seen by the jury (or, for that matter, by the defense).

Then, in *McMillan*, the Supreme Court approved a sentencing scheme in which, upon conviction, a judge (rather than a jury) decides if a certain fact (a "sentencing factor" in the language of *McMillan*) was proven by preponderance of the evidence (rather than upon proof beyond a reasonable doubt). The Court emphasized, however, that the factor at issue in *McMillan* did not alter the *maximum* penalty for the crime committed; it only limited the judge's discretion *within* the sentencing range that otherwise applied.

McMillan is far from the end of the story. In *Almendarez-Torres v. United States*, 523 U.S. 224, 118 S.Ct. 1219, 140 L.Ed.2d 350 (1998), the Court, 5–4 again, upheld the constitutionality of a federal statute that made it an offense, punishable by imprisonment of no more than *two* years, for a deported alien to be found in the United States. The statute further provided that if a judge determined by preponderance of the evidence that the deported alien had previously been convicted of an aggravated felony, the maximum sentence for illegally re-entering the United States was *twenty* years. The Court, this time per Justice Breyer, upheld Congress' right to treat recidivism—that is, the fact that the deported alien had previously been convicted of an aggravated felony—as a "sentencing factor" to be determined by the judge, by a preponderance of evidence, rather than by a jury upon proof beyond a reasonable doubt. The Court found it constitutionally irrelevant that the sentencing factor here enhanced the potential *maximum* sentence for an offense from two to twenty years, rather than simply limiting the judge's sentencing discretion within an already existing sentencing range (as in *McMillan*).

But, *Almendarez-Torres* is also not the end of the story. The *Apprendi* revolution was just two years away.

b. Sentencing as a More Formal Enterprise: The *Apprendi* Revolution

Introductory Comment

In *Jones v. United States*, 526 U.S. 227, 119 S.Ct. 1215, 143 L.Ed.2d 311 (1999), the Supreme Court considered a federal carjacking statute. Subsection (1) of the statute imposed a maximum penalty of fifteen years' imprisonment for carjacking; subsection (2) authorized a maximum punishment of twenty-five years if serious bodily injury occurred; and subsection (3) authorized life imprisonment or the death penalty if a death occurred. Under federal law, the "fact" that serious bodily injury (or death) occurred did not need to be alleged in the indictment, did not need to be submitted to the jury for proof, and did not need to be found to exist beyond a reasonable doubt. Instead, the judge determined the presence or absence of this critical fact by preponderance of the evidence during a post-conviction sentencing hearing. In still another 5–4 opinion, Justice Souter interpreted the carjacking statute as effectively defining three separate offenses. As such, "serious bodily injury" and "death" were elements of their respective offenses—not "sentencing facts"—which therefore had to be alleged in the indictment, proven beyond a reasonable doubt, and submitted to the jury for verdict.

Jones would not have been an especially momentous decision if all that the Court had done was interpret a specific federal statute. But, in dictum, it stated that if Congress had *not* intended to treat "serious bodily injury" and "death" as elements of the offense—if it *had* intended to allow these facts to be determined by a judge, as sentencing factors, by preponderance of the evidence—this *might* have violated the Constitution. Justice Souter wrote:

> [U]nder the Due Process Clause of the Fifth Amendment and the notice and jury trial guarantees of the Sixth Amendment, any fact (other than prior conviction) that increases the maximum penalty for a crime must be charged in an indictment, submitted to a jury, and proven beyond a reasonable doubt. Because our prior cases suggest rather than establish this principle, our concern about the Government's reading of the statute rises only to the level of doubt, not certainty.

Then, along came the following case: Dictum became a constitutional holding. A sentencing revolution was underway.

APPRENDI V. NEW JERSEY
Supreme Court of the United States, 2000.
530 U.S. 466, 120 S.Ct. 2348, 147 L.Ed.2d 435.

JUSTICE STEVENS delivered the opinion of the Court [joined by JUSTICES SCALIA, SOUTER, THOMAS, and GINSBURG].

A New Jersey statute classifies the possession of a firearm for an unlawful purpose as a "second-degree" offense. Such an offense is punishable by imprisonment for "between five years and 10 years." A separate statute, described by that State's Supreme Court as a "hate crime" law, provides for an "extended term" of imprisonment if the trial judge finds, by a preponderance of the evidence, that "the defendant in committing the crime acted with a purpose to intimidate an individual or group of individuals because of race, color, gender, handicap, religion, sexual orientation or ethnicity." The extended term authorized by the hate crime law for second-degree offenses is imprisonment for "between 10 and 20 years." [The trial judge sentenced Apprendi to a 12-year term of imprisonment.—Eds.]

The question presented is whether the Due Process Clause of the Fourteenth Amendment requires that a factual determination authorizing an increase in the maximum prison sentence for an offense from 10 to 20 years be made by a jury on the basis of proof beyond a reasonable doubt. * * *

II * * *

Our answer to that question was foreshadowed by our opinion in *Jones v. United States* [Introductory Comment, immediately preceding this case], construing a federal statute. We there noted that "under the Due Process Clause of the Fifth Amendment and the notice and jury trial guarantees of the Sixth Amendment, any fact (other than prior conviction) that increases the maximum penalty for a crime must be charged in an indictment, submitted to a jury, and proven beyond a reasonable doubt." The Fourteenth Amendment commands the same answer in this case involving a state statute.

III

* * * New Jersey threatened Apprendi with certain pains if he unlawfully possessed a weapon and with additional pains if he selected his victims with a purpose to intimidate them because of their race. As a matter of simple justice, it seems obvious that the procedural safeguards designed to protect Apprendi from unwarranted pains should apply equally to the two acts that New Jersey has singled out for punishment. Merely using the label "sentence enhancement" to describe the latter surely does not provide a principled basis for treating them differently.

At stake in this case are constitutional protections of surpassing importance: the proscription of any deprivation of liberty without "due process of law," and the [Sixth Amendment] guarantee that "in all criminal prosecutions, the accused shall enjoy the right to a speedy and public trial, by an impartial jury."[3] Taken together, these rights indisputably entitle a criminal defendant to "a jury determination that [he] is guilty of every element of the crime with which he is charged, beyond a reasonable doubt."

* * * [T]he historical foundation for our recognition of these principles extends down centuries into the common law. "To guard against a spirit of oppression and tyranny on the part of rulers," and "as the great bulwark of [our] civil and political liberties," 2 J. Story, Commentaries on the Constitution of the United States 540–541 (4th ed. 1873), trial by jury has been understood to require that "the truth of every accusation, whether preferred in the shape of indictment, information, or appeal, should afterwards be confirmed by the unanimous suffrage of twelve of

---

[3] Apprendi has not here asserted a constitutional claim based on the omission of any reference to sentence enhancement or racial bias in the indictment. * * * [The Fourteenth] Amendment has not, however, been construed to include the Fifth Amendment right to "presentment or indictment of a Grand Jury" * * *. We thus do not address the indictment question separately today.

[the defendant's] equals and neighbours * * *." 4 W. Blackstone, Commentaries on the Laws of England 343 (1769).

Equally well founded is the companion right to have the jury verdict based on proof beyond a reasonable doubt. * * *

Any possible distinction between an "element" of a felony offense and a "sentencing factor" was unknown to the practice of criminal indictment, trial by jury, and judgment by court as it existed during the years surrounding our Nation's founding. As a general rule, criminal proceedings were submitted to a jury after being initiated by an indictment containing "all the facts and circumstances which constitute the offence, * * * stated with such certainty and precision, that the defendant * * * may be enabled to determine the species of offence they constitute, in order that he may prepare his defence accordingly * * * *and that there may be no doubt as to the judgment which should be given*, if the defendant be convicted." J. Archbold, Pleading and Evidence in Criminal Cases 44 (15th ed. 1862) (emphasis added). The defendant's ability to predict with certainty the judgment from the face of the felony indictment flowed from the invariable linkage of punishment with crime.

Thus, with respect to the criminal law of felonious conduct, "the English trial judge of the later eighteenth century had very little explicit discretion in sentencing. The substantive criminal law tended to be sanction-specific; it prescribed a particular sentence for each offense. The judge was meant simply to impose that sentence (unless he thought in the circumstances that the sentence was so inappropriate that he should invoke the pardon process to commute it)." * * *

This practice at common law held true when indictments were issued pursuant to statute. Just as the circumstances of the crime and the intent of the defendant at the time of commission were often essential elements to be alleged in the indictment, so too were the circumstances mandating a particular punishment. "Where a statute annexes a higher degree of punishment to a common-law felony, if committed under particular circumstances, an indictment for the offence, in order to bring the defendant within that higher degree of punishment, must expressly charge it to have been committed under those circumstances, and must state the circumstances with certainty and precision." Archbold, Pleading and Evidence in Criminal Cases, at 51. If, then, "upon an indictment under the statute, the prosecutor prove the felony to have been committed, but fail in proving it to have been committed under the circumstances specified in the statute, the defendant shall be convicted of the common-law felony only."

We should be clear that nothing in this history suggests that it is impermissible for judges to exercise discretion—taking into consideration various factors relating both to offense and offender—in imposing a judgment *within the range* prescribed by statute. We have often noted that judges in this country have long exercised discretion of this nature in imposing sentence *within statutory limits* in the individual case. See, *e.g.*, *Williams v. New York* [p. 1407]. As in *Williams*, our periodic recognition of judges' broad discretion in sentencing * * * has been regularly accompanied by the qualification that that discretion was bound by the range of sentencing options prescribed by the legislature. * * *

We do not suggest that trial practices cannot change in the course of centuries and still remain true to the principles that emerged from the Framers' fears "that the jury right could be lost not only by gross denial, but by erosion." But practice must at least adhere to the basic principles undergirding the requirements of trying to a jury all facts necessary to constitute a statutory offense, and proving those facts beyond reasonable doubt. As we made clear in [*In re*] *Winship,* [397 U.S. 358, 90 S.Ct. 1068, 25 L.Ed.2d 368 (1970),] the "reasonable doubt" requirement "has [a] vital role in our criminal procedure for cogent reasons." * * *

Since *Winship*, we have made clear beyond peradventure that *Winship*'s due process and associated jury protections extend, to some degree, "to determinations that [go] not to a defendant's guilt or innocence, but simply to the length of his sentence." *Almendarez-Torres* (Scalia, J., dissenting). This was a primary lesson of *Mullaney v. Wilbur* [p. 1416, Note 1], in which we invalidated a Maine statute that presumed that a defendant who acted with an intent to kill possessed the "malice aforethought" necessary to constitute the State's murder offense (and therefore, was subject to that crime's associated punishment of life imprisonment). The statute placed the burden on the defendant of proving, in rebutting the statutory presumption, that he acted with a lesser degree of culpability, such as in the heat of passion, to win a reduction in the offense from murder to manslaughter (and thus a reduction of the maximum punishment of 20 years).

The State had posited in *Mullaney* that requiring a defendant to prove heat-of-passion intent to overcome a presumption of murderous intent did not implicate *Winship* protections because, upon conviction of either offense, the defendant would lose his liberty and face societal stigma just the same. Rejecting this argument, we acknowledged that criminal law "is concerned not only with guilt or innocence in the abstract, but also with the degree of criminal culpability" assessed. Because the "consequences" of a guilty verdict for murder and for manslaughter differed substantially, we dismissed the possibility that a State could circumvent the protections of *Winship* merely by "redefining the elements that constitute different crimes, characterizing them as factors that bear solely on the extent of punishment."

IV

It was in *McMillan v. Pennsylvania* [p. 1412] that this Court, for the first time, coined the term "sentencing factor" to refer to a fact that was not found by a jury but that could affect the sentence imposed by the judge. * * * Articulating for the first time, and then applying, a multifactor set of criteria for determining whether the *Winship* protections applied to bar such a system, we concluded that the Pennsylvania statute did not run afoul of our previous admonitions against relieving the State of its burden of proving guilt, or tailoring the mere form of a criminal statute solely to avoid *Winship*'s strictures.

We did not, however, there budge from the position that (1) constitutional limits exist to States' authority to define away facts necessary to constitute a criminal offense, and (2) that a state scheme that keeps from the jury facts that "expose [defendants] to greater or additional punishment" may raise serious constitutional concern. * * *[13]

Finally, as we made plain in *Jones* last Term, *Almendarez-Torres v. United States* [p. 1417, Note 3] represents at best an exceptional departure from the historic practice that we have described. * * *

Rejecting Almendarez-Torres' [constitutional] objection, we concluded that sentencing him to a term higher than that attached to the offense alleged in the indictment did not violate the strictures of *Winship* in that case. Because Almendarez-Torres had admitted the three earlier convictions for aggravated felonies—all of which had been entered pursuant to proceedings with substantial procedural safeguards of their own—no question concerning the right to a jury trial or the standard of proof that would apply to a contested issue of fact was before the Court. * * * [O]ur conclusion in *Almendarez-Torres* turned heavily upon the fact that the additional sentence to which the defendant was subject was "the prior commission of a serious crime." Both the certainty that procedural safeguards attached to any "fact" of prior conviction, and the reality that Almendarez-Torres did not challenge the accuracy of that "fact" in his case, mitigated the due process and Sixth Amendment concerns otherwise implicated in allowing a judge to determine a "fact" increasing punishment beyond the maximum of the statutory range.

Even though it is arguable that *Almendarez-Torres* was incorrectly decided, * * * we need not revisit [that case] for purposes of our decision today to treat the case as a narrow exception to the general rule we recalled at the outset. Given its unique facts, it surely does not warrant

---

[13] The principal dissent accuses us of today "overruling *McMillan*." We do not overrule *McMillan*. We limit its holding to cases that do not involve the imposition of a sentence more severe than the statutory maximum for the offense established by the jury's verdict—a limitation identified in the *McMillan* opinion itself. * * *

rejection of the otherwise uniform course of decision during the entire history of our jurisprudence.

In sum, * * * [o]ther than the fact of a prior conviction, any fact that increases the penalty for a crime beyond the prescribed statutory maximum must be submitted to a jury, and proved beyond a reasonable doubt. With that exception, we endorse the statement of the rule set forth in the concurring opinions in that case: "It is unconstitutional for a legislature to remove from the jury the assessment of facts that increase the prescribed range of penalties to which a criminal defendant is exposed. It is equally clear that such facts must be established by proof beyond a reasonable doubt."[16]

V * * *

New Jersey's defense of its hate crime enhancement statute has three primary components: (1) the required finding of biased purpose is not an "element" of a distinct hate crime offense, but rather the traditional "sentencing factor" of motive; (2) *McMillan* holds that the legislature can authorize a judge to find a traditional sentencing factor on the basis of a preponderance of the evidence; and (3) *Almendarez-Torres* extended *McMillan*'s holding to encompass factors that authorize a judge to impose a sentence beyond the maximum provided by the substantive statute under which a defendant is charged. None of these persuades us that the constitutional rule that emerges from our history and case law should incorporate an exception for this New Jersey statute.

---

[16] The principal dissent would reject the Court's rule as a "meaningless formalism," because it can conceive of hypothetical statutes that would comply with the rule and achieve the same result as the New Jersey statute. While a State could, hypothetically, undertake to revise its entire criminal code in the manner the dissent suggests—extending all statutory maximum sentences to, for example, 50 years and giving judges guided discretion as to a few specially selected factors within that range—this possibility seems remote. Among other reasons, structural democratic constraints exist to discourage legislatures from enacting penal statutes that expose every defendant convicted of, for example, weapons possession, to a maximum sentence exceeding that which is, in the legislature's judgment, generally proportional to the crime. This is as it should be. Our rule ensures that a State is obliged "to make its choices concerning the substantive content of its criminal laws with full awareness of the consequences, unable to mask substantive policy choices" of exposing all who are convicted to the maximum sentence it provides. *Patterson v. New York*, (Powell, J., dissenting). So exposed, "[t]he political check on potentially harsh legislative action is then more likely to operate." * * *

In all events, if such an extensive revision of the State's entire criminal code were enacted * * *, we would be required to question whether the revision was constitutional under this Court's prior decisions.

Finally, the principal dissent ignores the distinction the Court has often recognized between facts in aggravation of punishment and facts in mitigation. If facts found by a jury support a guilty verdict of murder, the judge is authorized by that jury verdict to sentence the defendant to the maximum sentence provided by the murder statute. If the defendant can escape the statutory maximum by showing, for example, that he is a war veteran, then a judge that finds the fact of veteran status is neither exposing the defendant to a deprivation of liberty greater than that authorized by the verdict according to statute, nor is the judge imposing upon the defendant a greater stigma than that accompanying the jury verdict alone. Core concerns animating the jury and burden-of-proof requirements are thus absent from such a scheme.

New Jersey's first point is nothing more than a disagreement with the rule we apply today. * * *

* * * Despite what appears to us the clear "elemental" nature of the factor here, the relevant inquiry is one not of form, but of effect—does the required finding expose the defendant to a greater punishment than that authorized by the jury's guilty verdict?[19]

* * * [T]he effect of New Jersey's sentencing "enhancement" here is unquestionably to turn a second-degree offense into a first-degree offense, under the State's own criminal code. The law thus runs directly into our warning in *Mullaney* that *Winship* is concerned as much with the category of substantive offense as "with the degree of criminal culpability" assessed. This concern flows not only from the historical pedigree of the jury and burden rights, but also from the powerful interests those rights serve. The degree of criminal culpability the legislature chooses to associate with particular, factually distinct conduct has significant implications both for a defendant's very liberty, and for the heightened stigma associated with an offense the legislature has selected as worthy of greater punishment.

The preceding discussion should make clear why the State's reliance on *McMillan* is * * * misplaced. * * * When a judge's finding based on a mere preponderance of the evidence authorizes an increase in the maximum punishment, it is appropriately characterized as "a tail which wags the dog of the substantive offense." * * *

New Jersey's reliance on *Almendarez-Torres* is also unavailing. The reasons supporting an exception from the general rule for the statute construed in that case do not apply to the New Jersey statute. * * * [T]here is a vast difference between accepting the validity of a prior judgment of conviction entered in a proceeding in which the defendant had the right to trial by jury and the right to require the prosecutor to prove guilt beyond a reasonable doubt, and allowing the judge to find the required fact under a lesser standard of proof. * * *

* * *

The New Jersey procedure challenged in this case is an unacceptable departure from the jury tradition that is an indispensable part of our criminal justice system. Accordingly, the judgment of the Supreme Court of New Jersey is reversed, and the case is remanded for further proceedings not inconsistent with this opinion.

---

[19] This is not to suggest that the term "sentencing factor" is devoid of meaning. The term appropriately describes a circumstance, which may be either aggravating or mitigating in character, that supports a specific sentence *within the range* authorized by the jury's finding that the defendant is guilty of a particular offense. On the other hand, when the term "sentence enhancement" is used to describe an increase beyond the maximum authorized statutory sentence, it is the functional equivalent of an element of a greater offense than the one covered by the jury's guilty verdict. * * *

JUSTICE SCALIA, concurring.

I feel the need to say a few words in response to Justice Breyer's dissent. It sketches an admirably fair and efficient scheme of criminal justice designed for a society that is prepared to leave criminal justice to the State. (Judges, it is sometimes necessary to remind ourselves, are part of the State—and an increasingly bureaucratic part of it, at that.) The founders of the American Republic were not prepared to leave it to the State, which is why the jury-trial guarantee was one of the least controversial provisions of the Bill of Rights. It has never been efficient; but it has always been free.

As for fairness, which Justice Breyer believes "in modern times" the jury cannot provide: I think it not unfair to tell a prospective felon that if he commits his contemplated crime he is exposing himself to a jail sentence of 30 years—and that if, upon conviction, he gets anything less than that he may thank the mercy of a tenderhearted judge * * * . Will there be disparities? Of course. But the criminal will never get more punishment than he bargained for when he did the crime, and his guilt of the crime (and hence the length of the sentence to which he is exposed) will be determined beyond a reasonable doubt by the unanimous vote of 12 of his fellow citizens.

In Justice Breyer's bureaucratic realm of perfect equity, by contrast, the facts that determine the length of sentence to which the defendant is exposed will be determined to exist (on a more-likely-than-not basis) by a single employee of the State. It is certainly arguable (Justice Breyer argues it) that this sacrifice of prior protections is worth it. But it is not arguable that, just because one thinks it is a better system, it must be, or is even more likely to be, the system envisioned by a Constitution that guarantees trial by jury. What ultimately demolishes the case for the dissenters is that they are unable to say what the right to trial by jury *does* guarantee if, as they assert, it does not guarantee—what it has been assumed to guarantee throughout our history—the right to have a jury determine those facts that determine the maximum sentence the law allows. They provide no coherent alternative.

Justice Breyer proceeds on the erroneous and all-too-common assumption that the Constitution means what we think it ought to mean. It does not; it means what it says. And the guarantee that "in all criminal prosecutions, the accused shall enjoy the right to * * * trial, by an impartial jury" has no intelligible content unless it means that all the facts which must exist in order to subject the defendant to a legally prescribed punishment *must* be found by the jury.

JUSTICE THOMAS, with whom JUSTICE SCALIA joins as to Parts I and II, concurring. * * *

I

This case turns on the seemingly simple question of what constitutes a "crime." Under the Federal Constitution, "the accused" has the right (1) "to be informed of the nature and cause of the accusation" (that is, the basis on which he is accused of a crime), (2) to be "held to answer for a capital, or otherwise infamous crime" only on an indictment or presentment of a grand jury, and (3) to be tried by "an impartial jury of the State and district wherein the crime shall have been committed." With the exception of the Grand Jury Clause, the Court has held that these protections apply in state prosecutions. Further, the Court has held that due process requires that the jury find beyond a reasonable doubt every fact necessary to constitute the crime.

All of these constitutional protections turn on determining which facts constitute the "crime"—that is, which facts are the "elements" or "ingredients" of a crime. * * *

* * * This question became more complicated following the Court's decision in *McMillan v. Pennsylvania,* which spawned a special sort of fact known as a sentencing enhancement. Such a fact increases a defendant's punishment but is not subject to the constitutional protections to which elements are subject. Justice O'Connor's dissent, in agreement with *McMillan* and *Almendarez-Torres v. United States,* takes the view that a legislature is free (within unspecified outer limits) to decree which facts are elements and which are sentencing enhancements.

Sentencing enhancements may be new creatures, but the question that they create for courts is not. Courts have long had to consider which facts are elements in order to determine the sufficiency of an accusation (usually an indictment). The answer that courts have provided regarding the accusation tells us what an element is, and it is then a simple matter to apply that answer to whatever constitutional right may be at issue in a case—here, *Winship* and the right to trial by jury. A long line of essentially uniform authority addressing accusations, and stretching from the earliest reported cases after the founding until well into the 20th century, establishes that the original understanding of which facts are elements was even broader than the rule that the Court adopts today.

This authority establishes that a "crime" includes every fact that is by law a basis for imposing or increasing punishment (in contrast with a fact that mitigates punishment). Thus, if the legislature defines some core crime and then provides for increasing the punishment of that crime upon a finding of some aggravating fact—of whatever sort, including the fact of a prior conviction—the core crime and the aggravating fact together constitute an aggravated crime, just as much as grand larceny is an aggravated form of petit larceny. The aggravating fact is an element of the aggravated crime. Similarly, if the legislature, rather than creating grades of crimes, has provided for setting the punishment of a crime based on some fact—such as a fine that is proportional to the value of stolen goods—that fact is also an element. * * *

II * * *

Cases from the founding to roughly the end of the Civil War establish the rule that I have described, applying it to all sorts of facts, including recidivism. [Justice Thomas' survey of federal and state case law is omitted.]

Without belaboring the point any further, I simply note that this traditional understanding—that a "crime" includes every fact that is by law a basis for imposing or increasing punishment—continued well into the 20th century, at least until the middle of the century. In fact, it is fair to say that *McMillan* began a revolution in the law regarding the definition of "crime." Today's decision, far from being a sharp break with the past, marks nothing more than a return to the *status quo ante*—the status quo that reflected the original meaning of the Fifth and Sixth Amendments.

III

The consequence of the above discussion for our decisions in *Almendarez-Torres* and *McMillan* should be plain enough, but a few points merit special mention. * * *

* * * [O]ne of the chief errors of *Almendarez-Torres*—an error to which I succumbed—was to attempt to discern whether a particular fact is traditionally (or typically) a basis for a sentencing court to increase an offender's sentence. For the reasons I have given, it should be clear that this approach just defines away the real issue. What matters is the way by which a fact enters into the sentence. If a fact is by law the basis for imposing or increasing punishment—for establishing or increasing the prosecution's entitlement—it is an element. * * * One reason frequently offered for treating recidivism differently, a reason on which we relied in *Almendarez-Torres*, is a concern for prejudicing the jury by informing it of the prior conviction. But this concern, of which earlier courts were well aware, does not make the traditional understanding of what an element is any less applicable to the fact of a prior conviction.

* * * [Moreover,] I think it clear that the common-law rule would cover the *McMillan* situation of a mandatory minimum sentence (in that case, for visible possession of a firearm during the commission of certain crimes). No doubt a defendant could, under such a scheme, find himself sentenced to the same term to which he could have been sentenced absent the mandatory minimum. * * * But it is equally true that his expected

punishment has increased as a result of the narrowed range and that the prosecution is empowered, by invoking the mandatory minimum, to require the judge to impose a higher punishment than he might wish. * * * Thus, the fact triggering the mandatory minimum is part of "the punishment sought to be inflicted" * * * . * * *

JUSTICE O'CONNOR, with whom THE CHIEF JUSTICE REHNQUIST, JUSTICE KENNEDY, and JUSTICE BREYER join, dissenting. * * *

I * * *

In one bold stroke the Court today casts aside our traditional cautious approach and instead embraces a universal and seemingly bright-line rule limiting the power of Congress and state legislatures to define criminal offenses and the sentences that follow from convictions thereunder. The Court states: "Other than the fact of a prior conviction, any fact that increases the penalty for a crime beyond the prescribed statutory maximum must be submitted to a jury, and proved beyond a reasonable doubt." In its opinion, the Court marshals virtually no authority to support its extraordinary rule. Indeed, it is remarkable that the Court cannot identify a single instance, in the over 200 years since the ratification of the Bill of Rights, that our Court has applied, as a constitutional requirement, the rule it announces today.

According to the Court, its constitutional rule "emerges from our history and case law." None of the history contained in the Court's opinion requires the rule it ultimately adopts. * * *

* * * [T]he Court asserts that its rule is supported by "our cases in this area." That the Court begins its review of our precedent with a quotation from a dissenting opinion speaks volumes about the support that actually can be drawn from our cases for the "increase in the maximum penalty" rule announced today. The Court then cites our decision in *Mullaney v. Wilbur* to demonstrate the "lesson" that due process and jury protections extend beyond those factual determinations that affect a defendant's guilt or innocence. * * * The Court chooses to ignore, however, the decision we issued two years later, *Patterson v. New York* [p. 1416, Note 1], which clearly rejected the Court's broad reading of *Mullaney.* * * *

Patterson is important because it plainly refutes the Court's expansive reading of *Mullaney*. Indeed, the defendant in *Patterson* characterized *Mullaney* exactly as the Court has today and we *rejected* that interpretation:

> "*Mullaney's* holding, it is argued, is that the State may not permit the blameworthiness of an act *or the severity of punishment authorized for its commission* to depend on the presence or absence of an identified fact without assuming the

burden of proving the presence or absence of that fact, as the case may be, beyond a reasonable doubt. In our view, the *Mullaney* holding should not be so broadly read." * * *

The case law from which the Court claims that its rule emerges consists of only one other decision—*McMillan v. Pennsylvania*. The Court's reliance on *McMillan* is also puzzling, given that our holding in that case points to the rejection of the Court's rule. * * *

* * * [I]t is incumbent on the Court not only to admit that it is overruling *McMillan*, but also to explain why such a course of action is appropriate under normal principles of *stare decisis*. * * *

II

That the Court's rule is unsupported by the history and case law it cites is reason enough to reject such a substantial departure from our settled jurisprudence. Significantly, the Court also fails to explain adequately why the Due Process Clauses of the Fifth and Fourteenth Amendments and the jury trial guarantee of the Sixth Amendment require application of its rule. Upon closer examination, it is possible that the Court's "increase in the maximum penalty" rule rests on a meaningless formalism that accords, at best, marginal protection for the constitutional rights that it seeks to effectuate.

Any discussion of either the constitutional necessity or the likely effect of the Court's rule must begin, of course, with an understanding of what exactly that rule is. * * * In fact, there appear to be several plausible interpretations of the constitutional principle on which the Court's decision rests.

* * * [U]nder one reading, the Court appears to hold that the Constitution requires that a fact be submitted to a jury and proved beyond a reasonable doubt only if that fact, as a formal matter, extends the range of punishment *beyond the prescribed statutory maximum*. A State could, however, remove from the jury (and subject to a standard of proof below "beyond a reasonable doubt") the assessment of those facts that define narrower ranges of punishment, within the overall statutory range, to which the defendant may be sentenced. Thus, apparently New Jersey could cure its sentencing scheme, and achieve virtually the same results, by drafting its weapons possession statute in the following manner: First, New Jersey could prescribe, in the weapons possession statute itself, a range of 5 to 20 years' imprisonment for one who commits that criminal offense. Second, New Jersey could provide that only those defendants convicted under the statute who are found by a judge, by a preponderance of the evidence, to have acted with a purpose to intimidate an individual on the basis of race may receive a sentence greater than 10 years' imprisonment. * * *

Under another reading of the Court's decision, it may mean only that the Constitution requires that a fact be submitted to a jury and proved beyond a reasonable doubt if it, as a formal matter, *increases the range of punishment beyond that which could legally be imposed absent that fact.* A State could, however, remove from the jury (and subject to a standard of proof below "beyond a reasonable doubt") the assessment of those facts that, as a formal matter, *decrease* the range of punishment *below that which could legally be imposed absent that fact.* Thus, consistent with our decision in *Patterson,* New Jersey could cure its sentencing scheme, and achieve virtually the same results, by drafting its weapons possession statute in the following manner: First, New Jersey could prescribe, in the weapons possession statute itself, a range of 5 to 20 years' imprisonment for one who commits that criminal offense. Second, New Jersey could provide that a defendant convicted under the statute whom a judge finds, by a preponderance of the evidence, *not* to have acted with a purpose to intimidate an individual on the basis of race may receive a sentence no greater than 10 years' imprisonment. * * *

If either of the above readings is all that the Court's decision means, "the Court's principle amounts to nothing more than chastising [the New Jersey Legislature] for failing to use the approved phrasing in expressing its intent as to how [unlawful weapons possession] should be punished." * * *

Given the pure formalism of the above readings of the Court's opinion, one suspects that the constitutional principle underlying its decision is more far reaching. The actual principle underlying the Court's decision may be that any fact (other than prior conviction) that has the effect, *in real terms,* of increasing the maximum punishment beyond an otherwise applicable range must be submitted to a jury and proved beyond a reasonable doubt. * * * The principle thus would apply not only to schemes like New Jersey's, under which a factual determination exposes the defendant to a sentence beyond the prescribed statutory maximum, but also to all determinate-sentencing schemes in which the length of a defendant's sentence within the statutory range turns on specific factual determinations (*e.g.,* the federal Sentencing Guidelines). * * *

I would reject any such principle. * * *

JUSTICE BREYER, with whom CHIEF JUSTICE REHNQUIST joins, dissenting. * * *

I * * *

* * * [I]t is important for present purposes to understand why *judges,* rather than *juries,* traditionally have determined the presence or absence of * * * sentence-affecting facts in any given case. And it is important to realize that the reason is not a theoretical one, but a practical one. It does

not reflect (Justice Scalia's opinion to the contrary notwithstanding) an ideal of procedural "fairness," but rather an administrative need for procedural *compromise*. There are, to put it simply, far too many potentially relevant sentencing factors to permit submission of all (or even many) of them to a jury. * * *

* * * [T]o require jury consideration of all such factors—say, during trial where the issue is guilt or innocence—could easily place the defendant in the awkward (and conceivably unfair) position of having to deny he committed the crime yet offer proof about how he committed it, *e.g.*, "I did not sell drugs, but I sold no more than 500 grams." And while special postverdict sentencing juries could cure this problem, they have seemed (but for capital cases) not worth their administrative costs. * * *

Finally, it is important to understand how a legislature decides which factual circumstances among all those potentially related to generally harmful behavior it should transform into elements of a statutorily defined crime (where they would become relevant to the guilt or innocence of an accused), and which factual circumstances it should leave to the sentencing process (where, as sentencing factors, they would help to determine the sentence imposed upon one who has been found guilty). Again, theory does not provide an answer. Legislatures, in defining crimes in terms of elements, have looked for guidance to common-law tradition, to history, and to current social need. And, traditionally, the Court has left legislatures considerable freedom to make the element determination. * * *

IV

I certainly do not believe that the present sentencing system is one of "perfect equity," and I am willing, consequently, to assume that the majority's rule would provide a degree of increased procedural protection in respect to those particular sentencing factors currently embodied in statutes. I nonetheless believe that any such increased protection provides little practical help and comes at too high a price. For one thing, by leaving mandatory minimum sentences untouched, the majority's rule simply encourages any legislature interested in asserting control over the sentencing process to do so by creating those minimums. That result would mean significantly less procedural fairness, not more.

For another thing, this Court's case law, prior to *Jones v. United States,* led legislatures to believe that they were permitted to increase a statutory maximum sentence on the basis of a sentencing factor. And legislatures may well have relied upon that belief.

* * * [T]he majority's rule creates serious uncertainty about the constitutionality of such statutes and about the constitutionality of the confinement of those punished under them. * * *

NOTES AND QUESTIONS

1. Constitutional issues aside—solely as a matter of sound public policy—do you believe jury sentencing is preferable to sentencing by judges? According to Judge Morris Hoffman:

> The modern case against jury sentencing typically relies on certain assumptions about the relative sentencing competence of judges and jurors. These assumptions are often expressed in various versions of the following four propositions: (1) judges are less susceptible to prejudice than jurors; (2) sentences imposed by judges are more uniform * * * ; (3) judges are more lenient than juries; and (4) jury sentencing encourages compromise verdicts.

Morris B. Hoffman, *The Case for Jury Sentencing*, 52 Duke L.J. 951 985–86 (2003).

Do you believe these arguments withstand scrutiny? Are there other arguments for or against jury sentencing that you would raise?

As a purely empirical matter, Judge Hoffman claims that social science research does not support the first claim (that judges are less susceptible to prejudice than juries). According to Hoffman, studies suggest that the risk of prejudice is heightened by leaving sentencing decisions to a single person (be that person a judge or layperson) than to leave the decision to a group of people. *Id.* at 986–87. In regard to uniformity-in-sentencing, the studies cited by Hoffman do not clearly support or disprove the argument for judicial sentencing. *Id.* at 987–88.

As for leniency—the third point listed above—Judge Hoffman cites an Alabama study that found that "judges were substantially harsher than their jury counterparts." *Id.* at 988. But, in a more recent study of sentencing in Arkansas and Virginia, a contrary result was reported: Jury sentences after a jury trial were both more variable *and* more severe than sentencing by a judge after a bench trial. Nancy J. King & Rosevelt L. Noble, *Jury Sentencing in Noncapital Cases: Comparing Severity and Variance with Judicial Sentences in Two States*, 2 J. Empirical Legal Stud. 331 (2005). And, there is a more recent analysis of federal cases, suggesting judicial leniency. See p. 1208, Note 6.

As to the fourth argument, the claim is that jury sentencing will result in more guilty verdicts, albeit more lenient sentences. Erik Lillquist, *The Puzzling Return of Jury Sentencing: Misgivings About Apprendi*, 82 N.C. L. Rev. 621, 692 (2004). The reasoning is that when jurors are deadlocked on the issue of guilt, if they know they will be imposing the sentence, those who would otherwise hold out for acquittal will vote for conviction in exchange for a reduced sentence. Several mock jury verdicts support this claim. Hoffman, *supra*, at 989. Advocates of jury sentencing respond that this concern can be avoided by requiring bifurcated trials (separate juries). Is that a suitable solution?

2. *The implications of Apprendi: judicial factfinding in capital cases.* In *Walton v. Arizona*, 497 U.S. 639, 110 S.Ct. 3047, 111 L.Ed.2d 511 (1990), the Supreme Court upheld a capital sentencing system that permitted judges, rather than juries, to find the specific aggravating factors justifying the imposition of death in capital sentencing proceedings.

In a deleted portion of Justice O'Connor's principal dissent in *Apprendi*, she predicted that the *Apprendi* rule would require the Court to overrule *Walton*. By a 7–2 vote, the Court did just that in Ring v. Arizona, 536 U.S. 584, 122 S.Ct. 2428, 153 L.Ed.2d 556 (2002). Justice Ginsburg concluded that "*Apprendi*'s reasoning is irreconcilable with *Walton*'s holding * * * ." Dissenters O'Connor and Rehnquist agreed with this proposition but stated that they would have overruled *Apprendi* and retained *Walton*.

According to the majority, "our Sixth Amendment jurisprudence cannot be home to both" *Apprendi* and *Walton*. "The right to trial by jury guaranteed by the Sixth Amendment would be senselessly diminished if it encompassed the factfinding necessary to increase a defendant's sentence by two years, but not the factfinding necessary to put him to death." *Walton* was overruled "to the extent that it allows a sentencing judge, sitting without a jury, to find an aggravating circumstance necessary for the imposition of the death penalty."

However, what if a jury *is* involved, but only is permitted to render an advisory recommendation on the death penalty? Under Florida law, the jury provides a recommendation, but the judge must independently find and weigh the aggravating and mitigating circumstances and render the ultimate sentencing judgment. The Court, with only Justice Alito dissenting, held that "Florida's sentencing scheme, which required the judge alone to find the existence of an aggravating circumstance," violates the *Apprendi* rule. Hurst v. Florida, 577 U.S. ___, 136 S.Ct. 616, 193 L.Ed.2d 504 (2016).

3. *The implications of Apprendi: Is McMillan v. Pennsylvania* (p. 1412) *still good law? Apprendi* placed in doubt *McMillan*'s continued vitality, as Justice Stevens virtually acknowledged in *Apprendi* (see footnote 13). After all, if the Sixth Amendment requires a jury (not a judge) to determine, beyond a reasonable doubt (and not by a lesser standard of proof), any fact that increases the *maximum* punishment of a defendant, why should the rule be different in regard to facts that increase the *minimum* punishment?

In *Harris v. United States*, 536 U.S. 545, 122 S.Ct. 2406, 153 L.Ed.2d 525 (2002), the Court ruled, 5–4, that *McMillan* remains good law, notwithstanding *Apprendi*. Justice Kennedy, writing for himself, Chief Justice Rehnquist, and Justices O'Connor and Scalia, explained:

> *McMillan* and *Apprendi* are consistent because there is a fundamental distinction between the factual findings that were at issue in those two cases. *Apprendi* said that any fact extending the defendant's sentence beyond the maximum authorized by the jury's verdict would have been considered an element of an aggravated crime—and thus the domain of the jury—by those who framed the

Bill of Rights. The same cannot be said of a fact increasing the mandatory minimum (but not extending the sentence beyond the statutory maximum), for the jury's verdict has authorized the judge to impose the minimum with or without the finding. As *McMillan* recognized, a statute may reserve this type of factual finding for the judge without violating the Constitution. * * *

Read together, *McMillan* and *Apprendi* mean that those facts setting the outer limits of a sentence, and of the judicial power to impose it, are the elements of the crime for the purposes of the constitutional analysis. Within the range authorized by the jury's verdict, however, the political system may channel judicial discretion—and rely upon judicial expertise—by requiring defendants to serve minimum terms after judges make certain factual findings. It is critical not to abandon that understanding at this late date.

Despite this reasoning, the required fifth vote for retaining *McMillan* came from Justice Breyer, a dissenter in *Apprendi*, who admitted that "I cannot easily distinguish *Apprendi* from this case in terms of logic." He voted to retain *McMillan*, however, because "extending *Apprendi* * * * would have adverse practical * * * consequences * * * ."

But, lo and behold, eleven years later, the Supreme Court overruled *Harris* in Alleyne v. United States, 570 U.S. ___, 133 S.Ct. 2151, 186 L.Ed.2d 314 (2013). In the 5–4 opinion, Justice Breyer switched sides, stating that although he "continue[s] to disagree with *Apprendi*, * * * *Apprendi* has now defined the relevant legal regime for an additional decade. And, in my view, the law should no longer tolerate the anomaly that the *Apprendi/Harris* distinction creates."

In *Alleyne*, the sentencing range supported by the jury's verdict was from five years to life imprisonment. The judge, however, found by a preponderance of the evidence that the defendant "brandished" a firearm during the offense, thus triggering a mandatory minimum sentence of seven years. Justice Thomas, writing for the Court, vacated the sentence on the ground that the distinction drawn in *Harris*,

> between facts that increase the statutory maximum and facts that increase only the mandatory minimum * * * is [a] distinction inconsistent with our decision in *Apprendi v. New Jersey*, and with the original meaning of the Sixth Amendment. Any fact that, by law, increases the penalty for a crime is an "element" [of the crime] that must be submitted to the jury and found beyond a reasonable doubt. Mandatory minimum sentences increase the penalty for a crime. It follows, then, that any fact that increases the mandatory minimum * * * must be submitted to the jury.

Justice Thomas went on to "take care to note what our holding does not entail." He stated that the holding in *Alleyne* "does not mean that any fact that influences judicial discretion must be found by a jury." Hearkening back to *Williams v. New York* (p. 1407), the Court stated that it does not violate the Constitution for judges to exercise discretion in imposing a judgment *within the range* prescribed by statute. In other words, in the context of a mandatory-minimum triggered by a finding of fact, *McMillan*'s understanding of the Sixth Amendment is no longer good law, but the case is still good law for the proposition that a judge can conduct discretionary fact-finding in a sentencing scheme that permits it. Jury sentencing is not required in that kind of sentencing scheme, and the judge may use the preponderance-of-proof standard and still comply with the due process clause.

4. *The further implications of Apprendi: the recidivism exception.* There is still another case that might seem in jeopardy in light of *Apprendi*. Specifically, is there now any justification for the recidivism exception (p. 1417, Note 3, *Almendarez-Torres*) to *Apprendi*? In James v. United States, 550 U.S. 192, 127 S.Ct. 1586, 167 L.Ed.2d 532 (2007), *J* pled guilty to being a felon in possession of a firearm, in violation of a federal statute for which the maximum punishment was ten years imprisonment. But, another federal statute mandated a minimum fifteen year sentence if *J* had three prior convictions for violent felonies. Although the primary issue in *James* was whether the petitioner's state conviction for attempted burglary constituted a "violent felony," Justice Alito, writing also for Chief Justice Roberts, and Justices Kennedy, Souter, and Breyer, dropped a footnote at the end of their majority opinion, stating:

> To the extent that [*J*] contends that the simple fact of his prior conviction was required to be found by a jury, his position is baseless. [*J*] admitted the fact of his prior conviction in his guilty plea, and in any case, we have held that prior convictions need not be treated as an element of the offense for Sixth Amendment purposes. *Almendarez-Torres v. United States.*

Thus, even though *J* admitted the fact of his prior conviction, the Court's additional language ("in any case * * * ") suggests that at least four current members of the Court (Justice Souter having retired from the Court) are prepared to continue to recognize the recidivism exception.

5. *And now come the guidelines?* One concern of the *Apprendi* dissenters was that the reasoning of *Apprendi* put the Federal Sentencing Guidelines—and, presumably, state sentencing guidelines systems—in jeopardy. They were correct, as the next case and Notes following it teach.

BLAKELY V. WASHINGTON
Supreme Court of the United States, 2004.
542 U.S. 296, 124 S.Ct. 2531, 159 L.Ed.2d 403.

JUSTICE SCALIA delivered the opinion of the Court [joined by JUSTICES STEVENS, SOUTER, THOMAS, and GINSBURG]. * * *

I * * *

The State charged petitioner with first-degree kidnaping. Upon reaching a plea agreement, however, it reduced the charge to second-degree kidnaping involving domestic violence and use of a firearm. Petitioner entered a guilty plea admitting the elements of second-degree kidnaping and the domestic-violence and firearm allegations, but no other relevant facts.

The case then proceeded to sentencing. In Washington, second-degree kidnaping is a class B felony. State law provides that "no person convicted of a [class B] felony shall be punished by confinement * * * exceeding * * * a term of ten years." Other provisions of state law, however, further limit the range of sentences a judge may impose. Washington's Sentencing Reform Act specifies, for petitioner's offense of second-degree kidnaping with a firearm, a "standard range" of 49 to 53 months. A judge may impose a sentence above the standard range if he finds "substantial and compelling reasons justifying an exceptional sentence." * * * When a judge imposes an exceptional sentence, he must set forth findings of fact and conclusions of law supporting it. A reviewing court will reverse the sentence if it finds that "under a clearly erroneous standard there is insufficient evidence in the record to support the reasons for imposing an exceptional sentence."

Pursuant to the plea agreement, the State recommended a sentence within the standard range of 49 to 53 months. After hearing [petitioner's wife's] description of the kidnaping, however, the judge rejected the State's recommendation and imposed an exceptional sentence of 90 months—37 months beyond the standard maximum. He justified the sentence on the ground that petitioner had acted with "deliberate cruelty," a statutorily enumerated ground for departure in domestic-violence cases.

Faced with an unexpected increase of more than three years in his sentence, petitioner objected. The judge accordingly conducted a 3-day bench hearing featuring testimony from petitioner, [his wife and son,] a police officer, and medical experts. After the hearing, he issued 32 findings of fact * * * . * * *

The judge adhered to his initial determination of deliberate cruelty.

Petitioner appealed, arguing that this sentencing procedure deprived him of his federal constitutional right to have a jury determine beyond a reasonable doubt all facts legally essential to his sentence. * * * We granted certiorari.

II

This case requires us to apply the rule we expressed in *Apprendi v. New Jersey*: "Other than the fact of a prior conviction, any fact that increases the penalty for a crime beyond the prescribed statutory maximum must be submitted to a jury, and proved beyond a reasonable doubt." * * *

In this case, petitioner was sentenced to more than three years above the 53-month statutory maximum of the standard range because he had acted with "deliberate cruelty." The facts supporting that finding were neither admitted by petitioner nor found by a jury. The State nevertheless contends that there was no *Apprendi* violation because the relevant "statutory maximum" is not 53 months, but the 10-year maximum for class B felonies. It observes that no exceptional sentence may exceed that limit. Our precedents make clear, however, that the "statutory maximum" for *Apprendi* purposes is the maximum sentence a judge may impose *solely on the basis of the facts reflected in the jury verdict or admitted by the defendant*. In other words, the relevant "statutory maximum" is not the maximum sentence a judge may impose after finding additional facts, but the maximum he may impose *without* any additional findings. When a judge inflicts punishment that the jury's verdict alone does not allow, the jury has not found all the facts "which the law makes essential to the punishment," and the judge exceeds his proper authority.

The judge in this case could not have imposed the exceptional 90-month sentence solely on the basis of the facts admitted in the guilty plea. Those facts alone were insufficient because, as the Washington Supreme Court has explained, "[a] reason offered to justify an exceptional sentence can be considered only if it takes into account factors other than those which are used in computing the standard range sentence for the offense," which in this case included the elements of second-degree kidnaping and the use of a firearm. Had the judge imposed the 90-month sentence solely on the basis of the plea, he would have been reversed. The "maximum sentence" is no more 10 years here than it was 20 years in *Apprendi* (because that is what the judge could have imposed upon finding a hate crime) * * * .

The State defends the sentence by drawing an analogy to those we upheld in *McMillan v. Pennsylvania,* [p. 1412], and *Williams v. New York,* [p. 1407]. Neither case is on point. *McMillan* involved a sentencing scheme that imposed a statutory *minimum* if a judge found a particular fact. We specifically noted that the statute "does not authorize a sentence in excess of that otherwise allowed for [the underlying] offense." *Williams* involved an indeterminate-sentencing regime that allowed a judge (but did not compel him) to rely on facts outside the trial record in determining whether to sentence a defendant to death. The judge could have "sentenced [the defendant] to death giving no reason at all." Thus, neither case involved a sentence greater than what state law authorized on the basis of the verdict alone. * * *

Because the State's sentencing procedure did not comply with the Sixth Amendment, petitioner's sentence is invalid.

III

Our commitment to *Apprendi* in this context reflects not just respect for longstanding precedent, but the need to give intelligible content to the right of jury trial. That right is no mere procedural formality, but a fundamental reservation of power in our constitutional structure. Just as suffrage ensures the people's ultimate control in the legislative and executive branches, jury trial is meant to ensure their control in the judiciary. *Apprendi* carries out this design by ensuring that the judge's authority to sentence derives wholly from the jury's verdict. Without that restriction, the jury would not exercise the control that the Framers intended. * * *

IV

By reversing the judgment below, we are not, as the State would have it, "finding determinate sentencing schemes unconstitutional." This case is not about whether determinate sentencing is constitutional, only about how it can be implemented in a way that respects the Sixth Amendment. Several policies prompted Washington's adoption of determinate sentencing, including proportionality to the gravity of the offense and parity among defendants. Nothing we have said impugns those salutary objectives.

Justice O'Connor argues that, because determinate sentencing schemes involving judicial factfinding entail less judicial discretion than indeterminate schemes, the constitutionality of the latter implies the constitutionality of the former. This argument is flawed * * * . [T]he Sixth Amendment by its terms is not a limitation on judicial power, but a reservation of jury power. It limits judicial power only to the extent that the claimed judicial power infringes on the province of the jury. Indeterminate sentencing does not do so. It increases judicial discretion, to be sure, but not at the expense of the jury's traditional function of finding the facts essential to lawful imposition of the penalty. Of course indeterminate schemes involve judicial factfinding, in that a judge (like a parole board) may implicitly rule on those facts he deems important to the exercise of his sentencing discretion. But the facts do not pertain to whether the defendant has a legal *right* to a lesser sentence—and that makes all the difference insofar as judicial impingement upon the traditional role of the jury is concerned. In a system that says the judge may punish burglary with 10 to 40 years, every burglar knows he is risking 40 years in jail. In a system that punishes burglary with a 10-year sentence, with another 30 added for use of a gun, the burglar who enters a home unarmed is *entitled* to no more than a 10-year sentence—and by reason of the Sixth Amendment the facts bearing upon that entitlement must be found by a jury. * * *

Justice Breyer argues that *Apprendi* works to the detriment of criminal defendants who plead guilty by depriving them of the opportunity to argue sentencing factors to a judge. But nothing prevents a defendant from waiving his *Apprendi* rights. When a defendant pleads guilty, the State is free to seek judicial sentence enhancements so long as the defendant either stipulates to the relevant facts or consents to judicial factfinding. If appropriate waivers are procured, States may continue to offer judicial factfinding as a matter of course to all defendants who plead guilty. Even a defendant who stands trial may consent to judicial factfinding as to sentence enhancements, which may well be in his interest if relevant evidence would prejudice him at trial. We do not understand how *Apprendi* can possibly work to the detriment of those who are free, if they think its costs outweigh its benefits, to render it inapplicable.[12]

Nor do we see any merit to Justice Breyer's contention that *Apprendi* is unfair to criminal defendants because, if States respond by enacting "17-element robbery crimes," prosecutors will have more elements with which to bargain. Bargaining already exists with regard to sentencing factors because defendants can either stipulate or contest the facts that make them applicable. If there is any difference between bargaining over sentencing factors and bargaining over elements, the latter probably favors the defendant. Every new element that a prosecutor can threaten to charge is also an element that a defendant can threaten to contest at trial and make the prosecutor prove beyond a reasonable doubt. Moreover, given the sprawling scope of most criminal codes, and the power to affect sentences by making (even nonbinding) sentencing recommendations, there is already no shortage of *in terrorem* tools at prosecutors' disposal. * * *

Justice Breyer also claims that *Apprendi* will attenuate the connection between "real criminal conduct and real punishment" by encouraging plea bargaining and by restricting alternatives to adversarial factfinding. The short answer to the former point (even assuming the

---

[12] Justice Breyer responds that States are not *required* to give defendants the option of waiving jury trial on some elements but not others. True enough. But why would the States that he asserts we are coercing into hard-heartedness—that is, States that *want* judge-pronounced determinate sentencing to be the norm but we won't let them—want to prevent a defendant from *choosing* that regime? * * *

questionable premise that *Apprendi* does encourage plea bargaining) is that the Sixth Amendment was not written for the benefit of those who choose to forgo its protection. It guarantees the *right* to jury trial. It does not guarantee that a particular number of jury trials will actually take place. That more defendants elect to waive that right * * * does not prove that a constitutional provision guaranteeing *availability* of that option is disserved.

Justice Breyer's more general argument—that *Apprendi* undermines alternatives to adversarial factfinding—is not so much a criticism of *Apprendi* as an assault on jury trial generally. His esteem for "non-adversarial" truth-seeking processes, supports just as well an argument against either. Our Constitution and the common-law traditions it entrenches, however, do not admit the contention that facts are better discovered by judicial inquisition than by adversarial testing before a jury. Justice Breyer may be convinced of the equity of the regime he favors, but his views are not the ones we are bound to uphold. * * *

JUSTICE O'CONNOR, with whom JUSTICE BREYER joins, and with whom THE CHIEF JUSTICE REHNQUIST and JUSTICE KENNEDY join as to all but Part IV–B, dissenting.

The legacy of today's opinion, whether intended or not, will be the consolidation of sentencing power in the State and Federal Judiciaries. The Court says to Congress and state legislatures: If you want to constrain the sentencing discretion of judges and bring some uniformity to sentencing, it will cost you—dearly. Congress and States, faced with the burdens imposed by the extension of *Apprendi* to the present context, will either trim or eliminate altogether their sentencing guidelines schemes and, with them, 20 years of sentencing reform. It is thus of little moment that the majority does not expressly declare guidelines schemes unconstitutional; for, as residents of "*Apprendi*-land" are fond of saying, "the relevant inquiry is one not of form, but of effect." The "effect" of today's decision will be greater judicial discretion and less uniformity in sentencing. Because I find it implausible that the Framers would have considered such a result to be required by the Due Process Clause or the Sixth Amendment, and because the practical consequences of today's decision may be disastrous, I respectfully dissent. * * *

II

Far from disregarding principles of due process and the jury trial right, as the majority today suggests, Washington's reform has served them. Before passage of the Act, a defendant charged with second degree kidnaping, like petitioner, had no idea whether he would receive a 10-year sentence or probation. The ultimate sentencing determination could turn as much on the idiosyncracies of a particular judge as on the specifics of the defendant's crime or background. A defendant did not know what facts, if any, about his offense or his history would be considered relevant by the sentencing judge or by the parole board. After passage of the Act, a defendant charged with second degree kidnaping knows what his presumptive sentence will be; he has a good idea of the types of factors that a sentencing judge can and will consider when deciding whether to sentence him outside that range; he is guaranteed meaningful appellate review to protect against an arbitrary sentence. Criminal defendants still face the same statutory maximum sentences, but they now at least know, much more than before, the real consequences of their actions.

Washington's move to a system of guided discretion has served equal protection principles as well. Over the past 20 years, there has been a substantial reduction in racial disparity in sentencing across the State. The reduction is directly traceable to the constraining effects of the guidelines * * * . * * *

The majority does not, because it cannot, disagree that determinate sentencing systems, like Washington's, serve important constitutional values. * * * But extension of *Apprendi* to the present context will impose significant costs on a legislature's determination that a particular fact, not historically an element, warrants a higher sentence. While not a constitutional prohibition on guidelines schemes, the majority's decision today exacts a substantial constitutional tax.

The costs are substantial and real. Under the majority's approach, any fact that increases the upper bound on a judge's sentencing discretion is an element of the offense. Thus, facts that historically have been taken into account by sentencing judges to assess a sentence within a broad range—such as drug quantity, role in the offense, risk of bodily harm—all must now be charged in an indictment and submitted to a jury, simply because it is the legislature, rather than the judge, that constrains the extent to which such facts may be used to impose a sentence within a pre-existing statutory range.

While that alone is enough to threaten the continued use of sentencing guidelines schemes, there are additional costs. For example, a legislature might rightly think that some factors bearing on sentencing, such as prior bad acts or criminal history, should not be considered in a jury's determination of a defendant's guilt—such "character evidence" has traditionally been off limits during the guilt phase of criminal proceedings because of its tendency to inflame the passions of the jury. If a legislature desires uniform consideration of such factors at sentencing, but does not want them to impact a jury's initial determination of guilt, the State may have to bear the additional expense of a separate, full-blown jury trial during the penalty phase proceeding. * * *

The majority may be correct that States and the Federal Government will be willing to bear some of these costs. But simple economics dictate that they will not, and cannot, bear them all. To the extent that they do not, there will be an inevitable increase in judicial discretion with all of its attendant failings.

III * * *

[I]t is difficult for me to discern what principle besides doctrinaire formalism actually motivates today's decision. The majority chides the *Apprendi* dissenters for preferring a nuanced interpretation of the Due Process Clause and Sixth Amendment jury trial guarantee that would generally defer to legislative labels while acknowledging the existence of constitutional constraints—what the majority calls the "the law must not go too far" approach. If indeed the choice is between adopting a balanced case-by-case approach that takes into consideration the values underlying the Bill of Rights, as well as the history of a particular sentencing reform law, and adopting a rigid rule that destroys everything in its path, I will choose the former. * * *

IV * * *

[B] * * *

What I have feared most has now come to pass: Over 20 years of sentencing reform are all but lost, and tens of thousands of criminal judgments are in jeopardy.

[The dissenting opinion of JUSTICE KENNEDY, with whom JUSTICE BREYER joined, is omitted.]

JUSTICE BREYER, with whom JUSTICE O'CONNOR joins, dissenting.

* * * In [the majority's] view, the Sixth Amendment * * * [requires that] a jury must find, not only the facts that make up the crime of which the offender is charged, but also all (punishment-increasing) facts about the *way* in which the offender carried out that crime.

It is not difficult to understand the impulse that produced this holding. Imagine a classic example—a statute (or mandatory sentencing guideline) that provides a 10-year sentence for ordinary bank robbery, but a 15-year sentence for bank robbery committed with a gun. One might ask why it should matter for jury trial purposes whether the statute (or guideline) labels the gun's presence (a) a *sentencing fact* about the way in which the offender carried out the *lesser* crime of ordinary bank robbery, or (b) a factual *element* of the *greater* crime of bank robbery with a gun? If the Sixth Amendment requires a jury finding about the gun in the latter circumstance, why should it not also require a jury to find the same fact in the former circumstance? The two sets of circumstances are functionally identical. In both instances, identical punishment follows from identical factual findings (related to, *e.g.,* a bank, a taking, a thing-of-value, force or threat of force, and a gun). The only difference between the two circumstances concerns a legislative (or Sentencing Commission) decision about which *label* ("sentencing fact" or "element of a greater crime") to affix to one of the facts, namely, the presence of the gun, that will lead to the greater sentence. Given the identity of circumstances apart from the label, the jury's traditional factfinding role, and the law's insistence upon treating like cases alike, why should the legislature's labeling choice make an important Sixth Amendment difference?

The Court in *Apprendi,* and now here, concludes that it should not make a difference. The Sixth Amendment's jury trial guarantee applies similarly to both. I agree with the majority's analysis, but not with its conclusion. That is to say, I agree that, classically speaking, the difference between a traditional sentencing factor and an element of a greater offense often comes down to a legislative choice about which label to affix. But I cannot jump from there to the conclusion that the Sixth Amendment always requires identical treatment of the two scenarios. That jump is fraught with consequences that threaten the fairness of our traditional criminal justice system * * * . * * *

I

The majority ignores the adverse consequences inherent in its conclusion. As a result of the majority's rule, sentencing must now take one of three forms, each of which risks either impracticality, unfairness, or harm to the jury trial right the majority purports to strengthen. This circumstance shows that the majority's Sixth Amendment interpretation cannot be right.

A

A first option for legislators is to create a simple, pure or nearly pure "charge offense" or "determinate" sentencing system. In such a system, an indictment would charge a few facts which, taken together, constitute a crime, such as robbery. Robbery would carry a single sentence, say, five years' imprisonment. And every person convicted of robbery would receive that sentence—just as, centuries ago, everyone convicted of almost any serious crime was sentenced to death.

Such a system assures uniformity, but at intolerable costs. First, simple determinate sentencing systems impose identical punishments on people who committed their crimes in very different ways. When dramatically different conduct ends up being punished the same way, an injustice has taken place. Simple determinate sentencing has the virtue of treating like cases alike, but it simultaneously fails to treat different cases differently. * * *

Second, in a world of statutorily fixed mandatory sentences for many crimes, determinate sentencing gives tremendous power to prosecutors to manipulate sentences through their choice of charges. Prosecutors can simply charge, or threaten to charge, defendants with crimes bearing higher mandatory sentences. Defendants, knowing that they will not have a chance to argue for a lower sentence in front of a judge, may plead to charges that they might otherwise contest. Considering that most criminal cases do not go to trial and resolution by plea bargaining is the norm, the rule of *Apprendi*, to the extent it results in a return to determinate sentencing, threatens serious unfairness.

B

A second option for legislators is to return to a system of indeterminate sentencing * * * . Under indeterminate systems, the length of the sentence is entirely or almost entirely within the discretion of the judge or of the parole board, which typically has broad power to decide when to release a prisoner.

When such systems were in vogue, they were criticized, and rightly so, for producing unfair disparities, including race-based disparities, in the punishment of similarly situated defendants. The length of time a person spent in prison appeared to depend on "what the judge ate for breakfast" on the day of sentencing, on which judge you got, or on other factors that should not have made a difference to the length of the sentence. And under such a system, the judge could vary the sentence greatly based upon his findings about how the defendant had committed the crime—findings that might not have been made by a "preponderance of the evidence," much less "beyond a reasonable doubt."

Returning to such a system would diminish the " 'reason' " the majority claims it is trying to uphold. It also would do little to "ensure [the] control" of what the majority calls "the peopl[e,]" *i.e.*, the jury, "in the judiciary," since "the people" would only decide the defendant's guilt, a finding with no effect on the duration of the sentence. While "the judge's authority to sentence" would formally derive from the jury's verdict, the jury would exercise little or no control over the sentence itself. It is difficult to see how such an outcome protects the structural safeguards the majority claims to be defending.

C

A third option is that which the Court seems to believe legislators will in fact take. That is the option of retaining structured schemes that attempt to punish similar conduct similarly and different conduct differently, but modifying them to conform to *Apprendi*'s dictates. Judges would be able to depart *downward* from presumptive sentences upon finding that mitigating factors were present, but would not be able to depart *upward* unless the prosecutor charged the aggravating fact to a jury and proved it beyond a reasonable doubt. The majority argues * * * that most legislatures will enact amendments along these lines in the face of the oncoming *Apprendi* train. It is therefore worth exploring how this option could work in practice, as well as the assumptions on which it depends.

1

This option can be implemented in one of two ways. The first way would be for legislatures to subdivide each crime into a list of complex crimes, each of which would be defined to include commonly found sentencing factors such as drug quantity, type of victim, presence of violence, degree of injury, use of gun, and so on. A legislature, for example, might enact a robbery statute, modeled on robbery sentencing guidelines, that increases punishment depending upon (1) the nature of the institution robbed, (2) the (a) presence of, (b) brandishing of, (c) other use of, a firearm, (3) making of a death threat, (4) presence of (a) ordinary, (b) serious, (c) permanent or life threatening, bodily injury, (5) abduction, (6) physical restraint, (7) taking of a firearm, (8) taking of drugs, (9) value of property loss, etc.

This possibility is, of course, merely a highly calibrated form of the "pure charge" system discussed in Part I–A. And it suffers from some of the same defects. The prosecutor, through control of the precise charge, controls the punishment, thereby marching the sentencing system directly away from, not toward, one important guideline goal: rough uniformity of punishment for those who engage in roughly the same *real* criminal conduct. The artificial (and consequently unfair) nature of the resulting sentence is aggravated by the fact that prosecutors must charge all relevant facts about the way the crime was committed before a presentence investigation examines the criminal conduct, perhaps before the trial itself, *i.e.,* before many of the facts relevant to punishment are known.

This "complex charge offense" system also prejudices defendants who seek trial, for it can put them in the untenable position of contesting material aggravating facts in the guilt phases of their trials. Consider a defendant who is charged, not with mere possession of cocaine, but with the specific offense of possession of more than 500 grams of cocaine. Or consider a defendant charged, not with murder, but with the new crime of murder using a machete. Or consider a defendant whom the prosecution wants to claim was a "supervisor," rather than an ordinary gang member. How can a Constitution that guarantees due process put these defendants, as a matter of course, in the position of arguing, "I did not sell drugs, and if I did, I did not sell more than 500 grams" or, "I did not kill him, and if I did, I did not use a machete," or "I did not engage in gang activity, and certainly not as a supervisor" to a single jury? * * *

The majority announces that there really is no problem here because "States may continue to offer judicial factfinding as a matter of course to all defendants who plead guilty" and defendants may "stipulate to the relevant facts or consent to judicial factfinding." The problem, of course, concerns defendants who do not want to plead guilty to those elements that, until recently, were commonly thought of as sentencing factors. As to those defendants, the fairness problem arises because States may very well decide that they will *not* permit defendants to carve subsets of facts out of the new, *Apprendi*-required 17-element robbery crime, seeking a judicial determination as to some of those facts and a jury determination as to others. Instead, States may simply require defendants to plead guilty to all 17 elements or proceed with a (likely prejudicial) trial on all 17 elements.

The majority does not deny that States may make this choice; it simply fails to understand *why* any State would want to exercise it. The answer is * * * that the alternative may prove too expensive and unwieldy for States to provide. States that offer defendants the option of judicial factfinding as to some facts (*i.e.,* sentencing facts), say, because of fairness concerns, will also have to offer the defendant a second sentencing jury— just as Kansas has done. I therefore turn to that alternative.

2

The second way to make sentencing guidelines *Apprendi*-compliant would be to require at least two juries for each defendant whenever aggravating facts are present: one jury to determine guilt of the crime charged, and an additional jury to try the disputed facts that, if found, would aggravate the sentence. Our experience with bifurcated trials in the capital punishment context suggests that requiring them for run-of-the-mill sentences would be costly, both in money and in judicial time and resources. * * * Indeed, cost and delay could lead legislatures to revert to the complex charge offense system described in Part I–C–1, *supra*.

[According to] an *amicus curiae* brief filed by the Kansas Appellate Defender Office, * * * a two-jury system has proved workable in Kansas. And that may be so. But in all likelihood, any such workability reflects an uncomfortable fact, a fact at which the majority hints, but whose constitutional implications it does not seem to grasp. The uncomfortable fact that could make the system seem workable—even desirable in the minds of some, including defense attorneys—is called "plea bargaining." The Court can announce that the Constitution requires at least two jury trials for each criminal defendant—one for guilt, another for sentencing— but only because it knows full well that more than 90% of defendants will not go to trial even once, much less insist on two or more trials.

What will be the consequences of the Court's holding for the 90% of defendants who do not go to trial? The truthful answer is that we do not know. Some defendants may receive bargaining advantages if the increased cost of the "double jury trial" guarantee makes prosecutors more willing to cede certain sentencing issues to the defense. Other defendants may be hurt if a "single-jury-decides-all" approach makes them more reluctant to risk a trial—perhaps because they want to argue that they did not know what was in the cocaine bag, that it was a small amount regardless, that they were unaware a confederate had a gun, etc.

At the least, the greater expense attached to trials and their greater complexity, taken together in the context of an overworked criminal justice system, will likely mean, other things being equal, fewer trials and a greater reliance upon plea bargaining—a system in which punishment is set not by judges or juries but by advocates acting under bargaining constraints. At the same time, the greater power of the prosecutor to control the punishment through the charge would likely weaken the relation between real conduct and real punishment as well. Even if the Court's holding does not further embed plea-bargaining practices (as I fear it will), its success depends upon the existence of present practice. I do not understand how the Sixth Amendment could *require* a sentencing system that will work in practice only if no more than a handful of defendants exercise their right to a jury trial.

The majority's only response is to state that "bargaining over elements * * * probably favors the defendant," adding that many criminal defense lawyers favor its position. But the basic problem is not one of "fairness" to defendants or, for that matter, "fairness" to prosecutors. Rather, it concerns the greater fairness of a sentencing system that a more uniform correspondence between real criminal conduct and real punishment helps to create. At a minimum, a two-jury system, by preventing a judge from taking account of an aggravating fact without the prosecutor's acquiescence, would undercut, if not nullify, legislative efforts to ensure through guidelines that punishments reflect a convicted offender's real criminal conduct, rather than that portion of the offender's conduct that a prosecutor decides to charge and prove. * * *

In these and other ways, the two-jury system would work a radical change in pre-existing criminal law. It is not surprising that this Court has never previously suggested that the Constitution—outside the unique context of the death penalty—might require bifurcated jury-based sentencing. And it is the impediment the Court's holding poses to legislative efforts to achieve that greater systematic fairness that casts doubt on its constitutional validity.

D

Is there a fourth option? Perhaps. Congress and state legislatures might, for example, rewrite their criminal codes, attaching astronomically high sentences to each crime, followed by long lists of mitigating facts, which, for the most part, would consist of the absence of aggravating facts. But political impediments to legislative action make such rewrites difficult to achieve; and it is difficult to see why the Sixth Amendment would require legislatures to undertake them.

It may also prove possible to find combinations of, or variations upon, my first three options. But I am unaware of any variation that does not involve (a) the shift of power to the prosecutor (weakening the connection between real conduct and real punishment) inherent in any charge offense system, (b) the lack of uniformity inherent in any system of pure judicial discretion, or (c) the complexity, expense, and increased reliance on plea bargains involved in a "two-jury" system. The simple fact is that the design of any fair sentencing system must involve efforts to make practical compromises among competing goals. The majority's reading of the Sixth Amendment makes the effort to find those compromises— already difficult—virtually impossible. * * *

IV

Now, let us return to the question I posed at the outset. Why does the Sixth Amendment permit a jury trial right (in respect to a particular fact) to depend upon a legislative labeling decision, namely, the legislative decision to label the fact a *sentencing fact*, instead of an *element of the crime?* The answer is that the fairness and effectiveness of a sentencing system, and the related fairness and effectiveness of the criminal justice system itself, depends upon the legislature's possessing the constitutional authority (within due process limits) to make that labeling decision. To restrict radically the legislature's power in this respect, as the majority interprets the Sixth Amendment to do, prevents the legislature from seeking sentencing systems that are consistent with, and indeed may help to advance, the Constitution's greater fairness goals.

* * * Whatever the faults of guidelines systems—and there are many—they are more likely to find their cure in legislation emerging from the experience of, and discussion among, all elements of the criminal justice community, than in a virtually unchangeable constitutional decision of this Court. * * *

NOTES AND QUESTIONS

1.   *The aftermath.* The *Blakely* decision was handed down on June 24, 2004. The effect was electric. (Justice O'Connor, speaking to an annual conference of the Ninth Circuit, characterized the decision, which "disgusted" her, as a "Number 10 earthquake to me.") Not only did state legislatures, governors, and state sentencing commissions almost immediately seek to determine *Blakely*'s likely effect on their own sentencing guideline systems, but the federal criminal justice system was turned upside down. Did *Blakely* spell the impending end of the Federal Sentencing Guidelines? Judges about

to sentence federal defendants were unsure what to do. Countless already-sentenced defendants wondered whether they had grounds for appeal. Consequently, the Supreme Court acted with extraordinary speed: On August 2, 2004, during the Court's summer recess, it granted writs of certiorari in two federal cases (one of which had not yet even been heard by the Court of Appeals), and ordered consolidated, expedited oral arguments in the two appeals on October 4, 2004, the first day of the 2004 Court Term. The questions presented on appeal were:

> "1. Whether the Sixth Amendment is violated by the imposition of an enhanced sentence under the United States Sentencing Guidelines based on the sentencing judge's determination of a fact (other than a prior conviction) that was not found by the jury or admitted by the defendant." [This question is discussed in Note 2, *infra*.]

> "2. If the answer to the first question is 'yes,' the following question is presented: whether, in a case in which the Guidelines would require the court to find a sentence-enhancing fact, the Sentencing Guidelines as a whole would be inapplicable * * * such that the sentencing court must exercise its discretion to sentence the defendant within the maximum and minimum set by statute for the offense of conviction." [This question is consider in Note 3, *infra*.]

The relevant facts in the cases the Supreme Court chose to hear were as follows: In the first case, Freddie Booker was charged with possession with intent to distribute at least fifty grams of cocaine base (crack). Having heard evidence that he had 92.5 grams in his duffel bag, the jury found him guilty of violating a statute that prescribed a minimum sentence of ten years in prison and a maximum sentence of life for that offense. Based on Booker's criminal history and the quantity of drugs found by the jury, the Sentencing Guidelines, which were mandatory, required the judge to select a "base" sentence of not less than 210 nor more than 262 months in prison. However, at a post-trial sentencing proceeding, the judge concluded by a preponderance of the evidence that Booker had possessed an additional 566 grams of crack and was guilty of obstructing justice. These findings mandated a far more severe sentence, between 360 months and life imprisonment. Instead of the sentence of 262 months that the judge could have imposed on the basis of the facts proved to the jury beyond a reasonable doubt, Booker received a thirty-year sentence. The Court of Appeals for the Seventh Circuit, however, held that in light of *Blakely*, this sentence violated the Sixth Amendment, and remanded with instructions to the District Court either to sentence respondent within the sentencing range supported by the jury's findings or to hold a separate sentencing hearing before a jury. The government appealed.

In the second appeal, Duncan Fanfan was charged with conspiracy to distribute and to possess with intent to distribute at least 500 grams of cocaine in violation of federal law. On these facts, the maximum sentence authorized by the jury verdict was imprisonment for seventy-eight months. Before sentencing, however, *Blakely* was handed down. The trial judge proceeded with a sentencing hearing at which he found, by preponderance of the evidence, additional facts that, under the Guidelines, would have authorized a sentence in the 188-to-235 month range. Because of *Blakely*, however, the judge concluded that he could not impose the heightened sentence, and instead imposed a sentence that fell within the range justified by the guilty verdict in the case. Again, the government appealed.

On January 12, 2005, the Supreme Court rendered its decision in these two cases. United States v. Booker, 543 U.S. 220, 125 S.Ct. 738, 160 L.Ed.2d 621 (2005). The result was at least as remarkable, and as complicated, as the cases that had preceded it.

2.   *United States v. Booker (part 1): the Sixth Amendment applies to the Federal Sentencing Guidelines.* The first remarkable feature of *Booker* is that there are two opinions of the Court. The first opinion of the Court answered the first of the two questions set out in Note 1. Justice Stevens, author of *Apprendi*, joined by the same justices who constituted the majority in *Apprendi* and *Blakely* (Justices Scalia, Souter, Thomas, and Ginsburg), delivered this part of the Court's opinion. Unsurprisingly, they held that both courts below "correctly concluded that the Sixth Amendment as construed in *Blakely* does apply to the [Federal] Sentencing Guidelines." As Stevens explained:

> Our precedents * * * make clear "that the 'statutory maximum' for *Apprendi* purposes is the maximum sentence a judge may impose *solely on the basis of the facts reflected in the jury verdict or admitted by the defendant."* * * *
>
> * * * [T]here is no distinction of constitutional significance between the Federal Sentencing Guidelines and the Washington procedures at issue in that case. * * * This conclusion rests on the premise, common to both systems, that the relevant sentencing rules are mandatory and impose binding requirements on all sentencing judges.
>
> If the Guidelines as currently written could be read as merely advisory provisions that recommended, rather than required, the selection of particular sentences in response to differing sets of facts, their use would not implicate the Sixth Amendment. We have never doubted the authority of a judge to exercise broad discretion in imposing a sentence within a statutory range. See *Williams* v. *New York* [p. 1407]. Indeed, everyone agrees that the constitutional issues presented by these cases would have been avoided entirely if Congress had omitted from the [Sentencing Reform Act of 1984] the provisions that make the Guidelines binding on district judges * * *. For when a trial judge exercises his discretion to select a specific sentence within a defined range, the defendant has no right to a jury determination of the facts that the judge deems relevant.

The Guidelines as written, however, are not advisory; they are mandatory and binding on all judges. While subsection (a) of § 3553 of the sentencing statute lists the Sentencing Guidelines as one factor to be considered in imposing a sentence, subsection (b) directs that the court "*shall* impose a sentence of the kind, and within the range" established by the Guidelines, subject to departures in specific, limited cases. Because they are binding on judges, we have consistently held that the Guidelines have the force and effect of laws. * * *

Accordingly, we reaffirm our holding in *Apprendi*: Any fact (other than a prior conviction) which is necessary to support a sentence exceeding the maximum authorized by the facts established by a plea of guilty or a jury verdict must be admitted by the defendant or proved to a jury beyond a reasonable doubt.

The *Apprendi* and *Blakely* dissenters, also predictably, dissented here. Justice Breyer, joined by Chief Justice Rehnquist and Justices O'Connor and Kennedy, largely repeated their earlier criticisms of the *Apprendi* rule.

And so, the answer to the Court's first question—"Whether the Sixth Amendment is violated by the imposition of an enhanced sentence under the United States Sentencing Guidelines based on the sentencing judge's determination of a fact (other than a prior conviction) that was not found by the jury or admitted by the defendant"—was "Yes."

3. *United States v. Booker (part 2): the Guidelines become discretionary.* The affirmative answer to the first question now compelled the Court to answer the second "cert question" set out in Note 1, which it characterized as the "remedy" issue.

One possible remedy was to declare the Federal Sentencing Guidelines, as a whole, unconstitutional. In short, the law would return to the pre-Guideline era when trial judges had unfettered discretion to sentence a defendant within the minimum and maximum penalties set by statute for the offense of conviction.

A second potential remedy was one that would ostensibly shift sentencing power from judges to juries. That remedy, in the words of Justice Breyer, was to

retain the Sentencing Act (and the Guidelines) as written, but * * * engraft onto the existing system today's Sixth Amendment "jury trial" requirement. The addition would change the Guidelines by preventing the sentencing court from increasing a sentence on the basis of a fact that the jury did not find (or that the offender did not admit).

This solution seemed to be the direction the Court was going in *Apprendi*, *Blakely*, and now *Booker*. It is the remedy Justice Stevens was prepared to announce for the Court majority here, but then something unusual happened—Justice Ginsburg switched sides on the remedy.

Justice Ginsburg joined the four *Apprendi*, *Blakely*, and *Booker* dissenters to form a new, "remedial" majority. Thus, although Justice Stevens and his majority found that the Guidelines violated the Sixth Amendment, the justices who *opposed* the recent line of cases (now along with Justice Ginsburg) had the opportunity to fashion the remedy! As explained by Justice Breyer, now writing the five-justice opinion of the Court on *this* issue: "The * * * approach, which we now adopt, * * * through severance and excision of two provisions [of the Guidelines] [is to] make the Guidelines system advisory while maintaining a strong connection between the sentence imposed and the offender's real conduct—a connection important to the increased uniformity of sentencing that Congress intended its Guidelines system to achieve."

Thus, the irony: Although the existing Guidelines violate the Sixth Amendment right-to-jury principles set out in *Blakely* and now *Booker*, the remedy is *not* to permit juries to determine sentencing facts necessary to increase a defendant's sentence under the Guidelines, but rather to give judges even greater discretion than they had prior to the Court's ruling, by making the federal guidelines discretionary rather than mandatory!

In the view of the Breyer remedial majority, the guidelines-as-discretionary remedy is "more compatible with the legislature's intent as embodied in the 1984 Sentencing Act" than Justice Stevens's proposed remedy. According to Breyer:

> We * * * do not believe that the entire statute must be invalidated. Most of the statute is perfectly valid. * * * Indeed, we must retain those portions of the Act that are (1) constitutionally valid, (2) capable of "functioning independently," and (3) consistent with Congress' basic objectives in enacting the statute.
>
> Application of these criteria indicates that we must sever and excise two specific statutory provisions: the provision that requires sentencing courts to impose a sentence within the applicable Guidelines range (in the absence of circumstances that justify a departure), see 18 U.S.C. § 3553(b)(1) (Supp. 2004), and the provision that sets forth standards of review on appeal, including *de novo* review of departures from the applicable Guidelines range, see § 3742(e) (main ed. and Supp. 2004). With these two sections excised * * * the remainder of the Act satisfies the Court's constitutional requirements.

So, what does this mean? Are judges now entirely free to roam where they choose, imposing sentences anywhere between the minimums and maximums set by Congress? And, how will an appellate court, called upon to decide whether a judge's sentence is permissible, conduct such a review? Justice Breyer explained:

> Without the "mandatory" provision, the Act nonetheless requires judges to take account of the Guidelines together with other

sentencing goals. The Act nonetheless requires judges to consider the Guidelines "sentencing range established for * * * the applicable category of offense committed by the applicable category of defendant," the pertinent Sentencing Commission policy statements, the need to avoid unwarranted sentencing disparities, and the need to provide restitution to victims. And the Act nonetheless requires judges to impose sentences that reflect the seriousness of the offense, promote respect for the law, provide just punishment, afford adequate deterrence, protect the public, and effectively provide the defendant with needed educational or vocational training and medical care.

Moreover, despite the absence of § 3553(b)(1), the Act continues to provide for appeals from sentencing decisions * * * . We concede that the excision of § 3553(b)(1) requires the excision of a different, appeals-related section, namely § 3742(e), which sets forth standards of review on appeal. * * *

Excision of § 3742(e), however, does not pose a critical problem for the handling of appeals. That is because, as we have previously held, a statute that does not *explicitly* set forth a standard of review may nonetheless do so *implicitly*. We infer appropriate review standards from related statutory language, the structure of the statute, and the "sound administration of justice." And in this instance those factors, in addition to the past two decades of appellate practice in cases involving departures, imply a practical standard of review already familiar to appellate courts: review for "unreasonableness."

4.   *The "new" Court's take on the Apprendi revolution.* As the preceding materials demonstrate, five justices—Stevens, Scalia, Souter, Thomas, and Ginsburg—were responsible for the sentencing "revolution" begun with *Apprendi*. Chief Justice Rehnquist, and Justices Breyer, Kennedy, and O'Connor opposed constitutionalization of the law. But, after *Booker*, two of the four dissenters—the Chief Justice who died, and Justice O'Connor who retired—were replaced by Chief Justice Roberts and Justice Alito, respectively. And, three of the "majority" justices (Souter, Stevens, and Scalia) are no longer on the Court, replaced by Sonia Sotomayor, Elena Kagan, and a justice not yet determined at the time this casebook went to press.

New justices Roberts and Alito had their first opportunity to rule on an *Apprendi* issue in Cunningham v. California, 549 U.S. 270, 127 S.Ct. 856, 166 L.Ed.2d 856 (2007), a case involving the constitutionality of California's determinate sentencing law. In *Cunningham*, Justice Ginsburg delivered an opinion in which the new Chief Justice joined the pro-*Apprendi* "regulars" (Stevens, Scalia, Souter, and Thomas) to declare the California law unconstitutional. Justice Alito dissented in *Cunningham*, along with anti-*Apprendi* justices Kennedy and Breyer.

Of additional interest in *Cunningham* is a separate dissenting opinion authored by Justice Kennedy and joined by Justice Breyer, which stated in part:

> In my view the *Apprendi* line of cases remains incorrect. Yet there may be a principled rationale permitting those cases to control within the central sphere of their concern, while reducing the collateral, widespread harm to the criminal justice system and the corrections process now resulting from the Court's wooden, unyielding insistence on expanding the *Apprendi* doctrine far beyond its necessary boundaries. * * *
>
> As dissenting opinions have suggested before, the Constitution ought not to be interpreted to strike down all aspects of sentencing systems that grant judicial discretion with some legislative direction and control. Judges and legislators must have the capacity to develop consistent standards, standards that individual juries empaneled for only a short time cannot elaborate in any permanent way. Judges and sentencing officials have a broad view and long-term commitment to correctional systems. Juries do not. Judicial officers and corrections professionals, under the guidance and control of the legislature, should be encouraged to participate in an ongoing manner to improve the various sentencing schemes in our country.
>
> This system of guided discretion would be permitted to a large extent if the Court confined the *Apprendi* rule to sentencing enhancements based on the nature of the offense. These would include, for example, the fact that a weapon was used; violence was employed; a stated amount of drugs or other contraband was involved; or the crime was motivated by the victim's race, gender, or other status protected by statute. Juries could consider these matters without serious disruption because these factors often are part of the statutory definition of an aggravated crime in any event and because the evidence to support these enhancements is likely to be a central part of the prosecution's case.
>
> On the other hand, judicial determination is appropriate with regard to factors exhibited by the defendant. These would include, for example, prior convictions; cooperation or noncooperation with law enforcement; remorse or the lack of it; or other aspects of the defendant's history bearing upon his background and contribution to the community. This is so even if the relevant facts were to be found by the judge by a preponderance of the evidence. These are facts that should be taken into account at sentencing but have little if any significance for whether the defendant committed the crime. See Berman & Bibas, Making Sentencing Sensible, 4 Ohio St. J.Crim.L. 37, 55–57 (2006).

The majority's only response to Justice Kennedy's suggestion was to indicate in a footnote that "*Apprendi* itself * * * leaves no room for the bifurcated approach Justice Kennedy proposes." This seems correct—the *Apprendi* rule applies to "any" fact that increases the penalty for a crime beyond the maximum sentence—but do you find Kennedy's suggestion a good middle approach?

5. *So, what does it mean to say that the Guidelines are now advisory?* What does this *really* mean as a practical matter? How is a district court supposed to use the "advisory" Guidelines? If the judge rejects the "advice" of the Guidelines, how is an appellate court supposed to evaluate the sentencing judge's departure from them? Justice Breyer provided the Court's first answer to such questions in *Booker* itself—essentially, "review for 'unreasonableness.' "

In 2007, the Supreme Court provided more guidance. First, in Rita v. United States, 551 U.S. 338, 127 S.Ct. 2456, 168 L.Ed.2d 203 (2007), the Court held that the law "permits" a court of appeal to "presume that a sentence imposed within a properly calculated United States Sentencing Guideline range is a reasonable sentence." However, Justice Breyer, writing for six members of the Court (Chief Justice Roberts and Justices Stevens, Kennedy, Ginsburg and Alito joined), explained that this presumption of reasonableness is *not* binding:

> It does not, like a trial-related evidentiary presumption, insist that one side, or the other, shoulder a particular burden of persuasion or proof lest they lose their case. Nor does the presumption reflect strong judicial deference of the kind that leads appeals courts to grant greater factfinding leeway to an expert agency than to a district judge. Rather, the presumption reflects the fact that, by the time an appeals court is considering a within-Guidelines sentence on review, *both* the sentencing judge and the Sentencing Commission will have reached the *same* conclusion as to the proper sentence in the particular case. That double determination significantly increases the likelihood that the sentence is a reasonable one.

Justice Breyer warned, however, that a "nonbinding appellate presumption that a Guidelines sentence is reasonable does not *require* the sentencing judge to impose that sentence."

Then, in Gall v. United States, 552 U.S. 38, 128 S.Ct. 586, 169 L.Ed.2d 445 (2007), the Supreme Court had the opportunity to consider a case in which a judge did *not* sentence a defendant within the Guidelines. In the case, defendant Gall pleaded guilty to participating in an ongoing conspiracy to distribute the controlled substance "Ecstasy" while he was a University of Iowa college student. Although Gall participated in the conspiracy for approximately six months, he voluntarily withdrew from it, graduated from the university, obtained gainful employment, and thereafter led a crime-free life until he was arrested for his years-earlier participation in the criminal enterprise. A presentence report recommended that Gall receive a sentence of 30-to-37 months in prison, but the judge instead sentenced the defendant to 36 months' probation, finding that probation reflected the seriousness of his offense, and that a prison sentence was unnecessary in light of Gall's voluntary withdrawal from the conspiracy and his "self-rehabilitation." The Eighth Circuit reversed this sentence, ruling that any sentence outside the Guidelines range must be supported by "extraordinary circumstances."

The Supreme Court, in turn, reversed the Eighth Circuit. In an opinion delivered by Justice Stevens and joined by all but two dissenters (Justices Thomas and Alito), the Court stated:

> As a result of our decision [in *Booker*], the Guidelines are now advisory, and appellate review of sentencing decisions is limited to determining whether they are reasonable. Our explanation of reasonableness review in the *Booker* opinion made it pellucidly clear that the familiar abuse-of-discretion standard of review now applies to appellate review of sentencing decisions.
>
> It is also clear that a district judge must give serious consideration to the extent of any departure from the Guidelines and must explain his conclusion that an unusually lenient or an unusually harsh sentence is appropriate in a particular case with sufficient justifications. For even though the Guidelines are advisory rather than mandatory, they are * * * the product of careful study based on extensive empirical evidence derived from the review of thousands of individual sentencing decisions.
>
> In reviewing the reasonableness of a sentence outside the Guidelines range, appellate courts may therefore take the degree of variance into account and consider the extent of a deviation from the Guidelines. We reject, however, an appellate rule that requires extraordinary circumstances to justify a sentence outside the Guidelines range. We also reject the use of a rigid mathematical formula that uses the percentage of a departure as the standard for determining the strength of the justifications required for a specific sentence. * * *
>
> As we explained in *Rita*, a district court should begin all sentencing proceedings by correctly calculating the applicable Guidelines range. As a matter of administration and to secure nationwide consistency, the Guidelines should be the starting point and the initial benchmark. The Guidelines are not the only consideration, however. Accordingly, after giving both parties an opportunity to argue for whatever sentence they deem appropriate, the district judge should then consider all of the § 3553(a) factors to determine whether they support the sentence requested by a party.[6]

---

[6]   Section 3553(a) lists seven factors that a sentencing court must consider. The first factor is a broad command to consider the nature and circumstances of the offense and the history and

In so doing, he may not presume that the Guidelines range is reasonable. He must make an individualized assessment based on the facts presented. If he decides that an outside-Guidelines sentence is warranted, he must consider the extent of the deviation and ensure that the justification is sufficiently compelling to support the degree of the variance. We find it uncontroversial that a major departure should be supported by a more significant justification than a minor one. After settling on the appropriate sentence, he must adequately explain the chosen sentence to allow for meaningful appellate review and to promote the perception of fair sentencing.

Regardless of whether the sentence imposed is inside or outside the Guidelines range, the appellate court must review the sentence under an abuse-of-discretion standard. It must first ensure that the district court committed no significant procedural error, such as failing to calculate (or improperly calculating) the Guidelines range, treating the Guidelines as mandatory, failing to consider the § 3553(a) factors, selecting a sentence based on clearly erroneous facts, or failing to adequately explain the chosen sentence—including an explanation for any deviation from the Guidelines range. Assuming that the district court's sentencing decision is procedurally sound, the appellate court should then consider the substantive reasonableness of the sentence imposed under an abuse-of-discretion standard. When conducting this review, the court will, of course, take into account the totality of the circumstances, including the extent of any variance from the Guidelines range. If the sentence is within the Guidelines range, the appellate court may, but is not required to, apply a presumption of reasonableness. But if the sentence is outside the Guidelines range, the court may not apply a presumption of unreasonableness. It may consider the extent of the deviation, but must give due deference to the district court's decision that the § 3553(a) factors, on a whole,

---

characteristics of the defendant. The second factor requires the consideration of the general purposes of sentencing, including:

the need for the sentence imposed—

(A) to reflect the seriousness of the offense, to promote respect for the law, and to provide just punishment for the offense;

(B) to afford adequate deterrence to criminal conduct;

(C) to protect the public from further crimes of the defendant; and

(D) to provide the defendant with needed educational or vocational training, medical care, or other correctional treatment in the most effective manner.

The third factor pertains to the kinds of sentences available; the fourth to the Sentencing Guidelines; the fifth to any relevant policy statement issued by the Sentencing Commission; the sixth to the need to avoid unwarranted sentence disparities; and the seventh to the need to provide restitution to any victim. Preceding this list is a general directive to impose a sentence sufficient, but not greater than necessary, to comply with the purposes of sentencing described in the second factor. The fact that § 3553(a) explicitly directs sentencing courts to consider the Guidelines supports the premise that district courts must begin their analysis with the Guidelines and remain cognizant of them throughout the sentencing process.

justify the extent of the variance. The fact that the appellate court might reasonably have concluded that a different sentence was appropriate is insufficient to justify reversal of the district court.

Practical considerations also underlie this legal principle. The sentencing judge is in a superior position to find facts and judge their import under § 3553(a) in the individual case. The judge sees and hears the evidence, makes credibility determinations, has full knowledge of the facts and gains insights not conveyed by the record. The sentencing judge has access to, and greater familiarity with, the individual case and the individual defendant before him than the Commission or the appeals court. Moreover, [d]istrict courts have an institutional advantage over appellate courts in making these sorts of determinations, especially as they see so many more Guidelines sentences than appellate courts do.

The Supreme Court held that the sentence imposed by the District Court here was a reasonable one and satisfied the abuse-of-discretion standard of review.

6.   *More on the role of rehabilitation in sentencing in the post-*Booker *world.* In the last Note (*Gall*), the Supreme Court held that a district court judge's sentence outside the Guidelines, based in part on the defendant's "self-rehabilitation" *before arrest*, was not unreasonable.

Consider this different scenario: A defendant's sentence is set aside on appeal, and by the time of re-sentencing, there is evidence of his *post-sentencing* rehabilitation. May the judge consider *this* evidence to support a *downward* variance from the Guidelines? In Pepper v. United States, 562 U.S. 476, 131 S.Ct. 1229, 179 L.Ed.2d 196 (2011), Justice Sotomayor described the post-sentencing facts of the case this way:

> At the time of his initial sentencing in 2004, Pepper was a 25-year-old drug addict who was unemployed, estranged from his family, and had recently sold drugs as part of a methamphetamine conspiracy. By the time of his * * * resentencing in 2009, Pepper had been drug-free for nearly five years, had attended college and achieved high grades, was a top employee at his job slated for a promotion, had re-established a relationship with his father, and was married and supporting his wife's daughter.

The trial judge took these facts into consideration in his downward variance, but the Eighth Circuit reversed, ruling in part that the Sentencing Reform Act and a specific sentencing guideline prohibited the district court's consideration of the defendant's post-sentencing rehabilitation.

The Supreme Court reversed. It held, 6–2, that in view of the fact *Booker* (p. 1451, Note 2) rendered the Federal Sentencing Guidelines advisory rather than mandatory, a downward variance can be supported by evidence of post-sentencing rehabilitation. Justice Sotomayor, writing for the majority, quoted *Williams v. New York* (p. 1407):

"It has been uniform and constant in the federal judicial tradition for the sentencing judge to consider every convicted person as an individual and every case as a unique study in the human failings that sometimes mitigate, sometimes magnify, the crime and the punishment to ensure." Underlying this tradition is the principle that "the punishment should fit the offender and not merely the crime."

* * * In particular, we have emphasized that "[h]ighly relevant—if not essential—to [the] selection of an appropriate sentence is the possession of the fullest information possible concerning the defendant's life and characteristics."

Justices Breyer and Alito wrote concurring opinions expressing concern with the language in the Sotomayor opinion. Breyer stated that citation to *Williams* was unhelpful: "That is because Congress in the Sentencing Reform Act of 1984—the law before us—disavowed the individualized approach to sentencing that that case followed." To Justice Breyer, the "question is whether a sentencing judge may *sometimes* take account of a (resentenced) offender's postsentencing rehabilitation—despite a Guideline policy statement that says *never*. I would find it reasonable for a judge to disregard the Guidelines' absolute prohibition" in a case of the sort presented here.

Justice Alito's partial concurrence and partial dissent was sharper in tone and suggested where his thoughts might be going:

Anyone familiar with the history of criminal sentencing in this country cannot fail to see the irony in the Court's praise for the sentencing scheme exemplified by *Williams*. By the time of the enactment of the Sentencing Reform Act in 1984, this scheme had fallen into widespread disrepute. * * *

Some language in today's opinion reads like a paean to that old regime, and I fear that it may be interpreted as sanctioning a move back toward a system that prevailed prior to 1984. If that occurs, I suspect that the day will come when the irrationality of that system is once again seen, and perhaps then the entire *Booker* line of cases will be reexamined.

7. *Concurrent versus consecutive sentences: The Apprendi revolution stalls.* In Oregon v. Ice, 555 U.S. 160, 129 S.Ct. 711, 172 L.Ed.2d 517 (2009), the Supreme Court considered a new *Apprendi* issue. Under Oregon law, a defendant tried and convicted of multiple offenses could not be sentenced to consecutive (instead of concurrent) sentences unless the judge—not a jury—found certain facts specified by statute. In *Ice*, the judge made such a factual finding, which resulted in an increase in the defendant's effective sentence from 90 months (his sentence if his convictions were served concurrently) to 340 months.

The Supreme Court, 5–4, held that the Oregon law, and thus the sentence Ice received, did *not* violate the Sixth Amendment. Justice Ginsburg explained why the majority refused to extend *Apprendi* to this situation:

> Most States continue the common-law tradition: They entrust to judges' unfettered discretion the decision whether sentences for discrete offenses shall be served consecutively or concurrently. In some States, sentences for multiple offenses are presumed to run consecutively, but sentencing judges may order concurrent sentences upon finding cause therefor. Other States, including Oregon, constrain judges' discretion by requiring them to find certain facts before imposing consecutive, rather than concurrent, sentences. It is undisputed that States may proceed on the first two tracks without transgressing the Sixth Amendment. The sole issue in dispute, then, is whether the Sixth Amendment, as construed in *Apprendi* and *Blakely*, precludes the mode of proceeding chosen by Oregon and several of her sister States. We hold, in light of historical practice and the authority of States over administration of their criminal justice systems, that the Sixth Amendment does not exclude Oregon's choice. * * *

> The Federal Constitution's jury-trial guarantee assigns the determination of certain facts to the jury's exclusive province. Under that guarantee, this Court held in *Apprendi*, "any fact that increases the penalty for a crime beyond the prescribed statutory maximum must be submitted to a jury, and proved beyond a reasonable doubt."

> [Justice Ginsburg summarized the *Apprendi* case law.] All of these decisions involved sentencing for a discrete crime, not—as here—for multiple offenses different in character or committed at different times.

> Our application of *Apprendi*'s rule must honor the "longstanding common-law practice" in which the rule is rooted. The rule's animating principle is the preservation of the jury's historic role as a bulwark between the State and the accused at the trial for an alleged offense. Guided by that principle, our opinions make clear that the Sixth Amendment does not countenance legislative encroachment on the jury's traditional domain. We accordingly considered whether the finding of a particular fact was understood as within "the domain of the jury * * * by those who framed the Bill of Rights." In undertaking this inquiry, we remain cognizant that administration of a discrete criminal justice system is among the basic sovereign prerogatives States retain.

> These twin considerations—historical practice and respect for state sovereignty—counsel against extending *Apprendi*'s rule to the imposition of sentences for discrete crimes. The decision to impose sentences consecutively is not within the jury function that "extends

down centuries into the common law." Instead, specification of the regime for administering multiple sentences has long been considered the prerogative of state legislatures. * * *

In light of this history, legislative reforms regarding the imposition of multiple sentences do not implicate the core concerns that prompted our decision in *Apprendi*. There is no encroachment here by the judge upon facts historically found by the jury, nor any threat to the jury's domain as a bulwark at trial between the State and the accused. Instead, the defendant—who historically may have faced consecutive sentences by default—has been granted by some modern legislatures statutory protections meant to temper the harshness of the historical practice.

Justice Scalia, with whom Chief Justice Roberts and Justices Souter and Thomas joined, would have none of it:

The rule of *Apprendi* is clear: Any fact—other than that of a prior conviction—that increases the maximum punishment to which a defendant may be sentenced must be admitted by the defendant or proved beyond a reasonable doubt to a jury. Oregon's sentencing scheme allows judges rather than juries to find the facts necessary to commit defendants to longer prison sentences, and thus directly contradicts what we held eight years ago and have reaffirmed several times since. The Court's justification of Oregon's scheme is a virtual copy of the dissents in those cases. * * *

* * * [T]he Court attempts to distinguish Oregon's sentencing scheme by reasoning that the rule of *Apprendi* applies only to the length of a sentence for an individual crime and not to the total sentence for a defendant. I cannot understand why we would make such a strange exception to the treasured right of trial by jury. Neither the reasoning of the *Apprendi* line of cases, nor any distinctive history of the factfinding necessary to imposition of consecutive sentences, nor (of course) logic supports such an odd rule.

We have taken pains to reject artificial limitations upon the facts subject to the jury-trial guarantee. We long ago made clear that the guarantee turns upon the penal consequences attached to the fact, and not to its formal definition as an element of the crime. *Mullaney v. Wilbur*, [p. 1416, Note 1]. * * *

This rule leaves no room for a formalistic distinction between facts bearing on the number of years of imprisonment that a defendant will serve for one count (subject to the rule of *Apprendi*) and facts bearing on how many years will be served in total (now not subject to *Apprendi*). * * * The decision to impose consecutive sentences alters the single consequence most important to convicted noncapital defendants: their date of release from prison. For many defendants, the difference between consecutive and concurrent sentences is more important than a jury verdict of innocence on any single count: Two consecutive 10-year sentences are in most circumstances a more severe punishment than any number of concurrent 10-year sentences.

To support its distinction-without-a-difference, the Court puts forward the same (the *very* same) arguments regarding the history of sentencing that were rejected by *Apprendi*. Here, it is entirely irrelevant that common-law judges had discretion to impose either consecutive or concurrent sentences, just as there it was entirely irrelevant that common-law judges had discretion to impose greater or lesser sentences (within the prescribed statutory maximum) for individual convictions. * * * Our concern here is precisely the same as our concern in *Apprendi*: What happens when a State breaks from the common-law practice of discretionary sentences and permits the imposition of an elevated sentence only upon the showing of extraordinary facts? In such a system, the defendant "is *entitled* to" the lighter sentence "and by reason of the Sixth Amendment[,] the facts bearing upon that entitlement must be found by a jury." *Blakely.* * * *

* * * The Court's reliance upon a distinction without a difference, and its repeated exhumation of arguments dead and buried by prior cases, seems to me the epitome of [an unprincipled rationale]. Today's opinion muddies the waters, and gives cause to doubt whether the Court is willing to stand by *Apprendi*'s interpretation of the Sixth Amendment jury-trial guarantee.

8.   *Apprendi and criminal fines.* Do the principles of *Apprendi* apply to criminal fines, or only to sentences of incarceration and death? The Court answered that question in Southern Union Co. v. United States, 567 U.S. ___, 132 S.Ct. 2344, 183 L.Ed.2d 318 (2012).

In *Southern Union*, the defendant corporation was convicted by a jury of violation of a federal environmental criminal statute that barred the knowing storing of liquid mercury without a permit. Violations of the statute were punishable by, among other things, a fine of $50,000 for each day of the violation. The trial judge concluded from the "content and context of the verdict all together"—the jury was never required to render a finding in this regard—that the jury found a 762-day violation and, therefore, fined the corporation according to that assumption. The Supreme Court, per Justice Sotomayor, ruled, 6–3, that *Apprendi* applies to fines:

[W]e see no principled basis under *Apprendi* for treating criminal fines differently [than punishment by imprisonment or death]. *Apprendi*'s "core concern" is to reserve to the jury "the determination of facts that warrant punishment for a specific statutory offense." That concern applies whether the sentence is a criminal fine or imprisonment or death. * * * [T]he amount of a fine, like the maximum term of imprisonment or eligibility for the death penalty, is often calculated by reference to particular facts. Sometimes, as here, the fact is the duration of a statutory violation; under other statutes it is the amount of the defendant's gain or victim's loss, or some other factor. In all such cases, requiring juries to find beyond a reasonable doubt facts that determine the fine's maximum amount is necessary to implement *Apprendi*'s "animating principle": the "preservation of the jury's historic role as a bulwark between the State and the accused at the trial for an alleged offense."

The justices who have previously demonstrated dislike for *Apprendi*—Justices Breyer, Kennedy, and Alito—dissented, contending that "the Sixth Amendment permits a sentencing judge to determine sentencing facts—facts that are not elements of the crime but are relevant only to the amount of the fine the judge will impose."

2. JUDICIAL VINDICTIVENESS IN SENTENCING

NORTH CAROLINA V. PEARCE

Supreme Court of the United States, 1969.
395 U.S. 711, 89 S.Ct. 2072, 23 L.Ed.2d 656.

MR. JUSTICE STEWART delivered the opinion of the Court [joined by CHIEF JUSTICE WARREN and JUSTICES DOUGLAS, BRENNAN, and MARSHALL].

When at the behest of the defendant a criminal conviction has been set aside and a new trial ordered, to what extent does the Constitution limit the imposition of a harsher sentence after conviction upon retrial? That is the question presented by these two cases.

In No. 413 the respondent Pearce was convicted in a North Carolina court upon a charge of assault with intent to commit rape. The trial judge sentenced him to prison for a term of 12 to 15 years. Several years later he initiated a state post-conviction proceeding which culminated in the reversal of his conviction by the Supreme Court of North Carolina, upon the ground that an involuntary confession had unconstitutionally been admitted in evidence against him. He was retried, convicted, and sentenced by the trial judge to an eight-year prison term, which, when added to the time Pearce had already spent in prison, the parties agree amounted to a longer total sentence than that originally imposed. * * *

In No. 418 the respondent Rice pleaded guilty in an Alabama trial court to four separate charges of second-degree burglary. He was sentenced to prison terms aggregating 10 years. Two and one-half years later the judgments were set aside in a state * * * proceeding, upon the ground that Rice had not been accorded his constitutional right to counsel. He was retried upon three of the charges, convicted, and sentenced to prison terms aggregating 25 years. No credit was given for the time he had spent in prison on the original judgments. * * *

The problem before us involves two related but analytically separate issues. One concerns the constitutional limitations upon the imposition of a more severe punishment after conviction for the same offense upon retrial. The other is the more limited question whether, in computing the new sentence, the Constitution requires that credit must be given for that part of the original sentence already served. * * *

We turn first to the more limited aspect of the question before us— whether the Constitution requires that, in computing the sentence imposed after conviction upon retrial, credit must be given for time served under the original sentence. [The Court held that the double jeopardy bar on "multiple punishments" for the same charge required that credit be given.] * * *

II.

* * * We turn * * * to consideration of the broader problem of what constitutional limitations there may be upon the general power of a judge to impose upon reconviction a longer prison sentence than the defendant originally received. * * *

* * * A trial judge is not constitutionally precluded * * * from imposing a new sentence, whether greater or less than the original sentence, in the light of events subsequent to the first trial that may have thrown new light upon the defendant's "life, health, habits, conduct, and mental and moral propensities." Such information may come to the judge's attention from evidence adduced at the second trial itself, from a new presentence investigation, from the defendant's prison record, or possibly from other sources. The freedom of a sentencing judge to consider the defendant's conduct subsequent to the first conviction in imposing a new sentence is no more than consonant with the principle, fully approved in *Williams v. New York*, [p. 1407], that a State may adopt the "prevalent modern philosophy of penology that the punishment should fit the offender and not merely the crime."

To say that there exists no absolute constitutional bar to the imposition of a more severe sentence upon retrial is not, however, to end the inquiry. There remains for consideration the impact of the Due Process Clause of the Fourteenth Amendment.

It can hardly be doubted that it would be a flagrant violation of the Fourteenth Amendment for a state trial court to follow an announced practice of imposing a heavier sentence upon every reconvicted defendant for the explicit purpose of punishing the defendant for his having succeeded in getting his original conviction set aside. Where, as in each of the cases before us, the original conviction has been set aside because of a constitutional error, the imposition of such a punishment, "penalizing those who choose to exercise" constitutional rights, "would be patently unconstitutional." And the very threat inherent in the existence of such a punitive policy would, with respect to those still in prison, serve to "chill the exercise of basic constitutional rights." But even if the first conviction has been set aside for nonconstitutional error, the imposition of a penalty upon the defendant for having successfully pursued a statutory right of appeal or collateral remedy would be no less a violation of due process of law. * * * A court is "without right to * * * put a price on an appeal. A defendant's exercise of a right of appeal must be free and unfettered. * * * [I]t is unfair to use the great power given to the court to determine sentence to place a defendant in the dilemma of making an unfree choice." * * *

Due process of law, then, requires that vindictiveness against a defendant for having successfully attacked his first conviction must play no part in the sentence he receives after a new trial. And since the fear of such vindictiveness may unconstitutionally deter a defendant's exercise of the right to appeal or collaterally attack his first conviction, due process also requires that a defendant be freed of apprehension of such a retaliatory motivation on the part of the sentencing judge.

In order to assure the absence of such a motivation, we have concluded that whenever a judge imposes a more severe sentence upon a defendant after a new trial, the reasons for his doing so must affirmatively appear. Those reasons must be based upon objective information concerning identifiable conduct on the part of the defendant occurring after the time of the original sentencing proceeding. And the factual data upon which the increased sentence is based must be made part of the record, so that the constitutional legitimacy of the increased sentence may be fully reviewed on appeal.

We dispose of the two cases before us in the light of these conclusions. [The Court found that no effort was made by the State in either case to justify the more severe sentences imposed. Therefore, the sentences violated the due process clause]. * * *

[JUSTICE DOUGLAS, with whom JUSTICE MARSHALL concurred, "agree[d] with the Court as to the reach of due process." JUSTICES BLACK and HARLAN, in separate opinions, concurred in part and dissented in part.]

MR. JUSTICE WHITE, concurring in part.

I join the Court's opinion except that in my view [the Court] should authorize an increased sentence on retrial based on any objective, identifiable factual data not known to the trial judge at the time of the original sentencing proceeding.

[The Court had only eight members when *Pearce* was decided.]

NOTES AND QUESTIONS

1.   *Actual versus presumed vindictiveness.* As the Supreme Court now explains *Pearce*, the rule announced in that case only creates a rebuttable presumption of vindictiveness. In Wasman v. United States, 468 U.S. 559, 104 S.Ct. 3217, 82 L.Ed.2d 424 (1984) Chief Justice Burger explained *Pearce* this way:

> If it was not clear from the Court's holding in *Pearce*, it is clear from our subsequent cases applying *Pearce* that due process does not in any sense forbid enhanced sentences or charges, but only enhancement motivated by *actual vindictiveness* toward the defendant for having exercised guaranteed rights. In [*North Carolina v.*] *Pearce* and *Blackledge* [*v. Perry*] [p. 907], the Court "presumed" that the increased sentence * * * [was] the product[ ] of actual vindictiveness aroused by the defendants' appeals. It held that the defendants' right to due process was violated not because the sentence[s] * * * were enhanced, but because there was no evidence introduced to rebut the presumption that actual vindictiveness was behind the increases; in other words, by operation of law, the increases were deemed motivated by vindictiveness. In [various post-*Pearce* cases] * * *—where the presumption was held not to apply—we made clear that a due process violation could be established only by proof of actual vindictiveness.

> In sum, where the presumption applies, the sentencing authority * * * must rebut the presumption that an increased sentence * * * resulted from vindictiveness; where the presumption does not apply, the defendant must affirmatively prove actual vindictiveness.

2.   *When does the presumption of vindictiveness apply?* No sooner did the Supreme Court decide *Pearce* than it began to find circumstances in which the presumption of vindictiveness does not apply. The Court limited the application of the *Pearce* rule to those circumstances in which there is a " 'reasonable likelihood' " that the increase in sentence is the product of actual vindictiveness on the part of the sentencing authority." Alabama v. Smith, 490 U.S. 794, 109 S.Ct. 2201, 104 L.Ed.2d 865 (1989) (quoting United States v. Goodwin, 457 U.S. 368, 102 S.Ct. 2485, 73 L.Ed.2d 74 (1982)).

For example, in Chaffin v. Stynchcombe, 412 U.S. 17, 93 S.Ct. 1977, 36 L.Ed.2d 714 (1973), the Court rejected the implementation of the *Pearce* rule in a case of jury sentencing. The Court said that the possibility of vindictiveness in such circumstances was "de minimis." As the Court has explained *Chaffin*, "[n]ot only was the second jury * * * unaware of the prior conviction, but in contrast to the judge * * * in *Pearce* * * *, it was thought unlikely that a jury would consider itself to have a 'personal stake' in a prior conviction or a 'motivation to engage in self-vindication.'" Wasman v. United States, 468 U.S. 559, 104 S.Ct. 3217, 82 L.Ed.2d 424 (1984).

Likewise, in Texas v. McCullough, 475 U.S. 134, 106 S.Ct. 976, 89 L.Ed.2d 104 (1986), the Supreme Court stated that the presumption was inapplicable because of "different sentencers"—a jury at the first trial, and a judge at the post-appeal second trial.

And, in Alabama v. Smith, 490 U.S. 794, 109 S.Ct. 2201, 104 L.Ed.2d 865 (1989), the Court overruled *Simpson v. Rice*, the companion case to *Pearce*. In *Smith*, as with *Rice*, the defendant pleaded guilty, succeeded in having his plea vacated on appeal, and then received a longer sentence after a subsequent trial and conviction. The Court ruled that "when a greater penalty is imposed after trial than was imposed after a prior guilty plea, the increase in sentence is not more likely than not attributable to the vindictiveness on the part of the sentencing judge."

3. *Overcoming the presumption.* When the *Pearce* presumption *does* apply, how may it be rebutted? *Pearce* itself offered an answer: "objective information concerning identifiable conduct on the part of the defendant occurring after the time of the original sentencing proceeding," all set out in the record by the sentencing judge at the second trial. Many observers and lower courts thought that this was the only way the presumption could be rebutted, but this has proven wrong. Here is what the Supreme Court announced in Texas v. McCullough, 475 U.S. 134, 106 S.Ct. 976, 89 L.ed.2d 104 (1986):

> *Pearce* permits "a sentencing authority [to] justify an increased sentence by affirmatively identifying relevant conduct or events that occurred subsequent to the original sentencing proceedings." This language, however, was never intended to describe exhaustively all of the possible circumstances in which a sentence increase could be justified. Restricting justifications for a sentence increase to *only* "events that occurred subsequent to the original sentencing proceedings" could in some circumstances lead to absurd results. The Solicitor General provides the following hypothetical example:
>
>> "Suppose * * * that a defendant is convicted of burglary, a non-violent, and apparently first, offense. He is sentenced to a short prison term or perhaps placed on probation. Following a successful appeal and a conviction on retrial, it is learned that the defendant has been using an alias and in fact has a long criminal record that includes other burglaries, several armed robbery convictions, and a conviction for murder committed in the course of a burglary. None of the reasons underlying *Pearce* in any way justifies the perverse result that the defendant receive no greater sentence in light of this information than he originally received when he was thought to be a first offender."

We agree with the Solicitor General and find nothing in *Pearce* that would require such a bizarre conclusion. Perhaps then the reach of *Pearce* is best captured in our statement in *United States v. Goodwin*, [457 U.S. 368, 102 S.Ct. 2485, 73 L.Ed.2d 74 (1982)]:

> "In sum, the Court [in *Pearce*] applied a presumption of vindictiveness, which may be overcome only by objective information * * * justifying the increased sentence."

Nothing in the Constitution requires a judge to ignore "objective information * * * justifying the increased sentence."

CHAPTER 18

DOUBLE JEOPARDY

■ ■ ■

"[N]o man is to be brought into jeopardy of his life, more than once, for the same offence." 4 W. Blackstone, Commentaries *329.

Introductory Comment

We can trace the right against double jeopardy to the ancient Greeks and Romans. A maxim found its way into church canons as early as 847 A.D. that "[n]ot even God judges twice for the same act." Early double jeopardy pleas in English law appear around 1200. The evolution of the common law of double jeopardy from that time until Blackstone is complex because of the overlapping systems of royal and ecclesiastical courts, as well as the diverging of tort remedies from criminal penalties. By the middle of the eighteenth century, however, Blackstone could write with confidence of the "universal maxim of the common law of England, that no man is to be brought into jeopardy of his life, more than once, for the same offence." 4 W. Blackstone, Commentaries *329.

Blackstone's language found its way, little changed, into the Fifth Amendment to the United States Constitution: "[N]or shall any person be subject for the same offence to be twice put in jeopardy of life or limb." Other than adding "or limb" to "life," the double jeopardy clause is substantively identical to Blackstone's maxim. Thus, it seems likely that the Framers meant to constitutionalize the English pleas of former conviction and former acquittal as jeopardy bars.

The right against double jeopardy was once a right of great importance, but it offers less protection today. In Blackstone's world, few common law crimes existed, and application of double jeopardy was easy and powerful. As Blackstone noted, a conviction of manslaughter barred an indictment for murder. But those were the only two felony homicide offenses in Blackstone's day. Today, a single criminal act often violates several criminal statutes and, as you will see, the Court's test for what is the "same offense" provides little protection. Defendants rarely win a double jeopardy claim when the prosecutor charges statutes that are facially different.

Moreover, a single criminal "event" can give rise to different counts of the same statutory offense based on different acts—*e.g.*, robbery of six victims standing close together. The Court's doctrine almost always permits multiple convictions based on multiple acts.

To be sure, prosecutors sometimes re-charge the same statutory offense based on the same act. Knowing of course about double jeopardy, prosecutors do this only when they believe the original trial did not end in a way that constituted a jeopardy bar. Convictions not vacated on appeal and acquittals are a jeopardy bar to another trial for the same offense. But mistrials and dismissals are not an obvious end to jeopardy and, indeed, the Court rarely permits those outcome to bar a new trial.

Modern double jeopardy protection has been further undermined by the Court's so-called "dual sovereignty" doctrine. The Court has concluded that Indian tribes, all fifty states, and the federal government are different sovereigns for the purpose of prosecuting crime. Thus, South Dakota, Minnesota, the Rosebud Sioux tribe, and the federal government could all prosecute the same crime—say, conspiracy to rob a federally-insured bank located off the reservation in South Dakota where the agreement occurred on the reservation and an overt act occurred in Minnesota.

What was once a formidable bar to government excess has now become largely a parlor game in which we pretty much know that the defendant will lose unless the prosecutor or judge makes a serious error. But lawyers must learn enough about double jeopardy law to know when a serious error has been made. Moreover, most states and the Justice Department provide broader double jeopardy protection than the Court has found in the Constitution. These protections draw on the same concepts that underlie the Court's doctrine.[a]

We begin with the "same offense" problem because all but one double jeopardy dimension crucially depends on the relevant offenses being the same offense.[b] If *X* robs *A* on Tuesday and *B* on Wednesday, or rapes *C* on Thursday and returns to kill her on Friday, double jeopardy will have nothing to say about trials or punishments for these separate crimes. But if *X* rapes and kills *C*, and the felony murder charge is based on the rape, ah, that is a harder question.

---

[a]   For a fuller elaboration of the history and doctrine of double jeopardy law, see George C. Thomas III, Double Jeopardy: The History, The Law (1998).

[b]   The one dimension that is indifferent to the "same offense" question is collateral estoppel. See *Ashe v. Swenson*, p. 1498.

A. THE "SAME OFFENSE" SARGASSO SEA

This Is Really Hard: Some Background Principles

"While the Clause itself simply states that no person shall 'be subject for the same offense to be twice put in jeopardy of life or limb,' the decisional law in the area is a veritable Sargasso Sea which could not fail to challenge the most intrepid judicial navigator." Albernaz v. United States, 450 U.S. 333, 101 S.Ct. 1137, 67 L.Ed.2d 275 (1981). Part of the Sargasso Sea is evaluating "sameness" in different statutory offenses, or in multiple counts of a single statutory offense. It is perhaps the most difficult double jeopardy issue, in part because the Court has not developed a clear, coherent set of principles, and in part because what might appear to be one question potentially contains a range of sub-issues.

The most obvious "same offense" question can be called the "definitional" question. For example, does the statutory offense of auto theft *define* the same double jeopardy offense as the statutory offense of joyriding? This question requires examining the elements of the statutory offenses.

In addition to the definitional question is what can be called the "unit of prosecution" issue. It is obvious that robbery is the same *definitional* offense as robbery. But what if the defendant, as in *Ashe v. Swenson*, p. 1498, robbed six victims in rapid succession? The Court noted in *Ashe* that six different robberies are six different "offenses" for purposes of double jeopardy. This question is largely (if not entirely) a substantive criminal law question. It requires that a court define carefully the scope of the proscribed conduct, and the purpose of the statutory offense, and lay the defendant's conduct over that definition to see how many "units" have occurred. Because robbery is designed to protect the safety and property of potential victims, each victim should constitute a different unit of prosecution, as *Ashe* suggested.

Two factors make the "unit of prosecution" analysis difficult. First, the scope of the substantive offense is often fuzzy. Battery, for example, is often defined as "offensive touching." If *D* grabs *V* by the arm and simultaneously hits *V* in the nose with his fist, is this one offensive touching or two? This is more difficult than the robbery example because in a sense the grabbing of *V*'s arm is incidental to, or subsumed within, the punch. When asked later how the battery was committed against him, *V* will almost certainly talk about the punch to the nose and not about being grabbed by the arm. Also making *V*'s case different from the robbery victims in *Ashe* is that *V* is the only victim of the offense. Yet a thug who commits many acts of violence on a single victim is surely guilty of more than one offense. Finding a principle, or even a norm, to guide this inquiry is extremely difficult.

The second problem with the "unit of prosecution" issue is that it can arise in conjunction with the definitional issue, causing courts sometimes to submerge the "unit of prosecution" issue into the definitional issue. Holding that auto theft and joyriding *define* the same double jeopardy offense does not end the "same offense" analysis. Perhaps the defendant operated the vehicle more than once. That would raise a "unit of prosecution" question: Is operating a stolen vehicle more than once a single unit of the "same offense" of auto theft/joyriding?

There are other problems. Because "unit of prosecution" is, at least initially, a question of substantive criminal law, it might seem that the legislature can make the unit as broad or as narrow as it wishes (consistent with due process and the Eighth Amendment prohibition of cruel and unusual punishment). If that is right, then the legislature could create a separate unit of joyriding for each day (or hour or minute) that a car is kept from its owner without permission, and the double jeopardy clause would have nothing to say about this division of conduct. Perhaps legislatively-authorized multiple convictions *in a single trial* pose only a question of proportional punishment. Perhaps double jeopardy is agnostic about the relationship between punishment and culpability. The Court in *Missouri v. Hunter*, p. 1489, has embraced that understanding, limited (so far at least) to multiple convictions in a single trial. Thus, as long as the legislature clearly indicates how it wishes a particular division of conduct divided into offenses, double jeopardy drops out of the picture when the issue is the amount of punishment.

But what if the prosecutor sought to use a narrow joyriding statute to prosecute each day of joyriding in successive trials? Stated differently, does the double jeopardy clause place any limit on how the legislature can define the "unit of prosecution" when the prosecutor is seeking convictions for those separate units in successive trials? The issue now is not the relationship between punishment and culpability but the procedures by which the punishment is imposed. The Court has yet to address the *Missouri v. Hunter* issue in successive prosecutions.

However double jeopardy is finally understood as a limit on the legislature, it clearly limits prosecutors and judges, thus ensuring that they operate within the "same offense" definitions created by the legislature. When this limitation is asserted in the context of a single trial, it is a claim that the judge is imposing too many convictions, and it is often loosely referred to as the "multiple punishment" doctrine. The usage is loose because the protection is against multiple *convictions*, rather than punishments. Two convictions for the same offense are not permitted even if no sentence is attached to one of the convictions. Ball v. United States, 470 U.S. 856, 105 S.Ct. 1668, 84 L.Ed.2d 740 (1985).

If all of this sounds too complicated for mere mortals, the blame belongs at the feet of the Court, not the casebook authors! We begin with one of the Court's first attempts to articulate a substantive vision of "same offense." It was a unanimous Court that included Justices Holmes and Brandeis. Notice that the case involves both the definitional and unit of prosecution issues.

BLOCKBURGER V. UNITED STATES

Supreme Court of the United States, 1932.
284 U.S. 299, 304, 52 S.Ct. 180, 182, 76 L.Ed. 306.

MR. JUSTICE SUTHERLAND delivered the opinion of the Court [joined by CHIEF JUSTICE HUGHES, and JUSTICES HOLMES, VAN DEVANTER, McREYNOLDS, BRANDEIS, BUTLER, STONE, and ROBERTS].

The petitioner was charged with violating [two] provisions of the Harrison Narcotic Act. The indictment contained five counts. The jury returned a verdict against petitioner upon the second, third, and fifth counts only. Each of these counts charged a sale of morphine hydrochloride to the same purchaser. The second count charged a sale on a specified day of ten grains of the drug not in or from the original stamped package; the third count charged a sale on the following day of eight grains of the drug not in or from the original stamped package; the fifth count charged the latter sale also as having been made not in pursuance of a written order of the purchaser as required by the statute. The court sentenced petitioner to five years' imprisonment and a fine of $2,000 upon each count, the terms of imprisonment to run consecutively; and this judgment was affirmed on appeal.

The principal contentions here made by petitioner are as follows: (1) That, upon the facts, the two sales charged in the second and third counts as having been made to the same person constitute a single offense; and (2) that the sale charged in the third count as having been made not from the original stamped package, and the same sale charged in the fifth count as having been made not in pursuance of a written order of the purchaser, constitute but one offense, for which only a single penalty lawfully may be imposed.

One. The sales charged in the second and third counts, although made to the same person, were distinct and separate sales made at different times. It appears from the evidence that, shortly after delivery of the drug which was the subject of the first sale, the purchaser paid for an additional quantity, which was delivered the next day. But the first sale had been consummated, and the payment for the additional drug, however closely following, was the initiation of a separate and distinct sale completed by its delivery.

The contention on behalf of petitioner is that these two sales, having been made to the same purchaser and following each other, with no substantial interval of time between the delivery of the drug in the first transaction and the payment for the second quantity sold, constitute a single continuing offense. The contention is unsound. The distinction between the transactions here involved and an offense continuous in its character is well settled, as was pointed out by this court in the case of *In re Snow*, 120 U.S. 274, 7 S.Ct. 556, 30 L.Ed. 658 (1887). There it was held that the offense of cohabiting with more than one woman was a continuous offense, and was committed, in the sense of the statute, where there was a living or dwelling together as husband and wife. * * *

The Narcotic Act does not create the offense of engaging in the business of selling the forbidden drugs, but penalizes any sale made in the absence of either of the qualifying requirements set forth. Each of several successive sales constitutes a distinct offense, however closely they may follow each other. The distinction stated by Mr. Wharton is that, "when the impulse is single, but one indictment lies, no matter how long the action may continue. If successive impulses are separately given, even though all unite in swelling a common stream of action, separate indictments lie." Wharton's Criminal Law (11th Ed.) § 34. Or, as stated in note 3 to that section, "The test is whether the individual acts are prohibited, or the course of action which they constitute. If the former, then each act is punishable separately. * * * If the latter, there can be but one penalty."

In the present case, the first transaction, resulting in a sale, had come to an end. The next sale was not the result of the original impulse, but of a fresh one—that is to say, of a new bargain. The question is controlled, not by the *Snow* Case, but by such cases as that of *Ebeling v. Morgan*, 237 U.S. 625, 35 S.Ct. 710, 59 L.Ed. 1151 (1915). There the accused was convicted under several counts of a willful tearing, etc., of mail bags with intent to rob. The court stated the question to be "whether one who, in the same transaction, tears or cuts successively mail bags of the United States used in conveyance of the mails, with intent to rob or steal any such mail, is guilty of a single offense, or of additional offenses because of each successive cutting with the criminal intent charged." Answering this question, the court, after quoting the statute:

> "These words plainly indicate that it was the intention of the lawmakers to protect each and every mail bag from felonious injury and mutilation. Whenever any one mail bag is thus torn, cut, or injured, the offense is complete. Although the transaction of cutting the mail bags was in a sense continuous, the complete statutory offense was committed every time a mail bag was cut in the manner described, with the intent charged. The offense as

to each separate bag was complete when that bag was cut, irrespective of any attack upon, or mutilation of, any other bag."

Two. Section 1 of the Narcotic Act creates the offense of selling any of the forbidden drugs except in or from the original stamped package; and section 2 creates the offense of selling any of such drugs not in pursuance of a written order of the person to whom the drug is sold. Thus, upon the face of the statute, two distinct offenses are created. Here there was but one sale, and the question is whether, both sections being violated by the same act, the accused committed two offenses or only one.

The statute is not aimed at sales of the forbidden drugs qua sales, a matter entirely beyond the authority of Congress, but at sales of such drugs in violation of the requirements set forth in sections 1 and 2, enacted as aids to the enforcement of the stamp tax imposed by the act.

Each of the offenses created requires proof of a different element. The applicable rule is that, where the same act or transaction constitutes a violation of two distinct statutory provisions, the test to be applied to determine whether there are two offenses or only one is whether each provision requires proof of an additional fact which the other does not. * * * Applying the test, we must conclude that here, although both sections were violated by the one sale, two offenses were committed. * * *

NOTES AND QUESTIONS

1. *Unit of prosecution and the rule of lenity.* One question before the Court was whether the two sales underlying counts two and three were different units of prosecution. In answering questions like this, the Court sometimes talks about a "rule of lenity." The rule of lenity is a subset of the rule of statutory interpretation that construes criminal statutes narrowly. Thus, courts should not convict a defendant of more offenses (more "units") than the legislature authorized. Whenever doubt exists about the number of convictions authorized, courts should resolve those doubts in favor of lenity.

The rule of lenity has venerable roots. For example, the issue in a 1777 English case was whether four sales of bread on Sunday were four violations of a statute that provided: "no tradesman or other person shall do or exercise any worldly labor, business, or work of their ordinary calling on the Lord's day." Each sale of bread could be an "exercise" of business—each sale did after all require different proof—but the King's Bench indulged a more lenient construction, finding that the intent of Parliament was to penalize "exercising his ordinary trade on the Lord's day." Selling baked goods on Sunday could be committed only once per Sunday, regardless of how many sales occurred that one day. Otherwise, the court observed, "if a tailor sews on the Lord's day, every stitch he takes is a separate offense." Crepps v. Durden, 2 Cowp. 640 (K.B. 1777). Judges in 1777 appreciated the extraordinary number of offenses that can exist if the "unit" of prohibited conduct is defined narrowly.

Blockburger distinguishes *In re Snow*, where Snow cohabited with the same women over an unbroken period of thirty-five months, all of which occurred before the first indictment. In rejecting the prosecution's division of this period into three different periods, the *Snow* Court said:

> The division of the two years and eleven months is wholly arbitrary. On the same principle, there might have been an indictment covering each of the thirty-five months, with imprisonment for seventeen years and a half and fines amounting to $10,500, or even an indictment covering every week, with imprisonment for 74 years and fines amounting to $44,400; and so on, *ad infinitum*, for smaller periods of time.

2. Why would two sales of narcotics, but not two sales of bread or thirty-five months of cohabitation, be different units of prosecution? Compare the unit of prosecution issue in *Blockburger* with the one in *Ebeling* (the mail bag case discussed in *Blockburger*)? Could *Blockburger* be right and *Ebeling* wrong? The Court quotes Wharton's treatise: "when the impulse is single, but one indictment lies, no matter how long the action may continue." Is this a helpful verbal formulation?

3. *The rule of lenity: modern examples.* A modern statement of the rule of lenity can be found in Prince v. United States, 352 U.S. 322, 77 S.Ct. 403, 1 L.Ed.2d 370 (1957), concluding that the Court recognizes a "policy of not attributing to Congress, in the enactment of criminal statutes, an intention to punish more severely than the language of its laws clearly imports in the light of pertinent legislative history." So, for example, it is a single offense to take two women across state lines in a single vehicle in violation of the Mann Act. Bell v. United States, 349 U.S. 81, 75 S.Ct. 620, 99 L.Ed. 905 (1955). Similarly, the Court held that thirty-two counts under the Fair Labor Standards Act were but three offenses. The Court said judges should treat "as one offense all violations that arise from that singleness of thought, purpose or action, which may be deemed a single 'impulse.'" United States v. Universal C.I.T. Credit Corp., 344 U.S. 218, 73 S.Ct. 227, 97 L.Ed. 260 (1952). The Court has suggested that a single assault against a federal officer is committed if one shot wounds two federal officers. Ladner v. United States, 358 U.S. 169, 79 S.Ct. 209, 3 L.Ed.2d 199 (1958).

4. *Problem: one more bottle of beer on the wall * * * .* A state ordinance prohibits "the sale of beer without a license." A prosecutor charges a beer seller with 1,800 counts of selling beer. Should a court uphold 1,800 convictions? Should this be governed by the *Blockburger* principle or the principle underlying *Crepps v. Durden*, Note 1? See State v. Broeder, 90 Mo.App. 169 (1901).

5. *The "definitional" same offense issue.* The second issue before the *Blockburger* Court was whether the very same sale of narcotics that violated two sections of the Harrison Act was one offense or two. Are you persuaded that Congress intended the sale of the same narcotics to be punished as two separate offenses? Do you think the *Blockburger* Court thought it was

explicating the double jeopardy clause or doing something a little less foundational?

Do you see how the Court's conception of congressional power in 1932 paved the way for this result?

Suppose a legislature identifies different aggravating circumstances that will turn robbery into first degree robbery. Section (b) makes it first degree robbery to rob a store after dark because it is more difficult to catch robbers at night. Section (c) makes it first degree robbery to commit a robbery while wearing a business suit because it is more difficult to catch robbers who look like business men. Now suppose our robber robs a store at night and while wearing a suit. Two double jeopardy offenses under *Blockburger*?

6. *How many trials are possible for the same conduct?* In Gore v. United States, 357 U.S. 386, 78 S.Ct. 1280, 2 L.Ed.2d 1405 (1958), Gore was charged with the same two narcotics offenses as in *Blockburger* plus an additional one: the sale of drugs knowing that they had been illegally imported. All three offenses were based on a single sale. After being convicted and sentenced consecutively for these offenses, Gore raised two arguments: first, Congress did not intend a single sale to result in three convictions and consecutive sentences; and, second, if Congress *did* intend that result, it was forbidden by the double jeopardy clause. By a vote of 5–4, the Court rejected both arguments. On congressional intent, the Court found that

> the various enactments by Congress extending over nearly half a century constitute a network of provisions, steadily tightened and enlarged, for grappling with a powerful, subtle and elusive enemy. If the legislation reveals anything, it reveals the determination of Congress to turn the screw of the criminal machinery—detection, prosecution and punishment—tighter and tighter.

Chief Justice Warren dissented from the Court's reading of legislative intent, drawing on the rule of lenity: "Where the legislature has failed to make its intention manifest, courts should proceed cautiously, remaining sensitive to the interests of defendant and society alike."

On the double jeopardy point, the Court concluded that *Blockburger* had settled the question. Justice Douglas, joined by Justice Black, argued that *Blockburger* should be overruled: "I think it is time that the Double Jeopardy Clause was liberally construed in light of its great historic purpose to protect the citizen from more than one trial for the same act."

Gore permits not only three convictions but also three successive prosecutions for the same sale or possession. A law review Note published in 1958 identified nine different federal narcotics laws that could in theory be violated with a single sale. Note, *Consecutive Sentences in Single Prosecutions: Judicial Multiplication of Statutory Penalties*, 67 Yale L.J. 916, 928 n.43 (1958). In the wake of the "war on drugs," that number is probably higher. Whatever Congress might have intended about cumulative punishments for a single sale, does it make sense to think that Congress intended to authorize nine different trials in which the same sale (and thus the same underlying culpability) would be proved again and again and again?

7. Under *Blockburger*, an offense with elements 1,2 is the same as an offense with element 1 or an offense with element 2, but not the same as an offense with elements 1,3. It seems sensible that offenses are functionally the same if proving offense (1,2) will always prove offense (2). In that case, offense (2) is a necessarily-included offense of offense (1,2), and it seems likely that a legislature would punish the greater offense more severely precisely because it has the additional element. Thus, to punish the necessarily-included offense along with the greater offense would exceed what the legislature authorized.

For an illuminating analysis of the law of lesser included offenses, state and federal, see James A. Shellenberger & James A. Strazzella, *The Lesser Included Offense Doctrine and the Constitution: The Development of Due Process and Double Jeopardy Remedies*, 79 Marq. L. Rev. 1 (1995).

That *Blockburger* produces a sensible outcome where one offense is necessarily included in another is not to say that the converse inference is correct—that the presence of *any* distinct element, such as wearing a business suit, is a good measure of intent to punish cumulatively. The Court would not have to accept as equally helpful both kinds of outcomes from the *Blockburger* test. It could decide that *Blockburger* works just fine to tell us when offenses are the same but that double jeopardy requires another test when *Blockburger* pronounces offenses to be different. With that in mind, pause over footnote 6 in the next case.

BROWN V. OHIO

Supreme Court of the United States, 1977.
432 U.S. 161, 97 S.Ct. 2221, 53 L.Ed.2d 187.

MR. JUSTICE POWELL delivered the opinion of the Court [joined by JUSTICES BRENNAN, STEWART, WHITE, MARSHALL, and STEVENS].

The question in this case is whether the Double Jeopardy Clause of the Fifth Amendment bars prosecution and punishment for the crime of stealing an automobile following prosecution and punishment for the lesser included offense of operating the same vehicle without the owner's consent.

I

On November 29, 1973, the petitioner, Nathaniel Brown, stole a 1965 Chevrolet from a parking lot in East Cleveland, Ohio. Nine days later, on December 8, 1973, Brown was caught driving the car in Wickliffe, Ohio. The Wickliffe police charged him with "joyriding"—taking or operating the car without the owner's consent * * * .[1] The complaint charged that "on or about December 8, 1973, * * * Nathaniel H. Brown did unlawfully and purposely take, drive or operate a certain motor vehicle to wit; a 1965 Chevrolet * * * without the consent of the owner one Gloria Ingram * * * ." Brown pleaded guilty to this charge and was sentenced to 30 days in jail and a $100 fine.

Upon his release from jail on January 8, 1974, Brown was returned to East Cleveland to face further charges, and on February 5 he was indicted by the Cuyahoga County grand jury. The indictment was in two counts, the first charging the theft of the car "on or about the 29th day of November 1973,"[2] * * * and the second charging joyriding on the same date * * * . A bill of particulars filed by the prosecuting attorney specified that

> "on or about the 29th day of November, 1973, * * * Nathaniel Brown unlawfully did steal a Chevrolet motor vehicle, and take, drive or operate such vehicle without the consent of the owner, Gloria Ingram * * * ."

Brown objected to both counts of the indictment on the basis of former jeopardy. [The prosecutor dismissed the joyriding count.]

* * * [T]he Cuyahoga County Court * * * overruled Brown's double jeopardy objections [to the auto theft count]. The court sentenced Brown to six months in jail but suspended the sentence and placed Brown on probation for one year.

The Ohio Court of Appeals affirmed. It held that under Ohio law the misdemeanor of joyriding was included in the felony of auto theft:

> "Every element of the crime of operating a motor vehicle without the consent of the owner is also an element of the crime of auto theft. 'The difference between the crime of stealing a motor vehicle, and operating a motor vehicle without the consent of the owner is that conviction for stealing requires proof of an intent on the part of the thief to *permanently* deprive the owner of possession.' * * * [T]he crime of operating a motor vehicle without the consent of the owner is a lesser included offense of auto theft. * * * "

Although this analysis led the court to agree with Brown that "for purposes of double jeopardy the two prosecutions involve the same

---

[1]   Section 4549.04(D) provided at the time: "No person shall purposely take, operate, or keep any motor vehicle without the consent of its owner." A violation was punishable as a misdemeanor. * * *

[2]   Section 4549.04(A) provided: "No person shall steal any motor vehicle." A violation was punishable as a felony.

statutory offense,"[4] it nonetheless held the second prosecution permissible:

> "The two prosecutions are based on two separate acts of the appellant, one which occurred on November 29th and one which occurred on December 8th. Since appellant has not shown that both prosecutions are based on the same act or transaction, the second prosecution is not barred by the double jeopardy clause."
> * * *

II

The Double Jeopardy Clause of the Fifth Amendment, applicable to the States through the Fourteenth, provides that no person shall "be subject for the same offence to be twice put in jeopardy of life or limb." It has long been understood that separate statutory crimes need not be identical—either in constituent elements or in actual proof—in order to be the same within the meaning of the constitutional prohibition. The principal question in this case is whether auto theft and joyriding, a greater and lesser included offense under Ohio law, constitute the "same offence" under the Double Jeopardy Clause.

Because it was designed originally to embody the protection of the common-law pleas of former jeopardy, the Fifth Amendment double jeopardy guarantee serves principally as a restraint on courts and prosecutors. The legislature remains free under the Double Jeopardy Clause to define crimes and fix punishments; but once the legislature has acted courts may not impose more than one punishment for the same offense and prosecutors ordinarily may not attempt to secure that punishment in more than one trial.

The Double Jeopardy Clause "protects against a second prosecution for the same offense after acquittal. It protects against a second prosecution for the same offense after conviction. And it protects against multiple punishments for the same offense." Where consecutive sentences are imposed at a single criminal trial, the role of the constitutional guarantee is limited to assuring that the court does not exceed its legislative authorization by imposing multiple punishments for the same offense. Where successive prosecutions are at stake, the guarantee serves "a constitutional policy of finality for the defendant's benefit." That policy protects the accused from attempts to relitigate the facts underlying a prior acquittal, see *Ashe v. Swenson* [p. 1498], and from attempts to secure additional punishment after a prior conviction and sentence.

---

[4] As the Ohio Court of Appeals recognized, the Wickliffe and Cuyahoga County prosecutions must be viewed as the acts of a single sovereign under the Double Jeopardy Clause.

The established test for determining whether two offenses are sufficiently distinguishable to permit the imposition of cumulative punishment was stated in *Blockburger v. United States*, [p. 1475]:

> "The applicable rule is that where the same act or transaction constitutes a violation of two distinct statutory provisions, the test to be applied to determine whether there are two offenses or only one, is whether each provision requires proof of a fact which the other does not * * * ."

This test emphasizes the elements of the two crimes. "If each requires proof of a fact that the other does not, the *Blockburger* test is satisfied, notwithstanding a substantial overlap in the proof offered to establish the crimes * * * ."

If two offenses are the same under this test for purposes of barring consecutive sentences at a single trial, they necessarily will be the same for purposes of barring successive prosecutions. Where the judge is forbidden to impose cumulative punishment for two crimes at the end of a single proceeding, the prosecutor is forbidden to strive for the same result in successive proceedings. Unless "each statute requires proof of an additional fact which the other does not," the Double Jeopardy Clause prohibits successive prosecutions as well as cumulative punishment.[6]

We are mindful that the Ohio courts "have the final authority to interpret * * * that State's legislation." Here the Ohio Court of Appeals has authoritatively defined the elements of the two Ohio crimes: Joyriding consists of taking or operating a vehicle without the owner's consent, and auto theft consists of joyriding with the intent permanently to deprive the owner of possession. Joyriding is the lesser included offense. The prosecutor who has established joyriding need only prove the requisite intent in order to establish auto theft; the prosecutor who has established auto theft necessarily has established joyriding as well.

Applying the *Blockburger* test, we agree with the Ohio Court of Appeals that joyriding and auto theft, as defined by the court, constitute "the same statutory offense" within the meaning of the Double Jeopardy Clause. For it is clearly *not* the case that "each [statute] requires proof of a fact which the other does not." As is invariably true of a greater and lesser included offense, the lesser offense—joyriding—requires no proof beyond that which is required for conviction of the greater—auto theft.

---

[6] The *Blockburger* test is not the only standard for determining whether successive prosecutions impermissibly involve the same offense. Even if two offenses are sufficiently different to permit the imposition of consecutive sentences, successive prosecutions will be barred in some circumstances where the second prosecution requires the relitigation of factual issues already resolved by the first. * * * [I]n *In re Nielsen*, 131 U.S. 176, 9 S.Ct. 672, 33 L.Ed. 118 (1889), the Court held that a conviction of a Mormon on a charge of cohabiting with his two wives over a 2½-year period barred a subsequent prosecution for adultery with one of them on the day following the end of that period. * * *

The greater offense is therefore by definition the "same" for purposes of double jeopardy as any lesser offense included in it.

This conclusion merely restates what has been this Court's understanding of the Double Jeopardy Clause at least since *In re Nielsen* was decided in 1889. In that case the Court endorsed the rule that

> "where * * * a person has been tried and convicted for a crime which has various incidents included in it, he cannot be a second time tried for one of those incidents without being twice put in jeopardy for the same offence."

Although in this formulation the conviction of the greater precedes the conviction of the lesser, the opinion makes it clear that the sequence is immaterial. * * * Whatever the sequence may be, the Fifth Amendment forbids successive prosecution and cumulative punishment for a greater and lesser included offense.[7]

III

After correctly holding that joyriding and auto theft are the same offense under the Double Jeopardy Clause, the Ohio Court of Appeals nevertheless concluded that Nathaniel Brown could be convicted of both crimes because the charges against him focused on different parts of his 9-day joyride. We hold a different view. The Double Jeopardy Clause is not such a fragile guarantee that prosecutors can avoid its limitations by the simple expedient of dividing a single crime into a series of temporal or spatial units. The applicable Ohio statutes, as written and as construed in this case, make the theft and operation of a single car a single offense. Although the Wickliffe and East Cleveland authorities may have had different perspectives on Brown's offense, it was still only one offense under Ohio law.[8] Accordingly, the specification of different dates in the two charges on which Brown was convicted cannot alter the fact that he was placed twice in jeopardy for the same offense in violation of the Fifth and Fourteenth Amendments. * * *

MR. JUSTICE BRENNAN, with whom MR. JUSTICE MARSHALL joins, concurring.

I join the Court's opinion, but in any event would reverse on the ground, not addressed by the Court, that the State did not prosecute petitioner in a single proceeding. I adhere to the view that the Double

---

[7]   An exception may exist where the State is unable to proceed on the more serious charge at the outset because the additional facts necessary to sustain that charge have not occurred or have not been discovered despite the exercise of due diligence.

[8]   We would have a different case if the Ohio Legislature had provided that joyriding is a separate offense for each day in which a motor vehicle is operated without the owner's consent. We also would have a different case if in sustaining Brown's second conviction the Ohio courts had construed the joyriding statute to have that effect. We then would have to decide whether the state courts' construction, applied retroactively in this case, was such "an unforeseeable judicial enlargement of a criminal statute" as to violate due process.

Jeopardy Clause of the Fifth Amendment, applied to the States through the Fourteenth Amendment, requires the prosecution in one proceeding, except in extremely limited circumstances not present here, of "all the charges against a defendant that grow out of a single criminal act, occurrence, episode, or transaction." In my view, the Court's suggestion [at n.8] that the Ohio Legislature might be free to make joyriding a separate and distinct offense for each day a motor vehicle is operated without the owner's consent would not affect the applicability of the single-transaction test. Though under some circumstances a legislature may divide a continuing course of conduct into discrete offenses, I would nevertheless hold that all charges growing out of conduct constituting a "single criminal act, occurrence, episode, or transaction" must be tried in a single proceeding.

MR. JUSTICE BLACKMUN, with whom THE CHIEF JUSTICE [BURGER] and MR. JUSTICE REHNQUIST join, dissenting. * * *

I, of course, have no quarrel with the Court's general double jeopardy analysis. I am unable to ignore as easily as the Court does, however, the specific finding of the Ohio Court of Appeals that the two prosecutions at issue here were based on petitioner's separate and distinct acts committed, respectively, on November 29 and on December 8, 1973.

Petitioner was convicted of operating a motor vehicle on December 8 without the owner's consent. He subsequently was convicted of taking and operating the same motor vehicle on November 29 without the owner's consent and with the intent permanently to deprive the owner of possession. It is possible, of course, that at some point the two acts would be so closely connected in time that the Double Jeopardy Clause would require treating them as one offense. This surely would be so with respect to the theft and any simultaneous unlawful operation. Furthermore, as a matter of statutory construction, the allowable unit of prosecution may be a course of conduct rather than the separate segments of such a course. I feel that neither of these approaches justifies the Court's result in the present case.

Nine days elapsed between the two incidents that are the basis of petitioner's convictions. During that time the automobile moved from East Cleveland to Wickliffe. It strains credulity to believe that petitioner was operating the vehicle every minute of those nine days. A time must have come when he stopped driving the car. When he operated it again nine days later in a different community, the Ohio courts could properly find, consistently with the Double Jeopardy Clause, that the acts were sufficiently distinct to justify a second prosecution. Only if the Clause requires the Ohio courts to hold that the allowable unit of prosecution is the course of conduct would the Court's result here be correct. On the facts of this case, no such requirement should be inferred, and the state courts should be free to construe Ohio's statute as they did.

This Court, I fear, gives undeserved emphasis to the Ohio Court of Appeals' passing observation that the Ohio misdemeanor of joyriding is an element of the Ohio felony of auto theft. That observation was merely a preliminary statement, indicating that the theft and any simultaneous unlawful operation were one and the same. But the Ohio Court of Appeals then went on flatly to hold that such simultaneity was not present here. Thus, it seems to me, the Ohio courts did precisely what this Court, [at n.8], professes to say they did not do.

In my view, we should not so willingly circumvent an authoritative Ohio holding as to Ohio law. I would affirm the judgment of the Court of Appeals.

NOTES AND QUESTIONS

1. *"Same offense" and "unit of prosecution" commingled.* Auto theft and joyriding, as construed by the Ohio courts in *Brown*, are an easy example of the same definitional *Blockburger* offense. Auto theft has an additional element, but joyriding is necessarily included and thus does not require proof of a fact not required for auto theft. What is less clear in *Brown*, and what provoked Justice Blackmun's dissent, is the "unit of prosecution" dimension of the joyriding "same offense" problem. It would not be the same offense for Brown to steal Abel's car, return it, and then steal it again the next day. This requires us to revisit, yet again, the "unit of prosecution" problem.

It is clear that two sales of narcotics are, as the Court held in *Blockburger*, two offenses. Each sale is a discrete harm. The "unit of prosecution" problem is harder in *Brown*—how many "units" of joyriding/auto theft occur when a thief keeps a car for nine days? Justice Blackmun is right that different acts of driving must have occurred during the nine-day joyride. But that misses the point of how physical acts in the universe manifest criminal blameworthiness. How many offenses of larceny is it to steal an item and keep it for nine days (or nine years)? The answer: one. If there is more than one "unit" of conduct in *Brown*, it must be because joyriding is a divisible offense even though auto theft is not divisible.

But why would the lesser offense be divisible if the greater offense, auto theft, is not divisible? The *Brown* majority seems to assume that the state court found only one unit of joyriding when the statute (footnote 1 in *Brown*) is violated by the operation of a single car. On that reading, it would only be one unit of auto theft/joyriding if Brown had kept the car for nine months and had driven it across country many times. Support for that reading of legislative intent comes in the following thought experiment: if it is one unit of auto theft to steal a car and keep it nine years, it would be bizarre to say that 1,000 units of joyriding occurred if Brown drove the car 1,000 times during the nine years. That would make joyriding potentially a much more serious offense than auto theft, or rape or robbery for that matter, with discretion of how many joyriding convictions to "stack" solely in the hands of the prosecutor. That is an unlikely reading of legislative intent on the unit of prosecution for joyriding.

2.   *A complicated application of Blockburger.* Whalen v. United States, 445 U.S. 684, 100 S.Ct. 1432, 63 L.Ed.2d 715 (1980), was a multiple punishment case in which the Court sought to divine congressional intent from an application of the *Blockburger* test to what is known as a "compound-predicate" statutory scheme—i.e., where a "compound" offense like felony murder uses "predicate" offenses to enhance culpability. The issue in *Whalen* was whether felony murder and the rape proved in the felony murder are the same offense under *Blockburger* and thus could sustain only one conviction.

> In the present case * * *, proof of rape is a necessary element of proof of the felony murder, and we are unpersuaded that this case should be treated differently from other cases in which one criminal offense requires proof of every element of another offense. There would be no question in this regard if Congress, instead of listing the six lesser included offenses in the alternative, had separately proscribed the six different species of felony murder under six statutory provisions. It is doubtful that Congress could have imagined that so formal a difference in drafting had any practical significance, and we ascribe none to it. To the extent that the Government's argument persuades us that the matter is not entirely free of doubt, the doubt must be resolved in favor of lenity.

> Justice Rehnquist dissented, noting that

> the *Blockburger* test, although useful in identifying statutes that define greater and lesser included offenses in the traditional sense, is less satisfactory, and perhaps even misdirected, when applied to statutes defining "compound" and "predicate" offenses. Strictly speaking, two crimes do not stand in the relationship of greater and lesser included offenses unless proof of the greater necessarily entails proof of the lesser. * * *

> If one tests the [statutes of felony murder and rape] in the abstract, one can see that rape is not a lesser included offense of felony murder, because proof of the latter will not necessarily require proof of the former. One can commit felony murder without rape and one can rape without committing felony murder.

Who gets the better of the argument? In seeking the best understanding of Congress's intent, who is right? Do you think Congress intended for someone who raped and then killed the victim to be convicted only of murder? Why or why not?

While *Whalen* could be understood as mere statutory construction, because it involved interpretation of a federal statute, the Court in a brief, unanimous per curiam opinion had previously held that robbery and felony murder based on robbery are the same offense when prosecuted successively in state court. See Harris v. Oklahoma, 433 U.S. 682, 97 S.Ct. 2912, 53 L.Ed.2d 1054 (1977).

3. A few commentators have criticized the *Blockburger* test as being too generous. One attack is that the "plain meaning" of "same offense" is "same statutory offense"—thus, the only offense that is the same as auto theft is auto theft. Akhil Reed Amar & Jonathan L. Marcus, *Double Jeopardy Law After Rodney King*, 95 Colum. L. Rev. 1 (1995). A second kind of attack is that *Blockburger* permits the more serious culpability to go unprosecuted if the State tries the less serious offense first, as was the case in *Brown*. Peter Westen & Richard Drubel, *Toward a General Theory of Double Jeopardy*, 1978 Sup. Ct. Rev. 81.

Supporters of the *Blockburger* test offer its clarity as a virtue. While it is clearer and easier to apply than any other test the Court has adopted or toyed with, it sometimes produces odd results. Consider the following problems.

4. *Problems.* Which of the following pairs of statutory offenses are the same offense under *Blockburger*? Each of these offenses is created in a separate statute.

A. Robbery inside a dwelling, and robbery in the nighttime (committed when *R* robbed one victim at night in a dwelling).

B. Robbery (forcible taking of property intending to deprive the owner permanently of possession) and larceny (taking property intending to deprive the owner permanently of possession).

C. Burglary (breaking and entering a dwelling with the intent to commit a felony inside), and larceny committed inside the dwelling.

D. Felony murder and premeditated murder.

E. Manslaughter by motor vehicle, which requires proof of reckless *mens rea*, and homicide by motor vehicle while intoxicated.

F. Larceny (taking property intending to deprive the owner permanently of possession), and wrongful diversion of electric current (diverting electric current so that it is not metered).

G. Rape (sexual intercourse accomplished by force or threat of force and without the consent of the victim), and statutory rape (sexual intercourse with a person younger than 16).

5. Whatever the virtues and defects of *Blockburger*, the Court held in 1993 that it was the only test to be applied when the issue is whether different statutes define the same double jeopardy offense. See United States v. Dixon, 509 U.S. 688, 113 S.Ct. 2849, 125 L.Ed.2d 556 (1993).

6. A bar against multiple convictions in one trial was unknown in Blackstone's day, but this "multiple punishment" doctrine is derivable from Blackstone's *autrefois convict* plea—why permit the prosecutor to do in one

trial what the double jeopardy clause forbids in successive trials? *Blockburger* was a single trial, multiple punishment case. The Court has since developed a more comprehensive theory of multiple punishment.

MISSOURI V. HUNTER

Supreme Court of the United States, 1983.
459 U.S. 359, 103 S.Ct. 673, 74 L.Ed.2d 535.

CHIEF JUSTICE BURGER delivered the opinion of the Court [joined by JUSTICES BRENNAN, WHITE, BLACKMUN, POWELL, REHNQUIST, and O'CONNOR].

We granted certiorari to consider whether the prosecution and conviction of a criminal defendant in a single trial on both a charge of "armed criminal action" and a charge of first-degree robbery—the underlying felony—violates the Double Jeopardy Clause of the Fifth Amendment.

I * * *

[The Missouri robbery statute] prescribes the punishment for robbery in the first degree and provides in pertinent part:

> "Every person convicted of robbery in the first degree by means of a dangerous and deadly weapon and every person convicted of robbery in the first degree by any other means shall be punished by imprisonment by the division of corrections for not less than five years * * * ."

[A separate statute] proscribes armed criminal action and provides in pertinent part:

> "[A]ny person who commits any felony under the laws of this state by, with, or through the use, assistance, or aid of a dangerous or deadly weapon is also guilty of the crime of armed criminal action and, upon conviction, shall be punished by imprisonment by the division of corrections for a term of not less than three years. The punishment imposed pursuant to this subsection shall be in addition to any punishment provided by law for the crime committed by, with, or through the use, assistance, or aid of a dangerous or deadly weapon. * * *

Pursuant to these statutes respondent was sentenced to concurrent terms of (a) 10 years' imprisonment for the robbery; (b) 15 years for armed criminal action; and (c) to a consecutive term of 5 years' imprisonment for assault, for a total of 20 years. * * *

II

* * * The Missouri Supreme Court concluded that under the test announced in *Blockburger*, armed criminal action and any underlying

offense are the "same offense" under the Fifth Amendment's Double Jeopardy Clause. That court acknowledged that the Missouri legislature had expressed its clear intent that a defendant should be subject to conviction and sentence under the armed criminal action statute in addition to any conviction and sentence for the underlying felony. The court nevertheless held that the Double Jeopardy Clause "prohibits imposing punishment for both armed criminal action and for the underlying felony." It then set aside the defendant's conviction for armed criminal action. * * *

[The United States Supreme Court had vacated and remanded a series of Missouri armed criminal action cases for reconsideration in light of two cases containing dicta that said the question of multiple punishment in a single trial was ultimately a question of legislative intent.] The Missouri court, however, remained unpersuaded, stating:

> "Until such time as the Supreme Court of the United States declares clearly and unequivocally that the Double Jeopardy Clause of the Fifth Amendment to the United States Constitution does not apply to the legislative branch of government, we cannot do other than what we perceive to be our duty to refuse to enforce multiple punishments for the same offense arising out of a single transaction." * * *

III

The Double Jeopardy Clause is cast explicitly in terms of being "twice put in jeopardy." We have consistently interpreted it " 'to protect an individual from being subjected to the hazards of trial and possible conviction more than once for an alleged offense.' " Because respondent has been subjected to only one trial, it is not contended that his right to be free from multiple trials for the same offense has been violated. Rather, the Missouri court vacated respondent's conviction for armed criminal action because of the statements of this Court that the Double Jeopardy Clause also "protects against multiple punishments for the same offense." Particularly in light of recent precedents of this Court, it is clear that the Missouri Supreme Court has misperceived the nature of the Double Jeopardy Clause's protection against multiple punishments. With respect to cumulative sentences imposed in a single trial, the Double Jeopardy Clause does no more than prevent the sentencing court from prescribing greater punishment than the legislature intended. * * *

Here, the Missouri Supreme Court has construed the two statutes at issue as defining the same crime. In addition, the Missouri Supreme Court has recognized that the legislature intended that punishment for violations of the statutes be cumulative. We are bound to accept the Missouri court's construction of that State's statutes. However, we are not bound by the Missouri Supreme Court's legal conclusion that these two statutes violate the Double Jeopardy Clause, and we reject its legal conclusion.

[S]imply because two criminal statutes may be construed to proscribe the same conduct under the *Blockburger* test does not mean that the Double Jeopardy Clause precludes the imposition, in a single trial, of cumulative punishments pursuant to those statutes. The [*Blockburger*] rule of statutory construction * * * is not a constitutional rule requiring courts to negate clearly expressed legislative intent. Thus far, we have utilized that rule only to limit a federal court's power to impose convictions and punishments when the will of Congress is not clear. Here, the Missouri Legislature has made its intent crystal clear. Legislatures, not courts, prescribe the scope of punishments.[5]

Where, as here, a legislature specifically authorizes cumulative punishment under two statutes, regardless of whether those two statutes proscribe the "same" conduct under *Blockburger*, a court's task of statutory construction is at an end and the prosecutor may seek and the trial court or jury may impose cumulative punishment under such statutes in a single trial. * * *

JUSTICE MARSHALL, with whom JUSTICE STEVENS joins, dissenting. * * *

A State has wide latitude to define crimes and to prescribe the punishment for a given crime. For example, a State is free to prescribe two different punishments (*e.g.*, a fine and a prison term) for a single offense. But the Constitution does not permit a State to punish as two crimes conduct that constitutes only one "offence" within the meaning of the Double Jeopardy Clause. For whenever a person is subjected to the risk that he will be convicted of a crime under state law, he is "put in jeopardy of life or limb." If the prohibition against being "twice put in jeopardy" for "the same offence" is to have any real meaning, a State cannot be allowed to convict a defendant two, three, or more times simply by enacting separate statutory provisions defining nominally distinct crimes. If the Double Jeopardy Clause imposed no restrictions on a legislature's power to authorize multiple punishment, there would be no limit to the number of convictions that a State could obtain on the basis of the same act, state of mind, and result. A State would be free to create substantively identical crimes differing only in name, or to create a series of greater and lesser included offenses, with the first crime a lesser included offense of the second, the second a lesser included offense of the third, and so on. * * *

[Q]uite apart from any sentence that is imposed, each separate criminal conviction typically has collateral consequences, in both the

---

[5]   This case presents only issues under the Double Jeopardy Clause.

jurisdiction in which the conviction is obtained and in other jurisdictions. The number of convictions is often critical to the collateral consequences that an individual faces. For example, a defendant who has only one prior conviction will generally not be subject to sentencing under a habitual offender statute.

Furthermore, each criminal conviction itself represents a pronouncement by the State that the defendant has engaged in conduct warranting the moral condemnation of the community. Because a criminal conviction constitutes a formal judgment of condemnation by the community, each additional conviction imposes an additional stigma and causes additional damage to the defendant's reputation.

A statutory scheme that permits the prosecution to obtain two convictions and two sentences therefore cannot be regarded as the equivalent of a statute that permits only a single conviction, whether or not that single conviction can result in a sentence of equal severity. * * *

In light of these considerations, the Double Jeopardy Clause cannot reasonably be interpreted to leave legislatures completely free to subject a defendant to the risk of multiple punishment on the basis of a single criminal transaction. In the context of multiple prosecutions, it is well established that the phrase "same offence" in the Double Jeopardy Clause has independent content—that two crimes that do not satisfy the *Blockburger* test constitute the "same offence" under the Double Jeopardy Clause regardless of the legislature's intent to treat them as separate offenses. Otherwise multiple prosecutions would be permissible whenever authorized by the legislature. The Court has long assumed that the *Blockburger* test is also a rule of constitutional stature in multiple-punishment cases, and I would not hesitate to hold that it is. If the prohibition against being "twice put in jeopardy" for "the same offence" is to provide meaningful protection, the phrase "the same offence" must have content independent of state law in both contexts. Since the Double Jeopardy Clause limits the power of all branches of government, including the legislature, there is no more reason to treat the test as simply a rule of statutory construction in multiple-punishment cases than there would be in multiple-prosecution cases. * * *

NOTES AND QUESTIONS

1. *Yet one more application of Blockburger.* Were the Missouri courts correct that armed criminal action and first degree robbery define the same offense under *Blockburger*?

2. *A weird legislature.* After *Hunter*, can a successful double jeopardy claim be made against two convictions under the following, somewhat weird, criminal statutes?

"R–1.01 *Robbery*. Robbery, as defined elsewhere in this code, shall be punished by ten years in prison, without possibility of parole.

"R–1.02 *Aggravated Robbery*. If R–1.01 is committed by displaying a deadly weapon, the actor shall be convicted twice of violating R–1.01, and shall be sentenced consecutively."

3.   Is there any reason for the double jeopardy clause to prohibit the kind of legislative drafting exemplified by Note 2? Is there a defensible definition of "same offense" that ignores the legislature's power "to define crimes and fix punishments," which the Court noted in *Brown v. Ohio*, p. 1480? More specifically, how is the example above different from the following:

"Z–1.01 *Robbery*. Robbery, as defined elsewhere in this code, shall be punished by ten years in prison, without possibility of parole.

"Z–1.02 *Aggravated Robbery*. It shall be aggravated robbery to violate Z–1.01 by displaying a deadly weapon. The sentence shall be twenty years in prison, without possibility of parole, and a conviction of Z–1.02 shall be treated as if it were two convictions (one for robbery and one for displaying a weapon during a robbery) for all purposes (including, but not limited to, habitual offender status)."

4.   *Can Hunter's rationale be cabined? Hunter* is limited to the single trial context, thus leaving unsettled whether the same deference to the legislature is appropriate in the successive prosecution context. For a time, the Court and commentators assumed that the legislature does not have complete freedom to define "same offense" in the context of successive prosecutions, often quoting Justice Black's eloquent dicta from *Green v. United States*, 355 U.S. 184, 78 S.Ct. 221, 2 L.Ed.2d 199 (1957):

[T]he State with all its resources and power should not be allowed to make repeated attempts to convict an individual for an alleged offense, thereby subjecting him to embarrassment, expense and ordeal and compelling him to live in a continuing state of anxiety and insecurity, as well as enhancing the possibility that even though innocent he may be found guilty.

But Black's rhetoric, eloquent though it is, ultimately begs the question about what constitutes "an alleged offense," as Michael Moore points out:

The time, expense, and embarrassment of a criminal trial are harms to every criminal defendant, but they are harms we obviously are and should be willing to inflict on a defendant sometimes, else we'd never prosecute anyone. Similarly, the knowing infliction of these harms on a defendant by a prosecutor cannot always amount to harassment; it is only where these harms are inflicted on a defendant for no good reason that a prosecutor is harassing a defendant. When offences are not truly the same, there is a good reason for a defendant to have to suffer the harms of criminal trials more than once, and there is a good reason for a prosecutor to knowingly inflict them more than once. That reason is "insuring that the guilty are punished." If a defendant has truly done more than one wrong, he deserves more than one punishment. Hence, conviction for an earlier wrong should not bar a second prosecution for the second wrong.

Michael S. Moore, Act and Crime 353 (1993). See also George C. Thomas III, *A Blameworthy Act Approach to the Double Jeopardy Same Offense Problem*, 83 Cal. L. Rev. 1027, 1049–1050 (1995) ("We might say that it is immoral to lie or cheat. But we cannot say that it is an 'offense,' in the criminal law sense or the double jeopardy sense, until the [legislature] has made it an offense").

The test case for whether the double jeopardy clause limits legislative authority to define offenses would be a *Hunter*-type case in which the offenses are tried separately. So far, that case has not reached the United States Supreme Court.

B. FORMER ACQUITTAL/COLLATERAL ESTOPPEL (ISSUE PRECLUSION)

Blackstone's plea of "former conviction" needs no separate treatment from what we saw in the last section on "same offense." A defendant cannot be convicted, or prosecuted, for the same offense more than once. But "former acquittal" raises additional issues, and we treat it separately here.

FONG FOO v. UNITED STATES

Supreme Court of the United States, 1962.
369 U.S. 141, 82 S.Ct. 671, 7 L.Ed.2d 629.

PER CURIAM [joined by CHIEF JUSTICE WARREN and JUSTICES BLACK, FRANKFURTER, DOUGLAS, HARLAN, BRENNAN, and STEWART].

The petitioners, a corporation and two of its employees, were brought to trial before a jury in a federal district court upon an indictment charging a conspiracy and the substantive offense of concealing material facts in a matter within the jurisdiction of an agency of the United States * * * . After seven days of what promised to be a long and complicated trial, three government witnesses had appeared and a fourth was in the process of testifying. At that point the district judge directed the jury to return verdicts of acquittal as to all the defendants, and a formal judgment of acquittal was subsequently entered.

The record shows that the district judge's action was based upon one or both of two grounds: supposed improper conduct on the part of the Assistant United States Attorney who was prosecuting the case, and a supposed lack of credibility in the testimony of the witnesses for the prosecution who had testified up to that point.

The Government filed a petition for a writ of mandamus in the Court of Appeals for the First Circuit, praying that the judgment of acquittal be vacated and the case reassigned for trial. The court granted the petition, upon the ground that under the circumstances revealed by the record the trial court was without power to direct the judgment in question. Judge Aldrich concurred separately, finding that the directed judgment of acquittal had been based solely on the supposed improper conduct of the prosecutor, and agreeing with his colleagues that the district judge was without power to direct an acquittal on that ground. * * *

* * * [The double jeopardy clause] is at the very root of the present case, and we cannot but conclude that the guaranty was violated when the Court of Appeals set aside the judgment of acquittal and directed that the petitioners be tried again for the same offense.

The petitioners were tried under a valid indictment in a federal court which had jurisdiction over them and over the subject matter. The trial did not terminate prior to the entry of judgment * * * . It terminated with the entry of a final judgment of acquittal as to each petitioner. The Court of Appeals thought, not without reason, that the acquittal was based upon an egregiously erroneous foundation. Nevertheless, "[t]he verdict of acquittal was final, and could not be reviewed * * * without putting [the petitioners] twice in jeopardy, and thereby violating the Constitution." * * *

MR. JUSTICE WHITTAKER took no part in the consideration or decision of these cases.

MR. JUSTICE HARLAN, concurring.

Were I able to find, as Judge Aldrich did, that the District Court's judgment of acquittal was based solely on the Assistant United States Attorney's *alleged* misconduct, I would think that a retrial of the petitioners would not be prevented by the Double Jeopardy Clause of the Fifth Amendment. Even assuming that a trial court may have power, in extreme circumstances, to direct a judgment of acquittal, instead of declaring a mistrial, because of a prosecutor's misconduct—a proposition which I seriously doubt—I do not think that such power existed in the circumstances of this case. But since an examination of the record leaves me unable, as it did the majority of the Court of Appeals, to attribute the action of the District Court to this factor alone, I concur in the judgment of reversal.

MR. JUSTICE CLARK, dissenting.

* * * The District Court under the circumstances here clearly had no power to direct a verdict of acquittal or to enter a judgment thereon. In

my view when a trial court has no power to direct such a verdict, the judgment based thereon is a nullity. The word "acquittal" in this context is no magic open sesame freeing in this case two persons and absolving a corporation from serious grand jury charges of fraud upon the Government. * * *

It is fundamental in our criminal jurisprudence that the public has a right to have a person who stands legally indicted by a grand jury publicly tried on the charge. No judge has the power before hearing the testimony proffered by the Government or at least canvassing the same to enter a judgment of acquittal and thus frustrate the Government in the performance of its duty to prosecute those who violate its law.

Here, as the United States Attorney advised the court, only three witnesses of the "many * * * to be heard from * * *" had testified. The court had only begun to hear what promised to be a protracted conspiracy case involving many witnesses. The Government had not rested. * * * At such a stage of the case the District Court had no power to prejudge the Government's proof—find it insufficient or unconvincing—and set the petitioners free. * * *

NOTES AND QUESTIONS

1. Does the Court hold in *Fong Foo* that any judgment called an "acquittal" by the trial judge is immune from scrutiny? What would be the reason to have such a rule? Is Justice Clark's dissent a better way to approach the problem of premature "acquittals"? Do you see any problem with Clark's solution?

What distinction does Justice Harlan draw in his concurring opinion? Why would he have dissented if the trial judge acted solely on the basis of the prosecutor's alleged misconduct? Is this a better rule than the majority or dissent?

2. *Bright line rules.* If you are attracted to the bright line nature of the *Fong Foo* rule, consider the hopefully unusual case in which the trial judge announced, after the jury is sworn: "Ms. Prosecutor, I don't like the color of your suit, and I'm entering a verdict of acquittal on that ground." Would you apply *Fong Foo* here? If not, why apply a bright line rule in *Fong Foo* itself?

3. If a judgment called an "acquittal" is always, or almost always, a bar to a new indictment, what would you expect the rule to be for verdicts that are in substance an acquittal even though called something else by the judge? Suppose a judge dismisses an indictment at the close of the State's case on the ground that the evidence was insufficient to convict? Does it matter whether the judge entitled the dismissal an "acquittal"? In United States v. Scott, 437 U.S. 82, 98 S.Ct. 2187, 57 L.Ed.2d 65 (1978), the Court held that the label of the dismissal is unimportant, noting that "[a] defendant is acquitted only when 'the ruling of the judge, whatever its label, actually

represents a resolution [in the defendant's favor], correct or not, of some or all of the factual elements of the offense charged.'"

4.   *When is an acquittal not an acquittal, part 1?* What if the defendant pays the judge $10,000 for an acquittal? Blackstone might have had fraudulent acquittals in mind when he limited the rule of former acquittal to cases "when a man is once *fairly* found not guilty upon any indictment." 4 W. Blackstone, Commentaries *329 (emphasis added). Writing a century and a half later, Bishop noted "direct English authority" and "numerous judicial *dicta*, English and American" for the proposition that a defendant who has bribed the judge has never been in jeopardy. 1 Bishop on Criminal Law 747, § 1009 (9th ed. 1923). Anne Bowen Poulin agrees that courts should ignore the acquittal and permit a second trial "if the prosecution establishes, beyond a reasonable doubt, that the acquittal was a product of a corrupt [judicial] process." Anne Bowen Poulin, *Double Jeopardy and Judicial Accountability: When Is an Acquittal Not an Acquittal?*, 27 Ariz. St. L.J. 953, 990 (1995). In these cases, the defendant has relinquished "any claim to a protected interest in the finality of the fact finder's verdict or in the termination of the stress and anxiety of the trial." *Id.* at 989. Professor Poulin argues that a similar exception should not be recognized when a defendant corrupts members of the jury; here, the corruption of the process is less profound, and it is much more difficult to obtain because, presumably, some or most of the jury are not corrupted.

David Rudstein recognizes that an acquittal obtained by fraud is a corruption of the process but argues that it happens so infrequently that "the game hardly seems worth the candle." David S. Rudstein, *Double Jeopardy and the Fraudulently-Obtained Acquittal*, 60 Mo. L. Rev. 607, 651 (1995). The "candle," as Professor Rudstein sees it, is the potential for harassment of acquitted defendants and the loss of finality of acquittals. The State could come forward years later, allege fraud, and force an acquitted defendant to defend the charge of fraud.

One state court has reached this issue, holding that double jeopardy does not forbid a second trial when the judge was bribed to return an acquittal. People v. Aleman, 281 Ill.App.3d 991, 217 Ill.Dec. 526, 667 N.E.2d 615 (1996). The court stressed the lack of "risk that is traditionally associated with a criminal prosecution."

Refer back to Note 3. Is *Aleman* consistent with the *Scott* definition of an acquittal?

5.   *When is an acquittal not an acquittal, part 2?* In Blueford v. Arkansas, 565 U.S. ___, 132 S.Ct. 2044, 182 L.Ed.2d 937 (2012), the state charged four homicide counts: capital murder, non-capital murder, manslaughter, and negligent homicide. When the jury told the judge it was deadlocked on manslaughter, the judge asked for "the count" on the two murder charges, and the forewoman said, "Oh we are unanimous" against guilt on both murder counts. The judge sent the jury back to deliberate further, but it was not able to reach a verdict on manslaughter. Rejecting

defense pleas to allow the jury to enter not guilty verdicts on murder, the judge granted a mistrial. The Court held that the announcement in open court did not constitute a verdict for double jeopardy purposes because it was still possible for the jury to change its mind on the murder counts when it resumed deliberations. See also United States v. Sanford, 429 U.S. 14, 97 S.Ct. 20, 50 L.Ed.2d 17 (1976) (*per curiam*) (a finding of insufficient evidence by a judge is not a verdict if it occurs after the jeopardy for the first trial has ended).

You will see later that had the jury resolved the deadlock on manslaughter by convicting Blueford of that offense, the effect would have been to acquit him implicitly of the murder charges. See p. 1503, Note 1. As he was not convicted of *anything*, there was more doubt about his guilt than in cases where there is a conviction of a lesser offense. Thus, Blueford argued that he should not be treated less favorably for double jeopardy purposes than a defendant who is convicted of a lesser charge. But the *Blueford* majority was not persuaded. Blueford's argument assumes "that the votes reported by the foreperson did not change, even though the jury deliberated further after that report. That assumption is unjustified, because the reported votes were * * * not final." Justice Sotomayor, joined by Justices Ginsburg and Kagan, dissented.

6.   *Bar of prosecution appeal.* Can the prosecution appeal an acquittal? Nothing in Blackstone's pleas in bar would prohibit the appeal (but of course there were no appeals in Blackstone's day). What common law double jeopardy prohibited was a second trial. Thus, one could construe the double jeopardy clause to permit the prosecution to appeal to clarify a point of law for future cases. Whether or not the State prevails on the point of law, the acquittal still stands, and double jeopardy forbids new proceedings for that offense. In the federal system, prosecution appeal is barred because it would fail the Article III requirement of "case and controversy," but some states permit these appeals. For thoughts on prosecution appeal, including discussion of where and why it is permitted, see James A. Strazzella, *The Relationship of Double Jeopardy to Prosecution Appeals*, 73 Notre Dame L. Rev. 1 (1997).

ASHE V. SWENSON[c]
Supreme Court of the United States, 1970.
397 U.S. 436, 90 S.Ct. 1189, 25 L.Ed.2d 469.

MR. JUSTICE STEWART delivered the opinion of the Court [joined by JUSTICES BLACK, DOUGLAS, HARLAN, BRENNAN, WHITE, and MARSHALL].

In *Benton v. Maryland*, 395 U.S. 784, 89 S.Ct. 2056, 23 L.Ed.2d 707 [1969], the Court held that the Fifth Amendment guarantee against double jeopardy is enforceable against the States through the Fourteenth

---

[c]   One seat was vacant when *Ashe* was argued and decided. Abe Fortas had resigned his seat in May, 1969, and Harry Blackmun was not sworn in to take that seat until June, 1970.

Amendment. The question in this case is whether the State of Missouri violated that guarantee when it prosecuted the petitioner a second time for armed robbery in the circumstances here presented.

Sometime in the early hours of the morning of January 10, 1960, six men were engaged in a poker game in the basement of the home of John Gladson at Lee's Summit, Missouri. Suddenly three or four masked men, armed with a shotgun and pistols, broke into the basement and robbed each of the poker players of money and various articles of personal property. The robbers—and it has never been clear whether there were three or four of them—then fled in a car belonging to one of the victims of the robbery. Shortly thereafter the stolen car was discovered in a field, and later that morning three men were arrested by a state trooper while they were walking on a highway not far from where the abandoned car had been found. The petitioner was arrested by another officer some distance away.

The four were subsequently charged with seven separate offenses— the armed robbery of each of the six poker players and the theft of the car. In May 1960 the petitioner went to trial on the charge of robbing Donald Knight, one of the participants in the poker game. At the trial the State called Knight and three of his fellow poker players as prosecution witnesses. Each of them described the circumstances of the holdup and itemized his own individual losses. The proof that an armed robbery had occurred and that personal property had been taken from Knight as well as from each of the others was unassailable. The testimony of the four victims in this regard was consistent both internally and with that of the others. But the State's evidence that the petitioner had been one of the robbers was weak. Two of the witnesses thought that there had been only three robbers altogether, and could not identify the petitioner as one of them. Another of the victims, who was the petitioner's uncle by marriage, said that at the "patrol station" he had positively identified each of the other three men accused of the holdup, but could say only that the petitioner's voice "sounded very much like" that of one of the robbers. The fourth participant in the poker game did identify the petitioner, but only by his "size and height, and his actions."

The cross-examination of these witnesses was brief, and it was aimed primarily at exposing the weakness of their identification testimony. Defense counsel made no attempt to question their testimony regarding the holdup itself or their claims as to their losses. Knight testified without contradiction that the robbers had stolen from him his watch, $250 in cash, and about $500 in checks. His billfold, which had been found by the police in the possession of one of the three other men accused of the robbery, was admitted in evidence. The defense offered no testimony and waived final argument.

The trial judge instructed the jury that if it found that the petitioner was one of the participants in the armed robbery, the theft of "any money" from Knight would sustain a conviction. He also instructed the jury that if the petitioner was one of the robbers, he was guilty under the law even if he had not personally robbed Knight. The jury—though not instructed to elaborate upon its verdict—found the petitioner "not guilty due to insufficient evidence."

Six weeks later the petitioner was brought to trial again, this time for the robbery of another participant in the poker game, a man named Roberts. The petitioner filed a motion to dismiss, based on his previous acquittal. The motion was overruled, and the second trial began. The witnesses were for the most part the same, though this time their testimony was substantially stronger on the issue of the petitioner's identity. For example, two witnesses who at the first trial had been wholly unable to identify the petitioner as one of the robbers, now testified that his features, size, and mannerisms matched those of one of their assailants. Another witness who before had identified the petitioner only by his size and actions now also remembered him by the unusual sound of his voice. The State further refined its case at the second trial by declining to call one of the participants in the poker game whose identification testimony at the first trial had been conspicuously negative. The case went to the jury on instructions virtually identical to those given at the first trial. This time the jury found the petitioner guilty, and he was sentenced to a 35-year term in the state penitentiary. * * *

[The Court noted that its earlier cases had never considered "whether collateral estoppel is an ingredient of the Fifth Amendment guarantee against double jeopardy."]

"Collateral estoppel" is an awkward phrase, but it stands for an extremely important principle in our adversary system of justice. It means simply that when an issue of ultimate fact has once been determined by a valid and final judgment, that issue cannot again be litigated between the same parties in any future lawsuit. Although first developed in civil litigation, collateral estoppel has been an established rule of federal criminal law at least since this Court's decision more than 50 years ago in *United States v. Oppenheimer*, 242 U.S. 85, 37 S.Ct. 68, 61 L.Ed. 161. As Mr. Justice Holmes put the matter in that case, "It cannot be that the safeguards of the person, so often and so rightly mentioned with solemn reverence, are less than those that protect from a liability in debt." As a rule of federal law, therefore, "[i]t is much too late to suggest that this principle is not fully applicable to a former judgment in a criminal case, either because of lack of 'mutuality' or because the judgment may reflect only a belief that the Government had not met the higher burden of proof exacted in such cases for the Government's evidence as a whole although not necessarily as to every link in the chain."

The federal decisions have made clear that the rule of collateral estoppel in criminal cases is not to be applied with the hypertechnical and archaic approach of a 19th century pleading book, but with realism and rationality. Where a previous judgment of acquittal was based upon a general verdict, as is usually the case, this approach requires a court to "examine the record of a prior proceeding, taking into account the pleadings, evidence, charge, and other relevant matter, and conclude whether a rational jury could have grounded its verdict upon an issue other than that which the defendant seeks to foreclose from consideration." The inquiry "must be set in a practical frame and viewed with an eye to all the circumstances of the proceedings." Any test more technically restrictive would, of course, simply amount to a rejection of the rule of collateral estoppel in criminal proceedings, at least in every case where the first judgment was based upon a general verdict of acquittal.

Straightforward application of the federal rule to the present case can lead to but one conclusion. For the record is utterly devoid of any indication that the first jury could rationally have found that an armed robbery had not occurred, or that Knight had not been a victim of that robbery. The single rationally conceivable issue in dispute before the jury was whether the petitioner had been one of the robbers. And the jury by its verdict found that he had not. The federal rule of law, therefore, would make a second prosecution for the robbery of Roberts wholly impermissible.

The ultimate question to be determined, then, in the light of *Benton v. Maryland*, is whether this established rule of federal law is embodied in the Fifth Amendment guarantee against double jeopardy. We do not hesitate to hold that it is. For whatever else that constitutional guarantee may embrace, it surely protects a man who has been acquitted from having to "run the gantlet" a second time. Green v. United States, 355 U.S. 184, 190, 78 S.Ct. 221, 225, 2 L.Ed.2d 199 (1957).

The question is not whether Missouri could validly charge the petitioner with six separate offenses for the robbery of the six poker players. It is not whether he could have received a total of six punishments if he had been convicted in a single trial of robbing the six victims. It is simply whether, after a jury determined by its verdict that the petitioner was not one of the robbers, the State could constitutionally hale him before a new jury to litigate that issue again.

After the first jury had acquitted the petitioner of robbing Knight, Missouri could certainly not have brought him to trial again upon that charge. Once a jury had determined upon conflicting testimony that there was at least a reasonable doubt that the petitioner was one of the robbers, the State could not present the same or different identification evidence in a second prosecution for the robbery of Knight in the hope that a different jury might find that evidence more convincing. The situation is constitutionally no different here, even though the second trial related to another victim of the same robbery. For the name of the victim, in the circumstances of this case, had no bearing whatever upon the issue of whether the petitioner was one of the robbers.

In this case the State in its brief has frankly conceded that following the petitioner's acquittal, it treated the first trial as no more than a dry run for the second prosecution: "No doubt the prosecutor felt the state had a provable case on the first charge and, when he lost, he did what every good attorney would do—he refined his presentation in light of the turn of events at the first trial." But this is precisely what the constitutional guarantee forbids. * * *

[The concurring opinions of JUSTICE BLACK, JUSTICE HARLAN, and JUSTICE BRENNAN are omitted.]

MR. CHIEF JUSTICE BURGER, dissenting.

* * * Nothing in the language or gloss previously placed on this provision of the Fifth Amendment remotely justifies the treatment that the Court today accords to the collateral-estoppel doctrine. Nothing in the purpose of the authors of the Constitution commands or even justifies what the Court decides today; this is truly a case of expanding a sound basic principle beyond the bounds—or needs—of its rational and legitimate objectives to preclude harassment of an accused. * * *

II * * *

The majority rests its holding in part on a series of cases beginning with *United States v. Oppenheimer*, which did not involve constitutional double jeopardy but applied collateral estoppel as developed in civil litigation to federal criminal prosecutions as a matter of this Court's supervisory power over the federal court system. The Court now finds the federal collateral estoppel rule to be an "ingredient" of the Fifth Amendment guarantee against double jeopardy and applies it to the States through the Fourteenth Amendment; this is an ingredient that eluded judges and justices for nearly two centuries.

The collateral-estoppel concept—originally a product only of civil litigation—is a strange mutant as it is transformed to control this criminal case. In civil cases the doctrine was justified as conserving judicial resources as well as those of the parties to the actions and additionally as providing the finality needed to plan for the future. It ordinarily applies to parties on each side of the litigation who have the same interest as or who are identical with the parties in the initial litigation. Here the complainant in the second trial is not the same as in the first even though the State is a party in both cases. Very properly, in criminal cases, finality and conservation of private, public, and judicial resources are lesser values than in civil litigation. Also, courts that have applied the collateral-estoppel concept to criminal actions would certainly not apply it to *both* parties, as is true in civil cases, *i.e.*, here, if Ashe had been convicted at the first trial, presumably no court would then hold that he was thereby foreclosed from litigating the identification issue at the second trial.

Perhaps, then, it comes as no surprise to find that the only expressed rationale for the majority's decision is that Ashe has "run the gantlet" once before. This is not a doctrine of the law or legal reasoning but a colorful and graphic phrase, which, as used originally in an opinion of the Court written by Mr. Justice Black, was intended to mean something entirely different. The full phrase is "run the gantlet *once on that charge* * * *"; it is to be found in *Green v. United States*, 355 U.S. 184, 190, 78 S.Ct. 221, 225 (1957), where no question of multiple crimes against multiple victims was involved. Green, having been found guilty of second degree murder on a charge of first degree, secured a new trial. This Court held nothing more than that Green, once put in jeopardy—once having "run the gantlet * * * *on that charge*"—of first degree murder, could not be compelled to defend against that charge again on retrial.

Today's step in this area of constitutional law ought not be taken on no more basis than casual reliance on the "gantlet" phrase lifted out of the context in which it was originally used. This is decision by slogan. * * *

Finally, the majority's opinion tells us "that the rule of collateral estoppel in criminal cases is not to be applied with the hypertechnical and archaic approach of a 19th century pleading book, but with realism and rationality."

With deference I am bound to pose the question: what is reasonable and rational about holding that an acquittal of Ashe for robbing Knight bars a trial for robbing Roberts? To borrow a phrase from the Court's opinion, what could conceivably be more "hypertechnical and archaic" and more like the stilted formalisms of 17th and 18th century common-law England, than to stretch jeopardy for robbing Knight into jeopardy for robbing Roberts? * * *

NOTES AND QUESTIONS

1.   *Implied acquittals.* Both the majority and Chief Justice Burger's dissent quote Green v. United States, 355 U.S. 184, 190, 78 S.Ct. 221, 225, 2 L.Ed.2d 199 (1957). The majority picks out the "run the gantlet" phrase in an analytical move that may justify Burger's charge of jurisprudence by

sloganeering. But Burger ignores a substantive parallel with *Green*. Green was charged with first degree murder and convicted of second degree murder. When his second degree murder conviction was overturned on appeal, the Court held that he could not be retried for first degree murder because the first jury's verdict of a lesser included offense amounted to an implicit acquittal of the greater offense. Was Ashe not implicitly acquitted of robbing all of the poker players?

2.   Chief Justice Burger is right that collateral estoppel is a further "gloss" on the tests that the Court has used to figure out when two offenses are the "same offense" under the double jeopardy clause. It is without doubt correct that the robbery of six individuals is six double jeopardy offenses of robbery even if committed in one "transaction"—the *Ashe* majority says as much and *Blockburger* compels this outcome—yet Ashe wins because of collateral estoppel. Do you see the conceptual relationship between *Ashe* and the other acquittal cases we have studied to this point? Doesn't *Ashe* apply the same principle as *Scott* (Note 4 following *Fong Foo*)?

3.   *Easy and hard cases.* Conceptually, the verdict in *Ashe* operated as a not guilty verdict on *all offenses* that require proof that Ashe was the robber. This requires an understanding of what facts are necessarily found in the defendant's favor by the acquitting jury. For an easy case, consider the defense of mistaken identity. A defendant acquitted in that trial cannot be tried for any crime that requires proof of his presence at the crime scene. Harris v. Washington, 404 U.S. 55, 92 S.Ct. 183, 30 L.Ed.2d 212 (1971) (*per curiam*).

But plenty of hard cases exist, too. In Ex parte Taylor, 101 S.W.3d 434 (Tex. Crim. App. 2002), the accused lost control of his car and both of the passengers died in the ensuing accident. He was charged with two counts of "intoxication manslaughter." In the trial of one count, evidence of alcohol consumption and his blood alcohol content was introduced, but the jury acquitted. The State then sought to try Taylor for the second death, this time using evidence of marijuana consumption. Permissible? Is there something you need to know before you can answer?

4.   *Clarifying Ashe.* The Court clarified the collateral estoppel terminology in Taylor v. Sturgell, 553 U.S. 880, 128 S.Ct. 2161, 171 L.Ed.2d 155 (2008), a civil case. In a footnote, the Court said that it intended to replace "collateral estoppel" with "issue preclusion." The new terminology puts the focus on what must be decided—whether a prior verdict precluded the State from prosecuting an issue in a new proceeding. In 2009, the Court applied "issue preclusion" in a way that clarifies the substance of the doctrine.

Begin with the facts of *Ashe* but assume that the first jury could not agree on a verdict and the judge declared a mistrial on account of a "hung jury." As you will shortly see (p. 1511, Note 6), the Court has held since 1824 that a mistrial based on a hung jury does not constitute a jeopardy bar to another trial for the very same offense. Thus, if the first jury had hung, rather than acquitting Ashe, the State could have recharged the robbery of Knight or, if it wished, one or more of the other poker players.

Now to a hypothetical that parallels the facts in Yeager v. United States, 557 U.S. 110, 129 S.Ct. 2360, 174 L.Ed.2d 78 (2009). What if in the case of the prosecution of the robberies of Knight and Player #2, the jury acquits as to Knight and is hung as to Player #2? A hung jury is not a bar to a new trial, but here the acquittal perhaps forecloses the possibility that Ashe was the robber. In *Yeager*, the Court held, 6–3, that the acquittal would operate as issue preclusion if the State sought to re-prosecute the count on which the jury was hung. Just as the *Powell* Court ignored the acquittal, the *Yeager* Court ignored the hung jury: "Courts properly avoid explorations into a jury's sovereign space, and for good reason. The jury's deliberations are secret and not subject to outside examination."

One way to read *Yeager* is that a hung jury is meaningless in the double jeopardy calculus because "the fact that a jury hangs is evidence of nothing— other than, of course, that it has failed to decide anything." This reading explains the rule since 1824 that a hung jury is not a jeopardy bar. A hung jury is nothing. Thus, the acquittal that accompanies the hung jury can be given preclusive effect.

What if the *Ashe* jury had acquitted on the robbery of Knight, convicted on the robbery of Player #2, and deadlocked on Players #3–#6? Recall *United States v. Powell*, p. 1385, Note 3.D, where the Court held that juries have the prerogative to return contradictory verdicts. But the effect of contradictory verdicts is that the acquittal loses its preclusive effect: "The problem is that the same jury reached inconsistent results; once that is established principles of collateral estoppel—which are predicated on the assumption that the jury acted rationally and found certain facts in reaching its verdict—are no longer useful." This language from *Powell* suggests that the acquittal of the robbery of Ashe would *not* bar a new trial for robbing Players #3–#6.

5. *Convictions as acquittals.* We saw in *Ashe* that an acquittal of one offense can sometimes "acquit" of another offense even though they are not the "same offense" under *Blockburger*. Oddly enough, even a conviction can sometimes function as an acquittal.

Suppose an appellate reversal reveals a fundamental weakness in the sufficiency of the State's case. As Chapter 19 will show, p. 1524, the necessary implication of an appellate finding of insufficient evidence is that no rational jury could have found the defendant guilty, and the judge should have granted an acquittal at the close of the case. In effect, the trial process failed the defendant. Not only did the jury fail to deliver an acquittal, but the trial judge failed to enter an acquittal to which the defendant was entitled. In that situation of double failure—a conviction based on insufficient evidence that the trial judge does not remedy—the Court held unanimously in Burks v. United States, 437 U.S. 1, 98 S.Ct. 2141, 57 L.Ed.2d 1 (1978), that double jeopardy bars a retrial. The Court reasoned that there is no reason to treat a defendant differently when the jury and judge fail her than she would have been treated if the jury and judge had done their job properly. Cf. Tibbs v. Florida, 457 U.S. 31, 102 S.Ct. 2211, 72 L.Ed.2d 652 (1982) (holding that a finding that a conviction is "against the weight of the evidence" is not a jeopardy bar).

C. THE MISTRIAL DOCTRINE

Not all trials end in verdict. Some end in a mistrial or dismissal prior to a formal verdict. The distinction between a mistrial and a dismissal is more procedural than substantive. A mistrial contemplates setting a new trial date for the same charge, while a dismissal requires the State to refile charges and begin again. In both cases, the lack of a verdict usually permits the State to bring the case again if it wishes. Occasionally, however, the grounds for granting a pre-verdict termination, or the way it is granted, will cause a court to find that the double jeopardy clause forbids a second trial.

A thorny question is what circumstances cause courts to treat pre-verdict trial endings as equivalent to a verdict. No complete answer exists. One clear category consists of cases in which the defendant's chance at an acquittal are undermined by the pre-verdict termination. Viewed this way, the mistrial doctrine is simply a prophylaxis to prevent avoidance of the former acquittal doctrine. The next case can be partly, but only partly, explained by "acquittal avoidance."

DOWNUM V. UNITED STATES
Supreme Court of the United States, 1963.
372 U.S. 734, 83 S.Ct. 1033, 10 L.Ed.2d 100.

MR. JUSTICE DOUGLAS delivered the opinion of the Court [joined by CHIEF JUSTICE WARREN and JUSTICES BLACK, BRENNAN, and GOLDBERG]. * * *

On the morning of April 25, 1961, the case was called for trial and both sides announced ready. A jury was selected and sworn and instructed to return at 2 p.m. When it returned, the prosecution asked that the jury be discharged because its key witness on Counts 6 and 7 was not present—one Rutledge * * * . Petitioner moved that Counts 6 and 7 be dismissed for want of prosecution and asked that the trial continue on the rest of the counts. This motion was denied and the judge discharged the jury over petitioner's objection. Two days later when the case was called again and a second jury impaneled, petitioner pleaded former jeopardy. His plea was overruled, a trial was had, and he was found guilty. * * *

The present case was one of a dozen set for call during the previous week, and those cases involved approximately 100 witnesses. Subpoenas for all of them, including Rutledge, had been delivered to the marshal for service. The day before the case was first called, the prosecutor's assistant checked with the marshal and learned that Rutledge's wife was going to let him know where her husband was, if she could find out. No word was received from her and no follow-up was made. The prosecution allowed the jury to be selected and sworn even though one of its key witnesses was absent and had not been found.

From *United States v. Perez*, 9 Wheat. 579, 6 L.Ed. 165, decided in 1824, to *Gori v. United States*, 367 U.S. 364, 81 S.Ct. 1523, 6 L.Ed.2d 901, decided in 1961, it has been agreed that there are occasions when a second trial may be had although the jury impaneled for the first trial was discharged without reaching a verdict and without the defendant's consent. The classic example is a mistrial because the jury is unable to agree. *United States v. Perez, supra*. In *Wade v. Hunter*, 336 U.S. 684, 69 S.Ct. 834, 93 L.Ed. 974 [1949], the tactical problems of an army in the field were held to justify the withdrawal of a court-martial proceeding and the commencement of another one on a later day. Discovery by the judge during a trial that a member or members of the jury were biased *pro* or *con* one side has been held to warrant discharge of the jury and direction of a new trial. At times the valued right of a defendant to have his trial completed by the particular tribunal summoned to sit in judgment on him may be subordinated to the public interest—when there is an imperious necessity to do so. Differences have arisen as to the application of the principle. Harassment of an accused by successive prosecutions or declaration of a mistrial so as to afford the prosecution a more favorable opportunity to convict are examples when jeopardy attaches. But those extreme cases do not mark the limits of the guarantee. The discretion to discharge the jury before it has reached a verdict is to be exercised "only in very extraordinary and striking circumstances," to use the words of Mr. Justice Story * * * . For the prohibition of the Double Jeopardy Clause is "not against being twice punished, but against being twice put in jeopardy."

The jury first selected to try petitioner and sworn was discharged because a prosecution witness had not been served with a summons and because no other arrangements had been made to assure his presence. That witness was essential only for two of the six counts concerning petitioner. Yet the prosecution opposed petitioner's motion to dismiss those two counts and to proceed with a trial on the other four counts—a motion the court denied. Here, as in *Wade v. Hunter, supra*, we refuse to say that the absence of witnesses "can never justify discontinuance of a trial." Each case must turn on its facts. On this record, however, we think what was said in *Cornero v. United States*, [48 F.2d 69 (9th Cir. 1931)], states the governing principle. There a trial was first continued because prosecution witnesses were not present, and when they had not been found at the time the case was again called, the jury was discharged. A plea of double jeopardy was sustained when a second jury was selected, the court saying:

> "The fact is that, when the district attorney impaneled the jury without first ascertaining whether or not his witnesses were present, he took a chance. While their absence might have justified a continuance of the case in view of the fact that they were under bond to appear at that time and place, the question presented here is entirely different from that involved in the exercise of the sound discretion of the trial court in granting a continuance in furtherance of justice. The situation presented is simply one where the district attorney entered upon the trial of the case without sufficient evidence to convict. This does not take the case out of the rule with reference to former jeopardy. There is no difference in principle between a discovery by the district attorney immediately after the jury was impaneled that his evidence was insufficient and a discovery after he had called some or all of his witnesses."

That view, which has some support in the authorities, is in our view the correct one. We resolve any doubt "in favor of the liberty of the citizen, rather than exercise what would be an unlimited, uncertain, and arbitrary judicial discretion." * * *

MR. JUSTICE CLARK, with whom MR. JUSTICE HARLAN, MR. JUSTICE STEWART and MR. JUSTICE WHITE join, dissenting. * * *

* * * Since the prosecutor was trying another case on the Tuesday morning that petitioner's case was called, he was unable immediately to contact the marshal and determine whether Mr. Rutledge was present, and he announced ready for trial without ascertaining this. The jury for petitioner's case was selected and then excused until 2 p.m., and the prosecutor proceeded to complete the hearing of his other case before noon. Then, upon checking with the marshal's office during the noon recess, the prosecutor discovered that Rutledge was not present. He immediately informed the judge in his chambers, and upon the opening of the afternoon session defense counsel was advised in open court that the key witness of the Government was not available and the case would have to go over a couple of days. * * *

The first jury had never begun to act in this case. Petitioner was never formally arraigned in the presence of the first jury, nor was any evidence presented or heard for or against him at that time, nor was he required to put on any defense. In addition, the second jury having been impaneled two days later, there was no continued or prolonged anxiety, nor was the petitioner caused any additional expense or embarrassment, deprived of any right or prejudiced in any way. Neither has petitioner contended that one jury was more or less favorable than the other.

The conclusions of the trial court and the Court of Appeals indicate that they viewed the circumstances in which the prosecutor found himself as having resulted from excusable oversight. There is no indication that the prosecutor's explanation was a mere cover for negligent preparation or that his action was in any way deliberate. There is nothing in the record that even suggests that the circumstances were used by the prosecutor for the purpose of securing a more favorable jury or in any way to take advantage of or to harass the petitioner. Indeed, it appears to be just one of those circumstances which often creep into a prosecutor's life as a result of inadvertence when many cases must be handled during a short trial period. * * *

As I see the problem, the issue is whether the action of the prosecutor in failing to check on the presence of his witness before allowing a jury to be sworn was of such moment that it constituted a deprival of the petitioner's rights and entitled him to a verdict of acquittal without any trial on the merits. Obviously under the facts here he suffered no such deprivation. Ever since *Perez* this Court has recognized that the "ends of public justice" must be considered in determining such a question. In this light I cannot see how this Court finds that the trial judge abused his discretion in affording the Government a two-day period in which to bring forward its key witness who, to its surprise, was found to be temporarily absent. I believe that the "ends of public justice," to which Mr. Justice Story referred in *Perez*, require that the Government have a fair opportunity to present the people's case and obtain adjudication on the merits, rather than that the criminal be turned free because of the harmless oversight of the prosecutor.

NOTES AND QUESTIONS

1.   Is *Downum* best explained as giving the defendant the acquittal that was perhaps avoided by the mistrial or is there a core right to have the case heard by the jury that had been sworn?

2.   What could the trial judge have done in *Downum* to avoid the double jeopardy problem?

3.   *When jeopardy "attaches."* A defendant cannot plead double jeopardy until one jeopardy has begun ("attached") and ended. It is obvious, and trivial, that jeopardy ends with a conviction or acquittal. The only time the issue of attachment and the end of jeopardy become important is in cases, like *Downum*, that terminate prior to a formal verdict. Notice that in *Downum*, the jury had been sworn but no witnesses had been called when the prosecutor obtained a mistrial. That point, the Court later held, is when jeopardy attaches in a jury trial. Crist v. Bretz, 437 U.S. 28, 98 S.Ct. 2156, 57 L.Ed.2d 24 (1978). The Court suggested in *Crist* that jeopardy attaches in a bench trial when the first witness was sworn, the point Montana had chosen for jury trials as well as bench trials. But *Crist* held the Montana law

unconstitutional as it applied to jury trials. Can you think of a reason to hold unconstitutional a state rule that jeopardy attaches in a jury trial case only when the first witness is sworn?

4.   *Problem: the judge who is quick on the trigger. J,* an accountant, is prosecuted for assisting the preparation of fraudulent income tax returns. The government has subpoenaed the taxpayers for whom *J* prepared the returns in question. The trial judge warns the first of these witnesses of his privilege against self-incrimination and, despite his willingness to testify, refuses to allow the testimony until he has consulted with a lawyer. Upon learning that the remaining witnesses were similarly situated, the judge declares a mistrial so abruptly that there is no opportunity for the prosecutor to suggest a continuance or for *J* to object to the discharge of the jury. Should double jeopardy forbid a second trial for this offense? United States v. Jorn, 400 U.S. 470, 91 S.Ct. 547, 27 L.Ed.2d 543 (1971) (plurality). Is this a form of "acquittal avoidance?"

5.   *Downum redux.* In Martinez v. Illinois, 572 U.S. ___, 134 S.Ct. 2070, 188 L.Ed.2d 1112 (2014) (per curiam), the inability of the State to secure the attendance of two witnesses complicated attempts to try the defendant. When the witnesses did not appear after repeated subpoenas, the trial court offered to dismiss the case before the jury was sworn. The prosecutor instead moved for a continuance, which the court denied, noting that the case would soon be four years old. The trial court announced that it would swear the jurors, and the prosecutor told the judge that "the State will not be participating in the trial. I wanted you to know that." The court responded: "Very well. We'll see how that works out."

The prosecutor refused to make an opening statement, and the defense moved for a judgment of acquittal, noting that the State had presented no evidence and had indicated its intention not to present evidence. The court gave the State an opportunity to reply; the prosecutor once again said that the State was not participating in the trial. The judge granted the motion for a judgment of acquittal.

The Illinois Appellate Court and Illinois Supreme Court held that jeopardy had never attached because the State did not participate in the trial and thus the defendant was not subjected to the risk of conviction. The state supreme court recognized that jeopardy "generally" attaches when the jury is sworn, but declared what happened in *Martinez* an exception to the general rule. It noted that "rigid, mechanical rules" should not govern the issue of when jeopardy attaches.

When Martinez filed his petition for certiorari, the State waived the right to reply, an appellate version of the prosecutor not participating in the trial. The State did, however, respond to the Court's request for a response, and the Court reversed the state courts without benefit of oral argument. One commentator said that deciding the case on the paper record was "the judicial version of a slap upside the back of Illinois' head."

The "slap" was a unanimous per curiam opinion that said, in effect, that a mechanical rule is needed here. Of course to say that jeopardy attaches is to say nothing of whether a defendant can be retried. What matters is the outcome of the attachment of jeopardy. Here, as in *Downum*, the prosecution presented no evidence. Unlike *Downum*, the trial judge in *Martinez* granted a judgment of acquittal based on its view that the State had failed to prove its case. As the Court put it tersely: "And because Martinez was acquitted, the State cannot retry him."

Notice that *Martinez* is not technically a mistrial case because the trial court granted a motion for acquittal. But the Supreme Court said in a footnote that the result would "probably" still have been the same had the judge granted a mistrial after the jury was sworn, citing *Downum,* because the absence of witnesses does not normally constitute adequate cause for a mistrial. When the cause of the mistrial is not lack of evidence, the mistrial doctrine is governed by what the Court has described as a "manifest necessity doctrine," the subject of the next Note

6. *Downum* is the only Supreme Court mistrial case with a majority opinion (a five-justice majority at that) in favor of the defendant. *Jorn* had no majority opinion. Thus, we have no clear rules that tell us when defendants will win a mistrial claim. We do, however, have a clear rule about when they will *lose*. The Court established in a Justice Story opinion in United States v. Perez, 22 U.S. (9 Wheat.) 579, 6 L.Ed. 165 (1824), that a mistrial based on a hung jury has no double jeopardy consequences, and the Court has never wavered from that rule.

When a mistrial is granted to cure a flawed trial, but without an inference of acquittal avoidance, there is no rule whatsoever. Even the norm here is fuzzy. The Court on occasion speaks of the "valued right of a defendant to have his trial completed by the particular jury summoned to sit in judgment against him." But the basis for this norm is not clear. Is it because of the expense and anxiety of having to start over? Presumably due process would not allow the prosecution to terminate a trial arbitrarily and force the defendant to defend again; thus, as far as this rationale is concerned, double jeopardy seems to add nothing to due process. Perhaps there is value in letting the defendant, rather than the prosecutor, decide whether to proceed to verdict, a value that is embedded in the double jeopardy clause.

7. *Mistrials and the Holy Roman Empire.* The Court has developed a sort of "test" for when another trial can follow a mistrial—the mistrial must have been "required by 'manifest necessity' or the 'ends of public justice.'" Putting content to those terms, of course, is far from easy. Indeed, Professor Stephen Schulhofer has concluded that the "manifest necessity" standard is a "thoroughly deceptive misnomer, perhaps not rivaled even by the Holy Roman Empire." Stephen J. Schulhofer, *Jeopardy and Mistrials*, 125 U. Pa. L. Rev. 449, 491 (1977).

In Illinois v. Somerville, 410 U.S. 458, 93 S.Ct. 1066, 35 L.Ed.2d 425 (1973), the prosecutor went to trial with an indictment that did not charge a crime under state law and could not be remedied by amendment. Thus, the only alternative to a mistrial was to proceed to verdict; if the verdict was a conviction, it would be subject to automatic reversal. After the jury was empaneled and sworn, but before any evidence had been presented, the judge granted the prosecutor's motion for mistrial. The Court held, 5–4, that the mistrial did not constitute a jeopardy bar. Can you distinguish *Somerville* from *Downum*?

The narrow holding in *Somerville* is consistent with *Downum*: A "trial judge properly exercises his discretion to declare a mistrial if an impartial verdict cannot be reached, or if a verdict of conviction could be reached but would have to be reversed on appeal due to an obvious procedural error in the trial."

But the dicta and analysis in *Somerville* repudiates the central tenet of *Downum*. Recall what the Court said in *Downum* about the exercise of discretion: "We resolve any doubt 'in favor of the liberty of the citizen, rather than exercise what would be an unlimited, uncertain, and arbitrary judicial discretion.' " The *Somerville* Court turned that proposition on its head, almost presuming that the trial court made the right decision. At one point, the Court said that the "broad discretion reserved to the trial judge" when considering a mistrial motion "has been consistently reiterated in decisions of this Court." To justify this departure from the *Downum* analysis, the Court quoted at length from Justice Story's 1824 opinion holding that a mistrial based on a hung jury did not bar a second trial.

> We think, that in all cases of this nature, the law has invested Courts of justice with the authority to discharge a jury from giving any verdict, whenever, in their opinion, taking all the circumstances into consideration, there is a manifest necessity for the act, or the ends of public justice would otherwise be defeated. They are to exercise a sound discretion on the subject; and it is impossible to define all the circumstances, which would render it proper to interfere. To be sure, the power ought to be used with the greatest caution, under urgent circumstances, and for very plain and obvious causes; and, in capital cases especially, Courts should be extremely careful how they interfere with any of the chances of life, in favour of the prisoner. But, after all, they have the right to order the discharge; and the security which the public have for the faithful, sound, and conscientious exercise of this discretion, rests, in this, as in other cases, upon the responsibility of the Judges, under their oaths of office.

United States v. Perez, 22 U.S. (9 Wheat.) 579, 6 L.Ed. 165 (1824).

For the *Somerville* dissent, the key to the case was that the mistrial was necessitated because of the prosecutor's error. In that way, *Somerville* is like *Downum*. As Justice White put it: "Judged by the standards of *Downum* and

Jorn I cannot find, in the words of the majority, an 'important countervailing interest of proper judicial administration' in this case; I cannot find 'manifest necessity' for a mistrial to compensate for prosecutorial mistake."

Which prosecutor's mistake—the one in *Downum* or the one in *Somerville*—is more egregious? But perhaps that is not the right question. Which mistake is more likely to provide the trial judge with "manifest necessity" to declare a mistrial?

8. *Defense motion for mistrial.* One might think that a *defense* motion for a mistrial would never create a jeopardy bar. After all, the defendant is getting what he requested. But imagine a case where the prosecutor is losing and *she creates grounds for a mistrial* that leave the defendant with little chance of a fair verdict. The most difficult case for defendants is when the prosecutor exposes the jury to improper, prejudicial information likely to lead them to vote guilty. Should there be a double jeopardy remedy in that kind of case?

In *Oregon v. Kennedy*, 456 U.S. 667, 102 S.Ct. 2083, 72 L.Ed.2d 416 (1982), the Court held that a defense motion for a mistrial constituted a jeopardy bar to a second trial when, but only when, "the governmental conduct in question is intended to 'goad' the defendant into moving for a mistrial."

Justice Stevens, writing for four members of the Court, concurred in the judgment in *Kennedy*. Stevens rejected the majority's "intent to goad" standard in favor of a more malleable standard based on overreaching: "To invoke the exception for overreaching, a court need not divine the exact motivation for the prosecutorial error. It is sufficient that the court is persuaded that egregious prosecutorial misconduct has rendered unmeaningful the defendant's choice to continue or to abort the proceeding."

Which standard do you prefer?

9. *Problem: the persistent prosecutor.* Pursuant to a defense *motion in limine*, the judge orders the prosecutor not to introduce three items of evidence in a child sexual abuse case, on the ground that the evidence would be highly prejudicial and not sufficiently probative. Toward the end of the trial, the prosecutor refers, at different times, to all three items of evidence. The defendant first objects and then moves for a mistrial. The judge sustains the objection, telling the prosecutor that his actions deserved a contempt of court citation, but denies the motion for mistrial. The jury convicts. On appeal, the conviction is reversed on the ground that the judge should have granted a mistrial. At a second trial, before a different judge, the same evidentiary order is entered and, amazingly, the prosecutor again refers to each item of evidence near the end of the trial. This time, the judge grants the defendant's mistrial motion. Will the defendant win a jeopardy claim against a third trial under the *Oregon v. Kennedy* (Note 8) standard? What about under Justice Stevens's standard in his concurring opinion?

10. Some states have rejected the *Kennedy* standard as an interpretation of their own constitutions, including Oregon on remand from the United States Supreme Court in *Kennedy*. See State v. Kennedy, 295 Or. 260, 666 P.2d 1316 (1983) (standard is whether prosecutor intended, or was indifferent to the danger of, a mistrial). In Bauder v. State, 921 S.W.2d 696 (Tex. Crim. App. 1996), the state court noted the temptation the prosecutor faces when he realizes he has a losing case. This prosecutor can improve his position by deliberately offering objectionable evidence which he believes will materially improve his chances to obtain a conviction. He might get a conviction or, if that fails, provoke a mistrial motion by the defense. Either way, he's better off than if he does not offer objectionable evidence. When that happens, the court wrote that "it seems to us that the prosecutor's specific intent, whether to cause a mistrial or to produce a necessarily unfair trial or simply to improve his own position in the case, is irrelevant. In our view, putting a defendant to this choice, even recklessly, is constitutionally indistinguishable from deliberately forcing him to choose a mistrial." See also Pool v. Superior Court, 139 Ariz. 98, 677 P.2d 261 (1984).

D. THE "DUAL SOVEREIGNTY" EXCEPTION TO EVERYTHING YOU HAVE LEARNED SO FAR

BARTKUS V. ILLINOIS

Supreme Court of the United States, 1959.
359 U.S. 121, 79 S.Ct. 676, 3 L.Ed.2d 684.

MR. JUSTICE FRANKFURTER delivered the opinion of the Court [joined by JUSTICES CLARK, HARLAN, WHITTAKER, and STEWART].

Petitioner was tried in the Federal District Court for the Northern District of Illinois on December 18, 1953, for robbery of a federally insured savings and loan association * * * . The case was tried to a jury and resulted in an acquittal. On January 8, 1954, an Illinois grand jury indicted Bartkus. The facts recited in the Illinois indictment were substantially identical to those contained in the prior federal indictment. The Illinois indictment charged that these facts constituted a violation of [an] Illinois * * * robbery statute. Bartkus was tried and convicted in the Criminal Court of Cook County and was sentenced to life imprisonment under the Illinois Habitual Criminal Statute.

The Illinois trial court considered and rejected petitioner's plea of *autrefois acquit*. * * *

The state and federal prosecutions were separately conducted. It is true that the agent of the Federal Bureau of Investigation who had conducted the investigation on behalf of the Federal Government turned over to the Illinois prosecuting officials all the evidence he had gathered against the petitioner. Concededly, some of that evidence had been gathered after acquittal in the federal court. The only other connection between the two trials is to be found in a suggestion that the federal sentencing of the accomplices who testified against petitioner in both trials was purposely continued by the federal court until after they testified in the state trial. The record establishes that the prosecution was undertaken by state prosecuting officials within their discretionary responsibility and on the basis of evidence that conduct contrary to the penal code of Illinois had occurred within their jurisdiction. It establishes also that federal officials acted in cooperation with state authorities, as is the conventional practice between the two sets of prosecutors throughout the country. It does not support the claim that the State of Illinois in bringing its prosecution was merely a tool of the federal authorities, who thereby avoided the prohibition of the Fifth Amendment against a retrial of a federal prosecution after an acquittal. It does not sustain a conclusion that the state prosecution was a sham and a cover for a federal prosecution, and thereby in essential fact another federal prosecution.

* * * The Fifth Amendment's proscription of double jeopardy has been invoked and rejected in over twenty cases of real or hypothetical successive state and federal prosecution cases before this Court. * * *

* * * [In Moore v. Illinois, 55 U.S. (14 How.) 13, 14 L.Ed. 306 (1852), the Court] gave definitive statement to the rule which had been evolving:

"An offence, in its legal signification, means the transgression of a law."

"Every citizen of the United States is also a citizen of a State or territory. He may be said to owe allegiance to two sovereigns, and may be liable to punishment for an infraction of the laws of either. The same act may be an offence or transgression of the laws of both."

"That either or both may (if they see fit) punish such an offender, cannot be doubted. Yet it cannot be truly averred that the offender has been twice punished for the same offence; but only that by one act he has committed two offences, for each of which he is justly punishable. He could not plead the punishment by one in bar to a conviction by the other."

* * * Indeed Mr. Justice Holmes once wrote of this rule that it "is too plain to need more than statement." * * *

The entire history of litigation and contention over the question of the imposition of a bar to a second prosecution by a government other than the one first prosecuting is a manifestation of the evolutionary unfolding of law. Today a number of States have statutes which bar a second prosecution if the defendant has been once tried by another government for a similar offense. A study of the cases under the New

York statute, which is typical of these laws, demonstrates that the task of determining when the federal and state statutes are so much alike that a prosecution under the former bars a prosecution under the latter is a difficult one. The proper solution of that problem frequently depends upon a judgment of the gravamen of the state statute. It depends also upon an understanding of the scope of the bar that has been historically granted in the State to prevent successive state prosecutions. Both these problems are ones with which the States are obviously more competent to deal than is this Court. Furthermore, the rules resulting will intimately affect the efforts of a State to develop a rational and just body of criminal law in the protection of its citizens. We ought not to utilize the Fourteenth Amendment to interfere with this development. Finally, experience such as that of New York may give aid to Congress in its consideration of adoption of similar provisions in individual federal criminal statutes or in the federal criminal code.

Precedent, experience, and reason alike support the conclusion that Alfonse Bartkus has not been deprived of due process of law by the State of Illinois. * * *

MR. JUSTICE BLACK, with whom THE CHIEF JUSTICE [WARREN] and MR. JUSTICE DOUGLAS concur, dissenting.

Petitioner, Bartkus, was indicted in a United States District Court for bank robbery. He was tried by a jury and acquitted. So far as appears the trial was conducted fairly by an able and conscientious judge. Later, Bartkus was indicted in an Illinois state court for the same bank robbery. This time he was convicted and sentenced to life imprisonment. His acquittal in the federal court would have barred a second trial in any court of the United States because of the provision in the Fifth Amendment that no person shall "be subject for the same offence to be twice put in jeopardy of life or limb." The Court today rejects Bartkus' contention that his state conviction after a federal acquittal violates the Fourteenth Amendment to our Constitution. I cannot agree.

* * * *United States v. Lanza*, decided in 1922, allowed federal conviction and punishment of a man who had been previously convicted and punished for the identical acts by one of our States. Today, for the first time in its history, this Court upholds the state conviction of a defendant who had been *acquitted* of the same offense in the federal courts. I would hold that a federal trial following either state acquittal or conviction is barred by the Double Jeopardy Clause of the Fifth Amendment. * * *

Fear and abhorrence of governmental power to try people twice for the same conduct is one of the oldest ideas found in western civilization. Its roots run deep into Greek and Roman times. Even in the Dark Ages, when so many other principles of justice were lost, the idea that one trial and one punishment were enough remained alive through the canon law and the teachings of the early Christian writers. By the thirteenth century it seems to have been firmly established in England, where it came to be considered as a "universal maxim of the common law." It is not surprising, therefore, that the principle was brought to this country by the earliest settlers as part of their heritage of freedom, and that it has been recognized here as fundamental again and again. Today it is found, in varying forms, not only in the Federal Constitution, but in the jurisprudence or constitutions of every State, as well as most foreign nations. It has, in fact, been described as a part of all advanced systems of law and as one of those universal principles "of reason, justice, and conscience, of which Cicero said: 'Nor is it one thing at Rome and another at Athens, one now and another in the future, but among all nations it is the same.'" While some writers have explained the opposition to double prosecutions by emphasizing the injustice inherent in two punishments for the same act, and others have stressed the dangers to the innocent from allowing the full power of the state to be brought against them in two trials, the basic and recurring theme has always simply been that it is wrong for a man to "be brought into Danger for the same Offence more than once." Few principles have been more deeply "rooted in the traditions and conscience of our people."

The Court apparently takes the position that a second trial for the same act is somehow less offensive if one of the trials is conducted by the Federal Government and the other by a State. Looked at from the standpoint of the individual who is being prosecuted, this notion is too subtle for me to grasp. If double punishment is what is feared, it hurts no less for two "Sovereigns" to inflict it than for one. If danger to the innocent is emphasized, that danger is surely no less when the power of State and Federal Governments is brought to bear on one man in two trials, than when one of these "Sovereigns" proceeds alone. In each case, inescapably, a man is forced to face danger twice for the same conduct.

The Court, without denying the almost universal abhorrence of such double prosecutions, nevertheless justifies the practice here in the name of "federalism." This, it seems to me, is a misuse and desecration of the concept. * * *

One may, I think, infer from the fewness of the cases [cited by the Court] that retrials after acquittal have been considered particularly obnoxious, worse even, in the eyes of many, than retrials after conviction. I doubt, in fact, if many practices which have been found to violate due process can boast of so little actual support. Yet it is on this meager basis that the Court must ultimately rest its finding that Bartkus' retrial does not violate fundamental principles "rooted in the traditions and conscience of our peoples." * * *

MR. JUSTICE BRENNAN, whom THE CHIEF JUSTICE [WARREN] and MR. JUSTICE DOUGLAS join, dissenting. * * *

I think that the record before us shows that the extent of participation of the federal authorities here constituted this state prosecution actually a second federal prosecution of Bartkus. * * *

To set aside this state conviction because infected with constitutional violations by federal officers implies no condemnation of the state processes as such. The conviction is set aside not because of any infirmities resulting from fault of the State but because it is the product of unconstitutional federal action. I cannot grasp the merit of an argument that protection against federal oppression in the circumstances shown by this record would do violence to the principles of federalism. * * *

NOTES AND QUESTIONS

1. In a companion case to *Bartkus*, the Court held that the federal government can prosecute the same conduct that underlies a state verdict. Abbate v. United States, 359 U.S. 187, 79 S.Ct. 666, 3 L.Ed.2d 729 (1959).

2. It is safe to say that the argument in favor of the majority's position is formalistic, while Justice Black and Justice Brennan make substantive arguments (which are very different from each other). Which approach do you prefer? Does the answer depend more on what you think the proper relationship is between the state and federal governments, or more on your view of the scope of double jeopardy protection?

Fewer than thirty years after the Bill of Rights was ratified, the Court noted the possibility that state and federal criminal statutes could proscribe the same conduct. In Houston v. Moore, 18 U.S. (5 Wheat.) 1, 5 L.Ed. 19 (1820), Justice Story argued that double jeopardy would forbid convictions under both statutes in that situation, but his view never commanded a majority of the Court.

3. Professor Sandra Guerra proposes that the dual sovereignty exception should not apply to crimes where the states and federal government have "multijurisdictional law enforcement efforts," *e.g.*, the federal-state cooperation in the "war on drugs."

> While the theory of "dual sovereignty" as derived from federalism principles has survived unchanged from the early twentieth century, in law enforcement the reality of a nation of separate sovereignties has steadily eroded. * * *

> * * * Ironically, the dual sovereignty doctrine rests on a federalist theory that envisions two separate and independent sovereigns, each of which has its respective laws that reflect its unique priorities and interests. The doctrine shows respect for each sovereign's right to vindicate its own interests without interference

from another sovereign. The irony lies in the fact that it is precisely in drug cases where this theory least reflects reality. In drug cases, multijurisdictional task forces bring the sovereigns together in a united effort against a common foe. At least in cases involving multijurisdictional law enforcement, therefore, the Court should reconsider its decision in *Bartkus*.

Sandra Guerra, *The Myth of Dual Sovereignty: Multijurisdictional Drug Law Enforcement and Double Jeopardy*, 73 N.C. L. Rev. 1159, 1163 & 1209 (1995).

4.   *Formalism rules.* Given the Court's formalistic reasoning in *Bartkus*, it will not surprise you that a verdict in an Indian tribal court does not bar a federal prosecution for the same offense. United States v. Wheeler, 435 U.S. 313, 98 S.Ct. 1079, 55 L.Ed.2d 303 (1978). Or that Alabama can prosecute for the same murder for which Georgia had already obtained a conviction. Heath v. Alabama, 474 U.S. 82, 106 S.Ct. 433, 88 L.Ed.2d 387 (1985). How did both states have jurisdiction? Why do you think Alabama prosecuted the case after a *conviction*? Is permitting the second trial to go forward here more or less troubling than what happened in *Bartkus*?

On the other hand, a state prosecution cannot follow a conviction of a municipal offense in municipal court. Waller v. Florida, 397 U.S. 387, 90 S.Ct. 1184, 25 L.Ed.2d 435 (1970). Do you see the formalistic difference? How do you think a prosecution by a territory, such as Puerto Rico, would be treated? See Puerto Rico v. Sanchez Valle, 579 U.S. ___, 136 S.Ct. 1863, 195 L.Ed.2d 179 (2016).

5.   *The Petite policy.* The Department of Justice operates under a self-imposed policy limiting its power to re-prosecute the conduct underlying a state verdict (or a prior federal verdict). The policy is known as the *Petite* policy after the first Supreme Court case to discuss the policy. Petite v. United States, 361 U.S. 529, 80 S.Ct. 450, 4 L.Ed.2d 490 (1960). It was issued by the Republican Attorney General less than two weeks after *Abbate* and *Bartkus*. The basic idea is that the federal government will not reprosecute the "same acts or transactions" unless the prior proceeding left substantial federal interests "demonstrably unvindicated." Moreover, "the Department will presume that a prior prosecution, regardless of result, has vindicated the relevant federal interest." Finally, when "a substantial question arises" whether the policy applies, the question "should be submitted to the appropriate Assistant Attorney General for resolution." United States Attorneys' Manual 9–2.031 (updated July, 2009).

Do you see a potential problem in plea bargaining when your client's conduct can be charged as both a state and federal crime?

6.   *The states react.* About half the states by statute bar a state trial following a federal verdict for the same offense. See George C. Thomas III, *A Blameworthy Act Approach to the Double Jeopardy Same Offense Problem*, 83 Cal. L. Rev. 1027, 1057 n.137 (1995). Though the "same offense" problem is as

difficult here as elsewhere, the salient point is that half the states rejected the Court's offer to proceed as separate sovereigns in this context.

7.   We have left much about double jeopardy insufficiently discussed or ignored entirely. For example, there is the issue of whether and when a civil sanction might be a double jeopardy penalty that would bar prosecution of its criminal analog. See Hudson v. United States, 522 U.S. 93, 118 S.Ct. 488, 139 L.Ed.2d 450 (1997). For two excellent critiques of the Court's recent analysis of this area of double jeopardy law, see Stanley E. Cox, *Halper's Continuing Double Jeopardy Implications: A Thorn By Any Other Name Would Prick as Deep*, 39 St.L.U.L.Rev. 1235 (1995); Susan R. Klein, *Civil In Rem Forfeiture and Double Jeopardy*, 82 Iowa L. Rev. 183 (1996). For a defense of what the Court has done, suggesting the Court has not gone far enough in recognizing that sanctions deemed civil by the legislature never violate double jeopardy, see Nancy J. King, *Portioning Punishment: Constitutional Limits on Successive and Excessive Penalties*, 144 U. Pa. L. Rev. 101 (1995). For an innovative way to avoid at least part of the double jeopardy/civil penalty problem, see David S. Rudstein, *Civil Penalties and Multiple Punishment Under the Double Jeopardy Clause: Some Unanswered Questions*, 46 Okla. L. Rev. 587 (1993).

Several issues surround sentencing and appeal. Does a sentence of a particular length "acquit" of a longer sentence that might be imposed in a second trial following appeal? No, because the "slate has been wiped clean" by the reversal of the first conviction. See North Carolina v. Pearce, 395 U.S. 711, 89 S.Ct. 2072, 23 L.Ed.2d 656 (1969).

Does a jury decision to impose a life sentence rather than the death penalty "acquit" of the death penalty, thus preventing the State from seeking the death penalty if the underlying conviction is reversed on appeal? See Bullington v. Missouri, 451 U.S. 430, 101 S.Ct. 1852, 68 L.Ed.2d 270 (1981) (holding yes).

8.   *And justice to all.* As you have seen in this chapter, England is the "mother" of modern double jeopardy law, having applied the principle as far back as 1200. In July, 2002, the British Home Secretary, speaking for the ruling Labor Party, proposed an exception to the double jeopardy principle. The goal is to "rebalance the criminal justice system in favor of the victim and bring justice to all." Warren Hoge, *Britain Plans Criminal Justice Changes to Favor the Victims*, New York Times, July 18, 2002, A8. These changes were enacted in 2003. See Criminal Justice Act 2003, ch. 44, §§ 75–80. While the details are quite complex, in sum English law now permits an acquittal to be quashed if the Director of Public Prosecutions consents to an appeal, and the Court of Appeals finds (1) "there is new and compelling evidence against the acquitted person in relation to the qualifying offence"; and (2) "it is in the public interest for the application to proceed." A "qualifying offense" is a serious offense, such as murder, manslaughter, rape, kidnaping, terrorism, arson endangering life, and certain drug offenses. *Id.*, at § 75, schedule 5, part 1.

Leaving aside the constitutional issues that would have to be faced in this country, is the English approach a good idea? Consider the case where DNA evidence conclusively demonstrates that the defendant was guilty of the murder of which he was acquitted.

CHAPTER 19

POST-TRIAL PROCESS: CORRECTING ERRONEOUS VERDICTS

■ ■ ■

In 1862 Anthony Trollope wrote with some amusement that he had discovered on his travels in Canada that the province of Ontario had just introduced a system of criminal appeals. He reassured his audience by adding that the local bench and bar thought the innovation unnecessary, even eccentric, and expected that it would soon be abandoned. This must rank as one of the major gaffes in criminal procedure prophecy.

—Graham Hughes, *The Decline of Habeas Corpus*, New York University Center for Research in Crime and Justice, 1990, at 1.

A. APPEAL

The complexity and range of issues that attend a criminal case require many decisions by lawyers on both sides—for example, whether to file motions to compel discovery, to resist discovery, to suppress evidence, to change venue, to join charges or defendants, to resist joinder, to dismiss the indictment on any of a variety of grounds. Moreover, the trial itself—relatively fast-paced and chock full of potential evidentiary objections—requires countless decisions on matters as mundane as whether to object to a leading question or as fundamental as whether to have the defendant testify after the State has rested its case. Any time a lawyer or judge is faced with a decision, a mistake can occur. The instructions the judge gives the jury are also a fertile source of error. Some errors rise to the level of constitutional or statutory violations of defendants' rights, and all of these errors are fair game for appeal although the doctrine of "harmless error" allows appellate courts to ignore errors in some cases.

The law school experience is dominated by appellate cases. You will probably read a thousand or more appellate cases by the time you graduate from law school. It might seem that appeals happen routinely or even automatically, perhaps as a way of providing cases for casebooks! Nothing could be farther from the truth. Perfecting an appeal is tedious, time-consuming work. It requires full knowledge of the relevant rules of procedure. For example, you must obtain a transcript of the proceedings, certify it as accurate, and file it with the court of appeals. If your client is indigent, the State must make a transcript available at no cost to you or your client—Griffin v. Illinois, 351 U.S. 12, 76 S.Ct. 585, 100 L.Ed. 891 (1956)—but the burden of ordering the transcript and making certain it is properly certified and filed will remain on you.

An appeal is not the only way to obtain relief from a conviction. Defense lawyers will often make a motion for acquittal, notwithstanding the jury's verdict, or a motion for a new trial or for arrest of judgment. If those motions fail, a notice of appeal is typically required to begin the appellate process.

As we will see in a death penalty case later in this chapter, p. 1588, Note 5, the failure to file a notice of appeal on time typically results in forfeiting the entire appeal. Thus, while learning and following the rules of procedure is boring work, its importance cannot be overestimated.

1. APPELLATE REVIEW OF EVIDENCE SUFFICIENCY

Throughout the book, you have seen examples of courts reversing convictions for various constitutional violations that have nothing to do with guilt or innocence—the classic example is when a court reverses a conviction because evidence was seized in violation of the Fourth Amendment. But one ground of appellate reversal goes directly to the concern about protecting innocent defendants—the right identified in In re Winship, 397 U.S. 358, 90 S.Ct. 1068, 25 L.Ed.2d 368 (1970), to be proven guilty beyond a reasonable doubt. Because we have devoted little attention to this particular constitutional right, and the effect of its denial, we use it to illustrate the appeal process.

JACKSON V. VIRGINIA
Supreme Court of the United States, 1979.
443 U.S. 307, 99 S.Ct. 2781, 61 L.Ed.2d 560.

MR. JUSTICE STEWART delivered the opinion of the Court [joined by JUSTICES BRENNAN, WHITE, MARSHALL, and BLACKMUN].

The Constitution prohibits the criminal conviction of any person except upon proof of guilt beyond a reasonable doubt. The question in this case is what standard is to be applied in a federal habeas corpus proceeding when the claim is made that a person has been convicted in a state court upon insufficient evidence. * * *

II

Our inquiry in this case is narrow. The petitioner has not seriously questioned any aspect of Virginia law governing the allocation of the burden of production or persuasion in a murder trial. As the record demonstrates, the judge sitting as factfinder in the petitioner's trial was aware that the State bore the burden of establishing the element of premeditation, and stated that he was applying the reasonable-doubt standard in his appraisal of the State's evidence. The petitioner, moreover, does not contest the conclusion of the Court of Appeals that under the "no evidence" rule of *Thompson v. Louisville*, [362 U.S. 199, 80 S.Ct. 624, 4 L.Ed.2d 654 (1960)],[a] his conviction of first-degree murder is sustainable. And he has not attacked the sufficiency of the evidence to support a conviction of second-degree murder. His sole constitutional claim, based squarely upon *Winship*, is that the District Court and the Court of Appeals were in error in not recognizing that the question to be decided in this case is whether any rational factfinder could have concluded beyond a reasonable doubt that the killing for which the petitioner was convicted was premeditated. The question thus raised goes to the basic nature of the constitutional right recognized in the *Winship* opinion.

III * * *

B

Although several of our cases have intimated that the factfinder's application of the reasonable-doubt standard to the evidence may present a federal question when a state conviction is challenged, the Federal Courts of Appeals have generally assumed that so long as the reasonable-doubt instruction has been given at trial, the no-evidence doctrine of *Thompson v. Louisville* remains the appropriate guide for a federal habeas corpus court to apply in assessing a state prisoner's challenge to his conviction as founded upon insufficient evidence. We cannot agree.

The *Winship* doctrine requires more than simply a trial ritual. A doctrine establishing so fundamental a substantive constitutional standard must also require that the factfinder will rationally apply that standard to the facts in evidence. A "reasonable doubt," at a minimum, is one based upon "reason." Yet a properly instructed jury may occasionally convict even when it can be said that no rational trier of fact could find guilt beyond a reasonable doubt, and the same may be said of a trial judge sitting as a jury. In a federal trial, such an occurrence has traditionally been deemed to require reversal of the conviction. Under *Winship*, which established proof beyond a reasonable doubt as an essential of Fourteenth Amendment due process, it follows that when such a conviction occurs in a state trial, it cannot constitutionally stand.

---

[a]   The Court in *Thompson* searched the record of a state conviction and concluded, "[W]e find no evidence whatever in the record to support these charges." The Court also concluded that it is "a violation of due process to convict and punish a man without evidence of his guilt." This standard was taken to mean that federal courts would not reweigh or reassess evidence of guilt and thus could reverse a conviction for lack of evidence only if the record contained no evidence of guilt. Eds.

A federal court has a duty to assess the historic facts when it is called upon to apply a constitutional standard to a conviction obtained in a state court. For example, on direct review of a state-court conviction, where the claim is made that an involuntary confession was used against the defendant, this Court reviews the facts to determine whether the confession was wrongly admitted in evidence. The same duty obtains in federal habeas corpus proceedings.

After *Winship* the critical inquiry on review of the sufficiency of the evidence to support a criminal conviction must be not simply to determine whether the jury was properly instructed, but to determine whether the record evidence could reasonably support a finding of guilt beyond a reasonable doubt. But this inquiry does not require a court to "ask itself whether it believes that the evidence at the trial established guilt beyond a reasonable doubt." Instead, the relevant question is whether, after viewing the evidence in the light most favorable to the prosecution, *any* rational trier of fact could have found the essential elements of the crime beyond a reasonable doubt. This familiar standard gives full play to the responsibility of the trier of fact fairly to resolve conflicts in the testimony, to weigh the evidence, and to draw reasonable inferences from basic facts to ultimate facts. Once a defendant has been found guilty of the crime charged, the factfinder's role as weigher of the evidence is preserved through a legal conclusion that upon judicial review *all of the evidence* is to be considered in the light most favorable to the prosecution. The criterion thus impinges upon "jury" discretion only to the extent necessary to guarantee the fundamental protection of due process of law.

That the *Thompson* "no evidence" rule is simply inadequate to protect against misapplications of the constitutional standard of reasonable doubt is readily apparent. "[A] mere modicum of evidence may satisfy a 'no evidence' standard * * * ." Any evidence that is relevant—that has any tendency to make the existence of an element of a crime slightly more probable than it would be without the evidence—could be deemed a "mere modicum." But it could not seriously be argued that such a "modicum" of evidence could by itself rationally support a conviction beyond a reasonable doubt. The *Thompson* doctrine simply fails to supply a workable or even a predictable standard for determining whether the due process command of *Winship* has been honored. * * *

MR. JUSTICE POWELL took no part in the consideration or decision of this case.

MR. JUSTICE STEVENS, with whom THE CHIEF JUSTICE [BURGER] and MR. JUSTICE REHNQUIST join, concurring in the judgment. * * *

II * * *

The primary reasoning of the Court in *Winship* is * * * inapplicable here. The Court noted in that case that the reasonable-doubt standard has the desirable effect of significantly reducing the risk of an inaccurate factfinding and thus of erroneous convictions, as well as of instilling confidence in the criminal justice system. In this case, however, it would be impossible (and the Court does not even try) to demonstrate that there is an appreciable risk that a factfinding made by a jury beyond a reasonable doubt, and twice reviewed by a trial judge in ruling on directed verdict and post-trial acquittal motions and by one or more levels of appellate courts on direct appeal, as well as by two federal habeas courts under the *Thompson* "no evidence" rule, is likely to be erroneous. Indeed, the very premise of *Winship* is that properly selected judges and properly instructed juries act rationally, that the former will tell the truth when they declare that they are convinced beyond a reasonable doubt and the latter will conscientiously obey and understand the reasonable-doubt instructions they receive before retiring to reach a verdict, and therefore that either factfinder will itself provide the necessary bulwark against erroneous factual determinations. To presume otherwise is to make light of *Winship*.

Having failed to identify the evil against which the rule is directed, and having failed to demonstrate how it follows from the analysis typically used in due process cases of this character, the Court places all of its reliance on a dry, and in my view incorrect, syllogism: If *Winship* requires the factfinder to apply a reasonable-doubt standard, then logic requires a reviewing judge to apply a like standard.

But, taken to its ultimate conclusion, this "logic" would require the reviewing court to "ask itself whether *it* believes that the evidence at the trial established guilt beyond a reasonable doubt." The Court, however, rejects this standard, as well as others that might be considered consistent with *Winship*. For example, it does not require the reviewing court to view just the evidence most favorable to the prosecution and then to decide whether that evidence convinced it beyond a reasonable doubt, nor whether, based on the entire record, rational triers of fact could be convinced of guilt beyond a reasonable doubt. Instead, and without explanation, it chooses a still narrower standard that merely asks whether, "after viewing the evidence in the light most favorable to the prosecution, *any* rational trier of fact could have found the essential elements of the crime beyond a reasonable doubt." It seems to me that if "logic" allows this choice after *Winship* it should also allow the presumption that the Court has rejected—that trial judges and juries will act rationally and honestly in applying the reasonable-doubt standard, at least so long as the trial is free of procedural error and the record contains evidence tending to prove each of the elements of the offense.

Time may prove that the rule the Court has adopted today is the wisest compromise between one extreme that maximizes the protection against the risk that innocent persons will be erroneously convicted and the other extreme that places the greatest faith in the ability of fair procedures to produce just verdicts. But the Court's opinion should not obscure the fact that its new rule is not logically compelled by the analysis or the holding in *Winship* or in any other precedent, or the fact that the rule reflects a new policy choice rather than the application of a pre-existing rule of law.

III * * *

The Court indicates [in an omitted part of the opinion] that the new standard to be applied by federal judges in habeas corpus proceedings may be substantially the same as the standard most state reviewing courts are already applying. The federal district courts are therefore being directed simply to duplicate the reviewing function that is now being performed adequately by state appellate courts. * * * [T]o assign a single federal district judge the responsibility of directly reviewing, and inevitably supervising, the most routine work of the highest courts of a State can only undermine the morale and the esteem of the state judiciary—particularly when the stated purpose of the additional layer of review is to determine whether the State's factfinder is "rational." Such consequences are intangible but nonetheless significant. * * *

NOTES AND QUESTIONS

1.   Justice Stevens' opinion concurring in the judgment in *Jackson* describes the majority's approach as a compromise between two extreme views that manifest the dichotomy between procedural and substantive fairness. Can you describe these two opposing positions?

2.   Which of the three positions—the two extremes and the compromise—do *you* think is required by due process?

3.   The Court in an omitted part of the opinion described how federal courts should treat conflicts in the record:

> [A] federal habeas corpus court faced with a record of historical facts that supports conflicting inferences must presume—even if it does not affirmatively appear in the record—that the trier of fact resolved any such conflicts in favor of the prosecution, and must defer to that resolution.

How would you apply that standard to the following child abuse case? The mother of the child testified that she saw the father spank the child on Monday, and she took the child to the doctor on Thursday when the bruises had not healed. The doctor testified for the State, but the prosecutor did not ask when the blows that caused the bruises were likely struck. On cross-examination, the defense elicited the doctor's medical opinion that the spanking on Monday did not cause the bruises because the bruises were too old—they were at least a week old. (The defense lawyer was willing to ask this question on cross-examination because he had engaged in a bit of informal discovery; he had phoned the doctor a few days prior to trial.) On re-direct, however, the prosecutor elicited a concession that it was possible, though unlikely, that the bruises were caused by the spanking on Monday.

When the defense cross-examined the mother, she was defensive and hostile. She lost her temper at several points. She admitted that she did not report the abuse until her mother saw the bruises ("I was trying to protect my husband"). She was vague about whether it was she or her mother who was caring for the child the week before when it was most likely that the blows were inflicted. She told inconsistent stories about the number of blows she observed and the intensity of the blows.

After the jury had deliberated about two hours, the foreman passed a note to the judge that they wanted to ask him a question. The judge called court back into session, and the jury foreman asked the judge, "Your Honor, may we indict the mother?" The judge appeared stunned and asked the question be repeated. The foreman asked it again. "No," the judge said. "You are not a grand jury. You may not indict anyone. Your only job is to decide the guilt or innocence of the defendant."

The jury retired to deliberate further. Thirty minutes later, the jury returned a guilty verdict of misdemeanor child abuse, and imposed a sentence of ninety days. Would this verdict be upheld on appeal using the *Thompson* no-evidence standard, as described in *Jackson*? What about under the *Jackson* standard itself? (You should assume that the facts did *not* create the possibility of the defendant being the accomplice of the mother.)

The Tennessee Court of Criminal Appeals upheld the conviction in an unpublished opinion. How would you write the opinion? How could a jury find probable cause to indict the mother if it simultaneously believed there was proof beyond a reasonable doubt that someone else committed the crime? Or is this not the relevant question under *Jackson*? In any event, the case was lost, the defendant served sixty days in the county jail (thirty days off for good behavior), and then remarried the woman whose testimony convicted him of a crime he probably did not commit.

4.   *Now try Texas on for size.* The Texas Court of Criminal Appeals recognized that *Jackson* does not forbid states from adopting standards of appellate review that are more favorable to defendants: "But while *Jackson v. Virginia* does impose upon the states a constitutional minimum legal sufficiency standard, it does not (and could not, consistent with principles of federalism) prevent the states from applying sufficiency standards that are more solicitous of defendants' rights." Watson v. State, 204 S.W.3d 404, 412 (Tex. Ct. Crim. App. 2006).

The standard of review that Texas adopted in 1996 asked two questions: (1) whether the evidence, although legally sufficient, is "so weak" that the jury verdict seems clearly wrong and manifestly unjust; and (2) whether the jury verdict, though legally sufficient, is nevertheless against the great weight and preponderance of the evidence. These questions are to be answered by viewing all of the evidence from a "neutral" standpoint, rather than, as in *Jackson*, in the light most favorable to the verdict. See Clewis v. State, 922 S.W.2d 126 (Tex. Ct. Crim. App. 1996).

Is the Texas standard different in practice from *Jackson*? Apply it to the facts in Note 3. In 2010, the Texas Court of Criminal Appeals overruled *Clewis*, holding that *Jackson* is "the only standard that a reviewing court should apply in determining whether the evidence is sufficient to support each element of a criminal offense." Brooks v. State, 323 S.W.3d 893 (Texas Ct. Crim. App. 2010).5. There is yet one more reason that courts are loathe to reverse convictions on the ground of insufficient evidence. As you saw in more detail in the last chapter, p. 1505, Note 5, the Court has held that a reversal on the grounds of insufficient evidence is functionally the same as an acquittal. Burks v. United States, 437 U.S. 1, 98 S.Ct. 2141, 57 L.Ed.2d 1 (1978).

5. *Flawed instructions.* Instructing juries on the meaning of reasonable doubt has proven difficult. Some courts still use a charge based on one given by Chief Justice Shaw of the Massachusetts Supreme Court in Commonwealth v. Webster, 59 Mass. 295 (1850). If the instruction does not communicate a sufficiently high standard of proof, it would constitute a due process violation under *Winship*. Determining whether that requisite verbal standard has been met is a challenge to legal and linguistic reasoning. Below are two instructions that reached the Supreme Court in 1990 and 1994. The Court held unanimously in a *per curiam* opinion that one of the instructions violated the due process clause. The Court held 7–2 that one of the instructions was permissible under due process. Can you choose between them?

[1] "Reasonable doubt" is such a doubt as would cause a reasonable and prudent person, in one of the graver and more dangerous transactions of life, to pause and hesitate before taking the represented facts as true and relying and acting thereon. It is such a doubt as will not permit you, after full, fair, and impartial consideration of all the evidence, to have an abiding conviction, to a moral certainty, of the guilt of the accused. At the same time, absolute or mathematical certainty is not required. You may be convinced of the truth of a fact beyond a reasonable doubt and yet be fully aware that possibly you may be mistaken. You may find an accused guilty upon the strong probabilities of the case, provided such probabilities are strong enough to exclude any doubt of his guilt that is reasonable. A reasonable doubt is an actual and substantial doubt reasonably arising from the evidence, from the facts or circumstances shown by the evidence, or from the lack of evidence on the part of the State, as distinguished from a doubt arising from mere possibility, from bare imagination, or from fanciful conjecture.

[2] If you entertain a reasonable doubt as to any fact or element necessary to constitute the defendant's guilt, it is your duty to give him the benefit of that doubt and return a verdict of not guilty. Even where the evidence demonstrates a probability of guilt, if it does not establish such guilt beyond a reasonable doubt, you must acquit the accused. This doubt, however, must be a reasonable one; that is one that is founded upon a real tangible substantial basis and not upon mere caprice and conjecture. It must be such doubt as would give rise to a grave uncertainty, raised in your mind by reasons of the unsatisfactory character of the evidence or lack thereof. A reasonable doubt is not a mere possible doubt. It is an actual substantial doubt. It is a doubt that a reasonable man can seriously entertain. What is required is not an absolute or mathematical certainty, but a moral certainty.

If you were the defendant, would you prefer one over the other? Can you write a better instruction?

2. HARMLESS ERROR

In Chapman v. California, 386 U.S. 18, 87 S.Ct. 824, 17 L.Ed.2d 705 (1967), the Court faced the issues of whether a violation of *Griffin v. California*, p. 1370, can ever be harmless and, "if so, was the error harmless in this case?" *Griffin*, you will recall, held that prosecutors could not comment on the failure of the accused to testify. The *Chapman* prosecutor violated *Griffin* in various ways in his closing argument. The California Constitution permitted judgments to be reversed only when "the error complained of has resulted in a miscarriage of justice." The California courts held that the *Griffin* violations did not constitute a "miscarriage of justice."

The Supreme Court reversed Chapman's conviction but rejected the position

that all federal constitutional errors, regardless of the facts and circumstances, must always be deemed harmful. Such a holding, as petitioners correctly point out, would require an automatic reversal of their convictions and make further discussion unnecessary. We decline to adopt any such rule. All 50 States have harmless-error statutes or rules, and the United States long ago through its Congress established for its courts the rule that judgments shall not be reversed for "errors or defects which do not affect the substantial rights of the parties." 28 U.S.C. § 2111. * * * All of these rules, state or federal, serve a very useful purpose insofar as they block setting aside convictions for small errors or defects that have little, if any, likelihood of having changed the result of the trial. We conclude that there may be some constitutional errors which in the setting of a particular case are so unimportant and insignificant that they may, consistent with the Federal Constitution, be deemed harmless, not requiring the automatic reversal of the conviction.

As for whether the error in question was harmless, the Court adopted the following standard: "whether there is a reasonable possibility that the evidence complained of might have contributed to the conviction." But the burden of proving that there was no reasonable possibility that the error was harmful, the Court held, should be on the State because it had benefitted from the error. The Court then held that "before a federal constitutional error can be held harmless, the court must be able to declare a belief that it was harmless beyond a reasonable doubt."

NOTES AND QUESTIONS

1.   *How can a violation of the federal Constitutional be harmless?* Professor Steven Goldberg estimated that 10% of all criminal appeals are resolved by a finding of harmless constitutional error. Steven H. Goldberg, *Harmless Error: Constitutional Sneak Thief*, 71 J. Crim. L. & Criminology 421 (1980). Using this estimate, in one of ten cases involving federal constitutional error, an appellate court will affirm the conviction notwithstanding the error. Professor Goldberg questions the concept of a "harmless" federal constitutional error:

> An appellate court defies common sense when it steps out of its traditional role as a reviewing court and attempts to operate as a primary factfinder. Appellate review of an entire trial transcript is an incredibly inefficient use of appellate court time. To pursue such a course in order to determine whether error is harmless, so that judicial economy might be served is not only ironic, it is nonsensical. * * * Unless the courts adopt a policy of total fact review first and legal issue second, the appellate court cannot begin the time-consuming task of fact review until it has taken the time to perform its traditional function of reviewing for and, in this case, finding error.

Id. at 429–30.

2.   *Approaches to harmless error.* Professor Martha Field discerned three quite different approaches to harmless error that appear in Supreme Court opinions during the first decade following *Chapman*:

> a)   The first approach focuses upon the erroneously admitted evidence (or other constitutional error) to ask whether it might have contributed to a guilty verdict.

> b)   The second approach asks whether, once erroneously admitted evidence is excluded, there remains overwhelming evidence to support the jury's verdict.

c) The third approach asks whether the tainted evidence is merely cumulative—that is, merely duplicative of some remaining evidence.

Supreme Court opinions often do not distinguish between these variant approaches, although the approach selected can change the disposition of many cases. At times the Court appears to have endorsed the second and third approaches to harmless error, although it sometimes seems to favor the first approach standing alone. I believe that harmlessness should be found only when either the first test or a carefully circumscribed version of the third is satisfied.

Martha A. Field, *Assessing the Harmlessness of Federal Constitutional Error—A Process in Need of a Rationale*, 125 U. Pa. L. Rev. 15, 16 (1976).

As you read the next case, consider which of Professor Field's approaches inform the various opinions.

ARIZONA V. FULMINANTE

Supreme Court of the United States, 1991.
499 U.S. 279, 111 S.Ct. 1246, 113 L.Ed.2d 302.

JUSTICE WHITE delivered an opinion, Parts I, II, and IV of which are the opinion of the Court, and Part III of which is a dissenting opinion. [JUSTICES MARSHALL, BLACKMUN, and STEVENS joined Parts I, II, III, and IV of that opinion. JUSTICE SCALIA joined Parts I and II. JUSTICE KENNEDY joined Parts I and IV.] * * * *

I

Early in the morning of September 14, 1982, Fulminante called the Mesa, Arizona, Police Department to report that his 11-year-old stepdaughter, Jeneane Michelle Hunt, was missing. He had been caring for Jeneane while his wife, Jeneane's mother, was in the hospital. Two days later, Jeneane's body was found in the desert east of Mesa. She had been shot twice in the head at close range with a large caliber weapon, and a ligature was around her neck. Because of the decomposed condition of the body, it was impossible to tell whether she had been sexually assaulted.

Fulminante's statements to police concerning Jeneane's disappearance and his relationship with her contained a number of inconsistencies, and he became a suspect in her killing. When no charges were filed against him, Fulminante left Arizona for New Jersey. Fulminante was later convicted in New Jersey on federal charges of possession of a firearm by a felon.

Fulminante was incarcerated in the Ray Brook Federal Correctional Institution in New York. There he became friends with another inmate,

Anthony Sarivola, then serving a 60-day sentence for extortion. The two men came to spend several hours a day together. Sarivola, a former police officer, had been involved in loansharking for organized crime but then became a paid informant for the Federal Bureau of Investigation. While at Ray Brook, he masqueraded as an organized crime figure. After becoming friends with Fulminante, Sarivola heard a rumor that Fulminante was suspected of killing a child in Arizona. Sarivola then raised the subject with Fulminante in several conversations, but Fulminante repeatedly denied any involvement in Jeneane's death. During one conversation, he told Sarivola that Jeneane had been killed by bikers looking for drugs; on another occasion, he said he did not know what had happened. Sarivola passed this information on to an agent of the Federal Bureau of Investigation, who instructed Sarivola to find out more.

Sarivola learned more one evening in October 1983, as he and Fulminante walked together around the prison track. Sarivola said that he knew Fulminante was "starting to get some tough treatment and whatnot" from other inmates because of the rumor. Sarivola offered to protect Fulminante from his fellow inmates, but told him, " 'You have to tell me about it,' you know. I mean, in other words, 'For me to give you any help.' " Fulminante then admitted to Sarivola that he had driven Jeneane to the desert on his motorcycle, where he choked her, sexually assaulted her, and made her beg for her life, before shooting her twice in the head. * * *

Prior to trial [for first-degree murder of Jeneane], Fulminante moved to suppress the statement he had given Sarivola in prison, as well as a second confession he had given to Donna Sarivola, then Anthony Sarivola's fiancee and later his wife, following his May 1984 release from prison. He asserted that the confession to Sarivola was coerced, and that the second confession was the "fruit" of the first. Following the hearing, the trial court denied the motion to suppress, specifically finding that, based on the stipulated facts, the confessions were voluntary. The State introduced both confessions as evidence at trial, and on December 19, 1985, Fulminante was convicted of Jeneane's murder. He was subsequently sentenced to death.

Fulminante appealed, arguing, among other things, that his confession to Sarivola was the product of coercion and that its admission at trial violated his rights to due process under the Fifth and Fourteenth Amendments to the United States Constitution. After considering the evidence at trial as well as the stipulated facts before the trial court on the motion to suppress, the Arizona Supreme Court held that the confession was coerced, but initially determined that the admission of the confession at trial was harmless error, because of the overwhelming nature of the evidence against Fulminante. Upon Fulminante's motion for reconsideration, however, the court ruled that this Court's precedent precluded the use of the harmless-error analysis in the case of a coerced confession. The court therefore reversed the conviction and ordered that Fulminante be retried without the use of the confession to Sarivola. * * *

II * * *

Although the question is a close one, we agree with the Arizona Supreme Court's conclusion that Fulminante's confession was coerced. * * * [For the coercion analysis, see Note 5, p. 610. Eds.]

III

Four of us, Justices Marshall, Blackmun, Stevens, and myself, would affirm the judgment of the Arizona Supreme Court on the ground that the harmless-error rule is inapplicable to erroneously admitted coerced confessions. We thus disagree with the Justices who have a contrary view.

The majority today abandons what until now the Court has regarded as the "axiomatic [proposition] that a defendant in a criminal case is deprived of due process of law if his conviction is founded, in whole or in part, upon an involuntary confession, without regard for the truth or falsity of the confession, and even though there is ample evidence aside from the confession to support the conviction." The Court has repeatedly stressed that the view that the admission of a coerced confession can be harmless error because of the other evidence to support the verdict is "an impermissible doctrine"; for "the admission in evidence, over objection, of the coerced confession vitiates the judgment because it violates the Due Process Clause of the Fourteenth Amendment." * * * [T]he rule was the same even when another confession of the defendant had been properly admitted into evidence. Today, a majority of the Court, without any justification overrules this vast body of precedent without a word and in so doing dislodges one of the fundamental tenets of our criminal justice system.

In extending to coerced confessions the harmless-error rule of *Chapman v. California*, p. 1361, the majority declares that because the Court has applied that analysis to numerous other "trial errors," there is no reason that it should not apply to an error of this nature as well. The four of us remain convinced, however, that we should abide by our cases that have refused to apply the harmless-error rule to coerced confessions, for a coerced confession is fundamentally different from other types of erroneously admitted evidence to which the rule has been applied. Indeed, as the majority concedes, *Chapman* itself recognized that prior cases "have indicated that there are some constitutional rights so basic to a fair trial that their infraction can *never* be treated as harmless error," and it placed in that category the constitutional rule against using a defendant's coerced confession against him at his criminal trial.

Moreover, cases since *Chapman* have reiterated the rule that using a defendant's coerced confession against him is a denial of due process of law regardless of the other evidence in the record aside from the confession.

Chapman specifically noted three constitutional errors that could not be categorized as harmless error: using a coerced confession against a defendant in a criminal trial, depriving a defendant of counsel, and trying a defendant before a biased judge. The majority attempts to distinguish the use of a coerced confession from the other two errors listed in *Chapman* * * * by drawing a meaningless dichotomy between "trial errors" and "structural defects" in the trial process. * * *

* * * This effort fails, for our jurisprudence on harmless error has not classified so neatly the errors at issue. For example, we have held susceptible to harmless-error analysis the failure to instruct the jury on the presumption of innocence, while finding it impossible to analyze in terms of harmless error the failure to instruct a jury on the reasonable-doubt standard. These cases cannot be reconciled by labeling the former "trial error" and the latter not, for both concern the exact same stage in the trial proceedings. Rather, these cases can be reconciled only by considering the nature of the right at issue and the effect of an error upon the trial. A jury instruction on the presumption of innocence is not constitutionally required in every case to satisfy due process, because such an instruction merely offers an additional safeguard beyond that provided by the constitutionally required instruction on reasonable doubt. While it may be possible to analyze as harmless the omission of a presumption of innocence instruction when the required reasonable-doubt instruction has been given, it is impossible to assess the effect on the jury of the omission of the more fundamental instruction on reasonable doubt. In addition, omission of a reasonable-doubt instruction, though a "trial error," distorts the very structure of the trial because it creates the risk that the jury will convict the defendant even if the State has not met its required burden of proof.

These same concerns counsel against applying harmless-error analysis to the admission of a coerced confession. A defendant's confession is "probably the most probative and damaging evidence that can be admitted against him," so damaging that a jury should not be expected to ignore it even if told to do so, and because in any event it is impossible to know what credit and weight the jury gave to the confession. Concededly, this reason is insufficient to justify a *per se* bar to the use of *any* confession. Thus, *Milton v. Wainwright*, 407 U.S. 371, 92 S.Ct. 2174, 33 L.Ed.2d 1 (1972), applied harmless-error analysis to a confession obtained and introduced in circumstances that violated the defendant's Sixth Amendment right to counsel. Similarly, the Courts of Appeals have held that the introduction of incriminating statements taken from defendants in violation of *Miranda v. Arizona,* 384 U.S. 436, 86 S.Ct. 1602, 16 L.Ed.2d 694 (1966), is subject to treatment as harmless error.

Nevertheless, in declaring that it is "impossible to create a meaningful distinction between confessions elicited in violation of the Sixth Amendment and those in violation of the Fourteenth Amendment," the majority overlooks the obvious. Neither *Milton v. Wainwright* nor any of the other cases upon which the majority relies involved a defendant's coerced confession, nor were there present in these cases the distinctive reasons underlying the exclusion of coerced incriminating statements of the defendant. First, some coerced confessions may be untrustworthy. Consequently, admission of coerced confessions may distort the truth-seeking function of the trial upon which the majority focuses. More importantly, however, the use of coerced confessions, "whether true or false," is forbidden "because the methods used to extract them offend an underlying principle in the enforcement of our criminal law: that ours is an accusatorial and not an inquisitorial system—a system in which the State must establish guilt by evidence independently and freely secured and may not by coercion prove its charge against an accused out of his own mouth." This reflects the "strongly felt attitude of our society that important human values are sacrificed where an agency of the government, in the course of securing a conviction, wrings a confession out of an accused against his will," as well as "the deep-rooted feeling that the police must obey the law while enforcing the law; that in the end life and liberty can be as much endangered from illegal methods used to convict those thought to be criminals as from the actual criminals themselves." Thus, permitting a coerced confession to be part of the evidence on which a jury is free to base its verdict of guilty is inconsistent with the thesis that ours is not an inquisitorial system of criminal justice.

As the majority concedes, there are other constitutional errors that invalidate a conviction even though there may be no reasonable doubt that the defendant is guilty and would be convicted absent the trial error. For example, a judge in a criminal trial "is prohibited from entering a judgment of conviction or directing the jury to come forward with such a verdict, regardless of how overwhelmingly the evidence may point in that direction." A defendant is entitled to counsel at trial, and as *Chapman* recognized, violating this right can never be harmless error. * * *

The search for truth is indeed central to our system of justice, but "certain constitutional rights are not, and should not be, subject to harmless-error analysis because those rights protect important values that are unrelated to the truth-seeking function of the trial." The right of a defendant not to have his coerced confession used against him is among those rights, for using a coerced confession "abort[s] the basic trial process" and "render[s] a trial fundamentally unfair."

For the foregoing reasons the four of us would adhere to the consistent line of authority that has recognized as a basic tenet of our criminal justice system, before and after both *Miranda* and *Chapman*, the prohibition against using a defendant's coerced confession against him at his criminal trial. *Stare decisis* is "of fundamental importance to the rule of law"; the majority offers no convincing reason for overturning our long line of decisions requiring the exclusion of coerced confessions.

IV

Since five Justices have determined that harmless-error analysis applies to coerced confessions, it becomes necessary to evaluate under that ruling the admissibility of Fulminante's confession to Sarivola. *Chapman v. California* made clear that "before a federal constitutional error can be held harmless, the court must be able to declare a belief that it was harmless beyond a reasonable doubt." The Court has the power to review the record *de novo* in order to determine an error's harmlessness. In so doing, it must be determined whether the State has met its burden of demonstrating that the admission of the confession to Sarivola did not contribute to Fulminante's conviction. Five of us are of the view that the State has not carried its burden and accordingly affirm the judgment of the court below reversing respondent's conviction.

A confession is like no other evidence. * * * "[T]he admissions of a defendant come from the actor himself, the most knowledgeable and unimpeachable source of information about his past conduct. Certainly, confessions have profound impact on the jury, so much so that we may justifiably doubt its ability to put them out of mind even if told to do so." While some statements by a defendant may concern isolated aspects of the crime or may be incriminating only when linked to other evidence, a full confession in which the defendant discloses the motive for and means of the crime may tempt the jury to rely upon that evidence alone in reaching its decision. In the case of a coerced confession such as that given by Fulminante to Sarivola, the risk that the confession is unreliable, coupled with the profound impact that the confession has upon the jury, requires a reviewing court to exercise extreme caution before determining that the admission of the confession at trial was harmless.

In the Arizona Supreme Court's initial opinion, in which it determined that harmless-error analysis could be applied to the confession, the court found that the admissible second confession to Donna Sarivola rendered the first confession to Anthony Sarivola cumulative. The court also noted that circumstantial physical evidence concerning the wounds, the ligature around Jeneane's neck, the location of the body, and the presence of motorcycle tracks at the scene corroborated the second confession. The court concluded that "due to the overwhelming evidence adduced from the second confession, if there had not been a first confession, the jury would still have had the same basic evidence to convict" Fulminante.

We have a quite different evaluation of the evidence. Our review of the record leads us to conclude that the State has failed to meet its burden of establishing, beyond a reasonable doubt, that the admission of Fulminante's confession to Anthony Sarivola was harmless error. Three considerations compel this result.

First, the transcript discloses that both the trial court and the State recognized that a successful prosecution depended on the jury believing the two confessions. Absent the confessions, it is unlikely that Fulminante would have been prosecuted at all, because the physical evidence from the scene and other circumstantial evidence would have been insufficient to convict. Indeed, no indictment was filed until nearly two years after the murder. Although the police had suspected Fulminante from the beginning, as the prosecutor acknowledged in his opening statement to the jury, "[W]hat brings us to Court, what makes this case fileable, and prosecutable and triable is that later, Mr. Fulminante confesses this crime to Anthony Sarivola and later, to Donna Sarivola, his wife." After trial began, during a renewed hearing on Fulminante's motion to suppress, the trial court opined, "You know, I think from what little I know about this trial, the character of this man [Sarivola] for truthfulness or untruthfulness and his credibility is the centerpiece of this case, is it not?" The prosecutor responded, "It's very important, there's no doubt." Finally, in his closing argument, the prosecutor prefaced his discussion of the two confessions by conceding: "[W]e have a lot of [circumstantial] evidence that indicates that this is our suspect, this is the fellow that did it, but it's a little short as far as saying that it's proof that he actually put the gun to the girl's head and killed her. So it's a little short of that. We recognize that."

Second, the jury's assessment of the confession to Donna Sarivola could easily have depended in large part on the presence of the confession to Anthony Sarivola. Absent the admission at trial of the first confession, the jurors might have found Donna Sarivola's story unbelievable. Fulminante's confession to Donna Sarivola allegedly occurred in May 1984, on the day he was released from Ray Brook, as she and Anthony Sarivola drove Fulminante from New York to Pennsylvania. Donna Sarivola testified that Fulminante, whom she had never before met, confessed in detail about Jeneane's brutal murder in response to her casual question concerning why he was going to visit friends in Pennsylvania instead of returning to his family in Arizona. Although she testified that she was "disgusted" by Fulminante's disclosures, she stated that she took no steps to notify authorities of what she had learned. In fact, she claimed that she barely discussed the matter with Anthony

Sarivola, who was in the car and overheard Fulminante's entire conversation with Donna. Despite her disgust for Fulminante, Donna Sarivola later went on a second trip with him. Although Sarivola informed authorities that he had driven Fulminante to Pennsylvania, he did not mention Donna's presence in the car or her conversation with Fulminante. Only when questioned by authorities in June 1985 did Anthony Sarivola belatedly recall the confession to Donna more than a year before, and only then did he ask if she would be willing to discuss the matter with authorities.

Although some of the details in the confession to Donna Sarivola were corroborated by circumstantial evidence, many, including details that Jeneane was choked and sexually assaulted, were not. As to other aspects of the second confession, including Fulminante's motive and state of mind, the *only* corroborating evidence was the first confession to Anthony Sarivola.[9] Thus, contrary to what the Arizona Supreme Court found, it is clear that the jury might have believed that the two confessions reinforced and corroborated each other. For this reason, one confession was not merely cumulative of the other. While in some cases two confessions, delivered on different occasions to different listeners, might be viewed as being independent of each other, it strains credulity to think that the jury so viewed the two confessions in this case, especially given the close relationship between Donna and Anthony Sarivola.

The jurors could also have believed that Donna Sarivola had a motive to lie about the confession in order to assist her husband. Anthony Sarivola received significant benefits from federal authorities, including payment for information, immunity from prosecution, and eventual placement in the federal Witness Protection Program. In addition, the jury might have found Donna motivated by her own desire for favorable treatment, for she, too, was ultimately placed in the Witness Protection Program.

Third, the admission of the first confession led to the admission of other evidence prejudicial to Fulminante. For example, the State

---

[9]   The inadmissible confession to Anthony Sarivola was itself subject to serious challenge. Sarivola's lack of moral integrity was demonstrated by his testimony that he had worked for organized crime during the time he was a uniformed police officer. His overzealous approach to gathering information for which he would be paid by authorities was revealed by his admission that he had fabricated a tape recording in connection with an earlier, unrelated FBI investigation. He received immunity in connection with the information he provided. His eagerness to get in and stay in the federal Witness Protection Program provided a motive for giving detailed information to authorities. During his first report of the confession, Sarivola failed to hint at numerous details concerning an alleged sexual assault on Jeneane; he mentioned them for the first time more than a year later during further interrogation, at which he also recalled, for the first time, the confession to Donna Sarivola. The impeaching effect of each of these factors was undoubtedly undercut by the presence of the second confession, which, not surprisingly, recounted a quite similar story and thus corroborated the first confession. Thus, each confession, though easily impeachable if viewed in isolation, became difficult to discount when viewed in conjunction with the other.

introduced evidence that Fulminante knew of Sarivola's connections with organized crime in an attempt to explain why Fulminante would have been motivated to confess to Sarivola in seeking protection. Absent the confession, this evidence would have had no relevance and would have been inadmissible at trial. The Arizona Supreme Court found that the evidence of Sarivola's connections with organized crime reflected on Sarivola's character, not Fulminante's, and noted that the evidence could have been used to impeach Sarivola. This analysis overlooks the fact that had the confession not been admitted, there would have been no reason for Sarivola to testify and thus no need to impeach his testimony. Moreover, we cannot agree that the evidence did not reflect on Fulminante's character as well, for it depicted him as someone who willingly sought out the company of criminals. It is quite possible that this evidence led the jury to view Fulminante as capable of murder. * * *

Because a majority of the Court has determined that Fulminante's confession to Anthony Sarivola was coerced and because a majority has determined that admitting this confession was not harmless beyond a reasonable doubt, we agree with the Arizona Supreme Court's conclusion that Fulminante is entitled to a new trial at which the confession is not admitted. * * *

CHIEF JUSTICE REHNQUIST, with whom JUSTICE O'CONNOR joins, JUSTICE KENNEDY and JUSTICE SOUTER join as to Parts I and II, and JUSTICE SCALIA joins as to Parts II and III, delivered the opinion of the Court with respect to Part II, and a dissenting opinion with respect to Parts I and III.

The Court today properly concludes that the admission of an "involuntary" confession at trial is subject to harmless error analysis. Nonetheless, the independent review of the record which we are required to make shows that respondent Fulminante's confession was not in fact involuntary. And even if the confession were deemed to be involuntary, the evidence offered at trial, including a second, untainted confession by Fulminante, supports the conclusion that any error here was certainly harmless.

[In Part I of Chief Justice Rehnquist's opinion, he and Justices O'Connor, Kennedy, and Souter concluded that on the facts in this case, "the Court today embraces a more expansive definition of [involuntariness] than is warranted by any of our decided cases."]

II

Since this Court's landmark decision in *Chapman v. California*, in which we adopted the general rule that a constitutional error does not automatically require reversal of a conviction, the Court has applied harmless-error analysis to a wide range of errors and has recognized that most constitutional errors can be harmless.

The common thread connecting these cases is that each involved "trial error"—error which occurred during the presentation of the case to the jury, and which may therefore be quantitatively assessed in the context of other evidence presented in order to determine whether its admission was harmless beyond a reasonable doubt. In applying harmless-error analysis to these many different constitutional violations, the Court has been faithful to the belief that the harmless-error doctrine is essential to preserve the "principle that the central purpose of a criminal trial is to decide the factual question of the defendant's guilt or innocence, and promotes public respect for the criminal process by focusing on the underlying fairness of the trial rather than on the virtually inevitable presence of immaterial error." * * *

It is on the basis of * * * language in *Chapman* that Justice White in dissent concludes that the principle of *stare decisis* requires us to hold that an involuntary confession is not subject to harmless-error analysis. We believe that there are several reasons which lead to a contrary conclusion. In the first place, the * * * language from *Chapman* does not by its terms adopt any such rule in that case. The language that "[a]lthough our prior cases have indicated," coupled with the relegation of the cases themselves to a footnote, is more appropriately regarded as a historical reference to the holdings of these cases. * * *

The admission of an involuntary confession—a classic "trial error"— is markedly different from the other two constitutional violations referred to in the *Chapman* footnote as not being subject to harmless-error analysis. One of those violations, involved in *Gideon v. Wainwright*, [p. 1043], was the total deprivation of the right to counsel at trial. The other violation, involved in *Tumey v. Ohio*, 273 U.S. 510, 47 S.Ct. 437, 71 L.Ed. 749 (1927), was a judge who was not impartial. These are structural defects in the constitution of the trial mechanism, which defy analysis by "harmless-error" standards. The entire conduct of the trial from beginning to end is obviously affected by the absence of counsel for a criminal defendant, just as it is by the presence on the bench of a judge who is not impartial. Since our decision in *Chapman*, other cases have added to the category of constitutional errors which are not subject to harmless error the following: unlawful exclusion of members of the defendant's race from a grand jury; the right to self-representation at trial; and the right to public trial. Each of these constitutional deprivations is a similar structural defect affecting the framework within which the trial proceeds, rather than simply an error in the trial process itself. "Without these basic protections, a criminal trial cannot reliably serve its function as a vehicle for determination of guilt or innocence, and no criminal punishment may be regarded as fundamentally fair."

It is evident from a comparison of the constitutional violations which we have held subject to harmless error, and those which we have held not, that involuntary statements or confessions belong in the former category. The admission of an involuntary confession is a "trial error," similar in both degree and kind to the erroneous admission of other types of evidence. The evidentiary impact of an involuntary confession, and its effect upon the composition of the record, is indistinguishable from that of a confession obtained in violation of the Sixth Amendment—of evidence seized in violation of the Fourth Amendment—or of a prosecutor's improper comment on a defendant's silence at trial in violation of the Fifth Amendment. When reviewing the erroneous admission of an involuntary confession, the appellate court, as it does with the admission of other forms of improperly admitted evidence, simply reviews the remainder of the evidence against the defendant to determine whether the admission of the confession was harmless beyond a reasonable doubt. * * *

Of course an involuntary confession may have a more dramatic effect on the course of a trial than do other trial errors—in particular cases it may be devastating to a defendant—but this simply means that a reviewing court will conclude in such a case that its admission was not harmless error; it is not a reason for eschewing the harmless-error test entirely. The Supreme Court of Arizona, in its first opinion in the present case, concluded that the admission of Fulminante's confession was harmless error. That court concluded that a second and more explicit confession of the crime made by Fulminante after he was released from prison was not tainted by the first confession, and that the second confession, together with physical evidence from the wounds (the victim had been shot twice in the head with a large calibre weapon at close range and a ligature was found around her neck) and other evidence introduced at trial rendered the admission of the first confession harmless beyond a reasonable doubt.

III

I would agree with the finding of the Supreme Court of Arizona in its initial opinion—in which it believed harmless-error analysis was applicable to the admission of involuntary confessions—that the admission of Fulminante's confession was harmless. Indeed, this seems to me to be a classic case of harmless error: a second confession giving more details of the crime than the first was admitted in evidence and found to be free of any constitutional objection. Accordingly, I would affirm the holding of the Supreme Court of Arizona in its initial opinion and reverse the judgment which it ultimately rendered in this case.

JUSTICE KENNEDY, concurring in the judgment.

For the reasons stated by the Chief Justice, I agree that Fulminante's confession to Anthony Sarivola was not coerced. In my view, the trial court did not err in admitting this testimony. A majority of the Court, however, finds the confession coerced and proceeds to consider whether harmless-error analysis may be used when a coerced confession has been admitted at trial. With the case in this posture, it is appropriate for me to address the harmless-error issue.

Again for the reasons stated by the Chief Justice, I agree that harmless-error analysis should apply in the case of a coerced confession. That said, the court conducting a harmless-error inquiry must appreciate the indelible impact a full confession may have on the trier of fact, as distinguished, for instance, from the impact of an isolated statement that incriminates the defendant only when connected with other evidence. If the jury believes that a defendant has admitted the crime, it doubtless will be tempted to rest its decision on that evidence alone, without careful consideration of the other evidence in the case. Apart, perhaps, from a videotape of the crime, one would have difficulty finding evidence more damaging to a criminal defendant's plea of innocence. For the reasons given by Justice White in Part IV of his opinion, I cannot with confidence find admission of Fulminante's confession to Anthony Sarivola to be harmless error.

The same majority of the Court does not agree on the three issues presented by the trial court's determination to admit Fulminante's first confession: whether the confession was inadmissible because coerced; whether harmless-error analysis is appropriate; and if so whether any error was harmless here. My own view that the confession was not coerced does not command a majority.

In the interests of providing a clear mandate to the Arizona Supreme Court in this capital case, I deem it proper to accept in the case now before us the holding of five Justices that the confession was coerced and inadmissible. I agree with a majority of the Court that admission of the confession could not be harmless error when viewed in light of all the other evidence; and so I concur in the judgment to affirm the ruling of the Arizona Supreme Court.

NOTES AND QUESTIONS

1.   Reread Professor Field's approaches to harmless error, p. 1532, Note 2. Which approach best describes Justice White's dissent on the issue of whether coerced confessions require automatic reversal? The majority opinion? Justice Kennedy's concurring opinion?

2.   Do you have doubt about whether Fulminante is guilty? What is the source of that doubt?

3.   Justice White's dissent in *Fulminante* noted that the Court had found "it impossible to analyze in terms of harmless error the failure to instruct a jury on the reasonable-doubt standard," citing *Jackson v. Virginia*, p. 1524. Though only dicta in *Jackson* and *Fulminante*, the Court later

turned the dicta into holding. Noting that the Sixth Amendment jury trial right is interrelated with the due process right to be found guilty beyond a reasonable doubt, Justice Scalia concluded for a unanimous Court that a jury improperly instructed on the standard of proof has not actually rendered a verdict.

> There being no jury verdict of guilty-beyond-a-reasonable-doubt, the question whether the *same* verdict of guilty-beyond-a-reasonable-doubt would have been rendered absent the constitutional error is utterly meaningless. There is no *object*, so to speak, upon which harmless error analysis can operate. The most an appellate court can conclude is that a jury *would surely have found* [the defendant] guilty beyond a reasonable doubt—not that the jury's actual finding of guilty beyond a reasonable doubt *would surely not have been different* absent the constitutional error. That is not enough. The Sixth Amendment requires more than appellate speculation about a hypothetical jury's action, or else directed verdicts for the State would be sustainable on appeal; it requires an actual jury finding of guilty.

Sullivan v. Louisiana, 508 U.S. 275, 113 S.Ct. 2078, 124 L.Ed.2d 182 (1993).

4.   What if a judge erroneously fails to instruct a jury on an essential element of an offense? In Neder v. United States, 527 U.S. 1, 119 S.Ct. 1827, 144 L.Ed.2d 35 (1999), the issue was whether that failure should be analyzed in terms of harmless error, or whether it discredits the verdict and thus necessarily requires automatic reversal of a defendant's conviction.

The defendant in *Neder*, relying on *Sullivan*, Note 5, argued that there was no difference between a jury being improperly instructed on the burden of proof beyond a reasonable doubt (*Sullivan*) and a jury not knowing of an element that it must find beyond a reasonable doubt. The Supreme Court conceded that *Sullivan* could reach the *Neder* situation, but it nonetheless rejected the argument, finding that earlier cases had already decided the issue. Thus, "an instruction that omits an element of the offense does not necessarily render a criminal trial fundamentally unfair or an unreliable vehicle for determining guilt or innocence." The Court reasoned that the failure to instruct on an element of an offense is different in kind from "such [structural] defects as the complete deprivation of counsel or trial before a biased judge."

Justice Scalia, joined by Justices Souter and Ginsburg, argued in dissent that "depriving a criminal defendant of the right to have the jury determine his guilt of the crime charged—which necessarily means his commission of every element of the crime charged—can never be harmless." With characteristic style, Scalia underlined the central importance of the right to a jury trial: "When this Court deals with the content of this guarantee—the only one to appear in both the body of the Constitution and the Bill of Rights—it is operating upon the spinal column of American democracy."

Professor Roger Fairfax agrees with Scalia: "Juries implement constitutional structure and serve as an important conduit for citizen influence on the criminal justice process and government generally." Thus, even when an elemental omission error is harmless to the defendant, it is "anything but harmless to the jury itself. * * * The only way to remedy and deter such injury to the jury is to treat such errors as structural error and automatically reverse convictions based upon fewer than all the elements of the charged crime." Roger A. Fairfax, Jr., *Harmless Constitutional Error and the Institutional Significance of the Jury*, 76 Fordham L. Rev. 2027, 2060 (2008).

Is the error in *Neder* distinguishable from *Sullivan*? If so, which error seems more troubling to you?

3. RETROACTIVITY

A problem with far-reaching consequences is retroactivity: If the Supreme Court creates a new criminal procedure rule or right, how should it be applied to other cases? Assume, for example, a new rule restricting police investigation in some way. Obviously, the new rule will be applied prospectively—to all cases that have not yet reached the stage of police investigation where the new rule is relevant. But should the new rule also be applied to cases that have passed that stage of police investigation? If so, there are three options: (1) cases that have not yet been tried; (2) cases that have not yet been tried or have resulted in a conviction not yet final because an appeal is pending; (3) all cases, regardless of whether the conviction is final and how long it has been final. The Court did not give much careful thought to retroactivity until the 1980s, but it poses a problem in fairness and equality.

Assume three convicted defendants, *M*, *F*, and *P* in three different states in 1964. All three appeal their convictions on the ground that the police failed to advise them that they could talk to a lawyer during interrogation. Each loses because the prevailing law in 1964 did not provide an automatic right to counsel during interrogation. *F* is in a state that provides expedited criminal appeals, and his certiorari petition reaches the United States Supreme Court at the end of the 1964 term. The Court denies certiorari, the time for filing a collateral attack expires, and his conviction is thus final.

M's petition reaches the Court at the beginning of the 1965 term, and the Court joins it with three other cases. On June 13, 1966, the Court reverses all four convictions, creating the new rule of *Miranda v. Arizona*, p. 625. *P*'s certiorari petition arrives in the fall of 1966 and his direct appeal is thus pending when *Miranda* is decided. Should *F* and *P* be given the benefit of the new rule?

It is obviously a difficult question. On the one hand, why treat *F* and *P* differently from *M* just because *M*'s case was one of the ones fished from the stream of roughly 8,000 certiorari petitions filed each year in the Supreme Court? On the other hand, why reverse hundreds of convictions for police failures when the police did not know they were required to give warnings?

The Court's first attempt to provide coherence to this area of criminal procedure was in Linkletter v. Walker, 381 U.S. 618, 85 S.Ct. 1731, 14 L.Ed.2d 601 (1965). The issue was whether to apply retroactively the holding in *Mapp v. Ohio*, p. 83, that States had to exclude evidence seized in violation of the Fourth Amendment. As the Court would later describe the three-prong test used in *Linkletter*, it required examining "the purpose of the exclusionary rule, the reliance of the States on prior law, and the effect on the administration of justice of a retroactive application of the exclusionary rule." Teague v. Lane, 489 U.S. 288, 109 S.Ct. 1060, 103 L.Ed.2d 334 (1989). Using this test, *Linkletter* held that *Mapp* would not be applied retroactively. *F* and *P* would both lose under *Linkletter*. See Johnson v. New Jersey, 384 U.S. 719, 86 S.Ct. 1772, 16 L.Ed.2d 882 (1966) (holding that *Miranda* applied only to cases where the trials began after the decision was announced).

The *Linkletter* doctrine was, to put it mildly, not entirely successful. As the Court itself conceded, commentators had "a veritable field day" with the doctrine, "with much of the discussion being 'more than mildly negative.'" The principal criticism was that "the *Linkletter* standard led to the disparate treatment of similarly situated defendants on direct review." So, for example, the Court held that *Miranda* would apply only "to trials commencing after that decision had been announced." Thus, *P* in the hypothetical above was treated differently from *M*, an "inequity" that "generated vehement criticism."

Teague explained how the Court had remedied this inequity in 1987:

> In *Griffith v. Kentucky*, 479 U.S. 314, 107 S.Ct. 708, 93 L.Ed.2d 649 (1987), we rejected as unprincipled and inequitable the *Linkletter* standard for cases pending on direct review at the time a new rule is announced, and adopted the first part of the retroactivity approach advocated by Justice Harlan. We agreed with Justice Harlan that "failure to apply a newly declared constitutional rule to criminal cases pending on direct review violates basic norms of constitutional adjudication." We gave two reasons for our decision. First, because we can only promulgate new rules in specific cases and cannot possibly decide all cases in which review is sought, "the integrity of judicial review" requires the application of the new rule to "all similar cases pending on direct review." * * * Second, because "selective application of new rules violates the principle of treating similarly situated defendants the same," we refused to continue to tolerate the

inequity that resulted from not applying new rules retroactively to defendants whose cases had not yet become final. Although new rules that constituted clear breaks with the past generally were not given retroactive effect under the *Linkletter* standard, we held that "a new rule for the conduct of criminal prosecutions is to be applied retroactively to all cases, state or federal, pending on direct review or not yet final, with no exception for cases in which the new rule constitutes a 'clear break' with the past."

NOTES AND QUESTIONS

1. Do you see how the *Griffith* retroactivity principle works? How would the *Miranda* retroactivity issue be decided for *F* and *P* in the earlier hypothetical? Is that a good outcome? In what ways is the current approach to retroactivity better than the *Linkletter* approach? Worse?

2. Do you think *Griffith* will constrain future Courts when considering whether to impose a new rule of constitutional criminal procedure on police?

3. *Cases pending.* Notice that the *Griffin* rule extends to all cases *pending* on direct appeal when the new rule is announced. Thus, the *end* of direct review is not the end of the defendant's ability to assert the new rule. He may assert it when collaterally attacking his conviction. Miller-El's case is a good example. It was pending when the Court decided *Batson v. Kentucky* (p. 1249). The Texas Court of Criminal Appeals remanded Miller-El's case to the trial court for new findings in light of *Batson*. Based on those findings, the state court rejected Miller-El's *Batson* claim, and the United States Supreme Court denied certiorari. Miller-El then filed a federal habeas corpus petition based in part on his already-rejected *Batson* claim.

The federal district court ruled against Miller-El, and the Fifth Circuit refused to hear his appeal on the *Batson* issue. The Supreme Court reversed the Fifth Circuit and ordered that court to reach the merits of the *Batson* claim. Miller-El v. Cockrell, 537 U.S. 322, 123 S.Ct. 1029, 154 L.Ed.2d 931 (2003). The Fifth Circuit reached the merits but ruled against Miller-El. He again appealed to the Supreme Court, which reversed the Fifth Circuit and held in his favor. Miller-El v. Dretke, 545 U.S. 231, 125 S.Ct. 2317, 162 L.Ed.2d 196 (2005). For a brief discussion of the lengthy litigation in Miller-El's case, see p. 1269, Note 17.

Batson was decided in 1986 and was a new rule. Miller-El's victory in the Supreme Court was in 2005, nineteen years after *Batson*. But because his case was pending on direct review when *Batson* was decided, he could use the new rule for as many appeals and collateral attacks as the law permitted him.

For an insightful analysis of the culture in which Miller-El's case lingered for eighteen years, see Sandra Guerra Thompson, *The Non-Discrimination Ideal of Hernandez v. Texas Confronts a "Culture" of*

Discrimination: The Amazing Story of Miller-El v. Texas, 25 Chicano-Latino L. Rev. 97 (2005).

4.   We quoted from *Teague v. Lane* to explain the Court's approach to retroactivity in the context of cases not yet final when the new rule is announced. The issue in *Teague*, however, was how to approach retroactivity in habeas cases when the conviction *has* become final. How do you think the Court resolved that issue? We will return to *Teague* after a brief introduction to the law of habeas corpus.

B.   FEDERAL HABEAS CORPUS

1.   HISTORY AND THEORY OF HABEAS CORPUS

GRAHAM HUGHES—THE DECLINE OF HABEAS CORPUS

New York University Center for Research in Crime and Justice (1990), 1–4.

[I]f an appeal is now thought to be a virtual due process component of a criminal prosecution, there is considerable disagreement about how far review need be carried. Disraeli said that "finality is not the language of politics." Wrong * * * !—at least for criminal justice politics and especially death politics, where "finality" is very much the current buzz word. A protracted review process is aggravating enough to many observers and judges even if the prisoner is already serving his prison sentence; but when he is cheating the gallows by lolling around for years in a death cell, apoplexy threatens.

Much of the wrath of the finality lobby has been directed against the use of the habeas corpus writ in federal courts to challenge state convictions. The considerable success of this campaign in severely restricting the range of habeas is one of the strongest examples of the current devaluation of constitutional rights. * * *

The outcome has been the momentous withdrawal of the federal courts from effective supervision of the national criminal justice systems. * * *

Habeas at first looks like a very unlikely tool for mounting a post-appeal challenge to a criminal conviction since, in its historical English form, it was always a decisive answer to a habeas petition by a prisoner to show that he was imprisoned pursuant to the judgment of a court with subject matter jurisdiction. While habeas was given a niche in Article I of the United States Constitution it was certainly not with any thought of its being a post-conviction remedy—as the Supreme Court made abundantly clear in 1830 in *Ex parte Watkins* [28 U.S. 193, 7 L.Ed. 650 (1830)], where they denied a habeas petition which challenged a federal conviction on the ground that the indictment did not disclose an offense known to the law. The record of a judgment of conviction by a court having jurisdiction over criminal matters was a final answer to the petition, said the Court. Whether the indictment properly made allegations of an offense known to the law was exactly the kind of question to be settled by the trial court.

Thus it was not the Magna Charta, nor later English history, nor the United States Constitution that launched habeas on its brilliant career as a post-conviction remedy. Rather, it was, in the first place, a statute of 1867, part of the efforts to impose a post-Civil War Reconstruction settlement. Responding to the imprisonment in southern states of former slaves and of Union officials, the 1867 Act made federal habeas available as a remedy to any state prisoner who was in custody in violation of the Constitution, laws or treaties of the United States.

In spite of the large promise of this statute, federal habeas in fact made little impact on state criminal justice for another century. There were many reasons for this slow take off. Most conspicuous was the long-held position that the guarantees applicable to criminal suspects and defendants contained in the Bill of Rights did not apply to the states. Second, the habeas process itself was severely restricted by a cluster of doctrines. These included: (1) a strong requirement to the effect that all available state remedies must be exhausted before federal habeas could lie. Since state post-conviction remedies were often a procedural maze that could tie up the prisoner for years, the effect was usually to exhaust the prisoner before reaching the federal court. (2) A strong procedural default approach to the effect that failure to timely raise a point at the state level was a good reason for federal as well as state courts to decline to review the matter. (3) Extreme respect for state court findings of fact.

In the 1960s all these barriers were either swept aside or at least reduced in height and difficulty. First, the incorporation of virtually all the guarantees and protections of the Bill of Rights into the due process clause of the Fourteenth Amendment made them applicable to the states. But by itself this enormous enlargement of the relevance of the federal Constitution to the criminal process of the states would have meant very little—for how was the federal presence to be asserted? The certiorari jurisdiction of the Supreme Court would constitute so sporadic an intervention that it could not be considered a serious, regular monitor of state court judgments.

To consummate the criminal procedure revolution of the 1960s, an everyday instrument was necessary and this lay to hand in the little used federal habeas jurisdiction under the 1867 Act. With habeas, every district court judge could be a surrogate Supreme Court to inquire into the constitutional propriety of the detention of a state prisoner. But habeas needed to be stripped of its doctrinal encumbrances to be fitted for this mission. This was largely accomplished in a great trilogy of cases in

1963, *Fay v. Noia* [372 U.S. 391, 435, 83 S.Ct. 822, 847, 9 L.Ed.2d 837 (1963)], *Townsend v. Sain* [372 U.S. 293, 83 S.Ct. 745, 9 L.Ed.2d 770 (1963)], and *Sanders v. United States* [373 U.S. 1, 83 S.Ct. 1068, 10 L.Ed.2d 148 (1963)].

These decisions, and especially the cornerstone opinion of Justice Brennan in *Fay v. Noia*, did the following things: (1) they made it clear that the doctrine requiring exhaustion of state remedies did not apply when a state remedy was ineffective or no longer available, even if that was due to the neglect of the prisoner; (2) they repudiated a strong procedural default doctrine and held that failure at the state level to raise an issue in timely fashion would only bar the petitioner from federal habeas if the failure amounted to a deliberate bypass or waiver; (3) they weakened the presumptive validity of state fact findings and made it easier to obtain a federal evidentiary hearing; (4) they made it clear that res judicata does not apply to habeas and set up a liberal approach to the filing of successive petitions.

Great as the changes were, they hardly resulted in a general gaol delivery. Certainly there was a sharp increase in the number of habeas petitions filed, though it remained minuscule as an overall percentage of state convictions. The great majority of petitions was always summarily dismissed and the rate of reversal of state convictions was never generally higher than 7% of the comparatively few petitions presented. (The dramatic exception is death penalty cases where the rate of reversal as to state sentencing procedures in federal habeas has been as high as 60%.) Nevertheless, many state courts continued to express concern and indignation over the federal overlordship that habeas courts were exercising, while conservative commentators and judges deplored the tendency of federal habeas to protract uncertainty about the final propriety of state convictions. * * *

[There would be a counter-revolution. It] began in 1976 when *Stone v. Powell* [428 U.S. 465, 96 S.Ct. 3037, 49 L.Ed.2d 1067 (1976)] expelled Fourth Amendment questions from the realm of habeas. It continued in 1977 when *Wainwright v. Sykes* [p. 1565] held that most constitutional rights may be inadvertently forfeited and only a few need be subjected to the more stringent standards that require a formal waiver. Most recently, in 1989, habeas has been maimed by the holding in *Teague v. Lane* [p. 1554] that the writ may only be used to declare or apply a "new" interpretation of a constitutional right if that right belongs to a very small group that has retroactive application. In this way habeas has been relegated to the strange task of enforcing yesterday's law.[b]

---

[b]   We present the material in this excerpt in a slightly reordered form; this paragraph is in a different place than it occupied in the original. Eds.

NOTES AND QUESTIONS

1.   A petition for a writ of habeas corpus is an original action instituted by the inmate as petitioner, usually naming the warden of the prison as defendant. Three of the federal statutes that govern the general procedure of filing a habeas petition are included in Supplement Appendix A: 28 U.S.C. § 2254 provides for habeas petitions from state prisoners; 28 U.S.C. § 2255 provides for habeas petitions from federal prisoners, and 28 U.S.C. § 2244 contains various limitations that apply to both state and federal habeas actions. In addition to these provisions, the Constitution provides, "The Privilege of the Writ of Habeas Corpus shall not be suspended, unless when in Cases of Rebellion or Invasion the public Safety may require it." Art. I, § 9, paragraph 2. Do you see an argument that this provision restricts, rather than guarantees, the right of habeas corpus?

2.   Compare 28 U.S.C. § 2254 with § 2255. Supp. App. A. Identify some of the ways in which the federal habeas statute defers to state courts. Based on Graham Hughes's explanation for the expansion of federal habeas, what do you think motivated Congress to include these provisions?

3.   *Fourth Amendment limitations in habeas review.* In Stone v. Powell, 428 U.S. 465, 96 S.Ct. 3037, 49 L.Ed.2d 1067 (1976), the Court held that federal courts have no power to review Fourth Amendment claims against state convictions as long as the state courts have "fully and fairly" considered the Fourth Amendment claim. Though "full and fair" consideration might require a federal court to make certain that the state courts were not flagrantly wrong on the merits, the doctrine has developed to require only that the state courts reach the merits of the Fourth Amendment issue.

Is *Stone v. Powell* consistent with 28 U.S.C. § 2254(a)? One way to harmonize the two is to conclude, as the Court has done on several occasions, that the exclusionary rule is not itself a constitutional requirement of the Fourth Amendment. Is there another way to read § 2254(a) so that it would permit the Supreme Court to carve out constitutional issues that are not justiciable in habeas? Assuming the exclusionary rule is a constitutional requirement, does § 2254(a) *require* federal courts to hear a Fourth Amendment claim?

4.   *The writ as reflective of deeper values.* In a perceptive student Note, Evans Wohlforth argues that the writ itself has no substantive content. Instead, it is a vessel in which the legal system pours its current conception of the relationship among the relevant legal actors.

> History shows that the writ is simultaneously a creature of statute, a constitutional imperative, and a fundamental precept of centuries of common law. It cuts across the conventional taxonomy of common law, constitutionalism, and legislative enactment. Like a three-legged stool, it rests equally on each of these primary sources of law.
>
> For centuries, the question of who should have the right to define the parameters of the writ has been settled by power

struggles. In England, the history of the writ paralleled the ascendancy of constitutional government over the raw power of the royal executive. In America, the writ has been a conduit through which power has ebbed and flowed between the federal and the state governments. Most recently, the writ has reflected the modern Court's attempt to create a "value-neutral" Constitution.

Throughout these institutional power struggles, a core concept has remained constant. By virtue of its unique power to free prisoners, the writ reflects the current division of power among society's institutions, including that of the Constitution itself. Observers of the apparent upheavals have often focused on the legislative or judicial authority to effect an alteration to the writ. In reality, however, where critics note an expansion or contraction of the writ's scope, they are actually observing a change in the status of the institution that wields it. * * *

The modern Court's use of habeas corpus reflects its own vision of the constitutional order. If federalism requires that federal rights be subordinate to other constitutional values, it is only natural that habeas corpus not be allowed to operate to thwart those other values. If value-neutral adjudication requires that constitutional rights are to be preserved only to the extent they serve other systemic or structural interests, then habeas will reflect this purposive view of constitutional rights.

As shown above, this is entirely consistent with the writ's history. The Court is doing no more than the common law courts of England or the Reconstruction Congress did in defining the scope of the writ as congruent with their vision of constitutional rights. The writ changes to reflect change in the underlying constitution, rather than effecting it.

Stone v. Powell illustrates this proposition starkly. Although often read as a case on the scope of habeas, the bulk of the opinion deals with the underlying issues of the Fourth Amendment and the exclusionary rule. *Stone* separated the remedy of excluding evidence searched or seized unconstitutionally from the constitutional guarantee itself. The *Stone* Court overruled the decision in *Mapp v. Ohio*, in which the Warren Court found that the exclusionary rule was required by the Fourth Amendment, was of constitutional origin, and, therefore, ran against the states. Thus, *Stone*'s holding that the exclusionary rule was not cognizable upon habeas review is incidental to the more important point that the rule is no longer within the Constitution.

Evans Wohlforth, Note, *Theories, A Meta-Theory, and Habeas Corpus*, 46 Rutgers L. Rev. 1395, 1412–13 (1994).

What would Evans Wohlforth say is the content of the Privilege of the Writ of Habeas Corpus guaranteed by Art. I, § 9, paragraph 2?

5.   *Other jurisdictional limitations?* The Court has so far not extended the *Stone v. Powell* limitation on habeas into other areas. The question of whether to deprive federal habeas courts of the jurisdiction to hear *Miranda* claims was settled by a 5–4 majority in Withrow v. Williams, 507 U.S. 680, 113 S.Ct. 1745, 123 L.Ed.2d 407 (1993). Writing for the majority in *Withrow*, Justice Souter concluded that the *Miranda* right was different in kind from the "right" to the exclusionary rule. Why would the Court restrict federal habeas in Fourth Amendment cases but leave the door open for *Miranda* claims?

One reason is Wohlforth's theory that the habeas point is "incidental to the more important point" about the underlying right. Under Wohlforth's theory, *Withrow v. Williams* in 1994 actually predicted the Court's holding in 2000 that *Miranda*, unlike the Fourth Amendment exclusionary rule, is part of the Constitution. See *Dickerson v. United States*, p. 670.

6.   *Other requirements.* As you can see from 28 U.S.C. § 2254(b)(1), the petitioner must be in custody and must have exhausted available state remedies. In most cases, these requirements are easily satisfied—your client is in prison and has been through every available state appellate or post-conviction level of review. Some quite technical issues arise in non-typical cases, which are beyond the scope of this work.

2.   RETROACTIVITY

Section A. considered the retroactivity problem in direct appeals, which the Court has now resolved by requiring *all* new rules to be fully retroactive to cases not yet final when the rule is announced. Habeas cases present a more difficult retroactivity question. Prior to the passage of the Antiterrorism and Effective Death Penalty Act of 1996, there was no time limit on filing habeas challenges to state convictions and reviewing courts were often faced with convictions several years old. (The time limit now is, generally, a year after the conviction becomes final.) Consider the effect of holding *Miranda* fully retroactive so that anyone still in prison could challenge his conviction on the ground that the police failed to provide warnings.

TEAGUE V. LANE
Supreme Court of the United States, 1989.
489 U.S. 288, 109 S.Ct. 1060, 103 L.Ed.2d 334.

JUSTICE O'CONNOR announced the judgment of the Court and delivered the opinion of the Court with respect to Parts I, II, and III [joined by CHIEF JUSTICE REHNQUIST and JUSTICES WHITE, SCALIA, AND KENNEDY] and an opinion with respect to Parts IV and V, in which THE CHIEF JUSTICE, JUSTICE SCALIA, and JUSTICE KENNEDY join. * * *

I

Petitioner, a black man, was convicted by an all-white Illinois jury of three counts of attempted murder, two counts of armed robbery, and one count of aggravated battery. During jury selection for petitioner's trial, the prosecutor used all 10 of his peremptory challenges to exclude blacks. * * *

On appeal, petitioner argued that the prosecutor's use of peremptory challenges denied him the right to be tried by a jury that was representative of the community. * * *

[After losing his state appeals, Teague filed a petition for a writ of habeas corpus in federal court.]

II

Petitioner's first contention is that he should receive the benefit of our decision in *Batson v. Kentucky*, [p. 1249] even though his conviction became final before *Batson* was decided. * * *

[*Batson* held that, under the Equal Protection Clause,] a defendant can establish a prima facie case by showing that he is a "member of a cognizable racial group," that the prosecutor exercised "peremptory challenges to remove from the venire members of the defendant's race," and that those "facts and any other relevant circumstances raise an inference that the prosecutor used that practice to exclude the veniremen from the petit jury on account of their race." Once the defendant makes out a prima facie case of discrimination, the burden shifts to the prosecutor "to come forward with a neutral explanation for challenging black jurors." * * *

[The Court rejected Teague's *Batson* argument, having already held in Allen v. Hardy, 478 U.S. 255, 106 S.Ct. 2878, 92 L.Ed.2d 199 (1986) (*per curiam*), that *Batson* would not be applied retroactively on collateral review of convictions that became final before *Batson*.]

IV

Petitioner's * * * final contention is that the Sixth Amendment's fair cross section requirement applies to the petit jury. * * * *Taylor v. Louisiana* [p. 1213] expressly stated that the fair cross section requirement does not apply to the petit jury. Petitioner nevertheless contends that the *ratio decidendi* of *Taylor* cannot be limited to the jury venire, and he urges adoption of a new rule. Because we hold that the rule urged by petitioner should not be applied retroactively to cases on collateral review, we decline to address petitioner's contention.

A * * *

In our view, the question "whether a decision [announcing a new rule should] be given prospective or retroactive effect should be faced at the time of [that] decision." Retroactivity is properly treated as a threshold question, for, once a new rule is applied to the defendant in the case announcing the rule, evenhanded justice requires that it be applied retroactively to all who are similarly situated. Thus, before deciding whether the fair cross section requirement should be extended to the petit jury, we should ask whether such a rule would be applied retroactively to the case at issue. * * *

It is admittedly often difficult to determine when a case announces a new rule, and we do not attempt to define the spectrum of what may or may not constitute a new rule for retroactivity purposes. In general, however, a case announces a new rule when it breaks new ground or imposes a new obligation on the States or the Federal Government. To put it differently, a case announces a new rule if the result was not *dictated* by precedent existing at the time the defendant's conviction becomes final. Given the strong language in *Taylor* and our statement in *Akins v. Texas*, 325 U.S. 398, 403, 65 S.Ct. 1276, 1279, 89 L.Ed. 1692 (1945), that "[f]airness in [jury] selection has never been held to require proportional representation of races upon a jury," application of the fair cross section requirement to the petit jury would be a new rule. * * *

B

Justice Harlan believed that new rules generally should not be applied retroactively to cases on collateral review. He argued that retroactivity for cases on collateral review could "be responsibly [determined] only by focusing, in the first instance, on the nature, function, and scope of the adjudicatory process in which such cases arise. The relevant frame of reference, in other words, is not the purpose of the new rule whose benefit the [defendant] seeks, but instead the purposes for which the writ of habeas corpus is made available." With regard to the nature of habeas corpus, Justice Harlan wrote:

> "Habeas corpus always has been a *collateral* remedy, providing an avenue for upsetting judgments that have become otherwise final. It is not designed as a substitute for direct review. The interest in leaving concluded litigation in a state of repose, that is, reducing the controversy to a final judgment not subject to further judicial revision, may quite legitimately be found by those responsible for defining the scope of the writ to outweigh in some, many, or most instances the competing interest in readjudicating convictions according to all legal standards in effect when a habeas petition is filed."

Given the "broad scope of constitutional issues cognizable on habeas," Justice Harlan argued that it is "sounder, in adjudicating habeas petitions, generally to apply the law prevailing at the time a conviction became final than it is to seek to dispose of [habeas] cases on the basis of intervening changes in constitutional interpretation." As he had explained * * * "the threat of habeas serves as a necessary additional incentive for trial and appellate courts throughout the land to conduct their proceedings in a manner consistent with established constitutional standards. In order to perform this deterrence function, * * * the habeas court need only apply the constitutional standards that prevailed at the time the original proceedings took place." * * *

We agree with Justice Harlan's description of the function of habeas corpus. "[T]he Court never has defined the scope of the writ simply by reference to a perceived need to assure that an individual accused of crime is afforded a trial free of constitutional error." Rather, we have recognized that interests of comity and finality must also be considered in determining the proper scope of habeas review. Thus, if a defendant fails to comply with state procedural rules and is barred from litigating a particular constitutional claim in state court, the claim can be considered on federal habeas only if the defendant shows cause for the default and actual prejudice resulting therefrom. * * *

These underlying considerations of finality find significant and compelling parallels in the criminal context. Application of constitutional rules not in existence at the time a conviction became final seriously undermines the principle of finality which is essential to the operation of our criminal justice system. Without finality, the criminal law is deprived of much of its deterrent effect. The fact that life and liberty are at stake in criminal prosecutions "shows only that 'conventional notions of finality' should not have *as much* place in criminal as in civil litigation, not that they should have *none*." * * *

* * * [T]he application of new rules to cases on collateral review * * * *continually* forces the States to marshal resources in order to keep in prison defendants whose trials and appeals conformed to then-existing constitutional standards. Furthermore, as we recognized in *Engle v. Isaac*, [456 U.S. 107, 102 S.Ct. 1558, 71 L.Ed.2d 783 (1982)] "[s]tate courts are understandably frustrated when they faithfully apply existing constitutional law only to have a federal court discover, during a [habeas] proceeding, new constitutional commands."

We find these criticisms to be persuasive, and we now adopt Justice Harlan's view of retroactivity for cases on collateral review. Unless they fall within an exception to the general rule, new constitutional rules of criminal procedure will not be applicable to those cases which have become final before the new rules are announced.

V

Petitioner's conviction became final in 1983. As a result, the rule petitioner urges would not be applicable to this case, which is on collateral review, unless it would fall within an exception.

The first exception suggested by Justice Harlan—that a new rule should be applied retroactively if it places "certain kinds of primary, private individual conduct beyond the power of the criminal law-making authority to proscribe," is not relevant here. Application of the fair cross section requirement to the petit jury would not accord constitutional protection to any primary activity whatsoever.

The second exception suggested by Justice Harlan—that a new rule should be applied retroactively if it requires the observance of "those procedures that * * * are 'implicit in the concept of ordered liberty,'" we apply with a modification. The language used by Justice Harlan * * * leaves no doubt that he meant the second exception to be reserved for watershed rules of criminal procedure:

> "Typically, it should be the case that any conviction free from federal constitutional error at the time it became final, will be found, upon reflection, to have been fundamentally fair and conducted under those procedures essential to the substance of a full hearing. However, in some situations it might be that time and growth in social capacity, as well as judicial perceptions of what we can rightly demand of the adjudicatory process, will properly alter our understanding of the *bedrock procedural elements* that must be found to vitiate the fairness of a particular conviction. For example, such, in my view, is the case with the right to counsel at trial now held a necessary condition precedent to any conviction for a serious crime." * * *

Because we operate from the premise that such procedures would be so central to an accurate determination of innocence or guilt, we believe it unlikely that many such components of basic due process have yet to emerge. We are also of the view that such rules are "best illustrated by recalling the classic grounds for the issuance of a writ of habeas corpus—that the proceeding was dominated by mob violence; that the prosecutor knowingly made use of perjured testimony; or that the conviction was based on a confession extorted from the defendant by brutal methods."

An examination of our decision in *Taylor* applying the fair cross section requirement to the jury venire leads inexorably to the conclusion that adoption of the rule petitioner urges would be a far cry from the kind of absolute prerequisite to fundamental fairness that is "implicit in the concept of ordered liberty." * * * Because the absence of a fair cross section on the jury venire does not undermine the fundamental fairness that must underlie a conviction or seriously diminish the likelihood of obtaining an accurate conviction, we conclude that a rule requiring that petit juries be composed of a fair cross section of the community would not be a "bedrock procedural element" that would be retroactively applied under the second exception we have articulated.

Were we to recognize the new rule urged by petitioner in this case, we would have to give petitioner the benefit of that new rule even though it would not be applied retroactively to others similarly situated. In the words of Justice Brennan, such an inequitable result would be "an unavoidable consequence of the necessity that constitutional adjudications not stand as mere dictum." But the harm caused by the failure to treat similarly situated defendants alike cannot be exaggerated: such inequitable treatment "hardly comports with the ideal of 'administration of justice with an even hand.'" Our refusal to allow such disparate treatment in the direct review context led us to adopt the first part of Justice Harlan's retroactivity approach [requiring new rules to be retroactive to all cases then on direct review]. "The fact that the new rule may constitute a clear break with the past has no bearing on the 'actual inequity that results' when only one of many similarly situated defendants receives the benefit of the new rule."

If there were no other way to avoid rendering advisory opinions, we might well agree that the inequitable treatment described above is "an insignificant cost for adherence to sound principles of decision-making." But there is a more principled way of dealing with the problem. We can simply refuse to announce a new rule in a given case unless the rule would be applied retroactively to the defendant in the case and to all others similarly situated. We think this approach is a sound one. Not only does it eliminate any problems of rendering advisory opinions, it also avoids the inequity resulting from the uneven application of new rules to similarly situated defendants. We therefore hold that, implicit in the retroactivity approach we adopt today, is the principle that habeas corpus cannot be used as a vehicle to create new constitutional rules of criminal procedure unless those rules would be applied retroactively to *all* defendants on collateral review through one of the two exceptions we have articulated. Because a decision extending the fair cross section requirement to the petit jury would not be applied retroactively to cases on collateral review under the approach we adopt today, we do not address petitioner's claim. * * *

[The opinions of JUSTICE WHITE, concurring in part and concurring in the judgment; JUSTICE BLACKMUN, concurring in part and concurring in the judgment; and JUSTICE STEVENS, with whom JUSTICE BLACKMUN joins as to Part I, concurring in part and concurring in the judgment, are omitted].

JUSTICE BRENNAN, with whom JUSTICE MARSHALL joins, dissenting. * * *

* * * Out of an exaggerated concern for treating similarly situated habeas petitioners the same, the plurality would for the first time preclude the federal courts from considering on collateral review a vast

range of important constitutional challenges; where those challenges have merit, it would bar the vindication of personal constitutional rights and deny society a check against further violations until the same claim is presented on direct review. In my view, the plurality's "blind adherence to the principle of treating like cases alike" amounts to "letting the tail wag the dog" when it stymies the resolution of substantial and unheralded constitutional questions. Because I cannot acquiesce in this unprecedented curtailment of the reach of the Great Writ, particularly in the absence of any discussion of these momentous changes by the parties or the lower courts, I dissent. * * *

II * * *

C

The plurality does not so much as mention *stare decisis*. Indeed, from the plurality's exposition of its new rule, one might infer that its novel fabrication will work no great change in the availability of federal collateral review of state convictions. Nothing could be further from the truth. Although the plurality declines to "define the spectrum of what may or may not constitute a new rule for retroactivity purposes," it does say that generally "a case announces a new rule when it breaks new ground or imposes a new obligation on the States or the Federal Government." Otherwise phrased, "a case announces a new rule if the result was not *dictated* by precedent existing at the time the defendant's conviction became final." This account is extremely broad. Few decisions on appeal or collateral review are "*dictated*" by what came before. Most such cases involve a question of law that is at least debatable, permitting a rational judge to resolve the case in more than one way. Virtually no case that prompts a dissent on the relevant legal point, for example, could be said to be "*dictated*" by prior decisions. By the plurality's test, therefore, a great many cases could only be heard on habeas if the rule urged by the petitioner fell within one of the two exceptions the plurality has sketched. Those exceptions, however, are narrow. Rules that place " 'certain kinds of primary, private individual conduct beyond the power of the criminal law-making authority to proscribe,' " are rare. And rules that would require "new procedures without which the likelihood of an accurate conviction is seriously diminished," are not appreciably more common. The plurality admits, in fact, that it "believe[s] it unlikely that many such components of basic due process have yet to emerge." The plurality's approach today can thus be expected to contract substantially the Great Writ's sweep.

Its impact is perhaps best illustrated by noting the abundance and variety of habeas cases we have decided in recent years that could never have been adjudicated had the plurality's new rule been in effect. * * *

* * * In *Estelle v. Smith*, 451 U.S. 454, 101 S.Ct. 1866, 68 L.Ed.2d 359 (1981), for example, we held that a psychiatrist who examined the defendant before trial without warning him that what he said could be used against him in a capital sentencing proceeding could not testify against him at such a proceeding. Under the plurality's newly fashioned rule, however, we could not have decided that case on the merits. The result can hardly be said to have been compelled by existing case law, and the exclusion of such testimony at sentencing cannot have influenced the jury's determination of the defendant's guilt or enhanced the likely accuracy of his sentence. Nor is *Estelle v. Smith* unique in that respect. [Justice Brennan cites a total of 18 cases in which the Court had reached the merits of an issue on habeas that would be a "new rule" under *Teague* and thus could not have been reached under the plurality's approach. These cases include Schneckloth v. Bustamonte, consent search, p. 352, Barker v. Wingo, speedy trial, p. 1010, and Ross v. Moffitt, counsel for indigents on discretionary appeal, p. 1065]

D

These are massive changes, unsupported by precedent. They also lack a reasonable foundation. By exaggerating the importance of treating like cases alike and granting relief to all identically positioned habeas petitioners or none, "the Court acts as if it has no choice but to follow a mechanical notion of fairness without pausing to consider 'sound principles of decisionmaking.'" Certainly it is desirable, in the interest of fairness, to accord the same treatment to all habeas petitioners with the same claims. Given a choice between deciding an issue on direct or collateral review that might result in a new rule of law that would not warrant retroactive application to persons on collateral review other than the petitioner who brought the claim, we should ordinarily grant certiorari and decide the question on direct review. Following our decision in *Griffith v. Kentucky*, a new rule would apply equally to all persons whose convictions had not become final before the rule was announced, whereas habeas petitioners other than the one whose case we decided might not benefit from such a rule if we adopted it on collateral review. Taking cases on direct review ahead of those on habeas is especially attractive because the retrial of habeas petitioners usually places a heavier burden on the States than the retrial of persons on direct review. Other things being equal, our concern for fairness and finality ought to therefore lead us to render our decision in a case that comes to us on direct review.

Other things are not always equal, however. Sometimes a claim which, if successful, would create a new rule not appropriate for retroactive application on collateral review is better presented by a habeas case than by one on direct review. In fact, sometimes the claim is *only* presented on collateral review. In that case, while we could forgo deciding the issue in the hope that it would eventually be presented squarely on direct review, that hope might be misplaced, and even if it were in time fulfilled, the opportunity to check constitutional violations and to further the evolution of our thinking in some area of the law would in the meanwhile have been lost. In addition, by preserving our right and that of the lower federal courts to hear such claims on collateral review, we would not discourage their litigation on federal habeas corpus and thus not deprive ourselves and society of the benefit of decisions by the lower federal courts when we must resolve these issues ourselves.

The plurality appears oblivious to these advantages of our settled approach to collateral review. Instead, it would deny itself these benefits because adherence to precedent would occasionally result in one habeas petitioner's obtaining redress while another petitioner with an identical claim could not qualify for relief. In my view, the uniform treatment of habeas petitioners is not worth the price the plurality is willing to pay. Permitting the federal courts to decide novel habeas claims not substantially related to guilt or innocence has profited our society immensely. Congress has not seen fit to withdraw those benefits by amending the statute that provides for them. And although a favorable decision for a petitioner might not extend to another prisoner whose identical claim has become final, it is at least arguably better that the wrong done to one person be righted than that none of the injuries inflicted on those whose convictions have become final be redressed, despite the resulting inequality in treatment. * * *

NOTES AND QUESTIONS

1.   *Teague now commands a majority.* Justice O'Connor's opinion refusing to reach claims for new rules in habeas proceedings mustered only four votes in *Teague.* Justice White concurred in the judgment on the ground that a more flexible approach was preferable to the Court's evolving doctrine that all new rules are applicable on direct review and never applicable in habeas. The next year, and without explanation, he joined the five-justice majority opinion in Butler v. McKellar, 494 U.S. 407, 110 S.Ct. 1212, 108 L.Ed.2d 347 (1990), that endorsed and clarified *Teague.*

2.   *When is a new case a "new rule"?* Notice that the Court defines "new rule" using two different formulations. Are these two ways of saying the same thing or is one harder to satisfy than the other?

3.   *Clarifying one of the Teague exceptions.* In Welch v. United States, 578 U.S. ___. 136 S.Ct. 1257. 194 L.Ed.2d 387 (2016), the issue was whether a habeas corpus petitioner could benefit from a later interpretation of a federal criminal statute that would have made it inapplicable to him. Though the interpretation of the statute was a new rule, because it was not dictated by precedent, the Court held, 8–1, that the habeas petitioner could prevail because the new rule was "substantive" rather than "procedural." A

procedural rule governs *how* a defendant is prosecuted. If the procedure changes after a conviction becomes final, a habeas corpus petitioner is generally not permitted to benefit from the new rule. He got the constitutional procedure that was in effect at the time of his conviction.

Substantive rules determine *whether* a defendant is guilty. A new substantive rule can place the petitioner's conduct beyond the power of the State to penalize. Welch's sentence was increased by application of a provision of the Armed Career Criminal Act of 1984 that was later held unconstitutional under the void-for-vagueness doctrine. Because Welch would not have been subject to the Armed Career Criminal Act if tried today, the Court held he was entitled to benefit from the new rule in his petition for habeas corpus.

Justice Thomas dissented, essentially arguing that this was a more expansive definition of the exception for new substantive rules than Justice Harlan intended. Thomas might be right as a matter of what Justice Harlan wrote, but it does seem unfair to make inmates like Welch serve the rest of a sentence that could *never have been imposed* if the statute had been correctly applied. Thus, the Court now understands *Teague* to permit habeas petitions based on new interpretations of laws that place the defendant's conduct outside the scope of what was proscribed.

4. *And what are "watershed rules of criminal procedure"?* In 2007, the Court held unanimously that the *Crawford v. Washington*, p. 1303, rule for applying the confrontation clause was a new rule—it after all rejected the analytical approach of a quarter century of confrontation clause cases—but that it was *not* a "watershed rule" exempt from *Teague*. Whorton v. Bockting, 549 U.S. 406, 127 S.Ct. 1173, 167 L.Ed.2d 1 (2007). A watershed rule "must itself constitute a previously unrecognized bedrock procedural element that is essential to the fairness of a proceeding." The *Whorton* Court used as a standard *Gideon v. Wainwright*, p. 1043, a case that held that indigents have a right to appointed counsel when charged with a felony. Noting that "*Gideon* effected a profound and 'sweeping' change," the Court concluded that the "*Crawford* rule simply lacks the 'primacy' and 'centrality' of the *Gideon* rule." Thus, Bockting, whose conviction was final when *Crawford* was decided, could not use *Crawford* to attack his conviction.

Schriro v. Summerlin, 542 U.S. 348, 124 S.Ct. 2519, 159 L.Ed.2d 442 (2004), presented the Court with a more difficult "watershed" issue. Ring v. Arizona, p. 1434, Note 2, held that the Sixth Amendment requires that juries, not judges, find the aggravating factors that justify imposition of the death penalty. Schriro's conviction had become final before the Court decided *Ring*. As *Ring* overruled a prior case, there can be no doubt that it was a new rule under *Teague*. The only way Schriro could benefit from the new rule is if it is one of the "watershed rules of criminal procedure" that are exempt from *Teague*.

The plurality in *Teague* said that watershed rules are "central to an accurate determination of innocence or guilt." The issue in *Schriro*, therefore, was whether the rule that only a jury can find aggravating factors in a death case is sufficiently central to "an accurate determination of innocence or guilt" to qualify for retroactive application in all cases. The Court, by a 5–4 margin, held that it was not. Schriro thus could not benefit from the new rule of *Ring*. The majority said that the question was not

> whether the Framers believed that juries are more accurate factfinders than judges (perhaps so—they certainly thought juries were more independent). Nor is the question whether juries actually *are* more accurate factfinders than judges (again, perhaps so). Rather, the question is whether judicial factfinding so "*seriously* diminishes" accuracy that there is an " 'impermissibly large risk' " of punishing conduct the law does not reach. The evidence is simply too equivocal to support that conclusion.

Justice Breyer's dissent argued that accuracy in part refers to whether the community would find that the defendant deserved the death penalty. Defined that way, he argued, having judges find aggravating factors in death cases *does* create an "impermissibly large risk" of executing someone whom the community would not have condemned to die. Breyer also noted the appearance of injustice created by the majority's holding. The community "will simply witness two individuals, both sentenced through the use of unconstitutional procedures, one individual going to his death, the other saved, all through an accident of timing." How, Breyer asked, "can the Court square this spectacle" with the principle that "any decision to impose the death sentence be, and appear to be, based on reason"?

It appears that Justice O'Connor was right when she said in *Teague* that it was "unlikely that many" watershed rules "have yet to emerge."

5. *The scope of Teague.* The *Teague* rule forbids the creation of new constitutional rules in habeas cases. What it does *not* forbid is the Court reaching the merits of a request for a new rule and then holding against petitioner. That is what happened in *Portuondo v. Agard*, p. 1377, Note 5. One of the habeas petitioner's arguments was based on the rule of *Griffin v. California*, p. 1370, that the prosecutor cannot comment on a defendant's failure to testify. But in *Portuondo*, the defendant *did* testify; his complaint was that the prosecutor commented about the advantage that he had in testifying last. Do you see why the petitioner *must have been* seeking to establish a new rule? The Court reached the merits of the *Griffin* argument and ruled that defendants have no right to keep the prosecutor from commenting on the defendant's advantage in testifying last. There was no mention of *Teague*.

3. PROCEDURAL DEFAULT—THE "CAUSE AND PREJUDICE" TEST

As lawyers too often learn the hard way, "procedural default" is what happens when a rule of procedure is not followed. For example, a lawyer procedurally defaults an evidentiary objection to a particular question if the objection is not made in a timely fashion. More importantly (and more frighteningly), the lawyer defaults a client's right to appeal if the notice of appeal is not filed as required. Typically, the remedy for procedural default is that the substance of the claim is defaulted. If the notice of appeal is not filed in time, the client's appeal cannot be heard, regardless of how meritorious it may be. The implications for procedural default in habeas cases are immense. As we saw in Chapter 14, many criminal defendants have mediocre lawyers. Many claims are defaulted. Should federal courts hear these claims? Does it matter if they are defaulted in state court, pursuant to state law, or federal court, pursuant to the federal law of default?

WAINWRIGHT V. SYKES
Supreme Court of the United States, 1977.
433 U.S. 72, 97 S.Ct. 2497, 53 L.Ed.2d 594.

MR. JUSTICE REHNQUIST delivered the opinion of the Court [joined by CHIEF JUSTICE BURGER, and JUSTICES STEWART, BLACKMUN, POWELL, and STEVENS].

We granted certiorari to consider the availability of federal habeas corpus to review a state convict's claim that testimony was admitted at his trial in violation of his rights under *Miranda v. Arizona*, p. 625, a claim which the Florida courts have previously refused to consider on the merits because of noncompliance with a state contemporaneous-objection rule [which required objections to be made at the time the evidence is offered for admission]. * * *

Respondent appealed his conviction, but apparently did not challenge the admissibility of the inculpatory statements. He later filed in the trial court a motion to vacate the conviction and, in the State District Court of Appeals and Supreme Court, petitions for habeas corpus. These filings, apparently for the first time, challenged the statements made to police on grounds of involuntariness. In all of these efforts respondent was unsuccessful.

Having failed in the Florida courts, respondent initiated the present action under 28 U.S.C. § 2254, asserting the inadmissibility of his statements by reason of his lack of understanding of the *Miranda* warnings. * * *

The simple legal question before the Court calls for a construction of the language of 28 U.S.C. § 2254(a), which provides that the federal courts shall entertain an application for a writ of habeas corpus "in behalf of a person in custody pursuant to the judgment of a state court only on the ground that he is in custody in violation of the Constitution or laws or treaties of the United States." But, to put it mildly, we do not write on a clean slate in construing this statutory provision. Its earliest counterpart, applicable only to prisoners detained by federal authority, is found in the Judiciary Act of 1789. Construing that statute for the Court in *Ex parte Watkins*, 3 Pet. 193, 202, 7 L.Ed. 650 (1830), Mr. Chief Justice Marshall said:

> "An imprisonment under a judgment cannot be unlawful, unless that judgment be an absolute nullity; and it is not a nullity if the Court has general jurisdiction of the subject, although it should be erroneous."

In 1867, Congress expanded the statutory language so as to make the writ available to one held in state as well as federal custody. For more than a century since the 1867 amendment, this Court has grappled with the relationship between the classical common-law writ of habeas corpus and the remedy provided in 28 U.S.C. § 2254. Sharp division within the Court has been manifested on more than one aspect of the perplexing problems which have been litigated in this connection. Where the habeas petitioner challenges a final judgment of conviction rendered by a state court, this Court has been called upon to decide no fewer than four different questions, all to a degree interrelated with one another: (1) What types of federal claims may a federal habeas court properly consider? (2) Where a federal claim is cognizable by a federal habeas court, to what extent must that court defer to a resolution of the claim in prior state proceedings? (3) To what extent must the petitioner who seeks federal habeas exhaust state remedies before resorting to the federal court? (4) In what instances will an adequate and independent state ground bar consideration of otherwise cognizable federal issues on federal habeas review?

Each of these four issues has spawned its share of litigation. With respect to the first, the rule laid down in *Ex parte Watkins*, *supra*, was gradually changed by judicial decisions expanding the availability of habeas relief beyond attacks focused narrowly on the jurisdiction of the sentencing court. * * *

There is no need to consider here in greater detail these first three areas of controversy attendant to federal habeas review of state convictions. Only the fourth area—the adequacy of state grounds to bar federal habeas review—is presented in this case. The foregoing discussion of the other three is pertinent here only as it illustrates this Court's historic willingness to overturn or modify its earlier views of the scope of the writ, even where the statutory language authorizing judicial action has remained unchanged.

As to the role of adequate and independent state grounds, it is a well-established principle of federalism that a state decision resting on an adequate foundation of state substantive law is immune from review in the federal courts. The application of this principle in the context of a federal habeas proceeding has therefore excluded from consideration any questions of state *substantive* law, and thus effectively barred federal habeas review where questions of that sort are either the only ones raised by a petitioner or are in themselves dispositive of his case. The area of controversy which has developed has concerned the reviewability of federal claims which the state court has declined to pass on because not presented in the manner prescribed by its *procedural* rules. The adequacy of such an independent state procedural ground to prevent federal habeas review of the underlying federal issue has been treated very differently than where the state-law ground is substantive. * * * .

In *Brown* [*v. Allen*, 344 U.S. 443, 73 S.Ct. 397, 97 L.Ed. 469 (1953)], petitioner Daniels' lawyer had failed to mail the appeal papers to the State Supreme Court on the last day provided by law for filing, and hand delivered them one day after that date. Citing the state rule requiring timely filing, the Supreme Court of North Carolina refused to hear the appeal. This Court * * * held that federal habeas was not available to review a constitutional claim which could not have been reviewed on direct appeal here because it rested on an independent and adequate state procedural ground.

In *Fay v. Noia*, [372 U.S. 391, 435, 83 S.Ct. 822, 847, 9 L.Ed.2d 837 (1963)], respondent Noia sought federal habeas to review a claim that his state-court conviction had resulted from the introduction of a coerced confession in violation of the Fifth Amendment to the United States Constitution. While the convictions of his two codefendants were reversed on that ground in collateral proceedings following their appeals, Noia did not appeal and the New York courts ruled that his subsequent *coram nobis* action was barred on account of that failure. This Court held that petitioner was nonetheless entitled to raise the claim in federal habeas, and thereby overruled its decision 10 years earlier in *Brown v. Allen, supra*:

> "[T]he doctrine under which state procedural defaults are held to constitute an adequate and independent state law ground barring direct Supreme Court review is not to be extended to limit the power granted the federal courts under the federal habeas statute."

As a matter of comity but not of federal power, the Court acknowledged "a limited discretion in the federal judge to deny relief * * * to an applicant who had deliberately by-passed the orderly procedure of the state courts and in so doing has forfeited his state court remedies." In so stating, the Court made clear that the waiver must be knowing and actual—" 'an intentional relinquishment or abandonment of a known right or privilege.' " Noting petitioner's "grisly choice" between acceptance of his life sentence and pursuit of an appeal which might culminate in a sentence of death, the Court concluded that there had been no deliberate bypass of the right to have the federal issues reviewed through a state appeal.

A decade later we decided Davis v. United States, [411 U.S. 233, 93 S.Ct. 1577, 36 L.Ed.2d 216 (1973)], in which a federal prisoner's application under 28 U.S.C. § 2255 sought for the first time to challenge the makeup of the grand jury which indicted him. The Government contended that he was barred by the requirement of Fed. Rule Crim. Proc. 12(b)(2) [now (b)(3)] providing that such challenges must be raised "by motion before trial." The Rule further provides that failure to so object constitutes a waiver of the objection, but that "the court for cause shown may grant relief from the waiver." We noted that the Rule "promulgated by this Court and, pursuant to 18 U.S.C. § 3771, 'adopted' by Congress, governs by its terms the manner in which the claims of defects in the institution of criminal proceedings may be waived," and held that this standard contained in the Rule, rather than the *Fay v. Noia* concept of waiver, should pertain in federal habeas as on direct review. Referring to previous constructions of Rule 12(b)(2) [now (b)(3)], we concluded that review of the claim should be barred on habeas, as on direct appeal, absent a showing of cause for the noncompliance and some showing of actual prejudice resulting from the alleged constitutional violation.

Last Term, in *Francis v. Henderson*, [425 U.S. 536, 96 S.Ct. 1708, 48 L.Ed.2d 149 (1976)], the rule of *Davis* was applied to the parallel case of a state procedural requirement that challenges to grand jury composition be raised before trial. The Court noted that there was power in the federal courts to entertain an application in such a case, but rested its holding on "considerations of comity and concerns for the orderly administration of criminal justice * * * ." While there was no counterpart provision of the state rule which allowed an exception upon some showing of cause, the Court concluded that the standard derived from the Federal Rule should nonetheless be applied in that context since " '[t]here is no reason to * * * give greater preclusive effect to procedural defaults by federal defendants than to similar defaults by state defendants.' " As applied to the federal petitions of state convicts, the *Davis* cause-and-prejudice standard was thus incorporated directly into the body of law governing the availability of federal habeas corpus review. * * *

[After examining Florida's contemporaneous objection rule, the Court concluded] that Florida procedure did, consistently with the United States Constitution, require that respondent's confession be challenged at trial or not at all, and thus his failure to timely object to its admission amounted to an independent and adequate state procedural ground which would have prevented direct review here. We thus come to the crux of this case. Shall the rule of *Francis v. Henderson*, *supra*, barring federal habeas review absent a showing of "cause" and "prejudice" attendant to a state procedural waiver, be applied to a waived objection to the admission of a confession at trial? We answer that question in the affirmative.

As earlier noted in the opinion, since *Brown v. Allen*, it has been the rule that the federal habeas petitioner who claims he is detained pursuant to a final judgment of a state court in violation of the United States Constitution is entitled to have the federal habeas court make its own independent determination of his federal claim, without being bound by the determination on the merits of that claim reached in the state proceedings. This rule of *Brown v. Allen* is in no way changed by our holding today. Rather, we deal only with contentions of federal law which were *not* resolved on the merits in the state proceeding due to respondent's failure to raise them there as required by state procedure. We leave open for resolution in future decisions the precise definition of the "cause"-and-"prejudice" standard, and note here only that it is narrower than the standard set forth in dicta in *Fay v. Noia*, which would make federal habeas review generally available to state convicts absent a knowing and deliberate waiver of the federal constitutional contention. It is the sweeping language of *Fay v. Noia*, going far beyond the facts of the case eliciting it, which we today reject.

The reasons for our rejection of it are several. The contemporaneous-objection rule itself is by no means peculiar to Florida, and deserves greater respect than *Fay* gives it, both for the fact that it is employed by a coordinate jurisdiction within the federal system and for the many interests which it serves in its own right. A contemporaneous objection enables the record to be made with respect to the constitutional claim when the recollections of witnesses are freshest, not years later in a federal habeas proceeding. It enables the judge who observed the demeanor of those witnesses to make the factual determinations necessary for properly deciding the federal constitutional question. While the 1966 amendment to § 2254 requires deference to be given to such determinations made by state courts, the determinations themselves are less apt to be made in the first instance if there is no contemporaneous objection to the admission of the evidence on federal constitutional grounds.

A contemporaneous-objection rule may lead to the exclusion of the evidence objected to, thereby making a major contribution to finality in criminal litigation. Without the evidence claimed to be vulnerable on federal constitutional grounds, the jury may acquit the defendant, and that will be the end of the case; or it may nonetheless convict the defendant, and he will have one less federal constitutional claim to assert in his federal habeas petition. If the state trial judge admits the evidence in question after a full hearing, the federal habeas court pursuant to the 1966 amendment to § 2254 will gain significant guidance from the state ruling in this regard. Subtler considerations as well militate in favor of honoring a state contemporaneous-objection rule. An objection on the spot may force the prosecution to take a hard look at its hole card, and even if the prosecutor thinks that the state trial judge will admit the evidence he must contemplate the possibility of reversal by the state appellate courts or the ultimate issuance of a federal writ of habeas corpus based on the impropriety of the state court's rejection of the federal constitutional claim.

We think that the rule of *Fay v. Noia*, broadly stated, may encourage "sandbagging" on the part of defense lawyers, who may take their chances on a verdict of not guilty in a state trial court with the intent to raise their constitutional claims in a federal habeas court if their initial gamble does not pay off. * * *

The failure of the federal habeas courts generally to require compliance with a contemporaneous-objection rule tends to detract from the perception of the trial of a criminal case in state court as a decisive and portentous event. A defendant has been accused of a serious crime, and this is the time and place set for him to be tried by a jury of his peers and found either guilty or not guilty by that jury. To the greatest extent possible all issues which bear on this charge should be determined in this proceeding: the accused is in the court-room, the jury is in the box, the judge is on the bench, and the witnesses, having been subpoenaed and duly sworn, await their turn to testify. Society's resources have been concentrated at that time and place in order to decide, within the limits of human fallibility, the question of guilt or innocence of one of its citizens. Any procedural rule which encourages the result that those proceedings be as free of error as possible is thoroughly desirable, and the contemporaneous-objection rule surely falls within this classification.

We believe the adoption of the *Francis* rule in this situation will have the salutary effect of making the state trial on the merits the "main event," so to speak, rather than a "tryout on the road" for what will later be the determinative federal habeas hearing. There is nothing in the Constitution or in the language of § 2254 which requires that the state trial on the issue of guilt or innocence be devoted largely to the testimony of fact witnesses directed to the elements of the state crime, while only later will there occur in a federal habeas hearing a full airing of the federal constitutional claims which were not raised in the state proceedings. If a criminal defendant thinks that an action of the state trial court is about to deprive him of a federal constitutional right there is every reason for his following state procedure in making known his objection.

The "cause"-and-"prejudice" exception of the *Francis* rule will afford an adequate guarantee, we think, that the rule will not prevent a federal habeas court from adjudicating for the first time the federal constitutional claim of a defendant who in the absence of such an adjudication will be the victim of a miscarriage of justice. Whatever precise content may be given those terms by later cases, we feel confident in holding without further elaboration that they do not exist here. Respondent has advanced no explanation whatever for his failure to object at trial, and, as the proceeding unfolded, the trial judge is certainly not to be faulted for failing to question the admission of the confession himself. The other evidence of guilt presented at trial, moreover, was substantial to a degree that would negate any possibility of actual prejudice resulting to the respondent from the admission of his inculpatory statement.

We accordingly [instruct the district court] to dismiss respondent's petition for a writ of habeas corpus. * * *

[The opinions of CHIEF JUSTICE BURGER, concurring; JUSTICE STEVENS, concurring; and JUSTICE WHITE, concurring in the judgment, are omitted.]

MR. JUSTICE BRENNAN, with whom MR. JUSTICE MARSHALL joins, dissenting. * * *

I

I begin with the threshold question: What is the meaning and import of a procedural default? If it could be assumed that a procedural default more often than not is the product of a defendant's conscious refusal to abide by the duly constituted, legitimate processes of the state courts, then I might agree that a regime of collateral review weighted in favor of a State's procedural rules would be warranted. *Fay*, however, recognized that such rarely is the case; and therein lies *Fay*'s basic unwillingness to embrace a view of habeas jurisdiction that results in "an airtight system of [procedural] forfeitures."

This, of course, is not to deny that there are times when the failure to heed a state procedural requirement stems from an intentional decision to avoid the presentation of constitutional claims to the state forum. *Fay* was not insensitive to this possibility. Indeed, the very purpose of its bypass test is to detect and enforce such intentional procedural forfeitures of outstanding constitutionally based claims. *Fay* does so through application of the longstanding rule used to test whether action or inaction on the part of a criminal defendant should be construed as a decision to surrender the assertion of rights secured by the Constitution: To be an effective waiver, there must be "an intentional relinquishment or abandonment of a known right or privilege." Incorporating this standard, *Fay* recognized that if one "understandingly and knowingly forewent the privilege of seeking to vindicate his federal claims in the state courts, whether for strategic, tactical or any other reasons that can fairly be described as the deliberate by-passing of state procedures, then it is open to the federal court on habeas to deny him all relief * * * ." For this reason, the Court's assertion that it "think[s]" that the *Fay* rule encourages intentional "sandbagging" on the part of the defense lawyers is without basis; certainly the Court points to no cases or commentary arising during the past 15 years of actual use of the *Fay* test to support this criticism. Rather, a consistent reading of case law demonstrates that the bypass formula has provided a workable vehicle for protecting the integrity of state rules in those instances when such protection would be both meaningful and just.

But having created the bypass exception to the availability of collateral review, *Fay* recognized that intentional, tactical forfeitures are not the norm upon which to build a rational system of federal habeas jurisdiction. In the ordinary case, litigants simply have no incentive to slight the state tribunal, since constitutional adjudication on the state and federal levels are not mutually exclusive. Under the regime of collateral review recognized since the days of *Brown v. Allen*, and enforced by the *Fay* bypass test, no rational lawyer would risk the "sandbagging" feared by the Court.[5] If a constitutional challenge is not properly raised on the state level, the explanation generally will be found elsewhere than in an intentional tactical decision.

In brief then, any realistic system of federal habeas corpus jurisdiction must be premised on the reality that the ordinary procedural default is born of the inadvertence, negligence, inexperience, or incompetence of trial counsel. The case under consideration today is typical. * * * [T]here is no basis for inferring that Sykes or his state trial lawyer was even aware of the existence of his claim under the Fifth Amendment; for this is not a case where the trial judge expressly drew the attention of the defense to a possible constitutional contention or procedural requirement, or where the defense signals its knowledge of a

---

[5] In brief, the defense lawyer would face two options: (1) He could elect to present his constitutional claims to the state courts in a proper fashion. If the state trial court is persuaded that a constitutional breach has occurred, the remedies dictated by the Constitution would be imposed, the defense would be bolstered, and the prosecution accordingly weakened, perhaps precluded altogether. If the state court rejects the properly tendered claims, the defense has lost nothing: Appellate review before the state courts and federal habeas consideration are preserved. (2) He could elect to "sandbag." This presumably means, first, that he would hold back the presentation of his constitutional claim to the trial court, thereby increasing the likelihood of a conviction since the prosecution would be able to present evidence that, while arguably constitutionally deficient, may be highly prejudicial to the defense. Second, he would thereby have forfeited all state review and remedies with respect to these claims (subject to whatever "plain error" rule is available). Third, to carry out his scheme he would now be compelled to deceive the federal habeas court and to convince the judge that he did not "deliberately bypass" the state procedures. If he loses on this gamble, all federal review would be barred, and his "sandbagging" would have resulted in nothing but the forfeiture of all judicial review of his client's claims. The Court, without substantiation, apparently believes that a meaningful number of lawyers are induced into option 2 by *Fay*. I do not. That belief simply offends common sense.

constitutional claim by abandoning a challenge previously raised. Rather, any realistic reading of the record demonstrates that we are faced here with a lawyer's simple error.

Fay's answer thus is plain: the bypass test simply refuses to credit what is essentially a lawyer's mistake as a forfeiture of constitutional rights. I persist in the belief that the interests of Sykes and the State of Florida are best rationalized by adherence to this test, and by declining to react to inadvertent defaults through the creation of an "airtight system of forfeitures." * * *

III * * *

Punishing a lawyer's unintentional errors by closing the federal courthouse door to his client is both a senseless and misdirected method of deterring the slighting of state rules. It is senseless because unplanned and unintentional action of any kind generally is not subject to deterrence; and, to the extent that it is hoped that a threatened sanction addressed to the defense will induce greater care and caution on the part of trial lawyers, thereby forestalling negligent conduct or error, the potential loss of all valuable state remedies would be sufficient to this end. And it is a misdirected sanction because even if the penalization of incompetence or carelessness will encourage more thorough legal training and trial preparation, the habeas applicant, as opposed to his lawyer, hardly is the proper recipient of such a penalty. Especially with fundamental constitutional rights at stake, no fictional relationship of principal-agent or the like can justify holding the criminal defendant accountable for the naked errors of his attorney. This is especially true when so many indigent defendants are without any realistic choice in selecting who ultimately represents them at trial. Indeed, if responsibility for error must be apportioned between the parties, it is the State, through its attorney's admissions and certification policies, that is more fairly held to blame for the fact that practicing lawyers too often are ill-prepared or ill-equipped to act carefully and knowledgeably when faced with decisions governed by state procedural requirements. * * *

NOTES AND QUESTIONS

1.   The majority and dissent operate from different premises about the reason to impose a cause-and-prejudice standard on claims lost by state procedural default. If you carefully articulate each premise, you will see why the two opinions disagree so fundamentally.

2.   The Court describes the various cases leading to *Wainwright v. Sykes.* Can you tell which was the crucial predecessor—the case that, once decided, doomed the *Fay* "deliberate by-pass" rule?

3.   Following *Wainwright,* the Court adopted "prejudice" inquiries as part of the test for ineffective assistance of counsel in *Strickland v.*

Washington, p. 1088 and as part of the test to determine whether the prosecution had a constitutional duty to disclose evidence to the defense, p. 969. In both these contexts, as well as in *Wainwright v. Sykes,* the defense must show a reasonable probability that, but for the particular error, the result of the proceeding would have been different. What do these tests suggest is the Court's conception of a "fair trial"?

4.   *An advertisement for computer searches.* Issac raised self-defense as an affirmative defense to murder. The judge instructed the jury, in accordance with well-settled state law, that Issac bore the burden of proving self-defense by a preponderance of the evidence. The state had a contemporaneous objection rule requiring defendants to object to jury instructions before the jury retires to deliberate. Issac's lawyer did not object. Later, in federal habeas, Issac wants to argue that the instruction violated his federal constitutional rights. Can Issac establish "cause" for the failure to object?

The ground for the objection not made at trial is that the instruction impermissibly shifted the burden of proof to the defendant, in violation of *In re Winship* and its progeny. *Winship* is touched on in *Jackson v. Virginia,* p. 1524. While *Winship* holds that the State bears the burden of proving a defendant guilty beyond a reasonable doubt, it did not investigate the relationship between this duty and the procedural mechanisms for allocating the burden of proof on particular issues. It was not until *Mullaney v. Wilbur,* 421 U.S. 684, 95 S.Ct. 1881, 44 L.Ed.2d 508 (1975), that burden-shifting devices were explicitly included within the reach of *Winship.*

Mullaney was decided three months before Isaac's trial but had yet to affect Ohio state law, which still approved the judicial instruction in question. The Supreme Court held that Isaac had procedurally defaulted the underlying substantive claim by not raising what his lawyer surely thought was an almost frivolous state law claim. Engle v. Isaac, 456 U.S. 107, 102 S.Ct. 1558, 71 L.Ed.2d 783 (1982). According to the Court, the "futility of presenting an objection to the state courts cannot alone constitute cause for a failure to object at trial." The Court noted that, prior to Isaac's trial, "numerous courts" in other states had held that *Winship* required the State to "bear the burden of disproving certain affirmative defenses." So be sure to do your homework. To preserve your client's substantive claims for habeas, you must know how courts in other states are applying federal precedents.

5.   *But not every failure to raise a claim is subject to Wainwright v. Sykes.* In Cone v. Bell, 556 U.S. 449, 129 S.Ct. 1769, 173 L.Ed.2d 701 (2009), Cone raised a *Brady* discovery claim for the first time thirteen years after his conviction had been affirmed on direct appeal and in state post-conviction proceedings. But the Supreme Court held that the *Brady* claim was neither waived nor defaulted because Cone did not become aware of the factual predicate for the claim until the thirteen-year mark when the State was forced to disclose the contents of the prosecutor's files to him. There was no

need to evaluate "cause" and "prejudice" because "Cone properly preserved and exhausted his *Brady* claim in the state court."

6.   *Reaping the fruit of Wainwright v. Sykes.* The procedural default rule also applies to the failure to raise issues on appeal. If a defendant raises an issue at trial, but fails to raise it at the first level of appeal, the issue is typically defaulted for the next level of appeal and, after *Wainwright*, any defaulted state claim is also defaulted for federal habeas unless the petitioner can meet the grueling standard of "cause" and "prejudice." Now that we know, from *Engle*, that one cannot always rely on state law as an excuse for failing to raise claims, what practice pointer does this suggest for lawyers representing defendants on appeal, particularly in death cases?

If you said, "Raise every plausible issue," that seems to be the view held by conscientious defense lawyers. But keep your wits about you. In one New Jersey death case, for example, defense lawyers raised 548 grounds for reversal in their petition for post-conviction relief. State v. Marshall, 148 N.J. 89, 690 A.2d 1 (1997). The petition and supporting documents encompassed more than 8,000 pages. Dismissing the appeal on the merits, the state court noted the "enormous institutional burden on this Court, diverting time and resources from the Court's other adjudicative and administrative responsibilities," and questioned "both the wisdom and necessity for so massive a presentation." The court said that it intended "emphatically" to "discourage the artificial fragmentation of claims for post-conviction relief purposes, even in capital cases."

Marshall, by the way, was turned into a made-for-television movie, "Blind Faith," which aired February 11, 1990 on NBC, starring Robert Urich as Robert Marshall.

SMITH V. MURRAY
Supreme Court of the United States, 1986.
477 U.S. 527, 106 S.Ct. 2661, 91 L.Ed.2d 434.

JUSTICE O'CONNOR delivered the opinion of the Court [joined by CHIEF JUSTICE BURGER, and JUSTICES WHITE, POWELL, and REHNQUIST].

We granted certiorari to decide whether and, if so, under what circumstances, a prosecutor may elicit testimony from a mental health professional concerning the content of an interview conducted to explore the possibility of presenting psychiatric defenses at trial. * * * On examination, however, we conclude that petitioner defaulted his underlying constitutional claim by failing to press it before the Supreme Court of Virginia on direct appeal. Accordingly, we decline to address the merits of petitioner's claims and affirm the judgment dismissing the petition for a writ of habeas corpus.

I

Following a jury trial, petitioner was convicted of the May 1977 murder of Audrey Weiler. * * *

Prior to the trial, petitioner's appointed counsel, David Pugh, had explored the possibility of presenting a number of psychiatric defenses. Towards that end, Mr. Pugh requested that the trial court appoint a private psychiatrist, Dr. Wendell Pile, to conduct an examination of petitioner. * * * During the course of the examination, Dr. Pile did in fact ask petitioner both about the murder and about prior incidents of deviant sexual conduct. Although petitioner initially declined to answer, he later stated that he had once torn the clothes off a girl on a school bus before deciding not to carry out his original plan to rape her. That information, together with a tentative diagnosis of "Sociopathic Personality; Sexual Deviation (rape)," was forwarded to the trial court, with copies sent both to Mr. Pugh and to the prosecutor who was trying the case for the Commonwealth. At no point prior to or during the interview did Dr. Pile inform petitioner that his statements might later be used against him or that he had the right to remain silent and to have counsel present if he so desired.

At the sentencing phase of the trial, the Commonwealth called Dr. Pile to the stand. Over the defense's objection, Dr. Pile described the incident on the school bus. On cross-examination, he repeated his earlier conclusion that petitioner was a "sociopathic personality." After examining a second psychiatrist, the Commonwealth introduced petitioner's criminal record into evidence. It revealed that he had been convicted of rape in 1973 and had been paroled from the penitentiary on that charge less than four months prior to raping and murdering Ms. Weiler. The defense then called 14 character witnesses, who testified that petitioner had been a regular churchgoer, a member of the choir, a conscientious student in high school, and a good soldier in Vietnam. After lengthy deliberation, the jury recommended that petitioner be sentenced to death.

Petitioner appealed his conviction and sentence to the Supreme Court of Virginia. In his brief he raised 13 separate claims, including a broad challenge to the constitutionality of Virginia's death penalty provisions, objections to several of the trial court's evidentiary rulings, and a challenge to the exclusion of a prospective juror during *voir dire*. Petitioner did not, however, assign any error concerning the admission of Dr. Pile's testimony. At a subsequent state postconviction hearing, Mr. Pugh explained that he had consciously decided not to pursue that claim after determining that "Virginia case law would [not] support our position at that particular time." Various objections to the Commonwealth's use of Dr. Pile's testimony were raised, however, in a brief filed by *amicus curiae* Post-Conviction Assistance Project of the University of Virginia Law School.

The Supreme Court of Virginia affirmed the conviction and sentence in all respects. In a footnote, it noted that, pursuant to a rule of the court, it had considered only those arguments advanced by *amicus* that concerned errors specifically assigned by the defendant himself. Accordingly, it did not address any issues concerning the prosecution's use of the psychiatric testimony. This Court denied the subsequent petition for certiorari, which, again, did not urge the claim that admission of Dr. Pile's testimony violated petitioner's rights under the Federal Constitution.

In 1979, petitioner sought a writ of habeas corpus in [state court]. For the first time since the trial, he argued that the admission of Dr. Pile's testimony violated his privilege against self-incrimination under the Fifth and Fourteenth Amendments to the Federal Constitution. The court ruled, however, that petitioner had forfeited the claim by failing to press it in earlier proceedings. At a subsequent evidentiary hearing, conducted solely on the issue of ineffective assistance of counsel, the court heard testimony concerning the reasons underlying Mr. Pugh's decision not to pursue the Fifth Amendment claim on appeal. On the basis of that testimony, the court found that Pugh and his assistant had researched the question, but had determined that the claim was unlikely to succeed. Thus, the court found, "counsel exercised reasonable judgment in deciding not to preserve the objection on appeal, and * * * this decision resulted from informed, professional deliberation." Petitioner appealed the denial of his habeas petition to the Supreme Court of Virginia, contending that the Circuit Court had erred in finding that his objection to the admission of Dr. Pile's testimony had been defaulted. The Supreme Court declined to accept the appeal, and we again denied certiorari.

Having exhausted state remedies, petitioner sought a writ of habeas corpus in the United States District Court * * * .

II * * *

We need not determine whether petitioner has carried his burden of showing actual prejudice from the allegedly improper admission of Dr. Pile's testimony, for we think it self-evident that he has failed to demonstrate cause for his noncompliance with Virginia's procedures. We have declined in the past to essay a comprehensive catalog of the circumstances that would justify a finding of cause. Our cases, however, leave no doubt that a deliberate, tactical decision not to pursue a particular claim is the very antithesis of the kind of circumstance that would warrant excusing a defendant's failure to adhere to a State's legitimate rules for the fair and orderly disposition of its criminal cases.

As the Court explained in *Reed* [*v. Ross*, 468 U.S. 1, 104 S.Ct. 2901, 82 L.Ed.2d 1 (1984)]:

> "[D]efense counsel may not make a tactical decision to forgo a procedural opportunity—for instance, to object at trial or to raise an issue on appeal—and then when he discovers that the tactic has been unsuccessful, pursue an alternative strategy in federal court. The encouragement of such conduct by a federal court on habeas corpus review would not only offend generally accepted principles of comity, but would undermine the accuracy and efficiency of the state judicial systems to the detriment of all concerned. Procedural defaults of this nature are, therefore, inexcusable, and cannot qualify as 'cause' for purposes of federal habeas corpus review."

Here the record unambiguously reveals that petitioner's counsel objected to the admission of Dr. Pile's testimony at trial and then consciously elected not to pursue that claim before the Supreme Court of Virginia. The basis for that decision was counsel's perception that the claim had little chance of success in the Virginia courts. With the benefit of hindsight, petitioner's counsel in this Court now contends that this perception proved to be incorrect. Even assuming that to be the case, however, a State's subsequent acceptance of an argument deliberately abandoned on direct appeal is irrelevant to the question whether the default should be excused on federal habeas. Indeed, it is the very prospect that a state court "may decide, upon reflection, that the contention is valid" that undergirds the established rule that "perceived futility alone cannot constitute cause," for "[a]llowing criminal defendants to deprive the state courts of [the] opportunity" to reconsider previously rejected constitutional claims is fundamentally at odds with the principles of comity that animate *Sykes* and its progeny.

Notwithstanding the deliberate nature of the decision not to pursue his objection to Dr. Pile's testimony on appeal—a course of conduct virtually dispositive of any effort to satisfy *Syke*'s "cause" requirement—petitioner contends that the default should be excused because Mr. Pugh's decision, though deliberate, was made in ignorance. Had he investigated the claim more fully, petitioner maintains, "it is inconceivable that he would have concluded that the claim was without merit or that he would have failed to raise it."

The argument is squarely foreclosed by our decision in [*Murray v.*] *Carrier* [, 477 U.S. 478, 106 S.Ct. 2639, 91 L.Ed.2d 397 (1986)], which holds that "the mere fact that counsel failed to recognize the factual or legal basis for a claim, or failed to raise the claim despite recognizing it, does not constitute cause for a procedural default." Nor can it seriously be maintained that the decision not to press the claim on appeal was an error of such magnitude that it rendered counsel's performance constitutionally deficient under the test of *Strickland v. Washington* [p. 1088]. *Carrier* reaffirmed that "the right to effective assistance of counsel * * * may in a particular case be violated by even an isolated error * * * if that error is sufficiently egregious and prejudicial." But counsel's deliberate decision not to pursue his objection to the admission of Dr. Pile's testimony falls far short of meeting that rigorous standard. After conducting a vigorous defense at both the guilt and sentencing phases of the trial, counsel surveyed the extensive transcript, researched a number of claims, and decided that, under the current state of the law, 13 were worth pursuing on direct appeal. This process of "winnowing out weaker arguments on appeal and focusing on" those more likely to prevail, far from being evidence of incompetence, is the hallmark of effective appellate advocacy. It will often be the case that even the most informed counsel will fail to anticipate a state appellate court's willingness to reconsider a prior holding or will underestimate the likelihood that a federal habeas court will repudiate an established state rule. But, as *Strickland v. Washington* made clear, "[a] fair assessment of attorney performance requires that every effort be made to eliminate the distorting effects of hindsight, to reconstruct the circumstances of counsel's challenged conduct, and to evaluate the conduct from counsel's perspective at the time." Viewed in light of Virginia law at the time Mr. Pugh submitted his opening brief to the Supreme Court of Virginia, the decision not to pursue his objection to the admission of Dr. Pile's testimony fell well within the "wide range of professionally competent assistance" required under the Sixth Amendment to the Federal Constitution.

Nor can petitioner rely on the novelty of his legal claim as "cause" for noncompliance with Virginia's rules. Petitioner contends that this Court's decisions in *Estelle v. Smith*, 451 U.S. 454, 101 S.Ct. 1866, 68 L.Ed.2d 359 (1981), and *Ake v. Oklahoma*, 470 U.S. 68, 105 S.Ct. 1087, 84 L.Ed.2d 53 (1985), which were decided well after the affirmance of his conviction and sentence on direct appeal, lend support to his position that Dr. Pile's testimony should have been excluded. But, as a comparison of *Reed* and *Engle* [*v. Isaac*, 456 U.S. 107, 102 S.Ct. 1558, 71 L.Ed.2d 783 (1982)] makes plain, the question is not whether subsequent legal developments have made counsel's task easier, but whether at the time of the default the claim was "available" at all. As petitioner has candidly conceded, various forms of the claim he now advances had been percolating in the lower courts for years at the time of his original appeal. Moreover, in this very case, an *amicus* before the Supreme Court of Virginia specifically argued that admission of Dr. Pile's testimony violated petitioner's rights under the Fifth and Sixth Amendments. Under these circumstances, it simply is not open to argument that the legal basis of the claim petitioner now presses on federal habeas was unavailable to counsel at the time of the direct appeal.

We conclude, therefore, that petitioner has not carried his burden of showing cause for noncompliance with Virginia's rules of procedure. That determination, however, does not end our inquiry. As we noted in *Engle* and reaffirmed in *Carrier*, " '[i]n appropriate cases' the principles of comity and finality that inform the concepts of cause and prejudice 'must yield to the imperative of correcting a fundamentally unjust incarceration.' " Accordingly, "where a constitutional violation has probably resulted in the conviction of one who is actually innocent, a federal habeas court may grant the writ even in the absence of a showing of cause for the procedural default."

We acknowledge that the concept of "actual," as distinct from "legal," innocence does not translate easily into the context of an alleged error at the sentencing phase of a trial on a capital offense. Nonetheless, we think it clear on this record that application of the cause and prejudice test will not result in a "fundamental miscarriage of justice." There is no allegation that the testimony about the school bus incident was false or in any way misleading. Nor can it be argued that the prospect that Dr. Pile might later testify against him had the effect of foreclosing meaningful exploration of psychiatric defenses. While that concern is a very real one in the abstract, here the record clearly shows that Dr. Pile did ask petitioner to discuss the crime he stood accused of committing as well as prior incidents of deviant sexual conduct. Although initially reluctant to do so, ultimately petitioner was forthcoming on both subjects. In short, the alleged constitutional error neither precluded the development of true facts nor resulted in the admission of false ones. Thus, even assuming that, as a legal matter, Dr. Pile's testimony should not have been presented to the jury, its admission did not serve to pervert the jury's deliberations concerning the ultimate question whether *in fact* petitioner constituted a continuing threat to society. Under these circumstances, we do not believe that refusal to consider the defaulted claim on federal habeas carries with it the risk of a manifest miscarriage of justice. * * *

JUSTICE STEVENS, with whom JUSTICE MARSHALL and JUSTICE BLACKMUN join and with whom JUSTICE BRENNAN joins as to Parts II and III, dissenting. [Parts I, II, and III are omitted. What follows is the introduction to the dissent. Eds.]

The record in this case unquestionably demonstrates that petitioner's constitutional claim is meritorious, and that there is a significant risk that he will be put to death *because* his constitutional rights were violated.

The Court does not take issue with this conclusion. It is willing to assume that (1) petitioner's Fifth Amendment right against compelled self-incrimination was violated; (2) his Eighth Amendment right to a fair, constitutionally sound sentencing proceeding was violated by the introduction of the evidence from that Fifth Amendment violation; and (3) those constitutional violations made the difference between life and death in the jury's consideration of his fate. Although the constitutional violations and issues were sufficiently serious that this Court decided to grant certiorari, and although the Court of Appeals for the Fourth Circuit decided the issue on the merits, this Court concludes that petitioner's presumably meritorious constitutional claim is procedurally barred and that petitioner must therefore be executed.

In my opinion, the Court should reach the merits of petitioner's argument. To the extent that there has been a procedural "default," it is exceedingly minor—perhaps a kind of "harmless" error. Petitioner's counsel raised a timely objection to the introduction of the evidence obtained in violation of the Fifth Amendment. A respected friend of the Court—the University of Virginia Law School's Post-Conviction Assistance Project—brought the issue to the attention of the Virginia Supreme Court in an extensive *amicus curiae* brief. Smith's counsel also raised the issue in state and federal habeas corpus proceedings, and, as noted, the Court of Appeals decided the case on the merits. Consistent with the well-established principle that appellate arguments should be carefully winnowed, however, Smith's counsel did not raise the Fifth Amendment issue in his original appeal to the Virginia Supreme Court— an unsurprising decision in view of the fact that a governing Virginia Supreme Court precedent, which was then entirely valid and only two years old, decisively barred the claim. * * *

I fear that the Court has lost its way in a procedural maze of its own creation and that it has grossly misevaluated the requirements of "law and justice" that are the federal court's statutory mission under the federal habeas corpus statute. * * *

NOTES AND QUESTIONS

1.   Which opinion would you have joined in *Smith*? Is it possible to rule in Smith's favor without undermining the relative clarity of the cause-and-prejudice test? The dissent in *Smith* expressed the issue in personal terms: "[T]here is a significant risk that [Smith] will be put to death *because* his constitutional rights were violated." Do you agree with this characterization?

The tone in Justice Stevens's dissent is sharply critical of the majority opinion. That federalism issues still provoke this kind of emotion over 200 years after ratification of the Constitution would, perhaps, not surprise the Framers.

2.   An additional issue would arise today if the Court were considering whether to grant certiorari in a case like *Smith*. What is that concern? Note the ground for granting certiorari.

3.   The Supreme Court obviously felt the underlying Fifth Amendment issue worthy of deciding, because it granted certiorari to decide this issue— yet the Court held that the failure to preserve it in the state courts was not ineffective assistance of counsel under *Strickland*. How can this be the best understanding of effective assistance of counsel? As Stephen Bright has put it, "[T]he result of *Sykes* and *Strickland* is that, so long as counsel is not so bad as to fall below the *Strickland* standard, the poorest level of representation at trial receives the least scrutiny in post-conviction review." Stephen B. Bright, *Death By Lottery—Procedural Bar of Constitutional Claims in Capital Cases Due to Inadequate Representation of Indigent Defendants*, 92 W. Va. L. Rev. 679, 692 (1990). Again in Bright's words: "The lax standard of *Strickland* and the strict procedural requirements of *Sykes* have become the gateposts on the road to legal condemnation." *Id.* at 683.

4.   *"Actual innocence" exception to Wainwright v. Sykes.* Notice the reference in *Smith* to an exception for "actual" innocence. The Court fleshed out this idea somewhat in Schlup v. Delo, 513 U.S. 298, 115 S.Ct. 851, 130 L.Ed.2d 808 (1995), reaching the question of what kind of showing a petitioner has to make to qualify for the "actual innocence" exception. When the claim is that the defaulted constitutional claim deprived the fact-finder of reliable, exculpatory evidence, the petitioner must show that "it is more likely than not that no reasonable juror would have convicted him in light of the new evidence." A more difficult standard applies when the claim is that the petitioner is "innocent" of the death penalty—*i.e.*, that though guilty of the crime, the defendant was not eligible for the death penalty. In that situation, the default is excused only if the petitioner shows "by clear and convincing evidence that but for a constitutional error no reasonable juror would find the petitioner eligible for the death penalty." Sawyer v. Whitley, 505 U.S. 333, 112 S.Ct. 2514, 120 L.Ed.2d 269 (1992). In neither *Schlup* nor *Sawyer* did the Court find the "actual innocence" exception met (in *Schlup* the Court remanded for the lower courts to apply the standard the Court had fashioned).

In *House v. Bell*, 547 U.S. 518, 126 S.Ct. 2064, 165 L.Ed.2d 1 (2006), the Court found enough evidence of "actual innocence" to avoid procedural default. House was convicted of capital murder. After losing his direct appeals, House filed a *pro se* petition for state post-conviction relief, raising ineffective assistance of counsel. A new lawyer was appointed for the post-conviction proceedings, and he added a claim of erroneous jury instructions. The trial judge dismissed the petition and, on appeal, the lawyer abandoned the ineffective assistance claim. After the appellate courts upheld the dismissal of House's petition, he filed a second post-conviction petition, raising the same ineffective assistance of counsel as before. The Tennessee courts held this claim defaulted for failure to preserve it on appeal of the first petition.

The State's case was based, in part, on forensic evidence—House's semen on the victim's clothes, and blood stains on his blue jeans that did not match his blood type. In the federal habeas proceedings, the defense established that the semen stains on the victim's clothes came from her husband, not from House, and that the blood on House's blue jeans could *not* have come from the victim. There was other evidence suggesting that House was innocent, including evidence that the victim's husband was the murderer, but also other evidence suggesting that House might be guilty. The Court weighed the evidence:

> This is not a case of conclusive exoneration. Some aspects of the State's evidence * * * still support an inference of guilt. Yet the central forensic proof connecting House to the crime—the blood and the semen—has been called into question, and House has put forward substantial evidence pointing to a different suspect. Accordingly, and although the issue is close, we conclude that this is the rare case where—had the jury heard all the conflicting testimony—it is more likely than not that no reasonable juror viewing the record as a whole would lack reasonable doubt.

5. *Something very wrong is taking place tonight.* Suppose a habeas petitioner, sentenced to death, makes only a single claim: he did not commit the crime. He does not contest the fairness of the trial, the sufficiency of the evidence, or any other procedural ground. Rather, he simply argues that while the circumstantial evidence was sufficient to meet the *Jackson* standard, p. 1524, someone else has now confessed to the crime, and he is therefore entitled to habeas relief because it would violate the United States Constitution to permit his conviction and death sentence to stand.

Does it? What specific provision? If you cannot find a constitutional provision that protects against the conviction of the actually innocent, then this petitioner's habeas petition must be dismissed because he raised no other issues. See Herrera v. Collins, 506 U.S. 390, 113 S.Ct. 853, 122 L.Ed.2d 203 (1993). *Herrera* suggested that federal habeas should not be available where the sole claim was factual innocence. Ultimately, however, the Court assumed that a sufficiently powerful showing of innocence would have made execution unconstitutional. Herrera's evidence did not meet that standard. Leonel Herrera was executed by the State of Texas on May 12, 1993. His last words were:

> I am innocent, innocent, innocent. And make no mistake about this. I owe society nothing. I would like to encourage all those who stood by me to continue the struggle for human rights and continue to help those who are innocent * * * . I am an innocent man. And something very wrong is taking place tonight.

Herrera died by lethal injection. Graczyk, "Man Executed for Killing Police Officer," Dallas Morning News, May 13, 1993. For three critiques of *Herrera*, see Susan Bandes, *Simple Murder: A Comment on the Legality of Executing the Innocent*, 44 Buff. L. Rev. 501 (1996) Vivian Berger, *Herrera v.*

Collins: The Gateway of Innocence for Death-Sentenced Prisoners Leads Nowhere, 35 Wm. & Mary L. Rev. 943 (1994); George C. Thomas III, Gordon G. Young, Keith Sharfman & Kate Briscoe, *Is It Ever Too Late For Innocence?: Finality, Efficiency, and Claims of Innocence*, 64 U. Pitt. L. Rev. 263 (2003).

6.   In *House v. Bell*, Note 4, the Court revisited the issue of whether "a truly persuasive demonstration of 'actual innocence' made after trial would render the execution of a defendant unconstitutional." Just as in *Herrera*, the Court left the question open but held "that whatever burden a hypothetical freestanding innocence claim would require, this petitioner has not satisfied it." Thus, House could present his defaulted ineffective assistance of counsel claim, because he met *that* innocence standard, but he could not win his habeas petition on the ground that he was innocent.

BARRY FRIEDMAN—A TALE OF TWO HABEAS
73 Minnesota Law Review 248 (1988), 256–61.

Assume defendants Tom, Dick, and Mary are tried individually for participation in the same crime. Differences among their cases result only from variations in the quality of their representation at trial or on appeal and the related decision to raise, or failure to raise, a claim of constitutional error committed in state court. This section will show that these differences lead to widely differing, rationally inexplicable dispositions of their habeas petitions by a federal court, despite the identical merits of their underlying constitutional claims.

Accused Tom retains the very best of criminal defense attorneys. His attorney raises every conceivable constitutional claim, but Tom is convicted nonetheless. Tom then files a federal habeas petition, seeking redetermination of any or all of the constitutional claims raised in state court. Under prevailing habeas doctrine, Tom is entitled to this broad review by the federal habeas court, and if Tom proves his case, he may obtain relief. If the habeas court finds constitutional error, the conviction will be reversed unless the state can bear the heavy burden of proving beyond a reasonable doubt that the error was harmless.

Compare Tom's situation with that of Dick, whose court-appointed counsel is fresh out of law school and unsure of what he is doing. Dick's lawyer tries his best, but fails to raise in state court a number of the constitutional claims that Tom's lawyer raised. After Dick is convicted, he seeks habeas relief, hoping to litigate the defaulted claims. Dick could face the burden of overcoming the default to obtain habeas review, under unfavorable standards developed for this purpose, but he need not worry about that burden because his attorney's performance was so deficient that it failed even to meet sixth amendment standards for effective assistance of counsel. Rather than trying to overcome the default, Dick simply will assert a sixth amendment claim in federal habeas court. Under the guise of his claim for ineffective assistance of counsel, Dick now may raise essentially the same issues as did Tom. For Dick to obtain relief, however, the Court's sixth amendment jurisprudence requires that he prove he suffered "actual prejudice" from his lawyer's failure to raise the claims raised by Tom's lawyer. Thus, even if Dick establishes the same state-court error that Tom established, Dick does not likewise shift to the state the burden to prove the error was harmless, but rather must himself show that but for the error he might not have been convicted.

In other words, Dick, under the rubric of a sixth amendment claim, in effect may raise any substantive claim Tom may raise by asserting that his attorney was ineffective in failing to raise that claim. But Dick is, in effect, penalized for having incompetent counsel in that he must bear the burden and prove a higher degree of materiality with regard to the error in order to have his conviction overturned.

Defendant Mary's plight is worse yet. Mary's lawyer is not very good, but not very bad either. Mary's lawyer is mediocre. Unfortunately, Mary's lawyer forgets to raise at least one of the constitutional claims raised by Tom's lawyer in state court. The neglected claim, however, is the claim Mary now believes to be her strongest, so she raises the claim in her petition for federal habeas review. Unlike Tom, Mary is not entitled automatically to a determination on the merits of this claim, because her lawyer procedurally defaulted it by failing to raise it properly in state court. Unlike Dick, Mary cannot obtain review of the constitutional claim through a claim for ineffective assistance of counsel because her lawyer's overall performance was not so deficient as to qualify her for relief under prevailing sixth amendment standards, despite the lawyer's failure to raise a meritorious constitutional claim. Finally, the federal court will not excuse Mary's procedural default, because *Smith*, [p. 1575], and *Carrier* allow Mary to litigate her claim *only* if she can prove that she actually is innocent. In other words, those with mediocre lawyers who fail to raise constitutional claims in conformity with state rules get no federal habeas relief unless they satisfy the heretofore unheard of burden of proving their own innocence.

In sum, current habeas jurisprudence produces the following inexplicable result. Prisoners whose lawyers raise and lose constitutional claims in state court may relitigate those claims in federal court and obtain relief under a relatively low standard of materiality. Prisoners with claims defaulted by a lawyer whose performance was constitutionally deficient also may obtain review on the merits of those claims in a federal court, but despite the fact that such prisoners are not responsible for counsels' failings, a higher materiality standard applies. Prisoners with defaulted claims who cannot establish ineffective assistance of counsel, who also are not responsible for their defaults, must prove actual innocence to obtain habeas review of their constitutional claims.

The seeming unfairness of this scenario is exacerbated when the undefined constitutional claim involved in the hypothetical above is given a name. Assume, for example, Tom, Dick, and Mary are trying to raise a fourth amendment claim before the federal habeas court. It turns out that Tom cannot raise the claim after all, because in *Stone v. Powell*, [428 U.S. 465, 96 S.Ct. 3037, 49 L.Ed.2d 1067 (1976)], the Court held that fourth amendment claims—alone among constitutional defects in state criminal proceedings—are barred from relitigation in habeas. For the same reason, Mary cannot raise the claim either. But Dick can raise the claim even though fourth amendment claims generally are not cognizable on habeas, because the rule changes if the claim was defaulted due to counsel's constitutionally deficient performance at trial.

Suppose, in contrast, the defendants are asserting that the state discriminated blatantly in selecting the grand jury: for example, the prosecutor intentionally excluded all blacks. Tom can raise the claim; indeed, under governing precedent such discrimination never can be harmless error. If he proves his claim on habeas review, Tom will obtain relief no matter what the state argues as to the materiality of the violation. Mary, however, will have her claim barred by the default holdings of *Smith* and *Carrier*, unless she can establish her actual innocence, which possibly would make relief on the grand jury claim appropriate. Whether Dick, with the grossly incompetent lawyer, will obtain relief remains uncertain.

These illustrations paint a picture of habeas that is difficult to fathom.

NOTES AND QUESTIONS

1.   What might the Court's response be to Friedman's claim that the disparate treatment in his hypothetical cases is "difficult to fathom"?

2.   *Antiterrorism and Effective Death Penalty Act.* Speaking in part about the Antiterrorism and Effective Death Penalty Act (AEDPA), Mark Tushnet and Larry Yackle begin their analysis by noting, "Criminals are not popular. No politician in recent memory has lost an election for being too tough on crime." Mark Tushnet & Larry Yackle, *Symbolic Statutes and Real Laws: The Pathologies of the Antiterrorism and Effective Death Penalty Act and the Prison Litigation Reform Act*, 47 Duke L.J. 1, 1 (1997).

In the main, AEDPA simply reinforced or clarified the changes the Court had already made in cases like *Wainwright v. Sykes*, p. 1565, and *Teague v. Lane*, p. 1554. In addition, AEDPA creates a powerful presumption that state courts correctly applied federal law. 28 U.S.C. § 2254 (d), Supp. App. A., provides that a federal habeas petition on behalf of a state prisoner "shall not be granted" as to any claim "adjudicated on the merits in State court" unless the adjudication

> (1) resulted in a decision that was contrary to, or involved an unreasonable application of, clearly established Federal law, as determined by the Supreme Court of the United States; or

> (2) resulted in a decision that was based on an unreasonable determination of the facts in light of the evidence presented in the State court proceeding.

In addition, AEDPA created a statute of limitations for habeas petitions. See 28 U.S.C. § 2244(d)(1) & 28 U.S.C. § 2255. Supp. App. A. Though how to "count" can be complicated, in most cases the time limit will be one year from the date the conviction becomes final.

3.   *Friedman updated.* Notice that Barry Friedman's article about Tom, Dick, and Mary was published in 1988, which is eons ago in terms of habeas law. For example, AEDPA now imposes a statute of limitations. But the central thrust of Friedman's excellent article remains accurate.

4.   One effect of AEDPA is to make it even more difficult to overturn state jury verdicts on the basis of lack of evidence. Recall that *Jackson v. Virginia*, p. 1524, held that convictions must be upheld on federal review if "any rational trier of fact" could have found guilt beyond a reasonable doubt. *Jackson* instructed federal courts to presume that any conflicts in the evidence were resolved by the fact-finder "in favor of the prosecution" and then required reviewing courts to "defer to that resolution." Now that AEDPA requires its own flavor of deference to state court judgments, habeas petitioners who seek federal review of state convictions on evidence sufficiency grounds face what amounts to a double presumption that their convictions were valid.

In Cavazos v. Smith, 565 U.S. ___, 132 S.Ct. 2, 181 L.Ed.2d 311 (2011), the jury convicted the defendant of killing her infant grand-daughter. The California courts affirmed the conviction, rejecting her *Jackson* insufficient-evidence claim. Smith's habeas petition asked the federal courts to reverse her conviction on the ground of insufficient evidence. The Ninth Circuit held that, since there was no direct evidence of guilt, the State failed to prove guilt beyond a reasonable doubt. Moreover, the Ninth Circuit held that the absence of direct evidence meant that the California courts had "unreasonably applied" *Jackson*, making reversal permissible under AEDPA.

The Court reversed the Ninth Circuit in a per curiam opinion. It noted *Jackson*'s requirement of a deferential review of factual findings and then wrote: "When the deference to state court decisions required by [AEDPA] is applied to the state court's already deferential review [under *Jackson*], there can be no doubt of the Ninth Circuit's error below." Justice Ginsburg, joined by Justice Breyer and Justice Sotomayor, dissented. At a minimum, the dissent argued, the Court owed the Ninth Circuit more than a summary dismissal, given the 1,500 page trial transcript that was the basis for the lower court's judgment.

5. *When lawyer errors can **never** be ineffective assistance.* In Coleman v. Thompson, 501 U.S. 722, 111 S.Ct. 2546, 115 L.Ed.2d 640 (1991), Coleman's conviction and death sentence were affirmed on appeal, and he filed a habeas petition in state court. After a two-day hearing, the trial judge ruled against Coleman on various constitutional grounds. Coleman's lawyer filed the notice of appeal three days after the filing deadline, which caused the state supreme court to throw out the appeal on the ground that it had been procedurally defaulted. In a federal habeas corpus action, Coleman argued that he could show "cause" for losing his appeal—ineffective assistance of counsel. Because the filing of documents on time is a widely-recognized core obligation that lawyers have to their clients, Coleman argued that even under *Strickland*, p. 1088, his lawyer was ineffective and thus he could show cause under *Smith v. Murray*, p. 1575.

Justice O'Connor's majority opinion got off to an ominous start from Coleman's perspective: "This is a case about federalism. It concerns the respect that federal courts owe the States and the States' procedural rules when reviewing the claims of state prisoners in federal habeas corpus."

As this beginning implied, Coleman lost. No matter how ineffective counsel was, Coleman's counsel could not be *constitutionally* ineffective because no Sixth Amendment right to counsel exists in state habeas actions (*Ross v. Moffitt*, p. 1065). No matter how grave the error was, the State was not responsible for it—it could not be "imputed to the State"—because there was no State failure to appoint competent counsel.

Justice Blackmun's dissent, joined by Justices Brennan and Stevens, accused the majority of "a sleight of logic that would be ironic if not for its tragic consequences"—i.e., that a state prisoner pursuing state collateral relief must bear the risk of his attorney's grave errors, even if those errors would otherwise constitute ineffective assistance of counsel. The end result is "that the prisoner will be executed without having presented his federal claims to a federal court."

Is the result in *Coleman* fair? Just? Suppose Coleman had not been "lucky" enough to have a lawyer working for him on his state habeas petition. Do you suppose Coleman would have missed the filing deadline?

6. *A narrow exception to Coleman v. Thompson.* In 2012, the Court held that a federal habeas petitioner could show cause when he alleges: (1) trial counsel was ineffective; (2) counsel in state collateral proceedings was ineffective in not raising the ineffectiveness of trial counsel; and (3) the state system did not permit defendants to raise ineffective assistance of counsel claims on direct review but only in state collateral proceedings. Martinez v. Ryan, 566 U.S. ___, 132 S.Ct. 1309, 182 L.Ed.2d 272 (2012). As the Court recognized, if there were no exception to *Coleman* in this context, no appellate court, state or federal, would ever hear the constitutional claims

waived by ineffective counsel. In Coleman's case, the state habeas judge heard his constitutional claims.

7.   *Coleman v. Thompson: the aftermath.* At the end, Coleman was represented by the highly-regarded Washington, D.C. firm of Arnold & Porter, which developed evidence casting suspicion on the victim's next-door neighbor, Bobby Donnie Ramey. Arnold & Porter included that information in court documents and released information to the press claiming that Coleman was innocent. As a consequence of this publicity, Ramey filed a $5 million dollar libel suit against Arnold & Porter. The firm reportedly settled the suit, rumored for a significant sum that represented the expected costs for the firm to defend itself. John C. Tucker, May God Have Mercy (1997).

Coleman was electrocuted in Virginia on May 22, 1992.

4.   CLOSING THOUGHTS

We began the book with an examination of the goals of the criminal process—accuracy, fairness, efficiency, and limiting the powers of government. In a sense, we are brought full circle by the Court's recent habeas cases. The Court's justification in limiting habeas review is that the petitioners have already received a fair trial and then a fair opportunity to have both state and federal courts review the trial record. Habeas is merely an added level of review that can be restricted to accommodate other goals without being unfair. A powerful reason to limit habeas review is the Court's view in the early 1990s that an additional layer of review is not necessarily any more accurate than the first or the second or the third.

This premise is called into question by DNA and other scientific testing that has now made it possible in some cases to know for certain that an innocent man is in prison or on death row. It seems likely that the DNA revolution will change the way convictions are reviewed. But DNA and other scientific testing, as powerful as it is, cannot avail defendants unless biological evidence exists on which the testing can be done. As most cases do not involve the opportunity for definitive scientific testing, criminal procedure will continue to struggle to find the right balance between the universal and the individual case. When should courts defer to outcomes of procedures likely to produce accurate outcomes in most cases, and when should courts pursue accuracy in each individual case even when it causes a substantial loss of finality and efficiency?

Nowhere is this balance more excruciating than in the law of habeas corpus. Unlike the Warren Court, which threw open the federal habeas doors for re-examination of convictions, the Burger and Rehnquist Courts have insisted that almost all petitioners who default claims are forever barred from habeas review. The Court makes an exception for petitioners who are probably innocent because here the goal of enhancing accuracy tilts the balance toward the petitioner. When the petitioner cannot make that showing, current law treats default generally as barring review, on the theory that, when all is said and done, a fair trial is a more important goal than a last layer of review. In part, this outlook reflects the view that, in the absence of scientific testing, we can never know when an outcome is accurate. But in part it reflects the view of the Court that providing a defendant with a fair chance to disprove the State's case at trial is the most important overall guarantee of constitutional criminal procedure. This was Matthew Hale's view of the English common law from his seventeenth century vantage point. See Hale, The History of the Common Law (1713). Unless the Court changes course again, the criminal procedure future may be its past.

INDEX

References are to Pages